1 MONTH OF
FREE
READING

at

www.ForgottenBooks.com

By purchasing this book you are
eligible for one month membership to
ForgottenBooks.com, giving you
unlimited access to our entire
collection of over 1,000,000 titles via
our web site and mobile apps.

To claim your free month visit:
www.forgottenbooks.com/free846125

ISBN 978-0-484-37939-7
PIBN 10846125

THE

GRAMMAR

OF

ENGLISH GRAMMARS,

WITH

AN INTRODUCTION

HISTORICAL AND CRITICAL;

THE WHOLE

METHODICALLY ARRANGED AND AMPLY ILLUSTRATED;

WITH

FORMS OF CORRECTING AND OF PARSING, IMPROPRIETIES FOR CORRECTION, EXAMPLES FOR
PARSING, QUESTIONS FOR EXAMINATION, EXERCISES FOR WRITING, OBSERVATIONS
FOR THE ADVANCED STUDENT, DECISIONS AND PROOFS FOR THE SETTLEMENT
OF DISPUTED POINTS, OCCASIONAL STRICTURES AND DEFENCES, AN
EXHIBITION OF THE SEVERAL METHODS OF ANALYSIS,

AND

A KEY TO THE ORAL EXERCISES:

TO WHICH ARE ADDED

FOUR APPENDIXES,

PERTAINING SEPARATELY TO THE FOUR PARTS OF GRAMMAR.

BY GOOLD BROWN,

FORMERLY PRINCIPAL OF AN ENGLISH AND CLASSICAL ACADEMY, NEW YORK; AUTHOR OF THE INSTITUTES OF
ENGLISH GRAMMAR, THE FIRST LINES OF ENGLISH GRAMMAR, ETC.

"So let great authors have their due, that Time, who is the author of authors, be not deprived of his due,
which is, farther and farther to discover truth."—LORD BACON.

NEW YORK:

PUBLISHED BY SAMUEL S. & WILLIAM WOOD,

No. 261 PEARL STREET,

1851.

Entered according to Act of Congress, in the year 1851,

By GOOLD BROWN,

In the Clerk's Office of the District Court of the District of Massachusetts.

BOSTON:
PRINTED BY DAMRELL & MOORE,
No. 16 Devonshire Street,
1850 and 1851.

PREFACE.

The present performance is, so far as the end could be reached, the fulfillment of a design, formed about twenty-seven years ago, of one day presenting to the world, if I might, something like a complete grammar of the English language;—not a mere work of criticism, nor yet a work too tame, indecisive, and uncritical; for, in books of either of these sorts, our libraries already abound;—not a mere philosophical investigation of what is general or universal in grammar, nor yet a minute detail of what forms only a part of our own philology; for either of these plans falls very far short of such a purpose;—not a mere grammatical compend, abstract, or compilation, sorting with other works already before the public; for, in the production of school grammars, the author had early performed his part; and, of small treatises on this subject, we have long had a superabundance rather than a lack.

After about fifteen years devoted chiefly to grammatical studies and exercises, during most of which time I had been alternately instructing youth in four different languages, thinking it practicable to effect some improvement upon the manuals which explain our own, I prepared and published, for the use of schools, a duodecimo volume of about three hundred pages; which, upon the presumption that its principles were conformable to the best usage, and well established thereby, I entitled, "the Institutes of English Grammar." Of this work, which, it is believed, has been gradually gaining in reputation and demand ever since its first publication in 1823, there is no occasion to say more here, than that it was the result of diligent study, and that it is, essentially, the nucleus, or the groundwork, of the present volume.

With much additional labour, the principles contained in the Institutes of English Grammar, have here been not only reaffirmed and rewritten, but occasionally improved in expression, or amplified in their details. New topics, new definitions, new rules, have also been added; and all parts of the subject have been illustrated by a multiplicity of new examples and exercises, which it has required a long time to amass and arrange. To the main doctrines, also, are here subjoined many new observations and criticisms, which are the results of no inconsiderable reading and reflection.

Regarding it as my business and calling, to work out the above-mentioned purpose as circumstances might permit, I have laid no claim to genius, none to infallibility; but I have endeavoured to be accurate, and aspired to be useful; and it is a part of my plan, that the reader of this volume shall never, through my fault, be left in doubt as to the origin of any thing it contains. It is but the duty of an author, to give every needful facility for a fair estimate of his work; and, whatever authority there may be for anonymous copying in works on grammar, the precedent is always bad.

The success of other labours, answerable to moderate wishes, has enabled me to pursue this task under favourable circumstances, and with an unselfish, independent aim. Not with vainglorious pride, but with reverent gratitude to God, I acknowledge this advantage, giving thanks for the signal mercy which has upborne me to the long-continued effort. Had the case been otherwise,—had the labours of the school-room been still demanded for my support,—the present large volume would never have appeared. I had desired some leisure for the completing of this design, and to it I scrupled not to sacrifice the profits of my main employment, as soon as it could be done without hazard of adding an other chapter to "the Calamities of Authors."

The nature and design of this treatise are perhaps sufficiently developed in connexion with the various topics which are successively treated of in the Introduction. That method of teaching, which I conceive to be the best, is also there described. And, in the Grammar itself, there will be found occasional directions concerning the manner of its use. I have hoped to facilitate the study of the English language, not by abridging our grammatical code, or by rejecting the common phraseology of its doctrines, but by extending the former, improving the latter, and establishing both;—but still more, by furnishing new illustrations of the subject, and arranging its vast number of particulars in such order that every item may be readily found.

An other important purpose, which, in the preparation of this work, has been borne constantly in mind, and judged worthy of very particular attention, was the attempt to settle, so far as the most patient investigation and the fullest exhibition of proofs could do it, the multitudinous and vexatious disputes which have hitherto divided the sentiments of teachers, and made the study of English grammar so uninviting, unsatisfactory, and unprofitable, to the student whose taste demands a reasonable degree of certainty.

"Whenever labour implies the exertion of thought, it does good, at least to the strong : when the saving of labour is a saving of thought, it enfeebles. The mind, like the body, is strengthened by hard exercise : but, to give this exercise all its salutary effect, it should be of a reasonable kind ; it should lead us to the perception of regularity, of order, of principle, of a law. When, after all the trouble we have taken, we merely find anomalies and confusion, we are disgusted with what is so uncongenial : and, as our higher faculties have not been called into action, they are not unlikely to be outgrown by the lower, and overborne as it were by the underwood of our minds. Hence, no doubt, one of the reasons why our language has been so much neglected, and why such scandalous ignorance prevails concerning its nature and history, is its unattractive, disheartening irregularity : none but Satan is fond of plunging into chaos."—*Philological Museum*, (Cambridge, Eng., 1832,) Vol. i, p. 666.

If there be any remedy for the neglect and ignorance here spoken of, it must be found in the more effectual teaching of English grammar. But the principles of grammar can never have any beneficial influence over any person's manner of speaking or writing, till by some process they are made so perfectly familiar, that he can apply them with all the readiness of a native power ; that is, till he can apply them not only to what has been said or written, but to whatever he is about to utter. They must present themselves to the mind as by intuition, and with the quickness of thought; so as to regulate his language before it proceeds from the lips or the pen. If they come only by tardy recollection, or are called to mind but as contingent after-thoughts, they are altogether too late ; and serve merely to mortify the speaker or writer, by reminding him of some deficiency or inaccuracy which there may then be no chance to amend.

But how shall, or can, this readiness be acquired? I answer, By a careful attention to such *exercises* as are fitted to bring the learner's knowledge into practice. The student will therefore find, that I have given him something to *do*, as well as something to *learn*. But, by the formules and directions in this work, he is very carefully shewn how to proceed ; and, if he be a tolerable reader, it will be his own fault, if he does not, by such aid, become a tolerable grammarian. The chief of these exercises are the *parsing* of what is right, and the *correcting* of what is wrong ; both, perhaps, equally important ; and I have intended to make them equally easy. To any real proficient in grammar, nothing can be more free from embarrassment, than the performance of these exercises, in all ordinary cases. For grammar, rightly learned, institutes in the mind a certain knowledge, or process of thought, concerning the sorts, properties, and relations, of all the words which can be presented in any intelligible sentence ; and, with the initiated, a perception of the construction will always instantly follow or accompany a discovery of the sense : and instantly, too, should there be a perception of the error, if any of the words are misspelled, misjoined, misapplied, —or are, in any way, unfaithful to the sense intended.

Thus it is the great end of grammar, to secure the power of apt expression, by causing the principles on which language is constructed, if not to be constantly present to the mind, at least to pass through it more rapidly than either pen or voice can utter words. And where this power resides, there cannot but be a proportionate degree of critical skill, or of ability to judge of the language of others. Present what you will, grammar directs the mind immediately to a consideration of the sense; and, if properly taught, always creates a discriminating taste which is not less offended by specious absurdities, than by the common blunders of clownishness. Every one who has any pretensions to this art, knows that, to *parse* a sentence, is but to resolve it according to one's understanding of its import ; and it is equally clear, that the power to *correct* an erroneous passage, usually demands or implies a knowledge of the author's thought.

But, if parsing and correcting are of so great practical importance as our first mention of them suggests, it may be well to be more explicit here concerning them. The pupil who cannot perform these exercises both accurately and fluently, is not truly prepared to perform them at all, and has no right to expect from any body a patient hearing. A slow and faltering rehearsal of words clearly prescribed, yet neither fairly remembered nor understandingly applied, is as foreign from parsing or correcting, as it is from elegance of diction. Divide and conquer, is the rule here, as in many other cases. Begin with what is simple ;

practise it till it becomes familiar; and then proceed. No child ever learned to speak by any other process. Hard things become easy by use; and skill is gained by little and little.

Of the whole method of parsing, it should be understood, that it is to be a critical exercise in utterance, as well as an evidence of previous study,—an exhibition of the learner's attainments in the practice, as well as in the theory, of grammar; and that, in any tolerable performance of this exercise, there must be an exact adherence to the truth of facts, as they occur in the example, and to the forms of expression, which are prescribed as models, in the book. For parsing is, in no degree, a work of invention; but wholly an exercise, an exertion of skill. It is, indeed, an exercise for all the powers of the mind, except the inventive faculty. Perception, judgement, reasoning, memory, and method, are indispensable to the performance. Nothing is to be guessed at, or devised, or uttered at random. If the learner can but rehearse the necessary definitions and rules, and perform the simplest exercise of judgement in their application, he cannot but perceive what he *must say* in order to speak the truth in parsing. His principal difficulty is in determining the parts of speech. To lessen this, the trial should commence with easy sentences, also with few of the definitions, and with definitions that have been perfectly learned. This difficulty being surmounted, let him follow the forms prescribed for the several praxes of this work, and he shall not err. The directions and examples given at the head of each exercise, will show him exactly the number, the order, and the proper phraseology, of the particulars to be stated; so that he may go through the explanation with every advantage which a book can afford. There is no hope of him whom these aids will not save from "plunging into chaos."

"Of all the works of man, language is the most enduring, and partakes the most of eternity. And, as our own language, so far as thought can project itself into the future, seems likely to be coeval with the world, and to spread vastly beyond even its present immeasurable limits, there cannot easily be a nobler object of ambition than to purify and better it."—*Philological Museum*, Vol. i, p. 665.

It was some ambition of the kind here meant, awakened by a discovery of the scandalous errors and defects which abound in all our common English grammars, that prompted me to undertake the present work. Now, by the bettering of a language, I understand little else than the extensive teaching of its just forms, according to analogy and the general custom of the most accurate writers. This teaching, however, may well embrace also, or be combined with, an exposition of the various forms of false grammar by which inaccurate writers have corrupted, if not the language itself, at least their own style in it.

With respect to our present English, I know not whether any other improvement of it ought to be attempted, than the avoiding and correcting of those improprieties and unwarrantable anomalies by which carelessness, ignorance, and affectation, are ever tending to debase it, and the careful teaching of its true grammar, according to its real importance in education. What further amendment is feasible, or is worthy to engage attention, I will not pretend to say; nor do I claim to have been competent to so much as was manifestly desirable within these limits. But what I lacked in ability, I have endeavoured to supply by diligence; and what I could conveniently strengthen by better authority than my own, I have not failed to support with all that was due, of names, guillemets, and references.

Like every other grammarian, I stake my reputation as an author, upon "a certain set of opinions," and a certain manner of exhibiting them, appealing to the good sense of my readers for the correctness of both. All contrary doctrines are unavoidably censured by him who attempts to sustain his own; but, to grammatical censures, no more importance ought to be attached than what belongs to grammar itself. He who cares not to be accurate in the use of language, is inconsistent with himself, if he be offended at verbal criticism; and he who is displeased at finding his opinions rejected, is equally so, if he cannot prove them to be well founded. It is only in cases susceptible of a rule, that any writer can be judged deficient. I can censure no man for differing from me, till I can show him a principle which he ought to follow. According to Lord Kames, the standard of taste, both in arts and in manners, is "the common sense of mankind," a principle founded in the universal conviction of a common nature in our species. (See *Elements of Criticism*, Chap. xxv, Vol. ii, p. 364.) If this is so, the doctrine applies to grammar as fully as to any thing about which criticism may concern itself.

But, to the discerning student or teacher, I owe an apology for the abundant condescension with which I have noticed in this volume the works of unskillful grammarians. For men of sense have no natural inclination to dwell upon palpable offences against taste and scholarship; nor can they be easily persuaded to approve the course of an author who makes it his business to criticise petty productions. And is it not a fact, that grammatical authorship has sunk so low, that no man who is capable of perceiving its multitudinous errors, dares now stoop to notice the most flagrant of its abuses, or the most successful of its abusers? And, the quackery which is now so prevalent, what can be a more natural effect, than a very general contempt for the study of grammar? My apology to the reader therefore is, that, as the honour of our language demands correctness in all the manuals prepared for schools, a just exposition of any that are lacking in this point, is a service due to the study of English grammar, if not to the authors in question.

The exposition, however, that I have made of the errors and defects of other writers, is only an incident, or underpart, of the scheme of this treatise. Nor have I anywhere exhibited blunders as one that takes delight in their discovery. My main design has been, to prepare a work which, by its own completeness and excellence, should deserve the title here chosen. But, a comprehensive code of false grammar being confessedly the most effectual means of teaching what is true, I have thought fit to supply this portion of my book, not from anonymous or uncertain sources, but from the actual text of other authors, and chiefly from the works of professed grammarians.

"In what regards the laws of grammatical purity," says Dr. Campbell, "the violation is much more conspicuous than the observance."—See *Philosophy of Rhetoric*, p. 190. It therefore falls in with my main purpose, to present to the public, in the following ample work, a condensed mass of special criticisms, such as is not elsewhere to be found in any language. And, if the littleness of the particulars to which the learner's attention is called, be reckoned an objection, the author last quoted has furnished for me, as well as for himself, a good apology. "The elements which enter into the composition of the hugest bodies, are subtile and inconsiderable. The rudiments of every art and science exhibit at first, to the learner, the appearance of littleness and insignificancy. And it is by attending to such reflections, as to a superficial observer would appear minute and hypercritical, that language must be improved, and eloquence perfected."—*Ib.* p. 244.

GOOLD BROWN.

LYNN, MASS., 1851.

TABLE OF CONTENTS.

INTRODUCTION.

THE GRAMMAR OF ENGLISH GRAMMARS.

PART I.—ORTHOGRAPHY.

PART II.—ETYMOLOGY.

THE KEY.—PART IV.—PROSODY.

A

DIGESTED CATALOGUE

OF

ENGLISH GRAMMARS AND GRAMMARIANS,

WITH SOME

COLLATERAL WORKS AND AUTHORITIES,

ESPECIALLY SUCH AS ARE CITED IN

THE GRAMMAR OF ENGLISH GRAMMARS.

ADAM, ALEXANDER, LL.D.; "Latin and English Grammar:" Edinburgh, 1772; Boston, 1803.

ADAMS, JOHN Q., LL.D.; "Lectures on Rhetoric and Oratory;" 2 vols., 8vo: Cambridge, N. E., 1810.

ADAMS, Rev. CHARLES, A. M.; English Grammar; 12mo, pp. 172: 1st Edition, Boston, 1838.

ADAMS, DANIEL, M. B.; English Grammar; 12mo, pp. 103: 3d Edition, Montpelier, Vt., 1814.

ADAMS, R.; English Grammar; 18mo, pp. 143: Leicester, Mass., 1st Ed , 1806; 5th Ed. 1821.

AICKIN, JOSEPH; English Grammar, 8vo: London, 1693.

AINSWORTH, ROBERT; Latin and English Dictionary, 4to: 1st Ed., 1736; revised Ed., Lond., 1823.

AINSWORTH, LUTHER; English Grammar; 12mo, pp. 144: 1st Ed., Providence, R. I., 1837.

ALDEN, ABNER, A. M.; "Grammar Made Easy;" 12mo, pp. 180: 1st Ed., Boston, 1811.

ALDEN, Rev. TIMOTHY, Jun.; English Grammar; 18mo, pp. 36: 1st Ed., Boston, 1811.

ALEXANDER, CALEB, A. M.; (1.) "Grammatical Elements," published before 1794. (2.) "A Grammatical Institute of the Latin Language;" 12mo, pp. 132: Worcester, Mass., 1794. (3.) "A Grammatical System of the English Language;" 12mo, pp. 96; written at Mendon, Mass., 1795: 10th Ed., Keene, N. H., 1814. Also, (4.) "An Introduction to Latin," 1795; and, (5.) "An Introduction to the Speaking and Writing of English."

ALEXANDER, SAMUEL; English Grammar; 18mo, pp. 216: 4th Edition, London, 1832.

ALGER, ISRAEL, Jun., A. M.; "Abridgment of Murray's E. Gram.," &c.; 18mo, pp. 125: Boston, 1824 and 1842.

ALLEN, Rev. WILLIAM, M. A.; "Grammar of the English Language," &c.; 18mo: London. Also, "The Elements of English Grammar," &c.; 12mo, pp. 457: London, 1813; 2d Ed., 1824.

ALLEN and CORNWELL; English Grammar; 18mo, pp. 162: 3d Edition, London, 1841.

ALLEN, D. CAVERNO ; "Grammatic Guide, or Common School Grammar;" 12mo, pp. 94: Syracuse, N. Y., 1847.

ANDREW, JAMES, LL.D.; English Grammar; 8vo, pp. 129: London, 1817.

ANDREWS & STODDARD; "A Grammar of the Latin Language;" 12mo, pp. 323: Boston, 1836; 11th Ed., 1845.

ANGELL, OLIVER, A. M.; English Grammar; 12mo, pp. 90: 1st Edition, Providence, R. I., 1830.

ANGUS, WILLIAM, M. A.; English Grammar; 12mo, pp. 255: 2d Edition, Glasgow, Scotland, 1807.

ANON.; "The British Grammar;" 8vo, pp. 281: London, (perhaps,) 1760; Boston, Mass., 1784.

ANON.; "A Comprehensive Grammar," &c.; 18mo, pp. 174: 3d Ed., Philadelphia, T. Dobson, 1789.

ANON.; "The Comic Grammar," &c.: London, 1840.

ANON.; "The Decoy," an English Grammar with Cuts; 12mo, pp. 33: New York, S. Wood & Sons, 1820.

ANON.; E. Gram.. "By T. C.;" 18mo, pp. 104: London, 1843.

ANON.; Grammar and Rhetoric; 12mo, pp. 221: London, 1776.

ANON.; "The English Tutor;" 8vo: London, 1747.

ANON.; English Grammar, 12mo: London, Boosey, 1795.

ANON.; English Grammar; 18mo, pp. 161: London, 1838·

ANON.; English Grammar; 18mo, pp. 85: London, 1838.

ANON.; An English Grammar, with Engravings; 18mo, pp. 16: London, 1820.

ANON.; English Grammar, pp. 84: 1st Ed., Huddersfield, 1817.

ANON.; "The Essentials of English Grammar;" 18mo, pp. 108: 3d Edition, London, 1821.

ANON.; English Grammar; 18mo, pp. 131: Albany, N. Y., 1819.

ANON.; (A. H. Maltby & Co. pub.;) Murray's Abridgement, "with Additions;" 18mo, pp. 120: Newhaven, Ct., 1822.

ANON.; (James Loring, pub.;) Murray's Abridgement, "with Alterations and Improvements; by a Teacher of Youth;" (Lawson Lyon;) 18mo, pp. 72: 14th Ed., Boston, 1821.

ANON.; "The Infant School Grammar;" (said to have been written by Mrs. Bethune;) 18mo, pp. 132: New York, 1830. Jonathan Seymour, proprietor.

ANON.; Pestalozzian Grammar; 12mo, pp. 60: Boston, 1830.

ANON.; Interrogative Grammar; 12mo, pp. 70: Boston, 1832.

ANON.; Grammar with Cuts; 18mo, pp. 108: Boston, 1830.

ANON.; "The Juvenile English Grammar;" 18mo, pp. 89: Boston, 1829. B. Perkins & Co., publishers and proprietors.

ANON.; "The Little Grammarian;" 18mo, pp. 108: 2d Edition, Boston, 1829.

ANON.; An Inductive Grammar; 12mo, pp. 185: Windsor, Vt., 1829.

ANON.; "A Concise Grammar of the English Language, attempted in Verse;" 18mo, pp. 63: 1st Edition, New York, 1825.

ANON.; "Edward's First Lessons in Grammar;" 18mo, pp. 108: 1st Ed., Boston, T. H. Webb & Co., 1843.

ANON.; "The First Lessons in English Grammar;" 18mo, pp. 90: 1st Edition, Boston, 1842.

ANON.; "A New Grammar of the English Language;" 12mo, pp. 124: New York, 1831; 2d Ed., Boston, 1834.

ANON.; "Enclytica, or the Principles of Universal Grammar;" 8vo, pp. 133: London, J. Booth, 1814.

ANON.; "The General Principles of Grammar, edited by a few Well-Wishers to Knowledge;" 18mo, pp. 76: Philadelphia, Lea & Blanchard, 1847.

ARNOLD, T. K., M. A.; English Grammar; 12mo, pp. 76: 2d Edition, London, 1841.

ASH, JOHN, LL. D.; "Grammatical Institutes;" 18mo, pp. 142: London, first published about 1763; New York, "A New Edition, Revised and Corrected," 1799.

BACON, CALEB, Teacher; "Murray's English Grammar Put into Questions and Answers;" 18mo, pp. 108: New York, 1st Edition, 1818; 6th Edition, 1823, 1827, and 1830.

BADGLEY, JONATHAN; English Grammar; 12mo, pp. 200: 1st Edition, Utica, N.Y., 1845. Suppressed for plagiarism from G. Brown.

BALCH, WILILAM S.; (1.) "Lectures on Language;" 12mo, pp. 252: Providence, 1838. (2.) "A Grammar of the English Language;" 12mo, pp. 140: 1st Edition, Boston, 1839.

BALDWIN, EDWARD; English Grammar; 18mo, pp. 148: London, 1810; 2d Ed., 1824.

BARBER, Dr. JONATHAN; "A Grammar of Elocution;" 12mo: Newhaven, 1830.

BARNARD, FREDERICK A. P., A. M.; "Analytic Grammar; with Symbolic Illustration;" 12mo, pp. 264: New York, 1836. This is a curious work, and remarkably well-written.

BARNES, DANIEL H., of N. Y.; "The Red Book," or Bearcroft's "Practical Orthography," Revised and Enlarged; 12mo, pp. 347: New York, 1828.

BARNES, W.; English Grammar; 18mo, pp. 120: London, 1842.

BARRETT, JOHN; "A Grammar of the English Language;" 18mo, pp. 214: 2d Ed., Boston, 1819.

BARRETT, SOLOMON, Jun.; "The Principles of Language;" 12mo, pp. 120: Albany, 1837. "The Principles of English Grammar;" 18mo, pp. 96; "Tenth Edition, Revised:" Utica, 1845.

BARRIE, ALEXANDER; English Grammar; 24to, pp. 54: Edinburgh, 9th Ed., 1800.

BARTLETT, MONTGOMERY R.; "The Common School Manual;" called in the Third or Philadelphia Edition, "The National School Manual;"—"in Four Parts," or Separate Volumes, 12mo: I, pp. 108; II, 302; III, 379; IV, promised "to consist of 450 or 500 pages." First three parts, "Second Edition," New York, 1830. A miserable jumble, in the successive pages of which, Grammar is mixed up with Spelling-columns, Reading-lessons, Arithmetic, Geometry, and the other supposed daily tasks of a school-boy!

BAILEY, N., Schoolmaster; "English and Latin Exercises;" 12mo, pp. 183: London, 18th Ed., 1798.

BAYLEY, ANSELM, LL.D.; English Grammar, 8vo: London, 1772.

BEALE, SOLON; English Grammar, 18mo, pp. 27: Bangor, Maine, 1833.

BEALL, ALEXANDER; English Grammar, 12mo: 1st Ed, Cincinnati, Ohio, 1841.

BEATTIE, JAMES, LL. D.; "Theory of Language:" London, 1783; Philadelphia, 1809. "Elements of Moral Science;" 12mo, pp. 572; Baltimore, 1813. See, in Part I, the sections which treat of "The Faculty of Speech," and the "Essentials of Language;" and, in Part IV, those which treat of "Rhetorick, Figures, Sentences, Style, and Poetry."

BECK, WILLIAM; "Outline of English Grammar;" very small, pp. 34: 3d Ed., London, 1829.

BRECHER, CATHARINE E.; English Grammar, 12mo, pp. 74: 1st Ed., Hartfort, Ct., 1829.

BELL, JOHN; English Grammar, 12mo, pp. 446: (2 vols.:) 1st Ed., Glasgow, 1769.

BELLAMY, ELIZABETH; English Grammar, 12mo: London, 1802.

BENEDICT, ——; English Grammar, 12mo, pp. 192: 1st Ed., Nicholasville, Ky., 1832.

BETTESWORTH, JOHN; English Grammar, 12mo: London, 1778.

BICKNELL, ALEXANDER, Esq.; "The Grammatical Wreath;" 18mo, pp. 304: London, 1790.

BINGHAM, CALEB, A.M.; "The Young Lady's Accidence;" 18mo, pp. 60: Boston, 1804; 20th Ed., 1815.

BLAIR, HUGH, D.D., F. R. S.; "Lectures on Rhetoric and Belles-Lettres;" 8vo, pp. 560: London, 1783; New York, 1819.

BLAIR, JOHN, D. D.; English Grammar; 12mo, pp. 146: 1st Ed., Philadelphia, 1831.

BLAIR, DAVID, Rev.; "A Practical Grammar of the English Language;" 18mo, pp. 167: 7th Ed., London, 1815.

BLAISDALE, SILAS; English Grammar; 18mo, pp. 88: 1st Ed., Boston, 1831.

BLISS, LEONARD, Jun.; English Grammar; 18mo, pp. 73: 1st Ed., Louisville, Ky., 1839.

BOBBITT, A.; English Grammar; 12mo, pp. 136: 1st Ed., London, 1833.

BOLLES, WILLIAM; (1.) "A Spelling-Book;" 12mo, pp. 180: Ster. Ed., N. London, 1831. (2.) "An Explanatory and Phonographic Pronouncing Dictionary of the English Language;" royal octavo, pp. 944: 8ter. Ed., New London, 1845.

BOOTH, DAVID; Introd. to Analytical Dict.; 8vo, pp. 168: London, 1814. Analytical Dictionary of the English Language: London, 1835. E. Grammar, 12mo: London, 1837.

BRACE, JOAB; "The Principles of English Grammar;" (vile theft from Lennie;) 18mo, pp. 144: 1st Edition, Philadelphia, 1839.

BRADLEY, JOSHUA, A. M.; "Youth's Literary Guide;" 12mo, pp. 192: 1st Ed., Windsor, Vt., 1815.

BRADLEY, Rev. C.; English Grammar; 12mo, pp. 148: York, Eng., 1810; 3d Ed., 1813.

BRIDEL, EDMUND, LL.D.; E. Gram., 4to: London, 1799.

BRIGHTLAND, JOHN, Pub.; "A Grammar of the English Tongue;" 12mo, pp. 300: 7th Ed., London, 1746.

BRITTAIN, Rev. LEWIS; English Grammar; 12mo, pp. 156: 2d Edition, London, 1790.

BROMLEY, WALTER; English Grammar; 18mo, pp. 104: 1st Ed., Halifax, N. S., 1822.

BROWN, GOOLD; (1.) "The Institutes of English Grammar;" 12mo, pp. 220—312: New York, 1st Ed., 1823; stereotyped in 1832, and again in 1846. (2.) "The First Lines of English Grammar:" early copies 18mo, late copies 12mo, pp. 108: New York, 1st Ed., 1823; stereotyped in 1827, and in 1844. (3.) "A Key to the Exercises for Writing, contained in the Institutes of English Grammar;" 12mo, pp. 51: New York, 1825. (4.) "A Catechism of English Grammar;" 18mo, pp. 72: New York, 1827. (5.) "A Compendious English Grammar;" 12mo, pp. 22: (in Part I of the Treasury of Knowledge:) New York, 1831. (6.) "The Grammar of English Grammars;" 8vo, pp. 1048: first printed in Boston in 1850 and 1851.

BROWN, JAMES; (1.) An Explanation of E. Grammar as taught by an Expensive Machine; 8vo, pp. 40: 1st Ed., Boston, 1815. (2.) "The American Grammar;" a Pamphlet; 12mo, pp. 48: Salem, N. Y., 1821. (3.) "An American Grammar;" 18mo, pp. 162: New York, 1821. (4.) "An Appeal from the British System of English Grammar to Common Sense;" 12mo, pp. 336: Philadelphia, 1837. (5.) "The American System of English Syntax;" 12mo, pp. 216: Philad., 1838. (6.) "An Exegesis of English Syntax;" 12mo, pp. 147: Philad., 1840. (7.) "The First Part of the American System of English Syntax;" 12mo, pp. 195: Boston, 1841. (8.) "An English Syntascope," a "Chart," and other fantastical works.

BROWN, RICHARD; English Grammar, 12mo: London, 1692.

BUCHANAN, JAMES; "A Regular English Syntax;" 12mo, pp. 196: 5th American Ed., Philad., 1792.

BUCKE, CHARLES; "A Classical Grammar of the E. Language;" 18mo, pp. 152: London, 1829.

BULLEN, Rev. H. ST. JOHN; English Grammar; 12mo, pp. 140: 1st Edition, London, 1797.

BULLIONS, Rev. PETER, D. D.; (1.) "Elements of the Greek Language;" (now called, "The Principles of Greek Grammar;") mostly a version of Dr. Moor's "Elementa Linguæ Græcæ:" 1st Ed., 1831. (2.) "The Principles of English Grammar;" (mostly copied from Lennie;) 12mo, pp. 187; 2d Ed., New York, 1837; 5th Ed., Revised, pp. 216, 1843. (3.) "The Principles of Latin Grammar;" (professedly, "upon the foundation of Ad-

am's Latin Grammar;") 12mo, pp. 312: Albany, 1841: 12th Ed., New York, 1846. (4.) "Practical Lessons in English Grammar;" 12mo, pp. 132: New York, 1844. (5.) "An Analytical and Practical Grammar of the English Language;" 12mo, pp. 240: 1st Ed., New York, 1849.

BULLOKAR, WILLIAM; (1.) "Booke at Large for the Amendment of Orthographie for English Speech." (2.) "A Bref Grammar for English:" London, 1586.

BURHANS, HEZEKIAH; "The Critical Pronouncing Spelling-Book;" 12mo, pp. 204: 1st Ed., Philad., 1823.

BURLES, EDWARD; E. Gram., 12mo: Lond., 1652.

BURN, JOHN; "A Practical Grammar of the E. Lang.;" 12mo, pp. 275: Glasgow, 1766; 10th Ed., 1810.

BURR, JONATHAN, A. M.; "A Compendium of Eng. Gram.;" 18mo, pp. 72: Boston, 1797,—1804,—1818.

BUTLER, CHARLES; E. Gram., 4to: Oxford, Eng., 1633.

BUTLER, NOBLE, A. M.; "A Practical Grammar of the E. Lang.;" 12mo, pp. 216: 1st Ed., Louisville, Ky., 1845. "Introductory Lessons in E. Grammar," 1845.

CAMPBELL, GEORGE, D. D., F. R. S.; "The Philosophy of Rhetoric;" 8vo, pp. 446: London, 1776: Philad., 1818.

CARDELL, WM. S.; (1.) An "Analytical Spelling-Book; (with Part of the "Story of Jack Halyard;") 12mo, pp. 192: (published at first under the fictitious name of "John Franklin Jones:") New York, 1823; 2d Ed., 1824. (2.) An "Essay on Language;" 12mo, pp. 203: New York, 1825. (3.) "Elements of English Grammar;" 18mo, pp. 141: New York, 1826; 3d Ed., Hartford, 1827. (4.) "Philosophic Grammar of the English Language;" 12mo, pp. 236: Philadelphia, 1827.

CAREY, JOHN; English Grammar; 12mo, pp. 220: 1st Ed., London, 1809.

CARTER, JOHN; E. Gram., 8vo: Leeds, 1773.

CHANDLER, JOSEPH R.; "A Grammar of the English Language;" 12mo, pp. 180: Philad., 1821. Rev. Ed., pp. 208, stereotyped, 1847.

CHAPIN, JOEL; English Grammar; 12mo, pp. 252: 1st Edition, Springfield, Mass., 1842.

CHESSMAN, DANIEL, A. M.; Murray Abridged; 18mo, pp. 24: 3d Ed., Hallowell, Me., 1821.

CHURCHILL, T. O.; "A New Grammar of the English Language;" 12mo, pp. 454: 1st Ed., London, 1823.

CLAPHAM, Rev. SAMUEL; E. Grammar: London, 1810.

CLARK, HENRY; E. Grammar; 4to: London, 1656.

CLARK, SCHUYLER; "The American Linguist, or Natural Grammar;" 12mo, pp. 240: Providence, 1830.

CLARK, S. W., A. M.; "A Practical Grammar," with "a System of Diagrams;" 12mo, pp. 218: 2d Ed., New York, 1848.

CLARK, WILLIAM; E. Gram.; 18mo: London, 1810.

COAR, THOMAS; "A Grammar of the English Tongue;" 12mo, pp. 276: 1st Ed., London, 1796.

COBB, ENOS; "Elements of the English Language;" 12mo, pp. 108: 1st Ed., Boston, 1820.

COBB, LYMAN, A. M.; (1.) A Spelling-Book according to J. Walker; "Revised Ed.:" Ithaca, N. Y. 1825. (2.) "Abridgment of Walker's Crit. Pron. Dict.:" Hartford, Ct.,

D

1829. (3.) "Juvenile Reader, Nos. 1, 2, 3, and Sequel:" New York, 1831. (4.) "The North American Reader;" 12mo, pp. 498: New York, 1835. (5.) "New Spelling-Book, in Six Parts;" 12mo, pp. 168: N. Y., 1843. (6.) An "Expositor," a "Miniature Lexicon," books of "Arithmetic, &c., &c."

COBBETT, WILLIAM; "A Grammar of the E. Language;" 12mo, New York and Lond., 1818; 18mo, N. Y., 1832.

COBBIN, INGRAM; English Grammar; 18mo, pp. 72: 20th Edition, London.

COCHRAN, PETER, A. B.; English Grammar; 18mo, pp. 71: 1st Ed., Boston, 1802.

COLET, Dr. JOHN, Dean of St. Paul's; the "English Introduction" to Lily's Grammar; dedicated to Lily in 1510. See Gram. of E. Gram., Introd., Chap. XI, ¶¶ 3, 4, and 5.

COMLY, JOHN; "English Grammar Made Easy;" 18mo, pp. 192: 6th Ed., Philad., 1815; 15th Ed., 1826.

COMSTOCK, ANDREW, M. D.; "A System of Elocution;" 12mo, pp. 364: Philadelphia, 1844. "A Treatise on Phonology;" 12mo, 1846: &c.

CONNEL, ROBERT; English Grammar; 18mo, pp. 162: Glasgow, 1831; 2d Ed., 1834.

CONNON, C. W., M. A.; English Grammar; 12mo, pp. 168: Edinburgh, 1845.

COOPER, Rev. JOAB GOLDSMITH, A. M.; (1.) "An Abridgment of Murray's English Grammar;" (largely stolen from G. Brown;) 12mo, pp. 200: Philadelphia, 1828. (2.) "A Plain and Practical English Grammar;" 12mo, pp. 210: Philad., 1831.

COOTE, C., LL.D.; on the English Language; 8vo, pp. 282: 1st Edition, London, 1788.

CORBET, JAMES; English Grammar; 24to, pp. 153: 1st Edition, Glasgow, 1743.

CORBET, JOHN; English Grammar; 12mo: Shrewsbury, England, 1784.

CORNELL, WILLIAM M.; English Grammar; 4to, pp. 12: 1st Edition, Boston, 1840.

CRANE, GEORGE; "The Principles of Language;" 12mo, pp. 264: 1st Ed., London, 1843.

CROCKER, ABRAHAM; E. Gr., 12mo: Lond., 1772.

CROMBIE, ALEXANDER, LL.D., F. R. S.; "A Treatise on the Etymology and Syntax of the English Language;" 8vo, pp. 425: London, 2d Ed., 1809; 4th Ed., 1836.

CUTLER, ANDREW, A. M.; "English Grammar and Parser;" 12mo, pp. 168: 1st Ed., Plainfield, Ct., 1841.

DALE, W. A. T.; a small "English Grammar;" 18mo, pp. 72: 1st Ed., Albany, N. Y., 1820.

DALTON, JOHN; "Elements of English Grammar;" 12mo, pp. 312: London, 1st Ed., 1801.

DAVENPORT, BISHOP; "English Grammar Simplified;" 18mo, pp. 139: 1st Ed., Wilmington, Del., 1830.

DAVIDSON, DAVID; a Syntactical Treatise, or Grammar; 12mo: London, 1823.

DAVIS, Rev. JOHN, A. M.; English Grammar; 18mo, pp. 188: 1st Ed., Belfast, Ireland, 1832.

DAVIS, PARDON; (1.) An Epitome of E. Gram.; 12mo, pp. 66: 1st Ed., Philad., 1818. (2.) "Modern Practical E. Gram.;" 12mo, pp. 175: 1st Ed., Philad., 1845.

DAY, PARSONS E.; "District School Grammar;" 18mo, pp. 120: 2d Ed., Ithaca, N. Y., 1844.

DAY, WILLIAM; "Punctuation Reduced to a System;" 18mo, pp. 147: 3d Ed., London, 1847.

DEARBORN, BENJAMIN; "The Columbian Grammar;" 12mo, pp. 140: 1st Ed., Boston, 1795.

DEL MAR, E.; Treatise on English Grammar; 12mo, pp. 115: 1st Ed., London, 1842.

DILWORTH, THOMAS; "A New Guide to the English Tongue;" 12mo, pp. 148: London; 1st Ed., 1740; 26th Ed., 1764; 40th Ed., (used by G. B.,) undated.

DOHERTY, HUGH; a Treatise on English Grammar; 8vo, pp. 240: 1st Ed., London, 1841.

D'ORSEY, ALEXANDER J. D.; (1.) A Duodecimo Grammar, in Two Parts; Part I, pp. 153; Part II, pp. 142: 1st Ed., Edinburgh, 1842. (2.) An Introduction to E. Gram.; 18mo, pp. 104: Edin., 1845.

DE SACY, A. J. SYLVESTER, Baron; "Principles of General Grammar;" translated from the French, by D. Fosdick, Jun.; 12mo, pp. 156: 1st American, from the 5th French Edition; Andover and New York, 1834.

"DESPAUTER, JOHN, a Flemish grammarian, whose books were, at one time, in great repute; he died in 1520."—Univ. Biog. Dict. Despauter's Latin Grammar, in Three Parts, —Etymology, Syntax, and Versification,—comprises 858 octavo pages. Dr. Adam says, in the "Preface to the Fourth Edition" of his Grammar, "The first complete edition of Despauter's Grammar was printed at Cologne, anno 1522; his Syntax had been published anno 1509." G. Brown's copy is a "complete edition," printed partly in 1517, and partly in 1518.

DEVIS, ELLEN; E. Gram.; 18mo, pp. 130: London and Dublin; 1st Ed., 1777; 17th Ed., 1825. Devis's Grammar, spoken of in D. Blair's Preface, as being too "comprehensive and minute," is doubtless an other and much larger work.

DRUMMOND, JOHN; English Grammar; 8vo: London, 1767.

DYCHE, THOMAS; English Grammar; 8vo, pp. 10: London, 1st Ed., 1710; 12th Ed., 1765.

EARL, MARY; English Grammar; 18mo, pp. 36: 1st Ed., Boston, 1816.

EDWARDS, Mrs. M. C.; English Grammar; 8vo: Brentford, England, 1796.

EGELSHEM, WELLS; English Grammar; 12mo: London, 1781.

ELMORE, D. W., A. M.; "English Grammar;" 18mo, pp. 18: 1st Ed., Troy, N. Y., 1830. A mere trifle.

ELPHINSTON, JAMES; on the English Language; 12mo, pp. 298: 1st Ed., Lond., 1766.

EMERSON, BENJAMIN D.; "The National Spelling-Book;" 12mo, pp. 168: Boston, 1828.

EMERY, J., A. B.; English Grammar; 18mo, pp. 39: 1st Ed., Wellsborough, Pa., 1829.

EMMONS, S. B.; "The Grammatical Instructer;" 12mo, pp. 160: 1st Ed., Boston, 1832. Worthless.

ENSELL, G.; "A Grammar of the English Language;" in English and Dutch; 8vo, pp. 612: Rotterdam, 1797.

EVEREST, Rev. CORNELIUS B.; "An English Grammar;" 12mo, pp. 270: 1st Ed., Norwich, Ct., 1835. Suppressed for plagiarism from G. Brown.

EVERETT, ERASTUS, A. M.; "A System of English Versification;" 12mo, pp. 198: 1st Ed., New York, 1848.

FARNUM, CALEB, Jun., A. M.; "Practical Grammar;" 12mo, pp. 124: 1st Edition, (suppressed for petty larcenies from G. Brown,) Providence, R. I., 1842; 2d Edition, (altered to evade the charge of plagiarism,) Boston, 1843.

FARRO, DANIEL; "The Royal British Grammar and Vocabulary;" 12mo, pp. 344: 1st Ed., London, 1754.

FELCH, W.; "A Comprehensive Grammar;" 12mo, pp. 122: 1st Edition, Boston, 1837. This author can see others' faults better than his own.

FELTON, OLIVER C.; "A Concise Manual of English Grammar;" 12mo, pp. 145: Salem, Mass., 1843.

FENNING, DANIEL; English Grammar; 12mo, pp. 224: 1st Ed., London, 1771.

FENWICK, JOHN; a 12mo Gram.: London, 1811.

FISHER, A.; "A Practical New Grammar;" 12mo, pp. 176: London; 1st Ed., 1753; 28th Ed., 1795; "a New Ed., Enlarged, Improved, and Corrected," (used by G. B.,) 1800.

FISK, ALLEN; (1.) Epitome of E. Gram.; 18mo, pp. 124: Hallowell, Me., 1821; 2d Ed., 1828. (2.) "Adam's Latin Grammar Simplified;" 8vo, pp. 190: New York, 1822; 2d Ed., 1824. (3.) "Murray's English Grammar Simplified;" 8vo, pp. 178: 1st Ed., Troy, N. Y., 1822.

FLEMING, CALEB; a 12mo Gram.: Lond., 1765.

FLETCHER, LEVI; English Grammar; 12mo, pp. 83: 1st Ed., Philadelphia, 1834.

FLETCHER, Rev. W.; English Gram.; 18mo, pp. 175: London; 1st Ed., 1828; 2d Ed., 1833.

FLINT, ABEL, A. M., and D. D.; "Murray's English Grammar Abridged;" 12mo, pp. 204: Hartford, Ct.; 1st Ed., 1807; 6th Ed., pp. 214, 1826.

FLINT, JOHN; "First Lessons in English Grammar;" 18mo, pp. 107: 1st Ed., New York, 1834.

FLOWER, M. and W. B.; English Grammar; 18mo, pp. 170: 1st Ed., London, 1844.

FOLKER, JOSEPH; "An Introduction to E. Gram.;" 12mo, pp. 34: Savannah, Ga., 1821.

FORMEY, M., M. D., S. E., &c., &c.; "Elementary Principles of the Belles-Lettres;"— "Translated from the French, by the late Mr. Sloper Forman;" 12mo, pp. 224: Glasgow, 1767.

FOWLE, WILLIAM BENTLEY; (1.) "The True English Grammar," [Part I;] 18mo, pp. 180: Boston, 1827. (2.) "The True English Grammar, Part II;" 18mo, pp. 97: Boston, 1829. (3.) "The Common School Grammar, Part I;" 12mo, pp 46: Boston, 1842. (4.) "The Common School Grammar, Part II;" 12mo, pp. 108: Boston, 1842.

FOWLER, WILLIAM C.; "English Grammar;" 8vo, pp. 675: 1st Edition, New York, 1850.

FRAZEE, Rev. BRADFORD; "An Improved Grammar;" 12mo, pp. 192: Philad., 1844; 8ter. Ed., 1845.

FRENCH, D'ARCY A.; English Grammar; 12mo, pp. 168: Baltimore, 1st Ed., 1831.

FROST, JOHN, A. M.; (1.) "Elements of English Grammar;" 18mo, pp. 108: 1st Ed., Boston, 1829. (2.) "A Practical English Grammar;" (with 89 Cuts;) 12mo, pp. 204: 1st Ed., Philadelphia, 1842.

FULLER, ALLEN; "Grammatical Exercises, being a plain and concise Method of teaching English Grammar;" 12mo, pp. 108: 1st Ed., Plymouth, Mass., 1822. A book of no value.

GARTLEY, G.; English Grammar; 18mo, pp. 225: 1st Edition, London, 1830.

GAY, ANTHELME; "A French Prosodical Grammar;" for English or American Students; 12mo, pp. 215: New York, 1795.

GIBBS, Prof. J. W., of Yale C.; on Dialects, Sounds, and Derivations. See about 126 pages, credited to this gentleman, in Prof. Fowler's large Grammar, of 1850.

GILBERT, ELI; a "Catechetical Grammar;" 18mo, pp. 124: 1st Ed., 1834; 2d Ed., New York, 1835.

GILCHRIST, JAMES; English Grammar; 8vo, pp. 269: 1st Edition, London, 1815.

GILES, JAMES; English Grammar; 12mo, pp. 152: London, 1804; 2d Ed., 1810.

GILES, Rev. T. A., A. M.; English Grammar; 12mo, London, 2d Ed., 1838.

GILL, ALEXANDER; English Grammar, treated in Latin; 4to: London, 1621.

GILLEADE, G.; English Grammar; 12mo, pp. 206: London; 1st Edition, 1816.

GIRAULT DU VIVIER, CH. P.; (1.) "La Grammaire des Grammaires;" two thick volumes, 8vo: Paris; 2d Ed., 1814. (2.) "Traité des Participes;" 8vo, pp. 84: 2d Ed., Paris, 1816.

GOLDSBURY, JOHN, A. M.; (1.) "The Common School Grammar;" 12mo, pp. 94: 1st Ed., Boston, 1842. (2.) "Sequel to the Common School Grammar;" 12mo, pp. 110: 1st Ed., Boston, 1842.

GOODENOW, SMITH B.; "A Systematic Text-Book of English Grammar;" 12mo, pp. 144: 1st Edition, Portland, 1839; 2d Edition, Boston, 1843.

GOUGH, JOHN and JAMES; English Grammar; 18mo, pp. 212: 2d Ed., Dublin, 1760.

GOULD, BENJAMIN A.; "Adam's Lat. Gram., with Improvements;" 12mo, pp. 300: Boston, 1829.

GRAHAM, G. F.; English Grammar; 12mo, pp. 134: 1st Ed., London, 1843.

GRANT, JOHN, A. M.; (1.) "Institutes of Latin Grammar;" 8vo, pp. 453: London, 1808. (2.) A Comprehensive English Grammar; 12mo, pp. 410: 1st Ed., London, 1813.

GRANVILLE, GEO.; E. Gram., 12mo: Lond., 1827.

GRAY, JAMES, D. D.; English Grammar; 18mo, pp. 144: 1st Ed., Baltimore, 1818.

GREEN, MATTHIAS; English Grammar; 12mo, pp. 148: 1st Ed., London, 1837.

GREEN, RICHARD W.; "Inductive Exercises in English Grammar;" 18mo, pp. 108: 1st Ed., New York, 1829; 5th Ed., Phila., 1834.

GREENE. ROSCOE G.; (1.) E. Gram.; 12mo, pp. 132: Hallowell, Me; 1st Ed., 1828; Ster. Ed., 1835. (2.) "A Practical Grammar of the English Language;" (with Diagrams of Moods;) 12mo: Portland, 1829. (3.) "A Grammatical Text-Book, being an Abstract of a Practical Gram, &c.;" 12mo, pp. 69: Boston, 1833.

GREENE, SAMUEL S.; (1.) "Analysis of Sentences;" 12mo, pp. 258: 1st Ed., Philadelphia, 1848. (2.) "First Lessons in Grammar;" 18mo, pp. 171: 1st Ed., Philad., 1848.

GREENLEAF, JEREMIAH; "Grammar Simplified;" 4to, pp. 48: New York; 3d Ed., 1821; 20th Ed., 1837.

GREENWOOD, JAMES; English Grammar; 12mo, pp. 315: London, 1711; 2d Ed, 1722.

GRENVILLE, A. S.; "Introduction to English Grammar;" 12mo, pp. 63: 1st Ed., Boston, 1822.

GRISCOM, JOHN, LL. D.; "Questions in English Grammar;" 18mo, pp. 42: 1st Ed., New York, 1821.

GURNEY, DAVID, A. M.; English Grammar; 18mo, pp. 72: Boston, 1801; 2d Ed., 1808.

GUY, JOSEPH, Jun.; "English School Grammar;" 18mo, pp. 143: 4th Ed., London, 1816.

HALL, Rev. S. R.; "The Grammatical Assistant;" 12mo, pp. 131: 1st Ed., Springfield, Mass , 1832.

HALL, WILLIAM; "Encyclopædia of English Grammar;" (by report ;) Ohio, 1850.

HALLOCK, EDWARD J., A. M.; "A Grammar of the English Language;" 12mo, pp. 251; 1st Ed., New York, 1842. A very inaccurate book, with sundry small plagiarisms from G. Brown.

HAMLIN, LORENZO F.; "English Grammar in Lectures;" 12mo, pp. 108: New York, 1831; Ster. Ed., 1832.

HAMMOND, SAMUEL; E. Gram.; 8vo: Lond., 1744.

HARRIS, JAMES, Esq.; "Hermes, or a Philosophical Inquiry concerning Universal Grammar;" 8vo, pp. 468: London, 1751: 6th Ed., 1806.

HARRISON, Mr.; "Rudiments of English Grammar;" 18mo, pp. 108: 9th American Ed., Philad., 1812.

HARRISON, Rev. MATTHEW, A. M.; "The Rise, Progress, and Present Structure of the English Language;" 12mo, pp. 393: Preface dated, Basingstoke, Eng., 1848; 1st American Ed., Philadelphia, 1850.

HART, JOHN S., A. M.; "English Grammar;" 12mo, pp. 192; 1st Ed., Philadelphia, 1845.

HARVEY, J.; English Grammar: Lond., 1841.

HAZEN, EDWARD, A. M.; "A Practical Grammar of the E. Language;" 12mo, pp. 240: New York, 1842.

HAZLITT, WILLIAM; English Grammar; 18mo, pp. 205: London, 1810.

HENDRICK, J. L., A. M.; "A Grammatical Manual;" 18mo, pp. 105: 1st Ed., Syracuse, N. Y., 1844.

HEWES, JOHN, A. M.; E. Gram.; 4to: London, 1624.

HEWETT, D.; English Grammar; folio, pp. 16: 1st Edition, New York. 1838.

HIGGINSON, Rev. T. E.; E. Gram.; 12mo: Dublin, 1803.

HILEY, RICHARD; "A Treatise on English Grammar," &c.: 12mo, pp. 269: 3d Ed., London, 1840. Hiley's Grammar Abridged; 18mo, pp. 196: London, 1843: 4th Ed., 1841.

HILL, J. H.; "On the Subjunctive Mood;" 8vo, pp. 63: 1st Ed., London, 1834.

HODGSON, Rev. ISAAC; English Grammar; 18mo, pp. 184: 1st Ed., London, 1770.

HOME, HENRY, Lord Kames; "Elements of Criticism;" 2 volumes 8vo, pp. 836: (3d American, from the 8th London Ed.:) New York, 1819. Also, "The Art of Thinking;" 12mo, pp. 284: (from the last London Ed.:) New York, 1818.

HORNSEY, JOHN; English Grammar; 12mo, pp. 144: York, England, 1793; 6th Ed., 1816.

HORT, W. JILLARD; English Grammar; 18mo, pp. 219: 1st Ed., London, 1822.

HOUGHTON, JOHN; E. Gram., 8vo: London, 1766.

HOUSTON, SAMUEL, A. B.; English Grammar; 12mo, pp. 48: 1st Ed., Harrisburgh, Pa., 1818.

HOWE, S. L.; English Grammar; 18mo: 1st Ed., Lancaster, Ohio, 1838.

HOWELL, JAMES; E. Gram., 12mo: London, 1662.

HULL, JOSEPH HERVEY; "E. Gram., by Lectures;" 12mo, pp. 72: 4th Ed., Boston, 1828.

HUMPHREY, ASA; (1.) "The English Prosody;" 12mo, pp. 175: 1st Ed., Boston, 1847. (2.) "The Rules of Punctuation;" with "Rules for the Use of Capitals;" 18mo, pp. 71: 1st Ed., Boston, 1847.

HURD, S. T.; E. Gram. ; 2d Ed., Boston, 1827.

HUTHERSAL, JOHN; E. Gram.; 18mo: Eng., 1814.

INGERSOLL, CHARLES M.: "Conversations on English Grammar;" 12mo, pp. 296: New York, 1821.

JAMIESON, ALEXANDER; "A Grammar of Rhetoric and Polite Literature;" 12mo, pp. 345: "The first American, from the last London Edition;" Newhaven, 1820.

JAUDON, DANIEL; "The Union Grammar;" 18mo, pp. 216: Philadelphia; 1st Ed., 1812; 4th, 1828.

JENKINS, AZARIAH; English Grammar; 12mo, pp. 256: 1st Ed., Rochester, N. Y., 1835.

JOEL, THOMAS; English Grammar; 12mo, pp. 78: 1st Ed., London, 1775.

JOHNSON, RICHARD; "Grammatical Commentaries;" (chiefly on Lily;) 8vo, pp. 436: London, 1706.

JOHNSON, SAMUEL, LL.D.; "A Dictionary of the English language;" in two thick volumes, 4to: 1st American, from the 11th London Edition; Philadelphia, 1818. To this work, are prefixed Johnson's "History of the English Language," pp. 29; and his "Grammar of the English Tongue," pp. 14.

JONES, JOSHUA; E. Gram.; 18mo: Phila., 1841.

JONSON, BEN;—see, in his Works, "The English Grammar, made by Ben Jonson, for the Benefit of all strangers, out of his Observation of the English Language, now spoken and in use:" London, 1634: 8vo, pp. 94; Lond., 1816.

JUDSON, ADONIRAM, Jun., A. B.; English Grammar; 12mo, pp. 56: 1st Ed., Boston, 1808.

KENNION, CHARLOTTE; English Grammar; 12mo, pp. 157: 1st Ed., London, 1842.

KILSON, ROGER; E. Gram.; 12mo: England, 1807.

KING, WALTER W.; English Grammar; 18mo, pp. 76: 1st Ed., London, 1841.

KIRKHAM, SAMUEL; "English Grammar in Familiar Lectures;" 12mo, pp. 144—228: 2d Ed., Harrisburgh, Pa., 1825; 12th Ed., New York, 1829.

KNOWLES, JOHN; "The Principles of English Grammar;" 12mo: 3d Ed., London, 1794.

KNOWLTON, JOSEPH; English Grammar; 18mo, pp. 84: Salem, Mass., 1818; 2d Ed., 1832.

LATHAM, R. G., A. M.; (l.) "The English Language;" 8vo, pp. 418: 1st Ed., London, 1841. (2.) "English Grammar;" 12mo, pp. 214: 1st Ed., London, 1843.

LEAVITT, DUDLEY; English Grammar; 24to, pp. 60: 1st Ed., Concord, N. H., 1826.

LENNIE, WILLIAM; "The Principles of English Grammar;" 18mo, pp. 142: 5th Ed., Edinburgh, 1819: 13th Ed., 1831.

LEWIS, ALONZO; "Lessons in English Grammar;" 18mo, pp. 50: 1st Ed., Boston, 1822.

LEWIS, JOHN; English Grammar; 18mo, pp. 48: 1st Ed., New York, 1818.

LEWIS, WILLIAM GREATHEAD; English Grammar; 18mo, pp. 204: 1st Ed., London, 1821.

LILY, WILLIAM; "Brevissima Institutio, seu Ratio Grammatices cognoscendæ;" large 18mo, pp. 140: London, 1793.

LINDSAY, Rev. JOHN, A. M.; English Grammar; 18mo, pp. 88: 1st Ed., London, 1842

LOCKE, JOHN, M. D.; small English Grammar; 18mo: 1st Ed., Cincinnati, Ohio, 1827.

LOUGHTON, WILLIAM; English Grammar; 12mo, pp. 194: 2d Ed., London, 1739.

LOVECHILD, Mrs.; English Grammar; 18mo, pp. 72: 40th Ed., London, 1842.

LOWTH, ROBERT, D. D.; "A Short Introduction to English Grammar;" 18mo, pp. 132: London, 1763;—Philadelphia, 1799;—Cambridge, Mass., 1838.

LYNDE, JOHN; English Grammar; 18mo, pp. 108: 1st Ed., Woodstock, Vt., 1821.

MACK, EVERED J.; "The Self-Instructor, and Practical English Grammar;" 12mo, pp. 180: 1st Ed., Springfield, Mass., 1835. An egregious plagiarism from G. Brown.

MACGOWAN, Rev. JAMES; English Grammar; 18mo, pp. 248: London, 1825.

MACKINTOSH, DUNCAN; "An Essay on English Grammar;" 8vo, pp. 239: Boston, 1797.

MACKILQUHEM, WILLIAM; English Grammar; 12mo: Glasgow, 1799.

MAITTAIRE, MICHAEL; English Grammar; 8vo, pp. 272: London, 1712.

MARCET, Mrs.; English Grammar; 18mo, pp. 331: 7th Ed., London, 1843.

MARTIN, BENJ.; English Grammar; 12mo: London, 1754.

MATHESON, JOHN; English Grammar; 18mo, pp. 138: 2d Ed., London, 1821.

MAUNDER, SAMUEL; Grammar prefixed to Dictionary; 12mo, pp. 20: 1st Ed., London, 1830.

MAVOR, WILLIAM; English Grammar; 18mo, pp. 70: 1st Ed., London, 1820.

M'CREADY, F.; 12mo Grammar: Philad., 1820.

M'CULLOCH, J. M., D. D.; "A Manual of English Grammar;" 18mo, pp. 188: 7th Ed., Edinburgh, 1841.

M'ELLIGOTT, JAMES N.; "Manual, Analytical and Synthetical, of Orthography and Definition;" 8vo, pp. 223: 1st Ed., New York, 1846. Also, "The Young Analyzer;" 12mo, pp. 54: New York, 1846.

MEILAN, MARK A.; English Grammar; 12mo: London, 1803.

MENDENHALL, WILLIAM; "The Classification of Words;" 12mo, pp. 36: Philad., 1814.

MENNYE, J.; "English Grammar;" 8vo, pp. 124: 1st Ed., New York, 1785.

MERCHY, BLANCHE; English Grammar; 12mo, 2 vols., pp. 248: 1st Ed., London, 1799.

MERCHANT, AARON M.; Murray's small Grammar, Enlarged; 18mo, pp. 216: N. Y., 1824.

MILLER, ALEXANDER; English Grammar; 12mo, pp. 119: 1st Ed., New York, 1795.

MILLER, The Misses; English Grammar; 18mo, pp. 63: 1st Ed., London, 1830.

MILLER, FERDINAND H.; "The Ready Grammarian;" square 12mo, pp. 24: Ithaca, New York, 1843.

MILLER, TOBIAS HAM; Murray's Abridgement, with Questions; 12mo, pp. 76: Portsmouth, N. H., 1823.

MILLIGAN, Rev. GEORGE; English Grammar; 18mo, pp. 72: Edin., 1831; 2d Ed., 1839.

MOORE, THOMAS; "Orthography and Pronunciation;" 12mo, pp. 176: London, 1810.

MORGAN, JONATHAN, Jun., A. B.; English Grammar; 12mo, pp. 405: 1st Ed., Hallowell, Me., 1814.

MORLEY, CHARLES, A. B.; "School Grammar;" 12mo, pp. 86: (with Cuts:) 1st Ed., Hartford, Ct., 1836.

MOREY, AMOS C.; English Grammar; 18mo, pp. 106: Albany, N. Y., 1829.

MULKEY, WILLIAM; "An Abridgment of Walker's Rules on the Sounds of the Letters;" 18mo, pp. 124: Boston, 1834. Fudge!

MURRAY, ALEXANDER, D. D.; "The History of European Languages;" in two vols., 8vo; pp. 800.

MURRAY, ALEXANDER, Schoolmaster; "Easy English Grammar;" 12mo, pp. 194: 3d Ed., London, 1793.

MURRAY, LINDLEY; (1.) "English Grammar, Adapted to the Different Classes of Learners;" 12mo, pp. 284: York, Eng., 1796; 2d Ed., 1796; 23d Ed., 1816. (2.) "Abridgment of Murray's English Grammar;" 18mo, pp. 105: "From the 30th English Ed.," New York, 1817. (3.) "An English Grammar;" in two volumes, octavo; pp. 684: 4th American, from the last English Ed.; New York, 1819. (4.) A Spelling-Book; 18mo, pp. 180: New York, 1819.

MYLINS, WM. F.; Gram., 12mo: England, 1809.

MYLNE, Rev. A., D. D.; English Grammar; 18mo, pp. 180: 11th Ed., Edinburgh, 1832.

NESBIT, A.; "An Introd. to English Parsing;" 18mo, pp. 213: 2d Ed., York, England, 1823.

NEWBURY, JOHN; English Grammar; 12mo, pp. 162: 5th Ed., London, 1787.

NIGHTINGALE, Rev. J.; English Grammar; 12mo, pp. 96: 1st Ed., London, 1822.

NIXON, H.; (1.) "The English Parser;" 12mo, pp. 164: 1st Ed., London, 1826. (2.) "New and Comprehensive English Grammar;" 12mo: 1st Ed., London, 1833.

NUTTING, RUFUS, A. M.; "A Practical Grammar;" 12mo, pp. 144: 3d Ed., Montpelier, Vt., 1826.

ODELL, J., A. M.; English Grammar; 12mo, pp. 205: 1st Ed, London, 1806.

OLIVER, EDWARD, D. D.; English Grammar; 12mo, pp. 178: 1st Ed., London, 1807.

OLIVER, SAMUEL; English Grammar; 8vo, pp. 377: 1st Ed., London, 1825.

PALMER, MARY; English Grammar; 12mo, pp. 48: New York, 1803.

PARKER, RICHARD GREEN; (1.) "Exercises in Composition;" 12mo, pp. 106: 3d Ed., Boston, 1833. (2.) "Aids to English Composition;" 12mo, pp. 418: 1st Ed., Boston, 1844.

PARKER and FOX; "Progressive Exercises in English Grammar;" in three separate parts, 12mo:—Part I, pp. 96; Boston, 1834: Part II, pp. 60; Boston, 1835: Part III, pp. 122; Boston, 1840.

PARKHURST, JOHN L.; (1.) A "Systematic Introduction to English Grammar;" 18mo, pp. 104: Concord, N. H., 1820; 2d Ed., 1824. (2.) "English Grammar for Beginners;" 18mo, pp. 180: 1st Ed., Andover, Mass., 1838.

PARSONS, SAMUEL H.; English Grammar; 18mo, pp. 107: 1st Ed., Philadelphia, 1836.

PEIRCE, JOHN; "The New American Spelling-Book," with "A Plain and Easy Introduction to English Grammar;" 12mo, pp. 200: 6th Ed., Philadelphia, 1804. This Grammar is mostly copied from Harrison's.

PEIRCE, OLIVER B.; "The Grammar of the English Language;" 12mo, pp. 384: 1st Ed., New York, 1839. Also, Abridgement of the same; 18mo, pp. 144: Boston, 1840.

PENGELLEY, EDWARD; English Gram.; 18mo, pp. 108: 1st Ed., London, 1840.

PERLEY, DANIEL, M. D.; "A Grammar of the E. Lang.:" 18mo, pp. 79: 1st Ed., Andover, Mass., 1834.

PERRY, WILLIAM; Grammar in Dict.; 12mo: Edinburgh, 1801.

PICKBOURN, JAMES; "Dissertation on the English Verb:" London, 1789.

PICKET, ALBERT; "Analytical School Grammar;" 18mo, pp. 252: New York, 1823; 2d Ed., 1824.

PINNOCK, W.; (1.) A Catechism of E. Gram.;

18mo, pp. 70: 18th Ed., London, 1825. (2.) A Comprehensive Grammar; 12mo, pp. 318: 1st Ed., London, 1829.

POND, ENOCH, D. D.; "Murray's System of Eng. Grammar, Improved;" 12mo, pp. 228: 5th Ed., Worcester, Mass., 1835. Also, under the same title, a petty Grammar with Cuts; 18mo, pp. 71: New Ed., Worcester, 1835.

POWERS, DANIEL, A. M.;' E. Grammar; 12mo, pp. 188: 1st Ed., West Brookfield, Mass., 1845.

PRIESTLEY, JOSEPH, LL.D.; "The Rudiments of E. Gram.;" 18mo, pp. 202: 3d Ed., London, 1772.

PUE, HUGH A.; English Grammar; 18mo, pp. 149: 1st Ed., Philadelphia, 1841.

PULLEN, P. H.; English Grammar; 12mo, pp. 321: London, 1820; 2d Ed., 1822.

PUTNAM, J. M.; "Eng. Gram.;" (Murray's, Modified;) 18mo, pp. 162: Concord, N. H., 1825; Ster., 1831.

PUTNAM, SAMUEL; "Putnam's Murray;" 18mo, pp. 108: Improved Ster. Ed.; Dover, N. H., 1828.

PUTSEY, Rev. W.; English Grammar; 18mo, pp. 211: London, 1821: 2d Ed., 1829.

RAND, ASA; "Teacher's Manual," &c.; 18mo, pp. 90: 1st Ed., Boston, 1832.

REED, CALEB, A. M.; English Grammar; 18mo, pp. 36: 1st Ed., Boston, 1821.

REID, A.; English Grammar; 18mo, pp. 46: 2d Ed., London, 1839.

REID, JOHN, M. D.; English Grammar; 12mo, pp. 68: 1st Ed., Glasgow, 1830.

RIGAN, JOHN; Grammar, 12mo: Dublin, 1823.

ROBBINS, MANASSEH; "Rudimental Lessons in Etym. and Synt.;" 12mo, pp. 70: Prov., R. I., 1826.

ROBINSON, JOHN; English Grammar; 12mo, pp. 95: 1st Ed., Maysville, 1830.

ROOMR, Rev. T.; Gram.; 12mo: Eng., 1813.

ROSS, ROBERT; an American Grammar; 12mo, pp. 199: 7th Ed., Hartford, Ct, 1782.

ROTHWELL, J.; English Grammar; 12mo: 2d Ed., London, 1797.

ROZZELL, WM.; English Grammar in Verse; 8vo: London, 1795.

RUSH, JAMES, M. D.; "Philosophy of the Human Voice;" 8vo: Philadelphia, 1833.

RUSSELL, Rev. J., D. D.; English Grammar; 18mo, pp. 168: London, 1835; 10th Ed., 1842.

RUSSELL, WILLIAM; (1.) "A Grammar of Composition;" 12mo, pp. 150: Newhaven, 1823. (2.) "Lessons in Enunciation:" Boston, 1841. (3.) "Orthophony; or the Cultivation of the Voice;" 12mo, pp. 300: Improved Ed., Boston, 1847.

RUSSELL, WILLIAM E.; "An Abridgment of Murray's Grammar;" 18mo, pp. 142: Hartford, 1819.

RYLAND, JOHN; English Grammar; 18mo, pp. 164: 1st Ed., Northampton, Eng., 1767.

SABINE, H., A. M.; English Grammar; 18mo, pp. 120: 1st Ed., London, 1702.

SANBORN, DYER H.; "An Analytical Grammar of the English Language;" 12mo, pp. 299: 1st Ed., Concord, N. H., 1836.

SANDERS, CHARLES W. and J. C.; "The Young Grammarian;" 12mo, pp. 120: Rochester, N. Y., 1847.

SCOTT, WILLIAM; Gram., 12mo: Edinb., 1777.

SEARLE, Rev. THOMAS; Grammar in Verse; 18mo, pp. 114: 1st Ed., London, 1822.

SHATFORD, W.; English Grammar; 18mo, pp. 104: 1st Ed., London, 1834.

SHAW, Rev. JOHN; English Grammar; 12mo, pp. 250: 4th Ed., London. 1793.

SHERIDAN, THOMAS, A. M.; (1.) "Lectures on Elocution;" 12mo, pp. 185: London, 1762; Troy, N. Y., 1803. (2.) "Lectures on the Art of Reading." (3.) "A Rhetorical Grammar;" square 12mo, pp. 73: 3d Ed., Philadelphia, 1789. (4.) "Elements of English;" 12mo, pp. 69: Dublin, 1789. (5.) "A Complete Dictionary of the English Language;" 1st Ed., 1780.

SHERMAN, JOHN; American Grammar; 12mo, pp. 323: 1st Ed., Trenton Falls, N.Y., 1826.

SIMMONITE, W. J.; English Grammar; 12mo, pp. 228: 1st Ed., London, 1841.

SKILLERN, R. S., A. M.; English Grammar; 12mo, pp. 184: 2d Ed., Gloucester, England, 1808.

SMART, B. H.; (1.) "A Practical Grammar of English Pronunciation;" 8vo: London, 1810. (2.) "The Accidence of English Grammar;" 12mo, pp. 52: London, 1841. (3.) "The Accidence and Principles of English Grammar;" 12mo, pp. 280: London, 1841.

SMETHAM, THOMAS; English Grammar; 12mo, pp. 168: 1st Ed., London, 1774.

SMITH, ELI; English Grammar; 18mo, pp. 108: 1st Ed., Philadelphia, 1812.

SMITH, JOHN; Grammar, 8vo: Norwich, Eng., 1816.

SMITH, PETER, A. M.; English Grammar; 18mo, pp. 176: 1st Ed., Edinburgh, 1826.

SMITH, Rev. THOMAS; (1.) Alderson's "Orthographical Exercises." Copied; 18mo, pp. 108: 15th Ed., London, 1819. (2.) "Smith's Edition of L. Murray's Grammar;" 18mo, pp. 128: London, 1832. Very petty authorship.

SMITH, ROSWELL C.; (1.) "English Grammar on the Inductive System;" 12mo, pp. 205: Boston, 1830; 2d Ed., 1831. (2.) "English Grammar on the Productive System;" 12mo, pp. 192: 2d Ed., New York, 1832. A sham.

SNYDER, W.; English Grammar; 12mo, pp. 164: 1st Ed., Winchester, Va., 1834.

SPALDING, CHARLES; English Grammar; 8vo, pp. 36: 1st Ed., Onondaga, N. Y., 1825.

SPEAR, MATTHEW P.; "The Teacher's Manual of E. Gram.;" 12mo, pp. 116: 1st Ed., Boston, 1845.

STANIFORD, DANIEL, A. M.; "Short but Comp. Gram.;" 12mo, pp. 96: Boston, 1807; 2d Ed., 1815.

STEARNS, GEORGE; English Grammar; 4to, pp. 17: 1st Ed., Boston, 1843.

STOCKWOOD, JOHN; Gram., 4to: London, 1590.

STORY, JOSHUA; English Grammar; 12mo, pp. 180: 1st Ed., Newcastle, Eng., 1778; 3d, 1783.

ST. QUENTIN, D., M. A.; "The Rudiments of General Gram.;" 12mo, pp. 163: Lond., 1812.

SUTCLIFFE, JOSEPH, A. M.; English Grammar; 12mo, pp. 262: London, 1815; 2d Ed., 1821.

SWETT, J, A. M.; English Grammar; 12mo, pp. 192: Claremont, N. H., 1843; 2d Ed., 1844.

TICKEN, WILLIAM; English Grammar; 12mo, pp. 147: 1st Ed., London, 1806.

TICKNOR, ELISHA, A. M.; English Grammar; 18mo, pp. 72: 3d Ed., Boston, 1794.

TOBITT, R.; "Grammatical Institutes;" (in Verse;) 12mo, pp. 72: 1st Ed., London, 1825.

TODD, LEWIS C.; English Grammar; 18mo, pp. 126: Fredonia, N. Y., 1826; 2d Ed., 1827.

TOOKE, JOHN HORNE, A. M.; "Epea Pteroenta; or, the Diversions of Purley;" 2 vols., 8vo; pp. 924: 1st American, from the 2d London Ed.; Philadelphia, 1806.

TOWER, DAVID B., A. M.; "Gradual Lessons in Grammar;" small 12mo, pp. 180: Boston, 1847.

TRINDER, WILLIAM M.; English Grammar; 12mo, pp. 116: 1st Ed., London, 1781.

TUCKER, BENJAMIN; "A Short Introd. to E. Gram.;" 18mo, pp. 36: 4th Ed., Phila., 1812.

TURNER, DANIEL, A. M.; English Grammar; 8vo: London, 1739.

TURNER, Rev. BRANDON, A.M.; Grammar from G. Brown's Inst.; 12mo, pp. 238: Lond., 1841.

TWITCHELL, MARK; English Grammar; 18mo, pp. 106: 1st Ed., Portland, Me., 1825.

USSHER, G. NEVILLE; E. Gram.; 12mo, pp. 132: London, 1787; 3d Amer. Ed., Exeter, N. H. 1804.

WALDO, JOHN; "Rudiments," 12mo; Philad., 1813: "Abridg't," 18mo, pp. 124; Philadelphia, 1814.

WALKER, JOHN; E. Gram., 12mo, pp. 118; London, 1805; Rhyming Dict., 12mo; Pronouncing Dict., 8vo; and other valuable works.

WALKER, WILLIAM, B. D.; (1.) "A Treatise of English Particles;" 12mo, pp. 488: London, 1653; 10th Ed., 1691. (2.) "The Art of Teaching Grammar;" large 18mo, pp. 226: 8th Ed., London, 1717.

WALLIS, JOHN, D. D.; E. Gram. in Latin; 8vo, pp. 281: Lond., 1653; 6th Ed., 1765.

WARD, H.; English Grammar; 12mo, pp. 151: Whitehaven, England, 1777.

WARD, JOHN, LL.D.; English Grammar; 12mo, pp. 238: London, 1758.

WARD, WILLIAM, A. M.; "A Practical Grammar; " 12mo, pp. 192: York, England, 1765.

WARE, JONATHAN, Esq.; "A New Introduction to E. Grammar;" 12mo, pp. 48: Windsor, Vt., 1814.

WASE, CHRISTOPHER, M. A.; "An Essay of a Practical Gram.; " 12mo, pp. 79: Lond., 1660.

WATT, THOMAS, A. M.; "Gram. Made Easy;" 18mo, pp. 92: Edinburgh, 1703; 5th Ed., 1742.

WEBBER, SAMUEL, A. M., M. D.; "An Introd. to E. Grammar;" 12mo, pp. 116: Cambridge, Mass., 1832.

WEBSTER, NOAH, LL.D.; (1.) "A Plain and Comprehensive Grammar;" 12mo, pp. 131: 6th Ed., Hartford, Ct., 1800. (2.) "A Philosophical and Practical Grammar;" 12mo, pp. 250: Newhaven, Ct., 1807. (3.) "Rudiments of English Grammar;" 18mo, pp. 87: New York, 1811. (4.) "An Improved Grammar of the E. L.;" 12mo, pp. 180: Newhaven, 1831. (5.) "An American Dictionary of the E. L.," 4to; and an Abridgement, 8vo.

WELD, ALLEN H., A. M.; "English Grammar Illustrated;" 12mo, pp. 228: Portland, Me., 1846; 2d Ed., 1847: "Abridged Edition," Boston, 1849.

WELLS, WILLIAM H., M. A.; "Wells's School Grammar;" 12mo, pp. 220: 1st Ed., Andover, 1846; "113th Thousand," 1850.

WHITE, Mr. JAMES; "The English Verb;" 8vo, pp. 302: 1st Ed., London, 1761.

WHITING, JOSEPH, A. M.; English Grammar; 12mo: Detroit, 1845.

WHITWORTH, T.; English Grammar; 12mo, pp. 216: 1st Ed., London, 1819.

WICKES, EDWARD WALTER; English Grammar; 18mo, pp. 196: 2d Ed., London, 1841.

WILBUR & LIVINGSTON; "The Grammatical Alphabet;" (with a Chart;) 18mo, pp. 36: 2d Ed., Albany, 1815.

WILBUR, JOSIAH; English Grammar; 12mo, pp. 132: Bellows Falls, N. H., 1815; 2d Ed. 1822.

WILCOX, A. F.; "A Catechetical and Practical Grammar;" 18mo, pp. 110: 1st Ed, Newhaven, Ct., 1828.

WILLARD, SAMUEL; English Grammar; 18mo, pp. 54: 1st Ed., Greenfield, Mass., 1816.

WILLIAMS, Mrs. HONORIA; English Grammar; 12mo, pp. 226: London, 1823; 3d Ed., 1826.

WILSON, CHARLES, D. D.; "Elements of Hebrew Grammar;" 8vo, pp. 398: 3d-Ed., London, 1802.

WILSON, GEORGE; English Grammar; 18mo: London, 1777.

WILSON, JAMES P., D. D.; "An Essay on Grammar;" 8vo, pp. 281: Philadelphia, 1817.

WILSON, JOHN; "A Treatise on English Punctuation;" 12mo, pp. 204: Boston, 1850.

WILSON, Rev. J.; English Grammar; 18mo, pp. 184: 3d Ed., Congleton, England, 1803.

WISEMAN, CHARLES; an English Grammar, 12mo: London, 1765.

WOOD, HELEN; English Grammar; 12mo, pp. 207: London, 1st Ed., 1827; 6th Ed., 1841.

WOOD, Rev. JAMES, D. D.; English Grammar, 12mo: London, 1778.

WOODWORTH, A.; "Grammar Demonstrated;" 12mo, pp. 72: 1st Ed., Auburn, N. Y., 1823.

WORCESTER, JOSEPH E.; "Universal and Critical Dictionary of the English Language;" 1st Ed., Boston, 1846.

WORCESTER, SAMUEL; "A First Book of English Grammar;" 18mo, pp. 36: Boston, 1831.

WRIGHT, ALBERT D.; "Analytical Orthography;" 18mo, pp. 112: 2d Ed., Cazenovia, N. Y., 1842.

WRIGHT, JOSEPH W.; "A Philosophical Grammar of the English Language;" 12mo, pp. 252: New York and London, 1838.

END OF THE CATALOGUE.

INTRODUCTION

HISTORICAL AND CRITICAL.

CHAPTER I.

OF THE SCIENCE OF GRAMMAR.

"Hæc de Grammatica quam brevissime potui : non ut omnia dicerem sectatus, (quod infinitum erat,) sed ut maxime necessaria."—QUINTILIAN. Lib. i, Cap. x.

1. LANGUAGE, in the proper sense of the term, is peculiar to man ; so that, without a miraculous assumption of human powers, none but human beings can make words the vehicle of thought. An imitation of some of the articulate sounds employed in speech, may be exhibited by parrots, and sometimes by domesticated ravens, and we know that almost all brute animals have their peculiar natural voices, by which they indicate their feelings, whether pleasing or painful. But *language* is an attribute of reason, and differs essentially not only from all brute voices, but even from all the chattering, jabbering, and babbling of our own species, in which there is not an intelligible meaning, with division of thought, and distinction of words.

2. Speech results from the joint exercise of the best and noblest faculties of human nature, from our rational understanding and our social affection ; and is, in the proper use of it, the peculiar ornament and distinction of man, whether we compare him with other orders in the creation, or view him as an individual preëminent among his fellows. Hence that science which makes known the nature and structure of speech, and immediately concerns the correct and elegant use of language, while it surpasses all the conceptions of the stupid or unlearned, and presents nothing that can seem desirable to the sensual and grovelling, has an intrinsic dignity which highly commends it to all persons of sense and taste, and makes it most a favourite with the most gifted minds. That science is Grammar. And though there be some geniuses who affect to despise the trammels of grammar rules, to whom it must be conceded that many things which have been unskillfully taught as such, deserve to be despised ; yet it is true, as Dr. Adam remarks, that, "The study of Grammar has been considered an object of great importance by the wisest men in all ages."—*Preface to Latin and English Gram.*, p iii.

3. Grammar bears to language several different relations, and acquires from each a nature leading to a different definition. *First*, It is to language, as knowl-

1

edge is to the thing known ; and as doctrine, to the truths it inculcates.   In these relations, grammar is a science.   It is the first of what have been called the seven sciences, or liberal branches of knowledge ; namely, grammar, logic, rhetoric, arithmetic, geometry, astronomy, and music. *Secondly*, It is as skill, to the thing to be done ; and as power, to the instruments it employs.   In these relations, grammar is an art ; and as such, has long been defined, "*ars rectè scribendi, rectèque loquendi*," the art of writing and speaking correctly. *Thirdly*, It is as navigation, to the ocean, which nautic skill alone enables men to traverse.   In this relation, theory and practice combine, and grammar becomes, like navigation, a practical science. *Fourthly*, It is as a chart, to a coast which we would visit.   In this relation, our grammar is a text-book, which we take as a guide, or use as a help to our own observation. *Fifthly*, It is as a single voyage, to the open sea, the highway of nations   Such is our meaning, when we speak of the grammar of a particular text or passage.

4. Again : Grammar is to language a sort of self-examination.   It turns the faculty of speech or writing upon itself for its own elucidation ; and makes the tongue or the pen explain the uses and abuses to which both are liable, as well as the nature and excellency of that power, of which these are the two grand instruments.   From this account, some may begin to think that in treating of grammar we are dealing with something too various and changeable for the understanding to grasp ; a dodging Proteus of the imagination, who is ever ready to assume some new shape, and elude the vigilance of the inquirer.   But let the reader or student do his part ; and, if he please, follow us with attention.   We will endeavour, with welded links, to bind this Proteus, in such a manner that he shall neither escape from our hold, nor fail to give to the consulter an intelligible and satisfactory response.   Be not discouraged, generous youth.   Hark to that sweet far-reaching note :

> " Sed, quanto ille magis formas se vertet in omnes,
>   Tanto, nate, magis contende tenacia vincla."
>   VIRGIL. Geor. IV, 411.

> " But thou, the more he varies forms, beware
>   To strain his fetters with a stricter care."   DRYDEN'S VIRGIL.

5. If for a moment we consider the good and the evil that are done in the world through the medium of speech, we shall with one voice acknowledge, that not only the faculty itself, but also the manner in which it is used, is of incalculable importance to the welfare of man.   But this reflection does not directly enhance our respect for grammar, because it is not to language as the vehicle of moral or of immoral sentiment, of good or of evil to mankind, that the attention of the grammarian is particularly directed.   A consideration of the subject in these relations, pertains rather to the moral philosopher.   Nor are the arts of logic and rhetoric now considered to be properly within the grammarian's province.   Modern science assigns to these their separate places, and restricts grammar, which at one period embraced all learning, to the knowledge of language, as respects its fitness to be the vehicle of any particular thought or sentiment which the speaker or writer may wish to convey by it.   Accordingly grammar is commonly defined, by writers upon the subject, in the special sense of an art—" the *art* of speaking or writing a language with propriety or correctness."—*Webster's Dict.*

6. Lily says, " Grammatica est rectè scribendi atque loquendi ars ;" that is, " Grammar is the art of writing and speaking correctly."   Despauter, too, in his definition, which is quoted in a preceding paragraph, not improperly placed writing first, as being that with which grammar is primarily concerned.   For it ought to be remembered, that over any fugitive colloquial dialect, which has never been fixed by visible signs, grammar has no control ; and that the speaking which the

art or science of grammar teaches, is exclusively that which has reference to a knowledge of letters. It is the certain tendency of writing, to improve speech. And in proportion as books are multiplied, and the knowledge of written language is diffused, local dialects, which are beneath the dignity of grammar, will always be found to grow fewer, and their differences less. There are, in the various parts of the world, many languages to which the art of grammar has never yet been applied; and to which, therefore, the definition or true idea of grammar, however general, does not properly extend. And even where it has been applied, and is now honoured as a popular branch of study, there is yet great room for improvement: barbarisms and solecisms have not been rebuked away as they deserve to be.

7. Melancthon says, "Grammatica est certa loquendi ac scribendi ratio, Latinis Latinè." Vossius, "Ars benè loquendi eóque et scribendi, atque id Latinis Latinè." Dr. Prat, "Grammatica est rectè loquendi atque scribendi ars." Ruddiman also, in his Institutes of Latin Grammar, reversed the terms writing and speaking, and defined grammar, "ars rectè loquendi scribendique;" and, either from mere imitation, or from the general observation that speech precedes writing, this arrangement of the words has been followed by most modern grammarians. Dr. Lowth embraces both terms in a more general one, and says, "Grammar is the art of rightly expressing our thoughts by words." It is, however, the province of grammar, to guide us not merely in the expression of our own thoughts, but also in our apprehension of the thoughts, and our interpretation of the words, of others. Hence, Perizonius, in commenting upon Sanctius's imperfect definition, "Grammatica est ars rectè loquendi," not improperly asks, "et quidni intelligendi et explicandi?" "and why not also of understanding and explaining?" Hence, too, the art of reading is virtually a part of grammar; for it is but the art of understanding and speaking correctly that which we have before us on paper. And Nugent has accordingly given us the following definition: "Grammar is the art of reading, speaking, and writing a language by rules." —Introduction to Dict. p. xii.*

8. The word rectè, rightly. truly, correctly, which occurs in most of the foregoing Latin definitions, is censured by the learned Richard Johnson, in his Grammatical Commentaries, on account of the vagueness of its meaning. He says, it is not only ambiguous by reason of its different uses in the Latin classics, but destitute of any signification proper to grammar. But even if this be true as regards its earlier application, it may well be questioned, whether by frequency of use it has not acquired a signification which makes it proper at the present time. The English word correctly seems to be less liable to such an objection; and either this brief term, or some other of like import, (as, "with correctness"—"with propriety,") is still usually employed to tell what grammar is. But can a boy learn by such means what it is, to speak and write grammatically? In one sense, he can; and in another, he cannot. He may derive, from any of these terms, some idea of grammar as distinguished from other arts; but no simple definition of this, or of any other art, can communicate to him that learns it, the skill of an artist.

9. R. Johnson speaks at large of the relation of words to each other in sentences, as constituting in his view the most essential part of grammar; and as

---

* Ben Jonson's notion of grammar, and of its parts, was as follows: "Grammar is the art of true and well-speaking a language: the writing is but an accident
The parts of grammar are
Etymology, } which is { the true notation of words,
Syntaxe, } the right ordering of them.
A word is a part of speech or note, whereby a thing is known or called; and consisteth of one or more letters.
A letter is an indivisible part of a syllable, whose prosody, or right sounding, is perceived by the power; the orthography, or right writing, by the form.
Prosody, and Orthography, are not parts of grammar, but diffused, like blood and spirits, through the whole."—Jonson's Gram. Book I.

being a point very much overlooked, or very badly explained, by grammarians in general. His censure is just. And it seems to be as applicable to nearly all the grammars now in use, as to those which he criticised a hundred and thirty years ago. But perhaps he gives to the relation of words, (which is merely their dependence on other words according to the sense,) an earlier introduction and a more prominent place, than it ought to have in a general system of grammar. To the right use of language, he makes four things to be necessary. In citing these, I vary the language, but not the substance or the order of his positions. *First*, That we should speak and write words according to the significations which belong to them : the teaching of which now pertains to lexicography, and not to grammar, except incidentally. "*Secondly*, That we should observe *the relations* that words have one to another in sentences, and represent those relations by such variations, and particles, as are usual with authors in that language." *Thirdly*, That we should acquire a knowledge of the proper sounds of the letters, and pay a due regard to accent in pronunciation. *Fourthly*, That we should learn to write words with their proper letters, spelling them as literary men generally do.

10. From these positions, (though he sets aside the first, as pertaining to lexicography, and not now to grammar, as it formerly did,) the learned critic deduces first his four parts of the subject, and then his definition of grammar. "Hence," says he, "there arise four parts of grammar ; *Analogy*, which treats of the several parts of speech, their definitions, accidents, and formations ; *Syntax*, which treats of the use of those things in construction, according to their relations ; *Orthography*, which treats of spelling ; and *Prosody*, which treats of accenting in pronunciation. So, then, the true definition of grammar is this : Grammar is the art of *expressing the relations* of things in construction, with due accent in speaking, and orthography in writing, according to the custom of those whose language we learn." Again he adds : "The word *relation* has other senses, taken by itself ; but yet the *relation of words one to another in a sentence*, has no other signification than what I intend by it, namely, of cause, effect, means, end, manner, instrument, object, adjunct, and the like ; which are names given by logicians to those relations under which the mind comprehends things, and therefore the most proper words to explain them to others. And if such things are too hard for children, then grammar is too hard ; for there neither is, nor can be, any grammar without them. And a little experience will satisfy any man, that the young will as easily apprehend them, as *gender, number, declension*, and other grammar-terms." See *R. Johnson's Grammatical Commentaries*, p. 4.

11. It is true, that *the relation of words*—by which I mean that connexion between them, which the train of thought forms and suggests—or that dependence which one word has on an other according to the sense—lies at the foundation of all syntax. No rule or principle of construction can ever have any applicability beyond the limits, or contrary to the order, of this relation. To see what it is in any given case, is but to 'understand the meaning of the phrase or sentence. And it is plain, that no word ever necessarily agrees with an other, with which it is not thus connected in the mind of him who uses it. No word ever governs an other, to which the sense does not direct it. No word is ever required to stand immediately before or after an other, to which it has not some relation according to the meaning of the passage. Here then are the relation, agreement, government, and arrangement, of words in sentences ; and these make up the whole of syntax—but not the whole of grammar. To this one part of grammar, therefore, the relation of words is central and fundamental ; in the other parts also, there are some things to which the consideration of it is incidental ; but there are many more, like spelling, pronunciation, derivation, and whatsoever belongs merely to letters, syllables, and the forms of words, with which it has, in fact, no connexion. The relation of words, therefore, should be clearly and fully explained in its proper place, under the head

of syntax; but the general idea of grammar will not be brought nearer to truth, by making it to be " the art of *expressing the relations* of things," &c.

12. The term *grammar* is derived from the Greek word γραμμα, a letter. The art or science to which this term is applied, had its origin, not in cursory speech, but in the practice of writing; and speech, which is first in the order of nature, is last with reference to grammar. The matter or common subject of grammar, is language in general; which, being of two kinds, *spoken* and *written*, consists of certain combinations either of sounds or of visible signs, employed for the expression of thought. Letters and sounds, though often heedlessly confounded in the definitions given of vowels, consonants, &c., are, in their own nature, very different things. They address themselves to different senses; the former, to the sight; the latter, to the hearing. Yet, by a peculiar relation arbitrarily established between them, and in consequence of an almost endless variety in the combinations of either, they coincide in a most admirable manner, to effect the great object for which language was bestowed or invented; namely, to furnish a sure medium for the communication of thought, and the preservation of knowledge.

13. All languages, however different, have many things in common. There are points of a philosophical character, which result alike from the analysis of any language, and are founded on the very nature of human thought, and that of the sounds or other signs which are used to express it. When such principles alone are taken as the subject of inquiry, and are treated, as they sometimes have been, without regard to any of the idioms of particular languages, they constitute what is called General, Philosophical, or Universal Grammar. But to teach, with Lindley Murray and some others, that " Grammar may be considered as *consisting of two species*, Universal and Particular," and that the latter merely "applies those general principles to a particular language," is to adopt a twofold absurdity at the outset.* For every cultivated language has its particular grammar, in which whatsoever is universal, is necessarily included; but of which, universal or general principles form only a part, and that comparatively small. We find therefore in grammar no "two species" of the same genus; nor is the science or art, as commonly defined and understood, susceptible of division into any proper and distinct sorts, except with reference to different languages—as when we speak of Greek, Latin, French, or English grammar.

14. There is, however, as I have suggested, a certain science or philosophy of language, which has been denominated Universal Grammar; being made up of those points only, in which many or all of the different languages preserved in books, are found to coincide. All speculative minds are fond of generalization; and, in the vastness of the views which may thus be taken of grammar, such may find an entertainment which they never felt in merely learning to speak and write

* Horne Tooke eagerly seized upon a part of this absurdity, to prove that Dr. Lowth, from whom Murray derived the idea, was utterly unprepared for what he undertook in the character of a grammarian: " Dr. Lowth, when he undertook to write his *Introduction*, with the best intention in the world, most assuredly sinned against his better judgment. For he begins most judiciously, thus—' Universal grammar explains the principles which are common to *all* languages. The grammar of any particular language *applies* those common principles to that particular language.' And yet, with *this clear truth* before his eyes, he boldly proceeds to give a *particular* grammar; without being himself possessed of one single principle of *universal grammar*.'—*Diversions of Purley*, Vol. 1. p. 224. If Dr. Lowth discredited his better judgement in attempting to write an English grammar, perhaps Murray, and his weaker copyists, have little honoured theirs, in supposing they were adequate to such a work. But I do not admit, that either Lowth or Murray " *begins most judiciously*," in speaking of Universal and Particular grammar in the manner above cited. The authors who have erred with this fundamental blunder, are strangely numerous. It is found in some of the most dissimilar systems that can be named. Even Oliver B. Peirce, who has a much lower opinion of Murray's *shift* in grammar than Tooke had of Lowth's, adopts this false notion with all implicitness, though he decks it in language more objectionable, and scorns to acknowledge whence he got it. See his *Gram.* p. 16. De Sacy, in his *Principles of General Grammar*, says, " All rules of Syntax relate to two things, *Agreement and Government*."—*Fosdick's Tr.* p. 108. And again: " None of these rules properly belong to General Grammar, to each language follows, in regard to the rules of Agreement and Government, a course peculiar to itself."—B p 39. " It is with Construction [i. e. Arrangement] as with Syntax. It follows no general rule common to all languages."—*Ibid.* According to these positions, which I do not admit to be strictly true, General or Universal Grammar has no principles of *Syntax* at all, whatever else it may have which Particular Grammar can assume and apply.

grammatically. But the pleasure of such contemplations is not the earliest or the most important fruit of the study. The first thing is, to know and understand the grammatical construction of our own language. Many may profit by this acquisition, who extend not their inquiries to the analogies or the idioms of other tongues. It is true, that every item of grammatical doctrine is the more worthy to be known and regarded, in proportion as it approaches to universality. But the principles of all practical grammar, whether universal or particular, common or peculiar, must first be learned in their application to some one language, before they can be distinguished into such classes; and it is manifest, both from reason and from experience, that the youth of any nation not destitute of a good book for the purpose, may best acquire a knowledge of those principles, from the grammatical study of their native tongue.

15. Universal or Philosophical Grammar is a large field for speculation and inquiry, and embraces many things which, though true enough in themselves, are unfit to be incorporated with any system of practical grammar, however comprehensive its plan. Many authors have erred here. With what is merely theoretical, such a system should have little to do. Philosophy, dealing in generalities, resolves speech not only as a whole into its constituent parts and separable elements, as anatomy shows the use and adaptation of the parts and joints of the human body; but also as a composite into its matter and form, as one may contemplate that same body in its entirety, yet as consisting of materials, some solid and some fluid, and these curiously modelled to a particular figure. Grammar, properly so called, requires only the former of these analyses; and in conducting the same, it descends to the thousand minute particulars which are necessary to be known in practice. Nor are such things to be despised as trivial and low: ignorance of what is common and elementary, is but the more disgraceful for being ignorance of mere rudiments. "Wherefore," says Quintilian, "they are little to be respected, who represent this art as mean and barren; in which, unless you faithfully lay the foundation for the future orator, whatever superstructure you raise will tumble into ruins. It is an art, necessary to the young, pleasant to the old, the sweet companion of the retired, and one which in reference to every kind of study has in itself more of utility than of show. Let no one therefore despise as inconsiderable the elements of grammar. Not because it is a great thing, to distinguish consonants from vowels, and afterwards divide them into semivowels and mutes; but because, to those who enter the interior parts of this temple of science, there will appear in many things a great subtilty, which is fit not only to sharpen the wits of youth, but also to exercise the loftiest erudition and science."—*De Instititione Oratoria*, Lib. i, Cap. iv.

16. Again, of the arts which spring from the composition of language. Here the art of logic, aiming solely at conviction, addresses the understanding with cool deductions of unvarnished truth; rhetoric, designing to move, in some particular direction, both the judgement and the sympathies of men, applies itself to the affections in order to persuade; and poetry, various in its character and tendency, solicits the imagination, with a view to delight, and in general also to instruct. But grammar, though intimately connected with all these, and essential to them in practice, is still too distinct from each to be identified with any of them. In regard to dignity and interest, these higher studies seem to have greatly the advantage over particular grammar; but who is willing to be an ungrammatical poet, orator, or logician? For him I do not write. But I would persuade my readers, that an acquaintance with that grammar which respects the genius of their vernacular tongue, is of primary importance to all who would cultivate a literary taste, and is a necessary introduction to the study of other languages. And it may here be observed, for the encouragement of the student, that as grammar is essentially the same thing in all languages, he who has well mastered that of his own, has overcome more than half the difficulty of learning an other; and he

whose knowledge of words is the most extensive, has the fewest obstacles to encounter in proceeding further.

17. It was the "original design" of grammar, says Dr. Adam, to facilitate "the acquisition of languages;" and, of all practical treatises on the subject, this is still the main purpose. In those books which are to prepare the learner to translate from one tongue into an other, seldom is any thing else attempted. In those also which profess to explain the right use of vernacular speech, must the same purpose be ever paramount, and the "original design" be kept in view. But the grammarian may teach many things incidentally. One cannot learn a language, without learning at the same time a great many opinions, facts, and principles, of some kind or other, which are necessarily embodied in it. For all language proceeds from, and is addressed to, the understanding; and he that perceives not the meaning of what he reads, makes no acquisition even of the language itself. To the science of grammar, the *nature of the ideas* conveyed by casual examples, is not very essential: to the learner, it is highly important. The best thoughts in the best diction should furnish the models for youthful study and imitation; because such language is not only the most worthy to be remembered, but the most easy to be understood. A distinction is also to be made between use and abuse. In nonsense, absurdity, or falsehood, there can never be any grammatical authority; because, however language may be abused, the usage which gives law to speech, is still that usage which is founded upon the *common sense* of mankind.

18. Grammar appeals to reason, as well as to authority; but to what extent it should do so, has been matter of dispute. "The knowledge of useful arts," says Sanctius, "is not an invention of human ingenuity, but an emanation from the Deity, descending from above for the use of man, as Minerva sprung from the brain of Jupiter. Wherefore, unless thou give thyself wholly to laborious research into the nature of things, and diligently examine the *causes* and *reasons* of the art thou teachest, believe me, thou shalt but see with other men's eyes, and hear with other men's ears. But the minds of many are preoccupied with a certain perverse opinion, or rather ignorant conceit, that in grammar, or the art of speaking, there are no causes, and that reason is scarcely to be appealed to for any thing;—than which idle notion, I know of nothing more foolish;—nothing can be thought of which is more offensive. Shall man, endowed with reason, do, say, or contrive any thing, without design, and without understanding? Hear the philosophers; who positively declare that nothing comes to pass without a cause. Hear Plato himself; who affirms that names and words subsist by nature, and contends that language is derived from nature, and not from art."

19. "I know," says he, "that the Aristotelians think otherwise; but no one will doubt that names, are the signs, and as it were the instruments, of things. But the instrument of any art is so adapted to that art, that for any other purpose it must seem unfit; thus with an auger we bore, and with a saw we cut wood; but we split stones with wedges, and wedges are driven with heavy mauls. We cannot therefore but believe that those who first gave names to things, did it with design; and this, I imagine, Aristotle himself understood when he said, *ad placitum nomina significare.* For those who contend that names were made by chance, are no less audacious than if they would endeavour to persuade us, that the whole order of the universe was framed together fortuitously."

20. "You will see," continues he, "that in the first language, whatever it was, the names of things were taken from Nature herself; but, though I cannot affirm this to have been the case in other tongues, yet I can easily persuade myself that in every tongue a reason can be rendered for the application of every name; and that this reason, though it is in many cases obscure, is nevertheless worthy of investigation. Many things which were not known to the earlier philosophers, were

brought to light by Plato ; after the death of Plato, many were discovered by Aristotle ; and Aristotle was ignorant of many which are now everywhere known. For truth lies hid, but nothing is more precious than truth. But you will say, ' How can there be any certain origin to names, when one and the same thing is called by different names, in the several parts of the world ?' I answer, of the same thing there may be different causes, of which some people may regard one, and others, an other. * * * There is therefore no doubt, that of all things, even of words, a reason is to be rendered : and if we know not what that reason is, when we are asked ; we ought rather to confess that we do not know, than to affirm that none can be given. I know that Scaliger thinks otherwise ; but this is the true account of the matter.''

21. '' These several observations,'' he remarks further, '' I have unwillingly brought together against those stubborn critics who, while they explode reason from grammar, insist so much on the testimonies of the learned. But have they never read Quintilian, who says, (Lib. i, Cap. 6,) that, ' Language is established by reason, antiquity, authority, and custom ?' He therefore does not exclude reason, but makes it the principal thing. Nay, in a manner, Laurentius, and other grammatists, even of their fooleries, are forward to offer *reasons*, such as they are. Moreover, use does not take place without reason ; otherwise, it ought to be called abuse, and not use. But from use authority derives all its force ; for when it recedes from use, authority becomes nothing: whence Cicero reproves Cœlius and Marcus Antonius for speaking according to their own fancy, and not according to use. But, ' Nothing can be lasting,' says Curtius, (Lib. iv,) ' which is not based upon reason.' It remains, therefore, that of all things the reason be first assigned ; and then, if it can be done, we may bring forward testimonies ; that the thing, having every advantage, may be made the more clear.''—*Sanctii Minerva*, Lib. i, Cap. 2.

22. Julius Cæsar Scaliger, from whose opinion Sanctius dissents above, seems to limit the science of grammar to bounds considerably too narrow, though he found within them room for the exercise of much ingenuity and learning. He says, '' Grammatica est scientia loquendi ex usu ; neque enim constituit regulas scientibus usûs modum, sed ex eorum statis frequentibusque usurpationibus colligit communem rationem loquendi, quam discentibus traderet.''—*De Causis L. Latinæ*, Lib. iv, Cap 76. '' Grammar is the science of speaking according to use ; for it does not establish rules for those who know the manner of use, but from the settled and frequent usages of these, gathers the common fashion of speaking, which it should deliver to learners.'' This limited view seems not only to exclude from the science the use of the pen, but to exempt the learned from any obligation to respect the rules prescribed for the initiation of the young. But I have said, and with abundant authority, that the acquisition of a good style of writing is the main purpose of the study ; and, surely, the proficients and adepts in the art can desire for themselves no such exemption. Men of genius, indeed, sometimes affect to despise the pettiness of all grammatical instructions ; but this can be nothing else than affectation, since the usage of the learned is confessedly the basis of all such instructions, and several of the loftiest of their own rank appear on the list of grammarians.

23. Quintilian, whose authority is appealed to above, belonged to that age in which the exegesis of histories, poems, and other writings, was considered an essential part of grammar. He therefore, as well as Diomedes, and other ancient writers, divided the grammarian's duties into two parts ; the one including what is now called grammar, and the other the explanation of authors, and the stigmatizing of the unworthy. Of the opinion referred to by Sanctius, it seems proper to make here an ampler citation. It shall be attempted in English, though the paragraph is not an easy one to translate. I understand the author to say, '' Speak-

ers, too, have their rules to observe; and writers, theirs. Language is established by reason, antiquity, authority, and custom. Of reason the chief ground is analogy, but sometimes etymology. Ancient things have a certain majesty, and, as I might say, religion, to commend them. Authority is wont to be sought from orators and historians; the necessity of metre mostly excuses the poets. When the judgement of the chief masters of eloquence passes for reason, even error seems right to those who follow great leaders. But, of the art of speaking, custom is the surest mistress; for speech is evidently to be used as money, which has upon it a public stamp. Yet all these things require a penetrating judgement, especially analogy; the force of which is, that one may refer what is doubtful, to something similar that is clearly established, and thus prove uncertain things by those which are sure."—*Quint. Inst. Orat.*, Lib. i, Cap. 6.

24. The science of grammar, whatever we may suppose to be its just limits, does not appear to have been better cultivated in proportion as its scope was narrowed. Nor has its application to our tongue, in particular, ever been made in such a manner, as to do *great* honour to the learning or the talents of him that attempted it. What is new to a nation, may be old to the world. The development of the intellectual powers of youth by instruction in the classics, as well as the improvement of their taste by the exhibition of what is elegant in literature, is continually engaging the attention of new masters, some of whom may seem to effect great improvements; but we must remember that the concern itself is of no recent origin. Plato and Aristotle, who were great masters both of grammar and of philosophy, taught these things ably at Athens, in the fourth century *before* Christ. Varro, the grammarian, usually styled the most learned of the Romans, was *contemporary* with the Saviour and his apostles. Quintilian lived in the *first* century of our era, and before he wrote his most celebrated book, taught a school twenty years in Rome, and received from the state a salary which made him rich. This "consummate guide of wayward youth," as the poet Martial called him, being neither ignorant of what had been done by others, nor disposed to think it a light task to prescribe the right use of his own language, was at first slow to undertake the work upon which his fame now reposes; and, after it was begun, diligent to execute it worthily, that it might turn both to his own honour, and to the real advancement of learning.

25. He says, at the commencement of his book: "After I had obtained a quiet release from those labours which for twenty years had devolved upon me as an instructor of youth, certain persons familiarly demanded of me, that I should compose something concerning the proper manner of speaking; but for a long time I withstood their solicitations, because I knew there were already illustrious authors in each language, by whom many things which might pertain to such a work, had been very diligently written, and left to posterity. But the reason which I thought would obtain for me an easier excuse, did but excite the more earnest entreaty; because, amidst the various opinions of earlier writers, some of whom were not even consistent with themselves, the choice had become difficult; so that my friends seemed to have a right to enjoin upon me, if not the labour of producing new instructions, at least that of judging concerning the old. But although I was persuaded not so much by the hope of supplying what was required, as by the shame of refusing, yet, as the matter opened itself before me, I undertook of my own accord a much greater task than had been imposed; that while I should thus oblige my very good friends by a fuller compliance, I might not enter a common path and tread only in the footsteps of others. For most other writers who have treated of the art of speaking, have proceeded in such a manner as if upon adepts in every other kind of doctrine they would lay the last touch in eloquence; either despising as little things the studies which we first learn, or thinking them not to fall to their share in the divi-

sion which should be made of the professions; or, what indeed is next to this, hoping no praise or thanks for their ingenuity about things which, although necessary, lie far from ostentation : the tops of buildings make a show, their foundations are unseen."—*Quintiliani de Inst. Orat , Proœmium.*

26. But the reader may ask, "What have all these things to do with English Grammar?" I answer, they help to show us whence and what it is. Some acquaintance with the history of grammar as a science, as well as some knowledge of the structure of other languages than our own, is necessary to him who professes to write for the advancement of this branch of learning — and for him also who would be a competent judge of what is thus professed. Grammar must not forget her origin. Criticism must not resign the protection of letters. The national literature of a country is in the keeping, not of the people at large, but of authors and teachers. But a grammarian presumes to be a judge of authorship, and a teacher of teachers; and is it to the honour of England or America, that in both countries so many are countenanced in this assumption of place, who can read no language but their mother tongue? English Grammar is not properly an indigenous production, either of this country or of Britain; because it is but a branch of the general science of philology—a new variety, or species, sprung up from the old stock long ago transplanted from the soil of Greece and Rome.

27. It is true, indeed, that neither any ancient system of grammatical instruction nor any grammar of an other language, however contrived, can be entirely applicable to the present state of our tongue; for languages must needs differ greatly one from an other, and even that which is called the same, may come in time to differ greatly from what it once was. But the general analogies of speech, which are the central principles of grammar, are but imperfectly seen by the man of one language. On the other hand, it is possible to know much of these general principles, and yet be very deficient in what is peculiar to our own tongue. Real improvement in the grammar of our language, must result from a view that is neither partial nor superficial. "Time, sorry artist," as was said of old, "makes all he handles worse." And Lord Bacon, seeming to have this adage in view, suggests : "If Time of course alter all things to the worse, and Wisdom and Counsel shall not alter them to the better, what shall be the end?"—*Bacon's Essays,* p. 64.

28. Hence the need that an able and discreet grammarian should now and then appear, who with skillful hand can effect those corrections which a change of fashion or the ignorance of authors may have made necessary; but if he is properly qualified for his task, he will do all this without a departure from any of the great principles of Universal Grammar. He will surely be very far from thinking, with a certain modern author, whom I shall notice in an other chapter, that, "He is bound to take words and explain them as he finds them in his day, *without any regard to their ancient construction and application.*"—*Kirkham's Gram.* p. 28. The whole history of every word, so far as he can ascertain it, will be the view under which he will judge of what is right or wrong in the language which he teaches. Etymology is neither the whole of this view, nor yet to be excluded from it. I concur not therefore with Dr. Campbell, who, to make out a strong case, extravagantly says, "It is *never from an attention to etymology,* which would frequently mislead us, but from custom, the only infallible guide in this matter, that the meanings of words in present use must be learnt."—*Philosophy of Rhetoric,* p. 188. Jamieson too, with an implicitness little to be commended, takes this passage from Campbell; and, with no other change than that of "*learnt*" to "*learned,*" publishes it as a corollary of his own.—*Grammar of Rhetoric,* p. 42. It is folly to state for truth what is so obviously wrong. Etymology and custom are seldom at odds; and where they are so, the latter can hardly be deemed infallible.

CHAPTER II.

OF GRAMMATICAL AUTHORSHIP.

———◆———

"Respondeo, dupliciter aliquem dici grammaticum, arte et professione. Grammatici vera arte paucissimi sunt: et hi magna laude digni sunt, ut patuit: hos non vituperant summi viri; quia ipse Plinius ejusmodi grammaticus fuit, et de arte grammatica libellos edidit. Et Gellius veræ grammaticæ fuit diligentissimus doctor; sic et ipse Datus. Alii sunt grammatici professione, et ii plerumque sunt ineptissimi; quia scribimus indocti doctique, et indignissimus quisque hanc sibi artem vindicat: ——— hos mastigias multis probris docti summo jure insectantur."—DESPAUTER. *Synt. fol.* 1.

———◆———

1. It is of primary importance in all discussions and expositions of doctrines, of any sort, to ascertain well the *principles* upon which our reasonings are to be founded, and to see that they be such as are immovably established in the nature of things; for error in first principles is fundamental, and he who builds upon an uncertain foundation, incurs at least a *hazard* of seeing his edifice overthrown. The lover of *truth* will be, at all times, diligent to seek it, firm to adhere to it, willing to submit to it, and ready to promote it; but even the truth may be urged unseasonably, and important facts are easily liable to be misjoined. It is proper, therefore, for every grammarian gravely to consider, whether and how far the principles of his philosophy, his politics, his morals, or his religion, ought to influence, or actually do influence, his theory of language, and his practical instructions respecting the right use of words. In practice, grammar is so interwoven with all else that is known, believed, learned, or spoken of among men, that to determine its own peculiar principles with due distinctness, seems to be one of the most difficult points of a grammarian's duty.

2 From misapprehension, narrowness of conception, or improper bias, in relation to this point, many authors have started wrong; denounced others with intemperate zeal; departed themselves from sound doctrine; and produced books which are disgraced not merely by occasional oversights, but by central and radical errors. Hence, too, have sprung up, in the name of grammar, many unprofitable discussions, and whimsical systems of teaching, calculated rather to embarrass than to inform the student. Mere collisions of opinion, conducted without any acknowledged standard to guide the judgement, never tend to real improvement. Grammar is unquestionably a branch of that universal philosophy by which the thoroughly educated mind is enlightened to see all things aright; for philosophy, in this sense of the term, is found in everything. Yet, properly speaking, the true grammarian is not a philosopher, nor can any man strengthen his title to the former character by claiming the latter; and it is certain, that a most disheartening proportion of what in our language has been published under the name of Philosophic Grammar, is equally remote from philosophy, from grammar, and from common sense.

3 True grammar is founded on the authority of reputable custom; and that custom, on the use which men make of their reason. The proofs of what is right are accumulative, and on many points there can be no dispute, because our proofs from the best usage, are both obvious and innumerable. On the other hand, the evidence of what is wrong is rather demonstrative; for when we would expose a particular error, we exhibit it in contrast with the established principle which it violates. He who formed the erroneous sentence, has in this case no alternative, but either to acknowledge the solecism, or to deny the authority of the rule. There are disputable principles in grammar, as there are moot points in law; but this circumstance affects no settled usage in either; and every person of sense

and taste will choose to express himself in the way least liable to censure. All are free indeed from positive constraint on their phraseology; for we do not speak or write by statutes. But the ground of instruction assumed in grammar, is similar to that upon which are established the maxims of *common law*, in jurisprudence. The ultimate principle, then, to which we appeal, as the only true standard of grammatical propriety, is that species of custom which critics denominate GOOD USE; that is, present, reputable, general use.

4. Yet a slight acquaintance with the history of grammar will suffice to show us, that it is much easier to acknowledge this principle, and to commend it in words, than to ascertain what it is, and abide by it in practice. Good use is that which is neither ancient nor recent, neither local nor foreign, neither vulgar nor pedantic; and it will be found that no few have in some way or other departed from it, even while they were pretending to record its dictates But it is not to be concealed, that in every living language, it is a matter of much inherent difficulty, to reach the standard of propriety, where usage is various; and to ascertain with clearness the decisions of custom, when we descend to minute details. Here is a field in which whatsoever is achieved by the pioneers of literature, can be appreciated only by thorough scholars; for the progress of improvement in any art or science, can be known only to those who can clearly compare its ruder with its more refined stages; and it often happens that what is effected with much labour, may be presented in a very small compass.

5. But the knowledge of grammar may *retrograde;* for whatever loses the vital principle of renovation and growth, tends to decay. And if mere copyists, compilers, abridgers, and modifiers, be encouraged as they now are, it surely will not advance. Style is liable to be antiquated by time, corrupted by innovation, debased by ignorance, perverted by conceit, impaired by negligence, and vitiated by caprice. And nothing but the living spirit of true authorship, and the application of just criticism, can counteract the natural tendency of these causes. English grammar is still in its infancy; and even bears, to the imagination of some, the appearance of a deformed and ugly dwarf among the liberal arts. Treatises are multiplied almost innumerably, but still the old errors survive. Names are rapidly added to our list of authors, while little or nothing is done for the science. Nay, while new blunders have been committed in every new book, old ones have been allowed to stand as by prescriptive right; and positions that were never true, and sentences that were never good English, have been published and republished under different names, till in our language grammar has become the most ungrammatical of all studies! "Imitators generally copy their originals in an inverse ratio of their merits; that is, by adding as much to their faults, as they lose of their merits."—KNIGHT, *on the Greek Alphabet*, p. 117.

> "Who to the life an exact piece would make,
> Must not from others' work a copy take."—*Cowley.*

6. All science is laid in the nature of things; and he only who seeks it there, can rightly guide others in the paths of knowledge. He alone can know whether his predecessors went right or wrong, who is capable of a judgement independent of theirs. But with what shameful servility have many false or faulty definitions and rules been copied and copied from one grammar to another, as if authority had canonized their errors, or none had eyes to see them! Whatsoever is dignified and fair. is also modest and reasonable; but modesty does not consist in having no opinion of one's own, nor reason in following with blind partiality the footsteps of others. Grammar unsupported by authority, is indeed mere fiction. But what apology is this, for that authorship which has produced so many grammars without originality? Shall he who cannot write for himself, improve upon him

who can? Shall he who cannot paint, retouch the canvass of Guido? Shall modest ingenuity be allowed only to imitators and to thieves? How many a prefatory argument issues virtually in this! It is not deference to merit, but impudent pretence, practising on the credulity of ignorance! Commonness alone exempts it from scrutiny, and the success it has, is but the wages of its own worthlessness! To read and be informed, is to make a proper use of books for the advancement of learning; but to assume to be an author by editing mere commonplaces and stolen criticisms, is equally beneath the ambition of a scholar and the honesty of a man.

> " 'T is true, the ancients we may rob with ease ;
> But who with that mean shift himself can please ? "
> *Sheffield, Duke of Buckingham.*

7. Grammar being a practical art, with the principles of which every intelligent person is more or less acquainted, it might be expected that a book written professedly on the subject, should exhibit some evidence of its author's skill. But it would seem that a multitude of bad or indifferent writers have judged themselves qualified to teach the art of speaking and writing well; so that correctness of language and neatness of style are as rarely to be found in grammars as in other books. Nay, I have before suggested that in no other science are the principles of good writing so frequently and so shamefully violated. The code of false grammar embraced in the following work, will go far to sustain this opinion. There have been, however, several excellent scholars, who have thought it an object not unworthy of their talents, to prescribe and elucidate the principles of English Grammar. But these, with scarcely any exception, have executed their inadequate designs, not as men engaged in their proper calling, but as mere literary almoners, descending for a day from their loftier purposes, to perform a service, needful indeed, and therefore approved, but very far from supplying all the aid that is requisite to a thorough knowledge of the subject. Even the most meritorious have left ample room for improvement, though some have evinced an ability which does honour to themselves, while it gives cause to regret their lack of an inducement to greater labour. The mere grammarian can neither aspire to praise, nor stipulate for a reward; and to those who were best qualified to write, the subject could offer no adequate motive for diligence.

8. Unlearned men, who neither make, nor can make, any pretensions to a knowledge of grammar as a study, if they show themselves modest in what they profess, are by no means to be despised or undervalued for the want of such knowledge. They are subject to no criticism, till they turn authors and write for the public. And even then they are to be treated gently, if they have any thing to communicate, which is worthy to be accepted in a homely dress. Grammatical inaccuracies are to be kindly excused, in all those from whom nothing better can be expected; for people are often under a necessity of appearing as speakers or writers, before they can have learned to write or speak grammatically. The body is more to be regarded than raiment; and the substance of an interesting message, may make the manner of it a little thing. Men of high purposes naturally spurn all that is comparatively low; or all that may seem nice, overwrought, ostentatious, or finical. Hence St. Paul, in writing to the Corinthians, suggests that the design of his preaching might have been defeated, had he affected the orator, and turned his attention to mere "excellency of speech," or "wisdom of words." But this view of things presents no more ground for neglecting grammar, and making coarse and vulgar example our model of speech, than for neglecting dress, and making baize and rags the fashionable costume. The same apostle exhorts Timothy to "hold fast the form of sound *words*," which he himself had taught him. Nor can it be denied that there is an obligation resting upon all men, to use speech fairly and understandingly. But let it be remembered, that all those upon whose opinions or

practices I am disposed to animadvert, are either professed grammarians and philosophers, or authors who, by extraordinary pretensions, have laid themselves under special obligations to be *accurate* in the use of language. " The *wise in heart* shall be called prudent ; and the *sweetness of the lips* increaseth learning."— *Prov.* xvi, 21. " The words of a man's mouth are as deep waters, and the wellspring of wisdom [is] as a flowing brook."—*Ib.* xviii, 4. " A fool's mouth is his destruction, and his lips are the snare of his soul."—*Ib.* xviii, 7.

9. The old maxim recorded by Bacon, " *Loquendum ut vulgus, sentiendum ut sapientes* "—" We should speak as the vulgar, but think as the wise," is not to be taken without some limitation. For whoever literally speaks as the vulgar, shall offend vastly too much with his tongue, to have either the understanding of the wise or the purity of the good. In all untrained and vulgar minds, the ambition of speaking well is but a dormant or very weak principle. Hence the great mass of uneducated people are lamentably careless of what they utter, both as to the matter and the manner ; and no few seem naturally prone to the constant imitation of low example, and some, to the practice of every abuse of which language is susceptible. Hence, as every scholar knows, the least scrupulous of our lexicographers notice many terms but to censure them as " *low*," and omit many more as being beneath their notice. Vulgarity of language, then, ever has been, and ever must be, repudiated by grammarians. Yet we have had pretenders to grammar, who could court the favour of the vulgar, though at the expense of all the daughters of Mnemosyne.

10. Hence the enormous insult to learning and the learned, conveyed in the following scornful quotations : " Grammarians, go to your *tailors* and *shoemakers,* and learn from them the *rational* art of constructing your grammars ! "—*Neef's Method of Education*, p. 62. " From a labyrinth without a clew, in which the *most enlightened scholars* of Europe have mazed themselves and misguided others, the author ventures to turn aside."—*Cardell's Gram.* 12 mo, p. 15. Again : " The *nations of unlettered men* so adapted their language to philosophic truth, that all physical and intellectual research can find no essential rule to reject or change."—*Ibid*, p. 91. I have shown that " the nations of unlettered men " are among that portion of the earth's population, upon whose language the genius of grammar has never yet condescended to look down ! That people who make no pretensions to learning, can furnish better models or instructions than " the most enlightened scholars," is an opinion which ought not to be disturbed by argument.

11. I regret to say, that even Dr. Webster, with all his obligations and pretensions to literature, has well-nigh taken ground with Neef and Cardell, as above cited ; and has not forborne to throw contempt, even on grammar as such, and on men of letters indiscriminately, by supposing the true principles of every language to be best observed and kept by the illiterate. What marvel then, that all his multifarious grammars of the English language are despised ? Having suggested that the learned must follow the practice of the populace, because they cannot control it, he adds : " Men of letters may revolt at this suggestion, but if they will attend to the history of our language, they will find the fact to be as here stated. It is commonly supposed that the tendency of this practice of unlettered men is *to corrupt the language.* But the fact is directly the reverse. I am prepared to prove, were it consistent with the nature of this work, that nineteen-twentieths *of all the corruptions* of our language, for five hundred years past, have been introduced by *authors* — men who have made alterations in particular idioms *which they did not understand.* The same remark is applicable to the *orthography* and *pronunciation.* The tendency of unlettered men is to *uniformity* — to *analogy ;* and so strong is this disposition, that the common people have actually converted some of our irregular verbs into regular ones. It is to unlettered people that we owe the disuse of *holpen, bounden, sitten,* and the use of the regular participles *swelled, helped, worked,* in place of the ancient ones. This popular tendency is not to be

contemned and disregarded, as some of the learned affect to *do ;* [this verb *'do'* is wrong, because *' to be contemned'* is passive ;] for it is governed by *the natural, primary principles of all languages,* to which we owe all their regularity and all their melody ; viz., a love of uniformity in words of a like character, and a preference of an easy natural pronunciation, and a desire to express the most ideas with the smallest number of words and syllables. It is a fortunate thing for language, that these *natural principles* generally prevail over arbitrary and artificial rules."— *Webster's Philosophical Gram.* p. 119; *Improved Gram.* p. 78. So much for *unlettered erudition !*

12. If every thing that has been taught under the name of grammar, is to be considered as belonging to the science, it will be impossible ever to determine in what estimation the study of it ought to be held ; for all that has ever been urged either for or against it, may, upon such a principle, be *proved* by reference to different authorities and irreconcilable opinions. But all who are studious to know, and content to follow, *the fashion* established by the concurrent authority of *the learned,*[*] may at least have some standard to refer to ; and if a grammarian's rules be based upon this authority, it must be considered the exclusive privilege of the unlearned to despise them — as it is of the unbred, to contemn the rules of civility. But who shall determine whether the doctrines contained in any given treatise are, or are not, based upon such authority ? Who shall decide whether the contributions which any individual may make to our grammatical code, are, or are not, consonant with the best usage ? For this, there is no tribunal but the mass of readers, of whom few perhaps are very competent judges. And here an author's reputation for erudition and judgement, may be available to him : it is the public voice in his favour. Yet every man is at liberty to form his own opinion, and to alter it whenever better knowledge leads him to think differently.

13. But the great misfortune is, that they who need instruction, are not qualified to choose their instructor ; and many who must make this choice for their children, have no adequate means of ascertaining either the qualifications of such as offer themselves, or the comparative merits of the different methods by which they profess to teach. Hence this great branch of learning, in itself too comprehensive for the genius or the life of any one man, has ever been open to as various and worthless a set of quacks and plagiaries as have ever figured in any other. There always have been some who knew this, and there may be many who know it now ; but the credulity and ignorance which expose so great a majority of mankind to deception and error, are not likely to be soon obviated. With every individual who is so fortunate as to receive any of the benefits of intellectual culture, the whole process of education must begin anew ; and, by all that sober minds can credit, the vision of human perfectibility is far enough from any national consummation.

14. Whatever any may think of their own ability, or however some might flout to find their errors censured or their pretensions disallowed ; whatever improvement may actually have been made, or however fondly we may listen to boasts and felicitations on that topic ; it is presumed, that the general ignorance on the subject of grammar, as above stated, is too obvious to be denied. What then is the remedy ? and to whom must our appeal be made ? Knowledge cannot be imposed by power, nor is there any domination in the republic of letters. The remedy lies solely in that zeal which can provoke to a generous emulation in the cause of literature ; and the appeal, which has recourse to the learning of the learned, and to the common

---

[*] " A very good judge has left us his opinion and determination in this matter ; that he ' would take for his rule in speaking, not what might happen to be the faulty caprice of the multitude, but the consent and agreement of learned men,' "— *Creighton's Dict.* p. 21. The " good judge " here spoken of, is Quintilian ; whose words on the point are these : " Necessarium est judicium, constituendumque imprimis, id ipsum quid sit, quod *consuetudinem* vocemus. In loquendo, non, si quid vitiose multis insederit, pro regula sermonis, accipiendum est. Ergo consuetudinem sermonis, vocabo *consensum eruditorum ;* sicut vivendi, consensum bonorum."—*Inst. Orat.,* l, 6.

sense of all, must be pressed home to conviction, till every false doctrine stand refuted, and every weak pretender exposed or neglected. Then shall Science honour them that honour her; and all her triumphs be told, all her instructions be delivered, in "sound speech that cannot be condemned."

15. A generous man is not unwilling to be corrected; and a just one cannot but desire to be set right in all things. Even over noisy gainsayers, a calm and dignified exhibition of true doctrine, has often more influence than ever openly appears. I have even seen the author of a faulty grammar heap upon his corrector more scorn and personal abuse than would fill a large newspaper, and immediately afterwards, in a new edition of his book, renounce the errors which had been pointed out to him, stealing the very language of his amendments from the man whom he had so grossly vilified! It is true that grammarians have ever disputed, and often with more acrimony than discretion. Those who, in elementary treatises, have meddled much with philological controversy, have well illustrated the couplet of Denham:

> "The tree of knowledge, blasted by disputes,
> Produces sapless leaves in stead of fruits."

16. Thus, then, as I have before suggested, we find among writers on grammar two numerous classes of authors, who have fallen into opposite errors, perhaps equally reprehensible; the visionaries, and the copyists. The former have ventured upon too much originality, the latter have attempted too little. "The science of philology," says Dr. Alexander Murray, "is not a frivolous study, fit to be conducted by ignorant pedants or visionary enthusiasts. It requires more qualifications to succeed in it, than are usually united in those who pursue it:—a sound penetrating judgement; habits of calm philosophical induction; an erudition various, extensive, and accurate; and a mind likewise, that can direct the knowledge expressed in words, to illustrate the nature of the signs which convey it.—"*Murray's History of European Languages*, Vol. ii, p. 333.

17. They who set aside the authority of custom, and judge every thing to be ungrammatical which appears to them to be unphilosophical, render the whole ground forever disputable, and weary themselves in beating the air. So various have been the notions of this sort of critics, that it would be difficult to mention an opinion not found in some of their books. Amidst this rage for speculation on a subject purely practical, various attempts have been made, to overthrow that system of instruction, which long use has rendered venerable, and long experience proved to be useful. But it is manifestly much easier to raise even plausible objections against this system, than to invent an other less objectionable. Such attempts have generally met the reception they deserved. Their history will give no encouragement to future innovators.

18. Again: While some have thus wasted their energies in excentric flights, vainly supposing that the learning of ages would give place to their whimsical theories; others, with more success, not better deserved, have multiplied grammars almost innumerably, by abridging or modifying the books they had used in childhood. So that they who are at all acquainted with the origin and character of the various compends thus introduced into our schools, cannot but desire to see them all displaced by some abler and better work, more honourable to its author and more useful to the public, more intelligible to students and more helpful to teachers. Books professedly published for the advancement of knowledge, are very frequently to be reckoned among its greatest impediments; for the interests of learning are no less injured by whimsical doctrines, than the rights of authorship by plagiarism. Too many of our grammars, profitable only to their makers and venders, are like weights attached to the heels of Hermes. It is discouraging to know the history of this science. But the multiplicity of treatises already in use, is a reason, not for silence, but for offering more. For, as Lord Bacon observes, the number of ill-

written books is not to be diminished by ceasing to write, but by writing others which, like Aaron's serpent, shall swallow up the spurious.*

19. I have said that some grammars have too much originality, and others too little. It may be added, that not a few are chargeable with both these faults at once. They are original, or at least anonymous, where there should have been given other authority than that of the compiler's name; and they are copies, or, at best, poor imitations, where the author should have shown himself capable of writing in a good style of his own. What then is the middle ground for the true grammarian? What is the kind, and what the degree, of originality, which are to be commended in works of this sort? In the first place, a grammarian must be a writer, an author, a man who observes and thinks for himself; and not a mere compiler, abridger, modifier, copyist, or plagiarist. Grammar is not the only subject upon which we allow no man to innovate in doctrine; why, then, should it be the only one upon which a man may make it a merit, to work up silently into a book of his own, the best materials found among the instructions of his predecessors and rivals? Some definitions and rules, which in the lapse of time and by frequency of use have become a sort of public property, the grammarian may perhaps be allowed to use at his pleasure; yet even upon these a man of any genius will be apt to set some impress peculiar to himself. But the doctrines of his work ought, in general, to be expressed in his own language, and illustrated by that of others. With respect to quotation, he has all the liberty of other writers, and no more; for, if a grammarian makes "use of his predecessors' labours," why should any one think with Murray, "it is scarcely necessary to apologize for" this, "or for *omitting to insert* their names?"—*Introd. to L. Murray's Gram. p.* 7.

20. The author of this volume would here take the liberty briefly to refer to his own procedure. His knowledge of what is *technical* in grammar, was of course chiefly derived from the writings of other grammarians; and to their concurrent opinions and practices, he has always had great respect; yet, in truth, not a line has he ever copied from any of them with a design to save the labour of composition. For, not to compile an English grammar from others already extant, but to compose one more directly from the sources of the art, was the task which he at first proposed to himself. Nor is there in all the present volume a single sentence, not regularly quoted, the authorship of which he supposes may now be ascribed to an other more properly than to himself. Where either authority or acknowledgement was requisite, names have been inserted. In the doctrinal parts of the volume, not only quotations from others, but most examples made for the occasion, are marked with guillemets, to distinguish them from the main text; while, to almost every thing which is really taken from any other known writer, a name or reference is added. For those citations, however, which there was occasion to repeat in different parts of the work, a single reference has sometimes been thought sufficient. This remark refers chiefly to the corrections in the Key, the references being given in the Exercises.

21. Though the theme is not one on which a man may hope to write well with little reflection, it is true that the parts of this treatise which have cost the author the most labor, are those which "consist chiefly of materials selected from the writings of others." These, however, are not the didactical portions of the book, but the proofs and examples; which, according to the custom of the ancient grammarians, ought to be taken from other authors. But so much have the makers of our modern grammars been allowed to presume upon the respect and acquiescence of their readers, that the ancient exactness on this point would often appear pedantic. Many phrases and sentences, either original with the writer, or common to every body, will therefore be found among the illustrations of the following work; for it

---

* " The opinion of plenty is amongst the causes of want; and the great quantity of books maketh a show rather of superfluity than lack; which surcharge, nevertheless, is not to be removed by making no more books, but by making more good books, which, as the serpent of Moses, might devour the serpents of the enchanters."—*Bacon.* In point of style, his lordship is here deficient; and he has also mixed and marred the figure which he uses. But the idea is a good one.

was not supposed that any reader would demand for every thing of this kind the authority of some great name. Anonymous examples are sufficient to elucidate principles, if not to establish them; and elucidation is often the sole purpose for which an example is needed.

22. It is obvious enough, that no writer on grammar has any right to propose himself as authority for what he teaches; for every language, being the common property of all who use it, ought to be carefully guarded against the caprices of individuals; and especially against that presumption which might attempt to impose erroneous or arbitrary definitions and rules. "Since the matter of which we are treating," says the philologist of Salamanca, "is to be verified, first by reason, and then by testimony and usage, none ought to wonder if we sometimes deviate from the track of great men; for, with whatever authority any grammarian may weigh with me, unless he shall have confirmed his assertions by reason, and also by examples, he shall win no confidence in respect to grammar. For, as Seneca says, Epistle 95, 'Grammarians are the *guardians*, not the *authors*, of language.'"— *Sanctii Minerva*, Lib. ii, Cap. 2. Yet, as what is intuitively seen to be true or false, is already sufficiently proved or detected, many points in grammar need nothing more than to be clearly stated and illustrated; nay, it would seem an injurious reflection on the understanding of the reader, to accumulate proofs of what cannot but be evident to all who speak the language.

23. Among men of the same profession, there is an unavoidable rivalry, so far as they become competitors for the same prize; but in competition there is nothing dishonourable, while excellence alone obtains distinction, and no advantage is sought by unfair means. It is evident that we ought to account him the best grammarian, who has the most completely executed the worthiest design. But no worthy design can need a false apology; and it is worse than idle to prevaricate. That is but a spurious modesty, which prompts a man to disclaim in one way what he assumes in an other—or to underrate the duties of his office, that he may boast of having "done all that could reasonably be expected." Whoever professes to have improved the science of English grammar, must claim to know more of the matter than the generality of English grammarians; and he who begins with saying, that "little can be expected" from the office he assumes, must be wrongfully contradicted, when he is held to have done much. Neither the ordinary power of speech, nor even the ability to write respectably on common topics, makes a man a critic among critics, or enables him to judge of literary merit. And if, by virtue of these qualifications alone, a man will become a grammarian or a connoisseur, he can hold the rank only by courtesy—a courtesy which is content to degrade the character, that his inferior pretensions may be accepted and honoured under the name.

24. By the force of a late popular example, still too widely influential, grammatical authorship has been reduced, in the view of many, to little or nothing more than a mere serving-up of materials anonymously borrowed; and, what is most remarkable, even for an indifferent performance of this low office, not only unnamed reviewers, but several writers of note, have not scrupled to bestow the highest praise of grammatical excellence! And thus the palm of superior skill in grammar, has been borne away by a *professed compiler;* who had so mean an opinion of what his theme required, as to deny it even the common courtesies of compilation! What marvel is it, that, under the wing of such authority, many writers have since sprung up, to improve upon this most happy design; while all who were competent to the task, have been discouraged from attempting any thing like a complete grammar of our language? What motive shall excite a man to long-continued diligence, where such notions prevail as give mastership no hope of preference, and where the praise of his ingenuity and the reward of his labour must needs be inconsiderable, till some honoured compiler usurp them both, and bring his "most useful matter" before the world under better auspices? If the love of learning supply such a motive, who that has generously yielded to the impulse, will not now, like Johnson, feel himself reduced to an "humble drudge"—or, like

Perizonius, apologize for the apparent folly of devoting his time to such a subject as grammar?

25. The first edition of the "Institutes of English Grammar," the doctrinal parts of which are embraced in the present more copious work, was published in the year 1823; since which time, (within the space of twelve years,) about forty new compends, mostly professing to be abstracts of *Murray*, with improvements, have been added to our list of English grammars. The author has examined as many as thirty of them, and seen advertisements of perhaps a dozen more. Being various in character, they will of course be variously estimated; but, so far as he can judge, they are, without exception, works of little or no real merit, and not likely to be much patronized or long preserved from oblivion. For which reason, he would have been inclined entirely to disregard the petty depredations which the writers of several of them have committed upon his earlier text, were it not possible, that by such a frittering-away of his work, he himself might one day seem to some to have copied that from others which was first taken from him. Trusting to make it manifest to men of learning, that in the production of the books which bear his name, far more has been done for the grammar of our language than any single hand had before achieved within the scope of practical philology, and that with perfect fairness towards other writers; he cannot but feel a wish that the integrity of his text should be preserved, whatever else may befall; and that the multitude of scribblers who judge it so needful to remodel Murray's defective compilation, would forbear to publish under his name or their own what they find only in the following pages.

26. The mere rivalry of their authorship is no subject of concern; but it is enough for any ingenuous man to have toiled for years in solitude to complete a work of public utility, without entering a warfare for life to defend and preserve it. Accidental coincidences in books are unfrequent, and not often such as to excite the suspicion of the most sensitive. But, though the criteria of plagiarism are neither obscure nor disputable, it is not easy, in this beaten track of literature, for persons of little reading to know what is, or is not, original. Dates must be accurately observed; and a multitude of minute things must be minutely compared. And who will undertake such a task but he that is personally interested? Of the thousands who are forced into the paths of learning, few ever care to know, by what pioneer, or with what labour, their way was cast up for them. And even of those who are honestly engaged in teaching, not many are adequate judges of the comparative merits of the great number of books on this subject. The common notions of mankind conform more easily to fashion than to truth; and even of some things within their reach, the majority seem content to take their opinions upon trust. Hence, it is vain to expect that that which is intrinsically best, will be everywhere preferred; or that which is meritoriously elaborate, adequately appreciated. But common sense might dictate, that learning is not encouraged or respected by those who, for the making of books, prefer a pair of scissors to the pen.

27. The fortune of a grammar is not always an accurate test of its merits. The goddess of the plenteous horn stands blindfold yet upon the floating prow; and, under her capricious favour, any pirate-craft, ill stowed with plunder, may sometimes speed as well, as barges richly laden from the golden mines of science. Far more are now afloat, and more are stranded on dry shelves, than can be here reported. But what this work contains, is candidly designed to qualify the reader to be himself a judge of what it *should* contain; and I will hope, so ample a report as this, being thought sufficient, will also meet his approbation. The favour of one discerning mind that comprehends my subject, is worth intrinsically more than that of half the nation: I mean, of course, the half of whom my gentle reader is not one.

> "They praise and they admire they know not what,
> And know not whom, but as one leads the other."—*Milton.*

CHAPTER III.

OF GRAMMATICAL SUCCESS AND FAME.

———◆———

" Non is ego sum, cui aut jucundum, aut adeo opus sit, de aliis detrahere, et hac viâ ad famam contendere. Melioribus artibus laudem parare didici. Itaque non libenter dico, quod præsens institutum dicere cogit."—Jo. Augusti Ernesti *Pref. ad Græcum Lexicon*, p. vii

———◆———

1. The real history of grammar is little known; and many erroneous impressions are entertained concerning it: because the story of the systems most generally received has never been fully told; and that of a multitude now gone to oblivion was never worth telling. In the distribution of grammatical fame, which has chiefly been made by the hand of interest, we have had a strange illustration of the saying: "Unto every one that hath shall be given, and he shall have abundance; but from him that hath not, shall be taken away even that which he hath." Some whom fortune has made popular, have been greatly overrated, if learning and talent are to be taken into the account; since it is manifest, that with no extraordinary claims to either, they have taken the very foremost rank among grammarians, and thrown the learning and talents of others into the shade, or made them tributary to their own success and popularity.

2. It is an ungrateful task to correct public opinion by showing the injustice of praise. Fame, though it may have been both unexpected and undeserved, is apt to be claimed and valued as part and parcel of a man's good name; and the dissenting critic, though ever-so candid, is liable to be thought an envious detractor. It would seem in general most prudent to leave mankind to find out for themselves how far any commendation bestowed on individuals is inconsistent with truth. But, be it remembered, that celebrity is not a virtue; nor, on the other hand, is experience the cheapest of teachers. A good man may not have done all things ably and well; and it is certainly no small mistake to estimate his character by the current value of his copy-rights. Criticism may destroy the reputation of a book, and not be inconsistent with a cordial respect for the private worth of its author. The reader will not be likely to be displeased with what is to be stated in this chapter, if he can believe, that no man's merit as a writer, may well be enhanced by ascribing to him that which he himself, for the protection of his own honour, has been constrained to disclaim. He cannot suppose that too much is alleged, if he will admit that a grammarian's fame should be thought safe enough in his *own keeping*. Are authors apt to undervalue their own performances? Or because proprietors and publishers may profit by the credit of a book, shall it be thought illiberal to criticise it? Is the author himself to be disbelieved, that the extravagant praises bestowed upon him may be justified? "Superlative commendation," says Dillwyn, "is near akin to *detraction*." (See his *Reflections*, p. 22.) Let him, therefore, who will charge detraction upon me, first understand wherein it consists. I shall criticise, freely, both the works of the living, and the doctrines of those who, to us, live only in their works; and if any man dislike this freedom, let him rebuke it, showing wherein it is wrong or unfair. The amiable author just quoted, says again: "Praise has so often proved an *impostor*, that it would be well, wherever we meet with it, to treat it as a vagrant."—*Ib.* p. 100. I go not so far as this; but that eulogy which one knows to be false, he cannot but reckon impertinent.

3. Few writers on grammar have been more noted than WILLIAM LILY and LINDLEY MURRAY. Others have left better monuments of their learning and talents, but none perhaps have had greater success and fame. The Latin grammar

which was for a long time most popular in England, has commonly been ascribed to the one ; and what the Imperial Review, in 1805, pronounced ''the best English grammar, beyond all comparison, that has yet appeared,'' was compiled by the other.   And doubtless they have both been rightly judged to excel the generality of those which they were intended to supersede ; and both, in their day, may have been highly serviceable to the cause of learning.   For all excellence is but comparative ; and to grant them this superiority, is neither to prefer them now, nor to justify the praise which has been bestowed upon their authorship.   As the science of grammar can never be taught without a book, or properly taught by any book which is not itself grammatical, it is of some importance both to teachers and to students, to make choice of the best.   Knowledge will not advance where grammars hold rank by prescription.   Yet it is possible that many, in learning to write and speak, may have derived no inconsiderable benefit from a book that is neither accurate nor complete.

4. With respect to time, these two grammarians were three centuries apart ; during which period, the English language received its most classical refinement, and the relative estimation of the two studies, Latin and English grammar, became in a great measure reversed.   Lily was an Englishman, born at Odiham,* in Hampshire, in 1466.   When he had arrived at manhood, he went on a pilgrimage to Jerusalem ; and while abroad studied some time at Rome, and also at Paris. On his return he was thought one of the most accomplished scholars in England. In 1510, Dr. John Colet, dean of St. Paul's church, in London, appointed him the first high master of St. Paul's School, then recently founded by this gentleman's munificence.   In this situation, Lily appears to have taught with great credit to himself till 1522, when he died of the plague, at the age of 56.   For the use of this school, he wrote and published certain parts of the grammar which has since borne his name.   Of the authorship of this work many curious particulars are stated in the preface by John Ward, which may be seen in the edition of 1793. Lily had able rivals, as well as learned coadjutors and friends.   By the aid of the latter, he took precedence of the former ; and his publications, though not voluminous, soon gained a general popularity.   So that when an arbitrary king saw fit to silence competition among the philologists, by becoming himself, as Sir Thomas Elliott says, ''the chiefe authour and setter-forth of an introduction into grammar, for the childrene of his lovynge subjects,'' Lily's Grammar was preferred for the basis of the standard.   Hence, after the publishing of it became a privilege patented by the crown, the book appears to have been honoured with a royal title, and to have been familiarly called King Henry's Grammar.

5. Prefixed to this book, there appears a very ancient epistle to the reader, which while it shows the reasons for this royal interference with grammar, shows also, what is worthy of remembrance, that guarded and maintained as it was, even royal interference was here ineffectual to its purpose.   It neither produced uniformity in the methods of teaching, nor, even for instruction in a dead language, entirely prevented the old manual from becoming diverse in its different editions. The style also may serve to illustrate what I have elsewhere said about the duties of a modern grammarian.   ''As for the diversitie of grammars, it is well and profitably taken awaie by the King's Majesties wisdome ; who, foreseeing the inconvenience, and favorably providing the remedie, caused one kind of grammar by sundry learned men to be diligently drawn, and so to be set out, only every where to be taught, for the use of learners, and for the hurt in changing of schoolemaisters.''   That is, to prevent the injury which schoolmasters were doing by a whimsical choice, or frequent changing, of grammars.   But, says the letter, ''The varietie of teaching is divers yet, and alwaies will be ; for that every schoolemaister liketh that he knoweth, and seeth not the use of that he knoweth not ; and there-

* Not, '' Oldham, in Hampshire,'' as the Universal Biographical Dictionary has it ; for Oldham is in Lancashire, and the name of Lily's birthplace has sometimes been spelled ''Odiam.''

fore judgeth that the most sufficient waie, which he seeth to be the readiest meane, and perfectest kinde, to bring a learner to have a thorough knowledge therein." The only remedy for such an evil then is, to teach those who are to be teachers, and to desert all who, for any whim of their own, desert sound doctrine.

6. But, to return. A law was made in England by Henry the Eighth, commanding Lily's Grammar only, (or that which has commonly been quoted as Lily's,) to be everywhere adopted and taught, as the common standard of grammatical instruction.* Being long kept in force by means of a special inquiry, directed to be made by the bishops at their stated visitations, this law, for three hundred years, imposed the book on all the established schools of the realm. Yet it is certain, that about one half of what has thus gone under the name of Lily, ("because," says one of the patentees, "he had *so considerable a hand* in the composition,) was written by Dr. Colet, by Erasmus, or by others who improved the work after Lily's death. And of the other half, it has been incidentally asserted in history, that neither the scheme nor the text was original. The Printer's Grammar, London, 1787, speaking of the art of type-foundery, says : "The Italians in a short time brought it to *that* perfection, that in the beginning of the year 1474, they cast a letter not much inferior to the best types of the present age ; as may be seen in a Latin Grammar, written by Omnibonus Leonicenus, and printed at Padua on the 14th of January, 1474 ; *from whom our grammarian, Lily, has taken the entire scheme of his Grammar, and transcribed the greatest part thereof, without paying any regard to the memory of this author.*" The historian then proceeds to speak about types. See also the same thing in the History of Printing, 8vo, London, 1770. This is the grammar which bears upon its title page : "*Quam solam Regia Majestas in omnibus scholis docendam præcipit.*"

7. Murray was an intelligent and very worthy man, to whose various labours in the compilation of books our schools are under many obligations. But in original thought and critical skill he fell far below most of " the authors to whom," he confesses, "the grammatical part of his compilation is *principally indebted for its materials ;* namely, Harris, Johnson, Lowth, Priestley, Beattie, Sheridan, Walker, Coote, Blair, and Campbell."—*Introd. to Lindley Murray's Gram.* p. 7. It is certain and evident that he entered upon his task with a very insufficient preparation. His biography, which was commenced by himself and completed by one of his most partial friends, informs us, that, " Grammar did not particularly engage his attention, until a short time previous to the publication of his first work on that subject ;" that, " His Grammar, as it appeared in the first edition, was completed in rather less than a year ;" that, " It was begun in the spring of 1794, and published in the spring of 1795 — though he had an intervening illness, which, for several weeks, stopped the progress of the work ;" and that, " The Exercises and Key were also composed in about a year."—*Life of L. Murray,* p. 188. From the very first sentence of his book, it appears that he entertained but a low and most erroneous idea of the duties of that sort of character in which he was about to come before the public.† He improperly imagined, as many others have done, that " little can be expected " from a modern grammarian, or (as he chose to express it) " from a *new compilation,* besides a careful selection of the most useful matter, and some degree of improvement in the mode of adapting it to the

---

* There are other Latin grammars now in use in England ; but what one is most popular, or whether any regard is still paid to this ancient edict or not, I cannot say. Dr. Adam, in his preface, dated 1793, speaking of Lily, says : " His Grammar was appointed, by an act *which is still in force,* to be taught in the established schools of England." I have somehow gained the impression, that the act is now totally disregarded.—G. Brown.

† For this there is an obvious reason, or apology, in what his biographer states, as " the humble origin of his Grammar ;" and it is such a reason as will go to confirm what I allege. This famous compilation was produced at the request of *two or three young teachers,* who had charge of a *small female school* in the neighbourhood of the author's residence ; and nothing could have been more unexpected to their friend and instructer, than that he, in consequence of this service, should become known the world over, as *Murray the Grammarian.* " In preparing the work, and consenting to its publication, he had no expectation that it would be used, except by the school for which it was designed, and two or three other schools conducted by persons who were also his friends."—*Life of L. Murray,* p. 250.

understanding, and the gradual progress of learners."—*Introd. to L. Murray's Gram.* 8vo, p. 5; 12mo, p. 3. As if, to be master of his own art—to think and write well himself, were no part of a grammarian's business! And again, as if the jewels of scholarship, thus carefully selected, could need a burnish or a foil from other hands than those which fashioned them!

8. Murray's general idea of the doctrines of grammar was judicious. He attempted no broad innovation on what had been previously taught; for he had neither the vanity to suppose he could give currency to novelties, nor the folly to waste his time in labours utterly nugatory. By turning his own abilities to their best account, he seems to have done much to promote and facilitate the study of our language. But his notion of grammatical authorship, cuts off from it all pretence to literary merit, for the sake of doing good; and, taken in any other sense than as a forced apology for his own assumptions, his language on this point is highly injurious towards the very authors whom he copied. To justify himself, he ungenerously places them, in common with others, under a degrading necessity which no able grammarian ever felt, and which every man of genius or learning must repudiate. If none of our older grammars disprove his assertion, it is time to have a new one that will; for, to expect the perfection of grammar from him who cannot treat the subject in a style at once original and pure, is absurd. He says, " The greater part of an English grammar *must necessarily be a compilation;*" and adds, with reference to his own, " originality belongs to but a small portion of it. This I have acknowledged; and I trust *this acknowledgement* will protect me from all attacks, grounded on any supposed unjust and irregular assumptions." This quotation is from a letter addressed by Murray to his American publishers, in 1811, after they had informed him of certain complaints respecting the liberties which he had taken in his work. See " *The Friend,*" vol. iii, p. 34.

9. The acknowledgement on which he thus relies, does not appear to have been made, till his grammar had gone through several editions. It was, however, at some period, introduced into his short preface, or " Introduction," in the following well-meant but singularly sophistical terms: " In *a work* which professes itself to be a *compilation,* and which, *from the nature and design of it,* must consist chiefly of materials selected from the writings of others, *it is scarcely necessary to apologize* for the use which the Compiler has made of his predecessors' labours, or for *omitting to insert* their names. *From the alterations* which have been frequently made in the sentiments and the language, to suit the connexion, and to adapt them to the particular purposes for which they are introduced; and, in many instances, *from the uncertainty to whom* the passages originally belonged, the insertion of names *could seldom be made with propriety.* But if this could have been generally done, a work of this nature *would derive no advantage from it,* equal to the inconvenience of crowding the pages with a repetition of names and references. It is, however, proper to acknowledge, in general terms, that the authors to whom the grammatical part of this compilation is principally indebted for its materials, are Harris, Johnson, Lowth, Priestley, Beattie, Sheridan, Walker, and Coote."—*Introd. Duodecimo Gram.* p. 4; *Octavo,* p. 7.

10. The fallacy, or absurdity, of this language sprung from necessity. An impossible case was to be made out. For compilation, though ever so fair, is not grammatical authorship. But some of the commenders of Murray have not only professed themselves satisfied with this general acknowledgement, but have found in it a candour and a liberality, a modesty and a diffidence, which, as they allege, ought to protect him from all animadversion. Are they friends to learning? Let them calmly consider what I reluctantly offer for its defence and promotion. In one of the recommendations appended to Murray's grammars, it is said, " They have nearly superseded every thing else of the kind, by concentrating the remarks of the best authors on the subject." But, in truth, with several of the best English grammars published previously to his own, Murray appears to have been totally

unacquainted. The chief, if not the only school grammars which were largely copied by him, were Lowth's and Priestley's, though others perhaps may have shared the fate of these in being "superseded" by his. It may be seen by inspection, that in copying these two authors, the compiler, agreeably to what he says above, omitted all names and references—even such as they had scrupulously inserted : and, at the outset, assumed to be himself the sole authority for all his doctrines and illustrations ; satisfying his own mind with making, some years afterwards, that general apology which we are now criticising. For if he so mutilated and altered the passages which he adopted, as to make it improper to add the names of their authors, upon what other authority than his own do they rest ? But if, on the other hand, he generally copied without alteration ; his examples are still anonymous, while his first reason for leaving them so, is plainly destroyed : because his position is thus far contradicted by the fact.

11. In his later editions, however, there are two opinions which the compiler thought proper to support by regular quotations ; and, now and then, in other instances, the name of an author appears. The two positions thus distinguished, are these : *First*, That the noun *means* is necessarily singular as well as plural, so that one cannot with propriety use the singular form, *mean*, to signify that by which an end is attained ; *Second*, That the subjunctive mood, to which he himself had previously given all the tenses without inflection, is not different in form from the indicative, except in the present tense. With regard to the latter point, I have shown, in its proper place, that he taught erroneously, both before and after he changed his opinion ; and concerning the former, the most that can be proved by quotations, is, that both *mean* and *means* for the singular number, long have been, and still are, in good use, or sanctioned by many elegant writers; so that either form may yet be considered grammatical, though the irregular can claim to be so, only when it is used in this particular sense. As to his second reason for the suppression of names, to wit, " the *uncertainty to whom* the passages originally belonged,"—to make the most of it, it is but partial and relative ; and, surely, no other grammar ever before so multiplied the difficulty in the eyes of teachers, and so widened the field for commonplace authorship, as has the compilation in question. The origin of a sentiment or passage may be uncertain to one man, and perfectly well known to an other. The embarrassment which a *compiler* may happen to find from this source, is worthy of little sympathy. For he cannot but know from what work he is taking any particular sentence or paragraph, and those parts of a *grammar*, which are new to the eye of a great grammarian, may very well be credited to him who claims to have written the book. I have thus disposed of his second reason for the omission of names and references, in compilations of grammar.

12. There remains one more : " A work of this nature *would derive no advantage from it*, equal to the inconvenience of crowding the pages with a repetition of names and references." With regard to a small work, in which the matter is to be very closely condensed, this argument has considerable force. But Murray has in general allowed himself very ample room, especially in his two octavoes. In these, and for the most part also in his duodecimoes, all needful references might easily have been added without increasing the size of his volumes, or injuring their appearance. In nine cases out of ten, the names would only have occupied what is now blank space. It is to be remembered, that these books do not differ much, except in quantity of paper. His octavo Grammar is but little more than a reprint, in a larger type, of the duodecimo Grammar, together with his Exercises and Key. The demand for this expensive publication has been comparatively small ; and it is chiefly to the others, that the author owes his popularity as a grammarian. As to the advantage which Murray or his work might have derived from an adherence on his part to the usual custom of compilers, *that* may be variously estimated. The remarks of the best grammarians or the

sentiments of the best authors, are hardly to be thought the more worthy of acceptance, for being concentrated in such a manner as to merge their authenticity in the fame of the copyist. Let me not be understood to suggest that this good man sought popularity at the expense of others; for I do not believe that either fame or interest was his motive. But the right of authors to the credit of their writings, is a delicate point; and, surely, his example would have been worthier of imitation, had he left no ground for the foregoing objections, and carefully barred the way to any such inference.

13. But let the first sentence of this apology be now considered. It is here suggested, that because this work is a compilation, even such an acknowledgement as the author makes, is " scarcely necessary." This is too much to say. Yet one may readily admit, that a compilation, " from the nature and design of it, must consist chiefly "—nay, *wholly*—" of materials selected from the writings of others." But what able grammarian would ever willingly throw himself upon the horns of such a dilemma ? The nature and design *of a book*, whatever they may be, are matters for which the author alone is answerable; but the nature and design *of grammar*, are no less repugnant to the strain of this apology, than to the vast number of errors and defects which were overlooked by Murray in his work of compilation. It is the express purpose of this practical science, to enable a man to write well himself. He that cannot do this, exhibits no excess of modesty when he claims to have " done all that could reasonably be expected in a work of this nature."—*L. Murray's Gram. Introd.* p. 9. He that sees with other men's eyes, is peculiarly liable to errors and inconsistencies : uniformity is seldom found in patchwork, or accuracy in secondhand literature. Correctness of language is in the mind, rather than in the hand or the tongue ; and, in order to secure it, some originality of thought is necessary. A delineation from new surveys is not the less original because the same region has been sketched before ; and how can he be the ablest of surveyors, who, through lack of skill or industry, does little more than transcribe the field-notes and copy the projections of his predecessors ?

14. This author's oversights are numerous. There is no part of the volume more accurate than that which he literally copied from Lowth. To the Short Introduction alone, he was indebted for more than a hundred and twenty paragraphs ; and even in these there are many things obviously erroneous. Many of the best practical notes were taken from Priestley ; yet it was he, at whose doctrines were pointed most of those " positions and discussions," which alone the author claims as original. To some of these reasonings, however, his own alterations may have given rise ; for, where he " persuades himself he is not destitute of originality," he is often arguing against the text of his own earlier editions. Webster's well-known complaints of Murray's unfairness, had a far better cause than requital ; for there was no generosity in ascribing them to peevishness, though the passages in question were not worth copying. On perspicuity and accuracy, about sixty pages were extracted from Blair ; and it requires no great critical acumen to discover, that they are miserably deficient in both. On the law of language, there are fifteen pages from Campbell ; which, with a few exceptions, are well written. The rules for spelling are the same as Walker's : the third one, however, is a gross blunder ; and the fourth, a needless repetition.

15. Were this a place for minute criticism, blemishes almost innumerable might be pointed out. It might easily be shown that almost every rule laid down in the book for the observance of the learner, was repeatedly violated by the hand of the master. Nor is there among all those who have since abridged or modified the work, an abler grammarian than he who compiled it. Who will pretend that Flint, Alden, Comly, Jaudon, Russell, Bacon, Lyon, Miller, Alger, Maltby, Ingersoll, Fisk, Greenleaf, Merchant, Kirkham, Cooper, R. G. Greene, Woodworth, Smith, or Frost, has exhibited greater skill ? It is curious to observe, how frequently a grammatical blunder committed by Murray, or some one of his predecessors, has

escaped the notice of all these, as well as of many others who have found it easier to copy him than to write for themselves. No man professing to have copied and improved Murray, can rationally be supposed to have greatly excelled him; for to pretend to have produced an *improved copy of a compilation*, is to claim a sort of authorship, even inferior to his, and utterly unworthy of any man who is able to prescribe and elucidate the principles of English grammar.

16. But Murray's grammatical works, being extolled in the reviews, and made common stock in trade, — being published, both in England and in America, by booksellers of the most extensive correspondence, and highly commended even by those who were most interested in the sale of them, — have been eminently successful with the public; and in the opinion of the world, success is the strongest proof of merit. Nor has the force of this argument been overlooked by those who have written in aid of his popularity. It is the strong point in most of the commendations which have been bestowed upon Murray as a grammarian. A recent eulogist computes, that, "at least five millions of copies of his various school-books have been printed;" particularly commends him for his "candour and liberality towards rival authors;" avers that, "he went on, examining and correcting his Grammar, through all its forty editions, till he brought it to a degree of perfection which will render it as permanent as the English language itself;" censures (and not without reason) the "presumption" of those "superficial critics" who have attempted to amend the work, and usurp his honours; and, regarding the compiler's confession of his indebtedness to others, but as a mark of "his exemplary diffidence of his own merits," adds, (in very bad English,) "Perhaps there never was an author whose success and fame were *more unexpected by himself than Lindley Murray.*"—*The Friend*, vol. iii, p. 33.

17. In a New-York edition of Murray's Grammar, printed in 1812, there was inserted a "Caution to the Public," by Collins & Co., his American correspondents and publishers, in which are set forth the unparalleled success and merit of the work, "as it came *in purity* from the pen of the author;" with an earnest remonstrance against the several *revised editions* which had appeared at Boston, Philadelphia, and other places, and against the unwarrantable liberties taken by American teachers, in altering the work, under pretence of improving it. In this article it is stated, "that *the whole* of these mutilated editions *have been seen* and examined by Lindley Murray himself, and that they have met with *his decided disapprobation.* Every rational mind," continue these gentlemen, "will agree with him, that, 'the *rights of living authors*, and the *interests of science and literature*, demand the abolition of this *ungenerous practice.*'" (See this also in *Murray's Key*, N. Y., 1811, p. iii.) Here, then, we have the opinion and feeling of Murray himself, upon this tender point of right. Here we see the tables turned, and other men judging it "scarcely necessary to apologize for the use which *they have made* of their predecessors' labours."

18. It is really remarkable to find an author and his admirers so much at variance, as are Murray and his commenders, in relation to his grammatical authorship; and yet, under what circumstances could men have stronger desires to avoid apparent contradiction? They, on the one side, claim for him the highest degree of merit as a grammarian; and continue to applaud his works as if nothing more could be desired in the study of English grammar—a branch of learning which some of them are willing emphatically to call "*his* science." He, on the contrary, to avert the charge of plagiarism, disclaims almost every thing in which any degree of literary merit consists; supposes it impossible to write an English grammar the greater part of which is not a "compilation;" acknowledges that originality belongs to but a small part of his own; trusts that such a general acknowledgement will protect him from all censure; suppresses the names of other writers, and leaves his examples to rest solely on his own authority; and, "contented with the great respectability of his private character and station, is satisfied with being *useful*

as an author."—*The Friend*, vol. iii, p. 33. By the high praises bestowed upon his works, his own voice is overborne : the trumpet of fame has drowned it. His liberal authorship is profitable in trade, and interest has power to swell and prolong the strain.

19. The name and character of Lindley Murray are too venerable to allow us to approach even the errors of his grammars, without some recognition of the respect due to his personal virtues and benevolent intentions. For the private virtues of Murray, I entertain as cordial a respect as any other man. Nothing is argued against these, even if it be proved that causes independent of true literary merit have given him his great and unexpected fame as a grammarian. It is not intended by the introduction of these notices, to impute to him any thing more or less than what his own words plainly imply ; except those inaccuracies and deficiencies which still disgrace his work as a literary performance, and which of course he did not discover. He himself knew that he had not brought the book to such perfection as has been ascribed to it ; for, by way of apology for his frequent alterations, he says, " Works of this nature admit of repeated improvements ; and are, perhaps, never complete." Necessity has urged this reasoning upon me. I am as far from any invidious feeling, or any sordid motive, as was Lindley Murray. But it is due to truth, to correct erroneous impressions ; and, in order to obtain from some an impartial examination of the following pages, it seemed necessary first to convince them, *that it is possible* to compose a better grammar than Murray's, without being particularly indebted to him. If this treatise is not such, a great deal of time has been thrown away upon a useless project ; and if it is, the achievement is no fit subject for either pride or envy. It differs from his, and from all the pretended amendments of his, as a new map, drawn from actual and minute surveys, differs from an old one, compiled chiefly from others still older and confessedly still more imperfect. The region and the scope are essentially the same ; the tracing and the colouring are more original ; and (if the reader can pardon the suggestion) perhaps more accurate and vivid.

20. He who makes a new grammar, does nothing for the advancement of learning, unless his performance excel all earlier ones designed for the same purpose ; and nothing for his own honour, unless such excellence result from the exercise of his own ingenuity and taste. A good style naturally commends itself to every reader—even to him who cannot tell why it is worthy of preference. Hence there is reason to believe, that the true principles of practical grammar, deduced from custom and sanctioned by time, will never be generally superseded by any thing which individual caprice may substitute. In the republic of letters, there will always be some who can distinguish merit ; and it is impossible that these should ever be converted to any whimsical theory of language, which goes to make void the learning of past ages. There will always be some who can discern the difference between originality of style, and innovation in doctrine,—between a due regard to the opinions of others, and an actual usurpation of their text ; and it is incredible that these should ever be satisfied with any mere compilation of grammar, or with any such authorship as either confesses or betrays the writer's own incompetence. For it is not true, that, " an English grammar must necessarily be," in any considerable degree, if at all, " a compilation ; " nay, on such a theme, and in " the grammatical part " of the work, all compilation beyond a fair use of authorities regularly quoted, or of materials either voluntarily furnished or free to all, most unavoidably implies — not conscious " ability," generously doing honour to rival merit — nor " exemplary diffidence," modestly veiling its own — but inadequate skill and inferior talents, bribing the public by the spoils of genius, and seeking precedence by such means as not even the purest desire of doing good can justify.

21. Among the professed copiers of Murray, there is not one to whom the foregoing remarks do not apply, as forcibly as to him. For no one of them all has

attempted any thing more honourable to himself, or more beneficial to the public, than what their master had before achieved; nor is there any one, who, with the same disinterestedness, has guarded his design from the imputation of a pecuniary motive. It is comical to observe what they say in their prefaces. Between praise to sustain their choice of a model, and blame to make room for their pretended amendments, they are often placed in as awkward a dilemma, as that which was contrived when grammar was identified with compilation. I should have much to say, were I to show them all in their true light.* Few of them have had such success as to be worthy of notice here; but the names of many will find frequent place in my code of false grammar. The one who seems to be now taking the lead in fame and revenue, filled with glad wonder at his own popularity, is SAMUEL KIRKHAM. Upon this gentleman's performance, I shall therefore bestow a few brief observations. If I do not overrate this author's literary importance, a fair exhibition of the character of his grammar, may be made an instructive lesson to some of our modern literati. The book is a striking sample of a numerous species.

22. Kirkham's treatise is entitled, " English Grammar *in Familiar Lectures,* accompanied by a *Compendium,*" that is, by a folded sheet. Of this work, of which I have recently seen copies purporting to be of the " sixty-seventh edition," and others again of the " hundred and fifth edition," each published at Baltimore in 1835, I can give no earlier account, than what may be derived from the " second edition, enlarged and much improved," which was published at Harrisburg in 1825. The preface, which appears to have been written for his *first* edition, is dated, " Fredericktown, Md., August 22, 1823." In it, there is no recognition of any obligation to Murray, or to any other grammarian in particular; but with the modest assumption, that the style of the " best philologists," needed to be retouched, the book is presented to the world under the following pretensions :

"The author of this production has endeavoured to condense *all the most important subject-matter of the whole science,* and present it in so small a compass that the learner can become familiarly acquainted with it in a *short time.* He makes but small pretensions to originality in theoretical matter. Most of the principles laid down, have been selected from our *best modern philologists.* If his work is entitled to any degree of *merit,* it is not on account of a judicious selection of principles and rules, but for the easy mode adopted of communicating *these* to the mind of the learner."—*Kirkham's Grammar,* 1825, p. 10.

23. It will be found on examination, that what this author regarded as " *all the most important subject-matter of the whole science* " *of grammar,* included nothing more than the most common elements of the orthography, etymology, and syntax, of the English tongue — beyond which his scholarship appears not to have extended. Whatsoever relates to derivation, to the sounds of the letters, to prosody, (as punctuation, utterance, figures, versification, and poetic diction,) found no place in ·his " comprehensive system of grammar; " nor do his later editions treat any of these things amply or well. In short, he treats nothing well; for he is a bad writer. Commencing his career of authorship under circumstances the most forbidding, yet receiving encouragement from commendations bestowed in pity, he proceeded, like a man of business, to profit mainly by the chance; and, without ever acquiring either the feelings or the habits of a scholar, soon learned by experience that, " It is much better to *write* than [to] *starve.*"—*Kirkham's Gram.* stereotyped, p. 89. It is cruel in any man, to look narrowly into the faults of an author who peddles a school-book for bread. The starveling wretch whose defence and plea are poverty and sickness, demands, and must have, in the name of humanity, an immunity from criticism, if not the patronage of the public. Far be it from me, to notice any such character, except with kindness and charity. Nor

---

* " Grammatici namque auctoritas per se nulla est; quum ex sola doctissimorum oratorum, historicorum, poetarum, et aliorum ideoneorum scriptorum observatione, constet ortam esse veram grammaticam. *Multa dicenda forent, si grammatistarum ineptias refellere vellem :* sed nulla est gloria praeterire asellos."—DESPAUTERII Praef. Art. Versif. fol. iii, 1517.

need I be told, that tenderness is due to the "*young;*" or that noble results sometimes follow unhopeful beginnings. These things are understood and duly appreciated. The gentleman was young once, even as he says; and I, his equal in years, was then, in authorship, as young—though, it were to be hoped, not quite so immature. But, as circumstances alter cases, so time and chance alter circumstances. Under no circumstances, however, can the artifices of quackery be thought excusable in him who claims to be the very greatest of modern grammarians. The niche that in the temple of learning belongs to any individual, can be no other than that which his own labours have purchased: here, his *own merit* alone must be his pedestal. If this critical sketch be uni::peachably *just*, its publication requires no further warrant. The correction has been forborne, till the subject of it has become rich, and popular, and proud; proud enough at least to have published his utter contempt for me and all my works. Yet not for this do I judge him worthy of notice here, but merely as an apt example of some men's grammatical success and fame. The ways and means to these grand results are what I purpose now to consider.

24. The common supposition, that the world is steadily advancing in knowledge and improvement, would seem to imply, that the man who could plausibly boast of being the most successful and most popular grammarian of the nineteenth century, cannot but be a scholar of such merit as to deserve some place, if not in the general literary history of his age, at least in the particular history of the science which he teaches. It will presently be seen that the author of " English Grammar in Familiar Lectures," boasts of a degree of success and popularity, which, in this age of the world, has no parallel. It is not intended on my part, to dispute any of his assertions on these points; but rather to take it for granted, that in reputation and revenue he is altogether as preëminent as he pretends to be. The character of his alleged *improvements*, however, I shall inspect with the eyes of one who means to know the certainty for himself; and, in this item of literary history, the reader shall see, in some sort, *what profit* there is in grammar. Is the common language of two of the largest and most enlightened nations on earth so little understood, and its true grammar so little known or appreciated, that one of the most unscholarly and incompetent of all pretenders to grammar can have found means to outrival all the grammarians who have preceded him? Have plagiarism and quackery become the only means of success in philology? Are there now instances to which an intelligent critic may point, and say, " This man, or that, though he can scarcely write a page of-good English, has patched up a grammar, by the help of Murray's text only, and thereby made himself rich?" Is there such a charm in the name of *Murray*, and the word *improvement*, that by these two implements alone, the obscurest of men, or the absurdest of teachers, may work his passage to fame; and then, perchance, by contrast of circumstances, grow conceited and arrogant, from the fortune of the undertaking? Let us see what we can find in Kirkham's Grammar, which will go to answer these questions.

25. Take first from one page of his " hundred and fifth edition," a few brief quotations, as a sample of his thoughts and style:

"They, however, who introduce *usages which depart from the analogy and philosophy* of a language, *are conspicuous* among the number of those who *form that language*, and have power to control it." " PRINCIPLE.—A principle in grammar is a *peculiar construction* of the language, sanctioned by good usage." " DEFINITION.—A definition in grammar is a *principle* of language expressed in a *definite form*." " RULE.—A rule describes *the peculiar construction* or circumstantial relation of words, *which* custom has established for our observance."—*Kirkham's Grammar*, p. 18.

Now, as " a rule describes a peculiar construction," and " a principle is a peculiar construction," and " a definition is a principle;" how, according to this grammarian, do a principle, a definition, and a rule, differ each from the others? From the rote here imposed, it is certainly not easier for the learner to conceive of all these things *distinctly*, than it is to understand how a departure from philosophy may make a man deservedly "*conspicuous.*" It were easy to multiply examples like these, showing the work to be deficient in clearness, the first requisite of style.

26. The following passages may serve as a specimen of the gentleman's taste, and grammatical accuracy; in one of which, he supposes the neuter verb *is* to express an *action*, and every *honest man* to be *long since dead!* So it stands in all his editions. Did his praisers think so too?

"It is correct to say, *The man eats, he eats;* but we cannot say, *The man dog eats, he dog eats.* Why not? Because the man *is here represented* as the possessor, and dog, the property, or thing possessed; and the genius of our language requires, that when we add *to the possessor*, the *thing* which *he* is represented as possessing, *the possessor shall* take a particular form to show ITS case, or relation to the property."—*Ib.* p. 52.

THE PRESENT TENSE.—"This tense *is* sometimes applied to represent the *actions* of persons *long since dead;* as, 'Seneca *reasons* and *moralizes* well; An HONEST MAN IS the noblest work of God.'"—*Ib.* p. 138.

PARTICIPLES.—"The term *Participle* comes from the Latin word *participio,* * which signifies to *partake.*"—"Participles are formed by adding to the verb the termination *ing, ed,* or *en.* *Ing* signifies the same as the noun *being.* When *postfixed* to the *noun-state* of the verb, the *compound word* thus formed, expresses a continued state of the *verbal denotement.* It implies that what is meant by the verb, is *being* continued."—*Ib.* p. 78. "All participles *are compound* in their meaning and office."—*Ib.* p. 79.

VERBS.—"Verbs express, not only *the state* or *manner of being,* but, likewise, all the different *actions* and *movements* of all creatures and things, whether animate or inanimate."—*Ib.* p. 62. "It can be easily shown, that from the noun and' verb, all the other parts of speech have sprung. Nay, more. *They* may even be reduced to *one.* *Verbs do not, in reality, express actions;* but they are intrinsically *the mere* NAMES *of actions.*"—*Ib.* p. 37.

PHILOSOPHICAL GRAMMAR.—"I have thought proper to intersperse through the pages of this work, under the head of '*Philosophical Notes,*' an entire system of grammatical principles as deduced from *what appears † to me to* be the *most rational and consistent* philosophical investigations."—*Ib.* p. 36. "Johnson, and Blair, and Lowth, *would have been laughed at,* had they essayed *to thrust any thing like our* modernized philosophical grammar *down the throats of their cotemporaries.*"—*Ib.* p. 143.

Is it not a pity, that "more than one hundred thousand children and youth" should be daily poring over language and logic like this?

27. For the sake of those who happily remain ignorant of this successful empiricism, it is desirable that the record and exposition of it be made brief. There is little danger that it will long survive its author. But the present subjects of it are sufficiently numerous to deserve some pity. The following is a sample of the gentleman's method of achieving what he both justly and exultingly supposes, that Johnson, or Blair, or Lowth, could not have effected. He scoffs at his own grave instructions, as if they had been the production of some *other* impostor. Can the fact be credited, that in the following instances, he speaks of *what he himself teaches?*"—of what he seriously pronounces "*most rational and consistent?*—of what is part and parcel of that philosophy of his, which he declares, "will *in general be found to accord* with the *practical theory* embraced in the body of his work?*" See *Kirkham's Gram.* p. 36.

"Call this '*philosophical parsing,*' on reasoning principles, according to the original laws of nature and of thought,' and *the pill will be swallowed,* by pedants and their dupes, with the greatest ease imaginable."—*Kirkham's Gram.* p. 144. "For the *satisfaction* of those teachers who prefer it, *and for their adoption, too,* a modernized philosophical theory of the moods and tenses is here presented. If it is not quite so convenient and useful as the old one, they need not hesitate to adopt it. It has the advantage of being *new;* and, moreover, it sounds *large,* and will make the *commonalty stars.* Let it be distinctly understood that you teach '[*Kirkham's*] *philosophical grammar,* founded on reason and common sense,' and you will pass for a very learned man, and

---

* The Latin word for *participle* is *participium,* which makes *participio* in the dative or the ablative case; but the Latin word for *partake* is *participo,* and not "*participio.*"—G. BROWN.

† This sentence is manifestly bad English : either the singular verb "*appears*" should be made plural, or the plural noun "*investigations*" should be made singular.—G. BROWN.

make all the good housewives wonder at the rapid march of intellect, and the vast improvements of the age."—*Ib. p.* 141.

28. The *pretty promises* with which these "Familiar Lectures" abound, are also worthy to be noticed here, as being among the peculiar attractions of the performance. The following may serve as a specimen :

"If you *proceed according to my instructions*, you will be sure to acquire a practical knowledge of Grammar in *a short time.*"—*Kirkham's Gram.* p. 49. "If you have sufficient *resolution to do this*, you will, in a short time, *perfectly understand* the nature and office of the different parts of speech, their various properties and relations, and the rules of syntax that apply to them ; *and, in a few weeks*, be able to speak and write accurately." —*Ib.* p. 62. "You will please to turn back and read over again *the whole five lectures.* You must exercise *a little* patience."—*Ib.* p. 82. "By studying these lectures with attention, you will acquire *more grammatical* knowledge in *three months*, than is commonly obtained in *two years.*"—*Ib.* p. 82. "I will conduct you *so smoothly through the moods and tenses*, and the conjugation of verbs, that, instead of finding yourself involved in obscurities and deep intricacies, you will scarcely find *an obstruction to impede* your progress."—*Ib.* p. 133. "The supposed Herculean task of learning to conjugate verbs, will be transformed into *a few hours of pleasant pastime.*"—*Ib.* p. 142. "By *examining carefully* the conjugation of the verb through this mood, you will find it *very easy.*"—*Ib.* p. 147. "By pursuing the following direction, you can, *in a very short time*, learn to conjugate any verb." —*Ib.* p. 147. "Although this mode of procedure *may, at first, appear to be laborious*, yet, as it is necessary, I trust you will not hesitate to adopt it. *My confidence in your perseverance*, induces me to recommend *any course* which I know will tend to facilitate your progress."—*Ib.* p. 148.

29. The grand boast of this author is, that he *has succeeded* in " pleasing himself and the public." He trusts to have " gained the latter point," to so great an extent, and with such security of tenure, that henceforth no man can safely question *the merit* of his performance. Happy mortal ! to whom that success which is the ground of his pride, is also the glittering ægis of his sure defence ! To this he points with exultation and self-applause, as if the prosperity of the wicked, or the popularity of an imposture, had never yet been heard of in this clever world ! [*] Upon *what* merit this success has been founded, my readers may judge, when I shall have finished this slight review of his work. Probably no other grammar was ever so industriously spread. Such was the author's perseverance in his measures to increase the demand for his book, that even the attainment of such accuracy as he was capable of, was less a subject of concern. For in an article designed " to ward off some of the arrows of criticism,"—an advertisement which, from the eleventh to the " one hundred and fifth edition," has been promising " to the *publick another and a better* edition,"—he plainly offers this urgent engagement, as " an apology for its defects :"

" The author is apprehensive that his work is *not yet as* accurate and *as* much simplified as it *may be.* If, however, the disadvantages of lingering under a broken constitution, and of being able to devote to this subject *only a small portion of his time*, snatched from the *active pursuits of a business life*, (active as far as imperfect health permits him to be,) are my apology for its defects, he hopes that the candid will set down *the apology to his credit.*—Not that he would beg a truce with the gentlemen *criticks* and reviewers. Any compromise with them would betray a want of *self-confidence* and *moral courage*, which he would by no means, be willing to avow."—*Kirkham's Gram.* (Adv. of 1829,) p. 7.

30. Now, to this painful struggle, this active contention between business and the vapours, let all *credit* be given, and all *sympathy* be added ; but, as an aid to the

[*] "What! a book have *no merit*, and yet be called for at the rate of *sixty thousand copies a year!* What a slander is this upon the public taste! What an insult to the understanding and discrimination of the good people of these United States! According to this reasoning, all the inhabitants of our land must be fools, except one man, and that man is GOOLD BROWN ! "—KIRKHAM *in the Knickerbocker,* Oct. 1837, p. 361. Well may the honest critic expect to be called a slanderer of " the public taste," and an insulter of the nation's " understanding." If both the merit of this vaunted book and the wisdom of its purchasers are to be measured and proved by the author's profits, or the publishers' account of sales ! But, possibly, between the intrinsic merit and the market value of some books there may be a difference. Lord Byron received from Murray his bookseller, nearly ten dollars a line for the fourth canto of Childe Harold, or about as much for every two lines, as Milton obtained for the whole of Paradise Lost. Is this the true ratio of the merit of these authors, or of the wisdom of the different ages in which they lived?

studies of healthy children, what better is the book, for any forbearance or favour that may have been won by this apology? It is well known, that, till *phrenology* became the common talk, the author's principal business was, to commend his own method of teaching *grammar*, and to turn this publication to profit. This honourable industry, aided as himself suggests, by " not much *less* than one thousand written recommendations," is said to have wrought for him, in a very few years, a degree of success and fame, at which both the eulogists of Murray and the friends of English grammar may hang their heads. As to a "*compromise*" with any critic or reviewer whom he cannot bribe, it is enough to say of that, it is morally impossible. Nor was it necessary for such an author to throw the gauntlet, to prove himself not lacking in "*self-confidence.*" He can show his "*moral courage,*" only by daring do right.

31. In 1829, after his book had gone through ten editions, and the demand for it had become so great as "to call forth twenty thousand copies during the year," the prudent author, intending to veer his course according to the *trade-wind*, thought it expedient to retract his former acknowledgement to " our best modern philologists," and to profess himself a modifier of the Great Compiler's code. Where then holds the anchor of his praise? Let the reader say, after weighing and comparing his various pretensions:

"Aware that there is, in the *publick* mind, a strong predilection for the doctrines contained in Mr. Murray's grammar, he has thought proper, not merely from motives of policy, but from choice, *to select his principles chiefly from that work;* and, moreover, to adopt, as far as consistent with his own views, *the language of that eminent philologist.* In no instance has he varied from him, unless he conceived that, in so doing, *some practical advantage* would be gained. He hopes, *therefore,* to escape the censure so frequently and so justly awarded to those *unfortunate innovators* who have not scrupled to alter, mutilate, and torture the text of that able writer, merely to gratify an itching propensity to figure in the world *as authors,* and gain an ephemeral popularity by arrogating to themselves *the credit due to another.*" *—Kirkham's Gram.,* 1829, p. 10.

32. Now these statements are either true or false; and I know not on which supposition they are most creditable to the writer. Had any Roman grammatist thus profited by the name of Varro or Quintilian, he would have been filled with constant dread of somewhere meeting the injured author's frowning shade! Surely, among the professed admirers of Murray, no other man, whether innovator or copyist, unfortunate or successful, is at all to be compared to this gentleman for the audacity with which he has " not scrupled to alter, mutilate, and torture, the text of that able writer." Murray simply intended to do good, and good that might descend to posterity; and this just and generous intention goes far to excuse even his errors. But Kirkham, speaking of posterity, scruples not to disavow and renounce all care for them, or for any thing which a coming age may think of his character: saying,

"My pretensions reach not so far. To the *present generation only,* I present my claims. Should it lend me a listening ear, and grant me its suffrages, *the height of my ambition* will be attained."—*Advertisement, in his Elocution,* p. 346.

His whole design is, therefore, upon the very face of it, a paltry scheme of present income. And, seeing his entered classes of boys and girls must soon have done with him, he has doubtless acted wisely, and quite in accordance with his own interest, to have made all possible haste in his career.

33. Being no rival with him in this race, and having no personal quarrel with

---

* Kirkham's real opinion of Murray cannot be known from this passage only. How able is that writer who is chargeable with the *greatest want* of taste and discernment? "In regard to the application of the final pause in reading blank verse, *nothing can betray a greater want of rhetorical taste and philosophical acumen,* than the directions of Mr. Murray."—*Kirkham's Elocution,* p. 145. Kirkham is indeed no judge either of the merits, or of the demerits, of Murray's writings; nor is it probable that this criticism originated with himself. But, since it appears in his name, let him have the credit of it, and of representing the compiler whom he calls " *that able writer* " and " *that eminent philologist,*" as an untasteful dunce, and a teacher of *nonsense:* "To say that, unless we 'make every *line* sensible to the ear,' we mar the melody, and suppress the numbers of the poet, is *all nonsense.*"—*Ibid.* See Murray's Grammar, on " Poetical Pauses," 8vo, p. 260; 12mo, 210.

him on any account, I would, for his sake, fain rejoice at his success, and withhold my criticisms; because he is said to have been liberal with his gains, and because he has not, like some others, copied me in stead of Murray. But the vindication of a greatly injured and perverted science, constrains me to say, on this occasion, that pretensions less consistent with themselves, or less sustained by taste and scholarship, have seldom, if ever, been promulgated in the name of grammar. I have, certainly, no intention to say more than is due to the uninformed and the misguided. For some who are ungenerous and prejudiced themselves, will not be unwilling to think me so; and even this freedom, backed and guarded as it is, by facts and proofs irrefragable, may still be ingeniously ascribed to an ill motive. To two thirds of the community, one grammar is just as good as an other; because they neither know, nor wish to know, more than may be learned from the very worst. An honest expression of sentiment against abuses of a literary nature, is little the fashion of these times; and the good people who purchase books upon the recommendations of others, may be slow to believe there is *no* merit where so much has been attributed. But facts may well be credited, in opposition to courteous flattery, when there are the author's own words and works to vouch for them in the face of day. Though a thousand of our great men may have helped a copier's weak copyist to take "some practical advantage" of the world's credulity, it is safe to aver, in the face of dignity still greater, that testimonials more fallacious have seldom mocked the cause of learning. They did not read his book.

34. Notwithstanding the author's change in his professions, the work is now essentially the same as it was at first; except that its errors and contradictions have been greatly multiplied, by the addition of new matter inconsistent with the old. He evidently cares not what doctrines he teaches, or whose; but, as various theories are noised abroad, seizes upon different opinions, and mixes them together, that his books may contain something to suit all parties. "*A System of Philosophical Grammar*," though but an idle speculation, even in his own account, and doubly absurd in him, as being flatly contradictory to his main text, has been thought worthy of insertion. And what his title-page denominates "*A New System of Punctuation*," though mostly in the very words of Murray, was next invented to supply a deficiency which he at length discovered. To admit these, and some other additions, the "comprehensive system of grammar" was gradually extended from 144 small duodecimo pages, to 228 of the ordinary size. And, in this compass, it was finally stereotyped in 1829; so that the ninety-four editions published since, have nothing new for history.

35. But the publication of an other work designed for schools, "*An Essay on Elocution*," shows the progress of the author's mind. Nothing can be more radically opposite, than are some of the elementary doctrines which this gentleman is now teaching; nothing, more strangely inconsistent, than are some of his declarations and professions. For instance: "A consonant is a letter that cannot be perfectly sounded without the help of a vowel."—*Kirkham's Gram.* p. 19. Again: "A consonant is not only capable of being perfectly sounded without the help of a vowel, but, moreover, of forming, like a vowel, a separate syllable."— *Kirkham's Elocution*, p. 32. Take a second example. He makes "ADJECTIVE PRONOUNS" a *prominent division* and *leading title*, in treating of the pronouns proper; defines the term in a manner peculiar to himself; prefers and uses it in all his parsing; and yet, by the third sentence of the story, the learner is conducted to this just conclusion: "Hence, such a thing as an *adjective-pronoun* cannot exist."—*Grammar*, p. 105. Once more. Upon his own rules, or such as he had borrowed, he comments thus, and comments *truly*, because he had either written them badly or made an ill choice: "But some of these rules are foolish, trifling, and unimportant."—*Elocution*, p 97. Again: "Rules 10 and 11, rest on a sandy foundation. They appear not to be based on the principles of the language."—

8

Grammar, p. 59. These are but specimens of his own frequent testimony against himself! Nor shall he find refuge in the impudent falsehood, that the things which I quote as his, are not his own.* These contradictory texts, and scores of others which might be added to them, are as rightfully his own, as any doctrine he has ever yet inculcated. But, upon the credulity of ignorance, his high-sounding certificates and unbounded boasting can impose any thing. They overrule all in favour of one of the worst grammars extant;—of which he says, "It is now studied by more than one hundred thousand children and youth; and is more extensively used than *all other English grammars* published in the United States."—*Elocution*, p. 347. The booksellers say, he receives from his publishers *ten cents a copy*, on this work, and that he reports the sale of *sixty thousand copies per annum*. Such has of late been his public boast. I have once had the story from his own lips, and of course congratulated him, though I dislike the book. Six thousand dollars a year, on this most miserable modification of Lindley Murray's Grammar! Be it so—or double, if he and the public please. Murray had so little originality in his work, or so little selfishness in his design, that he would not take any thing; and his may ultimately prove the better bargain.

36. A man may boast and bless himself as he pleases, his fortune, surely, can never be worthy of an other's envy, so long as he finds it inadequate to his own great merits, and unworthy of his own poor gratitude. As a grammarian, Kirkham claims to be second only to Lindley Murray; and says, "Since the days of Lowth, no other work on grammar, Murray's only excepted, has been so favourably received by the *publick* as his own. As a proof of this, he would mention, that within the last six years it has passed through *fifty* editions."—*Preface to Elocution*, p. 12. And, at the same time, and in the same preface, he complains, that, "Of all the labours done under the sun, the labours *of the pen* meet with the poorest reward." *Ibid.* p. 5. This too clearly favours the report, that his books were not written by himself, but by others whom he hired. Possibly, the anonymous helper may here have penned, not his employer's feeling, but a line of his own experience. But I choose to ascribe the passage to the professed author, and to hold him answerable for the inconsistency. Willing to illustrate by the best and fairest examples these fruitful means of grammatical fame, I am glad of his present success, which, through this record, shall become yet more famous. It is the only thing which makes him worthy of the notice here taken of him. But I cannot sympathize with his complaint, because he never sought any but "the poorest reward;" and more than all he sought, he found. In his last "Address to Teachers," he says, "He may doubtless be permitted emphatically to say with Prospero, '*Your breath has filled my sails.*'"—*Elocution*, p. 18. If this boasting has any truth in it, he ought to be satisfied. But it is written, "He that loveth silver, shall not be satisfied with silver; nor he that loveth abundance, with increase." Let him remember this.† He now announces three or four other works as forthcoming shortly. What these will achieve, the world will see. But I must confine myself to the Grammar.

37. In this volume, scarcely any thing is found where it might be expected. "The author," as he tells us in his preface, "has not followed the common 'artificial and unnatural arrangement adopted by most of his predecessors;' *yet he* has endeavoured to pursue a more judicious one, namely, '*the order of the understanding.*'"—*Grammar*, p. 12. But if this is the order of his understanding, he is greatly to be pitied. A book more confused in its plan, more wanting in method, more imperfect in distinctness of parts, more deficient in symmetry, or

* "Now, in these instances, I should be fair game, were it not for the *trifling* difference, that I happen to present the doctrines and notions of *other writers*, and NOT my own, as stated by my learned censor."—*Kirkham, in the Knickerbocker*, Oct. 1837, p. 360. If the instructions above cited are not his own, there is not, within the lids of either book, a penny's worth that is. His fruitful, copy-rights are void in law: the "learned censor's" pledge shall guaranty this issue.—G. B. 1838.

† I am sorry to observe that the gentleman, Phrenologist, as he professes to be, has so little *reverence* in his crown. He could not read the foregoing suggestion without scoffing at it. Biblical truth is not powerless, though the scornful may refuse its correction.—G. B. 1838.

more difficult of reference, shall not easily be found in stereotype. Let the reader try to follow us here. Bating twelve pages at the beginning, occupied by the title, recommendations, advertisement, contents, preface, hints to teachers, and advice to lecturers; and fifty-four at the end, embracing syntax, orthography, orthoëpy, provincialisms, prosody, punctuation, versification, rhetoric, figures of speech, and a Key, all in the sequence here given; the work consists of fourteen chapters of grammar, absurdly called " Familiar Lectures." The first treats of sundries, under half a dozen titles, but chiefly of Orthography; and the last is three pages and a half, of the most common remarks, on Derivation. In the remaining twelve, the Etymology and Syntax of the ten parts of speech are commingled; and an attempt is made, to teach simultaneously all that the author judged important in either. Hence he gives us, in a strange congeries, rules, remarks, illustrations, false syntax, systematic parsing, exercises in parsing, two different orders of notes, three different orders of questions, and a variety of other titles merely occasional. All these things, being additional to his main text, are to be connected, in the mind of the learner, with the parts of speech successively, in some new and inexplicable catenation found only in the arrangement of the lectures. The author himself could not see through the chaos. He accordingly made his table of contents a mere meagre alphabetical index. Having once attempted in vain to explain the order of his instructions, he actually gave the matter up in despair!

88. In length, these pretended lectures vary, from three or four pages, to eight-and-thirty. Their subjects run thus: 1. Language, Grammar, Orthography; 2. Nouns and Verbs; 3. Articles; 4. Adjectives; 5. Participles; 6. Adverbs; 7. Prepositions; 8. Pronouns; 9. Conjunctions; 10. Interjections and Nouns; 11. Moods and Tenses; 12. Irregular Verbs; 13. Auxiliary, Passive, and Defective Verbs; 14. Derivation. Which, now, is "more judicious," such confusion as this, or the arrangement which has been common from time immemorial? Who that has any respect for the human intellect, or whose powers of mind deserve any in return, will avouch this jumble to be "the order of the understanding?" Are the methods of science to be accounted mere hinderances to instruction? Has grammar really been made easy by this confounding of its parts? Or are we lured by the name, "Familiar Lectures,"—a term manifestly adopted as a mere decoy, and, with respect to the work itself, totally inappropriate? If these chapters have ever been actually delivered as a series of lectures, the reader must have been employed on some occasions eight or ten times as long as on others! "People," says Dr. Johnson, "have now-a-days got a strange opinion that every thing should be taught by lectures. Now, I cannot see that lectures can do so much good as a private reading of the books from which the lectures are taken. I know of nothing that can be best taught by lectures, except where experiments are to be shown. You may teach chymistry by lectures—you might teach the making of shoes by lectures."—Boswell's Life of Johnson.

89. With singular ignorance and untruth, this gentleman claims to have invented a better method of analysis than had ever been practised before. Of other grammars, his preface avers, "They have all overlooked what the author considers a very important object; namely, a systematick order of parsing."—Grammar, p. 9. And, in his "Hints to Teachers," presenting himself as a model, and his book as a paragon, he says: "By pursuing this system, he can, with less labour, advance a pupil farther in the practical knowledge of this abstruse science, in two months, than he could in one year, when he taught in the old way."—Grammar, p. 12. What his "old way" was, does not appear. Doubtless something sufficiently bad. And as to his new way, I shall hereafter have occasion to show that that is sufficiently bad also. But to this gasconade the simple-minded have given credit—because the author showed certificates that testified to his great success, and called him "amiable and modest!" But who can look into the book,

or into the writer's pretensions in regard to his predecessors, and conceive the meri
which has made him—" preëminent by so much odds ? "   Was Murray less praise
worthy, less amiable, or less modest?   In illustration of my topic, and for the sak
of literary justice, I have selected that honoured "*Compiler*" to show the abuse
of praise ; let the history of this his vaunting *modifier* cap the climax of vanity
In general, his amendments of " that eminent philologist," are not more skillfu
than the following touch upon an eminent dramatist ; and here, it is plain, he ha
mistaken two nouns for adjectives, and converted into bad English a beautifu
passage, the sentiment of which is worthy of an *author's* recollection :

> " The evil *deed* or *deeds* that men do, *lives* after them ;
>   The good *deed* or *deeds* *is* oft interred with their bones."*
>   *Kirkham's Grammar*, p. 75.

40. Lord Bacon observes, " Nothing is thought so easy a request to a great per
son as his letter ; and yet, if it be not in a good cause, it is so much out of hi
reputation."   It is to this mischievous facility of recommendation, this prostitute
influence of great names, that the inconvenient diversity of school-books, and th
continued use of bad ones, are in a great measure to be attributed.   It belongs t
those who understand the subjects of which authors profess to treat, to judge fairl
and fully of their works, and then to let the *reasons* of their judgement be known
For no one will question the fact, that a vast number of the school-books now i
use are either egregious plagiarisms or productions of no comparative merit
And, what is still more surprising and monstrous, presidents, governors, senators
and judges ; professors, doctors, clergymen, and lawyers ; a host of titled connois
seurs ; with incredible facility lend their names, not only to works of inferio
merit, but to the vilest thefts, and the wildest absurdities, palmed off upon thei
own and the public credulity, under pretence of improvement.   The man who thu
prefixes his letter of recommendation to an ill-written book, publishes, out of mer
courtesy, a direct impeachment of his own scholarship or integrity.   Yet, hov
often have we seen the honours of a high office, or even of a worthy name, prosti
tuted to give a temporary or local currency to a book which it would disgrace an
man of letters to quote !   With such encouragement, nonsense wrestles for th
seat of learning, exploded errors are republished as novelties, original writers ar
plundered by dunces, and men that understand nothing well, profess to teach al
sciences !

---

* Every schoolboy is familiar with the following lines, and rightly understands the words " *evil* " an
" *good* " to be *nouns*, and not *adjectives* :

> " The *evil* that men do, lives after them ;
>   The *good* is oft interred with their bones."—SHAKSPEARE.
>   *Julius Cæsar, Act* 8 : *Antony's Funeral Oration over Cæsar's Body*

Kirkham has vehemently censured me for *omitting the brackets* in which he encloses the words that h
supposes to be *understood* in this complet.   But he forgets two important circumstances : *First*, that I w
quoting, not the bard, but the grammatist ; *Second*, that a writer uses brackets, to distinguish *his* ow
amendments of what he quotes, and not those of an other man.   Hence the marks which he has used, woul
have been *improper* for me.   Their insertion does not make his reading of the passage *good English*, and
consequently, does not avert the point of my criticism.

The foregoing Review of Kirkham's Grammar, was published as an extract from my manuscript, by th
editors of the Knickerbocker, in their number for June, 1837.   Four months afterwards, with friendship
changed, they gave him the " justice " of appearing in their pages, in a long and virulent article against m
and my works, representing me, " with emphatic force," as " *a knave, a liar, and a pedant*."   The enmity t
that effusion I forgave ; because I bore him no personal ill-will, and was not selfish enough to quarrel for m
own sake.   Its *imbecility* clearly proved, that in this critique there is nothing *with which he could justly fin*
fault.   Perceiving that no point of this argument could be broken, he *changed the ground*, and satisfie
himself with despising, upbraiding, and vilifying the writer.   Of what *use* this was, others may judge.

This extraordinary grammarian survived the publication of my criticism about ten years ; and, it !
charitably hoped, died happily ; while I have had, for a period somewhat longer, all the benefits which h
earnest " *castigation* " was fit to confer.   It is not perceived, that what was written before these events, shou
now be altered or suppressed by reason of them.   With his pretended " defence," I shall now concern mys
no further than simply to deny one remarkable assertion contained in it ; which is this—that I, Goold Brow
" at the funeral of Aaron Ely," in 1830, " praised, and *highly* praised, this self-same Grammar, and declared
to be ' A GOOD WORK ! ' ! "—*Kirkham, in the Knickerbocker*, Oct. 1837, p. 362.   I treated him always courteous
and, on this solemn occasion, walked with him without disputing on grammar ; but, if this statement of h
has any reasonable foundation, I know not what it is.—G. B. in 1850.

41. All praise of excellence must needs be comparative, because the thing itself is so. To excel in grammar, is but to know better than others wherein grammatical excellence consists. Hence there is no fixed point of perfection beyond which such learning may not be carried. The limit to improvement is not so much in the nature of the subject, as in the powers of the mind, and in the inducements to exert them upon a theme so humble and so uninviting. Dr. Johnson suggests, in his masterly preface, "that a whole life cannot be spent upon syntax and etymology, and that even a whole life would not be sufficient." Who then will suppose, in the face of such facts and confessions as have been exhibited, that either in the faulty publications of Murray, or among the various modifications of them by other hands, we have any such work as deserves to be made a permanent standard of instruction in English grammar? With great sacrifices, both of pleasure and of interest, I have humbly endeavoured to supply this desideratum ; and it remains for other men to determine, and other times to know, what place shall be given to these my labours, in the general story of this branch of learning. Intending to develop not only the principles but also the history of grammar, I could not but speak of its authors. The writer who looks broadly at the past and the present, to give sound instruction to the future, must not judge of men by their shadows. If the truth, honestly told, diminish the stature of some, it does it merely by clearing the sight of the beholder. Real greatness cannot suffer loss by the dissipating of a vapour. If reputation has been raised upon the mist of ignorance, who but the builder shall lament its overthrow? If the works of grammarians are often ungrammatical, whose fault is this but their own? If *all* grammatical fame is little in itself, how can the abatement of what is undeserved of it be much? If the errors of some have long been tolerated, what right of the critic has been lost by nonuser? If the interests of Science have been sacrificed to Mammon, what rebuke can do injustice to the craft? Nay, let the broad-axe of the critic hew up to the line, till every beam in her temple be smooth and straight. For, "certainly, next to commending good writers, the greatest service to learning is, to expose the bad, who can only in that way be made of any use to it."* And if, among the makers of grammars, the scribblings of some, and the filchings of others, are discreditable alike to themselves and to their theme, let the reader consider, how great must be the intrinsic worth of that study which still maintains its credit in spite of all these abuses !

CHAPTER IV.

OF THE ORIGIN OF LANGUAGE.

—◆—

"Tot fallaciis obrutum, tot hallucinationibus demersum, tot adhuc tenebris circumfusum studium hocce mihi visum est, ut nihil satis tuto in hac materia præstari posse arbitratus sim, nisi nova quadam arte critica juvemur."—SCIPIO MAFFEIUS : *Cassiod. Complexiones*, p. XXX.

—◆—

1. The origin of things is, for many reasons, a peculiarly interesting point in their history. Among those who have thought fit to inquire into the prime origin of speech, it has been matter of dispute, whether we ought to consider it a special gift from Heaven, or an acquisition of industry—a natural endowment, or an artificial invention. Nor is any thing that has ever yet been said upon it, sufficient to set the question permanently at rest. That there is in some words, and perhaps in

* See *Notes to Pope's Dunciad*, Book II, ver. 140.

some of every language, a natural connexion between the sounds uttered and the things signified, cannot be denied ; yet, on the other hand, there is, in the use of words in general, so much to which nature affords no clew or index, that this whole process of communicating thought by speech, seems to be artificial. | Under an other head, I have already cited from Sanctius some opinions of the ancient grammarians and philosophers on this point. | With the reasoning of that zealous instructor, the following sentence from Dr. Blair very obviously accords : " To suppose words invented, or names given to things, in a manner purely arbitrary, without any ground or reason, is to suppose an effect without a cause. There must have always been some motive which led to the assignation of one name rather than an other."—*Rhet.*, Lect. vi, p. 55.

2. But, in their endeavours to explain the origin and early progress of language, several learned men, among whom is this celebrated lecturer, have needlessly perplexed both themselves and their readers, with sundry questions, assumptions, and reasonings, which are manifestly contrary to what has been made known to us on the best of all authority. What signifies it* for a man to tell us how nations rude and barbarous invented interjections first,† and then nouns, and then verbs,‡ and finally the other parts of speech ; when he himself confesses that he does not know whether language " can be considered a human invention at all ; " and when he believed, or ought to have believed, that the speech of the first man, though probably augmented by those who afterwards used it, was the one language of the earth for more than eighteen centuries? The task of inventing a language *de novo*, could surely have fallen upon no man but Adam ; and he, in the garden of Paradise, had doubtless some aids and facilities not common to every wild man of the woods.

3. The learned Doctor was equally puzzled to conceive, " either how society could form itself, previously to language, or how words could rise into a language, previously to society formed."—*Blair's Rhet.*, L. vi, p. 54. This too was but an idle perplexity, though thousands have gravely pored over it since, as a part of the study of rhetoric ; for, if neither could be previous to the other, they must have sprung up simultaneously. And it is a sort of slander upon our prime ancestor, to suggest, that, because he was " *the first*," he must have been " *the rudest*" of his race ; and that, " consequently, those first rudiments of speech," which alone the supposition allows to him or to his family, must have been poor and narrow."—*Blair's Rhet.* p. 54. It is far more reasonable to think, with a later author, that, " Adam had an insight into natural things far beyond the acutest philosopher, as may be gathered from his giving of names to all creatures, according to their different constitutions."—*Robinson's Scripture Characters*, p. 4.

4. But Dr. Blair is not alone in the view which he here takes. The same thing has been suggested by other learned men. Thus Dr. James P. Wilson, of Philadelphia, in an octavo published in 1817, says : " It is difficult to discern how communities could have existed without language, and equally so to discover how language could have obtained, in a peopled world, prior to society."—*Wilson's Essay on Gram.* p. 1. I know not how so many professed Christians, and some of them teachers of religion too, with the Bible in their hands, can reason upon this subject as they do. We find them, in their speculations, conspiring to represent primeval man, to use their own words, as a " *savage*, whose ' howl at the appearance of danger, and whose exclamations of joy at the sight of his prey, reit-

---

* A modern namesake of the Doctor's, the *Rev. David Blair*, has the following conception of the *utility* of these speculations : " To enable children to comprehend the *abstract idea* that all the words in a language consist but of *nine kinds*, it will be found useful to explain how *savage tribes*, who having *no language*, would first invent one, beginning with interjections and nouns, and proceeding from one part of speech to another, as their introduction might successively be called for by necessity or luxury."—*Blair's Pract. Gram.* Pref. p. vii.
† " Interjections, I *shewed*, or passionate exclamations, were *the first elements* of speech."—*Dr. Hugh Blair's Lectures*, p 57.
‡ " It is certain that the verb was invented before the noun, in all the languages of which a tolerable account has been procured, either in ancient or modern times."—*Dr. Alex. Murray's History of European Languages*, Vol. I, p. 326.

erated, or varied with the change of objects, were probably the origin of language.'
—*Booth's Analytical Dictionary.* In the dawn of society, ages may have passed
away, with little more converse than what these efforts would produce."—*Gardiner's Music of Nature,* p. 31. Here Gardiner quotes Booth with approbation,
and the latter, like Wilson, may have borrowed his ideas from Blair. Thus are
we taught by a multitude of guessers, grave, learned, and oracular, that the last
of the ten parts of speech was in fact the first: "*Interjections* are exceedingly
interesting in one respect. They are, there can be little doubt, *the oldest words
in all languages;* and may be considered the elements of speech."—*Bucke's
Classical Gram.* p. 78. On this point, however, Dr. Blair seems not to be quite
consistent with himself: "Those exclamations, therefore, which by grammarians
are called *interjections,* uttered in a strong and passionate manner, were, *beyond
doubt,* the first elements or beginnings of speech."—*Rhet.*, L. vi, p. 55. "The
names of sensible objects were, *in all languages,* the words most early introduced."
—*Rhet.*, L. xiv, p. 135. "The *names of sensible objects,*" says Murray too, "were
the words most early introduced."—*Octavo Gram.* p. 336. But what says the
Bible?

5. Revelation informs us that our first progenitor was not only endowed with
the faculty of speech, but, as it would appear, actually incited by the Deity to
exert that faculty in giving *names* to the objects by which he was surrounded.
"Out of the ground the Lord God formed every beast of the field and every fowl
of the air; and brought them unto Adam, to see what he would call them: and
whatsoever Adam called every living creature, that was the name thereof. And
Adam gave names to all cattle, and to the fowls of the air, and to every beast of
the field; but for Adam there was not found a help meet for him."—*Gen.* ii, 19, 20.
This account of the first naming of the other creatures by man, is apparently a
parenthesis in the story of the creation of woman, with which the second chapter
of Genesis concludes. But, in the preceding chapter, the Deity is represented
not only as calling all things into existence *by his Word;* but as *speaking to the
first human pair,* with reference to their increase in the earth, and to their dominion
over it, and over all the living creatures formed to inhabit it. So that the order of
the events cannot be clearly inferred from the order of the narration. The manner
of this communication to man, may also be a subject of doubt. Whether it was,
or was not, made by a voice of words, may be questioned. But, surely, that
Being who, in creating the world and its inhabitants, manifested his own infinite
wisdom, eternal power, and godhead, does not lack words, or any other means of
signification, if he will use them. And, in the inspired record of his work in the
beginning, he is certainly represented, not only as naming all things imperatively,
when he spoke them into being, but as expressly calling the light *Day,* the
darkness *Night,* the firmament *Heaven,* the dry land *Earth,* and the gatherings of
the mighty waters *Seas.* Dr. Thomas Hartwell Horne, in commending a work by
Dr. Ellis, concerning the origin of human wisdom and understanding, says: "It
shows satisfactorily, that religion *and language* entered the world by divine
revelation, without the aid of which, man had not been a rational or religious
creature."—*Study of the Scriptures,* vol. i, p. 4. "Plato attributes the primitive
words of the *first language* to a divine origin;" and Dr. Wilson remarks, "The
transition from silence to speech, implies an effort of the understanding too great for
man."—*Essay on Gram.* p. 1. Dr. Beattie says, "Mankind must have spoken in
all ages, the young constantly learning to speak by imitating those who were older;
and, if so, our first parents must have received this art, as well as some others, by
inspiration."—*Moral Science,* p. 27. Horne Tooke says, "I imagine that it is, *in
some measure,* with the vehicle of our thoughts, as with the vehicles for our bodies.
Necessity produced both."—*Diversions of Purley,* vol. ii, p. 20. Again:
"Language, it is true, *is an art,* and a glorious one; whose influence extends over
all the others, and in which finally all science whatever must centre: but an art

springing from necessity, and originally invented by artless men, who did not sit down like philosophers to invent it."—*Ib.* vol. i, p. 259.

6. Milton imagines Adam's first knowledge of speech, to have sprung from the hearing of his own voice; and that voice to have been raised, instinctively, or spontaneously, in an animated inquiry concerning his own origin—an inquiry in which he addresses to unintelligent objects, and inferior creatures, such questions as the Deity alone could answer:

> "Myself I then perused, and limb by limb
> Surveyed, and sometimes went, and sometimes ran
> With supple joints, as lively vigor led:
> But who I was, or where, or from what cause,
> Knew not; *to speak I tried, and forthwith spake;*
> *My tongue obeyed, and readily could name*
> *Whate'er I saw.* 'Thou Sun,' said I, 'fair light,
> And thou enlightened Earth, so fresh and gay,
> Ye Hills, and Dales, ye Rivers, Woods, and Plains;
> And ye that live and move, fair Creatures! tell,
> Tell, if ye saw, how came I thus, how here?
> Not of myself; by some great Maker then,
> In goodness and in power preëminent:
> Tell me how I may know him, how adore,
> From whom I have that thus I move and live,
> And feel that I am happier than I know.'"
>
> *Paradise Lost*, Book viii, l. 267.

But, to the imagination of a poet, a freedom is allowed, which belongs not to philosophy. We have not always the means of knowing how far he *literally* believes what he states.

7. My own opinion is, that language is partly natural and partly artificial. And, as the following quotation from the Greek of Ammonius will serve in some degree to illustrate it, I present the passage in English for the consideration of those who may prefer ancient to modern speculations: "In the same manner, therefore, as mere motion is from nature, but dancing is something positive; and as wood exists in nature, but a door is something positive; so is the mere utterance of vocal sound founded in nature, but the signification of ideas by nouns or verbs is something positive. And hence it is, that, as to the simple power of producing vocal sound—which is as it were the organ or instrument of the soul's faculties of knowledge or volition—as to this vocal power, I say, man seems to possess it from nature, in like manner as irrational animals; but as to the power of using significantly nouns or verbs, or sentences combining these, (which are not natural but positive,) this he possesses by way of peculiar eminence; because he alone of all mortal beings partakes of a soul which can move itself, and operate to the production of arts. So that, even in the utterance of sounds, the inventive power of the mind is discerned; as the various elegant compositions, both in metre, and without metre, abundantly prove."—*Ammon. de Interpr.* p. 51.[*]

8. Man was made for society; and from the first period of human existence the race were social. Monkish seclusion is manifestly unnatural; and the wild independence of the savage, is properly denominated a state of nature, only in contradistinction to that state in which the arts are cultivated. But to civilized life, or even to that which is in any degree social, language is absolutely necessary. There is therefore no danger that the language of any nation shall fall into disuse, till the people by whom it is spoken, shall either adopt some other, or become

---

[*] The Greek of this passage, together with a translation not very different from the foregoing, is given as a marginal note, in *Harris's Hermes*, Book III, Chap. 3d.

themselves extinct. When the latter event occurs, as is the case with the ancient Hebrew, Greek, and Latin, the language, if preserved at all from oblivion, becomes the more permanent; because the causes which are constantly tending to improve or deteriorate every living language, have ceased to operate upon those which are learned only from ancient books. The inflections which now compose the declensions and conjugations of the dead languages, and which indeed have ever constituted the peculiar characteristics of those forms of speech, must remain forever as they are.

9. When a nation changes its language, as did our forefathers in Britain, producing by a gradual amalgamation of materials drawn from various tongues a new one differing from all, the first stages of its grammar will of course be chaotic and rude. Uniformity springs from the steady application of rules; and polish is the work of taste and refinement. We may easily err by following the example of our early writers with more reverence than judgement; nor is it possible for us to do justice to the grammarians, whether early or late, without a knowledge both of the history and of the present state of the science which they profess to teach. I therefore think it proper rapidly to glance at many things remote indeed in time, yet nearer to my present purpose, and abundantly more worthy of the student's consideration, than a thousand matters which are taught for grammar by the authors of treatises professedly elementary.

10. As we have already seen, some have supposed that the formation of the first language must have been very slow and gradual. But of this they offer no proof, and from the pen of inspiration we seem to have testimony against it. Did Adam give names to all the creatures about him, and then allow those names to be immediately forgotten? Did not both he and his family continually use his original nouns in their social intercourse? and how could they use them, without other parts of speech to form them into sentences? Nay, do we not know from the Bible, that on several occasions our prime ancestor expressed himself like an intelligent man, and used all the parts of speech which are now considered *necessary?* What did he say, when his fit partner, the fairest and loveliest work of God, was presented to him? "This is now bone of my bones, and flesh of my flesh: she shall be called Woman, because she was taken out of Man." And again: Had he not other words than nouns, when he made answer concerning his transgression: "I heard thy voice in the garden, and I was afraid, because I was naked; and I hid myself?" What is it, then, but a groundless assumption. to make him and his immediate descendants ignorant savages, and to affirm, with Dr. Blair, that "their speech must have been poor and narrow?" It is not possible now to ascertain what degree of perfection the oral communication of the first age exhibited. But, as languages are now known to improve in proportion to the improvement of society in civilization and intelligence, and as we cannot reasonably suppose the first inhabitants of the earth to have been savages, it seems, I think, a plausible conjecture, that the primeval tongue was at least sufficient for all the ordinary intercourse of civilized men, living in the simple manner ascribed to our early ancestors in Scripture; and that, in many instances, human speech subsequently declined far below its original standard.

11. At any rate, let it be remembered that the first language spoken on earth, whatever it was, originated in Eden before the fall; that this "one language" which all men understood until the dispersion, is to be traced, not to the cries of savage hunters, echoed through the wilds and glades where Nimrod planted Babel, but to that eastern garden of God's own planting, wherein grew "every tree that is pleasant to the sight and good for food;" to that paradise into which the Lord God put the new-created man, "to dress it and to keep it." It was here that Adam and his partner learned to speak, while yet they stood blameless and blessed, entire and wanting nothing; free in the exercise of perfect faculties of body and mind, capable of acquiring knowledge through observation and experience, and also

favoured with immediate communications with their Maker. Yet Adam, having nothing which he did not receive, could not originally bring any real knowledge into the world with him, any more than men do now : this, in whatever degree attained, must be, and must always have been, either an acquisition of reason, or a revelation from God. And, according to the understanding of some, even in the beginning, "That was not first which is spiritual, but that which is natural ; and afterward that which is spiritual."—1 *Cor.* xv, 46. That is, the spirit of Christ, the second Adam, was bestowed on the first Adam, after his creation, as the life and the light of the immortal soul. For, "In *Him* was life, and the life was the light of men ;" a life which our first parents forfeited and lost on the day of their transgression. "It was undoubtedly in the light of this pure influence that Adam had such an intuitive discerning of the creation, as enabled him to give names to all creatures according to their several natures."—*Phipps on Man*, p. 4. A lapse from all this favour, into conscious guilt and misery ; a knowledge of good withdrawn, and of evil made too sure ; followed the first transgression. Abandoned then in great measure by superhuman aid, and left to contend with foes without and foes within, mankind became what history and observation prove them to have been ; and henceforth, by painful experience, and careful research, and cautious faith, and humble docility, must they gather the fruits of *knowledge ;* by a vain desire and false conceit of which, they had forfeited the tree of life. So runs the story

> " Of man's first disobedience, and the fruit
> Of that forbidden tree, whose mortal taste
> Brought death into the world, and all our wo,
> With loss of Eden, till one greater Man
> Restore us, and regain the blissful seat."

12. The analogy of words in the different languages now known, has been thought by many to be sufficiently frequent and clear to suggest the idea of their common origin. Their differences are indeed great ; but perhaps not greater, than the differences in the several races of men, all of whom, as revelation teaches, sprung from one common stock. From the same source we learn, that till the year of the world 1844, "The whole world was of one language, and of one speech."— *Gen.* xi, 1. At that period, the whole world of mankind consisted only of the descendants of the eight souls who had been saved in the ark, and so many of the eight as had survived the flood one hundred and eighty-eight years. Then occurred that remarkable intervention of the Deity, in which he was pleased to confound their language ; so that they could not understand one an other's speech, and were consequently scattered abroad upon the face of the earth. This, however, in the opinion of many learned men, does not prove the immediate formation of any new languages.

13. But, whether new languages were thus immediately formed or not, the event, in all probability, laid the foundation for that diversity which subsequently obtained among the languages of the different nations which sprung from the dispersion ; and hence it may be regarded as the remote cause of the differences which now exist. But for the immediate origin of the peculiar characteristical differences which distinguish the various languages now known, we are not able with much certainty to account. Nor is there even much plausibility in the speculations of those grammarians who have attempted to explain the order and manner in which the declensions, the moods, the tenses, or other leading features of the languages, were first introduced. They came into use before they could be generally known, and the partial introduction of them could seldom with propriety be made a subject of instruction or record, even if there were letters and learning at hand to do them this honour. And it is better to be content with ignorance, than to form such conjectures as imply any thing that is absurd or impossible. For

instance: Neilson's Theory of the Moods, published in the Classical Journal of 1819, though it exhibits ingenuity and learning, is liable to this strong objection.; that it proceeds on the supposition, that the moods of English verbs, and of several other derivative tongues, were invented in a certain order by persons, not speaking a language learned chiefly from their fathers, but uttering a new one as necessity prompted. But when or where, since the building of Babel, has this ever happened? That no dates are given, or places mentioned, the reader regrets, but he cannot marvel.

14. By what successive changes, our words in general, and especially the minor parts of speech, have become what we now find them, and what is their original and proper signification according to their derivation, the etymologist may often show to our entire satisfaction. Every word must have had its particular origin and history; and he who in such things can explain with certainty what is not commonly known, may do some service to science. But even here the utility of his curious inquiries may be overrated; and whenever, for the sake of some favourite theory, he ventures into the regions of conjecture, or allows himself to be seduced from the path of practical instruction, his errors are obstinate, and his guidance is peculiarly deceptive. Men fond of such speculations, and able to support them with some show of learning, have done more to unsettle the science of grammar, and to divert ingenious teachers from the best methods of instruction, than all other visionaries put together. Etymological inquiries are important, and I do not mean to censure or discourage them, merely as such; but the folly of supposing that in our language words must needs be of the same class, or part of speech, as that to which they may be traced in an other, deserves to be rebuked. The words *the* and *an* may be articles in English, though obviously traceable to something else in Saxon; and a learned man may, in my opinion, be better employed, than in contending that *if. though*, and *although*, are not conjunctions, but verbs!

15. Language is either oral or written; the question of its origin has consequently two parts. Having suggested what seemed necessary respecting the origin of *speech*, I now proceed to that of *writing*. Sheridan says, "We have in use *two kinds of language*, the spoken and the written: the one, the gift of God; the other, the invention of man."—*Elocution*, p. xiv. If this ascription of the two things to their sources, were as just as it is clear and emphatical, both parts of our question would seem to be resolved. But this great rhetorician either forgot his own doctrine, or did not mean what he here says. For he afterwards makes the former kind of language as much a work of art, as any one will suppose the latter to have been. In his sixth lecture, he comments on the *gift* of speech thus: "But still we are to observe, that nature did no more than furnish the power and means; *she did not give the language*, as in the case of the passions, but left it to the industry of men, to find out and agree upon such articulate sounds, as they should choose to make the symbols of their ideas."—*Ib*. p. 147. He even goes farther, and supposes certain *tones of the voice* to be things invented by man: "Accordingly, as she did not furnish the *words*, which were to be the symbols of his ideas; neither did she furnish the *tones*, which were to manifest, and communicate by their own virtue, the internal exertions and emotions, of such of his nobler faculties, as chiefly distinguish him from the brute species; but left them also, like words, to the care and invention of man."—*Ibidem*. On this branch of the subject, enough has already been presented.

16. By most authors, alphabetic writing is not only considered an artificial invention, but supposed to have been wholly unknown in the early ages of the world. Its antiquity, however, is great. Of this art, in which the science of grammar originated, we are not able to trace the commencement. Different nations have claimed the honour of the invention; and it is not decided, among the learned, to whom, or to what country, it belongs. It probably originated in Egypt. For, "The Egyptians," it is said, "paid divine honours to the Inventor of Letters,

whom they called *Theuth:* and Socrates, when he speaks of him, considers him
as a god, or a god-like man."—*British Gram.* p. 32.   Charles Bucke has it,
" That the first inventor of letters is supposed to have been *Memnon;* who was,
in consequence, fabled to be the son of Aurora, goddess of the morning."—*Bucke's
Classical Gram.* p. 5.   The ancients in general seem to have thought Phœnicia
the birthplace of Letters :

> " Phœnicians first, if ancient fame be true,
> The sacred mystery of letters knew ;
> They first, by sound, in various lines design'd,
> Express'd the meaning of the thinking mind ;
> The power of words by figures rude conveyed,
> And useful science everlasting made."
>
> *Rowe's Lucan,* B. iii, L 334.

17. Some, however, seem willing to think writing coeval with speech.   Thus
Bicknell, from Martin's Physico-Grammatical Essay : " We are told by Moses,
that Adam gave *names to every living creature;* * but how those names were
written, or what sort of characters he made use of, is not known to us ; nor indeed
whether Adam ever made use of a written language at all ; since we find no mention made of any in the sacred history."—*Bicknell's Gram.* Part ii, p. 5.   A
certain late writer on English grammar, with admirable flippancy, cuts this matter
short, as follows,—satisfying himself with pronouncing all speech to be natural, and
all writing artificial : " Of how many primary kinds is language ?   It is of two
kinds; natural or spoken, and artificial or written."—*Oliver B. Peirce's Gram.*
p. 15.   " Natural language is, to a limited extent, (the representation of the
passions,) common to brutes as well as man ; but artificial language, being the
work of invention, is peculiar to man."—*Idem,* p. 16.

18. The writings delivered to the Israelites by Moses, are more ancient than
any others now known.   In the thirty-first chapter of Exodus, it is said, that God
" gave unto Moses, upon Mount Sinai, two tables of testimony, tables of stone,
written with the finger of God."   And again, in the thirty-second : " The tables
were the work of God, and the writing *was the writing of God,* graven upon the
tables."   But these divine testimonies, thus miraculously written, do not appear to
have been the first writing ; for Moses had been previously commanded to write an
account of the victory over Amalek, " for a memorial in a book, and rehearse it
in the ears of Joshua."—*Exod.* xvii, 14.   This first battle of the Israelites
occurred in Rephidim, a place on the east side of the western gulf of the Red Sea,
at or near Horeb, but before they came to Sinai, upon the top of which, (on the
fiftieth day after their departure from Egypt,) Moses received the ten commandments of the law.

19. Some authors, however, among whom is Dr. Adam Clarke, suppose that in
this instance the order of the record is not to be inferred from the order of the record,
or that there is room to doubt whether the use of letters was here intended ; and
that there consequently remains a strong probability, that the sacred Decalogue, which
God himself delivered to Moses on Sinai, A. M. 2513, B. C. 1491, was " the
first writing *in alphabetical characters* ever exhibited to the world."   See *Clarke's
Succession of Sacred Literature,* vol. i, p. 24.   Dr. Scott, in his General Preface
to the Bible, seems likewise to favour the same opinion.   "Indeed," says he,
" there is some probability in the opinion, that the art of writing was first communicated by revelation, to Moses, in order to perpetuate, with certainty, those
facts, truths, and laws, which he was employed to deliver to Israel.   Learned men
find no traces of *literary,* or alphabetical, writing, in the history of the nations,
till long after the days of Moses ; unless the book of Job may be regarded as
an exception.   The art of expressing almost an infinite variety of sounds, by the

---

* † should be, " *to all living creatures;*" for each creature had, probably, but one name.—G. BROWN.

interchanges of a few letters, or marks, seems more like a discovery to man from heaven, than a human invention; and its beneficial effects, and almost absolute necessity, for the preservation and communication of true religion, favour the conjecture."—*Scott's Preface*, p xiv.

20. The time at which Cadmus, the Phœnician, introduced this art into Greece, cannot be precisely ascertained. There is no reason to believe it was antecedent to the time of Moses; some chronologists make it between two and three centuries later. Nor is it very probable, that Cadmus invented the sixteen letters of which he is said to have made use. His whole story is so wild a fable, that nothing certain can be inferred from it. Searching in vain for his stolen sister—his sister Europa, carried off by Jupiter—he found a wife in the daughter of Venus! Sowing the teeth of a dragon, which had devoured his companions, he saw them spring up to his aid a squadron of armed soldiers! In short, after a series of wonderful achievements and bitter misfortunes, loaded with grief and infirm with age, he prayed the gods to release him from the burden of such a life; and, in pity from above, both he and his beloved Hermionè were changed into serpents! History, however, has made him generous amends, by ascribing to him the invention of letters, and accounting him the worthy benefactor to whom the world owes all the benefits derived from literature. I would not willingly rob him of this honour. But I must confess, there is no feature of the story, which I can conceive to give any countenance to his claim; except that as the great progenitor of the race of authors, his sufferings correspond well with the calamities of which that unfortunate generation have always so largely partaken.

21. The benefits of this invention, if it may be considered an invention, are certainly very great. In oral discourse the graces of elegance are more lively and attractive, but well-written books are the grand instructers of mankind, the most enduring monuments of human greatness, and the proudest achievements of human intellect. "The chief glory of a nation," says Dr. Johnson, "arises from its authors." Literature is important, because it is subservient to all objects, even those of the very highest concern. Religion and morality, liberty and government, fame and happiness, are alike interested in the cause of letters. It was a saying of Pope Pius the Second, that, "Common men should esteem learning as silver, noblemen value it as gold, and princes prize it as jewels." The uses of learning are seen in every thing that is not itself useless.* It cannot be overrated, but where it is perverted; and whenever that occurs, the remedy is to be sought by opposing learning to learning, till the truth is manifest, and that which is reprehensible, is made to appear so.

22. I have said, learning cannot be overrated, but where it is perverted. But men may differ in their notions of what learning is; and, consequently, of what is, or is not, a perversion of it. And so far as this point may have reference to theology, and the things of God, it would seem that the Spirit of God alone can fully show us its bearings. If the illumination of the Spirit is necessary to an understanding and a reception of scriptural truth, is it not by an inference more erudite than reasonable, that some great men have presumed to limit to a verbal medium the communications of Him who is everywhere his own witness, and who still gives to his own holy oracles all their peculiar significance and authority? Some seem to think the Almighty has never given to men any notion of himself, except by words. "Many ideas," says the celebrated Edmund Burke, "have never been at all presented to the senses of any men *but by words*, as God,†

---

* "Modern Europe owes a principal share of its enlightened and moral state to the restoration of learning: the advantages which have accrued to history, religion, the philosophy of the mind, and the progress of society; the benefits which have resulted from the models of Greek and Roman taste—in short, all that a knowledge of the progress and attainments of man in past ages can bestow on the present, has reached it through the medium of philology."—*Dr. Murray's History of European Languages*, Vol. II, p. 335.

† "The idea of God is a development from within, and a matter of faith, not an induction from without, and a matter of proof. When Christianity has developed its correlative principles within us, then we find evidences of its truth everywhere; nature is full of them: but we cannot find them before, simply because we have no eye to find them with."—H. N. Hudson: *Dem. Rev. May*, 1845.

angels, devils, heaven, and hell, all of which have however a great influence over the passions."—*On the Sublime and* [*the*] *Beautiful*, p. 97. That God can never reveal facts or truths except by words, is a position with which I am by no means satisfied. Of the great truths of Christianity, Dr. Wayland, in his Elements of Moral Science, repeatedly avers, "All these being *facts*, can never be known, except *by language*, that is, by revelation."—*First Edition*, p. 132. Again : " All of them being of the *nature of facts*, they could be made known to man *in no other way than by language*."—*Ib.* p. 136. But it should be remembered, that these same facts were otherwise made known to the prophets; (1. Pet. i, 11;) and that which has been done, is not impossible, whether there is reason to expect it again or not. So of the Bible, Calvin says, " No man can have the least knowledge of true and sound doctrine, without having been a disciple of the Scripture."—*Institutes*, B. i, Ch. 6. Had Adam, Abel, Enoch, Noah, and Abraham, then, no such knowledge? And if they had, what Scripture taught them ? We ought to value the Scriptures too highly to say of them any thing that is *unscriptural*. I am, however, very far from supposing there is any *other doctrine* which can be safely substituted for the truths revealed of old, the truths contained in the Holy Scriptures of the Old and New Testaments :

> " Left only in those written records pure,
> Though not but by the Spirit understood."*—Milton.*

CHAPTER V.

OF THE POWER OF LANGUAGE.

" Quis huic studio literarum, quod profitentur ii, qui grammatici vocantur, penitus se dedidit, quin omnem illarum artium pæne infinitam *vim* et *materiam* scientiæ cogitatione comprehenderit?"—CICERO. *De Oratore*, Lib. i, 3.

1. The peculiar *power* of language is an other point worthy of particular consideration. The power of an instrument is virtually the power of him who wields it ; and, as language is used in common, by the wise and the foolish, the mighty and the impotent, the candid and the crafty, the righteous and the wicked, it may perhaps seem to the reader a difficult matter, to speak intelligibly of its *peculiar power.* I mean, by this phrase, its fitness or efficiency to or for the accomplishment of the purposes for which it is used. As it is the nature of an agent, to be the doer of something, so it is the nature of an instrument, to be that with which something is effected. To make signs, is to do something, and, like all other actions, necessarily implies an agent ; so all signs, being things by means of which other things are represented, are obviously the instruments of such representation. Words, then, which represent thoughts, are things in themselves ; but, as signs, they are relative to other things, as being the instruments of their communication or preservation. They are relative also to him who utters them, as well as to those who may happen to be instructed or deceived by them. " Was it Mirabeau, Mr.

* So far as mind, soul, or spirit, is a subject of natural science, (under whatever name,) it may of course be known naturally. To say to what extent theology may be considered a natural science, or how much knowledge of any kind may have been opened to men otherwise than by words, is not now in point. Dr. Campbell says, " Under the general term [*physiology*] I also comprehend *natural theology* and *psychology*, which, in my opinion, have been most unnaturally disjoined by philosophers. Spirit, which here comprises only the Supreme Being and the human soul, is surely as much included under the notion of natural object as a body is, and is knowable to the philosopher purely in the same way, by observation and experience."—*Philosophy of Rhetoric*, p. 66. It is quite unnecessary for the teacher of languages to lead his pupils into any speculations on this subject. It is equally foreign to the history of grammar and to the philosophy of rhetoric.

President, or what other master of the human passions, who has told us that words are things? They are indeed things, and things of mighty influence, not only in addresses to the passions and high-wrought feelings of mankind, but in the discussion of legal and political questions also; because a just conclusion is often avoided, or a false one reached, by the adroit substitution of one phrase or one word for an other."—*Daniel Webster, in Congress,* 1833.

2. To speak, is a moral action, the quality of which depends upon the motive, and for which we are strictly accountable. "But I say unto you, that every idle word that men shall speak, they shall give account thereof in the day of judgement; for by thy words thou shalt be justified, and by thy words thou shalt be condemned."—*Matt.* xii, 36, 37. To listen, or to refuse to listen, is a moral action also; and there is meaning in the injunction, "Take heed what ye hear."—*Mark,* iv, 24. But why is it, that so much of what is spoken or written, is spoken or written in vain? Is language impotent? It is sometimes employed for purposes with respect to which it is utterly so; and often they that use it, know not how insignificant, absurd, or ill-meaning a thing they make of it. What is said, with whatever inherent force or dignity, has neither power nor value to him who does not understand it;[*] and, as Professor Duncan observes, "No word can be to any man the sign of an idea, till that idea comes to have a real existence in his mind."—*Logic,* p. 62. In instruction, therefore, speech ought not to be regarded as the foundation or the essence of knowledge, but as the sign of it; for knowledge has its origin in the power of sensation, or reflection, or consciousness, and not in that of recording or communicating thought. Dr. Spurzheim was not the first to suggest, "It is time to abandon the immense error of supposing that words and precepts are sufficient to call internal feelings and intellectual faculties into active exercise."—*Spurzheim's Treatise on Education,* p. 94.

3. But to this it may be replied, When God wills, the signs of knowledge are knowledge; and words, when he gives the ability to understand them, may, in some sense, become—"spirit and life." See *John,* vi, 63. Where competent intellectual faculties exist, the intelligible signs of thought do move the mind to think; and to think sometimes with deep feelings too, whether of assent or dissent, of admiration or contempt. So wonderful a thing is a rational soul, that it is hard to say to what ends the language in which it speaks, may, or may not, be sufficient. Let experience determine. We are often unable to excite in others the sentiments which we would: words succeed or fail, as they are received or resisted. But let a scornful expression be addressed to a passionate man, will not the words "call internal feelings" into action? And how do feelings differ from thoughts?[†] Hear Dr. James Rush: "The human mind is the place of representation of all the existences of nature which are brought within the scope of the senses. The representatives are called ideas. These ideas are the simple passive pictures of things, or [else] they exist with an activity, capable of so affecting the physical organs as to induce us to seek the continuance of that which produces them, or to avoid it. This active or vivid class of ideas comprehends the passions. The

---

[*] "Except ye utter by the tongue words easy to be understood, how shall it be known what is spoken? for ye shall speak into the air. There are, it may be, so many kinds of voices in the world, and none of them is without signification. Therefore, if I know not the meaning of the voice, I shall be unto him that speaketh, a barbarian; and he that speaketh, shall be a barbarian unto me."—1 *Cor.* xiv, 9, 10, 11.

"It is impossible that our knowledge of words should outstrip our knowledge of things. It may, and often will, come short of it. Words may be remembered as sounds, but [they] cannot be understood as signs, whilst we remain unacquainted with the things signified."—*Campbell's Philosophy of Rhetoric,* p. 160.

"Words can excite only ideas already acquired, and if no previous ideas have been formed, they are mere unmeaning sounds."—*Spurzheim on Education,* p. 200.

[†] Sheridan the elocutionist makes this distinction: "All that passes in the mind of man, may be reduced to two classes, which I call ideas and emotions. By ideas, I mean all thoughts which rise, and pass in succession in the mind. By emotions, all exertions of the mind in arranging, combining, and separating its ideas; as well as the effects produced on all the mind itself by those ideas; from the more violent agitation of the passions, to the calmer feelings produced by the operation of the intellect and the fancy. In short, thought is the object of the one; internal feeling, of the other. That which serves to express the former, I call the language of ideas; and the latter, the language of emotions. Words are the signs of the one; tones, of the other. Without the use of these two sorts of language, it is impossible to communicate through the ear, all that passes in the mind of man."—*Sheridan's Art of Reading; Blair's Lectures,* p. 332.

functions of the mind here described, exist then in different forms and degrees, from the simple idea, to the highest energy of passion : and the terms, thought, sentiment, emotion, feeling, and passion, are but the verbal signs of these degrees and forms. Nor does there appear to be any line of classification, for separating thought from passion : since simple thoughts, without changing their nature, do, from interest or incitement, often assume the colour of passion."—*Philosophy of the Human Voice*, p. 328.

4. Lord Kames, in the Appendix to his Elements of Criticism, divides *the senses* into external and internal, defining *perception* to be the act by which through the former we know outward objects, and *consciousness* the act by which through the latter we know what is within the mind. An *idea*, according to his definition, (which he says is precise and accurate,) is, " That *perception* of a real object which *is raised* in the mind by the power of *memory.*" But among the real objects from which memory may raise ideas, he includes the workings of the mind itself, or whatever we remember of our former passions, emotions, thoughts, or designs. Such a definition, he imagines, might have saved Locke, Berkley, and their followers, from much vain speculation ; for with the ideal systems of these philosophers, or with those of Aristotle and Des Cartes, he by no means coincides. This author says, "As ideas are the chief materials employed in reasoning and reflecting, it is of consequence that their nature and differences be understood. It appears now that ideas may be distinguished into three kinds : first, Ideas derived from original perceptions, properly termed *ideas of memory;* second, Ideas communicated *by language* or other signs ; and third, Ideas *of imagination.* These ideas differ from each other in many respects ; but chiefly in respect to their *proceeding from different causes.* The first kind is derived from real existences that have been objects of our senses ; *language is the cause of the second,* or any other sign that has the same power with language ; and a man's imagination is to himself the cause of the third. It is scarce [ly] necessary to add, that an idea, originally of imagination, being conveyed to others by language or any other vehicle, becomes in their mind an idea of the second kind ; and again, that an idea of this kind, being afterwards recalled to the mind, becomes in that circumstance an idea of memory."—*El. of Crit.* Vol. ii, p. 384.

5. Whether, or how far, language is to the mind itself *the instrument of thought,* is a question of great importance in the philosophy of both. Our literature contains occasional assertions bearing upon this point, but I know of no full or able discussion of it.* Cardell's instructions proceed upon the supposition, that neither the reason of men, nor even that of superior intelligences, can ever operate independently of words. "Speech," says he, "is to the mind what action is to animal bodies. Its improvement is the improvement of our intellectual nature, and a duty to God who gave it."—*Essay on Language*, p. 3. Again : " An attentive investigation will show, that there is no way in which the individual mind can, within itself, to any extent, *combine its ideas,* but by the intervention of words. Every process of the reasoning powers, beyond the immediate perception of sensible objects, depends on the structure of speech ; and, in a great degree, according to the excellence of this *chief instrument of all mental operations,* will be the means of personal improvement, of the social transmission of thought, and the elevation of national character. From this, it may be laid down as a broad principle, that no individual can make great advances in intellectual improvement, beyond the bounds of a ready-formed language, as the necessary means of his progress."—*Ib.* p. 9. These positions might easily be offset by contrary speculations of minds of equal rank ; but I submit them to the reader, with the single suggestion, that the author is not remarkable for that sobriety of judgement which gives weight to opinions.

* "Language is *the great instrument*, by which all the faculties of the mind are brought forward, moulded, polished, and exerted."—*Sheridan's Elocution*, p. xiv.

6. We have seen, among the citations in a former chapter, that Sanctius says, "Names are the signs, and as it were *the instruments, of things*." But what he meant by "*instrumenta rerum*," is not very apparent. Dr. Adam says, "The principles of grammar may be traced from the progress of the mind in the acquisition of language. Children first express their feelings by motions and gestures of the body, by cries and tears. *This is*[*] the language of nature, and therefore universal. *It fitly represents*[†] the quickness of sentiment and thought, which are as instantaneous as the impression of light on the eye. Hence we always express our stronger feelings by these natural signs. But when we want to make known to others the particular conceptions of the mind, we must represent them by parts, we must divide and analyze them. We express *each part by certain signs*,[‡] and join these together, according to the order of their relations. Thus words are *both the instrument and signs*§ *of the division* of thought."—*Preface to Latin Gram.*

7. The utterance of words, or the making of signs of any sort, requires time;[‖] but it is here suggested by Dr. Adam, that sentiment and thought, though susceptible of being retained or recalled, naturally flash upon the mind with immeasurable quickness.[¶] If so, they must originate in something more spiritual than language. The Doctor does not affirm that words are the instruments of thought, but of *the division* of thought. But it is manifest, that if they effect this, they are not the only instruments by means of which the same thing may be done. The deaf and dumb, though uninstructed and utterly ignorant of language, can think ; and can, by rude signs of their own inventing, manifest a similar division, corresponding to the individuality of things. And what else can be meant by "*the division of thought*," than our notion of objects, as existing severally, or as being distinguishable into parts? There can, I think, be no such division respecting that which is perfectly pure and indivisible in its essence ; and, I would ask, is not simple continuity apt to exclude it from our conception of every thing which appears with uniform coherence? Dr. Beattie says, "It appears to me, that, as all things are individuals, all thoughts must be so too."—*Moral Science*, Chap. i, Sec. 1. If, then, our thoughts are thus divided, and consequently, as this author infers, have not in themselves any of that generality which belongs to the signification of common nouns, there is little need of any instrument to divide them further : the mind rather needs help, as Cardell suggests, " to combine its ideas."[**]

8. So far as language is a work of art, and not a thing conferred or imposed upon us by nature, there surely can be in it neither division nor union that was not first in the intellect for the manifestation of which it was formed. First, with respect to generalization. "The human mind," says Harris, " by an energy as

---

* It should be, "*These are.*"—G. B.   † It should be, "*They fitly represent.*"—G. B.

‡ This is badly expressed ; for, according to his own deduction, *each part* has but *one* sign. It should be, "We express *the several parts by as many several signs.*"—G. BROWN.

§ It would be better English to say, " the *instruments* and *the* signs."—G. BROWN.

‖ " Good speakers do not pronounce above three syllables in a second of time ; and generally only two and a half, taking in the necessary pauses."—*Steele's Melody of Speech.*

¶ The same idea is also conveyed in the following sentence from Dr. Campbell : " Whatever regards the analysis of the operations of the mind, *which is quicker than lightning in all her energies*, must in a great measure be abstruse and dark."—*Philosophy of Rhetoric*, p. 289. Yet this philosopher has given it as his opinion, " that we really *think by signs* as well as speak by them."—*Ib.* p. 284. To reconcile these two positions with each other, we must suppose that thinking by signs, or words, is a process infinitely more rapid than speech.

** That generalization or abstraction which gives to similar things a common name, is certainly no laborious exercise of intellect ; nor does any mind find difficulty in applying such a name to an individual by means of the article. The general sense and the particular are alike easy to the understanding, and I know not whether it is worth while to inquire which is first in order. Dr. Alexander Murray says, " It must be attentively remembered, that all terms run from a general to a particular sense. The work of abstraction, the ascent from individual feelings to classes of these, was finished before terms were invented. Man was silent till he had formed some ideas to communicate ; and association of his perceptions soon led him to think and reason in ordinary matters."— *Hist. of European Languages*, Vol. I, p. 94. And, in a note upon this passage, he adds : "This is to be understood of primitive or radical terms. By the assertion that man was silent till he had formed ideas to communicate, is not meant, that any of our species were originally destitute of the natural expressions of feeling or thought. All that it implies, is, that man had been subjected, during an uncertain period of time, to the impressions made on his senses by the material world, before he began to express the natural varieties of these by articulated sounds. * * * * * Though the abstraction which formed such classes, might be greatly aided or supported by the signs ; yet it were absurd to suppose that the sign was invented, till the sense demanded it."—*Ib.* p. 399.

spontaneous and familiar to its nature, as the seeing of colour is familiar to the eye, discerns at once what in many is one, what in things dissimilar and different is similar and the same."—*Hermes*, p. 362.   Secondly, with respect to division. Mechanical separations are limited : " But the mind surmounts all power of concretion ; and can place in the simplest manner every attribute by itself ; convex without concave ; colour without superficies ; superficies without body ; and body without its accidents : as distinctly each one, as though they had never been united. And thus it is, that it penetrates into the recesses of all things, not only dividing them as wholes, into their more conspicuous parts, but persisting till it even separate those elementary principles which, being blended together after a more mysterious manner, are united in the minutest part as much as in the mightiest whole."— *Harris's Hermes*, p. 307.

9. It is remarkable that this philosopher, who had so sublime conceptions of the powers of the human mind, and who has displayed such extraordinary acuteness in his investigations, has represented the formation of words, or the utterance of language, as equalling in speed the progress of our very thoughts ; while, as we have seen, an other author, of great name, avers, that thought is " as instantaneous as the impression of light on the eye."   Philosophy here too evidently nods.   In showing the advantage of words, as compared with pictures, Harris says, " If we consider the ease and speed with which words are formed,—an case which knows no trouble or fatigue, and a *speed which equals the progress of our very thoughts,*[*] —we may plainly perceive an answer to the question here proposed, Why, in the common intercourse of men with men, imitations have been rejected, and symbols preferred."—*Hermes*, p. 336.   Let us hear a third man, of equal note : " Words have been called *winged ;* and they well deserve that name, when their abbreviations are compared with the progress which speech could make without these inventions ; but, compared with the rapidity of thought, they have not *the smallest claim to that title.*   Philosophers have calculated the difference of velocity between sound and light ; but who will attempt to calculate the difference between speech and thought ! "—*Horne Tooke's Epea Pteroenta*, Vol. i, p. 23.

10. It is certain, that, in the admirable economy of the creation, natures subordinate are made, in a wonderful manner, subservient to the operations of the higher ; and that, accordingly, our first ideas are such as are conceived of things external and sensible.   Hence all men whose intellect appeals only to external sense, are prone to a philosophy which reverses the order of things pertaining to the mind, and tends to materialism, if not to atheism.   " But "—to refer again to Harris—" the intellectual scheme which never forgets Deity, postpones every thing corporeal to the primary mental Cause.   It is here it looks for the origin of intelligible ideas, even of those which exist in human capacities.   For though sensible objects may be the destined medium to awaken the dormant energies of man's understanding, yet are those energies themselves no more contained in sense, than the explosion of a cannon, in the spark which gave it fire.   In short, all minds that are, are similar and congenial ; and so too are their ideas, or intelligible forms. Were it otherwise, there could be no intercourse between man and man, or (what is more important) between man and God."—*Hermes*, p. 393.

11. A doctrine somewhat like this, is found in the Meditations of the emperor Marcus Aurelius Antoninus, though apparently repugnant to the polytheism commonly admitted by the Stoics, to whom he belonged : "The world, take it all together, is but one ; there is but one sort of matter to make it of, one God to govern it, and one law to guide it.   For, run through the whole system of rational

---

[*] Dr. Alexander Murray too, in accounting for the frequent abbreviations of words, seems to suggest the possibility of giving them the celerity of thought : " Contraction is a change which results from a propensity to make the signs *as rapid as the thoughts* which they express.   Harsh combinations soon suffer contraction. Very long words preserve only the principal, that is, the accented part.   If a nation accents its words on the last syllable, the preceding ones will often be short, and liable to contraction.   If it follow a contrary practice, the terminations are apt to decay."—*History of European Languages*, Vol. I, p. 172.

beings, and you will find reason and truth but single and the same. And thus beings of the same kind, and endued with the same reason, are made happy by the same exercises of it."—Book vii, Sec. 9. Again: " Let your soul receive the Deity as your blood does the air; for the influences of the one are no less vital, than those of the other. This correspondence is very practicable : for there is an ambient omnipresent Spirit, which lies as open and pervious to your mind, as the air you breathe, does to your lungs : but then you must remember to be disposed to draw it."—Book viii, Sec. 54; *Collier's Translation.*

12. Agreeably to these views, except that he makes a distinction between a natural and a supernatural idea of God, we find Barclay, the early defender of the Quakers, in an argument with a certain Dutch nobleman, philosophizing thus : " If the Scripture then be true, there is in men a supernatural idea of God, which altogether differs from this natural idea—I say, in all men ; because all men are capable of salvation, and consequently of enjoying this divine vision. Now this capacity consisteth herein, that they have such a supernatural idea in themselves * For if there were no such idea in them, it were impossible they should so know God ; for whatsoever is clearly and distinctly known, is known by its proper idea ; neither can it otherwise be clearly and distinctly known. *For the ideas of all things are divinely planted in our souls ;* for, as the better philosophy teacheth, they are not begotten in us by outward objects or outward causes, but only are by these outward things excited or stirred up. And this is true, not only in supernatural ideas of God and things divine, and in natural ideas of the natural principles of human understanding, and conclusions thence deduced by the strength of human reason ; but even in the ideas of outward objects, which are perceived by the outward senses : as that noble Christian philosopher Boëthius hath well observed ; to which also the Cartesian philosophy agreeth." I quote only to show the concurrence of others, with Harris's position. Barclay carries on his argument with much more of a similar import. See *Sewel's History,* folio, p. 620.

13. But the doctrine of ideas existing primarily in God, and being divinely planted in our souls, did not originate with Boëthius : it may be traced back a thousand years from his time, through the philosophy of Proclus, Zeno, Aristotle,† Plato, Socrates, Parmenides, and Pythagoras. It is absurd to suppose any production or effect to be more excellent than its cause. That which really produces motion, cannot itself be inert ; and that which actually causes the human mind to think and reason, cannot itself be devoid of intelligence. " For knowledge can alone produce knowledge."‡ A doctrine apparently at variance with this, has recently been taught, with great confidence, among the professed discoveries of *Phrenology.* How much truth there may be in this new "*science,*" as it is called, I am not prepared to say ; but, as sometimes held forth, it seems to me not only to clash with some of the most important principles of mental philosophy, but to make the power of thought the result of that which is in itself inert and unthinking. Assuming that the primitive faculties of the human understanding have not been known in earlier times, it professes to have discovered, in the physical organization of the brain, their proper source, or essential condition, and the true index to their measure, number, and distribution. In short, the leading phrenologists, by acknowledging no spiritual substance, virtually deny that ancient doctrine, " It is not in flesh to think, or bones to reason,"§ and make the mind either a material substance, or a mere mode without substantial being.

* " We cannot form a distinct idea of any *moral or intellectual quality,* unless we find some trace of it in ourselves."—*Beattie's Moral Science, Part Second, Natural Theology,* Chap. II, No 424.
† " Aristotle tells us that the world is a copy or transcript of those ideas which are in the mind of the first Being, and that those ideas which are in the mind of man, are a transcript of the world. To this we may add, that words are the transcript of those ideas which are in the mind of man, and that writing or printing are [is] the transcript of words."—*Addison, Spect. No.* 166.
‡ Bolingbroke on Retirement and Study, Letters on History, p. 364.
§ See this passage in " The Economy of Human Life," p. 105—a work feigned to be a compend of Chinese maxims, but now generally understood to have been written or compiled by *Robert Dodsley,* an eminent and ingenious bookseller in London.

14. "The doctrine of *immaterial substances*," says Dr. Spurzheim, "is not sufficiently amenable to the test of observation; it is founded on belief, and only supported by hypothesis."—*Phrenology*, Vol. i, p. 20. But it should be remembered, that our notion of material substance, is just as much a matter of hypothesis. All accidents, whether they be qualities or actions, we necessarily suppose to have some support; and this we call *substance*, deriving the term from the Latin, or *hypostasis*, if we choose to borrow from the Greek. But what this substance, or hypostasis, is, independently of its qualities or actions, we know not. This is clearly proved by Locke. What do we mean by *matter?* and what by *mind?* *Matter* is that which is solid, extended, divisible, and movable. *Mind* is that which thinks, and wills, and reasons, and worships. Here are qualities in the one case; operations in the other. Here are two definitions as totally distinct as any two can be; and he that sees not in them a difference of *substance*, sees it no-where: to him all natures are one; and that one, an absurd supposition.

15. In favour of what is urged by the phrenologists, it may perhaps be admitted, as a natural law, that, "If a picture of a visible object be formed upon the retina, and the impression be communicated, by the nerves, to the brain, *the result* will be an act of perception."—*Wayland's Moral Science*, p. 4. But it does not follow, nor did the writer of this sentence believe, that perception is a mere act or attribute of the organized matter of the brain. A material object can only occasion in our sensible organs a corporeal motion, which has not in it the nature of thought or perception; and upon what principle of causation, shall a man believe, in respect to vision, that the thing which he sees, is more properly the cause of the idea conceived of it, than is the light by which he beholds it, or the mind in which that idea is formed? Lord Kames avers, that, "*Colour*, which appears to the eye as spread upon a substance, has no existence *but in the mind* of the spectator."—*Elements of Criticism*, i, 178. And Cicero placed the perception, not only of colour, but of taste, of sound, of smell, and of touch, in the mind, rather than in the senses. "Illud est album, hoc dulce, canorum illud, hoc bene olens, hoc asperum: animo jam hæc tenemus comprehensa, non sensibus."—*Ciceronis Acad.* Lib. ii, 7. Dr. Beattie, however, says: "Colours inhere not in the coloured body, but in the light that falls upon it; * * * and the word *colour* denotes, an external thing, and never a sensation of the mind."—*Moral Science*, i, 54. Here is some difference of opinion; but however the thing may be, it does not affect my argument; which is, that to perceive or think is an act or attribute of our immaterial substance or nature, and not to be supposed the effect either of the objects perceived or of our own corporeal organization.

16. Divine wisdom has established the senses as the avenues through which our minds shall receive notices of the forms and qualities of external things; but the sublime conception of the ancients, that those forms and qualities had an abstract preëxistence in the divine mind, is a common doctrine of many English authors, as Milton, Cowper, Akenside, and others. For example: "Now if *Ens primum* be the cause of *entia a primo*, then he hath the Idea of them in him: for he made them by counsel, and not by necessity; for then he should have needed them, and they have a parhelion of that wisdom that is in his Idea."—*Richardson's Logic*, p. 16: Lond. 1657.

> "Then the Great Spirit, whom his works adore,
> Within his own deep essence view'd the forms,
> The forms eternal of created things."—AKENSIDE.
> *Pleasures of the Imagination*, Book i.

> "And in the school of sacred wisdom taught,
> To read his wonders, in whose thought the world,
> Fair as it is, existed ere it was."—COWPER.
> *Task: Winter Morning Walk*, p. 150.

> " Thence to behold this new-created world,
> The addition of his empire, how it show'd
> In prospect from his throne, how good, how fair,
> Answering his great idea."—MILTON.
>
> *Paradise Lost*, Book vii, line 554.

17. "Original Truth,"[*] says Harris, "having the most intimate connection with the *Supreme Intelligence*, may be said (as it were) to shine with unchangeable splendor, enlightening thoughout the universe every possible subject, by nature susceptible of its benign influence. Passions and other obstacles may prevent indeed its efficacy, as clouds and vapours may obscure the sun ; but itself neither admits diminution, nor change, because the darkness respects only particular percipients. Among *these* therefore we must look for ignorance and error, and for that *subordination of intelligence* which is their natural consequence. Partial views, the imperfections of sense ; inattention, idleness, the turbulence of passions ; education, local sentiments, opinions, and belief ; conspire in many instances to furnish us with ideas, some too general, some too partial, and (what is worse than all this) with many that are erroneous, and contrary to truth. These it behoves us to correct as far as possible, by cool suspense and candid examination. Thus by a connection perhaps little expected, the cause of *Letters*, and that of *Virtue*, appear to coincide ; it being the business of both, to examine our ideas, and to amend them by the standard of nature and of truth." See *Hermes*, p. 406.

18. Although it seems plain from our own consciousness, that the mind is an active self-moving principle or essence, yet capable of being moved, after its own manner, by other causes outward as well as inward ; and although it must be obvious to reflection, that all its ideas, perceptions, and emotions, are, with respect to itself, of a spiritual nature—bearing such a relation to the spiritual substance in which alone they appear, as bodily motion is seen to bear to material substances ; yet we know, from experience and observation, that they who are acquainted with words, are apt to think in words—that is, mentally to associate their internal conceptions with the verbal signs which they have learned to use. And though I do not conceive the position to be generally true, that words are to the mind itself the necessary instruments of thought, yet, in my apprehension, it cannot well be denied, that in some of its operations and intellectual reaches, the mind is greatly assisted by its own contrivances with respect to language. I refer not now to the communication of knowledge ; for, of this, language is admitted to be properly the instrument. But there seem to be some processes of thought, or calculation, in which the mind, by a wonderful artifice in the combination of terms, contrives to prevent embarrassment, and help itself forward in its conceptions, when the objects before it are in themselves perhaps infinite in number or variety.

19. We have an instance of this in numeration. No idea is more obvious or simple than that of unity, or one. By the continual addition of this, first to itself to make two, and then to each higher combination successively, we form a series of different numbers, which may go on to infinity. In the consideration of these, the mind would not be able to go far without the help of words, and those peculiarly fitted to the purpose. The understanding would lose itself in the multiplicity, were it not aided by that curious concatenation of names, which has been contrived for the several parts of the succession. As far as *twelve* we make use of simple unrelated terms. Thenceforward we apply derivatives and compounds, formed

---

[*] " Those philosophers whose ideas of *being* and *knowledge* are derived from *body* and *sensation*, have a short method to explain the nature of *Truth*. It is a *factitious* thing, made by every man for himself ; which comes and goes, just as it is remembered and forgot ; which in the order of things makes its appearance *the last* of all, being not only subsequent to sensible objects, but even to our sensations of them ! According to this hypothesis, there are many truths, which have been, and are no longer , others, that will be, and have not been yet ; and multitudes, that possibly may never exist at all. But there are other reasoners, who must surely have had very different notions ; those, I mean, who represent Truth not as *the last*, but as *the first* of beings ; who call it *immutable, eternal, omnipresent ;* attributes that all indicate something more than human."—*Harris's Hermes*, p. 408.

from these in their regular order, till we arrive at a *hundred*. This one new word, *hundred*, introduced to prevent confusion, has eight hundred and ninety-nine distinct repetitions in connexion with the preceding terms, and thus brings us to a *thousand*. Here the computation begins anew, runs through all the former combinations, and then extends forward, till the word *thousand* has been used nine hundred and ninety-nine thousand times; and then, for ten hundred thousand, we introduce the new word *million*. With this name we begin again as before, and proceed till we have used it a million of times, each combination denoting a number clearly distinguished from every other ; and then, in like manner, we begin and proceed, with *billions, trillions, quadrillions, quintillions,* &c , to any extent we please.

20. Now can any one suppose that words are not here, in some true sense, the instruments of thought, or of the intellectual process thus carried on ? Were all these different numbers to be distinguished directly by the mind itself, and denominated by terms destitute of this artificial connexion, it may well be doubted whether the greatest genius in the world would ever be able to do what any child may now effect by this orderly arrangement of words ; that is, to distinguish exactly the several stages of this long progression, and see at a glance how far it is from the beginning of the series. " The great art of knowledge," says Duncan, " lies in managing with skill the capacity of the intellect, and contriving such helps, as, if they strengthen not its natural powers, may yet expose them to no unnecessary fatigue. When ideas become very complex, and by the multiplicity of their parts grow too unwieldy to be dealt with in the lump, we must ease the view of the mind by taking them to pieces, and setting before it the several portions separately, one after an other. By this leisurely survey we are enabled to take in the whole ; and if we can draw it into such an orderly combination as will naturally lead the attention, step by step, in any succeeding consideration of the same idea, we shall have it ever at command, and with a single glance of thought be able to run over all its parts."—*Duncan's Logic*, p. 37. Hence we may infer the great importance of method in grammar ; the particulars of which, as Quintilian says, are infinite.*

21. Words are in themselves but audible or visible signs, mere arbitrary symbols, used, according to common practice and consent, as significant of our ideas or thoughts.† But so well are they fitted to be made at will the medium of mental conference, that nothing else can be conceived to equal them for this purpose. Yet it does not follow that they who have the greatest knowledge and command of words, have all they could desire in this respect. For language is in its own nature but an imperfect instrument, and even when tuned with the greatest skill, will often

---

* Of the best method of teaching grammar, I shall discourse in an other chapter. That methods radically different must lead to different results, is no more than every intelligent person will suppose. The formation of just methods of instruction, or true systems of science, is work for those minds which are capable of the most accurate and comprehensive views of the things to be taught. He that is capable of " originating and producing " truth, or true " ideas," if any but the Divine Being is so, has surely no need to be trained into such truth by any factitious scheme of education. In all that he thus originates, he is himself a *Novum Organon* of knowledge, and capable of teaching others, especially those officious men who would help him with their second hand authorship, and their paltry catechisms of common-places I allude here to the fundamental principle of what in some books is called " *The Productive System of Instruction*," and to those schemes of grammar which are professedly founded on it. We are told that, " The *leading principle* of this system, is that which its name indicates—that the child should be regarded not as a mere recipient of the ideas of others, but as an agent *capable of collecting, and originating, and producing* most of the ideas which are necessary for *its* education, when *presented with* the objects or the facts *from which* they may be derived "—*Smith's New Gram. Pref.* p 5: *Amer. Journal of Education, New Series*, Vol I, No. 6, Art 1. It ought to be enough for any teacher, or for any writer, if he finds his readers or his pupils ready *recipients* of the ideas which he aims to convey. What more they know, they can never owe to him, unless they learn it from him against his will : and what they happen to lack, of understanding or believing him, may very possibly be more his fault than theirs.

† Lindley Murray, anonymously copying somebody, I know not whom, says : " Words derive their meaning from the consent and practice of those who use them. *There is no necessary connexion between words and ideas.* The association between the sign and the thing signified, is purely arbitrary."—*Octavo Gram.* i, p. 139. The second assertion here made, is very far from being literally true. However arbitrary may be the use or application of words, their connexion with ideas is so necessary, that they cannot be words without it. Signification, as I shall hereafter prove, is a part of the very essence of a word, the most important element of its nature. And Murray himself says, " The understanding and language have a strict connexion "—*Ib.* i, p. 356. In this, he changes without amendment the words of Blair: " Logic and rhetoric have here, as in many other cases, a strict connexion."—*Blair's Rhet.* p. 120.

be found inadequate to convey the impression with which the mind may labour. Cicero, that great master of eloquence, frequently confessed, or declared, that words failed him. This, however, may be thought to have been uttered as a mere figure of speech; and some may say, that the imperfection I speak of, is but an incident of the common weakness or ignorance of human nature; and that if a man always knew what to say to an other in order to persuade or confute, to encourage or terrify him, he would always succeed, and no insufficiency of this kind would ever be felt or imagined. This also is plausible; but is the imperfection less, for being sometimes traceable to an ulterior source? Or is it certain that human languages used by perfect wisdom, would all be perfectly competent to their common purpose? And if some would be found less so than others, may there not be an insufficiency in the very nature of them all?

22. If there is imperfection in any instrument, there is so much the more need of care and skill in the use of it. Duncan, in concluding his chapter about words as signs of our ideas, says, "It is apparent, that we are sufficiently provided with the means of communicating our thoughts one to another; and that the mistakes so frequently complained of on this head, are wholly owing to ourselves, in not sufficiently defining the terms we use, or perhaps not connecting them with clear and determinate ideas."—*Logic*, p. 69. On the other hand, we find that some of the best and wisest of men confess the inadequacy of language, while they also deplore its misuse. But, whatever may be its inherent defects, or its culpable abuses, it is still to be honoured as almost the only medium for the communication of thought and the diffusion of knowledge. Bishop Butler remarks, in his Analogy of Religion, (a most valuable work, though defective in style,) "So likewise the imperfections attending the only method by which nature enables and directs us to communicate our thoughts to each other, are innumerable. Language is, in its very nature, inadequate, ambiguous, liable to infinite abuse, even from negligence; and so liable to it from design, that every man can deceive and betray by it."— Part ii, Chap. 3. Lord Kames, too, seconds this complaint, at least in part: "Lamentable is the imperfection of language, almost in every particular that falls not under external sense. I am talking of a matter exceedingly clear in the perception, and yet I find no small difficulty to express it clearly in words."— *Elements of Criticism*, i, p. 86. "All writers," says Sheridan, "seem to be under the influence of one common delusion, that by the help of words alone, they can communicate all that passes in their minds."—*Lectures on Elocution*, p. xi.

23. Addison also, in apologizing for Milton's frequent use of old words and foreign idioms, says, "I may further add, that Milton's sentiments and ideas were so wonderfully sublime, that it would have been impossible for him to have represented them in their full strength and beauty, without having recourse to these foreign assistances. *Our language sunk under him*, and was unequal to that greatness of soul which furnished him with such glorious conceptions."—*Spectator*, No. 297. This, however, Dr. Johnson seems to regard as a mere compliment to genius; for of Milton he says, "The truth is, that both in prose and verse, he had formed his style by a perverse and pedantick principle." But the grandeur of his thoughts is not denied by the critic; nor is his language censured without qualification. "Whatever be the faults of his diction, he cannot want the praise of copiousness and variety: he was master of his language in its full extent; and has selected the melodious words with such diligence, that from his book alone the Art of English Poetry might be learned."—*Johnson's Life of Milton: Lives*, p. 92.

24. As words abstractly considered are empty and vain, being in their nature mere signs, or tokens, which derive all their value from the ideas and feelings which they suggest; it is evident that he who would either speak or write well, must be furnished with something more than a knowledge of sounds and letters. Words fitly spoken are indeed both precious and beautiful—"like apples of gold in pictures of silver." But it is not for him whose soul is dark, whose designs are

selfish, whose affections are dead, or whose thoughts are vain, to say with the son of Amram, "My doctrine shall drop as the rain, my speech shall distil as the dew; as the small rain upon the tender herb, and as the showers upon the grass."—*Deut.* xxxii, 2. It is not for him to exhibit the true excellency of speech, because he cannot feel its power. It is not for him, whatever be the theme, to convince the judgement with deductions of reason, to fire the imagination with glowing imagery, or win with graceful words the willing ear of taste. His wisdom shall be silence, when men are present; for the soul of manly language, is the soul that thinks and feels as best becomes a man.

CHAPTER VI.

OF THE ORIGIN AND HISTORY OF THE ENGLISH LANGUAGE.

" Non mediocres enim tenebræ in sylva, ubi hæc captanda : neque eo, quo pervenire volumus semitæ tritæ : neque non in tramitibus quædam objecta, quæ euntem retinere possent."—VARRO. *De Lingua Latina*, Lib. iv, p. 4.

1. In order that we may set a just value upon the literary labours of those who, in former times, gave particular attention to the culture of the English language, and that we may the better judge of the credibility of modern pretensions to further improvements, it seems necessary that we should know something of the course of events through which its acknowledged melioration in earlier days took place. For, in this case, the extent of a man's knowledge is the strength of his argument. As Bacon quotes Aristotle, " Qui respiciunt ad pauca, de facili pronunciant." He that takes a narrow view, easily makes up his mind. But what is any opinion worth, if further knowledge of facts can confute it?

2. Whatsoever is successively varied, or has such a manner of existence as time can affect, must have had both an origin and a progress; and may have also its particular *history*, if the opportunity for writing it be not neglected. But such is the levity of mankind, that things of great moment are often left without memorial while the hand of Literature is busy to beguile the world with trifles or with fictions, with fancies or with lies. The rude and cursory languages of barbarous nations, till the genius of Grammar arise to their rescue, are among those transitory things which unsparing time is ever hurrying away, irrecoverably, to oblivion. Tradition knows not what they were; for of their changes she takes no account. Philosophy tells us, they are resolved into the variable, fleeting breath of the successive generations of those by whom they were spoken; whose kindred fate it was, to pass away unnoticed and nameless, lost in the elements from which they sprung.

3. Upon the history of the English language, darkness thickens as we tread back the course of time. The subject of our inquiry becomes, at every step, more difficult and less worthy. We have now a tract of English literature, both extensive and luminous; and though many modern writers, and no few even of our writers on grammar, are comparatively very deficient in style, it is safe to affirm that the English language in general has never been written or spoken with more propriety and elegance, than it is at the present day. Modern English we read with facility; and that which was good two centuries ago, though considerably antiquated, is still easily understood. The best way, therefore, to gain a practical knowledge of the changes which our language has undergone, is, to read some of

our older authors in retrograde order, till the style employed at times more and more remote, becomes in some degree familiar. Pursued in this manner, the study will be less difficult, and the labour of the curious inquirer, which may be suspended or resumed at pleasure, will be better repaid, than if he proceed in the order of history, and attempt at first the Saxon remains.

4. The value of a language as an object of study, depends chiefly on the character of the *books* which it contains; and, secondarily, on its connexion with others more worthy to be thoroughly known. In this instance, there are several circumstances which are calculated soon to discourage research. As our language took its rise during the barbarism of the dark ages, the books through which its early history must be traced, are not only few and meagre, but, in respect to grammar, unsettled and diverse. It is not to be expected that inquiries of this kind will ever engage the attention of any very considerable number of persons. Over the minds of the reading public, the attractions of novelty hold a much greater influence, than any thing that is to be discovered in the dusk of antiquity. All old books contain a greater or less number of obsolete words, and antiquated modes of expression, which puzzle the reader, and call him too frequently to his glossary. And even the most common terms, when they appear in their ancient, unsettled orthography, are often so disguised as not to be readily recognized.

5. These circumstances (the last of which should be a caution to us against innovations in spelling) retard the progress of the reader, impose a labour too great for the ardour of his curiosity, and soon dispose him to rest satisfied with an ignorance, which, being general, is not likely to expose him to censure. For these reasons, ancient authors are little read; and the real antiquary is considered a man of odd habits, who, by a singular propensity, is led into studies both unfashionable and fruitless—a man who ought to have been born in the days of old, that he might have spoken the language he is so curious to know, and have appeared in the costume of an age better suited to his taste.

6. But *Learning* is ever curious to explore the records of time, as well as the regions of space; and wherever her institutions flourish, she will amass her treasures, and spread them before her votaries. Difference of languages she easily overcomes; but the leaden reign of unlettered Ignorance defies her scrutiny. Hence, of one period of the world's history, she ever speaks with horror—that "long night of apostasy," during which, like a lone Sibyl, she hid her precious relics in solitary cells, and fleeing from degraded Christendom, sought refuge with the eastern caliphs. "This awful decline of true religion in the world carried with it almost every vestige of civil liberty, of classical literature, and of scientific knowledge; and it will generally be found in experience that they must all stand or fall together."—*Hints on Toleration*, p. 263. In the tenth century, beyond which we find nothing that bears much resemblance to the English language as now written, this mental darkness appears to have gathered to its deepest obscuration; and, at that period, England was sunk as low in ignorance, superstition, and depravity, as any other part of Europe.

7. The English language gradually varies as we trace it back, and becomes at length identified with the Anglo-Saxon; that is, with the dialect spoken by the Saxons after their settlement in England. These Saxons were a fierce, warlike, unlettered people from Germany; whom the ancient Britons had invited to their assistance against the Picts and Scots. Cruel and ignorant, like their Gothic kindred, who had but lately overrun the Roman empire, they came, not for the good of others, but to accommodate themselves. They accordingly seized the country; destroyed or enslaved the ancient inhabitants; or, more probably, drove the remnant of them into the mountains of Wales. Of Welsh or ancient British words, Charles Bucke, who says in his grammar that he took great pains to be accurate in his scale of derivation, enumerates but one hundred and eleven, as now found in our language; and Dr. Johnson, who makes them but ninety-five, argues from their

paucity, or almost total absence, that the Saxons could not have mingled at all with these people, or even have retained them in vassalage.

8. The ancient languages of France and of the British isles are said to have proceeded from an other language yet more ancient, called the *Celtic ;* so that, from one common source, are supposed to have sprung the present Welsh, the present Irish, and the present Highland Scotch.* The term *Celtic* Dr. Webster defines, as a noun, "The language of the Celts ;" and, as an adjective, "Pertaining to the primitive inhabitants of the south and west of Europe, or to the early inhabitants of Italy, Gaul, Spain, and Britain." What *unity,* according to this, there was, or could have been, in the ancient Celtic tongue, does not appear from books, nor is it easy to be conjectured.† Many ancient writers sustain this broad application of the term *Celtæ* or *Celts ;* which, according to Strabo's etymology of it, means horsemen, and seems to have been almost as general as our word *Indians.* But Cæsar informs us that the name was more particularly claimed by the people who, in his day, lived in France between the Seine and the Garonne, and who by the Romans were called *Galli,* or *Gauls.*

9. The *Celtic* tribes are said to have been the descendants of Gomer, the son of Japhet. The English historians agree that the first inhabitants of their island owed their origin and their language to the *Celtæ,* or Gauls, who settled on the opposite shore. Julius Cæsar, who invaded Britain about half a century before the Christian era, found the inhabitants ignorant of letters, and destitute of any history but oral tradition. To this, however, they paid great attention, teaching every thing in verse. Some of the Druids, it is said, spent twenty years in learning to repeat songs and hymns that were never committed to writing. These ancient priests, or diviners, are represented as having great power, and as exercising it in some respects beneficially ; but their horrid rites, with human sacrifices, provoked the Romans to destroy them. Smollett says, "Tiberius suppressed those human sacrifices in Gaul ; and Claudius destroyed the Druids of that country ; but they subsisted in Britain till the reign of Nero, when Paulus Suetonius reduced the island of Anglesey, which was the place of their retreat, and overwhelmed them with such unexpected and sudden destruction, that all their knowledge and tradition, conveyed to them in the songs of their predecessors, perished at once."— *Smollett's Hist. of Eng.* 4to, B. i, Ch. i, § 7.

10. The Romans considered Britain a province of their empire, for a period of about five hundred years ; but the northern part of the island was never entirely subdued by them, and not till Anno Domini 78, a hundred and thirty-three years after their first invasion of the country, had they completed their conquest of England. Letters and arts, so far at least as these are necessary to the purposes of war or government, the victors carried with them ; and under their auspices some knowledge of Christianity was, at a very early period, introduced into Britain. But it seems strange, that after all that is related of their conquests, settlements,

* "The language which is, at present, spoken throughout Great Britain, is neither the ancient primitive speech of the island, nor derived from it ; but is altogether of foreign origin. The language of the first inhabitants of our island, beyond doubt, was the Celtic, or Gaelic, common to them with Gaul ; from which country, it appears, by many circumstances, that Great Britain was peopled. This Celtic tongue, which is said to be very expressive and copious, and is, probably, one of the most ancient languages in the world, obtained once in most of the western regions of Europe. It was the language of Gaul, of Great Britain, of Ireland, and very probably, of Spain also ; till, in the course of those revolutions which by means of the conquests, first, of the Romans, and afterwards, of the northern nations, changed the government, speech, and, in a manner, the whole face of Europe, *this tongue was gradually obliterated ;* and now subsists only in the mountains of Wales, in the Highlands of Scotland, and among the wild Irish. For the Irish, the Welsh, and the Erse, are no other than different dialects of the same tongue, the ancient Celtic."—*Blair's Rhetoric,* Lect. IX, p. 85.

† With some writers, *the Celtic* language is *the Welsh ;* as may be seen by the following extract : "By this he requires an impossibility, since much the greater Part of Mankind can by no means spare 10 or 11 Years of their Lives in learning those dead Languages, to arrive at a perfect Knowledge of their own. But by this Gentleman's way of Arguing, we ought not only to be Masters of *Latin* and *Greek,* but of *Spanish, Italian, High-Dutch, Low-Dutch, French,* the *Old Saxon, Welsh, Runic, Gothic,* and *Islandic ;* since much the greater number of Words of common and general Use are derived from *those Tongues.* Nay, by the same way of Reasoning we may prove, that the *Romans* and *Greeks* did not understand their own Tongues, because they were not acquainted with *the Welsh,* or *ancient Celtic,* there being above 620 radical *Greek* Words derived from *the Celtic,* and of the Latin a much greater Number."—*Preface to Brightland's Grammar,* p. v.

cities, fortifications, buildings, seminaries, churches, laws, &c , they should at last have left the Britons in so helpless, degraded, and forlorn a condition. They *did not sow among them the seeds* of any permanent improvement.

11. The Roman government, being unable to sustain itself at home, withdrew its forces finally from Britain in the year 446, leaving the wretched inhabitants almost as savage as it found them, and in a situation even less desirable. Deprived of their native resources, their ancient independence of spirit, as well as of the laws, customs, institutions, and leaders, that had kept them together under their old dynasties, and now deserted by their foreign protectors, they were apparently. left at the mercy of blind fortune, the wretched vicissitudes of which there was none to foresee, none to resist. The glory of the Romans now passed away. The mighty fabric of their own proud empire crumbled into ruins. Civil liberty gave place to barbarism ; Christian truth, to papal superstition ; and the lights of science were put out by both. The shades of night gathered over all ; settling and condensing, " till almost every point of that wide horizon, over which the Sun of Righteousness had diffused his cheering rays, was enveloped in a darkness more awful and more portentous than that which of old descended upon rebellious Pharaoh and the callous sons of Ham."—*Hints on Toleration*, p. 310.

12. The Saxons entered Britain in the year 449. But what was the form of their language at that time, cannot now be known. It was a dialect of the *Gothic* or *Teutonic ;* which is considered the parent of all the northern tongues of Europe, except some few of Sclavonian origin. The only remaining monument of the Gothic language is a copy of the Gospels, translated by Ulphilas ; which is preserved at Upsal, and called, from its embellishments, *the Silver Book.* This old work has been three times printed in England. We possess not yet in America all the advantages which may be enjoyed by literary men in the land of our ancestors ; but the stores of literature, both ancient and modern, are somewhat more familiar to us, than is there supposed ; and the art of printing is fast equalizing, to all nations that cultivate learning, the privilege of drinking at its ancient fountains.

13. It is neither liberal nor just to argue unfavourably of the intellectual or the moral condition of any remote age or country, merely from our own ignorance of it. It is true, we can derive from no quarter a favourable opinion of the state of England after the Saxon invasion, and during the tumultuous and bloody government of the heptarchy. But I will not darken the picture through design. If justice were done to the few names—to Gildas the wise, the memorialist of his country's sufferings and censor of the nation's depravity, who appears a solitary star in the night of the sixth century—to the venerable Bede, the greatest theologian, best scholar, and only historian of the seventh—to Alcuin, the abbot of Canterbury, the luminary of the eighth—to Alfred the great, the glory of the ninth, great as a prince, and greater as a scholar, seen in the evening twilight of an age in which the clergy could not read ;—if justice were done to all such, we might find something. even in these dark and rugged times, if not to soften the grimness of the portrait, at least to give greater distinctness of feature.

14. In tracing the history of our language, Dr. Johnson, who does little more than give examples, cites as his first specimen of ancient English, a portion of king Alfred's paraphrase in imitation of Boëthius. But this language of Alfred's is not English ; but rather, as the learned doctor himself considered it, an example of the Anglo-Saxon in its highest state of purity. This dialect was first changed by admixture with words derived from the Danish and the Norman ; and, still being comparatively rude and meagre, afterwards received large accessions from the Latin, the French, the Greek, the Dutch—till, by gradual changes, which the etymologist may exhibit, there was at length produced a language bearing a sufficient resemblance to the present English, to deserve to be called English at this day.

15. The formation of our language cannot with propriety be dated earlier than the thirteenth century. It was then that a free and voluntary amalgamation of its

chief constituent materials took place ; and this was somewhat earlier than we date
the revival of learning. The English of the thirteenth century is scarcely
intelligible to the modern reader. Dr. Johnson calls it "a kind of intermediate
diction, neither Saxon nor English;" and says, that Sir John Gower, who wrote in
the latter part of the fourteenth century, was "the first of our authors who can be
properly said to have written English." Contemporary with Gower, the father of
English poetry, was the still greater poet, his disciple Chaucer; who embraced
many of the tenets of Wickliffe, and imbibed something of the spirit of the
reformation, which was now begun.

16. The literary history of the fourteenth and fifteenth centuries is full of
interest ; for it is delightful to trace the progress of great and obvious improvement.
The reformation of religion and the revival of learning were nearly simultaneous.
Yet individuals may have acted a conspicuous part in the latter, who had little to
do with the former; for great learning does not necessarily imply great piety,
though, as Dr. Johnson observes, "the Christian religion always implies or produces
a certain degree of civility and learning."—*Hist. Eng. Lang. before his 4to Dict.*
"The ordinary instructions of the clergy, both philosophical and religious, gradually
fell into contempt, as the Classics superseded the one, and the Holy Scriptures
expelled the other. The first of these changes was effected by *the early grammarians* of Europe ; and it gave considerable aid to the reformation, though it had
no immediate connexion with that event. The revival of the English Bible,
however, completed the work : and though its appearance was late, and its progress
was retarded in every possible manner, yet its dispersion was at length equally
rapid, extensive, and effectual."—*Constable's Miscellany,* Vol. xx, p. 75.

17. Peculiar honour is due to those who lead the way in whatever advances
human happiness. And, surely, our just admiration of the character of the
reformers must be not a little enhanced, when we consider what they did for
letters as well as for the church. Learning does not consist in useless jargon, in
a multitude of mere words, or in acute speculations remote from practice ; else the
seventeen folios of St. Thomas Aquinas, the angelical doctor of the thirteenth
century, and the profound disputations of his great rival, Duns Scotus the subtle,
for which they were revered in their own age, had not gained them the contempt
of all posterity. From such learning the lucid reasoning of the reformers delivered
the halls of instruction. The school divinity of the middle ages passed away before
the presence of that which these men learned from the Bible, as did in a later age
the Aristotelian philosophy before that which Bacon drew from nature.

18. Towards the latter part of the fourteenth century, Wickliffe furnished the
first entire translation of the Bible into English. In like manner did the Germans,
a hundred and fifty years after, receive it in their tongue from the hands of Luther;
who says, that at twenty years of age, he himself had not seen it in any language.
Wickliffe's English style is elegant for the age in which he lived, yet very different
from what is elegant now. This first English translation of the Bible, being made
about a hundred years before the introduction of printing into England, could not
have been very extensively circulated. A large specimen of it may be seen in
Dr. Johnson's History of the English Language. Wickliffe died in 1384. The
art of printing was invented about 1440, and first introduced into England, in
1468 ; but the first printed edition of the Bible in English, was executed in
Germany. It was completed, October 5th, 1535.

19. "Martin Luther, about the year 1517, first introduced metrical psalmody
into the service of the church, which not only kept alive the enthusiasm of the
reformers, but formed a rallying point for his followers. This practice spread in
all directions ; and it was not long ere six thousand persons were heard singing
together at St. Paul's Cross in London. Luther was a poet and musician ; but
the same talent existed not in his followers. Thirty years afterwards, Sternhold
versified fifty-one of the Psalms; and in 1562, with the help of Hopkins, he

completed the Psalter. These poetical effusions were chiefly sung to German melodies, which the good taste of Luther supplied: but the Puritans, in a subsequent age, nearly destroyed these germs of melody, assigning as a reason, that music should be so simplified as to suit all persons, and that all may join."— *Gardiner's Music of Nature*, p. 283.

20. "The schools and colleges of England in the fifteenth and sixteenth centuries were not governed by a system of education which would render their students very eminent either as scholars or as gentlemen: and the monasteries, which were used as seminaries, even until the reformation, taught only the corrupt Latin used by the ecclesiastics. The time however was approaching, when the united efforts of Stanbridge, Linacre, Sir John Cheke, Dean Colet, Erasmus, William Lily, Roger Ascham, &c., were successful in reviving the Latin tongue in all its purity; and even in exciting a taste for Greek in a nation the clergy of which opposed its introduction with the same vehemence which characterized their enmity to a reformation in religion. The very learned Erasmus, the first who undertook the teaching of the Greek language at Oxford, met with few friends to support him; notwithstanding Oxford was the seat of nearly all the learning in England."— *Constable's Miscellany*, Vol. xx, p. 146.

21. "The priests preached against it, as a very recent invention of the arch-enemy; and confounding in their misguided zeal, the very foundation of their faith, with the object of their resentment, they represented the New Testament itself as 'an impious and dangerous book,' because it was written in that heretical language. Even after the accession of Henry VIII., when Erasmus, who had quitted Oxford in disgust, returned under his especial patronage, with the support of several eminent scholars and powerful persons, his progress was still impeded, and the language opposed. The University was divided into parties, called Greeks and Trojans, the latter being the strongest, from being favoured by the monks; and the Greeks were driven from the streets, with hisses and other expressions of contempt. It was not therefore until Henry VIII. and cardinal Wolsey gave it their positive and powerful protection, that this persecuted language was allowed to be quietly studied, even in the institutions dedicated to learning."—*Ib.* p. 147.

22. These curious extracts are adduced to show the *spirit of the times*, and the obstacles then to be surmounted in the cause of learning. This popular opposition to Greek, did not spring from a patriotic design to prefer and encourage English literature; for the improvement of this was still later, and the great promoters of it were all of them classical scholars. They wrote in English, not because they preferred it, but because none but those who were bred in colleges, could read any thing else; and, even to this very day, the grammatical study of the English language is shamefully neglected in what are called the higher institutions of learning. In alleging this neglect, I speak comparatively. Every student, on entering upon the practical business of life, will find it of far more importance to him, to be skillful in the language of his own country than to be distinguished for any knowledge which the learned only can appreciate. "Will the greatest Mastership in Greek and Latin, or [the] translating [of] these Languages into English, avail for the Purpose of acquiring an elegant English Style? No—we know just the Reverse from woeful Experience! And, as Mr. Locke and the Spectator observe, Men who have threshed hard at Greek and Latin for ten or eleven years together, are very often deficient in their own Language."—*Preface to the British Gram.* 8vo, 1784, p. xxi.

23. That the progress of English literature in early times was slow, will not seem wonderful to those who consider what is affirmed of the progress of other arts, more immediately connected with the comforts of life. "Down to the reign of Elizabeth, the greater part of the houses in considerable towns, had no chimneys: the fire was kindled against the wall, and the smoke found its way out as well as it could, by the roof, the door, or the windows. The houses were mostly built of

wattling, plastered over with clay; and the beds were only straw pallets, with a log of wood for a pillow. In this respect, even the king fared no better than his subjects; for, in Henry the Eighth's time, we find directions, 'to examine every night the straw of the king's bed, that no daggers might be concealed therein.' A writer in 1577, speaking of the progress of luxury, mentions three things especially, that were 'marvellously altered for the worse in England;' the multitude of chimneys lately erected, the increase of lodgings, and the exchange of treen platters into pewter, and wooden spoons into silver and tin; and he complains bitterly that oak instead of willow was employed in the building of houses."— REV. ROYAL ROBBINS: *Outlines of History*, p. 377.

24. Shakspeare appeared in the reign of Elizabeth; outlived her thirteen years; and died in 1616, aged 52. The English language in his hands did not lack power or compass of expression. His writings are now more extensively read, than any others of that age; nor has any very considerable part of his phraseology yet become obsolete. But it ought to be known, that the printers or editors of the editions which are now read, have taken extensive liberty in modernizing his orthography, as well as that of other old authors still popular. How far such liberty is justifiable, it is difficult to say. Modern readers doubtless find a convenience in it. It is very desirable that the orthography of our language should be made uniform, and remain permanent. Great alterations cannot be suddenly introduced; and there is, in stability, an advantage which will counterbalance that of a slow approximation to regularity. Analogy may sometimes decide the form of variable words, but the concurrent usage of the learned must ever be respected, in this, as in every other part of grammar.

25. Among the earliest of the English grammarians, was Ben Jonson, the poet; who died in the year 1637, at the age of sixty-three. His grammar, (which Horne Tooke mistakingly calls "the *first* as well as the *best* English grammar,") is still extant, being published in the several editions of his works. It is a small treatise, and worthy of attention only as a matter of curiosity. It is written in prose, and designed chiefly for the aid of foreigners. Grammar is an unpoetical subject, and therefore not wisely treated, as it once very generally was, in verse. But every poet should be familiar with the art, because the formal principles of his own have always been considered as embraced in it. To its poets, too, every language must needs be particularly indebted; because their compositions, being in general more highly finished than works in prose, are supposed to present the language in its most agreeable form. In the preface to the Poems of Edmund Waller, published in 1690, the editor ventures to say, "He was, indeed, the Parent of English Verse, and the first that shewed us our Tongue had Beauty and Numbers in it. Our Language owes more to Him, than the French does to Cardinal Richelieu and the whole Academy. * * * * The Tongue came into His hands a rough diamond: he polished it first; and to *that* degree, that all artists since him have admired the workmanship, without pretending to mend it."— *British Poets*, Vol. ii, 1800: *Waller's Poems*, p. 4.

26. Dr. Johnson however, in his Lives of the Poets, abates this praise, that he may transfer the greater part of it to Dryden and Pope. He admits that, "After about half a century of forced thoughts and rugged metre, some advances towards nature and harmony had been already made by Waller and Denham;" but, in distributing the praise of this improvement, he adds, "It may be doubted whether Waller and Denham could have over-born [*overborne*] the prejudices which had long prevailed, and which even then were sheltered by the protection of Cowley. The new versification, as it was called, may be considered as owing its establishment to Dryden; from whose time it is apparent that English poetry has had no tendency to relapse to its former savageness."—*Johnson's Life of Dryden: Lives*, p. 206. To Pope, as the translator of Homer, he gives this praise: "His version may be said to have tuned the English tongue; for since its appearance no writer,

however deficient in other powers, has wanted melody."—*Life of Pope: Lives,*
p. 567. Such was the opinion of Johnson; but there are other critics who object
to the versification of Pope, that it is "monotonous and cloying." See, in Leigh
Hunt's Feast of the Poets, the following couplet, and a note upon it:

> "But ever since Pope spoil'd the ears of the town
> With his cuckoo-song verses half up and half down."

27. The unfortunate Charles I, as well as his father James I, was a lover and
promoter of letters. He was himself a good scholar, and wrote well in English,
for his time: he ascended the throne in 1625, and was beheaded in 1648. Nor
was Cromwell himself, with all his religious and military enthusiasm, wholly
insensible to *literary* merit. This century was distinguished by the writings of
Milton, Dryden, Waller, Cowley, Denham, Locke, and others; and the reign of
Charles II, which is embraced in it, has been considered by some "the Augustan
age of English literature." But that honour, if it may well be bestowed on any,
belongs rather to a later period. The best works produced in the eighteenth
century, are so generally known and so highly esteemed, that it would be lavish of
the narrow space allowed to this introduction, to speak particularly of their merits.
Some grammatical errors may be found in almost all books; but our language was,
in general, written with great purity and propriety by Addison, Swift, Pope,
Johnson, Lowth, Hume, Horne, and many other celebrated authors who flourished
in the last century. Nor was it much before this period, that the British writers
took any great pains to be accurate in the use of their own language:

> "Late, very late, correctness grew our care,
> When the tir'd nation breath'd from civil war."—*Pope.*

28. English books began to be printed in the early part of the sixteenth century;
and, as soon as a taste for reading was formed, the press threw open the flood-gates
of general knowledge, the streams of which are now pouring forth, in a copious,
increasing, but too often turbid tide, upon all the civilized nations of the earth.
This mighty engine afforded a means by which superior minds could act more
efficiently and more extensively upon society in general. And thus, by the
exertions of genius adorned with learning, our native tongue has been made the
polished vehicle of the most interesting truths, and of the most important discoveries; and has become a language copious, strong, refined, and capable of no
inconsiderable degree of harmony. Nay, it is esteemed by some who claim to be
competent judges, to be the strongest, the richest, the most elegant, and the most
susceptible of sublime imagery, of all the languages in the world.

CHAPTER VII.

CHANGES AND SPECIMENS OF THE ENGLISH LANGUAGE.

"Quot enim verba, et nonnunquam in deterius, hoc, quo vivimus, sæculo, partim aliquâ, partim nullâ
necessitate cogente, mutata sunt?"—ROB. AINSWORTH: *Lat. Dict. 4to, Pref.* p. xi.

1. In the use of language, every one chooses his words from that common stock
which he has learned, and applies them in practice according to his own habits and
notions. If the style of different writers of the same age is various, much greater
is the variety which appears in the productions of different ages. Hence the date

of a book may often be very plausibly conjectured from the peculiarities of its style. As to what is best in itself, or best adapted to the subject in hand, every writer must endeavour to become his own judge. He who, in any sort of composition, would write with a master's hand, must first apply himself to books with a scholar's diligence. He must think it worth his while to inform himself, that he may be critical. Desiring to give the student all the advantage, entertainment, and satisfaction, that can be expected from a work of this kind, I shall subjoin a few brief specimens in illustration of what has been said in the foregoing chapter. The order of time will be followed *inversely;* and, as Saxon characters are not very easily obtained, or very apt to be read, the Roman letters will be employed for the few examples to which the others would be more appropriate. But there are some peculiarities of ancient usage in English, which, for the information of the young reader, it is proper in the first place to explain.

2. With respect to the letters, there are *several changes* to be mentioned. (1.) The pages of old books are often crowded with capitals: it was at one time the custom to distinguish all nouns, and frequently verbs, or any other important words, by heading them with a great letter. (2.) The letter Ess, of the lower case, had till lately two forms, the long and the short, as f and s; the former very nearly resembling the small f, and the latter, its own capital. The short *s* was used *at the end of words,* and the long *ſ,* in other places; but the latter is now laid aside, in favour of the more distinctive form. (3.) The letters *I* and *J* were formerly considered as one and the same. Hence we find *hallelujah* for *halleluiah, Iohn* for *John, iudgement* for *judgement,* &c. And in many dictionaries, the words beginning with *J* are still mixed with those which begin with *I.* (4.) The letters *U* and *V* were mixed in like manner, and for the same reason; the latter being a consonant power given to the former, and at length distinguished from it by a different form. Or rather, the figure of the capital seems to have been at last appropriated to the one, and that of the small letter to the other. But in old books the forms of these two letters are continually confounded or transposed. Hence it is, that our *Double-u* is composed of two *Vees;* which, as we see in old books, were sometimes printed separately; as, VV or vv.

3. The *orthography* of our language, rude and unsettled as it still is in many respects, was formerly much more variable and diverse. In books a hundred years old or more, we often find the most common words spelled variously by the same writer, and even upon the very same page. With respect to the forms of words, a few particulars may here be noticed: (1.) The article *an,* from which the *n* was dropped before words beginning with a consonant sound, is often found in old books where *a* would be more proper; as, *an heart, an help, an hill, an one, an use.* (2.) Till the seventeenth century, the possessive case was written without the apostrophe; being formed at different times, in *es, is, ys,* or *s,* like the plural; and apparently without rule or uniformity in respect to the doubling of the final consonant: as *Goddes, Godes, Godis, Godys,* or *Gods,* for *God's;* so *mannes, mannis, mannys* or *mans,* for *man's.* Dr. Ash, whose English Grammar was in some repute in the latter part of the eighteenth century, argued against the use of the apostrophe, alleging that it was seldom used to distinguish the possessive case till about the beginning of that century; and he then prophesied that the time would come, when *correct writers would lay it aside again,* as a strange corruption, an improper "departure from the original formation" of that case of English nouns. And, among the speculations of these latter days, I have somewhere seen an attempt to disparage this useful sign, and explode it, as an unsightly thing *never well estab- lished.* It does not indeed, like a syllabic sign, inform the ear or affect the sound; but still it is useful, because it distinguishes to the eye, not only the *case,* but the *number,* of the nouns thus marked. Pronouns, being different in their declension, do not need it, and should therefore always be written without it.

4. The common usage of those who have spoken English, has always inclined rather to brevity than to melody; contraction and elision of the ancient terminations

of words, constitute no small part of the change which has taken place, or of the difference which perhaps always existed between the solemn and the familiar style. In respect to euphony, however, these terminations have certainly nothing to boast; nor does the earliest period of the language appear to be that in which they were the most generally used without contraction. That degree of smoothness of which the tongue was anciently susceptible, had certainly no alliance with these additional syllables. The long sonorous endings which constitute the declensions and conjugations of the most admired languages, and which seem to chime so well with the sublimity of the Greek, the majesty of the Latin, the sweetness of the Italian, the dignity of the Spanish, or the polish of the French, *never had* any place in English. The inflections given to our words never embraced any other vowel power than that of the short *e* or *i;* and even this we are inclined to dispense with, whenever we can; so that most of our grammatical inflections are, to the ear, nothing but consonants blended with the final syllables of the words to which they are added. *ing* for the first participle, *er* for the comparative degree, and *est* for the superlative, are indeed added as whole syllables; but the rest, as *d* or *ed* for preterits and perfect participles, *s* or *es* for the plural number of nouns, or for the third person singular of verbs, and *st* or *est* for the second person singular of verbs, nine times in ten, fall into the sound or syllable with which the primitive word terminates. English verbs, as they are now commonly used, run through their entire conjugation without acquiring a single syllable from inflection, except sometimes when the sound of *d, s,* or *st* cannot be added to them.

5. This simplicity, so characteristic of our modern English, as well as of the Saxon tongue, its proper parent, is attended with advantages that go far to compensate for all that is consequently lost in euphony, or in the liberty of transposition. Our formation of the moods and tenses, by means of a few separate auxiliaries, all monosyllabic, and mostly without inflection, is not only simple and easy, but beautiful, chaste, and strong. In my opinion, our grammarians have shown far more affection for the obsolete or obsolescent terminations *en, eth, est,* and *edst,* than they really deserve. Till the beginning of the sixteenth century, *en* was used to mark the plural number of verbs, as, *they sayen* for *they say;* after which, it appears to have been dropped. Before the beginning of the seventeenth century, *s* or *es* began to dispute with *th* or *eth* the right of forming the third person singular of verbs; and, as the Bible and other grave books used only the latter, a clear distinction obtained, between the solemn and the familiar style, which distinction is well known at this day. Thus we have, *He runs, walks, rides, reaches,* &c., for the one; and, *He runneth, walketh, rideth, reacheth,* &c., for the other. About the same time, or perhaps earlier, the use of the second person singular began to be avoided in polite conversation, by the substitution of the plural verb and pronoun; and, when used in poetry, it was often contracted, so as to prevent any syllabic increase. In old books, all verbs and participles that were intended to be contracted in pronunciation, were contracted also, in some way, by the writer: as, "*call'd, carry'd, sacrific'd;*" "*fly'st, ascrib'st, cry'dst;*" "*tost, curst, blest, finisht;*" and others innumerable. All these, and such as are like them, we now pronounce in the same way, but usually write differently; as, *called, carried, sacrificed; fliest, ascribest, criedst; tossed, cursed, blessed, finished.* Most of these topics will be further noticed in the Grammar.

I. ENGLISH OF THE NINETEENTH CENTURY.

6. *Queen Victoria's Answer to an Address.—Example written in* 1837.

"I thank you for your condolence upon the death of his late Majesty, for the justice which you render to his character, and to the measures of his reign, and for your warm congratulations upon my accession to the throne. I join in your prayers for the prosperity of my reign, the best security for which is to be found in reverence for our holy religion, and in the observance of its duties."—VICTORIA, *to the Friends' Society.*

5

7. *From President Adams's Eulogy on Lafayette.—Written in 1834.*

"Pronounce him one of the first men of his age, and you have yet not done him justice. Try him by that test to which he sought in vain to stimulate the vulgar and selfish spirit of Napoleon ; class him among the men who, to compare and seat themselves, must take in the compass of all ages ; turn back your eyes upon the records of time ; summon from the creation of the world to this day the mighty dead of every age and every clime ; and where, among the race of merely mortal men, shall one be found, who, as the benefactor of his kind, shall claim to take precedence of Lafayette?"— JOHN QUINCY ADAMS.

8. *From President Jackson's Proclamation against Nullification.—1832.*

"No, we have not erred ! The Constitution is still the object of our reverence, the bond of our Union, our defence in danger, the source of our prosperity in peace. It shall descend, as we have received it, uncorrupted by sophistical construction, to our posterity : and the sacrifices of local interest, of State prejudices, of personal animosities, that were made to bring it into existence, will again be patriotically offered for its support."—ANDREW JACKSON.

9. *From a Note on one of Robert Hall's Sermons.—Written about 1831.*

"After he had written down the striking apostrophe which occurs at about page 76 of most of the editions—'Eternal God ! on what are thine enemies intent ! what are those enterprises of guilt and horror, that, for the safety of their performers, require to be enveloped in a darkness which the eye of Heaven must not *penetrate !*'—he asked. 'Did I say *penetrate*, sir, when I preached it ?' 'Yes.' 'Do you think, sir, I may venture to alter it ? for no man who considered the force of the English language, would use a word of three syllables there, but from absolute necessity.' 'You are doubtless at liberty to alter it, if you think well.' 'Then be so good, sir, as to take your pencil, and for *penetrate* put *pierce ; pierce* is the word, sir, and the only word to be used there.' "—OLINTHUS GREGORY.

10. *King William's Answer to an Address.—Example written in 1830.*

"I thank you sincerely for your condolence with me, on account of the loss which I have sustained, in common with my people, by the death of my lamented brother, his late Majesty. The assurances which you have conveyed to me, of loyalty and affectionate attachment to my person, are very gratifying to my feelings. You may rely upon my favour and protection, and upon my anxious endeavours to promote morality and true piety among all classes of my subjects."—WILLIAM IV, *to the Friends.*

11. *Reign of George IV, 1830 back to 1820.—Example written in 1827.*

"That morning, thou, that slumbered[*] not before,
Nor slept, great Ocean ! laid thy waves to rest,
And hushed thy mighty minstrelsy.   No breath
Thy deep composure stirred, no fin, no oar ;
Like beauty newly dead, so calm, so still,
So lovely, thou, beneath the light that fell
From angel-chariots sentinelled on high,
Reposed, and listened, and saw thy living change,
Thy dead arise. Charybdis listened, and Scylla ;
And savage Euxine on the Thracian beach
Lay motionless : and every battle ship
Stood still ; and every ship of merchandise,
And all that sailed, of every name, stood still."
ROBERT POLLOK : *Course of Time*, Book VII, line 634—647.

---

[*] The author of this specimen, through a solemn and sublime poem in ten books, *generally simplified* the preterit verb of the second person singular, by omitting the termination *st* or *est*, whenever his measure did not require the additional syllable. But his tuneless editors have, in many instances, taken the rude liberty both to spoil his versification, and to publish under his name what he did not write. They have given him *bad prosody*, or unutterable *harshness of phraseology*, for the sake of what they conceived to be *grammar.* So *Kirkham*, in copying the foregoing passage, alters it as he will ; and alters it *differently*, when he happens to write some part of it twice ; as,

"That morning, thou, that *slumberedst* not before,
Nor *slept*, great Ocean ! *laidst* thy waves *at* rest,
And *hushed* thy mighty minstrelsy.'"—*Kirkham's Elocution*, p. 203.

Again :   "That morning, thou, that *slumber'dst* not before,
Nor *sleptst*, great Ocean, *laidst* thy waves *at* rest,
And *hush'dst* thy mighty minstrelsy.'—*Kirkham's Elocution*, p. 44.

II. ENGLISH OF THE EIGHTEENTH CENTURY.

12. *Reign of George III, 1820 back to 1760.—Example written in 1800.*

"There is, it will be confessed, a delicate sensibility to character, a sober desire of reputation, a wish to possess the esteem of the wise and good, felt by the purest minds, which is at the farthest remove from arrogance or vanity. The humility of a noble mind scarcely dares approve of itself, until it has secured the approbation of others. Very different is that restless desire of distinction, that passion for theatrical display, which inflames the heart and occupies the whole attention of vain men. • • • The truly good man is jealous over himself, lest the notoriety of his best actions, by blending itself with their motive, should diminish their value; the vain man performs the same actions for the sake of that notoriety. The good man quietly discharges his duty, and shuns ostentation; the vain man considers every good deed lost that is not publickly displayed. The one is intent upon realities, the other upon semblances: the one aims to *be* virtuous, the other to *appear* so."—ROBERT HALL: *Sermon on Modern Infidelity.*

13. *From Washington's Farewell Address.—Example written in 1796.*

"Of all the dispositions and habits which lead to political prosperity, Religion and Morality are indispensable supports. In vain would that man claim the tribute of patriotism, who should labour to subvert these great pillars of human happiness, these firmest props of the duties of men and citizens. The mere politician, equally with the pious man, ought to respect and cherish them. A volume could not trace all their connexions with private and publick felicity. Let it simply be asked, where is the security for property, for reputation, for life, if the sense of religious obligation desert the oaths which are the instruments of investigation in courts of justice? And let us with caution indulge the supposition, that morality can be maintained without religion. Whatever may be conceded to the influence of refined education on minds of a peculiar structure; reason and experience both forbid us to expect that national morality can prevail in exclusion of religious principle."—GEORGE WASHINGTON.

14. *From Dr. Johnson's Life of Addison.—Example written about 1780.*

"That he always wrote as he would think it necessary to write now, cannot be affirmed; his instructions were such as the character of his readers made proper. That general knowledge which now circulates in common talk, was in his time rarely to be found. Men not professing learning, were not ashamed of ignorance; and in the female world, any acquaintance with books was distinguished only to be censured. His purpose was to infuse literary curiosity, by gentle and unsuspected conveyance, into the gay, the idle, and the wealthy; he therefore presented knowledge in the most alluring form, not lofty and austere, but accessible and familiar. When he shewed them their defects, he shewed them likewise that they might easily be supplied. His attempt succeeded; inquiry was awakened, and comprehension expanded. An emulation of intellectual elegance was excited, and from this time to our own, life has been gradually exalted, and conversation purified and enlarged."—SAMUEL JOHNSON: *Lives*, p. 321.

15. *Reign of George II, 1760 back to 1727.—Example written in 1751.*

"We Britons in our time have been remarkable borrowers, as our *multiform* Language may sufficiently shew. Our Terms in *polite Literature* prove, that this came from *Greece;* our Terms in *Music* and *Painting*, that these came from *Italy;* our Phrases in *Cookery* and *War*, that we learnt these from the French; and our Phrases in *Navigation*, that we were taught by the *Flemings* and *Low Dutch*. These many and very different Sources of our Language may be the cause, why it is so deficient in *Regularity* and *Analogy*. Yet we have this advantage to compensate the defect, that what we want in *Elegance*, we gain in *Copiousness*, in which last respect few Languages will be found superior to our own."—JAMES HARRIS: *Hermes*, Book iii, Ch. v, p. 408.

16. *Reign of George I, 1727 back to 1714.—Example written about 1718.*

"There is a certain coldness and indifference in the phrases of our European languages, when they are compared with the Oriental forms of speech: and it happens very luckily, that the Hebrew idioms run into the English tongue, with a particular grace and beauty. Our language has received innumerable elegancies and improvements from that infusion of Hebraisms, which are derived to it out of the poetical passages in holy writ. They give a force and energy to our expressions, warm and animate our language, and convey our thoughts in more ardent and intense phrases, than any that are to be met with in our tongue."—JOSEPH ADDISON: *Evidences*, p. 192.

17. *Reign of Queen Anne*, 1714 to 1702.—*Example written in* 1708.

. " Some by old words to Fame have made pretence,
　Ancients in phrase, mere moderns in their sense ;
　Such labour'd nothings, in so strange a style,
　Amaze th' unlearn'd, and make the learned smile."
" In words, as fashions, the same rule will hold ;
　Alike fantastick, if too new or old :
　Be not the first by whom the new are try'd,
　Nor yet the last to lay the old aside."
　　　　　　　ALEXANDER POPE : *Essay on Criticism*, L 324—336.

III. ENGLISH OF THE SEVENTEENTH CENTURY.

18. *Reign of William III*, 1702 to 1689.—*Example published in* 1700.

" And when we fee a Man of *Milton's* Wit *Chime* in with fuch a *Herd*, and Help on the *Cry* againft *Hirelings !* We find How Eafie it is for *Folly* and *Knavery* to Meet. and that they are Near of Kin, tho they bear Different Afpects. Therefor fince *Milton* has put himfelf upon a *Level* with the *Quakers* in this, I will let them go together. And take as little Notice of his *Buffoonry*, as of their *Dulnefs* againft *Tythes.* Ther is nothing worth *Quoting* in his *Lampoon* againft the *Hirelings.* But what ther is of *Argument* in it, is fully Confider'd in what follows."—CHARLES LESLIE : *Divine Right of Tythes*, Pref. p. xi.

19. *Reign of James II*, 1689 back to 1685.—*Example written in* 1685.

" His conversation, wit, and parts,
His knowledge in the noblest useful arts,
　Were such, dead authors could not give ;
　But habitudes of those who live ;
Who, lighting him, did greater lights receive :
　He drain'd from all, and all they knew ;
His apprehension quick, his judgment true :
　That the most learn'd with shame confess
His knowledge more, his reading only less."
　　JOHN DRYDEN : *Ode to the Memory of Charles II ; Poems*, p. 84.

20. *Reign of Charles II*, 1685 to 1660.—*Example from a Letter to the Earl of Sunderland, dated, "Philadelphia, 28th 5th mo. July,* 1683.''

" And I will venture to say, that by the help of God, and such noble Friends, I will show a Province in seven years, equal to her neighbours of forty years planting. I have lay'd out the Province into Countys. Six are begun to be seated ; they lye on the great river, and are planted about six miles back. The town platt is a mile long, and two deep,—has a navigable river on each side, the least as broad as the Thames at Woolwych, from three to eight fathom water. There is built about eighty houses, and I have settled at least three hundred farmes contiguous to it."—WILLIAM PENN : *The Friend*, vii.

21. *From an Address or Dedication to Charles II.—Written in* 1675.

" There is no [other] king in the world, who can so experimentally testify of God's providence and goodness ; neither is there any [other], who rules so many free people, so many true Christians : which thing renders thy government more honourable, thyself more considerable, than the accession of many nations filled with slavish and superstitious souls."—ROBERT BARCLAY : *Apology*, p. viii.

22. The following example, from the commencement of *Paradise Lost*, first published in 1667, has been cited by several authors, to show how large a proportion of our language is of Saxon origin. The thirteen words in Italics are the only ones in this passage, which seem to have been derived from any other source.

" Of man's first *disobedience*, and the *fruit*
Of that forbidden tree, whose *mortal* taste
Brought death into the world, and all our woe,
With loss of *Eden* ; till one greater Man
Restore us, and *regain* the blissful *seat*,
Sing, heav'nly *Muse*, that on the *secret* top
Of *Oreb*, or of *Sinai*, didst *inspire*
That shepherd, who first taught the chosen seed,
In the beginning, how the Heav'ns and Earth
Rose out of *Chaos*."—MILTON : *Paradise Lost*, Book I.

23. *Examples written during Cromwell's Protectorate, 1660 to 1650.*

"The Queene was pleased to shew me the letter, the seale beinge a Roman eagle, havinge characters about it almost like the Grecke. This day, in the afternoone, the vice-chauncellor came to me and stayed about four hours with me; in which tyme we conversed upon the longe debates."—WHITELOCKE: *Bucke's Class. Gram.*, p. 149.

"I am yet heere, and have the States of Holland ingaged in a more than ordnary maner, to procure me audience of the States Generall. Whatever happen, the effects mast needes be good."—STRICKLAND: *Bucke's Classical Gram.*, p. 149.

24. *Reign of Charles I, 1648 to 1625.—Example from Ben Jonson's Grammar, written about 1634; but the orthography is more modern.*

"The second and third person singular of the present are made of the first, by adding *st* and *eth*; which last is sometimes shortened into *s*. It seemeth to have been poetical licence which first introduced this abbreviation of the third person into use; but our best grammarians have condemned it upon some occasions, though perhaps not to be absolutely banished the common and familiar style."

"The persons plural keep the termination of the first person singular. In former times, till about the reign of Henry the eighth, they were wont to be formed by adding *en*; thus, *loven, sayen, complainen*. But now (whatever is the cause) it hath quite grown out of use, and that other so generally prevailed, that I dare not presume to set this afoot again: albeit (to tell you my opinion) I am persuaded that the lack hereof well considered, will be found a great blemish to our tongue. For seeing *time* and *person* be, as it were, the right and left hand of a verb, what can the maiming bring else, but a lameness to the whole body?"—Book i, Chap. xvi.

25. *Reign of James I, 1625 to 1603.—From an Advertisement, dated 1608.*

"I svppose it altogether needlesse (Christian Reader) by commending M. VVilliam Perkins, the Author of this booke, to wooe your holy affection, which either himselfe in his life time by his Christian conversation hath woon in you, or sithence his death, the neuer-dying memorie of his excellent knowledge, his great humilitie, his sound religion, his feruent zeale, his painefull labours, in the Church of God, doe most iustly challenge at your hands: onely in one word, I dare be bold to say of him as in times past *Nazianzen* spake of *Athanasius*. His life was a good definition of a true minister and preacher of the Gospell."—*The Printer to the Reader.*

26. *Examples written about the end of Elizabeth's reign—1603.*

"Some say, That euer 'gainst that season comes
Wherein our Saviour's Birth is celebrated,
The Bird of Dawning singeth all night long;
And then, say they, no Spirit dares walk abroad:
The nights are wholsom, then no Planets strike,
No Fairy takes, nor Witch hath pow'r to charm;   -
So hallow'd and so gracious is the time."

SHAKSPEARE : *Hamlet.*

"The sea, with such a storme as his bare head
In hell-blacke night indur'd, would haue buoy'd up.
And quench'd the stelled fires.
Yet, poore old heart, he holpe the heuons to raine.
If wolues had at thy gate howl'd that sterne time,
Thou shouldst haue said, Good porter, turne the key."

SHAKSPEARE : *Lear.*

IV. ENGLISH OF THE SIXTEENTH CENTURY.

27. *Reign of Elizabeth, 1603 back to 1558.—Example written in 1592.*

"As for the soule, it is no accidentarie qualitie, but a spirituall and inuisible essence or nature, subsisting by it selfe. Which plainely appeares in that the soules of men haue beeing and continuance as well forth of the bodies of men as in the same; and are as wel subiect to torments as the bodie is. And whereas we can and doe put in practise sundrie actions of life, sense, motion, vnderstanding, we doe it onely by the power and vertue of the soule. Hence ariseth the difference betweene the soules of men, and beasts. The soules of men are substances : but the soules of other creatures seeme not to be substances ; because they haue no beeing out of the bodies in which they are."—WILLIAM PERKINS : *Theol. Works, folio*, p. 155.

28. *Examples written about the beginning of Elizabeth's reign.*—1558.

" Who can perswade, when treason is aboue reason ; and mighte ruleth righte ; and it is had for lawfull, whatsoever is lustfull ; and commotioners are better than commissioners ; and common woe is named common weale ?"—SIR JOHN CHEKE.

"If a yong jentleman will venture him selfe into the companie of ruffians, it is over great a jeopardie, lest their facions, maners, thoughts, taulke, and dedes, will verie sone be over like."—ROGER ASCHAM.

29. *Reign of Mary the Bigot,* 1558 to 1553.—*Example written about* 1555.

" And after that Philosophy had spoken these wordes the said companye of the musys poeticall beynge rebukyd and sad, caste downe their countenaunce to the grounde, and by blussyng confessed their shamefastnes, and went out of the dores. But I (that had my syght dull and blynd wyth wepyng, so that I knew not what woman this was hauyng soo great aucthoritie) was amasyd or astonyed, and lokyng downeward, towarde the ground, I began pryvyle to look what thyng she would saye ferther."—COLVILLE : *Version from Boethius : Johnson's Hist. of E. L.,* p. 29.

30. *Example referred by Dr. Johnson to the year* 1553.

" Pronunciation is an apte orderinge bothe of the voyce, countenaunce, and all the whole bodye, accordynge to the worthines of such woordes and mater as by speeche are declared. The vse hereof is suche for anye one that liketh to haue prayse for tellynge his tale in open assemblie, that hauing a good tongue, and a comelye countenaunce, he shal be thought to passe all other that haue not the like vtteraunce : thoughe they have muche better learning."—DR. WILSON : *Johnson's Hist. E. L.,* p. 45.

31. *Reign of Edward VI,* 1553 to 1547.—*Example written about* 1550.

" Who that will followe the graces manyfolde
Which are in vertue, shall finde ausuncement :
Wherefore ye fooles that in your sinne are bolde,
Ensue ye wisdome, and leaue your lewde intent,
Wisdome is the way of men most excellent :
Therefore haue done, and shortly spede your pace,
To quaynt your self and company with grace."
ALEXANDER BARCLAY : *Johnson's Hist. E. L.,* p. 44.

32. *Reign of Henry VIII,* 1547 to 1509.—*Example dated* 1541.

" Let hym that is angry euen at the fyrste consyder one of these thinges, that like as he is a man, so is also the other, with whom he is angry, and therefore it is as lefull for the other to be angry, as unto hym : and if he so be, than shall that anger be to hym displeasant, and stere hym more to be angrye."—SIR THOMAS ELLIOTT : *Castel of Helthe.*

33. *Example of the earliest English Blank Verse ; written about* 1540. The supposed author died in 1541, aged 38. The piece from which these lines are taken describes the death of *Zoroas,* an Egyptian astronomer, slain in Alexander's first battle with the Persians.

" The Persians waild such sapience to foregoe ;
And very sone the Macedonians wisht
He would have lived ; king Alexander selfe
Demde him a man unmete to dye at all ;
Who wonne like praise for conquest of his yre,
As for stoute men in field that day subdued,
Who princes taught how to discerne a man,
That in his head so rare a jewel beares ;
But over all those same Camenes,* those same
Divine Camenes, whose honour he procurde,
As tender parent doth his daughters weale,
Lamented, and for thankes, all that they can,
Do cherish hym deceast, and sett hym free,
From dark oblivion of devouring death."
Probably written by SIR THOMAS WYAT.

* *Camenes,* the *Muses,* whom Horace called *Camœnæ.* The former is an English plural from the latter, or from the Latin word *camena,* a muse or song. These lines are copied from Dr. Johnson's History of the English Language ; their *orthography* is, in some respects, *too modern* for the age to which they are assigned.

34. *A Letter written from prison, with a coal.* The writer, *Sir Thomas More,* whose works, both in prose and verse, were considered models of pure and elegant style, had been Chancellor of England, and the familiar confidant of Henry VIII, by whose order he was beheaded in 1535.

"Myne own good doughter, our Lorde be thanked, I am in good helthe of bodye, and in good quiet of minde: and of worldly thynges I no more desyer then I haue. I besesche hym make you all mery in the hope of heauen. And such thynges as I somewhat longed to talke with you all, concerning the worlde to come, our Lorde put theim into your myndes, as I truste he doth and better to by hys holy spirite: who blesse you and preserue you all. Written wyth a cole by your tender louing father, who in hys pore prayers forgetteth none of you all, nor your babes, nor your nources, nor your good husbandes, nor your good husbandes shrewde wyues, nor your fathers shrewde wyfe neither, nor our other frendes. And thus fare ye hartely well for lacke of paper. THOMAS MORE, knight."—*Johnson's Hist. E. Lang.,* p. 42.

35. *From More's Description of Richard III.—Probably written about* 1520.

"Richarde the third sonne, of whom we nowe entreate, was in witte and courage egall with either of them, in bodye and prowesse farre vnder them bothe, little of stature, ill fetured of limmes, croke backed, his left shoulder much higher than his right, hard fauoured of visage, and such as is in states called warlye, in other menne otherwise, he was malicious, wrathfull, enuious, and from afore his birth euer frowarde. * * * Hee was close and secrete, a deep dissimuler, lowlye of countreynaunce, arrogant of heart—dispitious and cruell, not for euill will alway, but after for ambicion, and either for the suretie and encrease of his estate. Frende and foo was muche what indifferent, where his aduauntage grew, he spared no mans deathe, whose life withstoode his purpose. He slew with his owne handes king Henry the sixt, being prisoner in the Tower."—SIR THOMAS MORE: *Johnson's History of the English Language,* p. 39.

36. *From his description of Fortune, written about the year* 1500.

"Fortune is stately, solemne, prowde, and hye :
And rychesse geueth, to haue seruyce therefore.
The nedy begger catcheth an half peny :
Some manne a thousande pounde, some lesse some more.
But for all that she kepeth euer in store,
From euery manne some parcell of his wyll,
That he may pray therfore and serue her styll.
 Some manne hath good, but chyldren hath he none.
Some manne hath both, but he can get none health.
Some hath al thre, but vp to honours trone,
Can he not crepe, by no maner of stelth.
To some she sendeth chyldren, ryches, welthe,
Honour, woorshyp, and reuerence all hys lyfe:
But yet she pyncheth hym with a shrewde wife."

SIR THOMAS MORE.

V. ENGLISH OF THE FIFTEENTH CENTURY.

37. *Example for the reign of Henry VII, who was crowned on Bosworth field,* 1485, *and who died in* 1509.

"Wherefor and forasmoche as we haue sent for our derrest wif, and for our derrest moder, to come unto us, and that we wold have your advis and counsail also in soche matiers as we haue to doo for the subduying of the rebelles, we praie you, that, yeving your due attendaunce vppon our said derrest wif and lady moder, ye come with thaym unto us; not failing herof as ye purpose to doo us plaisir. Yeven undre our signett, at our Castell of Kenelworth, the xiij daie of Maye."—HENRY VII : *Letter to the Earl of Ormond: Bucke's Classical Gram.,* p. 147.

38. *Example for the short reign of Richard III,—from* 1485 *to* 1483.

"Right reverend fader in God, right trusty and right wel-beloved, we grete yow wele, and wol and charge you that under oure greate seale, being in your warde, ye do make in all haist our lettres of proclamation severally to be directed unto the shirrefs of everie countie within this oure royaume."—RICHARD III : *Letter to his Chancellor.*

39. *Reign of Edward IV,—from* 1483 *to* 1461.—*Example written in* 1364.

"Forasmoche as we by divers meanes bene credebly enformed and undarstand for certyne, that owr greate adversary Henry, namingo hym selfe kynge of England, by the

malicoous counsoyle and exitacion of Margaret his wife, namynge hir selfe queene of
England, have conspired," &c.—EDWARD IV: *Letter of Privy Seal.*

40. *Examples for the reign of Henry VI.—from* 1461 *back to* 1422.

"When Nembroth [i. e. *Nimrod*] by Might, for his own Glorye, made and incorporate
the first Realme, and subduyd it to hymself by Tyrannye, he would not have it governyd
by any other Rule or Lawe, but by his own Will; by which and for th' accomplishment
thereof he made it. And therfor, though he had thus made a Realme, holy Scripture
denyd to cal hym a Kyng, *Quia Rex dicitur a Regendo*; Whych thyng he did not, but
oppressyd tho People by Myght."—SIR JOHN FORTESCUE.

41. *Example from Lydgate, a poetical Monk, who died in* 1440.

"Our life here short of wit the great dulnes
The heuy soule troubled with trauayle,
And of memorye the glasyng brotelnes,
Drede and vncunning haue made a strong batail
With wormes my spirite to assayle,
And with their subtil creping in most queint
Hath made my spirit in makyng for to feint."
            JOHN LYDGATE: *Fall of Princes*, Book III, Prol.

42 *Example for the reign of Henry V,—from* 1422 *back to* 1413.

"I wolle that the Duc of Orliance be kept stille withyn the Castil of Pontefret, with
owte goyng to Robertis place, or to any other disport, it is better he lak his disport then
we were disceyved. Of all the remanant dothe as ye thenketh."—*Letter of* HENRY V.

43. *Example for the reign of Henry IV,—from* 1413 *back to* 1400.

"Right heigh and myghty Prynce, my goode and gracious Lorde,—I recommaund
me to you as lowly as I kan or may with all my pouer hert, desiryng to hier goode and
gracious tydynges of your worshipful astate and welfare."—LORD GREY: *Letter to the
Prince of Wales: Bucke's Classical Gram.*, p. 145.

        VI. ENGLISH OF THE FOURTEENTH CENTURY.

44. *Reign of Richard II,* 1400 *back to* 1377.—*Example written in* 1391.

"Lytel Lowys my sonne, I perceve well by certaine evidences thyne abylyte to lerne
scyences, touching nombres and proporcions, and also well consydre I thy besye prayer
in especyal to lerne the tretyse of the *astrolabye.* Than for as moche as a philosopher
saithe, he wrapeth hym in his frende, that condiscendeth to the ryghtfull prayers of
his frende: therefore I have given the a sufficient astrolabye for oure orizont, compown-
ed after the latitude of Oxenforde: vpon the whiche by meditacion of this lytell tretise,
I purpose to teche the a certaine nombre of conclusions, pertainynge to this same in-
strament."—GEOFFREY CHAUCER: *Of the Astrolabe.*

45. *Example written about* 1385—*to be compared with that of* 1555, *on* p. 70.

"And thus this companie of muses iblamed casten wrothly the chere dounward to
the yerth, and shewing by rednesse their shame, thei passeden sorowfully the thresholde.
And I of whom the sight ploungeth in teres was darked, so that I ne might not know
what that woman was, of so Imperial aucthoritie, I woxe all abashed and stonied, and
cast my sight doune to the yerth, and began still for to abide what she would doen
afterward."—CHAUCER: *Version from Boethius: Johnson's Hist. of E. L.*, p. 29.

46. *Poetical Example—probably written before* 1380.

"O Socrates, thou stedfast champion;
She ne might nevir be thy turmentour,
Thou nevir dreddist her oppression,
Ne in her chere foundin thou no favour,
Thou knewe wele the disceipt of her colour,
And that her moste worship is for to lie,
I knowe her eke a false dissimulour,
For finally Fortune I doe defie."—CHAUCER.

47. *Reign of Edward III,* 1377 *to* 1327.—*Example written about* 1360.

"And eke full ofte a littell skare
Vpon a banke, er men be ware,
Let in the streme, whiche with gret peine,
If any man it shall restreine.
Where lawe failleth, errour groweth;
He is not wise, who that ne troweth."—SIR JOHN GOWER.

48. Example from Mandeville, the English traveller—written in 1356.

"And this storre that is toward the Northe, that wee clepen the lode sterre, ne appearethe not to hem. For whiche cause, men may wel perceyve, that the lond and the see ben of rownde schapp and forme. For the partie of the firmament schewethe in o contree, that schewethe not in another contree. And men may well preven be experience and sotyle compassement of wytt, that zif a man fond passages be schippes, that wolde go to serchen the world, men mighte go be schippe all aboute the world, and aboven and benethen. The whiche thing I prove thus, aftre that I have seyn. • • • Be the whiche I seye zou certeynly, that men may envirowne alle the erthe of alle the world, as wel undre as aboven, and turnen azen to his contree, that hadde companye and schippynge and conduyt: and alle weyes he scholde fynde men, londes, and yles, als wel as in this contree."—SIR JOHN MANDEVILLE: *Johnson's Hist. of E. L.,* p. 26.

49. Example from the Visions of Pierce Ploughman, 1350.

"In the somer season,
When hot was the Sun,
I shope me into shroubs,
As I a shepe were;

In habit as an harmet,
Vnholy of werkes,
Went wyde in this world
Wonders to heare."

50. Description of a Ship—referred to the reign of Edward II: 1327–1307.

"Such ne saw they never none,
For it was so gay begone, •
Every nayle with gold ygrave,
Of pure gold was his sklave,
Her mast was of ivory,
Of samyte her sayle wytly,

Her robes all of whyte sylk,
As whyte as ever was ony mylke.
The noble ship was without
With clothes of gold spread about
And her loft and her wyndlace
All of gold depaynted was."
ANONYMOUS: *Bucke's Gram.* p. 143.

51. From an Elegy on Edward I, who reigned till 1307 *from* 1272.

"Thah mi tonge were made of stel,
Ant min herte yzote of braa,
The goodness myht y never telle,
That with kyng Edward was:
Kyng, as thou art cleped conquerour,
In uch battaille thou hadest prys;
God bringe thi soule to the honour,
That ever wes ant ever ys.

Now is Edward of Carnavan
Kyng of Engelond al aplyght;
God lete him never be worse man
Then his fader, ne lasse myht,
To holden his pore men to ryht,
Ant understonde good counsail,
Al Engelond for to wysse and dyht;
Of gode knyhtes darh him nout fail."
ANON: *Percy's Reliques,* Vol. ii, p. 10.

VII. ENGLISH OF THE THIRTEENTH CENTURY.

52. Reign of Henry III, 1272 to 1216.—*Example from an old ballad entitled Richard of Almaigne;* which Percy says was "made by one of the adherents of Simon de Montfort, earl of Leicester, soon after the battle of Lewes, which was fought, May 14, 1264."—*Percy's Reliques,* Vol. ii.

"Sitteth alle stille, and herkneth to me;
The kyng of Almaigne, bi mi leaute,
Thritti thousent pound askede he
For te make the pees in the countre,
Ant so he dude more.
Richard, thah thou be ever trichard,
Trichten shalt thou never more."

53. In the following examples, I substitute Roman letters for the Saxon. At this period, we find the characters mixed. The style here is that which Johnson calls "a kind of intermediate diction, neither Saxon nor English." Of these historical rhymes, by *Robert of Gloucester,* the Doctor gives us more than two hundred lines; but he dates them no further than to say, that the author "is placed by the criticks in the thirteenth century."—*Hist. of Eng. Lang.,* p. 24.

"Alfred thys noble man, as in the ger of grace he nom
Eygte hondred and syxty and tuelue the kyndom.
Arst he adde at Rome ybe, and, vor ys grete wysdom,
The pope Leo hym blessede, tho he thuder com,
And the kynges croune of hys lond, that in this lond gut ys:
And he led hym to be kyng, ar he kyng were y wys.

An he was kyng of Engelond, of alle that ther come,
That vorst thus ylad was of the pope of Rome,
An suththe other after hym of the erchebyssopes echon."

"Clerc he was god ynou, and gut, as me telleth me,
He was more than ten ger old, ar he couthe ys abece.
Ac ys gode moder ofte smale gyftes hym tok,
Vor to byleue other ple, and loky on ys boke.
So that by por clergye ys rygt lawes he wonde,
That neuere er nere y mad to gouerny ys lond."
                    ROBERT OF GLOUCESTER : *Johnson's Hist. of E. L.*, p. 25.

54. *Reign of John, 1216 back to 1199.*—*Subject of Christ's Crucifixion.*

"I syke when y singe for sorewe that y se
When y with wypinge bihold upon the tre,
Ant se Jhesu the suete ys hert blod for-lete
            For the love of me;
Ys woundes waxen wete, thei wepen, still and mete,
            Marie reweth me."
                    ANON : *Bucks's Gram.* p. 142.

VIII. ENGLISH, OR ANGLO-SAXON, OF THE TWELFTH CENTURY.

55. *Reign of Richard I, 1199 back to 1189.*—*Owl and Nightingale.*

"Ich was in one sumere dale,
In one snive digele pale,
I herde ich hold grete tale,
An hule and one nightingale.
That plait was stif I stare and strong,
Sum wile softe I lud among.

An other again other sval
I let that wole mod ut al.
I either seide of otheres custe,
That alere worste that hi wuste
I hure and I hure of others songe
Hi hold plaiding futhe stronge."
                    ANON : *Bucks's Gram.* p. 142.

56. *Reign of Henry II, 1189 back to 1154.*—*Example dated* 1180.

"And of alle than folke
The wuneden ther on folde,
Wes thisses landes folke

Leodene hendest itald;
And alswa the wimmen
Wunliche on heowen."
                    GODRIC : *Bucks's Gram.* p. 141.

57. *Example from the Saxon Chronicle, written about* 1160.

"Micel hadde Henri king gadered gold & syluer, and na god ne dide me for his saule thar of. Tha the king Stephne to Engla-land com, tha macod he his gadering æt Oxene-ford, & thar he nam the biscop Roger of Seres-beri, and Alexander biscop of Lincoln, & te Canceler Roger hife neues, & dide ælle in prisun, til hi jafen up here castles. Tha the suikes undergæton that he milde man was & softe & god, & na justise ne dide; tha diden hi alle wunder." See *Johnson's Hist. of the Eng. Language*, p. 22.

58. *Reign of Stephen, 1154 to 1135.*—*Example written about this time.*

"Fur in see bi west Spaygne.
Is a lond ihone Cokaygne.
Ther nis lond under heuenriche.
Of wel of godnis hit iliche.
Thoy paradis be miri and briyt.
Cokaygne is of fairer siyt.

What is ther in paradis.
Bot grasse and flure and greneria.
Thoy ther be ioi and gret dute.
Ther nis met bot ænlic frute.
Ther nis halle bure no bench.
Bot watir manis thurst to quench."
                    ANON : *Johnson's Hist. Eng. Lang.* p. 22.

59. *Reign of Henry I, 1135 to 1100.*—*Part of an Anglo-Saxon Hymn.*

"Heuene & erthe & all that is,
Biloken is on his honde.
He deth al that his wille is,
On sea and ec on londe.

He is orde albuten orde,
And ende albuten ende.
He one is eure on eche stede,
Wende wer thu wende.

He is buuen us and binethen,
Biuoren and ec bihind.
Se man that Godes wille deth,
He mai hine aihwar uinde.

Eche rune he iherth,
And wot eche dede.
He durh sigth eches ithanc,
Wai hwat sel us to rede.

Se man neure nele don god,
Ne neure god lif leden,
Er deth & dom come to his dure,
He mai him sore adreden.

Hunger & thurst hete & chele,
Ecthe and all unhelthe,
Durh deth com on this midelard,
And other uniselthe.

Ne mai non herte hit ithenche,
Ne no tunge telle,
Hu muchele pinum and hu uele,
Bieth inne helle.

Louie God mid ure hierte,
And mid all ure mihte,
And ure emcristene swo us self,
Swo us lereth drihte."

ANON: *Johnson's Hist. Eng. Lang.* p. 21.

IX. ANGLO-SAXON OF THE ELEVENTH CENTURY, COMPARED WITH ENGLISH.

60. *Saxon.*—11th Century.*	*English.*—14th Century.	*English.*—17th Century.
LUCÆ, CAP. I.	LUK, CHAP. I.	LUKE, CHAP. I.
"5. On Herodes dagum Indea cynincges, wæs sum sacerd on naman Zacharias, of Abian tune : and his wif wæs of Aarones dohtrum, and hyre nama wæs Elizabeth.	"5. In the dayes of Eroude kyng of Judee ther was a prest Zacarye by name, of the sort of Abia : and his wyf was of the doughtris of Aaron, and hir name was Elizabeth.	"5. There was in the days of Herod the king of Judea, a certain priest named Zacharias, of the course of Abia : and his wife was of the daughters of Aaron, and her name was Elisabeth.
6. Sothlice hig wæron butu rihtwise beforan Gode, gangende on eallum his bebodum and rihtwisnessum, butan wrohte.	6. And bothe weren juste bifore God, goynge in alle the maundementis and justifyingis of the Lord, withouten playnt.	6. And they were both righteous before God, walking in all the commandments and ordinances of the Lord, blameless.
7. And hig næfdon nan bearn, fortham the Elizabeth wæs unberende ; and hy on hyra dagum butu forth-eodun.	7. And thei hadden no child, for Elizabeth was bareyn; and bothe weren of greet age in her dayes.	7. And they had no child, because that Elisabeth was barren; and they both were now well stricken in years.
8. Sothlice wæs geworden tha Zacharias hys sacerdhades breac on his gewrixles endebyrdnesse beforan Gode,	8. And it befel that whanne Zacarye schould do the office of presthod in the ordir of his course to fore God,	8. And it came to pass, that while he executed the priest's office before God in the order of his course,
9. Æfter gewunan thæs sacerdhades hlotes, he eode that he his offrunge sette, tha he on Godes tempel eode.	9. Aftir the custom of the presthood, he wente forth by lot, and entride into the temple to encensen.	9. According to the custom of the priest's office, his lot was to burn incense when he went into the temple of the Lord.
10. Eall werod thæs folces wæs ute gebiddende on thære offrunge timan.	10. And al the multitude of the puple was without forth and preyede in the our of encensaying.	10. And the whole multitude of the people were praying without at the time of incense.
11. Tha ætywde him Drihtnes engel standende on thæs weofodes swithran healfe.	11. And an aungel of the Lord spperide to him, and stood on the right half of the auter of encense.	11. And there appeared unto him an angel of the Lord, standing on the right side of the altar of incense.
12. Tha weard Zacharias gedrefed that geseonde, and him ege onhreas.	12. And Zacarye seyinge was afrayed, and drede fel upon him.	12. And when Zacharias saw him, he was troubled, and fear fell upon him.
13. Tha cwæth se engel him to, Ne ondræd thu the Zacharias; fortham thin ben is gehyred, and thin wif Elizabeth the sunu centh, and thu nemst hys naman Johannes."—*Saxon Gospels.*	13. And the aungel sayde to him, Zacarye, drede thou not; for thy preier is herd, and Elisabeth thi wif schal bere to thee a sone, and his name schal be clepid Jon." *Wickliffe's Bible*, 1380.	13. But the angel said unto him, Fear not, Zacharias; for thy prayer is heard, and thy wife Elisabeth shall bear thee a son, and thou shalt call his name John." *Common Bible*, 1610.

See Dr. Johnson's History of the English Language, in his Quarto Dictionary.

*The Saxon characters being known nowadays to but very few readers, I have thought proper to substitute for them, in the latter specimens of this chapter, the Roman; and, as the old use of colons and periods for the smallest pauses, is liable to mislead a common observer, the punctuation too has here been modernised.

X. ANGLO-SAXON IN THE TIME OF KING ALFRED.

61. Alfred the Great, was the youngest son of Ethelwolf, king of the West Saxons, and succeeded to the crown on the death of his brother Ethelred, in the year 871, being then twenty-two years old. He had scarcely time to attend the funeral of his brother, before he was called to the field to defend his country against the Danes. After a reign of more than twenty-eight years, rendered singularly glorious by great achievements under difficult circumstances, he died universally lamented, on the 28th of October, A.D. 900. By this prince the university of Oxford was founded, and provided with able teachers from the continent. His own great proficiency in learning, and his earnest efforts for its promotion, form a striking contrast with the ignorance which prevailed before. "In the ninth century, throughout the whole kingdom of the West Saxons, no man could be found who was scholar enough to instruct the young king Alfred, then a child, even in the first elements of reading: so that he was in his twelfth year before he could name the letters of the alphabet. When that renowned prince ascended the throne, he made it his study to draw his people out of the sloth and stupidity in which they lay; and became, as much by his own example as by the encouragement he gave to learned men, the great restorer of arts in his dominions."—*Life of Bacon.*

62. The language of eulogy must often be taken with some abatement: it does not usually present things in their due proportions. How far the foregoing quotation is true, I will not pretend to say; but what is called "the revival of learning," must not be supposed to have begun at so early a period as that of Alfred. The following is a brief specimen of the language in which that great man wrote; but, printed in Saxon characters, it would appear still less like English.

"On thære tide the Gotan of Siththiu mægthe with Romana rice gewin upahofon. and mith heora cyningum. Rædgota and Eallerica wæron hatne. Romane burig abræcon. and eall Italia rice that is betwux tham muntum and Sicilia tham calonde in anwald gerehton. and tha ægter tham foresprecenan cyningum Theodric feng to tham ilcan rice se Theodric wæs Amulinga. he wæs Cristen. theah he on tham Arrianiscan gedwolan durhwunode. He gehet Romanum his freondscype. swa that hi mostan heora ealdrichta wyrthe beon."—KING ALFRED: *Johnson's Hist. of E. L.*, 4to *Dict.* p. 17.

CHAPTER VIII.

OF THE GRAMMATICAL STUDY OF THE ENGLISH LANGUAGE.

"Grammatica quid est? ars recté scribendi rectéque loquendi; poetarum enarrationem continens; omnium scientiarum fons uberrimus. * * * Nostra ætas parum perita veterum, nimis brevi gyro grammaticum sepsit: at apud antiquos olim tantum auctoritas hic ordo habuit, ut censores essent et judices scriptorum omnium soli grammatici: quos ob id etiam Criticos vocabant."—DESPAUTER. *Præf. ad Synt.* fol. 1.

1. Such is the peculiar power of language, that there is scarcely any subject so trifling, that it may not thereby be plausibly magnified into something great; nor are there many things which cannot be ingeniously disparaged till they shall seem contemptible. Cicero goes further: "Nihil est tam incredibile quod non dicendo fiat probabile;"—"There is nothing so incredible that it may not by the power of language be made probable." The study of grammar has been often overrated, and still oftener injuriously decried. I shall neither join with those who would lessen in the public esteem that general system of doctrines, which from time immemorial has been taught as grammar; nor attempt, either by magnifying its prac-

tical results, or by decking it out with my own imaginings, to invest it with any artificial or extraneous importance.

2. I shall not follow the footsteps of *Neef*, who avers that, "Grammar and incongruity are identical things," and who, under pretence of reaching the same end by better means, scornfully rejects as nonsense every thing that others have taught under that name ; because I am convinced, that, of all methods of teaching, none goes farther than his, to prove the reproachful assertion true. Nor shall I imitate the declamation of *Cardell* ; who, at the commencement of his essay, recommends the general study of language on earth, from the consideration that, "The faculty of speech is the medium of social bliss for superior intelligences in an eternal world;"* and who, when he has exhausted censure in condemning the practical instructions of others, thus lavishes praise, in both his grammars, upon that formless, void, and incomprehensible theory of his own : "This application of words," says he, "in their endless use, by one plain rule, to all things which nouns can name, instead of being the fit subject of blind cavil, *is the most sublime theme presented to the intellect on earth. It is the practical intercourse of the soul, at once with its God, and with all parts of his works!"—Cardell's Gram.* 12mo, p. 87 ; *Gram.* 18mo, p. 49.

3 Here, indeed, a wide prospect opens before us ; but he who traces science, and teaches what is practically useful, must check imagination, and be content with sober truth.

> "For apt the mind or fancy is to rove
> Uncheck'd, and of her roving is no end."—MILTON.

Restricted within its proper limits, and viewed in its true light, the practical science of grammar has an intrinsic dignity and merit sufficient to throw back upon any man who dares openly assail it, the lasting stigma of folly and self-conceit. It is true, the judgements of men are fallible, and many opinions are liable to be reversed by better knowledge : but what has been long established by the unanimous concurrence of the learned, it can hardly be the part of a wise instructor now to dispute. The literary reformer who, with the last named gentleman, imagines "that the persons to whom the civilized world have looked up for instruction in language, were all wrong alike in the main points,"† intends no middle course of reformation, and must needs be a man either of great merit, or of little modesty.

4. The English language may now be regarded as the common inheritance of about fifty millions of people ; who are at least as highly distinguished for virtue, intelligence, and enterprise, as any other equal portion of the earth's population. All these are more or less interested in the purity, permanency, and right use of that language ; inasmuch as it is to be, not only the medium of mental intercourse with others for them and their children, but the vehicle of all they value, in the reversion of ancestral honour, or in the transmission of their own. It is even impertinent, to tell a man of any respectability, that the study of this his native language is an object of great importance and interest : if he does not, from these most obvious considerations, feel it to be so, the suggestion will be less likely to convince him, than to give offence, as conveying an implicit censure.

5. Every person who has any ambition to appear respectable among people of education, whether in conversation, in correspondence, in public speaking, or in print, must be aware of the absolute necessity of a competent knowledge of the language in which he attempts to express his thoughts. Many a ludicrous anecdote is told, of persons venturing to use words of which they did not know the

---

* Essay on language, by William S. Cardell, New York, 1825, p. 2. This writer was a great admirer of Horne Tooke, from whom he borrowed many of his notions of grammar, but not this extravagance. Speaking of the words *right* and *just*, the latter says, "They are applicable only to *man* ; *to whom alone* language belongs, and of whose sensations only words are the representatives."—*Diversions of Purley*, Vol. ii, p. 9.

† CARDELL: *Both Grammars*, p. 4.

proper application ; many a ridiculous blunder has been published to the lasting disgrace of the writer ; and so intimately does every man's reputation for sense depend upon his skill in the use of language, that it is scarcely possible to acquire the one without the other.   Who can tell how much of his own good or ill success, how much of the favour or disregard with which he himself has been treated, may have depended upon that skill or deficiency in grammar, of which, as often as he has either spoken or written, he must have afforded a certain and constant evidence ?*

6. I have before said, that to excel in grammar, is but to know better than others wherein grammatical excellence consists ; and, as this excellence, whether in the thing itself, or in him that attains to it, is merely comparative, there seems to be no fixed point of perfection beyond which such learning may not be carried.   In speaking or writing to different persons, and on different subjects, it is necessary to vary one's style with great nicety of address ; and in nothing does true genius more conspicuously appear, than in the facility with which it adopts the most appropriate expressions, leaving the critic no fault to expose, no word to amend. Such facility of course supposes an intimate knowledge of all words in common use, and also of the principles on which they are to be combined.

7. With a language which we are daily in the practice of hearing, speaking, reading, and writing, we may certainly acquire no inconsiderable acquaintance, without the formal study of its rules.   All the true principles of grammar were presumed to be known to the learned, before they were written for the aid of learners ; nor have they acquired any independent authority, by being recorded in a book, and denominated grammar.   The teaching of them, however, has tended in no small degree to settle and establish the construction of the language, to improve the style of our English writers, and to enable us to ascertain with more clearness the true standard of grammatical purity.   He who learns only by rote, may speak the words or phrases which he has thus acquired ; and he who has the genius to discern intuitively what is regular and proper, may have further aid from the analogies which he thus discovers ; but he who would add to such acquisitions the satisfaction of knowing what is right, must make the principles of language his study.

8. To produce an able and elegant writer, may require something more than a knowledge of grammar rules ; yet it is argument enough in favour of those rules, that without a knowledge of them no elegant and able writer is produced.   Who that considers the infinite number of phrases which words in their various combinations may form, and the utter impossibility that they should ever be recognised individually for the purposes of instruction and criticism, but must see the absolute necessity of dividing words into classes, and of showing, by general rules of formation and construction, the laws to which custom commonly subjects them, or from which she allows them in particular instances to deviate ?   Grammar, or the art of writing and speaking, must continue to be learned by some persons ; because it is of indispensable use to society.   And the only question is, whether children and youth shall acquire it by a regular process of study and method of instruction, or be left to glean it solely from their own occasional observation of the manner in which other people speak and write.

9. The practical solution of this question belongs chiefly to parents and guardians.   The opinions of teachers, to whose discretion the decision will sometimes be left, must have a certain degree of influence upon the public mind ; and the popular notions of the age, in respect to the relative value of different studies, will doubtless bias many to the adoption or the rejection of this.   A consideration of the point seems to be appropriate here, and I cannot forbear to commend the study to the favour of my readers ; leaving every one, of course, to choose how much he will be influenced by my advice, example, or arguments.   If past experience and

* "*Quoties dicimus, toties de nobis judicatur.*"—Cicero.   "As often as we speak, so often are we judged."

the history of education be taken for guides, the study of English grammar will not be neglected; and the method of its inculcation will become an object of particular inquiry and solicitude. The English language ought to be learned at school or in colleges, as other languages usually are; by the study of its grammar, accompanied with regular exercises of parsing, correcting, pointing, and scanning; and by the perusal of some of its most accurate writers, accompanied with stated exercises in composition and elocution. In books of criticism, our language is already more abundant than any other. Some of the best of these the student should peruse, as soon as he can understand and relish them. Such a course, pursued with regularity and diligence, will be found the most direct way of acquiring an English style at once pure, correct, and elegant.

10. If any intelligent man will represent English grammar otherwise than as one of the most useful branches of study, he may well be suspected of having formed his conceptions of the science, not from what it really is in itself, but from some of those miserable treatises which only caricature the subject, and of which it is rather an advantage to be ignorant. But who is so destitute of good sense as to deny, that a graceful and easy conversation in the private circle, a fluent and agreeable delivery in public speaking, a ready and natural utterance in reading, a pure and elegant style in composition, are accomplishments of a very high order? And yet of all these, the proper study of English grammar is the true foundation. This would never be denied or doubted, if young people did not find, under some other name, better models and more efficient instruction, than what was practised on them for grammar in the school-room. No disciple of an able grammarian can ever speak ill of grammar, unless he belong to that class of knaves who vilify what they despair to reach.

11. By taking proper advantage of the ductility of childhood, intelligent parents and judicious teachers may exercise over the studies, opinions, and habits of youth a strong and salutary control; and it will seldom be found in experience, that those who have been early taught to consider grammatical learning as worthy and manly, will change their opinion in after life. But the study of grammar is not so enticing that it may be disparaged in the hearing of the young, without injury. What would be the natural effect of the following sentence, which I quote from a late well-written religious homily? " The pedagogue and his dunce may exercise their wits correctly enough, in the way of grammatical analysis, on some splendid argument, or burst of eloquence, or thrilling descant, or poetic rapture, to the strain and soul of which not a fibre in their nature would yield a vibration."—*New-York Observer*, Vol. ix, p. 78.

12. Would not the bright boy who heard this from the lips of his reverend minister, be apt the next day to grow weary of the parsing lesson required by his schoolmaster? And yet what truth is there in the passage? One can no more judge of the fitness of language, without regard to the meaning conveyed by it, than of the fitness of a suit of clothes, without knowing for whom they were intended. The grand clew to the proper application of all syntactical rules, is *the sense;* and as any composition is faulty which does not rightly deliver the author's meaning, so every solution of a word or sentence is necessarily erroneous, in which that meaning is not carefully noticed and literally preserved. To parse rightly and fully, is nothing else than to understand rightly and explain fully; and whatsoever is well expressed, it is a shame either to misunderstand or to misinterpret.

13. This study, when properly conducted and liberally pursued, has an obvious tendency to dignify the whole character. How can he be a man of refined literary taste, who cannot speak and write his native language grammatically? And who will deny that every degree of improvement in literary taste tends to brighten and embellish the whole intellectual nature? The several powers of the mind are not so many distinct and separable agents, which are usually brought into exercise one

by one; and even if they were, there might be found, in a judicious prosecution of this study, a healthful employment for them all. The *imagination*, indeed, has nothing to do with the elements of grammar; but in the exercise of composition, young fancy may spread her wings as soon as they are fledged; and for this exercise the previous course of discipline will have furnished both language, taste, and sentiment.

14. The regular grammatical study of our language is a thing of recent origin. Fifty or sixty years ago, such an exercise was scarcely attempted in any of the schools, either in this country or in England.* Of this fact we have abundant evidence both from books, and from the testimony of our venerable fathers yet living. How often have these presented this as an apology for their own deficiencies, and endeavoured to excite us to greater diligence, by contrasting our opportunities with theirs! Is there not truth, is there not power, in the appeal? And are we not bound to avail ourselves of the privileges which they have provided, to build upon the foundations which their wisdom has laid, and to carry forward the work of improvement? Institutions can do nothing for us, unless the love of learning preside over and prevail in them. The discipline of our schools can never approach perfection, till those who conduct, and those who frequent them, are strongly actuated by that disposition of mind, which generously aspires to all attainable excellence.

15. To rouse this laudable spirit in the minds of our youth, and to satisfy its demands whenever it appears, ought to be the leading objects with those to whom is committed the important business of instruction. A dull teacher, wasting time in a school-room with a parcel of stupid or indolent boys, knows nothing of the satisfaction either of doing his own duty, or of exciting others to the performance of theirs. He settles down in a regular routine of humdrum exercises, dreading as an inconvenience even such change as proficiency in his pupils must bring on; and is well content to do little good for little money, in a profession which he honours with his services merely to escape starvation. He has, however, one merit: he pleases his patrons, and is perhaps the only man that can; for they must needs be of that class to whom moral restraint is tyranny, disobedience to teachers, as often right as wrong; and who, dreading the expense, even of a school-book, always judge those things to be cheapest, which cost the least and last the longest. What such a man, or such a neighbourhood, may think of English grammar, I shall not stop to ask.

16. To the following opinion from a writer of great merit, I am inclined to afford room here, because it deserves refutation, and, I am persuaded, is not so well founded as the generality of the doctrines with which it is presented to the public. "Since human knowledge is so much more extensive than the opportunity of individuals for acquiring it, it becomes of the greatest importance so to economise the opportunity as to make it subservient to the acquisition of as large and as valuable a portion as we can. It is not enough to show that a given branch of education is useful: you must show that it is the most useful that can be selected. Remembering this, I think it would be expedient to dispense with the formal study of English grammar,—a proposition which I doubt not many a teacher will hear with wonder and disapprobation. We learn the grammar in order that we may learn English; and we learn English whether we study grammars or not. Especially we *shall* acquire a competent knowledge of our own language, if other departments of our education *were* improved."

17. "A boy learns more English grammar by joining in an hour's conversation with educated people, than in poring for an hour over Murray or Horne Tooke.

---

* " Nor had he far to seek for the source of our impropriety in the use of words, when he should reflect that the study of our own language, has never been made a part of the education of our youth. Consequently, the use of words is got wholly by chance, according to the company that we keep, or the books that we read."—SHERIDAN'S ELOCUTION, *Introd.* p. viii, dated "July 10, 1762," 2d Amer. Ed.

If he is accustomed to such society and to the perusal of well-written books, he will learn English grammar, though he never sees a word about syntax ; and if he is not accustomed to such society and such reading, the ' grammar books ' at a a boarding-school will not teach it.   Men learn their own language by habit, and not by rules : and this is just what we might expect ; for the grammar of a language is itself formed from the prevalent habits of speech and writing.   A compiler of grammar first observes these habits, and then makes his rules : but if a person is himself familiar with the habits, why study the rules ?   I say nothing of grammar as a general science ; because, although the philosophy of language be a valuable branch of human knowledge, it were idle to expect that school-boys should understand it.   The objection is, to the system of attempting to teach children formally that which they will learn practically without teaching."—JONATHAN DYMOND : *Essays on Morality*, p. 195.

18. This opinion, proceeding from a man who has written upon human affairs with so much ability and practical good sense, is perhaps entitled to as much respect as any that has ever been urged against the study in question.   And so far as the objection bears upon those defective methods of instruction which experience has shown to be inefficient, or of little use, I am in no wise concerned to remove it. The reader of this treatise will find their faults not only admitted, but to a great extent purposely exposed ; while an attempt is here made, as well as in my earlier grammars, to introduce a method which it is hoped will better reach the end proposed. But it may easily be perceived that this author's proposition to dispense with the formal study of English grammar is founded upon an untenable assumption.   Whatever may be the advantages of those purer habits of speech, which the young naturally acquire from conversation with educated people, it is not true, that, without instruction directed to this end, they will of themselves become so well educated as to speak and write grammatically.   Their language may indeed be comparatively accurate and genteel, because it is learned of those who have paid some attention to the study ; but, as they cannot always be preserved from hearing vulgar and improper phraseology, or from seeing it in books, they cannot otherwise be guarded from improprieties of diction, than by a knowledge of the rules of grammar.   One might easily back this position by the citation of some scores of faulty sentences from the pen of this very able writer himself.

19. I imagine there can be no mistake in the opinion, that in exact proportion as the rules of grammar are unknown or neglected in any country, will corruptions and improprieties of language be there multiplied.   The "general science " of grammar, or "the philosophy of language," the author seems to exempt, and in some sort to commend ; and at the same time his proposition of exclusion is applied not merely to the school-grammars, but *a fortiori* to this science, under the notion that it is unintelligible to school-boys.   But why should any principle of grammar be the less intelligible on account of the extent of its application ?   Will a boy pretend that he cannot understand a rule of English grammar, because he is told that it holds good in all languages ?   Ancient etymologies, and other facts in literary history, must be taken by the young upon the credit of him who states them ; but the doctrines of general grammar are to the learner the easiest and the most important principles of the science.   And I know of nothing in the true philosophy of language, which, by proper definitions and examples, may not be made as intelligible to a boy, as are the principles of most other sciences.   The difficulty of instructing youth in any thing that pertains to language, lies not so much in the fact that its philosophy is above their comprehension, as in our own ignorance of certain parts of so vast an inquiry ;—in the great multiplicity of verbal signs ; the frequent contrariety of practice ; the inadequacy of memory ; the inveteracy of ill habits ; and the little interest that is felt when we speak merely of words.

20. The grammatical study of our language was early and strongly recommended

6

by Locke,[*] and other writers on education, whose character gave additional weight
to an opinion which they enforced by the clearest arguments.   But either for
want of a good grammar, or for lack of teachers skilled in the subject and sensible
of its importance, the general neglect so long complained of as a grievous imperfection in our methods of education, has been but recently and partially obviated.
" The attainment of a correct and elegant style," says Dr. Blair, " is an object
which demands application and labour.   If any imagine they can catch it merely
by the ear, or acquire it by the slight perusal of some of our good authors, they
will find themselves much disappointed.   The many errors, even in point of
grammar, the many offences against purity of language, which are committed by
writers who are far from being contemptible, demonstrate, that a *careful study* of
the language is previously requisite, in all who aim at writing it properly."—
Rhetoric, Lect ix, p. 91.

21. " To think justly, to write well, to speak agreeably, are the three great ends
of academic instruction.   The Universities will excuse me, if I observe, that both
are, in one respect or other, defective in these three capital points of education.
While in Cambridge the general application is turned altogether on speculative
knowledge, with little regard to polite letters, taste, or style ; in Oxford the whole
attention is directed towards classical correctness, without any sound foundation laid
in severe reasoning and philosophy.   In Cambridge and in Oxford, the art of
speaking agreeably is so far from being taught, that it is hardly talked or thought
of.   *These defects* naturally produce dry unaffecting compositions in the one ;
superficial taste and puerile elegance in the other ; ungracious or affected speech
in both."—Dr. Brown, 1757 : *Estimate*, Vol. ii, p. 44.

22. "A grammatical study of our own language makes no part of the ordinary
method of instruction, which we pass through in our childhood ; and it is very
seldom we apply ourselves to it afterward.   Yet the want of it will not be effectually supplied by any other advantages whatsoever.   Much practice in the polite
world, and a general acquaintance with the best authors, are good helps ; but alone
[they] will hardly be sufficient : We have writers, who have enjoyed these advantages in their full extent, and yet cannot be recommended as models of an accurate
style.   Much less then will, what is commonly called learning, serve the purpose ;
that is, a critical knowledge of ancient languages, and much reading of ancient
authors : The greatest critic and most able grammarian of the last age, when he
came to apply his learning and criticism to an English author, was frequently at a
loss in matters of ordinary use and common construction in his own vernacular
idiom."—Dr. Lowth, 1763 : *Pref. to Gram.* p. vi.

23. " To the pupils of our public schools the acquisition of their own language,
whenever it is undertaken, is an easy task.   For he who is acquainted with
several grammars already, finds no difficulty in adding one more to the number.
And this, no doubt, is one of the reasons why English engages so small a proportion of their time and attention.   It is not frequently read, and is still less
frequently written.   Its supposed facility, however, or some other cause, seems to
have drawn upon it such a degree of neglect as certainly cannot be praised.   The
students in those schools are often distinguished by their compositions in the
learned languages, before they can speak or write their own with correctness,
elegance, or fluency.   A classical scholar too often has his English style to form,

[*] " To Write and Speak correctly, gives a Grace, and gains a favourable Attention to what one has to say :
And since 'tis *English*, that an English Gentleman will have constant use of, that is the Language he should
chiefly Cultivate, and wherein most care should be taken to polish and perfect his Stile.   To speak or write
better *Latin* than *English*, may make a Man be talk'd of, but he would find it more to his purpose to Express
himself well in his own Tongue, that he uses every moment, than to have the vain Commendation of others
for a very insignificant quality.   This I find universally neglected, and no care taken any where to improve
Young Men in their own Language, that they may thoroughly understand and be Masters of it.   If any one
among us have a facility or purity more than ordinary in his Mother Tongue, it is owing to Chance, or his
Genius, or any thing, rather than to his Education or any care of his Teacher.   To Mind what *English* his
Pupil speaks or writes is below the Dignity of one bred up amongst *Greek* and *Latin*, though he have but
little of them himself.   These are the learned Languages fit only for learned Men to meddle with and teach :
English is the Language of the illiterate Vulgar."—*Locke, on Education*, p. 389; *Fourth Ed., London*, 1699.

when he should communicate his acquisitions to the world. In some instances it is never formed with success; and the defects of his expression either deter him from appearing before the public at all, or at least counteract in a great degree the influence of his work, and bring ridicule upon the author. Surely these evils might easily be prevented or diminished."—DR. BARROW: *Essays on Education*, London, 1804 ; Philad., 1825, p. 87.

24. " It is also said that those who know Latin and Greek generally express themselves with more clearness than those who do not receive a liberal education. It is indeed natural that those who cultivate their mental powers, write with more clearness than the uncultivated individual. The mental cultivation, however, may take place in the mother tongue as well as in Latin or Greek. Yet the spirit of the ancient languages, further is declared to be superior to that of the modern. I allow this to be the case ; but I do not find that the English style is improved by learning Greek. It is known that literal translations are miserably bad, and yet young scholars are taught to translate, word for word, faithful to their dictionaries. Hence those who do not make a peculiar study of their own language, will not improve in it by learning, in this manner, Greek and Latin. Is it not a pity to hear, what I have been told by the managers of one of the first institutions of Ireland, that it was easier to find ten teachers for Latin and Greek, than one for the English language, though they proposed double the salary to the latter ? Who can assure us that the Greek orators acquired their superiority by their acquaintance with foreign languages ; or, is it not obvious, on the other hand, that they learned ideas and expressed them in their mother tongue ? "—DR. SPURZHEIM : *On Education*, 1832, p. 107.

25. " Dictionaries were compiled, which comprised all the words, together with their several definitions, or the sense each one expresses and conveys to the mind. These words were analyzed and classed according to their essence, attributes, and functions. Grammar was made a rudiment leading to the principles of all thoughts, and teaching by simple examples, the general classification of words and their subdivisions in expressing the various conceptions of the mind. Grammar is then the key to the perfect understanding of languages ; without which we are left to wander all our lives in an intricate labyrinth, without being able to trace back again any part of our way."—*Chazotte's Essay on the Teaching of Languages*, p. 45. Again : " Had it not been for his dictionary and his grammar, which taught him the essence of all languages, and the natural subdivision of their component parts, he might have spent a life as long as Methuselah's, in learning words, without being able to attain to a degree of perfection in any of the languages."— *Ib.* p. 50. " Indeed, it is not easy to say, to what degree, and in how many different ways, both memory and judgement may be improved by an intimate acquaintance with grammar ; which is therefore, with good reason, made the first and fundamental part of literary education. The greatest orators, the most elegant scholars, and the most accomplished men of business, that have appeared in the world, of whom I need only mention Cæsar and Cicero, were not only studious of grammar, but most learned grammarians."—DR. BEATTIE : *Moral Science*, Vol. i, p. 107.

26. Here, as in many other parts of my work, I have chosen to be liberal of quotations ; not to show my reading, or to save the labour of composition, but to give the reader the satisfaction of some other authority than my own. In commending the study of English grammar, I do not mean to discountenance that degree of attention which in this country is paid to other languages ; but merely to use my feeble influence to carry forward a work of improvement, which, in my opinion, has been wisely begun, but not sufficiently sustained. In consequence of this improvement, the study of grammar, which was once prosecuted chiefly through the medium of the dead languages, and was regarded as the proper business of those only who were to be instructed in Latin and Greek, is now thought to be an appropriate exercise for children in elementary schools. And the

sentiment is now generally admitted, that even those who are afterwards to learn other languages, may best acquire a knowledge of the common principles of speech from the grammar of their vernacular tongue. This opinion appears to be confirmed by that experience which is at once the most satisfactory proof of what is feasible, and the only proper test of what is useful.

27. It must, however, be confessed, that an acquaintance with ancient and foreign literature is absolutely necessary for him who would become a thorough philologist or an accomplished scholar; and that the Latin language, the source of several of the modern tongues of Europe, being remarkably regular in its inflections and systematic in its construction, is in itself the most complete exemplar of the structure of speech, and the best foundation for the study of grammar in general. But, as the general principles of grammar are common to all languages, and as the only successful method of learning them, is, to commit to memory the definitions and rules which embrace them, it is reasonable to suppose that the language most intelligible to the learner, is the most suitable for the commencement of his grammatical studies. A competent knowledge of English grammar is also in itself a valuable attainment, which is within the easy reach of many young persons whose situation in life debars them from the pursuit of general literature.

28. The attention which has lately been given to the culture of the English language, by some who, in the character of critics or lexicographers, have laboured purposely to improve it, and by many others who, in various branches of knowledge, have tastefully adorned it with the works of their genius, has in a great measure redeemed it from that contempt in which it was formerly held in the halls of learning. But, as I have before suggested, it does not yet appear to be sufficiently attended to in the course of what is called a *liberal education*. Compared with other languages, the English exhibits both excellences and defects; but its flexibility, or power of accommodation to the tastes of different writers, is great; and when it is used with that mastership which belongs to learning and genius, it must be acknowledged there are few, if any, to which it ought on the whole to be considered inferior. But above all, it is *our own;* and, whatever we may know or think of other tongues, it can never be either patriotic or wise, for the learned men of the United States or of England to pride themselves chiefly upon them.

29. Our language is worthy to be assiduously studied by all who reside where it is spoken, and who have the means and the opportunity to become critically acquainted with it. To every such student it is vastly more important to be able to speak and write well in English, than to be distinguished for proficiency in the learned languages and yet ignorant of his own. It is certain that many from whom better things might be expected, are found miserably deficient in this respect. And their neglect of so desirable an accomplishment is the more remarkable and the more censurable on account of the facility with which those who are acquainted with the ancient languages may attain to excellence in their English style. "Whatever the advantages or defects of the English language be, as it is our own language, it deserves a high degree of our study and attention. * * * Whatever knowledge may be acquired by the study of other languages, it can never be communicated with advantage, unless by such as can write and speak their own language well."— DR. BLAIR: *Rhetoric*, Lect. ix, p. 91.

30. I am not of opinion that it is expedient to press this study to much extent, if at all, on those whom poverty or incapacity may have destined to situations in which they will never hear or think of it afterwards. The course of nature cannot be controlled; and fortune does not permit us to prescribe the same course of discipline for all. To speak the language which they have learned without study, and to read and write for the most common purposes of life, may be education enough for those who can be raised no higher. But it must be the desire of

every benevolent and intelligent man, to see the advantages of literary, as well as of moral culture, extended as far as possible among the people. And it is manifest, that in proportion as the precepts of the divine Redeemer are obeyed by the nations that profess his name, will all distinctions arising merely from the inequality of fortune be lessened or done away, and better opportunities be offered for the children of indigence to adorn themselves with the treasures of knowledge.

31. We may not be able to effect all that is desirable; but, favoured as our country is, with great facilities for carrying forward the work of improvement, in every thing which can contribute to national glory and prosperity, I would, in conclusion of this topic, submit—that a critical knowledge of our common language is a subject worthy of the particular attention of all who have the genius and the opportunity to attain it—that on the purity and propriety with which American authors write this language, the reputation of our national literature greatly depends—that in the preservation of it from all changes which ignorance may admit or affectation invent, we ought to unite as having one common interest —that a fixed and settled orthography is of great importance, as a means of preserving the etymology, history, and indentity of words—that a grammar freed from errors and defects, and embracing a complete code of definitions and illustrations, rules and exercises, is of primary importance to every student and a great aid to teachers—that as the vices of speech as well as of manners are contagious, it becomes those who have the care of youth, to be masters of the language in its purity and elegance, and to avoid as much as possible every thing that is reprehensible either in thought or expression.

CHAPTER IX.

OF THE BEST METHOD OF TEACHING GRAMMAR.

"Quomodo differunt grammaticus et grammatista? Grammaticus est qui diligenter, acute, scienterque possit dicere aut scribere, et poetas enarrare: idem literatus dicitur. Grammatista est qui barbaris literis obstrepit, et abusus pro usu est; Græcis Latinam dat etymologiam, et totus in nugis est: Latine dicitur literator."—DESPAUTER. Syn. fol. 1.

---

1. It is hardly to be supposed that any person can have a very clear conviction of the best method of doing a thing, who shall not first have acquired a pretty correct and adequate notion of the thing to be done. Arts must be taught by artists; sciences, by learned men; and, if Grammar is the science of words, the art of writing and speaking well, the best speakers and writers will be the best teachers of it, if they choose to direct their attention to so humble an employment. For, without disparagement of the many worthy men whom choice or necessity has made schoolmasters, it may be admitted that the low estimation in which schoolkeeping is commonly held, does mostly exclude from it the first order of talents, and the highest acquirements of scholarship. It is one strong proof of this, that we have heretofore been content to receive our digests of English grammar, either from men who had had no practical experience in the labours of a school-room, or from miserable modifiers and abridgers, destitute alike of learning and of industry, of judgement and of skill.

2. But, to have a correct and adequate notion of English grammar, and of the best method of learning or teaching it, is no light attainment. The critical knowledge of this subject lies in no narrow circle of observation; nor are there any precise limits to possible improvement. The simple definition in which the

general idea of the art is embraced, "Grammar is the art of writing and speaking correctly," however useful in order to fix the learner's conception, can scarcely give him a better knowledge of the thing itself, than he would have of the art of painting, when he had learned from Dr. Webster, that it is "the art of representing to the eye, by means of figures and colors, any object of sight, and sometimes emotions of the mind." The first would no more enable him to write a sonnet, than the second, to take his master's likeness. The force of this remark extends to all the technical divisions, definitions, rules, and arrangements of grammar; the learner may commit them all to memory, and know but very little about the art.

3. This fact, too frequently illustrated in practice, has been made the basis of the strongest argument ever raised against the study of grammar; and has been particularly urged against the ordinary technical method of teaching it, as if the whole of that laborious process were useless. It has led some men, even of the highest talents, to doubt the expediency of that method, under any circumstances, and either to discountenance the whole matter, or to invent other schemes by which they hoped to be more successful. The utter futility of the old accidence has been inferred from it, and urged, even in some well-written books, with all the plausibility of a fair and legitimate deduction. The hardships of children, compelled to learn what they did not understand, have been bewailed in prefaces and reviews; incredible things boasted by literary jugglers, have been believed by men of sense; and the sympathies of nature, with accumulated prejudices, have been excited against that method of teaching grammar, which after all will be found in experience to be at once the easiest, the shortest, and the best. I mean, essentially, the ancient positive method, which aims directly at the inculcation of principles.

4. It has been already admitted, that definitions and rules committed to memory and not reduced to practice, will never enable any one to speak and write correctly. But it does not follow, that to study grammar by learning its principles, or to teach it technically by formal lessons, is of no real utility. Surely not. For the same admission must be made with respect to the definitions and rules of every practical science in the world; and the technology of grammar is even more essential to a true knowledge of the subject, than that of almost any other art. "To proceed upon principles at first," says Dr. Barrow, "is the most compendious method of attaining every branch of knowledge; and the truths impressed upon the mind in the years of childhood, are ever afterwards the most firmly remembered, and the most readily applied."—*Essays*, p. 84. Reading, as I have said, is a part of grammar; and it is a part which must of course precede what is commonly called in the schools the study of grammar. Any person who can read, can learn from a book such simple facts as are within his comprehension; and we have it on the authority of Dr. Adam, that, "The principles of grammar are the first abstract truths which a young mind can comprehend."—*Pref. to Lat. Gram.* p. 4.

5. It is manifest, that, with respect to this branch of knowledge, the duties of the teacher will vary considerably, according to the age and attainments of his pupils, or according to each student's ability or inclination to profit by his printed guide. The business lies partly between the master and his scholar, and partly between the boy and his book. Among these it may be partitioned variously, and of course unwisely; for no general rule can precisely determine for all occasions what may be expected from each. The deficiencies of any one of the three must either be supplied by the extraordinary readiness of an other, or the attainment of the purpose be proportionably imperfect. What one fails to do, must either be done by an other, or left undone. After much observation, it seems to me, that the most proper mode of treating this science in schools, is, to throw the labour of its acquisition almost entirely upon the students; to require from them very accurate rehearsals as the only condition on which they shall be listened to; and to refer them to their books for the information which they need, and in general for the

solution of all their doubts. But then the teacher must see that he does not set them to grope their way through a wilderness of absurdities. He must know that they have a book, which not only contains the requisite information, but arranges it so that every item of it may be readily found. That knowledge may reasonably be required at their recitations, which culpable negligence alone could have prevented them from obtaining.

6. Most grammars, and especially those which are designed for the senior class of students, to whom a well-written book is a sufficient instructor, contain a large proportion of matter which is merely to be read by the learner. This is commonly distinguished in type from those more important doctrines which constitute the frame of the edifice. It is expected that the latter will receive a greater degree of attention. The only successful method of teaching grammar, is, to cause the principal definitions and rules to be committed thoroughly to memory, that they may ever afterwards be readily applied. Oral instruction may smoothe the way, and facilitate the labour of the learner; but the notion of communicating a competent knowledge of grammar without imposing this task, is disproved by universal experience. Nor will it avail any thing for the student to rehearse definitions and rules of which he makes no practical application. In etymology and syntax, he should be alternately exercised in learning small portions of his book, and then applying them in parsing, till the whole is rendered familiar. To a good reader, the achievement will be neither great nor difficult; and the exercise is well calculated to improve the memory and strengthen all the faculties of the mind.

7. The objection drawn from the alleged inefficiency of this method, lies solely against the practice of those teachers who disjoin the principles and the exercises of the art; and who, either through ignorance or negligence, impose only such tasks as leave the pupil to suppose, that the committing to memory of definitions and rules, constitutes the whole business of grammar.* Such a method is no less absurd in itself, than contrary to the practice of the best teachers from the very origin of the study. The epistle prefixed to King Henry's Grammar almost three centuries ago, and the very sensible preface to the old British Grammar, an octavo reprinted at Boston in 1784, give evidence enough that a better method of teaching has long been known. Nay, in my opinion, the very best method cannot be essentially different from that which has been longest in use, and is probably most known. But there is everywhere ample room for improvement. Perfection was never attained by the most learned of our ancestors, nor is it found in any of our schemes. English grammar can be better taught than it is now, or ever has been. Better scholarship would naturally produce this improvement, and it is easy to suppose a race of teachers more erudite and more zealous, than either we or they.

8. Where invention and discovery are precluded, there is little room for novelty. I have not laboured to introduce a system of grammar essentially new, but to improve the old and free it from abuses. The mode of instruction here recommended is the result of long and successful experience. There is nothing in it, which any person of common abilities will find it difficult to understand or adopt. It is the plain didactic method of definition and example, rule and praxis; which no man who means to teach grammar well, will ever desert, with the hope of finding an other

* A late author, in apologizing for his choice in publishing a grammar without forms of praxis, (that is, without any provision for a stated application of its principles by the learner,) describes the whole business of *Parsing* as a "dry and uninteresting recapitulation of the disposal of a few parts of speech, and their *often times told* positions and influence;" urges "the *unimportance* of parsing, *generally;*" and represents it to be only "a finical and ostentatious parade of practical pedantry."— *Wright's Philosophical Gram.* pp. 224 and 226. It would be no great mistake to imagine, that *this gentleman's system* of grammar, applied in any way to practice, could not fail to come under this unflattering description; but, to entertain this notion of parsing in general, is as great an error, as that which some writers have adopted on the other hand, of making this exercise their sole process of inculcation, and supposing it may profitably supersede both the usual arrangement of the principles of grammar and the practice of explaining them by definitions. It is asserted in Parkhurst's "English Grammar for Beginners, on the Inductive Method of Instruction," that, "to teach the child a definition at the outset, is beginning at the *wrong end*;" that, "with respect to all that goes under the name of etymology in grammar, it is learned chiefly by practice in parsing, and scarcely at all by the aid of definitions."—*Preface*, pp. 5 and 6.

more rational or more easy. This book itself will make any one a grammarian, who will take the trouble to observe and practice what it teaches ; and even if some instructors should not adopt the readiest means of making their pupils familiar with its contents, they will not fail to instruct by it as effectually as they can by any other. A hope is also indulged, that this work will be particularly useful to many who have passed the ordinary period allotted to education. Whoever is acquainted with the grammar of our language, so as to have some tolerable skill in teaching it, will here find almost every thing that is true in his own instructions, clearly embraced under its proper head, so as to be easy of reference. And perhaps there are few, however learned, who, on a perusal of the volume, would not be furnished with some important rules and facts which had not before occurred to their own observation.

9. The greatest peculiarity of the method is, that it requires the pupil to speak or write a great deal, and the teacher very little. But both should constantly remember that grammar is the art of speaking and writing well ; an art which can no more be acquired without practice, than that of dancing or swimming. And each should ever be careful to perform his part handsomely—without drawling, omitting, stopping, hesitating, faltering, miscalling, reiterating, stuttering, hurrying, slurring, mouthing, misquoting, mispronouncing, or any of the thousand faults which render utterance disagreeable and inelegant. It is the learner's diction that is to be improved ; and the system will be found well calculated to effect that object ; because it demands of him, not only to answer questions on grammar, but also to make a prompt and practical application of what he has just learned. If the class be tolerable readers, and have learned the art of attention, it will not be necessary for the teacher to say much ; and in general he ought not to take up the time by so doing. He should, however, carefully superintend their rehearsals ; give the word to the next when any one errs ; and order the exercise in such a manner that either his own voice, or the example of his best scholars, may gradually correct the ill habits of the awkward, till all learn to recite with clearness, understanding well what they say, and making it intelligible to others.

10. Without oral instruction and oral exercises, a correct habit of speaking our language can never be acquired ; but written rules, and exercises in writing, are perhaps quite as necessary, for the formation of a good style. All these should therefore be combined in our course of English grammar. And, in order to accomplish two objects at once, the written doctrines, or the definitions and rules of grammar, should statedly be made the subject of a critical exercise in utterance ; so that the boy who is parsing a word, or correcting a sentence, in the hearing of others, may impressively realize, that he is then and there exhibiting his own skill or deficiency in oral discourse. Perfect forms of parsing and correcting should be given him as models, with the understanding that the text before him is his only guide to their right application. It should be shown, that in parsing any particular word, or part of speech, there are just so many things to be said of it, and no more, and that these are to be said in the best manner : so that whoever tells fewer, omits something requisite ; whoever says more, inserts something irrelevant ; and whoever proceeds otherwise, either blunders in point of fact, or impairs the beauty of the given expression. I rely not upon what are called "Parsing Tables," but upon the precise forms of expression which are given in the book for the parsing of the several sorts of words. Because the questions, or abstract directions, which constitute the common parsing tables, are less intelligible to the learner than a practical example ; and more time must needs be consumed on them, in order to impress upon his memory the number and the sequence of the facts to be stated.

11. If a pupil happen to be naturally timid, there should certainly be no austerity of manner to embarrass his diffidence ; for no one can speak well, who feels afraid. But a far more common impediment to the true use of speech, is carelessness.

He who speaks before a school, in an exercise of this kind, should be made to feel that he is bound by every consideration of respect for himself, or for those who hear him, to proceed with his explanation or rehearsal, in a ready, clear, and intelligible manner. It should be strongly impressed upon him, that the grand object of the whole business, is his own practical improvement; that a habit of speaking clearly and agreeably, is itself one half of the great art of grammar; that to be slow and awkward in parsing, is unpardonable negligence, and a culpable waste of time; that to commit blunders in rehearsing grammar, is to speak badly about the art of speaking well; that his recitations must ever be limited to such things as he perfectly knows; that he must apply himself to his book, till he can proceed without mistake; finally, that he must watch and imitate the utterance of those who speak well, ever taking that for the best manner, in which there are the fewest things that could be *mimicked.**

12. The exercise of parsing should be commenced immediately after the first lesson of etymology—the lesson in which are contained the definitions of the ten parts of speech; and should be carried on progressively, till it embraces all the doctrines which are applicable to it. If it be performed according to the order prescribed in the following work, it will soon make the student perfectly familiar with all the primary definitions and rules of grammar. It asks no aid from a dictionary, if the performer knows the meaning of the words he is parsing; and very little from the teacher, if the forms in the grammar have received any tolerable share of attention. It requires just enough of thought to keep the mind attentive to what the lips are uttering; while it advances by such easy gradations and constant repetitions as leave the pupil utterly without excuse, if he does not know what to say. Being neither wholly extemporaneous nor wholly rehearsed by rote, it has more dignity than a school-boy's conversation, and more ease than a formal recitation, or declamation; and is therefore an exercise most calculated to induce a habit of uniting correctness with fluency in ordinary speech—a species of elocution as valuable as any other.†

13. Thus would I unite the practice with the theory of grammar; endeavouring to express its principles with all possible perspicuity, purity, and propriety of diction; retaining, as necessary parts of the subject, those technicalities which the pupil must needs learn in order to understand the disquisitions of grammarians in general; adopting every important feature of that system of doctrines which appears to have been longest and most generally taught; rejecting the multitudinous errors and inconsistencies with which unskillful hands have disgraced the science and perplexed the schools; remodelling every ancient definition and rule which it is possible to amend, in respect to style, or grammatical correctness; supplying the numerous and great deficiencies with which the most comprehensive treatises

* Hesitation in speech may arise from very different causes. If we do not consider this, our efforts to cure it may make it worse. In most instances, however, it may be overcome by proper treatment. "Stammering," says a late author, "is occasioned by an *over-effort to articulate*; for when the mind of the speaker is occupied with his subject as not to allow him to reflect upon his defect, he will talk without difficulty. All stammerers can sing, owing to the continuous sound, and the slight manner in which the consonants are sounded in singing; so a drunken man can run, though he cannot walk or stand still."—*Gardiner's Music of Nature,* p. 30.

"To think rightly, is of knowledge; to speak fluently, is of nature;
To read with profit, is of care; but to write aptly, is of practice."
Book of Thoughts, p. 140.

† "There is nothing more becoming [to] a *Gentleman,* or more useful in all the occurrences of life, than to be able, on any occasion, to speak well, and to the purpose."—*Locke, on Education,* § 171   "But yet, I would ask my reader, whether he doth not know a great many, who live upon their estates, and so, with the name, should have the qualities of Gentlemen, who cannot so much as tell a story as they should; much less speak clearly and persuasively in any business. This I think not to be so much their fault, as the fault of their education.—They have been taught *Rhetoric,* but yet never taught how to express themselves handsomely with their tongues or pens in the language they are always to use; as if the names of the figures embellish the discourses of those who understood the art of speaking, were the very art and skill of speaking well. *This, as all other things of practice, is to be learned, not by a few, or a great many rules given; but by exercise* and APPLICATION *according to* GOOD RULES, *or rather* PATTERNS, *till habits are got, and a facility of doing it well.*—*Ib.* § 189. The forms of parsing and correcting which the following work supplies, are *patterns,* for the performance of these practical "*exercises:*" and such patterns as ought to be implicitly followed, by every one who means to be a ready and correct speaker on these subjects.

published by earlier writers, are chargeable; adapting the code of instruction to
the present state of English literature, without giving countenance to any innovation not sanctioned by reputable use; labouring at once to extend and to facilitate
the study, without forgetting the proper limits of the science, or debasing its style
by puerilities.

14. These general views, it is hoped, will be found to have been steadily adhered
to throughout the following work. The author has not deviated much from the
principles adopted in the most approved grammars already in use; nor has he
acted the part of a servile copyist. It was not his design to introduce novelties,
but to form a practical digest of established rules. He has not laboured to subvert the general system of grammar, received from time immemorial; but to
improve upon it, in its present application to our tongue. That which is excellent,
may not be perfect; and amendment may be desirable, where subversion would
be ruinous. Believing that no theory can better explain the principles of our
language, and no contrivance afford greater facilities to the student, the writer has
in general adopted those doctrines which are already best known; and has contented himself with attempting little more than to supply the deficiencies of the system, and to free it from the reproach of being itself ungrammatical. This indeed
was task enough; for, to him, all the performances of his predecessors seemed
meagre and greatly deficient, compared with what he thought needful to be done.
The scope of his labours has been, to define, dispose, and exemplify those doctrines
anew; and, with a scrupulous regard to the best usage, to offer, on that authority,
some further contributions to the stock of grammatical knowledge.

15. Having devoted many years to studies of this nature, and being conversant
with most of the grammatical treatises already published, the author conceived
that the objects above referred to, might be better effected than they had been in
any work within his knowledge. And he persuades himself, that, however this
work may yet fall short of possible completeness, the improvements here offered
are neither few nor inconsiderable. He does not mean to conceal in any degree
his obligations to others, or to indulge in censure without discrimination. He has
no disposition to depreciate the labours, or to detract from the merits, of those who
have written ably upon this topic. He has studiously endeavoured to avail himself of all the light they have thrown upon the subject. With a view to further
improvements in the science, he has also resorted to the original sources of grammatical knowledge, and has not only critically considered what he has seen or heard of
our vernacular tongue, but has sought with some diligence the analogies of speech
in the structure of several other languages. If, therefore, the work now furnished
be thought worthy of preference, as exhibiting the best method of teaching grammar; he trusts it will be because it deviates least from sound doctrine, while, by
fair criticism upon others, it best supplies the means of choosing judiciously.

16. Of all methods of teaching grammar, that which has come nearest to what
is recommended above, has doubtless been the most successful; and whatever
objections may have been raised against it, it will probably be found on examination to be the most analogous to nature. It is analytic in respect to the doctrines
of grammar, synthetic in respect to the practice, and logical in respect to both.
It assumes the language as an object which the learner is capable of conceiving to
be one whole; begins with the classification of all its words, according to certain
grand differences which make the several parts of speech; then proceeds to divide
further, according to specific differences and qualities, till all the classes, properties,
and relations, of the words in any intelligible sentence, become obvious and
determinate: and he to whom these things are known, so that he can see at a
glance what is the construction of each word, and whether it is right or not, is a
good grammarian. The disposition of the human mind to generalize the objects of
thought, and to follow broad analogies in the use of words, discovers itself early,
and seems to be an inherent principle of our nature. Hence, in the language of

children and illiterate people, many words are regularly inflected even in opposition to the most common usage.

17. It has unfortunately become fashionable to inveigh against the necessary labour of learning by heart the essential principles of grammar, as a useless and intolerable drudgery. And this notion, with the vain hope of effecting the same purpose in an easier way, is giving countenance to modes of teaching well calculated to make superficial scholars. When those principles are properly defined, disposed, and exemplified, the labour of learning them is far less than has been represented ; and the habits of application induced by such a method of studying grammar, are of the utmost importance to the learner. Experience shows, that the task may be achieved during the years of childhood ; and that, by an early habit of study, the memory is so improved, as to render those exercises easy and familiar, which, at a later period, would be found very difficult and irksome. Upon this plan, and perhaps upon every other, some words will be learned before the ideas represented by them are fully comprehended, or the things spoken of are fully understood. But this seems necessarily to arise from the order of nature in the development of the mental faculties ; and an acquisition cannot be lightly esteemed, which has signally augmented and improved that faculty on which the pupil's future progress in knowledge depends.

18. The memory, indeed, should never be cultivated at the expense of the understanding ; as is the case, when the former is tasked with ill-devised lessons by which the latter is misled and bewildered. But truth, whether fully comprehended or not, has no perplexing inconsistencies. And it is manifest that that which does not in some respect surpass the understanding, can never enlighten it—can never awaken the spirit of inquiry or satisfy research. How often have men of observation profited by the remembrance of words which, at the time they heard them, they did not "*perfectly understand!*" We never study anything of which we imagine our knowledge to be perfect. To learn, and, to understand, are, with respect to any science or art, one and the same thing. With respect to difficult or unintelligible phraseology alone, are they different. He who by study has once stored his memory with the sound and appropriate language of any important doctrine, can never, without some folly or conceit akin to madness, repent of the acquisition. Milton, in his academy, professed to teach things rather than words ; and many others have made plausible profession of the same thing since. But it does not appear, that even in the hands of Milton, the attempt was crowned with any remarkable success. See *Dr. Barrow's Essays*, p. 85.

19. The vain pretensions of several modern simplifiers, contrivers of machines, charts, tables, diagrams, vincula, pictures, dialogues, familiar lectures, ocular analyses, tabular compendiums, inductive exercises, productive systems, intellectual methods, and various new theories, for the purpose of teaching grammar, may serve to deceive the ignorant, to amuse the visionary, and to excite the admiration of the credulous ; but none of these things has any favourable relation to that improvement which may justly be boasted as having taken place within the memory of the present generation. The definitions and rules which constitute the doctrines of grammar, may be variously expressed, arranged, illustrated, and applied ; and in the expression, arrangement, illustration, and application of them, there may be room for some amendment ; but no contrivance can ever relieve the pupil from the necessity of committing them thoroughly to memory. The experience of all antiquity is added to our own, in confirmation of this ; and the judicious teacher, though he will not shut his eyes to a real improvement, will be cautious of renouncing the practical lessons of hoary experience, for the futile notions of a vain projector.

20. Some have been beguiled with the idea, that great proficiency in grammar was to be made by means of a certain fanciful method of *induction*. But if the scheme does not communicate to those who are instructed by it, a better knowledge

of grammar than the contrivers themselves seem to have possessed, it will be found of little use.* By the happy method of Bacon, to lead philosophy into the common walks of life, into the ordinary business and language of men, is to improve the condition of humanity; but, in teaching grammar, to desert the plain didactic method of definition and example, rule and praxis, and pretend to lead children by philosophic induction into a knowledge of words, is to throw down the ladder of learning, that boys may imagine themselves to ascend it, while they are merely stilting over the low level upon which its fragments are cast.

21. The chief argument of these inductive grammarians is founded on the principle, that children cannot be instructed by means of any words which they do not perfectly understand. If this principle were strictly true, children could never be instructed by words at all. For no child ever fully understands a word the first time he hears or sees it; and it is rather by frequent repetition and use, than by any other process, that the meaning of words is commonly learned. Hence most people make use of many terms which they cannot very accurately explain, just as they do of many *things*, the real nature of which they do not comprehend. The first perception we have of any word, or other thing, when presented to the ear or the eye, gives us some knowledge of it. So to the signs of thought, as older persons use them, we soon attach some notion of what is meant; and the difference between this knowledge, and that which we call an understanding of the word or thing, is, for the most part, only in degree. Definitions and explanations are doubtless highly useful, but induction is not definition, and an understanding of words may be acquired without either; else no man could ever have made a dictionary. But, granting the principle to be true, it makes nothing for this puerile method of induction; because the regular process by definitions and examples is both shorter and easier, as well as more effectual. In a word, this whole scheme of inductive grammar is nothing else than a series of *leading* questions and *manufactured* answers; the former being generally as unfair as the latter are silly. It is a remarkable tissue of ill-laid premises and of forced illogical sequences.

22. Of a similar character is a certain work, entitled, "English Grammar on the *Productive System:* a method of instruction recently adopted in Germany and Switzerland." It is a work which certainly will be "*productive*" of no good to any body but the author and his publishers. The book is as destitute of taste, as of method; of authority, as of originality. It commences with "the *inductive* process," and after forty pages of such matter as is described above, becomes a "*productive* system," by means of a misnamed "RECAPITULATION;" which jumbles together the etymology and the syntax of the language, through seventy-six pages more. It is then made still more "*productive*," by the appropriation of a like space to a reprint of Murray's Syntax and Exercises, under the inappropriate title, "GENERAL OBSERVATIONS." To Prosody, including punctuation and the use of capitals, there are allotted six pages, at the end; and to Orthography, four lines, in the middle of the volume! (See. p. 41.) It is but just, to regard the *title* of this book, as being at once a libel and a lie; a libel upon the learning and good sense of Woodbridge;† and a practical lie, as conveying a false notion of the origin of what the volume contains.

23. What there is in Germany or Switzerland, that bears *any resemblance* to this misnamed system of English Grammar, remains to be shown. It would be prodigal of the reader's time, and inconsistent with the studied brevity of this work. to expose the fallacy of what is pretended in regard to the origin of this new method, Suffice it to say, that the anonymous and questionable account of the "Productive

---

* The principal claimants of "the Inductive Method" of Grammar, are Richard W. Green, Roswell C. Smith, John L. Parkhurst, Dyer H. Sanborn, Bradford Frazee, and Solomon Barrett, Jr.; a set of writers, differing indeed in their qualifications, but in general not a little deficient in what constitutes an accurate grammarian.

† William C. Woodbridge edited the Journal, and probably wrote the article, from which the author of "English Grammar on the Productive System" took his "Preface."

System of Instruction," which the author has borrowed from a "valuable periodical," to save himself the trouble of writing a preface, and, as he says, to "*assist* [the reader] in forming an opinion of the comparative merits of *the system*," is not only destitute of all authority, but is totally irrelevant, except to the whimsical *name* of his book. If every word of it be true, it is insufficient to give us even the slightest reason to suppose, that any thing analogous to his production ever had existence in either of those countries; and yet it is set forth on purpose to convey the idea that such a system "*now predominates*" in the schools of both. (See *Pref.* p. 5.) The infidel *Neef*, whose new method of education has been tried in our country, and with its promulgator forgot, was an accredited disciple of this boasted "productive school;" a zealous coadjutor with Pestalozzi himself, from whose halls he emanated to "teach the offspring of a free people"—to teach them the nature of things sensible, and a contempt for all the wisdom of *books*. And what similarity is there between his method of teaching and that of *Roswell C. Smith*, except their pretence to a common parentage, and that both are worthless?

24. The success of Smith's Inductive and Productive Grammars, and the fame perhaps of a certain "Grammar in Familiar Lectures," produced in 1836 a rival work from the hands of a gentleman in New Hampshire, entitled, "An Analytical Grammar of the English Language, embracing *the Inductive and Productive Methods of Teaching*, with *Familiar Explanations in the Lecture Style*," &c. This is a fair-looking duodecimo volume of three hundred pages, the character and pretensions of which, if they could be clearly stated, would throw further light upon the two fallacious schemes of teaching mentioned above. For the writer says, "This grammar professes *to combine* both the *Inductive* and *Productive* methods of imparting instruction, of which much has been said within a few years *past*."—*Preface*, p. iv. And again : "The inductive and productive methods of instruction contain the essence of modern improvements."—*Gram.* p. 139. In what these modern improvements consist, he does not inform us; but, it will be seen, that he himself claims the *copyright* of *all* the improvements which he allows to *English grammar* since the appearance of Murray in 1795. More than two hundred pretenders to such improvements, appear however within the time; nor is the grammarian of Holdgate the least positive of the claimants. This new purveyor for the public taste, dislikes the catering of his predecessor, who poached in the fields of Murray ; and, with a tacit censure upon *his productions*, has *honestly bought* the rarities which he has served up. In this he has the advantage. He is a better writer too than some who make grammars; though no adept at composition, and a total stranger to method. To call his work a "*system*," is a palpable misnomer ; to tell what it is, an impossibility. It is a grammatical chaos, bearing such a resemblance to Smith's or Kirkham's as one mass of confusion naturally bears to an other, yet differing from both in almost every thing that looks like order in any of the three.

25. The claimant of the combination says, "this new system of English grammar now offered to the public, embraces *the principles* of a ' Systematic Introduction to English Grammar,' by John L. Parkhurst ; and the *present author* is indebted to Mr. Parkhurst for a knowledge of *the manner* of applying the principles involved in *his peculiar method* of teaching grammatical science. He is also under obligations to Mr. Parkhurst for many useful hints received several years since while under his instruction.—The *copy right* of Parkhurst's Grammar has been purchased by the writer of this, who alone is responsible for the present application of *its definitions*. Parkhurst's Systematic Introduction to English Grammar has passed through two editions, and is *the first improved system* of English grammar that has appeared before the public *since the first introduction* of Lindley Murray's English Grammar."—*Sanborn's Gram. Preface*, p. iii. What, then, is "THE PRODUCTIVE SYSTEM?" and with whom did it originate? The thousands of gross blunders committed by its professors, prove at least that it is no system of writing grammat-

ically; and, whether it originated with Parkhurst or with Pestalozzi, with Sanborn or with Smith, as it is confessedly a method but "recently adopted," and, so far as appears, never fairly tested, so is it a method that needs only to be *known*, to be immediately and forever exploded.

26. The best instruction is that which ultimately gives the greatest facility and skill in practice; and grammar is best taught by that process which brings its doctrines most directly home to the habits as well as to the thoughts of the pupil—which the most effectually conquers inattention, and leaves the deepest impress of shame upon blundering ignorance. In the language of some men, there is a vividness, an energy, a power of expression, which penetrates even the soul of dullness, and leaves an impression both of words unknown and of sentiments unfelt before. Such men can teach; but he who kindly or indolently accommodates himself to ignorance, shall never be greatly instrumental in removing it. "The colloquial barbarisms of boys," says Dr. Barrow, "should never be suffered to pass without notice and censure. Provincial tones and accents, and all defects in articulation, should be corrected whenever they are heard; lest they grow into established habits, unknown, from their familiarity, to him who is guilty of them, and adopted by others, from the imitation of his manner, or their respect for his authority."— *Barrow's Essays on Education*, p. 88.

27. In the whole range of school exercises, there is none of greater importance than that of parsing; and yet perhaps there is none which is, in general, more defectively conducted. Scarcely less useful, as a means of instruction, is the practice of correcting false syntax orally, by regular and logical forms of argument; nor does this appear to have been more ably directed towards the purposes of discipline. There is so much to be done, in order to effect what is desirable in the management of these things; and so little prospect that education will ever be generally raised to a just appreciation of that study which, more than all others, forms the mind to habits of correct thinking; that, in reflecting upon the state of the science at the present time, and upon the means of its improvement, the author cannot but sympathize, in some degree, with the sadness of the learned Sanctius; who tells us, that he had "always lamented, and often with tears, that while other branches of learning were excellently taught, grammar, which is the foundation of all others, lay so much neglected, and that for this neglect there seemed to be no adequate remedy."— *Pref. to Minerva.* The grammatical use of language is in sweet alliance with the moral; and a similar regret seems to have prompted the following exclamation of the Christian poet:

> "Sacred Interpreter of human thought,
> How few respect or use thee as they ought!"—COWPER.

28. No directions, either oral or written, can ever enable the heedless and the unthinking to speak or write well. That must indeed be an admirable book, which can attract levity to sober reflection, teach thoughtlessness the true meaning of words, raise vulgarity from its fondness for low examples, awaken the spirit which attains to excellency of speech, and cause grammatical exercises to be skillfully managed, where teachers themselves are so often lamentably deficient in them. Yet something may be effected by means of better books, if better can be introduced. And what withstands?—Whatever there is of ignorance or error in relation to the premises. And is it arrogant to say there is much? Alas! in regard to this, as well as to many a weightier matter, one may too truly affirm, *Multa non sunt sicut multis videntur*—Many things are not as they seem to many. Common errors are apt to conceal themselves from the common mind; and the appeal to reason and just authority is often frustrated, because a wrong head defies both. But, apart from this, there are difficulties: multiplicity perplexes choice; inconvenience attends change; improvement requires effort; conflicting theories demand examination; the principles of the science are unprofitably dis-

puted; the end is often divorced from the means; and much that belies the title, has been published under the name.

29. It is certain, that the printed formularies most commonly furnished for the important exercises of parsing and correcting, are either so awkwardly written or so negligently followed, as to make grammar, in the mouths of our juvenile orators, little else than a crude and faltering jargon.   Murray evidently intended that his book of exercises should be constantly used with his grammar; but he made the examples in the former so dull and prolix, that few learners, if any, have ever gone through the series agreeably to his direction.   The publishing of them in a separate volume, has probably given rise to the absurd practice of endeavouring to teach his grammar without them.   The forms of parsing and correcting which this author furnishes, are also misplaced; and when found by the learner, are of little use.   They are so verbose, awkward, irregular, and deficient, that the pupil must be either a dull boy or utterly ignorant of grammar, if he cannot express the facts extemporaneously in better English.   They are also very meagre as a whole, and altogether inadequate to their purpose; many things that frequently occur in the language, not being at all exemplified in them, or even explained in the grammar itself.   When we consider how exceedingly important it is, that the business of a school should proceed without loss of time, and that, in the oral exercises here spoken of, each pupil should go through his part promptly, clearly, correctly, and fully, we cannot think it a light objection that these forms, so often to be repeated, are badly written.   Nor does the objection lie against this writer only: *Ab uno disce omnes.*   But the reader may demand some illustrations.*

30. First—from his etymological parsing: "O Virtue! how amiable thou art!" Here his form for the word *Virtue* is—"*Virtue* is a *common substantive, of the neuter* gender, *of the third* person, *in the* singular number, *and the* nominative case.*"—Mur. Gram.* 8vo, ii, p. 2.   It should have been—"*Virtue* is a *common noun,* personified *proper*, of the *second* person, singular number, *feminine* gender, and nominative case."   And then the definitions of all these things should have followed in regular numerical order.   He gives the class of this noun wrong, for virtue addressed becomes an individual; he gives the gender wrong, and in direct contradiction to what he says of the word in his section on gender; he gives the person wrong, as may be seen by the pronoun *thou*, which represents it; he repeats the definite article three times unnecessarily, and inserts two needless prepositions, making them different where the relation is precisely the same: and all this, in a sentence of two lines, to tell the properties of the noun *Virtue!*— But further: in etymological parsing, the definitions explaining the properties of

---

* Many other grammars, later than Murray's, have been published, some in England, some in America, and some in both countries; and among these there are, I think, a few in which a little improvement has been made, in the methods prescribed for the exercises of parsing and correcting.   In most, however, *nothing of the kind has been attempted.*   And, of the formularies which have been given, the best that I have seen, are still miserably defective, and worthy of all the censure that is expressed in the paragraph above; while others, that appear in works not entirely destitute of merit, are absolutely *much worse* than Murray's, and worthy to condemn to a speedy oblivion the books in which they are printed.   In lieu of forms of expression, clear, orderly, accurate, and full; such as a young parser might profitably imitate; such as an experienced teacher would be sure to approve; what have we!   A chaos of half-formed sentences, for the ignorant pupil to flounder in, an infinite abyss of blunders, which a world of criticism could not fully expose!   See, for example, the seven pages of parsing, in the neat little book entitled, "A Practical Grammar of the English Language, by the Rev. David Blair: Seventh Edition: London, 1815:" pp. 49 to 57.   I cannot consent to quote more than one short paragraph of the miserable jumble which these pages contain.   Yet the author is evidently a man of learning, and capable of writing well on some subjects, if not on this.   "Bless the Lord, O my soul!" *Paro:* "*Bless*, a verb, (repeat 97); active (repeat 99); active voice (102); *infinitive mood* (107); *third person,* and *being the nominative* (118); present tense (111); conjugate the verb after the pattern (129); its object is *Lord 30*."—*Blair's Gram.* p. 50.   Of the paragraphs referred to, I must take some notice: "107. The *imperative* mood commands or orders or intreats."—*Ib.* p. 19.   "118. The *second person* is always the pronoun *thou* or *you* in the singular, and *ye* or *you* in the plural."—*Ib.* p. 21.   "111. The *imperative* mood has no distinction of tense, and the *infinitive* has no distinction of persons."—*Ib.* p. 20.   Now the author should have said: "*Bless* is a redundant active-transitive verb, from *bless, blessed* or *blest, blessing, blessed* or *blest;* found in the imperative mood, present tense, second person, and singular number:" and, if he meant to parse the word *syntactically,* he should have added: "and agrees with its nominative *thou* understood; according to the rule which says, 'Every finite verb must agree with its subject, or nominative, in person and number.' because the meaning is—*Bless thou* the Lord."   This is the whole story.   But, in the form above, several things are false; many, superfluous; some, deficient; several, misplaced; nothing, right.   Not much better are the models furnished by *Kirkham, Smith, Lennie, Bullions,* and other late authors.

the parts of speech, ought to be regularly and rapidly rehearsed by the pupil, till all of them become perfectly familiar; and till he can discern, with the quickness of thought, what alone will be true for the full description of any word in any intelligible- sentence.   All these the author omits; and, on account of this omission, his whole method of etymological parsing is miserably deficient.*

31. Secondly—from his syntactical parsing : "*Vice* degrades us."   Here his form for the word *Vice* is— "*Vice* is a common substantive, *of* the third person, *in* the singular number, *and the* nominative case."—*Mur. Gram.* 8vo, ii, p. 9. Now, when the learner is told that this is the syntactical parsing of a noun, and the other the etymological, he will of course conclude, that to advance from the etymology to the syntax of this part of speech, is merely, *to omit the gender*—this being the only difference between the two forms.   But even this difference had no other origin than the compiler's carelessness in preparing his octavo book of exercises—the gender being inserted in the duodecimo.   And what then ?   Is the syntactical parsing of a noun to be precisely the same as the etymological ?   Never.   But Murray, and all who admire and follow his work, are content to parse many words by halves—making, or pretending to make, a necessary distinction, and yet often omitting, in both parts of the exercise, every thing which constitutes the difference.   He should here have said—"*Vice* is a common noun, of the third person, singular number, neuter gender, and nominative case: and is the subject of *degrades;* according to the rule which says, 'A noun or a pronoun which is the subject of a verb, must be in the nominative case.'   Because the meaning is—*vice degrades.*"   This is the whole description of the word, with its construction ; and to say less, is to leave the matter unfinished.

32. Thirdly—from his "Mode of verbally correcting erroneous sentences : " Take his first example : "The man is prudent which speaks little."   (How far silence is prudence, depends upon circumstances : I waive that question.)   The learner is here taught to say, "This sentence is incorrect ; because *which* is a pro-

* Of Dr. Bullions's forms of parsing, as exhibited in his English Grammar, which is a modification of Lennie's Grammar, it is difficult to say, whether they are most remarkable for their deficiencies, their redundancies, or their contrariety to other teachings of the same author or authors. Both Lennie and Bullions adopt the rule, that, "An *ellipsis is not allowable* when it would obscure the sentence, weaken its force, or be attended with an impropriety."—L. p. 91 ; B. p. 130. And the latter strengthens this doctrine with several additional observations, the first of which reads thus : " In general, *no word should be omitted* that is necessary to the *full and correct* construction, or even *harmony of* a sentence."—*Bullions, E. Gr.* 130. Now the parsing above alluded to, has been thought particularly commendable for its *brevity*—a quality certainly desirable, so far as it consists with the end of parsing, or with the more needful properties of a good style, clearness, accuracy, ease, and elegance.   But, if the foregoing rule and observation are true, the models furnished by these writers are not commendably brief, but miserably defective.   Their brevity is, in fact, such as renders them all *bad English* : and not only so, it makes them obviously inadequate to their purpose, as bringing into use but a part of the principles which the learner has studied.   It consists only in the omission of what ought to have been inserted.   For example, this short line, "*I lean upon the Lord*," is parsed by both of these gentlemen thus : "*I, the first personal* pronoun, masculine, or feminine, singular, the nominative—*lean*, a verb, *neuter*, first person singular, present, indicative—*upon*, a preposition—*the*, an article, the definite—*Lord*, a noun. masculine, singular, *the* objective, (governed by *upon.*)"—*Lennie's Principles of English Gram.* p. 51 ; *Bullions's*, 74.   This is a little sample of their etymological parsing, in which exercise they generally omit not only all the definitions or "reasons" of the various terms applied, but also all the following particulars : first, the verb *is*, and certain *definitives* and *connectives*, which are " necessary to the full and correct construction " of their sentences ; secondly, the distinction of nouns as *proper* or *common ;* thirdly, the *person* of nouns, *first, second,* or *third ;* fourthly, the words, *number, gender,* and *case*, which are necessary to the sense and construction of certain words used ; fifthly, the distinction of adjectives as belonging to *different classes ;* sixthly, the division of verbs as being *regular* or *irregular, redundant* or *defective ;* seventhly, sometimes, (Lennie excepted,) the division of verbs as *active, passive,* or *neuter :* eighthly, the words *mood* and *tense*, which Bullions, on page 131, pronounces " quite unnecessary," and inserts in his own formule on page 132 ; ninthly, the distinction of adverbs as expressing *time, place, degree,* or *manner :* tenthly, the distinction of conjunctions as *copulative* or *disjunctive :* lastly, the distinction of interjections as indicating *different emotions.*   All these things does their completest specimen of etymological parsing lack, while it is grossly encumbered with parentheses of syntax, which " *must be omitted* till the pupil get the *rules* of syntax."—*Lennie,* p. 51.   It is also vitiated with several absurdities, contradictions, and improper changes of expression : as, "*His, the third personal pronoun ;* " (B. p. 23 ;)—" *me, the first personal pronoun ;* " (*Id.* 74 :)—" *A,* The indefinite article ; " (*Id.* 73 ;)—" *a,* an article, the indefinite ; " (*Id.* 74 ;)—" When the *verb is passive,* parse thus : '*A verb active,* in the passive voice, *regular, irregular,*' &c."—*Bullions,* p. 131.   In stead of teaching sufficiently, as elements of etymological parsing, the definitions which belong to this exercise, and then dismissing them for the principles of syntax, Dr. Bullions encumbers his method of syntactical parsing with such a series of etymological questions and answers as cannot but make it one of the slowest, longest, and most tiresome ever invented.   He thinks that the pupil, after parsing any word syntactically, " *should be requested to assign* a *reason for every thing contained in his statement !* "—*Princ pl.s of* E. Grammar. p 131.   And the teacher is to ask questions as numerous as the reasons!   Such is the parsing of a text-book which has been pronounced " superior to any other, for use in our common schools "—" a complete grammar of the language, and available *for every purpose* for which Mr. Brown's can possibly be used."—*Ralph K. Finch's Report,* p. 12.

noun *of the neuter gender, and does not agree in gender* with its antecedent *man*, which is masculine. But a pronoun should agree with its antecedent in gender, &c. according to the fifth rule of syntax. *Which* should *therefore* be *who*, a relative pronoun, agreeing with its antecedent *man;* and the sentence should stand thus : ' The man is prudent *who* speaks little.' "—*Murray's Octavo Gram.* ii, p. 18; *Exercises*, 12mo, p. xii. Again : " ' After I visited Europe, I returned to America.' This sentence," says Murray, " *is not correct ;* because the verb *visited* is in the imperfect tense, and yet used here to express an action, not only past, but prior to the time referred to by the verb *returned*, to which it relates. By the thirteenth rule of syntax, when verbs are used that, in point of time, relate to each other, the order of time should be observed. The imperfect tense *visited* should therefore have been *had visited*, in the pluperfect tense, representing the action of *visiting*, not only as past, but also as prior to the time of *returning*. *The sentence corrected would stand thus :* 'After I *had visited* Europe, I returned to America.' "—*Gr.* ii, p. 19 ; *and Ex.* 12mo, p. xii. These are the first two examples of Murray's verbal corrections, and the only ones retained by Alger, in his *improved, recopy-righted edition* of Murray's Exercises. Yet, in each of them, is the argumentation palpably false ! In the former, truly, *which* should be *who;* but not because *which* is " of the *neuter gender ;*" but because the application of that relative to *persons*, is now nearly obsolete. Can any grammarian forget that, in speaking of brute animals, male or female, we commonly use *which*, and never *who?* But if *which* must needs be *neuter*, the world is wrong in this.—As for the latter example, it is right as it stands ; and the correction is, in some sort, tautological. The conjunctive adverb *after* makes one of the actions subsequent to the other, and gives to the *visiting* all the priority that is signified by the pluperfect tense. "*After* I *visited* Europe," is equivalent to "*When* I *had visited* Europe." The whole argument is therefore void.[*]

33. These few brief illustrations, out of thousands that might be adduced in proof of the faultiness of the common manuals, the author has reluctantly introduced, to show that even in the most popular books, with all the pretended improvements of revisers, the grammar of our language has never been treated with that care and ability which its importance demands. It is hardly to be supposed that men unused to a teacher's duties, can be qualified to compose such books as will most facilitate his labours. Practice is a better pilot than theory. And while, in respect to grammar, the consciousness of failure is constantly inducing changes from one system to an other, and almost daily giving birth to new expedients as constantly to end in the same disappointment ; perhaps the practical instructions of an experienced teacher, long and assiduously devoted to the study, may approve

[*] There are many other critics, besides Murray and Alger, who seem not to have observed the import of *after* and *before* in connexion with the tenses Dr. Bullions, on page 139th of his English Grammar, copied the foregoing example from Lennie, who took it from Murray. Even Richard Hiley, and William Harvey Wells, grammarians of more than ordinary tact, have been obviously misled by the false criticism above cited. One of Hiley's Rules of Syntax, with its illustration, stands thus : " In *the use of the different tenses*, we must particularly observe *to use that tense* which clearly and properly conveys the sense intended ; thus, instead of saying, 'After I *visited* Europe, I returned to America ;' we should say, 'After I *had visited* Europe, I returned to America.' "—*Hiley's Gram.* p 90. Upon this he thought it needful to comment thus : "After I *visited* Europe, I returned to America ;' *this sentence is incorrect ; visited* ought to be *had visited*, because the action *implied* by the verb *visited* was COMPLETED *before* the other past action *returned*."— p. 91. See nearly the same things in *Wells's School Grammar*, 1st Edition, p. 150 and 151; but his later editions are wisely altered. Since " *visited* and *was completed* " are of the same tense, the argument from the latter, if it proves any thing, proves the former to be *right*, and the proposed change needless, or perhaps worse than needless. " I *visited* Europe, *before* I *returned* to America," or " I *visited* Europe, *and afterwards returned* to America," is good English, and not to be improved by any change of tense ; yet here too we see the reading " *was completed before*" the return, or HAD BEEN COMPLETED *at the time* of the return. I say, "The Pluperfect Tense is that which expresses what *had taken* place *at some past time* mentioned : as, 'I *had seen* him, *when* I met you.' " Murray says, "The Pluperfect Tense represents a *thing* not only as past, but also as prior to some *other point of time* specified in the sentence: as, I *had finished* my letter *before* he arrived." Hiley says, " The *Past-Perfect* expresses an action or event which *was past before* some *other past action or event* mentioned in the sentence, *and to which* it refers ; as, I *had finished* my lessons *before* he came." With this, Wells appears to concur, his example being similar. It seems to me, that these last two definitions, and their example too, are bad ; because, by the help of *before* or *after*, " *the past before the past* " *may be* clearly expressed by the *simple past tense* : as, " I *finished* my letter *before* he arrived."—" I finished my lessons *before* he came." " He arrived soon *after* I *finished* the letter."—" Soon *after* it *was completed*, he came in."

themselves to many, as seasonably supplying the aid and guidance which they require.

34. From the doctrines of grammar, novelty is rigidly excluded. They consist of details to which taste can lend no charm, and genius no embellishment. A writer may express them with neatness and perspicuity—their importance alone can commend them to notice. Yet, in drawing his illustrations from the stores of literature, the grammarian may select some gems of thought, which will fasten on the memory a worthy sentiment, or relieve the dullness of minute instruction. Such examples have been taken from various authors, and interspersed through the following pages. The moral effect of early lessons being a point of the utmost importance, it is especially incumbent on all those who are endeavouring to confer the benefits of intellectual culture, to guard against the admission or the inculcation of any principle which may have an improper tendency, and be ultimately prejudicial to those whom they instruct. In preparing this treatise for publication, the author has been solicitous to avoid every thing that could be offensive to the most delicate and scrupulous reader; and of the several thousands of quotations introduced for the illustration or application of the principles of the science, he trusts that the greater part will be considered valuable on account of the sentiments they contain.

35. The nature of the subject almost entirely precludes invention. The author has, however, aimed at that kind and degree of originality which are to be commended in works of this sort. What these are, according to his view, he has sufficiently explained in a preceding chapter. And, though he has taken the liberty of a grammarian, to think for himself and write in a style of his own, he trusts it will be evident that few have excelled him in diligence of research, or have followed more implicitly the dictates of that authority which gives law to language. In criticising the critics and grammatists of the schools, he has taken them upon their own ground—showing their errors, for the most part, in contrast with the common principles which they themselves have taught; and has hoped to escape censure, in his turn, not by sheltering himself under the name of a popular master, but by a diligence which should secure to his writings at least the humble merit of self-consistency. His progress in composing this work has been slow, and not unattended with labour and difficulty. Amidst the contrarieties of opinion, that appear in the various treatises already before the public, and the perplexities inseparable from so complicated a subject, he has, after deliberate consideration, adopted those views and explanations which appeared to him the least liable to objection, and the most compatible with his ultimate object—the production of a work which should show, both extensively and accurately, what is, and what is not, good English.

36. The great art of meritorious authorship lies chiefly in the condensation of much valuable thought into few words. Although the author has here allowed himself ampler room than before, he has still been no less careful to store it with such information as he trusted would prevent the ingenious reader from wishing its compass less. He has compressed into this volume the most essential parts of a mass of materials in comparison with which the book is still exceedingly small. The effort to do this, has greatly multiplied his own labour and long delayed the promised publication; but in proportion as this object has been reached, the time and patience of the student must have been saved. Adequate compensation for this long toil, has never been expected. Whether from this performance any profit shall accrue to the author or not, is a matter of little consequence; he has neither written for bread, nor on the credit of its proceeds built castles in the air. His ambition was, to make an acceptable book, by which the higher class of students might be thoroughly instructed, and in which the eyes of the critical would find little to condemn.. He is too well versed in the history of his theme, too well aware of the precarious fortune of authors, to indulge in any confident anticipa-

tions of extraordinary success: yet he will not deny that his hopes are large, he'ng conscious of having cherished them with a liberality of feeling which cannot fear disappointment. In this temper he would invite the reader to a thorough perusal of these pages.

37. A grammar should speak for itself. In a work of this nature, every word or tittle which does not recommend the performance to the understanding and taste of the skillful, is, so far as it goes, a certificate against it. Yet if some small errors shall have escaped detection, let it be recollected that it is almost impossible to compose and print, with perfect accuracy, a work of this size, in which so many little things should be observed, remembered, and made exactly to correspond. There is no human vigilance which multiplicity may not sometimes baffle, and minuteness sometimes elude. To most persons grammar seems a dry and difficult subject; but there is a disposition of mind, to which what is arduous, is for that very reason alluring. "Quo difficilius, hoc praeclarius," says Cicero; "The more difficult, the more honourable." The merit of casting up a high-way in a rugged land, is proportionate not merely to the utility of the achievement, but to the magnitude of the obstacles to be overcome. The difficulties encountered in boyhood from the use of a miserable epitome and the deep impression of a few mortifying blunders made in public, first gave the author a fondness for grammar; circumstances having since favoured this turn of his genius, he has voluntarily pursued the study, with an assiduity which no man will ever imitate for the sake of pecuniary recompense.

CHAPTER X.

OF GRAMMATICAL DEFINITIONS.

Scientiam autem nusquam esse censebant, nisi in animi motionibus atque rationibus: quâ de causâ definitiones rerum probabant, et has ad omnia, de quibus disceptabatur, adhibebant."—CICERONIS Academica, Lib. i, 9.

1. "The first and highest philosophy," says Puffendorf, "is that which delivers the most accurate and comprehensive *definitions* of things." Had all the writers on English grammar been adepts in this philosophy, there would have been much less complaint of the difficulty and uncertainty of the study. "It is easy," says Murray, "to advance plausible objections against almost every definition, rule, and arrangement of grammar."—*Gram.* 8vo, p. 59. But, if this is true, as regards his, or any other work, the reason, I am persuaded, is far less inherent in the nature of the subject than many have supposed.* Objectionable definitions and rules are but evidences of the ignorance and incapacity of him

---

* Samuel Kirkham, whose grammar is briefly described in the third chapter of this introduction, boldly lays the blame of all his philological faults, upon our noble *language itself*; and even conceives, that a well-written and fault-less grammar cannot be a good one, because it will not accord with that reasonless jumble which he takes every existing language to be! How diligently he laboured to perfect his work, and with what zeal for truth and accuracy, may be guessed from the following citation: "The truth is, after all *which* can be done to render the definitions and rules of grammar comprehensive and accurate, they will still be found, when critically examined by men of learning and science, *more* or *less exceptionable. These exceptions and imperfections* are the unavoidable consequence of the *imperfections of the language.* Language as well as every thing else *of human invention,* will always be *imperfect.* Consequently, a perfect system of grammatical principles *would not suit it.* A perfect grammar will not be produced, until some perfect being writes it for a perfect language; and a perfect language will not be constructed, until some *super-human agency is* employed in its production. All grammatical principles and systems which are not *perfect* are *exceptionable."—Kirkham's Grammar,* p. 66. The unplausible sophistry of these strange remarks, and the palliation they afford to the multitudinous defects of the book which contains them, may be left, without further comment, to the judgment of the reader.

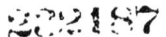

who frames them. And if the science of grammar has been so unskillfully treated that almost all its positions may be plausibly impugned, it is time for some attempt at a reformation of the code. The language is before us, and he who knows most about it, can best prescribe the rules which we ought to observe in the use of it. But how can we expect children to deduce from a few particulars an accurate notion of general principles and their exceptions, where learned doctors have so often faltered? Let the abettors of grammatical "*induction*" answer.

2. Nor let it be supposed a light matter to prescribe with certainty the principles of grammar. For, what is requisite to the performance? To know certainly, in the first place, what is the *best usage*. Nor is this all. Sense and memory must be keen, and tempered to retain their edge and hold, in spite of any difficulties which the subject may present. To understand things exactly as they are; to discern the differences by which they may be distinguished, and the resemblances by which they ought to be classified; to know, through the proper evidences of truth, that our ideas, or conceptions, are rightly conformable to the nature, properties, and relations, of the objects of which we think; to see how that which is complex may be resolved into its elements, and that which is simple may enter into combination; to observe how that which is consequent may be traced to its cause, and that which is regular be taught by rule; to learn from the custom of speech the proper connexion between words and ideas, so as to give to the former a just application, to the latter an adequate expression, and to things a just description; to have that penetration which discerns what terms, ideas, or things, are definable, and therefore capable of being taught, and what must be left to the teaching of nature: these are the essential qualifications for him who would form good definitions; these are the elements of that accuracy and comprehensiveness of thought, to which allusion has been made, and which are characteristic of "the first and highest philosophy."

· 3. Again, with reference to the cultivation of the mind, I would add: To observe accurately the appearances of things, and the significations of words; to learn first principles first, and proceed onward in such a manner that every new truth may help to enlighten and strengthen the understanding; and thus to comprehend gradually, according to our capacity, whatsoever may be brought within the scope of human intellect:—to do these things, I say. is, to ascend by sure steps, so far as we may, from the simplest elements of science—which, in fact, are our own, original, undefinable notices of things—towards the very topmost height of human wisdom and knowledge. The ancient saying, that truth lies hid, or in the bottom of a well, must not be taken without qualification; for "the first and highest philosophy" has many principles which even a child may understand. These several suggestions, the first of which the Baron de Puffendorf thought not unworthy to introduce his great work on the Law of Nature and of Nations, the reader, if he please, may bear in mind, as he peruses the following digest of the laws and usages of speech.

4. "Definitions," says Duncan, in his Elements of Logic, "are intended to make known the meaning of words standing for *complex ideas ;** and were we always careful to form those ideas exactly in our minds, and copy our definitions from that appearance, much of the confusion and obscurity complained of in languages might be prevented."—P. 70. Again he says: "The writings of the mathematicians are a clear proof, how much the advancement of human knowledge depends upon a right use of definitions."—P. 72. Mathematical science has been supposed to be, in its own nature, that which is best calculated to develop

---

* The phrase *complex ideas*, or *compound ideas*, has been used for the notions which we have of things consisting of different parts, or having various properties, so as to embrace some sort of plurality : thus our ideas of *all bodies* and *classes of things* are said to be complex or compound. *Simple ideas* are those in which the mind discovers no parts or plurality : such are the ideas of *heat, cold, blueness, redness, pleasure, pain, volition*, &c. But some writers have contended, that the *composition of ideas* is a fiction ; and that all the complexity, in any case, consists only in the use of a *general term* in lieu of many particular ones. Locke is on one side of this debate, Horne Tooke, on the other.

and strengthen the reasoning faculty ; but, as speech is emphatically *the discourse of reason*, I am persuaded, that had the grammarians been equally clear and logical in their instructions, their science would never have been accounted inferior in this respect.   Grammar is perhaps the most comprehensive of all studies ; but it is chiefly owing to the unskillfulness of instructors, and to the errors and defects of the systems in use, that it is commonly regarded as the most dry and difficult.

5. "Poor Scaliger (who well knew what a definition should be) from his own melancholy experience exclaimed —'*Nihil infelicius grammatico definitore!*' Nothing is more unhappy than the grammatical definer."—*Tooke's Diversions*, i, p. 288.   Nor do our later teachers appear to have been more fortunate in this matter.   A majority of all the definitions and rules contained in the great multitude of English grammars which I have examined, are, in some respect or other, erroneous.   The nature of their multitudinous faults, I must in general leave to the discernment of the reader, except the passages be such as may be suitably selected for examples of false syntax.   Enough, however, will be exhibited, in the course of this volume, to make the foregoing allegation credible ; and of the rest a more accurate judgement may perhaps be formed, when they shall have been compared with what this work will present as substitutes.   The importance of giving correct definitions to philological terms, and of stating with perfect accuracy whatsoever is to be learned as doctrine, has never been duly appreciated.   The grand source of the disheartening difficulties encountered by boys in the study of grammar, lies in their ignorance of the meaning of words.   This cause of embarrassment is not to be shunned and left untouched ; but, as far as possible, it ought to be removed.   In teaching grammar, or indeed any other science, we cannot avoid the use of many terms to which young learners may have attached no ideas.   Being little inclined or accustomed to reflection, they often hear, read, or even rehearse from memory, the plainest language that can be uttered, and yet have no very distinct apprehension of what it means.   What marvel then, that in a study abounding with terms taken in a peculiar or technical sense, many of which, in the common manuals, are either left undefined, or are explained but loosely or erroneously, they should often be greatly puzzled, and sometimes totally discouraged ?

6. *Simple ideas* are derived, not from teaching, but from sensation or consciousness ; but *complex ideas*, or the notions which we have of such things as consist of various parts, or such as stand in any known relations, are definable.   A person can have no better definition of *heat*, or of *motion*, than what he will naturally get by *moving* towards a *fire*.   Not so of our complex or general ideas, which constitute science.   The proper objects of scientific instruction consist in those genuine perceptions of pure mind, which form the true meaning of generic names, or common nouns ; and he who is properly qualified to teach, can for the most part readily tell what should be understood by such words.   But are not many teachers too careless here ?   For instance : a boy commencing the process of calculation, is first told, that, " Arithmetic is the art of computing by numbers," which sentence he partly understands ; but should he ask his teacher, " What is a *number*, in arithmetic?" what answer will he get ?   Were Goold Brown so asked, he would simply say, " *A number, in arithmetic, is an expression that tells how many ;* " for every expression that tells how many, is a number in arithmetic, and nothing else is.   But as no such definition is contained in *the books*,* there are ten chances to one, that, simple as the matter is, the readiest master you shall find, will give an erroneous answer.   Suppose the teacher should say, " That is a question which I have not thought of ; turn to your dictionary."   The boy reads

---

* Dilworth appears to have had a true *idea* of the thing, but he does not express it as a definition : " Q. Is an Unit or one, a Number ? A. An Unit is a number, *because it may properly answer the question how many!*"— *Schoolmaster's Assistant*, p. 2. A number in arithmetic, and a number in grammar, are totally different things. The *plural* number, as *men* or *horses*, does not tell *how many ;* nor does the word *singular* mean *one*, as the author of a recent grammar says it does. The *plural* number is one number, but it is not *the singular*. "The *Productive System*" teaches thus : " What does the word *singular* mean ? It means *one*."— *Smith's New Gram.* p. 7.

from Dr. Webster: " NUMBER—the designation of a unit in reference to other units, or in reckoning, counting, enumerating."—" Yes," replies the master, "that is it; Dr. Webster is unrivalled in giving definitions." Now, has the boy been instructed, or only puzzled? Can he conceive how the number *five* can be a *unit?* or how the word *five*, the figure 5, or the numeral letter V, is " the designation of a *unit?* " " He knows that each of these is a number, and that the oral monosyllable *five* is the same number, in an other form; but is still as much at a loss for a proper answer to his question, as if he had never seen either schoolmaster or dictionary. So is it with a vast number of the simplest things in grammar.

7. Since what we denominate scientific terms, are seldom, if ever, such as stand for ideas simple and undefinable; and since many of those which represent general ideas, or classes of objects, may be made to stand for more or fewer things, according to the author's notion of classification; it is sufficiently manifest that the only process by which instruction can effectually reach the understanding of the pupil and remove the difficulties spoken of, is that of delivering accurate definitions. These are requisite for the information and direction of the learner; and these must be thoroughly impressed upon his mind, as the only means by which he can know exactly how much and what he is to understand by our words. The power which we possess, of making known all our complex or general ideas of things by means of definitions, is a faculty wisely contrived in the nature of language, for the increase and spread of science; and, in the hands of the skillful, it is of vast avail to these ends. It is " the first and highest philosophy," instructing mankind, to think clearly and speak accurately; as well as to know definitely, in the unity and permanence of a general nature, those things which never could be known or spoken of as the individuals of an infinite and fleeting multitude.

8. And, without contradiction, the shortest and most successful way of teaching the young mind to distinguish things according to their proper differences, and to name or describe them aright, is, to tell in direct terms what they severally are. Cicero intimates that all instruction appealing to reason ought to proceed in this manner: " Omnis enim quæ à ratione suscipitur de re aliqua institutio, debet à *definitione* proficisci, ut intelligatur quid sit id, de quo disputetur.—*Off.* Lib. i, p. 4. Literally thus: " For all instruction which from reason is undertaken concerning any thing, ought to proceed from a *definition*, that it may be understood what the thing is, about which the speaker is arguing." Little advantage, however, will be derived from any definition, which is not, as Quintilian would have it, " Lucida et succincta rei descriptio"—a clear and brief description of the thing.

9. Let it here be observed that scientific definitions are of *things*, and not merely of *words;* or if equally of words *and* things, they are rather of nouns than of the other parts of speech. For a definition, in the proper sense of the term, consists not in a mere change or explanation of the verbal sign, but in a direct and true answer to the question, What is such or such a thing? In respect to its extent, it must with equal exactness include every thing which comes under the name, and exclude every thing which does not come under the name: then will it perfectly serve the purpose for which it is intended. To furnish such definitions, (as I have before suggested,) is work for those who are capable of great accuracy both of thought and expression. Those who would qualify themselves for teaching any particular branch of knowledge, should make it their first concern to acquire clear and accurate ideas of all things that ought to be embraced in their instructions. These ideas are to be gained, either by contemplation upon the things themselves as they are presented naturally, or by the study of those books in which they are rationally and clearly explained. Nor will such study ever be irksome to him whose generous desire after knowledge, is thus deservedly gratified.

10. But it must be understood, that although scientific definitions are said to be *of things*, they are not copied immediately from the real essence of the things, but are formed from the conceptions of the author's mind concerning that essence.

Hence, as Duncan justly remarks, "A mistaken idea never fails to occasion a mistake also in the definition." Hence, too, the common distinction of the logicians, between definitions of the *name* and definitions of the *thing*, seems to have little or no foundation. The former term they applied to those definitions which describe the objects of pure intellection, such as triangles, and other geometrical figures; the latter, to those which define objects actually existing in external nature. The mathematical definitions, so noted for their certainty and completeness, have been supposed to have some peculiar preëminence, as belonging to the former class. But, in fact the idea of a triangle exists as substantively in the mind, as that of a tree, if not indeed more so; and if I define these two objects, my description will, in either case, be equally a definition both of the name and of the thing; but in neither, is it copied from any thing else than that notion which I have conceived, of the common properties of all triangles or of all trees.

11. Infinitives, and some other terms not called nouns, may be taken abstractly or substantively, so as to admit of what may be considered a regular definition; thus the question, "What is it *to read?*" is nearly the same as, "What is *reading?*" "What is it *to be wise?*" is little different from, "What is *wisdom?*" and a true answer might be, in either case, a true definition. Nor are those mere translations or explanations of words, with which our dictionaries and vocabularies abound, to be dispensed with in teaching: they prepare the student to read various authors with facility, and furnish him with a better choice of terms, when he attempts to write. And in making such choice, let him remember, that as affectation of *hard* words makes composition ridiculous, so the affectation of *easy* and *common* ones may make it unmanly. But not to digress. With respect to grammar, we must sometimes content ourselves with such explications of its customary terms, as cannot claim to be perfect definitions; for the most common and familiar things are not always those which it is the most easy to define. When Dr. Johnson was asked, "What is *poetry?*" he replied, "Why, sir, it is easier to tell what it is not. We all know what *light* is: but it is not easy *to tell what it is.*"—*Boswell's Life of Johnson*, Vol. iii, p. 402. This was thought by the biographer to have been well and ingeniously said.

12. But whenever we encounter difficulties of this sort, it may be worth while to seek for their *cause.* If we find it, the understanding is no longer puzzled. Dr. Johnson seemed to his biographer, to show, by this ready answer, the acuteness of his wit and discernment. But did not the wit consist in adroitly excusing himself, by an illusory comparison? What analogy is there between the things which he compares? Of the difficulty of defining *poetry*, and the difficulty of defining *light*, the reasons are as different as are the two things themselves, *poetry* and *light*. The former is something so various and complex that it is hard to distinguish its essence from its accidents; the latter presents an idea so perfectly simple and unique that all men conceive of it exactly in the same way, while none can show wherein it essentially consists. But is it true, that, "We all know *what light is?*" Is it not rather true, that we know nothing at all about it, but what it is just as easy to tell as to think? We know it is that reflexible medium which enables us to see; and this is definition enough for all but the natively blind, to whom no definition perhaps can ever convey an adequate notion of its use in respect to sight.

13. If a person cannot tell what a thing is, it is commonly considered to be a fair inference, that he does not know. Will any grammarian say, "I know well enough what the thing is, but I cannot tell?" Yet, taken upon this common principle, the authors of our English grammars, (if in framing their definitions they have not been grossly wanting to themselves in the exercise of their own art,) may be charged, I think, with great ignorance, or great indistinctness of apprehension; and that, too, in relation to many things among the very simplest elements of their science. For example: Is it not a disgrace to a man of letters, to be

unable to tell accurately what a letter is? Yet to say, with Lowth, Murray, Churchill, and a hundred others of inferior name, that, "*A letter* is *the first principle* or *least part* of a word," is to utter what is neither good English nor true doctrine. The two articles *a* and *the* are here inconsistent with each other. "*A* letter " is *one* letter, *any* letter; but " *the first principle* of a word " is, surely, not one or any principle taken *indefinitely*. Equivocal as the phrase is, it must mean either *some particular principle*, or some particular *first* principle, of a word; and, taken either way, the assertion is false. For it is manifest, that *in no sense* can we affirm of *each* of the letters of a word, that it is " *the first principle* " of that word. Take, for instance, the word *man*. Is *m* the first principle of this word? You may answer, " Yes; for it is the first *letter* " Is *a* the first principle? " No; it is the *second*." But *n* too is a letter; and is *n* the first principle? " No; it is the *last!* " This grammatical error might have been avoided by saying, "*Letters* are the first principles, or least parts, of words." But still the definition would not be true, nor would it answer the question, What is a letter? The true answer to which is: "A letter is an alphabetic *character*, which commonly represents some elementary sound of human articulation, or speech."

14 This true definition sufficiently distinguishes letters from the marks used in punctuation, because the latter are not alphabetic, and they represent silence, rather than sound; and also from the Arabic figures used for numbers, because these are no part of any alphabet, and they represent certain entire words, none of which consists only of one letter, or of a single element of articulation. The same may be said of all the characters used for abbreviation; as, & for *and*, $ for *dollars*, or the marks peculiar to mathematicians, to astronomers, to druggists, &c. None of these are alphabetic, and they represent significant words, and not single elementary sounds: it would be great dullness, to assume that a word and an elementary sound are one and the same thing. But the reader will observe that this definition embraces *no idea* contained in the faulty one to which I am objecting; neither indeed could it, without a blunder. So wide from the mark is that notion of a letter, which the popularity of Dr. Lowth and his copyists has made a hundred fold more common than any other![*] According to an other erroneous definition given by these same gentlemen, " *Words* are articulate *sounds*, used by common consent, as signs of our ideas."—*Murray's Gram.* p. 22; *Kirkham's*, 20; *Ingersoll's*, 7; *Alger's*, 12; *Russell's*, 7; *Merchant's*, 9; *Fisk's*, 11; *Greenleaf's*, 20; and many others. See *Lowth's Gram.* p. 6; from which almost all authors have taken the notion, that words consist of " *sounds* " only. But letters are no principles or parts of *sounds* at all; unless you will either have visible marks to be sounds, or the sign to be a principle or part of the thing signified. Nor are they always principles or parts of *words*: we sometimes write what is *not a word*; as when, by letters, we denote pronunciation alone, or imitate brute voices. If words were formed of articulate sounds only, they could not exist in books, or be in any wise known to the deaf and dumb. These two primary definitions, then, are both false; and, taken together, they involve the absurdity of dividing things acknowledged to be indivisible. In utterance, we cannot divide consonants from their vowels; on paper, we can. Hence letters are the least parts of written language only; but the least parts of spoken words are syllables, and not letters. Every definition of a consonant implies this.

15 They who cannot define a letter or a word, may be expected to err in explaining other grammatical terms. In my opinion, nothing is well written, that

---

[*] It is truly astonishing that so great a majority of our grammarians could have been so blindly misled, as they have been, in this matter; and the more so, because a very good definition of a Letter was both published and republished, about the time at which Lowth's first appeared: viz., " What is a letter? A Letter is the Sign, Mark, or Character of a simple or uncompounded Sound. Are Letters Sounds? No. Letters are only the Signs or Symbols of Sounds, not the Sounds themselves."— *The British Grammar*, p. 8. See the very same words on the second page of *Buchanan's* " *English Syntax*," a work which was published as early as 1767.

can possibly be misunderstood; and if any definition be likely to *suggest* a wrong idea, this alone is enough to condemn it: nor does it justify the phraseology, to say, that a more reasonable construction can be put upon it. By Murray and others, the young learner is told, that, "A *vowel* is an articulate *sound*, that can be perfectly *uttered by itself;*" as if a vowel were nothing but a sound, and that a sort of echo, which can *utter itself;* and next, that, "A *consonant* is an articulate *sound*, which cannot be perfectly uttered *without the help of* a vowel." Now, by their own showing, every letter is either a vowel or a consonant; hence, according to these definitions, all the letters are articulate *sounds*. And, if so, what is a "silent letter?" It is a *silent articulate sound!* Again: ask a boy, "What is a *triphthong?*" He answers in the words of Murray, Weld, Pond, Smith, Adams, Kirkham, Merchant, Ingersoll, Bacon, Alger, and others: "A triphthong is the union of three vowels, *pronounced in like manner:* as *eau* in beau, *iew* in view." He accurately cites an entire paragraph from his grammar, but does he well conceive how the three vowels in *beau* or *view* are "pronounced *in like manner?*" Again: "A *syllable* is a *sound*, either simple or *compounded*, pronounced by a single impulse of the voice."—*Murray's Gram.* 8vo, p. 22. This definition resolves syllables into *sounds:* whereas their true elements are *letters*. It also mistakes the participle *compounded* for the adjective *compound;* whereas the latter only is the true reverse of *simple*. A compound sound is a sound composed of others which may be separated; a *sound compounded* is properly that which is made an ingredient with others, but which may itself be simple.

16. It is observable, that in their attempts to explain these prime elements of grammar, Murray, and many others who have copied him, overlook all *written* language; whereas their very science itself took its origin, name, and nature, from the invention of writing; and has consequently no bearing upon any dialect which has not been written. Their definitions absurdly resolve letters, vowels, consonants, syllables, and words, all into *sounds;* as if none of these things had any existence on paper, or any significance to those who read in silence. Hence, their explanations of all these elements, as well as of many other things equally essential to the study, are palpably erroneous. I attribute this to the carelessness with which men have compiled or made up books of grammar; and that carelessness to those various circumstances, already described, which have left diligence in a grammarian no hope of praise or reward. Without alluding here to my own books, no one being obliged to accuse himself, I doubt whether we have any school grammar that is much less objectionable in this respect, than Murray's; and yet I am greatly mistaken, if nine tenths of all the definitions in Murray's system are not faulty. "It was this sort of definitions, which made *Scaliger* say, ' *Nihil infelicius definitore grammatico.*'" See *Johnson's Gram. Com.* p. 351; *also paragraph 5th above.*

17. Nor can this objection be neutralized by saying, it is a mere matter of opinion—a mere prejudice originating in rivalry. For, though we have ample choice of terms, and may frequently assign to particular words a meaning and an explanation which are in some degree arbitrary; yet whenever we attempt to define things under the name which custom has positively fixed upon them, we are no longer left to arbitrary explications; but are bound to think and to say that only which shall commend itself to the understanding of others, as being altogether true to nature. When a word is well understood to denote a particular object or class of objects, the definition of it ought to be in strict conformity to what is known of the real being and properties of the thing or things contemplated. A definition of this kind is a proposition susceptible of proof and illustration; and therefore whatsoever is erroneously assumed to be the proper meaning of such a term, may be refuted. But those persons who take every thing upon trust, and choose both to learn and to teach mechanically, often become so slavishly habituated to the peculiar phraseology of their text-books, that, be the absurdity of a particular expres-

sion what it may, they can neither discover nor suspect any inaccuracy in it. It is also very natural even for minds more independent and acute, to regard with some reverence whatsoever was gravely impressed upon them in childhood. Hence the necessity that all school-books should proceed from skillful hands. Instruction should tell things as they are, and never falter through negligence.

18. I have admitted that definitions are not the only means by which a general knowledge of the import of language may be acquired; nor are they the only means by which the acquisition of such knowledge may be aided. To exhibit or point out *things* and tell their names, constitutes a large part of that instruction by which the meaning of words is conveyed to the young mind; and, in many cases, a mere change or apposition of terms may sufficiently explain our idea. But when we would guard against the possibility of misapprehension, and show precisely what is meant by a word, we must fairly define it. There are, however, in every language, many words which do not admit of a formal definition. ' The import of all definitive and connecting particles must be learned from usage, translation, or derivation; and nature reserves to herself the power of explaining the objects of our simple original perceptions. "All words standing for complex ideas are definable; but those by which we denote simple ideas, are not. For the perceptions of this latter class, having no other entrance into the mind, than by sensation or reflection, can be acquired only by experience."—*Duncan's Logic*, p. 63. "And thus we see, that as our simple ideas are the materials and foundation of knowledge, so the names of simple ideas may be considered as the elementary parts of language, beyond which we cannot trace the meaning and signification of words. When we come to them, we suppose the ideas for which they stand to be already known; or, if they are not, experience alone must be consulted, and not definitions or explications."—*Ibid.* p. 69.

19. But this is no apology for the defectiveness of any definition which might be made correct, or for the defectiveness of our English grammars, in the frequent omission of all explanation, and the more frequent adoption of some indirect form of expression. It is often much easier to make some loose observation upon what is meant by a given word or term in science, than to frame a faultless definition of the thing; because it is easier to refer to some of the relations, qualities, offices, or attributes of things, than to discern wherein their essence consists, so as to be able to tell directly and clearly what they are. The improvement of our grammatical code in this respect, was one of the principal objects which I thought it needful to attempt. when I first took up the pen as a grammarian. I cannot pretend to have seen, of course, every definition and rule which has been published on this subject; but, if I do not misjudge a service too humble for boasting, I have myself framed a greater number of new or improved ones, than all other English grammarians together. And not a few of them have, since their first publication in 1823, been complimented to a place in other grammars than my own. This is in good keeping with the authorship which has been spoken of in an other chapter; but I am constrained to say, it affords no proof that they were well written. If it did, the definitions and rules in Murray's grammar must undoubtedly be thought the most correct that ever have been given: they have been more frequently copied than any others.

20. But I have ventured to suggest, that nine tenths of this author's definitions are bad, or at least susceptible of some amendment. If this can be shown to the satisfaction of the reader, will he hope to find an other English grammar in which the eye of criticism may not detect errors and deficiencies with the same ease? My object is, to enforce attention to the proprieties of speech; and this is the very purpose of all grammar. To exhibit here all Murray's definitions, with criticisms upon them, would detain us too long. We must therefore be content to take a part of them as a sample. And, not to be accused of fixing only upon the worst, we will take a *series.* Let us then consider in their order his definitions of the

nine parts of speech;—for, calling the participle a verb, he reduces the sorts of words to that number. And though not one of his nine definitions now stands exactly as it did in his early editions, I think it may be said, that not one of them is now, if it ever has been, expressed grammatically.

21. FIRST DEFINITION :—"An Article is a word *prefixed* to substantives, *to point them out*, and to show how far *their*[*] signification extends."—*Murray, and others, from Lowth's Gram.* p. 10. This is obscure. In what manner, or in what respect, does an article point out substantives ? To point them out *as such*, or to show which words are substantives, seems at first view to be the meaning intended ; but it is said soon after, "*A* or *an* is used in a vague sense, to *point out* one single *thing* of the kind, in other respects *indeterminate ;* as, 'Give me *a* book ' ; 'Bring me *an* apple.' "—*Lowth*, p. 11 ; *Murray*, p. 31. And again : "It is *of the nature* of both the articles to determine or limit *the thing* spoken of."—*Murray's Gram.* 8vo, p. 170. Now, to point out *nouns* among the parts of speech, and to point out *things* as individuals of their class, are very different matters ; and which of these is the purpose for which articles are used, according to Lowth and Murray ? Their definition says the former, their explanations imply the latter ; and I am unable to determine which they really meant. The term *placed before* would have been better than "*prefixed ;*" because the latter commonly implies junction, as well as location. The word "*indeterminate*" is not a very easy one for a boy ; and, when he has found out what it means, he may possibly not know to which of the four preceding nouns, it ought to be referred :—"in a vague *sense*, to point out one single *thing* of the *kind*, in other *respects* indeterminate." What is this "vague sense ? " and what is it, that is "indeterminate ? "

22. SECOND DEFINITION :—"A Substantive or Noun is the name of any thing *that* exists, or of *which* we have any notion."—*Murray, and others*. According to his own syntax, this sentence of Murray's is wrong ; for he himself suggests, that when two or more relative clauses refer to the same antecedent, the same pronoun should be used in each Of clauses connected like these, this is true. He should therefore have said, "A Substantive, or Noun, is the name of any thing *which* exists, or of *which* we have any notion." His rule, however, though good against a text like this, is utterly wrong in regard to many others, and not very accurate in taking *two* for a "*series*," thus : " Whatever relative is used, in one of a *series* of clauses relating to the same antecedent, the same relative ought, generally to be used in *them all*. In the following sentence, *this rule is violated :* ' It is remarkable, that Holland, against *which* the war was undertaken, and *that*, in the very beginning, was reduced to the brink of destruction, lost nothing.' The clause ought to have been, 'and *which* in the very beginning.' "—*Murray's Gram.* 8vo, p. 155. But both the rule and the example, badly as they correspond, were borrowed from Priestley's Grammar, p. 102, where the text stands thus : " Whatever relative *be* used, in one of a *series* of clauses, relating to the same antecedent, the same ought to be used in *them all*. ' It is remarkable, that Holland,' " &c.

23. THIRD DEFINITION :—"An Adjective is a word added to a substantive, to express *its* quality."—*Lowth, Murray, Bullions, Pond, and others*. Here we have the choice of two meanings ; but neither of them is according to truth. It seems doubtful whether " *its* quality " is the *adjective's* quality, or the *substantive's ;* but in either sense, the phrase is false ; for an adjective is added to a noun, not to express any quality either of the adjective or of the noun, but to express some quality of the *thing signified* by the noun. But the definition is too much restricted ; for adjectives may be added to pronouns as well as to nouns, nor do they always express *quality*.

24. FOURTH DEFINITION :—"A Pronoun is a word used instead of a noun, to *avoid* the too frequent repetition of *the same word*."—*Dr. Ash's Gram.* p. 25 ;

---

[*] In Murray's octavo Grammar, this word is *the* in the first chapter, and *their* in the second ; in the duodecimo, it is *their* in both places.

Murray's, 28 and 50; *Felton's*, 18; *Alger's*, 18; *Bacon's*, 10; *and others.*
The latter part of this sentence is needless, and also contains several errors. 1.
The verb *avoid* is certainly very ill-chosen; because it implies intelligent agency,
and not that which is merely instrumental. 2. The article *the* is misemployed for
a; for, "*the* too frequent repetition," should mean *some particular* too frequent
repetition—an idea not intended here, and in itself not far from absurdity. 3.
The phrase, "*the same word*," may apply to the pronoun itself as well as to the
noun : in saying, "*I* came, *I* saw, *I* conquered," there is as frequent a repetition
of *the same word*, as in saying, "*Cæsar* came, *Cæsar* saw, *Cæsar* conquered."
If, therefore, the latter part of this definition must be retained, the whole should
be written thus : "A Pronoun is a word used *in stead* of a noun, to *prevent* too
frequent *a* repetition of *it*."

25. FIFTH DEFINITION :—"A Verb is a word which signifies *to be, to do*, or *to
suffer*."—*Lowth, Murray, and others.* NOTE :—"A verb may generally be
distinguished by *its making sense* with any of the personal pronouns, or the word
to before it."—*Murray, and others.* It is confessedly difficult to give a perfect
definition of a *verb;* and if, with Murray, we will have the participles to be verbs,
there must be no small difficulty in forming one that shall be tolerable. Against
the foregoing old explanation, it may be objected, that the phrase *to suffer*, being
now understood in a more limited sense than formerly, does not well express the
nature or import of a passive verb. I have said, "A Verb is a word that signifies
to be, to act, or *to be acted upon*." Children cannot readily understand, how
every thing that is in any way *acted upon*, may be said *to suffer*. The participle,
I think, should be taken as a distinct part of speech, and have its own definition.
The note added by Murray to his definition of a verb, would prove the participle
not to be included in this part of speech, and thus practically contradict his scheme.
It is also objectionable in respect to construction. The phrase "*by its making
sense*" is at least very questionable English ; for "*its making*" supposes *making*
to be a noun, and "*making sense*" supposes it to be an active participle. But
Lowth says, "Let it be either the one or the other, and abide by its own construction." Nay, the author himself, though he therein contradicts an other note of his
own, virtually condemns the phrase, by his caution to the learner against treating
words in *ing*, "as if they were of an *amphibious species*, partly nouns and partly
verbs."—*Murray's Gram.* 8vo, p. 193.

26. SIXTH DEFINITION :—"*An* Adverb is *a part of speech joined* to a verb,
an adjective, *and sometimes to* another adverb, to express some *quality* or *circumstance* respecting *it*."—*Murray's Gram.* p. 28 and 114. See *Dr. Ash's Gram.*
p. 47. This definition contains many errors ; some of which are gross blunders.
1. The first word, "*An*," is erroneously put for *The: an* adverb is *one* adverb,
not the whole class; and, if, "*An* adverb is *a part of speech*," any and every
adverb is a part of speech ; then, how many parts of speech are there? 2. The
word "*joined*" is not well chosen; for, with the exception of *cannot*, the adverb
is very rarely *joined* to the word to which it relates. 3. The want of a comma
before *joined*, perverts the construction; for the phrase, "*speech joined* to a
verb," is nonsense; and to suppose *joined* to relate to the noun *part*, is not much
better. 4. The word "*and*" should be *or;* because no adverb is ever added to
three or four different terms at once. 5. The word "*sometimes*" should be
omitted ; because it is needless, and because it is inconsistent with the only
conjunction which will make the definition true. 6. The preposition "*to*" should
either be inserted before "*an adjective*," or suppressed before the term which follows;
for when several words occur in the same construction, uniformity of expression is
desirable. 7. For the same reason, (if custom may be thus far conformed to
analogy,) the article "*an*" ought, in cases like this, if not always, to be separated
from the word *other;* thus, "An adverb is a word addded to *a* verb, *a* participle,
an adjective, or *an* other adverb." Were the eye not familiar with it, *another*

would be thought as irregular as *theother*. 8. The word "*quality*" is wrong; for no adverb ever expresses any *quality*, as such; qualities are expressed by *adjectives*, and never, in any direct manner, by adverbs. 9. The "*circumstances*" which we express by adverbs never belong to the *words*, as this definition avers that they do, but always to the *actions* or *qualities* which the words signify. 10. The pronoun *it*, according to Murray's second rule of syntax, ought to be *them*, and so it stands in his own early editions; but if *and* be changed to *or*, as I have said it should be, the pronoun *it* will be right.

27. SEVENTH DEFINITION :—"Prepositions serve to connect words with *one another*, and to show the relation *between them*."—*Lowth, Murray, and others*. This is only an observation, not a definition, as it ought to have been; nor does it at all distinguish the preposition from the conjunction. It does not reach the thing in question. Besides, it contains an actual solecism in the expression. The word "*between*" implies *but two* things; and the phrase "*one another*" is not applicable where there are but two. It should be, "to connect words with *each other*, and to show the *relation between* them;"—or else, "to connect words with *one or other*, and to show the *relations among* them." But the latter mode of expression would not apply to prepositions considered severally, but only to the whole class.

28. EIGHTH DEFINITION :—"*A* Conjunction is *a part of speech* that is *chiefly used* to connect sentences; so as, out of two *or more* sentences, to make but one: it sometimes connects only words."—*Murray, and others*. Here are more than thirty words, awkwardly and loosely strung together; and all that is said in them, might be much better expressed in half the number. For example : "A Conjunction is a word which connects other terms, and commonly of two sentences makes but one." But verbosity and want of unity are not the worst faults of this definition. We have three others to point out. 1. "*A* conjunction is" not "*a part of speech*; because *a* conjunction is *one* conjunction, and a part of speech is *a whole class*, or sort, of words. A similar error was noticed in Murray's definition of an adverb; and so common has this blunder become, that by a comparison of the definitions which different authors have given of the parts of speech, probably it will be found, that, by some hand or other, every one of the ten has been commenced in this way. 2. The words "*or more*" are erroneous, and ought to be omitted; for no one conjunction can connect more than two terms, in that consecutive order which the sense requires. Three or more simple sentences may indeed form a compound sentence; but, as they cannot be joined in a *cluster*, they must have two or more connectives. 3. The last clause erroneously suggests, that any or every conjunction "*sometimes connects only words;*" but the conjunctions which may connect only words, are not more than five, whereas those which connect only sentences are four times as many.

29. NINTH DEFINITION :—"Interjections are words *thrown in between the parts of a sentence*, to express the passions or emotions of the *speaker*; as, 'O Virtue! how amiable thou art!'"—*Murray, and many others*. This definition, which has been copied from grammar to grammar, and committed to memory millions of times, is obviously erroneous, and directly contradicted by the example. Interjections, though often enough thrown in between the parts of a *discourse*, are very rarely "thrown in between the parts of a *sentence*." They more frequently occur at the beginning of a sentence than any where else; and, in such cases, they do not come under this narrow definition. The author, at the head of his chapter on interjections, appends to this definition two other examples; both of which contradict it in like manner: "*Oh!* I have alienated my friend."—"*Alas!* I fear for life." Again: Interjections are used occasionally, in *written*, as well as in *oral* discourse; nor are they less indicative of the emotions of the *writer*, than of those "of the *speaker*."

30. I have thus exhibited, with all intentional fairness of criticism, the entire

series of these nine primary definitions ; and the reader may judge whether they sustain the praises which have been bestowed on the book,* or confirm the allegations which I have made against it. He will understand that my design is, here, as well as in the body of this work, to teach grammar practically, by *rectifying*, so far as I may, all sorts of mistakes either in it or respecting it ; to compose a book which, by a condensed exposition of such errors as are commonly found in other grammars, will at once show the need we have of a better, and be itself a fit substitute for the principal treatises which it censures. Grammatical errors are universally considered to be small game for critics. They must therefore be very closely grouped together, to be worth their room in this work. Of the tens of thousands who have learned for grammar a multitude of ungrammatical definitions and rules, comparatively few will ever know what I have to say of their acquisitions. But this I cannot help. To the readers of the present volume it is due, that its averments should be clearly illustrated by particular examples ; and it is reasonable that these should be taken from the most accredited sources, whether they do honour to their framers or not. My argument is only made so much the stronger, as the works which furnish its proofs, are the more esteemed, the more praised, or the more overrated.

31. Murray tells us, "There is no necessary connexion between words and ideas."—*Octavo Gram* i, 139. Though this, as I before observed, is not altogether true, he doubtless had very good reason to distinguish, in his teaching, "between *the sign* and *the thing signified*." Yet, in his own definitions and explanations, he frequently *confounds* these very things which he declares to be so widely different as not even to have a "necessary connexion" Errors of this kind are very common in all our English grammars Two instances occur in the following sentence ; which also contains an error in doctrine, and is moreover obscure, or rather, in its literal sense, palpably absurd : "To substantives belong gender, number, and case ; and *they* are *all of* the third person *when spoken of*, and of the second person *when spoken to*."—*Murray's Gram.* 38 ; *Alger's Murray*, 16 ; *Merchant's*, 23 ; *Bacon's*, 12 ; *Maltby's*, 12 ; *Lyon's*, 7 ; *Guy's*, 4 ; *Ingersoll's*, 26 ; *S Putnam's*, 13 ; *T. H Miller's*, 17 ; *Rev. T. Smith's*, 13. Who, but a child taught by language like this, would ever think of *speaking to a noun* ? or, that a noun of the second person *could not be spoken of*? or, that a noun cannot be put in the *first person*, so as to agree with *I* or *we* ? Murray himself once taught, that, "Pronouns *must always agree* with their antecedents, *and* the nouns for which they stand, in gender, number, and *person* ; " and he departed from a true and important principle of syntax, when he altered his rule to its present form. But I have said that the sentence above is obscure, or its meaning absurd. What does the pronoun "*they*" represent? "*Substantives*," according to the author's intent ; but "*gender, number*, and *case*," according to the obvious construction of the words. Let us try a parallel : "To scriveners belong pen, ink, and paper ; and *they* are all of primary importance when there is occasion to use them, and of none at all when they are not needed." Now, if this sentence is *obscure*, the other is not less so ; but, if this is perfectly *clear*, so that what is said is obviously and only what is intended, then it is equally clear, that what is said in the former, is gross absurdity, and that the words cannot reasonably be construed into the sense which the writer, and his copyists, designed.

32 All Murray's grammars, not excepting the two volumes octavo, are as *incomplete* as they are *inaccurate ;* being deficient in many things which are of so great importance that they should not be excluded from the very smallest epitome. For example : On the subject of the *numbers*, he attempted but one definition, and that is a fourfold solecism. He speaks of the *persons*, but gives neither definitions

nor explanations. In treating of the *genders*, he gives but one formal definition. His section on the *cases* contains no regular definition. On the *comparison* of adjectives, and on the *moods* and *tenses* of verbs, he is also satisfied with a very loose mode of teaching. The work as a whole exhibits more industry than literary taste, more benevolence of heart than distinctness of apprehension ; and, like all its kindred and progeny, fails to give to the principles of grammar that degree of clearness of which they are easily susceptible. The student does not know this, but he feels the effects of it, in the obscurity of his own views on the subject, and in the conscious uncertainty with which he applies those principles. In grammar, the terms *person, number, gender, case, mood, tense*, and many others, are used in a technical and peculiar sense ; and, in all scientific works, the sense of technical terms should be clearly and precisely defined. Nothing can be gained by substituting other names of modern invention ; for these also would need definitions as much as the old. We want to know the things themselves, and what they are most appropriately called. We want a book which will tell us, in proper order, and in the plainest manner, what all the elements of the science are.

33. What does he know of grammar, who cannot directly and properly answer such questions as these ?—" What are numbers, in grammar ? What is the singular number ? What is the plural number ? What are persons, in grammar ? What is the first person ? What is the second person ? What is the third person ? What are genders, in grammar ? What is the masculine gender ? What is the feminine gender ? What is the neuter gender ? What are cases, in grammar ? What is the nominative case ? What is the possessive case ? What is the objective case ?"—And yet the most complete acquaintance with every sentence or word of Murray's tedious compilation, may leave the student at a loss for a proper answer, not only to each of these questions, but also to many others equally simple and elementary ! A boy may learn by heart all that Murray ever published on the subject of grammar, and still be left to confound the numbers in grammar with numbers in arithmetic, or the persons in grammar with persons in civil life ! Nay, there are among the professed *improvers* of this system of grammar, men who have actually confounded these things, which are so totally different in their natures ! In "Smith's New Grammar on the Productive System," a work in which Murray is largely copied and strangely metamorphosed, there is an abundance of such confusion. For instance : "What is the meaning of the word *number* ? Number means *a sum that may be counted.*"—*R. C. Smith's New Gram* p. 7. From this, by a tissue of half a dozen similar absurdities, called *inductions*, the novice is brought to the conclusion that the numbers are two—as if there were in nature but two sums that might be counted ! There is no end to the sickening detail of such blunders. How many grammars tell us, that, "The first person is the *person who speaks ;* " that, "The second person is the *person spoken to ;* " and that, "the third person is the *person spoken of !* " As if the three persons of a verb, or other part of speech, were so many *intelligent beings !* As if, by exhibiting a word in the three persons, (as *go, goest, goes,*) we put it first *into the speaker*, then *into the hearer*, and then *into somebody else !* Nothing can be more abhorrent to grammar, or to sense, than such confusion. The things which are identified in each of these three definitions, are as unlike as Socrates and moonshine ! The one is a thinking being ; the other, a mere form peculiar to certain words. But Chandler, of Philadelphia, (" the Grammar King," forsooth !) without mistaking the grammatical persons for rational souls, has contrived to crowd into his definition of *person* more errors of conception and of language,— more insult to common sense.—than one could have believed it possible to put together in such space. And this ridiculous old twaddle, after six and twenty years, he has deliberately re-written and lately republished as something "adapted to the schools of America." It stands thus : "*Person is a distinction which is made in a noun between its representation of its object, either as spoken to, or*

spoken of."—Chandler's E. Grammar, Edition of 1821, p. 16 ; Ed. 1847, p. 21.

34. Grammarians have often failed in their definitions, because it is impossible to define certain terms in the way in which the description has been commonly attempted. He who undertakes what is impossible must necessarily fail ; and fail too, to the discredit of his ingenuity. It is manifest that whenever a generic name in the singular number is to be defined, the definition must be founded upon some property or properties common to all the particular things included under the term. Thus, if I would define a *globe*, a *wheel*, or a *pyramid*, my description must be taken, not from what is peculiar to one or an other of these things, but from those properties only which are common to all globes, all wheels, or all pyramids. But what property has *unity* in common with *plurality*, on which a definition of *number* may be founded ? What common property have the *three cases*, by which we can clearly define *case* ? What have the *three persons* in common, which, in a definition of *person*, could be made evident to a child ? Thus all the great classes of grammatical modifications, namely, *persons, numbers, genders, cases, moods*, and *tenses*, though they admit of easy, accurate, and obvious definitions in the plural, can scarcely be defined at all in the singular. I do not say, that the terms *person, number, gender, case, mood*, and *tense*, in their technical application to grammar, are all of them equally and absolutely undefinable in the singular ; but I say, that no definition, just in sense and suitable for a child, can ever be framed for any one of them. Among the thousand varied attempts of grammarians to explain them so, there are a hundred gross solecisms for every tolerable definition. For this, as I have shown, there is a very simple reason in the nature of the things.

35. But this reason, as well as many other truths equally important and equally clear, our common grammarians, have, so far as I know, every man of them overlooked. Consequently, even when they were aiming at the right thing, they frequently fell into gross errors of expression ; and, what is still more surprising, such errors have been entailed upon the very art of grammar, and the art of authorship itself, by the prevalence of an absurd notion, that modern writers on this subject can be meritorious authors without originality. Hence many a school-boy is daily rehearsing from his grammar-book what he might well be ashamed to have written. For example, the following definition from Murray's grammar, is found in perhaps a dozen other compends, all professing to teach the art of speaking and writing with propriety : "*Number is the consideration of an object, as one or more.*"[*] Yet

[*] For this definition, see *Murray's Gram.* 8vo, p. 40 ; *Duodecimo*, 41 ; *Smaller Gram.* 18 ; *Alger's*, 18 ; *Bacon's*, 15 ; *Frost's*, 8 ; *Ingersoll's*, 17 ; *A Teacher's*, 8 ; *Maltby's*, 14 ; *T. H. Miller's*, 20 ; *Pond's*, 18 ; *S. Putnam's*, 15 ; *Russell's*, 11 ; *Merchant's Murray*, 25 ; and *Worcester's Univ. and Crit. Dictionary*. Many other grammarians have attempted to define *number* ; with what success a few examples will show : (1.) "Number is the distinction of one from many."—*Allen's Gram.* p. 40 ; *Merchant's School Gram.* 28 ; *Greenleaf's*, 22 ; *Nutting's*, 17 ; *Picket's*, 19 ; *D. Adams's*, 31. (2.) "Number is the distinction of one from more."—*Fisher's Gram.* 51 ; *Alden's*, 7. (3.) "Number is the distinction of one from several or many."—*Coar's Gram.* p. 24. (4.) "Number is the distinction of one from more than one."—*Sanborn's Gram.* p. 24 ; *J Flint's*, 27 ; *Well's*, 52. (5.) "Number is the distinction of one from more than one, or many."—*Grant's Latin Gram.* p. 7. (6.) "What is number ? Number is the Distinction of one, from two, or many."—*British Gram.* p. 89 ; *Buchanan's*, 16. (7.) "You inquire, 'What is number ?' Merely this : the *distinction* of one from two, or many. Greek substantives have *three* numbers."—*Burke's Classical Gram.* p 38. All these authors say, that, in English, "there are *two numbers*, the singular and the plural." According to their explanations then, we have *two* "*distinctions of one from two, several, more, or many* :" and the Greeks, by adding a dual number, have *three!* Which, then, of the two or three modifications or forms, do they mean, when they say, "Number is *the distinction*," &c.? Or, if none of them, *what else* is meant? All these definitions had their origin in an old Latin one, which, although it is somewhat better, makes doubtful logic in its application : "NUMERUS est, unius et multorum distinctio. Numeri *igitur* sunt *duo* : Singularis et Pluralis."—*Ruddiman's Gram*, p 21. This means : (8.) "Number is a distinction of one and many. The numbers *therefore* are *two* : the Singular and the Plural." But we have yet other examples : as, (9.) "Number is the distinction of objects, as one or more."—*Kirkham's Gram.* p. 39. "The *distinction of objects as one*," is very much like "the *consideration of an object as more than one!*" (10.) "Number distinguishes objects as one or more."—*Cooper's Murray*, p. 21 ; *Practical Gram.* p 18. That is, number makes the plural to be either plural or singular for distinction's sake ! (11.) "Number is the distinction of *nouns* with regard to the *objects* signified, *as one* or *more*."—*Fisk's Murray*, p. 19. Here, too, number has "regard" to the same confusion ; while, by a gross error, its "distinction" is confined to "*nouns*" only ! (12.) "Number is *that property of a noun* by which it expresses *one* or *more* than one."—*Bullions's E. Gram.* p. 12 ; *Analyt Gram* 26. Here again number is improperly limited to "*a noun* :" and is said to be one sign of two, or either of two, incompatible ideas ! (13.) "Number shows *how many* are meant whether one or more."—*Smith's New Gram.* p. 45. This is not a *definition*, but a false assertion, in which Smith again confounds arithmetic with grammar ! *Wheat* and *oats* are of different numbers ; but neither of these numbers "means a *sum that may be counted*," or really "shows *how many* are meant." So of "*Man* in general, *Horses* in general, &c."—

this short sentence, as I have before suggested, is a fourfold solecism. *First*, the word " *number* " is wrong; because those modifications of language, which distinguish unity and plurality, cannot be jointly signified by it. *Secondly*, the word "*consideration*" is wrong; because *number* is not *consideration*, in any sense which can be put upon the terms: *condition, constitution, configuration*, or any other word beginning with *con*, would have done just as well. *Thirdly*, " the consideration of *an* object as *one*," is but idle waste of thought; for, that one thing is one,—that *an* object is *one* object,—every child knows by *intuition*, and not by "*consideration*." *Lastly*, to consider " *an* object as *more* " than one, is impossible; unless this admirable definition lead us into a misconception in so plain a case! So much for the art of " the grammatical definer."

36. Many other examples, equally faulty and equally common, might be quoted and criticised for the further proof and illustration of what I have alleged. But the reader will perhaps judge the foregoing to be sufficient. I have wished to be brief, and yet to give my arguments, and the neglected facts upon which they rest, their proper force upon the mind. Against such prejudices as may possibly arise from the authorship of rival publications, or from any interest in the success of one book rather than of an other, let both my judges and me be on our guard. I have intended to be fair; for captiousness is not criticism. If the reader perceives in these strictures any improper bias, he has a sort of discernment which it is my misfortune to lack. Against the compilers of grammars, I urge no conclusions at which any man can hesitate, who accedes to my preliminary remarks upon them; and these may be summed up in the following couplet of the poet Churchill:

> " To copy beauties, forfeits all pretence
> To fame;—to copy faults, is want of sense."

Brightland's Gram. p. 77. (14.) " Number is *the difference* in a *noun or pronoun*, to denote either a single thing or more than one."—*Davenport's Gram*. p. 14. This excludes the numbers of a *verb*, and makes the singular and the plural to be essentially one thing. (15.) " Number is a modification of nouns and verbs, according as the thing spoken of is represented, as, *one* or *more*, with regard to number."—*Burn's Gram*. p. 42. This also has many faults, which I leave to the discernment of the reader. (16.) " What is number? *number shows the distinction* of one from many."—*Wilcox's Gram*. p. 6. This is no answer to the question asked; besides, it is obviously worse than the first form, which has " *is*," for " *shows*." (17.) " What is Number? It is *the representation* of *objects* with respect to singleness, or plurality."—*O. B. Peirce's Gram*. p. 34. If there are two numbers, they are neither of them properly described in this definition, or in any of the preceding ones. There is a gross misconception, in taking each or either of them to be an alternate representation of two incompatible ideas. And this sort of error is far from being confined to the present subject; it runs through a vast number of the various definitions contained in our grammars. (18.) " *Number is the expression* of a *noun*, to indicate *one object or more than one*. Or, *Number is the expression* of unity or of more than unity."—*Hiley's Gram*. p. 14. How hard this author laboured to *think what number is*, and could not! (19.) " Number is the distinction *of unity and plurality* "—*Hart's E. Gram*. p. 40. Why say, " *distinction*," the *numbers*, or *distinctions*, being two? (20.) " Number is *the capacity of nouns* to represent either *one* or *more* than one object."—*Barrett's Revised Gram*. p. 40. (21.) " Number is *a property of the noun* which denotes *one* or *more* than one."—*Weld's Gram*. 2d Ed. p. 55. (22.) " Number is *a modification of nouns* to denote whether one object is meant, or more than one."—*Butler's Gram*. p. 19. Many of the grammarians have not attempted any definition of *number*, or of *the numbers*, though they speak of both the singular and the plural, and perhaps sometimes apply the term *number to the distinction* which is *in each*: for it is the property of the singular number, to distinguish unity from plurality; and of the plural, to distinguish plurality from unity. Among the authors who are thus silent, are Lily, Colet, Brightland, Harris, Lowth, Ash, Priestley, Bicknell, Adam, Gould, Harrison, Comly, Jaudon, Webster, Webber, Churchill, Sanborn, Leonie, Dalton, Blair, Cobbett, Cobb, A. Flint, Felch, Guy, Hall, and S. W. Clark. Adam and Gould, however, in explaining the properties of *verbs*, say: " *Number* marks *how many* we suppose to be, to us, or to suffer."—*A*. 80; *G*. 78.

CHAPTER XI.

BRIEF NOTICES OF THE SCHEMES OF CERTAIN GRAMMARS.

———◆———

"Sed ut perveniri ad summa nisi ex principiis non potest : ita, procedente jam opere, minima incipiunt esse quae prima sunt."—QUINTILIAN. Lib. x, Cap. 1, p. 560.

———◆———

1. The *history* of grammar, in the proper sense of the term, has heretofore been made no part of the study. I have imagined that many of its details might be profitable, not only to teachers, but to that class of learners for whose use this work is designed. Accordingly, in the preceding pages, there have been stated numerous facts properly historical, relating either to particular grammars, or to the changes and progress of this branch of instruction. These various details it is hoped will be more entertaining, and perhaps for that reason not less useful, than those explanations which belong merely to the construction and resolution of sentences. The attentive reader must have gathered from the foregoing chapters some idea of what the science owes to many individuals whose names are connected with it. But it seems proper to devote to this subject a few pages more, in order to give some further account of the origin and character of certain books.

2. The manuals by which grammar was first taught in English, were not properly English Grammars. They were translations of the Latin Accidence ; and were designed to aid British youth in acquiring a knowledge of the Latin language, rather than accuracy in the use of their own. The two languages were often combined in one book, for the purpose of teaching sometimes both together, and sometimes one through the medium of the other. The study of such works doubtless had a tendency to modify, and perhaps at that time to improve, the English style of those who used them. For not only must variety of knowledge have led to copiousness of expression, but the most cultivated minds would naturally be most apt to observe what was orderly in the use of speech. A language, indeed, after its proper form is well fixed by letters, must resist all introduction of foreign idioms, or become corrupted. Hence it is, that Dr. Johnson avers, "The great pest of speech is frequency of translation. No book was ever turned from one language into another, without imparting something of its native idiom ; this is the most mischievous and comprehensive innovation."— *Pref. to Joh. Dict.* 4to, p. 14. Without expressly controverting this opinion, or offering any justification of mere metaphrases, or literal translations, we may well assert, that the practice of comparing different languages, and seeking the most appropriate terms for a free version of what is ably written, is an excercise admirably calculated to familiarize and extend grammatical knowledge.

3. Of the class of books here referred to, that which I have mentioned in an other chapter, as Lily's or King Henry's Grammar, has been by far the most celebrated and the most influential. Concerning this treatise, it is stated, that its parts were not put together in the present form, until eighteen or twenty years after Lily's death. "The time when this work was completed," says the preface of 1793, "has been differently related by writers. Thomas Hayne places it in the year 1543, and Anthony Wood, in 1545. But neither of these accounts can be right ; for I have seen a beautiful copy, printed upon vellum, and illuminated, anno 1542, in quarto. And it may be doubted whether this was the first edition."—*John Ward, Pref.* p. vii. In an Introductory Lecture, read before the University of London in 1828, by Thomas Dale, professor of English literature, I find the following statement: "In this reign,"—the reign of Henry VIII, —"the study of grammar was reduced to a system, by the promulgation of many

grammatical treatises; one of which was esteemed of sufficient importance to be honoured with a royal name. It was called, 'The Grammar of King Henry the Eighth;' and to this, 'with other works, the young Shakspeare was probably indebted for some learning and much loyalty.' But the honour of producing the first English grammar is claimed by William Bullokar, who published, in the year 1586, 'A Bref Grammar for English,' being, to use his own words, 'the first Grammar for English that ever was, except my Grammar at large.'"

4. Ward's preface to Lily commences thus: " If we look back to the origin of our common *Latin Grammar*, we shall find it was no hasty performance, nor the work of a single person; but composed at different times by several eminent and learned men, till the whole was at length finished, and by the order of *King Henry* VIII.[,] brought into that form in which it has ever since continued. The *English introduction* was written by the reverend and learned Dr. *John Colet*, dean of St. *Paul's*, for the use of the school he had lately founded there; and was dedicated by him to *William Lily*, the first high master of that school, in the year 1510; for which reason it has usually gone by the name of *Paul's Accidence*. The substance of it remains the same, as at first; though it has been much altered in the manner of expression, and sometimes the order, with other improvements. The *English syntax* was the work of *Lily*, as appears by the title in the most ancient editions, which runs thus: *Gulielmi Lilii Angli Rudimenta*. But it has been greatly improved since his time, both with regard to the method, and an enlargement of double the quantity."

5. Paul's Accidence is therefore probably the oldest grammar that can now be found in our language. It is not, however, an English grammar; because, though written in antique English, and embracing many things which are as true of our language as of any other, it was particularly designed for the teaching of *Latin*. It begins thus: " In speech be these eight parts following: Noun, Pronoun, Verb, Participle, declined; Adverb, Conjunction, Preposition, Interjection, undeclined." This is the old platform of the Latin grammarians; which differs from that of the Greek grammars, only in having no Article, and in separating the Interjection from the class of Adverbs. Some Greek grammarians, however, separate the Adjective from the Noun, and include the Participle with the Verb: thus, "There are in Greek eight species of words, called Parts of Speech; viz. Article, Noun, Adjective, Pronoun, Verb, Adverb, Preposition, and Conjunction."— *Anthon's Valpy*, p. 18. With respect to our language, the plan of the Latin Accidence is manifestly inaccurate; nor can it be applied, without some variation, to the Greek. In both, as well as in all other languages that have *Articles*, the best amendment of it, and the nearest adherence to it, is, to make the Parts of Speech *ten*; namely, the Article, the Noun, the Adjective, the Pronoun, the Verb, the Participle, the Adverb, the Conjunction, the Preposition, and the Interjection.

6. The best Latin grammarians admit that the Adjective ought not to be called a Noun; and the best Greek grammarians, that the Interjections ought not to be included among Adverbs. With respect to Participles, a vast majority of grammarians in general, make them a distinct species, or part of speech; but, on this point, the English grammarians are about equally divided: nearly one half include them with the verbs, and a few call them adjectives. In grammar, it is wrong to deviate from the old groundwork, except for the sake of truth and improvement; and, in this case, to vary the series of parts, by suppressing one and substituting an other, is in fact a greater innovation, than to make the terms ten, by adding one and dividing an other. But our men of nine parts of speech innovated yet more: they added the Article, as did the Greeks; divided the Noun into Substantive and Adjective; and, without good reason, suppressed the Participle. And, of latter time, not a few have thrown the whole into confusion, to show the world "the order of [their] understanding." What was grammar fifty years ago, some

of these have not thought it worth their while to inquire! And the reader has seen, that, after all this, they can complacently talk of " the censure so frequently and so justly awarded to *unfortunate innovators*."—KIRKHAM'S *Gram.* p. 10.

7. The old scheme of the Latin grammarians has seldom, if ever, been *literally* followed in English; because its distribution of the parts of speech, as declined and undeclined, would not be true with respect to the English participle. With the omission of this unimportant distinction, it was, however, scrupulously retained by Dilworth, by the author of the British Grammar, by William Ward, by Buchanan, and by some others now little known, who chose to include both the article and the adjective with the noun, rather than to increase the number of the parts of speech beyond eight. Dr. Priestley says, "I shall adopt the *usual distribution* of words into eight classes; viz. Nouns, Adjectives, Pronouns, Verbs, Adverbs, Prepositions, Conjunctions, and Interjections.* I do this in compliance with the practice of most Grammarians; and because, *if any number, in a thing so arbitrary, must be fixed upon*, this seems to be as comprehensive and distinct as any. All the innovation I have made hath been to throw out the *Participle*, and substitute the *Adjective*, as more evidently a distinct part of speech."— *Rudiments of English Gram.* p. 3. All this comports well enough with Dr. Priestley's haste and carelessness; but it is not true, that he either adopted, " the usual distribution of words," or made an other " as comprehensive and distinct as any." His " *innovation*," too, which has since been countenanced by many other writers, I have already shown to be greater, than if, by a promotion of the article and the adjective, he had made the parts of speech ten. Dr. Beattie, who was Priestley's coeval, and a much better scholar, adopted this number without hesitation, and called every one of them by what is still its right name : " In English, there are *ten* sorts of words, which are all found in the following short sentence; ' I now see the good man coming; but, alas! he walks with difficulty.' *I* and *he* are pronouns; *now* is an adverb; *see* and *walks* are verbs; *the* is an article; *good*, an adjective; *man* and *difficulty* are nouns, the former substantive, the latter abstract; *coming* is a participle; *but*, a conjunction; *alas!* an interjection; *with*, a preposition. That no other sorts of words are necessary in language, will appear, when we have seen in what respects these are necessary."— *Beattie's Moral Science,* Vol. i, p. 80. This distribution is precisely that which the best *French* grammarians have *usually* adopted.

8. Dr. Johnson professes to adopt the division, the order, and the terms, " of the common grammarians, without inquiring whether a fitter distribution might not be found."—*Gram. before 4to Dict.* p. 1. But, in the Etymology of his Grammar, he makes no enumeration of the parts of speech, and treats only of articles, nouns, adjectives, pronouns, and verbs; to which if we add the others, according to the common grammarians, or according to his own Dictionary, the number will be *ten*. And this distribution, which was adopted by Dr. Ash about 1765, by Murray the schoolmaster about 1790, by Caleb Alexander in 1795, and approved by Dr. Adam in 1793, has since been very extensively followed; as may be seen in Dr. Crombie's treatise, in the Rev. Matt. Harrison's, and in the grammars of Harrison, Staniford, Alden, Coar, John Peirce, E. Devis, C. Adams, D. Adams, Chandler, Comly, Jaudon, Ingersoll, Hull, Fuller, Greenleaf, Kirkham, Ferd. H. Miller, Merchant, Mack, Nutting, Bucke, Beck, Barrett, Barnard, Maunder, Webber, Emmons, Hazen, Bingham, Sanders, and many others. Dr. Lowth's distribution is the same, except that he placed the adjective after the

---

* These are the parts of speech in some late grammars; as, Butler's, Day's, Frazee's, Fowle's New, Spear's, Weld's, Wells's, and the Well-wishers'. In Frost's Practical Grammar, the words of the language are said to be " divided into *right* classes," and the names are given thus : " *Noun, Article, Pronoun, Verb, Adverb, Preposition, Conjunction*, and *Interjection*."—P. 29. But the author afterwards treats of the *Adjective*, between the *Article* and the *Pronoun*, just as if he had forgotten to name it, and could not count nine with accuracy! In Perley's Grammar, the parts of speech are a different eight: " namely, *Nouns, Adjectives, Verbs, Adverbs, Prepositions, Conjunctions, Interjections*, and *Particles!*"—P. 8. S. W. Clark has Priestley's classes, but calls Interjections " Exclamations."

pronoun, the conjunction after the preposition, and, like Priestley, called the participle a verb, thus making the parts of speech *nine*. He also has been followed by many; among whom are Bicknell, Burn, Lennie, Mennye, Lindley Murray, Allen, Guy, Churchill, Wilson, Cobbett, Davis, David Blair, Davenport, Mendenhall, Wilcox, Picket, Pond, Russell, Bacon, Bullions, Brace, Hart, Lyon, Tob. H. Miller, Alger, A. Flint, Folker, S. Putnam, Cooper, Frost, Goldsbury, Hamlin, T. Smith, R. C. Smith, and Woodworth. But a third part of these, and as many more in the preceding list, are confessedly mere modifiers of Murray's compilation; and perhaps, in such a case, those have done best who have deviated least from the track of him whom they professed to follow.*

9. Some seem to have supposed, that by reducing the number of the parts of speech, and of the rules for their construction, the study of grammar would be rendered more easy and more profitable to the learner. But this, as would appear from the history of the science, is a mere retrogression towards the rudeness of its earlier stages. It is hardly worth while to dispute, whether there shall be nine parts of speech or ten; and perhaps enough has already been stated, to establish the expediency of assuming the latter number. Every word in the language must be included in some class, and nothing is gained by making the classes larger and less numerous. In all the artificial arrangements of science, distinctions are to be made according to the differences in things; and the simple question here is, what differences among words shall be at first regarded. To overlook, in our primary division, the difference between a verb and a participle, is merely to reserve for a subdivision, or subsequent explanation, a species of words which most grammarians have recognized as a distinct sort in their original classification.

10. It should be observed that the early period of grammatical science was far remote from the days in which *English* grammar originated. Many things which we now teach and defend as grammar, were taught and defended two thousand years ago, by the philosophers of Greece and Rome. Of the parts of speech, Quintilian, who lived in the first century of our era, gives the following account: "For the ancients, among whom were Aristotle† and Theodectes, treated only of verbs, nouns, and conjunctions: as the verb is what we say, and the noun, that of which we say it, they judged the power of discourse to be in *verbs*, and the matter in *nouns*, but the connexion in *conjunctions*. Little by little, the philosophers, and especially the Stoics, increased the number: first, to the conjunctions were added *articles*; afterwards, *prepositions*; to nouns, was added the *appellation*; then the *pronoun*; afterwards, as belonging to each verb, the *participle*; and, to verbs in common, *adverbs*. Our language [i.e. the *Latin*] does not require articles, wherefore they are scattered among the other parts of speech; but there is added to the foregoing the *interjection*. But some, on the authority of good authors, make the parts only eight; as Aristarchus, and, in our day, Palæmon; who have included the vocable, or appellation, with the noun, as a species of it. But they who make the noun one and the vocable an other, reckon nine. But there are also some who divide the vocable from the appellation; making the former to signify any thing manifest to sight or touch, as *house, bed*; and the latter, any thing to which either or both are wanting, as *wind, heaven, god, virtue*. They have also added the *asseveration* and the *attrectation*, which I do not approve. Whether the vocable or appellation should be included with the noun or not, as it is a matter of little consequence, I leave to the decision of others." See *Quintil. de Inst. Orat.* Lib. i, Cap. 4, § 24.

11. Several writers on English grammar, indulging a strange unsettlement of plan, seem not to have determined in their own minds, how many parts of speech

---

* Felton, who is confessedly a modifier of Murray, claims as a merit, "*the rejection of several useless parts of speech*," yet acknowledges "*nine*," and treats of *ten*; "viz., *Nouns, Pronouns, Verbs, Participles, Prepositions, Adjectives*, [*Articles*,] *Adverbs, Conjunctions, Exclamations*."—O. C. Felton's Gram. p. 5, and p. 9.

† Quintilian is at fault here; for, in some of his writings, if not generally, Aristotle recognized *four* parts of speech; *verbs, nouns, conjunctions*, and *articles*. See *Aristot. de Poetica*, Cap. xx.

there are, or ought to be. Among these are Horne Tooke, Webster, Dalton, Cardell, Green, and Cobb; and perhaps, from what he says above, we may add the name of Priestley. The present disputation about the sorts of words, has been chiefly owing to the writings of Horne Tooke, who explains the minor parts of speech as mere abbreviations, and rejects, with needless acrimony, the common classification. But many have mistaken the nature of his instructions, no less than that of the common grammarians. This author, in his third chapter, supposes his auditor to say, "But you have not all this while informed me *how many parts of speech* you mean to lay down." To whom he replies, "That shall be as you please. Either *two*, or *twenty*, or *more.*" Such looseness comported well enough with his particular purpose; because he meant to teach the derivation of words, and not to meddle at all with their construction. But who does not see that it is impossible to lay down rules for the *construction* of words, without first dividing them into the classes to which such rules apply? For example: if a man means to teach, that, "A verb must agree with its subject, or nominative, in person and number," must he not first show the learner *what words are verbs?* and ought he not to see in this rule a reason for not calling the participle a verb? Let the careless followers of Lowth and Priestley answer. Tooke did not care to preserve any parts of speech at all. His work is not a system of grammar; nor can it be made the basis of any regular scheme of grammatical instruction. He who will not grant that the same words may possibly be used as different parts of speech, must make his parts of speech either very few or very many. This author says, " I do not allow that *any* words change their nature in this manner, so as to belong sometimes to one part of speech, and sometimes to another, from the different ways of using them. I never could perceive any such fluctuation in any word whatever."—*Diversions of Purley*, Vol. i, p. 68.

12. From his own positive language, I·imagine this ingenious author never well considered what constitutes the sameness of words, or wherein lies the difference of the parts of speech; and, without understanding these things, a grammarian cannot but fall into errors, unless he will follow somebody that knows them. But Tooke confessedly contradicts and outfaces " *all other Grammarians*," in the passage just cited. Yet it is plain, that the whole science of grammar—or at least the whole of etymology and syntax, which are its two principal parts—is based upon a division of words into the parts of speech; a division which necessarily refers, in many instances, the same words to different sections according to the manner in which they are used. " Certains mots répondent ainsi, au même temps, à diverses parties d'oraison selon que la grammaire les emploie diversement."—*Buffier*, Art. 150. " Some words, from the different ways in which they are used, belong sometimes to one part of speech, sometimes to another."—*McCulloch's Gram.* p. 37. "And so say all other Grammarians."—*Tooke, as above.*

13. The history of *Dr. Webster*, as a grammarian, is singular. He is remarkable for his changeableness, yet always positive; for his inconsistency, yet very learned; for his zeal " to correct popular errors," yet often himself erroneous; for his fertility in resources, yet sometimes meagre; for his success as an author, yet never satisfied; for his boldness of innovation, yet fond of appealing to antiquity. His grammars are the least judicious, and at present the least popular, of his works. They consist of four or five different treatises, which for their mutual credit should never be compared: it is impossible to place any firm reliance upon the authority of a man who contradicts himself so much. Those who imagine that the last opinions of so learned a man must needs be right, will do well to wait, and see what will be his last: they cannot otherwise know to what his instructions will finally lead. Experience has already taught him the folly of many of his pretended improvements, and it is probable his last opinions of English grammar will be most conformable to that just authority with which he has ever been tampering. I do not say that he has not exhibited ingenuity as well as learning, or that he is

always wrong when he contradicts a majority of the English grammarians; but I may venture to say, he was wrong when he undertook to disturb the common scheme of the parts of speech, as well as when he resolved to spell all words exactly as they are pronounced.

14. It is not commonly known with how rash a hand this celebrated author has sometimes touched the most settled usages of our language. In 1790, which was seven years after the appearance of his first grammar, he published an octavo volume of more than four hundred pages, consisting of Essays, moral, historical, political, and literary, which might have done him credit, had he not spoiled his book by a grammatical whim about the reformation of orthography. Not perceiving that English literature, multiplied as it had been within two or three centuries, had acquired a stability in some degree corresponding to its growth, he foolishly imagined it was still as susceptible of change and improvement as in the days of its infancy. Let the reader pardon the length of this digression, if for the sake of any future schemer who may chance to adopt a similar conceit, I cite from the preface to this volume a specimen of the author's practice and reasoning. The ingenious attorney had the good sense quickly to abandon this project, and content himself with less glaring innovations; else he had never stood as he now does, in the estimation of the public. But there is the more need to record the example, because in one of the southern states the experiment has recently been tried again. A still abler member of the same profession, has renewed it but lately; and it is said there are yet remaining some converts to this notion of improvement. I copy literally, leaving all my readers and his to guess for themselves why he spelled "*writers*" with a *w* and "*riting*" without.

15. "During the course of ten or twelv yeers, I hav been laboring to correct popular errors, and to assist my yung brethren in the road to truth and virtue; my publications for these purposes hav been numerous; much time has been spent, which I do not regret, and much censure incurred, which my hart tells me I do not dezerv." * * * "The reeder wil obzerv that the *orthography* of the volum iz not uniform. The reezon iz, that many of the essays hav been published before, in the common orthography, and it would hav been a laborious task to copy the whole, for the sake of changing the spelling. In the essays ritten within the last yeer, a considerable change of spelling iz introduced by way of experiment. This liberty waz taken by the writers before the age of queen Elizabeth, and to this we are indebted for the preference of modern spelling over that of Gower and Chaucer. The man who admits that the change of *housbonde*, *mynde*, *ygone*, *moneth* into *husband*, *mind*, *gone*, *month*, iz an improovment, must acknowledge also the riting of *helth*, *breth*, *rong*, *tung*, *munth*, to be an improovment. There iz no alternativ. Every possible reezon that could ever be offered for altering the spelling of wurds, stil exists in ful force; and if a gradual reform should not be made in our language, it wil proov that we are less under the influence of reezon than our ancestors."—*Noah Webster's Essays*, Pref. p. xi.

16. But let us return, with our author, to the question of the parts of speech. I have shown that if we do not mean to adopt some less convenient scheme, we must count them *ten*, and preserve their ancient order as well as their ancient names. And, after all his vacillation in consequence of reading Horne Tooke, it would not be strange if Dr. Webster should come at last to the same conclusion. He was not very far from it in 1828, as may be shown by his own testimony, which he then took occasion to record. I will give his own words on the point: "There is great difficulty in devising a correct classification of the several sorts of words; and probably no classification that shall be simple and at the same time philosophically correct, can be invented. There are some words that do not strictly fall under any description of any class yet devised. Many attempts have been made and are still making to remedy this evil; but such schemes as I have seen, do not, in my apprehension, correct the defects of the old schemes, nor simplify the subject.

On the other hand, all that I have seen, serve only to obscure and embarrass the subject, by substituting new arrangements and new terms which are as incorrect as the old ones, and less intelligible. I have attentively viewed these subjects, in all the lights which my opportunities have afforded, and am convinced that the distribution of words, most generally received, *is the best that can be formed*, with some slight alterations adapted to the particular construction of the English language."

17. This passage is taken from the advertisement, or preface, to the Grammar which accompanies the author's edition of his great quarto Dictionary. Now the several schemes which bear his own name, were doubtless all of them among those which he had " *seen ;* " so that he here condemns them all collectively, as he had previously condemned some of them at each reformation. Nor is the last exempted. For although he here plainly gives his vote for that common scheme which he first condemned, he does not adopt it without "some slight alterations;" and in contriving these alterations he is inconsistent with his own professions. He makes the parts of speech *eight*, thus: "1. The name or noun; 2. The pronoun or substitute; 3. The adjective, attribute, or attributive; 4. The verb; 5. The adverb; 6. The preposition; 7. The connective or conjunction; 8. The exclamation or interjection." In his Rudiments of English Grammar, published in 1811, "to unfold the *true principles* of the language," his parts of speech were *seven ;* "viz. 1. Names or nouns; 2. Substitutes or pronouns; 3. Attributes or adjectives; 4. Verbs, with their participles; 5. Modifiers or adverbs; 6. Prepositions; 7. Connectives or conjunctions." In his Philosophical and Practical Grammar, published in 1807, a book which professes to teach "the *only legitimate principles*, and established usages," of the language, a twofold division of words is adopted; first, into two general classes, primary and secondary ; then into "*seven species* or parts of speech," the first two belonging to the former class, the other five to the latter ; thus: "1. Names or nouns; 2. Verbs; 3. Substitutes; 4. Attributes; 5. Modifiers; 6. Prepositions; 7. Connectives." In his "Improved Grammar of the English Language," published in 1831, the same scheme is retained, but the usual names are preferred.

18. How many different schemes of classification this author invented, I know not ; but he might well have saved himself the trouble of inventing any ; for, so far as appears, none of his last three grammars ever came to a second edition. In the sixth edition of his "Plain and Comprehensive Grammar, grounded on the *true principles* and idioms of the language," a work which his last grammatical preface affirms to have been originally fashioned "on the model of Lowth's," the parts of speech are reckoned "*six ;* nouns, articles, pronouns, adjectives, verbs, and abbreviations or particles." This work, which he says "was extensively used in the schools of this country," and continued to be in demand, he voluntarily suppressed ; because, after a profitable experiment of four and twenty years, he found it so far from being grounded on "true principles," that the whole scheme then appeared to him incorrigibly bad. And, judging from this sixth edition, printed in 1800, the only one which I have seen, I cannot but concur with him in the opinion. More than one half of the volume is a loose *Appendix* composed chiefly of notes taken from Lowth and Priestley; and there is a great want of method in what was meant for the body of the work. I imagine his several editions must have been different grammars with the same title ; for such things are of no uncommon occurrence, and I cannot otherwise account for the assertion that this book was compiled "on *the model of Lowth's*, and on the same principles as [those on which] Murray has constructed his."—*Advertisement in Webster's quarto Dict.*

19. In a treatise on grammar, a bad scheme is necessarily attended with inconveniences for which no merit in the execution can possibly compensate. The first thing, therefore, which a skillful teacher will notice in a work of this kind, is the arrangement. If he find any difficulty in discovering, at sight, what it is, he will

be sure it is bad; for a lucid order is what he has a right to expect from him who pretends to improve upon all the English grammarians. Dr. Webster is not the only reader of the EPEA PTEROENTA, who has been thereby prompted to meddle with the common scheme of grammar; nor is he the only one who has attempted to simplify the subject by reducing the parts of speech to *six*. John Dalton of Manchester, in 1801, in a small grammar which he dedicated to Horne Tooke, made them six, but not the same six. He would have them to be, nouns, pronouns, verbs, adverbs, conjunctions, and prepositions. This writer, like Brightland, Tooke, Fisher, and some others, insists on it that the articles are *adjectives*. Priestley, too, throwing them out of his classification, and leaving the learner to go almost through his book in ignorance of their rank, at length assigns them to the same class, in one of his notes. And so has Dr. Webster fixed them in his late valuable, but not faultless, dictionaries. But David Booth, an etymologist perhaps equally learned, in his "Introduction to an Analytical Dictionary of the English Language," declares them to be of the same species as the *pronouns*; from which he thinks it strange that they were ever separated! P. 21.

20. Now, what can be more idle, than for teachers to reject the common classification of words, and puzzle the heads of school-boys with speculations like these? It is easy to admit all that etymology can show to be true, and still justify the old arrangement of the elements of grammar. And if we depart from the common scheme, where shall we stop? Some have taught that the parts of speech are only *five*; as did the latter stoics, whose classes, according to Priscian and Harris, were these: articles, nouns appellative, nouns proper, verbs, and conjunctions. Others have made them *four*; as did Aristotle and the elder stoics, and, more recently, Milnes, Brightland, Harris, Ware, Fisher, and the author of a work on Universal Grammar, entitled Enclytica. Yet, in naming the four, each of these contrives to differ from *all the rest!* With Aristotle, they are, "nouns, verbs, articles, and conjunctions;" with Milnes, "nouns, adnouns, verbs, and particles;" with Brightland, "names, qualities, affirmations, and particles;" with Harris, "substantives, attributives, definitives, and connectives;" with Ware, "the name, the word, the assistant, the connective;" with Fisher, "names, qualities, verbs, and particles;" with the author of Enclytica, "names, verbs, modes, and connectives." But why make the classes so numerous as four? Many of the ancients, Greeks, Hebrews, and Arabians, according to Quintilian, made them *three*; and these three, according to Vossius, were nouns, verbs, and particles. "Veteres Arabes, Hebræi, et Græci, tres, non amplius, classes faciebant; 1. Nomen, 2. Verbum, 3. Particula seu Dictio."—*Voss. de Anal.* Lib. i, Cap. 1.

21. Nor is this number, *three*, quite destitute of modern supporters; though most of these come at it in an other way. D. St. Quentin, in his Rudiments of General Grammar, published in 1812, divides words into the "three general classes" last mentioned; viz., "1. Nouns, 2. Verbs, 3. Particles."—P. 5. Booth, who published the second edition of his etymological work in 1814, examining severally the ten parts of speech, and finding what he supposed to be the true origin of all the words in some of the classes, was led to throw one into an other, till he had destroyed seven of them. Then, resolving that each word ought to be classed according to the meaning which its etymology fixes upon it, he refers the number of classes to *nature*, thus: "If, then, each [word] has a *meaning*, and is capable of raising an idea in the mind, that idea must have its prototype in nature. It must either denote an *exertion*, and is therefore a *verb*; or a *quality*, and is, in that case, an *adjective*; or it must express an *assemblage* of qualities, such as is observed to belong to some individual object, and is, on this supposition, the *name* of such object, or a *noun*. * * * We have thus given an account of the different divisions of words, and have found that the whole may be classed under the three heads of Names, Qualities, and Actions; or Nouns, Adjectives, and Verbs."—*Introd. to Analyt. Dict.* p. 22.

22. This notion of the parts of speech, as the reader will presently see, found an advocate also in the author of the popular little story of Jack Halyard. It appears in his Philosophic Grammar published in Philadelphia in 1827. Whether the writer borrowed it from Booth, or was led into it by the light of "nature," I am unable to say : he does not appear to have derived it from the ancients. Now, if either he or the lexicographer has discovered in "nature" a prototype for this scheme of grammar, the discovery is only to be proved, and the schemes of all other grammarians, ancient or modern, must give place to it. For the reader will observe that this triad of parts is not that which is mentioned by Vossius and Quintilian. But authority may by found for reducing the number of the parts of speech yet lower. Plato, according to Harris, and the first inquirers into language, according to Horne Tooke, made them *two ;* nouns and verbs : which Crombie, Dalton, McCulloch, and some others, say, are the only parts essentially necessary for the communication of our thoughts. Those who know nothing about grammar, regard all words as of *one* class. To them, a word is simply a word ; and under what other name it may come, is no concern of theirs.

23. Towards this point, tends every attempt to simplify grammar by suppressing any of the *ten* parts of speech. Nothing is gained by it ; and it is a departure from the best authority. We see by what steps this kind of reasoning may descend ; and we have an admirable illustration of it in the several grammatical works of William S. Cardell. I shall mention them in the order in which they appeared ; and the reader may judge whether the author does not ultimately arrive at the conclusion to which the foregoing series is conducted. This writer, in his Essay on Language, reckons seven parts of speech ; in his New-York Grammar, six ; in his Hartford Grammar, three principal, with three others subordinate ; in his Philadelphia Grammar, three only—nouns, adjectives, and verbs. Here he alleges, "The unerring plan of *nature* has established three classes of perceptions, and consequently three parts of speech."—P. 171. He says this, as if he meant to abide by it. But, on his twenty-third page, we are told, "Every adjective is either a noun or a participle." Now, by his own showing, there are no participles : he makes them all adjectives, in each of his schemes. It follows, therefore, that all his adjectives, including what others call participles, are nouns. And this reduces his three parts of speech to two, in spite of "the unerring plan of *nature !*" But even this number is more than he well believed in ; for, on the twenty-first page of the book, he affirms, that, "All other terms are but derivative forms and new applications of *nouns.*" So simple a thing is this method of grammar ! But Neef, in his zeal for reformation, carries the anticlimax fairly off the brink ; and declares, "In the grammar which shall be the work of my pupils, there shall be found no nouns, no pronouns, no articles, no participles, no verbs, no prepositions, no conjunctions, no adverbs, no interjections, no gerunds, not even one single supine. Unmercifully shall they be banished from it."—*Neef's Method of Education*, p. 60.

24. When Cardell's system appeared, several respectable men, convinced by "his powerful demonstrations," admitted that he had made "many things in the *established doctrines* of the expounders of language appear sufficiently ridiculous ;"[*] and willingly lent him the influence of their names, trusting that his admirable scheme of English grammar, in which their ignorance saw nothing but new truth, would be speedily "perfected and generally embraced."[†] Being invited by the author to a discussion of his principles, I opposed them *in his presence*, both privately and publicly ; defending against him, not unsuccessfully, those doctrines which time and custom have sanctioned. And, what is remarkable, that candid opposition which Cardell himself had treated with respect, and parried in vain, was afterwards, by some of his converts, impeached of all unfairness, and even accused of wanting common sense. "No one," says Niebuhr, "ever over-

[*] *The Friend*, 1829, Vol. ii, p. 117.   [†] *The Friend*, Vol. ii, p. 105.

threw a literary idol, without provoking the anger of its worshipers."—*Philological Museum*, Vol. i, p. 489. The certificates given in commendation of this " set of opinions," though they had no extensive effect on the public, showed full well that the signers knew little of the history of grammar; and it is the continual repetition of such things, that induces me now to dwell upon its history, for the information of those who are so liable to be deceived by exploded errors republished as novelties. A eulogist says of Cardell, " He had adopted a set of opinions, which, to most of his readers, appeared *entirely new*." A reviewer proved, that all his pretended novelties are to be found in certain grammars now forgotten, or seldom read. The former replies, Then he [Cardell,] is right—and the man is no less stupid than abusive, who finds fault; for here is proof that the former "had highly respectable authority for almost every thing the has advanced!" See *The Friend*, Vol. ii, pp. 105 and 116, from which all the quotations in this paragraph, except one, are taken.

25. The reader may now be curious to know what these doctrines were. They were summed up by the reviewer, thus: " Our author pretends to have drawn principally from his own resources, in making up his books; and many may have supposed there is more *novelty* in them than there really is. For instance: 1. He classes the *articles* with *adjectives;* and so did Brightland, Tooke, Fisher, Dalton, and Webster. 2. He calls the *participles, adjectives;* and so did Brightland and Tooke. 3. He makes the *pronouns*, either *nouns* or *adjectives;* and so did Adam, Dalton, and others. 4. He distributes the *conjunctions* among the other parts of speech; and so did Tooke. 5. He rejects the *interjections;* and so did Valla, Sanctius, and Tooke. 6. He makes the *possessive case* an *adjective;* and so did Brightland. 7. He says our language has *no cases;* and so did Harris. 8. He calls *case, position;* and so did James Brown. 9. He reduces the adjectives to two classes, *defining* and *describing;* and so did Dalton. 10. He declares all *verbs* to be *active;* and so did Harris, (in his Hermes, Book i, Chap. ix,) though he admitted the *expediency* of the common division. and left to our author the absurdity of contending about it. Fisher also rejected the class of *neuter verbs*, and called them all *active*. 11. He reduces the *moods* to *three*, and the *tenses* to *three;* and so did Dalton, in the very same words. Fisher also made the *tenses three*, but said there *are no moods* in English. 12. He makes the *imperative mood* always *future;* and so did Harris, in 1751. Nor did the doctrine originate with him; for Brightland, a hundred years ago, [about 1706,] ascribed it to some of his predecessors. 13. He reduces the whole of our *syntax* to about *thirty lines;* and two thirds of these are useless; for Dr. Johnson expressed it quite as fully in *ten*. But their explanations are both good for nothing; and Wallis, more wisely, omitted it altogether."—*The Friend*, Vol. ii, p. 59.

26. Dr. Webster says, in a marginal note to the preface of his Philosophical Grammar, " Since the days of *Wallis*, who published a Grammar of the English Language, in Latin, in the reign of Charles II. [,] from which Johnson and Lowth borrowed most of their rules, *little improvement* has been made in English grammar Lowth supplied some valuable criticisms, most of which however respect obsolete phrases; but many of his criticisms are extremely erroneous, and they have had an ill effect, in perverting the true idioms of our language. Priestley furnished a number of new and useful observations on the peculiar phrases of the English language. To which may be added some good remarks of Blair and Campbell, interspersed with many errors. Murray, not having mounted to the original sources of information, and professing only to select and arrange the rules and criticisms of preceding writers, has furnished little or nothing new. Of the numerous compilations of inferior character, it may be affirmed, that they have added nothing to the stock of grammatical knowledge." And the concluding sentence of this work, as well as of his Improved Grammar, published in 1831,

extends the censure as follows : " It is not the English language only whose history and principles are yet to be illustrated ; but the grammars and dictionaries of all other languages, with which I have any acquaintance, must be revised and corrected, before their elements and true construction can be fully understood." In an advertisement to the grammar prefixed to his quarto American Dictionary, the Doctor is yet more severe upon books of this sort. " I close," says he, " with the single remark, that from all the observations I have been able to make, I am convinced the dictionaries and grammars which have been used in our seminaries of learning for the last forty or fifty years, are *so incorrect and imperfect* that they have introduced or sanctioned more errors than they have amended ; in other words, had the people of England and of these States been left to learn the pronunciation and construction of their vernacular language solely by tradition, and the reading of good authors, the language would have been spoken and written with more purity than it has been and now is, by those who have learned to adjust their language by the rules which dictionaries prescribe."

27. Little and much are but relative terms ; yet when we look back to the period in which English grammar was taught only in Latin, it seems extravagant to say, that " little improvement has been made " in it since. I have elsewhere expressed a more qualified sentiment. " That the grammar of our language has made considerable progress since the days of Swift, who wrote a petty treatise on the subject, is sufficiently evident ; but whoever considers what remains to be done, cannot but perceive how ridiculous are many of the boasts and felicitations which we have heard on that topic."* Some further notice will now be taken of that progress, and of the writers who have been commonly considered the chief promoters of it, but especially of such as have not been previously mentioned in a like connexion. Among these may be noticed *William Walker*, the preceptor of Sir Isaac Newton, a teacher and grammarian of extraordinary learning, who died in 1684. He has left us sundry monuments of his taste and critical skill : one is his " Treatise of English Particles,"—a work of great labour and merit, but useless to most people now-a-days, because it explains the English in Latin ; an other, his "Art of Teaching Improv'd,"—which is also an able treatise, and apparently well adapted to its object, " the Grounding of a Young Scholar in the Latin Tongue." In the latter, are mentioned other works of his, on " *Rhetorick*, and *Logick*," which I have not seen.

28. In 1706, *Richard Johnson* published an octavo volume of more than four hundred pages, entitled, " Grammatical Commentaries ; being an Apparatus to a New National Grammar : by way of animadversion upon the falsities, obscurities, redundancies and defects of Lily's System now in use." This is a work of great acuteness, labour, and learning ; and might be of signal use to any one who should undertake to prepare a new or improved Latin grammar : of which, in my opinion, we have yet urgent need. The English grammarian may also peruse it with advantage, if he has a good knowledge of Latin—and without such knowledge he must be ill prepared for his task. This work is spoken of and quoted by some of the early English grammarians ; but the hopes of the writer do not appear to have been realized. His book was not calculated to supply the place of the common one; for the author thought it impracticable to make a new grammar, suitable for boys, and at the same time to embrace in it proofs sufficient to remove the prejudices of teachers in favour of the old. King Henry's edict in support of Lily, was yet in force, backed by all the partiality which long habit creates ; and Johnson's learning, and labour, and zeal, were admired, and praised, and soon forgot.

29. Near the beginning of the last century, some of the generous wits of the reign of Queen Anne, seeing the need there was of greater attention to their vernacular language, and of a grammar more properly English than any then in

* See the Preface to my Compendious English Grammar in the American edition of *the Treasury of Knowledge*, Vol. I, p. 8.

ture, produced a book with which the later writers on the same subjects, would have done well to have made themselves better acquainted. It is entitled "A Grammar of the English Tongue ; with the Arts of Logick, Rhetorick, Poetry, &c. Illustrated with useful Notes ; giving the Grounds and Reasons of Grammar in General. The Whole making a Compleat System of an English Education. *Published by John Brightland*, for the Use of the Schools of Great Britain and Ireland." It is ingeniously recommended in a certificate by Sir Richard Steele, or the Tattler, under the fictitious name of Isaac Bickerstaff, Esq., and in a poem of forty-three lines, by Nahum Tate, poet laureate to her Majesty. It is a duodecimo volume of three hundred pages ; a work of no inconsiderable merit and originality ; and written in a style which, though not faultless, has scarcely been surpassed by any English grammarian since. I quote it as Brightland's :* who were the real authors, does not appear. It seems to be the work of more than one, and perhaps the writers of the Tattler were the men. My copy is of the seventh edition, London, printed for Henry Lintot, 1746. It is evidently the work of very skillful hands ; yet is it not in all respects well planned or well executed. It unwisely reduces the parts of speech to four ; gives them new names ; and rejects more of the old system than the schools could be made willing to give up. Hence it does not appear to have been very extensively adopted.

80. It is now about a hundred and thirty years, since *Dr. Swift*, in a public remonstrance addressed to the Earl of Oxford, complained of the imperfect state of our language, and alleged in particular, that " in many instances it offended against every part of grammar "† Fifty years afterward, *Dr. Lowth* seconded this complaint, and pressed it home upon the polite and the learned. " Does he mean," says the latter, " that the English language, as it is spoken by the politest part of the nation, and as it stands in the writings of the most approved authors, often offends against every part of grammar ? *Thus far, I am afraid the charge is true.*"—*Lowth's Gram. Pref.* p. iv. Yet the learned Doctor, to whom much praise has been justly ascribed for the encouragement which he gave to this neglected study, attempted nothing more than "A Short Introduction to English Grammar ;" which, he says, " was calculated for the learner *even of the lowest class :* " and those who would enter more deeply into the subject, he referred to *Harris ;* whose work is not an English grammar, but "A Philosophical Inquiry concerning Universal Grammar." Lowth's Grammar was first published in 1758. At the commencement of his preface, the reverend author, after acknowledging the enlargement, polish, and refinement, which the language had received during the preceding two hundred years, ventures to add, " but, whatever other improvements it may have received, it hath made *no advances* in grammatical accuracy." I do not quote this assertion to affirm it literally true, in all its apparent breadth ; but there is less reason to boast of the correctness even now attained, than to believe that the writers on grammar are not the authors who have in general come nearest

---

* Some say that Brightland himself was the writer of this grammar ; but to suppose him the sole author, hardly comports with its dedication to the Queen, by her " most Obedient and Dutiful *Subjects*, the *Authors ;*" or with the manner in which these are spoken of, in the following lines, by the laureate :

> " Then say what Thanks, what Praises must attend
> *The Gen'rous Wits*, who thus could condescend !
> Skill, that to Art's sublimest Orb can reach,
> Employ'd its humble Elements to Teach !
> Yet worthily Esteem'd, because we know
> To raise *Their* Country's Fame *they* stoop'd so low."—Tate.

† Dr. Campbell, in his Philosophy of Rhetoric, page 158th, makes a difficulty respecting the meaning of this passage ; cites it as an instance of the misapplication of the term *grammar*; and supposes the writer's notion of the thing to have been, " of grammar in the abstract, *an* universal archetype by which the particular grammars of all different tongues ought to be regulated." And adds, " If this was his meaning, I cannot say whether he is in the right or in the wrong, in this accusation. I acknowledge myself to be entirely ignorant of this ideal grammar." It would be more fair to suppose that Dr. Swift meant by " *grammar,*" the rules and principles according to which the English language ought to be spoken and written ; and, (as I shall hereafter show,) it is no great hyperbole to affirm, that every part of the code—nay, well-nigh every one of these rules and principles—is, in many instances, violated, if not by what may be called *the language itself,* at least by those speakers and writers who are under the strongest obligations to know and observe its true use.

to it in practice. ·Nor have the ablest authors always produced the best compends for the literary instruction of youth.

31. The treatises of the learned doctors Harris, Lowth, Johnson, Ash, Priestley, Horne Tooke, Crombie, Coote, and Webster, owe their celebrity not so much to their intrinsic fitness for school instruction, as to the literary reputation of the writers. Of *Harris's Hermes*, (which, in comparison with our common grammars, is indeed a work of much ingenuity and learning, full of interesting speculations, and written with great elegance both of style and method,) *Dr. Lowth* says, it is "the most beautiful and perfect example of analysis, that has been exhibited since the days of Aristotle."—*Pref. to Gram.* p. x. But these two authors, if their works be taken together, as the latter intended they should be, supply no sufficient course of English grammar. The instructions of the one are too limited, and those of the other are not specially directed to the subject.

32. *Dr. Johnson*, who was practically one of the greatest grammarians that ever lived, and who was very nearly coetaneous with both Harris and Lowth, speaks of the state of English grammar in the following terms: "I found our speech copious without order, and energetick *without rules:* wherever I turned my view, there was perplexity to be disentangled, and confusion to be regulated."—*Pref. to Dict.* p. 1. Again: "Having therefore *no assistance but from general grammar,* I applied myself to the perusal of our writers; and noting whatever might be of use to ascertain or illustrate any word or phrase, accumulated in time the materials of a dictionary."—*Ibid.* But it is not given to any one man to do every thing; else, Johnson had done it. His object was, to compile a dictionary, rather than to compose a grammar, of our language. To lexicography, grammar is necessary, as a preparation; but, as a purpose, it is merely incidental. Dr. Priestley speaks of Johnson thus: "I must not conclude this preface, without making my acknowledgements to Mr. *Johnson*, whose admirable dictionary has been of the greatest use to me in the study of our language. It is pity he had not formed as just, and as extensive an idea of English grammar. Perhaps this very useful work may still be reserved for his distinguished abilities in this way."—*Priestley's Gram.* p. xxiii. Dr. Johnson's English Grammar is all comprised in fourteen pages, and of course it is very deficient. The syntax he seems inclined entirely to omit, as (he says) Wallis did, and Ben Jonson had better done; but, for form's sake, he condescends to bestow upon it ten short lines.

33. My point here is, that the best grammarians have left much to be done by him who may choose to labour for the further improvement of English grammar; and that a man may well deserve comparative praise, who has not reached perfection in a science like this. Johnson himself committed many errors, some of which I shall hereafter expose; yet I cannot conceive that the following judgement of his works was penned without some bias of prejudice: "Johnson's merit ought not to be denied to him; but his dictionary is the most imperfect and faulty, and the least valuable *of any** of his productions; and that share of merit which it possesses, makes it by so much the more hurtful. I rejoice, however, that though the least valuable, he found it the most profitable: for I could never read his preface without shedding a tear. And yet it must be confessed, that his *grammar* and *history* and *dictionary* of what *he calls* the English language, are in all respects (except the bulk of the *latter†*) most truly contemptible performances; and a reproach to the learning and industry of a nation which could receive them with the slightest approbation. Nearly one third of this dictionary is as much the language of the Hottentots as of the English; and it would be no difficult matter so to translate any one of the plainest and most popular numbers of the *Spectator* into the language of this dictionary, that no mere Englishman, though well read in his own language,

* The phrase "*of any*" is here erroneous. These words ought to have been omitted; or the author should have said—"the least valuable of *all* his productions."

† This word *latter* should have been *last;* for *three* works are here spoken of.

would be able to comprehend one sentence of it. It appears to be a work of labour, and yet is in truth one of the most idle performances ever offered to the public; compiled by an author who possessed not one single requisite for the undertaking, and (being a publication of a set of booksellers) owing its success to that very circumstance which alone must make it impossible that it should deserve success."—*Tooke's Diversions of Purley*, Vol. i, p. 182.

34. Dr. Ash's "Grammatical Institutes, or Easy Introduction to Dr. Lowth's English Grammar, is a meagre performance, the ease of which consists in nothing but its brevity. Dr. Priestley, who in the preface to his third edition acknowledges his obligations to Johnson, and also to Lowth, thought it premature to attempt an English grammar; and contented himself with publishing a few brief "Rudiments," with a loose appendix consisting of "Notes and Observations, for the use of those who have made some proficiency in the language." He says, "With respect to our own language, there seems to be a kind of claim upon all who make use of it, to do something for its improvement; and the best thing we can do for this purpose at present, is, to exhibit its actual structure, and the varieties with which it is used. When these are once distinctly pointed out, and generally attended to, the best forms of speech, and those which are most agreeable to the analogy of the language, will soon recommend themselves, and come into general use; and when, by this means, the language shall be written with sufficient uniformity, we may hope to see a complete grammar of it. At present, *it is by no means ripe for such a work;* * but we may approximate to it very fast, if all persons who are qualified to make remarks upon it, will give a little attention to the subject. In such a case, a few years might be sufficient to complete it."—*Priestley's Gram. Pref.* p. xv. In point of time, both Ash and Priestley expressly claim priority to Lowth, for their first editions; but the former having allowed his work to be afterwards entitled an Introduction to Lowth's, and the latter having acknowledged some improvements in his from the same source, they have both been regarded as later authors.

35. The great work of the learned etymologist *John Horne Tooke*, consists of two octavo volumes, entitled, "EPEA PTEROENTA, or the Diversions of Purley." This work explains, with admirable sagacity, the origin and primitive import of many of the most common yet most obscure English words; and is, for that reason, a valuable performance. But as it contains nothing respecting the construction of the language, and embraces no proper system of grammatical doctrines, it is a great error to suppose that the common principles of practical grammar ought to give place to such instructions, or even be modelled according to what the author proves to be true in respect to the origin of particular words. The common grammarians were less confuted by him, than many of his readers have imagined; and it ought not to be forgotten that his purpose was as different from theirs, as are their schemes of Grammar from the plan of his critical "Diversions." In this connexion may be mentioned an other work of similar size and purpose, but more comprehensive in design; the "History of European Languages," by that astonishing linguist the late *Dr. Alexander Murray.* This work

* With this opinion concurred the learned James White, author of a Grammatical Essay on the English Verb, an octavo volume of more than three hundred pages, published in London in 1761. This author says, "Our Essays towards forming an English Grammar, have not been very many: from the reign of Queen Elizabeth, to that of Queen Ann, there are but Two that the author of the Present knows of; one in English by the renown'd Ben Jonson, and one in Latin by the learn'd Dr. Wallis. In the reign of Queen Ann indeed, there seems to have arisen a noble Spirit of ingenious Emulation in this Literary way; and to this we owe the treatises compos'd at that period for the use of schools, by Brightland, Greenwood, and Maittaire. But, since that time, nothing hath appear'd, that hath come to this Essayist's knowledge, deserving *to be taken any notice of as* tending to illustrate our Language by ascertaining the Grammar of it; except Anselm Bayly's Introduction to Languages, Johnson's Grammar prefix'd to the Abridgement of his Dictionary, and the late Dr. Ward's Essays upon the English Language.—These are all the Treatises he hath met with, relative to this subject; all which he hath perus'd very attentively, and made the best use of them in his power. But notwithstanding all these aids, something still remains to be done, at least it so appears to him, *preparatory to attempting with success the Grammar of our Language.* All our efforts of this kind seem to have been render'd ineffectual hitherto, chiefly by the prevalency of two false notions: one of which is, that our Verbs have no Moods; and the other, that our Language hath no Syntax."—*White's English Verb*, p. viii.

was left unfinished by its lamented author; but it will remain a monument of erudition never surpassed, acquired in spite of wants and difficulties as great as diligence ever surmounted. Like Tooke's volumes, it is however of little use to the mere English scholar. It can be read to advantage only by those who are acquainted with several other languages. The works of *Crombie* and *Coote* are more properly essays or dissertations, than elementary systems of grammar.

36 The number of English grammars has now become so very great, that not even a general idea of the comparative merits or defects of each can here be given. I have examined with some diligence all that I have had opportunity to obtain: but have heard of several which I have never yet seen. Whoever is curious to examine at large what has been published on this subject, and thus to qualify himself to judge the better of any new grammar, may easily make a collection of one or two hundred bearing different names. There are also many works not called grammars, from which our copyists have taken large portions of their compilations. Thus Murray confessedly copied from ten authors; five of whom are Beattie, Sheridan, Walker, Blair, and Campbell. Dr. Beattie, who acquired great celebrity as a teacher, poet, philosopher, and logician, was well skilled in grammar; but he treated the subject only in critical disquisitions, and not in any distinct elementary work adapted to general use. Sheridan and Walker, being lexicographers, confined themselves chiefly to orthography and pronunciation. Murray derived sundry principles from the writings of both; but the English Grammar prepared by the latter, was written, I think, several years later than Murray's. The learned doctors Blair and Campbell wrote on rhetoric, and not on the elementary parts of grammar. Of the two, the latter is by far the more accurate writer. Blair is fluent and easy, but he furnishes not a little false syntax; Campbell's Philosophy of Rhetoric is a very valuable treatise. To these, and five or six other authors whom I have noticed, was Lindley Murray "principally indebted for his materials." Thus far of the famous contributors to English grammar. The Lectures on Rhetoric and Oratory, delivered at Harvard University by John Quincy Adams, and published in two octavo volumes in 1810, are such as do credit even to that great man; but they descend less to verbal criticism, and enter less into the peculiar province of the grammarian, than do most other works of a similar title.

37. Some of the most respectable authors or compilers of more general systems of English grammar for the use of schools, are the writer of the British Grammar, Bicknell, Buchanan, William Ward, Alexander Murray the schoolmaster, Mennye, Fisher, Lindley Murray, Fenning, Allen, Grant, David Blair, Lennie, Guy, Churchill. To attempt any thing like a review or comparative estimate of these, would protract this introduction beyond all reasonable bounds; and still others would be excluded, which are perhaps better entitled to notice. Of mere modifiers and abridgers, the number is so great, and the merit or fame so little, that I will not trespass upon the reader's patience by any further mention of them or their works. Whoever takes an accurate and comprehensive view of the history and present state of this branch of learning, though he may not conclude, with Dr. Priestley, that it is premature to attempt a complete grammar of the language, can scarcely forbear to coincide with Dr. Barrow, in the opinion that among all the treatises heretofore produced no such grammar is found. "Some superfluities have been expunged, some mistakes have been rectified, and some obscurities have been cleared; still, however, that all the grammars used in our different schools, public as well as private, are disgraced by errors or defects, is a complaint as just as it is frequent and loud."—*Barrow's Essays*, p. 83.

38. Whether, in what I have been enabled to do, there will be found a remedy for this complaint, must be referred to the decision of others. Upon the probability of effecting this, I have been willing to stake some labour; how much, and with what merit, let the candid and discerning, when they shall have examined for themselves, judge. It is certain that we have hitherto had, of our language, no

complete grammar. The need of such a work I suppose to be at this time in no small degree felt, especially by those who conduct our higher institutions of learning; and my ambition has been to produce one which might deservedly stand along side of the Port-Royal Latin and Greek Grammars, or of the Grammaire des Grammaires of Girault du Vivier. If this work is unworthy to aspire to such rank, let the patrons of English literature remember that the achievement of my design is still a desideratum. We surely have no other book which might, in any sense, have been called "*the Grammar of English Grammars;*" none, which, either by excellence, or on account of the particular direction of its criticism, might take such a name. I have turned the eyes of Grammar, in an especial manner, upon the conduct of her own household; and if, from this volume, the reader acquire a more just idea of *the grammar* which is displayed in *English grammars*, he will discover at least one reason for the title which has been bestowed upon the work. Such as the book is, I present it to the public, without pride, without self-seeking, and without anxiety : knowing that most of my readers will be interested in estimating it *justly ;* that no true service, freely rendered to learning, can fail of its end ; and that no achievement merits aught with Him who graciously supplies all ability. The opinions expressed in it have been formed with candour, and are offered with submission. If in any thing they are erroneous, there are those who can detect their faults. In the language of an ancient master, I invite the correction of the candid : " Nos quoque, quantumcunque diligentes, cùm a candidis tùm a lividis carpemur : a candidis interdum justè ; quos oro, ut de erratis omnibus amicè me admoneant—erro nonnunquam quia homo sum."—*Despauter.*

GOOLD BROWN.

New York, 1836.

9

GRAMMAR

OF

ENGLISH GRAMMARS.

GRAMMAR, as an art, is the power of reading, writing, and speaking correctly. As an acquisition, it is the essential skill of scholarship. As a study, it is the practical science which teaches the right use of language.

An *English Grammar* is a book which professes to explain the nature and structure of the English language ; and to show, on just authority, what is, and what is not, good English.

ENGLISH GRAMMAR, in itself, is the art of reading, writing, and speaking the English language correctly. It implies, in the adept, such knowledge as enables him to avoid improprieties of speech ; to correct any errors that may occur in literary compositions ; and to parse, or explain grammatically, whatsoever is rightly written.

To read is to perceive what is written or printed, so as to understand the words, and be able to utter them with their proper sounds.

To write is to express words and thoughts by letters, or characters, made with a pen or other instrument.

To speak is to utter words orally, in order that they may be heard and understood.

Grammar, like every other liberal art, can be properly taught only by a regular analysis, or systematic elucidation, of its component parts or principles ; and these parts or principles must be made known chiefly by means of definitions and examples, rules and exercises.

A *perfect definition* of any thing or class of things is such a description of it, as distinguishes that entire thing or class from every thing else, by briefly telling *what it is*.

An *example* is a particular instance or model, serving to prove or illustrate some given proposition or truth.

A *rule of grammar* is some law, more or less general, by which custom regulates and prescribes the right use of language.

An *exercise* is some technical performance required of the learner in order to bring his knowledge and skill into practice.

LANGUAGE, in the primitive sense of the term, embraced only vocal expression, or human speech uttered by the mouth ; but after letters were invented to represent articulate sounds, language became twofold, *spoken* and *written ;* so that the term, *language,* now signifies, *any series of sounds or letters formed into words and employed for the expression of thought.*

Of the composition of language we have also two kinds, *prose* and *verse ;* the latter requiring a certain number and variety of syllables in each line, but the former being free from any such restraint.

The *least parts* of written language are letters ; of spoken language, syllables ; of language significant in each part, words ; of language combining thought, phrases ; of language subjoining sense, clauses ; of language completing sense, sentences.

A discourse, or narration, of any length, is but a series of sentences ; which, when written, must be separated by the proper points, that the meaning and relation of all the words may be quickly and clearly perceived by the reader, and the whole be uttered as the sense requires.

In extended compositions, a sentence is usually less than a paragraph ; a paragraph, less than a section; a section, less than a chapter ; a chapter, less than a book ; a book, less than a volume ; and a volume, less than the entire work.

The common order of *literary division,* then, is ; of a large work, into volumes ; of volumes, into books ; of books, into chapters ; of chapters, into sections ; of sections, into paragraphs ; of paragraphs, into sentences ; of sentences, into clauses ; of clauses, into phrases ; of phrases, into words ; of words, into syllables ; of syllables, into letters.

But it rarely happens that any one work requires the use of all these divisions ; and we often assume some natural distinction and order of parts, naming each as we find it ; and also subdivide into articles, verses, cantoes, stanzas, and other portions, as the nature of the subject suggests.

Grammar is divided into four parts ; namely, Orthography, Etymology, Syntax, and Prosody.

Orthography treats of letters, syllables, separate words, and spelling.

Etymology treats of the different *parts of speech,* with their classes and modifications.

Syntax treats of the relation, agreement, government, and arrangement of words in sentences.

Prosody treats of punctuation, utterance, figures, and versification.

OBSERVATIONS.

Obs. 1.—In the Introduction to this work, have been taken many views of the study, or general science, of grammar ; many notices of its history, with sundry criticisms upon its writers or critics ; and thus language has often been presented to the reader's consideration, either as a whole, or with broader scope than belongs to the teaching of its particular forms. We come now to the work of *analyzing* our own tongue, and of laying down those special rules and principles which should guide us in the use of it, whether in speech or in writing. The author intends to dissent from other grammarians no more than they are found to dissent from truth and reason ; nor will he expose their errors further than is necessary for the credit of the science and the information of the learner. A candid critic can have no satisfaction merely in finding fault with other men's performances. But the facts are not to be concealed, that many pretenders to grammar have shown themselves exceedingly superficial in their knowledge, as well as slovenly in their practice ; and that many vain composers of books have proved themselves *despisers* of this study, by the abundance of their inaccuracies, and the obviousness of their solecisms.

Obs. 2.—Some grammarians have taught that the word *language* is of much broader signification, than that which is given to it in the definition above. I confine it to speech and writing. For the propriety of this limitation, and against those authors who describe the thing otherwise, I appeal to the common sense of mankind. One late writer defines it thus : "LANGUAGE is *any means* by which one *person* communicates his *ideas to another."—Sanders's Spelling-Book*, p. 7. Dr. Webster goes much further, and says, "LANGUAGE, in its most extensive sense, is the instrument or means of communicating ideas *and affections* of the mind *and body*, from one *animal to another*. In this sense, *brutes possess the power of language;* for by various inarticulate sounds, they make known their wants, desires, and sufferings."—*Philosophical Gram.* p. 11; *Improved Gram.* p. 5. This latter definition the author of that vain book, "*the District School*," has adopted in his chapter on Grammar. Sheridan, the celebrated actor and orthoëpist, though he seems to confine language to the human species, gives it such an extension as to make words no necessary part of its essence. "The first thought," says he, "that would occur to every one, who had not properly considered the point, is, that language is composed of words. And yet, this is so far from being an adequate idea of language, that the point in which most men think its very essence to consist, is not even a necessary property of language. For language, in its full extent, means, any way or method whatsoever, by which *all that passes in the mind of one man*, may be manifested to another."—*Sheridan's Lectures on Elocution*, p. 129. Again: "I have already *shown*, that words are, in their own nature, *no essential part of language*, and are only considered so through custom."—*Ib.* p. 135.

OBS. 3.—According to S. Kirkham's notion, "LANGUAGE, in its most extensive sense, implies those signs by which *men and brutes*, communicate *to each other* their thoughts, affections and desires."—*Kirkham's English Gram.* p. 16. Again: "*The language of brutes* consists in the use of those inarticulate sounds by which they express *their thoughts and affections.*"—*Ib.* To me it seems a shameful abuse of speech, and a vile descent from the dignity of grammar, to make the voices of "*brutes*" any part of language, as taken in a literal sense. We might with far more propriety raise our conceptions of it to the spheres above, and construe literally the metaphors of David, who ascribes to the starry heavens, both "*speech*" and "*language*," "*voice*" and "*words*," daily "*uttered*" and everywhere "*heard*." See *Psalm* xix.

OBS. 4.—But, strange as it may seem, Kirkham, commencing his instructions with the foregoing definition of language, proceeds to divide it, agreeably to this notion, into two sorts, *natural* and *artificial;* and affirms that the former "is common both to man and brute," and that the language which is peculiar to man, the language which consists of *words*, is altogether an *artificial invention:* [*] thereby contradicting at once a host of the most celebrated grammarians and philosophers, and that without appearing to know it. But this is the less strange, since he immediately forgets his own definition and division of the subject, and as plainly contradicts himself. Without limiting the term at all, without excluding his fanciful "*language of brutes*," he says, on the next leaf, "*Language is conventional*, and not only *invented*, but, in its progressive advancement, *varied for purposes of practical convenience*. Hence it assumes *any and every form* which those who make use of it, choose to give it."—*Kirkham's Gram.* p. 18. This, though scarcely more rational than his "*natural language of men and brutes*," plainly annihilates that questionable section of grammatical science, whether brutal or human, by making all language a thing "*conventional*" and "*invented*." In short, it leaves no ground at all for any grammatical science of a positive character, because it resolves all forms of language into the irresponsible will of those who utter any words, sounds, or noises.

OBS. 5.—Nor is this gentleman more fortunate in his explanation of what may really be called language. On one page, he says, "*Spoken language*, or *speech*, is made up of articulate sounds uttered by the human voice."—*Kirkham's Gram.* p. 17. On the next, "The most important use of *that faculty called speech*, is, to convey our thoughts to others."—*Ib.* p. 18. Thus the grammarian who, in the same short paragraph, seems to "defy the ingenuity of man to give his words any other meaning than that which he himself intends *them to express*," (*Ib.* p. 19,) either writes so badly as to make any ordinary false syntax appear trivial, or actually conceives man to be the inventor of one of his own *faculties*. Nay, does he not make man the contriver of that "natural language" which he possesses "in common with the brutes?" a language "*The meaning of which*," he says, "*all the different animals perfectly understand?*" See his *Gram.* p. 16. And if this notion again be true, does it not follow, that a horse knows perfectly well what horned cattle mean by their bellowing, or a flock of geese by their gabbling? I should not have

_____

[*] A similar doctrine, however, is taught by no less an author than "the Rev. Alexander Crombie, LL. D.," who says, in the first paragraph of his introduction, "LANGUAGE consists of intelligible signs, and is the medium, by which *the mind* communicates *its thoughts*. It is either articulate, or inarticulate; artificial or natural. The former is peculiar to man; the latter is *common to all animals*. By inarticulate language, we mean those instinctive cries, by which the several tribes of inferior creatures are enabled to express their sensations and desires. By articulate language is understood a system of expression, composed of simple *sounds*, differently modified by the organs of speech, and variously combined."—*Treatise on the Etymology and Syntax of the English Language*, p. 1. See the same doctrine also in *Hiley's Gram.* p. 141. The language which "*is common to all animals*," can be no other than that in which Æsop's wolves and weasels, goats and grasshoppers, talked—a language quite too unreal for *grammar*. On the other hand, that which is composed of *sounds* only, and not of letters, includes but a mere fraction of the science.

noticed these things, had not the book which teaches them, been made popular by *a thousand* imposing attestations to its excellence and accuracy. For grammar has nothing at all to do with inarticulate voices, or the imaginary languages of *brutes.* It is scope enough for one science to explain all the languages, dialects, and speeches, that lay claim to *reason.* We need not enlarge the field, by descending

> "To beasts, whom * God on their creation-day
> Created mute to all articulate sound."—*Milton.*†

PART I.

ORTHOGRAPHY.

ORTHOGRAPHY treats of letters, syllables, separate words, and spelling.

CHAPTER I.—OF LETTERS.

A *Letter* is an alphabetic character, which commonly represents some elementary sound of the human voice.

An elementary sound of the human voice, is one of the simple sounds which compose a spoken language.

The sound of a letter is commonly called its *power:* when any letter of a word is not sounded, it is said to be *silent* or *mute.*

The letters in the English alphabet, are twenty-six; the simple sounds which they represent, are about thirty-six.

A knowledge of the letters consists in an acquaintance with these *four sorts of things;* their *names,* their *classes,* their *powers,* and their *forms.*

The letters are written, or printed, or painted, or engraved, in an infinite variety of shapes and sizes; and yet are always *the same,* because their names and powers do not change.

The following are some of the different sorts of types, or letters, with which every reader should be early acquainted:

1. The Roman : A a, B b, C c, D d, E e, F f, G g, H h, I i, J j, K k, L l, M m, N n, O o, P p, Q q, R r, S s, T t, U u, V v, W w, X x, Y y, Z z.

2. The Italic : *A a, B b, C c, D d, E e, F f, G g, H h, I i, J j, K k, L l, M m, N n, O o, P p, Q q, R r, S s, T t, U u, V v, W w, X x, Y y, Z z.*

3. The Script : *A a, B b, C c, D d, E e, F f, G g, H h, I i, J j, K k, L l, M m, N n, O o, P p, Q q, R r, S s, T t, U u, V v, W w, X x, Y y, Z z.*

4. The Old English : 𝕬 a, 𝕭 b, 𝕮 c, 𝕯 d, 𝕰 e, 𝕱 f, 𝕲 g, 𝕳 h, 𝕴 i, 𝕵 j, 𝕶 k, 𝕷 l, 𝕸 m, N n, 𝕺 o, 𝕻 p, 𝕼 q, 𝕽 r, S s, 𝕿 t, 𝖀 u, 𝖁 v, 𝖂 w, X x, 𝖄 y, Z z.

---

* The pronoun *whom* is not properly applicable to *beasts,* unless they are *personified:* the relative *which* would therefore have been preferable here.—G B.

† " The great difference between men and brutes, in the utterance of sound by the mouth, consists in the power of *articulation* in man, and the entire want of it in brutes."—*Webster's Improved Gram.* p. 8.

OBSERVATIONS.

Obs. 1.—A letter *consists* not in the figure only, or in the power only, but in the figure and power united; as an embassador consists not in the man only, or in the commission only, but in the man commissioned. The figure and the power, therefore, are necessary to constitute the letter; and a name is as necessary, to tell what it is. The *class* of a letter is determined by the nature of its power, or sound; as the embassador is plenipotentiary or otherwise, according to the extent of his commission. To all but the deaf and dumb, written language is the representative of that which is spoken; so that, in the view of people in general, the powers of the letters are habitually identified with their sounds, and are conceived to be nothing else. Hence any given sound, or modification of sound, which all men can produce at pleasure, when abitrarily associated with a written sign, or conventional character, constitutes what is called *a letter*. Thus we may produce the sounds of *a, e, o,* then, by a particular compression of the organs of utterance, modify them all, into *ba, be, bo,* or *fa, fe, fo;* and we shall see that *a, e,* and *o,* are letters of one sort, and *b* and *f,* of an other. By *elementary* or *articulate sounds,* * then, we mean not only the simple tones of the voice itself, but the modifying stops and turns which are given them in speech, and marked by letters : the real voices constituting vowels; and their modifications, consonants.

Obs. 2.—A mere mark to which no sound or power is ever given, cannot be a letter; though it may, like the marks used for punctuation, deserve a name and a place in grammar. Commas, semicolons, and the like, represent *silence*, rather than sounds, and are therefore not letters. Nor are the Arabic figures, which represent entire *words*, nor again any symbols standing for *things*, (as the astronomic marks for the sun, the moon, the planets,) to be confounded with letters; because the representative of any word or number, of any name or thing, differs widely in its power, from the sign of a simple elementary sound : i. e. from any constituent *part* of a written word. The first letter of a word or name does indeed sometimes stand for the whole, and is still a letter; but it is so, as being the first element of the word, and not as being the representative of the whole.

Obs. 3.—In their definitions of vowels and consonants, many grammarians have resolved letters into *sounds only;* as, "A Vowel is an articulate *sound*," &c.—"A Consonant is an articulate *sound*," &c.—*L. Murray's Gram.* p. 7. But this confounding of the visible signs with the things which they signify, is very far from being a true account of either. Besides, letters combined are capable of a certain mysterious power which is independent of all sound, though speech, doubtless, is what they properly represent. In practice, almost all the letters may occasionally happen to be *silent;* yet are they not, in these cases, necessarily useless. The deaf and dumb also, to whom none of the letters express or represent sounds, may be taught to read and write understandingly. They even learn in some way to distinguish the accented from the unaccented syllables, and to have some notion of *quantity*, or of something else equivalent to it; for some of them, it is said, can compose verses according to the rules of prosody. Hence it would appear, that the powers of the letters are not, of necessity, identified with their sounds; the things being in some respect distinguishable, though the terms are commonly taken as synonymous. The fact is, that a word, whether spoken or written, is of itself *significant*, whether its corresponding form be known or not. Hence, in the one form, it may be perfectly intelligible to the illiterate, and in the other, to the educated deaf and dumb; while, to the learned who hear and speak, either form immediately suggests the other, with the meaning common to both.

Obs. 4.—Our knowledge of letters rises no higher than to the forms used by the ancient Hebrews and Phœnicians. Moses is supposed to have written in characters which were nearly the same as those called Samaritan, but his writings have come to us in an alphabet more beautiful and regular, called the Chaldee or Chaldaic, which is said to have been made by Ezra the scribe, when he wrote out a new copy of the law, after the rebuilding of the temple. Cadmus carried the Phœnician alphabet into Greece, where it was subsequently altered and enlarged. The small letters were not

* Strictly speaking, an *articulate sound* is not a simple element of speech, but rather a complex one, whether syllable or word ; for *articulate* literally means *jointed*. But our grammarians in general, have applied the term to the sound of a letter, a syllable, or a word, indiscriminately : for which reason, it seems not very suitable to be used alone in describing any of the three. Sheridan says, "The essence of a syllable consists in *articulation only,* for every *articulate sound* of course forms a syllable."—*Lectures on Elocution*, p. 62. If he is right in this, not many of our letters—or, perhaps more properly, none of them—can singly represent *articulate* sounds. The looseness of this term induces me to adopt or prefer an other. "The Rev. W. Allen," who comes as near as any of our grammarians, to the true definition of a *letter*, says: 1. "The sounds used in language are called *articulate sounds*." 2. "A letter is a character used in printing or writing, to represent an *articulate* sound."—*Allen's Elements of E. Gram.* p. 2. Dr. Adam says: 1. "A letter is the mark of a *sound*, or of an *articulation* of sound." 2. "A vowel is properly called a *simple sound;* and the sounds formed by the concourse of vowels and consonants, *articulate sounds*."—*Latin and English Gram.* p. 1 and 2.

invented till about the seventh century of our era. The Latins, or Romans, derived most of their capitals from the Greeks; but their small letters, if they had any, were made afterwards among themselves. This alphabet underwent various changes, and received very great improvements, before it became that beautiful series of characters which we now use, under the name of *Roman letters.* Indeed these particular forms, which are now justly preferred by many nations, are said to have been adopted after the invention of printing. "The Roman letters were first used by Sweynheim and Pannartz, printers who settled at Rome, in 1467. The earliest work printed wholly in this character in England, is said to have been Lily's or Paul's Accidence, printed by Richard Pinson, 1518. The Italic letters were invented by Aldus Manutius at Rome, towards the close of the fifteenth century, and were first used in an edition of Virgil, in 1501."— *Constable's Miscellany,* Vol. xx, p. 147. The Saxon alphabet was mostly Roman. Not more than one quarter of the letters have other forms. But the changes, though few, give to a printed page a very different appearance. Under William the Conqueror, this alphabet was superseded by the modern Gothic, Old English, or Black letter; which, in its turn, happily gave place to the present Roman. The Germans still use a type similar to the Old English, but not so heavy.

Obs. 5.—I have suggested that a true knowledge of the letters implies an acquaintance with their *names,* their *classes,* their *powers,* and their *forms.* Under these four heads, therefore, I shall briefly present what seems most worthy of the learner's attention at first, and shall reserve for the appendix a more particular account of these important elements. The most common and the most useful things are not those about which we are in general most inquisitive. Hence many, who think themselves sufficiently acquainted with the letters, do in fact know but very little about them. If a person is able to read some easy book, he is apt to suppose he has no more to learn respecting the letters; or he neglects the minute study of these elements, because he sees what words they make, and can amuse himself with stories of things more interesting. But merely to understand common English, is a very small qualification for him who aspires to scholarship, and especially for a *teacher.* For one may do this, and even be a great reader, without ever being able to name the letters properly, or to pronounce such syllables as *ca, ce, ci, co, cu, cy,* without getting half of them wrong. No one can ever teach an art more perfectly than he has learned it; and if we neglect the *elements* of grammar, our attainments must needs be proportionately unsettled and superficial.

I. NAMES OF THE LETTERS.

The *names* of the letters, as now commonly spoken and written in English, are *A, Bee, Cee, Dee, E, Eff, Gee, Aitch, I, Jay, Kay, Ell, Em, En, O, Pee, Kue, Ar, Ess, Tee, U, Vee, Double-u, Ex, Wy, Zee.*

OBSERVATIONS.

Obs. 1.—With the learning and application of these names, our literary education begins; with a continual rehearsal of them in spelling, it is for a long time carried on; nor can we ever dispense with them, but by substituting others, or by ceasing to mention the things thus named. What is obviously indispensable, needs no proof of its importance. But I know not whether it has ever been noticed, that these names, like those of the days of the week, are worthy of particular distinction, for their own nature. They are words of a very peculiar kind, being nouns that are at once *both proper and common.* For, in respect to rank, character, and design, each letter is a thing strictly individual and identical—that is, it is ever one and the same; yet, in an other respect, it is a comprehensive sort, embracing individuals both various and numberless. Thus every B is a *b,* make it as you will; and can be nothing else than that same letter b, though you make it in a thousand different fashions, and multiply it after each pattern innumerably. Here, then, we see individuality combined at once with great diversity, and infinite multiplicity; and it is *to this combination,* that letters owe their wonderful power of transmitting thought. Their *names,* therefore, should always be written with capitals, as proper nouns; and should form the plural regularly, as ordinary appellatives. Thus: (if we adopt the names now most generally used in English schools:) *A, Aes; Bee, Bees; Cee, Cees; Dee, Dees; E, Ees; Eff, Effs; Gee, Gees; Aitch, Aitches; I, Ies; Jay, Jays; Kay, Kays; Ell, Ells; Em, Ems; En, Ens; O, Oes; Pee, Pees; Kue, Kues; Ar, Ars; Ess, Esses; Tee, Tees; U, Ues; Vee, Vees; Double-u, Double-ues; Ex, Exes; Wy, Wies; Zee, Zees.*

Obs. 2.—The names of the letters, as expressed in the modern languages, are mostly framed *with reference* to their powers, or sounds. Yet is there in English no letter of which the name is always identical with its power: for *A, E, I, O,* and *U,* are the only letters which can name themselves, and all these have other sounds than those which their names express. The simple powers of the other letters are so manifestly insufficient to form any name, and so palpable is the difference between the nature and the use of each, that did we not know how education has been trifled with, it would be hard to believe even Murray, when he says, "They are frequently confounded by writers on grammar. Observations and reasonings on the *name*, are often applied to explain the *nature* of a consonant; and by this means the student is led into error and perplexity."—*L. Murray's Gram.* 8vo, p. 8. The confounding of names with the things for which they stand, implies, unquestionably, great carelessness in the use of speech, and great indistinctness of apprehension in respect to things; yet so common is this error, that Murray himself has many times fallen into it.* Let the learner therefore be on his guard, remembering that grammar, both in its study and in its practice, requires the constant exercise of a rational discernment. Those letters which name themselves, take for their names those sounds which they usually represent at the end of an accented syllable; thus the names, *A, E, I, O, U*, are uttered with the sounds given to the same letters in the first syllables of the other names, *Abel, Enoch, Isaac, Obed, Urim;* or in the first syllables of the common words, *paper, penal, pilot, potent, pupil.* The other letters, most of which can never be perfectly sounded alone, have names in which their powers are combined with other sounds more vocal; as, *Bee, Cee, Dee,—Ell, Em, En,— Jay, Kay, Kue.* But in this respect the terms *Aitch* and *Double-u* are irregular; because they have no obvious reference to the powers of the letters thus named.

OBS. 3.—Letters, like all other things, must be learned and spoken of *by their names;* nor can they be spoken of otherwise; yet, as the simple characters are better known and more easily exhibited than their written names, the former are often substituted for the latter, and are read as the words for which they are assumed. Hence the orthography of these words has hitherto been left too much to mere fancy or caprice. Our dictionaries, by a strange oversight or negligence, do not recognize them as words; and writers have in general spelled them with very little regard to either authority or analogy. What they are, or ought to be, has therefore been treated as a trifling question: and, what is still more surprising, several authors of spelling-books make no mention at all of them; while others, here at the very threshold of instruction, teach falsely— giving "*ae*" for *Aitch*, "*er*" for *Ar*, "*oo*" or "*uu*" for *Double-u*, "*ye*" for *Wy*, and writing almost all the rest improperly. So that many persons who think themselves well educated, would be greatly puzzled to name on paper these simple elements of all learning. Nay, there can be found a hundred men who can readily write the alphabetic names which were in use two or three thousand years ago in Greece or Palestine, for one who can do the same thing with propriety, respecting those which we now employ so constantly in English:† and yet the words themselves are as familiar to every school-boy's lips as are the characters to his eye. This fact may help to convince us, that *the grammar* of our language has never yet been sufficiently taught. Among all the particulars which constitute this study, there are none which better deserve to be everywhere known, by proper and determinate names, than these prime elements of all written language.

OBS. 4.—Should it happen to be asked a hundred lustrums hence, what were the names of the letters in "the Augustan age of English literature," or in the days of William the Fourth and Andrew Jackson, I fear the learned of that day will be as much at a loss for an answer, as would most of our college tutors now, were they asked, by what series of names the Roman youth were taught to spell. Might not Quintilian or Varro have obliged many, by recording these? As it is, we are indebted

* Of this sort of blunder, the following false definition is an instance: "A *Vowel* is a letter, *the name of which* makes a full open sound."—*Lennie's Gr.* p. 6; *Brace's,* 7; *Hazen's,* 10 All this is just as true of a consonant as of a vowel. The comma too, used in this sentence, defeats even the sense which the writers intended. It is surely no description either of a vowel or of a consonant, to say, that it is a letter, and that the name of a letter makes a full open sound. Again, a late grammarian teaches, that the names of all the letters are nothing but *Roman capitals,* and then seems to inquire which of *these names* are *vowels,* thus: " Q. How many letters are in the alphabet? A. Twenty-six Q. What are their names? A A, B. C, D, E, F, G, H, I, J, K. L, M, N, O, P, Q, R, S, T, U, V, W, X, Y, Z. Q Which of *these* are called *Vowels?*" — *Fowle's Common School Gram. Part First,* p. 7. If my worthy friend Fowle had known or considered *what are the names* of the letters in English, he might have made a better beginning to his grammar than this.

† By the colloquial phrase, "*to a Tee,*" we mean, "to a *nicety,* to a *tittle,* a *jot,* an *iota.*" Had the British poet Cawthorn, himself a noted schoolmaster, known how to write the name of " T," he would probably have preferred it in the following couplet:

　　　" And swore by Varro's shade that he
　　　Conceiv'd the medal to a T."—*British Poets,* Vol. VII, p. 65.

Here the name would certainly be much fitter than the letter, because the text does not in reality speak of the letter. With the names of the Greek letters, the author was better acquainted; the same poem exhibits two of them, where the characters themselves are spoken of:

　　　" My eye can trace divinely true,
　　　In this dark curve a little Mu;
　　　And here, you see, there *seems* to lie
　　　The ruins of a Doric Xi."—*Ibidem.*

The critical reader will see that "*seems*" should be *seem,* to agree with its nominative "*ruins.*"

to Priscian, a grammarian of the sixth century, for almost all we know about them. But even the information which may be had, on this point, has been strangely overlooked by our common Latin grammarians.* What, but the greater care of earlier writers, has made the Greek names better known or more important than the Latin? In every nation that is not totally illiterate, custom must have established for the letters a certain set of names, which are *the only true ones*, and which are of course to be preferred to such as are local or unauthorized. In this, however, as in other things, use may sometimes vary, and possibly improve; but when its decisions are clear, no feeble reason should be allowed to disturb them. Every parent, therefore, who would have his children instructed to read and write the English language, should see that in the first place they learn to name the letters as they are commonly named in English. A Scotch gentleman of good education informs me, that the names of the letters, as he first learned them in a school in his own country, were these: "A, Ib, Ec, Id, E, Iff, Ig, Ich, I, Ij, Ik, Ill, Im, In, O, Ip, Kue, Ir, Iss, It, U, Iv, Double-u, Ix, Wy, Iz;" but that in the same school the English names are now used. It is to be hoped, that all teachers will in time abandon every such local usage, and name the letters *as they ought to be named;* and that the day will come, in which the regular English *orthography* of these terms, shall be steadily preferred, ignorance of it be thought a disgrace, and the makers of school-books feel no longer at liberty to alter names that are a thousand times better known than their own.

OBS. 5.—It is not in respect to their *orthography* alone, that these first words in literature demand inquiry and reflection: the *pronunciation* of some of them has often been taught erroneously, and, with respect to three or four of them, some writers have attempted to make an entire change from the customary forms which I have recorded. Whether the name of the first letter should be pronounced "*Aye*," as it is in England, "*Ah*," as it is in Ireland, or "*Aw*," as it is in Scotland, is a question which Walker has largely discussed, and clearly decided in favour of the first sound; and this decision accords with the universal practice of the schools in America. It is remarkable that this able critic, though he treated minutely of the letters, neglected the names of them all, except the first and the last. Of *Zee*, (which has also been called *Zed, Zad, Izzard, Uzzard*,)† he says, "Its common name is *izzard*, which Dr. Johnson explains into *s hard*; if, however, this is the meaning, it is a gross misnomer: for the *z* is not the hard, but the soft *s*; ‡ but as it has a less sharp, and therefore not so audible a sound, it is not impossible *but* it may mean *s surd*. *Zed*, borrowed from the French, is the more fashionable name of this letter; but, in my opinion, *not to be admitted, because the names of the letters ought to have no diversity.*"—*Walker's Principles*, No. 483. It is true, the name of a letter ought to be one, and in no respect diverse; but where diversity has already obtained, and become firmly rooted in custom, is it to be obviated by insisting upon what is old-fashioned, awkward, and inconvenient? Shall the better usage give place to the worse? Uniformity cannot be so reached. In this country, both *Zed* and *Izzard*, as well as the worse forms *Zad* and *Uzzard*, are now fairly superseded by the softer and better term *Zee;* and whoever will spell aloud, with each of these names, a few such words as *dizzy, mizzen, gizzard*, may easily perceive why none of the former can ever be brought again into use. I give up all four; *Zed* to the French, and the rest to oblivion.

OBS. 6.—By way of apology for noticing the name of the first letter, Walker observes, "If a diversity of names to vowels did not confound us in our spelling, or declaring to each other the component letters of a word, it would be entirely needless to enter into *so trifling a question* as the mere name of a letter; but when we find ourselves unable to convey signs to each other on account of this diversity of names, and that words themselves are endangered by an improper utterance of their component

---

* Lily, reckoning without the H, J, or V, speaks of the Latin letters as "*twenty-two;*" but *says nothing* concerning their names. Ruddiman, Adam, Grant, Gould, and others, who include the H, J, and V, rightly state the number to be "*twenty-five;*" but, concerning their names, are likewise *entirely silent*. Andrews and Stoddard, not admitting the K, teach thus: "The letters of the Latin language are *twenty-four*. They *have the same names* as the corresponding characters in English"—*Andrews and Stoddard's Latin Gram.* p.1. A later author speaks thus: "The Latin Alphabet consists of *twenty-five* letters, *the same in name* and form as the English, but without the *w*."—*Bullions's Latin Gram.* p. 1. It would probably be nearer to the truth, to say, "The Latin Alphabet, *like the French*, has no W; it consists of twenty-five letters, which are *the same in name* and form *as the French*." Will it be pretended that the French names and the English do not differ?

† "Z z, zed, more commonly called izzard or uzzard, that is, *s hard*."—*Dr. Johnson's Gram.* p. 1.
     "And how she sooth'd me when with study sad
     I labour'd on to reach the final Zad "—*Crabbe's Borough*, p. 228.

‡ William Bolles, in his new Dictionary, says of the letter Z: "Its sound is uniformly that of a *hard S*." The *name*, however, he pronounces as I do; though he writes it not *Zee* but *ze*; giving not the *orthography* of the name, as he should have done, but a mere index of its pronunciation. Walker proves by citations from Professor Ward and Dr. Wallis, that these authors considered the *sharp* or *hissing* sound of *s* the "*hard*" sound; and the *flat* sound, like that of z, its "*soft*" sound. See his *Dict.* 8vo, p. 58.

parts, it seems highly incumbent on us to attempt a uniformity in this point, which, insignificant as it may seem, is undoubtedly the foundation of a just and regular pronunciation."—*Dict. under A.* If diversity in this matter is so perplexing, what shall we say to those who are attempting innovations without assigning reasons, or even pretending authority? and if a knowledge of these names is the basis of a just pronunciation, what shall we think of him who will take no pains to ascertain how he ought to speak and write them? He who pretends to teach the proper fashion of speaking and writing, cannot deal honestly, if ever he silently prefer a suggested improvement, to any established and undisturbed usage of the language; for, in grammar, no individual authority can be a counterpoise to general custom. The best usage can never be that which is little known, nor can it be well ascertained and taught by him who knows little. Inquisitive minds are ever curious to learn the nature, origin, and causes of things; and that instruction is the most useful, which is best calculated to gratify this rational curiosity. This is my apology for dwelling so long upon the present topic.

Obs. 7.—The names originally given to the letters were not mere notations of sound, intended solely to express or make known the powers of the several characters then in use; nor ought even the modern names of our present letters, though formed with special reference to their sounds, to be considered such. Expressions of mere sound, such as the notations in a pronouncing dictionary, having no reference to what is meant by the sound, do not constitute words at all; because they are not those acknowledged signs to which a meaning has been attached, and are consequently without that significance which is an essential property of words. But, in every language, there must be a series of sounds by which the alphabetical characters are commonly known in speech; and which, as they are the acknowledged names of these particular objects, must be entitled to a place among *the words* of the language. It is a great error to judge otherwise; and a greater to make it a "trifling question" in grammar, whether a given letter shall be called by one name or by another. Who shall say that *Daleth, Delta,* and *Dee,* are not three *real words,* each equally important in the language to which it properly belongs? Such names have always been in use wherever literature has been cultivated; and as the forms and powers of the letters have been changed by the nations, and have become different in different languages, there has necessarily followed a change of the names. For, whatever inconvenience scholars may find in the diversity which has thence arisen, to name these elements in a set of foreign terms, inconsistent with the genius of the language to be learned, would surely be attended with a tenfold greater. We derived our letters, and their names too, from the Romans; but this is no good reason why the latter should be spelled and pronounced as we suppose they were spelled and pronounced in Rome.

Obs. 8.—The names of the twenty-two letters in Hebrew, are, without dispute, proper *words;* for they are not only significant of the letters thus named, but have in general, if not in every instance, some other meaning in that language. Thus the mysterious ciphers which the English reader meets with, and wonders over, as he reads the 119th Psalm, may be resolved, according to some of the Hebrew grammars, as follows:

א Aleph, A, an ox, or a leader; ב Beth, Bee, a house; ג Gimel, Gee, a camel; ד Daleth, Dee, a door; ה He, E, she, or behold; ו Vau, U, a hook, or a nail; ז Zain, Zee, armour; ח Cheth, or Heth, Aitch, a hedge; ט Teth, Tee, a serpent, or a scroll; י Jod, or Yod, I, or Wy, a hand shut; כ Caph, Cee, a hollow hand, or a cup; ל Lamed, Ell, an ox-goad; מ Mem, Em, a stain, or spot; נ Nun, En, a fish, or a snake; ס Samech, Ess, a basis, or support; ע Ain, or Oin, O, an eye, or a well; פ Pe, Pee, a lip, or mouth; צ Tzaddi, or Tsadhe, Tee-zee, (i. e. tz, or ts,) a hunter's pole; ק Koph, Kue, or Kay, an ape; ר Resch, or Resh, Ar, a head; ש Schin, or Sin, E's-aitch, or Ess, a tooth; ת Tau, or Thau, Tee, or Tee-aitch, a cross, or mark.

These English names of the Hebrew letters are written with much less uniformity than those of the Greek, because there has been more dispute respecting their powers. This is directly contrary to what one would have expected; since the Hebrew names are words originally significant of other things than the letters, and the Greek are not. The original pronunciation of both languages is admitted to be lost, or involved in so much obscurity that little can be positively affirmed about it; and yet, where least was known, grammarians have produced the most diversity; aiming at disputed sounds in the one case, but generally preferring a correspondence of letters in the other.

Obs. 9.—The word *alphabet* is derived from the first two names in the following series. The Greek letters are twenty-four; which are formed, named, and sounded, thus:

A α, Alpha, a; B β, Beta, b; Γ γ, Gamma, g hard; Δ δ, Delta, d; E ε Epsilon, e short; Z ζ, Zeta, z; H η, Eta, e long; Θ ϑ θ, Theta, th; I ι, Iota, i; K κ, Kappa, k;

Λ λ, Lambda, l; M μ, Mu, m; N ν, Nu, n; Ξ ξ, Xi, x; O ο, Omicron, o short; Η η, Pi, p; P ρ, Rho, r; Σ σ ς, Sigma, s; T τ, Tau, t; Υ υ, Upsilon, u; Φ φ, Phi, ph; X χ, Chi, ch; Ψ ψ, Psi, ps; Ω ω, Omega, o long.

Of these names, our English dictionaries explain the first and the last; and Webster has defined *Iota*, and *Zeta*, but without reference to the meaning of the former in Greek. *Beta*, *Delta*, *Lambda*, and perhaps some others, are also found in the etymologies or definitions of Johnson and Webster, both of whom spell the word *Lambda* and its derivative *lambdoidal* without the silent *b*, which is commonly, if not always, inserted by the authors of our Greek grammars, and which Worcester, more properly, retains.

OBS. 10.—The reader will observe that the foregoing names, whether Greek or Hebrew, are in general much less simple than those which our letters now bear; and if he has ever attempted to spell aloud in either of those languages, he cannot but be sensible of the great advantage which was gained when to each letter there was given a short name, expressive, as ours mostly are, of its ordinary power. This improvement appears to have been introduced by the Romans, whose names for the letters were even more simple than our own. But so negligent in respect to them have been the Latin grammarians, both ancient and modern, that few even of the learned can tell what they really were in that language; or how they differed, either in orthography or sound, from those of the English or the French, the Hebrew or the Greek. Most of them, however, may yet be ascertained from Priscian, and some others of note among the ancient philologists; so that by taking from later authors the names of those letters which were not used in old times, we can still furnish an entire list, concerning the accuracy of which there is not much room to dispute. It is probable that in the ancient pronunciation of Latin, *a* was commonly sounded as in *father; e* like the English *a; i* mostly like *e* long; *y* like *i* short; *c* generally and *g* always hard, as in *come* and *go*. But, as the original, native, or just pronunciation of a language is not necessary to an understanding of it when written, the existing nations have severally, in a great measure, accommodated themselves, in their manner of reading this and other ancient tongues.

OBS. 11.—As the Latin language is now printed, its letters are twenty-five. Like the French, it has all that belong to the English alphabet, except the *Double-u*. But, till the first Punic war, the Romans wrote C for G, and doubtless gave it the power as well as the place of the Gamma or Gimel. It then seems to have slid into K; but they used it also for S, as we do now. The ancient Saxons, generally pronounced C as K, but sometimes as Ch. Their G was either guttural, or like our Y. In some of the early English grammars the name of the latter is written *Ghee*. The letter F, when first invented, was called, from its shape, Digamma, and afterwards Ef. J, when it was first distinguished from I, was called by the Hebrew name Jod, and afterwards Je. V, when first distinguished from U, was called Vau, then Va, then Ve. Y, when the Romans first borrowed it from the Greeks, was called Ypsilon; and Z, from the same source, was called Zeta; and, as these two letters were used only in words of Greek origin, I know not whether they ever received from the Romans any shorter names. In Schneider's Latin Grammar, the letters are named in the following manner; except Je and Ve, which are omitted by this author: "A, Be, Ce, De, E, Ef, Ge, Ha, I, [Je,] Ka, El, Em, En, O, Pe, Cu, Er, Es, Te, U, [Ve,] Ix, Ypsilon, Zeta." And this I suppose to be the most proper way of writing their names *in Latin*, unless we have sufficient authority for shortening Ypsilon into Y, sounded as short *i*, and for changing Zeta into Ez.

OBS. 12.—In many, if not in all languages, the five vowels, A, E, I, O, U, name themselves; but they name themselves differently to the ear, according to the different ways of uttering them in different languages. And as the name of a consonant necessarily requires one or more vowels, that also may be affected in the same manner. But in every language there should be a known way both of writing and of speaking every name in the series; and that, if there is nothing to hinder, should be made conformable to *the genius of the language*. I do not say that the names above can be regularly declined in Latin; but in English it is as easy to speak of two Dees as of two trees, of two Kays as of two days, of two Exes as of two foxes, of two Effs as of two skiffs; and there ought to be no more difficulty about the correct way of writing the word in the one case, than in the other. In Dr. Sam. Prat's Latin Grammar, (an elaborate octavo, all Latin, published in London, 1722,) nine of the consonants are reckoned mutes; b, c, d, g, p, q, t, j, and v; and eight, semivowels; f, l, m, n, r, s, x, z. "All the mutes," says this author, "are named by placing *e* after them; as, be, ce, de, ge, except *q*, which ends in *u*." See p. 8. "The semivowels, beginning with *e*, end in themselves; as, **ef**, *ach*, el, em, en, er, es, *ex*, (or, as Priscian will have it, *ix*,) *eds*." See p. 9. This mostly accords with the names given in the preceding paragraph; and so far as it does not, I judge the author to be wrong. The reader will observe that the Doctor's explanation is neither very exact nor quite complete: K is a mute which is not enumerated, and the rule would make the name of it *Ke*, and not *Ka;*—H is not one of his eight semivowels, nor does the same *Ash* accord with his rule or seem like a Latin word;—the name of Z, according to his principle, would be *Ez* and not "*Eds*," although the letter may better indicate the *sound* which was then given to this letter.

OBS. 13.—If the history of these names exhibits diversity, so does that of almost all other terms; and yet there is some way of writing every word with correctness, and correctness tends to permanence. But Time, that establishes authority, destroys it also, when he fairly sanctions newer customs. To all names worthy to be known, it is natural to wish a perpetual uniformity; but if any one thinks the variableness of these to be peculiar, let him open the English Bible of the fourteenth century, and read a few verses, observing the names. For instance: "Forsothe whanne *Eroude* was to bringynge forth hym, in that nigt *Petir* was slepynge bitwixe tweyne knytis."—*Dedis*, (i. e. *Acts*,) xii, 6. "*Crist Thesu* that is to demynge the quyke and deed."—2 *Tim.* iv, 1. Since this was written for English, our language has changed much, and at the same time acquired, by means of the press, some aids to stability. I have recorded above the *true names* of the letters, as they are now used, with something of their history; and if there could be in human works any thing unchangeable, I should wish, (with due deference to all schemers and fault-finders,) that these names might remain the same forever.

OBS. 14.—If any change is desirable in our present names of the letters, it is that we may have a shorter and simpler term in stead of *Double-u*. But can we change this well known name? I imagine it would be about as easy to change *Alpha, Upsilon*, or *Omega*; and perhaps it would be as useful. Let Dr. Webster, or any defender of his spelling, try it. He never named the *English* letters rightly; long ago discarded the term *Double-u*; and is not yet tired of his experiment with "*oo*;" but thinks still to make the vowel sound of this letter its name. Yet he writes his new name wrong; has no authority for it but his own; and is, most certainly, reprehensible for the *innovation*.[*] If W is to be named as a vowel, it ought to *name itself*, as other vowels do, and not to take *two Oes* for its written name. Who that knows what it is, to name a letter, can think of naming *v* by double *o*? That it is possible for an ingenious man to misconceive this simple affair of naming the letters, may appear not only from the foregoing instance, but from the following quotation: "Among the thousand mismanagements of literary instruction, there is at the outset in the hornbook, *the pretence to represent elementary sounds* by syllables composed of two or more elements; as, *Be, Kay, Zed, Double-u*, and *Aitch*. These words are used in infancy, and through life, as *simple elements* in the process of synthetic spelling. If the definition of a *consonant* was made by the master from the practice of the child, it might suggest pity for the pedagogue, but should not make us forget the realities of nature."—*Dr. Rush, on the Philosophy of the Human Voice*, p. 52. This is a strange allegation to come from such a source. If I bid a boy spell the word *why*, he says, "Double-u, Aitch, Wy, *hwi*;" and knows that he has spelled and pronounced the word correctly. But if he conceives that the five syllables which form the three words, *Double-u*, and *Aitch*, and *Wy*, are the three simple sounds which he utters in pronouncing the word *why*, it is not because the hornbook, or the teacher of the hornbook, ever made any such blunder or "pretence;" but because, like some great philosophers, he is capable of misconceiving very plain things. Suppose he should take it into his head to follow Dr. Webster's books, and to say, "Oo, Ye, ye, *hwi*;" who, but these doctors, would imagine, that such spelling was supported either by "the realities of nature," or by the authority of custom? I shall retain both the old "definition of a consonant," and the usual names of the letters, notwithstanding the contemptuous pity it may excite in the minds of *such* critics.

II. CLASSES OF THE LETTERS.

The letters are divided into two general classes, *vowels* and *consonants*. A *vowel* is a letter which forms a perfect sound when uttered alone; as, *a, e, o*.

A *consonant* is a letter which cannot be perfectly uttered till joined to a vowel; as, *b, c, d*.[†]

The vowels are *a, e, i, o, u*, and sometimes *w* and *y*. All the other letters are consonants.

[*] Dr. Webster died in 1843. Most of this work was written while he was yet in vigour.

[†] This old definition John L. Parkhurst disputes;—says it "is *ambiguous*;"—questions whether it means, "that the name of such a letter, or the *simple sound*," requires a vowel! "If the latter," says he, "*the assertion is false*. The simple sounds, represented by the consonants, can be uttered separately, distinctly, and *perfectly*. It can be done with the utmost ease, even by a little child."—*Parkhurst's Inductive Gram. for Beginners*, p. 164. He must be one of those modern philosophers who delight to *make mouths* of these voiceless elements, to show how much may be done without sound from the larynx.

W or *y* is called a consonant when it precedes a vowel heard in the same syllable; as in *wine, twine, whine; ye, yet, youth :* in all other cases, these letters are vowels; as in *Yssel, Ystadt, yttria; newly, dewy, eyebrow.*

CLASSES OF CONSONANTS.

The consonants are divided, with respect to their powers, into *semivowels* and *mutes.*

A *semivowel* is a consonant which can be imperfectly sounded without a vowel, so that at the end of a syllable its sound may be protracted; as, *l, n, z,* in *al, an, az.*

A *mute* is a consonant which cannot be sounded at all without a vowel, and which at the end of a syllable suddenly stops the breath; as, *k, p, t,* in *ak, ap, at.*

The semivowels are *f, h, j, l, m, n, r, s, v, w, x, y, z,* and *c* and *g* soft: but *w* or *y* at the end of a syllable, is a vowel; and the sound of *c, f, g, h, j, s,* or *x,* can be protracted only as an *aspirate,* or strong breath.

Four of the semivowels, *l, m, n,* and *r,* are termed *liquids,* on account of the fluency of their sounds; and four others, *v, w, y,* and *z,* are likewise more vocal than the aspirates.

The mutes are eight; *b, d, k, p, q, t,* and *c* and *g* hard: three of these, *k, q,* and *c* hard, sound exactly alike: *b, d,* and *g* hard, stop the voice less suddenly than the rest.

OBSERVATIONS.

OBS. 1.—The foregoing division of the letters is of very great antiquity, and, in respect to its principal features, sanctioned by almost universal authority; yet if we examine it minutely, either with reference to the various opinions of the learned, or with regard to the essential differences among the things of which it speaks, it will not perhaps be found in all respects indisputably certain. It will however be of use, as a basis for some subsequent rules, and as a means of calling the attention of the learner to the manner in which he utters the sounds of the letters. A knowledge of about three dozen different elementary sounds is implied in the faculty of speech. The power of producing these sounds with distinctness, and of adapting them to the purposes for which language is used, constitutes perfection of utterance. Had we a perfect alphabet, consisting of one symbol, and only one, for each elementary sound; and a perfect method of spelling, freed from silent letters, and precisely adjusted to the most correct pronunciation of words; the process of learning to read would doubtless be greatly facilitated. And yet any attempt toward such a reformation, any change short of the introduction of some entirely new mode of writing, would be both unwise and impracticable. It would involve our laws and literature in utter confusion; because pronunciation is the least permanent part of language; and if the orthography of words were conformed entirely to this standard, their origin and meaning would, in many instances, be soon lost. We must therefore content ourselves to learn languages as they are, and to make the best use we can of our present imperfect system of alphabetic characters; and we may be the better satisfied to do this, because the deficiencies and redundancies of this alphabet are not yet so well ascertained, as to make it certain what a perfect one would be.

OBS. 2.—In order to have a right understanding of the letters, it is necessary to enumerate, as accurately as we can, the elementary *sounds* of the language; and to attend carefully to the manner in which these sounds are enunciated, as well as to the characters by which they are represented. The most unconcerned observer cannot but perceive that there are certain differences in the sounds, as well as in the shapes, of the letters; and yet under what heads they ought severally to be classed, or how many of them will fall under some particular name, it may occasionally puzzle a philosopher to tell. The student must consider what is proposed or asked, use his own senses, and judge for himself. With our lower-case alphabet before him, he can tell by his own eye, which are the long letters, and which the short ones; so let him learn by his own ear, which are the vowels, and which the consonants. The processes are alike simple; and, if he be neither blind nor deaf, he can do both about equally well. Thus he may know for a certainty, that *a* is a short letter, and *b* a long one; the former a vowel, the latter a consonant: and so of others. Yet as he may doubt whether *t* is a long letter or a short one, so he may be puzzled to say whether *w* and *y,* as heard in *we* and *ye,* are vowels or consonants: but neither of these difficulties should impair his confidence in any of his other decisions. If he attain by observation and practice a clear and perfect pronunciation of the letters, he will be able to class them for himself with as much accuracy as he will find in books.

OBS. 3.—Grammarians have generally agreed that every letter is either a vowel or a consonant; and also that there are among the latter some semivowels, some mutes, some aspirates, some liquids, some sharps, some flats, some labials, some dentals, some nasals, some palatals, and perhaps yet other species; but in enumerating the letters which belong to these several classes, they disagree so much as to make it no easy matter to ascertain what particular classification is best supported by their authority. I have adopted what I conceive to be the best authorized, and at the same time the most intelligible. He that dislikes the scheme, may do better, if he can. But let him with modesty determine what sort of discoveries may render our ancient anthorities questionable. Aristotle, three hundred and thirty years before Christ, divided the Greek letters into *vowels, semivowels,* and *mutes,* and declared that no syllable could be formed without a vowel. In the opinion of some neoterics, it has been reserved to our age, to detect the fallacy of this. But I would fain believe that the Stagirite knew as well what he was saying, as did Dr. James Rush, when, in 1827, he declared the doctrine of vowels and consonants to be "a misrepresentation." The latter philosopher resolves the letters into "*tonics, subtonics,* and *atonics;*" and avers that "consonants alone may form syllables." Indeed, I cannot but think the ancient doctrine better. For, to say that "consonants alone may form syllables," is as much as to say that consonants are not consonants, but vowels! To be consistent, the attempters of this reformation should never speak of vowels or consonants, semivowels or mutes; because they judge the terms inappropriate, and the classification absurd. They should therefore adhere strictly to their "tonics, subtonics, and atonics;" which classes, though apparently the same as vowels, semivowels, and mutes, are better adapted to their new and peculiar division of these elements. Thus, by reforming both language and philosophy at once, they may make what they will of either!

OBS. 4.—Some teach that w and y are always vowels: conceiving the former to be equivalent to oo, and the latter to i or e. Dr. Lowth says, " Y is always a vowel," and "W is either a vowel or a diphthong." Dr. Webster supposes w to be always " a vowel, a simple sound;" but admits that, "At the beginning of words, y is called an *articulation* or *consonant,* and *with some propriety perhaps,* as it brings the root of the tongue in close contact with the lower part of the palate, and nearly in the position to which the close g brings it."—*American Dict. Octavo.* But I follow Wallis, Brightland, Johnson, Walker, Murray, Worcester, and others, in considering both of them sometimes vowels and sometimes consonants. They are consonants at the beginning of words in English, because their sounds take the article a, and not an, before them; as, a wall, a yard, and not, an wall, an yard. But oo or the sound of e, requires an, and not a; as, an eel, an oxy boy.* At the end of a syllable we know they are vowels; but at the beginning, they are so squeezed in their pronunciation, as to follow a vowel without any hiatus, or difficulty of utterance; as, " O worthy youth! so young, so wise!"

OBS. 5.—Murray's rule, " W and y are consonants when they begin a word or syllable, but in every other situation they are vowels," which is found in Comly's book, Kirkham's, Merchant's, Ingersoll's, Fisk's, Hart's, Hiley's, Alger's, Bullions's, Pond's, S. Putnam's, Weld's, and in sundry other grammars, is favourable to my doctrine, but too badly conceived to be quoted here as authority. It *undesignedly* makes w a consonant in wine, and a vowel in twine; and y a consonant when it *forms* a syllable, as in dewy: for a letter that *forms* a syllable, "begins" it. But Kirkham has lately learned his letters anew; and, supposing he had Dr. Rush on his side, has philosophically taken their names for their sounds. He now calls y a "diphthong." But he is wrong here by his own showing: he should rather have called it a triphthong. He says, "By pronouncing in a very deliberate and perfectly natural manner, the letter y, (which is a diphthong,) he unpractised student will perceive, that the sound produced, is compound; being formed, at its opening, of the obscure sound of oo as heard in oo-ze, which sound rapidly slides into that of i, and then advances to that of ee as heard in e-ve, and on which it gradually passes off into silence."—Kirkham's Elocution, p. 75. Thus the "unpractised student" is taught that b-y spells buoy; or, if pronounced " very deliberately, boo-i-ee!"

_____

* This test of what is, or is not, a vowel sound or a consonant sound, is often appealed to, and is generally imagined to be a just one. Errors in the application of an or a are not unfrequent, but they do not affect the argument. It cannot be denied, that it is proper to use a, and not proper to use an, before the initial sound "w or y with a vowel following. And this rule holds good, whether the sound be expressed by these particular letters, or by others; as in the phrases, " a wonder, a one, a yew, a use, a ewer, a humour, a yielding vapour." But I have heard it contended, that these are vowel sounds, notwithstanding they require a; and w or u and y are always vowels, because even a vowel sound (it was said) requires a and not an, whenever an her vowel sound immediately follows it. Of this notion, the following examples are a sufficient refutation; a retrenchment, an aerial tour, an ailiad, an eyewink, an eyas, an iambus, an oasis, an o'ernight, an oil, an ewer, an owl, an ounce. The initial sound of yielding requires a, and not an; but those who call the y a vowel, say, it is equivalent to the unaccented long e. This does not seem to me to be exactly true; because the ther nowand requires an, and not a; as, "Athens, as well as Thebes, had an Eëtion."

Nay, this grammatist makes *b*, not a labial mute, as Walker, Webster, Cobb, and oth
have called it, but a nasal subtonic, or semivowel. He delights in protracting its "
tural murmur;" perhaps, in assuming its name for its sound; and, having proved,
"consonants are capable of forming syllables," finds no difficulty in mouthing this l
monosyllable *by* into *b-oo-i-ee!* In this way, it is the easiest thing in the world, for sn
man to outface Aristotle, or any other divider of the letters; for he *makes* the sound
which he judges. "Boy," says the teacher of Kirkham's Elocution, "describe the
tracted sound of *y*."—*Kirkham's Elocution*, p. 110. The pupil may answer, "That le
sir, has no longer or more complex sound, than what is heard in the word *eye*, or in
vowel *i*; but the book which I study, describes it otherwise. I know not whether I
make you understand it, but I will *tr-oo-i-ee*." If the word *try*, which the author
as an example, does not exhibit his "protracted sound of *y*," there is no word that de
the sound is a mere fiction, originating in strange ignorance.

Obs. 6.—In the large print above, I have explained the principal classes of the let
but not all that are spoken of in books. It is proper to inform the learner that
sharp consonants are *t*, and all others after which our contracted preterits and particip
require that *d* should be sounded like *t*; as in the words faced, reached, stuffed, laugh
triumphed, croaked, cracked, houghed, reaped, nipped, piqued, missed, wished, earth
betrothed, fixed. The *flat* or *smooth* consonants are *d*, and all others with which the pro
sound of *d* may be united; as in the words, daubed, judged, hugged, thronged, seal
filled, aimed, crammed, pained, planned, feared, marred, soothed, loved, dozed, buz
The *labials* are those consonants which are articulated chiefly by the lips; among whi
Dr. Webster reckons *b*, *f*, *m*, *p*, and *v*. But Dr. Rush says, *b* and *m* are nasals,
latter, "purely nasal."[*] The *dentals* are those consonants which are referred to
teeth; the *nasals* are those which are affected by the nose; and the *palatals* are th
which compress the palate, as *k* and hard *g*. But these last-named classes are no
much importance; nor have I thought it worth while to notice *minutely* the opini
of writers respecting the others, as whether *h* is a semivowel, or a mute, or neither.

Obs. 7.—The Cherokee alphabet, which was invented in 1821, by See-quo-yah,
George Guess, an ingenious but wholly illiterate Indian, contains eighty-five letters,
characters. But the sounds of the language are much fewer than ours; for the ch
acters represent, not simple tones and articulations, but *syllabic sounds*, and this num
is said to be sufficient to denote them all. But the different syllabic sounds in
language amount to some thousands. I suppose, from the account, that See-quo-y
writes his name, in his own language, with three letters; and that characters so us
would not require, and probably would not admit, such a division as that of vow
and consonants. One of the Cherokees, in a letter to the American Lyceum, sta
that a knowledge of this mode of writing is so easily acquired, that one who understa
and speaks the language, "can learn to read in a day; and, indeed," continues
writer, "I have known some to acquire the art in a single evening. It is only necess
to learn the different sounds of the characters, to be enabled to read at once. In
English language, we must not only first learn the letters, but to spell, before readin
but in Cherokee, all that is required, is, to learn the letters; for they have *sylli
sounds*, and by connecting different ones together, a word is formed: in which the
no art. All who understand the language can do so, and both read and write, so
as they can learn to trace with their fingers the forms of the characters. I sup
that more than one half of the Cherokees can read their own language, and are the
enabled to acquire much valuable information, with which they otherwise would
have been blessed."—*W. S. Coodey*, 1831.

Obs. 8.—From the foregoing account, it would appear that the Cherokee langu
a very peculiar one: its words must either be very few, or the proportion of polysyll
very great. The characters used in China and Japan, stand severally for *words*.
their number is said to be not less than seventy thousand; so that the study
whole life is scarcely sufficient to make a man thoroughly master of them. Syl
writing is represented by Dr. Blair as a great improvement upon the Chinese me
and yet as being far inferior to that which is properly *alphabetic*, like ours. "The
step, in this new progress," says he, "was the invention of an alphabet of syll
which probably preceded the invention of an alphabet of letters, among some
ancient nations; and which is said to be retained to this day, in Ethiopia, and
countries of India. By fixing upon a particular mark, or character, for every syl
in the language, the number of characters, necessary to be used in writing, was re

---

[*] Dr. Rush, in his Philosophy of the Human Voice, has exhibited some acuteness of observation, an
written with commendable originality. But his accuracy is certainly not greater than his confidenc
page 57th, he says, "The *m*, *n*, and *ng*, are purely nasal;" on page 401st, "Some of the tonic element
one of the subtonics, are made by *the assistance of the lips*; they are o-we, ee-ne, ou-r, and m."
intrinsic value of his work, I am not prepared or inclined to offer any opinion; I criticise him only so
he strikes at grammatical principles long established, and worthy still to be maintained.

within a much smaller compass than the number of words in the language.   Still, however, the number of characters was great; and must have continued to render both
reading and writing very laborious arts.   Till, at last, some happy genius arose, and
tracing the sounds made by the human voice, to their most simple elements, reduced
them to a very few *vowels and consonants ;* and, by affixing to each of these, the signs
which we now call letters, taught men how, by their combinations, to put in writing
all the different words, or combinations of sound, which they employed in speech.
By being reduced to this simplicity, the art of writing was brought to its highest state
of perfection ; and, in this state, we now enjoy it in all the countries of Europe."—
Blair's Rhetoric, Lect. VII, p. 68.

OBS. 9.—All certain knowledge of the sounds given to the letters by Moses and the
prophets having been long ago lost, a strange dispute has arisen, and been carried on
for centuries, concerning this question, " Whether the Hebrew letters are, or are not,
all consonants :" the vowels being supposed by some to be suppressed and understood ;
and not written, except by *points* of comparatively late invention.   The discussion of
such a question does not properly belong to English grammar ; but, on account of its
curiosity, as well as of its analogy to some of our present disputes, I mention it.   Dr.
Charles Wilson says, " After we have sufficiently known the figures and names of the
letters, the next step is, to learn to enunciate or to pronounce them, so as to produce
articulate sounds.   On this subject, which appears at first sight very plain and simple,
numberless contentions and varieties of opinion meet us at the threshold.   From the
earliest period of the invention of written characters to represent human language,
however more or less remote that time may be, it seems absolutely certain, that the distinction of letters into *vowels and consonants* must have obtained.   All the speculations
of the Greek grammarians assume this as a first principle."   Again : " I beg leave only
to premise this observation, that I absolutely and unequivocally deny the position, that
all the letters of the Hebrew alphabet are consonants ; and, after the most careful and
minute inquiry, give it as my opinion, that of the twenty-two letters of which the
Hebrew alphabet consists, five are vowels and seventeen are consonants.   The five vowels by name are, Aleph, He, Vau, Yod, and Ain."—*Wilson's Heb. Gram.* pp. 6 and 8.

III. POWERS OF THE LETTERS.

The *powers* of the letters are properly those elementary sounds which
their figures are used to represent ; but letters formed into words, are
capable of communicating thought independently of sound.

The simple elementary sounds of any language are few, commonly not
more than *thirty-six ;* [*] but they may be variously *combined,* so as to form
words innumerable.

Different vowel sounds, or vocal elements, are produced by opening the
mouth differently, and placing the tongue in a peculiar manner for each ;
but the voice may vary in loudness, pitch, or time, and still utter the same
vowel power.

The *vowel sounds* which form the basis of the English language, and
which ought therefore to be perfectly familiar to every one who speaks it,
are those which are heard at the beginning of the words, *ate, at, ah, all,
eel, ell, isle, ill, old, on, ooze, use, us,* and that of *u* in *bull.*

In the formation of syllables, some of these fourteen primary sounds may
be joined together, as in *ay, oil, out, owl ;* and all of them may be preceded or
followed by certain motions and positions of the lips and tongue, which will
severally convert them into other terms in speech.   Thus the same essential sounds may be changed into a new series of words by an *f ;* as, *fate,
fat, far, fall, feel, fell, file, fill, fold, fond, fool, fuse, fuss, full.*   Again,
into as many more with a *p ;* as, *pute, pat, par, pall, peel, pell, pile, pill,
pole, pond, pool, pule, purl, pull.*

[*] Dr. Comstock, by enumerating as elementary the sound of the diphthong *ou,* as in *our,* and the complex
power of *wh,* as in *what,* (which sounds ought not to be so reckoned,) makes the whole number of vocal
elements in English to be " *thirty-eight.*"   See *Comstock's Elocution, p.* 19.

Each of the vowel sounds may be variously expressed by letters. About half of them are sometimes words: the rest are seldom, if ever, used alone even to form syllables. But the reader may easily learn to utter them all, separately, according to the foregoing series. Let us note them as plainly as possible: eigh, ă, ah, awe, ēh, ĕ, eye, ĭ, oh, ŏ, oo, yew, ŭ, û.

Thus the eight long sounds, *eigh, ah, awe, eh, eye, oh, ooh, yew*, are, or may be, words; but the six less vocal, called the short vowel sounds, as in *at, et, it, ot, ut, put*, are commonly heard only in connexion with consonants; except the first, which is perhaps the most frequent sound of the vowel A or *a*—a sound sometimes given to the word *a*, perhaps most generally; as in the phrase, "twice ă day."

The simple *consonant sounds* in English are twenty-two: they are marked by *b, d, f, g hard, h, k, l, m, n, ng, p, r, s, sh, t, th sharp, th flat, v, w, y, z*, and *zh*. But *zh* is written only to show the sound of other letters; as of *s* in *pleasure*, or *z* in *azure*.

All these sounds are heard distinctly in the following words: *buy, die, fie, guy, high, kie, lie, my, nigh, eying, pie, rye, sigh, shy, tie, thigh, thy, vie, we, ye, zebra, seizure.* Again: most of them may be repeated in the same word, if not in the same syllable; as in *bibber, diddle, fifty, giggle, high-hung, cackle, lily, mimic, ninny, singing, pippin, mirror, hissest, flesh-brush, tittle, thinketh, thither, vivid, witwal, union,*[*] *dizzies, vision.*

· With us, the consonants J and X represent, not simple, but complex sounds: hence they are never doubled. J is equivalent to *dzh;* and X, either to *ks* or to *gz*. The former ends no English word, and the latter begins none. To the initial X of foreign words, we always give the simple sound of Z; as in *Xerxes, xebec*.

The consonants C and Q have no sounds peculiar to themselves. Q has always the power of *k*. C is hard, like *k*, before *a, o*, and *u;* and soft, like *s*, before *e, i*, and *y:* thus the syllables, *ca, ce, ci, co, cu, cy*, are pronounced, *ka, se, si, ko, ku, sy*. *S* before *c* preserves the former sound, but coalesces with the latter; hence the syllables, *sca, sce, sci, sco, scu, scy*, are sounded, *ska, se, si, sko, sku, sy*. *Ce* and *ci* have sometimes the sound of *sh;* as in *ocean, social*. *Ch* commonly represents the compound sound of *tsh;* as in *church*.

G, as well as C, has different sounds before different vowels. G is always hard, or guttural, before *a, o*, and *u;* and generally soft, like *j*, before *e, i*, or *y:* thus the syllables, *ga, ge, gi, go, gu, gy*, are pronounced *ga, je, ji, go, gu, jy*.

The possible combinations and mutations of the twenty-six letters of our alphabet, are many millions of millions. But those clusters which are unpronounceable, are useless. Of such as may be easily uttered, there are more than enough for all the purposes of useful writing, or the recording of speech.

Thus it is, that from principles so simple as about six and thirty plain elementary sounds, represented by characters still fewer, we derive such a variety of oral and written signs, as may suffice to explain or record all the sentiments and transactions of men in all ages.

---

[*] This word is commonly heard in two syllables, *yune'yun;* but if Walker is right in making it three, *yu'ne-un*, the sound of *y* consonant is heard in it but once. Worcester's notation is "*yūn'yun*." The long sound of *u* is *yu;* hence Walker calls it a "semi-consonant diphthong."

OBSERVATIONS.

Obs. 1.—A knowledge of sounds can be acquired, in the first instance, only by the ear. No description of the manner of their production, or of the differences which distinguish them, can be at all intelligible to him who has not already, by the sense of hearing, acquired a knowledge of both. What I here say of the sounds of the letters, must of course be addressed to those persons only who are able both to speak and to read English. Why then attempt instruction by a method which both ignorance and knowledge on the part of the pupil, must alike render useless? I have supposed some readers to have such an acquaintance with the powers of the letters, as is but loose and imperfect; sufficient for the accurate pronunciation of some words or syllables, but leaving them liable to mistakes in others; extending perhaps to all the sounds of the language, but not to a ready analysis or enumeration of them. Such persons may profit by a written description of the powers of the letters, though no such description can equal the clear impression of the living voice. Teachers, too, whose business it is to aid the articulation of the young, and, by a patient inculcation of elementary principles, to lay the foundation of an accurate pronunciation, may derive some assistance from any notation of these principles, which will help their memory, or that of the learner. The connexion between letters and sounds is altogether *arbitrary*; but a few positions, being assumed and made known, in respect to some characters, become easy standards for further instruction in respect to others of similar sound.

Obs. 2.—The importance of being instructed at an early age, to pronounce with distinctness and facility all the elementary sounds of one's native language, has been so frequently urged, and is so obvious in itself, that none but those who have been themselves neglected, will be likely to disregard the claims of their children in this respect.* But surely an accurate knowledge of the ordinary powers of the letters would be vastly more common, were there not much hereditary negligence respecting the manner in which these important rudiments are learned. The utterance of the illiterate may exhibit wit and native talent, but it is always more or less barbarous, because it is not aided by a knowledge of orthography. For pronunciation and orthography, however they may seem, in our language especially, to be often at variance, are certainly correlative: a true knowledge of either tends to the preservation of both. Each of the letters represents some one or more of the elementary sounds, exclusive of the rest; and each of the elementary sounds, though several of them are occasionally transferred, has some one or two letters to which it most properly or most frequently belongs. But borrowed, as our language has been, from a great variety of sources, to which it is desirable ever to retain the means of tracing it, there is certainly much apparent lack of correspondence between its oral and its written form. Still the discrepancies are few, when compared with the instances of exact conformity; and, if they are, as I suppose they are, unavoidable, it is as useless to complain of the trouble they occasion, as it is to think of forcing a reconciliation. The wranglers in this controversy, can never agree among themselves, whether orthography shall conform to pronunciation, or pronunciation to orthography. Nor does any one of them well know how our language would either sound or look, were he himself appointed sole arbiter of all variances between our spelling and our speech.

Obs. 3.—"Language," says Dr. Rush, "was long ago analyzed into its alphabetic elements. Wherever this analysis is known, the art of teaching language has, with the best success, been conducted upon the rudimental method." * * * "The art of reading consists in having all the vocal elements under complete command, that they may be properly applied, for the vivid and elegant delineation of the sense and sentiment of discourse."—*Philosophy of the Voice*, p. 346. Again, of "the pronunciation of the alphabetic elements," he says, "The least deviation *from the assumed standard* converts the listener into the critic: and I am surely speaking within bounds when I say, that for every miscalled element in discourse, ten succeeding words are lost to the greater part of an audience."—*Ibid*. p. 350. These quotations plainly imply both the practicability and the importance of teaching the pronunciation of our language analytically by means of its present orthography, and agreeably to the standard assumed by the grammarians. The first of them affirms that it has been done, "with the best success," according to some ancient method of dividing the letters and explaining their sounds. And yet, both before and afterwards, we find this same author complaining of our alphabet and its subdivisions, as if sense or philosophy must utterly repudiate both;

* "Children ought to be accustomed to speak loud, and to pronounce all possible sounds and articulations, even those of such foreign languages as they will be obliged to learn; for almost every language has its particular sounds which we pronounce with difficulty, if we have not been early accustomed to them. Accordingly, nations who have the greatest number of sounds in their speech, learn the most easily to pronounce foreign languages, since they know their articulations by having met with similar sounds in their own language."—*Spurzheim on Education*, p. 150.

and of our orthography, as if a ploughman might teach us to spell better: and, at the same time, he speaks of softening his censure through modesty. "The deficiencies, redundancies, and confusion, of the system of alphabetic characters in this language, prevent the adoption of its subdivisions in this essay."—*Ib.* p. 52. Of the specific sounds given to the letters, he says, "The first of these matters is under the rule of every body, and therefore is very properly to be excluded from the discussions of that philosophy which desires to be effectual in its instruction. How can we hope to establish a system of elemental pronunciation in a language, when great masters in criticism condemn at once every attempt, in so simple and useful a labour as the correction of its orthography!"—P. 256. Again: "I *deprecate noticing* the faults of speakers, in the pronunciation of the alphabetic elements. It is better for criticism to be modest on this point, till it has the sense or independence to make our alphabet and its uses, look more like the work of what is called—wise and transcendent humanity: till the pardonable variety of pronunciation, and the *true spelling by the vulgar*, have satirized into reformation that pen-craft which keeps up the troubles of orthography for no other purpose, as one can divine, than to boast of a very questionable merit as a criterion of education."—*Ib.* p. 383.

OBS. 4.—How far these views are compatible, the reader will judge. And it is hoped he will excuse the length of the extracts, from a consideration of the fact, that a great master of the "pen-craft" here ridiculed, a noted stickler for needless Kays and Ues now commonly rejected, while he boasts that his grammar, which he mostly copied from Murray's, is teaching the old explanation of the alphabetic elements to "more than one hundred thousand children and youth," is also vending under his own name an abstract of the new scheme of "*tonicks, subtonicks,* and *atonicks;*" and, in one breath, bestowing superlative praise on both, in order, as it would seem, to monopolize all inconsistency. "Among those who have successfully laboured in the philological field, *Mr. Lindley Murray* stands forth in bold relief, as undeniably at the head of the list."—*Kirkham's Elocution,* p. 12. "The modern candidate for oratorical fame, stands on very different, and far more advantageous, ground, than that occupied by the young and aspiring Athenian; especially since a *correct analysis of the vocal organs,* and a faithful record of their operations, have been given to the world by *Dr. James Rush,* of Philadelphia—a name that will *outlive* the unquarried marble of our mountains."—*Ibid.* p. 29. "But what is to be said when presumption pushes itself into the front ranks of elocution, and thoughtless friends undertake to support it? The fraud must go on, till presumption quarrels, as often happens, with its own friends, or with itself, and thus dissolves the spell of its merits."—*Rush, on the Voice,* p. 405.

OBS. 5.—The question respecting the *number* of simple or elementary sounds in our language, presents a remarkable puzzle: and it is idle, if not ridiculous, for any man to declaim about the imperfection of our alphabet and orthography, who does not show himself able to solve it. All these sounds may easily be written in a plain sentence of three or four lines upon almost any subject; and every one who can read, is familiar with them all, and with all the letters. Now it is either easy *to count* them, or it is difficult. If difficult, wherein does the difficulty lie? and how shall he who knows not what and how many they are, think himself capable of reforming our system of their alphabetic signs? If easy, why do so few pretend to know their number? and of those who do pretend to this knowledge, why are there so few that agree? A certain verse in the seventh chapter of Ezra, has been said to contain all the letters. It however contains no *j;* and, with respect to the sounds, it lacks that of *f,* that of *th sharp,* and that of *u* in *bull.* I will suggest a few additional words for these; and then both all the letters, and all the sounds, of the English language, will be found in the example; and most of them, many times over: "'And I, even I, Artaxerxes the king, do make a decree to all the treasurers' who 'are beyond the river, that whatsoever Ezra the priest, the scribe of the law of the God of heaven, shall require of you, it be done speedily' and faithfully, according to that which he shall enjoin." Some letters, and some sounds, are here used much more frequently than others; but, on an average, we have, in this short passage, each sound five times, and each letter eight. How often, then, does a man speak all the elements of his language, who reads well but one hour!

OBS. 6.—Of the number of elementary sounds in our language, different orthoëpists report differently; because they cannot always agree among themselves, wherein the identity or the simplicity, the sameness or the singleness, even of well-known sounds, consists; or because, if each is allowed to determine these points for himself, no one of them adheres strictly to his own decision. They may also, each for himself, have some peculiar way of utterance, which will confound some sounds which other men distinguish, or distinguish some which other men confound. For, as a man may write a very bad hand which shall still be legible, so he may utter many sounds improperly and still be understood. One may, in this way, make out a scheme of the alphabetic elements, which shall be true of his own pronunciation, and yet have obvious faults when tried by the best usage of English speech. It is desirable not to multiply these sounds beyond the number which a correct and elegant pronunciation of the language obviously requires. And what that number is, it seems to me not very difficult to ascertain; at least, I think we may fix it with sufficient accuracy for all practical purposes. But let it be remembered, that all who have hitherto attempted the enumeration, have deviated more or less from their own decisions concerning either the simplicity or the identity of sounds; but, most commonly, it appears to have been thought expedient to admit some exceptions concerning both. Thus the long or diphthongal sounds of *I* and *U*, are admitted by some, and excluded by others; the sound of *j*, or soft *g*, is reckoned as simple by some, and rejected as compound by others; so a part, if not all, of what are called the long and the short vowels, as heard in *ale* and *ell*, *arm* and *am*, *all* and *on*, *isle* or *eel* and *ill*, *tone* and *tun*, *pule* or *pool* and *pull*, have been declared essentially the same by some, and essentially different by others. Were we to recognize as elementary, no sounds but such as are unquestionably simple in themselves, and indisputably different in quality from all others, we should not have more sounds than letters: and this is a proof that we have characters enough, though the sounds are perhaps badly distributed among them.

OBS. 7.—I have enumerated *thirty-six* well known sounds, which, in compliance with general custom, and for convenience in teaching, I choose to regard as the oral elements of our language. There may be found some reputable authority for adding four or five more, and other authority as reputable, for striking from the list seven or eight of those already mentioned. For the sake of the general principle, which we always regard in writing, a principle of universal grammar, *that there can be no syllable without a vowel,* I am inclined to teach, with Brightland, Dr. Johnson, L. Murray, and others, that, in English, as in French, there is given to the vowel *e* a certain very obscure sound which approaches, but amounts not to an absolute suppression, though it is commonly so regarded by the writers of dictionaries. It may be exemplified in the words *oven, shovel, able;* * or in the unemphatic article *the* before a consonant, as in the sentence, "Take the nearest:" we do not hear it as *"thee nearest,"* nor as *"then earest,"* but more obscurely. There is also a feeble sound of *i* or *y* unaccented, which is equivalent to *ee* uttered feebly, as in the word *diversity.* This is the most common sound of *i* and of *y*. The vulgar are apt to let it fall into the more obscure sound of short *u.* As elegance of utterance depends much upon the preservation of this sound from such obtuseness, perhaps Walker and others have done well to mark it as *e* in *me;* though some suppose it to be peculiar, and others identify it with the short *i* in *fit.* Thirdly, a distinction is made by some writers, between the vowel sounds heard in *hate* and *bear,* which Sheridan and Walker consider to be the same. The apparent difference may perhaps result from the following consonant *r,* which is apt to affect the sound of the vowel which precedes it. Such words as *bear, care, dare, careful, parent,* are very liable to be corrupted in pronunciation, by too broad a sound of the *a;* and, as the multiplication of needless distinctions should be avoided, I do not approve of adding an other sound to a vowel which has already quite too many. Worcester, however, in his new Dictionary, and Wells, in his new Grammar, give to the vowel A *six* sounds in lieu of *four.*

OBS. 8.—Sheridan made the elements of his oratory *twenty-eight;* Jones followed him implicitly, and adopted the same number; † Walker recognized several more, but

* If it be admitted that the two semivowels *l* and *n* have vocality enough of their own to form a very feeble syllable, it will prove only that there are these exceptions of an important general rule. If the name of *Haydn* rhymes with *maiden,* it makes one exception to the rule of writing; but it is no part of the English language. The obscure sound of which I speak, is sometimes improperly confounded with that of short *u;* thus a recent writer, who professes great skill in respect to such matters, says, " One of the most common sounds in our language is that of the vowel *u,* as in the word *urn,* or as the diphthong *ea* in the word *earth,* for which we have no character. Writers have made various efforts to express it, as in *earth, both, mirth, worth, turf,* in which all the vowels are indiscriminately used in turn. ☞ *This defect has led to the absurd method of placing the vowel after the consonants, instead of between them, when a word terminates with this sound;* as in the following, *Bible, pure, centre, circle,* instead of *Bibel, puer, center, cirkel."—Gardiner's Music of Nature.* p. 498. " It would be a great step towards perfection to spell our words as they are pronounced ! "—*Ibid.* p. 499. How often do the reformers of language multiply the irregularities of which they complain !

† " The number of simple sounds in our tongue is twenty-eight, 9 Vowels and 19 Consonants. *H* is no letter, but merely a mark of aspiration."—*Jones's Prosodial Gram. before his Dict.* p 14.
" The number of simple vowel and consonant sounds in our tongue is twenty-eight, and one pure aspiration *h,* making in all twenty-nine."—*Bolles's Octavo Dict ,* Introd., p. 9.
" The number of *letters* in the English language is twenty-six; but the number of *elements* is thirty-eight."—*Comstock's Elocution,* p. 18. " There are thirty-eight elements in the English alphabet, and to represent those elements by appropriate characters, we should have thirty-eight letters. There is, then, a deficiency in our alphabet of twelve letters—and he who shall supply this imperfection, will be one of the greatest benefactors of the human race."—*Ib.* p 19. " Our alphabet is both redundant and defective C, *q.* and *x,* are respectively represented by *k* or *s, k,* and *ks,* or *gz;* and the remaining twenty-three letters are employed to represent *forty-one* elementary sounds."—*Wells's School Gram.* 1st. Ed p 36.

I know not whether he has anywhere told us *how many*; Lindley Murray enumerates *thirty-six*, and the same thirty-six that are given in the main text above. The eight sounds not counted by Sheridan are these : 1. The Italian *a*, as in *far*, *father*, which he reckoned but a lengthening of the *a* in *hat*; 2. The short *o*, as in *hot*, which he supposed to be but a shortening of the *a* in *hall*; 3. The diphthongal *i*, as in *isle*, which he thought but a quicker union of the sounds of the diphthong *oi*, but which, in my opinion, is rather a very quick union of the sounds *ah* and *ee* into *ay*, *I*;* 4. The long *u*, which is acknowledged to be equal to *yu* or *yew*, though perhaps a little different from *you* or *yoo*,† the sound given it by Walker; 5. The *u* heard in *pull*, which he considered but a shortening of *oo*; 6. The consonant *w*, which he conceived to be always a vowel, and equivalent to *oo*; 7. The consonant *y*, which he made equal to a short *ee*; 8. The consonant *h*, which he declared to be no letter, but a mere breathing. In all other respects, his scheme of the alphabetic elements agrees with that which is adopted in this work, and which is now most commonly taught.

OBS. 9.—The effect of *Quantity* in the prolation of the vowels, is a matter with which every reader ought to be experimentally acquainted. *Quantity* is simply the *time* of utterance, whether long or short. It is commonly spoken of with reference to *syllables*, because it belongs severally to all the distinct or numerable impulses of the voice, and to these only ; but, as vowels or diphthongs may be uttered alone, the notion of quantity is of course as applicable to them, as to any of the more complex sounds in which consonants are joined with them. All sounds imply time; because they are the transient effects of certain percussions which temporarily agitate the air, an element that tends to silence. When mighty winds have swept over sea and land, and the voice of the *Ocean* is raised, he speaks to the towering cliffs in the deep tones of a *long* quantity; the rolling billows, as they meet the shore, pronounce the long-drawn syllables of his majestic elocution. But see him again in gentler mood; stand upon the beach and listen to the rippling of his more frequent waves: he will teach you *short* quantity, as well as long. In common parlance, to avoid tediousness, to save time, and to adapt language to circumstances, we usually utter words with great rapidity, and in comparatively short quantity. But in oratory, and sometimes in ordinary reading, those sounds which are best fitted to fill and gratify the ear, should be sensibly protracted, especially in emphatic words; and even the shortest syllable, must be so lengthened as to be uttered with perfect clearness : otherwise the performance will be judged defective.

OBS. 10.—Some of the vowels are usually uttered in longer time than others; but whether the former are naturally long, and the latter naturally short, may be doubted: the common opinion is, that they are. But one author at least denies it; and says, " We must explode the pretended natural epithets *short* and *long* given to our vowels, independent on accent: and we must observe that our silent *e* final lengthens not its syllable, unless the preceding vowel be accented."—*Mackintosh's Essay on E. Gram.* p. 232. The distinction of long and short vowels which has generally obtained, and the correspondences which some writers have laboured to establish between them, have always been to me sources of much embarrassment. It would appear, that in one or two instances, sounds that differ only in length, or time, are commonly recognized as different elements; and that grammarians and orthoëpists, perceiving this, have attempted to carry out the analogy, and to find among what they call the long vowels a parent sound for each of the short ones. In doing this, they have either neglected to consult the ear, or have not chosen to abide by its verdict. I suppose the vowels heard in *pull* and *pool* would be necessarily identified, if the former were protracted or the latter shortened ; and perhaps there would be a like coalescence of those heard in *of* and *all*, were they tried in the same way, though I am not sure of it. In protracting the *e* in *met*, and the *i* in *ship*, ignorance or carelessness might perhaps, with the help of our orthoëpists, convert the former word into *mate* and the latter into *sheep*; and, as this would breed confusion in the language, the avoiding of the similarity may perhaps be a sufficient reason for confining these two sounds of *e* and *i*, to that short quantity in which they cannot be mistaken. But to suppose, as some do, that the protraction of *u* in *tun* would identify it with the *o* in *tone*, surpasses any notion I have of what stupidity may misconceive. With one or two exceptions, therefore, it appears to me that each of the pure vowel sounds is of such a nature, that it may be readily recognized by its own peculiar quality or tone, though it be made as long or as short as it is possible for any sound of the human voice to be. It is manifest that each of the vowel sounds heard in *ate*, *at*, *arm*, *all*,

---

* " When these sounds are openly pronounced, they produce the familiar accent *oy* : which, by the old English dramatic writers, was often expressed by *I*."—*Walker*. We still hear it so among the vulgar ; as, " *I*, *I*, air, presently ! " for " *Ay*, ay, air, presently ! " Shakspeare wrote,

" To sleepe, perchance to dreâme ; *I*, there's the rub."—*Bucke's Classical Gram.* p. 148.

† Walker pronounces *yew* and *you* precisely alike, " *yoo* ; " but, certainly, *ew* is not commonly equivalent to *oo*, though some make it so : thus Gardiner, in his scheme of the vowels, says, " *ew* equals *oo*, as in *news*, *neo*."—*Music of Nature*, p. 489. *Noo* for *new* is a *vulgarism*, to my ear.— G. *Brown*.

al, old, ooze, us, may be protracted to the entire extent of a full breath slowly expended, and still be precisely the same one simple sound;* and, on the contrary, that all but one may be shortened to the very minimum of vocality, and still be severally known without danger of mistake. The prolation of a pure vowel places the organs of utterance in that particular position which the sound of the letter requires, and then *holds them unmoved* till we have given to it all the length we choose.

OBS. 11.—In treating of the quantity and quality of the vowels, Walker says, "The first distinction of sound that seems to obtrude itself upon us when we utter the vowels, is a long and a short sound, according to the greater or less duration of time taken up in pronouncing them. This distinction is so obvious as to have been adopted in all languages, and is that to which we annex *clearer ideas than to any other ;* and though the short sounds of some vowels have not in our language been classed with sufficient accuracy with their parent long ones, yet this has bred but little confusion, as vowels long and short are always sufficiently distinguishable."—*Principles*, No. 63. Again : " But though the terms long and short, as applied to vowels, are pretty generally understood, an accurate ear will easily perceive that these terms do not always mean the long and short sounds of the respective vowels to which they are applied ; for, if we choose to be directed by the ear, in denominating vowels long or short, we must certainly give these appellations to those sounds only which have *exactly the same radical tone*, and differ only in the long or short emission of that tone."—*Ib.* No. 66. He then proceeds to state his opinion that the vowel sounds heard in the following words are thus correspondent : *tame, them ; car, carry ; wall, want ; dawn, gone ; theme, him ; tone*, nearly *tun ; pool, pull.* As to the long sounds of *i* or *y*, and of *u*, these two being diphthongal, he supposes the short sound of each to be no other than the short sound of its latter element *ee* or *oo*. Now to me most of this is exceedingly unsatisfactory ; and I have shown why.

OBS. 12.—If men's notions of the length and shortness of vowels are the clearest ideas they have in relation to the elements of speech, how comes it to pass that of all the disputable points in grammar, this is the most perplexed with contrarieties of opinion ? In coming before the world as an author, no man intends to place himself clearly in the wrong ; yet, on the simple powers of the letters, we have volumes of irreconcilable doctrines. A great connoisseur in things of this sort, who professes to have been long "in the habit of listening to sounds of every description, and that with more than ordinary attention," declares in a recent and expensive work, that "in every language we find the vowels *incorrectly classed ;*" and, in order to give to "the simple elements of English utterance" a better explanation than others have furnished, he devotes to a new analysis of our alphabet the ample space of twenty octavo pages, besides having several chapters on subjects connected with it. And what do his twenty pages amount to ? I will give the substance of them in ten lines, and the reader may judge. He does not tell us *how many* elementary sounds there are ; but, professing to arrange the vowels, long and short, "in the order in which they are naturally found," as well as to show of the consonants that the mutes and liquids form correspondents in regular pairs, he presents a scheme which I abbreviate as follows. VOWELS : 1. *A*, as in *all* and *what*, or *o*, as in *orifice* and *nŏt* ; 2. *U—ŭrn* and *hŭt*, or *lŏve* and *cŏme* ; 3. *O—vŏte* and *echŏ* ; 4. *A—ăh* and *hăt* ; 5. *A—hāzy*, no short sound ; 6. *E—ĕll* and *it* ; 7. *E—mĕrcy* and *mĕt* ; 8. *O—prōve* and *adŏ* ; 9. *OO—tōōl* and *fŏŏt* ; 10. *W—vow* and *law* ; 11. *Y—*(like the first *e —*) *syntax* and *duty*. DIPHTHONGS : 1. *I—*as *ah-ee* ; 2. *U—*as *ee-oo* ; 3. *OU—*as *au-oo*. CONSONANTS : 1. Mutes,—*c* or *z, f, h, k* or *g, p, t, th sharp, sh ;* 2. Liquids,—*l*, which has no corresponding mute, and *z, v, r, ng, m, n, th flat* and *j*, which severally correspond to the eight mutes in their order ; 3. Subliquids,—*g hard, b*, and *d*. See "Music of Nature," by *William Gardiner*, p. 480, and after.

OBS. 13.—Dr. Rush comes to the explanation of the powers of the letters as the confident first revealer of nature's management and wisdom ; and hopes to have laid the foundation of a system of instruction in reading and oratory, which, if adopted and perfected, "will beget a similarity of opinion and practice," and "be found to possess an excellence which must grow into sure and irreversible favour."—*Phil. of the Voice*, p. 404. "We have been willing," he says, "to believe, on faith alone, that nature is wise in the contrivance of speech. Let us now show, by our works of analysis, how she manages the *simple elements* of the voice, in the production of their unbounded combinations."—*Ibid.* p. 44. Again : "Every one, with peculiar self-satisfaction, thinks he reads well, and yet all read differently : there is, however, *but one mode* of reading well."—*Ib.* p. 403. That one mode, some say, his philosophy alone teaches. Of that, others may judge. I shall only notice here what seems to be his fundamental position, that, on all the vocal

---

* " As harmony is an inherent property of sound, the ear should be first called to the attention of *simple sounds ;* though, in reality, all are composed *of three*, so nicely blended as to *appear* but as one "—*Gardiner's Music of Nature*, p. 8. " Every sound is a mixture of three tones ; as much as a ray of light is composed of three prismatic colours."—*Ib.* p. 387.

elements of language, nature has stamped duplicity! To establish this extraordinary doctrine, he first attempts to prove, that "the letter *a*, as heard in the word *day*," combines two distinguishable yet inseparable sounds; that it is a compound of what he calls, with reference to vowels and syllables in general, "the radical and the vanishing movement of the voice," — a single and indivisible element in which "two sounds are heard continuously successive," the sounds of *a* and *e* as in *ale* and *eve*. He does not know that some grammarians have contended that *ay* in *day* is a proper diphthong, in which both the vowels are heard ; but, so pronouncing it himself, infers from the experiment, that there is no simpler sound of the vowel *a*. If this inference is not wrong, the word *shape* is to be pronounced *sha-epe*; and, in like manner, a multitude of other words will acquire a new element not commonly heard in them.

Obs. 14.—But the doctrine stops not here. The philosopher examines, in some similar way, the other simple vowel sounds, and finds a beginning and an end, a base and an apex, a radical and a vanishing movement, to them all ; and imagines a sufficient warrant from nature to divide them all "into two parts," and to convert most of them into diphthongs, as well as to include all diphthongs with them, as being altogether as simple and elementary. Thus he begins with confounding all distinction between diphthongs and simple vowels ; except that which he makes for himself when he admits "the radical and the vanish," the first half of a sound and the last, to have no difference in quality. This admission is made with respect to the vowels heard in *ooze, eel, err, end,* and *in*, which he calls, not diphthongs, but "monothongs." But in the *a* of *ale*, he hears *ā'-ee*; in that of *an*, *ă'-ĕ*; (that is, the short *a* followed by something of the sound of *e* in *err*;) in that of *art*, *ah'-ĕ*; in that of *all*, *awe'-ĕ*; in the *i* of *isle*, *ī'-ee*; in the *o* of *old*, *ō'-oo*; in the proper diphthong *ou, ou'-oo*; in the *oy* of *boy*, he knows not what. After his explanation of these mysteries, he says, "The seven radical sounds with their vanishes, which have been described, include, as far as I can perceive, all the elementary diphthongs of the English language."—*Ib.* p. 60. But all the sounds of the vowel *u*, whether diphthongal or simple, are excluded from his list, unless he means to represent one of them by the *e* in *err*; and the complex vowel sound heard in *voice* and *boy*, is confessedly omitted on account of a doubt whether it consists of two sounds or of three ! The elements which he enumerates are thirty-five ; but if *oi* is not a triphthong, they are to be thirty-six. Twelve are called "*Tonics*; and are heard in the usual sound of the separated *Italics*, in the following words : *A*-ll, *a*-rt, *a*-n, *a*-le, *ou*-r, *i*-sle, *o*-ld, *ee*-l, *oo*-ze, *e*-rr, *e*-nd, *i*-n."—*Ib.* p. 53. Fourteen are called "*Subtonics*; and are marked by the separated Italics in the following words : *B*-ow, *d*-are, *g*-ive, *v*-ile, *z*-one, *y*-e, *w*-o, *th*-en, *a*-*z*-ure, *si*-*ng*, *l*-ove, *m*-ay, *n*-ot, *r*-oe."—*Ib.* p. 54. Nine are called "*Atonics*; they are heard in the words, *U*-p, *ou*-*t*, *ar*-*k*, *i*-*f*, *ye*-*s*, *h*-e, *wh*-cat, *th*-in, *pu*-*sh*."—*Ib.* p. 56. My opinion of this scheme of the alphabet the reader will have anticipated.

IV. FORMS OF THE LETTERS.

In printed books of the English language, the Roman characters are generally employed ; sometimes, the *Italic ;* and occasionally, the 𝔒𝔩𝔡 𝔈𝔫𝔤𝔩𝔦𝔰𝔥 : but in handwriting, *Script letters* are used, the forms of which are peculiarly adapted to the pen.

Characters of different sorts or sizes should never be *needlessly mixed ;* because facility of reading, as well as the beauty of a book, depends much upon the regularity of its letters.

In the ordinary forms of the Roman letters, every thick stroke that slants, slants from the left to the right downwards, except the middle stroke in Z ; and every thin stroke that slants, slants from the left to the right upwards.

Italics are chiefly used to distinguish emphatic or remarkable words : in the Bible, they show what words were supplied by the translators.

In manuscripts, a single line drawn under a word is meant for Italics ; a double line, for small capitals ; a triple line, for full capitals.

In every kind of type or character, the letters have severally *two forms,* by which they are distinguished as *capitals* and *small letters.* Small letters constitute the body of every work ; and capitals are used for the sake of eminence and distinction.

The titles of books, and the heads of their principal divisions, are printed wholly in capitals. Showbills, painted signs, and short inscriptions, commonly appear best in full capitals.

Some of these are so copied in books; as, "I found an altar with this inscription, TO THE UNKNOWN GOD."—*Acts*, xvii, 23. "And they set up over his head, his accusation written, THIS IS JESUS, THE KING OF THE JEWS."—*Matt.* xxvii, 37.

RULES FOR THE USE OF CAPITALS.

RULE I.—OF BOOKS.

When particular books are mentioned by their names, the chief words in their titles begin with capitals, and the other letters are small; as, "Pope's Essay on Man"—"the Book of Common Prayer"—"the Scriptures of the Old and New Testaments."*

RULE II.—FIRST WORDS.

The first word of every distinct sentence, or of any clause separately numbered or paragraphed, should begin with a capital; as, "Rejoice evermore. Pray without ceasing. In every thing give thanks: for this is the will of God in Christ Jesus concerning you. Quench not the Spirit. Despise not prophesyings. Prove all things: hold fast that which is good."—1 *Thess.* v, 16—21.

"14. He has given his assent to their acts of pretended legislation :

15. *For* quartering large bodies of armed troops among us :
16. *For* protecting them, by a mock trial, from punishment for murders :
17. *For* cutting off our trade with all parts of the world :
18. *For* imposing taxes on us without our consent : " &c.
Declaration of American Independence.

RULE III.—OF DEITY.

All names of the Deity, and sometimes their emphatic substitutes, should begin with capitals; as, "God, Jehovah, the Almighty, the Supreme Being, Divine Providence, the Messiah, the Comforter, the Father, the Son, the Holy Spirit, the Lord of Sabaoth."

"The hope of my spirit turns trembling to Thee."—*Moore.*

RULE IV.—PROPER NAMES.

Proper names, of every description, should always begin with capitals; as, "Saul of Tarsus, Simon Peter, Judas Iscariot, England, London, the Strand, the Thames, the Pyrenees, the Vatican, the Greeks, the Argo and the Argonauts."

RULE V.—OF TITLES.

Titles of office or honour, and epithets of distinction, applied to persons, begin usually with capitals; as, "His Majesty William the Fourth, Chief Justice Marshall, Sir Matthew Hale, Dr. Johnson, the Rev. Dr. Chalmers, Lewis the Bold, Charles the Second, James the Less, St. Bartholomew, Pliny the Younger, Noah Webster, Jun., Esq."

RULE VI.—ONE CAPITAL.

Those compound proper names which by analogy incline to a union of their parts without a hyphen, should be so written, and have but one capital: as, "Eastport, Eastville, Westborough, Westfield, Westtown, Whitehall, Whitechurch, Whitehaven, Whiteplains, Mountmellick, Mountpleasant, Germantown, Germanflats,

* The titulary name of the sacred volume is "The Holy Bible." The word *Scripture*, or *Scriptures*, is a common name for the writings contained in this inestimable volume, and, in the book itself, is seldom distinguished by a capital; but, in other works, it seems proper in general to write it so, by way of eminence.

Blackrock, Redhook, Kinderhook, Newfoundland, Statenland, Newcastle, North-castle, Southbridge, Fairhaven, Dekalb, Deruyter, Lafayette, Macpherson."

RULE VII.—TWO CAPITALS.

The compounding of a name under one capital should be avoided when the general analogy of other similar terms suggests a separation under two; as, "The chief mountains of Ross-shire are Ben Chat, *Benchasker*, Ben Golich, Ben Nore, Ben Foskarg, and Ben Wyvis."—*Glasgow Geog.*, Vol. ii, p. 311. Write *Ben Chasker*. So, when the word *East, West, North*, or *South*, as part of a name denotes relative position, or when the word *New* distinguishes a place by contrast, we have generally separate words and two capitals; as, "East Greenwich, West Greenwich, North Bridgewater, South Bridgewater, New Jersey, New Hampshire."

RULE VIII.—COMPOUNDS.

When any adjective or common noun is made a distinct part of a compound proper name, it ought to begin with a capital; as, "The United States, the Argentine Republic, the Peak of Teneriffe, the Blue Ridge, the Little Pedee, Long Island, Jersey City, Lower Canada, Green Bay, Gretna Green, Land's End, the Gold Coast."

RULE IX.—APPOSITION.

When a common and a proper name are associated merely to explain each other, it is in general sufficient, if the proper name begin with a capital, and the appellative, with a small letter; as, "The prophet Elisha, Matthew the publican, the brook Cherith, the river Euphrates, the Ohio river, Warren county, Flatbush village, New York city."

RULE X.—PERSONIFICATIONS.

The name of an object personified, when it conveys an idea strictly individual, should begin with a capital; as, "Upon this, *Fancy* began again to bestir herself."—*Addison*. "Come, gentle *Spring*, ethereal mildness, come."—*Thomson*.

RULE XI.—DERIVATIVES.

Words derived from proper names, and having direct reference to particular persons, places, sects, or nations, should begin with capitals; as, "Platonic, Newtonian, Greek, or Grecian, Romish, or Roman, Italic, or Italian, German, or Germanic, Swedish, Turkish, Chinese, Genoese, French, Dutch, Scotch, Welsh:" so, perhaps, "to Platonize, Grecize, Romanize, Italicize, Latinize, or Frenchify."

RULE XII.—OF I AND O.

The words *I* and *O* should always be capitals; as, "Praise the Lord, O Jerusalem; praise thy God, O Zion."—*Psalm* cxlvii. "O wretched man that I am!"—"For that which I do, I allow not: for what I would, that do I not; but what I hate, that do I."—*Rom.* vii, 24 and 15.

RULE XIII.—OF POETRY.

Every line in poetry, except what is regarded as making but one verse with the preceding line, should begin with a capital; as,

"Our sons their fathers' failing language see,
And such as Chaucer is, shall Dryden be."—*Pope.*

Of the exception, some editions of the Psalms in Metre are full of examples; as,

"Happy the man whose tender care
relieves the poor distress'd!
When troubles compass him around,
the Lord shall give him rest."
Psalms with Com. Prayer, N. Y. 1819, Ps. xli.

RULE XIV.—OF EXAMPLES.

The first word of a full example, of a distinct speech, or of a direct quotation, should begin with a capital; as, "Remember this maxim: ' Know thyself.' ''— "Virgil says, ' Labour conquers all things.' ''—" Jesus answered them, Is it not written in your law, I said, Ye are gods ?''—*John*, x, 34. "Thou knowest the commandments, Do not commit adultery, Do not kill, Do not steal, Do not bear false witness, Honour thy father and thy mother."—*Luke*, xviii, 20.

RULE XV.—CHIEF WORDS.

Other words of particular importance, and such as denote the principal subjects treated of, may be distinguished by capitals; and names subscribed frequently have capitals throughout: as, "In its application to the Executive, with reference to the Legislative branch of the Government, the same rule of action should make the President ever anxious to avoid the exercise of any discretionary authority which can be regulated by Congress."—ANDREW JACKSON, 1835.

RULE XVI.—NEEDLESS CAPITALS.

Capitals are improper wherever there is not some special rule or reason for their use: a century ago books were disfigured by their frequency; as, "Many a Noble *Genius* is lost for want of *Education*. Which wou'd then be Much More Liberal. As it was when the *Church* Enjoy'd her *Possessions*. And *Learning* was, in the *Dark Ages*, Preserv'd almost only among the *Clergy*."—CHARLES LESLIE, 1700; *Divine Right of Tythes*, p. 228.

OBSERVATIONS.

OBS. 1.—The letters of the alphabet, read by their names, are equivalent to words. They are a sort of universal signs, by which we may mark and particularize objects of any sort, named or nameless; as, "To say, therefore, that while A and B are both quadrangular, A is more or less quadrangular than B, is absurd."—*Murray's Gram.* 56. Hence they are used in the sciences as symbols of an infinite variety of things or ideas, being construed both substantively and adjectively; as, "In ascending from the note C to D, the interval is equal to an inch; and from D to E, the same."— *Music of Nature*, p. 293. "We have only to imagine the G clef placed below it."—*Ib.* Any of their forms may be used for such purposes, but the custom of each science determines our choice. Thus Algebra employs small Italics; Music, Roman capitals; Geometry, for the most part, the same; Astronomy, Greek characters; and Grammar, in some part or other, every sort. Examples: "Then comes *answer* like an ABC book."—*Beauties of Shakspeare*, p. 97. "Then comes *question* like an *a, b, c*, book.—*Shakspeare*." See A, B, C, in *Johnson's quarto Dict.* Better :—"like an *A-Bee-Cee* book."

"For A, his magic pen evokes an O,
And turns the tide of Europe on the foe."—*Young*.

OBS. 2.—A lavish use of capitals defeats the very purpose for which the letters were distinguished in rank; and carelessness in respect to the rules which govern them, may sometimes misrepresent the writer's meaning. On many occasions, however, their use or disuse is arbitrary, and must be left to the judgement and taste of authors and printers. Instances of this kind will, for the most part, concern *chief words*, and come under the fifteenth rule above. In this grammar, the number of rules is increased; but the foregoing are still perhaps too few to establish an accurate uniformity. They will however tend to this desirable result; and if doubts arise in their application, the difficulties will be in particular examples only, and not in the general principles of the rules. For instance: In 1 Chron. xxix, 10th, some of our Bibles say, "Blessed be thou, LORD God of Israel our father, for ever and ever." Others say, "Blessed be thou, LORD God of Israel, our Father, for ever and ever." And others, "Blessed be thou, LORD God of Israel our Father, for ever and ever." The last is wrong, either in the capital F, or for lack of a comma after *Israel*. The others differ in meaning; because they construe the word *father*, or *Father*, differently. Which is right I know not. The first agrees with the Latin Vulgate, and the second, with the Greek text of the Septuagint; which two famous versions here disagree, without ambiguity in either.*

* "Benedictus es Domine Deus Israel patris nostri ab eterno in eternum."—*Vulgate.* "O Eternel! Dieu d'Israël, notre père, tu es béni de tout temps et à toujours."—*Common French Bible.* " Εὐλογητὸς εἶ Κύριε ὁ Θεὸς Ἰσραὴλ ὁ πατὴρ ἡμῶν ἀπὸ τοῦ αἰῶνος καὶ ἕως τοῦ αἰῶνος."—*Septuagint.*

OBS. 3.—The innumerable discrepancies in respect to capitals, which, to a greater or less extent, disgrace the very best editions of our most popular books, are a sufficient evidence of the want of better directions on this point. In amending the rules for this purpose, I have not been able entirely to satisfy myself; and therefore must needs fail to satisfy the very critical reader. But the public shall have the best instructions I can give. On Rule 1st, concerning *Books*, it may be observed, that when particular books or writings are mentioned by other terms than their real titles, the principle of the rule does not apply. Thus, one may call Paradise Lost, "Milton's *great poem ;*" or the Diversions of Purley, "the *etymological investigations* of Horne Tooke." So it is written in the Bible, "And there was delivered unto him *the book of the prophet* Esaias."—*Luke*, iv, 17. Because the name of Esaias, or Isaiah, seems to be the only proper title of his book.

OBS. 4.—On Rule 2d, concerning *First Words*, it may be observed, that the using of other points than the period, to separate sentences that are totally distinct in sense, as is sometimes practised in quoting, is no reason for the omission of capitals at the beginning of such sentences; but, rather, an obvious reason for their use. Our grammarians frequently manufacture a parcel of puerile examples, and, with the formality of apparent quotation, throw them together in the following manner: "He is above disguise ;" "we serve under a good master;" "he rules over a willing people;" "we should do nothing beneath our character."—*Murray's Gram.* p. 118. These sentences, and all others so related, should, unquestionably, begin with capitals. Of themselves, they are distinct enough to be separated by the period and a dash. With examples of one's own making, the quotation points may be used or not, as the writer pleases; but not on their insertion or omission, nor even on the quality of the separating point, depends in all cases the propriety or impropriety of using initial capitals. For example: "The Future Tense is the form of the verb which denotes future time ; as, John *will come,* you shall go, they will learn, the sun will rise to-morrow, he will return next week."—*Frazee's Improved Gram.* p. 38 ; *Old Edition*, 35. To say nothing of the punctuation here used, it is certain that the initial words, *you, they, the,* and *he,* should have commenced with capitals.

OBS. 5.—On Rule 3d, concerning *Names of Deity*, it may be observed, that the words *Lord* and *God* take the nature of proper names, only when they are used in reference to the Eternal Divinity. The former, as a title of honour to men, is usually written with a capital ; but, as a common appellative, with a small letter. The latter, when used with reference to any fabulous deity, or when made plural to speak of many, should seldom, if ever, begin with a capital ; for we do not write with a capital any common name which we do not mean to honour : as, "Though there be that are called *gods*, whether in heaven or in earth—as there be *gods* many, and *lords* many."—1 *Cor.* viii, 5. But a diversity of design or conception in respect to this kind of distinction, has produced great diversity concerning capitals, not only in original writings, but also in reprints and quotations, not excepting even the sacred books. Example: "The Lord is a great God, and a great King above all *Gods.*"—*Gurney's Essays,* p. 88. Perhaps the writer here exalts the inferior beings called gods, that he may honour the one true God the more; but the Bible, in four editions to which I have turned, gives the word *gods* no capital. See *Psalms,* xcv, 3. The word *Heaven* put for God, begins with a capital; but when taken literally, it commonly begins with a small letter. Several nouns occasionally connected with names of the Deity, are written with a very puzzling diversity : as, "The Lord of *Sabaoth;* "—"The Lord God of *hosts;* "—"The God of *armies;* "—"The Father of *goodness;* "—"The Giver of all *good;* "—"The Lord, the righteous *Judge.*" All these, and many more like them, are found sometimes with a capital, and sometimes without. *Sabaoth,* being a foreign word, and used only in this particular connexion, usually takes a capital; but the equivalent English words do not seem to require it. For " *Judge,*" in the last example, I would use a capital ; for " *good* " and " *goodness,*" in the preceding ones, the small letter : the one is an eminent name, the others are mere attributes. Alger writes, " *the Son of Man,*" with two capitals; others, perhaps more properly, " *the Son of man,*" with one—wherever that phrase occurs in the New Testament. But, in some editions, it has no capital at all.

OBS. 6.—On Rule 4th, concerning *Proper Names*, it may be observed, that the application of this principle supposes the learner to be able to distinguish between proper names and common appellatives. Of the difference between these two classes of words, almost every child that can speak, must have formed some idea. I once noticed that a very little boy, who knew no better than to call a pigeon a turkey because the creature had feathers, was sufficiently master of this distinction, to call many individuals by their several names, and to apply the common words, *man, woman, boy, girl,* &c., with that generality which belongs to them. There is, therefore, some very plain ground for this rule. But not all is plain, and I will not veil the cause of embarrassment. It is only an act of imposture, to pretend that grammar *is easy,* in stead of making it so. Innumerable instances occur, in which the following assertion is by no means true : " The distinction between a common and a proper noun is *very obvious*."—*Kirkham's Gram*. p. 22. Nor do the remarks of this author, or those of any other that I am acquainted with, remove any part of the difficulty. We are told by this gentleman, (in language incorrigibly bad,) that, " *Nouns* which denote the genus, species, or variety of beings or things, are always common ; as, *tree*, the genus ; *oak*, *ash*, *chestnut*, *poplar*, different species ; and *red oak*, *white oak*, *black oak*, varieties."—*Ib*. p. 32. Now, as it requires *but one noun* to denote either a genus or a species, I know not how to conceive of *those* "*nouns* which denote *the genus* of things," except as of other confusion and nonsense ; and, as for the three varieties of oak, there are surely no "*nouns*" here to denote them, unless he will have *red*, *white*, and *black* to be nouns. But what shall we say of—"the Red sea," the White sea, the Black sea;" or, with two capitals, " Red Sea, White Sea, Black Sea," and a thousand other similar terms, which are neither proper names unless they are written with capitals, nor written with capitals unless they are first judged to be proper names? The simple phrase, "the united states," has nothing of the nature of a proper name ; but what is the character of the term, when written with two capitals, "the United States?" If we contend that it is not then a proper name, we make our country anonymous. And what shall we say to those grammarians who contend, that " H*eaven*, *Hell*, *Earth*, *Sun*, and *Moon*, are proper names;" and that, as such, they should be written with capitals? See *Churchill's Gram*. p. 380.

Obs. 7.—It would seem that most, if not all, proper names had originally some common signification, and that very many of our ordinary words and phrases have been converted into proper names, merely by being applied to particular persons, places, or objects, and receiving the distinction of capitals. How many of the oceans, seas, lakes, capes, islands, mountains, states, counties, streets, institutions, buildings, and other things, which we constantly particularize, have no other proper names than such as are thus formed, and such as are still perhaps, in many instances, essentially appellative ! The difficulties respecting these will be further noticed below. A proper noun is the name of some particular individual, group, or people ; as, *Adam*, *Boston*, the *Hudson*, the *Azores*, the *Andes*, the *Romans*, the *Jews*, the *Jesuits*, the *Cherokees*. This is as good a definition as I can give of a proper noun or name. Thus we commonly distinguish the names of particular persons, places, nations, tribes, or sects, with capitals. Yet we name the sun, the moon, the equator, and many other particular objects, without a capital; for the word *the* may give a particular meaning to a common noun, without converting it into a proper name : but if we say *Sol*, for the sun, or *Luna*, for the moon, we write it with a capital. With some apparent inconsistency, we commonly write the word *Gentiles* with a capital, but *pagans*, *heathens*, and *negroes*, without : thus custom has marked these names with degradation. The names of the days of the week, and those of the months, however expressed, appear to me to partake of the nature of proper names, and to require capitals : as, *Sunday*, *Monday*, *Tuesday*, *Wednesday*, *Thursday*, *Friday*, *Saturday* ; or, as the Friends denominate them, *Firstday*, *Secondday*, *Thirdday*, *Fourthday*, *Fifthday*, *Sixthday*, *Seventhday*. So, if they will not use *January*, *February*, &c., they should write as proper names their *Firstmonth*, *Secondmonth*, &c. The Hebrew names for the months, were also proper nouns : to wit, Abib, Zif, Sivan, Thamuz, Ab, Elul, Tisri, Marchesvan, Chisleu, Tebeth, Shebat, Adar; the year, with the ancient Jews, beginning, as ours once did, in March.

Obs. 8.—On Rule 5th, concerning *Titles of Honour*, it may be observed, that names of office or rank, however high, do not require capitals merely as such; for, when we use them alone in their ordinary sense, or simply place them in apposition with proper names, without intending any particular honour, we begin them with a small letter : as, "the emperor Augustus ;"—" our mighty sovereign, Abbas Carascan ;"—" David the king ;"—" Tidal king of nations ;"—" Bonner, bishop of London ;"—" The sons of Eliphaz, the first-born son of Esau ; duke Teman, duke Omar, duke Zepho, duke Kenaz, duke Korah, duke Gatam, and duke Amalek."—*Gen*. xxxvi, 15. So, sometimes, in addresses in which even the greatest respect is intended to be shown : as, " O *sir*, we came indeed down at the first time to buy food "—*Gen*. xliii, 20. " O my *lord*, let thy servant, I pray thee, speak a word in my *lord's* ears."—*Gen*. xliv, 18. The Bible, which makes small account of worldly honours, seldom uses capitals under this rule ; but, in some editions, we find " Nehemiah the *Tirshatha*," and " Herod the *Tetrarch*," each with a needless capital. Murray, in whose illustrations the word *king* occurs nearly one hundred times, seldom honours his Majesty with a capital ; and, what is more, in all this mawkish mentioning of royalty, nothing is said of it *that is worth knowing*. Examples : "The *king* and the queen had put on their robes."—*Murray's Gram*. p. 154. " The *king*, with his life-guard, has just passed through the village."—*Ib*. 150. " The *king* of Great Britain's dominions."—*Ib*. 45. " On a sudden appeared the *king*."—*Ib*. 146. " Long live the *king* ! "—*Ib*. 146. " On which side soever the *king* cast his eyes."—*Ib*. 150. " It is the *king* of Great Britain's."—*Ib*. 176. " He desired to be their *king*."—*Ib*. 181. " They desired him to be their *king*."—*Ib.* 181. "He caused himself to be proclaimed *king*."—*Ib.* 182. These examples, and thousands more as simple and worthless, are among the pretended quotations by which this excellent man, thought "to promote the cause of virtue, as well as of learning ! "

Obs. 9.—On Rule 6th, concerning *One Capital for Compounds*, I would observe, that perhaps there is nothing more puzzling in grammar, than to find out, amidst all the diversity of random writing, and wild guess-work in printing, the true way in which the compound names of places should be written. For example : What in Greek was " *Ao Areios Pagos*," the *Martial Hill*, occurs twice in the New Testament : once, in the accusative case, " *ton Areion Pagon*," which is rendered *Areopagus ;* and once, in the genitive, " *tou Areiou Pagou*," which, in different copies of the English Bible is made *Mars' Hill, Mars' hill, Mars'-hill, Marshill, Mars Hill*, and perhaps *Mars hill.* But if *Mars* must needs be put in the possessive case, (which I doubt,) they are all wrong : for then it should be *Mars's Hill ;* as the name *Campus Martius* is rendered "*Mars's Field*," in Collier's Life of Marcus Antoninus. We often use nouns adjectively ; and *Areios* is an adjective : I would therefore write this name *Mars Hill*, as we write *Bunker Hill.* Again : *Whitehaven* and *Fairhaven* are commonly written with single capitals ; but, of six or seven *towns* called *Newhaven* or *New Haven*, some have the name in one word and some in two. *Haven* means *a harbour*, and the words, *New Haven*, written separately, would naturally be understood of a harbour : the close compound is obviously more suitable for the name of a city or town. In England, compounds of this kind are more used than in America ; and in both countries the tendency of common usage seems to be, to contract and consolidate such terms. Hence the British counties are almost all named by compounds ending with the word *shire ;* as, Nottinghamshire, Derbyshire, Staffordshire, Leicestershire, Northamptonshire, Warwickshire, Worcestershire, &c. But the best books we have, are full of discrepancies and errors in respect to names, whether foreign or domestic ; as, " *Ulswater* is somewhat smaller. The handsomest is *Derwentwater*."—*Balbi's Geog.* p. 212. " *Ullwater*, a lake of England," &c. " *Derwent-Water*, a lake in Cumberland," &c.—*Univ. Gazetteer.* " *Ullswater*, lake, Eng. situated partly in Westmoreland," &c.—*Worcester's Gaz.* " *Derwent Water*, lake, Eng. in Cumberland."—*Ibid.* These words, I suppose, should be written *Ullswater* and *Derwentwater.*

Obs. 10.—An affix, or termination, differs from a distinct word ; and is commonly understood otherwise, though it may consist of the same letters and have the same sound. Thus, if I were to write *Stow Bridge*, it would be understood of a *bridge ;* if *Stowbridge*, of a *town :* or the latter might even be the name of a *family.* So *Belleisle* is the proper name of a *strait ;* and *Belle Isle* of several different *islands* in France and America. Upon this plain distinction, and the manifest inconvenience of any violation of so clear an analogy of the language, depends the propriety of most of the corrections which I shall offer under Rule 6th. But if the inhabitants of any place choose to call their town a creek, a river, a harbour, or a bridge, and to think it officious in other men to pretend to know better, they may do as they please. If between them and their correctors there lie a mutual charge of misnomer, it is for the literary world to determine who is right. Important names are sometimes acquired by mere accident. Those which are totally inappropriate, no reasonable design can have bestowed. Thus a fancied resemblance between the island of Aquidneck, in Narraganset Bay, and that of Rhodes, in the Ægean Sea, has at length given to a *state*, or *republic*, which lies *chiefly on the main land*, the absurd name of *Rhode Island ;* so that now, to distinguish *Aquidneck* itself, geographers resort to the strange phrase, " *the Island of Rhode Island.*"—*Balbi.* The official title of this little republic, is, " *the State of Rhode Island and Providence Plantations.*" But this name is not only too long for popular use, but it is doubtful in its construction and meaning. It is capable of being understood in four different ways. 1. A stranger to the fact, would not learn from this phrase, that the " Providence Plantations " are included in the " State of Rhode Island," but would naturally infer the contrary. 2. The phrase, " Rhode Island and Providence Plantations," may be supposed to mean " Rhode Island [Plantations] and Providence Plantations." 3. It may be understood to mean " Rhode Island and Providence [i. e. two] Plantations." 4. It may be taken for "Rhode Island" [i. e. as an island] and the "Providence Plantations." Which, now, of all these did Charles the Second mean, when he gave the colony this name, with his charter, in 1663 ? It happened that he meant the last ; but I doubt whether any man in the state, except perhaps some learned lawyer, can *parse* the phrase, with any certainty of its true construction and meaning. This old title can never be used, except in law. To write the popular name *Rhodeisland*, as Dr. Webster has it,[*] would be some improvement upon it ; but to make it *Rhodeland*, or simply *Rhode*, would be much more appropriate. As for *Rhode Island*, it ought to mean nothing but the island ; and it is, in fact, *an abuse of language*, to apply it otherwise. In one of his para-

* Webster's old American Spelling-Book, p. 121.

ing lessons, Sanborn gives us for good English the following tautology : " *Rhode Island* derived its name from the *island* of *Rhode Island.*"—*Analytical Gram.* p. 37. Think of that sentence !

Obs. 11.—On Rules 7th and 8th, concerning *Two Capitals for Compounds*, I would observe, with a general reference to those *compound terms* which designate particular places or things, that it is often no easy matter to determine, either from custom or from analogy, whether such common words as may happen to be embraced in them, are to be accounted parts of compound proper names and written with capitals, or to be regarded as appellatives, requiring small letters according to Rule 9th. Again the question may be, whether they ought not to be joined to the foregoing word, according to Rule 6th. Let the numerous examples under these four rules be duly considered : for usage, in respect to each of them, is diverse ; so much so, that we not unfrequently find it contradictory, in the very same page, paragraph, or even sentence. Perhaps we may reach some principles of uniformity and consistency, by observing the several different kinds of phrases thus used. 1. We often add an adjective to an old proper name to make a new one, or to serve the purpose of distinction : as, New York, New Orleans, New England, New Bedford ; North America, South America ; Upper Canada, Lower Canada ; Great Pedee, Little Pedee ; East Cambridge, West Cambridge ; Troy, West Troy. All names of this class require two capitals : except a few which are joined together ; as *Northampton*, which is sometimes more analogically written *North Hampton*. 2. We often use the possessive case with some common noun after it ; as, Behring's Straits, Baffin's Bay, Cook's Inlet, Van Diemen's Land, Martha's Vineyard, Sacket's Harbour, Glenn's Falls. Names of this class generally have more than one capital ; and perhaps all of them should be written so, except such as coalesce ; as, Gravesend, Moorstown, the Crowsnest. 3. We sometimes use two common nouns with *of* between them ; as, the Cape of Good Hope, the Isle of Man, the Isles of Shoals, the Lake of the Woods, the Mountains of the Moon. Such nouns are usually written with more than one capital. I would therefore write "the Mount of Olives" in this manner, though it is not commonly found so in the Bible. 4. We often use an adjective and a common noun ; as, the Yellow sea, the Indian ocean, the White hills, Crooked lake, the Red river ; or, with two capitals, the Yellow Sea, the Indian Ocean, the White Hills, Crooked Lake, the Red River. In this class of names the adjective is the distinctive word, and always has a capital ; respecting the other term, usage is divided, but seems rather to favour two capitals. 5. We frequently put an appellative, or common noun, before or after a proper name ; as, New York city, Washington street, Plymouth county, Greenwich village. "The Carondelet canal extends from the city of New Orleans to the bayou St. John, connecting lake Pontchartrain with the Mississippi river."—*Balbi's Geog.* This is apposition. In phrases of this kind, the common noun often has a capital, but it seldom absolutely requires it ; and in general a small letter is more correct, except in some few instances in which the common noun is regarded as a permanent part of the name ; as in *Washington City, Jersey City*. 6. The words *Mount, Cape, Lake*, and *Bay*, are now generally written with capitals when connected with their proper names ; as, Mount Hope, Cape Cod, Lake Erie, Casco Bay. But they are not always so written, even in modern books ; and in the Bible we read of " mount Horeb, mount Sinai, mount Zion, mount Olivet," and many others, always with a single capital.

Obs. 12.—In modern compound names, the hyphen is now less frequently used than it was a few years ago. They seldom, if ever, need it, unless they are employed as adjectives ; and then there is a manifest propriety in inserting it. Thus the phrase, " the New London Bridge," can be understood only of a new bridge in London ; and if we intend by it a bridge in New London, we must say, " the New-London Bridge." So "the New York Directory " is not properly a directory for New York, but a new directory for York. I have seen several books with titles which, for this reason, were evidently erroneous. With respect to the ancient Scripture names, of this class, we find, in different editions of the Bible, as well as in other books, many discrepancies. The reader may see a very fair specimen of them, by comparing together the last two vocabularies of Walker's Key. He will there meet with an abundance of examples like these : "Uz'zen Shérah, Uzzen-shérah ; Talitha Cúmi, Talithacúmi ; Náthan Mélech, Náthan'-melech ; A'bel Mehólath, Abel-mehólah ; Házel Elpóni, Hazelepóni ; Az'noth Tábor, Aznoth-tábor ; Báal Ham'on, Baal-hámon ; Hámon Gog, Ham'ongog ; Báal Zébub, Báalz'ebub ; Shéthar Boz'näi, Shether-boz'näi ; Meródach Bal'adan, Merodach-bal'adan." All these glaring inconsistencies, and many more, has Dr. Webster restereotyped from Walker, in his octavo Dictionary ! I see no more need of the hyphen in such names, than in those of modern times. They ought, in some instances, to be joined together without it ; and, in others, to be written separately, with double capitals. But special regard should be had to the ancient text. The phrase, "Talitha, cumi "—i. e. "Damsel, arise "—is found in some Bibles, "Talitha-cumi ;" but this form of it is no more correct than either of those quoted above. See *Mark*, v, 41st, *in Griesbach's Greek Testament*, where a comma divides this expression.

OBS. 13.—On Rule 11th, concerning *Derivatives*, I would observe, that not only the proper adjectives, to which this rule more particularly refers, but also nouns, and even verbs, derived from such adjectives, are frequently, if not generally, written with an initial capital. Thus, from *Greece*, we have *Greek, Greeks, Greekish, Greekling, Grecize, Grecism, Grecian, Grecians, Grecianize.* So Murray, copying Blair, speaks of " *Latinized English ;*" and, again, of style strictly " *English*, without *Scotticisms* or *Gallicisms.*"— *Mur. Gram.* p. 295; *Blair's Lect.* p. 93. But it is questionable, how far this principle respecting capitals ought to be carried. The examples in Dr. Johnson's quarto Dictionary exhibit the words, *gallicisms, anglicisms, hebrician, latinize, latinized, judaized,* and *christianized,* without capitals; and the words *Latinisms, Grecisms, Hebraisms,* and *Frenchified,* under like circumstances, with them. Dr. Webster also defines *Romanize,* " To *Latinize ;* to conform to *Romish* opinions." In the examples of Johnson, there is a manifest inconsistency. Now, with respect to adjectives from proper names, and also to the nouns formed immediately from such adjectives, it is clear that they ought to have capitals : no one will contend that the words *American* and *Americans* should be written with a small *a* With respect to *Americanism, Gallicism,* and other similar words, there may be some room to doubt. But I prefer a capital for these. And, that we may have a uniform rule to go by, I would not stop here, but would write *Americanize* and *Americanized* with a capital also ; for it appears that custom is in favour of thus distinguishing nearly all verbs and participles of this kind, so long as they retain an obvious reference to their particular origin. But when any such word ceases to be understood as referring directly to the proper name, it may properly be written without a capital. Thus we write *jalap* from *Jalapa, hermetical* from *Hermes, hymeneal* from *Hymen, simony,* from *Simon, philippic* from *Philip ;* the verbs, to *hector,* to *romance,* to *japan,* to *christen,* to *philippize,* to *galvanize ;* and the adverbs *hermetically* and *jesuitically,* all without a capital : and perhaps *judaize, christianize,* and their derivatives, may join this class. Dr. Webster's octavo Dictionary mentions " the *prussic* acid" and "*prussian* blue," without a capital ; and so does Worcester's.

OBS. 14.—On Rule 12th, concerning *I* and *O*, it may be observed, that although many who occasionally write, are ignorant enough to violate this, as well as every other rule of grammar, yet no printer ever commits blunders of this sort. Consequently, the few erroneous examples which will be exhibited for correction under it, will not be undesigned mistakes. Among the errors of books, we do not find the printing of the words *I* and *O* in small characters ; but the confounding of *O* with the other interjection *oh,* is not uncommon even among grammarians. The latter has no concern with this rule, nor is it equivalent to the former, as a sign : *O* is a note of wishing, earnestness, and vocative address ; but *oh* is, properly, a sign of sorrow, pain, or surprise. In the following example, therefore, a line from Milton is perverted :

" *Oh* thou ! that with surpassing glory crowned ! "—*Bucke's Gram.* p. 88.

OBS. 15.—On Rule 13th, concerning *Poetry,* it may be observed, that the principle applies only to regular versification, which is the common form, if not the distinguishing mark, of poetical composition. And, in this, the practice of beginning every line with a capital is almost universal ; but I have seen some books in which it was whimsically disregarded. Such poetry as that of Macpherson's Ossian, or such as the common translation of the Psalms, is subjected neither to this rule, nor to the common laws of verse.

OBS. 16.—On Rule 14th, concerning *Examples, Speeches,* and *Quotations,* it may be observed, that the propriety of beginning these with a capital or otherwise, depends in some measure upon their form. One may suggest certain words by way of example, (as *see, saw, seeing, seen,*) and they will require no capital ; or he may sometimes write one half of a sentence in his own words, and quote the other with the gullemets and no capital ; but whatsoever is cited as being said with other relations of what is called *person,* requires something to distinguish it from the text into which it is woven. Thus Cobbett observes, that, " The French, in their Bible, say *Le Verbe,* where we say *The Word.*" — *E. Gram.* p. 21. Cobbett says *the whole* of this ; but he here refers one short phrase to the French nation, and an other to the English, not improperly beginning each with a capital, and further distinguishing them by Italics. Our common Bibles make no use of the quotation points, but rely solely upon capitals and the common points, to show where any particular speech begins or ends. In some instances, the insufficiency of these means is greatly felt, notwithstanding the extraordinary care of the original writers, in the use of introductory phrases. Murray says, " When a quotation is brought in obliquely after a comma, a capital is unnecessary : as, " Solomon observes, 'that pride goes before destruction.'" — *Octavo Gram.* p. 284. But, as the word ' *that* ' belongs not to Solomon, and the next word begins his assertion, I think we ught to write it, "Solomon observes, that, '*Pride goeth* before destruction.'" Or, if we do not mean to quote him literally, we may omit the guillemets, and say, "Solomon observes that pride goes before destruction."

IMPROPRIETIES FOR CORRECTION.

ERRORS RESPECTING CAPITALS.

☞ [The improprieties in the following examples are to be corrected orally by the learner, according to the formulas given, or according to others framed from them with such slight changes as the several quotations may require. A correct example will occasionally be admitted for the sake of contrast, or that the learner may see the quoted author's inconsistency. It will also serve as a block over which stupidity may stumble and wake up. But a full explanation of what is intended, will be afforded in the Key.]

UNDER RULE I. — OF BOOKS.

"Many a reader of the bible knows not who wrote the acts of the apostles." — *G. B.*

[FORMULE OF CORRECTION.—Not proper, because the words, *bible*, *acts*, and *apostles*, here begin with small letters. But, according to Rule 1st, "When particular books are mentioned by their names, the chief words in their titles begin with capitals, and the other *letters* are small." Therefore, "Bible" should begin with a capital B; and "Acts" and "Apostles," each with a large A.]

"The sons of Levi, the chief of the fathers, were written in the book of the chronicles." — SCOTT'S BIBLE: *Neh.* xii, 23. "Are they not written in the book of the acts of Solomon?" — SCOTT, ALGER: 1 *Kings*, xi, 41. "Are they not written in the book of the Chronicles of the kings of Israel?" — ALGER: 1 *Kings*, xxii, 39. "Are they not written in the book of the chronicles of the kings of Judah?" — SCOTT: *ib.* ver. 45. "Which were written in the law of Moses, and in the prophets, and in the psalms." — SCOTT: *Luke*, xxiv, p. 44. "The narrative of which may be seen in Josephus's History of the Jewish wars." — *Scott's Preface*, p ix. "This history of the Jewish war was Josephus's first work, and published about A. D. 75." — *Note to Josephus.* "'I have read,' says Photius, 'the chronology of Justus of Tiberias.'" — *Ib. Jos. Life.* "A philosophical grammar, written by James Harris, Esquire." — *Murray's Gram.* p. 34. "The reader is referred to Stroud's sketch of the slave laws." — *Anti-Slavery May.* i, 25. "But God has so made the bible that it interprets itself." — *Ib.* i, 78. "In 1562, with the help of Hopkins, he completed the psalter." — *Music of Nature*, p. 283. "Gardiner says this of *Sternhold*; of whom the universal biographical dictionary and the American encyclopedia affirm, that he died in 1549." — *Author.* "The title of a Book, to wit : 'English Grammar in familiar lectures,'" &c.—*Kirkham's Gram.* p. 2. "We had not, at that time, seen Mr. Kirkham's 'Grammar in familiar Lectures.'" — *Ib.* p. 3. "When you parse, you may spread the Compendium before you." — *Ib.* p. 53. "Whenever you parse, you may spread the compendium before you." — *Ib.* p. 113. "Adelung was the author of a grammatical and critical dictionary of the German language, and other works." — *Univ. Biog. Dict.* "Alley, William, author of 'the poor man's library,' and a translation of the Pentateuch, died in 1570." — *Ib.*

UNDER RULE II. — OF FIRST WORDS.

"Depart instantly : improve your time : forgive us our sins." — *Murray's Gram.* p. 61.

[FORMULE.—Not proper, because the words *improve* and *forgive* begin with small letters. But, according to Rule 2nd, "The first word of every distinct sentence should begin with a capital." Therefore, "Improve" should begin with a capital I; and "Forgive," with a capital F.]

EXAMPLES: "Gold is corrupting ; the sea is green ; a lion is bold." — *Mur. Gram.* p. 170 ; *et al.* Again : "It may rain ; he may go or stay ; he would walk ; they should learn." — *Ib.* p. 64 ; *et al.* Again : "Oh! I have alienated my friend ; alas ! I fear for life." — *Ib.* p. 128 ; *et al.* Again : "He went from London to York ;" "she is above disguise;" "they are supported by industry." — *Ib.* p. 28 ; *et al.* "On the foregoing examples, I have a word to say. they are better than a fair specimen of their kind. our grammars abound with worse illustrations. their models of English are generally spurious quotations. few of their proof-texts have any just parentage. goose-eyes are abundant ; but names scarce. who fathers the foundlings? nobody. then let their merit be nobody's, and their defects his who could write no better." — *Author.* "goose-eyes!" says a bright boy ; "pray, what are they? does this Mr. Author make new words when he pleases? *dead-eyes* are in a ship. they are blocks, with holes in them. -but what are goose-eyes in grammar?" ANSWER: "goose-eyes are quotation points. some of the Germans gave them this name, making a jest of their form. the French call them *guillemets*, from the name of their inventor."—*Author.* "*it* is a personal pronoun, of the third person singular."—*Comly's Gram.* 12th Ed. p. 126. "*ourselves* is a personal pronoun,

11

of the first person plural." — *Ib.* 138. " *thee* is a personal pronoun, of the second person singular." — *Ib.* 126. " *contentment* is a noun common, of the third person singular." — *Ib.* 128. " *wert* is a neuter verb, of the indicative mood, imperfect tense." — *Ib.* 129.

UNDER RULE III.—OF DEITY.

" O thou dispenser of life ! thy mercies are boundless."—*W. Allen's Gram.* p. 449.

[FORMULE—Not proper, because the word *dispenser* begins with a small letter. But, according to Rule 3d, " All names of the Deity, and sometimes their emphatic substitutes, should begin with capitals. Therefore, " Dispenser " should here begin with a capital D.]

" Shall not the judge of all the earth do right?"—SCOTT: *Gen.* xviii, 25. " And the spirit of God moved upon the face of the waters."—*Murray's Gram.* p. 330. It is the gift of him, who is the great author of good, and the Father of mercies."—*Ib.* 287. " This is thy god that brought thee up out of Egypt."—SCOTT, ALGER: *Neh.* ix, 18. " For the lord is our defence; and the holy one of Israel is our king." See *Psalm* lxxxix, 18. " By making him the responsible steward of heaven's bounties."—*Anti-Slavery Mag.* i, 29. " Which the Lord, the righteous judge, shall give me at that day."—SCOTT, FRIENDS: 2 *Tim.* iv, 8. " The cries of them • • • entered into the ears of the Lord of sabaoth." —SCOTT: *Jas.* v, 4. " In Horeb, the deity revealed himself to Moses, as the eternal I am, the self-existent one; and, after the first discouraging interview of his messengers with Pharaoh, he renewed his promise to them, by the awful name, jehovah—a name till then unknown, and one which the Jews always held it a fearful profanation to pronounce."—*Author.* " And god spake unto Moses, and said unto him, I am the lord: and I appeared unto Abraham, unto Isaac, and unto Jacob, by the name of god almighty; but by my name jehovah was I not known to them." See* *Exod.* vi, 2. " Thus saith the lord the king of Israel, and his redeemer the lord of hosts; I am the first, and I am the last; and besides me there is no god." See *Isa.* xliv, 6.

> " His impious race their blasphemy renew'd,
> And nature's king through nature's optics view'd."—*Dryden*, p. 90.

UNDER RULE IV.—OF PROPER NAMES.

" Islamism prescribes fasting during the month ramazan."—*Balbi's Geog.* p. 17.

[FORMULE.—Not proper, because the word *ramazan* here begins with a small letter. But, according to Rule 4th, " Proper names, of every description, should always begin with capitals." Therefore, " Ramazan " should begin with a capital R. The word is also misspelled: it should rather be *Ramadan.*]

" Near mecca, in arabia, is jebel nor, or the mountain of light, on the top of which the mussulmans erected a mosque, that they might perform their devotions where, according to their belief, mohammed received from the angel gabriel the first chapter of the Koran."—*Author.* " In the kaaba at mecca, there is a celebrated block of volcanic basalt, which the mohammedans venerate as the gift of gabriel to abraham, but their ancestors once held it to be an image of remphan, or saturn; so 'the image which fell down from jupiter,' to share with diana the homage of the ephesians, was probably nothing more than a meteoric stone."—*Id.* " When the lycaonians, at lystra, took paul and barnabas to be gods, they called the former mercury, on account of his eloquence, and the latter jupiter, for the greater dignity of his appearance."—*Id.* " Of the writings of the apostolic fathers of the first century, but few have come down to us; yet we have in those of barnabas, clement of rome, hermas, ignatius, and polycarp, very certain evidence of the authenticity of the New Testament, and the New Testament is a voucher for the old."—*Id.*

" It is said by tatian, that theagenes of rhegium, in the time of cambyses, atesimbrotus the thracian, antimachus the colophonian, herodotus of halicarnassus, dionysius the olynthian, ephorus of cumæ, philochorus the athenian, metaclides and chamæleon the peripatetics, and zenodotus, aristophanes, callimachus, crates, eratosthenes, aristarchus, and apollodorus, the grammarians, all wrote concerning the poetry, the birth, and the age of homer. (See *Coleridge's Introd.* p. 57.) Yet, for aught that now appears, the life of homer is as fabulous as that of hercules; and some have even suspected, that, as the son of jupiter and alcmena, has fathered the deeds of forty other herculeses, so this unfathered son of critheis, themisto, or whatever dame—this meleisgenes, mæ-

---

* Where the word " *See* " accompanies the reference, the reader may generally understand that the citation, whether right or wrong in regard to grammar, is not in all respects *exactly* as it will be found in the place referred to. Cases of this kind, however, will occur but seldom; and it is hoped the reason for admitting a few, will be sufficiently obvious Some rules are so generally known and observed, that one might search long for half a dozen examples of their undesigned violation. Wherever an error is made intentionally in the Exercises, the true reading and reference are to be expected in the Key.

onides, homer—the blind schoolmaster, and poet, of smyrna, chios, colophon, salamis, rhodes, argos, athens, or whatever place—has, by the help of lycurgus, solon, pisistratus, and other learned ancients, been made up of many poets or homers, and set so far aloft and aloof on old parnassus, as to become a god in the eyes of all greece, a wonder in those of all christendom."—*Author*.

> "Why so sagacious in your guesses?
> Your *effs*, and *tees*, and *arrs*, and *esses!*"—*Swift*.

UNDER RULE V.—OF TITLES.

"The king has conferred on him the title of duke."—*Murray's Key*, 8vo, p. 193.

[FORMULE.—Not proper, because the word *duke* begins with a small letter. But, according to Rule 5th, "Titles of office or honour, and epithets of distinction, applied to persons, begin usually with capitals." Therefore, "Duke" should here begin with a capital D.]

"At the court of queen Elizabeth."—*Murray's Gram. Oct.* p. 157; *Duod.* p. 126; *Fisk's*, 115; *et al.* "The laws of nature are, truly, what lord Bacon styles his aphorisms, laws of laws."—*Murray's Key*, p. 260. "Sixtus the fourth was, if I mistake not, a great collector of books."—*Ib.* p. 257. "Who at that time made up the court of king Charles the second."—*Murray's Gram.* p. 314. "In case of his majesty's dying without issue."—*Kirkham's Gram.* p. 181. "King Charles the first was beheaded in 1649."—*Allen's Gram.* p. 45. "He can no more impart or (to use lord Bacon's word,) *transmit* convictions."—*Kirkham's Eloc.* p. 220. "I reside at lord Stormont's, my old patron and benefactor."—*Murray's Gram.* p. 176. "We staid a month at lord Lyttleton's, the ornament of his country."—*Ib.* p. 177. "Whose prerogative is it? It is the king of Great Britain's;" "That is the duke of Bridgewater's canal;" "The bishop of Landaff's excellent book;" "The Lord mayor of London's authority."—*Ib.* p. 176. "Why call ye me lord, lord, and do not the things which I say?"—See GRIESBACH: *Luke*, vi, 46. "And of them he chose twelve, whom also he named apostles."—SCOTT: *Luke*, vi, 13. "And forthwith he came to Jesus, and said, Hail, master; and kissed him." See *the Greek: Matt.* xxvi, 49. "And he said, Nay, father Abraham: but if one went unto them from the dead, they will repent."—*Luke*, xvi, 30.

UNDER RULE VI.—OF ONE CAPITAL.

"Fall River, a village in Massachusetts, population 3431." See *Univ. Gaz.* p. 416.

[FORMULE.—Not proper, because the name *Fall River* is here written in two parts, and with two capitals. But, according to Rule 6th, "Those compound proper names which by analogy incline to a union of their parts without a hyphen, should be so written, and have but one capital." Therefore, *Fallriver*, as the name of a *town*, should be one word, and retain but one capital.]

"Dr. Anderson died at West Ham, in Essex, in 1808."—*Biog. Dict.* "Mad River, [the name of] two towns in Clark and Champaign counties, Ohio."—*Williams's Universal Gazetteer.* "White Creek, town of Washington county, N. York."—*Ib.* "Salt Creek, the name of four towns in different parts of Ohio."—*Ib.* "Salt Lick, a town of Fayette county, Pennsylvania."—*Ib.* "Yellow Creek, a town of Columbiana county, Ohio."—*Ib.* "White Clay, a hundred of New Castle county, Delaware."—*Ib.* "Newcastle, town and halfshire of Newcastle county, Delaware."—*Ib.* "Sing-Sing, a village of West Chester county, New York, situated in the town of Mount Pleasant."—*Ib.* "West Chester, a county of New York; also a town in Westchester county."—*Ib.* "West Town, a village of Orange county, New York."—*Ib.* "White Water, a town of Hamilton county, Ohio."—*Ib.* "White Water River, a considerable stream that rises in Indiana, and flowing southeasterly, unites with the Miami in Ohio."—*Ib.* "Black Water, a village of Hampshire, in England, and a town in Ireland."—*Ib.* "Black Water, the name of seven different rivers, in England, Ireland, and the United States."—*Ib.* "Red Hook, a town of Dutchess county, New York, on the Hudson."—*Ib* "Kinderhook, a town of Columbia county, New York, on the Hudson."—*Ib.* "New Fane, a town of Niagara county, New York."—*Ib.* "Lake Port, a town of Chicot county, Arkansas."—*Ib.* "Moose Head Lake, the chief source of the Kennebeck, in Maine."—*Ib.* "Macdonough, a county of Illinois, population (in 1830) 2,959."—*Ib.* p. 408. "Mc Donough, a county of Illinois, with a courthouse, at Macomb."—*Ib.* p. 185. "Half-Moon, the name of two towns, in New York and Pennsylvania; also of two bays in the West Indies." See *Worcester's Gaz.* "Le Bœuf, a town of Erie county, Pennsylvania, near a small lake of the same name."—*Ib.* "Charles City, James City, Elizabeth City, names of counties in Virginia, not cities, nor towns." See *Univ. Gas.* "The superior qualities of the waters of the Frome, here called Stroud water."—*Balbi's Geog.* p. 223.

UNDER RULE VII.—TWO CAPITALS.

"The Forth rises on the north side of Benlomond, and runs easterly."—*Glasg. Geog.*

[FORMULE.—Not proper, because the name " *Benlomond* " is compounded under one capital, contrary to the general analogy of other similar terms. But, according to Rule 7th, " The compounding of a name under one capital should be avoided when the general analogy of other similar terms suggests a separation under two." Therefore, " Ben Lomond " should be written with two capitals and no hyphen.]

"The red granite of Ben-nevis is said to be the finest in the world."—*Ib.* ii, 311. "Ben-more, in Perthshire, is 3,915 feet above the level of the sea."—*Ib.* 313. "The height of Bencleugh is 2,420 feet."—*Ib.* "In Sutherland and Caithness, are Ben Ormod, Ben Clibeg, Ben Grin, Ben Hope, and Ben Lugal."—*Ib.* 311. "Benvracky is 2,756 feet high; Ben-ledi, 3,009; and Ben-voirlich, 3,300."—*Ib.* 313. "The river Dochart gives the name of Glendochart to the vale through which it runs."—*Ib.* 314. "About ten miles from its source, the Tay diffuses itself into Lochdochart."—*Geog. altered.* LAKES:—"Lochard, Loch-Achray, Loch-Con, Loch-Doine, Loch-Katrine, Loch-Lomond, Loch-Voil."—*Scott's Lady of the Lake.* GLENS:—"Glenfinlas, Glen Fruin, Glen Luss, Ross-dhu, Leven-glen, Strath-Endrick, Strath-Gartney, Strath-Ire."—*Ib.* MOUNTAINS:—"Ben-an, Benharrow, Benledi, Ben-Lomond, Benvoirlich, Ben-venue, and sometimes Benvenue."—*Ib.* "Fenelon died in 1715, deeply lamented by all the inhabitants of the Low-countries."—*Murray's Sequel,* p. 322. "And Pharaoh-nechoh made Eliakim, the son of Josiah, king."—SCOTT, FRIENDS: 2 *Kings,* xxiii, 34. "Those who seem so merry and well pleased, call her *Good Fortune;* but the others, who weep and wring their hands, *Bad-fortune.*"—*Collier's Tablet of Cebes.*

UNDER RULE VIII.—OF COMPOUNDS.

"When Joab returned, and smote Edom in the valley of salt."—SCOTT: *Ps.* lx, *title.*

[FORMULE.—Not proper, because the words *valley* and *salt* begin with small letters. But, according to Rule 8th. " When any adjective or common noun is made a distinct part of a compound proper name, it ought to begin with a capital. Therefore, " Valley " should here begin with a capital V, and " Salt," with a capital S.]

"Then Paul stood in the midst of Mars' hill and said," &c.—SCOTT: *Acts,* xvii, 22. "And at night he went out, and abode in the mount that is called the mount of Olives." —*Luke,* xxi, 37. "Abgillus, son of the king of the Frisii, surnamed Prester John, was in the Holy land with Charlemagne."—*Univ. Biog. Dict.* "Cape Palmas, in Africa, divides the Grain coast from the Ivory coast."—*Dict. of Geog.* p. 125. "The North Esk, flowing from Loch-lee, falls into the sea three miles north of Montrose."—*Ib.* p. 232. "At Queen's ferry, the channel of the Forth is contracted by promontories on both coasts."—*Ib.* p. 233. "The Chestnut ridge is about twenty-five miles west of the Alleghanies, and Laurel ridge, ten miles further west."—*Bulbi's Geog* p. 65. "Washington City, the metropolis of the United States of America."—*W.'s Univ. Gaz.* p. 380. "Washington city, in the District of Columbia, population (in 1830) 18,826."—*Ib.* p. 408. "The loftiest peak of the white mountains, in new Hampshire, is called mount Washington."—*Author.* "Mount's bay, in the west of England, lies between the land's end and lizard point."—*Id.* "Salamis, an island of the Egean Sea, off the southern coast of the ancient Attica."—*Dict. of Geog.* "Rhodes, an island of the Egean sea, the largest and most easterly of the Cyclades."—*Ib.* "But he overthrew Pharaoh and his host in the Red sea."—BRUCE'S BIBLE: *Ps.* cxxxvi, 15. "But they provoked him at the sea, even at the Red sea."—SCOTT: *Ps.* cvi, 7.*

UNDER RULE IX.—OF APPOSITION.

"At that time, Herod the Tetrarch heard of the fame of Jesus."—ALGER: *Matt.* xiv, 1.

[FORMULE.—Not proper, because the word *Tetrarch* begins with a capital letter. But, according to Rule 8th, " When a common and a proper name are associated merely to explain each other, it is in general sufficient, if the proper name begin with a capital, and the appellative, with a small letter." Therefore, " tetrarch " should here begin with a small *t.*]

"Who has been more detested than Judas the Traitor?"—*Author.* "St. Luke, the Evangelist, was a physician of Antioch, and one of the converts of St. Paul."—*Id.* "Luther, the Reformer, began his bold career by preaching against papal indulgences."—*Id.* "The Poet Lydgate was a disciple and admirer of Chaucer: he died in 1440."—*Id.* "The Grammarian Varro, 'the most learned of the Romans,' wrote three books when he was eighty years old."—*Id.* "John Despauter, the great Grammarian of Flanders, whose works are still valued, died in 1520."—*Id.* "Nero, the Emperor and Tyrant of Rome, slew himself to avoid a worse death."—*Id.* "Cicero the Orator, 'the Father of his Country,' was assassinated at the age of 64."—*Id.*

* " Et irritaverunt ascendentes in mare, Mare rubrum."—*Latin Vulgate, folio, Psal.* cv. 7. This, I think, should have been " Mare Rubrum," with two capitals.—G. BROWN.

"Euripides, the Greek Tragedian, was born in the Island of Salamis, B. C. 476."—*Id.*
"I will say unto God my Rock, Why hast thou forgotten me?"—SCOTT: *Ps.* xlii, 9.
"Staten Island, an island of New York, nine miles below New York City."—*Univ. Gas.*
"When the son of Atreus, King of Men, and the noble Achilles first separated."—*Coleridge's Introd.* p. 83.

"Hermes, his Patron-God, those gifts bestow'd,
Whose shrine with weaning lambs he wont to load."—POPE: *Odys.* B. 19.

UNDER RULE X.—OF PERSONIFICATIONS.

"But wisdom is justified of all her children."—SCOTT, ALGER: *Luke*, vii, 35.

[FORMULE.—Not proper, because the word *wisdom* begins with a small letter. But, according to Rule 10th, "The name of an object personified, when it conveys an idea strictly individual, should begin with a capital." Therefore, "Wisdom" should here begin with a capital W.]

"Fortune and the church are generally put in the feminine gender."—*Murray's Gram.* i, p. 37. "Go to your natural religion; lay before her Mahomet, and his disciples."—*Blair's Rhetoric*, p. 157: See also *Murray's Gram.* i, 347. "O death! where is thy sting? O grave! where is thy victory?"—1 *Cor.* xv, 55; *Murray's Gram.* p. 348; *English Reader*, 31; *Merchant's Gram.* 212. "Ye cannot serve God and Mammon."—SCOTT, FRIENDS, ET AL: *Matt.* vi, 24. "Ye cannot serve God and mammon."—IIDEM: *Luke* xvi, 13. "This house was built as if suspicion herself had dictated the plan." See *Key.* "Poetry distinguishes herself from prose, by yielding to a musical law." See *Key.* "My beauteous deliverer thus uttered her divine instructions: 'My name is religion. I am the offspring of truth and love, and the parent of benevolence, hope, and joy. That monster, from whose power I have freed you, is called superstition: she is the child of discontent, and her followers are fear and sorrow.'" See *Key.* "Neither hope nor fear could enter the retreats; and habit had so absolute a power, that even conscience, if religion had employed her in their favour, would not have been able to force an entrance." See *Key.*

"In colleges and halls in ancient days,
There dwelt a sage called discipline."—*Wayland's M. Sci.* p. 368.

UNDER RULE XI.—OF DERIVATIVES.

"In English, I would have gallicisms avoided."—FELTON: *Johnson's Dict.*

[FORMULE.—Not proper, because the word *gallicisms* here begins with a small letter. But, according to Rule llth, "Words derived from proper names, and having direct reference to particular persons, places, sects, or nations, should begin with capitals." Therefore, "Gallicisms" should begin with a capital G.]

"Sallust was born in Italy, 85 years before the christian era."—*Murray's Seq.* 357. "Dr. Doddridge was not only a great man, but one of the most excellent and useful christians, and christian ministers."—*Ib.* 319. "They corrupt their style with untutored anglicisms."—MILTON: *in Johnson's Dict.* "Albert of Stade, author of a chronicle from the creation to 1286, a benedictine of the 13th century."—*Universal Biog. Dict.* "Graffio, a jesuit of Capua in the 16th century, author of two volumes on moral subjects."—*Ib.* "They frenchify and italianize words whenever they can." See *Key.* "He who sells a christian, sel s the grace of God."—*Anti-Slavery Mag.* p. 77. "The first persecution against the christians, under Nero, began A. D. 64."—*Gregory's Dict.* "P. Rapin, the jesuit, uniformly decides in favour of the Roman writers."—*Cobbett's Gram.* No. 171. "The Roman poet and epicurean philosopher Lucretius has said," &c.—*Cohen's Florida*, p. 107. Spell "calvinistic, atticism, gothicism, epicurism, jesuitism, sabianism, socinianism, anglican, anglicism, anglicize, vandalism, gallicism, romanise."—*Webster's El. Spelling-Book*, 130–133. "The large ternate bat."—*Webster's Dict. w.* ROASET; *Bolles's Dict. w.* ROSET.

"Church-ladders are not always mounted best
By learned clerks, and latinists profess'd."—*Cowper.*

UNDER RULE XII.—OF I AND O.

"Fall back, fall back; i have not room:—o! methinks i see a couple whom i should know."—*Lucian, varied.*

[FORMULE.—Not proper, because the word *I*, which occurs three times, and the word *O*, which occurs once, are here printed in letters of the lower case.* But, according to Rule 12th, "The words *I* and *O* should always be capitals." Therefore, each should be changed to a capital, as often as it occurs.]

"Nay, i live as i did, i think as i did, i love you as i did; but all these are to no purpose: the world will not live, think, or love, as i do."—*Swift, varied.* "Whither,

---

* The printers, from the manner in which they place their types before them, call the small letters "*lower-case letters*," or "*letters of the lower case.*"

o! whither shall i fly? o wretched prince! o cruel reverse of fortune! o father Micipsa! is this the consequence of thy generosity?"—*Sallust, varied.* "When i was a child, i spake as a child, i understood as a child, i thought as a child; but when i became a man, i put away childish things."—1 *Cor.* xiii, 11 : *varied.* "And i heard, but i understood not: then said i, o my Lord, what shall be the end of these things?"—*Dan.* xii, 8: *varied.* "Here am i; i think i am very good, and i am quite sure i am very happy, yet i never wrote a treatise in my life."—*Few Days in Athens, varied.* "Singular, Vocative, o master; Plural, Vocative, o masters."—*Bicknell's Gram.* p. 30.

"I, i am he; o father! rise, behold
Thy son, with twenty winters now grown old!" See *Pope's Odyssey.*

UNDER RULE XIII.—OF POETRY.

"Reason's whole pleasure, all the joys of sense,
lie in three words—health, peace, and competence;
but health consists with temperance alone,
and peace, O virtue! peace is all thy own."
            Pope's Essay on Man, a fine London Edition.

[FORMULE.—Not proper, because the last three lines of this example begin with small letters. But, according to Rule 13th, "Every line in poetry, except what is regarded as making but one verse with the preceding line, should begin with a capital." Therefore, the words, "Lie," "But," and "And," at the commencement of these lines, should severally begin with the capitals L, B, and A.]

"Observe the language well in all you write,
and swerve not from it in your loftiest flight.
The smoothest verse and the exactest sense
displease us, if ill English give offence:
a barbarous phrase no reader can approve;
nor bombast, noise, or affectation love.
In short, without pure language, what you write
can never yield us profit or delight.
Take time for thinking, never work in haste;
and value not yourself for writing fast."
            See *Dryden's Art of Poetry :—British Poets,* Vol. iii, p. 74.

UNDER RULE XIV.—OF EXAMPLES.

"The word *rather* is very properly used to express a small degree or excess of a quality: as, 'she is *rather* profuse in her expenses.'"—*Murray's Gram.* p. 47.

[FORMULE.—Not proper, because the word *she* begins with a small letter. But, according to Rule 14th, "The first word of a full example, of a distinct speech, or of a direct quotation, should begin with a capital." Therefore, the word "She" should here begin with a capital S.]

"*Neither* imports *not either;* that is, not one nor the other: as, 'neither of my friends was there.'"—*Murray's Gram.* p. 56. "When we say, 'he is a tall man,' 'this is a fair day,' we make some reference to the ordinary size of men, and to different weather."—*Ib.* p. 47. "We more readily say, 'A million of men,' than 'a thousand of men.'"—*Ib.* p. 169. "So in the instances, 'two and two are four;' 'the fifth and sixth volumes will complete the set of books.'"—*Ib.* p. 124. "The adjective may frequently either precede or follow it [the verb]: as, 'the man is *happy,*' or, '*happy* is the man:' 'The interview was *delightful;*' or, '*delightful* was the interview.'"—*Ib.* p. 168. "If we say, 'he writes a pen,' 'they ran the river,' 'the tower fell the Greeks,' 'Lambeth is Westminster-abbey,' [we speak absurdly;] and, it is evident, there is a vacancy which must be filled up by some connecting word: as thus, 'He writes *with* a pen;' 'they ran *towards* the river;' 'the tower fell *upon* the Greeks;' 'Lambeth is *over against* Westminster-abbey.'"—*Ib.* p. 118. "Let me repeat it;—he only is great, who has the habits of greatness."—*Murray's Key,* 241. "I say not unto thee, until seven times; but, until seventy times seven." See *Matt.* xviii, 22.

"The Panther smil'd at this; and when, said she,
Were those first councils disallow'd by me?"—*Dryden,* p. 95.

UNDER RULE XV.—OF CHIEF WORDS.

"The supreme council of the nation is called the divan."—*Balbi's Geog.* p. 360.

[FORMULE.—Not proper, because the word *divan* begins with a small letter. But, according to Rule 15th, "Other words of particular importance, and such as denote the principal subjects treated of, may be distinguished by capitals." Therefore, "Divan" should here begin with a capital D.]

"The British parliament is composed of king, lords, and commons."—*Murray's Key,* p. 184. "A popular orator in the House of Commons has a sort of patent for coining as many new terms as he pleases." See *Campbell's Rhet.* p. 169; *Murray's Gram.* 364.

"They may all be taken together, as one name; as, the *house of commons*."—*Merchant's School Gram.* p. 25. "Intrusted to persons in whom the parliament could 'confide."—*Murray's Gram.* 8vo, p. 202. "For 'The Lords' house,' it were certainly better to say, 'The house of lords;' and, in stead of 'The commons' vote,' to say, 'The votes of the commons.'" See *ib.* p. 177, 4th *Amer. Ed.;* also *Priestley's Gram.* p. 69. "The house of lords were so much influenced by these reasons." — *Murray's Gram.* 8vo, p. 152'; *Priestley's Gram.* 188. "Rhetoricians commonly divide them into two great classes; figures of words, and figures of thought. The former, figures of words, are commonly called tropes."—*Blair's Rhet.* p. 132. "Perhaps figures of imagination, and figures of passion, might be a more useful distribution."—*Ib.* p. 133. "Hitherto we have considered sentences, under the heads of perspicuity, unity, and strength."—*Ib.* p. 120.

"The word is then depos'd, and in this view,
　　You rule the scripture, not the scripture you."—*Dryden,* p. 95.

UNDER RULE XVI.—OF NEEDLESS CAPITALS.

"Be of good cheer: It is I; be not afraid."—ALGER: *Matt.* xiv, 27.

[FORMULE.—Not proper, because the word *B* begins with a capital *I*, for which their appears to be neither rule nor reason. But, according to Rule 16th, "Capitals are improper wherever there is not some special rule or reason for their use." Therefore, 'it' should here begin with a small letter, as Dr. Scott has it.]

"Between passion and lying, there is not a Finger's breadth."—*Murray's Key,* p. 240. "Can our Solicitude alter the course, or unravel the intricacy, of human events?'"—*Ib.* p. 242. "The last edition was carefully compared with the Original M. S."—*Ib.* p. 239. "And the governor asked him, saying, Art thou the King of the Jews?"—ALGER: *Matt.* xxvii, 11. "Let them be turned back for a reward of their shame, that say, Aha, Aha!'"—FRIENDS' BIBLE: *Ps.* lxx, 3. "Let them be desolate for a reward of their shame, that say unto me, Aha, aha!'"—IB.: *Ps.* xl, 15. "What think ye of Christ? whose Son is he? They say unto him, The Son of David. He saith unto them, How then doth David in Spirit call him Lord?"—SCOTT: *Matt.* xxii, 42, 43. "Among all Things in the Universe, direct your Worship to the Greatest: And which is that? T is that Being which Manages and Governs all the Rest."—*Meditations of M. Aurelius Antoninus,* p. 76. "As for Modesty and Good Faith, Truth and Justice, they have left this wicked World and retired to Heaven: And now what is it that can keep you here?"—*Ib.* p. 81.

"If Pulse of Verse, a Nation's Temper shows,
　　In keen Iambics English Metre flows."—*Brightland's Gram.* p. 151.

PROMISCUOUS ERRORS RESPECTING CAPITALS.

LESSON I.—MIXED.

"Come, gentle spring, Ethereal mildness, come."—*Gardiner's Music of Nature,* p. 411.

[FORMULE.—1. Not proper, because the word *spring* begins with a small letter. But, according to Rule 10th, "The name of an object personified, when it conveys an idea strictly individual, should begin with a capital." Therefore "Spring" should here begin with a capital S.
2. Not proper again, because the word *Ethereal* begins with a capital E, for which there appears to be neither rule nor reason. But, according to Rule 16th, "Capitals are improper whenever there is not some special rule or reason for their use" Therefore, "ethereal" should here begin with a small letter.]

As, "He is the Cicero of his age; he is reading the lives of the Twelve Cæsars."—*Murray's Gram.* p. 36. "In the History of Henry the fourth, by father Daniel, we are surprised at not finding him the great man."—*Priestley's Gram.* p. 151. "In the history of Henry the fourth, by Father Daniel, we are surprised at not finding him the great man."—*Murray's Gram.* p. 172; *Ingersoll's,* 187; *Fisk's,* 99. "Do not those same poor peasants use the Lever and the Wedge, and many other instruments?'"—*Murray,* 288; from *Harris,* 293. "Arithmetic is excellent for the gauging of Liquors; Geometry, for the measuring of Estates; Astronomy, for the making of Almanacks; and Grammar, perhaps, for the drawing of Bonds and Conveyances."—*Harris's Hermes,* p. 295. "The wars of Flanders, written in Latin by Famianus Strada, is a book of some note."—*Blair's Rhet.* p. 364. "William is a noun.—why? *was* is a verb.—why? *a* is an article—why? *very* is an adverb.—why?" &c.—*Merchant's School Gram.* p. 20. "In the beginning was the word, and that word was with God, and God was that word."—*Gwilt's Saxon Gram.* p. 49. "The greeks are numerous in thessaly, macedonia, romelia, and albania."—*Balbi, varied.* "He is styled by the Turks, Sultan (Mighty) or Padishah (lord)."—*Balbi's Geog.* p. 360. "I will ransom them from the power of the grave; I will redeem them from death: O death, I will be thy plagues;* O grave, I will be thy destruction."—SCOTT, ALGER, ET AL.: *Hosea*, xiii, 14. "Silver and Gold have I none; but such as I have, give I unto thee."—*Murray's Gram.* 8vo, p. 321. "Return, we beseech thee, O God of Hosts, look down from heaven, and behold, and visit this vine."—*Ib.* p. 342. "In the Attic Commonwealth, it was the privilege of every citizen to rail in public."—*Ib.* p. 316. "They assert that, in the phrases, 'give me *that*,' '*this* is John's,' and '*such* were *some* of you,' the words in italics are pronouns: but that, in the following phrases, they are not pronouns; '*this* book is instructive,' '*some* boys are ingenious,' '*my* health is declining,' '*our* hearts are deceitful,' &c."—*Ib.* p. 58. "And the coast bends again to the northwest, as far as Far Out head."—*Glasgow Geog.* Vol. ii, p. 308. Dr. Webster, and other makers of spelling-books, very improperly write "sunday, monday, tuesday, wednesday, thursday, friday, saturday," without capitals. See *Webster's Elementary Spelling-Book*, p. 85. "The commander in chief of the Turkish navy is styled the capitan-pasha."—*Balbi's Geog.* p. 360. "Shall we not much rather be in subjection unto the father of spirits, and live?"—SCOTT's BIBLE: *Heb.* xii, 9. "Shall we not much rather be in subjection unto the Father of Spirits, and live?"—FRIENDS' BIBLE: *Heb.* xii, 9. "He was more anxious to attain the character of a christian hero."—*Murray's Sequel*, p. 308. "Beautiful for situation, the joy of the whole earth, is mount Zion."—*Psalms*, xlviii, 2. "The Lord is my Helper, and I will not fear what man shall do unto me."—SCOTT: *Heb.* xiii, 6. "Make haste to help me, O LORD my Salvation."—SCOTT: *Ps.* xxxviii, 22.

"The City, which Thou seest, no other deem
Than great and glorious Rome, Queen of the Earth."
Harris's Hermes, p. 49.

LESSON II.—MIXED.

"That range of hills, known under the general name of mount Jura."—*Priestley's Gram.* p. 170. "He rebuked the Red sea also, and it was dried up."—SCOTT: *Ps.* cvi, 9. "Jesus went unto the mount of Olives."—*John*, viii. 1. "Milton's book, in reply to the *Defence of the king*, by Salmasius, gained him a thousand pounds from the parliament, and killed his antagonist with vexation." See *Murray's Sequel*, 343. "Mandeville, sir John, an Englishman, famous for his travels, born about 1300, died in 1372."—*Biog. Dict.* "Ettrick pen, a mountain in Selkirkshire, Scotland, height 2,200 feet."—*Glasgow Geog.* ii, p. 312. "The coast bends from Dungsby-head in a northwest direction to the promontory of Dunnet head."—*Ib.* p. 307. "Gen. Gaines ordered a detachment of near 300 men, under the command of Major Twiggs, to surround and take an Indian Village, called Fowl Town, about fourteen miles from fort Scott."—*Cohen's Florida*, p. 41. "And he took the damsel by the hand, and said unto her, Talitha Cumi."—ALGER: *Mark*, v, 4. "On religious subjects, a frequent recurrence of picture-language is attended with peculiar force."—*Murray's Gram.* p. 318. "Contemplated with gratitude to their Author, the Giver of all Good."—*Ib.* p. 289. "When he, the Spirit of Truth, is come, he will guide you into all truth."—*Ib.* p. 171; *Fisk*, 98; *Ingersoll*, 185. "See the lecture on verbs, rule XV. note 4."—*Fisk's E. Gram.* p. 117. "At the commencement of lecture II. I informed you that Etymology treats, 3dly, of derivation."—*Kirkham's Gram.* p. 171. "This VIII. lecture is a very important one." —*Ib.* p. 113. "Now read the XI. and XII. lectures *four or five* times over."—*Ib.* p. 152. "In 1752, he was advanced to the bench, under the title of lord Kames."—*Murray's Sequel*, p. 331. "One of his maxims was, 'know thyself.'"—*Lempriere's Dict. n. Chilo.* "Good master, what good thing shall I do, that I may have eternal life?" See *Matt.* xix, 16. "His best known works, however, are 'anecdotes of the earl of Chatham,' 2 vols. 4to., 3 vols. 8vo., and 'biographical, literary, and political anecdotes of several of the most eminent persons of the present age; never before printed,' 3 vols. 8vo. 1797." —*Univ. Biog. Dict. n. Almon.* "O gentle sleep, Nature's soft nurse, how have I frighted thee?"—*Merchant's School Gram.* p. 172. "O sleep, O gentle sleep, Nature's soft nurse," &c.—SINGER's SHAK. *Sec. Part of Hen. IV.*, Act. iii. "Sleep, gentle sleep, Nature's soft nurse," &c.—*Dodd's Beauties of Shakspeare*, p. 129.

"And Peace, O, Virtue ! Peace is all thy own."—*Pope's Works.* p. 379.
"And peace, O virtue ! peace is all thy own."—*Murray's Gram.* ii, 16.

LESSON III.—MIXED.

"Fenelon united the characters of a nobleman and a christian pastor. His book entitled ' An explication of the Maxims of the Saints concerning the interior life,' gave

---

*I imagine that " *plagues* " should here be *plague*, in the singular number, and not plural. " Ero *mors* tua, ô mors: morsus tuus ero, inferne."—*Vulgate*. "Ποῦ ἡ δίκη σου, θάνατε; ποῦ τὸ κέντρον σου, ᾅ᾽η;" —*Septuagint, ibid.*

considerable offence to the guardians of orthodoxy."—*Murray's Sequel*, p. 321. "When natural religion, who before was only a spectator, is introduced as speaking by the centurion's voice."—*Blair's Rhet.* p. 157. "You cannot deny, that the great mover and author of nature constantly explaineth himself to the eyes of men, by the sensible intervention of arbitrary signs, which have no similitude, or connexion, with the things signified."—*Berkley's Minute Philosopher*, p. 169. "The name of this letter is double U, its form, that of a double V."—*Wilson's Essay on Gram.* p. 19. "Murray, in his spelling book, wrote 'Charles-Town' with a Hyphen and two Capitals." See p. 101. "He also wrote 'european' without a capital." See p. 86. "They profess themselves to be pharisees, who are to be heard and not imitated."—*Calvin's Institutes, Ded.* p. 55. "Dr. Webster wrote both 'Newhaven' and 'Newyork' with single capitals." See his *American Spelling-Book*, p. 111. "Gayhead, the west point of Martha's Vineyard."—*Williams's Univ. Gaz.* Write "Craborchard, Eggharbor, Longisland, Perthamboy, Westhampton, Littlecompton, Newpaltz, Crownpoint, Fellspoint, Sandyhook, Portpenn, Portroyal, Portobello, and Portorico."—*Webster's American Spelling-Book*, 127–140. Write the names of the months: "january, february, march, april, may, june, july, august, september, october, november, december."—*Cobb's Standard Spelling-Book*, 21–40. Write the following names and words properly: "tuesday, wednesday, thursday, friday, saturday, saturn;—christ, christian, christmas, christendom, michaelmas, indian, bacchanals; — Easthampton, omega, johannes, aonian, levitical, deuteronomy, european."—*Cobb's Standard Spelling-Book, sundry places.*

> "Eight Letters in some Syllables we find,
> And no more Syllables in Words are joined."
>
> *Brightland's Gram.* p. 61.

CHAPTER II.— OF SYLLABLES.

A *Syllable* is one or more letters pronounced in one sound; and is either a word, or a part of a word: as, *a, an, ant.*

In every word there are as many syllables as there are distinct sounds; as, *gram-ma-ri-an.*

A word of one syllable is called a *monosyllable;* or word of two syllables, a *dissyllable;* a word of three syllables, a *trissyllable;* and a word of four or more syllables, a *polysyllable.*

Every vowel, except *w*, may form a syllable of itself; but the consonants belong to the vowels or diphthongs; and without a vowel no syllable can be formed.

DIPHTHONGS AND TRIPHTHONGS.

A *diphthong* is two vowels joined in one syllable; as, *ea* in *beat*, *ou* in *sound.*

A *proper diphthong*, is a diphthong in which both the vowels are sounded; as, *oi* in *voice.*

An *improper diphthong*, is a diphthong in which only one of the vowels is sounded; as, *oa* in *loaf.*

A *triphthong* is three vowels joined in one syllable; as, *eau* in *beau*, *iew* in *view.*

A *proper triphthong*, is a triphthong in which all the vowels are sounded; as, *uoy* in *buoy.*

An *improper triphthong*, is a triphthong in which only one or two of the vowels are sounded; as *eau* in *beauty*, *iou* in *anxious.*

The diphthongs in English are twenty-nine; embracing all but six of the thirty-five possible combinations of two vowels: *aa, ae, ai, ao, au, aw, ay,—ea, ee, ei, eo, eu, ew, ey,—ia, ie, (ii,) io, (iu, iw, iy,)—oa, oe, oi, oo, ou, ow, oy,—ua, ue, ui, uo, (uu, uw,) uy.*

Ten of these diphthongs, being variously sounded, may be either proper or improper; to wit, *ay,—ie,—oi, ou, ow,—ua, ue, ui, uo, uy.*

The proper diphthongs appear to be thirteen; *ay,—ia, ie, io,—oi, ou, ow, oy,—ua, ue, ui, uo, uy:* of which combinations, only three, *ia, io,* and *oy,* are invariably of this class.

The improper diphthongs are twenty-six; *aa, ae, ai, ao, au, aw, ay,— ea, ee, ei, eo, eu, ew, ey,—ie,—oa, oe, oi, oo, ou, ow,—ua, ue, ui, uo, uy.*

The only proper triphthong in English is *uoy,* as in *buoy, buoyant, buoyancy;* unless *uoi* in *quoit* may be considered a parallel instance.

The improper triphthongs are sixteen; *awe, uye, eau, eou, ewe, eye,—ieu, iew, iou,—oeu, owe,—uai, uaw, uay, uea, uee.*

SYLLABICATION.

In dividing words into syllables, we are chiefly to be directed by the ear; it may however be proper to observe, as far as practicable, the following rules.

RULE I.—CONSONANTS.

Consonants should generally be joined to the vowels or diphthongs which they modify in utterance; as, *An-ax-ag'-o-ras, ap-os-tol'-i-cal.*

RULE II.—VOWELS.

Two vowels, coming together, if they make not a diphthong, must be parted in dividing the syllables; as, *A-cha'-i-a, A-o'-ni-an, a-e'-ri-al.*

RULE III.—TERMINATIONS.

Derivative and grammatical terminations should generally be separated from the radical words to which they have been added; as, *harm-less, great-ly, connect-ed:* thus *count-er* and *coun-ter* are different words.

RULE IV.—PREFIXES.

Prefixes in general form separate syllables; as, *mis-place, out-ride, up-lift:* but if their own primitive meaning be disregarded, it may be otherwise; thus, *re-create,* and *rec'-reate, re-formation,* and *ref-ormation,* are words of different import.

RULE V.—COMPOUNDS.

Compounds, when divided, should be divided into the simple words which compose them; as, *boat-swain, foot-hold, never-the-less.*

RULE VI.—LINES FULL.

At the end of a line, a word may be divided, if necessary; but a syllable must never be broken.

· OBSERVATIONS.

OBS. 1.—The doctrine of English syllabication is attended with some difficulties; because its purposes are various, and its principles, often contradictory. The old rules, borrowed chiefly from grammars of other languages, and still retained in some of our own, are liable to very strong objections.* By aiming to divide on the vowels, and to

---

* "The usual rules for dividing [words into] syllables, are not only *arbitrary* but false and absurd. They contradict the very definition of a syllable given by the authors themselves. * * * * A syllable in pronunciation is an *indivisible* thing; and strange as it may appear, what is *indivisible* in utterance, is *divided* in writing; when the very purpose of dividing words into syllables in writing, is to lead the learner to a just pronunciation."—*Webster's Improved Gram.* p. 156; *Philosophical Gram.* 221.

force the consonants, as much as possible, into the beginning of syllables, they often pervert or misrepresent our pronunciation. Thus Murray, in his Spelling-Book, has "*gra-vel, fi-nish, me-lon, bro-ther, bo-dy, wi-dow, pri-son, a-va-rice, e-ve-ry, o-ran-ges, e-ne-my, me-di-cine, re-pre-sent, re-so-lu-tion,*" and a multitude of other words, divided upon a principle by which the young learner can scarcely fail to be led into error respecting their sounds. This method of division is therefore particularly reprehensible in such books as are designed to teach the true pronunciation of words; for which reason, it has been generally abandoned in our modern spelling-books and dictionaries: the authors of which have severally aimed at some sort of compromise between etymology and pronunciation; but they disagree so much, as to the manner of effecting it, that no two of them will be found alike, and very few, if any, entirely consistent with themselves.

OBS. 2.—The object of syllabication may be any one of the following four: 1. To enable a child to read unfamiliar words by spelling them; 2. To show the derivation or composition of words; 3. To exhibit the exact pronunciation of words; 4. To divide words properly, when it is necessary to break them at the ends of lines. With respect to the first of these objects, Walker observes, "When a child has made certain advances in reading, but is ignorant of the sound of many of the longer words, it may not be improper to lay down the common general rule to him, that a consonant between two vowels must go to the latter, and that two consonants coming together must be divided. *Farther than this it would be absurd to go with a child.*"—*Walker's Principles*, No. 539. Yet, as a caution be it recorded, that, in 1833, an itinerant lecturer from the South, who made it his business to teach what he calls in his title-page, "An *Abridgment* of Walker's Rules on the Sounds of the Letters,"—an *Abridgement*, which, he says in his preface, "will be found to contain, it is believed, all the important rules that are established by Walker, and to carry his principles *farther* than he himself has *done*"—befooled the Legislature of Massachusetts, the School Committee and Common Council of Boston, the professor of elocution at Harvard University, and many other equally wise men of the east, into the notion that English pronunciation could be conveniently taught to children, in "four or five days," by means of some three or four hundred rules of which the following is a specimen: "RULE 282. When a single consonant is preceded by a vowel under the preantepenultimate accent, and is followed by a vowel that is succeeded by a consonant, it belongs to the accented vowel."—*Mulkey's Abridgement of Walker's Rules*, p. 34.

OBS. 3.—A grosser specimen of literary quackery, than is the publication which I have just quoted, can scarcely be found in the world of letters. It censures "the principles laid down and illustrated by Walker," as "so elaborate and so verbose as to be wearisome to the scholar and useless to the child;" and yet declares them to be, "for the most part, the true rules of pronunciation, according to the analogy of the language."—*Mulkey's Preface*, p. 3. It professes to be an abridgement and simplification of those principles, especially adapted to the wants and capacities of children; and, at the same time, imposes upon the memory of the young learner twenty-nine rules for syllabication, similar to that which I have quoted above; whereas Walker himself, with all his verbosity, expressly declares it "*absurd*," to offer more than one or two, and those of the very simplest character. It is to be observed that the author teaches nothing but the elements of reading; nothing but the sounds of letters and syllables; nothing but a few simple fractions of the great science of grammar: and, for this purpose, he would conduct the learner through the following particulars, and have him remember them all: 1. *Fifteen distinctions* respecting the "classification and organic formation of the letters." 2. *Sixty-three rules* for "the sounds of the vowels, according to their relative positions." 3. *Sixty-four explanations* of "the different sounds of the diphthongs." 4. *Eighty-nine rules* for "the sounds of the consonants, according to position." 5. *Twenty-three heads*, embracing a hundred and fifty-six principles of accent. 6. *Twenty-nine "rules*" for dividing words into syllables." 7. *Thirty-three "additional principles;*" which are thrown together promiscuously, because he could not class them. 8. *Fifty-two pages* of "irregular words," forming particular exceptions to the foregoing rules. 9. *Twenty-eight pages* of notes extracted from Walker's Dictionary, and very prettily called "The Beauties of Walker." All this is Walker simplified for children!

OBS. 4.—Such is a brief sketch of Mulkey's system of orthoëpy; a work in which "he claims to have devised what has heretofore been a *desideratum*—a mode by which children in our common schools may be taught *the rules* for the pronunciation of their mother tongue."—*Preface*, p. 4. The faults of the book are so exceedingly numerous, that to point them out, would be more toil, than to write a volume of twice the size. And is it possible, that a system like this could find patronage in the metropolis of New England, in that proud centre of arts and sciences, and in the proudest halls of learning and of legislation? Examine the gentleman's credentials, and take your choice between the adoption of his plan, as a great improvement in the management of syllables, and the certain conclusion that great men may be greatly duped respecting them. Unless the public has been imposed upon by a worse fraud than mere literary quackery, the authorities I have mentioned did extensively patronize the scheme; and the Common Council of that learned city did order, November 14th, 1833, "That the School Committee be and they are hereby authorized to employ Mr. William Mulkey to give a course of Lectures on Orthoepy *to the several instructers of the public schools,* and that the sum of five hundred dollars is hereby appropriated for that purpose, and that the same amount be withdrawn from the reserved fund." See *Mulkey's Circular.*

Obs. 5.—Pronunciation is best taught to children by means of a good spelling-book; a book in which the words are arranged according to their analogies, and divided according to their proper sounds. Vocabularies, dictionaries, and glossaries, may also be serviceable to those who are sufficiently advanced to learn how to use them. With regard to the first of the abovenamed purposes of syllabication, I am almost ready to dissent even from the modest opinion of Walker himself; for ignorance can only guess at the pronunciation of words, till positive instruction comes in to give assurance; and it may be doubted whether even the simple rule or rules suggested by Walker would not about as often mislead the young reader as correct him. With regard to the second purpose, that of showing the derivation or composition of words, it is plain, that etymology, and not pronunciation, must here govern the division; and that it should go no further than to separate the constituent parts of each word; as, *ortho-graphy, theo-logy.* But when we divide for the third purpose, and intend to show what is the pronunciation of a word, we must, if possible, divide into such syllabic sounds as will exactly recompose the word, when put together again; as, *or-thog-ra-phy, the-ol-o-gy.* This being the most common purpose of syllabication, perhaps it would be well to give it a general preference; and adopt it whenever we can, not only in the composing of spelling-books and dictionaries, but also in the dividing of words at the ends of lines.

Obs. 6.—Dr. Lowth says, "The best and easiest rule, for dividing the syllables in spelling, is, to divide them as they are naturally divided in a right pronunciation; without regard to the derivation of words, or the possible combination of consonants at the beginning of a syllable."—*Lowth's Gram.* p. 5. And Walker approves of the principle, with respect to the third purpose mentioned above: "This," says that celebrated orthoepist, "is the method adopted by those who would convey the whole sound, by giving distinctly every part; and, when this is the object of syllabication, Dr. Lowth's rule is certainly to be followed."—*Walker's Principles,* No. 541. But this rule, which no one can apply till he has found out the pronunciation, will not always be practicable where that is known, and perhaps not always expedient where it is practicable. For example: the words *colonel, venison, transition, propitious,* cannot be so divided as to exhibit their pronunciation; and, in such as *acid, magic, pacify, legible, liquidate,* it may not be best to follow the rule, because there is some reasonable objection to terminating the first syllables of these words with *c, g,* and *q,* especially at the end of a line. The rule for terminations may also interfere with this, called "Lowth's;" as in *sizable, rising, dronish.*

Obs. 7.—For the dividing of words into syllables, I have given six rules, which are perhaps as many as will be useful. They are to be understood as general principles; and, as to the exceptions to be made in their application, or the settling of their conflicting claims to attention, these may be left to the judgement of each writer. The old principle of dividing by the eye, and not by the ear, I have rejected; and, with it, all but one of the five rules which the old grammarians gave for the purpose. "The divisions of the letters into syllables, should, unquestionably, be the same in written, as in spoken language; otherwise the learner is misguided, and seduced by false representations into injurious errors."—*Wilson's Essay on Gram.* p. 37. Through the influence of books in which the words are divided according to their sounds, the pronunciation of the language is daily becoming more and more uniform; and it may perhaps be reasonably hoped, that the general adoption of this method of syllabication, and a proper exposition of the occasional errors of ignorance, will one day obviate entirely the objection arising from the instability of the principle. For the old grammarians urged, that the scholar who had learned their rules should "strictly conform to them; and that he should industriously avoid *that random Method of dividing by the Ear,* which is subject to mere jumble, as it must be continually fluctuating according to the various Dialects of different Counties."—*British Grammar,* p. 47.

Obs. 8.—The important exercise of oral spelling is often very absurdly conducted. In many of our schools, it may be observed that the teacher, in giving out the words to be spelled, is not always careful to utter them with what he knows to be their true sounds, but frequently accommodates his pronunciation to the known or supposed ignorance of the scholar; and the latter is still more frequently allowed. to hurry through the process, without putting the syllables together as he proceeds; and, sometimes, without forming or distinguishing the syllables at all. Merely to pronounce a word and then name its letters, is an exceedingly imperfect mode of spelling; a mode in which far more is lost in respect to accuracy of speech, than is gained in respect to time. The syllables should not only be distinctly formed and pronounced, but pronounced as they are heard in the whole word; and each should be successively added to the preceding syllables, till the whole sound is formed by the reunion of all its parts. For example: *divisibility*. The scholar should say, "Dee I, de; Vee I Ess, viz, de-viz; I, de-viz-e; Bee I Ell, bil. de-viz-e-bil; I, de-viz-e-bil-e; Tee Wy, te, de-viz-e-bil-e-te." Again: *chicanery*. "Cee Aitch I, she; Cee A, ka, she-ka; En E Ar, nur, she-ka-nur; Wy, she-ka-nur-e." One of the chief advantages of oral spelling, is its tendency to promote accuracy of pronunciation; and this end it will reach, in proportion to the care and skill with which it is conducted. But oral spelling should not be relied on as the sole means of teaching orthography. It will not be found sufficient. The method of giving out words for practical spelling on slates or paper, or of reading something which is to be written again by the learner, is much to be commended, as a means of exercising those scholars who are so far advanced as to write legibly. This is called, in the schools, *dictation*.

IMPROPRIETIES FOR CORRECTION.

ERRORS IN SYLLABICATION.

LESSON I.—CONSONANTS.

1. Correct the division of the following words of two syllables: "ci-vil, co-lour, co-py, da-mask, do-zen, e-ver, fea-ther, ga-ther, hea-ven, hea-vy, ho-ney, le-mon, li-nen, mea-dow, mo-ney, ne-ver, o-live, o-range, o-ther, phea-sant, plea-sant, pu-nish, ra-ther, rea-dy, ri-ver, ro-bin, scho-lar, sho-vel, sto-mach, ti-mid, whi-ther."—*Murray's Spelling-Book*, N. Y. 1819, p. 43–50.

[FOURTLE.—Not proper, because the *v* in *ci-vil*, the *l* in *co-lour*, the *p* in *co-py*, &c., are written with the following vowel, but spoken with that which precedes. But, according to Rule 1st, "Consonants should generally be joined to the vowels or diphthongs which they modify in utterance." Therefore, these words should be divided thus: *civ-il, col-our, cop-y*, &c.]

2. Correct the division of the following words of three syllables: "be-ne-fit, ca-bi-net, ca-nis-ter, ca-ta-logue, cha-rac-ter, cha-ri-ty, co-vet-ous, di-li-gence, di-mi-ty, e-le-phant, e-vi-dent, e-ver-green, fri-vo-lous, ga-ther-ing, ge-ne-rous, go-vern-ess, go-vern-or, ho-nes-ty, ka-len-dar, la-ven-der, le-ve-ret, li-be-ral, me-mo-ry, mi-nis-ter, mo-dest-ly, no-vel-ty, no-bo-dy, pa-ra-dise, po-ver-ty, pre-sent-ly, pro-vi-dence, pro-per-ly, pri-son-er, ra-ven-ous, sa-tis-fy, se-ve-ral, se-pa-rate, tra-vel-ler, va-ga-bond;—con-si-der, con-ti-nue, de-li-ver, dis-co-ver, dis-fi-gure, dis-ho-nest, dis-tri-bute, in-ha-bit, me-cha-nic, what-e-ver;—re-com-mend, re-fu-gee, re-pri-mand."—*Murray: ib.* p. 67–83.

3. Correct the division of the following words of four syllables: "ca-ter-pil-lar, cha-ri-ta-ble, di-li-gent-ly, mi-se-ra-ble, pro-fit-a-ble, to-le-ra-ble;—be-ne-vo-lent, con-si-der-ate, di-mi-nu-tive, ex-pe-ri-ment, ex-tra-va-gant, in-ha-bi-tant, no-bi-li-ty, par-ti-cu-lar, pros-pe-ri-ty, ri-di-cu-lous, sin-ce-ri-ty;—de-mon-stra-tion, e-du-ca-tion, e-mu-la-tion, e-pi-de-mic, ma-le-fac-tor, ma-nu-fac-ture, me-mo-ran-dum, mo-de-ra-tor, pa-ra-ly-tic, pe-ni-ten-tial, re-sig-na-tion, sa-tis-fac-tion, se-mi-co-lon."—*Murray: ib.* p. 84–87.

4. Correct the division of the following words of five syllables: "a-bo-mi-na-ble, a-po-the-ca-ry, con-sid-e-ra-ble, ex-pla-na-to-ry, pre-pa-ra-to-ry;—a-ca-de-mi-cal, cu-ri-o-si-ty, ge-o-gra-phi-cal, ma-nu-fac-to-ry, sa-tis-fac-to-ry, me-ri-to-ri-ous;—cha-rac-te-ris-tic, e-pi-gram-ma-tic, ex-pe-ri-ment-al, po-ly-syl-la-ble, con-sid-e-ra-tion."—*Murray: ib.* p. 87–89.

5. Correct the division of the following proper names: "He-len, Leo-nard, Phi-lip, Ro-bert, Ho-race, Tho-mas;—Ca-ro-line, Ca-tha-rine, Da-ni-el, De-bo-rah, Do-ro-thy, Fre-de-rick, I-sa-bel, Jo-na-than, Ly-di-a, Ni-cho-las, O-li-ver, Sa-mu-el, Si-me-on, So-lo-mon, Ti-mo-thy, Va-len-tine;—A-me-ri-can, Bar-tho-lo-mew, E-li-za-beth, Na-tha-ni-el, Pe-ne-lo-pe, The-o-phi-lus."—*Murray: ib.* p. 98–101.

LESSON II.—MIXED.

1. Correct the division of the following words, by Rule 1st: "cap-rice, es-teem, dis-es-teem, ob-lige;—az-ure, mat-ron, pat-ron, phal-anx, sir-en, trait-or, trench-er, barb-er, burn-ish, garn-ish, tarn-ish, varn-ish, mark-et, musk-et, pamph-let;—brave-ry, knave-ry, slave-ry, eve-ning, scene-ry, bribe-ry, nice-ty, chi-cane-ry, ma-chine-ry, im-age-ry;—as-y-lum, hor-i-zon, fi-nan-cier, he-ro-ism,—sar-don-yx, scur-ril-ous,—com-e-di-an, post-e-ri-or."—*Webster's Spelling-Book.*

2. Correct the division of the following words by Rule 2d: "oy-er, fol-io, gen-ial, gen-ius, jun-ior, sa-tiate, vi-tiate;—am-bro-sia, cha-mel-ion, par-hel-ion, con-ven-ient, in-gen-ious, om-nis-cience, pe-cul-iar, so-cia-ble, par-tial-i-ty, pe-cun-ia-ry;—an-nun-ciate, e-nun-ciate, ap-pre-ciate, as-so-ciate, ex-pa-tiate, in-gra-tiate, in-i-tiate, li-cen-tiate, ne-go-tiate, no-vi-ciate, of-fi-ciate, pro-pi-tiate, sub-stan-tiate."—*Webster : Old Spelling-Book*, 86—91; *New*, 121—128.

3. Correct the division of the following words by Rule 3d: "dres-ser, has-ty, pas-try, sei-zure, rol-ler, jes-ter wea-ver, vam-per, han-dy, dros-sy, glos-sy, mo-ver, mo-ving, oo-zy, ful-ler, trus-ty, weigh-ty, noi-sy, drow-sy, swar-thy."—*Cobb's Standard Spelling-Book.* Again: "eas-tern, full-y, pull-et, rill-et, scan-ty, nee-dy."—*Webster.*

4. Correct the division of the following words by Rule 4th: "aw-ry,"—*Webster's Old Book*, 52; "ath-wart,"—*Ib.* 93; "pros-pect-ive,"—*Ib.* 66; "pa-renth-e-sis,"—*Ib.* 93; "res-ist-i-bil-i-ty,"—*Webster's New Book*, 93; "hem-is-pher-ic,"—*Ib.* 130; "mo-nos-tich, he-mis-tick,"*—*Walker's Dict.* 8vo; *Cobb*, 33; "tow-ards,"—*Cobb*, 48.

5. Correct the division of the following words by Rule 5th: "E'n-gland,"—*Murray's Spelling-Book*, p. 100; "a-no-ther,"—*Ib.* 71; "a-noth-er,"—*Emerson*, 76; "Be-thes-da, Beth-a-ba-ra,"—*Webster*, 141; *Cobb*, 159.

LESSON III.—MIXED.

1. Correct the division of the following words, according to their derivation : "ben-der, bles-sing, bras-sy, chaf-fy, chan-ter, clas-per, craf-ty, cur-dy, fen-der, fil-my, fus-ty, glas-sy, graf-ter, gras-sy, gus-ty, han-ded, mas-sy, mus-ky, rus-ty, swel-ling, tel-ler, tes-ted, thrif-ty, ves-ture."—*Cobb's Standard Spelling-Book.*

2. Correct the division of the following words, so as to give no wrong notion of their derivation and meaning : "barb-er, burn-ish, brisk-et, cank-er, chart-er, cuck-oo, furn-ish, garn-ish, guil-ty, hank-er, lust-y, port-al, tarn-ish, test-ate, test-y, trait-or, treat-y, varn-ish, vest-al, di-urn-al, e-tern-al, in-fern-al, in-tern-al, ma-tern-al, noo-turn-al, pa-tern-al."—*Webster's Elementary Spelling-Book.*

3. Correct the division of the following words, so as to convey no wrong idea of their pronunciation : "ar-mo-ry, ar-te-ry, butch-er-y, cook-e-ry, eb-o-ny, em-e-ry, ev-e-ry, fel-o-ny, fop-pe-ry, frip-pe-ry, gal-le-ry, his-to-ry, liv-e-ry, lot-te-ry, mock-e-ry, mys-te-ry, nun-ne-ry, or-re-ry, pil-lo-ry, quack-e-ry, sor-ce-ry, witch-e-ry."—*Ib.* 41–42.

4. Correct the division of the following words, and give to *n* before *k* the sound of *ng*: "ank-le, bask-et, blank-et, buck-le, cack-le, crank-le, crink-le, east-er, fick-le, freck-le, knuck-le, mark-et, monk-ey, port-ress, prick-le, poult-ice, punch-eon, qua-drant, qua-drate, squa-dron, rank-le, shack-le, sprink-le, tink-le, twink-le, wrink-le." —*Cobb's Standard Spelling-Book.*

5. Correct the division of the following words, with a proper regard to rules 1st and 3d : "a-scribe, bland-ish, bran-chy, clou-dy, dus-ty, drea-ry, eve-ning, faul-ty, fil-thy, fros-ty, gau-dy, gloo-my, heal-thy, hear-ken, hear-ty, hoa-ry, lea-ky, loung-er, mar-shy, migh-ty, mil-ky, naugh-ty, pas-sing, pit-cher, rea-dy, roc-ky, spee-dy, stea-dy, stor-my, thirs-ty, thor-ny, trus-ty, ves-try, wes-tern, weal-thy."—*Emerson's Spelling-Book*, 17–44.

CHAPTER III.— OF WORDS.

A *Word* is one or more syllables spoken or written as the sign of some idea, or of some manner of thought. Words are distinguished as *prim-itive* or *derivative*, and as *simple* or *compound*. The former division is called their *species;* the latter, their *figure.*

A *primitive* word is one that is not formed from any simpler word in the language ; as, *harm, great, connect.*

A *derivative* word is one that is formed from some simpler word in the language ; as, *harmless, greatly, connected, disconnect, unconnected.*

---

* This word, like *distich* and *monostich*, is from the Greek *stichos*, a verse; and is improperly spelled by Walker with a final *k.* It should be *hemistich*, with the accent on the first syllable. See *Webster, Scott, Perry, Worcester*, and others.

A *simple* word is one that is not compounded, not composed of other words; as, *watch, man, house, tower, never, the, less.*

A *compound* word is one that is composed of two or more simple words; as, *watchman, watchhouse, watchtower, nevertheless.*

Permanent compounds are consolidated; as, *bookseller, schoolmaster:* others, which may be called temporary compounds, are formed by the hyphen; as, *good-natured, negro-merchant.*

RULES FOR THE FIGURE OF WORDS.

RULE I.—COMPOUNDS.

Words regularly or analogically united, and commonly known as compounds, should never be needlessly broken apart. Thus, *steamboat, railroad, red-hot, well-being, new-coined,* are preferable to the phrases, *steam boat, rail road, red hot, well being, new coined;* and *toward us* is better than the old phrase, *to us ward.*

RULE II.—SIMPLES.

When the simple words would only form a regular phrase, of the same meaning, the compounding of any of them ought to be avoided. Thus, the compound *instead* is not to be commended, because the simple phrase, *in stead of,* is exactly like the other phrases, *in lieu of, in place of, in room of,* in which we write no compound.

RULE III.—THE SENSE.

Words otherwise liable to be misunderstood, must be joined together or written separately, as the sense and construction may happen to require. Thus, a *glass house* is a house made of glass, but a *glasshouse* is a house in which glass is made; so a *negro merchant* is a coloured trader, but a *negro-merchant* is a man who buys and sells negroes.

RULE IV.—ELLIPSES.

When two or more compounds are connected in one sentence, none of them should be split to make an ellipsis of half a word. Thus, " *six or seventeen* " should not be said for " *sixteen or seventeen ;* " nor ought we to say, " *calf, goat, and sheepskins,*" for " *calfskins, goatskins, and sheepskins.*" In the latter instance, however, it might be right to separate *all* the words; as in the phrase, " *soup, coffee,* and *tea* houses."—*Liberator,* x, 40.

RULE V.—THE HYPHEN.

When the parts of a compound do not fully coalesce, as *to-day, to-night, to-morrow ;* or when each retains its original accent, so that the compound has more than one, or one that is movable, as *first-born, hanger-on, laughter-loving, garlic-eater, butterfly-shell,* the hyphen should be inserted between them.

RULE VI.—NO HYPHEN.

When a compound has but one accented syllable in pronunciation, as *watchword, statesman, gentleman,* and the parts are such as admit of a complete coalescence, no hyphen should be inserted between them. Churchill, after much attention to this subject, writes thus: " The practical instruction of the *countinghouse* imparts a more thorough knowledge of *bookkeeping,* than all the fictitious transactions of a mere *schoolbook,* however carefully constructed to suit particular purposes."—*New Gram.* p. vii. But *counting-house,* having more stress on the last syllable than on the middle one, is usually written with the hyphen; and *book-*

keeping and *school-book*, though they may not need it, are oftener so formed than otherwise.

OBSERVATIONS.

Obs. 1.—Words are the least parts of significant language; that is, of language significant in each part; for to syllables, taken merely as syllables, no meaning belongs. But, to a word, signification of some sort or other, is essential; there can be no word without it; for a sign or symbol must needs represent or signify something. And as I cannot suppose words to represent external things, I have said "A *Word* is one or more syllables spoken or written as the sign of some *idea*." But of *what* ideas are the words of our language significant? Are we to say, "Of *all* ideas;" and to recognize as an English word every syllable, or combination of syllables, to which we know a meaning is attached? No. For this, in the first place, would confound one language with an other; and destroy a distinction which must ever be practically recognized, till all men shall again speak one language. In the next place, it would compel us to embrace among our words an infinitude of terms that are significant only of *local* ideas, such as men any where or at any time may have had concerning any of the individuals they have known, whether persons, places, or things. But, however important they may be in the eyes of men, the names of particular persons, places, or things, because they convey only particular ideas, do not properly belong to what we call *our language.* Lexicographers do not collect and define proper names, because they are beyond the limits of their art, and can be explained only from history. I do not say that proper names are to be excluded from grammar; but I would show wherein consists the superiority of general terms over these. For if our common words did not differ essentially from proper names, we could demonstrate nothing in science: we could not frame from them any general or affirmative proposition at all; because all our terms would be particular, and not general; and because every individual thing in nature must necessarily be forever itself only, and not an other.

Obs. 2.—Our common words, then, are the symbols neither of external particulars, nor merely of the sensible ideas which external particulars excite in our minds, but mainly of those general or universal ideas which belong rather to the intellect than to the senses. For intellection differs from sensation, somewhat as the understanding of a man differs from the perceptive faculty of a brute; and language, being framed for the reciprocal commerce of human minds, whose perceptions include both, is made to consist of signs of ideas both general and particular, yet without placing them on equal ground. Our general ideas—that is, our ideas conceived as common to many individuals, existing in any part of time, past, present, or future—such, for example, as belong to the words *man, horse, tree, cedar, wave, motion, strength, resist*—such ideas, I say, constitute that most excellent significance which belongs to words primarily, essentially, and immediately; whereas, our particular ideas, such as are conceived only of individual objects, which are infinite in number and ever fleeting, constitute a significance which belongs to language only secondarily, accidentally, and mediately. If we express the latter at all, we do it either by proper names, of which but very few ever become generally known, or by means of certain changeable limitations which are added to our general terms; whereby language, as Harris observes, "without wandering into infinitude, contrives how to denote things infinite."—*Hermes*, p. 346. The particular manner in which this is done, I shall show hereafter, in Etymology, when I come to treat of articles and definitives.

Obs. 3.—If we examine the structure of proper names, we shall find that most of them are compounds, the parts of which have, in very many instances, some general signification. Now a complete phrase commonly conveys some particular notion or conception of the mind; but, in this case, the signification of the general terms is restricted by the other words which are added to them. Thus *smith* is a more general term than *goldsmith;* and *goldsmith* is more general than *a goldsmith; a goldsmith*, than *the goldsmith; the goldsmith*, than *one Goldsmith; one Goldsmith*, than *Mr. Goldsmith; Mr. Goldsmith*, than *Oliver Goldsmith.* Thus we see that the simplest mode of designating particular persons or objects, is that of giving them *proper names;* but proper names must needs be so written, that they may be known as proper names, and not be mistaken for common terms. I have before observed, that we have some names which are both proper and common; and that these should be written with capitals, and should form the plural regularly. It is surprising that *the Friends*, who are in some respects particularly scrupulous about language, should so generally have overlooked the necessity there is, of *compounding* their numerical names of the months and days, and writing them uniformly with capitals, as proper names. For proper names they certainly are, in every thing but the form, whenever they are used without the article, and without those other terms which render their general idea particular. And the compound form with a capital, is as necessary for *Firstday, Secondday, Thirdday,* &c., as for *Sunday, Monday, Tuesday,* &c. "The first day of the week"—"The seventh day of the month"—"The second month of summer"—"The second month in the year," &c., are good English phrases, in which any compounding of the terms, or any additional use of capitals, would be improper; but, for common use, these phrases are found too long and too artificial. We must have a less cumbersome mode of specifying the months of the year and the days of the week. What then? Shall we merely throw away the terms of particularity, and, without substituting in their place the form of proper names, apply general terms to particular thoughts, and insist on it that this is right? And is not this precisely what is done by those who reject as heathenish the ordinary names of the months and days, and write "*first day*," for *Sunday,* in stead of "the first day of the week;" or "*second month*," for *February,* in stead of "the second month in the year;" and so forth? This phraseology may perhaps be well understood by those to whom it is familiar, but still it is an abuse of language, because it is inconsistent with the common acceptation of the terms. Example: "The departure of a ship will take place *every sixth day* with punctuality."—*Philadelphia Weekly Messenger.* The writer of this did not mean, "*every Friday;*" and it is absurd for the Friends so to understand it, or so to write, when that is what they mean.

OBS. 4.—In the ordinary business of life, it is generally desirable to express our meaning as briefly as possible; but legal phraseology is always full to the letter, and often redundant. Hence a merchant will write, "Nov. 24, 1837," or, "11 mo. 24th, 1837;" but a conveyancer will have it, "On the twenty-fourth day of November, one thousand eight hundred and thirty-seven"—or, perhaps, "On the twenty-fourth day of the eleventh month, in the year of our Lord one thousand eight hundred and thirty-seven." Accordingly we find that, in common daily use, all the names of the months, except *March, May, June,* and *July,* are abbreviated; thus, *Jan., Feb., Apr., Aug., Sept., Oct., Nov., Dec.* And sometimes even the Arabic number of the year is made yet shorter; as '37, for 1837; or 1835-6-7, for 1835, 1836, and 1837. In like manner, in constructing tables of time, we sometimes denote the days of the week by the simple initials of their names; as, S. for Sunday, M. for Monday, &c. But, for facility of abbreviation, the numerical names, whether of the months or of the days, are perhaps still more convenient. For, if we please, we may put the simple Arabic figures for them; though it is better to add *d* for *day,* and *mo.* for *month*: as, 1 d. 2 d. 3 d. &c.; 1 mo. 2 mo. 3 mo. &c. But, take which mode of naming we will, our ordinary expression of these things should be in neither extreme, but should avoid alike too great brevity and too great prolixity; and, therefore, it is best to make it a general rule in our literary compositions, to use the full form of proper names for the months and days, and to denote the years by Arabic figures written in full.

OBS. 5.—In considering the nature of words, I was once a little puzzled with a curious speculation, if I may not term it an important inquiry, concerning *the principle of their identity.* We often speak of "*the same words,*" and of "*different words;*" but wherein does the sameness or the difference of words consist? Not in their pronunciation; for the same word may be differently pronounced; as, *pāt'ron* or *pā'tron, măt'ron* or *mā'tron.* Not in their orthography; for the same word may be differently spelled; as, *favour* or *favor, music* or *musick, connexion* or *connection.* Not in their form of presentation; for the same word may be either spoken or written; and speech and writing present what we call *the same words,* in two ways totally different. Not in their meaning; for the same word may have different meanings, and different words may signify precisely the same thing. This sameness of words, then, must consist in something which is to be reconciled with great diversity. Yet every word is itself, and not an other; and every word must necessarily have some property peculiar to itself, by which it may be easily distinguished from every other. Were it not so, language would be unintelligible. But it *is* so; and, therefore, to mistake one word for an other, is universally thought to betray great ignorance or great negligence, though such mistakes are by no means of uncommon occurrence. But that the question about the identity of words is not a very easy one, may appear from the fact, that the learned often disagree about it in practice; as when one grammarian will have *an* and *a* to be two words, and an other will affirm them to be only different forms of one and the same word.

OBS. 6.—Let us see, then, if amidst all this diversity we can find that principle of sameness, by which a dispute of this kind ought to be settled. Now, although different words do generally differ in orthography, in pronunciation, and in meaning, so that an entire sameness implies one orthography, one pronunciation, and one meaning; yet some diversity is allowed in each of these respects, so that a sign differing from an other only in one, is not therefore a different word, or a sign agreeing with an other only in one, is not therefore the same word. It follows thence, that the principle of verbal identity, the principle which distinguishes every word from every other, lies in neither extreme: it lies in a narrower compass than in all three, and yet not singly in any one, but jointly in any two. So that signs differing in any two of these characteristics of a word, are different words; and signs agreeing in any two, are the same word. Consequently, if to any difference either of spelling or of sound we add a difference of signification everybody will immediately say, that we speak or write different words, and not the same: thus *dear*, beloved, and *deer*, an animal, are two such words as no one would think to be the same; and, in like manner, *use*, advantage, and *use*, to employ, will readily be called different words. Upon this principle, *an* and *a* are different words; yet, in conformity to old usage, and because the latter is in fact but an abridgement of the former, I have always treated them as one and the same article, though I have nowhere expressly called them the same word. But, to establish the principle above named, which appears to me the only one on which any such question can be resolved, or the identity of words be fixed at all, we must assume that every word has one right pronunciation, and only one; one just orthography, and only one; and some proper signification, which, though perhaps not always the same, is always a part of its essence. For when two words of different meaning are spelled or pronounced alike, not to maintain the second point of difference, against the double orthography or the double pronunciation of either, is to confound their identity at once, and to prove by the rule that two different words are one and the same, by first absurdly making them so.

OBS. 7.—In no part of grammar is usage more unsettled and variable than in that which relates to the *figure of words*. It is a point of which modern writers have taken but very little notice. Lily, and other ancient Latin grammarians, reckoned both species and figure among the grammatical accidents of nearly all the different parts of speech; and accordingly noticed them, in their Etymology, as things worthy to be thus made distinct topics, like numbers, genders, cases, moods, tenses, &c. But the manner of compounding words in Latin, and also in Greek, is always by consolidation. No use appears to have been made of the *hyphen*, in joining the words of those languages, though the name of the mark is a Greek compound, meaning "*under one.*" The compounding of words is one principal means of increasing their number; and the arbitrariness with which that is done or neglected in English, is sufficient of itself to make the number of our words a matter of great uncertainty. Such terms, however, having the advantage of explaining themselves in a much greater degree than others, have little need of definition; and when new things are formed, it is very natural and proper to give them new names of this sort: as, *steamboat*, *railroad*. The propriety or impropriety of these additions to the language, is not to be determined by dictionaries; for that must be settled by usage before any lexicographer will insert them. And so numerous, after all, are the discrepancies found in our best dictionaries, that many a word may have its day and grow obsolete, before a nation can learn from them the right way of spelling it; and many a fashionable thing may go entirely out of use, before a man can thus determine how to name it. *Railroads* are of so recent invention that I find the word in only one dictionary; and that one is wrong, in giving the word a hyphen, while half our printers are wrong, in keeping the words separate because *Johnson* did not compound them. But is it not more important, to know whether we ought to write *railroad*, or *rail-road*, or *rail road*, which we cannot learn from any of our dictionaries, than to find out whether we ought to write *rocklo*, or *roquelo*, or *roquelaur*, or *roquelaure*, which, in some form or other, is found in them all? The duke of Roquelaure is now forgotten, and his cloak is out of fashion.

OBS. 8.—No regular phrase, as I have taught in the second rule above, should be needlessly converted into a compound word, either by tacking its parts together with the hyphen, or by uniting them without a hyphen: for, in general, a phrase is one thing, and a word is an other; and they ought to be kept as distinct as possible.* But, when a whole phrase takes the relation of an *adjective*, the words must be compounded, and the hyphen becomes necessary; as, "An inexpressibly apt *bottle-of-small-beer* comparison."— *Peter Pindar.* The occasions for the compounding of words, are in general sufficiently plain, to any one who knows what is intended to be said; but, as we compound words, sometimes with the hyphen, and sometimes without, there is no small difficulty in ascertaining when to use this mark, and when to omit it. "Some settled rule for the use of the hyphen on these occasions, is much wanted. Modern printers have a strange predilection for it; using it on almost every possible occasion. Mr. L. Murray, who has only three lines on the subject, seems inclined to countenance this practice; which is, no doubt, convenient enough for those who do not like trouble. His words are: 'A

---

* According to Aristotle, the compounding of terms, or the writing of them as separate words, must needs be a matter of great importance to the sense. For he will have the parts of a compound noun, or of a compound verb, to be, like other syllables, destitute of any distinct signification in themselves, whatever may be their meaning when written separately. See his definitions of the parts of speech, in his *Poetics*, Chapter 20th of the Greek; or Goulston's Version in Latin, Chapter 12th.

Hyphen, marked thus - is employed in connecting compounded words: as, Lap-dog, tea-pot, pre-existence, self-love, to-morrow, mother-in-law.' Of his six examples, Johnson, our only acknowledged standard, gives the first and third without any separation between the syllables, *lapdog, preexistence*; his second and fifth as two distinct words each, *tea pot, to morrow*; and his sixth as three words, *mother in law*: so that only his fourth has the sanction of the lexicographer. There certainly can be no more reason for putting a hyphen after the common prefixes, than before the common affixes, *ness, ly,* and the rest."—*Churchill's Gram.* p. 374.

Obs. 9.—Again: "While it would be absurd, to sacrifice the established practice of all good authors to the ignorance of such readers [as could possibly mistake for a diphthong the two contiguous vowels in such words as *preexistence, cooperate,* and *reenter*]; it would unquestionably be advantageous, to have some principle to guide us in that labyrinth of words, in which the hyphen appears to have been admitted or rejected arbitrarily, or at hap-hazard. Thus, though we find in Johnson, *alms-basket, alms-giver,* with the hyphen; we have *almsdeed, almshouse, almsman,* without: and many similar examples of an unsettled practice might be adduced, sufficient to fill several pages. In this perplexity, is not the pronunciation of the words the best guide? In the English language, every word of more than one syllable is marked by an accent on some particular syllable. Some very long words indeed admit a secondary accent on *an other* syllable; but still this is much inferior, and leaves one leading accent prominent: as in *expos'tulatory.* Accordingly, when a compound has but one accented syllable in pronunciation, as *night'cap, bed'stead, broad'sword,* the two words have coalesced completely into one, and no hyphen should be admitted. On the other hand, when each of the radical words has an accent, as *Chris'tian-name', broad'-shoul'dered,* I think the hyphen should be used. *Good'-na'tured* is a compound epithet with two accents, and therefore requires the hyphen: in *good nature, good will,* and similar expressions, *good* is used simply as an adjective, and of course should remain distinct from the noun. Thus, too, when a noun is used adjectively, it should remain separate from the noun it modifies; as, a *gold ring,* a *silver buckle.* When two numerals are employed to express a number, without a conjunction between them, it is usual to connect them by a hyphen; as, *twenty-five, eighty-four*: but when the conjunction is inserted, the hyphen is as improper as it would be between other words connected by the conjunction. This, however, is a common abuse; and we often meet with *five-&-twenty, six-&-thirty,* and the like."—*Ib.* p. 376. Thus far Churchill: who appears to me, however, too hasty about the hyphen in compound numerals. For we write *one hundred, two hundred, three thousand,* &c., without either hyphen or conjunction; and as *five-and-twenty* is equivalent to *twenty-five,* and virtually but one word, the hyphen, if not absolutely necessary to the sense, is certainly not so very improper as he alleges. "*Christian name*" is as often written without the hyphen as with it, and perhaps as accurately.

IMPROPRIETIES FOR CORRECTION.

ERRORS IN THE FIGURE, OR FORM, OF WORDS.

UNDER RULE I.—OF COMPOUNDS.

"Professing to imitate Timon, the man hater."—*Goldsmith's Rome,* p. 161.

[FORMULE.—Not proper, because the compound term *manhater* is here made two words. But, according to Rule 1st, "Words regularly united, and commonly known as compounds, should never be needlessly broken apart." Therefore, *manhater* should be written as one word.]

"Men load hay with a pitch fork."—*Webster's New Spelling-Book,* p. 40. "A pear tree grows from the seed of a pear."—*Ib.* p. 33. "A tooth brush is good to brush your teeth."—*Ib.* p. 85. "The mail is opened at the post office."—*Ib.* p. 151. "The error seems to me two fold."—*Sanborn's Gram.* p. 230. "To pre-engage means to engage before hand."—*Webster's New Spelling-Book,* p. 82. "It is a mean act to deface the figures on a mile stone."—*Ib.* p. 88. "A grange is a farm and farm house."—*Ib.* p. 118. "It is no more right to steal apples or water melons, than money."—*Ib.* p. 118. "The awl is a tool used by shoemakers, and harness makers."—*Ib.* p. 150. "Twenty five cents are equal to one quarter of a dollar."—*Ib.* p. 107. "The blowing up of the Fulton at New York was a terrible disaster."—*Ib.* p. 54. "The elders also, and the bringers up of the children, sent to Jehu."—*Scott:* 2 *Kings,* x, 5. "Not with eye service, as men pleasers."—*Bickersteth, on Prayer,* p. 64. "A good natured and equitable construction of cases." — *Ash's Gram.* p. 138. "And purify your hearts, ye double minded."—*Gurney's Portable Evidences,* p. 115. "It is a mean spirited action to steal; i. e. to steal is a mean spirited action."—*Grammar of Alex. Murray, the schoolmaster,* p. 124. "There is, indeed, one form of orthography which is a kin to the subjunctive mood of the Latin tongue."—*Booth's Introd. to Dict.* p. 71. "To bring him into nearer connexion with real and everyday life."—*Philological Museum*, i, p. 469. "The common place, stale declamation of its revilers would be silenced."—*Ib.* i, p. 494. "She formed a very singular and unheard of project."—*Goldsmith's Rome*, p. 160. "He had many vigilant, though feeble talented, and mean spirited enemies."—ROBERTS VAUX: *The Friend*, vii, p. 74. "These old fashioned people would level our psalmody," &c.—*Music of Nature*, p. 292. "This slow shifting scenery in the theatre of harmony."—*Ib.* p. 398. "So we are assured from Scripture it self."—*Harris's Hermes*, p. 300. "The mind, being disheartened, then betakes its self to trifling."—*R. Johnson's Pref. to Gram. Com.* "Whose soever sins ye remit, they are remitted unto them."—*Beacon*, p. 115: SCOTT, ALGER, FRIENDS: *John*, xx, 23. "Tarry we our selves how we will."—*Walker's English Particles*, p. 161. "Manage your credit so, that you need neither swear your self, nor want a voucher."—*Collier's Antoninus*, p. 33. "Whereas song never conveys any of the above named sentiments."—*Rush, on the Voice*, p. 424. "I go on horse back."—*Guy's Gram.* p. 54. "This requires *purity*, in opposition to barbarous, obsolete, or new coined words."—*Adam's Gram.* p. 242 ; *Gould's*, 234. "May the Plough share shine."—*White's Eng. Verb*, p. 161. "Which way ever we consider it."—*Locke, on Ed.* p. 83.

> "Where e'er the silent (e) a Place obtains,
> The Voice foregoing, Length and softness gains."—*Brightland's Gr.* p. 15.

UNDER RULE II.—OF SIMPLES.

"It qualifies any of the four parts of speech abovenamed."—*Kirkham's Gram.* p. 83.

[FORMULE.—Not proper, because *abovenamed* is here unnecessarily made a compound. But, according to Rule 2d, " When the simple words would only form a regular phrase, of the same meaning, the compounding of any of them ought to be avoided." Therefore, *above* and *named* should here have been written as two words.]

"After awhile they put us out among the rude multitude."—*Fox's Journal*, i, p. 169. "It would be ashame, if your mind should falter and give in."—*Collier's Meditations of Antoninus*, p. 94. "They stared awhile in silence one upon another."—*Rasselas*, p. 73. "After passion has for awhile exercised its tyrannical sway."—*Murray's Gram.* ii, 135 and 267. "Though set within the same general-frame of intonation."—*Rush, on the Voice*, p. 389. "Which do not carry any of the natural vocal-signs of expression."—*Ib.* p. 329. "The measurable constructive-powers of a few associable constituents."—*Ib.* p. 343. "Before each accented syllable or emphatic monosyllabic-word."—*Ib.* p. 364. "One should not think too favourably of oneself." See *Murray's Gram.* i, p. 154. "Know ye not your ownselves, how that Jesus Christ is in you."—*Barclay's Works*, i, p. 355. "I judge not my ownself, for I know nothing of my own."—*Wayland's Moral Science*, p. 84. "Though they were in such a rage, I desired them to tarry awhile."—*Josephus*, v, p. 179. "*A* instead of *an* is now used before words beginning with *u* long."—*Murray's Gram.* p. 31. "John will have earned his wages the next new-year's day."—*Murray's Gram.* p. 82. "A new-year's-gift is a present made on the first day of the year." See *Johnson, Walker, Webster, et al.* "When he sat on the throne, distributing new-year's-gifts."—STILLINGFLEET, *in Johnson's Dict.* "St. Paul admonishes Timothy to refuse old-wives'-fables."—*Author.* "The world, take it altogether, is but one."—*Collier's Antoninus*, B. vii, Sec. 9. "In writings of this stamp we must accept of sound instead of sense."—*Murray's Gram.* p. 298. " A male-child, A female-child. Male-descendants, Female-descendants."—*Goldsbury's C. S. Gram.* p. 13 ; *Rev. T. Smith's Gram.* p. 15. " Male-servants, Female-servants. Male-relations, Female-relations."—*Felton's Gram.* p. 15.

> "Reserved and cautious, with no partial aim,
> My muse e'er sought to blast another's fame."—*Lloyd*, p. 162.

UNDER RULE III.—THE SENSE.

"Our discriminations of this matter have been but four footed instincts."—*Rush, on the Voice*, p. 291.

[*Formule.*—Not proper, because the term *four footed* is made two words, as if the instincts were four and footed. But, according to Rule 3d, " Words otherwise liable to be misunderstood, must be joined together, or written separately, as the sense and construction may happen to require." Therefore, *four-footed*, as it here means *quadruped*, or *having four feet*, should be one word]

"He is in the right, (says Clytus,) not to bear free born men at his table."—*Goldsmith's Greece*, ii, p. 128. "To the short seeing eye of man, the progress may appear little."—*The Friend*, ix, p. 377. "Knowledge and virtue are, emphatically, the stepping stone to individual distinction."—*Town's Analysis*, p. 5. "A tin peddler will sell tin vessels as he travels."—*Webster's New Spelling-Book*, p. 44. "The beams of a wood-house are held up by the posts and joists."—*Ib.* p. 39. "What you mean by *future tense adjective*, I can easily understand."—*Tooke's Diversions*, ii, p. 450. "The town has been for several days very well behaved."—*Spectator*, No. 532. "A *rounce* is the handle of a printing press."— *Webster's Dict.*; also *El. Spelling-Book*, p. 118. "The phraseology we call *thee and thouing* is not in so common use with us, as the *tutoyant* among the French."— *Walker's Dict. w. Thy.* "Hunting, and other out door sports, are generally pursued."—*Balbi's Geog.* p. 227. "Come unto me, all ye that labour and are heavy laden."—SCOTT, ALGER, FRIENDS: *Matt.* xi, 28. "God so loved the world, that he gave his only begotten Son to save it."—*Barclay's Works*, i, p. 71; *Scott's Bible, John*, iii, 16. "Jehovah is a prayer hearing God: Nineveh repented, and was spared."—*N. Y. Observer*, x, p. 90. "These are well pleasing to God, in all ranks and relations."—*Barclay's Works*, i, p. 73. "Whosoever cometh any thing near unto the tabernacle."—*Numb.* xvii, 13. "The words coalesce, when they have a long established association."—*Murray's Gram.* p. 169. "Open to me the gates of righteousness: I will go in to them."—OLD BIBLE: *Ps.* cxviii, 19. "He saw an angel of God coming into him." See *Acts*, x, 3. "The consequences of any action are to be considered in a two fold light."—*Wayland's Moral Science*, p. 108. "We commonly write two fold, three fold, four fold, and so on up to ten fold, without a hyphen; and, after that, we use one."—*Author.* See *Matt.* xiii, 8. "When the first mark is going off, he cries *turn!* the glass holder answers *done!*"—*Bowditch's Nav.* p. 128. "It is a kind of familiar shaking hands with all the vices."—*Maturin's Sermons*, p. 170. "She is a good natured woman ; " "James is self opinionated ; " "He is broken hearted." —*Wright's Gram.* p. 147. "These three examples apply to the *present tense* construction only."—*Ib.* p. 65. "So that it was like a game of hide and go seek."—*Edward's First Lessons in Grammar*, p. 90.

"That lowliness is young ambition's ladder,
Whereto the climber upward turns his face."—*Bucke's Gram.* p. 97.

UNDER RULE IV.—OF ELLIPSES.

"This building serves yet for a school and a meeting-house."

[FORMULE.—Not proper, because the compound word *schoolhouse* is here divided to avoid a repetition of the last half. But, according to Rule 4th, " When two or more compounds are connected in one sentence, none of them should be split to make an ellipsis of half a word." Therefore, " *school* " should be " *schoolhouse;* " thus, "This building serves yet for a *schoolhouse* and a meeting-house."]

"Schoolmasters and mistresses of honest friends [are] to be encouraged."—*N. E. Discipline*, p. xv. "We never assumed to ourselves a faith or worship-making-power." —*Barclay's Works*, i, p. 83. "Pot and pearl ashes are made from common ashes."—*Webster's New Spelling-Book*, p. 69. "Both the ten and eight syllable verses are iambics."— *Blair's Gram.* p. 121. "I say to myself, thou, he says to thy, to his self; &c."—*Dr. Murray's Hist. Europ. Lang.* ii, p. 121. "Or those who have esteemed themselves skilful, have tried for the mastery in two or four horse chariots."—*Zenobia*, i, p. 152. "I remember him barefooted and headed, running through the streets."—*Castle Rackrent*, p. 68. "Friends have the entire control of the school and dwelling-houses."—*The Friend*, vii, p. 231. "The meeting is held at the first mentioned place in the first month, at the last in the second, and so on."—*Ib.* p. 167. "Meetings for worship are held at the same hour on first and fourth days."—*Ib.* p. 230. "Every part of it, inside and out, is covered with gold leaf."—*Ib.* p. 404. "The Eastern Quarterly Meeting is held on the last seventh day in second, fifth, eighth, and eleventh month."—*Ib.* p. 87. "Trenton Preparative Meeting is held on the third fifth day in each month, at ten o'clock; meetings for worship at the same hour on first and fifth days."—*Ib.* p. 231. "Ketch, a vessel with two masts, a main and mizzen-mast."—*Webster's Dict.* "I only mean to suggest a doubt, whether nature has enlisted herself as a Cis or Trans-Atlantic partisan?"— *Jefferson's Notes*, p. 97. "By large hammers, like those used for paper and fullingmills, they beat their hemp."—MORTIMER: *in Johnston's Dict.* "Ant-hill, or Hillock, n. s. The small protuberances of earth, in which ants make their nests."—*Ib.* "It became necessary to substitute simple indicative terms called *pro-names* or *nouns*."—*Enclytica*, p. 16.

"Obscur'd, where highest woods, impenetrable
To star or sun-light, spread their umbrage broad."—*Milton.*

UNDER RULE V.—THE HYPHEN.

"*Evilthinking;* a noun, compounded of the noun *evil* and the imperfect participle *thinking;* singular number ;" &c.—*Churchill's Gram.* p. 180.

[FORMULE.—Not proper, because the word *evilthinking*, which has more than one accented syllable, is here compounded without the hyphen. But, according to Rule 5th, " When the parts of a compound do not fully coalesce, or when each retains its original accent, so that the compound has more than one, or one that is movable, the hyphen should be inserted between them." Therefore, the hyphen should be used in this word; thus, *evil-thinking.*]

" *Evilspeaking* ; a noun, compounded of the noun *evil* and the imperfect participle *speaking*."—*Ib.* " I am a tall, broadshouldered, impudent, black fellow."—SPECTATOR : *in Johnson's Dict.* " Ingratitude ! thou marblehearted fiend."—SHAK. : *ib.* " A popular licence is indeed the manyheaded tyranny."—SIDNEY : *ib.* " He from the manypeopled city flies."—SANDYS : *ib.* " He manylanguaged nations has surveyed."—POPE : *ib.* " The horsecucumber is the large green cucumber, and the best for the table."—MORTIMER : *ib.* " The bird of night did sit, even at noonday, upon the market-place."—SHAK. : *ib.* " These make a general gaoldelivery of souls, not for punishment."—SOUTH : *ib.* " Thy air, thou other goldbound brow, is like the first."—SHAK. : *ib.* " His person was deformed to the highest degree ; flatnosed, and blobberlipped."—L'ESTRANGE : *ib.* " He that defraudeth the labourer of his hire, is a bloodshedder."—ECCLUS. xxxiv, 22 : *ib.* " Bloodyminded, *adj.* from *bloody* and *mind.* Cruel ; inclined to blood-shed." See *John. Dict.* " Bluntwitted lord, ignoble in demeanour."—SHAK. : *ib.* " A young fellow with a bobwig and a black silken bag tied to it."—SPECTATOR : *ib.* " I have seen enough to confute all the boldfaced atheists of this age."—SHAK. : *ib.* " Before milkwhite, now purple with love's wound."—SHAK. : *ib.* " For what else is a redhot iron than fire ? and what else is a burning coal than redhot wood ?"—NEWTON : *ib.* " Pollevil is a large swelling, inflammation, or imposthume in the horse's poll, or nape of the neck just between the ears."—FARRIER : *ib.*

> " Quick-witted, brazenfac'd, with fluent tongues,
> Patient of labours, and dissembling wrongs."—DRYDEN : *ib.*

UNDER RULE VI.—NO HYPHEN.

" From his fond parent's eye a tear-drop fell."—*Snelling's Gift for Scribblers,* p. 43.

[FORMULE.—Not proper, because the word *tear-drop*, which has never any other than a full accent on the first syllable, is here compounded with the hyphen. But, according to Rule 6th, " When a compound has but one accented syllable in pronunciation, and the parts are such as admit of a complete coalescence, no hyphen should be inserted between them." Therefore, *teardrop* should be made a close compound.]

" How great, poor jack-daw, would thy sufferings be !"—*Ib.* p. 29. " Placed like a scare-crow in a field of corn."—*Ib.* p. 39. " Soup for the alms-house at a cent a quart." —*Ib.* p. 23. " Up into the watch-tower get, and see all things despoiled of fallacies."— DONNE : *Johnson's Dict. w. Lattice.* " In the day-time she sitteth in a watchtower, and flieth most by night."—BACON : *ib. w. Watchtower.* " In the daytime Fame sitteth in a watch-tower, and flieth most by night."—ID. : *ib. w. Daytime.* " The moral is the first business of the poet, as being the ground-work of his instruction."—DRYDEN : *ib. w. Moral.* " Madam's own hand the mouse-trap baited."—PRIOR : *ib. w. Mouse-trap.* " By the sinking of the air-shaft the air hath liberty to circulate."—RAY : *ib. w. Airshaft.* " The multiform and amazing operations of the air-pump and the loadstone."—WATTS : *ib. w. Multiform.* " Many of the fire-arms are named from animals."—*Ib. w. Musket.* " You might have trussed him and all his apparel into an eel-skin."—SHAK. : *ib. w. Truss.* " They may serve as land-marks, to shew what lies in the direct way of truth."—LOCKE : *ib. w. Landmark.* " A pack-horse is driven constantly in a narrow lane and dirty road."—*Id. ib. w. Lane.* " A mill-horse, still bound to go in one circle."—SIDNEY : *ib. w. Mill-horse.* " Of singing birds they have linnets, goldfinches, ruddocks, Canary-birds, black-birds, thrushes, and divers others."—CAREW : *ib. w. Goldfinch.* " Of singing birds, they have linnets, gold-finches, blackbirds, thrushes, and divers others."—ID. : *ib. w. Blackbird.* " Of singing birds, they have linnets, goldfinches, ruddocks, canary birds, blackbirds, thrushes, and divers other."—ID. : *ib. w. Canary bird.* " Cartridge, a case of paper or parchment filled with gun-powder."—*Johnson.*

> " Deep night, dark night, the silent of the night,
> The time of night when Troy was set on fire,
> The time when screech-owls cry, and ban-dogs howl."
>   SHAKSPEARE : *ib. w. Silent.*

" The time when screech-owls cry, and bandogs howl."
                    IDEM : *ib. w. Bandog.*

PROMISCUOUS ERRORS IN THE FIGURE OF WORDS.

LESSON I.—MIXED.

" They that live in glass-houses, should not throw stones."—*Old Adage.* " If a man profess Christianity in any manner or form soever."—*Watts,* p. 5. " For Cassius is a weary of the world."—SHAKSPEARE : *in Kirkham's Elocution,* p. 67. " By the coming together of more, the chains were fastened on."—*Walker's Particles,* p. 223. " Unto the carrying away of Jerusalem captive in the fifth month."—*Jer.* i, 3. " And the goings forth of the border shall be to Zedad."—*Numbers*, xxxiv, 8. "And the goings out of it shall be at Hazar-enan."—*Ib.* ver. 9. "For the taking place of effects, in a certain particular series."—*Dr. West, on Agency*, p. 39. "The letting go of which was the occasion of all that corruption."—*Dr. J. Owen.* "A falling off at the end always hurts greatly."—*Blair's Lect.* p. 126. "A falling off at the end is always injurious."—*Jamieson's Rhetoric*, p. 127. "As all holdings forth were courteously supposed to be trains of reasoning."—*Dr. Murray's Hist. Europ. Lang.* i, p. 333. "Whose goings forth have been from of old, from everlasting."—*Micah*, v, 2. "Some times the adjective becomes a substantive."—*Bradley's Gram.* p. 104. "It is very plain, I consider man as visited a new."—*Barclay's Works*, iii, p. 331. "Nor do I any where say, as he falsely insinuates."—*Ib.* p. 331. "Every where, any where, some where, no where."—*Alex. Murray's Gram.* p. 55. "The world hurries off a pace, and time is like a rapid river." —*Collier's Antoninus*, p. 58. "But to new model the paradoxes of ancient skepticism."— *Brown's Estimate*, i, p. 102. "The south east winds from the ocean invariably produce rain."—*Webster's Essays*, p. 369. "North west winds from the high lands produce cold clear weather."—*Ib.* "The greatest part of such tables would be of little use to English men."—*Priestley's Gram.* p. 155. "The ground floor of the east wing of Mulberry street meeting house was filled."—*The Friend*, vii, 232. "Prince Rupert's Drop. This singular production is made at the glass houses."—*Red Book*, p. 131.

"The lights and shades, whose well accorded strife
Gives all the strength and colour of our life."
Murray's Gram. p. 54 ; *Fisk's*, 65.

LESSON II.—MIXED.

"In the twenty and seventh year of Asa king of Judah did Zimri reign seven days in Tirzah."— 1 *Kings*, xvi, 15. "In the thirty and first year of Asa king of Judah, began Omri to reign over Israel."—*Ib.* xvi, 23. "He cannot so deceive himself as to fancy that he is able to do a rule of three sum."—*Foreign Quarterly Review.* "The best cod are those known under the name of Isle of Shoals dun fish."—*Balbi's Geog.* p. 26. "The soldiers, with down cast eyes, seemed to beg for mercy."—*Goldsmith's Greece*, ii, p. 142. "His head was covered with a coarse worn out piece of cloth."—*Ib.* p. 124. "Though they had lately received a reinforcement of a thousand heavy armed Spartans."—*Ib.* p. 38. "But he laid them by unopened ; and, with a smile, said, 'Business to morrow.'" —*Ib.* p. 7. "Chester monthly meeting is held at Moore's town, the third day following the second second day."—*The Friend*, vii, p. 124. "Eggharbour monthly meeting is held the first second day."—*Ib.* p. 124. "Little Egg Harbour Monthly Meeting is held at Tuckerton on the second fifth day in each month."—*Ib.* p. 231. "At three o'clock, on first day morning the 24th of eleventh month, 1834," &c.—*Ib.* p. 64. "In less than one-fourth part of the time usually devoted."—*Kirkham's Gram.* p. 4. "The pupil will not have occasion to use it one-tenth part as much."—*Ib.* p. 11. "The painter dips his paint brush in paint, to paint the carriage."—*Ib.* p. 28. "In an ancient English version of the New-Testament."—*Ib.* p. 74. "The little boy was bare headed."—*Red Book*, p. 36. "The man, being a little short sighted, did not immediately know him."—*Ib.* p. 40. "Picture frames are gilt with gold."—*Ib.* p. 44. "The park keeper killed one of the deer."—*Ib.* p. 44. "The fox was killed near the brick kiln."—*Ib.* p. 46. "Here comes Esther, with her milk pail."—*Ib.* p. 50. "The cabinet maker would not tell us."—*Ib.* p. 60. A fine thorn hedge extended along the edge of the hill.—*Ib.* p. 65. "If their private interests should be ever so little affected."—*Ib.* p. 73. "Unios are fresh water shells, vulgarly called fresh water clams."—*Ib.* p. 102.

"Did not each poet mourn his luckless doom,
Jostled by pedants out of elbow room."—*Lloyd*, p. 163.

LESSON III.—MIXED.

"The captive hovers a-while upon the sad remains."—PRIOR: *in Johnson's Dict. w. Hover.* "Constantia saw that the hand writing agreed with the contents of the letter."— ADDISON: *ib. w. Hand.* "They have put me in a silk night-gown, and a gaudy fool's cap." —ID.: *ib. w. Nightgown.* "Have you no more manners than to rail at Hocus, that has saved that clod-pated, numskull'd ninnyhammer of yours from ruin, and all his family?"—ARBUTHNOT: *ib. w. Ninnyhammer.* "A noble, that is, six shillings and eight-pence, is, and usually hath been paid."—BACON: *ib. w. Noble.* "The king of birds thick feather'd and with full-summed wings, fastened his talons east and west."—HOWEL: *ib. w. Full-summed.* "To morrow. This is an idiom of the same kind, supposing *morrow* to mean originally *morning* : as, *to night, to day*."—*Johnson's Dict.* 4to. "To-day goes away and to-morrow comes."—*Id. ib. w. Go*, No. 70. "Young children, who are tried in go carts, to keep their steps from sliding."—PRIOR : *ib. w. Go-cart.* "Which, followed well, would demonstrate them but goers backward."—SHAK.: *ib. w. Goer.* "Heaven's golden winged herald late he saw, to a poor Galilean virgin sent."—CRASHAW: *ib. w. Golden.* "My penthouse eye-brows and my shaggy beard offend your sight."— DRYDEN : *ib. w. Penthouse.* "The hungry lion would fain have been dealing with good horse-flesh."—L'ESTRANGE: *ib. w. Nag.* "A broad brimmed hat ensconced each careful head."—*Snelling's Gift*, p. 63. "With harsh vibrations of his three stringed lute."— *Ib.* p. 42. "They magnify a hundred fold an author's merit."—*Ib.* p. 14. "I'll nail them fast to some oft opened door."—*Ib.* p. 10. "Glossed over only with a saint-like show, still thou art bound to vice."—DRYDEN: *in Johnson's Dict. w. Gloss.* "Take of aqua-fortis two ounces, of quick-silver two drachms."—BACON : *ib. w. Charge.* "This rainbow never appears but when it rains in the sun-shine."—NEWTON : *ib. w. Rainbow.*

> "Not but there are, who merit others palms;
> Hopkins and Stern hold glad the heart with Psalms."
>
> *British Poets*, Lond. 1800, Vol. vi, p. 405.

CHAPTER IV.—OF SPELLING.

Spelling is the art of expressing words by their proper letters. This important art is to be acquired rather by means of the spelling-book or dictionary, and by observation in reading, than by the study of written rules; because what is proper or improper, depends chiefly upon usage.

The orthography of our language is attended with much uncertainty and perplexity: many words are variously spelled by the best scholars, and many others are not usually written according to the analogy of similar words. But to be ignorant of the orthography of such words as are spelled with uniformity, and frequently used, is justly considered disgraceful.

The following rules may prevent some embarrassment, and thus be of service to those who wish to be accurate.

RULES FOR SPELLING.

RULE I.—FINAL F, L, OR S.

Monosyllables ending in *f, l,* or *s*, preceded by a single vowel, double the final consonant; as *staff, mill, pass—muff, knell, gloss—off, hiss, puss.*

EXCEPTIONS. — The words *clef, if,* and *of,* are written with single *f;* and *as, gas, has, was, yes, his, is, this, us, pus,* and *thus,* with single *s.* So *bul,* for the flounder; *nul,* for *no,* in law; *sol,* for *sou* or *sun;* and *sal,* for *salt,* in chemistry, have but the single *l.*

OBS.—Because *sal, salis,* in Latin, doubles not the *l,* the chemists write *salify, salifiable, salification, saliferous, saline, salinous, saliniform, salifying,* &c., with single *l,* contrary to Rule 3d. But in *gas* they ought to double the *s;* for this is a word of their own invent-ing. Neither have they any plea for allowing it to form *gases* and *gaseous* with the *s* still single; for so they make it violate two general rules at once. If the singular cannot now be written *gass,* the plural should nevertheless be *gasses,* and the adjective should be *gasseous,* according to Rule 3d.

RULE II.—OTHER FINALS.

Words ending in any other consonant than *f, l,* or *s,* do not double the final let-ter; as, *mob, nod, dog, sum, sun, cup, cur, cut, fix, whiz.*

EXCEPTIONS.—We double the consonant in *abb, ebb, add, odd, egg, jagg, ragg, inn, err, burr, purr, butt, buzz, fuzz, yarr,* and some proper names. But we have also *ab* (*from*) and *ad* (*to*) for prefixes ; and *jag, rag, in, bur,* and *but,* are other words that conform to the rule.

RULE III.—DOUBLING.

Monosyllables, and words accented on the last syllable, when they end with a single consonant preceded by a single vowel, or by a vowel after *qu*, double their final consonant before an additional syllable that begins with a vowel: as, *rob, robbed, robber ; fop, foppish, foppery ; squat, squatter, squatting ; thin, thinner, thinnest ; swim, swimmer, swimming ; commit, committeth, committing, committed, committer, committee ; acquit, acquittal, acquittance, acquitted, acquitting, acquitteth.*

EXCEPTIONS.— 1. X final, being equivalent to *ks*, is never doubled : thus, from *mix*, we have *mixed, mixing*, and *mixer*. 2. When the derivative retains not the accent of the root, the final consonant is not always doubled : as, *prefer', pref'erence, pref'erable ; refer', ref'erence, ref'erable*, or *refer'rible ; infer', in'ference, in'ferable*, or *infer'rible ; transfer', a trans'fer, trans'ferable*, or *transfer'rible*. 3. But letters doubled in Latin, are usually doubled in English, without regard to accent, or to any other principle : as, Britain, *Britan'nic, Britannia ;* appeal, *appel'lant ;* argil, *argil'lous, argilla'ceous ;* cavil, *cav'illous, cavilla'tion ;* excel', *ex'cellent, ex'cellence ;* inflame', *inflam'mable, inflamma'tion.* See Observations 9 and 10, p. 190.

RULE IV.—NO DOUBLING.

A final consonant, when it is not preceded by a single vowel, or when the accent is not on the last syllable, should remain single before an additional syllable : as, *toil, toiling ; oil, oily ; visit, visited ; differ, differing ; peril, perilous ; viol, violist ; real, realize, realist ; dial, dialing, dialist ; equal, equalize, equality ; vitriol, vitriolic, vitriolate.*

EXCEPTIONS.— 1. The final *l* of words ending in *ol*, must be doubled before another vowel, lest the power of the *e* be mistaken, and a syllable be lost : as, *travel, traveller ; duel, duellist ; revel, revelling ; gravel, gravelly ; marvel, marvellous.* Yet the word *parallel*, having three Ells already, conforms to the rule in forming its derivatives ; as, *paralleling, paralleled*, and *unparalleled*. 2. Contrary to the preceding rule, the preterits, participles, and derivative nouns, of the few verbs ending in *al, il*, or *ol*, unaccented,— namely, *equal, rival, vial, marshal, victual, cavil, pencil, carol, gambol*, and *pistol*,—are usually allowed to double the *l*, though some dissent from the practice : as, *equalled, equalling ; rivalled, rivalling ; cavilled, cavilling, caviller ; carolled, carolling, caroller.* 3. When *ly* follows *l*, we have two Ells of course, but in fact no doubling : as, *real, really ; oral, orally ; cruel, cruelly ; civil, civilly ; cool, coolly ; wool, woolly.* 4. Compounds, though they often remove the principal accent from the point of duplication, always retain the double letter : as, *wit'snapper, kid'napper,*[*] *grass'hopper, duck'-legged, spur'-galled, hot'spurred, broad'-brimmed, hare'-lipped, half'-witted.* So, *compromitted* and *manumitted ;* but *benefited* is different.

RULE V.—FINAL CK.

Monosyllables and English verbs end not with *c*, but take *ck* for double *c :* as, *rack, wreck, rock, attack ;* but, in general, words derived from the learned languages need not the *k*, and common use discards it : as, *Italic, maniac, music, public.*

EXCEPTIONS.— The words *arc*, part of a circle ; *orc*, the name of a fish ; *lac*, a gum or resin ; and *sac*, or *soc*, a privilege, in old English law, are ended with *c* only. *Zinc* is, perhaps, better spelled *zink ; marc, mark ; disc, disk ;* and *talc, talck.*

RULE VI.—RETAINING.

Words ending with any double letter, preserve it double before any additional termination, not beginning with the same letter,† as in the following derivatives :

---

* Whether *worshipper* should follow this principle, or not, is questionable. If Dr. Webster is right in making *worship* a compound of *worth* and *ship*, he furnishes a reason against his own practice of using a single *p* in *worshiper, worshiped*, and *worshiping*. The Saxon word appears to have been *weorthscype*. But words ending in *ship* are *derivatives*, rather than compounds ; and therefore they seem to belong to the rule, rather than to the exception : as, "So we *followshiped* him."—*Herald of Freedom : Liberator*, ix, p. 68.

† When *ss* comes before *s*, or may be supposed to do so, or when *ll* comes before *l*, one of the letters is dropped that *three* of the same kind may not meet : as, *free, freer, freest, freeth, freed ; skill, skill-ss ; full, fully : droll, drolly.* And, as *burgess-ship, hostess-ship*, and *mistress-ship* are derivatives, and not compounds, I think they ought to follow the same principle, and be written *burgesship, hostesship, mistresship*. The proper

wooer, seeing, blissful, oddly, gruffly, equally, shelly, hilly, stiffness, illness, stillness, shrillness, fellness, smallness, drollness, freeness, grassless, passless, carelessness, recklessness, embarrassment, enfeoffment, agreement, agreeable.

EXCEPTIONS.— 1. Certain irregular derivatives in *t*, from verbs ending in *ll* or *ss*, as *dwelt* from *dwell, spelt* from *spell, shalt* from *shall, wilt* from *will, blest* from *bless, past* from *pass,* are exceptions to the foregoing rule. 2. If the word *pontiff* is properly spelled with two Effs, its eight derivatives are also exceptions to this rule; for they are severally spelled with one: as, *pontific, pontifical, pontificate,* &c. 3. The words *skillful, skillfully, willful, willfully, chillness, tallness, dullness,* and *fullness,* have generally been allowed to drop the second *l,* though all of them might well be made to conform to the general rule, agreeably to the orthography of Webster.

RULE VII.—RETAINING.

Words ending with any double letter, preserve it double in all derivatives formed from them by means of prefixes: as, *see, foresee ; feoff, enfeoff ; pass, repass ; press, depress ; miss, amiss ; call, recall ; stall, forestall ; thrall, inthrall ; spell, misspell ; tell, foretell ; sell, undersell ; add, superadd ; snuff, besnuff ; swell, overswell.*

OBSERVATION. — The words *enroll, unroll, miscall, befall, befell, bethrall, reinstall, disinthrall, fulfill,* and *twibill,* are very commonly written with one *l,* and made exceptions to this rule ; but those authors are in the right who retain the double letter.

RULE VIII.—FINAL LL.

Final *ll* is peculiar to monosyllables and their compounds, with the few derivatives formed from such roots by prefixes ; consequently, all other words that end in *l,* must be terminated with a single *l:* as, *cabal, logical, appal, excel, rebel, refel, dispel, extol, control, mogul, jackal, rascal, damsel, handsel, tinsel, tendril, tranquil, gambol, consul.*

OBSERVATION. — The words *annul, until, distil, extil,* and *instil,* are also properly spelled with one *l ;* for the monosyllables *null, till,* and *still* are not really their roots, but rather derivatives, or contractions of later growth. Webster, however, prefers *distill, extill,* and *instill* with *ll ;* and some have been disposed to add the other two.

RULE IX.—FINAL E.

The final *e* of a primitive word, when this letter is mute or obscure, is generally omitted before an additional termination beginning with a vowel : as, *remove, removal ; rate, ratable ; force, forcible ; true, truism ; rave, raving ; sue, suing ; eye, eying ; idle, idling ; centre, centring.*

EXCEPTIONS. — 1. Words ending in *ce* or *ge,* retain the *e* before *able* or *ous,* to preserve the soft sounds of *c* and *g:* as, *trace, traceable ; change, changeable ; outrage, outrageous.* 2. So, from *shoe,* we write *shoeing,* to preserve the sound of the root ; from *hoe, hoeing,* by apparent analogy ; and, from *singe, singeing ;* from *swinge, swingeing ;* from *tinge, tingeing ;* that they may not be confounded with *singing, swinging,* and *tinging.* 3. To compounds and prefixes, as *firearms, forearm, anteact, viceagent,* the rule does not apply ; and final *ee* remains double, by Rule VI, as in *disagreeable, disagreeing.*

RULE X.—FINAL E.

The final *e* of a primitive word is generally retained before an additional termination beginning with a consonant : as, *pale, paleness ; edge, edgeless ; judge, judgeship ; lodge, lodgement ; change, changeful ; infringe, infringement.*

---

form of *gall-less* is perhaps more doubtful. It ought not to be *gallless,* as Dr Webster has it ; and *galless,* the analogical form, is yet, so far as I know, without authority. But is it not preferable to the hyphened form, with three Ells, which has authority ? "GALL-LESS, *a.* Without gall or bitterness. *Cleaveland."—Chalmers, Bolles, Worcester.*

> "Ah! mild and *gall-less* dove,
> Which dost the pure and candid dwellings love,
>   Canst thou in Albion still delight ! "—*Cowley's Odes.*

Worcester's Dictionary has also the questionable word "*brilless.*" *Treen,* for *trees,* or for an adjective meaning *a tree's,* or *made of a tree,* is exhibited in several of our dictionaries, and pronounced as a monosyllable: but Dr Beattie, in his Poems, p. 84, has made it a dissyllable, with three like letters divided by a hyphen, thus :—

> "Plucking from *tree-en* bough her simple food."

EXCEPTIONS. — 1. When the *e* is preceded by a vowel, it is sometimes omitted; as in *duly, truly, awful, argument;* but much more frequently retained; as in *dueness, trueness, blueness, bluely, rueful, dueful, shoeless, eyeless.* 2. The word *wholly* is also an exception to the rule, for nobody writes it *wholely.* 3. Some will have *judgment, abridgment,* and *acknowledgment,* to be irreclaimable exceptions; but I write them with the *e,* upon the authority of Lowth, Beattie, Ainsworth, Walker, Cobb, Chalmers, and others: the French "*jugement,*" *judgement,* always retains the *e.*

RULE XI.—FINAL Y.

The final *y* of a primitive word, when preceded by a consonant, is generally changed into *i* before an additional termination: as, *merry, merrier, merriest, merrily, merriment; pity, pitied, pities, pitiest, pitiless, pitiful, pitiable; contrary, contrariness, contrarily.*

EXCEPTIONS. — 1. This rule applies to derivatives, but not to compounds: thus, we write *merciful,* and *mercy-seat; penniless,* and *pennyworth; scurviness,* and *scurvy-grass;* &c. But *ladyship* and *goodyship,* being unlike *secretaryship* and *suretiship; handicraft* and *handiwork,** unlike *handygripe* and *handystroke; babyship* and *babyhood,* unlike *stateliness* and *likelihood;* the distinction between derivatives and compounds, we see, is too nice a point to have been always accurately observed. 2. Before *ing* or *ish,* the *y* is retained to prevent the doubling of *i*: as, *pity, pitying; baby, babyish.* 3. Words ending in *ie,* dropping the *e* by Rule 9th, change the *i* into *y,* for the same reason: as, *die, dying; vie, trying; lie, lying.*

RULE XII.—FINAL Y.

The final *y* of a primitive word, when preceded by a vowel, should not be changed into *i* before any additional termination: as, *day, days; key, keys; guy, guys; valley, valleys; coy, coyly; cloy, cloys, cloyed; boy, boyish, boyhood; annoy, annoyer, annoyance; joy, joyless, joyful.*

EXCEPTIONS. — 1. From *lay, pay, say,* and *stay,* are formed *laid, paid, said,* and *staid;* but the regular words, *layed, payed, stayed,* are sometimes used. 2. *Raiment,* contracted from *arrayment,* is never written with the *y.* 3. *Daily* is more common than the regular form *dayly;* but *gayly, gayety,* and *gayness,* are justly superseding *gaily* and *gaiety.*

RULE XIII.—IZE AND ISE.

Words ending in *ize* or *ise* sounded alike, as in *wise* and *size,* generally take the *z* in all such as are essentially formed by means of the termination; and the *s* in monosyllables, and all such as are essentially formed by means of prefixes: as, *gormandize, apologize, brutalize, canonize, pilgrimize, philosophize, cauterize, anathematize, sympathize, disorganize,* with *z;* † *rise, arise, disguise, advise, derise, supervise, circumcise, despise, surmise, surprise, comprise, compromise, enterprise, presurmise,* with *s.*

EXCEPTIONS.—1. *Advertise, catechise, chastise, criticise,‡ exercise, exorcise,* and *merchandise.*

---

* *Handiwork, handicraft,* and *handicraftsman,* appear to have been corruptly written for *handwork, handcraft,* and *handcraftsman.* They were formerly in good use, and consequently obtained a place in our vocabulary, from which no lexicographer, so far as I know, has yet thought fit to discard them; but, being irregular, they are manifestly becoming obsolete, or at least showing a tendency to throw off these questionable forms. *Handcraft* and *handcraftsman* are now exhibited in some dictionaries; and *handiwork* seems likely to be resolved into *handy* and *work,* from which Johnson supposes it to have been formed. See Psalm xix, 1. The text is varied thus: " And the firmament *sheweth* his *handiwork.*" — *Johnson's Dict.* " And the firmament *sheweth* his *handy-work.*" — *Scott's Bible; Bruce's Bible; Harrison's Gram.* p. 88. " And the firmament *sheweth* his *handy work.*" — *Alger's Bible; Friends' Bible; Harrison's Gram.* p. 108.

† Here a word, formed from its root by means of the termination *ize,* afterwards assumes a prefix, to make a secondary derivative: thus, *organ, organize, disorganize.* In such a case, the latter derivative must of course be like the former; and I assume that the essential or primary formation of both from the word *organ* is by the termination *ize;* but it is easy to see that *disguise, demise, surmise,* and the like, are essentially or primarily formed by means of the prefixes, *dis, de,* and *sur.* As to *advertise, exercise, detonize,* and *recognize,* which I have noted among the exceptions, it is not easy to discover by which method we ought to suppose them to have been formed; but with respect to nearly all others, the distinction is very plain, and though there may be no *natural reason* for founding upon it such a rule as the foregoing, the voice of general custom is as clear in this as in most other points or principles of orthography, and, surely, some rule in this case is greatly needed

‡ *Criticise,* with *s,* is the orthography of Johnson, Walker, Webster, Jones, Scott, Bolles, Chalmers, Cobb, and others; and so did Worcester spell it in his Comprehensive Dictionary of 1831, but, in his Universal and Critical Dictionary of 1846, he wrote it with *z,* as did Bailey in his folio, about a hundred years ago. Here the *z* conforms to the foregoing rule, and the *s* does not.

are most commonly written with *s*; and *size, assize, capsize, analyze, overprice, detonize,* and *recognize,* with *z.* How many of them are real exceptions to the rule, it is difficult to say. 2. *Prize,* a thing taken, and *prize,* to esteem; *apprise,* to inform, and *apprize,* to value, or appraise, are often written either way, without this distinction of meaning, which some wish to establish. 3. The want of the foregoing rule has also made many words *variable,* which ought, unquestionably, to conform to the general principle.

RULE XIV.—COMPOUNDS.

Compounds generally retain the orthography of the simple words which compose them: as, *wherein, horseman, uphill, shellfish, knee-deep, kneedgrass, kneading-trough, innkeeper, skylight, plumtree, mandrill.*

EXCEPTIONS.— 1. In permanent compounds, or in any derivatives of which they are not the *roots,* the words *full* and *all* drop one *l;* as, *handful, careful, fulfill, always, although, withal :* in temporary compounds, they retain both; as, *full-eyed, chock-full,** *all-wise, save-all.* 2. So the prefix *mis* (if from *miss,* to err,) drops one *s;* but it is wrong to drop them both, as in Johnson's " *mispell* " and " *mispend,*" for *misspell* and *misspend.* 3. In the names of days, the word *mass* also drops one *s;* as, *Christmas, Candlemas, Lammas.* 4. The possessive case often drops the apostrophe; as in *herdsman, kitesfoot.* 5. One letter is dropped, if three of the same kind come together : as, *Rosshire, chaffinch ;* or else a hyphen is used: as, *Ross-shire, ill-looking, still-life.* 6. *Chilblain, welcome,* and *welfare,* drop one *l.* 7. *Shepherd, wherever,* and *whosever,* drop an *e ;* and *wherefore* and *therefore* assume one.

RULE XV.—USAGE.

Any word for the spelling of which we have no rule but usage, is written wrong if not spelled according to the usage which is most common among the learned: as, " The brewer grinds his malt before he *brues* his beer."—*Red Book,* p. 38.

OBSERVATIONS.

OBS. 1.— The foregoing rules aim at no wild and impracticable reformation of our orthography ; but, if carefully applied, they will do much to obviate its chief difficulties. Being made variable by the ignorance of some writers and the caprice of others, our spelling is now, and always has been, exceedingly irregular and unsettled. Uniformity and consistency can be attained in no other way, than by the steady application of rules and principles ; and these must be made as few and as general as the case will admit, that the memory of the learner may not be overmatched by their number or complexity. Rules founded on the analogy of similar words, and sanctioned by the usage of careful writers, must be taken as our guides; because common practice is often found to be capricious, contradictory, and uncertain. That errors and inconsistencies abound, even in the books which are proposed to the world as *standards* of English orthography, is a position which scarcely needs proof. It is true, to a greater or less extent, of all the spelling-books and dictionaries that I have seen, and probably of all that have ever been published. And as all authors are liable to mistakes, which others may copy, general rules should have more weight than particular examples to the contrary. " The right spelling of a word may be said to be that which agrees the best with its pronunciation, its etymology, and with the analogy of the particular class of words to which it belongs." — *Philological Museum,* Vol. i, p. 647.

OBS. 2.— I do not deny that great respect is due to the authority of our lexicographers, or that great improvement was made in the orthography of our language when Dr. Johnson put his hand to the work. But sometimes one man's authority may offset an other's; and he that is inconsistent with himself, destroys his own : for, surely, his example cannot be paramount to his principles. Much has been idly said, both for and against the adoption of Johnson's Dictionary, or Webster's, as *the criterion* of what is right or wrong in spelling ; but it would seem that no one man's learning is sufficiently extensive, or his memory sufficiently accurate, to be solely relied on to furnish *a standard* by which we may in all cases be governed. Johnson was generally right ; but, like other men, he was sometimes wrong. He erred sometimes in his *principles,* or in their application ; as when he adopted the *k* in such words as *rhetorick* and *demoniack;* or

---

* Like this, the compound *brim-full* ought to be written with a hyphen and accented on the last syllable ; but all our lexicographers have corrupted it into *brim′ful,* and, contrary to the authorities they quote, accented it on the first. Their noun *brim′fulness,* with a like accent, is also a corruption ; and the text of Shakspeare, which they quote for it, is nonsense, unless *brim* be there made a separate adjective : —

" With ample and *brim′fulness* of his force." — *Johnson's Dict. et al.*
" With *ample* and *brim′fullness* of his force," would be better.

when he inserted the *u* in such words as *governour, warriour, superiour*. Neither of these modes of spelling was ever generally adopted, in any thing like the number of words to which he applied them; or ever will be; though some indiscreet compilers are still zealously endeavouring to impose them upon the public, as the true way of spelling. He also erred sometimes *by accident*, or *oversight*; as when he spelled thus: "*recall* and *miscal, inthrall* and *bethral, windfall* and *downfall, laystall* and *thumbstal, waterfall* and *overfal, molehill* and *dunghill, windmill* and *twibil, uphill* and *downhil.*" This occasional excision of the letter *l* is reprehensible, because it is contrary to general analogy, and because both letters are necessary to preserve the sound, and show the derivation of the compound. Walker censures it as a "ridiculous irregularity," and lays the blame of it on the "*printers,*" and yet does not venture to correct it! See Johnson's Dictionary, first American edition, quarto: Walker's Pronouncing Dictionary, under the word *Dunghil;* and his Rhyming Dictionary, Introd. p. xv.

OBS. 3.—"Dr. Johnson's Dictionary" has been represented by some as having "nearly fixed the external form of our language." But Murray, who quotes this from Dr. Nares, admits, at the same time, that, "The orthography of a great number of English words, is far from being uniform, even amongst writers of distinction."— *Gram.* p. 25. And, after commending this work of Johnson's, as A STANDARD, from which, "it is earnestly to be hoped, that no author will henceforth, on light grounds, be tempted to innovate," he adds, "This Dictionary, however, contains some orthographical inconsistencies which ought to be rectified: such as, *immovable, moveable; chastely, chastness; fertileness, fertily; slimess, slyly; fearlessly, fearlesness; needlessness, needlessly.*"— *Ib.* In respect to the final *ck* and *our*, he also *intentionally departs from* THE STANDARD *which he thus commends;* preferring, in that, the authority of *Walker's Rhyming Dictionary*, from which he borrowed his rules for spelling. For, against the use of *k* at the end of words from the learned languages, and against the *u* in many words in which Johnson used it, we have the authority, not only of general usage now, but of many grammarians who were contemporary with Johnson, and of more than a dozen lexicographers, ancient or modern, among whom is Walker himself. In this, therefore, Murray's practice is right, and his commended standard dictionary, wrong.

OBS. 4.—Of words ending in *or* or *our*, we have about three hundred and twenty; of which not more than forty can now with any propriety be written with the latter termination. Aiming to write according to the best usage of the present day, I insert the *u* in so many of these words as now seem most familiar to the eye when so written; but I have no partiality for any letters that can well be spared; and if this book should ever, by any good fortune, happen to be reprinted, after *honour, labour, favour, behaviour,* and *endeavour*, shall have become as unfashionable as *authour, errour, terrour*, and *emperor*, are now, let the proof-reader strike out the useless letter not only from these words, but from all others which shall bear an equally antiquated appearance.

OBS. 5.—I have suggested the above-mentioned imperfections in *Dr. Johnson's* orthography, merely to justify the liberty which I take of spelling otherwise; and not with any view to give a preference to that of *Dr. Webster*, who is now contending for the honour of having furnished a more correct *standard*. For the latter author, though right in some things in which the former was wrong, is, on the whole, still more erroneous and inconsistent. In his various attempts at reformation in our orthography, he has spelled many hundreds of words in such a variety of ways, that he knows not at last which of them is right, and which are wrong. But in respect to *definitions*, he has done good service to our literature; nor have his critics been sufficiently just respecting what they call his "innovations." * To omit the *k* from such words as *publick*, or the *u* from such as *superiour*, is certainly *no innovation;* it is but ignorance that censures the general practice, under that name. The advocates for Johnson and opponents of Webster, who are now so zealously stickling for the *k* and the *u* in these cases, ought to know that they are contending for what was obsolete, or obsolescent, when Dr. Johnson was a boy.

OBS. 6.—I have before observed that some of the grammarians who were contemporary with Johnson, did not adopt his practice respecting the *k* or the *u*, in *publick, critick, errour, superiour*, &c. And indeed I am not sure there were any who did. Dr. Johnson was born in 1709, and he died in 1784. But Brightland's Grammar, which was written during the reign of Queen Anne, who died in 1714, in treating of the letter C, says, "If in any Word the harder Sound precedes (*e*), (*i*), or (*y*), (*k*) is either added or put in its Place; as, *Skill, Skin, Publick:* And tho' the additional (*k*) in the foregoing Word be an *old Way* of Spelling, yet it is now very justly left off, as being a superfluous Letter; for (*c*) at the End is always hard."— Seventh Edition, Lond. 1746, p. 37.

OBS. 7.—The three grammars of Ash, Priestley, and Lowth, all appeared, in their

* See Cobb's Critical Review of the Orthography of Webster.

first editions, about one time; all, if I mistake not, in the year 1758; and none of these learned doctors, it would seem, used the mode of spelling now in question. In Ash, of 1799, we have such orthography as this: "Italics, public, domestic, our traffic, music, quick; error, superior, warrior, authors, honour, humour, favour, behaviour." In Priestley, of 1772: "Iambics, dactyls, dactylic, anapæstic, monosyllabic, electric, public, critic; author, emperor's, superior; favour, labours, neighbours, laboured, vigour, endeavour; meagre, hillock, bailiwick, bishoprick, control, travelling." In Lowth, of 1799: "Comic, critic, characteristic, domestic; author, *favor, favored, endeavored, alledging,* foretells." Now all these are words in the spelling of which Johnson and Webster contradict each other; and if they are not all right, surely they would not, on the whole, be made more nearly right, by being conformed to either of these authorities exclusively. For THE BEST USAGE is the ultimate rule of grammar.

OBS. 8.— The old British Grammar, written before the American Revolution, and even before "*the Learned Mr. Samuel Johnson*" was doctorated, though it thus respectfully quotes that great scholar, does not follow him in the spelling of which I am treating. On the contrary, it abounds with examples of words ending in *ic* and *or*, and not in *ick* and *our*, as he wrote them; and I am confident, that, from that time to this, the former orthography has continued to be *more common than his.* Walker, the orthoëpist, who died in 1807, yielded the point respecting the *k*, and ended about four hundred and fifty words with *c* in his Rhyming Dictionary; but he thought it more of an innovation than it really was. In his Pronouncing Dictionary, he says, "It has been a custom, *within these twenty years,* to omit the *k* at the end of words, when preceded by *c.* This has introduced a *novelty* into the language, which is that of ending a word with an unusual letter," &c. "This omission of *k* is, however, too general to be counteracted, even by the authority of Johnson; but it is to be hoped it will be confined to words from the learned languages."— *Walker's Principles of Pronunciation*, No. 400. The tenth edition of Burn's Grammar, dated 1810, says, "It has become customary to omit *k* after *c* at the end of dissyllables and trissyllables, &c. as *music, arithmetic, logic;* but the *k* is retained in monosyllables; as, *back, deck, rick,* &c."— P. 25. James Buchanan, of whose English Syntax there had been five American editions in 1792, added no *k* to such words as *didactic, critic, classic,* of which he made frequent use; and though he wrote *honour, labour,* and the like, with *u,* as they are perhaps most generally written now, he inserted no *u* in *error, author,* or any of those words in which that letter would now be inconsistent with good taste.

OBS. 9.— Bicknell's Grammar, of 1790, treating of the letter *k,* says, "And for the same reason we have *dropt* it at the end of words after *c,* which is there always hard; as in *publick, logick,* &c. which are more elegantly written *public, logic.*"— Part ii, p. 13. Again: "It has heretofore joined with *c* at the end of words; as *publick, logick;* but, as before observed, being there quite superfluous, it is now left out."— *Ib.* p. 16. Horne Tooke's orthography was also agreeable to the rule which I have given on this subject. So is the usage of David Booth: "Formerly · a *k* was added, as, *rustick, politick, Arithmetick,* &c. but this is now in disuse."— *Booth's Introd. to Dict.* Lond. 1814, p. 80.

OBS. 10.—As the authors of many recent spelling-books— Cobb, Emerson, Burhans, Bolles, Sears, Marshall, Mott, and others — are now contending for this "*superfluous letter,*" in spite of all the authority against it, it seems proper briefly to notice their argument, lest the student be misled by it. It is summed up by one of them in the following words: "In regard to *k* after *c* at the end of words, it may be sufficient to say, that its omission has never been attempted, except in a *small portion* of the cases *where* it occurs; and that *it* tends to an erroneous pronunciation of derivatives, as in *mimick, mimicking,* where, if the *k* were omitted, *it* would read *mimicing;* and as *c* before *i* is always sounded like *s, it* must be pronounced *mimising.* Now, since *it* is never omitted in monosyllables, *where it* most frequently occurs, as in *block, clock,* &c., and *can be in a part only* of polysyllables, it is thought better to preserve it in all cases, by *which* we have one general rule, in place of *several* irregularities and exceptions that must follow its partial omission."— *Bolles's Spelling-Book,* p. 2. I need not tell the reader that these two sentences evince great want of care or skill in the art of grammar. But it is proper to inform him, that we have in our language eighty-six monosyllables which end with *ck,* and from them about fifty compounds or derivatives, which of course keep the same termination. To these may be added a dozen or more which seem to be of doubtful formation, such as *huckaback, pickapack, gimcrack, ticktack, picknick, barrack, knapsack, hollyhock, shamrock, hammock, hillock, hommock, bullock, roebuck.* But the verbs on which this argument is founded are only six; *attack, ransack, traffick, frolick, mimick,* and *physick;* and these, unquestionably, must either be spelled with the *k,* or must assume it in their derivatives. Now that useful class of words which are generally and properly written with final *c,* are about *four hundred and fifty* in number, and are all of them either adjectives or nouns of regular derivation from the learned languages, being words of more than one syllable, which have come to us from Greek or Latin roots. But what has the doubling of *c* by *k*, in our native monosyllables and their derivatives, to do with all these words of foreign origin? For the reason of the matter, we might as well double the *l*, as our ancestors did, in *naturall, temporall, spirituall*, &c.

OBS. 11.—The learner should observe that some letters incline much to a duplication, while some others are doubled but seldom, and some, never. Thus, among the vowels, *ee* and *oo* occur frequently; *aa* is used sometimes; *ii*, never—except in certain Latin words, (wherein the vowels are separately uttered,) such as *Horatii, Veii, iidem, genii*. Again, the doubling of *u* is precluded by the fact that we have a distinct letter called *Double-u*, which was made by joining two Vees, or two Ues, when the form for *u* was *v*. So, among the consonants, *f, l*, and *s*, incline more to duplication, than any others. These letters are double, not only at the end of those monosyllables which have but one vowel, as *staff, mill, pass*; but also under some other circumstances. According to general usage, final *f* is doubled after a single vowel, in almost all cases; as in *bailiff, caitiff, plaintiff, midriff, sheriff, tariff, mastiff*: yet not in *calif*, which is perhaps better written *caliph*. Final *l*, as may be seen by Rule 8th, admits not now of a duplication like this; but, by the exceptions to Rule 4th, it is frequently doubled when no other consonant would be; as in *travelling, grovelling*; unless, (contrary to the opinion of Lowth, Walker, and Webster,) we will have *fillipping, gossipping*, and *worshipping*, to be needful exceptions also.

OBS. 12.—Final *s* sometimes occurs single, as in *alas, atlas, bias*; and especially in Latin words, as *virus, impetus*; and when it is added to form plurals, as *verse, verses*: but this letter, too, is generally doubled at the end of primitive words of more than one syllable; as in *carcass, compass, cuirass, harass, trespass, embarrass*. On the contrary, the other consonants are seldom doubled, except when they come under Rule 3d. The letter *p*, however, is commonly doubled in some words, even when it forms a needless exception to Rule 4th; as in the derivatives from *fillip, gossip*, and perhaps also *worship*. This letter, too, was very frequently doubled in Greek; whence we have, from the name of Philip of Macedon, the words *Philippic* and *Philippize*, which, if spelled according to our rule for such derivatives, would, like *galloped* and *galloper, siruped* and *sirupy*, have but one *p*. We find them so written in some late dictionaries. But if *fillipped, gossipped*, and *worshipped*, with the other derivatives from the same roots, are just and necessary exceptions to Rule 4th, (which I do not admit,) so are these; and for a much stronger reason, as the classical scholar will think. In our language, or in words purely English, the letters *h, i, j, k, q, v, w, x*, and *y*, are, properly speaking, *never doubled*. Yet, in the forming of *compounds*, it may possibly happen, that two Aitches, two Kays, or even two Double-ues, or Wies shall come together; as in *withhold, brickkiln, slowworm, bayyarn*.

OBS. 13.—There are some words—as those which come from *metal, medal, coral, crystal, argil, axil, cavil, tranquil, pupil, papil*—in which the classical scholar is apt to violate the analogy of English derivation, by doubling the letter *l*, because he remembers the *ll* of their foreign roots, or their foreign correspondents. But let him also remember, that, if a knowledge of etymology may be shown by spelling metallic, metalliferous, metallography, metallurgic, metallurgist, metallurgy, medallic, medallion, crystallise, crystalline, argillous, argillaceous, axillar, axillary, cavillous, cavillation, papillate, papillous, papillary, tranquillity, and pupillary, with double *l*, ignorance of it must needs be implied in spelling metaline, metalist, metaloid, metaloidal, medalist, coralaceous, coraline, coralite, coralinite, coraloid, coraloidal, crystalite, argilite, argilitic, tranquilize, and pupilage, in like manner. But we cannot well double the *l* in the former, and not in the latter words. Here is a choice of difficulties. Etymology must govern orthography. But what etymology? our own, or that which is foreign? If we say, both, they disagree; and the mere English scholar cannot know when, or how far, to be guided by the latter. If a Latin diminutive, as *papilla* from *papula* or *papa, pupillus* from *pupus*, or *tranquillus* from *trans* and *quietus*, happen to double an *l*, must we forever cling to the reduplication, and that, in spite of our own rules to the contrary? Why is it more objectionable to change *pupillaris* to *pupilary*, than *pupillus* to *pupil*? or, to change *tranquillitas* to *tranquility*, than *tranquillus* to *tranquil*? And since *papilous, pupilage*, and *tranquilize* are formed from the English words, and not directly from the Latin, why is it not as improper to write them with double *l*, as to write *perilous, vassalage*, and *civilize*, in the same manner?

OBS. 14.—If the practice of the learned would allow us to follow the English rule here, I should incline to the opinion, that all the words which I have mentioned above, ought to be written with single *l*. Ainsworth exhibits the Latin word for *coral* in four forms, and the Greek word in three. Two of the Latin and two of the Greek have the *l* single; the others double it. He also spells "*coraliticus*" with one *l*, and defines it "A sort of white marble, called *coraline*."[*] The Spaniards, from whose *medalla*, we

---

[*] According to Littleton, the *coraliticus lapis* was a kind of Phrygian marble, "called *Coralius*, or by an

have *medal*; whose *argil** is *arcilla*, from the Latin *argilla*; and to whose *caviler*, Webster traces *cavil*; in all their derivatives from these Latin roots, *metallum*, metal — *coralium*, *corallium*, *curalium*, or *corallum*, coral — *crystallus* or *crystallum*, crystal — *pupillus*, pupil — and *tranquillus*, tranquil — follow their own rules, and write mostly with single *l*: as, *pupilero*, a teacher; *metalico*, metalic; *coralina (fem.)* coraline; *cristalino*, crystaline; *cristalizar*, crystalize; *traquilizar*, tranquilize; and *tranquilidad*, tranquility. And if we follow not ours, when or how shall the English scholar ever know why we spell as we do? For example, what can he make of the orthography of the following words, which I copy from our best dictionaries: equip', eq'uipage; wor'ship, wor'shipper; — peril, perilous; cavil, cavillous† ;—libel, libellous; quarrel, quarrelous ;—opal, opaline; metal, metalline‡ ;— coral, coralliform; crystal, crystalform; — dial, dialist; medal, medallist; — rascal, rascalion; medal, medallion; — moral, moralist, morality; metal, metallist, metallurgy; — civil, civilize, civility; tranquil, tranquillize, tranquillity; — novel, novelism, novelist, novelize; grovel, grovelling, grovelled, groveller?

OBS. 15.— The second clause of Murray's or Walker's 5th Rule for spelling, gives only a single *l* to each of the derivatives above named. § But it also treats in like manner many hundreds of words in which the *l* must certainly be doubled. And, as neither "the Compiler," nor any of his copiers, have paid any regard to their own principle, neither their doctrine nor their practice can be of much weight either way. Yet it is important to know to what words the rule is, or is not, applicable. In considering this vexatious question about the duplication of *l*, I was at first inclined to admit that, whenever final *l* has become single in English by dropping the second *l* of a foreign root, the word shall resume the *ll* in all derivatives formed from it by adding a termination beginning with a vowel; as, *beryllus*, *beryl*, *berylline*. This would, of course, double the *l* in nearly all the derivatives from *metal*, *medal*, &c. But what says custom? She constantly doubles the *l* in most of them; but wavers in respect to some, and in a few will have it single. Hence the difficulty of drawing a line by which we may abide without censure. *Pupil'lage* and *pupil'lary*, with *ll*, are according to *Walker's Rhyming Dictionary;* but Johnson spells them *pu'pilage* and *pu'pilary*, with single *l*; and Walker, in his Pronouncing Dictionary, has *pupilage* with one *l*, and *pupillary* with two. Again: both Johnson's and the Pronouncing Dictionary, give us *medallist* and *metallist* with *ll*, and are sustained by Webster and others; but Walker, in his Rhyming Dictionary, writes them *medalist* and *metalist*, with single *l*, like *dialist*, *formalist*, *cabalist*, *herbalist*, and twenty other such words. Farther: Webster doubles the *l* in all the derivatives of *metal*, *medal*, *coral*, *axil*, *argil*, and *papil*; but writes it single in all those of *crystal*, *cavil*, *pupil*, and *tranquil* — except *tranquillity*.

OBS. 16.— Dr. Webster also attempts, or pretends, to put in practice the hasty proposition of Walker, to spell with single *l* all derivatives from words ending in *l* not under the accent. "No letter," says Walker, "seems to be more frequently doubled improperly than *l*. Why we should write *libelling*, *levelling*, *revelling*, and yet *offering*, *suffering*, *reasoning*, I am totally at a loss to determine; and, unless *l* can give a better plea than any other letter in the alphabet, for being doubled in this situation, I must, in the style of Lucian, in his trial of the letter *T*, declare for an expulsion."— *Rhyming Dict.* p. x. This rash conception, being adopted by some men of still less caution, has wrought great mischief in our orthography. With respect to words ending in *el*, it is a good and sufficient reason for doubling the *l*, that the *e* may otherwise be supposed servile and silent. I have therefore made this termination a general exception to the rule against doubling. Besides, a large number of these words, being derived from foreign words in which the *l* was doubled, have a second reason for the duplication, as strong as that which has often induced these same authors to double that letter, as noticed above. Such are bordel, chapel, duel, fardel, gabel, gospel, gravel, lamel, label, libel, marvel, model, novel, parcel, quarrel, and spinel. Accordingly we find, that, in his work of expulsion, Dr. Webster has not unfrequently contradicted himself, and conformed to usage, by doubling the *l* where he probably intended to write it single. Thus, in the words bor-

other name *Rangarius*." But this substance seems to be different from all that are described by Webster, under the names of " coralline," " corallinite," and " corallite." See *Webster's Octave Dict.*

* The Greek word for argil is αργιλος, or αργιλλος, (from αργός, white,) meaning pure white earth; and is as often spelled with one Lambda as with two.

† Dr. Webster, with apparent propriety, writes *caviling* and *cavilous* with one *l*, like *dialing* and *perilous;* but he has in general no more uniformity than Johnson. In respect to the doubling of *l* final. He also, in some instances, accents similar words variously; as, *cor'alliform*, upon the first syllable, *metal'liform*, upon the second; *cav'ilous* and *pap'illous*, upon the first, *argil'lous*, upon the second; *ax'illar*, upon the first, *medul'lar*, upon the second. See *Webster's Octave Dict.*

‡ Perry wrote *crystaline*, *crystalize*, *crystalization*, *metaline*, *metalist*, *metalurgist*, and *metalurgy* · and these forms, as well as *crystalography*, *metalic*, *metalography*, and *metaliferous*, are noticed and preferred by the authors of the *Red Book*, on pp. 268 and 302.

§ "But if a diphthong precedes, or the accent is on the preceding syllable, the consonant remains single: as, to toil, toiling; to offer, an offering."—*Murray's Octavo Gram.* p. 24; *Walker's Rhym. Dict.* Introd. p. ix.

deller, chapellany, chapelling, gospellary, gospeller, gravelly, lamellate, lamellar, lamellarly, lamelliform, and spinellane, he has written the *l* double, while he has grossly corrupted many other similar words by forbearing the reduplication ; as, *traveler, groveling, duelist, marvelous,* and the like. In cases of such difficulty, we can never arrive at uniformity and consistency of practice, unless we resort to *principles,* and such principles as can be made intelligible to the *English* scholar. If any one is dissatisfied with the rules and exceptions which I have laid down, let him study the subject till he can furnish the schools with better.

Obs. 17.—We have in our language a very numerous class of adjectives ending in *able* or *ible,* as *affable, arable, tolerable, admissible, credible, infallible,* to the number of nine hundred or more. In respect to the proper form and signification of some of these, there occurs no small difficulty. *Able* is a common English word, the meaning of which is much better understood than its origin. Horne Tooke supposes it to have come from the Gothic noun *abal,* signifying *strength ;* and consequently avers, that it " has nothing to do with the Latin adjective *habilis, fit,* or *able,* from which our etymologists erroneously derive it."—*Diversions of Purley,* ii, p. 450. This I suppose the etymologists will dispute with him. But whatever may be its true derivation, no one can well deny that *able,* as a suffix, belongs most properly, if not exclusively, to *verbs ;* for most of the words formed by it, are plainly a sort of verbal adjectives. And it is evident that this author is right in supposing that English words of this termination, like the Latin verbals in *bilis,* have, or ought to have, such a signification as may justify the name which he gives them, of "*potential passive adjectives ;* " a signification in which the English and the Latin derivatives exactly correspond. Thus *dis'soluble* or *dissolv'able* does not mean *able to dissolve,* but *capable of being dissolved ;* and *divisible* or *dividable* does not mean *able to divide,* but *capable of being divided.*

Obs. 18.—As to the application of this suffix to nouns, when we consider the signification of the words thus formed, its propriety may well be doubted. It is true, however, that nouns do sometimes assume something of the nature of verbs, so as to give rise to adjectives that are of a participial character ; such, for instance, as *sainted, bigoted, conceited, gifted, tufted.* Again, of such as *hard-hearted, good-natured, cold-blooded,* we have an indefinite number. And perhaps, upon the same principle, the formation of such words as *actionable, companionable, exceptionable, marketable, merchantable, pasturable, treasonable,* and so forth, may be justified, if care be taken to use them in a sense analogous to that of the real verbals. But, surely, the meaning which is commonly attached to the words *amicable, changeable, fashionable, favourable, peaceable, reasonable, pleasurable, seasonable, suitable,* and some others, would never be guessed from their formation. Thus, *suitable* means *fitting* or *suiting,* and not *able to suit,* or *capable of being suited.*

Obs. 19.—Though all words that terminate in *able,* used as a suffix, are properly reckoned derivatives, rather than compounds, and in the former class the separate meaning of the parts united is much less regarded than in the latter ; yet, in the use of words of this formation, it would be well to have some respect to the general analogy of their signification as stated above ; and not to make derivatives of the same fashion convey meanings so very different as do some of these. Perhaps it is from some general notion of their impropriety, that several words of this doubtful character have already become obsolete, or are gradually falling into disuse : as, *accustomable, chanceable, concordable, conusable, customable, behoovable, leisurable, medicinable, personable, powerable, razorable, shapable, semblable, vengeable, veritable.* Still, there are several others, yet currently employed, which might better perhaps, for the same reason, give place to more regular terms : as, *amicable,* for *friendly* or *kind ; charitable,* for *benevolent* or *liberal ; colourable,* for *apparent* or *specious ; peaceable,* for *peaceful* or *unhostile ; pleasurable,* for *pleasing* or *delightful ; profitable,* for *gainful* or *lucrative ; sociable,* for *social* or *affable ; reasonable,* for *rational* or *just.*

Obs. 20.—In respect to the orthography of words ending in *able* or *ible,* it is sometimes difficult to determine which of these endings ought to be preferred ; as whether we ought to write *tenable* or *tenible, reversable* or *reversible, addable* or *addible.* In Latin, the termination is *bilis,* and the preceding vowel is determined by the *conjugation* to which the verb belongs. Thus, for verbs of the first conjugation, it is *a ;* as, from *arare,* to plough, *arabilis, arable,* tillable. For the second conjugation, it is *i ;* as, from *docēre,* to teach, *docibilis* or *docibis, docible* or *docile,* teachable. For the third conjugation, it is *i ;* as, from *vendēre,* to sell, *vendibilis, vendible,* salable. And, for the fourth conjugation, it is *i ;* as, from *sepelire,* to bury, *sepelibilis, sep'elible* [*], buriable. But from *solvo* and *volvo,* of the third conjugation, we have *ubilis, uble ;* as, *solubilis, sol'uble,* solvible or solvable ; *volubilis, vol'uble,* rollable. Hence the English words, *rev oluble, res'oluble, irres'oluble, dis'soluble, indis'soluble,* and *insol'uble.* Thus the Latin verbals in *bilis,* are a sufficient guide to the orthography of all such words as are traceable to them ; but the mere English scholar

[*] Johnson, Walker, and Webster, all spell this word *sep'tible ;* which is obviously wrong ; as is Johnson's derivation of it from *sepio,* to hedge in. *Sepio* would make, not this word, but *sepibilis* and *sepible,* hedgeable.

cannot avail himself of this aid; and of this sort of words we have a much greater number than were ever known in Latin. A few we have borrowed from the French: as, *tenable, capable, preferable, convertible;* and these we write as they are written in French. But the difficulty lies chiefly in those which are of English growth. For some of them are formed according to the model of the Latin verbals in *ibilis;* as *forcible, coercible, reducible, discernible:* and others are made by simply adding the suffix *able;* as *traceable, pronounceable, manageable, advisable, returnable.* The last are purely English; and yet they correspond in form with such as come from Latin verbals in *abilis.*

OBS. 21.—From these different modes of formation, with the choice of different roots, we have sometimes two or three words, differing in orthography and pronunciation, but conveying the same meaning; as, *divis'ible* and *divi'dable, des'picable* and *despi'sable, ref'erable* and *refer'rible, mis'cible* and *mix'able, dis'soluble, dissol'vible,* and *dissol'vable.* Hence, too, we have some words which seem to the mere English scholar to be spelled in a very contradictory manner, though each, perhaps, obeys the law of its own derivation; as, *peaceable* and *forcible, impierceable* and *coercible, marriageable* and *corrigible, damageable* and *eligible, changeable* and *tangible, chargeable* and *frangible, fencible* and *defensible, pref'erable* and *referrible, conversable* and *reversible, defendable* and *descendible, amendable* and *extendible, bendable* and *vendible, dividable* and *corrodible, returnable* and *discernible, indispensable* and *responsible, advisable* and *fusible, respectable* and *compatible, delectable* and *collectible, taxable* and *flexible.*

OBS. 22.—The American editor of the *Red Book,* to whom all these apparent inconsistencies seemed real blunders, has greatly exaggerated this difficulty in our orthography, and charged Johnson and Walker with having written all these words and many more, in this contradictory manner, *"without any apparent reason!"* He boldly avers, that, "The perpetual contradictions of the same or like words, *in all the books,* show that the authors had no distinct ideas of what is right, and what is wrong;" and ignorantly imagines, that, "The use of *ible* rather than *able, in any case,* originated in the necessity of keeping the soft sound of *c* and *g,* in the derivatives; and if *ible was confined* to that use, it would be an easy and simple rule."—*Red Book,* p. 170. Hence, he proposes to write *peacible* for *peaceable, tracible* for *traceable, changible* for *changeable, managible* for *manageable;* and so for all the rest that come from words ending in *ce* or *ge.* But, whatever advantage there might be in this, his "easy and simple rule" would work a revolution for which the world is not yet prepared. It would make *audible audable, fallible fallable, feasible feasable, terrible terrable, horrible horrable,* &c. No tyro can spell in a worse manner than this, even if he have no rule at all. And those who do not know enough of Latin grammar to profit by what I have said in the preceding observation, may console themselves with the reflection, that, in spelling these difficult words entirely by guess, they will not miss the way more than some have done who pretended to be critics. The rule given by John Burn, for *able* and *ible,* is less objectionable; but it is rendered useless by the great number of its exceptions.

OBS. 23.—As most of the rules for spelling refer to the final letters of our primitive words, it may be proper for the learner to know and remember, that not all the letters of the alphabet can assume that situation, and that some of them terminate words much more frequently than others. Thus, in Walker's Rhyming Dictionary, the letter *a* ends about 220 words; *b,* 160; *c,* 450; *d,* 1550; *e,* 7000; *f,* 140; *g,* 280; *h,* 400; *i,* 29; *j,* none; *k,* 550; *l,* 1900; *m,* 550; *n,* 3300; *o,* 200; *p,* 450; *q,* none; *r,* 2750; *s,* 3250; *t,* 3100; *u,* 14; *v,* none; *w,* 200; *x,* 100; *y,* 6000; *z,* 5. We have, then, three consonants, *j, q,* and *v,* which never end a word. And why not? With respect to *j* and *v,* the reason is plain from their history. These letters were formerly identified with *i* and *u,* which are not terminational letters. The vowel *i* ends no pure English word, except that which is formed of its own capital *I;* and the few words which end with *u* are all foreign, except *thou* and *you.* And not only so, the letter *j* is what was formerly called *i consonant;* and *v* is what was called *u consonant.* But it was the initial *i* and *u,* or the *i* and *u* which preceded an other vowel, and not those which followed one, that were converted into the consonants *j* and *v.* Hence, neither of these letters ever ends any English word, or is ever doubled. Nor do they unite with other consonants before or after a vowel: except that *v* is joined with *r* in a few words of French origin, as *livre, manœuvre;* or with *l* in some Dutch names, as *Watervleit.* Q ends no English word, because it is always followed by *u.* The French termination *que,* which is commonly retained in *pique, antique, critique, opaque, oblique, burlesque,* and *grotesque,* is equivalent to *k;* hence we write *packet, lackey, checker, risk, mask,* and *mosk,* rather than *paquet, laquey, chequer, risque, masque,* and *mosque.* And some authors write *burlesk* and *grotesk,* preferring *k* to *que.*

OBS. 24.—Thus we see that *j, q,* and *v,* are, for the most part, initial consonants only. Hence there is a harshness, if not an impropriety, in that syllabication which some have recently adopted, wherein they accommodate to the ear the division of such words as *maj-es-ty, proj-ect, traj-ect,—eq-ui-ty, liq-ui-date, ex-cheq-uer.* But *v,* in a similar situation, has now become familiar; as in *ev-er-y, ev-i-dence:* and it may also stand with *l* or *r*, in the division of such words as *solv-ing* and *serv-ing.* Of words ending in *ive*, Walker exhibits four hundred and fifty—exactly the same number that he spells with *ic.* And Horne Tooke, who derives *ive* from the Latin *ivus*, (q. d. *vis*,) and *ic* from the Greek *ιπος*, (q. d. *ιοχυς*,) both implying *power*, has well observed that there is a general correspondence of meaning between these two classes of adjectives—both being of "a potential active signification; as *purgative, vomitive, operative*, &c.; *cathartic, emetic, energetic*, &c."—*Diversions of Purley*, ii, p. 445. I have before observed, that Tooke spelled all this latter class of words without the final *k*; but he left it to Dr. Webster to suggest the reformation of striking the final *e* from the former.

OBS. 25.—In Dr. Webster's "Collection of Essays and *Fugitiv Peeces*," published in 1790, we find, among other equally ingenious improvements of our orthography, a general omission of the final *e* of all words ending in *ive*, or rather of all words ending in *ve*, preceded by a short vowel; as, "*primitiv, derivativ, extensiv, positiv, deserv, twelv, proov, luv, hav, giv, liv.*" This mode of spelling, had it been adopted by other learned men, would not only have made *v* a very frequent final consonant, but would have placed it in an other new and strange predicament, as being subject to reduplication. For he that will write *hav, giv*, and *liv*, must also, by a general rule of grammar, write *havving, givving*, and *livving.* And not only so, there will follow also, in the solemn style of the Bible, a change of *givest, livest, giveth*, and *liveth*, into *givvest, livvest, givveth*, and *livveth.* From all this it may appear, that a silent final *e* is not always quite so useless a thing as some may imagine. With a levity no less remarkable, does the author of the *Red Book* propose at once two different ways of reforming the orthography of such words as *pierceable, manageable*, and so forth; in one of which, the letter *j* would be brought into a new position, and subjected sometimes to reduplication. "It would be a useful improvement to change this *c* into *s*, and *g* into *j*;" as, *piersable, manajable*, &c. "Or they might assume *i*;" as, *piercible, managible*, &c.—*Red Book*, p. 170. Now would not this "useful improvement" give us such a word as *allejjable?* and would not one such monster be more offensive than all our present exceptions to Rule 9th? Out upon all such tampering with orthography!

OBS. 26.—If any thing could arrest the folly of innovators and dabbling reformers, it would be the history of former attempts to effect improvements similar to theirs. With this sort of history every one would do well to acquaint himself, before he proceeds to disfigure words by placing their written elements in any new predicament. If the orthography of the English language is ever reduced to greater regularity than it now exhibits, the reformation must be wrought by those who have no disposition either to exaggerate its present defects, or to undertake too much. Regard must be had to the origin, as well as to the sounds, of words. To many people, all silent letters seem superfluous; and all indirect modes of spelling, absurd. Hence, as the learner may perceive, a very large proportion of the variations and disputed points in spelling, are such as refer to the silent letters, which are retained by some writers and omitted by others. It is desirable that such as are useless and irregular should be always omitted; and such as are useful and regular always retained. The rules which I have laid down as principles of discrimination, are such as almost every reader will know to be generally true, and agreeable to present usage, though several of them have never before been printed in any grammar. Their application will strike out some letters which are often written, and retain some which are often omitted; but, if they err on either hand, I am confident they err less than any other set of rules ever yet formed for the same purpose. Walker, from whom Murray borrowed his rules for spelling, declares for an expulsion of the second *l* from *traveller, gambolled, grovelling, equalling, cavilling*, and all similar words; seems more willing to drop an *l* from *illness, stillness, shrillness, fellness*, and *drollness*, than to retain both in *smallness, tallness, chillness, dullness*, and *fullness*; makes it one of his orthographical aphorisms, that, "Words taken into composition often drop those letters which were superfluous in their simples; as, *Christmas, dunghil, handful*;" and, at the same time, chooses rather to restore the silent *e* to the ten derivatives from *move* and *prove*, from which Johnson dropped it, than to drop it from the ten similar words in which that author retained it! And not only so, he argues against the principle of his own aphorism; and says, "It is certainly to be feared that, if this pruning of our words of all the superfluous letters, as they are called, should be much farther indulged, we shall quickly antiquate our most respectable authors, and irreparably maim our language."—*Walker's Rhyming Dict.* p. xvii.

IMPROPRIETIES FOR CORRECTION.

ERRORS IN SPELLING.

UNDER RULE I.—OF FINAL F, L, OR S.

"He wil observe the moral law, in hiz conduct."—*Webster's Essays*, p. 320.

[FORMULES.—1. Not proper, because the word "*wil*" is here spelled with one *l*. But, according to Rule 1st, "Monosyllables ending in *f*, *l*, or *s*, preceded by a single vowel, double the final consonant." Therefore, this *l* should be doubled; thus, *will*.
2. Not proper again, because the word "*hiz*" is here spelled with *z*. But, according to the exceptions to Rule 1st, "The words *as*, *gas*, *has*, *was*, *yes*, *his*, &c.*, are written with single *s*." Therefore, this *z* should be *s*; thus, *his*.]

"A clif is a steep bank, or a precipitous rock." See *Rhyming Dict.* "A needy man's budget is ful of schemes."—*Old Adage.* "Few large publications in this country wil pay a printer."—*Noah Webster's Essays*, p. x. "I shal, with cheerfulness, resign my other papers to oblivion."—*Ib.* p. x. "The proposition waz suspended til the next session of the legislature."—*Ib.* p. 362. "Tenants for life wil make the most of lands for themselves."—*Ib.* p. 366. "While every thing iz left to lazy negroes, a state wil never be wel cultivated."—*Ib.* p. 367. "The heirs of the original proprietors stil hold the soil."—*Ib.* p. 349. "Say my annual profit on money loaned shal be six per cent.—*Ib.* p. 308. "No man would submit to the drudgery of business, if he could make money az fast by lying stil."—*Ib.* p. 310. "A man may az wel feed himself with a bodkin, az with a knife of the present fashion."—*Ib.* p. 400. "The clothes wil be ill washed, the food wil be badly cooked; and you wil be ashamed of your wife, if she iz not ashamed of herself."—*Ib.* p. 404. "He wil submit to the laws of the state, while he iz a member of it."—*Ib.* p. 320. "But wil our sage writers on law forever think by tradition?"—*Ib.* p. 318. "Some stil retain a sovereign power in their territories."—*Ib.* p. 298. "They sel images, prayers, the sound of bels, remission of sins, &c."—*Perkins's Theology*, p. 401. "And the law had sacrifices offered every day for the sins of al the people."—*Ib.* p. 406. "Then it may please the Lord, they shal find it to be a restorative."—*Ib.* p. 420. "Perdition is repentance put of til a future day."—*Old Maxim.* "The angels of God, which wil good and cannot wil evil, have nevertheless perfect liberty of wil."—*Perkins's Theology*, p. 716. "Secondly, this doctrine cuts off the excuse of al sin."—*Ib.* p. 717. "Knel, the sound of a bell rung at a funeral."—*Johnson* and *Walker.*

"If gold with dros or grain with chaf you find,
Select—and leave the chaf and dros behind."—*Author.*

UNDER RULE II.—OF OTHER FINALS.

"The mobb hath many heads, but no brains."—*Old Maxim.*

[FORMULE.—"Not proper, because the word "*mobb*" is here spelled with double *b*. But, according to Rule 2d, "Words ending in any other consonant than *f*, *l*, or *s*, do not double the final letter." Therefore, this *b* should be single; thus, *mob.*]

"Clamm, to clog with any glutinous or viscous matter."—*Johnson's Dict.* "Whurr, to pronounce the letter *r* with too much force."—*Ib.* "Flipp, a mixed liquor, consisting of beer and spirits sweetened."—*Ib.* "Glynn, a hollow between two mountains, a glen."—*Churchill's Grammar*, p. 22. "Lamm, to beat soundly with a cudgel or bludgeon."—*Walker's Dict.* "Bunn, a small cake, a simnel, a kind of sweet bread." See *ib.* "Brunett, a woman with a brown complexion."—*Ib.* and *Johnson's Dict.* "Wad'sett, an ancient tenure or lease of land in the Highlands of Scotland."—*Webster's Dict.* "To *dodd* sheep, is to cut the wool away about their tails."—*Ib.* "In *aliquem arietare*, Cic. To run full but at one."—*Walker's Particles*, p. 95. "Neither your policy nor your temper would permitt you to kill me."—*Philological Museum*, i, p. 427. "And admitt none but his own offspring to fill them."—*Ib.* i, p. 437. "The summ of all this Dispute is, that some make them Participles," &c.—*Johnson's Gram. Com.* p. 352. "As, the *whistling* of winds, the *buz* and *hum* of insects, the *hiss* of serpents, the *crash* of falling timber."—*Blair's Rhet.* p. 129; *Adam's Lat. Gram.* p. 247; *Gould's*, 238. "Vann, to winnow, or a fan for winnowing."—*Walker's Rhyming Dict.* "Creatures that buz, are very commonly such as will sting."—*Author.* "Begg, buy, or borrow; butt beware how you find."—*Id.* "It is better to have a house to lett, than a house to gett."—*Id.* "Let not your tongue cutt your throat."—*Old Precept.* "A little witt will save a fortunate man."—*Old Adage.* "There is many a slipp 'twixt the cup and the lipp."—*Id.* "Mothers' darlings make but milksopp heroes."—*Id.* "One eye-witness is worth tenn hearsays."—*Id.*

"The judge shall jobb, the bishop bite the town,
And mighty dukes pack cards for half a crown."—*Pope: in Joh. Dict. w. Pack.*

UNDER RULE III.—OF DOUBLING.

"Friz, to curl; frized, curled; frizing, curling."—*Webster's Dict.* 8vo, Ed. of 1829.

[FORMULE.—Not proper, because the words "*frized*" and "*frizing*" are here spelled with the single *z*, of their primitive *friz*. But, according to Rule 3d, "Monosyllables, and words accented on the last syllable, when they end with a single consonant, preceded by a single vowel, double their final consonant before an additional syllable that begins with a vowel." Therefore, this *z* should be doubled; thus, *frizzed*, *frizzing*.]

"The commercial interests served to foster the principles of Whigism."—*Payne's Geog.* ii, p. 511. "Their extreme indolence shunned every species of labour."—*Robertson's Amer.* i, p. 341. "In poverty and stripedness they attend their little meetings."—*The*

Friend, vii. p. 256. "In guiding and controling * the power you have thus obtained."—*Abbott's Teacher,* p. 15. "I began, Thou beganest, He began; We began, You began, They began."—*Alex. Murray's Gram.* p. 92. "Why does *began* change its ending; as, I began, Thou beganest?"—*Ib.* p. 93. "Truth and conscience cannot be controled by any methods of coercion."—*Hints on Toleration,* p. xvi. "Dr. Webster noded, when he wrote 'knit, kniter, and knitingneedle' without doubling the *t.*" See *El. Spelling-Book,* 1st Ed. p. 136. "A wag should have wit enough to know when other wags are quizing him."—*G. Brown.* "Bon'y, handsome, beautiful, merry."—*Walker's Rhym. Dict.* "Coquetish, practicing coquetry; after the manner of a jilt."—*Webster's Dict.* "Potage, a species of food, made of meat and vegetables boiled to softness in water." See *ib.* "Potager, from potage, a porringer, a small vessel for children's food." See *ib.* and *Worcester's.* "Compromit, compromited, compromiting; manumit, manumitted, manumitting."—*Webster.* "Inferible; that may be inferred or deduced from premises."—*Red Book,* p. 228. "Acids are either solid, liquid, or gaseous."—*Gregory's Dict. art. Chemistry.* "The spark will pass through the interrupted space between the two wires, and explode the gases."—*Ib.* "Do we sound *gases* and *gaseous* like *cases* and *caseous?* No: they are more like *glasses* and *osseous.*"—*G. Brown.* "I shall not need here to mention *Swiming,* when he is of an age able to learn."—*Locke, on Ed.* p. 12. "Why do lexicographers spell *thinnish* and *mannish* with two Ens, and *dimish* and *ramish* with one Em, each?" See *Joh.* and *Webster.* "*Gas* forms the plural regularly, *gases.*"—*O. B. Peirce's Gram.* p. 38. "Singular, Gas; Plural, Gases."—*S. W. Clark's Gram.* p. 47. "These are contractions from *sheded, bursted.*"—*Hiley's Grammar,* p. 45. "The Present Tense denotes what is occuring at the present time."—*Day's Gram.* p. 36, and p. 61. "The verb ending in *eth* is of the solemn or antiquated style; as, he loveth, he walketh, he runeth."—*P. Davis's Gram.* p. 34.

> "Thro' freedom's sons no more remonstrance rings,
> Degrading nobles and controling kings."—*Murray's Sequel,* p. 292.

UNDER RULE IV.—NO DOUBLING.

"A bigotted and tyrannical clergy will be feared."—*Brown's Estimate,* Vol. ii, p. 78.

[FORMULE.—Not proper, because the final *t* of *bigot* is here doubled in "*bigotted.*" But, according to Rule 4th, "A final consonant, when it is not preceded by a single vowel, or when the accent is not on the last syllable, should remain single before an additional syllable." Therefore, this *t* should be single; thus, *bigoted.*]

"Jacob worshipped his Creator, leaning on the top of his staff."—*Key in Merchant's Gram.* p. 185. "For it is all marvelously destitute of interest."—*Merchant's Criticisms.* "As, box, boxes; church, churches; lash, lashes; kiss, kisses; rebus, rebusses."—*Murray's Gram.* 12mo, p. 42. "Gossipping and lying go hand in hand."—*Old Maxim.* "The substance of the Criticisms on the Diversions of Purley was, with singular industry, gossipped by the present precious secretary of war, in Payne the bookseller's shop." See *Key.* "Worship makes worshipped, worshipper, worshipping; gossip, gossipped, gossipper, gossipping; fillip, filliped, fillipper, fillipping."—*Nix. Par.* p. 72. "I became as fidgetty as a fly in a milk-jug."—*Blackwood's Mag.* xl, p. 674. "That enormous error seems to be rivetted in popular opinion."—*Webster's Essays,* p. 364. "Whose mind is not biassed by personal attachments to a sovereign."—*Ib.* p. 318. "Laws against usury originated in a bigotted prejudice against the Jews."—*Ib.* p. 315. "The most critical period of life is usually between thirteen and seventeen."—*Ib.* p. 388. "Generalissimo, the chief commander of an army or military force." See *El. Spelling-book,* p. 93. "Tranquillize, to quiet, to make calm and peaceful."—*Ib.* p. 133. "Pommeled, beaten, bruised; having 'pommels, as a sword or dagger."—*Webster* and *Chalmers.* "From what a height does the jeweler look down upon his shoemaker!"—*Red Book,* p. 108. "You will have a verbal account from my friend and fellow traveler."—*Ib.* p. 155. "I observe that you have written the word *counseled* with one *l* only."—*Ib.* p. 173. "They were offended at such as combatted these notions."—*Robertson's America,* ii, p. 437." "From libel, come libeled, libeler, libeling, libelous; from grovel, groveled, groveler, groveling; from gravel, graveled and graveling." See *Webster's Dict.* "Woolliness, the state of being woolly."—*Ib.* "Yet he has spelled chappelling, bordeller, medallist, metalline, metallist, metallize, clavellated, &c. with *ll,* contrary to his rule."—*Cobb's Review of Webster,* p. 11. "Again, he has spelled cancelation and snively with single *l,* and cupellation, pannellation, wittolly, with *ll.*"—*Ib.* "Oilly, fatty, greasy, containing oil, glib."—*Rhyming Dict.* "Medallist, one curious in medals; Metallist, one skilled in metals."—*Johnson, Webster, Worcester, Cobb, et al.* "He is benefitted."—*Towne's Spelling-Book,* p. 5. "They traveled for pleasure."—*S. W. Clark's Gram.* p. 101.

> "Without you, what were man? A groveling herd,
> In darkness, wretchedness, and want enchain'd."—*Beattie's Minstrel,* p. 40.

---

* If the variable word *control, controvl,* or *controll,* is from *con* and *troul* or *troll,* it should be spelled with *ll,* by Rule 7th, and retain the *ll* by Rule 6th. Dr. Webster has it so, but he gives *control* also.

UNDER RULE V.—OF FINAL CK.

"He hopes, therefore, to be pardoned by the critick."—*Kirkham's Gram.* p. 10.

[FORMULE.—Not proper, because the word "*critick*" is here spelled with a final *k*. But, according to Rule 5th, "Monosyllables and English verbs end not with *c*, but take *ck* for double *c*; as, rack, wreck, rock, attack: but, in general, words derived from the learned languages need not the *k*, and common use discards it." Therefore, this *k* should be omitted; thus, *critic*.]

"The leading object of every publick speaker should be to persuade."—*Kirkham's Elocution,* p. 153. "May not four feet be as poetick as five; or fifteen feet, as poetick as fifty?"—*Ib.* p. 146. "Avoid all theatrical trick and mimickry, and especially all scholastick stiffness."—*Ib.* p. 154. "No one thinks of becoming skilled in dancing, or in musick, or in mathematicks, or logick, without long and close application to the subject." *Ib.* p. 152. "Caspar's sense of feeling, and susceptibility of metallick and magnetick excitement, were also very extraordinary."—*Ib.* p. 238. "Authorship has become a mania, or, perhaps I should say, an epidemick."—*Ib.* p. 6. "What can prevent this republick from soon raising a literary standard?"—*Ib.* p. 10. "Courteous reader, you may think me garrulous upon topicks quite foreign to the subject before me."—*Ib.* p. 11. "Of the Tonick, Subtonick, and Atonick elements."—*Ib.* p. 15. "The subtonick elements are inferiour to the tonicks in all the emphatick and elegant purposes of speech."—*Ib.* p. 32. "The nine atonicks, and the three abrupt subtonicks cause an interruption to the continuity of the syllabick impulse."—*Ib.* p. 37. "On scientifick principles, conjunctions and prepositions are but one part of speech."—*Kirkham's Gram.* p. 120. "That some inferior animals should be able to mimic human articulation, will not seem wonderful."—*Murray's Gram.* 8vo, Vol. i, p. 2.

> "When young, you led a life monastick,
> And wore a vest ecclesiastick;
> Now, in your age, you grow fantastick."—*Johnson's Dict.*

UNDER RULE VI.—OF RETAINING.

"Fearlesness, exemption from fear, intrepidity."—*Johnson's Dict.*

[FORMULE.—Not proper, because the word "*fearlesness*" is here allowed to drop one *s* of fearless. But, according to Rule 6th, "Words ending with any double letter, preserve it double before any additional termination not beginning with the same letter." Therefore, the other *s* should be inserted; thus, *fearlessness*.]

"Dreadlesness; fearlesness, intrepidity, undauntedness."—*Johnson's Dict.* "Regardlesly, without heed; Regardlesness, heedlessness, inattention."—*Ib.* "Blamelesly, innocently; Blamlesness, innocence."—*Ib.* "That is better than to be flattered into pride and carelesness."—TAYLOR: *Joh. Dict.* "Good fortunes began to breed a proud recklesness in them."—SIDNEY: *ib.* "See whether he lazily and listlesly dreams away his time."—LOCKE: *ib.* "It may be, the palate of the soul is indisposed by listlesness or sorrow."—TAYLOR: *ib.* "Pitilesly, without mercy; Pitilesness, unmercifulness."—*Johnson.* "What say you to such as these? abominable, accordable, agreable, &c."—*Tooke's Diversions,* ii, p. 432. "Artlesly; naturally, sincerely, without craft."—*Johnson.* "A chilness, or shivering of the body, generally precedes a fever."—*Murray's Key,* p. 167. "Smalness; littleness, minuteness, weakness."—*Rhyming Dict.* "Galless, a. free from gall or bitterness."—*Webster's Dict.* "Talness; height of stature, upright length with comparative slenderness." See *Johnson et al.* "Wilful; stubborn, contumacious, perverse, inflexible."—*Id.* "He guided them by the skilfulness of his hands."—*Psal.* lxxviii, 72. "The earth is the Lord's and the fulness thereof."—*Murray's Key,* p. 172. "What is now, is but an amasment of imaginary conceptions."—GLANVILLE: *Joh. Dict.* "Embarrasment; perplexity, entanglement." See *Littleton's Dict.* "The second is slothfulness, whereby they are performed slackly and carelesly."—*Perkins's Theology,* p. 729. "Instalment; induction into office; part of a large sum of money, to be paid at a particular time." See *Johnson's Dict.* "Inthralment; servitude, slavery."—*Ib.*

> "I, who at some times spend, at others spare,
> Divided between carelesness and care."—*Pope.*

RULE VII.—OF RETAINING.

"*Shall,* on the contrary, in the first person, simply foretels."—*Murray's Gram.* p. 88; *Ingersoll's,* 136; *Fisk's,* 78; *Jaudon's,* 59; *A. Flint's,* 42; *Wright's,* 90; *Bullions's,* 32.

[FORMULE.—Not proper, because the word "*foretels*" does not here retain the double *l* of *tell*. But, according to Rule 7th, "Words ending with any double letter, preserve it double in all derivatives formed from them by means of prefixes." Therefore, the other *l* should be inserted; thus, *foretells*.]

"There are a few compound irregular verbs, as *befal, bespeak, &c.*"—*Ash's Gram.* p. 46. "That we might frequently recal it to our memory."—*Calvin's Institutes,* p. 112. "The angels exercise a constant solicitude that no evil befal us."—*Ib.* p. 107. "Inthral; to enslave, to shackle, to reduce to servitude."—*Walker's Dict.* "He makes resolutions, and fulfils them by new ones."—*Red Book,* p. 138. "To enrol my humble name upon the list of authors on Elocution."—*Kirkham's Elocution*, p. 12. "Forestal; to antici-pate, to take up beforehand."—*Walker's Rhym. Dict.* "Miscal; to call wrong, to name improperly."—*Johnson.* "Bethral; to enslave, to reduce to bondage." See *id.* "Be-fal; to happen to, to come to pass."—*Rhym. Dict.* "Unrol; to open what is rolled or convolved."—*Johnson.* "Counterrol; to keep copies of accounts to prevent frauds." See *id.* "As Sisyphus uprols a rock, which constantly overpowers him at the summit." —*Author.* "Unwel; not well, indisposed, not in good health." See *Red Book,* 336. "Undersel; to defeat by selling for less, to sell cheaper than an other." See *id.* p. 332. "Inwal; to enclose or fortify with a wall." See *id.* p. 295. "Twibil; an instrument with two bills, or with a point and a blade; a pickaxe, a mattock, a halberd, a battle-axe." See *Dict.* "What you miscal their folly, is their care."—*Dryden.* "My heart will sigh when I miscal it so."—*Shakspeare.* "But if the arrangement recal one set of ideas more readily than another."—*Blair's Rhet.* p. 130.

> "'Tis done; and since 'tis done, 'tis past recal;
> And since 'tis part recal, must be forgotten."—*Dryden.*

UNDER RULE VIII.—OF FINAL LL.

"The righteous is taken away from the evill to come."—*Perkins's Works,* p. 417.

[FORMULE.—Not proper, because the word "*evill*" is here written with final *ll*. But, according to Rule 8th, "Final *ll* is peculiar to monosyllables and their compounds, with the few derivatives formed from such roots by prefixes; consequently, all other words that end in *l*, must be terminated with a single *l.*" Therefore, one *l* should be here omitted; thus, *evil.*]

"Patroll; to go the rounds in a camp or garrison, to march about and observe what passes."—*Webster's Amer. Dict.* 8vo. "Marshall; the chief officer of arms, one who regulates rank and order." See *Bailey's Dict.* "Weevill; a destructive grub that gets among corn." See *Rhym. Dict.* "It much excells all other studies and arts."—*Walker's Particles,* p. 217. "It is essential to all magnitudes, to be in one place."—*Perkins's Works,* p. 403. "By nature I was thy vassall, but Christ hath redeemed me."—*Ib.* p. 404. "Some, being in want, pray for temporall blessings."—*Ib.* p. 412. "And this the Lord doth, either in temporall or spirituall benefits."—*Ib.* p. 415. "He makes an idoll of them, by setting his heart on them."—*Ib.* p. 416. "This triall by desertion serveth for two purposes."—*Ib.* p. 420. "Moreover, this destruction is both perpetuall and terrible."—*Ib.* p. 726. "Giving to severall men several gifts, according to his good pleasure."—*Ib.* p. 731. "Untill; to some time, place, or degree, mentioned." See *Red Book,* p. 330. "Annull; to make void, to nullify, to abrogate, to abolish." "Nitric acid combined with argill, forms the nitrate of argill."—*Gregory's Dict. art. Chemistry.*

> "Let modest Foster, if he will, excell
> Ten Metropolitans in preaching well."—*Pope,* p. 414.

UNDER RULE IX.—OF FINAL E.

"Adjectives ending in *able* signify capacity; as, *comfortable, tenable, improveable.*"—*Priestley's Gram.* p. 33.

[FORMULE.—Not proper, because the word "*improveable*" here retains the final *e* of *improve.* But, accord-ing to Rule 9th, "The final *e* of a primitive word is generally omitted before an additional termination begin-ning with a vowel." Therefore, this *e* should be omitted; thus, *improvable.*]

"Their mildness and hospitality are ascribeable to a general administration of religious ordinances."—*Webster's Essays,* p. 336. "Retrench as much as possible with-out obscureing the sense."—*James Brown's American Gram.* 1821, p. 11. "Changable, subject to change; Unchangeable, immutable."—*Walker's Rhym. Dict.* "Tameable, susceptive of taming; Untameable, not to be tamed."—*Ib.* "Reconcileable, Unreconci-leable, Reconcileableness; Irreconcileable, Irreconcilably, Irreconcileableness."—*John-son's Dict.* "We have thought it most adviseable to pay him some little attention."—*Merchant's Criticisms.* "Proveable, that may be proved; Reprovable, blameable, worthy of reprehension."—*Walker's Dict.* "Moveable and Immovable, Moveably and Immov-ably, Moveables and Removal, Moveableness and Improvableness, Unremoveable and Unimprovable, Unremoveably and Removable, Proveable and Approvable, Irreprove-able and Reprovable, Unreproveable and Improvable, Unimproveableness and Improv-ably."—*Johnson's Dict.* "And with this cruelty you are chargable in some measure yourself."—*Collier's Antoninus,* p. 94. "Mothers would certainly resent it, as judgeing it proceeded from a low opinion of the genius of their sex."—*British Gram. Pref.* p. xxv. "Titheable, subject to the payment of tithes; Saleable, vendible, fit for sale; Loseable, possible to be lost; Sizeable, of reasonable bulk or size."—*Walker's Rhyming Dict.* "When he began this custom, he was puleing and very tender."—*Locke, on Ed.* p. 8.

> "The plate, coin, revenues, and moveables,
> Whereof our uncle Gaunt did stand possess'd."—*Shak.*

UNDER RULE X.—OF FINAL E.

"Diversly; in different ways, differently, variously."—*Rhym. Dict.*, and *Webster's.*

[FORMULE.—Not proper, because the word "*Diversly*" here omits the final *e* of its primitive word, *diverse.* But, according to Rule 10th, "The final *e* of a primitive word is generally retained before an additional termination beginning with a consonant." Therefore, this *e* should be retained; thus, *Diversely.*]

"The event thereof contains a wholesome instruction."—*Bacon's Wisdom of the Ancients*, p. 17. "Whence Scaliger falsly concluded that Articles were useless."—*Brightland's Gram.* p. 94. "The child that we have just seen is wholesomly fed."—*Murray's Key*, 8vo, p. 187. "Indeed, falshood and legerdemain sink the character of a prince."—*Collier's Antoninus*, p. 5. "In earnest, at this rate of managment, thou usest thyself very coarsly."—*Ib.* p. 19. "To give them an arrangment and diversity, as agreeable as the nature of the subject would admit."—*Murray's Pref. to Ex.* p. vi. "Alger's Grammar is only a trifling enlargment of Murray's little Abridgment."—*Author.* "You ask whether you are to retain or omit the mute *e* in the word judgment, abridgment, acknowledgment, lodgment, adjudgment, and prejudgment."—*Red Book*, p. 172. "Fertileness, fruitfulness; Fertily, fruitfully, abundantly."—*Johnson's Dict.* "Chastly, purely, without contamination; Chastness, chastity, purity."—*Ib.* and *Walker's.* "Rhymster, *n.* One who makes rhymes; a versifier; a mean poet."—*Johnson* and *Webster.* "It is therefore an heroical achievment to dispossess this imaginary monarch."—*Berkley's Minute Philos.* p. 151. "Whereby, is not meant the Present Time, as he imagins, but the Time Past."—*Johnson's Gram. Com.* p. 344. "So far is this word from affecting the noun, in regard to its definitness, that its own character of definitness or indefinitness, depends upon the noun to which it is prefixed."—*Webster's Philosophical Gram.* p. 20.

"Satire, by wholsome Lessons, wou'd reclaim,
    And heal their Vices to secure their Fame."—*Brightland's Gr.* p. 171.

UNDER RULE XI.—OF FINAL Y.

"Solon's the veryest fool in all the play."—*Dryden, from Persius*, p. 475.

[FORMULE.—Not proper, because the word "*veryest*" here retains the final *y* of its primitive *very.* But, according to Rule 11th, "The final *y* of a primitive word, when preceded by a consonant, is generally changed into *i* before an additional termination." Therefore, this *y* should be changed to *i*; thus, *veriest.*]

"Our author prides himself upon his great slyness and shrewdness."—*Merchant's Criticisms.* "This tense, then, implys also the signification of *Debeo.*"—*R. Johnson's Gram. Com.* p. 300. "That may be apply'd to a Subject, with respect to something accidental."—*Ib.* p. 133. "This latter accompanys his Note with a distinction."—*Ib.* p. 196. "This Rule is defective, and none of the Annotators have sufficiently supply'd it."—*Ib.* p. 204. "Though the fancy'd Supplement of Sanctius, Scioppius, Vossius, and Mariangelus, may take place."—*Ib.* p. 276. "Yet as to the commutableness of these two Tenses, which is deny'd likewise, they are all one."—*Ib.* p. 311. "Both these Tenses may represent a Futurity implyed by the dependence of the Clause."—*Ib.* p. 332. "Cry, cries, crying, cried, crier, decrial; Shy, shyer, shyest, shyly, shyness; Fly, flies, flying, flier, high-flier; Sly, slyer, slyest, slyly, slyness; Spy, spies, spying, spied, espial; Dry, drier, driest, dryly, dryness."—*Cobb's Dict.* "Cry, cried, crying, crier, cryer, decried, decrier, decrial; Shy, shyly, shily, shyness, shiness; Fly, flier, flyer, high-flyer; Sly, slily, slyly, sliness, slyness; Ply, plyer, plying, pliers, complied, complier; Dry, drier, dryer, dryly, dryness."—*Webster's Dict.* 8vo. "Cry, crier, decrier, decrial; Shy, shily, shyly, shiness, shyness; Fly, flier, flyer, high-flier; Sly, slily, slyly, sliness, slyness; Ply, pliers, plyers, plying, complier; Dry, drier, dryer, dryly, dryness."—*Chalmers's Abridgement of Todd's Johnson.* "I would sooner listen to the thrumming of a dandyzette at her piano."—*Kirkham's Elocution*, p. 24. "Send her away; for she cryeth after us."—*Felton's Gram.* p. 140. "Ivyed, *a.* Overgrown with ivy."—*Todd's Dict.*, and *Webster's.*

"Some dryly plain, without invention's aid,
    Write dull receipts how poems may be made."—*Pope.*

UNDER RULE XII.—OF FINAL Y.

"The gaiety of youth should be tempered by the precepts of age."—*Mur. Key*, p. 175.

[FORMULE.—Not proper, because the word "*gaiety*" does not here retain the final *y* of the primitive word gay. But, according to Rule 12th, "The final *y* of a primitive word, when preceded by a vowel, should not be changed into *i* before an additional termination." Therefore, this *y* should be retained; thus, *gayety.*]

"In the storm of 1703, two thousand stacks of chimnies were blown down, in and about London." See *Red Book*, p. 112. "And the vexation was not abated by the hacknied plea of haste."—*Ib.* p. 142. "The fourth sin of our daies is lukewarmness."—*Perkins's Works*, p. 725. "God hates the workers of iniquity, and destroies them that speak lies."—*Ib.* p. 723. "For, when he laies his hand upon us, we may not fret."—*Ib.* p. 726. "Care not for it; but if thou maiest be free, choose it rather."—*Ib.* p. 736. "Alexander Severus saith, 'He that buieth, must sell: I will not suffer buyers and sellers of offices.'"—*Ib.* p. 737. "With these measures fell in all monied men."—SWIFT: *Johnson's Dict.* "But rattling nonsense in full vollies breaks."—POPE: *ib. w. Volley.* "Vallies are the intervals betwixt mountains."—WOODWARD: *ib.* "The Hebrews had fifty-two journies or marches."—*Wood's Dict.* "It was not possible to manage or steer the gallies thus fastened together."—*Goldsmith's Greece,* ii, p. 106. "Turkies were not known to naturalists till after the discovery of America." See *Gregory's Dict.* "I would not have given it for a wilderness of monkies." See *Key.* "Men worked at embroidery, especially in abbies."—*Constable's Miscellany,* xxi, p. 101. "By which all purchasers or mortgagees may be secured of all monies they lay out."—TEMPLE: *Johnson's Dict.* "He would fly to the mines and the gallies for his recreation."—SOUTH: *ib.*

"Here pullies make the pond'rous oak ascend."—GAY: *ib.*

——— "You need my help, and you say,
Shylock, we would have monies."—SHAKSPEARE: *ib.*

UNDER RULE XIII.—OF IZE AND ISE.

"Will any able writer authorise other men to revise his works?"—*Author.*

[FORMULES.—1. Not proper, because the word "*authorise*" is here written with *s* in the last syllable, in stead of *z*. But according to Rule 13th, "Words ending in *ize* or *ise* sounded alike, as in *wise* and *size,* generally take the *z* in all such as are essentially formed by means of the termination." Therefore, this *s* should be *z;* thus, *authorize.*
2. Not proper again, because the word "*revise*" is here written with *z* in the last syllable, in lieu of *s.* But, according to Rule 13th, "Words ending in *ize* or *ise* sounded alike, as in *wise* and *size,* generally take the *z,* in monosyllables, and all such as are essentially formed by means of prefixes." Therefore, this *z* should be *s;* thus, *revise.*]

"It can be made as strong and expressive as this Latinised English."—*Murray's Gram.* p. 295. "Governed by the success or the failure of an enterprize."—*Ib.* ii, pp. 123 and 259. "Who have patronised the cause of justice against powerful oppressors." —*Ib.* pp. 94 and 228 ; *Merchant,* p. 199. "Yet custom authorises this use of it."—*Priestley's Gram.* p. 148. "They surprise myself, * * * and I even think the writers themselves will be surprized."—*Ib.* Pref. p. xi. "Let the interest rize to any sum which can be obtained."—*Webster's Essays,* p. 310. "To determin what interest shall arize on the use of money."—*Ib.* p. 313. "To direct the popular councils and check a rizing opposition."—*Ib.* p. 335. "Five were appointed to the immediate exercize of the office." — *Ib.* p. 340. "No man ever offers himself [as] a candidate by advertising."—*Ib.* p. 344. "They are honest and economical, but indolent, and destitute of enterprize."—*Ib.* p. 347. "I would however advize you to be cautious."—*Ib.* p. 404. "We are accountable for whatever we patronise in others."—*Murray's Key,* p. 175. "After he was baptized, and was solemnly admitted into the office."—*Perkins's Works,* p. 732. "He will find all, or most of them, comprized in the Exercises."—*British Gram.* Pref. p. v. "A quick and ready habit of methodising and regulating their thoughts."—*Ib.* p. xviii. "To tyrannise over the time and patience of his reader."—*Kirkham's Elocution,* p. iii. "Writers of dull books, however, if patronised at all, are rewarded beyond their deserts."—*Ib.* p. v. "A little reflection, will show the reader the propriety and the *reason* for emphasising the words marked."—*Ib.* p. 163. "The English Chronicle contains an account of a surprising cure."—*Red Book,* p. 61. "Dogmatise, to assert positively; Dogmatizer, an asserter, a magisterial teacher."—*Chalmers's Dict.* "And their inflections might now have been easily analysed."—*Murray's Gram.* 8vo, i, p. 113. "Authorize, disauthorize, and unauthorized; Temporize, contemporise, and extemporize."—*Walker's Dict.* "Legalise, equalise, methodise, sluggardize, womanise, humanize, patronise, cantonize, gluttonise, epitomise, anatomize, phlebotomise, sanctuarise, characterize, synonymise, recognise, detonize, colonise."—*Ibid.*

"This BEAUTY Sweetness always must comprize,
Which from the Subject, well express'd will rise."—*Brightland's Gr.* p. 164.

UNDER RULE XIV.—OF COMPOUNDS.

"The glory of the Lord shall be thy rereward."—COMMON BIBLES: *Isa.* lviii, 8.

[FORMULE.—Not proper, because the compound word "*rereward*" has not here the orthography of the two simple words *rear* and *ward,* which compose it. But, according to Rule 14th, "Compounds generally retain the orthography of the simple words which compose them." And. the accent being here unfixed, a hyphen is proper. Therefore, this word should be spelled thus, *rear-ward.*]

"A mere vaunt-courier to announce the coming of his master."—*Tooke's Diversions,* i, p. 49. "The parti-coloured shutter appeared to come close up before him."—*Kirkham's Elocution,* p. 233. "When the day broke upon this handfull of forlorn but dauntless spirits."—*Ib.* p. 245. "If, upon a plumbtree, peaches and apricots are ingrafted, no body will say they are the natural growth of the plumbtree."—*Berkley's Minute Philos.* p. 46. "The channel between Newfoundland and Labrador is called the Straits of Bellisle."—

Worcester's Gaz. "There being nothing that more exposes to Headach." *—Locke, on Education,* p. 6. "And, by a sleep, to say we end the heartach."—SHAK.: *in Joh. Dict.* "He that sleeps, feels not the toothach."—ID. *ibid.* "That the shoe must fit him, because it fitted his father and granfather."—*Philological Museum,* i, p. 431. "A single word, mispelt, in a letter, is sufficient to show, that you have received a defective education." —*Bucke's Gram.* p. 3. "Which mistatement the committee attributed to a failure of memory."—*Professors' Reasons,* p. 14. "Then he went through the Banquetting-House to the scaffold."—*Smollett's England,* Vol. iii, p. 345. "For the purpose of maintaining a clergyman and skoolmaster."—*Webster's Essays,* p. 355. "They however knew that the lands were claimed by Pensylvania."—*Ib.* p. 357. "But if you ask a reason, they immediately bid farewel to argument."—*Red Book,* p. 80. "Whom resist stedfast in the faith."—SCOTT: 1 *Peter,* v, 9. "And they continued stedfastly in the apostles' doctrine." —*Acts,* ii, 42. "Beware lest ye also fall from your own stedfastness."—2 *Peter,* iii, 17. "*Galiot,* or *galliott,* a Dutch vessel, carrying a main-mast and a mizen-mast."—*Web. Dict.* "Infinitive, to overflow; Preterit, overflowed; Participle, overflown."—*Cobbett's E. Gram.* (1818,) p. 61. "After they have mispent so much precious Time."—*British Gram.* p. xv. "Some say, two *handsfull;* some, two *handfulls;* and others, two *handfull.*"— *Alex. Murray's Gram.* p. 106. "Lapfull, as much as the lap can contain."—*Webster's Octavo Dict.* "Darefull, full of defiance."—*Walker's Rhym. Dict.* "The road to the blissfull regions, is as open to the peasant as to the king."—*Murray's Key,* 8vo, p. 167. "Misspel is *mis-spelt* in every Dictionary which I have seen."—*Barnes's Red Book,* p. 303. "Downfal; ruin, calamity, fall from rank or state."—*Johnson's Dict.* "The whole legislature likewize acts az a court."—*Webster's Essays,* p. 340. "It were better a milstone were hanged about his neck."—*Perkins's Works,* p. 731. "Plum-tree, a tree that produces plums; Hog-plumbtree, a tree."—*Webster's Dict.* "Trisyllables ending in *re* or *le,* accent the first syllable."—*Murray's Gram.* p. 238.

> "It happen'd on a summer's holiday,
> That to the greenwood shade he took his way."—*Churchill's Gr.* p. 135.

UNDER RULE XV.—OF USAGE.

"Nor are the modes of the Greek tongue more uniform."—*Murray's Gram.* p. 112.

[FORMULE.—Not proper, because the word "*modes*" is here written for *moods,* which is more common among the learned, and usually preferred by Murray himself. But, according to Rule 15th, "Any word for the spelling of which we have no rule but usage, is written wrong if not spelled according to the usage which is most common among the learned." Therefore, the latter form should be preferred; thus, *moods,* and not *modes.*]

"If we analize a conjunctive preterite, the rule will not appear to hold."—*Priestley's Gram.* p. 118. "No landholder would have been at that expence."—*Ib.* p. 116. "I went to see the child whilst they were putting on its cloaths."—*Ib.* p. 125. "This stile is ostentatious, and doth not suit grave writing."—*Ib.* p. 82. "The king of Israel, and Jehosophat the king of Judah, sat each on his throne."—*Mur. Gram.* p. 165, *twice; Merchant's,* 89; *Churchill's,* 300. "The king of Israel, and Jehosaphat the king of Judah, sat each on his throne."—*Lowth's Gram.* p. 90; *Harrison's,* 99; *Churchill's,* 138; *Wright's,* 148. "Lisias, speaking of his friends, promised to his father, never to abandon them."—*Murray's Gram.* ii, 121 and 253. "Some, to avoid this errour, run into it's opposite."—*Churchill's Gram.* p. 199. "Hope, the balm of life, sooths us under every misfortune."—*Merchant's Key,* p. 204. "Any judgement or decree might be heerd and reversed by the legislature."—*Webster's Essays,* p. 340. "A pathetic harang wil skreen from punishment any knave."—*Ib.* p. 341. "For the same reezon, the wimen would be improper judges."—*Ibid.* "Every person iz indulged in worshiping az he pleezes."—*Ib.* p. 345. "Most or all teechers are excluded from genteel company."—*Ib.* p. 362. "The Kristian religion, in its purity, iz the best institution on erth."—*Ib.* p. 364. "Neether clergymen nor human laws hav the leest authority over the conscience."—*Ib.* p. 363. "A gild is a society, fraternity, or corporation."—*Red Book,* p. 83. "Phillis was not able to unty the knot, and so she cut it."—*Ib.* p. 46. "An aker of land is the quantity of one hundred and sixty perches."—*Ib.* p. 93. "Oker is a fossil earth combined with the oxid of some metal."—*Ib.* p. 96. "Genii, when denoting aerial spirits : *Geniuses,* when signifying persons of genius."— *Mur.'s Gram.* i. p. 42. "Genii, when denoting aeriel spirits; *Geniuses,* when signifying persons of genius."—*Frost's Gram.* p. 9. "Genius, Plu. *geniuses,* men of wit; but *genii,* aerial beings."—*Nutting's Gram.* p. 18. "Acrisius, king of Argos, had a beautiful daughter, whose name was Danæ."—*Classic Tales,* p. 109. "Phæton was the son of Apollo and Clymene."—*Ib.* p. 152. "But, after all, I may not have reached the intended Gaol."—*Buchanan's Syntax,* Pref. p. xxvii. "'Pitticus was offered a large sum." Better : 'A large sum was offered to Pitticus.'—*Kirkham's Gram.* p. 187. "King Missipsi charged his

---

* *Ache,* and its plural, *aches,* appear to have been formerly pronounced like the name of the eighth letter, with its plural, *Aitch,* and *Aitches;* for the old poets made "*aches*" two syllables. But Johnson says of *ache,* a pain, it is "now *generally* written *ake,* and in the plural *akes,* of one syllable." See his *Quarto Dict.* So Walker : "It is now *almost universally* written *ake* and *akes.*" See Walker's *Principles,* No. 355. So Webster : "*Ake, less* properly written *ache.*" See his *Octavo Dict.* But Worcester seems rather to prefer *ache.*—G. B.

sons to respect the senate and people of Rome."—See *ib.* p. 161: "For example: Gallileo invented the telescope."—*Ib.* pp. 54 and 67. "Cathmor's warriours sleep in death."—*Ib.* p. 54. "For parsing will enable you to detect and correct errours in composition."—*Ib.* p. 50.

> "O'er barren mountains, o'er the flow'ry plain,
> Extends thy uncontroul'd and boundless reign."—*Dryden.*

PROMISCUOUS ERRORS IN SPELLING.

LESSON I.—MIXED.

"A bad author deserves better usage than a bad critick."—POPE: *Johnson's Dict. w. Former.* "Produce a single passage superiour to the speech of Logan, a Mingo chief, delivered to Lord Dunmore, when governour of Virginia."—*Kirkham's Elocution,* p. 247. "We have none synonimous to supply its place."—*Jamieson's Rhetoric,* p. 48. "There is a probability that the effect will be accellerated."—*Ib.* p. 48. "Nay, a regard to sound hath controuled the public choice."—*Ib.* p. 46. "Though learnt from the uninterrupted use of gutterel sounds."—*Ib.* p. 5. "It is by carefully filing off all roughness and inequaletics, that languages, like metals, must be polished."—*Ib.* p. 48. "That I have not mispent my time in the service of the community."—*Buchanan's Syntax,* Pref. xxviii. "The leaves of maiz are also called blades."—*Webster's El. Spelling-Book,* p. 43. "Who boast that they know what is past, and can foretel what is to come."—*Robertson's Amer.* i, p. 360. "Its tasteless dullness is interrupted by nothing but its perplexities."—*Abbott's Teacher,* p. 18. "Sentences constructed with the Johnsonian fullness and swell."—*Jamieson's Rhet.* p. 130. "The privilege of escaping from his prefatory dullness and prolixity."—*Kirkham's Elocution,* p. iv. "But in poetry this characteristick of dulness attains its full growth."—*Ib.* p. 72. "The leading characteristick consists in an increase of the force and fullness."—*Ib.* p. 71. "The character of this opening fulness and feebler vanish."—*Ib.* p. 31. "Who, in the fullness of unequalled power, would not believe himself the favourite of heaven?"—*Ib.* p. 181. "They marr one another, and distract him."—*Philological Museum,* i, p. 433. "Let a deaf worshipper of antiquity and an English prosodist settle this."—*Rush, on the voice,* p. 140. "This phillipic gave rise to my satirical reply in self-defence."—*Merchant's Criticisms.* "We here saw no inuendoes, no new sophistry, no falsehoods."—*Ib.* "A witty and humourous vein has often produced enemies."—*Murray's Key,* p. 173. "Cry holla! to thy tongue, I pr'ythee: it curvetts unseasonably."—*Shak.* "I said, in my slyest manner, 'Your health, sir.'"—*Blackwood's Mag.* xl, p. 679. "And attornies also travel the circuit in pursuite of business."—*Red Book,* p. 83. "Some whole counties in Virginia would hardly sel for the valu of the dets du from the inhabitants."—*Webster's Essays,* p. 361. "They were called the court of assistants, and exercized all powers legislativ and judicial."—*Ib.* p. 340. "Arithmetic is excellent for the guaging of liquors."—*Murray's Gram.* 8vo, p. 288. "Most of the inflections may be analysed in a way somewhat similar."—*Ib.* p. 112.

> "To epithets allots emphatic state,
> Whilst principals, ungrac'd, like lacquies wait."—*C. Churchill's Ros.* p. 8.

LESSON II.—MIXED.

"Hence it [less] is a privative word, denoting destitution; as, fatherless, faithless, pennyless."—*Webster's Dict. w. Less.* "Bay; red, or redish, inclining to a chesnut color."—*Same.* "To mimick, to imitate or ape for sport; a mimic, one who imitates or mimics."—*Ib.* "Counterroll, a counterpart or copy of the rolls; Counterrolment, a counter account."—*Ib.* "Millenium, the thousand years during which Satan shall be bound."—*Ib.* "Millenial, pertaining to the millenium, or to a thousand years."—*Ib.* "Thraldom; slavery, bondage, a state of servitude." See *Johnson's Dict.* "Brier, a prickly bush; Briery, rough, prickly, full of briers; Sweetbriar, a fragrant shrub." See *Johnson, Walker, Chalmers, Webster, and others.* "Will, in the second and third Persons, barely foretels."—*British Gram.* p. 132. "And therefor there is no Word false, but what is distinguished by Italics."—*Ib.* Pref. p. v. "What should be repeted is left to their Discretion."—*Ib.* p. iv. "Because they are abstracted or seperated from material Substances." *Ib.* p. ix. "All Motion is in Time, and therefor, where-ever it exists, implies Time as its Concommitant."—*Ib.* p. 140. "And illiterate grown persons are guilty of blameable spelling."—*Ib.* Pref. p. xiv. "They wil always be ignorant, and of ruf uncivil manners."—*Webster's Essays,* p. 346. "This fact wil hardly be beleeved in the northern states."—*Ib.* p. 367. "The province however waz harrassed with disputes."—*Ib.* p. 352. "So little concern haz the legislature for the interest of lerning."—*Ib.* p. 349. "The gentlemen wil not admit that a skoolmaster can be a gentleman." See *Ib.* p. 362. "Such absurd qui-pro-quoes cannot be too strenuously avoided."—*Churchill's Gram.* p. 205. "When we say, 'a man looks slyly,' we signify, that he assumes a sly look."—*Ib.* p. 339. "Peep; to look through a crevice; to look narrowly, closely, or slyly."—*Webster's Dict.* "Hence

the confession has become a hacknied proverb."—*Wayland's Moral Science*, p. 110. "Not to mention the more ornamental parts of guilding, varnish, &c."—*Tooke's Divers.* i, p. 20. "After this system of self-interest had been rivetted."—*Brown's Esti.* ii, p. 136. "Prejudice might have prevented the cordial approbation of a bigotted Jew."--SCOTT: *on Luke*, x.
" All twinkling with the dew-drop sheen,
The briar-rose fell in streamers green."—*Lady of the Lake*, p. 16.

LESSON III.—MIXED.

"The infinitive mode has commonly the sign *to* before it."—*Harrison's Gram.* p. 25. "Thus, it is adviseable to write *singeing*, from the verb to *singe*, by way of distinction from *singing*, the participle of the verb to *sing*."—*Ib.* p. 27. "Many verbs form both the preterite tense and the preterite participle irregularly."—*Ib.* p. 28. "Much must be left to every one's taste and judgment."—*Ib.* p. 67. "Verses of different lengths intermixed form a Pindarick poem."—*Priestley's Gram.* p. 44. "He'll surprize you."— *Frost's El. of Gram.* p. 88. "Unequalled archer! why was this concealed?"—KNOWLES: *ib.* p. 102. "So gaily curl the waves before each dashing prow."—BYRON: *ib.* p. 104. "When is a dipthong called a proper dipthong?"—*Infant School Gram.* p. 11. "How many *s* would goodness then end with? Three."—*Ib.* p. 33. "Q. What is a tripthong? *A.* A tripthong is the union of three vowels, pronounced in like manner."—*Bacon's Gram.* p. 7. "The verb, noun, or pronoun, is referred to the preceding terms taken separately."—*Ib.* p. 47. "The cubic foot of matter which occupies the center of the globe." —*Cardell's Gram.* 18mo, p. 47. "The wine imbibes oxigen, or the acidifying principle, from the air."—*Ib.* p. 62. "Charcoal, sulphur, and niter, make gun powder."—*Ib.* p. 90. "It would be readily understood, that the thing so labeled, was a bottle of Madeira wine."—*Ib.* p. 99. "They went their ways, one to his farm, an other to his merchandize."—*Ib.* p. 130. "A dipthong is the union of two vowels, sounded by a single impulse of the voice."—*Russell's Gram.* p. 7. "The professors of the Mahommedan religion are called Mussulmans."—*Maltby's Gram.* p. 73. "This shews that *let* is not a sign of the imperative mood, but a real verb."—*Ib.* p. 51. "Those preterites and participles, which are first mentioned in the list, seem to be the most eligible."—*Ib.* p. 47. "Monosyllables, for the most part, are compared by *er* and *est;* and dyssyllables by *more* and *most.*" —*Ib.* p. 19. "This termination, added to a noun, or adjective, changes it into a verb : as *modern*, to *modernise; a symbol*, to *symbolize.*"—*Churchill's Gram.* p. 24. "An Abridgment of Murray's Grammar, with additions from Webster, Ash, Tooke, and others."—*Maltby's title-page.* "For the sake of occupying the room more advantageously, the subject of Orthography is merely glanced at."—*Nutting's Gram.* p. 5. "So contended the accusers of Gallileo."—*O. B. Peirce's Gram.* 12mo, 1839, p. 380. "Murray says, 'They were *traveling past* when *we* met them.'"—*Peirce, ib.* p. 361. "They fulfil the only purposes for which they are designed."—*Ib.* p. 359. "On the fulfillment of the event."—*Ib.* p. 175. "Fullness consists in expressing every idea."—*Ib.* p. 291. "Consistently with fulness and perspicuity."—*Ib.* p. 337. "The word *verriest* is a gross corruption; as, 'He is the *verriest* fool on earth.'"—*Wright's Gram.* p. 202. "The sound will recal the idea of the object."—*Hiley's Gram.* p. 142. "Formed for great enterprizes."—*Bullions's Prin. of E. Gram.* p. 153. "The most important rules and definitions are printed in large type, *italicised.*"—*Hart's Gram.* p. 3. "HAMLETTED, *a.* Accustomed to a hamlet; countrified." —*Bolles's Dict.* and *Chalmers's.* "Singular, *spoonful, cup-full, coach-full, handful;* plural, *spoonfuls, cup-fulls, coach-fulls, handfuls.*"—*Bullions's Analyt. and Pract. Gram.* p. 27.
" Between Superlatives and following Names,
Of, by Grammatic Right, a Station claims."—*Brightland's Gram.* p. 146.

CHAPTER V.—QUESTIONS.

ORDER OF REHEARSAL, AND METHOD OF EXAMINATION.

☞ [The student ought to be able to answer with readiness, and in the words of the book, all the following questions on grammar. And if he has but lately commenced the study, it may be well to require of him a general rehearsal of this kind, before he proceeds to the correction of any part of the false grammar quoted in the foregoing chapters. At any rate, he should be master of so many of the definitions and rules as precede the part which he attempts to correct: because this knowledge is necessary to a creditable performance of the exercise. But those who are very quick at reading, may perform it *tolerably*, by consulting the book at the time, for what they do not remember. The answers to these questions will embrace all the main text of the work; and, if any further examination be thought necessary, extemporaneous questions may be framed for the purpose.]

LESSON I.—GRAMMAR.

1. What is the name, or title, of this book? 2. What is Grammar? 3. What is an English Grammar? 4. What is English Grammar, in itself? and what knowledge

does it imply ? 5. If grammar is the art of reading, writing, and speaking, define these actions. What is it, *to read ?* 6. What is it, *to write ?* 7. What is it, *to speak ?* 8. How is grammar to be taught, and by what means are its principles to be made known ? 9. What is a perfect definition ? 10. What is an example, as used in teaching ? 11. What is a rule of grammar ? 12. What is an exercise ? 13. What was language at first, and what is it now ? 14. Of what two kinds does the composition of language consist ? and how do they differ ? 15. What are the least parts of language ? 16. What has discourse to do with sentences? or sentences, with points ? 17. In extended compositions, what is the order of the parts, upwards from a sentence ? 18. What, then, is the common order of literary division, downwards, throughout ? 19. Are all literary works divided exactly in this way ? 20. How is Grammar divided ? 21. Of what does Orthography treat ? 22. Of what does Etymology treat ? 23. Of what does Syntax treat ? 24. Of what does Prosody treat ?

PART FIRST, ORTHOGRAPHY.

LESSON II.—LETTERS.

1. Of what does Orthography treat ? 2. What is a letter ? 3. What is an elementary sound of human voice, or speech ? 4. What name is given to the sound of a letter ? and what epithet, to a letter not sounded ? 5. How many letters are there in English ? and how many sounds do they represent ? 6. In what does a knowledge of the letters consist ? 7. What variety is there in the letters ? and how are they always the same ? 8. What different sorts of types, or letters, are used in English ? 9. What are the names of the letters in English ? 10. What are their names in both numbers, singular and plural ? 11. Into what general classes are the letters divided ? 12. What is a vowel ? 13. What is a consonant ? 14. What letters are vowels ? and what, consonants ? 15. When are *w* and *y* consonants ? and when, vowels ? 16. How are the consonants divided ? 17. What is a semivowel ? 18. What is a mute ? 19. What letters are reckoned semivowels? and how many of these are aspirates ? 20. What letters are called liquids ? and why ? 21. What letters are reckoned mutes ? and which of them are imperfect mutes ?

LESSON III.—SOUNDS.

1. What is meant, when we speak of the powers of the letters ? 2. Are the sounds of a language fewer than its words ? 3. How are different vowel sounds produced ? 4. What are the vowel sounds in English ? 5. How may these sounds be modified in the formation of syllables ? 6. Can you form a word upon each by means of an *f* ? 7. Will you try the series again with a *p* ? 8. How may the vowel sounds be written ? and how uttered when they are not words ? 9. Which of the vowel sounds form words ? and what of the rest ? 10. How many and what are the consonant sounds in English ? 11. In what series of words may all these sounds be heard ? 12. In what series of words may each of them be heard two or three times ? 13. What is said of the sounds of *j* and *z* ? 14. What is said of the sounds of *c* and *q* ? 15. What is said of *sc*, or *s* before *c* ? 16. What, of *ce, ci,* and *ch* ? 17. What sounds has the consonant *y* ? 18. In how many different ways can the letters of the alphabet be combined ? 19. What do we derive from these combinations of sounds and characters ?

LESSON IV.—CAPITALS.

1. What characters are employed in English ? 2. Why should the different sorts of letters be kept distinct ? 3. What is said of the slanting strokes in Roman letters ? 4. For what purpose are *Italics* chiefly used ? 5. In preparing a manuscript, how do we mark these things for the printer ? 6. What distinction of form belongs to each of the letters ? 7. What is said of small letters ? and why are capitals used ? 8. What things are commonly exhibited wholly in capitals ? 9. How many rules for capitals are given in this book ? and what are their titles ? 10. What says Rule 1st of *books ?* 11. What says Rule 2d of *first words ?* 12. What says Rule 3d of names *of Deity ?* 13. What says Rule 4th of *proper names ?* 14. What says Rule 5th of *titles ?* 15. What says Rule 6th of *one capital ?* 16. What says Rule 7th of *two capitals ?* 17. What says Rule 8th of *compounds ?* 18. What says Rule 9th of *apposition ?* 19. What says Rule 10th of *personifications ?* 20. What says Rule 11th of *derivatives ?* 21. What says Rule 12th of *I and O ?* 22. What says Rule 13th of *poetry ?* 23. What says Rule 14th of *examples ?* 24. What says Rule 15th of *chief words ?* 25. What says Rule 16th of *needless capitals ?*

[Now turn to the first chapter of Orthography, and correct the improprieties there quoted for the practical application of these rules]

LESSON V.—SYLLABLES.

1. What is a syllable ? 2. Can the syllables of a word be perceived by the ear ? 3. Under what names are words classed according to the number of their syllables ? 4. Which of the letters can form syllables of themselves? and which cannot ? 5. What is a diphthong ? 6. What is a proper diphthong ? 7. What is an improper diphthong ? 8. What is a triphthong ? 9. What is a proper triphthong ? 10. What is an improper

triphthong? 11. How many and what are the diphthongs in English? 12. How many and which of these are so variable in sound that they may be either proper or improper diphthongs? 13. How many and what are the proper diphthongs? 14. How many and what are the improper diphthongs? 15. Are proper triphthongs numerous in our language? 16. How many and what are the improper triphthongs? 17. What guide have we for dividing words into syllables? 18. How many special rules of syllabication are given in this book? and what are their titles, or subjects? 19. What says Rule 1st of *consonants?* 20. What says Rule 2d of *vowels?* 21. What says Rule 3d of *terminations?* 22. What says Rule 4th of *prefixes?* 23. What says Rule 5th of *compounds?* 24. What says Rule 6th of *lines full?*
[Now turn to the second chapter of Orthography, and correct the improprieties there quoted for the practical application of these rules.]

LESSON VI.—WORDS.

1. What is a word? 2. How are words distinguished in regard to *species* and *figure?* 3. What is a primitive word? 4. What is a derivative word? 5. What is a simple word? 6. What is a compound word? 7. How do permanent compounds differ from others? 8. How many rules for the figure of words are given in this book? and what are their titles, or subjects? 9. What says Rule 1st of *compounds?* 10. What says Rule 2d of *simples?* 11. What says Rule 3d of *the sense?* 12. What says Rule 4th of *ellipses?* 13. What says Rule 5th of *the hyphen?* 14. What says Rule 6th of *no hyphen?*
[Now turn to the third chapter of Orthography, and correct the improprieties there quoted for the practical application of these rules.]

LESSON VII.—SPELLING.

1. What is spelling? 2. How is this art to be acquired? and why so? 3. Why is it difficult to learn to spell accurately? 4. Is it then any disgrace to spell words erroneously? 5. What benefit may be expected from the rules for spelling? 6. How many rules for spelling are given in this book? and what are their titles, or subjects? 7. What says Rule 1st of *final f, l,* or *s?* 8. Can you mention the principal exceptions to this rule? 9. What says Rule 2d of *other finals?* 10. Are there any exceptions to this rule? 11. What says Rule 3d of the *doubling* of consonants? 12. Under what three heads are the exceptions to this rule noticed? 13. What says Rule 4th *against the doubling* of consonants? 14. Under what four heads are the apparent exceptions to this rule noticed? 15. What says Rule 5th of *final ck?* 16. What monosyllables, contrary to this rule, end with *c* only? 17. What says Rule 6th of the *retaining* of double letters before affixes? 18. Under what three heads are the exceptions to this rule noticed? 19. What says Rule 7th of the *retaining* of double letters after prefixes? 20. What observation is made respecting exceptions to this rule?

LESSON VIII.—SPELLING.

21. What says Rule 8th of *final ll,* and of *final l single?* 22. What words does this rule claim, which might seem to come under Rule 7th? and why? 23d What says Rule 9th of *final e omitted?* 24. Under what three heads are the exceptions, real or apparent, here noticed? 25. What says Rule 10th of *final e retained?* 26. Under what three heads are the exceptions to this rule noticed? 27. What says Rule 11th of *final y changed?* 28. Under what three heads are the limits and exceptions to this rule noticed? 29. What says Rule 12th of *final y unchanged?* 30. Under what three heads are the exceptions to this rule noticed? 31. What says Rule 13th of the terminations *ize* and *ise?* 32. Under what three heads are the apparent exceptions to this rule noticed? 33. What says Rule 14th of *compounds?* 34. Under what seven heads are the exceptions to this rule noticed? 35. What says Rule 15th of *usage,* as a law of spelling?
[Now turn to the fourth chapter of Orthography, and correct the improprieties there quoted for the practical application of these rules and their exceptions.]

CHAPTER VI.—FOR WRITING.

EXERCISES IN ORTHOGRAPHY.

☞ [The following examples of false orthography are inserted here, and not explained in the general Key, that they may be corrected by the pupil *in writing.* Some of the examples here quoted are less inaccurate than others, but all of them, except a few shown in contrast, are, in some respect or other, erroneous. It is supposed, that every student who can answer the questions contained in the preceding chapter, will readily discern wherein the errors lie, and be able to make the necessary corrections.]

EXERCISE I.—CAPITALS.

"Alexander the great killed his friend Clitus."—*Harrison's Gram.* p. 68. "The words in italics are parsed in the same manner."—*Maltby's Gram.* p. 69. "It may be read by those who do not understand latin."—*Barclay's Works,* iii, p. 262. "A roman *s* being added to a word in italics or small capitals."—*Churchill's Gram.* p. 215. "This is not simply a gallicism, but a corruption of the French *on;* itself a corruption."—*Ib.* p. 228.

"The Gallicism, '*it is me*,' is perpetually striking the ear in London."—*Ib.* p. 316. "'Almost nothing,' is a common scotticism, equally improper: it should be, 'scarcely any thing.'"—*Ib.* p. 333. "To use *learn* for *teach*, is a common Scotticism, that ought to be carefully avoided." See *ib.* p. 261. "A few observations on the subjunctive mood as it appears in our English bible."—*Wilcox's Gram.* p. 40. "The translators of the bible, have confounded two tenses, which in the original are uniformly kept distinct."—*Ib.* p. 40. "More like heaven on earth, than the holy land would have been."—*Anti-Slavery Mag.* i, p. 72. "There is now extant a poetical composition, called the golden verses of Pythagoras."—*Lempriere's Dict.* "Exercise of the Mind upon Theorems of Science, like generous and manly Exercise of the Body, tends to call forth and strengthen Nature's original Vigour."—*Harris's Hermes*, p. 295. "O that I could prevail on Christians to melt down, under the warm influence of brotherly love, all the distinctions of methodists, independents, baptists, anabaptists, arians, trinitarians, unitarians, in the glorious name of christians."—KNOX: *Churchill's Gram.* p. 173. "Pythagoras long ago remarked, 'that ability and necessity dwell near each other.'"—*Student's Manual*, p. 285. "The Latin Writers Decency neglect,
　　But modern Readers challenge more Respect."— *Brightland's Gram.* p. 172.

EXERCISE II.—SYLLABLES.

1. Correct *Bolles*, in the division of the following words: "Del-ia, Jul-ia, Lyd-ia, heigh-ten, pat-ron, ad-roit, worth-y, fath-er, fath-er-ly, mar-chi-o-ness, i-dent-ic-al, out-ra-ge-ous, ob-nox-i-ous, pro-di-gi-ous, tre-mend-ous, ob-liv-i-on, pe-cul-i-ar."— *Revised Spelling-Book:* New London, 1831.

2. Correct *Sears*, in the division of the following words: "A-quil-a, hear-ty, drea-ry, wor-my, hai-ry, thor-ny, phil-os-o-phy, dis-cov-e-ry, re-cov-e-ry, ad-diti-on, am-biti-on, au-spici-ous, fac-titi-ous, fla-giti-ous, fru-iti-on, sol-stiti-al, ab-o-liti-on."—*Standard Spelling-Book:* New Haven, 1826.

3. Correct *Bradley*, in the division of the following words: "Jes-ter, rai-ny, forg-e-ry, fin-e-ry, spic-e-ry, brib-e-ry, groc-e-ry, chi-can-e-ry, fer-riage, line-age; cri-ed, tri-ed, su-ed, slic-ed, forc-ed pledg-ed, sav-ed, dup-ed, strip-ed, touch-ed, trounc-ed."— *Improved Spelling-Book:* Windsor, 1815.

4. Correct *Burhans*, in the division of the following words: "Boar-der, brigh-ten, cei-ling, frigh-ten, glea-ner, lea-kage, suc-ker, mos-sy, fros-ty, twop-ence, pu-pill-ar-y, crit-i-call-y, gen-er-all-y, lit-er-all-y, log-i-call-y, trag-i-call-y, ar-ti-fici-al, po-liti-call-y, sloth-full-y, spite-full-y, re-all-y, sui-ta-ble, ta-mea-ble, flumm-er-y, neso-i-ence, shep-her-dess, trav-ell-er, re-pea-ter, re-pressi-on, suc-cessi-on, un-lear-ned." —*Critical Pronouncing Spelling-Book:* * Philadelphia, 1823.

5. Correct *Marshall*, in the division of the following words: "Trench-er, trunch-eon, lros-sy, glos-sy, glas-sy, gras-sy, dres-ses, pres-ses, cal-ling, chan-ging, en-chan-ging, con-ver-sing, mois-ture, join-ture, qua-drant, qua-drate, trans-gres-sor, dis-es-teem."— *New Spelling-Book:* New York, 1836.

6. Correct *Emerson*, in the division of the following words: "Dus-ty mis-ty, mar-shy, mil-ky, wes-tern, stor-my, nee-dy spee-dy, drea-ry, fros-ty, pas-sing, roc-ky, bran-chy, land-ish, pru-dish, eve-ning, a-noth-er."—*National Spelling-Book:* Boston, 1828.
"Two Vowels meeting, each with its full Sound,
　　Always to make Two Syllables are bound."—*Brightland's Gram.* p. 64.

EXERCISE III.—FIGURE OF WORDS.

"I was surprised by the return of my long lost brother."—*Parker's Exercises in English Composition,* p. 5. "Such singular and unheard of clemency cannot be passed over by me in silence."—*Ib.* p. 10. "I perceive my whole system excited by the potent stimulus of sun-shine."—*Ib.* p. 11. "To preserve the unity of a sentence, it is sometimes necessary to employ the case absolute, instead of the verb and conjunction."—*Ib.* p. 17. "Severity and hard hearted opinions accord with the temper of the times."—*Ib.* p. 18. "That poor man was put into the mad house."—*Ib.* p. 22. "This fellow must be put into the poor house."—*Ib.* p. 22. "I have seen the breast works and other defences of earth, that were thrown up."—*Ib.* p. 24. "Cloven footed animals are enabled to walk more easily on uneven ground."—*Ib.* p. 25. "Self conceit blasts the prospects of many youth."—*Ib.* p. 26. "Not a moment should elapse without bringing some thing to pass."—*Ib.* p. 36. "A school master decoyed the children of the principal citizens into the Roman camp."—*Ib.* p. 39. "The pupil may now write a description of the following objects. A school room. A steam boat. A writing desk. A dwelling house. A meeting house. A paper mill. A grist mill. A wind mill."—*Ib.* p. 45. "Every meta-

---

* This book has, probably, more *recommenders* than any other of the sort. I have not patience to count em accurately, but it would seem that *more than a thousand* of the great and learned have certified to the world, that they never before had seen so good a spelling-book! With personal knowledge of more than fifty the signers, G. B. refused to add his poor name, being ashamed of the mischievous facility with which very respectable men had loaned their signatures.

phor should be founded on a resemblance which is clear and striking; not far fetched, nor difficult to be discovered."—*Ib.* p. 49. "I was reclining in an arbour overhung with honey suckle and jessamine of the most exquisite fragrance."—*Ib.* p. 51. "The author of the following extract is speaking of the slave trade."—*Ib.* p. 60. "The all wise and benevolent Author of nature has so framed the soul of man, that he cannot but approve of virtue."—*Ib.* p. 74. "There is something of self denial in the very idea of it."—*Ib.* p. 75. "Age therefore requires a well spent youth to render it happy."—*Ib.* p. 76. "Pearl-ash requires much labour in its extraction from ashes."—*Ib.* p. 91. "*Club*, or *crump, footed,* Loripes; *Rough,* or *feather, footed,* Plumipes."—*Ainsworth's Dict.*

"The honey-bags steal from the humble bees,
And for night-tapers crop their waxen thighs."—SHAK.: *Joh.'s Dict. w. Glowworm.*
"The honeybags steal from the humblebees,
And for night tapers crop their waxen thighs."—SHAK.: *Joh.'s Dict. w. Humblebee.*
"The honey bags steal from the humble-bees,
And, for night tapers crop their waxen thighs."—*Dodd's Beauties of Shaks.* p. 51.

EXERCISE IV.—SPELLING.

"His antichamber, and room of audience, are little square chambers wainscoted."— ADDISON: *Johnson's Dict. w. Antechamber.* "Nobody will deem the quicksighted amongst them to have very enlarged views of ethicks."—LOCKE: *ib. w. Quicksighted.* "At the rate of this thick-skulled blunderhead, every plow-jobber shall take upon him to read upon divinity."—L'ESTRANGE: *ib. w. Blunderhead.* "On the topmast, the yards, and boltsprit would I flame distinctly." SHAK.: *ib. w. Bowsprit.* "This is the tune of our catch plaid by the picture of nobody."—ID. *ib. w. Nobody.* "Thy fall hath left a kind of blot to mark the fulfraught man."—ID. *ib. w. Fulfraught.* "Till blinded by some Jack o' Lanthorn sprite."—*Snelling's Gift,* p. 62. "The beauties you would have me eulogise."—*Ib.* p. 14. "They rail at me—I gaily laugh at them."—*Ib.* p. 13. "Which the king and his sister had intrusted to him withall."—*Josephus,* v, p. 143. "The terms of these emotions are by no means synonimous."—*Rush, on the Voice,* p. 336. "Lillied, *adj.* Embellished with lilies."—*Chalmers's Dict.* "They seize the compendious blessing without exertion and without reflexion."—*Philological Museum,* i, p. 428. "The first cry that rouses them from their torpour, is the cry that demands their blood."—*Ib.* p. 433. "It meets the wants of elementary schools and deserves to be patronised."—*Kirkham's Gram.* p. 5. "Whose attempts were paralysed by the hallowed sound."—*Music of Nature,* p. 270. "It would be an amusing investigation to analyse their language."— *Ib.* p. 200. "It is my father's will that I should take on me the hostess-ship of the day." SHAK.: in *Johnson's Dict.* "To retain the full apprehension of them undiminisht."— *Phil. Museum,* i, p. 468. "The ayes and noes were taken in the House of Commons." —*Anti-Slavery Mag.* i, p. 11. "Derivative words are formed by adding letters or syllables to primatives."—*Davenport's Gram.* p. 7. "The minister never was thus harrassed himself."—*Nelson, on Infidelity,* p. 6. "The most vehement politician thinks himself unbiassed in his judgment."—*Ib.* p. 17. "Mistress-ship, *n.* Female rule or dominion." —*Webster's Dict.*

"Thus forced to kneel, thus groveling to embrace
The scourge and ruin of my realm and race."—POPE: *Ash's Gram.* p. 83.

EXERCISE V.—MIXED.

"The quince tree is of a low stature; the branches are diffused and crooked."— MILLER: *Johnson's Dict.* "The greater slow worm, called also the blindworm, is commonly thought to be blind, because of the littleness of his eyes."—GREW: *ib.* "Oh Hocus! where art thou? It used to go in another guess manner in thy time."— ARBUTHNOT: *ib.* "One would not make a hotheaded crackbrained coxcomb forward for a scheme of moderation."—ID. *ib.* "As for you, colonel huff-cap, we shall try before a civil magistrate who's the greatest plotter."—DRYDEN: *ib. w. Huff.* "In like manner, Actions co-alesce with their Agents, and Passions with their Patients."—*Harris's Hermes,* p. 263. "These Sentiments are not unusual even with the Philosopher now a days."—*Ib.* p. 350. "As if the Marble were to fashion the Chizzle, and not the Chizzle the Marble."—*Ib.* p. 353. "I would not be understood, in what I have said, to under value Experiment."—*Ib.* p. 352. "How therefore is it that they approach nearly to Non-Entitys?"—*Ib.* p. 431. "Gluttonise, modernise, epitomise, barbarise, tyranise." —*Churchill's Gram.* pp. 31 and 42. "Now fair befal thee and thy noble house!"—SHAK.: *ib.* p. 241. "Nor do I think the error above-mentioned would have been so long indulged, &c."—*Ash's Gram.* p. 4. "The editor of the two editions above mentioned was pleased to give this little manuel to the public, &c."—*Ib.* p. 7. "The Note of Admiration denotes a modelation of the voice suited to the expression."—*Ib.* p. 16. "It always has some respect to the power of the agent; and is therefore properly stiled the potential mode."—*Ib.* p. 29. "Both these are supposed to be synonomous expressions."—*Ib.* p. 105. "An expence beyond what my circumstances admit."—DODDRIDGE: ib. p. 138. "There are four of them: the *Full-Point*, or *Period*; the *Colon*; the *Semi-Colon*; the *Comma*."—*Cobbett's E. Gram.* N. Y. 1818, p. 77. "There are many men, who have been at Latin-Schools for years, and who, at last, cannot write six sentences in English correctly."—*Ib.* p. 39. "But, figures of rhetorick are edge tools, and two edge tools too."—*Ib.* p. 182. "The horsechesnut grows into a goodly standard."—MORTIMER: *Johnson's Dict.* "Whereever *if* is to be used."—*O. B. Peirce's Gram.* p. 175.

"Peel'd, patch'd, and pyebald, linsey-woolsey brothers."—POPE: *Joh. Dict. w. Mummer.*
"Peel'd, patch'd, and piebald, linsey-woolsey brothers."—ID. *ib. w. Piebald.*

EXERCISE VI.—MIXED ERRORS.

"Pied, *adj.* [from *pie*.] Variegated; partycoloured."—*Johnson's Dict.* "Pie, [*pica*, Lat.] A magpie; a party-coloured bird."—*Ib.* "Gluy, *adj.* [from *glue*.] Viscous; tenacious; glutinous."—*Ib.* "Gluey, *a.* Viscous, glutinous. Glueyness, *n.* The quality of being gluey."—*Webster's Dict.* "Old Euclio, seeing a crow-scrat* upon the muck-hill, returned in all haste, taking it for an ill sign."—BURTON: *Johnson's Dict.* "Wars are begun by hairbrained† dissolute captains."—ID. *ib.* "A carot is a well known garden root."—*Red Book*, p. 60. "Natural philosophy, metaphysicks, ethicks, history, theology, and politicks, were familiar to him."—*Kirkham's Elocution*, p. 209. "The words in italicks and capitals, are emphatick."—*Ib.* p. 210. "It is still more exceptionable; Candles, Cherrys, Figs, and other sorts of Plumbs, being sold by Weight, and being Plurals."—*Johnson's Gram. Com.* p. 135. "If the End of Grammar be not to save that Trouble, and Expence of Time, I know not what it is good for."—*Ib.* p. 161. "Caule, Sheep Penns, or the like, has no Singular, according to Charisius."—*Ib.* p. 194. "These busi-bodies are like to such as reade bookes with intent onely to spie out the faults therof."—*Perkins's Works*, p. 741. "I think it every man's indispensible duty, to do all the service he can to his country."—*Locke, on Ed.* p. 4. "Either fretting it self into a troublesome Excess, or flaging into a downright want of Appetite."—*Ib.* p. 23. "And nobody would have a child cramed at breakfast."—*Ib.* p. 23. "Judgeship and judgment, lodgable and alledgeable, alledgement and abridgment, lodgment and infringement, enlargement and acknowledgment."—*Webster's Dict.* 8vo. "Huckster, *n. s.* One who sells goods by retail, or in small quantities; a pedler."—*Johnson's Dict.*

"He seeks bye-streets, and saves th' expensive coach."—GAY: *ib. w. Mortgage.*
"He seeks by-streets, and saves th' expensive coach."—GAY: *ib. w. By-street.*

EXERCISE VII.—MIXED ERRORS.

"Boys like a warm fire in a wintry day."—*Webster's El. Spelling-Book*, p. 62. "The lilly is a very pretty flower."—*Ib.* p. 62. "The potatoe is a native plant of America."—*Ib.* p. 60. "An anglicism is a peculiar mode of speech among the English."—*Ib.* p. 136. "Black berries and raspberries grow on briars."—*Ib.* p. 150. "You can broil a beef steak over the coals of fire."—*Ib.* p. 38. "Beef-steak, *n.* A steak or slice of beef for broiling."—*Webster's Dict.* "Beefsteak, *s.* a slice of beef for broiling."—*Treasury of Knowledge.* "As he must suffer in case of the fall of merchandize, he is entitled to the corresponding gain if merchandize rises."—*Wayland's Moral Science*, p. 258. "He is the worshipper of an hour, but the worldling for life."—*Maturin's Sermons*, p. 424. "Slyly hinting something to the disadvantage of great and honest men."—*Webster's Essays*, p. 329. "'Tis by this therefore that I Define the Verb; namely, that it is a Part of Speech, by which something is apply'd to another, as to its Subject."—*Johnson's Gram. Com.* p. 255. "It may sometimes throw a passing cloud over the bright hour of gaiety."—*Kirkham's Elocution*, p. 178. "To criticize, is to discover errors; and to crystalize implies to freeze or congele."—*Red Book*, p. 68. "The affectation of using the preterite instead of the participle, is peculiarly aukward; as, he has came."—*Priestley's Grammar*, p. 125. "They are moraly responsible for their individual conduct."—*Cardell's El. Gram.* p. 21. "An engine of sixty horse power, is deemed of equal force with a team of sixty horses."—*Red Book*, p. 113. "This, at fourpence per ounce, is two shillings and fourpence a week, or six pounds, one shilling and four pence a year."—*Ib.* p. 122. "The tru meening of parliament ix a meeting of barons or peers."—*Webster's Essays*, p. 276. "Several authorities seem at leest to favor this opinion."—*Ib.* p. 277. "That ix, as I hav explained the tru primitiv meening of the word."—*Ib.* p. 276. "The lords are peers of the relm; that ix, the ancient prescriptiv judges or barons."—*Ib.* p. 274.

"Falshood is folly, and 't is just to own
   The fault committed; this was mine alone."—*Pope, Odys.* B. xxii, l. 168.

---

* *Scrat, for scratch. The word is now obsolete, and may be altered by taking ch in the correction.*
† *"Hairbrained, adj. This should rather be written harebrained; unconstant, unsettled, wild as a hare."—Johnson's Dict. Webster writes it harebrained, as from hare and brain. Worcester, too, prefers this form.*

EXERCISE VIII.—MIXED ERRORS.

" A second verb so nearly synonimous with the first, is at best superfluous."—*Church-ill's Gram.* p. 332. "Indicate it, by some mark opposite [to] the word misspelt."—*Ab-bott's Teacher,* p. 74. " And succesfully controling the tendencies of mind."—*Ib.* p. 24. " It [the Monastick Life] looks very like what we call Childrens-Play."—[LESLIE'S] *Right of Tythes,* p. 236. " It seems rather lik Playing of Booty, to Please those Fools and Knaves."—*Ib.* Pref. p. vi. " And first I Name Milton, only for his Name, lest the Party should say, that I had not Consider'd his Performance against Tythes."—*Ib.* p. iv. " His Fancy was too Predominant for his Judgment. His Talent lay so much in Satyr that he hated Reasoning."—*Ib.* p. iv. " He has thrown away some of his Railery against Tythes, and the Church then underfoot."—*Ib.* p. v. " They Vey'd with one another in these things."—*Ib.* p. 220. " Epamanondas was far the most accomplished of the The-bans."—*Cooper's New Gram.* p. 27. " Whoever and Whichever, are thus declined. Sing. and Plur. *nom.* whoever, *poss.* whoseever, *obj.* whomever. Sing. and Plu. *nom.* whichever, *poss.* whoseever, *obj.* whichever."—*Ib.* p. 38. " WHEREEVER, *adv.* [*where* and *ever.*] At whatever place."—*Webster's Dict.* " They at length took possession of all the country south of the Welch mountains."—*Dobson's Comp. Gram.* p. 7. " Those Britains, who re-fused to submit to the foreign yoke, retired into Wales."—*Ib.* p. 6. " Religion is the most chearful thing in the world."—*Ib.* p. 43. " *Two* means the number two compleatly, whereas *second* means only the last of two, and so of all the rest."—*Ib.* p. 44. " Now send men to Joppa, and call for one Simon, whose sirname is Peter."—*Ib.* p. 96. (See *Acts,* x, 5.) " In French words, we use *enter* instead of *inter;* as, entertain, enterlace, enterprize."—*Ib.* p. 101. " Amphiology, i. e. a speech of uncertain or doubtful mean-ing."—*Ib.* p. 103. " Surprize; as, hah! hey day! what! strange!"—*Ib.* p. 109. " Names of the letters: ai bee see dee ee ef jee aitch eye jay kay el em en o pee cue ar ess tee you vee double u eks wi zed."—*Rev. W. Allen's Gram.* p. 3.

" I, O, and U, at th' End of Words require,
The silent *(e)*, the same do's (va) desire."—*Brightland's Gram.* p. 15.

EXERCISE IX.—MIXED ERRORS.

" *And* is written for *eaeend,* adding, ekeing."—*Dr. Murray's Hist. of Europ. Lang.* i, p. 222. " The Hindus have changed *ai* into *e,* sounded like *e* in *where.*"—*Ib.* ii, p. 121. " And therefor I would rather see the cruelest usurper than the mildest despot."—*Philological Museum,* i, p. 430. " Sufficiently distinct to prevent our marveling."—*Ib.* i, 477. " Possessed of this preheminence he disregarded the clamours of the people."—*Smollett's England,* iii, p. 222. " He himself, having communicated, administered the sacrament to some of the bye-standers."—*Ib.* p. 222. " The high fed astrology which it nurtured, is reduced to a skeleton on the leaf of an almanac."—*Cardell's Gram.* p. 6. " Fulton was an eminent engineer: he invented steam boats."—*Ib.* p. 30. " Then, in comes the be-nign latitude of the doctrine of good-will."—SOUTH: *in Johnson's Dict.* " Being very lucky in a pair of long lanthorn-jaws, he wrung his face into a hideous grimace."—SPEC-TATOR: *ib.* " Who had lived almost four-and-twenty years under so politick a king as his father."—BACON: *ib. w. Lowness.* " The children will answer; John's, or William's, or whose ever it may be."—*Infant School Gram.* p. 32. " It is found tolerably easy to apply them, by practising a little guess work."—*Cardell's Gram.* p. 91. " For between which two links could speech makers draw the division line?"—*Ib.* p. 50. " The won-derful activity of the rope dancer who stands on his head."—*Ib.* p. 56. " The brilliancy which the sun displays on its own disk, is sun shine."—*Ib.* p. 63. " A word of three syl-lables is termed a trisyllable."—*Murray's Gram.* p. 23; *Coar's,* 17; *Jaudon's,* 13; *Comly's,* 8; *Cooper's New Gr.* 8; *Kirkham's,* 20; *Picket's,* 10; *Alger's,* 12; *Blair's,* 7; *Guy's,* 2; *Bolles's Spelling-Book,* 161. See *Johnson's Dict.* " A word of three syllables is termed a trissyllable."—*British Gram.* p. 33; *Comprehensive Gram.* 23; *Bicknell's,* 17; *Allen's,* 31; *John Peirce's,* 149; *Lennie's,* 5; *Maltby's,* 8; *Ingersoll's,* 7; *Bradley's,* 66; *Davenport's,* 7; *Bucke's,* 16; *Bolles's Spelling-Book,* 91. See *Littleton's Lat. Dict.* (1.) " Will, in the first Persons, promises or threatens: But in the second and third Persons, it barely foretels." —*British Gram.* p. 132. (2.) " Will, in the first Persons, promises or threatens; but in the second and third Persons, it barely foretells."—*Buchanan's Gram.* p. 41. (3.) " Will, in the first person, promises, engages, or threatens. In the second and third persons, it merely foretels."—*Jaudon's Gram.* p. 59. (4.) " Will, in the first person singular and plural, promises or threatens; in the second and third persons, only foretells."—*Lowth's Gram.* p. 41. (5.) " Will, in the first person singular and plural, intimates resolution and promising; in the second and third person, only foretels."—*Murray's Gram.* p. 88; *Ingersoll's,* 136; *Fisk's,* 78; *A Flint's,* 42; *Bullions's,* 32; *Hamlin's,* 41; *Cooper's Abridg.* 50. ☞ *Murray's Second Edition* has it " *foretells.*" (6.) " Will, in the first person sin-gular and plural, expresses resolution and promising. In the second and third persons it only foretells."—*Comly's Gram.* p. 38; *E. Devis's,* 51; *Lennie's,* 22. (7.) " Will, in the first person, promises. In the second and third persons, it simply foretels."—*Maltby's Gram.* p. 24. (8.) " Will, in the first person implies resolution and promising; in the second and third, it foretells."—*Cooper's New Gram.* p. 51.   (9.) "*Will*, in the first person singular and plural, promises or threatens ; in the second and third persons, only foretels : *shall*, on the contrary, in the first person, simply foretels ; in the second and third persons, promises, commands, or threatens."—*Adam's Lat. and Eng. Gram.* p. 83.   (10.) "In the first person shall *foretels*, and will *promises* or *threatens*; but in the second and third persons *will* foretels, and *shall* promises or threatens."—*Blair's Gram.* p. 65.

> "If Mævius scribble in Apollo's spight,
>   There are who judge still worse than he can write."—*Pope.*

EXERCISE X.—MIXED ERRORS.

"I am liable to be charged that I latinize too much."—DRYDEN : *in Johnson's Dict.* "To mould him platonically to his own idea."—WOTTON : *ib.*   "I will marry a wife as beautiful as the houries, and as wise as Zobeide."—*Murray's E. Reader*, p. 148.   "I will marry a wife, beautiful as the Houries."—*Wilcox's Gram.* p. 65.   "The words in italics are all in the imperative mood."—*Maltby's Gram.* p. 71.   "Words Italicised, are emphatick, in various degrees."—*Kirkham's Elocution*, p. 173.   "Wherever two gg's come together, they are both hard."—*Buchanan's Gram.* p. 5.   "But these are rather silent (*o*)'s than obscure (*u*)'s."—*Brightland's Gram.* p. 19.   "That can be Guest at by us, only from the Consequences."—*Right of Tythes*, p. viii.   "He says he was glad that he had Baptized so few ; And asks them, Were ye Baptised in the Name of Paul ?"— *Ib.* p. ix.   "Therefor he Charg'd the Clergy with the Name of Hirelings."—*Ib.* p. viii. "On the fourth day before the first second day in each month."—*The Friend*, vii, p. 230. "We are not bound to adhere for ever to the terms, or to the meaning of terms, which were established by our ancestors."—*Murray's Gram.* p. 140.   "O ! learn from him to station quick eyed Prudence at the helm."—*Frost's El. of Gram.* p. 104.   "It pourtrays the serene landscape of a retired village."—*Music of Nature*, p. 421.   "By stating the fact, in a circumlocutary manner."—*Booth's Introd. to Dict.* p. 33.   "Time as an abstract being is a non-entity."—*Ib.* p. 29.   "From the difficulty of analysing the multiplied combinations of words."—*Ib.* p. 19.   "Drop those letters that are superfluous, as : handful, foretel."—*Cooper's Plain & Pract. Gram.* p. 10.   "Shall, in the first person, simply foretells." —*Ib.* p. 51.   "And the latter must evidently be so too, or, at least, cotemporary, with the act."—*Ib.* p. 60.   "The man has been traveling for five years."—*Ib.* p. 77.   "I shall not take up time in combatting their scruples."—*Blair's Rhet.* p. 320.   "In several of the chorusses of Euripides and Sophocles, we have the same kind of lyric poetry as in Pindar."—*Ib.* p. 398.   "Until the Statesman and Divine shall unite their efforts in forming the human mind, rather than in loping its excrescences, after it has been neglected."—*Webster's Essays*, p. 26.   "Where conviction could be followed only by a bigotted persistence in error."—*Ib.* p. 78.   "All the barons were entitled to a sect in the national council, in right of their baronys."—*Ib.* p. 260.   "Some knowlege of arithmetic is necessary for every lady."—*Ib.* p. 29.   "Upon this, [the system of chivalry,] were founded those romances of night-errantry."—*Blair's Rhet.* p. 374.   "The subject is, the atchievements of Charlemagne and his Peers, or Paladins."—*Ib.* p. 374.   "Aye, aye ; this slice to be sure outweighs the other."—*Blair's Reader*, p. 31.   "In the common phrase, *good-bye, bye* signifies *passing, going.* The phrase signifies, a good going, a prosperous passage, and is equivalent to *farewell.*"—*Webster's Dict.*   "Good-by, *adv.*—a contraction of *good be with you*—a familiar way of bidding farewell." See *Chalmers's Dict.* "Off he sprung, and did not so much as stop to say good bye to you."—*Blair's Reader*, p. 16.   "It no longer recals the notion of the action."—*Barnard's Gram.* p. 69.

> "Good-nature and good-sense must ever join ;
>   To err, is human ; to forgive, divine."—*Pope, Ess. on Crit.*

EXERCISE XI.—MIXED ERRORS.

"The practices in the art of carpentry are called planeing, sawing, mortising, scribing, moulding, &c."—*Blair's Reader*, p. 118.   "With her left hand, she guides the thread round the spindle, or rather round a spole which goes on the spindle."—*Ib.* p. 134. "Much suff'ring heroes next their honours claim."—POPE : *Johnson's Dict. w. Much.* "Vein healing verven, and head purging dill."—SPENSER : *ib. w. Head.*   "An, in old English, signifies *if*; as, '*an* it please your honor.' "—*Webster's Dict.*   "What, then, was the moral worth of these renouned leaders?"—*M'Ilvaine's Lect.* p. 460.   "Behold how every form of human misery is met by the self denying diligence of the benevolent."— *Ib.* p. 411.   "Reptiles, bats, and doleful creatures—jackalls, hyenas, and lions—inhabit the holes, and caverns, and marshes of the desolate city."—*Ib.* p. 270.   "ADAYS, *adv.*   On or in days; as, in the phrase, now *adays.*"—*Webster's Dict.*   "REFEREE, one to whom a thing is referred ; TRANSFEREE, the person to whom a transfer is made."—*Ib.*   "The Hospitallers were an order of knights who built a hospital at Jerusalem for pilgrims."—*Ib.*   "GERARD, Tom, or Tung, was the institutor and first grand master of the knights hospitalers : he died in 1120."—*Biog. Dict.*   "I had a purpose now to lead our many to the holy land."—

SHAK: *in Johnson's Dict.* "He turned their heart to hate his people, to deal subtilly with his servants."—*Psalms,* cv, 25. "In Dryden's ode of Alexander's Feast, the line, ' Fain, fain, fain, fain,' represents a gradual sinking of the mind."—*Kames, El. of Crit.* ii, p. 71. " The first of these lines is marvelously nonsensical."—*Jamieson's Rhet.* p. 117. " We have the nicely chiseled forms of an Apollo and a Venus, but it is the same cold marble still." —*Christian Spect.* viii, p. 201. "Death waves his mighty wand and paralyses all."—*Buck's Gram.* p. 35. " Fear God. Honor the patriot. Respect virtue."—*Kirkham's Gram.* p. 216. "Pontius Pilate being Governour of Judea, and Herod being Tetrarch of Galilee." —*Ib.* 189. See *Luke,* iii, 1. " AUCTIONIER, *n. s.* The person that manages an auction."— *Johnson's Dict.* "The earth put forth her primroses and days-eyes, to behold him."— HOWEL: *ib.* " *Musselman,* not being a compound of *man,* is *musselmans* in the plural."— *Lennie's Gram.* p. 9. "The absurdity of fatigueing them with a needless heap of grammar rules."—*Burgh's Dignity,* i, p. 147. "John was forced to sit with his arms a kimbo, to keep them asunder."—*ARBUTHNOT: Joh. Dict.* " To set the arms a kimbo, is to set the hands on the hips, with the elbows projecting outward."—*Webster's Dict.* " We almost uniformly confine the inflexion to the last or the latter noun."—*Maunder's Gram.* p. 2. "This is all souls day, fellows! Is it not?"—SHAK.: *in Joh. Dict.* · "The english physicians make use of troy-weight."—*Johnson's Dict.* "There is a certain number of ranks allowed to dukes, marquisses, and earls."—PEACHAM: *ib. w. Marquis.*

"How could you chide the young good natur'd prince,
And drive him from you with so stern an air."—ADDISON: *ib. w. Good,* 25.

EXERCISE XII.—MIXED ERRORS.

"In reading, every appearance of sing-song should be avoided."—*Sanborn's Gram.* p. 75. "If you are thoroughly acquainted with the inflexions of the verb."—*Ib.* p. 53. "The preterite of *read* is pronounced *red.*"—*Ib.* p. 48. "Humility opens a high way to dignity."— *Ib.* p. 15. "What is intricate must be unraveled."—*Ib.* p. 275. " Roger Bacon invented gun powder, A. D. 1280."—*Ib.* p. 277. "On which ever word we lay the emphasis."—*Murray's Gram.* 8vo, p. 243; 12mo, p. 195. "Each of the leaders was apprized of the Roman invasion."—*Nixon's Parser,* p. 123. "If I say, ' I *gallopped* from Islington to Holloway;' the verb is intransitive: if, 'I *gallopped* my *horse* from Islington to Holloway;' it is transitive."—*Churchill's Gram.* p. 238. "The reasonableness of setting a part one day in seven."—*The Friend,* iv, p. 240. " The promoters of paper money making reprobated this act."—*Webster's Essays,* p. 196. "There are five compound personal pronouns, which are derived from the five simple personal pronouns by adding to some of their cases the syllable *self* ; as, my-self, thy-self, him-self, her-self, it-self."—*Perley's Gram.* p. 16. "Possessives, my-own, thy-own, his-own, her-own, its-own, our-own, your-own, their-own."—*Ib. Declensions.* "Thy man servant and thy maid servant may rest, as well as thou."—*Sanborn's Gram.* p. 160. "How many right angles has an acute angled triangle?"—*Ib.* p. 220. "In the days of Jorum, king of Israel, flourished the prophet Elisha."—*Ib.* p. 148. " In the days of Jorum, king of Israel, Elisha, the prophet flourished."—*Ib.* p. 133. " Lodgable, *a.* Capable of affording a temporary abode." —*Webster's Octavo Dict.*—"Win me into the easy hearted man."—*Johnson's Quarto Dict.* "And then to end life, is the same as to dye."—*Milnes's Greek Gram.* p. 176. "Those usurping hectors who pretend to honour without religion, think the charge of a lie a blot not to be washed out but by blood."—SOUTH: *Joh. Dict.* "His gallies attending him, he pursues the unfortunate."—*Nixon's Parser,* p. 91. " This cannot fail to make us shyer of yielding our assent."—*Campbell's Rhet.* p. 117. "When he comes to the Italicised word, he should give it such a definition as its connection with the sentence may require."—*Claggett's Expositor,* p. vii. " Learn to distil from your lips all the honies of persuasion."—*Adams's Rhetoric,* Vol. i, p. 31. " To instill ideas of disgust and abhorrence against the Americans."—*Ib.* ii, 300. " Where prejudice has not acquired an uncontroled ascendency."—*Ib.* i, 31. " The uncontrolable propensity of his mind was undoubtedly to oratory."—*Ib.* i, 100. "The Brutus is a practical commentary upon the dialogues and the orator."—*Ib.* i, 120. " The oratorical partitions are a short elementary compendium." —*Ib.* i, 130. " You shall find hundreds of persons able to produce a crowd of good ideas upon any subject, for one that can marshall them to the best advantage."—*Ib.* i, 169. " In this lecture, you have the outline of all that the whole course will comprize." —*Ib.* i, 182. " He would have been stopped by a hint from the bench, that he was traveling out of the record."—*Ib.* i, 289. " To tell them that which should befal them in the last days."—*Ib.* ii, 308. " Where all is present, there is nothing past to recal."—*Ib.* ii, 358. " Whose due it is to drink the brimfull cup of God's eternal vengeance."— *Law and Grace,* p. 36.

"There, from the dead, centurions see him rise,
See, but struck down with horrible surprise!"—*Savage.*

"With seed of woes my heart brimful is charged."—SIDNEY: *Joh. Dict.*
" Our legions are brimful, our cause is ripe."—SHAKSPEARE: *ib.*

PART II.

ETYMOLOGY.

ETYMOLOGY treats of the different parts of speech, with their classes and modifications.

The *Parts of Speech* are the several kinds, or principal classes, into which words are divided by grammarians.

Classes, under the parts of speech, are the particular sorts into which the several kinds of words are subdivided.

Modifications are inflections, or changes, in the terminations, forms, or senses, of some kinds of words.

CHAPTER I.—PARTS OF SPEECH.

The Parts of Speech, or sorts of words, in English, are ten ; namely, the Article, the Noun, the Adjective, the Pronoun, the Verb, the Participle, the Adverb, the Conjunction, the Preposition, and the Interjection.

1. THE ARTICLE.

An Article is the word *the*, *an*, or *a*, which we put before nouns to limit their signification : as, *The* air, *the* stars ; *an* island, *a* ship.

2. THE NOUN.

A Noun is the name of any person, place, or thing, that can be known or mentioned : as, *George, York, man, apple, truth.*

3. THE ADJECTIVE.

An Adjective is a word added to a noun or pronoun, and generally expresses quality : as, A *wise* man ; a *new* book. You *two* are *diligent.*

4. THE PRONOUN.

A Pronoun is a word used in stead of a noun : as, The boy loves *his* book ; *he* has long lessons, and *he* learns *them* well.

5. THE VERB.

A Verb is a word that signifies *to be, to act,* or *to be acted upon : as,* I *am,* I *rule,* I *am ruled ;* I *love,* thou *lovest,* he *loves.*

6. THE PARTICIPLE.

A Participle is a word derived from a verb, participating the properties of a verb, and of an adjective or a noun ; and is generally formed by adding *ing, d,* or *ed,* to the verb : thus, from the verb *rule,* are formed three participles, two simple and one compound ; as, 1. *ruling,* 2. *ruled,* 8. *having ruled.*

7. THE ADVERB.

An Adverb is a word added to a verb, a participle, an adjective, or another adverb ; and generally expresses time, place, degree, or manner : as, They are *now here,* studying *very diligently.*

8. THE CONJUNCTION.

A Conjunction is a word used to connect words or sentences in construction, and to show the dependence of the terms so connected : as, " Thou *and* he are happy, *because* you are good."—*Murray.*

9. THE PREPOSITION.

A Preposition is a word used to express some relation of different things or thoughts to each other, and is generally placed before a noun or a pronoun: as, The paper lies *before* me *on* the desk.

10. THE INTERJECTION.

An Interjection is a word that is uttered merely to indicate some strong or sudden emotion of the mind: as, *Oh! alas! ah! poh! pshaw! avaunt! aha! hurrah!*

OBSERVATIONS.

OBS. 1.—The first thing to be learned in the study of this the second part of grammar, is the distribution of the words of the language into those principal sorts, or classes, which are denominated *the Parts of Speech.* This is a matter of some difficulty. And as no scheme which can be adopted, will be in all cases so plain that young beginners will not occasionally falter in its application, the teacher may sometimes find it expedient to refer his pupils to the following simple explanations, which are designed to aid their first and most difficult steps.

How can we know to what class, or part of speech, any word belongs? By learning the definitions of the ten parts of speech, and then observing how the word is written, and in what sense it is used. It is necessary also to observe, so far as we can, with what other words each particular one is capable of making sense.

1. Is it easy to distinguish an ARTICLE? If not always easy, it is generally so: *the, an,* and *a,* are the only English words called articles, and these are rarely any thing else. Because *as* and *a* have the same import, and are supposed to have the same origin, the articles are commonly reckoned two, but some count them as three.

2. How can we distinguish a NOUN? By means of the article before it, if there is one; as, *the house, an apple, a book*: or, by adding it to the phrase, "*I mentioned;*" as, "I mentioned *peace*"—"I mentioned *war*"—"I mentioned *slumber.*" Any word which thus makes complete sense, is, in that sense, a noun; because a noun is the *name* of any thing which can thus be mentioned by *a name.* Of English nouns, there are said to be as many as twenty-five or thirty thousand.

3. How can we distinguish an ADJECTIVE? By putting a noun after it, to see if the phrase will be sense. The noun *thing,* or its plural *things,* will suit almost any adjective; as, A *good* thing—A *bad* thing—A *little* thing—A *great* thing—*Few* things—*Many* things—*Some* things—*Fifty* things. Of adjectives, there are perhaps nine or ten thousand.

4. How can we distinguish a PRONOUN? By observing that its noun repeated makes the same sense. Thus, the example of the pronoun above, "The boy loves *his* book; *he* has long lessons, and *he* learns *them* well,"—very clearly means, "The boy loves *the boy's* book; *the boy* has long lessons, and *the boy* learns *those lessons* well." Here, then, by a disagreeable repetition of two nouns, we have the same sense without any pronoun; but it is obvious that the pronouns form a better mode of expression, because they prevent this awkward repetition. The different pronouns in English are twenty-four; and their variations in declension are thirty-two: so that the number of *words* of this class, is fifty-six.

5. How can we distinguish a VERB? By observing that it is usually the principal word in the sentence, and that without it there would be no assertion. It is the word which expresses what is affirmed or said of the person or thing mentioned; as, "Jesus *wept.*"—"Felix *trembled.*"—"The just *shall live* by faith." It will make sense when inflected with the pronouns; as, I *write,* thou *writ'st,* he *writes*; we *write,* you *write,* they *write.*—I *walk,* thou *walkest,* he *walks*; we *walk,* you *walk,* they *walk.* Of English verbs, some recent grammarians compute the number at eight thousand; others formerly reckoned them to be no more than four thousand three hundred.[*]

6. How can we distinguish a PARTICIPLE? By observing its derivation from the verb, and then placing it *after to be* or *having*; as, To be *writing,* Having *written*—To be *walking,* Having *walked*—To be *weeping,* Having *wept*—To be *studying,* Having *studied.* Of simple participles, there are twice as many as there are of simple or radical verbs; and the possible compounds are not less numerous than the simples, but they are much less frequently used.

7. How can we distinguish an ADVERB? By observing that it answers to the question, *When? Where? How much?* or *How?*—or serves to ask it; as, "He spoke fluently." How did he speak? *Fluently.* This word *fluently* is therefore an adverb: it tells *how* he spoke. Of adverbs, there are about two thousand six hundred; and four fifths of them end in *ly.*

8. How can we distinguish a CONJUNCTION? By observing what words or terms it joins together, or to what other conjunction it corresponds; as, "*Neither* wealth *nor* honor can heal a

---

[*] "The whole number of verbs in the English language, regular and irregular, simple and compounded, taken together, is about 4,300. See, in Dr. Ward's Essays on the English language, the catalogue of English verbs. The whole number of irregular verbs, the defective included, is about 176."—*Lowth's Gram.* Philad 1799, p. 59. Lindley Murray copied the first and the last of these three sentences, but made the latter number "about 177."—*Octavo Gram.* p. 109; *Duodecimo,* p. 98. In the latter work, he has this note: "The whole number of *words,* in the English language. is about thirty-five thousand."—*Ib.* Churchill says, "The whole number of verbs in the English language, according to Dr. Ward, is about 4,300. The irregulars, including the auxiliaries, scarcely exceed 200."—*New Gram.* p 113. An other late author has the following enumeration: "There are in the English language about twenty thousand five hundred nouns, forty pronouns, *eight thousand verbs,* nine thousand two hundred adnouns, two thousand six hundred adverbs, sixty-nine prepositions, nineteen conjunctions, and sixty-eight interjections; in all, above forty thousand words."—*Rev. David Blair's Gram.* p. 10. William Ward, M. A., in an old grammar *undated,* which speaks of Dr. Lowth's as one with which the public had "very *lately* been favoured," says: "There are *four Thousand and about five Hundred Verbs* in the English [language]."—*Ward's Practical Gram.* p. 52.

wounded conscience."—*Dilwyn's Ref.* p. 16. Or, it may be well to learn the whole list at once: *And, as, both, because, even, for, if, that, then, since, seeing, so: Or, nor, either, neither, than, though, although, yet, but, except, whether, lest, unless, save, provided, notwithstanding, whereas.* Of conjunctions, there are these twenty-nine in common use, and a few others now obsolete.

9. How can we distinguish a PREPOSITION? By observing that it will govern the pronoun *them*, and is not a verb or a participle; as, *About* them—*above* them—*across* them—*after* them—*against* them—*amidst* them—*among* them—*around* them—*at* them—*Before* them—*behind* them—*below* them—*beneath* them—*beside* them—*between* them—*beyond* them—*by* them—*For* them—*from* them—*In* them—*into* them, &c. Of the prepositions, there are about sixty now in common use.

10. How can we distinguish an INTERJECTION? By observing that it is an independent word or sound, uttered earnestly, and very often written with the note of exclamation; as, *Lo! behold! look! see! hark! hush! hist! mum!* Of interjections, there are sixty or seventy in common use, some of which are seldom found in books.

OBS. 2.—An accurate knowledge of words, and of their changes, is indispensable to a clear discernment of their proper combinations in sentences, according to the usage of the learned. Etymology, therefore, should be taught before syntax; but it should be chiefly taught by a direct analysis of entire sentences, and those so plainly written that the particular effect of every word may be clearly distinguished, and the meaning, whether intrinsic or relative, be discovered with precision. The parts of speech are usually named and defined with reference to the use of words *in sentences;* and, as the same word not unfrequently stands for several different parts of speech, the learner should be early taught to make for himself the proper application of the foregoing distribution, without recurrence to a dictionary, and without aid from his teacher. He who is endeavouring to acquaint himself with the grammar of a language which he can already read and understand, is placed in circumstances very different from those which attend the school-boy who is just beginning to construe some sentences of a foreign tongue. A frequent use of the dictionary may facilitate the progress of the one, while it delays that of the other. English grammar, it is hoped, may be learned directly from this book alone, with better success than can be expected when the attention of the learner is divided among several or many different works.

OBS. 3.—Dr. James P. Wilson, in speaking of the classification of words, observes, "The *names* of the distributive parts should either express, distinctly, the influence, which each class produces on sentences; or some other characteristic trait, by which the respective species of words may be distinguished, without danger of confusion. It is at least probable, that no distribution, sufficiently minute, can ever be made, of the parts of speech, which shall be wholly free from all objection. Hasty innovations, therefore, and crude conjectures, should not be permitted to disturb that course of grammatical instruction, which has been advancing in melioration, by the unremitting labours of thousands, through a series of ages."—*Wilson's Essay on Gram.* p. 66. Again: "The *number* of the parts of speech may be reduced, or enlarged, at pleasure; and the rules of syntax may be accommodated to such new arrangement. The best grammarians find it difficult, in practice, to distinguish, in some instances, adverbs, prepositions, and conjunctions; yet their effects are generally distinct. This inconvenience should be submitted to, since a less comprehensive distribution would be very unfavourable to a rational investigation of the meaning of English sentences."—*Ib.* p. 68. Again: "*As* and *so* have been also deemed substitutes, and resolved into other words. But if all abbreviations are to be restored to their primitive parts of speech, there will be a general revolution in the present systems of grammar; and the various improvements, which have sprung from convenience, or necessity, and been sanctioned by the usage of ancient times, must be retrenched, and anarchy in letters universally prevail."—*Ib.* p. 114.

OBS. 4.—I have elsewhere sufficiently shown why *ten* parts of speech are to be preferred to any other number, in English; and whatever diversity of opinion there may be respecting the class to which some particular words ought to be referred, I trust to make it obvious to good sense, that I have seldom erred from the course which is most expedient. 1. *Articles* are used with appellative nouns, sometimes to denote emphatically the species, but generally to designate individuals. 2. *Nouns* stand in discourse for persons, things, or abstract qualities. 3. *Adjectives* commonly express the concrete qualities of persons or things; but sometimes, their situation or number. 4. *Pronouns* are substitutes for names, or nouns; but they sometimes represent sentences. 5. *Verbs* assert, ask, or say something; and, for the most part, express action or motion. 6. *Participles* contain the essential meaning of their verbs, and commonly denote action, and imply time; but, apart from auxiliaries, they express that meaning either adjectively or substantively, and not with assertion. 7. *Adverbs* express the circumstances of time, of place, of degree, and of manner; the *when,* the *where,* the *how much,* and the *how.* 8. *Conjunctions* connect, sometimes words, and sometimes sentences, rarely phrases; and always show, either the manner in which one sentence or one phrase depends upon an other, or what connexion there is between two words that refer to a third. 9. *Prepositions* express the correspondent relations of things to things, of thoughts to thoughts, or of words to words; for these, if we speak truly, must be all the same in expression. 10. *Interjections* are either natural sounds or exclamatory words, used independently, and serving briefly to indicate the wishes or feelings of the speaker.

OBS. 5.—In the following passage, all the parts of speech are exemplified, and each is pointed out by the figure placed over the word: —

"The power of speech is a faculty peculiar to man; a faculty bestowed on him by his beneficent Creator, for the greatest and most excellent uses; but, alas! how often do we pervert it to the worst of purposes!" See *Lowth's Gram.* p. 7.

In this sentence, which has been adopted by Murray, Churchill, and others, we have the following parts of speech: 1. The words *the, a,* and *an,* are articles. 2. The words *power, speech, faculty, man, faculty, Creator, uses,* and *purposes,* are nouns. 3. The words *peculiar, beneficent, greatest, excellent,* and *worst,* are adjectives. 4. The words *him, his, we,* and *it,* are pronouns. 5. The words *is, do,* and *pervert,* are verbs. 6. The word *bestowed* is a participle. 7. The words *most, how*, and *often*, are adverbs. 8. The words *and* and *but* are conjunctions. 9. The words *of*, *to*, *on*, *by*, *for*, *to*, and *of*, are prepositions. 10. The word *alas!* is an interjection.

OBS. 6.—In speaking or writing, we of course bring together the different parts of speech just as they happen to be needed. Though a sentence of ordinary length usually embraces more than one half of them, it is not often that we find them *all* in so small a compass. Sentences sometimes abound in words of a particular kind, and are quite destitute of those of some other sort. The following examples will illustrate these remarks. (1.) ARTICLES: "*A* square is less beautiful than *a* circle; and *the* reason seems to be, that *the* attention is divided among *the* sides and angles of *a* square, whereas *the* circumference of *a* circle, being *a* single object, makes one entire impression."—*Kames, Elements of Crit.* i, p. 175. (2.) NOUNS: "A *number* of *things* destined for the same *use*, such as *windows*, *chairs*, *spoons*, *buttons*, cannot be too uniform; for, supposing their *figure* to be good, *utility* requires *uniformity*."—*Ib.* i, 176. (3.) ADJECTIVES: "Hence nothing *just*, *proper*, *decent*, *beautiful*, *proportioned*, or *grand*, is *risible*."—*Ib.* i, 229. (4.) PRONOUNS: "*I* must entreat the courteous reader to suspend *his* curiosity, and rather to consider *what* is written than *who they* are *that* write *it*."—*Addison, Spect.* No. 556. (5.) VERBS: "The least consideration *will inform* us how easy it *is* to *put* an ill-natured construction upon a word; and what perverse *turns* and expressions *spring* from an evil temper. Nothing *can be explained* to him who *will* not *understand*, nor *will* any thing *appear* right to the unreasonable."—*Cecil.* (6.) PARTICIPLES: "The Scriptures are an authoritative voice, *reproving*, *instructing*, and *warning* the world; and *declaring* the only means *ordained* and *provided* for *escaping* the awful penalties of sin."—*G. B.* (7.) ADVERBS: "The light of Scripture shines *steadily*, *purely*, *benignly*, *certainly*, *superlatively*."—*Dr. S. H. Cox.* (8.) CONJUNCTIONS: "Quietness *and* silence *both* become *and* befriend religious exercises. Clamour *and* violence often hinder, *but* never further, the work of God."—*Henry's Exposition.* (9.) PREPOSITIONS: "He has kept *among* us, *in* times *of* peace, standing armies, *without* the consent *of* our legislatures."—*Dec. of Indep.* (10.) INTERJECTIONS: "*Oh*, my dear strongbox! *Oh*, my lost guineas! *Oh*, poor, ruined, beggared old man! *Hoo! hoo! hoo!*"—*Moliere: Burgh's Art of Speaking*, p. 266.

EXAMPLES FOR PARSING.

Parsing is the resolving or explaining of a sentence, or of some related word or words, according to the definitions and rules of grammar. Parsing is to grammar what ciphering is to arithmetic.

A *Praxis* is a method of exercise, or a form of grammatical resolution, showing the learner how to proceed. The word is Greek, and literally signifies action, doing, practice, or formal use.

PRAXIS I.—ETYMOLOGICAL.

In the First Praxis, it is required of the pupil merely to distinguish and define the different parts of speech.

The definitions to be given in the First Praxis, are one, and only one, for each word, or part of speech. Thus:—

EXAMPLE PARSED.

"The patient ox submits to the yoke, and meekly performs the labour required of him."

The is an article. 1.* An article is the word *the*, *an*, or *a*, which we put before nouns to limit their signification.
Patient is an adjective. 1. An adjective is a word added to a noun or pronoun, and generally expresses quality.
Ox is a noun. 1. A noun is the name of any person, place, or thing, that can be known or mentioned.
Submits is a verb. 1. A verb is a word that signifies *to be*, *to act*, or *to be acted upon*.
To is a preposition. 1. A preposition is a word used to express some relation of different things or thoughts to each other, and is generally placed before a noun or a pronoun.
The is an article. 1. An article is the word *the*, *an*, or *a*, which we put before nouns to limit their signification.
Yoke is a noun. 1. A noun is the name of any person, place, or thing, that can be known or mentioned.
And is a conjunction. 1. A conjunction is a word used to connect words or sentences in construction, and to show the dependence of the terms so connected.
Meekly is an adverb. 1. An adverb is a word added to a verb, a participle, an adjective, or an other adverb; and generally expresses time, place, degree, or manner.
Performs is a verb. 1. A verb is a word that signifies *to be*, *to act*, or *to be acted upon*.
The is an article. 1. An article is the word *the*, *an*, or *a*, which we put before nouns to limit their signification.
Labour is a noun. 1. A noun is the name of any person, place, or thing, that can be known or mentioned.
Required is a participle. 1. A participle is a word derived from a verb, participating the properties of a verb, and of an adjective or a noun; and is generally formed by adding *ing*, *d*, or *ed*, to the verb.
Of is a preposition. 1. A preposition is a word used to express some relation of different things or thoughts to each other, and is generally placed before a noun or a pronoun.
Him is a pronoun. 1. A pronoun is a word used in stead of a noun.

---

* These definitions are numbered here, because each of them is the first of a series now begun. In class rehearsals, the pupils may be required to give the definitions in turn; and, to prevent any from losing the place, it is important that the numbers be mentioned. When all have become sufficiently familiar with the definitions, the exercise may be performed *without them*. They are to be read or repeated till faults disappear—or till the teacher is satisfied with the performance. He may then save time, by commanding his class to proceed more briefly; making such distinctions as are required in the praxis, but ceasing to explain the terms employed; that is, omitting all *the definitions, for brevity's sake*. This remark is applicable likewise to all the subsequent praxes of etymological parsing.

LESSON I.—PARSING.

"A nimble tongue often trips. The rule of the tongue is a great attainment. The language of truth is direct and plain. Truth is never evasive. Flattery is the food of vanity. A virtuous mind loathes flattery. Vain persons are an easy prey to parasites. Vanity easily mistakes sneers for smiles. The smiles of the world are deceitful. True friendship hath eternal views. A faithful friend is invaluable. Constancy in friendship denotes a generous mind. Adversity is the criterion of friendship. Love and fidelity are inseparable. Few know the value of a friend till they lose him. Justice is the first of all moral virtues. Let justice hold, and mercy turn, the scale. A judge is guilty who connives at guilt. Justice delayed is little better than justice denied. Vice is the deformity of man. Virtue is a source of constant cheerfulness. One vice is more expensive than many virtues. Wisdom, though serious, is never sullen. Youth is the season of improvement."—*Dillwyn's Reflections*, pp. 4–27.

"Oh! my ill-chang'd condition! oh, my fate!
    Did I lose heaven for this?"—*Cowley's Davideis.*

LESSON II.—PARSING.

"So prone is man to society, and so happy in it, that, to relish perpetual solitude, one must be an angel or a brute. In a solitary state, no creature is more timid than man; in society, none more bold. The number of offenders lessens the disgrace of the crime; for a common reproach is no reproach. A man is more unhappy in reproaching himself when guilty, than in being reproached by others when innocent. The pains of the mind are harder to bear than those of the body. Hope, in this mixed state of good and ill, is a blessing from heaven: the gift of prescience would be a curse. The first step towards vice, is, to make a mystery of what is innocent: whoever loves to hide, will soon or late have reason to hide. A man who gives his children a habit of industry, provides for them better than by giving them a stock of money. Our good and evil proceed from ourselves: death appeared terrible to Cicero, indifferent to Socrates, desirable to Cato."—*Home's Art of Thinking*, pp. 26–53.

"O thou most high transcendent gift of age!
    Youth from its folly thus to disengage."—*Denham's Age.*

LESSON III.—PARSING.

"Calm was the day, and the scene, delightful. We may expect a calm after a storm. To prevent passion is easier than to calm it."—*Murray's Ex.* p. 5. "Better is a little with content, than a great deal with anxiety. A little attention will rectify some errors. Unthinking persons care little for the future." See *ib.* "Still waters are commonly deepest. He laboured to still the tumult. Though he is out of danger, he is still afraid."—*Ib.* "Damp air is unwholesome. Guilt often casts a damp over our sprightliest hours. Soft bodies damp the sound much more than hard ones." —*Ib.* "The hail was very destructive. Hail, virtue! source of every good. We hail you as friends."—*Ib.* p. 6. "Much money makes no man happy. Think much, and speak little. He has seen much of the world." See *ib.* "Every being loves its like. We must make a like space between the lines. Behave like men. We are apt to like pernicious company."—*Ib.* "Give me more love, or more disdain."— *Carew.* "He loved Rachel more than Leah."—*Genesis.* "But how much that more is, he hath no distinct notion."—*Locke.*

"And my more having would be as a sauce
    To make me hunger more."—*Shakspeare.*

CHAPTER II.—ARTICLES.

An Article is the word *the*, *an*, or *a*, which we put before nouns to limit their signification: as, *The* air, *the* stars; *an* island, *a* ship.

An and *a*, being equivalent in meaning, are commonly reckoned *one and the same* article. *An* is used in preference to *a*, whenever the following word begins with a *vowel sound;* as, *An* art, *an* end, *an* heir. *an* inch, *an* ounce, *an* hour, *an* urn. *A* is used in preference to *an*, whenever the following word begins with a *consonant sound;* as, *A* man, *a* house, *a* wonder, *a* one, *a* yew, *a* use, *a* ewer. Thus the consonant sounds of *w* and *y*, even when expressed by other letters, require *a* and not *an* before them.

A common noun, when taken in its *widest sense*, usually admits no article: as, "A candid temper is proper for *man;* that is, for *all mankind*."—*Murray*.

In English, nouns without any article, or other definitive, are often used in a sense *indefinitely partitive:* as, "He took *bread*, and gave thanks."—*Acts*. That is, "*some bread*." "To buy *food* are thy servants come."—*Genesis*. That is, "*some food*." "There are *fishes* that have wings, and are not strangers to the airy region."—*Locke's Essay*, p. 322. That is, "*some fishes*."

"Words in which nothing but the *mere being* of any thing is implied, are used without articles: as, 'This is not *beer*, but *water;*' 'This is not *brass*, but *steel*.'" See *Dr. Johnson's Gram.* p. 5.

An or *a* before the genus, may refer to a *whole species;* and *the* before the species, may denote that whole species emphatically: as, "*A certain bird* is termed *the cuckoo*, from *the sound* which it emits.'—*Blair*.

But *an* or *a* is commonly used to denote individuals as *unknown*, or as not specially distinguished from others: as, "I see *an object* pass by, which I never saw till now; and I say, 'There goes *a beggar* with *a long beard*.'"—*Harris*.

And *the* is commonly used to denote individuals as *known*, or as specially distinguished from others: as, "*The* man departs, and returns a week after; and I say, 'There goes *the beggar* with *the long beard*.'"—*Id*.

The article *the* is applied to nouns of either number: as, "*The* man, *the* men;" "*The* good boy, *the* good boys."

The is commonly required before adjectives that are used by ellipsis as nouns: as, "*The young* are slaves to novelty; *the old*, to custom."—*Ld. Kames*.

The article *an* or *a* implies *unity*, or *one*, and of course belongs to nouns of the singular number only; as, *A* man,— *An* old man,— *A* good boy.

An or *a*, like *one*, sometimes gives a collective meaning to an adjective of number, when the noun following is plural; as, *A few days*,—*A hundred men*,—*One hundred pounds sterling*.

Articles should be *inserted* as often as the sense requires them; as, "Repeat the preterit and [*the*] perfect participle of the verb *to abide*."—Error in *Merchant's Gram.* p. 66.

Needless articles should be omitted; they seldom fail to pervert the sense: as, "*The* Rhine, *the* Danube, *the* Tanais, *the* Po, *the* Wolga, *the* Ganges, like many hundreds of similar *names*, rose not from any obscure jargon or irrational dialect."—Error in *Dr. Murray's Hist. of Europ. Lang.* Vol. i, p. 327.

The articles can seldom be put *one for the other*, without gross impropriety; and of course either is to be preferred to the other, as it better suits the sense: as, "*The* violation of this rule never fails to hurt and displease *a* reader."—Error in *Blair's Lectures*, p. 107. Say, "*A* violation of this rule never fails to displease *the* reader."

CLASSES.

The articles are distinguished as the *definite* and the *indefinite*.

I. The *definite article* is *the*, which denotes some particular thing or things; as, *The* boy, *the* oranges.

II. The *indefinite article* is *an* or *a*, which denotes one thing of a kind, but not any particular one ; as, *A* boy, *an* orange.

MODIFICATIONS.*

The English articles have no modifications, except that *an* is shortened into *a* before the sound of a consonant ; as, " In *an* epic poem, or *a* poem upon *an* elevated subject, *a* writer ought to avoid raising *a* simile on *a* low image."—*Ld. Kames.*

OBSERVATIONS.

Obs. 1.—No other words are so often employed as the articles. And, by reason of the various and very frequent occasions on which these definitives are required, no words are oftener misapplied ; none, oftener omitted or inserted erroneously. I shall therefore copiously illustrate both their *uses* and their *abuses ;* with the hope that every reader of this volume will think it worth his while to gain that knowledge which is requisite to the true use of these small but important words. Some parts of the explanation, however, must be deferred till we come to Syntax.

Obs. 2.—With the attempts of Tooke, Dalton, Webster, Cardell, Fowle, Wells,† Weld, Butler, Frazee, Perley, and other writers, to *degrade* the article from its ancient rank among the parts of speech, no judicious reader, duly acquainted with the subject, can, I think, be well pleased. An article is not properly an "*adjective*," as they would have it to be ; but it is a word of a peculiar sort —a *customary index* to the sense of nouns. It serves not merely to show the extent of signification, in which nouns are to be taken, but is often the principal, and sometimes the only mark, by which a word is known to have the sense and construction of a noun.

Obs. 3.—First let it be understood, that *an* or *a* is nearly equivalent in meaning to the numeral adjective *one*, but less emphatic ; and that *the* is nearly equivalent in meaning to the pronominal adjective *that* or *those*, but less emphatic. On *some* occasions, these adjectives may well be substituted for the articles ; but *not generally.* If the articles were generally equivalent to adjectives, or even if they were generally *like* them, they would *be* adjectives ; but, that adjectives may occasionally supply their places, is no argument at all for confounding the two parts of speech. Distinctions must be made, where differences exist ; and, that *a*, *an*, and *the*, do differ considerably from the other words which they most resemble, is shown even by some who judge " the distinctive name of *article* to be useless." See *Crombie's Treatise*, Chap. 2. The articles therefore must be distinguished, not only from adjectives, but from each other. For, though both are *articles*, each is an index *sui generis;* the one definite, the other indefinite. And as the words *that* and *one* cannot often be interchanged without a difference of meaning, so the definite article and the indefinite are seldom, if ever, interchangeable. To put one for the other, is therefore, in general, to put one *meaning* for an other : " *A* daughter of *a* poor man"—" *The* daughter of *the* poor man"—" *A* daughter of *the* poor man"—and, " *The* daughter of *a* poor man," are four phrases which certainly have four different and distinct significations. This difference between the two articles may be further illustrated by the following example : " That Jesus was *a* prophet sent from God, is one proposition ; that Jesus was *the* prophet, *the* Messiah, is an other ; and, though he certainly was both *a* prophet and *the* prophet, yet *the* foundations of *the* proof of these propositions are separate and distinct."—*Watson's Apology*, p. 105.

Obs. 4.—Common nouns are, for the most part, names of large classes of objects ; and, though what really constitutes the species must always be found entire in every individual, the several ob-

---

* The *modifications* which belong to the different parts of speech consist chiefly of the *inflections* or *changes* to which certain words are subject. But I use the term sometimes in a rather broader sense, as including not only *variations* of words, but, in certain instances, their *original forms*, and also such of their *relations* as serve to indicate peculiar properties. This is no questionable license in the use of the term ; for when the position of a word *modifies* its meaning, or changes its person or case, this effect is clearly a grammatical *modification*, though there be no absolute *inflection*. Lord Kames observes, " *That quality* which distinguishes one genus, one species, or even one individual, from an other, is termed a *modification :* thus the same particular that is termed a *property* or *quality*, when considered as belonging to an individual, or a class of individuals, is termed a *modification*, when considered as distinguishing the individual or the class from an other."—*Elements of Criticism*, Vol. ii. p. 392.

† Wells, having put the articles into the class of adjectives, produces authority as follows : " ' The words *a* or *an*, and *the*, are reckoned by *some* grammarians a separate part of speech ; but, as they in all respects come under the definition of the adjective, it is unnecessary, as well as *improper*, to rank them as a class by themselves.'— *Crane.*" To this he adds, " The articles are also ranked with adjectives by Priestley, E Oliver, Bell, Elphinston, M'Culloch, D'Orsey, Lindsay, Joel, Greenwood, Smetham, Dalton, King, Hort, Buchanan, Crane, J. Russell, Frazee, Cutler, Perley, Swett, Day, Goodenow, Willard, Robbins, Felton, Snyder, Butler, S. Barrett, Badgley, Hows, Wilsing, Davenport, Fowle, Weld, and others."—*Wells's School Gram.* p. 69. In this way, he may have made it seem to many, that, after thorough investigation, he had decided the point discreetly, and with preponderance of authority. For it is claimed as a " peculiar merit " of this grammar, that, " Every point of practical importance is *thoroughly investigated*, and reference is carefully made to the *researches* of preceding writers, in all cases which admit of being determined by *weight of authority*."—WILLIAM RUSSELL, *on the cover.* But, in this instance, as in sundry others, wherein he opposes the more common doctrine, and cites concurrent authors, both he and all his authorities are demonstrably in the wrong. For how can they be right, while reason, usage, and the prevailing opinion, are still against them ? If we have forty grammars which reject the articles as a part of speech, we have more than twice as many which recognise them as such ; among which are those of the following authors : viz., Adam, D. Adams, Ainsworth, Alden, Alger, Allen, Ash, Bacon, Barnard, Beattie, Beck, Bicknell, Bingham, Blair, Bucke, Bullions, Burn, Burr, Chandler, Churchill, Coar, Cobbett, Comly, Cooper, Davis, Dearborn, Everett, Farnum, Fisk, A Flint, Folker, Frost, R. G. Greene, Greenleaf, Guy, Hall, Hallock, Hart, Harrison, Matt. Harrison, Hazen, Hendrick, Hiley, Hull, Ingersoll, Jaudon, Johnson, Kirkham, Lennie, A. Lewis, Lowth, Maltby, Maunder, Mennye, Merchant, T. H. Miller, Murray Nixon, Nutting, Parker and Fox, John Peirce, Picket, Pond. S. Putnam, Russell, Sanborn, Sanders, R. C. Smith, Rev. T. Smith, Tower, Tucker, Walker, Webber, Wilcox, Wilson, Woodworth, J. M. Worcester, S. Worcester, Wright. The articles characterize our language more than some of the other parts of speech, and are worthy of distinction for many reasons, one of which is the very great *frequency* of their use.

jects thus arranged under one general name or idea, are in most instances susceptible of such a numerical distribution as gives rise to an other form of the noun, expressive of plurality ; as, *horse*, *horses*. Proper nouns, in their ordinary application, are, for the most part, names of particular individuals ; and as there is no plurality to a particular idea, or to an individual person or thing as distinguished from all others, so there is in general none to this class of nouns ; and no room for *further restriction by articles*. But we sometimes divert such nouns from their usual significa-tion, and consequently employ them with articles or in the plural form ; as, " I endeavoured to retain it nakedly in my mind, without regarding whether I had it from *an Aristotle* or a *Zoilus*, a *Newton* or a *Descartes*."—*Churchill's Gram.* Pref. p. 8. "It is not enough to have *Vitruviuses*, we must also have *Augustuses* to employ them."—*Bicknell's Gram.* Part ii, p. 61.
"*A Daniel* come to judgment! yea, *a Daniel!*"—SHAK. *Shylook.*
"Great Homer, in *th' Achilles*, whom he drew,
Sets not that one sole Person in our View."—*Brightland's Gram.* p. 183.

OBS. 5.—The article *an* or *a* usually denotes one out of several or many ; one of a sort of which there are more ; any one of that name, no matter which. Hence its effect upon a particular name, or proper noun, is *directly the reverse* of that which it has upon a common noun. It varies and fixes the meaning of both ; but while it restricts that of the latter, it enlarges that of the former. It reduces the general idea of the common noun to any one individual of the class : as, " *A man*; " that is, " *One man*, or *any man*." On the contrary, it extends the particular idea of the proper noun, and makes the word significant of a class, by supposing others to whom it will apply : as, " *A Nero;* " that is, " *Any Nero*, or *any cruel tyrant*." Sometimes, however, this article before a proper name, seems to leave the idea still particular ; but, if it really does so, the propriety of using it may be doubted: as, " No, not by *a John the Baptist* risen from the dead."—*Henry's Expos. Mark*, vi. "It was not solely owing to the madness and depravity of *a Tiberius*, a *Caligula*, a *Nero*, or a *Cara-calla*, that a cruel and sanguinary spirit, in their day, was so universal."—*M'Ilvaine's Evid.* p. 398.

OBS. 6.—With the definite article, the noun is applied, sometimes specifically, sometimes in-dividually, but always *definitely*, always distinctively. This article is demonstrative. It marks either the particular individual, or the particular species,—or, (if the noun be plural,) some parti-cular individuals of the species,—as being distinguished from all others. It sometimes refers to a thing as having been previously mentioned ; sometimes presumes upon the hearer's familiarity with the thing ; and sometimes indicates a limitation which is made by subsequent words connected with the noun. Such is the import of this article, that with it the singular number of the noun is often more comprehensive, and at the same time more specific, than the plural. Thus, if I say, " *The horse* is a noble animal," without otherwise intimating that I speak of some particular horse, the sentence will be understood to embrace collectively *that species* of animal ; and I shall be thought to mean, " Horses are noble animals." But if I say, " *The horses* are noble animals," I use an ex-pression so much more limited, as to include only a few ; it must mean some particular horses, which I distinguish from all the rest of the species. Such limitations should be made, whenever there is occasion for them ; but needless restrictions displease the imagination, and ought to be avoided ; because the mind naturally delights in terms as comprehensive as they may be, if also specific. Lindley Murray, though not uniform in his practice respecting this, seems to have thought it ne-cessary to use the plural in many sentences in which I should decidedly prefer the singular ; as, " That *the learners* may have no doubts."—*Murray's Octavo Gram.* i, p. 81. " The business will not be tedious to *the scholars*."—*Ib.* 81. " For the information of *the learners*."—*Ib.* 81. " It may afford instruction to *the learners*."—*Ib.* 110. " That this is the case, *the learners* will per-ceive by the following examples."—*Ib.* 326. " Some knowledge of it appears to be indispensable to *the scholars*."—*Ib.* 335.

OBS. 7.—Proper names of a plural form and signification, are almost always preceded by the de-finite article ; as, " *The Wesleys*," — " *The twelve Cæsars*,"—" *All the Howards*." So the names of particular nations, tribes, and sects ; as, *The Romans*, the *Jews*, the *Levites*, the *Stoics*. Like-wise the plural names of mountains ; as, *The Alps*, the *Apennines*, the *Pyrenees*, the *Andes*. Of plural names like these, and especially of such as designate tribes and sects, there is a very great number. Like other proper names, they must be distinguished from the ordinary words of the language, and accordingly they are always written with capitals ; but they partake so largely of the nature of common nouns, that it seems doubtful to which class they most properly belong. Hence they not only admit, but require the article ; while most other proper names are so definite in themselves, that the article, if put before them, would be needless, and therefore improper.
"*Nash, Rutledge, Jefferson*, in council great,
And *Jay*, and *Laurens* oped the rolls of fate ;
The *Livingstons*, fair freedoms generous band,
The *Lees*, the *Houstons*, fathers of the land."—*Barlow.*

OBS. 8.—In prose, the definite article is always used before names of rivers, unless the word *riv-er*, be added ; as, *The Delaware*, the *Hudson*, the *Connecticut*. But if the word *river* be added, the article becomes needless ; as, *Delaware river*, *Hudson river*, *Connecticut river*. Yet there seems to be no impropriety in using both ; as, *The Delaware river*, the *Hudson river*, the *Connecticut river*. And if the common noun be placed before the proper name, the article is again necessary ; as, *The river Delaware*, the *river Hudson*, the *river Connecticut*. In the first form of expression, however, the article has not usually been resolved by grammarians as relating to the proper name ; but these examples, and others of a similar character, have been supposed elliptical: as, " *The* [river] *Po-tomac*"—" *The* [ship] *Constitution*"—" *The* [steamboat] *Fulton*." Upon this supposition, the words in the first and fourth forms are to be parsed alike ; the article relating to the common noun, expressed or understood, and the proper noun being in apposition with the appellative. But in the second form, the apposition is reversed ; and, in the third, the proper name appears to be taken adjectively. Without the article, some names of rivers could not be understood ; as,
" No more *the Varus* and *the Atax* feel
" The lordly burden of the Latian keel."—*Rowe's Lucan*, i, p. 722.

OBS. 9.—The definite article is often used by way of eminence, to distinguish some particular individual emphatically, or to apply to him some characteristic name or quality : as, " *The Stagi-rite*"—that is, Aristotle; " *The Psalmist*"—that is, David; " *Alexander the Great*"—that is, (perhaps,) Alexander the Great *Monarch*, or Great *Hero*. So, sometimes, when the phrase relates to a collective body of men : as, "*The Honourable, the Legislature*"—"*The Honourable, the Senate*;" —that is, "The Honourable *Body*, the Legislature," &c. A similar application of the article in the following sentences, makes a most beautiful and expressive form of compliment : " These are the sacred feelings of thy heart, O Lyttleton, *the friend*."—*Thomson.* " The pride of swains Palemon was, *the generous* and *the rich.*"—*Id.* In this last example, the noun *man* is understood after "*generous*," and again after " *rich ;*" for, the article being an index to the noun, I conceive it to be improper ever to construe two articles as having reference to one unrepeated word. Dr. Priestley says, " We sometimes *repeat the article*, when the epithet precedes the substantive ; as, He was met by *the* worshipful *the* magistrates."—*Gram.* p. 148. It is true, we occasionally meet with such fulsome phraseology as this ; but the question is, how is it to be explained ? I imagine that the word *personages*, or something equivalent, must be understood after *worshipful*, and that the Doctor ought to have inserted a comma there.

OBS. 10.—In Greek, there is no article corresponding to our *an* or *a*, consequently *man* and *a man* are rendered alike ; the word, ἄνθρωπος may mean either. See, in the original, these texts : " There was *a man* sent from God," (*John*, i, 6,) and, " What is *man*, that thou art mindful of him ? "—*Heb.* ii, 6. So of other nouns. But the *definite* article of that language, which is exactly equivalent to our *the*, is a declinable word, making no small figure in grammar. It is varied by numbers, genders, and cases ; so that it assumes more than twenty different forms, and becomes susceptible of six and thirty different ways of *agreement*. But this article in English is perfectly simple, being entirely destitute of grammatical modifications, and consequently incapable of any form of grammatical agreement or disagreement—a circumstance of which many of our grammarians seem to be ignorant ; since they prescribe a rule, wherein they say, it " *agrees*," " *may agree*," or " *must agree*," with its noun. Nor has the indefinite article any variation of form, except the change from *an* to *a*, which has been made for the sake of brevity or euphony.

OBS. 11.—As *an* or *a* conveys the idea of unity, of course it applies to no other than nouns of the singular number. An *eagle* is one eagle, and the plural word *eagles* denotes more than one ; but what could possibly be meant by " *ans eagles*," if such a phrase were invented ? Harris very strangely says, " The Greeks have no article correspondent to *an* or *a*, but *supply its place by a* NEGATION *of their article*. And even in English, *where* the article *a* cannot be used, as *in* plurals, *its force is exprest by the same* NEGATION."—*Harris's Hermes*, p. 218. What a sample of grammar is this ! Besides several minor faults, we have here a *nonentity*, a NEGATION *of the Greek article*, made to occupy a place in language, and to express *force !* The force of what ? Of a plural *an* or *a !* of such a word as *ans* or *aes !* The error of the first of these sentences, Dr. Blair has copied entire into his eighth lecture.

OBS. 12.—The following rules of *agreement*, though found in many English grammars, are not only objectionable with respect to the sense intended, but so badly written as to be scarcely intelligible in any sense : 1. " The article *a* or *an agrees* with nouns *in* the singular number *only*, *individually, or collectively* : as, A Christian, an infidel, a score, a thousand." 2. " The definite article *the* may *agree* with nouns *in the singular* AND[*] *plural number* : as, The garden, the houses, the stars."—*Murray's Gram.* 8vo, p. 170 ; 12mo, 139 ; *Fisk's Murray*, 98 ; *a Teacher's*, 45. For the purpose of preventing any erroneous construction of the articles, these rules are utterly useless ; and for the purpose of syntactical parsing, or the grammatical resolution of this part of speech, they are awkward and inconvenient. The syntax of the articles may be much better expressed in this manner : " *Articles relate to the nouns which they limit ;*" for, in English, the bearing of the articles upon other words is properly that of simple *relation*, or dependence, according to the sense, and not that of *agreement*, not a similarity of distinctive modifications.

OBS. 13.—Among all the works of earlier grammarians, I have never yet found a book which taught correctly the *application* of the two forms of the indefinite article *an* or *a*. Murray, contrary to Johnson and Webster, considers *a* to be the original word, and *an* the euphonic derivative. He says : " *A* becomes *an* before a vowel, and before a silent *h*. But if the *h* be sounded, the *a* only is to be used."—*Murray's Gram.* p. 31. To this he adds, in a marginal note, " *A* instead of *an* is now used before words beginning with *u* long. It is used before *one*. *An* must be used before *words* WHERE the *h* is not silent, if the accent *is* on the second syllable ; as, *an* heroic action, *an* historical account."—*Ib.* This explanation, clumsy as it is, in the whole conception ; broken, prolix, deficient, and inaccurate as it is, both in style and doctrine ; has been copied and copied from grammar to grammar, as if no one could possibly better it. Besides several other faults, it contains a palpable misuse of the article itself : " *the h* " which is specified in the second and fifth sentences, is the " *silent h* " of the first sentence ; and this inaccurate specification gives us the two obvious solecisms of supposing, " *if the* [*silent*] *h be sounded*," and of *locating* " *words* WHERE *the* [*silent*] *h is not silent !* " In the word *humour*, and its derivatives, the *h* is silent, by all authority except Webster's ; and yet these words require *a* and not *an* before them.

OBS. 14.—It is the *sound* only, that governs the form of the article, and not the *letter* itself ; as, "Those which admit of the regular form, are marked with *an* R."—*Murray's Gram.* p. 107. " *A* heroic poem, written by Virgil."—*Webster's Dict.* " Every poem of the kind has no doubt a historical groundwork."—*Philological Museum*, i, p. 457. " *A* poet must be *a* naturalist and *a* historian."—*Coleridge's Introduction*, p. 111. Before *h* in an unaccented syllable, either form of the article may be used without offence to the ear ; and either may be made to appear preferable to the other, by merely aspirating the letter in a greater or less degree. But as the *h*, though ever so feebly aspirated has *something* of a consonant sound, I incline to think the article in this case ought to conform to the general principle : as, " *A* historical introduction has, generally, *a* happy effect to

* In Murray's Abridgement, and in his "Second Edition," 12mo, the connective in this place is " or ;" and so it is given by most of his amenders ; as in *Alger's Murray*, p. 58 ; *Alden's*, 89 ; *Bacon's*, 48 ; *Cooper's*, 111 ; *A. Fisk's*, 65 ; *Maltby's*, 60 ; *Miller's*, 67 ; *S. Putnam's*, 74 ; *Russell's*, 52 ; *T. Smith's*, 61. All these, and many more, repeat both of these rules.

rouse attention."—*Blair's Rhet.* p. 311. "He who would write heroic poems, should make his whole life *a heroic* poem." See *Life of Schiller*, p. 56. Within two lines of this quotation, the biographer speaks of "*an* heroic multitude!" The suppression of the sound of *h* being with Englishmen a very common fault in pronunciation, it is not desirable to increase the error, by using a form of the article which naturally leads to it. "How often do we hear *an air* metamorphosed into *a hair, a hat* into *a gnat*, and *a hero* into a *Nero!*"—*Churchill's Gram.* p. 205. Thus: "Neither of them had that bold and adventurous ambition which makes a conqueror *an hero.*"—*Bollingbroke, on History*, p. 174.

Obs. 15.—Some later grammarians are still more faulty than Murray, in their rules for the application of *an* or *a.* Thus Sanborn: "The vowels are *a, e, i, o,* and *u. An* should be used before words beginning *with any of these letters*, or with a silent *h.*"—*Analytical Gram.* p. 11. "*An* is used before words beginning with *u long* or with *h not silent*, when the accent is on the second syllable; as, *an united* people, *an historical* account, *an heroic* action."—*Ib.* p. 85. "*A* is used when the next word begins with a *consonant; an*, when it begins with a *vowel* or silent *h.*"—*Ib.* p. 129. If these rules were believed and followed, they would greatly multiply errors.

Obs. 16.—Whether the word *a* has been formed from *an*, or *an* from *a*, is a disputed point—or rather, a point on which our grammarians dogmatize differently. This, if it be worth the search, must be settled by consulting some genuine writings of the twelfth century. In the pure Saxon of an earlier date, the words *seldom occur;* and in that ancient dialect *an*, I believe, is used only as a declinable numerical adjective, and *a* only as a preposition. In the thirteenth century, both forms were in common use, in the sense now given them, as may be seen in the writings of Robert of Gloucester; though some writers of a much later date—or, at any rate, *one*, the celebrated Gawin Douglas, a Scottish bishop, who died of the plague in London, in 1522—constantly wrote *ane* for both *an* and *a:* as,

> "Be not ouer studyous to spy *ane* mote in myn E,
> That in gour awin *ane* ferrye bot can not se."—*Tooke's Diversions*, i, p. 124.

> "*Ane* uthir mache to him was socht and sperit;
> Bot thare was *nane* of all the rout that sterit.'—*Ib.* i, p. 160.

Obs. 17.—This, however, was a *Scotticism;* as is also the use of *æ* for *a:* Gower and Chaucer used *an* and *a* as we now use them. The Rev. J. M. M'Culloch, in an English grammar published lately in Edinburgh, says, "*A* and *an* were originally *æ* and *ane*, and were probably used at first simply to convey the idea of unity; as, *æ* man, *æ* ox."—*Manual of E. Gram.* p. 30. For this idea, and indeed for a great part of his book, he is indebted to Dr. Crombie; who says, "To signify unity, or one of a class, our forefathers employed *æ* or *ane;* as, *æ man, ane ox.*"—*Treatise on Etym. and Synt.* p. 53. These authors, like Webster, will have *a* and *an* to be *adjectives.* Dr. Johnson says, "*A*, an *article* set before nouns of the singular number; as, *a* man, *a* tree. This article has no plural signification. Before a word beginning with a vowel, it is written *an; as, an* ox, *an* egg; of which *a* is the contraction."—*Quarto Dict. w. A.*

Obs. 18.—Dr. Webster says, "*A* is also an abbreviation of the Saxon *an* or *ane, one*, used before words beginning with an articulation; as, *a* table *instead of an* table, or one table. *This is a modern change;* for, in Saxon, *an* was used before articulations as well as vowels; as, *an tid*, a time, *an gear*, a year."—*Webster's Octavo Dict.* A modern change, indeed! By his own showing in other works, it was made long before the English language existed! He says, "*An*, therefore, is the original English adjective or ordinal number *one;* and was never written *a* until after the Conquest."—*Webster's Philos. Gram.* p. 20; *Improved Gram.* 14. "*The Conquest*," means the Norman Conquest, in 1066; but English was not written till the thirteenth century. This author has long been idly contending, that *an* or *a* is not an *article*, but an *adjective;* and that it is not properly distinguished by the term "*indefinite.*" Murray has answered him well enough, but he will not be convinced.* See *Murray's Gram.* pp. 34 and 35. "If *a* and *one* were equal, we could not say, "*Such a one*"—"*What a one*"—"*Many a one*"—"*This one thing*;" and surely these are all good English, though *a* and *one* here admit no interchange.

Obs. 19.—*An* is sometimes a *conjunction*, signifying *if;* as, "Nay, *an* thou'lt mouthe, I'll rant as well as thou."—*Shak.* "*An* I have not ballads made on you all, and sung to fifty tunes, may a cup of sack be my poison."—*Id. Falstaff.* "But, *an* it were to do again, I should write again."—*Lord Byron's Letters.* "But *an* it be a long part, I can't remember it."—*Shakspeare: Burgh's Speaker*, p. 136.

Obs. 20.—In the New Testament, we meet with several such expressions as the following: "And his disciples were *an hungred*."—*Scott's Bible: Matt.* xii, 1. "When he was *an hungred.*"—*Ib.* xii, 3. "When he had need and was *an hungered.*"—*Ib. Mark*, ii, 25. Alger, the improver of Murray's Grammar, and editor of the Pronouncing Bible, taking this *an* to be the indefinite article, and perceiving that the *h* is sounded in *hungered*, changed the particle to *a* in all these passages; as, "And his disciples were *a hungered.*" But what sense he thought he had made of the sacred record, I know not. The Greek text, rendered word for word, is simply this: "*And his disciples hungered.*" And that the sentences above, taken either way, are *not good English*, must be obvious to every intelligent reader. *An*, as I apprehend, is here a mere *prefix*, which has somehow been mistaken in form, and erroneously disjoined from the following word. If so, the correction ought to be made after the fashion of the following passage from Bishop M'Ilvaine: "On a certain occasion, our Saviour was followed by five thousand men, into a desert place, where they were *enhungered.*"—*Lectures on Christianity*, p. 210.

Obs. 21.—The word *a*, when it does not denote one thing of a kind, is not an article, but a genuine *preposition;* being probably the same as the French *à*, signifying *to, at, on, in,* or *of:* as, "Who hath it? He that died *a* Wednesday."—*Shak.* That is, *on* Wednesday. So sometimes before plurals; as, "He carves *a* Sundays."—*Swift.* That is, *on* Sundays. "He is let out *a* nights."—*Id.* That is, *on* nights—like the following example: "A pack of rascals that walk the streets *on* nights."—*Id.* "He will knap the spears *a* pieces with his teeth."—*More's Antid.* That is, *in*

---

* When this was written, Dr. Webster was living.

ieces, or to pieces. So in the compound word *now-a-days*, where it means *on*; and in the proper ames, Thomas à Becket, Thomas à Kempis, Anthony à Wood, where it means *at* or *of*.

"Bot certainly the daisit blude *now on dayis*
Waxis dolf and dull throw myne unwieldy age."—*Douglas.*

OBS. 22.—As a preposition, *a* has now most generally become a *prefix*, or what the grammarians all an inseparable preposition: as in *abed*, in bed; *aboard*, on board; *abroad*, at large; *afire*, on re; *afore*, in front; *afoul*, in contact; *aloft*, on high; *aloud*, with loudness; *amain*, at main trength; *amidst*, in the midst; *akin*, of kin; *ajar*, unfastened; *ahead*, onward; *afield*, to the eld; *alee*, to the leeward; *anew*, of new, with renewal. "*A-nights*, he was in the practice of sleeping, :c.; but *a-days* he kept looking on the barren ocean, shedding tears."—*Dr. Murray's Hist. of Europ. .ang.* ii, p. 162. Compounds of this kind, in most instances, follow verbs, and are consequently ckoned adverbs; as, *To go astray—To turn aside—To soar aloft—To fall asleep.* But sometimes he antecedent term is a noun or a pronoun, and then they are as clearly adjectives; as, "Imagi- ation is like to work better upon sleeping men, than *men awake*."—*Lord Bacon.* "Man alive, id you ever make a *hornet afraid*, or catch a *weasel asleep?*" And sometimes the compound overns a noun or a pronoun after it, and then it is a preposition; as, "A bridge is laid *across* a iver."—*Webster's Dict.* "To break his bridge *athwart* the Hellespont."—*Bacon's Essays.*

"Where Ufens glides *along* the lowly lands,
Or the black water of Pomptina stands."—*Dryden.*

OBS. 23.—In several phrases, not yet to be accounted obsolete, this old preposition à still re- ains its place as a separate word; and none have been more perplexing to superficial grammar- ians, than those which are formed by using it before participles in *ing*; in which instances, the articles are in fact governed by it: for nothing is more common in our language, than for articles of this form to be governed by prepositions. For example, "You have set the cask *a* taking," and, "You have set the cask *to* leaking," are exactly equivalent, both in meaning and onstruction. "Forty and six years was this temple *in* building."—*John*, ii, 20. *Building* is not are a noun, but a participle; and *in* is here better than *a*, only because the phrase, *a building*, ight be taken for an article and a noun, meaning *an edifice.** Yet, in almost all cases, other repositions are, I think, to be preferred to à, if others equivalent to it can be found. Examples: 'Lastly, they go about to apologize for the long time their book hath been *a coming* out:" i. e. a *coming* out.—*Barclay's Works*, iii, p. 179. " And, for want of reason, he falls a *railing*:" i. e *to* ailing.—*Ib.* iii, 357. "That the soul should be this moment busy a *thinking*:" i. e. *at* or *in* hinking.—*Locke's Essay*, p. 78. "Which, once set a *going*, continue in the same steps:" i. e. *going.—Ib.* 284. "Those who contend for four per cent, have set men's mouths a *watering* or money:" i. e. *to* watering.—LOCKE: in Johnson's Dict. "Another falls a *ringing* a Pescennius tiger:" i. e. *to* ringing.—ADDISON: *ib.* "At least to set others a *thinking* upon the subject:" . e. *to* thinking.—*Johnson's Gram. Com.* p. 300. "Every one that could reach it, out off a iece, and fell a *eating*:" i. e. *to* eating.—*Newspaper.* "To go a *mothering*,† is to visit parents n Midlent Sunday."—*Webster's Dict. w. Mothering.* "Which we may find when we come a *fish- ng* here."—*Wotton.* "They go a *begging* to a bankrupt's door."—*Dryden.* "A *hunting* Chloe rent."—*Prior.* "They burst out a *laughing*."—*M. Edgeworth.* In the last six sentences, a eems more suitable than any other preposition would be: all it needs, is an accent to distinguish : from the article; as, à.

OBS. 24.—Dr. Alexander Murray says, "To be *a-seeking*, is the relic of the Saxon to be *on* or n seeking. What are you a-seeking? is *different* from, What are you seeking? It means more ally *the going on* with the process."—*Hist. Europ. Lang.* ii, p. 149. I disapprove of the hyphen n such terms as "*à seeking*," because it converts the preposition and participle into I know not

___

* In French, the preposition à, (*to*,) is always carefully distinguished from the verb a, (*has*,) by means of the rave accent, which is placed over the former for that purpose. But, in general also the Latin word *a*, (*from*,) is arked in the same way. But, with us, no appropriate sign has hitherto been adopted to distinguish the preposi- on *a* from the article *a*; though the Saxon *a*, (*to*,) is given by Johnson with an acute, even where no other *a* is und. Hence, in their ignorance, thousands of vulgar readers, and among them the authors of sundry grammars, ove constantly mistaken this preposition for an article. Examples: "Some adverbs are composed of *the article a* rained to nouns; as *a-side*, *a-thirst*, *a sleep*, *a-shore*, a-ground, &c."—*Comly's Gram.* p. 67. "Repeat some dverbs] that are composed of *the article a* and nouns."—*Kirkham's Gram.* p. 89. "To go a fishing;" "To o a hunting;" i. e. "to go on a fishing *voyage* or *business*;" "to go on a hunting *party*."—*Murray's Gram.* . 221; *Fisk's*, 147; *Ingersoll's*, 157; *Smith's*, 184; *Bullions's*, 129; *Merchant's*, 101; *Weld's*, 192, and others. That is interpretation is false and absurd, may be seen at once by any body who can read Latin; for, a *hunting*, *a* shing, &c., are expressed by the supine in *um*: as, "*Venatum ire.*"—Virg. Æn. I. e. "To go a hunting." "*Abeo* urnum."—Bezz. I. e. "I go a fishing."—*John*, xxi, 3. Every school-boy ought to know better than to call this *a* an rticle. "*A fishing* is equivalent to the infinitive *to fish*. For the Greek of the foregoing text' is 'Υπαγω αλιευειν, had is rendered by Montanus, "*Vado piscari*;" I. e. "*I go to fish*." One author ignorantly says, "The *article a* eems to have *no particular meaning*, and is *hardly proper* in such expressions as these. 'He went a-*hunting*.' he lies a-bed all day.'"—*Wilcox's Gram* p 59. No marvel, that he could not find the meaning of an *article* in his *a*.' With doltish and double inconsistency, Weld first calls this "The *article a* employed *in the sense of* a *reposition*," (*E. Gram.* p. 177,) and afterwards adopts Murray's interpretation as above cited! Some, too, have a absurd practice of joining this preposition to the partic ple; generally with the hyphen, but sometimes with- a. thus, "A-GOING, in motion; as, to set a mill agoing."—*Webster's Dict.* The doctor does not tell us what part f speech agoing is; but, certainly, "to set the mill *to* goin;," expresses just the same meaning, and is about as hen heard. In the burial-service of the Common Prayer Book, we read, "They are even as a*sleep*;" but, in the ntieth Psalm, from which this is taken, we find the text thus: "They are as a *sleep*:" that is, as a dream that i fled. Now these are very different readings, and cannot both be right.

† Here the lexicographer forgets his false etymology of *a* before the participle, and writes the words *separately*, the generality of authors always have done. *A* was used as a preposition long before the article *a* appeared in he language; and I doubt whether there is any truth at all in the common notions of its origin. Webster says, In the words *abed*, *ashore*, &c., and before *the* participles *acoming*, *agoing*, *ashooting*, [he should have said, 'and fter participles; as, a *coming*, a *going*, a *shooting*,'] a has been supposed a contraction of *on* or *at*. It may be so some cases; but with the participle, it is *sometimes* a contraction of the Saxon prefix *ge*, and *sometimes* per- aps of the Celtic *ag*."—*Improved Gram.* p. 175. See *Philos. Gram.* p. 244. What admirable learning is this! I, forsooth, is a *contraction* of *ge*! And this is the doctor's reason for *joining* it to the participle!

what; and it may be observed, in passing, that the want of it, in such as "*the going on,*" leaves us a loose and questionable word, which, by the conversion of the participle into a noun, becomes a nondescript in grammar. I dissent also from Dr. Murray, concerning the use of the preposition or prefix *a*, in examples like that which he has here chosen. After a *neuter verb*, this particle is unnecessary to the sense, and, I think, injurious to the construction. Except in poetry, which is measured by syllables, it may be omitted without any substitute; as, "I am *a* walking."—*Johnson's Dict. w. A.* "He had one only daughter, and she lay *a* dying."—*Luke,* viii, 42. "In the days of Noah, while the ark was *a* preparing."—1 *Pet.* iii, 20. "Though his unattentive thoughts be elsewhere *a* wandering."—*Locke's Essay,* p. 284. Say—"be wandering elsewhere;" and omit the *a*, in all such cases.

"And—when he thinks, good easy man, full surely
His greatness is *a* ripening—nips his root."—*Shak.*

OBS. 25.—"*A* has a peculiar signification, denoting the proportion of one thing to an other. Thus we say, The landlord hath a hundred *a* year; the ship's crew gained a thousand pounds *a* man."—*Johnson's Dict.* "After the rate of twenty leagues *a* day."—*Addison.* "And corn was at two sesterces *a* bushel."—*Duncan's Cicero,* p. 82. Whether *a* in this construction is the article or the preposition, seems to be questionable. Merchants are very much in the habit of supplying its place by the Latin preposition *per,* by; as, "Board, at $2 *per* week."—*Preston's Book-Keeping,* p. 44. "Long lawn, at $12 *per* piece."—*Dilworth's,* p. 63. "Cotton, at 2s. 6d. *per* pound."—*Morrison's,* p. 75. "Exchange, at 12d. *per* livre."—*Jackson's,* p. 73. It is to be observed that *an*, as well as *a*, is used in this manner; as, "The price is one dollar *an* ounce." Hence, I think, we may infer, that this is not the old preposition *a*, but the article *an* or *a*, used in the distributive sense of *each* or *every*, and that the noun is governed by a preposition understood: as, "He demands a dollar *an* hour:" i. e. a dollar *for each* hour.—"He comes twice *a* year:" i. e. twice *in every* year.— "He sent them to Lebanon, ten thousand *a* month by courses:" (1 *Kings,* v, 14:) i. e. ten thousand, *monthly;* or, as our merchants say, "*per month.*" Some grammarians have also remarked, that, "In mercantile accounts, we frequently see *a* put for *to*, in a very odd sort of way; as, 'Six bales marked 1 *a* 6.' The merchant means, 'marked *from* 1 *to* 6.' This is taken to be a relic of the Norman French, which was once the law and mercantile language of England; for, in French, *a*, with an accent, signifies *to* or *at*."—*Emmons's Gram.* p. 73. Modern merchants, in stead of accenting the *a*, commonly turn the end of it back; as, @.

OBS. 26.—Sometimes a numeral word with the indefinite article—as *a few, a great many, a dozen, a hundred, a thousand*—denotes an aggregate of several or many taken collectively, and yet is followed by a plural noun, denoting the sort or species of which this particular aggregate is a part: as, "A few small fishes"—"A great many mistakes"—"A dozen bottles of wine"—"A hundred lighted candles"—"A thousand miles off." Respecting the proper manner of explaining these phrases, grammarians differ in opinion. That the article relates not to the plural noun, but to the numeral word only, is very evident; but whether, in these instances, the words *few, many, dozen, hundred*, and *thousand*, are to be called nouns or adjectives, is matter of dispute. Lowth, Murray, and many others, call them *adjectives*, and suppose a peculiarity of construction in the article;—like that of the singular adjectives *every* and *one* in the phrases, "*Every* ten days" —"*One* seven times more."—*Dan.* iii, 19. Churchill and others call them *nouns*, and suppose the plurals which follow, to be always in the objective case governed by *of*, understood: as, "A few [of] years"—"A thousand [of] doors;"—like the phrases, "A *couple* of fowls"—"A *score* of fat bullocks."—*Churchill's Gram.* p. 279. Neither solution is free from difficulty. For example: "There are a great many adjectives."—*Dr. Adam.* Now, if *many* is here a singular nominative, and the only subject of the verb, what shall we do with *are?* and if it is a plural adjective, what shall we do with *a* and *great*. Taken in either of these ways, the construction is anomalous. One can hardly think the word "*adjectives*" to be here in the objective case, because the supposed ellipsis of the word *of* cannot be proved; and if *many* is a noun, the two words are perhaps in apposition, in the nominative. If I say, "*A thousand men* are on their way," the men are the *thousand*, and the thousand *is nothing but the men;* so that I see not why the relation of the terms may not be that of *apposition.* But if *authorities* are to decide the question, doubtless we must yield it to those who suppose the whole numeral phrase to be taken *adjectively;* as, "Most young Christians have, in the course of *half a dozen* years, time to read a *great many* pages."—*Young Christian,* p. 6.

"For harbour at *a thousand doors* they knock'd;
Not one of all *the thousand* but was lock'd."—*Dryden.*

OBS. 27.—The numeral words considered above, seem to have been originally adjectives, and such may be their most proper construction now; but all of them are susceptible of being construed as nouns, even if they are not such in the examples which have been cited. *Dozen,* or *hundred,* or *thousand,* when taken abstractly, is unquestionably a noun; for we often speak of *dozens, hundreds,* and *thousands. Few* and *many* never assume the plural form, because they have naturally a plural signification; and *a few* or *a great many* is not a collection so definite that we can well conceive of *fews* and *manies;* but both are sometimes construed substantively, though in modern English * it seems to be mostly by ellipsis of the noun. Example: "The praise of *the judicious few* is an ample compensation for the neglect of *the illiterate many.*"—*Churchill's Gram.* p. 278. Dr. Johnson says, the word *many* is remarkable in Saxon for its frequent use. The following are some of the examples in which he calls it a substantive, or noun: "After him the rascal *many* ran."—*Spenser.* "O thou fond *many*."—*Shakspeare.* "A care-craz'd mother of a *many* children."—*Id.* "And for thy sake have I shed *many* a tear."—*Id.* "The vulgar and the *many* are fit only to be led or driven."—*South.* "He is liable to a great *many* inconveniences every moment of his life."—*Tillotson.* "Seeing a great *many* in rich gowns, he was amazed."—*Addison.*

"There parting from the king, the chiefs divide,
And wheeling east and west, before their *many* ride."—*Dryden.*

* The following construction may be considered an *archaism*, or a form of expression that is now obsolete: "You have bestowed a many of kindnesses upon me."—*Walker's English Particles,* p. 278.

Obs. 28.—"On the principle here laid down, we may account for a peculiar use of the article with the adjective *few*, and some other diminutives. In saying, '*A few* of his adherents remained with him;' we insinuate, that they constituted a number sufficiently important to be formed into an aggregate : while, if the article be omitted, as, '*Few* of his adherents remained with him;' this implies, that he was nearly deserted, by representing them as individuals not worth reckoning up. A similar difference occurs between the phrases : 'He exhibited *a little* regard for his character;' and 'He exhibited *little* regard for his character.'"—*Churchill's Gram.* p. 279. The word *little*, in its most proper construction, is an adjective, signifying *small;* as, "He was *little* of stature."—*Luke.* "Is it not a *little* one ?"—*Genesis.* And in sentences like the following, it is also reckoned an adjective, though the article seems to relate to it, rather than to the subsequent noun ; or perhaps it may be taken as relating to them both : "Yet *a little* sleep, *a little* slumber, *a little* folding of the hands to sleep."—*Prov.* vi, 10; xxiv, 33. But, by a common ellipsis, it is used as a noun, both with and without the article; as, "*A little* that a righteous man hath, is better than the riches of many wicked."—*Psalms*, xxxvii, 16. "Better is *little* with the fear of the Lord, than great treasure and trouble therewith."—*Prov.* xv, 16. "He that despiseth little things, shall perish by *little* and *little*."—*Ecclesiasticus.* It is also used adverbially, both alone and with the article *a;* as, "The poor sleep *little*."—*Otway.* "Though they are *a little* astringent."—*Arbuthnot.* "When he had gone *a little* farther thence."—*Mark*, i, 19. "Let us vary the phrase [in] *a very little*" [degree].—*Kames*, Vol. ii, p. 163.

Obs. 29.—"As it is the nature of the articles to limit the signification of a word, they are applicable only to words expressing ideas capable of being individualized, or conceived of as single things or acts ; and nouns implying a general state, condition, or habit, must be used without the article. It is not vaguely therefore, but on fixed principles, that the article is omitted, or inserted, in such phrases as the following : 'in terror, in fear, in dread, in haste, in sickness, in pain, in trouble; in *a* fright, in *a* hurry, in *a* consumption ; *the* pain of his wound was great; her son's dissipated life was *a* great trouble to her.'"—*Churchill's Gram.* p. 127.

Obs. 30.—Though *the*, *an*, and *a*, are the only articles in our language, they are far from being the only definitives. Hence, while some have objected to the peculiar distinction bestowed upon these little words, firmly insisting on throwing them in among the common mass of adjectives ; others have taught, that the definitive adjectives—I know not how many—such as, *this, that, these, those, any, other, some, all, both, each, every, either, neither*—" are much more properly articles than any thing else."—*Hermes*, p 234. But, in spite of this opinion, it has somehow happened, that these definitive adjectives have very generally, and very absurdly, acquired the name of *pronouns.* Hence, we find Booth, who certainly excelled most other grammarians in learning and acuteness, marvelling that the *articles* "were ever separated from the class of *pronouns.*" To all this I reply, that *the*, *an*, and *a*, are worthy to be distinguished as *the only articles*, because they are not only used with much greater *frequency* than any other definitives, but are specially restricted to the limiting of the signification of nouns. Whereas the other definitives above mentioned are very often used to supply the place of their nouns ; that is, to represent them understood. For, in general, it is only by ellipsis of the noun after it, and not as the representative of a noun going before, that any one of these words assumes the appearance of a pronoun. Hence, they are not pronouns, but adjectives. Nor are they "more properly articles than any thing else;" for, "if the essence of an article be to define and ascertain" the meaning of a noun, this very conception of the thing necessarily supposes the noun to be used with it.

Obs. 31.—The following example, or explanation, may show what is meant by definitives. Let the general term be *man*, the plural of which is *men : A man*—one unknown or indefinite; *The man*—one known or particular; *The men*—some particular ones ; *Any man*—one indefinitely ; *A certain man*—one definitely ; *This man*—one near ; *That man*—one distant ; *These men*—several near; *Those men*—several distant; *Such a man*—one like some other; *Such men*—some like others ; *Many a man*—an multitude taken singly ; *Many men*—an indefinite multitude taken plurally ; *A thousand men*—a definite multitude ; *Every man*—all or each without exception ; *Each man*—both or all taken separately ; *Some man*—one, as opposed to none ; *Some men*—an indefinite number or part ; *All men*—the whole taken plurally ; *No men*—none of the sex ; *No man*—never one of the race.

EXAMPLES FOR PARSING.

PRAXIS II. — ETYMOLOGICAL.

In the Second Praxis, it is required of the pupil—to distinguish and define the different parts of speech, and to explain the ARTICLES *as definite or indefinite. The definitions to be given in the Second Praxis, are two for an article, and one for a noun, an adjective, a pronoun, a verb, a participle, an adverb, a conjunction, a preposition, or an interjection. Thus : —*

EXAMPLE PARSED.

"The task of a schoolmaster laboriously prompting and urging an indolent class, is worse than his who drives lazy horses along a sandy road."

The is the definite article 1 An article is the word *the, an,* or *a*, which we put before nouns to limit their signification. 2. The definite article is *the*, which denotes some particular thing or things.

task is a noun. 1. A noun is the name of any person, place, or thing, that can be known or mentioned.

of is a preposition. 1 A preposition is a word used to express some relation of different things or thoughts to each other, and is generally placed before a noun or a pronoun.

a is the indefinite article. 1. An article is the word *the, an,* or *a*, which we place before nouns to limit their signification. 2. The indefinite article is *an* or *a*, which denotes one thing of a kind, but not any particular one.

schoolmaster is a noun. 1. A noun is the name of any person, place, or thing, that can be known or mentioned.

15

Laboriously is an adverb. 1. An adverb is a word added to a verb, a participle, an adjective, or an other adverb ; and generally expresses time, place, degree, or manner.
Prompting is a participle. 1. A participle is a word derived from a verb, participating the properties of a verb, and of an adjective or a noun ; and is generally formed by adding *ing*, *d*, or *ed*, to the verb.
And is a conjunction. 1. A conjunction is a word used to connect words or sentences in construction, and to show the dependence of the terms so connected.
Urging is a participle. 1. A participle is a word derived from a verb, participating the properties of a verb, and of an adjective or a noun ; and is generally formed by adding *ing*, *d*, or *ed*, to the verb.
As is the indefinite article. 1. An article is the word *the*, *an*, or *a*, which we put before nouns to limit their signification. 2. The indefinite article is *an* or *a*, which denotes one thing of a kind, but not any particular one.
Indolent is an adjective. 1. An adjective is a word added to a noun or pronoun, and generally expresses quality.
Class is a noun. 1. A noun is the name of any person, place, or thing, that can be known or mentioned.
Is is a verb. 1. A verb is a word that signifies *to be*, *to act*, or *to be acted upon*.
Worse is an adjective. 1. An adjective is a word added to a noun or pronoun, and generally expresses quality.
Than is a conjunction. 1. A conjunction is a word used to connect words or sentences in construction, and to show the dependence of the terms so connected.
His is a pronoun. 1. A pronoun is a word used in stead of a noun.
Who is a pronoun. 1. A pronoun is a word used in stead of a noun.
Drives is a verb. 1. A verb is a word that signifies *to be*, *to act*, or *to be acted upon*.
Lazy is an adjective. 1. An adjective is a word added to a noun or pronoun, and generally expresses quality.
Horses is a noun. 1. A noun is the name of any person, place, or thing, that can be known or mentioned.
Along is a preposition. 1. A preposition is a word used to express some relation of different things or thoughts to each other, and is generally placed before a noun or a pronoun.
A is the indefinite article. 1. An article is the word *the*, *an*, or *a*, which we put before nouns to limit their signification. 2. The indefinite article is *an* or *a*, which denotes one thing of a kind, but not any particular one.
Sandy is an adjective. 1. An adjective is a word added to a noun or pronoun, and generally expresses quality.
Road is a noun. 1. A noun is the name of any person, place, or thing, that can be known or mentioned.

LESSON I.—PARSING.

" The Honourable, the Corporation of the city, granted the use of the common council chamber, for holding the Convention ; generously adding the privilege of occupying the rotunda, or the new court-room, if either would better suit the wishes of the committee."—*Journal of Literary Convention*, N. Y. 1830.

" When the whole is put for a part, or a part for the whole ; the genus for a species, or a species for the genus ; the singular number for the plural, or the plural for the singular ; and, in general, when any thing less, or any thing more, is put for the precise object meant ; the figure is called a Synecdoche." See *Blair's Rhet.* p. 141.

" The truth is, a representative, as an individual, is on a footing with other people ; but, as a representative of a State, he is invested with a share of the sovereign authority, and is so far a governor of the people." See *Webster's Essays*, p. 50.

" Knowledge is the fruit of mental labour—the food and the feast of the mind. In the pursuit of knowledge, the greater the excellence of the subject of inquiry, the deeper ought to be the interest, the more ardent the investigation, and the dearer to the mind the acquisition of the truth."—*Keith's Evidences*, p. 15.

" Canst thou, O partial Sleep ! give thy repose
To the wet seaboy in an hour so rude ? "—*Shakspeare.*

LESSON II.—PARSING.

" Every family has a master ; (or a mistress—I beg the ladies' pardon ;) a ship has a master ; when a house is to be built, there is a master ; when the highways are repairing, there is a master ; every little school has a master : the continent is a great school ; the boys are numerous, and full of roguish tricks ; and there is no master. The boys in this great school play truant, and there is no person to chastise them." See *Webster's Essays*, p. 128.

"A man who purposely rushes down a precipice and breaks his arm, has no right to say, that surgeons are an evil in society. A legislature may unjustly limit the surgeon's fee ; but the broken arm must be healed, and a surgeon is the only man to restore it." See *ib.* p. 135.

" But what new sympathies sprung up immediately where the gospel prevailed ! It was made the duty of the whole Christian community to provide for the stranger, the poor, the sick, the aged, the widow, and the orphan."—*M'Ilvaine's Evi.* p. 408.

" In the English language, the same word is often employed both as a noun and as a verb ; and sometimes as an adjective, and even as an adverb and a preposition also. Of this, *round* is an example." See *Churchill's Gram.* p. 24.

" The old oaken bucket, the iron-bound bucket,
The moss-covered bucket, arose from the well."— *Woodworth.*

LESSON III.—PARSING.

"Most of the objects in a natural landscape are beautiful, and some of them are grand : a flowing river, a spreading oak, a round hill, an extended plain, are delightful ; and even a rugged rock, and a barren heath, though in themselves disagreeable, contribute by contrast to the beauty of the whole." See *Kames's El. of Crit.* i, 185.

"An animal body is still more admirable, in the disposition of its several parts, and in their order and symmetry: there is not a bone, a muscle, a blood-vessel, a nerve, that hath not one corresponding to it on the opposite side ; and the same order is carried through the most minute parts." See *ib.* i, 271. "The constituent parts of a plant, the roots, the stem, the branches, the leaves, the fruit, are really different systems, united by a mutual dependence on each other."—*Ib.* i, 272.

"With respect to the form of this ornament, I observe, that a circle is a more agreeable figure than a square, a globe than a cube, and a cylinder than a parallelopip'edon. A column is a more agreeable figure than a pilaster ; and, for that reason, it ought to be preferred, all other circumstances being equal. An other reason concurs, that a column connected with a wall, which is a plain surface, makes a greater variety than a pilaster." See *ib.* ii, 352.

"But ah ! what myriads claim the bended knee !
Go, count the busy drops that swell the sea."—*Rogers.*

IMPROPRIETIES FOR CORRECTION.

ERRORS RESPECTING ARTICLES.

LESSON I.—ADAPT THE ARTICLES.

"Honour is an useful distinction in life."—*Milnes's Greek Gram.* p. vii.

[FORMULE.—Not proper, because the article *an* is used before *useful*, which begins with the sound of *yu*. But, according to a principle expressed on page 218th. "*A* is to be used whenever the following word begins with a consonant sound." Therefore, *an* should here be changed to *a* : thus, "Honour is a useful distinction in life."]

"No writer, therefore, ought to foment an humour of innovation."—*Jamieson's Rhet.* p. 55. "Conjunctions require a situation between the things of which they form an union."—*Ib.* p. 83. "Nothing is more easy than to mistake an *u* for an *a.*"—*Tooke's Diversions,* i, 130. "From making so ill an use of our innocent expressions."—*Wm. Penn.* "To grant thee an heavenly and incorruptible crown of glory."—*Sewel's Hist. Ded.* p . iv. "It in no wise follows, that such an one was able to predict."—*Ib.* p. viii. "With an harmless patience they have borne most heavy oppressions."—*Ib.* p. x. "My attendance was to make me an happier man."—*Spect.* No. 480. "On the wonderful nature of an human mind."—*Ib.* No. 554. "I have got an hussy of a maid, who is most craftily given to this."—*Ib.* No. 534. "Argus is said to have had an hundred eyes, some of which were always awake."—*Classic Stories,* p. 148. "Centiped, an hundred feet; centennial, consisting of a hundred years."—*Town's Analysis,* p. 19. "No good man, he thought, could be an heretic."—*Gilpin's Lives,* p. 72. "As, a Christian, an infidel, an heathen."—*Ash's Gram.* p. 50. "Of two or more words, usually joined by an hyphen."—*Blair's Gram.* p. 7. "We may consider the whole space of an hundred years as time present."—*Beattie: Murray's Gram.* p. 69. "In guarding against such an use of meats and drinks."—*Ash's Gram.* p. 138. "Worship is an homage due from man to his Creator."—*Annual Monitor for* 1836. "Then, an eulogium on the deceased was pronounced."—*Grimshaw's U. S.* p. 92. "But for Adam there was not found an help meet for him."—*Gen.* ii, 20. "My days are consumed like smoke, and my bones are burned as an hearth."—*Psalms,* cii, 3. "A foreigner and an hired servant shall not eat thereof."—*Exod.* xii, 45. "The hill of God is as the hill of Bashan ; an high hill, as the hill of Bashan."—*Psalms,* lxviii, 15. "But I do declare it to have been an holy offering, and such an one too as was to be once for all."—*Wm. Penn.* "An hope that does not make ashamed those that have it."—*Barclay's Works,* Vol. i, p. 75. "Where there is not an unity, we may exercise true charity."—*Ib.* i, 96. "Tell me, if in any of these such an union can be found ?"—*Brown's Estimate,* ii, 16.

"Such holy drops her tresses steeped,
Though 'twas an hero's eye that weeped."—*Sir W. Scott.*

LESSON II.—INSERT ARTICLES.

"This veil of flesh parts the visible and invisible world."—*Sherlock.*

[FORMULE —Not proper, because the article *the* is omitted before *invisible*, where the sense requires it . But, according to a suggestion on page 218th, "Articles should be inserted as often as the sense requires them." Therefore, *the* should be here supplied ; thus, "This veil of flesh parts the visible and *the* invisible world."]

"The copulative and disjunctive conjunctions operate differently on the verb."—*Mur-*

ray's Gram. ii, p. 286. "Every combination of a preposition and article with the noun."—*Ib.* i, 44. "*Either* signifies, 'the one or the other;' *neither* imports *not either*, that is, 'not one nor the other.'"—*Ib.* i, 56. "A noun of multitude may have a pronoun, or verb, agreeing with it, either of the singular or plural number."—*Bucke's Gram.* p. 90. "Copulative conjunctions are, principally, and, as, both, because, for, if, that, then, since, &c." See *ib.* 28. "The two real genders are the masculine and feminine."—*Ib.* 34. "In which a mute and liquid are represented by the same character, *th.*"—*Music of Nature*, p. 481. "They said, John Baptist hath sent us unto thee."—*Luke*, vii, 20. "They indeed remember the names of abundance of places."—*Spect.* No. 474. "Which created a great dispute between the young and old men."—*Goldsmith's Greece*, ii, p. 127. "Then shall be read the Apostles' or Nicene Creed."—*Com. Prayer*, p. 119. "The rules concerning the perfect tenses and supines of verbs are Lily's."—*King Henry's Gram.* p. iv. "It was read by the high and the low, the learned and illiterate."—*Johnson's Life of Swift.* "Most commonly, both the pronoun and verb are understood."—*Buchanan's Gram.* p. viii. "To signify the thick and slender enunciation of tone."—*Knight, on the Greek Alph.* p. 9. "The difference between a palatial and guttural aspirate is very small."—*Ib.* 12. "Leaving it to waver between the figurative and literal sense."—*Jamieson's Rhet.* p. 154. "Whatever verb will not admit of both an active and passive signification."—*Alex. Murray's Gram.* p. 31. "*The* is often set before adverbs in the comparative or superlative degree."—*Ib.* p. 15 ; *Kirkham's Gram.* 66. "Lest any should fear the effect of such a change upon the present or succeeding age of writers."—*Fowle's Common School Gram.* p. 5. "In all these measures, the accents are to be placed on even syllables ; and every line is, in general, more melodious, as this rule is more strictly observed."—*L. Murray's Octavo Gram.* p. 256 ; *Jamieson's Rhet.* 307. "How many numbers do nouns appear to have? Two, the singular and plural."—*Smith's New Gram.* p. 8. "How many persons? Three persons—the first, second, and third."—*Ib.* p. 10. "How many cases? Three—the nominative, possessive and objective."—*Ib.* p. 12.

> "Ah! what avails it me, the flocks to keep,
> Who lost my heart while I preserv'd sheep."
> POPE'S WORKS: *British Poets*, Vol. vi, p. 309 : Lond. 1800.

LESSON III.—OMIT ARTICLES.

"The negroes are all the descendants of Africans."—*Morse's Geog.*

[FORMULE.—Not proper, because the article *the* before *descendants*, is useless to the construction, and injurious to the sense. But, according to a principle on page 218th, "Needless articles should be omitted ; they seldom fail to pervert the sense." Therefore, *the* should be here omitted ; thus, "The negroes are all *descendants* of Africans."]

"A Sybarite was applied as a term of reproach to a man of dissolute manners."—*Morse's Ancient Geog.* p. 4. "The original signification of knave was a boy."—*Webster's El. Spell.* p. 136. "The meaning of these will be explained, for the greater clearness and precision." *Bucke's Gram.* p. 58. "What Sort of a Noun is Man? A Noun Substantive common."— *Buchanan's Gram.* p. 166. "Is *what* ever used as three kinds of a pronoun?"—*Kirkham's Gram.* p. 117. "They delighted in the having done it, as well as in the doing of it."— *Johnson's Gram. Com.* p. 344. "Both the parts of this rule are exemplified in the following sentences."—*Murray's Gram.* p. 174. "He has taught them to hope for another and a better world."—*S. L. Knapp.* "It was itself only preparatory to a future, a better, and perfect revelation."—*Keith's Evid.* p. 23. "*Es* then makes another and a distinct syllable."— *Brightland's Gram.* p. 17. "The eternal clamours of a selfish and a factious people."— *Brown's Estimate*, i, 74. "To those whose taste in Elocution is but a little cultivated."—*Kirkham's Eloc.* p. 65. "They considered they had but a Sort of a Gourd to rejoice in."—*Bennet's Memorial*, p. 333. "Now there was but one only such a bough, in a spacious and shady grove."—*Bacon's Wisdom*, p. 75. "Now the absurdity of this latter supposition will go a great way towards the making a man easy."—*Collier's Antoninus*, p. 131. "This is true of the mathematics, where the taste has but little to do."—*Todd's Student's Manual*, p. 331. "To stand prompter to a pausing, yet a ready comprehension."—*Rush, on the Voice*, p. 251. "Such an obedience as the yoked and the tortured negro is compelled to yield to the whip of the overseer."—*Chalmers's Serm.* p. 90. "For the gratification of a momentary and an unholy desire."—*Wayland's Mor. Sci.* p. 288. "The body is slenderly put together ; the mind a rambling sort of a thing."—*Collier's Antoninus*, p. 26. "The only nominative to the verb, is, *the officer.*"—*Murray's Gram.* ii, 22. "And though in the general it ought to be admitted, &c."—*Blair's Rhet.* p. 376. "Philosophical writing admits of a polished, a neat, and elegant style."—*Ib.* p. 367. "But notwithstanding this defect, Thomson is a strong and a beautiful describer."—*Ib.* p. 405. "So should he be sure to be ransomed, and a many poor men's lives saved."—*SHAK.: Hen.* v.

> "Who felt the wrong, or fear'd it, took the alarm,
> Appeal'd to Law, and Justice lent her arm."—*Pope*, p. 406.

LESSON IV.—CHANGE ARTICLES.

"To enable us to avoid the too frequent repetition of the same word."—*Bucke's Gr.* p. 52.

[FORMULE.—Not proper, because the article *the* is used to limit the meaning of "repetition," or "too frequent repetition," where *a* would better suit the sense. But, according to a principle on page 218th, "The articles can seldom be put one for the other, without gross impropriety ; and either is of course to be preferred to the other, as it better suits the sense." Therefore, "*the*" should be *a*, which, in this instance, ought to be placed after the adjective ; thus, "To enable us to avoid *too frequent a repetition* of the same word."]

"The former is commonly acquired in the third part of the time."—*Burn's Gram.* p. xi. "Sometimes the adjective becomes a substantive, and has another adjective joined to it : as, 'The chief good.' "—*L. Murray's Gram.* i, 169. "An articulate sound is the sound of the human voice, formed by the organs of speech."—*Ib.* i, 2 ; *Lowth's Gram.* 2 ; *T. Smith's*, 6. "Tense is the distinction of time : there are six tenses."—*Maunder's Gram.* p. 6. "In this case, the ellipsis of the last article would be improper."—*L. Murray's Gram.* i, p. 218. "Contrast has always the effect to make each of the contrasted objects appear in the stronger light."—*Ib.* i, 349 ; *Blair's Rhet.* p. 167. "These remarks may serve to show the great importance of the proper use of the article."—*Lowth's Gram.* p. 12 ; *Murray's*, i, 171. "'Archbishop Tillotson,' says an author of the History of England, 'died in this year.' "—*Blair's Rhet.* p. 107. "Pronouns are used instead of substantives, to prevent the too frequent repetition of them."—*Alex. Murray's Gram.* p. 22. "*That*, as a relative, seems to be introduced to save the too frequent repetition of *who* and *which*."—*Ib.* p. 23. "A pronoun is a word used instead of a noun to avoid the too frequent repetition of the same word."—*L. Murray's Gram.* i, p. 28. "*That* is often used as a relative, to prevent the too frequent repetition of *who* and *which*."—*Kirkham's Gram.* p. 109 ; *L. Murray's*, i, 53 ; *Ililey's*, 84. "His knees smote one against an other."—*Logan's Sermons.* "They stand now on one foot, then on another."—*Walker's Particles*, p. 259. "The Lord watch between me and thee, when we are absent one from another."—*Gen.* xxxi, 49. "Some have enumerated ten [parts of speech], making a participle a distinct part."—*L. Murray's Gram.* i, p. 29. "Nemesis rides upon an Hart, because a Hart is a most lively Creature."—*Bacon's Wisdom*, p. 50. "The transition of the voice from one vowel of the diphthong to another."—*Wilson's Essay on Gram.* p. 29. "So difficult it is to separate these two things from one another."—*Blair's Rhet.* p. 92. "Without the material breach of any rule."—*Ib.* p. 101. "The great source of a loose style, in opposition to precision, is the injudicious use of those words termed synonymous."—*Ib.* p. 97. "The great source of a loose style, in opposition to precision, is the injudicious use of the words termed *synonymous*."—*Murray's Gram.* i, p. 302. "Sometimes one article is improperly used for another."—*Sanborn's Gram.* p. 197.

"Satire of sense, alas ! can Sporus feel ?
Who breaks a butterfly upon a wheel ? "—*Pope*, p. 396.

LESSON V.—MIXED EXAMPLES.

"He hath no delight in the strength of an horse."—*Maturin's Sermons*, p. 311. "The head of it would be an universal monarch."—*Butler's Analogy*, p. 98. "Here they confound the material and formal object of faith."—*Barclay's Works*, iii, p. 57. "The Irish and Scotish Celtic are one language ; the Welsh, Cornish, and Armorican, are another."—*Dr. Murray's Hist.* ii, p. 316. "In an uniform and perspicuous manner."—*Ib.* i, 49. "Scripture, *n.* Appropriately, and by way of distinction, the books of the Old and New Testament ; the Bible."—*Webster's Dict.* "In two separate volumes, entitled the Old and the new Testaments."—*Wayland's Mor. Sci.* p. 139. "The Scriptures of the Old and New Testament contain a revelation."—*Ib.* "Q has ever an u after it ; which is not sounded in words derived from the French."—*Wilson's Essay*, p. 32. "What should we say of such an one ? That he is regenerate ? No."—*Hopkins's Prim. Ch.* p. 22. "Some grammarians subdivide vowels into the simple and the compound."—*Murray's Gram.* i, p. 8. "Emphasis has been further distinguished into the weaker and stronger emphasis."—*Ib.* i, 244. "Emphasis has also been divided into superior and the inferior emphasis."—*Ib.* i, 245. "Pronouns must agree with their antecedents, or nouns which they represent, in gender, number, and person."—*Merchant's Gram.* pp. 86, 111, and 130. "The adverb *where*, is often improperly used, for the relative pronoun and preposition."—*Ib.* 94. "The termination *ish* imports diminution, or lessening the quality."—*Ib.* 79. "In this train all their verses proceed : the one half of the line always answering to the other."—*Blair's Rhet.* p. 384. "To an height of prosperity and glory, unknown to any former age."—*Murray's Sequel*, p. 352. "*Hwile*, who, which, such as, such an one, is declined as follows."—*Gwilt's Saxon Gram.* p. 15. "When a vowel precedes *y*, an *s* only is required to form a plural."—*Bucke's Gram.* p. 40. "He is asked what sort of a word each is, whether a primitive, derivative, or compound." *British Gram.* p. vii. "It is obvious, that neither the 2d, 3d, nor 4th chapter of Matthew is the first ; consequently, there are not *four first* chapters."—*Churchill's Gram.* p. 306. "Some thought, which a writer wants art to introduce in its proper place."—*Blair's Rhet.* p. 109. "Groves and meadows are most pleasing in the spring."—*Ib.* 207. "The conflict between the carnal and spiritual mind, is often long."—*Gurney's Port. Ev.* p. 146. "A Philosophical Inquiry into the Origin of our Ideas of the Sublime and Beautiful."—*Burke's Title-page.*

"Silence, my muse ! make not these jewels cheap,
Exposing to the world too large an heap."—*Waller*, p. 113.

CHAPTER III.—NOUNS.

A Noun is the name of any person, place, or thing, that can be known or mentioned: as, *George, York, man, apple, truth.*

OBSERVATIONS.

OBS. 1.—All words and signs taken *technically*, (that is, independently of their meaning, and merely as things spoken of,) are *nouns;* or, rather, are *things* read and construed *as nouns:* as, "For this reason, I prefer *contémporary* to *cotémporary.*"—*Campbell's Rhet.* p. 175; *Murray's Gram.* i, p. 368. "I and J were formerly expressed by the same character; as were U and V."—*Allen's Gram.* p. 3. "*Us* is a personal pronoun."—*Murray.* "*Th* has two sounds."—*Id.* "The *'s* cannot be a contraction of *his*, because *'s* is put to *female* [feminine] nouns; as, *Woman's beauty, the Virgin's delicacy.*"—*Dr. Johnson's Gram.* "*Their* and *theirs* are the possessives likewise of *they*, when *they* is the plural of *it.*"—*Ib.* "Let B be a *now* or instant "—*Harris's Hermes*, p. 103. "In such case, I say that the instant B is the end of the time A B."—*Ib.* 103. "*A* is sometimes a noun; as, a great *A.*"—*Todd's Johnson.* "Formerly *sp* was cast in a piece, as *st's* are now."—*Hist. of Printing,* 1770. "I write to others than he will perhaps include in his *we.*"—*Barclay's Works,* iii, p. 455. "Here are no fewer than eight *ands* in one sentence."—*Blair's Rhet.* p. 112; *Murray's Gram.* i, p. 319. "Within this wooden *O;*" i. e. circle.—*Shak.*

OBS. 2.—In parsing, the learner must observe the sense and use of each word, and class it accordingly. Many words commonly belonging to other parts of speech are occasionally used as nouns; and, since it is the manner of its use, that determines any word to be of one part of speech rather than of an other, whatever word is used directly as a noun, must of course be parsed as such.

1. Adjectives made nouns: "The *Ancient* of days did sit."—*Bible.* "Of the *ancients.*"—*Swift.* "For such *impertinents.*"—*Steele.* "He is an *ignorant* in it."—*Id.* "In the luxuriance of an unbounded *picturesque.*"—*Jamieson.* "A source of the *sublime;*" i. e. of sublimity.—*Burke.* "The vast *immense* of space;" i. e. immensity.—*Murray.* "There is none his *like.*"—*Job,* xli. 33. "A *little* more than a *little*, is by *much* too *much.*"—*Shakspeare.* "And gladly make *much* of that entertainment."—*Sidney.* "A covetous man makes *the most* of what he has."—*L'Estrange.* "It has done *enough* for me."—*Pope.* "He had *enough* to do."—*Bacon.*

"*All* withers here; who *most* possess, are losers by their gain,
Stung by full proof, that bad at best, life's idle *all* is vain."—*Young.*
"Nor grudge I thee *the much* the Grecians give,
Nor murm'ring take *the little* I receive."—*Dryden.*

2. Pronouns made nouns: "A love of seeing the *what* and *how* of all about him."—STORY's LIFE OF FLAXMAN : *Pioneer,* i, p. 133. "The nameless HE, whose nod is Nature's birth."—*Young,* Night iv. "I was wont to load my *she* with knacks."—*Shak. Winter's Tale.* "Or any *he,* the proudest of thy sort."—*Shak.* "I am the happiest *she* in Kent."—*Steele.* "The *shes* of Italy."—*Shak.* "The *hes* in birds."—*Bacon.* "We should soon have as many *hes* and *shes* as the French."—*Cobbett's Gram.* ¶ 42. "If, for instance, we call a nation a *she,* or the sun a *he.*"—*Ib.* ¶ 198. "When I see many *its* in a page, I always tremble for the writer."—*Ib.* ¶ 196. "Let those two questionary petitioners try to do this with their *whos* and their *whiches.*"—SPECT.: *Ash's Gr.* p. 131.
"Such mortal drugs I have; but Mantua's law
Is death to any *he* that utters them."—*Shak.*

3. Verbs made nouns: "Avaunt all attitude, and *stare,* and *start* theatric."—*Cowper.* "A *maybe* of mercy is sufficient."—*Bridge.* "Which *cuts* are reckoned among the fractures."—*Wiseman.* "The officer erred in granting a *permit.*"—"Feel darts and charms, *attracts* and flames."—*Hudibras.* "You may know by the falling-off of the *come,* or sprout."—*Mortimer.* "And thou hast talk'd of *sallies* and *retires.*"—*Shak.*
"For all that else did come, were sure to fail;
Yet would he further none, but for *avail.*"—*Spenser.*

4. Participles made nouns: "For the *producing* of real happiness."—*Crabb.* "For the *crying* of the poor and the *sighing* of the needy. I will arise."—*Bible.* "Surely the *churning* of milk bringeth forth butter, and the *wringing* of the nose bringeth forth blood; so the *forcing* of wrath bringeth forth strife."—*Prov.* xxx, 33. "*Reading, writing,* and *ciphering,* are indispensable to civilized man."—"Hence was invented the distinction between *doing* and *permitting.*"—*Calvin's Inst.* p. 131. "Knowledge of the *past* comes next."—*Hermes,* p. 113. "I am my *beloved's,* and his desire is toward me "—*Sol. Song,* vii, 10. "Here's—a simple *coming-in* for one man."—*Shak.*
"What are thy rents? What are thy *comings-in?*
O Ceremony, show me but thy worth."—*Id.*

5. Adverbs made nouns: "In these cases we examine the *why,* the *what,* and the *how* of things."—*L'Estrange.* "If a point or *now* were extended, each of them would contain within itself infinite other points or *nows* "—*Hermes,* p. 102. "The *why* is plain as way to parish church."—*Shak.* "'Tis Heaven itself that points out an *hereafter.*"—*Addison.* "The dread of a *hereafter.*"—*Fuller.* "The murmur of the deep *amen.*"—*Sir W. Scott.* "For their *whereabouts* lieth in a mystery."—*Book of Thoughts,* p. 14. Better: "Their *whereabout* lieth," or, "Their *whereabouts lie,*" &c.
"Bid them farewell, Cordelia, though unkind;
Thou losest *here* a better *where* to find."—*Shak.*

6. Conjunctions made nouns: "The *if,* which is here employed, converts the sentence into a supposition."—*Blair's Rhet.* "Your *if* is the only peacemaker; much virtue is in *if.*"—*Shak.*
"So his Lordship decreed with a grave solemn tone,
Decisive and clear, without one *if* or *but*—
That whenever the Nose put his spectacles on,
By daylight or candlelight—Eyes should be shut."—*Cowper.*

7. Interjections or phrases made nouns : "Come away from all the *lo-heres!* and *lo theres!* "—
Sermon. "Will cuts him short with a '*What then?*'"—*Addison.* "With *hark* and *whoop*, and
wild *halloo*."—*Scott.* "And made a *pish* at chance and sufferance."—*Shak.*
"A single look more marks th' internal wo,
Than all the windings of the lengthen'd *oh*."—*Lloyd.*

CLASSES.

Nouns are divided into two general classes ; *proper* and *common.*

I. A *proper noun* is the name of some particular individual, or people, or
group; as, *Adam, Boston,* the *Hudson,* the *Romans,* the *Azores,* the *Alps.*

II. A *common noun* is the name of a sort, kind, or class, of beings or
things ; as, *Beast, bird, fish, insect, creatures, persons, children.*

The particular classes, *collective, abstract,* and *verbal,* are usually included among
common nouns.

1. A *collective noun,* or *noun of multitude,* is the name of many individuals together ; as, *Council, meeting, committee, flock.*

2. An *abstract noun* is the name of some particular quality considered apart from
its substance ; as, *Goodness, hardness, pride, frailty.*

3. A *verbal* or *participial noun* is the name of some action, or state of being ; and
is formed from a verb, like a participle, but employed as a noun : as, "The *triumphing* of the wicked is short."—*Job,* xx, 5.

OBSERVATIONS.

Obs. 1.—Through the influence of an article, a proper name sometimes acquires the import of
a common noun: as, "He is *the Cicero* of his age ;" that is, *the great orator.* "Many *a fiery
Alp ;*" that is, *high volcanic mountain.* "Such is the following application of famous names ;
a Solomon for a wise man, a Crœsus for a rich man, a Judas for a traitor, a Demosthenes for an
orator, and a Homer for a poet."—*Campbell's Rhet.* p. 326.
"Consideration, like an angel, came,
And whipp'd *th' offending Adam* out of him."—*Shak.*

Obs. 2.—A common noun, with the definite article before it, sometimes becomes proper : as,
The Park ; the Strand ; the Channel ; the Downs ; the United States.

Obs. 3.—The common name of a thing or quality personified, often becomes proper ; our conception of the object being changed by the figure of speech : as, "My power," said *Reason,* "is
to advise, not to compel."—*Johnson.* "Fair *Peace* her olive branch extends." For such a word,
the form of parsing should be like this : "*Peace* is a common noun, *personified proper;* of the
third person, singular number, *feminine gender,* and nominative case." Here the construction of
the word as a *proper noun,* and of the *feminine gender,* is the result of the personification, and
contrary to the literal usage.

MODIFICATIONS.

Nouns have modifications of four kinds ; namely, *Persons, Numbers,
Genders,* and *Cases.*

PERSONS.

Persons, in grammar, are modifications that distinguish the speaker, the
hearer, and the person or thing merely spoken of.

There are three persons ; the *first,* the *second,* and the *third.*

The *first person* is that which denotes the speaker or writer ; as, "*I Paul*
have written it."

The *second person* is that which denotes the hearer, or the person addressed ;
as, "*Robert,* who did this ?"

The *third person* is that which denotes the person or thing merely spoken
of ; as, "*James* loves his *book.*"

OBSERVATIONS.

Obs. 1 —The distinction of persons is founded on the different relations which the objects
mentioned in any discourse may bear to the discourse itself. The speaker or writer, being the
mover and maker of the communication, of course stands in the nearest or *first* of these relations.
The hearer or hearers, being personally present and directly addressed, evidently sustain the
next or *second* of these relations ; this relation is also that of the reader, when he peruses what is
addressed to himself in print or writing. Lastly, whatsoever or whosoever is merely menti ned in
the discourse, bears to it that more remote relation which constitutes the *third* person. The dis-

tinction of persons belongs to nouns, pronouns, and finite verbs; and to these it is always applied, either by peculiarity of form or construction, or by inference from the principles of concord. Pronouns are like their antecedents, and verbs are like their subjects, in person.

OBS. 2.—Of the persons, numbers, genders, cases, and some other grammatical modifications of words, it should be observed that they belong not exclusively to any one part of speech, but jointly and equally, to two or three. Hence, it is necessary that our *definitions* of these things be such as will apply to each of them in full, or under all circumstances; for the definitions ought to be as general in their application as are the things or properties defined. Any person, number, gender, case, or other grammatical modification, is really but one and the same thing, in whatever part of speech it may be found. This is plainly implied in the very nature of every form of syntactical agreement; and as plainly contradicted in one half, and probably more, of the definitions usually given of these things.

OBS. 3.—Let it be understood, that *persons, in grammar,* are not *words,* but mere forms, relations, or modifications of words; that they are things, thus named by a *figure; things* of the neuter gender, and not living souls. But persons, in common parlance, or in ordinary life, are *intelligent beings,* of one or the other sex. These objects, different as they are in their nature, are continually confounded by the makers of English grammars: as, "The *first* person is *the person who speaks.*" —*Comly's Gram* p. 17. So Bicknell, of London: "The *first* person speaks *of himself;* as, *I John take thee Elizabeth.* The *second* person has the speech directed *to him,* and is supposed to be present; as, *Thou Harry art a wicked fellow.* The *third* person is spoken of, or described, and supposed to be *absent;* as, *That Thomas is a good man.* And in the same manner the plural pronouns are used, when more than one are spoken of."—*Bicknell's Grammatical Wreath,* p. 50. "The person speaking is the first person; the person spoken to, the second; and the person spoken of, the third."—*Russell's Gram.* p. 16. "The first person is the speaker."—*Parker & Fox's Gram.* Part i, p. 6. "Person is that, which distinguishes a noun, *that speaks, one spoken to, or one spoken about.*"—*S. R. Hall's Gram.* p. 6. "A noun that speaks!" A noun "spoken to!" If ever one of Father Hall's nouns shall speak for itself, or answer when "spoken to," will it not reprove him? And how can the *first person* be "*the person* WHO *speaks,*" when every word of this phrase is of the *third* person? Most certainly, it *is not* HE, nor any one of his sort. If any body can boast of being "*the first person in grammar,*" I pray, *Who* is it? Is it not *I,* even *I?* Many grammarians say so. But nay: such authors know not what the first person in grammar is. The Rev. Charles Adams, with infinite absurdity, makes the three persons in grammar to be never any thing but *three nouns,* which hold a confabulation, thus: "Person is defined to be *that* which distinguishes a noun *that speaks, one spoken to, or one spoken of.* The *noun* that speaks [,] is the first person; as, *I, James,* was present. The *noun* that is spoken to, is the second person; as, *James,* were you present? The *noun* that is spoken of, is the third person; as, *James was* present."—*Adams's System of English Gram* p. 9. What can be a greater blunder, than to call the first person of a verb, of a pronoun, or even of a noun, "*the noun that speaks?*" What can be more absurd than are the following assertions? "*Nouns* are in the first person when *speaking.* Nouns are *of* the second person when *addressed or spoken to.*"—*O. C. Felton's Gram.* p. 9.

OBS. 4.—An other error, scarcely less gross than that which has just been noticed, is the very common one of identifying the three grammatical persons with certain *words,* called personal pronouns: as, "*I* is the first person, *thou* the second, *he, she* or *it,* the third."—*Smith's Productive Gram.* p. 53. "*I* is the first person, singular. *Thou* is the second person, singular. *He, she,* or *it,* is the third person, singular. *We* is the first person, plural. *Ye* or *you* is the second person, plural. *They* is the third person, plural."—*L. Murray's Gram.* p. 51; *Ingersoll's,* 54; *D. Adams's,* 37; *A. Flint's,* 18; *Kirkham's,* 98; *Cooper's,* 34; *T. H. Miller's,* 26; *Hull's,* 21; *Frost's,* 13; *Wilcox's,* 18; *Bacon's,* 19; *Alger's,* 22; *Maltby's,* 19; *Perley's,* 15; *S Putnam's,* 22. Now there is no more propriety in affirming, that "*I is the first person,*" than in declaring that *me, we, us, am, ourselves, we think, I write,* or any other word or phrase *of* the first person, *is* the first person. Yet Murray has given us no other definitions or explanations of the persons than the foregoing erroneous assertions; and, if I mistake not, all the rest who are here named, have been content to define them only as he did. Some others, however, have done still worse: as, "There are *three* personal pronouns; so called, because they denote the three persons, *who* are the subjects of *a* discourse, viz. 1st. *I, who* is the person *speaking;* 2d *thou, who is* spoken to; 3d *he she,* or *it, who* is spoken of, and their plurals, *we, ye* or *you, they.*"—*Bingham's Accidence,* 20th Ed., p. 7. Here the two kinds of error which I have just pointed out, are jumbled together. It is impossible to write *worse English* than this! Nor is the following much better: "Of the personal pronouns there are five, viz. *I.* in the first person, speaking: *Thou,* in the second person, spoken to; and *He, she. it,* in the third person, spoken of."—*Nutting's Gram.* p. 25.

OBS. 5.—In *written* language, the *first person* denotes the writer or author; and the *second,* the reader or person addressed: except when the writer describes not himself, but some one else, as uttering to an other the words which he records. This exception takes place more particularly in the writing of dialogues and dramas; in which the first and second persons are abundantly used, not as the representatives of the author and his reader, but as denoting the fictitious speakers and hearers that figure in each scene. But, in discourse, the grammatical persons may be changed without a change of the living subject. In the following sentence, the three grammatical persons are all of them used with reference to one and the same individual: "Say ye of *Him whom* the Father hath sanctified and sent into the world, *Thou blasphemest,* because *I said I am* the *Son* of God?"—*John,* x, 36.

OBS. 6.—The speaker seldom refers to himself *by name,* as the speaker; and, of the objects which there is occasion to name in discourse, but comparatively few are such as can ever be supposed to speak. Consequently, *nouns* are rarely used in the first person; and when they do assume this relation, a pronoun is commonly associated with them: as, "*I John*"—"*We Britons.*" These words I conceive to agree throughout, in person, number, gender, and case; though it must be confessed, that agreement like this is not always required between words in apposition. But some grammarians deny the first person to nouns altogether; others, with much more consistency, ascribe it ; * while very many are entirely silent on the subject. Yet it is plain that both the doctrine of concords, and the analogy of general grammar, require its admission. The reason of this may be seen in the following examples : " *Themistocles ad te veni.*" " I Themistocles have come to you."—*Grant's Lat. Gram.* p. 72. " *Adsum Troius Æneas.*"—Virgil. " *Romulus Rex regia arma offero.*"—Livy. " *Annibal peto pacem* "—Id. " *Callopius recensui.*" ' See *Terence's Comedies, at the end.* " *Paul,* an apostle, &c., unto Timothy, *my* own son in the faith."—1 Tim i, 1. Again, if the word *God* is of the second person, in the text, " Thou, *God,* seest me," why should any one deny that *Paul* is of the first person, in this one ? " *I Paul* have written it."—*Philemon,* 19. Or this ? " The salutation by the hand of *me Paul.*"—*Col* iv, 18. And so of the plural : "Of *you builders.*"—*Acts,* iv. 11. "Of *us the apostles.*"—*Pet.* iii, 2. How can it be pretended, that, in the phrase, " *I Paul,*" *I* is of the first person, as denoting the speaker, and *Paul,* of some other person, as denoting something or somebody that is *not* the speaker ? Let the admirers of Murray, Kirkham, Ingersoll, R. C. Smith, Comly; Greenleaf, Parkhurst, or of any others who teach this absurdity, answer.

OBS. 7.—As, in the direct application of what are called Christian names, there is a kind of familiarity, which on many occasions would seem to indicate a lack of proper respect ; so in a frequent and familiar use of the second person, as it is the placing of an other in the more intimate relation of the hearer, and one's self in that of the speaker, there is a sort of assumption which may seem less modest and respectful than to use the third person. In the following example, the patriarch Jacob uses both forms ; applying the term *servant* to himself, and to his brother Esau the term *lord* : " Let *my lord, I* pray *thee,* pass over before *his servant :* and *I* will lead on softly."—*Gen.* xxxiii, 14. For when a speaker or a writer does not choose to declare himself in the *first* person. or to address his hearer or reader in the *second,* he speaks of both or either in the *third.* Thus Moses relates what *Moses* did, and Cæsar records the achievements of *Cæsar.* So Judah humbly beseeches Joseph : " Let *thy servant* abide in stead of the lad a bondman to *my lord.*"—*Gen.* xliv, 33. And Abraham reverently intercedes with God : " Oh ! let not *the Lord* be angry, and I will speak."—*Gen.* xviii, 30. And the Psalmist prays : "*God* be merciful unto us, and bless us ; and cause *his* face to shine upon us."—*Ps.* lxvii, 1. So, on more common occasions : —

" As will the rest, so *willeth Winchester.*"—*Shak.*
" *Richard* of York, how *fares* our dearest *brother ?* "—*Id.*

OBS. 8.—When inanimate things are spoken to, they are *personified ;* and their names are put in the second person, because by the figure the objects are *supposed* to be capable of hearing : as, " What ailed thee, O *thou sea,* that thou fleddest ? *thou Jordan,* that thou wast driven back ? *Ye mountains,* that ye skipped like rams ; and *ye little hills;* like lambs ? Tremble, *thou earth,* at the presence of the Lord, at the presence of the God of Jacob."—*Psalms,* cxiv, 5–7.

NUMBERS.

Numbers, in grammar, are modifications that distinguish unity and plurality. There are two numbers ; the *singular* and the *plural.*

The *singular number* is that which denotes but one ; as, " The *boy learns.*"

The *plural number* is that which denotes more than one ; as, " The *boys learn.*"

The plural number *of nouns* is regularly formed by adding *s* or *es* to the singular : as, *book, books ; box, boxes ; sofa, sofas ; hero, heroes.*

When the singular ends in a sound which will unite with that of *s,* the plural is generally formed by adding *s only,* and the number of syllables is not increased : as, *pen, pens ; grape, grapes.*

But when the sound of *s* cannot be united with that of the primitive word, the regular plural adds *s* to final *e,* and *es* to other terminations, and forms a separate syllable : as, *page, pages ; fox, foxes.*

OBSERVATIONS.

OBS. 1.—The distinction of numbers serves merely to show whether we speak of one object, or of more. In some languages, as the Greek and the Arabic, there is a *dual* number, which denotes *two,* or a *pair ;* but in ours, this property of words, or class of modifications, extends no farther than to distinguish unity from plurality, and plurality from unity. It belongs to nouns, pronouns, and finite verbs ; and to these it is always applied, either by peculiarity of form, or by inference

* * If *I* or *we* is not before a name, it [the name] is of the first person : as, *I, N— N—, declare ; we, N— and M— do promise.*"—*Ward's Gram.* p. 88. "Nouns which relate to the person or persons *speaking,* are said to be of the *first* person : as, I, William, speak to you."—*Fowle's Common School Gram.* Part ii, p 22. The first person of nouns is admitted by Amsworth, Barnard, Brightland, Bullions, Butler, Cardell, Chandler, S. W. Clark, Cooper, Day, Emmons, Farnum. Felton, Fisk, John Flint, Fowle, Frazee, Gilbert, Goldsbury, R. G. Greene, Hall, Hallock, Hamlin, Hart, Hendrick, Hiley, Perley, Picket, Russell, Sanborn, Sanders, Smart, R C. Smith, Spear, Weld, Wells, Wilcox, and others. It is denied, either expressly or virtually, by Alger, Bacon. Comly, Davis, Dilworth, Greenleaf, Guy, Hazen, Ingersoll, Jaudon, Kirkham, L. Murray, Maltby, Merchant, Miller, Nutting, Parkhurst, & Putnam, Rev T. Smith, and others. Among the grammarians who do not appear to have noticed the persons of nouns at all, are Alden, Allen, Ash, Bicknell, Bingham, Blair, Buchanan, Bucke, Burn, Burr, Churchill, Coar, Cobb, Dalton, Dearborn, Abel Flint, B. W. Green, Harrison, Johnson, Lennie, Lowth, Mennye, Priestley, Standford, Ware, Webber, and Webster

from the principles of concord. Pronouns are like their antecedents, and verbs are like their subjects, in number.

OBS. 2.—The most common way of forming the plural of English nouns, is that of simply adding to them an *s*; which, when it unites with a sharp consonant, is always sharp, or hissing; and when it follows a vowel or a flat mute, is generally flat, like *z*: thus, in the words, *ships, skiffs, pits, rocks, depths, lakes, gulfs*, it is sharp; but in *seas, bays, rivers, hills, ponds, paths, rows, webs, flags*, it is flat. The terminations which always make the regular plural in *es*, with increase of syllables, are twelve; namely, *ce, ge, ch* soft, *che* soft, *sh, ss, s, se, x, xe, z,* and *ze*: as in *face, faces; age, ages; torch, torches; niche, niches; dish, dishes; kiss, kisses; rebus, rebuses; lens, lenses; chaise, chaises; corpse, corpses; nurse, nurses; box, boxes; axe, axes; phiz, phizzes; maze, mazes*. All other endings readily unite in sound either with the sharp or with the flat *s*, as they themselves are sharp or flat; and, to avoid an increase of syllables, we allow the final *e* mute to remain mute after that letter is added: thus, we always pronounce as monosyllables the words *babes, blades, strifes, tithes, yokes, scales, names, canes, ropes, shores, plates, doves,* and the like.

OBS. 3.—Though the irregular plurals of our language appear considerably numerous when brought together, they are in fact very few in comparison with the many thousands that are perfectly simple and regular. In some instances, however, usage is various in writing, though uniform in speech; an unsettlement peculiar to certain words that terminate in vowels: as, *Rabbis*, or *rabbies; octavos*, or *octavoes; attornies*, or *attorneys*. There are also some other difficulties respecting the plurals of nouns, and especially respecting those of foreign words; of compound terms; of names and titles; and of words redundant or deficient in regard to the numbers. What is most worthy of notice, respecting all these puzzling points of English grammar, is briefly contained in the following observations.

OBS. 4.—It is a general rule of English grammar, that all singular nouns ending with a vowel preceded by an other vowel, shall form the plural by simply assuming an *s*: as, *Plea, pleas; idea, ideas; hernia, hernias; bee, bees; lie, lies; foe, foes; shoe, shoes; cue, cues; eye, eyes; folio, folios; bamboo, bamboos; cuckoo, cuckoos; embryo, embryos; bureau, bureaus; purlieu, purlieus; sou, sous; view, views; straw, straws; play, plays; key, keys; medley, medleys; viceroy, viceroys; guy, guys*. To this rule, the plurals of words ending in *quy*, as *alloquies, colloquies, soliloquies,* are commonly made exceptions; because many have conceived that the *u*, in such instances, is a mere appendage to the *q*, or a consonant having the power of *w*, and not a vowel forming a diphthong with the *y*. All other deviations from the rule, as *monies* for *moneys, allies* for *alleys, vallies* for *valleys, chimnies* for *chimneys,* &c., are now usually condemned as errors. See Rule 12th for Spelling.

OBS. 5.—It is also a general principle, that nouns ending in *y* preceded by a consonant, change the *y* into *i*, and add *es* for the plural, without increase of syllables: as, *fly, flies; ally, allies; city, cities; colony, colonies*. So nouns in *i*, (so far as we have any that are susceptible of a change of number,) form the plural regularly by assuming *es*: as, *alkali, alkalies; salmagundi, salmagundies*. Common nouns ending in *y* preceded by a consonant, are numerous; and none of them deviate from the foregoing rule of forming the plural: thus, *duty, duties*. The termination added is *es*, and the *y* is changed into *i*, according to the general principle expressed in Rule 11th for Spelling. But, to this principle, or rule, some writers have supposed that *proper nouns* were to be accounted exceptions. And accordingly we sometimes find such names made plural by the mere addition of an *s*; as, "How come the *Pythagoras'*, [it should be, *the Pythagorases*,] the *Aristotles*, the *Tullys*, the *Livys*, to appear, even to us at this distance, as stars of the first magnitude in the vast fields of ether?"—*Burgh's Dignity*, Vol. i, p. 131. This doctrine, adopted from some of our older grammars, I was myself, at one period, inclined to countenance; (see *Institutes of English Gram*. p. 33, at the bottom;) but further observation having led me to suspect, there is more authority for changing the *y* than for retaining it, I shall by-and-by exhibit some examples of this change, and leave the reader to take his choice of the two forms, or principles.

OBS. 6.—The vowel *a*, at the end of a word, (except in the questionable term *huzza*, or when silent, as in *guinea*,) has always its Italian or middle sound, as heard in the interjection *aha!* a sound which readily unites with that of *s* flat, and which ought, in deliberate speech, to be carefully preserved in plurals from this ending: as, *Canada, the Canadas; cupola, cupolas; comma, commas; anathema, anathemas*. To pronounce the final *a* flat, as *Africay* for *Africa*, is a mark of vulgar ignorance.

OBS. 7.—The vowel *e* at the end of a word, is generally silent; and, even when otherwise, it remains single in plurals from this ending; the *es*, whenever the *e* is vocal, being sounded *eez*, or like the word *ease*: as, *apostrophe, apostrophes; epitome, epitomes; simile, similes*. This class of words being anomalous in respect to pronunciation, some authors have attempted to reform them, by changing the *e* to *y* in the singular, and writing *ies* for the plural: as, *apostrophy, apostrophies; epitomy, epitomies; simily, similies*. A reformation of some sort seems desirable here, and this has the advantage of being first proposed; but it is not extensively adopted, and perhaps never will be; for the vowel sound in question, is not exactly that of the terminations *y* and *ies*, but one which seems to require *ee*—a stronger sound than that of *y*, though similar to it.

OBS. 8.—For nouns ending in *o* preceded by a consonant, the regular method of forming the plural seems to be that of adding *es*; as in *bilboes, umboes, buboes, calicoes, moriscoes, gambadoes, barricadoes, fumadoes, carbonadoes, tornadoes, bravadoes, torpedoes, innuendoes, viragoes, mangoes, embargoes, cargoes, potargoes echoes, buffaloes, volcanoes, heroes, negroes, potatoes, manifestoes, mullatoes, stilettoes, woes*. In words of this class, the *e* appears to be useful as a means of preserving the right sound of the *o*; consequently, such of them as are the most frequently used, have become the most firmly fixed in this orthography. In practice, however, we find many similar nouns very frequently, if not uniformly, written with *s* only; as, *cantos, juntos, grottos, solos, quartos, octavos, duodecimos, tyros*. So that even the best scholars seem to have frequently doubted which termination they ought to regard as the *regular* one. The whole class includes more than one hundred words. Some, however, are seldom used in the plural; and others, never. *Wo* and *potato* are sometimes written *woe* and *potatoe*. This may have sprung from a notion, that has have the *e* in the plural, should have it also in the singular. But this principle has never carried out; and, being repugnant to derivation, it probably never will be. The only English appellatives that are established in *oe*, are the following fourteen : seven monosyllables, *doe, roe, shoe, sloe, sse, toe;* and seven longer words, *rockdoe, aloe, felloe, canoe, misletoe, tiptoe, .* The last is pronounced *dip'-lo-e* by Worcester; but Webster, Bolles, and some others, it as a word of two syllables only.

¶. 9—Established exceptions ought to be enumerated and treated as exceptions; but it is unwise to remember how to write some scores of words, so nearly alike as *fumadoes* and *gres-s, stilettos* and *palmettos,* if they are allowed to differ in termination, as these examples do in Johnson's Dictionary. Nay, for lack of a rule to guide his pen, even Johnson himself could not number the orthography of the common word *mangoes* well enough to *copy* it twice without inconsistency. This may be seen by his example from King, under the words *mango* and *potargo.* ¶, therefore, either termination is preferable to the uncertainty which must attend a division of class of words between the two; and since *es* has some claim to the preference, as being letter index to the sound; I shall make no exceptions to the principle, that common nouns ing *m o* preceded by a consonant take *es* for the plural. Murray says, " *Nouns which* end in *o e* sometimes *es* added, to form the plural; as, cargo, echo, hero, negro, manifesto, potato, and, wo: and sometimes only *s*; as, folio, nuncio, punctilio, seraglio."—*Octavo Gram.* p. 40. s amounts to nothing, unless it is to be inferred from his *examples,* that others like them in t are to take *s* or *es* accordingly; and this is what I teach, though it cannot be said that Murray maintains the principle.

¶¶. 10.—Proper names of *individuals,* strictly used as such, have no plural. But when several persons of the same name are spoken of, the noun becomes in some degree common, and admits of the plural form and an article; as, " *The Stuarts, the Cæsars.*"—*Allen's Gram.* p. 41. So also when such nouns are used to denote character; as, " *Solomons,* for wise men; *Neros,* for its. '—*Ib.* " Here we see it becomes a doubt which of the two *Herculeses,* was the monster-ler."—*Notes to Pope's Dunciad,* iv, 492. The proper names of *nations, tribes,* and *societies,* generally plural; and, except in a direct address, they are usually construed with the definite the ; as, " *The Greeks, the Athenians, the Jews, the Jesuits.*" But such words may take the singular form with the indefinite article, as often as we have occasion to speak of an individual of its people; as, " *A Greek, an Athenian, a Jew, a Jesuit.*"

¶¶. 11.—Proper names, when they form the plural, for the most part form it regularly, by assuming *s* or *es* according to the termination; as, *Carolina,* the *Carolinas; James,* the *Jameses.* Those which are only or chiefly plural, have, or ought to have, such terminations as are proper to distinguish them as plurals, so that the form for the singular may be inferred; as, " The *Tunguses* occupy nearly a third of Siberia."—*Balbi's Geog.* p. 379. Here the singular must certainly *Tungoose.* " The principal tribes are the *Pawnees,* the *Arrapahoes,* and the *Cumanches,* who a through the regions of the Platte, the Arkansaw, and the Norte."—*Ib.* p. 179. Here the plural may be supposed to be *a Pawnee, an Arrapaho,* and a *Cumanche.* " The Southern or Indian family comprised the *Cherokees, Creeks, Chickasaws, Choctaws, Seminoles,* and *Natchez.*" *Ib* p. 179. Here all are regular plurals, except the last; and this probably ought to be *Natchezes,* Jefferson spells it *Natchez,* the singular of which I do not know. Sometimes foreign words or their terminations have been improperly preferred to our own; which last are more intelligible, and therefore better; as, *Esquimaux,* to *Esquimaus; Knistenaux,* to *Knistenaus,* or *Crees; Sioux,* lows, or *Dakotahs; Iroquois,* to *Iroquoys,* or *Hurons.*

¶¶. 12.—Respecting the plurals of nouns ending in *i, o, u,* or *y,* preceded by a consonant, there present usage much uncertainty. As any vowel sound may be uttered with an *s,* many writers suppose these letters to require for plurals strictly regular, the *s* only; and to take *es* occasionally, way of exception. Others, (perhaps with more reason,) assume, that the most usual, regular, proper endings for the plural, in these instances, are *ies, oes,* and *ues*; as, *alkali, alkalies*; *, haloes; gnu, gnues; enemy, enemies.* This, I think, is right for common nouns. How far proper names are to be made exceptions, because they are proper names, is an other question. It certain that some of them are not to be excepted; as, for instance, *Alleghany,* the *Alleghanies*; *ly,* the Two *Sicilies; Ptolemy,* the *Ptolemies; Jehu,* the *Jehues.* So the names of tribes; as, *Missouries,* the *Otoes,* the *Winnebagoes.* Likewise, the *houries* and the *harpies;* which words, such not strictly proper names, are often written with a capital as such. Like these are *rabbies,* *es, mufties, sophies,* from which some writers omit the *e.* Johnson, Walker, and others, write *p* and *gypsies.* Webster, now writes *Gipsey* and *Gipseys;* Worcester prefers *Gypsy,* and probably *Gypsies:* Webster once wrote the plural *gypsies;* (see his *Essays,* p. 333;) and Johnson cites following line : —

" I, near yon stile, three sallow *gypsies* met."—*Gay.*

¶¶. 13—Proper names in *o* are commonly made plural by *s* only. Yet there seems to be the best reason for inserting the *e* in these, as in other nouns of the same ending; namely, to prevent *o o* from acquiring a short sound. " I apprehend," says Churchill, " it has been from an erroneous notion of proper names being unchangeable, that some, feeling the necessity of obviating this mispronunciation, have put an apostrophe between the *o* and the *s* in the plural, *in stead of an s*; *as Cato's, Nero's;* and on a similar principle, *Ajax's, Venus's;* thus using the possessive case regular for the nominative or objective plural. Harris says very properly, ' We have our *Marks* and our *Antonies:*' *Hermes,* B. 2, Ch. 4; for which these would have given us *Mark's* and *Antony's.*" *New Gram.* p. 206. Whatever may have been the motive for it, such a use of the apostrophe a gross impropriety. " In this quotation, [' From the Socrates's, the Plato's, and the Confucius's the age,'] the proper names should have been pluralized like common nouns; thus, From the *Socrateses,* the *Platoes,* and the *Confuciuses* of the age."—*Lennie's Gram.* p. 126; *Bullions's,* 142.

¶¶. 14.—The following are some examples of the plurals of proper names, which I submit to the judgment of the reader, in connexion with the foregoing observations: " The Romans had their plurals *Marci* and *Antonii,* as we in later days have our *Marks* and our *Anthonies.*"—*Harris's Hermes,* p. 40. " There seems to be more reason for such plurals, as the *Ptolemies, Scipios, Catos;*

or, to instance in more modern names, the *Howards, Pelhams,* and *Montagues*."—*Ib.* 40. " Near the family seat of the *Montgomeries* of Coil's-field."—*Burns's Poems,* Note, p. 7. " Tryphon, a surname of one of the *Ptolemies*."—*Lempriere's Dict.* " Sixteen of the *Tuberos,* with their wives and children, lived in a small house."—*Ib.* " What are the *Jupiters* and *Junos* of the heathens to such a God ?"—*Burgh's Dignity,* i, 234. " Also when we speak of more than one person of the same name ; as, the *Henries,* the *Edwards*."—*Cobbett's Gram.* ¶ 40. " She was descended from the *Percies* and the *Stanleys*."—*Lives of the Poets,* ii, 102. " Naples, or the *Two Sicilies*."—*Balbi's Geog.* p. 273. The word *India,* commonly makes the plural *Indies,* not *Indias ;* and, for *Ajaxes,* the poets write *Ajaces.* But Richard Hiley says, " Proper nouns, when pluralized, follow the same rules as common nouns ; as, Venus, the *Venuses ;* Ajax, the *Ajaxes ;* Cato, the *Catoes ;* Henry, the *Henries*."—*Hiley's E. Gram.* p. 18.

> " He ev'ry day from King to King can walk,
>   Of all our *Harries,* all our Edwards talk."—*Pope's Satires,* iv.

Obs. 15.—When a name and a title are to be used together in a plural sense, many persons are puzzled to determine whether the name, or the title, or both, should be in the plural form. For example—in speaking of two young ladies whose family name is Bell—whether to call them the *Miss Bells,* the *Misses Bell,* or the *Misses Bells.* To an inquiry on this point, a learned editor, who prefers the last, lately gave his answer thus : " There are two young ladies ; of course they are ' the *Misses.*' Their name is Bell ; of course there are two ' Bells.' Ergo, the correct phrase, in speaking of them, is—' the Misses Bells.' "—*N. Y. Com. Adv.* This puts the words in apposition ; and there is no question, that it is *formally* correct But still it is less agreeable to the ear, less frequently heard, and less approved by grammarians, than the first phrase ; which, if we may be allowed to assume that the two words may be taken together as a sort of compound, is correct also. Dr. Priestley says, " When a name has a title prefixed to it, as *Doctor, Miss, Master,* &c., the plural termination affects only the latter of the two words ; as, 'The two *Doctor Nettletons* '—' The two *Miss Thomsons ;*' though a strict analogy would plead for the alteration of the former word, and lead us to say, ' The two *Doctors Nettleton* '—' The two *Misses Thomson.* '"—*Priestley's Gram.* p. 59. The following quotations show the opinions of some other grammarians : " Two or more nouns in concordance, and forming one complex name, or a name and a title, have the plural termination annexed to the last only ; as, ' The *Miss Smiths* '—' The three *Doctor Simpsons* '—' The two *Master Wigginses.*' With a few exceptions, and those not parallel to the examples just given, we almost uniformly, in complex names, confine the inflection to the last or the latter noun."—*Dr. Crombie.* The foregoing opinion from Crombie, is quoted and seconded by Maunder, who adds the following examples : " Thus, Dr. Watts : ' May there not be *Sir Isaac Newtons* in every science ?'—' You must not suppose that the world is made up of *Lady Aurora Granvilles.* '"—*Maunder's Gram.* p. 2.

Obs. 16.—These writers do not seem to accord with W. L. Stone, the editor above quoted, nor would his reasoning apply well to several of their examples. Yet both opinions are right, if neither be carried too far. For when the words are in apposition, rather than in composition, the first name or title must be made plural, if it refer to more than one : as, " The *Misses Bell and Brown*" —" *Messrs. Lambert and Son*"—" The *Lords Calthorpe and Erskine*"—" The *Lords Bishops* of Durham and St David's"—" The *Knights Hospitalers* "—" The *Knights Templar.*"—" The *Knights Baronets.*" But this does not prove the other construction, which varies the last word only, to be irregular ; and, if it did, there is abundant authority for it. Nor is that which varies the first only, to be altogether condemned, though Dr. Priestley is unquestionably wrong respecting the " *strict analogy* " of which he speaks. The joining of a plural title to one singular noun, as, " *Misses Roy*"—" *The Misses Bell*"—" *The two Misses Thomson,*" produces a phrase which is in itself the *least analogous* of the three ; but " *The Misses Jane and Eliza Bell,*" is a phrase which nobody perhaps will undertake to amend. It appears, then, that each of these forms of expression may be right in some cases ; and each of them may be wrong, if improperly substituted for either of the others.

Obs. 17.—The following statements, though erroneous in several particulars, will show the opinions of some other grammarians, upon the foregoing point : " Proper nouns have the plural only when they refer to a race or family ; as, *The Campbells ;* or to several persons of the same name ; as, *The eight Henrys ; the two Mr. Bells ; the two Miss Browns ;* or, without the numeral, *the Miss Roys.* But in addressing letters in which both or all are equally concerned, and also when the names are different, we pluralize the *title,* (Mr. or Miss,) and write, *Misses* Brown ; *Misses* Roy ; *Messrs* (for Messieurs, Fr.) Guthrie and Tait."—*Lennie's Gram.* p. 7. " If we wish to distinguish the *unmarried* from the *married* Howards. If we wish to distinguish these Misses from other Misses, we call them the *Misses Howard.*"—*Fowle's Gram.* " To distinguish several persons of the same name and family from others of a different name and family, the *title,* and not the *proper name,* is varied to express the distinction ; as, the *Misses Story,* the *Messrs.* Story. The elliptical meaning is, the Misses and Messrs. *who are named* Story. To distinguish *unmarried* from *married* ladies, the *proper name,* and not the *title,* should be varied ; as, the *Miss Clarks.* When we mention more than one person of different names, the title should be expressed before each ; as, *Miss* Burns, *Miss* Parker, and *Miss* Hopkinson, were present."—*Sanborn's Gram.* p. 79. In the following examples from Pope's Works, the last word only is varied : " He paragons himself to two *Lord Chancellors* for law."—Vol. iii, p. 61. " Yearly panegyrics upon the *Lord Mayors.*"—*Ib.* p. 83.

> " Whence hapless Monsieur much complains at Paris
>   Of wrongs from Duchesses and *Lady Maries.*"—*Dunciad,* B. ii, l. 135.

Obs. 18.—The following eleven nouns in *f,* change the *f* into *v* and assume *es* for the plural : *sheaf, sheaves ; leaf, leaves ; loaf, loaves ; beef, beeves ; thief, thieves ; calf, calves ; half, halves ; elf, elves ; shelf, shelves ; self, selves ; wolf, wolves.* Three others in *fe* are similar : *life, lives ; knife, knives ; wife, wives.* These are specific exceptions to the general rule for plurals, and not a series of examples coming under a particular rule ; for, contrary to the instructions of nearly all our grammarians, there are more than twice as many words of the same endings, which take *s* only : as, *chiefs, kerchiefs, handkerchiefs, mischiefs, beliefs, misbeliefs, reliefs, bas-reliefs, briefs, waifs, griefs, clefs, semibrefs, oafs, waifs, coifs, gulfs, hoofs, roofs, proofs, reproofs, woofs, califs, turfs, scarfs, dwarfs, wharfs, fifes, strifes, safes.* The plural of *wharf* is sometimes written *wharves ;* but perhaps as frequently, and, if so, more accurately, *wharfs.* Examples and authorities : " *Wharf, wharfs.*"—*Brightland's Gram.* p. 80 ; *Wards,* 24 ; *Coar's,* 26 ; *Lennie's,* 7 ; *Bucke's,* 19. " There were not in London so many *wharfs,* or *keys,* for the landing of merchants' goods."—CHILD : *in Johnson's Dict.* "The *wharfs* of Boston are also worthy of notice."—*Balbi's Geog.* p. 37. "Between banks thickly clad with dwelling-houses, manufactories, and *wharfs.*"—*London Morn. Chronicle,* 1833. Nouns in *ff* take *s* only ; as, *skiffs, stuffs, gaffs.* But the plural of *staff* has hitherto been generally written *staves ;* a puzzling and useless anomaly, both in form and sound : for all the compounds of *staff* are regular ; as, *distaffs, whipstaffs, tipstaffs, flagstaffs, quarterstaffs :* and *staves* is the regular plural of *stave,* a word now in very common use with a different meaning, as every cooper and every musician knows. *Staffs* is now sometimes used ; as, " I saw the husbandmen bending over their *staffs.*"—*Lord Carnarvon.* "With their *staffs* in their hands for very age "—*Hope of Israel,* p. 16. "To distinguish between the two *staffs.*"—*Comstock's Elocution,* p. 43. In one instance, I observe, a very excellent scholar has written *selfs* for *selves,* but the latter is the established plural of *self :*

"Self-love would cease, or be dilated, when
We should behold as many *selfs* as men."—*Waller's Poems,* p. 55.

OBS. 19.—Of nouns purely English, the following thirteen are the only simple words that form distinct plurals not ending in *s* or *es,* and four of these are often regular : *man, men ; woman, women ; child, children ; brother, brethren* or *brothers ; ox, oxen ; goose, geese ; foot, feet ; tooth, teeth ; louse, lice ; mouse, mice ; die, dice* or *dies ; penny, pence* or *pennies ; pea, pease* or *peas.* The word *brethren* is now applied only to fellow-members of the same church or fraternity ; for sons of the same parents, we always use *brothers ;* and this form is sometimes employed in the other sense. *Dice* are spotted cubes for gaming ; *dies* are stamps for coining money, or for impressing metals. *Pence,* as *six pence,* refers to the amount of money in value ; *pennies* denotes the coins themselves. "We write *peas,* for two or more individual seeds ; but *pease,* for an indefinite number in quantity or bulk."—*Webster's Dict.* This last anomaly, I think, might well enough be spared ; the sound of the word being the same, and the distinction to the eye not always regarded. Why is it not as proper, to write an order for " a bushel of *peas,*" as for " a bushel of *beans ?* " "*Peas* and *beans* may be severed from the ground before they be quite dry."—*Cobbett's E. Gram.* ¶ 31.

OBS. 20.—When a compound, ending with any of the foregoing irregular words, is made plural, it follows the fashion of the word with which it ends : as, *Gentleman, gentlemen ; bondwoman, bondwomen; foster-child, foster-children; solan-goose, solan-geese; eyetooth, eyeteeth; woodlouse, woodlice ;* [*] *dormouse, dormice ; half-penny, half-pence, half-pennies.* In this way, these irregularities extend to many words ; though some of the metaphorical class, as *kite's-foot, colt's-foot, bear's-foot, lion's-foot,* being names of plants, have no plural. The word *man,* which is used the most frequently in this way, makes more than seventy such compounds. But there are some words of this ending, which, not being compounds of *man,* are regular : as, *German, Germans ; Turcoman, Turcomans ; Mussulman, Mussulmans ; talisman, talismans ; leman, lemans ; caiman, caimans.*

OBS. 21.—Compounds, in general, admit but one variation to form the plural, and that must be made in the principal word, rather than in the adjunct ; but where the terms differ little in importance, the genius of the language obviously inclines to a variation of the last only. Thus we write *fathers-in-law, sons-in-law, knights-errant, courts-martial, cousins-german, hangers-on, comings-in, goings-out, goings-forth,* varying the first ; and *manhaters, manstealers, manslayers, maneaters, mandrills, handfuls, spoonfuls, mouthfuls, pailfuls, outpourings, ingatherings, downsittings, overflowings,* varying the last. So, in many instances, when there is a less intimate connexion of the parts, and the words are written with a hyphen, if not separately, we choose to vary the latter or last : as, *fellow-servants, queen-consorts, three-per-cents, he-goats, she-bears, jack-a-d indies, jack-a-lanterns, piano-fortes.* The following mode of writing is irregular in two respects ; first, because the words are separated, and secondly, because both are varied : " Is it unreasonable to say with John Wesley, that ' *men buyers* are exactly on a level with *men stealers ?*'"—GOODELL'S LECT. II : *Liberator,* ix, 65. According to analogy, it ought to be : " *Manbuyers* are exactly on a level with *manstealers.*" J. W. Wright alleges, that, "The phrase, ' I want two *spoonfuls* or *handfuls,*' though common, is improperly constructed ;" and that, " we should say, ' Two *spoons* or *hands* full.' "—*Philos. Gram.* p. 222. From this opinion, I dissent : both authority and analogy favour the former mode of expressing the plural of such quantities.

OBS. 22.—There is neither difficulty nor uncertainty respecting the proper forms for the plurals of compound nouns in general ; but the two irregular words *man* and *woman* are often varied at the *beginning* of the looser kind of compounds, contrary to what appears to be the general analogy of similar words. Of the propriety of this, the reader may judge, when I shall have quoted a few examples : " Besides their *man-servants* and their *maid-servants.*"—*Nehemiah,* vii, 67. " And I have *oxen* and asses, flocks, and *men-servants,* and *women-servants.*"—*Gen.* xxxii, 5. " I gat me *men-singers,* and *women-singers,* and the delights of the sons of men."—*Ecclesiastes,* ii, 8. " And she brought forth a *man-child,* who was to rule all nations with a rod of iron."—*Rev.* xii, 5. " Why have ye done this, and saved the *men-children* alive ? "—*Exod.* i, 18. Such terms as these, if thought objectionable, may easily be avoided, by substituting for the former part of the compound the separate adjective *male* or *female ;* as, *male child, male children.* Or, for those of the third example, one might say, " *singing men* and *singing women,*" as in *Nehemiah,* vii, 67 ; for, in the ancient languages, the words are the same. Alger compounds " *singing-men* and *singing-women.*"

OBS. 23.—Some foreign compound terms, consisting of what are usually, in the language from which they come, distinct words and different parts of speech, are made plural in English, by the addition of *s* or *es* at the end. But, in all such cases, I think the hyphen should be inserted in the

---

[*] There are some singular compounds of the plural word *pence* which form their own plurals regularly ; as, *sixpence, sixpences.* " If you do not all show like gilt *twopences* to me."—SHAKSPEARE. " The *sorry stakes* of which are to be composed of the disputed difference in the value of two doubtful *sixpences.*"—GOODELL'S LECT.: *Liberator,* ix, 145.

compound, though it is the practice of many to omit it. Of this odd sort of words, I quote the following examples from Churchill; taking the liberty to insert the hyphen, which he omits: "*Ave-Maries, Te-Deums, camera-obscuras, agnus-castuses, habeas-corpuses, scire-faciases, hiccius-doccius-es, hocus-pocuses, ignis-fatuuses, chef-d'-œuvres, congé-d'-élires, flower-de-luces, louis-d'-ores, tête-à-têtes.*"—*Churchill's Gram.* p. 62.

OBS. 24.—Some nouns, from the nature of the things meant, have no plural. For, as there ought to be no word, or inflection of a word, for which we cannot conceive an appropriate meaning or use, it follows that whatever is of such a species that it cannot be taken in any plural sense, must naturally be named by a word which is singular only: as, *perry, cider, coffee, flax, hemp, fennel, tallow, pitch, gold, sloth, pride, meekness, eloquence.* But there are some things, which have in fact neither a comprehensible unity, nor any distinguishable plurality, and which may therefore be spoken of in either number; for the distinction of unity and plurality is, in such instances, merely verbal; and, whichever number we take, the word will be apt to want the other: as, *dregs,* or *sediment; riches,* or *wealth; pains,* or *toil; ethics,* or *moral philosophy; politics,* or *the science of government; belles-lettres,* or *polite literature.* So *darkness,* which in English appears to have no plural, is expressed in Latin by *tenebræ,* in French by *ténèbres,* which have no singular. It is necessary that every noun should be understood to be of one number or the other; for, in connecting it with a verb, or in supplying its place by a pronoun, we must assume it to be either singular or plural. And it is desirable that singulars and plurals should always abide by their appropriate forms, so that they may be thereby distinguished with readiness. But custom, which regulates this, as every thing else of the like nature, does not always adjust it well; or, at least, not always upon principles uniform in themselves and obvious to every intellect.

OBS. 25.—Nouns of multitude, when taken collectively, generally admit the regular plural form; which of course is understood with reference to the individuality of the whole collection, considered as one thing: but, when taken distributively, they have a plural signification without the form; and, in this case, their plurality refers to the individuals that compose the assemblage. Thus, a *council,* a *committee,* a *jury,* a *meeting,* a *society,* a *flock,* or a *herd,* is singular; and the regular plurals are *councils, committees, juries, meetings, societies, flocks, herds.* But these, and many similar words, may be taken plurally without the *s,* because a collective noun is the name of many individuals together. Hence we may say, "The *council were* unanimous."—"The *committee are* in consultation."—"The *jury were* unable to agree."—"The *meeting have shown their* discretion."—"The *society have settled their* dispute."—"The *flock are* widely scattered."—"The whole *herd were drowned* in the sea." The propriety of the last example seems questionable; because *whole* implies unity, and *were drowned* is plural. Where a purer concord can be effected, it may be well to avoid such a construction, though examples like it are not uncommon: as, "Clodius was acquitted by *a corrupt jury,* that had palpably taken shares of money before *they gave their* verdict."—*Bacon.* "And the *whole multitude* of the people *were praying* without, at the time of incense."—*Luke,* i, 10.

OBS. 26.—Nouns have, in some instances, a unity or plurality of meaning, which seems to be directly at variance with their form. Thus, *cattle,* for beasts of pasture, and *pulse,* for peas and beans, though in appearance singulars are generally, if not always, plural; and *summons, gallows, chintz, series, superficies, molasses, suds, hunks, jakes, trapes,* and *corps,* with the appearance of plurals, are generally, if not always, singular. Dr. Webster says that *cattle* is of both numbers; but wherein the oneness of cattle can consist, I know not. The Bible says, "God made—*cattle after their kind.*"—*Gen.* i, 25. Here *kind* is indeed singular, as if *cattle* were a natural genus of which one must be *a cattle;* as *sheep* are a natural genus of which one is *a sheep:* but whether properly expressed so or not, is questionable; perhaps it ought to be, "and cattle after their *kinds.*" Dr. Gillies says, in his History of Greece, "*Cattle was regarded* as the most convenient *measure* of value." This seems to me to be more inaccurate and unintelligible, than to say, "*Sheep was regarded* as the most convenient *measure* of value." And what would this mean? *Sheep* is not singular, unless limited to that number by some definitive word; and *cattle* I conceive to be incapable of any such limitation.

OBS. 27.—Of the last class of words above cited, some may assume an additional *es,* when taken plurally; as, *summonses, gallowses, chintses:* the rest either want the plural, or have it seldom and without change of form. *Corps,* a body of troops, is a French word, which, when singular, is pronounced *core,* and when plural, *cores.* But *corpse,* a dead body, is an English word, pronounced *korps,* and making the plural in two syllables, *corpses.* *Summonses* is given in Cobb's Dictionary as the plural of *summons;* but some authors have used the latter with a plural verb: as, "But Love's first *summons* seldom *are* obey'd."—*Waller's Poems,* p. 8. Dr. Johnson says this noun is from the verb *to summon;* and, if this is its origin, the singular ought to be *a summon,* and then *summons* would be a regular plural. But this "singular noun with a plural termination," as Webster describes it, more probably originated from the Latin verb *submoneas,* used in the writ, and came to us through the jargon of law, in which we sometimes hear men talk of "*summonsing* witnesses." The authorities for it, however, are good enough; as, "*This* present *summons.*"—SHAK.; *Joh. Dict.* "*This summons* he resolved to disobey."—FELL: *ib.* Chintz is called by Cobb a "substantive *plural,*" and defined as "cotton *cloths,* made in India;" but other lexicographers define it as singular, and Worcester (perhaps more properly) writes it *chintz.* Johnson cites Pope as speaking of "*a charming chintz,*" and I have somewhere seen the plural formed by adding *es.* "Of the Construction of single Words, or *Serieses* of Words."—*Ward's Gram.* p. 114. Walker, in his Elements of Elocution, makes frequent use of the word "*serieses,*" and of the phrase "*series of serieses.*" But most writers, I suppose, would doubt the propriety of this practice; because, in Latin, all nouns of the fifth declension, such as *caries, congeries, series, species, superficies,* make their nominative and vocative cases alike in both numbers. This, however, is no rule for writing English. Dr. Blair has used the word *species* in a plural sense; though I think he ought rather to have preferred the regular English word *kinds:* "The higher *species* of poetry seldom *admit* it."—*Rhet.* p. 403. *Specie,* meaning hard money, though derived or corrupted from *species,* is not the singular of that word; nor has it any occasion for a plural form, because we never speak of *a specie.* The plural of *gallows*, according to Dr. Webster, is *gallowses*; nor is that form without other authority, though some say, *gallows* is of both numbers and not to be varied: "*Gallowses* were occasionally put in order by the side of my windows."—*Leigh Hunt's Byron*, p. 369.

"Who would not guess there might be hopes,
　The fear of *gallowses* and ropes,
　Before their eyes, might reconcile
　Their animosities a while?"—*Hudibras*, p. 90.

OBS. 28.—Though the plural number is generally derived from the singular, and of course must as generally imply its existence, we have examples, and those not a few, in which the case is otherwise. Some nouns, because they signify such things as nature or art has made plural or double; some, because they have been formed from other parts of speech by means of the plural ending which belongs to nouns; and some, because they are compounds in which a plural word is principal, and put last, are commonly used in the plural number only, and have, in strict propriety, no singular. Though these three classes of plurals may not be perfectly separable, I shall endeavour to exhibit them in the order of this explanation.

1. Plurals in meaning and form: *analects, annals,*[*] *archives, ashes, assets, billiards, bowels, breeches, calends, cates, chops, clothes, compasses, crants, eaves, embers, estovers, forceps, giblets, goggles, greaves, hards* or *hurds, hemorrhoids, ides, matins, nippers, nones, obsequies, orgies,*[†] *piles, pincers* or *pinchers, pliers, reins, scissors, shears, skittles, snuffers, spectacles, teens, tongs, trowsers, tweezers, umbles, vespers, victuals.*

2. Plurals by formation, derived chiefly from adjectives: *acoustics, aeronautics, analytics, bitters, catoptrics, commons, conics, credentials, delicates, dioptrics, economics, ethics, extraordinaries, filings, fives, freshes, glanders, gnomonics, goods, hermeneutics, hustings, hydrodynamics, hydrostatics, hydraulics, hysterics, inwards, leavings, magnetics, mathematics, measles, mechanics, mnemonics, merils, metaphysics, middlings, movables, mumps, nuptials, optics, phonics, physics,*[‡] *pneumatics, poetics, politics, riches, rickets, settings, shambles, shatters, skimmings, spherics, staggers, statics, statistics, stays, strangles, sundries, sweepings, tactics, thanks, tidings, trappings, vives, vitals, wages,*[§] *withers, yellows.*

3. Plurals by composition: *backstairs, cocklestairs, firearms,*[‖] *headquarters, hotcockles, spatterdashes, self-affairs.* To these may be added the Latin words, *aborigines, antipodes, antes, antaci, amphiscii, anthropophagi, antiscii, ascii, literati, fauces, regalia,* and *credenda*, with the Italian *vermicelli,* and the French *belles-lettres* and *entremets.*

OBS. 29.—There are several nouns which are set down by some writers as wanting the singular, and by others as having it. Of this class are the following: *amends,*[¶] *ancients, avons, bots, catacombs, chives, cloves, cresses, dogsears, downs, dregs,*[**] *entrails, fetters, fireworks, greens, gyves, hatches, intestines, lees,*[††] *lungs, malanders, mallows, moderns, oats, orts, pleiads, premises, relics, remains, shackles, stilts, stairs, tares, vetches.* The fact is, that these words have, or ought to have, the singular, as often as there is any occasion to use it; and the same may, in general terms, be said of other nouns, respecting the formation of *the plural.*[‡‡] For where the idea of unity or plurality comes clearly before the mind, we are very apt to shape the word accordingly, without thinking much about the authorities we can quote for it.

OBS. 30.—In general, where both numbers exist in common use, there is some palpable oneness or individuality, to which the article *a* or *an* is applicable; the nature of the species is found entire in every individual of it; and a multiplication of the individuals gives rise to plurality in the name. But the nature of a mass, or of an indefinite multitude taken collectively, is not found in individuals as such; nor is the name, whether singular, as *gold*, or plural, as *ashes*, so understood. Hence, though every noun must be of one number or the other, there are many which have little or no need of both. Thus we commonly speak of *wheat, barley,* or *oats,* collectively; and very seldom find occasion for any other forms of these words. But chafferers at the corn-

[*] In the third canto of Lord Byron's Prophecy of Dante, this noun is used in the singular number:—
　"And ocean written o'er would not afford
　　　　Space for the *annal*, yet it shall go forth."

[†] "They never yet had separated for their daylight beds, without a climax to their *orgy*, something like the present scene."—*The Crock of Gold*, p. 13. "And straps never called upon to diminish that long whity-brown interval between shoe and *trowser*."—*Ib.* p. 24.

[‡] The noun *physic* properly signifies medicine, or the science of medicine; in which sense, it seems to have no plural. But Crombie and others cite one or two instances in which *physic* and *metaphysic* are used in the sense of the singular of *physics* and *metaphysics.* Several grammarians also quote some examples in which *physica, metaphysica, politics, optics,* and other similar names of sciences are used with verbs or pronouns of the singular number; but Dr. Crombie says, the plural construction of such words, "is more common, and more agreeable to analogy."—*On Etym. and Syntax,* p. 27.

[§] "Benjamin Franklin, following the occupation of a compositor in a printing-office, at a limited weekly *wage*," &c.—*Chambers' Edinburgh Journal*, No. 232.

[‖] Our lexicographers generally treat the word *firearms* as a close compound that has no singular. But some write it with a hyphen, as *fire-arms.* In fact the singular is sometimes used, but the way of writing it is unsettled. Dr. Johnson, in his Dictionary, defines a *carbine* as "a small sort of *fire arm*;" Webster has it, "a short gun, or *fire arm*;" Worcester, "a small *fire-arm*;" Cobb, "a sort of small *firearms.*" Webster uses "*fire-arm*," in defining "*stock.*"

[¶] "he, soon afterwards, he made a glorious *amend* for his fault, at the battle of Platæa."—*Hist. Reader*, p. 48.

[**] "There not a *dreg* of guilt defiles."—*Watts's Lyrics*, p. 27.

[††] In Young's Night Thoughts, (N. vii, l. 475,) *lee*, the singular of *lees*, is found; Webster and Bolles have also both forms in their dictionaries:—
　"Refine, exalt, throw down their poisonous *lee*,
　　And make them sparkle in the bowl of bliss."—*Young.*

[‡‡] J. W. Wright remarks, "Some nouns admit of no plural distinctions: as, *wine, wood, beer, sugar, tea, timber, fruit, meat, goodness, happiness,* and perhaps all nouns ending in *ness.*"—*Philos. Gram.* p. 189. If this learned author had been brought up in the *woods*, and had never read of Murray's "richer *wines*," or heard of Johnson's "dainty *meats*,"—never chaffered in the market about *sugars* and *teas*, or read in Isaiah that "all our *righteousnesses* are as filthy rags," or avowed, like Timothy, "a good profession before many *witnesses*,"—he might still have hewed the *timbers* of some rude cabin, and partaken of the wild *fruits* which nature affords. If these nine plurals are right, his assertion is nine times wrong, or misapplied by himself seven times in the ten.

market, in spite of Cobbett,[*] will talk about *wheats* and *barleys*, meaning different kinds[†] or qualities; and a gardener, if he pleases, will tell of an *oat*, (as does Milton, in his Lycidas,) meaning a single seed or plant. But, because *wheat* or *barley* generally means that sort of grain in mass, if he will mention a single kernel, he must call it a *grain of wheat* or a *barleycorn.* And these he may readily make plural, to specify any particular number; as, *five grains of wheat*, or *three barleycorns.*

Obs. 31.—My chief concern is with general principles, but the illustration of these requires many particular examples—even far more than I have room to quote. The word *amends* is represented by Murray and others, as being singular as well as plural; but Webster's late dictionaries exhibit *amend* as singular, and *amends* as plural, with definitions that needlessly differ, though not much. I judge "*an amends*" to be bad English; and prefer the regular singular, *an amend.* The word is of French origin, and is sometimes written in English with a needless final *e*; as, "But only to make a kind of honourable *amende* to God."—*Rollin's Ancient Hist.* Vol. ii, p. 24. The word *remains* Dr. Webster puts down as plural only, and yet uses it himself in the singular: "The creation of a Dictator, even for a few months, would have buried every *remain* of freedom." —*Webster's Essays*, p. 70. There are also other authorities for this usage, and also for some other nouns that are commonly thought to have no singular; as, "But Duelling is unlawful and murderous, a *remain* of the ancient Gothic barbarity."—*Brown's Divinity*, p. 26. "I grieve with the old, for so many additional inconveniencies, more than their small *remain* of life seemed destined to undergo."—Pope: *in Joh. Dict.* "A disjunctive syllogism is one whose major *premiss* is disjunctive."—*Hedge's Logic.* "Where should he have this gold? It is some poor fragment, some slender *ort* of his remainder."—Shak.: *Timon of Athens.*

Obs. 32.—There are several nouns which are usually alike in both numbers. Thus, *deer, folk, fry, gentry, grouse, hose, neat, sheep, swine, vermin,* and *rest,* (i. e. *the rest*, the others, the residue,) are regular singulars, but they are used also as plurals, and that more frequently. Again, *alms, aloes, bellows, means, news, odds, shambles,* and *species,* are proper plurals, but most of them are oftener construed as singulars. *Folk* and *fry* are collective nouns. *Folk* means *people*; a *folk, a people*: as, "The ants are *a people* not strong;"—"The conies are but *a feeble folk.*"—*Prov.* xxx, 25, 26. "He laid his hands on a few sick *folk*, and healed *them.*"—*Mark*, vi, 5. *Folks,* which ought to be the plural of *folk,* and equivalent to *peoples,* is now used with reference to a plurality of individuals, and the collective word seems liable to be entirely superseded by it. A *fry* is a swarm of young fishes, or of any other little creatures living in water: so called, perhaps, because their motions often make the surface *fry.* Several such swarms might properly be called *fries*; but this form can never be applied to the individuals, without interfering with the other. "So numerous *was the fry.*"—*Cowper.* "The *fry betake themselves* to the neighbouring pools." —*Quarterly Review.* "You cannot think more contemptuously of *these gentry* than *they* were thought of by the true prophets."—*Watson's Apology*, p. 93. "*Grouse,* a heathcock."—*Johnson.*
"The 'squires in scorn will fly the house
   For better game, and look for *grouse.*"—*Swift.*
"Here's an English tailor, come hither for stealing out of *a French hose.*"—*Shak.* "He, being in love, could not see to garter his *hose.*"—*Id.* Formerly, the plural was *hosen*: "Then these men were bound, in their coats, their *hosen,* and their hats."—*Dan.* iii, 21.
"Who both by his calf and his lamb will be known,
 ·   May well kill a *neat* and a *sheep* of his own."—*Tusser.*
"His droves of asses, camels, herds of *neat,*
   And flocks of *sheep,* grew shortly twice as great."—*Sandys.*
"As a jewel of gold in *a swine's* snout."—*Prov.* xi, 22. "A herd of *many swine,* feeding."— *Matt.* viii, 30. "An idle person only lives to spend his time, and eat the fruits of the earth, like a *vermin* or a wolf."—*Taylor.* "The head of a wolf, dried and hanged up, will scare away *vermin.*" *Bacon.* "Cheslip, a *small vermin* that lies under stones or tiles."—Skinner: *in Joh. and in Web. Dict.* "This is flour, the *rest is* bran."—"And the *rest were* blinded."—*Rom.* xi. 7. "The poor beggar hath a just demand of *an alms.*"—*Swift.* "Thine *alms are* come up for a memorial before God."—*Acts,* x, 4. "The draught of air performed the function of *a bellows.*"—*Robertson's Amer.* ii, 223. "As the *bellows do.*"—*Bicknell's Gram.* ii, 11. "The *bellows are* burned."—*Jer.* vi, 29. "Let a *gallows* be made."—*Esther,* v. 14 "*Millows are* very useful in medicine."— *Wood's Dict.* "*News,*" says Johnson, "is without the singular, unless it be considered as singular."—*Dict.* "So *is good news* from a fair country."—*Prov.* xxv, 25. "Evil *news rides* fast, while good *news baits.*"—*Milton.* "When Rhea heard *these news,* she fled "—*Raleigh.* "*News were brought* to the queen."—*Hume's Hist.* iv, 426. "The *news* I bring *are* afflicting, but the consolation with which *they are* attended, ought to moderate your grief."—*Gil Blas,* ii, p. 20. "Between these two cases there *are* great *odds.*"—*Hooker.* "Where the *odds is* considerable." *Campbell.* "Determining on which side the *odds lie.*"—*Locke.* "The greater *are the odds* that he mistakes his author."—*Johnson's Gram. Com.* p. 1. "Though thus *an odds* unequally they meet."—*Rowe's Lucan,* B. iv, l. 789. "Preeminent by *so much odds.*"—*Milton.* "To make a *shambles* of the parliament house."—*Shak.* "The earth has been, from the beginning, a great Aceldama, a *shambles* of blood."—*Christian's Vade-Mecum,* p. 6. "*A shambles*" sounds so inconsistent, I should rather say, "*A shamble.*" Johnson says, the etymology of the word is *uncertain*; Webster refers it to the Saxon *scamel*: it means *a butcher's stall,* a *meat market*; and there would seem to be no good reason for the *s,* unless more than one such place is intended. "Who sells his subjects to the *shambles* of a foreign power."—*Pitt.* "A special idea is called by the schools *a species.*"—*Watts.* "He intendeth the care of *species,* or common natures."—*Brown.*

---

[*] "I will not suppose it possible for my dear James to fall into either the company or the language of those persons who talk, and even write, about *barleys, wheats, clovers, flours, grasses,* and *malts.*"—*Cobbett's E. Gram.* p. 29.

[†] "It is a general rule, that all names of things measured or weighed, have no plural; for in them not number, but quality, is regarded: as, *wool, wine, oil.* When we speak, however, of different kinds, we use the plural: as, the coarser *wools,* the richer *wines,* the finer *oils.*"—*Murray's Gram.* p. 41.

"ALOE, (al'o) n.; plu. ALOES."—*Webster's Dict.* and *Worcester's.* "But it was *aloe* itself to lose the reward."—*Tupper's Crock of Gold*, p. 16.
"But high in amphitheatre above,
His arms the everlasting *aloes* threw."—*Campbell, G. of W.*, ii, 10.

OBS. 33.—There are some nouns, which, though really regular in respect to possessing the two forms for the two numbers, are not free from irregularity in the manner of their application. Thus *means* is the regular plural of *mean*; and, when the word is put for mediocrity, middle point, place, or degree, it takes both forms, each in its proper sense; but when it signifies things instrumental, or that which is used to effect an object, most writers use *means* for the singular as well as for the plural : as, "By *this means*,"—"By *that means*," with reference to one mediating cause; and, "By *these means*,"—"By *those means*," with reference to more than one. Dr. Johnson says the use of *means* for *mean* is not very grammatical; and, among his examples for the true use of the word, he has the following: "Pamela's noble heart would gratefully make known the valiant *mean* of her safety."—*Sidney.* "Their virtuous conversation was a *mean* to work the heathens' conversion."—*Hooker.* "Whether his wits should by that *mean* have been taken from him."—*Id.* "I'll devise a *mean* to draw the Moor out of the way."—*Shak.* "No place will please me so, no *mean* of death."—*Id.* "Nature is made better by no *mean*, but nature makes that *mean*."—*Id.* Dr. Lowth also questioned the propriety of construing *means* as singular, and referred to these same authors as authorities for preferring the regular form. Buchanan insists that *means* is right in the plural only; and that, "The singular should be used as perfectly analogous; by this *mean*, by that *mean*."—*English Syntax*, p. 103. Lord Kames, likewise, appears by his practice to have been of the same opinion : "Of this the child must be sensible intuitively, for it has no other *mean* of knowledge."—*Elements of Criticism*, Vol. i, p. 357. "And in both the same *mean* is employed."—*Ib.* ii, 271. Caleb Alexander, too, declares "*this means*," "*that means*," and "*a means*," to be "ungrammatical."—*Gram.* p. 58. But common usage has gone against the suggestions of these critics, and later grammarians have rather confirmed the irregularity, than attempted to reform it.

OBS. 34.—Murray quotes sixteen good authorities to prove that *means* may be singular; but whether it *ought* to be so or not, is still a disputable point. Principle is for the regular word *mean*, and good practice favours the irregularity, but is still divided. Cobbett, to the disgrace of grammar, says, "*Mean*, as a noun, is *never used in the singular*. It, like some other words, has broken loose from all principle and rule. By universal consent, it *is become always a plural*, whether used with *singular or plural* pronouns and articles, *or not*."—*Gram.* p. 144. This is as ungrammatical, as it is untrue. Both *mean* and *means* are sufficiently authorized in the singular : "The prospect which by this *mean* is opened to you."—*Melmoth's Cicero.* "Faith in this doctrine never terminates in itself, but is a *mean* to holiness as an end."—*Dr. Chalmers, Sermons*, p. v. "The *mean* of basely affronting him."—*Brown's Divinity*, p. 19. "They used every *mean* to prevent the re-establishment of their religion."—*Dr. Jamieson's Sacred Hist.* i, p. 20. "As a necessary *mean* to prepare men for the discharge of that duty."—*Bolingbroke, on Hist.* p. 153. "Greatest is the power of a *mean*, when its power is least suspected."—*Tupper's Book of Thoughts*, p. 37. "To the deliberative orator the reputation of unsullied virtue is not only useful, as a *mean* of promoting his general influence, it is also among his most efficient engines of persuasion, upon every individual occasion."—*J. Q. Adams's Lectures on Rhetoric and Oratory*, i, 352. "I would urge it upon you, as the most effectual *mean* of extending your respectability and usefulness in the world."—*Ib.* ii, 395. "Exercise will be admitted to be a necessary *mean* of improvement."—*Blair's Rhet.* p. 343. "And by *that mean* we have now an early prepossession in their favour."—*Ib.* p. 348. "To abolish all sacrifice by revealing a better *mean* of reconciliation."—*Keith's Evidences*, p. 46. "As a *mean* of destroying the distinction."—*Ib.* p. 3. "Which however is by no *mean* universally the case."—*Religious World Displayed*, Vol. iii, p. 155.

OBS. 35.—Again, there are some nouns, which, though they do not lack the regular plural form, are sometimes used in a plural sense without the plural termination. Thus *manner* makes the plural *manners*, which last is now generally used in the peculiar sense of behaviour, or deportment, but not always : it sometimes means methods, modes, or ways ; as, "At sundry times and in divers *manners*."—*Heb.* i, 1. "In the *manners* above mentioned."—*Butler's Analogy*, 100. "There be three *manners* of trials in England."—*Cowell: Joh. Dict. w. Jury.* "These two *manners* of representation."—*Lowth's Gram.* p. 15. "These are the three primary modes, or *manners*, of expression."—*Lowth's Gram.* p. 83. "In arrangement, too, various *manners* suit various styles."—*Campbell's Phil. of Rhet.* p. 172. "Between the two *manners*."—*Bolingbroke, on Hist.* p. 35. "Here are three different *manners* of asserting."—*Barnard's Gram.* p. 59. But *manner* has often been put for *sorts*, without the *s* ; as, "The tree of life, which bare *twelve manner* of fruits."—*Rev.* xxii, 2. "*All manner* of men assembled here in arms."—*Shak.* "*All manner* of outward advantages."—*Atterbury.* Milton used *kind* in the same way, but not very properly ; as, "*All kind* of living creatures."—*P. Lost*, B. iv, l. 286. This irregularity it would be well to avoid. *Manners* may still, perhaps, be proper for modes or ways ; and *all manner*, if allowed, must be taken in the sense of a collective noun ; but for sorts, kinds, classes, or species, I would use neither the plural nor the singular of this word. The word *heathen*, too, makes the regular plural *heathens*, and yet is often used in a plural sense without the *s* ; as, "Why do the *heathen* rage ?"—*Psalms*, ii, 1. "Christianity was formerly propagated among the *heathens*."—*Murray's Key*, 8vo, p. 217. The word *youth*, likewise, has the same peculiarities.

* So *pains* is the regular plural of *pain*, and, by Johnson, Webster, and other lexicographers, is recognized only as plural ; but Worcester inserts it among his stock words, with a comment, thus : "PAINS, n. Labor ; work ; toil ; care ; trouble. ☞ According to the best usage, the word *pains*, though of plural form, is used in these senses as singular, and is joined with a singular verb ; as, 'The pains they had taken *was* very great.' *Clarendon.* 'No pains *is* taken.' *Pope.* 'Great pains *is* taken.' *Priestley.* 'Much pains.' *Bolingbroke.*"— *Univ. and Crit. Dict.* The multiplication of anomalies of this kind is so undesirable, that nothing short of a very clear decision of Custom, against the use of the regular concord, can well justify the exception. Many such examples may be cited, but are they not examples of false syntax? I incline to think "the best usage" would still make all these verbs plural. Dr. Johnson cites the first example thus : "The *pains* they had taken *were* very great. *Clarendon.*"— *Quarto Dict. w. Pain.*

OBS. 36.—Under the present head come names of fishes, birds, or other things, when the application of the singular is extended from the individual to the species, so as to supersede the plural by assuming its construction: as, Sing. "A great *fish.*"—*Jonah,* i, 17. Plur. "For the multitude of *fishes.*"—*John,* xxi, 6. "A very great multitude of *fish.*"—*Ezekiel,* xlvii, 9 * The name of the genus being liable to this last construction, men seem to have thought that the species should follow; consequently, the regular plurals of some very common names of fishes are scarcely known at all. Hence some grammarians affirm, that *salmon, mackerel, herring, perch, tench,* and several others, are alike in both numbers, and ought never to be used in the plural form. I am not so fond of honouring these anomalies. Usage is here as unsettled, as it is arbitrary; and, if the expression of plurality is to be limited to either form exclusively, the regular plural ought certainly to be preferred. But, *for fish taken in bulk,* the singular form seems more appropriate; as, "These vessels take from thirty-eight to forty-five quintals of *cod* and *pollock,* and six thousand barrels of *mackerel,* yearly."—*Balbi's Geog.* p. 28.

OBS. 37.—The following examples will illustrate the unsettled usage just mentioned, and from them the reader may judge for himself what is right. In quoting at second-hand, I generally think it proper to make double references; and especially in citing authorities after Johnson, because he so often gives the same passages variously. But he himself is reckoned good authority in things literary. Be it so. I regret the many proofs of his fallibility. "Hear you this Triton of the *minnows* ?"—*Shak.* "The shoal of *herrings* was of an immense extent !"—*Murray's Key,* p. 185. "Buy my *herring* fresh."—*Swift: in Joh. Dict.* "In the fisheries of Maine, *cod, herring, mackerel, alewives, salmon,* and other *fish,* are taken."—*Balbi's Geog.* p. 23. "MEASE, s. The quantity of 500; as, a *mease* of *herrings.*"—*Webster's Dict.* "We shall have plenty of *mackerel* this season."—ADDISON: *in Joh. Dict.* "*Mackarel* is the same in both numbers. Gay has improperly *mackarels.*"—*Churchill's Gram.* p. 208. "They take *salmon* and *trouts* by groping and tickling them under the bellies."—CAREW: *in Joh. Dict.* "The pond will keep *trout* and *salmon* in their seasonable plight."—*Id. ib. w. Trout.* "Some *fish* are preserved fresh in vinegar, as *turbot.*" —*Id. ib. w. Turbot.* "Some *fish* are boiled and preserved fresh in vinegar, as *tunny* and *turbot.*" —*Id ib. w. Tunny.* "Of round *fish,* there are *brit, sprat, barn, smelts.*"—*Id. ib. w. Smelt.* "For *sprats* and *spurlings* for your house."—TUSSER: *ib. w. Spurling.* "The coast is plentifully stored with *pilchards, herrings,* and *haddock.*"—CAREW: *ib. w. Haddock.* "The coast is plentifully stored with round *fish, pilchard, herring, mackerel,* and *cod.*"—*Id. ib. w. Herring.* "The coast is plentifully stored with *shellfish, sea-hedgehogs, scallops, pilcherd, herring,* and *pollock.*"—*Id. ib. w. Pollock.* "A *roach* is a *fish* of no great reputation for his dainty taste. It is noted that *roaches* recover strength and grow a fortnight after spawning."—WALTON: *ib. w. Roach.* "A friend of mine stored a pond of three or four acres with *carps* and *tench.*"—HALE: *ib. w. Carp.* "Having stored a very great pond with *carps, tench,* and other *pond-fish,* and only put in two small *pikes,* this pair of tyrants in seven years devoured the whole.—*Id. ib. w. Tench.* "Singular, *tench;* plural, *tenches.*"—*Brightland's Gram.* p. 78. "The polar bear preys upon *seals, fish,* and the carcasses of *whales.*"—*Balbi's Geog.* p. 172. "*Trouts* and *salmons* swim against the stream."—BACON: *Ward's Gram.* p. 130.

> "'Tis true no *turbots* dignify my boards,
> But *gudgeons, flounders,* what my Thames affords."—*Pope.*

OBS. 38.—From the foregoing examples it would seem, if fish or fishes are often spoken of without a regular distinction of the grammatical numbers, it is not because the words are not susceptible of the inflection, but because there is some difference of meaning between the mere name of the sort and the distinct modification in regard to number. There are also other nouns in which a like difference may be observed. Some names of building materials, as *brick, stone, plank, joist,* though not destitute of regular plurals, as *bricks, stones, planks, joists,* and not unadapted to ideas distinctly singular, as *a brick, a stone, a plank, a joist,* are nevertheless sometimes used in a plural sense without the *s,* and sometimes in a sense which seems hardly to embrace the idea of either number; as, "Let us make *brick,* and burn *them* thoroughly."—*Gen.* xi, 3. "And they had *brick* for stone."—*Ib.* "The tale of *bricks.*"—*Exod.* v, 8 and 18. "Make *brick.*"—*Ib.* v, 16. "From your *bricks.*"—*Ib.* v, 19. "Upon altars of *brick.*"—*Isaiah,* lxv, 3. "The *bricks* are fallen down."—*Ib.* ix, 10. The same variety of usage occurs in respect to a few other words, and sometimes perhaps without good reason; as, "Vast numbers of sea *fowl* frequent the rocky cliffs."—*Balbi's Geog.* p. 231. "Bullocks, sheep, and *fowls.*"—*Ib.* p. 439. "*Cannon* is used alike in both numbers."—*Everett's Gram.* p. 48. "*Cannon* and *shot* may be used in the singular or plural sense."—*O. B. Peirce's Gram.* p. 37. "The column in the Place Vendome is one hundred and thirty-four feet high, and is made of the brass of the *cannons* taken from the Austrians and Prussians."—*Balbi's Geog.* p. 249. "As his *cannons* roar."—*Dryden's Poems,* p. 81. "Twenty *shot* of his greatest cannon."—CLARENDON: *Joh. Dict.* "Twenty *shots*" would here, I think, be more proper, though the word is not made plural when it means *little balls of lead.* "And *cannons* conquer armies."—*Hudibras,* Part III, Canto iii, l. 249.

> "Healths to both kings, attended with the roar
> Of *cannons* echoed from th' affrighted shore."—*Waller,* p. 7.

OBS. 39.—Of foreign nouns, many retain their original plural; a few are defective; and some are redundant, because the English form is also in use. Our writers have laid many languages under contribution, and thus furnished an abundance of irregular words, necessary to be explained, but never to be acknowledged as English till they conform to our own rules.

1. Of nouns in *a, saliva,* spittle, and *scoria,* dross, have no occasion for the plural; *lamina,* s

---

* "And the *fish* that *is* in the river shall die."—*Exod.* vii, 18. "And the *fish* that *was* in the river died."—*R.* 21. Here the construction is altogether in the singular, and yet the meaning seems to be plural This construction appears to be more objectionable, than the use of the word *fish* with a plural verb. The French Bible here corresponds with ours; but the Latin Vulgate, and the Greek Septuagint, have both the noun and the verb in the plural: as, "The *fishes* that *are* in the river,"—"The *fishes* that *were,*" &c. In our Bible, *fowl,* as well as *fish,* is sometimes plural; and yet both words, in some passages, have the plural form: as, "And *few* that may fly," &c.—*Gen.* i, 20. "I will consume the *fowls* of the heaven, and the *fishes* of the sea."—*Zeph.* i, 3.

thin plate, makes *laminæ*; *macula*, a spot, *maculæ*; *minutia*, a little thing, *minutiæ*; *nebula*, a mist, *nebulæ*; *siliqua*, a pod, *siliquæ*. *Dogma* makes *dogmas* or *dogmata*; *exanthema*, *exanthemas* or *exanthemata*; *miasm* or *miasma*, *miasms* or *miasmata*; *stigma*, *stigmas* or *stigmata*.

2. Of nouns in *um*, some have no need of the plural; as, *bdellium*, *decorum*, *elysium*, *equilibrium*, *guaiacum*, *laudanum*, *odium*, *opium*, *petroleum*, *serum*, *viaticum*. Some form it regularly; as, *asylums*, *compendiums*, *craniums*, *emporiums*, *encomiums*, *forums*, *frustums*, *lustrums*, *mausoleums*, *museums*, *pendulums*, *nostrums*, *rostrums*, *residuums*, *vacuums*. Others take either the English or the Latin plural; as, *desideratums* or *desiderata*, *mediums* or *media*, *menstruums* or *menstrua*, *memorandums* or *memoranda*, *spectrums* or *spectra*, *speculums* or *specula*, *stratums* or *strata*, *succedaneums* or *succedanea*, *trapeziums* or *trapezia*, *vinculums* or *vincula*. A few seem to have the Latin plural only: as, *arcanum*, *arcana*; *datum*, *data*; *effluvium*, *effluvia*; *erratum*, *errata*; *scholium*, *scholia*.

3. Of nouns in *us*, a few have no plural; as, *asparagus*, *calamus*, *mucus*. Some have only the Latin plural, which usually changes *us* to *i*; as, *alumnus*, *alumni*; *androgynus*, *androgyni*; *calculus*, *calculi*; *dracunculus*, *dracunculi*; *echinus*, *echini*; *magus*, *magi*. But such as have properly become English words, may form the plural regularly in *es*; as, *chorus*, *choruses*: so, *apparatus*, *bolus*, *callus*, *circus*, *fetus*, *focus*, *fucus*, *fungus*, *hiatus*, *ignoramus*, *impetus*, *incubus*, *isthmus*, *nautilus*, *nucleus*, *prospectus*, *rebus*, *sinus*, *surplus*. Five of these make the Latin plural like the singular; but the mere English scholar has no occasion to be told which they are. *Radius* makes the plural *radii* or *radiuses*. *Genius* has *genii*, for imaginary spirits, and *geniuses*, for men of wit. *Genus*, a sort, becomes *genera* in Latin, and *genuses* in English. *Denarius* makes, in the plural, *denarii* or *denariuses*.

4. Of nouns in *is*, some are regular; as, *trellis*, *trellises*: so, *annolis*, *butteris*, *caddis*, *dervis*, *iris*, *marquis*, *metropolis*, *portcullis*, *proboscis*. Some seem to have no need of the plural: as, *ambergris*, *aqua-fortis*, *arthritis*, *brewis*, *crasis*, *elephantiasis*, *genesis*, *orris*, *siriasis*, *tennis*. But most nouns of this ending follow the Greek or Latin form, which simply changes *is* to *es*: as, *amanuensis*, *amanuenses*; *analysis*, *analyses*; *antithesis*, *antitheses*; *axis*, *axes*; *basis*, *bases*; *crisis*, *crises*; *diæresis*, *diæreses*; *diesis*, *dieses*; *ellipsis*, *ellipses*; *emphasis*, *emphases*; *fascis*, *fasces*; *hypothesis*, *hypotheses*; *metamorphosis*, *metamorphoses*; *phasis*, *phases*; *praxis*, *praxes*; *synopsis*, *synopses*; *synthesis*, *syntheses*; *syrtis*, *syrtes*; *thesis*, *theses*. In some, however, the original plural is not so formed; but is made by changing *is* to *ides*: as, *aphis*, *aphides*; *apsis*, *apsides*; *ascaris*, *ascarides*; *bolis*, *bolides*; *cantharis*, *cantharides*; *chrysalis*, *chrysalides*; *ephemeris*, *ephemerides*; *epidermis*, *epidermides*. So *iris* and *proboscis*, which we make regular; and perhaps some of the foregoing may be made so too. Fisher writes *Praxises* for *praxes*, though not very properly. See his *Gram.* p. v. *Eques*, a Roman knight, makes *equites* in the plural.

5. Of nouns in *x*, there are few, if any, which ought not to form the plural regularly, when used as English words; though the Latins changed *x* to *ces*, and *ex* to *ices*, making the *s* sometimes long, and sometimes short: as, *apex*, *apices*, for *apexes*; *appendix*, *appendices*, for *appendixes*; *calix*, *calices*, for *calixes*; *calx*, *calces*, for *calxes*; *calyx*, *calyces*, for *calyxes*; *caudex*, *caudices*, for *caudexes*; *cicatrix*, *cicatrices*, for *cicatrixes*; *helix*, *helices*, for *helixes*; *index*, *indices*, for *indexes*; *matrix*, *matrices*, for *matrixes*; *quincunx*, *quincunces*, for *quincunxes*; *radix*, *radices*, for *radixes*; *varix*, *varices*, for *varixes*; *vertex*, *vertices*, for *vertexes*; *vortex*, *vortices*, for *vortexes*. Some Greek words in *x* change that letter to *ges*: as, *larynx*, *larynges*, for *larinxes*; *phalanx*, *phalanges*, for *phalanxes*. *Billet-doux*, from the French, is *billets-doux* in the plural.

6. Of nouns in *on*, derived from Greek, the greater part always form the plural regularly; as, *etymons*, *gnomons*, *ichneumons*, *myrmidons*, *phlegmons*, *trigons*, *tetragons*, *pentagons*, *hexagons*, *heptagons*, *octagons*, *enneagons*, *decagons*, *hendecagons*, *dodecagons*, *polygons*. So *trihedrons*, *tetrahedrons*, *pentahedrons*, &c., though some say, these last may end in *dra*, which I think improper. For a few words of this class, however, there are double plurals in use; as, *automata* or *automatons*, *criteria* or *criterions*, *parhelia* or *parhelions*; and the plural of *phenomenon* appears to be always *phenomena*.

7. The plural of *legumen* is *legumens* or *legumena*; of *stamen*, *stamens* or *stamina*; of *cherub*, *cherubs* or *cherubim*; of *seraph*, *seraphs* or *seraphim*; of *beau*, *beaus* or *beaux*; of *bandit*, *bandits* or *banditti*. The regular forms are in general preferable. The Hebrew plurals *cherubim* and *seraphim*, being sometimes mistaken for singulars, other plurals have been formed from them; as, "And over it the *cherubims* of glory."—*Acts*, ix, 5. "Then flew one of the *seraphims* unto me."—*Isaiah*, vi, 6. Dr. Campbell remarks: "We are authorized, both by use and by analogy, to say either *cherubs* and *seraphs*, according to the English idiom, or *cherubim* and *seraphim*, according to the oriental. The former suits better the familiar, the latter the solemn style. I shall add to this remark, "says he," that, as the words *cherubim* and *seraphim* are plural, the terms *cherubims* and *seraphims*, as expressing the plural, are quite improper."—*Phil.of Rhet.* p. 201.

OBS. 40.—When other parts of speech become nouns, they either want the plural, or form it regularly,[*] like common nouns of the same endings; as, "His affairs went on at *sizes* and *sevens*."—*Arbuthnot*. "Some mathematicians have proposed to compute by *twoes*; others, by *fours*; others, by *twelves*."—*Churchill's Gram.* p. 81. "Three *fourths*, nine *tenths*."—*Ib.* p. 230. "Time's *takings* and *leavings*."—*Barton*. "The *yeas* and *nays*."—*Newspaper*. "The *ays* and *noes*."—*Ib.* "*Oes* and *spangles*."—*Bacon*. "The *ins* and the *outs*."—*Newspaper*. "We find it more safe against

* Some authors, when they give to *mere words* the construction of plural nouns, are in the habit of writing them in the form of possessives singular; as, "They have of late, 'tis true, reformed, in some measure, the gouty joints and darning work of *whereunto's*, *whereby's*, *thereof's*, *therewith's*, and the rest of this kind."—*Shaftesbury*. "Here," says Dr. Crombie, "the genitive singular is *improperly* used for the objective case plural. It should be, *whereuntos*, *wherebys*, *thereofs*, *therewiths*."—*Treatise on Etym. and Synt.* p. 332. According to our rules, these words should rather be, *whereuntoes*, *wherebies*, *thereofs*, *therewiths*. "Any word, when used as the name of itself, becomes a noun."—*Goodenow's Gram.* p. 26. But some grammarians say, "The plural of words, considered as words *merely*, is formed by the apostrophe and *s*; as, ' Who, that has any taste, can endure the incessant, quick returns of the *also's*, and the *likewise's*, and the *moreover's*, and the *notwithstanding's*?'"—CAMPBELL."—*Wells's School Gram.* p. 54. Practice is not altogether in favour of this principle, and perhaps it would be better to decide with Crombie that such a use of the apostrophe is improper.

outs and *doubles*."—*Printer's Gram.* "His *ands* and his *ors*."—*Mott.* "One of the *buts*."—*Fowle.* "In raising the mirth of *stupids*."—*Steele.* "*Eatings, drinkings, wakings, sleepings, walkings, talkings, sayings, doings*—all were for the good of the public; there was not such a thing as a secret in the town."—LANDON: *Keepsake,* 1833. "Her innocent *forsooths* and *yesses*."—*Spect.* No. 266.

"Henceforth my wooing mind shall be expressed
In russet *yeas* and honest kersey *noes*."—SHAK. See *Johnson's Dict. w. Kersey.*

GENDERS.

Genders, in grammar, are modifications that distinguish objects in regard to sex.

There are three genders; the *masculine,* the *feminine,* and the *neuter.*

The *masculine gender* is that which denotes persons or animals of the male kind; as, *man, father, king.*

The *feminine gender* is that which denotes persons or animals of the female kind; as, *woman, mother, queen.*

The *neuter gender* is that which denotes things that are neither male nor female; as, *pen, ink, paper.*

Hence, names of males are masculine; names of females, feminine; and names of things inanimate, literally, neuter.

Masculine nouns make regular feminines, when their termination is changed to *ess:* as, *hunter, huntress; prince, princess; lion, lioness.*

OBSERVATIONS.

OBS. 1.—The different genders in grammar are founded on the natural distinction of sex in animals, and on the absence of sex in other things. In English, they belong only to nouns and pronouns; and to these they are usually applied, not arbitrarily, as in some other languages, but agreeably to the order of nature. From this we derive a very striking advantage over those who use the genders differently or without such rule; which is, that our pronouns are easy of application, and have a fine effect when objects are personified. Pronouns are of the same gender as the nouns for which they stand.

OBS. 2.—Many nouns are equally applicable to both sexes; as, *cousin, friend, neighbour, parent, person, servant.* The gender of these is usually determined by the context; and they are to be called masculine or feminine accordingly. To such words, some grammarians have applied the unnecessary and improper term *common gender.* Murray justly observes, "There is no such gender belonging to the language. The business of parsing can be effectually performed, without having recourse to a *common gender*."—*Gram.* 8vo, p. 39. The term is more useful, and less liable to objection, as applied to the learned languages; but with us it is plainly a solecism.

OBS. 3.—A great many of our grammars define gender to be "*the distinction of sex*," and then speak of a *common gender,* in which the two sexes are left *undistinguished;* and of the *neuter gender,* in which objects are treated as being of *neither sex.* These views of the matter are obviously inconsistent. Not genders, or *a* gender, do the writers undertake to define, but "gender" as a whole; and absurdly enough, too; because this whole of gender they immediately distribute into certain *other genders,* into genders of gender, or kinds of gender, and these not compatible with their definition. Thus Wells: "Gender is *the distinction of* objects with regard to sex. There are four genders;—the *masculine,* the *feminine,* the *common,* and the *neuter.*"—*School Gram.* 1st Ed. p. 49. [Those] "Nouns which are applicable *alike to both sexes,* are of the *common* gender."—*Ib.* This then is manifestly no gender under the foregoing definition, and the term *neuter* is made somewhat less appropriate by the adoption of a third denomination before it. Nor is there less absurdity in the phraseology with which Murray proposes to avoid the recognition of the *common gender:* "Thus we may say, *Parents* is a noun of the *masculine and feminine* gender; *Parent,* if doubtful, is of the *masculine or feminine* gender; and *Parent,* if the gender is known by the construction, is of the gender so ascertained."—*Gram.* 8vo, p. 39. According to this, we must have *five genders,* exclusive of that which is called *common;* namely, the *masculine,* the *feminine,* the *neuter,* the *androgynal,* and the *doubtful.*

OBS. 4.—It is plain that many writers on grammar have had but a confused notion of what a gender really is. Some of them, confounding gender with sex, deny that there are more than two genders, because there are only two sexes. Others, under a like mistake, resort occasionally, (as in the foregoing instance,) to an *androgynal,* and also to a *doubtful* gender: both of which are more objectionable than the *common gender* of the old grammarians; though this *common* "distinction with regard to sex," is, in our language, confessedly, no distinction at all. I assume, that there are in English the three genders, masculine, feminine, and neuter, and no more; and that every noun and every pronoun must needs be of some gender; consequently, of some one of these three. A gender is, literally, a sort, a kind, a sex. But genders, in grammar, are attributes of words, rather than of persons or things; whereas sexes are attributes, not of words, but of living creatures. He who understands this, will perceive that the absence of sex in some things, is as good a basis for a grammatical distinction, as the presence or the difference of it in others; nor can it be denied, that the neuter, according to my definition, is a gender, is a distinction "in *regard* to sex," though it does not embrace either of the sexes. There are therefore three genders, and only three.

OBS. 5.—Generic names, even when construed as masculine or feminine, often virtually include both sexes; as, "Hast thou given *the horse* strength? hast thou clothed *his* neck with thunder? Canst thou make *him* afraid as a grasshopper? the glory of *his* nostrils is terrible."—*Job*, xxxix, 19. Doth *the hawk* fly by thy wisdom, and stretch *her* wings toward the south? Doth *the eagle* mount up at thy command, and make *her* nest on high?"—*Ib.* ver. 26. These were called, by the old grammarians, *epicene* nouns—that is, *supercommon*; but they are to be parsed according to the gender of the pronoun that is put for them.

OBS. 6.—The gender of words, in many instances, is to be determined by the following principle of universal grammar.†‡ Those terms which are equally applicable to both sexes, (if they are not expressly applied to females,) and those plurals which are known to include both sexes, should be called masculine in parsing;, for, in all languages, the masculine gender is considered the most worthy, * and is generally employed when both sexes are included under one common term. Thus *parents* is always masculine, and must be represented by a masculine pronoun, for the gender of a word is a property indivisible, and that which refers to the male sex, always takes the lead in such cases. If one say, "Joseph took *the young child and his mother* by night, and fled with *them* into Egypt," the pronoun *them* will be masculine; but let "*his*" be changed to *its*, and the plural pronoun that follows, will be feminine. For the feminine gender takes precedence of the neuter, but not of the masculine; and it is not improper to speak of a young child without designating the sex. As for such singulars as *parent*, *friend*, *neighbour*, *thief*, *slave*, and many others, they are feminine when expressly applied to any of the female sex; but otherwise, masculine.

OBS. 7.—Nouns of multitude, when they convey the idea of unity or take the plural form, are of the neuter gender; but when they convey the idea of plurality without the form, they follow the gender of the individuals which compose the assemblage. Thus a *congress*, a *council*, a *committee*, a *jury*, a *sort*, or a *sex*, if taken collectively, is neuter; being represented in discourse by the neuter pronoun *it*: and the formal plurals, *congresses*, *councils*, *committees*, *juries*, *sorts*, *sexes*, of course, are neuter also. But, if I say, "The committee disgraced *themselves*," the noun and pronoun are presumed to be masculine, unless it be known that I am speaking of a committee of females. Again: "The *fair sex*, *whose* task is not to mingle in the labours of public life, have *their* own part assigned *them* to act."—*Comly's Gram.* p. 132. Here *sex*, and the three pronouns which have that word for their antecedent, are all feminine. Again: "*Each sex*, dressing *themselves* in the clothes of the other."—*Wood's Dictionary*, v. *Feast of Purim*. Here *sex*, and the pronoun which follows, are masculine; because, the male sex, as well as the female, is here spoken of plurally.

OBS. 8.—To *persons*, of every description, known or unknown, real or imaginary, we uniformly ascribe sex. † But, as personality implies intelligence, and sex supposes some obvious difference, a *young child* may be spoken of with distinction of sex or without, according to the notion of the speaker; as, "I went to see the *child* whilst they were putting on *its cloaths*."—*Priestley's Gram.* p. 125. "Because the *child* has no idea of any nurse besides *his* own."—*Ib.* p. 153. To *brute animals* also, the same distinction is generally applied, though with less uniformity. Some that are very small, have a gender which seems to be merely occasional and figurative; as, "Go to the *ant*, thou sluggard; consider *her* ways, and be wise."—*Prov.* vi, 6. "The *spider* taketh hold with *her* hands, and is in kings' palaces."—*Prov.* xxx, 28. So the *bee* is usually made feminine, being a little creature of admirable industry and economy. But, in general, irrational creatures whose sex is unknown, or unnecessary to be regarded, are spoken of as neuter; as, "And it became a *serpent*; and Moses fled from before *it*. And the Lord said unto Moses, Put forth thine hand, and take *it* by the tail. And he put forth his hand and caught *it*, and it became a rod in his hand."—*Exod.* iv, 3, 4. Here, although the word *serpent* is sometimes masculine, the neuter pronoun seems to be more proper. So of some imaginary creatures: as, "*Phenix*, the fowl which is said to exist single, and to rise again from *its* own ashes."—*Webster's Dict.* "So shall the *Phœnix* escape, with no stain on *its* plumage."—*Dr. Bartlett's Lect.* p. 10.

OBS. 9.—But this liberty of representing animals as of no sex, is often carried to a very questionable extent; as, "The *hare* sleeps with *its* eyes open."—*Barbauld.* "The *hedgehog*, as soon as *it* perceives *itself* attacked, rolls *itself* into a kind of ball, and presents nothing but *its* prickles to the foe "—*Blair's Reader*, p. 138. "The *panther* is a ferocious creature: like the tiger *it* seizes *its* prey by surprise."—*Ib.* p. 102. "The *leopard*, in *its* chace of prey, spares neither man nor beast."—*Ib.* p. 103. "If a man shall steal an *ox*, or a *sheep*, and kill *it*, or sell *it*."—*Exod.* xxii, 1. "A *dog* resists *its* instinct to run after a hare, because *it* recollects the beating *it* has previously received on that account. The *horse* avoids the stone at which *it* once has stumbled."—*Spurs-heim, on Education*, p. 3. "The *racehorse* is looked upon with pleasure; but it is the *warhorse*, that carries grandeur in *its* idea."—*Blair's Rhet.* p. 30.

OBS. 10.—The sexes are distinguished *by words*, in four different ways. First, by the use of different terminations: as, *Jew*, *Jewess*; *Julius*, *Julia*; *hero*, *heroine*. Secondly, by the use of entirely different names: as, *Henry*, *Mary*; *king*, *queen*. Thirdly, by compounds or phrases including some distinctive term: as, *Mr. Murray*, *Mrs. Murray*; *Englishman*, *Englishwoman*; *grandfather*,

* "The Supreme Being (*God*, Θεὸς, *Deus*, *Dieu*, &c.) is, in all languages, masculine; in as much as the masculine sex is the superior and more excellent; and as He is the Creator of all, the Father of gods and men."—*Harris's Hermes*, p. 54. This remark applies to all the direct names of the Deity, but the abstract idea of *Deity itself*, Τὸ Θεῖον, *Numen*, *Godhead*, or *Divinity*, is not masculine, but neuter. On this point, some notions have been published for grammar, that are too heterodox to be cited or criticised here. See *O. B. Peirce's Gram.* p 208.

† That is, we give them *sex*, if we mean to represent them *as persons*. In the following example, a character commonly esteemed feminine is represented as neuter, because the author would seem to doubt both the *sex* and the personality: "I don't know what a *witch* is, or what *it* was then."—*N. P. Rogers's Writings*, p. 154.

grandmother; landlord, landlady; merman, mermaid; servingman, servingmaid; man-servant, maid-servant; schoolmaster, schoolmistress; school-boy, school-girl; peacock, peahen; cock-sparrow, hen-sparrow; he-goat, she-goat; buck-rabbit, doe-rabbit; male elephant, female elephant; male convicts, female convicts. Fourthly, by the pronouns *he, his, him,* put for nouns masculine; and *she, her, hers,* for nouns feminine: as, "Ask *him* that fleeth, and *her* that escapeth, and say, What is done?"—*Jer.* xlviii, 19.

"O happy *peasant!* Oh unhappy *bard!*
His the mere tinsel, *hers* the rich reward."—*Cowper.*

OBS. 11.—For feminine nouns formed by inflection, the regular termination is *ess*; but the manner in which this ending is applied to the original or masculine noun, is not uniform:—

1. In some instances the syllable *ess* is simply added: as, *accuser, accuseress; advocate, advocatess; archer, archeress; author, authoress; avenger, avengeress; barber, barberess; baron, baroness; canon, canoness; cit, cittess;*[*] *coheir, coheiress; count, countess; deacon, deaconess; demon, demoness; diviner, divineress; doctor, doctoress; giant, giantess; god, goddess; guardian, guardianess; Hebrew, Hebrewess; heir, heiress; herd, herdess; hermit, hermitess; host, hostess; Jesuit, Jesuitess; Jew, Jewess; mayor, mayoress; Moabite, Moabitess; monarch, monarchess; pape, papess; or, pope, popess; patron, patroness; peer, peeress; poet, poetess; priest, priestess; prior, prioress; prophet, prophetess; regent, regentess; saint, saintess; shepherd, shepherdess; soldier, soldieress; tailor, tailoress; viscount, viscountess; warrior, warrioress.*

2. In other instances the termination is changed, and there is no increase of syllables: as, *abbot, abbess; actor, actress; adulator, adulatress; adulterer, adulteress; adventurer, adventuress; advoutrer, advoutress; ambassador, ambassadress; anchorite, anchoress; or, anachoret, anachoress; arbiter, arbitress; auditor, auditress; benefactor, benefactress; caterer, cateress, chanter, chantress; cloisterer, cloisteress; commander, commandress; conductor, conductress; creator, creatress; demander, demandress; detractor, detractress; eagle, eagless; editor, editress; elector, electress; emperor, emperess, or empress; emulator, emulatress; enchanter, enchantress; exactor, exactress; fautor, fautress; fornicator, fornicatress; fosterer, fosteress, or fostress; founder, foundress; governor, governess; huckster, huckstress; or, hucksterer, hucksteress; idolater, idolatress; inhabiter, inhabitress; instructor, instructress; inventor, inventress; launderer, laundress, or laundress; minister, ministress; monitor, monitress; murderer, murderess; negro, negress; offender, offendress; ogre, ogress; porter, portress; progenitor, progenitress; protector, protectress; proprietor, proprietress; pythonist, pythoness; seamster, seamstress; solicitor, solicitress; songster, songstress; sorcerer, sorceress; suitor, suitress; tiger, tigress; traitor, traitress; victor, victress; votary, votaress.*

3. In a few instances the feminine is formed as in Latin, by changing *or* to *rix*; but some of these have also the regular form, which ought to be preferred: as, *adjutor, adjutrix; administrator, administratrix; arbitrator, arbitratrix; coadjutor, coadjutrix; competitor, competitress,* or *competitrix; creditor, creditrix; director, directress,* or *directrix; executor, executress,* or *executrix; inheritor, inheritress,* or *inheritrix; mediator, mediatress,* or *mediatrix; orator, oratress,* or *oratrix; rector, rectress,* or *rectrix; spectator, spectatress,* or *spectatrix; testator, testatrix; tutor, tutoress,* or *tutress,* or *tutrix; deserter, desertress,* or *desertrice,* or *desertrix.*

4. The following are irregular words, in which the distinction of sex is chiefly made by the termination: *amoroso, amorosa; archduke, archduchess; chamberlain, chambermaid; duke, duchess; gaffer, gammer; goodman, goody; hero, heroine; landgrave, langravine; margrave, margravine; marquis, marchioness; palsgrave, palsgravine; sakeret, sakerhawk; sewer, sewster; sultan, sultana; tzar, tzarina; tyrant, tyfanness; widower, widow.*

OBS. 12.—The proper names of persons almost always designate their sex; for it has been found convenient to make the names of women different from those of men. We have also some appellatives which correspond to each other, distinguishing the sexes by their distinct application to each: as, *bachelor, maid; beau, belle; boy, girl; bridegroom, bride; brother, sister; buck, doe; boar, sow; bull, cow; cock, hen; colt, filly; dog, bitch; drake, duck; earl, countess; father, mother; friar, nun; gander, goose; grandsire, grandam; hart, roe; horse, mare; husband, wife; king, queen; lad, lass; lord, lady; male, female; man, woman; master, mistress;* Mister, Missis; (Mr. Mrs.;) *milter, spawner; monk, nun; nephew, niece; papa, mamma; rake, jilt; ram, ewe; ruff, reeve; sire, dam; sir, madam; sloven, slut; son, daughter; stag, hind; steer, heifer; swain, nymph; uncle, aunt; wizard, witch; youth, damsel; young man, maiden.*

OBS. 13.—The people of a particular country are commonly distinguished by some name derived from that of their country; as, *Americans, Africans, Egyptians, Russians, Turks.* Such words are sometimes called *gentile names.* There are also adjectives, of the same origin, if not the same form, which correspond with them. "Gentile names are for the most part considered as masculine, and the feminine is denoted by the gentile adjective and the noun *woman:* as, a *Spaniard,* a *Spanish woman;* a *Pole,* or *Polander,* a *Polish woman.* But, in a few instances, we always use a compound of the adjective with *man* or *woman:* as, an *Englishman,* an *Englishwoman;* a *Welshman,* a *Welshwoman;* an *Irishman,* an *Irishwoman;* a *Frenchman,* a *Frenchwoman;* a *Dutchman,* a *Dutchwoman:* and in these cases the adjective is employed as the collective noun; as, *the Dutch, the French,* &c. A *Scotchman,* and a *Scot,* are both in use; but the latter is not common in prose writers: though some employ it, and these generally adopt the plural, *Scots,* with the definite article, as the collective term."—*Churchill's New Gram.* p. 70.

OBS. 14.—The names of things without life, used literally, are always of the neuter gender: as, "When Cleopatra fled, Antony pursued her in a five-oared galley; and, coming along side of her *ship,* entered *it* without being seen by her."—*Goldsmith's Rome,* p. 160. "The *sun,* high as *it* is, has *its* business assigned; and so have the stars."—*Collier's Antoninus,* p. 138. But inanimate objects are often represented figuratively as having sex. Things remarkable for power,

---

[*] There is the same reason for doubling the *t* in *cittess,* as for doubling the *d* in *goddess.* See Rule 3d for Spelling. Yet Johnson, Todd, Webster, Bolles, Worcester, and others, spell it *citess,* with one *t.*
"Cits and *citesses* raise a joyful strain."—DRYDEN: *Joh. Dict.*

greatness, or sublimity, are spoken of as masculine; as, the *sun*, *time*, *death*, *sleep*, *fear*, *anger*, *winter*, *war*. Things beautiful, amiable, or prolific, are spoken of as feminine; as, a *ship*, the *moon*, the *earth*, *nature*, *fortune*, *knowledge*, *hope*, *spring*, *peace*. Figurative gender is indicated only by the personal pronouns of the singular number: as, " When we say of the *sun*, *He* is setting; or of a *ship*, *She* sails well."—*L. Murray*. For these two objects, the *sun* and a *ship*, this phraseology is so common, that the literal construction quoted above is rarely met with.

OBS. 15.— When any inanimate object or abstract quality is distinctly personified, and presented to the imagination in the character of a living and intelligent being, there is necessarily a change of the gender of the word; for, whenever personality is thus ascribed to what is literally neuter, there must be an assumption of one or the other sex: as, " *The Genius of Liberty* is awakened, and springs up; *she* sheds her divine light and creative powers upon the two hemispheres. A great *nation*, astonished at seeing *herself* free, stretches *her* arms from one extremity of the earth to the other, and embraces the first nation that became so."—*Abbé Fauchet*. But there is an inferior kind of personification, or of what is called such, in which, so far as appears, the gender remains neuter: as. " The following is an instance of personification and apostrophe united: ' O *thou sword* of the Lord! how long will it be ere *thou* be quiet? put *thyself* up into *thy* scabbard, rest, and be still! How can *it* be quiet, seeing the Lord hath given *it* a charge against Askelon, and against the sea-shore? there hath he appointed *it*.' "—*Murray's Gram.* p. 348. See *Jer.* xlvii, 6.

OBS. 16.— If what is called personification, does not always imply a change of gender and an ascription of sex, neither does a mere ascription of sex to what is literally of no sex, necessarily imply a personification; for there may be sex without personality, as we see in brute animals. Hence the gender of a brute animal personified in a fable, may be taken literally as before; and the gender which is figuratively ascribed to the *sun*, the *moon*, or a *ship*, is merely metaphorical. In the following sentence, *nature* is animated and made feminine by a metaphor, while a lifeless object bearing the name of *Venus*, is spoken of as neuter: " Like that conceit of old, which declared that the *Venus of Gnidos* was not the work of Praxiteles, since *nature herself* had concreted the boundary surface of *its* beauty."—*Rush, on the Voice*, p. xxv.

OBS. 17.— " In personifications regard must be had to propriety in determining the gender. Of most of the passions and moral qualities of man the ancients formed deities, as they did of various other things: and, when these are personified, they are usually made male or female, according as they were gods or goddesses in the pagan mythology. The same rule applies in other cases: and thus the planet Jupiter will be masculine; Venus, feminine: the ocean, *Oceānus*, masculine: rivers, months, and winds, the same: the names of places, countries, and islands, feminine."— *Churchill's Gram.* p. 71.

OBS. 18.— These suggestions are worthy of consideration, but, for the gender which ought to be adopted in personifications, there seems to be no absolute general rule, or none which English writers have observed with much uniformity. It is well, however, to consider what is most common in each particular case, and abide by it. In the following examples, the sex ascribed is not that under which these several objects are commonly figured; for which reason, the sentences are perhaps erroneous:—

" *Knowledge* is proud that *he* has learn'd so much;
  Wisdom is humble that *he* knows no more."—*Cowper*.
" But hoary *Winter*, unadorned and bare,
  Dwells in the dire retreat, and freezes there;
  There *she* assembles all *her* blackest storms,
  And the rude hail in rattling tempests forms.'—*Addison*.'
" *Her* pow'r extends o'er all things that have breath,
  A cruel tyrant, and *her* name is *Death*."—*Sheffield*.

CASES.

Cases, in grammar, are modifications that distinguish the relations of nouns or pronouns to other words.

There are three cases; the *nominative*, the *possessive*, and the *objective*.

The *nominative case* is that form or state of a noun or pronoun, which denotes the subject of a verb: as, The *boy* runs; *I* run.

The subject of a verb is that which answers to *who* or *what* before it; as, "The boy runs."—*Who* runs? "The *boy*." *Boy* is therefore here in the *nominative* case.

The *possessive case* is that form or state of a noun or pronoun, which denotes the relation of property: as, The *boy's* hat; *my* hat.

The possessive case of nouns is formed, in the singular number, by adding to the nominative *s preceded by an apostrophe;* and, in the plural, when the nominative ends in *s*, by adding *an apostrophe only:* as, singular, *boy's;* plural, *boys';* — sounded alike, but written differently.

The *objective case* is that form or state of a noun or pronoun which denotes the object of a verb, participle, or preposition: as, I know the *boy*, having seen *him* at *school;* and he knows *me*.

The object of a verb, participle, or preposition, is that which answers to *whom* or *what* after it ; as, " I know the boy."—I know *whom ?* " The *boy.*" *Boy* is therefore here in the *objective* case.

The nominative and the objective of nouns, are always alike in form, being distinguishable from each other only by their place in a sentence, or by their simple dependence according to the sense.

OBSERVATIONS.

OBS. 1.—The cases, in grammar, are founded on the different relations under which things are represented in discourse ; and from which the words acquire correspondent relations; or connexions and dependences according to the sense. In Latin, there are six cases; and in Greek, five. Consequently, the nouns and pronouns of those languages, and also their adjectives and participles, (which last are still further inflected by the three genders,) are varied by many different terminations unknown to our tongue. In English, those modifications or relations which we call *cases*, belong only to nouns and pronouns; nor are there ever more than three. Pronouns are not necessarily like their antecedents in case.

OBS. 2.—Because the infinitive mood, a phrase, or a sentence, may in some instances be made the subject of a verb, so as to stand in that relation in which the nominative case is most commonly found ; very many of our grammarians have deliberately represented all terms used in this manner, as being " *in the nominative case :*" as if, to sustain any one of the relations which are usually distinguished by a particular case, must necessarily constitute that modification itself. Many also will have participles, infinitives, phrases, and sentences, to be occasionally " *in the objective case :*" whereas it must be plain to every reader, that they are, all of them, *indeclinable* terms ; and that, if used in any relation common to nouns or pronouns, they assume that office, as participles, as infinitives, as phrases, or as sentences, and not as *cases*. They no more take the nature of cases, than they become nouns or pronouns. Yet Nixon, by assuming that *of*, with the word governed by it, constitutes a *possessive case*, contrives to give to participles, and even to the infinitive mood, *all three of the cases.* Of the infinitive, he says, "An examination of the first and second methods of parsing this mood, must naturally lead to the inference that *it is a substantive ;* and that, if it has the nominative case, it must also have the possessive and objective cases of a substantive. The fourth method proves its [capacity of] being in the possessive case: thus, 'A desire *to learn ;*' that is, '*of learning.*' When it follows a participle, or a verb, as by the fifth or [the] seventh method, it is in the objective case. Method sixth is analogous to the Case Absolute of a substantive."—*Nixon's Parser*, p. 83. If the infinitive mood is really a *declinable substantive*, none of our grammarians have placed it in the right chapter ; except that bold contemner of all grammatical and literary authority, Oliver B. Peirce. When will the cause of learning cease to have assailants and underminers among those who profess to serve it ? Thus every new grammatist, has some grand absurdity or other, peculiar to himself ; and what can be more gross, than to talk of English infinitives and participles as being in the *possessive case?*

OBS. 3.—It was long a subject of dispute among the grammarians, what number of cases an English noun should be supposed to have. Some, taking the Latin language for their model, and turning certain phrases into cases to fill up the deficits, were for having *six* in each number ; namely, the nominative, the genitive, the dative, the accusative, the vocative, and the ablative. Others, contending that a case in grammar could be nothing else than a terminational inflection, and observing that English nouns have but one case that differs from the nominative in form, denied that there were more than two, the nominative and the possessive. This was certainly an important question, touching a fundamental principle of our grammar ; and any erroneous opinion concerning it, might well go far to condemn the book that avouched it. Every intelligent teacher could see this. For what sense could be made of parsing, without supposing an objective case to nouns ? or what propriety could there be in making the words, *of*, and *to*, and *from*, govern or compose three different cases ? Again, with what truth can it be said, that nouns have *no cases* in English ? or what reason can be assigned for making more than three ?

OBS. 4.—Public opinion is now clear in the decision, that it is *expedient* to assign to English nouns three cases, and no more ; and, in a matter of this kind, what is expedient for the purpose of instruction, is right. Yet, from the works of our grammarians, may be quoted every conceivable notion, right or wrong, upon this point. Cardell, with Tooke and Gilchrist on his side, contends that English nouns have *no* cases. Brightland averred that they have neither cases nor genders.[*] Buchanan, and the author of the old British Grammar, assigned to them *one* case only, the possessive, or genitive. Dr. Adam also says, " In English, nouns have *only one* case, namely, the genitive, or possessive case."—*Latin and Eng. Gram.* p. 7. W. B. Fowle has two cases, but rejects the word *case :* " We use the simple term *agent* for a *noun that acts,* and *object* for the object of an action."—*Fowle's True Eng. Gram.* Part II, p. 68. Webber's Grammar, published at Cambridge in 1832, recognizes but *two* cases of nouns, declaring the objective to be " altogether superfluous."—P. 22 " Our substantives have no more cases than two."—*Jamieson's Rhet.* p. 14 "A Substantive doth not properly admit of more than two cases : the Nominative, and the Genitive."—*Ellen Devis's Gram.* p. 19. Dr. Webster, in his Philosophical Grammar, of 1807, and in his Improved Grammar, of 1831, teaches the same doctrine, but less positively. This assumption has also had the support of Lowth, Johnson, Priestley, Ash, Bicknell, Fisher, Dalton, and our celebrated Lindley Murray.[†]

---

[*] " But in the *English* we have *no Genders*, as has been seen in the foregoing Notes. The same may be said of *Cases* "—*Brightland's Gram.* Seventh Edition, Lond. 1746. p. 85.

[†] The Rev. David Blair so palpably contradicts himself in respect to this matter, that I know not which he favours most, two cases or three. In his main text, he adopts no objective, but says : " According to the sense or

ML

Obs. 5.—For the *true* doctrine of *three* cases, we have the authority of Murray, in his later editions: of Webster, in his "Plain and Comp. Grammar, grounded on *True Principles*," 1790; also in his "Rudiments of English Grammar," 1811; together with the united authority of Adams, Ainsworth, Alden, Alger, Bacon, Barnard, Bingham, Burr, Bullions, Butler, Churchill, Chandler, Cobbett, Comly, Cooper, Crombie, Davenport, Davis, Fisk, A. Flint, Frost, Guy, Hart, Hiley, Hull, Ingersoll, Jaudon, Kirkham, Lennie, Mack, M'Culloch, Maunder, Merchant, Nixon, Nutting, John Peirce, Perley, Picket, Russell, Smart, R. C. Smith, Rev. T. Smith, Wilcox, and I know not how many others.

Obs. 6.—Dearborn, in 1795, recognized *four* cases; "the nominative, the possessive, the objective, and the absolute." Charles Bucke, in his work misnamed "A Classical Grammar of the English Language," published in London in 1829, asserts, that, "Substantives in English do not vary their terminations;" yet he gives them *four* cases; "the nominative, the genitive, the accusative, and the vocative." So did Allen, in a grammar much more classical, dated, London, 1813. Hazen, in 1842, adopted "four cases; namely, the nominative, the possessive, the objective, and the independent."--*Hazen's Practical Grammar*, p. 35. So too, Goodenow, of Maine, makes the cases four: "the *subjective*,* the *possessive*, the *objective*, and the *absolute*."--*Text-Book*, p. 31. Goldsbury, of Cambridge, has also four: "the Nominative, the Possessive. the Objective, and the Vocative."—*Com. S. Gram.* p. 13. Three other recent grammarians,— Wells, of Andover,— Weld, of Portland,— and Clark, of Bloomfield, N. Y.—also adopt "*four* cases;—the *nominative*, the *possessive*, the *objective*, and the *independent*." —*Wells's Gram.* p. 57; *Weld's*, 60; *Clark's*, 49. The first of these gentlemen argues, that, "Since a noun or pronoun, used *independently*, cannot at the same time be employed as 'the subject of a verb,' there is a manifest impropriety in regarding it as a *nominative*." It might as well be urged, that a nominative after a verb, or in apposition with an other, is, for this reason, *not a nominative*. He also cites this argument: "'Is there not as much difference between the *nominative* and [the] *independent* case, as there is between the *nominative* and [the] *objective?* If so, why class them together as *one* case?'—*S. R. Hall*."—*Wells's School Gram.* p. 57. To this I answer, No. "The nominative is that case which *primely denotes the name* of any person or thing;" (*Burn's Gram.* p. 36;) and *this only* it is, that can be absolute, or independent, in English. This scheme of four cases is, in fact, a grave innovation. As authority for it, Wells cites Felton; and bids his readers, "See also Kennion, Parkhurst, Fowle, Flint, Goodenow, Bucke, Hazen, Goldsbury, Chapin, S. Alexander, and P. Smith."—Page 57. But is the fourth case of these authors *the same* as his? Is it a case which "has usually the nominative form," but admits occasionally of "*me*" and "*him*," and embraces objective nouns of "*time, measure, distance, direction*, or *place?*" No. Certainly one half of them, and probably more, give little or no countenance to *such* an independent case as he has adopted. Parkhurst admitted but three cases; though he thought *two others* "might be an improvement." What Fowle has said in support of Wells's four cases, I have sought with diligence, and not found. Felton's "independent case" is only what he absurdly calls, "*The noun or pronoun addressed*."—Page 91. Bucke and Goldsbury acknowledge "*the nominative case absolute;*" and none of the twelve, so far as I know, admit any objective word, or what others call objective, to be independent or absolute, except perhaps Goldsbury.

Obs. 7.—S. R. Hall, formerly principal of the Seminary for Teachers at Andover, (but no great grammarian,) in 1832, published a manual, called "The Grammatical Assistant;" in which he says, "There are *at least five cases*, belonging to English nouns, differing as much from *each* other, as the cases of Latin and Greek nouns. They may be called Nominative, Possessive, Objective, Independent and Absolute."—P. 7. O. B. Peirce will have both nouns and pronouns to be used in *five cases*, which he thus enumerates: "Four simple cases; the Subjective, Possessive, Objective, and the Independent; and the Twofold case."—*Gram* p. 42. But, on page 56th, he speaks of a "twofold *subjective* case," "the twofold *objective* case," and shows how the *possessive* may be twofold also; so that, without taking any of the Latin cases, or even all of Hall's, he really recognizes as many as seven, if not eight. Among the English grammars which assume all the *six cases* of the Latin Language, are Burn's, Coar's, Dilworth's, Mackintosh's, Mennye's, Wm. Ward's, and the "Comprehensive Grammar," a respectable little book, published by Dobson of Philadelphia, in 1789, but written by somebody in England.

Obs. 8.—Of the English grammars which can properly be said to be *now in use*, a very great majority agree in ascribing to nouns three cases, and three only. This, I am persuaded, is the best number, and susceptible of the best defence, whether we appeal to authority, or to other argument. The disputes of grammarians make no small part of the *history of grammar;* and in submitting to be guided by their decisions, it is proper for us to consider what *degree of certainty*

relation in which nouns are used, they are in the NOMINATIVE or [the] POSSESSIVE CASE, thus, *nom.* man; *poss.* man's." To this he adds the following marginal note · " In the English language, the distinction of the objective case is observable only in the pronouns. *Cases* being nothing but *inflections*, where inflections do not exist, there can be no grammatical distinction of cases, for the terms *inflection* and *case* are *perfectly synonymous* and convertible. As the English noun has *only one change* of termination, so *no other case* is here adopted. The objective case is noticed in the pronouns; and *in parsing nouns* it is easy to distinguish *subjects* from *objects*. A noun which *governs the verb* may be described as in the *nominative* case, and one governed by the verb, or following a preposition, as in the *objective case*."—*Blair's Practical Gram.*, *Seventh Edition*. London, 1815, p. 11. The terms *inflection* and *case* are not practically synonymous, and never were so in the grammars of the language from which they are derived. The man who rejects the objective case of English nouns, because it has not a form peculiar to itself alone, must reject the accusative and the vocative of all neuter nouns in Latin, for the same reason; and the ablative, too, must in general be discarded on the same principle. In some other parts of his book, Blair speaks of the objective case of nouns as familiarly as do other authors!

* This author says, "We choose to use the term *subjective* rather than *nominative*, because it is shorter, and because it conveys its meaning by its sound, whereas the latter word means, indeed, little or nothing in itself."—*Text-Book*, p. 68. This appears to me a foolish innovation, too much in the spirit of Oliver B. Peirce, who also adopts it. The person who knows not the meaning of the word *nominative*, will not be very likely to find out what is meant by *subjective;* especially as some learned grammarians, even such men as Dr. Crombie and Professor Bullions, often erroneously call the word which is governed by the verb its *subject*. Besides, if we say *subjective* and *objective*, in stead of *nominative* and *objective*, we shall inevitably change the accent of both, and give them a pronunciation hitherto unknown to the words.—G. BROWN.

there is in the rule, and what difference or concurrence there is among them: for, the teaching of any other than the best opinions, is not the teaching of science, come from what quarter it may. On the question respecting the objective case of nouns, Murray and Webster *changed sides with each other* ; and that, long after they first appeared as grammarians. Nor was this the only, or the most important instance, in which the different editions of the works of these two gentlemen, present them in opposition, both to themselves and to each other. "What cases are there in English? The *nominative*, which usually stands before a verb; as, the *boy* writes: The *possessive*, which takes an *s* with a *comma*, and denotes property; as, *John's* hat: The *objective*, which follows a verb or preposition: as, he honors *virtue*, or it is an honor to *him*."—*Webster's Plain and Comp. Gram , Sixth Edition*, 1800, p. 9. "But for convenience, the two positions of nouns, one *before*, the other *after* the verb, are called *cases*. There are then three cases, the *nominative*, *possessive*, and *objective*."—*Webster's Rudiments of Gram.*, 1811, p. 12. "In English therefore names have two cases only, the *nominative* or simple name, and the *possessive*."—*Webster's Philosoph. Gram.*, 1807, p. 32 : also his *Improved Gram.*, 1831, p. 24.

Obs. 9.—Murray altered his opinion after the tenth or eleventh edition of his duodecimo Grammar. His instructions stand thus: "In English, substantives have but two cases, the nominative, and [the] possessive or genitive."—*Murray's Gram.* 12mo, *Second Edition*, 1795, p. 35. "For the assertion, that there are in English but two cases of nouns, and three of pronouns, we have the authority of Lowth, Johnson, Priestley, &c. *names which are sufficient* to decide this point."—*Ib.* p. 36. "In English, substantives have three cases, the nominative, the possessive, and the objective."—*Murray's Gram.* 12mo, *Twenty-third Edition*, 1816, p. 44. "The author of this work *long doubted* the propriety of assigning to English substantives an *objective case:* but a renewed critical examination of the subject; an examination to which he was prompted by the extensive and increasing demand for the grammar, has produced in his mind a *full persuasion*, that the nouns of our language are entitled to this comprehensive objective case."—*Ib.* p. 46. If there is any credit in changing one's opinions, it is, doubtless, in changing them for the better; but, of all authors, a grammarian has the most need critically to examine his subject before he goes to the printer. "This case was adopted in the *twelfth edition* of the Grammar."—*Murray's Exercises*, 12mo, N. Y. 1818, p. viii.

Obs. 10. — The *possessive case* has occasioned no less dispute than the objective. On this vexed article of our grammar, custom has now become much more uniform than it was a century ago; and public opinion may be said to have settled most of the questions which have been agitated about it. Some individuals, however, are still dissatisfied. In the first place, against those who have thought otherwise, it is determined, by infinite odds of authority, that there *is such a case*, both of nouns and of pronouns. Many a common reader will wonder, who can have been ignorant enough to deny it. "The learned and sagacious Wallis, to whom every English grammarian owes a tribute of reverence, calls this modification of the noun an *adjective possessive ;* I think, with no more propriety than he might have applied the same to the Latin genitive."— *Dr. Johnson's Gram.* p. 5. Brightland also, who gave to *adjectives* the name of *qualities*, included all possessives among them, calling them "*Possessive Qualities*, or *Qualities of Possession.*"—*Brightland's Gram.* p. 90.

Obs. 11. — This exploded error, William S. Cardell, a few years ago, republished as a novelty ; for which, among other pretended improvements of a like sort, he received the ephemeral praise of some of our modern literati. William B. Fowle also teaches the same thing. See his *Common School Gram.* Part II, p. 104. In Felch's Grammar, too, published in Boston in 1837, an attempt is made, to revive this old doctrine ; but the author takes no notice of any of the above-named authorities, being probably ignorant of them all. His *reasoning* upon the point, does not appear to me to be worthy of a detailed answer.[*] That the possessive case of nouns is not an adjective, is demonstrable ; because it may have adjectives, of various kinds, relating to it : as, "*This old man's* daughter."—*Shak.* It may also govern an other possessive ; as, "*Peter's wife's* mother."—*Bible.* Here the former possessive is governed by the latter ; but, if both were adjectives, they would both relate to the noun *mother*, and so produce a confusion of ideas. Again, nouns of the possessive case have a distinction of number, which adjectives have not. In gender also, there lies a difference. Adjectives, whenever they are varied by gender or number, *agree with their nouns* in these respects. Not so with possessives ; as, "In the *Jews*' religion."—*Gal.* i, 13. "The *children's* bread."— *Mark*, vii, 27. "Some *men's* sins."—1 *Tim.* v, 24. "Other *men's* sins."—*Ib.* ver. 22.

Obs. 12. — Secondly, general custom has clearly determined that the possessive case of nouns is always to be written *with an apostrophe* : except in those few instances in which it is not governed singly by the noun following, but so connected with an other that both are governed jointly ; as, *Cato the Censor's* doctrine,—*Sir Walter Scott's* Works,—*Beaumont and Fletcher's Plays*. This custom of using the apostrophe, however, has been opposed by many. Brightland, and Buchanan, and the author of the British Grammar, and some late writers in the Philo-

---

[*] The authorities cited by Felch, for his doctrine of "*possessive adnouns*," amount to nothing. They are ostensibly two The first is a remark of Dr. Adam's : "'*John's book* was formerly written *Johnis book*. Some have thought the '*s* a contraction of *his*, but improperly. Others have imagined, with more justness, that, by the addition of the '*s*, the substantive is changed into a possessive adjective.'—*Adam's Latin and English Grammar.* p. 7 "—*Felch's Comp. Gram.* p. 26. Here Dr. Adam by no means concurs with what these " *others have imagined* ;" for, in the very same place, he declares the possessive case of nouns to be their *only case* The second is a dogmatical and inconsistent remark of some anonymous writer in some part of the "*American Journal of Education*," a work respectable indeed, but, on the subject of grammar, too often fantastical and heterodox. Felch thinks it not improper, to use the possessive case before participles ; in which situation, it denotes, not the owner of something, but the agent, subject, or recipient, of the action, being, or change. And what a jumble does he make, where he attempts to resolve this ungrammatical construction !—telling us, in almost the same breath, that, "The agent of a *nounal* verb [i. e. participle] is never expressed," but that, "Sometimes it [the *nounal* or *gerundial verb*] is *qualified*, in its *nounal capacity*, by a possessive adnoun indicative *of its agent* as a verb', as, there is nothing like one's *being* useful ; he doubted *their* HAVING it:" and then concluding, "Hence *it appears*, that the *present participle* may be used *as agent or object*, and yet retain its character as a verb."—*Felch's Comprehensive Gram.* p. 81. Alas for the schools, if the wise men of the East receive for grammar such utter confusion, and palpable self-contradiction, as this !

ogical Museum, are among those who have successively taught, that the possessive case should be formed *like the nominative plural*, by adding *s* when the pronunciation admits the sound, and *es* when the word acquires an additional syllable. Some of these approve of the apostrophe, and others do not. Thus Brightland gives some examples, which are contrary to his rule, adopting that strange custom of putting the *s* in Roman, and the name in Italic; "as, King *Charles's Court*, and *St. James's Park.*"—*Gram. of the English Tongue*, p. 91.

Obs. 13 — "The genitive case, in my opinion," says Dr. Ash, "might be much more properly formed by adding *s*, or when the pronunciation requires it, as, without an Apostrophe: as, *men, mens*; *Ox, Oxes*; *Horse, Horses*; *Ass, Asses.*"—*Ash's Gram.* p. 23. "To write *Ox's, Ass's, Fox's*, and at the same time pronounce it *Oxes, Asses, Foxes*, is such a departure from the original formation, at least in writing, and such an inconsistent use of the Apostrophe, as cannot be equalled perhaps in any other language."—*Ib.* Lowth, too, gives some countenance to this objection: 'It [i. e. '*God's grace* '] was formerly written '*Godis grace*;' we now always shorten it with an apostrophe; often *very improperly*, when we are obliged to pronounce it fully; as, '*Thomas's book*,' that is, '*Thomasis book*,' not '*Thomas his book*,' as it is commonly supposed."—*Lowth's Gram.* p. 17. Whatever weight there may be in this argument, the objection has been overruled by general custom. The convenience of distinguishing, even to the eye alone, the numbers and uses of the noun, is found too great to be relinquished. If the declension of English nouns is ever to be amended, it cannot be done in this way. It is understood by every reader, that the *apostrophic s* adds a syllable to the noun, whenever it will not unite with the sound in which the nominative ends; as, *torch's*, pronounced *torchiz*.

" Yet time ennobles or degrades each line;
       It brighten'd *Craggs's*, and may darken thine."—*Pope*.

Obs. 14.— The English possessive case unquestionably originated in that form of the Saxon genitive which terminates in *es*, examples of which may be found in almost any specimen of the Saxon tongue: as, "On *Herodes* dagum,"—"In *Herod's* days;"—"Of *Aarones* dohtrum,"—'Of *Aaron's* daughters."—*Luke*, i, 5. This ending was sometimes the same as that of the plural; and both were changed to *is* or *ys*, before they became what we now find them. This termination added a syllable to the word; and Lowth suggests, in the quotation above, that the apostrophe was introduced to shorten it. But some contend, that the use of this mark originated in a mistake. It appears from the testimony of Brightland, Johnson, Lowth, Priestley, and others, who have noticed the error in order to correct it, that an opinion was long entertained, that the termination *'s* was a contraction of the word *his*. It is certain that Addison thought so; for he expressly says it, in the 135th number of the Spectator. Accordingly he wrote, in lieu of the regular possessive, "My paper is *Ulysses his* bow."—*Guardian*, No. 98. " Of *Socrates his* rules of prayer."—*Spect.* No. 207. So Lowth quotes Pope: " By young *Telemachus his* blooming years."—*Gram.* p. 17.[*] There is also one late author who says, " The '*s* is a contraction of *his*, and was formerly written in full; as, William Russell *his* book."—*Goodenow's Gram.* p. 32. This is undoubtedly bad English; and always was so, however common may have been the erroneous notion which gave rise to it. But the apostrophe, whatever may have been its origin, is now the acknowledged distinctive mark of the possessive case of English nouns. The application of the '*s*, frequently to feminines, and sometimes to plurals, is proof positive that it is *not a contraction* of the pronoun *his*; as,

" Now Jove suspends his golden scales in air,
       Weighs the *men's* wits against the *Lady's* hair."—*Pope*, R. of L. v, 72.

Obs. 15.— Many of the old grammarians, and Guy among the moderns, represent the regular formation of the possessive case as being the same in both numbers, supposing generally in the plural an abbreviation of the word by the omission of the second or syllabic *s*. That is, they suppose that such terms as *eagles' wings, angels' visits*, were written for *eagles's wings, angels's visits*, &c. This view of the matter accounts well enough for the fashion of such plurals as *men's, women's, children's*, and makes them regular. But I find no evidence at all of the fact on which these authors presume; nor do I believe that the regular possessive plural was ever, in general, a syllable longer than the nominative. If it ever had been so, it would still be easy to prove the point, by quotations from ancient books. The general principle then is, that *the apostrophe forms the possessive case, with an s in the singular, and without it in the plural;* but there are some exceptions to this rule, on either hand; and these must be duly noticed.

Obs 16—The chief exceptions, or irregularities, in the formation of the possessive *singular*, are, I think, to be accounted mere poetic licenses; and seldom, if ever, to be allowed in prose. Churchill, (closely copying Lowth,) speaks of them thus: " In poetry the *s* is frequently omitted after proper names ending in *s* or *x*; as, 'The wrath of *Peleus'* son.' *Pope*. This is scarcely allowable in prose, though instances of it occur: as, '*Moses'* minister.' Josh. i, 1. '*Phinehas'* wife.' Sam., iv, 19. ' *Festus* came into *Felix'* room.' *Acts*, xxiv, 27. It was done in prose evidently to avoid the recurrence of a sibilant sound at the end of two following syllables; but this may as readily be obviated by using the preposition *of*, which is now commonly substituted for the possessive case in most instances."—*Churchill's New Gram.* p. 215. In Scott's Bible, Philadelphia, 1814, the texts here quoted are all of them corrected, thus: " *Moses's* minister,"—" *Phinehas's* wife,"—" *Felix's* room." But the phrase, " for *conscience* sake," (*Rom.* xiii, 5,) is there given without the apostrophe. Alger prints it, " for *conscience'* sake," which is better; and though not regular, it is a common form for this particular expression. Our common Bibles have this text. "And the weaned child shall put his hand on the *cockatrice'* den "—*Isaiah*, xi, 8. Alger, feeling this to be wrong, wrote it, " on the *cockatrice-den*."—*Pronouncing Bible*. Dr. Scott, in his reference Bible, makes this possessive regular, " on the *cockatrice's* den." This is right. The

---

[*] A critic's accuracy is sometimes liable to be brought into doubt, by subsequent alterations of the texts which he quotes. Many an error cited in this volume of criticism, may possibly not be found in some future edition of a book referred to; as several of those which were pointed out by Lowth, have disappeared from the places cited for them. Churchill also cites this line as above, (*New Gram.* p. 214;) but, in my edition of the Odyssey, Pope, the reading is this: " By lov'd *Telemachus's* blooming years! "—Book xi, l. 84.

Vulgate has it, "*in caverna reguli;*" which, however, is not classic Latin. After *z* also, the poets sometimes drop the *s*: as,

"Sad was the hour, and luckless was the day,
When first from *Shiraz'* walls I bent my way."—*Collins.*

OBS. 17.—A recent critic, who, I think, has not yet learned to speak or write the possessive case of *his own name* properly, assumes that the foregoing occasional or poetical forms are the only true ones for the possessive singular of such words. He says, "When the name *does end* with the sound of *s* or *z*, (no matter what letter represents the sound,) the possessive form is *made* by annexing only an apostrophe."—*O. B. Peirce's Gram.* p. 44. Agreeably to this rule, he letters his work, "*Peirce' Grammar*," and condemns, as bad English, the following examples and all others like them: "James *Otis'* letters, General *Gates'* command, General *Knox's* appointment, Gov. *Meigs's* promptness, Mr. *Williams's* oration, The *witness's* deposition."—*Ib.* p. 60. It is obvious that this gentleman's doctrine and criticism are as contrary to the common practice of all good authors, as they are to the common grammars, which he ridicules. Surely, such expressions as, "*Harris's* Hermes, *Philips's* Poems, *Prince's* Bay, *Prince's* Island, *Fox's* Journal, King *James's* edict, a *justice's* warrant, *Sphinx's* riddle, the *lynx's* beam, the *lass's* beauty," have authority enough to refute the cavil of this writer; who, being himself wrong, falsely charges the older grammarians, that, "their theories vary from the principles of the language correctly spoken or written."—*Ib.* p. 60. A much more judicious author treats this point of grammar as follows: "When the possessive noun is singular, and terminates with an *s*, another *s* is requisite after it, and the apostrophe must be placed between the two: as, ' *Dickens's* works,' —' *Harris's* wit.' "—*Day's Punctuation, Third London Edition,* p. 136. The following example, too, is right: "I would not yield to be your *house's* guest."—*Shakespeare.*

OBS. 18.—All *plural* nouns that differ from the singular without ending in *s*, form the possessive case in the same manner as the singular: as, *man's, men's; woman's, women's; child's, children's; brother's, brothers' or brethren's; ox's, oxen's; goose's, geese's.* In two or three words which are otherwise alike in both numbers, the apostrophe ought to follow the *s* in the plural, to distinguish it from the singular: as, the *sheep's* fleece, the *sheeps'* fleeces; a *neat's* tongue, *neats'* tongues; a *deer's* horns, a load of *deers'* horns.

OBS. 19.—Dr. Ash says, "Nouns of the plural number that end in *s*, will not very properly admit of the genitive case."—*Ash's Gram.* p. 54. And Dr. Priestley appears to have been of the same opinion. See his *Gram.* p. 69. Lowth too avers, that the sign of the possessive case is "never added to the plural number ending in *s*."—*Gram.* p. 18. Perhaps he thought the plural sign must involve an other *s*, like the singular. This however is not true, neither is Dr. Ash's assertion true; for the New Testament speaks as properly of "the *soldiers'* counsel," as of the "*centurion's* servant;" of "the scribes that were of the *Pharisees'* part," as of " *Paul's sister's* son." It would appear, however, that the possessive plural is less frequently used than the possessive singular; its place being much oftener supplied by the preposition *of* and the objective. We cannot say that either of them is absolutely necessary to the language; but they are both worthy to be commended, as furnishing an agreeable variety of expression.

"Then shall *man's* pride and dulness comprehend
His *actions', passions', being's* use and end."—*Pope.*

OBS. 20.—The apostrophe was introduced into the possessive case, at least for the singular number, in some part of the seventeenth century. Its adoption for the plural, appears to have been later: it is not much used in books a hundred years old. In Buchanan's "Regular English Syntax," which was written, I know not exactly when, but near the middle of the eighteenth century, I find the following paragraph: "We have certainly a Genitive Plural, though there has been no Mark to distinguish it. The Warriors Arms, i. e. the Arms of the Warriors, is as much a Genitive Plural, as the Warrior's Arms, for the Arms of the Warrior is a Genitive Singular. To distinguish this Genitive Plural, especially to Foreigners, we might use the Apostrophe reversed, thus, the Warrior's Arms, the Stone's End, for the End of the Stones, the Grocer's, Taylor's, Haberdasher's, &c. Company; for the Company of Grocers, Taylors, &c. The Surgeon's Hall, for the Hall of the Surgeons; the Rider's Names, for the Names of the Riders; and so of all Plural Possessives." See *Buchan. Synt.* p. 111. Our present form of the possessive plural, being unknown to this grammarian, must have had a later origin; nor can it have been, as some imagine it was, an abbreviation of a longer and more ancient form.

OBS. 21.—The apostrophic *s* has often been added to nouns *improperly;* the words formed by it not being intended for the possessive singular, but for the nominative or objective plural. Thus we find such authors as Addison and Swift, writing *Jacobus's* and *genius's*, for *Jacobuses* and *geniuses; idea's, toga's,* and *tunica's*, for *ideas, togas,* and *tunicas; enamorato's* and *virtuoso's*, for *enamoratoes* and *virtuosoes.* Errors of this kind, should be carefully avoided.

OBS. 22.—The apostrophe and *s* are sometimes added to mere characters, to denote plurality, and not the possessive case; as, two *a's*, three *b's*, four *9's.* These we cannot avoid, except by using the *names* of the things; as, two *Aes*, three *Bees*, four *Nines.* "Laced down the sides with little *c's.*"—*Steele.* "Whenever two *gg's* come together, they are both hard."—*Buchanan.* The names of *c* and *g*, plural, are *Cees* and *Gees.* Did these authors *know* the words, or did they not? To have learned the *names* of the letters, will be found on many occasions a great convenience, especially to critics. For example: "The pronunciation of these two consecutive *s's* is hard "—*Webber's Gram.* p. 21. Better: "*Esses.*" "*S* and *x*, however, are exceptions. They are pluralyzed by adding *es* preceded by a hyphen [-], as the *s-es*; the *x-es.*"—*O. B. Peirce's Gram.* p. 40. Better, use the *names, Ess* and *Ex*, and pluralize thus: "the *Esses*; the *Exes.*"

"Make Q's of answers, to waylay
What th' other party 's like to say."—*Hudibras,* P. III, C. ii, l. 951.

Here the cipher is to be read *Kues*, but it has not the meaning of this name merely. It is put either for the plural of Q, a *Question,* like D. D.'s, (read *Dee-Dees*,) for *Doctors of Divinity,* or else, more erroneously, for *cues*, the plural of *cue*, a turn which the next speaker catches.

OBS. 23.—In the following example, the apostrophe and *s* are used to give the sound of *s*

verb's termination, to words which the writer supposed were not properly verbs: "When a man in a soliloquy reasons with himself, and *pro's* and *con's,* and weighs all his designs."—*Congreve.* But here, "*proes* and *cons,*" would have been more accurate. "We put the ordered number of *m's* into our composing-stick."—*Printer's Gram.* Here "*Ems*" would have done as well. "All measures for *folio's* and *quarto's,* should be made to *m's* of the English body; all measures for *octavo's,* to Pica *m's.*"—*Ibid.* Here regularity requires, "*folios, quartoes, octavoes,*" and "*pica Ems.*" The verb *is,* when contracted, sometimes gives to its nominative the same form as that of the possessive case, it not being always spaced off for distinction, as it may be; as,
    "A *wit's* a feather, and a chief a rod;
    An honest *man's* the noblest work of God."—*Pope, on Man,* Ep. iv, l. 247.

OBS. 24.—As the *objective case of nouns* is to be distinguished from the nominative, only by the sense, relation, and position, of words in a sentence, the learner must acquire a habit of attending to these several things. Nor ought it to be a hardship to any reader to understand that which he thinks worth reading. It is seldom possible to mistake one of these cases for the other, without a total misconception of the author's meaning. The nominative denotes the agent, actor, or doer; the person or thing that is made the subject of an affirmation, negation, question, or supposition: its place, except in a question, is commonly *before* the verb. The objective, when governed by a verb or a participle, denotes the person on whom, or the thing on which, the action falls and terminates: it is commonly placed *after* the verb, participle, or preposition, which governs it. Nouns, then, by changing places, may change cases: as, "*Jonathan* loved *David;*" "*David* loved *Jonathan.*" Yet the case depends not entirely upon position; for any order in which the words cannot be misunderstood, is allowable: as, "Such tricks hath strong imagination."—*Shak.* Here the cases are known, because the meaning is plainly this: "Strong imagination hath such tricks." "To him give all the prophets witness."—*Acts,* x, 43. This is intelligible enough, and more forcible than the same meaning expressed thus: "All the prophets give witness to him." The *order* of the words never can affect the explanation to be given of them in parsing, unless it change the sense, and form them into a different sentence.

THE DECLENSION OF NOUNS.

The declension of a noun is a regular arrangement of its numbers and cases. Thus:—

EXAMPLE I. — FRIEND.

Sing.	Nom.	friend,	Plur.	Nom.	friends,
	Poss.	friend's,		Poss.	friends',
	Obj.	friend;		Obj.	friends.

EXAMPLE II. — MAN.

Sing.	Nom.	man,	Plur.	Nom.	men,
	Poss.	man's,		Poss.	men's,
	Obj.	man;		Obj.	men.

EXAMPLE III. — FOX.

Sing.	Nom.	fox,	Plur.	Nom.	foxes,
	Poss.	fox's,		Poss.	foxes',
	Obj.	fox;		Obj.	foxes.

EXAMPLE IV. — FLY.

Sing.	Nom.	fly,	Plur.	Nom.	flies,
	Poss.	fly's,		Poss.	flies',
	Obj.	fly;		Obj.	flies.

EXAMPLES FOR PARSING.

PRAXIS III. —ETYMOLOGICAL.

In the Third Praxis, it is required of the pupil—to distinguish and define the different parts of speech, and the classes and modifications of the ARTICLES and NOUNS.

The definitions to be given in the Third Praxis, are two for an article, six for a noun, and one for an adjective, a pronoun, a verb, a participle, an adverb, a conjunction, a preposition, or an interjection. Thus:—

EXAMPLE PARSED.

"The writings of Hannah More appear to me more praiseworthy than Scott's."

The is the definite article. 1. An article is the word *the, an,* or *a,* which we put before nouns to limit their signification. 2. The definite article is *the,* which denotes some particular thing or things.

Writings is a common noun, of the third person, plural number, neuter gender, and nominative case. 1. A noun is the name of any person, place, or thing. that can be known or mentioned. 2. A common noun is the name of a sort, kind, or class, of beings or things. 3. The third person is that which denotes the person or thing merely spoken of. 4. The plural number is that which denotes more than one. 5. The neuter gender is that which denotes things that are neither male nor female. 6. The nominative case is that form or state of a noun or pronoun, which denotes the subject of a verb.

Of is a preposition. 1. A preposition is a word used to express some relation of different things or thoughts to each other, and is generally placed before a noun or a pronoun.

Hannah More is a proper noun, of the third person, singular number, feminine gender, and objective case. 1. A noun is the name of any person, place, or thing, that can be known or mentioned. 2. A proper noun is the name of some particular individual, or people, or group. 3. The third person is that which denotes the person or thing merely spoken of. 4. The singular number is that which denotes but one. 5. The feminine gender is that which denotes persons or animals of the female kind. 6. The objective case is that form or state of a noun or pronoun, which denotes the object of a verb, participle, or preposition.

Appear is a verb. 1. A verb is a word that signifies *to be, to act, or to be acted upon.*

To is a preposition. 1. A preposition is a word used to express some relation of different things or thoughts to each other, and is generally placed before a noun or a pronoun.

Me is a pronoun. 1. A pronoun is a word used in stead of a noun.

More is an adverb. 1. An adverb is a word added to a verb, a participle, an adjective, or an other adverb; and generally expresses time, place, degree, or manner.

Praiseworthy is an adjective. 1. An adjective is a word added to a noun or pronoun, and generally expresses quality.

Than is a conjunction. 1. A conjunction is a word used to connect words or sentences in construction, and show the dependence of the terms so connected.

Scott's is a proper noun, of the third person, singular number, masculine gender, and possessive case. 1. A noun is the name of any person, place, or thing, that can be known or mentioned. 2. A proper noun is the name of some particular individual. or people, or group. 3. The third person is that which denotes the person or thing merely spoken of. 4. The singular number is that which denotes but one. 5. The masculine gender is that which denotes persons or animals of the male kind. 6. The possessive case is that form or state of a noun or pronoun, which denotes the relation of property.

LESSON I. — PARSING.

"The virtue of Alexander appears to me less vigorous than that of Socrates Socrates in Alexander's place I can readily conceive : Alexander in that of Socrates I cannot. Alexander will tell you, he can subdue the world : it was a greater work in Socrates to fulfill the duties of life. Worth consists most, not in great, but in good actions." — *Kames's Art of Thinking*, p. 70.

"No one should ever rise to speak in public, without forming to himself a just and strict idea of what suits his own age and character; what suits the subject, the hearers, the place, the occasion." — *Blair's Rhetoric*, p. 260.

"In the short space of little more than a century, the Greeks became such states-men, warriors, orators, historians, physicians, poets, critics, painters, sculptors architects, and, last of all, philosophers, that one can hardly help considering the golden period, as a providential event in honour of human nature, to show to what perfection the species might ascend." — *Harris's Hermes*, p. 417.

"Is genius yours ? Be yours a glorious end,
Be your king's, country's, truth's, religion's friend." — *Young*.

LESSON II.—PARSING.

"He that is called in the Lord, being a servant, is the Lord's freeman : likewise also, he that is called, being free, is Christ's servant." — 1 *Cor.* vii, 22.

"What will remain to the Alexanders, and the Cæsars, and the Jenghizes, and the Louises, and the Charleses, and the Napoleons, with whose 'glories' the idle voice of fame is filled ? " — *J. Dymond*.

"Good sense, clear ideas, perspicuity of language, and proper arrangement of words and thoughts, will always command attention." — *Blair's Rhet.* p. 174.

"A mother's tenderness and a father's care are nature's gifts for man's advan-tage. — Wisdom's precepts form the good man's interest and happiness." — *Murray's Key*, p. 194.

"A dancing-school among the Tuscaroras, is not a greater absurdity than a masquerade in America. A theatre, under the best regulations, is not essential to our happiness. It may afford entertainment to individuals ; but it is at the expense of private taste and public morals." — *Webster's Essays*, p. 86.

"Where dancing sunbeams on the waters played,
And verdant alders form'd a quivering shade." — *Pope*.

LESSON III.—PARSING.

"I have ever thought that advice to the young, unaccompanied by the routine honest employments, is like an attempt to make a shrub grow in a certain direction, by blowing it with a bellows." — *Webster's Essays*, p. 247.

"The Arabic characters for the writing of numbers, were introduced into Europe by Pope Sylvester II., in the eleventh century." — *Constable's Miscellany*.

"Emotions raised by inanimate objects, trees, rivers, buildings, pictures, arrive at perfection almost instantaneously; and they have a long endurance, a second view producing nearly the same pleasure with the first." — *Kames's Elements*, i, 108.

"There is great variety in the same plant, by the different appearances of its stem, branches, leaves, blossoms, fruit, size, and colour; and yet, when we trace that variety through different plants, especially of the same kind, there is discovered a surprising uniformity." — *Ib.* i, 273.

> "Attitude, action, air, pause, start, sigh, groan,
> He borrow'd, and made use of as his own." — *Churchill*.

> "I dread thee, fate, relentless and severe,
> With all a poet's, husband's, father's fear!" — *Burns*.

IMPROPRIETIES FOR CORRECTION.
ERRORS OF NOUNS.
LESSON I.—NUMBERS.

"All the ablest of the Jewish Rabbis acknowledge it." — *Wilson's Heb. Gram.* p. 7.

[FORMULE.—Not proper, because the word *Rabbi* is here made plural by the addition of *s* only. But, according to Observation 12th on the numbers, nouns in *i* ought rather to form the plural in *ies*. The capital *R*, too, is not necessary. Therefore, *Rabbis* should be *rabbies*, with *ies* and a small *r*.]

"Who has thoroughly imbibed the system of one or other of our Christian rabbis."—*Campbell's Rhet.* p. 378. "The seeming singularitys of reason soon wear off."—*Collier's Antoninus*, p. 47. "The chiefs and arikis or priests have the power of declaring a place or object taboo."—*Balbi's Geog.* p. 460. "Among the various tribes of this family, are the Pottawatomies, the Sacs and Foxes, or Saukis and Ottogamis."—*Ib.* p. 178. "The Shawnees, Kickapoos, Menomonies, Miamis and Delawares, are of the same region."—*Ib.* p. 178. The Mohegans and Abenaquis belonged also to this family."—*Ib.* p. 178. "One tribe of this family, the Winnebagos, formerly resided near lake Michigan."—*Ib.* p. 179. "The other tribes are the Ioways, the Otoes, the Missouris, the Quapaws."—*Ib.* p. 179. "The great Mexican family comprizes the Aztecs, Toltecs, and Tarascos."—*Ib.* p. 179. "The Mulattoes are born of negro and white parents; the Zambos, of Indians and negroes."—*Ib.* p. 165. "To have a place among the Alexanders, the Cæsars, the Lewis', or the Charles', the scourges and butchers of their fellow-creatures."—*Burgh's Dignity*, i, 132. "Which was the notion of the Platonic Philosophers and Jewish rabbii."—*Ib.* p. 248. "That they should relate to the whole body of virtuosos."—*Cobbett's E. Gram.* ¶ 212. "What thank have ye? for sinners also love those that love them."—*Luke*, vi, 32. "There are five ranks of nobility; dukes, marquesses, earls, viscounts, and barons."—*Balbi's Geog.* p. 228. "Acts, which were so well known to the two Charles's."—*Payne's Geog.* ii, 511. "Court Martials are held in all parts, for the trial of the blacks."—*Observer*, No. 468. "It becomes a common noun, and may have a plural number; as, the two *Davids*; the two *Scipios*, the two *Pompies*."—*Staniford's Gram.* p. 8. "The food of the rattlesnake is birds, squirrels, hare, rats, and reptiles."—*Balbi's Geog.* p. 177. "And let fowl multiply in the earth."—*Genesis*, i, 22. "Then we reached the hill-side where eight buffalo were grazing."—*Martineau's Amer.* i, 202. "*Corset, n.* a pair of bodice for a woman."—*Worcester's Dict.* 12mo. "As the *b's*; the *œ's*, the *doubleyu's*."—*O. B. Peirce's Gram.* p. 40. "Simplicity is the means between ostentation and rusticity."—*Pope's Pref. to Homer*. "You have disguised yourselves like tipstaves."—*Gil Blas*, i, 111. "But who, that hath any taste, can endure the incessant quick returns of the *also's*, and the *likewise's*, and the *moreover's*, and the *however's*, and the *notwithstanding's*?"—*Campbell's Rhet.* p. 439.

> "Sometimes, in mutual sly disguise,
> Let Aye's seem No's, and No's seem Aye's."—*Gay*, p. 431.

LESSON II.—CASES.

"For whose name sake, I have been made willing."—*Wm. Penn*.

[FORMULE.—Not proper, because the noun *name*, which is here meant for the possessive case singular, has not the true form of that case. But, according to a principle on page 247th, "The possessive case of nouns is formed, in the singular number, by adding to the nominative *s* preceded by an apostrophe; and, in the plural, when the nominative ends in *s*, by adding an apostrophe only." Therefore, *name* should be *name's*; thus, "For whose name's sake, I have been made willing."]

"Be governed by your conscience, and never ask any bodies leave to be honest."— *Collier's Antoninus*, p. 105. "To overlook nobodies me it or misbehaviour."—*Ib.* p. 9. "And Hector at last fights his way to the stern of Ajax' ship."—*Coleridge's Introd.*

p. 91. "Nothing is lazier, than to keep ones eye upon words without heeding their meaning."— *Philological Museum*, i, 645. "Sir William Joneses division of the day."— *Ib. Contents.* "I need only refer here to Vosses excellent account of it."— *Ib.* i, 465. "The beginning of Stesichoruses palinode has been preserved."—*Ib.* i, 442. "Though we have Tibulluses elegies, there is not a word in them about Glycera."—*Ib.* p. 446. "That Horace was at Thaliarchuses country-house."— *Ib.* i, 451. "That Sisyphuses foot-tub should have been still in existence."—*Ib.* i, 468. "How every thing went on in Horace's closet, and in Mecenases antechamber."— *Ib.* i, 458. "Who, for elegant brevities sake, put a participle for a verb."—*Walker's Particles*, p. 42. "The countries liberty being oppressed, we have no more to hope."—*Ib.* p. 73. "A brief but true account of this peoples' principles."— *Barclay's Pref.* "As, the Churche's Peace, or the Peace of the Church; Virgil's Æneid, or the Eneid of Virgil."— *British Gram.* p. 93. "As, Virgil's Æneid, for the Æneid of Virgil; the Church'es Peace, for the Peace of the Church."— *Buchanan's Syntax*, p. 18. "Which, with Hubner's Compend, and Wells' Geographia Classica, will be sufficient."— *Burgh's Dignity*, i, 155. "Witness Homer's speaking horses, scolding goddesses, and Jupiter enchanted with Venus' girdle."— *Ib.* i, 184. "Dr. Watts' Logic may with success be read and commented on to them."—*Ib.* p. 156. "Potter's Greek, and Kennet's Roman Antiquities, Strauchius' and Helvicus' Chronology."— *Ib.* p. 161. "*Sing.* Alice' friends, Felix' property; *Plur.* The Alices' friends, The Felixes' property."—*O. B. Peirce's Gram.* p. 46. "Such as Bacchus'es company,"—"at Bacchus'es festivals."— *Ainsworth's Dict. w. Thyrsus.* "Burn's inimitable *Tam o' Shanter* turns entirely upon such a circumstance."— *Scott's Lay, Notes*, p. 201. "Nominative, Men. Genitive, Mens. Objective, Men."—*Cutler's Gram.* p. 20. "Mens Happiness or Misery is most part of their own making."— *Locke, on Education*, p. 1. "That your Sons Cloths be never made strait, especially about the Breast."— *Ib.* p. 15. "Childrens Minds are narrow and weak."—*Ib.* p. 297. "I would not have little Children much tormented about Punctilio's, or Niceties of Breeding."—*Ib.* p. 90. "To fill his Head with suitable Idea's."—*Ib.* p. 113. "The Burgusdiscius's and the Scheiblers did not swarm in those Days, as they do now."—*Ib.* p. 163. "To see the various ways of dressing—a calve's head!"—*Shenstone*, Brit. Poets, Vol. vii, p. 143.

　　"He puts it on, and for decorum sake
　　Can wear it e'en as gracefully as she."—*Cowper's Task.*

LESSON III.—MIXED.

　　"Simon the witch was of this religion too."—*Bunyan's P. P.*, p. 123.

[FORMULE.—Not proper, because the feminine name *witch* is here applied to a man. But, according to the doctrine of genders, on page 244th, "Names of males are masculine; names of females, feminine;" &c. Therefore, *witch* should be *wizard*; thus, "Simon the *wizard*," &c.]

　　"Mammodis, *n.* Coarse, plain India muslins."—*Webster's Dict.* "Go on from single persons to families, that of the Pompeyes for instance."—*Collier's Antoninus*, p. 142. "By which the ancients were not able to account for phænomenas."—*Bailey's Ovid*, p. vi. "After this I married a wife who had lived at Crete, but a Jew by birth."—*Josephus's Life*, p. 194. "The very heathen are inexcusable for not worshipping him."—*Student's Manual*, p. 328. "Such poems as Camoen's Lusiad, Voltaire's Henriade, &c."—*Blair's Rhet.* p. 422. "My learned correspondent writes a word in defence of large scarves."—SPECT. *in Joh. Dict.* "The forerunners of an apoplexy are dulness, vertigos, tremblings."—ARBUTHNOT: *ib.* "*Vertigo* changes the *o* into *inēs*, making the plural *vertiginēs.*"—*Churchill's Gram.* p. 59. "*Noctambulo* changes the *o* into *ōnēs*, making the plural *noctambulōnēs.*"—*Ib.* p. 59. "What shall we say of noctambulos?—ARBUTHNOT: *in Joh. Dict.* "In the curious fretwork of rocks and grottos."—*Blair's Rhet.* p. 200. "Wharf makes the plural *wharves.*"—*Smith's Gram.* p. 45; *Merchant's*, 29; *Picket's*, 21; *Frost's*, 8. "A few cent's worth of maccaroni supplies all their wants."—*Balbi's Geog.* p. 275. "C sounds hard, like *k*, at the end of a word or syllables."—*Blair's Gram.* p. 4. "By which the virtuosi try The magnitude of every lie."—*Hudibras.* Quartos, octavos, shape the lessening pyre."—*Pope's Dunciad*, B. i, l. 162. "Perching within square royal rooves."—SIDNEY: *in Joh. Dict.* "Similies should, even in poetry, be used with moderation."—*Blair's Rhet.* p. 166. "Similies should never be taken from low or mean objects."—*Ib.* p. 167. "It were certainly better to say, 'The house of lords,' than 'the Lord's house.'"—*Murray's Gram.* 8vo. p. 177. "Read your answers. Unit figure? 'Five.' Ten's? 'Six.' Hundreds? 'Seven.'"—*Abbott's Teacher*, p. 79. "Alexander conquered Darius' army."—*Kirkham's Gram.* p. 58. "Three days time was requisite, to prepare matters."—*Brown's Estimate*, ii, 156. "So we say that Ciceros stile and Sallusts, were not one, nor Cesars and Livies, nor Homers and Hesiodus, nor Herodotus and Theucidides, nor Euripides and Aristophanes, nor Erasmus and Budeus stiles."—*Puttenham's Arte of English Poesie*, iii, 5. "*Lex* (i. e. *legs*) is no other than our ancestors past partciple *leg, laid down.*"—*Tooke's Diversions*, ii, 7. "Achaia's sons at Ilium slain for the Atride' sake."—*Cowper's Iliad.* "The corpse* of half her senate manure the fields of Thessaly."—*Addison's Cato.*

　　"Poisoning, without regard of fame or fear:
　　And spotted corpse are frequent on the bier."—*Dryden.*

* Corpse forms the plural regularly, corpses; as in 2 Kings, xix, 35: "In the morning, behold, they were all dead corpses."

CHAPTER IV.—ADJECTIVES.

An Adjective is a word added to a noun or pronoun, and generally expresses quality: as, A *wise* man; a *new* book. You *two* are *diligent*.

OBSERVATIONS.

OBS. 1.—Adjectives have been otherwise called attributes, attributives, qualities, adnouns; but none of these names is any better than the common one. Some writers have classed adjectives with verbs; because, with a neuter verb for the copula, they often form logical predicates: as, "Vices *are contagious*." The Latin grammarians usually class them with nouns; consequently their nouns are divided into nouns substantive and nouns adjective. With us, substantives are nouns; and adjectives form a part of speech by themselves. This is generally acknowledged to be a much better distribution. Adjectives cannot with propriety be called *nouns*, in any language; because they are not *the names* of the qualities which they signify. They must be *added* to nouns or pronouns in order to make sense. But if, in a just distribution of words, the term "*adjective nouns*" is needless and improper, the term "*adjective pronouns*" is, certainly, not less so: most of the words which Murray and others call by this name, are not pronouns, but adjectives.

OBS. 2.—The noun, or substantive, is a *name*, which makes sense of it-elf. The adjective is an adjunct to the noun or pronoun. It is a word added to denote quality, situation, quantity, number, form, tendency, or whatever else may characterize and distinguish the thing or things spoken of. Adjectives, therefore, are distinguished *from* nouns by their *relation to* them; a relation corresponding to that which qualities bear to things: so that no part of speech is more easily discriminated than the adjective. Again: English adjectives, as such, are all indeclinable. When, therefore, any words usually belonging to this class, are found to take either the plural or the possessive form, like substantive nouns, they are to be parsed as nouns. To abbreviate expression, we not unfrequently, in this manner, convert adjectives into nouns. Thus, in grammar, we often speak of *nominatives, possessives*, or *objectives*, meaning nouns or pronouns of the nominative, the possessive, or the objective case; of *positives, comparatives*, or *superlatives*, meaning adjectives of the positive, the comparative, or the superlative degree; of *infinitives, subjunctives*, or *imperatives*, meaning verbs of the infinitive, the subjunctive, or the imperative mood; and of *singulars, plurals*, and many other such things, in the same way. So a man's *superiors* or *inferiors* are persons superior or inferior to himself. His *betters* are persons better than he. *Others* are any persons or things distinguished from some that are named or referred to; as, "If you want enemies, excel *others*; if you want friends, let *others* excel you."—*Lacon*. All adjectives thus taken substantively, become *nouns*, and ought to be parsed as such, unless this word *others* is to be made an exception.

" Th' event is fear'd; should we again provoke
Our *stronger*, some worse way his wrath may find."—*Milton*, P. L. ii, 82.

OBS. 3.—Murray says, "Perhaps the words *former* and *latter* may be properly ranked amongst the demonstrative pronouns, *especially in many of their applications*. The following sentence may serve as an example: 'It was happy for the state, that Fabius continued in the command with Minutius: the *former's* phlegm was a check upon the *latter's* vivacity.' "—*Gram.* 8vo, p. 57. This I take to be bad English. *Former* and *latter* ought to be adjectives only; except when *former* means *maker*. And, if not so, it is too easy a way of multiplying pronouns, to manufacture two out of one single anonymous sentence. If it were said, "The deliberation *of the former* was a seasonable check upon the fiery temper *of the latter*," the words *former* and *latter* would seem to me not to be pronouns, but adjectives, each relating to the noun *commander* understood after it.

OBS. 4.—The sense and relation of words in sentences, as well as their particular form and meaning, must be considered in parsing, before the learner can say, with certainty, to what class they belong. Other parts of speech, and especially nouns and participles, by a change in their construction, may become adjectives. Thus, to denote the material of which a thing is formed, we very commonly make the name of the substance an adjective to that of the thing: as, A *gold* chain, a *silver* spoon, a *glass* pitcher, a *tin* basin, an *oak* plank, a *bass-wood* slab, a *whalebone* rod. This construction is in general correct, whenever the former word may be predicated of the latter; as, "The chain is gold."—"The spoon is silver." But we do not write *gold beater* for *goldbeater*, or *silver smith* for *silversmith*; because the beater is not gold, nor is the smith silver. This principle, however, is not universally observed; for we write *snowball, whitewash*, and many similar compounds, though the ball is snow, and the wash is white; and *linseed oil*, or *Newark cider*, may be a good phrase, though the former word cannot well be predicated of the latter. So in the following examples: "Let these *conversation* tones be the foundation of public pronunciation."—*Blair's Rhet.* p. 334. "A *muslin* flounce, made very full, would give a very agreeable *flirtation* air."—POPE: *Priestley's Gram.* p. 79.

" Come, calm Content, serene and sweet,
O gently guide my *pilgrim* feet
To find thy *hermit* cell."—*Barbauld*.

OBS. 5.—Murray says, "Various nouns placed before other nouns assume the nature of adjectives: as, sea fish, wine vessel, corn field, meadow ground, &c."—*Octavo Gram.* p. 48. This is, certainly, very lame instruction. If there is not palpable error in all his examples, the propriety of them all is at least questionable; and, to adopt and follow out their principle, would be, to tear apart some thousands of our most familiar compounds. "*Meadow ground*" may perhaps be a correct phrase, since the ground is meadow; it seems therefore preferable to the compound word *meadow-ground*. What he meant by "*wine vessel*," is doubtful:

17

that is, whether a ship or a cask, a flagon or a decanter. If we turn to our dictionaries, Webster has *sea-fish* and *wine-cask* with a hyphen, and *cornfield* without; while Johnson and others have *corn-field* with a hyphen, and *seafish* without. According to the rules for the figure of words, we ought to write them *seafish, winecask, cornfield.* What then becomes of the thousands of "adjectives" embraced in the "&c." quoted above ?

OBS. 6.—The pronouns *he* and *she,* when placed before or prefixed to nouns merely to denote their gender, appear to be used adjectively; as, "The male or *he* animals offered in sacrifice."—*Wood's Dict. w. Males.* "The most usual term is *he* or *she, male* or *female,* employed as an adjective : as, a *he bear,* a *she bear*; a *male elephant,* a *female elephant.*"—*Churchill's Gram.* p. 69. Most writers, however, think proper to insert a hyphen in the terms here referred to : as, *he-bear, she-bear,* the plurals of which are *he-bears* and *she-bears.* And, judging by the foregoing rule of predication, we must assume that this practice only is right. In the first example, the word *he* is useless; for the term *"male animals"* is sufficiently clear without it. It has been shown in the third chapter, that *he* and *she* are sometimes used as nouns; and that, as such, they may take the regular declension of nouns, making the plurals *hes* and *shes.* But whenever these words are used adjectively to denote gender, whether we choose to insert the hyphen or not, they are, without question, indeclinable. like other adjectives. In the following example, Sanborn will have *he* to be a noun in the *objective* case ; but I consider it rather, to be an adjective signifying *masculine.*

"(*Philosophy,* I say, and call *it He;*
For, whatsoe'er the painter's fancy be,
It a male-virtue seems to me.)"—*Cowley,* Brit. Poets, Vol. ii, p. 54.

OBS. 7.—Though verbs give rise to many adjectives, they seldom, if ever, become such by a mere change of construction. It is mostly by assuming an additional termination, that any verb is formed into an adjective : as in *teachable, moveable, oppressive, diffusive, prohibitory.* There are, however, about forty words ending in *ate,* which, without difference of form, are either verbs or adjectives; as, *aggregate, animate, appropriate, articulate, aspirate, associate, complicate, confederate, consummate, deliberate, desolate. effeminate, elate, incarnate, intimate, legitimate, moderate, ordinate, precipitate, prostrate, regenerate, reprobate, separate, sophisticate, subordinate.* This class of adjectives seems to be lessening. The participials in *ed,* are superseding some of them, at least in popular practice: as, *contaminated,* for *contaminate,* defiled ; *reiterated,* for *reiterate,* repeated ; *situated,* for *situate,* placed ; *attenuated,* for *attenuate,* made thin or slender. *Devote, exhaust,* and some other verbal forms, are occasionally used by the poets, in lieu of the participial forms, *devoted, exhausted,* &c.

OBS. 8.—Participles, which have naturally much resemblance to this part of speech, often drop their distinctive character, and become adjectives. This is usually the case whenever they stand immediately *before* the nouns to which they relate; as, A *pleasing* countenance, a *piercing* eye, an *accomplished* scholar, *an exalted* station. Many participial adjectives are derivatives formed from participles by the negative prefix *un,* which reverses the meaning of the primitive word; as, *undisturbed, undivided, unenlightened.* Most words of this kind differ of course from participles, because there are no such verbs as *to undisturb, to undivide,* &c. Yet they may be called participial adjectives, because they have the termination, and embrace the form, of participles. Nor should any participial adjective be needlessly varied from the true orthography of the participle: a distinction is, however, observed by some writers, between *past* and *passed, staid* and *stayed;* and some old words, as *drunken, stricken, shotten, rotten,* now obsolete as participles, are still retained as adjectives. This sort of words will be further noticed in the chapter on participles.

OBS. 9.—Adverbs are generally distinguished from adjectives, by the form, as well as by the construction, of the words. Yet, in instances not a few, the same word is capable of being used both adjectively and adverbially. In these cases, the scholar must determine the part of speech, by the construction alone; remembering that adjectives belong to nouns or pronouns only; and adverbs, to verbs. participles, adjectives, or other adverbs, only. The following examples from Scripture, will partially illustrate this point, which will be noticed again under the head of adverbs: "Is your father *well?*'"—*Gen.* xliii, 27. "Thou hast *well* said."—*John,* iv, 17. "He separateth *very* friends."—*Prov.* xvi, 9. "Esaias is *very* bold."—*Rom.* x, 20. "For a pretence, ye make *long* prayer."—*Matt.* xxiii, 14. "They that tarry *long* at the wine."—*Prov.* xxiii, 30. "It had not *much* earth."—*Mark,* iv, 5. "For she loved *much.*"—*Luke,* vii, 47.

OBS. 10.—Prepositions, in regard to their *construction,* differ from adjectives, almost exactly as active-transitive participles differ syntactically from adjectives: that is, in stead of being mere adjuncts to the words which follow them, they govern those words, and refer back to some other term ; which, in the usual order of speech, stands before them. Thus, if I say, "A *spreading* oak," *spreading* is an adjective relating to *oak ;* if, "A boy spreading hay," *spreading* is a participle, governing *hay,* and relating to *boy,* because the boy is the agent of the action. So, when Dr. Webster says, "The *off* horse in a team," *off* is an adjective, relating to the noun *horse;* but, in the phrase, "A man *off* his guard," *off* is a preposition, showing the relation between *man* and *guard,* and governing the latter. The following are other examples : "From the *above* speculations."—*Harris's Hermes,* p. 194. "An *after* period of life."—MARSHALL : *in Web. Dict.* "With some other of the *after* Judaical rites."—*Right of Tythes,* p. 86. "Whom this *beneath* world doth embrace and hug."—*Shak.* "Especially is *over* exertion made."—*Journal of Lit. Conv.* p. 119. "To both the *under* worlds."—*Hudibras.* "Please to pay to A. B. the amount of the *within* bill." Whether properly used or not, the words *above, after, beneath, over, under,* and *within,* are here unquestionably made *adjectives ;* yet every scholar knows, that they are generally prepositions, though sometimes adverbs.

CLASSES.

Adjectives may be divided into six classes ; namely, *common, proper, numeral, pronominal, participial,* and *compound.*

I. A *common adjective* is any ordinary epithet, or adjective denoting quality or situation; as, *Good, bad, peaceful, warlike—eastern, western, outer, inner,*

II. A *proper adjective* is an adjective formed from a proper name; as, *American, English, Platonic, Genoese.*

III. A *numeral adjective* is an adjective that expresses a definite number; as, *One, two, three, four, five, six,* &c.

IV. A *pronominal adjective* is a definitive word which may either accompany a noun, or represent it understood; as, "*All* join to guard what *each* desires to gain."—*Pope.* That is, "*All men* join to guard what *each man* desires to gain."

V. A *participial adjective* is one that has the form of a participle, but differs from it by rejecting the idea of time; as, "An *amusing* story,"—"A *lying* divination."

VI. A *compound adjective* is one that consists of two or more words joined together, either by the hyphen or solidly: as, *Nut-brown, laughter-loving, four-footed; threefold, lordlike, lovesick.*

OBSERVATIONS.

Obs. 1.—This distribution of the adjectives is no less easy to be applied, than necessary to a proper explanation in parsing. How many adjectives there are in the language, it is difficult to say; none of our dictionaries profess to exhibit all that are embraced in some of the foregoing classes. Of the Common Adjectives, there are probably not fewer than six thousand, exclusive of the common nouns which we refer to this class when they are used adjectively. Walker's Rhyming Dictionary contains five thousand or more, the greater part of which may be readily distinguished by their peculiar endings. Of those which end in *ous*, as *generous*, there are about 850. Of those in *y* or *ly*, as *shaggy, homely*, there are about 550. Of those in *ive*, as *deceptive*, there are about 400. Of those in *al*, as *autumnal*, there are about 550. Of those in *ical*, as *mechanical*, there are about 350. Of those in *able*, as *valuable*, there are about 600. Of those in *ible*, as *credible*, there are about 200. Of those in *ent*, as *different*, there are about 300. Of those in *ant*, as *abundant*, there are about 170. Of those in *less*, as *ceaseless*, there are about 220. Of those in *ful*, as *useful*, there are about 130. Of those in *ory*, as *explanatory*, there are about 200. Of those in *ish*, as *childish*, there are about 100. Of those in *ine*, as *masculine*, there are about 70. Of those in *en*, as *wooden*, there are about 50. Of those in *some*, as *quarrelsome*, there are about 30. These sixteen numbers, added together, make 4770.

Obs. 2.—The Proper Adjectives are, in many instances, capable of being converted into declinable nouns: as, *European, a European, the Europeans; Greek, a Greek, the Greeks; Asiatic, an Asiatic, the Asiatics.* But with the words *English, French, Dutch, Scotch, Welsh, Irish,* and in general all such as would acquire an additional syllable in their declension, the case is otherwise. The gentile noun has frequently fewer syllables than the adjective, but seldom more, unless derived from some different root. Examples: *Arabic, an Arab, the Arabs; Gallic, a Gaul, the Gauls; Danish, a Dane, the Danes; Moorish, a Moor, the Moors; Polish, a Pole, or Polander, the Poles; Swedish, a Swede, the Swedes; Turkish, a Turk, the Turks.* When we say, *the English, the French, the Dutch, the Scotch, the Welsh, the Irish,*—meaning, *the English people, the French people,* &c., many grammarians conceive that *English, French,* &c., are *indeclinable nouns.* But in my opinion, it is better to reckon them *adjectives*, relating to the noun *men* or *people* understood. Or if these words are nouns, so are a thousand others, after which there is the same ellipsis; as when we say, *the good, the great, .the wise, the learned.*[*] The principle would involve the inconvenience of multiplying our nouns of the singular form and a plural meaning, indefinitely. If they are nouns, they are, in this sense, plural only; and, in an other, they are singular only. For we can no more say, *an English, an Irish,* or *a French,* for *an Englishman, an Irishman,* or *a Frenchman;* than we can say, *an old, a selfish,* or *a rich,* for *an old man, a selfish man,* or *a rich man.* Yet, in distinguishing the *languages,* we call them *English, French, Dutch, Scotch, Welsh, Irish;* using the words, certainly, in no plural sense; and referring always the line of adjectives, where the gentile noun is different: as, *Arabic,* and not *Arab; Danish,* and not *Dane; Swedish,* and not *Swede.* In this sense, as well as in the former, Webster, Chalmers, and other modern lexicographers, call the words *nouns;* and the reader will perceive, that the objections offered before do not apply here. But Johnson, in his two quarto volumes, gives only two words of this sort, *English* and *Latin;* and both of

---

[*] Murray says, "An *adjective* put without a substantive, with the definite article before it, *becomes a substantive in sense and meaning,* and is *written as a substantive:* as, 'Providence rewards *the good,* and punishes *the bad.*'" If I understand this, it is very erroneous, and plainly contrary to the fact. I suppose the author to speak of *good persons* and *bad persons;* and, if he does, is there not an ellipsis in his language? How can it be said, that *good* and *bad* are here substantives, since they have a plural meaning and refuse the plural form? A word "*written as a substantive,*" unquestionably *is* a substantive; but neither of these is here entitled to that name. Yet Smith, and other satellites of Murray, endorse his doctrine; and say, that *good* and *bad* in this example, and all adjectives similarly circumstanced, "may be considered *nouns* in parsing."—*Smith's New Gram.* £2 "An adjective with the definite article before it, becomes *a noun,* (of the third person, plural number,) and must be parsed as such."—*R. G. Greene's Grammatical Text-Book,* p. 55.

these he calls *adjectives:* "ENGLISH, *adj.* Belonging to England; hence English* is the language of England." The word *Latin,* however, he makes a noun, when it means a schoolboy's exercise; for which usage he quotes, the following inaccurate example from Ascham: "He shall not use the common order in schools for making of *Latins.*"

OBS. 3.—Dr. Webster gives us explanations like these: "CHINESE, *n. sing.* and *plu.* A native of China; also the language of China."—"JAPANESE, *n.* A native of Japan; or the language of the inhabitants."—"GENOESE, *n. pl.* the people of Genoa in Italy. *Addison.*"—"DANISH, *n.* The language of the Danes."—"IRISH, *n.* l. A native of Ireland. 2. The language of the Irish; the Hiberno-Celtic." According to him, then, it is proper to say, *a Chinese, a Japanese,* or *an Irish;* but not, *a Genoese,* because he will have this word to be plural only! Again, if with him we call a native of Ireland *an Irish,* will not more than one be *Irishes?†* If a native of Japan be a *Japanese,* will not more than one be *Japaneses?* In short, is it not plain, that the words, *Chinese, Japanese, Portuguese, Maltese, Genoese, Milanese,* and all others of like formation, should follow one and the same rule? And if so, what is that rule? Is it not this:—that, like *English, French,* &c., they are always *adjectives;* except, perhaps, when they denote *languages?* There may possibly be some real authority from usage. for calling a native of China *a Chinese,*—of Japan *a Japanese,*—&c.; as there is also for the regular plurals, *Chinese, Japaneses,* &c.; but is it, in either case, good and sufficient authority? The like forms, it is acknowledged, are, on some occasions, mere adjectives; and, in modern usage, we do not find these words inflected, as they were formerly. Examples: "The *Chinese* are by no means a cleanly people, either in person or dress"—*Balbi's Geog.* p. 415. "The *Japanese* excel in working in copper, iron, and steel."—*Ib.* p. 419. "The *Portuguese* are of the same origin with the Spaniards."—*Ib.* p. 272. "By whom the undaunted *Tyrolese* are led."—*Wordsworth's Poems,* p 122. Again: "Amongst the *Portuguese,* 'tis so much a Fashion, and Emulation, amongst their Children, to *learn* to *Read,* and Write, that they cannot hinder them from it."—*Locke, on Education,* p. 271. "The *Maltese* do so, who harden the Bodies of their Children, and reconcile them to the Heat, by making them go stark Naked."—*Idem, Edition of* 1699, p. 5. "CHINESE, *n. s.* Used elliptically for the language and people of China: plural, *Chineses. Sir T. Herbert.*"—*Abridgement of Todd's Johnson.* This is certainly absurd. For if *Chinese* is used *elliptically* for the people of China, it is an *adjective,* and does not form the plural, *Chineses:* which is precisely what I urge concerning the whole class. These plural forms ought not to be imitated. Horne Tooke quotes some friend of his, as saying, "No, I will never descend with him beneath even *a Japanese:* and I remember what Voltaire remarks of *that country.*"—*Diversions of Purley,* i, 187. In this case, he ought, unquestionably, to have said—"beneath even *a native of Japan;*" because, whether *Japanese* be a noun or not, it is absurd to call *a Japanese, "that country."* Butler, in his Hudibras, somewhere uses the word *Chineses;* and it was, perhaps, in his day, common; but still, I say, it is contrary to analogy, and therefore wrong. Milton, too, has it:

"But in his way lights on the barren plains
　Of Sericana, where *Chineses‡* drive
　　With sails and wind their cany *waggons* light."—*Paradise Lost,* B. iii, l. 437.

OBS. 4.—The Numeral Adjectives are of three kinds; namely, *cardinal, ordinal,* and *multiplicative:* each kind running on in a series indefinitely. Thus:—

1. *Cardinal;* One, two, three, four, five, six, seven, eight, nine, ten, eleven, twelve, thirteen, fourteen, fifteen, sixteen, seventeen, eighteen, nineteen, twenty, twenty-one, twenty-two, &c.

2. *Ordinal;* First, second, third, fourth, fifth, sixth, seventh, eighth, ninth, tenth, eleventh, twelfth, thirteenth, fourteenth, fifteenth, sixteenth, seventeenth, eighteenth, nineteenth, twentieth, twenty-first, twenty-second, &c.

3. *Multiplicative;* Single or alone, double or twofold, triple or threefold, quadruple or fourfold, quintuple or fivefold, sextuple or sixfold, septuple or sevenfold, octuple or eightfold, &c. But high terms of this series are seldom used. All that occur above decuple or tenfold, are written with a hyphen, and are usually of round numbers only; as, thirty-fold, sixty-fold, hundred-fold.

OBS. 5.—A cardinal numeral denotes the whole number, but the corresponding ordinal denotes only the last one of that number, or, at the beginning of a series, the first of several or many. Thus: "*One* denotes simply the number *one,* without any regard to more; but *first* has respect to more, and so denotes only the first one of a greater number; and *two* means the number *two* completely; but *second,* the last one of *two:* and so of all the rest."—*Burn's Gram.* p. 54. A cardinal

---

* Here the word *English* appears to be used substantively, not by reason of the article, but rather because it *has no article;* for, when the definite article is used before such a word taken in the singular number, it seems to show that the noun *language* is understood. And it is remarkable, that before the names or epithets by which we distinguish the languages, this article may, in many instances, be either used or not used, repeated or not repeated, without any apparent impropriety: as, "This is the case with *the* Hebrew, French, Italian, and Spanish."—*Murray's Gram.* i, p. 36. Better, perhaps: "This is the case with *the* Hebrew, *the* French, *the* Italian, and *the* Spanish." But we may say: "This is the case with Hebrew, French, Italian, and Spanish" In the first of these forms, there appears to be an ellipsis of the plural noun *languages,* at the end of the sentence; in the second, an ellipsis of the singular noun *language,* after each of the national epithets; in the last, no ellipsis, but rather a substantive use of the words in question.

† The Doctor may, for aught I know, have taken his notion of this "*noun,*" from the language "of Dugald Dalgetty, boasting of his '5000 *Irishes* ' in the prison of Argyle." See *Letter of Wendell Phillips, in the Liberator,* Vol. XI, p. 211.

‡ Lindley Murray, or some ignorant printer of his octavo Grammar, has omitted this *s;* and thereby spoiled the prosody, if not the sense, of the line:

"Of Sericana, where *Chinese* drive," &c.—*Fourth American Ed.* p. 345.

If there was a design to correct the error of Milton's word, something should have been inserted. The common phrase, "*the Chinese,*" would give the sense, and the right number of syllables, but not the right accent. It would be sufficiently analogous with our mode of forming the words, *Englishmen, Frenchmen, Scotchmen, Dutchmen,* and *Irishmen,* and perhaps not unpoetical, to say:

"Of Sericana, where *Chinese-men* drive,
　With sails and wind, their cany *waggons* light."

number answers to the question, "*How many?*" An ordinal number answers to the question, "*Which one?*" or, "*What one?*" All the ordinal numbers, except *first, second, third,* and the compounds of these, as *twenty-first, twenty-second, twenty-third,* are formed directly from the cardinal numbers by means of the termination *th.* And as the primitives, in this case, are many of them either compound words, or phrases consisting of several words, it is to be observed, that the addition is made to the last term only. That is, of every compound ordinal number, the last term only is ordinal in form. Thus we say, *forty-ninth,* and not *fortieth-ninth;* nor could the meaning of the phrase, *four hundred and fiftieth,* be expressed by saying, *fourth hundredth and fiftieth;* for this, if it means any thing, speaks of three different numbers.

OBS. 6.—Some of the numerals are often used as *nouns;* and, as such, are regularly declined: as, *Ones, twoes, threes, fours, fives,* &c. So, *Fifths, sixths, sevenths, eighths, ninths, tenths,* &c. "The *seventy's* translation."—*Wilson's Hebrew Gram.* p. 32. "I will not do it for *forty's* sake."—*Gen.* xviii, 29. "I will not destroy it for *twenty's* sake."—*Ib.* ver 31. "For *ten's* sake."—*Ib.* ver. 32. "They sat down in ranks, by *hundreds,* and by *fifties.*"—*Mark,* vi, 40. "There are *millions* of truths that a man is not concerned to know."—*Locke.* With the compound numerals, such a construction is less common ; yet the denominator of a fraction may be a number of this sort: as, *seven twenty-fifths.* And here it may be observed, that, in stead of the ancient phraseology, as in 1 Chron. xxiv, 17th, "The *one and twentieth* to Jachin, the *two and twentieth* to Gamul, the *three and twentieth* to Delaiah, the *four and twentieth* to Maaziah," we now generally say, *the twenty-first, the twenty-second,* &c.; using the hyphen in all compounds till we arrive at *one hundred,* and then first introducing the word *and;* as, *one hundred and one,* or *one hundred and first,* &c.

OBS. 7.—The Pronominal Adjectives are comparatively very few ; but frequency of use gives them great importance in grammar. The following words are perhaps all that properly belong to this class, and several of these are much oftener something else : *All, any, both, certain, divers, each, either, else, enough, every, few, fewer, fewest, former, first, latter, last, little, less, least, many, more, most, much, neither, no or none, one, other, own, only, same, several, some, such, sundry, that, this, these, those, what, whatever, whatsoever, which, whichever, whichsoever.*[*] Of these forty-six words, seven are always singular, if the word *one* is not an exception ; namely, *each, either, every, neither, one, that, this :* and nine or ten others are always plural, if the word *many* is not an exception ; namely, *both, divers, few, fewer, fewest, many, several, sundry, these, those.* All the rest, like our common adjectives, are applicable to nouns of either number. *Else, every, only, no,* and *none,* are definitive words, which I have thought proper to call pronominal adjectives, though only the last can now with propriety be made to represent its noun understood. "Nor has Vossius, or any *else* that I know of, observed it."—*Johnson's Gram. Com.* p. 279. Say, "or any *one* else." Dr. Webster explains this word *else* thus : "ELSE, *a.* or *pron.* [Sax. *elles*] Other; one or something beside ; as, Who *else* is coming ?"—*Octavo Dict.* "Each and *every* of them," is an old phrase in which *every* is used pronominally, or with ellipsis of the word to which it refers; but, in common discourse, we now say, *every* one, *every* man, &c., never using the word *every* alone to suggest its noun. *Only* is perhaps most commonly an adverb; but it is still in frequent use as an adjective ; and in old books we sometimes find an ellipsis of the noun to which it belongs; as, "Neither are they the *only* [verbs] in which it is read."—*Johnson's Grammatical Commentaries,* p. 373. "But I think he is the *only* [one] of these Authors."—*Ib.* p. 193. *No* and *none* seem to be only different forms of the same adjective ; the former being used before a noun expressed, and the latter when the noun is understood, or not placed after the adjective ; as, "For *none* of us liveth to himself, and *no* man dieth to himself."—*Romans,* xiv, 7. *None* was anciently used *or no* before all words beginning with a vowel sound; as, "They are sottish children ; and they have *none* understanding."—*Jeremiah,* iv, 22. This practice is now obsolete. *None* is still used, when its noun precedes it ; as,

"Fools ! who from hence into the notion fall,
That *vice* or *virtue* there is *none* at all."—*Pope.*

OBS. 8.—Of the words given in the foregoing list as pronominal adjectives, about one third are

---

[*] The last six words are perhaps more frequently pronouns ; and some writers will have well-nigh all the rest to be pronouns also. "In like manner, in *the* English, there have been *rescued* from the adjectives, and classed with the pronouns, any, aught, each, every, many, none, one, other, some, such, that, those, this, these ; and by other writers, all, another, both, either, few, first, last, neither, and several "—*Wilson's Essay on Gram.* p. 106. Had the author said *wrested,* in stead of "*rescued,*" he would have taught a much better doctrine. These words are what Dr. Lowth correctly called "*Pronominal Adjectives.*"—*Lowth's Gram.* p. 24. This class of adjectives includes most of the words which Murray, Lennie, Bullions, Kirkham, and others, so absurdly denominate "*Adjective Pronouns.*" Their "Distributive Adjective Pronouns, *each, every, either, neither ;*" their "Demonstrative Adjective Pronouns, *this, that, these, those ;*" and their "Indefinite Adjective Pronouns, *some, other, any, one, all, such,* &c.," are every one of them here ; for they all are *Adjectives,* and not *Pronouns.* And it is obvious, that the corresponding words in Latin, Greek, or French, are adjectives likewise, and are, for the most part, so called ; so that, from General Grammar, or "the usages of other languages," arises an argument for ranking them as adjectives, rather than as pronouns. But the learned Dr. Bullions, after improperly assuming that every adjective *must "express the quality of a noun,"* and thence arguing that no such definitives can rightly be called *adjectives,* most absurdly suggests, that "*other languages,*" or "*the usages* of other languages," generally assign to these *English words* the place of *substitutes !* But so remarkable for self-contradiction, as well as other errors, is this gentleman's short note upon the classification of these words, that I shall present the whole of it for the reader's consideration.

"NOTE. The distributives, demonstratives, and indefinites, cannot strictly be called *pronouns;* since they never stand *instead* of nouns, but always *agree* with a *noun* expressed or understood: *Neither can they be properly called adjectives,* since they never express *the quality of a noun.* They are here classed *with pronouns,* in accordance with *the usages of other languages,* which *generally assign them this place.* All these, together with the *possessives,* in parsing, may *with sufficient propriety* be termed *adjectives,* being *uniformly regarded as such in* syntax."—*Bullions's Principles of English Gram.* p. 27. (See also his *Appendix* III, E. Gram p 199.) What a sample of grammatical instruction is here ! The pronominal adjectives "cannot properly be *called adjectives,*" but "they may with sufficient propriety be *termed adjectives !*" And so may "*the possessives,*" or *the personal pronouns in the possessive case !* "Here," i. e. in *Etymology,* they are all "*classed with pronouns ;*" but, in *Syntax,*" they are "*uniformly regarded as adjectives !*" Precious MODEL for the "Series of Grammars, English, Latin, and Greek, all on THE SAME PLAN ! "

sometimes used *adverbially*. They are the following: *All*, when it means *totally*; *any*, for *in any degree*; *else*, meaning *otherwise*; *enough*, signifying *sufficiently*; *first*, for *in the first place*; *last*, for *in the last place*; *little*, for *in a small degree*; *less*, for *in a smaller degree*; *least*, for *in the smallest degree*; *much*, for *in a great degree*; *more*, for *in a greater degree*; *most*, for *in the greatest degree*; *no*, or *none*, for *in no degree*; *only*, for *singly*, *merely*, *barely*; *what*, for *in what degree*, or *in how great a degree.* To these may perhaps be added the word *other*, when used as an alternative to *somehow*; as, "Somehow or *other* he will be favoured.—*Butler's Analogy*, p. 89. Here *other* seems to be put for *otherwise*; and yet the latter word would not be agreeable in such a sentence." "Somewhere or *other*," is a kindred phrase equally common, and equally good; or, rather, equally irregular and puzzling. Would it not be better, always to avoid both, by saying, in their stead, "In *some way or other*."—"In *some place or other*?" In the following examples, however, *other* seems to be used for *otherwise*, without such a connexion: "How is THAT used, *other* than as a Conjunction?"—*Ainsworth's Gram.* p. 88.

"Will it not be receiv'd that they have done 't?
—Who dares receive it *other*?"—SHAK.: Joh. Dict. w. Other.

OBS. 9.—*All* and *enough*, *little* and *much*, *more* and *less*, sometimes suggest the idea of quantity so abstractly, that we can hardly consider them as adjuncts to any other words; for which reason, they are, in this absolute sense, put down in our dictionaries as *nouns*. If nouns, however, they are never inflected by cases or numbers; nor do they in general admit the usual adjuncts or definitives of nouns.† Thus, we can neither say, *the all*, for *the whole*, nor *an enough*, for *a sufficiency*. And though *a little*, *the more*, and *the less*, are common phrases, the article does not here prove the following word to be a noun; because the expression may either be elliptical, or have the construction of an adverb: as, "Though *the more* abundantly I love you, *the less* I be loved."—2 Cor. xii, 15. Dr. Johnson seems to suppose that the partitive use of these words makes them nouns; as, "They have *much of the poetry* of Mecænas, but *little of his liberality*."—DRYDEN: *in Joh. Dict.* Upon this principle, however, adjectives innumerable would be made nouns; for we can just as well say, "Some *of the poetry*,"—"Any *of the poetry*,"—"The *best of Poetry*," &c. In all such expressions, the name of the thing divided, is understood in the partitive word; for a part of any thing must needs be of the same species as the whole. Nor was this great grammarian sufficiently attentive to adjuncts, in determining the parts of speech. *Nearly all*, *quite enough*, *so little*, *too much*, *vastly more*, *rather less*, and an abundance of similar phrases, are familiar to every body; in none of which, can any of these words of quantity, however abstract, be very properly reckoned nouns; because the preceding word is an adverb, and adverbs do not relate to any words that are literally nouns. All these may also be used partitively; as, "*Nearly all of us.*"

OBS. 10.—The following are some of Dr. Johnson's "*nouns*;" which, in connexion with the foregoing remarks, I would submit to the judgement of the reader: "'Then shall we be news-crammed.'—'*All* the better; we shall be the more remarkable.'"—SHAK.: *in Joh. Dict.* "*All* the fitter, Lentulus; our coming is not for salutation; we have business."—BEN JONSON: *ib.* "'Tis *enough* for me to have endeavoured the union of my country."—TEMPLE: *ib.* "Ye take too *much* upon you."—NUMBERS: *ib.* "The fate of love is such, that still it sees too *little* or too *much*."—DRYDEN: *ib.* "He thought not *much* to clothe his enemies."—MILTON: *ib.* "There remained not so *much* as one of them."—*Ib.* Exod. xiv, 28. "We will cut wood out of Lebanon, as *much* as thou shalt need."—*Ib.* 2 Chronicles. "The matter of the universe was created before the flood; if any *more* was created, then there must be as *much* annihilated to make room for it."—BURNET: *ib.* "The Lord do so, and much *more*, to Jonathan."—1 SAMUEL: *ib.* "They that would have *more* and *more*, can never have *enough*; no, not if a miracle should interpose to gratify their avarice."—L'ESTRANGE: *ib.* "They gathered some *more*, some *less*."—EXODUS: *ib.* "Thy servant knew nothing of this, *less* or *more*."—1 SAMUEL: *ib.* The first two examples above, Johnson explains thus: "That is, "*Every thing is the better*.""—"*Every thing is the fitter*." —*Quarto Dict.* The propriety of this solution may well be doubted; because the similar phrases, "So *much* the better,"—"*None* the fitter," would certainly be perverted, if resolved in the same way: *much* and *none* are here, very clearly, adverbs.

OBS. 11.—Whatever disposition may be made of the terms cited above, there are instances in which some of the same words can hardly be any thing else than nouns. Thus *all*, when it signifies *the whole*, or *every thing*, may be reckoned a noun; as, "Our *all* is at stake, and irretrievably lost, if we fail of success."—*Addison.* "A torch, snuff and *all*, goes out in a moment, when dipped in the vapour."—*Id.* "The first blast of wind laid it flat on the ground; nest, eagles, and *all*."—*L'Estrange.*

> "Finding, the wretched *all* they here can have,
> But present food, and but a future grave."—*Prior.*
> "And will she yet debase her eyes on me;
> On me, whose *all* not equals Edward's moiety?"—*Shak.*
> "Thou shalt be *all* in *all*, and I in thee,
> Forever; and in me all whom thou lov'st."—*Milton.*

---

* *Some*, for *somewhat*, or *in some degree*, appears to me a vulgarism; as, "This pause is generally *some* longer than that of a period."—*Sanborn's Gram.* p. 271. The word *what* seems to have been used adverbially in several different senses; in none of which is it much to be commended: as, "Though I forbear, *what* am I eased?"—Job, xvi, 6. "*What* advantageth it me?"—1 Cor. xv, 32. Here *what* means *in what degree*, *how much*? or *wherein*? "For *what* knowest thou, O wife, whether thou shalt save thy husband?"—1 Cor. vii, 16. Here *how* would have been better. "The enemy, having his country wasted, *what* by himself and *what* by the soldiers, findeth succour in no place."—*Spenser.* Here *what* means *partly*;—"wasted *partly* by himself and *partly* by the soldiers." This use of *what* was formerly very common, but is now, I think, obsolete. *What* before an adjective sometimes denotes with admiration the degree of the quality; and is called, by some, an *adverb*: as, "*What partial judges* are our love and hate!'"—*Dryden.* But here I take *what* to be an *adjective*; as when we say, *such* partial judges, *some* partial judges, &c. "*What* need I be forward with Death, that calls not on me?"—*Shakspeare.* Here *what* seems to be improperly put in place of *why.*

† Dr. Blair, in his Lectures on Rhetoric and Belles-Lettres, often uses the phrase "*this much*;" but it is, I think, more common to say "*thus much*," even when the term is used substantively.

OBS. 12.—There are yet some other words, which, by their construction alone, are to be distinguished from the pronominal adjectives. *Both*, when it stands as a correspondent to *and*, is reckoned a conjunction; as, "For *both* he that sanctifieth, *and* they who are sanctified, are all of one."—*Heb.* ii, 11. But, in sentences like the following, it seems to be an adjective, referring to the nouns which precede: "Language and manners are *both* established by the usage of people of fashion."—*Amer. Chesterfield*, p. 83. So *either*, corresponding to *or*, and *neither*, referring to *nor*, are conjunctions, and not adjectives. *Which* and *what*, with their compounds, *whichever* or *whichsoever*, *whatever* or *whatsoever*, though sometimes put before nouns as adjectives, are, for the most part, relative or interrogative pronouns. When the noun is used after them, they are adjectives; when it is omitted they are pronouns: as, "There is a witness of God, *which witness* gives true judgement."—*I. Penington.* Here the word *witness* might be omitted, and *which* would become a relative pronoun. Dr. Lowth says, "*Thy, my, her, our, your, their,* are pronominal adjectives."—*Gram.* p. 23. This I deny; and the reader may see my reasons, in the observations upon the declension of pronouns.

OBS. 13.—The words *one* and *other*, beside their primitive uses as adjectives, in which they still remain without inflection, are frequently employed as nouns, or as substitutes for nouns; and, in this substantive or pronominal character, they commonly have the regular declension of nouns, and are reckoned such by some grammarians; though others call them indefinite pronouns, and some, (among whom are Lowth and Comly,) leave them with the pronominal adjectives, even when they are declined in both numbers. Each of them may be preceded by either of the articles; and so general is the signification of the former, that almost any adjective may likewise come before it: as, *Any one, some one, such a one, many a one, a new one, an old one, an other one, the same one, the young ones, the little ones, the mighty ones, the wicked one, the Holy One, the Everlasting One.* So, like the French *on*, or *l'on*, the word *one*, without any adjective, is now very frequently used as a general or indefinite term for any man, or any person. In this sense, it is sometimes, unquestionably, to be preferred to a personal pronoun applied indefinitely: as, "Pure religion, and undefiled before God and the Father, is this, To visit the fatherless and widows in their affliction, and to keep *himself* [better, *one's self*] unspotted from the world."—*James*, i, 27. But, as its generality of meaning seems to form a sort of covering for egotism, some writers are tempted to make too frequent a use of it. Churehill ridicules this practice, by framing, or anonymously citing, the following sentence: "If *one* did but dare to abide by *one's* own judgement, *one's* language would be much more refined; but *one* fancies *one's self* obliged to follow, wherever the many choose to lead *one.*" See *Churchill's Gram.* p. 229. Here every scholar will concur with the critic in thinking, it would be better to say: "If *we* did but dare to abide by *our* own judgement, *our* language would be much more refined; but *we* fancy *ourselves* obliged to follow, wherever the many choose to lead *us.*" See *ib.*

OBS. 14.—Of the pronominal adjectives the following distribution has been made: "*Each, every,* and *either,* are called *distributives;* because, though they imply all the persons or things that make up a number, they consider them, not as one whole, but as taken separately. *This, that, former, latter, both, neither,* are termed *demonstratives;* because they point out precisely the subjects to which they relate. *This* has *these* for its plural; *that* has *those. This* and *that* are frequently put in opposition to each other; *this,* to express what is nearer in place or time; *that,* what is more remote. *All, any, one, other, some, such,* are termed *indefinite. Another* is merely *other* in the singular, with the indefinite article not kept separate from it.[*] *Other,* when not joined with a noun, is occasionally used both in the possessive case, and in the plural number: as,

'Teach me to feel an *other's* wo, to hide the fault I see;
That mercy I to *others* show, that mercy show to me.'—*Pope.*

Each other and *one another,* when used in conjunction, may be termed *reciprocals;* as they are employed to express a reciprocal action; the former, between two persons or things; the latter, *between*[†] more than two. The possessive cases of the personal pronouns have been also ranked under the head of pronominal adjectives, and styled *possessives;* but for this I see no good reason."—*Churchill's Gram.* p. 76.

OBS. 15.—The reciprocal terms *each other* and *one an other* divide, according to some mutual act or interchangeable relation, the persons or things spoken of, and are commonly of the singular number only. *Each other,* if rightly used, supposes two, and only two, to be acting and acted upon reciprocally; *one an other,* if not misapplied, supposes more than two, under like circumstances, and has an indefinite reference to all taken distributively: as, "Brutus and Aruns killed *each other.*" That is, *Each combatant* killed *the other.* "The disciples were commanded to love *one an other,* and to be willing to wash *one an other's* feet." That is, *All* the disciples were commanded to love *mutually;* for both terms, *one* and *other,* or *one disciple* and *an other disciple,* must be here understood as taken indefinitely. The reader will observe, that the two terms thus brought together, if taken substantively or pronominally in parsing, must be represented as being of *different cases;* or, if we take them adjectively, the noun, which is twice to be supplied, will necessarily be so.

[*] There seems to be no good reason for joining *an* and *other:* on the contrary, the phrase *an other* is always as properly two words, as the phrase *the other,* and more so. The latter, being long ago vulgarly contracted into *tother,* probably gave rise to the apparent contraction *another;* which many people nowadays are ignorant enough to divide wrong, and mispronounce. See "*a-no-ther*" in *Murray's Spelling-Book,* p. 71; and "*a-noth-er*" in *Emerson's,* p. 76. *An* here excludes any other article; and both analogy and consistency require that the words be separated. Their union, like that of the words *the* and *other,* has led sometimes to an improper repetition of the article; as, "*Another* such a man," for, "An other such man."—"Blind my hair up. As you yesterday? No, nor the t'other day."—BEN JOHNSON: *in Joh. Dict.* "He can not tell when he should take *the tone,* and when the *tother.*"—SIR T. MOORE: *Tooke's D. P.* Vol. ii, p. 448. That is—"when he should take *the one* and when *the other.*" Besides, the word *other* is declined, like a noun, and has the plural *others;* but the compounding of *another* constrains our grammarians to say, that this word "has no plural." All these difficulties will be removed by writing *an other* as two words. The printers chiefly rule this matter. To them, therefore, I refer it; with directions, not to unite these words for me, except where it has been done in the manuscript, for the sake of exactness in quotation.—G. BROWN.

[†] This is a misapplication of the word *between,* which cannot have reference to more than two things or parties: the term should have been *among.*—G. BROWN.

OBS. 16.—Misapplications of the foregoing reciprocal terms are very frequent in books, though it is strange that phrases so very common should not be rightly understood. Dr. Webster, among his explanations of the word *other*, has the following: "Correlative to *each*, and applicable to *any number* of individuals."—*Octavo Dict.* "*Other* is used as a substitute for a noun, and in this use has the plural number and the sign of the possessive case."—*Ib.* Now it is plain, that the word *other*, as a "correlative to *each*," may be so far "a substitute for a noun" as to take the form of the possessive case singular, and perhaps also the plural; as, "Look'd in *each other's* arms they lay." But, that the objective *other*, in any such relation, can convey a plural idea, or be so loosely applicable—" to *any number* of individuals," I must here deny. If it were so, there would be occasion, by the foregoing rule, to make it plural in form; as, "The ambitious strive to excel *each others.*" But this is not English. Nor can it be correct to say of more than two, "They all strive to excel *each other.*" Because the explanation must be, "*Each* strives to excel *other;*" and such a construction of the word *other*, is not agreeable to modern usage. *Each other* is therefore not equivalent to *one an other*, but nearer perhaps to *the one the other:* as, "The two generals are independent *the one of the other.*"—*Voltaire's Charles XII*, p. 67. "And these are contrary *the one to the other.*"—*Gal.* v, 17. "The necessary connexion *of the one with the other.*"—*Blair's Rhet.* p. 304. The latter phraseology, being definite and formal, is now seldom used, except the terms be separated by a verb or a preposition. It is a literal version of the French *l'un l'autre*, and in some instances to be preferred to *each other;* as,

"So fellest foes, whose plots have broke their sleep,
To take *the one the other*, by some chance."—*Shak.*

OBS. 17.—The Greek term for the reciprocals *each other* and *one an other*, is a certain plural derivative from ἄλλος, *other;* and is used in three cases, the genitive, ἀλλήλων, the dative, ἀλλήλοις, the accusative, ἀλλήλους / these being all the cases which the nature of the expression admits; and for all these we commonly use the *objective;*—that is, we put *each* or *one* before the objective *other.* Now these English terms, taken in a reciprocal sense, seldom, if ever, have any plural form; because the article in *one an other* admits of none; and *each other*, when applied to two persons or things, (as it almost always is,) does not require any. I have indeed seen, in some narrative, such an example as this: "The two men were ready to cut *each others' throats.*" But the meaning could not be, that each was ready to cut "*others' throats;*" and since, between the two, there was but one throat for *each* to cut, it would doubtless be more correct to say, "*each other's throat.*" So Burns, in touching a gentler passion, has an inaccurate elliptical expression:

"'Tis when a youthful, loving, modest pair,
In *others'* arms, breathe out the tender tale."—*Cotter's Sat. Night.*

He meant, "In *each other's* arms;" the apostrophe being misplaced, and the metre improperly allowed to exclude a word which the sense requires. Now, as to the plural of *each other*, although we do not use the objective, and say of many, "They love *each others,*" there appears to be some instances in which the possessive plural, *each others'*, would not be improper; as, "Sixteen ministers, who meet weekly at *each other's* houses."—*Johnson's Life of Swift.* Here the singular is wrong, because the governing noun implies a plurality of owners. "The citizens of different states should know *each others characters.*"—*Webster's Essays*, p. 35. This also is wrong, because no possessive sign is used. Either write, "*each others' characters,*" or say, "*one an other's character.*"

OBS. 18.—*One* and *other* are, in many instances, terms relative and partitive, rather than reciprocal; and, in this use, there seems to be an occasional demand for the plural form. In French, two parties are contrasted by *les uns—les autres;* a mode of expression seldom, if ever imitated in English. Thus: "Il les séparera les uns d'avec les autres." That is, "He shall separate them *some* from *others;*"—or, literally, "*the ones* from *the others.*" Our version is: "He shall separate them *one from an other.*"—*Matt.* xxv, 32. Beza has it: "Separabit eos *alteros ab alteris.*" The Vulgate: "Separabit eos *ab invicem.*" The Greek: "Ἀφοριεῖ αὐτοὺς ἀπ' ἀλλήλων." To separate many "*one from an other,*" seems, literally, to leave none of them together; and this is not, "as a shepherd divideth his sheep from the goats." To express such an idea with perfect propriety, in our language, therefore, we must resort to some other phraseology. In Campbell's version, we read: "And *out of them* he will separate *the good from the bad*, as a shepherd separateth *the* sheep from the goats." Better, perhaps, thus: "And he shall separate them, *the righteous from the wicked*, as a shepherd divideth his sheep from the goats."

OBS. 19.—Dr. Bullions says, "*One* and *other* refer to *the singular only.*"—*Eng. Gram.* p. 98. Of *ones* and *others* he takes no notice; nor is he sufficiently attentive to usage in respect to the roots. If there is any absurdity in giving a *plural* meaning to the singulars *one* and *other*, the following sentences need amendment: "The *one* preach Christ of contention; but *the other*, of love."—*Philippians*, i, 16. Here "*the one*" is put for "the one *class*," and "*the other*," for "the *other class;*" the ellipsis in the first instance not being a very proper one. "The confusion arises, when *the one* will put *their* sickle into *the other's* harvest."—*LESLEY: in Joh. Dict.* This may be corrected by saying, "*the one party,*" or "*the one nation,*" in stead of "*the one.*" "It is clear from Scripture, that Antichrist shall be permitted to work false miracles, and that they shall so counterfeit the true, that it will be hard to discern *the one* from *the other.*"—*Barclay's Works*, iii, 93. If in any case we may adopt the French construction above, "*the ones* from *the others,*" it will be proper here. Again: "I have seen *children* at a table, who, whatever was there, never asked for any thing, but contentedly took what was given them: and, at an other place, I have seen *others* cry for every thing they saw; they must be served out of every dish, and that first too. What made this vast difference, but this: That *one was* accustomed to have what *they* called or *cried* for; *the other* to go without it?"—*Locke, on Education*, p. 55. Here, (with *were* for *was*,) the terms of contrast ought rather to have been, *the ones—the others; the latter—the former; or, the importunate—the modest.* "Those nice shades, by which *virtues and vices* approach *each one another.*"—*Murray's Gram.* i, p. 350. This expression should be any thing, rather than what it is. Say, "By which *virtue and vice* approach *each other.*" Or: "By which certain virtues and vices *approximate—blend—become difficult of distinction.*"

OBS. 20.—"Most authors have given the name of *pronoun adjectives*, ['pronouns adjective,' or 'pronominal adjectives,'] to *my, mine; our, ours; thy, thine; your, yours; his, her, hers; their, theirs:* perhaps because they are followed by, or refer to, some substantive [expressed or understood after them]. But, were they adjectives, they must either express the quality of their substantive, or limit its extent: adjectives properly so called, do the first; definitive pronouns do the last. All adjectives [that are either singular or plural,] agree with their substantives in *number*; but I can say, 'They are *my books:*' *my* is singular, and *books* plural; therefore *my* is not an adjective. Besides, *my* does not express the *quality* of the books, but only ascertains the possessor, the same as the genitive or substantive does, to which it is similar. Examples: 'They are *my* books;'—'They are *John's* books;' &c."—*Alex. Murray's Gram.* p. 108.

OBS. 21.—To the class of Participial Adjectives, should be referred all such words as the following: (1.) The simple participles made adjectives by position; as, "A *rearing* lion,"—"A *raging* bear,"—"A *brawling* woman,"—"A *flattering* mouth,"—"An *understanding* heart,"—"*Burning* coals,"—"The *hearing* ear, and the *seeing* eye."—*Bible.* "A *troubled* fountain,"—"A *wounded* spirit,"—"An *appointed* time."—*Ib.* (2.) Words of a participial appearance, formed from nouns by adding *ed*; as, "The eve thy *sainted* mother died."—*W. Scott.* "What you write of me, would make me more *conceited*, than what I scribble myself."—*Pope.* (3.) Participles, or participial adjectives, reversed in sense by the prefix *un*; as, *unaspiring, unavailing, unbelieving, unbattered, uninjured, unbefriended.* (4.) Words of a participial form construed elliptically, as if they were nouns; as, "Among the *dying* and the dead."—"The *called* of Jesus Christ."—*Rom.* i, 6. "Dearly *beloved*, I beseech you."—1 *Pet.* ii, 11. "The *redeemed* of the Lord shall return."—*Isaiah*, li, 11. "They talk, to the grief of thy *wounded*."—*Psalms*, lxix, 26: *Margin.*

OBS. 22.—In the text, Prov. vii, 26, "She hath cast down many wounded," *wounded* is a participle; because the meaning is, "*many men wounded*," and not, "*many wounded men.*" Our Participial Adjectives are exceedingly numerous. It is not easy to ascertain how many there are of them; because almost any simple participle may be set before a noun, and thus become an adjective: as,

　　"Where *smiling* spring its earliest visit paid,
　　And *parting* summer's *ling'ring* blooms delay'd."—*Goldsmith.*

OBS. 23.—Compound Adjectives, being formed at pleasure, are both numerous and various. In their formation, however, certain analogies may be traced: (1.) Many of them are formed by joining an adjective to its noun, and giving to the latter the participial termination *ed;* as, *able-bodied, sharp-sighted, left-handed, full-faced, flat-nosed, thick-lipped, cloven-footed, high-heeled.* (2.) In some, two nouns are joined, the latter assuming *ed*, as above; as, *bell-shaped, hawk-nosed, eagle-sighted, lion-hearted, web-footed.* (3.) In some, the object of an active participle is placed before it; as, *money-getting, time-serving, self-consuming, cloud-compelling, fortune-hunting, sleep-disturbing.* (4.) Some, embracing numerals, form a series, though it is seldom carried far; as, *one-legged, two-legged, three-legged, four-legged.* So, *one-leaved, two-leaved, three-leaved, four-leaved:* or, perhaps better as Webster will have them, *one-leafed, two-leafed*, &c. But, upon the same principle, *short-lived*, should be *short-lifed*, and *long-lived, long-lifed.* (5.) In some, there is a combination of an adjective and a participle; as, *noble-looking, high-sounding, slow-moving, thorough-going, hard-finished, free-born, heavy-laden, only-begotten.* (6.) In some, we find an adverb and a participle united; as, *ever-living, ill-judging, well-pleasing, far-shooting, forth-issuing, back-sliding, ill-trained, down-trodden, above-mentioned.* (7.) Some consist of a noun and a participle which might be reversed with a preposition between them; as, *church-going, care-crazed, travel-soiled, blood-bespotted, dew-besprinkled.* (8.) A few, and those inelegant, terminate with a preposition; as, *unlooked-for, long-looked-for, unthought-of, unheard-of.* (9.) Some are phrases of many words, converted into one part of speech by the hyphen; as, "Where is the *ever-to-be-honoured* Chaucer?"—*Wordsworth.*

　　"And, with *God-only-knows-how-gotten* light,
　　Informs the nation what is wrong or right."—*Snelling's Gift for Scribblers*, p. 49.

OBS. 24.— Nouns derived from compound adjectives, are generally disapproved by good writers; yet we sometimes meet with them: as, *hard-heartedness*, for hardness of heart, or cruelty; *quick-sightedness*, for quickness of sight, or perspicacity; *worldly-mindedness*, for devotion to the world, or love of gain; *heavenly-mindedness*, for the love of God, or true piety. In speaking of ancestors or descendants, we take the noun, *father, mother, son, daughter,* or *child;* prefix the adjective *grand*, for the second generation; *great*, for the third; and then, sometimes, repeat the same, for degrees more remote: as, *father, grandfather, great-grandfather, great-great-grandfather.* "What would my *great-grandmother* say, thought I, could she know that thou art to be chopped up for fuel to warm the frigid fingers of her *great-great-great-granddaughters!*"—*T. H. Bayley.*

MODIFICATIONS.

Adjectives have, commonly, no modifications but *comparison.*

Comparison is a variation of the adjective, to express quality in different degrees: as, *hard, harder, hardest; soft, softer, softest.*

There are three degrees of comparison; the *positive*, the *comparative*, and the *superlative.*

The *positive degree* is that which is expressed by the adjective in its simple form: as, "An elephant is *large;* a mouse, *small;* a lion, *fierce* and *strong.*"

The *comparative degree* is that which is *more* or *less* than something contrasted with it: as, " A whale is *larger* than an elephant ; a mouse is *smaller* than a rat."

The *superlative degree* is that which is *most* or *least* of all included with it : as, " The whale is the *largest* of the animals that inhabit this globe ; the mouse is the *smallest* of all beasts."—*Dr. Johnson.*

Those adjectives whose signification does not admit of different degrees, cannot be compared ; as, *two, second, all, every, immortal, infinite.*

Those adjectives which may be varied in sense, but not in form, are compared by means of adverbs ; as, fruitful, *more* fruitful, *most* fruitful—fruitful, *less* fruitful, *least* fruitful.

OBSERVATIONS.

OBS. 1.—"Some scruple to call the positive a degree of comparison ; on the ground, that it does not imply either comparison, or degree. But no quality can exist, without existing in some degree : and, though the positive is very frequently used without reference to any other degree ; as it is *the standard,* with which other degrees of the quality are compared, it is certainly an essential object of the comparison. While these critics allow only two degrees, we might in fact with more propriety say, that there are five : 1, the quality in its standard state, or positive degree ; as *wise :* 2, in a higher state, or the comparative ascending ; *more wise :* 3, in a lower, or the comparative descending ; *less wise :* 4, in the highest state, or superlative ascending ; *most wise :* 5, in the lowest state, or superlative descending ; *least wise.* All grammarians, however, agree about the things themselves, and the forms used to express them ; though they differ about the names, by which these forms should be called : and as those names are practically best, which tend least to perplex the learner, I see no good reason here for deviating from what has been established by long custom."—*Churchill's Gram.* p. 231.

OBS. 2.—Churchill here writes plausibly enough, but it will be seen, both from his explanation, and from the foregoing definitions of the degrees of comparison, that there are but three. The comparative and the superlative may each be distinguishable into the ascending and the descending, as often as we prefer the adverbial form to the regular variation of the adjective itself ; but this imposes no necessity of classing and defining them otherwise than simply as the comparative and the superlative. The assumption of two comparatives and two superlatives, is not only contrary to the universal practice of the teachers of grammar ; but there is this conclusive argument against it—that the regular method of comparison has no degrees of diminution, and the form which has such degrees, is *no inflection* of the adjective. If there is any exception, it is in the words, *small, smaller, smallest,* and *little, less, least.* But of the smallness or littleness, considered abstractly, these, like all others, are degrees of increase, and not of diminution. *Smaller* is as completely opposite to *less small,* as *wiser* is to *less wise.* *Less* itself is a comparative descending, only when it diminishes some *other* quality : *less little,* if the phrase were proper, must needs be nearly equivalent to *greater* or *more.* Churchill, however, may be quite right in the following remark : " The comparative ascending of an adjective, and the comparative descending of an adjective expressing the opposite quality, are often considered synonymous, by those who do not discriminate nicely between ideas. But *less imprudent* does not imply precisely the same thing as *more prudent ;* or *more brave,* the same as *less cowardly.*"—*New Gram.* p. 231.

OBS. 3.—The definitions which I have given of the three degrees of comparison, are new. In short, I know not whether any other grammarian has ever given what may justly be called a *definition,* of any one of them. Here, as in most other parts of grammar, loose *remarks,* ill-written and untrue *assertions,* have sufficed. The explanations found in many English grammars are the following : " The positive state expresses the quality of an object, without any increase or diminution ; as, good, wise, great. The comparative degree increases or lessens the positive in signification ; as, wiser, greater, less wise. The superlative degree increases or lessens the positive to the highest or [the] lowest degree ; as, wisest, greatest, least wise. The simple word, or positive, becomes [the] comparative by adding *r* or *er ;* and the superlative by adding *st* or *est,* to the end of it. And the adverbs *more* and *most,* placed before the adjective, have the same effect ; as, wise, more wise, most wise."—*Murray's Grammar,* 2d Ed., 1795, p. 47. If a man wished to select some striking example of bad writing—of thoughts ill conceived, and not well expressed—he could not do better than take the foregoing : provided his auditors knew enough of grammar to answer the four simple questions here involved ; namely, What is the positive degree ? What is the comparative degree ? What is the superlative degree ? How are adjectives regularly compared ? To these questions I shall furnish *direct answers,* which the reader may compare with such as he can derive from the foregoing citation : the last two sentences of which Murray ought to have credited to Dr. Lowth ; for he copied them literally, except that he says, " the adverbs *more* AND *most,*" for the Doctor's phrase, " the adverbs *more* OR *most.*" See the whole also in *Kirkham's Grammar,* p. 72; in *Ingersoll's,* p. 35; in *Alger's,* p. 21; in *Bacon's,* p. 18; in *Russell's,* p. 14; in *Hamlin's,* p. 22; in *J. M. Putnam's,* p. 33; in *S. Putnam's,* p. 30; in *R. C. Smith's,* p. 51; in *Rev. T. Smith's,* p. 20.

OBS. 4.—In the five short sentences quoted above, there are more errors, than can possibly be enumerated in ten times the space. For example : (1.) If one should say of a piece of iron, " It grows cold or hot very rapidly," *cold* and *hot* could not be in the " *positive state,*" as they define it : because, either the " quality" or the " object," (I know not which,) is represented by them as " without any increase or diminution ;" and this would not, in the present case, be true of either ; for iron changes in bulk, by a change of temperature. (2.) What, in the first sentence, is erroneously called " the positive *state,*" in the second and the third, is called " the positive *degree ;*" and this again, in the fourth, is falsely indentified with "the simple word." Now, if we suppose the meaning to be, that "the positive state," "the positive degree," or "the simple word," is "without any increase or diminution;" this is expressly contradicted by three sentences out of the five, and implicitly, by one of the others. (3.) Not one of these sentences is true, in the most obvious sense of the words, if in any other; and yet the doctrines they were designed to teach, may have been, in general, correctly gathered from the examples. (4.) The phrase, "positive in signification," is not intelligible in the sense intended, without a comma after positive; and yet, in an armful of different English grammars which contain the passage, I find not one that has a point in that place. (5.) It is not more correct to say, that the comparative or the superlative degree "increases or lessens the positive," than it would be to aver, that the plural number increases or lessens the singular, or the feminine gender, the masculine. Nor does the superlative mean, what a certain learned Doctor understands by it—namely, "the greatest or least possible degree." If it did, "the thickest parts of his skull," for example, would imply small room for brains; "the thinnest," protect them ill, if there were any. (6.) It is improper to say, "The simple word becomes [the] comparative by adding r or er; and the superlative by adding st or est." The thought is wrong; and nearly all the words are misapplied; as, simple for primitive, adding for assuming, &c. (7.) Nor is it very wise to say, "the adverbs more and most, placed before the adjective, have the same effect:" because it ought to be known, that the effect of the one is very different from that of the other! "The same effect," cannot here be taken for any effect previously described; unless we will have it to be, that these words, more and most, "become comparative by adding r or er; and the superlative by adding st or est, to the end of them:" all of which is grossly absurd. (8.) The repetition of the word degree, in saying, "The superlative degree increases or lessens the positive to the highest or lowest degree," is a disagreeable tautology. Besides, unless it involves the additional error of presenting the same word in different senses, it makes one degree swell or diminish an other to itself; whereas, in the very next sentence, this singular agency is forgotten, and a second equally strange takes its place: "The positive becomes the superlative by adding st or est, to the end of it;" i. e. to the end of itself. Nothing can be more ungrammatical, than is much of the language by which grammar itself is now professedly taught!

OBS. 5.—It has been almost universally assumed by grammarians, that the positive degree is the only standard to which the other degrees can refer; though many seem to think, that the superlative always implies or includes the comparative, and is consequently inapplicable when only two things are spoken of. Neither of these positions is involved in any of the definitions which I have given above. The reader may think what he will about these points, after observing the several ways in which each form may be used. In the phrases, "greater than Solomon,"—"more than a bushel,"—"later than one o'clock," it is not immediately obvious that the positives great, much, and late, are the real terms of contrast. And how is it in the Latin phrases, "Dulcior melle, sweeter than honey,"—"Praestantior auro, better than gold?" These authors will resolve all such phrases thus: "greater, than Solomon was great,"—"more, than a bushel is much," &c. As the conjunction than never governs the objective case, it seems necessary to suppose an ellipsis of some verb after the noun which follows it as above; and possibly the foregoing solution, uncouth as it seems, may, for the English idiom, be the true one: as, "My Father is greater than I."—John, xiv, 28. That is, "My Father is greater than I am;"—or, perhaps, "than I am great." But if it appear that some degree of the same quality must always be contrasted with the comparative, there is still room to question whether this degree must always be that which we call the positive. Cicero, in exile, wrote to his wife: "Ego autem hoc miserior sum, quàm tu, quæ es miserrima, quòd ipsa calamitas communis est utriusque nostrùm, sed culpa mea propria est."—Epist. ad Fam. xiv, 3. "But in this I am more wretched, than thou, who art most wretched, that the calamity itself is common to us both, but the fault is all my own."

OBS. 6.—In my Institutes and First Lines of English Grammar, I used the following brief definitions: "The comparative degree is that which exceeds the positive; as, harder, softer, better." —"The superlative degree is that which is not exceeded; as, hardest, softest, best." And it is rather for the sake of suggesting to the learner the peculiar application of each of these degrees, than from any decided dissatisfaction with these expressions, that I now present others. The first, however, proceeds upon the common supposition, that the comparative degree of a quality, ascribed to any object, must needs be contrasted with the positive in some other, or with the positive in the same at an other time. This idea may be plausibly maintained, though it is certain that the positive term referred to, is seldom, if ever, allowed to appear. Besides, the comparative or the superlative may appear, and in such a manner as to be, or seem to be, in the point of contrast. Thus: "Objects near our view are apt to be thought greater than those of a larger size, that are more remote."—Locke's Essay, p. 186. Upon the principle above, the explanation here must be, that the meaning is—"greater than those of a larger size are thought great." "The poor man that loveth Christ, is richer than the richest man in the world, that hates him." —Bunyan's Pilgrim's Progress, p. 86. This must be "richer than the richest man is rich." The riches contemplated here, are of different sorts; and the comparative or the superlative of one sort, may be exceeded by either of these degrees of an other sort, though the same epithet be used for both. So in the following instances: "He that is higher than the highest regardeth; and there be higher than they."—Eccl. v, 8. That is, "He that is higher than the highest earthly dignitaries, regardeth; and there are higher authorities than these." "Fairer than aught imagined else fairest."—Pollok. "Sadder than saddest night."—Byron. It is evident that the superlative degree is not, in general, that which cannot be exceeded, but that which, in the actual state of the things included, "is not exceeded." Again, as soon as any given comparative or superlative is, by a further elevation or intension of the quality, surpassed and exceeded, that particular degree, whatever it was, becomes merely positive; for the positive degree of a quality, though it commonly includes the very lowest measure, and is understood to exceed nothing, may at any time equal the very highest. There is no paradox in all this, which is not also in the following simple examples: "Easier, indeed, I was, but far from easy."—Cowper's Life, p. 60.

"Who canst the wisest wiser make,
And babes as wise as they."—Cowper's Poems.

OBS. 7.—The relative nature of these degrees deserves to be further illustrated. (1.) It is plain, that the greatest degree of a quality in one thing, may be less than the least in an other; and, consequently, that the least degree in one thing, may be greater than the greatest in an other. Thus, the *heaviest* wood is *less heavy* than the *lightest* of the metals; and the *least valuable* of the metals is perhaps of *more value* than the *choicest* wood. (2.) The comparative degree may increase upon itself, and be repeated to show the gradation. Thus, a man may ascend into the air with a balloon, and rise *higher*, and *higher*, and *higher*, and *higher*, till he is out of sight. This is no uncommon form of expression, and the intension is from comparative to comparative. (3.) If a ladder be set up for use, one of its rounds will be *the highest*, and one other will be *the lowest*, or *least high*. And as that which is *highest*, is higher than all the rest, so every one will be *higher* than all below it. *The higher rounds*, if spoken of generally, and without definite contrast, will be those in the upper half; *the lower rounds*, referred to in like manner, will be those in the lower half, or those not far from the ground. *The highest rounds*, or *the lowest*, if we indulge such latitude of speech, will be those near the top or the bottom; there being, absolutely, or in *strictness* of language, but *one* of each. (4.) If *the highest* round be removed, or left uncounted, the next becomes the *highest*, though not *so high* as the former. For every one is *the highest* of the number which it completes. All admit this, till we come to *three*. And, as the third is *the highest of the three*, I see not why the second is not properly *the highest of the two*. Yet nearly all our grammarians condemn this phrase, and prefer "*the higher of the two*." But can they give a *reason* for their preference? That the comparative degree is implied between the positive and the superlative, so that there must needs be three terms before the latter is applicable, is a doctrine which I deny. And if the second is *the higher of the two*, because it is *higher than the first*; is it not also *the highest of the two*, because it *completes the number*? (5.) It is to be observed, too, that as our ordinal numeral *first*, denoting the one which begins a series, and having reference of course to more, is an adjective of the superlative degree, equivalent to *foremost*, of which it is perhaps a contraction; so *last* likewise, though no numeral, is a superlative also. (6.) These, like other superlatives, admit of a looser application, and may possibly include more than one thing at the beginning or the end of a series: as, "*The last years* of man are often helpless, like *the first*." (7.) With undoubted propriety, we may speak of *the first two, the last two, the first three, the last three*, &c.; but to say, *the two first, the two last*, &c., with this meaning, is obviously and needlessly inaccurate. "*The two first men* in the nation," may, I admit, be good English; but it can properly be meant only of *the two most eminent*. In specifying any part of a *series*, we ought rather to place the cardinal number after the ordinal. (8.) Many of the foregoing positions apply generally, to almost all adjectives that are susceptible of comparison. Thus, it is a common saying, "Take *the best first*, and *all* will be *best*." That is, remove that degree which is now superlative, and the epithet will descend to an other, "*the next best*."

OBS. 8.—It is a common assumption, maintained by almost all our grammarians, that the degrees which add to the adjective the terminations *er* and *est*, as well as those which are expressed by *more* and *most*, indicate an *increase*, or heightening, of the quality expressed by the positive. If such must needs be their import, it is certainly very improper, to apply them, as many do, to what can be only an approximation to the positive. Thus Dr. Blair: "Nothing that belongs to human nature, is *more universal* than the relish of beauty of one kind or other."—*Lectures*, p. 16. "In architecture, the Grecian models were long esteemed *the most perfect*."—*Ib.* p 20. Again: In his reprehension of Capernaum, the Saviour said, "It shall be *more tolerable* for the land of Sodom, in the day of judgement, than for thee."—*Matt.* xi, 24. Now, although ἀνεκτότερον, *more tolerable*, is in itself a good comparative, who would dare infer from this text, that in the day of judgement Capernaum shall fare *tolerably*, and Sodom, *still better?* There is much reason to think, that the essential nature of these grammatical degrees has not been well understood by those who have heretofore pretended to explain them. If we except those few approximations to sensible qualities, which are signified by such words as *whitish*, *greenish*, &c., there will be found no actual measure, or inherent degree of any quality, to which the simple form of the adjective is not applicable; or which, by the help of intensive adverbs of a positive character, it may not be made to express; and that, too, without becoming either comparative or superlative, in the technical sense of those terms. Thus *very white*, *exceedingly white*, *perfectly white*, are terms quite as significant as *whiter* and *whitest*, if not more so. Some grammarians, observing this, and knowing that the Romans often used their superlative in a sense merely intensive, as *altissimus* for *very high*, have needlessly divided our English superlative into two, "*the definite* and the *indefinite*;" giving the latter name to that degree which we mark by the adverb *very*, and the former to that which alone is properly called the superlative. Churchill does this: while, (as we have seen above,) in naming the degrees he pretends to prefer "what has been established by long custom."—*New Gram.* p. 231. By a strange oversight also, he failed to notice, that this doctrine interferes with his scheme of *five* degrees, and would clearly furnish him with *six*: to which if he had chosen to add the "*imperfect degree*" of Dr. Webster, (as *whitish*, *greenish*, &c.,) which is recognised by Johnson, Murray, and others, he might have had *seven*. But I hope my readers will by-and-by believe there is *no need* of more than *three*.

OBS. 9.—The true nature of the Comparative degree is this: it denotes either some *excess* or some *relative deficiency* of the quality, when one thing or party is compared with an other, in respect to what is in both: as, "Because the foolishness of God is *wiser* than men; and the weakness of God is *stronger* than men."—1 Cor. i, 25. "Few languages are, in fact, *more copious* than the English."—*Blair's Rhet.* p. 87. "Our style is *less compact* than that of the ancients."—*Ib.* p. 88. "They are counted to him *less* than nothing and vanity."—*Isaiah*, xl, 17. As the comparatives in a long *series* are necessarily many, and some of them *higher* than others, it may be asked, "How can the comparative degree, in this case, be merely 'that which exceeds *the positive?'* " Or, as our common grammarians prompt me here to say, "May not the comparative degree increase or lessen *the comparative*, in signification?" The latter form of the question they may answer for themselves; remembering that the comparative *may advance from the comparative*, step by step, from the second article in the series to the utmost. Thus, three is a higher or greater number than two; but four is higher than three; five, than four; and so on, *ad infinitum*.

My own form of the question I answer thus: "The *highest* of the *higher* is not *higher* than the rest are *higher*, but simply *higher* than they are *high*."

OBS. 10.—The true nature of the Superlative degree is this: it denotes, in a quality, *some extreme*, or *unsurpassed extent*. It may be used either absolutely, as being without bounds; or relatively, as being confined within any limits we choose to give it. It is equally applicable to that which is naturally unsurpassable, and to that which stands within the narrowest limits of comparison. The *heaviest* of *three feathers* would scarcely be thought a *heavy* thing, and yet the expression is proper; because the weight, whatever it is, is relatively *the greatest*. The *youngest* of three persons, may not be *very young*; nor need we suppose *the oldest* in a whole college to have arrived at *the greatest conceivable age*. What then shall be thought of the explanations which our grammarians have given of this degree of comparison? That of Murray I have already criticised. It is ascribed to him, not upon the supposition that he invented it; but because common sense continues to give place to the authority of his name in support of it. Comly, Russell, Alger, Ingersoll, Greenleaf, Fisk, Merchant, Kirkham, T. Smith, R. C. Smith, Hall, Hiley, and many others, have copied it into their grammars, as being better than any definition they could devise. Murray himself unquestionably took it from some obscure pedagogue among the old grammarians. Buchanan, who long preceded him, has nearly the same words: "The Superlative increases or diminishes the Positive in Signification, to the highest or [the] lowest Degree of all."—*English Syntax*, p. 28. If this must be taken for a grammatical definition, what definition shall grammar itself bear?

OBS. 11.—Let us see whether our later authors have done better. "The *superlative* expresses a quality in the greatest or [the] least *possible* degree; as, *wisest, coldest, least wise*."—*Webster's Old Gram*. p. 13. In his later speculations, this author conceives that the termination *ish* forms the *first* degree of comparison; as, "Imperfect, *dankish*," Pos. *dank*, Comp. *danker*, Superl. *dankest*. "There are therefore *four* degrees of comparison."—*Webster's Philosophical Gram*. p. 66. "The *fourth* denotes the utmost or [the] least degree of a quality; as, *bravest, wisest, poorest, smallest*. This is called the *superlative* degree."—*Ib.*; also his *Improved Gram.*, 1831, p. 47. "This degree is called the *Superlative degree*, from its raising the amount of the quality above that of all others."—*Webber's Gram.*, 1832, p. 26. It is not easy to quote, from any source, a worse sentence than this; if, indeed, so strange a jumble of words can be called a sentence. "*From its raising the amount*," is in itself a vicious and untranslatable phrase, here put for "*because it raises the amount;*" and who can conceive of the superlative degree, as "*raising the amount of the quality* above that of *all other qualities?*" Or, if it be supposed to mean, "above the amount of all other *degrees*," what is this amount? Is it that of one and one, the *positive* and the *comparative* added numerically? or is it the sum of all the quantities which these may indicate? Perhaps the author meant, "above the amount of all other *amounts*." If none of these absurdities is here taught, nothing is taught, and the words are nonsense. Again: "The *superlative degree* increases or diminishes the positive to the highest or [the] lowest degree *of which it is susceptible*." —*Bucke's Classical Gram*. p. 49. "The superlative degree is generally formed by adding *st* or *est* to the positive; and denotes *the greatest excess*."—*Nutting's Gram*. p. 33. "The superlative increases or diminishes the Signification of the Positive or Adjective, to a *very high* or a *very low* Degree."—*British Gram*. p. 97. What *excess* of skill, or what *very high degree* of acuteness, have the *brightest* and *best* of these grammarians exhibited? There must be some, if their definitions are true.

OBS. 12.—The common assertion of the grammarians, that the superlative degree is not applicable to *two* objects,* is not only unsupported by any reason in the nature of things, but it is contradicted in practice by almost every man who affirms it. Thus Maunder: "When only two persons or things are spoken of comparatively, to use the superlative is improper: as, 'Deborah, my dear, give those two boys a lump of sugar each; and let Dick's be the largest, because he spoke first.' This," says the critic, "should have been 'larger.'"—*Maunder's Gram*. p. 4. It is true, the comparative *might* here have been used; but the superlative is clearer, and more agreeable to custom. And how can "*largest*" be wrong, if "*first*" is right? "Let Dick's be the *larger*, because he spoke *sooner*," borders too much upon a different idea, that of *proportion*; as when we say, "*The sooner the better;*"—"*The more the merrier*." So Blair: "When only two things are compared, the comparative degree must be used, and not the superlative." — *Practical Gram*. p. 81. "A Trochee has the *first* syllable accented, and the *last* unaccented."—*Ib*. p. 118. "An Iambus has the *first* syllable unaccented, and the *last* accented."—*Ibid*. These two examples are found also in *Jamieson's Rhetoric*, p. 305; *Murray's Gram*. p. 253; *Kirkham's*, 219; *Bullions's*, 169; *Guy's*, 120; *Merchant's*, 166. So Hiley: "When *two* persons or things are compared, the *comparative* degree must be employed. When *three* or more persons or things are compared, the *superlative* must be used."—*Treatise on English Gram*. p. 78. Contradiction in practice: "Thomas is *wiser* than his *brothers*."—*Ib*. p. 79. Are not "*three* or *more* persons" here compared by "the comparative *wiser?*" "In an *Iambus* the *first* syllable is unaccented."—*Ib*. p. 123. An iambus has but *two* syllables; and this author expressly teaches that "*first*" is "superlative." —*Ib*. p. 21. So Sanborn: "The *positive* degree denotes *the simple form* of an adjective *without* any variation of meaning. The *comparative* degree increases or lessens the meaning *of the positive*, and denotes a comparison *between two* persons or things. The *superlative* degree increases or lessens the positive *to the greatest extent*, and denotes a comparison *between more than two* persons or things."—*Analytical Gram*. p. 30 and p. 86. These pretended definitions of the degrees of comparison embrace not only the absurdities which I have already censured in those of our

---

* I suppose that, in a comparison of *two*, any of the degrees may be accurately employed. The common usage is, to construe the positive with *as*, the comparative with *than*, and the superlative with *of*. But here custom allows us also to use the comparative with *of*, after the manner of the superlative; as, "This is *the better* of the two." It was but an odd whim of some old pedant, to find in this a reason for declaring it ungrammatical to say "This is *the best* of the two." In one grammar, I find the former construction *condemned*, and the latter approved, thus: "This is *the better* book of the two. Not correct, because the comparative state of the adjective, (*better*,) can not correspond with the preposition, *of*. The definite article, *the*, is likewise improperly applied to the comparative state; the sentence should stand thus, This is *the best* book of the two."—*Chandler's Gram.*; Ed. of 1821, p. 130; Ed. of 1847, p. 154.

common grammars, but several new ones peculiar to this author. Of the inconsistency of his doctrine and practice, take the following examples : " Which of two bodies, that move with the same velocity, will exercise the *greatest* power ? "—*Ib.* p. 93; and again, p. 208. " '*I* was offered a *dollar*,' —'*A dollar* was offered (to) *me.*' The *first* form should always be avoided."—*Ib.* p. 128. " Nouns in apposition generally annex the sign of the possessive case to the *last* ; as, ' For David my *servant's* sake.'—' John the *Baptist's* head.' *Bible.*"—*Ib.* p. 197.

OBS. 13.—So Murray: " We commonly say, ' This is the *weaker of the two* ;' or ' The *weakest* of the two :'* but the former is the regular mode of expression, because there are *only two* things compared."—*Octavo Gram.* i, 167.   What then of the following example : " Which of *those two* persons has *most* distinguished himself ? "—*Ib. Key*, ii, 187.   Again, in treating of the adjectives *this* and *that*, the same hand writes thus : " *This* refers to the *nearest* person or thing, and that to the *most distant* : as, ' *This* man is *more intelligent* than *that.*' *This* indicates the *latter*, or *last* mentioned ; *that*, the *former*, or *first* mentioned : as, ' Both wealth and poverty are temptations ; *that* tends to excite pride, *this*, discontent.'"—*Murray's Gram.* i, 56.   In the former part of this example, the superlative is twice applied where only two things are spoken of ; and, in the latter, it is twice made equivalent to the comparative, with a like reference. The following example shows the same equivalence : " *This* refers to the *last* mentioned or *nearer* thing, *that* to the *first* mentioned or *more* distant thing."—*Webber's Gram.* p. 31.   So Churchill : " The superlative should not be used, when only two persons or things are compared."—*New Gram.* p. 80. " In the *first* of these two sentences."—*Ib.* p. 162 ; *Lowth*, p. 120.   According to the rule, it should have been, " In the *former* of these two sentences ; " but this would be here ambiguous, because *former* might mean *maker*. " When our sentence consists of two members, the *longest* should, generally, be the concluding one."—*Blair's Rhet.* p. 117 : and *Jamieson's*, p. 99. " The *shortest* member being placed *first*, we carry it *more readily* in our memory as we proceed to the second."—*Ib. & Ib.* " Pray consider us, in this respect, as the *weakest* sex."—*Spect.* No. 533. In this last sentence, the comparative, *weaker*, would perhaps have been better ; because, not an absolute, but merely a comparative weakness is meant.

OBS. 14.—Hyperboles are very commonly expressed by comparatives or superlatives ; as, "My *little finger* shall be *thicker* than my *father's loins.*"—1 *Kings*, xii, 10. " Unto me, who am *less than the least* of all saints, is this grace given."—*Ephesians*, iii, 8. Sometimes, in thus heightening or lowering the object of his conception, the writer falls into a catachresis, solecism, or abuse of the grammatical degrees ; as, " Mustard-seed—which is *less than all the seeds* that be in the earth."—*Mark*, iv, 31. This expression is objectionable, because mustard-seed is a seed, and cannot be less than itself ; though that which is here spoken of, may perhaps have been " *the least of all seeds* :" and it is the same Greek phrase, that is thus rendered in Matt. xiii, 32. Murray has inserted in his Exercises, among " unintelligible and inconsistent words and phrases," the following example from Milton :

> " And, in the lowest deep, a lower deep
> Still threat'ning to devour me, opens wide."—*Exercises*, p. 122.

For this supposed inconsistency, he proposes in his Key the following amendment :

> " And, in the *lower* deep, *another* deep
> Still threat'ning to devour me, opens wide."—*Key*, p. 254.

But, in an other part of his book, he copies from Dr. Blair the same passage, with commendation : saying, " The following sentiments of *Satan in Milton*, as strongly as they are described, *contain nothing* but what is *natural and proper* :

> ' Me miserable ! which way shall I fly
> Infinite wrath, and infinite despair ?
> Which way I fly is Hell ; myself am Hell ;
> And in the lowest *depth*, a lower deep,
> Still threat'ning to devour me, opens wide,
> To which the Hell I suffer seems a Heaven.' *P. Lost.* B. iv, l. 73."
> *Blair's Lectures*, p. 153 ; *Murray's Grammar*, p. 352.

OBS. 15.—Milton's word, in the fourth line above, is *deep*, and not *depth*, as these authors here give it : nor was it very polite in them, to use a phraseology which comes so near to saying, the devil was in the poet. Alas for grammar ! accuracy in its teachers has become the most rare of all qualifications. As for Murray's correction above, I see not how it can please any one who chooses to think Hell a place of great depth. A descent into his " *lower* deep" and " *other* deep," might be a plunge less horrible than two or three successive slides in one of our western caverns ! But Milton supposes the arch-fiend might descend to the lowest *imaginable* depth of Hell, and there be liable to a still further fall of more tremendous extent. Fall whither ? Into the horrid and inconceivable profundity of the *bottomless pit!* What signifies it, to object to his language as " *unintelligible*," if it conveys his idea better than any other could ? In no human conception of what is infinite, can there be any real exaggeration. To amplify beyond the truth, is here impossible. Nor is there any superlation which can fix a limit to the idea of more and more in infinitude. Whatever literal absurdity there may be in it, the duplication seems greatly to augment what was even our greatest conception of the thing. Homer, with a like figure, though expressed in the positive degree, makes Jupiter threaten any rebel god, that he shall be thrown down from Olympus, to suffer the burning pains of the Tartarian gulf ; not in the centre, but,

> " *As deep* beneath th' infernal centre hurl'd,
> As from that centre to th' ethereal world."—*Pope's Iliad*, B. viii, l. 19.

---

* This example appears to have been borrowed from Campbell ; who, however, teaches a different doctrine from Murray, and clearly sustains my position : " Both degrees are in such cases used *indiscriminately.* We say *rightly*, either ' This is the weaker of the two,' or—' the weakest of the two.' "—*Philosophy of Rhetoric*, p 202. How positively do some other men contradict this ! "In comparing *two* persons or things, by means of an adjective, care must be taken, that the superlative state be not employed : We properly say, ' John is the *taller* of the two ;' but we *should not* say, ' John is the *tallest* of the two.' The reason is plain : we compare but *two* persons, and must therefore use the comparative state."—*Wright's Philosophical Gram.* p. 143. Rev. Matt. Harrison, too, insists on it, that the superlative must " have reference to more than two," and censures Dr. *Johnson* for not observing the rule. See *Harrison's English Language*, p. 255.

REGULAR COMPARISON.

Adjectives are regularly compared, when the comparative degree is expressed by adding *er*, and the superlative, by adding *est* to them: as, Pos. *great*, Comp. *greater*, Superl. *greatest*; Pos. *mild*, Comp. *milder*, Superl. *mildest*.

In the variation of adjectives, final consonants are doubled, final *e* is omitted, and final *y* is changed to *i*, agreeably to the rules for spelling: as, *hot, hotter, hottest; wide, wider, widest; happy, happier, happiest*.

The regular method of comparison belongs almost exclusively to monosyllables, with dissyllables ending in *w* or *y*, and such others as receive it and still have but one syllable after the accent: as, *fierce, fiercer, fiercest; narrow, narrower, narrowest; gloomy, gloomier, gloomiest; serene, serener, serenest; noble, nobler, noblest; gentle, gentler, gentlest*.

COMPARISON BY ADVERBS.

The two degrees of superiority may also be expressed with precisely the same import as above, by prefixing to the adjective the adverbs *more* and *most*: as, *wise, more wise, most wise; famous, more famous, most famous; amiable, more amiable, most amiable*.

The degrees of inferiority are expressed, in like manner, by the adverbs *less* and *least*: as, *wise, less wise, least wise; famous, less famous, least famous; amiable, less amiable, least amiable*. The regular method of comparison has, properly speaking, no degrees of this kind.

Nearly all adjectives that admit of different degrees, may be compared by means of the adverbs; but, for short words, the regular method is generally preferable: as, *quick, quicker, quickest;* rather than, *quick, more quick, most quick*.

OBSERVATIONS.

OBS. 1.—The genius of our language is particularly averse to the lengthening of long words by additional syllables; and, in the comparison of adjectives, *er* and *est* always add a syllable to the word, except it end in *le* after a mute. Thus, *free, freer, freest*, increases syllabically; but *ample, ampler, amplest*, does not. Whether any particular adjective admits of comparison or not, is a matter of reasoning from the sense of the term; by which method it shall be compared, is in some degree a matter of taste; though custom has decided that long words shall not be inflected, and for the shorter, there is generally an obvious bias in favour of one form rather than the other. Dr. Johnson says, "The comparison of adjectives is very *uncertain;* and being much regulated by commodiousness of utterance, or agreeableness of sound, is not easily reduced to rules. Monosyllables are commonly compared. Polysyllables, or words of more than two syllables, are seldom compared otherwise than by *more* and *most*. Dissyllables are seldom compared if they terminate in *ful, less, ing, ous, ed, id, al, ent, ain,* or *ive*."—*Gram. of the English Tongue,* p. 6. "When the positive contains but one syllable, the degrees are usually formed by adding *er* or *est*. When the positive contains two syllables, it is matter of taste which method you shall use in forming the degrees. The ear is, in this case, the best guide. But, when the positive contains more than two syllables, the degrees must be formed by the use of *more* and *most*. We may say, *tenderer* and *tenderest, pleasanter* and *pleasantest, prettier* and *prettiest;* but who could endure *delicater* and *delicatest?*"—*Cobbett's E. Gram.* ¶ 81. *Quiet, bitter, clever, sober,* and perhaps some others like them, are still regularly compared; but such words as *secretest, famousest, virtuousest, powerfullest,* which were used by Milton, have gone out of fashion. The following, though not very commonly used, are perhaps allowable. "Yet these are the two *commonest* occupations of mankind."—*Philological Museum,* i, 431. "Their *pleasantest* walks throughout life must be guarded by armed men."—*Ib.* i, 437. "Franklin possessed the rare talent of drawing useful lessons from the *commonest* occurrences."—*Murray's Sequel,* p. 323. "Unbidden guests are often *welcomest* when they are gone."—SHAK.: *in Joh. Dict.*
"There was a lad, th' *unluckiest* of his crew,
Was still contriving something bad, but new."—KING: *ib.*

OBS. 2.—I make a distinction between the regular comparison by *er* and *est,* and the comparison by adverbs; because, in a grammatical point of view, these two methods are totally different: the meaning, though the same, being expressed in the one case, by an inflection of the adjective; and in the other, by a phrase consisting of two different parts of speech. If the placing of an adverb before an adjective is to be called a grammatical modification or variation of the latter word, we shall have many other degrees than those which are enumerated above. The words may with much more propriety be parsed separately, the *degree* being ascribed to the *adverb*. The degrees in which qualities may exist in nature, are infinitely various; but the only degrees with which the grammarian is concerned, are those which our *variation* of the adjective or adverb enables us to express—including, as of course we must, the state or sense of the primitive word, as one. The reasoning which would make the positive degree to be *no degree,* would also make the nominative case, or the *casus rectus* of the Latins, to be *no case*.

OBS. 3.—Whenever the *adjective itself* denotes these degrees, and is duly varied in form to express them, they properly belong to it; as, *worthy, worthier, worthiest.* (Though no apology can be made for the frequent error of confounding the *degree of a quality,* with the *verbal sign* which expresses it.) If an *adverb* is employed for this purpose, that also is compared, and the two degrees thus formed or expressed, are properly its own; as, worthy, *more worthy, most worthy.* But these same degrees may be yet otherwise expressed; as, worthy, *in a higher degree* worthy, *in the highest degree* worthy. Here also the adjective *worthy* is virtually compared, as before; but only the adjective *high* is grammatically modified. There are also other adverbs, which. though not varied in themselves like *much, more, most,* may nevertheless have nearly the same effect upon the adjective; as, worthy, *comparatively* worthy, *superlatively* worthy. I make these remarks, because many grammarians have erroneously parsed the adverbs *more* and *most, less* and *least,* as parts of the adjective.

OBS. 4.—Harris, in his Hermes, or Philosophical Inquiry concerning Universal Grammar, has very unceremoniously pronounced the doctrine of three degrees of comparison, to be *absurd ;* and the author of the British Grammar, as he quotes the whole passage without offering any defence of that doctrine, seems to second the allegation. "Mr. Harris observes, that, 'There cannot well be more than two degrees; one to denote simple excess, and one to denote superlative. Were we indeed to introduce more degrees, we ought perhaps to introduce infinite, which is absurd. For why stop at a limited number, when in all subjects, susceptible of intension, the intermediate excesses are in a manner infinite? There are infinite degrees of *more white* between the first simple *white* and the superlative *whitest ;* the same may be said of *more great, more strong, more minute,* &c. The doctrine of grammarians about *three* such degrees, which they call the Positive, the Comparative, and the Superlative, must needs be absurd; both because in their Positive there is no comparison at all, and because their Superlative is a Comparative as much as their Comparative itself.' *Hermes,* p. 197."—*Brit. Gram.* p. 98. This objection is rashly urged. No comparison can be imagined without bringing together as many as two terms, and if the positive is one of these, it is a degree of comparison; though neither this nor the superlative is, for that reason,—"*a Comparative.*" Why we stop at three degrees, I have already shown: we have *three forms,* and only three.

OBS. 5.—"The termination *ish* may be accounted in some sort a degree of comparison, by which the signification is diminished below the positive, as *black, blackish,* or tending to blackness; *salt, saltish,* or having a little taste of salt:* they therefore admit of no comparison. This termination is seldom added but to words expressing sensible qualities, nor often to words of above one syllable, and is scarcely used in the solemn or sublime style."—*Dr. Johnson's Gram.* "The *first* [degree] denotes a slight degree of the quality, and is expressed by the termination *ish ;* as, *reddish, brownish, yellowish.* This may be denominated the *imperfect* degree of the attribute."—*Dr. Webster's Improved Gram.* p. 47. I doubt the correctness of the view taken above by Johnson, and dissent entirely from Webster, about his "*first degree*" of comparison." Of adjectives in *ish* we have perhaps a hundred; but nine out of ten of them are derived clearly from *nouns,* as, *boyish, girlish ;* and who can prove that *blackish, saltish, reddish, brownish,* and *yellowish,* are not also from the *nouns, black, salt, red, brown,* and *yellow?* or that "a *more reddish* tinge,"—"a *more saltish* taste," are not correct phrases? There is, I am persuaded, no good reason for noticing this termination as constituting a degree of comparison. All "double comparisons" are said to be ungrammatical; but, if *ish* forms a degree, it is such a degree as may be compared again: as,

"And seem *more learnedish* than those
That at a greater charge compose."—*Butler.*

OBS. 6.—Among the degrees of comparison, some have enumerated that of *equality ;* as when we say, "It is *as sweet as* honey." Here is indeed a comparison, but it is altogether in the *positive* degree, and needs no other name. This again refutes Harris; who says, that in the positive there is no comparison at all. But further: it is plain, that in this degree there may be comparisons of *inequality* also; as, "Molasses is *not so sweet as* honey."—"Civility is *not so slight* a matter as it is commonly thought."—*Art of Thinking,* p. 92. Nay, such comparisons may equal any superlative. Thus it is said, I think, in the Life of Robert Hall: "Probably no human being ever before suffered *so much* bodily pain." What a preëminence is here! and yet the form of the adjective is only that of the positive degree. "Nothing *so uncertain* as general reputation."—*Art of Thinking,* p. 50. "Nothing *so nauseous* as undistinguishing civility "—*Ib.* p. 88. These, likewise, would be strong expressions, if they were correct English. But, to my apprehension, every such comparison of equality involves a solecism, when, as it here happens, the former term includes the latter. The word *nothing* is a general negative, and *reputation* is a particular affirmative. The comparison of equality between them, is therefore certainly improper: because *nothing* cannot be equal to *something ;* and, reputation being something, and of course equal to itself, the proposition is evidently untrue. It ought to be, "Nothing is *more uncertain than* general reputation." This is the same as to say, "General reputation is *as uncertain as any* thing that can be named." Or else the former term should exempt the latter; as, "*Nothing else* —or, "No *other* thing, is *so uncertain as*" this popular honour, public esteem, or "*general reputation.*" And so of all similar examples.

OBS. 7.—In all comparisons, care must be taken to adapt the terms to the *degree* which is expressed by the adjective or adverb. The superlative degree requires that the object to which it

* Murray copied this passage literally, (though anonymously,) as far as the colon; and of course his book teaches us to account "*the termination ish,* in some sort, a *degree of comparison.*"—*Octavo Gram.* p. 47. But what is more absurd, than to think of accounting this, or any other suffix, "a *degree of comparison?*" The inaccuracy of the language is a sufficient proof of the haste with which Johnson adopted this notion, and of the blindness with which he has been followed. The passage is now found in most of our English grammars. Sanborn expresses the doctrine thus: "Adjectives terminating with *ish,* denote a degree of comparison less than the positive; as, *saltish, whitish, blackish* "—*Analytical Gram.* p. 87. But who does not know, that most adjectives of this ending are derived from *nouns,* and are compared only by adverbs, as *childish, foolish,* and so forth? Wilcox says, "Words ending in *ish,* generally express a slight degree; as, *reddish, bookish.*"—*Practical Gram.* p. 17. But who will suppose that *foolish* denotes but a slight degree of folly, or *bookish* but a slight fondness for books? And, with such an interpretation, what must be the meaning of *more bookish* or *most foolish?*

relates, be one of those with which it is compared; as, "*Eve* was *the fairest* of *women*." The comparative degree, on the contrary, requires that the object spoken of be not included among those with which it is compared; as, "*Eve* was *fairer* than any of *her daughters*." To take the inclusive term here, and say, "*Eve* was *fairer* than any *woman*," would be no less absurd. than Milton's assertion, that "*Eve* was *the fairest* of *her daughters*:" the former supposes that she was *not a woman*; the latter, that she was *one of her own daughters*. But Milton's solecism is double; he makes Adam *one of his own sons* :—

"Adam the goodliest man of men since born
His sons, the fairest of her daughters Eve."—*P. Lost*, B. iv, l. 324.

Obs. 8.—"Such adjectives," says Churchill, "as have in themselves a superlative significa-tion, or express qualities not susceptible of degrees, do not properly admit either the comparative or [the] superlative form. Under this rule may be included *all adjectives with a negative prefix*." —*New Gram.* p. 80. Again: "As *immediate* signifies instant, present with regard to time, Prior should not have written, ' *more* immediate.' *Dr. Johnson*."—*Ib.* p. 233. "Hooker has *unaptest;* Locke, *more uncorrupted;* Holder, *more undeceivable:* for these the proper expressions would have been the opposite signs without the negation; *least apt, less corrupted, less deceivable.* Watts speaks of 'a *most unpassable* barrier.' If he had simply said ' an unpassable barrier,' we should have understood it at once in the strongest sense, as a barrier impossible to be surmounted: but, by at-tempting to express something more, he gives an idea of something less; we perceive, that his *unpassable* means *difficult to pass*. This is the mischief of the propensity to exaggeration; which, striving after strength, sinks into weakness."—*Ib.* p 234.

Obs. 9.—The foregoing remarks from Churchill appear *in general* to have been dictated by good sense; but, if his own practice is right, there must be some exceptions to his rule respecting the comparison of adjectives with a negative prefix; for, in the phrase "*less imprudent*," which, ac-cording to a passage quoted before, he will have to be different from "*more prudent*," he himself furnishes an example of such comparison. In fact, very many words of that class are compared by good writers: as, "Nothing is *more unnecessary*."—*Lowth's Gram.* Pref. p. v. "What is yet *more unaccountable*."—ROGERS : *in Joh. Dict.* "It is hard to determine which is *most uneligible*." —*Id. ib.* "Where it appears the *most unbecoming* and *unnatural*."—ADDISON: *ib.* "Men of the best sense, and of the *most unblemished* lives."—*Id. ib.* "March and September are the *most unsettled* and *unequable* of seasons."—BENTLEY: *ib.* "Barcelona was taken by a *most unexpected* accident."—SWIFT: *ib.* "The *most barren* and *unpleasant*."—WOODWARD: *ib.* "O good, but *most unwise* patricians!"—SHAK.: *ib.* "*More unconstant* than the wind."—*Id. ib.* "We may say *more* or *less imperfect*."—*Murray's Gram.* p. 168. "Some of those [passions] which act with the *most irresistible* energy upon the hearts of mankind, are altogether omitted in the catalogue of Aristotle."—*Adams's Rhet.* i, 380. "The wrong of him who presumes to talk of owning me, is *too unmeasured* by kindness."—*Channing, on Emancipation*, p. 52. "Which, we are sensible, are *more inconclusive* than the rest."—*Blair's Rhet.* p. 319.

"Ere yet the salt of *most unrighteous* tears
Had left the flushing in her galled eyes."—*Shak.*

Obs. 10.—Comparison must not be considered a general property of adjectives. It belongs chiefly to the class which I call common adjectives, and is by no means applicable to all of these. *Common adjectives*, or epithets denoting quality, are perhaps more numerous than all the other classes put together. Many of these, and a few that are *pronominal*, may be varied by compari-son; and some *participial* adjectives may be compared by means of the adverbs. But adjectives formed from *proper names*, all the *numerals*, and most of the *compounds*, are in no way susceptible of comparison. All nouns used adjectively, as an *iron* bar, an *evening* school, a *mahogany* chair, a *South-Sea* dream, are also incapable of comparison. In the title of "His *Most Christian* Ma-jesty," the superlative adverb is applied to a *proper adjective;* but who will pretend that we ought to understand by it "*the highest degree*" of Christian attainment? It might seem uncourtly to suggest that this is "an abuse of the king's English," I shall therefore say no such thing. Pope compares the word *Christian*, in the following couplet :—

"Go, purified by flames ascend the sky,
My better and *more Christian* progeny."—*Dunciad*, B. i, l. 227.

IRREGULAR COMPARISON.

The following adjectives are compared irregularly : *good, better, best ; bad, evil,* or *ill, worse, worst; little, less, least ; much, more, most ; many, more, most.*

OBSERVATIONS.

Obs. 1.—In *English*, and also in *Latin*, most adjectives that denote *place* or *situation*, not only form the superlative irregularly, but are also either defective or redundant in comparison. Thus :

I. The following nine have more than one superlative : *far, farther, farthest, farmost* or *farther-most ; near, nearer, nearest* or *next ; fore, former, foremost* or *first ; hind, hinder, hindmost* or *hindermost ; in, inner, inmost* or *innermost ; out, outer* or *utter, outmost* or *utmost, outermost* or *ut-termost ; up, upper, upmost* or *uppermost ; low, lower, lowest* or *lowermost ; late, later* or *latter, la-test* or *last*.

II. The following five want the positive: [*aft*, adv.] *after, aftmost* or *aftermost ;* [*forth*, adv.] *further, furthest* or *furthermost ; hither, hithermost ; nether, nethermost ; under, undermost*.

III. The following want the comparative : *front, frontmost ; rear, rearmost ; head, headmost ; end, endmost ; top, topmost ; bottom, bottommost ; mid* or *middle, midst,*[*] *midmost* or *middlemost ;*

---

[*] *Midst* is a contraction of the regular superlative *middest*, used by Spenser, but now obsolete. *Midst,* also, seems to be obsolete as an adjective, though still frequently used as a noun ; as, " In the *midst*."—*Webster*. It is also a poetic contraction for the preposition *amidst*. In some cases it appears to be an adverb. In the following example it is equivalent to *middlemost*, and therefore an adjective : " Still greatest he *the midst*, Now dragon grown."—*Paradise Lost*, B. x, l. 528.

north, northmost; south, southmost; east, eastmost; west, westmost; northern, northernmost; southern, southernmost; eastern, easternmost; western, westernmost.

OBS. 2.—Many of these irregular words are not always used as adjectives, but oftener as nouns, adverbs, or prepositions. The sense in which they are employed, will show to what class they belong. The terms *fore* and *hind*, *front* and *rear*, *right* and *left*, *in* and *out*, *high* and *low*, *top* and *bottom*, *up* and *down*, *upper* and *under*, *mid* and *after*, all but the last pair, are in direct contrast with each other. Many of them are often joined in composition with other words; and some, when used as adjectives of place, are rarely separated from their nouns: as, *inland*, *outhouse*, *mid-sea*, *after-ages*. Practice is here so capricious, I find it difficult to determine whether the compounding of these terms is proper or not. It is a case about which he that inquires most, may perhaps be most in doubt. If the joining of the words prevents the possibility of mistaking the adjective for a preposition, it prevents also the separate classification of the adjective and the noun, and thus in some sense destroys the former by making the whole a noun. Dr. Webster writes thus: "FRONTROOM, *n.* A room or apartment in the *forepart* of a house. BACKROOM, *n.* A room behind the *front room*, or in the *back part* of the house."—*Octavo Dict.* So of many phrases by which people tell of turning things, or changing the position of their parts; as, *inside out*, *outside in*; *upside down*, *downside up*; *wrong* end *foremost*, *but-end foremost*; *forepart back*, *fore-end aft*; *hind* side *before*, *backside before*. Here all these contrasted particles seem to be adjectives of place or situation. What grammarians in general would choose to call them, it is hard to say; probably, many would satisfy themselves with calling the whole "*an adverbial phrase*,"—the common way of disposing of every thing which it is difficult to analyze. These, and the following examples from Scott, are a fair specimen of the uncertainty of present usage:

" The herds without a keeper strayed,
The plough was in *mid-furrow* staid."—*Lady of the Lake.*
" The eager huntsman knew his bound,
And in *mid chase* called off his hound."—*Ibidem.*

OBS. 3.—For the chief points of the compass, we have so many adjectives, and so many modes of varying or comparing them, that it is difficult to tell their number, or to know which to choose in practice. (1.) *North*, *south*, *east*, and *west*, are familiarly used both as nouns and as adjectives. From these it seems not improper to form superlatives, as above, by adding *most*; as, " From Aroar to Nebo, and the wild of *southmost* Abarim."—*Milton.* " There are no rivulets or springs in the island of Feror, the *westmost* of the Canaries."—*White's Nat. Hist.* (2.) These primitive terms may also be compared, in all three of the degrees, by the adverbs *farther* and *farthest*, or *further* and *furthest*; as, " Which is yet *farther west*."—*Bacon.* (3.) Though we never employ as separate words the comparatives *norther*, *souther*, *easter*, *wester*, we have *northerly*, *southerly*, *easterly*, and *westerly*, which seem to have been formed from such comparatives, by adding *ly*; and these four may be compared by the adverbs *more* and *most*, or *less* and *least*: as, " These hills give us a view of the *most easterly*, *southerly*, and *westerly* parts of England."—GRAUNT: in *Joh. Dict.* (4.) From these supposed comparatives likewise, some authors form the superlatives *northermost*, *southermost*, *eastermost*, and *westermost*; as, " From the *westermost* part of Oyster bay."—*Dr. Webster's Hist U. S.* p. 126. " And three miles southward of the *souther-most* part of said bay."—*Trumbull's Hist. of Amer.* Vol. i, p. 88. " Pockanocket was on the *westermost* line of Plymouth Colony."—*Ib.* p. 44. " As far as the *northermost* branch of the said bay or river."—*Ib.* p. 127. The propriety of these is at least questionable; and, as they are neither very necessary to the language, nor recognized by any of our lexicographers, I forbear to approve them. (5.) From the four primitives we have also a third series of positives, ending in *ern*; as, *northern*, *southern*, *eastern*, *western*. These, though they have no comparatives of their own, not only form superlatives by assuming the termination *most*, but are sometimes compared, perhaps in both degrees, by a separate use of the adverbs: as, "*Southernmost*, *a.* Furthest towards the south."—*Webster's Dict.* " Until it shall intersect the *northernmost* part of the thirty-first degree of north latitude."—*Articles of Peace.* " To the *north-westernmost* head of Connecticut river."—*Ib.* " Thence through the said lake to the *most north-western* point thereof."—*Ib.*

OBS. 4.—It may be remarked of the comparatives *former* and *latter* or *hinder*, *upper* and *under* or *nether*, *inner* and *outer* or *utter*, *after* and *hither*; as well as of the Latin *superior* and *inferior*, *anterior* and *posterior*, *interior* and *exterior*, *prior* and *ulterior*, *senior* and *junior*, *major* and *minor*; that they cannot, like other comparatives, be construed with the conjunction *than*. After all genuine English comparatives, this conjunction may occur, because it is the only fit word for introducing the latter term of comparison; but we never say, one thing is *former* or *latter*, *superior* or *inferior*, *than* an other. And so of all the rest here named. Again, no real comparative or superlative can ever need an other superadded to it; but *inferior* and *superior* convey ideas that do not always preclude the additional conception of *more* or *less*: as, " With respect to high and low notes, pronunciation is still *more inferior* to singing."—*Kames, Elements of Criticism*, Vol. ii, p. 73. " The mistakes which the *most superior* understanding is apt to fall into."—*West's Letters to a Young Lady*, p. 117.

OBS. 5.—Double comparatives and double superlatives, being in general awkward and unfashionable, as well as tautological, ought to be avoided. Examples: ' The duke of Milan, and his *more braver* daughter, could control thee."—*Shak. Tempest.* Say, " his *more gallant* daughter." "What in me was purchased, falls upon thee in a *more fairer* sort."—*Id. Henry IV.* Say, "*fairer*," or, " *more honest*;" for "*purchased*" here means *stolen*. " Changed to a *worser* shape thou canst not be."—*Id.* l *Hen.* VI. Say, " a *worse* shape"—or, " an *uglier* shape." " After the *most straitest* sect of our religion, I lived a Pharisee."—*Acts*, xxvi, 5. Say, " the *strictest* sect." 'Some say he's mad; others, that *lesser* hate him, do call it valiant fury."—*Shak.* Say, " others, that hate him *less*." In this last example, *lesser* is used adverbially, in which construction it is certainly incorrect. But against *lesser* as an adjective, some grammarians have spoken with more severity, than comports with a proper respect for authority. Dr. Johnson says, " LESSER, *adj.* A barbarous corruption of *less*, formed by the vulgar from the habit of terminating comparatives in *er ; afterward adopted by poets, and then by writers of prose, till it has all the authority which a mode originally erroneous can derive from custom.*"—*Quarto Dict.* With no great fairness, Churchill quotes this passage as far as the semicolon, and there stops. The position thus taken he further endeavours to strengthen, by saying, " *Worser,* though *not more barbarous,* offends the ear in a much greater degree, because it has not been so frequently used." —*New Gram.* p. 232. Example: " And God made two great lights; the greater light to rule the day, and the *lesser* light to rule the night."—*Gen.* i, 16. Kirkham, after making an *imitation* of this passage, remarks upon it: " *Lesser* is *as* incorrect as *badder, gooder, worser.*"—*Gram.* p. 77. The judgement of any critic who is ignorant enough to say this, is worthy only of contempt. *Lesser* is still frequently used by the most tasteful authors, both in verse and prose: as, " It is the glowing style of a man who is negligent of *lesser* graces."—*Blair's Rhet.* p. 189.

 " Athos, Olympus, Ætna, Atlas, made
  These hills seem things of *lesser* dignity."—*Byron.*

OBS. 6.—The adjective *little* is used in different senses; for it contrasts sometimes with *great,* and sometimes with *much. Lesser* appears to refer only to size. Hence *less* and *lesser* are not always equivalent terms. *Lesser* means *smaller,* and contrasts only with *greater. Less* contrasts sometimes with *greater,* but oftener with *more,* the comparative of *much ;* for, though it may mean *not so large,* its most common meaning is *not so much.* It ought to be observed, likewise, that *less* is not an adjective of *number,* though not unfrequently used as such. It does not mean *fewer,* and is therefore not properly employed in sentences like the following: " In all verbs, there are no *less* than three things implied at once."—*Blair's Rhet.* p. 81. " *Smaller* things than three," is nonsense; and so, in reality, is what the Doctor here says. *Less* is not the proper opposite to *more,* when *more* is the comparative of *many : few, fewer, fewest,* are the only words which contrast regularly with *many, more, most.* In the following text, these comparatives are rightly employed : " And to the *more* ye shall give the *more* inheritance, and to the *fewer* ye shall give the *less* inheritance."—*Numbers,* xxxiii, 54. But if writers will continue to use *less* for *fewer,* so that " *less cattle,*" for instance, may mean "*fewer cattle ;*" we shall be under a sort of necessity to retain *lesser,* in order to speak intelligibly : as, " It shall be for the sending forth of oxen, and for the treading of *lesser* cattle."—*Isaiah,* vii, 25. I have no partiality for the word *lesser,* neither will I make myself ridiculous by flouting at its rudeness. " This word," says Webster, " is a corruption, but [it is] too well established to be discarded. Authors always write the *Lesser* Asia." —*Octavo Dict.* " By the same reason, may a man punish the *lesser* breaches of that law."—*Locke.* " When we speak of the *lesser* differences among the tastes of men."—*Blair's Rhet.* p. 20. " In greater or *lesser* degrees of complexity."—*Burke, on Sublime,* p. 94. " The greater ought not to succumb to the *lesser.*"—*Dillwyn's Reflections,* p. 128. " To such productions, *lesser* composers must resort for ideas."—*Gardiner's Music of Nature,* p. 413.

 " The larger here, and there the *lesser* lambs,
  The new-fall'n young herd bleating for their dams."—*Pope.*

OBS. 7.—Our grammarians deny the comparison of many adjectives, from a false notion that they are already superlatives. Thus Allen : " Adjectives compounded with the Latin preposition *per,* are already superlative; as, *perfect, perennial, permanent,* &c."—*Elements of E. Gram.* p. 52. In reply to this, I would say, that nothing is *really superlative,* in English, but what has the form and construction of the superlative: as, " The *most permanent* of all dyes." No word beginning with *per,* is superlative by virtue of this *Latin prefix.* " Separate spirits, which are beings that have *perfecter* knowledge and greater happiness than we, must needs have also a *perfecter* way of communicating their thoughts than we have."—*Locke's Essay,* B. ii, Ch. 24, § 36. This mode of comparison is not now good, but it shows that *perfect* is no superlative. Thus Kirkham : " The *following* adjectives, and *many others,* are *always in the superlative degree ;* because, by expressing a quality in *the highest degree,* they carry in themselves a superlative signification : *chief, extreme, perfect, right, wrong, honest, just, true, correct, sincere, vast, immense, ceaseless, infinite, endless, unparalleled, universal, supreme, unlimited, omnipotent, all-wise, eternal.*"†—*Gram.* p. 73.

* What I here say, accords with the teaching of all our lexicographers and grammarians, except one dauntless critic, who has taken particular pains to put me, and some three or four others, on the defensive. This gentleman not only supposes *less* and *fewer, least* and *fewest,* to be sometimes equivalent in meaning, but actually exhibits them as being also etymologically of the same stock. *Less* and *least,* however, he refers to three different positives, and *more* and *most,* to four. And since, in one instance, he traces *less* and *more, least* and *most,* to the same primitive word, it follows of course, if he is right, that *more* is there equivalent to *less,* and *most* is equivalent to *least !* The following is a copy of this remarkable " DECLENSION ON INDEFINITE SPECIFYING ADNAMES," and just one half of the table is wrong : " *Some, more, most ; Some, less, least ;* Little, less, least ; Few, fewer or less, fewest or least ; Several, more, most ;* Much, more, most ; Many, more, most."—*Oliver B. Peirce's Gram.* p. 144.

† Murray himself had the same false notion concerning six of these adjectives, and perhaps all the rest; for his indefinite *andsoforths* may embrace just what the reader pleases to imagine. Let the following paragraph be compared with the observations and proofs which I shall offer: " Adjectives that have in themselves a superlative signification, do not properly admit of the superlative or [the] comparative form superadded : such as, ' Chief, extreme, perfect, right, universal, supreme,' &c. : which are sometimes improperly written, ' Chiefest, extremest, perfectest, rightest, most universal, most supreme,' &c. The following expressions are therefore improper. ' He sometimes claims admission to the *chiefest* offices;' ' The quarrel became *so universal* and national;' ' A method of attaining the *rightest* and greatest happiness.' The phrases, so perfect, so right, so extreme, so universal, &c. are incorrect; because they imply that one thing is less perfect, less extreme, &c. than another, which is *not possible.*"—*Murray's Gram.* 8vo, i, p. 167. For himself, a man may do as he pleases about comparing these adjectives : but whoever corrects others, on such principles as the foregoing, will have work enough on his hands. But the writer who seems to exceed all others, in error on this point, is *Joseph W. Wright.* In his " Philosophical Grammar," p. 51st, this author gives a list of *seventy-two* adjectives, which, he says, " admit of *no variation of state :*" I. e. are not compared. Among them are *round, flat, wet, dry, clear, pure, odd, free, plain, fair, chaste, blind,* and more than forty others, which are compared about as often as any words in the language. Dr. Blair is hypercritically censured by him, for saying " *most excellent,*" " *more false,*" "the *chastest* kind," " *more perfect,*" " *fuller, more full, fullest, most full, truest* and *most true ;*" Murray, for using " *quite wrong ;*" and Cobbett, for the phrase, " *perfect correctness.*" " Correctness," says the critic, " does not admit of *degrees of perfection.*"—*Ib.* pp. 143 and 151. But what does such a thinker know about correctness ? If this excellent quality cannot be *perfect,* surely nothing can. The words which Dr. Bullions thinks it " improper to compare," because he judges them to have " an absolute or superlative signification," are " *true, perfect, universal, chief, extreme, supreme,* &c."—no body knows how many. See *Principles of E. Gram.* p. 19 and p. 115.

So the Rev. David Blair: "The words *perfect, certain, infinite, universal, chief, supreme, right, true, extreme, superior,* and some others, which express a perfect and superlative sense in themselves, do not admit of comparison."—*English Gram.* p. 81. Now, according to Murray's definition, which Kirkham adopts, none of these words can be at all in the superlative degree. On the contrary, there are several among them, from which true superlatives are frequently and correctly formed. Where are the positives which are here supposed to be "*increased to the highest degree?*" Every real superlative in our language, except *best* and *worst, most* and *least, first* and *last,* with the still more irregular word *next,* is a derivative, formed from some other English word, by adding *est* or *most;* as, *truest, hindmost.* The propriety or impropriety of comparing the foregoing words, or any of the "*many others*" of which this author speaks, is to be determined according to their meaning, and according to the *usage of good writers,* and not by the dictation of a feeble pedant, or upon the supposition that if compared they would form "*double superlatives.*"

Obs. 8.—*Chief* is from the French word *chef,* the *head: chiefest* is therefore no more a double superlative than *headmost:* "But when the *headmost* foes appeared."—*Scott.* Nor are *chief* and *chiefest* equivalent terms: "Doeg an Edomite, the *chiefest* of the herdsmen."—1 *Samuel,* xxi, 7. "The *chief* of the herdsmen," would convey a different meaning; it ·would be either the *leader* of the herdsmen, or the *principal part* of them. *Chiefest,* however, has often been used where *chief* would have been better; as, "He sometimes denied admission to the *chiefest* officers of the army."—*Clarendon.* Let us look further at Kirkham's list of *absolute* "*superlatives.*"

Obs. 9.—*Extreme* is from the Latin superlative *extremus,* and of course its literal signification is not really susceptible of increase. Yet *extremest* has been used, and is still used, by some of the very best writers; as, "They thought it the *extremest* of evils."—*Bacon.* "That on the sea's *extremest* border stood."—*Addison.* "How, to *extremest* thrill of agony."—*Pollok,* B. viii, l. 270. "I go th' *extremest* remedy to prove."—*Dryden.* "In *extremest* poverty."—*Swift.* "The hairy fool stood on th' *extremest* verge of the swift brook, augmenting it with tears."—*Shak.* "While the *extremest* parts of the earth were meditating submission."—*Atterbury.* "His writings are poetical to the *extremest* boundaries of poetry."—*Adams's Rhetoric,* i, 87. In prose, this superlative is not now very common; but the poets still occasionally use it, for the sake of their measure; and it ought to be noticed that the simple adjective is *not partitive.* If we say, for the first example, "the *extreme* of evils;" we make the word a *noun,* and do not convey exactly the same idea that is there expressed.

Obs. 10.—*Perfect,* if taken in its strictest sense, must not be compared; but this word, like many others which mean most in the positive, is often used with a certain latitude of meaning, which renders its comparison by the adverbs not altogether inadmissible; nor is it destitute of authority, as I have already shown. (See Obs. 8th, p. 268.) "From the first rough sketches, to the *more perfect* draughts."—*Bolingbroke, on Hist.* p. 152. "The *most perfect.*"—*Adams's Lect. on Rhet.* i, 99 and 136; ii, 17 and 57: *Blair's Lect.* pp. 20 and 399. "The *most beautiful and perfect* example of analysis."—*Lowth's Gram. Pref.* p. 10. "The plainest, *most perfect,* and most useful manual."—*Bullions's E. Gram. Rec.* p. 7. "Our sight is the *most perfect,* and the most delightful, of all our senses."—*Addison, Spect.* No. 411; *Blair's Lect.* pp. 115 and 194; *Murray's Gram.* i 322. Here Murray anonymously copied Blair. "And to render natives *more perfect* in the knowledge of it."—*Campbell's Rhet.* p. 171; *Murray's Gram.* p. 366. Here Murray copied Campbell, the most accurate of all his masters. Whom did he copy when he said, "The phrases, *more perfect,* and *most perfect,* are improper?"—*Octavo Gram.* p. 168. But if these are wrong, so is the following sentence: "No poet has ever attained a *greater perfection* than Horace."—*Blair's Lect.* p. 398. And also this: "Why are we brought into the world *less perfect* in respect to our nature?"—*West's Letters to a Young Lady,* p. 220.

Obs. 11.—*Right* and *wrong* are not often compared by good writers; though we sometimes see such phrases as *more right* and *more wrong,* and such words as *rightest* and *wrongest:* "'Tis always in the *wrongest* sense."—*Butler.* "A method of attaining the *rightest* and greatest happiness."—PRICE: *Priestley's Gram.* p. 78. "It is no *more right* to steal apples, than it is to steal money."—*Webster's New Spelling-Book,* p. 118. There are equivalent expressions which seem preferable; as, *more proper, more erroneous, most proper, most erroneous.*

Obs. 12.—*Honest, just, true, correct, sincere,* and *vast,* may all be compared at pleasure. Pope's Essay on Criticism is *more correct* than any thing this modest pretender can write; and in it he may find the comparative *juster,* the superlatives *justest, truest, sincerest,* and the phrases, "*So vast* a throng,"—"*So vast* is art:" of all which are contrary to his teaching. "*Unjuster* dealing Is used in buying than in selling."—*Butler's Poems,* p. 163. "Iniquissimam pacem *justissimo* bello antefero."—*Cicero.* "I prefer the *unjustest* peace before the *justest* war."—*Walker's English Particles,* p. 68. The poet Cowley used the word *honestest;* which is not now very common. So Swift: "What *honester* folks never durst for their ears."—*The Yahoo's Overthrow.* So Junius: "The *honestest* and ablest men."—*Letter XVIII.* "The sentence would be *more correct* in the following form."—*Murray's Gram.* i, p. 223. "Elegance is chiefly gained by studying the *correctest* writers."—*Holmes's Rhetoric,* p. 27. *Honest* and *correct,* for the sake of euphony, require the adverbs; as, *more honest,* "*most correct.*"—*Lowth's Gram. Pref.* p. iv. *Vast, vaster, vastest,* are words as smooth, as *fast, faster, fastest;* and *more vast* is certainly as good English as *more just:* "Shall mortal man be *more just* than God?"—*Job.* iv, 17. "Wilt thou condemn him that is *most just?*"—*Ib.* xxxiv, 17. "More wise, more learn'd, *more just,* more-everything."—*Pope. Universal* is often compared by the adverbs, but certainly with no reënforcement of meaning: as, "One of the *most universal* precepts, is, that the orator himself should feel the passion."—*Adams's Rhet.* i, 379. "Though not *so universal.*"—*Ib.* ii, 311. "This experience is general, though not *so universal,* as the absence of memory in childhood."—*Ib.* ii, 362. "We can suppose no motive which would *more universally* operate."—*Dr. Blair's Rhet.* p. 55. "Music is known to have been *more universally* studied."—*Ib.* p. 123. "We shall not wonder, that his grammar has been *so universally* applauded."—*Walker's Recommendation in Murray's Gram.* ii, 306. "The pronoun *it* is the *most universal* of all the pronouns."—*Cutler's Gram.* p. 66. Thus much for one half of this critic's twenty-two "*superlatives.*" The rest are simply adjectives that are not susceptible of comparison: they are not "*superlatives*" at all. A man might just as well teach, that *good* is a superlative, and not susceptible of comparison, because "*there is none good but one.*"

Obs. 13.—Pronominal adjectives, when their nouns are expressed, simply relate to them, and have no modifications : except *this* and *that*, which form the plurals *these* and *those ;* and *much*, *many*, and a few others, which are compared. Examples : " Whence hath *this* man *this* wisdom, and *these* mighty works ?"—*Matt.* xiii, 54. " But *some* man will say, How are the dead raised up ? and with *what* body do they come ?"—1 *Cor.* xv, 35. "The *first* man Adam was made a living soul; the *last* Adam was made a quickening spirit."—*Ib.* 45. So, when one pronominal adjective " precedes an other, the former *must be taken* simply as an adjective ; as,
          " Those suns are set. O rise *some other* such !"—*Cowper's Task*, B. ii, 1. 252.

Obs. 14.—Pronominal adjectives when their nouns are not expressed, may be parsed as representing them in *person*, *number*, *gender*, and *case ;* but those who prefer it, may supply the ellipsis, and parse the adjective, *simply as an adjective*. Example: " He threatens *many*, who injures *one*."—*Kames*. Here it may be said, " *Many* is a pronominal adjective, meaning *many persons ;* of the third person, plural number, masculine gender, and objective case." Or those who will take the word simply as an adjective, may say, " *Many* is a pronominal adjective, of the positive degree, compared *many*, *more*, *most*, and relating to *persons* understood." And so of *"one*," which represents, or relates to, *person* understood. Either say, " *One* is a pronominal adjective, not compared," and give the *three definitions* accordingly; or else say, " One is a pronominal adjective, relating to *person* understood ; of the third person, singular number, masculine gender, and objective case," and give the *six definitions* accordingly.

Obs. 15.—*Elder* for *older*, and *eldest* for *oldest*, are still frequently used; though the ancient positive, *eld* for *old*, is now obsolete. Hence some have represented *old* as having a two-fold comparison ; and have placed it, not very properly, among the irregular adjectives. The comparatives *elder* and *better*, are often used as *nouns ;* so are the Latin comparatives *superior* and *inferior*, *interior* and *exterior*, *senior* and *junior*, *major* and *minor :* as, The *elder's* advice—One of the *elders* —His *betters*—Our *superiors*—The *interior* of the country—A handsome *exterior*—Your *seniors*— My *juniors*—A *major* in the army—He is yet a *minor*. The word *other*, which has something of the nature of a comparative, likewise takes the form of a noun, as before suggested ; and, in that form, the reader, if he will, may call it a noun: as, " What do ye more than *others ?*"—*Bible.* " God in thus much is bounded, that the evil hath he left unto an *other ;* and *that Dark Other* hath usurped the evil which Omnipotence laid down."—*Tupper's Book of Thoughts*, p. 45. Some call it a pronoun. But it seems to be pronominal, merely by ellipsis of the noun after it; although, unlike a mere adjective, it assumes the ending of the noun, to mark that ellipsis. Perhaps, therefore, the best explanation of it would be this : " *Others* is a pronominal adjective, having the form of a noun, and put for *other men ;* in the third person, plural number, masculine gender, and nominative case." The gender of this word varies, according to that of the contrasted term ; and the case, according to the relation which it bears to other words. In the following example, it is neuter and objective: (: "The fibres of this muscle act as those of *others*."—*Cheyne*. Here, " as *those* of *others*," means, " as *the fibres* of *other muscles*."

Obs. 16.—"Comparatives and superlatives seem sometimes to part with their relative nature, and only to retain their *intensive*, especially those which are formed by the superlative adverb *most ;* as, 'A *most learned* man,'—' A *most brave* man :' i. e. Not the bravest or the most learned man that ever was, but a man possessing bravery or learning in a very eminent degree." See *Alexander Murray's Gram.* p. 110. This use of the terms of comparison is thought by some not to be very grammatical.

Obs. 17.—Contractions of the superlative termination *est*, as *high'st* for *highest*, *bigg'st* for *biggest*, though sometimes used by the poets, are always inelegant, and may justly be considered grammatically improper. They occur most frequently in doggerel verse, like that of *Hudibras ;* the author of which work, wrote, in his droll fashion, not only the foregoing monosyllables, but *learned'st* for *most learned*, *activ'st* for *most active*, *desperat'st* for *most desperate*, *epidemical'st* for *most epidemical*, &c.

          " And th' *activ'st* fancies share as loose alloys,
          For want of equal weight to counterpoise."—*Butler's Poems.*
          " Who therefore finds the *artificial'st* fools
          Have not been chang'd i' th' cradle, but the schools."—*Ib.* p. 143.

Obs. 18.—Nouns used adjectively are not varied in number to agree with the nouns to which they relate, but what is singular or plural when used substantively, is without number when taken as an adjective : as, " One of the nine *sister* goddesses."—*Webster's Dict. w. Muse.* " He has money in a *savings* bank." The latter mode of expression is uncommon, and the term *savings-bank* is sometimes compounded, but the hyphen does not really affect the nature of the former word. It is doubtful, however, whether a plural noun can ever properly assume the character of an adjective ; because, if it is not then really the same as the possessive case, it will always be liable to be thought a false form of that case. What Johnson wrote *"fullers earth"* and *"fullers thistle*," Chalmers has *"fullers earth"* and *"fuller's thistle ;"* Webster, *"fuller's-earth"* and *"fuller's-thistle ;"* Ainsworth, *"fuller's earth"* and *"fuller's thistle ;"* Walker has only *"fullers-earth ;"* Worcester, *"fuller's-earth ;"* Cobb, *"fullers earth ;"* the Treasury of Knowledge, *"fullers'-earth."* So unsettled is this part of our grammar, that in many such cases it is difficult to say whether we ought to use the apostrophe, or the hyphen, or both, or neither. To insert neither, unless we make a close compound, is to use a plural noun adjectively ; which form, I think, is the most objectionable of all. See " *All souls day*,"—" *All-fools-day*,"—" *All-saints'-day*," &c., in the dictionaries. These may well be written " *All Souls' Day*," &c.

EXAMPLES FOR PARSING.

PRAXIS IV.—ETYMOLOGICAL.

In the Fourth Praxis, it is required of the pupil — to distinguish and define the different parts of speech, and the classes and modifications of the ARTICLES, NOUNS, *and* ADJECTIVES.

The definitions to be given in the Fourth Praxis, are two for an article, six for a noun, three for an adjective, and one for a pronoun, a verb, a participle, an adverb, a conjunction, a preposition, or an interjection. Thus :—

EXAMPLE PARSED.

" The best and most effectual method of teaching grammar, is precisely that of which the careless are least fond : teach learnedly, rebuking whatsoever is false, blundering, or unmannerly."

The is the definite article. 1. An article is the word *the, an,* or *a,* which we put before nouns to limit their signification. 2. The definite article is *the,* which denotes some particular thing or things.

Best is a common adjective, of the superlative degree ; compared irregularly, *good, better, best.* 1. An adjective is a word added to a noun or pronoun, and generally expresses quality. 2. A common adjective is any ordinary epithet, or adjective denoting quality or situation. 3. The superlative degree is that which is most or least of all included with it.

And is a conjunction. 1. A conjunction is a word used to connect words or sentences in construction, and to show the dependence of the terms so connected.

Most is an adverb. 1. An adverb is a word added to a verb, a participle, an adjective, or an other adverb ; and generally expresses time, place, degree, or manner.

Effectual is a common adjective, compared by means of the adverbs ; *effectual, more effectual, most effectual ;* or, *effectual, less effectual, least effectual.* 1. An adjective is a word added to a noun or pronoun, and generally expresses quality. 2. A common adjective is any ordinary epithet, or adjective denoting quality or situation. 3. Those adjectives which may be varied in sense, but not in form, are compared by means of adverbs.

Method is a common noun, of the third person, singular number, neuter gender, and objective case. 1. A noun is the name of any person, place, or thing, that can be known or mentioned. 2. A common noun is the name of a sort, kind, or class, of beings or things. 3. The third person is that which denotes the person or thing merely spoken of. 4. The singular number is that which denotes but one. 5. The neuter gender is that which denotes things that are neither male nor female. 6. The nominative case is that form or state of a noun or pronoun, which denotes the subject of a verb.

Of is a preposition. 1. A preposition is a word used to express some relation of different things or thoughts to each other, and is generally placed before a noun or a pronoun.

Teaching is a participle. 1. A participle is a word derived from a verb, participating the properties of a verb, and of an adjective or a noun ; and is generally formed by adding *ing, d,* or *ed,* to the verb.

Grammar is a common noun, of the third person, singular number, neuter gender, and objective case. 1. A noun is the name of any person, place, or thing, that can be known or mentioned. 2. A common noun is the name of a sort, kind, or class, of beings or things. 3. The third person is that which denotes the person or thing merely spoken of. 4. The singular number is that which denotes but one. 5. The neuter gender is that which denotes things that are neither male nor female. 6. The objective case is that form or state of a noun or pronoun, which denotes the object of a verb, participle, or preposition.

Is is a verb. 1. A verb is a word that signifies *to be, to act,* or *to be acted upon.*

Precisely is an adverb. 1. An adverb is a word added to a verb, a participle, an adjective, or an other adverb ; and generally expresses time, place, degree, or manner.

That is a pronominal adjective, not compared ; standing for *that method,* in the third person, singular number, neuter gender, and nominative case. [See Obs. 14th, p. 277.] 1. An adjective is a word added to a noun or pronoun, and generally expresses quality. 2. A pronominal adjective is a definitive word which may either accompany its noun or represent it understood. 3. The third person is that which denotes the person or thing merely spoken of. 4. The singular number is that which denotes but one. 5. The neuter gender is that which denotes things that are neither male nor female. 6. The nominative case is that form or state of a noun or pronoun, which denotes the subject of a verb.

Of is a preposition. 1. A preposition is a word used to express some relation of different things or thoughts to each other, and is generally placed before a noun or a pronoun.

Which is a pronoun. 1. A pronoun is a word used in stead of a noun.

The is the definite article. 1. An article is the word *the, an,* or *a,* which we put before nouns to limit their signification. 2. The definite article is *the,* which denotes some particular thing or things.

Careless is a common adjective, compared by means of the adverbs ; *careless, more careless, most careless ;* or, *careless, less careless, least careless.* 1. An adjective is a word added to a noun or pronoun, and generally expresses quality. 2. A common adjective is any ordinary epithet, or adjective denoting quality or situation. 3. Those adjectives which may be varied in sense, but not in form, are compared by means of adverbs.

Are is a verb. 1. A verb is a word that signifies *to be, to act,* or *to be acted upon.*

Least is an adverb. 1. An adverb is a word added to a verb, a participle, an adjective, or an other adverb ; and generally expresses time, place, degree, or manner.

Fond is a common adjective, compared regularly, *fond, fonder, fondest* ; but here made superlative by the adverb *least.* 1. An adjective is a word added to a noun or pronoun, and generally expresses quality. 2. A common adjective is any ordinary epithet, or adjective denoting quality or situation. 3. The superlative degree is that which is most or least of all included with it.

Teach is a verb. 1. A verb is a word that signifies *to be, to act, or to be acted upon.*

Learnedly is an adverb. 1. An adverb is a word added to a verb, a participle, an adjective, or an other adverb ; and generally expresses time, place, degree, or manner.

Rebuking is a participle. 1. A participle is a word derived from a verb, participating the properties of a verb, and of an adjective or a noun ; and is generally formed by adding *ing, d,* or *ed,* to the verb.

Whatsoever is a pronoun. 1. A pronoun is a word used in stead of a noun.

Is is a verb. 1. A verb is a word that signifies *to be, to act,* or *to be acted upon.*

False is a common adjective, of the positive degree ; compared regularly, *false, falser, falsest.* 1. An adjective is a word added to a noun or pronoun, and generally expresses quality. 2. A common adjective is any ordinary epithet, or adjective denoting quality or situation. 3. The positive degree is that which is expressed by the adjective in its simple form.

Blundering is a participial adjective, compared by means of the adverbs ; *blundering, more blundering, most blundering ;* or, *blundering, less blundering, least blundering.* 1. An adjective is a word added to a noun or pronoun, and generally expresses quality. 2. A participial adjective is one that has the form of a participle, but differs from it by rejecting the idea of time. 3. Those adjectives which may be varied in sense, but not in form, are compared by means of adverbs.

is a conjunction. 1. A conjunction is a word used to connect words or sentences in construction, and to show the dependence of the terms so connected.

Unmannerly is a common adjective, compared by means of the adverbs; *unmannerly, more unmannerly, most unmannerly;* or, *unmannerly, less unmannerly, least unmannerly.*   1. An adjective is a word added to a noun or pronoun, and generally expresses quality.   2. A common adjective is any ordinary epithet, or adjective denoting quality or situation.   3. Those adjectives which may be varied in sense, but not in form, are compared by means of adverbs.

LESSON I. — PARSING.

" The noblest and most beneficial invention of which human ingenuity can boast, is that of writing."—*Robertson's America*, Vol. ii, p. 193.

" Charlemagne was the tallest, the handsomest, and the strongest man of his time ; his appearance was truly majestic, and he had surprising agility in all sorts of manly exercises."—*Stories of France*, p. 19.

" Money, like other things, is more or less valuable, as it is less or more plentiful."—*Beattie's Moral Science*, p. 378.

" The right way of acting, is, in a moral sense, as much a reality, in the mind of an ordinary man, as the straight or the right road."—*Dr. Murray's Hist. Lang.* i, 118.

" The full period of several members possesses most dignity and modulation, and conveys also the greatest degree of force, by admitting the closest compression of thought."—*Jamieson's Rhet.* p. 79.

" His great master, Demosthenes, in addressing popular audiences, never had recourse to a similar expedient.   He avoided redundancies, as equivocal and feeble. He aimed only to make the deepest and most efficient impression ; and he employed for this purpose, the plainest, the fewest, and the most emphatic words."—*Ibid.* p. 68.

" The high eloquence which I have last mentioned, is always the offspring of passion.   A man actuated by a strong passion, becomes much greater than he is at other times.   He is conscious of more strength and ·force ; he utters greater sentiments, conceives higher designs, and executes them with a boldness and felicity, of which, on other occasions, he could not think himself capable."—*Blair's Rhet.* p. 236.

" His words bore sterling weight, nervous and strong,
   In manly tides of sense they roll'd along."—*Churchill.*
" To make the humble proud, the proud submiss,
   Wiser the wisest, and the brave more brave."—*W. S. Landor.*

LESSON II. — PARSING.

" I am satisfied that in this, as in all cases, it is best, safest, as well as most right and honorable, to speak freely and plainly."—*Channing's Letter to Clay*, p. 4.

" The gospel, when preached with the Holy Ghost sent down from heaven, through the wonder-working power of God, can make the proud humble, the selfish disinterested, the worldly heavenly, the sensual pure."—*Christian Experience*, p. 399.

" I am so much the better, as I am the liker* the best ; and so much the holier, as I am more conformable to the holiest, or rather to Him who is holiness itself."—*Bp. Beveridge.*

" Whether any thing in Christianity appears to them probable, or improbable ; consistent, or inconsistent ; agreeable to what they should have expected, or the contrary ; wise and good, or ridiculous and useless ; is perfectly irrelevant."—*M'Ilvaine's Evidences*, p. 523.

" God's providence is higher, and deeper, and larger, and stronger, than all the skill of his adversaries ; and his pleasure shall be accomplished in their overthrow, except they repent and become his friends."—*Cox, on Christianity*, p. 445.

" A just relish of what is beautiful, proper, elegant, and ornamental, in writing or painting, in architecture or gardening, is a fine preparation for the same just relish of these qualities in character and behaviour.   To the man who has acquired a taste so acute and accomplished, every action wrong or improper must be highly disgustful : if, in any instance, the overbearing power of passion sway him from his duty, he re-

* The regular comparison of this word, (*like, liker, likest*,) seems to be obsolete, or nearly so.   It is seldom met with, except in old books : yet we say, *more like*, or *most like, less like*, or *least like*.   " To lay the flock with whom he is, is *likest* to Christ."—*Barclay's Works*, Vol. 1, p. 180.   " Of Godlike pow'r ? for *likest* Gods they seem'd."—*Milton*, P. L. vi, l. 301.

turns to it with redoubled resolution never to be swayed a second time."—*Kames, Elements of Criticism*, Vol. i, p. 25.

 "In grave Quintilian's copious work, we find
 The justest rules and clearest method join'd."—*Pope, on Crit.*

LESSON III. — PARSING.

 "There are several sorts of scandalous tempers ; some malicious, and some effeminate ; others obstinate, brutish, and savage. Some humours are childish and silly ; some, false, and others, scurrilous ; some, mercenary, and some, tyrannical."—*Collier's Antoninus*, p. 52.

 "Words are obviously voluntary signs : and they are also arbitrary; excepting a few simple sounds expressive of certain internal emotions, which sounds being the same in all languages, must be the work of nature : thus the unpremeditated tones of admiration are the same in all men."—*Kames, Elements of Crit.* i, 347.

 "A stately and majestic air requires sumptuous apparel, which ought not to be gaudy, nor crowded with little ornaments. A woman of consummate beauty can bear to be highly adorned, and yet shows best in a plain dress."—*Ib.* p. 279. "Of all external objects a graceful person is the most agreeable. But in vain will a person attempt to be graceful, who is deficient in amiable qualities."—*Ib.* p. 299.

 "The faults of a writer of acknowledged excellence are more dangerous, because the influence of his example is more extensive ; and the interest of learning requires that they should be discovered and stigmatized, before they have the sanction of antiquity bestowed upon them, and become precedents of indisputable authority."—*Dr. Johnson, Rambler*, Vol. ii, No. 93.

 "Judges ought to be more learned than witty, more reverend than plausible, and more advised than confident ; above all things, integrity is their portion and proper virtue."—*Bacon's Essays*, p. 145.

 "The wisest nations, having the most and best ideas, will consequently have the best and most copious languages."—*Harris's Hermes*, p. 408.

 Here we trace the operation of powerful causes, while we remain ignorant of their nature ; but every thing goes on with such regularity and harmony, as to give a striking and convincing proof of a combining directing intelligence."—*Life of W. Allen*, Vol. i, p. 170.

 "The wisest, unexperienced, will be ever
 Timorous and loth, with novice modesty,
 Irresolute, unhardy, unadventurous."—*Milton.*

IMPROPRIETIES FOR CORRECTION.

ERRORS OF ADJECTIVES.

LESSON I.—DEGREES.

 "I have the real excuse of the honestest sort of bankrupts."—*Cowley's Preface*, p. viii.

 [FORMULE.—Not proper, because the adjective *honestest* is harshly compared by *est*. But, according to a principle stated on page 271st, concerning the regular degrees, "This method of comparison is to be applied only to monosyllables, and to dissyllables of a smooth termination, or such as receive it and still have but one syllable after the accent." Therefore, *honestest* should be *most honest* ; thus, "I have the real excuse of the *most honest* sort of bankrupts."]

 "The honourablest part of talk, is, to give the occasion."—*Bacon's Essays*, p. 90. "To give him one of his own modestest proverbs."—*Barclay's Works*, iii, 340. "Our language is now certainly properer and more natural, than it was formerly."—*Bp. Burnet.* "Which will be of most and frequentest use to him in the world."—*Locke, on Education*, p. 163. "The same is notified in the notablest places in the diocese."—*Whitgift.* "But it was the dreadfullest sight that ever I saw."—*Pilgrim's Progress*, p. 70. "Four of the ancientest, soberest, and discreetest of the brethren, chosen for the occasion, shall regulate it."—*Locke, on Church Gov.* "Nor can there be any clear understanding of any Roman author, especially of ancienter time, without this skill."—*Walker's Particles*, p. x. "Far the learnedest of the Greeks."—*Ib.* p. 120. "The learneder thou art, the humbler be thou."—*Ib.* p. 228. "He is none of the best or honestest."—*Ib.* p. 274. "The properest methods of communicating it to others."—*Burn's Gram.* Pref. p. viii. "What heaven's great King hath powerfullest to send against us."—*Paradise Lost.* "Benedict is not the unhopefullest husband that I know."—*SHAK.: in Joh. Dict.* "That he should immediately do all the meanest and triflingest things himself."—RAY: *in Johnson's Gram.* p. 6. " I shall be named among the famousest of women."—MILTON's *Samson Agonistes: ib.* "Those have the inventivest heads for all purposes."—ASCHAM: *ib.* " The wretcheder are the contemners of all helps."—BEN JONSON: *ib.* " I will now deliver a few of the properest and naturallest considerations that belong to this piece."—WOTTON: *ib.* " The mortalest poisons practised by the West Indians, have some mixture of the blood, fat, or flesh of man."—BACON: *ib.* " He so won upon him, that he rendered him one of the faithfulest and most affectionate allies the Medes ever had."—*Rollin,* ii, 71. " ' You see before you,' says he to him, ' the most devoted servant, and the faithfullest ally, you ever had.'"—*Ib.* ii, 79. " I chose the flourishing'st tree in all the park."—*Cowley.* " Which he placed, I think, some centuries backwarder than Julius Africanus thought fit to place it afterwards."—*Bolingbroke, on History,* p. 53. " The Tiber, the notedst river of Italy."—*Littleton's Dict.*

"To fartherest shores the ambrosial spirit flies."—*Cutler's Gram.* p. 140.

───"That what she wills to do or say,
　Seems wisest, virtuousest, discreetest, best."—*Milton,* B. viii, l. 550.

LESSON II. MIXED.

"During the three or four first years of its existence."—*Taylor's District School,* p. 27.

[FORMULE.—Not proper, because the cardinal numbers *three* and *four* are put before the ordinal *first.* But, according to the 7th part of Obs. 7th, page 268th, " In specifying any part of a series, we ought to place the cardinal number after the ordinal." Therefore the words *three* and *four* should be placed after *first* ; thus, " During the *first three* or *four* years of its existence."]

"To the first of these divisions, my ten last lectures have been devoted."—*Adams's Rhet.* Vol. i, p. 391. " There are in the twenty-four states not less than sixty thousand common schools."—*Taylor's District School,* p. 38. " I know of nothing which gives teachers so much trouble as this want of firmness."—*Ib.* p. 57. " I know of nothing that throws such darkness over the line which separates right from wrong."—*Ib.* p. 58. " None need this purity and simplicity of language and thought so much as the common school instructer." —*Ib.* p. 64. " I know of no periodical that is so valuable to the teacher as the Annals of Education."—*Ib.* p. 67. "Are not these schools of the highest importance ? Should not every individual feel the deepest interest in their character and condition ?"—*Ib.* p. 78. " If instruction were made a profession, teachers would feel a sympathy for each other."—*Ib.* p. 93. "Nothing is so likely to interest children as novelty and change."—*Ib.* p. 131. " I know of no labour which affords so much happiness as that of the teacher's."—*Ib.* p. 136. "Their school exercises are the most pleasant and agreeable of any that they engage in." —*Ib.* p. 136. " I know of no exercise so beneficial to the pupil as that of drawing maps." —*Ib.* p. 176. " I know of nothing in which our district schools are so defective as they are in the art of teaching grammar."—*Ib.* p. 196. " I know of nothing so easily acquired as history."—*Ib.* p. 206. " I know of nothing for which scholars usually have such an abhorrence, as composition."—*Ib.* p. 210. " There is nothing in our fellow-men that we should respect with so much sacredness as their good name."—*Ib.* p. 307. " Sure never any thing was so unbred as that odious man."—CONGREVE: *in Joh. Dict.* "In the dialogue between the mariner and the shade of the deceast."—*Philological Museum,* i, 466. " These master-works would still be less excellent and finisht."—*Ib.* i, 469. " Every attempt to staylace the language of polisht conversation, renders our phraseology inelegant and clumsy."—*Ib.* i, 678. " Here are a few of the unpleasant'st words that ever blotted paper." —SHAK.: *in Joh. Dict.* " With the most easy, undisobliging transitions."—BROOME: *ib.* "Fear is, of all affections, the unaptest to admit any conference with reason."—HOOKER: *ib.* "Most chymists think glass a body more undestroyable than gold itself."—BOYLE: *ib.* "To part with unhackt edges, and bear back our barge undinted."—SHAK.: *ib.* " Erasmus, who was an unbigotted Roman Catholic, was transported with this passage."—ADDISON: *ib.* " There are no less than two words, with any of which the sentence might have terminated."—*Campbell's Rhet.* p. 397. " The one preach Christ of contention ; but the other, of love."—*Philippians,* i, 16. " Hence we find less discontent and heart-burnings, than where the subjects are unequally burdened."—*Art of Thinking,* p. 56.

" The serpent, subtil'st beast of all the field,
　I knew; but not with human voice indu'd."—MILTON: *ib. w. Human.*

" How much more grievous would our lives appear,
　To reach th'eighth hundred, than the eightieth year ?"—*Denham,* B. P., ii, 244.

LESSON III. MIXED.

"Brutus engaged with Aruns ; and so fierce was the attack, that they pierced one another at the same time."—*Lempriere's Dict.*

[FORMULE.—Not proper, because the phrase *one another* is here applied to two persons only, the words *an* and *other* being needlessly compounded. But, according to Observation 15th, on the Classes of Adjectives, *each other* must be applied to two persons or things, and *one an other* to more than *two.* Therefore *one another* should here be *each other* ; thus, " Brutus engaged with Aruns ; and so fierce was the attack, that they pierced *each other* at the same time."]

"Her two brothers were one after another turned into stone."—*Art of Thinking,* p. 194.

"Nouns are often used as adjectives ; as, A *gold*-ring, a *silver*-cup."—*Lennie's Gram.* p. 14.
"Fire and water destroy one another."—*Wanostrocht's Gram.* p. 82. "Two negatives in English destroy one another, or are equivalent to an affirmative."—*Lowth's Gram.* p. 94 ; *E. Devis's,* 111 ; *Mack's,* 147 ; *Murray's,* 198 ; *Churchill's,* 148 ; *Putnam's,* 135 ; *C. Adams's,* 102 ; *Hamlin's,* 79 ; *Alger's,* 66 ; *Fisk's,* 140 ; *Ingersoll's,* 207 ; and *many others.* "Two negatives destroy one another, and are generally equivalent to an affirmative."—*Kirkham's Gram.* p. 191 ; *Felton's,* 85. "Two negatives destroy one another and make an affirmative." —*J. Flint's Gram.* p. 79. "Two negatives destroy one another, being equivalent to an affirmative."—*Frost's El. of E. Gram.* p. 48. "Two objects, resembling one another, are pre- sented to the imagination."—*Parker's Exercises in Comp.* p. 47. "Mankind, in order to hold converse with each other, found it necessary to give names to objects."—*Kirkham's Gram.* p. 42. "Words are derived from each other* in various ways."—*Cooper's Gram.* p. 108. "There are many other ways of deriving words from one another."—*Murray's Gram.* p. 131. "When several verbs connected by conjunctions, succeed each other in a sentence, the auxiliary is usually omitted except with the first."—*Frost's Gram.* p. 91. "Two or more verbs, having the same nominative case, and immediately following one another, are also separated by commas."†—*Murray's Gram.* p. 270 ; *C. Adams's,* 126 ; *Russell's,* 113 ; and others. "Two or more adverbs immediately succeeding each other, must be separated by commas." —*Same Grammars.* "If, however, the members succeeding each other, are very closely con- nected, the comma is unnecessary."—*Murray's Gram.* p. 273 ; *Comly's,* 152 ; *and others.* "Gratitude, when exerted towards one another, naturally produces a very pleasing sensa- tion in the mind of a grateful man."—*Mur.* p. 287. "Several verbs in the infinitive mood, having a common dependence, and succeeding one another, are also divided by commas." —*Comly's Gram.* p. 153. "The several words of which it consists, have so near a relation to each other."—*Murray's Gram.* p. 268 ; *Comly's,* 144 ; *Russell's,* 111 ; *and others.* "When two or more verbs have the same nominative, and immediately follow one another, or two or more adverbs immediately succeed one another, they must be separated by commas."— *Comly's Gram.* p. 145. "Nouns frequently succeed each other, meaning the same thing." —*Sanborn's Gram.* p. 63. "And these two tenses may tl us answer one another."—*John- son's Gram. Com.* p. 322. "Or some other relation which two objects bear to one another." —*Jamieson's Rhet.* p. 149. "That the heathens tolerated each other, is allowed."—*Gospel its own Witness,* p. 76. "And yet these two persons love one another tenderly."—*Murray's E. Reader,* p. 112. "In the six hundredth and first year."—*Gen.* viii, 13. "Nor is this arguing of his but a reiterate clamour."—*Barclay's Works,* i, 260. "In severals of them the inward life of Christianity is to be found."—*Ib.* iii, 272. "Though Alvarez, Despauterius, and other, allow it not to be Plural."—*Johnson's Gram. Com.* p. 169. "Even the most dissi- pate and shameless blushed at the sight."—*Lemp. Dict. w. Antiochus.* "We feel a superior satisfaction in surveying the life of animals, than that of vegetables."—*Jamieson's Rhet.* 172. "But this man is so full fraughted with malice."—*Barclay's Works,* iii, 265. "That I sug- gest some things concerning the properest means."—*Blair's Rhet.* p. 337.

 "So hand in hand they pass'd, the loveliest pair
  That ever since in love's embraces met."—*Milton,* P. L., B. iv, L 321.
 "Aim at the high'est, without the high'est attain'd
  Will be for thee no sitting, or not long."—*Id.* P. R., B. iv, l, 106.

CHAPTER V.—PRONOUNS.

A Pronoun is a word used instead of a noun : as, The boy loves *his* book; *he* has long lessons, and *he* learns *them* well.

The pronouns in our language are twenty-four ; and their variations are thirty-two : so that the number of *words* of this class, is fifty-six.

OBSERVATIONS.

Obs. 1.—The word for which a pronoun stands, is called its *antecedent,* because it usually pre- cedes the pronoun. But some have limited the term *antecedent* to the word represented by a re- lative pronoun. There can be no propriety in this, unless we will have every pronoun to be a rela-

---

*This example, and several others that follow it, are no ordinary solecisms ; they are downright Irish bulls, making actions or relations reciprocal, where reciprocity is *utterly* unimaginable. Two words can no more be "*derived from each other,*" than two living creatures can have received their existence from each other. So, two things can never "*succeed each other,*" except they alternate or move in a circle ; and a greater number in trals, can "*follow one an other*" only in some imperfect sense, not at all reciprocal. In some instances, therefore, the best form of correction will be, to reject the reciprocal terms altogether.—G. BROWN.
† This doctrine of punctuation, if not absolutely false in itself, is here very badly taught. When *only two words,* of any sort, occur in the same construction, they seldom require the comma ; and never can they need *more than one,* whereas these grammarians, by their plural word "*commas,*" suggest a constant demand for two or more.—G. BROWN.

tive, when it stands for a noun which precedes it; and, if so, it should be called something else, when the noun is to be found elsewhere. In the example above, *his* and *he* represent *boy*, and *them* represents *lessons*; and these nouns are as truly the antecedents to the pronouns, as any can be. Yet *his*, *he*, and *them*, in our most approved grammars, are not called relative pronouns, but personal.

Obs. 2.—Every pronoun may be explained as standing for the *name* of something, for the *thing itself* unnamed, or for a *former pronoun*; and, with the noun, pronoun, or thing, for which it stands, every pronoun must agree in person, number, and gender. The exceptions to this, whether apparent or real, are very few; and, as their occurrence is unfrequent, there will be little occasion to notice them till we come to syntax. But if the student will observe the use and import of pronouns, he may easily see, that some of them are put *substantively*, for nouns not previously introduced; some, *relatively*, for nouns or pronouns going before; some, *adjectively*, for nouns that must follow them in any explanation which can be made of the sense. These three modes of substitution, are very different, each from the others. Yet they do not serve for an accurate division of the pronouns; because it often happens, that a substitute which commonly represents the noun in one of these ways, will sometimes represent it in an other.

Obs. 3.—The pronouns *I* and *thou*, in their different modifications, stand immediately for persons that are, in general, sufficiently known without being named; (*I* meaning *the speaker*, and *thou*, *the hearer*;) their antecedents, or nouns, are therefore generally *understood*. The other personal pronouns, also, are sometimes taken in a general and demonstrative sense, to denote persons or things not previously mentioned; as, "*He* that hath knowledge, spareth his words." —*Bible*. Here *he* is equivalent to *the man*, or *the person*. "The care of posterity is most in *them* that have no posterity."—*Bacon*. Here *them* is equivalent to *those persons*. "How far do you call *it* to such a place?"—*Priestley's Gram.* p. 85. Here *it*, according to Priestley, is put for *the distance*. "For the priest's lips should keep knowledge, and *they* should seek the law at his mouth."—*Malachi*, ii, 7. Here *they* is put indefinitely for *men* or *people*. So *who* and *which*, though called relatives, do not always relate to a noun or pronoun going before them; for *who* may be a direct substitute for *what person*; and *which* may mean *which person*, or *which thing*: as, "And he that was healed, wist not *who* it was."—*John*, v, 13. That is, "*The man who* was healed, knew not *what person* it was." "I care not *which* you take; they are so much alike, one cannot tell *which* is *which*."

Obs. 4.—A pronoun with which a question is asked, usually stands for some person or thing unknown to the speaker; the noun, therefore, cannot occur before it, but may be used after it or in place of it. Examples: "In the grave, *who* shall give thee thanks?"—*Ps.* vi, 5. Here the word *who* is equivalent to *what person*, taken interrogatively. "*Which* of you convinceth me of sin?"—*John*, viii, 48. That is, "*Which man* of you?" "Master, *what* shall we do?"—*Luke*, iii, 12. That is, "*What act*, or *thing?*" These solutions, however, convert *which* and *what* into *adjectives*: and, in fact, as they have no inflections for the numbers and cases, there is reason to think them at all times essentially such. We call them pronouns, to avoid the inconvenience of supposing and supplying an infinite multitude of ellipses. But *who*, though often equivalent (as above) to an adjective and a noun, is never itself used adjectively; it is always a pronoun.

Obs. 5.—In respect to *who* or *whom*, it sometimes makes little or no difference to the sense, whether we take it as a demonstrative pronoun equivalent to *what person*, or suppose it to relate to an antecedent understood before it: as, "Even so the Son quickeneth *whom* he will."—*John*, v, 21. That is—"*what persons* he will," or, "*those persons* whom he will;" for the Greek word for *whom*, is, in this instance, plural. The former is a shorter explanation of the meaning, but the latter I take to be the true account of the construction; for, by the other, we make *whom* a double relative, and the object of two governing words at once. So, perhaps, of the following example, which Dr. Johnson cites under the word *who*, to show what he calls its "*disjunctive* sense:"—

> "There thou tellst *of* kings, and *who* aspire;
> *Who* fall, *who* rise, *who* triumph, *who* do moan."—*Daniel*.

Obs. 6.—It sometimes happens that the real antecedent, or the term which in the order of the sense must stand before the pronoun, is not placed antecedently to it, in the order given to the words: as, "It is written, To *whom* he was not spoken of, *they* shall see; and they that have not heard, shall understand."—*Romans*, xv, 21. Here the sense is, "*They* to *whom* he was not spoken of, shall see." Whoever takes the passage otherwise, totally misunderstands it. And yet the same order of the words might be used to signify, "They shall see *to whom* (that is, *to what persons*) he was not spoken of." Transpositions of this kind, as well as of every other, occur most frequently in poetry. The following example is from an Essay on Satire, printed with Pope's Works, but written by one of his friends:—

> "*Whose* is the crime, the scandal too be *theirs*;
> The knave and fool are their own libellers."—*J. Brown*.

Obs. 7.—The personal and the interrogative pronouns often stand in construction as the antecedents to other pronouns: as, "*He* also *that* is slothful in his work, is brother to *him that* is a great waster."—*Prov.* xviii, 9. Here *he* and *him* are each equivalent to *the man*, and each is taken as the antecedent to the relative which follows it. "For both *he that* sanctifieth, and *they who* are sanctified, are all of one: for which cause, *he* is not ashamed to call *them* brethren."— *Heb.* ii, 11. Here *he* and *they* may be considered the antecedents to *that* and *who*, of the first clause, and also to *he* and *them*, of the second. So the interrogative *who* may be the antecedent to the relative *that*; as, "*Who that* has any moral sense, dares tell lies?" Here *who*, being equivalent to *what person*, is the term with which the other pronoun agrees. Nay, an interrogative pronoun, (or the noun which is implied in it,) may be the antecedent to a *personal* pronoun; as, "*Who* hath first given to Him, and it shall be recompensed to *him* again?"—*Romans*, xi, 35. Here the idea is, "*What person* hath first given *any thing* to the Lord, so that it ought to be repaid *him?* that is, "so that *the gift* ought to be recompensed from Heaven to *the giver?*" In the following example, the first pronoun is the antecedent to all the rest:—

> "And *he that* never doubted of *his* state,
> *He* may perhaps—perhaps *he* may—too late."—*Cowper*.

OBS. 8.—So the personal pronouns of the *possessive* case, (which some call adjectives,) are sometimes represented by relatives, though less frequently than their primitives : as, "How different, O Ortogrul, is *thy* condition, *who* art doomed to the perpetual torments of unsatisfied desire!"—*Dr. Johnson.* Here *who* is of the second person, singular, masculine ; and represents the antecedent pronoun *thy :* for *thy* is a pronoun, and not (as some writers will have it) an adjective. Examples like this, disprove the doctrine of those grammarians who say that *my, his, her, its,* and their plurals, *our, your, their,* are adjectives. For, if they were mere adjectives they could not thus be made antecedents. Examples of this construction are sufficiently common, and sufficiently clear, to settle that point, unless they can be better explained in some other way. Take an instance or two more : " And they are written for *our* admonition, upon *whom* the end of the world are come."—1 *Cor.* x, 11.

> " Be thou the first true merit to befriend ;
> *His* praise is lost, *who* stays till all commend."—*Pope.*

CLASSES.

Pronouns are divided into three classes ; *personal, relative,* and *interrogative.*

I. A *personal pronoun* is a pronoun that shows, by its form, of what person it is ; as, " Whether *it*[*] were *I* or *they,* so *we* preach, and so *ye* believed."—1 *Cor.* xv, 11.

The simple personal pronouns are five : namely, *I,* of the first person; *thou,* of the second person ; *he, she,* and *it,* of the third person.

The compound personal pronouns are also five : namely, *myself,* of the first person ; *thyself,* of the second person ; *himself, herself,* and *itself,* of the third person.

II. A *relative pronoun* is a pronoun that represents an antecedent word or phrase, and connects different clauses of a sentence ; as, " No people can be great, *who* have ceased to be virtuous."—*Dr. Johnson.*

The relative pronouns are *who, which, what, that, as,* and the compounds *whoever* or *whosoever, whichever* or *whichsoever, whatever* or *whatsoever.*†

What is a kind of *double relative,* equivalent to *that which* or *those which;* and is to be parsed, first as antecedent, and then as relative : as, " This is *what* I wanted ; that is to say, *the thing which* I wanted."—*L. Murray.*

III. An *interrogative pronoun* is a pronoun with which a question is asked; as, " *Who* touched my clothes ? "—*Mark,* v, 30.

The interrogative pronouns are *who, which,* and *what ;* being the same in form as relatives.

Who demands a person's name ; *which,* that a person or thing be distinguished from others ; *what,* the name of a thing, or a person's occupation and character.

OBSERVATIONS.

OBS. 1.—The pronouns *I* and *myself, thou* and *thyself,* with their inflections, are literally applicable to persons only ; but, *figuratively,* they represent brutes, or whatever else the human imagination invests with speech and reason. The latter use of them, though literal perhaps is every thing *but person,* constitutes the purest kind of personification. For example : " The *trees* went forth on a time to anoint a king over them : and they said unto the *olive-tree,* ' Reign *thou* over *us.*' But the *olive-tree* said unto them, ' Should *I* leave *my* fatness, wherewith by *me* they honour God and man, and go to be promoted over the trees ?' " See *Judges,* ix, from 8 to 16.

OBS. 2.—The pronouns *he* and *himself, she* and *herself,* with their inflections, are literally applicable to persons and to brutes, and to these only ; if applied to lifeless objects, they animate them, and are figurative *in gender,* though literal perhaps in every other respect. For example : " A *diamond* of beauty and lustre, observing at *his* side in the same cabinet, not only many other

---

[*] Some grammarians exclude the word *it* from the list of personal pronouns, because it does not convey the idea of that personality which consists in *individual intelligence.* On the other hand, they will have *who* to be a personal pronoun, because it is literally applied to *persons only,* or intelligent beings. But I judge them to be wrong in respect to both ; and, had they given *definitions* of their several classes of pronouns, they might perhaps have found out that the word *it* is always personal, in a grammatical sense, and *who,* either relative or interrogative.

† " *Whoso* and *whatso* are found in old authors, but are now out of use."—*Churchill's Gram.* p. 76. These antiquated words are equivalent in import to *whosoever* and *whatsoever.* The former, *whoso,* being used many times in the Bible, and occasionally also by the poets, as by Cowper, Whittier, and others, can hardly be said to be obsolete ; though Wells, like Churchill, pronounced it so, in his first edition.

gems, but even a *loadstone*, began to question the latter how *he* came there—*he*, *who* appeared to be no better than a mere flint, a sorry rusty-looking pebble, without the least shining quality to advance *him* to such honour; and concluded with desiring *him* to keep *his* distance, and to pay a proper respect to *his* superiors."—*Kames's Art of Thinking*, p. 226.

OBS. 3.—The pronoun *it*, as it carries in itself no such idea as that of personality, or sex, or life, is chiefly used with reference to things inanimate; yet the word is, in a certain way, applicable to animals, or even to persons; though it does not, in itself, present them as such. Thus we say, "*It is I;*"—"*It was they;*"—"*It was you;*"—"*It was your agent;*"—" *It is your bull* that has killed one of my oxen." In examples of this kind, the word *it* is simply demonstrative; meaning, *the thing or subject spoken of*. That subject, whatever it be in itself, may be introduced again after the verb, in any person, number, or gender, that suits it. But, as the verb agrees with the pronoun *it*, the word which follows, can in no sense be made, as Dr. Priestley will have it to be, the *antecedent* to that pronoun. Besides, it is contrary to the nature of what is primarily demonstrative, to represent a preceding word of any kind. The Doctor absurdly says, " Not only things, but persons, may be the *antecedent* to this pronoun; as, *Who is it ? Is it not Thomas ?* i. e. *Who is the person? Is not he Thomas ?*"—*Priestley's Gram.* p. 85. In these examples, the terms are transposed by interrogation; but that circumstance, though it may have helped to deceive this author and his copiers, affects not my assertion.

OBS. 4.—The pronoun *who* is usually applied only to persons. Its application to brutes or to things is improper, unless we mean to personify them. But *whose*, the possessive case of this relative, is sometimes used to supply the place of the possessive case, otherwise wanting, to the relative *which*. Examples : " The mutes are those consonants *whose* sounds cannot be protracted."—*Murray's Gram.* p. 9. " Philosophy, *whose* end is, to instruct us in the knowledge of nature."—*Ib.* p. 54 ; *Campbell's Rhet.* 421. " Those adverbs are compared *whose* primitives are obsolete."—*Adam's Latin Gram.* p. 150. " After a sentence *whose* sense is complete in itself, a period is used."—*Nutting's Gram.* p. 124. " We remember best those things *whose* parts are methodically disposed, and mutually connected."—*Beattie's Moral Science*, i, 59. " Is there any other doctrine *whose* followers are punished ?"—ADDISON : *Murray's Gram.* p. 54 ; *Lowth's*, p. 26.
" The question, *whose* solution I require,
Is, what the sex of women most desire."—DRYDEN : *Lowth*, p. 25.

OBS. 5.—Buchanan, as well as Lowth, condemns the foregoing use of *whose*, except in grave poetry : saying, " This manner of *personification* adds an air of dignity to the higher and more solemn kind of poetry, but it is highly improper in the lower kind, or in prose."—*Buchanan's English Syntax*, p. 73. And, of the last two examples above quoted, he says, " It ought to be *of which*, in both places: i. e. The followers *of which*; the solution *of which*."—*Ib.* p. 73. The truth is, that no personification is here intended. Hence it may be better to avoid, if we can, this use of *whose*, as seeming to imply what we do not mean. But Buchanan himself (stealing the text of an older author) has furnished at least one example as objectionable as any of the foregoing : " Prepositions are naturally placed betwixt the Words *whose* Relation and Dependence each of them is to express."—*English Syntax*, p. 90; *British Gram.* p. 201. I dislike this construction, and yet sometimes adopt it, for want of an other as good. It is too much, to say with Churchill, that " this practice is now discountenanced by all correct writers."—*New Gram.* p. 226. Grammarians would perhaps differ less, if they would read more. Dr. Campbell commends the use of *whose* for *of which*, as an improvement suggested by good taste, and established by abundant authority. See *Philosophy of Rhetoric*, p. 420. " WHOSE, the possessive or genitive case of *who* or *which*; applied to persons or things."—*Webster's Octavo Dict.* " *Whose* is well authorized by good usage, as the possessive of *which*."—*Sanborn's Gram.* p. 69. " Nor is any language complete, *whose* verbs have not tenses."—*Harris's Hermes*.
"———— ' Past and future, are the wings
On *whose* support, harmoniously conjoined,
Moves the great spirit of human knowledge.'—MS."
Wordsworth's Preface to his Poems, p. xviii.

OBS. 6.—The relative *which*, though formerly applied to persons and made equivalent to *who*, is now confined to brute animals and inanimate things. Thus, " Our Father *which* art in heaven," is not now reckoned good English; it should be, " Our Father *who* art in heaven." In this, as well as in many other things, the custom of speech has changed; so that what was once right, is now ungrammatical. The use of *which* for *who* is very common in the Bible, and in other books of the seventeenth century; but all good writers now avoid the construction. It occurs seventy-five times in the third chapter of Luke; as, "Joseph, *which* was the son of Heli, *which* was the son of Matthat," &c. &c. After a personal term taken by metonymy for a thing, *which* is not improper; as, " Of the particular *author which* he is studying."—*Gallaudet*. And as an interrogative or a demonstrative pronoun or adjective, the word *which* is still applicable to persons, as formerly; as, " *Which* of you all ?"—" *Which man* of you all ?"—" There arose a reasoning among them, *which* of them should be greatest."—*Luke*, ix, 46. " Two fair twins—the puzzled strangers, *which* is *which*, inquire."—*Tickel*.

OBS. 7.—If *which*, as a direct relative, is inapplicable to persons, *who* ought to be preferred to it in all personifications: as,
" The seal is set. Now welcome thou dread power,
Nameless, yet thus omnipotent, *which* here
Walk'st in the shadow of the midnight hour."
BYRON : *Childe Harold's Pilgrimage*, Cant. iv, st. 138.
What sort of personage is here imagined and addressed, I will not pretend to say; but it should seem, that *who* would be more proper than *which*, though less agreeable in sound before the word *here*. In one of his notes on this word, Churchill has fallen into a strange error. He will have *who* to represent *a horse !* and that, in such a sense as would require *which* and not *who*, even for a person. As he prints the masculine pronoun in Italics, perhaps he thought, with Murray and

Webster, that *which* must needs be " of the *neuter gender*."[*] He says, "In the following passage, *which* seems to be used *instead* of *who*:—
    ' Between two horses, *which* doth bear *him* best;
    I have, perhaps, some shallow spirit of judgment.'
                                    SHAK., 1 *Hen.* VI."—*Churchill's Gram.* p. 226.

OBS. 8.—The pronoun *what* is usually applied to things only. It has a twofold relation, and is often used (by ellipsis of the noun) both as antecedent and as relative, in the form of a single word; being equivalent to *that which*, or *the thing which*,—*those which*, or *the things which*. In this double relation, *what* represents two cases at the same time: as, " He is ashamed of *what* he has done;" that is, " of what [*thing* or *action*] he has done;"—or, " of *that* [thing or action] *which* he has done." Here are two objectives. The two cases are sometimes alike, sometimes different; for either of them may be the nominative, and either, the objective. Examples: " The dread of censure ought not to prevail over *what is* proper."—*Kames, El. of Crit.* Vol. i, p. 252. "The public ear will not easily *bear what is* slovenly and incorrect."—*Blair's Rhet.* p. 12. " He who buys *what he* does not need, will often need *what* he cannot buy."—*Student's Manual*, p. 290. " *What* is just, is honest; and again, *what* is honest, is just."—*Cicero.* " He that hath an ear, let him hear *what* the Spirit saith unto the churches."—*Rev.* ii, 7, 11, 17, 29 ; iii, 6, 13, 22.

OBS. 9.—This pronoun, *what*, is usually of the singular number, though sometimes plural: as, " I must turn to the faults, or *what appear* such to me."—*Byron.* " All distortions and mimicries, as such, are *what raise* aversion instead of pleasure."—*Steele.* " Purified indeed from *what appear* to be its real defects."—*Wordsworth's Pref.* p. xix. " Every single impression, made even by the same object, is distinguishable from *what* have gone before, and from *what* succeed."—*Kames, El. of Crit.* Vol. i, p. 107. "Sensible people express no thoughts but *what* make some figure."—*Ib.* Vol. i, p. 399. The following example, which makes *what* both singular and plural at once, is a manifest solecism: " *What has* since followed *are* but natural consequences."—*J. C. CALHOUN, Speech in U. S. Senate*, March 4, 1850. Here *has* should be *have;* or else the form should be this : " *What has* since followed, *is* but *a* natural *consequence.*"

OBS. 10.—The common import of this remarkable pronoun, *what*, is, as we see in the foregoing examples, twofold; but some instances occur, in which it does not appear to have this double construction, but to be simply declaratory ; and many, in which the word is simply an adjective: as, " *What* a strange run of luck I have had to-day ! "—*Columbian Orator*, p. 233. Here *what* is a more adjective; and, in the following examples, a pronoun indefinite;—
    " I tell thee *what*, corporal, I could tear her."—*Shak.*
    " He knows *what* 's *what*, and that 's as high
        As metaphysic wit can fly."—*Hudibras.*

OBS. 11.—*What* is sometimes used both as an adjective and as a relative at the same time, and is placed before the noun which it represents; being equivalent to the adjective *any* or *all*, and the simple relative *who, which*,[†] or *that* : as, " *What* money we had, was taken away." That is, "*Any* money *who* enters, dies." " *What* man but enters, dies." That is, "*Any man who* enters, dies." " It was agreed that *what* goods were aboard his vessels, should be landed."—*Mickle's India*, p. 89. " *What* appearances of worth afterwards succeeded, were drawn from thence."—*Internal Policy of Great Britain*, p. 196. That is, "*All the* appearances of worth, *which* afterwards succeeded."—*Priestley's Gram.* p. 93. Indeed, this pronoun does not admit of being construed after a noun, as a simple relative: none but the most illiterate ever seriously use it so. *What* put for *who* or *which*, is therefore a ludicrous vulgarism; as, " The aspiring youth *what* fired the Ephesian dome."—*Jester.* The word used as above, however, does not always preclude the introduction of a personal pronoun before the subsequent verb; as,
    " *What* god but enters yon forbidden field,
        Who yields assistance, or but wills to yield,
        Back to the skies with shame *he* shall be driven,
        Gash'd with dishonest wounds, the scorn of heaven."—*Pope's Homer.*

OBS. 12.—The compound *whatever* or *whatsoever* has the same peculiarities of construction as has the simpler word *what* : as, " Whatever word expresses an affirmation, or assertion, is a verb ; or thus, *Whatever* word, with a noun or pronoun before or after it, makes full sense, is a verb."—*Adam's Latin Gram.* p. 78. That is, "*Any word which* expresses," &c. " We will certainly do *whatsoever* thing goeth forth out of our own mouth."—*Jeremiah*, xliv, 17. That is—"*any* thing, or *every* thing, *which*." "*Whatever* sounds are difficult in pronunciation, are, in the same proportion, harsh and painful to the ear."—*Blair's Rhet.* p. 121; *Murray's Gram.* p. 325. " *Whatsoever* things were written aforetime, were written for our learning."—*Romans*, xv, 4. In all these examples, the word *whatever* or *whatsoever* appears to be used both adjectively and relatively. There are instances, however, in which the relation of this term is not twofold, but simple: as, " *Whatever* useful or engaging endowments we possess, virtue is requisite in order to their shining with proper lustre."—*English Reader*, p. 23. Here *whatever* is simply an adjective. "The declarations contained in them [the Scriptures] rest on the authority of *God himself;* and there can be no appeal from them to any other authority *whatsoever*."—*London Epistle*, 1836. Here *whatsoever* may

_____

[*] " 'The man is prudent which speaks little.' This sentence is incorrect, because *which* is a pronoun of the neuter gender."—*Murray's Exercises*, p. 18. " *Which* is also a relative, but it is of [the] neuter gender. It is also interrogative."—*Webster's Improved Gram.* p. 26. For oversights like these, I cannot account The relative *which* is of *all the genders*, as every body ought to know, who has ever heard of the *horse which* Alexander rode, of the *ass which* spoke to Balaam, or of any of the *animals which* Noah had with him in the ark.

[†] The word *which* also, when taken in its *discriminative* sense, (i. e. to distinguish some persons or things from others,) may have a construction of this sort; and, by ellipsis of the noun after it, it may likewise bear a resemblance to the double relative *what* : as, " I shall now give you two passages; and request you to point out *which* words are mono-syllables, *which* dis-syllables, *which* tris-syllables, and *which* poly-syllables."—*Buck's Gram.* p. 16. Here, indeed, the word *what* might be substituted for *which*; because that also has a discriminative sense. Either would be right; but the author might have presented the same words and thoughts rather more accurately, thus: " I shall now give you two passages; and request you to point out which words are monosyllables; which, dissyllables; which, trissyllables; and which, polysyllables."

be parsed either as an adjective relating to *authority*, or as an emphatic pronoun in apposition with its noun, like *himself* in the preceding clause. In this general explanatory sense, *whatsoever* may be applied to persons as well as to things; as, " I should be sorry if it entered into the imagination of *any person whatsoever*, that I was preferred to all other patrons."—*Duncan's Cicero*, p. 11. Here the word *whomsoever* might have been used.

Obs. 13.—But there is an other construction to be here explained, in which *whatever* or *whatsoever* appears to be a *double relative*, or a term which includes both antecedent and relative; as, "*Whatever* purifies, fortifies also the heart."—*English Reader*, p. 23. That is, "*All that* purifies—or, *Every thing which* purifies—fortifies also the heart." "*Whatsoever* he doeth, shall prosper."—*Psal.* i, 3. That is, "*All that* he doeth—or, *All the things which* he doeth—shall prosper." This construction, however, may be supposed elliptical. The Latin expression is, "*Omnia quæcumque faciet prosperabuntur.*"—*Vulgate.* The Greek is similar: "Καὶ πάντα ὅσα ἂν ποιῇ κατευοδωθήσεται."—*Septuagint.* It is doubtless by some sort of ellipsis which familiarity of use inclines us to overlook, that *what*, *whatever*, and *whatsoever*, which are essentially adjectives, have become susceptible of this double construction as pronouns. But it is questionable what particular ellipsis we ought here to suppose, or whether any; and certainly, we ought always to avoid the supposing of an ellipsis, if we can.[*] Now if we say the meaning is, " Whatsoever *things* he doeth, shall prosper;" this, though analogous to other expressions, does not simplify the construction. If we will have it to be, " Whatsoever *things* he doeth, *they* shall prosper;" the pronoun *they* appears to be pleonastic. So is the word *it*, in the text, " *Whatsoever* he saith unto you, do *it*."—*John*, ii, 5. If we say the full phrase is, "*All things* whatsoever he doeth, shall prosper;" this presents, to an English ear, a still more obvious pleonasm. It may be, too, a *borrowed idiom*, found nowhere but in translations; as, "*All things whatsoever* ye shall ask in prayer, believing, ye shall receive."—*Matt.* xxi, 22. From these views, there seems to be some objection to any and every method of parsing the above-mentioned construction as *elliptical*. The learner may therefore say, in such instances, that *whatever* or *whatsoever* is a double relative, including both antecedent and relative; and parse it, first as antecedent, in connexion with the latter verb, and then as relative, in connexion with the former. But let him observe that the order of the verbs may be the reverse of the foregoing; as, " Ye are my friends, if ye *do* whatsoever I *command* you."—*John*, xv, 14. That is, according to the Greek, " If ye do whatsoever I command *to* you;" though it would be better English to say, " If ye do whatsoever I command you *to do*." In the following example, however, it seems proper to recognize an ellipsis; nay, the omissions in the construction of the last line, are as many as three or four:—

> " Expatiate with glad step, and choose at will
> *Whate'er* bright *spoils* the florid earth contains,
> *Whate'er* the *waters*, or the liquid *air*."—*Akenside.*

Obs. 14.—As the simple word *who* differs from *which* and *what*, in being always a declinable pronoun; so its compounds differ from theirs, in being incapable of either of the double constructions above described. Yet *whoever* and *whoso* or *whosoever*, as well as *whichever* and *whichsoever*, *whatever* and *whatsoever*, derive, from the affix which is added, or from the peculiarity of their syntax, an unlimited signification—or a signification which is limited only by the following verb;

---

[*] As for Butler's method of parsing these words by *always recognizing a noun as being* " UNDERSTOOD" *before them,*—a method by which, according to his publishers' notice, " The ordinary unphilosophical explanation of this class of words is discarded, and a simple, intelligible, common-sense view of the matter now *for the first time* substituted,"—I know not what novelty there is in it, that is not also just so much *error*. " Compare," says he, " these two sentences : ' I saw *whom* I wanted to see ;' ' I saw *what* I wanted to see.' If *what* in the latter is equivalent to *that which*, or *the thing which*, *whom* in the former is equivalent to *him whom*, or *the person whom*."—*Butler's Practical Gram.* p. 51. The former example being simply elliptical of the antecedent, he judges the latter to be so too; and infers, " that *what* is nothing more than a relative pronoun, and includes nothing else."—*Ib.* This conclusion is not well drawn, because the two examples are *not analogous*; and whoever thus finds " that *what* is nothing more than a relative," ought also to find it is something less,—a mere *adjective*. " I saw *the person whom* I wanted to see," is a sentence that *can scarcely spare* the antecedent and retain the sense ; " I saw *what* I wanted to see," is one which *cannot receive* an antecedent, without changing both the sense and the construction. One may say, " I saw *what things* I wanted to see ;" but this, in stead of giving *what* an antecedent, makes it an *adjective*, while it *retains the force of a relative*. Or he *may insert* a noun before *what*, agreeably to the solution of Butler ; as, " I saw *the things*, what I wanted to see :" or, if he please, both before and after ; as, " I saw *the things*, what *things* I wanted to see." But still, in either case, *what* is no " simple relative ;" for it here seems equivalent to the phrase, *so many as*. Or, again, he may omit the comma, and say, " I saw *the thing* what I wanted to see ;" but this, if it be not a vulgarism, will only mean, " I saw *the thing to be* what I wanted to see." So that this method of parsing the pronoun *what*, is manifestly no improvement, but rather a perversion and misinterpretation.

But, for further proof of his position, Butler adduces instances of what he calls " *the relative* THAT *with the antecedent omitted*. A few examples of this," he says, " will help us to ascertain the nature of *what*. ' We speak *that* we do know.' *Bible*. [John, iii, 11] ' I am *that* I am.' *Bible*. [Exod. iii, 14] ' Eschew *that* wicked is.' *Gower*. ' Is it possible he should know what he is, and be *that* he is?' *Shakspeare*. ' Gather the sequel by *that* went before.' *Id.* In these examples," continues he, " *that* is a relative; and is *exactly synonymous* with *what*. No one would contend that *that* stands for itself and its antecedent at the same time. The antecedent is omitted, *because it is indefinite*, OR EASILY SUPPLIED."—*Butler's Practical Gram.* p. 52 ; *Bullions's Analytical and Practical Gram.* p. 233. Converted at his wisest age, by these false arguments, so as to renounce and gainsay the doctrine taught almost universally, and hitherto spread industriously by himself, in the words of Lennie, that, " *What* is a compound relative, including both the relative and the antecedent," Dr. Bullions now most absurdly urges, that, " *The truth is, what is a simple relative*, having, wherever used, *like all other relatives*, BUT ONE CASE ; but * * * that it always refers to a *general antecedent, omitted*, BUT EASILY SUPPLIED *by the mind*," though " *not* UNDERSTOOD, *in the ordinary sense* of that expression."—*Analyt. and Pract. Gram.* of 1849, p. 51. Accordingly, though he differs from Butler about this matter of " *the ordinary sense*," he cites the foregoing suggestions of this author, with the following compliment: " These remarks appear to me *just*, and *conclusive on this point* "—*Ib.* p. 233. But there must, I think, be many to whom they will appear far otherwise. These elliptical uses of *that* are all of them bad or questionable English ; because, the ellipsis being such as may be supplied in two or three different ways, the true construction is doubtful, the true meaning not exactly determined by the words. It is quite as easy and natural to take " *that*" to be here a demonstrative term, having the relative *which* understood after it, as to suppose it " a relative," with an antecedent to be supplied before it. Since there would not be the same uncertainty, if *what* were in these cases substituted for *that*, it is evident that the terms are not " *exactly synonymous* ;" but, even if they were so, exact synonymy would not evince a sameness of construction.

and, as some general term, such as *any person*, or *all persons*, is implied as the antecedent, they are commonly connected with other words as if they stood for two cases at once: as, "*Whoever* seeks, shall find." That is, "*Any person who* seeks, shall find." But as the case of this compound, like that of the simple word *who*, *whose*, or *whom*, is known and determined by its form, it is necessary, in parsing, to treat this phraseology as being elliptical. The compounds of *who* do not, therefore, actually stand for two cases, though some grammarians affirm that they do.[*] Example: "The soldiers made proclamation, that they would sell the empire to *whoever* would purchase it at the highest price."—*Goldsmith's Rome*, p. 231. That is—"to *any man who* would purchase it." The affix *ever* or *soever* becomes unnecessary when the ellipsis is supplied; and this fact, it must be confessed, is a plausible argument against the supposition of an ellipsis. But the supposing of an antecedent understood, is here unavoidable: because the preposition *to* cannot govern the nominative case, and the word *whoever* cannot be an objective. And so in all other instances in which the two cases are different: as, "He bids *whoever* is athirst, to come."—*Jenks's Devotions*, p. 151. "Elizabeth publicly threatened, that she would have the head of *who-ever* had advised it."—HUME: *in Priestley's Gram.* p. 104.

OBS. 15.—If it is necessary in parsing to supply the antecedent to *whoever* or *whosoever*, when two *different* cases are represented, it is but analogous and reasonable to supply it also when two *similar* cases occur: as, "*Whoever* borrows money, *is bound* in conscience to repay it."—*Paley*. "*Whoever* is eager to find excuses for vice and folly, *will find* his own backwardness to practise them much diminished."—*Chapone*. "*Whoever* examines his own imperfections, *will cease* to be fastidious; *whoever* restrains humour and caprice, *will cease* to be squeamish."—*Crabb's Synonymes*. In all these examples, we have the word in the third person, singular number, masculine gender, and nominative case. And here it is most commonly found. It is always of the third person; and, though its number *may be* plural; its gender, feminine; its case, possessive or objective; we do not often use it in any of these ways. In some instances, the latter verb is attended with an other pronoun, which represents the same person or persons; as, "And *whosoever* will, let *him* take of the water of life freely."—*Rev.* xxii, 17. The case of this compound relative always depends upon what follows it, and not upon what precedes; as, "Or ask of *whomsoever* he has taught."—*Cowper*. That is—"of *any person* whom he has taught." In the following text, we have the possessive plural: "*Whosesoever* sins ye remit, they are remitted unto *them*."—*John*, xx, 23. That is, "*Whatever persons'* sins."

OBS. 16.—In such phraseology as the following, there is a stiffness which ought to be avoided: "For *whomever* God loves, he loves *them* in Christ, and no otherways."—*Barclay's Works*, Vol. iii, p. 215. Better: "For *all whom* God loves, he loves in Christ, and no *otherwise*." "When the Father draws, *whomever* he draws, may come."—*Penington*. Better: "When the Father draws, *all whom* he draws, (or, *every one whom* he draws,) may come." A modern critic of immense promise cites the following clause as being found in the Bible: "But he loveth *whomsoever* followeth after righteousness."—*O. B. Peirce's Gram.* p. 72. It is lamentable to see the unfaithfulness of this gentleman's quotations. About half of them are spurious; and I am confident that this one is neither Scripture nor good English. The compound relative, being the subject of *followeth*, should be in the nominative case; for the object of the verb *loveth* is the antecedent *every one*, understood. But the idea may be better expressed, without any ellipsis, thus: "He loveth *every one who* followeth after righteousness." The following example from the same hand is also wrong, and the author's rule and reasoning connected with it, are utterly fallacious: "I will give the reward to *whomsoever* will apprehend the rogue."—*Ib.* p. 256. Much better say, "*to any one who*;" but, if you choose the compound word, by all analogy, and all good authority, it must here be *whoever* or *whosoever*. The shorter compound *whoso*, which occurs very frequently in the Bible, is now almost obsolete in prose, but still sometimes used by the poets. It has the same meaning as *whosoever*, but appears to have been confined to the nominative singular; and *whatso* is still more rare: as, "*Whoso* diggeth a pit, shall fall therein."—*Prov.* xxvi, 27.

> "Which *whoso* tastes, can be enslaved no more."—*Cowper*.

> "On their intended journey to proceed,
> And over night *whatso* thereto did need."—*Hubbard*.

OBS. 17.—The relative *that* is applied indifferently to persons, to brute animals, and to inanimate things. But the word *that* is not always a relative pronoun. It is sometimes a pronoun, sometimes an adjective, and sometimes a conjunction. I call it not a demonstrative pronoun and also a relative; because, in the sense in which Murray and others have styled it a "demonstrative adjective *pronoun*," it is a pronominal *adjective*, and it is better to call it so. (1.) It is a *relative pronoun* whenever it is equivalent to *who*, *whom*, or *which*: as, "There is not a *just man* upon earth, *that* doeth good, and sinneth not."—*Eccl.* vii, 20. "It was diverse from all the *beasts that* were before it."—*Dan.* vii, 7. "And he had a *name* written, *that* no man knew but he himself."—*Rev.* xix, 12. (2.) It is a *pronominal adjective* whenever it relates to a noun expressed or understood after it: as, "Thus with violence shall *that* great *city*, Babylon, be thrown down."—*Rev.* xviii, 21. "Behold *that* [thing] which I have seen."—*Eccl.* v, 18. "And they said, · What is *that*[†] [matter] to us? See thou to *that*' [matter]."—*Matt.* xxvii, 4. (3.) In its other uses, it is

---

[*] See this erroneous doctrine in Kirkham's Grammar. p. 112; in Wells's, p. 74; in Sanborn's, p. 71, p. 96, and p. 177; in Cooper's, p. 88; in O. B. Peirce's, p. 70. These writers show a great fondness for this complex mode of parsing. But, in fact, no pronoun, not even the word *what*, has any double construction of cases from a real or absolute necessity; but merely because, the noun being suppressed, yet having a representative, we choose rather to understand and parse its representative doubly, than to supply the ellipsis. No pronoun includes "both the antecedent and the relative," by virtue of its own *composition*, or of its own derivation, as a word. No pronoun can properly be called "*compound*" merely because it has a double construction, and is equivalent to two other words. These positions, if true, as I am sure they are, will refute sundry assertions that are contained in the above-named grammars.

[†] Here the demonstrative word *that*, as well as the phrase *that matter*, which I form to explain its construction, unquestionably refers back to Judas's confession, that he had sinned; but still, as the word has not the connecting power of a relative pronoun, its true character is *that* of an adjective, and not *that* of a pronoun. This pronominal adjective is very often mixed with some such ellipsis, and *that* to repeat the import of various kinds of words and phrases; as, "God shall help her, and *that* right early."—*Psal.* xlvi, 5. "Nay, ye do wrong, and defraud, and *that* your brethren."—1 *Cor.* vi, 8. "I'll know your business, *that* I will."—*Shakspeare*.

a *conjunction;* and, as such, it most commonly makes what follows it, the purpose, object, or final cause, of what precedes it: as, "I read *that* I may learn."—*Dr. Adam.* "Ye men of Athens, I perceive *that* in all things ye are too superstitious."—*St. Paul.* "Live well, *that* you may die well."—*Anon.* "Take heed *that* thou speak not to Jacob."—*Genesis.* "Judge not, *that* ye be not judged."—*Matthew.*

OBS. 18.—The word *that,* or indeed any other word, should never be so used as to leave the part of speech uncertain; as, "For in the day *that* thou eatest thereof, thou shalt surely die."—*Gen.* ii, 17. Here *that* seems to be a relative *pronoun,* representing *day,* in the third person, singular, neuter; yet, in other respects, it seems to be a *conjunction,* because there is nothing to determine its case. Better: "For in the day *on which* thou eatest thereof, thou shalt surely die." This mongrel construction of the word *that,* were its justification possible, is common enough in our language to be made good English. But it must needs be condemned, because it renders the character of the term ambiguous, and is such a grammatical difficulty as puts the parser at a dead nonplus. Examples: (1.) "But *at the same time* THAT men are giving their orders, God on his part is likewise giving his."—*Rollin's Hist.* ii, 106. Here the phrase, "*at the same time that,*" is only equivalent to the adverb *while;* and yet it is incomplete, because it means, "*at the same time at which,*" or, "*at the very time at which.*" (2.) "The author of this work, *at the same time* THAT he has endeavoured to avoid a plan, *which may be* too concise or too extensive, defective in its parts or irregular in the disposition of them, has studied to render his *subject* sufficiently easy, intelligible, and comprehensive."—*Murray's Gram., Introd.,* p. 1. This sentence, which is no unfair specimen of its author's original style, needs three corrections: 1. For "*at the same time that,*" say *while:* 2. Drop the phrase, "*which may be,*" because it is at least useless: 3. For "*subject,*" read *treatise,* or *compilation.* You will thus have tolerable diction. Again: (3.) "The participles of active verbs *act upon objects* and govern them in the objective case, in the same manner *that* the verbs *do,* from which they are derived. *A participle* in the nature of an adjective, belongs or refers to *nouns* or *pronouns* in the same manner *that* adjectives *do;* and *when it will admit* the degrees of comparison, *it is called* a participial *adjective.*"—*Sanborn's Gram.* p. 38. This is the style of a gentleman of no ordinary pretensions, one who thinks he has produced the best grammar that has ever appeared in our language. To me, however, his work suggests an abundance of questions like these; each of which would palpably involve him in a dilemma: What is here meant by "*objects,*" the *words,* or the *things?* if the former, how are they acted upon? if the latter, how are they governed? If "*a participle* is called an *adjective,*" which is it, an adjective, or a participle? If "*a participle refers* to *nouns* or *pronouns,*" *how many* of these are required by the relation? When does a *participle*" admit the degrees of comparison?" How shall we parse the word *that* in the foregoing sentences?

OBS. 19.—The word *as,* though usually a conjunction or an adverb, has sometimes the construction of a relative pronoun, especially after *such, so many,* or *as many;* and, whatever the antecedent *noun* may be, this is the *only fit relative* to follow any of these terms in a restrictive sense. Examples: "We have been accustomed to repose on its veracity with *such* humble confidence *as* suppresses curiosity."—*Johnson's Life of Cowley.* "The malcontents made *such* demands *as* none but a tyrant could refuse."—*Bolingbroke, on Hist.* Let. 7. "The Lord added to the church daily *such* [persons] *as* should be saved."—*Acts,* ii, 47. "And *as many as* were ordained to eternal life, believed."—*Acts,* xiii, 48. "*As many as* I love, I rebuke and chasten."—*Rev.* iii, 19. "Know ye not, that *so many* of us *as* were baptized into Jesus Christ, were baptized into his death?"—*Rom.* vi, 3. "For *as many* of you *as* have been baptized into Christ, have put on Christ."—*Gal.* iii, 27. "A syllable, is *so many* letters *as* are spoken with one motion of the voice." —*Perley's Gram.* p. 8. "The compound tenses are *such as* cannot be formed without an auxiliary verb."—*Murray's Gram.* p. 91. "Send him *such* books *as* will please him."—*Webster's Improved Gram.* p. 37. "In referring to *such* a division of the day *as* is past, we use the imperfect."—*Murray's Gram.* p. 70. "Participles have the *same* government *as* the verbs from which they are derived."—*Ib.* Rule xiv. "Participles have *the same* government *as* the verbs *have* from which they are derived."—*Sanborn's Gram.* p. 94. In some of these examples, *as* is in the nominative case, and in others, in the objective; in some, it is of the masculine gender, and in others, it is neuter; in some, it is of the plural number, and in others, it is singular: but in all, it is of the third person; and in all, its person, number, gender, and case, are as obvious as those of any invariable pronoun can be.

OBS. 20.—Some writers—(the most popular are Webster, Bullions, Wells, and Chandler—)imagine that *as,* in such sentences as the foregoing, can be made a conjunction, and not a pronoun, if we will allow them to consider the phraseology elliptical. Of the example for which I am indebted to him, Dr. Webster says, "*As* must be considered as the nominative to *will please,* or we must suppose an ellipsis of several words: as, 'Send him such books *as the books which* will please him, or *as those which* will please him.'"—*Improved Gram.* p. 37. This pretended explanation must be rejected as an absurdity. In either form of it, *two* nominatives are idly imagined between *as* and its verb; and, I ask, of what is the first one the subject? If you say, "*Of are* understood," making the phrase, "such books *as the books are;*" does not *as* bear the same relation to this new verb *are,* that is found in the pronoun *who,* when one says, "Tell him *who* you *are?*" If so, *as* is a pronoun still; so that, thus far, you gain nothing. And if you will have the whole explanation to be, "Send him such books as *the books are books which* will please him;" you multiply words, and finally arrive at nothing, but tautology and nonsense. Wells, not condescending to show his pupils what he would supply after this *as,* thinks it sufficient to say, the word is "followed by an ellipsis of one or more words required to complete the construction; as, 'He was the father of all such *as* [   ] handle the harp and organ.'—*Gen.* 4: 21."—*Wells's School Gram.* 1st Ed. p. 164; 3d Ed. p. 172.

OBS. 21.—Chandler exhibits the sentence, "*These are not such as are worn;*" and, in parsing it, expounds the words *as* and *are,* thus; the crotchets being his, not mine: "*as . . . . .* is an *adverb, connecting* the two sentences, in comparing them. [*It is a fault* of some, that they make *as* a pronoun, when, in a comparative sentence, it corresponds with *such,* and is immediately followed by a verb, as in the sentence now given. This is probably done *from an ignorance* of the real nominative to the verb. The sentence *should stand thus*: ' These (*perhaps* bonnets) are not such (bonnets) *as* (those bonnets) are (which are) worn.' Then] *are* . . . . is the substantive verb, third person, plural number, indicative mood, present tense, and agrees with the noun *bonnets*, understood."—*Chandler's Common School Gram.* p. 162. All this bears the marks of shallow flippancy. No part of it is accurate. " *Are worn*," which the critic unwarrantably divides by his misplaced curves and uncouth impletions, is a passive verb, agreeing with the pronoun *as*. But the text itself is faulty, being unintelligible through lack of a noun; for, of things that *may be* " *worn*," there are a thousand different sorts. Is it not ridiculous, for a great grammarian to offer, as a model for parsing, what he himself, "*from an ignorance* of the real nominative," can only interpret with a "*perhaps*!" But the noun which this author supplies, the meaning which he guesses that he had, he here very improperly stows away within a pair of *crotchets*. Nor is it true, that " the sentence *should stand*" as above exhibited ; for the tautological correction not only has the very extreme of awkwardness, but still makes *as* a pronoun, a nominative, belonging after *are*: so that the phrase, " *as are worn*," is only encumbered and perverted by the verbose addition made. So of an other example given by this expounder, in which *as* is an objective : " He is exactly such a man *as* I saw."—*Chandler's Com. Sch. Gram.* p. 163. Here *as* is the object of *saw*. But the author says, " The sentence, however, *should stand thus*: ' He is exactly such a man *as* that person *was* whom I saw.' "—*Ibid.* This inelegant alteration makes *as* a nominative dependent on *was*.

OBS. 22.—The use of *as* for a relative pronoun, is almost entirely confined to those connexions in which no other relative would be proper ; hence few instances occur, of its absolute equivalence to *who*, *which*, or *that*, by which to establish its claim to the same rank. Examples like the following, however, go far to prove it, if proof be necessary ; because *who* and *which* are here employed, where *as* is certainly now required by all good usage : " It is not only convenient, but absolutely needful, that there be certain meetings at certain places and times, *as* may best suit the convenience of *such*, *who* may be most particularly concerned in them."—*Barclay's Works*, Vol. i, p. 495. " Which, no doubt, will be found obligatory upon all *such*, *who* have a sense and feeling of the mind of the Spirit."—*Ib.* i, p. 578. " Condemning or removing *such* things, *which* in themselves are evil."—*Ib.* i, p. 511. In these citations, not only are *who* and *which* improperly used for *as*, but the *commas* before them are also improper, because the relatives are intended to be taken in a restrictive sense. " If there be *such that* walk disorderly now."—*Ib.* i, p. 488. Here *that* ought to be *as ;* or else *such* ought to be *persons*, or *those*. " When such virtues, *as which* still accompany the truth, are necessarily supposed to be wanting."—*Ib.* i, p. 502. Here *which*, and the comma before *as*, should both be expunged. " I shall raise in their minds the same course of thought *as* has taken possession of my own."—*Duncan's Logic*, p. 61. " The pronoun must be in the same case *as* the antecedent would be *in*, if substituted for it."—*Murray's Gram.* p. 181. " The verb must therefore have the same construction *as* it has in the following sentence."—*Murray's Key*, p. 190. Here *as* is exactly equivalent to the relative *that*, and either may be used with equal propriety. We cannot avoid the conclusion, therefore, that, as the latter word is sometimes a conjunction and sometimes a pronoun, so is the former.

OBS. 23.—The relatives *that* and *as* have this peculiarity ; that, unlike *whom* and *which*, they never follow the word on which their case depends : nor indeed can any simple relative be so placed, except it be governed by a preposition or an infinitive. Thus, it is said, (John, xiii, 29th,) " Buy those things *that* we have need *of ;*" so we may say, " Buy such things *as* we have need of." But we cannot say, " Buy those things *of that* we have need ;" or, " *Buy* such things *of as* we have need." Though we may say, " Buy those things *of which* we have need," as well as, " Buy those things *which* we have need *of ;*" or, " Admit those persons *of whom* we have need," as well as, " Admit those persons *whom* we have need *of*." By this it appears that *that* and *as* have a closer connexion with their antecedents than the other relatives require : a circumstance worthy to have been better remembered by some critics. " Again, *that* and *as* are used rather differently. When *that* is used, the verb must be repeated ; as, ' Participles *require* the same government, *that* their verbs *require*.'—' James *showed* the same credulity, *that* his minister *showed*.' But when *as* is used, the verb generally may, or may not be repeated ; as, ' Participles *require* the same government *as* their verbs *require*;' or, ' *as* their verbs *require*.'—' James *showed* the same credulity *as* his minister ;' or, ' *as* his minister *showed* :' the second nominative *minister* being parsed as the nominative to the same verb *showed* understood."—*Nixon's Parser*, p. 140.*

OBS. 24.—The terminating of a sentence with a preposition, or other small particle, is in general undignified, though perhaps not otherwise improper. Hence the above-named inflexibility in the construction of *that* and *as*, sometimes induces an ellipsis of the governing word designed ; and is occasionally attended with some difficulty respecting the choice of our terms. Examples : " The answer is always in the same case *that* the interrogative word *is*."—*Sanborn's Gram.* p. 70. Here is a faulty termination ; and with it a more faulty ellipsis. In stead of ending the sentence with *is in*, say, " The answer always *agrees* in case *with* the interrogative word." Again : " The relative is of the same person *with* the antecedent."—*Lowth's Gram.* p. 101. This sentence is wrong, because the person of the relative is not really *identical with* the antecedent. " The relative is of the same person *as* the antecedent."—*Murray's Gram.* p. 154. Here the writer means—"*as* the antecedent *is of*." " A neuter verb becomes active, when followed by a noun of the same signification *with* its own."—*Sanborn's Gram.* p. 127. Here *same* is wrong, or else the last three words are useless. It would therefore be improper to say—" *of the same* signification *as* its own." The expression ought to be—"*of* a signification *similar to* its own." " Ode

* Dr. Bullions has undertaken to prove, " That the word *as* should not be considered a relative in any circumstances." The force of his five great arguments to this end, the reader may well conceive of, when he has compared the following one with what is shown in the 22d and 23d observations above : " 3. As *can never be used as a substitute for another relative pronoun*, nor *another relative pronoun as a substitute for it*. If, then, it is a relative pronoun, it is, to say the least, a very unaccommodating one."—*Bullions's Analytical and Practical Gram. of 1849*, p. 233.

is, *in Greek*, the same *with* song or hymn."—*Blair's Rhet.* p. 396. *Song* being no Greek word, I cannot think the foregoing expression accurate, though one might say, "Ode is *identical with* song or hymn." Would it not be better to say, "Ode is the same *as* song or hymn?" That is, "Ode is, *literally*, the same *thing that* song or hymn *is?*" "Treatises of philosophy, ought not to be composed in the *same* style *with* orations."—*Blair's Rhet.* p. 175. Here neither *with* nor *as* can be proper; because *orations* are not a *style*. Expunge *same*; and say—"in the style of orations."

OBS. 25.—Few writers are sufficiently careful in their choice and management of relatives. In the following instance, Murray and others violate a special rule of their own grammars, by using *whom* for *that* "after an adjective of the superlative degree :" "Modifying them acording to the genius of that tongue, and the established practice of *the best* speakers and writers *by whom* it is used."—*Octavo Gram.* p. 1; *Fisk's,* p. 11; *et al.* According to Priestley and himself, the great Compiler is here in an error. The rule is perhaps too stringent; but whoever teaches it, should keep it. If he did not like to say, "*the best* speakers and writers *that* it is used *by ;*" he ought to have said, "*the best* speakers and writers *that use it.*" Or, rather, he ought to have said *nothing* after the word "writers;" because the whole relative clause is here weak and useless. Yet how many of the amenders of this grammar have not had perspicacity enough, either to omit the *e*xpression, or to correct it according to the author's own rule!

OBS. 26.—Relative pronouns are capable of being taken in two very different senses : the one, *restrictive* of the general idea suggested by the antecedent; the other, *resumptive* of that idea, in the full import of the term—or, in whatever extent the previous definitives allow. The distinction between these two senses, important as it is, is frequently made to depend solely upon the insertion or the omission of *a comma.* Thus, if I say, "Men who grasp after riches, are never satisfied ;" the relative *who* is taken restrictively, and I am understood to speak *only of the avaricious.* But, if I say, "Men, who grasp after riches, are never satisfied ;" by separating the terms *men* and *who,* I declare *all men* to be covetous and unsatisfied. For the former sense, the relative *that* is preferable to *who;* and I shall presently show why. This example, in the latter form, is found in Sanborn's Grammar, page 142d : but whether the author meant what he says, or not, I doubt. Like many other unskillful writers, he has paid little regard to the above-mentioned distinction; and, in some instances, his meaning cannot have been what his words declare : as, "A prism is a solid, whose sides are all parallelograms."—*Analytical Gram.* p. 142. This, as it stands, is no definition of a prism, but an assertion of two things ; that a prism is a solid, and that all the sides of a solid are parallelograms. Erase the comma, and the words will describe the prism as a peculiar kind of solid; because *whose* will then be taken in the restrictive sense. This sense, however, may be conveyed even with a comma before the relative ; as, "Some fictitious histories yet remain, *that* were composed during the decline of the Roman empire."—*Blair's Rhet.* p. 374. This does not suggest that there are no other fictitious histories now extant, than such as were composed during the decline of the Roman empire ; but I submit it to the reader, whether the word *which,* if here put for *that,* would not convey this idea.

OBS. 27.—Upon this point, many philologists are open to criticism ; and none more so, than the recent author above cited. By his own plain showing, this grammarian has no conception of the difference of meaning, upon which the foregoing distinction is founded. What marvel, then, that he falls into errors, both of doctrine and of practice ? But, if no such difference exists, or none that is worthy of a critic's notice ; then the error is mine, and it is vain to distinguish between the restrictive and the resumptive sense of relative pronouns. For example : "The boy that desires to assist his companions, deserves respect."—*G. Brown.* "That boy, who desires to assist his companions, deserves respect."—*D. H. Sanborn.* According to my notion, these two sentences clearly convey two very different meanings ; the relative, in the former, being restrictive, but, in the latter, resumptive of the sense of the antecedent. But of the latter example this author says, "The clause, 'who desires to assist his companions,' with the relative *who* at its head, *explains or tells what boy deserves respect ;* and, like a conjunction, connects this clause to the noun *boy.*" —*Analytical Gram.* p. 69. He therefore takes it in a restrictive sense, as if this sentence were exact:y equivalent to the former. But he adds, "A relative pronoun is resolvable into a personal pronoun and a conjunction. The sentence would then read, 'That boy desires to assist his companions, *and he* deserves respect.'' The relative pronoun governs the nearer verb, and the antecedent the more distant one."—*Ib.* p. 69. Now, concerning the restrictive relative, this doctrine of equivalence does not hold good ; and, besides, the explanation here given, not only contradicts his former declaration of the sense he intended, but, with other seeming contradiction, joins the antecedent to the nearer verb, and the substituted pronoun to the more distant.

OBS. 28.—Again, the following principles of this author's punctuation are no less indicative of his false views of this matter : "RULE XIV.—Relative pronouns in the nominative or [*the*] objective case, are preceded by commas, when the clause which the relative *connects* [,] ends a sentence ; as, 'Sweetness of temper is a quality, which reflects a lustre on every accomplishment.'—*B. Greenleaf.* 'Self [-] denial is the sacrifice [,] which virtue must make.' [—*L. Murray.*] The comma is om:tted before the relative, when the verb which the antecedent governs, follows the relative clause ; as, 'He that suffers by imposture, *has* too often his virtue more impaired than his fortune.' —*Johnson.*" See *Sanborn's Analytical Gram.* p. 269. Such are some of our author's principles— "the essence of modern improvements." His practice, though often wrong, is none the worse for contradicting these doctrines. Nay, his proudest boast is ungrammatical, though peradventure not the less believed : "*No* [other] *grammar in the language* probably contains so great a quantity of *condensed and* useful matter with so little superfluity."—*Sanborn's Preface,* p. v.

OBS. 29.—Murray's rule for the punctuation of relatives, (a rule which he chiefly copied from Lowth,) recognizes virtually the distinction which I have made above ; but, in assuming that relatives "*generally*" require a comma before them, it erroneously suggests that the resumptive sense is more common than the restrictive. Churchill, on the contrary, as wrongly makes it an essential characteristic of *all* relatives, "to limit or explain the words to which they refer." See his *New Gram.* p. 74. The fact is, that relatives are so generally restrictive, that not one half of them are thus pointed; though some that do restrict their antecedent, nevertheless admit the point. This may be seen by the first example given us by Murray : " Relative pronouns are connective words, and *generally* admit a comma before them : as, ' He preaches sublimely, *who* lives a sober, righteous, and pious life.' But when two members, or *phrases*, [say *clauses*,] are closely connected by a relative, restraining the general notion of the antecedent to a particular sense, *the comma should be omitted*: as, ' *Self-denial* is the *sacrifice which* virtue must make ;' ' *A man who* is of a detracting spirit, will misconstrue the most innocent *words that* can be put together.' In the latter example, the assertion is not of ' a man in general,' but of ' a man who is of a detracting spirit ;' and therefore *they* [say *the pronoun and its antecedent*] should not be separated."—*Murray's Gram. Octavo*, p. 273; *Ingersoll's*, 285; *Comly's*, 152. This reasoning, strictly applied, would exclude the comma before *who* in the first example above; but, as the pronoun does not " closely" or immediately follow its antecedent, the comma is allowed, though it is not much needed. Not so, when the sense is resumptive: as, " The *additions, which* are very considerable, are chiefly *such as* are calcuated to obviate objections." See *Murray's Gram.* p. ix. Here the comma is essential to the meaning. Without it, *which* would be equivalent to *that ;* with it, *which* is equivalent to *and they.* But this latter meaning, as I imagine, cannot be expressed by the relative *that.*

OBS. 30.—Into the unfortunate example which Sanborn took from Murray, I have inserted the comma for him ; not because it is necessary or right, but because his rule requires it: " *Self denial* is the *sacrifice*," &c. The author of " a complete system of grammar," might better contradict even Murray, than himself. But why was this text admired? and why have *Greene, Bullions, Hiley, Hart*, and others, also copied it ? A *sacrifice* is something devoted and lost, for the sake of a greater good; and, *if Virtue sacrifice self-denial*, what will she do, but run into indulgence ? The great sacrifice which she demands of men, is rather that of their *self-love.* Wm. B. Russell has it, " *Self defence* is the sacrifice which virtue must make !"—*Russell's Abridgement of Murray's Gram.* p. 116. Bishop Butler tells us, " It is indeed *ridiculous* to assert, that *self-denial is essential to virtue and piety ;* but it would have been nearer the truth, though not strictly the truth itself, to have said, that it is essential to discipline and improvement."—*Analogy of Religion*, p. 123.

OBS. 31.—The relative *that*, though usually reckoned equivalent to *who* or *which*, evidently differs from both, in being more generally, and perhaps more appropriately, taken in the restrictive sense. It ought therefore, for distinction's sake, to be preferred to *who* or *which*, whenever an antecedent not otherwise limited, is to be restricted by the relative clause; as, " *Men that* grasp after riches, are never satisfied."—" I love *wisdom that* is gay and civilized."—*Art of Thinking*, p. 34. This phraseology leaves not the limitation of the meaning to depend solely upon the absence of a pause after the antecedent; because the relative *that* is seldom, if ever, used by good writers in any other than a restrictive sense. Again : " A man of a polite imagination is let into a great many pleasures *that* the vulgar are not capable of receiving."—*Addison, Spect.* No 411. Here, too, according to my notion, *that* is obviously preferable to *which* ; though a great critic, very widely known, has taken some pains to establish a different opinion. The " many pleasures" here spoken of, are no otherwise defined, than as being such as " the vulgar are not capable of receiving." The writer did not mean to deny that the vulgar are capable of receiving a great many pleasures ; but, certainly, if *that* were changed to *which*, this would be the meaning conveyed, unless the reader were very careful to avoid a pause where he would be apt to make one. I therefore prefer Addison's expression to that which Dr. Blair would substitute.

OBS. 32.—The style of Addison is more than once censured by Dr. Blair, for the frequency with which the relative *that* occurs in it, where the learned lecturer would have used *which*. The reasons assigned by the critic are these : " *Which* is a much more definitive word than *that*, being never employed in any other way than as a relative ; whereas *that* is a word of many senses ; sometimes a demonstrative pronoun, often a conjunction. In some cases we are indeed obliged to use *that* for a relative, in order to avoid *the* ungraceful repetition of *which* in the same sentence. But when we are laid under no necessity of this kind, *which* is always the preferable word, and certainly was so in this sentence : '*Pleasures which* the vulgar are not capable of receiving,' is much better than '*pleasures that* the vulgar are not capable of receiving.'"—*Blair's Rhetoric*, Lect. xx, p. 200. Now the facts are these: (1.) That *that* is the more definitive or restrictive word of the two. (2.) That the word *which* has as many different senses and uses as the word *that*. (3.) That not the repetition of *which* or *who* in a series of clauses, but a *needless change* of the relative, is ungraceful. (4.) That the necessity of using *that* rather than *which* or *who*, depends, not upon what is here supposed, but upon the different senses which these words usually convey. (5.) That as there is always some reason of choice, *that* is sometimes to be preferred ; *which*, sometimes ; and *who*, sometimes : as, " It is not the man *who* has merely taught, or *who* has taught long, or *who* is able to point out defects in authors, *that* is capable of enlightening the world in the respective sciences *which* have engaged his attention ; but the man *who* has taught *well*."—*Kirkham's Elocution*, p. 7.

OBS. 33.—Blair's Rhetoric consists of forty-seven lectures ; four of which are devoted to a critical examination of the style of Addison, as exhibited in four successive papers of the Spectator. The remarks of the professor are in general judicious ; but, seeing his work is made a common textbook for students of " Belles Lettres," it is a pity to find it so liable to reprehension on the score of inaccuracy. Among the passages which are criticised in the twenty-first lecture, there is one in which the essayist speaks of the effects of *novelty* as follows :—

' It is this *which* bestows charms on a monster, and makes even the imperfections of nature please us. It is this *that* recommends variety, where the mind is every instant called off to something new, and the attention not suffered to dwell too long and waste itself on any particular object. It is this, likewise, *that* improves what is great or beautiful, and makes it afford the mind a double entertainment.'—*Spectator*, No. 412.

This passage is deservedly praised by the critic, for its " perspicuity, grace, and harmony ;" but, in using different relatives under like circumstances, the writer has hardly done justice to his own good taste. Blair's remark is this : " His frequent use of *that*, instead of *which*, is another peculiarity of his style; but, on this occasion in particular, [it] cannot be much commended, as, ' It is this *which*,' seems, in every view, to be better than, ' It is this *that*,' three times repeated."—*Lect.* xxi, p. 207. What is here meant by "*every view*," may, I suppose, be seen in the corresponding criticism which is noticed in my last observation above; and I am greatly deceived, if, in this instance also, the relative *that* is not better than *which*, and more agreeable to polite usage. The direct relative which corresponds to the introductory pronoun *it* and *an other antecedent*, should, I think, be *that*, and not *who* or *which* : as, " It is not ye *that* speak."—*Matt.* x, 20. "It is thou, Lord, *who* hast the hearts of all men in thy hands, *that* turnest the hearts of any to show me favour."—*Jenks's Prayers*, p. 278. Here *who* has reference to *thou* or *Lord* only; but *that* has some respect to the pronoun *it*, though it agrees in person and gender with *thou*. A similar example is cited at the close of the preceding observation; and I submit it to the reader, whether the word *that*, as it there occurs, is not the *only fit word* for the place it occupies. So in the following examples : "There are *Words*, *which* are *not Verbs*, *that* signify actions and passions, and even things transient."—*Brightland's Gram.* p. 100. "It is the universal taste of mankind, *which* is subject to no such changing modes, *that* alone is entitled to possess any authority."—*Blair's Rhetoric*, p. 286.

OBS. 34.—Sometimes the broad import of an antecedent is *doubly restricted*, first by one relative clause, and then by an other; as, "And all *that dwell upon the earth*, shall worship him, *whose names are not written in the book of life*."—*Rev.* xiii, 8. "And then, like true Thames-Watermen, they abuse every man *that* passes by, *who* is better dressed than themselves."—*Brown's Estimate*, Vol. ii, p. 10. Here *and*, or *if he*, would be as good as " *who* ; " for the connective only serves to carry the restriction into narrower limits. Sometimes the limit fixed by one clause, is *extended* by an other; as, " There is no evil *that you may suffer*, or *that you may expect to suffer*, *which* prayer is not the appointed means to alleviate."—*Bickersteth, on Prayer*, p. 16 Here *which* resumes the idea of " *evil*," in the extent last determined ; or rather, in that which is fixed by either clause, since the limits of both are embraced in the assertion. And, in the two limiting clauses, the same pronoun was requisite, on account of their joint relation ; but the clause which assumes a different relation, is rightly introduced by a different pronoun. This is also the case in the following examples: "For there is no condemnation to those *that* are in Christ Jesus, *who* walk not after the flesh, but after the Spirit."—*Barclay's Works*, Vol. i, p. 432. " I will tell thee the mystery of the woman, and of the beast *that* carrieth her, *which* hath the seven heads and ten horns "—*Rev.* xvii, 7. Here the restrictive sense is well expressed by one relative, and the resumptive by an other. When neither of these senses is intended by the writer, *any* form of the relative must needs be improper: as, " The greatest genius *which runs* through the arts and sciences, takes a kind of tincture from them, and falls unavoidably into imitation."—*Addison, Spect.* No. 160. Here, as I suppose, *which runs* should be *in running*. What else can the author have meant?

OBS. 35.—Having now, as I imagine, clearly shown the difference between the restrictive and the resumptive sense of a relative pronoun, and the absolute necessity of making such a choice of words as will express that sense only which we intend; I hope the learner will see, by these observations, not merely that clearness requires the occasional use of each of our five relatives, *who*, *which*, *what*, *that*, and *as*; but that this distinction in the meaning, is a very common principle by which to determine what is, and what is not, good English. Thus *that* and *as* are appropriately our *restrictive* relatives, though *who* and *which* are sometimes used restrictively; but, in a *resumptive* sense, *who* or *which* is required, and required even after those terms which usually demand *that* or *as* : thus, " We are vexed at the unlucky chance, and go away dissatisfied. *Such* impressions, *which* ought not to be cherished, are a sufficient reason for excluding stories of that kind from the theatre."—*Kames, El. of Crit.* ii, 279. Here *which* is proper to the sense intended ; but *such* requires *as*, when the latter term limits the meaning of the former. In sentences like the following, *who* or *which* may be used in lieu of *that* ; whether with any advantage or not, the reader may judge : " You seize the critical moment *that* is favourable to emotion."—*Blair's Rhet.* p. 321. "*An* historian *that* would instruct us, must know when to be concise."—*Ib.* p. 359. " Seneca has been censured for the affectation *that* appears in his style."—*Ib.* p. 367. " Such as the prodigies *that* attended the death of Julius Cæsar."—*Ib.* p. 401. " By unfolding those principles *that* ought to govern the taste of every individual."—*Kames's Dedication to El. of Crit.* " But I am sure he has that *that* is better than an estate."—*Spect.* No. 475. " There are two properties, *that* characterize and essentially distinguish relative pronouns."—*Churchill's Gram.* p. 74. By these examples, it may be seen, that Dr. Blair often forgot or disregarded his own doctrine respecting the use of this relative ; though he was oftener led, by the error of that doctrine, to substitute *which* for *that* improperly.

OBS. 36.—*Whether* was formerly used as an interrogative pronoun, in which sense it always referred to one of two things ; as, "Ye fools and blind! for *whether* is greater, the gold, or the temple that sanctifieth the gold ?"—*Matt.* xxiii, 17. This usage is now obsolete; and, in stead of it, we say, "*Which* is greater ?" But as a disjunctive conjunction, corresponding to *or*, the word *whether* is still in good repute ; as, " Resolve *whether* you will go or not."—*Webster's Dict.* In this sense of the term, some choose to call *whether* an *adverb*.

OBS. 37.—In the view of some writers, interrogative pronouns differ from relatives chiefly in this ; that, as the subject referred to is unknown to the speaker, they do not relate to a *preceding* noun, but to something which is to be expressed in the answer to the question. It is certain that their *person*, *number*, and *gender*, are not regulated by an antecedent noun ; but by what the speaker supposes or knows of a subject which may, or may not, agree with them in these respects : as, "*What* lies there ?" Answer, " Two *men* asleep." Here *what*, standing for *what thing*, is of the third person, singular number, and neuter gender;. but *men*, which is the term that answers to it, is of the third person, plural, masculine. There is therefore no necessary agreement between the question and the answer, in any of those properties in which a pronoun usually agrees with its noun. Yet some grammarians will have interrogatives to agree with these " *subsequents*," as relatives agree with their *antecedents*. The answer, it must be granted, commonly contains a noun, corresponding in some respects to the interrogative pronoun, and agreeing with it *in case;* but this noun cannot be supposed to control the interrogation, nor is it, in any sense, the word for which the pronoun stands. For every pronoun must needs stand for something that is uttered or conceived by the same speaker; nor can any question be answered, until its meaning is understood. Interrogative pronouns must therefore be explained as direct substitutes for such other terms as one might use in stead of them. Thus *who* means *what person?*

"*Who* taught that heav'n-directed spire to rise?
The Man of Ross, each lisping babe replies."—*Pope.*

OBS. 38.—In the classification of the pronouns, and indeed in the whole treatment of them, almost all our English grammars are miserably faulty, and greatly at variance. In some forty or fifty, which I have examined on this point, the few words which constitute this part of speech, have more than twenty different modes of distribution. (1.) Cardell says, "There is but one kind of pronouns."—*Elements of Gram.* p. 30. (2.) D. Adams, Greenleaf, Nutting, and Weld, will have two kinds; "*personal* and *relative.*" (3.) Dr. Webster's "Substitutes, or pronouns, are of two kinds:" the one, "called *personal;*" the other, without name or number. See *Improved Gram.* p. 24. (4.) Many have fixed upon three sorts; "*personal, relative,* and *adjective;*" with a subdivision of the last. Of these is Lindley Murray, in his late editions, with his amenders, Ainsworth, Alger, Bacon, Bullions, Fisk, A. Flint, Frost, Guy, Hall, Kirkham, Lennie, Merchant, Picket, Pond, and S. Putnam. (5.) Kirkham, however, changes the order of the classes; thus, "*personal, adjective,* and *relative;*" and, with ridiculous absurdity, makes *mine, thine, hers, ours, yours,* and *theirs* to be "*compounds.*" (6.) Churchill adopts the plan of "*personal, relative,* and *adjective* pronouns;" and then destroys it by a valid argument. (7.) Comly, Wilcox, Wells, and Perley, have these three classes; "*personal, relative,* and *interrogative:*" and this division is right. (8.) Sanborn makes the following bull: "The *general* divisions of pronouns are *into personal, relative, interrogative,* and *several sub-divisions.*"—*Analytical Gram.* p. 91. (9.) Jaudon has these three kinds; "*personal, relative,* and *distributive.*" (10.) Robbins, these; "*simple, conjunctive,* and *interrogative.*" (11.) Lindley Murray, in his early editions, had these four; *personal, possessive, relative,* and *adjective.*" (12.) Bucke has these; "*personal, relative, interrogative,* and *adjective.*" (13.) Ingersoll, these; "*personal, adjective, relative,* and *interrogative.*" (14.) Buchanan; "*personal, demonstrative, relative,* and *interrogative.*" (15.) Coar; "*personal, possessive* or *pronominal adjectives, demonstrative,* and *relative.*" (16.) Bicknell; "*personal, possessive, relative,* and *demonstrative.*" (17.) Cobbett; "*personal, relative, demonstrative,* and *indefinite.*" (18.) M'Culloch; "*personal, possessive, relative,* and *reciprocal.*" (19.) Staniford has five; "*personal, relative, interrogative, definitive,* and *distributive.*" (20.) Alexander, six; "*personal, relative, demonstrative, interrogative, definitive,* and *adjective.*" (21.) Cooper, in 1828, had five; "*personal, relative, possessive, definite,* and *indefinite.*" (22.) Cooper, in 1831, six; "*personal, relative, definite, indefinite, possessive,* and *possessive pronominal adjectives.*" (23.) Dr. Crombie says: "Pronouns may be divided into *Substantive,* and *Adjective; Personal,* and *Impersonal; Relative,* and *Interrogative.*" (24.) Alden has seven sorts; "*personal, possessive, relative, interrogative, distributive, demonstrative,* and *indefinite.*" (25.) Smith has many kinds, and treats them so badly that nobody can count them. In respect to definitions, too, most of these writers are shamefully inaccurate, or deficient. Hence the filling up of their classes is often as bad as the arrangement. For instance, four and twenty of them will have interrogative pronouns to be relatives; but who that knows what a relative pronoun is, can coincide with them in opinion? Dr. Crombie thinks, "that interrogatives are strictly relatives;" and yet divides the two classes with his own hand!

MODIFICATIONS.

Pronouns have the same modifications as nouns; namely, *Persons, Numbers, Genders,* and *Cases.* Definitions universally applicable have already been given of all these things; it is therefore unnecessary to define them again in this place.

OBSERVATIONS.

OBS. 1.—In the personal pronouns, most of these properties are distinguished by the words themselves; in the relative and the interrogative pronouns, they are ascertained chiefly by means of the antecedent and the verb. Interrogative pronouns, however, as-well-as the relatives *which, what, as,* and all the compounds of *who, which,* and *what,* are always of the third person. Even in etymological parsing, some regard must be had to the syntactical relations of words. By *modifications,* we commonly mean actual changes in the forms of words, by which their grammatical properties are inherently distinguished; but, in all languages, the distinguishable properties of words are somewhat more numerous than their actual variations of form; there being certain principles of universal grammar, which cause the person, number, gender, or case, of some words, to be inferred from their relation to others; or, what is nearly the same thing, from the sense which is conveyed by the sentence. Hence, if in a particular instance it happen, that some, or even all, of these properties, are without any index in the form of the pronoun itself, they are still to be ascribed in parsing, because they may be easily and certainly discovered from the construction. For example: in the following text, it is just as easy to discern the *genders* of the pronouns, as the *cases* of the nouns; and both are known and asserted to be what they are, upon principles of mere inference: "For what knowest *thou,* O *wife,* whether *thou* shalt save *thy husband?* or how knowest *thou,* O *man,* whether *thou* shalt save *thy wife?*"—1 *Cor.* vii, 16. Again: "*Who* betrayed *her* companion? Not *I.*"—*Murray's Key,* p 211. Here *her* being of the feminine gender, it is the inference of every reader, that *who* and *I* are so too; but whether the word *companion* is masculine or feminine, is not so obvious.

OBS. 2.—The personal pronouns of the first and second persons, are equally applicable to both sexes; and should be considered masculine or feminine, according to the known application of them. [See *Levizac's French Gram.* p. 73.] The speaker and the hearer, being present to each other, of course know the sex to which they respectively belong; and, whenever they appear in narrative or dialogue, we are told who they are. In *Latin,* an adjective or a participle relating to these pronouns, is varied *to agree* with them in *number, gender,* and *case.* This is a sufficient proof, that *ego, I,* and *tu, thou,* are not destitute of gender, though neither the Latin words nor the English are themselves varied to express it:—

> " *Miseræ* hoc tamen unum
> Exequere, Anna, *mihi: solam* nam perfidus ille
> *Te* colere, arcanos etiam tibi credere sensus;
> *Sola* viri molles aditus et tempora nôras."—*Virgil.*

OBS. 3.—Many English grammarians, and Murray at their head, deny the first person of nouns, and the gender of pronouns of the first and second persons; and at the same time teach, that, "Pronouns must always agree with their antecedents, *and* the nouns for which they stand, in *gender, number,* and *person*." (*Murray's Gr.* 2d *Ed.* p. 111; *Rev. T. Smith's,* p. 60:) and further, with redundance of expression, that, "The relative is of the same person *with* the antecedent, and the verb agrees with it accordingly."—*Same.* These quotations form Murray's fifth rule of syntax, as it stands in his early editions.* In some of his revisings, the author erased the word *person* from the former sentence, and changed *with* to *as* in the latter. But other pronouns than relatives, agree with their nouns in person; so that his first alteration was not for the better, though Ingersoll, Kirkham, Alger, Bacon, J. Greenleaf, and some others, have been very careful to follow him in it. And why did he never discern, that the above-named principles of his etymology are both of them contradicted by this rule of his syntax, and one of them by his rule as it now stands? It is manifest, that no two words can possibly *agree* in any property which belongs not to both. Else what *is* agreement? Nay, no two things in nature, can in any wise agree, accord, or be alike, but by having some quality or accident in common. How strange a contradiction then is this! And what a compliment to learning, that it is still found in well-nigh all our grammars!

OBS. 4.—If there were truth in what Murray and others affirm, that "Gender has respect only to the third person singular of the pronouns, *he, she, it,*"† no two words could ever agree in gender; because there can be no such agreement between any two of the words here mentioned, and the assertion is, that gender has respect to no others. But, admitting that neither the author nor the numerous copiers of this false sentence ever meant to deny that gender has respect to *nouns,* they do deny that it has respect to any other *pronouns* than these; whereas I affirm that it ought to be recognised as a property of *all* pronouns, as well as of all nouns. Not that the gender of either is in all instances invariably fixed by the *forms* of the particular words; but there is in general, if not in every possible case, some principle of grammar, on which the gender of any noun or pronoun in a sentence may be readily ascertained. Is it not plain, that if we know who speaks or writes, who hears or is addressed, we know also the gender of the pronouns which are applied to these persons? The poet of The Task looked upon his mother's picture, and expressed his tender recollections of a deceased parent by way of *address;* and will any one pretend, that the pronouns which he applied to himself and to her, are either of the same gender, or of no gender? If we take neither of these assumptions, must we not say, they are of different genders? In this instance, then, let the parser call those of the first person, masculine; and those of the second, feminine:—

> " *My* mother! when *I* learned that *thou* wast dead,
> Say, wast *thou* conscious of the tears *I* shed?"—*Cowper.*

OBS. 5.—That the pronouns of the first and second persons are sometimes masculine and sometimes feminine, is perfectly certain; but whether they can or cannot be neuter, is a question difficult to be decided. To things inanimate they are only applied *figuratively;* and the question is, whether the figure always necessarily changes the gender of the antecedent noun. We assume the general principle, that the noun and its pronoun are always of the same gender; and we know that when inanimate objects are personified in the third person, they are usually represented as masculine or feminine, the gender being changed by the figure. But when a lifeless object is spoken to in the second person, or represented as speaking in the first, as the pronouns here employed are in themselves without distinction of gender, no such change can be proved by the mere words; and, if we allow that it would be needless to *imagine* it where the words do not prove it, the gender of these pronouns must in such cases be neuter, because we have no ground to think it otherwise. Examples: "And Jesus answered and said unto *it,* [the barren *figtree,*] No man eat fruit of *thee* hereafter forever."—*Mark,* xi, 14. "O *earth,* cover not *thou* my blood."— *Job,* xvi, 18. "O *thou sword* of the Lord, how long will it be *thou* be quiet?"—*Jeremiah,* xlvii, 6. In these instances, the objects addressed do not appear to be figuratively invested with the attribute of sex. So likewise with respect to the first person. If, in the following example, *gold* and *diamond* are neuter, so is the pronoun *me;* and, if not neuter, of what gender are they? The personification indicates no other.

> " Where thy true treasure? Gold says, 'Not in *me;*'
> And, 'Not in *me,*' the diamond. Gold is poor."—*Young.*

* The latter part of this awkward and complex rule was copied from Lowth's Grammar, p. 101. Dr. Ash's rule is, " *Pronouns* must always *agree* with the *nouns* for which they *refer,* in *Number, person,* and *gender*."—*Grammatical Institutes,* p 54. I quote this *exactly as it stands* in the book: the Italics are his, not mine. Roswell C. Smith appears to be ignorant of the change which Murray made in his fifth rule; for he still publishes as Murray's a principle of concord which the latter rejected as early as 1806: "RULE V. Corresponding with Murray's Grammar, RULE V. *Pronouns must agree with the nouns for which they stand, in gender, number,* AND PERSON."—*Smith's New Gram* p. 130. So *Allen Fisk,* in his "Murray's English Grammar Simplified," p. 111; *Aaron M. Merchant,* in his "*Abridgment* of Murray's English Grammar, Revised, *Enlarged* and *Improved,*" p. 79; and *the Rev. J. G. Cooper,* in his "Abridgment of Murray's English Grammar," p. 113; where, from the titles, every reader would expect to find the latest doctrines of Murray, and not what he had so long ago renounced or changed.

† L. Murray's Gram. 8vo, p. 51; 12mo, 51; 18mo, 22; D. Adams's, 37; Alger's, 21; Bacon's, 19; Fisk's, 20; Kirkham's, 97; Merchant's Murray, 85; Merchant's American Gram. 40; T. H. Miller's Gram. 26; Pond's, 26; S. Putnam's, 22; Russell's, 16; Rev. T. Smith's, 22.

THE DECLENSION OF PRONOUNS.

The declension of a pronoun is a regular arrangement of its numbers and cases.

I. SIMPLE PERSONALS.

The simple personal pronouns are thus declined :—

I, *of the* FIRST PERSON, *any of the genders.**

Sing.	Nom.	I,	Plur.	Nom.	we,
	Poss.	my, *or* mine,†		Poss.	our, *or* ours,
	Obj.	me ;		Obj.	us.

THOU, *of the* SECOND PERSON, *any of the genders.*

Sing.	Nom.	thou,‡	Plur.	Nom.	ye, *or* you,
	Poss.	thy, *or* thine,		Poss.	your, *or* yours,
	Obj.	thee ;		Obj.	you, *or* ye.§

HE, *of the* THIRD PERSON, *masculine gender.*

Sing.	Nom.	he,	Plur.	Nom.	they,
	Poss.	his,		Poss.	their, *or* theirs,
	Obj.	him ;		Obj.	them.

SHE, *of the* THIRD PERSON, *feminine gender.*

Sing.	Nom.	she,	Plur.	Nom.	they,
	Poss.	her, *or* hers,		Poss.	their, *or* theirs,
	Obj.	her ;		Obj.	them.

IT, *of the* THIRD PERSON, *neuter gender.*

Sing.	Nom.	it,	Plur.	Nom.	they,
	Poss.	its,		Poss.	their, *or* theirs,
	Obj.	it ;		Obj.	them.

II. COMPOUND PERSONALS.

The word *self*, added to the simple personal pronouns, forms the class of *compound personal pronouns ;* which are used when an action reverts upon the agent, and also when some persons are to be distinguished from others : as, sing. *myself*, plur. *ourselves ;* sing. *thyself*, plur. *yourselves ;* sing. *himself*, plur. *themselves ;* sing. *herself*, plur. *themselves ;* sing. *itself*, plur. *themselves.* They all want the possessive case, and are alike in the nominative and objective. Thus :—

MYSELF, *of the* FIRST PERSON,‖ *any of the genders.*

Sing.	Nom.	myself,	Plur.	Nom.	ourselves,
	Poss.	——,		Poss.	——,
	Obj.	myself ;		Obj.	ourselves.

* Dr. Crombie, and some others, represent *I* and *thou*, with their inflections, as being "*masculine and feminine*." Lennie, M'Culloch, and others, represent them as being "masculine *or* feminine." But, if either of them can have an antecedent that is *neuter*, neither of these views is strictly correct. (See *Obs.* 5th, above.) Mackintosh says, "We use *our, your, their*, in speaking of a thing or things belonging to plural nouns of *any gender*."—*Essay on English Gram.* p. 149.

† "It is perfectly plain, then, that *my* and *mine* are but different forms of the same word, as are *a* and *an*. *Mine*, for the sake of euphony, or from custom, stands for the possessive case without a noun ; but must be changed for *my* when the noun is expressed : and *my*, for a similar reason, stands before a noun, but must be changed for *mine* when the noun is dropped. * * * *Mine* and *my, thine* and *thy*, will, therefore, be considered in this book, as different forms of the possessive case from *I* and *Thou.* And the same rule will be extended to *her* and *hers, our* and *ours, your* and *yours, their* and *theirs* "—*Barnard's Analytic Grammar*, p 142.

‡ It has long been fashionable, in the ordinary intercourse of the world, to substitute the plural form of this pronoun for the singular through all the cases. Thus, by the figure ENALLAGE, "*you are*," for instance, is commonly put for "*thou art*." See Observations 20th and 21st, below ; also Figures of Syntax, in Part IV.

§ The original nominative was *ye*, which is still the only nominative of the solemn style ; and the original objective was *you*, which is still the only objective that our grammarians in general acknowledge. But, whether grammatical or not, *ye* is now very often used, in a familiar way, for the objective case (See Observations 22d and 23d, upon the declensions of pronouns.) T. Dilworth gave both cases alike : "*Nom.* Ye *or* you," "*Acc.* [or *Obj.*] Ye *or* you."—His *New Guide*, p. 98. Dr. Campbell says, "I am inclined to prefer that use which makes *ye* invariably the nominative plural of the personal pronoun *thou*, and *you* the accusative, when applied to an actual plurality."—*Philosophy of Rhetoric*, p. 174. No grammarian, however, discards *you* as a nominative of "actual plurality ;" and the present casual practice of putting *ye* in the objective, has prevailed to some extent for at least two centuries : as,
　　　　"Your change approaches, when all these delights
　　　　　　Will vanish and deliver *ye* to woe."—*Milton*, P. L., B. iv, l. 367.

‖ Dr. Young has, in one instance, and with very doubtful propriety, converted this pronoun into the *second person*, by addressing himself thus :—
　　　　"O *thou, myself!* abroad our counsels roam
　　　　And, like ill husbands, take no care at home."—*Love of Fame* Sat. II, l. 271.

THYSELF, *of the* SECOND PERSON, *any of the genders.*

Sing.			Plur.		
Nom.	thyself, *		Nom.	yourselves,	
Poss.	——,		Poss.	————,	
Obj.	thyself;		Obj.	yourselves.	

HIMSELF, *of the* THIRD PERSON, *masculine gender.*

Sing.			Plur.		
Nom.	himself,		Nom.	themselves,	
Poss.	——,		Poss.	————,	
Obj.	himself;		Obj.	themselves.	

HERSELF, *of the* THIRD PERSON, *feminine gender.*

Sing.			Plur.		
Nom.	herself,		Nom.	themselves,	
Poss.	——,		Poss.	————,	
Obj.	herself;		Obj.	themselves.	

ITSELF, *of the* THIRD PERSON, *neuter gender.*

Sing.			Plur.		
Nom.	itself,		Nom.	themselves,	
Poss.	——,		Poss.	————,	
Obj.	itself;		Obj.	themselves.	

III. RELATIVES AND INTERROGATIVES.

The relative and the interrogative pronouns are thus declined :—

WHO, *literally applied to persons only.*

Sing.		Plur.	
Nom.	who,	Nom.	who,
Poss.	whose,	Poss.	whose,
Obj.	whom;	Obj.	whom.

WHICH, *applied to animals and things.*

Sing.		Plur.	
Nom.	which,	Nom.	which,
Poss.	†——,	Poss.	——,
Obj.	which;	Obj.	which.

WHAT, *applied ordinarily to things only.‡*

Sing.		Plur.	
Nom.	what,	Nom.	what,
Poss.	——,	Poss.	——,
Obj.	what;	Obj.	what.

* The fashion of using the plural number for the singular, or *you* for *thou*, has also substituted *yourself* for *thyself*, in common discourse. In poetry, in prayer, in Scripture, and in the familiar language of the Friends, the original compound is still retained; but the poets use either term, according to the gravity or the lightness of their style. But *yourself*, like the regal compound *ourself*, though apparently of the singular number, and always applied to one person only, is, in its very nature, an anomalous and ungrammatical word; for it can neither mean more than one, nor agree with a pronoun or a verb that is singular. Swift indeed wrote : " Conversation is but carving ; carve for all, *yourself is starving.*" But he wrote erroneously, and his meaning is doubtful : probably he meant, "To carve for all, is, to *starve yourself.*" The compound personals, when they are nominatives before the verb, are commonly associated with the simple; as, "*I myself* also *am* a man."—*Acts.* x, 16. "That *thou thyself art* a guide."—*Rom.* ii, 19. "If it stand, as *you yourself* still *do.*"—*Shakspeare.* "That *you yourself are much* condemned."—*Id.* And, if the simple pronoun be omitted, the compound still requires the same form of the verb; as, "Which way I fly is Hell; *myself am* Hell."—*Milton.* The following example is different: "I love mankind; and in a monarchy myself *is* all that I can love."—*Life of Schiller, Follen's Pref* p. x. Dr. Follen objects to the British version, " Myself *were* all that I could love ;" and, if his own is good English, the verb *is* agrees with *all*, and not with *myself*. *Is* is of the third person: hence, "*myself is*," or, "*yourself is*," cannot be good syntax ; nor does any one say, "*yourself art*," or, "*ourself am*," but rather, "*yourself are*;" as, "Captain, *yourself are* the fittest "—*Dryden.* But to call this a "concord," is to turn a third part of the language upside-down; because, by analogy, it confounds, to such extent at least, the plural number with the singular through all our verbs : that is, if *ourself* and *yourself* are singulars, and not rather plurals put for singulars by a figure of syntax. But the words are, in some few instances, written separately : and then both the meaning and the construction are different: as, "Your *self is* sacred, profane *it* not."—*The Dial*, Vol. i, p. 86. Perhaps the word *myself* above ought rather to have been two words ; thus, "And, in a monarchy, *my self is all* that I can love." The two words here differ in person and case, perhaps also in gender ; and, in the preceding instance, they differ in person, number, gender, and case. But the compound always follows the person, number, and gender of its first part, and only the case of its last. The notion of some grammarians, (to wit, of Wells, and the sixty-eight others whom he cites for it,) that *you* and *your* are made singular by usage, is demonstrably untrue. Do *we, our,* and *us*, become actually singular, as often as a king or a critic applies them to himself? No; for nothing can be worse syntax than, *we am, we was,* or *you was*, though some contend for this last construction.

† *Whose* is sometimes used as the possessive case of *which*; as, "A religion *whose* origin is divine."—*Blair.* See Observations 4th and 5th. on the Classes of Pronouns.

‡ After *but*, as in the following sentence, the double relative *what* is sometimes applied to persons; and it is here equivalent to *the friend who* :—

> " Lorenzo, pride repress ; nor hope to find
> A friend, but *what* has found a friend in thee."— *Young.*

THAT, *applied to persons, animals, and things.*

Sing.	Nom.	that,	Plur.	Nom.	that,
	Poss.	——,		Poss.	——,
	Obj.	that ;		Obj.	that.

AS, *applied to persons, animals, and things.*

Sing.	Nom.	as,	Plur.	Nom.	as,
	Poss.	—,		Poss.	—,
	Obj.	as ;		Obj.	as.

IV. COMPOUND RELATIVES.

The compound relative pronouns, *whoever* or *whosoever, whichever* or *whichsoever,* and *whatever* or *whatsoever,*[*] are declined in the same manner as the simples, *who, which, what.* Thus :—

WHOEVER or WHOSOEVER, *applied only to persons.*

Sing.	Nom.	whoever,	Plur.	Nom.	whoever,
	Poss.	whosever,		Poss.	whosever,
	Obj.	whomever ;		Obj.	whomever.
Sing.	Nom.	whosoever,	Plur.	Nom.	whosoever,
	Poss.	whosesoever,		Poss.	whosesoever,
	Obj.	whomsoever ;		Obj.	whomsoever.

WHICHEVER or WHICHSOEVER, *applied to persons, animals, and things.*

Sing.	Nom.	whichever,	Plur.	Nom.	whichever,
	Poss.	————,		Poss.	————,
	Obj.	whichever ;		Obj.	whichever.
Sing.	Nom.	whichsoever,	Plur.	Nom.	whichsoever,
	Poss.	————,		Poss.	————,
	Obj.	whichsoever ;		Obj.	whichsoever.

WHATEVER or WHATSOEVER, *applied ordinarily to things only.*

Sing.	Nom.	whatever,	Plur.	Nom.	whatever,
	Poss.	————,		Poss.	————,
	Obj.	whatever ;		Obj.	whatever.
Sing.	Nom.	whatsoever,	Plur.	Nom.	whatsoever,
	Poss.	————,		Poss.	————,
	Obj.	whatsoever ;		Obj.	whatsoever.

OBSERVATIONS.

OBS. 1.—Most of the personal pronouns have two forms of the possessive case, in each number : as, *my* or *mine, our* or *ours; thy* or *thine, your* or *yours; her* or *hers, their* or *theirs.* The former is used before a noun expressed, or when nothing but an adjective intervenes; the latter, when the governing noun is understood, or is so placed that a repetition of it is implied in or after the pronoun : as, " *My* powers are *thine;* be *thine* alone The glory of my song."—*Montgomery.* " State what *mine* and *your* principles are."—*Legh Richmond, to his Daughters.* Better, perhaps : " State what *my* principles and *yours* are ; "—" State what *your* principles and *mine* are ; "—or, " State what are *my* principles and *your own.*"
> " Resign'd he fell ; superior to the dart
> That quench'd its rage in *yours* and *Britain's* heart."—*J. Brown.*
> " Behold ! to *yours* and *my* surprise,
> These trifles to a volume rise."—*Lloyd,* p. 186.

OBS. 2.—Possibly, when the same persons or things stand in a joint relation of this kind to different individuals or parties, it may be proper to connect two of the simple possessives to express it ; though this construction can seldom, if ever, be necessary, because any such

---

[*] Of all these compounds, L. Murray very improperly says, " They are *seldom used* in modern style."—*Octavo Gram.* p. 54; also *Fisk's,* p. 65. None of them are yet obsolete, though the shorter forms seem to be now generally preferred. The following suggestion of Cobbett's is erroneous ; because it implies that the shorter forms are innovations and faults ; and because the author carelessly speaks of them as one thing only : " We *sometimes* omit the *so,* and say, *whoever, whomever, whatever,* and even *whoever.* *It is a mere abbreviation.* The *so* is understood : and, it is best not to omit to write it."—*Eng. Gram.* ¶ 209. R. C. Smith dismisses the compound relatives with three lines ; and these he closes with the following notion : " *They are not often used !*"—*New Gram.* p 61.

expression as *thy and her sister*, *my and his duty*, if not erroneous, can mean nothing but *your sister, our duty*, &c. But some examples occur, the propriety of which it is worth while to consider: as, "I am sure it will be a pleasure to you to hear that she proves worthy of her father, worthy of you, and of *your and her* ancestors."—*Spectator*, No. 525. This sentence is from a version of Pliny's letter to his wife's aunt; and, as the ancestors of the two individuals are here the same, the phraseology may be allowable. But had the aunt commended her niece to Pliny, she should have said, "worthy of you, and of *your* ancestors and , *hers*." "Is it *her* or *his* honour that is tarnished? It is not *hers*, but *his*."—*Murray's Gram.* p. 175. This question I take to be bad English. It ought to be, "Is it *her* honour, or *his*, that is tarnished?" Her honour and his honour cannot be one and the same thing. This example was framed by Murray to illustrate that idle and puzzling distinction which he and some others make between "possessive adjective pronouns" and "the genitive case of the personal pronouns;" and, if I understand him, the author will here have *her* and *his* to be of the former class, and *hers* and *his* of the latter. It were a better use of time, to learn how to employ such words correctly. Unquestionably, they are of the same class and the same case, and would be every way equivalent, if the first form were fit to be used elliptically. For example: "The same phrensy had hindered the Dutch from improving to *their* *and* to the common advantage the public misfortunes of France."—*Bolingbroke, on Hist.* p. 309. Here the possessive case *their* appears to be governed by *advantage* understood, and therefore it would perhaps be better to say, *theirs*, or *their own*. But in the following instance, *our* may be proper, because both possessives appear to be governed by one and the same noun:—

"Although 'twas *our* and *their* opinion
Each other's church was but a Rimmon."—*Hudibras*.

OBS. 3.—*Mine* and *thine* were formerly preferred to *my* and *thy*, before all words beginning with a vowel sound; or rather, *mine* and *thine* were the original forms,* and *my* and *thy* were first substituted for them before consonants, and afterwards before vowels: as, "But it was thou, a man *mine* equal, *my* guide, and *mine* acquaintance."—*Psalms*, lv, 13. "*Thy* prayers and *thine* alms are come up for a memorial before God."—*Acts*, x, 4. When the Bible was translated, either form appears to have been used before the letter *h*; as, "Hath not *my hand* made all these things?"—*Acts*, vii, 50. "By stretching forth *thine hand* to heal."—*Acts*, iv, 30. According to present practice, *my* and *thy* are in general to be preferred before all nouns, without regard to the sounds of letters. The use of the other forms, in the manner here noticed, has now become obsolete; or, at least, antiquated, and peculiar to the poets. We occasionally meet with it in modern verse, though not very frequently, and only where the melody of the line seems to require it: as,

"Time writes no wrinkle on *thine* azure brow."—*Byron*.
"Deign on the passing world to turn *thine* eyes."—*Johnson*.
"*Mine* eyes beheld the messenger divine."—*Lusiad*.
"*Thine* ardent symphony sublime and high."—*Sir W. Scott*.

OBS. 4.—The possessives *mine, thine, hers, ours, yours, theirs*, usually denote possession, or the relation of property, with an *ellipsis* of the name of the thing possessed; as, "My sword and *yours* are kin."—*Shakspeare*. Here *yours* means *your sword*. "You may imagine what kind of faith *theirs* was."—*Bacon*. Here *theirs* means *their faith*. "He ran headlong into his own ruin whilst he endeavoured to precipitate *ours*."—*Bolingbroke*. Here *ours* means *our ruin*. "Every one that heareth these sayings of *mine*."—*Matt.* vii, 26. Here *mine* means *my sayings*. "Sing unto the Lord, O ye saints of *his*."—*Psalms*, xxx, 4. Here *his* means *his saints*. The noun which governs the possessive, is here *understood* after it, being inferred from that which precedes, as it is in all the foregoing instances. "And the man of *thine*, whom I shall not cut off from *mine* altar, shall be to consume *thine* eyes, and to grieve *thine* heart."—1 *Samuel*, ii, 33. Here *thine*, in the first phrase, means *thy men*; but, in the subsequent parts of the sentence, both *mine* and *thine* mean neither more nor less than *thy* and *my*, because there is no ellipsis. *Of* before the possessive case, governs the noun which is understood after this case; and is always taken in a *partitive* sense, and not as the sign of the possessive relation: as, "When we say, 'a soldier *of* the *king's*,' we mean, 'one *of* the king's *soldiers*.'"—*Webster's Improved Gram.* p. 29. There is therefore an ellipsis of the word *soldiers*, in the former phrase. So, in the following example, *mine* is used elliptically for *my feet*; or rather, *feet* is understood after *mine*, though *mine feet* is no longer good English, for reasons before stated:—

"Ere I absolve thee, stoop! that on thy neck
Levelled with earth this *foot of mine* may tread."—*Wordsworth*.

OBS. 5.—Respecting the *possessive case* of the simple personal pronouns, there appears among our grammarians a strange diversity of sentiment. Yet is there but one view of

* Sanborn, with strange ignorance of the history of these words, teaches thus: "*Mine* and *thine* appear to have been formed from *my* and *thy* by changing *y* into *i* and adding *n*, and then subjoining *e* to retain the long sound of the vowel"—*Analytical Gram.* p. 92. This false notion, as we learn from his guillemets and a remark in his preface, he borrowed from "Parkhurst's Systematic Introduction." Dr. Lowth says, "The Saxon *Ic* hath the possessive case *Min; Thu*, possessive *Thin; He*, possessive *His*: From which our possessive cases of the same pronouns are taken *without alteration*."—*Lowth's Gram.* p. 28.

the matter, that has in it either truth or reason, consistency or plausibility. And, in the opinion of any judicious teacher, an erroneous classification of words so common and so important as these, may well go far to condemn any system of grammar in which it is found. A pronoun agrees in person, number, and gender, with the noun *for which it is a substitute;* and, if it is in the possessive case, it is usually governed by *an other noun* expressed or implied after it. That is, if it denotes possession, it stands for the name of the possessor, and is governed by the name of the thing possessed. Now do not *my, thy, his, her, our, your, their,* and *mine, thine, hers, its, ours, yours, theirs,* all equally denote possession? and do they not severally show by their forms the person, the number, and sometimes also the gender, of whomever or whatever they make to be the possessor? If they do, they are all of them *pronouns,* and nothing else; all found in the *possessive case,* and nowhere else. It is true, that in Latin, Greek, and some other languages, there are not only genitive cases corresponding to these possessives, but also certain declinable adjectives which we render in English by these same words: that is, by *my* or *mine, our* or *ours; thy* or *thine, your* or *yours; &c.* But this circumstance affords no valid argument for considering any of these English terms to be mere adjectives; and, say what we will, it is plain that they have not the signification of adjectives, nor can we ascribe to them the construction of adjectives, without making their grammatical agreement to be what it very manifestly is not. They never agree, in any respect, with the nouns which *follow* them, unless it be by mere accident. This view of the matter is sustained by the authority of many of our English grammars; as may be seen by the declensions given by Ash, C. Adams, Ainsworth, Barnard, Buchanan, Bicknell, Blair, Burn, Butler, Comly, Churchill, Cobbett, Dalton, Davenport, Dearborn, Farnum, A. Flint, Fowler, Frost, Gilbert, Greenleaf, Hamlin, Hiley, Kirkham, Merchant, Murray the schoolmaster, Parkhurst, Picket, Russell, Sanborn, Sanders, R. C. Smith, Wilcox.

OBS. 6.—In opposition to the classification and doctrine adopted above, many of our grammarians teach, that *my, thy, his, her, our, your, their,* are adjectives or " adjective pronouns;" and that *mine, thine, hers, its, ours, yours, theirs,* are personal pronouns in the possessive case. Among the supporters of this notion, are D. Adams, Alden, Alger, Allen, Bacon, Barrett, Bingham, Bucke, Bullions, Cutler, Fisk, Frost, (in his small Grammar,) Guy, Hall, Hart, Harrison, Ingersoll, Jaudon, Lennie, Lowth, Miller, L. Murray, Pond, T. Smith, Spear, Staniford, Webber, Woodworth. The authority of all these names, however, amounts to little more than that of one man; for Murray pretended to follow Lowth, and nearly all the rest copied Murray. Dr. Lowth says, " *Thy, my, her, our, your, their,* are pronominal adjectives; but *his,* (that is, *he's,*) *her's, our's, your's, their's,* have evidently the form of the possessive case: And, by analogy, *mine, thine,* may be esteemed of the same rank."—*Lowth's Gram.* p. 23. But why did he not see, that by the same analogy, and also by the sense and meaning of the words, as well as by their distinctions of person, number, and gender, all the other six are entitled to " the same rank?" Are not the forms of *my, thy, her, our, your, their,* as fit to denote the relation of property, and to be called the possessive case, as *mine, thine, his,* or any others? In grammar, all needless distinctions are reprehensible. And where shall we find a more blamable one than this? It seems to have been based merely upon the false notion, that the possessive case of pronouns ought to be formed like that of nouns; whereas custom has clearly decided that they shall always be different: the former must never be written with an apostrophe; and the latter, never without it. Contrary to all good usage, however, the Doctor here writes " *her's, our's, your's, their's,*" each with a needless apostrophe. Perhaps he thought it would serve to strengthen his position; and help to refute what some affirmed, that *all* these words are adjectives.

OBS. 7.—Respecting *mine, thine,* and *his,* Lowth and L. Murray disagree. The latter will have them to be sometimes " *possessive pronouns,*" and sometimes " *possessive cases.*" An admirable distinction this for a great author to make! too slippery for even the inventor's own hold, and utterly unintelligible to those who do not know its history! In short, these authors disagree also concerning *my, thy, her, our, your, their;* and where two leaders of a party are at odds with each other, and each is in the wrong, what is to be expected from their followers? Perceiving that Lowth was wrong in calling these words " *pronominal adjectives,*" Murray changed the term to " *possessive pronouns,*" still retaining the class entire; and accordingly taught, in his early editions, that, " There are *four kinds* of pronouns, viz. the personal, *the possessive, the* relative, and *the* adjective pronouns."—*Murray's Gram.,* 2d Edition, p. 37. " The Possessive Pronouns are such as principally relate to possession or property. There are seven of them; viz. *my, thy, his, her, our, your, their.* The possessives *his, mine, thine,* may be accounted either *possessive pronouns,* or the *possessive cases* of their respective personal pronouns."—*Ib.* p. 40. He next idly demonstrates that these seven words may come before nouns of any number or case, without variation; then, forgetting his own distinction, adds, " When they are separated from the noun, all of them, except *his,* vary *their terminations;* as, this hat is *mine,* and the other is *thine;* those trinkets are *hers;* this house is *ours,* and that is *yours; theirs* is more commodious than *ours.*"—*Ib.* p. 40. Thus all his personal pronouns of the possessive case, he then made to be inflections of pronouns of *a different class!* What are they now? Seek the answer under the head of that gross solecism, "*Adjective Pronouns.*" You may find it in one half of our English grammars.

OBS. 8.—Any considerable error in the classing of words, does not stand alone; it naturally brings others in its train. Murray's " *Adjective Pronouns*," (which he now subdivides into four little classes, *possessive, distributive, demonstrative,* and *indefinite,*) being all of them misnamed and misplaced in his etymology, have led both him and many others into strange errors in syntax. The *possessives only* are "pronouns;" and these are pronouns of the possessive *case*. As such, they agree with the *antecedent* nouns for which they stand, in *person, number,* and *gender;* and are governed, like all other possessives, by the nouns which follow them. The rest are *not pronouns,* but pronominal *adjectives;* and, as such, they relate to nouns expressed or understood *after them.* Accordingly, they have none of the abovementioned qualities, except that the words *this* and *that* form the plurals *these* and *those.* Or, if we choose to ascribe to a pronominal adjective all the properties of the noun understood, it is merely for the sake of brevity in parsing. The difference, then, between a "pronominal adjective" and an "adjective pronoun" should seem to be this; that the one is *an adjective,* and the other *a pronoun:* it is like the difference between a *horserace* and a *racehorse.* What can be hoped from the grammarian who cannot discern it? And what can be made of rules and examples like the following? "Adjective *pronouns* must agree, in number, with *their substantives:* as, ' *This* book, *these* books; *that* sort, *those* sorts; *another* road, *other* roads.' "—*Murray's Gram.,* Rule viii, *Late Editions; Alger's Murray,* p. 66; *Alden's,* 85; *Bacon's,* 48; *Maltby's,* 59; *Miller's,* 66; *Merchant's,* 81; *S. Putnam's,* 70; *and others.* "Pronominal *adjectives* must agree with *their nouns* in gender, number, and person; thus, ' *My son,* hear the instructions of *thy* father.' ' Call the *labourers,* and give them *their* hire.' "—*Maunder's Gram.,* Rule xvii. Here Murray gives a rule for *pronouns,* and illustrates it by *adjectives;* and Maunder, as ingeniously blunders in reverse: he gives a rule for *adjectives,* and illustrates it by *pronouns.* But what do they mean by " *their substantives,*" or " *their nouns?*" As applicable to *pronouns,* the phrase should mean *nouns antecedent;* as applicable to *adjectives,* it should mean *nouns subsequent.* Both these rules are therefore false, and fit only to bewilder; and the examples to both are totally inapplicable. Murray's was once essentially right, but he afterwards corrupted it, and a multitude of his admirers have since copied the perversion. It formerly stood thus: "The pronominal adjectives *this* and *that,* &c. and the numbers* *one, two,* &c. must agree in number with their substantives: as, ' This book, these books; that sort, those sorts; one girl, ten girls; another road, other roads."—*Murray's Gram.,* Rule viii, 2d Ed., 1796.

OBS. 9.—Among our grammarians, some of considerable note have contended, that the personal pronouns have but *two cases,* the nominative and the objective. Of this class, may be reckoned Brightland, Dr. Johnson, Fisher, Mennye, Cardell, Cooper, Dr. Jas. P. Wilson, W. B. Fowle, and, according to his late grammars, Dr. Webster. But, in contriving what to make of *my* or *mine, our* or *ours, thy* or *thine, your* or *yours, his, her* or *hers, its,* and *their* or *theirs,* they are as far from any agreement, or even from self-consistency, as the cleverest of them could ever imagine. To the person, the number, the gender, and the case, of each of these words, they either profess themselves to be total strangers, or else prove themselves so, by the absurdities they teach. Brightland calls them " Possessive Qualities, or Qualities of Possession;" in which class he also embraces all *nouns* of the possessive case. Johnson calls them pronouns; and then says of them, "The possessive *pronouns,* like *other adjectives,* are without cases or change of termination."—*Gram.* p. 6. Fisher calls them " Personal Possessive Qualities;" admits the person and number of *my, our,* &c.; but supposes *mine, ours,* &c. to supply the place of *the nouns which govern them!* Mennye makes them one of his three classes of pronouns, " *personal, possessive,* and *relative;*" giving to both forms the rank which Murray once gave, and which Allen now gives, to the first form only. Cardell places them among his " defining adjectives." With Fowle, these, and all other possessives, are " possessive adjectives." Cooper, in his grammar of 1828, copies the last scheme of Murray: in that of 1831, he avers that the personal pronouns " want the possessive case." Now, like Webster and Wilson, he will have *mine, thine, hers, ours, yours,* and *theirs,* to be pronouns of the nominative or the objective case. Dividing the pronouns into six general classes, he makes these the fifth; calling them " Possessive Pronouns," but preferring in a note the monstrous name, " *Possessive Pronouns Substitute.*" His sixth class are what he calls, " The Possessive Pronominal *Adjectives;*" namely, " *my, thy, his, her, our, your, their, its, own,* and sometimes *mine* and *thine.*"—*Cooper's Pl. and Pr. Gram.* p. 43. But all these he has, unquestionably, either misplaced or misnamed; while he tells us, that, " Simplicity of arrangement should be the object of every compiler."—*Ib.* p. 33. Dr. Perley, (in whose scheme of grammar all the pronouns are *nouns,*) will have *my, thy, his, her, its, our, your,* and *their,* to be in the possessive case; but of *mine, thine, hers, ours, yours,* and *theirs,* he says, " These may be called *Desiderative Personal Pronouns.*"—*Perley's Gram.* p. 15.

OBS. 10.—Kirkham, though he professes to follow Murray, declines the simple personal pronouns as I have declined them; and argues admirably, that *my, thy, his,* &c., are pronouns of the possessive case, because, "They always *stand for nouns in the possessive case.*" But he afterwards palpably contradicts both himself and the common opinion of all former gram-

---

* This word should have been *numerals,* for two or three reasons. The author speaks of the *numeral adjectives;* and to say " the *numbers* must agree in *number* with their substantives," is tautological.—G. BROWN.

marians, in referring *mine, thine, hers,* &c., to the class of *"Compound Personal Pronouns."* Nay, as if to outdo even himself in absurdity, he first makes *mine, thine, hers, ours,* &c., to be compounds, by assuming that, "These *pluralizing adjuncts, n* and *s,* were, no doubt, formerly detached from the pronouns with which they now coalesce;" and then, because he finds in each of his supposed compounds the signification of a pronoun and its governing noun, reassumes, in parsing them, the very principle of error, on which he condemns their common classification. He says, "They should be parsed *as two words."* He also supposes them to represent the nouns *which govern them*—nouns with which they do not agree in any respect! Thus is he wrong in almost every thing he says about them. See *Kirkham's Gram.* p. 99, p. 101, and p. 104. Goodenow, too, a still later writer, adopts the major part of all this absurdity. He will have *my, thy, his, her, its, our, your, their,* for the possessive case of his personal pronouns; but *mine, thine, hers, ours, yours, theirs,* he calls *"compound possessive pronouns,* in the subjective or [the] objective case."—*Text-Book of E. Gram.* p. 33. Thus he introduces a new class, unknown to his primary division of the pronouns, and not included in his scheme of their declension. Fuller, too, in a grammar produced at Plymouth, Mass. in 1822, did nearly the same thing. He called *I, thou, he, she,* and *it,* with their plurals, *"antecedent* pronouns;" took *my, thy, his, her,* &c., for their *only* possessive forms in his declension; and, having passed from them by the space of just half his book, added: "Sometimes to prevent the repetition of the same word, an *antecedent pronoun in the possessive case,* is made to represent, both the pronoun and a noun; as, 'That book is *mine* '—i. e. ' *my book.*' MINE is a *compound antecedent pronoun,* and is equivalent to *my* book. Then parse *my,* and *book,* as though they were both expressed."—*Fuller's Gram.* p. 71.

OBS. 11.—Amidst all this diversity of doctrine at the very centre of grammar, who shall so fix its principles that our schoolmasters and schoolmistresses may know *what to believe and teach?* Not he that speculates without regard to other men's views; nor yet he that makes it a merit to follow implicitly "the footsteps of" *one only.* The true principles of grammar are with the learned; and that man is in the wrong, with whom the *most* learned will not, in general, coincide. Contradiction of falsities, is necessary to the maintenance of truth; correction of errors, to the success of science. But not every man's errors can be so considerable as to deserve correction from other hands than his own. Misinstruction in grammar has for this reason generally escaped censure. I do not wish any one to coincide with me merely through ignorance of what others inculcate. If doctors of divinity and doctors of laws will contradict themselves in teaching grammar, so far as they do so, the lovers of consistency will find it necessary to deviate from their track. Respecting these pronouns, I learned in childhood, from Webster, a doctrine which he now declares to be false. This was nearly the same as Lowth's, which is quoted in the sixth observation above. But, instead of correcting its faults, this zealous reformer has but run into others still greater. Now, with equal reproach to his etymology, his syntax, and his logic, he denies that our pronouns have any form of the possessive case at all. But grant the obvious fact, that *substitution* is one thing and *ellipsis* an other, and his whole argument is easily overthrown; for it is only by confounding these, that he reaches his absurd conclusion.

OBS. 12.—Dr. Webster's doctrine now is, that none of the English pronouns have more than two cases. He says, " *Mine, thine, his, hers, yours,* and *theirs,* are *usually considered as* [being of] the possessive case. But the *three first* are either attributes, and used with nouns, or they are substitutes. The *three last* are always substitutes, used in the place of names WHICH ARE UNDERSTOOD."—"That *mine, thine, his,* [*ours,*] *yours, hers,* and *theirs,* do not constitute a possessive case, is demonstrable; for they are constantly used as the nominatives to verbs and as the objectives after verbs and prepositions, as in the following passages. 'Whether it could perform its operations of thinking and memory out of a body organized as *ours is.*'—*Locke.* ' The reason is, that his subject is generally things; *theirs,* on the contrary, *is* persons.'—*Camp. Rhet.* ' Therefore leave your forest of beasts for *ours* of brutes, called men.'—*Wycherley to Pope.* It is needless to multiply proofs. We observe these *pretended possessives* uniformly used as nominatives or objectives.* Should it be said that *a*

---

* Cardell assails the common doctrine of the grammarians on this point, with similar assertions, and still more earnestness. See his *Essay on Language,* p. 89. The notion that " these *pretended possessives* [are] uniformly used as *nominatives or objectives*"—though demonstrably absurd, and confessedly repugnant to what is " *usually considered*" to be their true explanation—was adopted by Jaudon, in 1812; and has recently found several new advocates; among whom are Davis, Felch, Goodenow, Hazen, Smart, Weld, and Wells. There is, however, much diversity, as well as much inaccuracy, in their several expositions of the matter. Smart inserts in his declensions, as the only forms of the possessive case, the words of which he afterwards speaks thus: " The following *possessive cases* of the personal pronouns, (See page vii,) *must be called* PERSONAL PRONOUNS POSSESSIVE: *mine, thine, his, hers, ours, yours, theirs.* For these words are always used *substantively,* so as to include the meaning of some noun in the third person singular or plural, in the nominative or the objective case. Thus, if *we are speaking* of books, and say [,] ' *Mine* are here,' *mine* means *my books,* [☞] and it must be deemed a personal pronoun *possessive* in the *third* person *plural,* and *nominative* to the verb *are.*"—*Smart's Accidence,* p. xxii. If to say, these " *possessive cases* must be called a *class* of pronouns, used *substantively,* and deemed *nominatives or objectives,*" is not absurd, then nothing can be. Nor is any thing in grammar more certain, than that the pronoun " *mine* " can only be used by the speaker or writer, to denote himself or herself as the owner of something. It is therefore of the *first* person, *singular* number, *masculine* (or feminine) gender, and *possessive case;* being governed by the name of the thing or things possessed. This name is, of course, always *known;* and, if known and not expressed, it is " *understood.*" For sometimes a word is repeated to the mind, and clearly understood, where " it cannot properly be" expressed; as, " And he came and sought *fruit* thereon, and found *none.*"—*Luke,* xiii, 6. Wells opposes this doctrine, citing a

noun is understood; I reply, *this cannot be true,"* &c.—*Philosophical Gram.* p. 35; *Improved Gram.* p. 26. Now, whether it be true or not, this very position is expressly affirmed by the Doctor himself, in the citation above; though he is, unquestionably, wrong in suggesting that the pronouns are " used *in the place* of [those] names WHICH ARE UNDERSTOOD." They are used in the place of other names—the names of *the possessors;* and are governed by those which he here both admits and denies to be " understood."

OBS. 13.—The other arguments of Dr. Webster against the possessive case of pronouns, may perhaps be more easily answered than some readers imagine. The first is drawn from the fact that conjunctions connect like cases. " Besides, in three passages just quoted, the word *yours* is joined by a connective *to a name* in the same case; ' To ensure *yours* and *their immortality.'* ' The easiest part of *yours* and *my design.'* ' *My sword* and *yours* are kin.' Will any person pretend that the connective here joins different cases ?"—*Improved Gram.* p. 28; *Philosophical Gram.* p. 36. I answer, No. But it is falsely assumed that *yours* is here connected by *and* to *immortality,* to *design,* or to *sword;* because these words are again severally understood after *yours:* or, if otherwise, the two pronouns alone are connected by *and,* so that the proof is rather, that *their* and *my* are in the possessive case. The second argument is drawn from the use of the preposition *of* before the possessive. " For we say correctly, 'an acquaintance *of yours, ours,* or *theirs'—of* being the sign of the possessive; but if the words in themselves are possessives, then there must be two signs of the same case, which is absurd."—*Improved Gram.* p. 28; *Phil. Gr.* 36. I deny that *of* is here the sign of the possessive, and affirm that it is taken partitively, in all examples of this sort. " I know my sheep, and am known *of mine,"* is not of this kind; because *of* here means *by*—a sense in which the word is antiquated. In recurring afterwards to this argument, the Doctor misquotes the following texts, and avers that they " are evidently meant to include the *whole number:* ' Sing *to* the Lord, *all* ye saints *of his.'—Ps.* 30, 4. ' *He* that heareth these sayings *of mine.'—Matt. 7."—Improved Gram.* p. 29; *Phil. Gr.* 38. If he is right about the meaning, however, the passages are mistranslated, as well as misquoted : they ought to be, "Sing *unto* the Lord, O ye his *Saints."—" Every one* that heareth *these* my *sayings."* But when a definitive particle precedes the noun, it is very common with us, to introduce the possessive elliptically after it; and what Dr. Wilson means by suggesting that it is erroneous, I know not : " When the preposition *of* precedes *mine, ours, yours,* &c. the *errour* lies, not in this, that there are double possessive cases, but in forming an implication of a noun, which the substitute already denotes, together with the persons."—*Essay on Gram.* p. 110.

OBS. 14.—In his Syllabus of English Grammar, Dr. Wilson teaches thus : " *My, our, thy, your, his, her, its, their, whose,* and *whosoever* are possessive pronominal *adjectives.* *Ours, yours, hers,* and *theirs* are *pronoun substantives,* used either as subjects, or [as] objects; as singulars, or [as] plurals; and are substituted both for [the names of] the possessors, and [for those of the] things possessed. *His, its, whose, mine,* and *thine,* are sometimes used as *such substantives;* but also are at other times *pronominal possessive* adjectives."—*Wilson's Syllabus,* p. x. Now compare with these three positions, the following three from the same learned author. " In Hebrew, the *adjective* generally agrees with its noun in gender and number, but *pronouns* follow the gender of their antecedents, and not of the nouns with which they stand. So in English, *my, thy, his, her, its, our, your,* and *their,* agree with the nouns they represent, in number, gender, and person. But *adjectives,* having no change expressive of number, gender, or case, cannot accord with their nouns."—*Wilson's Essay on*

passage from Webster, as above, and also imitating his argument. This author acknowledges three classes of pronouns—" personal, relative, and interrogative ;" and then, excluding these words from their true place among personals of the possessive case, absurdly makes them a *supernumerary class of possessive nominatives or objectives;* " *Mine, thine, his, ours, yours,* and *theirs,* are POSSESSIVE PRONOUNS, used in construction either as *nominatives or objectives;* as. ' Your pleasures are past, *mine* are to come.' Here the word *mine,* which is used as a substitute for *my pleasures,* is the subject of the verb *are."—Wells's School Gram.* p. 71 ; 118 Ed. p. 78. Now the question to find the subject of the verb *are,* is, " My *what* are to come ?" Ans. " *pleasures.*" But the author proceeds to argue in a note thus : " *Mine, thine,* etc. are often parsed as pronouns in the possessive case, *and governed by nouns understood.* Thus, in the sentence, ' This book is mine,' the *word mine* is said to *possess book.* That the word *book* is *not here understood,* is obvious from the fact, that, when it is supplied, the phrase becomes not ' *mine* book,' but ' my book,' the pronoun being changed from *mine* to *my;* so that we are made, by this practice, to parse *mine* as *possessing a word* understood, before which it cannot properly be used. The word *mine* is here evidently employed as a substitute for the two words, *my* and *book."—Wells, ibid.* This note appears to me to be, in many respects, faulty. In the first place, its whole design was, to disprove what is true. For, barring the mere difference of *person,* the author's example above is equal to this : " Your pleasures are past, *W. H.* Wells's are to come." The ellipsis of " *pleasures,*" is evident in both. But *ellipsis* is not *substitution ;* no, nor is *equivalence. Mine,* when it suggests an ellipsis of the governing noun, is *equivalent* to *my and that noun;* but certainly, not " *a substitute for the two words.*" It is a substitute, or pronoun, for the *name of the speaker or writer;* and so is *my;* both forms representing, and always agreeing with, that name or person only. No possessive agrees with what governs it; but every pronoun ought to agree with that for which it stands. Secondly, if the note above cited does not aver, in its first sentence, that the pronouns in question *are* " *governed by nouns understood,*" it comes much nearer to saying this, than a writer should who mean to deny it. In the third place, the example, " This book is mine," is not a good one for its purpose. The word " *mine*" may be regularly parsed as a possessive, without supposing any ellipsis ; for " *book,*" the name of the thing possessed, is given, and in obvious connexion with it. And further, the matter affirmed is *ownership,* requiring *different cases ;* and not the *ownership* of something under different names, which must be put in the *same case.* In the fourth place, to mistake *regimen* for possession, and thence speak of *one word* " *as possessing*" an other, a mode of expression occurring twice in the foregoing note, is not only unscholarlike, but positively absurd. But, possibly, the author may have meant by it, so ridicule the choice phraseology of the following Rule : " A noun or pronoun in the possessive case, is governed by *the noun it possesses.*"—*Kirkham's Gram.* p. 181; *Frazee's,* 1844, p. 25.

Gram. p. 192.   "*Ours, yours, hers,* and *theirs,* are most usually considered possessive cases of personal pronouns; but they are, more probably, possessive substitutes, not adjectives, but *nouns.*"—*Ib.* p. 109.   "Nor can *mine* or *thine,* with any more propriety than *ours, yours,* &c. be joined to any noun, as possessive adjectives and possessive cases may."—*Ib.* p. 110. Whoever understands these instructions, cannot but see their inconsistency.

OBS. 15.—Murray argues at some length, without naming his opponents, that the words which he assumes to be such, are really personal pronouns standing rightfully in the possessive case; and that, "they should not, on the slight pretence of their differing from nouns, be dispossessed of the right and privilege, which, from time immemorial they have enjoyed."—*Octavo Gram.* p. 53.   Churchill as ably shows, that the corresponding terms, which Lowth calls *pronominal adjectives,* and which Murray and others will have to be *pronouns of no case,* are justly entitled to the same rank.   "If *mine, thine, hers, ours, yours, theirs,* be the possessive case; *my, thy, her, our, your, their,* must be the same.   Whether we say, 'It is *John's* book,' or, 'The book is *John's;*' *John's* is not less the possessive case in one instance, than it is in the other.   If we say, 'It is *his* book,' or, 'The book is *his;*' 'It is *her* book,' or, 'The book is *hers;*' 'It is *my* book,' or, 'The book is *mine;*' 'It is *your* book,' or, 'The book is *yours;*' are not these parallel instances ?   Custom has established it as a law, that this case of the pronoun shall drop its original termination, for the sake of euphony, when it precedes the noun that governs it; retaining it only where the noun is understood: but this certainly makes no alteration in the nature of the word; so that either *my* is as much a possessive case as *mine;* or *mine* and *my* are equally pronominal adjectives."— *Churchill's New Gram.* p. 221.   "Mr. Murray considers the phrases, '*our desire,*' '*your intention,*' '*their resignation,*' as instances of plural adjectives *agreeing* with singular nouns ; and consequently exceptions to the general (may we not say *universal?*) rule: but if *they* [the words our, your, *their,*] be, as is attempted to be proved above, the possessive cases of pronouns, no rule is here violated."—*Ib.* p. 224.

OBS. 16.—One strong argument, touching this much-disputed point of grammar, was incidentally noticed in the observations upon antecedents: an adjective cannot give person, number, and gender, to a relative pronoun; because, in our language, adjectives do not possess these qualities ; nor indeed in any other, except as they take them by immediate agreement with nouns or pronouns in the same clause.   But it is undeniable, that *my, thy, his, her, our, your, their,* do sometimes stand as antecedents, and give person, number, and gender to relatives, which head other clauses.   For the learner should remember, that, "When a relative pronoun is used, the sentence is divided into two parts; viz. the *antecedent* sentence, or that which contains the *antecedent;* and the *relative* sentence, containing the *relative.*"—*Nixon's Parser,* p. 123.   We need not here deny, that Terence's Latin, as quoted in the grammars, "Omnes laudare fortunas *meas, qui* haberem gnatum tali ingenio præditum," is quite as intelligible syntax, as can literally be made of it in English—"That all would praise *my* fortunes, *who* had a son endued with such a genius." For, whether the Latin be good or not, it affords no argument against us, except that of a supposed analogy ; nor does the literality of the version prove, at all points, either the accuracy or the sameness of the construction.

OBS. 17.—Surely, without some imperative reason, we ought not, in English, to resort to such an assumption as is contained in the following Rule : " Sometimes the relative *agrees* in person with that pronoun substantive, from which the possessive pronoun adjective is derived ; as, Pity *my* condition, *who* am so destitute.   I rejoice at *thy* lot, *who art* so fortunate.   We lament *his* fate, *who is* so unwary.   Beware of *her* cunning, *who is* so deceitful. Commiserate *our* condition, *who are* so poor.   Tremble at *your* negligence, *who are* so careless.   It shall be *their* property, *who are* so diligent.   We are rejoicing at *thy* lot, *who hast been* so fortunate."—*Nixon's Parser,* p. 142.   In his explanation of the last of these sentences, the author says, " *Who* is a relative pronoun ; in the masculine gender, singular number, second person, and agrees with *thee,* implied in the adjective *thy.*   RULE.—Sometimes the relative agrees in person, &c.   And it is the nominative to the verb *hast been.*   RULE.— When no nominative comes between the relative and the verb, the relative is the nominative to the verb."—*Ib.* p. 143.   A pupil of G. Brown's would have said, " *Who* is a relative pronoun ; representing '*thy,*' or the person addressed, in the second person, singular number, and masculine gender ; according to the rule which says, ' A pronoun must agree with its antecedent, or the noun or pronoun which it represents, in person, number, and gender:' and is in the nominative case, being the subject of *hast been ;* according to the rule which says, ' A noun or a pronoun which is the subject of a finite verb, must be in the nominative case.'   Because the meaning is—*who hast been ;* that is, *thy* lot, or the lot *of thee, who hast been.*"

OBS. 18.—Because the possessive case of a noun or pronoun is usually equivalent · meaning to the preposition *of* and the objective case, some grammarians, mistaking equivalence of meaning for sameness of case, have asserted that all our possessives ha double form.   Thus Nixon: " When the particle *of* comes between two substantives sig fying different things, it is not to be considered a preposition, but *the sign of the substant being in the possessive case,* equally as if the apostrophic *s* had been affixed to it ; as, ·

skill *of Cæsar,'* or *' Cæsar's* skill.' "—*English Parser,* p. 38. " When the apostrophic *s* is used, the genitive is the former of the two substantives; as, *' John's* house :' but when the particle *of* is used, it is the latter; as, *'* The house *of John.'* "—*Ib.* p. 46. The work here quoted is adapted to two different grammars; namely, Murray's and Allen's. These the author doubtless conceived to be the best English grammars extant. And it is not a little remarkable, that both of these authors, as well as many others, teach in such a faulty manner, that their intentions upon this point may be matter of dispute. " When Murray, Allen, and others, say, ' we make use of the particle of to express the *relation* of the genitive,' the ambiguity of their assertion leaves it in doubt whether or not they considered the substantive which is preceded by *of* and an other substantive, as in the *genitive* case."—*Nixon's English Parser,* p. 38. Resolving this doubt according to his own fancy, Nixon makes the possessive case of our personal pronouns to be as follows : " *mine* or *of me, ours* or *of us; thine* or *of thee, yours* or *of you; his* or *of him, theirs* or *of them; hers* or *of her, theirs* or *of them; its* or *of it, theirs* or *of them.*"—*English Parser,* p. 43. This doctrine gives us a form of declension that is both complex and deficient. It is therefore more objectionable than almost any of those which are criticised above. The arguments and authorities on which the author rests his position, are not thought likely to gain many converts; for which reason, I dismiss the subject, without citing or answering them.

OBS. 19.—In old books, we sometimes find the word *I* written for the adverb *ay, yes* : as, " To dye, to sleepe; To sleepe, perchance to dreame; *I,* there's the rub."—*Shakspeare, Old Copies.* The British Grammar, printed in 1784, and the Grammar of Murray the schoolmaster, published some years earlier than Lindley Murray's, say : " We use *I* as an Answer, in a familiar, careless, or merry Way; as, 'I, I, Sir, I, I; ' but to use *ay,* is accounted *rude,* especially to our Betters." See *Brit. Gram.* p. 198. The age of this rudeness, or incivility, if it ever existed, has long passed away; and the fashion seems to be so changed, that to write or utter *I* for *ay,* would now in its turn be " accounted *rude* "—the rudeness of ignorance—a false orthography, or a false pronunciation. In the word *ay,* the two sounds of *ah-ee* are plainly heard; in the sound of *I,* the same elements are more quickly blended. When this sound is suddenly repeated, some writers make a new word of it, which must be called an *interjection* : as, " ' Pray, answer me a question or two.' ' *Ey, ey,* as many as you please, cousin Bridget, an they be not too hard.' "—*Burgh's Speaker,* p. 99. " *Ey, ey,* 'tis so; she's out of her head, poor thing."—*Ib.* p. 100. This is probably a corruption of *ay,* which is often doubled in the same manner : thus,

" *Ay, ay,* Antipholus, look strange, and frown."—*Shakspeare.*

OBS. 20.—The common fashion of address being nowadays altogether in the plural form, the pronouns, *thou, thy, thine, thee,* and *thyself,* have become unfamiliar to most people, especially to the vulgar and uneducated. These words are now confined almost exclusively to the writings of the poets, to the language of the Friends, to the Holy Scriptures, and to the solemn services of religion. They are, however, the *only genuine* representatives of the second person singular, in English; and to displace them from that rank in grammar, or to present *you, your,* and *yours* as being literally singular, though countenanced by several late writers, is a useless and pernicious innovation. It is sufficient for the information of the learner, and far more consistent with learning and taste, to say, that the plural is fashionably used *for the singular,* by a figure of syntax; for, in all correct usage of this sort, the *verb* is plural, as well as the pronoun—Dr. Webster's fourteen authorities to the contrary notwithstanding. For, surely, " You *was* " cannot be considered good English, merely because that number of respectable writers have happened, on some particular occasions, to adopt the phrase; and even if we must needs concede this point, and grant to the Doctor and his converts, that " You *was* is *primitive* and *correct,*" the example no more proves that *you* is singular, than that *was* is plural. And what is one single irregular preterit, compared with all the verbs in the language?

OBS. 21.—In our present authorized version of the Bible, the numbers and cases of the second person are kept remarkably distinct,[*] the pronouns being always used in the following manner : *thou* for the nominative, *thy* or *thine* for the possessive, and *thee* for the objective, singular; *ye* for the nominative, *your* or *yours* for the possessive, and *you* for the objective, plural. Yet, before that version was made, fashionable usage had commonly substituted *you* for *ye,* making the former word nominative as well as objective, and applying it to one hearer as well as to more. And subsequently, as it appears, the religious sect that entertained a scruple about applying *you* to an individual, fell for the most part into an ungrammatical practice of putting *thee* for *thou;* making, in like manner, the objective pronoun to be both nominative and objective; or, at least, using it very commonly so in their conversation. Their manner of speaking, however, was not—or, certainly, with the present

---

[*] In respect to the *numbers,* the following text is an uncouth exception : " Pass *ye* away, *thou* inhabitant of Saphir."—*Micah,* i, 11. The singular and the plural are here strangely confounded. Perhaps the reading should be, " Pass *thou* away, O inhabitant of Saphir." Nor is the Bible free from *abrupt transitions* from one number to the other, or from one person to an other, which are neither agreeable nor strictly grammatical; as, " Brethren, if a man be overtaken in a fault, *ye which* [*who*] are spiritual, restore such an [a] one in the spirit of meekness; considering *thyself,* lest *thou* also be tempted."—*Gal.* vi, 1. " Ye that put far away the evil day, and cause the seat of violence to come near; that lie upon beds of ivory, and stretch *themselves* upon *their* couches," &c.—*Amos,* vi, 3.

generation of their successors, is not—as some grammarians represent it to be, that formal and antique phraseology which we call *the solemn style.*[*] They make no more use of the pronoun *ye,* or of the verbal termination *eth,* than do people of fashion ; nor do they, in using the pronoun *thou,* or their improper nominative *thee,* ordinarily inflect with *st* or *est* the preterits or the auxiliaries of the accompanying verbs, as is done in the solemn style. Indeed, to use the solemn style familiarly, would be, to turn it into burlesque ; as when Peter Pindar "*telleth what he troweth.*"[†] And let those who think with Murray, that our present version of the Scriptures is *the best standard* of English grammar,[‡] remember that in it they have no warrant for substituting *s* or *es* for the old termination *eth,* any more than for ceasing to use the solemn style of the second person familiarly. That version was good in its day, yet it shows but very imperfectly what the English language now is. Can we consistently take for our present standard, a style which does not allow us to use *you* in the nominative case, or *its* for the possessive ? And again is not a simplification of the verb as necessary and proper in the familiar use of the second person singular, as in that of the third ? This latter question I shall discuss in a future chapter.

Obs. 22.—The use of the pronoun *ye* in the nominative case, is now mostly confined to the solemn style ;[§] but the use of it in the objective, which is disallowed in the solemn style, and nowhere approved by our grammarians, is nevertheless *common* when no emphasis falls upon the word : as,

> "When you're unmarried, never load *ye*
> With jewels ; they may incommode *ye.*"—*Dr. King,* p. 384.

Upon this point, Dr. Lowth observes, "Some writers have used *ye* as the objective case plural of the pronoun of the second person, very improperly and ungrammatically ; [as,]

> 'The more shame for *ye :* holy men I thought *ye.*' Shak. Hen. VIII.
> 'But tyrants dread *ye,* lest your just decree
> Transfer the pow'r, and set the people free.' Prior.
> 'His wrath, which one day will destroy *ye* both.' Milt. P. L. ii. 734.

Milton uses the same manner of expression in a few other places of his Paradise Lost, and more frequently in his [smaller] poems. *It may, perhaps, be allowed in the comic and burlesque style,* which often imitates a vulgar and incorrect pronunciation ; but in the serious and solemn style, *no authority is sufficient* to justify so manifest a solecism."—*Lowth's Gram.* p. 22. Churchill copies this remark, and adds ; "Dryden has *you* as the nominative, and *ye* as the objective, in the same passage : ‖

> 'What gain *you,* by forbidding it to teaze *ye ?*
> It now can neither trouble *ye.* nor please *ye.*'

Was this from a notion, that *you* and *ye,* thus employed, were more analogous to *thou* and *thee* in the singular number ?"—*Churchill's Gram.* p. 225. I answer, No ; but, more probably, from a notion, that the two words, being now confessedly equivalent in the one case, might as well be made so in the other : just as the Friends, in using *thee* for *you,* are carelessly converting the former word into a nominative, to the exclusion of *thou* ; because the latter has generally been made so, to the exclusion of *ye.* When the confounding of such distinctions is begun, who knows where it will end ? With like ignorance, some writers suppose, that the fashion of using the plural for the singular is a sufficient warrant for putting the singular for the plural : as,

> "The joys of love, are they not doubly *thine,*
> *Ye poor !* whose health, whose spirits ne'er decline ?"—*Southwick's Pleas. of Poverty.*
> "But, *Neatherds,* go look to the kine,
> Their cribs with fresh fodder supply ;
> The task of compassion be *thine,*
> For herbage the pastures deny."—*Perfect's Poems,* p. 5.

Obs. 23.—When used in a burlesque or ludicrous manner, the pronoun *ye* is sometimes a

---

[*] "The solemn style is used, chiefly, in the Bible and in prayer. The Society of Friends *retain it in common parlance.* It consists in using *thou* in the singular number, and *ye* in the plural, instead of using *you* in both numbers as in the familiar style. * * * The third person singular (of verbs) ends with *th* or *eth,* which affects only the present indicative, and *hath* of the perfect. The second person, singular, ends with *st, est,* or *t* only."—*Sanborn's Gram.* p. 58. "In [the] solemn and poetic styles, *mine, thine,* and *thy,* are used ; and THIS *is the style adopted by the Friends' society.* In common discourse it appears very stiff and affected."—*Bartlett's C. S. Man'l,* Part II, p. 71.

[†] "And of the History of his being *lost* in a Blanket, *he saith,* 'Here, Scriblerus, *thou leesest* in what *thou assertest* concerning the blanket : It was not a blanket, but a rug.' Curliad, p. 26.'—*Notes to Pope's Dunciad,* B. ii, verse 8. A vulgar idea solemnly expressed, is ludicrous. Uttered in familiar terms, it is simply vulgar : as, "You lie, Scriblerus, in what *you* say about the blanket."

[‡] "Notwithstanding these verbal mistakes, the Bible, for the size of it, is the most accurate grammatical composition that we have in the English language. The authority of several eminent grammarians might be adduced in support of this assertion, but it may be sufficient to mention only that of Dr. Lowth, who says, 'The present translation of the Bible, is *the best standard* of the English language.'"—*Murray's Gram.* 8vo, p. 166. I revere the Bible vastly too much to be pleased with an imitation of its peculiar style, in any man's ordinary speech or writing.—G. Brown.

[§] "*Ye,* except in the solemn style, is *obsolete ;* but it is used in the language of tragedy, to express contempt : as, 'When *ye* shall know what Margaret knows, *ye* may not be so thankful.' Franklin."—*Allen's Gram.* p. 57. "The second person plural had *formerly* YE *both in the nominative and the objective.* This form is *now obsolete in the objective, and nearly obsolete in the nominative.*"—*Hart's Gram.* p. 55.

‖ So has Milton : —

> "To waste it all myself, and leave *ye* none !
> So disinherited how would *you* bless me !"—*Par. Lost.* B. x, l. 820.

mere expletive; or, perhaps, intended rather as an objective governed by a preposition understood. But, in such a construction, I see no reason to prefer it to the regular objective *you:* as,

"He'll laugh ye, dance ye, sing ye, vault, look gay,
And ruffle all the ladies in his play."—*King*, p. 574.

Some grammarians, who will have *you* to be singular as well as plural, ignorantly tell us, that "*ye* always means more than one." But the fact is, that when *ye* was in common use, it was as frequently applied to one person as *you:* thus,

"Farewell my doughter lady Margarete,
God wotte full oft it grieued hath my mynde,
That *ye* should go where we should seldome mete:
Now am I gone, and haue left *you* behynde."—*Sir T. More*, 1503.

In the following example, *ye* is used for *thee*, the objective singular; and that by one whose knowledge of the English language, is said to have been unsurpassed:—

"Proud Baronet of Nova Scotia!
The Dean and Spaniard must reproach *ye*."—*Swift*.

So in the story of the Chameleon:—

"'Tis green, 'tis green, Sir, I assure *ye*."—*Merrick*.

Thus we have *ye* not only for the nominative in both numbers, but at length for the objective in both; *ye* and *you* being made everywhere equivalent, by very many writers. Indeed this pronoun has been so frequently used for the objective case, that one may well doubt any grammarian's authority to condemn it in that construction. Yet I cannot but think it ill-chosen in the third line below, though right in the first:—

"*Ye!* who have traced the Pilgrim to the scene
Which is his last, if in your memories dwell
A thought which once was his, if on *ye* swell
A single recollection, not in vain
He wore his sandal-shoon, and scallop-shell."—*Byron*.

OBS. 24.—The three pronouns of the third person, *he, she,* and *it,* have always formed their plural number after one and the same manner, *they, their* or *theirs, them*. Or, rather, these plural words, which appear not to be regular derivations from any of the singulars, have ever been applied alike to them all. But *it,* the neuter pronoun singular, had formerly no variation of cases, and is still alike in the nominative and the objective. The possessive *its* is of comparatively recent origin. In our common Bible, the word is not found, except by misprint; nor do other writings of the same age contain it. The phrase, *of it,* was often used as an equivalent; as, "And it had three ribs in the mouth *of it* between the teeth *of it*."—*Dan.* vii, 5. That is—"in *its* mouth, between *its* teeth." But, as a possessive case was sometimes necessary, our ancestors used to borrow one; commonly from the masculine, though sometimes from the feminine. This produced what now appears a strange confusion of the genders: as, "*Learning* hath *his* infancy, when *it* is but beginning, and almost childish; then *his* youth, when *it* is luxuriant and juvenile; then *his* strength of years, when *it* is solid and reduced; and lastly *his* old age, when *it* waxeth dry and exhaust."—*Bacon's Essays*, p. 58. "Of beaten work shall the *candlestick* be made: *his* shaft, and *his* branches, *his* bowls, *his* knops, and *his* flowers, shall be of the same."—*Exodus*, xxv, 31. "They came and emptied the *chest*, and took *it* and carried *it* to *his* place again."—2 *Chron*. xxiv, 11, "Look not thou upon the *wine*, when *it* is red, when it giveth *his* colour in the cup, when *it* moveth *itself* aright."—*Prov*. xxiii, 31. "The *tree* is known by *his* fruit."—*Matt*. xii, 33. "When thou tillest the ground, *it* shall not henceforth yield unto thee *her* strength."—*Gen*. iv, 12. "He that pricketh the heart, maketh *it* to show *her* knowledge."—*Eccl*. xxii, 19. Shakspeare rarely, if ever, used *its*; and his style is sometimes obscure for the want of it: as,

"There is no *vice* so simple, but assumes
Some mark of virtue on *his* outward parts."—*Merch. of Venice*.

"The name of Cassius honours this corruption,
And *chastisement* doth therefore hide *his* head."—*Jul. Cæs.* Act iv.

OBS. 25.—The possessive case of pronouns should never be written with an apostrophe. A few pronominal adjectives taken substantively receive it; but the construction which it gives them, seems to make them nouns: as, one's, other's, and, according to Murray, *former's* and *latter's*. The real pronouns that end in *s*, as *his, hers, its, ours, yours, theirs,* though true possessives after their kind, have no occasion for this mark, nor does good usage admit it. Churchill, with equal disregard of consistency and authority, gives it to one of them, and denies it to the rest. Referring to the classification of these words as possessives, and of *my, thy, her, our, your, their,* as adjectives, he says: "It seems as if the termination in *s* had led to the distinction: but no one will contend, that *ours* is the possessive case of *our*, or *theirs* of *their*; though *ours, yours, hers,* and *theirs,* are often very improperly spelt with an apostrophe, a fault not always imputable to the printer; while in *it's,* which is unquestionably the possessive case of *it,* the apostrophe, by a strange perverseness, is almost always omitted."—*Churchill's Gram*. p. 222. The charge of strange perverseness may, in this instance, I think, be retorted upon the critic; and that, to the fair exculpation of those who choose to conform to the general usage which offends him.

OBS. 26.—Of the compound personal pronouns, this author gives the following account: "*Self*, in the plural *selves*, a noun, is often combined with the personal pronouns, in order to express emphasis, or opposition, or the identity of the subject and [the] object of a verb; and thus forms a pronoun *relative*: as, 'I did it *myself*;' 'he was not *himself*, when he said so;' 'the envious torment *themselves* more than others.' Formerly *self* and *selves* were used simply as nouns, and governed the pronoun, which was kept distinct from *it* [them] in the possessive case: but since *they* [the pronoun and the noun] have coalesced into one word, *they* [the compounds] are used only in the following forms: for the first person, *myself*, *ourselves*; for the second, *thyself*, or *yourself*, *yourselves*; for the third, *himself*, *herself*, *itself*, *themselves*: except in the regal style, in which, as generally in the second person, the singular noun is added to the plural pronoun, [making] *ourself*. Each of these is *the same is all three cases*."—*Churchill's Gram.* p. 75. In a note referring to the close of this explanation, he adds: "*Own* also is often employed with the possessive cases of the personal pronouns by way of emphasis, or opposition; but separately, as an adjective, and not combining with them to form *a relative*: as, 'I did it of *my own* free will;' 'Did he do it with *his own* hand?'"—*Ib.* p. 227.

OBS. 27.—The preceding instructions, faulty and ungrammatical as they are, seem to be the best that our writers have furnished upon this point. To detect falsities and blunders, is half the grammarian's duty. The pronouns of which the term *self* or *selves* forms a part, are used, not for the connecting of different clauses of a sentence, but for the purpose of emphatic distinction in the sense. In calling them "*relatives*," Churchill is wrong, even by his own showing. They have not the characteristics which he himself ascribes to relatives; but are compound personal pronouns, and nothing else. He is also manifestly wrong in asserting, that they are severally "the same in all three cases." From the very nature of their composition, the possessive case is alike impossible to them all. To express ownership with emphasis or distinction, we employ neither these compounds nor any others; but always use the simple possessives with the separate adjective *own*: as, "With *my own* eyes,"—"By *thy own* confession,"—"To *his own* house,"—"For *her own* father,"—"By *its own* weight,"—"To save *our own* lives,"—"For *your own* sake,"—"In *their own* cause."

OBS. 28.—The phrases, *my own*, *thy own*, *his own*, and so forth, Dr. Perley, in his little Grammar, has improperly converted by the hyphen into compound words: calling them the possessive forms of *myself*, *thyself*, *himself*, and so forth; as if one set of compounds could constitute the possessive case of an other! And again, as if the making of eight new pronouns for two great nations, were as slight a feat, as the inserting of so many hyphens! The word *own*, anciently written *owen*, is an *adjective*; from an old form of the perfect participle of the verb *to owe*; which verb, according to Lowth and others, once signified *to possess*. It is equivalent to *due*, *proper*, or *peculiar*; and, in its present use as an adjective, it stands nowhere else than between the possessive case and the name of the thing possessed: as "The Boy's *Own* Book,"—"Christ's *own* words,"—"Solomon's *own* and only son." Dr. Johnson, while he acknowledges the above-mentioned derivation, very strangely calls *own* a noun substantive; and, with not much more accuracy, says: "This is a word of no other use than as it is added to the possessive pronouns, *my*, *thy*, *his*, *our*, *your*, *their*."—*Quart. Dict. w. Own.* O. B. Peirce, with obvious untruth, says, "*Own* is used in combination with a name or substitute, and as *a part of it*, to constitute it emphatic."—*Gram.* p. 63. He writes it separately, but parses it as a part of the possessive noun or pronoun which precedes it.

OBS. 29.—The word *self* was originally *an adjective*, signifying *same*, *very*, or *particular*; but, when used alone, it is now generally *a noun*. This may have occasioned the diversity which appears in the formation of the compound personal pronouns. Dr. Johnson, in his great Dictionary, calls *self* a pronoun; but he explains it as being both adjective and substantive, admitting that, "Its primary signification seems to be that of an adjective."—Again he observes, "*Myself*, *himself*, *themselves*, and the rest, may, contrary to the analogy of *my*, *him*, *them*, be used as nominatives." *Hisself*, *itsself*, and *theirselves*, would be more analogical than *himself*, *itself*, *themselves*; but custom has rejected the former, and established the latter. When an adjective qualifies the term *self*, the pronouns are written separately in the possessive case; as, *My single self*—*My own self*—*His own self*—*Their own selves*. So anciently, without an adjective: as, "A man shall have diffused his life, *his self*, and his whole concernments so far, that he can weep his sorrows with an other's eyes."—*Sou.* "Something valuable for *its self* without view to any thing farther."—*Harris's Hermes*, p. 29. "That they would willingly, and of *their selves* endeavour to keep a perpetual chastity."—*Stat. Ed. VI, in Lowth's Gram.* p. 26. "Why I should either *imploy my self* in that study, put others upon it."—*Walker's English Particles*, p. xiv. "It is no matter whether you do it by your proctor, or by *your self*."—*Ib.* p. 96. The compound *oneself* is sometimes written in stead of the phrase *one's self*; but the latter is preferable, and more common. Even *self*, when written as two words, may possibly be right in some instances; as,

"Scorn'd be the wretch that quits his genial bowl,
His loves, his friendships, ev'n *his self*, resigns;
Perverts the sacred instinct of his soul,
And to a ducat's dirty sphere confines."—SHENSTONE: *Brit. Poets*, Vol. vii, p. 107.

OBS. 30.—In poetry, and even in some compositions not woven into regular numbers, the simple personal pronouns are not unfrequently used, for brevity's sake, in a reciprocal sense; that is, in stead of the compound personal pronouns, which are the proper reciprocals: as, "Wash *you*, make *you* clean."—*Isaiah*, i, 16. "I made *me* great works; I builded *me* houses; I planted *me* vineyards; I made *me* gardens and orchards."—*Ecclesiastes*, ii, 4. "Thou shalt surely clothe *thee* with them all as with an ornament, and bind them on *thee* as a bride doeth."—*Isaiah*, xlix, 18. Compare with these the more regular expression: "As a bridegroom decketh *himself* with ornaments, and as a bride adorneth *herself* with jewels."—*Isaiah*, lxi, 10. This phraseology is almost always preferable in prose; the other is a poetical license, or peculiarity: as,

"I turn *me* from the martial roar."—*Scott's L. L.*, p. 97.
"Hush *thee*, poor maiden, and be still."—*Ib.* p. 110.
"Firmer he roots *him* the ruder it blow."—*Ib.* p. 49.

Obs. 31.—To accommodate the writers of verse, the word *ever* is frequently contracted into *e'er*, pronounced like the monosyllable *air*. An easy extension of this license, gives us similar contractions of all the compound relative pronouns; as, *whoe'er* or *whosoe'er*, *whose'er* or *whosesoe'er*, *whome'er* or *whomsoe'er*, *whiche'er* or *whichsoe'er*, *whate'er* or *whatsoe'er*. The character and properties of these compounds are explained, perhaps sufficiently, in the observations upon the *classes* of pronouns. Some of them are commonly parsed as representing two cases at once; there being, in fact, an ellipsis of the noun, before or after them: as,

"Each art he prompts, each charm he can create,
Whate'er he gives, *are given* for you to hate."—*Pope's Dunciad.*

Obs. 32.—For a form of parsing the double relative *what*, or its compound *whatever* or *whatsoever*, it is the custom of some teachers, to suggest equivalent words, and then proceed to explain these, in lieu of the word in question. This is the method of *Russell's Gram.* p. 99; of *Merchant's*, p. 110; of *Kirkham's*, p. 111; of *Gilbert's*, p. 92. But it should be remembered that equivalence of meaning is not sameness of grammatical construction; and, even if the construction be the same, to parse other equivalent words, is not really to parse the text that is given. A good parser, with the liberty to supply obvious ellipses, should know how to explain all good English *as it stands;* and for a teacher to pervert good English into false doctrine, must needs seem the very worst kind of ignorance. What can be more fantastical than the following etymology, or more absurd than the following directions for parsing? "*What* is compounded of *which that*. These words have been contracted and made to coalesce, a part of the orthography of both being still retained: *what*—*wh*[*ich*—*t*]*hat;* (*which-that*.) Anciently it appeared in the varying forms, *tha qua, qua tha, qu'tha, quthat, quhat, hwat,* and finally *what*."—*Kirkham's Gram.* p. 111. This bald pedantry of "*tha qua, qua tha,*" was secretly borrowed from the grammatical speculations of William S. Cardell:[*] the "*which-that*" notion contradicts it, and is partly of the borrower's own invention. If *what* is a compound, it was compounded more than a thousand years ago; and, of course, long before any part of the English language existed as such. King Alfred used it, as he found it, in the Saxon form of *hwæt.* The Scotch afterwards spelled it *quhat.* Our English grammarians have *improperly* called it a compound; ánd Kirkham, still more absurdly. calls the word *others* a compound, and *mine, thine, ours, yours, &c.* compounds.[†]

Obs. 33.—According to this gentleman's notion of things, there is, within the little circle of the word *what*, a very curious play of antecedent parts and parts relative—a dodging contra-dance of *which that* and *that which*, with *things which*, and so forth. Thus: "When *what* is a *compound relative* you must always parse it *as two words;* that is, you must parse the antecedent part *as a noun*, and give it case; the relative part you may *analyze* like any other relative, giving it a case likewise. Example: 'I will try *what* (that which) can be

* "The word *what* is a *compound* of *two specifying adjectives*, each, of course, referring to a *noun*, expressed or understood. It is equivalent to *the which; that which; which that;* or *that that;* used also in the plural. At different periods, and in different authors, it appears in the varying forms, *tha qua, qua tha, qu'tha, quthat, quhat, hwat,* and *what*. This word is found in other forms; but it is needless to multiply them."—*Cardell's Essay on Language*, p. 86.
† This author's distribution of the pronouns, of which I have taken some notice in Obs. 10th above. is remarkable for its inconsistencies and absurdities. First he avers, " Pronouns are *generally* divided into three kinds, the *Personal*, the *Adjective*, and the *Relative* pronouns. *They are all known by the lists*."—*Kirkham's Gram.* p. 96. These short sentences are far from being accurate, clear, or true. He should have made the several kinds *known*, by a good definition of each. But this was work to which he did not find himself adequate. And if we look to his *lists* for the particular words of each kind, we shall get little satisfaction. Of the *Personal* pronouns, he says, " There are *five* of them; *I, thou, he, she, it*."—*Ib.* p. 97. These are *simple* words, and in their declension they are properly multiplied to forty. (See *Ib.* p 99.) Next he seems to double the number, thus: " When *self* is added to the personal pronouns, as himself, myself, itself, themselves, &c. they are called *Compound Personal Pronouns*."—*Ib.* p. 99. Then he asserts that *mine, thine, his, hers, ours, yours,* and *theirs*, are compounds of *ne* or *s* with *mi, thi, hi,* &c.; that their application invariably "gives them a compound character;" and that, "They may, therefore, be properly denominated *Compound Personal Pronouns*."—*Ib.* p. 101. Next he comes to his *Adjective* pronouns; and, after proving that he has grossly misplaced and misnamed every one of them, he gives his *lists* of the three kinds of these. His *Relative* pronouns are *who, which,* and *that.* " *What* is generally a *compound* relative."—*Ib.* p. 111. The compounds of *who, which,* and *what,* with *ever* or *soever*, he calls "*compound pronouns*, but not compound relatives."—*Ib.* pp. 110 and 112. Lastly he discovers, that, "Tru'h and simplicity " have been shamefully neglected in this his third section of pronouns; that, " Of the words called ' *relatives*,' *who* only is a pronoun, and this is strictly *personal*." that, " It ought to be classed with the personal pronouns;" and that, "*Which, that,* and *what*, are always *adjectives*. They never *stand for*, but always *belong to* nouns, either *expressed* or implied."—*Ib.* p. 114. What admirable teachings are these!

found in female delicacy.' Here *that*, the antecedent part of *what*, is in the obj. case, governed by the verb ' will try ;' *which*, the relative part, is in the nom. case to ' can be found.' 'I have heard *what* (i. e. *that which*, or *the thing which*) has been alleged.'"—*Kirkham's Gram*. p. 111. Here, we see, the author's " *which-that*" becomes *that which*, or something else. But this is not a full view of his method. The following vile rigmarole is a further sample of that " *New Systematick Order of Parsing*," by virtue of which he so very complacently and successfully sets himself above all other grammarians: " ' *From what* is recorded, he appears, &c.' *What* is a comp. rel. pron. including both the antecedent and the relative, and is equivalent to *that which*, or the *thing which*.—*Thing*, the antecedent part of *what*, is a noun, the name of a thing—com. the name of a species—neuter gender, it has no sex—third person, spoken of—sing. number, it implies but one—and in the obj. case, it is the object of the relation expressed by the prep. ' from,' and gov. by it : RULE 31. (Repeat the Rule, and *every other Rule* to which I refer.) *Which*, the relative part of *what*, is a pronoun, a word used instead of a noun—relative, it relates to ' thing' for its antecedent—neut. gender, third person, sing. number, because the antecedent is with which it agrees, according to RULE 14. *Rel. pron*. &c. *Which* is *in* the nom. case to the verb ' is recorded,' agreeably to RULE 15. *The relative is the nominative case to the verb, when no nominative comes between it and the verb*." —*Kirkham's Gram*. p. 113.

OBS. 34.—The distinction which has been made by Murray and others, between etymological parsing and syntactical—or, between that exercise which simply classifies and describes the words of a sentence, and that which adds to this the principles of their construction— is rejected by Kirkham, and also by Ingersoll, Fuller, Smith, Sanborn, Mack, and some others, it being altogether irreconcilable with their several modes of confounding the two main parts of grammar. If such a distinction is serviceable, the want of it is one of the inherent faults of the schemes which they have adopted. But, since "grammar is the art of speaking and writing with *propriety*," who that really values clearness and accuracy of expression, can think the want of them excusable in *models* prescribed for the exercise of parsing? And is it not better to maintain the distinction above named, than to interlace our syntactical parsing with broken allusions to the definitions which pertain to etymology? If it is, this new mode of parsing, which Kirkham claims to have invented, and Smith pretends to have got from Germany, whatever boast may be made of it, is essentially defective and very immethodical.* This remark applies not merely to the forms above cited, respecting the pronoun *what*, but to the whole method of parsing adopted by the author of " *English Grammar in Familiar Lectures*."

OBS. 35.—The forms of etymological parsing which I have adopted, being designed to train the pupil, in the first place, by a succession of easy steps, to a rapid and accurate description of the several species of words, and a ready habit of fully defining the technical terms employed in such descriptions, will be found to differ more from the forms of syntactical parsing, than do those of perhaps any other grammarian. The definitions, which constitute so large a portion of the former, being omitted as soon as they are thoroughly learned, give place in the latter to the facts and principles of syntax. Thus have we fullness in the one part, conciseness in the other, order and distinctness in both. The separation of etymology from syntax, however, though judiciously adopted by almost all grammarians, is in itself a mere matter of convenience. No one will pretend that these two parts of grammar are in their nature *totally* distinct and independent. Hence, though a due regard to method demands the maintenance of this ancient and still usual division of the subject, we not unfrequently, in treating of the classes and modifications of words, exhibit contingently some of the principles of their construction. This, however, is very different from a purposed blending of the two parts, than which nothing can be more unwise.

OBS. 36.—The great peculiarity of the pronoun *what*, or of its compound *whatever* or *whatsoever*, is a peculiarity of construction, rather than of etymology. Hence, in etymological parsing, it may be sufficient to notice it only as a relative, though the construction be double. It is in fact a relative; but it is one that reverses the order of the antecedent,

* "It is now proper to give some *examples of the manner* in which the learners should be exercised. in order to improve their knowledge, and to render it familiar to them. *This* is called *parsing*. The nature of the subject, as well as the adaptation of it to learners, requires *that it should be divided* into two parts : viz parsing, as it respects etymology alone ; and parsing, as it respects both etymology and syntax."—*Murray's Gram. Octavo*, Vol. i, p. 225. How very little real respect for the opinions of Murray, has been entertained by these self-seeking magnifiers and modifiers of his work!
What Murray calls " *Syntactical Parsing*," is sometimes called " *Construing*," especially by those who will have *Parsing* to be nothing more than an etymological exercise. A late author says, " The practice of *Construing* differs from that of parsing, in the extension of its objects. Parsing merely indicates the parts of speech and their accidents, but construing searches for and points out their syntactical relations."—*D. Blair's Gram*. p 44. Here the distinction which Murray judged to be necessary, is still more strongly marked and insisted on. And though I see no utility in restricting the word *Parsing* to a mere description of the parts of speech with their accidents, and no impropriety in calling the latter branch of the exercise " *Syntactical Parsing* ;" I cannot but think there is such a necessity for the division, as forms a very grave argument against those tangled schemes of grammar which do not admit of it. Blair is grossly inconsistent with himself. For, after drawing his distinction between Parsing and Construing, as above, he takes no further notice of the latter ; but, having filled up seven pages with his most wretched mode of " PARSING," adds, in an emphatic note : " *The Teacher should direct the Pupil to* CONSTRUE, IN THE SAME MANNER, *any passage from* MY CLASS-BOOK, *or other Work, at the rate of three or four lines per day*."—*D. Blair's Gram*. p. 56.

whenever the noun is inserted with it. But as the noun is usually suppressed, and as the supplying of it is attended with an obvious difficulty, arising from the transposition, we cut the matter short, by declaring the word to have, as it appears to have, a double syntactical relation. Of the foregoing example, therefore—viz., "From *what* is recorded," &c.,—a pupil of mine, in parsing *etymologically* would say thus : "*What* is a relative pronoun, of the third person, singular number, neuter gender, and nominative case. 1. A pronoun is a word used in stead of a noun. 2. A relative pronoun is a pronoun that represents an antecedent word or phrase, and connects different clauses of a sentence. 3. The third person is that which denotes the person or thing merely spoken of. 4. The singular number is that which denotes but one. 5. The neuter gender is that which denotes things that are neither male nor female. 6. The nominative case is that form or state of a noun or pronoun, which denotes the subject of a verb." In parsing *syntactically*, he would say thus : "*What* is a double relative, including both antecedent and relative, being equivalent to *that which*. As *antecedent*, it is of the third person, singular number, neuter gender, and objective case ; being *governed* by *from* ; according to the rule which says, ' A Noun or a Pronoun made the object of a preposition, is governed by it in the objective case.' Because the meaning is—*from what*. As *relative*, it is of the third person, singular number, neuter gender, and nominative case ; being the subject of *is recorded* ; according to the rule which says, ' A Noun or a Pronoun which is the subject of a finite verb, must be in the nominative case.' Because the meaning is—*what is recorded*."

OBS. 37.—The word *what*, when uttered independently as a mark of surprise, or as the prelude to an emphatic question which it does not ask, becomes an interjection ; and, as such, is to be parsed merely as other interjections are parsed : as, "*What!* came the word of God out from you ? or came it unto you only ?"—1 *Cor.* xiv, 36. "*What!* know ye not that your body is the temple of the Holy Ghost which is in you, which ye have of God ?"—1 *Cor.* vi, 19. " But *what!* is thy servant a dog, that he should do this great thing ?"—2 *Kings*, viii, 13. " *What!* are you so ambitious of a man's good word, who perhaps in an hour's time shall curse himself to the pit of hell ?"—*Collier's Antoninus*, p. 152.

> "*What!* up and down, carv'd like an apple-tart ?"—*Shakspeare.*
> "*What!* can you lull the winged winds asleep ?"—*Campbell.*

EXAMPLES FOR PARSING.

PRAXIS V.—ETYMOLOGICAL.

In the Fifth Praxis, it is required of the pupil—to distinguish and define the different parts of speech, and the classes and modifications of the ARTICLES, NOUNS, ADJECTIVES, and PRONOUNS.

The definitions to be given in the Fifth Praxis, are two for an article, six for a noun, three for an adjective, six for a pronoun, and one for a verb, a participle, an adverb, a conjunction, a preposition, or an interjection. Thus :—

EXAMPLE PARSED.

" Nay but, O man, who art thou that repliest against God ? Shall the thing formed say to him that formed it, Why hast thou made me thus ?"—*Rom.* ix, 20.

Nay is an adverb. 1. An adverb is a word added to a verb, a participle, an adjective, or an other adverb ; and generally expresses time, place, degree, or manner.
But is a conjunction. 1. A conjunction is a word used to connect words or sentences in construction, and to show the dependence of the terms so connected.
O is an interjection. 1. An interjection is a word that is uttered merely to indicate some strong or sudden emotion of the mind.
Man is a common noun, of the second person, singular number, masculine gender, and nominative case. 1. A noun is the name of any person, place, or thing, that can be known or mentioned. 2. A common noun is the name of a sort, kind, or class, of beings or things. 3. The second person is that which denotes the hearer, or the person addressed. 4. The singular number is that which denotes but one. 5. The masculine gender is that which denotes persons or animals of the male kind. 6. The nominative case is that form or state of a noun or pronoun, which denotes the subject of a verb.
Who is an interrogative pronoun, of the third person, singular number, masculine gender, and nominative case. 1. A pronoun is a word used in stead of a noun. 2. An interrogative pronoun is a pronoun with which a question is asked. 3. The third person is that which denotes the person or thing merely spoken of. 4. The singular number is that which denotes but one. 5. The masculine gender is that which denotes persons or animals of the male kind. 6. The nominative case is that form or state of a noun or pronoun which denotes the subject of a verb.
Art is a verb. 1. A verb is a word that signifies *to be, to act*, or *to be acted upon*.
Thou is a personal pronoun, of the second person, singular number, masculine gender, and nominative case. 1. A personal pronoun is a word used in stead of a noun. 2. A personal pronoun is a pronoun that shows, by its form, of what person it is. 3 The second person is that which denotes the hearer, or the person addressed. 4. The singular number is that which denotes but one. 5. The masculine gender is that which denotes persons or animals of the male kind. 6. The nominative case is that form or state of a noun or pronoun which denotes the subject of a verb.

That is a relative pronoun, of the second person, singular number, masculine gender, and nominative case.   1. A pronoun is a word used in stead of a noun.   2. A relative pronoun is a pronoun that represents an antecedent word or phrase, and connects different clauses of a sentence.   3. The second person is that which denotes the hearer, or the person addressed.   4. The singular number is that which denotes but one.   5. The masculine gender is that which denotes persons or animals of the male kind.   6. The nominative case is that form or state of a noun or pronoun, which denotes the subject of a verb.

Repliest is a verb.   1. A verb is a word that signifies *to be, to act,* or *to be acted upon.*

Against is a preposition.   1. A preposition is a word used to express some relation of different things or thoughts to each other, and is generally placed before a noun or a pronoun.

God is a proper noun, of the third person, singular number, masculine gender, and objective case.   1. A noun is the name of any person, place, or thing, that can be known or mentioned.   2. A proper noun is the name of some particular individual, or people, or group.   3. The third person is that which denotes the person or thing merely spoken of.   4. The singular number is that which denotes but one.   5. The masculine gender is that which denotes persons or animals of the male kind.   6. The objective case is that form or state of a noun or pronoun, which denotes the object of a verb, participle, or preposition.

Shall is a verb, auxiliary to *say,* and may be taken with it.

The is the definite article.   1. An article is the word *the, an,* or *a,* which we put before nouns to limit their signification.   2. The definite article is *the,* which denotes some particular thing or things.

Thing is a common noun, of the third person, singular number, neuter gender, and nominative case.   1. A noun is the name of any person, place, or thing, that can be known or mentioned.   2. A common noun is the name of a sort, kind, or class, of beings or things.   3. The third person is that which denotes the person or thing merely spoken of.   4. The singular number is that which denotes but one.   5. The neuter gender is that which denotes things that are neither male nor female.   6. The nominative case is that form or state of a noun or pronoun, which denotes the subject of a verb.

Formed is a participle.   1. A participle is a word derived from a verb, participating the properties of a verb, and of an adjective or a noun ; and is generally formed by adding *ing, d,* or *ed,* to the verb.

Say, or *shall say,* is a verb.   1. A verb is a word that signifies *to be, to act,* or *to be acted upon.*

To is a preposition.   1. A preposition is a word used to express some relation of different things or thoughts to each other, and is generally placed before a noun or a pronoun.

Him is a personal pronoun, of the third person, singular number, masculine gender, and objective case.   1. A pronoun is a word used in stead of a noun.   2. A personal pronoun is a pronoun that shows, by its form, of what person it is.   3. The third person is that which denotes the person or thing merely spoken of.   4. The singular number is that which denotes but one.   5. The masculine gender is that which denotes persons or animals of the male kind.   6 The objective case is that form or state of a noun or pronoun which denotes the object of a verb, participle, or preposition.

That is a relative pronoun, of the third person, singular number, masculine gender, and nominative case.   1. A pronoun is a word used in stead of a noun.   2. A relative pronoun is a pronoun that represents an antecedent word or phrase, and connects different clauses of a sentence.   3. The third person is that which denotes the person or thing merely spoken of.   4. The singular number is that which denotes but one.   5. The masculine gender is that which denotes persons or animals of the male kind.   6. The nominative case is that form or state of a noun or pronoun, which denotes the subject of a verb.

Formed is a verb.   1. A verb is a word that signifies *to be, to act, or to be acted upon.*

It is a personal pronoun, of the third person, singular number, neuter gender, and objective case.   1. A pronoun is a word used in stead of a noun.   2. A personal pronoun is a pronoun that shows, by its form, of what person it is.   3. The third person is that which denotes the person or thing merely spoken of.   4. The singular number is that which denotes but one.   5. The neuter gender is that which denotes things that are neither male nor female.   6. The objective case is that form or state of a noun or pronoun, which denotes the object of a verb, participle, or preposition.

Why is an adverb.   1. An adverb is a word added to a verb, a participle, an adjective, or an other adverb ; and generally expresses time, place, degree, or manner.

Hast is a verb, auxiliary to *made,* and may be taken with it.

Thou is a personal pronoun, of the second person, singular number, masculine gender, and nominative case.   1. A pronoun is a word used in stead of a noun.   2. A personal pronoun is a pronoun that shows, by its form, of what person it is.   3. The second person is that which denotes the hearer, or the person addressed.   4. The singular number is that which denotes but one.   5. The masculine gender is that which denotes persons or animals of the male kind.   6. The nominative case is that form or state of a noun or pronoun, which denotes the subject of a verb.

Made, or *hast made,* is a verb.   1. A verb is a word that signifies *to be, to act,* or *to be acted upon.*

Me is a personal pronoun, of the first person, singular number, neuter gender, and objective case.   1. A pronoun is a word used in stead of a noun.   2. A personal pronoun is a pronoun that shows, by its form, of what person it is.   3. The first person is that which denotes the speaker or writer.   4. The singular number is that which denotes but one.   5. The neuter gender is that which denotes things that are neither male nor female.   6. The objective case is that form or state of a noun or pronoun which denotes the object of a verb, participle, or preposition.

Thus is an adverb.   1. An adverb is a word added to a verb, a participle, an adjective, or an other adverb ; and generally expresses time, place, degree, or manner.

LESSON I. — PARSING.

"Every man has undoubtedly an inward perception of the celestial goodness by which he is quickened.   But, if to attain some ideas of God, it be not necessary for us to go beyond ourselves, what an unpardonable indolence is it in those who will not descend into themselves that they may find him ?"—*Calvin's Institutes,* B. i, Ch. 5.

"Jesus answered, If I honour myself, my honour is nothing : it is my Father that honoureth me ; of whom ye say, that he is your God : yet ye have not known him ; but I know him."—*John,* x, 54.

"What ! have ye not houses to eat and to drink in ? or despise ye the church of God, and shame them that have not ? What shall I say to you ? shall I praise you in this ? I praise you not."—1 *Cor.* xi, 22.

"We know not what we ought to wish for, but He who made us, knows."—*Burgh's Dignity,* Vol. ii, p. 20.

"And who is he that will harm you, if ye be followers of that which is good?"—1 *Peter.* iii, 13.

"For we dare not make ourselves of the number, or compare ourselves with some that commend themselves : but they, measuring themselves by themselves, and comparing themselves among themselves, are not wise."—2 *Cor.* x, 12.

"Whatever is humane, is wise ; whatever is wise, is just ; whatever is wise, just, and humane, will be found the true interest of states."—*Dr. Rush, on Punishments*, p. 19.

"But, methinks, we cannot answer it to ourselves, as-well-as to our Maker, that we should live and die ignorant of ourselves, and thereby of him, and of the obligations which we are under to him for ourselves."—*William Penn.*

"But where shall wisdom be found ? and where is the place of understanding ? The depth saith, ' It is not in me ;' and the sea saith, ' It is not with me.' Destruction and death say, ' We have heard the fame thereof with our ears.' " See *Job*, xxviii, 12, 14, 22 ; and *Blair's Lect.* p. 417.

> "I still had hopes, my latest hours to crown,
> Amidst these humble bow'rs to lay me down."—*Goldsmith.*

> "Why dost thou then suggest to me distrust,
> Knowing who I am, as I know who thou art ?"—*Milton*, P. R.

Lesson II. — Parsing.

"I would, methinks, have so much to say for myself, that if I fell into the hands of him who treated me ill, he should be sensible when he did so : his conscience should be on my side, whatever became of his inclination."—*Steele, Spect.* No. 522.

"A boy should understand his mother tongue well before he enters upon the study of a dead language ; or, at any rate, he should be made perfect master of the meaning of all the words which are necessary to furnish him with a translation of the particular author which he is studying."—*Gallaudet, Lit. Conv.* p. 206.

"No discipline is more suitable to man, or more congruous to the dignity of his nature, than that which refines his taste, and leads him to distinguish, in every subject, what is regular, what is orderly, what is suitable, and what is fit and proper."—*Kames's El. of Crit.* i, 275.

"Simple thoughts are what arise naturally ; what the occasion or the subject suggests unsought ; and what, when once suggested, are easily apprehended by all. Refinement in writing, expresses a less natural and [less] obvious train of thought."—*Blair's Rhet.* p. 184.

"Where the story of an epic poem is founded on truth, no circumstances must be added, but such as connect naturally with what are known to be true : history may be supplied, but it must not be contradicted."—See *Kames's El. of Crit.* ii, 280.

"Others, I am told, pretend to have been once his friends. Surely they are their enemies, who say so ; for nothing can be more odious than to treat a friend as they have treated him. But of this I cannot persuade myself, when I consider the constant and eternal aversion of all bad writers to a good one."—*Cleland, in Defence of Pope.*

> "From side to side he struts, he smiles, he prates,
> And seems to wonder what's become of Yates."—*Churchill.*

> "Alas ! what sorrows gloom'd that parting day,
> That call'd them from their native walks away !"—*Goldsmith.*

Lesson III. — Parsing.

"It is involved in the nature of man, that he cannot be indifferent to an event that concerns him or any of his connexions : if it be fortunate, it gives him joy ; if unfortunate, it gives him sorrow."—*Kames's El. of Crit.* i, 62.

"I knew a man who had relinquished the sea for a country life : in the corner of his garden he reared an artificial mount with a level summit, resembling most accurately a quarter-deck, not only in shape, but in size ; and here he generally walked."—*Ib.* p. 328.

"I mean, when we are angry with our Maker. For against whom else is it that our displeasure is pointed, when we murmur at the distribution of things here, either because our own condition is less agreeable than we would have it, or because that of others is more prosperous than we imagine they deserve?"—*Archbishop Secker*.

"Things cannot charge into the soul, or force us upon any opinions about them; they stand aloof and are quiet. It is our fancy that makes them operate and gall us; it is we that rate them, and give them their bulk and value."—*Collier's Antoninus*, p. 212.

"What is your opinion of truth, good-nature, and sobriety? Do any of these virtues stand in need of a good word; or are they the worse for a bad one? I hope a diamond will shine ne'er the less for a man's silence about the worth of it."—*Ib*. p. 49.

"Those words which were formerly current and proper, have now become obsolete and barbarous. Alas! this is not all: fame tarnishes in time too; and men grow out of fashion, as well as languages."—*Ib*. p. 55.

"O Luxury! thou curs'd by Heaven's decree,
How ill exchang'd are things like these for thee!"—*Goldsmith*.

"O, then, how blind to all that truth requires,
Who think it freedom when a part aspires!"—*Id*.

IMPROPRIETIES FOR CORRECTION.

ERRORS OF PRONOUNS.

LESSON I.—RELATIVES.

"At the same time that we attend to this pause, every appearance of sing-song and tone must be carefully guarded against."—*Murray's English Reader*, p. xx.

[FORMULE.—Not proper, because the word *that* has not clearly the construction either of a pronoun or of a conjunction. But, according to Observation 18th, on the Classes of Pronouns, "The word *that*, or indeed any other word, should never be so used as to leave the part of speech uncertain." Therefore, the expression should be altered; thus, "*While* we attend to this pause, every appearance of *singsong* must be carefully *avoid-d*."]

"For thou shalt go to all that I shall send thee."—*Jeremiah*, i, 7; *Gurney's Obs.* p. 223. "Ah! how happy would it have been for me, had I spent in retirement these twenty-three years that I have possessed my kingdom."—See *Sanborn's Gram.* p. 212. "In the same manner that relative pronouns and their antecedents are usually parsed."—*Ib.* p. 71. "Parse or mention all the other nouns in the parsing examples, in the same manner that you do the word in the form of parsing."—*Ib.* p. 8. "The passive verb will always be of the person and number that the verb *be* is, of which it is in part composed."—*Ib.* p. 53. "You have been taught that a verb must always be of the same person and number that its nominative is."—*Ib.* p. 68. "A relative pronoun, also, must always be of the same person, number, and even gender that its antecedent is."—*Ib.* p. 68. "The subsequent is always in the same case that the word is, which asks the question."—*Ib.* p. 95. "One sometimes represents an antecedent noun in the same definite manner that personal pronouns do."—*Ib.* p. 98. "The mind being carried forward to the time that an event happens, easily conceives it to be present."—*Ib.* p. 107. "*Save* and *saving* are parsed in the same manner that *except* and *excepting* are."—*Ib.* p. 123. "Adverbs describe, qualify, or modify the meaning of a verb in the same manner that adjectives do nouns."—*Ib.* p. 16. "The third person singular of verbs, is formed in the same manner, that the plural number of nouns is."—*Ib.* p. 41. "He saith further: 'that the apostles did not anew baptize such persons, that had been baptized with the baptism of John.'"—*Barclay's Works*, i, 292. "For we which live, are always delivered unto death for Jesus' sake."—*2 Cor.* iv, 11. "For they, which believe in God, must be careful to maintain good works."—*Barclay's Works*, i, 431. "Nor yet of those which teach things which they ought not, for filthy lucre's sake."—*Ib.* i, 435. "So as to hold such bound in heaven, whom they bind on earth, and such loosed in heaven, whom they loose on earth."—*Ib.* i, 478. "Now, if it be an evil to do any thing out of strife; then such things that are seen so to be done, are they not to be avoided and forsaken?"—*Ib.* i, 522. "All such who satisfy themselves not with the superficies of religion."—*Ib.* ii, 23. "And he is the same in substance, what he was upon earth, both in spirit, soul and body."—*Ib.* iii, 98. "And those that do not thus, are such, to whom the Church of Rome can have no charity."—*Ib.* iii, 204. "Before his book he placeth a great list of that he accounts the blasphemous assertions of the Quakers."—*Ib.* iii, 257. "And this is that he should have proved."—*Ib.* iii, 322. "Three of which were at that time actual students of philosophy in the university."—*Ib.* iii, 180. "Therefore it is not lawful for any whatsoever * * * to force the consciences of others."—*Ib.* ii, 13. "What is the cause that the former days were better than these?"—*Eccl.* vii, 10. "In the same manner that the term *my* depends on the name *books*."—*O. B. Peirce's Gram.* p. 54. "In the same manner as the term *house* depends on the relative *near*."—*Ib.* p. 58. "James died on the day that Henry returned."—*Ib.* p. 177.

LESSON II. — DECLENSIONS.

"*Other* makes the plural *others*, when it is found without it's substantive."—*Priestley's Gram.* p. 12.

[FORMULE.—Not proper, because the pronoun *it's* is written with an apostrophe. But, according to Observation 25th, on the Declensions of Pronouns, "The possessive case of pronouns should never be written with an apostrophe." Therefore, this apostrophe should be omitted; thus, "*Other* makes the plural *others*, when it is found without *its* substantive."]

"But *his, her's, our's, your's, their's*, have evidently the form of the possessive case."—*Lowth's Gram.* p. 23. "To the Saxon possessive cases, *hire, ure, eower, hira*, (that is, *her's, our's, your's, their's*,) we have added the *s*, the characteristic of the possessive case of nouns."—*Ib.* p. 23. "Upon the name of Jesus Christ our Lord, both their's and our's."—FRIENDS' BIBLE: 1 *Cor.* i, 2. "In this Place *His* Hand is clearly preferable either to *Her's* or *It's*.*—*Harris's Hermes*, p. 59. "That roguish leer of your's makes a pretty woman's heart ake."—ADDISON: in *Joh. Dict.* "Lest by any means this liberty of your's become a stumbling-block."—FRIENDS' BIBLE: 1 *Cor.* viii, 9. "First person: Sing. I, mine, me; Plur. we, our's, us "—*Wilbur and Livingston's Gram.* p. 16. "Second person: Sing. thou, thine, thee; Plur. ye or you, your's, you."—*Ib.* "Third person: Sing. she, her's, her; Plur. they, their's, them."—*Ib.* "So shall ye serve strangers in a land that is not your's."—SCOTT ET AL.: *Jer.* v, 19. "Second person, Singular: Nom. thou or you, Poss. thine or yours, Obj. thee or you."—*Frost's El. of E. Gram.* p. 13. "Second person, Dual: Nom. Gyt, ye two; Gen. Incer, of ye two; Dat. Inc, incrum, to ye two; Acc. Inc, ye two; Voc. Eala inc, O ye two; Abl. Inc, incrum, from ye two."—*Gwilt's Saxon Gram.* p. 12. "Second person, Plural: Nom. Ge, ye; Gen. Eower, of ye; Dat. Eow, to ye; Acc. Eow, ye; Voc. Eala ge, O ye; Abl. Eow. from ye."—*Ib.* (*written in* 1829.) "These words are, *mine, thine, his, her's, our's, your's, their's*, and *whose*."—*Cardell's Essay*, p. 88. "This house is *our's*, and that is *your's*. *Their's* is very commodious."—*Ib.* p. 90. "And they shall eat up thine harvest, and thy bread: they shall eat up thy flocks and thine herds."—*Jeremiah*, v, 17. "*Whoever* and *Whichever* are thus declined. *Sing.* and *Plu. nom.* whoever, *poss.* whoseever, *obj.* whomever. *Sing.* and *Plu. nom.* whichever, *poss.* whoseever, *obj.* whichever."—*Cooper's Plain and Practical Gram.* p. 38. "The compound personal pronouns are thus declined; *Sing. N.* Myself, *P.* my-own, *O.* myself; *Plur. N.* ourselves, *P.* our-own, *O.* ourselves. *Sing. N.* Thyself or yourself, *P.* thy-own or your-own, *O.* thyself or yourself;" &c.—*Perley's Gram.* p. 16. "Every one of us, each for hisself, laboured how to recover him."—SIDNEY: in *Priestley's Gram.* p. 96. "Unless when ideas of their opposites manifestly suggest their selves."—*Wright's Gram.* p. 49. "It not only exists in time, but is time its self."—*Ib.* p. 75. "A position which the action its self will palpably deny."—*Ib.* p. 102. "A difficulty sometimes presents its self."—*Ib.* p. 165. "They are sometimes explanations in their selves."—*Ib.* p. 249. "Our's, Your's, Their's, Her's, It's."—*S. Barrett's Gram.* p. 24.

"Their's the wild chace of false felicities;
His, the compos'd possession of the true."—*Murray's E. Reader*, p. 216.

LESSON III. — MIXED.

"It is the boast of Americans, without distinction of parties, that their government is the most free and perfect, which exists on the earth."—*Dr. Allen's Lectures*, p. 18.

[FORMULE.—Not proper, because the relative *which* is here intended to be taken in a restrictive sense. But, according to Observation 26th, on the Classes of Pronouns, and (others that follow it,) the word *who* or *which*, with a comma before it, does not usually limit the preceding term. Therefore, *which* should be *that*, and the comma should be omitted; thus,—" that their government is the most free and perfect *that* exists on the earth."]

"Children, who are dutiful to their parents, enjoy great prosperity."—*Sanborn's Gram.* p. 69. "The scholar, who improves his time, sets an example worthy of imitation."—*Ib.* p. 69. "Nouns and pronouns, which signify the same person, place, or thing, agree in case."—*Cooper's Gram.* p. 115. "An interrogative sentence is one, which asks a question."—*Ib.* p. 114. "In the use of words and phrases, which in point of time relate to each other, a due regard to *that relation* should be *observed*."—*Ib.* p. 146; see L. *Murray's* Rule xiii. "The same observations, which have been made respecting the effect of the article and participle, appear to be applicable to the pronoun and participle."—*Murray's Gram.* p. 193. "The reason that they have not the same use of them in reading, may be traced to the very defective and erroneous method, in which the art of reading is taught."—*Ib.* p. 252. "Since the time that reason began to exert her powers, thought, during our waking hours, has been active in every breast, without a moment's suspension or pause."—*Murray's Key*, p. 271; *Merchant's Gram.* 212. "In speaking of such who greatly delight in the same."—*Notes to Duncan*, 177. "Except such to whom the king shall hold out the golden sceptre, that he may live."—*Esther*, iv, 11. "But the same day that Lot went out of Sodom, it rained fire and brimstone from heaven, and destroyed them all."—*Luke*, xvii, 29. "In the next place I will explain several cases of nouns and pronouns which have not yet come under our notice."

* This is a comment upon the following quotation from Milton, where *Hers* for *His* would be a gross barbarism:
    "Should intermitted vengeance arm again
    His red right hand to plague us."—*Par. Lost*, ii, 174.

—*Kirkham's Gram.* p. 129. "Three natural distinctions of time are all which can exist."—*Hall's Gram.* p. 15. "We have exhibited such only as are obviously distinct; and which seem to be sufficient, and not more than sufficient."—*Murray's Gram.* p. 68; *Hall's, 14.* "This point encloses a part of a sentence which may be omitted without materially injuring the connexion of the other members."—*Hall's Gram.* p. 39. "Consonants are letters, which cannot be sounded without the aid of a Vowel."—*Bucke's Gram.* p. 9. "Words are not simple sounds, but sounds, which convey a meaning to the mind."—*Ib.* p. 16. "Nature's postures are always easy; and which is more, nothing but your own will can put you out of them."—*Collier's Antoninus,* p. 197. "Therefore ought we to examine our ownselves, and prove our ownselves."—*Barclay's Works,* i, 426. "Certainly it had been much more natural, to have divided Active Verbs into *Immanent,* or such whose Action is terminated in it self, and *Transient,* or such whose Action is terminated in something without it self."—*Johnson's Gram. Com.* p. 273. "This is such an advantage which no other lexicon will afford." —DR. TAYLOR: *in Pike's Lex.* p. iv. "For these reasons, such liberties are taken in the Hebrew tongue with those words as are of the most general and frequent use."—*Pike's Heb. Lexicon,* p. 184. "At the same time that we object to the laws, which the antiquarian in language would impose upon us, we must enter our protest against those authors, who are too fond of innovations."—*Murray's Gram.* Vol. i, p. 136.

CHAPTER VI.—VERBS.

A Verb is a word that signifies *to be, to act,* or *to be acted upon :* as, I *am,* I *rule,* I *am ruled ;* I *love,* thou *lovest,* he *loves.*

VERBS are so called, from the Latin *Verbum,* a *Word;* because the verb is that word which most essentially contains what is said in any clause or sentence.

An English verb has four CHIEF TERMS, or PRINCIPAL PARTS, ever needful to be ascertained in the first place ; namely, the *Present,* the *Preterit,* the *Imperfect Participle,* and the *Perfect Participle.*

The *Present* is that form of the verb, which is the root of all the rest ; the verb itself; or that simple term which we should look for in a dictionary: as, *be, act, rule, love, defend, terminate.*

The *Preterit* is that simple form of the verb, which denotes time past ; and which is always connected with some noun or pronoun, denoting the subject of the assertion : as, *I was, I acted, I ruled, I loved, I defended.*

The *Imperfect Participle* is that which ends commonly[*] in *ing,* and implies a *continuance* of the being, action, or passion : as, *being, acting, ruling, loving, defending, terminating.*

The *Perfect Participle* is that which ends commonly in *ed* or *en,* and implies a *completion* of the being, action, or passion : as, *been, acted, ruled, loved.*

CLASSES.

Verbs are divided, with respect to their *form,* into four classes ; *regular* and *irregular, redundant* and *defective.*

I. A *regular verb* is a verb that forms the preterit and the perfect participle by assuming *d* or *ed ;* as, *love, loved, loving, loved.*

II. An *irregular verb* is a verb that does not form the preterit and the perfect participle by assuming *d* or *ed ;* as, *see, saw, seeing, seen.*

III. A *redundant verb* is a verb that forms the preterit or the perfect

---

[*] The Imperfect Participle, *when simple,* or when taken as one of the four principal terms constituting the verb or springing from it, ends *always* in *ing.* But, in a subsequent chapter, I include under this name the first participle of the passive verb ; and this, in our language, is always a compound, and the latter term of it does not end in *ing:* as, "In all languages, indeed, examples are to be found of adjectives *being compared* whose signification admits neither intension nor remission."—CROMBIE, *on Etym. and Syntax,* p. 106 According to most of our writers on English grammar, the Present or Imperfect Participle Passive is *always* a compound of *being* and the form of the perfect participle ; as, *being loved, being seen.* But some represent it to have *two* forms. one of which is always simple ; as, " *Obeyed, or being obeyed,*"—*Sanborn's Analytical Gram.* p. 55: " Loved or being loved,"— *Parkhurst's Grammar for Beginners,* p. 110 : " *Loved, or, being loved,*"—*Clark's Practical Gram.* p 83. I here concur with the majority, who in no instance take the participle in *ed* or *en,* alone, for the Imperfect.

participle in two ways or more, and so as to be both regular and irregular; as, *thrive, thrived* or *throve, thriving, thrived* or *thriven.*

IV. A *defective verb* is a verb that forms no participles, and is used in but few of the moods and tenses; as, *beware, ought, quoth.*

Verbs are divided again, with respect to their *signification*, into four classes; *active-transitive, active-intransitive, passive,* and *neuter.*

I. An *active-transitive verb* is a verb that expresses an action which has some person or thing for its object; as, " Cain *slew Abel.*"—" Cassius *loved Brutus.*"

II. An *active-intransitive verb* is a verb that expresses an action which has no person or thing for its object; as, " John *walks.*"—" Jesus *wept.*"

III. A *passive verb* is a verb that represents its subject, or what the nominative expresses, as being acted upon; as, " I *am compelled.*"—" Cæsar *was slain.*"

IV. A *neuter verb* is a verb that expresses neither action nor passion, but simply being, or a state of being; as, " There *was light.*"—" The babe *sleeps.*"

OBSERVATIONS.

Obs. 1.—So various have been the views of our grammarians, respecting this complex and most important part of speech, that almost every thing that is contained in any theory or distribution of the English verbs, may be considered a matter of opinion and of dispute. Nay, the essential nature of a verb, in Universal Grammar, has never yet been determined by any received definition that can be considered unobjectionable. The greatest and most acute philologists confess that a faultless definition of this part of speech, is difficult, if not impossible, to be formed. Horne Tooke, at the close of his Diversions of Purley, cites with contempt nearly a dozen different attempts at a definition, some Latin, some English, some French; then, with the abruptness of affected disgust, breaks off the catalogue and the conversation together, leaving his readers to guess, if they can, what he conceived a verb to be. He might have added some scores of others, and probably would have been as little satisfied with any one of them. A definition like that which is given above, may answer in some degree the purpose of distinction; but, after all, we must judge what is, and what is not a verb, chiefly from our own observation of the sense and use of words.*

Obs. 2.—Whether *participles* ought to be called verbs or not, is a question that has been much disputed, and is still variously decided; nor is it possible to settle it in any way not liable to some serious objections. The same may perhaps be said of all the forms called *infinitives.* If the essence of a verb be made to consist in affirmation, predication, or assertion, (as it is in many grammars,) neither infinitives nor participles can be reckoned verbs, without a manifest breach of the definition. Yet are the former almost universally treated as verbs, and by some as the only pure verbs; nor do all deny them this rank, who say that affirmation is *essential* to a verb. Participles, when unconnected with auxiliaries, are most commonly considered a separate part of speech; but in the formation of many of our moods and tenses, we take them as *constituent parts of the verb.* If there is absurdity in this, there is more in undertaking to avoid it; and the inconvenience should be submitted to, since it amounts to little or nothing in practice. With auxiliaries, then, participles *are verbs:* without auxiliaries, they are *not verbs,* but form a separate part of speech.

Obs. 3.—The number of verbs in our language, amounts unquestionably to four or five thousand; some say, (perhaps truly,) to eight thousand. All these, whatever be the number, are confessedly *regular* in their formation, except about two hundred. For, though the catalogues in our grammars give the number somewhat variously, all the irregular, redundant, and defective verbs, put together, are *commonly* reckoned fewer than two hundred. I admit, in all, two hundred and nineteen. The regular verbs, therefore, are vastly more numerous than those which deviate from the stated form. But, since many of the latter are words of very frequent occurrence, the irregular verbs appear exceedingly numerous in practice, and consequently require a great deal of attention. The defective verbs being very few, and most of these few being mere auxiliaries, which are never parsed separately, there is little occasion to treat them as a distinct class; though Murray and others have ranked them so, and perhaps it is best to follow their example. The redundant verbs,

---

* In the following examples, "*he*" and "*she*" are converted into verbs; as "*thou*" sometimes is, in the writings of Shakspeare, and others: " Is it not an impulse of selfishness or of a depraved nature to *he* and *she* inanimate objects?"—*Cutler's English Gram.* p. 16. Dr. Bullions, who has heretofore published several of the worst definitions of the verb anywhere extant, has now perhaps one of the best: " A VERB is a word used to express the *act, being,* or *state* of its subject."—*Analyt. & Pract. Gram.* p. 59. Yet it is not very obvious, that "*he*" and "*she*" are here verbs under this definition.

which are regular in one form and irregular in an other, being of course always found written-either one way or the other, as each author chooses, may be, and commonly have been, referred in parsing to the class of regular or irregular verbs accordingly. But, as their number is considerable, and their character peculiar, there may be some advantage in making them a separate class. Besides, the definition of an irregular verb, as given in any of our grammars, seems to exclude all such as *may* form the preterit and the perfect participle by assuming *d* or *ed*.

OBS. 4.—In most grammars and dictionaries, verbs are divided, with respect to their signification, into three classes only; *active, passive,* and *neuter*. In such a division, the class of *active* verbs includes those only which are *active-transitive*, and all the *active-intransitive* verbs are called *neuter*. But, in the division adopted above, *active-intransitive* verbs are made a distinct class; and those only are regarded as neuter, which imply a state of existence without action. When, therefore, we speak of verbs without reference to their regimen, we may, if we please, apply the simple term *active* to all those which express *action,* whether *transitive* or *intransitive*. "We *act* whenever we *do* any thing; but we *may act* without *doing* any thing."—*Crabb's Synonymes*.

OBS. 5.—Among the many English grammars in which verbs are divided, as above mentioned, into *active, passive,* and *neuter*, only, are those of the following writers: Lowth, Murray, Ainsworth, Alden, Allen, Alger, Bacon, Bicknell, Blair, Bullions, (at first,) Charles Adams, Bucke, Cobbett, Dilworth, A. Flint, Frost, (at first,) Greenleaf, Hall, Johnson,* Lennie, Picket, Pond, Sanborn, R. C. Smith, Rev. T. Smith, and Wright. These authors, and many more, agree, that, "A *verb neuter* expresses neither action nor passion, but being, or a state of being."—*L. Murray*. Yet, according to their scheme, such words as *walk, run, swim, fly, strive, struggle, wrestle, contend,* are verbs *neuter*. In view of this palpable absurdity, I cannot but think it was a useful improvement upon the once popular scheme of English grammar, to make active-intransitive verbs a distinct class, and to apply the term *neuter* to those few only which accord with the foregoing definition. This had been done before the days of Lindley Murray, as may be seen in Buchanan's English Syntax, p. 56, and in the old British Grammar, p. 153, each published many years before the appearance of his work;† and it has often been done since, and is preferred even by many of the professed admirers and followers of Murray; as may be seen in the grammars of Comly, Fisk, Merchant, Kirkham, and others.

OBS. 6.—Murray himself quotes this improved distribution, and with some appearance of approbation; but strangely imagines it must needs be *inconvenient* in practice. Had he been a schoolmaster, he could hardly have so judged. He says, "Verbs have been distinguished by some writers, into the following kinds :—

"1st. *Active-transitive*, or those which denote an action that passes from the agent to some object : as, Cæsar conquered Pompey.

"2d. *Active-intransitive*, or those which express that kind of action, which has no effect upon any thing beyond itself: as, Cæsar walked.

"3d. *Passive*, or those which express, not action, but passion, whether pleasing or painful : as, Portia was loved ; Pompey was conquered.

"4th. *Neuter*, or those which express an attribute that consists neither in action nor passion : as, Cæsar stood.

"This appears to be an orderly arrangement. But if the class of *active-intransitive* verbs were admitted, *it would rather perplex* than assist the learner : for the difference between verbs active and neuter, as transitive and intransitive is easy and obvious : but the difference between verbs absolutely neuter and [those which are] intransitively active, is not always clear. It is, indeed, often *very difficult*, if not impossible to be ascertained."—*Murray's Gram.* 8vo, p. 60.‡

* Dr. Johnson says, " English verbs are active, as *I love;* or neuter, as *I languish.* The neuters are formed like the actives. The passive voice is formed by joining the participle preterit to the substantive verb, as *I am loved.*" He also observes, " Most verbs signifying *action* may likewise signify *condition* or *habit*, and become *neuters* ; as, *I love,* I am in love ; *I strike,* I am now striking."—*Gram. with his Quarto Dict.* p. 7.

† The doctrine here referred to, appears in both works in the very same words : to wit, " English Verbs are either Active, Passive, or Neuter. There are two sorts of Active Verbs, viz. *active-transitive* and *active-intransitive* Verbs."—*British Gram.* p. 153 ; *Buchanan's*, 56. Buchanan was in this case the copyist

‡ " The distinction between verbs absolutely neuter, as *to sleep,* and verbs active intransitive, as *to walk,* though *founded in* NATURE *and* TRUTH, is of little use in grammar. Indeed it would rather perplex than assist the learner ; for the difference between verbs active and [verbs] neuter, as transitive and intransitive, is easy and obvious ; but the difference between verbs absolutely neuter and [those which are] intransitively active is not always clear. The however these latter may differ in nature, the construction of them both is the same ; and grammar is not so much concerned with their *real*, as with their *grammatical* properties."—*Lowth's Gram.* p 30. But are not " TRUTH, NATURE, and REALITY," worthy to be preferred to any instructions that contradict them ? If they are, the good doctor and his worthy copyist have here made an ill choice. It is not only for the sake of these properties, that I retain a distinction which these grammarians, and others above named, reject ; but for the sake of avoiding the untruth, confusion, and absurdity, into which one must fall by calling all active-intransitive verbs *neuter*. The distinction of active verbs, as being either transitive or intransitive, is also necessarily retained. But the suggestion, that this distinction is more " *easy and obvious*" than the other, is altogether an error. The really neuter verbs, being very few, occasion little or no difficulty. But very many active verbs, perhaps a large majority, are sometimes used intransitively ; and of those which our lexicographers record as being always transitive, not a few are occasionally found without any object, either expressed or clearly suggested : as, " He *convinces*, but he does not *elevate nor animate.*"—*Blair's Rhet.* p. 242. " The child *imitates*, and *commits* to memory ; whilst the riper

Obs. 7.—The following note, from a book written on purpose to apply the principles of Murray's Grammar, and of Allen's, (the two best of the foregoing two dozen,) may serve as an offset to the reason above assigned for rejecting the class of active-intransitive verbs: "It is possible that some teachers may look upon the nice distinction here made, between the active *transitive* and the active *intransitive* verbs, as totally unnecessary. They may, perhaps, rank the latter with the neuter verbs. The author had his choice of difficulties: on the one hand, he was aware that his arrangement might not suit the views of the abovementioned persons; and, on the other, he was so sensible of the inaccuracy of their system, and of its clashing with the definitions, as well as rules, laid down in almost every grammar, that he was unwilling to bring before the public a work containing so well-known and manifest an error. Of what use can Murray's definition of the *active* verb be, to one who endeavours to prove the propriety of thus assigning an epithet to the various parts of speech, in the course of parsing? He says, ' A verb active expresses an action, and necessarily implies an agent, and an object acted upon.' In the sentence, 'William hastens away,' the active intransitive verb *hastens* has indeed an *agent*, ' William,' but where is the *object?* Again, he says, ' Active verbs govern the objective case ;' although it is clear it is not the *active* meaning of the verb which requires the objective case, but the *transitive*, and that only. He adds, ' A verb neuter expresses *neither action nor passion*, but being, or a state of being:' and the accuracy of this definition is borne out by the assent of perhaps every other grammarian. If, with this clear and forcible definition before our eyes, we proceed to class *active* intransitive verbs with neuter verbs, and direct our pupils to prove such a classification by reciting Murray's definition of the *neuter* verb, we may indeed expect from a thinking pupil the remonstrance which was actually made to a teacher on that system, while parsing the verb ' *to run.*' ' Sir,' asks the boy, ' does not *to run* imply action, for it always makes me perspire ? ' "—*Nixon's English Parser*, p. 9.

Obs. 8.—For the consideration of those classical scholars who may think we are bound by the authority of *general usage*, to adhere to the old division of verbs into active, passive, and neuter. it may be proper to say, that the distribution of the verbs in Latin, has been as much a matter of dispute among the great grammarians of that language, as has the distribution of English verbs, more recently, among ourselves; and often the points at issue were precisely the same.[*] To explain here the different views of the very old grammarians, as Charisius, Donatus, Servius, Priscian ; or even to notice the opinions of later critics, as Sanctius, Scioppius, Vossius, Perizonius; might seem perhaps a needless departure from what the student of mere English grammar is concerned to know. The curious, however, may find interesting citations from all these authors, under the corresponding head, in some of our Latin grammars. See *Prat's Grammatica Latina*, 8vo, London, 1722. It is certain that the division of *active* verbs, into *transitive* and *intransitive*—or, (what is the same thing,) into "*absolute* and *transitive*"—or, into "*immanent* and *transient*"—is of a very ancient date. The notion of calling *passive* verbs *transitive*, when used in their ordinary and proper construction, as some now do, is, I think, a *modern* one, and no small error.

up *digests*, and thinks independently."—*Dr. Lieber, Lit. Conv.* p. 313. Of examples like these, three different views may be taken; and it is *very questionable* which is the right one : First, that these verbs are here *intransitive*, though they are not commonly so ; *Second*, that they are *transitive*, and have objects understood ; *Third*, that they are used *improperly*, because no determinate objects are given them. If we assume the second opinion or the last, the full or the correct expressions may be these : "He convinces *the judgement*, but he does not elevate *the imagination*, or animate *the feelings*."—"The child imitates *others*, and commits *words* to memory ; whilst the riper age digests *facts or truths*, and thinks independently." These verbs are here *transitive*, but are they so above ? Those grammarians who, supposing no other distinction important, make of verbs but two classes, *transitive* and *intransitive*, are still as much at variance, and as much at fault, as others, (and often more so,) when they come to draw the line of this distinction. To "*requires*" an objective, to "*govern*" an objective, to "*admit*" an objective, and to "*have*" an objective, are criterions considerably different. Then it is questionable, whether infinitives, participles, or sentences, must or can have the effect of objectives. One author says, "If a verb has any objective case *expressed*, it is transitive : if it has none, it is intransitive. *Verbs which* appear transitive in their nature, may frequently be used intransitively."—*Chandler's Old Gram.* p. 32 ; his *Common School Gram.* p. 48. An other says, "A *transitive* verb *asserts* action which *does or can*, terminate on some object."—*Frazee's Gram.* p. 29. An other avers, "There are two classes of verbs *perfectly distinct* from each other, viz : Those which *do*, and those which *do not*, govern an objective case." And his definition is, "A *Transitive Verb* is one which *requires* an objective case after it."—*Hart's E. Gram.* p. 62. Both Frazee and Hart reckon the *passive* verb *transitive !* And the latter teaches, that, "*Transitive* verbs in English, are sometimes used *without an objective case* ; as, The apple *tastes sweet*!"—*Hart's Gram.* p. 73.

[*] In the hands of some gentlemen, "the Principles of Latin Grammar," and "the Principles of English Grammar,"—are equally pliable, or changeable ; and, what is very remarkable, a comparison of different editions will show, that the fundamental doctrines of a whole "*Series* of Grammars, English, Latin, and Greek," may so change in a single lustrum, as to rest upon authorities altogether different. Dr. Bullions's grammars, a few years ago, like those of his great oracles, Adam, Murray, and Lennie, divided verbs into " three kinds, *Active*, *Passive*, and *Neuter*." Now they divide them into two only, " *Transitive* and *Intransitive* ;" and absurdly aver, that, " *Verbs in the passive form are as really transitive as in the active form*."—*Prin. of E. Gram.* 1843. p. 200. Now, as if no verb could be plural, and no transitive act could be future, conditional, in progress, or left undone, they define thus : "A *Transitive* verb expresses an *act done* by one person or thing to another."—*Ib.* p. 29 ; *Analyt. and Pract. Gram.* 60 ; *Latin Gram.* 77. Now, the division which so lately as 1842 was pronounced by the Doctor to be "more useful than any other," and advantageously accordant with "most dictionaries of the English language," (see his *Fourth Edition*, p. 20,) is wholly rejected from this notable "*Series*." Now, the "*vexed question*" about "the classification of verbs," which, at some revision still later, drew from this author whole pages of weak arguments for his faulty *changes*, is complacently supposed to have been *well settled* in his favour ! Of this matter, now, in 1849, he speaks thus : " The division of verbs into transitive and intransitive has been so generally adopted and approved by the best grammarians, that any discussion of the subject is now unnecessary."—*Bullions's Analyt. and Pract. Gram.*, p. 59.

OBS. 9.—Dr. Adam's distribution of verbs, is apparently the same as the first part of Murray's; and his definitions are also in nearly the same words. But he adds, "The verb *Active* is also called *Transitive*, when the action *passeth over* to the object, or hath an effect on some other thing; as, *scribo literas*, I write letters : but when the action is confined within the agent, and *passeth not over* to any object, it is called *Intransitive*; as, *ambulo*, I walk; *curro*, I run : ☞ which are likewise called *Neuter Verbs.*"—*Adam's Latin and English Gram.* p. 79. But he had just before said, "A *Neuter* verb properly expresses neither action nor passion, but *simply the being, state, or condition* of things; as, *dormio*, I sleep; *sedeo*, I sit."—*Ibid.* Verbs of motion or action, then, must needs be as improperly called neuter, in Latin, as in English. Nor is this author's arrangement orderly in other respects; for he treats of "*Deponent* and *Common* Verbs," of "*Irregular* Verbs," of "*Defective* Verbs," and of "*Impersonal* Verbs," none of which had he mentioned in his distribution. Nor are the late revisers of his grammar any more methodical.

OBS. 10.—The division of our verbs into *active-transitive, active-intransitive, passive,* and *neuter,* must be understood to have reference not only to their *signification* as of themselves, but also to their *construction* with respect to the government of an objective word after them. The latter is in fact their most important distinction, though made *with reference* to a different part of speech. The classical scholar, too, being familiar with the forms of Latin and Greek verbs, will doubtless think it a convenience, to have the arrangement as nearly correspondent to those ancient forms, as the nature of our language will admit. This is perhaps the strongest argument for the recognition of the class of *passive verbs* in English. Some grammarians, choosing to parse the passive participle separately, reject this class of verbs altogether; and, forming their division of the rest with reference to the construction alone, make but two classes, *transitive* and *intransitive.* Such is the distribution adopted by C. Alexander, D. Adams, Bingham, Chandler, E. Cobb, Harrison, Nutting, and John Peirce; and supported also by some British writers, among whom are M'Culloch and Grant. Such too was the distribution of Webster, in his Plain and Comprehensive Grammar, as published in 1800. He then taught: "We have no *passive* verb in the language; and those which are called *neuter* are mostly *active.*"—Page 14. But subsequently, in his Philosophical, Abridged, and Improved Grammars, he recognized "a more natural and comprehensive division" of verbs, "into *transitive, intransitive,* and *passive.*"—*Webster's Rudiments,* p. 20. This, in reality, differs but little from the old division into *active, passive,* and *neuter.* In some grammars of recent date, as Churchill's, Butler's, S. W. Clark's, Frazee's, Hart's, Hendrick's, Perley's, Weld's, Wells's, and the *improved* treatises of Bullions and Frost, verbs are said to be of *two* kinds only, *transitive* and *intransitive;* but these authors allow to transitive verbs a "passive form," or "passive voice,"—absurdly making all passive verbs transitive, and all neuters intransitive, as if *action* were expressed by both. For this most faulty classification, Dr. Bullions pretends the authority of "Mr. Webster;" and Frazee, that of "Webster, Bullions, and others."—*Gram.* p. 30. But if Dr. Webster ever taught the absurd doctrine *that passive verbs are transitive,* he has contradicted it far too much to have any weight in its favour.

OBS. 11.—Dalton makes only two classes; and these he will have to be *active* and *passive;* an arrangement for which he might have quoted Scaliger, Sanctius, and Scioppius. Ash and Coar recognize but two, which they call *active* and *neuter.* This was also the scheme of Bullions, in his Principles of E. Gram., 4th Edition, 1842. Priestley and Maunder have two, which they call *transitive* and *neuter;* but Maunder, like some named above, will have transitive verbs to be susceptible of an active and a passive voice, and Priestley virtually asserts the same. Cooper, Day, Davis, Hazen, Hiley, Webster, Wells, (in his 1st Edition,) and Wilcox, have three classes; *transitive, intransitive,* and *passive.* Sanders's Grammar has *three;* "*Transitive, Intransitive,* and *Neuter;*" and two voices, *both transitive* Jaudon has four; *transitive, intransitive, auxiliary,* and *passive.* Burn has four; *active, passive, neuter,* and *substantive.* Cardell labours hard to prove that all verbs are *both active and transitive;* and for this, he might have desired their aid, he might have cited several ancient authorities.[*] Cutler avers, "*All verbs are active;*" yet he divides them "into *active transitive, active intransitive,* and *participial verbs.*"—*Grammar and Parser,* p. 31. Some grammarians, appearing to think all the foregoing modes of division useless, attempt nothing of the kind. William Ward, in 1765, rejected all such classification, but recognized three voices: "Active, Passive, and Middle : as, *I call, I am called, I am calling.*" Farnum, in 1842, acknowledged the first two of these voices, but made no division of verbs into classes.

OBS. 12.—If we admit the class of *active-intransitive* verbs, that of verbs *neuter* will unquestionably be very small. And this refutes Murray's objection, that the learner will "often" be puzzled to know which is which. Nor can it be of any consequence, if he happen in some instances to decide wrong. To *be,* to *exist,* to *remain,* to *seem,* to *lie,* to *sleep,* to *rest,* to *belong,* to *appertain,* and perhaps a few more, may best be called *neuter;* though some grammarians, as may be inferred from what is said above, deny that there are any neuter

---

[*] This late writer seems to have published his doctrine on this point as a *novelty;* and several teachers ignorantly received and admired it as such : I have briefly shown, in the Introduction to this work, how easily they were deceived. "By this, that Question may be resolv'd, whether every Verb not Passive governs always an Accusative, at least understood : 'Tis the *Opinion of some very able* GRAMMARIANS, but for our Parts we dont think it."—*Grammar published by John Brightland,* 7th Ed., London, 1746, p. 115.

verbs in any language. "Verba Neutra, ait Sanctius, nullo pacto esse possunt; quia, teste Aristotele, omnis motus, actio, vel passio, nihil medium est."—*Prat's Lat. Gram.* p. 117. John Grant, in his Institutes of Latin Grammar, recognizes in the verbs of that language the distinction which Murray supposes to be so "very difficult" in those of our own; and, without falling into the error of Sanctius, or of Lily,* respecting neuter verbs, judiciously confines the term to such as are neuter in reality.

OBS. 13.—Active-transitive verbs, in English, generally require, that the agent or doer of the action be expressed *before* them in the nominative case, and the object or receiver of the action, *after* them in the objective; as, "Cæsar *conquered* Pompey." Passive verbs, which are never primitives, but always derived from active-transitive verbs, (in order to form sentences of like import from natural opposites in voice and sense,) reverse this order, change the cases of the nouns, and denote that the subject, named before them, is affected by the action; while the agent follows, being introduced by the preposition *by*: as, "Pompey *was conquered by* Cæsar." But, as our passive verb always consists of two or more separable parts, this order is liable to be varied, especially in poetry; as,

"How many things *by season seasoned are*
　　To their right praise and true perfection!"—*Shakspeare.*
"Experience *is by industry achieved,*
　　And *perfected by* the swift *course* of time."—*Id.*

OBS. 14.—Most active verbs may be used either transitively or intransitively. Active verbs are transitive, whenever there is any person or thing expressed or clearly implied on which the action terminates; as, "I *knew* him well, and every truant *knew*."—*Goldsmith.* When they do not govern such an object, they are intransitive, whatever may be their power on other occasions; as, "The grand elementary principles of pleasure, by which he *moves*, and *feels*, and *lives*, and *moves*."—*Wordsworth's Pref.* p. xxiii. "The Father *originates* and *elects.* The Son *mediates* and *atones.* The Holy Spirit *regenerates* and *sanctifies.*"—*Gurney's Portable Evidences*, p. 66. "Spectators *remark*, judges *decide*, parties *watch*."—*Blair's Rhet.* p. 271. "In a sermon, a preacher *may explain, demonstrate, infer, exhort, admonish, comfort.*"—*Alexander's Gram.* p. 91.

OBS. 15.—Some verbs may be used in either an active or a neuter sense. In the sentence, "Here I rest," *rest* is a neuter verb; but in the sentence, "Here I rest my hopes," *rest* is an active-transitive verb, and governs *hopes.* And, a few that are always active in a grammatical sense, as necessarily requiring an object after them, do not always indicate such an exertion of force as we commonly call *action.* Such perhaps are the verbs to *have*, to *possess*, to *owe*, to *cost*; as, "They *have* no wine."—"The house *has* a portico."—"The man *possesses* no real estate."—"A son *owes* help and honour to his father."—*Holyday.* "The picture *cost* a crown."—*Wright*, p. 181. Yet possibly even these may be sometimes rather active-intransitive; as, "I can bear my part; 'tis my occupation: *have* at it with you."—*Shakspeare.* "Kings *have* to deal with their neighbours."—*Bacon.* "She will not let instructions enter where folly now *possesses.*"—*Shakspeare.*

"Thou hast deserv'd more love than I can show;
　　But 'tis thy fate to give, and mine to *owe.*"—*Dryden.*

OBS. 16.—An active-intransitive verb, followed by a preposition and its object, will sometimes admit of being put into the passive form; the object of the preposition being assumed for the nominative, and the preposition itself being retained with the verb, as an adverb: as, (*Active,*) "They *laughed* at him."—(*Passive,*) "He *was laughed at.*" "For some time the nonconformists *were connived at.*"—*Robertson's America*, Vol. ii, p. 414. "Every man *shall be dealt* equitably *with.*"—*Butler's Analogy*, p. 212. "If a church *would be looked up to*, it must stand high."—*Parker's Idea*, p. 15.

OBS. 17.—In some instances, what is commonly considered the active form of the verb, is used in a passive sense; and, still oftener, as we have no other passive form that so well denotes continuance, we employ the participle in *ing* in that sense also: as, "I'll teach you all what's *owing* to your Queen."—*Dryden.* That is—what is *due*, or *owed.* "The books continue *selling*; i. e. *upon the sale*, or *to be sold.*"—*Priestley's Gram.* 111. "So we say the brass is *forging*; i. e. *at the forging*, or in [*being forged.*]"—*Ib.* "They are to *blame*; i. e. *to be blamed.*"—*Ib.* Hence some grammarians seem to think, that in our language the distinction between active and passive verbs is of little consequence: "Mr. Grant, however, observes, p. 65, 'The component parts of the English verb, or name of action, are few, simple, and natural; they consist of three words, as *plough, ploughing, ploughed.* Now these words, and their inflections, may be employed either actively or passively. Actively, 'They *plough* the fields; they *are ploughing* the fields; they *ploughed*, or *have ploughed*, the fields.' Passively, 'The fields *plough* well; the fields *are ploughing*; the fields *are ploughed.*'" This passive use of the present tense

---

* Upon this point, Richard Johnson cites and criticises Lily's system thus: "'A Verb Neuter endeth in *o* or *m*, and cannot take *r* to make *him* a Passive; as, *Curro*, I run; *Sum*, I am.'—*Grammar, Eng.* p. 13. This Definition, is founded upon the Notion abovementioned, viz. That none but Transitives are Verbs Active, which is contrary to the reason of Things, and the common sense of Mankind. And what can shock a Child more, of any Ingenuity, than to be told, That *Ambulo* and *Curro* are Verbs Neuter; that is, to speak according to the common Apprehensions of Mankind, that they signifie neither to do, nor suffer."—*Johnson's Grammatical Commentaries*, 8vo, London, 1706, p. 273.

and participle is, however, restricted to what he denominates verbs of *external, material*, or *mechanical* action;' and not to be extended to verbs of *sensation* and *perception*; e. g. *love, feel, see*, &c."—*Nutting's Gram.* p. 40.

MODIFICATIONS.

Verbs have modifications of four kinds; namely, *Moods, Tenses, Persons*, and *Numbers*.

MOODS.

Moods* are different forms of the verb, each of which expresses the being, action, or passion, in some particular manner.

There are five moods; the *Infinitive*, the *Indicative*, the *Potential*, the *Subjunctive*, and the *Imperative*.

The *Infinitive mood* is that form of the verb, which expresses the being, action, or passion, in an unlimited manner, and without person or number: as, "To *die*,—to *sleep*;—To *sleep!*—perchance, to *dream!*"

The *Indicative mood* is that form of the verb, which simply indicates or declares a thing: as, I *write*; you *know*: or asks a question; as, "*Do* you *know?*"—"*Know* ye not?"

The *Potential mood* is that form of the verb, which expresses the power, liberty, possibility, or necessity, of the being, action, or passion: as, "I *can walk*; he *may ride*; we *must go*."

The *Subjunctive mood* is that form of the verb, which represents the being, action, or passion, as conditional, doubtful, and contingent: as, "If thou *go*, see that thou *offend* not."—"See thou *do* it not."—*Rev.* xix, 10.

The *Imperative mood* is that form of the verb, which is used in commanding, exhorting, entreating, or permitting: as, "*Depart* thou."—"*Be comforted*."—"*Forgive* me."—"*Go* in peace."

OBSERVATIONS.

OBS. 1.—The *Infinitive* mood is so called in opposition to the other moods, in which the verb is said to be *finite*. In all the other moods, the verb has a strict connexion, and necessary agreement in person and number, with some subject or nominative, expressed or understood; but the infinitive is the mere verb, without any such agreement, and has no power of completing sense with a noun. In the nature of things, however, all being, action, or passion, not contemplated abstractly as *a thing*, belongs to something that is, or acts, or is acted upon. Accordingly infinitives have, in most instances, a *reference* to some subject of this kind; though their grammatical dependence connects them more frequently with some other term. The infinitive mood, in English, is distinguished by the preposition *to;* which, with a few exceptions, immediately precedes it, and may be said to govern it. In dictionaries, and grammars, *to* is often used as a mere *index*, to distinguish verbs from the other parts of speech. But this little word has no more claim to be ranked as a part of the verb, than has the conjunction *if*, which is the sign of the subjunctive. It is the nature of a preposition, to show the relation of different things, thoughts, or words, to each other; and this "sign of the infinitive" may well be parsed separately as a preposition, since in most instances it manifestly shows the relation between the infinitive verb and some other term. Besides, by most of our grammarians, the present tense of the infinitive mood is declared to be the *radical form* of the verb; but this doctrine must be plainly untrue, upon the supposition that this tense is a compound.

OBS. 2.—The *Indicative* mood is so called because its chief use is, to *indicate*, or declare positively, whatever one wishes to say. It is that form of the verb, which we always employ when we affirm or deny any thing in a direct and independent manner. It is more frequently used, and has a greater number of tenses, than any other mood; and is also, in our language, the only one in which the principal verb is varied in termination. It is not however, on all occasions, confined to its primary use; else it would be simply and only declarative. But we use it sometimes interrogatively, sometimes conditionally; and each of these uses is different from a simple declaration. Indeed, the difference between a ques-

* Murray says, "*Mood* or *Mode* is a particular form of the verb, showing the manner in which the being, action, or passion is represented."—*Octavo Gram.* p. 68. By many grammarians, the term *Mode* is preferred to *Mood;* but the latter is, for this use, the more distinctive, and by far the more common word. In some treatises on grammar, as well as in books of logic, certain *parts of speech*, as *adjectives* and *adverbs*, are called *Modes*, because they qualify or modify other terms. E. g. "Thus all the parts of speech are reducible to four; viz., *Names, Verbs, Modes, Connectives*."—*Enclytica, or Universal Gram.* p. 8. "*Modes* are naturally divided, by their attribution to names or verbs, into *adnames* and *adverbs*."—*Ibid.* p. 24. After making this application of the name *modes*, was it not improper for the learned author to call the *moods* also "*modes?*"

tion and an assertion is practically very great. Hence some of the old grammarians made the form of inquiry a separate mood, which they called the *Interrogative Mood*. But, as these different expressions are distinguished, not by any difference of form in the verb itself, but merely by a different order of the words, it has been found most convenient in practice, to treat them as one mood susceptible of different senses.

OBS. 3.—The *Potential* mood is so called because the leading idea expressed by it, is that of the *power* of performing some action. This mood is known by the signs *may, can, must, might, could, would,* and *should*. Some of these auxiliaries convey other ideas than that of power in the agent; but there is no occasion to explain them severally here. The potential mood, like the indicative, may be used in asking a question; as, "*Must I budge?* *must I observe* you? *must I stand* and *crouch* under your testy humour?"—*Shakspeare*. No question can be asked in any other mood than these two. By some grammarians, the potential mood has been included in the subjunctive, because its meaning is often expressed in Latin by what in that language is called the subjunctive. By others, it has been entirely rejected, because all its tenses are compound, and it has been thought the words could as well be parsed separately. Neither of these opinions is sufficiently prevalent, or sufficiently plausible, to deserve a laboured refutation. On the other hand, James White, in his Essay on the English Verb, (London, 1761,) divided this mood into the following five: namely, "the *Elective*," denoted by *may* or *might;* "the *Potential*," by *can* or *could;* "the *Determinative*," by *would;* "the *Obligative*," by *should;* and "the *Compulsive*," by *must*. Such a distribution is needlessly minute. Most of these can as well be spared as those other "moods, *Interrogative, Optative, Promissive, Hortative, Precative,* &c.", which Murray mentions only to reject. See his *Octavo Gram.* p. 68.

OBS. 4.—The *Subjunctive* mood is so called because it is always *subjoined* to an other verb, and usually denotes some doubtful contingency, or some supposition contrary to fact. The manner of its dependence is commonly denoted by one of the following conjunctions; *if, that, though, lest, unless*. The indicative and potential moods, in all their tenses, may be used in the same dependent manner, to express any positive or potential condition; but this seems not to be a sufficient reason for considering them as parts of the subjunctive mood. In short, the idea of a "subjunctive mood in the indicative form," (which is adopted by Chandler, Frazee, Fisk, S. S. Greene, Comly, Ingersoll, R. C. Smith, Sanborn, Mack, Butler, Hart, Weld, and others,) is utterly inconsistent with any just notion of what a mood is; and the suggestion, which we frequently meet with, that the regular indicative or potential mood may be *thrown into the subjunctive* by merely prefixing a conjunction, is something worse than nonsense. Indeed, no mood can ever be made *a part of an other*, without the grossest confusion and absurdity. Yet, strange as it is, some celebrated authors, misled by an *if*, have tangled together three of them, producing such a snarl of tenses as never yet can have been understood without being thought ridiculous. See *Murray's Grammar*, and others that agree with his late editions.

OBS. 5.—In regard to the number and form of the tenses which should constitute the *subjunctive mood* in English, our grammarians are greatly at variance; and some, supposing its distinctive parts to be but elliptical forms of the indicative or the potential,* even deny the existence of such a mood altogether. On this point, the instructions published by Lindley Murray, however commended and copied, are most remarkably vague and inconsistent.† The early editions of his Grammar gave to this mood *six tenses*, none of which had any of the personal inflections; consequently there was, in all the tenses, *some difference* between it and the indicative. His later editions, on the contrary, make the subjunctive exactly like the indicative, except in the present tense, and in the choice of auxiliaries for the second-future. Both ways, he goes too far. And while at last he restricts the *distinctive form* of the subjunctive to narrower bounds than he ought, and argues against, "If thou loved, If thou knew," &c., he gives to this mood not only the last five tenses of the indicative, but also all those of the potential, with its multiplied auxiliaries; alleging, "that as the indicative mood *is converted into* the subjunctive, by the expression of a condition, motive, wish, supposition, &c.‡ being superadded to it, so the potential mood may, in like manner,

* "We have, in English, no genuine subjunctive mood, except the preterimperfect, if I *were*, if thou *wert*, &c. of the verb *to be*. [See Notes and Observations on the Third Example of Conjugation, in this chapter.] The phrase termed the *subjunctive mood*, is elliptical; *shall, may*, &c. being understood; as, 'Though hand (shall) join in hand, the wicked shall not be unpunished.' 'If it (may) be possible, live peaceably with all.' Scriptures."—*Rev. W. Allen's Gram.*, p. 61. Such expressions as, "If thou *do love*, If he *do love*," appear to disprove this doctrine. [See Notes and Remarks on the Subjunctive of the First Example conjugated below.]

† "Mr. Murray has changed his opinion, as often as Laban changed Jacob's wages. In the edition we print from, we find *shall* and *will* used, in each person of the *first* and *second* future tenses of the subjunctive, but he now states that in the second future tense, *shalt, shall*, should be used instead of *wilt, will*. Perhaps this is *the only improvement* he has made in his Grammar since 1796."—*Rev. T. Smith's Edition of Lindley Murray's English Gram.* p. 67.

‡ Notwithstanding this expression, Murray did not teach, as do many modern grammarians, that *inflected forms of the present tense*, such as, "If he *thinks* so," "Unless he *deceives* me," "If thou *lov'st* me," are of the subjunctive mood; though, when he rejected his changeless forms of the other tenses of this mood, he *improperly* put as many indicatives in their places. With him, and his numerous followers, the ending determines the mood in one term, while the conjunction controls it in the other five: he argues, "that in cases wherein contingency and futurity do not occur, it is not proper to turn the verb from its signification of present time, *nor to vary* [he means, or to forbear to change] its form or termination. ☞ *The verb would then be in the indicative mood, whatever conjunctions might attend it.*"—*L. Murray's Gram.* 8vo, p. 208; 12mo, p. 167.

be turned into the subjunctive."—*Octavo Gram.* p. 82. According to this, the subjunctive mood of every regular verb embraces, in one voice, as many as one hundred and thirty-eight different expressions; and it may happen, that in one single tense a verb shall have no fewer than fifteen different forms in each person and number. Six times fifteen are ninety; and so many are the several phrases which now compose Murray's pluperfect tense of the subjunctive mood of the verb *to strow*—a tense which most grammarians very properly reject as needless! But this is not all. The scheme not only confounds the moods and utterly overwhelms the learner with its multiplicity, but condemns as bad English what the author himself once adopted and taught for the imperfect tense of the subjunctive mood, "If thou *loved*, If thou *knew*," &c., wherein he was sustained by Dr. Priestley, by Harrison, by Caleb Alexander, by John Burn, by Alexander Murray, the schoolmaster, and by others of high authority. Dr. Johnson, indeed, made the preterit subjunctive like the indicative; and this may have induced the author to change his plan, and inflect this part of the verb with *st*. But Dr. Alexander Murray, a greater linguist than either of them, very positively declares this to be wrong: "When such words as *if, though, unless, except, whether,* and the like, are used before verbs, they lose their terminations of *est, eth,* and *s*, in those persons which commonly have them. No speaker of good English, expressing himself conditionally, says, Though thou *fallest,* or Though he *falls,* but, Though thou *fall,* and Though he *fall;* nor, Though thou *camest,* but, Though, or although, thou *came.*"—*History of European Languages,* Vol. i, p. 55.

OBS. 6.—Nothing is more important in the grammar of any language, than a knowledge of the *true forms* of its verbs. Nothing is more difficult in the grammar of our own, than to learn, in this instance and some others, what forms we ought to prefer. Yet some authors tell us, and Dr. Lowth among the rest, that our language is wonderfully simple and easy. Perhaps it is so. But do not its "simplicity and facility" appear greatest to those who know least about it?—i. e. least of its grammar, and least of its history? In citing a passage from the eighteenth chapter of Ezekiel, Lord Kames has taken the liberty to change the word *hath* to *have* seven times in one sentence. This he did, upon the supposition that the subjunctive mood has a perfect tense which differs from that of the indicative; and for such an idea he had the authority of Dr. Johnson's Grammar, and others. The sentence is this: "But if he *be* a robber, a shedder of blood; if he *have* eaten upon the mountains, and defiled his neighbour's wife; if he *have* oppressed the poor and needy, *have* spoiled by violence, *have* not restored the pledge, *have lift* up his eyes to idols, *have* given forth upon usury, and *have* taken increase: shall he live? he shall not live."—*Elements of Criticism,* Vol. ii, p. 261. Now, is this good English, or is it not? One might cite about half of our grammarians in favour of this reading, and the other half against it; with Murray, the most noted of all, first on one side, and then on the other. Similar puzzles may be presented concerning three or four other tenses, which are sometimes ascribed, and sometimes denied, to this mood. It seems to me, after much examination, that the subjunctive mood in English should have *two tenses,* and no more; the *present* and the *imperfect.* The present tense of this mood naturally implies contingency and futurity, while the imperfect here becomes an *aorist,* and serves to suppose a case as a mere supposition, a case contrary to fact. Consequently the foregoing sentence, if expressed by the subjunctive at all, ought to be written thus: "But if he *be* a robber, a shedder of blood; if he *eat* upon the mountains, and *defile* his neighbour's wife; if he *oppress* the poor and needy, *spoil* by violence, *restore* not the pledge, *lift* up his eyes to idols, *give* forth upon usury, and *take* increase; shall he live? he shall not live."

OBS. 7.—"Grammarians *generally* make a present and a past time under the subjunctive mode."—*Cobbett's Gram.* ¶ 100. These are the tenses which are given to the subjunctive by *Blair,* in his "*Practical Grammar.*" If any one will give to this mood *more tenses* than these, the five which are adopted by *Staniford,* are perhaps the least objectionable: namely, "*Present,* If thou love, or do love; *Imperfect,* If thou loved, or did love; *Perfect,* If thou have loved; *Pluperfect,* If thou had loved; *Future,* If thou should or would love."—*Staniford's Gram.* p. 22. But there are no sufficient reasons for even this extension of its tenses. —Fisk, speaking of this mood, says: "Lowth restricts it entirely to the present tense."— "Uniformity on this point is highly desirable."—"On this subject, we adopt the opinion of Dr. Lowth."—*English Grammar Simplified,* p. 70. His desire of uniformity he has both hazarded and backed by a palpable misstatement. The learned Doctor's subjunctive mood, in the second person singular, is this: "*Present time.* Thou love; AND, Thou *mayest love. Past time.* Thou *mightest* love; AND, Thou *couldst,* &c. love; and have loved."—*Lowth's Gram.* p. 38. But Fisk's subjunctive runs thus: "*Indic. form,* If thou lovest; *varied form,* If thou love." And again: "*Present tense,* If thou art, If thou be; *Imperfect tense,* If thou wast, If thou wert."—*Fisk's Grammar Simplified,* p. 70. His very definition of the subjunctive mood is illustrated *only by the indicative;* as, "If thou *walkest.*"—"I will perform the operation, if he *desires* it."—*Ib.* p. 69. Comly's subjunctive mood, except in some of his early editions, stands thus: "*Present tense,* If thou lovest; *Imperfect tense,* If thou lovedst or loved; *First future tense,* If thou (shalt) love."—*Eleventh Ed.* p. 41. This author teaches, that the indicative or potential, when preceded by an *if,* "should be *parsed in* the *subjunctive* mood."—*Ib.* p. 42. Of what is in fact the true subjunctive, he says: "*Some writers* use the singular number in the present tense of the subjunctive mood, without any variation; as, '*if I love,* if thou *love,* if he *love.*' But this usage *must be ranked amongst the anomalies* of our language."—*Ib.* p. 41. Cooper, in his pretended "Abridgment of Murray's Grammar, Philad. 1828," gave to the subjunctive mood the following form, which contains all six of the tenses: "2d pers. If thou love, If thou do love, If thou loved, If thou did love, If thou have loved, If thou had loved, If thou shall (or will) love, If thou shall (or will) have loved." This is almost exactly what Murray at first adopted, and afterwards rejected; though it is probable, from the abridger's preface, that the latter was ignorant of this fact. Soon afterwards, a perusal of Dr Wilson's Essay on Grammar dashed from the reverend gentleman's mind the whole of this fabric; and in his "Plain and Practical Grammar, Philad. 1831," he acknowledges but four moods, and concludes some pages of argument thus: "From the above considerations, it will appear *to every sound grammarian,* that our language does not admit a subjunctive mode, at least, separate and distinct from the indicative and potential."—*Cooper's New Gram.* p. 63.

OBS. 8.—The true *Subjunctive* mood, in English, is virtually rejected by some later grammarians, who nevertheless acknowledge under that name a greater number and variety of forms than have ever been claimed for it in any other tongue. All that is peculiar to the Subjunctive, all that should constitute it a distinct mood, they represent as an archaism, an obsolete or antiquated mode of expression, while they willingly give to it every form of both the indicative and the potential, the two other moods which sometimes follow an *if.* Thus Wells, in his strange entanglement of the moods, not only gives to the subjunctive, as well as to the indicative, a "Simple" or "Common Form," and a "Potential Form;" not only recognizes in each an "Auxiliary Form," and a "Progressive Form;" but encumbers the whole with distinctions of style,—with what he calls the "Common Style," and the "Ancient Style;" or the "Solemn Style," and the "Familiar Style:" yet, after all, his own example of the Subjunctive, "Take heed, lest any man *deceive* you," is obviously different from all these, and not explainable under any of his paradigms! Nor is it truly consonant with any part of his theory, which is this: "The subjunctive of all verbs except *be,* takes *the same form as the indicative.* Good writers were formerly much accustomed *to drop* the personal termination in the *subjunctive present,* and write 'If he *have,*' 'If he *deny,*' etc., for 'If he *has,*' 'If he *denies,*' etc.; but this termination is now *generally retained,* unless an *auxiliary is understood.* Thus, 'If he *hear,*' may properly be used for 'If he *shall hear*' or 'If he *should hear,*' but not for 'If he *hears.*'"—*Wells's School Gram.* p. 83; 3d Ed. p. 87. Now every position here taken is demonstrably absurd. How could "good writers" indite "much" bad English by *dropping* from the subjunctive an indicative ending which never belonged to it? And how can a needless "auxiliary" be "*understood,*" on the principle of equivalence, where, by awkwardly changing a mood or tense, it only helps some grammatical theorist to convert good English into bad, or to pervert a text? The phrases above may all be right, or all be wrong, according to the correctness or incorrectness of their application: when each is used as best it may be, there is no exact equivalence. And this is true of half a dozen more of the same sort; as, "If he *does hear,*"—"If he *do hear,*"—"If he *is hearing,*"—"If he *be hearing,*"—"If he *shall be hearing,*"—"If he *should be hearing.*"

OBS. 9.—Similar to Wells's, are the subjunctive forms of Allen H. Weld. Mistaking *annex* to signify *prefix,* this author teaches thus: "ANNEX *if, though, unless, suppose, admit, grant, allow,* or any word implying a *condition,* to each tense of *the Indicative and Potential modes,* to form the subjunctive; as, If thou lovest or love. If he loves, or love. Formerly it was customary to *omit the terminations* in the second and third persons of the present tense of the Subjunctive mode. But now the terminations are *generally retained,* except when the ellipsis of *shall* or *should* is implied; as, If he obey, i. e., if he *shall,* or *should* obey." —*Weld's Grammar, Abridged Edition,* p. 71. Again: "*In general,* the form of the verb in the Subjunctive, *is the same as that of the Indicative;* but an *elliptical form* in the second and third *person* [persons] singular, is used in the following instances: (1.) *Future contingency* is expressed by the *omission of the Indicative termination;* as, If he go, for, if he *shall* go. Though he slay me, i. e., though he *should* slay me. (2.) *Lest* and *that* annexed to a command are followed by the *elliptical form* of the Subjunctive; as, Love not sleep [,] lest thou *come* to poverty. (3.) *If* with *but* following it, when futurity is denoted, requires the *elliptical form;* as, If he *do* but *touch* the hills, they shall smoke."—*Ib.* p. 126. As for this scheme, errors and inconsistencies mark every part of it. First, the rule for forming the subjunctive is false, and is plainly contradicted *by all that is true* in the examples: "*If thou love,*" or, "*If he love,*" contains not the form of the indicative. Secondly, no terminations have ever been "generally" omitted from, or retained in, the form of the subjunctive present; because that part of the mood, as commonly exhibited, is well known to be made of the *radical verb,* without inflection. One might as well talk of suffixes for the imperative, "*Love thou,*" or "*Do* thou love." Thirdly, *shall* or *should* can never be really implied in the subjunctive present; because the supposed ellipsis, needless and unexampled, would change the tense, the mood, and commonly also the meaning. "If he *shall,*" properly implies a condition of *future certainty;* "If he *should,*" a supposition of *duty:* the true subjunctive suggests neither of these. Fourthly, "the ellipsis of *shall* or *should*," is most absurdly called above, "the omission of the *Indicative termination.*" Fifthly, it is very strangely supposed, that to omit what pertains to the *indicative* or the *potential* mood, will produce an "elliptical form *of the Subjunctive.*" Sixthly, such examples as the last, "If he do but *touch* the hills," having the auxiliary *do* not inflected as in the indicative, disprove the whole theory.

Obs. 10.—In J. R. Chandler's grammars, are taken nearly the same views of the "Subjunctive or Conditional Mood," that have just been noticed. "This mood," we are told, "is *only* the indicative *or* potential mood, with the word *if* placed before the nominative case."—*Gram. of 1821*, p. 48; *Gram. of 1847*, p. 73. Yet, of even *this*, the author has said, in the former edition, "It would, perhaps, be *better to abolish the use* of the subjunctive mood entirely. *Its use* is a continual source of dispute among grammarians, and of perplexity to scholars."—Page 33. The suppositive verb *were*,—(as, "*Were* I a king,"—"If I *were* a king,"—) which this author formerly rejected, preferring *was*, is now, after six and twenty years, replaced in his own examples; and yet he still attempts to *disgrace it*, by falsely representing it as being only "the indicative *plural*" very grossly misapplied! See *Chandler's Common School Gram.* p. 77.

Obs. 11.—The *Imperative* mood is so called because it is chiefly used in *commanding*. It is that brief form of the verb, by which we directly urge upon others our claims and wishes. But the nature of this urging varies according to the relation of the parties. We command inferiors; exhort equals; entreat superiors; permit whom we will;—and all by this same imperative form of the verb. In answer to a request, the imperative implies nothing more than permission. The will of a superior may also be urged imperatively by the indicative future. This form is particularly common in solemn prohibitions; as, "Thou *shalt not kill*. * * * Thou *shalt not steal.*"—*Exodus*, xx, 13 and 15. Of the ten commandments, eight are negative, and all these are indicative in form. The other two are in the imperative mood : "*Remember* the sabbath day to keep it holy. *Honour* thy father and thy mother."—*Ib.* But, the imperative form may also be negative : as, "*Touch not*; *taste not*; *handle not.*"—*Colossians*, ii, 21.

TENSES.

Tenses are those modifications of the verb, which distinguish time.

There are six tenses; the *Present*, the *Imperfect*, the *Perfect*, the *Pluperfect*, the *First-future*, and the *Second-future*.

The *Present tense* is that which expresses what *now exists*, or *is taking* place : as, " I *hear* a noise; somebody *is coming.*"

The *Imperfect tense* is that which expresses what *took place*, or *was occurring*, in time fully past : as, " I *saw* him yesterday, and *hailed* him as he *was passing.*"

The *Perfect tense* is that which expresses what *has taken* place, within some period of time not yet fully past : as, " I *have seen* him to-day ; something *must have detained* him."

The *Pluperfect tense* is that which expresses what *had taken* place, at some past time mentioned : as, " I *had seen* him, when I met you."

The *First-future tense* is that which expresses what *will take* place hereafter : as, " I *shall see* him again, and I *will inform* him."

The *Second-future tense* is that which expresses what *will have taken* place, at some future time mentioned : as, I *shall have seen* him by to-morrow noon."

OBSERVATIONS.

Obs. 1.—The terms here defined are the names usually given to those parts of the verb to which they are in this work applied; and though some of them are not so strictly appropriate as scientific names ought to be, it is thought inexpedient to change them. In many old grammars, and even in the early editions of Murray, the three past tenses are called the *Preterimperfect*, *Preterperfect*, and *Preterpluperfect*. From these names, the term *Preter*, (which is from the Latin preposition *præter*, meaning *beside*, *beyond*, or *past*,) has well been dropped for the sake of brevity.

Obs. 2.—The distinctive epithet *Imperfect*, or *Preterimperfect*, appears to have been much less accurately employed by the explainers of our language, than it was by the Latin grammarians from whom it was borrowed. That tense which passes in our schools for the *Imperfect*, (as, I *slept*, *did sleep*, or *was sleeping*,) is in fact *more completely past*, than that which we call the *Perfect*. Murray indeed has attempted to show that the name is right; and, for the sake of consistency, one could wish he had succeeded. But every scholar must observe, that the simple preterit, which is the first form of this tense, and is never found in any other, as often as the sentence is declarative, tells what *happened* within some period of time *fully past*, as *last week, last year*; whereas the perfect tense is used to express what *has happened* within some period of time *not yet fully past*, as *this week, this year*. As to the completeness of the action, there is no difference; for what *has been done* to-day, is as *completely done*, as what *was achieved* a year ago. Hence it is obvious that the term *Imperfect* has no other applicability to the English tense so called, than what it may have derived from the participle in *ing*, which we use in translating the Latin imperfect tense: as, *Dormiebam, I was sleeping; Legebam, I was reading; Docebam, I was teaching.* And if for this reason the whole English tense, with all its variety of forms in the different moods, "may, with propriety, be denominated *imperfect*;" surely, the participle itself should be so denominated *a fortiori*: for it always conveys this same idea, of " *action not finished*," be the tense of its accompanying auxiliary what it may.

Obs. 3.—The tenses do not all express time with equal precision; nor can the whole number in any language supersede the necessity of adverbs of time, much less of dates, and of nouns that express periods of duration. The tenses of the indicative mood, are the most definite; and, for this reason, as well as for some others, the explanations of all these modifications of the verb, are made with particular reference to that mood. Some suppose the compound or participial form, as *I am writing*, to be more definite in time, than the simple form, as *I write*, or the emphatic form, as *I do write*; and accordingly they divide all the tenses into *Indefinite* and *Definite*. Of this division Dr. Webster seems to claim the invention; for he gravely accuses Murray of copying it unjustly from him, though the latter acknowledges in a note upon his text, it " is, *in part*, taken from Webster's Grammar."—*Murray's Octavo Gram.* p. 73. The distribution, as it stands in either work, is not worth quarrelling about: it is evidently more cumbersome than useful. Nor, after all, is it true that the compound form is more definite in time than the other. For example: " Dionysius, tyrant of Syracuse, *was always betraying* his unhappiness."—*Art of Thinking*, p. 123. Now, if *was betraying* were a more definite tense than *betrayed*, surely the adverb "*always*" would require the latter, rather than the former.

Obs. 4.—The present tense, of the indicative mood, expresses not only what is now actually going on, but general truths, and customary actions: as, " Vice *produces* misery."—" He *hastens* to repent, who *gives* sentence quickly."—*Grant's Lat. Gram.* p. 71. " Among the Parthians, the signal *is given* by the drum, and not by the trumpet."—*Justin.* Deceased authors may be spoken of in the present tense, because they seem to live in their works; as, " Seneca *reasons* and *moralizes* well."—*Murray.* " Women *talk* better than men, from the superior shape of their tongues: an ancient writer *speaks* of their loquacity three thousand years ago.—*Gardiner's Music of Nature*, p. 27.

Obs. 5.—The text, John, viii, 58, " Before Abraham *was*, I *am*," is a literal Grecism, and not to be cited as an example of pure English: our idiom would seem to require, " Before Abraham *was*, I *existed*." In animated narrative, however, the present tense is often substituted for the past, by the figure *enallage*. In such cases, past tenses and present may occur together; because the latter are used merely to bring past events more vividly before us: as, " Ulysses *wakes*, not knowing where he *was*."—*Pope.* " The dictator *flies* forward to the cavalry, beseeching them to dismount from their horses. They *obeyed*; they *dismount*, *rush* onward, and for vancouriers *show* their bucklers."—*Livy.* On this principle, perhaps, the following couplet, which Murray condemns as bad English, may be justified:—

　　　　" Him portion'd maids, apprentic'd orphans blest,
　　　　The young who *labour*, and the old who *rest*." See *Murray's Key*, R. 13.

Obs. 6.—The present tense of the subjunctive mood, and that of the indicative when preceded by *as soon as, after, before, till*, or *when*, is generally used with reference to future time; as, " If he *ask* a fish, will he give him a serpent? "—*Matt.* vii, 10. " If I *will* that he *tarry* till I *come*, what is that to thee? Follow thou me."—*John*, xxi, 22. " When he *arrives*, I will send for you." The imperative mood has but one tense, and that is always present with regard to the giving of the command; though what is commanded, must be done in the future, if done at all. So the subjunctive may convey a present supposition of what the will of another may make uncertain: as, " If thou *count* me therefore a partner, *receive* him as myself."—*St. Paul to Philemon*, 17. The perfect indicative, like the present, is sometimes used with reference to time that is relatively future; as, " He will be fatigued before he *has walked* a mile."—" My lips shall utter praise, when thou *hast taught* me thy statutes."—*Psalms*, cxix, 170. " Marvel not at this: for the hour is coming, in the which all that *are* in the graves, shall hear his voice, and shall come forth; they that *have done* good, unto the resurrection of life; and they that *have done* evil, unto the resurrection of damnation."—*John*, v, 28.

Obs. 7.—What is called the *present* infinitive, can scarcely be said to express any particular time.[*] It is usually dependent on an other verb, and therefore relative in time. It may be connected with any tense of any mood: as, " I *intend to do* it; I *intended to do* it; I *have intended to do* it; I *had intended to do* it;" &c. For want of a better mode of expression, we often use the infinitive to denote futurity, especially when it seems to be

[*] " The infinitive mood, as ' *to shine*,' may be called the name of the verb; it carries *neither time nor affirmation*; but simply expresses that attribute, action, or state of things, which is to be the subject of the other moods and tenses."—*Blair's Lectures*, p. 81. By the word " *subject* " the Doctor does not here mean the *nominative* to the other moods and tenses, but the *material of* them, or that which is formed into them.

taken adjectively; as, "The time *to come*,"—"The world *to come*,"—"Rapture yet *to be.*" This, sometimes with the awkward addition of *about*, is the only substitute we have for the Latin future participle in *rus*, as *venturus, to come*, or *about to come*. This phraseology, according to Horne Tooke, (see *Diversions of Purley*, Vol. ii, p. 457,) is no fitter than that of our ancestors, who for this purpose used the same preposition, but put the participle in *ing* after it, in lieu of the radical verb, which we choose to employ: as, " Generacions of eddris, who shewide to you to fle fro wraththe *to comynge ?* "—*Matt*. iii, 7. Common Version: " O generation of vipers ! who hath warned you to flee from the wrath *to come ?* " " Art thou that art *to comynge*, ether abiden we an other ? "—*Matt*. xi, 3. Common Version: " Art thou he that *should come*, or do we look for another ? " " Sotheli there the ship was *to puttyng out* the charge."—*Dedis*, xxi, 3. Common Version: " For there the ship was *to unlade* her burden."—*Acts*, xxi, 3. Churchill, after changing the names of the two infinitive tenses to "*Future imperfect*" and "*Future perfect*," adds the following note: "The tenses of the infinitive mood are usually termed *present* and *preterperfect* : but this is certainly improper; for they are so completely future, that what is called the present tense of the infinitive mood is often employed simply to express futurity; as, 'The life *to come*.'"—*New Gram*. p. 249.

Obs. 8.—The pluperfect tense, when used conditionally, in stead of expressing what actually *had taken place* at a past time, almost always implies that the action thus supposed *never was performed;* on the contrary, if the supposition be made in a *negative form*, it suggests that the event *had occurred:* as, "Lord, if thou *hadst been here*, my brother *had not died*."—*John*, xi, 32. " If I *had not come* and spoken unto them, they *had not had* sin ; but now they have no cloak for their sin."—*John*, xv, 22. " If thou *hadst known*, even thou, at least in this thy day, the things which belong unto thy peace ! But now they are hid from thine eyes."—*Luke*, xix, 42. The supposition is sometimes indicated by a mere transposition of the verb and its subject ; in which case, the conjunction *if* is omitted : as, " *Had ye believed* Moses, ye would have believed me."—*John*, v, 46.

> " *Had I but fought* as wont, one thrust
> *Had laid* De Wilton in the dust."—*Scott*.

Obs. 9.—In the language of prophecy we find the past tenses very often substituted for the future, especially when the prediction is remarkably clear and specific. Man is a creature of present knowledge only ; but it is certain, that He who sees the end from the beginning, has sometimes revealed to him, and by him, things deep in futurity. Thus the sacred seer who is esteemed the most eloquent of the ancient prophets, more than *seven hundred years* before the events occurred, spoke of the vicarious sufferings of Christ as of things already past, and even then described them in the phraseology of historical facts : " Surely he *hath borne* our griefs, *and carried* our sorrows : yet we *did esteem* him stricken, smitten of God, and afflicted. But he *was wounded* for our transgressions ; he *was bruised* for our iniquities : the chastisement of our peace *was* upon him ; and by his stripes we are healed."—*Isaiah*, liii, 4 and 5. Multiplied instances of a similar application of the past tenses to future events, occur in the Bible, especially in the writings of this prophet.

PERSONS AND NUMBERS.

The person and number of a verb are those modifications in which it agrees with its subject or nominative.

In each number, there are three persons ; and in each person, two numbers : thus,

Singular.		*Plural.*	
1st per. I	love,	1st per. We	love,
2d per. Thou	lovest,	2d per. You	love,
3d per. He	loves ;	3d per. They	love.

Definitions universally applicable have already been given of all these things ; it is therefore unnecessary to define them again in this place.

Where the verb is varied, the second person singular is regularly formed by adding *st* or *est* to the first person ; and the third person singular, in like manner, by adding *s* or *es :* as, I *see*, thou *seest*, he *sees ;* I *give*, thou *givest*, he *gives ;* I *go*, thou *goest*, he *goes ;* I *fly*, thou *fliest*, he *flies ;* I *vex*, thou *vexest*, he *vexes ;* I *lose*, thou *losest*, he *loses*.

Where the verb is not varied to denote its person and number, these properties are inferred from its subject or nominative : as, If I *love*, if thou *love*, if he *love ;* if we *love*, if you *love*, if they *love*.

OBSERVATIONS.

Obs. 1.—It is considered a principle of Universal Grammar, that a finite verb must agree with its subject or nominative in person and number. Upon this principle, we ascribe to every such verb the person and number of the nominative word, whether the verb itself be literally modified by the relation or not. The doctrine must be constantly taught and observed, in every language in which the verbs have *any variations* of this kind. But suppose an instance of a language in which all the verbs were entirely destitute of such inflections; the principle, as regards that language, must drop. Finite verbs, in such a case, would still relate to their subjects, or nominatives, agreeably to the sense; but they would certainly be rendered incapable of adding to this relation any agreement or disagreement. So the concords which belong to adjectives and participles in Latin and Greek, are rejected in English, and there remains to these parts of speech nothing but a simple relation to their nouns according to the sense. And by the fashionable substitution of *you* for *thou*, the concord of English verbs with their nominatives, is made to depend, in common practice, on little more than one single terminational *s*, which is used to mark one person of one number of one tense of one mood of each verb. So near does this practice bring us to the dropping of what is yet called a universal principle of grammar.*

OBS. 2.—In most languages, there are in each tense, through all the moods of every verb, six different terminations to distinguish the different persons and numbers. This will be well understood by every one who has ever glanced at the verbs as exhibited in any Latin, Greek, French, Spanish, or Italian grammar. To explain it to others, a brief example shall be given: (with the remark, that the Latin pronouns, here inserted, are seldom expressed, except for emphasis:) "*Ego amo*, I love; *Tu amas*, Thou lovest; *Ille amat*, He loves; *Nos amamus*, We love; *Vos amatis*, You love; *Illi amant*, They love." Hence it may be perceived, that the paucity of variations in the English verb, is a very striking peculiarity of our language. Whether we are gainers or losers by this simplicity, is a question for learned idleness to discuss. The common people who speak English, have far less inclination to add new endings to our verbs, than to drop or avoid all the remains of the old. Lowth and Murray tell us, "This scanty provision of terminations *is sufficient* for all the purposes of discourse; and that, "*For this reason*, the plural termination in *en*, (they *loven*, they *weren*,) formerly in use, was laid aside as *unnecessary*, and has long been obsolete."—*Lowth's Gram.* p. 31; *Murray's*, 63.

OBS. 3.—Though modern usage, especially in common conversation, evidently inclines to drop or shun all unnecessary suffixes and inflections, still it is true, that the English verb in some of its parts, varies its termination, to distinguish, or agree with, the different persons and numbers. The change is, however, principally confined to the second and third persons singular of the present tense of the indicative mood, and to the auxiliaries *hast* and *has* of the perfect. In the ancient biblical style, now used only on solemn occasions, the second person singular is distinguished through all the tenses of the indicative and potential moods. And as the use of the pronoun *thou* is now mostly confined to the solemn style, the terminations of that style are retained in connexion with it, through all the following examples of the conjugation of verbs. In the plural number, there is no variation of ending, to denote the different persons; and the verb in the three persons plural, (with the two exceptions *are* and *were*, from *am* and *was*,) is the same as in the first person singular. Nor does the use of *you* for the singular, warrant its connexion with any other than the plural form of the verb. This strange and needless confusion of the numbers, is, in all languages that indulge it, a practical inconvenience. It would doubtless have been much better, had *thou* and *you* still kept their respective places—the one, nominative singular—the other, objective plural—as they appear in the Bible. But as the English verb is always attended by a noun or a pronoun, expressing the subject of the affirmation, no ambiguity arises from the want of particular terminations in the verb, to distinguish the different persons and numbers.

OBS. 4.—Although our language, in its ordinary use, exhibits the verbs in such forms only, as will make, when put together, but a very simple conjugation; there is probably no other language on earth, in which it would be so difficult for a learned grammarian to fix, settle, and exhibit, to the satisfaction of himself and others, the principles, paradigms, rules, and exceptions, which are necessary for a full and just exhibition of this part of speech. This difficulty is owing, partly to incompatibilities or unsettled boundaries between the solemn and the familiar style; partly

---

* Some grammarians absurdly deny that persons and numbers are properties of verbs at all: not indeed because our verbs have so few inflections, or because these authors wish to discard the little distinction that remains; but because they have some fanciful conception, that these properties cannot pertain to a verb. Yet, when they come to their syntax, they all forget, that if a verb has no person and number, it cannot agree with a nominative in these respects. Thus KIRKHAM: "*Person*, strictly speaking, is a quality that belongs *not to verbs*, but to nouns and pronouns. We say, however, that the verb *must agree* with its nominative in *person*, as well as in number."—*Gram. in Familiar Lect.* p. 46. So J. W. WRIGHT: "In truth, number and person *are not properties of verbs.* Mr. Murray grants, that, 'in philosophical strictness, both number and person might (say, *may*) be excluded from every verb, as they are, in fact, the properties of substantives, not a part of the essence of the verb.'"—*Philosophical Gram.* p. 68. This author's rule of syntax for verbs, makes them agree with their nominatives, not in person and number, but in *termination*, or else in *nobody knows what:* "A Verb *must vary its terminations*, so as to agree with the nominative to which it is connected."—*Ib.* p. 168. But Murray's rule is, "A verb must agree with its nominative case in *number and person:*" and this doctrine is directly repugnant to that interpretation of his words above, by which these gentlemen have so egregiously misled themselves and others. Undoubtedly, both the numbers and the persons of all English verbs might be abolished, and the language would still be intelligible. But while any such distinctions remain, and the verb is actually modified to form them, they belong as properly to this part of speech as they can to any other. De Sacy says, "The distinction of number *occurs in* the verb;" and then adds, "yet this distinction does not properly *belong to* the verb, as it signifies nothing which can be numbered."—*Fosdick's Version*, p. 64 This deceptive reason is only a new form of the blunder which I have once exposed, of confounding the numbers in grammar with numbers in arithmetic. J. M. Putnam, after repeating what is above cited from Murray, adds: "The terms *number* and *person*, as applied to the verb are *figurative*. The properties which belong to one thing, for convenience' sake are ascribed to another."—*Gram.* p. 49. Kirkham imagines, if ten men *build* a house, or *navigate* a ship round the world, they perform just "*ten actions*," and no more. "Common sense teaches you," says he, "that *there must be as many actions as there are actors;* and that the verb when it has no form or ending to show it, is as strictly plural, as when it has. So, in the phrase, '*We walk*,' the verb *walk* is [of the] first person, because it expresses the *actions* performed by the *speakers.* The verb, then, when correctly written, always agrees, *in sense*, with its nominative in number and person."—*Kirkham's Gram.* p. 47. It seems to me, that these authors do not very well know what persons or numbers, in grammar, are.

to differences in the same style between ancient usage and modern; partly to interfering claims of new and old forms of the preterit and the perfect participle; partly to the conflicting notions of different grammarians respecting the subjunctive mood; and partly to the blind tenacity with which many writers adhere to rugged derivatives, and prefer unutterable contractions to smooth and easy abbreviations. For example: a clergyman says to a lucky gamester, (1.) "*You dwell* in a house which *you* neither *planned* nor *built.*" A member of the Society of Friends would say, (2.) "*Thou dwellst* in a house which *thou* neither *planned* nor *built.*" Or, if not a scholar, as likely as not, (3.) "*Thee dwells* in a house which *thee* neither *planned* nor *built.*" The old or solemn style would be, (4.) "*Thou dwellest* in a house which *thou* neither *plannedst* nor *buildedst.*" Some untasteful and overgrammatical poet will have it, (5.) "*Thou dwell'st* in halls *thou* neither *plann'dst* nor *build'dst.*" The doctrines of Murray's Grammar, and of most others, would require, (6.) "*Thou dwellest* in a house which thou neither *plannedst* nor *builtest.*" Or, (according to this author's method of avoiding unpleasant sounds,) the more complex form, (7.) "*Thou dost dwell* in a house which *thou* neither *didst plan* nor *didst build.*" Out of these an other poet will make the line, (9.) "*Dost dwell* in halls which *thou* nor *plann'dst* nor *built'st.*" An other, more tastefully, would drop the *st* of the preterit, and contract the present, as in the second instance above: thus,

(10.) "*Thou dwellst* in halls *thou* neither *planned* nor *built,*
    And *revelst* there in riches won by guilt."

Obs. 5.—Now let all these ten different forms of saying the same thing, by the same verbs, in the same mood, and the same two tenses, be considered. Let it also be noticed, that for these same verbs within these limits, there are yet other forms, of a *complex* kind; as, "*You do dwell,*" or, "*You are dwelling ;*" used in lieu of, "*Thou dost dwell,*" or, "*Thou art dwelling :*" so, "*You did plan,*" or, "*You were planning;*" used in lieu of, "*Thou didst plan,*" or, "*Thou wast planning.*" Take into the account the opinion of Dr. Webster and others, that, "*You was planning,*" or, "*You was building,*" is a still better form for the singular number; and well "established by national usage, both here and in England."—*Improved Gram.* p. 25. Add the less inaccurate practice of some, who use *was* and *did* familiarly with *thou;* as, "*Thou was planning, did thou build?*" Multiply all this variety tenfold, with a view to the other moods and tenses of these three verbs, *dwell, plan,* and *build;* then extend the product, whatever it is, from these three common words, to *all* the verbs in the English language. You will thus begin to have some idea of the difficulty mentioned in the preceding observation. But this is only a part of it; for all these things relate only to the second person singular of the verb. The double question is, Which of these forms ought to be approved and taught for that person and number? and which of them ought to be censured and rejected as bad English? This question is perhaps as important, as any that can arise in English grammar. With a few candid observations by way of illustration, it will be left to the judgement of the reader.

Obs. 6.—The history of *youyouing* and *thoutheeing* appears to be this. Persons in high stations, being usually surrounded by attendants, it became, many centuries ago, a species of court flattery, to address individuals of this class, in the plural number, as if a great man were something more than one person. In this way, the notion of greatness was agreeably *multiplied*, and those who laid claim to such honour, soon began to think themselves insulted whenever they were addressed with any other than the plural pronoun.* Humbler people yielded through fear of offence; and the practice extended, in time, to all ranks of society: so that at present the customary mode of familiar as well as complimentary address, is altogether plural; both the verb and the pronoun being used in that form.† This practice, which confounds one of the most important distinctions of the language, affords a striking instance of the power of fashion. It has made propriety itself *seem* improper. But shall it be allowed, in the present state of things, to confound our conjugations and overturn our grammar? Is it right to introduce it into our paradigms, as the only form of the second person singular, that modern usage acknowledges? Or is it expedient to augment by it that multiplicity of other forms, which must either take this same place or be utterly rejected? With due deference to those grammarians who have adopted one or the other of these methods, the author of this work answers all these questions decidedly in the negative. It is not to be denied, that the use of the plural *for the singular* is now so common as to form the *customary mode* of address to individuals of every rank. The Society of Friends, or Quakers, however, continue to employ the singular number in familiar discourse; and custom, which has now destroyed the compliment of the plural, has removed also the supposed opprobrium of the singular, and placed it on an equality with the plural in point of respect. The singular is universally employed in reference to the Supreme Being; and is generally preferred in poetry. It is the language of Scripture, and of the Prayer-Book; and is consistently retained in nearly all our grammars; though not always, perhaps, consistently treated.

Obs. 7.—Whatever is fashionable in speech, the mere disciples of fashion will always approve; and, probably, they will think it justifiable to despise or neglect all that is otherwise. These may be contented with the sole use of such forms of address as, "*You, you, sir ;*"—"*You, you, madam.*" But the literati who so neglect all the services of religion, as to forget that these are yet conducted in English independently of all this fashionable youyouing, must needs be poor judges of what

---

* John Despauter, whose ample Grammar of the Latin language appeared in its third edition in 1517, represents this practice as a corruption originating in false pride, and maintained by the wickedness of hungry flatterers. On the twentieth leaf of his Syntax, he says, "Videntur hodie Christiani superbiores, quam olim ethnici imperatores, qui dii haberi voluerunt; nam hi nunquam inviti audierunt pronomina *tu, tibi, tuus.* Quæ si hodie alicui monachorum antistiti, aut decano, aut pontifici dicantur aut scribantur, videbitur ita loquens aut scribens blasphemasse, et anathemate dignus: nec tamen Abbas, aut pontifex, tam ægre feret, quam Malchi, aut famelici gnathones, his assistentes, et vociferantes, *Sic loqueris, aut scribis, pontifici?*" Quintilianus et Donatus dicunt barbarismum, aut solœcismum esse, siquis uni dicat, *Salvete.*" The learned Erasmus also ridiculed this practice, calling those who adopted it, "*vositatores,*" or *youyouers.*

† "By a *perversion* of language the pronoun *you* is almost invariably used for the second person singular, as well as plural; always, however, retaining the plural verb; as, 'My friend, you *write* a good hand.' *Thou* is confined to a solemn style, or [to] poetical compositions."—*Chandler's Grammar,* Edition of 1821, p. 41; Ed. of 1847, p. 66.

belongs to their own justification, either as grammarians or as moral agents. A fashion by virtue of which millions of youth are now growing up in ignorance of that form of address which, in their own tongue, is most appropriate to poetry, and alone adapted to prayer, is perhaps not quite so light a matter as some people imagine. It is at least so far from being a good reason for displacing that form from the paradigms of our verbs in a grammar, that indeed no better needs be offered for tenaciously retaining it. Many children may thus learn at school what all should know, and what there is little chance for them to learn elsewhere. Not all that presume to minister in religion, are well acquainted with what is called the solemn style. Not all that presume to explain it in grammars, do know what it is. A late work, which boasted the patronage of De Witt Clinton, and through the influence of false praise came nigh to be imposed by a law of New York on all the common schools of that State; and which, being subsequently sold in Philadelphia for a great price, was there republished under the name of the "National School Manual;" gives the following account of this part of grammar: "In the solemn and poetic styles, the second person singular, in both the above tenses, is thou; and the second person plural, is ye, or you. The verb, to agree with the second person singular, changes its termination. Thus: 2d person, sing. Pres. Tense, Thou walkest, or *Thou walketh*. Imperfect Tense, Thou walkedst. In the third person singular, in *the above styles*, the verb has sometimes *a different* termination; as, Present Tense, He, she, or *it walks* or walketh. The *above form of inflection* may be applied *to all verbs* used in the solemn *or* poetic *styles*; but for ordinary purposes, I have supposed it proper to employ the form of the verb, adopted in common conversation, as least perplexing to young minds."—*Bartlett's Common School Manual*, Part ii, p. 114. What can be hoped from an author who is ignorant enough to think "*Thou walketh*" is good English? or from one who tells us, that "*It walks*" is of the solemn style? or from one who does not know that *you* is never a *nominative*, in the style of the Bible?

OBS. 8.—Nowhere on earth is fashion more completely mistress of all the tastes and usages of society, than in France. Though the common French Bible still retains the form of the second person singular, which in that language is shorter and perhaps smoother than the plural; yet even that sacred book, or at least the New Testament, and that by different persons, has been translated into more fashionable French, and printed at Paris, and also at New York, with the form of address everywhere plural; as, "Jesus anticipated him, saying, 'What *do you think*, Simon? of whom do the kings of the earth take taxes and tribute?'"—*Matt.* xvii, 24. "And, going to prayers, they said, 'O Lord, *you who know* the hearts of all men, show which of these two *you have chosen*.'"—*Acts,* i, 24. This is one step further in the progress of politeness, than has yet been taken in English. The French grammarians however, so far as I perceive, have never yet disturbed the ancient order of their conjugations and declensions, by inserting the plural verb and pronoun in place of the singular; and, in the familiarity of friendship, or of domestic life, the practice which is denominated *tutoyant*, or *thoutheeing*, is far more prevalent in France than in England. Also, in the prayers of the French, the second person singular appears to be yet generally preserved, as it is in those of the English and the Americans. The less frequent use of it in the familiar conversation of the latter, is very probably owing to the general impression, that it cannot be used with propriety, except in the solemn style. Of this matter, those who have laid it aside themselves, cannot with much modesty pretend to judge for those who have not; or, if they may, there is still a question, how far it is right to lay it aside. The following lines are a sort of translation from Horace; and I submit it to the reader, whether it is comely for a Christian divine to be less reverent toward God, than a heathen poet; and whether the plural language here used, does not lack the reverence of the original, which is singular:—

"Preserve, Almighty Providence!
 Just what *you gave* me, competence."—*Swift.*

OBS. 9.—The terms, *solemn style, familiar style, modern style, ancient style, legal style, regal style, nautic style, common style,* and the like, as used in grammar, imply no certain divisions of the language; but are designed merely to distinguish, in a general way, the *occasions* on which some particular forms of expression may be considered proper, or the *times* to which they belong. For what is grammatical sometimes, may not be so always. It would not be easy to tell, definitely, in what any one of these styles consists; because they all belong to one language, and the number or nature of the peculiarities of each is not precisely fixed. But whatever is acknowledged to be peculiar to any one, is consequently understood to be improper for any other: or, at least, the same phraseology cannot belong to styles of an opposite character; and words of general use belong to no particular style.* For example: "So then it is not of him that *willeth*, nor of him that *runneth*, but of God that *showeth* mercy."—*Rom.* ix, 16. If the termination *eth* is not obsolete, as some say it is, all verbs to which this ending is added, are of the solemn style; for the common or familiar expression would here be this: "So then it is not of him that *wills*, nor of him that *runs*, but of God that *shows* mercy." Ben Jonson, in his grammar, endeavoured to arrest this change of *eth* to *s*; and, according to Lindley Murray, (Octavo Gram. p. 90,) Addison also injudiciously disapproved it. In spite of all such objectors, however, some future grammarian will probably have to say of the singular ending *eth*, as Lowth and Murray have already said of the plural *en*: "It was laid aside as unnecessary."

* In regard to the inflection of our verbs, William B. Fowle, who is something of an antiquarian in grammar, and who professes now to be "conservative" of the popular system, makes a threefold distinction of style, thus: "English verbs have three Styles [,] or Modes, [;] called [the] *Familiar*, [the] *Solemn* [,] and [the] *Ancient*. The *familiar style*, or mode, is that used in common conversation; as, you *see*, he *fears*. The solemn style, or mode, is that used in the Bible, and in prayer; as, Thou *seest*, he *feareth*. The ancient style, or mode, now little used, allows no change in the second and third person, [persons,] singular, of the verb, and generally follows the word *if, though, lest,* or *whether*; as, if thou *see*; though he *fear*; lest he *be* angry; whether he *go* or *stay*."—*Fowle's Common School Grammar*, Part Second, p. 44. Among his subsequent examples of the *Solemn style*, he gives the following: "Thou *lovest,* Thou *lovedst,* Thou *art,* Thou *wast,* Thou *hast,* Thou *hadst,* Thou *dost* or *dost,* Thou *didst*." And, as corresponding examples of the *Ancient style*, he has these forms: "Thou *love,* Thou *loved,* Thou *or you be,* Thou *wert,* Thou *have,* Thou *had,* Thou *do,* Thou *did*."—*Ib.*, pp. 44-50. This distinction and this arrangement do not appear to me to be altogether warranted by facts. The necessary distinction of *moods,* this author rejects; confounding the *Subjunctive* with the *Indicative,* in order to furnish out this useless and fanciful contrast of his *Solemn* and *Ancient styles.*

Obs. 10.—Of the origin of the personal terminations of English verbs, that eminent etymologist Dr. Alexander Murray, gives the following account: "The readers of our modern tongue may be reminded, that the terminations, *est, eth*, and *s*, in our verbs, as in *layest, layeth*, and *laid'd*, or *laidest*; are the faded *remains of the pronouns* which were formerly joined to the verb itself, and placed the language, in respect of concise expression, on a level with the Greek, Latin, and Sanscrit, its sister dialects."—*History of European Languages*, Vol. i, p. 52. According to this, since other signs of the persons and numbers are now employed with the verb, it is not strange that there should appear a tendency to lay aside such of these endings as are least agreeable and least necessary. Any change of this kind will of course occur first in the familiar style. For example: "Thou *wentest* in to men uncircumcised, and *didst eat* with them."—*Acts*, xi, 1. "These things write I unto thee, that thou *mayest* know how thou *oughtest* to behave thyself in the house of God."—1 *Tim.* iii, 15. These forms, by universal consent, are now of the solemn style; and, consequently, are really good English in no other. For nobody, I suppose, will yet pretend that the inflection of our preterits and auxiliaries by *st*, or *est*, is entirely *obsolete*;* and surely no person of any literary taste ever uses the foregoing forms familiarly. The termination *est*, however, has *in some instances* become obsolete; or has faded into *st* or *t*, even in the solemn style. Thus, (if indeed, such forms ever were in good use,) *diddest* has become *didst; havest, hast; haddest, hadst; shallest, shalt; willest, wilt*; and *cannest, canst. Mayest, mightest, couldest, wouldest*, and *shouldest*, are occasionally found in books not ancient; but *mayst, mightst, couldst, wouldst*, and *shouldst*, are abundantly more common, and all are peculiar to the solemn style. "*Must, burst, durst, thrust, blest, curst, past, lost, list, crept, kept, girt, built, felt, dwelt, left, bereft*, and many other verbs of similar endings, are seldom, if ever, found encumbered with an additional *est*. For the rule which requires this ending, has always had many exceptions that have not been noticed by grammarians.† Thus Shakspeare wrote even in the present tense, "Do as thou *list*," and not "Do as thou *listest*." Possibly, however, *list* may here be reckoned of the subjunctive mood; but the following example from Byron is certainly in the indicative:—

"And thou, who never yet of human wrong
  Lost the unbalanced scale, great Nemesis!"—*Harold*, C. iv, st. 132.

Obs. 11.—Any phraseology that is really obsolete, is no longer fit to be imitated even in the solemn style; and what was never good English, is no more to be respected in that style, than in any other. Thus: "Art not thou that Egyptian, *which* before these days *madest* an uproar, and *leddest* out into the wilderness four thousand men that were murderers?"—*Acts*, xxi, 38. Here, (I think,) the version ought to be, "Art not thou that Egyptian, *who* a while ago *made* an uproar, and *led* out into the wilderness four thousand men, that were murderers?" If so, there is in this no occasion to make a difference between the solemn and the familiar style. But what is the familiar form of expression for the texts cited before? The fashionable will say, it is this: "*You went* in to men uncircumcised, and *did eat* with them."—"I write these things *to you*, that *you may know* how *you ought* to behave *yourself* in the house of God." But this is not *literally* of the singular number: it is no more singular, than *vos* in Latin, or *vous* in French, or *we* used for *I* in English, is singular. And if there remains to us any other form, that is both singular and grammatical, it is unquestionably the following: "*Thou went* in to men uncircumcised, and *did eat* with them."—"I write these things to *thee*, that thou *may know* how thou *ought* to behave *thyself* in the house of God." The acknowledged doctrine of all the teachers of English grammar, that the inflection of our auxiliaries and preterits by *st* or *est* is peculiar to "the solemn style," leaves us no other alternative, than either to grant the propriety of here dropping the suffix for the familiar style, or to rob our language of any familiar use of the pronoun *thou* forever. Who, then, are here the neologists, the innovators, the impairers of the language? And which is the greater *innovation*, merely to drop, on familiar occasions, or *when it suits our style*, one obsolescent verbal termination,—a termination often dropped *of old* as well as now,—or to strike from the conjugations of all our verbs one sixth part of their entire scheme?

"O mother myn, that cleaped *were* Argyve,
  Wo worth that day that thou me *bare* on lyue."—*Chaucer*.

Obs. 12.—The grammatical propriety of distinguishing from the solemn style both of the forms presented above, must be evident to every one who considers with candour the reasons, analogies, and authorities, for this distinction. The support of the latter is very far from resting solely on the practice of a particular sect; though this, if they would forbear to corrupt the pronoun while they simplify the verb, would deserve much more consideration than has ever been allowed it. Which of these modes of address is the more grammatical, it is useless to dispute; since fashion

---

* In that monstrous jumble and perversion of Murray's doctrines, entitled, "English Grammar on the Productive System, by Roswell C. Smith," *you* is everywhere preferred to *thou*, and the verbs are conjugated *without the latter pronoun*. At the close of his paradigms, however, the author inserts a few lines respecting " *these obsolete conjugations*," with the pronoun *thou*; for a further account of which, he refers the learner, *with a sneer*, to the common grammars in the schools. See the work, p. 79. He must needs be a remarkable grammarian, with whom Scripture, poetry, and prayer, are all "*obsolete!*" Again: "*Thou* in the singular *is obsolete*, except among the Society of Friends; and *ye* is an *obsolete* plural!"—*Guy's School Gram.* p. 26. In an other late grammar, professedly "constructed upon the *basis* of Murray's, by the Rev. *Charles Adams*, A. M., Principal of Newbury Seminary," the second person singular is everywhere superseded by the plural; the former being silently dropped from all his twenty pages of conjugations, without so much as a hint, or a saving clause, respecting it; and the latter, which is put in its stead, is falsely called *singular*. By his pupils, all forms of the verb that agree only with *thou*, will of course be conceived to be either obsolete or barbarous, and consequently ungrammatical. Whether or not the reverend gentleman makes any account of the Bible or of prayer, does not appear; he cites some poetry, in which there are examples that cannot be reconciled with his "System of English Grammar." Parkhurst, in his late "Grammar for Beginners," tells us that, "Such words as are used in the Bible, and not used in common books, are called *obsolete!*"—P. 146. Among these, he reckons all the distinctive forms of the second person singular, and all the "peculiarities" which "constitute what is commonly called the *Solemn Style*." —Ib. p. 148. Yet, with no great consistency, he adds: "This style *is always used* in prayer, and is *frequently used* in poetry."—*Ibid.* Joab Brace, Jun., may be supposed to have the same notion of what is obsolete; for he too has perverted all Lennie's examples of the verb, as Smith and Adams did Murray's.

† Coar gives *durst* in the "Indicative mood," thus: "I durst, *thou durst*, he durst;" &c.—*Coar's E. Gram.* p. 115. But when he comes to *wist*, he does not know what the second person singular should be, and so he leaves it out: "I wist, ———, he wist; we wist, ye wist, they wist."—*Coar's E. Gram.* p. 116

rules the one, and a scruple of conscience is sometimes alleged for the other. A candid critic will consequently allow all to take their choice. It is enough for him, if he can demonstrate to the candid inquirer, what phraseology is in any view allowable, and what is for any good reason reprehensible. That the use of the plural for the singular is ungrammatical, it is neither discreet nor available to affirm; yet, surely, it did not originate in any regard to grammar rules. Murray the schoolmaster, whose English Grammar appeared some years before that of Lindley Murray, speaks of it as follows: "*Thou*, the second person singular, though *strictly grammatical*, is seldom used, except in addresses to God, in poetry, and by the people called Quakers. In all other cases, *a fondness for foreign manners*,* and the power of custom, have given a sanction to the use of *you*, for the second person singular, though *contrary to grammar*,† and attended with this particular inconveniency, that a plural verb must be used to agree with the pronoun in number, and both applied to a *single person*; as, *you are*, or *you were*,—not *you wast*, or *you was*."—*Third Edition*, Lond. 1793, p. 34. This author everywhere exhibits the auxiliaries, *mayst*, *mightst*, *couldst*, *wouldst*, and *shouldst*, as words of one syllable; and also observes, in a marginal note, "Some writers begin to say, '*Thou may*, *thou might*,' &c."—*Ib.* p. 36. Examples of this are not very uncommon: "Thou *shall* want ere I want."—*Old Motto; Scott's Lay*, Note 1st to Canto 3. "Thyself the mournful tale *shall* tell."—*Felton's Gram.* p. 20.

> "One sole condition would I dare suggest,
> That *thou would save* me from my own request."—*Jane Taylor.*

OBS. 13.—In respect to the second person singular, the grammar of Lindley Murray makes no distinction between the solemn and the familiar style; recognizes in no way the fashionable substitution of *you* for *thou*; and, so far as I perceive, takes it for granted, that every one who pretends to speak or write grammatically, must always, in addressing an individual, employ the singular pronoun, and inflect the verb with *st* or *est*, except in the imperative mood and the subjunctive present. This is the more remarkable, because the author was a valued member of the Society of Friends; and doubtless his own daily practice contradicted his doctrine, as palpably as does that of every other member of the Society. And many a schoolmaster, taking that work for his text-book, or some other as faulty, is now doing precisely the same thing. But what a teacher is he, who dares not justify as a grammarian that which he constantly practices as a man! What a scholar is he, who can be led by a false criticism or a false custom, to condemn his own usage and that of every body else! What a casuist is he, who dares pretend conscience for practising that which he knows and acknowledges to be wrong! If to speak in the second person singular without inflecting our preterits and auxiliaries, is a censurable corruption of the language, the Friends have no alternative but to relinquish their scruple about the application of *you* to one person; for none but the adult and learned can ever speak after the manner of ancient books: children and common people can no more be brought to speak agreeably to any antiquated forms of the English language, than according to the imperishable models of Greek and Latin. He who traces the history of our vernacular tongue, will find it has either simplified or entirely dropped several of its ancient terminations; and that the *st* or *est* of the second person singular, *never was adopted* in any thing like the extent to which our modern grammarians have attempted to impose it. "Thus becoming unused to inflections, we lost the perception of their meaning and nature."—*Philological Museum*, i, 669. "You cannot make a whole people all at once talk in a different tongue from that which it has been used to talk in: you cannot force it to unlearn the words it has learnt from its fathers, in order to learn a set of newfangled words out of [a grammar or] a dictionary."—*Ib.* i, 650. Nor can you, in this instance, restrain our poets from transgressing the doctrine of Lowth and Murray:—

> "Come, thou pure Light, which first in Eden *glowed*,
> And *threw* thy splendor round man's calm abode."—*Alonzo Lewis.*

OBS. 14.—That which has passed away from familiar practice, may still be right in the solemn style, and may there remain till it becomes obsolete. But no obsolescent termination has ever yet been recalled into the popular service. This is as true in other languages as in our own: "In almost every word of the Greek," says a learned author, "we meet with contractions and abbreviations; but, I believe, the flexions of no language allow of extension or amplification. In our own we may write *sleeped* or *slept*, as the metre of a line or the rhythm of a period may require; but by no license may we write *sleepeed*."—*Knight, on the Greek Alphabet*, 4to, p. 107. But, if after contracting *sleeped* into *slept*, we add an *est* and make *sleptest*, is there not here an extension of the word from one syllable to two? Is there not an amplification that is at once novel, disagreeable, unauthorized, and unnecessary? Nay, even in the regular and established change, as of *loved* to *lovedst*, is there not a syllabic increase, which is unpleasant to the ear, and unsuited to familiar speech? Now, to what extent do these questions apply to the verbs of our language? Lindley Murray, it is presumed, had no conception of that extent; or of the weight of the objec-

---

* For the substitution of *you* for *thou*, our grammarians assign various causes. That which is most commonly given in modern books, is certainly not the original one, because it concerns no other language than ours: "In order to avoid the unpleasant formality which accompanies the use of *thou* with a correspondent verb, its plural *you*, is usually adopted in familiar conversation; as, Charles, *will* you walk? instead of—*wilt thou* walk? You *read too fast*, instead of—*thou readest* too fast."—*Jaudon's Gram.* p. 38.

† This position, as may be seen above, I do not suppose it competent for any critic to maintain. The use of *you* for *thou* is no more "contrary to grammar," than the use of *we* for *I*; which, it seems, is grammatical enough for all editors, compilers, and crowned heads, if not for others. But both are *figures of syntax*; and, as such, they stand upon the same footing. Their only contrariety to grammar consists in this, that the words are not the literal *representatives* of the number for which they are put. But in what a posture does the grammarian place himself, who condemns, as bad *English*, that phraseology which he constantly and purposely uses? The author of the following remark, as well as all who have praised his work, ought immediately to adopt the style of the Friends, or Quakers: "The word *thou*, in grammatical construction, is preferable to *you*, in the second person singular: however, custom has familiarized the latter, and consequently made it more general, though BAD GRAMMAR. To say, '*You are a man*,' is NOT GRAMMATICAL LANGUAGE; the word *you* having reference to a *plural noun* only. It should be, '*Thou art a man*.'"—*Wright's Philosoph. Gram.* p. 55. This author, like Lindley Murray and many others, continually calls *himself* WE; and it is probable, that neither he, nor any one of his sixty reverend commenders, *dares address* any man otherwise than by the above-mentioned "BAD GRAMMAR!"

tion which is implied in the second. With respect to a vast number of our most common verbs, he himself never knew, nor does the greatest grammarian now living know, in what way he ought to form the simple past tense in the second person singular, otherwise than by the mere uninflected preterit with the pronoun *thou.* Is *thou sleepedst* or *thou sleptest, thou leavedst* or *thou leftest, thou feeledst* or *thou feltest, thou dealedst* or *thou dealtest, thou tossedst* or *thou tostest, thou losedst* or *thou lostest, thou payedst* or *thou paidest, thou layedst* or *thou laidest,* better English than *thou slept, thou left, thou felt, thou dealt, thou tossed, thou lost, thou paid, thou laid?* And, if so, of the two forms in each instance, which is the right one? and why? The Bible has "*saidst*" and "*layedst*; Dr. Alexander Murray, "*laid'st*" and "*laidest!*" Since the inflection of our preterits has never been orderly, and is now decaying and waxing old, shall we labour to recall what is so nearly ready to vanish away?

> "Tremendous Sea! what time *thou lifted* up
> Thy waves on high, and with thy winds and storms
> Strange pastime *took,* and *shook* thy mighty sides
> Indignantly, the pride of navies fell."—*Pollok,* B. vii, l. 611.

OBS. 15.—Whatever difficulty there is in ascertaining the true form of the preterit itself, not only remains, but is augmented, when *st* or *est* is to be added for the second person of it. For, since we use sometimes one and sometimes the other of these endings; (as, said*st*, sawe*st*, bid*est*, knewe*st*, loved*st*, went*est*;) there is yet need of some rule to show which we ought to prefer. The variable formation or orthography of verbs in the simple past tense, has always been one of the greatest difficulties that the learners of our language have had to encounter. At present, there is a strong tendency to terminate as many as we can of them in *ed,* which is the only regular ending. The pronunciation of this ending, however, is at least threefold; as in *remembered, repented, relinquished.* Here the added sounds are, first *d,* then *ed,* then *t;* and the effect of adding *st,* whenever the *ed* is sounded like *t,* will certainly be a perversion of what is established as the true pronunciation of the language. For the solemn and the familiar pronunciation of *ed* unquestionably differ. The present tendency to a regular orthography, ought rather to be encouraged than thwarted; but the preferring of *mixed* to *mixt, whipped* to *whipt, worked* to *wrought, kneeled* to *knelt,* and so forth, does not make *mixedst, whippedst, workedst, kneeledst,* and the like, any more fit for modern English, than are *mixtest, whiptest, wroughtest, kneltest, burntest, dweltest, heldest, giltest,* and many more of the like stamp. And what can be more absurd than for a grammarian to insist upon forming a great parcel of these strange and crabbed words for which he can quote no good authority? Nothing; except it be for a poet or a rhetorician to huddle together great parcels of consonants which no mortal man can utter,* (as *lov'dst, lurk'dst, shrugg'dst,*) and call them "*words.*" Example: "The clump of *subtonick* and *atonick* elements at the termination of *such words* as the following, is frequently, to the no small injury of articulation, particularly slighted: couldst, wouldst, hadst, prob'st, *prob'dst,* hurl'st, *hurl'dst,* arm'st, *arm'dst,* want'st, *want'dst,* burn'st, *burn'dst,* bark'st, *bark'dst,* bubbl'st, *bubbl'dst,* troubbl'st, *troubbl'dst.*"—*Kirkham's Elocution,* p. 42. The word *trouble* may receive the additional sound of *st,* but this gentleman does not here *spell* so accurately as a great author should. Nor did they who penned the following lines, write here as poets should:—

> "Of old thou *build'st* thy throne on righteousness."—*Pollok's C. of T.,* B. vi, l. 638.
> "For though thou *work'dst* my mother's ill."—*Byron's Parasina.*
> "Thou thyself *doat'dst* on womankind, admiring."—*Milton's P. R.,* B. ii, l. 175.
> "But he, the sev'nth from thee, whom thou *beheldst.*"—*Id. P. L.,* B. xi, l. 700.
> "Shall build a wondrous ark, as thou *beheldst.*"—*Id. ib.* B. xi, l. 819.
> "Thou, who *inform'd'st* this clay with active fire!"—*Savage's Poems,* p. 247.
> "Thy valiantness was mine, thou *suck'dst* it from me."—*Shak. Coriol.* Act iii.
> "This cloth thou *dipp'dst* in blood of my sweet boy."—*Id. Henry VI,* P. i.
> "Great Queen of arms, whose favour Tydeus won;
> As thou *defend'st* the sire, defend the son."—*Pope, Iliad,* B. x, l. 337.

OBS. 16.—Dr. Lowth, whose popular little Grammar was written in or about 1758, made no scruple to hem up both the poets and the Friends at once, by a criticism which I must needs consider more dogmatical than true; and which, from the suppression of what is least objectionable in it, has become, in other hands, the source of still greater errors: "*Thou* is the polite, and even *in the familiar style is disused,* and the plural *you* is employed instead of it; we say, *you have,* not *thou hast.* Though in this case, we apply *you* to a single person, yet the verb too *must agree with it in the plural number*; it must necessarily be, *you have,* not *you hast. You was* is an enormous solecism, † and yet authors of the first rank have inadvertently fallen into it. * * * On the contrary, the solemn style admits not of *you* for a single person. This *hath led* Mr. Pope into *a great impropriety* in the beginning of his Messiah:—

> ' O thou my voice inspire,
> Who *touch'd* Isaiah's hallow'd lips with fire!'

---

* "We are always given to cut our words short; and, *with very few exceptions,* you find people writing *'ov'd, mov'd, wal'd;* instead of *loved, moved, walked.* They wish to make the *pen* correspond with the *tongue.* From *lov'd, mov'd, walk'd,* it is very easy to slide into *levt, movt, walkt.* And this has been the case with regard to *curst, dealt, dwelt, leapt helps,* and many others in the last inserted list. It is just as proper to say *jumpt,* as it is to say *leapt;* and just as proper to say *walkt* as either; and thus we might go on till the orthography of the whole language were changed. When the love of contraction came to operate on such verbs as *to burst* and *to light,* it found such a clump of consonants already at the end of the words, that it could add none. It could not enable the organs even of English speech to pronounce *burst'd, light'd.* It, therefore, made really short work of it, and dropping the last syllable altogether, wrote, *burst, light,* (rather, *lit,*) in the past time and passive participle."—*Cobbett's English Gram.* ¶ 109. How could the man who saw all this, insist on adding *st* for the *second person,* where not even the *d* of the past tense could be articulated? Am I to be called an innovator, because I do not like in conversation such *new and unauthorized* words as *littest, leaptest, curstest?* or a corrupter of the language, because I do not admire in poetry such unutterable monstrosities as, *light'dst, leap'dst, curs'dst?* The novelism, with the corruption too, is wholly theirs who stickle for these awkward forms.

† "You *were,* not you *was,* for you *was* seems to be as ungrammatical, as you *hast* would be. For the pronoun *you* being confessedly plural, its correspondent verb ought to be plural."—*John Burn's Gram.* 10th Ed. p. 72.

The solemnity of the style would not admit of *you* for *thou*, in the pronoun ; nor the measure of the verse *touchedst*, or *didst touch*, in the verb, as it *indispensably ought to be*, in the one or the other of these two forms ; *you*, who *touched*, or *thou*, who *touchedst*, or *didst touch*.

          ' Just of *thy* word, in every thought sincere ;
      Who *knew* no wish, but what the world might hear.'—Pope.

It ought to be *your* in the first line, or *knewest* in the second. In order to avoid this *grammatical inconvenience*, the two distinct forms of *thou* and *you*, are often used promiscuously by our modern poets, in the same paragraph, and even in the same sentence, very inelegantly and improperly :—

      ' Now, now, I seize, I clasp *thy* charms ;
      And now *you* burst, ah, cruel ! from my arms.'—Pope."—*Lowth's English Gram.* p. 34.

Obs. 17.—The points of Dr. Lowth's doctrine which are not sufficiently true, are the following : First, it is not true, that *thou*, in the familiar style, is *totally disused*, and the plural *you* employed universally in its stead ; though Churchill, and others, besides the good bishop, seem to represent it so. It is now nearly two hundred years since the rise of the Society of Friends : and, whatever may have been the practice of others before or since, it is certain, that from their rise to the present day, there have been, at every point of time, many thousands who made no use of *you* for *thou*; and, but for the clumsy forms which most grammarians hold to be indispensable to verbs of the second person singular, the beautiful, distinctive, and poetical words, *thou, thyself, thy, thine*, and *thee*, would certainly be in no danger yet of becoming obsolete. Nor can they, indeed, at any rate, become so, till the fairest branches of the Christian Church shall wither ; or, what should seem so gracious omen, her bishops and clergy learn *to pray in the plural number*, for fashion's sake. Secondly, it is not true, that, " *thou*, who *touch'd*," ought *indispensably* to be, " *thou*, who *touchedst*, or *didst touch*." It is far better to dispense with the inflection, in such a case, than either to impose it, or to resort to the plural pronoun. The "grammatical inconvenience" of dropping the *st* or *est* of a preterit, even in the solemn style, cannot be great, and may be altogether imaginary ; that of imposing it, except in solemn prose, is not only real, but is often insuperable. It is not very agreeable, however, to see it added to some verbs, and dropped from others, in the same sentence : as,

" Thou, who *didst call* the Furies from the abyss,
  And round Orestes *bade* them howl and hiss."—*Byron's Childe Harold*, Canto iv, st. 132.

" Thou *satt'st* from age to age insatiate,
  And *drank* the blood of men, and *gorged* their flesh."—*Pollok's Course of Time*, B. vii, l. 700.

Obs. 18.—We see then, that, according to Dr. Lowth and others, *the only good English* in which one can address an individual on any ordinary occasion, is *you* with a plural verb : and that, according to Lindley Murray and others, *the only good English* for the same purpose, is *thou* with a verb inflected with *st* or *est*. Both parties to this pointed contradiction, are more or less in the wrong. The respect of the Friends for those systems of grammar which deny them the familiar use of the pronoun *thou*, is certainly not more remarkable, than the respect of the world for those which condemn the substitution of the plural *you*. Let grammar be a true record of existing facts, and all such contradictions must vanish. And, certainly, these great masters here contradict each other, in what every one who reads English, ought to know. They agree, however, in requiring, as indispensable to grammar, what is not only inconvenient, but absolutely impossible. For what " the measure of verse *will not admit*," cannot be used in poetry ; and what may possibly be crowded into it, will often be far from ornamental. Yet our youth have been taught to spoil the versification of Pope and others, after the following manner : " Who *touch'd* Isaiah's hallow'd lips with fire." Say, " Who *touchedst* or *didst touch*."—*Murray's Key*, 8vo, p. 180. " For thee that *ever felt* another's wo." Say, " *Didst feel*."—Ib. " Who *knew* no wish but what the world might hear." Say, " Who *knewest* or *didst know*."—Ib. " Who all my sense *confin'd*." Say, " *Confinedst* or *didst confine*."—Ib, p. 186. " Yet *gave* me in this dark estate." Say, " *Gavedst* or *didst give*."—Ib. " *Left* free the human will."—Pope. Murray's criticism extends not to this line, but by the analogy, we must say, " *Leavedst* or *leftest*." Now it would be easier to fill a volume with such quotations, and such corrections, than to find sufficient authority to prove one such word as *gavedst, leavedst*, or *leftest*, to be really good English. If Lord Byron is authority for " *work'dst*," he is authority also for dropping the *st*, even where it might be added :—

          —"Thou, who with thy frown
  Annihilated senates."—*Childe Harold's Pilgrimage*, Canto iv, st. 83.

Obs. 19.—According to Dr. Lowth, as well as Coar and some others, those preterits in which *ed* is sounded like *t*, " admit the change of *ed* into *t* ; as, *snatcht, checkt, snapt, mixt*, dropping also one of the double letters, *dwelt, past*."—*Lowth's Gram.* p. 46. If this principle were generally adopted, the number of our regular verbs would be greatly diminished, and irregularities would be indefinitely increased. What confusion the practice must make in the language, especially when we come to inflect this part of the verb with *st* or *est*, has already been suggested. Yet an ingenious and learned writer, an able contributor to the Philological Museum, published at Cambridge, England, in 1832 ; tracing the history of this class of derivatives, and finding that after the *ed* was contracted in pronunciation, several eminent writers, as Spenser, Milton, and others, adopted in most instances a contracted form of orthography ; has seriously endeavoured to bring us back to their practice. From these authors, he cites an abundance of such contractions as the following : 1. " Stowd, hewd, subdewd, joyd, cald, expeld, compeld, spoild, kild, seemd, benumbd, armd, redeemd, staind, shund, paynd, stird, appeard, perceivd, resolvd, obeyd, equald, foyld, hurld, ruind, joynd, scatterd, witherd," and others ending in *d*. 2. " Clapt, whipt, worshipt, lopt, stopt, stampt, pickt, knockt, linkt, puft, stuft, hist, kist, abasht, brusht, astonisht, vanquisht, confest, talkt, twitcht," and many others ending in *t*. This scheme divides our regular verbs into three classes ; leaving but very few of them to be written as they now are. It proceeds upon the principle of accommodating our orthography to the familiar, rather than to the solemn pronunciation of the language. " This," as Dr. Johnson observes, " is to measure by a shadow." It is, whatever show of learning or authority may support it, a pernicious innovation. The critic says, " I have not ventured to follow the example of Spenser and Milton throughout, but have merely attempted to revive the old form of the preterit in *t*."—*Phil. Museum*, Vol. i, p. 663. " We ought not however to stop here," he thinks ; and suggests that it would be no small improvement, " to write *leveld* for *levelled*, *enameld* for *enamelled*, *reformd* for *reformed*," &c.

OBS. 20.—If the multiplication of irregular preterits, as above described, is a grammatical error of great magnitude ; the forcing of our old and well-known irregular verbs into regular forms that are seldom if ever used, is an opposite error nearly as great. And, in either case, there is the same embarrassment respecting the formation of the second person. Thus *Cobbett*, in his English Grammar in a Series of Letters, has dogmatically given us a list of *seventy* verbs, which, he says, are, " by some persons, *erroneously deemed irregular ;*" and has included in it the words, *blow, build, cast, cling, creep, freeze, draw, throw,* and the like, to the number of *sixty ;* so that he is really right in no more than one seventh part of his catalogue. And, what is more strange, for several of the irregularities which he censures, his own authority may be quoted from the early editions of this very book : as, " For you could have *thrown* about seeds."—Edition of 1818, p. 13. " For you could have *throwed* about seeds."—Edition of 1832, p. 13. " A tree is *blown* down."— Ed. of 1818, p. 27. " A tree is *blowed* down."—Ed. of 1832, p. 25. " It *froze* hard last night. Now, what was it that *froze* so hard ? "—Ed. of 1818, p. 38. " It *freezed* hard last night. Now, what was it that *freezed* so hard ?"—Ed. of 1832, p. 35. A whole page of such contradictions may be quoted from this one grammarian, showing that *he did not know* what form of the preterit he ought to prefer. From such an instructor, who can find out what is good English, and what is not ? Respecting the inflections of the verb, this author says, " There are three persons : *but, our verbs have no variation in their spelling, except for the third person singular.*"—*Cobbett's E. Gram.* ¶ 88. Again : " Observe, however, that, in our language, there is no very great use in this distinction of modes ; because, for the most part, our little *signs* do the business, and *they never vary in the letters of which they are composed.*"—*Ib.* ¶ 95. One would suppose, from these remarks, that Cobbett meant to dismiss the pronoun *thou* entirely from his conjugations. Not so at all. In direct contradiction to himself, he proceeds to inflect the verb as follows : " I work, *Thou workest,* He works ; &c. I worked, *Thou workedst,* He worked ; &c. I shall or will work, *Thou shalt or wilt work,* He shall or will work ;" &c.—*Ib.* ¶ 98. All the *compound* tenses, except the future, he rejects, as things which " can only serve to fill up a book."

OBS. 21.—It is a common but erroneous opinion of our grammarians, that the unsyllabic suffix *st*, wherever found, is a modern contraction of the syllable *est*. No writer, however, thinks it always necessary to remind his readers of this, by inserting the sign of contraction ; though English books are not a little disfigured by questionable apostrophes inserted for no other reason. Dr. Lowth says, " The nature of our language, the accent and pronunciation of it, [incline] us to contract even all our regular verbs : thus *loved*, *turned*, are commonly pronounced in one syllable *lov'd*, *turn'd :* and the second person, which was originally in three syllables, *lovedest*, *turnedest*, is [say has] now become a dissyllable, *lovedst*, *turnedst.*"—*Lowth's Gram.* p. 45 ; *Hiley's*, 45 ; *Churchill's*, 104. See also *Priestley's Gram.* p. 114 ; and *Coar's*, p. 102. This latter doctrine, with all its vouchers, still needs confirmation. What is it but an idle conjecture ? If it were true, a few quotations might easily prove it ; but when, and by whom, have any such words as *lovedest*, *turnedest*, ever been used ? For aught I see, the simple *st* is as complete and as old a termination for the second person singular of an English verb, as *est ;* indeed, it appears to be *older :* and, for the preterit, it is, and (I believe) *always has been*, the *most* regular, if not the *only* regular, addition. If *sufferedest*, *woundedest*, and *killedest*, are words more regular than *sufferedst*, *woundedst*, *killedst*, then are *heardest*, *knewest*, *slewest*, *sawest*, *rannest*, *mettest*, *swammest*, and the like, more regular than *heardst*, *knewst*, *slewst*, *sawst*, *ranst*, *metst*, *swamst*, *satst*, *saidst*, *ledst*, *fledst*. *toldst*, and so forth ; but not otherwise.* So, in the solemn style, we write *seemest*, *deemest*, *swimmest*, like *seemeth*, *deemeth*, *swimmeth*, and so forth ; but, when we use the form which has no increase of syllables, why is an apostrophe more necessary in the second per-

---

* Among grammarians, as well as among other writers, there is some diversity of usage concerning the personal inflections of verbs ; while nearly all, nowadays, remove the chief occasion for any such diversity, by denying with a fashionable bigotry the possibility of any grammatical use of the pronoun *thou* in a familiar style. To illustrate this, I will cite Cooper and Wells—two modern authors who earnestly agree to account *you* and its verb literally singular, and *thou* altogether erroneous, in common discourse : except that *Wells* allows the phrase, " *If thou art*," for " *Common style.*"— *School Gram.* p. 100.

1. Cooper, improperly referring *all* inflection of the verb to the grave or solemn style, says: " In the colloquial or familiar style, we observe *no change.* The same is the case in the plural number." He then proceeds thus : " In the second person of the present of the indicative, in the *solemn style*, the verb takes *st* or *est ;* and in the third person *th* or *eth*, as : *thou hast, thou lovest, thou teachest ; he hath, he loveth, he goeth.* In the colloquial or *familiar style*, the verb *does not vary* in the second person ; and in the third person, it ends in *s* or *es*, as : *he loves, he teaches, he does.* The indefinite, [i. e. the preterit,] in the second person singular of the indicative, is the grave style, ends in *est*, as : *thou taughtest, thou wentest.* ☞ But, *in those verbs, where* the sound of *st* will unite with the last syllable of the verb, the vowel is omitted, as : *thou lovedst, thou heardst, thou didst.*"—*Cooper's Murray*, p. 60 ; *Plain and Practical Gram.* p. 59. This, the reader will see, is somewhat contradictory ; for the colloquial style varies the verb by " *s* or *es*," and *taught'st* may be uttered without the *e*. As for " *lovedst*," I deny that any vowel " *is omitted*" from it ; but possibly one may be, as *lov'dst.*

2. Wells's account of the same thing is this : " In the simple form of the present and past indicative, the second person singular of the *solemn style* ends regularly in *st* or *est*, as, thou *seest*, thou *hearest*, thou *sawest*, thou *heardest ;* and the third person singular of the present, in *s* or *es*, as, he *hears*, he *wishes*, and also in *th* or *eth*, as, he *saith*, he *loveth.* In the simple form of the present indicative, the third person singular of the *common* or *familiar style*, ends in *s* or *es* ; as, he *sleeps* ; he *rises.* The first person singular of the *solemn style*, and the first and second persons singular of the *common style*, have *the same form* as the three persons plural."—*Wells's School Grammar*, 1st Ed. p. 88 ; 3d Ed. p. 86. This, too, is both defective and inconsistent. It does not tell when to add *est*, and when, *st* only. It does not show what the *regular preterit*, as *freed* or *loved*, should make with *thou :* whether *freedest* and *lovedest*, by assuming the syllable *est ;* *fre-edst* and *lov-edst*, by increasing syllabically from assuming *st* only ; or *freedst* and *lov'dst*, or *lovedst*, still to be uttered as monosyllables. It absurdly makes " *s*," or " *es*" a sign of two opposite styles. (See Obs. 9th, above.) And it does not except " *I am, I was, If I am, If I was, If thou art, I am loved*," and so forth, from requiring " the same form, [*are* or *were*,] as the three persons plural." This author prefers " *heardest ;*" the other, " *heardst*," which I think better warranted :—

" And *heardst* thou why he drew his blade ?
Heardst thou that shameful word and blow
Brought Roderick's vengeance on his foe ?"—*Scott, L. L.*, C. v, st. 6.

son, than in the third?—in *seemst, deemst, swimst,* than in *seems, deems, swims?* When final *e* is dropped from the verb, the case is different ; as,

> " Thou *cutst* my head off with a golden axe,
> And *smil'st* upon the stroke that murders me."—*Shakspeare.*

Obs. 22.—Dr. Lowth supposes the verbal termination *s* or *es* to have come from a contraction of *eth.* He says, " Sometimes, by the rapidity of our pronunciation, the vowels are shortened or lost ; and the consonants, which are thrown together, do not coalesce with one another, and are therefore changed into others of the same organ, or of a kindred species. This occasions a farther deviation from *the regular form :* thus, *loveth, turneth,* are contracted into *lov'th, turn'th,* and these, for easier pronunciation, *immediately* become *loves, turns.*"—*Lowth's Gram.* p. 46 ; *Hiley's,* 45. This etymology may possibly be just, but certainly such contractions as are here spoken of, were not very common in Lowth's age, or even in that of Ben Jonson, who resisted the *s.* Nor is the sound of sharp *th* very obviously akin to flat *s.* The change would have been less violent, if *lov'st* and *turnst* had become *loves* and *turns ;* as some people nowadays are apt to change them, though doubtless this is a grammatical error : as,

> " And wheresoe'er thou *casts* thy view."—*Cowley.*
> " Nor thou that *flings* me floundering from thy back."—*Bat. of Frogs and Mice,* l. 123.
> " Thou *sitt'st* on high, and *measures* destinies."—*Pollok, Course of Time,* B. vi, l. 668.

Obs. 23.—Possibly, those personal terminations of the verb which do not form syllables, are mere contractions or relics of *est* and *eth,* which are syllables ; but it is perhaps not quite so easy to prove them so, as some authors imagine. In the oldest specimens given by Dr. Johnson in his History of the English Language,—specimens bearing a much earlier date than the English language can claim,—even in what he calls " Saxon in its highest state of purity," both *st* and *th* are often added to verbs, without forming additional syllables, and without any sign of contraction. Nor were verbs of the second person singular always inflected of old, in those parts to which *est* was afterwards very commonly added. Examples : " Buton ic wat thæt thu *hæfst* thara wæpna."—*King Alfred.* " But I know that thou *hast* those weapons." " Thæt thu *oncnawe* thara worda sothfæstnesse. of tham the thu *gelæred eart.*"—*Lucæ,* i, 4. " That thou *mightest know* the certainty of those things wherein thou *hast been instructed.*"—*Luke,* i, 4. " And thu *nemst* his naman Johannes."—*Lucæ,* i, 13. "And his name *schal be clepid* Jon."—*Wickliffe's Version.* "And thou *shalt call* his name John."—*Luke,* i, 13. "And he ne *drincth* win ne beor." —*Lucæ,* i, 15. " He *schal* not *drinke* wyn ne sydyr."—*Wickliffe.* " And *shall drink* neither wine nor strong drink."—*Luke,* i, 15. "And nu thu *bist* suwigende. and thu *sprecan* ne *miht* oth thone dæg the thas thing *gewurthath.* fortham thu minum wordum ne *gelyfdest.* tha *beoth* on hyra timan *gefyllede.*"—*Lucæ,* i, 20. "And lo, thou *schalt be* doumbe, and thou *schalt* not mowe *speke,* til into the day in which these thingis *schulen be don,* for thou *hast* not *beleved* to my wordis, whiche *schulen be fulfild* in her tyme."—*Wickliffe.* " And, behold, thou *shalt* be dumb, and not able to speak, until the day *that* * these things *shall be performed,* because thou *believest* not my words, which *shall be fulfilled* in their season."—*Luke,* i, 20.

> " In chaungyng of her course, the chaunge *shewth* this,
> Vp *startth* a knaue, and downe there *falth* a knight."—*Sir Thomas More.*

Obs. 24.—The corollary towards which the foregoing observations are directed, is this. As most of the peculiar terminations by which the second person singular is properly distinguished in the solemn style, are not only difficult of utterance, but are quaint and formal in conversation ; the preterits and auxiliaries of our verbs are seldom varied in familiar discourse, and the present is generally simplified by contraction, or by the adding of *st* without increase of syllables. A distinction between the solemn and the familiar style, has long been admitted, in the pronunciation of the termination *ed,* and in the ending of the verb in the third person singular ; and it is evidently according to good taste and the best usage, to admit such a distinction in the second person singular. In the familiar use of the second person singular, the verb is usually varied only in the present tense of the indicative mood, and in the auxiliary *hast* of the perfect. This method of varying the verb renders the second person singular analogous to the third, and accords with the practice of the most intelligent of those who retain the common use of this distinctive and consistent mode of address. It disencumbers their familiar dialect of a multitude of harsh and useless terminations, which serve only, when uttered, to give an uncouth prominency to words not often emphatic ; and, without impairing the strength or perspicuity of the language, increases its harmony, and reduces the form of the verb in the second person singular nearly to the same simplicity as in the other persons and numbers. It may serve also, in some instances, to justify the poets, in those abbreviations for which they have been so unreasonably censured by Lowth, Murray, and some other grammarians : as,

> "And thou their natures *knowst.* and *gave* them names,
> Needless to thee repeated."—*Milton,* P. L., Book vii, line 494.

Obs. 25.—The writings of the Friends, being mostly of a grave cast, afford but few examples of their customary mode of forming the verb in connexion with the pronoun *thou,* in familiar discourse. The following may serve to illustrate it : " Suitable to the office thou *layst* claim to."— R. BARCLAY'S *Works,* Vol. i, p. 27. " Notwithstanding thou *may have* sentiments opposite to mine."—THOMAS STORY. " To devote all thou *had* to his service ;"—" If thou *should come ;*"— " What thou *said ;*"—" Thou kindly *contributed ;*"—" The epistle which thou *sent* me ;"— " Thou *would* perhaps *allow ;*"—" If thou *submitted ;*"—" Since thou *left ;*"—" Should thou *act ;*" —" Thou *may be* ready ;"—" That thou *had met ;*"—" That thou *had intimated ;*"—" Before thou *puts* " [putst] ;—" What thou *meets* " [meetst] ;—" If thou *had made ;*"—" I observed thou *was ;*"—" That thou *might put* thy trust ;"—" Thou *had been* at my house."—JOHN KENDALL. " Thou *may be* plundered ;"—" That thou *may feel ;*"—" Though thou *waited* long, and *sought* him ;"—" I hope thou *will bear* my style ;"—" Thou also *knows* " [knowst] ;—" Thou *grew* up ;"—" I wish thou *would* yet *take* my counsel."—STEPHEN CRISP. " Thou *manifested* thy tender regard, *stretched* forth thy delivering hand, and *fed* and *sustained* us."—SAMUEL FOTHER-

* Better, as Wickliffe has it, " the day *in which ;*" though, after nouns of time, the relative *that* is often used, like the Latin ablative *quo* or *quâ,* as being equivalent to *in which* or *on which.*

GILL. The writer has met with thousands that used the second person singular in conversation, but never with any one that employed, on ordinary occasions, all the regular endings of the solemn style. The simplification of the second person singular, which, to a greater or less extent, is everywhere adopted by the Friends, and which is here defined and explained, removes from each verb eighteen of these peculiar terminations; and, (if the number of English verbs be, as stated by several grammarians, 8000,) disburdens their familiar dialect of 144,000 of these awkward and useless appendages.* This simplification is supported by usage as extensive as the familiar use of the pronoun *thou;* and is also in accordance with the canons of criticism: "The *first* canon on this subject is, All words and phrases which are remarkably harsh and unharmonious, and not absolutely necessary, should be rejected." See *Campbell's Philosophy of Rhetoric,* B. ii, Ch. ii, Sec. 2, Canon Sixth, p. 181. See also, in the same work, (B. iii, Ch. iv, Sec. 2d,) an *express defence* of "those elisions whereby the sound is improved;" especially of the suppression of the "feeble vowel in the last syllable of the preterits of our regular verbs;" and of "such abbreviations" as "the eagerness of conveying one's sentiments, the rapidity and ease of utterance, necessarily produce, in the dialect of conversation."—Pages 426 and 427. Lord Kames says, "That the English tongue, originally harsh, is at present much softened by dropping many *redundant consonants,* is undoubtedly true: that it is not capable of being further mellowed without suffering in its force and energy, will scarce be thought by any one who possesses an ear."—*Elements of Criticism,* Vol. ii, p. 12.

OBS. 26.—The following examples are from a letter of an African Prince, translated by Dr. Desaguillier of Cambridge, England, in 1743, and published in a London newspaper: "I lie there too upon the bed *thou presented* me;"—"After *thou left* me, in thy swimming house;"—"Those good things *thou presented* me;"—"When *thou spake* to the Great Spirit and his Son." If it is desirable that our language should retain this power of a simple literal version of what in others may be familiarly expressed by the second person singular, it is clear that our grammarians must not continue to dogmatize according to the letter of some authors hitherto popular. But not every popular grammar condemns such phraseology as the foregoing. "I improved, Thou improved*st*, &c. This termination of the second person preterit, on account of its harshness, *is seldom used,* and especially in the irregular verbs."—*Harrison's Gram.* p. 26. "The termination *est,* annexed to the preter tenses of verbs, is, at best. a very harsh one, when it is contracted, according to our general custom of throwing out the *e;* as *learnedst,* for *learnedest;* and especially, if it be again contracted into one syllable, *as it is commonly pronounced,* and made *learndst.* * * * I believe a writer or speaker would have recourse to any periphrasis rather than say *keptest,* or *keptst.* * * * Indeed this harsh termination *est* is *generally quite dropped in common conversation,* and sometimes by the poets, in writing."—*Priestley's Gram.* p. 115. The fact is, it never was added with much uniformity. Examples: "But like the hell hounde *thou waxed* full furious, expressyng thy malice when *thou* to honour *stied.*"—FABIAN'S CHRONICLE, V. ii, p. 522: in *Tooke's Divers.,* V. ii, p. 232

    "Thou from the arctic regions *came.* Perhaps
      Thou *noticed* on thy way a little orb,
      Attended by one moon—her lamp by night."—*Pollok,* B. ii, l. 5.

    "'So I believ'd.'—'No, Abel! to thy grief,
      So thou *relinquish'd* all that was belief."—*Crabbe, Borough,* p. 279.

OBS. 27.—L. Murray, and his numerous copyists, Ingersoll, Greenleaf, Kirkham, Fisk, Flint, Comly, Alger, and the rest; though they insist on it, that the *st* of the second person can never be dispensed with, except in the imperative mood and some parts of the subjunctive; are not altogether insensible of that monstrous harshness which their doctrine imposes upon the language. Some of them tell us to avoid this by preferring the auxiliaries *dost* and *didst:* as *dost burst,* for *burstest; didst check,* for *checkedst.* This recommendation proceeds on the supposition that *dost* and *didst* are smoother syllables than *est* and *edst;* which is not true: *didst learn* is harsher than either *learnedst* or *learntest;* and all three of them are intolerable in common discourse. Nor is the "*energy,* or *positiveness,*" which grammarians ascribe to these auxiliaries, always appropriate. Except in a question, *dost* and *didst,* like *do, does,* and *did,* are usually signs of *emphasis;* and therefore unfit to be substituted for the *st, est,* or *edst,* of an unemphatic verb. Kirkham, who, as we have seen, graces his Elocution with such unutterable things, as "*prob'dst, hurl'dst, arm'dst, want'dst, burn'dst, bark'dst, bubbl'dst, troubl'dst,*" attributes the use of the plural for the singular, to a design of avoiding the ruggedness of the latter. "In order to avoid the disagreeable harshness of sound, occasioned by the frequent recurrence of the terminations *est, edst,* in the adaptation of our verbs to the nominative *thou,* a *modern innovation* which substitutes *you* for *thou,* in familiar style, has generally been adopted. This innovation contributes greatly to the harmony of our colloquial style. *You* was formerly restricted to the plural number; but now it is employed to

<hr/>

* It is not a little strange, that some men, who *never have seen or heard* such words as their own rules would produce for the second person singular of many hundreds of our most common verbs, will nevertheless pertinaciously insist, that it is wrong to countenance in this matter any departure from the style of King James's Bible. One of the very rashest and wildest of modern innovators,—a critic who, but for the sake of those who still speak in this person and number, would gladly consign the pronoun *thou,* and all its attendant verbal forms, to utter oblivion,—thus treats this subject and me: "The Quakers, or Friends, however, use *thou,* and its attendant form of the *asserter,* in conversation. FOR THEIR BENEFIT, *thou* is given, in this work, in all the varieties of inflection; (in some of which it could not properly be used in an address to the Deity;; for THEY ARE MOST EGREGIOUSLY in the use of *thou,* with the form of the *asserter* which follows *he* or *they,* and are countenanced in their errors by G. Brown, who, instead of 'disburdening *the language* of 144,000 useless *distinctions,' increases* their number just 144,000."—*Oliver B. Peirce's Gram.* p. 85. Among people of sense, converts are made by teaching, and reasoning, and proving; but this man's disciples must yield to the balderdash of a *false speller, false quoter,* and *false asserter!* This author says, that "*dropt*" is the past tense of "*drop;*" (p. 118;) let him prove, for example. that *droptest* is not a clumsy *innovation,* and that *droppedst* is not a formal *archaism,* and then tell of the egregious error of adopting neither of these forms in common conversation. The following, with its many common contractions, is the language of POPE; and I ask this, or any other opponent of my doctrine, TO SHOW HOW SUCH VERBS ARE RIGHTLY FORMED, either for poetry or for conversation, in *the second person singular.*

    "It *fled,* I *follow'd;* now in hope, now pain;
    It *stopt,* I *stopt;* it *mov'd,* I *mov'd* again.
    At last it *fixt,* 'twas on what plant it *pleas'd,*
    And where it *fix'd,* the beauteous bird I *seis'd.*"—*Dunciad,* B. IV, l. 427.

represent either a singular or a plural noun."—*Kirkham's Gram.* p. 99. A *modern innovation,* for sooth ! Does not every body know it was current four hundred years ago, or more ? Certainly, both *ye* and *you* were applied in this manner, to the great, as early as the fourteenth century. Chaucer sometimes used them so, and he died in 1400. Sir T. More uses them so, in a piece dated 1503.

> " O dere cosyn, Dan Johan, she sayde,
> What eyleth *you* so rathe to aryse ?"—*Chaucer.*

Shakspeare most commonly uses *thou,* but he sometimes has *you* in stead of it. Thus, he makes Portia say to Butus :

> " *You* suddenly arose, and walk'd about,
> Musing, and sighing, with *your* arms across ;
> And when I ask'd *you* what the matter was,
> *You* star'd upon me with ungentle looks."—*J. Cæsar,* Act ii, Sc. 2.

OBS. 28.—" There is a natural tendency in all languages to throw out the rugged parts which improper consonants produce, and to preserve those which are melodious and agreeable to the ear."—*Gardiner's Music of Nature,* p. 29. " The English tongue, so remarkable for its grammatical simplicity, is loaded with a great variety of dull unmeaning terminations. Mr. Sheridan attributes this defect, to an utter inattention to what is easy to the organs of speech and agreeable to the ear ; and further adds, that, ' the French having been adopted as the language of the court, no notice was taken of the spelling or pronunciation of our words, until the reign of queen Anne.' So little was spelling attended to in the time of Elizabeth, that Dr. Johnson informs us, that on referring to Shakspeare's will, to determine how his name was spelt, he was found to have written it himself [in] no *less* [fewer] than three different ways."—*Ib.* p. 477. In old books, our participial or verbal termination *ed,* is found written in about a dozen different ways ; as, *ed, de, d, t, id, it, yd, yt, ede, od, ud.* For *est* and *eth,* we find sometimes the consonants only ; sometimes, *ist* or *yst, ith* or *yth ;* sometimes, for the latter, *oth* or *ath ;* and sometimes the ending was omitted altogether. In early times also the *th* was an ending for verbs of the third person plural, as well as for those of the third person singular ;[*] and, in the imperative mood, it was applied to the second person, both singular and plural : as,

> "*Demith* thyself, that *demist* other's dede ;
> And trouthe she shall deliver, it's no drede."—*Chaucer.*

OBS. 29.—It must be obvious to every one who has much acquaintance with the history of our language, that this part of its grammar has always been quite as unsettled as it is now ; and, however we may wish to establish its principles, it is idle to teach for absolute certainty that which every man's knowledge may confute. Let those who desire to see our forms of conjugation as sure as those of other tongues. study to exemplify in their own practice what tends to uniformity. The best that can be done by the author of a grammar, is, to exhibit usage, as it has been, and as it is ; pointing out to the learner what is most fashionable, as well as what is most orderly and agreeable. If by these means the usage of writers and speakers cannot be fixed to what is fittest for their occasions, and therefore most grammatical, there is in grammar no remedy for their inaccuracies ; as there is none for the blunders of dull opinionists, none for the absurdities of Ignorance stalled in the seats of Learning. Some grammarians say, that, whenever the preterit of an irregular verb is like the present, it should take *edst* for the second person singular. This rule, (which is adopted by Walker, in his Principles, No. 372,) gives us such words as *cast-edst, cost-edst, bid-dedst, burst-edst, cut-tedst, hit-tedst, let-tedst, put-tedst, hurt-edst, rid-dedst, shed-dedst, &c.* The few examples which may be adduced from ancient writings, in support of this principle, are undoubtedly formed in the usual manner from regular preterits now obsolete ; and if this were not the case, no person of taste could think of employing, on any occasion, derivatives so uncouth. Dr. Johnson has justly remarked, that " the chief defect of our language, is ruggedness and asperity." And this defect, as some of the foregoing remarks have shown, is peculiarly obvious, when even the regular termination of the second person singular is added to our preterits. Accordingly, we find numerous instances among the poets, both ancient and modern, in which that termination is omitted. See Percy's Reliques of Ancient Poetry, everywhere.

> " Thou, who of old the prophet's eye *unscaled.*"—*Pollok.*
> " Thou *saw* the fields laid bare and waste."—*Burns.*[†]

---

[*] The Rev. W. Allen, in his English Grammar, p. 132, says : " *Yth* and *eth* (from the Saxon *íaδ*) were formerly, *plural terminations ;* as, ' Manners *makyth* man.' William of Wykeham's motto. 'After long advisement, they *taketh* upon them to try the matter.' Stapleton's Translation of Bede. ' Doctrine and discourse *maketh* nature less importune.' Bacon." The use of *eth* as a plural termination of verbs, was evidently earlier than the use of *es* for the same purpose. Even the latter is utterly obsolete, and the former can scarcely have been *English.* The Anglo-Saxon verb *lufian,* or *lufigean,* to love, appears to have been inflected with the several pronouns thus : Ic lufige, Thu lufast, He lufath, We lufiath, Ge lufiath, Hi lufiath. The form in Old English was this : I love, Thou lovest, He loveth, We loven, Ye loven, They loven. Dr. Priestley remarks, (though in my opinion unadvisedly,) that, " Nouns of a plural form, but of a singular signification, require a singular construction ; as, mathematicks is a useful study. This observation will likewise," says he, " in some measure, vindicate the grammatical propriety of the famous saying of William of Wykeham, Manners *maketh* man."—*Priestley's Gram.* p. 189. I know not what *half-way* vindication there can be, for any such construction. *Manners* and *mathematics* are not nouns of the singular number, and therefore both *is* and *maketh* are wrong. I judge it better English to say, " Mathematics *are* a useful study."—" Manners *make* the man." But perhaps both ideas may be still better expressed by a change of the nominative, thus : " The *study* of mathematics *is* useful."— " *Behaviour* makes the man."

[†] What the state of our literature would have been, had no author attempted any thing on English grammar, must of course be a matter of mere conjecture, and not of any positive " conviction." It is my opinion, that, with all their faults, most of the books and essays in which this subject has been handled, have been in some degree beneficial, and a few of them highly so ; and that, without their influence, our language must have been much more chaotic and indeterminable than it now is. But a late writer says, and, with respect to *some* of our verbal terminations, says wisely : " It is my *sincere conviction* that fewer irregularities would have crept into the language had no grammars existed, than have been authorised by grammarians ; for it should be understood that the first of our grammarians, finding that good writers differed upon many points, instead of endeavouring to reconcile these discrepancies, absolutely perpetuated them by *citing opposite usages, and giving high authorities for both.* To this we owe all the irregularities which exists in the personal terminations of verbs, some of the best early writers using them promiscuously, some using them *uniformly,* and others making *no use* of them ; and really they are *of no use but to puzzle children and foreigners,* perplex poets, and furnish an awkward dialect to that exemplary sort

Obs. 30.—With the familiar form of the second person singular, those who constantly put *you* for *thou* can have no concern ; and many may think it unworthy of notice, because Murray has said nothing about it : others will hastily pronounce it bad English, because they have learned at school some scheme of the verb, which implies that this must needs be wrong.   It is this partial learning which makes so much explanation here necessary. The formation of this part of speech, form it as you will, is *central to grammar*, and cannot but be very important.   Our language can never entirely drop the pronoun *thou*, and its derivatives, *thy, thine, thee, thyself*, without great injury, especially to its poetry   Nor can the distinct syllabic utterance of the termination *ed* be now generally practised, except in solemn prose.   It is therefore better, not to insist on those old verbal forms against which there are so many objections, than to exclude the pronoun of the second person singular from all such usage, whether familiar or poetical, as will not admit them.   It is true that on most occasions *you* may be substituted for *thou*, without much inconvenience ; and so may *we* be substituted for *I*, with just as much propriety ; though Dr. Perley thinks the latter usage " is not to be encouraged."—*Gram.* p. 28.   Our authors and editors, like kings and emperors, are making *we* for *I* their most constant mode of expression.   They renounce their individuality to avoid egotism.   And when all men shall have adopted this enallage, the fault indeed will be banished, or metamorphosed, but with it will go an other sixth part of every English conjugation. The pronouns in the following couplet are put for the first person singular, the second person singular, and the second person plural; yet nobody will understand them so, but by their antecedents:

" Right trusty, and so forth—*we* let *you* to know
We are very ill used by *you mortals* below."—*Swift.*

Obs. 31.—It is remarkable that some, who forbear to use the plural for the singular in the second person, adopt it without scruple, in the first.   The figure is the same in both ; and in both, sufficiently common.   Neither practice is worthy to be made more general than it now is.   If *thou* should not be totally sacrificed to what was once a vain compliment, neither should *I*, to what is now an occasional, and perhaps a vain assumption.   Lindley Murray, who does not appear to have used *you* for *thou*, and who was sometimes singularly careful to periphrase and avoid the latter, nowhere in his grammar speaks of himself in the first person singular.   He is often " the *Compiler* ;" rarely, " the *Author ;*" generally, " We :" as, " *We* have distributed these parts of grammar, in the mode which *we* think most correct and intelligible."—*Octavo Gram.* p. 58. " *We* shall not pursue this subject any further."—*Ib.* p. 62. " *We* shall close these remarks on the tenses."—*Ib.* p. 76. " *We* presume no solid objection can be made."—*Ib.* p. 78. " The observations which *we* have made."—*Ib.* p. 100. " *We* shall produce a remarkable example of this beauty from Milton."—*Ib.* p. 331. " *We* have now given sufficient openings into this subject."—*Ib.* p. 334.   This usage has authority enough ; for it was not uncommon even among the old Latin grammarians ; but he must be a slender scholar, who thinks the pronoun *we* thereby becomes *singular*.   What advantage or fitness there is in thus putting *we* for *I*, the reader may judge. Dr. Blair did not hesitate to use *I*, as often as he had occasion ; neither did Lowth, or Johnson, or Walker, or Webster: as, " *I* shall produce a remarkable example of this beauty from Milton."—*Blair's Rhet.* p. 129.   " *I* have now given sufficient openings into this subject."—*Ib.* p. 131.   So in Lowth's Preface: " *I* believe,"—" *I* am persuaded,"—" *I* am sure,"—" *I* think,"—" *I* am afraid,"—" *I* will not take upon *me* to say."

. Obs. 32.—Intending to be critical without hostility, and explicit without partiality, I write not for or against any sect, or any man; but to teach all who desire to know *the grammar* of our tongue.   The student must distinctly understand, that it is necessary to speak and write differently, according to the different circumstances or occasions of writing.   Who is he that will pretend that the solemn style of the Bible may be used in familiar discourse, without a mouthing affectation ?   In preaching, the ancient terminations of *est* for the second person singular and *eth* for the third, as well as *ed* pronounced as a separate syllable for the preterit, are admitted to be generally in better taste than the smoother forms of the familiar style ; because the latter, though now frequently heard in religious assemblies, are not so well suited to the dignity and gravity of a sermon or a prayer.   In grave poetry also, especially when it treats of scriptural subjects, to which *you* put for *thou* is obviously unsuitable, the personal terminations of the verb, though from the earliest times to the present day they have usually been contracted and often omitted by the poets, ought still perhaps to be considered grammatically necessary, whenever they can be uttered, agreeably to the notion of our tuneless critics.   The critical objection to their elision, however, can have no very firm foundation while it is admitted by some of the objectors themselves, that, " Writers *generally* have recourse to this mode of expression, that they may avoid harsh terminations."—*Irving's Elements of English Composition*, p. 12.   But if writers of good authority, such as Pope, Byron, and Pollok, have sometimes had recourse to this method of simplifying the verb, even in compositions of a grave cast, the elision may, with tenfold stronger reason, be admitted in familiar writing or discourse, on the authority of general custom among those who choose to employ the pronoun *thou* in conversation.

" But thou, false Arcite, never *shall* obtain," &c.—*Dryden, Fables.*
" These goods *thyself can* on thyself bestow."—*Id. in Joh. Dict.*
" What I show, *thy self may* freely on thyself bestow."—*Id. Lowth's Gram.* p. 26.
" That thou *might* Fortune to thy side engage."—*Prior.*
" Of all thou ever *conquered*, none was left."—*Pollok*, B. vii, l. 760.
" And touch me trembling, as thou *touched* the man,"—&c.—*Id.* B. x. l. 60.

Obs. 33.—Some of the Friends (perhaps from an idea that it is less formal) misemploy *thee* for *of Christians*, who in every thing else study simplicity."—*Fowle's True E. Gram.* Part II, p 26.   Wells, a still later writer, gives this unsafe rule : " *When the past tense is a monosyllable not ending in a single vowel,* the second person singular of the solemn style is generally formed by the addition of *est* ; as *heardest, fleddest, toakest. Hadst, wast, saidst,* and *didst*, are exceptions."—*Wells's School Gram.* 1st Ed. p. 106 ; 3d Ed p. 110 ; 12th Ed. p. 115.   Now the termination *d* or *ed* commonly adds no syllable ; so that the regular past tense of any monosyllabic verb is, with a few exceptions, a monosyllable still ; as, *freed, feed, loved, feared, planned, turned* : and how would these sound with *est* added, which Lowth, Hiley, Churchill, and some others erroneously claim as having pertained to such preterits anciently ?   Again, if *heard* is a contraction of *heared*, and *fled*, of *fleed*, as seems probable ; then are *heardst* and *fledst*, which are sometimes used, more regular than *heardest, fleddest* : so of many other preterits.

thou; and often join it to the third person of the verb in stead of the second. Such expressions as, *thee does, thee is, thee has, thee thinks,* &c., are double solecisms; they set all grammar at defiance. Again, many persons who are not ignorant of grammar, and who employ the pronoun aright, sometimes improperly sacrifice concord to a slight improvement in sound, and give to the verb the ending of the third person, for that of the second. Three or four instances of this, occur in the examples which have been already quoted. See also the following, and many more, in the works of the poet Burns; who says of himself. "Though it cost the schoolmaster some thrashings, I made an excellent English scholar; and, by the time I was ten or eleven years of age, I was a critic in substantives, VERBS, and particles:"—"But when thou *pours;*"—"There thou *shines* chief;"—"Thou *clears* the head;"—"Thou *strings* the nerves;"—"Thou *brightens* black despair;"—"Thou *comes;*"—"Thou *travels* far;"—"Now *thou's* turned out;"—"Unseen thou *lurks;*"—"O thou pale orb that silent *shines.*" This mode of simplifying the verb, confounds the persons; and, as it has little advantage in sound, over the regular contracted form of the second person, it ought to be avoided. With this author it may be, perhaps, a Scotticism: as,

"Thou *paints* auld nature to the nines,
In thy sweet Caledonian lines."—*Burns to Ramsay.*

"Thou *paintst old* nature," would be about as smooth poetry, and certainly much better English. This confounding of the persons of the verb, however, is no modern peculiarity. It appears to be about as old as the use of *s* for *th* or *eth.* Spenser, the great English poet of the sixteenth century, may be cited in proof: as,

"Siker, *thou's* but a lazy loord,
And *rekes* much of thy swinke."—*Joh. Dict. w. Loord.*

OBS. 34.—In the solemn style, (except in poetry, which usually contracts these forms,) the second person singular of the present indicative, and that of the irregular preterits, commonly end in *est,* pronounced as a separate syllable, and requiring the duplication of the final consonant, according to Rule 3d for Spelling: as, I *run,* thou *runnest;* I *ran,* thou *rannest.* But as the termination *ed,* in solemn discourse, constitutes a syllable, the regular preterits form the second person singular by assuming *st,* without further increase of syllables: as, I *loved,* thou *lovedst;* not, "*lovedest,*" as Chandler made it in his English Grammar, p. 41, Edition of 1821; and as Wells's rule, above cited, if literally taken, would make it. *Dost* and *hast,* and the three irregular preterits, *wast, didst,* and *hadst,* are permanently contracted; though *doest* and *diddest* are sometimes seen in old books. *Saidst* is more common, and perhaps more regular, than *saidest.* *Werest* has long been contracted into *wert:* "I would thou *werest* either cold or hot."—*W. Perkins,* 1608.[*] The auxiliaries *shall* and *will* change the final *l* to *t,* and become *shalt* and *wilt.* To the auxiliaries, *may, can, might, could, would,* and *should,* the termination *est* was formerly added; but they are now generally written with *st* only, and pronounced as monosyllables, even in solemn discourse. Murray, in quoting the Scriptures, very often changes *mayest* to *mayst, mightest* to *mightst,* &c. Some other permanent contractions are occasionally met with, in what many grammarians call the solemn style; as *bidst* for *biddest, fledst* for *fleddest, satst* for *sattest:*

"Riding sublime, thou *bidst* the world adore,
And humblest nature with thy northern blast."—*Thomson.*
"Fly thither whence thou *fledst.*"—*Milton, P. L.,* B. iv, l. 963.
"Unspeakable, who *sitst* above these heavens."—*Id. ib.* B. v, l. 156.
"Why *satst* thou like an enemy in wait?"—*Id. ib.* B. iv, l. 825.

OBS. 35.—The formation of the third person singular of verbs, is *now* precisely the same as that of the plural number of nouns: as, *love, loves; show, shows; boast, boasts; fly, flies; reach, reaches.* This form began to be used about the beginning of the sixteenth century. The ending seems once to have been *es,* sounded as *s* or *z:* as,

"And thus I see among these pleasant thynges
Eche care *decayes,* and yet my sorrow *sprynges.*"—*Earl of Surry.*
"With throte yrent, he *roares,* he *lyeth* along."—*Sir T. Wyat.*
"He *dyeth,* he is all dead, he *pantes,* he *restes.*"—*Id.* 1540.

In all these instances, the *e* before the *s* has become improper. The *es* does not here form a syllable; neither does the *eth,* in "*lyeth*" and "*dyeth.*" In very ancient times, the third person singular appears to have been formed by adding *th* or *eth* nearly as we now add *s* or *es.* [†] Afterwards, as in our common Bible, it was formed by adding *th* to verbs ending in *e,* and *eth* to all others; as, "For he that *eateth* and *drinketh* unworthily, *eateth* and *drinketh* damnation to himself."—1 *Cor.* xi, 29. "He *quickeneth* man, who is dead in trespasses and sins; he *keepeth* alive the quickened soul, and *leadeth* it in the paths of life; he *scattereth, subdueth,* and *conquereth* the enemies of the soul."—*I. Penington.* This method of inflection, as now pronounced, always adds a syllable to the verb. It is entirely confined to the solemn style, and is little used. *Doth, hath,* and *saith,* appear to be permanent contractions of verbs thus formed. In the days of Shakspeare, both terminations were common, and he often mixed them, in a way which is not very proper now: as, "The equality of mercy is not strained;

It *droppeth,* as the gentle rain from heaven
Upon the place beneath: it is twice bless'd;
It *blesseth* him that *gives,* and him that *takes.*"—*Merchant of Venice.*

---

[*] Chaucer appears not to have inflected this word in the second person: "Also ryght as *thou were* ensample of meche folde errour, righte so thou must be ensample of manifold correction."—*Testament of Love.* "Rennin and crie as *thou were* wode."—*House of Fame.* So others: "I wolde *thou were* cold or hoot."—WICKLIFFE'S VERSION OF THE APOCALYPSE. "I wolde *thou were* cold or hote"—VERSION OF EDWARD VI: Tooke, Vol. ii, p. 276. See Rev. iii, 15: "I would *thou wert* cold or hot."—COMMON VERSION.

[†] See evidences of the *antiquity* of this practice, in the examples under the twenty-third observation above. According to Churchill, it has had some local continuance even to the present time. For, in a remark upon Lowth's contractions, *lov'th, turn'th,* this author says. "There are *still in use in some country places,* the third person singular of verbs in general being formed by the addition of the sound *th* simply, not making an additional syllable."—*Churchill's Gram.* p. 255. So the *eth* in the following example adds no syllable:—

"Death *goeth* about the field, rejoicing mickle
To see a sword that so surpass'd his sickle."
Harrington's Ariosto, B xiii: see *Singer's Shak.* Vol. ii, p. 296.

OBS. 36.—When the second person singular is employed in familiar discourse, with any regard to correctness, it is usually formed in a manner strictly analogous to that which is now adopted in the third person singular. When the verb ends with a sound which will unite with that of *st* or *s*, the second person singular is formed by adding *st* only, and the third, by adding *s* only; and the number of syllables is not increased: as, I *read*, thou *readst*, he *reads*; I *know*, thou *knowest*, he *knows*; I *take*, thou *takest*, he *takes*; I *free*, thou *freest*, he *frees*. For, when the verb ends in mute *e*, no termination renders this *e* vocal in the familiar style, if a synæresis can take place. To prevent their readers from ignorantly assuming the pronunciation of the solemn style, the poets have generally marked such words with an apostrophe: as,

> "Look what thy soul holds dear, imagine it
> To lie the way thou *go'st*, not whence thou *com'st*."—*Shak.*

OBS. 37.—But when the verb ends in a sound which will not unite with that of *st* or *s*, the second and third persons are formed by adding *est* and *es*; or, if the first person end in mute *e*, the *st* and *s* render that *e* vocal; so that the verb acquires an additional syllable: as, I *trace*, thou *tracest*, he *traces*; I *pass*, thou *passest*, he *passes*; I *fix*, thou *fixest*, he *fixes*; I *preach*, thou *preachest*, he *preaches*; I *blush*, thou *blushest*, he *blushes*; I *judge*, thou *judgest*, he *judges*. But verbs ending in *o* or *y* preceded by a consonant, do not exactly follow either of the foregoing rules. In these, *y* is changed into *i*, and, to both *o* and *i*, *st* and *es* are added without increase of syllables: as, I *go*, thou *goest*, he *goes*; I *undo*, thou *undoest*, * he *undoes*; I *fly*, thou *fliest*, he *flies*; I *pity*, thou *pitiest*, he *pities*. Thus, in the following lines, *goest* must be pronounced like *ghost*; otherwise, we spoil the measure of the verse:

> "Thou *goest* not now with battle, and the voice
> Of war, as once against the rebel hosts;
> Thou *goest* a Judge, and *findst* the guilty bound:
> Thou *goest* to prove, condemn, acquit, reward."—*Pollok*, B. x.

In solemn prose, however, the termination is here made a separate syllable: as, I *go*, thou *goest*, he *goeth*; I *undo*, thou *undoest*, he *undoeth*; I *fly*, thou *fliest*, he *flieth*; I *pity*, thou *pitiest*, he *pitieth*.

OBS. 38.—The auxiliaries *do*, *dost*, *does*,—(pronounced *doo*, *dust*, *duz*; and not as the words *dough*, *dosed*, *doze*,—) am, art, is,—have, hast, has,—being also in frequent use as principal verbs of the present tense, retain their peculiar forms, with distinction of person and number, when they help to form the compound tenses of other verbs. The other auxiliaries are not varied, or ought not to be varied, except in the solemn style. Example of the familiar use: "That thou *may* be found truly owning it."—*Barclay's Works*, Vol. i, p. 234.

OBS. 39.—The only regular terminations that are added to English verbs, are *ing*, *d* or *ed*, *st* or *est*, *s* or *es*, *th* or *eth*.† Ing, and *th* or *eth*, always add a syllable to the verb; except in *doth, hath, saith.*‡ The rest, whenever their sound will unite with that of the final syllable of the verb, are usually added without increasing the number of syllables; otherwise, they are separately pronounced. In solemn discourse, however, *ed* and *est* are by most speakers uttered distinctly in all cases; except sometimes when a vowel precedes: as in *sanctified*, *glorified*, which are pronounced as three syllables only. Yet, in spite of this analogy, many readers will have *sanctifiest* and *glorifiest* to be words of four syllables. If this pronunciation is proper, it is only so in solemn prose. The prosody of verse will show how many syllables the poets make: as,

> "Thou *diedst*, a most rare boy, of melancholy!"—*Shak. Cymb.* Act iv, sc. 2.
> "Had not a voice thus warn'd me: What thou *seest*,
> What there thou *seest*, fair creature, is thyself."—*Milton*, B. iv, l. 467.
> "By those thou *wooedst* from death to endless life."—*Pollok*, B. ix, l. 7.
> "Attend: that thou art happy, owe to God;
> That thou *continuest* such, owe to thyself."—*Milton*, B. v, l. 520.

OBS. 40.—If the grave and full form of the second person singular must needs be supposed to

---

* The second person singular of the simple verb *do*, is now usually written *dost*, and read *dust*; being permanently contracted in orthography, as well as in pronunciation. And perhaps the compounds may follow; as, Thou *undost*, *outdost*, *misdost*, *overdost*, &c. But exceptions to exceptions are puzzling, even when they conform to the general rule. The Bible has *dost* and *doth* for auxiliaries, and *doest* and *doeth* for principal verbs.

† N. Butler avers, "The only regular terminations added to verbs are *est*, *s*, *ed*, *edst*, and *ing*."—*Butler's Practical Gram.* p. 81. But he adds, in a marginal note, this information: "The third person singular of the present formerly ended in *eth*. This termination is still sometimes used in the solemn style. Contractions sometimes take place; as, *sayst* for *sayest*."—*Ibid.* This statement not only imposes a vast deal of *needless irregularity* upon the few inflections admitted by the English verb, but is, so far as it disagrees with mine, a causeless innovation. The terminations rejected, or here regarded as irregular, are *d*, *st*, *es*, *th*, and *eth*; while *edst*, which is plainly a combination of *ed* and *st*,—the past ending of the verb with the personal inflection,—is assumed to be one single and regular termination which I had overlooked! It has long been an almost universal doctrine of our grammarians, that regular verbs form their preterits and perfect participles by adding *d* to final *e*, and *ed* to any other radical ending. Such is the teaching of Blair, Brightland, Bullions, Churchill, Coar, Comly, Cooper, Fowle, Frazee, Ingersoll, Kirkham, Lennie, Murray, Weld, Wells, Sanborn, and others, a great multitude. But this author alleges, that, "*Loved* is not formed by adding *d* to *love*, but by adding *ed*, and dropping *e* from *love*."—*Butler's Answer to Brown.* Any one is at liberty to think this, if he will. But I see not the use of playing thus with mute *Ees*, adding one to drop an other, and often pretending to drop two under one apostrophe, as in *lov'd*, *lov'st*! To suppose that the second person of the regular preterit, as *lovedst*, is not formed by adding *st* to the first person, is contrary to the analogy of other verbs, and is something worse than an idle whim. And why should the formation of the third person be called *irregular* when it requires *es*, as in *flies*, *denies*, *goes*, *vetoes*, *wishes*, *preaches*, and so forth? In forming *flies* from *fly*, Butler changes "*y* into *ie*," on page 20th, adding *s* only; and, on page 11th, "into *y*" only, adding *es*. Uniformity would be better.

‡ Cooper says, "The termination *eth* is commonly contracted into *th*, to prevent the addition of a syllable to the verb, as: *doeth*, *doth*."—*Plain and Practical Gram.* p 59. This, with reference to modern usage, is plainly erroneous For, when *s* or *es* was substituted for *th* or *eth*, and the familiar use of the latter ceased, this mode of inflecting the verb without increasing its syllables, ceased also, or at least became unusual. It appears that the inflecting of verbs with *th* without a vowel, as well as with *st* without a vowel, was more common in very ancient times than subsequently. Our grammarians of the last century seem to have been more willing to *encumber* the language with syllabic endings, than to *simplify* it by avoiding them. See Observations, 21st, 22d, and 23d, above.

end rather with the syllable *est* than with *st* only, it is certain that this form may be *contracted*, whenever the verb ends in a sound which will unite with that of *st*. The poets generally employ the briefer or contracted forms ; but they seem not to have adopted a uniform and consistent method of writing them. Some usually insert the apostrophe, and, after a single vowel, double the final consonant before *st* ; as, *hold'st, bidd'st, said'st, ledd'st, wedd'st, trimm'st, may'st, might'st*, and so forth: others, in numerous instances, add *st* only, and form permanent contractions ; as, *holdst, bidst, saidst, ledst, wedst, trimst, mayst, mightst*, and so forth. Some retain the vowel *e*, in the termination of certain words, and suppress a preceding one ; as, *quick'nest, happ'nest, scatt'rest, rend'rest, rend'redst, slumb'rest, slumb'redst*: others contract the termination of such words, and insert the apostrophe ; as, *quicken'st, happen'st, scatter'st, render'st, render'dst, slumber'st, slumber'dst*. The nature and idiom of our language, " the accent and pronunciation of it," incline us to abbreviate or " contract even all our regular verbs ;" so as to avoid, if possible, an increase of syllables in the inflection of them. Accordingly, several terminations which formerly constituted distinct syllables, have been either wholly dropped, or blended with the final syllables of the verbs to which they are added. Thus the plural termination *en* has become entirely obsolete ; *th* or *eth* is no longer in common use ; *ed* is contracted in pronunciation ; the ancient *ys* or *is*, of the third person singular, is changed to *s* or *es*, and is usually added without increase of syllables ; and *st* or *est* has, in part, adopted the analogy. So that the proper mode of forming these contractions of the second person singular, seems to be, to add *st* only ; and to insert no apostrophe, unless a vowel is suppressed from the verb to which this termination is added : as, *thinkst, sayst, bidst, sitst, satst, lov'st, lov'dst, slumberst, slumber'dst*.

"And know, for that thou *slumberst* on the guard,
   Thou shalt be made to answer at the bar."—*Cotton.*

OBS. 41.—No man deserves more praise for his attention to English pronunciation, than John Walker. His Pronouncing Dictionary was, for a long period, the best standard of orthoëpy, that our schools possessed. But he seems to me to have missed a figure, in preferring such words as *quick'nest, strength'nest*, to the smoother and more regular forms, *quickenst, strengthenst*. It is true that these are rough words, in any form you can give them ; but let us remember, that needless apostrophes are as rough to the eye, as needless *st's* to the ear. Our common grammarians are disposed to encumber the language with as many of both as they can find any excuse for, and vastly more than can be sustained by any good argument. In words that are well understood to be contracted in pronunciation, the apostrophe is now less frequently used than it was formerly. Walker says, " This contraction of the participial *ed*, and the verbal *en*, is so fixed an idiom of our pronunciation, that to alter it, would be to alter the sound of the whole language. It must, however, be regretted that it subjects our tongue to some of the most hissing, snapping, clashing, grinding sounds that ever grated the ears of a Vandal: thus, *rasped, scratched, wrenched, bridled, fangled, birchen, hardened, strengthened, quickened*, &c. almost frighten us when written as they are actually pronounced, as *raspt, scratcht, wrencht, bridl'd, fangl'd, birch'n, strength'n'd, quick'n'd*, &c. : they become still more formidable when used contractedly in the solemn style, which never ought to be the case ; for here instead of *thou strength'n'st* or *strength'n'd'st, thou quick'n'st* or *quick'n'd'st*, we ought to pronounce *thou strength'nest* or *strength'nedst, thou quick'nest*, or *quick'-nedst*, which are sufficiently harsh of all conscience."—*Principles*, No. 359. Here are too many apostrophes ; for it does not appear that such words as *strengthenedest* and *quickenedest* ever existed, except in the imagination of certain grammarians. In solemn prose one may write, *thou quickenest, thou strengthenest*, or, *thou quickenedst, thou strengthenedst* ; but, in the familiar style, or in poetry, it is better to write, *thou quickenst, thou strengthenst, thou quickened, thou strengthened*. This is language which it is possible to utter ; and it is foolish to strangle ourselves with strings of rough consonants, merely because they are insisted on by some superficial grammarians. Is it not strange, is it not incredible, that the same hand should have written the two following lines, in the same sentence ? Surely, the printer has been at fault.

" With noiseless foot, thou *walkedst* the vales of earth"—
" Most honourable thou *appeared*, and most
   To be desired."—*Pollok's Course of Time*, B. ix, l. 18, and l. 24.

OBS. 42.—It was once a very common practice, to retain the final *y*, in contractions of the preterit or of the second person of most verbs that end in *y*, and to add the consonant terminations *d, st*, and *dst*, with an apostrophe before each ; as, *try'd* for *tried, reply'd* for *replied, try'st* for *triest, try'dst* for *triedst*. Thus Milton :—

" Thou following *cry'dst* aloud, Return, fair Eve ;
   Whom *fly'st* thou ? whom thou *fly'st*, of him thou art."—P. L., B. iv, l. 481.

This usage, though it may have been of some advantage as an index to the pronunciation of the words, is a palpable departure from the common rule for spelling such derivatives. That rule is, " The final *y* of a primitive word, when preceded by a consonant, is changed into *i* before an additional termination." The works of the British poets, except those of the present century, abound with contractions like the foregoing ; but late authors, or their printers, have returned to the rule ; and the former practice is wearing out and becoming obsolete. Of regular verbs that end in *ay, ey*, or *oy*, we have more than half a hundred ; all of which usually retain the *y* in their derivatives, agreeably to an other of the rules for spelling. The preterits of these we form by adding *ed* without increase of syllables ; as, *display, displayed ; survey, surveyed ; enjoy, enjoyed*. These also, in both tenses, may take *st* without increase of syllables ; as, *display'st, display'dst ; survey'st, survey'dst ; enjoy'st, enjoy'dst*. All these forms, and such as these, are still commonly considered contractions, and therefore written with the apostrophe ; but if the termination *st* is sufficient of itself to mark the second person singular, as it certainly is considered to be as regards one half of them, and as it certainly was in the Saxon tongue still more generally, then for the other half there is no need of the apostrophe, because nothing is omitted. *Est*, like *es*, is generally a syllabic termination ; but *st*, like *s*, is not. As signs of the third person, the *s* and the *es* are always considered equivalent ; and, as signs of the second person, the *st* and the *est* are sometimes, and ought to be always, considered so too. To all verbs that admit the sound, we add the *s* without marking it as a contraction for *es* ; and there seems to be no reason at all against adding the *st* in like manner, whenever we choose to form the second person without adding the syllable to the verb. The foregoing observations I commend to the particular consideration of all those who hope to write such English as shall do them honour—to every one who, from a spark of literary ambition, may say of himself,

———" I twine
My hopes of being remembered in my line
With my land's language."—*Byron's C. Harold,* Canto iv, st. 9.

THE CONJUGATION OF VERBS.

The conjugation of a verb is a regular arrangement of its moods, tenses, persons, numbers, and participles.

There are four PRINCIPAL PARTS in the conjugation of every simple and complete verb ; namely, the *Present,* the *Preterit,* the *Imperfect Participle,* and the *Perfect Participle.** A verb which wants any of these parts, is called *defective :* such are most of the auxiliaries.

An *auxiliary* is a short verb prefixed to one of the principal parts of an other verb, to express some particular mode and time of the being, action, or passion. The auxiliaries are *do, be, have, shall, will, may, can,* and *must,* with their variations.

OBSERVATIONS.

OBS. 1 —The *present,* or the verb in the present tense, is radically the same in all the moods, and is the part from which all the rest are formed. The present infinitive is commonly considered *the root,* or *simplest form,* of the English verb. We usually place the *preposition* TO *before* it ; but never when with an auxiliary it forms a compound tense that is not infinitive : there are also some other exceptions. which plainly show, that the word *to* is neither a part of the verb, as Cobbett, R. C. Smith, S. Kirkham, and Wells, say it is ; nor a part of the infinitive mood, as Hart and many others will have it to be, but a distinct *preposition.* (See, in the *Syntax* of this work, Observations on Rule 18th.) The preterit and the perfect participle are regularly formed by adding *d* or *ed,* and the imperfect participle by adding *ing,* to the present.

OBS. 2.—The moods and tenses, in English, are formed partly by inflections, or changes made in the verb itself, and partly by the combination of the verb or its participle, with a few short verbs, called *auxiliaries,* or *helping verbs.* This view of the subject, though disputed by some, is sustained by such a preponderance both of authority and of reason, that I shall not trouble the reader with any refutation of those who object to it. Murray the schoolmaster observes, " In the English language, the times and modes of verbs are expressed in a perfect, easy, and beautiful manner, by the aid of a few little words called *auxiliaries,* or *helping verbs.* The possibility of a thing is expressed by *can* or *could ;* the liberty to do a thing, by *may* or *might ;* the inclination of the will, by *will* or *would ;* the necessity of a thing, by *must* or *ought, shall* or *should.* The preposition *to* is never expressed after the helping verbs, except after *ought.*"—*Alex. Murray's Gram.* p. 112. See nearly the same words in *Buchanan's English Syntax,* p. 36 ; and in *the British Gram.* p. 125.

OBS. 3 —These authors are wrong in calling *ought* a helping verb, and so is Oliver B. Peirce, in calling " *ought to,*" and " *ought to have*" auxiliaries ; for no auxiliary ever admits the preposition *to* after it or into it : and Murray of Holdgate is no less in fault, for calling *let* an auxiliary ; because no mere auxiliary ever governs the objective case. The sentences, " He *ought* to *help* you," and " *Let* him *help* you," severally involve two different moods : they are equivalent to, " It *is his duty* to *help* you ;"—" *Permit* him *to help* you." Hence *ought* and *let* are not auxiliaries, but principal verbs.

OBS 4 —Though most of the auxiliaries are defective, when compared with other verbs : yet these three, *do, be,* and *have,* being also principal verbs, are complete : but the participles of *do* and *have* are not used as auxiliaries ; unless *having,* which helps to form the third or "compound perfect" participle, (as *having loved,*) may be considered such. The other auxiliaries have no participles.

OBS. 5 —English verbs are principally conjugated by means of auxiliaries ; the only tenses which can be formed by the simple verb, being the present and the imperfect ; as I *love,* I *loved.* And even here an auxiliary is usually preferred in questions and negations ; as, "*Do* you love ?"— "You *do* not *love.*" "*Did* he *love ?*"—" He *did* not *love.*" "*Do* I not yet *grieve ?*"—"*Did* she not *die ?*" All the other tenses, even in their simplest form, are compounds.

OBS. 6.—Dr. Johnson says, "*Do* is sometimes used superfluously, as *I* do *love, I* did *love ;* simply for *I love,* or *I loved ;* but this is considered as a *vitious* mode of speech."—*Gram. in* 4to *Dict.* p. 8. He also somewhere tells us, that these auxiliaries " are not proper before *be* and *have ;*" as, "*I do be,*" for *I am ;* "*I did have,*" for *I had.* The latter remark is generally true, and it ought to

* These are what William Ward, in his Practical Grammar, written about 1765, denominated " the CAPITAL FORMS, or ROOTS, of the English Verb." Their number too is the same " And these Roots," says he, " are considered as FOUR in each verb ; although in many verbs two of them are alike, and in some few three are alike." —P. 50. Few modern grammarians have been careful to display these Chief Terms, or Principal Parts, properly. Many say nothing about them. Some speak of *three,* and name them faultily. Thus Wells : " The three *principal parts* of a verb are the *present tense,* the *past tense,* and the *perfect participle.*"—*School Gram.* 113th Ed. p. 92. Now a whole " tense " is something more than one verbal form, and Wells's " perfect participle " includes the auxiliary " *having.*" Hence, in stead of *write, wrote, written,* (the true principal parts of a certain verb,) one might take under Wells's description, either of these threes, both entirely false : *am writing, did write,* and *having written ;* or, *do write, wrotest,* and *having written.* But *writing,* being the root of the " Progressive Form of the Verb," is far more worthy to be here counted a chief term, than *wrote,* the preterit, which occurs only in one tense, and never receives an auxiliary. So of other verbs. This sort of treatment of the Principal Parts, is a very grave defect in sundry schemes of grammar.

remembered;* but, in the *imperative mood, be* and *have* will admit the emphatic word *do*
fore them : as, " Now *do be* careful ; "—"*Do have* a little discretion." Sanborn repeatedly puts
before *be*, in this mood : as, "*Do* you *be*. *Do* you *be* guarded. *Do* thou *be*. *Do* thou *be* guarded."
Analytical Gram. p. 150. "*Do* thou *be* watchful."—*Ib.* p. 155. In these instances, he must
ve forgotten that he had elsewhere said positively, that. "*Do*, as an auxiliary, *is never used* with
e verb *be* or *am*."—*Ib.* p. 112. In the other moods, it is seldom proper before *be ;* but it is sometimes
sed before *have*, especially with a negative : as, " Those modes of charity which *do not have* in view
e cultivation of moral excellence, are essentially defective."—*Wayland's Moral Science*, p. 428.
Surely, the law of God, whether natural or revealed, *does not have* respect merely to the external
nduct of men."—*Stuart's Commentary on Romans*, p. 158. " And each day of our lives *do we*
we occasion to see and lament it."—*Dr. Bartlett's Lecture on Health*, p. 5. " Verbs, in them-
lves considered, *do not have* person and number."—*R. C. Smith's New Gram.* p. 21. [This notion
f Smith's is absurd. Kirkham taught the same as regards " person."] In the following example,
ter *be* is used for *is*,—the auxiliary *is*,—and perhaps allowably : " It is certain from scripture, that
e same person *does* in the course of life many times offend and *be* forgiven."—*West's Letters*
o *a Young Lady*, p. 182.

OBS. 7.—In the compound tenses, there is never any variation of ending for the different persons
nd numbers, except in the *first auxiliary :* as, "Thou *wilt have finished* it;" not, "Thou *wilt*
ast finishedst it ;" for this is nonsense. And even for the former, it is better to say, in the familiar
tyle, "Thou *will have finished* it ;" for it is characteristic of many of the *auxiliaries*, that, unlike
ther verbs, they are not varied by *s* or *eth*, in the third person singular, and never by *st* or *est*, in
e second person singular, except in the solemn style. Thus all the auxiliaries of the potential
ood, as well as *shall* and *will* of the indicative, are without inflection in the third person singular,
hough *will*, as a principal verb, makes *wills* or *willeth*, as well as *willest*, in the indicative present.
ence there appears a tendency in the language, to confine the inflection of its verbs to *this tense*
ly ; and to the auxiliary *have, hast, has*, which is essentially present, though used with a par-
ciple to form the perfect. *Do, dost, does*, and *am, art, is*, whether used as auxiliaries or as
rincipal verbs, are always of the indicative present.

OBS. 8.—The word *need*,—(though, as a principal verb and transitive, it is unquestionably both
egular and complete,—having all the requisite parts, *need, needed, needing, needed*,—and being
ecessarily inflected in the indicative present, as, I *need*, thou *needst* or *needest*, he *needs* or
eedeth,—) is so frequently used without inflection, when placed before an other verb to express a
ecessity of the being, action, or passion, that one may well question whether it has not become,
nder these circumstances, an *auxiliary* of the potential mood ; and therefore proper to be used,
ke all the other auxiliaries of this mood, without change of termination. I have not yet know-
gly used it so myself, nor does it appear to have been classed with the auxiliaries, by any of our
rammarians, except Webster.† I shall therefore not presume to say now, with positiveness, that
deserves this rank ; (though I incline to think it does ;) but rather quote such instances as have
curred to me in reading, and leave the student to take his choice, whether to condemn as bad
aglish the uninflected examples, or to justify them in this manner. " He that can swim. *need* not
espair to fly."—*Johnson's Rasselas*, p. 29. " One therefore *needs* not expect to do it."—*Kirkham's*
locution, p. 155. " In so doing I should only record some vain opinions of this age, which a
ture one *need* not know."—*Rush, on the Voice*, p. 345. " That a boy *needs* not be kept at
hool."—LINDSEY : *in Kirkham's Elocution*, p. 164. " No man *need* promise, unless he please."—
ayland's Moral Science, p. 312. " What better reason *needs* be given ?"—*Campbell's Rhet.* p. 51.
He *need* assign no other reason for his conduct."—*Wayland, ib.* p. 214. " Now there is nothing
at a man *needs* be ashamed of in all this."—*Collier's Antoninus*, p. 45. " No notice *need* be
ken of the advantages."—*Walker's Rhyming Dict.* Vol. ii, p. 304. " Yet it *needs* not be
peated."—*Bicknell's Gram.* Part ii, p. 51. " He *need* not be anxious."—*Greenleaf's Gram.*
mplified, p. 38. " He *needs* not be afraid."—*Fisk's Gram. Simplified*, p. 124. " He who will
ot learn to spell, *needs* not learn to write."—*Red Book*, p. 22. " The heeder *need* be under no
ar."—*Greenleaf's Gram.* p. 38.‡ " More *need* not be said about it."—*Cobbett's E. Gram.* ¶ 272.
The object *needs* not be expressed."—*Booth's Introd. to Dict.* p. 37. " Indeed, there *need* be no
ich thing."—*Fosdick's De Sacy*, p. 71. " This *needs* to be illustrated."—*Ib.* p. 81. "And no
rt of the sentence *need* be omitted."—*Parkhurst's Grammar for Beginners*, p. 114. " The learner
eds *to* know what sort of words are called verbs."—*Ib.* p. 6. " No one *need* be apprehensive of
ffering by faults of this kind."—*Sheridan's Elocution*, p. 171. " The student who has bought
ly of the former copies *needs* not repent."—*Dr. Johnson, Adv. to Dict.* " He *need* not enumerate
eir names."—*Edward's First Lessons in Grammar*, p. 38. "A quotation consisting of a word
two only *need* not begin with a capital."—*Churchill's Gram.* p. 383. " Their sex is commonly
own, and *needs* not *to* be marked."—*Ib.* p. 72; *Murray's Octavo Gram.* 51. " One *need* only
en Lord Clarendon's history, to find examples every where."—*Blair's Rhet.* p. 108. " Their sex
commonly known, and *needs* not be marked."—*Lowth's Gram.* p. 21; *Murray's Duodecimo*
ram. p. 51. " Nobody *need* be afraid he shall not have scope enough."—LOCKE: *in Sanborn's*
ram. p 163. " No part of the science of language, *needs to be ever* uninteresting to the purer."—*Nutting's Gram.* p. vii. " The exact amount of knowledge is not, and *need* not be,

* A grammarian should know better, than to exhibit, *as a paradigm* for school-boys, such English as the fol-
wing "I do have, Thou dost have, He does have; We do have, You do have, They do have "—*Everest's*
um. p. 106. " I did have, Thou didst have, He did have ; We did have, You did have, They did have."—
· p. 107. I know not whether any one has yet thought of conjugating the verb *be* after this fashion ; but the
empt to introduce. " *am being, is being*," &c., is an innovation much worse.

† Hiley borrows from Webster the remark, that, "*Need*, when intransitive, is formed *like an auxiliary*, and is
lowed by a verb. without the prefix *to :* as, ' He *need* go no farther.' "—*Hiley's Gram.* p. 90; *Webster's Imp.*
em. p 127 ; *Pulos. Gram.* p. 178. But he forbears to class it with the auxiliaries, and even contradicts him-
f, by a subsequent remark taken from Dr. Campbell, that, for the sake of " ANALOGY, ' *he needs*,' ' *he dares*,' are
lerable to ' *he need*, ' *he dare*.' "—*Hiley's Gram* p 146 ; *Campbell's Rhet.* p. 175.

‡ This grammarian here uses *need* for the third person singular, designedly, and makes a remark for the justifi-
ion of the practice ; but he neither calls the word an auxiliary, nor cites any other than anonymous examples,
ich are, perhaps, of his own invention.

great."—*Todd's Student's Manual*, p. 44. "He *needs to* act under a motive which is all-perva —*Ib.* p. 375. "What *need* be said, will not occupy a long space."—*Ib.* p. 344. "The r *needs* not always be used."—*Bucke's Gram.* p. 96. "Such as he *need* not be ashamed of."— *ing's Gift for Scribblers*, p. 23.

"*Needst* thou—*need* any one on earth—despair ? "—*Ib.* p.32.
"Take timely counsel; if your dire disease
Admits no cure, it *needs* not *to* displease."—*Ib.* p. 14.

OBS. 9.—If *need* is to be recognized as an auxiliary of the potential mood, it must be stood to belong to two tenses; the present and the perfect; like *may, can,* and *must*: as, "I not *go,* He *need* not *have gone ;* Thou *need* not *go,* Thou *need* not *have gone ;*" or, in the : style, "Thou *needst* not *go,* Thou *needst* not *have gone.*" If, on the contrary, we will ha be always a principal verb, the distinction of time should belong to itself, and also the dist of person and number, in the parts which require it: as, "He *needs* not go, He *needs* t Thou *needst* not go, Thou *needed* not go;" or, in the solemn style, "Thou *needest* not go *needest* not go." Whether it can be right to say, "He *needed* not *have gone,*" is at least tionable. From the observations of Murray, upon relative tenses, under his thirteenth : syntax, it seems fair to infer that he would have judged this phraseology erroneous. Agai *needs* not *have gone,*" appears to be yet more objectionable, though for the same reason. . "He *need* not *have gone,*" is a correct expression, *need* is clearly proved to be an *auxilia* the three words taken together must form *the potential perfect.* And so of the plural: ! argument is from the connexion of the tenses, and not merely from the tendency of auxil reject inflection : as, "They *need* not *have been* under great concern about their public aff *Hutchinson's History,* i, 194. From these examples, it may be seen that an auxiliary and a pal verb have some *essential difference ;* though those who dislike the doctrine of cea tenses, pretend not to discern any. Take some further citations; a few of which are em in respect to time. And observe also that the regular verb sometimes admits the prepos after it : "'There is great dignity in being waited for,' said one who had the habit of tan and who *had* not much else of which he *need* be vain."—*Student's Manual,* p. 64. "But he not *have gone* so far for more instances."—*Johnson's Gram. Com.* p. 143. "He *need* n: la 'perhaps the virtue.'"—*Sedgwick's Economy,* p. 196. "I *needed* not *to ask* how she felt' *bott's Young Christian,* p. 84. "It *need* not *have been* so."—*Ib.* p. 111. "The most una dating politician *need* not absolutely *want* friends."—*Hunt's Feast of the Poets,* p. ii.. " therefore *needs* not be introduced with much precaution."—*Campbell's Rhet.* p. 326. "W obscurer term *needs to* be explained by one that is clearer."—*Ib.* p. 367. "Though, if she li younger, she *need* not *have known* it."—*West's Letters,* p. 120. "Nothing *need* be said, so they were the *most perfect* barbarisms."—*Blair's Rhet.* p. 470. "He *need* not go."—*'i e* *Gram.* p. 36. "He *needed* but use the word *body.*"—LOCKE: *in Joh. Dict.* "He *need* t i quired to use them."—*Parker's Eng. Composition,* p. 50. "The last consonant of *ej* not be doubled."—*Dr. Webster.* "It *needs* the less *to be inforced.*"—*Brown's Esti.* "Of these pieces of his, we *shall not need to give* any particular account."—*Seneca's M* *rc* "And therefore I *shall need say* the less of them."—*Scougal,* p. 101. "This compound words *need* occasion no surprise."—*Cardell's Essay on Language,* p. 87.
"Therefore stay, thou *needst* not *to* be gone."—*Shakspeare.*
"Thou *need* na *start* awa sae hasty."—*Burns. Poems,* p. 15.
"Thou *need* na *jouk* behind the hallan."—*Id. ib.* p. 67.

OBS. 10.—The auxiliaries, except *must,* which is invariable, have severally two forms .t to tense, or time; and when inflected in the second and third persons singular, are usually in the following manner : —

[TO DO.

PRESENT TENSE ; AND SIGN OF THE INDICATIVE PRESENT.
Sing. I do, thou dost, he does ;   *Plur.* We do, you do, they do.

IMPERFECT TENSE ; AND SIGN OF THE INDICATIVE IMPERFECT.
Sing. I did, thou didst, he did ;   *Plur.* We did, you did, they did.

TO BE.

PRESENT TENSE ; AND SIGN OF THE INDICATIVE PRESENT.
Sing. I am, thou art, he is ;   *Plur.* We are, you are, they are.

IMPERFECT TENSE ; AND SIGN OF THE INDICATIVE IMPERFECT.
Sing. I was, thou wast, he was ;   *Plur.* We were, you were, they were.

TO HAVE.

PRESENT TENSE ; BUT SIGN OF THE INDICATIVE PERFECT.
Sing. I have, thou hast, he has ;   *Plur.* We have, you have, they have.

IMPERFECT TENSE ; BUT SIGN OF THE INDICATIVE PLUPERFECT.
Sing. I had, thou hadst, he had ;   *Plur.* We had, you had, they had.

SHALL AND WILL.

These auxiliaries have distinct meanings, and, as signs of the future, they are inter thus :

PRESENT TENSE ; BUT SIGNS OF THE INDICATIVE FIRST-FUTURE.

1. Simply to express a future action or event : —
Sing. I shall, thou wilt, he will ;   *Plur.* We shall, you will, they wi..

2. To express a promise, command, or threat : —
Sing. I will, thou shalt, he shall ;   *Plur.* We will, you shall, they shall.

IMPERFECT TENSE; BUT, AS SIGNS, AORIST, OR INDEFINITE.

1. Used with reference to duty or expediency:—

s. I should, thou shouldst, he should; *Plur.* We should, you should, they should.

2. Used with reference to volition or desire:—

g. I would, thou wouldst, he would; *Plur.* We would, you would, they would.

MAY.

PRESENT TENSE; AND SIGN OF THE POTENTIAL PRESENT.

Sing. I may, thou mayst, he may; *Plur.* We may, you may, they may.

IMPERFECT TENSE; AND SIGN OF THE POTENTIAL IMPERFECT.

g. I might, thou mightst, he might; *Plur.* We might, you might, they might.

CAN.

PRESENT TENSE; AND SIGN OF THE POTENTIAL PRESENT.

Sing. I can, thou canst, he can; *Plur.* We can, you can, they can.

IMPERFECT TENSE; AND SIGN OF THE POTENTIAL IMPERFECT.

Sing. I could, thou couldst, he could; *Plur.* We could, you could, they could.

MUST.

PRESENT TENSE; AND SIGN OF THE POTENTIAL PRESENT.

Sing. I must, thou must, he must; *Plur.* We must, you must, they must.

must is ever used in the sense of the Imperfect tense, or Preterit, the form is the same as the Present: this word is entirely invariable.

.II.—Several of the auxiliaries are occasionally used as mere expletives, being quite unnecessary to the sense: as, 1. Do and DID: "And it is night, wherein all the beasts of the forest do forth."—*Psalms.* civ, 20. "And ye, that on the sands with printless feet *do* chase the flying, and *do* fly him when he comes back."—*Shak.* "And if a man *did* need a poison —*la* This needless use of *do* and *did* is now avoided by good writers. 2. SHALL, SHOULD, &c. "'Men *shall* deal unadvisedly sometimes, which after-hours give leisure to repent I *should* advise you to proceed. I *should* think it would succeed. He it *should* seem, thinks he."—*W. Allen's Gram.* p. 65. "I *could* wish you to go."—*Ib.* p. 71. 3. WILL, &c. The two are nearly of the same character, but not exactly: "The isle is full of noises; sometimes a sound twanging instruments *will* hum about mine ears."—*Shak.* "In their evening she *would* steal in amongst them."—*Barbauld.*

"His listless length at noontide *would* he stretch."—*Gray.*

.III.—As our old writers often formed the infinitive in *en*, so they sometimes dropped the *n* of the perfect participle. Hence we find, in the infancy of the language, *done* used also for *done;* and that by the same hand, with like changes in other verbs: as, "Thou hast done."—*Chaucer.* "As he was wont to *done.*"—*Id.* "The treson that to women *I. —Id.* "For to *ben* honourable and free."—*Id.* "I am sworn to *holden* it secre."— "Our nature God hath to him *unyte.*"—*Douglas.* "None otherwise negligent than I *you* might not *bee.*"—*Id.* See *W. Allen's E. Gram.* p. 97.

"But netheless the thynge is *do,*
That fals god was soone *go.*"—GOWER: *H. Tooke,* Vol. i, p. 376.

.IV.—*May* is from the Anglo-Saxon *mægan,* to be able. In the parent language also, it is an auxiliary. It is exhibited by Fortescue, as a principal verb; 'They shall *may* do it: they shall be able (to) do it.'"—*W. Allen's Gram.* p. 70. "*May not,* was formerly used *as,* 'Graces for which we *may not* cease to sue.' Hooker."—*Ib.* p. 91. "*May* frequently expresses doubt of the fact; as, 'I *may* have the book in my library, but I think I have it is used also, to express doubt, or a consequence, with a future signification; as, 'I *power* the use of my limbs, but I see little probability of it.'—'That they *may* receive me be buried.' *Luke,* xvi, 4."—*Churchill's Gram.* p. 247. In these latter instances, the *potent* is akin to the subjunctive. Hence Lowth and others improperly call "*I may* is the subjunctive mood. Others, for the same reason, and with as little propriety, deny to it any subjunctive mood; alleging an ellipsis in every thing that bears that name: 'If I *may*) be possible, live peaceably with all men.' Scriptures."—*W. Allen's Gram.* p. 61. *May* is a sign of wishing, and consequently occurs often in prayer: as, "*May* it be thy good will.'—'O that it *may* please thee;"—"*Mayst* thou be pleased." Hence the potential is like the imperative: the phrases, "Thy will be done,"—"May thy will be done,"— "will done,"—"Let thy will be done,"—are alike in meaning, but not in mood or confine.

.V.—*Can,* to be able, is etymologically the same as the regular verbs *ken,* to see, and *con,* most of them being derived from the Saxon *connan* or *cunnan,* to know: whence also the *cunning,* which was formerly a participle. In the following example *will* and *can* are forms. "In evil, the best condition is, not *to will;* the second, not *to can.*"—*Ld. Bacon.* As *can* which signifies knowledge, may also signify power, appears from these examples: 'I *should not know how,* (i. e. *could* not.) 'Ασφαλισασθε ως οιδατε, Strengthen it how, (i. e. as you *can.*) *Nescio* mentiri, I *know not how to* (i. e. *I cannot*) *Lily's Gram.* p. 71. *Shall,* Saxon *sceal,* originally signified to *owe;* for which reason *it really* means *ought.* In the following example from Chaucer, *shall* is a principal verb in its original meaning:

"For, by the faith I *shall* to God, I wene,
Was neuer straungir none in hir degre."—*W. Allen's Gram.* p. 64.

.VI.—*Do* and *did* are auxiliary only to the present infinitive, or the radical verb; as, *do throw,* *did throw,* thus the mood of *do throw* or *to throw* is marked by *do* or *to.* *Be,* in all its parts, is with either of the simple participles; as, *to be throwing, to be thrown; I am throwing, I threw,* and so, through the whole conjugation. *Have* and *had,* in their literal use, are

auxiliary to the perfect participle only; as, *have thrown, had thrown. Have* is from the $
habban, to possess; and, from the nature of the perfect participle, the tenses thus formed, sq
in general a completion of the action. The French idiom is similar to this: as, *J'ai ru, i have
Shall* and *should, will* and *would, may* and *might, can* and *could, must,* and also *need,* (if w
the last a helping verb,) are severally auxiliary to both forms of the infinitive, and to these t
as, *shall throw, shall have thrown; should throw, should have thrown;* and so of all the rest.

Obs. 16.—The form of the indicative pluperfect is sometimes used in lieu of the potentia
perfect; as, "If all the world could have seen it, the wo *had been* universal."—*Shakspeare*
is, "*would have been* universal." "I *had been* drowned, but that the shore was shallow."—*Id.* That is—"I *should have been drowned.*" This mode of expression may be re
to the figure *enallage,* in which one word or one modification is used for an other. For
this is the use of *were* for *would be:* "It *were* injustice to deny the execution of the l
any individual;" that is, "it *would be* injustice."—*Murray's Grammar,* p. 89. In som
stances, *were* and *had been* seem to have the same import; as, "Good *were* it for that man
had never been born."—*Mark,* xiv, 21. "It *had been* good for that man if he had not been b
Matt. xxvi, 24. In prose, all these licenses are needless, if not absolutely improper. In p
their brevity may commend them to preference; but to this style, I think, they ought to b
fined: as,

> "That *had been* just, replied the reverend bard;
> But done, fair youth, thou ne'er *hadst met* me here."—*Pollok.*
> "The keystones of the arch!—though all were o'er,
> For us repeopled *were* the solitary shore."—*Byron.*

Obs. 17.—With an adverb of comparison or preference, as *better, rather, best, as lief,* or a
the auxiliary *had* seems sometimes to be used before the infinitive to form the pa
imperfect or pluperfect: as, "He that loses by getting, *had better lose* than get."—*Penn's M*
"Other prepositions *had better have been substituted.*"—*Priestley's Gram.* p. 166. "I had
say."—*Lowth: ib.* p. 110. "It compels me to think of that which I *had rather forged.*"—l
steth, on Prayer, p. 25. "You *had much better say* nothing upon the subject."—*Webster, i B*
p. 147. "I *had much rather show* thee what hopes thou hast before thee."—*Baxter* "
rather speak five words with my understanding, than ten thousand words in an unknown tu
—1 *Cor.* xiv, 19. "I knew a gentleman in America who told me '*how much rather* he te
woman than the man he is."—*Martineau's Society in America,* Vol. i. p. 153. "I *had* as
as not."—*Webster's Dict. w. Lief.* "I *had as lieve* the town crier spoke my lines."—*Shak. B*
"We *had best leave* nature to her own operations."—*Kames, El. of Crit.* Vol. i, p. 310 "
method *had he best take?*"—*Harris's Hermes,* p. ix. These are equivalent to the phrases
better lose—might better have been substituted—*would* as lief say—*would* rather forget—migh
better say—*would* much rather show—*would* rather speak—how much rather he *would* li—
as lief go—*should* best leave—*might* he best take; and, for the sake of regularity, these latter
ought to be preferred, as they sometimes are: thus, "For my own part, I *would rather* cut
a tree in all its luxuriancy."—*Addison, Spect.* No. 414; *Blair's Rhet.* p. 223. The followin
struction is different: "Augustus *had like to* have been slain."—*S. Butler.* Here *had* sign
verb of the indicative imperfect. The following examples appear to be positively err
"Much that was said, *had better remained* unsaid."—*N. Y. Observer.* Say, "*might better*
mained." "A man that is lifting a weight, if he put not sufficient strength to it, *had* e te
none at all."—*Baxter.* Say, "*might as well put.*" "You *were better pour* off the first if
and use the latter."—*Bacon.* Say, "*might better pour;*" or, if you prefer it, "*had better*
Shakspeare has an expression which is still worse:—

> "Or, by the worth of mine eternal soul,
> Thou *hadst been better have been born* a dog."—*Beauties,* p. 295.

Obs. 18.—The form of conjugating the active verb, is often called the *Active* Voice, and
the passive verb, the *Passive Voice.* These terms are borrowed from the Latin and Greek gram
and, except as serving to diversify expression, are of little or no use in English grammar.
grammarians deny that there is any propriety in them, with respect to any language. B
after showing that the import of the verb does not always follow its form of voice, adds
must, therefore, carefully distinguish the Voice of a Verb from its signification. To
the distinction, I denominate that an *Active* Verb which contains an Attribute in which the
is considered as performed by the Subject; and that a *Passive* Verb which contains an Attr
which the action is considered as suffered by the Subject, and performed upon it by su
I call that voice a *Subjective* Voice which is generally appropriated to the Active Verb, and t
Objective Voice which is generally appropriated to the Passive Verb. As to the Neuter V
they possess a peculiar form, I call it a *Neuter* Voice."—*Fosdick's Translation,* p. 99.

Obs. 19.—A recognition of the difference between actives and passives, in our original
tion of verbs with respect to their signification—a principle of division very properly ado p
a great majority of our grammars and dictionaries, but opinionately rejected by Webster,
and sundry late grammarians,—renders it unnecessary, if not improper, to place Voices, the
Voice and the Passive, among the *modifications* of our verbs, or to speak of them as se
conjugations. So must it be in respect to "a Neuter Voice," or any other distinction.
classification involves. The significant characteristic is not overlooked; the distinct is
neglected as nonessential; but it is transferred to a different category. Hence I cannot
approve of the following remark, which "the Rev. W. Allen" appears to cite with appr
"'The distinction of active or passive,' says the accurate Mr. Jones, '*is not essential* t
In the infancy of language, it was, in all probability, not known. In Hebrew, the distinc
imperfectly exists, and, in the early periods of it, probably did not exist at all. In A
only distinction which obtains, arises from the vowel points, a late invention compar
antiquity of that language. And in our own tongue, the names of *active* and *passive* we
remained unknown, if they had not been learnt in Latin.'"—*Allen's Elements o' E
Gram.* p. 96.

. 30.—By *the conjugation* of a verb, some teachers choose to understand nothing more than
mine of its principal parts ; giving to the arrangement of its numbers and persons, through
e moods and tenses, the name of *declension*. This is a misapplication of terms, and the
tion is as needless, as it is contrary to general usage. Dr. Bullions, long silent concerning principal parts, seems now to make a singular distinction between "*conjugating*" and "*con-
n*." H.s *conjugations* include the moods, tenses, and inflections of verbs ; but he teaches
it with some inaccuracy, as follows : "The principal parts of the verb are the *Present indicative Past indicative* and the *Past participle*. The mentioning of these parts is called
MATING THE VERB."—*Analyt. and Pract. Gram.*, 1849, p. 80.

31.—English verbs having but very few inflections to indicate to what part of the scheme
words and tenses they pertain, it is found convenient to insert in our conjugations the prepo-
to, to mark the infinitive ; personal *pronouns*, to distinguish the persons and numbers ; the
ation *if*, to denote the subjunctive mood ; and the adverb *not*, to show the form of negation.
these additions, or indexes, a verb may be conjugated in *four ways* :—

firmatively ; as, I write, I do write, or, I am writing ; and so on.

agatively ; as, I write not, I do not write, or, I am not writing.

interrogatively ; as, Write I ? Do I write ? or, Am I writing ?

interrogatively and negatively ; as, Write I not ? Do I not write ? or, Am I not writing ?

1. SIMPLE FORM, ACTIVE OR NEUTER.

e simplest form of an English conjugation, is that which makes the
nt and imperfect tenses without auxiliaries ; but, even in these, auxiliaries
required for the potential mood, and are often preferred for the indicative.

FIRST EXAMPLE.

The regular active verb LOVE, conjugated affirmatively.

PRINCIPAL PARTS.

Present.	*Preterit.*	*Imperfect Participle.*	*Perfect Participle.*
Love.	Loved.	Loving.	Loved.

INFINITIVE MOOD.*

infinitive mood is that form of the verb, which expresses the being, action, or passion,
unlimited manner, and without person or number. It is used only in the present and
t tenses.

PRESENT TENSE.

tense is the *root*, or *radical verb* ; and is usually preceded by the preposition *to*, which
its relation to some other word : thus,

To love.

PERFECT TENSE.

tense prefixes the auxiliary *have* to the perfect participle ; and, like the infinitive
t, is usually preceded by the preposition *to* : thus,

To have loved.

INDICATIVE MOOD.

indicative mood is that form of the verb, which simply indicates or declares a thing,
is a question. It is used in all the tenses.

PRESENT TENSE.

present indicative, in its simple form, is essentially the same as the present infinitive,
this verb ; except that the verb *be* has *am* in the indicative.

1. The simple form of the present tense is varied thus : —

Singular.		*Plural.*	
1st person, I	love,	1st person, We	love,
2d person, Thou	lovest,	2d person, You	love,
3d person, He	loves ;	3d person, They	love.

This tense may also be formed by prefixing the auxiliary *do* to the verb : thus,

Singular.		*Plural.*	
1. I	do love,	1. We do love,	
2. Thou dost love,		2. You do love,	
3. He	does love ;	3. They do love.	

The substantive form, or, as it is commonly termed, *infinitive mood*, contains at the same time the essence
of meaning, and the literal root on which all inflections of the verb are to be grafted. This character
seems to the infinitive in all languages, it [this mood] ought to precede the [other] moods of verbs,
instead made to follow them, as is absurdly practised in almost all grammatical systems."—*Enclytica*, p. 14.

IMPERFECT TENSE.

This tense, in its simple form is *the preterit*; which, in all regular verbs, adds *d* or the present, but in others is formed variously.

1. The simple form of the imperfect tense is varied thus:—

Singular.	*Plural.*
1. I loved,	1. We loved,
2. Thou lovedst,	2. You loved,
3. He loved ;	3. They loved.

2. This tense may also be formed by prefixing the auxiliary *did* to the present: the

Singular.	*Plural.*
1. I did love,	1. We did love,
2. Thou didst love,	2. You did love,
3. He did love ;	3. They did love.

PERFECT TENSE.

This tense prefixes the auxiliary *have* to the perfect participle: thus,

Singular.	*Plural.*
1. I have loved,	1. We have loved,
2. Thou hast loved,	2. You have loved,
3. He has loved ;	3. They have loved.

PLUPERFECT TENSE.

This tense prefixes the auxiliary *had* to the perfect participle: thus,

Singular.	*Plural.*
1. I had loved,	1. We had loved,
2. Thou hadst loved,	2. You had loved,
3. He had loved ;	3. They had loved.

FIRST-FUTURE TENSE.

This tense prefixes the auxiliary *shall* or *will* to the present: thus,

1. Simply to express a future action or event :—

Singular.	*Plural.*
1. I shall love,	1. We shall love,
2. Thou wilt love,	2. You will love,
3. He will love ;	3. They will love.

2. To express a promise, volition, command, or threat :—

Singular.	*Plural.*
1. I will love,	1. We will love,
2. Thou shalt love,	2. You shall love,
3. He shall love ;	3. They shall love.

SECOND-FUTURE TENSE.

This tense prefixes the auxiliaries *shall have* or *will have* to the perfect participle: thus

Singular.	*Plural.*
1. I shall have loved,	1. We shall have loved,
2. Thou wilt have loved,	2. You will have loved,
3. He will have loved ;	3. They will have loved.

OBS.—The auxiliary *shall* may also be used in the second and third persons of this tense, wh preceded by a conjunction expressing condition or contingency ; as, "*If he shall have comple the work by midsummer.*"—*L. Murray's Gram.* p. 80. So, with the conjunctive adverb *when*; " Then cometh the end, *when he shall have delivered* up the kingdom to God, even the Fath *when* he *shall have put* down all rule and all authority and power."—1 *Cor.* xv, 24. And perha *will* may here be used in the first person to express a promise, though such usage, I *think*, seldo occurs. Professor Fowler has given to this tense, first, the "*Predictive*" form, as exhibit above, and then a form which he calls "*Promissive*," and in which the auxiliaries are varied thu " Singular. 1. I *will* have taken. 2. Thou *shalt* have taken, you *shall* have taken. 3. He *sh* have taken. Plural. 1. We *will* have taken. 2. Ye *or* you *shall* have taken. 3. He [say *The shall* have taken."—*Fowler's E. Gram.* 8vo, N. Y. 1850, p. 231. But the other instances ju cited show that such a form is not always promissory.

POTENTIAL MOOD.

s potential mood is that form of the verb, which expresses the power, liberty, possibility sessity of the being, action, or passion. It is used in the first four tenses; but the tial *imperfect* is properly an *aorist*: its time is very indeterminate; as, "He *would be* d of sensibility were he not greatly satisfied."—*Lord Kames, El. of Crit.* Vol. i, p. 11.

PRESENT TENSE.

This tense prefixes the auxiliary *may, can,* or *must,* to the radical verb: thus,

Singular.	*Plural.*
1. I may love,	1. We may love,
2. Thou mayst love,	2. You may love,
3. He may love ;	3. They may love.

IMPERFECT TENSE.

is tense prefixes the auxiliary *might, could, would,* or *should,* to the radical verb: thus

Singular.	*Plural.*
1. I might love,	1. We might love,
2. Thou mightst love,	2. You might love,
3. He might love ;	3. They might love.

PERFECT TENSE.

is tense prefixes the auxiliaries, *may have, can have,* or *must have,* to the perfect parti-
: thus,

Singular.	*Plural.*
1. I may have loved,	1. We may have loved,
2. Thou mayst have loved,	2. You may have loved,
3. He may have loved ;	3. They may have loved.

PLUPERFECT TENSE.

is tense prefixes the auxiliaries, *might have, could have, would have,* or *should have,* to the
: participle: thus,

Singular.	*Plural.*
1. I might have loved,	1. We might have loved,
2. Thou mightst have loved,	2. You might have loved,
3. He might have loved ;	3. They might have loved.

SUBJUNCTIVE MOOD.

s subjunctive mood is that form of the verb, which represents the being, action, or
a. as conditional, doubtful, or contingent. This mood is generally preceded by a
action; as, *if, that, though, lest, unless, except.* But sometimes, especially in poetry, it
sed by a mere placing of the verb before the nominative; as, "*Were I,*" for, "*If I
*"—"*Had he,*" for, "*If he had ;*"—"*Fall we,*" for, "*If we fall ;*"—"*Knew they,*" for, "*If
we.*" It does not vary its termination at all, in the different persons.* It is used in
resent, and sometimes in the imperfect tense; rarely—and perhaps never *properly*—in
other. As this mood can be used only in a dependent clause, the *time* implied in its
is always relative, and generally indefinite; as,

> "It shall be in eternal restless change,
>   Self-fed, and self-consum'd : *if this fail,*
>   The pillar'd firmament is rottenness."—*Milton, Comus,* l. 596.

---

f this, I mean, that the verb in all the persons, both singular and plural, is *the same in form.* But Lindley
s. When he speaks of *not varying* or *not changing* the termination of the verb, most absurdly means by it,
the verb is *inflected,* just as it is in the indicative or the potential mood ; and when he speaks of *changes* or
loss of *termination,* he means, that the verb *remains the same* as in the first person singular ! For exam-
"The second person singular of the imperfect tense in the subjunctive mood, is also *very frequently varied in*
poetics : as, ' If thou *loved* him truly, thou wouldst obey him.' "—*Murray's Gram.* 8vo, p. 209. " The
law of the potential mood, when applied to the subjunctive, *do not change* the termination of the second
singular ; as, " If thou *mayst* or *canst* go."—*Ib.* p. 210. " Some authors think, that the termination of
the *should be varied :* as, I advise thee, that thou *may* beware."—*Ib.* p. 210. " When the circum-
of *contingency* and *futurity* concur, it is proper *to vary* the terminations of the second and third persons
..."—*Ib.* 210. " It may be considered as a rule, that *the changes of termination are necessary,* when these
circumstances concur."—*Ib.* p. 207. " It may be considered as a rule, that *no changes of terminations are ne-*
when these two circumstances concur."—*Ingersoll's Gram.* p. 264 Now Murray and Ingersoll here *mean*
by the same thing ! Whose fault is that ! If Murray's, he has committed many such. But, in this matter,
contradicted not only by Ingersoll, but, on one occasion, by himself. For he declares it to be an opinion in
he concurs, " That the definition and nature of the subjunctive mood, have *no reference* to change of termi-
ation"—*Murray's Gram.* 8vo, p. 211. And yet, amidst his strange blunders, he seems to have ascribed the *meaning*
the verb has in this mood, *to the inflections* which it receives *in the indicative :* saying, " That part of the verb
grammarians call the present tense of the subjunctive mood, has a future signification. *This is effected by*
the terminations of the second and third persons singular *of the indicative !*"—*Ib.* p. 207. But the absurd-
which he really means to teach, is, that the subjunctive mood *is derived from the indicative,*—the primitive or
al verb, *from its derivatives or branches !*

PRESENT TENSE.

This tense is generally used to express some condition on which a future action or event is affirmed. It is therefore erroneously considered by some grammarians, as an elliptical form of the future.

Singular.	*Plural.*
1. If I love,	1. If we love,
2. If Thou love,	2. If you love,
3. If He love ;	3. If they love.

OBS.—In this tense, the auxiliary *do* is sometimes employed ; as, "If thou *do prosper* my way."—*Genesis*, xxiv, 42. "If he *do* not *utter* it."—*Leviticus*, v, 1. "If he *do* but *intimate* his desire."—*Murray's Key*, p. 207. "If he *do promise*, he will certainly perform."—*Ib.* p. 208. "An event which, if it ever *do occur*, must occur in some future period."—*Hiley's Gram.* (3d Ed. Lond.) p. 89. "If he *do* but *promise*, thou art safe."—*Ib.* 89.

> "Till old experience *do attain*
> To something like prophetic strain."—MILTON : *Il Penseroso.*

These examples, if they are right, prove the tense to be *present*, and not *future*, as Hiley and some others suppose it to be.

IMPERFECT TENSE.

This tense, like the imperfect of the potential mood, with which it is frequently connected, is properly an aorist, or indefinite tense ; for it may refer to time past, present, or future; as, "If therefore perfection *were* by the Levitical priesthood, what further need *was there* that an other priest *should rise?*"—*Heb.* vii, 11. "They must be viewed *exactly* in the same light, as if the intention to purchase *now existed.*"—*Murray's Parsing Exercises*, p. 24. "If it *were* possible, they *shall deceive* the very elect."—*Matt.* xxiv, 24. "If the whole body *were* an eye, where *were* the hearing ?"—1 *Corinthians*, xii, 17. "If the thankful *refrained*, it *would be* pain and grief to them."—*Atterbury.*

Singular.	*Plural.*
1. If I loved,	1. If we loved,
2. If thou loved,	2. If you loved,
3. If he loved ;	3. If they loved.

OBS.—In this tense, the auxiliary *did* is sometimes employed. The subjunctive may here be distinguished from the indicative, by these circumstances ; namely, that the time is indefinite, and that the supposition is always contrary to the fact : as, "Great is the number of those who might attain to true wisdom, if they *did not already think* themselves wise."—*Dillwyn's Reflections*, p. 36. This implies that they *do think* themselves wise ; but an indicative supposition or concession—(as, "Though they *did not think* themselves wise, they were so—") accords with the fact, and with the literal time of the tense,—here time past. The subjunctive imperfect, suggesting the idea of what is not, and known by the sense, is sometimes introduced without any of the usual *signs* ; as, "In a society of perfect men, *where all understood* what was morally right, *and were determined* to act accordingly, it is obvious, that human laws, or even human organization to enforce God's laws, would be altogether unnecessary, and could serve no valuable purpose."—PRES. SHANNON : *Examiner*, No. 78.

IMPERATIVE MOOD.

The imperative mood is that form of the verb, which is used in commanding, exhorting, entreating, or permitting. It is commonly used only in the second person of the present tense.

PRESENT TENSE.

Singular.	2. Love [thou,]	or Do thou love ;
Plural.	2. Love [ye *or* you,]	or Do you love.

OBS.—In the Greek language, which has three numbers, the imperative mood is used in the second and third persons of them all ; and has also several different tenses, some of which cannot be clearly rendered in English. In Latin, this mood has a distinct form for the third person, both singular and plural. In Italian, Spanish, and French, the first person plural is also given. Imitations of some of these forms are occasionally employed in English, particularly by the poets. Such imitations must be referred to this mood, unless by ellipsis and transposition we make them out to be something else ; and against this there are strong objections. Again, as imprecation on one's self is not impossible, the first person singular may be added ; so that this mood *may possibly have* all the persons and numbers. Examples : "*Come we* now to his translation of the Iliad."—*Pope's Pref. to Dunciad.* "*Proceed we* therefore in our subject."—*Ib.* "*Blessed be he* that blesseth thee."—*Gen.* xxvii, 29. "Thy *kingdom come.*"—*Matt.* vi, 10. "But *pass we* that."—*W. Scott.* "Third person : *Be he, Be they.*"—*Churchill's Gram.* p. 92.

> "My soul, *turn* from them—*turn we* to survey," &c.—*Goldsmith.*
> "Then *turn we* to her latest tribune's name."—*Byron.*
> "Where'er the eye could light these words you read :
> '*Who comes* this way—*behold*, and *fear* to sin!'"—*Pollok.*
> "*Fall he* that must, beneath his rival's arms,
> And *live the rest*, secure of future harms."—*Pope.*
> "*Cursed be I* that did so !—All the *charms*
> Of Sycorax, toads, beetles, bats, *light* on you !"—*Shakspeare.*
> "*Have done* thy charms, thou hateful wither'd hag ! "—*Idem.*

PARTICIPLES.

1. *The Imperfect.*	2. *The Perfect.*	3. *The Preperfect.*
Loving.	Loved.	Having loved.

SYNOPSIS OF THE FIRST EXAMPLE.

FIRST PERSON SINGULAR.

IND. I love *or* do love, I loved *or* did love, I have loved, I had loved, I shall *or* will love, I shall *or* will have loved. POT. I may, can, *or* must love; I might, could, would, *or* should love; I may, can, *or* must have loved; I might, could, would, *or* should have loved. SUBJ. If I love, If I loved.

SECOND PERSON SINGULAR.

IND. Thou lovest *or* dost love, Thou lovedst *or* didst love, Thou hast loved, Thou hadst loved, Thou shalt *or* wilt love, Thou shalt *or* wilt have loved. POT. Thou mayst, canst, *or* must love; Thou mightst, couldst, wouldst, *or* shouldst love; Thou mayst, canst, *or* must have loved; Thou mightst, couldst, wouldst, *or* shouldst have loved. SUBJ. If thou love, If thou loved. IMP. Love [thou,] *or* Do thou love.

THIRD PERSON SINGULAR.

IND. He loves *or* does love, He loved *or* did love, He has loved, He had loved, He shall *or* will love, He shall *or* will have loved. POT. He may, can, *or* must love; He might, could, would, *or* should love; He may, can, *or* must have loved; He might, could, would, or should have loved. SUBJ. If he love, If he loved.

FIRST PERSON PLURAL.

IND. We love *or* do love, We loved *or* did love, We have loved, We had loved, We shall *or* will love. We shall *or* will have loved. POT. We may, can, *or* must love, We might, could, would, *or* should love; We may, can, *or* must have loved; We might, could, would, *or* should have loved. SUBJ. If we love, If we loved.

SECOND PERSON PLURAL.

IND. You love *or* do love, You loved *or* did love, You have loved, You had loved, You shall *or* will love, You shall *or* will have loved. POT. You may, can, *or* must love; You might, could, would, *or* should love; You may, can, *or* must have loved; You might, could, would, *or* should have loved. SUBJ. If you love, If you loved. IMP. Love [ye *or* you,] *or* Do you love.

THIRD PERSON PLURAL.

IND. They love *or* do love, They loved *or* did love, They have loved, They had loved, They shall *or* will love, They shall *or* will have loved. POT. They may, can, *or* must love; They might, could, would, *or* should love; They may, can, *or* must have loved; They might, could, would, *or* should have loved. SUBJ. If they love, If they loved.

FAMILIAR FORM WITH 'THOU.'

NOTE.—In the familiar style, the second person singular of this verb, is usually and more properly formed thus: IND. Thou lov'st *or* dost love, Thou loved *or* did love, Thou hast loved, Thou had loved, Thou shall *or* will love, Thou shall *or* will have loved. POT. Thou may, can, *or* must love; Thou might, could, would, *or* should love; Thou may, can, *or* must have loved; Thou might, could, would, *or* should have loved. SUBJ. If thou love, If thou loved. IMP. Love [thou,] *or* Do thou love.

SECOND EXAMPLE.

The irregular active verb SEE, conjugated affirmatively.

PRINCIPAL PARTS.

Present.	*Preterit.*	*Imp. Participle.*	*Perf. Participle.*
See.	Saw.	Seeing.	Seen.

INFINITIVE MOOD.

PRESENT TENSE.

To see.

23

PERFECT TENSE.
To have seen.

INDICATIVE MOOD.
PRESENT TENSE.

Singular.
1. I   see,
2. Thou seest,
3. He   sees ;

Plural.
1. We see,
2. You see,
3. They see.

IMPERFECT TENSE.

Singular.
1. I   saw,
2. Thou sawest,
3. He   saw ;

Plural.
1. We saw,
2. You saw,
3. They saw.

PERFECT TENSE.

Singular.
1. I   have seen,
2. Thou hast seen,
3. He   has seen ;

Plural.
1. We have seen,
2. You have seen,
3. They have seen.

PLUPERFECT TENSE.

Singular.
1. I   had seen,
2. Thou hadst seen,
3. He   had seen ;

Plural.
1. We had seen,
2. You had seen,
3. They had seen.

FIRST-FUTURE TENSE.

Singular.
1. I   shall see,
2. Thou wilt see,
3. He   will see ;

Plural.
1. We shall see,
2. You will see,
3. They will see.

SECOND-FUTURE TENSE.

Singular.
1. I   shall have seen,
2. Thou wilt have seen,
3. He   will have seen ;

Plural.
1. We   shall have seen,
2. You   will have seen,
3. They will have seen.

POTENTIAL MOOD.
PRESENT TENSE.

Singular.
1. I   may see,
2. Thou mayst see,
3. He   may see ;

Plural.
1. We may see,
2. You may see,
3. They may see.

IMPERFECT TENSE.

Singular.
1. I   might see,
2. Thou mightst see,
3. He   might see ;

Plural.
1. We might see,
2. You might see,
3. They might see.

PERFECT TENSE.

Singular.
1. I   may have seen,
2. Thou mayst have seen,
3. He   may have seen ;

Plural.
1. We may have seen,
2. You may have seen,
3. They may have seen.

PLUPERFECT TENSE.

Singular.

1. I   might have seen,
2. Thou mightst have seen,
3. He   might have seen ;

Plural.

1. We   might have seen,
2. You might have seen,
3. They might have seen.

SUBJUNCTIVE MOOD.

PRESENT TENSE.

Singular.

1. If I   see,
2. If thou see,
3. If he   see ;

Plural.

1. If we   see,
2. If you see,
3. If they see.

IMPERFECT TENSE.

Singular.

1. If I   saw,
2. If thou saw,
3. If he   saw ;

Plural.

1. If we   saw,
2. If you saw,
3. If they saw.

IMPERATIVE MOOD.

PRESENT TENSE.

Singular. 2. See [thou,]   *or* Do thou see ;
Plural.   2. See [ye *or* you,] *or* Do you see.

PARTICIPLES.

1. *The Imperfect.*   2. *The Perfect.*   8. *The Preperfect.*
   Seeing.   Seen.   Having seen.

NOTES.

NOTE I.—The student ought to be able to rehearse the form of a verb, not only according to the order of the entire conjugation, but also according to the synopsis of the several persons and numbers. One sixth part of the paradigm, thus recited, gives in general a fair sample of the whole ; and, in class recitations, this mode of rehearsal will save much time : as, IND. I see *or* do see, I saw *or* did see, I have seen, I had seen, I shall *or* will see, I shall *or* will have seen. POT. I may, can, *or* must see ; I might, could, would, *or* should see ; I may, can, *or* must have seen ; I might, could, would, *or* should have seen. SUBJ. If I see, If I saw.

NOTE II.—In the familiar style, the second person singular of this verb is usually and more properly formed thus : IND. Thou seest *or* dost see, Thou saw *or* did see, Thou hast seen, Thou had seen, Thou shall *or* will see, Thou shall or will have seen. POT. Thou may, can, *or* must see : Thou might, could, would, *or* should see ; Thou may, can, *or* must have seen ; Thou might, could, would, *or* should have seen. SUBJ. If thou see, If thou saw. IMP. See [thou,] *or* Do thou see.

THIRD EXAMPLE.

The irregular neuter verb BE, conjugated affirmatively.

PRINCIPAL PARTS.

Present.   *Preterit.*   *Imp. Participle.*   *Perf. Participle.*
Be.   Was.   Being.   Been.

INFINITIVE MOOD.

PRESENT TENSE.
To be.

PERFECT TENSE.
To have been.

INDICATIVE MOOD.

PRESENT TENSE.

Singular.

1. I   am,
2. Thou art,
3. He   is ;

Plural.

1. We   are,
2. You are,
3. They are.

IMPERFECT TENSE.

Singular.	*Plural.*
1. I was,	1. We were,
2. Thou wast, (*or* wert,)*	2. You were,
3. He was;	3. They were.

PERFECT TENSE.

Singular.	*Plural.*
1. I have been,	1. We have been,
2. Thou hast been,	2. You have been,
3. He has been;	3. They have been.

PLUPERFECT TENSE.

Singular.	*Plural.*
1. I had been,	1. We had been,
2. Thou hadst been,	2. You had been,
3. He had been;	3. They had been.

FIRST-FUTURE TENSE.

Singular.	*Plural.*
1. I shall be,	1. We shall be,
2. Thou wilt be,	2. You will be,
3. He will be;	3. They will be.

SECOND-FUTURE TENSE.

Singular.	*Plural.*
1. I shall have been,	1. We shall have been,
2. Thou wilt have been,	2. You will have been,
3. He will have been;	3. They will have been.

POTENTIAL MOOD.

PRESENT TENSE.

Singular.	*Plural.*
1. I may be,	1. We may be,
2. Thou mayst be,	2. You may be,
3. He may be;	3. They may be.

IMPERFECT TENSE.

Singular.	*Plural.*
1. I might be,	1. We might be,
2. Thou mightst be,	2. You might be,
3. He might be;	3. They might be.

PERFECT TENSE.

Singular.	*Plural.*
1. I may have been,	1. We may have been,
2. Thou mayst have been,	2. You may have been,
3. He may have been;	3. They may have been.

PLUPERFECT TENSE.

Singular.	*Plural.*
1. I might have been,	1. We might have been,
2. Thou mightst have been,	2. You might have been,
3. He might have been;	3. They might have been.

SUBJUNCTIVE MOOD.

PRESENT TENSE.

Singular.	*Plural.*
1. If I be,	1. If we be,
2. If thou be,	2. If you be,
3. If he be;	3. If they be.

---

* *Wert* is sometimes used in lieu of *wast*; and, in such instances, both by authority and by analogy, it appears to belong here, if anywhere. See Obs. 2d and 3d, below.

IMPERFECT TENSE.

Singular.		*Plural.*
1. If I were,*		1. If we were,
2. If thou were, (*or* wert,)†		2. If you were,
3. If he were ;		3. If they were.

IMPERATIVE MOOD.

PRESENT TENSE.

Singular. 2. Be [thou,]   *or* Do thou be ;
Plural.   2. Be [ye *or* you,] *or* Do you be.

PARTICIPLES.

1. *The Imperfect.*	2. *The Perfect.*	3. *The Preperfect.*
Being.	Been.	Having been.

FAMILIAR FORM WITH 'THOU.'

NOTE.—In the familiar style, the second person singular of this verb, is usually and more properly formed thus : IND. Thou art, Thou was, Thou hast been, Thou had been, Thou shall *or* will be, Thou shall *or* will have been. POT. Thou may, can, *or* must be ; Thou might, could, would, *or* should be ; Thou may, can, *or* must have been ; Thou might, could, would, *or* should have been. SUBJ. If thou be, If thou were. IMP. Be [thou,] *or* Do thou be.

OBSERVATIONS.

OBS. 1.—It appears that *be*, as well as *am*, was formerly used for the indicative present : as, " I be, Thou beest, He be ; We be, Ye be, They be." See *Brightland's Gram.* p. 114. Dr. Lowth, whose Grammar is still preferred at Harvard University, gives both forms, thus : " I am, Thou art, He is ; We are, Ye are, They are. Or, I be, Thou beest, He *is* ; We be, Ye be, They be." To the third person singular, he subjoins the following example and remark : " ' I think it *be* thine indeed, for thou liest in it.' Shak. Hamlet. *Be*, in the singular number of this time and mode, especially in the third person, is obsolete ; and *is become* somewhat antiquated *in the plural*."—*Lowth's Gram.* p. 36. Dr. Johnson gives this tense thus : "*Sing.* I am ; thou art ; he is ; *Plur.* We are, *or* be ; ye are, *or* be ; they are, *or* be." And adds, " The plural *be* is now little in use."—*Gram. in Johnson's Dict.* p. 8. The Bible commonly has *am, art, is*, and *are*, but not always ; the indicative *be* occurs in some places : as, " We *be* twelve brethren."—*Gen.* xlii, 32. "What *be* these two olive branches ?"—*Zech.* iv, 12. Some traces of this usage still occur in poetry : as,

" There *be* more things to greet the heart and eyes
    In Arno's dome of Art's most princely shrine,
  Where Sculpture with her rainbow sister vies ;
    There *be* more marvels yet—but not for mine."—*Byron's Childe Harold*, Canto iv, st. 61.

OBS. 2.—Respecting the verb *wert*, it is not easy to determine whether it is most properly of the indicative mood only, or of the subjunctive only, or of both, or of neither. The *regular* and *analogical* form for the indicative, is " Thou *wast* ;" and for the subjunctive, " If thou *were*." Brightland exhibits, " I *was* or *were*, Thou *wast* or *wert*, He *was* or *were*," without distinction of mood, for the three persons singular ; and, for the plural, *were* only. Dr. Johnson gives us, for the indicative, " Thou wast, *or* wert ;" with the remark, "*Wert* is properly of the *conjunctive* mood, and ought not to be used in the indicative."—*Johnson's Gram.* p. 8. In his conjunctive (or subjunctive) mood, he has, " Thou *beest*," and " Thou *wert*." So Milton wrote, " If thou *beest* he."—*P. Lost*, B. i, l. 84. Likewise Shakspeare : " If thou *beest* Stephano."—*Tempest.* This inflection of *be* is obsolete : all now say, " If thou *be*." But *wert* is still in use, to some extent, *for both moods* ; being generally placed by the grammarians in the subjunctive only, but much oftener written for the indicative : as, "Whate'er thou art or *wert*."—*Byron's Harold*, Canto iv, st. 115. " O thou that *wert* so happy !"—*Ib.* st. 109. " Vainly *wert* thou wed."—*Ib.* st. 169.

OBS. 3.—Dr. Lowth gave to this verb, BE, that form of the subjunctive mood, which it now has in most of our grammars ; appending to it the following examples and questions : " ' Before the

───────────

* Some grammarians, regardless of the general usage of authors, prefer *was* to *were* in the singular number of this tense of the subjunctive mood. In the following remark, the tense is named " *present*," and this preference is urged with some critical extravagance : "*Was*, though the past tense of the indicative mood, expresses the *present* of the hypothetical ; as, ' I wish that I *was* well.' *The use of this hypothetical form* of the subjunctive mood, *has given rise to a form of expression wholly unwarranted by the rules of grammar*. When the verb *was* is to be used in the *present tense singular*, in this form of the subjunctive mood, the ear is often pained with a *plural were*, as, ' *Were I* your master'—' *Were he* compelled to do it,' &c. This has become so common that some of the best grammars of the language furnish authority for the *barbarism*, and even in the second person supply *wert*, as a convenient accompaniment. If such a conjugation is admitted, we may expect soon to see Shakspeare's '*thou beest*' in full use."—*Chandler's Gram.* Ed. of 1821, p. 55. In "*Chandler's Common School Grammar*," of 1847, the language of this paragraph is somewhat softened, but the substance is still retained. See the latter work, p. 80.

† " If I were, If *thou were*, If he were."—*Harrison's Gram.* p. 81. " If, or though, I were loved. If, or though, *thou were*, or *wert* loved. If, or though, he were loved."—*Bicknell's Gram.* Part i, p. 69. " If, though, &c. I were burned, *thou were* burned or you were burned, he were burned."—*Buchanan's Gram.* p. 53. " Though *thou were*. Some say, ' though thou *wert*.' "—*Mackintosh's Gram.* p. 178. " If or though I were. If or though *thou were*. If or though he *were*."—*St. Quentin's General Gram.* p. 86. " If I was, Thou wast, or You was or were, He was. Or thus : If I were, Thou wert, or You was or were, He were."—*Webster's Philosophical Gram.* p. 96 ; *Improved Gram.* p. 64. " PRESENT TENSE. Before, &c. I *be* ; thou *beest*, or you *be* ; he, she, or it, *be* : We, you *or ye*, they, *be*. PAST TENSE. Before, &c. I *were* ; thou *wert*, or you *were* ; he, she, or it, *were* : We, you or *ye*, they, *were*."—WHITE, *on the English Verb*, p. 52.

sun, Before the Heavens, thou *wert.'—Milton.* 'Remember what thou *wert.'—Dryden.* 'I knew thou *wert* not slow to hear.'—*Addison.* 'Thou who of old *wert* sent to Israel's court.'—*Prior.* 'All this thou *wert.'—Pope.* 'Thou, Stella, *wert* no longer young.'—*Swift.* Shall we, in deference to these great authorities," asks the Doctor, "allow *wert* to be the same with *wast,* and common to the indicative and [the] subjunctive mood? or rather abide by the practice of our best ancient writers; the propriety of the language, which requires, as far as may be, distinct forms, for different moods; and the analogy of formation in each mood; I *was,* thou *wast;* I *were,* thou *wert?* all which conspire to make *wert* peculiar to the subjunctive mood."—*Lowth's Gram.* p. 37; *Churchill's,* p. 251. I have before shown, that several of the "best ancient writers" *did not inflect* the verb *were,* but wrote "*thou were;*" and, surely, "the analogy of formation," requires that the subjunctive *be not inflected.* Hence" the propriety which requires distinct forms," requires not *wert,* in either mood. Why then should we make this contraction of the old indicative form *werest,* a *solitary exception,* by fixing it in the subjunctive only, and that in opposition to the best authorities that ever used it? It is worthier to take rank-with its kindred *beest,* and be called an *archaism.*

OBS. 4.—The chief characteristical difference between the indicative and the subjunctive mood, is, that in the latter the verb is *not inflected at all,* in the different persons: as, IND. "Thou *magnifest* his work." SUBJ. "Remember that thou *magnify* his work."—*Job,* xxxvi, 24. IND. "He *cuts* off, *shuts* up, and *gathers* together." SUBJ. "If he *cut* off, and *shut* up, 'or *gather* together, then who can hinder him?"—*Job,* xi, 10. There is also a difference of meaning. The Indicative, "If he *was,*" admits the *fact;* the Subjunctive, "If he *were,*" supposes that he was not. These moods may therefore be distinguished by the sense, even when their forms are alike: as, "Though *it thundered,* it did not rain."—"Though *it thundered,* he would not hear it." The indicative assumption here is, "Though it *did thunder,*" or, "Though there *was thunder;*" the subjunctive, "Though it *should thunder,*" or, "Though there *were* thunder." These senses are clearly different. Writers however are continually confounding these moods; some in one way, some in another. Thus S. R. Hall, the teacher of a *Seminary for Teachers:* "SUBJ. *Present Tense.* 1. If I be, *or* am, 2. If thou be, *or* art, 3. If he be, *or* is; 1. If we be, *or* are, 2. If ye *or* you be, *or* are, 3. If they be, *or* are. *Imperfect Tense.* 1. If I were, *or* was, 2. If thou wert, *or* wast, 3. If he were, *or* was; 1. If we were, 2. If ye *or* you were, 3. If they were."—*Hall's Grammatical Assistant,* p. 17. Again: "SUBJ. *Present Tense.* 1. If I love, 2. If thou *lovest,* 3. If he love;" &c. "The remaining tenses of this *mode,* are, *in general,* similar to the correspondent tenses of the Indicative *mode, only* with the conjunction prefixed."—*Ib.* p. 20. Dr. Johnson observes, "The indicative and conjunctive moods are by modern writers frequently confounded; or rather the conjunctive is wholly neglected, when some convenience of versification does not invite its revival. It is used among the purer writers of former times; as, 'Doubtless thou art our father, though Abraham *be* ignorant of us, and Israel *acknowledge* us not.'"—*Gram. in Joh. Dict.* p. 9. To neglect the subjunctive mood, or to confound it with the indicative, is to augment several of the worst faults of the language.

II. COMPOUND OR PROGRESSIVE FORM.

Active and neuter verbs may also be conjugated, by adding the Imperfect Participle to the auxiliary verb BE, through all its changes; as, "I *am writing* a letter."—"He *is sitting* idle."—"They *are going.*" This form of the verb denotes a *continuance* of the action or state of being, and is, on many occasions, preferable to the simple form of the verb.

FOURTH EXAMPLE.

The irregular active verb READ, conjugated affirmatively, in the Compound Form.

PRINCIPAL PARTS OF THE SIMPLE VERB.

Present.	*Preterit.*	*Imp. Participle.*	*Perf. Participle.*
Read.	Read.	Reading.	Read.

INFINITIVE MOOD.

PRESENT TENSE.
To be reading.

PERFECT TENSE.
To have been reading.

INDICATIVE MOOD.

PRESENT TENSE.

Singular.	*Plural.*
1. I am reading,	1. We are reading,
2. Thou art reading,	2. You are reading,
3. He is reading;	3. They are reading.

IMPERFECT TENSE.

Singular.	*Plural.*
1. I was reading,	1. We were reading,
2. Thou wast reading,	2. You were reading,
3. He was reading ;	3. They were reading.

PERFECT TENSE.

Singular.	*Plural.*
1. I have been reading,	1. We have been reading,
2. Thou hast been reading,	2. You have been reading,
3. He has been reading ;	3. They have been reading.

PLUPERFECT TENSE.

Singular.	*Plural.*
I. I had been reading,	1. We had been reading,
2. Thou hadst been reading,	2. You had been reading,
3. He had been reading ;	3. They had been reading.

FIRST-FUTURE TENSE.

Singular.	*Plural.*
1. I shall be reading,	1. We shall be reading,
2. Thou wilt be reading, .	2. You will be reading,
3. He will be reading ;	3. They will be reading.

SECOND-FUTURE TENSE.

Singular.	*Plural.*
1. I shall have been reading,	1. We shall have been reading,
2. Thou wilt have been reading,	2. You will have been reading,
3. He will have been reading ;	3. They will have been reading.

POTENTIAL MOOD.

PRESENT TENSE.

Singular.	*Plural.*
1. I may be reading,	1. We may be reading,
2. Thou mayst be reading,	2. You may be reading,
3. He may be reading ;	3. They may be reading.

IMPERFECT TENSE.

Singular.	*Plural.*
1. I might be reading,	1. We might be reading,
2. Thou mightst be reading,	2. You might be reading,
3. He might be reading ;	3. They might be reading.

PERFECT TENSE.

Singular.	*Plural.*
1. I may have been reading,	1. We may have been reading,
2. Thou mayst have been reading,	2. You may have been reading,
3. He may have been reading ;	3. They may have been reading.

PLUPERFECT TENSE.

Singular.	*Plural.*
1. I might have been reading,	1. We might have been reading,
2. Thou mightst have been reading,	2. You might have been reading,
3. He might have been reading ;	3. They might have been reading.

SUBJUNCTIVE MOOD.

PRESENT TENSE.

Singular.	*Plural.*
1. If I be reading,	1. If we be reading,
2. If thou be reading,	2. If you be reading,
3. If he be reading ;	3. If they be reading.

IMPERFECT TENSE.

Singular.	*Plural.*
1. If I were reading,	1. If we were reading,
2. If thou were reading,	2. If you were reading,
3. If he were reading ;	3. If they were reading.

IMPERATIVE MOOD.

Sing. 2. Be [thou] reading, *or* Do thou be reading ;
Plur. 2. Be [ye *or* you] reading, *or* Do you be reading.

PARTICIPLES.

1. *The Imperfect.* 2. *The Perfect.* 3. *The Preperfect.*
Being reading, ———— Having been reading.

FAMILIAR FORM WITH 'THOU.'

NOTE.—In the familiar style, the second person singular of this verb, is usually and more properly formed thus : IND. Thou art reading, Thou was reading, Thou hast been reading, Thou had been reading, Thou shall *or* will be reading, Thou shall *or* will have been reading. POT. Thou may, can, *or* must be reading ; Thou might, could, would, *or* should be reading ; Thou may, can, *or* must have been reading ; Thou might, could, would, *or* should have been reading. SUBJ. If thou be reading, If thou were reading. IND. Be [thou,] reading, *or* Do thou be reading.

OBSERVATIONS.

OBS. 1.—Those verbs which, in their simple form, imply continuance, do not admit the compound form : thus we say, " I *respect* him ; " but not, " I am *respecting* him." This compound form seems to imply that kind of action, which is susceptible of intermissions and renewals. Affections of the mind or heart are supposed to last ; or, rather, actions of this kind are complete as soon as they exist. Hence, *to love, to hate, to desire, to fear, to forget, to remember,* and many other such verbs, are *incapable* of this method of conjugation.* It is true, we often find in *grammars* such models, as, " I *was loving,* Thou *wast loving,* He *was loving,*" &c. But this language, to express what the authors intend by it, is not English. " He *was loving,*" can only mean, " He was *affectionate* : " in which sense, loving is an adjective, and susceptible of comparison. Who, in common parlance, has ever said, " He *was loving me,*" or any thing like it ? Yet some have improperly published various examples, or even whole conjugations, of this spurious sort. See such in *Adam's Gram.* p. 91 ; *Gould's Adam,* 83 ; *Bullions's English Gram.* 52 ; *his Analyt. and Pract. Gram.* 92 ; *Chandler's New Gram.* 85 and 86 ; *Clark's,* 80 ; *Cooper's Plain and Practical,* 70 ; *Frazee's Improved,* 66 and 69 ; *S. S. Greene's,* 234 ; *Guy's,* 25 ; *Hallock's,* 103 ; *Hart's,* 88 ; *Hendrick's,* 38 ; *Lennie's,* 31 ; *Lowth's,* 40 ; *Harrison's,* 34 ; *Perley's,* 36.

OBS. 2.—Verbs of this form have sometimes a *passive* signification ; as, " The books *are now selling.*"—*Allen's Gram.* p. 82. "As the money *was paying* down."—*Ainsworth's Dict. w. As.* "It requires no motion in the organs whilst it *is forming.*"—*Murray's Gram.* p. 8. "Those works are long *forming* which must always last."—*Dr. Chetwood.* "While the work of the temple *was carrying* on."—*Dr. J. Owen.* "The designs of Providence *are carrying* on."—*Bp. Butler.* "A scheme, which *has been carrying* on, and *is* still *carrying* on."—*Id. Analogy,* p. 188. "We are permitted to know nothing of what *is transacting* in the regions above us."—*Dr. Blair.* "While these things *were transacting* in Germany."—*Russell's Modern Europe,* Part First, Let. 59. "As he *was carrying* to execution, he demanded to be heard."—*Goldsmith's Greece,* Vol. i, p. 163. "To declare that the action *was doing* or done."—*Booth's Introd.* p. 28. "It *is doing* by thousands now."—*Abbott's Young Christian,* p. 121. "While the experiment *was making,* he was watching every movement."—*Ib.* p. 309. "A series of communications from heaven, which had *been making* for fifteen hundred years."—*Ib.* p. 166. "Plutarch's Lives *are re-printing.*"—*L. Murray's Gram.* 8vo, p. 64. "My Lives *are reprinting.*"—*DR. JOHNSON : Worcester's Univ. and Crit. Dict.* p. xlvi. "All this *has been transacting* within 130 miles of London."—*BYRON : Perley's Gram.* p. 37. "When the heart *is corroding* by vexations."—*Student's Manual,* p. 336. "The padlocks for our lips *are forging.*"—*WHITTIER : Liberator,* No. 993. "When his throat *is cutting.*"—*Collier's Antoninus.* "While your story *is telling.*"—*Adams's Rhet.* i, 425. "But the seeds of it *were sowing* some time before."—*Bolingbroke, on History,* p. 168. "As soon as it was formed, nay even whilst it *was forming.*"—*Ib.* p. 163. "Strange schemes of private ambition *were formed and forming* there."—*Ib.* p. 291. "Even when it *was making and made.*"—*Ib.* 299. "Which have been made and *are making.*"—*HENRY CLAY : Liberator,* ix, p. 141. "And they *are* in measure *sanctified, or* sanctifying,* by the power thereof."—*Barclay's Works,* i, 537. "Which *is* now *accomplishing* amongst

---

* The text in Acts, xxii, 20th, " I also *was standing* by, and *consenting* unto his death," ought rather to be, " I also *stood* by, and *consented* to his death ; " but the present reading is, thus far, a literal version from the Greek, though the verb "*kept,*" that follows, is not. Montanus renders it literally : " Et ipse *eram astans, et consentiens* interemptioni ejus, et *custodiens* vestimenta interficientium illum." Beza makes it better Latin thus : " Ego quoque *adstabam,* et unâ *assentiebar* cædi ipsius, et *custodiebam* pallia eorum qui interimebant eum." Other examples of a questionable or improper use of the progressive form may occasionally be found in good authors ; as, "A promising boy of six years of age, *was missing* by his parents."—*Whittier, Stranger in Lowell,* p. 100. *Missing, wanting,* and *willing,* after the verb *to be,* are commonly reckoned participial *adjectives* ; but here " *was missing*" is made a passive verb, equivalent to *was missed,* which, perhaps, would better express the meaning. To *miss,* to perceive the absence of, is such an act of the mind, as seems unsuited to the compound form, *to be missing* ; and, if we cannot say, " The mother *was missing* her son," I think we ought not to use the same form passively, as above.

the uncivilised countries of the earth."—*Chalmers, Sermons*, p. 281. "Who *are ruining*, or *ruined*, [in] this way."—*Locke, on Ed.* p. 155. "Whilst they *were undoing*."—*Ibid.* "Whether he was employing fire *to* consume [something]," or *was* himself *consuming* by fire."—*Crombie, on Etym. and Syntax.* p. 148. "At home, the greatest exertions *are making* to promote its progress."—*Sheridan's Elocution*, p. iv. "With those [sounds] which *are uttering*."—*Ib.* p. 125. "Orders *are now concerting* for the dismissal of all officers of the Revenue marine."—*Providence Journal*, Feb. 1, 1850. Expressions of this kind are condemned by some critics, under the notion that the participle in *ing* must never be passive; but the usage is unquestionably for far better authority, and, according to my apprehension, in far better taste, than the more complex phraseology which some late writers adopt in its stead; as, "The books *are* now *being sold*."—"In all the towns about Cork, the whiskey shops *are being closed*, and soup, coffee, and tea houses [are] *establishing* generally."—*Dublin Evening Post*, 1840.

OBS. 3.—The question here is, Which is the most correct expression, "While the bridge *was building*,"—"While the bridge was *a* building,"—or, "While the bridge *was being built?*" And again, Are they all wrong? If none of these is right, we must reject them all, and say, "While *they were building* the bridge;"—"While the bridge *was in process of erection;*"—or resort to some other equivalent phrase. Dr. Johnson, after noticing the compound form of active-intransitives, as, "I *am going*,"—"She *is dying*,"—"The tempest *is raging*,"—"I *have been walking*," and so forth, adds: "There is *another* manner of using the active participle, which gives it a *passive* signification:* as, The grammar is now printing, *Grammatica jam nunc chartis imprimitur*. The brass is forging, *Æra excuduntur*. This is, in my opinion," says he, "a *vitious* expression, probably corrupted from a phrase more pure, but now somewhat obsolete: The book is *a* printing, The brass is *a* forging; *a* being properly *at*, and *printing* and *forging* verbal nouns signifying action, according to the analogy of this language.'—*Gram. in Joh. Dict.* p. 9.

OBS. 4.—*A* is certainly sometimes a *preposition;* and, as such, it may govern a participle, and that without converting it into a "*verbal noun.*" But that such phraseology ought to be preferred to what is exhibited with so many authorities, in a preceding paragraph, and with an example from Johnson among the rest, I am not prepared to concede. As to the notion of introducing a new and more complex passive form of conjugation, as, "The bridge *is being built*," "The bridge *was being built*," and so forth, it is one of the most absurd and monstrous innovations ever thought of. Yet some two or three men, who seem to delight in huge absurdities, declare that this "*modern innovation is likely to supersede*" the simpler mode of expression. Thus, instead of, "The work *is now publishing*," they choose to say, "The work is *now being published*."—*Kirkham's Gram.* p. 82. This is certainly no better English than, "The work *was being published*, *has been being published*, *had been being published*, *shall* or *will be being published*, *shall* or *will have been being published;*" and so on, through all the moods and tenses. What a language shall we have when our verbs are thus conjugated!

OBS. 5.—A certain *Irish* critic, who even outdoes in rashness the above-cited American, having recently arrived in New York, has republished a grammar, in which he not only repudiates the passive use of the participle in *ing*, but denies the usual passive form of the present tense, "*I am loved, I am smitten*," &c., as taught by Murray and others, to be good English; and tells us that the true form is, "*I am being loved, I am being smitten,*" &c. See the 98th and 103rd pages of *Joseph W. Wright's Philosophical Grammar*, (*Edition of* 1838,) dedicated "TO COMMON SENSE!" † But both are offeset, if not refuted, by the following observations from a source decidedly better: "It has lately become common to use the present participle *passive* [,] to express the suffering of an action as *continuing*, instead of the participle in -*ing* in the passive sense; thus, instead of, 'The house *is building*,' we now very frequently hear, 'The house *is being built*.' This mode of expression, besides being awkward, is incorrect, and *does not express the idea intended*. This will be obvious, I think, from the following considerations.

"1. The expression, '*is being*,' is equivalent to '*is*,' and expresses no more; just as, '*is loving*,' is equivalent to, '*loves*.' Hence. '*is being built*,' is precisely equivalent to, '*is built*.'

"2. '*Built*,' is a perfect participle; and therefore cannot, in any connexion, express an action, or the suffering of an action, *now in progress*. The verb *to be*, signifies *to exist;* '*being*,' therefore, is equivalent to '*existing*.' If then we substitute the synonyme, the nature of the expression will be obvious; thus, 'the house is *being built*,' is, in other words, 'the house is *existing built*,'.

---

* Some grammarians, contrary to the common opinion, suppose the verbs here spoken of, to have, not a *passive*, but a *neuter* signification. Thus, Joseph Guy, Jun., of London: "*Active* verbs often take a *neuter* sense; as, A house is building; here, *is building* is used in a *neuter* signification, because it has no object after it. By this rule are explained such sentences as, Application is wanting; The grammar is printing; The lottery is drawing; it is flying, &c."—*Guy's English Gram.* p. 21. "*Neuter*," here, as in many other places, is meant to include the *active-intransitives.* "*Is flying*" is of this class; and "*is wanting*," corresponding to the Latin *caret*, appears to be *neuter*; but the rest seem rather to be passives. Tried, however, by the usual criterion,—the naming of the *agent*," which, it is said, "a verb passive necessarily implies,"—what may at first seem progressive passives, may not always be found such. "*Most* verbs signifying *action*," says Dr. Johnson, "may likewise signify con-*dition*, or *habit*, and become *neuters*, [i. e *active-intransitives;*] as, *I love*, I am in love; *I strike*, I am in love; *I strike*, I am now striking."—*Gram. before Quarto Dict.* p. 7. So *sell, form, make,* and many others, usually transitive, have sometimes an ctive-intransitive sense which nearly approaches the passive, and of which *are selling*, is *forming*, *are making*, and the like, may be only equivalent expressions. For example: "It is cold, and ice *forms* rapidly—*is forming* rapidly—or *is formed* rapidly." Here, with little difference of meaning, is the appearance of both voices, the active and the Passive; while "*is forming*," which some will have for an example of "the *Middle* voice," may be referred to either. If the following passive construction is right, *is wanting* or *are wanting* may be a verb of three or four different sorts: "Reflections that may drive away despair, *cannot be wanting by him*, who considers,"—*Johnson's Rambler*, No 129: *Wright's Gram.* p. 196.

† Dr. Bullions, in his grammar of 1849, says, "Nobody would think of saying, 'He is being loved'—! This result being desired.'"—*Analyt. and Pract. Gram.* p. 237. But, according to J. W. Wright, whose superiority in grammar has sixty-two titled vouchers, this unheard of barbarism is, for the present passive, precisely and solely that one ought to say! Nor is it, in fact, any more barbarous, or more foreign from usage, than the spurious example which the Doctor himself takes for a model in the active voice: "I *am loving*, Thou *art loving*, &c, ; *have been loving*, Thou *hast been loving*, &c."—*A. and P. Gr.* p. 92. So: "James *is loving* me."—*Ib.* p. 285.

or more simply as before, 'the house *is built*;' plainly importing an action not *progressing*, but now *existing in a finished state*.

"3. If the expression, '*is being built*,' be a correct form of the present indicative passive, then it must be equally correct to say in the perfect, '*has been being built*;' in the past perfect, '*had been being built*;' in the present infinitive, '*to be being built*;' in the perfect infinitive, '*to have been being built*;' and in the present participle, '*being being built*;' which all will admit to be ex pressions as incorrect as they are inelegant, but precisely analogous to that which now begins to prevail."—*Bullions's Principles of English Gram.* p. 58.

OBS. 6.—It may be replied, that the verbs *to be* and *to exist* are not always synonymous; because the former is often a mere auxiliary, or a mere copula, whereas the latter always means something positive, as *to be in being, to be extant.* Thus we may speak of a thing as *being destroyed*, or may say, it *is annihilated*; but we can by no means speak of it as *existing destroyed*, or say, it *exists annihilated*. The first argument above is also nugatory. These drawbacks, however, do not wholly destroy the force of the foregoing criticism, or at all extenuate the obvious tautology and impropriety of such phrases as, *is being, was being*, &c. The gentlemen who affirm that this new form of conjugation "*is being introduced* into the language," (since they allow participles to follow possessive pronouns) may very fairly be asked, "What evidence have you of *its being being introduced*?" Nor can they, on their own principles, either object to the monstrous phraseology of this question, or tell how to better it!

OBS. 7.—D. H. Sanborn, an other recent writer, has very emphatically censured this innovation, as follows: "English and American writers have of late introduced a new kind of phraseology, which has become quite prevalent in the periodical and popular publications of the day. Their intention, doubtless, is, to supersede the use of the verb in the *definite form*, when it has a passive signification. They say, 'The ship is *being* built,'—' time is *being wasted*,'—' the work is *being advanced*,' instead of, 'the ship *is building*, time *is wasting*, the work *is advancing*.' Such a phraseology is a solecism too palpable to receive any favor; it is at war with the practice of the most distinguished writers in the English language, such as Dr. Johnson and Addison. When an individual says, 'a house is being burned,' he declares that a house is *existing, burned*, which is impossible; for *being* means *existing*, and *burned*, *consumed by fire*. The house ceases to exist as such, after it is consumed by fire. But when he says, 'a house *is burning*,' we understand that it *is consuming by fire*; instead of inaccuracy, doubt, and ambiguity, we have a form of expression perfectly intelligible, beautiful, definite, and appropriate."—*Sanborn's Analytical Gram.* p. 102.

OBS. 8.—Dr. Perley speaks of this usage thus: "An attempt has been made of late to introduce a kind of passive participial voice; as, 'The temple is being built.' This ought not to be encouraged. For, besides being an innovation, it is less convenient than the use of the present participle in the passive sense. *Being built* signifies action *finished*; and how can, *Is being built*, signify an action *unfinished*?"—*Perley's Gram.* p. 37.

OBS. 9.—The question now before us has drawn forth, on either side, a deal of ill scholarship and false logic, of which it would be tedious to give even a synopsis. Concerning the import of some of our most common words and phrases, these ingenious masters,—Bullions, Sanborn, and Perley,—severally assert some things which seem not to be exactly true. It is remarkable that critics can err in expounding terms so central to the language, and so familiar to all ears, as "*be, being, being built, burned, being burned, is, is burned, to be burned*," and the like. That *to be* and *to exist*, or their like derivatives, such as *being* and *existing*, *is* and *exists*, cannot always explain each other, is sufficiently shown above; and thereby is refuted Sanborn's chief argument, that, "*is being burned*," involves the contradiction of "*existing, burned*," or "*consumed by fire*." According to his reasoning, as well as that of Bullions, *is burned* must mean *exists consumed*: *was burned, existed consumed*; and thus our whole passive conjugation would often be found made up of bald absurdities! That this new *unco-passive* form conflicts with the older and better usage of taking the progressive form sometimes passively, is doubtless a good argument against the innovation; but that "Johnson and Addison" are fit representatives of the older "practice" in this case, may be doubted. I know not that the latter has any where make use of such phraseology; and one or two examples from the former are scarcely an offset to his positive verdict against the usage. See OBS. 3rd, above.

OBS. 10.—As to what is called "*the present* or *the imperfect participle passive*,"—as, "*being burned*," or "*being burnt*,"—if it is rightly interpreted in *any* of the foregoing citations, it is, beyond question, very improperly *thus* named. In participles, *ing* denotes *continuance*: thus *being* usually means *continuing to be*; *loving, continuing to love*; *building, continuing to build*,—or (as taken passively) *continuing to be built*: i. e., (in words which express the sense more precisely and certainly,) *continuing to be in process of construction*. What then is "*being built*," but "*continuing to be built*," the same, or nearly the same, as "*building*" taken passively? True it is, that *built*, when alone, being a perfect participle, does not mean "*in process of construction*," but rather, "*constructed*," which intimates *completion*; yet, in the foregoing passive phrases, and others like them, as well as in all examples of this unco-passive voice, continuance of the passive state being first suggested, and cessation of the act being either regarded as future or disregarded, the imperfect participle passive is for the most part received as equivalent to the simple imperfect used in a passive sense. But Dr. Bullions, who, after making "*is being built* precisely equivalent to *is built*," classes the two participles differently, and both erroneously,—the one as a "*present* participle," and the other, of late, as a "*past*,"—has also said above, "'*Built*,' is a *perfect* participle; and THEREFORE cannot, *in any connexion*, express an action, or the suffering of an action, *now in progress*." And Dr. Perley, who also calls the compound of *being* a "*present* participle, argues thus: "*Being built* signifies an *action finished*; and how can *Is being built*, signify an *action unfinished*?" To expound a *passive* term *actively*, or as "*signifying action*," is, at any rate, a near approach to absurdity; and I shall presently show that the fore-cited notion of "*a perfect participle*," now half abandoned by Bullions himself, has been the seed of the very worst form of that ridiculous neology which the good Doctor was opposing.

OBS. 11.—These criticisms being based upon the *meaning* of certain participles, either alone or phrases, and the particular terms spoken of being chiefly meant to represent *classes*, what is d of them may be understood of their *kinds.* Hence the appropriate *naming* of the kinds, so as convey no false idea of any participle's import, is justly brought into view; and I may be allowed say here, that, for the first participle passive, which begins with "*being,*" the epithet "*Imper- x*" is better than "*Present,*" because this compound participle denotes, not always what is *sent,* but always *the state* of something by which an action *is, or was, or will be, undergone or dergoing*—a *state continuing,* or so regarded, though perhaps the action causative may be end- —or sometimes perhaps imagined only, and not yet really begun. With a marvellous insta- ity of doctrine, for the professed systematizer of different languages and grammars, Dr. Bullions s recently changed his names of the second and third participles, in both voices, from "*Per- t*" and "*Compound Perfect,*" to "*Past*" and "*Perfect.*" His notion now is, that, "*The Per- t participle is always compound*; as, *Having finished, Having been finished.*"—*Bullions's Analyst. d Pract. Grammar,* 1849, p. 77. And what was the "*Perfect*" before, in his several books, is w called the "*Past;*" though, with this change, he has deliberately made an other which is re- gnant to it: this participle, being the basis of three tenses always, and of all the tenses some- nes, is now allowed by the Doctor to lend the term "*perfect*" to the three,—"*Present-perfect, ust-perfect, Future-perfect,*"—even when itself is named otherwise!

Obs. 12.—From the erroneous conception, that a perfect participle must, in every connexion, ex- tes "*action finished,*" *action past,*—or perhaps from only a moiety of this great error,—the notion at such a participle cannot, in connexion with an auxiliary, constitute a passive verb of the *present use,*—J. W. Wright, above mentioned, has not very unnaturally reasoned, that, "The expression, *am loved,*" which Mr. Murray has employed to exhibit the passive conjugation of the *present tense,* ay much more *feasibly* represent *past* than *present* time." See *Wright's Philosophical Gram.* 99. Accordingly, in his own paradigm of the passive verb, he has formed *this tense* solely from hat he calls the participle *present,* thus: "I am *being smitten,* Thou art *being smitten,*" &c.—*Ib.* 98. His "*Passed Tense,*" too, for some reason which I do not discover, he distinguishes above the st by a *double form,* thus: "I *was smitten, or being smitten;* Thou *wast smitten, or being smit- n*;" &c.—P. 99. In his opinion, "Few will object to *the propriety* of the more familiar phrase- logy, '*I am in the* ACT,—or, *suffering the* ACTION *of* BEING SMITTEN:' and yet," says he, "in ihstance and effect, it is wholly the same as, '*I am being smitten,*' which is THE TRUE FORM of ie verb in the *present* tense of the *passive voice!*"—*Ibid.* Had we not met with some similar ex- ressions of English or American blunderers, "the *act or action of being smitten,*" would be ac- ounted a downright Irish bull; and as to this ultra notion of neologizing all our passive verbs, y the addition of "*being,*"—with the author's cool talk of "*the presentation of this theory, and he*] *consequent suppression of that hitherto employed,*"—there is a transcendency in it, worthy of he most sublime aspirant among grammatical new-fanglers.

Obs. 13.—But, with all its boldness of innovation, Wright's Philosophical Grammar is not a ttle *self-contradictory* in its treatment of the passive verb. The entire "suppression" of the sual form of its present tense, did not always appear, even to this author, quite so easy and asonable a matter, as the foregoing citations would seem to represent it. The passive use of he participle in *ing,* he has easily disposed of: despite innumerable authorities for it, one false ssertion, of seven syllables, suffices to make it quite impossible.* But the usual passive form, hich, with some show of truth, is accused of not having always precisely the same meaning as he progressive used passively,—that is, of not always denoting *continuance in the state of receiving ntinued action,*—and which is, for that remarkable reason, judged worthy of *rejection,* is neverthe- ss admitted to have, in very many instances, a conformity to this idea, and therefore to "belong hus far] to the present tense."—P. 103. This contradicts to an indefinite extent, the proposi- ion for its rejection. It is observable also, that the same examples, '*I am loved*' and '*I am smit- n,*'—the same "*tolerated, but erroneous forms,*" (so called on page 103,) that are given as ecimens of what he would reject,—though at first pronounced "*equivalent* in grammatical con- truction," censured for the same pretended error, and proposed to be changed alike to "*the true rm*" by the insertion of "*being,*"—are subsequently declared to "belong to" different classes nd different tenses. "*I am loved,*" is referred to that "numerous" class of verbs, which "*de- til* ACTION *of prior, but retained, endured, and continued existence;* and therefore, in this sense, *long to the present tense.*" But "*I am smitten,*" is idly reckoned of an opposite class, (said y Dr. Bullions to be "perhaps the greater number,") whose "ACTIONS described are neither *con- nuous* in their nature, nor *progressive* in their duration; but, on the contrary, *completed and per- cted* · and [which] are consequently descriptive of *passed* time and ACTION."—*Wright's Gram.* p. 03. Again: "In what instance soever this latter form and signification *can* be introduced, *their nport should be, and, indeed, ought to be, supplied by the perfect tense construction:*—for example, '*am smitten,*' [should] be, '*I have been smitten.*'"—*Ib.* Here is self-contradiction indefinitely ex- taded *in an other way.* Many a good phrase, if not every one, that the author's first suggestion rould turn to the unco-passive form, his present "*remedy*" would about as absurdly convert into the perfect tense."

Obs. 14.—But Wright's inconsistency, about this matter, ends not here: it runs through all he ays of it; for, in this instance, error and inconsistency constitute his whole story. In one lace, he anticipates and answers a question thus: "To what tense do the constructions, 'I am leased;' 'He is expected:' '*I am smitten;*' 'He is bound;' belong?" We answer:—*So far as*

---

* "Suppose a criminal to be *enduring* the operation of binding:—Shall we say, with Mr. Murray,—'The criminal *binding!*' If so, HE MUST BE BINDING SOMETHING,—a circumstance, in effect, quite opposed to the fact present- d. Shall we then say, as he does, in the *present tense* conjugation of his passive verb,—'The criminal is bound?' f so, the *action* of binding, which the criminal is suffering, will be represented as completed,—a position which he action is *self* will palpably deny." See *Wright's Phil. Gram.* p. 102. It is folly for a man to puzzle himself r others thus, with *fictitious examples,* imagined on purpose to make *good usage seem wrong.* There is bad ummar enough, for all useful purposes, in the actual writings of valued authors; but who can show, by any roch, that the English language, as heretofore written, is so miserably inadequate to our wants, that we need n the strange neologism, "The criminal *is being bound,*" or any thing similar?

these and like constructions are applicable to the delineation of *continuous* and *retained* ACTION, they express *present* time; and must be treated accordingly."—P. 103. This seems to intimate that even, '*I am smitten*,' and its likes, as they stand, may have some good claim to be of the present tense; which suggestion is contrary to several others made by the author. To expound this, or any other passive term, *passively*, never enters his mind: with him, as with sundry others, "ACTION," "*finished* ACTION," or "*progressive* ACTION," is all any *passive* verb or participle ever means! No marvel, that awkward perversions of the forms of utterance and the principles of grammar should follow such interpretation. In Wright's syntax a very queer distinction is apparently made between a passive verb, and the participle chiefly constituting it; and here, too, through a fancied ellipsis of "*being*" before the latter, most, if not all, of his other positions concerning passives, are again disastrously overthrown by something worse—a word "*imperceptibly understood.*" "'*I am smitten;*' '*I was smitten;*' &c., are," he says, "the *universally acknowledged forms* of the VERBS in these tenses, in the passive voice :—not of the PARTICIPLE. In all verbal constructions of the character of which we have hitherto treated, (see page 103) *and, where the* ACTIONS described are *continuous* in their *operations*,—the participle BEING is *imperceptibly omitted, by ellipsis.*"—P. 144.

OBS. 15.—Dr. Bullions has stated, that, "The present participle active, and the present participle passive, are *not counterparts* to each other in signification; [,] the one signifying the present doing, and the other the present suffering of an action, [;] for the latter *always intimates the present being of an* ACT, *not in progress, but completed.*"—*Prin. of Eng. Gram.* p. 58. In this, he errs no less grossly than in his idea of the "*action* or the suffering" expressed by "a *perfect* participle," as cited in OBS. 5th above; namely, that it must have *ceased.* Worse interpretation, or balder absurdity, is scarcely to be met with; and yet the reverend Doctor, great linguist as he should be, was here only trying to think and tell the common import of a very common sort of English participles; such as, "*being loved*" and "*being seen*." In grammar, "*an act*," that has "*present being*," can be nothing else than an act now doing, or "*in progress;*" and if, "*the present being of an* ACT *not in progress*," were here a possible thought, it surely could not be intimated by any *such* participle. In Acts, i, 3 and 4, it is stated, that our Saviour showed himself to the apostles, "alive after his passion, by many infallible proofs, *being seen* of them forty days, and *speaking* of the things *pertaining* to the kingdom of God: and, *being assembled* together with them commanded them that they should not depart from Jerusalem." Now, of these misnamed "*present* participles," we have here one "*active*," one "*passive*," and two others—(one in each form—) that are *neuter;* but *no present time*, except what is in the indefinite date of "*pertaining*." The events are past, and were so in the days of St. Luke. Yet each of the participles denotes *continuance:* not, indeed, in or to the *present time*, but *for a time.* "*Being seen*" means *continuing to be seen;* and, in this instance, the period of the continuance was "forty days" of time past. But, according to the above-cited "*principle of English Grammar*," so long and so widely inculcated by "the Rev. Peter Bullions, D. D., Professor of Languages," &c.,—a central principle of interpretation, presumed by him to hold "*always*,"—this participle must intimate "*the present being of an act, not in progress, but completed;*" —that is, "*the present being of*" the apostles' act *in formerly seeing the risen Saviour!*

OBS. 16.—This grammarian has lately taken a deal of needless pains to sustain, by a studied division of verbs into two classes, similar to those which are mentioned in OBS. 13th above, a part of the philosophy of J. W. Wright, concerning our usual form of passives in the present tense. But, as he now will have it, that the two voices sometimes tally as counterparts, it is plain that he adheres but partially to his former erroneous conception of a perfect or "past" participle, and the terms which hold it "in any connexion." The awkward substitutes proposed by the Irish critic, he does not indeed countenance; but argues against them still, and, in some respects, very justly. The doctrine now common to these authors, on this point, is the highly important one, that, in respect to half our verbs, what we commonly take for the passive present, *is not such*—that, in "the *second* class, (perhaps the greater number,) the *present-passive* implies that *the act expressed by the active voice has ceased.* Thus, 'The house is built.' * * * Strictly speaking, then," says the Doctor, "the PAST PARTICIPLE with the verb TO BE *is not the present tense in the passive voice of verbs thus used;* that is, this form does not express passively the *doing* of the act.'—*Bullions's Analyt. and Pract. Grammar,* Ed. of 1849, p. 235. Thus far these two authors agree; except that Wright seems to have avoided the incongruity of *calling* that "*the present-passive*" which he *denies* to be such. But the Doctor, approving none of this practitioner's "remedies," and being less solicitous to provide other treatment than expulsion for the thousands of present passives which both deem spurious, adds, as from the chair, this verdict: "These verbs either *have no present-passive*, or it is made by annexing the participle in *ing*, in its passive sense, to the verb *to be;* as, 'The house *is building*.'"—*Ib.* p. 236.

OBS. 17.—It would seem, that Dr. Bullions thinks, and in reality Wright also, that nothing can be a present passive, but what "*expresses passively the* DOING *of the act.*" This is about as wise, as to try to imagine every active verb to *express actively the receiving of an act!* It borders exceedingly hard upon absurdity; it very much resembles the nonsense of "*expressing receptively the giving of something!*" Besides, the word "DOING," being used substantively, does not determine well what is here meant; which is, I suppose, *continuance*, or an *unfinished state* of the act received—an idea which seems adapted to the participle in *ing*, but which it is certainly no fault of a participle ending in *d, t,* or *n*, not to suggest. To "*express passively the doing of the act,*" if the language means anything rational, may be, simply to say, that the act *is* or *was done.* For "*doings*" are, as often as any-wise, "*things done*," as *buildings* are *fabrics built*; and "*is built*," and "*am smitten*," the gentlemen's choice examples of *false passives*, and of "*actions finished*,"— though neither of them necessarily intimates either continuance or cessation of the act suffered, or, if it did, would be the less or the more passive or present,—may, in such a sense, "express the *doing* of the act," if any passives can :—nay, the "finished act" has such completion as may be stated with degrees of progress or of frequency; as, "The house *is partly built.*"—"I am *oftener smitten.*" There is, undoubtedly, some difference between the assertions, "The house *is building,*" and, "The house *is partly built*;" though, for practical purposes, perhaps, we need not always very nice in choosing between them. For the sake of variety, however, if for nothing else, it is to be hoped, the doctrine above-cited, which limits half our passive verbs of the present tense, *to the progressive form only*, will not soon be generally approved. It impairs the language more than neo-passives are likely ever to corrupt it.

OBS. 18.—"'No *startling novelties* have been introduced," says the preface to the "Analytical and Practical Grammar of the English Language." To have shunned all shocking innovations, only to have exercised common prudence. It is not pretended, that any of the Doctor's errors are remarked upon, or elsewhere in this treatise, will *startle* any body; but, if errors exist, even plausible guise, it may not be amiss, if I tell of them. To suppose every verb or participle to be either *"transitive"* or *" intransitive,"* setting all *passives* with the former sort, all *neuters* with the latter; (p. 59;)—to define the *transitive* verb or participle as expressing always *"an act* DONE *by one person or thing to another;"* (p. 60;)—to say, after making passive verbs transitive, "The object of a transitive verb is in the *objective case,"* and, "A verb that does not make sense with an objective after it, is intransitive;" (p. 60;)—to insist upon a precise and almost universal *identity of meaning*" in terms so obviously *contrasted* as are the two voices, "active" and " passive;" (pp. 95 and 235;)—to allege, as a general principle, "that whether we use the active, or the passive voice, *the meaning is the same,* except in some cases in the present tense;" (p. 67;)—to attribute to the verbs naturally opposite in voice and sense, that sameness of meaning which is observable only in certain *whole sentences* formed from them; (pp. 67, 95, and 235;)—to assume that each " VOICE is particular *form of the verb,"* yet make it include *two cases,* and often a preposition before one of them; (pp. 66, 67, and 95;)—to pretend from the words, "The PASSIVE VOICE represents the object of the verb as *acted upon,"* (p. 67,) that, *"According to the* DEFINITION, the passive voice expresses, passively, *the same thing* that the active does actively;" (p. 235;)—to affirm that, " 'Cæsar *conquered* Gaul,' and ' Gaul *was conquered* by Cæsar,' express *precisely the same idea,"*—and then say, "It will be felt at once that the expressions, ' Cæsar *conquers* Gaul,' and ' Gaul *is conquered by* Cæsar," *do not express the same thing ;"* (p. 235;)—to deny that passive verbs or neuter are worthy to constitute a distinct class, yet profess to find, in one single tense of the former, such a difference of meaning as warrants a general division of verbs in respect to it; (*ib.;*)—to announce, in old English, that, *" In regard to this matter* [,] there are evidently TWO CLASSES of verbs; namely, those *whose* present-passive expresses precisely the same thing, passively, as the active voice does actively, and those *in which it* does not:" (*ib.* :)—to do these several things, as they have been done, is, to set forth, not " novelties " only, but errors and inconsistencies.

OBS. 19.—Dr. Bullions still adheres to his old argument, that *being* after its own verb must be void of meaning; or, in his own words, "that *is being built,* if it mean anything, can mean nothing more than *is built,* which is not the idea intended to be expressed."—*Analyt. and Pract. Gram.* p. 237. He had said, (as cited in OBS. 5th above,) " The expression, ' *is being,*' is equivalent to *is,* and expresses *no more*; just as, ' *is loving,*' is equivalent to ' *loves.*' Hence, ' *is being built,*' is precisely equivalent to ' *is built.*'"—*Principles of E. Gram.* p. 58. He has now discovered " that *there is no progressive form* of the verb *to be,* and no need of it:" and that, " hence, there *is no such expression* in English as *is being.*"—*Analyt. and Pract. Gram.* p. 236. He should have noticed also, that " *is loving*" is not an authorized " equivalent to *loves ;*" and, further, that the error of saying " *is being built,*" is only in the relation of the *first two words* to each other. If *is being*" and " *is loving*" are left unused for the same reason, the truth may be, that *is itself,* like *loves,* commonly denotes " *continuance ;*" and that *being* after it, in stead of being necessary to repeat, can only be awkwardly tautologous. This is, in fact, THE GRAND OBJECTION to the new phraseology—" *is being practised*"—" *am being smitten*"—and the like. Were there no danger that petty writers would one day seize upon it with like avidity, an other innovation, exactly similar to this in every thing but tense—similar in awkwardness, in tautology, in unmistakableness—might here be uttered for the sake of illustration. Some men conceive, that " The *perfect participle* is always compound; as, *having seen, having written ;*"—and that the simple word, *seen* or *written,* had originally, and still ought to have, only a passive construction. For such views, they find authorities. Hence, in lieu of the common phrases, " *had we seen,*" " *we have written,*" they adopt such English as this : "*Had we having seen* you, we should have stopped."—" *We have wrong written* but just now, to our correspondent." Now, "*We are being smitten,*" is no better grammar than this ;—and no worse : " The idea intended " is in no great jeopardy in either case.

OBS. 20.—J. R. Chandler, of Philadelphia, in his Common School Grammar of 1847, has earnestly undertaken the *defence* of this new and much-mooted passive expression; which he calls " *the definite Passive Voice,*" or " *the Passive Voice of the Definite Form.*" He admits it, however, to be a form that " does not *sound well,*"—a " *novelty* that strikes the ear unpleasantly ;" but he will have the defect to be, not in the tautologous conceit of " *is being,*" " *was being,*" " *has been being,*" and the like, but in everybody's organ of hearing,—supposing all ears corrupted, " from infancy," to a distaste for correct speech, by " the habit of *hearing* and using words *ungrammatically !*" See p. 89. Claiming this new form as " *the true passive,*" in just contrast with the progressive active, he not only rebukes all attempts " to evade " the use of it, " by some real or supposed equivalent, but also declares, that, " The attempt to deprive the transitive definite verb of [this] *passive*;*voice,* is *to strike at the foundation of the language,* and *to strip it of one of its most important qualities ;* that of making both actor and sufferer, each in turn and at pleasure, the subject of conversation."—*Ibid.* Concerning *equivalents,* he evidently argues fallaciously ; for he urges, that the using of them " *does not dispense with the necessity of the definite passive voice.*"—P. 88. But it is plain, that, of the many fair substitutes which may in most cases be found, if any one is preferred, its form, and all the rest, are of course rejected for the time.

OBS. 21.—By Chandler, as well as others, this new passive form is justified only on the supposition, that the simple participle in *ing* can never with propriety be used passively. No plausible argument, indeed, can be framed for it, without the assumption, that the simpler form, when used in the same sense, *is ungrammatical.* But this is, in fact, a begging of the main question ; and that, in opposition to abundant authority for the usage condemned. (See OBS. 3d, above.) This author pretends that, "*The RULE of all grammarians declares the verb is, and a present participle (is building, or is writing), to be in the active voice*" only.—P. 88. (I add the word "*only*," but this is what he means, else he merely quibbles.) Now in this he is wrong, and so are the several grammarians who support the principle of this imaginary "*RULE*." The opinion of critics in general would be better represented by the following suggestions of the Rev. W. Allen: "When the English verb does not signify *mental affection*, the distinction of voice is often disregarded: thus we say, *actively*, they *were selling* fruit; and, *passively*, the books *are* now *selling*. The same remark applies to the participle used as a noun: as, actively, *drawing* is an elegant amusement, *building* is expensive; and, passively, his *drawings* are good, this is a fine *building*."—*Allen's Elements of E. Gram.* p. 82.

OBS. 22.—Chandler admits, that, "When it is said, 'The house *is building*,' the meaning is easily obtained; though," he strangely insists, "*it is exactly opposite to the assertion.*"—P. 59. He endeavours to show, moreover, by a fictitious example made for the purpose, that the progressive form, if used in both voices, will be liable to ambiguity. It may be so in some instances; but, were there weight enough in the objection to condemn the passive usage altogether, one would suppose there might be found, somewhere, an *actual example or two* of the abuse. Not concurring with Dr. Bullions in the notion that the active voice and the passive usually "express precisely the same thing," this critic concludes his argument with the following sentence: "There is an *important difference* between *doing* and *suffering*; and *that difference is grammatically shown* by the appropriate use of the active and passive voices of a verb."—*Chandler's Common School Gram.* p. 89.

OBS. 23.—The opinion given at the close of OBS. 2d above, was first published in 1833. An opposite doctrine, with the suggestion that it is "*improper* to say, 'the house *is building*,' instead of 'the house *is being built*,'"—is found on page 64th of the Rev. David Blair's Grammar, of 1815, —"Seventh Edition," with a preface dated, "*October 20th*, 1814." To any grammarian who wrote at a period much earlier than that, the question about *unco-passives* never occurred. Many critics have passed judgement upon them since, and so generally with reprobation, that the man must have more hardihood than sense, who will yet disgust his readers or hearers with them.[*] That "This new form has been used by *some respectable writers*," we need not deny; but let us look at the given "*instances* of it: 'For these who *are being educated* in our seminaries.' R. SOUTHEY. —'*It was being uttered.*' COLERIDGE.—'The foundation *was being laid.*' BRIT. CRITIC."— *English Grammar with Worcester's Univ. and Crit. Dict.* p. xlvi. Here, for the first example, it would be much better to say, "For those who *are educated*,"†—or, "who *are receiving their education*;" for the others, "It *was uttering*,"—"*was uttered*,"—or, "*was in uttering*."—"The foundation *was laying*,"—"*was laid*,"—or, "*was about being laid.*" Worcester's opinion of the "new form" is to be inferred from his manner of naming it in the following sentence: "Within a *few years, a strange and awkward neologism* has been introduced, by which the *present passive participle* is substituted, in such cases as the above, for the participle in *ing*."—*Ibid.* He has two instances more, in each of which the phrase is linked with an expression of disapprobation; "'It [τετυπμενος] signifies properly, though *in uncouth English*, one who *is being beaten.*' ABP. WHATELY.—The bridge *is being built*, and other phrases of the like kind, *have pained* the eye.' D. BOOTH."—*Ibid.*

OBS. 24.—Richard Hiley, in the third edition of his Grammar, published in London, in 1840, after showing the passive use of the participle in *ing*, proceeds thus: "No ambiguity arises, we presume, from the use of the participle in this manner. To avoid, however, affixing a passive signification to the participle in *ing*, an attempt has lately been made to substitute the passive participle in its place. Thus instead of 'The house was *building*,' 'The work is *printing*,' we sometimes hear, 'The house was *being built*,' 'The work is *being printed*.' But this mode is contrary to the English idiom, and has not yet obtained the sanction of reputable authority."—*Hiley's Gram.* p. 30.

OBS. 25.—Professor Hart, of Philadelphia, whose English Grammar was first published in 1845, justly prefers the usage which takes the progressive form occasionally in a passive sense; but, in arguing against the new substitute, he evidently remoulds the early reasoning of Dr. Bullions errors and all; a part of which he introduces thus: "I know the correctness of this mode of expression has lately been very much assailed, and an attempt, to some extent successful, has

---

[*] It is a very strange event in the history of English grammar, that such a controversy as this should have arisen; but a stranger one still, that, after all that has been said, more argument is needed. Some men, who hope to be valued as scholars, yet stickle for an odd phrase, which critics have denounced as follows: "But the history of the language scarcely affords a parallel to the excruciating refinement '*is being*,' and its unmerciful variations. We hope, and indeed believe, that it has not received the sanction of any grammar adopted in our popular education, as it certainly never will of any writer of just pretensions to scholarship."—*The True Sun, N. Y.*, April 16, 1846.

† Education is a work of continuance, yet completed, like many others, as fast as it goes on. It is not, like the act of loving or hating, so complete at the first moment as not to admit the progressive form of the verb; for we may say of a lad, "I am *educating* him for the law;" and possibly, "He is *educating* for the law;" though to so well as, "He *is to be educated* for the law." But, to suppose that "*is educated*" or "*are educated*" implies necessarily a *cessation of the educating*, is a mistake. That conception is right, only when *educated* is taken adjectively. The phrase, "those who *are educated* in our seminaries," hardly includes such as *have been educated* there in times past; much less does it apply to these exclusively, as some seem to think. "*Being*," as inserted by Southey, is therefore quite *needless*: so is it *often*, in this new phraseology, the best correction being its mere omission.

‡ Worcester has also this citation: "The Eclectic Review remarks, 'That a need of this phrase, *or an equivalent one*, is felt, is sufficiently proved by the extent to which it is used by educated persons and respectable writers.' —*Gram. before Dict.* p. xlvi. Sundry phrases, equivalent in sense to this new voice, have long been in the, are, of course, still needed; something from among them being always, by every accurate writer, still preferred. But this awkward innovation, use it who will, can no more be justified by plea of "*need*," than can every other hackneyed solecism extant. Even the Archbishop, if quoted right by Worcester, has descended to "*uncouth English*," without either necessity or propriety, having thereby only misexpounded a very common Greek word, a "perfect or pluperfect" participle, which means "*beaten, struck, or having been beaten.*"—G. BROWN.

a made [,] to introduce the form [,] '*is being built.*' But, in the first place, the old mode of passion is a well established usage of the language, being found in our best and most correct ers. Secondly, *is being built* does not convey *the idea intended,* [;] namely [,] that of *progres-action. Is being,* taken together, means simply *is,* just as *is writing* means *writes ;* therefore, *being built* means *is built,* a perfect and not a progressive ACTION. Or, if *being* [and] *built* be put together, *they signify an* ACTION COMPLETE, and the phrase means, as before, *the house is* (its) *being built.*"—*Hart's Gram.* p. 76. The last three sentences here are liable to many objections, some of which are suggested above.

26.—It is important, that the central phraseology of our language be so understood, as not *misinterpreted with credit,* or falsely expounded by popular critics and teachers. Hence and of *exposition* are the more particularly noticed in these observations. In "*being built,*" Hart, like sundry authors named above, finds nothing but "ACTION COMPLETE." Without this, Butler interprets better, when he says, "'The house *is built,*' denotes an *existing state,* than a *completed action.*" But this author, too, in his next three sentences, utters as many as; for he adds: "The name of the agent *cannot be expressed* in phrases of this kind. We may say, 'The house is built *by* John.' When we say, 'The house is built *by* mechanics,' we express an *existing state.*"—*Butler's Practical Gram.* p. 80. Unquestionably, "*is built by* mechanics," expresses *nothing else* than the "*existing state*" of being "built by mechanics," either with an affirmation:—that is, the "existing state" of receiving the action of mechanics, framed of "the house." And, in my judgement, one may very well say, "*The house is built by* us;" meaning, "*John is building the house.*" St. Paul says, "Every house *is builded by* a MAN."—*Heb.* iii, 4. In this text, the common "name of the agent" is "expressed."

27.—Wells and Weld, whose grammars date from 1846, being remarkably chary of finding thing wrong in "respectable writers," hazard no opinion of their own, concerning the correct-or incorrectness of either of the usages under discussion. They do not always see absurdity the approbation of opposites; yet one should here, perhaps, count them with the majorities allow. The latter says, "The participle in *ing* is sometimes used passively: as, forty and years was this temple in *building* ; not in *being built.*"—*Weld's English Gram.* 2d Ed. p. 170. Here, means to suggest, that "*in being built*" would "not" be good English, he teaches very openly ; if his thought is, that this phrase would "not" express the sense of the former one, *building,*" he palpably contradicts his own position ! But he proceeds, in a note, thus: "The self expression, *is being built, is being committed,* &c., is almost universally condemned by grammarians; but it is *sometimes* met with in respectable writers. It occurs most frequently in paper paragraphs, and in hasty compositions."—*Ibid.* Wells comments thus: "Different have long existed among critics respecting this passive use of the imperfect participle. Some respectable writers substitute *the compound passive participle*; as, 'The house is *being* built,' 'The book is *being printed.*' But the prevailing practice of the best authors is in favor of simple form; as, 'The house is *building.*' "—*Wells's School Gram.* 1st Ed. p. 148; 113th p. 161.

28.—S. W. Clark, in the second edition of his Practical Grammar, stereotyped and pub-lished in New York in 1848, appears to favour the insertion of "*being*" into passive verbs; but instructions are so obscure, so often inaccurate, and so incompatible one with an other, that it hard to say, with certainty, what he approves. In one place, he has this position: "The Passive of a verb is formed by adding *the Passive Participle* of that verb, to the verb *be.* EXAMPLES I am loved. I am feared. They *are* worshipped."—Page 69. In an other, he has this: "When object is to be represented as receiving the action, *the Passive Participle* should be used. EXAMPLE—Henry's *lesson* is BEING RECITED."—P. 132. Now these two positions utterly con-tradict each other; for they are equally general, and "*the Passive Participle*" is first one thing, then an other. Again, he has the following assertions, both false: "The Present (or First) Participle always ends in *ing,* and is *limited to the Active Voice.* The Past (or Second) Participle regular Verbs ends in *d* or *ed,* and is *limited to the Passive Voice.*"—P. 131. Afterwards, in [defiance] of the fancied limitation, he acknowledges the passive use of the participle in *ing,* and that this is "*authority*" for it; but, at the same time, most absurdly supposes the word to predicate action," and also to be *wrong*: saying, "*Action* is *sometimes* predicated of a *passive* subject. EXAMPLE—'The *house is building*'.. for.. 'The *house is being built,*'.. which means.. " The house *being built.*" On this, he remarks thus: "This is one of the instances in which *Authority* is against *Philosophy.* For an *act* cannot *properly* be predicated of a *passive agent.* Many good men properly reject this idiom. 'Mansfield's prophecy *is being realized.*'—MICHELET'S LUTHER." *Clark's Practical Gram.* p. 133. It may require some study to learn from this *which idiom it is,*

Clark has also the following citations, which most probably accord with his own opinions, though the first is inconvenient : "The propriety of these *imperfect passive tenses* has been *doubted by almost all* our gramma-rians, though I believe but few of them have written many pages without condescending to make use of them." Fisk says, 'One of the greatest defects of the English tongue, with regard to the verb, seems to be the want of a *perfect passive participle.*' And yet he uses the imperfect participle in a passive *sense* as often as most others.—*Fiskburn's Dissertation on the English Verb.*

Several other expressions of this sort now and then occur, such as the new-fangled and most uncouth solecism, 'is done,' for the good old English idiomatic expression, 'is doing,'—an absurd periphrasis, driving out a bold and pithy turn of the English language."—*N. A. Review.* See *Wells's Grammar,* 1850, p. 161.

"The term, "*imperfect passive tenses,*" seems not a very accurate one; because the present, the perfect, &c., included. Fiskburn applies it to any passive tenses formed from the simple "imperfect participle;" but the phrase, "passive verbs in the progressive form," would better express the meaning. The term, "*compound pas-participle,*" which Wells applies above to "*being built,*" "*being printed,*" and the like, is also both unusual and awkward. Most readers would sooner understand by it the form, *having been built, having been printed,* &c. The author's mode of naming participles is always either very awkward or not distinctive. His scheme makes it necessary to add here, for each of these forms, a third epithet, referring to his main distinction, of "*imperfect* and *perfect* passive," as, "the compound *imperfect* participle *passive,*" and "the compound *perfect* participle *passive.*" Is "*being built*" or "*being printed,*" but "an *imperfect passive participle ?*" Was this, or something else, the Venture of Bentlia?

that these " many good writers reject :" but the grammarian who can talk of " *a passive act*
without perceiving that the phrase is self-contradictory and absurd, may well be expected to m
tain a " Philosophy " which is against "Authority,"and likewise to prefer a ridiculous innova
to good and established usage.

Obs. 29.—As most verbs are susceptible of both forms, the simple active and the compou
progressive, and likewise of a transitive and an intransitive sense in each ; and as many, when u
intransitively, may have a meaning which is scarcely distinguishable from that of the passive fa
it often happens that this substitution of the imperfect participle passive for the simple impe
in *ing*, is quite needless, even when the latter is not considered passive. For example: "Se
the following paragraph, how widely the bane *is being circulated !* "—*Liberator*, No. 999, p. 34. 1
is circulating would be better ; and so would *is circulated*. Nor would either of these much
the sense, if at all ; for *"circulate"* may mean, according to Webster," *to be diffused*," or, as J
son and Worcester have it, " *to be dispersed*."

III. FORM OF PASSIVE VERBS.

Passive verbs, in English, are always of a compound form ; being m
from active-transitive verbs, by adding the Perfect Participle to the auxili
verb BE, through all its changes : thus from the active-transitive verb *l*
is formed the passive verb *be loved*.

FIFTH EXAMPLE.

The regular passive verb BE LOVED, conjugated affirmatively.

PRINCIPAL PARTS OF THE ACTIVE VERB.

Present.	*Preterit.*	*Imp. Participle.*	*Perf. Particip*
Love.	Loved.	Loving.	Loved.

INFINITIVE MOOD.

PRESENT TENSE.
To be loved.

PERFECT TENSE.
To have been loved.

INDICATIVE MOOD.

PRESENT TENSE.

Singular.	*Plural.*
1. I am loved,	1. We are loved,
2. Thou art loved,	2. You are loved,
3. He is loved ;	3. They are loved.

IMPERFECT TENSE.

Singular.	*Plural.*
1. I was loved,	1. We were loved,
2. Thou wast loved,	2. You were loved,
3. He was loved ;	3. They were loved.

PERFECT TENSE.

Singular.	*Plural.*
1. I have been loved,	1. We have been loved,
2. Thou hast been loved,	2. You have been loved,
3. He has been loved ;	3. They have been loved.

PLUPERFECT TENSE.

Singular.	*Plural.*
1. I had been loved,	1. We had been loved,
2. Thou hadst been loved,	2. You had been loved,
3. He had been loved ;	3. They had been loved.

FIRST-FUTURE TENSE.

Singular.	*Plural.*
1. I shall be loved,	1. We shall be loved,
2. Thou wilt be loved,	2. You will be loved,
3. He will be loved ;	3. They will be loved.

SECOND-FUTURE TENSE.

Singular.
1. I　　shall have been loved,
2. Thou wilt have been loved,
3. He　　will have been loved;

Plural.
1. We　shall have been loved,
2. You　will have been loved,
3. They will have been loved.

POTENTIAL MOOD.

PRESENT TENSE.

Singular.
1. I　　may　be loved,
2. Thou mayst be loved,
3. He　may　be loved;

Plural.
1. We　may be loved,
2. You　may be loved,
3. They may be loved.

IMPERFECT TENSE.

Singular.
1. I　　might　be loved,
2. Thou mightst be loved,
3. He　　might　be loved;

Plural.
1. We　might be loved,
2. You　might be loved,
3. They might be loved.

PERFECT TENSE.

Singular.
1. I　　may　have been loved,
2. Thou mayst have been loved,
3. He　may　have been loved;

Plural.
1. We　may have been loved,
2. You　may have been loved,
3. They may have been loved.

PLUPERFECT TENSE.

Singular.
1. I　　might　have been loved,
2. Thou mightst have been loved,
3. He　　might　have been loved;

Plural.
1. Wo　might have been loved,
2. You　might have been loved,
3. They might have been loved.

SUBJUNCTIVE MOOD.

PRESENT TENSE.

Singular.
1. If I　　be loved,
2. If thou be loved,
3. If he　be loved;

Plural.
1. If we　be loved,
2. If you　be loved,
3. If they be loved.

IMPERFECT TENSE.

Singular.
1. If I　　were loved,
2. If thou were loved,
3. If he　were loved;

Plural.
1. If we　were loved,
2. If you　were loved,
3. If they were loved.

IMPERATIVE MOOD.

PRESENT TENSE.

Singular. 2. Be　[thou] loved,　*or* Do thou be loved;
Plural. 2. Be [ye or you] loved,　*or* Do you be loved.

PARTICIPLES.

1. *The Imperfect.*　2. *The Perfect.*　3. *The Preperfect.*
Being loved.　　　Loved.　　　Having been loved.

FAMILIAR FORM WITH 'THOU.'

NOTE.—In the familiar style, the second person singular of this verb, is usually and more properly formed thus: IND. Thou art loved, Thou was loved, Thou hast been loved, Thou had been loved, Thou shall or will be loved, Thou shall or will have been loved. POT. Thou may, can, *or* must be loved; Thou might, could, would, *or* should be loved; Thou may, can, *or* must have been loved; Thou might, could, would, *or* should have been loved. SUBJ. If thou be loved, If thou were loved. IMP. Be [thou] loved, *or* Do thou be loved.

OBSERVATIONS.

OBS. 1.—A few active-intransitive verbs, that signify mere motion, change of place, or change of condition, may be put into this form, with a *neuter* signification; making not *passive* but *neuter*

24

verbs, which express nothing more than the state which results from the change: as, "*I am come.*"—"*She is gone.*"—"*He is risen.*"—"*They are fallen.*" These are what Dr. Johnson and some others call "*neuter passives;*" a name which never was very proper, and for which we have no frequent use.

OBS. 2.—Most neuter verbs of the passive form, such as, "*am grown, art become, is lain, are flown, are vanished, are departed, was sat, were arrived,*" may now be considered errors of conjugation, or perhaps of syntax. In the verb, *to be mistaken,* there is an irregularity which ought to be particularly noticed. When applied to *persons,* this verb is commonly taken in a *neuter* sense, and signifies, *to be in error, to be wrong;* as, "I am *mistaken,* thou *art mistaken,* he *is mistaken.*" But, when used of *things,* it is a proper passive verb, and signifies *to be misunderstood,* or *to be taken wrong;* as, "The sense of the passage *is mistaken;* that is, not rightly understood." See *Webster's Dict. w.* Mistaken. "I have known a shadow across a brook *to be mistaken* for a footbridge."

OBS. 3.—Passive verbs may be easily distinguished from neuter verbs of the same form, by a reference to the agent or instrument, common to the former class, but not to the latter. This frequently is, and always may be, expressed after *passive* verbs; but never is, and never can be, expressed after *neuter* verbs: as, "The thief has been caught *by the officer.*"—"Pens are made *with a knife.*" Here the verbs are passive; but, "*I am not yet ascended,*" (John, xx, 17,) is not passive, because it does not convey the idea of being ascended *by* some one's agency.

OBS. 4.—Our ancient writers, after the manner of the French, very frequently employed this mode of conjugation in a neuter sense; but, with a very few exceptions, present usage is clearly in favour of the auxiliary *have* in preference to *be,* whenever the verb formed with the perfect participle is not passive; as, "They *have* arrived,"—not, "They *are* arrived." Hence such examples as the following, are not now good English: "All these reasons *are* now ceased."—*Butler's Analogy,* p. 157. Say, "*have* now ceased." "It *is* not got beyond the reach of his faculties."—*Ib.* p. 158. Say, "*had* not got." "Which *is* now grown wholly obsolete."—*Churchill's Gram.* p. 330. Say, "*has* now grown." "And when he *was* entered into a ship."—*Bible.* Say, "*had* entered."—"What *is* become of decency and virtue?"—*Murray's Key,* p. 196. Say, "*has* become."

OBS. 5.—Dr. Priestley says, "It seems *not to have been determined* by the English grammarians, whether the *passive* participles of verbs neuter require the auxiliary *am* or *have* before them. The French, in this case, confine themselves strictly to the former. 'What *has become* of national liberty?' Hume's History, Vol. 6. p. 254. The French would say, *what is become;* and, in this instance, perhaps, with more propriety."—*Priestley's Gram.* p. 128. It is no marvel that those writers who have not rightly made up their minds upon this point of English grammar, should consequently fall into many mistakes. The perfect participle of a neuter verb is not "*passive,*" as the doctor seems to suppose it to be; and the mode of conjugation which he here inclines to prefer, is a mere *Gallicism,* which is fast wearing out from our language, and is even now but little countenanced by good writers.

OBS. 6.—There are a few verbs of the passive form which seem to imply that a person's own mind is the agent that actuates him; as, "The editor *is rejoiced* to think," &c.—*Juvenile Keepsake.* "I am *resolved* what to do."—*Luke,* xvi, 4. "He *was resolved* on going to the city to reside."—*Comly's Gram.* p. 114. "James *was resolved* not to indulge himself."—*Murray's Key,* ii, 220. "He *is inclined* to go."—"He *is determined* to go."—"He *is bent* on going." These are properly passive verbs, notwithstanding there are active forms which are nearly equivalent to most of them; as, "The editor *rejoices* to think."—"I *know* what to do."—"He *had resolved* on going."—"James *resolved* not to indulge himself." So in the phrase, "I am *ashamed* to beg," we seem to have a passive verb of this sort; but, the verb *to ashame* being now obsolete, *ashamed* is commonly reckoned an *adjective.* Yet we cannot put it before a noun, after the usual manner of adjectives. *To be indebted,* is an other expression of the same kind. In the following example, "*am remember'd*" is used for *do remember,* and, in my opinion, *inaccurately:*

> "He said mine eyes were black, and my hair black;
> And, now I am *remember'd,* scorn'd at me."—*Shakspeare.*

IV. FORM OF NEGATION.

A verb is conjugated *negatively,* by placing the adverb *not* after it, or after the first auxiliary; but the infinitive and participles take the negative first: as, Not to love, Not to have loved; Not loving, Not loved, Not having loved.

FIRST PERSON SINGULAR.

IND. I love not, *or* I do not love; I loved not, *or* I did not love; I have not loved; I had not loved; I shall not, *or* will not, love; I shall not, *or* will not, have loved. POT. I may, can, *or* must not love; I might, could, would, *or* should not love; I may, can, *or* must not have loved; I might, could, would, *or* should not have loved. SUBJ. If I love not, If I loved not.

SECOND PERSON SINGULAR.

SOLEMN STYLE:—IND. Thou lovest not, *or* Thou dost not love; Thou lovedst not, *or* Thou didst not love; Thou hast not loved; Thou hadst not loved; Thou shalt not, *or* wilt not, love; Thou shalt not, *or* wilt not, have loved. POT. Thou mayst, canst, *or* must not love; Thou mightst, couldst, wouldst, *or* shouldst not love; Thou mayst, canst, or must not have loved; Thou mightst, couldst, wouldst, or shouldst not have loved. Subj. If thou love not, If thou loved not. Imp. Love [thou] not, or Do thou not love.

FAMILIAR STYLE:—IND. Thou lov'st not, or Thou dost not love; Thou loved not, or Thou did not love; Thou hast not loved; Thou had not loved; Thou shall not, or will not, love; Thou shall not, or will not, have loved. Pot. Thou may, can, or must not love; Thou might, could, would, or should not love; Thou may, can, or must not have loved; Thou might, could, would, or should not have loved. Subj. If thou love not, If thou loved not. Imp. Love [thou] not, or Do [thou] not love.

THIRD PERSON SINGULAR.

IND. He loves not, or He does not love; He loved not, or He did not love; He has not loved; He had not loved; He shall not, or will not, love; He shall not, or will not, have loved. Pot. He may, can, or must not love; He might, could, would, or should not love; He may, can, or must not have loved; He might, could, would, or should not have loved. Subj. If he love not, If he loved not.

V. FORM OF QUESTION.

A verb is conjugated *interrogatively*, in the indicative and potential moods, by placing the nominative after it, or after the first auxiliary: as,

FIRST PERSON SINGULAR.

IND. Love I? or Do I love? Loved I? or Did I love? Have I loved? Had I loved? Shall I love? Shall I have loved? Pot. May, can, or must I love? Might, could, would, or should I love? May, can, or must I have loved? Might, could, would, or should I have loved?

SECOND PERSON SINGULAR.

SOLEMN STYLE:—IND. Lovest thou? or Dost thou love? Lovedst thou? or Didst thou love? Hast thou loved? Hadst thou loved? Wilt thou love? Wilt thou have loved? Pot. Mayst, canst, or must thou love? Mightst, couldst, wouldst, or shouldst thou love? Mayst, canst, or must thou have loved? Mightst, couldst, wouldst, or shouldst thou have loved?

FAMILIAR STYLE:—IND. Lov'st thou? or Dost thou love? Loved thou? or Did thou love? Hast thou loved? Had thou loved? Will thou love? Will thou have loved? Pot. May, can, or must thou love? Might, could, would, or should thou love? May, can, or must thou have loved? Might, could, would, or should thou have loved?

THIRD PERSON SINGULAR.

IND. Loves he? or Does he love? Loved he? or Did he love? Has he loved? Had he loved? Shall or will he love? Will he have loved? Pot. May, can, or must he love? Might, could, would, or should he love? May, can, or must he have loved? Might, could, would, or should he have loved?

VI. FORM OF QUESTION WITH NEGATION.

A verb is conjugated *interrogatively and negatively*, in the indicative and potential moods, by placing the nominative and the adverb *not* after the verb, or after the first auxiliary: as,

FIRST PERSON PLURAL.

IND. Love we not? or Do we not love? Loved we not? or Did we not love? Have we not loved? Had we not loved? Shall we not love? Shall we not have loved? Pot. May, can, or must we not love? Might, could, would, or should we not love? May, can, or must we not have loved? Might, could, would, or should we not have loved?

SECOND PERSON PLURAL.

IND. See ye not? or Do you not see? Saw ye not? or Did you not see? Have you not seen? Had you not seen? Will you not see? Will you not have seen?

Pot. May, can, *or* must you not see? Might, could, would, *or* should you not see? May, can, *or* must you not have seen? Might, could, would, *or* should you not have seen?

THIRD PERSON PLURAL.

Ind. Are they not loved? Were they not loved? Have they not been loved? Had they not been loved? Shall *or* will they not be loved? Will they not have been loved? May, can, *or* must they not be loved? Might, could, would, *or* should they not be loved? May, can, *or* must they not have been loved? Might, could, would, *or* should they not have been loved?

OBSERVATIONS.

Obs. 1.—In a familiar question or negation, the compound or auxiliary form of the verb is, in general, preferable to the simple: as, "No man lives to purpose, who *does not live* for posterity."—*Dr. Wayland.* It is indeed so much more common, as to seem the only proper mode of expression: as, "*Do I say* these things as a man?"—"*Do you think* that we excuse ourselves?"—"*Do you not know* that a little leaven *leavens* the whole lump?"—"*Dost thou revile?*" &c. But in the solemn or the poetic style, though either may be used, the simple form is more dignified, and perhaps more graceful: as, "*Say I* these things as a man?"—1 *Cor.* ix, 8. "*Think ye* that we excuse ourselves?"—2 *Cor.* xii, 19. "*Know ye not* that a little leaven *leaveneth* the whole lump?"—1 *Cor.* v, 6. "*Revilest thou* God's high priest?"—*Acts.* "King Agrippa, *believest thou* the prophets?"—*Ib.* "*Understandest thou* what thou readest?"—*Ib.* "Of whom *speaketh* the prophet this?"—*Id.* "And the man of God said, Where *fell it?*"—2 *Kings,* vi, 6.
"What! *heard ye not* of lowland war?"—*Sir W. Scott, L. L.*
"*Seems he not,* Malise, like a ghost?"—*Id. L. of Lake.*
"Where *thinkst thou* he is now? *Stands he,* or *sits he?*
    Or *does he walk?* or *is he* on his horse?"—*Shak. Ant. and Cleop.*

Obs. 2.—In interrogative sentences, the auxiliaries *shall* and *will* are not always capable of being applied to the different persons agreeably to their use in simple declarations: thus, "*Will I go?*" is a question which there never can be any occasion to ask in its literal sense; because none knows better than I, what my will or wish is. But "*Shall I go?*" may properly be asked; because *shall* here refers to *duty,* and asks to know what is agreeable to the will of an other. In questions, the first person generally requires *shall;* the second, *will;* the third admits of both: but, in the second-future, the third, used interrogatively, seems to require *will* only. Yet, in that figurative kind of interrogation which is sometimes used to declare a negative, there may be occasional exceptions to these principles; as, "*Will I eat* the flesh of bulls, or drink the blood of goats?"—*Psalms,* l, 13. That is, *I will not eat,* &c.

Obs. 3.—*Cannot* is not properly one word, but two: in parsing, the adverb must be taken separately, and the auxiliary be explained with its principal. When power is denied, *can* and *not* are now *generally united*—perhaps in order to prevent ambiguity; as, "I *cannot* go." But when the power is affirmed, and something else is denied, the words are written separately; as, "The Christian apologist *can not merely* expose the utter baseness of the infidel assertion, but he has positive ground for erecting an opposite and confronting assertion in its place."—*Dr. Chalmers.* The junction of these terms, however, is not of much importance to the sense: and, as it is plainly contrary to analogy, some writers,—(as Dr. Webster, in his late or "improved" works; Dr. Bullions, in his; Prof. W. C. Fowler, in his new "English Grammar," 8vo; J. R. Chandler, W. S. Cardell, O. B. Peirce,—)always separate them. And, indeed, why should we write, "I *cannot* go, Thou *canst not* go, He *cannot* go?" Apart from the custom, we have just as good reason to join *not* to *canst* as to *can;* and sometimes its union with the latter is a gross error: as, "He *cannot only* make a way to escape, but with the injunction to duty can infuse the power to perform."—*Maturin's Sermons,* p. 287. The fear of ambiguity never prevents us from disjoining *can* and *not* whenever we wish to put a word between them: as, "Though the waves thereof toss themselves, yet *can* they *not* prevail; though they roar, yet *can* they *not* pass over it."—*Jeremiah,* v, 22. "Which then I *can* resist *not.*"—*Byron's Manfred,* p. 1.
    "*Can I not* mountain maiden spy,
    But she must bear the Douglas eye?"—*Scott.*

Obs. 4.—In negative questions, the adverb *not* is sometimes placed before the nominative, and sometimes after it: as, "Told *not I* thee?"—*Numb.* xxiii, 26. "Spake *I not* also to thy messengers?"—*Ib.* xxiv, 12. "*Cannot I* do with you as this potter?"—*Jer.* xviii, 6. "Art *not thou* a seer?"—2 *Sam* xv, 27. "Did *not Israel* know?"—*Rom.* x, 19. "Have *they not* heard?"—*Ib.* 18 "Do *not they* blaspheme that worthy name?"—*James,* ii, 7. This adverb, like every other, should be placed where it will sound most agreeably, and best suit the sense. Dr. Priestley imagined that it could not properly come before the nominative. He says, "When the nominative case is put after the verb, on account of *an* interrogation, *no other word* should be interposed between them. [EXAMPLES:] 'May *not we* here say with Lucretius?'—*Addison on Medals,* p. 29. May *we not* say? 'Is *not it* he.' [?] Smollett's *Voltaire,* Vol. 18, p. 152. Is *it not* he. [?]"—*Priestley's Gram.* p. 177.

Obs. 5.—In grave discourse, or in oratory, the adverb *not* is spoken as distinctly as other words; but, *ordinarily,* when placed before the nominative, it is rapidly slurred over in utterance and the *o* is not heard. In fact, it is *generally* (though inclegantly) contracted in familiar conversation, and joined to the auxiliary: as, Ind. Don't they do it? Didn't they do it? Haven't they done it? Hadn't they done it? Shan't, or won't they do it? Won't they have done it? Pot. Mayn't, can't, *or* mustn't they do it? Mightn't, couldn't, wouldn't, *or* shouldn't they do it? Mayn't, can't, *or* mustn't they have done it? Mightn't, couldn't, wouldn't, *or* shouldn't they have done it?

OBS. 6.—Well-educated people commonly utter their words with more distinctness and fullness than the vulgar, yet without adopting ordinarily the long-drawn syllables of poets and orators or the solemn phraseology of preachers and prophets. Whatever may be thought of the grammatical propriety of such contractions as the foregoing, no one who has ever observed how the English language is usually spoken, will doubt their commonness, or their antiquity. And it may be observed, that, in the use of these forms, the distinction of persons and numbers in the verb, is almost, if not entirely, dropped. Thus *don't* is used for *dost not* or *does not*, as properly as for *do not ;* and, "*Thou can't* do it, or *shan't* do it," is as good English as, "*He can't* do it, or *shan't* do it." *Will*, according to Webster, was anciently written *woll :* hence *won't* acquired the *o*, which is long in Walker's orthoëpy. *Haven't*, which cannot be used for *has not* or *hast not*, is still further contracted by the vulgar, and spoken *ha'n't*, which serves for all three. These forms are sometimes found in books; as, "WONT, a contraction of *woll not*, that is, *will not*."—*Webster's Dict*. "HA'NT, a contraction of *have not* or *has not*."—*Id*. "WONT, (wònt or wŭnt,) A contraction of *would not :*—used for *will* not."—*Worcester's Dict*. "HA'N'T, (hănt or hänt,) A vulgar contraction for *has not*, or *have not*."—*Id*. In the writing of such contractions, the apostrophe is not always used; though some think it necessary for distinction's sake: as, "Which is equivalent, because what *can't* be done *won't* be done."—*Johnson's Gram. Com*. p. 312.

IRREGULAR VERBS.

An *irregular verb* is a verb that does not form the preterit and the perfect participle by assuming *d* or *ed ;* as, *see, saw, seeing, seen*. Of this class of verbs there are about one hundred and ten, beside their several derivatives and compounds.

OBSERVATIONS.

OBS. 1.—Regular verbs form their preterits and perfect participles, by adding *d* to final *e*, and *ed* to all other terminations; the final consonant of the verb being sometimes doubled, (as in *dropped*,) and final *y* sometimes changed to *i*, (as in *cried*,) agreeably to the rules for spelling in such cases. The verb *hear, heard, hearing, heard*, adds *d* to *r* and is therefore irregular. *Heard* is pronounced *hĕrd* by all our lexicographers, except *Webster :* who formerly wrote it *heerd*, and still pronounces it so; alleging, in despite of universal usage against him, that it is written "more correctly *heared*."—*Octavo Dict*., 1829. Such pronunciation would doubtless require this last orthography, "*heared ;*" but both are, in fact, about as fanciful as his former mode of spelling, which ran thus : "*Az* I had *heerd* suggested by *frends* or indifferent *reeders*."—*Dr. Webster's Essays, Preface*, p. 10.

OBS. 2.—When a verb ends in a sharp consonant, *t* is sometimes improperly substituted for *ed*, making the preterit and the perfect participle irregular in spelling, when they are not so in sound ; as, *distrest* for *distressed*, *tost* for *tossed*, *mixt* for *mixed*, *crackt* for *cracked*. These contractions are now generally treated as *errors* in writing; and the verbs are accordingly (with a few exceptions) accounted regular. Lord Kames commends Dean Swift for having done "all in his power to restore the syllable *ed ;*" says, he "possessed, if any man ever did, the true genius of the English tongue ;" and thinks that in rejecting these ugly contractions, "he well deserves to be imitated."—*Elements of Criticism*, Vol. ii, p. 12. The regular orthography is indeed to be preferred in all such cases; but the writing of *ed* restores no syllable, except in solemn discourse; and, after all, the poems of Swift have so very many of these irregular contractions in *t*, that one can hardly believe his lordship had ever read them. Since the days of these critics still more has been done towards the restoration of the *ed*, in orthography, though not in sound ; but, even at this present time, our poets not unfrequently write, *est* for *essed* or *ess'd*, in forming the preterits or participles of verbs that end in the syllable *ess*. This is an ill practice, which needlessly multiplies our redundant verbs, and greatly embarrasses what it seems at first to simplify : as,

"O friend! I know not which way I must look
   For comfort, being, as I am, *opprest*,
To think that now our life is only *drest*
   For show."—*Wordsworth's Poetical Works*, 8vo, p. 119.

OBS. 3.—When the verb ends with a smooth consonant, the substitution of *t* for *ed* produces an irregularity in sound, as well as in writing. In some such irregularities, the poets are indulged for the sake of rhyme ; but the best speakers and writers of prose prefer the regular form, wherever good use has sanctioned it : thus *learned* is better than *learnt ; burned*, than *burnt ; penned*, than *pent ; absorbed*, than *absorbt ; spelled*, than *spelt ; smelled*, than *smelt*. So many of this sort of words as are allowably contracted, belong to the class of redundant verbs, among which they may be seen in a subsequent table.

OBS. 4.—Several of the irregular verbs are variously used by the best authors ; redundant forms are occasionally given to some verbs, without sufficient authority ; and many preterits and participles which were formerly in good use, are now obsolete, or becoming so. The *simple* irregular verbs in English are about one hundred and ten, and they are nearly all monosyllables. They are derived from the Saxon, in which language they are also, for the most part, irregular.

OBS. 5.—The following alphabetical list exhibits the simple irregular verbs, as they are *now generally* used. In this list, those preterits and participles which are supposed to be preferable, and best supported by authorities, are placed first. Nearly all compounds that follow the form of their simple verbs, or derivatives that follow their primitives, are here purposely omitted. *Welcome* and *behave* are always regular, and therefore belong not here. Some words which are obsolete, have also been omitted, that the learner might not mistake them for words in present use. Some of those which are placed last, are now little used.

LIST OF THE IRREGULAR VERBS.

Present.	Preterit.	Imperfect Participle.	Perfect Participle.
Arise,	arose,	arising,	arisen.
Be,	was,	being,	been.
Bear,	bore *or* bare,	bearing,	borne *or* born. *
Beat,	beat,	beating,	beaten *or* beat.
Begin,	began *or* begun, †	beginning,	begun.
Behold,	beheld,	beholding,	beheld.
Beset,	beset,	besetting,	beset.
Bestead,	bestead,	besteading,	bestead.‡
Bid,	bid *or* bade,	bidding,	bidden *or* bid.
Bind,	bound,	binding,	bound.
Bite,	bit,	biting,	bitten *or* bit.
Bleed,	bled,	bleeding,	bled.
Break,	broke,§	breaking,	broken.
Breed,	bred,	breeding,	bred.
Bring,	brought,	bringing,	brought.
Buy,	bought,	buying,	bought.
Cast,	cast,	casting,	cast.
Chide,	chid,	chiding,	chidden *or* chid.
Choose,	chose,	choosing,	chosen.
Cleave, ‖	cleft *or* clove,	cleaving,	cleft *or* cloven.
Cling,	clung,	clinging,	clung.
Come,	came,	coming,	come.
Cost,	cost,	costing,	cost.
Cut,	cut,	cutting,	cut.
Do,	did,	doing,	done.
Draw,	drew,	drawing,	drawn.
Drink,	drank,	drinking,	drunk, *or* drank. ¶
Drive,	drove,	driving,	driven.

Borne usually signifies *carried ; born* signifies *brought forth.* J. E. Worcester, the lexicographer, speaks of these two participles thus : "☞ The participle *born* is used in the passive form, and *borne* in the active form, [with reference to birth] ; as, ' He was *born* blind,' *John* ix. ; ' The barren hath *borne* seven,' 1 *Sam.* ii. This distinction between *born* and *borne*, though not recognised by grammarians, is in accordance with common usage, at least in this country. In many editions of the Bible it is recognized ; and in many it is not. It seems to have been more commonly recognized in American, than in English, editions."—*Worcester's Universal and Critical Dict. w. Bear.* In five, out of seven good American editions of the Bible among my books, the latter text is, "The barren hath *born* seven ;" in two, it is as above, "hath *borne*." In Johnson's Quarto Dictionary, the perfect participle of *bear* is given erroneously, "*bore*, or *born ;*" and that of *forbear*, which should be *forborne*, is found, both in his columns and in his preface. "*forborn*."

† According to Murray, Lennie, Bullions, and some others, to use *begun* for *began* or *run* for *ran*, is improper ; but Webster gives *run* as well as *ran* for the preterit, and *begun* may be used in like manner, on the authority of Dryden, Pope, and Parnell.

‡ "And they shall pass through it, hardly *bestead*, and hungry "—*Isaiah*, viii, 21.

§ "*Brake* [for the preterit of *Break*] seems now obsolescent."—*Dr. Crombie, Etymo'. and Syntax*, p. 193. Some recent grammarians, however, retain it ; among whom are Bullions and M'Culloch. Wells retains it, but marks it as, "*Obsolete ;*" as he does also the preterits *bare, clave, drave, gat, slang, spake, span, spat, sware, tare, writ ;* and the participles *hovn, loaden, rid* from *ride, spitten, stricken*, and *writ.* In this he is not altogether consistent. Forms really obsolete belong not to any modern list of irregular verbs ; and even such as are archaic and obsolescent, it is sometimes better to omit. If "*loaden*," for example, is now out of use, why should "*load, unload, and overload*," be placed, as they are by this author, among "irregular verbs ;" while *freight* and *distract*, in spite of *fraught* and *distraught*, are reckoned regular ? "*Rid*," for *rode* or *ridden*, though admitted by Worcester, appears to me a low vulgarism.

‖ *Cleave*, to split, is most commonly, if not always, irregular, as above ; *cleave*, to stick, or adhere, is regular, but *clave* was formerly used in the preterit : as, "The men of Judah *clave* unto their king."—*Samuel.*

¶ Respecting the preterit and the perfect participle of this verb, *drink*, our grammarians are greatly at variance Dr. Johnson says, " preter. *drank* or *drunk* ; part. pass. *drunk* or *drunken*." Dr. Webster : " pret. and pp. *drank.* Old pret. and pp. *drunk* ; pp. *drunken*." Lowth : " pret. *drank* ; part. *drunk* or *drunken*." So Stanford, Webber, and others. Murray has it : " Imperf. *drank*, Perf. Part. *drunk*." So Comly, Lennie, Bullions, Blair, Butler, Frost, Felton, Goldsbury, and many others. Churchill cites the text, " Serve me till I have eaten and *drunken* ;" and observes, "*Drunken* is now used only as an adjective. The *impropriety* of using the preterimperfect [*drank*] for the participle of this verb is very common."—*New Gram.* p. 261. Sanborn gives both forms for the participle,

Present.	Preterit.	Imperfect Participle.	Perfect Participle.
Eat,	ate or ĕat,	eating,	eaten or eat.
Fall,	fell,	falling,	fallen.
Feed,	fed,	feeding,	fed.
Feel,	felt,	feeling,	felt.
Fight,	fought,	fighting,	fought.
Find,	found,	finding,	found.
Flee,	fled,	fleeing,	fled.
Fling,	flung,	flinging,	flung,
Fly,	flew,	flying,	flown.
Forbear,	forbore,	forbearing,	forborne.
Forsake,	forsook,	forsaking,	forsaken.
Get,	got,	getting,	got or gotten.
Give,	gave,	giving,	given.
Go,	went,	going,	gone.
Grow,	grew,	growing,	grown.
Have,	had,	having,	had.
Hear,	heard,	hearing,	heard.
Hide,	hid,	hiding,	hidden or hid.
Hit,	hit,	hitting,	hit.
Hold,	held,	holding,	held.*
Hurt,	hurt,	hurting,	hurt.†
Keep,	kept,‡	keeping,	kept.
Know,	knew,	knowing,	known.
Lead,	led,	leading,	led.
Leave,	left,	leaving,	left.
Lend,	lent,	lending,	lent.
Let,	let,	letting,	let.
Lie,§	lay,	lying,	lain.
Lose,	lost,	losing,	lost.
Make,	made,	making,	made.
Meet,	met,	meeting,	met.
Outdo,	outdid,	outdoing,	outdone.
Put,	put,	putting,	put.
Read,	rĕad,	reading,	rĕad.
Rend,	rent,	rending,	rent.‖
Rid,	rid,	ridding,	rid.
Ride,	rode,	riding,	ridden or rode.
Ring,	rung or rang,	ringing,	rung.
Rise,	rose,	rising,	risen.
Run,	ran or run,	running,	run.

preferring *drunk* to *drunk*. Kirkham prefers *drunk* to *drank*; but contradicts himself in a note, by unconsciously making *drunk* an adjective: "The men were *drunk*; i. e. inebriated. The toasts were *drank*."—*Gram.* p. 149. Cardell, in his Grammar, gives, " *drink, drank, drunk*; " but in his story of Jack Halyard, on page 59, he wrote, "had *drinked*: " and this, according to Fowle's True English Grammar, is not incorrect. The preponderance of authority is yet in favour of saying, " had *drunk*; but *drank* seems to be a word of greater delicacy, and perhaps it is sufficiently authorized. A hundred late writers may be quoted for it, and some that were popular in the days of Johnson. " In the choice of what is fit to be eaten and *drank*."—*Beattie's Moral Science*, Vol. i, p. 51. " Which I had no sooner *drank*."—*Addison, Tatler*, No. 181.
  　　" Thy brother's blood the thirsty earth hath *drank*,
  　　Broach'd with the steely point of Clifford's lance."—*Shakspeare*.
* "*Holden* is not in general use ; and is chiefly employed by attorneys."—*Crombie, on Etymology and Syn.* p. 196. Wells marks this word as, "*Obsolescent*."—*School Gram.* p. 103.
† " I have been found guilty of killing cats I never *hurted*."—*Roderick Random*, Vol. i, p. 8.
‡ " They *keeped* aloof as they passed her bye."—*J. Hogg, Pilgrims of the Sun*, p. 19.
§ *Lie*, to be at rest, is irregular, as above ; but *lie*, to utter falsehood, is regular, as follows : lie, lied, lying, lied.
  　　" Thus said, at least, my mountain guide,
  　　Though deep, perchance, the villain *lied*."—*Scott's Lady of the Lake*.
‖ Perhaps there is authority sufficient to place the verb *rend* among those which are redundant.
  　　" Where'er its cloudy veil was *rended*."—*Whittier's Moll Pitcher*.
  　　" Mortal, my message is for thee ; thy chain to earth is *rended* ;
  　　I bear thee to eternity ; prepare ! thy course is ended."—*The Amulet*.
  　　" Come as the winds come, when forests are *rended*."—*Sir W. Scott*.
  　　" The hunger pangs her sons which *rended*."—*NEW QUARTERLY REVIEW : Examiner*, No. 119.

Present.	Preterit.	Imperfect Participle.	Perfect Participle.
Say,	said,	saying,	said.*
See,	saw,	seeing,	seen.
Seek,	sought,	seeking,	sought.
Sell,	sold,	selling,	sold.
Send,	sent,	sending,	sent.
Set,	set,	setting,	set.
Shed,	shed,	shedding,	shed.
Shoe,	shod,	shoeing,	shod.†
Shoot,	shot,	shooting,	shot.
Shut,	shut,	shutting,	shut.
Shred,	shred,	shredding,	shred.
Shrink,	shrunk *or* shrank,	shrinking,	shrunk.
Sing,	sung *or* sang,‡	singing,	sung.
Sink,	sunk *or* sank,	sinking,	sunk.
Sit,	sat,	sitting,	sat.§
Slay,	slew,	slaying,	slain.
Sling,	slung,	slinging,	slung.
Slink,	slunk *or* slank,	slinking,	slunk.
Smite,	smote,	smiting,	smitten *or* smit.
Speak,	spoke,	speaking,	spoken.
Spend,	spent,	spending,	spent.
Spin,	spun,	spinning,	spun.
Spit,	spit *or* spat,	spitting,	spit *or* spitten.
Spread,	spread,	spreading,	spread.
Spring,	sprung *or* sprang,	springing,	sprung.
Stand,	stood,	standing,	stood.
Steal,	stole,	stealing,	stolen.
Stick,	stuck,	sticking,	stuck.
Sting,	stung,	stinging,	stung.
Stink,	stunk *or* stank,	stinking,	stunk.
Stride,	strode *or* strid,	striding,	stridden *or* strid.‖
Strike,	struck,	striking,	struck *or* stricken.
Swear,	swore,	swearing,	sworn.
Swim,	swum *or* swam,	swimming,	swum.
Swing,	swung *or* swang,	swinging,	swung.
Take,	took,	taking,	taken.

* We find now and then an instance in which *gainsay* is made regular : as, " It can neither be *rivalled* nor *gainsayed*."—*Chapman's Sermons to Presbyterians*, p. 36. Perhaps it would be as well to follow Webster here, in writing *rivaled* with one *l*; and the analogy of the simple verb *say*, in forming this compound irregularly, *gainsaid*. Usage warrants the latter, however, better than the former.

† " Shoe, *shoed* or shod, shoeing, *shoed* or shod."—*Old Gram. by W. Ward*, p. 64 ; and *Fowle's True English Gram*. p. 46.

‡ "A Murray has rejected *sung* as the *Preterit*, and L. Murray has rejected *sang*. Each *Preterit*, however, rests on good authority. The same observation may be made, respecting *sank* and *sunk*. Respecting the *preterits* which have a *a* or *u*, as *slang*, or *slung*, *sank*, or *sunk*, it would be better were the former only to be used, as the *Preterits* and Participle would thus be discriminated."—*Dr. Crombie, on Etymology and Syntax*, p. 199. The *preterits* which this critic thus prefers, are *rang, sang, slang, sprang, swang, sank, shrank, slank, stank, swam*, and *span* for *spun*. In respect to them all, I think he makes an ill choice. According to his own showing, *fling, string*, and *sting*, always make the preterit and the participle alike ; and this is the obvious tendency of the language, in all these words. I reject *slang* and *span*, as derivatives from *sling* and *spin* ; because, in such a sense, they are obsolete, and the words have other uses. Lindley Murray, *in his early editions*, rejected *sang, sank, slang, swang, shrank, slank, stank*, and *span* ; and, at the same time, preferred *rang, sprang*, and *swam*, to *rung, sprung*, and *swum*. In his later copies, he gave the preference to the *u*, in all these words ; but restored *sang* and *sank*, which Crombie names above, still omitting the other six, which did not happen to be mentioned to him.

§ *Sate* for the preterit of *sit*, and *sitten* for the perfect participle, are, in my opinion, obsolete, or no longer in good use. Yet several recent grammarians prefer *sitten* to *sat* ; among whom are Crombie, Lennie, Bullions, and M'Culloch. Dr. Crombie says, " *Sitten*, though formerly in use, is now obsolescent. Laudable attempts, however, have been made to restore it."—*On Etymol. and Syntax*, p. 199. Lennie says. " Many authors, both here and in America, use *sate* as the Past time of *sit* ; but this is improper, for it is apt to be confounded with *sate* to glut. *Sitten* and *spitten* are preferable [to *sat* and *spit*,] though obsolescent."—*Principles of E. Gram*. p. 45. Bullions says, " *Sitten* and *spitten* are nearly obsolete, though preferable to *sat* and *spit*."—*Principles of E. Gram*. p. 64. M'Culloch gives these verbs in the following form : " Sit, sat, sitten *or* sat. Spit, spit *or* spat, spit *or* spitten."—*Manual of E. Gram*. p. 65.

‖ " He will find the political hobby which he has *bestrided* no child's nag."—*The Vanguard, a Newspaper*.
" Through the pressed nostril, spectacle-*bestrid*."—*Cowper*.
" A lank haired hunter *strided*."—*Whittier's Sabbath Scene*.

Present.	Preterit.	Imperfect Participle.	Perfect Participle.
Teach,	taught,	teaching,	taught.
Tear,	tore,	tearing,	torn.
Tell,	told,	telling,	told.
Think,	thought,	thinking,	thought.
Thrust,	thrust,	thrusting,	thrust.
Tread,	trod,	treading,	trodden or trod.
Wear,	wore,	wearing,	worn.
Win,	won,	winning,	won.
Write,	wrote,	writing,	written.*

REDUNDANT VERBS.

A *redundant verb* is a verb that forms the preterit or the perfect participle in two or more ways, and so as to be both regular and irregular; as, *Thrive, thrived* or *throve, thriving, thrived* or *thriven.* Of this class of verbs, there are about ninety-five, beside sundry derivatives and compounds.

OBSERVATIONS.

OBS. 1.—Those irregular verbs which have more than one form for the preterit or for the perfect participle, are in some sense redundant; but, as there is no occasion to make a distinct class of such as have double forms that are never regular, these redundancies are either included in the preceding list of the simple irregular verbs, or omitted as being improper to be now recognized for good English. Several examples of the latter kind, including both innovations and archaisms, will appear among the improprieties for correction, at the end of this chapter. A few old preterits or participles may perhaps be accounted good English in the solemn style, which are not so in the familiar: as, "And none *spake* a word unto him."—*Job,* ii, 13. "When I *brake* the five loaves."—*Mark,* viii, 19. "And he *drave* them from the judgement-seat."—*Acts,* xviii, 16. "Serve me till I have *eaten* and *drunken*."—*Luke,* xvii, 8. "It was not possible that he should be *holden* of it."—*Acts,* ii, 24. "Thou *castedst* them down into destruction."—*Psal.* lxxiii, 18. "Behold, I was *shapen* in iniquity."—*Ib.* li, 5. "A meat-offering *baken* in the oven."—*Leviticus,* ii, 4. "With *casted* slough, and fresh celerity."—SHAK. *Henry V.*
"Thy dreadful vow, *loaden* with death."—ADDISON: *in Joh. Dict.*

OBS. 2.—The verb *bet* is given in Worcester's Dictionary as being always regular: "BET, *v. a.* [*i.* BETTED; *pp.* BETTING, BETTED.] To wager; to lay a wager or bet. SHAK."—*Octavo Dict.* In Ainsworth's Grammar, it is given as being always irregular: "*Present,* Bet; *Imperfect,* Bet; *Participle,* Bet."—Page 36. On the authority of these, and of some others cited in OBS. 6th below, I have put it with the redundant verbs. The verb *prove* is redundant, if *proven,* which is noticed by Webster, Bolles, and Worcester, is an admissible word. "The participle *proven* is used in Scotland and in some parts of the United States, and sometimes, though rarely, in England.—'There is a mighty difference between *not proven* and *disproven.*' DR. TH. CHALMERS. 'Not *proven.*' QU. REV."—*Worcester's Universal and Critical Dict.* The verbs *bless* and *dress* are to be considered redundant, according to the authority of Worcester, Webster, Bolles, and others. Cobbett will have the verbs, *cast, chide, cling, draw, grow, shred, sling, slink, spring, sting, stride, swim, swing,* and *thrust,* to be always regular; but I find no sufficient authority for allowing to any of them a regular form; and therefore leave them, where they always have been, in the list of simple irregulars. These fourteen verbs are a part of the long list of *seventy* which this author says, "are, by some persons, *erroneously* deemed irregular." Of the following *ten* only, is his assertion true; namely, *dip, help, leap, load, overflow, slip, snow, stamp, strip, whip.* These ten ought always to be formed regularly; for all their irregularities may well be reckoned obsolete. After these deductions from this most erroneous catalogue, there remain forty-four other very common verbs, to be disposed of contrary to this author's instructions. All but two of these I shall place in the list of *redundant* verbs; though for the use of *throwed* I find no written authority but his and William B. Fowle's. The two which I do not consider redundant are *spit* and *strew,* of which it may be proper to take more particular notice.

OBS. 3.—*Spit,* to stab, or to put upon a spit, is regular; as, "I *spitted frogs,* I crushed a

---

* In the age of Pope, *writ* was frequently used both for the participle and for the preterit of this verb. It is now either obsolete or peculiar to the poets. In prose it seems vulgar: as, "He *writ* it, at least, published it, in 1670."—*Barclay's Works,* Vol. i, p. 77.
  "He who, supreme in judgement, as in wit,
  Might boldly censure, as he boldly *writ.*"—Pope, *Ess. on Crit.*
Dr. Crombie remarked, more than thirty years ago, that, "*Wrote* as the Participle [of *Write*,] is generally disused, and likewise *writ.*"—*Treatise on Etym. and Synt.* p. 202.

heap of emmets."—*Dryden*. *Spit*, to throw out saliva, is irregular, and most properly formed thus: *spit, spit, spitting, spit*. "*Spat* is obsolete."—*Webster's Dict*. It is used in the Bible; as, "He *spat* on the ground, and made clay of the spittle."—*John*, ix, 6. L. Murray gives this verb thus: "Pres. *Spit*; Imp. *spit, spat*: Perf. Part. *spit, spitten*." NOTE: "*Spitten* is nearly obsolete."—*Octavo Gram*. p. 106. Sanborn has it thus: "Pres. *Spit*; Imp. *spit*; Pres. Part. *spitting*; Perf. Part. *spit, spat*."—*Analytical Gram*. p. 48. Cobbett, at first, taking it in the form, "to *spit*, I *spat, spitten*," placed it among the seventy which he so erroneously thought should be made regular; afterwards he left it only in his list of irregulars, thus: "to *spit*, I *spit, spitten*."—*Cobbett's E. Gram*. of 1832, p. 54. Churchill, in 1823, preferring the older forms, gave it thus: "*Spit, spat* or *spit, spitten* or *spit*."—*New Gram*. p. 111. NOTE:—"Johnson gives *spat* as the preterimperfect, and *spit* or *spitted* as the participle of this verb, when it means to pierce through with a pointed instrument: but in this sense, I believe, it is always regular; while, on the other hand, the regular form is now never used, when it signifies to eject from the mouth; though we find in *Luke*, xviii, 32, 'He shall be *spitted* on.'"—*Churchill's New Gram*. p. 264. This text ought to have been, "He shall be *spit* upon."

OBS. 4.—*To strew* is in fact nothing else than an other mode of spelling the verb *to strow*; as *shew* is an obsolete form for *show*; but if we pronounce the two forms differently, we make them different words. Walker, and some others, pronounce them alike, *stro*: Sheridan, Jones, Jameson, and Webster, distinguish them in utterance, *stroo* and *stro*. This is convenient for the sake of rhyme, and perhaps therefore preferable. But *strew*, I incline to think, is properly a regular verb only, though Wells and Worcester give it otherwise: if *strewn* has ever been proper, it seems now to be obsolete. EXAMPLES: "Others cut down branches from the trees, and *strewed* them in the way."—*Matt*. xxi, 8. "Gathering where thou hast not *strewed*."—*Matt*. xxv, 24.

> "Their name, their years, *spelt* by th' unletter'd *muse*,
> The place of fame and elegy supply:
> And many a *holy text* around she *strews*,
> That teach the rustic moralist to die."—*Gray*.

OBS. 5.—The list which I give below, prepared with great care, exhibits the redundant verbs, as they are now generally used, or as they may be used without grammatical impropriety.[*] Those forms which are supposed to be preferable, and best supported by authorities, are placed first. No words are inserted here, but such as some modern authors countenance. L. Murray recognizes *bereaved, catched, dealed, digged, dwelled, hanged, knitted, shined, spilled*; and, in his early editions, he approved of *bended, builded, creeped, weaved, worked, wringed*. His two larger books now tell us, "The Compiler *has not inserted* such verbs as *learnt, spelt, spilt*, &c. which are improperly terminated by *t*, instead of *ed*."—*Octavo Gram*. p. 107; *Duodecimo*, p. 97. But if he did not, in all his grammars, insert, "*Spill, spilt*, R. *spilt*, R.," (pp. 106, 96,) preferring the irregular form to the regular, somebody else has done it for him. And, what is remarkable, many of his *amenders*, as if misled by some evil genius, have contradicted themselves in precisely the same way! Ingersoll, Fisk, Merchant, and Hart, republish exactly the foregoing words, and severally become "The Compiler" of the same erroneous catalogue! Kirkham prefers *spilt* to *spilled*, and then declares the word to be "*improperly* terminated by *t* instead of *ed*."—*Gram*. p. 151. Greenleaf, who condemns *learnt* and *spelt*, thinks *dwelt* and *spilt* are "the *only established* forms;" yet he will have *dwell* and *spill* to be "*regular*" verbs, as well as "*irregular!*"—*Gram. Simp*. p. 29. Webber prefers *spilled* to *spilt*; but Picket admits only the latter. Cobbett and Sanborn prefer *bereaved, builded, dealed, digged, dreamed, hanged*, and *knitted*, to *bereft, built, dealt, dug, dreamt, hung*, and *knit*. The former prefers *creeped* to *crept*, and *freezed* to *froze*; the latter, *slitted* to *slit, wringed* to *wrung*; and both consider, "I *bended*," "I *bursted*," and "I *blowed*," to be good modern English. W. Allen acknowledges *freezed* and *slided*; and, like Webster, prefers *hove* to *hoven*: but the latter justly prefers *heaved* to both. EXAMP.: "The supple kinsman *slided* to the helm."—*New Timon*. "The rogues *slided* me into the river."—*Shak*. "And the sand *slided* from beneath my feet."—DR. JOHNSON: *in Murray's Sequel*, p. 179. "Wherewith she *freez'd* her foes to congeal'd stone."—*Milton's Comus*, l. 449. "It *freezed* hard last night. Now, what was it that *freezed* so hard?"—*Emmons's Gram*. p. 25. "Far hence lies, ever *freez'd*, the northern main."—*Savage's Wanderer*, l. 57. "Has he not taught, *beseeched*, and *shed* abroad the Spirit unconfined?"—*Pollok's Course of Time*, B. x, l. 275.

OBS. 6.—D. Blair supposes *catched* to be an "erroneous" word and unauthorized: "I *catch'd* it," for "I *caught* it," he sets down for a "*vulgarism*."—*E. Gram*. p. 111. But *catched* is used by some of the most celebrated authors. Dearborn prefers the regular form of *creep*: "*creep, creeped* or *crept, creeped* or *crept*."—*Columbian Gram*. p. 38. I adopt no man's opinions implicitly; copy nothing without examination; but, *to prove all my decisions to be right*, would be an endless task. I shall do as much as ought to be expected, toward showing that they are so. It is to be remembered, that the *poets*, as well as the *vulgar*, use

---

[*] A word is not necessarily *ungrammatical* by reason of having a rival form that is more common. The regular words, *beseeched, blowed, bursted, digged, freezed, bereaved, hanged, meaned, sawed, showed, stringed, weeped*, I admit for good English, though we find them all condemned by some critics.

some forms which a *gentleman* would be likely to avoid, unless he meant to quote or imitate: as,

> "So *clomb* the first grand thief into God's fold;
> So since into his church lewd hirelings climb."—*Milton, P. L.*, B. iv, l. 192.

> "He *shore* his sheep, and, having packed the wool,
> Sent them unguarded to the hill of wolves."—*Pollok, C. of T.*, B. vi, l. 306.

> ——"The King of heav'n
> Bar'd his red arm, and launching from the sky
> His *writhen* bolt, not shaking empty smoke,
> Down to the deep abyss the flaming felon *strook*."—*Dryden.*

OBS. 7.—The following are examples in proof of some of the forms acknowledged below: "Where etiquette and precedence *abided* far away."—*Paulding's Westward-Ho!* p. 6. "But there were no secrets where Mrs. Judith Paddock *abided*."—*Ib.* p. 8. "They *abided* by the forms of government established by the charters."—*John Q: Adams, Oration*, 1831. "I have *abode* consequences often enough in the course of my life."—*Id. Speech*, 1839. "I *awaked* up last of all."—*Ecclus.* xxxiii, 16. "For this are my knees *bended* before the God of the spirits of all flesh."—*Wm. Penn.* "There was never a prince *bereaved* of his dependencies," &c.—*Bacon.* "Madam, you have *bereft* me of all words."—*Shakspeare.* "Reave, *reaved* or *reft*, reaving, *reaved* or *reft.* Bereave is similar."—*Ward's Practical Gram.* p. 65. "And let them tell their tales of woful ages, long ago *betid*."—*Shak.* "Of every nation *blent*, and every age."—*Pollok, C. of T.*, B. vii, p. 153. "I *builded* me houses."—*Ecclesiastes*, ii, 4. "For every house is *builded* by some man; but he that *built* all things is God."—*Heb.* iii, 4. "What thy hands *builded* not, thy wisdom gained."—*Milton's P. L.*, x, 373. "Present, *bet*; Past, *bet*; Participle, *bet.*"—*Mackintosh's Gram.* p. 197; *Alexander's*, 38. "John of Gaunt loved him well, and *betted* much upon his head."—*Shakspeare: Joh. Dict. w. Bet.* "He lost every earthly thing he *betted*."—*Prior: ib.* "A seraph *kneeled.*"—*Pollok, C. T.*, p. 95.

> "At first, he declared he himself would be *blowed*,
> Ere his conscience with such a foul crime he would load."—*J. R. Lowell.*

"They are *catched* without art or industry."—*Robertson's Amer.* Vol. i, p. 302. "Apt to be *catched* and dazzled."—*Blair's Rhet.* p. 26. "The lion being *catched* in a net."—*Art of Thinking*, p. 232. "In their self-will they *digged* down a wall."—*Gen.* xlix, 6. "The royal mother instantly *dove* to the bottom and brought up her babe unharmed."—*Trumbull's America*, i, 144. "The learned have *diven* into the secrets of nature."—*Carnot: Columbian Orator*, p. 82. "They have *awoke* from that ignorance in which they had *slept.*"—*London Encyclopedia.* "And he *slept* and *dreamed* the second time."—*Gen.* xli, 5. "So I *awoke.*"—*Ib.* 21. "But he *hanged* the chief baker."—*Gen.* xl, 22. "Make as if you *hanged* yourself."—*Arbuthnot: in Joh. Dict.* "Graven by art and man's device."—*Acts*, xvii, 29. "*Grav'd* on the stone beneath yon aged thorn."—*Gray.* "That the tooth of usury may be *grinded.*"—*Lord Bacon.* "And he *built* the inner court with three rows of *hewed* stone."—1 *Kings*, vi, 36. "A thing by which matter is *hewed.*"—*Dr. Murray's Hist. of Europ. Lang.* Vol. i, p. 378. "SCAGD or SCAD *meaned* distinction, dividing."—*Ib.* i, 114. "He only *meaned* to acknowledge him to be an extraordinary person."—*Lowth's Gram.* p. 12. "The determines what particular thing is *meaned.*"—*Ib.* p. 11. "If Hermia *mean'd* to say Lysander lied."—*Shak.* "As if I *meaned* not the first but the second creation."—*Barclay's Works*, iii, 289. "From some stones have rivers *bursted* forth."—*Sale's Koran*, Vol. i, p. 14.

> "So move we on; I only *meant*
> To show the reed on which you *leant.*"—*Scott, L. L.*, C. v, st. 11.

OBS. 8.—*Layed*, *payed*, and *stayed*, are now less common than *laid*, *paid*, and *staid*; but perhaps not less correct, since they are the same words in a more regular and not uncommon orthography: "Thou takest up that [which] thou *layedst* not down."—*Friends' Bible, Smith's, Bruce's: Luke*, xix, 21. Scott's Bible, in this place, has "*layest*," which is wrong in tense. "Thou *layedst* affliction upon our loins."—*Friends' Bible: Psalms*, lxvi, 11. "Thou *laidest* affliction upon our loins."—*Scott's Bible, and Bruce's.* "Thou *laidst* affliction upon our loins."—*Smith's Bible, Stereotyped by J. Howe.* "Which gently *lay'd* my knighthood on my shoulder."—*Singer's Shakspeare: Richard II*, Act i, Sc. 1. "But no regard was *payed* to his remonstrance."—*Smollett's England*, Vol. iii, p. 212. "Therefore the heaven over you is *stayed* from dew, and the earth is *stayed* from her fruit."—*Haggai*, i, 10. "STAY, i. STAYED or STAID; pp. STAYING, STAYED or STAID."—*Worcester's Univ. and Crit. Dict.* "Now Jonathan and Ahimaaz *stayed* by En-rogel."—2 *Sam.* xvii, 17. "This day have I *payed* my vows."—*Friends' Bible: Prov.* vii, 14. Scott's Bible has "*paid.*" "They not only *stayed* for their resort, but discharged divers."—*Hayward: in Joh. Dict.* "I *stayed* till the latest grapes were ripe."—*Waller's Dedication.* "To lay is regular, and has in the past time and participle *layed* or *laid.*"—*Lowth's Gram.* p. 54. "To the flood, that *stay'd* her flight."—*Milton's Comus*, l. 832. "All rude, all waste, and desolate is *lay'd.*"—*Rowe's Lucan*, B. ix, l. 1636. "And he smote thrice, and *stayed.*"—2 *Kings*, xiii, 18.

> "When Cobham, generous as the noble peer
> That wears his honours, *pay'd* the fatal price
> Of virtue blooming, ere the storms were *laid.*"—*Shenstone*, p. 167.

OBS. 9.—By the foregoing citations, *lay*, *pay*, and *stay*, are clearly proved to be redundant. But, in nearly all our English grammars, *lay* and *pay* are represented as being always irregular; and *stay* is as often, and as improperly, supposed to be always regular. Other examples in proof of the list: "I *lit* my pipe with the paper."—*Addison*.

"While he whom learning, habits, all prevent,
    Is largely *mulct* for each impediment."—*Crabbe, Bor.* p. 102.
"And then the chapel—night and morn to pray,
    Or *mulct* and threaten'd if he kept away."—*Ib.* p. 162.

"A small space is formed, in which the breath is *pent* up."—*Gardiner's Music of Nature*, p. 493. "*Pen*, when it means to write, is always regular. Boyle has *penned* in the sense of confined."—*Churchill's Gram.* p. 261. "*Rapped* with admiration."—HOOKER: *Joh. Dict.* "And being *rapt* with the love of his beauty."—*Id. ib.* "And *rapt* in secret studies."—SHAK.: *ib.* "I'm *rapt* with joy."—ADDISON: *ib.* "*Roast* with fire."—FRIENDS' BIBLE: *Exod.* xii, 8 and 9. "*Roasted* with fire."—SCOTT's BIBLE: *Exod.* xii, 8 and 9. "Upon them hath the light *shined*."—*Isaiah*, ix, 2. "The earth *shined* with his glory."—*Ezekiel*, xliii, 2. "After that he had *showed* wonders."—*Acts*, vii, 36. "Those things which God before had *showed*."—*Acts*, iii, 18. "As shall be *shewed* in Syntax."—*Johnson's Gram. Com.* p. 28. "I have *shown* you, that the *two first* may be dismissed."—*Cobbett's E. Gram.* ¶ 10. "And in this struggle were *sowed* the seeds of the revolution."—*Everett's Address*, p. 16. "Your favour *showed* to the performance, has given me boldness."—*Jenks's Prayers, Ded.* "Yes, so have I *strived* to preach the gospel."—*Rom.* xv, 20. "Art thou, like the adder, *waxen* deaf?"—*Shakspeare*. "*Hamstring'd* behind, unhappy Gyges died."—*Dryden*. "In Syracusa was I born and *wed*."—*Shakspeare*. "And thou art *wedded* to calamity."—*Id.* "I saw thee first, and *wedded* thee."—*Milton*. "Sprung the rank weed, and *thrived* with large increase."—*Pope*. "Some errors never would have *thriven*, had it not been for learned refutation."—*Book of Thoughts*, p. 34. "Under your care they have *thriven*."—*Junius*, p. 5. "Fixed by being rolled closely, compacted, *knitted*."—*Dr. Murray's Hist.* Vol. i, p. 374. "With kind converse and skill has *weaved*."—*Prior*. "Though I shall be *wetted* to the skin."—*Sandford and Merton*, p. 64. "I *speeded* hither with the very extremest inch of possibility."—*Shakspeare*. "And pure grief *shore* his old thread in twain."—*Id.* "And must I ravel out my *weaved-up* follies?"—*Id. Rich. II.* "Tells how the drudging Goblin *sweet*."—*Milton's L'Allegro.* "Weave, wove or *weaved*, weaving, wove, *weaved*, or woven."—*Ward's Gram.* p. 67.

"Thou who beneath the frown of fate hast stood,
    And in thy dreadful agony *sweat* blood."—*Young*, p. 238.

OBS. 10.—The verb *to shake* is now seldom used in any other than the irregular form, *shake*, *shook*, *shaking*, *shaken*; and, in this form only, is it recognized by our principal grammarians and lexicographers, except that Johnson improperly acknowledges *shook* as well as *shaken* for the perfect participle: as, "I've *shook* it off."—DRYDEN: *Joh. Dict.* But the regular form, *shake*, *shaked*, *shaking*, *shaked*, appears to have been used by some writers of high reputation; and, if the verb is not now properly redundant, it formerly was so. Examples regular: "The frame and huge foundation of the earth *shak'd* like a coward."—SHAKSPEARE: *Hen. IV.* "I am he that is so *love-shaked*."—*Id. As You Like it.* "A sly and constant knave, not to be *shak'd* off."—*Id. Cymbeline: Joh. Dict.* "I thought he would have *shaked* it off."—*Tattler: ib.* "To the very point I *shaked* my head at."—*Spectator*, No. 4. "From the ruin'd roof of *shak'd* Olympus."—*Milton's Poems.* "None hath *shak'd* it off."—*Walker's English Particles*, p. 89. "They *shaked* their heads."—*Psalms*, cix, 25. Dr. Crombie says, "Story, in his Grammar, has, *most unwarrantably*, asserted, that the Participle of this Verb should be *shaked*."—ON ETYMOLOGY AND SYNTAX, p. 198. Fowle, on the contrary, pronounces *shaked* to be right. See *True English Gram.* p. 46.

OBS. 11.—All former lists of our irregular and redundant verbs are, in many respects, defective and erroneous; nor is it claimed for those which are here presented, that they are absolutely perfect. I trust, however, they are much nearer to perfection, than are any earlier ones. Among the many individuals who have published schemes of these verbs, none have been more respected and followed than Lowth, Murray, and Crombie; yet are these authors' lists severally faulty in respect to as many as sixty or seventy of the words in question, though the whole number does not amount to two hundred. By Lowth, eight verbs are made redundant, which I think are now regular only: namely, *bake*, *climb*, *fold*, *help*, *load*, *owe*, *wash*. By Crombie, as many: to wit, *bake*, *climb*, *freight*, *help*, *lift*, *load*, *shape*, *writhe*. By Murray, two: *load* and *shape*. With Crombie, and in general with the others too, twenty-seven verbs are always irregular, which I think are sometimes regular, and therefore redundant: *abide*, *beseech*, *blow*, *burst*, *creep*, *freeze*, *grind*, *lade*, *lay*, *pay*, *rive*, *seethe*, *shake*, *show*, *sleep*, *slide*, *speed*, *string*, *strive*, *strow*, *sweat*, *thrive*, *throw*, *weave*, *weep*, *wind*, *wring*. Again, there are, I think, more than twenty redundant verbs which are treated by Crombie,—and, with one or two exceptions, by Lowth and Murray also—as if they were always regular: namely, *betide*, *blend*, *bless*, *burn*, *dive*, *dream*, *dress*, *geld*, *kneel*, *lean*, *leap*, *learn*, *mean*, *mulct*, *pass*, *pen*, *plead*, *prove*, *reave*, *smell*, *spell*, *stave*, *stay*, *sweep*, *wake*, *whet*, *wont*. Crombie's list contains the auxiliaries, which properly belong to a different table. Erroneous as it is, in all these things, and more, it is introduced by the author with the following praise, in bad English : "*Verbs, which* depart from this rule, are called Irregular, *of which* I believe the subsequent enumeration to be *nearly complete.*"—TREATISE ON ETYM. AND SYNT. p. 192.

OBS. 12.—Dr. Johnson, in his Grammar of the English Tongue, recognizes two forms which would make *teach* and *reach* redundant. But *teached* is now "obsolete," and *rought* is "old," according to his own Dictionary. Of *loaded* and *loaden,* which he gives as participles of *load,* the regular form only appears to be now in good use. For the redundant forms of many words in the foregoing list, as of *abode* or *abided, awaked* or *awoke, besought* or *beseeched, caught* or *catched, hewed* or *hewn, mowed* or *mown, laded* or *laden, seethed* or *sod, sheared* or *shore, sowed* or *sown, waked* or *woke, wove* or *weaved,* his authority may be added to that of others already cited. In Dearborn's Columbian Grammar, published in Boston in 1795, the year in which Lindley Murray's Grammar first appeared in York, no fewer than thirty verbs are made redundant, which are not so represented by Murray. Of these I have retained eighteen in the following list, and left the other twelve to be now considered always regular. The thirty are these : "bake, *bend, build, burn,* climb, *creep, dream,* fold, freight, *geld,* heat, *heave,* help, *lay, leap,* lift, *light,* melt, owe, *quit,* rent, rot, *seethe, spell, split, strive,* wash, *weave, wet, work."* See *Dearborn's Gram.* p. 37—45.

LIST OF THE REDUNDANT VERBS.

Present.	Preterit.	Imperfect Participle.	Perfect Participle.
Abide,	abode *or* abided,	abiding,	abode *or* abided.
Awake,	awaked *or* awoke,	awaking,	awaked *or* awoke.
Belay,	belayed *or* belaid,	belaying,	belayed *or* belaid.
Bend,	bent *or* bended,	bending,	bent *or* bended.
Bereave,	bereft *or* bereaved,	bereaving,	bereft *or* bereaved.
Beseech,	besought *or* beseeched,	beseeching,	besought *or* beseeched.
Bet,	betted *or* bet,	betting,	betted *or* bet.
Betide,	betided *or* betid,	betiding,	betided *or* betid.
Blend,	blended *or* blent,	blending,	blended *or* blent.
Bless,	blessed *or* blest,	blessing,	blessed *or* blest.
Blow,	blew *or* blowed,	blowing,	blown *or* blowed.
Build,	built *or* builded,	building,	built *or* builded.
Burn,	burned *or* burnt,	burning,	burned *or* burnt.
Burst,	burst *or* bursted,	bursting,	burst *or* bursted.
Catch,	caught *or* catched,	catching,	caught *or* catched.
Clothe,	clothed *or* clad,	clothing,	clothed *or* clad.
Creep,	crept *or* creeped,	creeping,	crept *or* creeped.
Crow,	crowed *or* crew,	crowing,	crowed.
✓Curse,	cursed *or* curst,	cursing,	cursed *or* curst.
Dare,	dared *or* durst,	daring,	dared.
Deal,	dealt *or* dealed,	dealing,	dealt *or* dealed.
Dig,	dug *or* digged, .	digging,	dug *or* digged.
Dive,	dived *or* dove,	diving,	dived *or* diven.
Dream,	dreamed *or* dreamt,	dreaming,	dreamed *or* dreamt.
Dress,	dressed *or* drest,	dressing,	dressed *or* drest.
Dwell,	dwelt *or* dwelled,	dwelling,	dwelt *or* dwelled.
Freeze,	froze *or* freezed,	freezing,	frozen *or* freezed.
Geld,	gelded *or* gelt,	gelding,	gelded *or* gelt.
Gild,	gilded *or* gilt,	gilding,	gilded *or* gilt.
Gird,	girded *or* girt,	girding,	girded *or* girt.
Grave,	graved,	graving,	graved *or* graven.
Grind,	ground *or* grinded,	grinding,	ground *or* grinded.
Hang,	hung *or* hanged,	hanging,	hung *or* hanged.
Heave,	heaved *or* hove,	heaving,	heaved *or* hoven.
Hew,	hewed,	hewing,	hewed *or* hewn.
Kneel,	kneeled *or* knelt,	kneeling,	kneeled *or* knelt.
Knit,	knit *or* knitted,	knitting,	knit *or* knitted.
Lade,	laded,	lading,	laded *or* laden.
Lay,	laid *or* layed,	laying,	laid *or* layed.
Lean,	leaned *or* lĕant,	leaning,	leaned *or* lĕant.

Present.	Preterit.	Imperfect Participle.	Perfect Participle.
Leap,	leaped or lĕapt,	leaping,	lĕaped or lĕapt.*
Learn,	learned or learnt,	learning,	learned or learnt.
Light,	lighted or lit,	lighting,	lighted or lit.
Mean,	meant or meaned,	meaning,	meant or meaned.
Mow,	mowed,	mowing,	mowed or mown.
Mulct,	mulcted or mulct,	mulcting,	mulcted or mulct.
Pass,	passed or past,	passing,	passed or past.
·Pay,	paid or payed,	paying,	paid or payed.
Pen, (to coop,)	penned or pent,	penning,	penned or pent.
Plead,	pleaded or pled,	pleading,	pleaded or pled.
Prove,	proved,	proving,	proved or proven.
Quit,	quitted or quit,	quitting,	quitted or quit.†
Rap,	rapped or rapt,	rapping,	rapped or rapt.
Reave,	reft or reaved,	reaving,	reft or reaved.
Rive,	rived,	riving,	riven or rived.
Roast,	roasted or roast,	roasting,	roasted or roast.
Saw,	sawed,	sawing,	sawed or sawn.
Seethe,	seethed or sod,	seething,	seethed or sodden.
Shake,	shook or shaked,	shaking,	shaken or shaked.
Shape,	shaped,	shaping,	shaped or shapen.
Shave,	shaved,	shaving,	shaved or shaven.
·Shear,	sheared or shore,	shearing,	sheared or shorn.
Shine,	shined or shone,	shining,	shined or shone.
Show,	showed,	showing,	showed or shown.
Sleep,	slept or sleeped,	sleeping,	slept or sleeped.
Slide,	slid or slided,	sliding,	slidden, slid, or slided
Slit,	slitted or slit,	slitting,	slitted or slit.
Smell,	smelled or smelt,	smelling,	smelled or smelt.
Sow,	sowed,	sowing,	sowed or sown.
Speed,	sped or speeded,	speeding,	sped or speeded.
Spell,	spelled or spelt,	spelling,	spelled or spelt.
Spill,	spilled or spilt,	spilling,	spilled or spilt.
Split,	split or splitted,	splitting,	split or splitted.‡
Spoil,	spoiled or spoilt,	spoiling,	spoiled or spoilt.
Stave,	stove or staved,	staving,	stove or staved.
Stay,	staid or stayed,	staying,	staid or stayed.
String,	strung or stringed,	stringing,	strung or stringed.
Strive,	strived or strove,	striving,	strived or striven.
Strow,	strowed,	strowing,	strowed or strown.
Sweat,	sweated or sweat,	sweating,	sweated or sweat.
Sweep.	swept or sweeped,	sweeping,	swept or sweeped.
Swell,	swelled,	swelling,	swelled or swollen.
Thrive,	thrived or throve,	thriving,	thrived or thriven.
Throw,	threw or throwed,	throwing,	thrown or throwed.
Wake,	waked or woke,	waking,	waked or woke.
Wax,	waxed,	waxing,	waxed or waxen.
Weave,	wove or weaved,	weaving,	woven or weaved.

* "And the man in whom the evil spirit was, leapt on them."—FRIENDS' BIBLE: Acts, xix, 16. In the Bible, and several others, the word is "leaped." Walker says, "The past time of this verb is generally written with the diphthong short; and if so, it ought to be spelled leapt, rhyming with kept."—Dict. w. Leap. Webster, who improperly pronounces leaped in two ways, "lĕpt or lēpt," misquotes Walker, as saying, "It out'to be spelled lept."—Universal and Critical Dict. w. Leap. In the solemn style, leapèd is, of course, two syllables: for leapedst or leaptst, I know not that either can be found.

† Acquit is almost always formed regularly, thus: acquit, acquitted, acquitting, acquitted. But, like quit, sometimes found in an irregular form also; which, if it be allowable, will make it redundant: as, "To be acquit from my continual smart."—SPENSER: Johnson's Dict. "The writer holds himself acquit of all charges in regard."—Judd, on the Revolutionary War, p. 5.

‡ "Not know my voice! O, time's extremity! Hast thou so crack'd and splitted my poor tongue?"—SHAK.: Com. of E.

Present.	Preterit.	Imperfect Participle.	Perfect Participle.
Wed,	wedded or wed,	wedding,	wedded or wed.
Weep,	wept or weeped,	weeping,	wept or weeped.
Wet,	wet or wetted,	wetting,	wet or wetted.
Whet,	whetted or whet,	whetting,	whetted or whet.*
Wind,	wound or winded,	winding,	wound or winded.
Wont,	wont or wonted,	wonting,	wont or wonted.
Work,	worked or wrought,	working,	worked or wrought.
Wring,	wringed or wrung,	wringing,	wringed or wrung.†

DEFECTIVE VERBS.

A *defective verb* is a verb that forms no participles, and is used in but few of the moods and tenses; as, *beware, ought, quoth.*

OBSERVATIONS.

Obs. 1.—When any of the principal parts of a verb are wanting, the tenses usually derived from those parts are also, of course, wanting. All the auxiliaries, except *do, be,* and *have,* if we compare them with other verbs, are defective ; but, *as auxiliaries,* they lack nothing ; for no complete verb is used throughout as an auxiliary, except *be.* And since an auxiliary differs essentially from a principal verb, the propriety of referring *may, can, must,* and *shall,* to the class of defective verbs, is at least questionable. In parsing there is never any occasion to *call* them defective verbs, because they are always taken together with their principals. And though we may technically say, that their participles are " *wanting,*" it is manifest that none are *needed.*'

Obs. 2.—*Will* is sometimes used as a principal verb, and as such it is regular and complete ; *will, willed, willing, willed :* as, " His Majesty *willed* that they should attend."—*Clarendon.* "He *wills* for them a happiness of a far more exalted and enduring nature."—*Gurney.* "Whether thou *willest* it to be a minister to our pleasure."—*Harris.* "I *will ;* be thou clean."—*Luke,* v, 13. "Nevertheless, not as I *will,* but as thou *wilt.*"—*Matt.* xxvi, 39. "To *will* is present with me."—*Rom.* vii, 18. But *would* is sometimes also a principal verb ; as, "What *would* this man ?"—*Pope.* "*Would* God that all the Lord's people were prophets."—*Numb.* xi, 29. "And Israel *would* none of me."—*Psalm,* lxxxi, 11. If we refer this indefinite preterit to the same root, *will* becomes redundant : *will, willed* or *would, willing, willed.* In respect to time, *would* is less definite than *willed,* though both are called preterits. It is common, and perhaps best, to consider them distinct verbs. The latter only can be a participle : as,

"How rarely does it meet with this time's guise,
When man was *will'd* to love his enemies !"—*Shakspeare.*

Obs. 3.—The remaining defective verbs are only five or six questionable terms, which our grammarians know not well how else to explain ; some of them being now nearly obsolete, and others never having been very proper. *Begone* is a needless coalition of *be* and *gone,* better written separately, unless Dr. Johnson is right in calling the compound an *interjection :* as,

"*Begone !* the goddess cries with stern disdain,
Begone ! nor dare the hallow'd stream to stain."—*Addison.*

Beware also seems to be a needless compound of *be* and the old adjective *ware,* wary, aware, cautious. Both these are, of course, used only in those forms of expression in which *be* is proper ; as, "*Beware* of dogs, beware of evil workers, beware of the concision."—*Philippians,* iii, 2. "But we *must bewaret* of carrying our attention to this beauty too far."—*Blair's Rhet.* p. 119. These words were formerly separated : as, "Of whom *be* thou *ware* also."—1 *Tim.* iv, 15. "They *were ware* of it."—FRIENDS' BIBLE, and ALGER'S: *Acts,* xiii, 6. "They were *aware* of it."—SCOTT'S BIBLE: *ib.* "And in an hour *that* he is not *ware* of him."—*Johnson's Dict. w. Ware.* "And in an hour that he is not *aware* of."—COMMON BIBLES: *Matt.* xxiv, 50. "Bid her well *be ware* and still erect."—MILTON: *in Johnson's Dict.* "That even Silence *was took* ere she *was ware.*"—*Id. Comus,* line 558. The adjective *ware* is now said to be " *obsolete ;*" but the propriety of this assertion depends upon that of forming such a defective verb. What is the use of doing so ?

* *What* is made redundant in Webster's American Dictionary, as well as in Wells's Grammar ; but I can hardly affirm that the irregular form of it is well authorized.

† In S. W. Clark's Practical Grammar, first published in 1847—a work of high pretensions, and prepared expressly " for the education of Teachers "—*sixty-three* out of the foregoing ninety-five Redundant Verbs, are treated as having no regular or no irregular forms. (1.) The following twenty-nine are *omitted* by this author, as if they *were always regular :* belay, bet, betide, blend, bless, curse, dive, dress, geld, lean, leap, learn, mulct, pass, pen, plead, prove, rap, reave, roast, seethe, smell, spoil, stave, stay, wake, wed, whet, wont. (2.) The following thirty-four are *given* by him as being *always irregular ;* abide, bend, beseech, blow, burst, catch, chide, creep, deal, freeze, grind, hang, knit, lade, lay, mean, pay, shake, sleep, slide, speed, spell, spill, split, string, strive, sweat, sweep, thrive, throw, weave, weep, wet, wind. Thirty-two of the ninety-five are made redundant by him, though not so called in his book.

In Wells's School Grammar, " the 113th Thousand," dated 1850, the deficiencies of the foregoing kinds, if I am right, are about fifty. This author's " List of Irregular Verbs" has forty-four Redundants, to which he assigns a regular form as well as an irregular. He is here about as much nearer right than Clark, as this number surpasses thirty-two, and comes towards ninety-five. The words about which they differ, are—*pen, seethe,* and *whet,* of the former number ; and *catch, deal, hang, knit, spell, spill, sweat,* and *thrive,* of the latter.

‡ In the following example, there is a different phraseology, which seems not so well suited to the sense : "But we *must be aware* of imagining, that we render style strong and expressive, by a constant and multiplied use of epithets."—*Blair's Rhet.* p. 281. Here, in stead of " *be aware,*" the author should have said, " *beware,*" or " *be ware :*" that is, be *wary,* or *cautious ;* for *aware* means *apprised,* or *informed,* a sense very different from the other.

"This to disclose is all thy guardian can;
    Beware of all, but most *beware* of man."—*Pope.*

The words written separately will always have the same meaning, unless we omit the preposition *of*, and suppose the compound to be a *transitive* verb. In this case, the argument for compounding the terms appears to be valid; as,

"*Beware* the public *laughter* of the town;
    Thou springst a-leak already in thy crown."—*Dryden.*

OBS. 4.—The words *ought* and *own*, without question, were originally parts of the redundant verb *to owe*; thus: owe, owed or ought, owing, owed or own. But both have long been disjoined from this connexion, and hence owe has become regular. *Own*, as now used, is either a pronominal adjective, as, "my *own* hand," or a regular verb thence derived, as, "to *own* a house." *Ought*, under the name of a *defective verb*, is now generally thought to be properly used, in this one form, in all the persons and numbers of the present and the imperfect tense of the indicative and subjunctive moods. Or, if it is really of one tense only, it is plainly an aorist; and hence the time must be specified by the infinitive that follows: as, "He *ought* to *go*; He *ought* to *have gone*." "If thou *ought* to *go*; If thou *ought* to *have gone*." Being originally a preterit, it never occurs in the infinitive mood, and is entirely invariable, except in the solemn style, where we find *oughtest* in both tenses; as, "How thou *oughtest* to *behave* thyself."—1 *Tim.* iii, 16. "Thou *oughtest* therefore to *have put* my money to the exchangers."—*Matt.* xxiv, 27. We never say, or have said, "He, she, or it, *oughts* or *oughteth*." Yet we manifestly use this verb in the present tense, and in the third person singular; as, "Discourse *ought always to begin* with a clear proposition."—*Blair's Rhet.* p. 217. I have already observed that some grammarians improperly call *ought* an auxiliary. The learned authors of Brightland's Grammar, (which is dedicated to Queen Anne,) did so; and also affirmed that *must* and *ought* "have only the *present time*," and are alike *invariable*. "It is *now* quite obsolete to say, *thou oughtest*; for *ought* now changes its ending no more than *must*."—*Brightland's Gram.*, (approved by Isaac Bickerstaff, Esq.,) p. 112.

"*Do, will*, and *shall, must*, OUGHT, and *may*,
    Have, am, or *be*, this Doctrine will display."—*Ib.* p. 107.

OBS. 5.—*Wis*, preterit *wist*, to know, to think, to suppose, to imagine, appears to be now nearly or quite obsolete; but it may be proper to explain it, because it is found in the Bible: as, "I *wist* not, brethren, that he was the high priest."—*Acts*, xxiii, 5. "He himself *wist* not that his face shone.'"—*Life of Schiller*, p. iv. *Wit*, to know, and *wot*, knew, are also obsolete, except in the phrase *to wit*; which, being taken abstractly, is equivalent to the adverb *namely*, or to the phrase, *that is to say*. The phrase, "*we do you to wit*," (in 2 Cor. viii, 1st,) means, "we *inform* you." Churchill gives the present tense of this verb three forms, *weet, wit*, and *wot*; and there seems to have been some authority for them all: as, "He was, *to weet*, a little roguish page."—*Thomson.* "But little *wotteth* he the might of the means his folly despiseth."—*Tupper's Book of Thoughts*, p. 35. *To wit*, used alone, to indicate a thing spoken of, (as the French use their infinitive, *savoir, à savoir*, or the phrase, *c'est à savoir*,) is undoubtedly an elliptical expression: probably for, "*I give you to wit*;" i. e. "I give you *to know*." *Trow*, to think, occurs in the Bible; as, "I *trow* not."—*N. Test.* And Coar gives it as a defective verb; and only in the first person singular of the present indicative, "*I trow*." Webster and Worcester mark the word as obsolete; but Sir W. Scott, in the Lady of the Lake, has this line:

"Thinkst thou he trow'd thine omen ought?"—*Canto* iv, stanza 10.

Quoth and *quod*, for *say, saith*, or *said*, are obsolete, or used only in ludicrous language. Webster supposes these words to be equivalent, and each confined to the first and third persons of the present and imperfect tenses of the indicative mood. Johnson says, that, "*quoth you*," as used by Sidney, is irregular; but Tooke assures us, that "The *th* in quoth, does not designate the third person."—D. P. ii, 323. They are each invariable, and always placed before the nominative: as, *quoth I, quoth he.*

"Yea, so sayst thou, (*quod* Troylus,) alas!"—*Chaucer.*
    "I feare, *quod* he, it wyll not be."—*Sir T. More.*
    "Stranger, go! Heaven be thy guide!
    Quod the beadsman of Nith-side."—*Burns.*

OBS. 6.—*Methinks*, (i. e., *to me it* thinks,) for I think, or, it seems to me, with its preterit *methought*, (i. e., *to me it* thought,) is called by Dr. Johnson an "ungrammatical word." He imagined it to be "a Norman corruption, the French being apt to confound *me* and *I*."—*Joh. Dict.* It is indeed a puzzling anomaly in our language, though not without some Anglo-Saxon or Latin parallels; and, like its kindred, "me *seemeth*," or "*meseems*," is little worthy to be countenanced, though often used by Dryden, Pope, Addison, and other good writers. Our lexicographers call it an *impersonal verb*, because, being compounded with an objective, it cannot have a nominative expressed. It is nearly equivalent to the adverb *apparently*; and if impersonal, it is also defective; for it has no participles,—no "*methinking*," and no participial construction of "*methought*;" though Webster's Octavo Dictionary absurdly suggests that the latter word may be used as a participle. In the Bible, we find the following text: "*Me thinketh* the running of the foremost is like the running of Ahimaaz."—2 *Sam.* xviii, 27. And Milton improperly makes *thought* an impersonal verb, apparently governing the separate objective pronoun *him*; as,

"*Him thought* he by the brook of Cherith stood."—*P. R.*, B. ii, l. 264.

OBS. 7.—Some verbs from the nature of the subjects to which they refer, are chiefly confined to the third person singular; as, "It *rains*; it *snows*; it *freezes*; it *hails*; it *lightens*; it *thunders*. These have been called *impersonal verbs*; because the neuter pronoun it, which is commonly used before them, does not seem to represent any noun, but, in connexion with the verb, merely to express a state of things. They are however, in fact, neither impersonal nor defective. Some. or all of them, may possibly take some other nominative, if not a different person; as, "The Lord *rained* upon Sodom, and upon Gomorrah, brimstone and fire."—*Gen.* xix, 24. "The God of glory *thundereth*."—*Psalms*, xxix, 3. "*Canst thou thunder* with a voice like him?"—*Job.*

xl, 9. In short, as Harris observes, "The doctrine of Impersonal Verbs has been justly rejected by the best grammarians, both ancient and modern."—*Hermes*, p. 175.

OBS. 8.—By some writers, words of this kind are called *Monopersonal Verbs; that is,* verbs *one person.* This name, though not very properly compounded, is perhaps more fit than the other but we have little occasion to speak of these verbs as a distinct class in our language. Dr. Mur ray says, "What is called an impersonal verb, is not so; for *lic-et, juv-at,* and *opport-et,* have *Tha, that thing.* or *it,* in their composition."—*History of European Languages,* Vol. ii, p. 146 *Ail, irk,* and *behoove,* are regular verbs and transitive; but they are used only in the third person singular: as, "What *ails* you?"—"It *irks* me."—"It *behooves* you." The last two are obsolescent or at least not in very common use. In Latin, *passive* verbs, or neuters of the passive form, are often used impersonally, or without an obvious nominative; and this elliptical construction is sometimes imitated in English, especially by the poets: as,

"Meanwhile, ere thus *was sinn'd* and *judg'd* on earth,
Within the gates of Hell sat Sin and Death. '—*Milton, P. L.,* B. x, l. 230.
"Forthwith on all sides to his aid *was run*
By angels many and strong, who interpos'd."—*Id.* B. vi, l. 335.

LIST OF THE DEFECTIVE VERBS.

Present.	Preterit.	Present.	Preterit.
Beware,	————.	Shall,	should.
Can,	could.	Will,*	would.
May,	might.	Quoth,	quoth.
Methinks,	methought.	Wis,	wist.†
Must,	must.‡	Wit,	wot.
Ought,	ought.‡		

EXAMPLES FOR PARSING.

PRAXIS VI. — ETYMOLOGICAL.

In the Sixth Praxis, it is required of the pupil—to distinguish and define the different parts of speech, and the classes and modifications of the ARTICLES, NOUNS, ADJECTIVES, PRONOUNS, *and* VERBS.

The definitions to be given in the Sixth Praxis, are two for an article, six for noun, three for an adjective, six for a pronoun, seven for a verb finite, five for an infinitive, and one for a participle, an adverb, a conjunction, a preposition, or an interjection. Thus:—

EXAMPLE PARSED.

"The freedom of choice seems essential to happiness; because, properly speaking, that is not our own which is imposed upon us."—*Dillwyn's Reflections,* p. 109.

The is the definite article. 1. An article is the word *the, an,* or *a,* which we put before nouns to limit their signification. 2. The definite article is *the,* which denotes some particular thing or things.

Freedom is a common noun, of the third person, singular number, neuter gender, and nominative case. 1. A noun is the name of any person, place, or thing, that can be known or mentioned. 2. A common noun is the name of a sort, kind, or class, of beings or things. 3. The third person is that which denotes the person or thing merely spoken of. 4. The singular number is that which denotes but one. 5. The neuter gender is that which denotes things that are neither male nor female. 6. The nominative case is that form or state of a noun or pronoun, which denotes the subject of a verb.

Of is a preposition. 1. A preposition is a word used to express some relation of different things or thoughts to each other, and is generally placed before a noun or a pronoun.

Choice is a common noun, of the third person, singular number, neuter gender, and objective case. 1. A noun is the name of any person, place, or thing, that can be known or mentioned. 2. A common noun is the name of a sort, kind, or class, of beings or things. 3. The third person is that which denotes the person or thing merely spoken of. 4. The singular number is that which denotes but one. 5. The neuter gender is that which denotes things that are neither male nor female. 6. The objective case is that form or state of a noun or pronoun, which denotes the object of a verb, participle, or preposition.

Seems is a regular neuter verb, from *seem, seemed, seeming, seemed ;* found in the indicative mood, present tense, third person, and singular number. 1. A verb is a word that signifies *to be, to act,* or *to be acted upon.* 2. A regular verb is a verb that forms the preterit and the perfect participle by assuming *d* or *ed.* 3. A neuter verb is a verb that expresses neither action nor passion, but simply being, or a state of being. 4. The indicative mood is that form of the verb, which simply indicates or declares a thing, or asks a question. 5.

* Dr. Crombie contends that *must* and *ought* are used only in the present tense. (See his *Treatise,* p. 204.) In this he is wrong, especially with regard to the latter word. Lennie, and his copyist Bullions, adopt the same notice ; but Murray, and many others, suppose them to have, both a present and [a] past signification."

† Dr. Crombie says, " This Verb, as an auxiliary, is *inflexible ;* thus we say, 'he *will* go ;' and 'he *wills to* go.'"—*Treatise on Etym. and Syntax,* p. 208. He should have confined his remarks to the *familiar style,* in which all the auxiliaries, except *do, be,* and *have,* are inflexible. For, in the solemn style, we do not say, " Thou *wilt* go," but, " Thou *wilt* go."

‡ "HAD-I-WIST. A proverbial expression, *Oh* that I had known. *Gower.*"—*Chalmer's Dict.* also *Webster's* In this phrase, which is here needlessly compounded, and not very properly explained, we see *wist* used as a *perfect participle.* But the word is obsolete. "*Had I wist,*" is therefore an obsolete phrase, meaning, If I had known, or, "O that I had known."

The *present tense* is that which expresses what now exists, or is taking place. 6. The *third person* is that which denotes the person or thing merely spoken of. 7. The *singular number* is that which denotes but one.

Essential is a common adjective, compared by means of the adverbs; *essential, more essential, most essential; or, essential, less essential, least essential.* 1. An adjective is a word added to a noun or pronoun, and generally expresses quality. 2. A common adjective is any ordinary epithet, or adjective denoting quality or situation. 3. Those adjectives which may be varied in sense, but not in form, are compared by means of adverbs.

To is a preposition. 1. A preposition is a word used to express some relation of different things or thoughts to each other, and is generally placed before a noun or a pronoun.

Happiness is a common noun, of the third person, singular number, neuter gender, and objective case. 1. A noun is the name of any person, place, or thing, that can be known or mentioned. 2. A common noun is the name of a sort, kind, or class, of beings or things. 3. The third person is that which denotes the person or thing merely spoken of. 4. The singular number is that which denotes but one. 5. The neuter gender is that which denotes things that are neither male nor female. 6. The objective case is that form or state of a noun or pronoun which denotes the object of a verb, participle, or preposition.

Because is a conjunction. 1. A conjunction is a word used to connect words or sentences in construction, and to show the dependence of the terms so connected.

Properly is an adverb. 1. An adverb is a word added to a verb, a participle, an adjective, or an other adverb; and generally expresses time, place, degree, or manner.

Speaking is a participle. 1. A participle is a word derived from a verb, participating the properties of a verb, and of an adjective or a noun; and is generally formed by adding *ing, d*, or *ed*, to the verb.

That is a pronominal adjective, not compared; standing for *that thing*, in the third person, singular number, neuter gender, and nominative case. [See Obs. 14th, p. 277.] 1. An adjective is a word added to a noun or pronoun, and generally expresses quality. 2. A pronominal adjective is a definitive word which may either accompany its noun, or represent it understood. 3. The third person is that which denotes the person or thing merely spoken of. 4. The singular number is that which denotes but one. 5. The neuter gender is that which denotes things that are neither male nor female. 6. The nominative case is that form or state of a noun or pronoun, which denotes the subject of a verb.

Is is an irregular neuter verb, from *be, was, being, been;* found in the indicative mood, present tense, third person, and singular number. 1. A verb is a word that signifies *to be, to act,* or *to be acted upon.* 2. An irregular verb is a verb that does not form the preterit and the perfect participle by assuming *d* or *ed.* 3. A neuter verb is a verb that expresses neither action nor passion, but simply being, or a state of being. 4. The indicative mood is that form of the verb, which simply indicates or declares a thing, or asks a question. 5. The present tense is that which expresses what now exists, or is taking place. 6. The third person is that which denotes the person or thing merely spoken of. 7. The singular number is that which denotes but one.

Not is an adverb. 1. An adverb is a word added to a verb, a participle, an adjective, or an other adverb; and generally expresses time, place, degree, or manner.

Our is a personal pronoun, of the first person, plural number, masculine gender, and possessive case. 1. A pronoun is a word used in stead of a noun. 2. A personal pronoun is a pronoun that shows, by its form, of what person it is. 3. The first person is that which denotes the speaker or writer. 4. The plural number is that which denotes more than one. 5. The masculine gender is that which denotes persons or animals of the male kind. 6. The possessive case is that form or state of a noun or pronoun, which denotes the relation of property.

Own is a pronominal adjective, not compared. 1. An adjective is a word added to a noun or pronoun, and generally expresses quality. 2. A pronominal adjective is a definitive word which may either accompany its noun, or represent it understood. 3. Those adjectives whose signification does not admit of different degrees cannot be compared.

Which is a relative pronoun, of the third person, singular number, neuter gender, and nominative case. 1. A pronoun is a word used in stead of a noun. 2. A relative pronoun is a pronoun that represents an antecedent word or phrase, and connects different clauses of a sentence. 3. The third person is that which denotes the person or thing merely spoken of. 4. The singular number is that which denotes but one. 5. The neuter gender is that which denotes things that are neither male nor female. 6. The nominative case is that form or state of a noun or pronoun which denotes the subject of a verb.

Is imposed is a regular passive verb, from the active verb, *impose, imposed, imposing, imposed,*— passive, *to be imposed;* found in the indicative mood, present tense, third person, and singular number. 1. A verb is a word that signifies *to be, to act,* or *to be acted upon.* 2. A regular verb is a verb that forms the preterit and the perfect participle by assuming *d* or *ed.* 3. A passive verb is a verb that represents the subject, or what the nominative expresses, as being acted upon. 4. The indicative mood is that form of the verb which simply indicates or declares a thing, or asks a question. 5. The present tense is that which expresses what now exists, or is taking place. 6. The third person is that which denotes the person or thing merely spoken of. 7. The singular number is that which denotes but one.

Upon is a preposition. 1. A preposition is a word used to express some relation of different things or thoughts to each other, and is generally placed before a noun or a pronoun.

Us is a personal pronoun, of the first person, plural number, masculine gender, and objective case. 1. A pronoun is a word used in stead of a noun. 2. A personal pronoun is a pronoun that shows, by its form, of what person it is. 3. The first person is that which denotes the speaker or writer. 4. The plural number is that which denotes more than one. 5. The masculine gender is that which denotes persons or animals of the male kind. 6. The objective case is that form or state of a noun or pronoun, which denotes the object of a verb, participle, or preposition.

LESSON I. — PARSING.

"He has desires after the kingdom, and makes no question but it shall be his; he wills, runs, strives, believes, hopes, prays, reads scriptures, observes duties, and regards ordinances."—*Penington,* ii, 124.

"Wo unto you, lawyers! for ye have taken away the key of knowledge: ye enter not in yourselves, and them that were entering in ye hindered."—*Luke,* xi, 52.

"Above all other liberties, give me the liberty to know, to utter, and to argue freely, according to my conscience."—*Milton.*

"Eloquence is to be looked for only in free states. Longinus illustrates this observation with a great deal of beauty. 'Liberty,' he remarks, 'is the nurse of true genius; it animates the spirit, and invigorates the hopes, of men; it excites honourable emulation, and a desire of excelling in every art.' "—*Blair's Rhet.* p. 237.

"None of the faculties common to man and the lower animals, conceives the idea of civil liberty, any more than that of religion."—*Spurzheim, on Education,* p. 259.

"Whoever is not able, or does not dare, to think, or does not feel contradictions and absurdities, is unfit for a refined religion and civil liberty."—*Ib.* p. 258.

"The too great number of journals, and the extreme partiality of their authors, have much discredited them. A man must have great talents to please all sorts of readers;

and it is impossible to please all authors, who, generally speaking, cannot bear with the most judicious and most decent criticisms."—*Formey's Belles-Letters*, p. 170.

" Son of man, I have broken the arm of Pharaoh king of Egypt ; and, lo, it shall not be bound up to be healed, to put a roller to bind it, to make it strong to hold the sword."—*Ezekiel*, xxx, 21.

> " Yet he was humble, kind, forgiving, meek,
> Easy to be entreated, gracious, mild ;
> And, with all patience and affection, taught,
> Rebuked, persuaded, solaced, counselled, warned."—*Pollok*, B. ix.

LESSON II.—PARSING.

" What is coming, will come ; what is proceeding onward, verges towards completion."—*Dr. Murray's Europ. Lang.* i, 324. " Sir, if it had not been for the art of printing, we should now have had no learning at all ; for books would have perished faster than they could have been transcribed."—*Dr. Johnson's Life*, iii, 400.

" Passionate reproofs are like medicines given scalding hot : the patient cannot take them. If we wish to do good to those whom we rebuke, we should labour for meekness of wisdom, and use soft words and hard arguments."—*Dodd.*

" My prayer for you is, that God may guide you by his counsel, and in the end bring you to glory : to this purpose, attend diligently to the dictates of his good spirit, which you may hear within you ; for Christ saith, ' He that dwelleth with you, shall be in you.' And, as you hear and obey him, he will conduct you through this troublous world, in ways of truth and righteousness, and land you at last in the habitations of everlasting rest and peace with the Lord, to praise him for ever and ever."—*T. Gurin.*

" By matter, we mean, that which is tangible, extended, and divisible ; by mind, that which perceives, reflects, wills, and reasons. These properties are wholly dissimilar and admit of no comparison. To pretend that mind is matter, is to propose a contradiction in terms ; and is just as absurd, as to pretend that matter is mind."—*Gurney's Portable Evidence*, p. 78.

" If any one should think all this to be of little importance, I desire him to consider what he would think, if vice had, essentially, and in its nature, these advantageous tendencies, or if virtue had essentially the direct contrary ones."—*Butler*, p. 99.

" No man can write simpler and stronger English than the celebrated Boz, and this renders us the more annoyed at those manifold vulgarities and slipshod errors, which unhappily have of late years so disfigured his productions."—LIVING AUTHORS OF ENGLAND : *The Examiner*, No. 119.

> " Here Havard, all serene, in the same strains,
> Loves, hates, and rages, triumphs, and complains."—*Churchill*, p. 3.

> " Let Satire, then, her proper object know,
> And ere she strike, be sure she strike a foe."—*John Brown.*

LESSON III.—PARSING.

" The Author of nature has as truly directed that vicious actions, considered as mischievous to society, should be punished, and has as clearly put mankind under a necessity of thus punishing them, as he has directed and necessitated us to preserve our lives by food."—*Butler's Analogy*, p. 88.

" An author may injure his works by altering, and even amending, the successive editions : the first impression sinks the deepest, and with the credulous it can rarely be effaced ; nay, he will be vainly employed who endeavours to eradicate it."—*Werter*, p. 82.

" It is well ordered, that even the most innocent blunder is not committed with impunity ; because, were errors licensed where they do no hurt, inattention would grow into habit, and be the occasion of much hurt."—*Kames, El. of Crit.* i, 285.

" The force of language consists in raising complete images ; which have the effect to transport the reader, as by magic, into the very place of the important action, and to convert him as it were into a spectator, beholding every thing that passes."—*Id. ib.* ii, 241.

"An orator should not put forth all his strength at the beginning, but should rise and grow upon us, as his discourse advances."—*Blair's Rhet.* p. 309.

"When a talent is given to any one, an account is opened with the giver of it, who appoints a day in which he will arrive and 'redemand his own with usury.'"—*West's Letters to a Young Lady*, p. 74.

"Go, and reclaim the sinner, instruct the ignorant, soften the obdurate, and (as occasion shall demand) cheer, depress, repel, allure, disturb, assuage, console, or terrify."—*Jerningham's Essay on Eloquence*, p. 97.

> "If all the year were playing holydays,
> To sport would be as tedious as to work :
> But when they seldom come, they wish'd-for come,
> And nothing pleaseth but rare accidents."—*Shak. Hen. V.*

"The man that once did sell the lion's skin
While the beast liv'd, was kill'd with hunting him."—*Id. Joh. Dict. w. Beast.*

IMPROPRIETIES FOR CORRECTION.

ERRORS OF VERBS.

LESSON I.—PRETERITS.

"In speaking on a matter which toucht their hearts."—*Philological Museum*, Vol. i, p. 441.

[FORMULE.—Not proper, because the verb *toucht* is terminated in *t*. But, according to Observation 2nd, on the irregular verbs, *touch* is regular. Therefore, this *t* should be changed to *ed*; thus, " In speaking on a matter which *touched* their hearts."]

"Though Horace publisht it some time after."—*Ib.* i, 444. "The best subjects with which the Greek models furnish him."—*Ib.* i, 444. "Since he attacht no thought to it." —*Ib.* i, 645. "By what slow steps the Greek alphabet reacht its perfection."—*Ib.* i, 651. "Because Goethe wisht to erect an affectionate memorial."—*Ib.* i, 469. "But the Saxon forms soon dropt away."—*Ib.* i, 668. "It speaks of all the towns that perisht in the age of Philip."—*Ib.* i, 252. "This enricht the written language with new words."—*Ib.* i, 668. "He merely furnisht his friend with matter for laughter."—*Ib.* i, 479. "A cloud arose and stopt the light."—*Swift's Poems*, p. 313. "She slipt *spadills* in her breast."—*Ib.* p. 371. "I guest the hand."—*Ib.* p. 372. "The tyrant stript me to the skin : My skin he flay'd, my hair he cropt; At head and foot my body lopt."—*Ib. On a Pen*, p. 338. "I see the greatest owls in you, That ever screecht or ever flew."—*Ib.* p. 403. "I sate with delight, From morning till night."—*Ib.* p. 367. "Dick nimbly skipt the gutter."—*Ib.* p. 375. "In at the pantry door this morn I slipt."—*Ib.* p. 369. "Nobody living ever toucht me, but you."—*Walker's Particles*, p. 92. "*Present*, I ship; *Past*, I shipped or shipt; *Participle*, shipped or shipt."— *Murray the schoolmaster, Gram.* p. 31. "Then the king arose, and tare his garments."—*2 Sam.* xiii, 31. "When he lift up his foot, he knew not where he should set it next."—*Bunyan.* "He lift up his spear against eight hundred, whom he slew at one time."—*2 Sam. : in Joh. Dict.* "Upon this chaos rid the distressed ark."—*BURNET : ib.* "On whose foolish honesty, my practices rid easy."—*SHAK. : ib.* "That form of the first or primogenial Earth, which rise immediately out of chaos."—*BURNET : ib.* "Sir, how come it you have holp to make this rescue?"—*SHAK. : in Joh. Dict.* "He sware he had rather lose all his father's images than that table."—*PREACHAM : ib.* "When our language dropt its ancient terminations."— *Dr. Murray's Hist.* ii, 5. "When themselves they vilify'd."—*Milton, P. L.*, xi, 515. "But I choosed rather to do thus."—*Barclay's Works*, i, 456. "When he plead against the parsons."—*School History*, p. 168. "And he that saw it, bear record."—*Cutler's Gram*, p. 72. "An irregular verb has one more variation, as drive, drivest, drives, drivedst, drove, driving, driven."—*REV. MATT. HARRISON, on the English Language*, p. 260. "Beside that village Hannibal pitcht his camp."—*Walker's Particles*, p. 79. "He fetcht it even from Tmolus."—*Ib.* p. 114. "He supt with his morning gown on."—*Ib.* p. 285. "There stampt her sacred name." —*Barlow's Columbiad*, B. i, l. 233.

> "Fixt on the view the great discoverer stood,
> And thus addrest the messenger of good."—*Barlow*, B. i, l. 658.

LESSON II.—MIXED.

"Three freemen were being tried at the date of our last information."—*Newspaper.*

[FORMULE.—Not proper, because the participle *being* is used after its own verb *were*. But, according to Observation 4th, on the compound form of conjugation, this complex passive form is an absurd innovation. Therefore, the expression should be changed; thus, " Three freemen *were on trial*"—or, " *were receiving their trial*— at the date of our last information."]

"While the house was being built, many of the tribe arrived."—*Ross Cox's Travels*, p. 102.

"But a foundation has been laid in Zion, and the church is being built upon it."—*The Friend*, ix, 377. "And one fourth of the people are being educated."—*East India Magazine.* "The present, or that which is now being done."—*Beck's Gram.* p. 13. "A new church, called the Pantheon, is just being completed in an expensive style."—*G. A. Thompson's Guatemala*, p. 467. "When I last saw him, he was grown considerably."—*Murray's Key*, p. 223 ; *Merchant's*, 198. "I know what a rugged and dangerous path I am got into."—*Duncan's Cicero*, p. 83. "You were as good preach ease to one on the rack."—*Locke's Essay*, p. 285. "Thou hast heard me, and art become my salvation."—*Psal.* cxviii, 21. "While the Elementary Spelling-Book was being prepared for the press."—*L. Cobb's Review*, p. vi. "Language is become, in modern times, more correct and accurate."—*Jamieson's Rhet.* p. 16. "If the plan have been executed in any measure answerable to the author's wishes."—*Robbins's Hist.* p. 3. "The vial of wrath is still being poured out on the seat of the beast."—*Christian Experience*, p. 409. "Christianity was become the generally adopted and established religion of the whole Roman Empire."—*Gurney's Essays*, p. 35. "Who wrote before the first century was elapsed."—*Ib.* p. 13. "The original and analogical form is grown quite obsolete."—*Lowth's Gram.* p. 56. "Their love, and their hatred, and their envy, are perished."—*Murray's Gram.* i, 149. "The poems were got abroad and in a great many hands."—*Pref. to Waller.* "It is more harmonious, as well as more correct, to say, 'the bubble is almost bursted."—*Cobbett's E. Gram.* ¶ 109. "I drave my suitor from his mad humour of love."—*Shak.* "Se viriliter expedivit. (*Cicero.*) He hath plaid the man."—*Walker's Particles*, p. 214. "Wilt thou kill me, as thou diddest the Egyptian yesterday?"—*Friends' Bible* : *Acts*, vii, 28. "And we, methoughts, look'd up t'him from our hill."—*Cowley's Davideis*, B. iii, l. 386. "I fear thou doest not think as much of best things as thou oughtest."—*Memoir of M. C. Thomas*, p. 34. "When this work was being commenced."—*Wright's Gram.* p. 10. "Exercises and Key to this work are being prepared."—*Ib.* p. 12. "James is loved, or being loved by John."—*Ib.* p. 64. "Or that which is being exhibited."—*Ib.* p. 77. "He was being smitten."—*Ib.* 78. "In the passive state we say, 'I am being loved.'"—*Ib.* p. 80. "Subjunctive Mood : If I am being smitten, If thou art being smitten, If he is being smitten."—*Ib.* p. 100. "I will not be able to convince you how superficial the reformation is."—*Chalmers's Sermons*, p. 88. "I said to myself, I will be obliged to expose the folly."—*Chazotte's Essay*, p. 3. "When Clodius, had he meant to return that day to Rome, must have been arrived."—*Adams's Rhetoric*, i, 418. "That the fact has been done, is being done, or shall or will be done."—*O. B. Peirce's Gram.* pp. 347 and 356. "Am I being instructed?"—*Wright's Gram.* p. 70. "I am choosing him."—*Ib.* p. 112. "John, who was respecting his father, was obedient to his commands."—*Barrett's Revised Gram.* p. 69. "The region echos to the clash of arms."—*Beattie's Poems*, p. 63.

"And sitt' st on high, and mak'st creation's top
Thy footstool ; and behold'st below thee, all."—*Pollok*, B. vi, l. 663.

"And see if thou can'st punish sin, and let
Mankind go free. Thou fail'st—be not surprised."—*Id.* B. ii, l. 118.

LESSON III.—MIXED.

"What follows, had better been wanting altogether."—*Blair's Rhet.* p. 201.

[FORMULE.—Not proper, because the phrase *had better been*, is used in the sense of the potential pluperfect. But, according to Observation 17th, on the conjugations, this substitution of one form for another is of questionable propriety. Therefore, the regular form should here be preferred ; thus, "What follows, *might better have been* wanting altogether."]

"This member of the sentence had much better have been omitted altogether."—*Ib.* p. 212. "One or [the] other of them, therefore, had better have been omitted."—*Ib.* p. 212. "The whole of this last member of the sentence had better have been dropped."—*Ib.* p. 112. "In this case, they had much better be omitted."—*Ib.* p. 173. "He had better have said 'the productions.'"—*Ib.* p. 220. "The Greeks have ascribed the origin of poetry to Orpheus, Linus, and Musæus."—*Ib.* p. 377. "It has been noticed long ago, that all these fictitious names have the same number of syllables."—*Phil. Museum*, i, 471. "When I found that he had committed nothing worthy of death, I have determined to send him."—*Acts*, xxv, 25. "I had rather be a door-keeper in the house of my God."—*Ps.* lxxxiv, 10. "As for such, I wish the Lord open their eyes."—*Barclay's Works*, iii, 263. "It would a made our passidge over the river very difficult."—*Walley, in 1692.* "We should not a been able to have carried our great guns."—*Id.* "Others would a questioned our prudence, if we had." See *Hutchinson's Hist. of Mass.* i, 478. "Beware thou bee'st not BECÆSAR'D ; i. e. Beware that thou dost not dwindle into a mere Cæsar."—*Harris's Hermes*, p. 183. "Thou raisedest thy voice to record the stratagems of needy heroes."—ARBUTHNOT : *in Joh. Dict. w. Scalade.* "Life hurrys off apace : thine is almost up already."—*Collier's Antoninus*, p. 19. "'How unfortunate has this accident made me !' crys such a one."—*Ib.* p. 60. "The muse that soft and sickly wooes the ear."—*Pollok*, i, 13. "A man were better relate himself to a statue."—*Bacon.* "I heard thee say but now, thou lik'dst not that."—*Shak.* "In my whole course of wooing, thou cried'st, *Indeed !*"—*Id.* "But our ears are

grown familiar with *I have wrote, I have drank,* &c., which are altogether as ungrammatical."
—*Lowth's Gram.* p. 63; *Churchill's,* 114. "The court was sat before Sir Roger came."—
Addison, Spect. No. 122. "She need be no more with the jaundice possest."—*Swift's Poems,*
p. 346. "Besides, you found fault with our victuals one day that you was here."—*Ib.* p. 333.
"If spirit of other sort, So minded, have o'erleap'd these earthly bounds."—*Milton,* P. L.,
B. iv, 1. 582. "It should have been more rational to have forborn this."—*Barclay's Works,*
Vol. iii, p. 265. "A student is not master of it till he have seen all these."—*Dr. Murray's
Life,* p. 55. "The said justice shall summons the party."—*Brevard's Digest.* "Now what
is become of thy former wit and humour?"—*Spect.* No. 532. "Young stranger, whither
wand'rest thou?"—*Burns,* p. 29. "SUBJ.: *Pres.* If I love, If thou lovest, If he love. *Imp.*
If I loved, If thou lovedst, If he loved."—*Merchant's Gram.* p. 51. "SUBJ.: If I do not love,
If thou dost not love, If he does not love;" &c.—*Ib.* p. 56. "If he have committed sins, they
shall be forgiven him."—*James,* v, 15. "Subjunctive Mood of the verb *to call,* second person
singular: If Thou callest. If Thou calledst. If Thou hast called. If Thou hadst called.
If Thou call. If Thou shalt or wilt have called."—*Hiley's Gram.* p. 41. "Subjunctive Mood
of the verb *to love,* second person singular: If thou love. If thou do love. If thou lovedst.
If thou didst love. If thou hast loved. If thou hadst loved. If thou shalt or wilt love.
If thou shalt or wilt have loved."—*Bullions's E. Gram.* p. 46. "I was; thou wast, or you
was; he, she, or it was: We, you or ye, they, were."—*White, on the English Verb,* p. 51.
"I taught, thou taughtedst, he taught."—*Coar's English Gram.* p. 66. "We say, *if it
rains, suppose it rains,* lest *it should rain,* unless *it rains.* This manner of speaking is called
the SUBJUNCTIVE mode."—*Weld's Gram.* 2d Ed. p. 72; Abridged Ed. 59. "He is arrived at
what is deemed the age of manhood."—*Priestley's Gram.* 163. "He had much better have
let it alone."—*Tooke's Diversions,* i, 43. "He were better be without it."—*Locke, on Education,* p. 105. "Hadest not thou been by."—*Beauties of Shak.* p. 107. "I learned geography,
Thou learnedest arithmetick. He learned grammar."—*Fuller's Gram.* p. 34. "Till the
sound is ceased."—*Sheridan's Elocution,* p. 126. "Present, die; Preterit, died; Perf. Participle, dead."—*British Gram.* p. 158; *Buchanan's,* 58; *Priestley's,* 48; *Ash's,* 45; *Fisher's,*
71; *Bicknell's,* 73.

"Thou bowed'st thy glorious head to none, feared'st none."—*Pollok,* B. viii, l. 603.
"Thou look'st upon thy boy as though thou guessedst it."—*N. A. Reader,* p. 320.
"As once thou slept'st, while she to life was form'd."—*Milt. P. L.,* B. xi, l. 369.
    "Who finds the partridge in the puttock's nest,
    But may imagine how the bird was dead?"—*Shak.: Joh. Dict.*
"Which might have well becom'd the best of men."—*Id. Ant. and Cleop.*

CHAPTER VII.—PARTICIPLES.

A Participle is a word derived from a verb, participating the properties of a
verb, and of an adjective or a noun; and is generally formed by adding *ing,
d,* or *ed,* to the verb: thus, from the verb *rule,* are formed three participles,
two simple and one compound; as, 1. *ruling,* 2. *ruled,* 3. *having ruled.*

OBSERVATIONS.

OBS. 1.—Almost all verbs and participles seem to have their very essence in *motion,* or
the privation of motion—in *acting,* or *ceasing to act.* And to all motion and rest, *time* and *place*
are necessary concomitants; nor are the ideas of *degree* and *manner* often irrelevant. Hence
the use of *tenses* and of *adverbs.* For whatsoever comes to pass, must come to pass *sometime* and *somewhere;* and, in every event, something must be affected *somewhat* and
somehow. Hence it is evident that those grammarians are right, who say, that "all participles *imply time.*" But it does not follow, that the *English* participles *divide* time, like the
tenses of a verb, and *specify* the period of action; on the contrary, it is certain and manifest,
that they do not. The phrase, "*men labouring,*" conveys no other idea than that of *labourers at work;* it no more suggests the *time,* than the *place, degree,* or *manner,* of their work.
All these circumstances require *other words* to express them; as, "Men now here *awkwardly*
labouring *much* to little purpose." Again: "*Thenceforward* will men, *there* labouring *hard*
and *honourably,* be looked down upon by dronish lordlings."

OBS. 2.—Participles retain the *essential meaning* of their verbs; and, *like* verbs, are either
active-transitive, active-intransitive, passive, or *neuter,* in their signification. For this reason,
many have classed them with the verbs. But their *formal meaning* is obviously different.
They convey no affirmation, but usually relate to nouns or pronouns, *like adjectives,* except
when they are joined with auxiliaries to form the compound tenses of their verbs; or when
they have in part the nature of substantives, like the Latin gerunds. Hence some have injudiciously ranked them with the adjectives. The most discreet writers have commonly

assigned them a separate place among the parts of speech; because, in spite of all opposite usages, experience has shown that it is expedient to do so.

OBS. 3.—According to the doctrine of Harris, all words denoting the *attributes* of things, are either verbs, or participles, or adjectives. Some attributes have their essence in motion : as, *to walk, to run, to fly, to strike, to live* ; or, *walking, running, flying, striking, living*. Others have it in the privation of motion : as, *to stop, to rest, to cease, to die* ; or, *stopping, resting, ceasing, dying*. And there are others which have nothing to do with either motion or its privation ; but have their essence in the quantity, quality, or situation of things : as, *great* and *small, white* and *black, wise* and *foolish, eastern* and *western*. These last terms are adjectives ; and those which denote motion or its privation, are either verbs or participles, according to their formal meaning ; that is, according to their manner of attribution. See *Hermes*, p. 95. Verbs commonly say or affirm something of their subjects ; as, "*The babe wept.*" Participles suggest the action or attribute without affirmation ; as, "*A babe weeping,*"—"*An act regretted.*"

OBS. 4.—A verb, then, being expressive of some attribute, which it ascribes to the thing or person named as its subject ; of time, which it divides and specifies by the tenses ; and also, (with the exception of the infinitive,) of an assertion or affirmation ; if we take away the affirmation and the distinction of tenses, there will remain the attribute and the general notion of time ; and these form the essence of an English participle. So that a participle is something less than a verb, though derived immediately from it ; and something more than an adjective, or mere attribute, though its manner of attribution is commonly the same. Hence, though the participle by rejecting the idea of time may pass almost insensibly into an adjective, and become truly a participial adjective ; yet the participle and the adjective are by no means one and the same part of speech, as some will have them to be. There is always an essential difference in their meaning. For instance : there is a difference between *a thinking man* and *a man thinking* ; between *a bragging fellow* and *a fellow bragging* ; between *a fast-sailing ship* and *a ship sailing fast*. A thinking man, a bragging fellow, or a fast-sailing ship, is contemplated as being habitually or permanently such ; a man thinking, a fellow bragging, or a ship sailing fast, is contemplated as performing a particular act ; and this must embrace a period of *time*, whether that time be specified or not. John Locke was a *thinking man* ; but we should directly contradict his own doctrine, to suppose him *always thinking*.

OBS. 5.—The English participles are all derived from the *roots* of their respective verbs, and do not, like those of some other languages, take their names from the *tenses*. On the contrary, they are reckoned among the principal parts in the conjugation of their verbs, and many of the tenses are formed from them. In the compound forms of conjugation, they are found alike *in all the tenses*. They do not therefore, of themselves, express any particular time ; but they denote the state of the being, action, or passion, in regard to its progress or completion. This I conceive to be their principal distinction. Respecting the participles in *Latin*, it has been matter of dispute, whether those which are called the *present* and the *perfect*, are really so in respect to time or not. Sanctius denies it. In *Greek*, the distinction of tenses in the participles is more apparent ; yet even here the time to which they refer, does not always correspond to their names. See remarks on the Participles in the *Port Royal Latin and Greek Grammars.*

OBS. 6.—Horne Tooke supposes our participles in *ed* to express time past, and those in *ing* to have no signification of time. He says, " I did not mean to deny the adsignification of time to *all* the participles ; though I continue to withhold it from that which is called the *participle present.*"—*Diversions of Purley*, Vol. ii, p. 415. Upon the same point, he afterwards adds, " I am neither new nor singular : for Sanctius both asserted and proved it by numerous instances in the Latin. Such as, ' Et *abfui proficiscens* in Græciam.' *Cicero*. ' Sed postquam amans *accessit* pretium pollicens.' *Terent*. ' Ultro ad eam *venies indicans* te amare.' *Terent*. ' Turnum *fugientem* hæc terra videbit.' *Virg*."—*Tooke's Div*. ii, 420. Again : " And thus I have given you my opinion concerning what is called the *present participle*. Which I think improperly so called ; because I take it to be merely the simple verb *adjectived*, without any adsignification of *manner* or *time*."—*Tooke's Div*. Vol. ii, p. 423.

OBS. 7.—I do not agree with this author, either in limiting participles in *ed* to time past, or in denying all signification of time to those in *ing* ; but I admit that what is commonly called the *present participle*, is not very properly so denominated, either in English or in Latin, or perhaps in any language. With us, however, this participle is certainly, in very many instances, something else than " merely the simple verb *adjectived*." For, in the first place, it is often of a complex character, as *being loved, being seen*, in which two verbs are " *adjectived*" together, and that by different terminations. Yet do these words as perfectly coalesce in respect to time, as to everything else ; and *being loved* or *being seen* is confessedly as much a " *present*" participle, as *being*, or *loving*, or *seeing*—neither form being solely confined to what now is. Again, our participle in *ing* stands not only for the present participle of the Latin or Greek grammarians, but also for the Latin gerund, and often for the Greek infinitive used substantively ; so that by this ending, the English verb is not only *adjectived*, but also *substantived*, if one may so speak. For the participle when governed by a preposition, partakes not of the qualities "of a verb and an *adjective*," but rather of those of a verb and a *noun*.

CLASSES.

English verbs, not defective, have severally three participles ;[*] which have been very variously denominated, perhaps the most accurately thus : the *Imperfect*, the *Perfect*, and the *Preperfect*. Or, as their order is undisputed, they may be conveniently called the *First*, the *Second*, and the *Third*.

I. The *Imperfect participle* is that which ends commonly in *ing*, and implies a *continuance* of the being, action, or passion : as, *being, acting, ruling, loving, defending, terminating*.

II. The *Perfect participle* is that which ends commonly in *ed* or *en*,and implies a *completion* of the being, action, or passion : as, *been, acted, ruled, loved, defended, terminated*.

III. The *Preperfect participle* is that which takes the sign *having*, and implies a *previous completion* of the being, action, or passion : as, *having loved, having seen, having written ; having been loved, having been writing, having been written*.

The *First* or *Imperfect* Participle, when simple, is always formed by adding *ing* to the radical verb ; as, *look, looking :* when compound, it is formed by prefixing *being* to some other simple participle ; as, *being reading, being read, being completed*.

The *Second* or *Perfect* Participle is always simple, and is regularly formed by adding *d* or *ed* to the radical verb : those verbs from which it is formed otherwise, are either irregular or redundant.

The *Third* or *Preperfect* Participle is always compound, and is formed by prefixing *having* to the perfect, when the compound is double, and *having been* to the perfect or the imperfect, when the compound is triple : as, *having spoken, having been spoken, having been speaking*.

OBSERVATIONS.

Obs. 1.—Some have supposed that both the simple participles denote present *time ;* some have supposed that the one denotes present, and the other, past time ; some have supposed that the first denotes no time, and the second, time past ; some have supposed that neither has any regard to time ; and some have supposed that both are of *all* times. In regard to the distinction of *voice*, or the manner of their signification, some have supposed the one to be active, and the other to be passive ; some have supposed the participle in *ing* to be active or neuter, and the other active or passive ; and some have supposed that either of them may be active, passive, or neuter. Nor is there any more unanimity among grammarians, in respect to the participles. Hence several different names have been loosely given to each of the participles : and sometimes with manifest impropriety ; as when Buchanan, in his conjugations, calls *being*, "Active,"—and *been, having been, having had*, "Passive." Learned men may differ in opinion respecting the nature of words, but grammar can never well deserve the name of *science*, till at least an ordinary share of reason and knowledge appears in the language of those who teach it.

Obs. 2.—The First participle has been called the Present, the Progressive, the Imperfect, the Simple Imperfect, the Indefinite, the Active, the Present Active, the Present Passive, the Present Neuter, and, in the passive voice, the Preterimperfect, the Compound

---

[*] That is, passive verbs, as well as others, have three participles for each ; so that, from one active-transitive root, there come *six* participles—three active, and three passive. Those numerous grammarians who, like Lindley Murray, make passive verbs a distinct class, for the most part, very properly state the participles of a verb to be "*three ;*" but, to represent the two voices as modifications of one species of verbs, and then say, "The Participles are *three*," as many recent writers do, is manifestly absurd ; *because two threes should be six*. Thus, for example, Dr. Bullions : "In English [,] the *transitive* verb has always *two voice*, the Active and [the] Passive."—*Prin. of E. Gram.* p. 38. "The Participles are *three*, [;] the Present, the *Perfect*, and the *Compound Perfect*."—*P.* T. 57. Again : "*Transitive* verbs have two voices, called the *Active* and the *Passive*."—*Bullions's Analytical Pract. Gram.* p. 66. Verbs have *three* participles—the *present*, the *past*, and the *perfect* ; as, *loving, loved, having loved*, in the active voice : AND *being loved, loved, having been loved*, in the passive."—*Ib.* p. 76. Now either not all these are the participles of *one* verb, or that verb has *more than three*. Take your choice. Redundant verbs usually have *duplicate forms* of all the participles except the Imperfect Active ; as, *lighting, lighted* or *lit, having lighted* or *having lit ;* so again, *being lighted* or *being lit, lighted* or *lit, having been lighted* or *having been lit*.

Imperfect, the Compound Passive, the Passive.   The SECOND, which, though it is always but *one word*, some authors treat as being *two participles*, or *three*, has been called the Perfect, the Preter, the Preterperfect, the Imperfect, the Simple Perfect, the Past, the Simple past, the Preterit, the Passive, the Present Passive, the Perfect Active, the Past Active, the Auxiliary Perfect, the Perfect Passive, the Perfect Neuter, the Simple Perfect Active, the Simple Perfect Passive.   The THIRD has been called the Compound, the Compound Active, the Compound Passive, the Compound Perfect, the Compound Perfect Active, the Compound Perfect Passive, the Compound Preter, the Present, the Present Perfect, the Past, the Past Compound, the Compound Past, the Prior-perfect, the Prior-present, the Perfect, the Pluperfect, the Preterperfect, the Preperfect.*   In teaching others to speak and write well, it becomes us to express our doctrines in the most suitable terms ; but the application of a name is of no great consequence, so that the thing itself be rightly understood by the learner.   Grammar should be taught in a style at once neat and plain, clear and brief.   Upon the choice of his terms, the writer of this work has bestowed much reflection ; yet he finds it impossible either to please everybody, or to explain, without intolerable prolixity, all the reasons for preference.

OBS. 3.—The participle in *ing* represents the action or state as *continuing* and ever *incomplete ;* it is therefore rightly termed the IMPERFECT participle : whereas the participle in *ed* always, or at least usually, has reference to the action as *done* and *complete ;* and is, by proper contradistinction, called the PERFECT participle.   It is hardly necessary to add, that the terms *perfect* and *imperfect*, as thus applied to the English participles, have no reference

* The diversity in the *application* of these names, and in the number or nature of the participles recognised in different grammars, is quite as remarkable as that of the names themselves.   To prepare a general synopsis of this discordant teaching, no man will probably think it worth his while.   The following are a few examples of it :

1. " How many Participles, are there ; There are two, the Active Participle which ends in (ing), as burning, and the Passive Participle which ends in (ed) as, burned."—*The British Grammar*, p. 140.   In this book, the participles of *Be* are named thus : "ACTIVE.   Being.   PASSIVE.   Been, having been."—*Ib.* p. 188.

2. " How many *Sorts* of Participles are there ? *A.* Two ; the Active Participle, that ends always in *ing* ; as, *loving*, and the Passive Participle, that ends always in *ed, t, or n ;* as, *loved, taught, slain.*"—*Fisher's Practical New Gram.* p. 75.

3. "ACTIVE VOICE.   *Participles.* Present, calling.   Past, having called.   Future, being about to call.   PASSIVE VOICE.   Present, being called.   Past, having been called.   Future, being about to be called."—*Ward's Practical Gram.* pp. 55 and 59.

4. ACT. " Present, loving ; Perfect, loved ; Past, having loved."—*Lowth's Gram.* p. 89.   The participles *passive* are not given by Lowth ; but, by inference from his rule for forming " the passive verb," they must be these : " Present, being loved ; Perfect, loved, or been loved ; Past. having been loved." See *Lowth's Gram.* p. 44.

5. "ACT. V. *Present,* Loving.   Past, Loved.   *Perfect,* Having loved.   PAS. V. *Pres.* Being loved.   *Past.* Loved.   *Perf.* Having been loved."—*Lennie's Gram.* pp. 25 and 33 ; *Bullions's Analyt. and Pract, Gram.* 37 and 95.   This is Bullions's *revised* scheme. and much worse than his former one copied from Murray.

6. ACT. "*Present.* Loving.   *Perfect.* Loved.   *Compound Perfect,* Having loved." PAS. "*Present.* Being loved.   *Perfect or Passive.* Loved.   *Compound Perfect.* Having been loved."—*L. Murray's late editions,* pp. 98 and 99 ; *Hart's Gram.* 85 and 88 ; *Bullions's Principles of E. Gram.* pp. 47 and 55.   No form or name of the first participle passive was adopted by Murray in his early editions.

7. ACT. " *Present.* Pursuing.   Perfect.   Pursued.   Compound perfect.   Having pursued." PAS. "*Present and Perfect.* Pursued, or being pursued.   Compound Perfect.   Having been pursued."—*Rev. W. Allen's Gram.* pp. 92 and 93   Here the first two passive forms, and their names too, are thrown together ; the former as equivalents, the latter as coalescents.

8. " TRANSITIVE. *Pres.* Loving, *Perf.* Having loved.   PASSIVE. *Pres.* Loved or Being loved, *Perf.* Having been loved."—*Parkhurst's Gram. for Beginners*, p. 110.   Here the second active form is wanting ; and the second passive is confounded with the first.

9. ACT. " *Imperfect,* Loving [;] *Perfect,* Having loved [.]" PAS. "*Imperfect,* Being loved [;] *Perfect,* Loved, Having been loved."—*Wells's School Gram.* pp. 99 and 101.   Here, too, the second active is not given ; the third is called by the name of the second ; and the second passive is confounded with the *third*, as if they were but forms of the same thing.

10. ACT. "*Imperfect,* (*Present,*) Loving.   *Perfect,* Having loved.   *Auxiliary Perfect,* Loved." PAS. "*Imperfect,* (*Present,*) Being loved.   *Perfect,* Having been loved.   *Passive,* Loved."—*N. Butler's Pract. Gram.* pp. 84 and 91.   Here the common order of most of the participles is very improperly disturbed, and as many are misnamed.

11. ACT. " *Present,* Loving [;] *Perfect,* Loved [;] Comp. *Perf.* Having loved [.] " PAS. " *Present,* Being loved [;] *Perfect,* Loved, or been loved [;] *Compound Perfect,* Having been loved."—*Frazee's Improved Gram.* 68 and 73.   Here the second participle passive has two forms, one of which, " *been loved,*" is not commonly recognised, except as part of some passive verb or preperfect participle.

12. ACT. V. "*Imperfect,* Seeing.   *Perfect,* Seen.   *Compound,* Having seen." PAS. V. "*Preterimperfect,* Being seen.   *Preterperfect,* Having been seen."—*Churchill's New Gram.* p. 102.   Here the chief and radical passive participle is lacking, and neither of the compounds is well named.

13. ACT. "*Present,* Loving, [;] *Past,* Loved, [;] *Com. Past,* Having loved." PAS. "*Present,* Being loved. [;] *Past,* Loved. [;] *Com. Past.* [,] Having been loved."—*Felton's Analyt. and Pract. Gram.*, of 1843, pp. 37 and 60.

14. ACT. " *Present.* [,] Loving. [;] Perfect. Loved. Compound Perfect. Having loved." PAS. " Perfect or Passive. Loved   Compound Perfect. Having been loved."—*Bicknell's Gram. Lond.* 1790, Part I, pp. 66 and 70 ; *L. Murray's* 2d *Edition*, York, 1796, pp. 72 and 77.   Here "*Being loved,*" is not noticed.

15. "*Participles. Active Voice. Present.* Loving.   *Past.* Loved, or having loved.   *Participles. Passive Voice. Present.* Being loved.   *Past.* Having been loved."—*John Burn's Practical Gram.* p. 70.   Here the chief Passive term, "Loved," is omitted, and two of the active forms are confounded.

16. "*Present,* loving, *Past,* loved, *Compound*, having loved."—*S. W. Clark's Practical Gram.* of 1848, p. 71.   "ACT. VOICE.—*Present* ... Loving [;] *Compound* [,] Having loved ...... Having been *loving.*"—*Ib.* p. 81.   "PAS. VOICE.— *Present* ..... Loved, or, being loved [;] *Compound* ..... Having been loved [:] *Compound* ..... Having been loved."—*Ib.* p. 88.   "Th Compound Participle consists of *the* Participle of a principal verb, added to the word *having*, or *being*, or to the two words *having been.*   Examples — Having loved—*being loved*— having been loved."—*Ib.* p. 71.   Here the second extract is *deficient*, as may be seen by comparing it with the first ; and the fourth is *grossly erroneous*, as is shown by the third.   The participles, too, are misnamed throughout.

The reader may observe that the *punctuation* of the foregoing examples is very discrepant.   I have, in brackets, suggested some corrections, but have not attempted a general adjustment of it.

to *time*, or to those *tenses* of the verb which are usually (but not very accurately) named by these epithets. The terms *present* and *past*, which some still prefer to *imperfect* and *perfect*, do denote *time*, and are in a kind of oblique contradistinction; but how well they apply to the participles, may be seen by the following texts: "God *was* in Christ, *reconciling* the world unto himself."—"We pray you in Christ's stead, *be* ye *reconciled* to God."—St. Paul: 2 *Cor.* v, 19, 20. Here *reconciling* refers to the death of Christ, and *reconciled*, to the desired conversion of the Corinthians; and if we call the former a *present* participle, and the latter a *past*, we nominally reverse the order of time in respect to the events, and egregiously misapply both terms.

Obs. 4.—Though the participle in *ing* has, by many, been called the *Present* participle, it is as applicable to past or future, as to present time; otherwise, such expressions as, "I *had been writing*,"—"I *shall be writing*," would be solecisms. It has also been called, almost as frequently, the *Active* participle. But it is not always active, even when derived from an active verb; for such expressions as, "The goods are *selling*,"—"The ships are now *building*," are in use, and not without good authority: as, "And hope to allay, by rational discourse, the pain of his joints *tearing* asunder."—*Locke's Essay*, p. 285. "Insensible of the designs now *forming* by Philip."—*Goldsmith's Greece*, ii, 48. "The improved edition now *publishing*."—Bp. Halifax: *Pref. to Butler*. "The present tense expresses an action now *doing*."—*Emmons's Gram.* p. 40. The distinguishing characteristic of this participle is, that it denotes an unfinished and progressive state of the being, action, or passion; it is therefore properly denominated the Imperfect participle. If the term were applied with reference to *time*, it would be no more objectionable than the word *present*, and would be equally supported by the usage of the Greek linguists. I am no more inclined to "*innovation*," than are the pedants who, for the choice here made, have ignorantly brought the false charge against me. This name, authorized by Beattie and Pickbourn, is approved by Lindley Murray,* and adopted by several of the more recent grammarians. See the works of Dr. Crombie, J. Grant, T. O. Churchill, R. Hiley, B. H. Smart, M. Harrison, and G. Lewis, published in London; and J. M. M'Culloch's Grammar, published in Edinburgh; also some American grammars, as E. Hazen's, N. Butler's, D. B. Tower's, W. H. Wells's, the Sanderses'.

Obs. 5.—The participle in *ed*, as is mentioned above, usually denotes a *completion* of the being, action, or passion, and should therefore be denominated the Perfect participle. But this completion may be spoken of as present, past, or future; for the participle itself has no tenses, and makes no distinction of time, nor should the name be supposed to refer to the perfect tense. The conjugation of any passive verb, is a sufficient proof of all this: nor is the proof invalidated by resolving verbs of this kind into their component parts. Of the participle in *ed* applied to *present* time, the following is an example: "Such a course would be less likely to produce injury to health, than the *present course pursued* at our colleges."—*Literary Convention*, p. 118. Tooke's notion of grammatical time, appears to have been in several respects a strange one: he accords with those who call this a *past* participle, and denies to the other not only the name and notion of *a tense*, but even the *general idea* of time. In speaking of the old participial termination *and* or *ende*, †which our Anglo-Saxon ancestors used where we write *ing*, he says, "I do not allow that there are any *present* participles, or any *present tense* of the verb."‡—*Diversions of Purley*, Vol. ii, p. 41.

Obs. 6.—The *Perfect* participle of transitive verbs, being used in the formation of passive verbs, is sometimes called the *Passive* participle. It usually has in itself a passive signification, except when it is used in forming the compound tenses of the active verb. Hence the difference between the sentences, "I have written a letter," and, "I have a letter writ-

---

* "The *most unexceptionable* distinction *which* grammarians make between the participles, is, that the one points to the continuation of the action, passion, or state denoted by the verb; and the other, to the completion of it. Thus, the present participle signifies *imperfect* action, or action begun and not ended: as, 'I am *writing* a letter.' The past participle signifies action *perfected*, or finished: as, 'I have *written* a letter.'—'The letter is written.'"—*Murray's Grammar*, 8vo, p. 65. "The first [participle] expresses a *continuation*; the other, a *completion*."—*W. Allen's Grammar*, 12mo, London, 1813. "The idea which this participle [e. g. '*tearing*'] really expresses, is simply that of the *continuance* of an action in an *incomplete* or *unfinished* state. The action may belong to time *present*, to time *past*, or to time *future*. The participle which denotes the *completion* of an action, as *torn*, is called the *perfect* participle; because it represents the action as *perfected* or *finished*."—*Barnard's Analytic Gram.* p. 51. Emmons stealthily copies from my Institutes as many as ten lines in defence of the term '*Imperfect*,' and yet, in his conjugations, he calls the participle in *ing*, "*Present*." This seems inconsistent. See his "*Grammatical Instructer*," p. 61.

† "The ancient termination (from the Anglo-Saxon) was *and*; as, 'His *schynand* sword.' Douglas. And sometimes *ende*; as, 'She, betwene the deth and life, *Swounende* lay full othe.' Gower."—*W. Allen's Gram.* p. 88. "The present Participle, in Saxon, was formed by *ande*, *ende*, or *onde*; and, by cutting off the final *e*, it acquired a Substantive signification, and extended the idea to the agent: as, *alysende*, freeing, and *alysend*, a redeemer. *freonde*, loving or friendly, and *freond*, a lover or a friend."—*Booth's Introd. to Dict.* p. 76.

‡ William B. Fowle, a modern disciple of Tooke, treats the subject of grammatical time rather more strangely than his master. Thus: "How many times or tenses have verbs? *Two*, [the] present and [the] *past*." To this he immediately adds in a note: "We *do not believe* in a past any more than a future tense of verbs."—*The True English Gram.* p. 80. So, between these two authors, our verbs will retain no tenses at all. Indeed, by his two tenses, Fowle only meant to recognize the two simple forms of an English verb. For he says, in an other place, "We repeat our conviction that no verb in itself expresses time of any sort."—*Ib.* p. 69.

ten ; " the former being equivalent to *Scripsi literas*, and the latter to *Sunt mihi literæ scripta*. But there are many perfect participles which cannot with any propriety be called passive. Such are all those which come from intransitive or neuter verbs ; and also those which so often occur in the tenses of verbs not passive. I have already noticed some instances of this misnomer ; and it is better to preclude it altogether, by adhering to the true name of this participle, THE PERFECT. Nor is that entirely true which some assert, " that this participle in the *active* is only found in combination ;" that, " Whenever it stands alone to be parsed as a Participle, it is passive."—*Hart's English Gram.* p. 75. See *Bullions's Analyt. and Pract. Gram.* p. 77. " Rebelled," in the following examples, cannot with any propriety be called a *passive* participle :

> " *Rebelled*, did I not send them terms of peace,
> Which not my justice, but my mercy asked ? "—*Pollok*, x, 253.
> " Arm'd with thy might, rid Heav'n of these *rebell'd*,
> To their prepar'd ill mansion driven down."—*Milton*, vi, 737.

OBS. 7.—The third participle has most generally been called the *Compound* or the *Compound perfect*. The latter of these terms seems to be rather objectionable on account of its length ; and against the former it may be urged that, in the compound forms of conjugation, the first or imperfect participle is a compound : as, *being writing, being seen*. Dr. Adam calls *having loved* the *perfect* participle *active*, which he says must be rendered in Latin by the *pluperfect* of the subjunctive ; " as, he having loved, *quum amavisset ;*" (*Lat. and Eng. Gram.* p. 140 ;) but it is manifest that the perfect participle of the verb *to love*, whether active or passive, is the simple word *loved*, and not this compound. Dr. Adam, in fact, if he denies this, only contradicts himself ; for, in his paradigms of the English Active Voice, he gives the participles as two only, and both simple, thus : "*Present*, Loving ; *Perfect*, Loved : "—"*Present*, Having ; *Perfect*, Had." So of the Neuter Verb : "*Present*, Being ; *Perfect*, Been."—*Ib.* pp. 81 and 82. His scheme of either names or forms is no model of accuracy. On the very next page, unless there is a misprint in several editions, he calls the *Second* participle the " *imperfect ;*" saying, "The whole of the passive voice in English is formed by the auxiliary verb *to be*, and the participle *imperfect* ; as, *I am loved, I was loved, &c.*" Further : " In many verbs," he adds, " the *present* participle also is used in a passive sense ; as, *These things are doing, were doing*, &c. ; *The house is building, was building, &c.*"—*Ib.* p. 83. N. Butler, in his Practical Grammar, of 1845, names, and counts, and orders, the participles very oddly : " Every verb," he says, " has *two* participles—the *imperfect* and the *perfect*."—P. 78. Yet, for the verb *love*, he finds these six ; two " IMPERFECT, *Loving* and *Being loved ;*" two " PERFECT, *Having loved* and *Having been loved ;*" one " AUXILIARY PERFECT, *Loved*," of the "*Active Voice ;*" and one " PASSIVE, *Loved*," of the " *Passive Voice.*" Many old writers erroneously represent the participle in *ing* as always active, and the participle in *ed* or *en* as always passive ; and some, among whom is Buchanan, making no distinction between the simple perfect *loved* and the compound *having loved*, place the latter with the former, and call it passive also. The absurdity of this is manifest : for *having loved* or *having seen* is active ; *having been* or *having sat* is neuter ; and *having been loved* or *having been seen* is passive. Again, the triple compound, *having been writing*, is active ; and *having been sitting* is neuter ; but if one speak of goods as *having been selling* low, a similar compound is passive.

OBS. 8.—Now all the compound participles which begin with *having* are essentially alike ; and, as a class of terms, they ought to have a name adapted to their nature, and expressive of their leading characteristic. *Having loved* differs from the simple participle *loved*, in signification as well as in form ; and, if this participle is to be named with reference to its *meaning*, there is no more suitable term for it, than the epithet PREPERFECT,—a word which explains itself, like *prepaid* or *prerequisite*. Of the many other names, the most correct one is PLUPERFECT,— which is a term of very nearly the same meaning. Not because this compound is really of the pluperfect *tense*, but because it always denotes being, action, or passion, that is, or was, or will be, *completed before* the doing or being of something else ; and, of course, when the latter thing is represented as past, the participle must correspond to the pluperfect tense of its verb ; as, " *Having explained* her views, it was necessary she should expatiate on the vanity and futility of the enjoyments promised by Pleasure."—*Jamieson's Rhet.* p. 181. Here *having explained* is exactly equivalent to *when she had explained*. Again : " I may say, *He had commanded*, and we obeyed ; or, *He having commanded*, we obeyed."—*Felch's Comprehensive Gram.* p. ix. Here the two phrases in Italics correspond in import, though not in construction.

OBS. 9.—*Pluperfect* is a derivative contracted from the Latin *plusquam-perfectum*, and literally signifies *more than complete*, or *beyond the perfect ;* i. e., (as confirmed by use,) *antecedently finished*, or *completed before*. It is the usual name of our fourth tense ; is likewise applicable to a corresponding tense in other tongues ; and is a word familiar to every scholar. Yet several grammarians,—too ready, perhaps, for innovation,—have shown their willingness to discard it altogether. Bullions, Butler, Hiley, Perley, Wells, and some others, call the English pluperfect *tense*, the *past-perfect*, and understand either epithet to mean—" *completed at* or *before* a certain *past* time ;" (*Bullions's E. Gram.* p. 39 ;) that is—

"*finished or past, at* some *past* time."—*Butler's Pract. Gram.* p. 72. The relation of the *tense* is *before the past,* but the epithet *pluperfect* is not necessarily limited to this relation, any more than what is *perfect* is necessarily past. Butler has urged, that, "*Pluperfect* does not mean *completed before,*" but is only "a technical name of a particular tense;" and, arguing from this erroneous assumption, has convinced himself, "It would be as correct to call this the *second future* participle as the *pluperfect.*"—*Ib.* p. 79. The technical name, as limited to the past, is *preterpluperfect,* from the older term *præteritum plusquam perfectum;* so *preterperfect,* from *præteritum perfectum,* i. e. *past perfect,* is the name of an *other* tense, now called the *perfect:* wherefore the substitution of *past-perfect* for *pluperfect* is the less to be commended. There may be a convenience in having the name of the tense to differ from that of the participle, and this alone induces me to prefer *preperfect* to *pluperfect* for the name of the latter.

OBS. 10.—From the participle in *ed* or *en,* we form three tenses, which the above-named authors call *perfect ;*—"the *present-perfect,* the *past-perfect,* and the *future-perfect ;*"—as, *have seen, had seen, will have seen.* Now it is, doubtless, the *participle,* that gives to these their *perfectness ;* while diversity in the auxiliaries makes their difference of time. Yet it is assumed by Butler, that, in general, the simple participle in *ed* or *en,* "does not denote an action *done* and *completed,*" and is not to be called *perfect ;* (p. 80 ;)—that, "If we wish to express by a participle, an action *completed at any time,* we use the compound form, and *this is* THE *perfect participle ;*" (p. 79 ;)— that, "*The characteristic* of the participle in *ed* is, that it implies the *reception* of an action ;" (p. 79 ;)—that, hence, it should be called *the passive,* though it "is *usually* called the *perfect* participle ;" (p. 79 ;) —that, "The use of *this participle* in the *perfect tenses* of the active voice should not be taken into consideration in giving it a name or a definition ;" (p. 80 ;)—that its *active, neuter,* or *intransitive* use is not a primitive idiom of the language, but the result of a gradual *change* of the term from the passive to the active voice ; (p. 80 ;)—that, "the participle *has changed* its mode of signification, so that, instead of being passive, it is now active in sense ;" (p. 105 ;)—that, "having changed its original meaning so entirely, it should not be considered *the same* participle ;" (p. 78 ;)—that, "in such cases, it is *a perfect* participle," and, "for the sake of distinction [,] this may be called the *auxiliary perfect* participle."—*Ib.* These speculations I briefly throw before the reader, without designing much comment upon them. It will be perceived that they are, in several respects, contradictory one to an other. The author himself names the participle in reference to a usage which he says, "should not be taken into consideration ;" and names it absurdly too ; for he calls that "the *auxiliary,*" which is manifestly the *principal* term. He also identifies as one what he professes to distinguish as two.

OBS. 11.—Participles often become *adjectives,* and are construed before nouns to denote quality. The terms so converted form the class of *participial adjectives.* Words of a participial form may be regarded as adjectives, under the following circumstances : 1. When they reject the idea of time, and denote something customary or habitual, rather than a transient act or state ; as, "A *lying* rogue,"—i. e., one addicted to lying. 2. When they admit adverbs of comparison ; as, "A *more learned* man." 3. When they are compounded with something that does not belong to the verb ; as, "*unfeeling, unfelt :*" there is no verb *to unfeel ;* therefore these words cannot be participles. Adjectives are generally placed before their nouns ; participles, after them. The words beginning with *un,* in the following lines may be classed with participial adjectives :

"No king, no subject was ; unscutcheoned all ;
Uncrowned, unplumed, unhelmed, unpedigreed ;
Unlaced, uncoroneted, unbestarred."—*Pollok, C. of T.,* B. viii, l. 89.

OBS. 12.—Participles in *ing* often become *nouns.* When preceded by an article, an adjective or a noun or pronoun of the possessive case, they are construed as nouns ; and, if wholly such, have neither adverbs nor active regimen : as, "He laugheth at *the shaking* of a spear."—*Job,* xli, 29. "There is *no searching* of *his understanding.*"—*Isaiah,* xl, 28. "In *their setting* of their threshold by my threshold."—*Ezekiel,* xliii, 8. "That any man should make *my glorying* void."—1 *Cor.* ix, 15. The terms so converted form the class of *verbal* or *participial nouns.* But some late authors—(J. S. Hart, S. S. Greene, W. H. Wells, and others—) have given the name of participial nouns to many *participles,*—such participles, often, as retain all their verbal properties and adjuncts, and merely partake of some syntactical resemblance to nouns. Now, since the chief characteristics of such words are from the verb, and are incompatible with the specific nature of a noun, it is clearly improper to call them *nouns.* There are, in the popular use of participles, certain mixed constructions which are reprehensible ; yet it is the peculiar nature of a *participle,* to participate the properties of other parts of speech,—of the verb and adjective,—of the verb and noun,—or sometimes, perhaps, of all three. A participle immediately preceded by a preposition, is not converted into a noun, but remains a participle, and therefore retains its adverb, and also its government of the objective case ; as, "I thank you *for helping him so seasonably.*" Participles in this construction correspond with the Latin gerund, and are sometimes called *gerundives.*

Obs. 13.—To distinguish the participle from the participial noun, the learner should observe the following four things: 1. Nouns take articles and adjectives before them; participles, as such, do not. 2. Nouns may govern the possessive case before them, but not the objective after them; participles may govern the objective case, but not so properly the possessive. 3. Nouns, if they have adverbs, require the hyphen; participles take adverbs separately, as do their verbs. 4. Participial nouns express actions as things, and are sometimes declined like other nouns; participles usually refer actions to their agents or recipients, and have in English no grammatical modifications of any kind.

Obs. 14.—To distinguish the perfect participle from the preterit of the same form, observe *the sense*, and see which of the auxiliary forms will express it: thus, *loved* for *being loved*, is a participle; but *loved* for *did love*, is a preterit verb. So *held* for *did hold*, *stung* for *did sting*, *taught* for *did teach*, and the like, are irregular verbs; but *held* for *being held*, *stung* for *being stung*, *taught* for *being taught*, and the like, are perfect participles.

Obs. 15.—Though the English participles have no inflections, and are consequently incapable of any grammatical agreement or disagreement, those which are simple, are sometimes elegantly taken in a plural sense, with the apparent construction of *nouns*; but, under these circumstances, they are in reality neither nouns nor participles, but participial adjectives construed elliptically, as other adjectives often are, and relating to plural nouns understood. The ellipsis is sometimes of a singular noun, though very rarely, and much less properly. Examples: "To them who are *the called* according to his purpose."—*Rom.* x, 28. That is—" the called *ones* or *persons*." "God is not the God of *the dead*, but of *the living*." —*Matt.* xxii, 32. " Neither is it found in the land of *the living*."—*Job*, xxviii, 13. "*The living, the living, he* shall praise thee, as I do this day."—*Isaiah*, xxxviii, 19. "Till we are made fit to live and reign with him and *all his redeemed*, in the heavenly glory forever."—*Jenks's Prayers*, p 18.

> " *Ye blessed* of my Father, come, *ye just*,
>   Enter the joy eternal of your Lord."—*Pollok*, B. x, l. 591.
> "Depart from me, *ye cursed*, into the fire
>   Prepared eternal in the gulf of Hell."—*Id.* B. x, l. 449.

EXAMPLES FOR PARSING.

PRAXIS VII.—ETYMOLOGICAL.

In the Seventh Praxis it is required of the pupil—to distinguish and define the different parts of speech, and the classes and modifications of the ARTICLES, NOUNS, ADJECTIVES, PRONOUNS, VERBS, *and* PARTICIPLES.

The definitions to be given in the Seventh Praxis, are two for an article, six for a noun, three for an adjective, six for a pronoun, seven for a verb finite, five for an infinitive, two for a participle,—and one for an adverb, a conjunction, a preposition, or an interjection. Thus:—

EXAMPLE PARSED.

" Religion, rightly understood and practised, has the purest of all joys attending it."

Religion is a common noun, of the third person, singular number, neuter gender, and nominative case. 1. A noun is the name of any person, place, or thing, that can be known or mentioned. 2. A common noun is the name of a sort, kind, or class, of beings or things. 3. The third person is that which denotes the person or thing merely spoken of. 4. The singular number is that which denotes but one. 5. The neuter gender is that which denotes things that are neither male nor female. 6. The nominative case is that form or state of a noun or pronoun, which denotes the subject of a verb.

Rightly is an adverb. 1. An adverb is a word added to a verb, a participle, an adjective, or an other adverb; and generally expresses time, place, degree, or manner.

Understood is a perfect participle, from the irregular active-transitive verb, *understand, understood, sometimes understanding, understood*. 1. A participle is a word derived from a verb, participating the properties of a verb, and of an adjective or a noun; and is generally formed by adding *ing*, *d*, or *ed*, to the verb. 2. The perfect participle is that which ends commonly in *ed* or *en*, and implies a completion of the being, action, or passion.

And is a conjunction. 1. A conjunction is a word used to connect words or sentences in construction, and to show the dependence of the terms so connected.

Practised is a perfect participle, from the regular active-transitive verb, *practise, practised, practising, practised*. 1. A participle is a word derived from a verb, participating the properties of a verb, and of an adjective or a noun; and is generally formed by adding *ing*, *d*, or *ed*, to the verb. 2. The perfect participle is that which ends commonly in *ed* or *en*, and implies a completion of the being, action, or passion.

Has is an irregular active-transitive verb, from *have, had, having, had*; found in the indicative mood, present tense, third person, and singular number. 1. A verb is a word that signifies *to be*, *to act*, or *to be acted upon*. 2. An irregular verb is a verb that does not form the preterit and the perfect participle by assuming *d* or *ed*. 3. An active-transitive verb is a verb that expresses an action which has some person or thing for its object. 4. The indicative mood is that form of the verb, which simply indicates or declares a thing, or asks a question. 5. The present tense is that which expresses what now exists, or is taking place. 6. The third person is that which denotes the person or thing merely spoken of. 7. The singular number is that which denotes but one.

The is the definite article. 1. An article is the word *the*, *an*, or *a*, which we put before nouns to limit their signification. 2. The definite article is *the*, which denotes some particular thing or things.

Purest is a common adjective, of the superlative degree; compared regularly, *pure, purer, purest*. 1. An adjective is a word added to a noun or pronoun, and generally expresses quality. 2. A common adjective is any ordinary epithet, or adjective denoting quality or situation. 3. The superlative degree is that which is *most* or *least* of all included with it.

Of is a preposition. 1. A preposition is a word used to express some relation of different things or thoughts to each other, and is generally placed before a noun or a pronoun.
All is a pronominal adjective, not compared. 1. An adjective is a word added to a noun or pronoun, and generally expresses quality. 2. A pronominal adjective is a definitive word which may either accompany its noun or represent it understood. 3. Those adjectives whose signification does not admit of different degrees, cannot be compared.
Joys is a common noun, of the third person, plural number, neuter gender, and objective case. 1. A noun is the name of any person, place, or thing, that can be known or mentioned. 2. A common noun is the name of a sort, kind, or class, of beings or things. 3. The third person is that which denotes the person or thing merely spoken of. 4. The plural number is that which denotes more than one. 5. The neuter gender is that which denotes things that are neither male nor female. 6. The objective case is that form or state of a noun or pronoun, which denotes the object of a verb, participle, or preposition.
Attending is an imperfect participle, from the regular active-transitive verb, *attend, attended, attending, attended.* 1. A participle is a word derived from a verb, participating the properties of a verb, and of an adjective or a noun; and is generally formed by adding *ing, d,* or *ed,* to the verb. 2. The imperfect participle is that which ends commonly in *ing,* and implies a continuance of the being, action, or passion.
It is a personal pronoun, of the third person, singular number, neuter gender, and objective case. 1. A pronoun is a word used in stead of a noun. 2. A personal pronoun is a pronoun that shows, by its form, of what person it is. 3. The third person is that which denotes the person or thing merely spoken of. 4. The singular number is that which denotes but one. 5. The neuter gender is that which denotes things that are neither male nor female. 6. The objective case is that form or state of a noun or pronoun, which denotes the object of a verb, participle, or preposition.

LESSON I.—PARSING.

"A Verb is a word whereby something or other is represented as existing, possessing, acting, or being acted upon, at some particular time, past, present, or future; and this in various manners."—*White, on the English Verb,* p. 1.

" Error is a savage, lurking about on the twilight borders of the circle illuminated by truth, ready to rush in and take possession, the moment her lamp grows dim."—*Beecher.*

" The science of criticism may be considered as a middle link, connecting the different parts of education into a regular chain."—*Ld. Kames, El. of Crit.,* p. xxii.

" When I see a man walking, a tree growing, or cattle grazing, I cannot doubt but that these objects are really what they appear to be. Nature determines us to rely on the veracity of our senses; for otherwise they could not in any degree answer their end, that of laying open things existing and passing around us."—*Id. ib.* i, 85.

" But, advancing farther in life, and inured by degrees to the crooked ways of men; pressing through the crowd, and the bustle of the world; obliged to contend with this man's craft, and that man's scorn; accustomed, sometimes, to conceal their sentiments, and often to stifle their feelings; they become at last hardened in heart, and familiar with corruption."—BLAIR: *Murray's Sequel,* p. 140.

> " Laugh'd at, he laughs again; and stricken hard,
> Turns to his stroke his adamantine scales,
> That fear no discipline of human hands."—*Cowper's Task,* p. 47.

LESSON II.—PARSING.

" Thus shame and remorse united in the ungrateful person, and indignation united with hatred in the hearts of others, are the punishments provided by nature for injustice."—*Kames, El. of Crit.* Vol. i, p. 288.

"Viewing man as under the influence of novelty, would one suspect that custom also should influence him?—Human nature, diversified with many and various springs of action, is wonderfully, and, indulging the expresssion, intricately constructed."—*Id. ib.* i, 325.

" Dryden frequently introduces three or four persons speaking upon the same subject, each throwing out his own notions separately, without regarding what is said by the rest."—*Id. ib.* ii, 294.

" Nothing is more studied in Chinese gardens, than to raise wonder or surprise. Sometimes one is led insensibly into a dark cavern, terminating unexpectedly in a landscape enriched with all that nature affords the most delicious."—*Id. ib.* ii, 334.

" The answer to the objection here implied, is obvious, even on the supposition of the questions put being answered in the affirmative."—*Prof. Vethake.*

" As birds flying, so will the Lord of hosts defend Jerusalem; defending also, he will deliver it; and, passing over, he will preserve it."—*Isaiah,* xxxi, 5.

> "Here, by the bonds of nature feebly held,
> Minds combat minds, repelling and repell'd."—*Goldsmith.*

> " Suffolk first died, and York, all haggled over,
> Comes to him where in gore he lay insteeped."—*Shakspeare.*

LESSON III.—PARSING.

"Every change in the state of things is considered as an effect, indicating the agency, characterizing the kind, and measuring the degree, of its cause."—*Dr. Murray, Hist. of Eu. L.*, i, 179.

"Having loved his own who were in the world, he loved them unto the end. And supper being ended, (the devil having now put it into the heart of Judas Iscariot, Simon's son, to betray him,) Jesus, knowing that the Father had given all things into his hand, and that he had come from God and was going to God, arose from supper, and laid aside his coat, and, taking a towel, girded himself: then he poured some water into a basin, and began to wash the disciples' feet, and to wipe them with the towel with which he was girded."—See *John*, xiii.

"Spiritual desertion is naturally and judicially incurred by sin. It is the withdrawal of that divine unction which enriches the acquiescent soul with moral power and pleasure. The subtraction leaves the mind enervated, obscured, confused, degraded, and distracted."—HOMO: *N. Y. Observer.*

"Giving no offence in any thing, but in all things approving ourselves as the ministers of God: as unknown, and yet well known; as dying, and, behold, we live; as chastened, and not killed; as sorrowful, yet always rejoicing; as poor, yet making many rich; as having nothing, and yet possessing all things."—2 *Cor.* vi.

"O may th' indulgence of a father's love,
Pour'd forth on me, be doubled from above."—*Young.*

IMPROPRIETIES FOR CORRECTION.

ERRORS OF PARTICIPLES.

☞ [As the principles upon which our participles ought to be formed, were necessarily anticipated in the preceding chapter on verbs, the reader must recur to that chapter for the doctrines by which the following errors are to be corrected. The great length of that chapter seemed a good reason for separating these examples from it, and it was also thought, that such words as are erroneously written for participles, should, for the sake of order, be chiefly noticed in this place. In many of these examples, however, the participle is not really a separate part of speech, but is in fact taken with an auxiliary to form some compound tense of its verb.]

LESSON I.—IRREGULARS.

"Many of your readers have mistook that passage."—*Steele, Spect.*, No. 544.

[FORMULA.—Not proper, because the preterit verb *mistook* is here used for the perfect participle. But, according to the table of irregular verbs, we ought to say, *mistake*, *mistook*, *mistaking*, *mistaken*; after the form of the simple verb, *take*, *took*, *taking*, *taken*. Therefore, the sentence should be amended thus: "Many of your readers have mistaken that passage."]

"Had not my dog of a steward ran away."—*Addison, Spect.* "None should be admitted, except he had broke his collar-bone thrice."—*Spect.* No. 474. "We could not know what was wrote at twenty."—*Pref. to Waller.* "I have wrote, thou hast wrote, he has wrote; we have wrote, ye have wrote, they have wrote."—*Ash's Gram.* p. 62. "As if God had spoke his last words there to his people."—*Barclay's Works*, i, 462. "I had like to have came in that ship myself."—*N. Y. Observer*, No. 453. "Our ships and vessels being drove out of the harbour by a storm."—*Hutchinson's Hist. of Mass.*, i, 470. "He will endeavour to write as the ancient author would have wrote, had he writ in the same language."—*Bolingbroke, on Hist.* i, 68. "When his doctrines grew too strong to be shook by his enemies."—*Atterbury.* "The immortal mind that hath forsook Her mansion."—*Milton.* "Grease that's sweaten from the murderer's gibbet, throw into the flame."—*Shak. Macbeth.* The court also was chided for allowing such questions to be put."—*Col. Stone, on Freemasonry*, p. 470. "He would have spoke."—*Milton, P. L.*, B. x, l. 517. "Words interwove with sighs found out their way."—*Id. ib.* i, 621. "Those kings and potentates who have strove."—*Id. Eiconoclast*, xvii. "That even Silence was took."—*Id. Comus*, l. 557. "And envious Darkness, ere they could return, had stole them from me."—*Id. Comus*, l. 195. "I have chose this perfect man."—*Id. P. R.*, B. i, l. 165. "I will scarce think you have swam in a gondola."—*Shak. As You Like It.* "The fragrant brier was wove between."—*Dryden, Fables.* "Then finish what you have began."—*Id. Poems*, ii, 172. "But now the years a numerous train have ran."—*Pope's Odyssey*, B. xi, l. 555. "Repeats your verses wrote on glasses."—*Prior.* "Who by turns have rose."—*Id.* "Which from great authors I have took."—*Id. Alma.* Ev'n there he should have fell."—*Id. Solomon.*

"The sun has rose, and gone to bed,
Just as if Partridge were not dead."—*Swift.*

"And though no marriage words are spoke,
They part not till the ring is broke."—*Id. Riddles.*

LESSON II.—REGULARS.

"When the word is stript of all the terminations."—*Dr. Murray's Hist. of En. L.*, i. 319.

[FORMULE.—Not proper, because the participle *stript* is terminated in *t*. But, according to Observation 2d, on the irregular verbs, *stript* is regular. Therefore, this *t* should be changed to *ed*; and the final *p* should be doubled, according to Rule 3d for Spelling: thus, "When the word is *stripped* of all the terminations."]

"Forgive him, Tom; his head is crackt."—*Swift's Poems*, p. 397. "For 'tis the sport, to have the engineer hoist with his own petar."—*Hamlet*, Act 3. "As great as they are, I was nurst by their mother."—*Swift's Poems*, p. 310. "If he should now be cry'd down since his change."—*Ib.* p. 306. "Dipt over head and ears—in debt."—*Ib.* p. 312. "We see the nation's credit crackt."—*Ib.* p. 312. "Because they find their pockets pickt."—*Ib.* p. 338. "O what a pleasure mixt with pain!"—*Ib.* p. 373. "And only with her Brother linkt."—*Ib.* p. 387. "Because he ne'er a thought allow'd, That might not be confest."—*Ib.* p. 361. "My love to Sheelah is more firmly fixt."—*Ib.* p. 369. "The observations annext to them will be intelligible."—*Philological Museum*, Vol. i, p. 457. "Those eyes are always fixt on the general principles."—*Ib.* i, 458. "Laborious conjectures will be banisht from our commentaries."—*Ib.* i, 459. "Tiridates was dethroned, and Phraates was reestablisht in his stead."—*Ib.* i, 462. "A Roman who was attacht to Augustus."—*Ib.* i, 466. "Nor should I have spoken of it, unless Baxter had talkt about two such."—*Ib.* i, 467. "And the reformers of language have generally rusht on."—*Ib.* i, 649. "Three centuries and a half had then elapst since the date."—*Ib.* i, 249. "Of such criteria, as has been remarkt already, there is an abundance."—*Ib.* i, 261. "The English have surpast every other nation in their services."—*Ib.* i, 306. "The party addrest is next in dignity to the speaker."—*Harris's Hermes*, p. 66. "To which we are many times helpt."—*Walker's Particles*, p. 13. "But for him, I should have lookt well enough to myself."—*Ib.* p. 88. "Why are you vext, Lady? why do frown?"—*Milton, Comus*, l. 667. "Obtruding false rules prankt in reason's garb."—*Ib.* l. 759, "But, like David equipt in Saul's armour, it is encumbered and oppressed."—*Campbell's Rhet.* p. 378.

"And when their merchants are blown up, and crackt,
    Whole towns are cast away in storms, and wreckt."—*Butler*, p. 163.

LESSON III.—MIXED.

"The lands are holden in free and common soccage."—*Trumbull's Hist.* i, 133.

[FORMULE.—Not proper, because the participle *holden* is not in that form which present usage authorizes. But, according to the table of irregular verbs, the four parts of the verb *to hold*, as now used, are *hold, held, holding, held*. Therefore, *holden* should be *held*; thus, "The lands are *held* in free and common soccage."]

"A stroke is drawed under such words."—*Cobbett's E. Grammar*, Edition of 1832, ¶ 154. "It is striked even, with a strickle."—*Walker's Particles*, p. 115. "Whilst I was wandring, without any care, beyond my bounds."—*Ib.* p. 83. "When one would do something, unless hindred by something present."—*Johnson's Gram. Com.* p. 311. "It is used potentially, but not so as to be rendred by these signs."—*Ib.* p. 320. "Now who would dote upon things hurryed down the stream thus fast?"—*Collier's Antoninus*, p. 89. "Heaven hath timely try'd their growth."—*Milton, Comus*, l. 970. "O! ye mistook, ye should have snatcht his wand."—*Ib.* p. 815. "Of true virgin here distrest."—*Ib.* p. 905. "So that they have at last come to be substitute in the stead of it."—*Barclay's Works*, i, 339. "Though ye have lien among the pots."—*Psal.* lxviii, 13. "And, lo, in her mouth was an olive-leaf pluckt off."—FRIENDS' BIBLE, and BRUCE'S: *Gen.* viii, 11. "Brutus and Cassius Are rid, like madmen, through the gates of Rome."—*Shak.* "He shall be spitted on."—*Luke*, xviii, 32. "And are not the countries so overflown still situate between the tropics?"—*Bentley's Sermons.* "Not trickt and frounc't as she was wont, But kercheft in a comely cloud."—*Milton, Il Penseroso*, l. 123. "To satisfy his rigor, Satisfy'd never."—*Id. P. L.*, B. x. l. 804. "With him there crucify'd."—*Id. P. L.*, B. xii, l. 417. "Th' earth cumber'd, and the wing'd air darkt with plumes."—*Id. Comus*, l. 730. "And now their way to Earth they had descry'd."—*Id. P. L.*, B. x, l. 325. "Not so thick swarm'd once the soil Bedropt with blood of Gorgon."—*Ib.* B. x, l. 527. "And in a troubled sea of passion tost."—*Ib.* B. x, l. 718. "The cause, alas, is quickly guest."—*Swift's Poems*, p. 404. "The kettle to the top was hoist."—*Ib.* p. 274. "In chains thy syllables are linkt."—*Ib.* p. 318. "Rather than thus be overtopt, Would you not wish their laurels cropt?"—*Ib.* 415. "The hyphen, or conjoiner, is a little line, drawed to connect words, or parts of words."—*Cobbett's Gram.*, 1832, ¶150. "In the other manners of dependence, this general rule is sometimes broke."—*Joh. Gram. Com.* p. 334. "Some intransitive verbs may be rendered transitive by means of a preposition prefixt to them."—*Grant's Lat. Gram.* p. 66. "Whoever now should place the accent on the first syllable of *Valerius*, would set every body a-laughing."—*Walker's Dict.* "Being mocked, scourged, spitted on, and crucified."—*Gurney's Essays*, p. 40.

"For rhyme in Greece or Rome was never known,
    Till by barbarian deluges o'erflown."—*Roscommon.*
"In my own Thames may I be drownded,
    If e'er I stoop beneath a crown'd-head."—*Swift.*

CHAPTER VIII.—ADVERBS.

An Adverb is a word added to a verb, a participle, an adjective, or an other adverb ; and generally expresses time, place, degree, or manner : as, They are *now here*, studying *very diligently.*

OBSERVATIONS.

Obs. 1.—Adverbs briefly express what would otherwise require several words : as, *Now*, for *at this time* ;—*Here*, for *in this place* ;—*Very*, for *in a high degree* ;—*Diligently*, for *in an industrious manner.* Thus the meaning of almost any adverb, may be explained by some phrase beginning with a preposition and ending with a noun.

Obs. 2.—There are several customary combinations of short words, which are used adverbially, and which some grammarians do not analyze in parsing ; as, *not at all, at length, in fine, in full, at least, at present, at once, this once, in vain, no doubt, on board.* But all words that convey distinct ideas, and rightly retain their individuality, ought to be taken separately in parsing. With the liberty of supposing a few ellipses, an ingenious parser will seldom find occasion to speak of "adverbial phrases." In these instances, *length, doubt, fine,* and *board,* are unquestionably nouns ; *once*, too, is used as a noun ; *full* and *all* may be parsed either as nouns, or as adjectives whose nouns are understood ; *at least,* is, *at the least measure ; at present,* is, *at the present time ;* and *in vain,* is, *in a vain course, or manner.*

Obs. 3.—A phrase is a combination of two or more separable parts of speech, the *parsing* of which of course implies their separation. And though the division of our language into words, and the division of its words into parts of speech, have never yet been made exactly to correspond, it is certainly desirable to bring them as near together as possible. Hence such terms as *everywhere, anywhere, nowadays, forever, everso, to-day, to-morrow, by-and-by, inside-out, upside-down,* if they are to be parsed simply as adverbs, ought to be compounded, and not written as phrases.

Obs. 4.—Under nearly all the different classes of words, some particular instances may be quoted, in which other parts of speech seem to take the nature of adverbs, so as either to *become* such, or to be apparently used *for* them. (1.) ARTICLES : "This may appear incredible, but it is not *the* less true."—*Dr. Murray's Hist.* i, 337. "The other party was *a* little coy."—*D. Webster.* (2.) NOUNS : "And scrutiny became *stone*[*] blind."—*Cowper.* "He will come *home to-morrow.*"—*Clark.* "They were travelling *post* when he met them."—*Murray's Gram.* p. 69. "And with a vengeance sent from Media *post* to Egypt."—*Milton, P. L.,* B. iv, l. 170. "That I should care *a groat* whether he likes the work or not."—*Kirkham.* "It has snowed terribly all night, and is *vengeance* cold."—*Swift.* (3.) ADJECTIVES : "Drink *deep,* or taste not."—*Pope.* "A place *wondrous* deep."—*Webster's Dict.* "That fools should be so *deep* contemplative."—*Shak.* "A man may speak *louder* or *softer* in the same key ; when he speaks *higher* or *lower,* he changes his key."—*Sheridan's Elocution,* p. 116. (4.) PRONOUNS : "*What* am I eased ?"—*Job.* "*What* have I offended thee ?"—*Gen.* xx, 9. "He is *somewhat* arrogant."—*Dryden.* (5.) VERBS : "*Smack* went the whip, round went the wheels."—*Cowper.* "For then the farmers came *jog, jog,* along the miry road."—*Id.* "*Crack!* went something on deck."—*Robinson Crusoe.* "Then straight went the yard *slap* over their noddle."—*Arbuthnot.* (6.) PARTICIPLES : "Like medicines given *scalding* hot."—*Dodd.* "My clothes are almost *dripping* wet."—*Swift.* "In came Squire South, stark, *staring* mad."—*Arbuthnot.* "An *exceeding* high mountain."—*Matt.* iv, 8. "How sweet, how *passing* sweet, the hour to me ! "—*Ch. Observer.* "When we act *according* to our duty."—*Dr. Johnson.* "A man was famous *according* as he had lifted up axes upon the thick trees."—*Psal.* lxxiv, 5. (7.) CONJUNCTIONS : "Look, *as* I blow this feather from my face."—*Shak.* "Not at all, or *but* very gently."—*Locke.* "He was *but* born to try the lot of man."—*Pope.* (8.) PREPOSITIONS : "They shall go *in* and *out.*"—*Bible.* "From going *to* and fro in the earth, and walking *up* and *down* in it."—*Ib.* These are actually *adverbs,* and not prepositions, because they govern nothing. (9.) INTERJECTIONS are never used as adverbs, though the Greek grammarians refer them nearly all to this class. The using of other words for adverbs, (i. e. the adverbial use of any words that we do not actually call adverbs,) may be referred to the figure *enallage :* [†] as,

"*Tramp, tramp,* across the land they speed,
Splash, splash, across the sea."—*Burger.*

---

[*] " STONE'-BLIND," " STONE'-COLD," and " STONE'-DEAD," are given in Worcester's Dictionary, as compound *adjectives* ; and this is perhaps their best classification ; but, if I mistake not, they are usually accented quite as strongly on the latter syllable, as on the former, being spoken rather as two emphatic words. A similar example from Sigourney, " I saw an infant *marble cold,*" is given by Frazee under this Note : "Adjectives sometimes belong to other adjectives ; as, ' *red hot* iron.' "—*Improved Gram.* p. 141. But Webster himself, from whom this doctrine and the example are borrowed, (see his Rule XIX,) makes " RED'-HOT" but one word in his Dictionary ; and Worcester gives it as one word, in a less proper form, even without a hyphen, " RED-HOT."

[†] " OF ENALLAGE.—The construction which may be reduced to this figure in English, chiefly appears when one part of speech is used with the power and effect of another."—*Ward's English Gram.* p. 150.

Obs. 5.—As other parts of speech seem sometimes to take the nature of adverbs, so adverbs sometimes, either really or apparently, assume the nature of other parts of speech. (1.) Of NOUNS: as, "A committee is not needed merely to say *Yes* or *No*; that will do very little good; the *yes* or the *no* must be accompanied and supported by reasons."—*Dr. M'-Cartee.* "Shall I tell you *why*? Ay, sir, and *wherefore*; for, they say, every *why* hath a *wherefore*."—*Shak.* (2.) Of ADJECTIVES: as, "Nebuchadnezzar invaded the country, and reduced it to an *almost* desert."—*Wood's Dict. w. Moab.* "The *then* bishop of London, Dr. Laud, attended on his Majesty."—*Clarendon.* "With *upward* speed his agile wings he spread."—*Prior.* "She lights the *downward* heaven, and rises there."—*Dryden.* (3.) Of PRONOUNS: as, "He liked the ground *whereon* she trod."—*Milton.* "*Wherein* have you been galled by the king?"—*Shak.* "O how unlike the place from *whence* they fell!"—*Par. Lost,* B. i, l. 75. Here *whereon* is exactly equivalent in sense to *on which*; *wherein,* to *in what*, and *whence,* to *which*: but none of them are actually reckoned pronouns. (4.) Of VERBS: as, "If he be hungry more than wanton, bread alone will *down*."—*Locke.* "To *down* proud hearts that would not willing die."—*Sidney.* "She never could *away* with me."—*Shak.* "*Away*, and glister like the god of war."—*Id.* "*Up*, get ye out of this place."—*Gen.* xix, 14. (5.) Of CONJUNCTIONS: as, "I, *even* I, am he."—*Isaiah,* xliii, 25. "If I will that he tarry *till* I come."—*John*, xxi, 22. "I will go and see him *before* I die."—*Gen.* xlv, 28. "*Before* I go *whence* I shall not return."—*Job*, x, 21. (6.) Of PREPOSITIONS: as, "Superior to any that are dug *out* the ground."—*Eames's Lect.* p. 28. "Who act *so counter* heavenly mercy's plan."—*Burns.* Better perhaps, "*out of*" and "*counter* to." (7.) Of INTERJECTIONS: as, "*Up*, up, Glentarkin! rouse thee, ho!"—*Scott.* "*Down, down,* cried Mar, your lances *down*!"—*Id.* "*Off!* or I fly for ever from thy sight."—*Smith.*

Obs. 6.—In these last examples, *up,* and *down,* and *off,* have perhaps as much resemblance to imperative verbs, as to interjections; but they need not be referred to either of these classes, because by supplying a verb we may easily parse them as adverbs. I neither adopt the notion of Horne Tooke, that the same word cannot belong to different parts of speech, nor refer every word to that class to which it may at first sight appear to belong; for both of these methods are impracticable and absurd. The essential nature of each part of speech, and every important peculiarity of its individual terms, it is hoped, will be sufficiently explained in some part or other of this work; but, as the classification of words often depends upon their *construction,* some explanations that go to determine the parts of speech, must be looked for under the head of Syntax.

Obs. 7.—The proper classification, or subdivision, of adverbs, though it does not appear to have been discovered by any of our earlier grammarians, is certainly very clearly indicated by the meaning and nature of the words themselves. The four important circumstances of any event or assertion, are the *when,* the *where,* the *how-much,* and the *how;* or the *time,* the *place,* the *degree,* and the *manner.* These four are the things which we usually express by adverbs. And seldom, if ever, do we find any adverb the notion of which does not correspond to that of *sometime, somewhere, somewhat,* or *somehow.* Hence the general classes of this sort of words ought to be formed under these four heads. The classification heretofore most commonly adopted in English grammars, has every fault which the spirit of awkwardness could possibly give it. The head of it is this: "Adverbs, *though very numerous,* may be reduced to *certain* classes, the *chief* of which are *those of* Number, Order, Place, Time, Quantity, Manner or Quality, Doubt, Affirmation, Negation, Interrogation, and Comparison."—*Murray's Gram.* p. 115; *Comly's,* 66; *Kirkham's,* 86; *R. C. Smith's.* 34; *Hall's,* 26; *and others.*

CLASSES.

Adverbs may be reduced to four general classes; namely, adverbs of *time,* of *place,* of *degree,* and of *manner.* Besides these, it is proper to distinguish the particular class of *conjunctive* adverbs.

I. Adverbs of *time* are those which answer to the question, *When? How long? How soon?* or, *How often?* including these which ask.

Obs.—Adverbs of time may be subdivided as follows:—

1. Of time present; as, *Now, yet, to-day, nowadays, presently, instantly, immediately, straightway, directly, forthwith.*

2. Of time past; as, *Already, just now, lately, recently, yesterday, formerly, anciently, once, heretofore, hitherto, since, till now, long ago, erewhile, erst.*

3. Of time to come; as, *To-morrow, hereafter, henceforth, henceforward, by-and-by, soon, erelong, shortly.*

4. Of time relative; as, *When, then, first, just, before, after, while, whilst, meanwhile, as, till, until, seasonably, betimes, early, late, whenever, afterward, afterwards, otherwhile, otherwhiles.*

5. Of time absolute; as, *Always, ever, never, aye, eternally, forever, perpetually, continually, incessantly, endlessly, evermore, everlastingly.*

6. Of time repeated; as, *Often, oft, again, occasionally, frequently, sometimes, seldom, rarely, daily, weekly, monthly, yearly, annually, once, twice, thrice,* or *three times.* Above this, we use

only the phrases, *four times, five times, six times*, &c. Whether these ought to be reckoned adverbs or not, is questionable: *times*, for *repetitions*, may be supposed a noun.

II. Adverbs of *place* are those which answer to the question, *Where? Whither? Whence?* or, *Whereabout?* including these which ask.

Obs.—Adverbs of place may be subdivided as follows:—

1. Of place in which; as, *Where, here, there, yonder, above, below, about, around, somewhere, anywhere, elsewhere, otherwhere, everywhere, nowhere, wherever, wheresoever, within, without, whereabout, whereabouts, hereabout, hereabouts, thereabout, thereabouts.*

2. Of place to which; as, *Whither, hither, thither, in, up, down, back, forth, aside, ashore, abroad, aloft, home, homewards, inwards, upwards, downwards, backwards, forwards. Inward, homeward, upward, downward, backward,* and *forward*, are also adverbs, as well as adjectives; but some critics, for distinction's sake, choose to use these only as adjectives.

3. Of place from which; as, *Whence, hence, thence, away, out, off, far, remotely.*

4. Of the order of place; as, *First, secondly, thirdly, fourthly*, &c. Thus, *secondly* means *in the second place; thirdly, in the third place;* &c. For order, or rank, implies place, though it may consist of relative degrees.

III. Adverbs of *degree* are those which answer to the question, *How much? How little?* or to the idea of *more or less*.

Obs.—Adverbs of degree may be subdivided as follows:—

1. Of excess or abundance; as, *Much, more, most, too, very, greatly, far, besides; chiefly, principally, mainly, mostly, generally; entirely, full, fully, completely, perfectly, wholly, totally, altogether, all, quite, clear, stark; exceedingly, excessively, extravagantly, intolerably; immeasurably, inconceivably, infinitely.*

2. Of equality or sufficiency; as, *Enough, sufficiently, competently, adequately, proportionally, equally, so, as, even, just, exactly, precisely.*

3. Of deficiency or abatement; as, *Little, less, least, scarcely, hardly, scantly, scantily, merely, barely, only, but, partly, partially, nearly, almost, well-nigh, not quite.*

4. Of quantity in the abstract; as, *How*, (meaning, *in what degree*,) *however, howsoever, everso, something, anything, nothing, a groat, a sixpence, a sou-markee,* and other nouns of quantity used adverbially.

IV. Adverbs of *manner* are those which answer to the question, *How?* or, by affirming, denying, or doubting, show *how* a subject is regarded.

Obs.—Adverbs of manner may be subdivided as follows:—

1. Of manner from quality; as, *Well, ill, wisely, foolishly, justly, wickedly,* and many others formed by adding *ly* to adjectives of quality. *Ly* is a contraction of *like;* and is the most common termination of English adverbs. When added to nouns, it forms adjectives; but some few of these are also used adverbially: as, *daily, weekly, monthly,* which denote time.

2. Of affirmation or assent; as, *Yes, yea, ay, verily, truly, indeed, surely, certainly, doubtless, undoubtedly, assuredly, certes, forsooth,* * *amen.*

3. Of negation; as, *No, nay, not, nowise, noway, noways, nohow.*

4. Of doubt or uncertainty; as, *Perhaps, haply, possibly, perchance, peradventure, may-be.*

5. Of mode or way; as, *Thus, so, how, somehow, nohow, anyhow, however, howsoever, like, else, otherwise, across, together, apart, asunder, namely, particularly, necessarily, hesitatingly, trippingly, extempore, headlong, lengthwise.*

V. *Conjunctive adverbs* are those which perform the office of conjunctions, and serve to connect sentences, as well as to express some circumstance of time, place, degree, or the like. This class embraces a few words not strictly belonging to any of the others: as, (1.) The adverbs of cause; *why, wherefore, therefore;* but the last two of these are often called conjunctions. (2.) The pronominal compounds; *herein, therein, wherein,* &c.; in which the former term is a substitute, and virtually governed by the enclitic particle.

OBSERVATIONS.

Obs. 1.—Conjunctive adverbs often relate equally to two verbs in different clauses, on which account it is the more necessary to distinguish them from others; as, "And they feared *when* they heard that they were Romans."—*Acts*, xvi. 38. Here *when* is a conjunctive adverb of time, and relates equally to *feared* and to *heard*. "The right of coming on the shore for their purposes in general, *as* and *when* they please."—*Holroyd*. Here *as* is a conjunctive adverb of manner, and *when*, of time; both relating equally to *coming* and to *please*.

Obs. 2.—The following words are the most frequently used as conjunctive adverbs: *after, again, also, as, before, besides, consequently, else, ere, even, furthermore, hence, how, however, moreover, nevertheless, otherwise, since, so, still, till, then, thence, therefore, too, until, when, where, wherefore, whither,* and *while,* or *whilst*.

Obs. 3.—Adverbs of *time, place,* and *manner,* are generally connected with verbs or participles; those of *degree* are more frequently placed before adjectives or adverbs: the latter, however, some-

---

* *Forsooth* is literally a word of affirmation or assent, meaning *for truth*, but it is now almost always used ironically: as, "In those gentlemen whom the world *forsooth* calls wise and solid, there is generally either a moroseness that persecutes, or a dullness that tires you."—*Home's Art of Thinking,* p. 24.

times denote the measure of actions or effects; as, "And I wept *much*."—*Rev.* v, 4. "And Isaac trembled *very exceedingly*."—*Gen.* xxvii, 33. " Writers who had felt *less*, would have said *more*."—*Fuller.*

> " Victors and vanquished, in the various field,
> Nor *wholly* overcome, nor *wholly* yield."—*Dryden.*

OBS. 4.—The adverbs *here, there,* and *where,* when compounded with prepositions, have the force of pronouns, or of pronominal adjectives: as, *Hereby,* for *by this; thereby,* for *by that, whereby,* for *by which,* or *by what.* The prepositions which may be subjoined in this manner, are only the short words, *at, by, for, from, in, into, of, on, to, unto, under, upon,* and *with.* Compounds of this kind, although they partake the nature of pronouns with respect to the nouns going before, are still properly reckoned adverbs, because they relate as such to the verbs which follow them; as, " You take my life, when you do take the means *whereby* I live."—*Shak.* Here *whereby* is a conjunctive adverb, representing *means,* and relating to the verb *live.*[*] This mode of expression is now somewhat antiquated, though still frequently used by good authors, and especially by the poets.

OBS. 5.—The adverbs, *when, where, whither, whence, how, why, wherefore, wherein, whereof, whereby,* and other like compounds of *where,* are sometimes used as *interrogatives ;* but, as such, they still severally belong to the classes under which they are placed in the foregoing distribution, except that words of interrogation are not at the same time connectives. These adverbs, and the three pronouns, *who, which,* and *what,* are the only interrogative words in the language; but questions may be asked without any of them, and all have other uses than to ask questions.

OBS. 6.—The conjunctive adverbs, *when, where, whither, whence, how,* and *why,* are sometimes so employed as to partake of the nature of *pronouns,* being used as a sort of *special relatives,* which refer back to antecedent nouns of *time, place, manner,* or *cause,* according to their own respective meanings; yet being adverbs, because they relate as such, to the verbs which follow them: as, " In the *day when* God shall judge the secrets of men."—*Rom.* ii, 16. " In a *time when* thou mayest be found."—*Psal.* xxxii, 6. " I sought for some time what I at length found here, a *place where* all real wants might be easily supplied."—*Dr. Johnson.* " To that *part of the* mountain *where* the declivity began to grow craggy."—*Id.* " At *Canterbury, whither* some voice had run before."—*Wotton.* " Look unto the *rock whence* ye are hewn, and to the hole of the *pit whence* ye are digged."—*Isaiah,* li, 1. " We may remark three different *sources whence* it arises."—*Blair's Rhet.* p. 163. " I'll tell you a *way how* you may live your time over again."—*Collier's Antoninus,* p. 108. "A crude account of the *method how* they perceive truth."—*Harris's Hermes,* p. 404. " The *order how* the Psalter is appointed to be read "—*Common Prayer.* " In the same reasoning we see the *cause, why* no substantive is susceptible of these comparative degrees."—*Hermes,* p. 201. " There seems no *reason why* it should not work prosperously."—*Society in America,* p. 68. " There are strong *reasons why* an extension of her territory would be injurious to her."—*Ib.* "An other *reason why* it deserved to be more studied."—*Blair's Rhet.* p. 123. " The *end why* God hath ordained faith, is, that his free grace might be glorified."—*Goodwin.*

OBS. 7.—The direct use of adverbs for pronouns, is often, if not generally, inelegant; and, except the expression may be thereby agreeably shortened, it ought to be considered ungrammatical. The following examples, and perhaps also some of the foregoing, are susceptible of improvement: " Youth is *the time, when* we are young."—*Sanborn's Gram.* p. 120. Say rather, " Youth is *that part of life which* succeeds to childhood." " The boy gave a satisfactory *reason why* he was tardy."—*Ibid.* Say rather, "The boy gave a satisfactory reason *for his tardiness.*" " The several *sources from whence* these pleasures are derived."—*Murray's Key,* p. 258. Say rather—" sources from *which.*" " In *cases where* it is only said, that a question has been asked."—*Kirkham's Gram.* p. 217. Say, " In *those cases in which.*" " To the false rhetoric of the *age when* he lived."—*Harris's Hermes,* p. 415. Say rather—" of the age *in which* he lived."

OBS. 8.—When a conjunctive adverb is equivalent to both an antecedent and a relative, the construction seems to be less objectionable, and the brevity of the expression affords an additional reason for preferring it, especially in poetry: as, " But the Son of man hath not *where* to lay his head."—*Matt.* viii, 20. " There might they see *whence* Po and Ister came."—*Hoole's Tasso.* " Tell *how* he formed your shining frame."—*Ogilvie.* " The wind bloweth *where* it listeth, and thou hearest the sound thereof, but canst not tell *whence* it cometh, and *whither* it goeth."—*John,* iii, 8. In this construction, the adverb is sometimes preceded by a preposition; the noun being, in fact, *understood:* as,

> " Sinks, like a sea-weed, *into whence* she rose."—*Byron.*
> " Here Machiavelli's earth return'd *to whence* it rose."—*Id.*

OBS. 9.—The conjunctive adverb *so,* very often expresses the sense of some word or phrase going before; as, " Wheresoever the speech is corrupted, *so* is the mind."—*Seneca's Morals,* p. 267. That is, the mind is *also corrupted.* " I consider grandeur and sublimity, as terms synonymous, or nearly *so.*"—*Blair's Rhet.* p. 29. The following sentence is grossly wrong, because the import of this adverb was not well observed by the writer : " We have now come to *far the most complicated* part of speech ; and one which is sometimes rendered *still more so,* than the nature of our language requires."—*Nutting's Gram.* p. 38. *So,* in some instances, repeats the import of a preceding *noun,* and consequently partakes the nature of a *pronoun;* as,

> " We think our fathers *fools,* so wise we grow;
> Our wiser sons, no doubt, will think us *so.*"—*Pope, on Crit.*

OBS. 10.—" *Since* is often improperly used for *ago* : as, ' When were you in France ?—Twenty

---

[*] In most instances, however, the words *hereof, thereof,* and *whereof,* are placed after *nouns,* and have nothing to do with any *verb.* They are therefore not properly *adverbs,* though all our grammarians and lexicographers call them so. Nor are they *adjectives;* because they are not used *adjectively,* but rather in the sense of a pronoun governed by *of;* or, what is nearly the same thing, in the sense of the possessive or genitive case. Example: "And the fame *hereof* went abroad."—*Matt.* ix, 26. That is, " the fame *of this miracle;*" which last is a better expression, the other being obsolete, or worthy to be so, on account of its irregularity.

years *since.*' It ought to be, 'Twenty years *ago.*' *Since* may be admitted to supply the place of *ago that:* it being equally correct to say, " It is twenty years *since* I was in F ance;' and, ' It is twenty years *ago, that* I was in France.' "—*Churchill's Gram.* p. 337. The difference between *since* and *ago* is clearly this : the former, being either a preposition or a conjunctive adverb, cannot with strict propriety be used *adjectively ;* the latter, being in reality an old participle, naturally comes after a noun, in the sense of an adjective ; as, *a year ago, a month ago, a week ago.* "*Go,· ago, ygo, gon, agon, gone, agone,* are all used indiscriminately by our old English writers as the past participle of the verb *to go.*"—*Tooke's Diversions,* Vol. i, p. 376. " Three days *agone,* I fell sick."—1 *Samuel,* xxx, 13.

MODIFICATIONS.

Adverbs have no modifications, except that a few are compared, after the manner of adjectives : as, *soon, sooner, soonest; often, oftener, oftenest;* * *long, longer, longest ; fast, faster, fastest.*

The following are irregularly compared : *well, better, best ; badly* or *ill, worse, worst ; little, less, least ; much, more, most ; far, farther, farthest ; forth, further, furthest. Rath, rather, rathest,* is now used only in the comparative.

OBSERVATIONS.

Obs. 1.—Most adverbs that are formed from adjectives by the addition of *ly,* will admit the comparative adverbs *more* and *most, less* and *least,* before them : as, *wisely, more wisely, most wisely ; culpably, less culpably, least culpably.* This is virtually a comparison of the latter adverb, but the grammatical inflection, or degree, belongs only to the former ; and the words being written separately, it is certainly most proper to parse them separately, ascribing the degree of comparison to the word which expresses it. As comparison does not belong to adverbs in general, it should not be mentioned in parsing, except in the case of those few which are varied by it.

Obs. 2.—In the works of Milton, and occasionally in those of some other poets of his age,[†] adverbs of two syllables, ending in *ly,* are not only compared regularly, like adjectives of the same ending, but are used in the measure of iambic verse as if they still formed only two syllables. Examples : —
" But God hath *wiselier* arm'd his vengeful ire."—*P. Lost,* B. x, l. 1022.
" Destroyers *rightlier* call'd and plagues of men."—*Ib.* B. xi, l. 699.
"And on his quest, where *likeliest* he might find."—*Ib.* B. ix, l. 414.
" Now *amplier* known thy Saviour and thy Lord."—*Ib.* B. xii, l. 544.
"Though thou wert *firmlier* fasten'd than a rock."—*Sam. Agon.* l. 1398.
" Not rustic, as before, but *seemlier* clad."—*P. Reg.* B. ii, l. 299.
———————————" Whereof to thee anon
Plainlier shall be reveal'd."—*Paradise Lost,* B. xii, l. 150.
———" To show what coast thy sluggish crare
Might *easiliest* harbour in."—*Shakspeare, Cymb.* Act IV.
" Shall not myself be *kindlier* mov'd than thou art ?"—*Id. Tempest,* Act V.
" But *earthlier* happy is the rose distill'd."—*Id. M. S. N. Dream,* Act I.

Obs. 3.—The usage just cited is clearly analogical, and has the obvious advantage of adding to the flexibility of the language, while it also multiplies its distinctive forms. If carried out as it might be, it would furnish to poets and orators an ampler choice of phraseology, and at the same time, obviate in a great measure the necessity of using the same words both adjectively and adverbially. The words which are now commonly used in this twofold character, are principally monosyllables ; and, of adjectives, monosyllables are the class which we oftenest compare by *er* and *est :* next to which come dissyllables ending in *y ;* as, *holy, happy, lovely.* But if to any monosyllable we add *ly* to form an adverb, we have of course a dissyllable ending in *y ;* and if adverbs of this class may be compared regularly, after the manner of adjectives, there can be little or no occasion to use the primitive word otherwise than as an adjective. But, according to present usage, few adverbs are ever compared by inflection, except such words as may also be used adjectively. For example : *cleanly, comely, deadly, early, kindly, kingly, likely, lively, princely, seemly, weakly,* may all be thus compared ; and, according to Johnson and Webster, they may all be used either adjectively

* *Seldom* is sometimes compared in this manner, though not frequently ; as, " This kind of verse occurs the *seldomest,* but has a happy effect in diversifying the melody."—*Blair's Rhet.* p. 335. In former days, this word, as well as its correlative *often,* was sometimes used *adjectively ;* as, "Thine *often* infirmities."—1 *Tim.* v, 23. "I hope God's Book hath not been my *seldomest* lectures."—*Queen Elizabeth,* 1566. John Walker has regularly compared the adverb *forward :* in describing the letter L, he speaks of the tip of the tongue as being "brought a little *forwarder* to the teeth."—*Pron. Dict. Princip.* No 55.
† A few instances of the *regular inflection* of adverbs ending in *ly,* may be met with in *modern* compositions, as in the following comparisons : " As melodies will sometimes ring *sweetlier* in the echo."—*The Dial,* Vol. i, p. 6. " I remember no poet whose writings would *safelier* stand the test."—*Coleridge's Biog. Lit.* Vol. ii, p. 53.

or adverbially. Again: *late, later, latest*, is commonly contrasted in both senses, with *early, earlier, earliest*; but if *lately, latelier, lateliest*, were adopted in the adverbial contrast, *early* and *late, earlier* and *later, earliest* and *latest*, might be contrasted as adjectives only.

OBS. 4.—The using of adjectives for adverbs, is *in general* a plain violation of grammar. Example: "*To* is a preposition, governing the verb *sell*, in the infinitive mood, *agreeable* to Rule 18, which says, The preposition *To* governs the infinitive mood."—*Comly's Gram.* p. 137. Here *agreeable* ought to be *agreeably*; an adverb, relating to the participle *governing*. Again, the using of adverbs for adjectives, is a fault as gross. Example: "Apprehending the nominative to be put *absolutely*."—*Murray's Gram.* p. 155. Here *absolutely* ought to be *absolute*; an adjective, relating to the word *nominative*. But, *in poetry*, there is not only a frequent substitution of quality for manner, in such a way that the adjective may still be parsed adjectively; but sometimes also what *appears* to be (whether right or wrong) a direct use of adjectives for adverbs, especially in the higher degrees of comparison: as,

"*Firmer* he roots him the *ruder* it blow."—*Scott, L. of L.*, C. ii, st. 19.
"True ease in writing comes from art, not chance,
    As those move *easiest* who have learn'd to dance."—*Pope, Ess. on Crit.*
"And also now the sluggard *soundest* slept."—*Pollok, C. of T.*, B. vi, l. 257.
"In them is *plainest* taught, and *easiest* learnt,
    What makes a nation happy, and keeps it so."—*Milton, P. R.*, B. iv, l. 361.

OBS. 5.—No use of words can be *right*, that actually confounds the parts of speech; but in many instances, according to present practice, the same words may be used either adjectively or adverbially. *Firmer* and *ruder* are not adverbs, but adjectives. In the example above, they may, I think, be ranked with the instances in which quality is poetically substituted for manner, and be parsed as relating to the pronouns which follow them. A similar usage occurs in Latin, and is considered elegant. *Easiest*, as used above by Pope, may perhaps be parsed upon the same principle; that is, as relating to *those*, or to *persons* understood before the verb *move*. But *soundest, plainest*, and *easiest*, as in the latter quotations, cannot be otherwise explained than as being adverbs. *Plain* and *sound*, according to our dictionaries, are used both adjectively and adverbially; and, if their superlatives are not misapplied in these instances, it is because the words are adverbs, and regularly compared as such. *Easy*, though sometimes used adverbially by reputable writers, is presented by our lexicographers as an adjective only; and if the latter are right, Milton's use of *easiest* in the sense and construction of *most easily*, must be considered an error in grammar. And besides, according to his own practice, he ought to have preferred *plainliest* to *plainest*, in the adverbial sense of *most plainly*.

OBS. 6.—Beside the instances already mentioned, of words used both adjectively and adverbially, our dictionaries exhibit many primitive terms which are to be referred to the one class or the other, according to their construction; as, *soon, late, high, low, quick, slack, hard, soft, wide, close, clear, thick, full, scant, long, short, clean, near, scarce, sure, fast*; to which may as well be added, *slow, loud*, and *deep*; all susceptible of the regular form of comparison, and all regularly convertible into adverbs in *ly*; though *soonly* and *longly* are now obsolete, and *fastly*, which means *firmly*, is seldom used. In short, it is, probably, from an idea, that no adverbs are to be compared by *er* and *est* unless the same words may also be used adjectively, that we do not thus compare *lately, highly, quickly, loudly*, &c., after the example of Milton. But, however custom may sanction the adverbial construction of the foregoing simple terms, the distinctive form of the adverb is in general to be preferred, especially in prose. For example: "The more it was complained of, the *louder* it was praised."—*Daniel Webster, in Congress*, 1837. If it would seem quaint to say, "The *loudlier* it was praised," it would perhaps be better to say, "The *more loudly* it was praised;" for our critics have not acknowledged *loud* or *louder* to be an adverb. Nor have *slow* and *deep* been so called. Dr. Johnson cites the following line to illustrate the latter as an *adjective*:

"Drink hellebore, my boy! drink *deep*, and scour thy brain. DRYDEN."—*Joh. Dict. w. Deep.*
"Drink hellebore, my boy! drink deep, and *purge* thy brain."—*Dryd. IV Sat. of Persius.*

OBS. 7.—In some instances, even in prose, it makes little or no difference to the sense, whether we use adjectives referring to the nouns, or adverbs of like import, having reference to the verbs: as, "The whole conception is conveyed *clear* and *strong* to the mind."—*Blair's Rhet.* p. 138. Here *clear* and *strong* are adjectives, referring to *conception*; but we might as well say, "The whole conception is conveyed *clearly* and *strongly* to the mind." "Against a power that exists *independent* of their own choice."—*Webster's Essays*, p. 46. Here we might as well say, "exists *independently*;" for the independence of the power, in whichever way it is expressed, is nothing but *the manner* of its *existence*. "This work goeth *fast* on and prospereth."—*Ezra.* "Skill comes so *slow*, and life so *fast* doth fly."—*Davies.* Dr. Johnson here takes *fast* and *slow* to be adjectives, but he might just as well have called them adverbs, so far as their meaning or construction is concerned. For what here qualifies the things spoken of, is nothing but the *manner* of their *motion*; and this might as well be expressed by the words, *rapidly, slowly, swiftly*. Yet it ought to be observed, that this does not prove the equivalent words to be adverbs, and not adjectives. Our philologists have often been led into errors by the argument of equivalence.

EXAMPLES FOR PARSING.

PRAXIS VIII.—ETYMOLOGICAL.

In the Eighth Praxis, it is required of the pupil—to distinguish and define the different parts of speech, and the classes and modifications of the ARTICLES, NOUNS, ADJECTIVES, PRONOUNS, VERBS, PARTICIPLES, and ADVERBS.

The definitions to be given in the Eighth Praxis, are two for an article, six for a noun, three for an adjective, six for a pronoun, seven for a verb finite, five for an infinitive, two for a participle, two (and sometimes three) for an adverb,— and one for a conjunction, a preposition, or an interjection. Thus :—

EXAMPLE PARSED.

" When was it that Rome attracted most strongly the admiration of mankind ? " —*R. G. Harper.*

When is an adverb of time. 1. An adverb is a word added to a verb, a participle, an adjective, or an other adverb ; and generally expresses time, place, degree. or manner. 2. Adverbs of time are those which answer to the question, *When ? How long ? How soon ?* or *How often ?* including these which ask.

Was is an irregular neuter verb, from *be, was, being, bern* ; found in the indicative mood, imperfect tense, third person, and singular number. 1. A verb is a word that signifies *to be, to act,* or *to be acted upon.* 2. An irregular verb is a verb that does not form the preterit and the perfect participle by assuming *d* or *ed.* 3. A neuter verb is a verb that expresses neither action nor passion, but simply being, or a state of being. 4. The indicative mood is that form of the verb, which simply indicates or declares a thing, or asks a question. 5. The imperfect tense is that which expresses what took place, or was occurring, in time fully past. 6. The third person is that which denotes the person or thing merely spoken of. 7. The singular number is that which denotes but one.

It is a personal pronoun, of the third person, singular number, neuter gender, and nominative case. 1. A pronoun is a word used in stead of a noun. 2. A personal pronoun is a pronoun that shows, by its form, of what person it is. 3. The third person is that which denotes the person or thing merely spoken of. 4. The singular number is that which denotes but one. 5. The neuter gender is that which denotes things that are neither male nor female. 6. The nominative case is that form or state of a noun or pronoun, which denotes the subject of a verb.

That is a conjunction. 1. A conjunction is a word used to connect words or sentences in construction, and to show the dependence of the terms so connected.

Rome is a proper noun, of the third person, singular number, personified feminine, and nominative case. 1. A noun is the name of any person, place, or thing, that can be known or mentioned. 2. A proper noun is the name of some particular individual, or people, or group. 3. The third person is that which denotes the person or thing merely spoken of. 4. The singular number is that which denotes but one. 5. The feminine gender is that which denotes persons or animals of the female kind. 6. The nominative case is that form or state of a noun or pronoun, which denotes the subject of a verb.

Attracted is a regular active-transitive verb, from *attract, attracted, attracting, attracted* ; found in the indicative mood, imperfect tense, third person, and singular number. 1. A verb is a word that signifies *to be, to act,* or *to be acted upon.* 2. A regular verb is a verb that forms the preterit and the perfect participle by assuming *d* or *ed.* 3. An active-transitive verb is a verb that expresses an action which has some person or thing for its object. 4. The indicative mood is that form of the verb, which simply indicates or declares a thing, or asks a question. 5. The imperfect tense is that which expresses what took place, or was occurring, in time fully past. 6. The third person is that which denotes the person or thing merely spoken of. 7. The singular number is that which denotes but one.

Most is an adverb of degree, compared, *much, more, most,* and found in the superlative. 1. An adverb is a word added to a verb, a participle, an adjective, or an other adverb ; and generally expresses time, place, degree, or manner. 2. Adverbs of degree are those which answer to the question, *How much ? How little ?* or to the idea of *more* or *less.* 3. The superlative degree is that which is *most* of *least* of all included with it.

Strongly is an adverb of manner. 1. An adverb is a word added to a verb, a participle, an adjective, or an other adverb ; and generally expresses time, place, degree, or manner. 2. Adverbs of manner are those which answer to the question, *How ?* or, by affirming, denying, or doubting, show *how* a subject is regarded.

The is the definite article. 1. An article is the word *the, an,* or *a,* which we put before nouns to limit their signification. 2. The definite article is *the,* which denotes some particular thing or things.

Admiration is a common noun, of the third person, singular number, neuter gender, and objective case. 1. A noun is the name of any person, place, or thing, that can be known or mentioned. 2. A common noun is the name of a sort, kind, or class, of beings or things. 3. The third person is that which denotes the person or thing merely spoken of. 4. The singular number is that which denotes but one. 5. The neuter gender is that which denotes the object of a verb, participle, or preposition.

Of is a preposition. 1. A preposition is a word used to express some relation of different things or thoughts to each other, and is generally placed before a noun or a pronoun.

Mankind is a common noun, collective, of the third person, conveying the idea of plurality, masculine gender, and objective case. 1. A noun is the name of any person, place, or thing, that can be known or mentioned. 2. A collective noun, or noun of multitude, is the name of many individuals together. 3. The third person is that which denotes the person or thing merely spoken of. 4. The plural number is that which denotes more than one. 5. The masculine gender is that which denotes persons or animals of the male kind. 6. The objective case is that form or state of a noun or pronoun, which denotes the object of a verb, participle, or preposition.

LESSON I.—PARSING.

" Wisely, therefore, is it ordered, and agreeably to the system of Providence, that we should have nature for our instructor."—*Kames, El. of Crit.* i, 358.

" It is surprising, how quickly, and for the most part how correctly, we judge of character from external appearance."—*Id. ib.* i, 359.

" The members of a period connected by proper copulatives, glide smoothly and gently along, and are a proof of sedateness and leisure in the speaker."—*Id. ib.* ii, 88.

" Antithesis ought only to be occasionally studied, when it is naturally demanded by the comparison or opposition of objects."—*Jamieson's Rhet.* p. 102.

" Did men always think clearly, and were they at the same time fully masters of the language in which they write, there would be occasion for few rules."—*Ib.* 102.

"Rhetoric, or oratory, is the art of speaking justly, methodically, floridly, and copiously, upon any subject, in order to touch the passions, and to persuade."—*Bradley's Literary Guide*, p. 155.

"The more closely we follow the natural order of any subject we may be investigating, the more satisfactorily and explicitly will that subject be opened to our understanding."—*Gurney's Essays*, p. 160.

> "Why should we doubt of that, whereof our sense
> Finds demonstration from experience ?
> Our minds are here, and there, below, above ;
> Nothing that's mortal, can so swiftly move."—*Denham.*

LESSON II.—PARSING.

"If we can discern particularly and precisely what it is, which is most directly obedience or disobedience to the will and commands of God ; what is truly morally beautiful, or really and adsolutely deformed ; the question concerning liberty, as far as it respects ethics, or morality, will be sufficiently decided."—*West, on Agency*, p. xiii.

"Thus it was true, historically, individually, philosophically, and universally, that they did not like to retain God in their knowledge."—*Cox, on Christianity*, p. 327.

"We refer to Jeremiah Evarts and Gordon Hall. They had their imperfections, and against them they struggled discreetly, constantly, successfully, until they were fitted to ascend to their rest."—*N. Y. Observer*, Feb. 2d, 1833.

"Seek not proud riches ; but such as thou mayst get justly, use soberly, distribute cheerfully, and leave contentedly."—*Ld. Bacon.*

"There are also some particularly grievous sins, of which conscience justly accuses us ; sins committed more or less presumptuously and willingly, deliberately and repeatedly."—*Bickersteth, on Prayer*, p. 59.

"And herein I apprehend myself now to suffer wrongfully, being slanderously reported, falsely accused, shamefully and despitefully used, and hated without a cause."—*Jenks's Prayers*, p. 173.

> "Of perfect knowledge, see, the dawning light
> Foretells a noon most exquisitely bright !
> Here, springs of endless joy are breaking forth !
> There, buds the promise of celestial worth ! "—*Young.*

LESSON III.—PARSING.

"A true friend unbosoms freely, advises justly, assists readily, adventures boldly, takes all patiently, defends courageously, and continues a friend unchangeably."—*Penn's Maxims.*

"That mind must be wonderfully narrow, that is wholly wrapped up in itself ; but this is too visibly the character of most human minds."—*Burgh's Dignity*, ii, 35.

"There is not a man living, who wishes more sincerely than I do, to see a plan adopted for the abolition of slavery ; but there is only one proper and effectual mode by which it can be accomplished, and that is, by legislative authority.—*Geo. Washington*, 1786.

"Sloth has frequently and justly been denominated the rust of the soul. The habit is easily acquired ; or, rather, it is a part of our very nature to be indolent."—*Student's Manual*, p. 176.

"I am aware how improper it is to talk much of my wife ; never reflecting how much more improper it is to talk much of myself."—*Home's Art of Thinking*, p. 89.

"Howbeit whereinsoever any is bold, (I speak foolishly,) I am bold also. Are they Hebrews? so am I. Are they Israelites? so am I. Are they the seed of Abraham? so am I. Are they ministers of Christ? (I speak as a fool,) I am more."—*2 Cor.* xi.

> "Oh, speak the wondrous man ! how mild, how calm,
> How greatly humble, how divinely good,
> How firm establish'd on eternal truth."—*Thomson.*

IMPROPRIETIES FOR CORRECTION.

ERRORS RESPECTING ADVERBS.

"We can much easier form the conception of a fierce combat."—*Blair's Rhet.* p. 167.

[FORMULE.—Not proper, because the adjective *easier* is used as an adverb, to qualify the verb *can form*. But, according to Observation 4th on the Modifications of Adverbs, "The using of adjectives for adverbs, is in general a plain violation of grammar." Therefore, *easier* should be *more easily*; thus, "We can much *more easily* form the conception of a fierce combat."]

"When he was restored, agreeable to the treaty, he was a perfect savage."—*Webster's Essays*, p. 235. "How I shall acquit myself suitable to the importance of the trial."—*Duncan's Cic.* p. 85. "Can any thing show your holiness how unworthy you treat mankind?"—*Spect.* No. 497. "In what other [language,] consistent with reason and common sense, can you go about to explain it to him?"—*Lowth's Gram. Pref.* p. viii. "Agreeable to this rule, the short vowel Sheva has two characters."—*Wilson's Hebrew Gram.* p. 46. "We shall give a remarkable fine example of this figure."—*Murray's Gram.* p. 347. "All of which is most abominable false."—*Barclay's Works*, iii, 431. "He heaped up great riches, but passed his time miserable."—*Murray's Key*, 8vo, ii, 202. "He is never satisfied with expressing any thing clearly and simple."—*Blair's Rhet.* p. 96. "Attentive only to exhibit his ideas clear and exact, he appears dry."—*Ib.* p. 100. "Such words as have the most liquids and vowels, glide the softest."—*Ib.* p. 129. "The simplest points, such as are easiest apprehended."—*Ib.* p. 312. "Too historical, to be accounted a perfect regular epic poem."—*Ib.* p. 441. "Putting after them the oblique case, agreeable to the French construction."—*Priestley's Gram.* p. 108. "Where the train proceeds with an extreme slow pace."—*Kames, El. of Crit.* i, 151. "So as scarce to give an appearance of succession."—*Ib.* i, 152. "That concord between sound and sense, which is perceived in some expressions independent of artful pronunciation."—*Ib.* ii, 63. "Cornaro had become very corpulent, previous to the adoption of his temperate habits."—*Hitchcock, on Dysp.* p. 396. "Bread, which is a solid and tolerable hard substance."—*Sandford and Merton*, p. 38. "To command every body that was not dressed as fine as himself."—*Ib.* p. 19. "Many of them have scarce outlived their authors."—*Pref. to Lily's Gram.* p. ix. "Their labour, indeed, did not penetrate very deep."—*Wilson's Heb. Gram.* p. 30. "The people are miserable poor, and subsist on fish."—*Hume's Hist.* ii, 433. "A scale, which I took great pains, some years since, to make."—*Bucke's Gram.* p. 81. "There is no truth on earth so well established as the truth of the Bible."—*Taylor's District School*, p. 288. "I know of no work so much wanted as the one Mr. Taylor has now furnished."—*Dr. Nott: ib.* p. ii. "And therefore their requests are seldom and reasonable."—*Taylor: ib.* p. 58. "Questions are easier proposed than rightly answered."—*Dillwyn's Reflections*, p. 19. "Often reflect on the advantages you possess, and on the source from whence they are all derived."—*Murray's Gram.* p. 374. "If there be no special Rule which requires it to be put forwarder."—*Milnes's Greek Gram.* p. 234. "The Masculine and Neuter have the same Dialect in all Numbers, especially when they end the same."—*Ib.* p. 259.

"And children are more busy in their play
Than those that wisely'st pass their time away."—*Butler*, p. 163.

CHAPTER IX.—CONJUNCTIONS.

A Conjunction is a word used to connect words or sentences in construction, and to show the dependence of the terms so connected: as, "Thou *and* he are happy, *because* you are good."—*Murray.*

OBSERVATIONS.

OBS. 1.—Our connective words are of four kinds; namely, relative pronouns, conjunctive adverbs, * conjunctions, and prepositions. These have a certain resemblance to one an other, so far as they are all of them *connectives*; yet there are also characteristical differences by which they may in general be easily distinguished. Relative pronouns represent ante-

---

* De Sacy, in his Principles of General Grammar, calls the relative pronouns "*Conjunctive Adjectives.*" See Fosdick's Translation, p. 57. He also says, "The words *who, which*, etc. are not the only words which connect the function of a Conjunction with another design. There are Conjunctive *Nouns* and *Adverbs*, as well as Adjectives; and a characteristic of these words is, that we can substitute for them another form of expression in which shall be found the words *who, which*, etc. Thus, *when, where, what, how, as*, and many others, are Conjunctive words: [as,] 'I shall finish *when* I please;' that is, 'I shall finish *at the time at which* I please'—'I know not *where* I am;' i. e. 'I know not *the place in which* I am.'"—*Ib.* p. 58. In respect to the conjunctive adverb, this is well enough, so far as it goes; but the word *who* appears to me to be a pronoun, and not an adjective; and of his "*Conjunctive Nouns*," he ought to have given us some examples, if he knew of any.

cedents, and stand in those relations which we call cases; conjunctive adverbs assume the connective power in addition to their adverbial character, and consequently sustain a double relation; conjunctions, (except the introductory correspondents,) join words or sentences together, showing their relation either to each other or to something else; prepositions, though naturally subject themselves to something going before, assume the government of the terms which follow them, and in this they differ from all the rest.

Obs. 2.—Conjunctions do not express any of the real objects of the understanding, whether things, qualities, or actions, but rather the several modes of connexion or contrast under which these objects are contemplated. Hence conjunctions were said by Aristotle and his followers to be in themselves "devoid of signification;" a notion which Harris, with no great propriety, has adopted in his faulty definition* of this part of speech. It is the office of this class of particles, to link together words, phrases, or sentences, that would otherwise appear as loose shreds, or unconnected aphorisms; and thus, by various forms of dependence, to give to discourse such continuity as may fit it to convey a connected train of thought or reasoning. The skill or inability of a writer may as strikingly appear in his management of these little connectives, as in that of the longest and most significant words in the language.

> "The current is often evinced by the straws,
> And the course of the wind by the flight of a feather;
> So a speaker is known by his *ands* and his *ors*,
> Those stitches that fasten his patchwork together."—*Robert F. Mott.*

Obs. 3.—Conjunctions sometimes connect entire sentences, and sometimes particular words or phrases only. When one whole sentence is closely linked with an other, both become clauses or members of a more complex sentence; and when one word or phrase is coupled with an other, both have in general a common dependence upon some other word in the same sentence. In etymological parsing, it may be sufficient to name the conjunction as such, and repeat the definition above; but, in syntactical parsing, the learner should always specify the terms connected. In many instances, however, he may conveniently abbreviate his explanation, by parsing the conjunction as connecting "what precedes and what follows;" ·or, if the terms are transposed, as connecting its own clause to the second, to the third, or to some other clause in the context.

Obs. 4.—However easy it may appear, for even the young parser to *name the terms which* in any given instance are connected by the conjunction, and of course to know for himself *what these terms are,*—that is, to know what the conjunction does, or does not, connect,—it is certain that a multitude of grammarians and philosophers, great and small, from Aristotle down to the latest modifier of Murray, or borrower from his text, have been constantly contradicting one an other, if not themselves, in relation to this matter. Harris avers, that "the Conjunction connects, *not Words, but Sentences;*" and frames his definition accordingly: See *Hermes,* p. 237. This doctrine is true of *some* of the conjunctions, but it is by no means true of them *all.* He adds, in a note, "Grammarians have usually considered the Conjunction as connecting rather single Parts of Speech, than whole Sentences, and that too with the addition of like with like, Tense with Tense, Number with Number, Case with Case, &c. This *Sanctius* justly explodes."—*Ib.* p. 238. If such has been the usual doctrine of the grammarians, they have erred on the one side, as much as our philosopher, and his learned authorities, on the other. For, in this instance, Harris's quotations of Latin and Greek writers, prove only that Sanctius, Scaliger, Apollonius, and Aristotle, held the same error that he himself had adopted;—the error which Latham and others now inculcate, that, "There are always *two propositions* where there is one Conjunction."—*Fowler's E. Gram.* 8vo, 1850, p. 557.

Obs. 5.—The common doctrine of L. Murray and others, that, "Conjunctions connect the same moods and tenses of verbs, and cases of nouns and pronouns," is not only badly expressed, but is pointedly at variance with their previous doctrine, that, "Conjunctions very often unite sentences, when they appear to unite only words; as in the following instances: 'Duty *and* interest forbid vicious indulgences;' 'Wisdom *or* folly governs us.' Each of these forms of expression," they absurdly say, "contains two sentences."—*Murray's Gram.* p. 124; *Smith's,* 95; *Fisk's,* 84; *Ingersoll's,* 81. By "*the same moods, tenses,* or *cases,*" we must needs here understand some *one mood, tense,* or *case,* in which the connected words *agree;* and, if the conjunction has any thing to do with this agreement, or sameness of mood, tense, or case, it must be because words only, and not sentences, are connected by it. Now, *if, that, though, lest, unless,* or any other conjunction that introduces the subjunctive, will almost always be found to connect different moods, or rather to subjoin one sentence to another in which there is a different mood. On the contrary, *and, as, even, than, or,* and *nor,* though they may connect sentences, do, in very many instances, connect words only; as, "The *king and queen* are an amiable pair."—*Murray.* "And a being of *more than human* dignity stood before me."—*Dr. Johnson.* It cannot be plausibly pretended, that *and* and *than,* in these two examples, connect clauses or sentences. So *and* and *or,* in the examples above, con-

---

* "Now the Definition of a CONJUNCTION is as follows—a *Part of Speech, void of Signification itself, but so formed as to help Signification, by making* TWO *or more significant Sentences to be* ONE *significant Sentence.*"—Harris's *Hermes,* 6th Edition, London, p. 238.

nect the nouns only, and not "sentences:" else our common rules for the agreement of verbs or pronouns with words connected, are nothing but bald absurdities. It is idle to say, that the construction and meaning are not *what they appear to be;* and it is certainly absurd to contend, that conjunctions always connect sentences; or always, words only. One author very strangely conceives, that, "Conjunctions may be said either always to connect words only, or always to connect sentences, *according to the view which may be taken of them* in analyzing."—*Nutting's Gram.* p. 77.

Obs. 6.—"Several words belonging to other parts of speech, are occasionally used as conjunctions. Such are the following: *provided, except,* verbs; *both,* an adjective; *either, neither, that,* pronouns; *being, seeing,* participles; *before, since, for,* prepositions. I will do it, *provided* you lend some help. Here *provided* is a conjunction, that connects the two sentences. 'Paul said, *Except* these abide in the ship, ye cannot be saved.' Here *except* is a conjunction. *Excepting* is also used as a participle and conjunction. '*Being* this reception of the gospel was so anciently foretold.'—*Bishop Pearson.* '*Seeing* all the congregation are holy.' —*Bible.* Here *being* and *seeing* are used as conjunctions."—*Alexander's Gram.* p. 50. The foregoing remark, though worthy of some attention, is not altogether accurate. *Before,* when it connects sentences, is not a conjunction, but a conjunctive adverb. *Provided,* as cited above, resembles not the verb, but the perfect participle. *Either* and *neither,* when they are not conjunctions, are pronominal adjectives, rather than pronouns. And, to say, that, "words *belonging to other parts of speech,* are used as *conjunctions,*" is a sort of solecism, which leaves the learner in doubt to what class they *really* belong. *Being,* and *being that,* were formerly used in the sense of *because, since,* or *seeing that;* (Lat. *cùm, quoniam,* or *quando;*) but this usage is now obsolete. So there is an uncommon or obsolete use of *without,* in the sense of *unless,* or *except;* (Lat. *nisi;*) as, "He cannot rise *without* he be helped."—*Walker's Particles,* p. 425. "Non potest *nisi* adjutus exsurgere."—*Seneca.*

CLASSES.

Conjunctions are divided into two general classes, *copulative* and *disjunctive;* and a few of each class are particularly distinguished from the rest, as being *corresponsive.*

I. A *copulative conjunction* is a conjunction that denotes an addition, a cause, a consequence, or a supposition: as, "He *and* I shall not dispute; *for, if* he has any choice, I shall readily grant it."

II. A *disjunctive conjunction* is a conjunction that denotes opposition of meaning: as, "*Though* he were dead, *yet* shall he live."—*St. John's Gospel.* "Be not faithless, *but* believing."—*Id.*

III. The *corresponsive conjunctions* are those which are used in pairs, so that the latter answers to the former: as, "John came *neither* eating *nor* drinking."—*Matt.* xi, 18. "But *if* I cast out devils by the Spirit of God, *then* the kingdom of God is come unto you."—*Ib.* xii, 28.

LIST OF THE CONJUNCTIONS.

! b Copulatives: *And, as, both, because, even, for, if, that, then, since, seeing, so.*

2. The Disjunctives: *Or, nor, either, neither, than, though, although, yet, but, except, whether, lest, unless, save, provided, notwithstanding, whereas.*

3. The Corresponsives: *Both — and; as — as; as — so; if — then; either —or; neither—nor; whether—or; though,* or *although—yet.*

OBSERVATIONS.

Obs. 1.—By some writers, the words, *also, since, too, then, therefore,* and *wherefore,* are placed among the copulative conjunctions; and *as, so, still, however,* and *albeit,* among the disjunctive: but Johnson and Webster have marked most of these terms as *adverbs* only. It is perhaps of little moment, by which name they are called; for, in some instances, conjunctions and conjunctive adverbs do not differ very essentially. *As, so, even, then, yet,* and *but,* seem to belong sometimes to the one part of speech, and sometimes to the other. I call them adverbs when they chiefly express time, manner, or degree; and conjunctions, when they appear to be mere connectives. *As, yet,* and *but,* are generally conjunctions; but *so, even,* and *then,* are almost always adverbs. *Seeing* and *provided,* when used as connectives, are more properly conjunctions than any thing else; though Johnson ranks them with the adverbs, and Webster, by supposing many awkward ellipses, keeps them with the participles. Examples: "For these are not drunken, as ye suppose, *seeing* it is but the third hour of the day."—*Acts*, ii, 15. "The senate shall have power to adjourn themselves, *provided* such adjournment shall not exceed two days at a time."—*Constitution of New Hampshire.*

OBS. 2.—*Since*, when it governs a noun after it, is a preposition: as, "Hast thou commanded the morning *since* thy *days?*"—*Job. Albeit* is equivalent in sense to *although*, and is properly a conjunction; but this old compound is now nearly or quite obsolete. *As* is sometimes a relative pronoun, sometimes a conjunctive adverb, and sometimes a copulative conjunction. Example of the last: "We present ourselves *as* petitioners." If *as* is ever disjunctive, it is not so here; nor can we parse it as an adverb, because it comes between two words that are essentially in apposition. The equivalent Latin term *quasi* is called an adverb, but, in such a case, not very properly: as, "Et colles *quasi* pulverem pones;"— "And thou shalt make the hills *as* chaff."—*Isaiah*, xli, 15. So *even*, which in English is frequently a sign of emphatic repetition, seems sometimes to be rather a conjunction than an adverb: as, "I, *even* I, am the Lord."—*Isaiah*, xliii, 11.

OBS. 3.—*Save* and *saving*, when they denote exception, are not adverbs, as Johnson denominates them, or a verb and a participle, as Webster supposes them to be, but disjunctive conjunctions; and, as such, they take the same case after as before them: as, "All the conspirators, *save* only *he*, did that they did, in envy of great Cæsar."—*Shak.* "All this world's glory seemeth vain, and all their shows but shadows, *saving she.*"—*Spenser.* "Israel burned none of them, *save Hazor* only."—*Joshua*, xi, 13. "And none of them was cleansed, *saving Naaman* the Syrian."—*Luke*, iv, 27. *Save* is not here a transitive verb, for Hazor was not *saved* in any sense, but utterly destroyed; nor is Naaman here spoken of as *being saved by an other leper*, but as being cleansed when others were not. These two conjunctions are now little used; and therefore the propriety of setting the nominative after them and treating them as conjunctions, is the more apt to be doubted. The Rev. Matt. Harrison, after citing five examples, four of which have the nominative with *save*, adds, without naming the part of speech, or assigning any reason, this decision, which I think erroneous: "In all these passages, *save* requires after it the objective case." His five examples are these: "All, *save I*, were at rest, and enjoyment."—*Frankenstein.* "There was no stranger with us, in the house, *save we* two."—1 *Kings*, iii, 18.

"And nothing wanting is, *save she*, alas!"—DRUMMOND *of Hawthornden.*

"When all slept sound, *save she*, who bore them both."—ROGERS, *Italy*, p. 108.

"And all were gone, *save him*, who now kept guard."—*Ibid.* p. 185.

OBS. 4.—The conjunction *if* is sometimes used in the Bible to express, not a supposition of what follows it, but an emphatic negation: as, "I have sworn in my wrath, *if* they shall enter into my rest."—*Heb.* iv, 3. That is, *that they shall not enter.* The same peculiarity is found in the Greek text, and also in the Latin, and other versions. *Or*, in the obsolete phrase "*or ever*," is not properly a conjunction, but a conjunctive adverb of time, meaning *before.* It is supposed to be a corruption of *ere*: as, "I was set up from everlasting, from the beginning, *or ever* the earth was."—*Prov.* viii, 23. "And we, *or ever* he come near, are ready to kill him."—*Acts*, xxiii, 15. This term derives no support from the original text.

OBS. 5.—There are some peculiar phrases, or combinations of words, which have the force of conjunctions, and which it is not very easy to analyze satisfactorily in parsing: as, "And *for all* there were so many, yet was not the net broken."—*John*, xxi, 11. Here *for all* is equivalent to *although*, or *notwithstanding*; either of which words would have been more elegant. *Nevertheless* is composed of three words, and is usually reckoned a conjunctive adverb; but it might as well be called a disjunctive conjunction, for it is obviously equivalent to *yet, but*, or *notwithstanding*; as, "I am crucified with Christ: *nevertheless* I live; *yet* not I, *but* Christ liveth in me."—*Gal.* ii, 20. Here, for *nevertheless* and *but*, we have in the Greek the same particle δὶ. "Each man's mind has some peculiarity, *as well as* his face."—*Locke.* "Relative pronouns, *as well as* conjunctions, serve to connect sentences." —*Murray's Gram.* p. 124. Here the first *as* corresponds to the second, but *well* not being used in the literal sense of an adverb, some judicious grammarians take the whole phrase as a conjunction. It is, however, susceptible of division: as, "It is adorned with admirable pieces of sculpture, *as well* modern, *as* ancient."—*Addison.*

OBS. 6.—So the phrases, *for as much as, in as much as, in so much that*, if taken collectively, have the nature of conjunctions; yet they contain within themselves correspondent terms and several different parts of speech. The words are sometimes printed separately, and sometimes partly together. Of late years, *forasmuch, inasmuch, insomuch*, have been usually compounded, and called adverbs. They might as well, perhaps, be called conjunctions, as they were by some of our old grammarians; for two conjunctions sometimes come together: as, "Answering their questions, *as if* * it were a matter that needed it."—

---

* Whether these, or any other conjunctions that come together, ought to be parsed together, is doubtful. I am not in favour of taking any words together, that can well be parsed separately. Goodenow, who defines a *phrase* to be " the union of two or more words having the *nature and construction of a single word*," finds an immense number of these *unions*, which he cannot, or does not, analyze. As examples of "a *conjunctional phrase*," he

Locke. "These should be at first gently treated, *as though* we expected an imposthuma-tion."—*Sharp.* "But there are many things which we must acknowledge to be true, *not-withstanding that* we cannot comprehend them."—*Beattie's Moral Science,* p. 211. "There is no difference, *except that* some are heavier than others."—"We may be playful, *and yet* innocent ; grave, *and yet* corrupt."—*Murray's Key,* p. 166.

Obs. 7.—Conjunctions have no grammatical modifications, and are consequently in-capable of any formal agreement or disagreement with other words ; yet their import as connectives, copulative or disjunctive, must be carefully observed, lest we write or speak them improperly. Example of error : "Prepositions are *generally set before* nouns *and* pro-nouns."—*Wilbur's Gram.* p. 20. Here *and* should be *or ; because,* although a preposition usually governs a noun *or* a pronoun, it seldom governs both at once. And besides, the assertion above seems very naturally to mean, that nouns and pronouns are *generally pre-ceded* by prepositions—as gross an error as dullness could invent ! L. Murray also says of prepositions : "They are, *for the most part,* put before nouns *and* pronouns."—*Gram.* p. 117. So Felton : "They *generally stand before* nouns *and* pronouns."—*Analytic and Prac. Gram.* p. 61. The blunder however came originally from Lowth, and out of the following ad-mirable enigma : "Prepositions, *standing by themselves in construction,* are put before nouns *and* pronouns ; and sometimes after verbs ; but *in this sort of composition* they are *chiefly prefixed* to verbs : as, *to outgo, to overcome.*"—*Lowth's Gram.* p. 66.

Obs. 8.—The opposition suggested by the disjunctive particle *or,* is sometimes merely nominal, or verbal : as, "That object is a triangle, *or* figure contained under three right lines."—*Harris.* "So if we say, that figure is a sphere, *or* a globe, *or* a ball."—*Id. Hermes,* p. 258. In these cases, the disjunction consists in nothing but an alternative of words ; for the terms connected describe or name the same thing. For this sense of *or,* the Latins had a peculiar particle, *sive,* which they called *Subdisjunctiva,* a *Subdisjunctive :* as, "Alexander *sive* Paris ; Mars *sive* Mavors."—*Harris's Hermes,* p. 258. In English, the conjunction *or* is very frequently equivocal : as, "They were both more ancient than Zoroaster *or* Zerdusht." —*Campbell's Rhet.* p. 250 ; *Murray's Gram.* p. 297. Here, if the reader does not happen to know that *Zoroaster* and *Zerdusht* mean the same person, he will be very likely to mistake the sense. To avoid this ambiguity, we substitute, (in judicial proceedings,) the Latin ad-verb *alias, otherwise ;* using it as a conjunction subdisjunctive, in lieu of *or,* or the Latin *sive :* as, "Alexander, *alias* Ellick."—" Simson, *alias* Smith, *alias* Baker."—*Johnson's Dict.*

EXAMPLES FOR PARSING.

PRAXIS IX. — ETYMOLOGICAL.

In the Ninth Praxis, it is required of the pupil—to distinguish and define the different parts of speech, and the classes and modifications of the ARTICLES, NOUNS, ADJECTIVES, PRONOUNS, VERBS, PARTICIPLES, ADVERBS, *and* CON-JUNCTIONS.

The definitions to be given in the Ninth Praxis, are two for an article, six for a noun, three for an adjective. six for a pronoun, seven for a verb finite, five for an infinitive, two for a participle, two (and sometimes three) for an adverb, two for a conjunction,—and one for a preposition, or an interjection. Thus :—

EXAMPLE PARSED.

"If thou hast done a good deed, boast not of it."—*Maxims.*

If is a copulative conjunction. 1. A conjunction is a word used to connect words or sentences in construction, and to show the dependence of the terms so connected 2. A copulative conjunction is a conjunction that denotes an addition, a cause, a consequence, or a supposition.

Thou is a personal pronoun, of the second person, singular number, masculine gender, and nominative case. 1. A pronoun is a word used in stead of a noun. 2. A personal pronoun is a pronoun that shows, by its form, of what person it is. 3. The second person is that which denotes the hearer, or the person addressed. 4. The singular number is that which denotes but one. 5. The masculine gender is that which denotes persons or animals of the male kind. 6. The nominative case is that form or state of a noun or pronoun, which denotes the subject of a verb.

Hast done is an irregular active-transitive verb, from *do, did, doing, done ;* found in the indicative mood, per-fect tense, second person, and singular number. 1. A verb is a word that signifies *to be, to act,* or *to be acted* upon. 2. An irregular verb is a verb that does not form the preterit and the perfect participle by assuming *d* or *ed.* 3. An active-transitive verb is a verb that expresses an action which has some person or thing for its object. 4. The indicative mood is that form of the verb, which simply indicates or declares a thing, or asks a question. 5. The perfect tense is that which expresses what has taken place, within some period of time not yet fully past. 6. The second person is that which denotes the hearer, or the person addressed. 7. The singular number is that which denotes but one.

A is the indefinite article. 1. An article is the word *the, an,* or *a,* which we put before nouns to limit their sig-nification. 2. The indefinite article is *an* or *a,* which denotes one thing of a kind, but not any particular one.

Good is a common adjective, of the positive degree ; compared irregularly, *good, better, best.* 1. An adjective is a word added to a noun or pronoun, and generally expresses quality. 2. A common adjective is any

gives "as if" and "as though."—Gram. p. 26. But when he comes to speak of *ellipsis,* he says : "After the con-junctions *than, as, but,* &c., some words are generally understood ; as, "We have more than [*that is which*] will suffice ;' 'He acted as [*he would act*] *if* he were mad.' "—*Ib.* p. 41. This doctrine is plainly repugnant to the other.

ordinary epithet, or adjective denoting quality or situation.   3. The positive degree is that which is expressed by the adjective in its simple form.

Deed is a common noun, of the third person, singular number, neuter gender, and objective case.   1. A noun is the name of any person, place, or thing, that can be known or mentioned.   2. A common noun is the name of a sort, kind, or class, of beings or things.   3. The third person is that which denotes the person or thing merely spoken of.   4. The singular number is that which denotes but one.   5. The neuter gender is that which denotes things that are neither male nor female.   6. The objective case is that form or state of a noun or pronoun, which denotes the object of a verb, participle, or preposition.

Boast is a regular active-intransitive verb, from *boast, boasted, boasting, boasted*; found in the imperative mood, present tense, second person, and singular number.   1. A verb is a word that signifies *to be, to act*, or *to be acted upon*.   2. A regular verb is a verb that forms the preterit and the perfect participle by assuming *d* or *ed*.   3. An active-intransitive verb is a verb that expresses an action which has no person or thing for its object.   4. The imperative mood is that form of the verb, which is used in commanding, exhorting, entreating, or permitting.   5. The present tense is that which expresses what now exists, or is taking place.   6. The second person is that which denotes the hearer, or the person addressed.   7. The singular number is that which denotes but one.

Not is an adverb of manner, expressing negation.   1. An adverb is a word added to a verb, a participle, an adjective, or an other adverb; and generally expresses time, place, degree, or manner.   2. Adverbs of manner are those which answer to the question, *How ?* or, by affirming, denying, or doubting, show *how* a subject is regarded.

Of is a preposition.   1. A preposition is a word used to express some relation of different things or thoughts to each other, and is generally placed before a noun or a pronoun.

It is a personal pronoun, of the third person, singular number, neuter gender, and objective case.   1. A pronoun is a word used in stead of a noun.   2. A personal pronoun is a pronoun that shows, by its form, of what person it is.   3. The third person is that which denotes the person or thing merely spoken of.   4. The singular number is that which denotes but one.   5. The neuter gender is that which denotes things that are neither male nor female.   6. The objective case is that form or state of a noun or pronoun which denotes the object of a verb, participle, or preposition.

LESSON I.—PARSING.

" In all gratifications, disgust ever lies nearest to the highest pleasures ; and therefore let us not marvel, if this is peculiarly the case in eloquence.   By glancing at either poets or orators, we may easily satisfy ourselves, that neither a poem nor an oration which aims continually at what is fine, showy, and sparkling, can please us long. Wherefore, though we may wish for the frequent praise of having expressed ourselves well and properly, we should not covet repeated applause for being bright and splendid."—CICERO, *de Oratore*.

" The foundation of eloquence, as well as of every other high attainment, is practical wisdom.   For it happens in oratory, as in life, that nothing is more difficult, than to discern what is proper and becoming.   Through lack of such discernment, gross faults are very often committed.   For neither to all ranks, fortunes, and ages, nor to every time, place, and auditory, can the same style either of language or of sentiment be adapted.   In every part of a discourse, as in every part of life, we must consider what is suitable and decent ; and this must be determined with reference both to the matter in question, and to the personal character of those who speak and those who hear."—CICERO, *Orator ad Brutum*.

" So spake th' Omnipotent, and with his words
   All seem'd well pleas'd ; all seem'd, but were not all."—*Milton*.

LESSON II.—PARSING.

"A square, though not more regular than a hexagon or an octagon, is more beautiful than either : for what reason, but that a square is more simple, and the attention is less divided ? "—*Kames, El. of Crit.* i, 175.

" We see the material universe in motion ; but matter is inert ; and, so far as we know, nothing can move it but mind : therefore God is a spirit.   We do not mean that his nature is the same as that of our soul ; for it is infinitely more excellent.   But we mean, that he possesses intelligence and active power in supreme perfection ; and, as these qualities do not belong to matter, which is neither active nor intelligent, we must refer them to that which is not matter, but mind."—*Beattie's Moral Science*, p. 210.

" Men are generally permitted to publish books, and contradict others, and even themselves, as they please, with as little danger of being confuted, as of being understood."—*Boyle*.

" Common reports, if ridiculous rather than dangerous, are best refuted by neglect." —*Kames's Thinking*, p. 76.   " No man is so foolish, but that he may give good counsel at a time ; no man so wise, but he may err, if he take no counsel but his own."—*Ib.* p. 97.

" Young heads are giddy, and young hearts are warm,
   And make mistakes for manhood to reform."—*Cowper*.

LESSON III.—PARSING.

"The Nouns denote substances, and those either natural, artificial, or abstract. They moreover denote things either general, or special, or particular. The Pronouns, their substitutes, are either prepositive, or subjunctive."—*Harris's Hermes*, p. 85.

"In a thought, generally speaking, there is at least one capital object considered as acting or as suffering. This object is expressed by a substantive noun : its action is expressed by an active verb ; and the thing affected by the action is expressed by another substantive noun : its suffering, or passive state, is expressed by a passive verb ; and the thing that acts upon it, by a substantive noun. Beside these, which are the capital parts of a sentence, or period, there are generally underparts ; each of the substantives, as well as the verb, may be qualified : time, place, purpose, motive, means, instrument, and a thousand other circumstances, may be necessary to complete the thought."—*Kames, El. of Crit.* ii, 34.

" Yet those whom pride and dullness join to blind,
To narrow cares and narrow space confined,
Though with big titles each his fellow greets,
Are but to wits, as scavengers to streets."—*Mallet.*

IMPROPRIETIES FOR CORRECTION.

ERRORS RESPECTING CONJUNCTIONS.

"A *Verb* is so called from the Latin *verbum*, or *word*."—*Bucke's Classical Gram.* p. 56.

[FORMULE.—Not proper, because the conjunction *or*, connecting *verbum* and *word*, supposes the latter to be *Latin*. But, according to Observation 7th, on the Classes of Conjunctions, " The import of connectives, copulative or disjunctive, must be carefully observed, lest we write or speak them improperly." In this instance, *or* should be changed to *a* ; thus, " A *Verb* is so called from the Latin *verbum, a word :* " that is, " which means, a *word*."]

" References are often marked by letters and figures."—*Gould's Adam's Gram.* p. 283. (1.) "A Conjunction is a word which joins words and sentences together."—*Lennie's E. Gram.* p. 51 ; *Bullions's*, 70 ; *Brace's*, 57.   (2.) "A conjunction is used to connect words and sentences together."—*Smith's New Gram.* p. 37.   (3.) "A conjunction is used to connect words and sentences."—*Maunder's Gram.* p. 1.   (4.) " Conjunctions are words used to join words and sentences."—*Wilcox's Gram.* p. 3.   (5.) "A Conjunction is a word used to connect words and sentences."—*M'Culloch's Gram.* p. 36 ; *Hart's*, 92 ; *Day's*, 10. (6.) "A conjunction joins words and sentences together."—*Mackintosh's Gram.* p. 115 ; *Hiley's*, 10 and 53. (7.) " The Conjunction joins words and sentences together."—*L. Murray's Gram.* 2d *Edition*, p. 28.   (8.) " Conjunctions connect words and sentences to each other."—*Ib.* p. 123. *Improved Gram.* 81.   (9.) " Conjunctions connect words and sentences."—*Wilcox's Gram.* p. 80 ; *Wells's*, 1st Ed. 159 and 168.   (10.) "The conjunction is a part of speech used to connect words and sentences."—*Weld's Gram.* 2d Ed. p. 49.   (11.) "A conjunction is a word used to connect words and sentences together."—*Fowler's E. Gram.* § 329.   (12.) "Connectives are words which unite words and sentences in construction."—*Webster's Philos. Gram.* p. 123 ; *Improved Gram.* 81.   " English Grammar is miserably taught in our district schools ; the teachers know but little or nothing about it."—*Taylor's District School*, p. 48.   " Least, instead of preventing, you draw on Diseases."—*Locke, on Ed.* p. 40.   "The definite article *the* is frequently applied to adverbs in the comparative and superlative degree."—*Murray's Gram.* p. 33 ; *Ingersoll's*, 33 ; *Lennie's*, 6 ; *Bullions's*, 8 ; *Fisk's*, 53 ; and others.   " When nouns naturally neuter are converted into masculine and feminine."—*Murray's Gram.* 8vo, p. 38. "This form of the perfect tense represents an action completely past, and often at no great distance, but not specified."—*Ib.* p. 74.   "The Conjunction Copulative serves to connect or to continue a sentence, by expressing an addition, a supposition, a cause, &c."—*Ib.* p. 123. "The Conjunction Disjunctive serves, not only to connect and continue the sentence, but also to express opposition of meaning in different degrees."—*Ib.* p. 123.   " Whether we open the volumes of our divines, philosophers, historians, or artists, we shall find that they abound with all the terms necessary to communicate their observations and discoveries."—*Ib.* p. 138.   " When a disjunctive occurs between a singular noun, or pronoun, and a plural one, the verb is made to agree with the plural noun and pronoun."—*Ib.* p. 152 : *R. C. Smith, Alger, Comly, Merchant, Picket, et al.*   " Pronouns must always agree with their antecedents, and the nouns for which they stand, in gender and number."—*Murray's Gram.* p. 154.   " Verbs neuter do not act upon, or govern, nouns and pronouns."—*Ib.* p. 179.   "And the auxiliary both of the present and past imperfect times."—*Ib.* p. 72.   "If this rule should not appear to apply to every example, which has been produced, nor to others which might be adduced."—*Ib.* p. 216.   "An emphatical pause is made, after something has been said of peculiar moment, and on which we desire to fix the hearer's attention."—*Ib.* p. 248 ; *Hart's Gram.* 175.   "An imperfect phrase contains no assertion, or does not amount to a proposition or sentence."—*Murray's Gram.* p. 267. "The word was in the mouth of every one, but for all that, the subject may still be a secret."—*Ib.* p. 213. "A word it was in the mouth of every one, but for all that, as to its precise and definite idea, this may still be a secret."—*Harris's Three Treatises,* p. 5. "It cannot be otherwise, in regard that the French prosody differs from that of every other country in Europe."—*Smollett's Voltaire,* ix, 306.. "So gradually as to allow its being engrafted on a subtonic."—*Rush, on the Voice,* p. 255. "Where the Chelsea or Malden bridges now are."—*Judge Parker.* "Adverbs are words joined to verbs, participles, adjectives, and other adverbs.—*Smith's Productive Gram.* p. 92. "I could not have told you, who the hermit was, nor on what mountain he lived."—*Bucke's Classical Gram,* p. 32. "*Am,* or *be* (for they are the same) naturally, or in themselves signify *being.*"—*Brightland's Gram.* p. 113. "Words are distinct sounds, by which we express our thoughts and ideas."—*Infant School Gram.* p. 13. "His fears will detect him, but he shall not escape."—*Comly's Gram.* p. 64. "*Whose* is equally applicable to persons or things."—WEBSTER: *in Sanborn's Gram.* p. 95. "One negative destroys another, or is equivalent to an affirmative."—*Bullions, Eng. Gram.* p. 118.

> "No sooner does he peep into
> The world, but he has done his do."—*Hudibras.*

CHAPTER X.—PREPOSITIONS.

A Preposition is a word used to express some relation of different things or thoughts to each other, and is generally placed before a noun or a pronoun; as, "The paper lies *before* me *on* the desk."

OBSERVATIONS.

OBS. 1.—The relations of things to things in nature, or of words to words in discourse, are infinite in number, if not also in variety. But just classification may make even infinites the subjects of sure science. Every *relation* of course implies more objects, and more terms, than one; for any one thing, considered merely in itself, is taken independently, abstractly, irrelatively, as if it had no relation or dependence. In all correct language, the grammatical relation of the *words* corresponds exactly to the relation of the *things* or *ideas* expressed; for the relation of words, is their dependence, or connexion, *according to the sense.* This relation is oftentimes immediate, as of one word to an other, without the intervention of a preposition; but it is seldom, if ever, reciprocally equal; because dependence implies subordination; and mere adjunction is a sort of inferiority.

OBS. 2.—To a preposition, the *antecedent* term may be a noun, an adjective, a pronoun, a verb, a participle, or an adverb; and the *subsequent* term may be a noun, a pronoun, a pronominal adjective, an infinitive verb, or a participle. In some instances, also, as in the phrases, *in vain, on high, at once, till now, for ever, by how much, until then, from thence, from above,* we find adjectives used elliptically, and adverbs substantively, after the preposition. But, in phrases of an adverbial character, what is elsewhere a preposition often becomes an adverb. Now, if prepositions are concerned in expressing the various relations of so many of the different parts of speech, multiplied, as these relations must be, by that endless variety of combinations which may be given to the terms; and if the sense of the writer or speaker is necessarily mistaken, as often as any of these relations are misunderstood, or their terms misconceived; how shall we estimate the importance of a right explanation, and a right use, of this part of speech?

OBS. 3.—The grammarian whom Lowth compliments, as excelling all others, in "acuteness of investigation, perspicuity of explication, and elegance of method;" and as surpassing all but Aristotle, in the beauty and perfectness of his philological analysis; commences his chapter on conjunctions in the following manner: "Connectives are the subject of what follows; which, *according as* they connect *either Sentences or Words,* are called by the different *Names* of *Conjunctions* or *Prepositions.* Of these Names, that of the Preposition is taken from a *mere accident,* as *it* commonly stands in connection before *the Part, which it connects.* The name of the Conjunction, as is evident, has reference to its essential character. Of these two we shall consider the Conjunction *first,* because it connects, *not Words,* but Sentences."—*Harris's Hermes,* p. 237.

OBS. 4.—In point of order, it is not amiss to treat conjunctions before prepositions; though this is not the method of Lowth, or of Murray. But, to any one who is well acquainted with these two parts of speech, the foregoing passage cannot but appear, in three sentences out of the four, both defective in style and erroneous in doctrine. It is true, that conjunctions generally connect sentences, and that prepositions as generally express relations between particular words: but it is true also, that conjunctions *often* connect words only; and that prepositions, by governing antecedents, relatives, or even personal pronouns, may serve to subjoin sentences to sentences, as well as to determine the relation and construction of the particular words which they govern. Example : " The path seems now plain and even, *but* there are asperities and pitfalls, *over which* Religion only can conduct you."—*Dr. John-son.* Here are three simple sentences, which are made members of one compound sentence, by means of *but* and *over which;* while two of these members, clauses, or subdivisions, contain particular words connected by *and.*

Obs. 5.—In one respect, the preposition is the *simplest* of all the parts of speech : in our common schemes of grammar, is has neither classes nor modifications. Every connective word that governs an object after it, is called a preposition, *because it does so;* and in etymological parsing, to name the preposition as such, and define the name, is, perhaps, all that is necessary. But in syntactical parsing, in which we are to omit the definitions, and state the construction, we ought to explain what terms the preposition connects, and to give a rule adapted to this office of the particle. It is a palpable defect in nearly all our grammars, that their syntax contains NO SUCH RULE. " Prepositions govern the objective case," is a rule for *the objective case,* and not for the syntax of *prepositions.* " Prepositions show the relations of words, and of the things or thoughts expressed by them," is the principle for the latter ; a principle which we cannot neglect, without a shameful lameness in our interpretation ;—that is, when we pretend to parse syntactically.

Obs. 6.—Prepositions and their objects very often precede the words on which they depend, and sometimes at a great distance. Of this we have an example, at the opening of Milton's Paradise Lost ; where "*Of,*" the first word, depends on "*Sing,*" in the sixth line below ; for the meaning is—"*Sing of man's first disobedience,*" &c. To find the terms of the relation, is to find the *meaning* of the passage ; a very useful exercise, provided the words have a meaning which is worth knowing. The following text has for centuries afforded ground of dispute, because it is doubtful in the original, as well as in many of the versions, whether the preposition *in* (i. e. "*in the regeneration*") refers back to *have followed,* or forward to the last verb *shall sit :* "Verily I say unto you that ye who have followed me, *in* the regeneration, when the Son of man shall sit *in* the throne of his glory, ye also shall sit upon twelve thrones, judging the twelve tribes of Israel."—*Matt.* xix, 28. The second *in* is manifestly wrong : the Greek word is *ἐπὶ, on* or *upon; i. e.* "*upon* the throne of his glory."

Obs. 7.—The prepositions have, from their own nature, or from custom, such an *adaptation* to particular terms and relations, that they can seldom be used one for an other without manifest impropriety. Example of error : " Proper seasons should be allotted *for* retirement."—*Murray's Key,* p. 173. We do not say " *allotted for,*" but " *allotted to :*" hence *for* is either wrong in itself or misplaced. Such errors always vex an intelligent reader. He sees the terms mismatched, the intended connexion doubtful, the sense obscured, and wishes the author could have valued his own meaning enough to have made it intelligible ; —that is, (to speak technically,) enough to have made it a certain clew to his syntax. We can neither parse nor correct what we do not understand. Did the writer mean, " Proper seasons should be *allotted to* retirement ?"—or, " Proper *seasons for* retirement should be allotted ?"—or, " Seasons *proper for* retirement should be allotted ?" Every expression is incorrigibly bad, the *meaning* of which cannot be known. Expression ? Nay, expression it is not, but only a mock utterance or an abortive attempt at expression.

Obs. 8.—Harris observes, in substance, though in other words, that almost all the prepositions were originally formed to denote relation of *place ;* that this class of relations is primary, being that which natural bodies maintain at all times one to another ; that in the continuity of place these bodies form the universe, or visible whole ; that we have some prepositions to denote the *contiguous* relation of bodies, and others for the *detached* relation ; and that both have, by degrees, been extended from local relations, to the relations of subjects incorporeal. He appears also to assume, that, in such examples as the following,— "Caius *walketh with* a staff ;"—"The statue *stood upon* a pedestal ;"—"The river *ran over* a sand ;"—" He *is going to* Italy ;"—"The sun *is risen above* the hills ;"—"These figs *came from* Turkey ;"—the antecedent term of the relation is not the verb, but the noun or pronoun before it. See *Hermes,* pp. 266 and 267. Now the true antecedent is, unquestionably, that word which, in the order of the sense, the preposition should immediately follow : and a verb, a participle, or an adjective, may sustain this relation, just a well as a substantive. "*The man spoke of colour,*" does not mean, "*The man of colour spoke ;*" nor does, "*The member from Delaware replied,*" mean, "*The member replied from Delaware.*"

Obs. 9.—To make this matter more clear, it may be proper to observe further, that what I call the order of the sense, is not always that order of the words which is fittest to express the sense of a whole period ; and that the true antecedent is that word to which the preposition and its object would naturally be subjoined, were there nothing to interfere with such an arrangement. In practice it often happens, that the preposition and its object cannot be placed immediately after the word on which they depend, and which they would naturally follow. For example : " She hates the means *by which* she lives." That is, " She hates the means which she *lives by.*" Here we cannot say, " She hates the means she *lives by which ;*" and yet, in regard to the preposition *by,* this is really the order of the sense.

Again: "Though thou shouldest bray a fool *in a mortar among wheat with a pestle*, yet will not his foolishness depart from him."—*Prov.* xxvii, 22. Here is no transposition to affect our understanding of the prepositions, yet there is liability to error, because the words which immediately precede some of them, are not their true antecedents: the text does not really speak of "*a mortar among wheat*," or of "*wheat with a pestle*." To what then are the *mortar,* the *wheat,* and the *pestle,* to be mentally subjoined? If all of them, to any one thing, it must be to the *action* suggested by the verb *bray,* and not to its object *fool;* for the text does not speak of "*a fool with a pestle,*" though it does *seem* to speak of "*a fool in a mortar,* and *among wheat.*" Indeed, in this instance, as in many others, the verb and its object are so closely associated that it makes but little difference in regard to the sense, whether you take both of them together, or either of them separately, as the antecedent to the preposition. But, as the instrument of an action is with the agent rather than with the object, if you will have the substantives alone for antecedents, the natural order of the sense must be supposed to be this: "Though *thou with* a pestle shouldest bray a *fool in* a mortar [and] *among wheat,* yet will not his *foolishness from* him depart." This gives to each of the prepositions an antecedent different from that which I should assign. Sanborn observes, "There seem to be *two kinds* of relation expressed by prepositions,—an *existing* and a *connecting* relation."—*Analyt. Gram.* p. 225. The latter, he adds, "*is the most important.*"—*Ib.* p. 226. But it is the former that admits nothing but *nouns* for antecedents. Others besides Harris may have adopted this notion, but I have never been one of the number, though a certain author scruples not to charge the error upon me. See *O. B. Peirce's Grammar*, p. 165.

OBS. 10.—It is a very common error among grammarians, and the source of innumerable discrepancies in doctrine, as well as one of the chief means of maintaining their interminable disputes, that they suppose *ellipses* at their own pleasure, and supply in every given instance just what words their fancies may suggest. In this work, I adopt for myself, and also recommend to others, the contrary course of avoiding on all occasions the supposition of any *needless* ellipses. Not only may the same preposition govern more than one object, but there may also be more than one antecedent word, bearing a joint relation to that which is governed by the preposition. (1.) Examples of joint objects: "There is an inseparable connexion BETWEEN *piety and virtue.*"—*Murray's Key*, 8vo, p. 171. "In the conduct of Parmenio, a mixture OF *wisdom and folly* was very conspicuous."—*Ib.* p. 179. "True happiness is an enemy TO *pomp and noise.*"—*Ib.* p. 171. (2.) "Examples of joint antecedents: "In unity consist the *welfare and security* OF every society."—*Ib.* p. 182. "It is our duty to be *just and kind* TO our fellow-creatures, and to be *pious and faithful* TO Him that made us."—*Ib.* p. 181. "If the author did not mean to speak of being *pious to God* as well as *faithful to Him,* he has written incorrectly: a comma after *pious,* would alter both the sense and the construction. So the text, "For I am meek, and lowly in heart," is commonly perverted in our Bibles, for want of a comma after *meek.* The Saviour did not say, he was *meek in heart:* the Greek may be *very literally* rendered thus: "For gentle am I, and humble in heart."

OBS. 11.—Many writers seem to suppose, that no preposition can govern more than one object. Thus L. Murray, and his followers: "The ellipsis of the *preposition,* as well as of the verb, is seen in the following instances: 'He went into the abbeys, halls, and public buildings;' that is, 'He went into the abbeys, he went into the halls, and he went into the public buildings.'—'He also went through all the streets, and lanes of the city;' that is, 'Through all the streets, and through all the lanes, &c."—*Murray's Gram.* 8vo, p. 219. See the same interpretations in *Ingersoll's Gram.* p. 155; *Merchant's,* 100; *Picket's,* 211; *Alger's,* 73; *Fisk's,* 147; *Guy's,* 91; *Adams's,* 82; *R. C. Smith's,* 183; *Hamlin's,* 105; *Putnam's,* 139; *Weld's,* 292. Now it is plain, that in neither of these examples is there any such ellipsis at all. Of the three prepositions, the first governs three nouns; the second, two; and the third, one only. But the last, (which is *of,*) has two antecedents, *streets* and *lanes,* the comma after *streets* being wrong; for the author does not speak of all the streets in the world, but of *all the streets and lanes* of a particular city. Dr. Ash has the same example without the comma, and supposes in it only an ellipsis of the preposition *through,* and even that supposition is absurd. He also furnished the former example, to show an ellipsis, not of the verb *went,* but only of the preposition *into;* and in this too he was utterly wrong. See *Ash's Grammar,* p. 100. Bicknell also, whose grammar appeared five years before Murray's, confessedly copied the same examples from Ash; and repeated, not the verb and its nominative, but only the prepositions *through* and *into,* agreeably to Ash's erroneous notion. See his *Grammatical Wreath,* Part i, p. 124. Again the principles of Murray's supposed ellipses, are as inconsistent with each other, as they are severally absurd. Had the author explained the second example according to his notion of the first, he should have made it to mean, 'He also *went* through all the streets *of the city,* and *he also went* through all the lanes *of the city.*' What a pretty idea is this for a principle of grammar! And what a multitude of admirers are pretending to carry it out in parsing! One of the latest writers on grammar says, that, "*Between him and me,*" signifies, "*Between him, and between me!*"—*Wright's Philosophical Gram.* p. 206. And an other absurdly resolves a simple sentence into a compound one, thus: "'There was a difficulty between John, and his brother.' That is, there was a difficulty between John, and *there was a difficulty between* his brother."—*James Brown's English Syntax,* p. 127; and again, p. 130.

OBS. 12.—Two prepositions are not unfrequently connected by a conjunction, and that for different purposes, thus : (1.) To express two different relations at once ; as, "The picture of my travels *in and around* Michigan."—*Society in America*, i, 231. (2.) To suggest an alternative in the relation affirmed ; as, "The action will be fully accomplished *at or before* the time."—*Murray's Gram.* i, 72. Again : "The First Future Tense represents the action as yet to come, *either with or without* respect to the precise time."—*Ib. Felton's Gram.* p. 23. *With* and *without* being direct opposites, this alternative is a thing of course, and the phrase is an idle truism. (3.) To express two relations so as to affirm the one and deny the other ; as, "Captain, yourself are the fittest to live and reign not *over*, but next and immediately *under* the people."—*Dryden.* Here, perhaps, "*the people*" may be understood after *over*. (4.) To suggest a mere alternative of words ; as, "NEGATIVELY, adv. *With or by* denial."—*Webster's Dict.* (5.) To add a similar word, for aid or force ; as, "Hence adverbs of time were necessary, *over and above* the tenses."—See *Murray's Gram.* p. 116. "To take effect *from and after* the first day of May."—*Newspaper.*

OBS. 13.—In some instances, two prepositions come directly together, so as jointly to express a sort of compound relation between what precedes the one and what follows the other : as, "And they shall sever the wicked *from among* the just."—*Matt.* xiii, 49. "Moses brought out all the rods *from before* the Lord."—*Numb.* xvii, 9. "Come out *from among* them."—*2 Cor.* vi, 17. "From Judea, and *from beyond* Jordan."—*Matt.* iv, 25. "Nor a law-giver *from between* his feet."—*Gen.* xlix, 10. Thus the preposition *from*, being itself adapted to the ideas of motion and separation, easily coincides with any preposition of place, to express this sort of relation ; the terms however have a limited application, being used only between *a verb* and *a noun*, because the relation itself is between *motion* and the *place* of its beginning : as, "The sand *slided from beneath* my feet."—*Dr. Johnson.* In this manner, we may form *complex prepositions* beginning with *from*, to the number of *about* thirty ; as, *from amidst, from around, from before, from behind*, &c. Besides these, there are several others, of a more questionable character, which are sometimes referred to the same class ; as, *according to, as to, as for, because of, instead of, off of, out of, over against*, and *round about.* Most or all of these are sometimes resolved in a different way, upon the assumption that the former word is an adverb ; yet we occasionally find some of them compounded by the hyphen : as, "Pompey's lieutenants, Afranius and Petreius, who lay *over-against* him, decamp suddenly."—*Rowe's Lucan*, Argument to B. iv. But the common fashion is, to write them separately ; as, "One thing is set *over against* an other."—*Bible.*

OBS. 14.—It is not easy to fix a principle by which prepositions may in all cases be distinguished from adverbs. The latter, we say, do not govern the objective case ; and if we add, that the former do *severally* require some object after them, it is clear that any word which precedes a preposition, must needs be something else than a preposition. But this destroys all the doctrine of the preceding paragraph, and admits of no such thing as a *complex preposition* ; whereas that doctrine is acknowledged, to some extent or other, by every one of our grammarians, not excepting even those whose counter-assertions leave no room for it. Under these circumstances, I see no better way, than to refer the student to the definitions of these parts of speech, to exhibit examples in all needful variety, and then let him judge for himself what disposition ought to be made of those words which different grammarians parse differently.

OBS. 15.—If our prepositions were to be divided into classes, the most useful distinction would be, to divide them into *Single* and *Double.* The distinction which some writers make, who divide them into "*Separable* and *Inseparable*," is of no use at all in parsing, because the latter are mere syllables ; and the idea of S. R. Hall, who divides them into "*Possessive* and *Relative*," is positively absurd ; for he can show us only *one* of the former kind, and that one, (the word *of*,) is not always such. A *Double Preposition*, if such a thing is admissible, is one that consists of two words which in syntactical parsing must be taken together, because they jointly express the relation between two other terms ; as, "The waters were dried up *from off* the earth."—*Gen.* viii, 13. "The clergy kept this charge *from off* us."—*Leslie, on Tithes*, p. 221. "Confidence in an unfaithful man in time of trouble, is like a broken tooth, and a foot *out of* joint."—*Prov.* xxv, 19. "The beam *out of* the timber shall answer it."—*Hab.* ii, 11. *Off* and *out* are most commonly adverbs, but neither of them can be called an adverb here.

OBS. 16.—Again, if *according to* or *as to* is a preposition, then is *according* or *as* a preposition also, although it does not of itself govern the objective case. *As*, thus used, is called a conjunction by some, an adverb by others. Dr. Webster considers *according* to be always a participle, and expressly says, "It is never a preposition."—*Octavo Dict.* The following is an instance in which, if it is not a preposition, it is a participle : "This is a construction not *according* to the rules of grammar."—*Murray's Gram.* Vol. ii, p. 22. But *according to* and *contrary to* are expressed in Latin and Greek by single prepositions ; and if *to* alone is the preposition in English, then both *according* and *contrary* must, in many instances, be adverbs. Example : "For dost thou sit as judging me *according* to the law, and *contrary to* law command me to be smitten ?" (See the Greek of Acts, xxiii, 3.) *Contrary*, though literally an adjective, is often made either an adverb, or a part of a complex preposition, unless the grammarians are generally in error respecting it : as, " He dares not act *contrary to* his instructions."—*Murray's Key*, p. 179.

OBS. 17.—J. W. Wright, with some appearance of analogy on his side, but none of usage, everywhere adds *ly* to the questionable word *according*; as, "We are usually estimated *accordingly to* our company."—*Philosophical Gram.* p. 127. "*Accordingly to* the forms in which they are employed."—*Ib.* p. 137. "*Accordingly to* the above principles, the *adjective* ACCORDING (or *agreeable*) is frequently, but improperly, substituted for the adverb ACCORD-INGLY (or *agreeably*.)"—*Ib.* p. 145. The word *contrary* he does not notice; but, on the same principle, he would doubtless say, "He dares not act *contrarily to* his instructions." We say indeed, "He acted *agreeably to* his instructions;"—and not, "He acted *agreeable* to his instructions." It must also be admitted, that the adverbs *accordingly* and *contrarily* are both of them good English words. If these were adopted, where the character of *according* and *contrary* is disputable, there would indeed be no longer any occasion to call these latter either adverbs or prepositions. But the fact is, that *no good writers have yet preferred them*, in such phrases; and the adverbial ending *ly* gives an additional syllable to a word that seems already quite too long.

OBS. 18.—*Instead* is reckoned an adverb by some, a preposition by others; and a few write *instead-of* with a needless hyphen. The best way of settling the grammatical question respecting this term, is, to write the noun *stead* as a separate word, governed by *in*. Bating the respect that is due to anomalous usage, there would be more propriety in compounding *in quest of*, *in lieu of*, and many similar phrases. For *stead* is not always followed by *of*, nor always preceded by *in*, nor always made part of a compound. We say, *in our stead*, *in your stead*, *in their stead*, &c.; but *lieu*, which has the same meaning as *stead*, is much more limited in construction. Examples: "In the *stead* of sinners, He, a divine and human person, suffered."—*Barnes's Notes*. "Christ suffered in *the place* and *stead* of sinners."—*Ib.* "*For*, in its primary sense, is *pro*, *loco alterius*, in *the stead* or *place* of another." —*Lowth's Gram.* p. 65.

"If it may stand him more in *stead* to lie."—*Milt. P. L.*, B. i, l. 473.
" But here thy sword can do thee little *stead*."—*Id. Comus*, l. 611.

OBS. 19.—*From forth* and *from out* are two poetical phrases, apparently synonymous, in which there is a fanciful transposition of the terms, and perhaps a change of *forth* and *out* from adverbs to prepositions. Each phrase is equivalent in meaning to *out of* or *out from*. *Forth*, under other circumstances, is never a preposition; though *out*, perhaps, may be. We speak as familiarly of going *out doors*, as of going *up stairs*, or *down cellar*. Hence *from out* may be parsed as a complex preposition, though the other phrase should seem to be a mere example of hyperbaton:

"I saw *from out* the wave her structures rise."—*Byron*.
"Peeping *from forth* their alleys green."—*Collins*.

OBS. 20.—"*Out of* and *as to*," says one grammarian, " are properly prepositions, although they are double words. They may be called *compound* prepositions."—*Cooper's Gram.* p. 103. I have called the *complex* prepositions *double* rather than *compound*, because several of the single prepositions are compound words; as, *into*, *notwithstanding*, *overthwart*, *throughout*, *upon*, *within*, *without*. And even some of these may follow the preposition *from*; as, "If he shall have removed *from within* the limits of this state." But *in* and *to*, *up* and *on*, *with* and *in*, are not always compounded when they come together, because the sense may positively demand that the former be taken as an adverb, and the latter only as a preposition: as, "I will come *in to* him, and will sup with him."—*Rev.* iii, 20 "A statue of Venus was set *up on* Mount Calvary."—*M'Ilvaine's Lectures*, p. 332. "The troubles which we meet *with in* the world."—*Blair*. And even two prepositions may be brought together without union or coalescence; because the object of the first one may be expressed or understood *before* it: as, "The man whom you spoke *with in* the street;" —"The treatment you complain *of on* this occasion;"—"The house that you live *in in* the summer;"—"Such a dress as she had *on in* the evening."

OBS. 21.—Some grammarians assume, that, "Two prepositions in immediate succession require a noun to be *understood* between them; as, 'Hard by, a cottage chimney smokes, *From betwixt* two aged oaks.'—' The mingling notes came softened *from below*.' "— *Nutting's Gram.* p. 105. This author would probably understand here—" From *the space* betwixt two aged oaks;"—"came softened from *the region* below *us*." But he did not consider all the examples that are included in his proposition; nor did he rightly regard even those which he cites. The doctrine will be found a very awkward one in practice; and an other objection to it is, that most of the ellipses which it supposes, are entirely imaginary. If there were truth in his assumption, the compounding of prepositions would be positively precluded. The terms *over-against* and *round-about* are sometimes written with the hyphen, and perhaps it would be well if all the complex prepositions were regularly compounded; but, as I before suggested, such is not the present fashion of writing them, and the general usage is not to be controlled by what any individual may think.

OBS. 22.—Instances may, doubtless, occur, in which the object of a preposition is suppressed by ellipsis, when an other preposition follows, so as to bring together two that do not denote a compound relation, and do not, in any wise, form one complex preposition. Of such suppression, the following is an example; and, I think, a double one: "They take pronouns *after instead of before* them."—*Fowler, E. Gram.* § 521. This may be interpreted to mean, and probably does mean—"They take pronouns after *them* in *stead* of *taking them* before them."

OBS. 23.—In some instances, the words, *in, on, of, for, to, with,* and others commonly reckoned prepositions, are used after infinitives or participles, in a sort of *adverbial* construction, because they do not govern any objective; yet not exactly in the usual sense of adverbs, because they evidently express the relation between the verb or participle and a nominative or objective going before. Examples: "Houses are built to live *in,* and not to look *on;* therefore let use be preferred before uniformity, except where both may be had."—*Ld. Kames.* "These are not mysteries for ordinary readers to be let *into.*"—ADDISON: *Joh. Dict. w. Let.* "Heaven is worth dying *for,* though earth is not worth living *for.*"—*R. Hall.* "What! have ye not houses to eat and to drink *in?*"—1 *Cor.* xi, 22. This is a very peculiar idiom of our language; and if we say, "Have ye not houses *in which* to eat and to drink?" we form *an other* which is not much less so. Greek: "Μὴ γὰρ οἰκίας οὐκ ἔχετε εἰς τὸ ἐσθίειν καὶ πίνειν;" Latin: "Num enim domos non habetis ad manducandum et bibendum?"—*Leusden.* "N'avez vous pas des maisons pour manger et pour boire?"—*French Bible.*[*]

OBS. 24.—In OBS. 10th, of Chapter Fourth, on Adjectives, it was shown, that words of *place,* (such as, *above, below, beneath, under,* and the like,) are sometimes set before nouns in the character of adjectives, and not of prepositions: as, "In the *above* list"—"From the *above* list."—*Bullions, E. Gram.* p. 70. To the class of adjectives also, rather than to that of adverbs, may some such words be referred, when, without governing the objective case, they are put *after* nouns to signify place: as, "The *way* of life is *above* to the wise, that he may depart from *hell beneath.*"—*Prov.* xv, 24. "Of any thing that is in *heaven above,* or that is in the *earth beneath.*" —*Exod.* xx, 4.

> "Say first, of *God above* or *man below,*
> What can we reason but from what we know?"—*Pope.*

LIST OF THE PREPOSITIONS.

The following are the principal prepositions arranged alphabetically: *Aboard, about, above, across, after, against, along, amid* or *amidst, among* or *amongst, around, at, athwart;—Bating, before, behind, below, beneath, beside* or *besides, between* or *betwixt, beyond, by;—Concerning;—Down, during;—Ere, except, excepting;—For, from;—In, into;—Mid* or *midst;—Notwithstanding;—Of, off,*[†] *on, out, over, overthwart;—Past, pending;—Respecting, round;—Since;—Through, throughout, till, to, touching, toward* or *towards;—Under, underneath, until, unto, up, upon;—With, within, without.*

OBSERVATIONS.

OBS. 1.—Grammarians differ considerably in their tables of the English prepositions. Nor are they all of one opinion, concerning either the characteristics of this part of speech, or the particular instances in which the acknowledged properties of a preposition are to be found. Some teach that, "Every preposition requires an *objective case* after it."—*Lennie,* p. 50; *Bullions, Prin. of E. Gram.* p. 69. In opposition to this, I suppose that the preposition *to* may take an *infinitive verb* after it; that *about* also may be a preposition, in the phrase, "*about to write;*" that *about, above, after, against, by, for, from, in, of,* and some other prepositions, may govern *participles,* as such; (i. e. without making them nouns, or cases;) and, lastly, that after a preposition an *adverb* is sometimes construed substantively, and yet is indeclinable; as, *for once, from afar, from above, at unawares.*

OBS. 2.—The writers just quoted, proceed to say: "When a *preposition does not govern* an objective case, it becomes an adverb; as, 'He rides *about.*' But in such phrases as, *cast up, hold out, fall on,* the words *up, out,* and *on,* must be considered as *a part of the verb,* rather than as prepositions or adverbs."—*Lennie's Prin. of E. Gram.* p. 50; *Bullions's,* p. 59; *his Analyt. and P. Gram.* p. 109. Both these sentences are erroneous: the one, more particularly so, in expression; the other, in doctrine. As the preposition is chiefly distinguished by its regimen, it is absurd to speak of it as governing nothing; yet it does not always govern the objective case, for participles and infinitives have no cases. *About, up, out,* and *on,* as here cited, are all of them *adverbs;* and so are all other particles that thus qualify verbs, without governing any thing. L. Murray grossly errs where he assumes, that, "The distinct component parts of such phrases as, *to cast up, to fall on, to bear out, to give over,* &c., are *no guide* to the sense of the whole." Surely, "to cast *up*" is to cast *somehow,* though the meaning of the phrase may be "*to compute.*" By this author,

---

[*] Of the construction noticed in this observation, the Rev. Matt. Harrison cites a good example; pronounces it elliptical; and scarcely forbears to condemn it as bad English: "*In the following sentence, the relative pronoun* is three times omitted:—'Is there a God to swear *by,* and is there none to believe *in,* none to trust *to?*'—*Letters and Essays, Anonymous. By, in,* and *to,* as prepositions, stand alone, *denuded of the relatives* to which they apply. The sentence presents no attractions worthy of imitation. It exhibits a license carried to the extreme point of endurance."—*Harrison's English Language,* p. 196.

[†] "An ellipsis of *from* after the adverb *off* has caused the latter word sometimes to be inserted *incorrectly* among the prepositions. Ex. 'off (from) his horse.'"—*Hart's Gram.* p. 96. *Off* and *on* are opposites; and, in a sentence like the following, I see no more need of inserting "*from*" after the former, than *to* after the latter: "Thou shalt not come down *off* that bed *on* which thou art gone up."—2 *Kings,* i, 16.

and some others, all *such adverbs* are absurdly called *prepositions*, and are also as absurdly declared to be *parts* of the preceding verbs! See *Murray's Gram.* p. 117; *W. Allen's*, 179; *Kirkham's*, 96; *R. C. Smith's*, 93; *Fisk's*, 86; *Butler's*, 63; *Wells's*, 146.

Obs. 3.—In comparing the different English grammars now in use, we often find the primary distinction of the parts of speech, and every thing that depends upon it, greatly perplexed by the *fancied ellipses*, and *forced constructions*, to which their authors resort. Thus Kirkham: "Prepositions are sometimes erroneously called adverbs, when their nouns are understood. 'He rides *about ;*' that is, about the *town, country*, or some-*thing* else. 'She was *near* [the *act* or *misfortune* of] falling;' 'But do not *after* [that *time* or *event*] lay the blame on me.' 'He came *down* [the *ascent*] from the hill;' 'They lifted him *up* [the *ascent*] out of the pit.' 'The angels *above ;*' —above *us*—'Above these lower *heavens*, to us invisible, or dimly seen.'"—*Gram.* p. 89. The errors of this passage are almost as numerous as the words ; and those to which the doctrine leads are absolutely innumerable. That *up* and *down*, with verbs of motion, imply ascent and descent, as *wisely* and *foolishly* imply wisdom and folly, is not to be denied ; but the grammatical bathos of coming "*down* [the *ascent*] *from the hill*" *of science*, should startle those whose faces are directed upward! *Downward ascent* is a movement worthy only of Kirkham, and his Irish rival, Joseph W. Wright. The *brackets* here used are Kirkham's, not mine.

Obs. 4.—"Some of the *prepositions*," says L. Murray, "have the *appearance and effect* of conjunctions : as, 'After their prisons were thrown open,' &c. 'Before I die;' 'They made haste to be prepared *against* their friends arrived :' but if the noun *time*, which *is understood*, be added, they will lose their *conjunctive form :* as, 'After [*the time when*] their prisons,' &c."—*Octavo Gram.* p. 119. Here, *after, before*, and *against*, are neither conjunctions nor prepositions, but conjunctive *adverbs of time*, referring to the verbs which follow them, and also, when the sentences are completed, to others antecedent. The awkward addition of "*the time when*," is a sheer perversion. If *after, before*, and the like, can ever be adverbs, they are so here, and not conjunctions, or prepositions.

Obs. 5.—But the great Compiler proceeds: "The *prepositions, after, before, above, beneath*, and several others, sometimes *appear to be adverbs*, and may be *so considered :* as, 'They had their reward soon *after ;*' 'He died not long *before ;*' 'He dwells *above ;*' but if the nouns *time* and *place* be added, they will lose their adverbial form : as, 'He died not long *before that time,*' &c."—*Ib.* Now, I say, when any of the foregoing words "*appear* to be adverbs," they *are* adverbs, and, if adverbs, then not prepositions. But to consider prepositions to be adverbs, as Murray here does, or seems to do ; and to suppose "the NOUNS *time* AND *place*" to be understood in the several examples here cited, as he also does, or seems to do ; are singly such absurdities as no grammarian should fail to detect, and together such a knot of blunders, as ought to be wondered at, even in the Compiler's humblest copyist. In the following text, there is neither preposition nor ellipsis:

"Above, below, without, within, around,
Confus'd, unnumber'd multitudes are found."—*Pope, on Fame.*

Obs. 6.—It comports with the name and design of this work, which is a broad synopsis of grammatical criticism, to notice here one other absurdity ; namely, the doctrine of "*sentential nouns.*" There is something of this in several late grammars : as, "The prepositions after, before, ere, since, till, and until, frequently govern *sentential* nouns ; and after, before, since, notwithstanding, and some others, frequently govern a noun or pronoun *understood*. A preposition governing a sentential noun, is, by Murray and others, considered a *conjunction ;* and a preposition governing a noun understood, an *adverb*."—J. L. PARKHURST: *in Sanborn's Gram.* p. 123. "Example: 'He will, *before he dies*, sway the sceptre.' *He dies* is a sentential noun, third person, singular number ; and is governed by *before ; before he dies*, being equivalent in meaning to *before his death*."—*Sanborn, Gram.* p. 176. "'*After they had waited* a long time, they departed.' After *waiting*."—*Ib.* This last solution supposes the phrase, "*waiting a long time*," or at least the participle *waiting*, to be a *noun ;* for, upon the author's principle of equivalence, "*they had waited*," will otherwise be a "*sentential*" participle—a thing however as good and as classical as the other!

Obs. 7.—If a preposition can ever be justly said to take a sentence for its object, it is chiefly in certain ancient expressions, like the following : "For *in that* he died, he died unto sin once ; but *in that* he liveth, he liveth unto God."—*Rom.* vi, 10. "My Spirit shall not always strive with man, *for that* he also is flesh."—*Gen.* vi, 3. "For, *after that*, in the wisdom of God, the world by wisdom knew not God, it pleased God by the foolishness of preaching to save them that believe." —1 *Cor.* i, 21. Here, *in, for*, and *after*, are all followed by the word *that ;* which Tooke, Webster, Frazee, and some others, will have to be "a substitute," or "pronoun," representing the sentence which follows it, and governed by the preposition. But *that*, in this sense, is usually, and perhaps more properly, reckoned a conjunction. And if we take it so, *in, for*, and *after*, (unless the last be an adverb,) must either be reckoned conjunctions also, or be supposed to govern sentences. The expressions however are little used ; because "*in that*" is nearly equivalent to *as ;* "*for that*" can be better expressed by *because ;* and "*after that*," which is equivalent to *inasmuch, postquam*, may well be rendered by the term, *seeing that*, or *since*. "*Before that* Philip called thee*," is a similar example ; but "*that*" is here needless, and "*before*" may be parsed as a conjunctive adverb of time. I have one example more : "But, *besides that* he attempted it formerly with no success, it is certain the Venetians keep too watchful an eye," &c.—*Addison*. This is good English, but the word "*besides*," if it be not a conjunction, may as well be called an adverb, as a preposition.

Obs. 8.—There are but few words in the list of prepositions, that are not sometimes used as being of some other part of speech. Thus *bating, excepting, concerning, touching, respecting, during, pending*, and a part of the compound *notwithstanding*, are literally participles ; and some writers, in opposition to general custom, refer them always to their original class. Unlike most other prepositions, they do not refer to *place*, but rather to *action, state*, or *duration ;* for, even as prepositions, they are still allied to participles. Yet to suppose them always participles, as would Dr. Webster and some others, is impracticable. Examples: "They speak *concerning* virtue."— *Bullions, Prin. of E. Gram.* p. 69. Here *concerning* cannot be a participle, because its antecedent term is a *verb*, and the meaning is, "they *speak of* virtue." "They are bound *during life :*" that is, *durante vitâ*, life continuing, or, as long as life lasts. So, "*Notwithstanding this ;*" i. e. "*hos non obstante*," this not hindering. Here the nature of the construction seems to depend on the order of the words. "Since he had succeeded, *notwithstanding them*, peaceably to the throne."—*Bolingbroke, on Hist.* p. 31. "This is a correct English idiom, Dr. Lowth's *criticism* to the contrary *notwithstanding.*"—*Webster's Improved Gram.* p. 85. In the phrase, "*notwithstanding them,*" the former word is clearly a preposition governing the latter ; but Dr. Webster doubtless supposed the word "*criticism*" to be in the nominative case, put absolute with the participle : and so it would have been, had he written *not withstanding* as two words, like "*non obstante ;*" but the compound word *notwithstanding* is not a participle, because there is no verb to *notwithstand.* But *notwithstanding*, when placed before a nominative, or before the conjunction *that*, is a conjunction, and, as such, must be rendered in Latin by *tamen*, yet, *quamvis*, although, or *nihilominus*, nevertheless.

OBS. 9.—*For*, when it signifies *because*, is a conjunction : as, "Boast not thyself of to-morrow; *for* thou knowest not what a day may bring forth."—*Prov.* xxvii, 1. *For* has this meaning, and, according to Dr. Johnson, is a conjunction, when it precedes *that* ; as, "Yet *for that* the worst men are most ready to remove, I would wish them chosen by descretion of wise men."—*Spenser.* The phrase, as I have before suggested, is almost obsolete ; but Murray, in one place, adopts it from Dr. Beattie : "*For that* those parts of the verb are not properly called tenses."—*Octavo Gram.* p. 75. How he would have parsed it, does not appear. But both words are connectives. And, from the analogy of those terms which serve as links to other terms, I should incline to take *for that*, *in that*, *after that*, and *besides that*, (in which a known conjunction is put last,) as complex conjunctions ; and also, to take *as for*, *as to*, and *because of*, (in which a known preposition is put last,) as complex prepositions. But there are other regular and equivalent expressions that might in general to be preferred to any or all of these.

OBS. 10.—Several words besides those contained in the list above, are (or have been) occasionally employed in English as prepositions : as, *A*, (chiefly used before participles,) *abaft*, *adown*, *afore*, *aloft*, *aloof*, *alongside*, *anear*, *aneath*, *anent*, *aslant*, *aslope*, *astride*, *atween*, *atwixt*, *bmouth*, *bywest*, *cross*, *dehors*, *despite*, *inside*, *left-hand*, *maugre*, *minus*, *onto*, *opposite*, *outside*, *per*, *plus*, *sans*, *spite*, *thorough*, *traverse*, *versus*, *via*, *withal*, *withinside*.

OBS. 11.—Dr. Lowth says, "the particle *a* before participles, in the phrases, *a* coming, *a* going, *a* walking, *a* shooting, &c. and before nouns, as *a*-bed, *a*-board, *a*-shore, *a*-foot, &c. seems to be *a true and genuine preposition*, a little disguised by familiar use and quick pronunciation. Dr. Wallis supposes it to be the preposition *at*. I rather think it is the preposition *on*."—*Lowth's Gram.* p. 65 ; *Churchill's*, 268. There is no need of supposing it to be either. It is not from *on* ; for in Saxon it sometimes accompanied *on :* as in the phrase, "*on à weoruld ;*" that is, "*on to ages ;*" or, as Wickliffe rendered it, "*into worldis ;*" or, as our version has it, "*for ever.*" See *Luke,* i, 55. This preposition was in use long before either *a* or *an*, as an article, appeared in its present form in the language ; and, for ought I can discover, it may be as old as either *on* or *at*. *An*, too, is found to have had at times the sense and construction of *in* or *on* ; and this usage is, beyond doubt, older than that which makes it an article. *On*, however, was an exceedingly common preposition in Saxon, being used almost always where we now put *on*, *in*, *into*, *upon*, or *among*, and sometimes, for *with* or *by* ; so, sometimes, where *a* was afterwards used : thus, "What in the Saxon Gospel of John, is, 'Ic wylle gan *on* fixoth,' is, in the English version, 'I go *a* fishing.' Chap. xxi, ver. 3." See *Lowth's Gram.* p. 65 ; *Churchill's*, 269. And *a* is now sometimes equivalent to *on* ; as, "He would have a learned University make Barbarisms *a* purpose."—*Bentley, Diss. on Phalaris*, p. 223. That is,—"*on* purpose." How absurdly then do some grammarians interpret the forgoing text!—"I go *on* a fishing."—*Alden's Gram.* p. 117. "I go on *a* fishing *voyage or business.*"—*Murray's Gram.* p. 221 ; *Merchant's*, 101. "It may not be improper," says Churchill in another place, "to observe here, that the preposition *on*, is too frequently pronounced as if it were the vowel *a*, in ordinary conversation ; and this corruption *is* [has] become so prevalent, that I have even met with 'laid it *a oneside*' in a periodical publication. It should have been '*on one side*,' if the expression were meant to be particular ; '*aside*,' if general."—*New Gram.* p. 345. By these writers, *a* is also supposed to be sometimes a corruption of *of :* as, "Much in the same manner, Thomas *of* Becket, by very frequent and familiar use, became Thomas *a* Becket ; and one *of the* clock, or perhaps *on the* clock, is written, one o'clock, but pronounced, one *a* clock. The phrases with *a* before a participle are out of use in the solemn style; but still prevail in familiar discourse. They are established by long usage, and good authority; and there seems to be no reason, why they should be utterly rejected."—*Lowth's Gram.* p. 66. "Much in the same manner, John *of* Nokes, and John *of* Styles, become John *a* Nokes, and John *a* Styles: and one *of the* clock, or rather *on the* clock, is written one o'clock, but pronounced one *a* clock. The phrases with *a* before participles, are out of use in the solemn style ; but still prevail in familiar discourse."—*Churchill's New Gram.* p. 269.

OBS. 12.—The following are *examples* of the less usual prepositions, *a*, and others that begin with *a :* "And he set—three thousand and six hundred overseers to set the people *a* work."—*2 Chron.* ii, 18. "Who goeth *a* warfare any time at his own charges ?"—*1 Cor.* ix, 7. "And the mixed multitude that was among them fell *a* lusting."—*Num.* xi, 4.

"And sweet Billy Dimond, *a* patting his hair up."—*Feast of the Poets*, p. 17.
"The god fell *a* laughing to see his mistake."—*Ib.* p. 18.
"You'd have thought 'twas the bishops or judges *a* coming."—*Ib.* p. 22.
"A place on the lower deck, *abaft* the mainmast."—*Gregory's Dict.* "A moment gazed *adown* the dale."—*Scott, L. L.* p. 10. "*Adown* Strath-Gartney's valley broad."—*Ib.* p. 84. "For *afore* the harvest, when the bud is perfect," &c.—*Isaiah*, xviii, 5. "Where the great luminary *aloof* the vulgar constellations thick." See *Milton's Paradise Lost*, B. iii, l. 576. "The great luminary *aloft* the vulgar constellations thick."—*Johnson's Dict. w. Aloft.* "Captain Falconer having previously gone *alongside* the Constitution."—*Newspaper.* "Seventeen ships sailed for New England, and *aboard* these above fifteen hundred persons."—*Robertson's Amer.* ii, 429. "There

is a willow grows *askant* the brook:" Or, as in some editions: "There is a willow grows *aslant* the brook."—SHAK. *Hamlet*, Act iv, 7. "*Aslant* the dew-bright earth."—*Thomson*. "Swift as meteors glide *aslope* a summer eve."—*Fenton*. "*Aneath* the heavy rain."—*James Hogg*. "With his magic spectacles *astride* his nose."—*Merchant's Criticisms*.

> "*Atween* his downy wings be furnished, there."—*Wordsworth's Poems*, p. 147.
> "And there a season *atween* June and May."—*Castle of Indolence*, C. i, st. 2.

OBS. 13.—The following are examples of rather unusual prepositions beginning with *b*, *c*, or *d*: "Or where wild-meeting oceans boil *besouth* Magellan."—*Burns*. "Whereupon grew that *by-word*, used by the Irish, that they dwelt *by-west* the law, *which* dwelt beyond the river *of the Bar-row*."—DAVIES: *in Joh. Dict.* Here Johnson calls *by-west* a noun substantive, and Webster, as improperly, marks it for an adverb. No hyphen is needed in *byword* or *bywest*. The first sylla-ble of the latter is pronounced *be*, and ought to be written so, if "*besouth*" is right.

> "From Cephalenia *cross* the surgy main
> Philœtius late arrived, a faithful swain."—*Pope*, *Odys.*, B. xx, l. 234.
> "And *cross* their limits cut a sloping way,
> Which the twelve signs in beauteous order sway."—*Dryden's Virgil*.

"A fox was taking a walk one night *cross* a village."—*L'Estrange*. "The enemy had cut down great trees *cross* the ways."—*Knolles*. "DEHORS,' prep. [Fr.] Without; as, '*dehors* the land.' Blackstone."—*Worcester's Dict.* 8vo. "You have believed, *despite* too our physical conforma-tion."—*Bulwer*.

> "And Roderick shall his welcome make,
> *Despite* old spleen, for Douglas' sake."—*Scott, L. L.*, C. ii, st. 26.

OBS. 14.—The following quotations illustrate further the list of unusual prepositions: "And she would be often weeping *inside* the room while George was amusing himself without."—*Anna Ross*, p. 81. "Several nuts grow closely together, *inside* this prickly covering."—*Jacob Abbott*. "An other boy asked why the peachstone was not *outside* the peach."—*Id.* "As if listening to the sounds *withinside* it."—*Gardiner's Music of Nature*, p. 214. "Sir Knight, you well might mark the mound, *Left hand* the town."—*Scott's Marmion*. "Thus Butler, *maugre* his wicked in-tention, sent them home again."—*Sewel's Hist.* p. 256. "And, *maugre* all that can be said in its favour."—*Stone, on Freemasonry*, p. 121. "And, *maugre* the authority of Sterne, I even doubt its benevolence."—*West's Letters*, p. 29.

> "I through the ample air in triumph high
> Shall lead Hell captive *maugre* Hell."—*Milton's P. L.*, B. iii, l. 255.

"When Mr. Seaman arose in the morning, he found himself *minus* his coat, vest, pocket-hand-kerchief, and tobacco-box."—*Newspaper*. "Throw some coals *onto* the fire."—FORBY: *Worcester's Dict. w. Onto.* "Flour, at $4 *per* barrel."—*Preston's Book-Keeping.* "Which amount, *per* invoice, to $4000."—*Ib.* "*To Smiths* is the substantive *Smiths*, *plus* the preposition *to*."—*Fowler's E. Gram.* § 33. "The Mayor of Lynn *versus* Turner."—*Cowper's Reports*, p. 86. "Slaves were imported from Africa, *via* Cuba."—*Society in America*, i, 327. "*Pending* the discussion of this subject, a memorial was presented."—*Gov. Everett.*

> "Darts his experienced eye and soon *traverse*
> The whole battalion views their order due."—*Milton.*
> "Because, when *thorough* deserts vast
> And regions desolate they past."—*Hudibras.*

OBS. 15.—*Minus*, less, *plus*, more, *per*, by, *versus*, towards, or against, and *vid*, by the way of, are Latin words; and it is not very consistent with the *purity* of our tongue, to use them as above. *Sans*, without, is French, and not now heard with us. *Afore* for *before*, *atween* for *between*, *trav-erse* for *across*, *thorough* for *through*, and *withal* for *with*, are obsolete. *Withal* was never placed before its object, but was once very common at the end of a sentence. I think it not properly a preposition, but rather an adverb. It occurs in Shakspeare, and so does *sans*; as,

> "I did laugh, *sans* intermission, an hour by his dial."—*As You Like It.*
> "I pr'ythee, *whom* doth he trot *withal?*"—*Ib.*
> "*Sans* teeth, *sans* eyes, *sans* taste, *sans* every thing."—*Ib.*

OBS. 16.—Of the propriety and the nature of such expressions as the following, the reader may now judge for himself: "In consideration of what passes sometimes *within-side* of those vehicles."—*Spectator*, No. 533. "Watch over yourself, and let nothing throw you *off from* your guard."—*Dis-trict School*, p. 54. "The windows broken, the door *off from* the hinges, the roof open and leaky."—*Ib.* p. 71. "He was always a shrewd observer of men, *in and out of* power."—*Knapp's Life of Burr*, p. viii. "Who had never been broken *in to* the experience of sea voyages."—*Timothy Flint.* "And there came a fire *out from before* the Lord."—*Leviticus*, ix, 24. "Because eight readers *out of* ten, it is believed, forget it."—*Brown's Estimate*, ii, 32. "Fifty days after the *Pass-over*, and *their coming out of* Egypt."—*Watts's Script. Hist.* p. 57. "As the mountains are *round about* Jerusalem, so the Lord is *round about* his people."—*Psal.* cxxv, 2. "Literally, 'I proceeded *forth from out of* God and am come.' "—*Gurney's Essays*, p. 161. "But he that came *down from* (or *from out of*) heaven."—*Ibid.*

> "Here none the last funereal rights receive;
> To be cast *forth the* camp, is all their friends can give."—*Rowe's Lucan*, vi, 166.

EXAMPLES FOR PARSING.

PRAXIS X.—ETYMOLOGICAL.

In the Tenth Praxis, it is required of the pupil—to distinguish and define the different parts of speech, and the classes and modifications of the ARTICLES, NOUNS, ADJECTIVES, PRONOUNS, VERBS, PARTICIPLES, ADVERBS, CONJUNCTIONS, *and* PREPOSITIONS.

The definitions to be given in the Tenth Praxis, are two for an article, six for a noun, three for an adjective, six for a pronoun, seven for a verb finite, five for an infinitive, two for a participle, two (and sometimes three) for an adverb, two for a conjunction, one for a preposition, and one for an interjection.   Thus:—

EXAMPLE PARSED.

"Never adventure on too near an approach to what is evil."—*Maxims.*

Never is an adverb of time. 1. An adverb is a word added to a verb, a participle, an adjective, or an other adverb; and generally expresses time, place, degree, or manner. 2. Adverbs of time are those which answer to the question, *When ? How long ? How soon ?* or, *How often ?* including these which ask.

Adventure is a regular active-intransitive verb, from *adventure, adventured, adventuring, adventured ;* found in the imperative mood, present tense, second person, singular (or it may be plural) number. 1. A verb is a word that signifies *to be, to act,* or *to be acted upon.* 2. A regular verb is a verb that forms the preterit and the perfect participle by assuming *d* or *ed.* 3. An active-intransitive verb is a verb that expresses an action that has no person or thing for its object. 4. The imperative mood is that form of the verb which is used in commanding, exhorting, entreating, or permitting. 5. The present tense is that which expresses what now exists, or is taking place. 6. The second person is that which denotes the hearer, or the person addressed. 7. The singular number is that which denotes but one.

On is a preposition. 1. A preposition is a word used to express some relation of different things or thoughts to each other, and is generally placed before a noun or a pronoun.

Too is an adverb of degree. 1. An adverb is a word added to a verb, a participle, an adjective, or an other adverb; and generally expresses time, place, degree, or manner. 2. Adverbs of degree are those which answer to the question, *How much ? How little ?* or to the idea of *more or less.*

Near is a common adjective, of the positive degree; compared, *near, nearer, nearest* or *next.* 1. An adjective is a word added to a noun or pronoun, and generally expresses quality. 2. A common adjective is any ordinary epithet, or adjective denoting quality or situation. 3. The positive degree is that which is expressed by the adjective in its simple form.

An is the indefinite article. 1. An article is the word *the, an,* or *a,* which we put before nouns to limit their signification. 2. The indefinite article is *an* or *a,* which denotes one thing of a kind, but not any particular one.

Approach is a common noun, of the third person, singular number, neuter gender, and objective case. 1. A noun is the name of any person, place, or thing, that can be known or mentioned. 2. A common noun is the name of a sort, kind, or class, of beings or things. 3. The third person is that which denotes the person or thing merely spoken of. 4. The singular number is that which denotes but one. 5. The neuter gender is that which denotes things that are neither male nor female. 6. The objective case is that form or state of a noun or pronoun which denotes the object of a verb, participle, or preposition.

To is a preposition. 1. A preposition is a word used to express some relation of different things or thoughts to each other, and is generally placed before a noun or a pronoun.

What is a relative pronoun, of the third person, singular number, neuter gender, and nominative case. 1. A pronoun is a word used in stead of a noun. 2. A relative pronoun is a pronoun that represents an antecedent word or phrase, and connects different clauses of a sentence. 3. The third person is that which denotes the person or thing merely spoken of. 4. The singular number is that which denotes but one. 5. The neuter gender is that which denotes things that are neither male nor female. 6. The nominative case is that form or state of a noun or pronoun, which denotes the subject of a verb.

Is is an irregular neuter verb, from *be, was, being, been ;* found in the indicative mood, present tense, third person, and singular number. 1. A verb is a word that signifies *to be, to act,* or *to be acted upon.* 2. An irregular verb is a verb that does not form the preterit and the perfect participle by assuming *d* or *ed.* 3. A neuter verb is a verb that expresses neither action nor passion, but simply being, or a state of being. 4. The indicative mood is that form of a verb, which simply indicates or declares a thing, or asks a question. 5. The present tense is that which expresses what now exists, or is taking place. 6. The third person is that which denotes the person or thing merely spoken of. 7. The singular number is that which denotes but one.

Evil is a common adjective, of the positive degree; compared irregularly, *bad, evil,* or *ill, worse, worst.* 1. An adjective is a word added to a noun or pronoun, and generally expresses quality. 2. A common adjective is any ordinary epithet, or adjective denoting quality or situation. 3. The positive degree is that which is expressed by the adjective in its simple form.

LESSON I.—PARSING.

"My Lord, I do here, in the name of all the learned and polite persons of the nation, complain to your Lordship, as first minister, that our language is imperfect ; that its daily improvements are by no means in proportion to its daily corruptions ; that the pretenders to polish and refine it, have chiefly multiplied abuses and absurdities ; and that, in many instances, it offends against every part of grammar."—*Dean Swift, to the Earl of Oxford.*

"Swift must be allowed to have been a good judge of this matter ; to which he was himself very attentive, both in his own writings, and in his remarks upon those of his friends : He is one of the most correct, and perhaps [he is] the best, of our prose writers.   Indeed the justness of this complaint, *as* far as I can find, *hath* never yet been questioned ; and yet no effectual method *hath* hitherto been taken to redress the grievance which was the object of it."—*Lowth's Gram.* p. iv.

"The only proper use to be made of the blemishes which occur in the writings of such authors, is, to point out to those who apply themselves to the study of composition, some of the rules which they ought to observe for avoiding such errors ; and to render them sensible of the necessity of strict attention to language and style."—*Blair's Rhet.* p. 233.

"Thee, therefore, and with thee myself I weep,
For thee and me I mourn in anguish deep."—*Pope's Homer.*

LESSON II.—PARSING.

"The southern corner of Europe, comprehended between the thirty-sixth and fortieth degrees of latitude, bordering on Epirus and Macedonia towards the north, and on other sides surrounded by the sea, was inhabited, above eighteen centuries before the Christian era, by many small tribes of hunters and shepherds, among whom the Pelasgi and Hellenes were the most numerous and powerful."—*Gillies, Gr.* p. 12.

"In a vigorous exertion of memory, ideal presence is exceedingly distinct: thus, when a man, entirely occupied with some event that made a deep impression, forgets himself, he perceives every thing as passing before him, and has a consciousness of presence, similar to that of a spectator."—*Kames, El. of Crit.* i, 88.

"Each planet revolves about its own axis in a given time; and each moves round the sun, in an orbit nearly circular, and in a time proportioned to its distance. Their velocities, directed by an established law, are perpetually changing by regular accelerations and retardations."—*Ib.* i, 271.

"You may as well go about to turn the sun to ice by fanning in his face with a peacock's feather."—*Shak.*

"*Ch. Justice.* I sent for you, when there were matters against you for your life, to come speak with me. *Falstaff.* As I was then advised by my learned counsel in the laws of this land-service, I did not come."—*Id.* 2. Hen. IV, Act i, Sc. 2.

"It is surprising to see the images of the mind stamped upon the aspect; to see the cheeks take the die of the passions and appear in all the colours of thought."—*Collier.*

> —————"Even from out thy slime
> The monsters of the deep are made."—*Byron.*

LESSON III.—PARSING.

"With a mind weary of conjecture, fatigued by doubt, sick of disputation, eager for knowledge, anxious for certainty, and unable to attain it by the best use of my reason in matters of the utmost importance, I *have* long ago turned my thoughts to an impartial examination of the proofs on which revealed religion is grounded, and I am convinced of its truth."—*Bp. Watson's Apology,* p. 69.

"The sceptre shall not depart from Judah, nor a lawgiver from between his feet, until Shiloh come; and unto him shall the gathering of the people be."—*Gen.* xlix, 10.

"Again, ye have heard that it hath been said by them of old time, thou shalt not forswear thyself, but shalt perform unto the Lord thine oaths. But I say unto you, Swear not at all: neither by heaven; for it is God's throne: nor by the earth; for it is his footstool: neither by Jerusalem; for it is the city of the great King. Neither shalt thou swear by thy head; because thou canst not make one hair white or black."—*Matt.* v, 33—36.

"Refined manners, and polite behaviour, must not be deemed altogether artificial: men who, inured to the sweets of society, cultivate humanity, find an elegant pleasure in preferring others, and making them happy, of which the proud, the selfish, scarcely have a conception."—*Kames, El. of Crit.* i, 105.

> "Bacchus, that first from out the purple grape
> Crush'd the sweet poison of misused wine."—*Milton.*

IMPROPRIETIES FOR CORRECTION.

ERRORS RESPECTING PREPOSITIONS.

"Nouns are often formed by participles."—*L. Murray's Index, Octavo Gram.* ii, 290.

[FORMULE.—Not proper, because the relation here intended, between *are forms* / and *participles,* is not well signified by the preposition *by.* But, according to Observation 7th, on this part of speech, "The prepositions have, from their own nature, or from custom, such an adaptation to particular terms and relations, that they can seldom be used one for an other without manifest impropriety." This relation would be better expressed by *from;* thus, "Nouns are often formed *from* participles."]

"What tenses are formed on the perfect participle?"—*Ingersoll's Gram.* p. 104. "Which tense is formed on the present?"—*Ibid.* "When a noun or pronoun is placed before a participle, independently on the rest of the sentence," &c.—*Ib.* p. 150; *Murray,* 145; and others. "If the addition consists in two or more words."—*Murray's Gram.* p. 176 ; *Ingersoll's*, 177. "The infinitive mood is often made absolute, or used independently on the rest of the sentence."—*Mur.* p. 184 ; *Ing.* 244 ; and others. "For the great satisfaction of the reader, we shall present him with a variety of false constructions."—*Murray's Gram.* p. 189. "For your satisfaction, I shall present you with a variety of false constructions."—*Ingersoll's Gram.* p. 258. "I shall here present you with a scale of derivation."—*Bucke's Gram.* p. 81. "These two manners of representation in respect of number."—*Lowth's Gram.* p. 15 ; *Churchill's*, 57. "There are certain adjectives, which seem to be derived without any variation from verbs."—*Lowth's Gram.* p. 89. "Or disqualify us for receiving instruction or reproof of others."—*Murray's Key*, 8vo, p. 253. "For being more studious than any other pupil of the school."—*Ib.* p. 226. "From misunderstanding the directions, we lost our way."—*Ib.* p. 201. "These people reduced the greater part of the island to their own power."—*Ib.* p. 261.* "The principal accent distinguishes one syllable in a word from the rest."—*Murray's Gram.* p. 236. "Just numbers are in unison to the human mind."—*Ib.* p. 298. "We must accept of sound instead of sense."—*Ib.* p. 298. "Also, instead for *consultation*, he uses *consult.*"—*Priestley's Gram.* p. 143. "This ablative seems to be governed of a preposition understood."—*Walker's Particles*, p. 268. "That my father may not hear on't by some means or other."—*Ib.* p. 257. "And, besides, my wife would hear on't by some means."—*Ib.* p. 81. "For insisting in a requisition so odious to them." —*Robertson's Amer.* i, 206. "Based in the great self-evident truths of liberty and equality."—*Scholar's Manual.* "Very little knowledge of their nature is acquired by the spelling book."—*Murray's Gram.* p. 21. "They do not cut it off: except in a few words ; as, *due, duly*, &c."—*Ib.* p. 24. "Whether passing in such time, or then finished."—*Lowth's Gram.* p. 31. "It hath disgusted hundreds of that confession."—*Barclay's Works*, iii, 269. "But they have egregiously fallen in that inconvenience."—*Ib.* iii, 73. "For is not this to set nature a work ?"—*Ib.* i, 270. "And surely that which should set all its springs a-work, is God."—ATTERBURY: *in Blair's Rhet.* p. 298. "He could not end his treatise without a panegyric of modern learning."—TEMPLE: *ib.* p. 110. "These are entirely independent on the modulation of the voice."—*Walker's Elocution*, p. 308. "It is dear of a penny. It is cheap of twenty pounds."—*Walker's Particles*, p. 274. "It will be despatched, in most occasions, without resting."—*Locke.* "'O, the pain the bliss in dying.'"—*Kirkham's Gram.* p. 129. "When [he is] presented with the objects or the facts."—*Smith's Productive Gram.* p. 5. "I will now present you with a synopsis."—*Ib.* p. 25. "The conjunction disjunctive connects sentences, by expressing opposition of meaning in various degrees."—*Ib.* p. 38. "I shall now present you with a few lines."—*Bucke's Classical Gram.* p. 13. "Common names of Substantives are those, which stand for things generally."—*Ib.* p. 31. "Adjectives in the English language admit no variety in gender, number, or case whatever, except that of the degrees of comparison."—*Ib.* p. 48. "Participles are adjectives formed of verbs."—*Ib.* p. 63. "I do love to walk out of a fine summer's evening."—*Ib.* p. 97. "An *Ellipsis*, when applied to grammar, is the elegant omission of one or more words in a sentence."—*Merchant's Gram.* p. 99. "The prefix *to* is generally placed before verbs in the infinitive mood, but before the following verbs it is properly omitted ; (viz.) *bid, make, see, dare, need, hear, feel*, and *let* ; as, He *bid* me *do* it ; He *made* me *learn* ; &c."—*Ib. Stereotype Edition*, p. 91 ; *Old Edition*, 85. "The infinitive sometimes follows *than*, after a comparison ; as, I wish nothing more, *than to know* his fate."—*Ib.* p. 92. See *Murray's Gram.* 8vo, i, 184. "Or by prefixing the adverbs *more* or *less*, in the comparative, and *most* or *least*, in the superlative."—*Merchant's Gram.* p. 36. "A pronoun is a word used instead of a noun."—*Ib.* p. 17 ; *Comly*, 15. "In monosyllables the Comparative is regularly formed by adding *r* or *er*."—*Perley's Gram.* p. 21. "He has particularly named these, in distinction to others."—*Harris's Hermes*, p. vi. "To revive the decaying taste of antient Literature."—*Ib.* p. xv. "He found the greatest difficulty of writing."—HUME: *in Priestley's Gram.* p. 159.

> "And the tear that is wip'd with a little address
> May be followed perhaps with a smile."
> *Webster's American Spelling-Book*, p. 78 ; and *Murray's E. Reader*, p. 212.

CHAPTER XI. — INTERJECTIONS.

An Interjection is a word that is uttered merely to indicate some strong or sudden emotion of the mind : as, *Oh ! alas ! ah ! poh ! pshaw ! avaunt ! aha ! hurrah !*

* "Who consequently reduced the *greatest* part of the island TO their own power."—*Swift, on the English Tongue.* "We can say, that *one nation reduces another* TO *subjection*. But when *dominion* or *power* is used, we always, as [so] far as I know, say, *reduce* UNDER *their power*" [or *dominion*].—*Blair's Rhet.* p. 229.

OBSERVATIONS.

OBS. 1.—Of pure interjections but few are admitted into books. Unimpassioned writings reject this part of speech altogether. As words or sounds of this kind serve rather to indicate feeling than to express thought, they seldom have any definable signification. Their use also is so variable, that there can be no very accurate classification of them. Some significant words, perhaps more properly belonging to other classes, are sometimes ranked with interjections, when uttered with emotion and in an unconnected manner; as, *strange! prodigious! indeed!* Wells says, "*Other parts of speech,* used by way of exclamation, are *properly regarded as interjections;* as, *hark! surprising! mercy!* "—*School Gram.* 1846, p. 110. This is an evident absurdity; because it directly confounds the classes which it speaks of as being different. Nor is it right to say, "*Other parts of speech* are frequently used *to perform the office* of interjections."—*Wells,* 1850, p. 120.

OBS. 2.—The word *interjection* comes to us from the Latin name *interjectio,* the root of which is the verb *interjicio,* to throw between, to interject. Interjections are so called because they are usually thrown in between *the parts of discourse,* without any syntactical connexion with other words. Dr. Lowth, in his haste, happened to describe them as a kind of natural sounds "thrown in between the parts *of a sentence;*" and this strange blunder has been copied into almost every definition that has been given of the Interjection since. See Murray's Grammar and others. Webster's Dictionary defines it as, "A word thrown in between *words connected in construction;*" but of all the parts of speech none are less frequently found in this situation.

OBS. 3.—The following is a fair sample of "Smith's *New Grammar,*"—i. e. of "English Grammar on the *Productive System,*"—a new effort of quackery to scarf up with cobwebs the eyes of common sense: "Q. When I exclaim. 'Oh! I have ruined my friend,' 'Alas! I fear for life,' *which words* here appear to be thrown in *between the sentences,* to express passion or feeling? Ans. *Oh! Alas!* Q. What does *interjection* mean? Ans. *Thrown between.* Q. What name, then, shall we give such words as *oh! alas!* &c.? Ans. INTERJECTIONS. Q. What, then, are interjections? Ans. Interjections are words thrown in *between the parts of sentences,* to express the passions or sudden feelings of the speaker. Q. How may an interjection generally be known? Ans. By *its taking* an exclamation *point* after it: [as,] '*Oh!* I have alienated my friend.'"—*R. C. Smith's New Grammar,* p. 39. Of the interjection, this author gives, in his examples for parsing, *fifteen* other instances; but nothing can be more obvious, than that not more than one of the whole fifteen stands either "between sentences" or between the parts of any sentence! (See *New Gram.* pp. 40 and 96.) Can he be a competent grammarian, who does not know the meaning of *between;* or who, knowing it, misapplies so very plain a word?

OBS. 4.—The Interjection, which is idly claimed by sundry writers to have been the first of words at the origin of language, is now very constantly set down, among the parts of speech, as the last of the series. But, for the name of this the last of the ten sorts of words, some of our grammarians have adopted the term *exclamation.* Of the old and usual term *interjection,* a recent writer justly says, "This name is preferable to that of *exclamation,* for some exclamations are not interjections, and some interjections are not exclamations."—*Fowler's E. Gram.* § 333.

LIST OF THE INTERJECTIONS.

The following are the principal interjections arranged according to the emotions which they are generally intended to indicate: (1.) Of joy; *eigh! hey! io!* (2.) Of praise; *well-done! good! bravo!* (3.) Of sorrow; *oh! ah! alas! alack! hoo! welladay!* or *welaway!* (4.) Of wonder; *heigh! ha! strange! indeed! whew! hoity-toity! hoida! zounds! egad! my stars!* (5.) Of wishing, earnestness, or vocative address; (often with a noun or pronoun in the nominative absolute;) *O!* (6.) Of pain or fear; *oh! O dear! ah! eh!* (7.) Of contempt; *fudge! pugh! poh! pshaw! pish! tush! tut! humph!* (8.) Of aversion; *foh! faugh! fie! fy! foy!* * *off! begone! avaunt! aroynt! whew!* (9.) Of calling aloud; *ho! what ho! soho! hollo! halloo! hoy! ahoy!* (10.) Of exultation; *ah! aha! huzza! hey! heyday! hurrah!* (11.) Of laughter; *ha, ha, ha; he, he, he.* (12.) Of salutation; *welcome! hail! all-hail!* (13.) Of calling to attention; *ho! lo! behold! look! see! hark! la! law!* † (14.) Of calling to silence; *hush! hist! whist! 'st! aw! mum!* (15.) Of surprise or horror; *oh! ha! hah! what!* (16.) Of languor or weariness; *heigh-ho! heigh-ho-hum!* (17.) Of stopping; *hold! soft! avast! whoh!* (18.) Of parting; *farewell! adieu!* (19.) Of knowing or detecting; *oho! ahah! ay-ay!* (20.) Of interrogating; *eh? ha?* ‡ *hey?*

---

* "*O foy,* don't misapprehend me; I don't say so."—DOUBLE DEALER: *Kames, El. of Crit.* i, 305.

† According to Walker and Webster, *la* is pronounced *law;* and, if they are right in this, the latter is only a false mode of spelling. But I set down both, because both are found in books, and because I incline to think the former is from the French *la,* which is pronounced *lah.* Johnson and Webster make *lo* and *lo* synonymous; deriving *lo* from the Saxon *la,* and *la* either from *lo* or from the French *la.* "*Law,* how you joke, cousin."—*Columbian Orator,* p. 178. "*Law* me! the very ghosts are come now!"—*Ibid.* "*Law,* sister Betty! I am glad to see you!"—*Ibid.*

"*La* you! if you speak ill of the devil,
How he takes it at heart!"—SHAKSPEARE: *Joh. Dict. w. La.*

‡ The interjection of interrogating, being placed at the end, either after a question, or after something which it converts into a question, is usually marked with its own separate *eroteme;* as, "But this is even so: eh?"—*Newspaper.* "Is 't not drown'd i' the last rain? Ha?"—*Shakspeare.* "Does Bridget paint still, Pompey? Ha?"—*Id.* "Suits my complexion—hey gal? so I think."—*Yankee Schoolmaster.* Sometimes we see it divided only by a comma, from the preceding question; as, "What dost thou think of this doctrine, friend Gurth, ha?"—SCOTT'S IVANHOE: *Fowler's E. Gram.* § 29.

OBSERVATIONS.

OBS. 1.—With the interjections, may perhaps be reckoned *haw* and *gee*, the imperative words of teamsters driving cattle; and other similar sounds, useful under certain circumstances, but seldom found in books. Besides these, and all the foregoing, there are several others, too often heard, which are unworthy to be considered parts of a cultivated language. The frequent use of interjections savours more of thoughtlessness than of sensibility. Philosophical writing and dispassionate discourse exclude them altogether. Yet are there several words of this kind, which in earnest utterance, animated poetry, or impassioned declamation, are not only natural, but exceedingly expressive: as, " Lift up thy voice, O daughter of Gallim; cause it to be heard unto Laish, O poor Anathoth."—*Isaiah*, x, 30. "*Alas, alas*, that great city Babylon, that mighty city! for in one hour is thy judgement come."—*Rev.* xviii, 10.

"*Ah me!* forbear, returns the queen, forbear;
Oh! talk not, talk not of vain beauty's care."—*Odyssey*, B. xviii, l. 310.

OBS. 2.—Interjections, being in general little else than mere natural voices or cries, must of course be adapted to the sentiments which are uttered with them, and never carelessly confounded one with an other when we express them on paper. The adverb *ay* is sometimes improperly written for the interjection *ah*; as, *ay me!* for *ah me!* and still oftener we find *oh*, an interjection of sorrow, pain, or surprise,* written in stead of *O*, the proper sign of wishing, earnestness, or vocative address: as,

"*Oh* Happiness! our being's end and aim! '—*Pope, Ess. Ep.* iv, l. 1.
" And peace, *oh* Virtue! peace is all thy own."—*Id. ib. Ep.* iv. l. 82.
"*Oh* stay, O pride of Greece! Ulysses, stay!
O cease thy course, and listen to our lay !"—*Odys.* B. xii, l. 222.

OBS. 3.—The chief characteristics of the interjection are independence, exclamation, and the want of any definable signification. Yet not all the words or signs which we refer to this class, will be found to coincide in all these marks of an interjection. Indeed the last, (the want of a tional meaning,) would seem to exclude them from the language; for *words* must needs be significant of something. Hence many grammarians deny that mere sounds of the voice have any ore claim to be reckoned among the parts of speech, than the neighing of a horse, or the lowing of a cow. There is some reason in this; but in fact the reference which these sounds have the feelings of those who utter them, is to some extent instinctively understood; and does nstitute a sort of significance, though we cannot really define it. And, as their use in lange, or in connexion with language, makes it necessary to assign them a place in grammar, it certainly more proper to treat them as above, than to follow the plan of the Greek gramrians, most of whom throw all the interjections into the class of *adverbs*.

OBS. 4.—Significant words uttered independently, after the manner of interjections, ought in eral, perhaps, to be referred to their original classes; for all such expressions may be supposed elliptical: as, "*Order!* gentlemen, *order!*" i. e. " Come to order,"—or, " Keep order." "*Silence!*" i. e. " Preserve silence." "*Out! out!*" i. e. " Get out,"—or, " Clear out!" (See Obs. 5th and 6th, upon Adverbs.)

"Charge, Chester, charge! *On*, Stanley, *on!*
Were the last words of Marmion."—*Scott*.

OBS. 5.—In some instances, interjections seem to be taken substantively and made nouns ; ̄as, " I may sit in a corner, and cry *hey-ho* for a husband."—*Shak.*

So, according to James White, in his Essay on the Verb, is the word *fie*, in the following example:

"If you deny me, *fie* upon your law."—SHAK.: *White's Verb*, p. 163.

EXAMPLES FOR PARSING.

PRAXIS XI.—ETYMOLOGICAL.

In the Eleventh Praxis, it is required of the pupil—to distinguish and define the different parts of speech, and ALL their classes and modifications.

The definitions to be given in the Eleventh Praxis, are, two for an article, six for a noun, three for an adjective, six for a pronoun, seven for a verb finite, five for an infinitive, two for a participle, two (and sometimes three) for an adverb, two for a conjunction, one for a preposition, and two for an interjection. Thus:—

EXAMPLE PARSED.

" O ! sooner shall the earth and stars fall into chaos ! "

) Is an interjection, indicating earnestness. 1. An interjection is a word that is uttered merely to indicate some strong or sudden emotion of the mind. 2. The interjection of wishing, earnestness, or vocative address, is O.

Sooner is an adverb of time, of the comparative degree; compared, *soon, sooner, soonest*. 1. An adverb is a word added to a verb, a participle, an adjective, or an other adverb; and generally expresses time, place, degree, or manner. 2. Adverbs of time are those which answer to the question, *When ? How long ? How soon ?* or, *How often ?* including these which ask. 3. The comparative degree is that which is more or less than something contrasted with it.

Shall is an auxiliary to *fall*. 1. An auxiliary is a short verb prefixed to one of the principal parts of an other verb, to express some particular mode and time of the being, action, or passion.

* Though *oh* and *ah* are most commonly used as signs of these depressing passions, it must be confessed that hey are sometimes employed by reputable writers, as marks of cheerfulness or exultation; as, "*Ah*, pleasant *roof*," &c.— *Cowper's Task*, p. 179. " Merrily *oh!* merrily *oh!*"—*Moore's Tyrolese Song*. " Cheerily *oh! heartily oh!*"—B. But even if this usage be supposed to be right, there is still some difference between these rords and the interjection O: if there were not, we might dispense with the latter, and substitute one of the former; but this would certainly change the import of many an invocation.

The is the definite article. 1. An article is the word *the, an,* or *a,* which we put before nouns to limit their signification. 2. The definite article is *the,* which denotes some particular thing or things.

Earth is a common noun, of the third person, singular number, neuter gender, and nominative case. 1. A noun is the name of any person, place, or thing, that can be known or mentioned. 2. A common noun is the name of a sort, kind, or class, of beings or things. 3. The third person is that which denotes the person or thing merely spoken of. 4. The singular number is that which denotes but one. 5. The neuter gender is that which denotes things that are neither male nor female. 6. The nominative case is that form or state of a noun or pronoun, which denotes the subject of a verb.

And is a copulative conjunction. 1. A conjunction is a word used to connect words or sentences in construction, and to show the dependence of the terms so connected. 2. A copulative conjunction is a conjunction that denotes an addition, a cause, a consequence, or a supposition.

Stars is a common noun, of the third person, plural number, neuter gender, and nominative case. 1. A noun is the name of any person, place, or thing, that can be known or mentioned. 2. A common noun is the name of a sort, kind, or class, of beings or things. 3. The third person is that which denotes the person or thing merely spoken of. 4. The plural number is that which denotes more than one. 5. The neuter gender is that which denotes things that are neither male nor female. 6. The nominative case is that form or state of a noun or pronoun, which denotes the subject of a verb.

Fell, or *Shall fall,* is an irregular active-intransitive verb, from *fall, fell, falling, fallen ;* found in the indicative mood, first-future tense, third person, and plural number. 1. A verb is a word that signifies *to be, to act,* or *to be acted upon.* 2. An irregular verb is a verb that does not form the preterit and the perfect participle by assuming *d* or *ed.* 3. An active-intransitive verb is a verb that expresses an action which has no person or thing for its object. 4. The indicative mood is that form of the verb, which simply indicates or declares a thing, or asks a question. 5. The first-future tense is that which expresses what will take place hereafter. 6. The third person is that which denotes the person or thing merely spoken of. 7. The plural number is that which denotes more than one.

Into is a preposition. 1. A preposition is a word used to express some relation of different things or thoughts to each other, and is generally placed before a noun or a pronoun.

Chaos is a common noun, of the third person, singular number, neuter gender, and objective case. 1. A noun is the name of any person, place, or thing, that can be known or mentioned. 2. A common noun is the name of a sort, kind, or class, of beings or things. 3. The third person is that which denotes the person or thing merely spoken of. 4. The singular number is that which denotes but one. 5. The neuter gender is that which denotes things that are neither male nor female. 6. The objective case is that form or state of a noun or pronoun which denotes the object of a verb, participle, or preposition.

LESSON I.—PARSING.

"Ah ! St. Anthony preserve me !—Ah—ah—eh—eh !—Why—why—after all, your hand is not so co-o-o-old, neither. Of the two, it is rather warmer than my own. Can it be, though, that you are not dead ?" "Not I."—MOLIERE : *in Burgh's Speaker,* p. 232.

"I'll make you change your cuckoo note, you old philosophical humdrum, you—[*Beats him*]—I will—[*Beats him*]. I'll make you say somewhat else than, 'All things are doubtful ; all things are uncertain ;'—[*Beats him*] I will, you old fusty pedant." "Ah !—oh !—eh !—What, beat a philosopher !—Ah !—oh !—oh ! "—MOLIERE : *ib.* p. 247.

"What ! will these hands never be clean ?—No more of that, my lord ; no more of that. You mar all with this starting." * * * " Here is the smell of blood still.—All the perfumes of Arabia will not sweeten this little hand. Oh ! oh ! oh !"—*Shak., Macbeth,* Act V, Sc 1.

"Ha ! at the gates what grisly forms appear !
What dismal shrieks of laughter wound the ear ! "—*Merry.*

LESSON II.—PARSING.

"Yet this may be the situation of some now known to us.—O frightful thought ! O horrible image ! Forbid it, O Father of mercy ! If it be possible, let no creature of thine ever be the object of that wrath, against which the strength of thy whole creation united, would stand but as the moth against the thunderbolt ! "—*Burgh's Speaker,* p. 289.

"If it be so, our God, whom we serve, is able to deliver us from the burning fiery furnace ; and he will deliver us out of thine hand, O king. But if not, be it known unto thee, O king, that we will not serve thy gods, nor worship the golden image which thou hast set up."—*Daniel,* iii, 17 and 18.

"Grant me patience, just Heaven !—Of all the cants which are canted in this canting world—though the cant of hypocrites may be the worst—the cant of criticism is the most tormenting ! "—*Sterne.*

"Ah, no ! Achilles meets a shameful fate,
Oh ! how unworthy of the brave and great."—*Pope.*

LESSON III.—PARSING.

"O let not thy heart despise me ! thou whom experience has not taught that it is misery to lose that which it is not happiness to possess."—*Dr. Johnson.*

"Disguise thyself as thou wilt, still, Slavery ! still thou art a bitter draught ; and though thousands in all ages have been made to drink of thee, thou art no less bitter on that account."—*Sterne.*

" Put it out of the power of truth to give you an ill character ; and if any body reports you not to be an honest or a good man, let your practice give him the lie. This is all very feasible."—*Antoninus.*

" Oh that men should put an enemy into their mouths to steal away their brains! that we should, with joy, pleasance, revel, and applause, transform ourselves into beasts ! "—*Shakspeare.*

"All these afar off stood, crying, Alas !
　　　Alas ! and wept, and gnashed their teeth, and groaned ;
　　　And with the owl, that on her ruins sat,
　　　Made dolorous concert in the ear of Night."—*Pollok.*

" Snatch'd in thy prime ! alas, the stroke were mild,
　　　Had my frail form obey'd the fate's decree !
　　　Blest were my lot, O Cynthio ! O my child !
　　　Had Heaven so pleas'd, and I had died for thee ! "—*Shenstone.*

IMPROPRIETIES FOR CORRECTION.

ERRORS RESPECTING INTERJECTIONS.

"Of chance or change, oh let not man complain."—*Bucke's Classical Gram.* p. 85.

[FORMULE.—Not proper, because the interjection *oh*, a sign of sorrow, pain, or surprise, is here used to indicate mere earnestness. But, according to the list of interjections, or Obs. 2d under it, the interjection of wishing, earnestness, or vocative address, is *O*, and not *oh.* Therefore, *oh* should here be *O ;* thus, " Of chance or change, O let not man complain."—*Beattie's Minstrel,* B. ii, l. 1.]

" O thou persecutor ! Oh ye hypocrites."—*Merchant's Gram.* p. 99 ; *et al.* "Oh! thou, who touchedst Isaiah's hallowed lips with fire."—*Ib.* (*Key,*) p. 197. "Oh! happy we, surrounded by so many blessings."—*Ib.* (*Exercises,*) p. 138. "Oh! thou, who art so unmindful of thy duty."—*Ib.* (*Key,*) p. 196. "If I am wrong, oh teach my heart To find that better way."—*Pope's Works.* "Heus ! evocate huc Davum. *Ter.* Hoe! call Davus out hither."—*Walker's Particles,* p. 155. "It was represented by an analogy, (Oh, how inadequate !) which was borrowed from the religion of paganism."—*Murray's Gram.* p. 281. "Oh that Ishmael might live before thee!"—ALGER'S BIBLE: *Gen.* xvii, 18. "And he said unto him, Oh let not the Lord be angry, and I will speak."—FRIENDS' BIBLE: *Gen.* xviii, 30. "And he said, Oh let not the Lord be angry."—ID. and SCOTT'S : *ib.* ver. 32. "Oh, my lord, let thy servant, I pray thee, speak a word."—FRIENDS' BIBLE, and ALGER'S : *Gen.* xliv, 18. "Oh, Virtue! how amiable thou art! I fear, alas! for my life."—*Fisk's Gram.* p. 89. "Ay me, they little know How dearly I abide that boast so vain."—*Milton's P. L.,* B. iv, L 86. "Oh! that I had digged myself a cave."—FLETCHER : *in Bucke's Gram.* p. 78. "O, my good lord ! thy comfort comes too late."—SHAK. : *ib.* p. 78. "The vocative takes no article ; it is distinguished thus : O Pedro, Oh Peter ! O Dios, Oh God ! " —*Bucke's Gram.* p. 43. "Oh, o ! But, the relative is always the same."—*Cobbett's Eng. Gram.* 1st Ed. p. 127. "Oh, oh! But, the relative is always the same."—*Id.* Edition of 1832, p. 116. "Ah hail, ye happy men !"—*Jaudon's Gram.* p. 116. "Oh that I had wings like a dove !"—FRIENDS' BIBLE, and ALGER'S : *Ps.* lv, 6. "Oh Glorious hope! O Blessed abode !"—*O. B. Peirce's Gram.* p. 183. "Alas, Friends, how joyous is your presence." —*Rev. T. Smith's Gram.* p. 87. "Oh, blissful days ! Ah me! how soon ye pass ! "—*Parker and Fox's Gram.* Part I, p. 16 ; Part III, p. 29.

　　　"Oh golden days ! oh bright unvalued hours !
　　　What bliss (did ye but know that bliss) were yours ! "—*Barbauld.*

" Ay me ! what perils do environ
　　　The man that meddles with cold iron ! "—*Hudibras.*

CHAPTER XII.—QUESTIONS.

ORDER OF REHEARSAL, AND METHOD OF EXAMINATION.

PART SECOND, ETYMOLOGY.

☞ [The following questions refer almost wholly to the main text of the Etymology of this work, and are such as every student should be able to answer with readiness and accuracy, before he proceeds to any subsequent part of the study or the exercises of English grammar.]

LESSON I.—PARTS OF SPEECH.

1. Of what does Etymology treat ? 2. What is meant by the term, "*Parts of Speech?*" 3. What are *Classes,* under the parts of speech ? 4. What are *Modifications?* 5. How

many and what are the parts of speech? 6. What is an article? 7. What is a noun? 8. What is an adjective? 9. What is a pronoun? 10. What is a verb? 11. What is a participle? 12. What is an adverb? 13. What is a conjunction? 14. What is a preposition? 15. What is an interjection?

LESSON II.—PARSING.

1. What is *Parsing?* and what relation does it bear to grammar? 2. What is a *Praxis?* and what is said of the word? 3. What is required of the pupil in the FIRST PRAXIS? 4. How many definitions are here to be given for each part of speech? 5. How is the following example parsed? "The patient ox submits to the yoke, and meekly performs the labour required of him."

[Now parse, in like manner, the three lessons of the *First Chapter*, or the *First Praxis*.]

LESSON III.—ARTICLES.

1. What is an ARTICLE? 2. Are *an* and *a* different articles, or the same? 3. When ought *an* to be used, and what are the examples? 4. When should *a* be used, and what are the examples? 5. What form of the article do the sounds of *w* and *y* require? 6. Can you repeat the alphabet, with *an* or *a* before the name of each letter? 7. Will you name the ten parts of speech, with *an* or *a* before each name? 8. When does a common noun not admit an article? 9. How is the sense of nouns commonly made indefinitely partitive? 10. Does the mere being of a thing demand the use of articles? 11. Can articles ever be used when we mean to speak of a whole species? 12. But how does *an* or *a* commonly limit the sense? 13. And how does *the* commonly limit the sense? 14. Which number does *the* limit, the singular or the plural? 15. When is *the* required before adjectives? 16. Why is *an* or *a* not applicable to plurals? 17. What is said of *an* or *a* before an adjective of number? 18. When, or how often, should articles be inserted? 19. What is said of needless articles? 20. What is the effect of putting one article for the other, and how shall we know which to choose? 21. How are the two articles distinguished in grammar? 22. Which is the definite article, and what does it denote? 23. Which is the indefinite article, and what does it denote? 24. What modifications have the articles?

LESSON IV.—PARSING.

1. What is required of the pupil in the SECOND PRAXIS? 2. How many definitions are here to be given for each part of speech? 3. How is the following example parsed? "The task of a schoolmaster laboriously prompting and urging an indolent class, is worse than his who drives lazy horses along a sandy road."

[Now parse, in like manner, the three lessons of the *Second Chapter*, or the *Second Praxis*; and then, if you ·please, you may correct orally the five lessons of *bad English*, with which the Second Chapter concludes.]

LESSON V.—NOUNS.

1. What is a NOUN, and what are the examples given? 2. Into what general classes are nouns divided? 3. What is a proper noun? 4. What is a common noun? 5. What particular classes are included among common nouns? 6. What is a collective noun? 7. What is an abstract noun? 8. What is a verbal or participial noun? 9. What modifications have nouns? 10. What are *Persons*, in grammar? 11. How many persons are there, and what are they called? 12. What is the first person? 13. What is the second person? 14. What is the third person? 15. What are *Numbers*, in grammar? 16. How many numbers are there, and what are they called? 17. What is the singular number? 18. What is the plural number? 19. How is the plural number of nouns regularly formed? 20. How is the regular plural formed without increase of syllables? 21. How is the regular plural formed when the word gains a syllable?

LESSON VI.—NOUNS.

1. What are *Genders*, in grammar? 2. How many genders are there, and what are they called? 3. What is the masculine gender? 4. What is the feminine gender? 5. What is the neuter gender? 6. What nouns, then, are masculine? what, feminine? and what, neuter? 7. What inflection of English nouns regularly changes their gender? 8. On what are the different genders founded, and to what parts of speech do they belong? 9. When the noun is such as may be applied to either sex, how is the gender usually determined? 10. What principle of universal grammar determines the gender when both sexes are taken together? 11. What is said of the gender of nouns of multitude? 12. Under what circumstances is it common to disregard the distinction of sex? 13. In how many ways are the sexes distinguished in grammar? 14. When the gender is figurative, how is it indicated? 15. What are *Cases*, in grammar? 16. How many cases are there, and what are they called? 17. What is the nominative case? 18. What is the subject of a verb? 19. What is the possessive case? 20. How is the possessive case of nouns formed? 21. What is the objective case? 22. What is the object of a verb, participle, or preposition? 23. What two cases of nouns are alike in form, and how are they distinguished? 24. What is the declension of a noun? 25. How do you decline the nouns, *friend, man, fox,* and *fly?*

LESSON VII.—PARSING.

1. What is required of the pupil in the THIRD PRAXIS? 2. How many definitions are here to be given for each part of speech? 3. How is the following example parsed? "The writings of Hannah More appear to me more praise-worthy than Scott's."

[Now parse, in like manner, the three lessons of the *Third Chapter*, or the *Third Praxis*; and then, if you please, you may correct orally the three lessons of bad *English*, with which the Third Chapter concludes.]

LESSON VIII.—ADJECTIVES.

1. What is an ADJECTIVE, and what are the examples given? 2. Into what classes may adjectives be divided? 3. What is a common adjective? 4. What is a proper adjective? 5. What is a numeral adjective? 6. What is a pronominal adjective? 7. What is a participial adjective? 8. What is a compound adjective? 9. What modifications have adjectives? 10. What is comparison, in grammar? 11. How many and what are the degrees of comparison? 12. What is the positive degree? 13. What is the comparative degree? 14. What is the superlative degree? 15. What adjectives cannot be compared? 16. What adjectives are compared by means of adverbs? 17. How are adjectives regularly compared? 18. What principles of spelling must be observed in the comparing of adjectives? 19. To what adjectives is the regular method of comparison, by *er* and *est*, applicable? 20. Is there any other method of expressing the degrees of comparison? 21. How are the degrees of diminution, or inferiority, expressed? 22. Has the regular method of comparison any degrees of this kind? 23. Do we ever compare by adverbs those adjectives which can be compared by *er* and *est*? 24. How do you compare *good? bad, evil,* or *ill? little? much? many?* 25. How do you compare *far? near? fore? hind? in? out? up? low? late?* 26. What words want the positive? 27. What words want the comparative?

LESSON IX.—PARSING.

1. What is required of the pupil in the FOURTH PRAXIS? 2. How many definitions are here to be given for each part of speech? 3. How is the following example parsed? "The best and most effectual method of teaching grammar, is precisely that of which the careless are least fond: teach learnedly, rebuking whatsoever is false, blundering, or unmannerly."

[Now parse, in like manner, the three lessons of the *Fourth Chapter*, or the *Fourth Praxis*; and then, if you please, you may correct orally the three lessons of bad *English*, with which the Fourth Chapter concludes.]

LESSON X.—PRONOUNS.

1. What is a PRONOUN, and what is the example given? 2. How many pronouns are there? 3. How are pronouns divided? 4. What is a personal pronoun? 5. How many and what are the simple personal pronouns? 6. How many and what are the compound personal pronouns? 7. What is a relative pronoun? 8. Which are the relative pronouns? 9. What peculiarity has the relative *what?* 10. What is an interrogative pronoun? 11. Which are the interrogative pronouns? 12. Do *who, which,* and *what,* all ask the same question? 13. What modifications have pronouns? 14. Why are not these things defined under the head of pronouns? 15. What is the declension of a pronoun? 16. How do you decline the pronoun *I? Thou? He? She? It?* 17. What is said of the compound personal pronouns? 18. How do you decline the pronoun *Myself? Thyself? Himself? Herself? Itself?* 19. Are the interrogative pronouns declined like the simple relatives? 20. How do you decline *Who? Which? What? That? As?* 21. Have the compound relative pronouns any declension? 22. How do you decline *Whoever? Whosoever? Whichever? Whichsoever? Whatever? Whatsoever?*

LESSON XI.—PARSING.

1. What is required of the pupil in the FIFTH PRAXIS? 2. How many definitions are here to be given for each part of speech? 3. How is the following example parsed? "Nay but, O man, who art thou that repliest against God? Shall the thing formed say to him that formed it, Why hast thou made me thus?"

[Now parse, in like manner, the three lessons of the *Fifth Chapter*, or the *Fifth Praxis*; and then, if you please, you may correct orally the three lessons of bad *English*, with which the Fifth Chapter concludes.]

LESSON XII.—VERBS.

1. What is a VERB, and what are the examples given? 2. Why are *verbs* called by that name? 3. Respecting an English verb, what things are to be sought in the first place? 4. What is *the Present?* 5. What is *the Preterit?* 6. What is *the Imperfect Participle?* 7. What is *the Perfect Participle?* 8. How are verbs divided, with respect to their form? 9. What is a regular verb? 10. What is an irregular verb? 11. What is a redundant verb? 12. What is a defective verb? 13. How are verbs divided, with respect to their signification? 14. What is an active-transitive verb? 15. What is an active-intransitive verb? 16. What is a passive verb? 17. What is a neuter verb? 18. What modifications have verbs? 19. What are *Moods,* in grammar? 20. How many moods are there, and what are they called? 21. What is the infinitive mood? 22. What is the indicative mood? 23. What is the potential mood? 24. What is the subjunctive mood? 25. What is the imperative mood?

LESSON XIII.—VERBS.

1. What are *Tenses*, in grammar? 2. How many tenses are there, and what are they called? 3. What is the present tense? 4. What is the imperfect tense? 5. What is the perfect tense? 6. What is the pluperfect tense? 7. What is the first-future tense? 8. What is the second-future tense? 9. What are the *Person* and *Number* of a verb? 10. How many persons and numbers belong to verbs? 11. Why are not these things defined under the head of verbs? 12. How are the second and third persons singular distinctively formed? 13. How are the person and number of a verb ascertained, where no peculiar ending is employed to mark them? 14. What is the conjugation of a verb? 15. What are the PRINCIPAL PARTS in the conjugation of a verb? 16. What is a verb called which wants some of these parts? 17. What is an auxiliary, in grammar? 18. 'What verbs are used as auxiliaries? 19. What are the inflections of the verb *do*, in its simple tenses? 20. What are the inflections of the verb *be*, in its simple tenses? 21. What are the inflections of the verb *have*, in its simple tenses? 22. What are the inflections and uses of *shall* and *will*? 23. What are the inflections and uses of *may*? 24. What are the inflections and uses of *can*? 25. What are the uses of *must*, which is uninflected? 26. To what style is the inflecting of *shall, will, may, can, should, would, might*, and *could*, now restricted?

LESSON XIV.—VERBS.

1. What is the simplest form of an English conjugation? 2. What is the first example of conjugation? 3. What are the principal parts of the verb LOVE? 4. How many and what tenses has the *infinitive* mood?—the *indicative*?—the *potential*?—the *subjunctive*?—the *imperative*? 9. What is the verb LOVE in the *Infinitive*, present?—perfect?—*Indicative*, present?—imperfect?—perfect?—pluperfect?—first-future?—second-future?—*Potential*, present?—imperfect?—perfect?—pluperfect?—*Subjunctive*, present?—imperfect?—*Imperative*, present? 24. What are its participles?

LESSON XV.—VERBS.

1. What is the synopsis of the verb LOVE, in the first person singular?—second person singular, solemn style?—third person singular?—first person plural?—second person plural? —third person plural? 7. If the second person singular of this verb be used familiarly, how should it be formed?

LESSON XVI.—VERBS.

1. What is the second example of conjugation? 2. What are the principal parts? 3. How is the verb SEE conjugated throughout? 4. How do you form a synopsis of the verb *see*, with the pronoun *I? thou? he? we? you? they?*

LESSON XVII.—VERBS.

1. What is the third example of conjugation? 2. What are the principal parts? 3. How is the verb BE conjugated? 4. How do you form a synopsis of the verb *be*, with the nominative *I? thou? he? we? you? they? the man? the men?*

LESSON XVIII.—VERBS.

1. What is the compound form of conjugating active or neuter verbs? 2. What peculiar meaning does this form convey? 3. What is the fourth example of conjugation? 4. What are the principal parts of the simple verb READ? 5. How is the verb READ conjugated in the compound form? 6. How do you form a synopsis of the verb BE READING, with the nominative *I? thou? he? we? you? they? the boy? the boys?*

LESSON XIX.—VERBS.

1. How are passive verbs formed? 2. What is the fifth example of conjugation. 3. How is the passive verb BE LOVED conjugated throughout? 4. How do you form a synopsis of the verb BE LOVED, with the nominative *I? thou? he? we? you? they? the child? the children?*

LESSON XX.—VERBS.

1. How is a verb conjugated negatively? 2. How is the form of negation exemplified by the verb *love* in the first person singular? 3. What is the form of negation for the solemn style, second person singular? 4. What is the form for the familiar style? 5. What is the negative form of the verb *love* with the pronoun *he?* 6. How is the verb conjugated interrogatively? 7. What is the interrogative form of the verb *love* with the pronoun *I?* 8. What is the form of question in the solemn style, with this verb in the second person singular? 9. How are such questions asked in the familiar style? 10. What is the interrogative form of the verb *love* with the pronoun *he?* 11. How is a verb conjugated interrogatively and negatively? 12. How is the negative question exemplified in the first person plural? 13. How is the negative question exemplified in the second person plural? 14. How is the like synopsis formed in the third person plural?

Lesson XXI.—Verbs.

1. What is an irregular verb? 2. How many simple irregular verbs are there? 3. What are the principal parts of the following verbs : Arise, be, bear, beat, begin, behold, beset, bestead, bid, bind, bite, bleed, break, breed, bring, buy, cast, chide, choose, cleave, cling, come, cost, cut, do, draw, drink, drive, eat, fall, feed, feel, fight, find, flee, fling, fly, forbear, forsake, get, give, go, grow, have, hear, hide, hit, hold, hurt, keep, know, lead, leave, lend, let, lie, lose, make, meet, outdo, put, read, rend, rid, ride, ring, rise, run, say, see, seek, sell, send, set, shed, shoe, shoot, shut, shred, shrink, sing, sink, sit, slay, sling, slink, smite, speak, spend, spin, spit, spread, spring, stand, steal, stick, sting, stink, stride, strike, swear, swim, swing, take, teach, tear, tell, think, thrust, tread, wear, win, write?

Lesson XXII.—Verbs.

1. What is a redundant verb? 2. How many redundant verbs are there? 3. What are the principal parts of the following verbs : Abide, awake, belay, bend, bereave, beseech, bet, betide, blend, bless, blow, build, burn, burst, catch, clothe, creep, crow, curse, dare, deal, dig, dive, dream, dress, dwell, freeze, geld, gild, gird, grave, grind, hang, heave, hew, kneel, knit, lade, lay, lean, leap, learn, light, mean, mow, mulct, pass, pay, pen, plead, prove, quit, rap, reave, rive, roast, saw, seethe, shake, shape, shave, shear, shine, show, sleep, slide, slit, smell, sow, speed, spell, spill, split, spoil, stave, stay, string, strive, strow, sweat, sweep, swell, thrive, throw, wake, wax, weave, wed, weep, wet, whet, wind, wont, work, wring? 4. What is a defective verb? 5. What verbs are defective?

Lesson XXIII.—Parsing.

1. What is required of the pupil in the Sixth Praxis? 2. How many definitions are here to be given for each part of speech? 3. How is the following example parsed? " The freedom of choice seems essential to happiness ; because, properly speaking, that is not our own which is imposed upon us."

[Now parse, in like manner, the three lessons of the *Sixth Chapter*, or the *Sixth Praxis*; and then, if you please, you may correct orally the three lessons of *bad English*, with which the Sixth Chapter concludes.]

Lesson XXIV.—Participles.

1. What is a Participle, and how is it generally formed? 2. How many kinds of participles are there, and what are they called? 3. What is the imperfect participle? 4. What is the perfect participle? 5. What is the preperfect participle? 6. How is the first or imperfect participle formed? 7. How is the second or perfect participle formed? 8. How is the third or preperfect participle formed? 9. What are the participles of the following verbs, according to the simplest form of conjugation : Repeat, study, return, mourn, seem, rejoice, appear, approach, suppose, think, set, come, rain, stand, know, deceive?

Lesson XXV.—Parsing.

1. What is required of the pupil in the Seventh Praxis? 2. How many definitions are here to be given for each part of speech? 3. How is the following example parsed? " Religion, rightly understood and practised, has the purest of all joys attending it."

[Now parse, in like manner, the three lessons of the *Seventh Chapter*, or the *Seventh Praxis*; and then, if you please, you may correct orally the three lessons of *bad English*, with which the Seventh Chapter concludes.]

Lesson XXVI.—Adverbs.

1. What is an Adverb, and what is the example given? 2. To what general classes may adverbs be reduced? 3. What are adverbs of time? 4. What are adverbs of place? 5. What are adverbs of degree? 6. What are adverbs of manner? 7. What are conjunctive adverbs? 8. Are all the conjunctive adverbs included in the first four classes? 9. How may the adverbs of time be subdivided? 10. How may the adverbs of place be subdivided? 11. How may the adverbs of degree be subdivided? 12. How may the adverbs of manner be subdivided? 13. What modifications have adverbs? 14. How do we compare *well, badly* or *ill, little, much, far,* and *forth?* 15. Of what degree is the adverb *rather?* 16. What is said of the comparison of adverbs by *more* and *most, less* and *least?*

Lesson XXVII.—Parsing.

1. What is required of the pupil in the Eighth Praxis? 2. How many definitions are here to be given for each part of speech? 3. How is the following example parsed? " When was it that Rome attracted most strongly the admiration of mankind? "

[Now parse, in like manner, the three lessons of the *Eighth Chapter*, or the *Eighth Praxis*; and then, if you please, you may correct orally the lesson of *bad English*, with which the Eighth Chapter concludes.]

Lesson XXVIII.—Conjunctions.

1. What is a Conjunction, and what is the example given? 2. Have we any connective words besides the conjunctions? 3. How do relative pronouns differ from other connectives? 4. How do conjunctive adverbs differ from other connectives? 5. How do conjunctions differ from other connectives? 6. How do prepositions differ from other connectives?

7. How are the conjunctions divided? 8. What is a copulative conjunction? 9. What is a disjunctive conjunction? 10. What are corresponsive conjunctions? 11. Which are the copulative conjunctions? 12. Which are the disjunctive conjunctions? 13. Which are the corresponsive conjunctions?

LESSON XXIX.—PARSING.

1. What is required of the pupil in the NINTH PRAXIS? 2. How many definitions are here to be given for each part of speech? 3. How is the following example parsed? "If thou hast done a good deed, boast not of it."

[Now parse, in like manner, the three lessons of the *Ninth Chapter*, or the *Ninth Praxis;* and then, if you please, you may correct orally the lesson of *bad English*, with which the Ninth Chapter concludes.]

LESSON XXX.—PREPOSITIONS.

1. What is a PREPOSITION, and what is the example given? 2. Are the prepositions divided into classes? 3. Have prepositions any grammatical modifications? 4. How are the prepositions arranged in the list? 5. What are the prepositions beginning with *a?*—with *b?*—with *c?*—with *d?*—with *e?*—with *f?*—with *i?*—with *m?*—with *n?*—with *o?*—with *p?* —with *r?*—with *s?*—with *t?*—with *u?*—with *w?* 21. Does this list contain all the words that are ever used in English as prepositions?

LESSON XXXI.—PARSING.

1. What is required of the pupil in the TENTH PRAXIS? 2. How many definitions are here to be given for each part of speech? 3. How is the following example parsed? "Never adventure on too near an approach to what is evil."

[Now parse, in like manner, the three lessons of the *Tenth Chapter*, or the *Tenth Praxis;* and then, if you please, you may correct orally the lesson of *bad English*, with which the Tenth Chapter concludes.]

LESSON XXXII.—INTERJECTIONS.

1. What is an INTERJECTION, and what are the examples given? 2. Why are interjections so called? 3. How are the interjections arranged in the list? 4. What are the interjections of joy?—of praise?—of sorrow?—of wonder?—of wishing or earnestness?—of pain or fear?—of contempt?—of aversion?—of calling aloud?—of exultation?—of laughter?—of salutation?—of calling to attention?—of calling to silence?—of surprise or horror?—of languor?—of stopping?—of parting?—of knowing or detecting?—of interroga.ing?

LESSON XXXIII.—PARSING.

1. What is required of the pupil in the ELEVENTH PRAXIS? 2. How many definitions are here given for each part of speech? 3. How is the following example parsed? "O! sooner shall the earth and stars fall into chaos!"

[Now parse, in like manner, the three lessons of the *Eleventh Chapter*, or the *Eleventh Praxis;* and then, if you please, you may correct orally the lesson of *bad English*, with which the Eleventh Chapter concludes.]

CHAPTER XIII.—FOR WRITING.
EXERCISES IN ETYMOLOGY.

☞ [When the pupil has become familiar with the different parts of speech, and their classes and modifications, and has been sufficiently exercised in etymological parsing and correcting, he should *write out* the following exercises; for speech and writing afford us different modes of testing the proficiency of students, and exercises in both are necessary to a complete course of English Grammar.]

EXERCISE I.—ARTICLES.

1. Prefix the definite article to each of the following nouns: path, paths; loss, losses; name, names; page, pages; want, wants; doubt, doubts; votary, votaries.

2. Prefix the indefinite article to each of the following nouns: age, error, idea, omen, urn, arch, bird, cage, dream, empire, farm, grain, horse, idol, jay, king, lady, man, novice, opinion, pony, quail, raven, sample, trade, uncle, vessel, window, youth, zone, whirlwind, union, onion, unit, eagle, house, honour, hour, herald, habitation, hospital, harper, harpoon, ewer, eye, humour.

3. Insert the definite article rightly in the following phrases: George Second—fair appearance—part first—reasons most obvious—good man—wide circle—man of honour—man of world—old books—common people—same person—smaller piece—rich and poor—first and last—all time—great excess—nine muses—how rich reward—so small number—all ancient writers—in nature of things—much better course.

4. Insert the indefinite article rightly in each of the following phrases: new name—very quick motion—other sheep—such power—what instance—great weight—such worthy cause —to great difference—high honour—humble station—universal law—what strange event— so deep interest—as firm hope—so great wit—humorous story—such person—few dollars— little reflection.

EXERCISE II.—NOUNS.

1. Write the plurals of the following nouns : town, country, case, pin, needle, harp, pen, sex, rush, arch, marsh, monarch, blemish, distich, princess, gas, bias, stigma, wo, grotto, folio, punctilio, ally, duty, toy, money, entry, valley, volley, half, dwarf, strife, knife, roof, muff, staff, chief, sheaf, mouse, penny, ox, foot, erratum, axis, thesis, criterion, bolus, rebus, son-in-law, pailful, man-servant, fellow-citizen.

2. Write the feminines corresponding to the following nouns : earl, friar, stag, lord, duke, marquis, hero, executor, nephew, heir, actor, enchanter, hunter, prince, traitor, lion, arbiter, tutor, songster, abbot, master, uncle, widower, son, landgrave.

3. Write the possessive case singular, of the following nouns : table, leaf, boy, torch, park, porch, portico, lynx, calf, sheep, wolf, echo, folly, cavern, father-in-law, court-martial, precipice, countess, lordship.

4. Write the possessive case plural, of the following nouns : priest, tutor, scholar, mountain, city, courtier, judge, citizen, woman, servant, writer, grandmother.

5. Write the possessive case, both singular and plural, of the following nouns : body, fancy, lady, attorney, negro, nuncio, life, brother, deer, child, wife, goose, beau, envoy, distaff, hero, thief, wretch.

EXERCISE III.—ADJECTIVES.

1. Annex a suitable noun to each of the following adjectives, without repeating any word : good, great, tall, wise, strong, dark, dangerous, dismal, drowsy, twenty, true, difficult, pale, livid, ripe, delicious, stormy, rainy, convenient, heavy, disastrous, terrible, necessary. Thus — good *manners*, &c.

2. Place a suitable adjective before each of the following nouns, without repeating any word : man, son, merchant, work, fence, fear, poverty, picture, prince, delay, suspense, devices, follies, actions. Thus—*wise* man, &c.

3. Write the forms in which the following adjectives are compared by inflection, or change of form : black, bright, short, white, old, high, wet, big, few, lovely, dry, fat, good, bad, little, much, many, far, true, just, vast.

4. Write the forms in which the following adjectives are compared, using the adverbs of increase : delightful, comfortable, agreeable, pleasant, fortunate, valuable, wretched, vivid, timid, poignant, excellent, sincere, honest, correct.

5. Write the forms in which the following adjectives are compared, using the comparative adverbs of inferiority or diminution : objectionable, formidable, forcible, comely, pleasing, obvious, censurable, prudent, imprudent, imperfect, pleasant, unpleasant.

EXERCISE IV.—PRONOUNS.

1. Write the nominative plural of the following pronouns : I, thou, he, she, it, who, which, what, that, as.

2. Write the objective singular of the following pronouns : I, thou, he, she, it, who, which, what, that, as.

3. Write the following words in their customary and proper forms : he's, her's, it's, our's your's, their's, who's, meself, hisself, theirselves.

4. Write together in declension the following pronouns, according to the agreement of each two : I myself, thou thyself, he himself, she herself, it itself.

5. Re-write the following sentences, and make them good English : " Nor is the criminal binding any thing : but was, his self, being bound."—*Wright's Gram.* p. 193. " The writer surely did not mean, that the work was preparing its self."—*Ib.* "May, or *can*, in its self, denotes possibility."—*Ib.* p. 216. " Consequently those in connection with the remaining pronouns respectively, should be written,—he, *his self*;—she, *her self*;—ye or you, *your selves*; they, *their selves*."—*Ib.* p. 154. " Lest their beacons be lost to the view, and their selves wrecked on the shoals of destruction."—*Ib.* p. 155. " In the regal style, as generally in the second person, the singular noun is added to the plural pronoun, *ourself*." —*Churchill's Gram.* p. 76. " Each has it's peculiar advantages."—*Ib.* p. 283. " Who his ownself bare our sins in his own body on the tree."—*The Friend*, iv, 302. " It is difficult to look inwardly on oneself."—*Journal of N. Y. Lit. Convention*, p. 267.

EXERCISE V.—VERBS.

1. Write the four principal parts of each of the following verbs : slip, thrill, caress, force, release, crop, try, die, obey, delay, destroy, deny, buy, come, do, feed, lie, say, huzza, pretend, deliver, arrest.

2. Write the following preterits each in its appropriate form : exprest, stript, dropt, jumpt, prest, topt, whipt, linkt, propt, fixt, crost, stept, distrest, gusht, confest, snapt, shipt, kist, discust, lackt.

3. Write the following verbs in the indicative mood, present tense, second person singular : move, strive, please, reach, confess, fix, deny, survive, know, go, outdo, close, lose, pursue, defend, surpass, conquer, deliver, enlighten, protect, polish.

4. Write the following verbs in the indicative mood, present tense, third person singular :

leave, seem, search, impeach, fear, redress, comply, bestow, do, woo, sue, view, allure, rely, beset, release, be, bias, compel, degrade, efface, garnish, handle, induce.

5. Write the following verbs in the subjunctive mood, present tense, in the three persons singular : serve, shun, turn, learn, find, wish, throw, dream, possess, detest, disarm, allow, pretend, expose, alarm, deprive, transgress.

EXERCISE VI.—VERBS.

1. Write a synopsis of the first person singular of the active verb *amuse*, conjugated affirmatively.

2. Write a synopsis of the second person singular of the neuter verb *sit*, conjugated affirmatively in the solemn style.

3. Write a synopsis of the third person singular of the active verb *speak*, conjugated affirmatively in the compound form.

4. Write a synopsis of the first person plural of the passive verb *be reduced*, conjugated affirmatively.

5. Write a synopsis of the second person plural of the active verb *lose*, conjugated negatively.

6. Write a synopsis of the third person plural of the neuter verb *stand*, conjugated interrogatively.

7. Write a synopsis of the first person singular of the active verb *derive*, conjugated interrogatively and negatively.

EXERCISE VII.—PARTICIPLES.

1 Write the simple imperfect participles of the following verbs : belong, provoke, degrade, impress, fly, do, survey, vie, coo, let, hit, put, defer, differ, remember.

2. Write the perfect participles of the following verbs : turn, burn, learn, deem, crowd, choose, draw, hear, lend, sweep, tear, thrust, steal, write, delay, imply, exist.

3. Write the preperfect participles of the following verbs : depend, dare, deny, value, forsake, bear, set, sit, lay, mix, speak, sleep, allot.

4. Write the following participles each in its appropriate form : dipt, deckt, markt, equipt, ingulft, embarrast, astonisht, tost, embost, absorpt, attackt, gasht, soakt, hackt.

5. Write the regular participles which are now generally preferred to the following irregular ones : blent, blest, clad, curst, diven, drest, graven, hoven, hewn, knelt, leant, leapt, learnt, lit, mown, mulct, past, pent, quit, riven, roast, sawn, sodden, shaven, shorn, sown, striven, strown, sweat, swollen, thriven, waxen.

6. Write the irregular participles which are commonly preferred to the following regular ones : abided, bended, builded, bursted, catched, creeped, dealed, digged, dwelled, freezed, grinded, knitted, layed, meaned, payed, reaved, slided, speeded, splitted, stringed, sweeped, throwed, weaved, weeped, winded.

EXERCISE VIII.—ADVERBS, &c.

1. Compare the following adverbs : soon, often, long, fast, near, early, well, badly or ill, little, much, far, forth.

2. Place the comparative adverbs of increase before each of the following adverbs : purely, fairly, sweetly, earnestly, patiently, completely, fortunately, profitably, easily.

3. Place the comparative adverbs of diminution before each of the following adverbs : secretly, slily, liberally, favourably, powerfully, solemnly.

4. Insert suitable conjunctions in place of the following dashes : Love—fidelity are inseparable. Be shy of parties—factions. Do well—boast not. Improve time—it flies. There would be few paupers—no time were lost. Be not proud—thou art human. I saw —it was necessary. Wisdom is better—wealth. Neither he—I can do it. Wisdom—folly governs us. Take care—thou fall. Though I should boast—am I nothing.

5. Insert suitable prepositions in place of the following dashes : Plead—the dumb. Qualify thyself—action—study. Think often—the worth—time. Live—peace—all men. Keep—compass. Jest not—serious subjects. Take no part—slander. Guilt starts—its own shadow. Grudge not—giving. Go not—sleep—malice. Debate not—temptation. Depend not—the stores—others. Contend not—trifles. Many fall—grasping—things—their reach. Be deaf—detraction.

6. Correct the following sentences, and adapt the interjections to the emotions expressed by the other words : Aha ! aha ! I am undone. Hey ! io ! I am tired. Ho ! be still. Avaunt ! this way. Ah ! what nonsense. Heigh-ho ! I am delighted. Hist ! it is contemptible. Oh ! for that sympathetic glow ! Ah ! what withering phantoms glare !

PART III.

SYNTAX.

SYNTAX treats of the relation, agreement, government, and arrangement, of words in sentences.

The *relation* of words is their reference to other words, or their dependence according to the sense.

The *agreement* of words is their similarity in person, number, gender, case, mood, tense, or form.

The *government* of words is that power which one word has over an other, to cause it to assume some particular modification.

The *arrangement* of words is their collocation, or relative position, in a sentence.

CHAPTER I.—SENTENCES.

A *sentence* is an assemblage of words, making complete sense, and always containing a nominative and a verb; as, " Reward sweetens labour."

The *principal parts* of a sentence are usually three; namely, the SUBJECT, or nominative,—the attribute, or finite VERB,—and the case put after, or the OBJECT* governed by the verb: as, "*Crimes deserve punishment.*"

The *other* or *subordinate parts* depend upon these, either as primary or as secondary *adjuncts;* as, "*High* crimes *justly* deserve *very severe* punishments."

Sentences are of two kinds, *simple* and *compound.*†

A *simple sentence* is a sentence which consists of one single assertion, supposition, command, question, or exclamation; as, " David and Jonathan loved each other."—" If thine enemy hunger."—" Do violence to no man."—"Am I not an apostle? "—1 *Cor.* ix, 1. " What immortal glory shall I have acquired! "—HOOKE: *Mur. Seq.* p. 71.

A *compound sentence* is a sentence which consists of two or more simple ones either expressly or tacitly connected; as, " Send men to Joppa, *and* call for Simon, *whose* surname is Peter ; *who* shall tell thee words, *whereby* thou and all thy house shall be saved."—*Acts*, xi, 13. " The more the works of Cowper are read, the more his readers will find reason to admire the variety and the extent, the graces and the energy, of his literary talents."—HAYLEY: *Mur. Seq.* p. 250.

A *clause*, or *member*, is a subdivision of a compound sentence; and is itself a sentence, either simple or compound: as, " If thine enemy be hungry, give him bread to eat ; if he be thirsty, give him water to drink."—*Prov.* xxv, 21.‡

---

* This position is denied by some grammarians. One recent author says, " The *object* cannot properly be called one of the principal parts of a sentence ; as it belongs only to some sentences, and then is dependent on the verb, which it modifies or explains "—*Goodenow's Gram.* p. 87. This is consistent enough with the notion, that, "An infinitive, with or without a substantive, may be *the object of a transitive verb;* as, ' I wish *to ride;* ' ' I wish you *to ride.*' "—*Ib.* p 87. Or, with the *contrary* notion, that, " An infinitive may be *the object of a preposition*, expressed or understood ; as, 'I wish *for you to ride.*' "—*Ibid.* But if the object governed by the verb, is always a mere qualifying adjunct, a mere " explanation of the attribute," (*Ib.* p. 28,) how differs it from an adverb ? " Adverbs are words *added to verbs,* and sometimes to other words, to *qualify* their meaning."—*Ib.* p. 28 And if infinitives, and other mere *adjuncts,* may be the objects which make verbs transitive, how shall a transitive verb be known ? The fact is, that the *true* object of the transitive verb *is one of the principal parts* of the sentence, and that the infinitive mood cannot properly be reckoned such an object.

† Some writers distinguish sentences as being of *three* kinds, *simple,* and *complex,* and *compound;* but, in this work, care has not in general been taken to discriminate between complex sentences and compound. A late author states the difference thus: " A sentence containing but one proposition is *simple;* a sentence containing two propositions, one of which modifies the other, is *complex;* a sentence containing two propositions which in no way modify each other, is *compound.*"—*Greene's Analysis*, p. 8. The term *compound,* as applied to sentences, is not usually so restricted.

‡ The terms *clause* and *member,* in grammar, appear to have been generally used as words synonymous; but some authors have thought it convenient to discriminate them, as having different senses. Hiley says, " Those

A *phrase* is two or more words which express some relation of different ideas, but no entire proposition ; as, " By the means appointed."—" To be plain with you."—" Having loved his own."

Words that are omitted by *ellipsis*, and that are necessarily understood in order to complete the construction, (and only such,) must be supplied in parsing.

The *leading principles* to be observed in the construction of sentences, are embraced in the following twenty-four rules, which are arranged, as nearly as possible, in the order of the parts of speech.

THE RULES OF SYNTAX.

RULE I.—ARTICLES.

Articles relate to the nouns which they limit.

RULE II.—NOMINATIVES.

A Noun or a Pronoun which is the subject of a finite verb, must be in the nominative case.

RULE III.—APPOSITION.

A Noun or a personal Pronoun used to explain a preceding noun or pronoun, is put, by apposition, in the same case.

RULE IV.—POSSESSIVES.

A Noun or a Pronoun in the possessive case, is governed by the name of the thing possessed.

RULE V.—OBJECTIVES.

A Noun or a Pronoun made the object of an active-transitive verb or participle, is governed by it in the objective case.

RULE VI.—SAME CASES.

A Noun or a Pronoun put after a verb or participle not transitive, agrees in case with a preceding noun or pronoun referring to the same thing.

RULE VII.—OBJECTIVES.

A Noun or a Pronoun made the object of a preposition, is governed by it in the objective case.

RULE VIII.—NOM. ABSOLUTE.

A Noun or a Pronoun is put absolute in the nominative, when its case depends on no other word.

RULE IX.—ADJECTIVES.

Adjectives relate to nouns or pronouns.

RULE X.—PRONOUNS.

A Pronoun must agree with its antecedent, or the noun or pronoun which it represents, in person, number, and gender.

---

parts of a sentence which are separated by commas, are called *clauses;* and those separated by semicolons, are called *members.*"—*Hiley's Gram.* p. 66. W. Allen too confines the former term to simple members : " A compound sentence is formed by uniting two or more simple sentences ; as, Man is mortal, and life is uncertain. Each of these simple sentences is called a *clause.* When the *members* of a compound sentence are complex, they are subdivided into *clauses ;* as, Virtue leads to honor, and insures true happiness ; but vice degrades the understanding, and is succeeded by infamy."—*Allen's Gram.* p. 128. By some authors, the terms *clause* and *phrase* are often carelessly confounded, each being applied with no sort of regard to its proper import. Thus, where L. Murray and his copyists expound their text about " the pupil's composing frequently," even the minor phrase, " *composing frequently,*" is absurdly called a *clause ;* " an entire *clause* of a sentence." See *Murray's Gram.* p. 179; *Alger's,* 61; *Fisk's,* 108; *Ingersoll's,* 180; *Merchant's,* 84; R. C. *Smith's,* 152; *Weld's,* 2d Ed., 150. The term *sentence* also is sometimes grossly misapplied. Thus, by R. C. Smith, the phrases "*James and William,*" " *Thomas and John,*" and others similar, are called " sentences."—*Smith's New Gram.* pp. 9 and 10. So Weld absurdly writes as follows : " A *whole sentence* is frequently the object of a preposition ; as, ' The crime of being a young man.' *Being a young man,* is the object of the preposition *of.*"—*Weld's E. Gram.* 2d Edition, p. 42. The phrase " *being a young man,*" here depends upon " *of ;*" but this preposition governs nothing but the participle " *being.*" The construction of the word " *man* " is explained below, in Obs. 7th on Rule 6th, of Same Cases.

RULE XI.—PRONOUNS.

When the antecedent is a collective noun conveying the idea of plurality, the Pronoun must agree with it in the plural number.

RULE XII.—PRONOUNS.

When a Pronoun has two or more antecedents connected by *and*, it must agree with them jointly in the plural, because they are taken together.

RULE XIII.—PRONOUNS.

When a Pronoun has two or more antecedents connected by *or* or *nor*, it must agree with them singly, and not as if taken together.

RULE XIV.—FINITE VERBS.

Every finite verb must agree with its subject, or nominative, in person and number.

RULE XV.—FINITE VERBS.

When the nominative is a collective noun conveying the idea of plurality, the Verb must agree with it in the plural number.

RULE XVI.—FINITE VERBS.

When a Verb has two or more nominatives connected by *and*, it must agree with them jointly in the plural, because they are taken together.

RULE XVII.—FINITE VERBS.

When a Verb has two or more nominatives connected by *or* or *nor*, it must agree with them singly, and not as if taken together.

RULE XVIII.—INFINITIVES.

The preposition TO governs the Infinitive mood, and commonly connects it to a finite verb.

RULE XIX.—INFINITIVES.

The active verbs, *bid, dare, feel, hear, let, make, need, see*, and their participles, usually take the Infinitive after them without the preposition TO.

RULE XX.—PARTICIPLES.

Participles relate to nouns or pronouns, or else are governed by prepositions.

RULE XXI.—ADVERBS.

Adverbs relate to verbs, participles, adjectives, or other adverbs.

RULE XXII.—CONJUNCTIONS.

Conjunctions connect words, sentences, or parts of sentences.

RULE XXIII.—PREPOSITIONS.

Prepositions show the relations of words, and of the things or thoughts expressed by them.

RULE XXIV.—INTERJECTIONS.

Interjections have no dependent construction ; they are put absolute, either alone, or with other words.

GENERAL OR CRITICAL OBSERVATIONS ON SYNTAX.

OBS. 1.—An explanation of the relation, agreement, government, and arrangement, of words in sentences, constitutes that part of grammar which we call *Syntax*. But many grammarians, representing this branch of their subject as consisting of two parts only, "*concord* and *government*," say little or nothing of the *relation* and *arrangement* of words, except as these are involved in the others. The four things are essentially different in their nature, as may be seen by the definitions given above, yet not so distinct in practice that they can well be made the basis of any perfect division of the rules of syntax. I have therefore, on this occasion, preferred the order of the parts of speech; each of which will form a chapter in the Syntax of this work, as each forms a chapter in the Etymology.

Obs. 2.—*Agreement* and *concord* are one and the same thing. *Relation* and *agreement*, though different, may yet coincide, and be taken together. The latter is moreover naturally allied to the former. Seven of the ten parts of speech are, with a few exceptions, incapable of any agreement: of these the *relation* and *use* must be explained in parsing; and all *requisite agreement* between any of the rest, is confined to words that *relate* to each other. For one word may *relate* to an other and not *agree* with it; but there is never any *necessary agreement* between words that have not a *relation* one to the other, or a connexion according to the sense. Any similarity happening between unconnected words, is no syntactical concord, though it may rank the terms in the same class etymologically.

Obs. 3.—From these observations it may be seen, that the most important and most comprehensive principle of English syntax, is the simple *Relation* of words, according to the sense. To this head alone ought to be referred all the rules of construction by which our articles, our nominatives, our adjectives, our participles, our adverbs, our conjunctions, our prepositions, and our interjections, are to be parsed. To the ordinary syntactical use of any of these, no rules of concord, government, or position, can at all apply. Yet so defective and erroneous are the schemes of syntax which are commonly found in our English grammars, that *no rules of simple relation*, none by which any of the above-named parts of speech can be consistently parsed, are in general to be found in them. If there are any exceptions to this censure, they are very few, and in treatises still marked with glaring defects in regard to the syntax of some of these parts of speech.

Obs. 4.—Grammarians, of course, do not utter falsehoods intentionally; but it is lamentable to see how often they pervert doctrine by untruths uttered ignorantly. It is the design of this pandect, to make every one who reads it, an intelligent judge of the *perversions*, as well as of the true doctrines, of English grammar. The following citations will show him the scope and parts which have commonly been assigned to our syntax: "The construction of sentences depends principally upon the *concord* or *agreement*, and the *regimen* or *government*, of words."—*Lowth's Gram.* p. 68; *Churchill's*, 120. "Words in sentences have a *twofold relation* to one another; namely, that of *Concord* or Agreement; and that of *Government* or Influence."—*Dr. Adam's Latin and English Grammar*, p. 151. "The third part of Grammar is SYNTAX, which treats of the *agreement and construction* of words in a sentence."—*R. G. Greene's Grammatical Text-Book*, p. 15. "Syntax principally consists of two parts, *Concord* and *Government*."—*Murray's Gram.* p. 142; *Ingersoll's*, 170; *Alger's*, 51; *R. C. Smith's*, 169; and many others. "Syntax consists of two parts, *Concord* and *Government*."—*Kirkham's Gram.* p. 175; *Wright's*, 124. "The Rules of Syntax may all be included under three heads, *Concord, Government*, and *Position*."—*Bullions's E Gram.* p. 87. "*Position* means *the place* which a word occupies in a sentence."—*Ib.* "These rules may be mostly ranked under the two heads of *agreement* and *government*; the remainder may be termed *miscellaneous*."—*Nutting's Gram.* p. 92. "Syntax treats of the agreement, government and proper arrangement of words in *a sentence*."—*Frost's El. of Gram.* p. 43. This last-named author, in touching the text of my books, has often *corrupted* it, as he does here; but my definitions of *the tenses* he copied without marring them much. The borrowing occurred as early as 1828, and I add this notice now, lest any should suppose *me* the plagiarist.

Obs. 5.—Most of our English grammars have *more* rules of syntax than are needed, and yet are very deficient in *such* as are needed. To say, as some do, that articles, adjectives, and participles, *agree* with nouns, is to teach Greek or Latin syntax, and not English. To throw, as Nutting does, the whole syntax of adverbs into a remark on *such a rule of agreement*, is to choose disorder for its own sake. To say, with Frost, Hall, Smith, Perley, Kirkham, Sanborn, Rand, and others, "The nominative case *governs* the verb in number and person," and again, "A verb *must agree* with its nominative case in number and person," is to confound the meaning of *government* and *agreement*, to say the same thing in different words, and to leave the subject of a verb still without a rule: for rules of government are applicable only to the words *governed*, and nothing ever agrees with that which governs it.* To say, with Murray and others, "Participles have the same government as the verbs from which they are derived," is to say nothing by which either verbs or participles may be parsed, or any of their errors corrected: those many grammarians, therefore, who make this their only rule for participles, leave them all without any syntax. To say, with Murray, Alger, and others, "Adverbs, *though they have no government of case, tense*, &c. require an appropriate *situation* in the sentence," is to squander words at random, and leave the important question unanswered, "To what do adverbs relate?" To say again, with the same gentlemen, "Conjunctions connect the *same moods and tenses of verbs, and cases of* nouns and pronouns," is to put an ungrammatical, obscure, and useless assertion, in the place

---

* In the very nature of things, all *agreement* consists in concurrence, correspondence, conformity, similarity, sameness, equality; but *government* is direction, control, regulation, restraint, influence, authoritative requisition, with the implication of inequality. That these properties ought to be so far distinguished in grammar, as never to be supposed to coexist in the same terms and under the same circumstances, must be manifest to every reasoner. Some grammarians who seem to have been not always unaware of this, have nevertheless egregiously forgotten it at times. Thus Nutting, in the following remark, expresses a true doctrine, though he has written it with no great accuracy: "A word *in parsing* never governs the same word *which* it qualifies, or with which it agrees."—*Practical Gram.* p. 108. Yet, in his syntax, in which he pretends to separate agreement from government, he frames his first rule under the latter head thus: "The nominative case *governs* a verb."—*Ib* p. 96. Lindley Murray recognizes no such government as this; but seems to suppose his rule for the agreement of a verb with its nominative to be sufficient: for both verb and nominative He appears, however, not to have known that a word does not agree syntactically with an other that governs it; for, in his Exercises, he has given an, apparently from his own pen, the following *untrue*, but otherwise not very objectionable sentence: "On these occasions, the pronoun is *governed by, and consequently agrees with*, the preceding word."—*Exercises*, 8vo, ii, 70. This he corrects thus: "On these occasions, the pronoun is governed by the preceding word, *and consequently agrees with it*."—*Key*, 8vo, ii, 204. The amendments most needed he overlooks; for the thought is not just, and the two verbs which are here connected with one and the same nominative, are different in form. See the same example, with the same variation of it, in *Smith's New Gram.* p. 167; and, without the change, in *Ingersoll's*, p. 233; and *Fisk's*, 141.

of an important rule. To say merely, "Prepositions govern the objective case," is to rest all the syntax of prepositions, on a rule which never applies to them, but which is meant only for one of the constructions of the objective case. To say, as many do, "Interjections *require* the objective case of a pronoun of the first person after them, and the nominative case of the second," is to tell what is utterly false as the words stand, and by no means true in the sense which the authors intend. Finally, to suppose, with Murray, that, "the Interjection *does not require a distinct, appropriate rule*," is in admirable keeping with all the foregoing quotations, and especially with his notion of what it *does* require; namely, "the *objective case* of the first person:" but who dares deny that the following exclamation is good English?

> "O wretched *we*! why were we hurried down ,
> This lubric and adulterate age!"—*Dryden.*

OBS. 6.—The *truth* of any doctrine in science, can be nothing else than its conformity to facts, or to the nature of things; and chiefly by what he knows of the things themselves, must any one judge of what others say concerning them. Erroneous or inadequate views, confused or inconsistent statements, are the peculiar property of those who advance them; they have, in reality, no relationship to science itself, because they originate in ignorance; but all science is knowledge—it is knowledge methodized. What general rules are requisite for the syntactical parsing of the several parts of speech in English, may be seen at once by any one who will consider for a moment the usual construction of each. The correction of false syntax, in its various forms, will require more—yes, five times as many; but such of these as answer only the latter purpose, are, I think, better reserved for notes under the principal rules. The doctrines which I conceive most worthy to form the leading canons of our syntax, are those which are expressed in the twenty-four rules above. If other authors prefer more, or fewer, or different principles for their chief rules, I must suppose, it is because they have studied the subject less. Biased, as we may be, both by our knowledge and by our ignorance, it is easy for men to differ respecting matters of *expediency*; but that clearness, order, and consistency, are both *expedient*, and *requisite*, in didactic compositions, is what none can doubt.

OBS. 7.—Those English grammarians who tell us, as above, that syntax is divided into *parts*, or included under a certain number of *heads*, have almost universally contradicted themselves by treating the subject without any regard to such a division; and, at the same time, not a few have somehow been led into the gross error of supposing broad principles of concord or government where no such things exist. For example, they have invented general RULES like these: "The adjective *agrees* with its noun in number, case, and gender."—*Bingham's English Gram.* p. 40. "Interjections *govern* the nominative case, and sometimes the objective; as, 'O thou! alas me!'"—*Ib.* p. 43. "Adjectives *agree* with their nouns in number."—*Wilbur and Livingston's Gram* p. 22. "Participles *agree* with their nouns in number."—*Ib.* p. 23. "Every adjective *agrees in number* with some substantive expressed or understood."—*Hiley's Gram.* Rule 8th, p. 77. "The article THE *agrees* with nouns in either number: as, *The wood, the woods* "—*Bucke's Classical Grammar of the English Language,* p. 84. "O! oh! ah! *require* the accusative case of a pronoun in the first person after them: as '*Ah me!*' But when the second person is used, *it requires* a nominative case: as, '*O thou!*'"—*Ib.* p 87. "Two or more Nominatives in the singular number, connected by the Conjunction *or, nor,* EITHER, NEITHER, *govern* a singular Verb. But Pronouns singular, of different persons, joined by *or,* EITHER, *nor,* NEITHER, *govern* a plural Verb."—*Ib.* p. 94. "One Nominative frequently *governs* many Verbs."—*Ib* p 95 "Participles are sometimes *governed* by the article."—*Murray's Gram.* 8vo, p. 192. "An adverb, an adjective, or a participle, may involve in itself the force of a *preposition, and govern* the objective case."—*Nutting's Gram.* p. 99. "The nominative case *governs* the verb."*—*Greenleaf's Gram.* p. 32; *Kirkham's,* 176; and others. "The nominative case *comes before* the verb"—*Bingham's Gram* p 38; *Wilbur and Livingston's,* 23. "The Verb TO BE, *always governs* a Nominative, unless it be of the Infinitive Mood."—*Buchanan's Syntax.* p. 94. "A verb in the infinitive mood *may be governed* by a verb, noun, adjective, participle, or pronoun."—*Kirkham's Gram.* p. 187. Or, (as a substitute for the foregoing rule,) say, according to this author: "A verb in the infinitive mood, *refers to* some noun or pronoun, as its subject or actor "—*Ib.* p. 188. Now what does he know of English grammar, who supposes any of these rules to be worthy of the place which they hold, or have held, in the halls of instruction?"

OBS. 8.—It is a very common fault with the compilers of English grammars, to join together in the same rule the syntax of different parts of speech, uniting laws that must ever be applied separately in parsing. For example: "RULE XI. Articles and adjectives *relate to nouns* expressed or understood; and the adjectives *this, that, one, two,* must agree in number with the nouns to which they relate."—*Comly's Gram.* p. 87. Now, in parsing an *article,* why should the learner have to tell all this story about *adjectives?* Such a mode of expressing the rule, is certainly in bad taste; and, after all, the syntax of adjectives is not here comprised, for they often relate to pronouns. "RULE III. Every adjective and participle *belongs* to some noun or pronoun expressed or understood."—*Frost's El. of Gram.* p 44. Here a compiler who in his etymology supposes participles to be *verbs,* allows them no other construction than that of *adjectives.* His rule implicitly denies that they can either be parts of their verbs in the formation of *tenses,* or be governed by prepositions in the character of *gerunds.* To suppose that a *noun may* govern the objective case, is both absurd in itself, and contrary to all authority; yet, among his

---

* It has been the notion of some grammarians, that *the verb governs the nominative before it.* This is an old rule, which seems to have been very much forgotten by modern authors; though doubtless it is as true, and as worthy to be perpetuated, as that which supposes the nominative to govern the verb: "Omne verbum personale finiti modi regit ante se expresse vel subaudite ejusdem numeri et personae nominativum vel aliquid pro nominativo: ut, *ego scribo, tu legis, ille auscultat.*"—DESPAUTERII SYNT. fol xvi. This Despauter was a laborious author, who, within fifty years after the introduction of printing, complains that he found his task heavy, on account of the immense number of books and opinions which he had to consult: "Necdum tamen huic operi ultimam manum alter imposui, quam Apelles olim picturis: siquidem aptius exire, quum in multis tum in hac arte est difficillimum, *propter librorum legendorum immensitatem,* et opinionum innumeram diversitatem."—*Ibid. Epist. Apologetica,* A. D. 1513. But if, for this reason, the task was heavy *then,* what is it *now*!

forty-nine rules, this author has the following: "RULE XXV. A participial *noun* is sometimes governed by a preposition and *may govern an objective case;* as, 'George is too fond *of wasting time* in trifles.'"—*Frost's El. of Gram.* p. 47. Here again is the fault of which I am speaking, two rules in one; and this fault is combined with an other still worse. *Wasting* is a participle, governed by *of;* and *time* is a noun, governed by *wasting.* The latter is a declinable word, and found in the objective case; the former is indeclinable, and found in no case. It is an error to suppose that cases are the only things which are susceptible of being governed; nor is the brief rule, "Prepositions govern the objective case," so very clear a maxim as never to be misapprehended. If the learner infer from it, that *all* prepositions must necessarily govern the objective case, or that the objective case is *always* governed by a preposition, he will be led into a great mistake.

OBS. 9. This error of crowding things together, is still more conspicuous in the following examples: "RULE IV. Every article, adjective, and participle, *must qualify* some noun, or pronoun, either expressed or understood."—*Nutting's Gram.* p. 94. "RULE IX. The objective case is governed by a transitive verb or a preposition, usually coming before it."—*Ib.* p. 98. Here an author who separates participles from verbs, has attempted first to compress the entire syntax of three different parts of speech into one short rule; and, secondly, to embrace all the forms of dependence, incident to objective nouns and pronouns, in an other as short. This brevity is a poor exchange for the order and distribution which it prevents—especially as none of its objects are here reached. Articles do not relate to pronouns, unless the obsolete phrase *the which* is to be revived;[*] participles have other constructions than those which adjectives admit; there are exceptions to the rules which tie articles to nouns, and adjectives to nouns or pronouns; and the objective case may not only be governed by a participle, but may be put in apposition with an other objective. The objective case in English usually stands for the Latin genitive, dative, accusative, and ablative; hence any rule that shall embrace the whole construction of this one case, will be the sole counterpart to four fifths of all the rules in any code of Latin syntax. For I imagine the construction of these four oblique cases, will be found to occupy at least that proportion of the syntactical rules and notes in any Latin grammar that can be found. Such rules, however, are often placed under false or equivocal titles;[†] as if they contained the construction of the *governing* words, rather than that of the *governed.* And this latter error, again, has been transferred to most of our English grammars, to the exclusion of any rule for the proper construction of participles, of adverbs, of conjunctions, of prepositions, or of interjections. See the syntax of Murray and his copyists, whose treatment of these parts of speech is noticed in the fifth observation above.

OBS. 10.—It is doubtless most convenient, that, in all rules for the construction of *cases,* nouns and pronouns be taken together; because the very same doctrines apply equally well to both, and a case is as distinct a thing in the mind, as a part of speech. This method, therefore, I have myself pursued; and it has indeed the authority of all grammarians—not excepting those who violate its principles by adopting two special rules for the relative pronoun, which are not needed. These special rules, which I shall notice again hereafter, may be seen in Murray's Rule 6th, which is double, and contains them both. The most complex rule that I have admitted, is that which embraces the government of objectives by verbs and participles. The regimen by verbs, and the regimen by participles, may not improperly be reckoned distinct principles; but the near alliance of participles to their verbs, seems to be a sufficient reason for preferring one rule to two, in this instance.

OBS. 11.—An other common fault in the treatment of this part of grammar, is the practice of making many of the rules *double,* or even *triple,* in their form. Of L. Murray's twenty-two rules, for instance, there are six which severally consist of two distinct paragraphs; and one is composed of three such parts, with examples under each. Five others, though simple in their form, are complex in their doctrine, and liable to the objections which have been urged above against this characteristic. These twelve, therefore, I either reject entirely from my catalogue, or divide and simplify to fit them for their purpose. In short, by comparing the twenty-two rules which were adopted by this popular grammarian, with the twenty-four which are given in this work, the reader may see, that twelve of the former have pleased me too little to have any place at all among the latter, and that none of the remaining ten have been thought worthy to be copied without considerable alteration. Nor are the rules which I adopt, more nearly coincident with those of any other writer. I do not proffer to the schools the second-hand instructions of a mere compiler. In his twenty-two rules, independently of their examples, Murray has used six hundred and seventeen words, thus giving an average of twenty-eight words to each rule; whereas in the twenty-four rules which are presented above, the words are but four hundred and thirty-six, making

---

* Nutting's rule certainly implies that *articles* may relate to *pronouns,* though he gives no example, nor can he give any that is now good English; but he may, if be pleases, quote some other modern grammatists, who teach the same false doctrine: as, "RULE 11. *The article refers to its noun* (OR PRONOUN) *to limit its signification."*—R. G. Greene's Grammatical Text-Book, p. 18. Greene's two grammars are used extensively in the state of Maine, but they appear to be little known anywhere else. This author professes to inculcate "the principles established by Lindley Murray." If veracity, on this point, is worth any thing, it is a pity that in both books there are so many points which, like the foregoing parenthesis, belie this profession. He followed here *Ingersoll's* RULE IV, which is this: "*The article refers to a noun* OR PRONOUN, *expressed or understood, to limit its signification."*—Conversations on E. Gram. p. 186.

† It is truly a matter of surprise to find under what *titles* or *heads,* many of the rules of syntax have been set, by some of the best scholars that have ever written on grammar. In this respect, the Latin and Greek grammarians are particularly censurable; but it better suits my purpose to give an example or two from one of the ablest of the English. Thus that elegant scholar the Rev. W. Allen: "SYNTAX OF NOUNS. 825. A verb agrees with its nominative case in number and person."—*Elements of E. Gram.* p. 131. This is in no wise the syntax of *Nouns,* but rather that of *the Verb.* Again: "SYNTAX OF VERBS. 405. Active Verbs govern the accusative case; as, I love *him.* We saw *them.* God rules the *world."*—*Ib.* p. 161. This is not properly the syntax of *Verbs,* but rather that of *Nouns* or *Pronouns* in the accusative or objective case. Any one who has but the least sense of order, must see the propriety of referring the rule to that sort of words to which it is applied in parsing, and not to some other. Verbs are never parsed or construed by the latter of these rules, nor nouns by the former.

the average less than nineteen. And yet I have not only divided some of his propositions and extended others, but, by rejecting what was useless or erroneous, and filling up the deficiencies which mark his code, I have delivered twice the amount of doctrine in two thirds of the space, and furnished eleven important rules which are not contained in his grammar. Thus much, in this place, to those who so frequently ask, "Wherein does your book differ from Murray's?"

OBS. 12.—Of all the systems of syntax, or of grammar, which it has been my fortune to examine, a book which was first published by Robinson and Franklin of New York in 1839, a fair-looking duodecimo volume of 384 pages, under the brief but rather ostentatious title, "THE GRAMMAR *of the English Language*," is, I think, the most faulty — the most remarkable for the magnitude, multitude, and variety, of its strange errors, inconsistencies, and defects. This singular performance is the work of *Oliver B. Peirce*, an itinerant lecturer on grammar, who dates his preface at "Rome, N. Y., December 29th, 1838." Its leading characteristic is boastful innovation; it being full of acknowledged "contempt for the works of other writers."—P. 379. It lays "claim to *singularity*" as a merit, and boasts of a new thing under the sun — "in a theory RADICALLY NEW, *a Grammar of the English Language;* something which I believe," says the author, "has NEVER BEFORE BEEN FOUND."—P. 9. The old scholastic notion, that because Custom is the arbitress of speech, novelty is excluded from grammar, this hopeful reformer thoroughly condemns; "repudiating this sentiment to the full extent of it," (*ib.*) and "writing his theory as though he had never seen a book, entitled an English Grammar."—*Ib.* And, for all the ends of good learning, it would have been as well or better, if he never had. His passion for novelty has led him not only to abandon or misapply, in an unprecedented degree, the usual terms of the art, but to disregard in many instances its most unquestionable principles, universal as well as particular. His parts of speech are the following ten: "Names, Substitutes, *Asserters,* Adnames, Modifiers, Relatives, Connectives, Interrogatives, Repliers, and Exclamations."—*The Gram.* p. 20. His *names* are nouns; his *substitutes* are pronouns, and any adjectives whose nouns are not expressed; his *asserters* are verbs and participles, though the latter assert nothing; his *adnames* are articles, adjectives whose nouns or pronouns are expressed, and adverbs that relate to adjectives; his *modifiers* are such adverbs as "modify the sense *or sound* of a whole sentence;" his *relatives* are prepositions, some of which *govern no object;* his *connectives* are conjunctions, with certain adverbs and phrases; his *interrogatives* and *repliers* are new parts of speech, very lamely explained; his *exclamations* are interjections, and "*phrases used independently;*" as, O hapless choice!"—*The Gram.* p. 22. In parsing, he finds a world of "*accommodatives;*" as, "John is more than *five years* older than William."—*Ib.* p. 202. Here he calls the whole phrase "*more than five years,*" "a secondary *adname;*" i. e. *adjective.* But, in the phrase, "*more than five years* afterwards," he would call the same words "a secondary *modifier;*" i. e. *adverb.*—*Ib.* p. 203. And, in the phrase, "*more than five years* before the war," he would call them "a secondary *relative;*" i. e. *preposition.*—*Ib.* p. 204. And so of other phrases innumerable. His cases are five, two of which are new, "the *Independent,*" and "the *Twofold* case." His "*independent case*" is sometimes the nominative in form, as "*thou*" and "*she;*" (p. 62;) sometimes the objective, as, "*me*" and "*him;*" (p. 62 and p. 199;) sometimes erroneously supposed to be the subject of a finite verb; while *his nominative* is sometimes as erroneously said to have *no verb.* His code of syntax has two sorts of rules, Analytical and Synthetical. The former are professedly seventeen in number; but, many of them consisting of two, three, or four distinct parts, their real number is more properly thirty-four. The latter are reckoned forty-five; but if we count their separate parts, they are fifty-six: and these with the others make *ninety.* I shall not particularize their faults. All of them are whimsically conceived and badly written. In short, had the author artfully designed to turn English grammar into a subject of contempt and ridicule, by as ugly a caricature of it as he could possibly invent, he could never have hit the mark more exactly than he has done in this "*new theory*" — this rash production, on which he so sincerely prides himself. Alone as he is, in well-nigh all his opinions, behold how prettily he talks of "COMMON SENSE, the only sure foundation of any theory!" and says, "On this imperishable foundation—this rock of eternal endurance—I rear my superstructure, *the edifice of scientific truth,* the temple of Grammatical consistency!"—*Peirce's Preface,* p. 7.

OBS. 13.—For the teaching of different languages, it has been thought very desirable to have "a Series of grammars, Greek, Latin, English, &c., all, so far as general principles are concerned, upon the same plan, and as nearly in the same words as the genius of the languages would permit." See *Bullions's Principles of E. Gram.* 2d Ed. pp. iv and vi. This scheme necessarily demands a minute comparison not only of the several languages themselves, but also of the various grammars in which their principles, whether general or particular, are developed. For by no other means can it be ascertained to what extent uniformity of this kind will be either profitable to the learner, or consistent with truth. Some books have been published, which, it is pretended, are thus accommodated to one an other, and to the languages of which they treat. But, in view of the fact, that the Latin or the Greek grammars now extant, (to say nothing of the French, Spanish, and others,) are almost as various and as faulty as the English, I am apprehensive that this is a desideratum not soon to be realized—a design more plausible in the prospectus, than feasible in the attempt. At any rate, the grammars of different languages must needs differ as much as do the languages themselves, otherwise some of their principles will of course be false; and we have already seen that the nonobservance of this has been a fruitful source of error in respect to English syntax. The achievement, however, is not altogether impossible, if a man of competent learning will devote to it a sufficient degree of labour. But the mere revising or altering of some one grammar in each language, can scarcely amount to any thing more than a pretence of improvement. Waiving the pettiness of compiling upon the basis of another man's compilation, the foundation of a good grammar for any language, must be both deeper and broader than all the works which Professor Bullions has selected to build upon: for the Greek, than Dr. Moor's "*Elementa Linguæ Græcæ;*" for the Latin, than Dr. Adam's "*Rudiments of Latin and English Grammar;*" for the English, than Murray's "*English Grammar,*" or Lennie's "*Principles of English Grammar;*" which last work, in fact, the learned gen-

tleman preferred, though he pretends to have mended the code of Murray. But, certain
Lennie never supposed himself a copyist of Murray; nor was he to much extent an imitator of
him, either in method or in style.

OBS. 14.—We have, then, in this new American form of "*The Principles of English Grammar*,"
Lennie's very compact little book, altered, enlarged, and bearing on its title-page (which is
erwise in the very words of Lennie) an other author's name, and, in its early editions, the
and self-accusing inscription, "(ON THE PLAN OF MURRAY'S GRAMMAR.)" And this
claiming to have been approved " by the most competent judges," now challenges the praise
only of being " better adapted to the use of academies and schools *than any yet published*,"
of so presenting "*the rules and principles of general grammar*, as that they may apply to.
in perfect harmony with, *the grammars of the dead languages*."—*Recommendations*, p. iv.
are admirable professions for a critical author to publish; especially, as every rule or princi
General Grammar, condemning as it must whoever violates it, cannot but " be in *perfect har*
with " every thing that is true. In this model for all grammars, Latin, Greek, &c., the doct
of punctuation, of abbreviations, and of capital letters, and also sections on the rhetorical
sions of a discourse, the different kinds of composition, the different kinds of prose composi
and the different kinds of poetry, are made *parts of the Syntax*; while his hints for correct
elegant writing, and his section on the composition of letters and themes, which other wri
suppose to belong rather to syntax, are here subjoined as *parts of Prosody*. In the exercise
parsing appended to his *Etymology*, the Doctor furnishes *twenty-five Rules of Syntax*, which
says, " are not intended to be committed to memory, but to be used as directions to the
ginner in parsing the exercises under them."—*E. Gram.* p. 75. Then, for his syntax prope
copies from Lennie, with some alterations, *thirty-four other rules*, nine of which are double,
all are jumbled together by both authors, without any regard to the distinction of concord and
ernment, so common in the grammars of the dead languages, and even, so far as I can disce
without any principle of arrangement whatever. They profess indeed to have placed those
first, which are easiest to learn, and oftenest to be applied; but the syntax of *articles*, w
even on this principle should have formed the first of the series, is placed by Lennie as the th
fourth rule, and by his amender as the thirty-second. To all this complexity, the latter
twenty-two Special Rules, with an abundance of "*Notes*," "*Observations*," and "*Remarks*," d
guished by these titles, on some principle which no one but the author can understand. La
his *method of syntactical parsing* is not only mixed up with etymological questions and ans
but his *directions* for it, with their *exemplification*, are perplexingly at variance with his
specimen of the performance. See pages 131 and 133. So much for this grand scheme.

OBS. 15.—Strictures like the foregoing, did they not involve the defence of grammar it
so as to bear upon interests more important than the success or failure of an elementary b
might well be withheld through motives of charity, economy, and peace. There is many a gr
mar now extant, concerning which a truly critical reader may know more at first sight, than
did he that made it. What such a reader will be inclined to rate beneath criticism, an other
haps will confidently pronounce above it. If my remarks are just, let the one approve them
the other's sake. For what becomes of the teaching of grammar, when that which is reco
as the most excellent method, must be exempted from censure by reason of its utter worthl
ness? And what becomes of Universal Syntax, when the imperfect systems of the Latin
Greek grammars, in stead of being amended, are modelled to the grossest faults of what
worthless in our own?*

OBS. 16.—What arrangement of Latin or Greek syntax may be best in itself, I am not
concerned to show. Lily did not divide his, as others have divided the subject since; but
stated briefly his *three concords*, and then proceeded to what he called *the construction* of
several parts of speech, taking them in their order. The three concords of Lily are the follow
(1.) Of the *Nominative and Verb*; to which the accusative before an infinitive, and the colle
noun with a plural verb, are reckoned exceptions; while the agreement of a verb or pro
with two or more nouns, is referred to the figure *syllepsis*. (2.) Of the *Substantive and Adjecti*
under which the agreement of participles, and of some pronouns, is placed in the form of a

---

* What " the Series of Grammars, English, Latin, and Greek, ON THE SAME PLAN," will ultimately be,—
many treatises for each or any of the languages it will probably contain,—what uniformity will be found in
distribution of their several sorts and sizes,—or what sameness they will have, except that which is bestowed
the binders,—cannot yet be stated with any certainty. It appears now, in 1850, that the scheme has thus
resulted in the production of *three remarkably different grammars*, for the English part of the series, and
more, a Latin grammar and a Greek, which resemble each other, or any of these, as little. In these works, abo
changes and discrepances, sometimes indicating a great *unsettlement* of " principles " or " plan," and often
citing our special wonder at the extraordinary *variety* of teaching, which has been claimed to be, " as nearly
the same words as the *genius of the language* would permit!" In what *should* have been uniform, and
might have been so, these grammars are rather remarkably diverse! Uniformity in the order, number, or pl
ology of the Rules of Syntax, even for our own language, seems scarcely yet to have entered this " SAME PLAN
at all! The "onward progress of English grammar," or, rather. of the author's studies therein, has alrea
within " fifteen years," greatly varied, from the *first model* of the "*Series*," his own idea of a good gramm
and, though such changes bar consistency, a future progress, real or imaginary, may likewise, with as good re
son, vary it yet as much more. In the preface to the work of 1849, it is said : " This, though *not resemble*
different from the former, is yet in some respects a new work. It has been almost *entirely rewritten*." An
again : " The Syntax is *much fuller* than in the former work; and though *the rules are not different*, they a
arranged in a *different order*." So it is proved, that the model needed remodelling; and that the Syntax, esp
cially, was defective, in matter as well as in order. The suggestions, that " *the rules are not different*," and "t
works, " *not essentially* " so, will sound best to those who shall never compare them. The old code has thirty-fo
chief, and twenty-two " special rules ; " the new has twenty-six " special," and one " general rule
Among all these, we shall scarcely find *exact sameness* preserved in so many as half a dozen instances. Of th
old thirty-four, *fourteen only* were judged worthy to remain as principal rules; and two of these have no clai
as all to such rank, one of them being quite useless. Of the *twenty* now made chief, five are new to " the Seri
of Grammars," and three of these exceedingly resemble as many of mine; five are slightly altered, and fiv
greatly, from their predecessors among the old; one is the first half of an old rule; one is an old subordina
rule, altered and elevated; and *three are as they were before*, their numbers and relative positions excepted!

(2.) Of the *Relative and Antecedent*; after which the two special rules for the *cases* of relatives are given as underparts. Dr. Adam divided his syntax into two parts; of Simple Sentences, and of Compound Sentences. His three concords are the following: (1.) Of one *Substantive with an Other*; which construction is placed by Lily and many others among the figures of syntax, and is called *apposition*. (2.) Of an *Adjective with a Substantive*; under which principle, we are told to take adjective pronouns and participles. (3.) Of a *Verb with a Nominative*; under which, the collective noun with a verb of either number, is noticed in an observation. The construction of relatives, of conjunctions, of comparatives, and of words put absolute, this author reserves for the second part of his syntax; and the agreement of plural verbs or pronouns with joint nominatives or antecedents, which Ruddiman places in an observation on his *four concords*, is here absurdly reckoned a part of the construction of conjunctions. Various divisions and subdivisions of the Latin syntax, with special dispositions of some particular principles of it, may be seen in the elaborate grammars of Despauter, Prat, Ruddiman, Grant, and other writers. And here it may be proper to observe, that, the mixing of syntax with etymology, after the manner of Ingersoll, Kirkham, R. W. Green, R. C. Smith, Sanborn, Felton, Parkhurst, Parker and Fox, and others, is a modern innovation, pernicious to both; either topic being sufficiently comprehensive, and sufficiently difficult, when they are treated separately; and each having, in some instances, employed the pens of able writers almost to the exclusion of the other.

OBS. 17.—The syntax of any language must needs conform to the peculiarities of its etymology, and also be consistent with itself; for all will expect better things of a scholar, than to lay down positions in one part of his grammar, that are irreconcilable with what he has stated in an other. The English language, having few inflections, has also few concords or agreements, and still fewer governments. Articles, adjectives, and participles, which in many other languages agree with their nouns in gender, number, and case, have usually, in English, no modifications in which they *can agree* with their nouns. Yet *Lowth* says, "The adjective in English, having no variation of gender and number, *cannot but agree* with the substantive in these respects."—*Short Introd. to Gram.* p. 86. What then is the *agreement* of words? Can it be any thing else than their *similarity* in some common property or modification? And is it not obvious, that no two things in nature can at all *agree*, or *be alike*, except in some quality or accident which belongs to each of them? Yet how often have *Murray* and others, as well as *Lowth*, forgotten this! To give one instance out of many: "*Gender* has respect only to the third person singular of the pronouns, *he, she, it*."—*Murray, J. Peirce, Flint, Lyon, Bacon, Russell, Fisk, Maltby, Alger, Miller, Merchant, Kirkham*, and other careless copyists. Yet, according to these same gentlemen, "Gender is the *distinction of nouns*, with regard to sex;" and, "Pronouns *must always agree* with their antecedents, *and the nouns* for which they stand, *in gender*." Now, not one of these three careless assertions can possibly be reconciled with either of the others!

OBS. 18.—*Government* has respect only to nouns, pronouns, verbs, participles, and prepositions; the other five parts of speech neither govern nor are governed. The *governing* words may be either nouns, or verbs, or participles, or prepositions; the words *governed* are either nouns, or pronouns, or verbs, or participles. In parsing, the learner must remember that the rules of government are not to be applied to the *governing* words, but to those which *are governed*; and which, for the sake of brevity, are often technically named after the particular form or modification assumed; as, *possessives, objectives, infinitives, gerundives*. These are the only things in English, that can properly be said to be subject to government; and these are always so, in their own names; unless we except such infinitives as stand in the place of nominatives. *Gerundives* are participles governed by prepositions; but, there being little or no occasion to distinguish these from other participles, we seldom use this name. The Latin *Gerund* differs from a participle, and the English *Gerundive* differs from a participial noun. The participial noun may be the subject or the object of a verb, or may govern the possessive case before it, like any other noun; but the true English gerundive, being essentially a participle, and governing an object after it, like any other participle, is itself governed only by a preposition. At least, this is its usual and allowed construction, and no other is acknowledged to be indisputably right.

OBS. 19.—The simple *Relations* of words in English, (or those several *uses* of the parts of speech which we may refer to this head,) are the following nine: (1.) Of Articles to nouns, by Rule 1st; (2.) Of Nominatives to verbs, by Rule 2d; (3.) Of Nominatives absolute or independent, by Rule 8th; (4.) Of Adjectives to nouns or pronouns, by Rule 9th; (5.) Of Participles to nouns or pronouns, by Rule 20th; (6.) Of Adverbs to verbs, participles, &c., by Rule 21st; (7.) Of Conjunctions as connecting words, phrases, or sentences, by Rule 22nd; (8.) Of Prepositions as showing the relations of things, by Rule 23d; (9.) Of Interjections as being used independently, by Rule 24th.

OBS. 20.—The syntactical *Agreements* in English, though actually much fewer than those which occur in Latin, Greek, or French, may easily be so reckoned as to amount to double, or even triple, the number usually spoken of by the old grammarians. The twenty-four rules above, embrace the following ten heads, which may not improperly be taken for so many distinct concords: (1.) Of a Noun or Pronoun in direct apposition with an other, by Rule 3d; (2.) Of a Noun or Pronoun after a verb or participle not transitive, by Rule 6th; (3.) Of a Pronoun with its antecedent, by Rule 10th; (4.) Of a Pronoun with a collective noun, by Rule 11th; (5.) Of a Pronoun with joint antecedents, by Rule 12th; (6.) Of a Pronoun with disjunct antecedents, by Rule 13th; (7.) Of a Verb with its nominative, by Rule 14th; (8.) Of a Verb with a collective noun, by Rule 15th; (9.) Of a Verb with joint nominatives, by Rule 16th; (10.) Of a Verb with disjunct nominatives, by Rule 17th. To these may be added two other *special* concords, less common and less important, which will be explained in *notes* under the rules: (11.) Of one Verb with an other, in mood, tense, and form, when two are connected so as to agree with the same nominative; (12.) Of Adjectives that imply unity or plurality, with their nouns, in number.

OBS. 21.—Again, by a different mode of reckoning them, the concords, or the *general principles* of agreement, in our language, may be made to be only three or four; and some of those much *less general*, than they are in other languages: (1.) *Words in apposition agree in case*, according to

Rule 3d; of which principle, Rule 6th may be considered a modification. (2.) *Pronouns agree with their nouns, in person, number, and gender,* according to Rule 10th; of which principle, Rules 11th, 12th, and 13th, may be reckoned modifications. (3) *Verbs agree with their nominatives, in person and number,* according to Rule 14th; of which principle, Rules 15th, 16th, and 17th, and the occasional agreement of one verb with an other, may be esteemed mere modifications. (4.) *Some adjectives agree with their nouns in number.* These make up the twelve concords above enumerated.

OBS. 22.—The rules of *Government* in the best Latin grammars are about sixty; and these are usually distributed (though not very properly) under three heads; " 1. Of Nouns. 2. Of Verbs. 3. Of Words indeclinable."—*Grant's Lat. Gram.* p. 170. " Regimen est triplex; 1. Nominum. 2. Verborum. 3. Vocum indeclinabilium."—*Ruddiman's Gram.* p. 138. This division of the subject brings all the *titles* of the rules wrong. For example, if the rule be, " Active verbs govern the accusative case," this is not properly " the government *of verbs,*" but rather the government *of the accusative* by verbs. At least, such titles are *equivocal,* and likely to mislead the learner. The governments in English are only seven, and these are expressed, perhaps with sufficient distinctness, in six of the foregoing rules : (1.) Of Possessives by nouns, in Rule 4th; (2.) Of Objectives by verbs, in Rule 5th; (3.) Of Objectives by participles, in Rule 5th; (4.) Of Objectives by prepositions, in Rule 7th; (5.) Of Infinitives by the preposition *to,* in Rule 18th; (6.) Of Infinitives by the verbs *bid, dare,* &c., in Rule 19th; (7.) Of Participles by prepositions, in Rule 20th.

OBS. 23.—The *Arrangement* of words, (which will be sufficiently treated of in the observations hereafter to be made on the several rules of construction,) is an important part of syntax, in which not only the beauty but the propriety of language is intimately concerned, and to which particular attention should therefore be paid in composition. But it is to be remembered, that the mere collocation of words in a sentence never affects the method of parsing them : on the contrary, the same words, however placed, are always to be parsed in precisely the same way, so long as they express precisely the same meaning. In order to show that we have parsed any part of an inverted or difficult sentence rightly, we are at liberty to declare the meaning by any arrangement which will make the construction more obvious, provided we retain both the sense and all the words unaltered; but to drop or alter any word, is to pervert the text under pretence of resolving it, and to make a mockery of parsing. Grammar rightly learned, enables one to understand both the sense and the construction of whatsoever is rightly written ; and he who reads what he does not understand, reads to little purpose. With great indignity to the muses, several pretenders to grammar have foolishly taught, that, " In parsing poetry, in order to *come at the meaning* of the author, the learner will find it necessary to transpose his language."—*Kirkham's Gram.* p. 166. See also the books of *Merchant, Wilcox, O. B. Peirce, Hull, Smith, Felton,* and others, to the same effect. To what purpose can he *transpose* the words of a sentence, who does not first see what they mean, and how to explain or parse them as they stand ?

OBS. 24.—Errors innumerable have been introduced into the common modes of parsing, through a false notion of what constitutes a *simple sentence.* Lowth, Adam, Murray, Gould, Smith, Ingersoll, Comly, Lennie, Hiley, Bullions, Wells, and many others, say, " A simple sentence has in it *but one subject,* and *one finite verb* : as, ' Life is short.' "—*L. Murray's Gram.* p. 141. In accordance with this assertion, some assume, that, " Every nominative *has its own verb* expressed or understood;" and that, " Every verb (except in the infinitive mood and participles) *has its own nominative* expressed or understood."—*Bullions's E. Gram.* p. 87. The adopters of these dogmas, of course think it right to *supply* a nominative whenever they do not find a separate one expressed for every finite verb, and a verb whenever they do not find a separate one expressed for every nominative. This mode of interpretation not only precludes the agreement of a verb with two or more nominatives, so as to render nugatory two of the most important rules of these very gentlemen's syntax; but, what is worse, it perverts many a plain, simple, and perfect sentence, to a form which its author did not choose, and a meaning which he never intended. Suppose, for example, the text to be, " A good constitution and good laws make good subjects."—*Webster's Essays,* p. 152. Does not the verb *make* agree with *constitution* and *laws,* taken conjointly ? and is it not a *perversion* of the sentence to interpret it otherwise ? Away then with all this *needless subaudition!* But while we thus deny that there can be a true ellipsis of what is not necessary to the construction, it is not to be denied that there *are* true ellipses, and in some men's style very many. The assumption of O. B. Peirce, that no correct sentence is elliptical, and his impracticable project of a grammar founded on this principle, are among the grossest of possible absurdities.

OBS. 25.—Dr. Wilson says, " There may be several subjects to the same verb, several verbs to the same subject, or several objects to the same verb, and the sentence be simple. But when the sentence remains simple, the same verb must be differently affected by its several adjuncts, or the sense liable to be altered by a separation. If the verb or the subject *be* affected in the same manner, or the sentence *is* resolvable into more, it is compounded. Thus, ' Violet, indigo, blue, green, yellow, orange, and red, mixed in due proportion, produce white,' is a simple sentence, for the subject is indivisible. But, ' Violet, indigo, blue, green, yellow, orange, and red, are refrangible rays of light,' is a compound sentence, and may be separated into seven."—*Essay on Gram.* p. 186. The propriety of the distinction here made, is at least questionable; and I incline to consider the second example a simple sentence, as well as the first; because what the writer calls a separation into seven, involves a change of *are* to *is,* and of *rays* to *ray,* as well as a sevenfold repetition of this altered predicate, "*is a refrangible ray of light.*" But the parser, in interpreting the words of others, and expounding the construction of what is written, has no right to alter any thing in this manner. Nor do I admit that he has a right to insert or repeat any thing *needlessly;* for the nature of a sentence, or the syntax of some of its words, may often be altered without change of the sense, or of any word for an other: as, " 'A wall seven feet high;' that is, 'A wall *which is* seven feet high.' "—*Hiley's Gram.* p. 109. " ' He spoke and acted prudently; ' that is, ' He spoke *prudently,* and *he* acted prudently.' "—*Ibid.* " ' He spoke and acted wisely; '

that is, 'He spoke *wisely*, and *he* acted wisely.'"—*Murray's Gram.* p. 219; *Alger's*, 70; *R. C. Smith's*, 183; *Weld's*, 192; and others. By this notion of ellipsis, the connexion or joint relation of words is destroyed.

OBS. 26.—Dr. Adam, who thought the division of sentences into simple and compound, of sufficient importance to be made the basis of a general division of syntax into two parts, has defined a simple sentence to be, "that which has but one nominative, and one finite verb;" and a compound sentence, "that which has more than one nominative, or one finite verb." And of the latter he gives the following erroneous and self-contradictory account: "A compound sentence is made up of two or more simple sentences or *phrases*, and is commonly called a *Period*. The parts of which a compound sentence consists, are called *Members* or *Clauses*. In every compound sentence there are either several subjects and one attribute, or several attributes and one subject, or both several subjects and several attributes; that is, there are either several nominatives applied to the same verb, or several verbs applied to the same nominative, or both. Every verb marks a judgment or attribute, and every attribute must have a subject. There must, therefore, be in every sentence or period, as many propositions as there are verbs of a finite mode. Sentences are compounded by means of relatives and conjunctions; as, Happy is the man *who* loveth religion, *and* practiseth virtue."—*Adam's Gram.* p. 202; *Gould's*, 199; and others.

OBS. 27.—Now if every compound sentence consists of such parts, members, or clauses, as are in themselves sentences, either simple or compound, either elliptical or complete; it is plain, in the first place, that the term "*phrases*" is misapplied above, because a phrase is properly only a part of some simple sentence. And if "a simple sentence is that which has but one nominative and one finite verb," and "a compound sentence is made up of two or more simple sentences," it follows, since "all sentences are either simple or compound," that, *in no sentence, can there be* "either several nominatives applied to the same verb, or several verbs applied to the same nominative." What, therefore, this author regarded as *the characteristic* of all compound sentences, is, according to his own previous positions, utterly impossible to any sentence. Nor is it less repugnant to his subsequent doctrine, that, "Sentences are compounded by means of *relatives* and *conjunctions;*" for, according to his notion. "A conjunction is an indeclinable word, which serves to join *sentences* together."—*Adam's Gram.* p. 149. It is assumed, that, "In every *sentence* there must be a verb and a nominative expressed or understood."—*Ib.* p. 151. Now if there happen to be two nominatives to one verb, as when it was said, "Even the *winds* and the *sea* obey him;" this cannot be anything more than a simple sentence; because one single verb is a thing indivisible, and how can we suppose it to form the most essential part of two different sentences at once?

OBS. 28.—The distinction, or real difference, between those simple sentences in which two or more nominatives or verbs are taken conjointly, and those compound sentences in which there is an ellipsis of some of the nominatives or verbs, is not always easy to be known or fixed; because, in many instances, a supposed *ellipsis*, without at all affecting the sense, may obviously change the construction, and consequently the nature of the sentence. For example: "And they all forsook him, and [they all] fled."—*Mark*, xiv, 50. Some will say, that the words in brackets are here *understood*. I may deny it, because they are needless; and nothing needless can form a true ellipsis. To the supplying of useless words, if we admit the principle, there may be no end; and the notion that conjunctions join sentences only, opens a wide door for it. For example: "And that man was perfect and upright, and one that feared God, and eschewed evil."—*Job*, i, 1. No additional words will make this clause any plainer, and none are really necessary to the construction; yet some grammarians will parse it with the following impletions, or more: "And that man was a perfect *man*, and *he was an* upright *man*, and *he was* one *man* that feared God, and *that* eschewed *evil things.*" It is easy to see how this liberty of interpretation, or of interpolation, will change simple sentences to compound sentences, as well as alter the nature and relation of many particular words; and at the same time, it takes away totally those peculiarities of construction by which Dr. Adam and others would recognize a sentence as being compound. What then? are there not two kinds of sentences? Yes, truly; but these authors are wrong in their notions and definitions of both. Joint nominatives or joint verbs may occur in either; but they belong primarily to some simple sentences, and only for that reason are found in any that are compound. A sentence, too, may possibly be made compound, when a simple one would express the whole meaning as well or better; as, "And [David] smote the Philistines from Geba *until thou come* to Gazer." —*2 Sam.* v, 25. Here, if we omit the words in Italics, the sentence will become simple, not elliptical.

THE ANALYZING OF SENTENCES.

To analyze a sentence, is, to resolve it into some species of constituent parts, but most properly into words, its first significant elements, and to point out their several relations and powers in the given connexion.

The component parts of a sentence are *members, clauses, phrases,* or *words.* Some sentences, which are short and simple, can only be divided into their words; others, which are long and complex, may be resolved into parts again and again divisible.

Of analysis applicable to sentences, there are several different methods; and, so far as their difference may compatibly aid the application of different principles of the science of grammar, there may be an advantage in the occasional use of each.

29

FIRST METHOD OF ANALYSIS.

Sentences not simple may be reduced to their constituent members, clauses, or simple sentences; and the means by which these are united, may be shown. Thus :—

EXAMPLE ANALYZED.

"Even the Atheist, who tells us that the universe is self-existent and indestructible—even he, who, instead of seeing the traces of a manifold wisdom in its manifold varieties, sees nothing in them all but the exquisite structures and the lofty dimensions of materialism—even he, who would despoil creation of its God, cannot look upon its golden suns, and their accompanying systems, without the solemn impression of a magnificence that fixes and overpowers him."—DR. CHALMERS, *Discourses on Revelation and Astronomy*, p. 231.

ANALYSIS.—This is a compound sentence, consisting of three complex members, which are separated by the two dashes. The three members are united in one sentence, by a suspension of the sense at each dash, and by two virtual repetitions of the subject, "*Atheist*," through the pronoun "*he*," put in the same case, and representing this noun. The sense mainly intended is not brought out till the period ends. Each of the three members is complex, because each has not only a relative clause, commencing with "*who*," but also an antecedent verb which makes sense with "*cannot look*," &c. The first of these relative clauses involves also a subordinate, supplementary clause,—"*the universe is self-existent and indestructible*,"—introduced after the verb "*tells*" by the conjunction "*that*." The last phrase, "*without the solemn impression*," &c., which is subjoined by "*without*" to "*cannot look*," embraces likewise a subordinate, relative clause,—"*that fixes and overpowers him*,"—which has two verbs; the whole, antecedent and all, being but an adjunct of an adjunct, yet an essential element of the sentence.

SECOND METHOD OF ANALYSIS.

Simple sentences, or the simple members of compound sentences, may be resolved into their PRINCIPAL and their SUBORDINATE PARTS; the subject, the verb, and the case put after or governed by the verb, being first pointed out as the principal parts; and the other words being then detailed as adjuncts to these, according to THE SENSE, or as adjuncts to adjuncts. Thus :—

EXAMPLE ANALYZED.

"Fear naturally quickens the flight of guilt. Rasselas could not catch the fugitive, with his utmost efforts; but, resolving to weary, by perseverance, him whom he could not surpass in speed, he pressed on till the foot of the mountain stopped his course."—DR. JOHNSON, *Rasselas*, p. 23.

ANALYSIS.—The first period here is a simple sentence. Its principal parts are—*Fear, quickens, flight; Fear* being the subject, *quickens* the verb, and *flight* the object. *Fear* has no adjunct; *naturally* is an adjunct of *quickens; the* and *of guilt* are adjuncts of *flight.* The second period is composed of several clauses, or simple members, united. The first of these is also a simple sentence, having three principal parts—*Rasselas, could catch,* and *fugitive;* their subject, the verb, and its object, in their order. *Not* is added to *could catch,* reversing the meaning; *the* is an adjunct to *fugitive; with* joins its phrase to *could not catch;* but *his* and *utmost* are adjuncts of *efforts.* The word *but* connects the two chief members as parts of one sentence. "*Resolving to weary*," is an adjunct to the pronoun *he,* which stands before *pressed.* "*By perseverance*," is an adjunct to *weary.* *Him* is governed by *weary,* and is the antecedent to *whom.* "*Whom he could not surpass in speed*," is a relative clause, or subordinate simple member, having three principal parts—*he, could surpass,* and *whom. Not* and *in speed* are adjuncts to the verb *could surpass.* "*He pressed on*," is another simple member, or sentence, and the chief clause here used, the others being subjoined to this. Its principal parts are two, *he* and *pressed;* the latter taking the particle *on* as an adjunct, and being intransitive. The words dependent on the nominative *he,* (to wit, *resolving,* &c.,) have already been mentioned. *Till* is a conjunctive adverb of time, connecting the concluding clause to *pressed on.* "*The foot of the mountain stopped his course*," is a subordinate clause and simple member, whose principal parts are—the subject *foot,* the verb *stopped,* and the object *course.* The adjuncts of *foot* are *the* and *of the mountain;* the verb in this sentence has no adjunct but *course,* which is better reckoned a principal word; lastly, *his* is an adjunct to *course,* and governed by it.

THIRD METHOD OF ANALYSIS.

Sentences may be partially analyzed by a resolution into their SUBJECTS and their PREDICATES, a method which some late grammarians have borrowed from the logicians; the grammatical subject with its adjuncts, being taken for the logical subject; and the finite verb, which some call the grammatical predicate, being, with*

---

* "The grammatical predicate is a verb."—*Butler's Pract. Gram.*, 1845, p. 135. "The grammatical predicate is a finite verb."—*Wells's School Gram.*, 1850, p. 185. "The grammatical predicate is either a verb alone, or the copula *sum* [some part of the verb *be*] with a noun or adjective."—*Andrews and Stoddard's Lat. Gram.* p. 162. "The predicate consists of two parts,—the verb, or copula, and that which is asserted by it, called the *attribute;* as, 'Snow *is* white.' "—*Greene's Analysis,* p. 15. "The grammatical predicate consists of the *attribute* and *copula,* not modified by other words."—*Bullions, Analyt. and Pract. Gram.* p. 129. "The logical predicate is the grammatical, with all the words or phrases that modify it."—*Ib.* p. 130. "The *Grammatical predicate* is the word or words containing the whole affirmation, made respecting the subject."—*Bullions, Latin Gram.* p. 209. "Every proposition necessarily consists of these three parts; [the *subject,* the *predicate,* and the *copula;*] but then it is not alike needful, that they be all severally expressed in words; because the copula *is often included* in the term of the

its subsequent case and the adjuncts of both, denominated the predicate, or the logical predicate. Thus:—

EXAMPLE ANALYZED.

"Such is the emptiness of human enjoyment, that we are always impatient of the present. Attainment is followed by neglect, and possession, by disgust. Few moments are more pleasing than those in which the mind is concerting measures for a new undertaking. From the first hint that wakens the fancy, to the hour of actual execution, all is improvement and progress, triumph and felicity."—DR. JOHNSON, *Rambler.*

ANALYSIS.—Here the first period is a compound sentence, containing two clauses, which are connected by *that*. In the first clause, *emptiness* is the grammatical subject, and " *the emptiness of human enjoyment*," is the logical. *Is* some would call the grammatical predicate, and " Such is," or *is such*, the logical; but the latter consists, as the majority teach, of " the copula " *is*, and " the attribute," or " predicate," *such*. In the second clause, the subject is *we*; which is unmodified, and in which therefore the logical form and the grammatical coincide and are the same. *Are* may here be called the grammatical predicate; and " *are always impatient of the present*," the logical. The second period, too, is a compound sentence, having two clauses, which are connected by *and*. *Attainment* is the subject of the former; and, " *is followed by neglect*," is the predicate. In the latter, *possession* alone is the subject; and, " [*is followed*] *by disgust*," is the predicate; the verb *is followed* being understood at the comma. The third period, likewise, is a compound, having three parts, with the two connectives *than* and *which*. Here we have *moments* for the first grammatical subject, and *Few moments* for the logical; then, *are* for the grammatical predicate, and *are more pleasing* for the logical: or, if we choose to say so, for " the copula and the attribute." " *Than those*," is an elliptical member, meaning, " than *are* those *moments*," or, " than those *moments are pleasing* ;" both subject and predicate are wholly suppressed, except that *those* is reckoned a part of the logical subject. In *which* is an adjunct of *is concerting*, and serves well to connect the members, because *which* represents *those*, i. e. *those* moments. *Mind*, or the *mind*, is the next subject of affirmation; and *is concerting*, or, " *is concerting measures for a new undertaking*," is the predicate, or matter affirmed. Lastly, the fourth period, like the rest, is compound. The phrases commencing with *From* and *to*, describe a period of time, and are adjuncts of the verb *is*. The former contains a subordinate relative clause, of which *that* (representing *hint*) is the subject, and *wakens*, or *wakens the fancy*, the predicate. Of the principal clause, the word *all*, taken as a noun, is the subject, whether grammatical or logical; and " the copula," or " grammatical predicate," *is*, becomes, with its adjuncts and the nominatives following, the logical predicate.

FOURTH METHOD OF ANALYSIS.

All syntax is founded on the RELATION *of words one to an other, and the* CONNEXION *of clauses and phrases, according to* THE SENSE. *Hence sentences may be, in some sort, analyzed, and perhaps profitably, by the tracing of such relation or connexion, from link to link, through a series of words, beginning and ending with such as are somewhat remote from each other, yet within the period. Thus:—*

EXAMPLES ANALYZED.

1. " Swift would say, ' The thing has not life enough in it to keep it sweet ;' Johnson, ' The creature possesses not vitality sufficient to preserve it from putrefaction.' " —MATT. HARRISON, *on the English Language*, p. 102.

ANALYSIS.—What is the general sense of this passage ? and what, the chain of connexion between the words *Swift* and *putrefaction*? The period is designed to show, that Swift preferred words of Saxon origin ; and Johnson, of Latin. It has in contrast two coördinate members, tacitly connected ; the verb *would say* being understood after *Johnson*, and perhaps also the particle *but*, after the semicolon. *Swift* is the subject of *would say*; and *would say* introduces the clause after it, as what would be said. The relates to *thing*; *thing* is the subject of *has*; *has* is qualified by *not*, and governs *life*; *life* is qualified by the adjective *enough*, and by the phrase, *in it* ; *enough* is antecedent to *to* ; *to* governs *keep*; *keep* governs *it*, which stands for *the thing* ; and *it*, in lieu of *the thing*, is qualified by *sweet*. The chief members are connected either by standing in contrast as members, or by *but*, understood before *Johnson*. *Johnson* is the subject of *would say*, understood ; and this *would say*, again introduces a clause, as what would be said. The relates to *creature* ; *creature* is the subject of *possesses*; *possesses* is qualified by *not*, and governs *vitality*; *vitality* is qualified by *sufficient* ; *sufficient* is antecedent to *to* ; *to* governs *preserve* ; *preserve* governs *it*, and is antecedent to *from* ; and *from* governs *putrefaction*.

2. " There is one Being to whom we can look with a perfect conviction of finding that security, which nothing about us can give, and which nothing about us can take away."—GREENWOOD : *Wells's School Gram.* p. 192.*

predicate ; as when we say, he sits; which imports the same as, he is sitting."—Duncan's Logic, p. 105. In respect to this Third Method of Analysis, it is questionable, whether a noun or an adjective which follows the verb and forms part of the assertion, is to be included in " the grammatical predicate " or not. Wells says, No : " It would destroy at once all distinction between the grammatical and the logical predicate."—School Gram. p. 185. An other question is, whether the copula (is, was, or the like,) which the logicians discriminate, should be included as part of the logical predicate, when it occurs as a distinct word. The prevalent practice of the grammatical analyzers is, so to include it—a practice which in itself is not very " logical." The distinction of subjects and predicates as " grammatical and logical," is but a recent one. In some grammars, the partition used in logic is copied without change, except perhaps of words : as, " There are, in sentences, a subject, a predicate, and a copula."—Jos. R. CHANDLER, Gram. of 1821, p. 108 ; Gram. of 1847, p. 110.

** I cite this example from Wells, for the purpose of explaining it without the several errors which that gentleman's " Model " inculcates. He suggests that and connects, not the two relative clauses, as such, but the two verbs can give and can take ; and that the connexion between away and is must be traced through the former, and its object which. These positions, I think, are wrong. He also uses here, as elsewhere, the expressions, " which relates it," and, " which is related by," each in a very unusual, and perhaps an unauthorized, sense. His formula*

ANALYSIS.—What is the general structure of this passage? and what, the chain of connexion "between the words *away* and *is?*" The period is a complex sentence, having four clauses, all connected together by relatives; the second, by *whom*, to the first and chief clause, "*There is one Being;*" the third and the fourth, to the second, by *which* and *which;* but the last two, having the same antecedent, *security*, and being coördinate, are also connected one to the other by *and*. As to "the chain of connexion," *Away* relates to *can take;* *can take* agrees with its nominative *nothing*, and governs *which;* *which* represents *security; security* is governed by *finding; finding* is governed by *of; of* refers back to *conviction; conviction* is governed by *with; with* refers back to *can look; can look* agrees with *we*, and is, in sense, the antecedent of *to; to* governs *whom; whom* represents *Being;* and *Being* is the subject of *is*.

FIFTH METHOD OF ANALYSIS.

The best and most thorough method of analysis is that of COMPLETE SYNTACTICAL PARSING *; a method which, for the sake of order and brevity, should ever be kept free from all mixture of etymological definitions or reasons, but which may be preceded or followed by any of the foregoing schemes of resolution, if the teacher choose to require any such preliminary or subsidiary exposition. This method is fully illustrated in the Twelfth Praxis below.*

OBSERVATIONS ON METHODS OF ANALYSIS.

OBS. 1.—The almost infinite variety in the forms of sentences, will sometimes throw difficulty in the way of the analyzer, be his scheme or his skill what it may. The last four or five observations of the preceding series have shown, that the distinction of sentences as *simple* or *compound*, which constitutes the chief point of the First Method of Analysis above, is not always plain, even to the learned. The definitions and examples which I have given, will make it *generally* so; and, where it is otherwise, the question or puzzle, it is presumed, cannot often be of much practical importance. If the difference be not obvious, it can hardly be a momentous error, to mistake a phrase for an elliptical clause, or to call such a clause a phrase.

OBS. 2.—The Second Method above is, I think, easier of application than any of the rest; and, if other analysis than the regular method of parsing seem desirable, this will probably be found as useful as any. There is, in many of our popular grammars, some recognition of the principles of this analysis—some mention of " the *principal parts* of a sentence," in accordance with what are so called above,—and also, in a few, some succinct account of the parts called " *adjuncts;* " but there seems to have been no prevalent practice of applying these principles, in any stated or well-digested manner. Lowth, Murray, Alger, W. Allen, Hart, Hiley, Ingersoll, Wells, and others, tell of these " PRINCIPAL PARTS; "—Lowth calling them, " the *agent*, the *attribute*, and the *object;* " (*Gram.* p. 72;)—Murray, and his copyists, Alger, Ingersoll, and others, calling them, " the *subject*, the *attribute*, and the *object;* "—Hiley and Hart calling them, " the *subject* or *nominative*, the *attribute* or *verb*, and the *object;* "—Allen calling them, " the *nominative*, the *verb*, and (if the verb is active) the *accusative* governed by the verb; " and also saying, " The *nominative* is sometimes called, the *subject;* the verb, the *attribute;* and the accusative, the *object;* "—Wells calling them, " the *subject* or *nominative*, the *verb*, and the *object;* " and also recognizing the "*adjuncts*," as a species which "embraces all the words of a simple sentence [,] except the *principal parts;* "—yet not more than two of them all appearing to have taken any thought, and they but little, about the formal *application* of their common doctrine. In Allen's English Grammar, which is one of the best, and likewise in Wells's, this reduction of all connected words, or parts of speech, into " the principal parts " and " the adjuncts," is fully recognized; the adjuncts, too, are discriminated by Allen, as " either primary or secondary," nor are their more particular species or relations overlooked; but I find no method prescribed for the analysis intended, except what Wells adopted in his early editions but has since changed to an other or abandoned, and no other allusion to it by Allen, than this Note, which, with some appearance of intrusion, is appended to his " Method of Parsing the Infinitive Mood: "—" The pupil *may now begin to analyse* [*analyze*] the sentences, by distinguishing the principal words and their adjuncts."—*W. Allen's E. Gram.* p. 258.

OBS. 3.—These authors in general, and many more, tell us, with some variation of words, that the agent, subject, or nominative, is that of which something is said, affirmed, or denied; that the attribute, verb, or predicate, is that which is said, affirmed, or denied, of the subject; and that the object, accusative, or case sequent, is that which is introduced by the finite verb, or affected by the action affirmed. Lowth says, " In English the nominative case, denoting the agent, usually goes before the verb, or attribution; and the objective case, denoting the object, follows the verb active."—*Short Introd.* p. 72. Murray copies, but not literally, thus: " The nominative denotes the subject, and usually goes before the verb [,] or attribute; and the word or *phrase*, denoting the object, follows the verb: as, 'A wise man governs his passions.' Here, *a wise man* is the subject; *governs*, the attribute, or thing affirmed; and *his passions*, the object."—*Murray's Octavo,* p. 142; *Duodecimo,* 115. To include thus the adjuncts with their principals, as the logicians do, is *here* manifestly improper; because it unites what the grammatical analyzer is chiefly concerned to separate, and tends to defeat the main purpose for which " THE PRINCIPAL PARTS " are so named and distinguished.

OBS. 4.—The Third Method of Analysis, described above, is an attempt very briefly to epitomize the chief elements of a great scheme—to give, in a nutshell, the substance of what our grammarians have borrowed from the logicians, then mixed with something of their own, next

reads thus: "*Away* modifies *can take; can take* is CONNECTED with *can give* by *and;* WHICH is governed by *can give*, and relates to *security; security* is the object of *finding, which* is RELATED BY *of* to *conviction; conviction* is the object of with, *which* RELATES IT to *can look; to* expresses the relation between *whom* and *can look*, and *whom* relates to *Being*, which is the subject of *is*."—*Wells's School Gram.*, 113th. Ed., p. 192. Neither this nor the subsequent method has been often called " *analysis;* " for, in grammar, each user of this term has commonly applied it to some one method only — the method preferred by himself.

amplified with small details, and, in some instances, branched out and extended to enormous bulk and length. Of course, they have not failed to set forth the comparative merits of this scheme in a sufficiently favourable light. The two ingenious gentlemen who seem to have been chiefly instrumental in making it popular, say in their preface, "The rules of syntax contained in this work result directly from the analysis of propositions, and of compound sentences; and for this reason the student should make himself perfectly familiar with the sections relating to *subject* and *predicate*, and should be able readily to analyse sentences, whether simple or compound, and to explain their structure and connection. * * * This exercise *should always precede* the more minute and subsidiary labor of parsing. If the latter be conducted, as it often is, independently of previous analysis, the *principal advantage* to be derived from the study of language, as an intellectual exercise, will inevitably be lost."—*Latin Grammar of Andrews and Stoddard*, p. vi. N. Butler, who bestows upon this subject about a dozen duodecimo pages, says in his preface, "The rules for the analysis of sentences, which is a *very useful and interesting* exercise, have been taken from Andrews' and Stoddard's Latin Grammar, some changes and additions being made."—*Butler's Practical Gram.* p. iv.*

Obs. 5.—Wells, in the early copies of his School Grammar, as has been hinted, adopted a method of analysis similar to the *Second* one prescribed above; yet referred, even from the first, to "Andrews and Stoddard's Latin Grammar," and to "De Sacy's General Grammar," as if these were authorities for what he then inculcated. Subsequently, *he changed his scheme*, from that of *Parts Principal* and *Adjuncts*, to one of *Subjects* and *Predicates*, "either grammatical or logical," also "either simple or compound;"—to one resembling Andrews and Stoddard's, yet differing from it, often, as to what constitutes a "grammatical predicate;"—to one resembling the *Third Method* above, yet differing from it, (as does Andrews and Stoddard's,) in taking the logical subject and predicate *before* the grammatical. "The chapter on Analysis," said he then, "has been revised and enlarged with great care, and will be found to embody *all the most important* principles on this subject [,] *which* are contained in the works of De Sacy, Andrews and Stoddard, Kühner, Crosby, and Crane. It is gratifying to observe that the attention of teachers is now so generally directed *to this important mode* of investigating the structure of our language, *in connection with* the ordinary exercises of *etymological* and syntactical parsing."—*Wells's School Gram.*, New Ed., 1850, p. iv.

Obs. 6.—In view of the fact, that Wells's chief mode of sentential analysis had just undergone an almost total metamorphosis, a change plausible perhaps, but of doubtful utility,—that, up to the date of the words just cited, and afterwards, so far and so long as any copies of his early "Thousands" remain in use, the author himself has earnestly directed attention to a method which he now means henceforth to abandon,—in this view, the praise and gratulation expressed above seem singular. If it has been found practicable, to slide "the attention of teachers," and their approbation too, adroitly over from one "important mode of investigating the structure of our language," to an other;—if "it is gratifying to observe," that the direction thus given to public opinion sustains itself so well, and "is so generally" acquiesced in;—if it is proved, that the stereotyped praise of one system of analysis may, without alteration, be so transferred to an other, as to answer the double purpose of commending and superseding;—it is not improbable that the author's next new plates will bear the stamp of yet *other* "most important principles" of analysis. This process is here recommended to be used "*in connection with* the ordinary exercises of *etymological* and syntactical parsing,"—exercises, which, in Wells's Grammar, are generally, and very improperly, commingled; and if, to these, may be profitably conjoined either his present or his former scheme of analysis, it were well, had he somewhere put them together and shown how.

Obs. 7.—But there are other passages of the School Grammar, so little suited to this notion of "*connection*," that one can hardly believe the word ought to be taken in what seems its only sense. "Advanced classes should attend less to the common *Order of Parsing*, and more to the *Analysis* of language."—*Wells's Grammar*, "3d Thousand," p. 125; "113th Thousand," p. 132. This implies, what is probably true of the etymological exercise, that parsing is more rudimental than the other forms of analysis. It also intimates, what is not so clear, that pupils rightly instructed must advance from the former to the latter, as to something more worthy of their intellectual powers. The passage is used with reference to either form of analysis adopted by the author. So the following comparison, in which Parsing is plainly disparaged, stands permanently at the head of "the chapter on Analysis," to commend first one mode, and then an other: "It is particularly desirable that pupils *should pass as early as practicable from the formalities of* common PARSING, to the *more important* exercise of ANALYZING critically the structure of language. The mechanical routine of technical parsing is peculiarly liable to become monotonous and dull, while *the practice of explaining the various relations and offices of words in a sentence*, is adapted to call the mind of the learner into constant and vigorous action, and can hardly fail of exciting the deepest interest."—*Wells's Gram.* 3d Th. p. 181; 113th Th. p. 184.

Obs. 8.—An ill scheme of *parsing*, or an ill use of a good one, is almost as unlucky in grammar, as an ill method of *ciphering*, or an ill use of a good one, would be in arithmetic. From the strong contrast cited above, one might suspect that, in selecting, devising, or using, a technical process for the exercising of learners in the principles of etymology and syntax, this author had been less fortunate than the generality of his fellows. Not only is it implied, that parsing is no critical analysis, but even what is set *in opposition* to the "mechanical routine," may very well serve for

---

* The possessive phrase here should be, "*Andrews and Stoddard's*," as Wells and others write it. The adding of the apostrophe to the former name is wrong, even by the better half of Butler's own absurd and self-contradictory Rule: to wit, " When two or more nouns in the possessive case are connected by *and*, the possessive termination *should be added to each of them*; as, 'These are John's and Eliza's books.' But, if objects are possessed in common by two or more, and the nouns are closely connected without any intervening words, the possessive termination *is added to the last noun only*; as, 'These are John and Eliza's books.' "—*Butler's Practical Gram.* p. 168. The sign twice used implies two governing nouns: "John's and Eliza's books " = " John's books and Eliza's;" " Andrews' and Stoddard's Latin Grammar " = " Andrews' (or Andrews's) Latin Grammar and Stoddard's."

a definition of Syntactical Parsing—"*the practice of explaining the various relations and offices of words in a sentence!*" If this "practice," well ordered, can be at once interesting and profitable to the learner, so may parsing. Nor, after all, is even this author's mode of parsing, defective though it is in several respects, less "important" to the users of his book, or less valued by teachers, than the analysis which he sets above it.

OBS. 9.—S. S. Greene, a public teacher in Boston, who, in answer to a supposed "demand for a *more philosophical plan* of teaching the English language," has entered in earnest upon the "Analysis of Sentences," having devoted to one method of it more than the space of two hundred duodecimo pages, speaks of analysis and of parsing, thus: "The resolving of a sentence into its elements, or of any complex element into the parts which compose it, is called *analysis*."—*Greene's Analysis*, p. 14. "Parsing consists in naming a part of speech, giving its modifications, relation, agreement or dependence, and the rule for its construction. *Analysis* consists in pointing out the words or groups of words which constitute the elements of a sentence. Analysis *should precede* parsing."—*Ib.* p. 26. "A large proportion of the elements of sentences are not single words, but combinations or groups of words. These groups perform the office of the *substantive*, the *adjective*, or the *adverb*, and, in some one of these relations, enter in as the component parts of a sentence. The pupil who learns to determine the elements of a sentence, *must, therefore, learn the force of these combinations before* he separates them into the single words which compose them. *This advantage* is wholly lost *in* the ordinary methods of parsing."—*Ib.* p. 3.

OBS. 10.—On these passages, it may be remarked in the first place, that the distinction attempted between analysis and parsing is by no means clear, or well drawn. Nor indeed could it be; because parsing is a species of analysis. The first assertion would be just as true as it is now, were the former word substituted for the latter: thus, "The resolving of a sentence into its elements, or of any complex element into the *parts* which compose it, is called *parsing*." Next, the "*Parsing*" spoken of in the second sentence, is *Syntactical* Parsing only; and, without a limitation of the species, neither this assertion nor the one concerning precedence is sufficiently true. Again, the suggestion, that, "*Analysis* consists in *pointing out* the words or groups of words which *constitute the elements* of a sentence," has nothing distinctive in it; and, without some idea of the author's peculiar system of "elements," previously impressed upon the mind, is scarcely, if at all, intelligible. Lastly, that a pupil must *understand* a sentence,—or, what is the same thing, "learn the force of the words combined,"—before he can be sure of parsing each word rightly, is a very plain and certain truth; but what "advantage" over parsing this truth gives to the lesser analysis, which deals with "groups," it is not easy to discover. If the author had any clear idea of "*this advantage*," he has conveyed no such conception to his readers.

OBS. 11.—Greene's Analysis is the most expanded form of the Third Method above. Its nucleus, or germinating kernel, was the old partition of *subject* and *predicate*, derived from the art of logic. Its chief principles may be briefly stated thus: Sentences, which are simple, or complex, or compound, are made up of *words, phrases*, and *clauses*—three grand classes of elements, called the *first*, the *second*, and the *third* class. From these, each sentence must have two elements; the *Subject*, or Substantive element, and the *Predicate*, or Predicative element, which are principal; and a sentence *may* have five, the subordinates being the Adjective element, the Objective element, and the Adverbial element. The five elements have sundry modifications and subdivisions. Each of the five may, like a sentence, be simple, or complex, or compound; and each may be of any of the three grand classes. The development of this scheme forms a volume, not small. The system is plausible, ingenious, methodical, mostly true, and somewhat elaborate; but it is neither very useful nor very accurate. It seems too much like a great tree, beautiful, symmetrical, and full of leaves, but raised or desired only for fruit, yet bearing little, and some of that little not of good quality, but knurly or bitter. The chief end of a grammar, designed for our tongue, is, to show what is, and what is not, good English. To this end, the system in question does not appear to be well adapted.

OBS. 12.—Dr. Bullions, the projector of the "Series of Grammars, English, Latin, and Greek, all *on the same plan*," inserted in his Latin Grammar, of 1841, a short sketch of the new analysis by "subjects and predicates," "grammatical and logical," the scheme used by Andrews and Stoddard; but his English Grammar, which appeared in 1834, was too early for this "new and improved method of investigating" language. In his later English Grammar, of 1849, however, paying little regard to *sameness of* "*plan*" or conformity of definitions, he carefully devoted to this matter the space of fifteen pages, placing the subject, not injudiciously, in the first part of his syntax, and referring to it thus in his Preface: "The subject of ANALYSIS, wholly omitted in the former work, is here introduced in its proper place; and to an extent in accordance with its importance."—*Bullions, Analyt. and Pract. Gram.* p. 3.

OBS. 13.—In applying any of the different methods of analysis, as a school exercise, it will in general perhaps be best to use each *separately*; the teacher directing which one is to be applied, and to what examples. The selections prepared for the stated praxes of this work, will be found as suitable as any. Analysis of sentences is a central and essential matter in the teaching or the study of grammar; but the truest and the most important of the sentential analyses is *parsing*; which, because it is a method distinguished by a technical name of its own, is not commonly denominated analysis. The relation which other methods should bear to *parsing*, is, as we have seen, variously stated by different authors. *Etymological* parsing and *Syntactical* are, or ought to be, distinct exercises. The former, being the most simple, the most elementary, and also requisite to be used before the pupil is prepared for the latter, should, without doubt, take precedence of all the rest, and be made familiar in the first place. Those who say, "*Analysis should precede parsing*," will scarcely find the application of other analysis practicable, till this is somewhat known. But *Syntactical Parsing* being, when complete in form, the most thorough process of grammatical resolution, it seems proper to have introduced the other methods before it, as above. It can hardly be said that any of these are *necessary* to this exercise, or to one an other; yet in a full course of grammatical instruction, each may at times be usefully employed.

OBS. 14.—Dr. Bullions suggests, that, "*Analysis* should precede *Syntactical parsing*, because, till we know the parts and elements of a sentence, we can not understand their relations, nor intelligently combine them into one consistent whole."—*Analytical and Pract. Gram.* p. 114. This reason is entirely fictitious and truthless ; for the *words* of a sentence are intuitively known to be its "parts and elements ;" and, to "*understand* their relations," is as necessary to one form of analysis as to an other ; but, "intelligently to *combine* them," is no part of the parser's duty : this belongs to the *writer* ; and where he has not done it, he must be criticised and censured, as one that knows not well what he says. In W. Allen's Grammar, as in Wells's, Syntactical parsing and Etymological are not divided. Wells intersperses his "Exercises in Parsing," at seven points of his Syntax, and places "the chapter on Analysis," at the end of it. Allen treats first of the several parts of grammar, didactically ; then presents a series of exercises adapted to the various heads of the whole. At the beginning of these, are fourteen "Methods of Parsing," which show, successively, the properties and construction of his nine parts of speech ; and, *at the ninth method*, which resolves *infinitives*, it is proposed that the pupil begin to apply a method of analysis similar to the Second one above.

EXAMPLES FOR PARSING.

PRAXIS XII. — SYNTACTICAL.

The grand clew to all syntactical parsing is THE SENSE *; and as any composition is faulty which does not rightly deliver the author's meaning, so every solution of a word or sentence is necessarily erroneous, in which that meaning is not carefully noticed and literally preserved.*

In all complete syntactical parsing, it is required of the pupil—to distinguish the different parts of speech and their classes ; to mention their modifications in order ; to point out their relation, agreement, or government ; and to apply the Rules of Syntax. Thus :—

EXAMPLE PARSED.

"A young man studious to know his duty, and honestly bent on doing it, will find himself led away from the sin or folly in which the multitude thoughtlessly indulge themselves ; but, ah ! poor fallen human nature ! what conflicts are thy portion, when inclination and habit—a rebel and a traitor—exert their sway against our only saving principle ! "

A is the indefinite article : and relates to *man*, or *young man* ; according to Rule 1st, which says, "Articles relate to the nouns which they limit." Because the meaning is—*a man—a young man.*

Young is a common adjective, of the positive degree, compared regularly, *young, younger, youngest:* and relates to *man* ; according to Rule 9th, which says, "Adjectives relate to nouns or pronouns." Because the meaning is—*young man.*

Man is a common noun, of the third person, singular number, masculine gender, and nominative case : and is the subject of *will find* ; according to Rule 2d, which says, "A noun or a pronoun which is the subject of a finite verb, must be in the nominative case." Because the meaning is—*man will find.*

Studious is a common adjective, compared by means of the adverbs ; *studious, more studious, most studious* ; or, *studious, less studious, least studious* ; and relates to *man* ; according to Rule 9th, which says, "Adjectives relate to nouns or pronouns." Because the meaning is—*man studious.*

To is a preposition : and shows the relation between *studious* and *know* ; according to Rule 23d, which says, "Prepositions show the relations of words, and of the things or thoughts expressed by them." Because the meaning is—*studious to know.*

Know is an irregular active-transitive verb, from *know, knew, knowing, known* ; found in the infinitive mood, present tense—no person, or number : and is governed by *to* ; according to Rule 18th, which says, "The preposition *to* governs the infinitive mood, and commonly connects it to a finite verb." Because the meaning is—*to know.*

His is a personal pronoun, representing *man*, in the third person, singular number, and masculine gender ; according to Rule 10th, which says, "A pronoun must agree with its antecedent, or the noun or pronoun which it represents, in person, number, and gender :" and is in the possessive case, being governed by *duty* ; according to Rule 4th, which says, "A noun or a pronoun in the possessive case, is governed by the name of the thing possessed." Because the meaning is—*his duty*—i. e. the *young man's duty.*

Duty is a common noun, of the third person, singular number, neuter gender, and objective case : and is governed by *know* ; according to Rule 5th, which says, "A noun or a pronoun made the object of an active-transitive verb or participle, is governed by it in the objective case." Because the meaning is—to *know his duty.*

And is a copulative conjunction : and connects the phrase which follows it, to that which precedes ; according to Rule 22d, which says, "Conjunctions connect words, sentences, or parts of sentences." Because the meaning is—studious to know his duty, *and* honestly bent, &c.

Honestly is an adverb of manner : and relates to *bent* ; according to Rule 21st, which says, "Adverbs relate to verbs, participles, adjectives, or other adverbs." Because the meaning is—*honestly bent.*

Bent is a perfect participle, from the redundant active-transitive verb, *bend, bent or bended, bending, bent or bended:* and relates to *man* ; according to Rule 20th, which says, "Participles relate to nouns or pronouns, or else are governed by prepositions." Because the meaning is—*man bent.*

On is a preposition : and shows the relation between *bent* and *doing* ; according to Rule 23d, which says, "Prepositions show the relations of words, and of the things or thoughts expressed by them." Because the

Himself is a compound personal pronoun, representing *man*, in the third person, singular number, and masculine gender; according to Rule 10th, which says, "A pronoun must agree with its antecedent, or the noun or pronoun which it represents, in person, number, and gender:" and is in the objective case, being governed by *will find*; according to Rule 5th, which says, "A noun or a pronoun made the object of an active-transitive verb or participle, is governed by it in the objective case." Because the meaning is—*will find himself*—i. e. his own mind or person.

Led is a perfect participle, from the irregular active-transitive verb, *lead, led, leading, led*; and relates to *himself*; according to Rule 20th, which says, "Participles relate to nouns or pronouns, or else are governed by prepositions." Because the meaning is—*himself led*.

Away is an adverb of place: and relates to *led*; according to Rule 21st, which says, "Adverbs relate to verbs, participles, adjectives, or other adverbs." Because the meaning is—*led away*.

From is a preposition: and shows the relation between *led* and *sin or folly*; according to Rule 23d, which says, "Prepositions show the relations of words, and of the things or thoughts expressed by them." Because the meaning is—*led from sin or folly*.

The is the definite article: and relates to *sin* and *folly*; according to Rule 1st, which says, "Articles relate to the nouns which they limit." Because the meaning is—*the sin or folly*.

Sin is a common noun, of the third person, singular number, neuter gender, and objective case: and is governed by *from*; according to Rule 7th, which says, "A noun or a pronoun made the object of a preposition, is governed by it in the objective case." Because the meaning is—*from sin*.

Or is a disjunctive conjunction: and connects *sin* and *folly*; according to Rule 22d, which says, "Conjunctions connect words, sentences, or parts of sentences." Because the meaning is—*sin or folly*.

Folly is a common noun, of the third person, singular number, neuter gender, and objective case: and is connected by *or* to *sin*, and governed by the same preposition *from*; according to Rule 7th, which says, "A noun or a pronoun made the object of a preposition, is governed by it in the objective case." Because the meaning is—*from sin or folly*.

In is a preposition: and shows the relation between *indulge* and *which*; according to Rule 23d, which says, "Prepositions show the relations of words, and of the things or thoughts expressed by them." Because the meaning is—*indulge in which*—or, *which they indulge in*.

Which is a relative pronoun, representing *sin or folly*, in the third person, singular number, and neuter gender; according to Rule 13th, which says, "When a pronoun has two or more antecedents connected by *or* or *nor*, it must agree with them singly, and not as if taken together:" and is in the objective case, being governed by *in*; according to Rule 7th, which says, "A noun or a pronoun made the object of a preposition, is governed by it in the objective case." Because the meaning is—*in which*—i. e. *in which sin or folly*.

The is the definite article: and relates to *multitude*; according to Rule 1st, which says, "Articles relate to the nouns which they limit." Because the meaning is—*the multitude*.

Multitude is a common noun, collective, of the third person, conveying the idea of plurality, masculine gender, and nominative case: and is the subject of *indulge*; according to Rule 2d, which says, "A noun or a pronoun which is the subject of a finite verb, must be in the nominative case." Because the meaning is—*multitude indulge*.

Thoughtlessly is an adverb of manner: and relates to *indulge*; according to Rule 21st, which says, "Adverbs relate to verbs, participles, adjectives, or other adverbs." Because the meaning is—*thoughtlessly indulge*.

Indulge is a regular active-transitive verb, from *indulge, indulged, indulging, indulged*; found in the indicative mood, present tense, third person, and plural number: and agrees with its nominative *multitude*; according to Rule 15th, which says, "When the nominative is a collective noun conveying the idea of plurality, the verb must agree with it in the plural number." Because the meaning is—*multitude indulge*.

Themselves is a compound personal pronoun, representing *multitude*, in the third person, plural number, and masculine gender; according to Rule 11th, which says, "When the antecedent is a collective noun conveying the idea of plurality, the pronoun must agree with it in the plural number:" and is in the objective case, being governed by *indulge*; according to Rule 5th, which says, "A noun or a pronoun made the object of an active-transitive verb or participle, is governed by it in the objective case." Because the meaning is—*indulge themselves*—i. e. the individuals of the multitude indulge themselves.

But is a disjunctive conjunction: and connects what precedes and what follows; according to Rule 22d, which says, "Conjunctions connect words, sentences, or parts of sentences." Because the meaning is—A young man, &c. *but*, ah! &c.

Ah is an interjection, indicating sorrow: and is used independently; according to Rule 24th, which says, "Interjections have no dependent construction: they are put absolute, either alone, or with other words." Because the meaning is—*ah!*—unconnected with the rest of the sentence.

Poor is a common adjective, of the positive degree, compared regularly, *poor, poorer, poorest*; and relates to *nature*; according to Rule 9th, which says, "Adjectives relate to nouns or pronouns." Because the meaning is—*poor human nature*.

Fallen is a participial adjective, compared (perhaps) by adverbs: and relates to *nature*; according to Rule 9th, which says, "Adjectives relate to nouns or pronouns." Because the meaning is—*fallen nature*.

Human is a common adjective, not compared: and relates to *nature*; according to Rule 9th, which says, "Adjectives relate to nouns or pronouns." Because the meaning is—*human nature*.

Nature is a common noun, of the second person, singular number, neuter gender, and nominative case: and is put absolute by direct address: according to Rule 5th, which says, "A noun or a pronoun is put absolute in the nominative, when its case depends on no other word." Because the meaning is—*poor fallen human nature!*—the noun being unconnected with any verb.

What is a pronominal adjective, not compared: and relates to *conflicts*; according to Rule 9th, which says, "Adjectives relate to nouns or pronouns." Because the meaning is—*what conflicts*.

Conflicts is a common noun, of the third person, plural number, neuter gender, and nominative case: and is the subject of *are*; according to Rule 2d, which says, "A noun or a pronoun which is the subject of a finite verb, must be in the nominative case." Because the meaning is—*conflicts are*.

Are is an irregular neuter verb, from *be, was, being, been*; found in the indicative mood, present tense, third person, and plural number: and agrees with its nominative *conflicts*; according to Rule 14th, which says, "Every finite verb must agree with its subject, or nominative, in person and number." Because the meaning is—*conflicts are*.

Thy is a personal pronoun, representing *nature*, in the second person, singular number, and neuter gender; according to Rule 10th, which says, "A pronoun must agree with its antecedent, or the noun or pronoun which it represents, in person, number, and gender:" and is in the possessive case, being governed by *portion*; according to Rule 4th, which says, "A noun or a pronoun in the possessive case, is governed by the name of the thing possessed." Because the meaning is—*thy portion*.

Portion is a common noun, of the third person, singular number, neuter gender, and nominative case: and is put after *are*, in agreement with *conflicts*; according to Rule 6th, which says, "A noun or a pronoun put after a verb or participle not transitive, agrees in case with a preceding noun or pronoun referring to the same thing." Because the meaning is—*conflicts are thy portion*.

When is a conjunctive adverb of time: and relates to the two verbs, *are* and *exert*; according to Rule 21st, which says, "Adverbs relate to verbs, participles, adjectives, or other adverbs." Because the meaning is—what conflicts are thy portion, *when* inclination and habit *exert*, &c.

Inclination is a common noun, of the third person, singular number, neuter gender, and nominative case: and is one of the subjects of *exert*; according to Rule 2d, which says, "A noun or a pronoun which is the subject of a finite verb, must be in the nominative case." Because the meaning is—*inclination and habit exert*.

And is a copulative conjunction: and connects *inclination* and *habit*; according to Rule 22d, which says, "Conjunctions connect words, sentences, or parts of sentences." Because the meaning is—*inclination and habit*.

Habit is a common noun, of the third person, singular number, neuter gender, and nominative case: and is one of the subjects of *exert*; according to Rule 2d, which says, "A noun or a pronoun which is the subject of a finite verb, must be in the nominative case." Because the meaning is—*inclination and habit exert*.

A is the indefinite article: and relates to *rebel*; according to Rule 1st, which says, "Articles relate to the nouns which they limit." Because the meaning is—*a rebel*.

Rebel is a common noun, of the third person, singular number, masculine gender, and nominative case: and is put in apposition with *inclination*; according to Rule 3d, which says, "A noun or a personal pronoun used to explain a preceding noun or pronoun, is put, by apposition, in the same case." Because the meaning is—*inclination, a rebel*.

And is a copulative conjunction: and connects *rebel* and *traitor;* according to Rule 22d, which says, "Conjunctions connect words, sentences, or parts of sentences." Because the meaning is—*a rebel and a traitor.*
A is the indefinite article: and relates to *traitor;* according to Rule 1st, which says, "Articles relate to the nouns which they limit." Because the meaning is—*a traitor.*
Traitor is a common noun, of the third person, singular number, masculine gender, and nominative case: and is put in apposition with *habit;* according to Rule 3d, which says, "A noun or a personal pronoun used to explain a preceding noun or pronoun, is put, by apposition, in the same case." Because the meaning is—*habit, a traitor.*
Exert is a regular active-transitive verb, from *exert, exerted, exerting, exerted:* found in the indicative mood, present tense, third person, and plural number: and agrees with its two nominatives *inclination and habit;* according to Rule 16th, which says, "When a verb has two or more nominatives connected by *and,* it must agree with them jointly in the plural, because they are taken together." Because the meaning is—*inclination and habit exert.*
Their is a personal pronoun, representing *inclination and habit,* in the third person, plural number, and neuter gender; according to Rule 12th, which says, "When a pronoun has two or more antecedents connected by *and,* it must agree with them jointly in the plural, because they are taken together:" and is in the possessive case, being governed by *sway;* according to Rule 4th, which says, "A noun or a pronoun in the possessive case, is governed by the name of the thing possessed." Because the meaning is—*their sway*—i. e. the *sway of inclination and habit.*
Sway is a common noun, of the third person, singular number, neuter gender, and objective case: and is governed by *exert;* according to Rule 5th, which says, "A noun or a pronoun made the object of an active-transitive verb or participle, is governed by it in the objective case." Because the meaning is—*exert sway.*
Against is a preposition: and shows the relation between *exert* and *principle;* according to Rule 23d, which says, "Prepositions show the relations of words, and of the things or thoughts expressed by them." Because the meaning is—*exert against principle.*
Our is a personal pronoun, representing *the speakers,* in the first person, plural number, and masculine gender; according to Rule 10th, which says, "A pronoun must agree with its antecedent, or the noun or pronoun which it represents, in person, number, and gender:" and is in the possessive case, being governed by *principle;* according to Rule 4th, which says, "A noun or a pronoun in the possessive case, is governed by the name of the thing possessed." Because the meaning is—*our principle*—i. e. the *speakers' principle.*
Only is a pronominal adjective, not compared: and relates to *principle;* according to Rule 9th, which says, "Adjectives relate to nouns or pronouns." Because the meaning is—*only principle.*
Saving is a participial adjective, compared by adverbs when it means *frugal,* but not compared in the sense here intended: and relates to *principle;* according to Rule 9th, which says, "Adjectives relate to nouns or pronouns." Because the meaning is—*saving principle.*
Principle is a common noun, of the third person, singular number, neuter gender, and objective case: and is governed by *against;* according to Rule 7th, which says, "A noun or a pronoun made the object of a preposition, is governed by it in the objective case." Because the meaning is—*against principle.*

LESSON I.—ARTICLES.

"In English heroic verse, the capital pause of every line, is determined by the sense to be after the fourth, the fifth, the sixth or the seventh syllable."—*Kames, El. of Crit.* ii, 105.

"When, in considering the structure of a tree or a plant, we observe how all the parts, the roots, the stem, the bark, and the leaves, are suited to the growth and nutriment of the whole; when we survey all the parts and members of a living animal; or when we examine any of the curious works of art—such as a clock, a ship, or any nice machine; the pleasure which we have in the survey, is wholly founded on this sense of beauty."—*Blair's Rhet.* p. 49.

"It never can proceed from a good taste, to make a teaspoon resemble the leaf of a tree; for such a form is inconsistent with the destination of a teaspoon."—*Kames, El. of Crit.* ii, 351.

"In an epic poem, a history, an oration, or any work of genius, we always require a fitness, or an adjustment of means to the end which the author is supposed to have in view."—*Blair's Rhet.* p. 50.

"Rhetoric, Logic, and Grammar, are three arts that should always walk hand in hand. The first is the art of speaking eloquently; the second, that of thinking well; and the third, that of speaking with propriety."—*Formey's Belles-Lettres,* p. 114.

"Spring hangs her infant blossoms on the trees,
Rock'd in the cradle of the western breeze."—*Cowper.*

LESSON II.—NOUNS.

"There goes a rumour, that I am to be banished. And let the sentence come, if God so will. The other side of the sea is my Father's ground, as well as this side."—*Rutherford.*

"Gentlemen, there is something on earth greater than arbitrary or despotic power. The lightning has its power, and the whirlwind has its power, and the earthquake has its power. But there is something among men more capable of shaking despotic power, than lightning, whirlwind, or earthquake; that is—the threatened indignation of the whole civilized world."—*Daniel Webster.*

"And Isaac sent away Jacob; and he went to Padan Aram, unto Laban, son of Bethuel the Syrian, and brother of Rebecca, Jacob's and Esau's mother."—See *Gen.* xxviii, 5.

"The purpose you undertake is dangerous." "Why that is certain : it is dangerous to take a cold, to sleep, to drink : but I tell you, my Lord fool, out of this nettle danger, we pluck this flower safety."—*Shakspeare.*

"And towards the Jews alone, one of the noblest charters of liberty on earth—*Magna Charta*, the Briton's boast—legalized an act of injustice."—*Keith's Evidences*, p. 74.

"Were Demosthenes's Philippics spoken in a British assembly, in a similar conjuncture of affairs, they would convince and persuade at this day. The rapid style, the vehement reasoning, the disdain, anger, boldness, freedom, which perpetually animate them, would render their success infallible over any modern assembly. I question whether the same can be said of Cicero's orations ; whose eloquence, however beautiful, and however well suited to the Roman taste, yet borders oftener on declamation, and is more remote from the manner in which we now expect to hear real business and causes of importance treated."—*Blair's Rhet.* p. 248.

"In fact, every attempt to present on paper the splendid effects of impassioned eloquence, is like gathering up dewdrops, which appear jewels and pearls on the grass, but run to water in the hand : the essence and the elements remain, but the grace, the sparkle, and the form, are gone."—*Montgomery's Life of Spencer.*

"As in life true dignity must be founded on character, not on dress and appearance ; so in language the dignity of composition must arise from sentiment and thought, not from ornament."—*Blair's Rhet.* p. 144.

"And man, whose heaven-erected face the smiles of love adorn,
Man's inhumanity to man makes countless thousands mourn."—*Burns.*

"Ah wretched man ! unmindful of thy end !
A moment's glory ! and what fates attend ! "—*Pope, Iliad,* B. xvii, l. 231.

LESSON III.—ADJECTIVES.

"Embarrassed, obscure, and feeble sentences, are generally, if not always, the result of embarrassed, obscure, and feeble thought."—*Blair's Rhet.* p. 120.

"Upon this ground, we prefer a simple and natural, to an artificial and affected style ; a regular and well-connected story, to loose and scattered narratives ; a catastrophe which is tender and pathetic, to one which leaves us unmoved."—*Ib.* p. 23.

"A thorough good taste may well be considered as a power compounded of natural sensibility to beauty, and of improved understanding."—*Ib.* p. 18.

"Of all writings, ancient or modern, the sacred Scriptures afford us the highest instances of the sublime. The descriptions of the Deity, in them, are wonderfully noble ; both from the grandeur of the object, and the manner of representing it."—*Ib.* p. 36.

"It is not the authority of any one person, or of a few, be they ever so eminent, that can establish one form of speech in preference to another. Nothing but the general practice of good writers and good speakers can do it."—*Priestley's Gram.* p. 107.

"What other means are there to attract love and esteem so effectual as a virtuous course of life ? If a man be just and beneficent, if he be temperate, modest, and prudent, he will infallibly gain the esteem and love of all who know him."—*Kames, El. of Crit.* i, 167.

"But there are likewise, it must be owned, people in the world, whom it is easy to make worse by rough usage, and not easy to make better by any other."—*Abp. Secker.*

"The great comprehensive truth written in letters of living light on every page of our history—the language addressed by every past age of New England to all future ages, is this : Human happiness has no perfect security but freedom ;—freedom, none but virtue ;—virtue, none but knowledge : and neither freedom, nor virtue, nor knowledge, has any vigour or immortal hope, except in the principles of the Christian faith, and in the sanctions of the Christian religion."—*President Quincy.*

"For bliss, as thou hast part, to me is bliss ;
Tedious, unshared with thee, and odious soon."—*P. Lost,* B. ix, l. 880.

LESSON IV.—PRONOUNS.

"There is but one governor whose sight we cannot escape, whose power we cannot resist: a sense of His presence and of duty to Him, will accomplish more than all the laws and penalties which can be devised without it."—*Woodbridge, Lit. C.* p. 154.

"Every voluntary society must judge who shall be members of their body, and enjoy fellowship with them in their peculiar privileges."—*Watts.*

"Poetry and impassioned eloquence are the only sources from which the living growth of a language springs; and even if in their vehemence they bring down some mountain rubbish along with them, this sinks to the bottom, and the pure stream flows along over it."—*Philological Museum,* i, 645.

"This use is bounded by the province, county, or district, which gives name to the dialect, and beyond which its peculiarities are sometimes unintelligible, and always ridiculous."—*Campbell's Rhet.* p. 163.

"Every thing that happens, is both a cause and an effect; being the effect of what goes before, and the cause of what follows."—*Kames, El. of Crit.* ii, 297.

"Withhold not good from them to whom it is due, when it is in the power of thine hand to do it."—*Prov.* iii, 27.

"Yet there is no difficulty at all in ascertaining the idea. * * * By reflecting upon that which is myself now, and that which was myself twenty years ago, I discern they are not two, but one and the same self."—*Butler's Analogy,* p. 271.

"If you will replace what has been long expunged from the language, and extirpate what is firmly rooted, undoubtedly you yourself become an innovator."—*Campbell's Rhet.* p. 167; *Murray's Gram.* 364.

"To speak as others speak, is one of those tacit obligations, annexed to the condition of living in society, which we are bound in conscience to fulfill, though we have never ratified them by any express promise; because, if they were disregarded, society would be impossible, and human happiness at an end."—See *Murray's Gram.* 8vo, p. 139.

"In England *thou* was in current use until, perhaps, near the commencement of the seventeenth century, though it was getting to be regarded as somewhat disrespectful. At Walter Raleigh's trial, Coke, when argument and evidence failed him, insulted the defendant by applying to him the term *thou.* 'All that Lord Cobham did,' he cried, 'was at *thy* instigation, *thou* viper! for I *thou* thee, *thou* traitor!'"—*Fowler's E. Gram.* § 220.

> "Th' Egyptian crown I to your hands remit;
> And with it take his heart who offers it."—*Shakspeare.*

LESSON V.—VERBS.

"Sensuality contaminates the body, depresses the understanding, deadens the moral feelings of the heart, and degrades man from his rank in the creation."—*Murray's Key,* ii, p. 231.

"When a writer reasons, we look only for perspicuity; when he describes, we expect embellishment; when he divides, or relates, we desire plainness and simplicity."—*Blair's Rhet.* p. 144.

"Livy and Herodotus are diffuse; Thucydides and Sallust are succinct; yet all of them are agreeable."—*Ib.* p. 178.

"Whenever petulant ignorance, pride, malice, malignity, or envy, interposes to cloud or sully his fame, I will take upon me to pronounce that the eclipse will not last long."—*Dr. Delany.*

"She said she had nothing to say, for she was resigned, and I knew all she knew that concerned us in this world; but she desired to be alone, that in the presence of God only, she might without interruption do her last duty to me."—*Spect.* No. 520.

"Wisdom and truth, the offspring of the sky, are immortal; while cunning and deception, the meteors of the earth, after glittering for a moment, must pass away."—*Robert Hall.* "See, I have this day set thee over the nations, and over the kingdoms, to root out, and to pull down, and to destroy, and to throw down, to build, and to plant."—*Jeremiah,* i, 10.

"God might command the stones to be made bread, or the clouds to rain it; but he chooses rather to leave mankind to till, to sow, to reap, to gather into barns, to grind, to knead, to bake, and then to eat."—*London Quarterly Review.*

"Eloquence is no invention of the schools. Nature teaches every man to be eloquent, when he is much in earnest. Place him in some critical situation, let him have some great interest at stake, and you will see him lay hold of the most effectual means of persuasion."—*Blair's Rhet.* p. 235.

"It is difficult to possess great fame and great ease at the same time. Fame, like fire, is with difficulty kindled, is easily increased, but dies away if not continually fed. To preserve fame alive, every enterprise ought to be a pledge of others, so as to keep mankind in constant expectation."—*Art of Thinking,* p. 50.

"Pope, finding little advantage from external help, resolved thenceforward to direct himself, and at twelve formed a plan of study which he completed with little other incitement than the desire of excellence."—*Johnson's Lives of Poets,* p. 498.

　　"Loose, then, from earth the grasp of fond desire,
　　Weigh anchor, and some happier clime explore."—*Young.*

Lesson VI.—Participles.

"The child, affrighted with the view of his father's helmet and crest, and clinging to the nurse; Hector, putting off his helmet, taking the child into his arms, and offering up a prayer for him; Andromache, receiving back the child with a smile of pleasure, and at the same instant bursting into tears; form the most natural and affecting picture that can possibly be imagined."—*Blair's Rhet.* p. 435.

"The truth of being, and the truth of knowing are one; differing no more than the direct beam and the beam reflected."—*Ld. Bacon.* "Verbs denote states of being, considered as beginning, continuing, ending, being renewed, destroyed, and again repeated, so as to suit any occasion."—*William Ward's Gram.* p. 41.

"We take it for granted, that we have a competent knowledge and skill, and that we are able to acquit ourselves properly, in our native tongue; a faculty, solely acquired by use, conducted by habit, and tried by the ear, carries us on without reflection."—*Lowth's Gram* p. vi.

"I mean the teacher himself; who, stunned with the hum, and suffocated with the closeness of his school-room, has spent the whole day in controlling petulance, exciting indifference to action, striving to enlighten stupidity, and labouring to soften obstinacy."—*Sir W. Scott.*

"The inquisitive mind, beginning with criticism, the most agreeable of all amusements, and finding no obstruction in its progress, advances far into the sensitive part of our nature; and gains imperceptibly a thorough knowledge of the human heart, of its desires, and of every motive to action."—*Kames, El. of Crit.* i, 42.

　　"They please, are pleased; they give to get esteem;
　　Till, seeming blest, they grow to what they seem."—*Goldsmith.*

Lesson VII.—Adverbs.

"How cheerfully, how freely, how regularly, how constantly, how unweariedly, how powerfully, how extensively, he communicateth his convincing, his enlightening, his heart-penetrating, warming, and melting; his soul-quickening, healing, refreshing, directing, and fructifying influence!"—*Brown's Metaphors,* p. 96.

"The passage, I grant, requires to be well and naturally read, in order to be promptly comprehended; but surely there are very few passages worth comprehending, either of verse or prose, that can be promptly understood, when they are read unnaturally and ill."—*Thelwall's Lect.* "They waste life in what are called good resolutions — partial efforts at reformation, feebly commenced, heartlessly conducted, and hopelessly concluded."—*Maturin's Sermons,* p. 262.

"A man may, in respect of grammatical purity, speak unexceptionably, and yet speak obscurely and ambiguously; and though we cannot say, that a man may speak properly, and at the same time speak unintelligibly, yet this last case falls more naterally to be considered as an offence against perspicuity, than as a violation of propriety."—*Jamieson's Rhet.* p. 104.

"Ye are witnesses, and God also, how holily and justly and unblamably we behaved ourselves among you that believe."—1 *Thes.* ii, 10.

"The question is·not, whether they know what is said of Christ in the Scriptures; but whether they know it savingly, truly, livingly, powerfully."—*Penington's Works*, iii, 28.

> "How gladly would the man recall to life
> The boy's neglected sire! a mother too,
> That softer friend, perhaps more gladly still,
> Might he demand them at the gates of death!"—*Cowper.*

Lesson VIII.—Conjunctions.

"Every person's safety requires that he should submit to be governed; for if one man may do harm without suffering punishment, every man has the same right, and no person can be safe."—*Webster's Essays*, p. 88.

"When it becomes a practice to collect debts by law, it is a proof of corruption and degeneracy among the people. Laws and courts are necessary, to settle controverted points between man and man; but a man should pay an acknowledged debt, not because there is a law to oblige him, but because it is just and honest, and because he has promised to pay it."—*Ib.* p. 42.

"The liar, and only the liar, is invariably and universally despised, abandoned, and disowned. It is therefore natural to expect, that a crime thus generally detested, should be generally avoided."—*Hawkesworth.*

"When a man swears to the truth of his tale, he tacitly acknowledges that his bare word does not deserve credit. A swearer will lie, and a liar is not to be believed even upon his oath; nor is he believed, when he happens to speak the truth."—*Red Book*, p. 108.

"John Adams replied, 'I know Great Britain has determined on her system, and that very determination determines me on mine. You know I have been constant and uniform in opposition to her measures. The die is now cast. I have passed the Rubicon. Sink or swim, live or die, survive or perish with my country, is my unalterable determination.'"—*Seward's Life of John Quincy Adams*, p. 26.

"I returned, and saw under the sun that the race is not to the swift, nor the battle to the strong, neither yet bread to the wise, nor yet riches to men of understanding, nor yet favour to men of skill; but time and chance happen to them all."—*Ecclesiastes*, ix, 11.

> "Little, alas! is all the good I can;
> A man oppress'd, dependent, yet a man."—*Pope, Odys.* B. xiv, p. 70.

Lesson IX.—Prepositions.

"He who legislates only for a party, is engraving his name on the adamantine pillar of his country's history, to be gazed on forever as an object of universal detestation."—*Wayland's Moral Science*, p. 401.

"The Greek language, in the hands of the orator, the poet, and the historian, must be allowed to bear away the palm from every other known in the world; but to that only, in my opinion, need our own yield the precedence."—*Barrow's Essays*, p. 91.

"For my part, I am convinced that the method of teaching which approaches most nearly to the method of investigation, is incomparably the best; since, not content with serving up a few barren and lifeless truths, it leads to the stock on which they grew."—*Burke, on Taste*, p. 37.   Better—"on which *truths grow.*"

"All that I have done in this difficult part of grammar, concerning the proper use of prepositions, has been to make a few general remarks upon the subject; and then to give a collection of instances, that have occurred to me, of the improper use of some of them."—*Priestley's Gram.* p. 155.

"This is not an age of encouragement for works of elaborate research and real utility. The genius of the trade of literature is necessarily unfriendly to such productions."—*Thelwall's Lect.* p. 102.

"At length, at the end of a range of trees, I saw three figures seated on a bank of moss, with a silent brook creeping at their feet."—*Steele.*

"Thou rather, with thy sharp and sulph'rous bolt,
Splitst the unwedgeable and gnarled oak."—*Shakspeare.*

LESSON X.—INTERJECTIONS.

"Hear the word of the Lord, O king of Judah, that sittest upon the throne of David; thou, and thy servants, and thy people that enter in by these gates: thus saith the Lord, Execute ye judgement and righteousness, and deliver the spoiled out of the hand of the oppressor."—*Jeremiah,* xxii, 2, 3.

"Therefore, thus saith the Lord concerning Jehoiakim the son of Josiah king of Judah, They shall not lament for him, saying, Ah my brother! or, Ah sister! they shall not lament for him, saying, Ah lord! or, Ah his glory! He shall be buried with the burial of an ass, drawn and cast forth beyond the gates of Jerusalem."—*Jer.* xxii, 18, 19.

"O thou afflicted, tossed with tempest, and not comforted, behold, I will lay thy stones with fair colours, and lay thy foundations with sapphires."—*Isaiah,* liii, 11.

"O prince! O friend! lo! here thy Medon stands;
Ah! stop the hero's unresisted hands."—*Pope, Odys.* B. xxii, l. 417.
"When, lo! descending to our hero's aid,
Jove's daughter Pallas, war's triumphant maid!"—*Ib.* B. xxii, l. 222.
"O friends! oh ever exercised in care!
Hear Heaven's commands, and reverence what ye hear!"—*Ib.* B. xii, l. 324.
"Too daring prince! ah, whither dost thou run?
Ah, too forgetful of thy wife and son!"—*Pope's Iliad,* B. vi, l. 510.

CHAPTER II.—ARTICLES.

In this chapter, and those which follow it, the Rules of Syntax are again exhibited, in the order of the parts of speech, with Examples, Exceptions, Observations, Notes, and False Syntax. The Notes are all of them, in form and character, subordinate rules of syntax, designed for the detection of errors. The correction of the False Syntax placed under the rules and notes, will form an *oral exercise,* similar to that of parsing, and perhaps more useful.[*]

RULE I.—ARTICLES.

Articles relate to the nouns which they limit:[†] as, "At *a* little distance from *the* ruins of *the* abbey, stands *an* aged elm."

"See *the* blind beggar dance, *the* cripple sing,
The sot a hero, lunatic *a* king."—*Pope's Essay,* Ep. ii, l. 268.

---

[*] "I will not take upon me to say, whether we have any Grammar that sufficiently instructs us by rule and example; but I am sure we have none, that in the manner here attempted, teaches us what is right, by showing what is wrong; though this perhaps may prove *the more useful and effectual method* of instruction."—*Lowth's Gram. Pref.* p. viii.

[†] With the possessive case and its governing noun, we use but *one article;* and sometimes it seems questionable, to which of the two that article properly relates: as, "This is one of *the* Hebrews' children."—*Exodus,* ii, 6. The sentence is plainly equivalent to the following, which has two articles: "This is one of *the children of the* Hebrews." Not because the one article is equivalent to the two, or because it relates to both of the nouns; but because the possessive relation itself makes one of the nouns sufficiently definite. Now, if we change the latter construction back into the former, it is the noun *children* that drops its article; it is therefore the other to which the remaining article relates. But we sometimes find examples in which the same analogy does not hold. Thus, "*a summer's day*," means, "*a day of summer;*" and we should hardly pronounce it equivalent to "*the day of a summer.*" So the questionable phrase, "*a three days' journey,*" means, "*a journey of three days;*" and, whether the construction be right or wrong, the article *a* cannot be said to relate to the plural noun. Possibly such a phrase as, "*the three years' war,*" might mean, "*the war of three years;*" so that the article must relate to the latter noun. But in general it is the latter noun that is rendered definite by the possessive relation: thus the phrase, "*man's works,*" is equivalent to "*the works* of man," not to "works *of the man;*" so, "*the man's works,*" is equivalent, not to, "the works of man," but to "*the works of the man.*"

EXCEPTION FIRST.

The definite article used *intensively*, may relate to an *adjective* or *adverb* of the comparative or the superlative degree; as, "A land which was *the mightiest*."—*Byron*. "*The farther* they proceeded, *the greater* appeared their alacrity."—*Dr. Johnson.* "He chooses it *the rather*." —*Cowper.* See Obs. 10th, below.

EXCEPTION SECOND.

The indefinite article is sometimes used to give a collective meaning to what seems a *plural adjective of number*; as, "Thou hast *a few* names even in Sardis."—*Rev.* iii, 4. "There are *a thousand* things which crowd into my memory."—*Spectator*, No. 468. "The centurion commanded *a hundred* men."—*Webster.* See Etymology, Articles, Obs. 26.

OBSERVATIONS ON RULE I.

OBS. 1.—The article is a kind of *index*, usually pointing to some noun; and it is a general, if not a universal, principle, that no one noun admits of more than one article. Hence, two or more articles in a sentence are signs of two or more nouns; and hence too, by a very convenient ellipsis, an article before an adjective is often made to relate to a noun *understood*; as, "*The* grave [*people*] rebuke *the* gay [*people*], and *the* gay [*people*] mock *the* grave" [*people*].—*Maturin's Sermons*, p. 103. "*The* wise [*persons*] shall inherit glory."—*Prov.* iii, 35. "*The* vile [*person*] will talk villainy."—*Coleridge's Lay Sermons*, p. 105: see *Isaiah*, xxxii, 6. "The testimony of the Lord is sure, making wise *the* simple" [*ones*].—*Psal.* xix, 7. "*The* Old [*Testament*] and the New Testament are alike authentic."—"*The* animal [*world*] and the vegetable world are adapted to each other."—"*An* epic [*poem*] and a dramatic poem *are* the same in substance."—*Ld. Kames, El. of Crit.* ii, 274. "The neuter verb is conjugated like *the* active" [*verb*].—*Murray's Gram.* p. 99. "Each section is supposed to contain a heavy [*portion*] and a light portion; the heavy [*portion*] being the accented syllable, and the light [*portion*] the unaccented" [*syllable*].—*Rush, on the Voice*, p. 364.

OBS. 2.—Our language does not, like the French, *require a repetition* of the article before every noun in a series; because the same article may serve to limit the signification of several nouns, provided they all stand in the same construction. Hence the following sentence is bad English : "The understanding and language have a strict connexion."—*Murray's Gram.* i, p. 356. The sense of the former noun only was meant to be limited. The expression therefore should have been, "*Language and the understanding* have a strict connexion," or, "The understanding *has* a strict connexion *with language.*" In some instances, one article *seems* to limit the sense of several nouns that are not all in the same construction, thus : "As it proves a greater or smaller obstruction to *the* speaker's or *writer's* aim."—*Campbell's Rhet.* p. 200. That is — "to *the* aim of *the* speaker or *the* writer." It is, in fact, the possessive, that limits the other nouns ; for, "*a man's foes*," means, "*the* foes of *a* man ;" and, "*man's wisdom*," means, "*the* wisdom of man." The governing noun cannot have an article immediately before it. Yet the omission of articles, when it occurs, is not properly *by ellipsis*, as some grammarians declare it to be ; for there never can be a proper ellipsis of an article, when there is not also an ellipsis of its noun. Ellipsis supposes the omitted words to be necessary to the construction, when they are not so to the sense ; and this, it would seem, cannot be the case with a mere article. If such a sign be in any wise necessary, it ought to be used ; and if not needed in any respect, it cannot be said to be *understood*. The definite article being generally required before adjectives that are used by ellipsis as nouns, we in this case repeat it before every term in a series ; as, "They are singled out from among their fellows, as *the* kind, *the* amiable, *the* sweet-tempered, *the* upright."—*Dr. Chalmers.*

> "*The* great, *the* gay, shall they partake
> The heav'n that thou alone canst make?"—*Cowper.*

OBS. 3.—The article precedes its noun, and is never, by itself, placed after it ; as, "Passion is *the* drunkenness of *the* mind."—*Southey.* When an *adjective* likewise precedes the noun, the article is usually placed *before the adjective*, that its power of limitation may extend over that also ; as, "*A concise* writer compresses his thoughts into *the fewest* possible words."—*Blair's Rhet.* p. 176.

> "*The* private path, *the* secret acts of men,
> If noble, far *the noblest* of their lives."—*Young.*

OBS. 4.—The relative position of the article and the adjective is seldom a matter of indifference. Thus, it is good English to say, "*both the men,*" or, "*the two men ;*" but we can by no means say, "*the both men,*" or, "*two the men.*" Again, the two phrases, "*half a dollar,*" and "*a half dollar,*" though both good, are by no means equivalent. Of the pronominal adjectives, some exclude the article ; some precede it ; and some follow it, like other adjectives. The word *same* is seldom, if ever used without the definite article or some stronger definitive before it ; as, "On *the same* day,"—"In *that same* hour,"—"*These same* gentlemen." After the adjective *both*, the definite article *may* be used, but it is generally *unnecessary*, and this is a sufficient reason for omitting it : as, "The following sentences will fully exemplify, to the young grammarian, *both the parts* of this rule."—*Murray's Gram.* i, p. 192.

Say, "*both parts*." The adjective *few* may be used either with or without an article, but not with the same import: as, "*The few* who were present, were in the secret;" i. e. All then present, knew the thing. "*Few* that were present, were in the secret;" i. e. Not many then present knew the thing. "When I say, 'There were *few* men with him,' I speak diminutively, and mean to represent them as inconsiderable; whereas, when I say, 'There were *a few* men with him,' I evidently intend to make the most of them."—*Murray's Gram.* p. 171. See Etymology, Articles, Obs. 28.

Obs. 5.—The pronominal adjectives which exclude the article, are *any, each, either, every, much, neither, no,* or *none, some, this, that, these, those.* The pronominal adjectives which precede the article, are *all, both, many, such,* and *what;* as, "*All the* world,"—"*Both the* judges," —"*Many a* ° mile,"—"*Such a* chasm,"—"*What a* freak." In like manner, any adjective of quality, when its meaning is limited by the adverb *too, so, as,* or *how,* is put before the article; as, "*Too great a* study of strength, is found to betray writers into a harsh manner." —*Blair's Rhet.* p. 179. "Like *many an* other poor wretch, I now suffer *all the* ill consequences of *so foolish an* indulgence." "*Such a* gift is *too small* a reward for *so great a* labour." —*Brightland's Gram.* p. 95. "Here flows *as clear a* stream as any in Greece. *How beautiful a* prospect is here!"—*Bicknell's Gram.* Part ii, p. 52. The pronominal adjectives which follow the article, are *few, former, first, latter, last, little, one, others,* and *same;* as, "An author might lean either to *the one* [*style*] or to *the other,* and yet be beautiful."—*Blair's Rhet.* p. 179. *Many,* like *few,* sometimes follows the article; as, "*The many* favours which we have received."—"In conversation, for *many a man,* they say, *a many men.*"—*Johnson's Dict.* In this order of the words, *a* seems awkward and needless: as,

"Told of *a many* thousand warlike French."—*Shak.*

Obs. 6.—When the adjective is preceded by any other adverb than *too, so, as,* or *how,* the article is almost always placed before the adverb: as, "One of *the* most complete models;"— "*An* equally important question;"—"*An* exceedingly rough passage;"—"*A* very important difference." The adverb *quite,* however, may be placed either before or after the article, though perhaps with a difference of construction: as, "This *is quite a* different thing;"—or, "This is *a quite different* thing." "Finding it *quite an* other thing;"—or, "Finding it *a quite other* thing."—*Locke, on Ed.* p. 153. Sometimes *two adverbs* intervene between the article and the adjective; as, "We had a *rather more* explicit account of the Novii."—*Philol. Museum,* i, 458. But when an other adverb follows *too, so, as,* or *how,* the three words should be placed either before the article or after the noun; as, "Who stands there in *so purely poetical* a light."—*Ib.* i, 449. Better, perhaps: "*In a light so purely poetical.*"

Obs. 7.—The definitives *this, that,* and some others, though they supersede the article *as* or *a,* may be followed by the adjective *one;* for we say, "*this one thing,*" but not "*this a thing.*" Yet, in the following sentence, *this* and *a* being separated by other words, appear to relate to the same noun: "For who is able to judge *this* thy so great *a* people?"—1 *Kings,* iii, 9. But we may suppose the noun *people* to be understood after *this.* Again, the following example, if it is not wrong, has an ellipsis of the word *use* after the first *a:*

"For highest cordials all their virtue lose
    By a too frequent and too bold a use."—*Pomfret.*

Obs. 8.—When the adjective is placed *after* the noun, the article generally retains its place *before* the noun, and is not repeated before the adjective: as, "*A* man *ignorant* of astronomy;"—"*The* primrose *pale.*" In *Greek,* when an adjective is placed after its noun, if the article is applied to the noun, it is repeated before the adjective; as, "Ἡ πόλις ἡ μεγάλη,"—"*The* city *the* great;" i. e. "The great city."

Obs. 9.—Articles, according to their own definition and nature, come *before* their nouns; but the definite article and an adjective seem sometimes to be placed after the noun to which they both relate: as, "Section *the Fourth;*"—"Henry *the Eighth.*" Such examples, however, may possibly be supposed elliptical; as, "Section, *the fourth division* of the chapter;"—"Henry, *the eighth king* of that name:" and, if they are so, the article, in *English,* can never be placed after its noun, nor can two articles ever properly relate to one noun, in any particular construction of it. Priestley observes, "Some writers affect to *transpose* these words, and place the numeral adjective first; [as,] '*The first Henry.*' Hume's History, Vol. i, p. 497. This construction is common with this writer, but there seems to be a *want of dignity* in it."—*Rudiments of E. Gram.* p. 150. Dr. Webster cites the word *Great,* in "*Alexander the Great,*" as a *name,* or *part* of a name; that is, he gives it as an instance of "*cognomination.*" See his *American Dict.* 8vo. And if this is right, the article may be said to relate to the epithet only, as it appears to do. For, if the word is taken substantively, there is certainly no ellipsis; neither is there any transposition in putting it last, but rather, as Priestley suggests, in putting it first.

Obs. 10.—The definite article is often prefixed to *comparatives* and *superlatives;* and its effect is, as Murray observes, (in the words of Lowth,) "to mark the degree *the more* strongly, and to define it *the more* precisely: as, '*The more* I examine it, *the better* I like it.'

_____

° Horne Tooke says, "The *use* of A after the word MANY is a corruption for *of;* and has no connexion whatever with the *article* A, i. e. *one.*"—*Diversions of Purley,* Vol. ii, p. 334. With this conjecture of the learned etymologist, I do not concur: it is hardly worth while to state here, what may be urged pro and con.

'I like this *the least* of any.'"—*Murray's Gram.* p. 33; *Lowth's*, 14. "For neither if we eat, are we *the better*; neither if we eat not, are we *the worse.*"—1 *Cor.* viii, 8. "One is not *the more* agreeable to me for loving beef, as I do; nor *the less* agreeable for preferring mutton."—*Kames, El. of Crit.* Vol. ii, p. 365. "They are not the men in the nation, *the most* difficult to be replaced."—*Priestley's Gram.* p. 148. In these instances, the article seems to be used *adverbially*, and to relate only to the *adjective* or *adverb* following it. (See observation fourth, on the Etymology of Adverbs.) Yet none of our grammarians have actually reckoned *the* an adverb. After the *adjective*, the noun might perhaps be supplied; but when the word *the* is added to an *adverb*, we must either call it an adverb, or make an exception to Rule 1st above: and if an exception is to be made, the brief form which I have given, cannot well be improved. For even if a noun be understood, it may not appear that the article relates to it, rather than to the degree of the quality. Thus: "*The* deeper the well, *the* clearer the water." This Dr. Ash supposes to mean, "The deeper *well* the well *is*, the clearer *water* the water *is*."—*Ash's Gram.* p. 107. But does the text specify a *particular* "deeper well" or "clearer water?" I think not. To what then does *the* refer, but to the proportionate degree of *deeper* and *clearer?*

OBS. 11.—The article *the* is sometimes elegantly used, after an idiom common in the French language, in lieu of a possessive pronoun; as, "He looked him full in *the* face; i. e. in *his* face."—*Priestley's Gram.* p. 150. "Men who have not bowed *the* knee to the image of Baal."—*Rom.* xi, 4. That is, *their knees.*

OBS. 12.—The article *an* or *a*, because it implies unity, is applicable to nouns of the singular number only; yet a collective noun, being singular in form, is sometimes preceded by this article even when it conveys the idea of plurality and takes a plural verb: as, "There *are* a very great *number* [of adverbs] ending in *ly*."—*Buchanan's Syntax*, p. 63. "A *plurality* of them *are* sometimes felt at the same instant."—*Kames, El. of Crit.* Vol. i, p. 114. In support of this construction, it would be easy to adduce a great multitude of examples from the most reputable writers; but still, as it seems not very consistent, to take any word plurally after restricting it to the singular, we ought rather to avoid this if we can, and prefer words that literally agree in number: as, "Of adverbs there *are* very *many* ending in *ly*."—"*More than one* of them *are* sometimes felt at the same instant." The word *plurality*, like other collective nouns, is literally singular; as, "To produce the latter, a *plurality* of objects *is* necessary."—*Kames, El. of Crit.* Vol. i, p. 224.

OBS. 13.—Respecting the form of the indefinite article, present practice differs a little from that of our ancient writers. *An* was formerly used before all words beginning with *h*, and before several other words which are now pronounced in such a manner as to require *a*: thus, we read in the Bible, "*An* help,"—"*an* house,"—"*an* hundred,"—"*an* one,"—"*an* ewer,"—"*an* usurer;" whereas we now say, "*A* help,"—"*a* house,"—"*a* hundred," —"*a* one,"—"*a* ewer,"—"*a* usurer."

OBS. 14.—Before the word *humble*, with its compounds and derivatives, some use *an*, and others, *a*; according to their practice, in this instance, of sounding or suppressing the aspiration. Webster and Jameson sound the *h*, and consequently prefer *a*; as, "But *a humbling* image is not always necessary to produce that effect."—*Kames, El. of Crit.* i, 205. "O what a blessing is *a humble* mind!"—*Christian Experience*, p. 342. But Sheridan, Walker, Perry, Jones, and perhaps a majority of fashionable speakers, leave the *h* silent, and would consequently say, "*An humbling* image,"—"*an humble* mind,"—&c.

OBS. 15.—An observance of the principles on which the article is to be repeated or not repeated in a sentence, is of very great moment in respect to accuracy of composition. These principles are briefly stated in the notes below, but it is proper that the learner should know the reasons of the distinctions which are there made. By a repetition of the article before several adjectives in the same construction, a repetition of the noun is implied; but without a repetition of the article, the adjectives, in all fairness of interpretation, are confined to one and the same noun: as, "No figures will render *a cold* or *an empty* composition interesting."—*Blair's Rhet.* p. 134. Here the author speaks of a cold composition and an empty composition as different things. "*The* metaphorical and *the* literal meaning *are* improperly mixéd."—*Murray's Gram.* p. 339. Here the verb *are* has two nominatives, one of which is expressed, and the other understood. "But *the* third and *the* last of these [forms] *are* seldom used."—*Adam's Lat. Gram.* p. 186. Here the verb "*are used*" has two nominatives, both of which are understood; namely, "the third *form*" and "the last *form*." Again: "*The* original and *present* signification *is* always retained."—*Dr. Murray's Hist. of Lang.* Vol. ii, p. 149. Here *one signification* is characterized as being both original and present. "*A loose and verbose* manner never *fails* to create disgust."—*Blair's Rhet.* p. 261. That is, *one manner*, loose and verbose. "To give a short and yet clear and plain answer to this proposition."—*Barclay's Works*, Vol. i, p. 533. That is, *one answer, short, clear, and plain*; for the conjunctions in the text connect nothing but the adjectives.

OBS. 16.—To avoid repetition, even of the little word *the*, we sometimes, with one article, join *inconsistent* qualities to a *plural noun*;—that is, when the adjectives so differ as to individualize the things, we sometimes make the noun plural, in stead of repeating the article: as, "*The* north and south *poles*;" in stead of, "*The* north and *the* south *pole*."—

"*The* indicative and potential *moods ;*" in stead of, "*The* indicative and *the* potential *mood.*" —"*The* Old and New *Testaments ;*" in stead of, "*The* Old and *the* New *Testament.*" But, in any such case, to repeat the article when the noun is made plural, is a huge blunder; because it implies a repetition of the plural noun. And again, not to repeat the article when the noun is singular, is also wrong; because it forces the adjectives to coalesce in describing one and the same thing. Thus, to say, "*The* north and south *pole,*" is certainly wrong, unless we mean by it, *one pole,* or *slender stick of wood,* pointing north and south; and again, to say, "*The* north and *the* south *poles,*" is also wrong, unless we mean by it, *several poles at the north* and *others at the south.* So the phrase, "*The* Old and New *Testament,*" is wrong, because we have not *one Testament that is both Old and New ;* and again, "*The* Old and *the* New *Testaments,*" is wrong, because we have not *several Old Testaments and several New ones :* at least we have them not in the Bible.

OBS. 17.—Sometimes a noun that *admits no article,* is preceded by adjectives that do not describe the same thing; as, "Never to jumble *metaphorical and plain language* together."— *Blair's Rhet.* p. 146. This means, "*metaphorical language* and *plain language ;*" and, for the sake of perfect clearness, it would perhaps be better to express it so. "For as *intrinsic and relative beauty* must often be blended in the same building, it becomes a difficult task to attain *both* in any perfection."—*Kames, El. of Crit.* Vol. ii, p. 330. That is, "*intrinsic beauty* and *relative beauty* must often be blended ; and this phraseology would be better. "In correspondence to that distinction of *male and female sex.*"—*Blair's Rhet.* p. 74 This may be expressed as well or better, in half a dozen other ways ; for the article may be added, or the noun may be made plural, with or without the article, and before or after the adjectives. "They make no distinction between causes of civil and criminal jurisdiction."—*Adams's Rhet.* Vol. i, p. 302. This means—"between causes of civil and *causes of* criminal jurisdiction ; and, for the sake of perspicuity, it ought to have been so written,— or, still better, *thus :* "They make no distinction between civil causes and criminal."

NOTES TO RULE I.

NOTE I.—When the indefinite article is required, *a* should always be used before the sound of a consonant, and *an,* before that of a vowel ; as, "With the talents of an angel, *a* man may be a fool."—*Young.*

NOTE. II.—The article *an* or *a* must never be so used as to relate, or even seem to relate, to a plural noun. The following sentence is therefore faulty : "I invited her to spend a day in viewing *a seat and gardens.*"—*Rambler,* No. 34. Say, "a seat and *its* gardens."

NOTE III —When nouns are joined in construction, with different adjuncts, different dependence, or positive contrast, the article, if it belong at all to the latter, must be repeated. The following sentence is therefore inaccurate : "She never considered the quality, but merit of her visitors."—*Wm. Penn.* Say, "*the* merit." So the article in brackets is absolutely necessary to the sense and propriety of the following phrase, though not inserted by the learned author : "The Latin introduced between the Conquest and [*the*] reign of Henry the Eighth."—*Fowler's E. Gram.* 8vo, 1850, p. 42.

NOTE IV.—When adjectives are connected, and the qualities belong to things individually different, though of the same name, the article should be repeated : as, "*A* black and *a* white horse ;" i. e. *two horses,* one black and the other white. "*The* north and *the* south line ;" i. e. *two lines,* running east and west.

NOTE V.—When adjectives are connected, and the qualities all belong to the same thing or things, the article should not be repeated : as, "*A* black and white horse ;" i. e. *one* horse, *piebald.* "*The* north and south line ;" i. e. *one line,* running north and south, like a meridian.

NOTE VI.—When two or more individual things of the same name are distinguished by adjectives that cannot unite to describe the same thing, the article must be added to each if the noun be singular, and to the first only if the noun follow them in the plural : as, "*The* nominative and *the* objective *case ;*" or, "*The* nominative and objective *cases.*"—"*The* third, *the* fifth, *the* seventh, and *the* eighth *chapter ;*" or, "*The* third, fifth, seventh, and eighth *chapters.*" *

---

* *Churchill* rashly condemns this construction, and still more rashly proposes to make the noun singular without repeating the article. See his *New Gram.* p. 311. But he sometimes happily forgets his own doctrine; as, "In fact, *the second and fourth lines* here stamp the character of the measure."—*Ib.* p. 391. O. B. Peirce says, "'Joram's *second* and *third daughters,*' must mean, if it means any thing, his *second daughters* and *third daughters ;* and, 'the *first* and *second verses,*' if it means any thing, must represent the *first verses* and the *second*

NOTE VII.—When two phrases of the same sentence have any special correspondence with each other, the article, if used in the former, is in general required also in the latter: as, "For ye know neither *the* day nor *the* hour."—*Matt.* xxv, 18. "Neither *the* cold nor *the* fervid are formed for friendship."—*Murray's Key,* p. 209. "The vail of the temple was rent in twain, from *the* top to *the* bottom."—*Matt.* xxvii, 51.

NOTE VIII.—When a special correspondence is formed between individual epithets, the noun which follows must not be made plural; because the article, in such a case, cannot be repeated as the construction of correspondents requires. Thus, it is improper to say, "Both *the* first and second *editions,*" or, "Both *the* first and *the* second *editions,*" for the accurate phrase, "Both *the* first and *the* second *edition* ; and still worse to say, "Neither *the* Old nor New *Testaments,*" or, "Neither *the* Old nor *the* New *Testaments,*" for the just expression, "Neither *the* Old nor *the* New *Testament.*" Yet we may say, "Neither *the* old nor *the* new *statutes,*" or, "Both *the* early and *the* late *editions ;*" for here the epithets severally apply to more than one thing.

NOTE IX.—In a series of three or more terms, if the article is used with any, it should in general be added either to every one, or else to the first only. The following phrase is therefore inaccurate: "Through their attention to the helm, the sails, or rigging."—*Brown's Estimate,* Vol. i, p. 11. Say, "*the* rigging."

NOTE X.—As the article *an* or *a* denotes "*one thing of a kind,*" it should not be used as we use *the,* to denote emphatically a *whole kind ;* and again, when the species is said to be *of the genus,* no article should be used to limit the latter. Thus some will say, "*A* jay is a sort of *a bird ;*" whereas they ought to say, "*The* jay is a sort *of bird.*" Because it is absurd to suggest, that *one jay* is *a sort of one bird.* Yet we may say, "*The* jay is *a bird,*" or, "*A* jay is *a bird ;*" because, as every species is one under the genus, so every individual is one under both.

NOTE XI.—The article should not be used before the names of virtues, vices, passions, arts, or sciences, in their general sense; before terms that are strictly limited by other definitives; or before any noun whose signification is sufficiently definite without it: as, "*Falsehood* is odious."—"*Iron* is useful."—"*Beauty* is vain."— "*Admiration* is useless, when it is not supported by *domestic worth.*"—*Webster's Essays,* p. 30.

NOTE XII.—When titles are mentioned merely as titles; or names of things, merely as names or words; the article should not be used before them: as, "He is styled *Marquis ;*" not, "*the* Marquis," or, "*a* Marquis."—"Ought a teacher to call his pupil *Master ?*"—"*Thames* is derived from the Latin name *Tamĕsis.*"

NOTE XIII.—When a comparison or an alternative is made with two nouns, if both of them refer to the same subject, the article should not be inserted before the latter; if to different subjects, it should not be omitted: thus, if we say, "He is a better teacher than poet," we compare different qualifications of the same man; but if we say, "He is a better teacher than *a* poet," we speak of different men, in regard to the same qualification.

NOTE XIV.—The definite article, or some other definitive, (as *this, that, these, those,*) is generally required before the antecedent to the pronoun *who* or *which* in a restrictive clause; as, "All *the* men *who* were present, agreed to it."—*W. Allen's*

verses."—*Peirce's English Gram.* p. 263. According to my notion, this interpretation is as false and hypercritical, as is the rule by which the author professes to show what is right. He might have been better employed in explaining some of his own phraseology, such as, " the *indefinite-past and present* of the *declarative mode.*"—*Ib.* p. 100. The critic who writes such stuff as this, may well be a misinterpreter of good common English. It is plain, that the two examples which he thus distorts, are neither obscure nor inelegant. But, in an alternative of single things, the article *must be repeated,* and a plural noun is improper; as, " But they do not receive *the* Nicene or *the* Athanasian *creeds.*"—*Adam's Religious World,* Vol. ii, p. 105. Say, " *creed.*" So in an enumeration; as, " There are three participles : *the* present, *the* perfect, and *the* compound perfect *participles.*"—*Ingersoll's Gram.* p. 43. Expunge this last word, " *participles.*" Sometimes a sentence is wrong, not as being in itself a solecism, but as being unadapted to the author's thought. Example : " Other tendencies will be noticed in the Etymological and Syntactical part."—*Fowler's E. Gram.,* N. Y., 1850. p. 75. This implies, what appears not to be true, that the author meant to treat Etymology and Syntax *together* in a single part of his work. Had he put an *s* to the noun " *part,*" he might have been understood in either of two other ways, but not in this. To make sure of his meaning, therefore, he should have said—" in the Etymological *Part* and *the* Syntactical."

Gram. p. 145. "*The thoughts which* passion suggests are always plain and obvious ones."—*Blair's Rhet.* p. 468. "*The things which* are impossible with men, are possible with God."—*Luke,* xviii, 27. See Etymology, Chap. V, Obs. 26th, &c., on Classes of Pronouns.

NOTE XV.—The article is generally required in that construction which converts a participle into a verbal or participial noun; as, "*The completing of* this, by the *working-out of* sin inherent, must be by the power and spirit of Christ in the heart." —*Wm. Penn.* "They shall be *an abhorring* unto all flesh."—*Isaiah,* lxvi, 24. "For *the dedicating of* the altar."—*Numb.* vii, 11.

NOTE XVI.—The article should not be added to any participle that is not taken in all other respects as a noun; as, "For *the dedicating* the altar."—"He made a mistake in *the giving* out the text." Expunge *the*, and let *dedicating* and *giving* here stand as participles only; for in the construction of nouns, they must have not only a definitive before them, but the preposition *of* after them.

NOTE XVII.—The false syntax of articles properly includes every passage in which there is any faulty insertion, omission, choice, or position, of this part of speech. For example: "When the verb is *a* passive, the agent and object change places."— *Lowth's Gram.* p. 73. Better: "When the verb is *passive*, the agent and *the* object change places." "Comparisons used by the sacred poets, are generally short."— *Russell's Gram.* p. 87. Better: "*The* comparisons," &c. "Pronoun means *for* noun, and *is used to avoid the* too frequent repetition of *the* noun."—*Infant School Gram.* p. 89. Say rather: "*The* pronoun *is put* for *a* noun, and is used to *prevent* too frequent *a* repetition of the noun." Or: "*The word* PRONOUN means *for* noun; and *a pronoun* is used to *prevent* too frequent *a* repetition of *some* noun."

IMPROPRIETIES FOR CORRECTION.

FALSE SYNTAX UNDER RULE I.

☞ [The examples of False Syntax placed under the rules and notes, are to be corrected *orally* by the pupil, according to the formules given, or according to others framed in like manner, and adapted to the several nets.]

EXAMPLES UNDER NOTE I.—AN OR A.

"I have seen an horrible thing in the house of Israel."—*Hosea,* vi, 10.

[FORMULE.—Not proper, because the article *an* is used before *horrible,* which begins with the sound of the consonant *h.* But, according to Note 1st, under Rule 1st, "When the indefinite article is required, *a* should always be used before the sound of a consonant, and *an*, before that of a vowel." Therefore, *an* should be *a*; thus, "I have seen *a* horrible thing in the house of Israel."]

"There is an harshness in the following sentences."—*Priestley's Gram.* p. 188. "Indeed, such an one is not to be looked for."—*Blair's Rhet.* p. 27. "If each of you will be disposed to approve himself an useful citizen."—*Ib.* p. 263. "Land with them had acquired almost an European value."—*Webster's Essays,* p. 325. "He endeavoured to find out an wholesome remedy."—*Neef's Method of Ed.* p. 3. "At no time have we attended an Yearly Meeting more to our own satisfaction."—*The Friend,* v, 224. "Addison was not an humourist in character."—*Kames, El. of Crit.* i, 303. "Ah me! what an one was he?"—*Lily's Gram.* p. 49. "He was such an one as I never saw."—*Ib.* "No man can be a good preacher, who is not an useful one."—*Blair's Rhet.* p. 283. "An usage which is too frequent with Mr. Addison."—*Ib.* p. 200. "Nobody joins the voice of a sheep with the shape of an horse."—*Locke's Essay,* p. 298. "An universality seems to be aimed at by the omission of the article."—*Priestley's Gram.* p. 154. "Architecture is an useful as well as a fine art."—*Kames, El. of Crit.* ii, 335. "Because the same individual conjunctions do not preserve an uniform signification."—*Nutting's Gram.* p. 78. "Such a work required the patience and assiduity of an hermit."—*Johnson's Life of Morin.* "Resentment is an union of sorrow with malignity."—*Rambler,* No. 185. "His bravery, we know, was an high courage of blasphemy."—*Pope.* "Hyssop; a herb of bitter taste."—*Pike's Heb. Lex.* p. 3.

"On each enervate string they taught the note
To pant, or tremble through an Eunuch's throat."—*Pope.*

UNDER NOTE II.—AN OR A WITH PLURALS.

"At a sessions of the court in March, it was moved," &c.—*Hutchinson's Hist. of Mass.* i, 61. "I shall relate my conversations, of which I kept a memoranda."—*Duchess D'Abrantes,* p. 26. "I took another dictionary, and with a scissors cut out, for instance, the word ABACUS."— *A. B. Johnson's Plan of a Dict.* p. 12. "A person very meet seemed he for the purpose, of a forty-five years old."—*Gardiner's Music of Nature,* p. 338. "And it came to pass about an eight days after these sayings."—*Luke,* ix, 28. "There were slain of them upon a three thousand men."—1 *Mac.* iv, 15. "Until I had gained the top of these white mountains, which seemed another Alps of snow."—*Addison, Tat.* No. 161. "To make them a satisfactory amends for all the losses they had sustained."—*Goldsmith's Greece*, p. 187. "As a first fruits of many more that shall be gathered."—*Barclay's Works*, i, 506. "It makes indeed a little amends, by inciting us to oblige people."—*Sheffield's Works*, ii, 229. "A large and lightsome back-stairs leads up to an entry above."—*Ib.* p. 260. "Peace of mind is an honourable amends for the sacrifices of interest."—*Murray's Gram.* p. 162; *Smith's*, 138. "With such a spirit and sentiments were hostilities carried on."—*Robertson's America*, i, 166. "In the midst of a thick woods, he had long lived a voluntary recluse."—*G. B.* "The flats look almost like a young woods."—*Morning Chronicle.* "As we went on, the country for a little ways improved, but scantily."—*Essex County Freeman*, Vol. ii. No. 11. "Whereby the Jews were permitted to return into their own country, after a seventy years captivity at Babylon."—*Rollin's An. Hist.* Vol. ii, p. 20. "He did not go a great ways into the country."—*Gilbert's Gram.* p. 85.

　　　　"A large amends by fortune's hand is made,
　　　　And the lost Punic blood is well repay'd."—*Rowe's Lucan*, iv, 1241.

UNDER NOTE III.—NOUNS CONNECTED.

"As where a landscape is conjoined with the music of birds and odour of flowers."—*Kames, El. of Crit.* i, 117. "The last order resembles the second in the mildness of its accent, and softness of its pause."—*Ib.* ii, 113. "Before the use of the loadstone or knowledge of the compass."—*Dryden.* "The perfect participle and imperfect tense ought not to be confounded."—*Murray's Gram.* ii, 292. "In proportion as the taste of a poet, or orator, becomes more refined."—*Blair's Rhet.* p. 27. "A situation can never be intricate, as long as there is an angel, devil, or musician, to lend a helping hand."—*Kames, El. of Crit.* ii, 285. "Avoid rude sports: an eye is soon lost, or bone broken."—"Not a word was uttered, nor sign given."—*Brown's Inst.* p. 125. "I despise not the doer, but deed."—*Ibid.* "For the sake of an easier pronunciation and more agreeable sound."—*Lowth.* "The levity as well as loquacity of the Greeks made them incapable of keeping up the true standard of history."—*Bolingbroke, on Hist.* p. 115.

UNDER NOTE IV.—ADJECTIVES CONNECTED.

"It is proper that the vowels be a long and short one."—*Murray's Gram.* p. 327. "Whether the person mentioned was seen by the speaker a long or short time before."—*Ib.* p. 70; *Fisk's*, 72. "There are three genders, Masculine, Feminine, and Neuter."—*Adam's Lat. Gram.* p. 8. "The numbers are two; Singular and Plural."—*Ib.* p. 80; *Gould's*, 77. "The persons are three; First, Second, [and] Third."—*Adam, et al.* "Nouns and pronouns have three cases; the nominative, possessive, and objective."—*Comly's Gram.* p. 19; *Ingersoll's*, 21. "Verbs have five moods; namely, the Indicative, Potential, Subjunctive, Imperative, and Infinitive."—*Bullions's E. Gram.* p. 35; *Lennie's*, 20. "How many numbers have pronouns? Two, the singular and plural."—*Bradley's Gram.* p. 82. "To distinguish between an interrogative and exclamatory sentence."—*Murray's Gram.* p. 280; *Comly's*, 163; *Ingersoll's*, 292. "The first and last of which are compounded members."—*Lowth's Gram.* p. 123. "In the last lecture, I treated of the concise and diffuse, the nervous and feeble manner."—*Blair's Rhet.* p. 183. "The passive and neuter verbs, I shall reserve for some future conversation."—*Ingersoll's Gram.* p. 69. "There are two voices; the Active and Passive."—*Adam's Gram.* p. 59; *Gould's*, 87. "*Whose* is rather the poetical than regular genitive of *which*."—*Dr. Johnson's Gram.* p. 7. "To feel the force of a compound, or derivative word."—*Town's Analysis*, p. 4. "To preserve the distinctive uses of the copulative and disjunctive conjunctions."—*Murray's Gram.* p. 150; *Ingersoll's*, 233. "E has a long and short sound in most languages."—*Bicknell's Gram.* Part ii, p. 13. "When the figurative and literal sense are mixed and jumbled together."—*Blair's Rhet.* p. 151. "The Hebrew, with which the Canaanitish and Phœnician stand in connection."—CONANT: *Fowler's E. Gram.* 8vo, 1850, p. 28. "The languages of Scandinavia proper, the Norwegian and Swedish.—*Fowler, ib.* p. 31.

UNDER NOTE V.—ADJECTIVES CONNECTED.

"The path of truth is a plain and a safe path."—*Murray's Key*, p. 236. "Directions for acquiring a just and a happy elocution."—*Kirkham's Elocution*, p. 144. "Its leading object is to adopt a correct and an easy method."—*Kirkham's Gram.* p. 9. "How can it choose but wither in a long and a sharp winter."—*Cowley's Pref.* p. vi. "Into a dark and a distant unknown."—*Chalmers, on Astronomy*, p. 230. "When the bold and the strong enslaved his fellow man."—*Chazotte's Essay*, p. 21. "We now proceed to consider the things most essential to an accurate and a perfect sentence."—*Murray's Gram.* p. 306. "And hence arises a second and a very considerable source of the improvement of taste."—*Blair's Rhet.* p. 18. "Novelty produces in the mind a vivid and an agreeable emotion."—*Ib.* p. 50. "The deepest and the bitterest feeling still is, the separation."—*Dr. M'Rie.* "A great and a good man looks beyond time."—*Brown's Institutes*, p. 125. "They made but a weak and an ineffectual resistance."—*Ib.* "The light and the worthless kernels will float."—*Ib.* "I rejoice that there is an other and a better world."—*Ib.* For he is determined to *revise* his work, and present to the publick another and a better edition."—*Kirkham's Gram.* p. 7. "He hoped that this title would secure him an ample and an independent authority."—*Murray's Gram.* p. 172: see *Priestley's,* 147. "There is however another and a more limited sense."—*Adams's Rhet.* Vol. ii, p. 232.

UNDER NOTE VI.—ARTICLES OR PLURALS.

"This distinction forms, what are called the diffuse and the concise styles."—*Blair's Rhet.* p. 176. "Two different modes of speaking, distinguished at first by the denominations of the Attic and the Asiatic manners."—*Adams's Rhet.* Vol. i, p. 83. "But the great design of uniting the Spanish and the French monarchies under the former was laid."—*Bolingbroke, on History,* p. 180. "In the solemn and the poetic styles, it [*do* or *did*] is often rejected."—*W. Allen's Gram.* p. 68. "They cannot be at the same time in the objective and the nominative cases."—*Murray's Gram.* 8vo, p. 151 ; *Ingersoll's,* 239 ; *R. C. Smith's,* 127. "They are named the POSITIVE, the COMPARATIVE, and the SUPERLATIVE degrees."—*Smart's Accidence,* p. 27. "Certain Adverbs are capable of taking an Inflection, namely, that of the comparative and the superlative degrees."—*Fowler's E. Gram.* 8vo, 1850, § 321. "In the subjunctive mood, the present and the imperfect tenses often carry with them a future sense."—*L. Murray's Gram.* p. 187 ; *Fisk's,* 131. "The imperfect, the perfect, the pluperfect, and the first future tenses of this mood, are conjugated like the same tenses of the indicative."—*Kirkham's Gram.* p. 145. "What rules apply in parsing personal pronouns of the second and third person ?"—*Ib.* p. 116. "Nouns are sometimes in the nominative or objective case after the neuter verb to *be,* or after an active-intransitive or passive verb."—*Ib.* p. 55. "The verb varies its endings in the singular in order to agree in form with the first, second, and third person of its nominative."—*Ib.* p. 47. "They are identical in effect, with the radical and the vanishing stresses."—*Rush, on the Voice,* p. 339. "In a sonnet the first, fourth, fifth, and eighth line rhyme to each other : so do the second, third, sixth, and seventh line ; the ninth, eleventh, and thirtenth, line ; and the tenth, twelfth, and fourteenth line."—*Churchill's Gram.* p. 311. "The iron and the golden ages are run ; youth and manhood are departed."—*Wright's Athens,* p. 74. "If, as you say, the iron and the golden ages are past, the youth and the manhood of the world."—*Ib.* "An Exposition of the Old and New Testament."—*Matthew Henry's Title-page.* "The names and order of the books of the Old and New Testament."—*Friends' Bible,* p. 2 ; *Bruce's,* p. 2 ; *et al.* "In the second and third person of that tense."—*L. Murray's Gram.* p. 81. "And who still unites in himself the human and the divine natures."—*Gurney's Evidences,* p. 59. "Among whom arose the Italian, the Spanish, the French, and the English languages."—*L. Murray's Gram.* 8vo, p. 111. "Whence arise these two, the singular and the plural Numbers."—*Burn's Gram.* p. 32.

UNDER NOTE VII.—CORRESPONDENT TERMS.

"Neither the definitions, nor examples, are entirely the same with his."—*Ward's Pref. to Lily's Gram.* p. vi. "Because it makes a discordance between the thought and expression."—*Kames, El. of Crit.* ii, 24. "Between the adjective and following substantive."—*Ib.* ii, 104. "Thus, Athens became both the repository and nursery of learning."—*Chazotte's Essay,* p. 28. "But the French pilfered from both the Greek and Latin."—*Ib.* p. 102. "He shows that Christ is both the power and wisdom of God."—*The Friend,* x, 414. "That he might be Lord both of the dead and living."—*Rom.* xiv, 9. "This is neither the obvious nor grammatical meaning of his words."—*Blair's Rhet.* p. 209. "Sometimes both the accusative and infinitive are understood."—*Adam's Gram.* p. 155; *Gould's,* 158. "In some cases we can use either the nominative or accusative promiscuously."—*Adam,* p. 156 ; *Gould,* 159. "Both the former and latter substantive are sometimes to be understood."—*Adam,* p. 157 ; *Gould,* 160. "Many whereof have escaped both the commentator and poet himself."—*Pope.* "The verbs *must* and *ought* have both a present and past signification."—*Murray's Gram.* p. 108. "How shall we distinguish between the friends and enemies of the government ? "—*Webster's Essays,* p. 352. "Both the ecclesiastic and secular powers concurred in those measures."—*Campbell's Rhet.* p. 260. "As the period has a beginning and end within itself it implies an inflexion."—*Adams's Rhet.* ii, 245. "Such as ought to subsist between a principal and accessory."—*Kames, on Crit.* i, 39.

UNDER NOTE VIII.—CORRESPONDENCE PECULIAR.

"When both the upward and the downward slides occur in pronouncing a syllable, they are called a *Circumflex* or *Wave.*"—*Kirkham's Elocution,* pp. 75 and 104. "The word *that* is used both in the nominative and objective cases."—*Sanborn's Gram.* p. 69. "But all the other moods and tenses of the verbs, both in the active and passive voices, are conjugated at large."—*Murray's Gram.* 8vo, p. 81. "Some writers on Grammar object to the propriety of admitting the second future, in both the indicative and subjunctive moods."—*Ib.* p. 82. "The same conjunction governing both the indicative and the subjunctive moods, in the same sentence, and in the same circumstances, seems to be a great impropriety."—*Ib.* p. 207. "The true distinction between the subjunctive and the indicative moods in this tense."—*Ib.* p. 208. "I doubt of his capacity to teach either the French or English languages."—*Chazotte's Essay,* p. 7. "It is as necessary to make a distinction between the active transitive and the active intransitive forms of the verb, as between the active and passive forms."—*Nixon's Parser*, p. 13.

UNDER NOTE IX.—A SERIES OF TERMS.

"As comprehending the terms uttered by the artist, the mechanic, and husbandman."—*Chazotte's Essay*, p. 24. "They may be divided into four classes—the Humanists, Philanthropists, Pestalozzian and the Productive Schools."—*Smith's New Gram.* p. iii. "Verbs have six tenses, the Present, the Imperfect, the Perfect, the Pluperfect, and the First and Second Future tenses."—*Kirkham's Gram.* p. 138 ; *L. Murray's*, 68 ; *R.C. Smith's*, 27 ; *Alger's*, 28. "*Is* is an irregular verb neuter, indicative mood, present tense, and the third person singular."—*Murray's Gram.* Vol. ii, p. 2. "*Should give* is an irregular verb active, in the potential mood, the imperfect tense, and the first person plural."—*Ibid.* "*Us* is a personal pronoun, first person plural, and in the objective case."—*Ibid.* "*Them* is a personal pronoun, of the third person, the plural number, and in the objective case."—*Ibid.* "It is surprising that the Jewish critics, with all their skill in dots, points, and accents, never had the ingenuity to invent a point of interrogation, of admiration, or a parenthesis."—*Wilson's Hebrew Gram.* p. 47. "The fifth, sixth, seventh, and the eighth verse."—*O. B. Peirce's Gram.* p. 263. "Substitutes have three persons ; the First, Second, and the Third."—*Ib.* p. 34. "*John's* is a proper noun, of the masculine gender, the third person, singular number, possessive case, and governed by *wife*, by Rule I."—*Smith's New Gram.* p. 48. "Nouns in the English language have three cases ; the nominative, the possessive, and objective."—*Barrett's Gram.* p. 13 ; *Alexander's*, 11. "The Potential [mood] has four [tenses], viz. the Present, the Imperfect, the Perfect, and Pluperfect."—*Ingersoll's Gram.* p. 96.

"Where Science, Law, and Liberty depend,
And own the patron, patriot, and the friend."—*Savage, to Walpole.*

UNDER NOTE X.—SPECIES AND GENUS.

"A pronoun is a part of speech put for a noun."—*Paul's Accidence*, p. 11. "A verb is a part of speech declined with mood and tense."—*Ib.* p. 15. "A participle is a part of speech derived of a verb."—*Ib.* p. 38. "An adverb is a part of speech joined to verbs to declare their signification."—*Ib.* p. 40. "A conjunction is a part of speech that joineth sentences together."—*Ib.* p. 41. "A preposition is a part of speech most commonly set before other parts."—*Ib.* p. 42. "An interjection is a part of speech, which betokeneth a sudden motion or passion of the mind."—*Ib.* p. 44. "An enigma or riddle is also a species of allegory."—*Blair's Rhet.* p. 151; *Murray's Gram.* 343. "We may take from the Scriptures a very fine example of an allegory."—*Ib.* Blair, 151; *Mur.* 341. "And thus have you exhibited a sort of a sketch of art."—*Harris : in Priestley's Gram.* p. 176. "We may 'imagine a subtle kind of a reasoning,' as Mr. Harris acutely observes."—*Churchill's Gram.* p. 71. "But, before entering on these, I shall give one instance of a very beautiful metaphor, that I may show the figure to full advantage."—*Blair's Rhet.* p. 143. "Aristotle, in his Poetics, uses metaphor in this extended sense, for any figurative meaning imposed upon a word ; as a whole put for the part, or a part for a whole ; the species for the genus, or a genus for the species."—*Ib.* p. 142. "It shows what kind of an apple it is of which we are speaking."—*Kirkham's Gram.* p. 69. "Cleon was another sort of a man."—*Goldsmith's Greece*, Vol. i, p. 124. "To keep off his right wing, as a kind of a reserved body."—*Ib.* ii, 12. "This part of speech is called a verb."—*Mack's Gram.* p. 70. "What sort of a thing is it ?"—*Hiley's Gram.* p. 20. "What sort of a charm do they possess ?"—*Bullions's Principles of E. Gram.* p. 73.

"Dear Welsted, mark, in dirty hole,
That painful animal, a Mole."—*Note to Dunciad*, B. ii, l. 207.

UNDER NOTE XI.—ARTICLES NOT REQUISITE.

"Either thou or the boys were in the fault."—*Comly's Key, in Gram.* p. 174. "It may, at the first view, appear to be too general."—*Murray's Gram.* p. 222; *Ingersoll's*, 275. "When the verb has a reference to future time."—*Ib. M.* p. 207 ; *Ing.* 264. "No; they are the language of imagination rather than of a passion."—*Blair's Rhet.* p. 165. "The dislike of the English Grammar, which has so generally prevailed, can only be attributed to the intricacy of syntax."—*Russell's Gram.* p. iv. "Is that ornament in a good taste ?"—*Kames, El. of Crit.* ii, 326. "There are not many fountains in a good taste."—*Ib.* ii, 329. "And I persecuted this way unto the death."—*Acts*, xxii, 4. "The sense of the feeling can, indeed, give us the idea of extension."—*Blair's Rhet.* p. 196. "The distributive adjective pronouns, *each, every, either*, agree with the nouns, pronouns, and verbs, of the singular number only."—*Murray's Gram.* p. 165; *Lowth's*, 89. "Expressing by one word, what might, by a circumlocution, be resolved into two or more words belonging to the other parts of speech."—*Blair's Rhet.* p. 84. "By the certain muscles which operate all at the same time."—*Murray's Gram.* p. 19. "It is sufficient here to have observed thus much in the general concerning them."—*Campbell's Rhet.* p. 112. "Nothing disgusts us sooner than the empty pomp of language."—*Murray's Gram.* p. 319.

UNDER NOTE XII.—TITLES AND NAMES.

"He is entitled to the appellation of a gentleman."—*Brown's Inst.* p. 126. "Cromwell assumed the title of a Protector."—*Ib.* "Her father is honoured with the title of an Earl." —*Ib.* "The chief magistrate is styled a President."—*Ib.* "The highest title in the state is that of the Governor."—*Ib.* "That boy is known by the name of the Idler."—*Murray's Key,* 8vo, p. 205. "The one styled the Mufti, is the head of the ministers of law and religion."—*Balbi's Geog.* p. 360. "Ranging all that possessed them under one class, he called that whole class, *a tree.*"—*Blair's Rhet.* p. 73. "For the oak, the pine, and the ash, were names of whole classes of objects."—*Ib.* p. 73. "It is of little importance whether we give to some particular mode of expression the name of a trope, or of a figure."—*Ib.* p. 133. "The collision of a vowel with itself is the most ungracious of all combinations, and has been doomed to peculiar reprobation under the name of an hiatus."—*J. Q. Adams's Rhet.* Vol. ii, p. 217. "We hesitate to determine, whether the *Tyrant* alone, is the nominative, or whether the nominative includes the spy."—*Cobbett's E. Gram.* ¶ 246. "Hence originated the customary abbreviation of *twelve months,* into a *twelvemonth; seven nights into se'night; fourteen nights* into a *fortnight.*"—*Webster's Improved Gram.* p. 105.

UNDER NOTE XIII.—COMPARISONS AND ALTERNATIVES.

"He is a better writer than a reader."—*W. Allen's False Syntax, Gram.* p. 332. "He was an abler mathematician than a linguist."—*Ib.* "I should rather have an orange than apple."—*Brown's Inst.* p. 126. "He was no less able a negotiator, than a courageous warrior."—*Smollett's Voltaire,* Vol. i, p. 181. "In an epic poem we pardon many negligences that would not be permitted in a sonnet or epigram."—*Kames, El. of Crit.* Vol. i, p. 186. "That figure is a sphere, or a globe, or a ball."—*Harris's Hermes,* p. 258.

UNDER NOTE XIV.—ANTECEDENTS TO WHO OR WHICH.

"Carriages which were formerly in use, were very clumsy."—*Inst.* p. 126. "The place is not mentioned by geographers who wrote at that time."—*Ib.* "Questions which a person asks himself in contemplation, ought to be terminated by points of interrogation."—*Murray's Gram.* p. 279; *Comly's,* 162; *Ingersoll's,* 291. "The work is designed for the use of persons, who may think it merits a place in their Libraries."—*Murray's Gram.* 8vo, p. iii. "That persons who think confusedly, should express themselves obscurely, is not to be wondered at."—*Ib.* p. 298. "Grammarians who limit the number to two, or at most to three, do not reflect."—*Ib.* p. 75. "Substantives which end in *ics,* are those that signify profession."—*Ib.* p. 132. "To these may be added verbs, which chiefly among the poets govern the dative."—*Adam's Gram.* p. 170; *Gould's,* 171. "Consonants are letters, which cannot be sounded without the aid of a vowel."—*Bucke's Gram.* p. 9. "To employ the curiosity of persons who are skilled in grammar."—*Murray's Gram. Pref.* p. iii. "This rule refers only to nouns and pronouns, which have the same bearing or relation."—*Ib.* i. p. 204. "So that things which are seen, were not made of things which do appear."—*Heb.* xi, 3. "Man is an imitative creature: he may utter sounds, which he has heard."—*Wilson's Essay on Gram.* p. 21. "But men, whose business is wholly domestic, have little or no use for any language but their own."—*Webster's Essays,* p. 5.

UNDER NOTE XV.—PARTICIPIAL NOUNS.

"Great benefit may be reaped from reading of histories."—*Sewel's Hist.* p. iii. "And some attempts were made towards writing of history."—*Bolingbroke, on Hist.* p. 110. "It is Invading of the Priest's Office for any other to Offer it."—*Right of Tythes,* p. 200. "And thus far of forming of verbs."—*Walker's Art of Teaching,* p. 35. "And without shedding of blood is no remission."—*Heb.* ix, 22. "For making of measures we have the best method here in England."—*Printer's Gram.* "This is really both admitting and denying, at once."—*Butler's Analogy,* p. 72. "And hence the origin of making of parliaments."—*Brown's Estimate,* Vol. i, p. 71. "Next thou objectest, that having of saving light and grace presupposes conversion. But that I deny: for, on the contrary, conversion presupposeth having light and grace."—*Barclay's Works,* Vol. i, p. 143. "They cried down wearing of rings and other superfluities, as we do."—*Ib.* i, 236. "Whose adorning, let it not be that outward adorning of plaiting the hair, and of wearing of gold, or of putting on of apparel."—1 *Peter,* iii, 3. "In spelling of derivative Words, the Primitive must be kept whole."—*British Gram.* p. 50; *Buchanan's Syntax,* 9. "And the princes offered for dedicating of the altar."—*Numbers,* vii, 10. "Boasting is not only telling of lies, but also many unseemly truths."—*Sheffield's Works,* ii, 244. "We freely confess that forbearing of prayer in the wicked is sinful."—*Barclay,* i, 316. "For revealing of a secret, there is no remedy."—*Inst. E. Gram.* p. 126. "He turned all his thoughts to composing of laws for the good of the state."—*Rollin's Ancient Hist.* Vol. ii, p. 38.

UNDER NOTE XVI.—PARTICIPLES, NOT NOUNS.

"It is salvation to be kept from falling into a pit, as truly as to be taken out of it after the falling in."—*Barclay,* i, 210. "For in the receiving and embracing the testimony of truth, they felt their souls eased."—*Ib.* i, 469. "True regularity does not consist in the having but a single rule, and forcing every thing to conform to it."—*Philol. Museum,* i, 664. "To the man of the world, this sound of glad tidings appears only an idle tale, and not worth the attending to."—*Life of Tho.* Say, p. 144. "To be the deliverer of the captive Jews, by the ordering their temple to be rebuilt," &c.—*Rollin,* ii, 124. "And for the preserving them from being defiled."—*N. E. Discipline,* p. 133. "A wise man will avoid the showing any excellence in trifles."—*Art of Thinking,* p. 80. "Hirsutus had no other reason for the valuing a book."—*Rambler,* No. 177 ; *Wright's Gram.* p. 190. "To the being heard with satisfaction, it is necessary that the speaker should deliver himself with ease."—*Sheridan's Elocution,* p. 114. "And to the being well heard, and clearly understood, a good and distinct articulation contributes more, than power of voice."—*Ib.* p. 117.

"*Potential* means the having power or will ;

As, If you *would* improve, you *should* be still."—*Tobitt's Gram.* p. 31.

UNDER NOTE XVII.—VARIOUS ERRORS.

"For the same reason, a neuter verb cannot become a passive."—*Lowth's Gram.* p. 74. "The period is the whole sentence complete in itself."—*Ib.* p. 115. "The colon or member is a chief constructive part, or greater division of a sentence."—*Ib.* "The semicolon or half member, is a less constructive part or subdivision, of a sentence or member."—*Ib.* "A sentence or member is again subdivided into commas or segments."—*Ib.* p. 116. "The first error that I would mention, is, a too general attention to the dead languages, with a neglect of our own."—*Webster's Essays,* p. 3. "One third of the importations would supply the demands of people."—*Ib.* p. 119. "And especially in grave stile."—*Priestley's Gram.* p. 72. "By too eager pursuit, he ran a great risk of being disappointed."—*Murray's Key, Octavo Gram.* Vol. ii, p. 201. "Letters are divided into vowels and consonants."—*Murray's Gram.* i, p. 7 ; *and others.* "Consonants are divided into mutes and semivowels."—*Ib.* i, 8 ; *and others.* "The first of these forms is most agreeable to the English idiom."—*Ib.* i, 176. "If they gain, it is a too dear rate."—*Barclay's Works,* i, 504. "A pronoun is a word used instead of a noun, to prevent a too frequent repetition of it."—*Maunder's Gram.* p. 1. "This vulgar error might perhaps arise from a too partial fondness for the Latin."—*Dr. Ash's Gram. Pref.* p. iv. "The groans which a too heavy load extorts from her."—*Hitchcock, on Dyspepsy,* p. 50. "The numbers [of a verb] are, of course, singular and plural."—*Bucke's Gram.* p. 58. "To brook no meanness, and to stoop to no dissimulation, are the indications of a great mind."—*Murray's Key,* ii, 236. "This mode of expression rather suits familiar than grave style."—*Murray's Gram.* i, 198. "This use of the word rather suits familiar and low style."—*Priestley's Gram.* p. 134. "According to the nature of the composition the one or other may be predominant."—*Blair's Rhet.* p. 102. "Yet the commonness of such sentences prevents in a great measure a too early expectation of the end."—*Campbell's Rhet.* p. 411. "An eulogy or a philippic may be pronounced by an individual of one nation upon the subject of another."—*Adams's Rhet.* i, 298. "A French sermon, is for most part, a warm animated exhortation."—*Blair's Rhet.* p. 288. "I do not envy those who think slavery no very pitiable a lot."—*Channing, on Emancipation,* p. 52. "The auxiliary and principal united, constitute a tense."—*Murray's Gram.* i, 75. "There are some verbs which are defective with respect to persons."—*Ib.* i, 109. "In youth, the habits of industry are most easily acquired."—*Murray's Key,* ii, 235. "Apostrophe (') is used in place of a letter left out."—*Bullions, Eng. Gram.* p. 156.

CHAPTER III.—CASES, OR NOUNS.

The rules for the construction of Nouns, or Cases, are seven ; hence this chapter, according to the order adopted above, reviews the series of rules from the second rule to the eighth, inclusively. Though *Nouns* are here the topic, all these seven rules apply alike to *Nouns and to Pronouns ;* that is, to all the words of our language which are susceptible of *Cases.*

RULE II.—NOMINATIVES.

A Noun or a Pronoun which is the subject of a finite verb, must be in the nominative case : as, " The *Pharisees* also, *who* were covetous, heard all these things ; and *they* derided him."—*Luke,* xvi, 14. " But where the *meekness* of self-knowledge veileth the front of self-respect, there look *thou* for the man whom *none* can know but *they* will honour.—*Book of Thoughts,* p. 66.

" Dost *thou* mourn Philander's fate ?

I know *thou* sayst it : says thy *life* the same ? "—*Young,* N. ii, l. 22.

OBSERVATIONS ON RULE II.

OBS. 1.—To this rule, there are *no exceptions;* and nearly all nominatives, or far the greater part, are to be parsed by it. There are however *four* different ways of disposing of the nominative case. *First,* it is generally *the subject of a verb,* according to Rule 2d. *Secondly,* it may be put *in apposition* with an other nominative, according to Rule 3d. *Thirdly,* it may be put after a verb or a participle *not transitive,* according to Rule 6th. *Fourthly,* it may be put *absolute,* or may help to form a *phrase that is independent* of the rest of the sentence, according to Rule 8th.

OBS. 2.—The subject, or nominative, is generally placed *before* the verb; as, "*Peace dawned* upon his mind."—*Johnson.* "*What is written* in the law ?"—*Bible.* But, in the following nine cases, the subject of the verb is usually placed *after* it, or after the first auxiliary :

1. When a question is asked without an interrogative pronoun in the nominative case; as, "*Shall mortals be* implacable ? "—*Hooke.* "What *art thou doing?* "—*Id.* "How many loaves *have ye?* "—*Bible.* "*Are they* Israelites ? so am *I.*"—*Ib.*

2. When the verb is in the imperative mood; as, "*Go thou.*"—"*Come ye.*" But, with this mood, the pronoun is very often omitted and understood; as, " Philip saith unto him, *Come* and *see.*" —*John,* i, 46. "And he saith unto them, *Be* not *affrighted.*"—*Mark,* xvi, 5.

3. When an earnest wish, or other strong feeling, is expressed; as, "*May she be* happy !"— "How *were we struck !* "—*Young.* " Not as the world giveth, *give I* unto you."—*Bible.*

4. When a supposition is made without the conjunction *if;* as, "*Had they known* it ;" for, "*If* they had known it."—"*Were it* true ;" for, "*If* it were true."—"*Could we draw* by the covering of the grave ;" for, "*If* we could draw," &c.

5. When *neither* or *nor,* signifying and *not,* precedes the verb; as, " This was his fear; *nor was his apprehension* groundless."—'' Ye shall not eat of it, *neither shall ye touch* it."—*Gen.* iii, 3.

6. When, for the sake of emphasis, some word or words are placed before the verb, which more naturally come after it; as, " Here *am I.*"—" Narrow *is the way.*"—" Silver and gold *have I* none; but such as I have, *give I* thee."—*Bible.*

7. When the verb has no regimen, and is itself emphatical; as, "*Echo the mountains* round."— *Thomson.* "After the Light Infantry *marched* the *Grenadiers,* then *followed* the *Horse.*"—*Buchanan's Syntax,* p. 71.

8. When the verbs, *say, answer, reply,* and the like, introduce the parts of a dialogue; as, "'Son of affliction,' *said Omar,* 'who art thou ?' 'My name,' *replied* the *stranger,* 'is Hassan.'" —*Dr. Johnson.*

9. When the adverb *there* precedes the verb; as, " There *lived* a man."—*Montgomery.* "In all worldly joys, there *is* a secret *wound* "—*Owen.* This use of *there,* the general introductory adverb of place, is idiomatic, and somewhat different from the use of the same word in reference to a particular locality; as, " Because *there* was much water *there.*"—*John,* iii, 23.

OBS. 3.—In exclamations, and some other forms of expression, a few verbs are liable to be suppressed, the ellipsis being obvious; as, "How different [is] this from the philosophy of Greece and Rome !"—DR. BEATTIE: *Murray's Sequel,* p. 127. "What a lively picture [is here] of the most disinterested and active benevolence !"—HERVEY: *ib.* p. 94. "When Adam [spake] thus to Eve."—MILTON: *Paradise Lost,* B. iv, l. 610.

OBS. 4.—Though we often use nouns in the nominative case to show whom we address, yet the imperative verb takes no other nominative of the second person, than the simple personal pronoun, *thou, ye,* or *you,* expressed or understood. It would seem that some, who ought to know better, are liable to mistake for the subject of such a verb, the noun which we put absolute in the nominative by direct address. Of this gross error the following is an example : "*Study boys.* In this sentence," (says its author,) " *study* is a verb of the second person, plural number, and agrees with its nominative case, *boys*—according to the rule : A verb must agree with its nominative case in number and person. *Boys* is a noun *of* the second person, plural number, masculine gender, *in* the nominative case *to* the verb *study.*"—*Ingersoll's Gram.* p. 17.* Now the fact is, that this laconic address, of three syllables, is written wrong ; being made bad English, for want of a comma between the two words. Without this mark, *boys* must be an objective, governed by *study ;* and with it, a nominative, put absolute by direct address. But, in either case, *study* agrees with *ye* or *you* understood, and has not the noun for its subject, or nominative.

OBS. 5.—Some authors say, and if the first person be no exception, say truly : " The nominative case to a verb, unless it be a pronoun, is always of the *third* person."—*Churchill's Gram.* p. 141. But W. B. Fowle will have all pronouns to be *adjectives.* Consequently all his verbs, of every sort, agree with *nouns* "expressed or understood." This, and every other absurd theory of language, can easily be made out, by means of a few perversions, which may be called *corrections,* and a sufficient number of interpolations, made under pretence of filling up ellipses. Thus, according to this author, "*They fear,*" means, " They *things spoken of* fear."—*True Eng. Gram.* p. 33. And, "*John, open* the door," or, "*Boys, stop* your noise," admits no comma. And, " Be grateful, ye children," and, " Be ye grateful children," are, in his view, every way equivalent : the comma in the former being, in his opinion, needless. See *ib.* p. 39.

OBS. 6 —Though the nominative and objective cases of nouns do not differ in form, it is nevertheless, in the opinion of many of our grammarians, improper to place any noun in both relations at once, because this produces a confusion in the syntax of the word. Examples : " He then goes

---

* Oliver B. Peirce, in his new theory of grammar, not only adopts Ingersoll's error, but adds others to it. He supposes no ellipsis, and declares it grossly improper ever to insert the pronoun. According to him. the following text is wrong : "*My son, despise not thou* the chastening of the Lord."—*Heb.* xii, 5. See *Peirce's Gram.* p. 255. Of this gentleman's book I shall say the less, because its faults are so many and so obvious. Yet this is " *The Grammar of the English Language,*" and claims to be the *only* work which is worthy to be called an English Grammar. "The first and only Grammar of the English Language !"—*Ib.* p. 10. In punctuation, it is a very chaos, as one might guess from the following Rule : "*A word* of the second person, and in the *subjective* case, must have a semicolon after it ; as, John ; hear me "—*Ib.* p 282. Behold his practice ! "John, beware "—P. 84. "Children, study."—P. 80. "Henry ; study."—P. 249. "Pupil ; parse."—P. 211 ; and many other places. "Be thou, or do thou be writing? Be ye or you, or do ye or you be writing?"—P. 110. According to his Rule, this tense requires six semicolons ; but the author points it with two commas and two notes of interrogation !

on to declare that there are, and distinguish of, four *manners* of saying *Per se.*"—*Walker's Trea-tise of Particles*, p. xii. Better: "He then proceeds to show, that *per se* is susceptible of four different senses." "In just allegory *and* similitude there is always a propriety, or, if you choose to call it, *congruity*, in the literal sense, as well as a distinct meaning or sentiment suggested, which is called the figurative sense."—*Campbell's Philosophy of Rhetoric*, p. 291. Better: "In just allegory *or* similitude, there is always a propriety—or, if you choose to call it *so*, a *congruity* —in the literal sense," &c. "It must then be meant of his sins who *makes*, not of his who *becomes*, the convert."—*Atterbury's Sermons*, i, 2. Better: "It must then be meant of his sins who *makes the convert*, not of his who *becomes converted.*" "Eye *hath* not *seen*, nor ear *heard*, neither *have entered* into the heart of man, *the things* which God hath prepared for them that love him."—1 *Cor.* ii, 9. A more regular construction would be: "Eye hath not seen, nor ear heard, neither *hath it* entered into the heart of man to *conceive*, the things which God hath prepared for them that love him." The following example, from Pope, may perhaps be conceded to the poet, as an allowable ellipsis of the words "*a friend*," after *is* :

"In who obtain defence, or who defend ;
In him who *is*, or him who *finds, a friend.*"—*Essay on Man*, Ep. iv, l. 60.

Dr. Lowth cites the last three examples, without suggesting any forms of correction ; and says of them, "There seems to be an impropriety in these sentences in which the same noun stands in a double capacity, performing at the same time the offices *both of the* nominative and objective case."—*Lowth's Gram.* p. 73. He should have said—"*of both the* nominative and *the* objective case." Dr. Webster, citing the line, "In him who is, and him who finds, a friend," adds, "Lowth condemns this use of the noun in the nominative and objective at the same time ; but *without reason*, as the cases are not distinguished in English."—*Improved Gram.* p. 175.

OBS. 7.—In Latin and Greek, the accusative before the infinitive, is often reckoned *the subject of* the latter verb ; and is accordingly parsed by a sort of exception to the foregoing rule—or rather, to that general rule of concord which the grammarians apply to the verb and its nomina-tive. This construction is translated into English, and other modern tongues, sometimes literally, or nearly so, but much oftener, by a nominative and a finite verb. Example : "Εἶπεν αὐτὸν φωνηθῆναι."—*Mark*, x. 49. "Ait illum vocari."—*Leusden.* "Jussit eum vocari."—*Beza.* "Præcepit illum vocari."—*Vulgate.* "He commanded him to be called."—*English Bible.* "He commanded that he should be called."—*Milnes's Gr. Gram.* p. 143. "Il dit qu'on l'appelât."—*French Bible.* "He bid that somebody should call him." "Il commanda qu'on le fit venir."—*Nouveau Test.* Paris, 1812. "He commanded that they should *make him come* ;" that is, "*lead him* or *bring him.*" "Il commanda qu'on l'appelât."—*De Sacy's N. Test.*

OBS. 8.—In English, the objective case before the infinitive mood, although it may truly denote the agent of the infinitive action, or the subject of the infinitive passion, is nevertheless taken as the object of the preceding verb, participle, or preposition. Accordingly our language does not admit a literal translation of the above-mentioned construction, except the preceding verb be such as can be interpreted transitively. "*Gaudeo te valère*," "I am glad that thou art well," can-not be translated more literally ; because, "I am glad thee to be well," would not be good Eng-lish. "*Aiunt regem adventāre*," "They say the king is coming," may be otherwise rendered "They *declare* the king to be coming ;" but neither version is entirely literal ; the objective being retained only by a change of *aiunt, say*, into such a verb as will govern the noun.

OBS. 9.—The following sentence is a literal imitation of the Latin accusative before the infini-tive, and for that reason it is not good English : "But experience teacheth us, *both these opinions to be* alike ridiculous."—*Barclay's Works*, Vol. i, p. 262. It should be, "But experience *teaches us, that both these opinions are* alike ridiculous." The verbs *believe, think, imagine*, and others expressing *mental action*, I suppose to be capable of governing nouns or pronouns in the objective case, and consequently of being interpreted transitively. Hence I deny the correctness of the following explanation : "RULE XXIV. The objective case precedes the infinitive mode ; [as,] 'I *believe* your *brother to be* a good man.' Here *believe* does not govern brother, in the objective case, because it is not the object after it. *Brother*, in the objective case, third person singular, precedes the neuter verb *to be*, in the infinitive mode, present time, third person singular."— S. *Barrett's Gram* p. 135. This author teaches that, "The *infinitive mode agrees* with the objective *case* in number and person."—*Ibid.* Which doctrine is denied ; because the infinitive has no number or person, in any language. Nor do I see why the noun *brother*, in the foregoing exam-ple, may not be both the object of the active verb *believe*, and the subject of the neuter infinitive *to be*, at the same time ; for the subject of the infinitive, if the infinitive can be said to have a subject, is not necessarily in the nominative case, or necessarily independent of what precedes.

OBS. 10.—There are many teachers of English grammar, who still adhere to the principle of the Latin and Greek grammarians, which refers the accusative or objective to the latter verb, and supposes the former to be intransitive, or to govern only the infinitive. Thus Nixon : "The objective case is frequently put before the infinitive mood, as its subject ; as, 'Suffer *me* to de-part.' "*—English Parser*, p. 34. "When an objective case stands before an infinitive mood, as 'I understood *it* to be him,' 'Suffer *me* to depart,' such objective should be parsed, not as gov-erned by the preceding verb, but as the objective case before the infinitive ; that is, *the subject of* it. The reason of this is—the former verb can govern one object only, and that is (in such sen-tences) the infinitive mood ; the interv⸱ning objective being the subject of the infinitive following, and not governed by the former verb ; as, in that instance, it *would be governing* two objects."— *Ib. Note.†*

* In Butler's Practical Grammar, first published in 1845, this doctrine is taught as a *novelty*. His publishers, in their circular letter, speak of it as one of "the *peculiar advantages* of this grammar over preceding works," and as an important matter, "*heretofore altogether omitted by grammarians!*" Wells cites Butler in support of his *false* principle: "A verb in the infinitive is *often* preceded by a noun or pronoun in the objective, which has *no direct depen·tence* on any other word. Examples :—' Columbus ordered a strong *fortress* of wood and *plaster to be erected.*'—*Irving.* ' Its favors here should make *us tremble* '—*Young.*" See *Wells's School Gram.* p 147.

† "Sometimes indeed *the verb hath two regimens*, and then *the preposition is necessary* to one of them , as, ' I *address myself to* my judges.'"—*Campbell's Philosophy of Rhetoric*, p. 178. Here the verb *address* governs the

Obs. 11.—The notion that one verb governs an other in the infinitive, just as a transitive verb governs a noun, and so that it cannot also govern an objective case, is not only contradictory to my scheme of parsing the infinitive mood, but is also false in itself, and repugnant to the principles of General Grammar. In Greek and Latin, it is certainly no uncommon thing for a verb to govern two cases at once; and even the accusative before the infinitive is sometimes governed by the preceding verb, as the objective before the infinitive naturally is in English. But, in regard to construction, every language differs more or less from every other; hence each must have its own syntax, and abide by its own rules. In regard to the point here in question, the reader may compare the following examples: *"Ἔχω ἀνάγκην ἐξελθεῖν."—Luke*, xiv, 18. "Habeo necesse exire."—*Leusden.* English: "I have *occasion to go* away." Again: *"Ὁ ἔχων ὦτα ἀκούειν, ἀκουέτω."—Luke*, xiv, 35. "Habens aures audiendi, audiat."—*Leusden.* "Qui habet aures ad audiendum, audiat."—*Beza.* English: "He that hath *ears to hear,* let *him hear.*" But our most frequent use of the infinitive after the objective, is in sentences that must not be similarly constructed in Latin or Greek; * as, "And he commanded the *porter to watch.*"—*Mark*, xiii, 34. "And he delivered *Jesus to be crucified.*"—*Mark*, xv, 15. "And they led *him* out *to crucify* him."—*Mark*, xv, 20. "We heard *him say.*"—*Mark*, xiv, 58. "That I might make *thee know.*"—*Prov.* xxii, 21.

Obs. 12.—If our language does really admit any thing like the accusative before the infinitive, in the sense of a positive subject at the head of a clause, it is only in some prospective descriptions like the following: "Let certain studies be prescribed to be pursued during the freshman year; *some* of these to be attended to by the whole class; with regard to others, a *choice* to be allowed; *which*, when made by the student, (the parent or guardian sanctioning it,) to be binding during the freshman year: the same *plan* to be adopted with regard to the studies of the succeeding years."—GALLAUDET: *Journal of the N. Y. Literary Convention*, p. 118. Here the four words, *some, choice, which,* and *plan,* may apppear to a Latinist to be so many objectives, or accusatives, placed before infinitives, and used to describe that state of things which the author would promote. If objectives they are, we may still suppose them to be governed by *let, would have,* or something of the kind, understood: as, "*Let* some of these be attended to;" or, "Some of these I *would have* to be attended to," &c. The relative *which* might with more propriety be made nominative, by changing "*to* be binding" to "*shall* be binding;" and as to the rest, it is very doubtful whether they are not now nominatives, rather than objectives. The infinitive, as used above, is a mere substitute for the Latin future participle; and any English noun or pronoun put absolute with a participle, is in the nominative case. English relatives are rarely, if ever, put absolute in this manner: and this may be the reason why the construction of *which,* in the sentence above, seems awkward. Besides, it is certain that the other pronouns are sometimes put absolute with the infinitive; and that, in the nominative case, not the objective: as,

"And *I to be* a corporal in his field,
And wear his colours like a tumbler's hoop!
What? *I! I love! I sue! I seek* a wife!"—*Shak. Love's Labour Lost.*

IMPROPRIETIES FOR CORRECTION.

FALSE SYNTAX UNDER RULE II.

THE SUBJECT OF A FINITE VERB.

"The whole need not a physician, but them that are sick."—*Bunyan's Law & Gr.* p. iv.

[FORMULE.—Not proper, because the objective pronoun *them* is here made the subject of the verb *need,* understood. But, according to Rule 2d, "A noun or a pronoun which is the subject of a finite verb, must be in the nominative case." Therefore, *them* should be *they;* thus, "The whole need not a physician, but *they* that are sick."]

"He will in no[t]wise cast out whomsoever cometh unto him."—*Robert Hall.* "He feared the enemy might fall upon his men, whom he saw were off their guard."—*Hutchinson's Massachusetts,* ii, 133. "Whomsoever shall compel thee to go a mile, go with him twain."—*Dymond's Essays,* p. 48. "The idea's of the author have been conversant with the faults of other writers."—*Swift's T. T.* p. 55. "You are a much greater loser than me by his death."

pronoun *myself,* and is also the antecedent to the preposition *to;* and the construction would be similar, if the preposition governed the infinitive or a participle: as, "I prepared myself *to swim;*" or, "I prepared myself *for* swimming." But, in any of these cases, it is not very accurate, to say, "*the verb has two regimens;*" for the latter term is properly the regimen of the *preposition.* Cardell, by robbing the prepositions, and supposing ellipses, found *two regimens for every verb.* W. Allen, on the contrary, (from whom Nixon gathered his doctrine above,) by giving the "accusative" to the infinitive, makes a multitude of our active-transitive verbs "*neuter.*" See *Allen's Gram.* p. 166. But Nixon absurdly calls the verb "active-transitive," *because it governs the infinitive;* i. e. as he supposes—and, except when *to* is not used, *erroneously* supposes

* A certain *new theorist,* who very innocently fogs himself and his credulous readers with a deal of impertinent pedantry. after denouncing my doctrine that *to* before the infinitive is a *preposition,* appeals to me thus: "Let me ask you, G. B.—Is not the infinitive in Latin *the same* as in *the English?* Thus, I desire *to teach Latin*—Ego Cupio *docere.* I saw Abel *come*—Ego videbam Abelem *venire.* The same principle is recognized by the Greek grammars and those of most of the modern languages."—O B. Peirce's Gram. p. 358. Of this gentleman I know nothing but from what appears in his book—a work of immeasurable and ill-founded vanity—a whimsical, dogmatical, blundering performance This short sample of his Latin, *with six puerile errors in seven words,*) is proof positive that he knows nothing of that language, whatever may be his attainments in Greek, or the other tongues of which he tells. To his question, I answer emphatically, NO. In Latin, "One verb governs an other in the infinitive; as, Cupio *discere,* I desire *to learn.*"—Adam's Gram. p. 181 This government never admits the intervention of a preposition. "I saw Abel come," has no preposition; but the Latin of it is, "*Vidi Abelem venientem,*" and not what is given above: or, according to St. Jerome and others, who wrote, "*Abel venientem,*" without declension. we ought rather to say, "*Vidi Abel venientem.*" If they are right, "*Ego videbam Abelem venire,*" is every word of it wrong!

—*Swift to Pope*, l. 63. "Such peccadillo's pass with him for pious frauds."—*Barclay's Works*, Vol. iii, p. 279. "In whom I am nearly concerned, and whom I know would be very apt to justify my whole procedure."—*Ib.* i, 560. "Do not think such a man as me contemptible for my garb."—*Addison.* "His wealth and him bid adieu to each other."—*Priestley's Gram.* p. 107. "So that, 'He is greater than *me*,' will be more grammatical than, 'He is greater than *I*.'"—*Ib.* p. 106. "The Jesuits had more interests at court than him."—*Smollett: in Pr. Gram.* p. 106.* "Tell the Cardinal that I understand poetry better than him."—*Id. ib.* "An inhabitant of Crim Tartary was far more happy than him." *Id. ib.* "My father and him have been very intimate since."—*Fair American*, ii, 53. "Who was the agent, and whom the object struck or kissed?"—*Infant School Gram.* p. 32. "To find the person whom he imagined was concealed there."—*Kirkham's Elocution*, p. 225. "He offered a great recompense to whomsoever would help him."—*Hume: in Pr. Gram.* p. 104. "They would be under the dominion, absolute and unlimited, of whomsoever might exercise the right of judgement."—*Gov. Haynes's Speech, in 1832.* "They had promised to accept whomsoever should be born in Wales."—*Stories by Croker.* "We sorrow not as them that have no hope."—*Maturin's Sermons*, p. 27. "If he suffers, he suffers as them that have no hope."—*Ib.* p. 32. "We acknowledge that he, and him only, hath been our peacemaker."—*Gratton.* "And what can be better than him that made it?"—*Jenks's Prayers*, p. 329. None of his school-fellows is more beloved than him."—*Cooper's Gram.* p. 42. "Solomon, who was wiser than them all."—*Watson's Apology*, p. 76. "Those whom the Jews thought were the last to be saved, first entered the kingdom of God."—*Eleventh Hour, Tract*, No. 4. "A stone is heavy, and the sand weighty; but a fool's wrath is heavier than them both."—*Prov.* xxvii, 3. "A man of business, in good company, is hardly more insupportable than her they call a notable woman."—*Steele, Spect.* "The king of the Sarmatians, whom we may imagine was no small prince, restored him a hundred thousand Roman prisoners."—*Life of Antoninus*, p. 83. "Such notions would be avowed at this time by none but rosicrucians, and fanatics as mad as them."—*Bolingbroke's Ph. Tr.* p. 24. "Unless, as I said, Messieurs, you are the masters, and not me."—*Basil Hall: Harrison's E. Lang.* p. 173. "We had drawn up against peaceable travellers, who must have been as glad as us to escape." —*Burnes's Travels: ibid.* Stimulated, in turn, by their approbation and that of better judges than them, she turned to their literature with redoubled energy."—*Quarterly Review: Life of H. More: ibid.* "I know not whom else are expected."—*Scott's Pirate: ibid.* "He is great, but truth is greater than us all."—*Horace Mann, in Congress, 1850.* "Him I accuse has entered."—*Fowler's E. Gram.* § 482: see *Shakspeare's Coriolanus*, Act V, sc. 5.

"Scotland and thee did each in other live."—*Dryden's Po.* Vol. ii, p. 220.
"We are alone; here's none but thee and I."—*Shak.* 2 Hen. VI.
"Me rather had, my heart might feel your love,
Than my unpleas'd eye see your courtesy."—*Idem: Joh. Dict.*
"Tell me, in sadness, whom is she you love?—*Id. Romeo and Juliet*, A. I, sc. 1.
"Better leave undone, than by our deeds acquire
Too high a fame, when him we serve's away."—*Shak. Ant. and Cleop.*

RULE III.—APPOSITION.

A Noun or a personal Pronoun used to explain a preceding noun or pronoun, is put, by apposition, in the same case: as, "But it is really *I*, your old *friend* and *neighbour*, *Piso*, late a *dweller* upon the Cœlian hill, who am now basking in the warm skies of Palmyra."—*Zenobia.*

"But *he*, our gracious *Master*, kind as just,
Knowing our frame, remembers we are dust."—*Barbauld.*

OBSERVATIONS ON RULE III.

Obs. 1.—*Apposition* is that peculiar relation which one noun or pronoun bears to an other, when two or more are placed together in the same case, and used to designate the same person or thing: as, "*Cicero* the *orator*;"—"The *prophet Joel*;"—"*He* of Gath, *Goliah*;"—"Which ye *yourselves* do know;"—"To make *him king*;"—"To give his *life* a *ransom* for many;"—"I made the *ground* my *bed*;"—"*I*, thy *schoolmaster*;"—"*We* the *People* of the United States." This placing-together of nouns and pronouns in the same case, was reckoned by the old grammarians a *figure of syntax*; and from them it received, in their elaborate detail of the grammatical and rhetorical figures, its present name of *apposition*. They reckoned it a species of *ellipsis*, and supplied between the words, the participle *being*, the infinitive *to be*, or some other part of their "*substantive verb*:" as, "Cicero *being* the orator;"—"To make him *to be* king;"—"I *who am* thy schoolmaster." But the later Latin grammarians have usually placed it among their regular concords; some calling it the first concord, while others make it the last, in the series; and

* Priestley cites these examples as *authorities*, not as *false syntax*. The errors which I thus quote at secondhand from other grammarians, and mark with double references, are in general such as the first quoters have allowed, and made themselves responsible for; but this is not the case in every instance. Such credit has sometimes, though rarely, been given, where the expression was disapproved.—G. BROWN.

some, with no great regard to consistency, treating it both as a figure and as a regular concord, at the same time.

Obs. 2.—Some English grammarians teach, " that the words in the cases preceding and following the verb *to be*, may be said to be *in apposition* to each other."—*Murray's Gram.* 8vo, p. 181; *R. C. Smith's*, 155; *Fisk's*, 126; *Ingersoll's*, 146; *Merchant's*, 91. But this is entirely repugnant to the doctrine, that apposition is a *figure;* nor is it at all consistent with the original meaning of the word *apposition;* because it assumes that the literal reading, when the supposed ellipsis is supplied, is *apposition* still. The old distinction, however, between apposition and same cases, is *generally* preserved in our grammars, and is worthy ever to be so. The rule for *some cases* applies to all nouns or pronouns that are put after verbs or participles not transitive, and that are made to agree in case with other nouns or pronouns going before, and meaning the same thing. But some teachers who observe this distinction with reference to the neuter verb *be*, and to certain passive verbs of *naming, appointing*, and the like, absurdly break it down in relation to other verbs, neuter or active-intransitive. Thus Nixon: "Nouns in apposition are in the same case; as, '*Hortensius* died a *martyr;*' '*Sydney* lived the shepherd's *friend*.' "—*English Parser*, p. 54. It is remarkable that *all* this author's examples of " *nominatives in apposition*," (and he gives eighteen in the exercise,) are precisely of this sort, in which there is really *no apposition at all.*

Obs. 3.—In the exercise of parsing, rule third should be applied only to the *explanatory term;* because the case of the *principal term* depends on its relation to the rest of the sentence, and comes under some other rule. In certain instances, too, it is better to waive the analysis which *might* be made under rule third, and to take both or all the terms together, under the rule for the main relation. Thus, the several proper names which distinguish an individual, are always in apposition, and should be taken together in parsing; as, *William Pitt—Marcus Tullius Cicero*. It may, I think, be proper to include with the personal names, some titles also; as, *Lord Bacon—Sir Isaac Newton*. Wm. E. Russell and Jonathan Ware, (two American authors of no great note,) in parsing the name of "*George Washington*," absurdly take the former word as an *adjective* belonging to the latter. See *Russell's Gram.* p. 100; and *Ware's*, 17. R. C. Smith does the same, both with honorary titles, and with baptismal or Christian names. See his *New Gram.* p. 97. And one English writer, in explaining the phrases, *John Wickliffe's influence*," "*Robert Bruce's exertions*," and the like, will have the first nouns to be governed by the last, and the intermediate ones to be distinct possessives *in apposition* with the former. See *Nixon's English Parser*, p. 59. Wm. B. Fowle, in his "True English Grammar," takes all titles, all given names, all possessives, and all pronouns, to be adjectives. According to him, this class embraces more than half the words in the language. A later writer than any of these says, " The proper noun is *philosophically* an adjective. Nouns common or proper, of similar or dissimilar import, *may be parsed as adjectives*, when they become qualifying or distinguishing words; as, *President* Madison,—*Doctor* Johnson,—*Mr.* Webster,—*Esq.* Carleton,—*Miss* Gould,—*Professor* Ware,—*lake* Erie,—the *Pacific* ocean,—*Franklin* House,—*Union* street."—*Sanborn's Gram.* p. 134. I dissent from all these views, at least so far as not to divide a *man's name* in parsing it. A person will sometimes have such a multitude of names, that it would be a flagrant waste of time, to parse them all separately; for example, that wonderful doctor, *Paracelsus*, who called himself, "*Aureolus Philippus Theophrastus Bombastus Paracelsus de Hoenheim*."—*Univ. Biog. Dict.*

Obs. 4.—A very common rule for apposition in Latin, is this: "Substantives signifying the same thing, agree in case."—*Adam's Latin Gram.* p. 156. The same has also been applied to our language: "Substantives denoting the same person or thing, agree in case."—*Bullions's E. Gram.* p. 102. This rule is, for two reasons, very faulty: first, because the apposition of *pronouns* seems not to be included in it; secondly, because two nouns that are not in the same case, do sometimes "signify" or "denote" the same thing. Thus, "*the city of London*," means only the *city* London; "*the land of Egypt*," is only *Egypt;* and "*the person of Richard*," is *Richard himself*. Dr. Webster defines apposition to be, "The placing of two nouns in the same case, without a connecting word between them."—*Octavo Dict.* This, too, excludes the pronouns, and has exceptions, both various and numerous. In the first place, the apposition may be of more than two nouns, without any connective; as, "*Ezra the priest*, the *scribe* of the law."—*Ezra*, vii, 21. Secondly, two nouns connected by a conjunction, may both be put in apposition with a preceding noun or pronoun; as, "God hath made that same *Jesus*, whom ye have crucified, both *Lord* and *Christ*."—*Acts*, ii, 36. "Who made *me* a *judge* or a *divider* over you."—*Luke*, xii, 14. Thirdly, the apposition may be of two nouns immediately connected by *and*, provided the two words denote but one person or thing; as, "This great *philosopher and statesman* was bred a printer." Fourthly, it may be of two words connected by *as*, expressing the idea of a partial or assumed identity; as, "Yet count *him* not *as* an *enemy*, but admonish *him as* a brother."—2 *Thess.* iii, 15. "So that *he, as* God, sitteth in the temple of God."—*Ib.* ii, 4. Fifthly, it may perhaps be of two words connected by *than;* as, "He left *them* no more *than* dead *men*."—*Law and Grace*, p. 23. Lastly, there is a near resemblance to apposition, when two equivalent nouns are connected by *or;* as, "The back of the hedgehog is covered with *prickles, or spines*."—*Webster's Dict.*

Obs. 5.—To the rule for apposition, as I have expressed it, there are properly *no exceptions*. But there are many puzzling examples of construction under it, some of which are but little short of exceptions; and upon such of these as are most likely to embarrass the learner, some further observations shall be made. The rule supposes the first word to be the principal term, with which the other word, or subsequent noun or pronoun, is in apposition; and it generally is so: but the *explanatory* word is sometimes placed first, especially among the poets; as,

"From bright'ning fields of ether fair disclos'd,
     Child of the sun, refulgent *Summer* comes."—*Thomson.*

Obs. 6.—The pronouns of the *first* and *second* persons are often placed before nouns merely to distinguish their person; as, "*I John* saw these things."—*Bible.* "But what is this to *you receivers!*" —*Clarkson's Essay on Slavery*, p. 103. "His praise, ye *brooks*, attune."—*Thomson.* In this case of apposition, the words are in general closely united, and either of them may be taken as the explanatory term. The learner will find it easier to parse *the noun* by rule third; or *both nouns*, if there be two: as, "*I* thy *father-in-law Jethro* am come unto thee."—*Exod.* xviii, 6. There are many other examples, in which it is of no moment, which of the terms we take for the principal; and to all such the rule may be applied literally: as, "Thy *son Benhadad king* of Syria hath sent me to thee."—2 *Kings*, viii, 9.

Obs. 7.—When two or more nouns of the *possessive case* are put in apposition, the possessive termination added to one, denotes the case of both or all: as, "For *Herodias'* sake, his *brother Philip's wife*."—*Matt.* xiv. 3; *Mark*, vi, 17. Here *wife* is in apposition with *Herodias'*, and *brother* with *Philip's*; consequently all these words are reckoned to be in the possessive case. The Greek text, which is better, stands essentially thus: "For the sake of Herodias, the wife of Philip his brother." "For *Jacob* my *servant's* sake, and *Israel* mine *elect*."—*Isaiah*, xlv, 4. Here, as *Jacob* and *Israel* are only different names for the same person or nation, the four nouns in Italics are, according to the rule, all made possessives by the one sign used; but the construction is not to be commended: it would be better to say, "For *the* sake *of* Jacob my servant, and Israel mine elect." "With *Hyrcanus* the high *priest's* consent."—*Wood's Dict. w. Herod.* "I called at *Smith's*, the *bookseller*; or, at *Smith* the *bookseller's*."—*Bullions's E. Gram.* p. 105. Two words, each having the possessive sign, can never be in apposition one with the other; because that sign has immediate reference to the governing noun expressed or understood after it; and if it be repeated, separate governing nouns will be implied, and the apposition will be destroyed.•

Obs. 8.—If the foregoing remark is just, the apposition of two nouns in the possessive case, requires the possessive sign to be added to that noun which immediately precedes the governing word, whether expressed or understood, and positively excludes it from the other. The sign of the case is added, sometimes to the former, and sometimes to the latter noun, but never to both: or, if added to both, the two words are no longer in apposition. Example: "And for that reason they ascribe to him a great part of his *father Nimrod's*, or *Belus's* actions."—*Rollin's An. Hist.* Vol. ii, p. 6. Here *father* and *Nimrod's* are in strict apposition; but if *actions* governs *Belus's*, the same word is implied to govern *Nimrod's*, and the two names are not in apposition, though they are in the same case and mean the same person.

Obs. 9.—Dr. Priestley says, "Some would say, 'I left the parcel at Mr. *Smith's* the *bookseller*;' others, ' at Mr. *Smith* the *bookseller's*;' and perhaps others, at ' Mr. *Smith's* the *bookseller's*.' The last of these forms is most agreeable to the Latin idiom, but the first seems to be more natural in ours; and if the addition consist [*consists*, says Murray,] of two or more words, *the case seems to be very clear*; as, 'I left the parcel at Mr. *Smith's* the *bookseller and stationer*;' i. e. at Mr. Smith's, *who is a* bookseller and stationer."—*Priestley's Gram.* p. 70. Here the examples, if rightly pointed, *would all be right*; but the ellipsis supposed, not only destroys the apposition, but converts the explanatory noun into a nominative. And in the phrase, "*at Mr. Smith's, the bookseller's*," there is no apposition, except that of *Mr.* with *Smith's*; for the governing noun *house* or *store* is understood as clearly after the one possessive sign as after the other. Churchill imagines that in Murray's example, "I reside at Lord *Stormont's*, my old *patron* and *benefactor*," the last two nouns are in the nominative after "*who was*," understood; and also erroneously suggests, that their joint apposition with *Stormont's* might be secured, by saying, less elegantly, "I reside at Lord *Stormont's*, my old patron and *benefactor's*."—*Churchill's New Gram.* p. 285. Lindley Murray, who tacitly takes from Priestley all that is quoted above, except the term "*Mr.*," and the notion of an elipsis of "*who is*," assumes each of the three forms as an instance of apposition, but pronounces the first only to be "correct and proper." If, then, the first is elliptical, as Priestley suggests, and the others are ungrammatical, as Murray pretends to prove, we cannot have in reality any such construction as the apposition of two possessives; for the sign of the case cannot possibly be added in more than these three ways. But Murray does not adhere at all to his own decision, as may be seen by his subsequent remarks and examples, on the same page: as, "The *emperor Leopold's*;"—"*Dionysius* the *tyrant's*;"—"For *David* my *servant's* sake;" "Give me here *John* the *Baptist's* head;"—"Paul the *apostle's* advice." See *Murray's Gram.* 8vo, p. 176; *Smith's New Gram.* p. 150; and others.

Obs. 10.—An explanatory noun without the possessive sign, seems sometimes to be put in apposition with a *pronoun of the possessive case*; and, if introduced by the conjunction *as*, it may either precede or follow the pronoun: thus, "I rejoice in *your* success *as* an *instructer*."—*Sanborn's Gram.* p. 244. "*As* an *author*, his 'Adventurer' is *his* capital work."—*Murray's Sequel*, p. 329.

"Thus shall mankind *his* guardian care engage,
The promised *father* of a future age."—*Pope*.

But possibly such examples may be otherwise explained on the principle of ellipsis; as, [*He being*] "the promised *father*," &c. "As [*he was*] an *author*," &c. "As [*you are*] an *instructer*."

Obs. 11.—When a noun or pronoun *is repeated* for the sake of emphasis, or for the adding of an epithet, the word which is repeated may properly be said to be in apposition with that which is first introduced; or, if not, the repetition itself implies sameness of case: as, "They have forsaken

_____

• Lindley Murray thought it not impracticable to put two or more nouns in apposition and add the possessive sign to each; nor did he imagine there would often be any positive impropriety in so doing. His words, on this point, are these: "On the other hand, the application of the *genitive* sign to both or all of the nouns in apposition, would be *generally* harsh and displeasing, and *perhaps in some cases incorrect*: as, 'The Emperor's Leopold's'; King's George's; Charles's the Second's; The parcel was left at Smith's, the bookseller's and stationer's.'"—*Octavo Gram.* p. 177. Whether he imagined *any of these* to be "*incorrect*" or not, does not appear! Under the next rule, I shall give a short note which will show them *all* to be so. The author, however, after presenting these uncouth fictions, which show nothing but his own deficiency in grammar, has done the world the favour not to pronounce them *very convenient* phrases; for he continues the paragraph as follows: "The rules which we have endeavoured to elucidate, will prevent the *inconveniences* of both these modes of expression; and they appear to be *simple, perspicuous*, and *consistent* with the idiom of the language."—*Ib.* This undeserved praise of his own rules, he might as well have left to some other hand. They have had the fortune, however, to please sundry critics, and to become the prey of many thieves; but are certainly very deficient in the three qualities here named; and, taken together with their illustrations, they form little else than a tissue of errors, partly his own, and partly copied from Lowth and Priestley.

me, the *fountain* of living waters, and hewed them out *cisterns*, broken *cisterns*, that can hold no water."—*Jer.* ii, 13.

> "I find the total of their hopes and fears
> *Dreams*, empty *dreams*."—*Cowper's Task*, p. 71.

OBS. 12.—A noun is sometimes put, as it were, in apposition to a *sentence;* being used (perhaps elliptically) to sum up the whole idea in one emphatic word, or short phrase. But, in such instances, the noun can seldom be said to have any positive relation that may determine its case; and, if alone, it will of course be in the nominative, by reason of its independence. Examples: "He permitted me to consult his library,—a *kindness* which I shall not forget."—*W. Allen's Gram.* p. 143. "I have offended reputation; a most unnoble *swerving*."—*Shakspeare.* "I want a hero, —an uncommon *want*."—*Byron.* "Lopez took up the sonnet, and after reading it several times, frankly acknowledged that he did not understand it himself; a *discovery* which the poet probably never made before."—*Campbell's Rhet.* p. 280.

> "In Christian hearts O for a pagan zeal!
> A needful, but opprobrious *prayer!*"—*Young*, N. ix, l. 995.
> "Great standing *miracle*, that Heav'n assign'd
> Its only thinking thing this turn of mind."—*Pope.*

OBS. 13.—A *distributive* term in the singular number, is frequently construed in apposition with a comprehensive plural; as, "*They* reap vanity, *every one* with his neighbour."—*Bible.* "Go ye *every man* unto his city."—*Ibid.* So likewise with two or more singular nouns which are taken conjointly; as, "The *Son and Spirit* have *each* his proper office."—*Butler's Analogy*, p. 163. And sometimes a *plural* word is emphatically put after a series of particulars comprehended under it; as, "Ambition, interest, glory, *all* concurred."—*Letters on Chivalry*, p. 11. "Royalists, republicans, churchmen, sectaries, courtiers, patriots, *all parties* concurred in the illusion." —*Hume's History*, Vol. viii, p. 73. The foregoing examples are plain, but similar expressions sometimes require care, lest the distributive or collective term be so placed that its construction and meaning may be misapprehended. Examples: "We have *turned every one* to his own way." —*Isaiah*, liii, 6. Better: "*We have every one* turned to his own way." "For in many things we *offend all*."—*James*, iii, 2. Better: "For in many things *we all* offend." The latter readings doubtless convey the *true sense* of these texts. To the relation of apposition, it may be proper also to refer the construction of a singular noun taken in a distributive sense and repeated after *by* to denote order; as, "*They* went out *one* by one."—*Bible.* "Our whole *company, man by* man, ventured in."—*Goldsmith.* "To examine a *book, page* by page; to search a *place, house* by house."—*Ward's Gram.* p. 106. So too, perhaps, when the parts of a thing explain the whole; as,

> "But those that sleep, and think not on their sins,
> Pinch *them, arms, legs, backs, shoulders, sides,* and *shins*."—*Shak.*

OBS. 14.—To express a reciprocal action or relation, the pronominal adjectives *each other* and *one an other* are employed: as, "They love *each other;*"—"They love *one an other*." The words, separately considered, are singular; but, taken together, they imply plurality; and they can be properly construed only after plurals, or singulars taken conjointly. *Each other* is usually applied to two persons or things; and *one an other*, to more than two. The impropriety of applying them otherwise, is noticed elsewhere; (see, in Part II, Obs. 15th, on the Classes of Adjectives;) so that we have here to examine only their relations of *case*. The terms, though reciprocal and closely united, are seldom or never in the same construction. If such expressions be analyzed, *each* and *one* will generally appear to be in the nominative case, and *other* in the objective; as, "They love *each other;*" i. e. *each loves the other*. "They love *one an other;*" i. e. any or every *one* loves any or every *other*. *Each* and *one* (—if the words be taken as cases, and not adjectively,)—are properly in agreement or apposition with *they*, and *other* is governed by the verb. The terms, however, admit of other constructions; as, "Be ye helpers *one* of an *other*."—*Bible.* Here *one* is in apposition with *ye*, and *other* is governed by *of*. "Ye are *one* an *other's* joy."—*Ib.* Here *one* is in apposition with *ye*, and *other's* is in the possessive case, being governed by *joy*. "Love will make you *one* an *other's* joy." Here *one* is in the objective case, being in apposition with *you*, and *other's* is governed as before. "*Men's* confidence in *one an other;*"—"*Their* dependence *one* upon an *other*." Here the word *one* appears to be in apposition with the possessive going before; for it has already been shown, that words standing in that relation *never take the possessive sign*. But if its location after the preposition must make it objective, the *whole* object is the complex term, "*one an other*." "Grudge not *one against an other*."—*James*, v, 9. "Ne vous plaignez point *les uns des autres*."—*French Bible.* "Ne auspirate *alius* adversus *alium*."—*Beza.* "Ne ingemiscite adversus *alii alios*."—*Leusden.* "Μὴ στενάζετε κατ' ἀλλήλων."—*Greek New Testament.*

OBS. 15.—The construction of the Latin terms *alius alium, alii alios*, &c., with that of the French *l'un l'autre, l'un de l'autre*, &c., appears, at first view, sufficiently to confirm the doctrine of the preceding observation; but, besides the frequent use, in Latin and Greek, of a reciprocal *adverb* to express the meaning of *one an other* or *each other*, there are, from each of these languages, some analogical arguments for taking the English terms together as compounds. The most common term in Greek for *one an other*, (Ἀλλήλων dat. ἀλλήλοις, αις, οις, acc. ἀλλήλους, ab ἄλλος, *alius*,) is a single derivative word, the case of which is known by its termination; and *each other* is sometimes expressed in Latin by a compound: as, "Et osculantes se *alterutrum*, fleverunt pariter."—*Vulgate.* That is: "And kissing *each other*, they wept together." As the text speaks of but two persons, our translators have not expressed it well in the common version: "And they kissed *one an other*, and wept *one* with an *other*."—1 *Sam.* xx, 41. *Alterutrum* is composed of a nominative and an accusative, like *each-other;* and, in the nature of things, there is no reason why the former should be compounded, and the latter not. Ordinarily, these seems to be no need of compounding either of them. But some examples occur, in which it is not easy to parse *each other* and *one an other* otherwise than as compounds: as, "He only recommended this, and not the washing of *one another's* feet."—*Barclay's Works*, Vol. iii, p. 142.

"The Temple late two brother sergeants saw,
Who deem'd *each other oracles* of law."—*Pope*, B. ii, Ep. 2.*

Obs. 16.—The *common* and the *proper* name of an object are very often associated, and put in apposition; as, "*The river Thames*,"—"*The ship Albion*,"—"*The poet Cowper*,"—"*Lake Erie*," —"*Cape May*,"—"*Mount Atlas*." But, in English, the proper name of a *place*, when accompanied by the common name, is generally put in the objective case, and preceded by *of*; as, "The city *of* New York,"—"The land *of* Canaan,"—"The island *of* Cuba,"—"The peninsula *of* Yucatan." Yet in some instances, even of this kind, the immediate apposition is preferred; as, "That the *city Sepphoris* should be subordinate to the *city Tiberias*."—*Life of Josephus*, p. 142. In the following sentence, the preposition *of* is at least needless: "The law delighteth herself in the number *of* twelve; and the number *of* twelve is much respected in holy writ."—*Coke, on Juries*. Two or three late grammarians, supposing *of* always to indicate a possessive relation between one thing and an other, contend that it is no less improper, to say, "The city *of* London, the city *of* New Haven, the month *of* March, the islands *of* Cuba and Hispaniola, the towns *of* Exeter and Dover," than to say, "King *of* Solomon, Titus *of* the Roman Emperor, Paul *of* the apostle, or, Cicero *of* the orator."—See *Barrett's Gram.* p. 101; *Emmons's*, 16. I cannot but think there is some mistake in their mode of finding out what is proper or improper in grammar. Emmons scarcely achieved two pages more, before he forgot his criticism, and adopted the phrase, "in the city *of* New Haven."—*Gram.* p. 19.

Obs. 17.—When an object acquires a new name or character from the action of a verb, the new appellation is put in apposition with the object of the active verb, and in the nominative after the passive: as, "They named the *child John*;"—"The child was named *John*."—"They elected *him president*;"—"He was elected *president*." After the active verb, the acquired name must be parsed by Rule 3d; after the passive, by Rule 6th. In the following example, the pronominal adjective *some*, or the noun *men* understood after it, is the direct object of the verb *gave*, and the nouns expressed are in apposition with it: "And he gave *some, apostles*; and *some, prophets*; and *some, evangelists*; and *some, pastors* and *teachers*."—*Ephesians*, iv, 11. That is, "He *bestowed some* [men] as *apostles*; and *some* as *prophets*; and *some* as *evangelists*; and *some* as *pastors* and *teachers*." The common reader might easily mistake the meaning and construction of this text, in two different ways; for he might take *some* to be either a *dative case*, meaning *to some persons*, or an adjective to the nouns which are here expressed. The punctuation, however, is calculated to show that the nouns are in apposition with *some*, or *some men*, in what the Latins call *the accusative case*. But the version ought to be amended by the insertion of *as*, which would here be an express sign of the apposition intended.

Obs. 18.—Some authors teach that words in apposition must agree in person, number, and gender, as well as in case; but such agreement the following examples show not to be always necessary: "The *Franks, a people* of Germany."—*W. Allen's Gram*. "The Kenite *tribe*, the *descendants* of Hobab."—*Milman's Hist. of the Jews*. "But how can you a *soul*, still either hunger or thirst?"—*Lucian's Dialogues*, p 14. "Who seized the wife of *me* his *host*, and fled.—*Ib*. p. 16.

"Thy gloomy *grandeurs* (Nature's most august,
Inspiring *aspect!*) claim a grateful verse."—*Young*, N. ix, l. 566.

IMPROPRIETIES FOR CORRECTION.

FALSE SYNTAX UNDER RULE III.

ERRORS OF WORDS IN APPOSITION.

"Now, therefore, come thou, let us make a covenant, I and thou."—*Gen.* xxxi, 44.

[FORMULE.—Not proper, because the pronouns *I* and *thou*, of the nominative case, are here put in apposition with the preceding pronoun *us*, which is objective. But, according to Rule 3d, "A noun or a personal pronoun, used to explain a preceding noun or pronoun, is put, by apposition, in the same case." Therefore, *I* and *thou* should be *thee* and *me*; (the first person, in our idiom, being usually put last;) thus, "Now, therefore, come thou, let *us* make a covenant, *thee* and *me*."]

"Now, therefore, come thou, we will make a covenant, thee and me."—*Variation of Gen.*

---

* In Professor Fowler's recent and copious work, "The English Language in its Elements and Forms," our present *Reciprocals* are called, not *Pronominal Adjectives*, but "*Pronouns*," and are spoken of, in the first instance, thus: "§ 248. A RECIPROCAL PRONOUN is *one* that implies the mutual action of different agents. EACH OTHER, and ONE ANOTHER, are our reciprocal forms, *which are treated exactly as if they were compound pronouns*, taking for their genitives, *each other's, one another's*. Each other is properly used of *two*, and *one another* of *more*." The definition here given takes for granted what is at least disputable, that "*each other*," or "*one another*," is not a *phrase*, but is merely "*one pronoun*." But, to none of his three important positions here taken, does the author himself at all adhere. In § 451, at Note 8, he teaches thus: "'They love each other.' Here *each* is in the nominative case in apposition with *they*, and *other* is in the objective case. 'They helped one another.' Here *one* is in apposition with *they*, and *another* is in the objective case." Now, by this mode of parsing, the reciprocal terms "are treated," not as "compound pronouns," but as phrases consisting of distinct or separable words: and, as being separate or separable words, whether they be Adjectives or Pronouns, they conform not to his definition above. Out of the sundry instances in which, according to his own showing, he has misapplied one or the other of these phrases, I cite the following: (1.) "The *two* ideas of Science and Art differ from *one another* as the understanding differs from the will."—*Fowler's Gram.* 1850, § 180. Say—"from *each other*;" or—"*one* from the *other*." (2.) "THOU, THY, THEE, are etymologically related to *each other*."—*Ib.* § 216. Say—"to *one* another;" because there are *more* than *two*." (3.) "Till within some centuries, the Germans, like the French and the English, addressed *each other* in familiar conversation by the Second Person Singular."—*Ib.* § 231. Say—"addressed *one as another*." (4.) "*Two* sentences are, on the other hand, connected in the way of co-ordination [,] when they are not thus dependent one upon *another*."—*Ib.* § 332. Say—"upon *each other*;" or—"*one* upon *the other*;" because there are but two. (5.) "These *two* rivers are at a great distance from one *another*."—*Ib.* § 617. Say—"from *each other*;" or—"*one from* the *other*." (6.) "The trees [in the *Forest of Bombast*] are close, spreading, and twined into *each other*."—*Ib.* § 617. Say—"into *one an other*."

"The word came not to Esau, the hunter, that stayed not at home; but to Jacob, the plain man, he that dwelt in tents."—*Wm. Penn.* "Not to every man, but to the man God, (i. e.) he that is led by the spirit of God."—*Barclay's Works,* i, 266. "For, admittin God 'to be a creditor, or he to whom the debt should be paid, and Christ he that satisf or pays it on the behalf of man the debtor, this question will arise, whether he paid th debt as God, or man, or both?"—*Wm. Penn.* "This Lord Jesus Christ, the heavenly M the Emmanuel, God with us, we own and believe in: he whom the high priests rag against," &c.—*George Fox.* "Christ, and Him crucified, was the Alpha and Omega of his addresses, the fountain and foundation of his hope and labour."—*Experience of Paul,* 399. "'Christ and Him crucified' is the head, and the only head, of the church."—*De son's Sermon.* "But if 'Christ and Him crucified' are the burden of the ministry, su disastrous results are all avoided."—*Ib.* "He never let fall the least intimation, that himse or any other person, whomsoever, was the object of worship."—*Hannah Adams's View,* 250. "Let the elders that rule well, be counted worthy of double honour, especially th who labour in the word and doctrine."—*1 Tim.* v, 17. "Our Shepherd, him who is styl King of saints, will assuredly give his saints the victory."—*Sermon.* "It may seem o to talk of *we subscribers.*"—*Fowle's True Eng. Gram.* p. 20. "And they shall have none bury them, them, their wives, nor their sons, nor their daughters; for I will pour the wickedness upon them."—*Jeremiah,* xiv, 16. "Yet I supposed it necessary to send to y Epaphroditus, my brother, and companion in labour, and fellow-soldier, but your messe ger, and he that ministered to my wants."—*Philippians,* ii, 25.

"Amidst the tumult of the routed train,
The sons of false Antimachus were slain;
He, who for bribes his faithless counsels sold,
And voted Helen's stay for Paris' gold."—*Pope, Iliad,* B. xi, l. 161.
"See the vile King his iron sceptre bear —
His only praise attends the pious Heir;
He, in whose soul the virtues all conspire,
The best good son, from the worst wicked sire."—Dr. LOWTH: *Union Poems,* p. 1
"Then from thy lips poured forth a joyful song
To thy Redeemer!—yea, it poured along
In most melodious energy of praise,
To God, the Saviour, he of ancient days."—*Arm Chair,* p. 15.

RULE IV.—POSSESSIVES.

A Noun or a Pronoun in the possessive case, is governed by the name o the thing possessed: as, "*God's* mercy prolongs *man's* life."—*Allen.*

"*Theirs* is the vanity, the learning *thine;*
Touch'd by *thy* hand, ag* in *Rome's* glories shine."—*Pope.*

OBSERVATIONS ON RULE IV.

OBS. 1.—Though the *ordinary* syntax of the possessive case is sufficiently plain and easy there is perhaps, among all the puzzling and disputable points of grammar, nothing more diffi cult of decision, than are some questions that occur respecting the right management of the case. That its usual construction is both clearly and properly stated in the foregoing rule, is what none will doubt or deny. But how many and what exceptions to this rule ought to be allowed, or whether any are justly demanded or not, are matters about which there may be much diversity of opinion. Having heretofore published the rule without any express exceptions, I am not now convinced that it is best to add any; yet are there three different modes of expression which might be plausibly exhibited in that character. Two of these would concern only the parser; and, for that reason, they seem not to be very important. The other involves the ap proval or reprehension of a great multitude of very common expressions, concerning which our ablest grammarians differ in opinion, and our most popular digest plainly contradicts itself. These points are; *first,* the apposition of possessives, and the supposed ellipses which may affect that construction; *second y,* the government of the possessive case after *is, was,* &c., when the ownership of a thing is simply affirmed or denied; *thirdly,* the government of the possessive by a participle. *as such*—that is, while it retains the government and adjuncts of a participle.

OBS. 2.—The apposition of one possessive with an other, (as, "For *David* my *servant's* sake,") might doubtless be consistently made a formal exception to the direct government of the posses sive by its controlling noun. But this apposition is only a sameness of construction, so that what governs the one, virtually governs the other. And if the case of any noun or pronoun is known and determined by the rule or relation of apposition, there can be no need of an exception to the foregoing rule for the purpose of parsing it, since that purpose is already answered by rule third. If the reader, by supposing an ellipsis which I should not, will resolve any given instance of this kind into something else than apposition, I have already shown him that some great gram marians have differed in the same way before. Useless ellipses, however, should never be sup posed; and such *perhaps* is the following: "At Mr. Smith's [*who is*] the bookseller."—See Dr. *Priestley's Gram.* p. 71.

OBS 3.—In all our Latin grammars, the verb *sum, fui, esse,* to be, is said (though not with strict propriety) sometimes to *signify* possession, property, or duty, and in that sense to govern the genitive case: as, "*Est regis;*"—"It is the king's."—"*Hominis est errare;*"—"It is man's to err."—"*Pecus est Meliboei;*"—"The flock is Meliboeus's." And sometimes, with like import, this verb, expressed or understood, may govern the dative; as, "*Ego* [sum] *dilecto meo, et dilectus meus* [est] *mihi.*"—*Vulgate.* "I am my beloved's, and my beloved is mine."—*Solomon's Song,* vi, 3. Here, as both the genitive and the dative are expressed in English by the possessive, if the former are governed by the verb, there seems to be precisely the same reason from the nature of the expression, and an additional one from analogy, for considering the latter to be so too. But all the annotators upon the Latin syntax suggest, that the genitive thus put after *sum* or *est,* is really governed, not by the verb, but by some *noun understood;* and with this idea, of an ellipsis in the construction, all our English grammarians appear to unite. They might not, however, find it very easy to tell by what noun the word *beloved's* or *mine* is governed, in the last example above; and so of many others, which are used in the same way: as, "There shall nothing die of all that is the *children's* of Israel."—*Exod.* ix, 4. The Latin here is, "Ut nihil omninò pereat ex his *quæ pertinent ad* filios Israël."—*Vulgate.* That is,—"of all those *which belong to* the children of Israel."

> "For thou art *Freedom's* now—and *Fame's,*
> One of the few, the immortal names
> That were not born to die."—HALLECK: *Marco Bozzaris.*

OBS. 4.—Although the possessive case is always intrinsically an *adjunct,* and therefore incapable of being used or comprehended in any sense that is positively abstract; yet we see that there are instances in which it is used with a certain degree of abstraction,—that is, with an actual separation from the name of the thing possessed; and that accordingly there are, in the simple personal pronouns, (where such a distinction is most needed,) two different forms of the case; the one adapted to the concrete, and the other to the abstract construction. That form of the pronoun, however, which is equivalent in sense to the concrete and the noun, is still the possessive case, and nothing more; as, "And all *mine* are *thine,* and *thine* are *mine.*"—*John,* xvii, 10. For if we suppose this equivalence to prove such a pronoun to be something more than the possessive case, as do some grammarians, we must suppose the same thing respecting the possessive case of a noun, whenever the relation of ownership or possession is simply affirmed or denied with such a noun put last: as, "For all things are *yours;* and ye are *Christ's;* and Christ is *God's.*"—1 *Cor.* iii, 21. By the second example placed under the rule, I meant to suggest, that the possessive case, when placed before or after this verb, (*be,*) *might* be parsed as being governed by the nominative; as we may suppose "*theirs*" to be governed by "*vanity,*" and "*thine*" by "*learning,*" these nouns being the names of the things possessed. But then we encounter a difficulty, whenever a *pronoun* happens to be the nominative; as, "Therefore glorify God in your body, and in your spirit, *which are God's.*"—1 *Cor.* vi, 20. Here the common resort would be to some ellipsis; and yet it must be confessed, that this mode of interpretation cannot but make some difference in the sense: as, "If ye be *Christ's,* then are ye Abraham's seed."—*Gal.* iii, 29. Here some may think the meaning to be, "If ye be *Christ's seed,* or *children.*" But a truer version of the text would be, "If ye *are of Christ,* then are ye Abraham's seed."—"Que si vous *êtes à Christ,* vous êtes donc la postérité d'Abraham."—*French Bible.*

OBS. 5.—Possession is the having of something, and if the possessive case is always an adjunct, referring either directly or indirectly to that which constitutes it a possessive, it would seem but reasonable, to limit the government of this case to that part of speech which is understood *substantively*—that is, to "the *name* of the thing possessed." Yet, in violation of this restriction, many grammarians admit, that a *participle,* with the regimen and adjuncts of a participle, may govern the possessive case; and some of them, at the same time, with astonishing inconsistency, aver, that the possessive case before a participle converts the latter into a noun, and necessarily deprives it of its regimen. Whether participles are worthy to form an exception to my rule or not, this palpable contradiction is one of the gravest faults of L. Murray's code of syntax. After copying from Lowth the doctrine that a participle with an *article* before it becomes a noun, and must drop the government and adjuncts of a participle, this author informs us, that the same principles are applicable to the *pronoun* and participle: as, "Much depends on *their observing of* the rule, and error will be the consequence of *their neglecting of* it;" in stead of, "*their observing the rule,*" and "*their neglecting it.*" And this doctrine he applies, with yet more positiveness, to the *noun* and participle; as if the error were still more glaring, to make an active participle govern a possessive *noun:* saying, "We shall perceive this *more clearly,* if we substitute a noun for the pronoun: as, 'Much depends upon *Tyro's observing of* the rule,' &c.; which is the same as, 'Much depends on Tyro's *observance* of the rule.' But, as this construction sounds rather *harshly,* it would, in general, be better to express the sentiment in the following, or some other form: 'Much depends on the *rule's being observed;* and error will be the consequence of *its being neglected:*' or—'on *observing the rule;* and—*of neglecting it.*'"—*Murray's Gram.* 8vo, p. 193; *Ingersoll's,* 199; and others.

OBS. 6.—Here it is assumed, that "*their observing the rule,*" or "*Tyro's observing the rule,*" is an ungrammatical phrase; and, several different methods being suggested for its correction, a preference is at length given to what is perhaps not less objectionable than the original phrase itself. The last form offered, "*on observing the rule,*" &c., is indeed correct enough in itself; but, as a substitute for the other, it is both inaccurate and insufficient. It merely omits the possessive case, and leaves the action of the participle undetermined in respect to the agent. For the possessive case before a real participle, denotes not the possessor of something, as in other instances, but the agent of the action, or the subject of the being or passion; and the simple question here is, whether this extraordinary use of the possessive case is, or is not, such an idiom of our language as ought to be justified. Participles may become nouns, if we choose to use them substantively; but can they govern the possessive case before them, while they govern also the objective after them, or while they have a participial meaning which is qualified by adverbs? If they can, Lowth, Murray, and others, are wrong in supposing the foregoing phrases to be ungrammatical, and in teaching that the possessive case before a participle converts it into a noun; and if they cannot, Priestley, Murray, Hiley, Wells, Weld, and others, are wrong in supposing that a participle, or a phrase beginning with a participle, may properly govern the possessive case. Compare Murray's seventh note under his Rule 10th, with the second under his Rule 14th. The same contradiction is taught by many other compilers. See *Smith's New Grammar*, pp. 152 and 162; *Comly's Gram.* 91 and 106; *Ingersoll's*, 180 and 199.

OBS. 7.—Concerning one of the forms of expression which Murray approves and prefers, among his corrections above, the learned doctors Lowth and Campbell appear to have formed very different opinions. The latter, in the chapter which, in his Philosophy of Rhetoric, he devotes to disputed points in syntax, says: "There is only one other observation of Dr. Lowth, on which, before I conclude this article, I must beg leave to offer some remarks. 'Phrases like the following, though very common, are improper: Much depends upon the *rule's being observed;* and error will be the consequence of *its being neglected.* For here *is* a noun *and* a pronoun representing it, each in the possessive case, that is, under the government of another noun, but without other noun to govern it: for *being observed,* and *being neglected,* are not nouns: nor can you supply the place of the possessive case by the preposition *of* before the noun or pronoun.'* For my part," continues Campbell, "notwithstanding what is here very speciously urged, I am not satisfied that there is any fault in the phrases censured. They appear to me to be perfectly in the idiom of our tongue, and such as on some occasions could not easily be avoided, unless by recurring to circumlocution, an expedient which invariably tends to enervate the expression."— *Philosophy of Rhetoric,* B. ii, Ch. iv, p. 234.

OBS. 8.—Dr. Campbell, if I understand his argument, defends the foregoing expressions against the objections of Dr. Lowth, not on the ground that participles as such may govern the possessive case, but on the supposition that as the simple active participle may become a noun, and in that character govern the possessive case, so may the passive participle, and with equal propriety, notwithstanding it consists of two or more words, which must in this construction be considered as forming "one compound noun." I am not sure that he means to confine himself strictly to this latter ground, but if he does, his position cannot be said in any respect to contravene my rule for the possessive case. I do not, however, agree with him, either in the opinion which he offers, or in the negative which he attempts to prove. In view of the two examples, "Much depends upon the *rule's being observed,*" and, "Much depends upon *their observing of the rule,*" he says: "Now, although I allow both *the* modes of expression to be good, I think the first *simpler and better* than the second." Then, denying all faults, he proceeds: "Let us consider whether the former be liable to *any objections,* which do not equally affect the latter." But in his argument, he considers only the objections offered by Lowth, which indeed he sufficiently refutes. Now to me there appear to be other objections, which are better founded. In the first place, the two sentences are not equivalent in meaning; hence the preference suggested by this critic and others, is absurd. Secondly, a compound noun formed of two or three words without any hyphen, is at best such an anomaly, as we ought rather to avoid than to prefer. If these considerations do not positively condemn the former construction, they ought at least to prevent it from displacing the latter; and seldom is either to be preferred to the regular noun, which we can limit by the article or the possessive at pleasure: as, "Much depends on *an observance* of the rule."— "Much depends on *their observance* of the rule." Now these two sentences are equivalent to the two former, but not to each other; and, *vice versa:* that is, the two former are equivalent to these, but not to each other.†

OBS. 9.—From Dr. Campbell's commendation of Lowth, as having "given some excellent directions for preserving the proper distinction between the noun and the gerund,"—that is, between the participial noun and the participle,—it is fair to infer that he meant to preserve it himself; and yet, in the argument above mentioned, he appears to have carelessly framed one ambiguous or very erroneous sentence, from which, as I imagine, his views of this matter have been misconceived, and by which Murray and all his modifiers have been furnished with an example wherewith to confound this distinction, and also to contradict themselves. The sentence is this: "Much will depend on *your pupil's composing,* but more on *his reading* frequently."— *Philos. of Rhet.* p. 235. Volumes innumerable have gone abroad, into our schools and elsewhere, which pronounce this sentence to be "correct and proper." But after all, what does it mean? Does the adverb *"frequently"* qualify the verb *"will depend,"* expressed in the sentence? or *"will depend,"* understood after *more?* or both? or neither? Or does this adverb qualify the action of *"reading?"* or the action of *"composing?"* or both? or neither? But *composing* and *reading,* if they are mere *nouns,* cannot properly be qualified by any adverb; and, if they are called participles, the question recurs respecting the possessives. Besides, *composing,* as a Participle, is commonly *transitive;* nor is it very fit for a noun, without some adjunct. And, when participles become nouns, their government (it is said) falls upon *of,* and their adverbs are usually

---

* For this quotation, Dr. Campbell gives, in his margin, the following reference: "Introduction, &c. Sentences, Note on the 6th Phrase." But in my edition of Dr. Lowth's Introduction to English Grammar, (a Philadelphia edition of 1799,) I do *not find* the passage. Perhaps it has been omitted in consequence of Campbell's criticism, of which I here cite but a part.—G. BROWN.

† By some grammarians it is presumed to be consistent with the nature of *participles* to govern the possessive case; and Hiley, if he is to be understood *literally,* assumes it as an "*established principle,*" that they *all do so!* "*Participles* govern nouns and pronouns in the possessive case, and at the same time, if derived from transitive verbs, *require* the noun or pronoun following to be in the objective case, *without the intervention of the preposition of;* as, 'Much depends on *William's observing the rule,* and error will be the consequence of *his neglecting it;*' or, 'Much *will* depend on the *rule's being observed by William,* and error will be the consequence of *its being neglected.*'"—*Hiley's Gram.* p. 94. These sentences, without doubt, are nearly equivalent to each other in meaning. To make them exactly so, "*depends*" or "*will depend*" must be changed in tense, and "*its being neglected*" must be "*its being neglected by him.*" But who that has looked at the facts in the case, or informed himself on the points here in dispute, will maintain that either the awkward phraseology of the latter example, or the mixed and questionable construction of the former, or the extensive rule under which they are here presented, is among "the established principles and best usages of the English language?"—Ib. p. 1.

converted into adjectives; as, "Much will depend on your *pupil's composing of themes*; but more, on *his frequent reading*." This may not be the author's meaning, for the example was originally composed as a mere mock sentence, or by way of "*experiment*;" and one may doubt whether its meaning was ever at all thought of by the philosopher. But, to make it a respectable example, some correction there must be; for, surely, no man can have any clear idea to communicate, which he cannot better express, than by imitating this loose phraseology. It is scarcely more correct, than to say, "Much will depend on *an author's using*, but more on *his learning* frequently." Yet is it commended as a *model*, either entire or in part, by Murray, Ingersoll, Fisk, R. C. Smith, Cooper, Lennie, Hiley, Bullions, C. Adams, A. H. Weld, and I know not how many other school critics.

Obs. 10.—That singular notion, so common in our grammars, that a participle and its adjuncts may form "*one name*," or "*substantive phrase*," and so govern the possessive case, where it is presumed the participle itself could not, is an invention worthy to have been always ascribed to its true author. For this doctrine, as I suppose, our grammarians are indebted to Dr. Priestley. In his grammar it stands thus: "When an *entire clause* of a sentence, beginning with a participle of the present tense, is used as one name, or to express one idea, or circumstance, the noun on which it depends may be put in the genitive case. Thus, instead of saying, *What is the meaning of this lady holding up her train*, i. e. *what is the meaning of the lady in holding up her train*, we may say, *What is the meaning of this* lady's *holding up her train*; just as we say, *What is the meaning of this lady's dress*, &c. So we may either say, *I remember* it being *reckoned a great exploit*; or, perhaps more elegantly, *I remember* its being *reckoned*, &c."—*Priestley's Gram.* p. 69. Now, to say nothing of errors in punctuation, capitals, &c., there is scarcely any thing in all this passage, that is either conceived or worded properly. Yet, coming from a Doctor of Laws, and Fellow of the Royal Society, it is readily adopted by Murray, and for his sake by others; and so, with all its blunders, the vain gloss passes uncensured into the schools, as a rule and model for elegant composition. Dr. Priestley pretends to appreciate the difference between participles and participial nouns, but he rather contrives a fanciful distinction in the sense, than a real one in the construction. His only note on this point,—a note about the "*horse running to-day*," and the "*horse's running* to-day,"—I shall leave till we come to the syntax of participles.

Obs. 11.—Having prepared the reader to understand the origin of what is to follow, I now cite from L. Murray's code a paragraph which appears to be contradictory to his own doctrine, as suggested in the fifth observation above; and not only so, it is irreconcilable with any proper distinction between the participle and the participial noun. "When an *entire clause* of a sentence, beginning with a participle of the present tense, is used as *one name*, or to express one idea or circumstance, the *noun on which it depends* may be put in the *genitive* case; thus, *instead* of saying, 'What is the reason of this *person* dismissing his servant so hastily?' *that* is, 'What is the reason of this person, *in* dismissing his servant so hastily?' we *may* say, and *perhaps* ought to say, 'What is the reason of this *person's* dismissing *of* his servant *so hastily?*' Just as we say, 'What is the reason of this person's *hasty dismission* of his servant?' So also, we say, 'I remember it being reckoned a great exploit;' or more properly, 'I remember *its* being reckoned,' &c. The following sentence is *correct and proper*: 'Much will depend on *the pupil's composing*, but more on *his reading* frequently.' It would not be accurate to say, 'Much will depend on the *pupil composing*,' &c. We also properly say; 'This will be the *effect of the pupil's composing* frequently;' instead of, 'Of the *pupil composing* frequently.' The *participle*, in such constructions, *does the office* of a substantive; and it should therefore have a CORRESPONDENT REGIMEN."—*Murray's Gram.* Rule X, Note 7; *Ingersoll's*, p. 180; *Fisk's*, 108; *R. C. Smith's*, 152; *Alger's*, 61; *Merchant's*, 84. See also *Weld's Gram.* 2d Ed., p. 150; "Abridged Ed.," 117.[*]

Obs. 12.—Now, if it were as easy to prove that a participle, as such, or (what amounts to the same thing) a phrase beginning with a participle, ought never to govern the possessive case, as it is to show that every part and parcel of the foregoing citations from Priestley, Murray, and

---

[*] What, in Weld's "Abridged Edition," is improperly called a "participial *noun*," was, in his "original work," still more erroneously termed "a participial *clause*." This gentleman, who has lately amended his general rule for possessives by wrongfully copying or imitating mine, has also as widely varied his conception of the *participial* —"*object possessed*;" but, in my judgement, a change still greater might not be amiss. "The possessive is often governed by a participial *clause*; as, much will depend on the *pupil's composing* frequently. *Pupil's* is governed by the clause, '*composing frequently*.' NOTE.—The sign ('s) should be annexed to the word governed by the *participial clause* following it."—*Weld's Gram.* 2d Edition, p. 150. Again: "The possessive is often governed by a participial *noun*; as, Much will depend on the *pupil's composing* frequently. *Pupil's* is governed by the participial *noun composing*. NOTE.—The sign ('s) should be annexed to the word governed by the *participial noun* following it."—*Weld's Gram. Abridged*, p. 117. Choosing the possessive case, where, both by analogy and by authority, the objective would be quite as grammatical, if not more so; destroying, as far as possible, all syntactical distinction between the participle and the participial noun, by confounding them purposely, even in name; this author, like Wells, whom he too often imitates, takes no notice of the question here discussed, and seems quite unconscious that participles partly made nouns *can produce* false syntax. To the foregoing instructions, he subjoins the following comment, as a marginal note: "*The participle used as a noun, still retains its verbal properties*, and may govern the objective case, or be modified by an adverb or adjunct, like the verb from which it is derived."—*Ibid.* When one part of speech is said to be *used as an other*, the learner may be greatly puzzled to understand *to which class* the given word belongs. If "*the participle used as a noun*, still retains its verbal properties," it is, manifestly, not a noun, but a participle still; not a participial noun, but a *nounal participle*, whether the thing be allowable or not. Hence the teachings just cited are inconsistent. Wells says, "*Participles* are often used *in the sense of nouns*; as, 'There was again the *smacking* of whips, the *clattering* of hoofs, and the *glittering* of harness.'—IRVING."—*School Gram.* p. 154. This is not well stated; because these are participial *nouns*, and not "*participles*." What Wells calls "participial nouns," differ from these, and are *all* spurious, *all* mongrels, *all* participles rather than nouns. In regard to possessives before participles, no instructions appear to be more defective than those of this gentleman. His sole rule supposes the pupil always to know when and why the possessive is *proper*, and only instructs him *not to form it without the sign*: It is this: "When a noun or a pronoun, preceding a *participle used as a noun*, is *properly* in the possessive case, the sign of possession should not be omitted."—*School Gram.* p. 121. All the examples put under this rule, are inappropriate: each will mislead the learner. Those which are called "*Correct*," are, I think, erroneous; and those which are called "*False Syntax*," the adding of the possessive sign will not amend.

others, is both weakly conceived and badly written, I should neither have detained the reader so long on this topic, nor ever have placed it among the most puzzling points of grammar. Let it be observed, that what these writers absurdly call "*an entire* CLAUSE *of a sentence*," is found on examination to be some *short* PHRASE, the participle with its adjuncts, or even the participle alone, or with a single adverb only; as, "holding up her train,"—"dismissing his servant so hastily,"—"composing,"—"reading frequently,"—"composing frequently." And each of these, with an opposite error as great, they will have to be "*one name*," and to convey but "*one idea*;" supposing that by virtue of this imaginary *oneness*, it may govern the possessive case, and signify something which a "lady," or a "person," or a "pupil," may consistently *possess*. And then, to be wrong in every thing, they suggest that any noun on which such a participle, with its adjuncts, "depends, *may be put* in the *genitive case*;" whereas, such a change is seldom, if ever, admissible, and in our language, no participle *ever can depend* on any other than the nominative or the objective case. Every participle so depending is an adjunct to the noun; and every possessive, in its turn, is an adjunct to the word which governs it. In respect to construction, no terms differ more than a participle which governs the possessive case, and a participle which does not. These different constructions the contrivers of the foregoing rule, here take to be equivalent in meaning; whereas they elsewhere pretend to find in them quite different significations. The meaning is sometimes very different, and sometimes very similar; but seldom, if ever, are the terms convertible. And even if they were so, and the difference were nothing, would it not be better to adhere, where we can, to the analogy of General Grammar? In Greek and Latin, a participle may agree with a noun in the genitive case; but, if we regard analogy, that genitive must be Englished, not by the possessive case, but by *of* and the objective; as, "'Επεὶ δοκιμὴν ζητεῖτε τοῦ ἐν ἐμοὶ λαλοῦντος Χριστοῦ.'"—"Quandoquidem experimentum quæritis in me loquentis Christi."—*Beza.* "Since ye seek a proof of *Christ speaking* in me."—2 *Cor.* xiii, 3. We might here, perhaps, say, "*of Christ's speaking* in me," but is not the other form better? The French version is, "Puisque vous cherchez une preuve *que Christ parle* par moi;" and this, too, might be imitated in English: "Since ye seek a proof *that Christ speaks* by me."

OBS. 13.—As prepositions very naturally govern any of our participles except the simple perfect, it undoubtedly seems agreeable to our idiom not to disturb this government, when we would express the subject or agent of the being, action, or passion, between the preposition and the participle. Hence we find that the doer or the sufferer of the action is usually made its possessor, whenever the sense does not positively demand a different reading. Against this construction there is seldom any objection, if the participle be taken entirely as a noun, so that it may be called a participial noun; as, "Much depends *on their observing of* the rule."—*Lowth, Campbell,* and *L. Murray.* On the other hand, the participle after the objective is unobjectionable, if the noun or pronoun be the leading word in sense; as, "It would be idle to profess an apprehension of serious *evil resulting* in any respect from the utmost *publicity being given* to its contents."—*London Eclectic Review,* 1816. "The following is a beautiful instance of the *sound* of words *corresponding* to motion."—*Murray's Gram.* i, p. 333. "We shall discover many *things partaking* of both those characters."—*West's Letters,* p. 182. "To a *person following* the vulgar mode of omitting the comma."—*Churchill's Gram.* p. 365. But, in comparing the different constructions above noticed, writers are frequently puzzled to determine, and frequently too do they err in determining, which word shall be made the adjunct, and which the leading term. Now, wherever there is much doubt which of the two forms ought to be preferred, I think we may well conclude that both are wrong; especially, if there can easily be found for the idea an other expression that is undoubtedly clear and correct. Examples: "These appear to be instances of the present *participle being used* passively."—*Murray's Gram.* p. 64. "These are examples of the past *participle being applied* in an active sense."—*Ib.* 64. "We have some examples of *adverbs being used* for substantives."—*Priestley's Gram.* p. 134; *Murray's,* 198; *Ingersoll's,* 205; *Fisk's,* 140; *Smith's,* 165. "By a *noun, pronoun,* or *adjective, being prefixed* to the substantive." —*Murray's Gram.* p. 39; also *Ingersoll's, Fisk's, Alger's, Maltby's, Merchant's, Bacon's,* and others. Here, if their own rule is good for any thing, these authors ought rather to have preferred the possessive case; but strike out the word *being,* which is not necessary to the sense, and all question about the construction vanishes. Or if any body will justify these examples as they stand, let him observe that there are written, without number, in the same sense on the same principle; as, "Much depends *on the rule being observed.*"—"Much will depend *on the pupil composing frequently.*" Again: "Cyrus did not wait for the *Babylonians coming* to attack him."—*Rollin,* ii, 86. "Cyrus did not wait for the *Babylonians' coming* to attack him." That is—"for *their* coming," and not, "for *them* coming;" but much better than either: "Cyrus did not wait for the Babylonians *to come and* attack him." Again: "To prevent his *army's being* enclosed and hemmed in."—*Rollin,* ii, 89. "To prevent his *army being* enclosed and hemmed in." Both are wrong. Say, "To prevent his *army from being* enclosed and hemmed in." Again: "As a sign of *God's fulfilling* the promise."—*Rollin,* ii, 23. "As a sign of *God fulfilling* the promise." Both are objectionable. Say, "As a sign *that God would fulfil* the promise." Again: "There is affirmative evidence for *Moses's being* the author of these books."—*Bp. Watson's Apology,* p. 28. "The first argument you produce against *Moses being* the author of these books."—*Ib.* p. 29. Both are bad. Say,—"for *Moses as being* the author"—"against *Moses as being* the author, &c.

OBS. 14.—Now, although thousands of sentences might easily be quoted, in which the possessive case is *actually* governed by a participle, and that participle not taken in every respect as a noun; yet I imagine, there are, of this kind, few examples, if any, the meaning of which might not be *better expressed* in some other way. There are surely none among all the examples which are presented by Priestley, Murray, and others, under their rule above. Nor would a thousand such as are there given, amount to any proof of the rule. They are all of them *unreal* or *feigned* sentences, made up for the occasion, and, like most others that are produced in the same way, made up badly—made up after some ungrammatical model. If a gentleman could possibly demand a *lady's meaning* in such an act as *the holding-up of her train,* he certainly would use none of Priestley's three questions; but would probably say, "Madam, *what do you mean* by holding up your train?" It was folly for the doctor to ask *an other person*, as if an other could *guess* her meaning better than he. The text is therefore not to be corrected by inserting a hyphen and an *of*, after Murray's doctrine before cited; as, "What is the meaning of this *lady's holding-up of* her train?" Murray did well to reject this example, but as a specimen of English, his own is no better. The question which he asks, ought to have been, "*Why did this person dismiss* his servant so hastily?" Fisk has it in the following form: "What is the reason of this *person's dismissing his servant* so hastily?"—*English Grammar Simplified*, p. 108. This amender of grammars omits the *of* which Murray and others scrupulously insert to govern the noun *servant*, and boldly avows at once, what their rule implies, that, "Participles are sometimes used both as verbs and as nouns at the same time; as, 'By the *mind's changing the object*,' &c."—*Ib.* p. 134; so *Emmons's Gram.* p. 64. But he errs as much as they, and contradicts both himself and them. For one ought rather to say, "By the *mind's changing of* the object;" else *changing*, which "does the office of a noun," has not truly "a correspondent regimen." Yet *of* is useless after *dismissing*, unless we take away the *adverb* by which the participle is prevented from becoming a noun. "*Dismissing of* his servant *so hastily*," is in itself an ungrammatical phrase; and nothing but to omit either the preposition or the two adverbs, can possibly make it right. Without the latter, it may follow the possessive; but without the former, our *most approved grammars* say it cannot. Some critics, however, object to the *of*, because the *dismissing* is not *the servant's act*; but this, as I shall hereafter show, is no valid objection: they stickle for a false rule.

Obs. 15.—Thus these authors, differing from one an other as they do, and each contradicting himself and some of the rest, are, as it would seem, all wrong in respect to the whole matter at issue. For whether the phrase in question be like Priestley's, or like Murray's, or like Fisk's, it is still, according to the best authorities, unfit to govern the possessive case; because, in stead of being a substantive, it is something more than a participle, and yet they take it substantively. They form this phrase in many different fashions, and yet each man of them pretends that what he approves, is just like the construction of a regular noun: "*Just as we say*, 'What is the reason of this person's *hasty dismission of* his servant.'"—*Murray, Fisk, and others.* "*Just as we say*, 'What is the meaning of this lady's *dress*,' &c."—*Priestley.* The *meaning* of a *lady's dress*, forsooth! The illustration is worthy of the doctrine taught. "*An entire clause of a sentence*," substantively possessed, is sufficiently like "*the meaning of a lady's dress*, &c." Cobbett despised *andeoforths*, for their lack of meaning; and I find none in this one, unless it be, "*of tinsel and of fustian*." This gloss therefore I wholly disapprove, judging the position more tenable, to deny, if we consequently must, that either a phrase or a participle, as such, can consistently govern the possessive case. For whatever word or term gives rise to the direct relation of property, and is rightly made to govern the possessive case, ought in reason to be a *noun*—ought to be the *name* of some substance, quality, state, action, passion, being, or thing. When therefore other parts of speech assume this relation, they naturally *become nouns*; as, "Against the day of *my burying*."—*John*, xii, 7. "Till the day of *his showing* unto Israel."—*Luke*, i, 80. "By *my own showing*."—*Cowper, Life*, p. 22. "By a fortune of *my own getting*."—*Ib.* "Let *your yea* be yea, and *your nay* nay."—*James*, v, 12. "Prate of *my whereabout*."—*Shak.*

Obs. 16.—The government of possessives by "*entire clauses*," or "*substantive phrases*," as they are sometimes called, I am persuaded, may best be disposed of, in almost every instance, by charging the construction with impropriety or awkwardness, and substituting for it some better phraseology. For example, our grammars abound with sentences like the following, and call them good English: (1.) "So we may either say, 'I remember *it being* reckoned a great exploit;' or perhaps more elegantly, 'I remember *its being* reckoned a great exploit.'"—*Priestley, Murray, and others.* Here both modes are wrong; the latter, especially; because it violates a general rule of syntax, in regard to the case of the noun *exploit*. Say, "I remember *it was* reckoned a great exploit." Again: (2.) "We also properly say, 'This will be the effect of the *pupil's composing* frequently.'"—*Murray's Gram.* p. 179; *and others.* Better, "This will be the effect, *if the pupil compose* frequently." But this sentence is *fictitious*, and one may doubt whether good authors can be found who use *compose* or *composing* as being intransitive. (3.) "What can be the reason of the *committee's having delayed* this business?"—*Murray's Key*, p. 223. Say, "*Why have the committee* delayed this business?" (4.) "What can be the cause of the *parliament's neglecting* so important a business?"—*Ib.* p. 195. Say, "*Why does the parliament neglect* so important a business?" (5.) "The time of *William's making* the experiment, at length arrived."—*Ib.* p. 195. Say, "The time *for William to make* the experiment, at length arrived." (6.) "I hope this is the last time of *my acting* so imprudently."—*Ib.* p. 263. Say, "I hope *I shall never again act* so imprudently." (7.) "If I were to give a reason for *their looking* so well, it would be, that they rise early."—*Ib.* p. 263. Say, "I should attribute *their healthful appearance* to their early rising." (8.) "The tutor said, that diligence and application to study were necessary to *our becoming* good scholars."—*Cooper's Gram.* p. 145. Here is an anomaly in the construction of the noun *scholars*. Say, "The tutor said, that *diligent application* to study *was* necessary to our *success in learning*." (9.) "The reason of *his having acted in the manner he did*, was not fully explained."—*Murray's Key*, p. 263. This author has a very singular mode of giving "STRENGTH" to weak sentences. The faulty text here was, "The reason why he acted in the manner he did, was not fully explained."—*Murray's Exercises*, p. 131. This is much better than the other, but I should choose to say, "The reason of *his conduct* was not fully explained." For, surely, the "one idea or circumstance" of his "having acted in the manner *in which* he did *act*," may be quite as forcibly named by the one word *conduct*, as by all this verbiage, this "substantive phrase," or "entire clause," of such cumbrous length.

Obs. 17.—The foregoing observations tend to show, that the government of possessives by participles, is in general a construction little to be commended, if at all allowed. I thus narrow down the application of the principle, but do not hereby determine it to be altogether wrong. There are other arguments, both for and against the doctrine, which must be taken into the account, before we can fully decide the question. The double construction which may be given to infinitive verbs; the Greek idiom which allows to such verbs an article before them and an objective after them; the mixed character of the Latin gerund, part noun, part verb; the use or substitution of the participle in English for the gerund in Latin;—all these afford so many reasons by analogy, for allowing that our participle—except it be the perfect—since it participates the properties of a verb and a noun, as well as those of a verb and an adjective, may unite in itself a double construction, and be taken substantively in one relation, and participially in an other. Accordingly some grammarians so define it; and many writers so use it; both parties disregarding the distinction between the participle and the participial noun, and justifying the construction of the former, not only as a proper participle after its noun, and as a gerundive after its preposition; not only as a participial adjective before its noun, and as a participial noun, in the regular syntax of a noun; but also as a mixed term, in the double character of noun and participle at once. Nor are these its only uses; for, after an auxiliary, it is the main verb; and in a few instances, it passes into a preposition, an adverb, or something else. Thus have we from the verb a single derivative, which fairly ranks with about half the different parts of speech, and takes distinct constructions even more numerous; and yet these authors scruple not to make of it a hybridous thing, neither participle nor noun, but constructively both. "But this," says Lowth, "is inconsistent; let it be either the one or the other, and abide by its proper construction."— *Gram.* p. 82. And so say I—as asserting the general principle, and leaving the reader to judge of its exceptions. Because, without this mongrel character, the participle in our language has a multiplicity of uses unparalleled in any other; and because it seldom happens that the idea intended by this double construction may not be otherwise expressed more elegantly. But if it sometimes seem proper that the gerundive participle should be allowed to govern the possessive case, no exception to my rule is needed for the *parsing* of such possessive; because whatever is invested with such government, whether rightly or wrongly, is assumed as "the name of something possessed."

Obs. 18.—The reader may have observed, that in the use of participial nouns the distinction of *voice* in the participle is sometimes disregarded. Thus, "Against the day of my *burying*," means, "Against the day of my *being buried*." But in this instance the usual noun *burial* or *funeral* would have been better than either: "Against the day of *my burial*." I. e. "In diem *funerationis meæ*."—*Beza.* "In diem *sepulturæ meæ*."—*Leusden.* "'Εις τὶν ἱμέραν τοῦ ἐταφιασμοῦ μου."— *John*, xii, 7. In an other text, this noun is very properly used for the Greek infinitive, and the Latin gerund; as, "For my burial."—*Matt.* xxvi, 12. "Ad *funerandum* me."—*Beza.* "Ad *sepeliendum* me."—*Leusden.* Literally: "For burying me." "Πρὸς τὸ ταφιάσαι με." Nearly: "For to have me buried." Not all that is allowable, is commendable; and if either of the uncompounded terms be found a fit substitute for the compound participial noun, it is better to dispense with the latter, on account of its dissimilarity to other nouns: as, "Which only proceed upon the *question's being begged*."—*Barclay's Works*, Vol. iii, p. 361. Better, "Which only proceed upon a *begging of the question*." "The *king's having conquered* in the battle, established his throne."—*Nixon's Parser*, p. 128. Better, "The king's *conquering* in the battle;" for, in the participial noun, the distinction of *tense*, or of previous *completion*, is as needless as that of *voice*. "The *fleet's having sailed* prevented mutiny."—*Ib.* p. 78. Better, "The *sailing of the fleet*,"—or, "The *fleet's sailing*," &c. "The *prince's being murdered* excited their pity."—*Ibid.* Better, "The prince's *murder* excited their *indignation*."

Obs. 19.—In some instances, as it appears, not a little difficulty is experienced by our grammarians, respecting the addition or the omission of the possessive sign, the terminational apostrophic *s*, which in nouns is the ordinary index of the possessive case. Let it be remembered that every possessive is governed, or ought to be governed, by some noun expressed or understood, except such as (without the possessive sign) are put in apposition with others so governed; and for every possessive termination there must be a separate governing word, which, if it is not expressed, is shown by the possessive sign to be understood. The possessive sign itself *may* and *must* be omitted in certain cases; but, because it can never be inserted or discarded without suggesting or discarding a governing noun, it is never omitted *by ellipsis*, as Buchanan, Murray, Nixon, and many others, erroneously teach. The four lines of Note 2d below, are sufficient to show, in every instance, when it must be used, and when omitted; but Murray, after as many octavo pages on the point, still leaves it perplexed and undetermined. If a person knows what he means to say, let him express it according to the Note, and he will not fail to use just as many apostrophes and Esses as he ought. How absurd then is that common doctrine of ignorance, which Nixon has gathered from Allen and Murray, his chief oracles! "If *several* nouns in the *genitive* case, are immediately connected by a *conjunction*, the apostrophic *s* is annexed *to the last*, but *understood to the rest*; as, Neither *John* (i. e. John's) nor *Eliza's* books."—*English Parser*, p. 115. The author gives fifteen other examples like this, all of them bad English, or at any rate, not adapted to the sense which he intends!

Obs. 20.—The possessive case generally comes *immediately before* the governing noun, expressed or understood; as, "All *nature's* difference keeps all *nature's* peace."—*Pope.* "*Lady!* be *thine* [i. e. *thy walk*] the Christian's walk."—*Chr. Observer.* "Some of Æschylus's [plays] and Euripides's plays are opened in this manner."—*Blair's Rhet.* p. 459. And in this order one possessive sometimes governs another: as, "Peter's wife's mother;"—"Paul's sister's son."— *Bible.* But, to this general principle of arrangement, there are some exceptions: as,

1. When the governing noun has an adjective, this may intervene; as, "Flora's earliest smells."—*Milton.* "Of man's first disobedience."—*Id.* In the following phrase from the Spectator, "Of Will's last night's lecture," it is not very clear, whether *Will's* is governed by *night's* or by *lecture;* yet it violates a general principle of our grammar, to suppose the latter; because, on this supposition, two possessives, each having the sign, will be governed by one noun.

2. When the possession is affirmed or denied; as, "The book is *mine*, and not *John's*." But here the governing noun *may be supplied* in its proper place; and, in some such instances, it *must* be, else a pronoun or the verb will be the only governing word: as, "Ye are *Christ's* [disciples, or people]; and Christ is *God's*" [son].—*St. Paul.* Whether this phraseology is thus elliptical or not, is questionable. See Obs. 4th, in this series.

3. When the case occurs without the sign, either by apposition or by connexion; as, "In her *brother Absalom's* house."—*Bible.* "*David* and *Jonathan's* friendship."—*Allen.* "*Adam* and *Eve's* morning hymn."—*Dr. Ash.* "Behold, the heaven, and the heaven of heavens, is the Lord's thy God."—*Deut.* x, 14. "For *peace* and *quiet's* sake."—*Cowper.* "To the beginning of King James the First's reign."—*Bolingbroke, on Hist.* p. 32.

OBS. 21.—The possessive case is in general (though not always) equivalent to the preposition *of* and *the objective*; as, "*Of* Judas Iscariot, *Simon's* son."—*John*, xiii, 2. "*To* Judas Iscariot, the son *of Simon.*"—*Ib.* xiii, 26. On account of this one-sided equivalence, many grammarians erroneously reckon the latter to be a "*genitive case*" as well as the former. But they ought to remember, that the preposition is used more frequently than the possessive, and in a variety of senses that cannot be interpreted by this case; as, "*Of* some *of* the books *of* each *of* these classes *of* literature, a catalogue will be given at the end *of* the work."—*L. Murray's Gram.* p. 178. Murray calls this a "laborious mode of expression," and doubtless it might be a little improved by substituting *in* for the third *of*; but my argument is, that the meaning conveyed cannot be expressed by possessives. The notion that *of* forms a genitive case, led Priestley to suggest, that our language admits a "*double genitive*;" as, "This book of my *friend's.*"—*Priestley's Gram.* p. 71. "It is a discovery *of Sir Isaac Newton's.*"—*Ib.* p. 72. "This exactness *of his.*" —*STERNE: ib.* The doctrine has since passed into nearly all our grammars; yet is there no double case here, as I shall presently show.

OBS. 22.—Where the governing noun cannot be easily mistaken, it is often omitted by ellipsis: as, "At the alderman's" [*house*];—"St. Paul's" [*church*];—"A book of my brother's" [*books*];—"A subject of the emperor's" [*subjects*];—"A friend of mine;" i. e., one *of my friends.* "Shall we say that Sacrificing was a pure invention of *Adam's*, or of *Cain or Abel's?*"—*Leslie, on Tythes,* p. 93. That is—of Adam's *inventions*, or of Cain or Abel's *inventions.* The Rev. David Blair, unable to resolve this phraseology to his own satisfaction, absurdly sets it down among what he calls "ERRONEOUS OR VULGAR PHRASES." His examples are these: "A poem of Pope's;"—"A soldier of the king's;"—"That is a horse of my father's."—*Blair's Practical Gram.* p. 110, 111. He ought to have supplied the plural nouns, *poems, soldiers, horses.* This is the true explanation of all the "double genitives" which our grammarians discover; for when the first noun is *partitive*, it naturally suggests more or other things of the same kind, belonging to this possessor; and when such is not the meaning, this construction is improper. In the following example, the noun *eyes* is understood after *his*:

"Ev'n *his*, the *warrior's eyes*, were forced to yield,
That saw, without a tear, Pharsalia's field."—*Rowe's Lucan,* B. viii, l. 144.

OBS. 23.—When two or more nouns of the possessive form are in any way connected, they usually refer to things individually different but of the same name; and when such is the meaning, the governing noun, which we always suppress somewhere to avoid tautology, is *understood* wherever the sign is added without it; as, "A *father's* or *mother's sister* is an aunt."—*Dr. Webster.* That is, "A *father's sister* or a mother's sister is an aunt." "In the same commemorative acts of the senate, *were* thy name, thy *father's*, thy *brother's*, and the *emperor's.*"— *Zenobia,* Vol. i, p. 231.

"From Stiles's pocket into *Nokes's*" [pocket].—*Hudibras,* B. iii, C. iii, l. 715.

"Add *Nature's, Custom's, Reason's,* Passion's strife."—*Pope, Brit. Poets,* Vol. vi, p. 383.

OBS. 24.—The possessive sign is sometimes annexed to that part of a compound name, which is, of itself, in the objective case; as, "At his *father-in-law's* residence." "Here, "*At the residence of his father-in-law,*" would be quite as agreeable; and, as for the plural, one would hardly think of saying, "Men's wedding parties are usually held at their *fathers-in-law's* houses." When the compound is formed with *of*, to prevent a repetition of this particle, the possessive sign is sometimes added as above; and yet the hyphen is not commonly inserted in the phrase, as I think it ought to be. Examples: "The duke of Bridgewater's canal;"—"The bishop of Landaff's excellent book;"—"The Lord mayor of London's authority;"—"The captain of the guard's house."—*Murray's Gram.* p. 176. "The Bishop of Cambray's writings on eloquence."—*Blair's Rhet.* p. 346. "The bard of Lomond's lay is done."—*Queen's Wake,* p. 99. "For the kingdom of God's sake."—*Luke,* xviii, 29. "Of the children of Israel's half."—*Numbers,* xxxi, 30. From these examples it would seem, that the possessive sign has a less intimate alliance with the possessive case, than with the governing noun; or, at any rate, a dependence less close than that of the objective noun which here assumes it. And since the two nouns here so intimately joined by *of*, cannot be explained separately as forming two cases, but must be parsed together as *one name* governed in the usual way, I should either adopt some other phraseology, or write the compound term with hyphens, thus: "The *Duke-of-Bridgewater's* canal; "—"The *Bishop-of-Landaff's* excellent book;"—"The *Bard-of-Lomond's* lay is done." But there is commonly some better mode of correcting such phrases. With deference to Murray and others, "*The King of Great Britain's* prerogative,"[*] is but an untoward way of saying, "*The prerogative of the British King;*" and, "*The Lord mayor of London's authority,*" may quite as well be written, "*The authority of London's Lord Mayor.*" Blair, who for brevity robs the *Arch*bishop of half his title, might as well have said, "*Fenelon's* writings on eloquence." "*Propter regnum Dei,*" might have been rendered, "For the kingdom *of God;*"—"For *the sake of* the kingdom of God;"

---

[*] It is remarkable, that Lindley Murray, with all his care in revising his work, did not see the *inconsistency* of his instructions in relation to phrases of this kind. First he copies Lowth's doctrine, literally and anonymously, from the Doctor's 17th page, thus: "When the thing to which *another is said to belong*, is expressed by a circumlocution, or by *many terms*, the sign of the possessive case *is commonly added to the last* term: as, 'The *king of Great Britain's* dominions.'"—*Murray's Gram.* 8vo, p. 45. Afterwards he condemns this: "The word in the *genitive* case is frequently PLACED IMPROPERLY: as, 'This fact appears from Dr. *Pearson of Birmingham's* experiments.' *It* should be, 'from the experiments of Dr. *Pearson* of Birmingham.'"—*Ib.* p. 175. And again he makes it *necessary*: "A phrase in which the words are so connected and dependent, as to admit of no pause before the *conclusion, necessarily requires* the genitive sign *at or near the end of the phrase*: as, 'Whose prerogative is it? It is the *king of* Great Britain's;' 'That is the *duke of Bridgewater's* canal;'" &c.—*Ib.* p. 176. Is there not *contradiction* in these instructions?

—or, "For the sake of *God's* kingdom." And in lieu of the other text, we might say, "Of the *Israelites'* half."

OBS. 25.—"Little explanatory circumstances," says Priestley, "are particularly awkward between the *genitive* case, and the word which usually follows it; as, 'She began to extol the farmer's, *as she called him*, excellent understanding.' Harriet Watson, Vol. i, p. 27."—*Priestley's Gram.* p 174. Murray assumes this remark, and adds respecting the example, "It ought to be, 'the excellent understanding of the farmer, as she called him.'"—*Murray's Gram.* p. 175. Intersertions of this kind are as uncommon as they are uncouth. Murray, it seems, found none for his Exercises, but made up a couple to suit his purpose. The following might have answered as well for an other: "Monsieur D'acier observes, that Zeno's (the Founder of the Sect,) opinion was Fair and Defensible in these Points."—*Collier's Antoninus*, p. ii.

OBS. 26.—It is so usual a practice in our language, to put the possessive sign always and only where the two terms of the possessive relation meet, that this ending is liable to be added to any adjunct which can be taken as a part of the former noun or name; as, (1.) "The *court-martial's* violent proceedings." Here the plural would be *courts-martial;* but the possessive sign must be at the end. (2.) "In *Henry the Eighth's* time."—*Walker's Key, Introd.* p. 11. This phrase can be justified, only by supposing the adjective a part of the name. Better, "In the time of Henry the Eighth." (3.) "And strengthened with a *year* or *two's* age."—*Locke, on Education.* p. 6. Here *two's* is put for *two years;* and, I think, improperly; because the sign is such as suits the former noun, and not the plural. Better, "And strengthened with a *year's age* or *more.*" The word *two* however is declinable as a noun, and possibly it may be so taken in Locke's phrase (4.) "This rule is often infringed, by the *case absolute's not being properly distinguished* from certain forms of expression apparently *similar* to it."—*Murray's Gram.* p. 155. *Fisk's,* 113; *Ingersoll's,* 210. Here the possessive sign, being appended to a distinct adjective, and followed by nothing that can be called a noun, is employed as absurdly as it well can be. Say, "This rule is often infringed by an improper use of the nominative absolute;" for this is precisely what these authors mean. (5.) "The participle is distinguished from the adjective by the *former's expressing the idea of time,* and the *latter's denoting only a quality.*"—*Murray's Gram.* p. 65; *Fisk's,* 82; *Ingersoll's,* 45; *Emmons's,* 64; *Alger's,* 28. This is liable to nearly the same objections. Say, "The participle differs from an adjective by expressing the idea of time, whereas the adjective denotes only a quality." (6.) "The relatives *that* and *as* differ from *who* and *which* in the *former's not being immediately joined* to the governing word."—*Nixon's Parser.* p. 140. This is still worse, because *former's,* which is like a singular noun, has here a plural meaning; namely, "in *the former terms' not being,*" &c. Say—"in *that the former never follow* the governing word."

OBS. 27.—The possessive termination is so far from being liable to suppression *by ellipsis,* agreeably to the nonsense of those interpreters who will have it to be "*understood*" wherever the case occurs without it, that on the contrary it is sometimes retained where there is an actual suppression of the noun to which it belongs. This appears to be the case whenever the pronominal adjectives *former* and *latter* are inflected, as above. The inflection of these, however, seems to be needless, and may well be reckoned improper. But, in the following line, the adjective elegantly takes the sign; because there is an ellipsis of both nouns: *poor's* being put for *poor man's,* and the governing noun *joys* being understood after it: "The *rich man's joys* increase, the *poor's* decay."—*Goldsmith.* So, in the following example, *guilty's* is put for *guilty person's:*

> "Yet, wise and righteous ever, scorns to hear
> The fool's fond wishes, or the *guilty's* prayer."—*Rowe's Lucan,* B. v, l. 155.

This is a poetical license; and others of a like nature are sometimes met with. Our poets use the possessive case much more frequently than prose writers, and occasionally inflect words that are altogether invariable in prose; as,

> "Eager that last great chance of war he waits,
> Where *either's* fall determines *both their* fates."—*Ibid.* B. vi, l. 13.

OBS. 28.—To avoid a concurrence of hissing sounds, the *s* of the possessive singular is sometimes omitted, and the apostrophe alone retained to mark the case; as, "For *conscience'* sake."—*Bible* "*Moses'* minister."—*Ib.* "*Felix'* room."—*Ib.* "*Achilles'* wrath."—*Pope.* "*Shews'* walls."—*Collins.* "*Epicurus'* sty."—*Beattie.* "*Douglas'* daughter."—*Scott.* "For *Douglas'* sake."—*Ib.* "To his *mistress'* eyebrow."—*Shak.* This is a sort of poetic license, as is suggested in the 16th Observation upon the Cases of Nouns, in the Etymology. But in prose the elision should be very sparingly indulged; it is in general less agreeable, as well as less proper, than the regular form. Where is the propriety of saying, *Hicks' Sermons, Barnes' Notes, Kames' Elements, Adams' Lectures, Josephus' Works,* while we so uniformly say, *in Charles's reign, St. James's Palace,* and the like? The following examples are right: "At *Westminster* and *Hicks's* Hall."—*Hudibras.* "Lord *Kames's* Elements of Criticism."—*Murray's Sequel,* p. 331. "Of *Rubens's* allegorical pictures."—*Hazlitt.* "With respect to *Burns's* early education."—*Dugald Stewart.* "*Isocrates's* pomp;"—"*Demosthenes's* life."—*Blair's Rhet.* p. 242. "The repose of *Epicurus's* gods."—*Wilson's Heb. Gram.* p. 93.

> "To *Douglas's* obscure abode."—*Scott, L. L.,* C. iii, st. 28.
> "Such was the *Douglas's* command."—*Id. ib.,* C. ii, st. 36.

OBS. 29.—Some of our grammarians, drawing broad conclusions from a few particular examples, falsely teach as follows: "When a singular noun ends in *ss,* the apostrophe only is added; as, 'For *goodness'* sake:' except the word *witness;* as, 'The *witness's* testimony.' When a noun in the possessive case ends in *ence,* the *s* is omitted, but the apostrophe is retained; as, 'For *conscience'* sake.'"—*Kirkham's Gram.* p. 49; *Hamlin's,* 16; *Smith's New Gram.* 47.[*] Of principles

---

[*] A late grammarian tells us: "*In* nouns ending in *es* and *ss,* the other *s* is not added; as, *Charles' hat, Goodness'* sake."—*Wilcox's Gram.* p. 11. He should rather have said, "*To* nouns ending in *es* or *ss,* the other *s* is not added." But his doctrine is worse than his syntax; and, what is remarkable, he himself forgets it in the course of a few minutes, thus: "Decline *Charles.* Nom. *Charles,* Poss. *Charles's,* Obj. *Charles.*"—*Ib.* p. 62.

rences very much like these, is the whole system of "*Inductive Grammar*" essentially up. But is it not plain that *heiress's, abbess's, peeress's, countess's,* and many other words of the form, are as good English as *witness's?* Did not Jane West write justly, "She made apt to look in at the dear *dutchess's?*"—*Letters to a Lady,* p. 95. Does not the Bible speak by of "*an ass's head,*" sold at a great price ?—2 *Kings,* vi, 25. Is Burns also wrong, about *his lassie,*" and "*miss's bonnet?*"—*Poems,* p. 44. Or did Scott write inaccurately, guide "Led slowly through the *pass's* jaws?"—*Lady of the Lake,* p. 121. So much for that is the rule for the termination *ence,* or (as Smith has it) *nce,* more true. *Prince's* and *are* as good possessives as any; and so are the following :

> "That vice should triumph, virtue vice obey ;
> This sprung some doubt of *Providence's* sway."—*Parnell.*
> "And sweet *Benevolence's* mild command "—*Lord Lyttelton.*
> "I heard the *lance's* shivering crash,
>   As when the whirlwind rends the ash."—*Sir Walter Scott*

30.—The most common rule now in use for the construction of the possessive case, is a shred of old code of Latin grammar : " One substantive governs *another,* signifying a different thing, possessive or genitive case."—*L. Murray's Rule X.* This canon not only leaves occasion for doubt one respecting pronouns of the possessive case, but it is also obscure in its phraseology, negligent of the various modes in which nouns may come together in English. All nouns objectively, and many that are compounded together, seem to form exceptions to it. But who all or enumerate these *exceptions?* Different combinations of nouns have so often little or absence of meaning, or of relation to each other, and so frequently is the very same vocal ex- written variously by our best scholars, and ablest lexicographers, that in many ordinary as it seems scarcely possible to determine who or what is right. Thus, on the au- of Johnson, one might write, *a stone's cast,* or *stone's throw ;* but Webster has it, *stones- times-throw ;* Maunder, *stonecast, stonethrow ;* Chalmers, *stonecast ;* Worcester, *stone's- So* Johnson and Chalmers write *stonesmickle,* a bird ; Webster has it *stone's-mickle ;* yet refer to Ainsworth as their authority, and his word is *stone-smickle :* Littleton has it *smich.* Johnson and Chalmers write, *popeseye* and *sheep's eye ;* Walker, Maunder, and Webster, *popeseye* and *sheep's-eye ;* Scott has *pope's-eye* and *sheepseye ;* Webster, *pope's-eye* and *eye, bird-eye* and *birds-eye.* Ainsworth has *goat's beard,* for the name of a plant ; John- *godbeard ;* Webster, *goat-beard* and *goat's-beard* Ainsworth has *prince's feather,* for the with ; Johnson, Chalmers, Walker, and Maunder, write it *prince's-feather ;* Webster and Worcester, *prince's-feather ;* Bolles has it *prince's feather ;* and here they are all wrong, for the should be *prince's-feather.* There are hundreds more of such terms ; all as uncertain in orthography as these.

31.—While descrepancies like the foregoing abound in our best dictionaries, none of our can supply any hints tending to show which of these various forms we ought to prefer. the following suggestions, together with the six Rules for the Figure of Words, in Part may enable the reader to decide these questions with sufficient accuracy. (1.) Two short nouns are apt to unite in a permanent compound, when the former, taking the sole accent, as the main purpose or chief characteristic of the thing named by the latter ; as, *teacup,* ink. *daystar, horseman, sheepfold, houndfish, hourglass.* (2.) Temporary compounds of a nature may be formed with the hyphen, when there remain two accented syllables ; as, *well, bosom-friend, fellow-servant, horse-chestnut, goat-marjoram, marsh-marigold.* (3.) former of two nouns, if it be not plural, may be taken adjectively, in any relation that differs opposition and from possession ; as, "The *silver* cup."—"The *parent* birds,"—"My *pil- ket.*"—"Thy *hermit* cell,"—"Two *brother* sergeants." (4.) The possessive case and its long noun, combining to form a *literal* name, may be joined together without either hy- or apostrophe : as, *tradesman, ratsbane, doomsday, kinswoman, craftsmaster.* (5.) The posses- case and its governing noun, combining to form a *metaphorical* name, should be written both apostrophe and hyphen ; as, *Job's-tears, Jew's ear, bear's-foot, colt's-tooth, sheep's-head, fish-ball, crab's-eyes, hound's-tongue, king's spear, lady's-slipper, lady's-bedstraw,* &c. (6.) The more case and its governing noun, combining to form an *adjective,* whether literal or meta- phorical, should generally be written with both apostrophe and hyphen ; as, "*Neat's-foot* oil,"— *"calf's-foot* jelly."—"A *carp's-tongue* drill,"—"A *bird's-eye* view,"—"The *states'-rights* party,"— *"camel's-hair* shawl." But a triple compound noun may be *formed* with one hyphen only : *"a doomsday-book ;* " (—*Joh. Dict.;*) "An *armscad lift.*" Cardell, who will have all posses- to be adjectives, writes an example thus: "John's *camel's hair* girdle."—*Elements of Eng.* p. 39. This is as if *John's camel* had a *hair girdle!* (7.) When the possessive case and governing noun merely help to form a regular phrase, the compounding of them in any fashion be reckoned improper ; thus the phrases, *a day's work, at death's door, on New Year's Day, year's gift, All Souls' Day, All Saints' Day, All Fools' Day, the saints' bell, the heart's blood, day's meat,* though often written otherwise, may best stand as they do here.

32.—The existence of a permanent compound of any two words, does not necessarily pre- the use of the possessive relation between the same words. Thus, we may speak of a *horse's* or *a goat's skin,* notwithstanding there are such words as *horseshoe* and *goatskin.* E. g. " That upon the *housetops.*"—ALGER'S BIBLE. *Matt.* x, 27. " Unpeg the basket on the *house's* "—*Beauties of Sh sh,* p. 238. Webster defines *frostnail,* (which, under the word *cork,* he erro- only writes *frost nail,*) "A nail driven into *a horse-shoe,* to prevent *the horse* from slipping on " Worcester has it, "A nail driven into *a horse's shoe,* to prevent *his slipping on the ice.*" ance, "A nail with a *prominent head driven into the horse's shoes,* that it may pierce the ice." under, "A nail with a *sharp head driven* into the *horses' shoes* in frosty weather." None of these compounds is very well written. Say rather, "A *spur-headed* nail driven into *a horse's shoe* to went him *from slipping.*" There is commonly some difference, and sometimes a very great one, seen the compound noun and the possessive relation, and also between the radical compound that of the possessive. Thus a *harelip* is not a *hare's lip,* nor is a *headman* a *headsman,* or *heart-ease heart's-ease.* So, according to the books, a *cat-head,* a *cat's-head,* and a *cat's h* three very different things; yet what Webster writes, *cat-tail,* Johnson, *cats-tail,* Wal others, *cat's-tail,* means but the same thing, though not a *cat's tail.* Johnson's " *h Jews-ear, lady-mantle,* and *lady-bedstraw,*" are no more proper, than Webster's " *bear's-x foot, lady's mantle,* and *lady's bed-straw.*" All these are wrong.

OBS. 33.—Particular examples, both of proper distinction, and of blind irregularity, a the heads above suggested, may be quoted and multiplied indefinitely, even from our literary authorities; but, since nothing can be settled but by the force of *principles,* he wl be accurate, must resort to rules,—must consider what is analogical, and, in all doubtful ca this the preference. But, in grammar, particular analogies are to respected, as we. a which are more general. For example, the noun *side,* in that relation which should sec quire the preceding noun to be in the possessive case, is usually compounded with it, the being used where the compound has more than two syllables, but not with two only; as, *hillside, roadside, wayside, seaside, river-side, water-side, mountain-side.* Some instances separate construction occur, but they are rare: as, "And her maidens walked along by the *side.*"—*Exodus,* ii, 5. After this noun also, the possessive preposition *of* is sometimes a as, "On this *side* the river;"—(*Bible;*) "On this *side* Trent."—*Cowell.* Better, " Or *of* the river," &c. "Blind Bartimeus sat by the *highway side,* begging."—*Mark,* x, 4 Alger more properly writes "*highway-side.*" In Rev. xiv, 20th, we have the unusual cc "*horse-bridles.*" The text ought to have been rendered, "even unto the *horses' bridles.* "usque ad frænos equorum." Greek, "ἄχρι τῶν χαλινῶν τῶν ἵππων."

OBS. 34.—Correlatives, as father and son, husband and wife, naturally possess ead hence such combinations as, *father's son,* and *son's father,* though correct enough in their redundant in expression. The whole and a part are a sort of correlatives, but the whole t possess its parts, more properly than any of the parts, the whole. Yet we seldom put th in the possessive case before its part, or parts, but rather express the relation by *of;* as, ter *of* a dollar," rather than, " a *dollar's* quarter." After the noun *half,* we usually a this preposition, if an article intervene; as, "*half a dollar,*" rather than, "half *of* a or " a *dollar's* half." So we may say, "*half the way,*" for "half of the way;" but w say, "*half us,*" for "half of us." In the phrase, "*a half dollar,*" the word *half* is an ad and a very different meaning is conveyed. Yet the compounds *half-pint* and *half-ps* sometimes used to signify, the *quantity* of half a pint, the *value* of *half a penny.* In measure, or time, the part is sometimes made possessive of the whole; as, "a *pound's* a *yard's* length, an *hour's* time." On the contrary, we do not say, "*weight's* pound, yard, or *time's* hour;" nor yet, "a pound *of* weight, a yard *of* length;" and rarely do "an hour *of* time." *Pound* and *yard* having other uses, we sometimes say, "a pound a yard *in* length;" though scarcely, "an hour *in* time."

OBS. 35.—Between a portion of time and its correlative action, passion, or being, the dive relation is interchangeable; so that either term may be the principal, and either, the a as, "*Three years'* hard work," or, "Three years *of hard work.*" Sometimes we may e either term in either form; as, "During the *ten years'* war,"—"During the ten years *of* "During the war *of ten years,*"—"During the *war's* ten years." Hence some writers ceiving why either word should make the other its governed adjunct, place both upon a if they were in apposition; as, "Three *days time.*"—*Brown's Estimate,* Vol. ii, p. 156. few *years preparation.*"—*Blair's Rhet.* p. 341. "Of forty *years planting.*"—*Wm. Penn* account, of five *years standing.*" If these phrases were correct, it would also be correct "*one day time,*"—"*one year preparation,*"—"*one year planting,*"—"*of one year standard* all these are manifestly bad English; and, by analogy, so are the others.

OBS. 36.—Any noun of weight, measure, or time, put immediately before an other, if a in the possessive case, will naturally be understood *adjectively;* as, "No person can, only, give to an other an adequate idea of a *pound weight,* or [a] *foot rule.*"—*Grxxr.* This phraseology can, with propriety, refer only to the weight or the rule with which w or measure; it cannot signify *a pound in weight,* or *a foot in length,* though it is very p that the author intended the latter. When the noun *times* is used before an other acc of multiplication, there may be supposed an ellipsis of the preposition *of* between the " as when we divide by the word *half;* as, "An hour is sixty *times the length* of a minute *ray's Gram.* p. 48. "Thirty seconds are *half the length* of a minute." That is,—"h length,"—"sixty times *of* the length."

NOTES TO RULE IV.

NOTE I.—In the syntax of the possessive case, its appropriate form, sing plural, should be observed, agreeably to the sense and declension of the word. write *John's, men's, hers, its, ours, yours, theirs,* ; and not, *Johns, mens', her our's, your's, their's.*

NOTE II.—When nouns of the possessive case are connected by conjul or put in apposition, the sign of possession must always be annexed to *sxe* such only, as immediately precede the governing noun, expressed or undersa "*John* and *Eliza's* teacher is a man of more learning than *James's* or *Anir* —"For *David* my *servant's* sake."—*Bible.* "For my sake and the *gospel's* "Lost in *love's* and *friendship's* smile."—*Scott.*

NOTE III.—The relation of property may also be expressed by the prepo and the objective; as, "The *will of* man," for "*man's will.*" Of these fol should adopt that which will render the sentence the most perspicuous and agreeable ; and, by the use of both, avoid an unpleasant repetition of either.

NOTE IV.—A noun governing the possessive plural, should not, by a forced agreement, be made plural, when its own sense does not require it ; as, "For *our parts*,"—"Were I in *your places:*" for we may with propriety say, "*Our part, your place*, or *your condition;*" as well as, "*Our desire, yourintention, their resignation.*"—*L. Murray's Gram.* p. 169. A noun taken figuratively may also be singular, when the literal meaning would require the plural : such expressions as *their face, their neck, their hand, their head, their heart, our mouth, our life*, are frequent in the Scriptures, and not improper.

NOTE V.—The possessive case should not be needlessly used before a participle that is not taken in other respects as a noun. The following phrase is therefore wrong: "Adopted by the Goths in *their* pronouncing the Greek."—*Walker's Key*, p. 17. Expunge *their*. Again : "Here we speak of *their* becoming both in form and signification passive."—*Campbell's Rhet.* p. 226. Say rather, "Here we speak of *them as becoming passive*, both in form and signification."

IMPROPRIETIES FOR CORRECTION.

FALSE SYNTAX UNDER RULE IV.

EXAMPLES UNDER NOTE I. — THE POSSESSIVE FORM.

"*Mans* chief good is an upright mind." See *Brown's Institutes of E. Gram.* p. 179.

[FORMULE.—Not proper, because the noun *mans*, which is intended for the possessive singular of *man*, has not the appropriate form of that case and number. But, according to Note 1st under Rule 4th, "In the syntax of the possessive case, its appropriate form, singular or plural, should be observed, agreeably to the sense and declension of the word." Therefore, *mans* should be *man's*, with the apostrophe before the *s* ; thus, "*Man's* chief good is an upright mind."]

"The translator of Mallets History has the following note."—*Webster's Essays*, p. 263. "The act, while it gave five years full pay to the officers, allowed but one year's pay to the privates."—*Ib.* p. 184. "For the study of English is preceded by several years attention to Latin and Greek."—*Ib.* p. 7. "The first, the Court Baron, is the freeholders or yeomens court."—*Coke, Litt.* p. 74. "I affirm, that Vaugelas' definition labours under an essential defect."—*Campbell's Rhet.* p. 163. "I affirm, that Vangelas's definition labours under an essential defect."—*Murray's Octavo Gram.*, Fourth Amer. Ed., Vol. ii, p. 360.[*] "There is a chorus in Aristophane's plays."—*Blair's Rhet.* p. 480. "It denotes the same conception in my mind as in their's."—*Duncan's Logic*, p. 65. "This afterwards enabled him to read Hicke's Saxon Grammar."—*Life of Dr. Murray*, p. 76. "I will not do it for Jonas sake."—*Dr. Ash's Gram.* p. 56. "I arose, and asked if those charming infants were her's."—*Werter*, p. 21. "They divide their time between milliners shops and taverns."—*Brown's Estimate*, Vol. i, p. 65. "The angels adoring of Adam is also mentioned in the Talmud."—*Sale's Koran*, p. 6. "Quarrels arose from the winners insulting of those who lost."—*Ib.* p. 171. "The vacancy, occasioned by Mr. Adams' resignation."—*Adams's Rhet.* Vol. i, p. vii. "Read for instance Junius' address, commonly called his letter to the king."—*Ib.* i, 225. "A perpetual struggle against the tide of Hortensius' influence."—*Ib.* ii, 23. "Which, for distinction sake, I shall put down severally."—*Johnson's Gram. Com.* p. 302. "The fifth case is in a clause signifying the matter of ones fear."—*Ib.* p. 312. "And they took counsel, and bought with them the potters' field."—*ALGER'S BIBLE : Matt.* xxvii, 7. "Arise for thy servant's help, and redeem them for thy mercy's sake."—*Jenks's Prayers*, p. 65. "Shall not their cattle, and their substance, and every beast of their's be ours ? "—SCOTT'S BIBLE : *Gen.* xxxiv, 23. "And every beast of their's, be our's ? "—FRIENDS' BIBLE : *Ib.* "It's regular plural, *bullaces*, is used by Bacon."—*Churchill's Gram.* p. 213. "Mordecai walked every day before the court of the womens house."—SCOTT'S BIBLE : *Esther*, i, 11. "Behold, they that wear soft clothing are in king's houses."—IR. and FRIENDS' BIBLE : *Matt.* xi, 8 : also *Webster's Imp. Gram.* p. 173. "Then Jethro, Moses' father-in-law, took Zipporah, Moses' wife, and her two sons; and Jethro, Moses' father-in-law, came, with his sons and his wife, unto Moses."—ALGER'S BIBLE, and THE FRIENDS' : *Exod.* xviii, 2–5. "King James' translators merely revised former translations."—*Rev. B. Frazee's Gram.* p. 137. "May they be like corn on houses tops."—*White, on the English Verb*, p. 160.

"And for his Maker's image sake exempt."—*Par. Lost*, B. xi, l. 514.

"By all the fame acquir'd in ten years war."—*Rowe's Lucan*, B. i, l. 674.

"Nor glad vile poets with true critics gore."—*Pope's Dunciad*, p. 175.

"Man only of a softer mold is made,
Not for his fellow's ruin, but their aid."—*Dryden's Poems*, p. 92.

---

[*] VAUGELAS was a noted French critic, who died in 1650. In Murray's Grammar, the name is more than once mistaken. On page 359th, of the edition above cited, it is printed "*Vangelas.*"—G. BROWN.

UNDER NOTE II. — POSSESSIVES CONNECTED.

"It was necessary to have both the physician, and the surgeon's advice."—*Co* and *Pr. Gram.* p. 140. "This out-side fashionableness of the Taylor or Tire-making."—*Locke, on Education,* p. 49. "Some pretending to be of Paul's party. Apollos, others of Cephas, and others, pretending yet higher, to be of Christ's."—*Dict. w. Apollos.* "Nor is it less certain that Spenser's and Milton's spelling agree with our pronunciation."—*Philol. Museum,* i, 661. "Law's, Edwards', and Watts' of the Divine Dispensations."—*Burgh's Dignity,* Vol. i, p. 193. "And who was Saviour, and the Prophets?"—*Bayly's Works,* p. 600. "Without any impedime own, or his parents or guardians will."—*Literary Convention,* p. 145. "James neither the boy * nor the girl's distress."—*Nixon's Parser,* p. 116. "John regard the master nor the pupil's advantage."—*Ib.* p. 117. "You reward neither the ma woman's labours."—*Ib.* "She examines neither James nor John's conduct."—*P.* pitiest neither the servant nor the master's injuries."—*Ib.* "We promote Englar land's happiness."—*Ib.* "Were Cain and Abel's occupation the same?"—*Brow* 179. "Were Cain's and Abel's occupations the same?"—*Ib.* "What was Sir Andrew's employment?"—*Author.* "Till he can read himself Sanctii Minc Scioppius and Perizonius's Notes."—*Locke, on Education,* p. 295.

> "And love's and friendship's finely-pointed dart
> Falls blunted from each indurated heart."—*Goldsmith.*

UNDER NOTE III. — CHOICE OF FORMS.

"But some degree of trouble is all men's portion."—*Murray's Key,* p. 218 ; *M* 197. "With his father's and mother's names upon the blank leaf."—*Corner-St* "The general, in the army's name, published a declaration."—*HUME : in Priest* p. 69. "The Commons' vote."—*Id. ib.* "The Lords' house."—*Id. ib.* "A coll writers faults."—*SWIFT: ib.* p. 68. "After ten years wars."—*Id. ib.* "Profession testation of such practices as his predecessors."—*Notes to the Dunciad.* "By th shall have ended my years office."—*Walker's Particles,* p. 104. "For Herodias' brother Philip's wife."—*Mark,* vi, 17. "For Herodias's sake, his brother Philip's *Murray's Key.* p. 194. "I endure all things for the elect's sakes, that they may al salvation."—*FRIENDS' BIBLE: 2 Tim.* ii, 10. "For the elects' sakes."—*Scott* "For the elect's sake."—*ALGER's BIBLE, and BRUCE'S.* "He was Louis the Si son's heir."—*W. Allen's Exercises, Gram.* p. 329. "The throne we honour is the chil people."—"An account of the proceedings of the court of Alexander."—*As* tutor of a person of fashion's child !"—*Gil Blas,* Vol. i, p. 20. "It is curious that this sentence of the Bishop is, itself, ungrammatical !"—*Cobbett's E. Gram.* troops broke into Leopold the emperor's palace."—*Nixon's Parser,* p. 59. "The was called by Eldon the judge's desire."—*Ibid.* "Peter's, John's, and Andrew's tion was that of fishermen."—*Brace's Gram.* p. 79. "The venerable president of t Academy's debility has lately increased."—*Maunder's Gram.* p. 12.

UNDER NOTE IV. — POSSESSIVES PLURAL.

"God hath not given us our reasons to no purpose."—*Barclay's Works,* Vol. "For our sakes, no doubt, this is written."—*1 Cor.* ix, 10. "Are not health and of body desirable for their own sakes?"—*Hermes,* p. 296 ; *Murray's Gram.* 259. sailors who were boiling their dinners upon the shore."—*Day's Sandford and Mer* "And they in their turns were subdued by others."—*Pinnock's Geography,* p. 12. try on our parts is not superseded by God's grace."—*Arrowsmith.* "Their Health may be pretty well secur'd."—*Locke, on Education,* p. 51. "Though he was ri our sakes he became poor."—*Murray's Gram.* p. 211. "It were to be wished, his had been as wise on their parts."—*Harris's Hermes,* p. 60. "The Arabs are co by the ancients for being most exact to their words, and respectful to their law *Sale's Koran.* "That is, as a reward of some exertion on our parts."—*Gurney's* p. 86. "So that it went ill with Moses for their sakes."—*Psalms,* cvi, 32. "All have their parts in the burning lake."—*Watts,* p. 33. "For our own sakes thine."—*Pref. to Waller's Poems,* p. 3. "By discovering their abilities to detect errors."—*Murray's Gram.* Vol. ii, p. iv.

> "This world I do renounce; and, in your sights,
> Shake patiently my great affliction off."—*Beauties of Shak.* p. 263.

"If your relenting angers yield to treat,
> Pompey and thou, in safety, here may meet."—*Rowe's Lucan,* B. iii, L

UNDER NOTE V. — POSSESSIVES WITH PARTICIPLES.

"This will encourage him to proceed without his acquiring the prejudice."— *Gram.* p. 5. "And the notice which they give of an action's being completed or n

---

* Nixon parses *boy,* as being "in the possessive case, governed by *distress* understood;" and for "coupled by *nor* to *boy,*" according to the Rule, "Conjunctions connect the same cases." Thus one word ten wrong ; the other, parsed wrong: and so of all his examples above.—G. BROWN.

pleted."—*L. Murray's Gram.* p. 72; *Alger's*, 30. "Some obstacle or impediment that prevents its taking place."—*Priestley's Gram.* p. 38; *Alex. Murray's*, 37. "They have apostolical authority for their so frequently urging the seeking of the Spirit."—*The Friend*, Vol. xii, p. 54. "Here then is a wide field for reason's exerting its powers in relation to the objects of taste."—*Blair's Rhet.* p. 18. "Now this they derive altogether from their having a greater capacity of imitation and description."—*Ib.* p. 51. "This is one clear reason of their paying a greater attention to that construction."—*Ib.* p. 123. "The dialogue part had also a modulation of its own, which was capable of its being set to notes."—*Ib.* p. 471. "What is the reason of our being often so frigid and unpersuasive in public discourse?"— *Ib.* p. 334. "Which is only a preparation for his leading his forces directly upon us."—*Ib.* p. 264. "The nonsense about *which's* relating to things only, and having no declension, needs no refutation."—*Fowle's True E. Gram.* p. 18. "Who, upon his breaking it open, found nothing but the following inscription."—*Rollin*, Vol. ii, p. 33. "A prince will quickly have reason to repent his having exalted one person so high."—*Id.* ii, 116. "Notwith- standing it's being the immediate subject of his discourse."—*Churchill's Gram.* p. 294. "With our definition of its being synonymous with *time*."—*Booth's Introd.* p. 29. "It will considerably increase the danger of our being deceived."—*Campbell's Rhet.* p. 293. "His beauties can never be mentioned without their suggesting his blemishes also."—*Blair's Rhet.* p. 442. "No example has ever been adduced of a man's conscientiously approving of an action, because of its badness."—*Gurney's Evidences*, p. 90. "The last episode of the angel's shewing Adam the fate of his posterity, is happily imagined."—*Blair's Rhet.* p. 452. "And the news came to my son, of his and the bride being in Dublin."—*Castle Rackrent*, p. 44. "There is no room for the mind's exerting any great effort."—*Blair's Rhet.* p. 32. "One would imagine, that these criticks never so much as heard of Homer's having written first."—*Pope's Preface to Homer.* "Condemn the book, for its not being a geography."—*O. B. Peirce's Gram.* p. 317. "There will be in many words a transition from their being the figurative to their being the proper signs of certain ideas."—*Camp- bell's Rhet.* p. 322. "The doctrine of the Pope's being the only source of ecclesiastical power."—*Religious World*, ii, 290. "This has been the more expedient from the work's being designed for the benefit of private learners."—*Murray's Exercises, Introd.* p. v. "This was occasioned by the Grammar's having been *set up*, and not admitting of enlargement." —*Ib. Advertisement*, p. ix.

RULE V.—OBJECTIVES.

A Noun or a Pronoun made the object of an active-transitive verb or par- ticiple, is governed by it in the objective case: as, " I found *her* assisting *him*."—" Having finished the *work*, I submit *it*."

" Preventing *fame*, misfortune lends him *wings*,
And Pompey's self his own sad *story* brings."—*Rowe's Lucan*, B. viii, l. 66.

OBSERVATIONS ON RULE V.

Obs. 1.—To this rule there are no exceptions; but to the old one adopted by Murray and others, "Active verbs govern the objective case," there are more than any writer will ever think it worth his while to enumerate. In point of brevity, the latter has the advantage, but in noth- ing else; for, as a general rule for NOUNS AND PRONOUNS, this old brief assertion is very defec- tive; and, as a rule for "THE SYNTAX OF VERBS," under which head it has been oftener ranked, it is entirely useless and inapplicable. As there are four different constructions to which the nominative case is liable, so there are four in which the objective may be found; and two of these are common to both; namely, *apposition*, and *sameness of case*. Every objective is governed by some *verb* or *participle*, according to Rule 5th, or by some *preposition*, according to Rule 7th; except such as are put in *apposition* with others, according to Rule 3d, or after an infinitive or a participle *not transitive*, according to Rule 6th: as, "Mistaking *one* for the *other*, they took *him*, a sturdy *fellow*, called *Red Billy*, to be *me*." Here is every construction which the objective case can have; except, perhaps, that in which, as an expression of time, place, measure, or man- ner, it is taken after the fashion of an *adverb*, the governing preposition being suppressed, or, as some say, no governing word being needed. Of this exception, the following quotations may serve for examples: "It holds on by a single button round my neck, *cloak fashion*."—EDGE- WORTH'S *Castle Rackrent*, p. 17. A man quite at leisure to parse all his words, would have said, "*in the* fashion *of a* cloak." Again: "He does not care the *rind of a* lemon for her all the while."—*Ib.* p. 108. "We turn our eyes *this way* or *that way*."—*Webster's Philos. Gram.* p. 172; *Frazee's Gram.* 157. Among his instances of "*the objective case restrictive*," or of the noun "used in the objective, without a governing word," Dr. Bullions gives this: "Let us go *home*." But, according to the better opinion of Worcester, *home* is here an *adverb*, and not a noun. See Obs. 6th on Rule 7th.

Obs. 2.—The objective case *generally follows* the governing word: as, "And Joseph knew his *brethren*, but they knew not *him*."—*Gen.* xlii, 8. But when it is emphatic, it often precedes the nominative: as, "*Me* he restored to mine office, and *him* he hanged."—*Gen.* xli, 13. "*John* have I beheaded."—*Luke*, ix, 9. "But *me* ye have not always."—*Matt.* xxvi, 11. "*Him* walking on a sunny hill he found."—*Milton.* In poetry, the objective is sometimes placed between the nominative and the verb; as,

"His daring foe securely *him* defied."—*Milton.*
"Much he the *place* admir'd, the person more."—*Id.*
"The broom its yellow *leaf* hath shed."—*Langhorne.*

If the nominative be a pronoun which cannot be mistaken for an objective, the words may possibly change places; as, "*Silver* and *gold* have *I* none." "Created *thing* nought valued *he* nor shunn'd."—*Milton,* B. ii, 1. 679. But such a transposition of *two nouns* can scarcely fail to render the meaning doubtful or obscure; as,

"This *pow'r* has *praise,* that virtue scarce can warm,
Till fame supplies the universal charm."—*Dr. Johnson.*

A relative or an interrogative pronoun is commonly placed at the head of its clause, and of course it precedes the verb which governs it; as, "I am Jesus, *whom* thou persecutest."—*Acts,* ix, 5. "*Which* of the prophets have not your fathers persecuted?"—*Ib.* vii, 52.

"Before their Clauses plac'd, by settled use,
The Relatives these Clauses introduce."—*Ward's Gram.* p. 86.

OBS. 3.—Every active-transitive verb or participle has some *noun* or *pronoun* for its object, or some *pronominal adjective* which assumes the relation of the objective case. Though verbs are often followed by the infinitive mood, or a dependent clause, forming a part of the logical predicate; yet these terms, being commonly introduced by a connecting particle, do not form *such an object* as is contemplated in our definition of a transitive verb. Its government of *the objective,* is the only proper criterion of this sort of verb. If, in the sentence, "Boys *love* to play," the former verb is transitive, as several respectable grammarians affirm; why not also in a thousand others; as, "Boys *like* to play;"—"Boys *delight* to play;"—"Boys *long* to play;"—"The boys *seem* to play;"—"The boys *cease* to play;"—"The boys *ought* to play;"—"The boys *go out* to play;"—"The boys *are gone out* to play;"—"The boys *are allowed* to play;" and the like? The construction in all is precisely the same, and the infinitive may follow one kind of verb just as well as an other. How then can the mere addition of this mood make *any* verb transitive? or where, on such a principle, can the line of distinction for transitive verbs be drawn? The infinitive, *in fact,* is governed by the preposition *to;* and the preceding verb, if it has no other object, is intransitive. It must, however, be confessed that some verbs which thus take the infinitive after them, cannot otherwise be intransitive; as, "A great mind *disdains to hold* any thing by courtesy."—*Johnson's Life of Swift.* "They *require to be distinguished* by a comma."—*Murray's Gram.* p. 272.

OBS. 4.—A transitive verb, as I have elsewhere shown, may both govern the objective case, and be followed by an infinitive also; as, "*What* have I *to do* with thee?"—*John,* ii, 4. This question, as one would naturally take it, implies, "I have *nothing to do* with thee;" and, by analogy, *what* is governed by *have,* and not by *do;* so that the latter verb, though not commonly intransitive, appears to be so here. Indeed the infinitive mood is often used without an objective, when every other part of the same verb would require one. Maunder's rule is, "Transitive verbs and participles govern *either* the objective case *or* the infinitive *mode.*"—*Comprehensive Gram.* p. 14. Murray teaches, not only that, "The *infinitive mood* does the office of a substantive in the objective case; as, 'Boys love *to play;*'" but that, "The *participle* with its adjuncts, may be considered as a substantive phrase *in the objective case,* governed by the preposition or verb; as, 'He studied to avoid *expressing himself too severely.*'"—See his *Octavo Gram.* pp. 184 and 194. And again: "*Part of a sentence,* as well as a noun or pronoun, may be said to be *in the objective case,* or to be put objectively, *governed* by the active verb; as, 'We sometimes see *virtue in distress,* but we should consider *how great will be her ultimate reward.*' Sentences or phrases under this circumstance, may be termed *objective sentences* or *phrases.*"—*Ib.* p. 180.

OBS. 5.—If we admit that sentences, parts of sentences, infinitives, participles with their adjuncts, and other phrases, as well as nouns and pronouns, may be "*in the objective case;*" it will be no easy matter, either to define this case, or to determine what words do, or do not, govern it.* The construction of infinitives and participles will be noticed hereafter. But on one of

* Wells, whose Grammar, in its first edition, divides verbs into "*transitive, intransitive,* and *passive;*" but whose late editions absurdly make all passives transitive; says, in his third edition, "A *transitive verb* is a verb that *has some noun or pronoun* for its object;" (p. 78:) adopts, in his syntax, the old dogma, "Transitive verbs govern the objective case;" (3d Ed. p. 154;) and to this rule subjoins a series of remarks, so singularly fit to puzzle or mislead the learner, and withal so successful in winning the approbation of committees and teachers, that it may be worth while to notice most of them here.

"REM. 1.—A sentence or phrase *often* supplies the place of a noun or pronoun in the objective case; as, 'You see *how few of these men have returned.*'"—*Wells's School Gram.,* "Third Thousand," p. 154; late Ed. § 215. According to this, must we not suppose verbs to be often transitive, when *not made so* by the author's *definition?* And if "*see*" is here transitive, would not other forms, such as *are told, have been told,* or *are aware,* be just as much so, if put in its place?

"REM. 2.—An *intransitive* verb may be used to *govern an objective,* when the verb and the noun depending upon it are of kindred signification; as, '*To live* a blameless *life;*'—'*To run* a *race.*'"—*Ib.* Here verbs are absurdly called "*intransitive,*" when, both in fact and by the foregoing definition, they are clearly transitive; or, at least, are, by many teachers, supposed to be so.

"REM. 3.—Idiomatic expressions sometimes occur in which *intransitive* verbs are followed by *objectives depending upon them;* as, '*To look the subject* fully in the face.'—*Channing.* 'They *laughed him to scorn.*'—*Matt.* 9: 24. 'And *talked the night* away.'—*Goldsmith.*"—*Ib.* Here, again, verbs evidently *made transitive by the construction,* are, with strange inconsistency, called "*intransitive.*" By these three remarks together, the distinction between transitives and intransitives must needs be extensively *obscured* in the mind of the learner.

"REM. 4.—Transitive verbs of *asking, giving, teaching, and some others,* are often employed to govern *two* objectives; as, '*Ask him* his opinion;'—'This experience *taught me* a valuable *lesson.*'—'*Spare me* yet this bitter cup.'—*Hemans.* 'I thrice *presented him* a kingly *crown.*'—*Shakspeare.*"—*Ib.* This rule not only jumbles together several different constructions, such as would require different cases in Latin or Greek, but is evidently repugnant to *the sense* of many of the passages to which it is meant to be applied. Wells thinks, the practice of supplying a preposition, "is, in many cases, arbitrary, and does violence to an important and well established

Murray's examples I would here observe, that the direct use of the infinitive for an objective noun is a manifest *Grecism*; as, "For to will is present with me; but *to perform* that which is good, I find not."—*Octavo Gram.* p. 184.   That is, "*the performance of* that which is good, I find not."   Or perhaps we may supply a noun after the verb, and take this text to mean, "But to perform that which is good, I find not *the ability*."   Our Bible has it, "But *how* to perform that which is good, I find not;" as if *the manner* in which he might do good, was what the apostle found not: but Murray cites it differently, omitting the word *how*, as we see above.   All active verbs to which something is subjoined by *when, where, whence, how*, or *why*, must be accounted intransitive, unless we suppose them to govern such nouns of time, place, degree, manner, or cause, as correspond to these connectives; as, "I *know why* she blushed."   Here we might supply the noun *reason*, as, "I know *the reason* why she blushed;" but the word is needless, and I should rather parse *know* as being intransitive.   As for "*virtue in distress*," if this is an "*objective phrase*," and not to be analyzed, we have millions of the same sort; but, if one should say, "*Virtue in distress* excites pity," the *same* phrase would demonstrate the absurdity of Murray's doctrine, because the two nouns here take *two different cases.*

OBS. 6.—The word *that*, which is often employed to introduce a dependent clause, is, by some grammarians, considered as a *pronoun*, representing the clause which follows it; as, "I know *that* Messias cometh."—*John*, iv, 25. This text they would explain to mean, "*Messias cometh*, I know *that*;" and their opinion seems to be warranted both by the origin and by the usual import of the particle.   But, in conformity to general custom, and to his own views of the practical purposes of grammatical analysis, the author has ranked it with the conjunctions.   And he thinks it better, to call those verbs intransitive, which are followed by *that* and a dependent clause, than to supply the very frequent ellipses which the other explanation supposes.   To explain it as a conjunction, connecting an active-transitive verb and its object, as several respectable grammarians do, appears to involve some inconsistency.   If *that* is a conjunction, it connects what precedes and what follows; but a transitive verb should exercise a direct government, without the intervention of a conjunction.   On the other hand, the word *that* has not, in any such sentence, the inherent nature of a pronoun.   The transposition above, makes it only a *pronominal*

idiom of the language."—*Ib*. But how can any idiom be violated by a mode of parsing, which merely expounds its *true meaning?* If the dative case has the meaning of *to*, and the ablative has the meaning of *from*, how can they be expounded, in English, but by suggesting the *particle*, where it is omitted? For example: "Spare me yet [*from*] this bitter cup."—"Spare [*to*] me yet this joyous cup." This author says, "*The rule* for the government of two objectives by a verb, without the aid of a preposition, is adopted by Webster, Murray, Alexander, Frazee, Nutting, Perley, Goldsbury, J. M. Putnam, Hamlin, Flower, Crane, Brace, and many others."—*Ib.* Yet, if I mistake not, the weight of authority is vastly against it. *Such a rule as this*, is not extensively approved; and even some of the names here given, are improperly cited. Lindley Murray's remark, "Some of our verbs appear to govern two words in the objective case," is applied only to *words in apposition*, and wrong even there; Perley's rule is only of "*Some* verbs of *asking* and *teaching*;" and Nutting's note, "It *sometimes happens* that one can neither deny it, nor tell how much it means.

"REM. 5.—Verbs of *asking, giving, teaching*, and *some others*, are often employed in the passive voice *to govern* a noun or pronoun; as, 'He was asked his opinion'—*Johnson*. 'He *had been refused shelter*.'—*Irving*."—*Ib* p. 155, § 215. Passive *governing* is not far from absurdity. Here, by way of illustration, we have examples of *two sorts*; the one elliptical, the other solecistical. The former text appears to mean, "He was asked *for* his opinion;"—or, "He was asked *to give* his opinion:" the latter should have been, "*Shelter had been refused* him;"—i. e. "*to* him." Of the seven instances cited by the author, five at least are of the latter kind, and therefore to be condemned; and it is to be observed, that when they are *corrected*, and the right word is made *nominative*, the passive government, by Wells's own showing, becomes nothing but the ellipsis of a preposition. Having just given a *rule*, by which all his various examples are assumed to be regular and right, he very inconsistently adds this note: "*This form* of expression is *anomalous*, and *might*, in many cases, be improved. Thus, *instead* of saying, 'He was offered a seat in the council,' it would be preferable to say, 'A seat in the council was offered [to] him.'"—*Ib.* p. 155, § 215. By admitting here the ellipsis of the preposition *to*, he evidently refutes the doctrine of his own text, so far as it relates to *passive government*, and, by implication, the doctrine of his fourth remark also. For the ellipsis of *to*, before "*him*," is just as evident in the active expression, "I thrice *presented him* a kingly crown." as in the passive, "A kingly crown *was thrice presented him*." It is absurd to deny it in either. Having offset *himself*, Wells as ingeniously balances his *authorities, pro and con*; but, the *elliptical* examples being *allowable*, he should not have said that I and others "*condemn this usage altogether.*"

"REM. 6.—The passive voice of a verb is sometimes used in connection with a *preposition*, forming a compound *passive verb*; as, 'He *was listened to*.'—'Nor is this to be scoffed at.'—This is a tendency to be guarded against.'—'A bitter persecution *was carried on*.'—*Hallam*."—*Ib.* p. 155, § 215. The words here called "*prepositions*," are *adverbs*. Prepositions they cannot be; because they have no subsequent term. Nor is it either necessary or proper, to call them parts of the verb: "*was carried on*," is no more a "compound verb," than "*was carried off*," or "*was carried forward*." and the like.

"REM. 7.—Idiomatic expressions sometimes occur in which a noun in the objective is preceded by a passive verb, and followed by a *preposition used adverbially*. EXAMPLES: 'Vocal and instrumental music *were made use of*.'—*Addison*. 'The third, and fifth, *were taken possession of* at half past eight.'—*Southey*. 'The Pinta *was soon lost sight of* in the darkness of the night.'—*Irving*."—*Ib.* p. 155, § 215. As it is by the manner of their use, that we distinguish prepositions and adverbs, it seems no more proper to speak of "*a preposition used adverbially*," than of "*an adverb used prepositionally*." But even if the former phrase is right and the thing conceivable, here is no instance of it; for "*of*" here modifies no verb, adjective, or adverb. The construction is an unparsable synchysis, a vile snarl, which no grammarian should hesitate to condemn. These examples may each be corrected in several ways: 1. Say—"*were used*;"—"*were taken into possession*;"—"*was soon lost from sight*." 2. Say—"They made use of music, *both* vocal and instrumental."—"Of the third, *the* fourth, and *the* fifth, *they took possession* at half past eight."—"Of the Pinta *they* soon lost sight," &c. 3. Say—"Use *was also* made of *both* vocal and instrumental music."—"Possession of the third, *the* fourth, and the fifth, *was taken* at half past eight."—"The Pinta soon *disappeared* in the darkness of the night." Here, again, Wells puzzles his pupil, with a note which half justifies and half condemns the awkward usage in question. See *School Gram.* 1st Ed. p. 147; 3d Ed. 156; late Ed. § 215.

"REM. 8.—There are *some* verbs which may be used either transitively or intransitively; as, 'He *will return* in a week.' 'He *will return* the book.'"—*Ib.* p. 147; 156; &c. According to Dr. Johnson, this is true of "*most* verbs," and Lindley Murray asserts it of "*many*." There are, I think, but *few* which may *not*, in some phraseology or other, be used both ways. Hence the rule, "*Transitive verbs govern the objective case*." or, as Wells now has it, "*Transitive verbs*, in the active voice, govern the objective case," (§ 215,) rests only upon a distinction which *itself creates*, between transitives and intransitives; and therefore it amounts to little.

adjective; as, "Messias cometh, I know *that fact.*" And in many instances such a solution is impracticable; as, "The people sought him, and came unto him, and stayed him, *that* he should not depart from them."—*Luke*, iv, 42. Here, to prove *that* to be a pronoun, the disciples of Tooke and Webster must resort to more than one imaginary ellipsis, and to such an inversion as will scarcely leave the sense in sight.

OBS. 7.—In some instances the action of a transitive verb gives to its direct object an additional name, which is also in the objective case, the two words being in apposition; as, "Thy saints proclaim *thee king.*"—*Cowper.* "And God called the *firmament Heaven.*"—*Bible.* "Ordering them to make *themselves masters* of a certain steep eminence."—*Rollin*, ii, 67. And, in such a construction, the direct object is sometimes placed before the verb; though the name which results from the action, cannot be so placed: as, "And *Simon* he surnamed *Peter.*"—*Mark*, iii, 15. "*Him* that overcometh will I make a *pillar* in the temple of my God."—*Rev.* iii, 12. Some grammarians seem not to have considered this phraseology as coming within the rule of apposition. Thus Webster: "We have some verbs which *govern two words* in the objective case; as,

> 'Did I request thee, maker, from my clay
> To mold *me man?*'—*Milton*, 10, 744.

'God seems to have made him *what* he was.'—*Philosophical Gram.* p. 170; *Improved Gram.* p. 120. See also *Weld's Gram.* 2d Ed. p. 154; "Abridged Ed." p. 119; and *Fowler's E. Gram.* § 450. So Murray: "Some of our verbs *appear to govern two words* in the objective case; as, 'The Author of my being formed *me man.*' —'They desired me to call *them brethren.*'—'He seems to have made *him what* he was.'"—*Octavo Gram.* p. 183. Yet this latter writer says, that in the sentence, "They appointed *me executor,*" and others like it, "the verb *to be is understood.*"—*Ib.* p. 182. These then, according to his own showing, are instances of apposition; but I pronounce them such, without either confounding same cases with apposition, or making the latter a species of ellipsis. See Obs. 1st and 2d, under Rule 3d.

OBS. 8.—In general, if not always, when a verb is followed by two objectives which are neither in apposition nor connected by a conjunction, one of them is governed by a preposition understood; as, "I paid [to] *him* the *money.*"—"They offered [to] *me a seat.*"—"He asked [of] *them* the *question.*"—"I yielded, and unlock'd [to] *her* all my *heart.*"—*Milton.* In expressing such sentences passively, the object of the preposition is sometimes erroneously assumed for the nominative; as, "He was paid *the money,*" in stead of, "*The money* was paid [to] *him.*"—"I was offered *a seat,*" in stead of, "*A seat* was offered [to] *me.*" This kind of error is censured by Murray more than once, and yet he himself has, in very many instances, fallen into it. His first criticism on it, is in the following words: "We sometimes meet with such expressions as these: 'They were asked a question;' 'They were offered a pardon;' 'He had been left a great estate by his father.' In these *phrases*, verbs passive are made to govern the objective case. This license *is not to be approved.* The expressions should be: 'A question was put to them;' 'A pardon was offered to them;' 'His father left him a great estate.'"—*L. Murray's Octavo Gram.* p. 183. See Obs. 12, below.

OBS. 9.—In the Latin syntax, verbs of *asking* and *teaching* are said to govern two accusatives; as, "*Posce Deum veniam,* Beg pardon of God."—*Grant's Latin Gram.* p. 207. "*Docuit me grammaticam,* He taught me grammar."—*Grant, Adam, and others.* And again: "When a verb in the active voice governs two cases, in the passive it retains the latter case; as, *Doceor grammaticam,* I am taught grammar."—*Adam's Gram.* p. 177. These writers however suggest, that in reality the *latter* accusative is governed, not by the verb, but by a preposition understood. In general the English idiom *does not coincide* with what occurs in Latin under these rules. We commonly insert a preposition to govern one or the other of the terms. But we sometimes leave to the verb the objective of the person, and sometimes that of the thing; and after the two verbs *ask* and *teach,* we sometimes *seem* to leave both: as, "When thou dost *ask me* blessing, I'll kneel down, and *ask of thee* forgiveness."—*Shakspeare.* "In long journeys, *ask your master leave* to give ale to the horses."—*Swift.* "And he *asked them of* their welfare."—*Gen.* xliii, 27. "They *asked of him* the parable."—*Mark*, iv, 10. ("*Interrogárunt eum de parabolâ.*"—*Beza.*) "And asking *them questions.*"—*Luke*, ii, 46. "But *teach them* thy *sons.*"—*Deut.* iv, 9. "*Teach them* diligently *unto* thy *children.*"—*Ib.* vi, 7. "Ye shall *teach them* your *children.*"—*Ib* xi, 19. "Shall any *teach God knowledge?*"—*Job*, xxi, 22. "I will *teach you* the *fear* of the Lord."—*Psal.* xxxiv, 11. "He will *teach us of* his *ways.*"—*Isaiah*, ii, 3; *Micah*, iv, 2. "Let him that *is taught* in the *word,* communicate."—*Gal.* vi, 6.

OBS. 10.—After a careful review of the various instances in which more than one noun or pronoun may possibly be supposed to be under the government of a single active verb in English, I incline to the opinion that none of our verbs ought to be parsed as actually governing two cases, except such as are followed by two objectives connected by a conjunction. Consequently I do not admit, that any passive verb can properly govern an objective noun or pronoun. Of the ancient Saxon dative case, and of what was once considered the government of two cases, there yet appear some evident remains in our language; as, "Give *him bread* to eat."—"Bread shall be given *him.*"—*Bible.* But here, by almost universal consent, the indirect object is referred to the government of a "preposition understood;" and in many instances this sort of ellipsis is certainly no elegance: as, "Give [to] truth and virtue the *same arms which* you give [to] vice and falsehood, and the former are likely to prevail."—*Blair's Rhet.* p. 235. The questionable expres-

---

* To these examples, Webster adds *two others,* of a *different sort,* with a comment, thus: "'Ask *him* his *opinion;*' 'You have asked *me* the *news.*' Will it be said that the latter phrases are elliptical, for 'ask *of* him his opinion?' I apprehend this to be a mistake. According to the true idea of the government of a transitive verb, *him* must be the *object* in the phrase under consideration, as much as in this, 'Ask *him* for a guinea;' or in this, 'ask him to go.'"—*Ibid. ut supra;* Fraze's *Gram.* p. 152; *Fowler's,* p. 480. If, for the reason here stated, it is a "mistake" to supply *of* in the foregoing instances, it does not follow that they are not elliptical. On the contrary, if they are analogous to, "Ask him *for* a guinea;" or, "Ask him *to go;*" it is manifest that the construction must be this: "Ask him [*for*] his opinion;" or, "Ask him [*to tell*] his opinion." So that the question resolves itself into this: What is the best way of *supplying the ellipsis,* when two objectives thus occur after *ask?*—G. BROWN.

sion, "*Ask me blessing*," if interpreted analogically, must mean, "Ask *for* me a blessing," which is more correct and explicit; or, if *me* be not supposed a dative, (and it does not appear to be so, above,) the sentence is still wrong, and the correction must be, "Ask *of* me a blessing," or "Ask my blessing." So, "Ask your *master leave*," ought rather to be, "Ask *of* your master leave," "Ask your master *for* leave," or, "Ask your *master's* leave." The example from Mark ought to be, "They asked *him about* the parable." Again, the elliptical sentence, "Teach them thy sons," is less perspicuous, and therefore less accurate, than the full expression, "Teach them *to* thy sons." *To teach* is to tell things *to* persons, or to instruct persons *in* things; *to ask* is to request or demand things *of* or *from* persons, or to interrogate or solicit persons *about* or *for* things. These verbs cannot be proved to govern two cases in English, because it is more analogical and more reasonable to supply a preposition, (if the author omits it,) to govern one or the other of the objects.

OBS. 11.—Some writers erroneously allow passive verbs to govern the objective in English, not only where they imagine our idiom to coincide with the Latin, but even where they know that it does not. Thus Dr. Crombie: "Whatever is put in the accusative case after the verb, must be the nominative to it in the passive voice, while the other case is retained under the government of the verb, and cannot become its nominative. Thus, ' I persuade you *to* this or *of* this,' *Persuadeo hoc tibi.* Here, the person persuaded is expressed in the dative case, and cannot, therefore, be the nominative to the passive verb. We must, therefore, say, *Hoc tibi persuadetur*, ' You are persuaded *of* this;' not, *Tu persuaderis.* He trusted me *with* this affair,' or ' He believed me *in* this,' *Hoc mihi credidit.*—Passively, *Hoc mihi creditum est.* ' I told you this,' *Hoc tibi dixi.* 'YOU WERE TOLD THIS,' *Hoc tibi dictum est;* not, *Tu dictus es.*" [No, surely: for, ' *Tu dictus es*,' means, ' You were called,' or, ' Thou art reputed;'—and, if followed by any case, it must be the *nominative*.] "It is the more necessary to attend to this rule, and to these distinctions, as the idioms of the two languages do not always concur. Thus, *Hoc tibi dictum est*, means not only 'This was told *to* you,' but ' YOU WERE TOLD THIS.' *Liber mihi a patre promissus est*, means both 'A book was promised (*to*) me by my father,' and ' I WAS PROMISED A BOOK.' *Is primùm rogatus est sententiam*, ' He was first asked *for* his opinion,' and ' An opinion was first asked *of* him;' 'In which last the accusative of the person becomes, in Latin, the nominative in the passive voice." See *Grant's Latin Gram.* p. 210.

OBS. 12.—Murray's *second* censure upon passive government, is this: "The following sentences, which give [to] the passive voice the regimen of an active verb, *are very irregular, and by no means to be imitated.* ' The bishops and abbots *were allowed their seats* in the house of lords.' ' *Thrasea was forbidden the presence* of the emperor.' ' He *was shown* that *very story* in one of his own books.'[*] These sentences should have been; ' The bishops and abbots were allowed *to have* (or *to take*) their seats in the house of lords;' or, ' Seats in the house of lords were allowed *to* the bishops and abbots:' ' Thrasea was forbidden *to approach* the presence of the emperor;' or, ' The presence of the emperor was forbidden *to* Thrasea:' ' That very story was shown *to* him in one of his own books.' "—*Octavo Gram.* p. 223. See Obs. 8, above. One late grammarian, whose style is on the whole highly commendable for its purity and accuracy, forbears to condemn the phraseology here spoken of; and, though he does not expressly defend and justify it, he seems disposed to let it pass, with the license of the following canon. "For convenience, it may be well to state it as a rule, that—*Passive verbs govern an objective, when the nominative to the passive verb is not the proper object of the active voice.*"—*Barnard's Analytic Gram.* p. 134. Another asserts the government of two cases by very many of our active verbs, and the government of one by almost any passive verb, according to the following rules : " Verbs of teaching, giving, and some others of a similar nature, govern two objectives, the one of a person and the other of a thing; as, He taught *me grammar* : His tutor gave *him a lesson* : He promised *me a reward*. A passive verb may govern an objective, when the words immediately preceding and following it, do not refer to the same thing; as, Henry *was offered* a *dollar* by his father to induce him to remain."—*J. M. Putnam's Gram.* pp. 110 and 112.

OBS. 13.—The common dogmas, that an active verb must govern an object, and that a neuter or intransitive verb must not, amount to nothing as directions to the composer; because the classification of verbs depends upon this very matter, whether they have, or have not, an object after them; and no general principle has been, or can be, furnished beforehand, by which their fitness or unfitness for taking such government can be determined. This must depend upon usage, and usage must conform to the sense intended. Very many verbs—probably a vast majority—govern an object sometimes, but not always: many that are commonly intransitive or neuter, are not in all their uses so; and many that are commonly transitive, have sometimes no apparent regimen. The distinction, then, in our dictionaries, of verbs active and neuter, or transitive and intransitive, serves scarcely any other purpose, than to show how the presence or absence of the objective case, affects the meaning of the word. In some instances the signification of the verb seems almost merged in that of its object; as, *to lay hold, to make use, to take care.* In others, the transitive character of the word is partial; as, "He *paid* my *board; I *told* you* so." Some verbs will govern any objective whatever; as, *to name, to mention.* What is there that *cannot be named* or *mentioned*? Others again are restricted to one noun, or to a few; as, *to transgress a law*, or *rule.* What can be transgressed, but a law, a limit, or something equivalent? Some verbs will govern a kindred noun, or its pronoun, but scarcely any other; as, "He *lived* a virtuous *life*."—"Hear, I pray you, this *dream which I have dreamed.*"—*Gen.* xxxvii, 6. "I will also command the clouds that they *rain* no *rain* upon it."—*Isaiah*, v, 6.

OBS. 14.—Our grammarians, when they come to determine what verbs are properly transitive, and what are not so, do not in all instances agree in opinion. In short, plain as they think the matter, they are much at odds. Many of them say, that, " In the phrases, ' To dream a dream,'

---

* These examples Murray borrowed from Webster, who published them, with *references*, under his 34th Rule. With too little faith in the corrective power of grammar, the Doctor remarks upon the construction as follows : "This idiom is outrageously anomalous, but perhaps incorrigible."—*Webster's Philos. Gram.* p. 180; *Imp. Gr.* 128.

'To live a virtuous life,' 'To run a race,' 'To walk a horse,' 'To dance a child,' the verbs assume a *transitive* character, and in these cases may be denominated active."—See *Guy's Gram.* p. 21; *Murray's,* 180; *Ingersoll's,* 183; *Fisk's,* 123; *Smith's,* 153. This decision is undoubtedly just; yet a late writer has taken a deal of pains to find fault with it, and to persuade his readers, that, "No verb is active in *any sense,* or under *any construction,* that will not, in *every sense,* permit the objective case of a personal pronoun after it."—*Wright's Gram.* p. 174. Wells absurdly supposes, "An *intransitive* verb may be *used to govern* an objective."—*Gram.* p. 145. Some imagine that verbs of mental action, such as *conceive, think, believe,* &c., are not properly transitive; and, if they find an object after such a verb, they choose to supply a preposition to govern it: as, "I conceived it (*of* it) in that light."—*Guy's Gram.* p. 21. "Did you conceive (of) him to be me?"—*Ib.* p. 28. With this idea, few will probably concur.

OBS. 15.—We sometimes find the pronoun *me* needlessly thrown in after a verb that either governs some other object or is not properly transitive, at least in respect to this word; as, "It ascends *me* into the brain; dries *me* there all the foolish, dull, and crudy vapours."—*Shakspeare's Falstaff.* "Then the vital commoners and inland petty spirits muster *me* all to their captain, the heart."—*Id.* This is a faulty relic of our old Saxon dative case. So of the second person: "Fare *you* well, Falstaff."—*Shak.* Here *you* was written for the objective case, but it seems now to have become the nominative to the verb *fare.* "Fare *thee* well."—*W. Scott.* "Farewell *to* thee."—*Id.* These expressions were once equivalent in syntax; but they are hardly so now; and, in lieu of the former, it would seem better English to say, "Fare *thou* well." Again: "Turn *thee* aside to thy right hand or to thy left, and lay *thee* hold on one of the young men, and take *thee* his armour."—2 *Sam.* ii, 21. If any modern author had written this, our critics would have guessed he had learned from some of the Quakers to misemploy *thee* for *thou.* The construction is an imitation of the French reciprocal or reflected verbs. It ought to be thus: "Turn *thou* aside to thy right hand or to thy left, and *lay hold* on one of the young men, and take *to thyself* his armour." So of the third person: "The king soon found reason to repent *him of his* provoking such dangerous enemies."—HUME: *Murray's Gram.* i, p. 180. Here both of the pronouns are worse than useless, though Murray discerned but one error.

"Good Margaret, *run thee* into the parlour;
There thou shalt find my cousin Beatrice."—SHAK.: *Much Ado.*

NOTES TO RULE V.

NOTE I.—Those verbs or participles which require a regimen, or which signify action that must terminate transitively, should not be used without an object; as, "She *affects* [kindness,] in order to *ingratiate* [herself] with you."—"I *must caution* [you,] at the same time, against a servile imitation of any author whatever." —*Blair's Rhet.* p. 192.

NOTE II.—Those verbs and participles which do not admit an object, or which express action that terminates in themselves, or with the doer, should not be used transitively; as, "The planters *grow* cotton." Say *raise, produce,* or *cultivate.* "Dare you speak lightly of the law, or move that, in a criminal trial, judges should advance one step beyond *what* it permits them *to go?*"—*Blair's Rhet.* p. 278. Say,—"beyond *the point to which* it permits them to go."

NOTE III.—No transitive verb or participle should assume a government to which its own meaning is not adapted; as, "*Thou* is a pronoun, a word used *instead* of a noun—personal, it *personates* 'man.'"—*Kirkham's Gram.* p. 131. Say, "It *represents* man." "Where *a string* of such sentences *succeed each other.*"—*Blair's Rhet.* p. 168. Say, "Where *many* such sentences *come in succession.*"

NOTE IV.—The passive verb should always take for its subject or nominative the direct object of the active-transitive verb from which it is derived; as, (Active,) "They denied me this privilege." (Passive,) "This *privilege* was denied *me;*" not, "*I* was denied this *privilege:*" for *me* may be governed by *to* understood, but *privilege* cannot, nor can any other regimen be found for it.

NOTE V.—Passive verbs should never be made to govern the objective case, because the receiving of an action supposes it to terminate on the subject or nominative.* Errors: "Sometimes it *is made use of* to give a small degree of emphasis."— *L. Murray's Gram.* 8vo, p. 197. Say, "Sometimes it *is used,*" &c. "His female

---

* This seems to be a reasonable principle of syntax, and yet I find it contradicted, or a principle opposite to it set up, by some modern teachers of note, who venture to justify all those abnormal phrases which I here condemn as errors. Thus Fowler: "Note 5. When a Verb with its Accusative case, is *equivalent to a single verb,* it may take this accusative after it in the passive voice; as, 'This *has been put an end to.*'"—*Fowler's English Language,* 8vo, § 552. Now what is this, but an effort to teach bad English by rule?—and by such a rule, too, *as is vastly* mere general than even the great class of terms which it was designed to include? And yet this rule, broad as it is, does not apply at all to the example given! For "*put an end,*" without the important word "*to,*" is not equivalent to *stop* or *terminate.* Nor is the example right. One ought rather to say, "This has been *ended;*" or, "This has been *stopped.*" See the marginal Note to Obs. 5th, above.

characters *have been found fault with* as insipid."—*Hazlitt's Lect.* p. 111. Say,—
"*have been censured; or,—"have been blamed, decried, dispraised, or condemned.*"

NOTE VI.—The perfect participle, as such, should never be made to govern any objective term; because, without an active auxiliary, its signification is almost always passive: as, "We shall set down the characters *made use of* to represent all the elementary sounds."—*L. Murray's Gram.* p. 5; *Fisk's,* 34. Say,—"the characters *employed,* or *used.*"

NOTE VII.—As the different cases in English are not always distinguished by their form, care must be taken lest their construction be found equivocal, or ambiguous; as, "And we shall always *find our sentences acquire* more vigour and energy when thus retrenched."—*Blair's Rhet.* p. 111. Say, "We shall always find *that* our sentences acquire more vigour," &c.; or, "We shall always find our sentences *to* acquire more vigour and energy when thus retrenched."

NOTE VIII.—In the language of our Bible, rightly quoted or printed, *ye* is not found in the objective case, nor *you* in the nominative; scriptural texts that preserve not this distinction of cases, are consequently to be considered inaccurate.

IMPROPRIETIES FOR CORRECTION.

FALSE SYNTAX UNDER RULE V.

UNDER THE RULE ITSELF.—THE OBJECTIVE FORM.

"Who should I meet the other day but my old friend!"—*Spectator,* No. 32.

[FORMULE.—Not proper, because the pronoun *who* is in the nominative case, and is used as the object of the active-transitive verb *should meet.* But, according to Rule 5th, "A noun or a pronoun made the object of an active-transitive verb or participle, is governed by it in the objective case." Therefore, *who* should be *whom;* thus, "*Whom* should I meet," &c.]

"Let not him boast that puts on his armour, but he that takes it off."—*Barclay's Works,* iii, 262.   "Let none touch it, but they who are clean."—*Sale's Koran,* 95.   "Let the sea roar, and the fullness thereof; the world, and they that dwell therein."—*Psalms,* xcviii, 7. "Pray be private, and careful who you trust."—*Mrs. Goffe's Letter.*   "How shall the people know who to entrust with their property and their liberties?"—*District School,* p. 301. "The chaplain entreated my comrade and I to dress as well as possible."—*World Displayed,* i, 163.   "He that cometh unto me, I will in no wise cast out."—*Tract,* No. 3, p. 6.   "Who, during this preparation, they constantly and solemnly invoke."—*Hope of Israel,* p. 84. "Whoever or whatever owes us, is Debtor; whoever or whatever we owe, is Creditor."—*Marsh's Book-Keeping,* p. 23.   "Declaring the curricle was his, and he should have who he chose in it."—*Anna Ross,* p. 147.   "The fact is, Burke is the only one of all the host of brilliant contemporaries who we can rank as a first-rate orator."—*The Knickerbocker,* May, 1833.   "Thus you see, how naturally the Fribbles and the Daffodils have produced the Messalina's of our time."—*Brown's Estimate,* ii, 53.   "They would find in the Roman list both the Scipio's."—*Ib.* ii, 76.   "He found his wife's clothes on fire, and she just expiring."—*New-York Observer.*   "To present ye holy, unblameable, and unreproveable in his sight."—*Barclay's Works,* i, 353.   "Let the distributer do his duty with simplicity; the superintendent, with diligence; he who performs offices of compassion, with cheerfulness." —*Stuart's Romans,* xii, 9.   "If the crew rail at the master of the vessel, who will they mind?"—*Collier's Antoninus,* p. 106.   "He having none but them, they having none but hee."—DRAYTON's *Polyolbion.*

> "Thou, nature, partial nature, I arraign!
> Of thy caprice maternal I complain."—*Burns's Poems,* p. 50.

> "Nor knows he who it is his arms pursue
> With eager clasps, but loves he knows not who."—*Addison's,* p. 218.

UNDER NOTE I.—OF VERBS TRANSITIVE.

"When it gives that sense, and also connects, it is a conjunction."—*L. Murray's Gram.* p. 116.   "Though thou wilt not acknowledge, thou canst not deny the fact."—*Murray's Key,* p. 209.   "They *specify,* like many other adjectives, and *connect* sentences."—*Kirkham's Gram.* p. 114.   "The violation of this rule tends so much to perplex and obscure, that it is safer to err by too many short sentences."—*Murray's Gram.* p. 312.   "A few *Exercises* are subjoined to each important definition, for him to *practice* upon as he proceeds in committing."—*Nutting's Gram.* 3d Ed. p. vii.   "A verb signifying actively governs the accusative." —*Adam's Gram.* p. 171; *Gould's,* 172; *Grant's,* 199; and others.   "Or, any word that will *conjugate,* is a verb."—*Kirkham's Gram.* p. 44.   "In these two concluding sentences, the author, hastening to finish, appears to write rather carelessly."—*Blair's Rhet.* p. 216.

"He simply reasons on one side of the question, and then finishes."—*Ib.* p. 306. "Praise to God teaches to be humble· and lowly ourselves."—ATTERBURY: *ib.* p. 304. "This author has endeavored to surpass."—*Green's Inductive Gram.* p. 54. "Idleness and plexure fateeg as soon as bizziness."—*Noah Webster's Essays*, p. 402. "And, in conjugating, you must pay particular attention to the manner in which these signs are applied."—*Kirkham's Gram.* p. 140. "He said Virginia would have emancipated long ago."—*The Liberator*, ix, 33. "And having in a readiness to revenge all disobedience."—2 *Cor.* x, 6. "However, in these cases, custom generally determines."—*Wright's Gram.* p. 50. "In proof, let the following cases demonstrate."—*Ib.* p. 46. "We must surprise, that he should so speedily have forgotten his first principles."—*Ib.* p. 147. "How should we surprise at the expression, 'This is a *soft* question!'"—*Ib.* p. 219. "And such as prefer, can parse it as a possessive adjective."—*Goodenow's Gram.* p. 89. "To assign all the reasons, that induced to deviate from other grammarians, would lead to a needless prolixity."—*Alexander's Gram.* p. 4. "The Indicative mood simply indicates or declares."—*Farnum's Gram.* p. 33.

UNDER NOTE II.—OF VERBS INTRANSITIVE.

"In his seventh chapter he expatiateth himself at great length."—*Barclay's Works*, iii, 350. "He quarrelleth my bringing some testimonies of antiquity, agreeing with what I say."—*Ib.* iii, 373. "Repenting him of his design."—*Hume's Hist.* ii, 56. "Henry knew, that an excommunication could not fail of operating the most dangerous effects."—*Ib.* ii, 165. "The popular lords did not fail to enlarge themselves on the subject."—*Macaulay's Hist.* iii, 177. "He is always master of his subject; and seems to play himself with it."—*Blair's Rhet.* p. 445. "But as soon as it comes the length of disease, all his secret infirmities shew themselves."—*Ib.* p. 256. "No man repented him of his wickedness."—*Jeremiah*, viii, 6. "Go thee one way or other, either on the right hand, or on the left."—*Ezekiel*, xxi, 16. "He lies him down by the rivers side."—*Walker's Particles*, p. 99. "My desire has been for some years past, to retire myself to some of our American plantations."—*Cowley's Pref. to his Poems*, p. vii. "I fear me thou wilt shrink from the payment of it."—*Zenobia*, i, 76. "We never recur an idea, without acquiring some combination."—*Rippingham's Art of Speaking*, p. xxxii.

"Yet more; the stroke of death he must abide,
Then lies him meekly down fast by his brethren's side."—*Milton.*

UNDER NOTE III.—OF VERBS MISAPPLIED.

"A parliament forfeited all those who had borne arms against the king."—*Hume's Hist.* ii, 223. "The practice of forfeiting ships which had been wrecked."—*Ib.* i, 500. "The nearer his military successes approached him to the throne."—*Ib.* v. 383. "In the next example, you personifies *ladies*, therefore it is plural."—*Kirkham's Gram.* p. 103. "The first *its* personates vale; the second *its* represents stream."—*Ib.* p. 103. "Pronouns do not always avoid the repetition of nouns."—*Ib.* p. 96. "*Very* is an adverb of comparison, it compares the adjective *good*."—*Ib.* p. 88. "You will please to commit the following paragraph."—*Ib.* p. 140. "Even the Greek and Latin passive verbs require an auxiliary to conjugate some of their tenses."—*Murray's Gram.* p. 100. "The deponent verbs, in Latin, require also an auxiliary to conjugate several of their tenses."—*Ib.* p. 100. "I have no doubt he made as wise and true proverbs, as any body has done since."—*Ib.* p. 145. "A uniform variety assumes as many set forms as Proteus had shapes."—*Kirkham's Elocution*, p. 72. "When words in apposition follow each other in quick succession."—*Nixon's Parser*, p. 57. "Where such sentences frequently succeed each other."—*L. Murray's Gram.* p. 349. "Wisdom leads us to speak and act what is most proper."—*Blair's Rhet.* p. 99; *Murray's Gram.* i, 303.

"*Jul.* Art thou not Romeo, and a Montague?
Rom. Neither, fair saint, if either thee dislike."—*Shak.*

UNDER NOTE IV.—OF PASSIVE VERBS.

"We too must be allowed the privilege of forming our own laws."—*L. Murray's Gram.* p. 134. "For we are not only allowed the use of all the ancient poetic feet," &c.—*Ib.* p. 259; *Kirkham's Elocution*, 143; *Jamieson's Rhet.* 310. "By what code of morals am I denied the right and privilege?"—*Dr. Bartlett's Lect.* p. 4. "The children of Israel have alone been denied the possession of it."—*Keith's Evidences*, p. 68. "At York fifteen hundred Jews were refused all quarter."—*Ib.* p. 73. "He would teach the French language in three lessons, provided he was paid fifty-five dollars in advance."—*Chasette's Essay*, p. 4. "And when he was demanded of the Pharisees, when the kingdom of God should come."—*Luke*, xvii, 20. "I have been shown a book."—*Campbell's Rhet.* p. 392. "John Horne Tooke was refused admission only because he had been in holy orders."—*Diversions of Purley*, i, 60. "Mr. Horne Tooke having taken orders, he was refused admission to the bar."—*Churchill's Gram.* p. 145. "Its reference to place is lost sight of."—*Bullions's E. Gram.* p. 116. "What striking lesson are we taught by the tenor of this history?"—*Bush's Questions*, p. 71. "He had been left, by a friend, no less than eighty thousand pounds."—*Priestley's Gram.* p. 112. "Where there are many things to be done, each must be allowed its share of time and labour."—*Johnson's Pref. to Dict.* p. xiii. "Presenting the subject in a far more practical form than it has been heretofore given."—*Kirkham's Phrenology*, p. v. "If a being of entire impartiality should be shown the two companies."—*Scott's Pref. to Bible*, p. vii. "He was offered the command of the British army."—*Grimshaw's Hist.* p. 81. "Who had been unexpectedly left a considerable sum."—*Johnson's Life of Goldsmith.* "Whether a maid or a widow may be granted such a privilege."—*Spectator*, No. 536. "Happily all these affected terms have been denied the public suffrage."—*Campbell's Rhet.* p. 199. "Let him next be shewn the parsing table."—*Nutting's Gram.* p. viii. "Thence, he may be shown the use of the Analyzing Table."—*Ib.* p. ix. "Pittacus was offered a great sum of money."—*Sanborn's Gram.* p. 228. "He had been allowed more time for study."—*Ib.* p. 229. "If the walks were a little taken care of that lie between them."—*Addison, Spect.* No. 414. "Suppose I am offered an office or a bribe."—*Pierpont's Discourse*, Jan. 27, 1839.

"Am I one chaste, one last-embrace deny'd?
Shall I not lay me by his clay-cold side?"—*Rowe's Lucan*, B. ix, l. 103.

UNDER NOTE V.—PASSIVE VERBS TRANSITIVE.

"The preposition *to* is made use of before nouns of place, when they follow verbs and participles of motion."—*Murray's Gram.* p. 203; *Ingersoll's*, 231; *Greenleaf's*, 35; *Fisk's*, 143; *Smith's*, 170; *Guy's*, 90; *Fowler's*, 555. "They were refused entrance into the house."—*Murray's Key*, ii, 204. "Their separate signification has been lost sight of."—*Horne Tooke*, ii, 422. "But, whenever *ye* is made use of, it must be in the nominative, and never in the objective, case."—*Cobbett's Gram.* ¶ 58. "It is said, that more persons than one are paid handsome salaries, for taking care to see acts of parliament properly worded."—*Churchill's Gram.* p. 334. "The following Rudiments of English Grammar, have been made use of in the University of Pennsylvania."—DR. ROGERS: *in Harrison's Gram.* p. 2. "It never should be lost sight of."—*Newman's Rhetoric*, p. 19. "A very curious fact hath been taken notice of by those expert metaphysicians."—*Campbell's Rhet.* p. 281. "The archbishop interfered that Michelet's lectures might be put a stop to."—*The Friend*, ix, 378. "The disturbances in Gottengen have been entirely put an end to."—*Daily Advertiser.* "Besides those that are taken notice of in these exceptions."—*Priestley's Gram.* p. 6. "As one, two, or three auxiliary verbs are made use of."—*Ib.* p. 24. "The arguments which have been made use of."—*Addison's Evidences*, p. 32. "The circumstance is properly taken notice of by the author."—*Blair's Rhet.* p. 217. "Patagonia has never been taken possession of by any European nation."—*Cumming's Geog.* p. 62. "He will be found fault withal no more, i. e. not hereafter."—*Walker's Particles*, p. 226. "The thing was to be put an end to somehow."—*Leigh Hunt's Byron*, p. 15. "In 1798, the Papal Territory was taken possession of by the French."—*Pinnock's Geog.* p. 223. "The idea has not for a moment been lost sight of by the Board."—*Common School Journal*, i, 37. "I shall easily be excused the labour of more transcription."—*Johnson's Life of Dryden.* "If I may be allowed that expression."—*Campbell's Rhet.* p. 259, and 288. "If without offence I may be indulged the observation."—*Ib.* p. 295. "There are other characters, which are frequently made use of in composition."—*Murray's Gram.* p. 281; *Ingersoll's*, 293. "Such unaccountable infirmities might be in many, perhaps in most, cases got the better of."—*Beattie's Moral Science*, i, 153. "Which ought never to be had recourse to."—*Ib.* i, 186. "That the widows may be taken care of."—*Barclay's Works*, i, 499. "Other cavils will yet be taken notice of."—*Pope's Pref. to Homer.* "Which implies, that all christians are offered eternal salvation."—*West's Letters*, p. 149. "Yet even the dogs are allowed the crumbs which fall from their master's table."—*Campbell's Gospels, Matt.* xv, 27. "For we say the light within must be taken heed unto."—*Barclay's Works*, i, 148. "This sound of *a* is taken notice of in Steele's Grammar."—*Walker's Dict.* p. 22. "One came to be paid ten guineas for a pair of silver buckles."—*Castle Rackrent*, p. 104. "Let him, therefore, be carefully shewn the application of the several questions in the table."—*Nutting's Gram.* p. 8. "After a few times, it is no longer taken notice of by the hearers."—*Sheridan's Lect.* p. 182. "It will not admit of the same excuse, nor be allowed the same indulgence, by people of any discernment."—*Ibid.* "Inanimate things may be made property of."—*Beattie's M. Sci.* p. 355.

"And, when he's bid a liberaller price,
Will not be sluggish in the work, nor nice."—*Butler's Poems*, p. 162.

UNDER NOTE VI.—OF PERFECT PARTICIPLES.

"All the words made use of to denote spiritual and intellectual things, are in their origin metaphors."—*Campbell's Rhet.* p. 330. "A reply to an argument commonly made use of by unbelievers."—*Blair's Rhet.* p. 293. "It was heretofore the only form made use of in the preter tenses."—*Dr. Ash's Gram.* p. 47. "Of the points, and other characters made use of in writing."—*Ib.* p. xv. "If *thy* be the personal pronoun made use of."—*Walker's Dict.* "The Conjunction is a word made use of to connect sentences."—*Burn's Gram.* p. 28. "The points made use of to answer these purposes are the four following."—*Harrison's Gram.* p. 67. "*Incense* signifies perfumes exhaled by fire, and made use of in religious ceremonies."—*Murray's Key*, p. 171. "In most of his orations, there is too much art; even carried the length of ostentation."—*Blair's Rhet.* p. 246. "To illustrate the great truth, so often lost sight of in our times."—*Common School Journal*, i, 88. "The principal figures, made use of to affect the heart, are Exclamation, Confession, Deprecation, Commination, and Imprecation."—*Formey's Belles-Lettres*, p. 133. "Disgusted at the odious artifices made use of by the Judge."—*Junius*, p. 13. "The whole reasons of our being allotted a condition, out of which so much wickedness and misery would in fact arise."—*Butler's Analogy*, p. 109. "Some characteristical circumstance being generally invented or laid hold of."—*Kames, El. of Crit.* ii, 246.

"And *by* is likewise us'd with Names that shew
The Means made use of, or the Method how."—*Ward's Gram.* p. 105.

UNDER NOTE VII.—CONSTRUCTIONS AMBIGUOUS.

"Many adverbs admit of degrees of comparison as well as adjectives."—*Priestley's Gram.* p. 133. "But the author, who, by the number and reputation of his works, formed our language more than any one, into its present state, is Dryden."—*Blair's Rhet.* p. 180. "In some States, Courts of Admiralty have no juries, nor Courts of Chancery at all."—*Webster's Essays*, p. 146. "I feel myself grateful to my friend."—*Murray's Key*, p. 276. "This requires a writer to have, himself, a very clear apprehension of the object he means to present to us."—*Blair's Rhet.* p. 94. "Sense has its own harmony, as well as sound."—*Ib.* p. 127. "The apostrophe denotes the omission of an *i* which was formerly inserted, and made an addition of a syllable to the word."—*Priestley's Gram.* p. 67. "There are few, whom I can refer to, with more advantage than Mr. Addison."—*Blair's Rhet.* p. 139. "DEATH, in *theology*, [is a] perpetual separation from God, and eternal torments."—*Webster's Dict.* "That could inform the *traveler* as well as the old man himself!"—*O. B. Peirce's Gram.* p. 345.

UNDER NOTE VIII.—YE AND YOU IN SCRIPTURE.

"Ye daughters of Rabbah, gird ye with sackcloth."—ALGER'S BIBLE: *Jer.* xlix, 3. "Wash ye, make you clean."—*Brown's Concordance, w. Wash.* "Strip ye, and make ye bare, and gird sackcloth upon your loins."—ALGER'S BIBLE: *Isaiah*, xxxii, 11. "You are not ashamed that you make yourselves strange to me."—FRIENDS' BIBLE: *Job*, xix, 3. "You are not ashamed that ye make yourselves strange to me."—ALGER'S BIBLE: *ib.* "If you knew the gift of God."—*Brown's Concordance, w. Knew.* "Depart from me, ye workers of iniquity, I know ye not."—*Penington's Works*, ii, 122.

RULE VI.—SAME CASES.

A Noun or a Pronoun put after a verb or participle not transitive, agrees in case with a preceding noun or pronoun referring to the same thing: as, "*It* is *I.*"—"*These* are *they.*"—"The *child* was named *John.*"—"*It* could not be *he.*"—"The *Lord* sitteth *King* forever."—*Psalms*, xxix, 10.

"What war could ravish, commerce could bestow,
And *he* return'd a *friend*, *who* came a *foe*."—*Pope*, Ep. iii, l. 206.

OBSERVATIONS ON RULE VI.

OBS. 1.—Active-transitive verbs, and their imperfect and pluperfect participles, always govern the objective case; but active-intransitive, passive, and neuter verbs, and their participles, take the same case after as before them, when both words refer to the same thing. The latter are rightly supposed *not to govern* * any case; nor are they in general followed by any noun or pronoun. But, because they are not transitive, some of them become connectives to such words as are in the same case and signify the same thing. That is, their finite tenses may be followed by a nominative, and their infinitives and participles by a nominative or an objective, *agreeing* with a noun or a pronoun which precedes them. The cases are the same, because the person or thing is one; as, "*I* am *he.*"—"*Thou* art *Peter.*"—"Civil *government* being the sole *object* of forming societies, its administration must be conducted by common consent."—*Jefferson's Notes*, p. 129. Identity is both the foundation and the characteristic of this construction. We chiefly use it to affirm or deny, to suggest or question, the *sameness* of things; but sometimes *figuratively*, to illustrate the relations of persons or things by comparison: † as, "*I* am the true *vine*, and my *Father* is the *husbandman.*"—*John*, xv, 1. "*I* am the *vine*, *ye* are the *branches.*"—*John*, xv, 5. Even the names of direct opposites, are sometimes put in the same case, under this rule; as,

"By such a change thy *darkness* is made *light*,
Thy *chaos order*, and thy *weakness might*."—*Cowper*, Vol. i, p. 88.

OBS. 2.—In this rule, the terms *after* and *preceding* refer rather to the order of the sense and construction, than to the mere *placing* of the words; for the words in fact admit of various posi-

---

* Some, however, have conceived the putting of the same case after the verb as before it, to be *government*; as, "Neuter verbs occasionally govern either the nominative or [the] objective case, after them."—*Alexander's Gram.* p. 54. "The verb to *be*, *always* governs a Nominative, unless it be of the Infinitive Mood."—*Buchanan's Gram.* p. 94. This latter assertion is, in fact, monstrously untrue, and also solecistical.

† Not unfrequently the conjunction *as* intervenes between these "same cases," as it may also between words in apposition; as, "He then is *as* the head, and we *as* the members; he the vine, and we the branches."—*Barclay's Works*, Vol. ii, p. 189.

tions. The proper subject of the verb is the nominative *to* it, or *before* it, by Rule 2d ; and the other nominative, however placed, is understood to be that which comes *after* it, by Rule 6th. In general, however, the proper subject *precedes* the verb, and the other word *follows* it, agreeably to the literal sense of the rule. But when the proper subject is placed after the verb, as in certain instances specified in the second observation under Rule 2d, the explanatory nominative is commonly introduced still later ; as, "But be *thou* an *example* of the believers."—1 *Tim.* iv, 12. "But what ! is thy *servant* a *dog* ?"—2 *Kings*, viii, 13. "And so would I, were *I Parmenio*."—*Goldsmith.* "O Conloch's daughter ! is *it thou* ?"—*Ossian.* But in the following example, on the contrary, there is a transposition of the entire lines, and the verb agrees with the two nominatives in the latter :

> "To thee *were* solemn *toys* or empty *show*,
> The *robes* of pleasure and the *veils* of wo."—*Dr. Johnson.*

OBS. 3.—In interrogative sentences, the terms are usually transposed,* or both are placed after the verb ; as, "Am *I* a *Jew* ?"—*John*, xviii, 35. "Art *thou* a *king* then ?"—*Ib.* ver. 37. " *What* is *truth* ?"—*Ib.* ver. 38. " *Who* art *thou* ?"—*Ib.* i, 19. "Art *thou Elias* ?"—*Ib.* i, 21. "Tell me, Alciphron, is not *distance* a *line* turned endwise to the eye ?"—*Berkley's Dialogues*, p. 161.

> " Whence, and *what* art *thou*, execrable shape ? "—*Milton.*
> " Art *thou* that traitor *angel* ? art *thou he* ? "—*Idem.*

OBS. 4.—In a declarative sentence also, there may be a rhetorical or poetical transposition of one or both of the terms ; as, "And I *thy victim* now remain."—*Francis's Horace*, ii, 45. " To thy own *dogs* a *prey* thou shalt be made."—*Pope's Homer.* "I was eyes to the blind, and *feet* was *I* to the lame."—*Job*, xxix, 15. " Far other *scene* is *Thrasymené* now."—*Byron.* In the following sentence, the latter term is palpably misplaced : " It does not clearly appear at first *what the antecedent is* to *they*."—*Blair's Rhet.* p. 218. Say rather : " It does not clearly appear at first, *what is the antecedent* to [the pronoun] *they*." In examples transposed like the following, there is an elegant ellipsis of the verb to which the pronoun is nominative ; as, *am, art*, &c.

> " When pain and anguish wring the brow,
> A ministering *angel thou*."—*Scott's Marmion.*
> " The forum's champion, and the people's chief,
> Her new-born *Numa thou*—with reign, alas ! too brief."—*Byron.*
> " For this commission'd, I forsook the sky—
> Nay, cease to kneel—thy *fellow-servant I*."—*Parnell.*

OBS. 5.—In some peculiar constructions, both words naturally come *before* the verb ; as, " I know not *who she is*."—" *Who* did you say *it* was ? "—"I know not how to tell thee *who I am*."—*Romeo.* " Inquire thou whose *son* the *stripling* is."—1 *Sam.* xvii, 56. " Man would not be the creature *which he* now is."—*Blair.* " I could not guess *who it* should be."—*Addison.* And they are sometimes placed in this manner by *hyperbaton*, or transposition ; as, " Yet *he it* is."—*Young.* " No contemptible *orator he* was."—*Dr. Blair.* " *He it* is to whom I shall give a sop."—*John*, xiii, 26. "And a very noble *personage Cato* is."—*Blair's Rhet.* p. 457. " *Clouds they* are without water."—*Jude*, 12.

> " Of worm or serpent kind it *something* looked,
> But monstrous, with a thousand snaky heads."—*Pollok*, B. i, l. 183.

OBS. 6.—As infinitives and participles have no nominatives of their own, such of them as are not transitive in their nature, may take *different* cases after them ; and, in order to determine what case it is that follows them, the learner must carefully observe what preceding word denotes the same person or thing, and apply the principle of the rule accordingly. This word being often remote, and sometimes understood, the *sense* is the only clew to the construction: Examples : " *Who* then can bear the thought of being an *outcast* from his presence ? "—*Addison.* Here *outcast* agrees with *who*, as well as with *thought*. "*I* cannot help being so passionate an *admirer* as I am."—*Steele.* Here *admirer* agrees with *I*. " To recommend *what* the soberer part of mankind look upon to be a *trifle*."—*Steele.* Here *trifle* agrees with *what* as relative, the objective governed by *upon*. "*It* would be a romantic *madness*, for a *man* to be a *lord* in his closet."—*Id.* Here *madness* is in the nominative case, agreeing with *it ;* and *lord*, in the objective, agreeing with *man.* " To affect to be a *lord* in one's closet, would be a romantic *madness.*" In this sentence also, *lord* is in the objective, after *to be ;* and *madness*, in the nominative, after *would be.*

> " ' My dear *Tibullus* !' if that will not do,
> Let *me* be *Horace*, and be *Ovid you*."—*Pope*, B. ii, Ep. ii, 143.

OBS. 7.—An active-intransitive or a neuter participle in *ing*, when governed by a preposition, is often followed by a noun or a pronoun the case of which depends not on the preposition, but on the case which goes before. Example : "The *Jews* were in a particular manner ridiculed *for being* a credulous *people*."—*Addison's Evidences*, p. 28. Here *people* is in the nominative case, agreeing with *Jews.* Again : " The learned pagans ridiculed the *Jews* for *being* a credulous *people*." Here *people* is in the objective case, because the preceding noun *Jews* is so. In both instances the preposition *for* governs the participle *being*, and nothing else. " The atrocious crime of *being* a young *man*, I shall neither attempt to palliate or deny."—PITT: *Bullions's E. Gram.* p. 82 ; *S. S. Greene's*, 174. Sanborn has this text, with "*nor*" for "*or*."—*Analytical Gram.* p. 190. This example has been erroneously cited, as one in which the case of the noun after the participle is *not determined* by its relation to any other word. Sanborn absurdly supposes it to be "in the *nominative independent*." Bullions as strangely tells us, "it may correctly be called the

---

* " 'Whose house is that ?' This sentence, before it is parsed, *should be transposed ;* thus, 'Whose is that house ?' The same observation applies to every sentence of a similar construction."—*Chandler's old Gram.* p. 93. This instruction is worse than nonsense ; for it teaches the pupil to parse every word in the sentence *wrong !* The author proceeds to explain *Whose*, as " qualifying *house*, understood ;" *is*, as agreeing " with its nominative, *house* ;" *that*, as " qualifying *house* ;" and *house*, as " nominative case to the verb. *is*." Nothing of this is *true* of the original question. For, in that, *Whose* is governed by *house ; house* is nominative after *is ;* is agrees with *house* understood ; and *that* relates to *house* understood. The meaning is, " Whose house is that house ?" or, in the order of a declarative sentence, " That house is whose house ?"

objective indefinite"—like *me* in the following example: "He was not sure *of its being me*."—*Bullions's E. Gram.* p. 82. This latter text I take to be *bad English.* It should be, "He was not sure *of it as being me;*" or, "He was not sure *that it was I.*" But, in the text above, there is an evident transposition. The syntactical order is this: "*I* shall neither deny *nor* attempt to palliate the atrocious crime of being a young man." The words man and *I* refer to the same person, and are therefore in the same case, according to the rule which I have given above.

OBS. 8.—S. S. Greene, in his late Grammar, improperly denominates this case after the participle *being,* "the *predicate-nominative,*" and imagines that it necessarily remains a nominative even when a possessive case precedes the participle. If he were right in this, there would be an important exception to Rule 6th above. But so singularly absurd is his doctrine about "*abridged predicates,*" that in general the *abridging* shows an *increase* of syllables, and often a conversion of good English into bad. For example: "*It* [the predicate] remains *unchanged in the nominative,* when, with the participle of the copula, *it* becomes a *verbal noun,* limited by the possessive case of the subject; as, 'That he was a foreigner prevented his election' = '*His* being a *foreigner* prevented his election.'"—*Greene's Analysis,* p. 160. Here the number of syllables is unaltered; but *foreigner* is very improperly called "a verbal noun," and an example which only lacks a comma, is changed to what Wells rightly calls an "*anomalous expression,*" and one wherein that author supposes *foreigner* and *his* to be necessarily in the same case. But Greene varies this example into other "*abridged forms,*" thus: "I knew *that he was a foreigner,*" = "I knew *his being,* or *of his being a foreigner.*" "The fact *that he was a foreigner,* = *of his being a foreigner,* was undeniable." "*When he was first called a foreigner,* = *on his being first called a foreigner,* his anger was excited."—*Ib.* p. 171. All these changes *enlarge,* rather than abridge, the expression; and, at the same time, make it questionable English, to say the least of it.

OBS. 9.—In some examples, the adverb *there* precedes the participle, and we evidently have nothing by which to determine the case that follows; as, "These judges were twelve in number: Was this *owing to there being* twelve primary *deities* among the Gothic nations?"—*Webster's Essays,* p. 263. Say rather: "Was this *because there were* twelve primary deities among the Gothic nations?" "How many are injured by Adam's fall, that know nothing of *there ever being* such a *man* in the world!"—*Barclay's Apology,* p. 185. Say rather,—"*who know not that there ever was* such a man in the world!"

OBS. 10.—In some other examples, we find a possessive before the participle and a doubtful case after it; as, "This our Saviour himself was pleased to make use of as the strongest argument of *his* being the promised *Messiah.*"—*Addison's Evidences,* p. 81. "But my chief affliction consisted in *my* being singled out from all the other boys, by a lad about fifteen years of age, as a proper *object* upon whom he might let loose the cruelty of his temper."—*Cowper's Memoir,* p. 14. "Τοῦ πατρὸς [ὄντος] ὄνου εὐθὺς ὑπεμνήσθη. He had some sort of recollection of his *father's being* an *ass.*"—*Collectanea Græca Minora, Note,* p. 7. This construction, though not uncommon, is anomalous in more respects than one. Whether or not it is worthy to form an exception to the rule of *same cases,* or even to that of *possessives,* the reader may judge from the observations made on it under the latter. I should rather devise some way to avoid it, if any can be found—and I believe there can; as, "This our Saviour himself was pleased to *advance* as the strongest *proof that he was* the promised Messiah."—"But my chief affliction consisted in *this, that I was* singled out," &c. The story of the mule is, "*He seemed to recollect on a sudden that his father was an ass.*" This is the proper meaning of the Greek text above; but the construction is different, the Greek nouns being genitives in apposition.

OBS. 11.—A noun in the nominative case sometimes follows a finite verb, when the equivalent subject that stands before the verb, is not a noun or pronoun, but a phrase or a sentence which supplies the place of a nominative; as, "That the barons and freeholders derived their authority from kings, is wholly a *mistake.*"—*Webster's Essays,* p. 277. "To speak of a slave as a member of civil society, may, by some, be regarded a *solecism.*"—*Stroud's Sketch,* p. 65. Here *mistake* and *solecism* are as plainly nominatives, as if the preceding subjects had been declinable words.

OBS. 12.—When a noun is put after an abstract infinitive that is not transitive, it appears necessarily to be in the objective case,* though not governed by the verb; for if we supply any noun

---

* 1. In Latin, the *accusative* case is used after such a verb, because an other word in the same case is understood before it; as, "*Facĕre quæ libet, ID est [hominem] esse regem.*"—SALLUST. "To do what he pleases, THAT is [for a man] to be a *king.*" If Professor Bullions had understood Latin, or Greek, or English, as well as his commenders imagine, he might have discovered what construction of cases we have in the following instances: "It is an honour [for a *man*] to be the *author* of such a work."—*Bullions's Eng. Gram.* p. 82. "To be *surely* for a stranger [,] is dangerous."—*Ib.* "Not to know what happened before you were born, is to be always a *child.*" —*Ib.* "Nescire quid acciderit antequam natus es, est semper esse *puerum.*"—*Ib.* "Ἔστι τῶν αἰσχρῶν... τόπων, ὧν ἡμῖν ποτὲ κύριοι φαίνεσθαι προϊεμένους." "It is a shame to be seen giving up countries of which we were once masters."—DEMOSTHENES: *ib.* What support these examples give to this grammarian's *new* notion of "*the objective indefinite,*" or to his still later seizure of Greene's doctrine of "*the predicate-nominative,*" the learned reader may judge. All the Latin and Greek grammarians suppose an *ellipsis,* in such instances; but some moderns are careless enough of that, and of the analogy of General Grammar in this case, to have seconded the Doctor in his absurdity. See *Farnum's Practical Gram.* p. 23; and *S. W. Clark's,* p. 149.

2. Professor Hart has an indecisive remark on this construction, as follows: "Sometimes a verb in the infinitive mood has a noun after it without any other noun before it; as, 'To be a good *man,* is not so easy a thing as many people imagine.' Here '*man*' may be parsed as used *indefinitely* after the verb *to be.* It is not easy to say in what *case* the noun is in such sentences. The analogy of the Latin would seem to indicate the *objective.*—Thus, 'Not to know what happened in past years, is to be always a *child,*' Latin, 'semper esse *puerum.*' In like manner, in English, we may say, '*Its* being *me, need* make no change in your determination.'"—*Hart's English Gram.* p. 127.

3. These learned authors thus differ about what certainly admits of no other solution than that which is given in the Observation above. To parse the nouns in question, "*as used indefinitely,*" without case, and to call them "*objectives indefinite,*" without agreement or government, are two methods equally repugnant to reason. The last suggestion of Hart's is also a false argument for a true position. The phrases, "*Its being me,*" and "*To be a good man,*" are far from being constructed "*in like manner.*" The former is manifestly bad English; because *Its* and *me* are not in the same case. But S. S. Greene would say, "*Its being I,* is right." For in a similar instance,

to which such infinitive may be supposed to refer, it must be introduced before the verb by the preposition *for*: as, "To be an *Englishman* in London, a *Frenchman* in Paris, a *Spaniard* in Madrid, is no easy matter; and yet it is necessary."—*Home's Art of Thinking*, p. 89. That is, "*For a traveller* to be an *Englishman* in London," &c. "It is certainly as easy to be a *scholar*, as a *gamester*."—*Harris's Hermes*, p. 425. That is, "It is as easy *for a young man* to be a *scholar*, as it is *for him to be a gamester*." "To be an eloquent *speaker*, in the proper sense of the *word*, is far from being a common or an easy *attainment*."—*Blair's Rhet.* p. 337. Here *attainment* is in the nominative, after *is*—or, rather, after *being*, for it follows both; and *speaker*, in the objective after *to be*. "It is almost as hard a thing [for a *man*] to be a *poet* in despite of fortune, as it is [for *one* to be a *poet*] in despite of nature."—*Cowley's Preface to his Poems*, p. vii.

OBS. 13.—Where precision is necessary, loose or abstract infinitives are improper; as, "But *to be precise*, signifies, that *they* express *that* idea, and *no more*."—*Blair's Rhet.* p. 94; *Murray's Gram.* 301; *Jamieson's Rhet.* 64. Say rather: "But, *for an author's words to be precise*, signifies, that they express *his exact* idea, and *nothing* more *or less*."

OBS. 14.—The principal verbs that take the same case after as before them, except those which are passive, are the following: to be, to stand, to sit, to lie, to live, to grow, to become, to turn, to commence, to die, to expire, to come, to go, to range, to wander, to return, to seem, to appear, to remain, to continue, to reign. There are doubtless some others, which admit of such a construction; and of some of these, it is to be observed, that they are sometimes transitive, and govern the objective: as, "To *commence* a suit."—*Johnson*. "O *continue* thy loving kindness unto them."—*Psalm*, xxxvi, 10. "A feather will *turn* the scale."—*Shak*. "*Return* him a trespass offering."—1 *Samuel*. "For it *becomes* me so to speak."—*Dryden*. But their construction with like cases is easily distinguished by the sense; as, "When *I* commenced *author*, my aim was to amuse."—*Kames, El. of Crit.* ii, 286. "*Men* continue men's *destroyers*."—*Nixon's Parser*, p. 56. "'Tis most just, that *thou* turn *rascal*."—*Shak. Timon of Athens*. "He went out *mate*, but *he* returned *captain*."—*Murray's Gram.* p. 182. "After this event *he* became *physician* to the king."—*Ib.* That is, "When I *began to be* an author," &c.

"Ev'n mean *self-love* becomes, by force divine,
The *scale* to measure others' wants by thine."—*Pope*.

OBS. 15.—The common instructions of our English grammars, in relation to the subject of the preceding rule, are exceedingly erroneous and defective. For example: "The verb TO BE, has *always* a nominative case after it, *unless it be* in the infinitive *mode*."—*Lowth's Gram.* p. 77. "The verb TO BE *requires* the same case after it as before it."—*Churchill's Gram.* p. 142. "The verb TO BE, through all its variations, *has* the same case after it, as *that* which *next* precedes it."—*Murray's Gram.* p. 181; *Alger's*, 62; *Merchant's*, 91; *Putnam's*, 116; *Smith's*, 97; and many others. "The verb TO BE has *usually* the same case after it, as that which *immediately* precedes it."—*Hall's Gram.* p. 31. "*Neuter verbs have* the same case after them, as that which *next* precedes them."—*Folker's Gram.* p. 14. "*Passive verbs which signify naming*, and others of a *similar* nature, have the same case *before and after* them."—*Murray's Gram.* p. 182. "A Noun or Pronoun used in predication with a verb, is in the Independent Case. EXAMPLES—'Thou art a *scholar*.' 'It is *I*.' 'God is *love*.'"—*S. W. Clark's Pract. Gram.* p. 149. So many and monstrous are the faults of these rules, that nothing but very learned and reverend authority, could possibly impose such teaching anywhere. The first, though written by Lowth, is not a whit wiser, than to say, "The preposition *to* has *always* an infinitive mood after it, *unless it be* a preposition." And this latter absurdity is even a better rule for all infinitives, than the former for all predicated nominatives. Nor is there much more fitness in any of the rest. "The verb TO BE, *through all*," or even *in any*, of its parts, has neither "*always*" nor *usually* a case "*expressed* or *understood*" after it; and, even when there *is* a noun or a pronoun put after it, the case is, in very many instances, not to be determined by that which "*next*" or "*immediately*" precedes the verb. Examples: "A *sect of freethinkers* is a *sum* of ciphers."—*Bentley*. "And *I* am this *day* weak, though anointed *king*."—2 *Sam.* iii, 39. "*What* made *Luther* a great *man*, was *his* unshaken *reliance* on God."—*Kortz's Life of Luther*, p. 13. "The devil offers his service; *he* is sent with a positive *commission* to be a lying *spirit* in the mouth of all the prophets."—*Calvin's Institutes*, p. 131. It is perfectly certain that in these four texts, the words, *sum, king, reliance*, and *spirit*, are *nominatives*, after the verb or participle; and not *objectives*, as they must be, if there were any truth in the common assertion, "that the two cases, which, in the construction of the sentence, are *the next* before and after it, must always be alike."—*Smith's New Gram.* p. 98. Not only may the nominative before the verb be followed by an objective, but the nominative after it may be preceded by a possessive; as, "Amos, the herdsman of *Tekoa*, was not a *prophet's* son."—"It is the *king's* chapel, and it is the *king's* court."—*Amos*, vii, 13. How ignorant then must that person be, who cannot see the falsity of the instructions above cited! How careless the reader who overlooks it!

NOTES TO RULE VI.

NOTE I.—The putting of a noun in an unknown case after a participle or a participial noun, produces an anomaly which it seems better to avoid; for the cases ought to be *clear*, even in exceptions to the common rules of construction. Examples: 1. "WIDOWHOOD, *n*. The state *of being a widow*."—*Webster's Dict.* Say rather, "WIDOWHOOD, *n*. The state of a widow."—*Johnson, Walker, Worcester*. (2.) "I had a suspicion of the *fellow's* being a *swindler*." Say rather, "I had a suspicion

be has this conclusion: "Hence, in *abridging* the following proposition, 'I was not aware *that it was he*,' we should say '*of its being he*,' not '*his*' nor '*him*.'"—*Greene's Analysis*, 1st Ed. p. 171. When *bring* becomes a noun, no case after it appears to be very proper; but this author, thus "*abridging*" four syllables *into five*, produces an anomalous construction which it would be much better to avoid.

that the fellow was a swindler." (3.) "To prevent *its* being a dry *detail* of terms."—*Buck.* Better, "To prevent *it from* being a dry detail of terms."*

NOTE II.—The nominative which follows a verb or participle, ought to accord in signification, either literally or figuratively, with the preceding term which is taken for a sign of the same thing. Errors: (1.) "*To be convicted* of bribery, was then a *crime* altogether unpardonable."—*Blair's Rhet.* p. 265. *To be convicted* of a crime is not the crime itself; say, therefore, "*Bribery* was then a *crime* altogether unpardonable." (2.) "The second person is the *object* of the Imperative."—*Murray's Gram. Index,* ii, 292. Say rather, "The second person is the *subject* of the imperative;" for the *object* of a verb is the word governed by it, and not its nominative.

IMPROPRIETIES FOR CORRECTION.

FALSE SYNTAX UNDER RULE VI.

UNDER THE RULE ITSELF.—OF PROPER IDENTITY.

"Who would not say, 'If it be *me,*' rather than, If it be *I?*"—*Priestley's Gram.* p. 105.

[FORMULE.—Not proper, because the pronoun *me,* which comes after the neuter verb *be,* is in the objective case, and does not agree with the pronoun *it,* the verb's nominative,† which refers to the same thing. But, according to Rule 6th, "A noun or a pronoun put after a verb or participle not transitive, agrees in case with a preceding noun or pronoun referring to the same thing." Therefore, *me* should be *I;* thus, "Who would not say, 'If it be *I,*' rather than, 'If it be *me?*'"]

"Who is there? It is me."—*Priestley, ib.* p. 104. "It is him."—*Id. ib.* 104. "Are these the houses you were speaking of? Yes, they are them."—*Id. ib.* 104. "It is not me they are in love with."—*Addison's Spect.* No. 290; *Priestley's Gram.* p. 104; and *Campbell's Rhet.* p. 203. "It cannot be me."—SWIFT: *Priestley's Gram.* p. 104. "To that which once was thee."—PRIOR: *ib.* 104. "There is but one man that she can have, and that is me."—CLARISSA: *ib.* 104. "We enter, as it were, into his body, and become, in some measure, him."—ADAM SMITH: *ib.* p. 105. "Art thou proud yet? Ay, that I am not thee."—*Shak.* Timon. "He knew not whom they were."—*Milnes, Greek Gram.* p. 234. "Who do ye think me to be?"—*Priestley's Gram.* p. 108. "Whom do men say that I, the Son of man, am?"—*Matt.* xvi, 13. "But whom say ye that I am?"—*Ib.* xvi, 15. "Whom think ye that I am? I am not he."—*Acts,* xiii, 25. "No; I am mistaken; I perceive it is not the person whom I supposed it was."—*Winter in London,* ii, 66. "And while it is Him I serve, life is not without value."—*Zenobia,* i, 76. "Without ever dreaming it was him."—*Life of Charles XII,* p. 271. "Or he was not the illiterate personage whom he affected to be."—*Montgomery's Lect.* "Yet was he him, who was to be the greatest apostle of the Gentiles."—*Barclay's Works,* i, 540. "Sweet was the thrilling ecstasy; I know not if 'twas love, or thee."—*Queen's Wake,* p. 14. "Time was, when none would cry, that oaf was me."—*Dryden, Prol.* "No matter where the vanquish'd be, nor whom."—*Rowe's Lucan,* B. i, l. 676. "No, I little thought it had been him."—*Life of Gratton.* "That reverence and godly fear, whose object is 'Him who can destroy both body and soul in hell.'"—*Maturin's Sermons,* p. 312. "It is us that they seek to please, or rather to astonish."—*West's Letters,* p. 28. "Let the same be she that thou hast appointed for thy servant Isaac."—*Gen.* xxiv.

---

* Parkhurst and Sanborn, by what they call "A NEW RULE," attempt to determine the doubtful or unknown case which this note censures, and to justify the construction as being well-authorised and hardly avoidable. Their rule is this: "A noun following a neuter or [a] passive participial noun, is in the *nominative independent.* A noun or pronoun in the *possessive case,* always precedes the participial noun, either *expressed* or *understood,* signifying the same thing as the noun does that follows it." To this new and exceptionable dogma, Sanborn adds: "This form of expression is one of the most common idioms of the language, and *in general composition cannot* be well avoided. In confirmation of the statement made, various authorities are subjoined. Two grammarians only, to our knowledge, have remarked on this phraseology: 'Participles are sometimes preceded by a possessive case and followed by a nominative; as, There is no doubt of *his* being a great *statesman.*' B. GREENLEAF. 'We sometimes find a participle that takes the same case after as before it, converted into a verbal noun, and the latter word retained unchanged in connexion with it; as, I have some recollection of his *father's* being a *judge.*' GOOLD BROWN."—*Sanborn's Analytical Gram.* p. 189. On what principle the words *statesman* and *judge* can be affirmed to be in the nominative case, I see not; and certainly they are not nominatives "*independent,*" because the word *being,* after which they stand, is not itself independent. It is true, the phraseology is common enough to be good English: but I dislike it; and if this citation from me, was meant for a confirmation of the reasoning or dogmatism preceding, it is not made with fairness, because my *opinion* of the construction is omitted by the quoter. See *Institutes of English Gram.* p. 162. In an other late grammar,—a shameful work, because it is in great measure a tissue of petty larcenies from my Institutes, with alterations for the worse,—I find the following absurd "Note," or Rule: "An infinitive or participle is often followed by a substantive *explanatory* of an *indefinite* person or thing. The substantive is then in the *objective case,* and may be called the *objective after the infinitive,* or *participle;* [as,] It is an honor to be the *author* of such a work. His being a great *man,* did not make him a happy man. By being an obedient *child,* you will secure the approbation of your parents."—*Farnum's Practical Gram.* 1st Ed p. 25. The first of these examples is elliptical; (see Obs. 12th above, and the Marginal Note;) the second is bad English—or, at any rate, directly repugnant to the rule for same cases; and the third parsed wrong by the rule: "*child*" is in the nominative case. See Obs. 7th above.

† When the preceding case is not "*the verb's nominative,*" this phrase must of course be omitted; and when the word which is to be corrected, does not literally follow the verb, it may be proper to say, "*constructively follows,*" in lieu of the phrase, "*comes after.*"

14. "Although I knew it to be he."—*Dickens's Notes*, p. 9.   "Dear gentle youth, is't none but thee?"—*Dorset's Poems*, p. 4.   "Whom do they say it is?"—*Fowler's E. Gram.* § 493. "These are her garb, not her; they but express
Her form, her semblance, her appropriate dress."—*Hannah More.*

UNDER NOTE I.—THE CASE DOUBTFUL.

"I had no knowledge of there being any connexion between them."—*Stone, on Freemasonry*, p. 25. "To promote iniquity in others, is nearly the same as being the actors of it ourselves."—*Murray's Key*, p. 170. "It must arise from feeling delicately ourselves."—*Blair's Rhet.* p. 330 ; *Murray's Gram.* 248. "By reason of there not having been exercised a competent physical power for their enforcement."—*Mass. Legislature*, 1839. "PUPILAGE, *n.* The state of being a scholar."—*Johnson, Walker, Webster, Worcester.* "Then the other part's being the definition would make it include all verbs of every description."—*O. B. Peirce's Gram.* p. 343. "John's being my friend,* saved me from inconvenience."—*Ib.* p. 201. "William's having become a judge, changed his whole demeanor."—*Ib.* p. 201. "William's having been a teacher, was the cause of the interest which he felt."—*Ib.* p. 216. "The being but one among many stifleth the chidings of conscience."—*Book of Thoughts*, p. 131. "As for its being esteemed a close translation, I doubt not many have been led into that error by the shortness of it."—*Pope's Pref. to Homer.* "All presumption of death's being the destruction of living bodies, must go upon supposition that they are compounded, and so discerptible."—*Butler's Analogy*, p. 68. "This argues rather their being proper names." —*Churchill's Gram.* p. 382. "But may it not be retorted, that its being a gratification is that which excites our resentment?"—*Campbell's Rhet.* p. 145. "Under the common notion, of its being a system of the whole poetical art."—*Blair's Rhet.* p. 401. "Whose time or other circumstances forbid their becoming classical scholars."—*Literary Convention*, p. 113. "It would preclude the notion of his being a merely fictitious personage."—*Philological Museum*, i, 446. "For, or under pretence of their being heretics or infidels."—*The Catholic Oath:* Geo. III, 31st. "We may here add Dr. Horne's sermon on Christ's being the Object of religious Adoration."—*Relig. World*, Vol. ii, p. 200. "To say nothing of Dr. Priestley's being a strenuous advocate," &c.—*Ib.* ii, 207. "By virtue of Adam's being their public head."—*Ib.* ii, 233. "Objections against there being any such moral plan as this." —*Butler's Analogy*, p. 57. "A greater instance of a man's being a blockhead."—*Spect.* No. 520. "We may insure or promote its being a happy state of existence to ourselves."— *Gurney's Evidences*, p. 86. "By its often falling a victim to the same kind of unnatural treatment."—*Kirkham's Elocution*, p. 41. "Their appearing foolishness is no presumption against this."—*Butler's Analogy*, p. 189. "But what arises from their being offences; *i. e.* from their being liable to be perverted."—*Ib.* p. 185. "And he entered into a certain man's house, named Justus, one that worshipped God."—*Acts*, xviii, 7.

UNDER NOTE II.—OF FALSE IDENTIFICATION.

"But to be popular, he observes, is an ambiguous word."—*Blair's Rhet.* p. 307. "The infinitive mood, or part of a sentence, is often the nominative case to a verb."—*L. Murray's Index, Octavo Gram.* Vol. ii, p. 290. "When any person, in speaking, introduces his own name, it is the first person; as, 'I, James, of the city of Boston.'"—*R. C. Smith's New Gram.* p. 43. "The name of the person spoken to, is the second person; as, 'James, come to me.'"—*Ibid.* "The name of the person or thing spoken of, or about, is the third person; as, 'James has come.'"—*Ibid.* "The object [of a passive verb] is always its subject or nominative case."—*Ib.* p. 62. "When a noun is in the nominative case to an active verb, it is the actor."—*Kirkham's Gram.* p. 44. "And the person commanded, is its nominative."—*Ingersoll's Gram.* p. 120. "The first person is that who speaks."—*Pasquier's Levizac*, p. 91. "The Conjugation of a Verb is its different variations or inflections throughout the Moods and Tenses."—*Wright's Gram.* p. 80. "The first person is the speaker. The second person is the one spoken to. The third person is the one spoken of."—*Parker and Fox's Gram.* Part i, p. 6 ; *Hiley's*, 18. "The first person is the one that speaks, or the speaker."—*Sanborn's Gram.* pp. 23 and 75. "The second person is the one that is spoken to, or addressed."—*Ibid.* "The third person is the one that is spoken of, or that is the topic of conversation."—*Ibid.* "*I*, is the first person Singular. *We*, is the first person Plural."—*Murray's Gram.* p. 51; *Alger's, Ingersoll's*, and *many others.* "*Thou*, is the second person Singular. *Ye* or *you*, is the second person Plural.'—*Ibid.* "*He, she*, or *it*, is the third person Singular. *They*, is the third person Plural."—*Ibid.* "The nominative case is the actor, or subject of the verb."—*Kirkham's Gram.* p. 43. "The noun *John* is the actor,

---

* The author of this example supposes *friend* to be in the nominative case, though *John's* is in the possessive, and both words denote the same person. But this is not only contrary to the general rule for same cases, but contrary to his own application of one of his own rules. Example : "*Maria's* duty, as a *teacher*, is, to instruct her pupils." Here, he says, "*Teacher* is in the *possessive* case, from its relation to the name *Maria*, denoting the same object."—*Peirce's Gram.* p. 211. This explanation, indeed, is scarcely intelligible, on account of its grammatical inaccuracy. He means, however, that, "*Teacher* is in the *possessive* case, from its relation to the name *Maria's*, the two words denoting the same object." No word can be possessive "from its relation to the name *Maria*," except by standing immediately before it, in the usual manner of possessives.

therefore John is in the nominative case."—*Ibid.* "The actor is always the nominative case."—*Smith's New Gram.* p. 62. "The nominative case is always the agent or actor." *Mack's Gram.* p. 67. "Tell the part of speech each name is."—*J. Flint's Gram.* p. "What number is *boy?* Why? What number is *pens?* Why?"—*Ib.* p. 27. "The speaker is the first person, the person spoken to, the second person, and the person or thing spoken of, is the third person."—*Ib.* p. 26. "What nouns are masculine gender? All males are masculine gender."—*Ib.* p. 28. "An interjection is a sudden emotion of the mind." *Barrett's Gram.* p. 62.

RULE VII. — OBJECTIVES.

A Noun or a Pronoun made the object of a preposition, is governed by in the objective case: as, "The temple of *fame* stands upon the *grave:* flame that burns upon its *altars,* is kindled from the *ashes* of great men. —*Hazlitt.*

    "Life is His gift, from *whom* whate'er life needs,
      With ev'ry good and perfect *gift,* proceeds."—*Cowper,* Vol. i, p. 9

OBSERVATIONS ON RULE VII.

OBS. 1.—To this rule there are no exceptions; for prepositions, in English, govern no other case than the objective.* But the learner should observe, that most of our prepositions may be the *imperfect participle* for their object, and some, the *pluperfect,* or *preperfect;* as, "On opening the trial, they accused him *of having defrauded* them."—"A quick wit, a nice judgment, he could not raise this man *above being received* only upon the foot *of contributing* to mirth and diversion."—*Steele.* And the preposition *to* is often followed by an *infinitive verb;* as, "When a sort of wind is said *to whistle,* and an other *to roar;* when a serpent is said *to hiss,* a fly *to hum,* and falling timber *to crash;* when a stream is said *to flow,* and hail *to rattle;* the analogy between the word and the thing signified, is plainly discernible."—*Blair's Rhet.* p. 55. But let it not be supposed that participles or infinitives, when they are governed by prepositions, are therefore in the *objective case;* for case is no attribute of either of these classes of words: they are indeclinable in English, whatever be the relations they assume. They are governed *as participles,* or *as infinitives,* and not *as cases.* The mere fact of government is so far from *creating* the modification governed, that it necessarily presupposes it to exist, and that it is something cognizable in etymology.

OBS. 2.—The brief assertion, that, "Prepositions govern the objective case," which till very lately our grammarians have universally adopted as their sole rule for both terms, the governed and the governed,—the preposition and its object,—is, in respect to both, somewhat exceptionable, being but partially and lamely applicable to either. It neither explains the connecting nature of the preposition, nor applies to all objectives, nor embraces all the terms which a preposition may govern. It is true, that prepositions, when they introduce declinable words, or words that have cases, always govern the objective; but the rule is liable to be misunderstood, and is in fact often misapplied, as if it meant something more than this. Besides, in no other instance do grammarians attempt to parse both the governing word and the governed, by one and the same rule. I have therefore placed the *objects* of this government here, where they belong in the order of the parts of speech, expressing the rule in such terms as cannot be mistaken; and have also given, in its proper place, a distinct rule for the construction of the preposition itself. See Rule 23d.

OBS. 3.—Prepositions are sometimes *elliptically* construed with *adjectives,* the real object of the relation being thought to be some objective noun understood: as, *in vain,* in *secret, at first, on high;* i. e. *in a vain manner, in secret places, at the first time,* on *high places.* Such phrases usually imply time, place, degree, or manner, and are equivalent to adverbs. In parsing, the learner may supply the ellipsis.

OBS. 4.—In some phrases, a preposition seems to govern a *perfect participle;* but these expressions are perhaps rather to be explained as being elliptical: as, "To give it up *for lost;*"—"To take that for *granted* which is disputed."—*Murray's Gram.* Vol. i, p. 109. That is, perhaps, "To give it up for *a thing* lost;"—"To take that for *a thing* granted," &c. In the following passage, the words *ought* and *should* are employed in such a manner that it is difficult to say to what part of speech they belong: "It is that very character of *ought* and *should* which makes justice a law to us; and the same character is applicable to propriety, though perhaps more faintly than justice."—*Kames, El. of Crit.* Vol. i, p. 286. The meaning seems to be, "It is that very character of *being owed* and *required, that* makes justice a law to us;" and this mode of expression it is more easy to be *parsed,* is perhaps more grammatical than his Lordship's.

OBS. 5.—In some instances, prepositions precede *adverbs;* as, *at once, at unawares, from from above, till now, till very lately, for once, for ever.* Here the adverb, though an ind

---

* Dr. Webster, who was ever ready to justify almost any usage for which he could find half a dozen authorities, absurdly supposes, that *who* may sometimes be rightly preferred to *whom,* as the object of a tion. His remark is this: "In the use of *who* as an interrogative, there is an *apparent deviation* from construction — it being used *without distinction of case;* as, '*Who* do you speak *to?*' '*Who* is she married '*Who* is this reserved *for?*' '*Who* was it made *by?*' This idiom is not merely colloquial: it is found in the language of our best authors."—*Webster's Philosophical Gram.* p. 194; his *Improved Gram.* p. 136. "In this '*Who* do you speak *to?*' there is a *deviation* from regular construction; but the practice of thus using in certain familiar phrases, seems to be *established* by the best authors."—*Webster's Rudiments of E. Gram.* p. 72. Almost any other solecism may be quite as well justified as this. The present work shows, in fact, a great mass of authorities for many of the incongruities which it ventures to rebuke.

word, appears to be made *the object* of the preposition. It is in fact used substantively, and governed by the preposition. The term *forever* is often written as one word, and, as such, is obviously an adverb. The rest are what some writers would call *adverbial phrases ;* a term not very consistent with itself, or with the true idea of *parsing.* If different parts of speech are to be taken together as having the nature of an adverb, they ought rather to coalesce and be united; for the verb to *parse,* being derived from the Latin *pars,* a *part,* implies in general a distinct recognition of the elements or words of every phrase or sentence.

OBS. 6.—Nouns of *time, measure, distance,* or *value,* have often so direct a relation to verbs or adjectives, that the prepositions which are supposed to govern them, are usually suppressed ; as, "We rode *sixty miles* that *day.*" That is,—"*through* sixty miles *on* that day." "The country is not *a farthing* richer."—*Webster's Essays,* p. 122. That is,—"richer *by* a farthing." "The error has been copied *times* without number."—*Ib.* p. 281. That is,—"on or *at* times *innumerable.*" "A row of columns *ten feet* high, and a row *twice that height,* require different proportions."—*Kames, El. of Crit.* ii, 344. That is,—"high *to* ten feet," and, "a row *of* twice that height." "*Altus sex pedes,* High on or *at* six feet."—*Dr. Murray's Hist. of Europ. Lang.* ii, 150. All such nouns are in the *objective case,* and, in parsing them, the learner may supply the ellipsis ; * or, perhaps it might be as well, to say, as do B. H. Smart and some others, that the noun is an objective of time, measure, or value, taken *adverbially,* and relating directly to the verb or adjective qualified by it. Such expressions as, "A board *of* six feet *long,*"—"A boy *of* twelve years *old,*" are wrong. Either strike out the *of,* or say, "A board of six feet *in length,*"—"A boy of twelve years *of age ;*" because this preposition is not suited to the adjective, nor is the adjective fit to qualify the time or measure.

OBS. 7.—After the adjectives *like, near,* and *nigh,* the preposition *to* or *unto* is often understood ; † as, "It is *like* [to or *unto*] silver."—*Allen.* "How *like* the former."—*Dryden.* "*Near* yonder copse."—*Goldsmith.* "*Nigh* this recess."—*Garth.* As similarity and proximity are *relations,* and not *qualities,* it might seem proper to call *like, near,* and *nigh,* prepositions ; and some grammarians have so classed the last two. Dr. Johnson seems to be inconsistent in calling *near* a preposition, in the phrase, "So *near* thy heart," and an adjective, in the phrase, "Being *near* their master." See his *Quarto Dict.* I have not placed them with the prepositions, for the following four reasons : (1.) Because they are sometimes *compared ;* (2.) Because they sometimes have *adverbs* evidently relating to them ; (3.) Because the preposition *to* or *unto* is sometimes expressed after them ; and (4.) Because the words which *usually* stand for them in the learned languages, are clearly *adjectives.‡* But *like,* when it expresses similarity of *manner,* and *near* and *nigh,* when they express proximity of *degree,* are adverbs.

OBS. 8.—The word *worth* is often followed by an objective, or a participle, which it appears to govern ; as, "If your arguments produce no conviction, they are *worth* nothing to me."—*Beattie.* "To reign is *worth* ambition."—*Milton.* "This is life indeed, life *worth* preserving."—*Addison.* It is not easy to determine to what part of speech *worth* here belongs. Dr. Johnson calls it an *adjective,* but says nothing of the *object* after it, which some suppose to be governed by *of* understood. In this supposition, it is gratuitously assumed, that *worth* is equivalent to *worthy,* after which *of* should be expressed ; as, "Whatsoever is *worthy of* their love, is *worth* their anger."—*Denham.* But as *worth* appears to have no certain characteristic of an adjective, some call it a *noun,* and suppose a double ellipsis ; as, "My knife is worth a shilling ;" i. e. "My knife is *of the* worth *of* a shilling."—*Kirkham's Gram.* p. 163. "'The book is worth that *sum ;*' that is,

* Grammarians differ much as to the proper mode of parsing such nouns. Wells says, "This is *the case independent by ellipsis.*"—*School Gram.* p. 123. But the idea of *such* a case is a flat absurdity. Ellipsis occurs only where something, not uttered, is implied ; and where a *preposition* is thus wanting, the noun is, of course, its *object ;* and therefore *not independent.* Webster, with too much contempt for the opinion of "Lowth, followed by the *whole tribe of writers* on this subject," declares it "a palpable error," to suppose "prepositions to be understood before these expressions ;" and, by two new rules, his 23d and 28th, teaches, that, "Names of measure or dimension, followed by an adjective," and "Names of certain portions of time and space, and especially words denoting continuance of time or progression, are used *without a governing word.*"—*Philos. Gram.* pp. 165 and 171 ; *Imp. Gram.* 116 and 122 ; *Rudiments,* 65 and 67. But this is no account at all of the *construction,* or of the *case* of the noun. As the nominative, or the case which we may use independently, is never a subject of government, the phrase, "*without a governing word,*" implies that the case is *objective ;* and how can this case be known, except by the discovery of some "governing word," of which it is the *object?* We find, however, many such rules as the following : "Nouns of time, distance, and degree, are put in the objective case without a preposition."—*Nutting's Gram.* p. 100. "Nouns which denote time, quantity, measure, distance, value, or direction are often put in the objective case without a preposition."—*Weld's Gram.* p. 153 ; "Abridged Ed." 118. "Names signifying duration, extension, quantity, quality, and valuation, are in the objective case without a governing word."—*Frazee's Gram.* p. 154. *Bullions,* too, has a similar rule. To estimate these rules aright, one should observe how often the nouns in question are found *with* a governing word. Weld, of late, contradicts himself by *admitting the ellipsis ;* and then, inconsistently with his admission, most absurdly *denies the frequent use* of the preposition with nouns of *time, quantity,* &c. "Before words of this description, *the ellipsis of a preposition is obvious.* But it is *seldom proper to use* the preposition before such words."—*Weld's "Abridged Edition,"* p. 118.

† Professor Fowler absurdly says, "*Nigh, near, next, like,* when followed by the objective case. *may be regarded either* as Prepositions or as Adjectives, *to* being understood."—*Fowler's E. Gram.* 8vo, 1850. § 458, Note 7. Now, "*to* being understood," it is plain that no one of these words can be accounted a preposition, but by supposing the preposition to be complex, and to be partly suppressed. This can be nothing better than an idle whim ; and, since the classification of words as parts of speech, is always positive and exclusive, to refer any particular word indecisively to "either" of two classes, is certainly no better *teaching,* than to say, "I do not know of which sort it is ; call it what you please !"

‡ The following examples may illustrate these points : "These verbs, and all others *like* to them, were *like* them."—*Dr. Murray's Hist. of Europ. Lang.* Vol. ii, p. 128. "The old German, and even the modern German, are much *liker* to the Visigothic than they are to the dialect of the Edda."—*Ib.* i, 330. "Proximus finem, *nighest* the end."—*Ib.* ii, 150. "Let us now come *nearer* to our own language."—*Dr. Blair's Rhet.* p. 85. "This looks *very like* a paradox."—*BEATTIE : Murray's Gram.* i, p. 118. "He was *near* [to] falling."—*Ib.* p. 116. Murray, who puts *near* into his list of prepositions, gives this example to show how "*prepositions become adverbs :*' 'There was none ever before *like unto* it."—*Stone, on Masonry,* p. 5.

"And earthly power doth then show *likest* God's,
     When mercy *seasons* justice."—*Beauties of Shakspeare,* p. 46.

' The book is (*the*) worth (*of*) that *sum*;' 'It is worth *while*;' that is, 'It is (*the*) worth (*of the*) while.'"—*Nixon's Parser*, p. 54. This is still less satisfactory; * and as the whole appears to be mere guess-work, I see no good reason why *worth* is not a *preposition*, governing the noun or participle.† If an *adverb* precede *worth*, it may as well be referred to the foregoing verb, as when it occurs before any other preposition: as, "It is richly worth the money."—"It *lies directly before* your door." Or if we admit that an adverb sometimes relates to this word, the same thing may be as true of other prepositions: as, "And this is a lesson which, to the greatest part of mankind, is, I think, *very well worth* learning."—*Blair's Rhet.* p. 303. "He sees let down from the ceiling, *exactly over* his head, a glittering sword, hung by a single hair."—*Murray's E. Reader*, p. 33.

OBS. 9.—Both Dr. Johnson and Horne Tooke, (who never agreed if they could help it,) unite in saying that *worth*, in the phrases, "Wo *worth* the man,"—"Wo *worth* the day," and the like, is from the imperative of the Saxon verb *wyrthan* or *weorthan*, to *be*; i. e. "Wo *be* [*to*] the man," or, "Wo *betide* the man," &c. And the latter affirms, that, as the preposition *by* is from the imperative of *beon*, to *be*, so *with*, (though admitted to be sometimes from *withan*, to join) is often no other than this same imperative verb *wyrth* or *worth*: if so, the three words *by*, *with*, and *worth*, were originally synonymous, and should now be referred at least to one and the same class. The *dative case*, or oblique object, which they governed as *Saxon verbs*, becomes their proper object, when taken as *English prepositions*; and in this also they appear to be alike. *Worth*, then, when it signifies *value*, is a common noun; but when it signifies *equal in value to*, it governs an objective, and has the usual characteristics of a preposition. Instances may perhaps be found in which *worth* is an adjective, meaning *valuable* or *useful*, as in the following lines:

"They glow'd, and grew more intimate with God,
More *worth* to men, more joyous to themselves."—*Young*, N. IX, 1. 988.

In one instance, the poet Campbell appears to have used the word *worthless* as a preposition:

"Eyes a mutual soul confessing,
Soon you'll make them grow
Dim, and *worthless* your *possessing*,
Not with age, but woe!"

OBS. 10.—After verbs of *giving*, *paying*, *procuring*, and some others, there is usually an ellipsis of *to* or *for* before the objective of the person; as, "Give [*to*] *him* water to drink."—"Buy [*for*] *me* a knife."—"Pay [*to*] *them* their wages." So in the exclamation, "Wo is *me!*" meaning, "Wo is *to* me!" This ellipsis occurs chiefly before the personal pronouns, and before such nouns as come between the verb and its direct object; as, "Whosoever killeth you, will think that he doeth [*to*] *God* service."—*John*, xvi, 2. "Who brought [*to*] her *masters* much gain by soothsaying."—*Acts*, xvi, 16. "Because he gave not [*to*] *God* the glory."—*Ib.* xii, 23. "Give [*to*] *me* leave to allow [*to*] *myself* no respite from labour."—*Spect.* No. 454. "And the sons of Joseph, which were born [*to*] *him* in Egypt, were two souls."—*Gen.* xlvi, 27. This elliptical construction of a few objectives, is what remains to us of the ancient Saxon dative case. If the order of the words be changed, the preposition must be inserted; as, "Pray do my service *to* his majesty."—*Shak.* The doctrine inculcated by several of our grammarians, that, "Verbs of *asking*, *giving*, *teaching*, and *some others*, are often employed to govern two objectives." (*Wells,* § 215,) I have, under a preceding rule, discountenanced; preferring the supposition, which appears to have greater weight of authority, as well as stronger support from reason, that, in the instances cited in proof of such government, a preposition is, in fact, understood. Upon this question of ellipsis, depends, in all such instances, our manner of parsing one of the objective words.

OBS. 11.—In *dates*, as they are usually written, there is much abbreviation; and several nouns of place and time are set down in the objective case, without the prepositions which govern them: as, "New York, Wednesday, 20th October, 1830."—*Journal of Literary Convention.* That is, "*At* New York, *on* Wednesday, *the* 20th *day of* October, *in the year* 1830."

NOTE TO RULE VII.

An objective noun of time or measure, if it qualifies a subsequent adjective, must not also be made an adjunct to a preceding noun; as, "To an infant *of* only two or three years *old*."—*Dr. Wayland.* Expunge *of*, or for *old* write *of age*. The following is right: "The vast army of the Canaanites, *nine hundred chariots strong*, covered the level plain of Esdraelon."—*Milman's Jews*, Vol. i, p. 159. See Obs. 6th above.

---

* Wright's notion of this construction is positively absurd and self-contradictory. In the sentence, "My cane is worth a shilling," he takes the word *worth* to be a noun "in *apposition* to the word *shilling*." And to prove it so, he puts the sentence successively into these four forms: "My cane is *worth* or *value* for a shilling;"—"The *worth* or *value* of my cane is a shilling;"—"My cane is a *shilling's worth*;"—"My cane is *the worth of* a shilling."—*Philosophical Gram.* p. 150. In all these transmutations, *worth* is unquestionably a noun; but in none of them, is it in apposition with the word *shilling*; and he is quite mistaken in supposing that they "indispensably prove the word in question to be a noun." There are other authors, who, with equal confidence, and equal absurdity, call *worth* a verb. For example: "A noun, which signifies the price, is put in the objective case, without a preposition; as, 'my book is *worth* twenty shillings.' Is *worth* is a *neuter verb*, and answers to the *latin* verb *valet*."—*Barrett's Gram.* p. 188. I do not deny that the phrase "*is worth*" is a just version of the verb *valet*; but this equivalence in import, is no proof at all that *worth* is a verb. *Prodest* is a Latin verb, which signifies "*is profitable to*:" but who will thence infer, that *profitable to* is a verb?

† In J. R. Chandler's English Grammar, as published in 1821, the word *worth* appears in the list of prepositions; but the revised list, in his edition of 1847, does not contain it. In both books, however, it is expressly parsed as a preposition; and, in expounding the sentence, "The book is worth a dollar," the author makes this remark: "*Worth* has been called an adjective by some, and a noun by others: *worth*, however, in this sentence expresses a relation by value, and is so far a preposition; and no ellipsis, which may be formed, would change the nature of the word, without giving the sentence a different meaning."—*Chandler's Gram.* Old Ed. p. 155; New Ed. p. 181.

IMPROPRIETIES FOR CORRECTION.

FALSE SYNTAX UNDER RULE VII.

UNDER THE RULE ITSELF.—OF THE OBJECTIVE IN FORM.

"But I do not remember who they were for."—*Abbott's Teacher*, p. 265.

[FORMULE.—Not proper, because the pronoun *who* is in the nominative case, and is made the object of the preposition *for*. But, according to Rule 7th, "A noun or a pronoun made the object of a preposition, is governed by it in the objective case." Therefore, *who* should be *whom*; thus, "But I do not remember *whom* they were for."]

"But if you can't help it, who do you complain of?"—*Collier's Antoninus*, p. 137. "Who was it from? and what was it about?"—*Edgeworth's Frank*, p. 72. "I have plenty of victuals, and, between you and I, something in a corner."—*Day's Sandford and Merton*. "The upper one, who I am now about to speak of."—*Hunt's Byron*, p. 311. "And to poor we, thine enmity's most capital."—*Beauties of Shakspeare*, p. 201. "Which thou dost confess, were fit for thee to use, as they to claim."—*Ib.* p. 196. "To beg of thee, it is my more dishonour, than thou of them."—*Ib.* p. 197. "There are still a few who, like thou and I, drink nothing but water."—*Gil Blas*, Vol. i, p. 104. "Thus, I *shall* fall; Thou *shalt* love thy neighbour; He *shall* be rewarded, express no resolution on the part of *I, thou, he*."—*Lennie's E. Gram.* p. 22; *Bullions's*, 32. "So saucy with the hand of she here—What's her name?"—*Shak. Ant. and Cleop.* Act iii, Sc. 11. "All debts are cleared between you and I."—*Id. Merchant of Venice*, Act iii, Sc. 2. "Her price is paid, and she is sold like thou."—*Milman's Fall of Jerusalem*. "Search through all the most flourishing era's of Greece."—*Brown's Estimate*, ii, 16. "The family of the Rudolph's had been long distinguished."—*The Friend*, Vol. v, p. 54. "It will do well enough for you and I."—*Castle Rackrent*, p. 120. "The public will soon discriminate between him who is the sycophant, and he who is the teacher."—*Chazotte's Essay*, p. 10. "We are still much at a loss who civil power belongs to."—*Locke*. "What do you call it? and who does it belong to?"—*Collier's Cebes*. "He had received no lessons from the Socrates's, the Plato's, and the Confucius's of the age."—*Haller's Letters*. "I cannot tell who to compare them to."—*Bunyan's P. P.*, p. 128. "I see there was some resemblance betwixt this good man and I."—*Pilgrim's Progress*, p. 298. "They by that means have brought themselves into the hands and house of I do not know who."—*Ib.* p. 196. "But at length she said there was a great deal of difference between Mr. Cotton and we."—*Hutchinson's Mass.* ii, 430. "So you must ride on horseback after we."*—Mrs. GILPIN: *Cowper*, i, 275. "A separation must soon take place between our minister and I."—*Werter*, p. 109. "When she exclaimed on Hastings, you, and I."—*Shakspeare*. "To who? to thee? What art thou?"—*Id.* "That they should always bear the certain marks who they came from."—*Butler's Analogy*, p. 221.

"This life has joys for you and I,
And joys that riches ne'er could buy."—*Burns*.

UNDER THE NOTE.—OF TIME OR MEASURE.

"Such as almost every child of ten years old knows."—*Town's Analysis*, p. 4. "One winter's school of four months, will carry any industrious scholar, of ten or twelve years old, completely through this book."—*Ib.* p. 12. "A boy of six years old may be taught to speak as correctly, as Cicero did before the Roman Senate."—*Webster's Essays*, p. 27. "A lad of about twelve years old, who was taken captive by the Indians."—*Ib.* p. 235. "Of nothing else but that individual white figure of five inches long which is before him."—*Campbell's Rhet.* p. 288. "Where lies the fault, that boys of eight or ten years old, are with great difficulty made to understand any of its principles?"—*Guy's Gram.* p. v. "Where language of three centuries old is employed."—*Booth's Introd. to Dict.* p. 21. "Let a gallows be made of fifty cubits high."—*Esther*, v, 14. "I say to this child of nine years old bring me that hat, he hastens and brings it me."—*Osborn's Key*, p. 3. "He laid a floor twelve feet long, and nine feet wide; that is, over the extent *of* twelve feet long, and *of* nine feet wide."—*Merchant's School Gram.* p. 95. "The Goulah people are a tribe of about fifty thousand strong."—*Examiner*, No. 71.

RULE VIII.—NOM. ABSOLUTE.

A Noun or a Pronoun is put absolute in the nominative, when its case depends on no other word: as, "*He failing*, who shall meet success?"—"Your *fathers*, where are they? and the *prophets*, do they live forever?"—*Zech.* i, 5. "Or *I* only and *Barnabas*, have not we power to forbear

---

* Cowper here purposely makes Mrs. Gilpin use bad English; but this is no reason why a school-boy may not be taught to correct it. Dr. Priestley supposed that the word *we*, in the example, "To poor *we*, thine enmity," &c., was also used by Shakspeare, "in a droll humorous way."—*Gram.* p. 108. He surely did not know the connexion of the text. It is in "Volumnia's *pathetic* speech" to her victorious son. See *Coriolanus*, Act V, Sc. 8.

working?"—1 *Cor.* ix, 6. " Nay but, *O man*, who art thou that repliest against God?"—*Rom.* ix, 20. "O rare *we!*"—*Cowper.* " Miserable *they!*"—*Thomson.*

> " The *hour* conceal'd, and so remote the *fear,*
> Death still draws nearer, never seeming near."—*Pope.*

OBSERVATIONS ON RULE VIII.

Obs. 1.—Many grammarians make an idle distinction between the nominative *absolute* and the nominative *independent,* as if these epithets were not synonymous; and, at the same time, they are miserably deficient in directions for disposing of the words so employed. Their two rules do not embrace more than one half of those *frequent* examples in which the case of the noun or pronoun depends on no other word. Of course, the remaining half cannot be parsed by any of the rules which they give. The lack of a comprehensive rule, like the one above, is a great and glaring defect in all the English grammars that the author has seen, except his own, and such as are indebted to him for such a rule. It is proper, however, that the different forms of expression which are embraced in this general rule, should be discriminated, one from an other, by the scholar: let him therefore, in parsing any nominative absolute, tell *how it is put so;* whether with a *participle,* by direct *address,* by *pleonasm,* or by *exclamation.* For, in discourse, a noun or a pronoun is put absolute in the nominative, after *four modes,* or under the following *four circumstances:* (of which Murray's "case absolute," or "nominative absolute," contains only the first:)

I. When, *with a participle,* it is used to express a cause, or a concomitant fact; as, "I say, *this being so,* the *law being broken,* justice takes place."—*Law and Grace,* p. 27. " *Pontius Pilate being* governor of Judea, and *Herod being* tetrarch of Galilee, and his *brother* Philip tetrarch of Iturea," &c.—*Luke,* iii, 1. " *I being* in the way, the Lord led me to the house of my master's brethren."—*Gen.* xxiv, 27.

> ———" While shame, *thou looking on,*
> Shame to be overcome or overreach'd,
> Would utmost vigor raise."—*Milton, P. L.,* B. ix, l. 312.

II. When, *by direct address,* it is put in the second person, and set off from the verb, by a comma or an exclamation point; as, "At length, *Seged,* reflect and be wise."—*Dr. Johnson.* "It may be, *drunkard, swearer, liar, thief,* thou dost not think of this "—*Law and Grace,* p. 27.

> "*This said,* he form'd thee, *Adam!* thee, *O man!*
> *Dust* of the ground, and in thy nostrils breath'd
> The breath of life."—*Milton's Paradise Lost,* B vii, l. 524.

III. When, *by pleonasm,* it is introduced abruptly for the sake of emphasis, and is not made the subject or the object of any verb; as, "*He that hath,* to him shall be given."—*Mark,* iv, 25. "*He that is holy,* let him be holy still."—*Rev.* xxii, 11. "*God,* a troop shall overcome him."—*Gen.* xlix, 19. "The *north* and the *south,* thou hast created them."—*Psalms,* lxxxix, 12. "And *they that have believing masters,* let them not despise them."—1 *Tim.* vi, 2. "And the *leper in whom the plague is,* his clothes shall be rent, and his head bare."—*Levit.* xiii, 45. " *They who serve me* with adoration,—I am in them, and they [are] in me."—R. W. Emerson: *Liberator,* No. 904.

> ———" What may this mean,
> That thou, dead corse, again in complete steel,
> Revisitst thus the glimpses of the moon,
> Making night hideous; and, *we fools of nature,**
> So horribly to shake our disposition
> With thoughts beyond the reaches of our souls?"—*Shak. Hamlet.*

IV. When, *by mere exclamation,* it is used without address, and without other words expressed or implied to give it construction; as, "And the Lord passed by before him, and proclaimed, *the Lord, the Lord God,* merciful and gracious, long-suffering, and abundant in goodness and truth." *Exodus,* xxxiv, 6. " O *the depth* of the riches both of the wisdom and knowledge of God!"— *Rom.* xi, 33. "I should not like to see her limping back, Poor *beast!*"—*Southey.*

> "Oh! deep enchanting *prelude* to repose,
> The *dawn* of bliss, the *twilight* of our woes!"—*Campbell.*

Obs. 2.—The nominative put absolute with a participle, is often equivalent to a dependent clause commencing with *when, while, if, since,* or *because.* Thus, "I being a child," may be equal to, "When I was a child," or, "Because I was a child." Here, in lieu of the nominative, the Greeks used the genitive case, and the Latins, the ablative. Thus, the phrase, "Καὶ ὑστερήσαντος οἴνου," "*And the wine failing,*" is rendered by Montanus, "*Et deficiente vino;*" but by Beza, "*Et cum defecisset vinum;*" and in our Bible, "*And when they wanted wine.*"—*John,* ii, 3. After a noun or a pronoun thus put absolute, the participle *being* is frequently understood, especially if an adjective or a like case come after the participle; as,

> "They left their bones beneath unfriendly skies,
> His worthless absolution [*being*] all the prize."—*Cowper,* Vol. i, p. 84.
> "Alike in ignorance, *his reason* [———] *such,*
> Whether he thinks too little or too much."—*Pope, on Man.*

Obs. 3.—The case which is put absolute in addresses or invocations, is what in the Latin and Greek grammars is called *the Vocative.* Richard Johnson says, "The only use of the Vocative

---

* Dr. Enfield misunderstood this passage; and, in copying it into his Speaker, (a very popular school-book,) he has perverted the text, by changing *we* to *us:* as if the meaning were, "Making us fools of nature." But it is plain, that all "*fools of nature*" must be fools of nature's own making, and not persons temporarily frighted out of their wits by a ghost; nor does the meaning of the last two lines comport with any objective construction of this pronoun. See *Enfield's Speaker,* p. 364.

Case, is, to call upon a Person, or a thing put Personally, which we speak to, to give notice to what we direct our Speech; and this is therefore, properly speaking, the *only Case absolute or independent* which we may make use of without respect to any other Word."—*Gram. Commentaries,* p. 131. This remark, however, applies not justly to our language; for, with us, the vocative case, is unknown, or not distinguished from the nominative. In English, all nouns of the second person are either put absolute in the nominative, according to Rule 8th, or in apposition with their own pronouns placed before them, according to Rule 3d: as, " This is the stone which was set at nought of *you builders* "—*Acts,* iv, 11. " How much rather ought *you receivers* to be considered as abandoned and execrable ! "—*Clarkson's Essay,* p. 114.

> " Peace ! *minion,* peace ! it boots not me to hear
> The selfish counsel of *you hangers-on.*"—*Brown's Inst.* p. 189.

> "*Ye Sylphs* and *Sylphids,* to your chief give ear;
> Fays, Faries, Genii, Elves, and Dæmons, hear ! "—*Pope, R. L.* ii, 74.

Obs. 4.—The case of nouns used in exclamations, or in mottoes and abbreviated sayings, often depends, or may be conceived to depend, on something *understood;* and, when their construction can be satisfactorily explained on the principle of ellipsis, they are *not put absolute,* unless the ellipsis be that of the participle. The following examples may perhaps be resolved in this manner, though the expressions will lose much of their vivacity : "A *horse! a horse!* my *kingdom* for a horse ! "—*Shak.* "And he said unto his father, My *head!* my *head!*"—2 *Kings,* iv, 19. "And Samson said, With the jaw-bone of an ass, *heaps* upon heaps, with the jaw of an ass, have I slain a thousand men."—*Judges,* xv, 16. " Ye have heard that it hath been said, An *eye* for an eye, and a *tooth* for a tooth."—*Matt.* v, 38. " *Peace,* be still."—*Mark,* iv, 39. " One God, *world* without end. Amen."—*Com. Prayer.*

> "*My fan,* let others say, who laugh at toil;
> Fan! hood! glove! scarf! is her laconic style."—*Young.*

Obs. 5.—" Such Expressions as, *Hand to Hand, Face to Face, Foot to Foot,* are of the nature of Adverbs, and are of elliptical Construction : For the Meaning is, *Hand* OPPOSED *to Hand, &c.*"— *W. Ward's Gram.* p 100. This learned and ingenious author seems to suppose the former noun to be here put absolute with a participle understood; and this is probably the best way of explaining the construction both of that word and of the preposition that follows it. So Samson's phrase, " *heaps upon heaps,*" may mean, " heaps *being piled* upon heaps; " and Scott's, " *man to man,* and *steel to steel,*" may be interpreted, " *man being opposed* to man, and *steel being opposed* to steel: "

> " Now, man to man, and steel to steel,
> A chieftain's vengeance thou shalt feel."—*Lady of the Lake.*

Obs. 6.—Cobbett, after his own hasty and dogmatical manner, rejects the whole theory of nominatives absolute, and teaches his "soldiers, sailors, apprentices, and ploughboys," that, " The supposition, that there can be a noun, or pronoun, which has reference to *no verb,* and *no preposition,* is certainly a mistake."—*Cobbett's E. Gram.* ¶ 201. To sustain his position, he lays violent hands upon the plain truth, and even trips himself up in the act. Thus : " For want of a little thought, as to the matter immediately before us, some grammarians have found out ' *an absolute case,*' as they call it; and Mr. Lindley Murray gives an instance of it in these words : ' *Shame being lost,* all virtue is lost.' The full meaning of this sentence is this : ' *It being,* or *the state of things being such, that* shame *is* lost, all virtue is lost.' "—*Cobbett's E. Gram.* ¶ 191. Again : "There must, you will bear in mind, always be a verb expressed or understood. One would think, that this was not the case in [some instances: as,] ' *Sir,* I beg you to give me a bit of bread.' The sentence which follows the *Sir,* is complete; but the *Sir* appears to stand wholly without connexion. However, the full meaning is this : ' I beg you, *who are a Sir,* to give me a bit of bread.' Now, if you take time to reflect a little on this matter, you will never be puzzled for a moment by those detached words, to suit which grammarians have invented *vocative cases* and *cases absolute,* and a great many other appellations, with which they puzzle themselves, and confuse and bewilder and torment those who read their books."—*Ib.* Let. xix, ¶¶ 225 and 226. All this is just like Cobbett. But, let his admirers reflect on the matter as long as they please, the two *independent* nominatives *it* and *state,* in the text, "*It being,* or the *state* of things *being such,*" will forever stand a glaring confutation both of his doctrine and of his censure : " the *case absolute* " is there still ! He has, in fact, only converted the *single* example into a *double* one !

Obs. 7.—The Irish philologer, J. W. Wright, is even more confident than Cobbett, in denouncing " *the case absolute;* " and more severe in his reprehension of " Grammarians in general, and Lowth and Murray in particular," for entertaining the idea of such a case. " Surprise must cease," says he, " on an acquaintance with the fact, that persons who imbibe such fantastical doctrine *should be destitute of sterling information* on the subject of English grammar.—The English language is a stranger to this case. *We* speak thus, with confidence, conscious of the justness of *our* opinion :—an opinion, not precipitately formed, but one which is the result of mature and deliberate inquiry. ' *Shame being lost,* all virtue is lost :' The meaning of this is,— ' *When* shame *is being lost,* all virtue is lost.' Here, the words *is being lost* form *the true present tense* of the passive voice; in which voice, all verbs, thus expressed, are *unsuspectedly* situated : thus, *agreeing* with the noun *shame,* as the nominative of the first member of the sentence."— *Wright's Philosophical Gram.* p. 192. With all his deliberation, this gentleman has committed one oversight here, which, as it goes to contradict his scheme of the passive verb, some of his sixty venerable commenders ought to have pointed out to him. My old friend, the " Professor of *Elocution* in Columbia College," who finds by this work of " superior excellence," that " the nature of the *verb,* the most difficult part of grammar, has been, at length, *satisfactorily explained,*" ought by no means, after his " very attentive examination " of the book, to have left this service to me. In the clause, " all virtue *is lost,*" the passive verb " *is lost*" has the form which Murray gave it—the form which, till within a year or two, *all men* supposed to be the only right one; but, according to this new philosophy of the language, all men have been as much in error in this matter, as in their notion of the nominative absolute. If Wright's theory of the verb is correct, the only just form of the foregoing expression is, "all virtue *is being lost.*" If this central position is untenable, his management of the nominative absolute falls of course. To me, the inserting of the word *being* into all our passive verbs, seems the most monstrous absurdity ever broached in the name of grammar. The threescore certifiers to the accuracy of that theory, have, I trow, only recorded themselves as so many *ignoramuses;* for there are more than three-score myriads of better judgements against them.

IMPROPRIETIES FOR CORRECTION.

FALSE SYNTAX UNDER RULE VIII.

NOUNS OR PRONOUNS PUT ABSOLUTE.

"Him having ended his discourse, the assembly dispersed."—*Brown's Inst.* p. 190.

[FORMULE.—Not proper, because the pronoun *him*, whose case depends on no other word, is in the objective case. But, according to Rule 8th, "A noun or a pronoun is put absolute in the nominative, when its case depends on no other word." Therefore, *him* should be *he;* thus, "*He* having ended his discourse, the assembly dispersed."]

"Me being young, they deceived me."—*Inst. E. Gram.* p. 190. "Them refusing to comply, I withdrew."—*Ib.* "Thee being present, he would not tell what he knew."—*Ib.* "The child is lost; and me, whither shall I go?"—*Ib.* "Oh! happy us, surrounded with so many blessings."—*Murray's Key*, p. 187; *Merchant's*, 197; *Smith's New Gram.* 96; *Farnum's*, 63. "'Thee too! Brutus, my son!' cried Cæsar overcome."—*Brown's Inst.* p. 190. "Thee! Maria! and so late! and who is thy companion?"—*New-York Mirror*, Vol. x, p. 353. "How swiftly our time passes away! and ah! us, how little concerned to improve it!"—*Comly's Gram. Key*, p. 192.

"There all thy gifts and graces we display,
Thee, only thee, directing all our way."

CHAPTER IV.—ADJECTIVES.

The syntax of the English Adjective is fully embraced in the following brief rule, together with the exceptions, observations, and notes, which are, in due order, subjoined.

RULE IX.—ADJECTIVES.

Adjectives relate to nouns or pronouns: as, "*Miserable* comforters are ye *all.*"—*Job*, xvi, 2. "*No worldly* enjoyments are *adequate* to the *high* desires and powers of an *immortal* spirit."—*Blair.*

"Whatever faction's *partial* notions are,
No hand is wholly *innocent* in war."—*Rowe's Lucan*, B. vii, l. 191.

EXCEPTION FIRST.

An adjective sometimes relates to a *phrase* or *sentence* which is made the subject of an intervening verb; as, "*To insult the afflicted*, is *impious.*"—*Dillwyn.* "*That he should refuse*, is not *strange.*"—"*To err is human.*" Murray says, "*Human* belongs to its substantive '*nature*' understood."—*Gram.* p. 233. From this I dissent.

EXCEPTION SECOND.

In combined arithmetical numbers, one adjective often relates *to an other*, and the whole phrase, to a subsequent noun; as, "*One thousand four hundred and fifty-six* men."—"Six dollars and *eighty-seven and a half* cents for *every five* days' service."—"In the *one hundred and twenty-second* year."—"*One seven* times more than it was wont to be heated."—*Daniel*, iii, 19.

EXCEPTION THIRD.

With an infinitive or a participle denoting being or action in the abstract, an adjective is sometimes also taken *abstractly;* (that is, without reference to any particular noun, pronoun, or other subject;) as, "To be *sincere*, is to be *wise*, *innocent*, and *safe.*"—*Hawkesworth.* "*Capacity* marks the abstract quality of being *able* to receive or hold."—*Crabb's Synonymes.* "Indeed, the main secret of being *sublime*, is to say great things in few and plain words."—*Hiley's Gram.* p. 215. "Concerning being *free* from sin in heaven, there is no question."—*Barclay's Works*, iii, 437. Better: "Concerning *freedom* from sin," &c.

EXCEPTION FOURTH.

Adjectives are sometimes substituted for their corresponding abstract nouns; (perhaps, in most instances, *elliptically*, like Greek neuters;) as, "The sensations of *sublime* and *beau-*

tiful are not always distinguished by very distant boundaries."—*Blair's Rhet.* p. 47. That is, "of *sublimity* and *beauty.*" "The faults opposite to *the sublime* are chiefly two: *the frigid*, and *the bombast.*"—*Ib.* p. 44. Better: "The faults opposite to *sublimity*, are chiefly two; *frigidity* and *bombast.*" "Yet the ruling character of the nation was that of *barbarous* and *cruel.*"—*Brown's Estimate,* ii. 26. That is, "of *barbarity* and *cruelty.*" "In a word, *agreeable* and *disagreeable* are qualities of the objects we perceive;" &c.—*Kames, El. of Crit.* i, 99. "*Polished,* or *refined,* was the idea which the author had in view."—*Blair's Rhet.* p. 219.

OBSERVATIONS ON RULE IX.

Obs. 1.—Adjectives often relate to nouns or pronouns *understood;* as, "A new sorrow recalls *all* the *former*" [sorrows].—*Art of Thinking,* p. 31. [The place] "*Farthest* from him is best."—*Milton, P. L.* "To whom they all gave heed, from the *least* [person] to the *greatest*" [person].—*Acts,* viii, 10. "The Lord your God is God of gods, and Lord of lords, a great God, a *mighty* [God], and a *terrible*" [God].—*Deut.* x, 17. "Every one can distinguish an *angry* from a *placid,* a *cheerful* from a *melancholy,* a *thoughtful* from a *thoughtless,* and a *dull* from a penetrating, countenance."—*Beattie's Moral Science,* p. 192. Here the word *countenance* is understood *seven* times; for eight different countenances are spoken of. "He came unto his *own* [possessions], and his *own* [men] received him not."—*John,* i, 11 The *Rev. J. G. Cooper,* has it: "He came unto his own (*creatures,*) and his own (*creatures*) received him not."—*Pl. and Pract. Gram.* p. 44. This ambitious editor of Virgil, abridger of Murray, expounder of the Bible, and author of several "new and improved" grammars, (of different languages,) should have understood this text, notwithstanding the obscurity of our version. "Εἰς τὰ ἴδια ἦλθε, καὶ οἱ ἴδιοι αὐτὸν οὐ παρέλαβον."—"In *propria* venit, et *proprii* eum non receperunt."—*Montanus.* "Ad *sua* venit, et *sui* eum non exceperunt."—*Beza.* "Il est venu *chez soi;* et *les siens* ne l'ont point reçu."—*French Bible.* Sometimes the construction of the adjective involves an ellipsis of *several words,* and those perhaps the principal parts of the clause; as, "The sea appeared to be agitated more than [in that degree *which* is] *usual.*"—*Murray's Key,* 8vo, p. 217. "During the course of the sentence, the scene should be changed as little as [in the least] *possible*" [*degree*].—*Blair's Rhet.* p. 107; *Murray's Gram.* 8vo, p. 312.

"Presumptuous man! the reason wouldst thou find,
Why [thou art] form'd so *weak,* so *little,* and so *blind?*"—*Pope.*

Obs. 2.—Because *qualities* belong only to *things,* most grammarians teach, that, "*Adjectives* are capable of being added *to nouns only.*"—*Buchanan's Syntax,* p. 26. Or, as Murray expresses the doctrine: "Every adjective, and every adjective pronoun, *belongs to a substantive,* expressed or understood."—*Octavo Gram.* p. 161. "The adjective *always* relates to *a substantive.*"—*Ib.* p. 169. This teaching, which is alike repugnant to the true *definition* of an adjective, to the *true rule* for its construction, and to *all the exceptions* to this rule, is but a sample of that hasty sort of induction, which is ever jumping to false conclusions for want of a fair comprehension of the facts in point. The position would not be tenable, even if all our *pronouns* were admitted to be *nouns,* or "*substantives;*" and, if these two parts of speech are to be distinguished, the consequence must be, that Murray supposes a countless number of unnecessary and absurd *ellipses.* It is sufficiently evident, that in the construction of sentences, adjectives often relate immediately to *pronouns,* and only through them to the nouns which they represent. Examples: "I should like to know who has been carried off, except *poor dear me.*"—*Byron.* "To *poor us* there is not much hope remaining."—*Murray's Key,* 8vo, p. 204. "It is the final pause *which alone,* on many occasions, marks the difference between prose and verse."—*Murray's Gram.* p. 260. "And sometimes after *them both* "—*Ib.* p. 196. "All men hail'd *me happy* "—*Milton.* "To receive *unhappy me.*"—*Dryden.* "Superior to *them all.*"—*Blair's Rhet.* p. 419. "*They* returned to their own country, *full* of the discoveries which they had made."—*Ib.* p. 350. "*All ye* are brethren."—*Matt.* xxiii, 8. "And *him only* shalt thou serve."—*Matt.* iv, 10.

"Go *wiser thou,* and in thy scale of sense
Weigh thy opinion against Providence."—*Pope.*

Obs. 3.—When an adjective follows a finite verb, and is not followed by a noun, it generally relates to the subject of the verb; as, "*I am glad* that the *door* is made *wide.*"—"An unbounded *prospect* doth not long continue *agreeable.*"—*Kames, El. of Crit.* i, 244 "Every thing which is *false, vicious,* or *unworthy,* is despicable to him, though all the world should approve it."—*Spectator,* No. 520. Here *false, vicious,* and *unworthy,* relate to *which;* and *despicable* relates to *thing.* The practice of Murray and his followers, of supplying a "substantive" in all such cases, is absurd. "When the Adjective forms the *Attribute* of a Proposition, it belongs to the noun [or pronoun] which serves as the *Subject* of the Proposition, and cannot be joined to any other noun, since it is of the Subject that we affirm the quality expressed by this Adjective."—*De Sacy, on General Gram.* p. 37. In some peculiar phrases, however, such as, *to fall short of, to make bold with, to set light by,* the adjective has such a connexion with the verb, that it may seem questionable how it ought to be explained in parsing. Examples: (1.) "This latter mode of expression falls *short* of the force and vehemence of the former."—*L. Murray's Gram.* p. 353. Some will suppose the word *short* to be here used *adverbially,* or to qualify *falls* only; but perhaps it may as well be parsed as an adjective relating to "*mode,*" the nominative. (2.) "And that I have made so *bold* with thy glorious Majesty."—*Jenks's Prayers,* p. 156. This expression is perhaps elliptical: it may mean, "that I have made *myself* so bold," &c. (3.) "Cursed be he that *setteth light* by his father or his mother: and all the people shall say, Amen."—*Deut.* xxvii, 16. This may mean, "that *setteth* light *esteem* or *estimation,*" &c.

Obs. 4.—When an adjective follows an infinitive or a participle, the noun or pronoun to which it relates, is sometimes before it, and sometimes after it, and often considerably remote; as, "A real gentleman cannot but practice those virtues *which,* by an intimate knowledge of mankind, he has found to be *useful* to them."—"He [a melancholy enthusiast] thinks *himself* obliged in duty to be *sad* and *disconsolate.*"—*Addison.* "He is scandalized at *youth* for being *lively,* and at *childhood* for being *playful*."—*Id.* "But growing *weary* of one who almost walked him out of breath, *he* left him for Horace and Anacreon."—*Steele.*

OBS. 5.—Adjectives preceded by the definite article, are often used, by *ellipsis, as nouns; as, the learned,* for, *learned men.* Such phrases usually designate those classes of persons or things, which are characterized by the qualities they express; and this, the reader must observe, is a use quite different from that *substitution* of adjectives for nouns, which is noticed in the fourth exception above. In *our* language, the several senses in which adjectives may thus be taken, are not distinguished with that clearness which the inflections of other tongues secure. Thus, *the noble, the vile, the excellent,* or *the beautiful,* may be put for three extra constructions: first, for *noble persons, vile persons,* &c.; secondly, for *the noble man, the vile man,* &c.; thirdly, for the abstract qualities, *nobility, vileness, excellence, beauty.* The last-named usage forms an exception to the rule; in the other two the noun is understood, and should be supplied by the parser. Such terms, if elliptical, are most commonly of the plural number, and refer to the word *persons* or *things* understood; as, "*The careless* and *the imprudent, the giddy* and *the fickle, the ungrateful* and *the interested,* everywhere meet us."—*Blair.* Here the noun *persons* is to be six times supplied. "Wherever there is taste, *the witty* and *the humorous* make themselves perceived."—*Campbell's Rhet.* p. 21. Here the author meant, simply, the qualities *wit* and *humour,* and he ought to have used these words, because the others are equivocal, and are more naturally conceived to refer to persons. In the following couplet, the noun *places* or *things* is understood after "*open,*" and again after "*covert,*" which last word is sometimes misprinted "*coverts:*"

"Together let us beat this ample field,
Try what *the open,* what *the covert,* yield."—*Pope, on Man.*

OBS. 6.—The adjective, in English, is generally placed immediately *before its noun;* as, "*Vain* man! is grandeur given to *gay* attire ?"—*Beattie.* Those adjectives which relate to *pronouns,* most commonly follow them; as. "They left *me weary* on a grassy turf."—*Milton.* But to both these general rules there are many exceptions; for the position of an adjective may be varied by a variety of circumstances, not excepting the mere convenience of emphasis: as, "And Jehu said, Unto *which* of *all us ?*"—*2 Kings,* ix, 5. In the following instances the adjective is placed *after the word* to which it relates:

1. When other words depend on the adjective, or stand before it to qualify it; as, "A mind *conscious of right,*"—"A wall *three feet thick,*"—"A body of troops *fifty thousand strong.*"

2. When the quality results from an action, or receives its application through a verb or participle; as, "Virtue renders *life happy.*"—"He was in Tirzah, drinking *himself drunk* in the house of Arza."—*1 Kings,* xvi, 9. "All men agree to call *vinegar sour, honey sweet,* and *aloes bitter.*"—*Burke, on Taste,* p. 38. "God made *thee perfect,* not *immutable.*"—*Milton.*

3. When the quality excites admiration, and the adjective would thus be more clearly distinctive; as, "Goodness *infinite,*"—"Wisdom *unsearchable.*"—*Murray.*

4. When a verb comes between the adjective and the noun; as, "Truth stands *independent of* all external things."—*Burgh.* "Honour is not *seemly* for a fool."—*Solomon.*

5. When the adjective is formed by means of the prefix *a;* as, *afraid, alert, alike, alive, alone, asleep, awake, aware, averse, ashamed, askew.* To these may be added a few other words; as, *else, enough, extant, extinct, fraught, pursuant.*

6. When the adjective has the nature, but not the form, of a participle; as, "A queen *regnant,*" —"The prince *regent,*"—"The heir *apparent,*"—"A lion, not *rampant,* but *couchant* or *dormant,*"— "For the time then *present*"

OBS. 7.—In some instances, the adjective may *either precede or follow* its noun; and the writer may take his choice, in respect to its position: as,

1. In *poetry*—provided the sense be obvious; as,

——————"Wilt thou to the *isles*
Atlantic, to the rich *Hesperian clime,*
Fly in the train of Autumn ?"—*Akenside, P. of I.* Book i, p. 27.

——————"Wilt thou fly
With laughing Autumn to the *Atlantic isles,*
And range with him *th' Hesperian field !*"—*Id. Bucke's Gram.* p. 120.

2. When technical usage favours one order, and common usage an other; as, "A notary *public,*" or, "A *public* notary ;"—"The heir *presumptive,*" or, "The *presumptive* heir." See *Johnson's Dict* and *Webster's.*

3. When an adverb precedes the adjective; as, "A Being *infinitely wise,*" or, "An *infinitely wise* Being." Murray, Comly, and others, here approve only the former order; but the latter is certainly not ungrammatical.

4. When several adjectives belong to the same noun; as, "A woman, *modest, sensible,* and *virtuous,*" or, "A *modest, sensible,* and *virtuous* woman." Here again, Murray, Comly, and others, approve only the former order; but I judge the latter to be quite as good.

5. When the adjective is emphatic, it may be *foremost* in the sentence, though the natural order of the words would bring it last; as, "*Weighty* is the anger of the righteous."—*Bible.* "*Blessed* are the pure in heart."—*Ib.* "*Great* is the earth, *high* is the heaven, *swift* is the sun in his course."—*1 Esdras,* iv, 34. "The more *laborious* the life is, *the less populous* is the country." —*Goldsmith's Essays,* p. 151.

OBS. 8.—By an ellipsis of the noun, an adjective with a preposition before it, is sometimes equivalent to an adverb; as, "*In particular;*" that is, "*In a particular manner;*" equivalent to *particularly.* So "*in general*" is equivalent to *generally.* It has already been suggested, that, in parsing, the scholar should here supply the ellipsis. See Obs. 3d, under Rule vii.

OBS. 9.—Though English adjectives are, for the most part, incapable of any *agreement,* yet such of them as denote unity or plurality, ought in general to have nouns of the same number; as, *this man, one man, two men, many men.*[*] In phrases of this form, the rule is well observed;

---

[*] In Clark's Practical Grammar, of 1849, is found this NOTE: "The Noun should correspond in number with the Adjectives. EXAMPLES—A two feet ruler. A ten feet pole."—P. 165. These examples are wrong: the doc-

but in some peculiar ways of numbering things, it is commonly disregarded; for certain nouns are taken in a plural sense without assuming the plural termination. Thus people talk of many *loads* of cheese,—many *sail* of vessels,—many *stand* of arms,—many *head* of cattle,—many *dozen* of eggs,—many *brace* of partridges,—many *pair* of shoes. So we read in the Bible of " two hundred *pennyworth* of bread," and " twelve *manner* of fruits." In all such phraseology, there is, in regard to the *form* of the latter word, an evident disagreement of the adjective with its immediate noun: but sometimes, (where the preposition *of* does not occur,) expressions that seem somewhat like these may be elliptical: as when historians tell of many *thousand foot* soldiers), or *many hundred horse* (troops). To denote a collective number, a singular adjective may precede a plural one; as, "*One* hundred men," — "*Every* six weeks." And to denote plurality, the adjective *many* may, in like manner, precede *an* or *a* with a singular noun; as, "The Odyssey entertains us with *many a wonderful adventure*, and *many a landscape* of nature."—*Blair's Rhet.* p 436 " There *starts up many* a writer."—*Kames, El. of Crit.* i, 306.

" Full *many a flower is born* to blush unseen,
And waste its sweetness on the desert air."—*Gray.*

OBS 10.—Though *this* and *that* cannot relate to plurals, many writers do not hesitate to place them before singulars taken conjointly, which are equivalent to plurals; as, "*This power and will* do necessarily produce that which man is empowered to do."—*Sale's Koran,* i, 229. "*That purity and self denial* which are essential to the support of virtue."—*Murray's Key,* 8vo, p. 218. "*This modesty and decency* were looked upon by them as a law of nature."—*Rollin's Hist.* ii, 45. Here the plural forms, *these* and *those*, cannot be substituted; but the singular may be repeated, if the repetition be thought necessary. Yet, when these same pronominal adjectives are placed after the nouns to suggest the things again, they must be made plural; as, "*Modesty and decency* were thus carefully guarded, for *these* were looked upon as being enjoined by the law of nature."

OBS. 11.—In prose, the use of adjectives for adverbs is improper; but, in poetry, an adjective relating to the noun or pronoun, is sometimes elegantly used in stead of an adverb qualifying the verb or participle; as, "*Gradual* sinks the breeze Into a perfect calm."—*Thomson's Seasons,* p. . "To Thee I bend the knee; to Thee my thoughts *Continual* climb."—*Ib.* p. 48. "As on he walks *Graceful*, and crows defiance."—*Ib.* p. 56. "As through the falling glooms *Pensive* I stray."—*Ib.* p. 80. "They, *sportive,* wheel; or, sailing down the stream, Are snatch'd *immediate* By the quick-eyed trout."—*Ib* p. 82. "*Incessant* still you flow."—*Ib.* p. 91. " The shatter'd clouds *Tumultuous* rove, the interminable sky *Sublimer* swells."—*Ib.* p. 116. In order to determine, in difficult cases, whether an adjective or an adverb is required, the learner should carefully attend to the definitions of these parts of speech and consider whether, in the case in question, *quality* is to be expressed, or *manner:* if the former, an adjective is always proper; if the latter, an adverb. That is, in this case, the adverb, though not always required in poetry, is specially requisite in prose. The following examples will illustrate this point: " She looks *cold*;"—" She looks *coldly* on him "—" I sat *silent*;"—" I sat *silently* musing."—" Stand *firm*; maintain your cause *firmly*." See *Etymology,* Chap. viii, Obs. 4th, 5th, 6th, and 7th, on the Modifications of Adverbs.

OBS 12.—In English, an adjective and its noun are often taken as a sort of compound term, to which other adjectives may be added; as, "An *old man*; a *good* old man; a very *learned, judicious,* good old man."—*L. Murray's Gram.* p. 169; *Brit. Gram.* 195; *Buchanan's,* 79. "Of an *other determinate positive new* birth, subsequent to baptism, we know nothing."—*West's Letters,* p. 183. When adjectives are thus accumulated, the subsequent ones should convey such ideas as the former may consistently qual fy, otherwise the expression will be objectionable. Thus the ordinal adjectives *first, second, third, next,* and *last,* may qualify the cardinal numbers, but they cannot very properly be qualified by them. When, therefore, we specify any part of a series, the cardinal adjective ought, by good right, to follow the ordinal, and not, as in the following phrase, be placed before it: " In reading the *nine last chapters* of John."—*Fuller.* Properly speaking, there is but one last chapter in any book. Say, therefore, " the *last nine* chapters;" for, out of the twenty-one chapters in John, a man may select several different nines. (See *Etymology,* Chap. iv, Obs. 7th, on the Degrees of Comparison.) When one of the adjectives merely qualifies the other, they should be joined together by a hyphen; as, "A *red-hot* iron,"— "A *dead-ripe* melon " And when both or all refer equally and solely to the noun, they ought either to be connected by a conjunction, or to be separated by a comma. The following example is therefore faulty: " It is the business of an epic poet, to form a *probable interesting* tale."— *Blair's Rhet.* p. 427. Say, "probable *and* interesting;" or else insert a comma in lieu of the conjunction.

"Around him wide a sable army stand,
A *low-born, cell-bred, selfish, servile* band."—*Dunciad,* B. ii, l. 355.

OBS. 13.—Dr. Priestley has observed: " There is a remarkable ambiguity in the use of the negative adjective *no*; and I do not see," says he, "how it can be remedied in any language. If I say, '*No laws are better than the English,*' it is only my known sentiments that can inform a person whether I mean to praise, or dispraise them."—*Priestley's Gram.* p. 136. It may not be possible to remove the ambiguity from the phraseology here cited, but it is easy enough to avoid the form, and say in stead of it, "*The English laws are worse than none,*" or, "*The English laws are as good as any*;" and, in neither of these expressions, is there any ambiguity, though the other may doubtless be taken in either of these senses. Such an ambiguity is sometimes used on purpose; as when one man says of another, " He is no small knave;" or, " He is no small fool."

_____, is misapplied in both. With this author, a, as well as *two* or *ten,* is an *adjective* of number; and, since two differ in number, what sort of concord or construction do the four words in each of these phrases make? Here a numeral and a noun are united to form a *compound adjective,* we commonly, if not always, use the latter in its primitive or singular form; as, "A *twopenny* toy,"—" a *twofold* error,"—" *three-coat* plastering,"—" a *threepenny* loaf,"—" a *foursquare* figure,"—" of *twenty-horse* power." And no carpenter hesitates to say, " a *twofoot* rule,"—" a *tenfoot* pole:" which phrases are right; while Clark's are not only unusual, but unanalogical, ungrammatical.

NOTES TO RULE IX.

NOTE I.—Adjectives that imply unity or plurality, must agree with their nouns in number : as, "*That sort, those sorts ;*"—"*This hand, these hands.*"*

NOTE II.—When the adjective is necessarily plural, or necessarily singular, the noun should be made so too: as, "*Twenty pounds,*" not, "Twenty *pound ;*"—"*Four feet* long." not, "Four *foot* long ;"—"*One session,*" not, "One *sessions.*"

NOTE III.—The reciprocal expression, *one an other,* should not be applied to two objects, nor *each other,* or *one the other,* to more than two; as, "Verse and prose, on some occasions, run into *one another,* like light and shade."—*Blair's Rhet.* p. 377 ; *Jamieson's,* 298. Say, "into *each other.*" "For mankind have always been butchering *each other.*"—*Webster's Essays,* p. 151. Say, "*one an other.*" See *Etymology,* Chap. iv, Obs. 15th, 16th, 17th, and 18th, on the Classes of Adjectives.

NOTE IV.—When the comparative degree is employed with *than,* the latter term of comparison should *never include* the former; nor the former the latter : as, "*Iron is more useful* than *all the metals.*"—"*All the metals* are *less useful* than *iron.*" In either case, it should be, "all the *other* metals."

NOTE V.—When the superlative degree is employed, the latter term of comparison, which is introduced by *of,* should *never exclude* the former; as, "A fondness for show, is, of all *other* follies, the most vain." Here the word *other* should be expunged ; for this latter term must *include* the former : that is, the fondness for show must be one of the follies of which it is the vainest.

NOTE VI.—When equality is denied, or inequality affirmed, neither term of the comparison should *ever include* the other; because every thing must needs be equal to itself, and it is absurd to suggest that a part surpasses the whole : as, "*No writings whatever* abound *so much* with the bold and animated figures, *as the sacred books.*"—*Blair's Rhet.* p. 414. Say, "No *other* writings whatever ;" because the sacred books *are* "*writings.*" See *Etymology,* Chap. iv, Obs. 6th, on Regular Comparison.

NOTE VII.—Comparative terminations, and adverbs of degree, should not be applied to adjectives that are not susceptible of comparison ; and all double comparatives and double superlatives should be avoided : as, "*So universal* a complaint :" say rather, "*So general.*"—"Some *less nobler* plunder :" say, "*less noble.*"—"The *most straitest* sect :" expunge *most.* See *Etymology,* Chap. iv, from Obs. 5th to Obs. 13th, on Irregular Comparison.

NOTE VIII.—When adjectives are connected by *and, or,* or *nor,* the shortest and simplest should in general be placed first; as, "He is *older* and *more respectable* than his brother." To say, "*more respectable* and *older,*" would be obviously inelegant. as possibly involving the inaccuracy of "*more older.*"

NOTE IX.—When one adjective is superadded to an other without a conjunction expressed or understood, the most distinguishing quality must be expressed next to the noun, and the latter must be such as the former may consistently qualify ; as, "An *agreeable young* man," not, "A *young agreeable* man."—"The art of speaking, like *all other* practical arts, may be facilitated by rules."—*Enfield's Speaker,* p. 10. Example of error : "The Anglo-Saxon language possessed, for the *two first* persons, a *Dual* number."—*Fowler's E. Gram.* 1850, p. 59. Say, "the *first two* persons :" for the second of three can hardly be one of *the first*; and "*two first,*" with the *second* and *third* added, will clearly make *more* than three. See Obs. 12th, above.

NOTE X.—In prose, the use of adjectives for adverbs, is a vulgar error ; the adverb alone being proper, when *manner* or *degree* is to be expressed. and not *quality :* as, "He writes *elegant ;*" say, "*elegantly.*"—"It is a *remarkable* good likeness ;" say, "*remarkably* good."

---

* Certain adjectives that differ in number, are sometimes connected disjunctively by *or* or *than,* while the noun literally agrees with that which immediately precedes it, and with the other merely by implication or supplement, under the figure which is called *zeugma* : as, "Two or more nouns joined together by *one* or *more copulative* conjunctions."—*Lowth's Gram.* p. 75 ; *L Murray's,* 2d Ed. p. 106. "He speaks not to *one* or a *few judges,* but to a large assembly."—*Blair's Rhet.* p. 280. "*More* than *one* object at a time."—*Murray's Gram.* 8vo, p. 301. See Obs. 10th on Rule 17th.

NOTE XI.—The pronoun *them* should never be used as an adjective, in lieu of *those*: say, "I bought *those* books;" not, "*them* books." This also is a vulgar error, and chiefly confined to the conversation of the unlearned.*

NOTE XII.—When the pronominal adjectives, *this* and *that*, or *these* and *those*, are contrasted; *this* or *these* should represent the latter of the antecedent terms, and *that* or *those*, the former: as,

"And, reason raise o'er instinct as you can,
In *this* 'tis God directs, in *that* 'tis man."—*Pope*.

"Farewell my friends! farewell my foes!
My peace with *these*, my love with *those!*"—*Burns*.

NOTE XIII.—The pronominal adjectives *either* and *neither*, in strict propriety of syntax, relate to two things only; when more are referred to, *any* and *none*, or *any one* and *no one*, should be used in stead of them: as, "*Any* of the three," or, "*Any one* of the three;" not, "*Either* of the three."—"*None* of the four," or, "*No one* of the four;" not, "*Neither* of the four."†

NOTE XIV.—The adjective *whole* must not be used in a plural sense, for *all; nor less*, in the sense of *fewer;* nor *more* or *most*, in any ambiguous construction, where it may be either an adverb of degree, or an adjective of number or quantity: as, "Almost the *whole* inhabitants were present."—*Hume:* see *Priestley's Gram.* p. 190.‡ Say, "Almost *all* the inhabitants." "No *less* than three dictionaries have been published to correct it."—*Dr. Webster*. Say, "No *fewer*." "This trade enriched some *people more* than them."—*Murray's Gram.* i, p. 215. This passage is not clear in its import: it may have either of two meanings. Say, "This trade enriched some *other* people, *besides* them." Or, "This trade enriched some *others* more than *it did* them."

NOTE XV.—Participial adjectives retain the termination, but not the government of participles; when, therefore, they are followed by the objective case, a preposition must be inserted to govern it: as, "The man who is most *sparing of* his words, is generally most *deserving of* attention."

NOTE XVI.—When the figure of any adjective affects the syntax and sense of the sentence, care must be taken to give to the word or words that form, simple or compound, which suits the true meaning and construction. Examples: "He is *forehead bald*, yet he is clean."—FRIENDS' BIBLE: *Lev.* xiii, 41. Say, "*forehead-bald*."—ALGER'S BIBLE, and SCOTT'S. "From such phrases as, '*New England scenery*,' convenience requires the *omission* of the hyphen."—*Sanborn's Gram* p. 89. This is a false notion. Without the hyphen, the phrase properly means, "*New scenery in England;*" but *New-England scenery* is scenery in New England. "'*Many coloured wings*,' means *many wings which are coloured;* but ' *many coloured wings*,' means *wings of many colours*."—*Blair's Gram.* p. 116.

---

* The learned William B. Fowle strangely imagines all pronouns to be *adjectives*, belonging to noun-expressed or understood after them; as, "*We* kings require *them* (subjects) to obey *us* (kings)."—*The True English Gram.* p. 21. "*They* grammarians, [i. e] *those* grammarians. *They* is an other spelling of *the*, and of course means *this, that, these, those*, as the case may be."—*Ibid.* According to him, then, "*them* grammarians," for "*those* grammarians," is perfectly good English; and so is "*they* grammarians," though the vulgar do not take care to *very this adjective*, "as the case may be." His notion of subjoining a noun to every pronoun, is a fit counterpart to that of some other grammarians, who imagine an ellipsis of a pronoun after almost every noun. Thus: "The personal *Relatives*, for the most part, *are suppressed* when the Noun is expressed: as, Man (he) is the Lord of this lower World. Woman (she) is the fairest Part of the Creation. The Palace (it) stands on a Hill. Men and Women (they) are rational Creatures."—*British Gram.* p. 284: *Buchanan's*, 131. It would have been worth a great deal to some men, to have known *what an Ellipsis is;* and the man who shall yet make such knowledge common, ought to be forever honoured in the schools.

† "An illegitimate and ungrammatical use of these words, *either* and *neither*, has lately been creeping into the language, in the application of these terms to a plurality of objects; as, '*Twenty* ruffians broke into the house, but *neither* of them could be recognized.' 'Here are *fifty* pens, you will find that *either* of them will do.'"—MATT. HARRISON, *on the English Language*, p. 199. "*Either* and *neither*, applied to any number more than *one* of two objects, is a mere solecism. and one of late introduction."—*Ib.* p. 200. Say, "*Either* OR *neither*," &c.—G. B.

‡ Dr. Priestley censures this construction, on the ground, that the word *whole* is an "*attribute of unity*," and therefore improperly added to a plural noun. But, in fact, this adjective is not *necessarily* singular, nor is *all necessarily* plural. Yet there is a difference between the words: *whole* is equivalent to *all* only when the noun is singular; for then only do *entireness* and *totality* coincide. A man may say, "*the whole thing*," when he means, "*all the thing;*" but he must not call *all things, whole things*. In the following example, *all* is put for *whole*, and taken substantively; but the expression is a quaint one, because the article and preposition seem needless: "Which doth encompass and embrace the *all* of things."—*The Dial*, Vol. i, p. 59.

IMPROPRIETIES FOR CORRECTION.

FALSE SYNTAX UNDER RULE IX.

EXAMPLES UNDER NOTE I.—AGREEMENT OF ADJECTIVES.

"I am not recommending these kind of sufferings to your liking."—BP. SHERLOCK: *Lowth's Gram.* p. 87.

[FORMULE.—Not proper, because the adjective *these* is plural, and does not agree with its noun *kind*, which is singular. But, according to Note 1st under Rule 9th. "Adjectives that imply unity or plurality, must agree with their nouns in number." Therefore, *these* should be *this*; thus, "I am not recommending *this* kind of sufferings."]

"I have not been to London this five years."—*Webster's Philos. Gram.* p. 152. "These kind of verbs are more expressive than their radicals."—*Dr. Murray's Hist. of Lang.* Vol. ii, p. 163. "Few of us would be less corrupted than kings are, were we, like them, beset with flatterers, and poisoned with that vermin."—*Art of Thinking,* p. 66. "But it seems this literati had been very ill rewarded for their ingenious labours."—*Roderick Random,* Vol. ii, p. 87. "If I had not left off troubling myself about those kind of things."—*Swift.* "For these sort of things are usually join'd to the most noted fortune."—*Bacon's Essays,* p. 101. "The nature of that riches and long-suffering is, to lead to repentance."—*Barclay's Works,* iii, 380. "I fancy they are these kind of gods, which Horace mentions."—*Addison, on Medals,* p. 74. "During that eight days they are prohibited from touching the skin."—*Hope of Israel,* p. 78. "Besides, he had not much provisions left for his army."—*Goldsmith's Greece,* i, 86. "Are you not ashamed to have no other thoughts than that of amassing wealth, and of acquiring glory, credit, and dignities?"—*Ib.* p. 192. "It distinguisheth still more remarkably the feelings of the former from that of the latter."—*Kames, El. of Crit.* Vol. i p. xvii. "And this good tidings of the reign shall be published through all the world."—*Campbell's Gospels, Matt.* xxiv, 14. "This twenty years have I been with thee."—*Gen.* xxxi, 38. "In these kind of expressions some words seem to be understood."—*Walker's Particles,* p. 179. "He thought these kind of excesses indicative of greatness."—*Hunt's Byron,* p. 117. "These sort of fellows are very numerous."—*Spect. No.* 486. "Whereas these sort of men cannot give account of their faith."—*Barclay's Works,* i, 444. "But the question is, whether that be the words."—*Ib.* iii, 321. "So that these sort of Expressions are not properly Optative."—*Johnson's Gram. Com.* p. 276. "Many things are not that which they appear to be."—*Sanborn's Gram.* p. 176. "So that every possible means are used."—*Formey's Belles-Lettres,* p. iv.

"We have strict statutes, and most biting laws,
    Which for this nineteen years we have let sleep."—*Shak.*
"They could not speak; and so I left them both,
    To bear this tidings to the bloody king."—*Id. Richard III.*

UNDER NOTE II.—OF FIXED NUMBERS.

"Why, I think she cannot be above six foot two inches high."—*Spect. No.* 533. "The world is pretty regular for about forty rod east and ten west."—*Ib. No.* 535. "The standard being more than two foot above it."—*Bacon: Joh. Dict. w. Standard.* "Supposing, (among other Things) he saw two Suns, and two Thebes."—*Bacon's Wisdom,* p. 25. "On the right hand we go into a parlour thirty three foot by thirty nine."—*Sheffield's Works,* ii, 258. "Three pound of gold went to one shield."—1 *Kings,* x, 17. "Such an assemblage of men as there appears to have been at that sessions."—*The Friend,* x, 389. "And, truly, he hath saved me this pains."—*Barclay's Works,* ii, 266. "Within this three mile may you see it coming."—*Shak.: Joh. Dict. w. Mile.* "Most of the churches, not all, had one or more ruling elder."—*Hutchinson's Hist. of Mass.* i, 375. "While a Minute Philosopher, not six foot high, attempts to dethrone the Monarch of the universe."—*Berkley's Alciphron,* p. 151. "The wall is ten foot high."—*Harrison's Gram.* p. 50. "The stalls must be ten foot broad."—*Walker's Particles,* p. 201. "A close prisoner in a room twenty foot square, being at the north side of his chamber, is at liberty to walk twenty foot southward, not to walk twenty foot northward."—*Locke: Joh. Dict. w. Northward.* "Nor, after all this pains and industry, did they think themselves qualified."—*Columbian Orator,* p. 13. "No less than thirteen gypsies were condemned at one Suffolk assizes, and executed."—*Webster's Essays,* p. 333. "The king was petitioned to appoint one, or more, person, or persons."—MACAULAY: *Priestley's Gram.* p. 194. "He carries weight! he rides a race! 'Tis for a thousand pound!"—*Cowper's Poems,* i, 279. "They carry three tire of guns at the head, and at the stern there are two tire of guns."—*Joh. Dict. w. Galleass.* "The verses consist of two sort of rhymes."—*Formey's Belles-Lettres,* p. 112. "A present of 40 camel's load of the most precious things of Syria."—*Wood's Dict.* Vol. i, p. 162. "A large grammar, that shall extend to every minutiæ."—*S. Barrett's Gram.,* Tenth Ed., Pref. p. iii.

"So many spots, like næves on Venus' soil,
    One jewel set off with so many foil."—*Dryden.*
"For, of the lower end, two handful
    It had devour'd, it was so manful."—*Hudibras,* i, 365.

UNDER NOTE III.—OF RECIPROCALS.

"That *shall* and *will* might be substituted for one another."—*Priestley's Gram.* p. 131. "We use not *shall* and *will* promiscuously for one another."—*Brightland's Gram.* 110. "But I wish to distinguish the three high ones from each other also."—*Fowle's True Eng. Gram.* p. 13. "Or on some other relation, which two objects bear to one another."—*Blair's Rhet.* p. 142. "Yet the two words lie so near to one another in meaning, that, in the present case, any one of them, perhaps would have been sufficient."—*Ib.* p. 203. "Both orators use great liberties with one another."—*Ib.* p. 244. "That greater separation of the two sexes from one another."—*Ib.* 466. "Most of whom live remote from each other."—*Webster's Essays,* p. 39. "Teachers like to see their pupils polite to each other." —*Webster's El. Spelling-Book,* p. 28. "In a little time, he and I must keep company with one another only."—*Spect.* No. 474. "Thoughts and circumstances crowd upon each other."—*Kames, El. of Crit.* i, 32. "They cannot see how the ancient Greeks could understand each other."—*Literary Convention,* p. 96. "The spirit of the poet, the patriot, and the prophet, vied with each other in his breast."—*Hazlitt's Lect.* p. 112. "Athamas and Ino loved one another."—*Classic Tales,* p. 91. "Where two things are compared or contrasted to one another."—*Blair's Rhet.* p. 119. "Where two things are compared, or contrasted, with one another."—*Murray's Gram.* i, p. 324. "In the classification of words, almost all writers differ from each other."—*Bullions, E. Gram.* p. iv.

"I will not trouble thee, my child. Farewell;
We'll no more meet; no more see one another."—*Shak. Lear.*

UNDER NOTE IV.—OF COMPARATIVES.

"Errours in Education should be less indulged than any."—*Locke, on Ed.* p. iv. "This was less his case than any man's that ever wrote."—*Pref. to Waller.* "This trade enriched some people more than it enriched them."*—*Murray's Gram.* i, p. 215. "The Chaldee alphabet, in which the Old Testament has reached us, is more beautiful than any ancient character known."—*Wilson's Essay,* p. 5. "The Christian religion gives a more lovely character of God, than any religion ever did."—*Murray's Key,* p. 169. "The temple of Cholula was deemed more holy than any in New Spain."—*Robertson's America,* ii, 477. "Cibber grants it to be a better poem of its kind than ever was writ."—*Pope.* "Shakspeare is more faithful to the true language of nature, than any writer."—*Blair's Rhet.* p. 468. "One son I had—one, more than all my sons, the strength of Troy."—*Cowper's Homer.* "Now Israel loved Joseph more than all his children, because he was the son of his old age."—*Gen.* xxxvii, 3.

UNDER NOTE V.—OF SUPERLATIVES.

"Of all other simpletons, he was the greatest."—*Nutting's English Idioms.* "Of all other beings, man has certainly the greatest reason for gratitude."—*Ibid. Gram.* p. 110. "This lady is the prettiest of all her sisters."—*Peyton's Elements of Eng. Lang.* p. 39. "The relation which, of all others, is by far the most fruitful of tropes, I have not yet mentioned." —*Blair's Rhet.* p. 141. "He studied Greek the most of any nobleman."—*Walker's Particles,* p. 231. "And indeed that was the qualification of all others most wanted at that time."—*Goldsmith's Greece,* ii, 35. "Yet we deny that the knowledge of him, as outwardly crucified, is the best of all other knowledge of him."—*Barclay's Works,* i, 144. "Our ideas of numbers are of all others the most accurate and distinct."—*Duncan's Logic,* p. 35. "This indeed is of all others the case when it can be least necessary to name the agent."—*J. Q. Adams's Rhet.* i, 231. "The period, to which you have arrived, is perhaps the most critical and important of any moment of your lives."—*Ib.* i, 394. "Perry's royal octavo is esteemed the best of any pronouncing Dictionary yet known."—*Red Book,* p. x. "This is the tenth persecution, and of all the foregoing, the most bloody."—*Sammes's Antiquities,* Chap. xiii. "The English tongue is the most susceptible of sublime imagery, of any language in the world."—See *Bucke's Gram.* p. 141. "Homer is universally allowed to have had the greatest Invention of any writer whatever."—*Pope's Preface to Homer.* "In a version of this particular work, which most of any other seems to require a venerable antique cast."—*Ib.* "Because I think him the best informed of any naturalist who has ever written."—*Jefferson's Notes,* p. 82. "Man is capable of being the most social of any animal."—*Sheridan's Elocution,* p. 145. "It is of all others that which most moves us."—*Ib.* 158. "Which of all others, is the most necessary article."—*Ib.* p. 166.

"Quoth he 'this gambol thou advisest,
Is, of all others, the unwisest.' "—*Hudibras,* iii, 316.

UNDER NOTE VI.—INCLUSIVE TERMS.

"Noah and his family outlived all the people who lived before the flood."—*Webster's El. Spelling-Book,* p. 101. "I think it superior to any work of that nature we have yet had."—*Dr. Blair's Rec. in Murray's Gram.* Vol. ii, p. 300. "We have had no grammar-

This is not a mere repetition of the last example cited under Note 14th above; but it is Murray's interpretation of the text there quoted. Both forms are faulty, but not in the same way.—G. BROWN.

who has employed so much labour and judgment upon our native language, as the author of these volumes."—*British Critic, ib.* ii, 299. "No persons feel so much the distresses of others, as they who have experienced distress themselves."—*Murray's Key,* 8vo, p. 227. "Never was any people so much infatuated as the Jewish nation."—*Ib.* p. 185; *Frazee's Gram.* 135. "No tongue is so full of connective particles as the Greek."—*Blair's Rhet.* p. 85. "Never sovereign was so much beloved by the people."—*Murray's Exercises,* R. xv, p. 68. "No sovereign was ever so much beloved by the people."—*Murray's Key,* p. 202. "Nothing ever affected her so much as this misconduct of her child."—*Ib.* p. 203; *Merchant's,* 195. "Of all the figures of speech, none comes so near to painting as metaphor." —*Blair's Rhet.* p. 142; *Jamieson's,* 149. "I know none so happy in his metaphors as Mr. Addison."—*Blair's Rhet.* p. 150. "Of all the English authors, none is so happy in his metaphors as Addison."—*Jamieson's Rhet.* p. 157. "Perhaps no writer in the world was ever so frugal of his words as Aristotle."—*Blair,* p. 177; *Jamieson,* 251. "Never was any writer so happy in that concise spirited style as Mr. Pope."—*Blair's Rhet.* p. 403. "In the harmonious structure and disposition of periods, no writer whatever, ancient or modern, equals Cicero."—*Blair,* 121; *Jamieson,* 123. "Nothing delights me so much as the works of nature."—*Murray's Gram.* i, p. 150. "No person was ever so perplexed as he has been to-day."—*Murray's Key,* ii, 216. "In no case are writers so apt to err as in the position of the word *only.*"—*Maunder's Gram.* p. 15. "For nothing is so tiresome as perpetual uniformity."—*Blair's Rhet.* p. 102.

"No writing lifts exalted man so high,
As sacred and soul-moving poesy."—*Sheffield.*

UNDER NOTE VII.—EXTRA COMPARISONS.

"How much more are ye better than the fowls!"—*Luke,* xii, 24. "Do not thou hasten above the Most Highest."—2 *Esdras,* iv, 34. "This word *peer* is most principally used for the nobility of the realm."—*Cowell.* "Because the same is not only most universally received," &c.—*Barclay's Works,* i, 447. "This is, I say, not the best and most principal evidence."—*Ib.* iii, 41. "Offer unto God thanksgiving, and pay thy vows unto the Most Highest."—*The Psalter,* Ps. l, 14. "The holy place of the tabernacle of the Most Highest." —*Ib.* Ps. xlvi, 4. "As boys should be educated with temperance, so the first greatest lesson that should be taught them is to admire frugality."—*Goldsmith's Essays,* p. 152. "More universal terms are put for such as are more restricted."—*Brown's Metaphors,* p. 11. "This was the most unkindest cut of all."—*Dodd's Beauties of Shak.* p. 251; *Singer's Shak.* ii, 264. "To take the basest and most poorest shape."—*Dodd's Shak.* p. 261. "I'll forbear: and am fallen out with my more headier will."—*Ib.* p. 262. "The power of the Most Highest guard thee from sin."—*Percival, on Apostolic Succession,* p. 90. "Which title had been more truer, if the dictionary had been in Latin and Welch."—VERSTEGAN: *Harrison's E. Lang,* p. 254. "The waters are more sooner and harder frozen, than more further upward, within the inlands."—*Id. ib.* "At every descent, the worst may become more worse."—H. MANN: *Louisville Examiner,* 8vo, Vol. i, p. 149.

"Or as a moat defensive to a house
Against the envy of less happier lands."—*Shakspeare.*
"A dreadful quiet felt, and worser far
Than arms, a sullen interval of war."—*Dryden.*

UNDER NOTE VIII.—ADJECTIVES CONNECTED.

"It breaks forth in its most energetick, impassioned, and highest strain."—*Kirkham's Elocution,* p. 66. "He has fallen into the most gross and vilest sort of railing."—*Barclay's Works,* iii, 261. "To receive that more general and higher instruction which the public affords."—*District School,* p. 281. "If the best things have the perfectest and best operations."—HOOKER: *Joh. Dict.* "It became the plainest and most elegant, the most splendid and richest," of all languages. See *Bucke's Gram.* p. 140. "But the most frequent and the principal use of pauses, is, to mark the divisions of the sense."—*Blair's Rhet.* p. 331; *Murray's Gram.* 248. "That every thing belonging to ourselves is the perfectest and the best."—*Clarkson's Prize Essay,* p. 189. "And to instruct their pupils in the most thorough and best manner."—*Report of a School Committee.*

UNDER NOTE IX.—ADJECTIVES SUPERADDED.

"The Father is figured out as an old venerable man."—*Dr. Brownlee's Controversy.* "There never was exhibited such another masterpiece of ghostly assurance."—*Id.* "After the three first sentences, the question is entirely lost."—*Spect.* No. 476. "The four last parts of speech are commonly called particles."—*Alex. Murray's Gram.* p. 14. "The two last chapters will not be found deficient in this respect."—*Student's Manual,* p. 6. "Write upon your slates a list of the ten first nouns."—*Abbott's Teacher,* p. 85. "We have a few remains of other two Greek poets in the pastoral style, Moschus and Bion."—*Blair's Rhet.* p. 393. "The nine first chapters of the book of Proverbs are highly poetical."—*Ib.* p. 417. "For of these five l.eads, only the two first have any particular relation to the sublime."— *Ib.* p. 35. "The resembling sounds of the two last syllables give a ludicrous air to the whole."—*Kames, El. of Crit.* ii, 69. "The three last are arbitrary."—*Ib.* p. 72. "But in the phrase 'She hangs the curtains,' the verb *hangs* is a transitive active verb."—*Comly's Gram.* p. 30. "If our definition of a verb, and the arrangement of transitive or intransitive active, passive, and neuter verbs, are properly understood."—*Ib.*, 15th Ed., p. 30. "These two last lines have an embarrassing construction."—*Rush, on the Voice*, p. 160. "God was provoked to drown them all, but Noah and other seven persons."—*Wood's Dict.* ii, 129. "The *six first* books of the Æneid are extremely beautiful."—*Formey's Belles-Lettres*, p. 27. "A few more instances only can be given here."—*Murray's Gram.* p. 131. "A few more years will obliterate every vestige of a subjunctive form."—*Nutting's Gram.* p. 46. "Some define them to be verbs devoid of the two first persons."—*Crombie's Treatise*, p. 205. "In such another Essay-tract as this."—*White's English Verb*, p. 302. "But we fear that not such another man is to be found."—Rev. Ed. Irving: *on Horne's Psalms*, p. xxiii.

> "Oh such another sleep, that I might see
> But such another man!"—Shak. *Antony and Cleopatra*.

Under Note X.—Adjectives for Adverbs.

"*The* is an article, relating to the noun *balm*, agreeable to Rule 11."—*Comly's Gram.* p. 133. "*Wise* is an adjective relating to the noun *man's*, agreeable to Rule 11th."—*Ibid.* 12th Ed. often. "To whom I observed, that the beer was extreme good."—*Goldsmith's Essays*, p. 127. "He writes remarkably elegant."—*O. B. Peirce's Gram.* p. 152. "John behaves truly civil to all men."—*Ib.* p. 153. "All the sorts of words hitherto considered have each of them some meaning, even when taken separate."—*Beattie's Moral Science*, i, 44. "He behaved himself conformable to that blessed example."—*Sprat's Sermons*, p. 80. "Marvellous graceful."—*Clarendon, Life*, p. 18. "The Queen having changed her ministry suitable to her wisdom."—*Swift, Exam.* No. 21. "The assertions of this author are easier detected."—*Swift:* censured in *Lowth's Gram.* p. 93. "The characteristic of his sect allowed him to affirm no stronger than that."—*Bentley: ibid.* "If one author had spoken nobler and loftier than an other."—*Id. ib.* "Xenophon says express."—*Id. ib.* "I can never think so very mean of him."—*Id. ib.* "To convince all that are ungodly among them, o all their ungodly deeds, which they have ungodly committed."—*Jude*, 15th: *ib.* "I think it very masterly written."—*Swift to Pope*, Let. 74: *ib.* "The whole design must refer to the golden age, which it lively represents."—*Addison, on Medals: ib.* "Agreeable to this, we read of names being blotted out of God's book."—Burder: approved in *Webster's Impr. Gram.* p. 107; *Frazee's*, 140; *Maltby's*, 93. "Agreeable to the law of nature, children are bound to support their indigent parents."—*Webster's Imp. Gram.* p. 109. "Words taken independent of their meaning are parsed as nouns of the neuter gender."—*Maltby's Gr.* 96. "Conceit in weakest bodies strongest works."—*Beaut. of Shak.* p. 236.

Under Note XI.—THEM for THOSE.

"Though he was not known by them letters, or the name Christ."—*Wm. Bayly's Works*, p. 94. "In a gig, or some of them things."—*Edgeworth's Castle Rackrent*, p. 35. "When cross-examined by them lawyers."—*Ib.* p. 93. "As the custom in them cases is."—*Ib.* p. 101. "If you'd have listened to them slanders."—*Ib.* p. 115. "The old people were telling stories about them fairies, but to the best of my judgment there's nothing in it."—*Ib.* p. 188. "And is it not a pity that the Quakers have no better authority to substantiate their principles than the testimony of them old Pharisees?"—*Hibbard's Errors of the Quakers*, p. 107.

Under Note XII.—THIS and THAT.

"Hope is as strong an incentive to action, as fear: this is the anticipation of good, that of evil."—*Brown's Institutes*, p. 135. "The poor want some advantages which the rich enjoy; but we should not therefore account those happy, and these miserable."—*Ib.*

> "Ellen and Margaret, fearfully, 　Then turned their ghastly look each one,
> Sought comfort in each other's eye; 　This to her sire, that to her son."—
> *Scott's Lady of the Lake*, Canto ii, Stanza 29.

> "Six youthful sons, as many blooming maids,
> In one sad day beheld the Stygian shades;
> These by Apollo's silver bow were slain,
> Those Cynthia's arrows stretched upon the plain."—*Pope, Il.* xxiv, 760.

> "Memory and forecast just returns engage,
> This pointing back to youth, that on to age."—See *Key*.

Under Note XIII.—EITHER and NEITHER.

"These make the three great subjects of discussion among mankind; truth, duty, and interest. But the arguments directed towards either of them are generically distinct."—*Blair's Rhet.* p. 318. "A thousand other deviations may be made, and still either of them may be correct in principle. For these divisions and their technical terms, are all arbitrary."—*R. W. Green's Inductive Gram.* p. vi. "Thus it appears, that our alphabet is deficient, as it has but seven vowels, to represent thirteen different sounds; and has no letter to represent either of five simple consonant sounds."—*Churchill's Gram.* p. 19. "Then neither of these [five] verbs can be neuter."—*Oliver B. Peirce's Gram.* p. 343. "And the *asserter* is in neither of the four already mentioned."—*Ib.* p. 356. "As it is not in either of these four."—*Ib.* p. 356. "See whether or not the word comes within the definition of either of the other three simple cases."—*Ib.* p. 51. "Neither of the ten was there."—*Frazee's Gram.* p. 108. "Here are ten oranges, take either of them."—*Ib.* p. 102. "There are three modes, by either of which recollection will generally be supplied; inclination, practice, and association."—*Rippingham's Art of Speaking,* p. xxix. "Words not reducible to either of the three preceding heads."—*Fowler's E. Gram* 8vo, 1850, pp. 335 and 340. "Now a sentence may be analyzed in reference to either of these [four] classes."—*Ib.* p. 577.

UNDER NOTE XIV.—WHOLE, LESS, MORE, AND MOST.

"Does not all proceed from the law, which regulates the whole departments of the state?" *Blair's Rhet.* p. 278. "A messenger relates to Theseus the whole particulars."—*Kames, El. of Crit.* Vol. ii, p. 313. "There are no less than twenty diphthongs in the English language." —*Dr. Ash's Gram.* p. xii. "The Redcross Knight runs through the whole steps of the Christian life."—*Spectator,* No. 540. "There were not less than fifty or sixty persons present." —*Teachers' Report.* "Greater experience, and more cultivated society, abate the warmth of imagination, and chasten the manner of expression."—*Blair's Rhet.* p. 152; *Murray's Gram.* i, 351. "By which means knowledge, much more than oratory, is become the principal requisite."—*Blair's Rhet.* p. 254. "No less than seven illustrious cities disputed the right of having given birth to the greatest of poets."—*Lemp. Dict. n. Homer.* "Temperance, more than medicines, is the proper means of curing many diseases."—*Murray's Key,* 8vo, p. 222. "I do not suppose, that we Britons want genius, more than our neighbours."—*Ib.* p. 215. "In which he saith, he has found no less than twelve untruths."—*Barclay's Works,* i, 460. "The several places of rendezvous were concerted, and the whole operations fixed." HUME: see *Priestley's Gram.* p. 190. "In these rigid opinions the whole sectaries concurred."—*Id. ib.* "Out of whose modifications have been made most complex modes."— LOCKE: *Sanborn's Gram.* p. 148. "The Chinese vary each of their words on no less than five different tones."—*Blair's Rhet.* p. 58. "These people, though they possess more shining qualities, are not so proud as he is, nor so vain as she."—*Murray's Key,* 8vo, p. 211. "'Tis certain, we believe ourselves more, after we have made a thorough Inquiry into the Thing."—*Brightland's Gram.* p. 244. "As well as the whole Course and Reasons of the Operation."—*Ib.* "Those rules and principles which are of most practical advantage."— *Newman's Rhet.* p. 4. "And there shall be no more curse."—*Rev.* xxii, 3. "And there shall be no more death."—*Rev.* xxi, 4. "But in recompense, we have more pleasing pictures of ancient manners."—*Blair's Rhet.* p. 436. "Our language has suffered more injurious changes in America, since the British army landed on our shores, than it had suffered before, in the period of three centuries."—*Webster's Essays,* Ed. of 1790, p. 96. "The whole conveniences of life are derived from mutual aid and support in society."—*Kames, El. of Crit.* Vol. i, p. 166.

UNDER NOTE XV.—PARTICIPIAL ADJECTIVES.

"To such as think the nature of it deserving their attention."—*Butler's Analogy,* p. 34. "In all points, more deserving the approbation of their readers."—*Keepsake,* 1830. "But to give way to childish sensations was unbecoming our nature."—*Lempriere's Dict. n. Zeno.* "The following extracts are deserving the serious perusal of all."—*The Friend,* Vol. v, p. 135. "No inquiry into wisdom, however superficial, is undeserving attention."—*Bulwer's Disowned,* ii, 95. "The opinions of illustrious men are deserving great consideration."—*Porter's Family Journal,* p. 3. "And resolutely keep its laws, Uncaring consequences."—*Burns's Works,* ii, 43. "This is an item that is deserving more attention."—*Goodell's Lectures.*

"Leave then thy joys, unsuiting such an age,
To a fresh comer, and resign the stage."—*Dryden.*

UNDER NOTE XVI.—FIGURE OF ADJECTIVES.

"The tall dark mountains and the deep toned seas."—*Sanborn's Gram.* p. 278. "O! learn from him To station quick eyed Prudence at the helm."—ANON.: *Frost's El. of Gram.* p. 104. "He went in a one horse chaise."—*Blair's Gram.* p. 113. "It ought to be, 'in a one horse chaise.'"—*Dr. Crombie's Treatise,* p. 334. "These are marked with the above mentioned letters."—*Felker's Gram.* p. 4. "A many headed faction."—*Ware's Gram.* p. 18. "Lest there should be no authority in any popular grammars for the perhaps heaven inspired effort."—*Fowle's True English Gram.* Part 2d, p. 25. "Common metre stanzas consist of four Iambic lines; one of eight, and the next of six syllables. They were formerly written in two fourteen syllable lines."—*Goodenow's Gram.* p. 69. "Short metre stanzas consist of four Iambic lines; the third of eight, the rest of six syllables."—*Ibid.* "Particular metre stanzas consist of six Iambic lines; the third and sixth of six syllables, the rest of eight."—*Ibid.* "Hallelujah metre stanzas consist of six Iambic lines; the last two of eight syllables, and the rest of six."—*Ibid.* "Long metre stanzas are merely the union of four Iambic lines, of ten syllables each."—*Ibid.* "A majesty more commanding than is to be found among the rest of the Old Testament poets.'"—*Blair's Rhet.* p. 418.

" You sulphurous and thought executed fires,
  Vaunt couriers to oak cleaving thunderbolts,
  Singe my white head! And thou, all shaking thunder
  Strike flat the thick rotundity o' the world!"—*Beauties of Shak.* p. 264.

CHAPTER V.—PRONOUNS.

The rules for the agreement of Pronouns with their antecedents are four; hence this chapter extends from the tenth rule to the thirteenth, inclusively. The *cases* of Pronouns are embraced with those of nouns, in the seven rules of the third chapter.

RULE X.—PRONOUNS.

A Pronoun must agree with its antecedent, or the noun or pronoun which it represents, in person, number, and gender : * as, " This is the friend of *whom I* spoke ; *he* has just arrived."—" This is the book *which I* bought ; *it* is an excellent work."—" *Ye,* therefore, *who* love mercy, teach *your* sons to love *it* too."—*Cowper.*

" Speak *thou, whose* thoughts at humble peace repine,
  Shall Wolsey's wealth with Wolsey's end be *thine?* "—*Dr. Johnson.*

EXCEPTION FIRST.

When a pronoun stands for some person or thing *indefinite,* or *unknown to the speaker,* this rule is not *strictly* applicable; because the person, number, and gender, are rather assumed in the pronoun, than regulated by an antecedent: as, " I do not care *who* knows it."—*Steele.* "*Who* touched me? Tell me *who* it was."—" We have no knowledge how, or by *whom,* it is inhabited."—ABBOT: *Joh. Dict.*

EXCEPTION SECOND.

The neuter pronoun *it* may be applied to a young child, or to other creatures masculine or feminine by nature, when they are not obviously distinguishable with regard to sex; as, " Which is the real friend to the *child,* the person who gives *it* the sweetmeats, or the person who, considering only *its* health, resists *its* importunities?"—*Opie.* " He loads the *animal* he is showing me, with so many trappings and collars, that I cannot distinctly view *it.*"—*Murray's Gram.* p. 301. " The *nightingale* sings most sweetly when *it* sings in the night."—*Bucke's Gram.* p. 52.

EXCEPTION THIRD.

The pronoun *it* is often used without a definite reference to any antecedent, and is sometimes a mere expletive, and sometimes the representative of an action expressed afterwards by a verb; as, " Whether she grapple *it* with the pride of philosophy."—*Chalmers.* " Seeking to lord *it* over God's heritage."—*The Friend,* vii, 253. "*It* is not for kings, O Lemuel, *it* is not for kings *to drink* wine, nor for princes strong drink."—*Prov.* xxxi, 4. " Having no temptation to *it,* God cannot *act unjustly* without defiling his nature."—*Brown's Divinity,* p. 11. " Come, and trip *it* as you go, On the light fantastic toe."—*Milton.*

EXCEPTION FOURTH.

A singular antecedent with the adjective *many,* sometimes admits a plural pronoun, but never in the same clause; as, " Hard has been the fate of *many* a great *genius,* that while *they* have conferred immortality on others, *they* have wanted themselves some friend to embalm their names to posterity."—*Welwood's Pref. to Rowe's Lucan.*

" In Hawick twinkled *many a light,*
  Behind him soon *they* set in night."—*W. Scott.*

EXCEPTION FIFTH.

When a plural pronoun is put by enallagè for the singular, it does not agree with its noun in number, because it still requires a plural verb; as, " *We* [Lindley Murray] *have followed* those authors, who appear to have given them the most natural and intelligible distribu-

---

* Some authors erroneously say, "A *personal* pronoun does not always agree in person with its antecedent; as, 'John said, *I* will do it.'"—*Goodenow's Gram.* " When I say, ' Go, and say to those children, *you* must come in,' you perceive that the noun children is of the *third* person, but the pronoun *you* is of the *second;* yet *you* stands for *children.*"—*Ingersoll's Gram.* p. 54. Here are different speakers, with separate speeches; and these critics are manifestly deceived by the circumstance. It is not to be supposed, that the nouns represented by one speaker's pronouns, are to be found or sought, in what an other speaker utters. The pronoun *I* does not here stand for the noun *John* which is of the third person; it is John's own word, representing himself as the speaker. The meaning is, "*I myself, John,* of the *first person,* will do it." Nor does *you* stand for *children* as spoken *of* by Ingersoll; but for *children* of the *second person,* uttered or implied in the address of his messenger: as, " *Children, you must come in.*"

tion."—*Murray's Gram.* 8vo, p. 29. "*We shall close our* remarks on this subject, by introducing the sentiments of Dr. Johnson respecting it."—*Ib.* " My lord, *you know* I love *you.*"—*Shakspeare.*

EXCEPTION SIXTH.

The pronoun sometimes disagrees with its antecedent in one sense, because it takes it in an other; as, " I have perused Mr. Johnson's *Grammatical Commentaries,* and find *it* • a very laborious, learned, and useful Work."— *Tho. Knipe,* D. D. "*Lamps* is of the plural number, because *it* means more than one."—*Smith's New Gram.* p. 8. "*Man* is of the masculine gender, because *it* is the name of a male."—*Ib.* "The *Utica Sentinel* says *it* has not heard whether the wounds are dangerous."—*Evening Post.* (Better: "The *editor* of the Utica Sentinel says, *he* has not heard," &c.) "There is little *Benjamin* with *their* ruler."—*Psalms,* lxviii, 27.

> "*Her* end when *emulation* misses,
> *She* turns to envy, stings, and hisses."—*Swift's Poems,* p. 415.

OBSERVATIONS ON RULE. X.

OBS. 1.— Respecting a pronoun, the main thing is, that the reader perceive clearly *for what it stands;* and next, that he do not misapprehend *its relation of case.* For the sake of completeness and uniformity in parsing, it is, I think, expedient to apply the foregoing rule not only to those pronouns which have obvious antecedents expressed, but also to such as are not accompanied by the nouns for which they stand. Even those which are put for persons or things unknown or indefinite, may be said to agree with whatever is meant by them; that is, with such nouns as their own properties indicate. For the reader will naturally understand something by every pronoun, unless it be a mere expletive, and without any antecedent. For example: " It would depend upon *who* the forty were."— *Trial at Steubenville,* p. 50. Here *who* is an indefinite relative, equivalent to *what persons;* of the third person, plural, masculine; and is in the nominative case after *were,* by Rule 6th. For the full construction seems to be this : " It would depend upon *the persons who* the forty were." So *which,* for *which person,* or *which thing,* (if we call it a pronoun rather than an adjective,) may be said to have the properties of the noun *person* or *thing* understood; as,
> " His notions fitted things so well,
> That *which* was *which* he could not tell."— *Hudibras.*

OBS. 2.— The pronoun *we* is used by the speaker to represent himself and others, and is therefore plural. But it is sometimes used, by a sort of fiction, in stead of the singular, to intimate that the speaker is not alone in his opinions; or, perhaps more frequently, to evade the charge of egotism; for this modest assumption of plurality seems most common with those who have something else to assume: as, "And so lately as 1809, Pope Pius VII, in communicating his ' own dear son,' Napoleon, whom he crowned and blessed, says: '*We,* unworthy as *we* are, represent the God of peace.' "— *Dr. Brownlee.* Monarchs sometimes prefer *we* to *I,* in immediate connexion with a singular noun; as, "*We Alexander,* Autocrat of all the Russias."—"*We the Emperor* of China," &c.— *Economy of Human Life,* p. vi. They also employ the anomalous compound *ourself,* which is not often used by other people; as, " Witness *ourself* at Westminster, 28 day of April, in the tenth year of *our* reign. CHARLES.'
> "*Ourself* to hoary Nestor will repair."—*Pope, Iliad,* B. x, l. 65.

OBS. 3.— The pronoun *you,* though originally and properly plural, is now generally applied alike to one person or to more. Several observations upon this fashionable substitution of the plural number for the singular, will be found in the fifth and sixth chapters of Etymology. This usage, however it may seem to involve a solecism, is established by that authority against which the mere grammarian has scarcely a right to remonstrate. Alexander Murray, the schoolmaster, observes, " When language was plain and simple, the English always said *thou,* when speaking to a single person. But when an affected politeness, and a fondness for continental manners and customs began to take place, persons of rank and fashion said *you* in stead of *thou.* The innovation gained ground, and custom gave sanction to the change, and stamped it with the authority of law."— *English Gram.* Third Edition, 1793, p. 107. This respectable grammarian acknowledged both *thou* and *you* to be of the second person singular. I do not, however, think it necessary or advisable to do this, or to encumber the conjugations, as some have done, by introducing the latter pronoun, and the corresponding form of the verb, as singular.† It is manifestly better to say, that the plural is used *for the singular,* by the figure *Enallagè.* For if *you* has literally become singular by virtue of this substitution, *we* also is singular for the same reason, as often as it is substituted for *I;* else the authority of innumerable authors, editors, compilers, and crowned heads, is insufficient to make it so. And again, if *you* and the corresponding form of the verb are literally of *the second person singular,* (as Wells contends, with an array of more than sixty names

---

* The propriety of this construction is questionable. See Obs. 2d on Rule 14th.

† Among the authors who have committed this great fault, are, Alden, the Allens, O. Adams, the author of the British Grammar, Buchanan, Cooper, Cutler, Davis, Dilworth, Felton, Fisher, Fowler, Frazee, Goldsbury, Hallock, Hall, M'Culloch, Morley, J Putnam, Russell, Sanborn, R. C. Smith, Weld, Wells, Webster, and White. " *You is* plural, whether it refer to only one individual, or to more."— *Dr. Crombie, on Etym. and Synt.* p. 240. " The word *you,* even when applied to one person, *is plural,* and should never be connected with a singular verb."—*Alexander's Gram.* p. 58; *Emmons's,* 26. " *You is* of the Plural Number, even though used as the Name of a single Person."— *W. Ward's Gram.* p. 88. "Altho' the Second Person Singular in both Times be marked with *thou,* to distinguish it from the Plural, yet we, out of Complaisance, though we speak but to one particular Person, use the *Plural you,* and never thou, but when we address ourselves to Almighty God, or when we speak in an emphatical Manner, or make a distinct and particular Application to a Person."—*British Gram.* p. 126 ; *Buchanan's,* 27. " But *you,* tho' applied to a single Person, requires a *Plural Verb,* the same as ye ; as, *you love,* not *you lovest* or *loves;* you *were,* not *you was* or *wast.*"—*Buchanan's Gram.* p. 87.

of English grammarians to prove it,) then, by their own rule of concord, since *thou* and its verb are still generally retained in the same place by these grammarians, a verb that agrees with one of these nominatives, must also agree with the other; so that *you hast* and *thou have, you seest* and *thou see*, may be, so far as appears from *their* instructions, as good a concord as can be made of these words!

OBS. 4.—The putting of *you* for *thou* has introduced the anomalous compound *yourself*, which is now very generally used in stead of *thyself*. In this instance, as in the less frequent adoption of *ourself* for *myself*, Fashion so tramples upon the laws of grammar, that it is scarcely possible to frame an intelligible exception in her favour. These pronouns are essentially singular, both in form and meaning; and yet they cannot be used with *I* or *thou*, with *me* or *thee*, or with any verb that is literally singular; as, "*I ourself am :*" but, on the contrary, they must be connected only with such plural terms as are put for the singular; as, "*We ouself are king* "—"Undoubtedly *you yourself become* an innovator."—*L. Murray's Gram.* p. 364; *Campbell's Rhet.* 167.

"Try touch, or sight, or smell; try what *you will,*
    You strangely *find* nought but *yourself* alone."—*Pollok, C. of T.*, B. i, l. 162.

OBS. 5.—Such terms of address, as *your Majesty, your Highness, your Lordship, your Honour*; are sometimes followed by verbs and pronouns of the second person plural, substituted for the singular; and sometimes by words literally singular, and of the third person, with no other figure than a substitution of *who* for *which :* as, "Wherein *your Lordship, who shines* with so much distinction in the noblest assembly in the world, peculiarly *excels.*"—*Dedication of Sale's Koran.* "We have good cause to give *your Highness* the first place ; *who*, by a continued series of favours, *have obliged* us, not only while *you moved* in a lower orb, but since the Lord hath called *your Highness* to supreme authority."—*Massachusetts to Cromwell,* in 1654.

OBS. 6.—The general usage of the French is like that of the English, *you* for *thou ;* but Spanish, Portuguese, or German politeness requires that the third person be substituted for the second. And when they would be very courteous, the Germans use also the plural for the singular, as *they* for *thou.* Thus they have a fourfold method of addressing a person: as, *they*, denoting the highest degree of respect; *he*, a less degree; *you*, a degree still less ; and *thou*, none at all, or absolute reproach. Yet, even among them, the last is used as a term of endearment to children, and of veneration to God! *Thou*, in English, still retains its place firmly, and without dispute, in all addresses to the Supreme Being; but in respect to the *first person*, an observant clergyman has suggested the following dilemma : "Some men will be pained, if a minister says *we* in the pulpit ; and others will quarrel with him, if he says *I.*"—*Abbott's Young Christian,* p. 268.

OBS. 7.—Any extensive perversion of the common words of a language from their original and proper use, is doubtless a matter of considerable moment. These changes in the use of the pronouns, being some of them evidently a sort of complimentary fictions, some religious people have made it a matter of conscience to abstain from them, and have published their reasons for so doing. But the *moral objections* which may lie against such or any other applications of words, do not come within the grammarian's province. Let every one consider for himself the moral bearing of what he utters: not forgetting the text, "But I say unto you, that *every idle word* that men shall speak, they shall give account thereof in the day of judgement; for *by thy words* thou shalt be justified, and *by thy words* thou shalt be condemned."—*Matt.* xii, 36 and 37. What scruples this declaration *ought to raise*, it is not my business to define. But if such be God's law, what shall be the reckoning of those who make no conscience of uttering continually, or when they will, not idle words only, but expressions the most absurd, insignificant, false, exaggerated, vulgar, indecent, injurious, wicked, sophistical, unprincipled, ungentle, and perhaps blasphemous, or profane?

OBS. 8.—The agreement of pronouns with their antecedents, it is necessary to observe, is liable to be controlled or affected by several of the figures of rhetoric. A noun used figuratively often suggests two different senses, the one literal, and the other tropical; and the agreement of the pronoun must be sometimes with this, and sometimes with that, according to the nature of the trope. If the reader be unacquainted with tropes and figures, he should turn to the explanation of them in Part Fourth of this work; but almost every one knows something about them, and such as must here be named, will perhaps be made sufficiently intelligible by the examples. There seems to be no occasion to introduce under this head more than four; namely, personification, metaphor, metonymy, and synecdoche.

OBS. 9.—When a pronoun represents the name of an inanimate object *personified*, it agrees with its antecedent in the figurative, and not in the literal sense; as, "There were others whose crime it was rather to neglect *Reason* than to disobey *her.*"—*Dr. Johnson.* "*Penance* dreams *her* life away."—*Rogers.* "Grim *Darkness* furls *his* leaden shroud."—*Id.* Here if the pronoun were made neuter, the personification would be destroyed; as, "By the progress which *England* had already made in navigation and commerce, *it* was now prepared for advancing farther."—*Robertson's America,* Vol. ii, p. 341. If the pronoun *it* was here intended to represent *England*, the feminine *she* would have been much better; and, if such was not the author's meaning, the sentence has some worse fault than the agreement of a pronoun with its noun in a wrong sense.

OBS. 10.—When the antecedent is applied *metaphorically*, the pronoun usually agrees with it in a literal, and not in its figurative sense; as, "Pitt was the *pillar which* upheld the state."—"The *monarch* of mountains rears *his* snowy head."—"The *stone which* the builders rejected."—*Matt.* xxi, 42. According to this rule, *which* would be better than *whom*, in the following text: "I considered the horns, and, behold, there came up among them an other *little horn*, before *whom* there were three of the first horns plucked up by the roots."—*Daniel,* vii, 8. In *Rom.* ix, 1, there is something similar: "Behold, I lay in Sion a *stumbling-stone* and *rock* of offence: and *whosoever* believeth *on him* shall not be ashamed." Here the *stone* or *rock* is a metaphor for *Christ*, and the pronoun *him* may be referred to the sixth exception above; but the construction is not agreeable, because it is not regular: it would be more grammatical, to change *on him* to *thereon*. In the following example, the noun "*wolves*," which literally requires *which*, and not *who*, is used metaphorically for *selfish priests* ; and, in the relative, the figurative or personal sense is allowed to prevail :

> "*Wolves* shall succeed for teachers, grievous *wolves,*
> *Who* all the sacred mysteries of Heaven
> To their own vile advantages shall turn."—*Milton, P. L.,* B. xii, l. 508.

This seems to me somewhat forced and catachrestical. So too, and worse, the following ; which makes a *star* rise and *speak* :

> "So *spake* our *Morning star* then in *his rise,*
> And *looking* round on every side *beheld*
> A pathless desert, dusk with horrid shades."—*Id. P. R.,* B. i, l. 294.

OBS. 11.—When the antecedent is put by *metonymy* for a noun of different properties, the pronoun sometimes agrees with it in the figurative, and sometimes in the literal sense ; as, "When *Israel* was a child, then I loved *him,* and called my son out of Egypt. As they called *them,* so *they* went from them : [i. e. When Moses and the prophets called the *Israelites,* they often refused to hear :] *they* sacrificed unto Baalim, and burnt incense to graven images. I taught *Ephraim* also **to** go, taking *them* by *their* arms ; but *they* knew not that I healed *them.*"—*Hosea,* xi, 1, 2, 3. The mixture and obscurity which are here, ought not to be imitated. The name of a man, put for the nation or tribe of his descendants, may have a pronoun of either number, and a nation may be figuratively represented as feminine ; but a mingling of different genders or numbers ought to be avoided ; as, "*Moab* is spoiled, and gone up out of *her* cities, and *his* chosen young men are gone down to the slaughter."—*Jeremiah,* xlviii, 15.

> "The wolf, who [say *that*] from the nightly fold,
> Fierce drags the bleating *prey,* ne'er drunk *her* milk,
> Nor wore *her* warming fleece."—*Thomson's Seasons.*

> "That each may fill the circle mark'd by *Heaven,*
> *Who* sees with equal eye, as God of all,
> A hero perish or a sparrow fall."—*Pope's Essay on Man.*

> "And *heaven* beholds *its* image in his breast."—*Ib.*

> "Such fate to suffering *worth* is given,
> *Who* long with wants and woes has striven."—*Burns.*

OBS. 12.—When the antecedent is put by *synecdoche* for more or less than it literally signifies, the pronoun agrees with it in the figurative, and not in the literal sense ; as,

> "A dauntless *soul* erect, *who* smiled on death."—*Thomson.*

> "But to the generous still improving *mind,*
> *That* gives the hopeless heart to sing for joy,
> To *him* the long review of ordered life
> Is inward rapture only to be felt."—*Id. Seasons.*

OBS. 13.—Pronouns usually *follow* the words which they represent ; but this order is sometimes reversed : as, "*Whom* the cap fits, let *him* put it on."—"Hark ! *they* whisper ; *angels* say," &c.— *Pope.* "*Thou,* O Lord, art a God full of compassion."—*Old Test.* And in some cases of apposition, the pronoun naturally comes first ; as, "*I Tertius*"—"*Ye lawyers.*" The pronoun *it,* likewise, very often precedes the clause or phrase which it represents ; as, "Is *it* not manifest, that the generality of people speak and write very badly ?"—*Campbell's Rhet.* p. 160 ; *Murray's Gram.* i, 358. This arrangement is too natural to be called a transposition. The most common form of the real inversion is that of the antecedent and relative in poetry ; as,

> "*Who* stops to plunder at this signal hour,
> The birds shall tear *him,* and the dogs devour."—POPE : *Iliad,* xv. 400.

OBS. 14.—A pronoun sometimes represents a *phrase* or a *sentence* ; and in this case the pronoun is always in the third person singular neuter : as, "Surely the Lord is in this place, and I knew *it* not."—*Gen.* xxviii, 10. "Yet men can go on to vilify or disregard Christianity ; *which* is to talk and act as if they had a demonstration of its falsehood."—*Butler's Analogy,* p. 269. "When *it* is asked wherein personal identity consists, the answer should be the same as if *it* were asked, wherein consists similitude or equality."—*Ib.* p. 270. "Also, that the soul be without knowledge, *it* is not good."—*Prov.* xix, 2. In this last example, the pronoun is not really necessary. "That the soul be without knowledge, *is* not good."—*Jenks's Prayers,* p. 144. Sometimes an infinitive verb is taken as an antecedent ; as, "He will not be able *to think,* without *which it* is impertinent *to read* ; nor *to act,* without *which it* is impertinent *to think.*"—*Bolingbroke, on History,* p. 163.

OBS. 15.—When a pronoun follows two words, having a neuter verb between them, and both referring to the same thing, it may represent either of them, but not often with the same meaning ; as, 1. "I am the man, who command." Here, *who command* belongs to the subject *I,* and the meaning is, "I who command, am the man." (The latter expression places the relative nearer to its antecedent, and is therefore preferable.) 2. "I am the man who commands." Here, *who commands* belongs to the predicate *man,* and the meaning is, "I am the commander." Again : "I perceive thou art a pupil, *who possessest* good talents"—*Cooper's Pl. and Pract. Gram.* p. 136. Here the construction corresponds not to the perception, which is, of the pupil's talents. Say, therefore, "I perceive thou art a *pupil possessing* (or, *who possessest*) good talents."

OBS. 16.—After the expletive *it,* which may be employed to introduce a noun or a pronoun of any person, number, or gender, the above-mentioned distinction is generally disregarded ; and the relative is most commonly made to agree with the latter word, especially if this word be of the first or the second person : as, "*It* is no more *I that* do it."—*Rom.* vii, 20. "For *it* is not *ye that speak.*" —*Matt.* x, 20. The propriety of this construction is questionable. In the following examples, the relative agrees with the *it,* and not with the subsequent nouns : "*It* is the combined *excellencies* of all the denominations *that gives* to her her winning beauty and her powerful charms."—*Bible Society's Report,* 1838, p. 89. "*It* is *purity* and *neatness* of expression *which is* chiefly to be studied."—*Blair's Rhet.* p. 271. "*It is not the difficulty* of the language, but on the contrary the *simplicity and facility* of it, *that occasions* this neglect."—*Lowth's Gram.* p. vi. "*It is a wise head* and *a good heart that constitutes* a great man."—*Child's Instructor,* p. 22.

OBS. 17.—The pronoun *it* very frequently refers to something mentioned subsequently in the sentence; as, "*It* is useless *to complain* of what is irremediable." This pronoun is a necessary expletive at the commencement of any sentence in which the verb is followed by a phrase or a clause which, by transposition, might be made the subject of the verb; as, "*It* is impossible *to please every one.*"—*W. Allen's Gram.* "*It* was requisite *that the papers should be* sent.—*Ib.* The following example is censured by the Rev. Matt. Harrison: "*It* is *really curious, the course* which balls will sometimes take."—*Abernethy's Lectures.* "This awkward expression," says the critic, "might have been avoided by saying, ' The course which balls will sometimes take is really curious."—*Harrison, on the English Language,* p. 147. If the construction is objectionable, it may, in this instance, be altered thus: " It is really curious, *to observe* the course which balls will sometimes take!" So, it appears, we may avoid a *pleonasm* by an *addition.* But he finds a worse example: saying, "Again, in an article *from* the ' New Monthly,' No. 103, we meet with the same form of expression, *but with an aggravated aspect :*—' It is incredible, the number of apothecaries' shops, presenting themselves.' It would be quite as easy to say, ' The number of apothecaries' shops, presenting themselves, is incredible.' "—*Ib.* p. 147. This, too, may take an infinitive, " *to tell,*" or " *to behold ;* " for there is no more extravagance in doubting one's eyes, than in declaring one's own statement " incredible." But I am not sure that the original form is not allowable. In the following line, we seem to have something like it :
" It curled not Tweed alone, that breeze."—*Sir W. Scott.*

OBS. 18.—*Relative* and *interrogative* pronouns are placed at or near the beginning of their own clauses; and the learner must observe that, through all their cases, they almost invariably retain this situation in the sentence, and are found before their verbs even when the order of the construction would reverse this arrangement: as, " He *who* preserves me, to *whom* I owe my being, *whose* I am, and *whom* I serve, is eternal."—*Murray,* p. 159. " He *whom* you seek."—*Lowth.*
" The good must merit God's peculiar care ;
But *who,* but God, can tell us *who* they are ? "—*Pope.*

OBS. 19.—A *relative* pronoun, being the representative of some antecedent word or phrase, derives from this relation its person, number, and gender, but not its case. By taking an other relation of case, it helps to form an other clause ; and, by retaining the essential meaning of its antecedent, serves to connect this clause to that in which the antecedent is found. No relative, therefore, can ever be used in an independent simple sentence, or be made the subject of a subjunctive verb, or be put in apposition with any noun or pronoun ; but, like other connectives, this pronoun belongs at the head of a clause in a compound sentence, and excludes conjunctions, except when two such clauses are to be joined together, as in the following example: " I should be glad, at least, of an easy companion, *who* may tell me his thoughts, *and* to *whom* I may communicate mine."—*Goldsmith's Essays,* p. 196.

OBS. 20.—The two *special rules* commonly given by the grammarians, for the construction of relatives, are not only unnecessary,[*] but faulty. I shall notice them only to show my reasons for discarding them. With whom they originated, it is difficult to say. Paul's Accidence has them, and if Dean Colet, the supposed writer, did not take them from some earlier author, they must have been first taught by *him,* about the year 1510 ; and it is certain that they have been copied into almost every grammar published since. The first one is faulty, because, " *When there cometh no nominative case between the relative and the verb, the relative shall* [not always] *be the nominative case to the verb ;* " as may be seen by the following examples : " Many are the works of human industry, *which* hardly granted to the same man."—*Dr. Johnson's Adv. to Dict.* " They aim at his removal ; *which* there is reason to fear they will effect."— "*Which* to avoid, I cut them off."—*Shak. Hen. IV.* The second rule is faulty, because, "*When there cometh a nominative case between the relative and the verb, the relative shall* [not always] *be such case as the verb will have after* it ; " as may be seen by the following examples: " The author has not advanced any instances, *which* he does not think *are* pertinent."—*Murray's Gram.* i, 192. "*Which* we have reason to think *was* the case with the Greek and Latin."—*Ib.* 112. " Is this your son, *who* ye say *was born* blind ? "—*John,* ix, 19. The case of the relative cannot be accurately determined by any rules of mere location. It may be nominative to a verb afar off, or it may be objective with a verb immediately following ; as, ' *Which* I do not find that there ever *was.*"— *Knight, on the Greek Alphabet,* p. 31. "And our chief reason for believing *which* is that our ancestors did so before us."—*Philological Museum,* i, 641. Both these particular rules are useless, because the general rules for the cases, as given in chapter third above, are applicable to relatives, sufficient to all the purpose, and not liable to any exceptions.

OBS. 21.—In syntactical parsing, each word, in general, is to be resolved by some *one* rule ; but the parsing of a pronoun commonly requires *two* ; one for its agreement with the noun or nouns for which it stands, and an other for its case. The rule of agreement will be one of the four which are embraced in this present chapter ; and the rule for the case will be one of the seven which compose chapter third. So that the whole syntax of pronouns requires the application of eleven different rules, while that of nouns or verbs is embraced in six or seven, and that of any other part of speech, in one only. In respect to their cases, relatives and interrogatives admit of every construction common to nouns, or to the personal pronouns, except apposition. This is proved by the following examples:
1. Nominatives by Rule 2d: "I *who* write ;— Thou *who* writest ;— He *who* writes ;—The animal *which* runs."—*Dr. Adam.* " He *that* spareth his rod, hateth his son."—*Solomon.* " He *who* does any thing *which* he knows *is* wrong, ventures on dangerous ground."—"*What* will become of us without religion ? "—*Blair.* " Here I determined to wait the hand of death ; *which,*

I hope, when at last it comes, *will fall* lightly upon me."—*Dr. Johnson.* "*What is* sudden and unaccountable, *serves* to confound."—*Crabb.* "They only are wise, *who are* wise to salvation." —*Goodwin.*

2. Nominatives by Rule 6th: (i. e. words parsed as nominatives after the verbs, though most transposed:) "*Who* art thou?"—*Bible.* "*What* were we?"—*Ib.* " Do not tell them *who* I am —" Let him be *who* he may, he is not the honest fellow *that* he seemed."—'The general body of mankind is neither *what* it was designed, nor *what* it ought to be."

3. Nominatives absolute by Rule 8th: "There are certain bounds to imprudence, *which* being *transgressed,* there remains no place for repentance in the natural course of things."—*Bp. Butler.* "*Which being so,* it need not be any wonder, why I should."—*Walker's Particles, Pref.* p. x. "He offered an apology, *which not being admitted,* he became submissive."—*Murray's Key,* 202. This construction of the relative is a *Latinism,* and very seldom used by the best *English* writers.

4. Possessives by Rule 4th: "The chief man of the island, *whose* name was Publius."—*Acts.* "Despair, a cruel tyrant, from *whose* prisons none can escape."—*Dr. Johnson.* "To contemplate on Him *whose* yoke is easy and *whose* burden is light."—*Steele.*

5. Objectives by Rule 5th: "Those *whom* she persuaded."—*Dr. Johnson.* "The cloak that I left at Troas."—*St. Paul.* "By the things *which* he suffered."—*Id.* "A man *whom* there is reason to suspect."—"*What* are we to do?"—*Burke.* "Love refuses nothing *that* love sends." —*Gurnall.* "The first thing, says he, is, to choose some maxim or point of morality; to indicate *which,* is to be the design of his work."—*Blair's Rhet.* p. 421. "*Whomsoever* you please appoint."—*Lowth.* "*Whatsoever* he doeth, shall prosper."—*Bible.* "*What* we are afraid to do before men, we should be afraid to think before God."—*Sibs.* "Shall I hide from Abraham the thing *which* I do?"—*Gen.* xviii, 32. "Shall I hide from Abraham *what* I am going to do?" "Call imperfection *what* thou fanciest such."—*Pope.*

6. Objectives by Rule 6th: (i. e. pronouns parsed as objectives after neuter verbs, though they stand before them:) "He is not the man *that* I took him to be."—"*Whom* did you suppose me to be?"—"If the lad ever become *what* you wish him to be."

7. Objectives by Rule 7th: "To *whom* shall we go?"—*Bible.* "The laws by *which* the world is governed, are general."—*Bp. Butler.* "*Whom* he looks upon as his defender."—*Addison.* "That secret heaviness of heart *which* unthinking men are subject to."—*Id.* "I cannot but think the loss of such talents *as* the man of *whom* I am speaking was master of, a more melancholy instance."—*Steele.* "Grammar is the solid foundation upon *which* all other science rests." —*Buchanan's Eng. Synt.* p. xx.

OBS. 22.—In familiar language, the relative of the objective case is frequently *understood;* as, "The man [*whom*] I trust."—*Cowper.* "Here is the letter [*which*] I received." So in the following sentences: "This is the man they hate. These are the goods they bought. Are these the Gods they worship? Is this the woman you saw?"—*Ash's Gram.* p. 96. This ellipsis seems allowable only in the familiar style. In grave writing, or deliberate discourse, it is much better to express this relative. The omission of it is often attended with some obscurity; as, "The next error [*that*] I shall mention [,] is a capital one."—*Kames, El. of Crit.* ii, 157. "It is little [*that*] we know of the divine perfections."—*Scougal,* p. 94. "The faith [*which*] we give to memory, may be thought, on a superficial view, to be resolvable into consciousness, as well as that [*which*] we give to the immediate impressions of sense."—*Campbell's Rhet.* p. 53. "We speak that [*which*] we do know, and testify that [*which*] we have seen."—*John,* iii, 11. The omission of a relative in the nominative case, is almost always inelegant; as, "This is the worst thing [that] could happen."—"There were several things [*which*] brought it upon me."—*Pilgrim's Progress,* p. 162. The latter ellipsis may occur after *but* or *than,* and it is also sometimes allowed in poetry; as, [There is] "No person of reflection but [who] must be sensible, that an incident makes a stronger impression on an eye-witness, than when heard at second hand."—*Kames, El. of Crit.* ii, 257.

> "In this 'tis God directs, in that 'tis man."—*Pope, on Man.*
> "Abuse on all he lov'd, or lov'd him, spread."—*Id. to Arbuthnot.*
> "There's nothing blackens like the ink of fools."—*Id. to Augustus.*

OBS. 23.—The *antecedent* is sometimes suppressed, especially in poetry; as, "Who will, may be a judge."—*Churchill.* "How shall I curse [*him* or *them*] whom God hath not cursed?"—*Numbers,* xxiii, 8. "There are, indeed, [some persons] who seem disposed to extend her authority much farther."—*Campbell's Philosophy of Rhet* p. 187.

> [*He*] "Who lives to nature, rarely can be poor;
> [*He*] Who lives to fancy, never can be rich."—*Young.*
> "Serious should be an author's final views;
> [*They*] Who write for pure amusement, ne'er amuse."—*Id.*

OBS. 24.—*Which,* as well as *who,* was formerly applied to persons; as, "Our *Father which* art in heaven."—*Bible.* "Pray for *them which* despitefully use you."—*Luke,* vi, 28. And, as to the former example here cited, some British critics, without preferring the archaism, have accused "The Americans" of "poor criticism," in that they "have changed *which* into *who,* as being more consonant to the rules of Grammar" Falsely imagining, that *which* and *who,* with the same antecedent, can be of different *genders,* they allege, that, "The use of the *neuter* pronoun carried with it a certain vagueness and sublimity, not inappropriate in reminding us that our worship is addressed to a Being, infinite, and superior to all distinctions applicable to material objects."— *Men and Manners in America:* quoted and endorsed by the REV. MATT. HARRISON, in his treatise on the English Language, p. 191. This is all fancy; and, in my opinion, absurd. It is just like the religious prejudice which could discern "a singular propriety" in "the double superlative *most highest.*"—*Lowth's Gram.* p. 28. But *which* may still be applied to a young child, if sex and intelligence be disregarded; as, "The *child which* died." Or even to adults, when they are spoken of without regard to a distinct personality or identity; as, "*Which* of you will go?"— "Crabb knoweth not *which* is *which,* himself or his parodist."—*Leigh Hunt.*

OBS. 25.—A proper name taken merely as a name, or an appellative taken in any sense not strictly personal, must be represented by *which,* and not by *who;* as, "Herod—*which* is but an other name for cruelty."—"In every prescription of duty, God proposeth himself as a rewarder; that he is only to those that please him."—*Dr. J. Owen. Which* would perhaps be more proper than *whom,* in the following passage: "They did not destroy the *nations,* concerning *whom* the Lord commanded them."—*Psalm,* cvi, 34. Dr. Blair has preferred it in the following instance: "My lion and my pillar are sufficiently interpreted by the mention of *Achilles* and the *minister,* which I join to them."—*Lectures,* p. 151. He meant, "*whose names I connect with theirs;*" and that, that he joined the *person* of Achilles to a lion, or that of a minister to a pillar.

OBS. 26.—When two or more relative clauses pertain to the same antecedent, if they are connected by a conjunction, the same relative ought to be employed in each, agreeably to the doctrine of the seventh note below; but if no conjunction is expressed or understood between them, the pronoun ought rather to be different; as, "There are many things *that* you can speak of, which cannot be seen."—*R. W. Green's Gram.* p. 11. This distinction is noticed in the fifth chapter of Etymology, Obs. 29th, on the Classes of Pronouns. Dr. Priestley says, "Whatever relative is used, in a *series* of clauses, relating to the same antecedent, the same ought to be used in them all. 'It is remarkable, that *Holland,* against *which* the war was undertaken, *and that,* in the very beginning, was reduced to the brink of destruction, lost nothing.'—*Universal History,* Vol. 25, p. 9. It ought to have been, *and which in the very beginning.*"—*Priestley's Gram.* p. 102. L. Murray, (as I have shown in the Introduction, Ch. x, ¶ 22,) assumes all this, without references; taking as a salvo the word *"generally,"* which merely impairs the certainty of the rule:—"the same relative ought *generally* to be used in them all."—*Octavo Gram.* p. 155. And, of *who* and *that,* Cobbett says: "Either may do; but both *never* ought to be relatives of the same antecedent in the same sentence."—*Gram.* ¶ 202. The inaccuracy of these rules is as great as that of the phraseology which is corrected under them. In the following sentence, the first relative only is restrictive, and consequently the other may be different: "These were the officers *that* were called *decemviri,* and *who* signalized themselves afterwards so gloriously upon all occasions."—*Rollin's Hist.* ii, 62. See also in *Rev.* x, 6th, a similar example without the conjunction.

OBS. 27.—In conversation, the possessive pronoun *your* is sometimes used in a droll way, being shortened into *yur* in pronunciation, and nothing more being meant by it, than might be expressed by the article *an* or *a:* as, "Rich honesty dwells, like *your* miser, sir, in a poor house; *your* pearl in *your* foul oyster."—*Shakspeare.*

NOTES TO RULE X.

NOTE I.—A pronoun should not be introduced in connexion with words that belong are properly to the antecedent, or to an other pronoun; as, "And then there is not use for *Pallas her* glass."—*Bacon's Wisdom,* p. 22. Say—"for *Pallas's* glass."

"My *banks they* are furnish'd with bees,
Whose murmur invites one to sleep."—*Shenstone,* p. 284.

This last instance, however, is only an example of *pleonasm;* which is allowable and frequent in *animated discourse,* but inelegant in any other. Our grammarians have condemned it too positively. It occurs sundry times in the Bible; as, "Know ye that the LORD *he is* God."—*Psalms,* c, 8.

NOTE II.—A change of number in the second person, or even a promiscuous use of *ye* and *you* in the same case and the same style, is inelegant, and ought to be avoided; as, "*You* wept, and I for *thee.*"—"Harry, said my lord, don't cry; I'll give you something towards *thy* loss."—*Swift's Poems,* p 267. "*Ye sons* of sloth, ye offspring of darkness, awake from your sleep."—*Brown's Metaphors,* p. 96. Our poets have very often adopted the former solecism, to accommodate their measure! or to avoid the harshness of the old verb in the second person singular: as,

Thy heart is yet blameless, O fly while *you may.*"—*Queen's Wake,* p. 46.

"Oh! Peggy, Peggy, when *thou goest* to brew,
Consider well what *you're* about to do."—*King's Poems,* p. 594.

"As in that lov'd Athenian bower,
You learn'd an all-commanding power,
Thy mimic soul, O nymph endear'd!
Can well recall what then it heard."—*Collins, Ode to Music.*

NOTE III.—The relative *who* is applied only to persons, and to animals or things personified; and *which,* to brute animals and inanimate things spoken of literally: "The *judge who* presided;"—"The old *crab who* advised the young one;"—The horse *which* ran away;"—"The *book which* was given me."

NOTE IV.—Nouns of multitude, unless they express persons directly as such, would not be represented by the relative *who:* to say, "The *family whom* I visited," would hardly be proper; *that* would here be better. When such nouns are strictly of the neuter gender, *which* may represent them; as, "The *committees which* were

appointed." But where the idea of rationality is predominant, *who* or *whom* se
not to be improper; as, "The conclusion of the Iliad is like the exit of a great
out of *company whom* he has entertained magnificently."—*Cowper.* "A la
only the expression of the desire of a *multitude who* have power to punish."—*Bro*
Philosophy of the Mind.

NOTE V.—In general, the pronoun must so agree with its antecedent as to pre
the same idea, and never in such a manner as to confound the name with the t
signified, or any two things with each other. Examples: "*Jane* is in the nomina
case, because *it* leads the sentence."—*Infant School Gram.* p. 80. Here *it* re
sents *the word* "*Jane*," and not *the person Jane.* "What mark or sign is put
master to show that *he* is in the possessive case? Spell *it.*"—*Ib.* p. 32. Her
word "*master*" is most absurdly confounded with *the man;* and that to accommo
grammar to a child's comprehension!

NOTE VI.—The relative *that* may be applied either to persons or to things
the following cases, it is more appropriate than *who, whom,* or *which;* and oug
be preferred, unless it be necessary to use a preposition before the relative:—
After an adjective of the superlative degree, when the relative clause is restricti
as, "He was the *first that* came."—"He was the *fittest* person *that* could the
found."—*Campbell's Rhet.* p. 422. "The Greeks were the *greatest* reasoners
ever appeared in the world."—BEATTIE: *Murray's Gram.* p. 127. (2.) After
adjective *same,* when the relative clause is restrictive; as, "He is the *same* man
you saw before."—*Priestley's Gram.* p. 101; *Murray's,* 156; *Campbell's R*
422. (3.) After the antecedent *who;* as, "Who *that* is a sincere friend to it,
look with indifference upon attempts to shake the foundation of the fabric?"—W
ington. (4.) After two or more antecedents that demand a relative adapted bot
persons and to things; as, "He spoke largely of the *men and things that* be
seen."—"When some particular *person or thing* is spoken of, *that* ought to be
distinctly marked."—*Murray's Gram.* p. 51. (5.) After an unlimited antece
which the relative clause is designed to restrict; as, "*Thoughts that* breathe,
words that burn."—*Gray.* "*Music that* accords with the present tone of mind
on that account, doubly agreeable."—*Kames, El. of Crit.* ii, 311. "For Theocr
descends sometimes into *ideas that* are gross and mean."—*Blair's Rhet.* p. 3
(6.) After any antecedent introduced by the expletive *it;* as, "*It* is *you that* suf
—"It was I, and not he, *that* did it."—*Churchill's Gram.* p. 142. "It was
he † *that* they were so angry with."—*Murray's Exercises,* R. 17. "*It* was
Gavius alone *that* Verres meant to insult."—*Blair's Rhet.* p. 325. (7.) An
general, wherever the propriety of *who* or *which* is doubtful; as, "The little d
that was placed in the midst."

NOTE VII.—When two or more relative clauses connected by a conjunction
a similar dependence in respect to the antecedent, the same pronoun must be emp
in each; as, "O thou, *who* art, and *who* wast, and *who* art to come!"—"
they shall spread them before the sun, and the moon, and all the host of hea
whom they have loved, and *whom* they have served, and after *whom* they
walked, and *whom* they have sought, and *whom* they have worshiped."—*Jer.* vii

NOTE VIII.—The relative, and the preposition governing it, should not be omit
when they are necessary to the sense intended, or to a proper connexion of the p
of the sentence; as, "He is still in the situation you saw him." Better thus:"
is still in the situation *in which* you saw him."

---

* This rule, in all its parts, is to be applied chiefly, if not solely, to such relative clauses as are taken
restrictive sense; for, in the *resumptive* sense of the relative, *who* or *which* may be more proper than
"Abraham solemnly adjures his *most faithful* servant, *whom* he despatches to Charran on this matrimonial
sion for his son, to discharge his mission with all fidelity."—*Milman's Jews,* i, 21. See Etymology, chap
Obs. 23d, 24th, &c., on the Classes of Pronouns.

† Murray imagined this sentence to be bad English. He very strangely mistook the pronoun *he* for the ch
of the preposition *with;* and accordingly condemned the text, under the rule, "Prepositions govern the *obj*
case." So of the following: "It is not I he is engaged with."—*Murray's Exercises,* R. 17. Better "It is
that he is engaged with." Here is no violation of the foregoing rule, or of any other; and both render m
even Murray's form of the latter, are quite as good as his proposed substitutes: "It was not *with him* that t
were so angry."—*Murray's Key,* p. 51. "It is not *with me* he is engaged."—*Ib.* In these fancied correc
the phrases *with him* and *with me* have a very awkward and questionable position: it seems doubtful, whe
they depend on *was* and *is,* or on *angry* and *engaged.*

NOTE IX.—After certain nouns, of time, place, manner, or cause, the conjunctive adverbs *when, where, whither, whence, how,* and *why,* are a sort of special relatives; but no such adverb should be used where a preposition and a relative pronoun would better express the relation of the terms: as, "A cause *where* justice is so much concerned." Say, "A cause *in which.*" See Etymology, Obs. 6th, 7th, and 8th, on the Classes of Adverbs.

NOTE X.—Where a pronoun or a pronominal adjective will not express the meaning clearly, the noun must be repeated, or inserted in stead of it: as, "We see the beautiful variety of colour in the rainbow, and are led to consider the cause of *it.*" Say,—"the cause of *that variety;*" because the *it* may mean *the variety, the colour,* or *the rainbow.*

NOTE XI.—To prevent ambiguity or obscurity, the relative should, in general, be placed as near as possible to the antecedent. The following sentence is therefore faulty: "He is like a beast of prey, that is void of compassion." Better thus: "He that is void of compassion, is like a beast of prey."

NOTE XII.—The pronoun *what* should never be used in stead of the conjunction *that;* as, "Think no man so perfect but *what* he may err." This is a vulgar fault. Say,—"but *that* he may err."

NOTE XIII.—A pronoun should never be used to represent *an adjective,*—except the pronominal adjectives, and others taken substantively; because a pronoun can neither express a concrete quality as such, nor convert it properly into an abstract: as, "Be *attentive;* without *which* you will learn nothing." Better thus: "Be attentive; *for without attention* you will learn nothing."

NOTE XIV.—Though the relative *which* may in some instances stand for a phrase or a sentence, it is seldom, if ever, a fit representative of an indicative assertion; as, "The man opposed me, *which* was anticipated."—*Nixon's Parser,* p. 127. Say,— "*but his opposition* was anticipated." Or: "The man opposed me, *as* was anticipated." Or:—"*as I expected he would.*" Again: "The captain disobeys orders, *which* is punished."—*Ib.* p. 128. This is an other factitious sentence, formed after the same model, and too erroneous for correction: none but a conceited grammatist could ever have framed such a construction.

NOTE XV.—The possessive pronouns, *my, thy, his, her, its,* &c., should be inserted or repeated as often as the sense or construction of the sentence requires them; their omission, like that of the articles, can scarcely in any instance constitute a proper ellipsis: as, "Of Princeton and vicinity."—Say, "Of Princeton and *its* vicinity." "The man and wife."—Say, "The man and *his* wife." "Many verbs vary both their signification and construction."—*Adam's Gram.* p. 170; *Gould's,* 171. Say,—"and *their* construction."

NOTE XVI.—In the correcting of any discord between the antecedent and its pronoun, if the latter for any sufficient reason is most proper as it stands, the former must be changed to accord with it: as, "Let us discuss what relates to *each particular* in *their* order :—*its* order."—*Priestley's Gram.* p. 193. Better thus: "Let us discuss what relates to *the several particulars,* in *their* order." For the *order* of things implies plurality.

IMPROPRIETIES FOR CORRECTION.

FALSE SYNTAX UNDER RULE X.

UNDER THE RULE ITSELF.—OF AGREEMENT.

"The subject is to be joined with his predicate."—BP. WILKINS: *Lowth's Gram.* p. 42.

[FORMULE.—Not proper, because the pronoun *his* is of the masculine gender, and does not correctly represent its antecedent noun *subject,* which is of the third person, singular, neuter. But, according to Rule 10th, "A pronoun must agree with its antecedent, or the noun or pronoun which it represents, in person, number, and gender." Therefore, *his* should be *its;* thus, "The subject is to be joined with *its* predicate."]

"Every one must judge of their own feelings."—*Byron's Letters.* "Every one in the family should know their duty."—*Wm. Penn.* "To introduce its possessor into 'that way in which it should go.'"—*Infant School Gram.* p. v. "Do not they say, every true believer has the Spirit of God in them?"—*Barclay's Works,* iii, 388. "There is none in their natural state righteous, no not one."—*Wood's Dict. of Bible*, ii, 129. "If ye were of the world world would love his own."—*John*, xv, 19. "His form had not yet lost all her ori brightness."—*Milton*. "No one will answer as if I were their friend or companion *Steele, Spect*. No. 534. "But in lowliness of mind let each esteem other better than the selves."—*Philippians*, ii, 3. "And let none of you imagine evil in your hearts again neighbour."—*Zechariah*, viii, 17. "For every tree is known by his own fruit."—*Luke*, "But she fell to laughing, like one out of their right mind."—*Castle Rackrent*, p. 51. " these systems, so far from having any tendency to make men better, have a manifest dency to make him worse."—*Wayland's Moral Science*, p. 123. "And nobody else w make that city their refuge any more."—*Josephus's Life*, p. 158. "What is quantity, respects syllables or words ? It is that time which is occupied in pronouncing it."—I *ley's Gram*. p. 108. "In such expressions the adjective so much resembles an adverb meaning, that they are usually parsed as such."—*Bullions, E. Gram*. p. 103. "The tong like a race-horse ; which runs the faster the less weight it carries."—ADDISON : *Ju. Murray's Key*, Rule 8. "As two thoughtless boys were trying to see which could lif greatest weight with their jaws, one of them had several of his firm-set teeth wrenched their sockets."—*Newspaper*. "Everybody nowadays publishes memoirs ; everybody recollections which they think worthy of recording."—*Duchess D'Abrantes*, p. 25. "I body trembled for themselves or their friends."—*Goldsmith's Greece*, i, 171.

    "A steed comes at morning : no rider is there ;
    But its bridle is red with the sign of despair."—*Campbell*.

UNDER NOTE I.—PRONOUNS WRONG OR NEEDLESS.

"Charles loves to study ; but John, alas ! he is very idle."—*Merchant's School Gram*. "Or what man is there of you, whom if his son ask bread, will he give him a stone ?"— vii, 9. "Who, instead of going about doing good, they are perpetually intent upon mischief."—*Tillotson*. "Whom ye delivered up, and denied him in the presence of tius Pilate."—*Acts*, iii, 13. "Whom, when they had washed, they laid her in an chamber."—*Acts*, ix, 37. "Then Manasseh knew that the Lord he was God."—2 Ch xxxiii, 13. "Whatever a man conceives clearly, he may, if he will be at the trouble, into distinct propositions, and express it clearly to others."—*Murray's Gram*. 8vo, p "But to that point of time which he has chosen, the painter being entirely confined cannot exhibit various stages of the same action."—*Blair's Rhet*. p. 62. "It is without proof at all what he subjoins."—*Barclay's Works*, i, 301. "George Fox his Testimony cerning Robert Barclay."—*Ib*. i, 111. "According to the author of the Postscript advice."—*Ib*. iii, 263. "These things seem as ugly to the Eye of their Meditati those Æthiopians pictur'd in Nemesis her Pitcher."—*Bacon's Wisdom of the Ancients*, "Moreover, there is always a twofold Condition propounded with Sphynx her Ænigm *Ib*. p. 73. "Whoever believeth not therein, they shall perish."—*Sale's Koran*, p "When, at Sestius his entreaty, I had been at his house."—*Walker's Particles*, p

    "There high on Sipylus his shaggy brow,
    She stands, her own sad monument of woe."—*Pope's Homer*, B. xxiv, l. 777.

UNDER NOTE II.—CHANGE OF NUMBER.

"So will I send upon you famine, and evil beasts, and they shall bereave thee."—E v, 17. "Why do you plead so much for it ? why do ye preach it up ?"—*Barclay's* i, 180. "Since thou hast decreed that I shall bear man, your darling."—*Esther's Lessons in Gram*. p. 106. "You have my book and I have thine ; i. e. thy book."—*ter's Gram*., 1821, p. 22. "Neither art thou such a one as to be ignorant of what are."—*Bullions, Lat. Gram*. p. 70. "Return, thou backsliding Israel, saith the Lord, will not cause mine anger to fall upon you."—*Jeremiah*, iii, 12. "The Almighty, until to cut thee off in the fullness of iniquity, has sent me to give you warning."—*Art of T ing*, p. 278. "Wert thou born only for pleasure ? were you never to do any thing !"—*lier's Antoninus*, p. 63. "Thou shalt be required to go to God, to die, and give up account."—BARNES's NOTES : on *Luke*, xii, 20. "And canst thou expect to behold resplendent glory of the Creator ? would not such a sight annihilate you ?"—*Milton*. the prophet had commanded thee to do some great thing, would you have refused *Common School Journal*, i, 80. "Art thou penitent ? Evince your sincerity by br forth fruits meet for repentance."—*Christian's Vade-Mecum*, p. 117. "I will call thee dear son : I remember all your tenderness."—*Classic Tales*, p. 8. "So do thou, my open your ears, and your eyes."—*Wright's Athens*, p. 83. "I promise you, this was en to discourage thee."—*Pilgrim's Progress*, p. 446. "Ere you remark an other's sin, Bid own conscience look within."—*Gay*. "Permit that I share in thy woe, The privileg you refuse ?"—*Perfect's Poems*, p. 6. "Ah ! Strephon, how can you despise Her who w out thy pity dies ?"—*Swift's Poems*, p. 340.

    "Thy verses, friend, are Kidderminster stuff,
    And I must own, you've measur'd out enough."—*Shenstone*.
    "This day, dear Bec, is thy nativity ;
    Had Fate a luckier one, she'd give it ye."—*Swift*.

UNDER NOTE III.—WHO AND WHICH.

"Exactly like so many puppets, who are moved by wires."—*Blair's Rhet.* p. 462. "They are my servants, which I brought forth out of the land of Egypt."—*Leviticus*, xxv, 42. "Behold I and the children which God hath given me."—*Heb.* ii, 13; *Webster's Bible, and others.* "And he sent Eliakim which was over the household, and Shebna the scribe."—*2 Kings*, xix, 2. "In a short time the streets were cleared of the corpses who filled them."—*M'Ilvaine's Lect.* p. 411. "They are not of those which teach things which they ought not, for filthy lucre's sake."—*Barclay's Works*, i, 435. "As a lion among the beasts of the forest, as a young lion among the flocks of sheep; who, if he go through, both treadeth down and teareth in pieces."—*Micah*, v, 8. "Frequented by every fowl whom nature has taught to dip the wing in water."—*Rasselas*, p. 10. "He had two sons, one of which was adopted by the family of Maximus."—*Lempriere, w. Æmylius.* "And the ants, who are collected by the smell, are burned by fire."—*The Friend*, xii, 49. "They being the agents, to which this thing was trusted."—*Nixon's Parser*, p. 139. "A packhorse who is driven constantly forwards and backwards to market."—*Locke: Joh. Dict.* "By instructing children, the affection of which will be increased."—*Nixon's Parser*, p. 136. "He had a comely young woman which travelled with him."—*Hutchinson's Hist.* i, 29. "A butterfly, which thought himself an accomplished traveller, happened to light upon a beehive."—*Inst.* p. 143. "It is an enormous elephant of stone, who disgorges from his uplifted trunk a vast but graceful shower."—*Zenobia*, i, 150. "He was met by a dolphin, who sometimes swam before him, and sometimes behind him."—*Edward's First Lessons in Gram.* p. 34.

"That Cæsar's horse, who, as fame goes, | Was not by half so tender-hoofed,
Had corns upon his feet and toes, | Nor trod upon the ground so soft."—*Hudibras*, p. 6.

UNDER NOTE IV.—NOUNS OF MULTITUDE.

"He instructed and fed the crowds who surrounded him."—*Murray's Exercises*, p. 52. "The court, who gives currency to manners, ought to be exemplary."—*Ibid.* "Nor does he describe classes of sinners who do not exist."—*Anti-Slavery Magazine*, i, 27. "Because the nations among whom they took their rise, were not savage."—*Murray's Gram.* p. 113. "Among nations who are in the first and rude periods of society."—*Blair's Rhet.* p. 60. "The martial spirit of those nations, among whom the feudal government prevailed."—*Ib.* p. 374. "France who was in alliance with Sweden."—*Smollett's Voltaire*, vi, 187. "That faction in England who most powerfully opposed his arbitrary pretensions."—*Mrs. Macaulay's Hist.* iii, 21. "We may say, 'the crowd, *who* was going up the street.'"—*Cobbett's Gram.* ¶ 204. "Such members of the Convention who formed this Lyceum, as have subscribed this Constitution."—*New-York Lyceum.*

UNDER NOTE V.—CONFUSION OF SENSES.

"The possessor shall take a particular form to show its case."—*Kirkham's Gram.* p. 53. "Of which reasons the principal one is, that no Noun, properly so called, implies its own Presence."—*Harris's Hermes*, p. 76. "Boston is a proper noun, which distinguishes it from other cities."—*Sanborn's Gram.* p. 22. "Conjunction means union, or joining together. It is used to join or unite either words or sentences."—*Ib.* p. 20. "The word *interjection* means *thrown among*. It is interspersed among other words to express sudden or strong emotion."—*Ib.* p. 21. "*Indeed*, or in very deed, may better be written separately, as they formerly were."—*Cardell's Gram.* 12mo, p. 89. "*Alexander*, on the contrary, is a particular name, and is restricted to distinguish him alone."—*Jamieson's Rhet.* p. 25. "As an indication that nature itself had changed her course."—*Hist. of America*, p. 9. "Of removing from the United States and her territories the free people of colour."—*Jenifer.* "So that *gh* may be said not to have their proper sound."—*Webster's El. Spelling-Book*, p. 10. "Are we to welcome the loathsome harlot, and introduce it to our children?"—*Maturin's Sermons*, p. 167. "The first question is this, 'Is reputable, national, and present use, which, for brevity's sake, I shall hereafter simply denominate good use, always uniform in her decisions?'"—*Campbell's Rhet.* p. 171. "Time is always masculine, on account of its mighty efficacy. Virtue is feminine from its beauty, and its being the object of love."—*Murray's Gram.* p. 37; *Blair's*, 125; *Sanborn's*, 189; *Emmons's*, 13; *Putnam's*, 25; *Fisk's*, 57; *Ingersoll's*, 26; *Greenleaf's*, 21. See also *Blair's Rhet.* p. 53. "When you speak to a person or thing, it is in the second person."—*Bartlett's Manual*, Part ii. p. 27. "You now know the noun, for it means name."—*Ibid.* "T. What do you see? P. A book. T. Spell it."—*R. W. Green's Gram.* p. 12. "T. What do you see now? P. Two books. T. Spell them."—*Ibid.* "If the United States lose her rights as a nation."—*Liberator*, Vol. ix, p. 24. "When a person or thing is addressed or spoken to, it is in the second person."—*Frost's El. of Gram.* p. 7. "When a person or thing is spoken of, it is in the third person."—*Ibid.* "The ox, that ploughs the ground, has the same plural termination also, *oxen*."—*Bucke's Classical Gram.* p. 40.

"Hail, happy States! thine is the blissful seat,
Where nature's gifts and art's improvements meet."
EVERETT: *Columbian Orator*, p. 239.

UNDER NOTE VI.—THE RELATIVE THAT.

(1.) "This is the most useful art which men possess."—*Murray's Key. 8vo*, p. 275. "The earliest accounts which history gives us concerning all nations, bear testimony to these facts."—*Blair's Rhet.* p. 379; *Jamieson's*, 300. "Mr. Addison was the first who attempted a regular inquiry" [into the pleasures of taste].—*Blair's Rhet.* p. 28. "One of the first who introduced it was Montesquieu."—*Murray's Gram.* p. 125. "Massillon is perhaps the most eloquent writer of sermons which modern times have produced."—*Blair's Rhet.* 289. "The greatest barber who ever lived, is our guiding star and prototype."—*Hart's Figaro*, No. 6.

(2.) "When prepositions are subjoined to nouns, they are generally the same which are subjoined to the verbs, from which the nouns are derived."—*Priestley's Gram.* p. 146. "The same proportions which are agreeable in a model, are not agreeable in a large building."—*Kames, El. of Crit.* ii, 343. "The same ornaments, which we admire in a private apartment, are unseemly in a temple."—*Murray's Gram.* p. 128. "The same whom John saw also in the sun."—*Milton, P. L.*, B. iii, l. 623.

(3.) "Who can ever be easy, who is reproached with his own ill conduct?"—*Thomas à Kempis*, p. 72. "Who is she who comes clothed in a robe of green?"—*Inst.* p. 143. "Who has either sense or civility, does not perceive the vileness of profanity?"

(4.) "The second person denotes the person or thing which is spoken to."—*Compendium in Kirkham's Gram.* "The third person denotes the person or thing which is spoken of."—*Ibid.* "A passive verb denotes action received or endured by the person or thing which is its nominative."—*Ibid. and Gram.* p. 157. "The princes and states who had neglected or favoured the growth of this power."—*Bolingbroke, on History*, p. 222. "The nominative expresses the name of the person or thing which acts, or which is the subject of discourse." —*Hiley's Gram.* p. 19.

(5.) "Authors who deal in long sentences, are very apt to be faulty."—*Blair's Rhet.* p. 108. "Writers who deal in long sentences, are very apt to be faulty."—*Murray's Gram.* p. 313. "The neuter gender denotes objects which are neither male nor female."—*Merchant's Gram.* p. 26. "The neuter gender denotes things which have no sex."—*Kirkham's Compendium.* "Nouns which denote objects neither male nor female, are of the neuter gender." —*Wells's Gram.* 1st Ed. p. 49. "Objects and ideas which have been long familiar, make too faint an impression to give an agreeable exercise to our faculties."—*Blair's Rhet.* p. 58. "Cases which custom has left dubious, are certainly within the grammarian's province."—*Murray's Gram.* p. 164. "Substantives which end in *ery*, signify action or habit."—*Ib.* p. 132. "After all which can be done to render the definitions and rules of grammar accurate," &c.—*Ib.* p. 36. "Possibly, all which I have said, is known and taught."—*A. B. Johnson's Plan of a Dict.* p. 15.

(6.) "It is a strong and manly style which should chiefly be studied."—*Blair's Rhet.* p. 261. "It is this which chiefly makes a division appear neat and elegant."—*Ib.* p. 313. "I hope it is not I with whom he is displeased."—*Murray's Key*, R. 17. "When it is this alone which renders the sentence obscure."—*Campbell's Rhet.* p. 242. "This sort of full and ample assertion, '*it is this which*,' is fit to be used when a proposition of importance is laid down."—*Blair's Rhet.* p. 197. "She is the person whom I understood it to have been." See *Murray's Gram.* p. 181. "Was it thou, or the wind, who shut the door?"—*Inst.* p. 143. "It was not I who shut it."—*Ib.*

(7.) "He is not the person who it seemed he was."—*Murray's Gram.* p. 181; *Ingersoll's*, 147. "He is really the person who he appeared to be."—*Same.* "She is not now the woman whom they represented her to have been."—*Same.* "An only child, is one who has neither brother nor sister; a child alone, is one who is left by itself."—*Blair's Rhet.* p. 98; *Jamieson's*, 71; *Murray's Gram.* 303.

UNDER NOTE VII.—RELATIVE CLAUSES CONNECTED.

(1.) "A Substantive, or Noun, is the name of a thing; of whatever we conceive in any way to subsist, or of which we have any notion."—*Lowth's Gram.* p. 14. (2.) "A Substantive or noun is the name of any thing that exists, or of which we have any notion."— *L. Murray's Gram.* p. 27; *Alger's*, 15; *Bacon's*, 9; *E. Devis's*, 8; *A. Flint's*, 10; *Folker's*, 5; *Hamlin's*, 9; *Ingersoll's*, 14; *Merchant's*, 25; *Pond's*, 15; *S. Putnam's*, 10; *Rand's*, 9; *Russell's*, 9; *T. Smith's*, 12; and others. (3.) "A substantive or noun is the name of any person, place, or thing that exists, or of which we can have an idea."—*Frost's El. of E. Gram.* p. 6. (4.) "A noun is the name of anything that exists, or of which we form an idea."—*Hallock's Gram.* p. 37. (5.) "A Noun is the name of any person, place, object, or thing, that exists, or which we may conceive to exist."—*D. C. Allen's Grammatic Guide*, p. 19. (6.) "The name of every thing that exists, or of which we can form any notion, is a noun."—*Fisk's Murray's Gram.* p. 56. (7.) "An allegory is the representation of some one thing by an other that resembles it, and which is made to stand for it."—*Murray's Gram.* p. 341. (8.) "Had he exhibited such sentences as contained ideas inapplicable to young minds, or which were of a trivial or injurious nature."—*Murray's Gram.* Vol. ii, p. v. (9.) "Man would have others obey him, even his own kind; but he will not obey God, that is so much above him, and who made him."—*Penn's Maxims.* (10.) "But what we may consider here, and which few Persons have taken Notice of, is," &c.—*Brightland's Gram.* p. 117. (11.) "The Compiler has not inserted such verbs as are irregular only in familiar writing or discourse, and which are improperly terminated by *t*, instead of *ed*."—*Murray's Gram.* p. 107; *Fisk's*, 81; *Hart's*, 68; *Ingersoll's*, 104; *Merchant's*, 63. (12.) "The remaining parts of speech, which are called the indeclinable parts, or that admit of no variations, will not detain us long."—*Blair's Rhet.* p. 84.

UNDER NOTE VIII.—THE RELATIVE AND PREPOSITION.

"In the temper of mind he was then."—*Addison, Spect.* No. 54. "To bring them into the condition I am at present."—*Spect.* No. 520. "In the posture I lay."—*Swift's Gulliver.* "In the sense it is sometimes taken."—*Barclay's Works*, i, 527. "Tools and utensils are said to be *right*, when they serve for the uses they were made."—*Collier's Antoninus*, p. 99. "If, in the extreme danger I now am, I do not imitate the behaviour of those," &c.—*Goldsmith's Greece*, i, 193. "News was brought, that Darius was but twenty miles from the place they then were."—*Ib.* ii, 113. "Alexander, upon hearing this news, continued four days in the place he then was."—*Ib.* ii, 113. "To read, in the best manner it is now taught."—*L. Murray's Gram.* p. 246. "It may be expedient to give a few directions as to the manner it should be studied."—*Hallock's Gram.* p. 9. "Participles are words derived from verbs, and convey an idea of the acting of an agent, or the suffering of an object, with the time it happens."—*Alex. Murray's Gram.* p. 50.

> "Had I but serv'd my God with half the zeal
> I serv'd my king, he would not in mine age
> Have left me naked to mine enemies."—*Beauties of Shak.* p. 173.

UNDER NOTE IX.—ADVERBS FOR RELATIVES.

"In compositions where pronunciation has no place."—*Blair's Rhet.* p. 101. "They framed a protestation, where they repeated their claims."—*Hume's Hist.* "Which have reference to Substances, where Sex never had existence."—*Harris's Hermes*, p. 43. "Which denote substances where sex never had existence."—*Murray's Gram.* p. 38; *Fisk's*, 57. "There is no rule given how truth may be found out."—*Walker's Particles*, p. 160. "The nature of the objects whence they are taken."—*Blair's Rhet.* p. 165. "That darkness of character, where we can see no heart."—*Murray's Key*, 8vo, p. 236. "The states where they negotiated."—*Formey's Belles-Lettres*, p. 169. "Till the motives whence men act be known."—*Beattie's Moral Science*, p. 262. "He assigns the principles whence their power of pleasing flows."—*Blair's Rhet.* p. 19. "But I went on, and so finished this History in that form as it now appears."—*Sewel's Preface*, p. v. "By prepositions we express the cause why, the instrument by which, wherewith, or the manner how a thing is done."— *Alex. Murray's Gram.* p. 128; *John Burn's*, 121. "They are not such in the language whence they are derived."—*Town's Analysis*, p. 13. "I find it very hard to persuade several, that their passions are affected by words from whence they have no ideas."—*Burke, on the Sublime*, p. 95. "The known end, then, why we are placed in a state of so much affliction, hazard, and difficulty, is our improvement in virtue and piety."—*Butler's Anal.* p. 109.

> "Yet such his acts, as Grecks unborn shall tell,
> And curse the battle where their fathers fell."—*Pope, Il.* B. x, l. 61.

UNDER NOTE X.—REPEAT THE NOUN.

"Youth may be thoughtful, but it is not very common."—*Webster's El. Spelling-Book*, p. 85. "A proper name is that given to one person or thing."—*Bartlett's School Manual*, ii, 27. "A common name is that given to many things of the same sort."—*Ibid.* "This rule is often violated; some instances of which are annexed."—*Murray's Gram.* p. 149; *Ingersoll's*, 237. "This is altogether careless writing. It renders style often obscure, always embarrassed and inelegant."—*Blair's Rhet.* p. 106. "Every inversion which is not governed by this rule, will be disrelished by every one of taste."—*Kames, El. of Crit.* ii, 62. "A proper diphthong is that in which both the vowels are sounded."—*Murray's Gram.* p. 9; *Alger's*, 11; *Bacon's*, 8; *Merchant's*, 9; *Hiley's*, 3; and others. "An improper Diphthong is one in which only one of the two Vowels is sounded."—*Lennie's Gram.* p. 5. "Abraham, Isaac, Jacob, and his descendants, are called Hebrews."—*Wood's Dict.* "Every word in our language, of more than one syllable, has one of them distinguished from the rest in this manner."—*Murray's Gram.* p. 236. "Two consonants proper to begin a word must not be separated; as, fa-ble, sti-fle. But when they come between two vowels, and are such as cannot begin a word, they must be divided; as, ut-most, un-der."—*Ib.* p. 22. "Shall the intellect alone feel no pleasures in its energy, when we allow them to the grossest energies of appetite and sense?"—*Harris's Hermes*, p. 298; *Murray's Gram.* 289. "No man hath a propensity to vice as such: on the contrary, a wicked deed disgusts him, and makes him abhor the author."—*Kames, El. of Crit.* i, 66. "The same that belong to nouns, belong also to pronouns."—*Greenleaf's Gram.* p. 8. "What is Language? It is the means of communicating thoughts from one to another."—*O. B. Peirce's Gram.* p. 15. "A simple word is that which is not made up of more than one."—*Adam's Gram.* p. 4; *Gould's,* p. 4. "A compound word is that which is made up of two or more words."—*Ib.* "When a conjunction is to be supplied, it is called Asyndeton."—*Adam's Gram.* p. 235.

UNDER NOTE XI.—PLACE OF THE RELATIVE.

"It gives a meaning to words, which they would not have."—*Murray's Gram.* p. 244. "There are many words, in the English language, that are sometimes used as adjectives, and sometimes as adverbs."—*Ib.* p. 114. "Which do not more effectually show the varied intentions of the mind, than the auxiliaries do which are used to form the potential mood."—*Ib.* p. 67. "These accents make different impressions on the mind, which will be the subject of a following speculation."—*Kames, El. of Crit.* ii, 108. "And others very much differed from the writer's words, to whom they were ascribed."—*Pref. to Lily's Gram.* p. xii. "Where there is nothing in the sense which requires the last sound to be elevated, an easy fall will be proper."—*Murray's Gram.* i, p. 250; *Bullions's E. Gram.* 167. "Then is an ellipsis of the verb in the last clause, which, when you supply, you find it necessary to use the adverb not."—*Campbell's Rhet.* p. 176; *Murray's Gram.* 368. "*Study* is singular number, because its nominative *I* is, with which it agrees."—*Smith's New Gram.* p. 21. "John is the person, or, thou art who is in error."—*Wright's Gram.* p. 136. "For he hath made him to be sin for us, who knew no sin."—*2 Cor.* v, 21.

"Take that of me, my friend, who have the power
To seal the accuser's lips."—*Beauties of Shakspeare,* p. 268.

UNDER NOTE XII.—WHAT FOR THAT.

"I had no idea but what the story was true."—*Brown's Inst.* p. 144. "The post-boy is not so weary but what he can whistle."—*Ib.* "He had no intimation but what the men were honest."—*Ib.* "Neither Lady Haversham nor Miss Mildmay will ever believe, but what I have been entirely to blame." See *Priestley's Gram.* p. 93. "I am not satisfied, but what the integrity of our friends is more essential to our welfare than their knowledge of the world."—*Ibid.* "There is, indeed, nothing in poetry, so entertaining or descriptive, but what a didactic writer of genius may be allowed to introduce in some part of his work."—*Blair's Rhet.* p. 401. "Brasidas, being bit by a mouse he had catched, let it slip out of his fingers: 'No creature, (says he,) is so contemptible but what may provide for its own safety, if it have courage.'"—PLUTARCH : *Kames, El. of Crit.* Vol. i, p. 81.

UNDER NOTE XIII.—ADJECTIVES FOR ANTECEDENTS.

"In narration, Homer is, at all times, remarkably concise, which renders him lively and agreeable."—*Blair's Rhet.* p. 435. "It is usual to talk of a nervous, a feeble, or a spirited style; which are plainly the characters of a writer's manner of thinking."—*Ib.* p. 92. "It is too violent an alteration, if any alteration were necessary, which none is."—*Knight, on the Greek Alphabet,* p. 134. "Some men are too ignorant to be humble, without which there can be no docility."—*Berkley's Alciphron,* p. 385. "Judas declared him innocent; which he could not be, had he in any respect deceived the disciples."—*Porteus.* "They supposed him to be innocent, which he certainly was not."—*Murray's Gram.* i, p. 50; *Emmons's,* 25. "They accounted him honest, which he certainly was not."—*Felch's Comp. Gram.* p. 39. "Be accurate in all you say or do; for it is important in all the concerns of life."—*Brown's Inst.* p. 145. "Every law supposes the transgressor to be wicked; which indeed he is, if the law is just."—*Ib.* "To be pure in heart, pious, and benevolent, which all may be, constitutes human happiness."—*Murray's Gram.* p. 232. "To be dexterous in danger, is a virtue; but to court danger to show it, is weakness."—*Penn's Maxims.*

UNDER NOTE XIV.—SENTENCES FOR ANTECEDENTS.

"This seems not so allowable in prose; which the following erroneous examples will demonstrate."—*Murray's Gram.* p. 175. "The accent is laid upon the last syllable of a word; which is favourable to the melody."—*Kames, El. of Crit.* ii, 86. "Every line consists of ten syllables, five short and five long; from which there are but two exceptions, both of them rare."—*Ib.* ii, 89. "The soldiers refused obedience, which has been explained."—*Nixon's Parser,* p. 128. "Cæsar overcame Pompey, which was lamented."—*Ib.* "The crowd hailed William, which was expected."—*Ib.* "The tribunes resisted Scipio, which was anticipated."—*Ib.* "The censors reproved vice, which was admired."—*Ib.* "The generals neglected discipline, which has been proved."—*Ib.* "There would be two nominatives to the verb was, which is improper."—*Adam's Lat. Gram.* p. 205; *Gould's,* 202. "His friend bore the abuse very patiently; which served to increase his rudeness: it produced, at length, contempt and insolence."—*Murray's Gram.* i, p. 50; *Emmons's,* 25. "Almost all compounded sentences, are more or less elliptical; some examples of which may be seen under the different parts of speech."—*Murray's Gram.* p. 217; *Guy's,* 90; *R. C. Smith's,* 190; *Ingersoll's,* 153; *Fisk's,* 144; *J. M. Putnam's,* 137; *Weld's,* 190.

UNDER NOTE XV.—REPEAT THE PRONOUN.

"In things of Nature's workmanship, whether we regard their internal or external structure, beauty and design are equally conspicuous."—*Kames, El. of Crit.* i, 269. "It puzzles the reader, by making him doubt whether the word ought to be taken in its proper or figurative sense."—*Ib.* ii, 231. "Neither my obligations to the muses, nor expectations from them, are so great."—*Cowley's Preface.* "The Fifth Annual Report of the Anti-Slavery Society of Ferrisburgh and vicinity."—*Liberator,* ix, 69. "Meaning taste in its figurative as well as proper sense."—*Kames, El. of Crit.* ii, 360. "Every measure in which either your personal or political character is concerned."—*Junius, Let.* ix. "A jealous, righteous God has often punished such in themselves or offspring."—*Extracts,* p. 179. "Hence their civil and religious history are inseparable."—*Milman's Jews,* i, 7. "Esau thus carelessly threw away both his civil and religious inheritance."—*Ib.* i, 24. "This intelligence excited not only our hopes, but fears likewise."—*Jaudon's Gram.* p. 170. "In what manner our defect of principle and ruling manners have completed the ruin of the national spirit of union."—*Brown's Estimate,* i, 77. "Considering her descent, her connexion, and present intercourse."—*Webster's Essays,* p. 85. "His own and wife's wardrobe are packed up in a firkin."—*Parker and Fox's Gram.* Part i, p. 73.

UNDER NOTE XVI.—CHANGE THE ANTECEDENT.

"The sound of *e* and *o* long, in their due degrees, will be preserved, and clearly distinguished."—*Murray's Gram.* 8vo, p. 242. "If any person should be inclined to think," &c., "the author takes the liberty to suggest to them," &c.—*Ib.* Pref. p. iv. "And he walked in all the ways of Asa his father; he turned not aside from it."—*1 Kings,* xxii, 43. "If ye from your hearts forgive not every one his brother their trespasses."—*Matt.* xviii, 35. "Nobody ever fancied they were slighted by him, or had the courage to think themselves his betters."—*Collier's Antoninus,* p. 8. "And Rebekah took goodly raiment of her eldest son Esau, which were with her in the house, and put them upon Jacob her younger son."— *Gen.* xxvii, 15. "Where all the attention of man is given to their own indulgence."— *Maturin's Sermons,* p. 181. "The idea of a *father* is a notion superinduced to the substance, or man—let man be what it will."—*Locke's Essay,* i, 219. "Leaving every one to do as they list."—*Barclay's Works,* i, 460. "Each body performed his part handsomely."— *J. Flint's Gram.* p. 15. "This block of marble rests on two layers of stone, bound together with lead, which, however, has not prevented the Arabs from forcing out several of them."— *Parker and Fox's Gram.* Part i, p. 72.

"Love gives to every power a double power,
Above their functions and their offices."—*Shakspeare.*

RULE XI.—PRONOUNS.

When the antecedent is a collective noun conveying the idea of plurality, the Pronoun must agree with it in the plural number: as, "The *council* were divided in *their* sentiments."—"The Christian *world* are beginning to awake out of *their* slumber."—*C. Simeon.* "Whatever Adam's *posterity* lost through him, that and more *they* gain in Christ."—*J. Phipps.*

"To this, one pathway gently-winding leads,
Where march a *train* with baskets on *their* heads."—*Pope, Il.* B. xviii, l. 657.

OBSERVATIONS ON RULE XI.

OBS. 1.—The collective noun, or noun of multitude, being a name that signifies many, may in general be taken in either of two ways, according to the intention of the user: that is, either with reference to the *aggregate* as one thing, in which sense it will accord with the neuter pronoun *it* or *which;* or with reference to the *individuals,* so as to accord with a plural pronoun *they, their, them,* or *who,* masculine, or feminine, as the individuals of the assemblage may happen to be. The noun itself, being literally singular both in form and in fact, has not unfrequently some article or adjective before it that implies unity; so that the interpretation of it in a plural sense by the pronoun or verb, was perhaps not improperly regarded by the old grammarians as an example of the figure *syllepsis:* as, "Liberty should reach every individual of *a people,* as *they* all share one common nature."—*Spectator,* No. 287.

"Thus urg'd the chief; *a generous troop appears,*
Who spread *their* bucklers and advance *their* spears."—*Pope, Iliad,* B. xi, l. 720.

OBS. 2.—Many of our grammarians say, "When a noun of multitude is preceded by a definitive word, which clearly limits the sense to an aggregate with an idea of unity, it requires a verb and pronoun to agree with it in the singular number."—*Murray's Gram.* p. 153; *Ingersoll's,* 249; *Fisk's,* 122; *Fowler's,* 528. But this principle, I apprehend, cannot be sustained by an appeal to general usage. The instances in practice are not few, in which both these senses are clearly indicated with regard to the same noun; as, "*Each House* shall keep a journal of *its* proceedings, and from time to time publish the same, excepting such parts as may in *their* judgement require secrecy."—*Constitution of the United States,* Art. i, Sec. 5. "I mean *that part* of mankind *who are known* by the name of women's men, or beaux."—*Addison, Spect.* No. 536. "*A set* of men *who are* common enough in the world."—*Ibid.* "It is vain for a *people* to expect to be free, unless *they* are first willing to be virtuous."—*Wayland's Moral Science,* p. 397. "For *this people's* heart is waxed gross, and *their* ears are dull of hearing, and *their* eyes *they* have closed."—*Matt.* xiii, 15. *"This enemy* had now enlarged *their* confederacy, and made *themselves* more formidable than before."—*Life of Antoninus,* p. 62.

 " Thus from the tents the fervent *legion swarms,*
  So loud *their* clamour, and so keen *their* arms."—*Pope, Iliad,* B. xvi, l. 320.

 OBS. 3.—Most collective nouns of the neuter gender, may take the regular plural form, and be represented by a pronoun in the third person, plural, neuter; as, "The *nations* will enforce *their* laws." This construction comes under Rule 10th, as does also the singular, "The *nation* will enforce *its* laws;" for, in either case, the agreement is entirely literal. Half of Murray's Rule 4th is therefore needless. To Rule 11th above, there are properly no exceptions; because the number of the pronoun is itself the index to the sense in which the antecedent is therein taken. It does not follow however, but that there may be violations of the rule, or of the notes under it, by the adoption of one number when the other would be more correct, or in better taste. A collection of things inanimate, as a fleet, a heap, a tier, a bundle, is seldom, if ever, taken distributively, with a plural pronoun. For a further elucidation of the construction of collective nouns, see Rule 15th, and the observations under it.

NOTES TO RULE XI.

NOTE. I.—A collective noun conveying the idea of unity, requires a pronoun in the third person, singular, neuter; as, "When a legislative *body* makes laws, *it* acts for *itself* only; but when *it* makes grants or contracts, *it* acts as a party."—*Webster's Essays,* p. 40. "A civilized *people* has no right to violate *its* solemn obligations, because the other party is uncivilized."—*Wayland's Moral Science,* p. 314.

NOTE II.—When a collective noun is followed by two or more words which must each in some sense agree with it, uniformity of number is commonly preferable to diversity, and especially to such a mixture as puts the singular both before and after the plural; as, " *That* ingenious nation *who have done* so much honour to modern literature, *possesses,* in an eminent degree, the talent of narration."—*Blair's Rhet.* p. 364. Better: " *which has done.*"

IMPROPRIETIES FOR CORRECTION.

FALSE SYNTAX UNDER RULE XI.

UNDER THE RULE ITSELF.—THE IDEA OF PLURALITY.

"The jury will be confined till it agrees on a verdict."—*Brown's Inst.* p. 145.

[FORMULE.—Not proper, because the pronoun *it* is of the singular number, and does not correctly represent its antecedent *jury,* which is a collective noun conveying rather the idea of plurality. But, according to Rule 11th, "When the antecedent is a collective noun conveying the idea of plurality, the pronoun must agree with it in the plural number." Therefore, *it* should be *they;* thus, " The jury will be confined till *they* agree on a verdict."]

"And mankind directed its first cares towards the needful."—*Formey's Belles-Lettres,* p. 114. "It is difficult to deceive a free people respecting its true interest.—*Life of Charles XII,* p. 67. "All the virtues of mankind are to be counted upon a few fingers, but his follies and vices are innumerable."—*Swift.* "Every sect saith, ' Give me liberty :' but give it him, and to his power, he will not yield it to any body else."—*Oliver Cromwell.* " Behold, the people shall rise up as a great lion, and lift up himself as a young lion."—*Numbers,* xxiii, 24. "For all flesh had corrupted his way upon the earth."—*Gen.* vi, 12. "There happened to the army a very strange accident, which put it in great consternation."—*Goldsmith.*

UNDER NOTE I.—THE IDEA OF UNITY.

"The meeting went on in their business as a united body."—*Foster's Report,* i, 69. "Every religious association has an undoubted right to adopt a creed for themselves."—*Gould's Advocate,* iii, 405. "It would therefore be extremely difficult to raise an insurrection in that State against their own government."—*Webster's Essays,* p. 104. "The mode in which a Lyceum can apply themselves in effecting a reform in common schools."—*New York Lyceum.* "Hath a nation changed their gods, which are yet no gods ? "—*Jeremiah,* ii, 11. "In the holy scriptures each of the twelve tribes of Israel is often called by the name of the patriarch, from whom they descended."—*J. Q. Adams's Rhet.* ii, 331.

UNDER NOTE II.—UNIFORMITY OF NUMBER.

"A nation, by the reparation of their own wrongs, achieves a triumph more glorious than any field of blood can ever give."—*J. Q. Adams.* " The English nation, from which we descended, have been gaining their liberties inch by inch."—*Webster's Essays,* p. 46. " If a Yearly Meeting should undertake to alter its fundamental doctrines, is there any power in the society to prevent their doing so ? "—*Foster's Report,* i, 96. "There is a generation that curseth their father, and doth not bless their mother."—*Proverbs,* xxx, 11. " There is a generation that are pure in their own eyes, and yet is not washed from their filthiness —*Ib.* xxx, 12. " He hath not beheld iniquity in Jacob, neither hath he seen perverseness in Israel : the Lord his God is with him, and the shout of a king is among them."—*Numb* xxiii, 21. "My people hath forgotten me, they have burnt incense to vanity."—*Jer.* xviii, 15. "When a quarterly meeting hath come to a judgment respecting any difference, relative to any monthly meeting belonging to them," &c.—*Extracts,* p. 195 ; *N. E. Discip.* p. 118. "The number of such compositions is every day increasing, and appear to be limited only by the pleasure or conveniency of the writer."—*Booth's Introd. to Dict.* p. 37. "The church of Christ hath the same power now as ever, and are led by the same Spirit into the same practices."—*Barclay's Works,* i, 477. "The army, whom its chief had thus abandoned, pursued meanwhile their miserable march."—*Lockhart's Napoleon,* ii, 165.

RULE XII.—PRONOUNS.

When a Pronoun has two or more antecedents connected by *and*, it must agree with them jointly in the plural, because they are taken together : as, "*Minos* and *Thales* sung to the lyre the laws which *they* composed."—STRABO : *Blair's Rhet.* p. 379. "*Saul* and *Jonathan* were lovely and pleasant in *their* lives, and in *their* death *they* were not divided."—*2 Sam.* i, 23.

" *Rhesus* and *Rhodius* then unite *their* rills,
Caresus roaring down the stony hills."—*Pope, Il.* B. xii, l. 17.

EXCEPTION FIRST.

When two or more antecedents connected by *and* serve merely to describe one person or thing, they are either in apposition or equivalent to one name, and do not require a plural pronoun ; as, "This great *philosopher* and *statesman* continued in public life till *his* eighty-second year."—"The same *Spirit, light,* and *life, which enlighteneth,* also sanctifieth, and there is not an other."—*Penington.* "My *Constantius* and *Philetus* confesseth me two years older when I writ *it.*"—*Cowley's Preface.* "Remember these, O *Jacob* and *Israel!* for *thou* art my servant."—*Isaiah,* xliv. 21. "In that *strength* and *cogency which renders* eloquence powerful."—*Blair's Rhet.* p. 252.

EXCEPTION SECOND.

When two antecedents connected by *and* are emphatically distinguished, they belong to different propositions, and, if singular, do not require a plural pronoun ; as, "The *butler,* and *not the baker,* was restored to *his* office."—"The *good man,* and the *sinner too,* shall have *his* reward."—"*Truth,* and *truth only,* is worth seeking for *its* own sake."—"It is *the sense* in which the word is used, and *not the letters* of which it is composed, *that determines* what is the part of speech to which it belongs."—*Cobbett's Gram.* ¶ 130.

EXCEPTION THIRD.

When two or more antecedents connected by *and* are preceded by the adjective *each, every,* or *no,* they are taken separately, and do not require a plural pronoun ; as "*Every plant* and *every tree* produces others after *its* own kind."—"It is the cause of *every reproach* and *distress* which *has attended* your government."—*Junius, Let.* xxxv. But if the latter be a collective noun, the pronoun may be plural ; as, "*Each minister* and *each church* act according to *their* own impressions."—*Dr. M'Cartee.*

OBSERVATIONS ON RULE XII.

OBS. 1.—When the antecedents are of *different persons,* the first person is preferred to the second, and the second to the third ; as, *John,* and *thou,* and *I,* are attached to *our* country."—"*John* and *thou* are attached to *your* country."—"The Lord open some light, and show both *you* and *me our* inheritance !"—*Baxter.* "*Thou* and thy *sons* with thee *shall bear* the iniquity of *your* priesthood."—*Numbers,* xviii, 1.

" For all are friends in heaven ; all faithful friends ;
And many friendships in the days of Time
Begun, are lasting here, and growing still :
So grows *ours* evermore, both *theirs and mine.*"—*Pollok, C. of T.,* B. v, l. 335.

OBS. 2.—The *gender* of pronouns, except in the third person singular, is distinguished only by their antecedents. In expressing that of a pronoun which has antecedents of *different* genders, the masculine should be preferred to the feminine, and the feminine to the neuter. The parser of English should remember, that this is a principle of General Grammar.

OBS. 3.—When two words are taken separately as nominatives, they ought not to be united in the same sentence as antecedents. In the following example, therefore, *them* should be *it :* "The first has a lenis, and the other an asper over *them.*"—*Printer's Gram.* p. 246. Better thus : "The first has a lenis *over it,* and the other, an asper."

OBS. 4.—Nouns that stand as nominatives or antecedents, are sometimes taken conjointly when there is no conjunction expressed ; as, "The historian, the orator, the philosopher, *address themselves* primarily to the understanding : *their* direct aim is, to inform, to persuade, to instruct."—*Blair's Rhet.* p. 377. The copulative *and* may here be said to be understood, because the verb and the pronouns are plural ; but it seems better *in general,* either to introduce the connective word, or to take the nouns disjunctively : as, "They have all the copiousness, the fervour, the inculcating method, that *is* allowable and graceful in an orator ; perhaps too much of *it* for a writer."—*Blair's Rhet.* p. 343. To this, however, there may be exceptions,—cases in which the plural form is to be preferred,—especially in poetry; as,

"Faith, justice, heaven itself, now *quit their* hold,
When to false fame the captive heart is sold."—*Brown, on Satire.*

Obs. 5.—When two or more antecedents connected by *and* are nominally alike, one or more of them may be *understood*; and, in such a case, the pronoun must still be plural, as agreeing with all the nouns, whether expressed or implied: as, "But intellectual and moral culture ought to go hand in hand; *they* will greatly help each other."—*Dr. Weeks.* Here *they* stands for *intellectual culture* and *moral culture.* The following example is incorrect: "The Commanding or Unlimited *mode,* may be used in an absolute sense, or without a name or substitute on which it can depend."—*O. B. Pierce's Gram.* p. 80. Change *it* to *they,* or *and* to *or.* See Note 6th to Rule 16th.

IMPROPRIETIES FOR CORRECTION.

FALSE SYNTAX UNDER RULE XII.

PRONOUNS WITH ANTECEDENTS CONNECTED BY AND.

"Discontent and sorrow manifested itself in his countenance."—*Brown's Inst.* p. 146.

[FORMULE.—Not proper, because the pronoun *itself* is of the singular number, and does not correctly represent its two antecedents *discontent* and *sorrow,* which are connected by *and,* and taken conjointly. But, according to Rule 12th, "When a pronoun has two or more antecedents connected by *and,* it must agree with them jointly in the plural, because they are taken together." Therefore, *itself* should be *themselves*; thus, "Discontent and sorrow manifested *themselves* in his countenance."]

"Both conversation and public speaking became more simple and plain, such as we now find it."—*Blair's Rhet.* p. 59. "Idleness and ignorance, if it be suffered to proceed, &c."—JOHNSON: *Priestley's Gram.* p. 186. "Avoid questions and strife; it shows a busy and contentious disposition."—*Wm. Penn.* "To receive the gifts and benefits of God with thanksgiving, and witness it blessed and sanctified to us by the word and prayer, is owned by us."—*Barclay's Works,* i, 213. "Both minister and magistrate are compelled to chose between his duty and his reputation."—*Junius,* p. 9. "All the sincerity, truth, and faithfulness, or disposition of heart or conscience to approve it, found among rational creatures, necessarily originate from God."—*Brown's Divinity,* p. 12. "Your levity and heedlessness, if it continue, will prevent all substantial improvement."—*Brown's Inst.* p. 147. "Poverty and obscurity will oppress him only who esteems it oppressive."—*Ib.* "Good sense and refined policy are obvious to few, because it cannot be discovered but by a train of reflection."—*Ib.* "Avoid haughtiness of behaviour, and affectation of manners: it implies a want of solid merit."—*Ib.* "If love and unity continue, it will make you partakers of one an other's joy."—*Ib.* "Suffer not jealousy and distrust to enter: it will destroy, like a canker, every germ of friendship."—*Ib.* "Hatred and animosity are inconsistent with Christian charity: guard, therefore, against the slightest indulgence of it."—*Ib.* "Every man is entitled to liberty of conscience, and freedom of opinion, if he does not pervert it to the injury of others."—*Ib.*

"With the azure and vermilion
Which is mix'd for my pavilion."—*Byron's Manfred,* p. 9.

RULE XIII. — PRONOUNS.

When a Pronoun has two or more antecedents connected by *or* or *nor,* it must agree with them singly, and not as if taken together: as, "*James or John* will favour us with *his* company."—"Neither *wealth* nor *honour* can secure the happiness of *its* votaries."

"What *virtue* or what mental *grace,*
But men unqualified and base
        Will boast *it* their possession?"—*Cowper, on Friendship.*

OBSERVATIONS ON RULE XIII.

Obs. 1.—When two or more *singular* antecedents are connected by *or* or *nor,* the pronoun which represents them, ought in general to be singular, because *or* and *nor* are disjunctives; and, to form a complete concord, the nouns ought also to be of the same person and gender, that the pronoun may agree in all respects with each of them. But when *plural* nouns are connected in this manner, the pronoun will of course be plural, though it still agrees with the antecedents singly; as, "Neither *riches* nor *honours* ever satisfy *their* pursuers." Sometimes, when different numbers occur together, we find the plural noun put last, and the pronoun made plural after both, especially if this noun is a mere substitute for the other; as,

"What's *justice* to a man, or *laws,*
That never comes within *their* claws?"—*Hudibras.*

Obs. 2.—When antecedents of different persons, numbers, or genders, are connected by *or* or *nor,* they cannot very properly be represented by any pronoun that is not applicable to each of them. The following sentences are therefore inaccurate; or at least they contradict the teachings of their own authors: "Either *thou or I* am greatly mistaken, in *our judgment* on this subject."—*Murray's Key*, p. 184. "Your character, which *I, or any other writer*, may now value *ourselves* by (upon) drawing."—SWIFT: *Lowth's Gram.* p. 96. "Either *you or I* will be in *our* place in due time."—*Cooper's Gram.* p. 127. But different pronouns may be so connected as to refer to such antecedents taken separately; as, "By requiring greater labour from such *slave or slaves*, than *he or she or they* are able to perform."—*Prince's Digest.* Or, if the gender only be different, the masculine may involve the feminine by implication; as, "If a man smite the eye of his *servant*, or the eye of his *maid*, that it perish, he shall let *him* go free for *his* eye's sake."—*Exodus*, xxi, 26.

OBS. 3.—It is however very common to resort to the plural number in such instances as the foregoing, because our plural pronouns are alike in all the genders; as, "When either *man or woman* shall separate *themselves* to vow a vow of a Nazarite."—*Numbers*, vi, 2. "Then shalt thou bring forth *that man or that woman* unto thy gates, and shalt stone *them* with stones, till *they* die."—*Deut.* xvii, 5. "Not on outward charms could *he or she* build *their* pretensions to please."—*Opie, on Lying*, p. 148. "Complimenting either *man or woman* on agreeable qualities which *they* do not possess, in hopes of imposing on *their* credulity."—*Ib.* p. 108. "*Avidien*, or his *wife*, (no matter which,) *sell their* presented partridges and fruits."—*Pope*, Sat. ii, l. 50. "Beginning with Latin or Greek hexameter, *which are* the same."—*Kames, El. of Crit.* i, 79.

"Did ever *Proteus, Merlin*, any *witch*,
Transform *themselves* so strangely as the rich?"—*Pope*, Ep. i, l. 152.

OBS. 4.—From the observations and examples above, it may be perceived, that whenever there is a difference of person, number, or gender, in antecedents connected disjunctively, there is an inherent difficulty respecting the form of the pronoun personal. The best mode of meeting this inconvenience, or of avoiding it by a change of the phraseology, may be different on different occasions. The disjunctive connexion of explicit pronouns is the most correct, but it savours too much of legal precision and wordiness to be always eligible. Commonly an ingenious mind may invent some better expression, and yet avoid any syntactical anomaly. In Latin, when nouns are connected by the conjunctions which correspond to *or* or *nor*, the pronoun or verb is so often made plural, that no such principle as that of the foregoing Rule, or of Rule 17th, is taught by the common grammars of that language. How such usage can be logically right however, it is difficult to imagine. Lowth, Murray, Webster, and most other English grammarians, teach, that, "The conjunction disjunctive has an effect contrary to that of the copulative; and, as the verb, noun, or pronoun, is referred to the preceding terms taken separately, it must be in the singular number."—*Lowth's Gram.* p. 75; *L. Murray's*, 151; *Churchill's*, 142; *W. Allen's*, 133; *Lennie's*, 83; *and many others.* If there is any allowable exception to this principle, it is for the adoption of the plural when the concord cannot be made by any one pronoun singular; as, "If I value my friend's *wife or son* upon account of *their* connexion with him."—*Kames, El. of Crit.* i, 73. "Do not drink wine nor strong drink, *thou nor thy sons* with thee, when *ye* go into the tabernacle of the congregation."—*Levit.* x, 8. These examples, though they do not accord with the preceding rule, seem not to be susceptible of any change for the better. There are also some other modes of expression, in which nouns that are connected disjunctively, may afterwards be represented together; as, "*Foppery* is a sort of folly much more contagious THAN *pedantry*; but as *they* result alike from affectation, *they* deserve alike to be proscribed."—*Campbell's Rhet.* p. 217.

IMPROPRIETIES FOR CORRECTION.

FALSE SYNTAX UNDER RULE XIII.

PRONOUNS WITH ANTECEDENTS CONNECTED BY OR OR NOR.

"Neither prelate nor priest can give their flocks any decisive evidence that you are lawful pastors."—*Dr. Brownlee.*

[FORMULE.—Not proper, because the pronoun *their* is of the plural number, and does not correctly represent its two antecedents *prelate* and *priest*, which are connected by *nor*, and taken disjunctively. But, according to Rule 13th, "When a pronoun has two or more antecedents connected by *or* or *nor*, it must agree with them singly, and not as if taken together." Therefore, *their* should be *his*; thus, "Neither prelate nor priest can give *his* flocks any decisive evidence that you are lawful pastors"]

"And is there a heart of parent or of child, that does not beat and burn within them?"—*Maturin's Sermons*, p. 367. "This is just as if an eye or a foot should demand a salary for their service to the body."—*Collier's Antoninus*, p. 178. "If thy hand or thy foot offend thee, cut them off, and cast them from thee."—*Matt.* xviii, 8. "The same might as well be said of Virgil, or any great author, whose general character will infallibly raise many casual additions to their reputation."—*Pope's Pref. to Homer.* "Either James or John, one of them, will come."—*Smith's New Gram.* p. 37. "Even a rugged rock or barren heath, though in themselves disagreeable, contribute by contrast to the beauty of the whole."—*Kames, El. of Crit.* i, 185. "That neither Count Rechteren nor Monsieur Mesnager had behaved themselves right in this affair."—*Spect.* No. 481. "If an Aristotle, a Pythagoras, or a Galileo, suffer for their opinions, they are 'martyrs.'"—*Gospel its own Witness*, p. 80. "If an ox gore a man or a woman, that they die; then the ox shall be surely stoned."—*Exodus*, xxi, 28. "She was calling out to one or an other, at every step, that a Habit was ensnaring them."—DR. JOHNSON: *Murray's Sequel*, 181. "Here is a Task put upon Children, that neither this Author, nor any other have yet undergone themselves."—*Johnson's Gram. Com.* p. 162. "Hence, if an adjective or participle be subjoined to the verb, when of the singular number, they will agree both in gender and number with the collective noun."—*Adam's Lat. Gram.* p. 154; *Gould's,* 158. "And if you can find a diphthong, or a triphthong, be pleased to point them out too."—*Buck's Classical Gram.* p. 16. "And if you can find a diphthong, or a triphthong, a trissyllable, or a polysyllable, point them respectively out."—*Ib.* p. 25. "The false refuges in which the atheist or the sceptic have intrenched themselves."—*Christian Spect.* viii, 185. "While the man or woman thus assisted by art expects their charms will be imputed to nature alone."—*Opie,* 141. "When you press a watch, or pull a clock, they answer your question with precision; for they repeat exactly the hour of the day, and tell you neither more nor less than you desire to know."—*Bolingbroke, on History,* p. 102.

" Not the Mogul, or Czar of Muscovy,
 Not Prester John, or Cham of Tartary,
 Are in their houses Monarch more than I."—KING: *Brit. Poets,* Vol. iii, p. 611.

CHAPTER VI.—VERBS.

In this work, the syntax of Verbs is embraced in six consecutive rules, with the necessary exceptions, notes, and observations, under them; hence this chapter extends from the fourteenth to the twentieth rule in the series.

RULE XIV.—FINITE VERBS.

Every finite Verb must agree with its subject, or nominative, in person and number: as, "I *know;* thou *knowest,* or *knowest; he *knows,* or *knoweth.*"— " The bird *flies;* the birds *fly.*"

" Our fathers' fertile *fields* by slaves *are till'd,*
 And *Rome* with dregs of foreign lands *is fill'd.*"
                                —*Rowe's Lucan,* B. vii, l. 600.

OBSERVATIONS ON RULE XIV.

OBS. 1.—To this general rule for the verb, there are properly *no exceptions;* * and all the special rules that follow, which prescribe the concord of verbs in particular instances, virtually accord with it. Every *finite verb,* (that is, every verb *not in the infinitive* mood,) must have some noun, pronoun, or phrase equivalent, known as the *subject* of the being, action, or passion; † and with this subject, whether expressed or understood, the verb must agree in person and number. The infinitive mood, as it does not unite with a nominative to form an assertion, is of course exempt

* In their speculations on the *personal pronouns,* grammarians sometimes contrive, by a sort of abstraction, to reduce all the persons to the *third;* that is, the author or speaker puts *I,* not for himself in particular, but for any one who utters the word, and *thou,* not for his particular hearer or reader, but for any one who is addressed; and, conceiving of these as persons merely spoken of by himself, he puts the verb in the third person, and not in the first or second: as, "*I* is the speaker, *thou* [is] the hearer, and *he, she,* or *it,* is the person or thing spoken of. All denote *qualities of existence,* but such qualities as make different impressions on the mind. *I* is the being of *consciousness, thou* [is the being] of *perception,* and *he* of *memory.*"—*Booth's Introd.* p. 44. This is such syntax as I should not choose to imitate; nor is it very proper to say, that the three persons in grammar " denote *qualities of existence.*" But, supposing the phraseology to be correct, it is no *real* exception to the foregoing rule of concord; for *I* and *thou* are here made to be pronouns of the *third* person. So in the following example, which I take to be bad English: " I, or the person who speaks, *is* the first person; you, *is* the second; he, she, or it, is the third person singular."—*Bartlett's Manual,* Part ii, p. 70. Again, in the following; which is perhaps a little better: " The person '*I' is spoken of* as acted upon."—*Bullions, Prin. of E. Gram.,* 3d Edition, p. 29. But there is a manifest absurdity in saying, with this learned " Professor of Languages," that the pronouns of the different persons are those persons: as, "*I is the first person,* and denotes the speaker. *Thou is the second,* and denotes the person spoken to."—*Ib.* p. 22.

† (1.) Concerning the verb *need,* Dr. Webster has the following note: " In the use of this verb there is another irregularity, which is peculiar, the verb being *without a nominative,* expressed or implied. ' Whereof here *needs* no account.'—*Milt. P. L.* 4. 235. There is no evidence of the fact, and there *needs* none. This is an established use of *need.*"—*Philos. Gram.* p. 178; *Improved Gram.* 127; *Greenleaf's Gram. Simp.* p. 38; *Fowler's E. Gram.* p. 537. " Established use?" To be sure, it is " an established use;" but the learned Doctor's comment is a most unconscionable blunder,—a pedantic violation of a sure principle of Universal Grammar,—a perversion worthy only of the veriest ignoramus. Yet Greenleaf profitably publishes it, with other plagiarisms, for " Grammar Simplified!" Now the verb " *needs,*" like the Latin *eget,* signifying *is necessary,* is here not active, but neuter; and has the nominative set *after it,* as any verb must, when the adverb *there* or *here* is before it. The verbs *need* and *want* may have the same construction, and can have no other, when the word *there,* and not a nominative, precedes them; as, " Peradventure *there shall lack few* of the fifty righteous."—*Gen.* xviii, 28. There is therefore neither " *irregularity,*" nor any thing " *peculiar,*" in thus placing the verb and its nominative.

(2.) Yet have we other grammarians, who, with astonishing facility, have allowed themselves to be misled, and whose books are now misleading the schools, in regard to this very simple matter. Thus Wells: " The *transitive* verbs *need* and *want,* are sometimes employed in a general sense, *without a nominative,* expressed or implied. *Examples:*—' There *needed* a new dispensation.'—*Caleb Cushing.* ' There *needs* no better picture.'—*Irving.* ' There *wanted* not patrons to stand up.'—*Sparks.* ' Nor did there *want* Cornice, or frieze.'—*Milton.*"—*Wells's School Gram.* 1st Ed. p. 141; 118th Ed. p. 154. In my edition of Milton, the text is, " Nor did *they want* Cornice or frieze."—*P. L.,* B. i, l. 715, 716. This reading makes *want* a " transitive" verb, but the other makes it neuter, with the nominative following it. Again, thus Weld: " *A verb in the imperative mode,* and the *transitive* verbs *need, want,* and *require,* sometimes appear to be used indefinitely, *without a nominative;* as, *let there be* from any such agreement. These may be considered principles of Universal Grammar. The Greeks, however, had a strange custom of using a plural noun of the neuter gender, with a verb of the third person singular; and, in both Greek and Latin, the infinitive mood with an accusative before it was often equivalent to a finite verb with its nominative. In English, we have *neither of these usages*; and plural nouns, even when they denote no absolute plurality, (as *shears, scissors, trowsers, pantaloons, tongs*,) require plural verbs or pronouns: as, "Your *shears come* too late, to clip the bird's wings."—SIDNEY: *Churchill's Gram.* p. 30.

OBS. 2.—When a book that bears a plural title, is spoken of as one thing, there is sometimes presented an *apparent exception* to the foregoing rule; as, "The *Pleasures* of Memory *was published* in the year 1792, and became at once popular."—*Allan Cunningham.* "The '*Sentiments* of a Church-of-England Man' *is written* with great coolness, moderation, ease, and perspicuity."—*Johnson's Life of Swift.* "The '*Pleasures* of Hope' *is* a splendid poem; *it* was written for perpetuity."—*Samuel L. Knapp.* In these instances, there is, I apprehend, an improper ellipsis of the common noun, with which each sentence ought to commence; as, "The *poem* entitled,"—"The *work* entitled," &c. But the plural title sometimes controls the form of the verb; as, "My *Lives* are reprinting."—*Dr. Johnson.*

OBS. 3.—In the figurative use of the present tense for the past or imperfect, the vulgar have a habit of putting the third person singular with the pronoun *I*; as, "*Thinks I* to myself."—*Rev. J. Marriott.* "O, *says I*, Jacky, are you at that work?"—*Day's Sandford and Merton.* "Huzza! huzza! Sir Condy Rackrent forever, was the first thing *I hears* in the morning."—*Edgeworth's Castle Rackrent*, p. 97. This vulgarism is to be avoided, not by a simple omission of the terminational *s*, but rather by the use of the literal preterit: as, "*Thought* I to myself;"—"O, *said* I;"—"The first thing I *heard*." The same mode of correction is also proper, when, under like circumstances, there occurs a disagreement in number; as, "After the election was over, there *comes shoals* of people from all parts."—*Castle Rackrent*, p. 103. "Didn't ye hear it? *says they* that were looking on."—*Ib.* p. 147. Write, "there *came*,"—"*said they*."

OBS. 4.—It has already been noticed, that the article *a*, or a singular adjective, sometimes precedes an arithmetical number with a plural noun; as, "*A thousand years* in thy sight *are* but as yesterday."—*Psalms*, xc, 4. So we might say, "*One* thousand years *are*,"—"*Each* thousand years *are*,"—"*Every* thousand years *are*," &c. But it would not be proper to say, "*A* thousand years *is*," or, "*Every* thousand years *is*;" because the noun *years* is plainly plural, and the anomaly of putting a singular verb after it, is both needless and unauthorized. Yet, to this general rule for the verb, the author of a certain "English Grammar *on the Productive System*," (a strange perversion of Murray's compilation, and a mere catch-penny work, now extensively used in New England,) is endeavouring to establish, by his own bare word, the following exception: "*Every* is sometimes associated with a plural noun, in which case the verb must be singular; as, "*Every* hundred years *constitutes* a century."—*Smith's New Gram.* p. 103. His *reason* is this; that the phrase containing the nominative, "*signifies a single period of time*, and is, therefore, *in reality* singular."—*Ib.* Cutler also, a more recent writer, seems to have imbibed the same notion; for he gives the following sentence as an example of "false construction: Every hundred years *are* called a century."—*Cutler's Grammar and Parser*, p. 145. But, according to this argument, no plural verb could ever be used with any *definite number* of the parts of time; for any three years, forty years, or threescore years and ten, are as single a period of time, as "every hundred years," "every four years," or "every twenty-four hours." Nor is it true, that, "*Every* is sometimes associated with a plural noun;" for "*every years*," or "*every hours*," would be worse than nonsense. I, therefore, acknowledge no such exception; but, discarding the principle of the note, put this author's pretended *corrections* among my quotations of *false syntax*.

OBS. 5.—Different verbs always have different subjects, expressed or understood; except when two or more verbs are connected in the same construction, or when the same word is repeated for the sake of emphasis. But let not the reader believe the common doctrine of our grammarians, respecting either the ellipsis of nominatives or the ellipsis of verbs. In the text, "The man was old and crafty," Murray sees no connexion of the ideas of age and craftiness, but thinks the text a *compound sentence*, containing two nominatives and two verbs; i. e. "The man was old, and

light; There *required* haste in the business; There *needs* no argument for proving, &c. There *wanted* not men who would, &c. The last expressions have an *active form with a passive sense*, and should perhaps rather be considered *elliptical* than *wanting a nominative*; as, "*haste is required, no argument is needed*, &c."—Weld's English Grammar Illustrated, p. 143. Is there anywhere, in print, viler pedantry than this? The only elliptical example, "*Let* there be light," — a kind of sentence from which the nominative is *usually suppressed*, — is here absurdly represented as *being full*, yet without a subject for its verb; while other examples, which are full, and in which the nominative *must follow* the verb, because the adverb "*there*" precedes, are first denied to have nominatives, and then most bunglingly tortured with false ellipses, to prove that they have them!

(3.) The idea of a command *wherein no person or thing is commanded*, seems to have originated with Webster, by whom it has been taught, since 1807, as follows: "In some cases, the imperative verb is used without a definite nominative."—*Philos. Gram.*, p. 141; *Impr. Gram.* 96; *Rudiments*, 60. See the same words in *Frazee's Gram.* p. 132. Wells has something similar: "A verb in the imperative is sometimes used *absolutely*, having no direct reference to any particular subject expressed or implied; as, 'And God said, *Let* there be light.'"—*School Gram.* p. 141. But, when this command was uttered to the dark waves of primeval chaos, it must have meant, "*Do ye let light be there*." What else could it mean? There may frequently be difficulty in determining what or who is addressed by the imperative *let*, but there seems to be more in affirming that it has no subject. Nutting, puzzled with this word, makes the following dubious and unsatisfactory suggestion: "Perhaps it may be, in many cases, equivalent to *may*; or it may be termed itself an *imperative mode impersonal*; that is, containing a command or an entreaty addressed to no particular person."—*Nutting's Practical Gram.* p. 47.

(4.) These several errors, about the "Imperative used Absolutely," with "no subject addressed," as in "*Let there be light*," and the Indicative "verbs NEED and WANT, employed without a nominative, either expressed or implied," are again carefully reiterated by the learned Professor Fowler, in his great text-book of philology "in its *Elements* and *Forms*,"—called, rather extravagantly, an "English Grammar." See, in his edition of 1850, § 507, Note 3 and Note 7; also § 520, Note 2. Wells's authorities for "Imperatives Absolute," are, "Frazee, Allen and Cornwell, Nutting, Lynde, and Chapin;" and, with reference to "NEED and WANT," he says, "See Webster, Perley, and Ingersoll."—*School Gram.*, 1850, § 209.

the man was crafty." * And all his other instances of "the ellipsis of the verb," are equally fanciful! See his *Octavo Gram.* p. 219; *Duodecimo*, 175. In the text, "God loves, protects, supports, and rewards the righteous," there are four verbs in *the same construction*, agreeing with the same nominative, and governing the same object; but Buchanan and others expound it, "God loves, and God protects, and God supports, and God rewards the righteous."—*English Syntax*, p. 76; *British Gram.* 192. This also is fanciful and inconsistent. If the nominative is here "*elegantly understood* to each verb," so is the objective, which they do not repeat. "And again," they immediately add, "the *verb* is often understood to its noun or nouns; as, He dreams of gibbets, halters, racks, daggers, &c. i. e. He dreams of gibbets, and he dreams of halters, &c."—*Same works and places*. In none of these examples is there any occasion to suppose an ellipsis, if we admit that two or more words *can* be connected in the same construction!

OBS. 6.—Verbs in the imperative mood commonly agree with the pronoun *thou, ye*, or *you*, understood after them; as, "*Heal* [ye] the sick, *cleanse* [ye] the lepers, *raise* [ye] the dead, *cast* [ye] out devils."—*Matt.* x, 8. "*Trust* God and *be* doing, and *leave* the rest with him."—*Dr. Sibs.* When the doer of a thing must first proceed to the place of action, we sometimes use *go* or *come* before an other verb, without any conjunction between the two; as, "Son, *go work* today in my vineyard."—*Matt.* xxi, 28. "*Come see* a man who [has] told me all things that ever I did."—*John*, iv, 29. "He ordered his soldiers to *go murder* every child about Bethlehem, or near it."—*Wood's Dict. of Bible, w. Herod.* "Take a present in thine hand, and *go meet* the man of God."—*2 Kings*, viii, 8. "I will *go see* if he be at home."—*Walker's Particles*, p. 169.

OBS. 7.—The *place* of the verb has reference mainly to that of the subject with which it agrees, and that of the object which it governs; and as the arrangement of these, with the instances in which they come before or after the verb, has already been noticed, the position of the latter seems to require no further explanation. See Obs. 2d under Rule 2d, and Obs. 2d under Rule 5th.

OBS. 8.—The infinitive mood, a phrase, or a sentence, (and, according to some authors, the participle in *ing*, or a phrase beginning with this participle,) is sometimes the proper subject of a verb, being equivalent to a nominative of the third person singular; as, "To play *is* pleasant."—*Lowth's Gram.* p. 80. "To write well, *is* difficult; to speak eloquently, *is* still more difficult."—*Blair's Rhet.* p. 81. "To take men off from prayer, *tends* to irreligiousness, *is* granted."—*Barclay's Works*, i, 214. "To educate a child perfectly, *requires* profounder thought, greater wisdom, than to govern a state."—*Channing's Self-Culture*, p. 30. "To determine these points, *belongs* to good sense."—*Blair's Rhet.* p. 321. "How far the change would contribute to his welfare, *comes* to be considered."—*Id. Sermons.* "That too much care does hurt in any of our tasks, *is* a doctrine so flattering to indolence, that we ought to receive it with extreme caution."—*Life of Schiller*, p. 148. "That there is no disputing about taste, *is* a saying so generally received *as* to have become a proverb."—*Kames, El. of Crit.* ii, 360. "For what purpose they embarked, *is* not yet known."—"To live in sin and yet to believe the forgiveness of sin, *is* utterly impossible."—*Dr. J. Owen.*

> "There shallow draughts intoxicate the brain,
> But drinking largely *sobers* us again."—*Pope.*

OBS. 9.—The same meaning will be expressed, if the pronoun *it* be placed before the verb, and the infinitive, phrase, or sentence, after it; as, "*It* is pleasant *to play*."—"*It* is difficult *to write well* ;" &c. The construction of the following sentences is rendered defective by the omission of this pronoun: "Why do ye that which [*it*] is not lawful to do on the sabbath days?"—*Luke*, vi, 2. "The show-bread, which [*it*] is not lawful to eat, but for the priests only."—*Ib.* vi, 4. "We have done that which [*it*] was our duty to do."—*Ib.* xvii, 10. Here the relative *which* ought to be in the objective case, governed by the infinitives; but the omission of the word *it* makes this relative the nominative to *is* or *was*, and leaves *to do* and *to eat* without any regimen. This is not ellipsis, but error. It is an accidental gap into which a side piece falls, and leaves a breach elsewhere. The following is somewhat like it, though what falls in, appears to leave no chasm: "From this deduction, [*it*] *may be easily seen* how it comes to pass, that personification makes so great a figure."—*Blair's Rhet.* p. 155. "Whether the author had any meaning in this expression, or what it was, [*it*] *is not easy* to determine."—*Murray's Gram.* i, p. 296. "That warm climates should accelerate the growth of the human body, and shorten its duration, [*it*] *is very reasonable* to believe."—*Ib.* p. 144. These also need the pronoun, though Murray thought them complete without it.

OBS. 10.—When the infinitive mood is made the subject of a finite verb, it is most commonly used to express action or state in the abstract; as, "*To be* contents his natural desire."—*Pope.* Here *to be* stands for simple *existence* ; or if for the existence *of the Indian*, of whom the author speaks, that relation is merely implied. "*To define* ridicule, has puzzled and vexed every critic."—*Kames, El. of Crit.* i. 300. Here "*to define*" expresses an action quite as distinct from any agent, as would the participial noun; as, "The *defining* of ridicule," &c. In connexion with the infinitive, a concrete quality may also be taken as an abstract; as, "*To be good is to be happy.*" Here *good* and *happy* express the quality of *goodness* and the state of *happiness* considered abstractly; and therefore these adjectives do not relate to any particular noun. So also the passive infinitive, or a perfect participle taken in a passive sense; as, "*To be satisfied with a little*, is the greatest wisdom."—"*To appear discouraged*, is the way to become so." Here the *satisfaction* and the *discouragement* are considered abstractly, and without reference to any particular person. (See Obs. 12th and 13th on Rule 6th.) So too, apparently, the participles *doing* and *suffering*, as well as the adjective *weak*, in the following example:

> "Fallen Cherub, to be *weak* is miserable,
> *Doing* or *suffering*."—*Milton's Paradise Lost.*

---

* This interpretation, and others like it, are given not only by *Murray*, but by many other grammarians, one of whom at least was earlier than he. See *Bicknell's Gram.* Vol. 1, p. 123; *Ingersoll's*, 153; *Guy's*, 91; *Alger's*, 73; *Merchant's*, 100; *Picket's*, 211; *Fisk's*, 146; *D. Adams's*, 81; *R. C. Smith's*, 182.

Obs. 11.—When the action or state is to be expressly limited to one class of beings, or to a particular person or thing, without making the verb finite; the noun or pronoun may be introduced before the infinitive by the preposition *for*: as, "*For men to search* their own glory, is not glory."—*Prov.* xxv, 27. "*For a prince to be reduced* by villany to my distressful circumstances, is calamity enough."—*Translation of Sallust.* "*For holy persons to be humble*, is as hard, as *for a prince to submit* himself to be guided by tutors."—TAYLOR: *Priestley's Gram.* p. 132; *Murray's*, 184. But such a limitation is sometimes implied, when the expression itself is general; as, "*Not to know me*, argues thyself unknown."—*Milton.* That is, "*For thee* not to know me." The phrase is put for, "*Thy ignorance of me;*" for an other's ignorance would be no argument in regard to the individual addressed. "*I, to bear this*, that never knew but better, *is* some burden."—*Beauties of Shak.* p. 327. Here the infinitive *to bear*, which is the subject of the verb *is*, is limited in sense by the pronoun *I*, which is put absolute in the nominative, though perhaps *improperly*; because, "*For me to bear this*," &c., will convey the same meaning, in a form much more common, and perhaps more grammatical. In the following couplet, there is an ellipsis of the infinitive; for the phrase, "fool with fool," means, "*for* fool *to contend* with fool," or, "for one fool to contend with an other:"

"Blockheads with reason wicked wits abhor,
But *fool with fool* is barb'rous civil war."—*Pope, Dunciad*, B. iii, l. 175.

Obs. 12.—The objective noun or pronoun thus introduced by *for* before the infinitive, was erroneously called by Priestley, *the subject of the affirmation;*" (Gram. p. 132;) and Murray, Ingersoll, and others, have blindly copied the blunder. See *Murray's Gram.* p. 184; *Ingersoll's*, 244. Again, Ingersoll says, "The infinitive mood, or part of a sentence, is sometimes the subject of a verb, *and is, therefore, its* NOMINATIVE."—*Conversations on English Gram.* p. 246. To this erroneous deduction, the phraseology used by Murray and others too plainly gives countenance: "The infinitive mood, or part of a sentence, is sometimes put *as the nominative case* to the verb."—*Murray's Gram.* p. 144; *Fisk's*, 123; *Kirkham's*, 188; *Lennie's*, 99; *Bullions's*, 89; and many more. Now the objective before the infinitive may not improperly be called *the subject* of this form of the verb, as the nominative is, of the finite; but to call it "the subject *of the affirmation*," is plainly absurd; because no infinitive, in English, ever expresses an affirmation. And again, if a whole phrase or sentence is made the subject of a *finite* verb, or of an affirmation, no one word contained in it, can singly claim this title. Nor can the whole, by virtue of this relation, be said to be "in the *nominative case;*" because, in the nature of things, neither phrases nor sentences are capable of being declined by cases.

Obs. 13.—Any phrase or sentence which is made the subject of a finite verb, must be taken in the sense of *one thing*, and be spoken of as *a whole*; so that the verb's agreement with it, in the third person singular, is not an exception to Rule 14th, but a construction in which the verb may be parsed by that rule. For any one thing merely spoken of, is of the third person singular, whatever may be the nature of its parts. Not every phrase or sentence, however, is fit to be made the subject of a verb;—that is, if its own import, and not the mere expression, is the thing whereof we affirm. Thus Dr. Ash's example for this very construction, " a *sentence* made the subject of a verb," is, I think, a palpable solecism: "The King and Queen appearing in public *was* the cause of my going."—*Ash's Gram.* p. 52. What is here before the verb *was*, is no " *sentence;*" but a mere phrase, and such a one as we should expect to see used independently, if any regard were had to its own import. The Doctor would tell us what "was *the cause* of his going:" and here he has two nominatives, which are equivalent to the plural *they*; q. d. "*They* appearing in public *was* the cause." But such a construction is not English. It is an other sample of the false illustration which grammar receives from those who *invent* the proof-texts which they ought to quote.

Obs. 14.—One of Murray's examples of what he erroneously terms " *nominative sentences*," i. e., "sentences or clauses constituting the subject of an affirmation," is the following: "A desire to excel others in learning and virtue [,] *is* commendable."—*Gram.* 8vo, p. 144. Here the verb *is* agrees regularly with the noun *desire*, and with that only; the whole text being merely a simple sentence, and totally irrelevant to the doctrine which it accompanies.[*] But the great "Compiler" supposes the adjuncts of this noun to be parts of the nominative, and imagines the verb to agree with all that precedes it. Yet, soon after, he expends upon the ninth rule of Webster's Philosophical Grammar a whole page of useless criticism, to show that the adjuncts of a noun are not to be taken as parts of the nominative; and that, when objectives are thus subjoined, "the assertion grammatically respects the first nouns only."—*Ib.* p. 148. I say *useless*, because the

[*] The same may be said of Dr. Webster's "*nominative sentences;*" three fourths of which are nothing but phrases that include a nominative with which the following verb agrees. And who does not know, that to call the adjuncts of any thing "an *essential part* of it," is a flat absurdity? An *adjunct* is "something added to another, but not *essentially* a part of it."—*Webster's Dict.* But, says the Doctor, "Attributes and other words often make ah *essential part* of the nominative; [as,] '*Our* IDEAS *of* eternity CAN as nothing but an infinite succession of moments of duration.'—LOCKE. '*A wise* SON MAKETH a glad father; but a *foolish* SON is the heaviness of his mother.' Abstract the name from its attribute, and the proposition cannot always be true. '*He that gathereth in summer* is a wise son.' Take away the description, '*that gathereth in summer*,' and the affirmation ceases to be true, or becomes inapplicable. These sentences or clauses thus *constituting* the subject of a affirmation, may be termed *nominative sentences*."—*Improved Gram.* p. 96. This teaching reminds me of the Doctor's own exclamation: "What strange work has been made with Grammar!"—*Ib.* p. 94; *Philos. Gram.* 198. In Nesbit's English Parsing, a book designed mainly for "a Key to Murray's Exercises in Parsing," the following example is thus expounded: "The smooth stream, the serene atmosphere, [and] the mild zephyr, are the proper emblems of a gentle temper, and a peaceful life."—*Murray's Exercises*, p. 8. "*The smooth stream, the serene atmosphere, the wild zephyr*, is part of a sentence, *which* is the *nominative case* to the verb ' are.' *Are* is an irregular verb neuter, in the indicative mood, the present tense, the third person plural, and *agrees with the aforementioned part of a sentence*, as its nominative case."—*Introduction to English Parsing*, p. 137. On this principle of analysis, all the rules that speak of nominatives or antecedents connected by conjunctions, may be dispensed with, as useless; and the doctrine, that a verb which has a phrase or sentence for its subject, must be *singular*, is palpably contradicted, and supposed erroneous!

truth of the doctrine is so very plain. Some, however, may imagine an example like the following to be an exception to it; but I do not, because I think the true nominative suppressed:

"By force they could not introduce these gods;
For *ten to one* in former days *was* odds."—*Dryden's Poems*, p. 38.

OBS. 15.—Dr. Webster's ninth rule is this: "When the nominative consists of several words, and the last of the names is in the plural number, the verb is commonly in the plural also; as, 'A part of the exports *consist* of raw silk.' 'The number of oysters *increase*.' GOLDSMITH. 'Such as the train of our ideas *have lodged* in our memories.' LOCKE. 'The greater part of philosophers *have acknowledged* the excellence of this government.' ANACHARSIS."—*Philos. Gram.* p. 146; *Impr. Gram.* 100. The last of these examples Murray omits; the second he changes thus: "A number of men and women *were* present." But all of them his reasoning condemns as ungrammatical. He thinks them wrong, upon the principle, that the verbs, being plural, do not agree with the first nouns only. Webster, on the contrary, judges them all to be right; and, upon this same principle, conceives that his rule must be so too. He did not retract or alter the doctrine after he saw the criticism, but republished it verbatim, in his "Improved Grammar," of 1831. Both err, and neither convinces the other.

OBS. 16.—In this instance, as Webster and Murray both teach erroneously, whoever follows either, will be led into many mistakes. The fact is, that some of the foregoing examples, though perhaps not all, are perfectly right; and hundreds more, of a similar character, might be quoted, which no true grammarian would presume to condemn. But what have these to do with the monstrous absurdity of supposing objective adjuncts to be "parts of the actual nominative?" The words, "*part*," "*number*," "*train*," and the like, are *collective nouns*; and, as such, they often have plural verbs in agreement with them. To say "A *number* of men and women *were* present,". is as correct as to say, "A very great *number* of our words *are* plainly derived from the Latin."—*Blair's Rhet.* p 86. Murray's criticism therefore, since it does not exempt these examples from the censure justly laid upon Webster's rule, will certainly mislead the learner. And again the rule, being utterly wrong in principle, will justify blunders like these: "The truth of the narratives *have* never been disputed;"—"The virtue of these men and women *are* indeed exemplary."—*Murray's Gram.* p. 148. In one of his notes, Murray suggests, that the article *an* or *a* before a collective noun must confine the verb to the singular number; as, "A *great number* of men and women *was* collected."—*Ib.* p. 153. But this doctrine he sometimes forgot or disregarded; as, "But if *a number* of interrogative or exclamatory sentences *are thrown* into one general group."—*Ib.* p. 284; *Comly*, 166; *Fisk*, 160; *Ingersoll*, 295.

OBS. 17.—Cobbett, in a long paragraph, (the 245th of his English Grammar,) stoutly denies that any *relative pronoun* can ever be the nominative to a verb; and, to maintain this absurdity, he will have the relative and its antecedent to be always alike in *case*, the only thing in which they are always independent of each other. To prove his point, he first frames these examples: "The men *who are* here, the man *who is* here; the cocks *that crow*, the cock *that crows*;" and then asks, "Now, if the relative be the nominative, why do the verbs *change*, seeing that here is no change in the relative?" He seems ignorant of the axiom, that two things severally equal to a third, are also equal to each other: and accordingly, to answer his own question, resorts to a new principle: "The verb is continually varying. Why does it vary? Because it *disregards the relative* and goes and finds the antecedent, and accommodates its number to that."—*Ibid.* To this wild doctrine, one erratic Irishman yields a full assent; and, in one American grammatist, we find a partial and unintentional concurrence with it.[*] But the fact is, the relative agrees with the antecedent, and the verb agrees with the relative: hence all three of the words are alike in person and number. But between the case of the relative and that of the antecedent, there never is, or can be, in our language, any sort of connexion or interference. The words belong to different clauses; and, if both be nominatives, they must be the subjects of different verbs: or, if the noun be sometimes put absolute in the nominative, the pronoun is still left to its own verb. But Cobbett concludes his observation thus: "You will observe, therefore, that, when I, in the etymology and syntax as relating to relative pronouns, speak of relatives as being in the nominative case, I mean, that they relate to nouns or to personal pronouns, *which are in that case*. The same observation applies *to the other cases*."—*Ib.* ¶ 245. This suggestion betrays in the critic an unaccountable ignorance of his subject.

OBS. 18.—Nothing is more certain, than that the relatives, *who*, *which*, *what*, *that*, and *as*, are often nominatives, and the only subjects of the verbs which follow them: as, "The Lord will show *who are* his, and *who is* holy."—*Numbers*, xvi. 5. "Hardly is there any person, but *who*, on such occasions, *is disposed* to be serious."—*Blair's Rhet.* p. 469. "Much of the merit of Mr. Addison's Cato depends upon that moral turn of thought *which distinguishes* it."—*Ib.* 469. "Admit not a single word but *what is* necessary."—*Ib.* p. 313. "The pleader must say nothing but *what is* true; and, at the same time, he must avoid saying any thing *that will hurt* his cause."—*Ib.* 312. "I proceed to mention such *as appear* to me most material."—*Ib.* p. 126. After *but* or *than*, there is sometimes an ellipsis of the relative, and perhaps also of the antecedent; as, "There is no

---

[*] "No Relative can become a Nominative to a Verb."—*Joseph W. Wright's Philosophical Grammar*, p. 162. "A *personal* pronoun becomes a nominative, though a *relative* does not."—*Ib.* p. 153. This teacher is criticised by the other as follows: "Wright says, that 'Personal pronouns may be in the nominative case,' and that 'relative pronouns can not be.' Yet he declines his relatives thus: 'Nominative case, *who*; possessive, *whose*; objective, *whom*!'"—*Oliver B. Peirce's Grammar*, p. 381. This latter author here sees the palpable inconsistency of the former, and accordingly treats *who*, *which*, *what*, *whatever*, &c., as relative pronouns of the nominative case—or, as he calls them, "connective substitutes in the subjective form;" but when *what* or *whatever* precedes its noun, or when *as* is preferred to *who* or *which*, he refers both verbs to the noun itself, and adopts the very principle by which Cobbett and Wright erroneously parse the verbs which belong to the relatives, *who*, *which*, and *that*: as, "Whatever honesty will adhere to strict principles of honesty, will find his reward in himself."—*Peirce's Gram.* p. 55. Here Peirce considers *whatever* to be a mere adjective, and *man* the subject of *will adhere* and *will find*. "Such persons as write grammar, should, themselves, be grammarians."—*Ib.* p. 330. Here he declares *as* to be no pronoun, but "a modifying connective," i. e. conjunction; and supposes *persons* to be the direct subject of *write* as well as of *should be*: as if a conjunction could connect a verb and its nominative!

heart *but must feel* them."—*Blair's Rhet.* p. 469.   "There is no one *but must be* sensible of the extravagance."—*Ib.* p. 479.   "Since we may date from it a more general and a more concerted opposition to France *than there had been* before."—*Bolingbroke, on Hist.* p. 213.   That is, " than *what* there had been before;"—or, " than *any opposition which* there had been before." " John has more fruit *than can be gathered* in a week."—*O. B. Peirce's Gram.* pp. 196 and 331. I suppose this sentence to mean, " John has more fruit than *what* can be gathered in a week." But the author of it denies that it is elliptical, and seems to suppose that *can be gathered* agrees with *John.*   Part of his comment stands thus : " The above sentence—' John has more fruit than can be gathered in a week'—in every respect full and *perfect*—must, to be *grammatical!* according to *all* the ' old theories,' stand, John has more fruit than *that fruit is which, or which fruit* can be gathered in a week ! ! !"—*Ib.* 331.   What shall be done with the headless critic who thus mistakes exclamation points for arguments, and multiplies his confidence in proportion to his fallacies and errors ?

OBS. 19.—In a question, the nominative *I* or *thou* put after the verb, controls the agreement, in preference to the interrogative *who, which,* or *what,* put before it ; as, "*Who am I? What am I? Who art thou? What art thou?*" And, by analogy, this seems to be the case with all plurals ; as, "*Who are we? Who are you? Who are they? What are these?*" But sometimes the interrogative pronoun is the only nominative used ; and then the verb, whether singular or plural, must agree with this nominative, in the third person, and not, as Cobbett avers, with an antecedent understood : as, "*Who is* in the house ? *Who are* in the house ? *Who strikes* the iron ? *Who strike* the iron ? *Who was* in the street ? *Who were* in the street ?"—*Cobbett's Gram.* ¶ 245.   All the interrogative pronouns may be used in either number, but, in examples like the following, I imagine the singular to be more proper than the plural : "*What have become* of our previous customs ?"—*Hunt's Byron,* p. 121.   " And *what have become* of my resolutions to return to God ?"—*Young Christian,* 2d Ed., p. 91.   When two nominatives of different properties come after the verb, the first controls the agreement, and neither the plural number nor the most worthy person is always preferred ; as, " *Is it I? Is it thou? Is it they?*"

OBS. 20.—The verb after a relative sometimes has the appearance of disagreeing with its nominative, because the writer and his reader disagree in their conceptions of its mood.   When a relative clause is subjoined to what is itself subjunctive or conditional, some writers suppose that the latter verb should be put in the subjunctive mood ; as, " If there be any intrigue *which stand* separate and independent."—*Blair's Rhet.* p. 457.   " The man also would be of considerable use, who should vigilantly attend to every illegal practice *that were beginning* to prevail."—*Campbell's Rhet.* p. 171.   But I have elsewhere shown, that relatives, in English, are not compatible with the subjunctive mood ; and it is certain, that no other mood than the indicative or the potential is commonly used after them.   Say therefore, " If there be any intrigue *which stands,*" &c.   In assuming to himself the other text, Murray's says, "*That* man also would be of considerable use, who should vigilantly attend to every illegal practice *that was* beginning to prevail."—*Octavo Gram.* p. 356.   But this seems too positive.   The potential imperfect would be better : viz., " that *might begin* to prevail."

OBS. 21.—The termination *st* or *est*, with which the second person singular of the verb is formed in the indicative present, and, for the solemn style, in the imperfect also ; and the termination *s* or *es*, with which the third person singular is formed in the indicative present, and only there ; are signs of the mood and tense, as well as of the person and number, of the verb.   They are not applicable to a future uncertainty, or to any mere supposition in which we would leave the time indefinite and make the action hypothetical ; because they are commonly understood to fix the time of the verb to the present or the past, and to assume the action as either doing or done. For this reason, our best writers have always omitted those terminations, when they intended to represent the action as being doubtful and contingent as well as conditional.   And this omission constitutes the whole *formal* difference between the indicative and the subjunctive mood.   The *essential* difference has, by almost all grammarians, been conceived to extend somewhat further ; for, if it were confined strictly within the limits of the literal variation, the subjunctive mood would embrace only two or three words in the whole formation of each verb.   After the example of Priestley, Dr. Murray, A. Murray, Harrison, Alexander, and others, I have given to it all the persons of the two simple tenses, singular and plural ; and, for various reasons, I am decidedly of the opinion, that these are its most proper limits.   The perfect and pluperfect tenses, being past, cannot express what is really contingent or uncertain ; and since, in expressing conditionally what may or may not happen, we use the subjunctive present as embracing the future indefinitely, there is no need of any formal futures for this mood.   The comprehensive brevity of this form of the verb, is what chiefly commends it.   It is not an elliptical form of the future, as some affirm it to be ; nor equivalent to the indicative present, as others will have it ; but a *true subjunctive,* though its distinctive parts are chiefly confined to the second and third persons singular of the simple verb : as, " Though *thou wash* thee with nitre."—*Jer.* ii, 22.   " It is just, O great king ! that a *murderer perish.*"—*Corneille.*   " This single *crime,* in my judgment, *were* sufficient to condemn him."—*Duncan's Cicero,* p. 82.   " Beware that *thou bring* not my son thither."—BIBLE : *Ward's Gram.* p. 128.   " See [that] *thou tell* no man."—*Id. ib.*   These examples can hardly be resolved into any thing else than the subjunctive mood.

NOTES TO RULE XIV.

NOTE I.—When the nominative is a relative pronoun, the verb must agree with it in person and number, according to the pronoun's agreement with its true antecedent or antecedents.   Example of error : " The second book [of the Æneid] is one of the greatest masterpieces *that ever was executed* by any hand."—*Blair's Rhet.* p. 439. Here the true antecedent is *masterpieces,* and not the word *one* ; but *was executed* is singular, and "by any *hand*" implies but one agent.   Either say, "It is one of the greatest *masterpieces that* ever *were executed;*" or else, "It is *the greatest masterpiece that* ever *was executed by any hand*"   But these assertions differ much in their import.

NOTE II.—"The adjuncts of the nominative do not control its agreement with the verb; as, Six months' *interest was* due.   The *progress* of his forces *was* impeded." —*W. Allen's Gram.* p. 131.   "The *ship*, with all her furniture, was destroyed." —*Murray's Gram.* p. 150.   "All *appearances* of modesty *are* favourable and pre-possessing.—*Blair's Rhet.* p. 308.   "The *power* of relishing natural enjoyments *is* soon gone.*'—Fuller, on the Gospel,* p. 185.

NOTE III.—Any phrase, sentence, mere word, or other sign, taken as one whole, and made the subject of an assertion, requires a verb in the third person singular; as, "To lie *is* base."—*Adam's Gram.* p. 154.   "When, to read and write, *was* of itself an honorary distinction."—*Hazlitt's Lect.* p. 40.   "To admit a God and then refuse to worship him, *is* a modern and inconsistent practice."—*Fuller, on the Gospel,* p. 30.   "*We is* a personal pronoun."—*L. Murray's Gram.* p. 227.   "*Th has* two sounds."—*Ib.* p. 161.   "The *'s is* annexed to each."—*Bucke's Gram.* p. 89. "*Ld. stands* for *lord.*"—*Webster's American Dict.* 8vo.

NOTE IV.—The pronominal adjectives, *each, one,* *either,* and *neither,* are always in the third person singular; and, when they are the leading words in their clauses, they require verbs and pronouns to agree with them accordingly: as, "*Each* of you *is* entitled to *his* share."—"Let no *one* deceive *himself.*"

NOTE V.—A neuter or a passive verb between two nominatives should be made to agree with that which precedes it ;† as, "Words *are* wind:" except when the terms are transposed, and the proper subject is put after the verb by *question* or *hyperbaton;* as, "His pavilion *were* dark *waters* and thick *clouds* of the sky."—*Bible.* "Who *art thou?*"—*Ib.*   "The wages of sin *is* death."—*Ib. Murray, Comly,* and others.   But, of this last example, Churchill says, "*Wages are* the subject, of which it is affirmed, that *they are* death."—*New Gram.* p. 314.   If so, *is* ought to be *are;* unless Dr. Webster is right, who imagines *wages* to be *singular,* and cites this example to prove it so.   See his *Improved Gram.* p. 21.

NOTE VI.—When the verb cannot well be made singular, the nominative should be made plural, that they may agree: or, if the verb cannot be plural, let the nominative be singular.   Example of error: "For *every one* of them *know* their several duties."—*Hope of Israel,* p. 72.   Say, "For *all* of them know their several duties."

NOTE VII.—When the verb has different forms, that forms should be adopted, which is the most consistent with present and reputable usage in the style employed: thus, to say familiarly, "The clock *hath stricken;*"—"Thou *laughedst* and *talkedst,*

---

* Professor Fowler says, "*One* when contrasted with *other,* sometimes represents *plural* nouns; as, 'The reason why the *one* are ordinarily taken for real qualities, and the *other* for bare powers, seems to be.'—LOCKE."—*Fowler's E. Gram.* 8vo, 1850, p. 242.   This doctrine is, I think, erroneous; and the example, too, is defective.   For, if *one* may be *plural,* we have no distinctive definition or notion of either number.   "*One*" and "*other*" are not here to be regarded as the leading words in their clauses; they are mere adjectives, each referring to the collective noun *class* or *species,* understood, which should have been expressed after the former.   See Etym. Obs. 10, p. 288.

† Dr. Priestley says, "It is a rule, I believe, in all grammars, that when a verb comes between two nouns, either of which may be understood as the subject of the affirmation, that it may agree with either of them; but some regard must be had to that which is more naturally the subject of it, as also to that which stands next to the verb; for if no regard be paid to these circumstances, the construction will be harsh: (as,) *Minced pies was regarded as* a profane and superstitious viand by the sectaries.   *Hume's Hist.*   A great *cause* of the low state of industry *were* the restraints put upon it.   *Ib.*   By this term *was* understood, such *persons* as invented, or drew up rules for themselves and the world."—*English Gram. with Notes,* p. 189.   The Doctor evidently supposed all these examples to be *bad English,* or at least *harsh in their construction.*   And the first two unquestionably are so; while the last, whether right or wrong, has nothing at all to do with his rule: it has but one nominative, and that appears to be part of a definition, and not the true subject of the verb.   Nor, indeed, is the first any more relevant; because Hume's "*viand*" cannot possibly be taken "*as the subject* of the affirmation."   Lindley Murray, who literally copies Priestley's note, (all but the first line and the last,) rejects these two examples, substituting for the former, "His *meat was* locusts and wild honey," and for the latter, "The *wages* of sin *is* death"   He very evidently supposes all three of his examples to be *good English.*   In this, according to Churchill, he is at fault in two instances out of the three; and still more so, in regard to the note, or rule, itself.   In stead of being "a rule in all grammars," it is (so far as I know) found only in these authors, and such as have implicitly copied it from Murray.   Among these last, are Alger, Ingersoll, R. C. Smith, Fisk, and Merchant.   Churchill, who cites it only as Murray's, and yet expends two pages of criticism upon it, very justly says: "To make that the nominative case, (or subject of the affirmation,] which happens to stand nearest to the verb, appears to me to be on a par with the blunder pointed out in note 204th;" [that is, of making the verb agree with an objective case which happens to stand nearer to it, than its subject, or nominative.]—*Churchill's New Gram.* p. 313.

when thou *oughtest* to have been silent ; "—" He *readeth* and *writeth*, but he *doth* not cipher," would be no better, than to use *don't*, *won't*, *can't*, *shan't*, and *didn't*, in preaching.

NOTE VIII.—Every finite verb not in the imperative mood, should have a separate nominative expressed ; as, "*I came, I saw, I conquered :*" except when the verb is repeated for the sake of emphasis, or connected to an other in the same construction, or put after *but* or *than ;* as, " Not an eminent orator has lived *but is* an example of it." —*Ware.* " Where more is meant *than meets* the ear."—*Milton's Allegro.* (See Obs. 5th and Obs. 18th above.)

> " They *bud, blow, wither, fall,* and *die.*"—*Watts.*
> " That evermore his teeth they *chatter,*
> *Chatter, chatter, chatter* still."—*Wordsworth.*

NOTE IX.—A future contingency is best expressed by a verb in the subjunctive present ; and a mere supposition, with indefinite time, by a verb in the subjunctive imperfect ; but a conditional circumstance assumed as a fact, requires the indicative mood :* as, " If thou *forsake* him, he will cast thee off forever."—*Bible.* " If it *were* not so, I would have told you."—*Ib.* " If thou *went*, nothing would be gained."— " Though he *is* poor, he is contented."—"Though he *was* rich, yet for your sakes he became poor."—2 *Cor.* viii, 9.

NOTE X.—In general, every such use or extension of the subjunctive mood, as the reader will be likely to mistake for a discord between the verb and its nominative, ought to be avoided as an impropriety : as, " We are not sensible of disproportion, till the difference between the quantities compared *become* the most striking circumstance." —*Kames, El. of Crit.* ii, 341. Say rather, " *becomes ;*" which is indicative. " Till the general preference of certain forms *have been declared.*"—*Priestley's Gram. Pref.* p. xvii. Say, " *has been declared ;*" for " *preference*" is here the nominative, and Dr. Priestley himself recognizes no other subjunctive tenses than the present and the imperfect ; as, " If thou *love,* If thou *loved.*"—*Ib.* p. 16.

IMPROPRIETIES FOR CORRECTION.

FALSE SYNTAX UNDER RULE XIV.

UNDER THE RULE ITSELF.—VERB AFTER THE NOMINATIVE.

" Before you left Sicily, you was reconciled to Verres."—*Duncan's Cicero,* p. 19.

[FORMULE.—Not proper, because the passive verb *was reconciled* is of the singular number, and does not agree with its nominative *you*, which is of the second person plural. But, according to Rule 14th, " Every finite verb must agree with its subject, or nominative, in person and number." Therefore, *was reconciled* should be *were reconciled* ; thus, " Before you left Sicily, you *were reconciled* to Verres."]

" Knowing that you was my old master's good friend."—*Spect.* No. 517. " When the judge dare not act, where is the loser's remedy ?"—*Webster's Essays,* p. 131. " Which extends it no farther than the variation of the verb extend."—*Murray's Gram.* 8vo, Vol. i, p. 211. " They presently dry without hurt, as myself hath often proved."—*Roger Williams.* " Whose goings forth hath been from of old, from everlasting."—*Keith's Evidences.* " You was paid to fight against Alexander, not to rail at him."—*Porter's Analysis,* p. 70. " Where more than one part of speech is almost always concerned."—*Churchill's Gram. Pref.* p. viii. " Nothing less than murders, rapines, and conflagrations, employ their thoughts."—*Duncan's Cicero,* p. 175. " I wondered where you was, my dear."—*Lloyd's Poems,* p. 185. " When thou most sweetly sings."—*Drummond of Hawthornden.* " Who dare, at the present day, avow himself equal to the task ?"—*Music of Nature,* p. 11. " Every body are very kind to her, and not discourteous to me."—*Byron's Letters.* " As to what thou says respecting the diversity of opinions."—*The Friend,* Vol. ix, p. 45. " Thy nature, immortality, who knowest ?"—*Everest's Gram.* p. 38. " The natural distinction of sex in animals gives rise to what, in grammar, is called genders."—*Ib.* p. 51. " Some pains has likewise been taken."—*Scott's Pref. to Bible.* " And many a steed in his stables were

---

* " If the excellence of Dryden's works *was lessened* by his indigence, their number was increased."—*Dr. Johnson.* This is an example of the proper and necessary use of the indicative mood after an *if*, the matter of the condition being regarded as a fact. But Dr. Webster, who prefers the indicative *too often*, has the following note upon it : " If Johnson had followed the common grammars, or even his own, which is prefixed to his Dictionary, he would have written *were*—' If the excellence of Dryden's works *were* lessened '—Fortunately this great man, led by usage rather than by books, wrote *correct English, instead of grammar.*"—*Philosophical Gram.* p. 236. Now this is as absurd, as it is characteristic of the grammar from which it is taken. Each form is right sometimes, and neither can be used for the other, without error.

seen."—*Penwarne's Poems*, p. 108. "They was forced to eat what never was esteemed food."—*Josephus's Jewish War*, B. i, Ch. i, § 7. "This that yourself hath spoken, I desire that they may take their oaths upon."—*Hutchinson's Mass.* ii, 435. "By men whose experience best qualify them to judge."—*Committee on Literature, N. Y. Legislature.* "He dare venture to kill and destroy several other kinds of fish."—*Johnson's Dict. w. Perch.* "If a gudgeon meet a roach, He dare not venture to approach."—*Swift: Ib. w. Roach.* "Which thou endeavours to establish unto thyself."—*Barclay's Works,* i, 164. "But they pray together much oftener than thou insinuates."—*Ib.* i, 215. "Of people of all denominations, over whom thou presideth."—*The Friend,* Vol. v, p. 198. "I can produce ladies and gentlemen whose progress have been astonishing."—*Chazotts, on Teaching Lang.* p. 52. "Which of these two kinds of vice are more criminal?"—*Brown's Estimate,* ii, 115. "Every twenty-four hours affords to us the vicissitudes of day and night."—*Smith's New Gram.* p. 103. "Every four years adds another day."—*Ib.* "Every error I could find, Have my busy muse employed."—*Swift's Poems,* p. 335. "A studious scholar deserve the approbation of his teacher."—*Sanborn's Gram.* p. 226. "Perfect submission to the rules of a school indicate good breeding."—*Ib.* p. 37. "A comparison in which more than two is concerned." —*Bullions, E. Gram.* p. 114. "By the facilities which artificial language afford them."—*O. B. Peirce's Gram.* p. 16. "Now thyself hath lost both lop and top."—*Spenser: Joh. Dict. w. Lop.* "Glad tidings is brought to the poor."—*Campbell's Gospels: Luke,* vii, 23. "Upon which, all that is pleasurable, or affecting in elocution, chiefly depend."—*Sheridan's Elocution,* p. 129. "No pains has been spared to render this work complete."—*Bullions, Lat. Gram. Pref.* p. iv. "The United States contains more than a twentieth part of the land of this globe."—*De Witt Clinton: Cobb's N. Amer. Reader,* p. 173. "I am mindful that myself is (or am) strong."—*Fowler's E. Gram.* § 500. "Myself *is* (not *am*) weak; thyself *is* (not *art*) weak."—*Ib.* § 479.

"How pale each worshipful and reverend guest
　Rise from a clergy or a city feast!"—*Pope,* Sat. ii, l. 75.

UNDER THE RULE ITSELF.—VERB BEFORE THE NOMINATIVE.

"Where was you born? In London."—*Buchanan's Syntax,* p. 133. "There is frequent occasions for commas."—*Ingersoll's Gram.* p. 281. "There necessarily follows from thence, these plain and unquestionable consequences."—*Priestley's Gram.* p. 191. "And to this impression contribute the redoubled effort."—*Kames, El. of Crit.* ii, 112. "Or if he was, was there no spiritual men then?"—*Barclay's Works,* iii, 86. "So by these two also is signified their contrary principles."—*Ib.* iii, 200. "In the motions made with the hands, consist the chief part of gesture in speaking."—*Blair's Rhet.* p. 336. "Dare he assume the name of a popular magistrate?"—*Duncan's Cicero,* p. 140. "There was no damages as in England, and so Scott lost his wager."—*Byron.* "In fact there exists such resemblances." —*Kames, El. of Crit.* ii, 64. "To him giveth all the prophets witness."—*Crowdson's Beam,* p. 79. "That there was so many witnesses and actors."—*Addison's Evidences,* p. 37. "How does this man's definitions stand affected?"—*Collier's Antoninus,* p. 136. "Whence comes all the powers and prerogatives of rational beings?"—*Ib.* p. 144. "Nor does the Scriptures cited by thee prove thy intent."—*Barclay's Works,* i, 155. "Nor do the Scripture cited by thee prove the contrary."—*Ib.* i, 211. "Why then cite thou a Scripture which is so plain and clear for it?"—*Ib.* i, 163. "But what saith the Scriptures as to respect of persons among Christians?"—*Ib.* i, 404. "But in the mind of man, while in the savage state, there seems to be hardly any ideas but what enter by the senses."—*Robertson's America,* i, 289. "What sounds have each of the vowels?"—*Griscom's Questions.* "Out of this has grown up aristocracies, monarchies, despotisms, tyrannies."—*Brownson's Elwood,* p. 222. "And there was taken up, of fragments that remained to them, twelve baskets."—*Luke,* ix, 17. "There seems to be but two general classes."—*Day's Gram.* p. 3. "Hence arises the six forms of expressing time."—*Ib.* p. 37. "There seems to be no other words required."—*Chandler's Gram.* p. 28. "If there is two, the second increment is the syllable next the last."—*Bullions, Lat. Gram.,* 12th Ed., p. 281. "Hence arises the following advantages."—*Id. Analyt. and Pract. Gram.,* 1849, p. 67. "There is no data by which it can be estimated."—*J. C. Calhoun's Speech,* March 4, 1850. "To this class belong the Chinese [language], in which we have nothing but naked roots."—*Fowler's E. Gram.* 8vo, 1850, p. 27. "There was several other grotesque figures that presented themselves."—*Spect. No.* 173. "In these consist that sovereign good which ancient sages so much extol."—*Percival's Tales,* ii, 221. "Here comes those I have done good to against my will."—*Shak. Shrew.* "Where there is more than one auxiliary."—*O. B. Peirce's Gram.* p. 80.

"On me to cast those eyes where shine nobility."—*Sidney: Joh. Dict.*
"Here's half-pence in plenty, for one you'll have twenty."—*Swift's Poems,* p. 347.
"Ah, Jockey, ill advises thou, I wis,
　To think of songs at such a time as this."—*Churchill,* p. 18.

UNDER NOTE I.—THE RELATIVE AND VERB.

"Thou who loves us, wilt protect us still."—*Alex. Murray's Gram.* p. 67. "To use that endearing language, Our Father, who is in heaven."—*Bates's Doctrines,* p. 103. "Resembling the passions that produceth these actions."—*Kames, El. of Crit.* i, 157. "Except *dwarf, grief, hoof, muff,* &c. which takes *s* to make the plural."—*Ash's Gram.* p. 19. "As the cattle that goeth before me and the children be able to endure."—*Gen.* xxxiii, 14. "Where is the man who dare affirm that such an action is mad?"—*Werter.* "The ninth book of Livy affords one of the most beautiful exemplifications of historical painting, that is any where to be met with."—*Blair's Rhet.* p. 360. "In some studies too, that relate to taste and fine writing, which is our object," &c.—*Ib.* p. 349. "Of those affecting situations, which makes man's heart feel for man."—*Ib.* p. 464. "We see very plainly, that it is neither Osmyn, nor Jane Shore, that speak."—*Ib.* p. 468. "It should assume that briskness and ease, which is suited to the freedom of dialogue."—*Ib.* p. 469. "Yet they grant, that none ought to be admitted into the ministry, but such as is truly pious."—*Barclay's Works,* iii, 147. "This letter is one of the best that has been written about Lord Byron."—*Hunt's Byron,* p. 119. "Thus, besides what was sunk, the Athenians took above two hundred ships."—*Goldsmith's Greece,* i, 102. "To have made and declared such orders as was necessary."—*Hutchinson's Hist.* i, 470. "The idea of such a collection of men as make an army."—*Locke's Essay,* p. 217. "I'm not the first that have been wretched."—*Southern's Fn. Ad.* Act 2. "And the faint sparks of it, which is in the angels, are concealed from our view."—*Calvin's Institutes,* B. i, Ch. 11. "The subjects are of such a nature, as allow room for much diversity of taste and sentiment."—*Blair's Rhet. Pref.* p. 5. "It is in order to propose examples of such perfection, as are not to be found in the real examples of society." —*Formey's Belles-Lettres,* p. 16. "I do not believe that he would amuse himself with such fooleries as has been attributed to him."—*Ib.* p. 218. "That shepherd, who first taughtst the chosen seed."—*O. B. Peirce's Gram.* p. 238. "With respect to the vehemence and warmth which is allowed in popular eloquence."—*Blair's Rhet.* p. 261. "Ambition is one of those passions that is never to be satisfied."—*Home's Art of Thinking,* p. 36. "Thou wast he that leddest out and broughtest in Israel."—1 *Chron.* xi, 2. "Art thou the man of God that camest from Judah?"—1 *Kings,* xiii, 14.

> "How beauty is excell'd by manly grace
> And wisdom, which alone is truly fair."—*Milton,* B. iv, l. 490.

> "What art thou, speak, that on designs unknown,
> While others sleep, thus range the camp alone?"—*Pope, Il.* x. 90.

UNDER NOTE II.—NOMINATIVE WITH ADJUNCTS.

"The literal sense of the words are, that the action had been done."—*Dr. Murray's Hist. of Lang.* i, 65. "The rapidity of his movements were beyond example."—*Wells's Hist.* p. 161. 'Murray's Grammar, together with his Exercises and Key, have nearly superseded every thing else of the kind."—*Evan's Rec.: Murray's Gram.* 8vo, ii, 305. "The mechanism of clocks and watches were totally unknown."—*Hume: Priestley's Gram.* p. 193. "The *it,* together with the verb *to be,* express states of being."—*Cobbett's Eng. Gram.* ¶ 190. "Hence it is, that the profuse variety of objects in some natural landscapes, neither breed confusion nor fatigue."—*Kames, El. of Crit.* i, 266. "Such a clatter of sounds indicate rage and ferocity."—*Music of Nature,* p. 195. "One of the fields make threescore square yards, and the other only fifty-five."—*Duncan's Logic,* p. 8. "The happy effects of this fable is worth attending to."—*Bailey's Ovid,* p. x. "Yet the glorious serenity of its parting rays still linger with us."—*Gould's Advocate.* "Enough of its form and force are retained to render them uneasy."—*Maturin's Sermons,* p. 261. "The works of nature, in this respect, is extremely regular."—*Dr. Pratt's Werter.* "No small addition of exotic and foreign words and phrases have been made by commerce."—*Bicknell's Gram.* Part ii, p. 10. "The dialect of some nouns are taken notice of in the notes."—*Milnes, Greek Gram.* p. 255. "It has been said, that a discovery of the full resources of the arts, afford the means of debasement, or of perversion."—*Rush, on the Voice,* p. xxvii. "By which means the Order of the Words are disturbed."—*Holmes's Rhet.* B. i, p. 57. "The twofold influence of these and the others require the asserter to be in the plural form."—*O. B. Peirce's Gram.* p. 251. "And each of these afford employment."—*Percival's Tales,* Vol. ii, p. 175. "The pronunciation of the vowels are best explained under the rules relative to the consonants."—*Coar's Gram.* p. 7. 'The judicial power of these courts extend to all cases in law and equity."—*Hall and Baker's School Hist.* p. 286. "One of you have stolen my money."—*Rational Humorist,* p. 45. 'Such redundancy of epithets, instead of pleasing, produce satiety and disgust."—*Kames, El of Crit.* ii, 256. "It has been alleged, that a compliance with the rules of Rhetoric, tend to cramp the mind."—*Hiley's Gram.,* 3d Ed., p. 187. "Each of these are presented to us in different relations."—*Hendrick's Gram.,* 1st Ed., p. 34. "The past tense of these verbs, *should, would, might, could,* are very indefinite with respect to time."—*Bullions, E. Gram.,* 2d Ed., p. 33; 5th Ed., p. 31. "The power of the words, which are said to govern this mood, are distinctly understood."—*Chandler's Gram.,* Ed. of 1821, p. 33.

> "And now, at length, the fated term of years
> The world's desire have brought, and lo! the God appears."
> —*Dr. Lowth, on "the Genealogy of Christ,"*

> "Variety of Numbers still belong
> To the soft Melody of Ode or Song."—*Brightland's Gram.* p. 170.

UNDER NOTE III.—COMPOSITE OR CONVERTED SUBJECTS.

"Many are the works of human industry, which to begin and finish are hardly granted to the same man."—*Johnson, Adv. to Dict.* "To lay down rules for these are as ineffacious."—*Dr. Pratt's Werter,* p. 19. "To profess regard, and to act *differently,* discover a base mind."—*Murray's Key,* ii, p. 206. See also *Bullions's E. Gram.* 82 and 112; *Lennie's,* 58. "To magnify to the height of wonder things great, new, and admirable, extremely please the mind of man."—*Fisher's Gram.* p. 152. "In this passage, *according as* are used in a manner which is very common."—*Webster's Philosophical Gram.* p. 183. "*A cause de* are called a preposition; *a cause que,* a conjunction."—DR. WEBSTER: *Knickerbroker,* 1836. "To these are given to speak in the name of the Lord."—*The Friend,* vii, 256. "While *wheat* has no plural, *oats* have seldom any singular."—*Cobbett's E. Gram.* ¶ 41. "He cannot assert that *l* are inserted in *fullness* to denote the sound of *u.*"—*Cobb's Review of Webster,* p. 11. "*s* have the power of *k.*"—*Gould's Adam's Gram.* p. 2. "*ti,* before a vowel, and unaccented, have the sound of *si* or *ci.*"—*Ibid.* "In words derived from the French, as *chagrin, chicanery,* and *chaise, ch* are sounded like *sh.*"—*Bucke's Gram.* p. 10. "But in the word *schism, schismatic,* &c. the *ch* are silent."—*Ibid.* "*Ph* are always sounded like *f,* at the beginning of words."—*Bucke's Gram.* "*Ph* have the sound of *f* as in *philosophy.*"—*Webster's El. Spelling-Book,* p. 11. "*Sh* have one sound only as in *shall.*"—*Ib.* "*Th* have two sounds."—*Ib.* "*x* have the sound of *sk,* before *a, o, u,* and *r.*"—*Ib.* "*Aw,* have the sound of *a* in *hall.*"—*Bolles's Spelling-Book,* p. vi. "*Ew,* sound like *u.*"—*Ib.* "*Ow,* when both sounded, have the sound of *ou.*"—*Ib.* "*Ui,* when both pronounced in one syllable sound like *wi* in *languid.*"—*Ib.*

"*Ui* three several Sorts of Sound express,
   As *Guile, rebuild, Bruise* and *Recruit* confess."—*Brightland's Gram.* p. 34.

UNDER NOTE IV.—EACH, ONE, EITHER, AND NEITHER.

"When each of the letters which compose this word, have been learned."—*Dr. Weeks, on Orthog.* p. 22. "As neither of us deny that both Homer and Virgil have great beauties."—*Blair's Rhet.* p. 21. "Yet neither of them are remarkable for precision."—*Ib.* p. 95. "How far each of the three great epic poets have distinguished themselves."—*Ib.* p. 427. "Each of these produce a separate agreeable sensation."—*Ib.* p. 48. "On the Lord's day every one of us Christians keep the sabbath."—*Tr. of Irenæus.* "And each of them bear the image of purity and holiness."—*Hope of Israel,* p. 81. "Were either of these meetings ever acknowledged or recognized?"—*Foster's Report,* i, 96. "Whilst neither of these letters exist in the Eugubian inscription."—*Knight, on Greek Alph.* p. 122. "And neither of them are properly termed indefinite."—*Wilson's Essay on Gram.* p. 88. "As likewise of the several subjects, which have in effect each their verb."—*Lowth's Gram.* p. 120. "Sometimes when the word ends in *s,* neither of the signs are used."—*Alex. Murray's Gram.* p. 21. "And as neither of these manners offend the ear."—*Walker's Dict. Pref.* p. 5. "Neither of these two Tenses are confined to this signification only."—*Johnson's Gram. Com.* p. 339. "But neither of these circumstances are intended here."—*Tooke's Diversions,* ii, 237. "So that all are indebted to each, and each are dependent upon all."—*Am. Bible Society's Rep.* 1836, p. 89. "And yet neither of them express any more action in this case than they did in the other."—*Bullions, E. Gram.* p. 201. "Each of these expressions denote action."—*Halleck's Gram.* p. 74. "Neither of these moods seem to be defined by distinct boundaries."—*Butler's Practical Gram.* p. 66. "Neither of these solutions are correct."—*Bullions, Lat. Gram.* p. 236. "Neither bear any sign of case at all."—*Fowler's E. Gram.* 8vo, 1850, § 217.
   "Each in their turn like Banquo's monarch stalk."—*Byron.*
   "And tell what each of them by th'other lose."—*Shak. Cori.* iii, 2.

UNDER NOTE V.—VERB BETWEEN TWO NOMINATIVES.

"The quarrels of lovers is a renewal of love."—*Adam's Lat. Gram.* p. 156; *Alexander's,* 49; *Gould's,* 159; *Bullions's,* 206. "Two dots, one placed above the other, is called *Shva.*"—*Dr. Wilson's Heb. Gram.* p. 43. "A few centuries, more or less, is a matter of small consequence."—*Ib.* p. 31. "Pictures were the first step towards the art of writing. Hieroglyphicks was the second step."—*Parker's English Composition,* p. 27. "The comeliness of youth are modesty and frankness; of age, condescension and dignity."—*Murray's Key,* 8vo, p. 166. "Merit and good works is the end of man's motion."—*Lord Bacon.* "Divers philosophers hold that the lips is parcel of the mind."—*Shakspeare.* "The clothing of the natives were the skins of wild beasts."—*Indian Wars,* p. 92. "Prepossessions in favor of our nativ town, is not a matter of surprise."—*Webster's Essays,* p. 217. "Two shillings and six pence is half a crown, but not a half crown."—*Priestley's Gram.* p. 150; *Bicknell's,* ii, 53. "Two vowels, pronounced by a single impulse of the voice, and uniting in one sound, is called a dipthong."—*Cooper's Pl. and Pr. Gram.* p. 1. "Two or more sentences united together is called a Compound Sentence."—*P. E. Day's District School Gram.* p. 10. "Two or more words rightly put together, but not completing an entire proposition, is called a Phrase."—*Ibid.* "But the common Number of Times are five."—*The British Grammar,* p. 122. "Technical terms, injudiciously introduced, is another source of darkness in composition."—*Jamieson's Rhet.* p. 107. "The United States is the great middle division of North America."—*Morse's Geog.* p. 44. "A great cause of the low state of industry were the restraints put upon it."—HUME; *Murray's Gram.* p. 145; *Ingersoll's,* 172; *Sanborn's,* 192; *Smith's,* 123; and others. "Here two tall ships becomes the victor's prey."—*Rowe's Lucan,* B. ii, L. 1098. "The expenses incident to an outfit is surely no object."—*The Friend,* Vol. iii, p. 200.

" Perhaps their loves, or else their sheep,
        Was all that did their silly thoughts so busy keep."—*Milton.*

UNDER NOTE VI.—CHANGE THE NOMINATIVE.

"Much pains has been taken to explain all the kinds of words."—*Infant School Gram.* p. 128. "Not less [*time*] than three years are spent in attaining this faculty."—*Music of Nature,* p. 28. "Where this night are met in state Many a friend to gratulate His wish'd presence."—*Milton's Comus,* l. 948. "Peace! my darling, here's no danger, Here's no oxen near thy bed."—*Watts.* "But every one of these are mere conjectures, and some of them very unhappy ones."—*Coleridge's Introduction,* p. 61. "The old theorists, calling the Interrogatives and Repliers, *adverbs,* is only a part of their regular system of naming words."—*O. B. Peirce's Gram.* p. 374. "Where a series of sentences occur, place them in the order in which the facts occur."—*Ib.* p. 264. "And that the whole in conjunction make a regular chain of causes and effects."—*Kames, El. of Crit.* ii, 275. "The origin of the Grecian, and Roman republics, though equally involved in the obscurities and uncertainties of fabulous events, present one remarkable distinction."—*Adams's Rhet.* i, 95. "In these respects, mankind is left by nature an unformed, unfinished creature."—*Butler's Analogy,* p. 144. "The scripture are the oracles of God himself."—HOOKER: *Joh. Dict. w. Oracle.* "And at our gates are all manner of pleasant fruits."—*Solomon's Song,* vii, 13. "The preterit of *pluck, look,* and *toss* are, in speech, pronounced *pluckt, lookt, tosst.*"—*Fowler's E. Gram.* 1850, § 68.

" Severe the doom that length of days impose,
    To stand sad witness of unnumber'd woes!"—*Melmoth.*

UNDER NOTE VII.—ADAPT FORM TO STYLE.

1. *Forms not proper for the Common or Familiar Style.*

"Was it thou that buildedst that house?"—*Inst.* p. 151. "That boy writeth very elegantly."—*Ib.* "Couldest not thou write without blotting thy book?"—*Ib.* "Thinkest thou not it will rain to-day?"—*Ib.* "Doth not your cousin intend to visit you?"—*Ib.* "That boy hath torn my book."—*Ib.* "Was it thou that spreadest the hay?"—*Ib.* "Was it James, or thou, that didst let him in?"—*Ib.* "He dareth not say a word."—*Ib.* "Thou stoodest in my way and hinderedst me."—*Ib.*

"Whom see I?—Whom seest thou now?—Whom sees he?—Whom lovest thou most?—What dost thou to-day?—What person seest thou teaching that boy?—He hath two new knives.—Which road takest thou?—What child teaches he?"—*Ingersoll's Gram.* p. 66. "Thou, who makest my shoes, sellest many more."—*Ib.* p. 67.

"The English language hath been much cultivated during the last two hundred years. It hath been considerably polished and refined."—*Lowth's Gram.* Pref. p. iii. "This *stile* is ostentatious, and doth not suit grave writing."—*Priestley's Gram.* p. 82. "But custom hath now appropriated *who* to persons, and *which* to things."—*Ib.* p. 97. "The indicative mood sheweth or declareth; as, *Ego amo,* I love: or else asketh a question; as, *Amas tu?* Dost thou love?"—*Paul's Accidence,* Ed. of 1793, p. 16. "Though thou canst not do much for the cause, thou mayst and shouldst do something."—*Murray's Gram.* p. 143. "The support of so many of his relations, was a heavy tax; but thou knowest he paid it cheerfully."—*Murray's Key,* R. 1, p. 180. "It may, and often doth, come short of it."—*Campbell's Rhetoric,* p. 160.

" 'Twas thou, who, while thou seem'dst to chide,
    To give me all thy pittance tried."—*Mitford's Blanch,* p. 78.

2. *Forms not proper for the Solemn or Biblical Style.*

"The Lord has prepar'd his throne in the heavens; and his kingdom rules over all."—"Thou answer'd them, O Lord our God: thou was a God that forgave them, though thou took vengeance of their inventions."—"Then thou spoke in vision to thy Holy One, and said, I have laid help upon one that is mighty."—"So then, it is not of him that wills, nor of him that runs, but of God that shows mercy; who dispenses his blessings, whether temporal or spiritual, as seems good in his sight."

" Thou, the mean while, was blending with my thought;
    Yea, with my life, and life's own secret joy."—*Coleridge.*

UNDER NOTE VIII.—EXPRESS THE NOMINATIVE.

"Who is here so base, that would be a bondman?"—*Beauties of Shakspeare,* p. 249. "Who is here so rude, that would not be a Roman?"—*Ib.* "There is not a sparrow falls to the ground without his notice."—*Murray's Gram.* p. 300. "In order to adjust them so,

as shall consist equally with the perspicuity and the strength of the period."—*Ib.*
Blair's Rhet. 118. "But, sometimes, there is a verb comes in."—*Cobbett's English*
¶ 248. "Mr. Prince has a genius would prompt him to better things."—*Spectator, I*
"It is this removes that impenetrable mist."—*Harris's Hermes*, p. 362. "By the p
given him for his courage."—*Locke, on Education*, p. 214. "There is no man would
welcome here."—*Steele, Spect.* No. 544. "Between an antecedent and a consequ
what goes before, and immediately follows."—*Blair's Rhet.* p. 141. "And as connect
what goes before and follows."—*Ib.* p. 354. "There is no man doth a wrong for the
sake."—*Lord Bacon.* "All the various miseries of life, which people bring upon the
by negligence and folly, and might have been avoided by proper care, are instances o
—*Butler's Analogy*, p. 108. "Ancient philosophers have taught many things in f
morality, so far at least as respect justice and goodness towards our fellow-creat
Gospel its own Witness, p. 56. "Indeed, if there be any such, have been, or appear
us, as suppose, there is not a wise man among us all, nor an honest man, that is
judge betwixt his brethren; we shall not covet to meddle in their matter."—*I*
Works, i, 504. "There were that drew back; there were that made shipwreck c
yea, there were that brought in damnable heresies."—*Ib.* i, 466. "The nature of t
rendered this plan altogether proper, and in similar situations is fit to be imitated."—
Rhet. p. 274. "This is an idiom to which our language is strongly inclined, a
formerly very prevalent."—*Churchill's Gram.* p. 150. "His roots are wrapped ab
heap, and seeth the place of stones."—*Job*, viii, 17.

"New-York, Fifthmonth 3d, 15.

"Dear friend, Am sorry to hear of thy loss; but hope it may be retrieved. Sh
happy to render thee any assistance in my power. Shall call to see thee to-
morning. Accept assurances of my regard. A

"New-York, May 3d, P. M., 18.

"Dear sir, Have just received the kind note favoured me with this morning; and
forbear to express my gratitude to you. On further information, find have not
much as at first supposed; and believe shall still be able to meet all my engag
Should, however, be happy to see you. Accept, dear sir, my most cordial thanks.
—See *Brown's Institutes*, p. 151.

"Will martial flames forever fire thy mind,
And never, never be to Heaven resign'd?"—*Pope, Odys.* xii, 145.

UNDER NOTE IX.—APPLICATION OF MOODS.
First Clause of the Note.—For the Subjunctive Present.

"He will not be pardoned, unless he repents."—*Brown's Institutes*, p. 191.

[FORMULE.—Not proper, because the verb *repents*, which is here used to express a future contingency i
indicative mood. But, according to the first clause of Note 9th to Rule 14th, "A future contingency
expressed by a verb in the subjunctive present." Therefore, *repents* should be *repent*; thus, "He wi
pardoned, unless he *repent*."]

"If thou findest any kernelwort in this marshy meadow, bring it to me."—*Neef's I
of Teaching*, p. 258. "If thou leavest the room, do not forget to shut that drawer.
p. 246. "If thou graspest it stoutly, thou wilt not be hurt."—*Ib.* p. 106. "On con
that he comes, I will consent to stay."—*Murray's Exerc.* p. 74. "If he is but discre
will succeed."—*Inst.* p. 191. "Take heed that thou speakest not to Jacob."—*Ib.*
thou castest me off, I shall be miserable."—*Ib.* "Send them to me if thou pleasest.
"Watch the door of thy lips, lest thou utterest folly."—*Ib.* "Though a liar speak
truth, he will hardly be believed."—*Common School Manual*, ii, 124. "I will go un
should be ill."—*Murray's Gram.* p. 300. "If the word or words understood are say
the true construction will be apparent."—*Murray's Exercises in Parsing*, p. 21. "I
thou shalt see the propriety of the measure, we shall not desire thy support."—*M.
Key*, p. 209. "Unless thou shouldst make a timely retreat, the danger will be una
ble."—*Ib.* p. 209. "We may live happily, though our possessions are small."—*Ib.*
"If they are carefully studied, they will enable the student to parse all the exercis
Ib., Note, p. 165. "If the accent is fairly preserved on the proper syllable, this dr
sound will never be heard."—*Murray's Gram.* p. 242. "One phrase may, in point of
be equivalent to another, though its grammatical nature is essentially different."—
108. "If any man obeyeth not our word by this epistle, note that man."—*Dr. W.*
Bible. "Thy skill will be the greater, if thou hittest it."—*Putnam's Analytical R.
204. "Thy skill will be the greater if thou hit'st it."—*Cobb's N. A. Reader*, p. 321.
shall overtake him though he should run."—*Priestley's Gram.* p. 118; *Murray's,
Smith's*, 173. "We shall be disgusted if he gives us too much."—*Blair's Rhet.* p. 34
"What is't to thee, if he neglect thy urn,
Or without spices lets thy body burn."—*Dryden: Joh. Dict. w. What.*

Second Clause of Note IX.—For the Subjunctive Imperfect.

"And so would I, if I was he."—*Brown's Institutes*, p. 191.

[FORMULE.—Not proper, because the verb *was*, which is here used to express a mere supposition, with indefinite time, is in the indicative mood. But, according to the second clause of Note 9th to Rule 14th, "A mere *supposition*, with indefinite time, is best expressed by a verb in the subjunctive imperfect." Therefore, *was* should be *were;* thus, "And so would I, if I *were* he."]

"If I was a Greek, I should resist Turkish despotism."—*Cardell's Elements of Gram.* p. 80. "If he was to go, he would attend to your business."—*Ib.* p. 81. "If thou feltest as I do, we should soon decide."—*Inst.* p. 191. "Though thou sheddest thy blood in the cause, it would but prove thee sincerely a fool."—*Ib.* "If thou lovedst him, there would be more evidence of it."—*Ib.* "If thou couldst convince him, he would not act accordingly."—*Murray's Key*, p. 209. "If there was no liberty, there would be no real crime."—*Formey's Belles-Lettres*, p. 118. "If the house was burnt down, the case would be the same."—*Foster's Report*, i, 89. "As if the mind was not always in action, when it prefers any thing !"—*West, on Agency*, p. 38. "Suppose I was to say, ' Light is a body.' "—*Harris's Hermes*, p. 78. "If either oxygen or azote was omitted, life would be destroyed."—*Gurney's Evidences*, p. 155. "The verb *dare* is sometimes used as if it was an auxiliary."—*Priestley's Gram.* p. 132. "A certain lady, whom I could name, if it was necessary."—*Spectator*, No. 536. "If the *e* was dropped, *c* and *g* would assume their hard sounds."—*Buchanan's Syntax*, p. 10. "He would no more comprehend it, than if it was the speech of a Hottentot."—*Neef's Sketch*, p. 112. "If thou knewest the gift of God," &c.—*John*, iv, 10. "I wish I was at home."—*O. B. Peirce's Gram.* p. 260. "Fact alone does not constitute right : if it does, general warrants were lawful."—*Junius, Let.* xliv, p. 205. "Thou look'st upon thy boy as though thou guessest it."—*Putnam's Analytical Reader*, p. 202. "Thou look'st upon thy boy as though thou guessedst it."—*Cobb's N. A. Reader*, p. 320. "He fought as if he had contended for life."—*Hiley's Gram.* p. 92. "He fought as if he had been contending for his life."—*Ib.* 92.

"The dewdrop glistens on thy leaf, As if thou seem'st to shed a tear ;	As if thou knew'st my tale of grief, Felt all my sufferings severe."—*Alex. Letham.*

Last Clause of Note IX.—For the Indicative Mood.

"If he know the way, he does not need a guide."—*Brown's Institutes*, p. 191.

[FORMULE.—Not proper, because the verb *know*, which is used to express a conditional circumstance assumed as a fact, is in the subjunctive mood. But, according to the last clause of Note 9th to Rule 14th, "A conditional circumstance assumed as a fact, requires the indicative mood." Therefore, *know* should be *knows;* thus, " If he *knows* the way, he does not need a guide."]

"And if there be no difference, one of them must be superfluous, and ought to be rejected."—*Murray's Gram.* p. 149. "I cannot say that I admire this construction, though it be much used."—*Priestley's Gram.* p. 172. "We are disappointed, if the verb do not immediately follow it."—*Ib.* p. 177. "If it were they who acted so ungratefully, they are doubly in fault."—*Murray's Key*, 8vo, p. 223. "If art become apparent, it disgusts the reader."—*Jamieson's Rhet.* p. 80. "Though perspicuity be more properly a rhetorical than a grammatical quality, I thought it better to include it in this book."—*Campbell's Rhet.* p. 233. "Although the efficient cause be obscure, the final cause of those sensations lies open."—*Blair's Rhet.* p. 29. "Although the barrenness of language, and the want of words be doubtless one cause of the invention of tropes."—*Ib.* p. 135. "Though it enforce not its instructions, yet it furnishes us with a greater variety."—*Ib.* p. 353. "In other cases, though the idea be one, the words remain quite separate."—*Priestley's Gram.* p. 140. "Though the Form of our Language be more simple, and has that peculiar Beauty."—*Buchanan's Syntax*, p. v. "Human works are of no significancy till they be completed."—*Kames, El. of Crit.* i, 245. "Our disgust lessens gradually till it vanish altogether."—*Ib.* i, 338. "And our relish improves by use, till it arrive at perfection."—*Ib.* i, 338. "So long as he keep himself in his own proper element."—*COKE: Ib.* i, 233. "Whether this translation were ever published or not I am wholly ignorant."—*Sale's Koran*, i, 13. "It is false to affirm, ' As it is day, it is light,' unless it actually be day."—*Harris's Hermes*, p. 246. "But we may at midnight affirm, 'If it be day, it is light.' "—*Ibid.* "If the Bible be true, it is a volume of unspeakable interest."—*Dickinson.* "Though he were a son, yet learned he obedience by the things which he suffered."—*Heb.* v, 8. "If David then call him Lord, how is he his son ?"—*Matt.* xxii, 45.

"'Tis hard to say, if greater want of skill
 Appear in writing or in judging ill."—*Pope, Ess. on Crit.*

UNDER NOTE X.—FALSE SUBJUNCTIVES.

"If a man have built a house, the house is his."—*Wayland's Moral Science*, p. 286.

[FORMULE.—Not proper, because the verb *have built*, which extends the subjunctive mood into the perfect tense, has the appearance of disagreeing with its nominative *man*. But, according to Note 10th to Rule 14th, "Every such use or extension of the subjunctive mood, as the reader will be likely to mistake for a discord between the verb and its nominative, ought to be avoided as an impropriety." Therefore, *have built* should be *has built;* thus, "If a man *has built* a house, the house is his."]

"If God have required them of him, as is the fact, he has time."—*Ib.* p. 351. "Unless a previous understanding to the contrary have been had with the Principal."—*Berrian's Circular*, p. 5. "O if thou have Hid them in some flowery cave."—*Milton's Comus*, l. 239. "O if Jove's will Have link'd that amorous power to thy soft lay."—*Milton, Sonnet* 1. "SUBJUNCTIVE MOOD: If thou love, If thou loved, If thou have loved, If thou had loved, If thou shall or will love, If thou shall or will have loved."—*L. Murray's Gram*. 2d Ed. p. 71; *Cooper's Murray*, 58; *D. Adams's Gram*. 48; and others. "Till religion, the pilot of the soul, have lent thee her unfathomable coil."—*Tupper's Thoughts*, p. 170. "Whether nature or art contribute most to form an orator, is a trifling inquiry."—*Blair's Rhet*. p. 338. "Year after year steals something from us; till the decaying fabric totter of itself, and crumble at length into dust."—*Murray's Key*, 8vo, p. 225. "If spiritual pride have not entirely vanquished humility."—*West's Letters*, p. 184. "Whether he have gored a son, or have gored a daughter."—*Exodus*, xxi, 31. "It is doubtful whether the object introduced by way of simile, relate to what goes before, or to what follows."—*Kames, El. of Crit*. ii, 45.

> "And bridle in thy headlong wave,
> Till thou our summons answer'd have."—*Milt. Comus*, l. 887.

RULE XV.—FINITE VERBS.

When the nominative is a collective noun conveying the idea of plurality, the Verb must agree with it in the plural number: as, "The *council were divided*."—"The *college* of cardinals *are* the electors of the pope."—*Murray's Key*, p. 176. "Quintus Curtius relates, that *a number* of them *were drowned* in the river Lycus."—*Home's Art of Thinking*, p. 125.

"Yon *host come* learn'd in academic rules."—*Rowe's Lucan*, vii, 401.

"While heaven's high *host* on hallelujahs *live*."—*Young's N. Th*. iv, 378.

OBSERVATIONS ON RULE XV.

OBS. 1.—To this rule there are *no exceptions;* because, the collective noun being a name which even in the singular number "signifies *many*," the verb which agrees with it, can never properly be singular, unless the collection be taken literally as one aggregate, and not as "conveying the idea of plurality." Thus, the collective noun singular being in general susceptible of two senses, and consequently admitting two modes of concord, the form of the verb, whether singular or plural, becomes the principal index to the particular sense in which the nominative is taken. After such a noun, we can use either a singular verb, agreeing with it literally, strictly, formally, according to Rule 14th; or a plural one, agreeing with it figuratively, virtually, ideally, according to Rule 15th. So, when the collective noun is an antecedent, the relative having in itself no distinction of the numbers, its verb becomes the index to the sense of all three; as, "Wherefore lift up thy prayer for the *remnant that* IS *left*."—*Isaiah*, xxxvii, 4. "Wherefore lift up thy prayer for the *remnant that* ARE *left*."—*2 Kings*, xix, 4. Ordinarily the word *remnant* conveys no idea of plurality; but, it being here applied to persons, and having a meaning to which the mere singular neuter noun is not well adapted, the latter construction is preferable to the former. The Greek version varies more in the two places here cited; being plural in Isaiah, and singular in Kings. The Latin Vulgate, in both, is, "*pro reliquiis quæ repertæ sunt:*" i.e., "for the remains, or remnants, that are found."

OBS. 2.—Dr. Adam's rule is this: "A collective noun may be joined with a verb either of the singular or of the plural number; as, *Multitudo stat*, or *stant; the multitude stands, or stand*." —*Latin and English Gram*. p. 154. To this doctrine, Lowth, Murray, and others, add: "Yet not without regard to the *import of the word*, as conveying *unity or plurality of idea*."—*Lowth*, p. 74; *Murray*, 152. If these latter authors mean, that collective nouns are permanently divided in import, so that some are invariably determined to the idea of unity, and others to that of plurality, they are wrong in principle; for, as Dr. Adam remarks, "A collective noun, when joined with a verb singular, expresses many considered as one whole; but when joined with a verb plural, it signifies many separately, or as individuals."—*Adam's Gram*. p. 154. And if this alone is what their addition means, it is purposely useless; and so, for all the purposes of parsing, is the singular half of the rule itself. Kirkham divides this rule into two, one for "unity of idea," and the other for "plurality of idea," shows how each is to be applied in parsing, according to his "*systematick order;*" and then, turning round with a gallant tilt at his own work, condemns both, as idle fabrications, which it were "better to reject than to retain;" alleging that, "The existence of such a thing as 'unity or plurality of idea,' as applicable to nouns of this class, is *doubtful*."— *Kirkham's Gram*. p. 59. How then shall a plural verb or pronoun after a collective noun, be parsed, seeing it does not agree with the noun by the ordinary rule of agreement? Will any one say, that every such construction is *bad English?* If this cannot be maintained, rules eleventh and fifteenth of this series are necessary. But when the noun conveys the idea of unity or takes the plural form, the verb or pronoun has no other than a literal agreement by the common rule; as,

> "A *priesthood*, such *as* Baal's *was* of old,
> A *people*, such *as* never *was* till now."—*Cowper*.

OBS. 3.—Of the construction of the verb and collective noun, a late British author gives the following account: "Collective nouns are substantives *which* signify *many in the singular number*. Collective nouns are of two sorts: 1. Those which cannot become plural like other substantives; as, nobility, mankind, &c. 2. Those which can be made plural by the usual rules for a substantive ; as, 'A multitude, multitudes ; a crowd, crowds ;' &c. Substantives which imply plurality in the singular number, and consequently have no other plural, generally require a plural verb. They are cattle, cavalry, clergy, commonalty, gentry, laity, mankind, nobility, peasantry, people, populace, public, rabble, &c. [:] as, 'The public *are* informed.' Collective nouns which form a regular plural, such as, number, numbers ; multitude, multitudes ; have, like all other substantives, a singular verb, when they are in the singular number ; and a plural verb, when they are in the plural number ; as, ' A number of people *is* assembled ; Numbers *are* assembled.'—' The fleet *was* dispersed ; a *part* of it *was* injured ; the several *parts are* now collected.' "—*Nixon's Parser*, p. 120. To this, his main text, the author appends a note, from which the following passages are extracted : "There are few persons acquainted with Grammar, who may not have noticed, in many authors as well as speakers, an irregularity in supposing collective nouns to have, at one time, a singular meaning, and consequently to require a singular verb ; and, at an other time, to have a plural meaning, and therefore to require a plural verb. This irregularity appears to have arisen from the want of a clear idea of the nature of a collective noun. This defect the author has endeavoured to supply ; and, upon his definition, he has founded the two rules above. It is allowed on all sides that, hitherto, no satisfactory rules have been produced to enable the pupil to ascertain, with any degree of certainty, when a collective noun should have a singular verb, and when a plural one. A rule that simply tells its examiner, that when a collective noun in the nominative case conveys the idea of unity, its verb should be singular ; and when it implies plurality, its verb should be plural, is of very little value ; for such a rule will prove the *pupil's being in the right*, whether he *should* put the verb in the singular or the plural.'"—*Ibid.*

OBS. 4.—The foregoing explanation has many faults ; and whoever trusts to it, or to any thing like it, will certainly be very much misled. In the first place, it is remarkable that an author who could suspect in others " the *want of a clear idea* of the nature of a collective noun," should have hoped to supply the defect by a definition so ambiguous and ill-written as is the one above. Secondly, his subdivision of this class of nouns into two sorts, is both baseless and nugatory ; for that plurality which has reference to the individuals of an assemblage, has no manner of connexion or affinity with that which refers to more than one such aggregate ; nor is there any interference of the one with the other, or any ground at all for supposing that the absence of the latter is, has been, or ought to be, the occasion for adopting the former. Hence, thirdly, his two rules, (though, so far as they go, they seem not untrue in themselves,) by their limitation under this false division, exclude and deny the true construction of the verb with the greater part of our collective nouns. For, fourthly, the first of these rules rashly presumes that any collective noun which in the singular number implies a plurality of individuals, is consequently destitute of any other plural ; and the second accordingly supposes that no such nouns as, council, committee, jury, meeting, society, assembly, court, college, company, army, host, band, retinue, train, multitude, number, part, half, portion, majority, minority, remainder, set, sort, kind, class, nation, tribe, family, race, and a hundred more, can ever be properly used with a plural verb, except when they assume the plural form. To prove the falsity of this supposition, is needless. And, finally, the objection which this author advances against the common rules, is very far from proving them useless, or not greatly preferable to his own. If they do not in every instance enable the student to ascertain with certainty which form of concord he ought to prefer, it is only because no rules can possibly tell a man precisely when he ought to entertain the idea of unity, and when that of plurality. In some instances, these ideas are unavoidably mixed or associated, so that it is of little or no consequence which form of the verb we prefer ; as, " Behold, the *people* IS *one*, and *they have all* one language."—*Gen.* xi, 6.

" Well, if a king's a lion, at the least
  The *people* ARE *a* many-headed *beast*."—*Pope*, Epist. i, l. 120.

OBS.—5. Lindley Murray says, " On many occasions, *where* a noun of multitude is used, it is very difficult to decide, whether the verb should be in the singular, or in the plural number ; and this difficulty has induced some grammarians to cut the knot at once, and to assert that every noun of multitude must always be considered as conveying the idea of unity."—*Octavo Gram.* p. 153. What these occasions, or who these grammarians, are, I know not ; but it is certain that the difficulty here imagined does not concern the application of such rules as require the verb and pronoun to conform to the sense intended ; and, where there is no apparent impropriety in adopting either number, there is no occasion to raise a scruple as to which is right. To cut knots by dogmatism, and to tie them by sophistry, are employments equally vain. It cannot be denied that there are in every multitude both a unity and a plurality, one or the other of which must be preferred as the principle of concord for the verb or the pronoun, or for both. Nor is the number of nouns small, or their use unfrequent, which, according to our best authors, admit of either construction ; though Kirkham assails and repudiates *his own rules*, because, " Their application is quite limited."—*Grammar in Familiar Lectures*, p. 59.

OBS. 6.—Murray's doctrine seems to be, not that collective nouns are generally susceptible of two senses in respect to number, but that some naturally convey the idea of unity, others, that of plurality, and a few, either of these senses. The last, which are probably ten times more numerous than all the rest, he somehow merges or forgets, so as to speak of *two classes* only : saying, " Some nouns of multitude certainly convey to the mind an idea of plurality, others, that of a whole as one thing, and others again, sometimes that of unity, and sometimes that of plurality. On this ground, it is warrantable, and consistent with the nature of things, to apply a plural verb and pronoun *to the one class*, and a singular verb and pronoun *to the other*. We shall immediately perceive the *impropriety* of the following constructions : ' The clergy *has* withdrawn *itself* from the temporal courts ;' ' The assembly *was* divided in *its* opinion ;' &c."—*Octavo Gram.* p. 153. The simple fact is, that *clergy, assembly*, and perhaps every other collective noun, may sometimes convey the idea of unity, and sometimes that of plurality ; but an "*opinion*" or a voluntary " *withdrawing* " is a *personal* act or quality ; *wherefore* it is here more consistent to adopt the plural sense and construction, in which alone we take the collection as individuals, or persons.

36

OBS. 7.—Although a uniformity of number is generally preferable to diversity, in the construction of words that refer to the same collective noun; and although many grammarians deny that any departure from such uniformity is allowable; yet, if the singular be put first, a plural pronoun may sometimes follow without obvious impropriety: as, "So Judah *was* carried away out of *their* land."—2 *Kings*, xxv, 21. "Israel *is* reproved and threatened for *their* impiety and idolatry."—*Friends' Bible, Hosea*, x. "There *is* the enemy *who wait* to give us battle."—*Murray's Introductory Reader*, p. 36. When the idea of plurality predominates in the author's mind, a plural verb is sometimes used *before* a collective noun that has the singular article *an* or *a*; as, "There *are a sort* of authors, *who seem* to take up with appearances."—*Addison.* "Here *are a number* of facts or incidents leading to the end in view."—*Kames, El. of Crit.* ii, 296. "There *are a great number* of exceedingly good writers among the French."—*Maunder's Gram.* p. 11.
        "There in the forum *swarm a numerous train,*
        The subject of debate a townsman slain."—*Pope, Iliad*, B. xviii, l. 578.

OBS. 8.—Collective nouns, when they are merely *partitive* of the plural, like the words *sort* and *number* above, are usually connected with a plural verb, even though they have a singular definitive; as, "And *this sort* of adverbs commonly *admit* of Comparison."—*Buchanan's English Syntax*, p. 64. Here, perhaps, it would be better to say, "*Adverbs of this sort* commonly *admit* of comparison." "*A part* of the exports *consist* of raw silk."—*Webster's Improved Gram.* p. 100. This construction is censured by Murray, in his octavo Gram. p. 148; where we are told, that the verb should agree with the first noun only. Dr. Webster alludes to this circumstance, in *improving* his grammar, and admits that, "A part of the exports *consists*, seems to be more correct."—*Improved Gram.* p. 100. Yet he retains his original text, and obviously thinks it a light thing, that, "in some cases," his rules or examples "may not be vindicable." (See Obs. 14th, 15th, and 16th, on Rule 14th, of this code.) It would, I think, be better to say, "The exports *consist* partly of raw silk." Again: "*A multitude* of Latin words *have*, of late, been poured in upon us."—*Blair's Rhet.* p. 94. Better, perhaps: "*Latin words, in great multitude*, have, of late, been poured in upon us." So: "For *the bulk* of *writers* are very apt to confound them with each other."—*Ib.* p. 97. Better: "For *most writers* are very apt to confound them with each other." In the following example, (here cited as *Kames* has it, *El. of Crit.* ii, 247,) either the verb *is*, or the phrase, "*There are some moveless men*," might as well have been used:
        "There *are a sort* of men, whose visages
        Do cream and mantle like a standing pond."—*Shak.*

OBS. 9.—Collections of *things* are much less frequently and less properly regarded as individuals, or under the idea of plurality, than collections of *persons*. This distinction may account for the difference of construction in the two clauses of the following example; though I rather doubt whether a plural verb ought to be used in the former: "The *number* of commissioned *officers* in the guards *are* to the marching regiments as one to eleven: the *number* of *regiments* given to the guards, compared with those given to the line, *is* about three to one."—*Junius*, p. 147. Whenever the multitude is spoken of with reference to a personal act or quality, the verb ought, as I before suggested, to be in the plural number; as, "The public *are informed*."—"The plaintiff's counsel *have assumed* a difficult task."—"The committee *were instructed* to prepare a remonstrance." "The English nation *declare* they are grossly injured by *their* representatives."—*Junius*, p. 147. "One particular class of men *are* permitted to call *themselves* the King's friends."—*Id.* p. 176. "The Ministry *have* realized the compendious ideas of Caligula."—*Id.* p. 177. It is in accordance with this principle, that the following sentences have plural verbs and pronouns, though their definitives are singular, and perhaps ought to be singular: "So depraved *were that people* whom in their history we so much admire."—HUME: *M'Ilvaine's Lect.* p. 400. "Oh, *this people have sinned* a great sin, and have made them gods of gold."—*Exodus*, xxxii, 31. "*This people* thus gathered *have* not wanted those trials."—*Barclay's Works*, i, 460. The following examples, among others, are censured by Priestley, Murray, and the copyists of the latter, without sufficient discrimination, and for a reason which I think fallacious; namely, "because the ideas they represent seem not to be sufficiently divided in the mind:"—"The court of Rome *were* not without solicitude."—*Hume.* "The house of Lords *were* so much influenced by these reasons."—*Id.* See *Priestley's Gram.* p. 188; *Murray's*, 152; *R. C. Smith's*, 129; *Ingersoll's*, 248; and others.

OBS. 10.—In general, a collective noun, unless it be made plural in form, no more admits a plural adjective before it, than any other singular noun. Hence the impropriety of putting *these* or *those* before *kind* or *sort*; as, "*These kind* of knaves I know."—*Shakspeare.* Hence, too, I infer that *cattle* is not a collective noun, as Nixon would have it to be, but an irregular plural which has no singular; because we can say *these cattle* or *those cattle*, but neither a bullock nor a herd is ever called *a cattle*, *this cattle*, or *that cattle*. And if "*cavalry, clergy, commonalty*," &c., were like this word, they would all be plurals also, and not "substantives which imply plurality in the singular number, and consequently have no other plural." Whence it appears, that the writer who most broadly charges others with not understanding the nature of a collective noun, has most of all misconceived it himself. If there are not *many clergies*, it is because *the clergy* is one body, with one Head, and not because it is in a particular sense many. And, since the forms of words are not necessarily confined to things that exist, who shall say that the plural word *clergies*, as I have just used it, is not good English?

OBS. 11.—If we say, "*these people*," "*these gentry*," "*these folk*," we make *people, gentry*, and *folk*, not only irregular plurals, but plurals to which there are no correspondent singulars; for, by these phrases, we must mean certain individuals, and not more than one people, gentry, or folk. But these names are sometimes collective nouns singular; and, as such, they may have verbs of either number, according to the sense; and may also form regular plurals, as *peoples*, and *folks*; though we seldom, if ever, speak of *gentries*; and *folks* is now often irregularly applied to persons, as if one person were a *folk*. So *troops* is sometimes irregularly, if not improperly, put for *soldiers*, as if a soldier were a *troop*; as, "While those gallant *troops*, by *whom* every hazardous, every laborious service is performed, are left to perish."—*Junius*, p 147. In

Genesis, xxvii, 29th, we read, "Let *people* serve thee, and nations bow down to thee." But, according to the Vulgate, it ought to be, "Let *peoples* serve thee, and nations bow down to thee;" according to the Septuagint, "Let *nations* serve thee, and *rulers* bow down to thee." Among Murray's "instances of false syntax," we find the text, "This people draweth near to me with their mouth," &c.—*Octavo Gram.* Vol. ii, p. 49. This is corrected in his Key, thus: "*These* people *drew* near to me with their mouth."—*Ib.* ii, 185. The Bible has it: "This people *draw near me* with their mouth."—*Isaiah*, xxix, 13. And again: "This people *draweth nigh unto* me with their mouth."—*Matt.* xv, 8. Dr. Priestley thought it ought to be, "This people *draws* nigh unto me with their *mouths.*"—*Priestley's Gram.* p. 63. The second evangelist omits some words: "This people *honoureth* me with their lips, but *their heart* is far from me."—*Mark*, vii, 6. In my opinion, the plural verb is here to be preferred; because the pronoun *their* is plural, and the worship spoken of was a personal rather than a national act. Yet the adjective *this* must be retained, if the text specify the Jews as a people. As to the words *mouth* and *heart*, they are to be understood figuratively of *speech* and *love;* and I agree not with Priestley, that the plural number must necessarily be used. See Note 4th to Rule 4th.

OBS. 12.—In making an assertion concerning a number or quantity with some indefinite excess or allowance, we seem sometimes to take for the subject of the verb what is really the object of a preposition; as, "In a sermon, there *may be* from three to five, or six heads."—*Blair's Rhet.* p. 313. "In those of Germany, there *are* from eight to twelve professors."—*Dwight, Lit. Convention*, p. 138. "About a million and a half *was subscribed* in a few days."—*N. Y. Daily Advertiser.* "About one hundred feet of the Muncy dam *has been swept* off."—*N. Y. Observer.* "Upwards of one hundred thousand dollars *have been appropriated.*"—*Newspaper.* "But I fear there *are* between twenty and thirty of them."—*Tooke's Diversions*, ii, 441. "Besides which, there *are* upwards of fifty smaller islands."—*Balbi's Geog.* p. 30. "On board of which *embarked* upwards of three hundred passengers."—*Robertson's Amer.* ii, 419. The propriety of using *above* or *upwards of* for *more than*, is questionable, but the practice is not uncommon. When there is a preposition before what seems at first to be the subject of the verb, as in the foregoing instances, I imagine there is an ellipsis of the word *number, amount, sum*, or *quantity;* the first of which words is a collective noun and may have a verb either singular or plural: as, "In a sermon, there may be *any number* from three to five or six heads." This is awkward, to be sure; but what does the Doctor's sentence *mean*, unless it is, that there *may be an optional number* of heads, varying from three to six?

OBS. 13.—Dr. Webster says, "When an aggregate amount is expressed by the plural names of the particulars composing that amount, the verb may be in the singular number; as, 'There *was* more than a hundred and fifty thousand pounds sterling.' *Mavor's Voyages.*" To this he adds, "However repugnant to the principles of grammar this may seem at first view, the practice is correct; for the affirmation is not made of the individual parts or divisions named, the *pounds*, but of the entire sum or amount."—*Philosophical Gram.* p. 146; *Improved Gram.* p. 100. The fact is, that the Doctor here, as in some other instances, deduces a false rule from a correct usage. It is plain that either the word *more*, taken substantively, or the noun to which it relates as an adjective, is the only nominative to the verb *was*. Mavor does not affirm that there *were* a hundred and fifty thousand pounds; but that there *was more*—i. e., more *money* than so many pounds *are*, or *amount to*. Oliver B. Peirce, too, falls into a multitude of strange errors respecting the nature of *more than*, and the construction of other words that accompany these. See his "Analytical Rules," and the manner in which he applies them, in "*The Grammar*," p. 195 *et seq.*

NOTE TO RULE XV.

A collective noun conveying the idea of unity, requires a verb in the third person singular; and generally admits also the regular plural construction: as, "His *army was* defeated."—"His *armies were* defeated."

IMPROPRIETIES FOR CORRECTION.

FALSE SYNTAX UNDER RULE XV.

UNDER THE RULE ITSELF.—THE IDEA OF PLURALITY.

"The gentry is punctilious in their etiquette."

[FORMULE.—Not proper, because the verb *is* is of the singular number, and does not correctly agree with its nominative *gentry*, which is a collective noun conveying rather the idea of plurality. But, according to Rule 15th, "When the nominative is a collective noun conveying the idea of plurality, the verb must agree with it in the plural number." Therefore, *is* should be *are;* thus, "The gentry *are* punctilious in their etiquette."]

"In France the peasantry goes barefoot, and the middle sort makes use of wooden shoes."—HARVEY: *Priestley's Gram.* p. 188. "The people rejoices in that which should cause sorrow."—See *Murray's Exercises*, p. 49. "My people is foolish, they have not known me."—*Jer.* iv, 22; *Lowth's Gram.* 75. "For the people speaks, but does not write."—*Philological Museum*, i, 646. "So that all the people that was in the camp, trembled."—*Exodus*, xix, 16. "No company likes to confess that they are ignorant."—*Student's Manual*, p. 217. "Far the greater part of their captives was anciently sacrificed."—*Robertson's America*, i, 339. "Above one half of them was cut off before the return of spring."—*Ib.* ii, 419. "The other class, termed Figures of Thought, supposes the words to be used in their proper and literal meaning."—*Blair's Rhet.* p. 133; *Murray's Gram.* 337. "A multitude of words in their dialect approaches to the Teutonic form, and therefore afford excellent assistance."—*Dr. Murray's Hist. of Lang.* i, 148. "A great majority of our authors is defective in manner."—*James Brown's Crit.*　"The greater part of these new-coined words has been rejected."—*Tooke's Diversions*, ii, 445.　"The greater part of the words it contains is subject to certain modifications and inflections."—*The Friend*, ii, 123.　"While all our youth prefers her to the rest."—*Waller's Poems*, p. 17.　"Mankind is appointed to live in a future state." —*Butler's Analogy*, p. 57.　"The greater part of human kind speaks and acts wholly by imitation."—*Wright's Gram.* p. 169.　"The greatest part of human gratifications approaches so nearly to vice."—*Ibid.*

"While still the busy world is treading o'er
　The paths they trod five thousand years before."—*Young.*

UNDER THE NOTE.—THE IDEA OF UNITY.

"In old English this species of words were numerous."—*Dr. Murray's Hist. of Lang.* ii, 6. "And a series of exercises in false grammar are introduced towards the end."—*Frost's El. of E. Gram.* p. iv.　"And a jury, in conformity with the same idea, were anciently called *homagium*, the homage, or manhood."—*Webster's Essays*, p. 296.　"With respect to the former, there are indeed plenty of means."—*Kames, El. of Crit.* ii, 319.　"The number of school districts have increased since the last year."—*Gov. Throop*, 1832.　"The Yearly Meeting have purchased with its funds these publications."—*Foster's Reports*, i, 76.　"Have the legislature power to prohibit assemblies?"—*Wm. Sullivan.*　"So that the whole number of the streets were fifty."—*Rollin's Ancient Hist.* ii, 8.　"The number of inhabitants were not more than four millions."—SMOLLETT: see *Priestley's Gram.* p. 193.　"The House of Commons were of small weight."—HUME: *Ib.* p. 188.　"The assembly of the wicked have enclosed me."—*Psal.* xxii, 16; *Lowth's Gram.* p. 75.　"Every kind of convenience and comfort are provided."—*Com. School Journal*, i, 24.　"Amidst the great decrease of the inhabitants in Spain, the body of the clergy have suffered no diminution; but has rather been gradually increasing."—*Payne's Geog.* ii, 418.　"Small as the number of inhabitants are, yet their poverty is extreme."—*Ib.* ii, 417.　"The number of the names were about one hundred and twenty."—*Ware's Gram.* p. 12: see *Acts*, i, 15.

RULE XVI. — FINITE VERBS.

When a Verb has two or more nominatives connected by *and*, it must agree with them jointly in the plural, because they are taken together: as, "True rhetoric *and* sound logic *are* very nearly allied."—*Blair's Rhet.* p. 11. "Aggression *and* injury in no case *justify* retaliation."—*Wayland's Moral Science*, p. 406.

"Judges *and* senates *have been bought* for gold,
　Esteem *and* love *were* never to be sold."—*Pope.*

EXCEPTION FIRST.

When two nominatives connected by *and* serve merely to describe one person or thing, they are either in apposition or equivalent to one name, and do not require a plural verb; as, "Immediately *comes* a hue and cry after a gang of theives."—*L'Estrange.*　"The *hue and cry* of the country *pursues* him."—*Junius*, Letter xxiii.　"Flesh and blood [i. e. man, or man's nature,] *hath not revealed* it unto thee."—*Matt.* xvi, 17.　"Descent and fall to us *is* adverse."—*Milton, P. L.* ii, 76.　"This *philosopher* and *poet was banished* from his country." —"Such a *Saviour* and *Redeemer is* actually *provided* for us."—*Gurney's Essays*, p. 336. "Let us then declare what great things our *God and Saviour has done* for us."—*Dr. Scott, on Luke* viii.　"*Toll, tribute*, and *custom, was paid* unto them."—*Ezra*, iv, 20.

"Whose icy *current* and compulsive *course*
　Ne'er *feels* retiring ebb, but *keeps* due on."—*Shakspeare.*

EXCEPTION SECOND.

When two nominatives connected by *and*, are emphatically distinguished, they belong to different propositions, and, if singular, do not require a plural verb; as, "*Ambition*, and not the *safety* of the state, *was* concerned."—*Goldsmith.*　"*Consanguinity*, and not *affinity*, is the ground of the prohibition."—*Webster's Essays*, p. 324.　"But a *modification*, and oftentimes a total *change, takes* place."—*Maunder.*　"*Somewhat*, and, in many circumstances, a great *deal* too, *is put* upon us."—*Butler's Analogy*, p. 108.　"*Disgrace*, and perhaps *ruin, was* the certain consequence of attempting the latter."—*Robertson's America*, i, 434.

"*Ay*, and *no* too, *was* no good divinity."—*Shakspeare.*
"*Love*, and *love only, is* the loan for love."—*Young.*

EXCEPTION THIRD.

When two or more nominatives connected by *and* are preceded by the adjective *each, every*, or *no*, they are taken separately, and do not require a plural verb; as, "When *no part* of their substance, and *no one* of their properties, *is* the same."—*Bp. Butler.*　"Every limb and feature *appears* with its respective grace."—*Steele.* "Every person, and every occurrence, *is held* in the most favourable light."—*Murray's Key*, p. 190. "Each worm, and each insect, *is* a marvel of creative power."

> "Whose every look and gesture *was* a joke
> To clapping theatres and shouting crowds."—*Young.*

. EXCEPTION FOURTH.

When the verb separates its nominatives, it agrees with that which precedes it, and is understood to the rest; as, "The *earth is* the Lord's, and the *fullness* thereof."—*Murray's Exercises*, p. 36.

> "*Disdain forbids* me, and my *dread* of shame."—*Milton.*
> "————Forth in the pleasing spring,
> Thy *beauty walks*, thy *tenderness*, and *love*."—*Thomson.*

OBSERVATIONS ON RULE XVI.

OBS. 1.—According to Lindley Murray, (who, in all his compilation, from whatever learned authorities, refers us to *no places* in any book but his own,) "Dr. Blair observes, that 'two or more substantives, joined by a copulative, *must always require* the verb or pronoun to which they *refer*, to be *placed* in the plural number:' and this," continues the great Compiler, "is the *general sentiment* of English grammarians."—*Murray's Gram.* i, p. 150. The same thing is stated in many other grammars : thus, *Ingersoll* has the very same words, on the 238th page of his book ; and *R. C. Smith* says, "Dr. Blair *very justly* observes," &c.—*Productive Gram.* p. 126. I therefore doubt not, the learned rhetorician has somewhere made some such remark ; though I can neither supply the reference which these gentlemen omit, nor vouch for the accuracy of their quotation. But I trust to make it very clear, that so many grammarians as hold this sentiment, are no great readers, to say the least of them. Murray himself acknowledges *one* exception to this principle, and unconsciously furnishes examples of one or two more ; but, in stead of placing the former in his Grammar, and under the rule, where the learner would be likely to notice it, he makes it an obscure and almost unintelligible note, in the *margin of his Key*, referring by an asterisk to the following correction : "Every man and every woman *was* numbered."—*Murray's Gram.* 8vo, Vol. ii, p. 190. To justify this phraseology, he talks thus : "*Whatever number* of nouns may be connected *by a conjunction with the pronoun* EVERY, this *pronoun* is as applicable to *the whole mass* of them, as to any *one of the nouns* ; and *therefore* the verb is correctly put in the singular number, and *refers to the whole* separately and individually considered."—*Ib.* So much, then, for "*the pronoun* EVERY!" But, without other exceptions, what shall be done with the following texts from Murray himself? "The flock, *and* not the fleece, *is*, or *ought* to be the object of the shepherd's care."—*Ib.* ii, 184. "This prodigy of learning, this scholar, critic, *and* antiquary, *was* entirely destitute of breeding and civility."—*Ib.* ii, 217. And, in the following line, what conjunction appears, or what is the difference between "horror" and "black despair," that the verb should be made plural ?

> "What black despair, what horror, *fill* his *mind*!"—*Ib.* ii, 183.
> "What black despair, what horror *fills* his *heart*!"—*Thomson.*[*]

OBS. 2.—Besides the many examples which may justly come under the four exceptions above specified, there are several questionable but customary expressions, which have some appearance of being deviations from this rule, but which may perhaps be reasonably explained on the principle of ellipsis : as, "All work and no play, *makes* Jack a dull boy."—"Slow and steady often *outtravels* haste."—*Dillwyn's Reflections*, p. 23. "Little and often *fills* the purse."—*Treasury of Knowledge*, Part i, p. 446. "Fair and softly *goes* far." These maxims, by universal custom, lay claim to a singular verb ; and, for my part, I know not how they can well be considered either real exceptions to the foregoing rule, or real inaccuracies under it ; for, in most of them, the words connected are not *nouns*; and those which are so, may not be nominatives. And it is clear, that every exception must have some specific character by which it may be distinguished ; else it destroys the rule, in stead of confirming it, as known exceptions are said to do. Murray appears to have thought the singular verb *wrong*; for, among his examples for parsing, he has, "Fair and softly *go* far," which instance is no more entitled to a plural verb than the rest. See his *Octavo Gram.* Vol. ii, p. 5. Why not suppose them all to be elliptical? Their meaning may be as follows : "*To have* all work and no play, *makes* Jack a dull boy."—"*What is* slow and steady, often *outtravels* haste."—"*To put in* little and often, *fills* the purse."—"*What proceeds* fair and softly, *goes* far." The following line from Shakspeare appears to be still more elliptical:

> "Poor and content *is* rich, and rich enough."—*Othello.*

This may be supposed to mean, "*He who is* poor and content," &c. In the following sentence again, we may suppose an ellipsis of the phrase *To have*, at the beginning ; though here, perhaps, to have pluralized the verb, would have been as well :

> "One eye on death and one full fix'd on heaven,
> *Becomes* a mortal and immortal man."—*Young.*

OBS. 3.—The names of two persons are not unfrequently used jointly as the name of their story; in which sense, they must have a singular verb, if they have any : as, "Prior's *Henry and Emma contains* an other beautiful example."—*Jamieson's Rhetoric*, p. 179. I somewhat hesitate to call this

---

[*] In his *English Reader*, (Part II, Chap. 5th, Sec. 7th,) Murray has this line in its proper form, as it here stands in the words of Thomson ; but, in his *Grammar*, he corrupted it, first in his *Exercises*, and then still more in his *Key*. Among his examples of "*False Syntax*," it stands thus :
"What black despair, what horror, *fills* his *mind*!"—*Exercises*, Rule 2.
So the error is propagated in the name of *Learning*, and this verse goes from grammar to grammar, as one that must have a "*plural*" verb. See *Ingersoll's Gram.* p. 242; *Smith's New Gram.* p. 127; *Fisk's Gram.* p. 120; *Weld's E. Gram.* p. 189.

an exception to the foregoing rule, because here too the phraseology may be supposed elliptical. The meaning is, "Prior's *little poem, entitled,* 'Henry and Emma,' contains," &c.;—or, "Prior's *story of* Henry and Emma contains," &c. And, if the first expression is only an abbreviation of one of these, the construction of the verb *contains* may be referred to Rule 14th. See Exception 1st to Rule 12th, and Obs. 2d on Rule 14th.

OBS. 4.—The conjunction *and,* by which alone we can with propriety connect different words to make them joint nominatives or joint antecedents, is sometimes suppressed and *understood;* but then its effect is the same, as if it were inserted: though a singular verb might sometimes be quite as proper in the same sentences, because it would merely imply a disjunctive conjunction or none at all: as, "The high breach of trust, the notorious corruption, *are stated* in the strongest terms."—*Junius,* Let. xx. "Envy, self-will, jealousy, pride, often *reign* there."— *Abbott's Corner Stone,* p. 111. (See Obs. 4th on Rule 12th.)

"Art, empire, earth itself, to change *are* doomed."—*Beattie.*
"Her heart, her mind, her love, *is* his alone."—*Cowley.*

In all the foregoing examples, a singular verb might have been used without impropriety; or the last, which is singular, might have been plural. But the following couplet evidently requires a plural verb, and is therefore correct as the poet wrote it; both because the latter noun is plural, and because the conjunction *and* is understood between the two. Yet a late grammarian, perceiving no difference between the joys of sense and the pleasure of reason, not only changes "*lie*" to "*lies,*" but uses the perversion for a *proof text,* under a rule which refers the verb to the first noun only, and requires it to be singular. See *Oliver B. Peirce's Gram.* p. 250.

"Reason's whole pleasure, all the joys of sense,
Lie in three words—health, peace, and competence."—*Pope's Ess.* Ep. iv, l. 80.

OBS. 5.—When the speaker changes his nominative to take a stronger expression, he commonly uses no conjunction; but, putting the verb in agreement with the noun which is next to it, he leaves the other to an implied concord with its proper form of the same verb: as, "The man whose *designs,* whose *whole conduct, tends* to reduce me to subjection, that man is at war with me, though not a blow has yet been given, nor a sword drawn."—*Blair's Rhet.* p. 265. "All *Greece,* all the barbarian *world, is* too narrow for this man's ambition."—*Ibid.* "This *self-command,* this *exertion* of reason in the midst of passion, *has* a wonderful effect both to please and to persuade."—*Ib.* p. 260. "In the mutual influence of body and soul, there *is a wisdom,* a *wonderful wisdom,* which we cannot fathom."—*Murray's Gram.* Vol. i, p. 150. If the principle here stated is just, Murray has written the following models erroneously: "Virtue, honour, nay, even self-interest, *conspire* to recommend the measure."—*Ib.* p. 150. "Patriotism, morality, every public and private consideration, *demand* our submission to just and lawful government."— *Ibid.* In this latter instance, I should prefer the singular verb *demands;* and in the former, the expression ought to be otherwise altered, thus: "Virtue, honour, *and* interest, *all conspire* to recommend the measure." Or thus: "Virtue, honour—nay, even self-interest, *recommends* the measure." On this principle, too, Thomson was right, and this critic wrong, in the example cited at the close of the first observation above. This construction is again recurred to by Murray, in the second chapter of his Exercises; where he explicitly condemns the following sentence because the verb is singular: "Prudence, policy, nay, his own true interest, strongly *recommends* the line of conduct proposed to him."—*Octavo Gram.* Vol. ii, p. 22.

OBS. 6.—When two or more nominatives are in apposition with a preceding one which they explain, the verb must agree with the first word only, because the others are adjuncts to this, and not joint subjects to the verb; as, "Loudd, the ancient Lydda and Diospolis, *appears* like a place lately ravaged by fire and sword."—*Keith's Evidences,* p. 93. "Beattie, James,—a philosopher and poet,—*was* born in Scotland, in the year 1735."—*Murray's Sequel,* p. 306. "For, the quantity, the length, and shortness of our syllables, *is* not, by any means, so fixed."—*Blair's Rhet.* p. 124. This principle, like the preceding one, persuades me again to dissent from Murray, who corrects or *perverts* the following sentence, by changing *originates* to *originate:* "All that makes a figure on the great theatre of the world; the employments of the busy, the enterprises of the ambitious, and the exploits of the warlike; the virtues which form the happiness, and the crimes which occasion the misery of mankind; *originates* in that silent and secret recess of thought, which is hidden from every human eye."—See *Murray's Octavo Gram.* Vol. ii, p. 181; or his *Duodecimo Key,* p. 21. The true subject of this proposition is the noun *all,* which is singular; and the other nominatives are subordinate to this, and merely explanatory of it.

OBS. 7.—Dr. Webster says, "*Enumeration* and addition of numbers are *usually* expressed in the singular *number;* [as,] two and two *is* four; seven and nine *is* sixteen; that is, *the sum of* seven and nine *is* sixteen. But modern usage inclines to reject the use of the verb in the singular number, in these and similar phrases."—*Improved Gram.* p. 106. Among its many faults, this passage exhibits a virtual contradiction. For what "*modern usage* inclines to reject," can hardly be the fashion in which any ideas "*are usually expressed.*" Besides, I may safely aver, that this is a kind of phraseology which all correct usage always did reject. It is not only a gross vulgarism, but a plain and palpable violation of the foregoing rule of syntax; and, as such it must be reputed, if the rule has any propriety at all. What "*enumeration*" has to do with it, is more than I can tell. But Dr. Webster once admired and commended this mode of speech, as one of the "wonderful proofs of ingenuity in the *framers* of language;" and laboured to defend it as being "correct upon principle;" that is, upon the principle that "*the sum of*" is understood to be the subject of the affirmation, when one says, "Two *and* two *is* four," in stead of, "Two and two *are* four."—See *Webster's Philosophical Gram.* p. 153. This seems to me a "wonderful proof" of *ignorance* in a very learned man.

OBS. 8.—In Greek and Latin, the verb frequently agrees with the nearest nominative, and is understood to the rest; and this construction is sometimes imitated in English, especially if the nouns follow the verb: as, "Νυνὶ δὲ ΜΕΝΕΙ πίστις, ἐλπὶς, ἀγάπη, τὰ τρία ταῦτα."—"Nunc vero *manet* fides, spes, charitas; tria hæc."—"Now *abideth* faith, hope, charity; these three."—1 *Cor.* xiii, 13. "And now *abideth* confession, prayer, and praise, these three; but the greatest of these is praise."—ATTERBURY: *Blair's Rhet.* p. 300. The propriety of this usage, so far as our language is concerned, I doubt. It seems to open a door for numerous deviations from the foregoing rule, and deviations of such a sort, that if they are to be considered exceptions, one can hardly tell why. The practice, however, is not uncommon, especially if there are more nouns than two, and each is emphatic; as, "Wonderful *was* the patience, fortitude, self-denial, *and* bravery of our ancestors."—*Webster's Hist. of U. S.* p. 118. "It is the very thing I would have you make out; for therein *consists* the force, and use, and nature of language."—*Berkley's Alciphron*, p. 161. "There *is* the proper noun, and the common noun. There *is* the singular noun, and the plural noun."—*Emmons's Gram.* p. 11. "From him *proceeds* power, sanctification, truth, grace, and every other blessing we can conceive."—*Calvin's Institutes*, B. i, Ch. 13. "To what purpose *cometh* there to me incense from Sheba, *and* the sweet cane from a far country?"—*Jer.* vi, 20. "For thine *is* the kingdom, *and* the power, *and* the glory, forever."—*Matt.* vi, 13. In all these instances, the plural verb might have been used; and yet perhaps the singular may be justified, on the ground that there is a distinct and emphatic enumeration of the nouns. Thus, it would be proper to say, "Thine *are* the kingdom, the power, and the glory;" but this construction seems less emphatic than the preceding, which means, "For thine is the kingdom, *thine is* the power, and *thine is* the glory, forever;" and this repetition is still more emphatic, and perhaps more proper, than the elliptical form. The repetition of the conjunction "*and*," in the original text as above, adds time and emphasis to the reading, and makes the singular verb more proper than it would otherwise be; for which reason, the following form, in which the Rev. Dr. Bullions has set the sentence down for bad English, is in some sort a *perversion* of the Scripture: "Thine is the kingdom, the power, and the glory."—*Bullions's E. Gram.* p. 141.

OBS. 9.—When the nominatives are of different *persons*, the verb agrees with the first person in preference to the second, and with the second in preference to the third; for *thou* and *I*, or *he*, *thou*, and *I*, are equivalent to *we*; and *thou* and *he* are equivalent to *you*: as, "Why speakest thou any more of thy matters? I have said, *thou* and *Ziba divide* the land."—2 *Sam.* xix, 29. That is, "divide *ye* the land." "And *live thou* and thy *children* of the rest."—2 *Kings*, iv, 7. "That *I* and thy *people have found* grace in thy sight."—*Exodus*, xxxiii, 16. "*I* and my *kingdom are* guiltless."—2 *Sam.* iii, 28. "*I*, and *you*, and *Piso* perhaps too, *are* in a state of dissatisfaction."—*Zenobia*, i, 114.

> "Then *I*, and *you*, and *all* of us, *fell* down.
> Whilst bloody treason flourish'd over *us*."—*Shak.*, J. *Cæsar*.

OBS. 10.—When two or more nominatives connected by *and* are of the same form but distinguished by adjectives or possessives, one or more of them may be omitted by ellipsis, but the verb must be plural, and agree with them all; as, "A literary, a scientific, a wealthy, and a poor man, *were assembled* in one room."—*Peirce's Gram.* p. 263. Here four different men are clearly spoken of. "Else the rising and the falling emphasis *are* the same."—*Knowles's Elocutionist*, p. 33. Here the noun *emphasis* is understood after *rising.* "The singular and [the] plural form *seem* to be confounded."—*Lowth's Gram.* p. 22. Here the noun *form* is presented to the mind twice; and therefore the article should have been repeated. See Obs. 15th on Rule 1st. "My farm and William's *are* adjacent to each other."—*Peirce's Gram.* p. 220. Here the noun *farm* is understood after the possessive *William's*, though the author of the sentence foolishly attempts to explain it otherwise. "Seth's, Richard's, and Edmund's *farms*, are those which their fathers left them."— *Ib.* p. 257. Here the noun *farms* is understood after *Seth's*, and again after *Richard's*; so that the sentence is written wrong, unless each man had more than one farm. "*Was* not Demosthenes's style, and his master Plato's, perfectly Attic; and yet none more lofty?"—*Milnes's Greek Gram.* p. 241. Here *style* is understood after *Plato's*; wherefore *was* should rather be *were*, or else *and* should be changed to *as well as.* But the text, as it stands, is not much unlike some of the exceptions noticed above. "The character of a fop, and of a rough warrior, *are* no where more successfully contrasted."—*Kames, El. of Crit.* Vol. i, p. 236. Here the ellipsis is not very proper. Say, "the character of a fop, and *that* of a rough warrior," &c. Again: "We may observe, that the eloquence of the bar, of the legislature, and of public assemblies, *are* seldom *or ever* found united *to high perfection* in the same person."—*J. Q. Adams's Rhet.* Vol. i, p. 256. Here the ellipsis cannot so well be avoided by means of the pronominal adjective *that*, and therefore it may be thought more excusable; but I should prefer a repetition of the nominative: as, "We may observe, that the eloquence of the bar, *the eloquence* of the legislature, and *the eloquence* of public assemblies, are seldom *if ever* found united, *in any high degree*, in the same person."

OBS. 11.—The conjunction *as*, when it connects nominatives that are in *apposition*, or significant of the same person or thing, is commonly placed at the beginning of the sentence, so that the verb agrees with its proper nominative following the explanatory word; thus, "*As a poet, he holds* a high rank."—*Murray's Sequel*, p. 355. "*As a poet, Addison claims* a high praise."—*Ib.* p. 304. "*As a model* of English prose, his *writings merit* the greatest praise."—*Ib.* p. 305. But when this conjunction denotes a *comparison* between different persons or things signified by two nominatives, there must be two verbs 'expressed or understood, each agreeing with its own subject; as, "Such *writers* as he [is,] *have* no reputation worth any man's envy."*

> "Such *men* as he [is] *be* never at heart's ease
> Whiles they behold a greater than themselves."—*Shakspeare.*

OBS. 12.—When two nominatives are connected by *as well as*, *but*, or *save*, they must in fact have two verbs, though in most instances only one is expressed; as, "Such is the mutual dependence of words in sentences, that several *others*, as well as [is] the *adjective*, *are* not to be used alone."—*Dr. Wilson's Essay*, p. 99. "The Constitution was to be the one fundamental law of the land, to which *all*, as well *States* as *people*, should submit."—W. I. BOWDITCH: *Liberator*, No. 984. "As well those which history, as those which experience *offers* to our reflection."—*Bolingbroke, on History*, p. 85. Here the words "*offers to our reflection*" are understood after "*history*."

---

* S. W. Clark, by reckoning "*as*" a "*preposition*," perverts the construction of sentences like this, and inserts a wrong case after the conjunction. See *Clark's Practical Grammar*, pp. 92 and 178; also *this Syntax*, Obs. 6 and Obs. 18, on Conjunctions.

"*None* but *He* who discerns futurity, *could have foretold* and described all these things."—*Keith's Evidences*, p. 62. "That there *was* in those times no other *writer*, of any degree of eminence, save *he* himself."—*Pope's Works*, Vol. iii, p. 43.

"I do entreat you not a man depart,
Save *I* alone, till Antony have spoke."—*Shak.*, *J. Cæsar.*

OBS. 13.—Some grammarians say, that *but* and *save*, when they denote exception, should govern the objective case as *prepositions.* But this idea is, without doubt, contrary to the current usage of the best authors, either ancient or modern. Wherefore I think it evident that these grammarians err. The objective case of *nouns* being like the nominative, the point can be proved only by the *pronouns ;* as, "There is none *but he* alone."—*Perkins's Theology*, 1608. "There is none other *but he.*"—*Mark*, xii, 32. (This text is good authority as regards the *case,* though it is incorrect in an other respect : it should have been, "There is *none but* he," or else, "There is *no* other *than he.*") "No man hath ascended up to heaven, *but he* that came down from heaven."—*John*, iii, 13. "Not that any man hath seen the father, *save he* which is of God."—*John*, vi, 46. "Few can, *save he* and *I.*"—*Byron's Werner.* "There is none justified, *but he* that is in measure sanctified."—*Pennington.* *Save,* as a conjunction, is nearly obsolete.

OBS. 14.—In Rev. ii, 17th, we read, "Which no man knoweth, *saving he* that receiveth it;" and again, xiii, 17th, "That no man might buy or sell, *save he* that had the mark." The following text is inaccurate, but not in the construction of the nominative *they :* "All men cannot receive this saying, *save they* to whom it is given."—*Matt.* xix, 11. The version ought to have been, "*Not all* men can receive this saying, *but they only* to whom it is given :" i. e., "they only *can receive it,* to whom *there is given power to receive it.*" Of *but* with a nominative, examples may be multiplied indefinitely. The following are as good as any : "There is no God *but He.*"—*Sale's Koran*, p. 27. "The former none *but He* could execute."—*Maturin's Sermons*, p. 317. "There was nobody at home then *but I.*"—*Walker's Particles*, p. 95. "A fact, of which as none *but he* could be conscious, [so] none *but he* could be the publisher of it."—*Pope's Works*, Vol. iii, p. 117. "Few *but they* who are involved in the vices, are involved in the irreligion of the times."—*Brown's Estimate*, i, 101.

"I claim my right. No Grecian prince but *I*
Has power this bow to grant, or to deny."—*Pope, Odys.* B. xxi, l. 272.
"Thus she, and none *but she,* th' insulting rage
Of heretics oppos'd from age to age."—*Dryden's Poems*, p. 98.

In opposition to all these authorities, and many more that might be added, we have, with now and then a text of false syntax, the absurd opinion of perhaps *a score or two* of our grammarians; one of whom imagines he has found in the following couplet from Swift, an example to the purpose ; but he forgets that the verb *let* governs the *objective* case :

"Let *none* but *him* who rules the thunder,
Attempt to part these twain asunder."—*Perley's Gram.* p. 62.

OBS. 15.—It is truly a wonder, that so many professed critics should not see the absurdity of taking *but* and *save* for "*prepositions,*" when this can be done only by condemning the current usage of nearly all good authors, as well as the common opinion of most grammarians; and the greater is the wonder, because they seem to do it innocently, or to teach it childishly, as not knowing that they cannot justify both sides, when the question lies between opposite and contradictory principles. By this sort of simplicity, which approves of errors, if much practised, and of opposites, when authorities may be found for them, no work, perhaps, is more strikingly characterized, than the School Grammar of W. H. Wells. This author says, "The use of *but* as a preposition is *approved* by J. E. Worcester, John Walker, R. C. Smith, Picket, Hiley, Angus, Lynde, Hull, Powers, Spear, Farnum, Fowle, Goldsbury, Perley, Cobb, Badgley, Cooper, Jones, Davis, Beall, Hendrick, Hazen, and Goodenow."—*School Gram.*, 1850, p. 178. But what if all these authors do prefer, "*but him,*" and "*save him,*" where ten times as many would say, "*but he,*" "*save he!*" Is it therefore difficult to determine which party is right ? Or is it proper for a grammarian to name sundry authorities on both sides, excite doubt in the mind of his reader, and leave the matter *unsettled?* "The use of *but* as a preposition," he also states, "is *discountenanced* by G. Brown, Sanborn, Murray, S. Oliver, and several other grammarians. (See also an able article in the Mass. Common School Journal, Vol. ii, p. 19.)"—*School Gram.* p. 178.

OBS. 16.—Wells passes no censure on the use of nominatives after *but* and *save;* does not intimate which case is fittest to follow these words ; gives no false syntax under his rule for the regimen of prepositions ; but inserts there the following brief remarks and examples :

"REM. 3.—The word *save* is frequently used to perform the office of a preposition ; as,
'And all desisted, all *save him* alone.'—*Wordsworth.*"

"REM. 4.—*But* is sometimes employed as a preposition, in the sense of *except ;* as,
'The boy stood on the burning deck,
Whence all *but him* had fled.'—*Hemans.*"—*Ib.* p. 167.

Now, "BUT," says Worcester, as well as Tooke and others, was "originally *bot,* contracted from *be out :*" and, if this notion of its etymology is just, it must certainly be followed by the nominative case, rather than by the objective; for the imperative *be* or *be out* governs no case, admits no additional term but a nominative—an obvious and important fact, quite overlooked by those who call *but* a preposition. According to Allen H. Weld, *but* and *save* "are *commonly* considered *prepositions,*" but "are *more commonly* termed *conjunctions !*" This author repeats Wells's examples of "*save him*" and "*but him,*" as being *right ;* and mixes them with opposite examples of "*save he,*" "*but he,*" "*save I,*" which he thinks to be *more right!*—*Weld's Gr.* p. 187.

OBS. 17.—Professor Fowler, too, an other author remarkable for a facility of embracing incompatibles, contraries, or dubieties, not only condemns as "false syntax" the use of *save* for an exceptive conjunction, (§ 587, ¶ 28,) but cites approvingly from Latham the following very strange absurdity : "One and the same word, in one and the same sentence, may be a Conjunction or [a] Preposition, as the case may be : [as,] All fled *but* John."—*Fowler's E. Gram.* 8vo, 1850, § 555. This is equivalent to saying, that "one and the same sentence" *may be two different sentences ;* may, without error, be understood in two different senses ; may be rightly taken, resolved, and parsed, in two different ways! Nay, it is equivalent to a denial of the old logical position, that, "It is impossible for a thing *to be* and *not be* at the same time;" for it supposes "*but*," in the instance given, to be at once both a conjunction and *not* a conjunction, both a preposition and *not* a preposition, "*as the case may be!*" It is true, that "one and the same word" may sometimes be differently parsed *by different grammarians*, and possibly even an adept may doubt who or what is right. But what ambiguity of construction, or what diversity of interpretation, proceeding from the same hand, can these admissions be supposed to warrant? The foregoing citation is a boyish attempt to justify different modes of parsing the same expression, on the ground that the expression itself is equivocal. "All fled *but John*," is thought to mean equally well, "All fled *but he*," and, "All fled *but him*;" while these latter expressions are erroneously presumed to be alike good English, and to have a difference of meaning corresponding to their difference of construction. Now, what is equivocal, or ambiguous, being therefore erroneous, is to be *corrected*, rather than parsed in any way. But I deny both the ambiguity and the difference of meaning which these critics profess to find among the said phrases. "*John fled not, but all the rest fled*," is virtually what is told us in each of them; but, in the form, "All fled but *him*," it is told ungrammatically; in the other two, correctly.

OBS. 18.—In Latin, *cum* with an ablative, sometimes has, or is supposed to have, the force of the conjunction *et* with a nominative; as, "*Dux cum aliquot principibus capiuntur.*"—LIVY: *W. Allen's Gram.* p. 131. In imitation of this construction, some English writers have substituted *with* for *and*, and varied the verb accordingly; as, "A long course of time, *with* a variety of accidents and circumstances, *are* requisite to produce those revolutions."—HUME: *Allen's Gram.* p. 131; *Ware's*, 12; *Priestley's*, 186. This phraseology, though censured by Allen, was expressly approved by Priestley, who introduced the present example, as his proof text under the following observation: "It is not necessary that the two *subjects of an affirmation* should stand in the very same construction, to require the verb to be in the plural number. If one of them be made to depend upon the other *by a connecting particle*, it may, *in some cases*, have the same force, as if it were independent of it."—*Priestley's Gram.* p. 186. Lindley Murray, on the contrary, condemns this doctrine, and after citing the same example with others, says: "It is however, proper to observe, that these modes of expression do not appear to be warranted by *the just principles* of construction."—*Octavo Gram.* p. 150. He then proceeds to prove his point, by alleging that the preposition governs the objective case in English, and the ablative in Latin, and that what is so governed, cannot be the nominative, or any part of it. All this is true enough, but still some men who know it perfectly well, will now and then write as if they did not believe it. And so it was with the writers of Latin and Greek. They sometimes wrote bad syntax; and the grammarians have not always seen and censured their errors as they ought. Since the preposition makes its object only an adjunct of the preceding noun, or of something else, I imagine that any construction which thus assumes two different cases as joint nominatives or joint antecedents, must needs be inherently faulty.

OBS. 19.—Dr. Adam simply remarks, "The plural is sometimes used after the preposition *cum* put for *et*; as, *Remo cum fratre Quirinus jura dabunt*, Virg."—*Latin and English Gram.* p. 207; *Gould's Adam's Latin Gram.* p. 204; *W. Allen's English Gram.* 131. This example is not fairly cited; though many have adopted the perversion, as if they knew no better. Alexander has it in a worse form still: "Quirinus, cum fratre, jura dabunt."—*Latin Gram.* p. 47. Virgil's words are, "*Cana* FIDES, *et* VESTA, *Remo cum fratre Quirinus, Jura dabunt.*"—*Æneid*, B. i, l. 296. Nor is *cum* here "put for *et*," unless we suppose also an antiptosis of *Remo fratre* for *Remus frater*; and then what shall the literal reading be, and how shall the rules of syntax be accommodated to such changes? Fair examples, that bear upon the point, may, however, be adduced from good authors, and in various languages; but the question is, are they *correct* in syntax? Thus Dr. Robertson: "The palace of Pizarro, *together with* the houses of several of his adherents, *were* pillaged by the soldiers."—*Hist. of Amer.* Vol. ii, p. 133. To me, this appears plainly ungrammatical; and, certainly, there are ways enough in which it may be corrected. First, with the present connective retained, "*were*" ought to be *was*. Secondly, if *were* be retained, "*together with*" ought to be changed to *and*, or *and also*. Thirdly, we may well change both, and say, "The palace of Pizarro, *as well as* the houses of several of his adherents, *was* pillaged by the soldiers." Again, in Mark, ix, 4th, we read: "And there appeared *unto* them Elias, *with* Moses; and *they* were talking with Jesus." If this text meant that *the three disciples* were talking with Jesus, it would be right as it stands; but St. Matthew has it, "And, behold, there appeared unto them *Moses and Elias, talking* with him;" and our version in Luke is, "And, behold, there talked with him two men, which were Moses and Elias."—Chap. ix, 30. By these corresponding texts, then, we learn, that the pronoun *they*, which our translators inserted, was meant for "*Elias with Moses;*" but the Greek verb for "*appeared*," as used by Mark, is *singular*, and agrees only with *Elias*. "Καὶ ὤφθη αὐτοῖς Ἠλίας σὺν Μωσεῖ· καὶ ἦσαν συλλαλοῦντες τῷ Ἰησοῦ."—"Et apparuit illis Elias cum Mose, et erant colloquentes Jesu."—*Montanus*. "Et visus est eis Elias cum Mose, qui colloquebantur cum Jesu."—*Beza*. This is as discrepant as our version, though not so ambiguous. The French Bible avoids the incongruity: "Et ils virent paroître *Moyse et Elie*, qui s'entretenoient avec Jésus." That is, "And there appeared to them *Moses and Elias*, who were talking with Jesus." Perhaps the closest and best version of the Greek would be, "And there appeared to them Elias, with Moses;[*] and *these two* were talking with Jesus." There is, in our Bible, an other instance of the construction now in question; but it has no support from the Septuagint, the Vulgate, or the French: to wit, "The second [lot came forth] to Gedaliah, *who with* his brethren and sons *were* twelve."—1 *Chron.* xxv, 9. Better: "*and he*, his brethren, and *his sons*, were twelve."

[*] Murray gives us the following text for false grammar, under the head of *Strength:* "And Elias with Moses appeared to them."—*Exercises*, 8vo, p. 185. This he corrects thus: "And *there appeared to them* Elias with Moses."—*Key*, 8vo, p. 266. He omits the comma after *Elias*, which some copies of the Bible contain, and others do not. Whether he supposed the verb *appeared* to be singular or plural, I cannot tell; and he did not extend his quotation to the pronoun *they*, which immediately follows, and in which alone the incongruity lies.

OBS. 20.—Cobbett, who, though he wrote several grammars, was but a very superficial grammarian, seems never to have doubted the propriety of putting *with* for *and*; and yet he was confessedly not a little puzzled to find out when to use a singular, and when a plural verb, after a nominative with such "a sort of addition made to it." The 246th paragraph of his English Grammar is a long and fruitless attempt to fix a rule for the guidance of the learner in this matter. After dashing off a culpable example, "Sidmouth, *with* Oliver the *spy*, *have* brought Brandreth to the block;" or, as his late editions have it, "The *Tyrant, with* the *Spy, have* brought *Peter* to the block;" he adds: "We hesitate which to employ, the singular or the plural verb; that is to say, *has* or *have*. The meaning must be our guide. If we mean, that the act has been done by the Tyrant himself, and that the spy has been a mere involuntary agent, then we ought to use the singular; but if we believe, that the spy has been a co-operator, an associate, an accomplice, then we must use the plural verb." Ay, truly; but must we not also, in the latter case, use *and*, and not *with?* After some further illustrations, he says: "When *with* means *along with, together with, in company with*, and the like, it is nearly the same as *and*; and then the plural verb must be used: [as,] 'He, with his brothers, *are* able to do much.' Not, '*is* able to do much.' If the pronoun be used instead of *brothers*, it will be in the objective case: 'He, *with them, are* able to do much.' But this is *no impediment* to the including of the noun (represented by *them*) in the nominative." I wonder what would be an impediment to the absurdities of such a dogmatist! The following is his last example: "'Zeal, with discretion, *do* much;' and not '*does* much;' for we mean, on the contrary, that it *does nothing.* It is the meaning that must determine which of the numbers we ought to employ." This author's examples are all fictions of his own, and such of them as here have a plural verb, are wrong. His rule is also wrong, and contrary to the best authority. St. Paul says to Timothy, "Godliness *with* contentment *is* great gain:"—1 *Tim.* vi, 6. This text is right; but Cobbett's principle would go to prove it erroneous. Is he the only man who has ever had a right notion of its *meaning?* or is he not rather at fault in his interpretations?

OBS. 21.—There is one other apparent exception to Rule 16th, (or perhaps a real one,) in which there is either an ellipsis of the preposition *with*, or else the verb is made singular because the first noun only is its true subject, and the others are explanatory nominatives to which the same verb must be understood in the plural number; as, "A torch, snuff and all, *goes out* in a moment, when dipped in the vapour."—ADDISON: *in Johnson's Dict. w. All.* "Down *comes* the *tree*, nest, eagles, and all."—See *All, ibidem.* Here *goes* and *comes* are necessarily made singular, the former agreeing with *torch* and the latter with *tree*; and, if the other nouns, which are like an explanatory parenthesis, are nominatives, as they appear to me to be, they must be subjects of *go* and *come* understood. Cobbett teaches us to say, "The bag, *with* the guineas and dollars in it, *were* stolen," and not, *was* stolen. "For," says he, "if we say *was* stolen, it is possible for us to mean, that the *bag only* was stolen."—*English Gram.* ¶ 246. And I suppose he would say, "The bag, guineas, dollars, and all, *were* stolen," and not, "*was* stolen;" for here a rule of syntax might be urged, in addition to his false argument from the sense. But the meaning of the former sentence is, "The bag was stolen, with the guineas and dollars in it;" and the meaning of the latter is, "The bag was stolen, guineas, dollars, and all." "Nor can there be any doubt about the meaning, place the words which way you will; and whatever, in either case, may be the true construction of the words in the parenthetical or explanatory phrase, they should not, I think, prevent the verb from agreeing with the first noun only. But if the other nouns intervene without affecting this concord, and without a preposition to govern them, it may be well to distinguish them in the punctuation; as, "The bag, (guineas, dollars, and all,) was stolen."

NOTES TO RULE XVI.

NOTE I.—When the conjunction *and* between two nominatives appears to require a plural verb, but such form of the verb is not agreeable, it is better to reject or change the connective, that the verb may stand correctly in the singular number; as, "There *is* a peculiar force *and* beauty in this figure."—*Kames, El. of Crit.* ii, 224. Better: "There is a peculiar force, *as well as a* peculiar beauty, in this figure." "What *means* this restless stir *and* commotion of mind?"—*Murray's Key*, 8vo, p. 242. Better: "What means this restless stir, *this* commotion of mind?"

NOTE II.—When two subjects or antecedents are connected, one of which is taken affirmatively, and the other negatively, they belong to different propositions; and the verb or pronoun must agree with the affirmative subject, and be understood to the other: as, "Diligent *industry*, and not mean savings, *produces* honourable competence."—"Not a loud voice, but strong *proofs bring* conviction."—"My *poverty*, but not my will, *consents*."—*Shakspeare.*

NOTE III.—When two subjects or antecedents are connected by *as well as, but,* or *save*, they belong to different propositions; and, (unless one of them is preceded by the adverb *not*,) the verb and pronoun must agree with the former and be understood to the latter: as, "*Veracity*, as well as justice, *is* to be our rule of life."—*Butler's Analogy*, p. 283. "The lowest *mechanic*, as well as the richest citizen, *may boast* that thousands of *his* fellow-creatures are employed for *him*."—*Percival's Tales*, ii, 177. "These *principles*, as well as every just rule of criticism, *are founded* upon the sensitive part of our nature."—*Kames, El. of Crit.* Vol. i, p.

xxvi. *"Nothing,* but wailings, *was* heard."—*"None,* but thou, *can aid* us."—"No mortal *man,* save he," &c., "*had e'er survived* to say *he* saw."—*Sir W. Scott.*

NOTE IV.—When two or more subjects or antecedents are preceded by the adjective *each, every,* or *no,* they are taken separately; and, (except *no* be followed by a plural noun,) they require the verb and pronoun to be in the singular number: as, "No rank, no honour, no fortune, no condition in life, *makes* the guilty mind happy."— "Every phrase and every figure *which* he uses, *tends* to render the picture more lively and complete."—*Blair's Rhet.* p. 179.

"And every sense, and every heart, *is* joy."—*Thomson.*
"Each beast, each insect, happy in *its* own."—*Pope.*

NOTE V.—When any words or terms are to be taken conjointly as subjects or antecedents, the conjunction *and,* (in preference to *with, or, nor,* or any thing else,) must connect them. The following sentence is therefore inaccurate; *with* should be *and;* or else *were* should be *was :* "One of them, [the] wife of Thomas Cole, *with* her husband, *were* shot down, the others escaped."—*Hutchinson's Hist.* Vol. ii, p. 86. So, in the following couplet, *or* should be *and,* or else *engines* should be *engine :*
"What if the head, the eye, *or* ear, repined
To serve mere *engines* to the ruling mind?"—*Pope.*

NOTE VI.—Improper omissions must be supplied; but when there occurs a true ellipsis in the construction of joint nominatives or joint antecedents, the verb or pronoun must agree with them in the plural, just as if all the words were expressed: as, "The *second* and the *third Epistle* of John *are* each but one short chapter."—"The metaphorical and the literal meaning *are* improperly mixed."—*Murray's Gram.* p. 339. "The Doctrine of Words, separately consider'd, and in a Sentence, *are* Things distinct enough."—*Brightland's Gram.* Pref. p. iv. Better perhaps: "The doctrine of words separately considered, and *that of words* in a sentence, *are* things distinct enough."

"The *Curii's* and the *Camilli's* little *field*
To vast extended territories *yield.*"—*Rowe's Lucan,* B. i, l. 320.

NOTE VII.—Two or more distinct subject phrases connected by *and,* require a plural verb, and generally a plural noun too, if a nominative follow the verb; as, "*To be wise in our own eyes, to be wise in the opinion of the world,* and *to be wise in the sight of our Creator,* are three things so very different, as rarely to coincide."— *Blair.* "'*This picture of my friend,*' and '*This picture of my friend's,*' suggest very different ideas."—*Priestley's Gram.* p. 71; *Murray's,* i, 178.

"Read of this burgess—on the stone *appear,*
How worthy he! how virtuous! and how dear!"—*Crabbe.*

IMPROPRIETIES FOR CORRECTION.

FALSE SYNTAX UNDER RULE XVI.

UNDER THE RULE ITSELF.—THE VERB AFTER JOINT NOMINATIVES.

"So much ability and merit is seldom found."—*Murray's Key,* 12mo, p. 18; *Merchant's School Gram.* p. 190.

[FORMULE.—Not proper, because the verb *is* is in the singular number, and does not correctly agree with its two nominatives, *ability* and *merit,* which are connected by *and,* and taken conjointly. But, according to Rule 16th, "When a verb has two or more nominatives connected by *and,* it must agree with them jointly in the plural, because they are taken together." Therefore, *is* should be *are ;* thus, "So much ability and merit *are* seldom found." Or : "So much ability and *so much merit are* seldom found."]

"The syntax and etymology of the language is thus spread before the learner."—*Bullions's English Gram.* 2d Edition, Rec. p. iii. "Dr. Johnson tells us, that in English poetry the accent and the quantity of syllables is the same thing."—*J. Q. Adams's Rhet.* ii, 213. "Their general scope and tendency, having never been clearly apprehended, is not remembered at all."—*Murray's Gram.* i, p. 126. "The soil and sovereignty was not purchased of the natives."—*Knapp's Lect. on Amer. Lit.* p. 55. "The boldness, freedom, and variety of our blank verse, is infinitely more favourable than rhyme, to all kinds of sublime poetry."— *Blair's Rhet.* p. 40. "The vivacity and sensibility of the Greeks seems to have been much greater than ours."—*Ib.* p. 253. "For sometimes the Mood and Tense is signified by the Verb, sometimes they are signified of the Verb by something else."—*Johnson's Gram. Com.*

p. 254. "The Verb and the Noun making a complete Sense, which the Participle
Noun does not."—*Ib.* p. 255. "The growth and decay of passions and emotions,
through all their mazes, is a subject too extensive for an undertaking like the pre
Kames, El. of Crit. i, 108. "The true meaning and etymology of some of his wo
lost."—*Knight, on the Greek Alph.* p. 37. "When the force and direction of person
is no longer understood."—*Junius,* p. 5. "The frame and condition of man admi
other principle."—*Brown's Estimate,* ii, 54. "Some considerable time and care wa
sary."—*Ib.* ii, 150. "In consequence of this idea, much ridicule and censure h
thrown upon Milton."—*Blair's Rhet.* p. 428. "With rational beings, mature and m
the same thing."—*Collier's Antoninus,* p. 111. "And the flax and the barley was s
—*Exod.* ix, 31. "The colon, and semicolon, divides a period, this with, and that
a connective."—*J. Ware's Gram.* p. 27. "Consequently wherever space and time i
there God must also be."—*Sir Isaac Newton.* "As the past tense and perfect pa
of *love* ends in *ed,* it is regular."—*Chandler's Gram.* p. 40; *New Edition,* p. 66. "
usual arrangement and nomenclature prevents this from being readily seen."—
Practical Gram. p. 3. "*Do* and *did* simply implies opposition or emphasis."—*Aler. M
Gram.* p. 41. "*I* and *another* make *we,* plural ; *Thou* and *another* is as much as *yc,*
or *it* and *another* make *they.*"—*Ib.* p. 124. "I and another, is as much as (we t
Person Plural ; Thou and another, is as much as (ye) the second Person Plural ; H
or it, and another, is as much as (they) the third Person Plural."—*British Gram.*
Buchanan's Syntax, p. 76. "God and thou art two, and thou and thy neighbour a
—*The Love Conquest,* p. 25. "Just as *on* and *a* has arisen out of the numeral *one.*"—
E. Gram. 8vo, 1850, § 200. "The tone and style of each of them, particularly the f
the last, is very different."—*Blair's Rhet.* p. 246. "Even as the roebuck and the
eaten."—*Deut.* xiii, 22. "Then I may conclude that two and three makes not 5
Barclay's Works, iii, 354. "Which at sundry times thou and thy brethren hast re
from us."—*Ib.* i, 165. "Two and two is four, and one is five."—*Pope: Lives of the
p. 490. "Humility and knowledge with poor apparel, excels pride and ignorance
costly array."—*Day's Gram. Parsing Lesson,* p. 100. "A page and a half has been
to the section on composition."—*Bullions's E. Gram.,* 5th Ed., Pref. p. vii. "Accura
expertness in this exercise is an important acquisition."—*Ib.* p. 71.

  "Woods and groves are of thy dressing,
  Hill and dale doth boast thy blessing."—*Milton's Poems,* p. 139.

UNDER THE RULE ITSELF.—THE VERB BEFORE JOINT NOMINATIVES.

"There is a good and a bad, a right and a wrong in taste, as in other things."—
Rhet. p. 21. "Whence has arisen much stiffness and affectation."—*Ib.* p. 133. "
error is owing, in a great measure, that intricacy and harshness, in his figurative lan
which I before remarked."—*Ib.* p. 150; *Jamieson's Rhet.* 157. "Hence, in his
Thoughts, there prevails an obscurity and hardness in his style."—*Blair's Rhet.*
"There is, however, in that work much good sense, and excellent criticism."—*Ib.
"There is too much low wit and scurrility in Plautus."—*Ib.* p. 481. "There is t
reasoning and refinement; too much pomp and studied beauty in them."—*Ib.*
"Hence arises the structure and characteristic expression of exclamation."—*Rush,
Voice,* p. 229. "And such pilots is he and his brethren, according to their own conf
—*Barclay's Works,* iii, 314. "Of whom is Hymeneus and Philetus; who concern
truth have erred."—*2 Tim.* ii, 17. "Of whom is Hymeneus and Alexander; whom
delivered unto Satan."—*1 Tim.* i, 20. "And so was James and John, the sons of Zeb
—*Luke,* v, 10. "Out of the same mouth proceedeth blessing and cursing."—*Jam.,
"Out of the mouth of the Most High proceedeth not evil and good."—*Lam.* iii, 38.
which there is most plainly a right and a wrong."—*Butler's Analogy,* p. 215. "
sentence there is both an actor and an object."—*Smith's Inductive Gram.* p. 14. "
breast-plate was placed the mysterious Urim and Thummim."—*Milman's Jews,
"What is the gender, number, and person of those in the first?"—*Smith's Productive
p. 19. "There seems to be a familiarity and want of dignity in it."—*Priestley's Gr
150. "It has been often asked, what is Latin and Greek?"—*Literary Convention,
"For where does beauty and high wit But in your constellation meet?"—*Hudibras,
"Thence to the land where flows Ganges and Indus."—*Paradise Lost,* B. ix, L 81.
these foundations seems to rest the midnight riot and dissipation of modern assembl
Brown's Estimate, ii, 46. "But what has disease, deformity, and filth, upon whi
thoughts can be allured to dwell?"—*Johnson's Life of Swift,* p. 492. "How is the 5
and number of the relative known?"—*Bullions, Practical Lessons,* p. 32.

  "High rides the sun, thick rolls the dust,
  And feebler speeds the blow and thrust."—*Sir W. Scott.*

UNDER NOTE I.—CHANGE THE CONNECTIVE.

"In every language, there prevails a certain structure and analogy of parts, which
derstood to give foundation to the most reputable usage."—*Blair's Rhet.* p. 90. "

runs through his whole manner, a stiffness and affectation, which renders him very unfit to be considered a general model."—*Ib.* p. 102. "But where declamation and improvement in speech is the sole aim."—*Ib.* p. 257. "For it is by these chiefly, that the train of thought, the course of reasoning, and the whole progress of the mind, in continued discourse of all kinds, is laid open."—*Lowth's Gram.* p. 103. "In all writing and discourse, the proper composition and structure of sentences is of the highest importance."—*Blair's Rhet.* p. 101. "Here the wishful look and expectation of the beggar naturally leads to a vivid conception of that which was the object of his thoughts."—*Campbell's Rhet.* p. 386. "Who say, that the outward naming of Christ, and signing with the cross, puts away devils."—*Barclay's Works*, i, 146. "By which an oath and penalty was to be imposed upon the members."—*Junius*, p. 6. "Light and knowledge, in what manner soever afforded us, is equally from God."—*Butler's Analogy*, p. 264. "For instance, sickness and untimely death is the consequence of intemperance."—*Ib.* p. 78. "When grief, and blood ill-tempered vexeth him."—*Beauties of Shakspeare*, p. 256. "Does continuity and connexion create sympathy and relation in the parts of the body?"—*Collier's Antoninus*, p. 111. "His greatest concern, and highest enjoyment, was to be approved in the sight of his Creator."—*Murray's Key*, p. 224. "Know ye not that there is a prince and a great man fallen this day in Israel?"—*2 Sam.* iii, 38. "What is vice and wickedness? No rarity, you may depend on it."—*Collier's Antoninus*, p. 107. "There is also the fear and apprehension of it."—*Butler's Analogy*, p. 87. "The apostrophe and *s*, (*'s*) is an abbreviation for *is*, the termination of the old English genitive."—*Bullions, E. Gram.* p. 17. "*Ti, ce,* and *ci,* when followed by a vowel, usually has the sound of *sh*; as in *partial, special, ocean.*"—*Weld's Gram.* p. 15.

> "Bitter constraint and sad occasion dear
> Compels me to disturb your season due."—*Milton's Lycidas.*
> "Debauches and excess, though with less noise,
> As great a portion of mankind destroys."—*Waller*, p. 55.

UNDER NOTE II.—AFFIRMATION WITH NEGATION.

"Wisdom, and not wealth, procure esteem."—*Brown's Inst.* p. 156. "Prudence, and not pomp, are the basis of his fame."—*Ib.* "Not fear, but labour have overcome him."—*Ib.* "The decency, and not the abstinence, make the difference."—*Ib.* "Not her beauty, but her talents attracts attention."—*Ib.* "It is her talents, and not her beauty, that attracts attention."—*Ib.* "It is her beauty, and not her talents, that attract attention."—*Ib.*

> "His belly, not his brains, this impulse give:
> He'll grow immortal; for he cannot live."—*Young, to Pope.*

UNDER NOTE III.—AS WELL AS, BUT, or SAVE.

"Common sense as well as piety tell us these are proper."—*Family Commentary*, p. 64. "For without it the critic, as well as the undertaker, ignorant of any rule, have nothing left but to abandon themselves to chance."—*Kames, El. of Crit.* i, 42. "And accordingly hatred as well as love are extinguished by long absence."—*Ib.* i, 113. "But at every turn the richest melody as well as the sublimest sentiments are conspicuous."—*Ib.* ii, 121. "But it, as well as the lines immediately subsequent, defy all translation."—*Coleridge's Introduction*, p. 96. "But their religion, as well as their customs, and manners, were strangely misrepresented."—BOLINGBROKE ON HISTORY, p. 123: *Priestley's Gram.* p. 192; *Murray's Exercises*, p. 47. "But his jealous policy, as well as the fatal antipathy of Fonseca, were conspicuous."—*Robertson's America*, i, 191. "When their extent as well as their value were unknown."—*Ib.* ii, 138. "The Etymology, as well as the Syntax, of the more difficult parts of speech are reserved for his attention [at a later period]."—*Parker and Fox's E. Gram.* Part i, p. 3. "What I myself owe to him, no one but myself know."—See *Wright's Athens*, p. 96. "None, but thou, O mighty prince! canst avert the blow."—*Inst.* p. 156. "Nothing, but frivolous amusements, please the indolent."—*Ib.*

> "Nought, save the gurglings of the rill, were heard."—*G. B.*
> "All songsters, save the hooting owl, was mute."—*G. B.*

UNDER NOTE IV.—EACH, EVERY, or NO.

"Give every word, and every member, their due weight and force."—*Blair's Rhet.* p. 110. "And to one of these belong every noun, and every third person of every verb."—*Wilson's Essay on Gram.* p. 74. "No law, no restraint, no regulation, are required to keep him in bounds."—*Literary Convention*, p. 260. "By that time, every window and every door in the street were full of heads."—*N. Y. Observer*, No. 503. "Every system of religion, and every school of philosophy, stand back from this field, and leave Jesus Christ alone, the solitary example."—*The Corner Stone*, p. 17. "Each day, and each hour, bring their portion of duty."—*Inst.* p. 156. "And every one that was in distress, and every one that was in debt, and every one that was discontented, gathered themselves unto him."—*1 Sam.* xxii, 2. "Every private Christian and member of the church ought to read and peruse the Scriptures, that they may know their faith and belief founded upon them."—*Barclay's Works*, i, 340. "And every mountain and island were moved out of their places."—*Rev.* vi, 14.

> "No bandit fierce, no tyrant mad with pride,
> No cavern'd hermit rest self-satisfied."

UNDER NOTE V.—WITH, OR, &c. FOR AND.

"The side A, with the sides B and C, compose the triangle."—*Tobitt's Gram.*
Felch's, 69; *Ware's*, 12. "The stream, the rock, or the tree, must each of the r
forth, so as to make a figure in the imagination."—*Blair's Rhet.* p. 390. "While th
euphony, constitute, finally, the whole."—*O. B. Peirce's Gram.* p. 293. "The bag. w
guineas and dollars in it, were stolen."—*Cobbett's E. Gram.* ¶ 246. "Sobriety, wit
industry and talent, enable a man to perform great deeds."—*Ib.* ¶ 246. "The *it.* ?
with the verb *to be*, express states of being."—*Ib.* ¶ 190. "Where Leonidas the
king, with his chosen band, fighting for their country, were cut off to the last r
Kames, El. of Crit. Vol. i, p. 203. "And Leah also, with her children, came near an
themselves."—*Gen.* xxxiii, 7. "The First or Second will, either of them, by the
coalesce with the Third, but not with each other."—*Harris's Hermes*, p. 74. "The
must centre in the query, whether Tragedy or Comedy are hurtful and dangerous
sentations?"—*Formey's Belles-Lettres*, p. 215. "Grief as well as joy are infectio
emotions they raise in the spectator resemble them perfectly."—*Kames, El. of Crit.*
"But in all other words the *Qu* are both sounded."—*Ensell's Gram.* p. 16. "*Qu* (wh
always together) have the sound of *kü* or *k*, as in *queen, opaque*."—*Goodenow's Gram*
"In this selection the *ai* form distinct syllables."—*Walker's Key*, p. 290. "And a c
able village, with gardens, fields, &c. extend around on each side of the square."—*L*
Vol. ix, p. 140. "Affection, or interest, guide our notions and behaviour in the
life; imagination and passion affect the sentiments that we entertain in matters of ta
Jamieson's Rhet. p. 171. " She heard none of those intimations of her defects, whic
petulance, or anger, produce among children."—*Rambler*, No. 189. "The King.
Lords and Commons, constitute an excellent form of government."—*Crombie's Tr.*
242. "If we say, 'I am the man, who commands you,' the relative clause, w
antecedent *man*, form the predicate."—*Ib.* p. 266.

"The spacious firmament on high,	And spangled heav'ns, a shining fra
With all the blue ethereal sky,	Their great Original proclaim."—A

Murray's Key, p. 174; *Day's Gram.* p. 92; *Farnum's*,

UNDER NOTE VI.—ELLIPTICAL CONSTRUCTIONS.

"There is a reputable and a disreputable practice."—*Adams's Rhet.* Vol. i, p. 350.
and this man was born in her."—*Milton's Psalms*, lxxxvii. "This and that man w
in her."—*Psal.* lxxxvii, 5. "This and that man was born there."—*Hendrick's Gram*
"Thus *le* in *lego* and *legi* seem to be sounded equally long."—*Adam's Gram.* p. 253:
243. ."A distinct and an accurate articulation forms the groundwork of good deliv
Kirkham's Elocution, p. 25. "How is vocal and written language understood?"—
Sanders, Spelling-Book, p. 7. "The good, the wise, and the learned man is an orn
human society."—*Bartlett's Reader*. "On some points, the expression of song and sp
identical."—*Rush, on the Voice*, p. 425. "To every room there was an open an
passage."—*Johnson's Rasselas*, p. 13. "There is such a thing as tru and false taste,
latter as often directs fashion, as the former."—*Webster's Essays*, p. 401. "There is
thing as a prudent and imprudent institution of life, with regard to our health
affairs."—*Butler's Analogy*, p. 210. "The lot of the outcasts of Israel and the disp
Judah, however different in one respect, have in another corresponded with
exactness."—*Hope of Israel*, p. 301. "On these final syllables the radical and v
movement is performed."—*Rush, on the Voice*, p. 64. "To be young or old, good,
the contrary, are physical or moral events."—SPURZHEIM: *Felch's Comp. Gram.* p.
eloquence of George Whitfield and of John Wesley was of a very different charac
from the other."—*Dr. Sharp*. "The affinity of *m* for the series *b*, and of *n* for the
give occasion for other Euphonic changes."—*Fowler's E. Gram.* § 77.

"Pylades' soul, and mad Orestes', was
In these, if we believe Pythagoras."—*Cowley's Poems*, p. 3.

UNDER NOTE VII.—DISTINCT SUBJECT PHRASES.

"To be moderate in our views, and to proceed temperately in the pursuit of them
best way to ensure success."—*Murray's Key*, 8vo, p. 206. "To be of any species,
have a right to the name of that species, is all one."—*Locke's Essay*, p. 300. " With
to will and to do is the same."—*Jamieson's Sacred History*, Vol. ii, p. 22. "To profe
to possess, is very different things."—*Inst.* p. 156. "To do justly, to love mercy,
walk humbly with God, is duties of universal obligation."—*Ib.* "To be round or
to be solid or fluid, to be large or small, and to be moved swiftly or slowly, is all
alien from the nature of thought."—*Ib.* "The resolving of a sentence into its ele
or parts of speech and stating the Accidents which belong to these, is called Pars
Bullions, Pract. Lessons, p. 9. "To spin and to weave, to knit and to sew, was once
employment; but now to dress and catch a beau, is all she calls enjoyment."—*Lyon*
Vol. 8, No. 1.

RULE XVII. — FINITE VERBS.

When a Verb has two or more nominatives connected by *or* or *nor*, it must agree with them singly, and not as if taken together: as, " Fear *or* jealousy *affects* him.—*W. Allen's Gram.* p. 133. " Nor eye, *nor* listening ear, an object *finds:* creation sleeps."—*Young.* " Neither character *nor* dialogue *was* yet understood."—*L. Murray's Gram.* p. 151.

" The wife, where danger *or* dishonour *lurks*,
    Safest and seemliest by her husband stays."—*Milton, P. L.*, ix, 267.

OBSERVATIONS ON RULE XVII.

Obs. 1.—To this rule, so far as its application is practicable, there are properly no exceptions; for, *or* and *nor* being disjunctive conjunctions, the nominatives are of course to assume the verb separately, and as agreeing with each. Such agreement seems to be positively required by the alternativeness of the expression. Yet the ancient grammarians seldom, if at all, insisted on it. In Latin and Greek, a plural verb is often employed with singular nominatives thus connected; as,

" Tunc nec mens mihi, nec color
    Certa sede *manent*."—HORACE. See *W. Allen's Gram.* p. 133.

" Ἐὰν δὲ ἀδελφὸς ἢ ἀδελφὴ γυμνοὶ ὑπάρχωσι, καὶ λειπόμενοι ὦσι τῆς ἐφημέρου τροφῆς."—*James,* ii, 15. And the best scholars have sometimes *improperly* imitated this construction in English; as, " Neither Virgil nor Homer *were* deficient in any of the former beauties."—DRYDEN'S PREFACE: *Brit. Poets,* Vol. iii, p. 168. " Neither Saxon nor Roman *have availed* to add any idea to his [Plato's] categories."—R. W. EMERSON: *Liberator*, No. 996.

" He comes—nor want *nor* cold his course *delay*:
    Hide, blushing Glory! hide Pultowa's day."—*Dr. Johnson.*
" No monstrous height, *or* breadth, *or* length, *appear*;
    The whole at once is bold and regular."—*Pope, on Crit.* 1. 250.

Obs. 2.—When two collective nouns of the singular form are connected by *or* or *nor*, the verb may agree with them in the plural number, because such agreement is adapted to each of them, according to Rule 15th; as, " Why *mankind*, or such a *part* of mankind, *are* placed in this condition."—*Butler's Analogy,* p. 213. " But neither the *Board* of Control nor the *Court* of Directors *have* any scruples about sanctioning the abuses of which I have spoken."—*Glory and Shame of England,* Vol. ii, p. 70.

Obs. 3.—When a verb has nominatives of different persons or numbers, connected by *or* or *nor*, an explicit concord with each is impossible; because the verb cannot be of different persons or numbers at the same time; nor is it so, even when its form is made the same in all the persons and numbers: thus, " I, thou, [or] he, *may affirm; we, ye, or they, may affirm.*"—*Beattie's Moral Science,* p. 36. Respecting the proper management of the verb when its nominatives thus disagree, the views of our grammarians are not exactly coincident. Few however are ignorant enough, or rash enough, to deny that there may be an implicit or implied concord in such cases, —a zeugma of the verb in English, as well as of the verb or of the adjective in Latin or Greek. Of this, the following is a brief example: " But *he nor I feel* more."—*Dr. Young,* Night iii, p. 36. And I shall by-and-by add others—enough, I hope, to confute those false critics who condemn all such phraseology.

Obs. 4.—W. Allen's rule is this: " If the nominatives are of different numbers or persons, the verb agrees with *the last*; as, he or his *brothers were* there; neither you *nor I am* concerned."—*English Gram.* p. 133. Lindley Murray, and others, say: (1.) " When singular pronouns, or a noun and pronoun, of different *persons*, are disjunctively connected, the verb must agree with that person which is placed *nearest to it:* as, 'I or thou *art* to blame;' ' Thou or I *am* in fault;' 'I, or thou, or he, *is* the author of it;' 'George or I am the person.' But it would be better to say; 'Either I am to blame, or thou art,' &c. (2.) When a disjunctive occurs between a singular noun, *or* pronoun, and a plural one, the verb is made to agree with the *plural* noun *and* pronoun: as, 'Neither poverty nor riches *were* injurious to him;' 'I or they *were* offended by it.' But in this case, the plural noun or pronoun, when *it* can conveniently be *done*, should be placed next to the verb."—*Murray's Gram.* 8vo, p. 151; *Smith's New Gram.* 128; *Alger's Gram. 54*; *Comly's,* 78 and 79; *Merchant's,* 86; *Picket's,* 175; and many more. There are other grammarians who teach, that the verb must agree with the nominative which is placed next to it, whether this be singular or plural; as, " Neither the servants nor the master *is* respected;"—" Neither the master nor the servants *are* respected."—*Alexander Murray's Gram.* p. 65. " But if neither the writings nor the author *is* in existence, the Imperfect should be used."—*Sanborn's Gram.* p. 107.

Obs. 5.—On this point, a new author has just given us the following precept and criticism: " Never connect by *or*, or *nor*, two or more names or substitutes that have the same *asserter* [i. e. verb] depending on them for sense, if when taken separately, they require different forms of the *asserters.* Examples. ' Neither you nor I *am concerned*. Either he or thou *wast* there. Either they *or* he is faulty.' These examples are as erroneous as it would be to say, ' Neither *you am* concerned, nor am I.' ' Either he *wast* there, or thou wast.' ' Either *they is* faulty, or *he is*.' The sentences should stand thus—' Neither of us *is* concerned,' or, ' neither *are you* concerned, nor am I.' ' Either *he was* there, or *thou wast*.' ' Either *they are* faulty, or *he is*.' They are, however, in all their impropriety, writen according to the principles of Goold Brown's *grammar!* and the theories of most of the former writers."—*Oliver B. Peirce's Gram.* p. 252. We shall see by-and-by who is right.

OBS. 6.—Cobbett also—while he approves of such English as, "He, *with them, are able much,*" for, "*He and they are able to do much*"—condemns expressly every possible exam which the verb has not a full and explicit concord with each of its nominatives, if they ar nected by *or* or *nor*. His doctrine is this : " If nominatives of different *members* present selves, we must not give them a verb which *disagrees* with either the one or the other. We not say : 'Neither the halter *nor* the bayonets *are* sufficient to prevent us from obtain rights.' We must avoid this bad grammar by using a different form of words : as, ' We an prevented from obtaining our rights by neither the halter nor the bayonets.' And, wh e we *wish* to write bad grammar, if we can express our meaning in good grammar ?"—*Cob's Gram.* ¶ 242. This question would have more force, if the correction here offered did n-t e a meaning *widely different* from that of the sentence corrected. But he goes on : " We i say, ' They or I am in fault ; I, or they, or he, *is* the author of it ; George or I am the w Mr. Lindley Murray says, that we *may* use these phrases ; and that we have only to til that the verb agree with that person which *is placed nearest* to it ; but, he says also, that i-t be *better* to avoid such phrases by giving a different turn to our words. I do not like to le i thing to chance or to discretion, when we have a *clear principle* for our guide."—*Ib.* ¶ 24 author's " clear principle" is merely his own confident assumption, that every form of a g : or implied agreement, every thing which the old grammarians denominated *zeugma*, is at e be condemned as a solecism. He is however supported by an other late writer of much g merit. See *Churchill's New Gram.* pp. 142 and 312.

OBS. 7.—If, in lieu of their fictitious examples, our grammarians would give us actua! q tions from reputable authors, their instructions would doubtless gain something in accura still more in authority. "*I or they were offended by it,*" and, "*I, or thou, or he, is the auth* r are expressions that I shall not defend. They imply an *egotistical* speaker, who either d know, or will not tell, whether he *is offended* or not,—whether he *is the author* or not' l there are expressions that are unobjectionable, and yet not conformable to any of the rul quoted. That nominatives may be correctly connected by *or* or *nor* without an expres i ment of the verb with each of them, is a point which can be proved to as full certainty as t any other in grammar ; Churchill, Cobbett, and Peirce to the contrary notwithstanding with which of the nominatives the verb shall expressly agree, or to which of them it may properly be understood, is a matter not easy to be settled by any *sure* general rule. N o lack of such a rule a very important defect, though the inculcation of a false or imperfe i may be. So judged at least the ancient grammarians, who noticed and named almost ev ry sible form of the zeugma, without censuring any as being ungrammatical. In the Instit English Grammar, I noted first the usual form of this concord, and then the allowable e tions ; but a few late writers, we see, denounce every form of it, exceptions and all : and, v ing alone in their notions of the figure, value their own authority more than that of all critics together.

OBS. 8.—In English, as in other languages, when a verb has discordant nominatives con disjunctively, it most commonly agrees expressly with that which is nearest, and only by t cation, with the more remote ; as, " When some word or words *are* dependent on the attr a —*Webster's Philos. Gram.* p. 153. " To the first of these qualities, dulness or refinement dangerous enemies."—*Brown's Estimate,* Vol. ii, p. 15. " He hazards his own life with t his enemy, and one or both *are* very *honorably* murdered."—*Webster's Essays,* p. 235. " I n sequence is, that they frown upon every one whose faults or negligence *interrupts* or *relax* s lessons."—*W. C. Woodbridge : Lit. Conv.* p. 114. " Good intentions, or at least sincerity i pose, *was* never denied her."—*West's Letters,* p. 43. " Yet this proves not that either he or w them to be the rule."—*Barclay's Works,* i, 157. " First clear yourselves of popery be f or thou *dost throw* it upon us."—*Ib.* i, 169. "*Is* the gospel or glad tidings of this salvation br nigh unto all ?"—*Ib.* i, 362. " Being persuaded, that either they, or their cause, *is* am g *Ib.* i, 504. " And the reader may judge whether he or I *do* most fully acknowledge man s —*Ib.* iii, 332. " To do justice to the Ministry, they have not yet pretended that any one. s two, of the three Estates, *have* power to make a new law, without the concurrence of the th r *Junius,* Letter xvii. " The forest, or hunting-grounds, *are* deemed the property of the tri *Robertson's America,* i, 313. " Birth or titles *confer* no preëminence."—*Ib.* i, 184. " Ne th bacco nor hides *were* imported from Caraccas into Spain."—*Ib.* ii, 507. " The keys or *swi* sel of the maple *has* two large side-wings."—*The Friend,* vii, 97. "An example or two *are* cient to illustrate the general observation."—*Dr. Murray's Hist. of Lang.* i, 58.

> " Not thou, nor those thy factious arts engage,
> *Shall* reap that harvest of rebellious rage."—*Dryden,* p. 60.

OBS. 9.—But when the remoter nominative is the principal word, and the nearer one i pressed parenthetically, the verb agrees literally with the former, and only by implicat e the latter ; as, " One example, (or ten,) *says* nothing against it."—*Leigh Hunt.* "And w i future ages,) *may* possibly *have* a proof of it."—*Bp. Butler.* So, when the alternative a i in the *words,* not in the *thought,* the former term is sometimes considered the princi pal and is therefore allowed to control the verb ; but there is always a harshness in this mixt u different numbers, and, to render such a construction tolerable, it is necessary to read the i term like a parenthesis, and make the former emphatic : as, "A *parenthesis,* or brackets, con s two angular strokes, or hooks, enclosing one or more words."—*Whiting's Reader,* p. 5 " show us that our own *schemes,* or prudence, *have* no share in our advancements."—*A i* " The Mexican *figures,* or picture-writing, *represent* things, not words ; *they* exhibit ima g eye, not ideas to the understanding."—*Murray's Gram.* p. 243 ; *English Reader,* p. xiii. "A t vancore, *Koprah,* or dried cocoa-nut kernels, *is* monopolised by government."—*Maunder* s c p. 12. " The *Scriptures,* or Bible, *are* the only authentic source."—*Bp. Tomline's* Ess a

> " Nor foes nor fortune *take* this power away ;
> And is my Abelard less kind than *they ?*"—*Pope,* p. 334.

OBS. 10.—The English adjective being indeclinable, we have no examples of some of the f of zeugma which occur in Latin and Greek. But adjectives differing in *number,* are som t connected without a repetition of the noun; and, in the agreement of the verb, the noun which is understood, is less apt to be regarded than that which is expressed, though the latter be more remote; as, "There *are one or two* small *irregularities* to be noted."—*Lowth's Gram.* p. 63. "There *are one or two persons*, and but one or two."—*Hazlitt's Lectures.* "There *are one or two* others."—*Crombie's Treatise*, p. 206. "There *are one or two*."—*Blair's Rhet.* p. 319. "There *are one or more* seminaries in every province."—*H. E. Dwight: Lit. Conv.* p. 133. "Whether *one or more* of the clauses *are* to be considered the nominative case."—*Murray's Gram.* i, p. 160. "So that, I believe, there *is* not *more* than *one* genuine example extant."—*Knight, on the Greek Alphabet*, p. 10. "There *is*, properly, no *more* than *one* pause or rest in the sentence."—*Murray's Gram.* i, p. 329; *Blair's Rhet.* p. 125. "Sometimes a small *letter or two is* added to the capital."—*Adam's Lat. Gram.* p. 223; *Gould's*, 283. Among the examples in the seventh paragraph above, there is one like this last, but with a plural verb; and if either is objectionable, *is* should here be *are*. The preceding example, too, is such as I would not imitate. To L. Murray, the following sentence seemed false syntax, because *one* does not agree with *persons*: "He saw *one or more persons* enter the garden."—*Murray's Exercises*, Rule 8th, p. 54. In his Key, he has it thus: "He saw one *person*, or *more than one*, enter the garden."—*Oct. Gram.* Vol. ii, p. 189. To me, this stiff *correction*, which many later grammarians have copied, seems worse than none. And the effect of the principle may be noticed in Murray's style elsewhere; as, "When *a semicolon, or more than one*, have preceded."—*Octavo Gram.* i, p. 277; *Ingersoll's Gram.* p. 288. Here a ready writer would be very apt to prefer one of the following phrases: "When a semicolon *or two* have preceded."—"When *one or two* semicolons have preceded,"—"When *one or more semicolons* have preceded." It is better to write by guess, than to become systematically awkward in expression.

OBS. 11.—In Greek and Latin, the pronoun of the first person, according to our critics, is *generally* placed first; as, "Ἐγὼ καὶ σὺ τὰ δίκαια ποιήσομεν. Xen."—*Milnes's Gr. Gram.* p. 120." That is, "*Ego et tu justa faciemus.*" Again: "*Ego et Cicero valemus.* Cic."—*Buchanan's Pref.* p. x; *Adam's Gram.* 206; *Gould's*, 203. "I and Cicero are well."—*Ib.* But, in English, a modest speaker usually gives to others the precedence, and mentions himself last; as, "He, or thou, or I, must go."—"Thou and I will do what is right."—" Cicero and I are well."—*Dr. Adam.* Yet, in speaking of himself and his *dependants*, a person most commonly takes rank before them; as, "Your inestimable letters supported *myself, my wife*, and *children*, in adversity."—*Lucien Bonaparte, Charlemagne*, p. v. "And I shall be destroyed, *I and my house*."—*Gen.* xxxiv, 30. And in acknowledging a fault, misfortune, or censure, any speaker may assume the first place; as, "Both *I and thou* are in the fault."—*Adam's Gram.* p. 207. "Both *I and you* are in fault."—*Buchanan's Syntax*, p. ix. "Trusty did not do it; *I and Robert* did it."—*Edgeworth's Stories.*
"With critic scales, weighs out the partial wit,
　　What *I*, or *you*, or *he*, or *no one* writ."—*Lloyd's Poems*, p. 162.

OBS. 12.—According to the theory of this work, verbs themselves are not unfrequently connected, one to an other, by *and, or*, or *nor*; so that two or more of them, being properly in the same construction, may be parsed as agreeing with the same nominative: as, "So that the blind and dumb [*man*] both *spake* and *saw*."—*Matt.* xii, 22. "That no one *might buy or sell*."—*Rev.* xiii, 17. "Which *see* not, nor *hear*, nor *know*."—*Dan.* v, 23. We have certainly very many examples like these, in which it is neither convenient nor necessary to suppose an ellipsis of the nominative before the latter verb, or before all but the first, as most of our grammarians do, whenever they find two or more finite verbs connected in this manner. It is true, the nominative may, in most instances, be repeated without injury to the sense; but this fact is no proof of such an ellipsis; because many a sentence which is not incomplete, may possibly take additional words without change of meaning. But these authors, (as I have already suggested under the head of conjunctions,) have not been very careful of their own consistency. If they teach, that, "Every finite verb has its own separate nominative, either expressed or implied," which idea Murray and others seem to have gathered from Lowth; or if they say, that, "Conjunctions really unite sentences, when they appear to unite only words," which notion they may have acquired from Harris; what room is there for that common assertion, that, "Conjunctions connect the same moods and tenses of verbs," which is a part of Murray's eighteenth rule, and found in most of our grammars? For no agreement is usually required between verbs that have separate nominatives; and if we supply a nominative wherever we do not find one for each verb, then in fact no two verbs will ever be connected by any conjunction.

OBS. 13.—What agreement there must be, between verbs that are in the same construction, it is not easy to determine with certainty. Some of the Latin grammarians tell us, that certain conjunctions connect "sometimes similar moods and tenses, and sometimes similar moods but different tenses." See *Prat's Grammatica Latina, Octavo*, Part ii, p. 95. Ruddiman, Adam, and Grant, omit the concord of tenses, and enumerate certain conjunctions which "couple like cases and moods." But all of them acknowledge some exceptions to their rules. The instructions of Lindley Murray and others, on this point, may be summed up in the following canon: "When verbs are connected by a conjunction, they must either agree in mood, tense, and form, or have

---

* This order of the persons, is *not universally* maintained in those languages. The words of Mary to her son, "Thy *father and I* have sought thee sorrowing," seem very properly to give the precedence to her husband; and this is their arrangement in St. Luke's Greek, and in the Latin versions, as well as in others.

† The hackneyed example, "*I and Cicero are well*,"—"*Ego et Cicero valemus*,"—which makes such a figure in the grammars, both Latin and English, and yet is ascribed to Cicero himself, deserves a word of explanation. Cicero the orator, having with him his young son Marcus Cicero at Athens, while his beloved daughter Tullia was with her mother in Italy, thus wrote to his wife, Terentia: "*Si tu, et Tullia, lux nostra, valetis; ego, et suavissimus Cicero, valemus.*"—*EPIST. AD FAM.* Lib. xiv, Ep. v. That is, "If thou, and Tullia, our joy, are well; I, and the sweet lad Cicero, are likewise well." This literal translation is good English, and not to be amended by inversion; for a father is not expected to give precedence to his child. But, when I was a boy, the text and version of Dr. Adam puzzled me not a little; because I could not conceive how Cicero could ever have said, "*I and Cicero are well.*" The garbled citation is now much oftener read than the original. See it in *Crombie's Treatise*, p. 243; *M'Culloch's Gram.* p 158; and others.

separate nominatives expressed." This rule, (with a considerable exception to it, which other authors had not noticed,) was adopted by myself in the Institutes of English Grammar, and also retained in the Brief Abstract of that work, entitled, The First Lines of English Grammar. It there stands as the thirteenth in the series of principal rules : but, as there is no occasion to refer to it in the exercise of parsing, I now think, a less prominent place may suit it as well or better. The principle may be considered as being less certain and less important than most of the usual rules of syntax : I shall therefore both modify the expression of it, and place it among the notes of the present code. See Notes 5th and 6th below.

Obs. 14.—By the agreement of verbs with each other in *form*, it is meant, that the simple form and the compound, the familiar form and the solemn, the affirmative form and the negative, or the active form and the passive, are not to be connected without a repetition of the nominative. With respect to *our* language, this part of the rule is doubtless as important, and as true, as any other. A thorough agreement, then, in mood, tense, and form, is *generally* required, when verbs are connected by *and*, *or*, or *nor*; and, under each part of this concord, there may be cited certain errors which ought to be avoided, as will by-and-by be shown. But, at the same time, there seem to be many allowable violations of the rule, some or other of which may perhaps form exceptions to every part of it. For example, the *tense* may be varied, as it often is in Latin : thus, "As the general state of religion *has been*, *is*, or *shall be*, affected by them."—*Butler's Analogy*, p. 241. "Thou art righteous, O Lord, which *art*, and *wast*, and *shalt be*, because thou hast judged thus."—*Rev.* xvi, 5. In the former of these examples, a repetition of the nominative would not be agreeable; in the latter, it would perhaps be an improvement: as, "*who* art, and *who wast*, and *who* shalt be." (I here change the pronoun, because the relative *which* is not now applied as above.) "This dedication may serve for almost any book, that *has been*, or *shall be* published." —*Campbell's Rhet.* p. 207 ; *Murray's Gram.* p. 222. "It ought to be, '*has been*, *is*, or *shall be*, published.'"—*Crombie's Treatise*, p. 383. "Truth and good sense *are* firm, and *will establish* themselves."—*Blair's Rhet.* p. 286. "Whereas Milton *followed* a different plan, and *has given* a tragic conclusion to a poem otherwise epic in its form."—*Ib.* p. 428. "I am certain, that such *are not*, nor ever *were*, the tenets of the church of England."—*West's Letters*, p. 148. "They *deserve*, and *will meet with*, no regard."—*Blair's Rhet.* p. 109.

> "Whoever thinks a faultless piece to see,
> Thinks what ne'er *was*, nor *is*, nor e'er *shall be*."—*Pope, on Crit.*

Obs. 15.—So verbs differing in *mood* or *form* may sometimes agree with the same nominative, if the simplest verb be placed first—rarely, I think, if the words stand in any other order : as, "One *may be* free from affectation and *not have* merit."—*Blair's Rhet.* p. 189. "There *is*, and *can be*, no other person."—*Murray's Key*, 8vo, p. 224. "To see what *is*, and *is allowed* to be, the plain natural rule."—*Butler's Analogy*, p. 284. "This great experiment *has worked*, and *is working*, well, every way well."—BRADBURN : *Liberator*, ix, 162. "This edition of Mr. Murray's works on English Grammar, *deserves* a place in Libraries, and *will not fail* to obtain it."—BRITISH CRITIC: *Murray's Gram.* 8vo, ii, 299.

> "What nothing earthly *gives*, or *can destroy*."—*Pope.*
> "Some *are*, and *must be*, greater than the rest."—*Id.*

Obs. 16.—Since most of the tenses of an English verb are composed of two or more words, to prevent a needless or disagreeable repetition of auxiliaries, participles, and principal verbs, those parts which are common to two or more verbs in the same sentence, are generally expressed to the first, and understood to the rest ; or reserved, and put last, as the common supplement of each : as, "To which they *do* or *can extend*."—*Butler's Analogy*, p. 77. "He *may*, as any one *may*, if he *will*, incur an infamous execution from the hands of civil justice."—*Ib.* p. 82. "All that has usurped the name of virtue, and [*has*] deceived us by its semblance, must be a mockery and a delusion."—*Dr. Chalmers.* "Human praise, and human eloquence, may acknowledge it, but the Discerner of the heart never will" [*acknowledge it*].—*Id.* "We use thee not so hardly, as prouder livers do" [*use thee*].—*Shak.* "Which they might have foreseen and [*might have*] avoided."—*Butler.* "Every sincere endeavour to amend, shall be assisted, [*shall be*] accepted, and [*shall be*] rewarded."—*Carter.* "Behold, I thought, He will surely come out to me, and [*will*] stand and [*will*] call on the name of the Lord his God, and [*will*] strike his hand over the place, and [*will*] recover the leper."—*2 Kings*, v, 11. "They mean to, and will, hear patiently." —*Salem Register.* That is, "They mean to hear patiently, and they will hear patiently."

> "Virtue *may be assail'd*, but never *hurt*,
> *Surpris'd* by unjust force, but not *inthrall'd*."—*Milton.*
> "Mortals whose pleasures are their only care,
> First wish to be *imposed on*, and then *are*."—*Cowper.*

Obs. 17.—From the foregoing examples, it may be seen, that the complex and divisible structure of the English moods and tenses, produces, when verbs are connected together, a striking peculiarity of construction in our language, as compared with the nearest corresponding construction in Latin or Greek. For we can connect different auxiliaries, participles, or principal verbs, without repeating, and apparently without connecting, the other parts of the mood or tense. And although it is commonly supposed that these parts are necessarily understood wherever they are not repeated, there are sentences, and those not a few, in which we cannot express them, without inserting also an additional nominative, and producing distinct clauses ; as, "*Should* it not *be taken* up and *pursued*?"—*Dr. Chalmers.* "Where thieves *do* not *break* through nor *steal*."—*Matt.* vi, 20. "None present *could* either *read* or *explain* the writing."—*Wood's Dict.* Vol. i, p. 159. Thus we sometimes make a single auxiliary an index to the mood and tense of more than one verb.

Obs. 18.—The verb *do*, which is sometimes an auxiliary and sometimes a principal verb, is thought by some grammarians to be also fitly made a *substitute* for other verbs, as a pronoun is for nouns ; but this doctrine has not been taught with accuracy, and the practice under it will in many instances be found to involve a solecism. In this kind of substitution, there must either be a true ellipsis of the principal verb, so that *do* is only an auxiliary ; or else the verb *do*, with its *object* or *adverb*, if it need one, must exactly correspond to an action described before; so that to speak of *doing this* or *thus*, is merely the shortest way of repeating the idea: as, "He *loves* not plays, as thou *dost*, Antony."—*Shak.* That is, "as thou *dost love plays.*" "This fellow is wise enough *to play the fool*; and, *to do that* well, craves a kind of wit."—*Id.* Here, "*to do that,*" is, "*to play the fool.*" "I will not *do it*, if I find thirty there."—*Gen.* xviii, 30. Do what? Destroy the city, as had been threatened. Where *do* is an auxiliary, there is no real substitution; and, in the other instances, it is not properly the verb *do*, that is the substitute, but rather the word that follows it—or perhaps, both. For, since every action consists in *doing something* or in *doing somehow*, this general verb *do*, with *this, that, it, thus*, or *so*, to identify the action, may assume the import of many a longer phrase. But care must be taken not to substitute this verb for any term to which it is not equivalent; as, "The *a* is certainly to be sounded as the English *do*."—*Walker's Dict. w. A.* Say, "as the English sound *it*;" for *do* is here absurd, and grossly solecistical. "The duke had not behaved with that loyalty with which he ought to have *done.*" —*Lowth's Gram.* p. 111; *Murray's*, i, 212; *Churchill's*, 355; *Fisk's*, 137; *Ingersoll's*, 269. Say, "with which he ought to have *behaved*;" for, to have *done* with loyalty, is not what was meant —far from it. Clarendon wrote the text thus: "The Duke had not behaved with that loyalty, *as* he ought to have done." This should have been corrected, not by changing "*as*" to "*with which*," but by saying—"with that loyalty *which* he ought to have *observed*;" or, "*which would have become him.*"

OBS. 19.—It is little to the credit of our grammarians, to find so many of them thus concurring in the same obvious error, and even making bad English worse. The very examples which have hitherto been given to prove that *do* may be a substitute for other verbs, are *none of them in point*, and all of them have been constantly and shamefully *misinterpreted*. Thus: "They [*do* and *did*] sometimes also supply the place of *another verb*, and make the repetition of it, in the same or a subsequent sentence, unnecessary: as, 'You attend not to your studies as he *does*;' (i. e. as he *attends*, &c.) 'I shall come if I can; but if I *do not*, please to excuse me;' (i. e. if I *come* not.)"—*L. Murray's Gram.* Vol. i, p. 88; *R. C. Smith's*, 88; *Ingersoll's*, 135; *Fisk's*, 78; *A. Flint's*, 41; *Hiley's*, 30. This remark, but not the examples, was taken from *Lowth's Gram.* p. 41. Churchill varies it thus, and retains Lowth's example: "It [i. e. *do*] is used also, to supply the *place of another verb*, in order to avoid the repetition of it: as, 'He *loves* not plays, As thou *dost*, Antony.' SHAKS."—*New Gram.* p. 96. Greenleaf says, "To prevent the repetition of *one or more verbs*, in the same, or [a] following sentence, we frequently make use of *do* AND *did*; as, 'Jack learns the English language as fast as Henry *does*;' that is, 'as fast as Henry learns.' 'I shall come if I can; but if I *do* not, please to excuse me;' that is, 'if I *come* not.'" —*Gram. Simplified*, p, 27. Sanborn says, "*Do* is also used *instead of another verb*, and not unfrequently instead of both *the verb and its object*; as, 'he *loves work* as well as you *do*;' that is, as well as you *love work*."—*Analyt. Gram.* p. 112. Now all these interpretations are wrong; the word *do, dost*, or *does*, being simply an auxiliary, after which the principal verb (with its object where it has one) is *understood*. But the first example is *bad English*, and its explanation is still worse. For, "*As he attends*, &c.," means, "As *he* attends *to your studies!*" And what good sense is there in this? The sentence ought to have been, "You do not attend to your studies, as he does *to his*." That is—"as he does *attend* to his *studies*." This plainly shows that there is, in the text, no real substitution of *does* for *attends*. So of all other examples exhibited in our grammars. under this head: there is nothing to the purpose, in any of them; the common principle of *ellipsis* resolves them all. Yet, strange to say, in the latest and most learned of this sort of text-books, we find the same sham example, fictitious and solecistical as it is, still blindly repeated, to show that "*does*" is not in its own place, as an auxiliary, but "supplies the place of another verb."—*Fowler's E. Gram.* 8vo, 1850, p. 265.

NOTES TO RULE XVII.

NOTE I.—When a verb has nominatives of different persons or numbers,* connected by *or* or *nor*, it must agree with the nearest, (unless an other be the principal term,) and must be understood to the rest, in the person and number required; as, "Neither you nor I *am* concerned."—*W. Allen.* "That neither they nor ye also die."—*Numb.* xviii, 3.

"But neither god, nor shrine, nor mystic rite,
Their city, nor her walls, his soul *delight*."—*Rowe's Lucan*, B. x, l. 26.

NOTE II.—But, since all nominatives that require different forms of the verb, virtually produce separate clauses or propositions, it is better to complete the concord whenever we conveniently can, by expressing the verb or its auxiliary in connexion with each of them; as, "Either thou *art* to blame, or I *am*."—*Comly's Gram.* p. 78. "Neither *were* their numbers, nor *was* their destination, known."—*W. Allen's Gram.* p. 134. So in clauses connected by *and*: as, "But declamation *is* idle, and *murmurs* fruitless."—*Webster's Essays*, p. 82. Say,—"and murmurs *are* fruitless."

NOTE III.—In English, the speaker should always mention himself last; unless

---

* Two singulars connected by *and*, when they form a part of such a disjunction, are still equivalent to a plural; and are to be treated as such, in the syntax of the verb. Hence the following construction appears to be inaccurate: "A single consonant or *a mute and a liquid* before an accented vowel, *is* joined to that vowel."— *Dr. Bullions, Lat. Gram.* p. xi.

his own superior dignity, or the confessional nature of the expression, warrant him in taking the precedence : as, "*Thou or I* must go."—"He then addressed his discourse to *my father and me.*"—"*Ellen and I* will seek, apart, the refuge of some forest cell."—*Scott.* See Obs. 11th above.

NOTE IV.—Two or more distinct subject phrases connected by *or* or *nor*, require a singular verb ; and, if a nominative come after the verb, that must be singular also : as, " That a drunkard should be poor, *or* that a fop should be ignorant, *is* not strange."—" To give an affront, or to take one tamely, *is* no *mark* of a great mind." So, when the phrases are unconnected : as, " To spread suspicion, to invent calumnies, to propagate scandal, *requires* neither labour nor courage."—*Rambler*, No. 183.

NOTE V.—In general, when *verbs* are connected by *and*, *or*, or *nor*, they must either agree in mood, tense, and form, or the simplest in form must be placed first ; as, " So Sennacherib king of Assyria *departed*, and *went* and *returned*, and *dwelt* at Nineveh."—*Isaiah*, xxxvii, 37.   " For if I *be* an offender, or *have committed* any thing worthy of death, I refuse not to die."—*Acts*, xxv, 11.

NOTE VI.—In stead of conjoining discordant verbs, it is in general better to repeat the nominative or insert a new one ; as, " He was greatly heated, and [*he*] *drank* with avidity."—*Murray's Key*, 8vo, p. 201.   "A person may be great or rich by chance ; but *cannot be* wise or good, without taking pains for it."—*Ib.* p. 200. Say,—" but *no one can be* wise or good, without taking pains for it."

NOTE VII.—A mixture of the forms of the solemn style and the familiar, is inelegant, whether the verbs refer to the same nominative or have different ones expressed ; as, " What *appears* tottering and in hazard of tumbling, *produceth* in the spectator the painful emotion of fear."—*Kames, El. of Crit.* ii, 356.   "And the milkmaid *singeth* blithe, And the mower *whets* his sithe."—*Milton's Allegro*, l. 65 and 66.

NOTE VIII.—To use different moods under precisely the same circumstances, is improper, even if the verbs have separate nominatives ; as, " Bating that one *speak* and an other *answers*, it is quite the same."—*Blair's Rhet.* p. 368.   Say,—" that one *speaks* ; " for both the speaking and the answering are assumed as facts.

NOTE IX.—When two terms are connected, which involve different forms of the same verb, such parts of the compound tenses as are not common to both forms, should be inserted in full : except sometimes after the auxiliary *do* ; as, "And then he *falls*, as I *do.*"—*Shak.* That is, " as I *do fall.*"   The following sentences are therefore faulty : " I think myself highly obliged *to make* his fortune, as he *has* mine."— *Spect.* No. 474.   Say,—" as he *has made* mine."   " Every attempt to remove them, *has*, and likely *will prove* unsuccessful."—*Gay's Prosodical Gram.* p. 4.   Say, —" *has proved*, and likely *will prove*, unsuccessful."

NOTE X.—The verb *do* must never be substituted for any term to which its own meaning is not adapted ; nor is there any use in putting it for a preceding verb that is equally short : as, " When we see how confidently men rest on groundless surmises in reference to their own souls, we cannot wonder that they *do it* in reference to others."—*Simeon.*   Better :—" that they *so rest* in reference to *the souls of* others ; " for this repeats the idea with more exactness.

NOTE XI.—The preterit should not be employed to form the compound tenses of the verb ; nor should the perfect participle be used for the preterit or confounded with the present.   Thus : say, " To have *gone*," not, " To have *went* ; " and, " I *did* so," not, " I *done* so ; " or, " He *saw* them," not, " He *seen* them."   Again : say not, " It was *lift* or *hoist* up ; " but, " It was *lifted* or *hoisted* up."

NOTE XII.—Care should be taken, to give every verb or participle its appropiate form, and not to confound those which resemble each other ; as, *to flee* and *to fly*, *to lay* and *to lie*, *to sit* and *to set*, *to fall* and *to fell*, &c.   Thus : say, " He *lay* by the fire ; " not, " He *laid* by the fire ; "—" He *has become* rich ; " not, " He *is become* rich ; "—" I *would* rather *stay* ; " not, " I *had* rather *stay.*"

NOTE XIII.—In the syntax of words that express time, whether they be verbs, adverbs, or nouns, the order and fitness of time should be observed, that the tenses may be used according to their import.   Thus : in stead of," I *have seen* him *last week* ; "

say, " I *saw* him *last week* ; "—and, in stead of, " I *saw* him *this week* ; " say, " I *have seen* him *this week*." So, in stead of, " I *told* you *already* ; " or, " I have *told* you *before* ; " say, " I *have told* you *already* ; "—" I *told* you *before*."

ͬ NOTE XIV.—Verbs of commanding, desiring, expecting, hoping, intending, permitting, and some others, in all their tenses, refer to actions or events, relatively present or future : one should therefore say, " I hoped you *would come* ; " not, " I hoped you *would have come* ; "—and, " I intended *to do* it ; " not, " I intended *to have done* it ; "—&c.

NOTE XV.—Propositions that are as true now as they ever were or will be, should generally be expressed in the present tense : as, " He seemed hardly to know, that two and two *make* four ; " not, " *made*."—*Blair's Gram.* p. 65. " He will tell you, that whatever *is, is* right." Sometimes the present tense is improper with the conjunction *that*, though it would be quite proper without it ; as, " Others said, *That* it *is* Elias. And others said, *That* it *is* a prophet."—*Mark*, vi, 15. Here *That* should be omitted, or else *is* should be *was*. The capital *T* is also improper.

IMPROPRIETIES FOR CORRECTION.

FALSE SYNTAX UNDER RULE XVII.

UNDER THE RULE ITSELF.—NOMINATIVES CONNECTED BY OR.

" We do not know in what either reason or instinct consist."—*Rambler*, No. 41.

[FORMULE.—Not proper, because the verb *consist* is of the plural number, and does not correctly agree with its two nominatives, *reason* and *instinct*, which are connected by *or*, and taken disjunctively. But, according to Rule 17th, " When a verb has two or more nominatives connected by *or* or *nor*, it must agree with them singly, and not as if taken together." Therefore, *consist* should be *consists* ; thus, " We do not know in what either reason or instinct *consists*."]

"A noun or a pronoun joined with a participle, constitute a nominative case absolute."—*Bicknell's Gram.* Part ii, p. 50. "The relative will be of that case, which the verb or noun following, or the preposition going before, use to govern."—*Dr. Adam's Gram.* p. 203. "Which the verb or noun following, or the preposition going before, usually govern."—*Gould's Adam's Gram.* p. 200.[*] " In the different modes of pronunciation which habit or caprice give rise to."—*Knight, on the Greek Alphabet*, p. 14. " By which he, or his deputy, were authorized to cut down any trees in Whittlebury forest."—*Junius*, p. 251. " Wherever objects were to be named, in which sound, noise, or motion were concerned, the imitation by words was abundantly obvious."—*Blair's Rhet.* p. 55. " The pleasure or pain resulting from a train of perceptions in different circumstances, are a beautiful contrivance of nature for valuable purposes."—*Kames, El. of Crit.* i, 262. " Because their foolish vanity or their criminal ambition represent the principles by which they are influenced, as absolutely perfect."—*Life of Madame De Staël*, p. 2. " Hence naturally arise indifference or aversion between the parties."—*Brown's Estimate*, ii, 37. "A penitent unbeliever, or an impenitent believer, are characters no where to be found."—*Tract*, No. 183. " Copying whatever is peculiar in the talk of all those whose birth or fortune entitle them to imitation."—*Rambler*, No. 194. " Where love, hatred, fear, or contempt, are often of decisive influence."—*Duncan's Cicero*, p. 119. "A lucky anecdote or an enlivening tale relieve the folio page."—*D'Israeli's Curiosities*, Vol. i, p. 15. " For outward matter or event, fashion not the character within."—*Book of Thoughts*, p. 37. " Yet sometimes we have seen that wine, or chance, have warmed cold brains."—*Dryden's Poems*, p. 76. " Motion is a Genus ; Flight, a Species ; this Flight or that Flight are Individuals."—*Harris's Hermes*, p. 38. " When *et, aut, vel, sive,* or *nec,* are joined to different members of the same sentence."—*Adam's Lat. and Eng. Gram.* p. 206 ; *Gould's Lat. Gram.* 203 ; *Grant's*, 266. " Wisdom or folly govern us."—*Fisk's English Gram.* p. 84. "*A* or *an* are styled indefinite articles."—*Folker's Gram.* p. 4. "A rusty nail, or a crooked pin, shoot up into prodigies."—*Spectator*, No. 7. "Are either the subject or the predicate in the second sentence modified ? "—*Fowler's E. Gram.* 8vo, 1850, p. 578, § 589.

" Praise from a friend, or censure from a foe,
    Are lost on hearers that our merits know."—*Pope, Iliad*, B. x, l. 293.

UNDER THE RULE ITSELF.—NOMINATIVES CONNECTED BY NOR.

"Neither he nor she have spoken to him."—*Perrin's Gram.* p. 237. " For want of a process of events, neither knowledge nor elegance preserve the reader from weariness."—*Johnson : in Crabb's Syn.* p. 511. " Neither history nor tradition furnish such information."—*Robertson's Amer.* Vol. i, p. 2. " Neither the form nor power of the liquids have varied materially."—*Knight, on the Greek Alph.* p. 16. " Where neither noise nor motion are

[*] Murray the schoolmaster has it, " *used to govern.*"—*English Gram.* p. 64. He puts the verb in a *wrong tense*. Dr. Bullions has it, " *usually governs.*"—*Lat. Gram.* p. 202. This is right.—G. B.

concerned."—*Blair's Rhet.* p. 55. "Neither Charles nor his brother were qualified to support such a system."—*Junius*, p. 260. "When, therefore, neither the liveliness of representation, nor the warmth of passion, serve, as it were, to cover the trespass, it is not safe to leave the beaten track."—*Campbell's Rhet.* p. 381. "In many countries called Christian, neither Christianity, nor its evidence, are fairly laid before men."—*Butler's Analogy*, p. 269. "Neither the intellect nor the heart are capable of being driven."—*Abbott's Teacher*, p. 20. "Throughout this hymn, neither Apollo nor Diana are in any way connected with the Sun or Moon."—*Coleridge's Introd.* p. 199. "Of which, neither he, nor this Grammar, take any notice."—*Johnson's Gram. Com.* p. 346. "Neither their solicitude nor their foresight extend so far."—*Robertson's Amer.* Vol. i, p. 287. "Neither Gomara, nor Oviedo, nor Herrera, consider Ojeda, or his companion Vespucci, as the first discoverers of the continent of America."—*Ib.* Vol. i, p. 471. "Neither the general situation of our colonies, nor that particular distress which forced the inhabitants of Boston to take up arms, have been thought worthy of a moment's consideration."—*Junius*, p. 174.

"Nor War nor Wisdom yield our Jews delight,
They will not study, and they dare not fight."—*Crabbe's Borough*, p. 50.
"Nor time nor chance breed such confusions yet,
Nor are the mean so rais'd, nor sunk the great."—*Rowe's Lucan*, B. iii, l. 213.

UNDER NOTE I.—NOMINATIVES THAT DISAGREE.

"The definite article *the*, designates what particular thing or things is meant."—*Merchant's School Gram.* p. 23 and p. 33. "Sometimes a word or words necessary to complete the grammatical construction of a sentence, is not expressed, but omitted by ellipsis."—*Burr's Gram.* p. 26. "Ellipsis, or abbreviations, is the wheels of language."—*Mauder's Gram.* p. 12. "The conditions or tenor of none of them appear at this day."—*Hutchinson's Hist. of Mass.* Vol. i, p. 16. "Neither men nor money were wanting for the service."—*Ib.* Vol. i, p. 279. "Either our own feelings, or the representation of those of others, require frequent emphatic distinction."—*Barber's Exercises*, p. 13. "Either Atoms and Chance, or Nature are uppermost: now I am for the latter part of the disjunction."—*Collier's Antoninus*, p. 181. "Their riches or poverty are generally proportioned to their activity or indolence."—*Ross Cox's Narrative.* "Concerning the other part of him, neither you nor he seem to have entertained an idea."—*Bp. Horne.* "Whose earnings or income are so small."—*N. E. Discipline*, p. 130. "Neither riches nor fame render a man happy."—*Day's Gram.* p. 71. "The references to the pages, always point to the first volume, unless the Exercises or Key are mentioned."—*Murray's Gram.* Vol. ii, p. 283.

UNDER NOTE II.—COMPLETE THE CONCORD.

"My lord, you wrong my father; nor he nor I are capable of harbouring a thought against your peace."—*Walpole.* "There was no division of acts; no pauses or interval between them; but the stage was continually full; occupied either by the actors, or the chorus."—*Blair's Rhet.* p. 463. "Every word ending in B, P, F, as also many in V, are of this order."—*Dr. Murray's Hist. of Lang.* i, 73. "As proud as we are of human reason, nothing can be more absurd than the general system of human life and human knowledge." —*Bolingbroke, on Hist.* p. 347. "By which the body of sin and death is done away, and we cleansed."—*Barclay's Works*, i, 165. "And those were already converted, and regeneration begun in them."—*Ib.* iii, 433. "For I am an old man, and my wife well stricken in years" —*Luke*, i, 18. "Who is my mother, or my brethren?"—*Mark*, iii, 33. "Lebanon is not sufficient to burn, nor the beasts thereof sufficient for a burnt-offering."—*Isaiah*, xl, 16. "Information has been obtained, and some trials made."—*Society in America*, i, 308. "It is as obvious, and its causes more easily understood."—*Webster's Essays*, p. 84. "All languages furnish examples of this kind, and the English as many as any other."—*Priestley's Gram.* p. 157. "The winters are long, and the cold intense."—*Morse's Geog.* p. 39. "How have I hated instruction, and my heart despised reproof!"—*Prov.* v, 12. "The vestals were abolished by Theodosius the Great, and the fire of Vesta extinguished."—*Lempriere, v. Vestales.* "Riches beget pride; pride, impatience."—*Bullions's Practical Lessons*, p. 89. "Grammar is not reasoning, any more than organization is thought, or letters sounds."— *Enclytica*, p. 90. "Words are implements, and grammar a machine."—*Ib.* p. 91.

UNDER NOTE III.—PLACE OF THE FIRST PERSON.

"I or thou art the person who must undertake the business proposed."—*Murray's Key. 8vo*, p. 184. "I and he were there."—*Dr. Ash's Gram.* p. 51. "And we dreamed a dream in one night, I and he."—*Gen.* xli, 11. "If my views remain the same as mine and his were in 1833."—GOODELL: *Liberator*, ix, 148. "I and my father were riding out."—*Inst.* p. 166. "The premiums were given to me and George."—*Ib.* "I and Jane are invited."— *Ib.* "They ought to invite me and my sister."—*Ib.* "I and you intend going."—*Guy's Gram.* p. 55. "I and John are going to Town."—*British Gram.* p. 193. "I, and he are sick. I, and thou are well."—*James Brown's American Gram.*, Boston Edition of 1841, p. 123. "I, and he is. I, and thou art. I, and he writes."—*Ib.* p. 126. "I, and they are well. I, thou, and she were walking."—*Ib.* p. 127.

UNDER NOTE IV.—DISTINCT SUBJECT PHRASES.

"To practice tale-bearing, or even to countenance it, are great injustice."—*Brown's Inst.* p. 159. "To reveal secrets, or to betray one's friends, are contemptible perfidy."—*Ib.* "To write all substantives with capital letters, or to exclude them from adjectives derived from proper names, may perhaps be thought offences too small for animadversion; but the evil of innovation is always something."—*Dr. Barrow's Essays*, p. 88. "To live in such families, or to have such servants, are blessings from God."—*Family Commentary*, p. 64. "How they portioned out the country, what revolutions they experienced, or what wars they maintained, are utterly unknown."—*Goldsmith's Greece*, Vol. i. p. 4. "To speak or to write perspicuously and agreeably, are attainments of the utmost consequence to all who purpose, either by speech or writing, to address the public."—*Blair's Rhet.* p. 11.

UNDER NOTE V.—MAKE THE VERBS AGREE.

"Doth he not leave the ninety and nine, and goeth into the mountains, and seeketh that which is gone astray?"—*Matt.* xviii, 12. "Did he not fear the Lord, and besought the Lord, and the Lord repented him of the evil which he had pronounced?"—*Jer.* xxvi, 19. "And dost thou open thine eyes upon such an one, and bringest me into judgement with thee?"—*Job*, xiv, 3. "If any man among you seem to be religious, and bridleth not his tongue, but deceiveth his own heart, this man's religion is vain."—*James*, i, 26. "If thou sell aught unto thy neighbour, or buyest aught of thy neighbour's hand, ye shall not oppress one an other."—*Leviticus*, xxv, 14. "And if thy brother that dwelleth by thee, shall have become poor, and be sold to thee, thou shalt not compel him to serve as a bond servant."—WEBSTER's BIBLE: *Lev.* xxv, 39. "If thou bring thy gift to the altar, and there rememberest that thy brother hath aught against thee," &c.—*Matt.* v, 23. "Anthea was content to call a coach, and crossed the brook."—*Rambler*, No. 34. "It is either totally suppressed, or appears in its lowest and most imperfect form."—*Blair's Rhet.* p. 23. "But if any man be a worshiper of God, and doeth his will, him he heareth."—*John*, ix, 31. "Whereby his righteousness and obedience, death and sufferings without, become profitable unto us, and is made ours."—*Barclay's Works*, i, 164. "Who ought to have been here before thee, and object, if they had aught against me."—*Acts*, xxiv, 19.

"Yes! thy proud lords, unpitied land, shall see
That man hath yet a soul, and dare be free."—Campbell.

UNDER NOTE VI.—USE SEPARATE NOMINATIVES.

"*H* is only an aspiration or breathing; and sometimes at the beginning of a word is not sounded at all."—*Lowth's Gram.* p. 4. "Man was made for society, and ought to extend his good will to all men."—*Ib.* p. 12; *Murray's*, i, 170. "There is, and must be, a supreme being, of infinite goodness, power, and wisdom, who created and supports them."—*Beattie's Moral Science*, p. 201. "Were you not affrighted, and mistook a spirit for a body?"—*Watson's Apology*, p. 122. "The latter noun or pronoun is not governed by the conjunction *than* or *as*, but agrees with the verb, or is governed by the verb or the preposition, expressed or understood."—*Murray's Gram.* p. 214; *Russell's*, 103; *Bacon's*, 51; *Alger's*, 71; *R. C. Smith's*, 179. "He had mistaken his true interests, and found himself forsaken."—*Murray's Key*, 8vo, p. 201. "The amputation was exceedingly well performed, and saved the patient's life."—*Ib.* p. 191. "The intentions of some of these philosophers, nay, of many [,] might have been, and probably were good."—*Ib.* p. 216. "This may be true, and yet will not justify the practice."—*Webster's Essays*, p. 33. "From the practice of those who have had a liberal education, and are therefore presumed to be best acquainted with men and things."—*Campbell's Rhet.* p. 161. "For those energies and bounties which created and preserve the universe."—*J. Q. Adams's Rhet.* i, 327. "I shall make it once for all, and hope it will be afterwards remembered."—*Blair's Lect.* p. 45. "This consequence is drawn too abruptly, and needed more explanation."—*Ib.* p. 229. "They must be used with more caution, and require more preparation."—*Ib.* p. 153. "The apostrophe denotes the omission of an *i*, which was formerly inserted, and made an addition of a syllable to the word."—*Priestley's Gram.* p. 67. "The succession may be rendered more various or more uniform, but in one shape or an other is unavoidable."—*Kames, El. of Crit.* i, 253. "It excites neither terror nor compassion, nor is agreeable in any respect."—*Ib.* ii, 277.

"Cheap vulgar arts, whose narrowness affords
No flight for thoughts, but poorly stick at words."—Denham.

UNDER NOTE VII.—MIXTURE OF DIFFERENT STYLES.

"Let us read the living page, whose every character delighteth and instructs us."—*Maunder's Gram.* p. 5. "For if it be in any degree obscure, it puzzles, and doth not please."—*Kames, El. of Crit.* ii, 357. "When a speaker addresseth himself to the understanding, he proposes the instruction of his hearers."—*Campbell's Rhet.* p. 13. "As the wine which strengthens and refresheth the heart."—*H. Adams's View*, p. 221. "This truth he wrappeth in an allegory, and feigns that one of the goddesses had taken up her abode with the other."—*Pope's Works*, iii, 46. "God searcheth and understands the heart."—

Thomas à Kempis. "The grace of God, that brings salvation hath appeared to all men."—*Barclay's Works*, i, 366. "Also we speak not in the words, which man's wisdom teaches; but which the Holy Ghost teacheth."—*Ib.* i, 388. "But he hath an objection, which he urgeth, and by which he thinks to overturn all."—*Ib.* iii, 327. "In that it gives them not that comfort and joy which it giveth unto them who love it."—*Ib.* i, 142. "Thou here misunderstood the place and misappliedst it."—*Ib.* iii, 38. "Like the barren heath in the desert, which knoweth not when good comes."—*Friends' Extracts*, p. 128; *N. E. Discip.* p. 75. "It speaketh of the time past, but shews that something was then doing, but not quite finished."—*E. Devis's Gram.* p. 42. "It subsists in spite of them; it advanceth unobserved."—PASCAL: *Addison's Evidences*, p. 17.

"But where is he, the Pilgrim of my song?—
Methinks he cometh late and tarries long."—*Byron*, Cant. iv, St. 164.

UNDER NOTE VIII.—CONFUSION OF MOODS.

"If a man have a hundred sheep, and one of them is gone astray, &c."—*Kirkham's Gram.* p. 227 with 197. "As a speaker advances in his discourse, especially if it be somewhat impassioned, and increases in energy and earnestness, a higher and louder tone will naturally steal upon him."—*Kirkham's Elocution*, p. 68. "If one man esteem a day above another, and another esteemeth every day alike; let every man be fully persuaded in his own mind."—*Barclay's Works*, i, 439. "If there be but one body of legislators, it is no better than a tyranny; if there are only two, there will want a casting voice."—*Addison, Spect.* No. 287. "Should you come up this way, and I am still here, you need not be assured how glad I shall be to see you."—*Ld. Byron.* "If he repent and becomes holy, let him enjoy God and heaven."—*Brownson's Elwood*, p. 248. "If thy fellow approach thee, naked and destitute, and thou shouldst say unto him, 'Depart in peace; be you warmed and filled;' and yet shouldst give him not those things that are needful to him, what benevolence is there in thy conduct?"—*Kirkham's Elocution*, p. 108.

"Get on your nightgown, lest occasion calls us,
And show us to be watchers."—*Beauties of Shakspeare*, p. 278.

"But if it climb, with your assisting hands,
The Trojan walls, and in the city stands."—*Dryden's Virgil*, ii, 145.

———————————————"Though Heaven's king
Ride on thy wings, and thou with thy compeers,
Us'd to the yoke, draw'st his triumphant wheels."—*Milton, P. L.* iv, l. 973.

"Us'd to the yoke, *draw'dst* his triumphant wheels."—*Lowth's Gram.* p. 106.

UNDER NOTE IX.—IMPROPER ELLIPSES.

"Indeed we have seriously wondered that Murray should leave some things as he has."—*Education Reporter.* "Which they neither have nor can do."—*Barclay's Works*, iii, 73. "The Lord hath, and doth, and will reveal his will to his people, and hath and doth raise up members of his body," &c.—*Ib.* i, 484. "We see then, that the Lord hath, and doth give such."—*Ib.* i, 484. "Towards those that have or do declare themselves members."—*Ib.* i, 494. "For which we can, and have given our sufficient reasons."—*Ib.* i, 507. "When we mention the several properties of the different words in sentences, in the same manner as we have those of *William's*, above, what is the exercise called?"—*Smith's New Gram.* p. 12. "It is, however to be doubted whether this peculiarity of the Greek idiom, ever has or will obtain extensively in the English."—*Nutting's Gram.* p. 47. "Why did not the Greeks and Romans abound in auxiliary words as much as we?"—*Murray's Gram.* i, p. 111. "Who delivers his sentiments in earnest, as they ought to be in order to move and persuade."—*Kirkham's Elocution*, p. 151.

UNDER NOTE X.—DO, USED AS A SUBSTITUTE.

"And I would avoid it altogether, if it could be done."—*Kames, El. of Crit.* i, 36. "Such a sentiment from a man expiring of his wounds, is truly heroic, and must elevate the mind to the greatest height that can be done by a single expression."—*Ib.* i, 204. "Successive images making thus deeper and deeper impressions, must elevate more than any single image can do."—*Ib.* i, 205. "Besides making a deeper impression than can be done by cool reasoning."—*Ib.* ii, 273. "Yet a poet, by the force of genius alone, can rise higher than a public speaker can do."—*Blair's Rhet.* p. 338. "And the very same reason that has induced several grammarians to go so far as they have done, should have induced them to go farther."—*Priestley's Gram. Pref.* p. vii. "The pupil should commit the first section perfectly, before he does the second part of grammar."—*Bradley's Gram.* p. 77. "The Greek *ch* was pronounced hard, as we now do in *chord*."—*Booth's Introd. to Dict.* p. 61. "They pronounce the syllables in a different manner from what they do at other times."—*Murray's Eng. Reader*, p. xi. "And give him the formal cool reception that Simon had done."—*Dr. Scott, on Luke* vii. "I do not say, as some have done."—*Bolingbroke, on Hist.* p. 271. "If he suppose the first, he may do the last."—*Barclay's Works*, iii, 406. "Who are now despising Christ in his inward appearance, as the Jews of old did him in his outward."—*Ib.* i, 506. "That text of Revelations must not be understood, as he doth it."—*Ib.* iii, 309. "Till the mode of parsing the noun is so familiar to him, that he can do it readily."—*Smith's New Gram.* p. 13. "Perhaps it is running the same course which Rome had done before."—*Middleton's Life of Cicero.* "It ought even on this ground to be avoided; which may easily be done by a different construction."—*Churchill's Gram.* p. 312. "These two languages are now pronounced in England as no other nation in Europe does besides."—*Creighton's Dict.* p. xi. "Germany ran the same risk that Italy had done."—*Murray's Key,* 8vo, p. 211 : see *Priestley's Gram.* p. 196.

UNDER NOTE XI.—PRETERITS AND PARTICIPLES.

"The Beggars themselves will be broke in a trice."—*Swift's Poems,* p. 347. "The hoop is hoist above his nose."—*Ib.* p. 404. "My heart was lift up in the ways of the Lord. 2 CHRON."—*Joh. Dict. w. Lift.* "Who sin so oft have mourned, Yet to temptation ran."—*Burns.* "Who would not have let them appeared."—*Steele.* "He would have had you sought for ease at the hands of Mr. Legality."—*Pilgrim's Progress,* p. 31. "From me his madding mind is start, And wooes the widow's daughter of the glen."—*SPENSER : Joh. Dict. w. Glen.* "The man has spoke, and still speaks."—*Ash's Gram.* p. 54. "For you have but mistook me all this while."—*Beauties of Shak.* p. 114. "And will you rent our ancient love asunder ?"—*Ib.* p. 52. "Mr. Birney has plead the inexpediency of passing such resolutions."—*Liberator,* Vol. xiii, p. 194. "Who have wore out their years in such most painful Labours."—*Littleton's Dict. Pref.* "And in the conclusion you were chose probationer."—*Spectator,* No. 32.

"How she was lost, took captive, made a slave ;
And how against him set that should her save."—*Bunyan.*

UNDER NOTE XII.—VERBS CONFOUNDED.

"But Moses preferred to wile away his time."—*Parker's English Composition,* p. 15. "His face shown with the rays of the sun."—*Calvin's Inst.* 4to, p. 76. "Whom they had sat at defiance so lately."—*Bolingbroke, on Hist.* p. 320. "And when he was set, his disciples came unto him."—*Matt.* v, 1. "When he was set down on the judgement-seat."—*Ib.* xxvii, 19. "And when they had kindled a fire in the midst of the hall, and were set down together, Peter sat down among them."—*Luke,* xxii, 55. "So after he had washed their feet, and had taken his garments, and was set down again, he said unto them, Know ye what I have done to you ?"—*John,* xiii, 12. "Even as I also overcame, and am set down with my Father in his throne."—*Rev.* iii, 21. "We have such an high priest, who is set on the right hand of the throne of the Majesty in the heavens."—*Heb.* viii, 1. "And is set down at the right hand of the throne of God."—*Ib.* xii, 2.* "He sat on foot a furious persecution."—*Payne's Geog.* ii, 418. "There layeth an obligation upon the saints, to help such."—*Barclay's Works,* i, 389. "There let him lay."—*Byron's Pilgrimage,* C. iv, st. 180. "Nothing but moss, and shrubs, and stinted trees, can grow upon it."—*Morse's Geog.* p. 43. "Who had lain out considerable sums purely to distinguish themselves."—*Goldsmith's Greece,* i, 132. "Whereunto the righteous fly and are safe."—*Barclay's Works,* i, 146. "He raiseth from supper, and laid aside his garments."—*Ib.* i, 438. "Whither—Oh ! whither shall I fly ?"—*Murray's English Reader,* p. 123. "Flying from an adopted murderer."—*Ib.* p. 122. "To you I fly for refuge."—*Ib.* p. 124. "The sign that should warn his disciples to fly from approaching ruin."—*Keith's Evidences,* p. 62. "In one she sets as a prototype for exact imitation."—*Rush, on the Voice,* p. xxiii. "In which some only bleat, bark, mew, winnow, and bray, a little better than others."—*Ib.* p. 90. "Who represented to him the unreasonableness of being effected with such unmanly fears."—*Rollin's Hist.* ii, 106. "Thou sawedst every action."—*Guy's School Gram.* p. 46. "I taught, thou taughtedst, he or she taught."—*Coar's Gram.* p. 79. "Valerian is taken by Sapor and flead alive, A. D. 260."—*Lempriere's Chron. Table, Dict.* p. xix. "What a fine vehicle is it now become for all conceptions of the mind !"—*Blair's Rhet.* p. 139. "What are become of so many productions ?"—*Volney's Ruins,* p. 8. "What are become of those ages of abundance and of life ?"—*Keith's Evidences,* p. 107. "The Spartan admiral was sailed to the Hellespont." —*Goldsmith's Greece,* i, 159. "As soon as he was landed, the multitude thronged about

---

* The two verbs *to sit* and *to set* are in general quite different in their meaning; but the passive verb *to be set* sometimes comes pretty near to the sense of the former, which is for the most part neuter. Hence, we not only find the Latin word *sedeo,* to sit, used in the sense of *being set,* as, "Ingens cœna *sedet,*" "A huge supper is *set,*" *Juv.* 2, 119 ; but, in the seven texts above, our translators have used *is set, was set,* &c., with reference to the personal posture of *sitting.* This, in the opinion of Dr. Lowth and some others, is erroneous. "*Set,*" says the Doctor, "can be no part of the verb *to sit.* If it belong to the verb *to set,* the translation in these passages is wrong. For *to set,* signifies *to place,* but without any designation of the *posture* of the person placed; which is a circumstance of importance, expressed by the original."—*Lowth's Gram.* p. 58 ; *Churchill's,* 265. These gentlemen cite three of these seven examples, and refer to the other four ; but they do not tell us how they would amend any of them — except that they prefer *sitten* to *sat,* vainly endeavouring to restore an old participle which is certainly obsolete. If any critic dislike my version of the last two texts, because I use the present tense for what in the Greek is the first aorist ; let him notice that this has been done in both by our translators, and in one by those of the Vulgate. In the preceding example, too, the same aorist is rendered, "am *set,*" and by Beza, "*sedeo ;*" though Montanus and the Vulgate render it literally by "*sedi,*" as I do by *sat.* See *Key to False Syntax,* Rule XVII, Note xii.

him."—*Ib.* i, 160. "Cyrus was arrived at Sardis."—*Ib.* i, 161. "Whose year was expired."—*Ib.* i, 162. "It had better have been, ' that faction which.' "—*Priestley's Gram.* p. 97. "This people is become a great nation."—*Murray's Gram.* p. 153 ; *Ingersoll's,* 249. "And here we are got into the region of ornament."—*Blair's Rhet.* p. 181. "The ungraceful parenthesis which follows, had far better have been avoided."—*Ib.* p. 215. "Who forced him under water, and there held him until drounded."—*Indian Wars,* p. 56.

"I had much rather be myself the slave,
    And wear the bonds, than fasten them on him."—*Cowper.*

UNDER NOTE XIII.—WORDS THAT EXPRESS TIME.

"I had finished my letter before my brother arrived."—*Kirkham's Gram.* p. 139. "I had written before I received his letter."—*Blair's Rhet.* p. 82. "From what has been formerly delivered."—*Ib.* p. 182. "Arts were of late introduced among them."—*Ib.* p. 245. "I am not of opinion that such rules can be of much use, unless persons saw them exemplified."—*Ib.* p. 336. "If we use the noun itself, we should say, ' This composition is John's.' "—*Murray's Gram.* p. 174. " But if the assertion referred to something, that is not always the same, or supposed to be so, the past tense must be applied."—*Ib.* p. 191. "They told him, that Jesus of Nazareth passeth by."—*Luke,* xviii, 37. "There is no particular intimation but that I continued to work, even to the present moment."—*R. W. Green's Gram.* p. 39. "Generally, as was observed already, it is but hinted in a single word or phrase."—*Campbell's Rhet.* p. 36. "The wittiness of the passage was already illustrated."—*Ib.* p. 36. "As was observed already."—*Ib.* p. 56. "It was said already in general."—*Ib.* p. 95. "As I hinted already."—*Ib.* p. 134. "What I believe was hinted once already."—*Ib.* p. 148. " It is obvious, as hath been hinted formerly, that this is but an artificial and arbitrary connexion."—*Ib.* p. 282. "They have done anciently a great deal of hurt."—*Bolingbroke, on Hist.* p. 109. "Then said Paul, I knew not, brethren, that he is the High Priest."—*Dr. Webster's Bible :* Acts, xxiii, 5. "Most prepositions originally denote the relation of place, and have been thence transferred to denote by similitude other relations."—*Lowth's Gram.* p. 65; *Churchill's,* 116. "His gift was but a poor offering, when we consider his estate."—*Murray's Key,* 8vo, p. 194. "If he should succeed, and should obtain his end, he will not be the happier for it."—*Murray's Gram.* i, p. 207. "These are torrents that swell to-day, and have spent themselves by to-morrow."—*Blair's Rhet.* p. 286. "Who have called that wheat to-day, which they have called tares to-morrow."—*Barclay's Works,* iii, 168. " He thought it had been one of his tenants."—*Ib.* i, 11. "But if one went unto them from the dead, they will repent."—*Luke,* xvi, 30. "Neither will they be persuaded, though one rose from the dead."—*Ib. verse* 31. "But it is while men alept, that the archenemy has always sown his tares."—*The Friend,* x, 351. "Crescens would not fail to have exposed him."—*Addison's Evidences,* p. 30.

"Bent was his bow, the Grecian hearts to wound ;
    Fierce as he mov'd, his silver shafts resound."—*Pope, Iliad,* B. i, l. 64.

UNDER NOTE XIV.—VERBS OF COMMANDING, &c.

"Had I commanded you to have done this, you would have thought hard of it."—*G. B.* "I found him better than I expected to have found him."—*Priestley's Gram.* p. 126. "There are several smaller faults, which I at first intended to have enumerated."—*Webster's Essays,* p. 246. "Antithesis, therefore, may, on many occasions, be employed to advantage in order to strengthen the impression which we intend that any object should make."—*Blair's Rhet.* p. 168. "The girl said, if her master would but have let her had money, she might have been well long ago."—See *Priestley's Gram.* p. 127. "Nor is there the least ground to fear, that we should be cramped here within too narrow limits."—*Campbell's Rhet.* p. 163 ; *Murray's Gram.* i, 360. "The Romans, flushed with success, expected to have retaken it."—*Hooke's Hist.* p. 37. "I would not have let fallen an unseasonable pleasantry in the venerable presence of Misery, to be entitled to all the wit that ever Rabelais scattered."—*Sterne : Enfield's Speaker,* p. 54. "We expected that he would have arrived last night."—*Inst.* p. 192. "Our friends intended to have met us."—*Ib.* "We hoped to have seen you."—*Ib.* "He would not have been allowed to have entered."—*Ib.*

UNDER NOTE XV.—PERMANENT PROPOSITIONS.

"Cicero maintained that whatsoever was useful was good."—" I observed that love constituted the whole moral chracter of God."—*Dwight.* "Thinking that one gained nothing by being a good man."—*Voltaire.* "I have already told you that I was a gentleman."—*Fontaine.* "If I should ask, whether ice and water were two distinct species of things."—*Locke.* "A stranger to the poem would not easily discover that this was verse."—*Murray's Gram,* 12mo, p. 260. "The doctor affirmed, that fever always produced thirst."—*Inst.* p. 192. "The ancients asserted, that virtue was its own reward."—*Ib.* "They should not have repeated the error, of insisting that the infinitive was a mere noun."—*Diversions of Purley,* Vol. i, p. 288. "It was observed in Chap. III, that the distinctive *or* had a double use."—*Churchill's Gram.* p. 154. "Two young gentlemen, who have made a discovery that there was no God."—*Swift.*

RULE XVIII. — INFINITIVES.

The preposition TO governs the Infinitive mood, and commonly connects it to a finite verb: as, "I desire TO *learn*."—*Dr. Adam.* "Of me the Roman people have many pledges, which I must strive, with my utmost endeavours, TO *preserve*, TO *defend*, TO *confirm*, and TO *redeem*."—*Duncan's Cicero*, p. 41.

"What if the foot, ordain'd the dust TO *tread*,
Or hand TO *toil*, aspir'd TO *be* the head?"—*Pope.*

OBSERVATIONS ON RULE XVIII.

OBS. 1.—No word is more variously explained by grammarians, than this word TO, which is put before the verb in the infinitive mood. Johnson, Walker, Scott, Todd, and some other lexicographers, call it an *adverb*; but, in explaining its use, they say it denotes certain *relations*, which it is not the office of an adverb to express. (See the word in *Johnson's Quarto Dictionary*.) D. St. Quentin, in his Rudiments of General Grammar, says, "*To*, before a verb, is an *adverb*;" and yet his "*Adverbs* are words that are joined to verbs or adjectives, and express some *circumstance* or *quality*." See pp. 33 and 39. Lowth, Priestley, Fisher, L. Murray, Webster, Wilson, S. W. Clark, Coar, Comly, Blair, Felch, Fisk, Greenleaf, Hart, Weld, Webber, and others, call it a *preposition*; and some of these ascribe to it the government of the verb, while others do not. Lowth says, "The *preposition* TO, placed before the verb, *makes* the infinitive mood."—*Short Gram.* p. 42. "Now this," says Horne Tooke, "is manifestly not so: for TO placed before the verb *loveth*, will not make the infinitive mood. He would have said more truly, that TO placed before some *nouns*, makes *verbs*."—*Diversions of Purley*, Vol. i, p. 287.

OBS. 2.—Skinner, in his *Canones Etymologici*, calls this TO "an *equivocal article*."—*Tooks*, *ib.* i, 288. Nutting, a late American grammarian, says: "The *sign* TO, is no other than the Greek article *to*; as, *to agapan* [, to love]; or, as some say, it is the Saxon *do*."—*Practical Gram.* p. 66. Thus, by suggesting two false and inconsistent derivations, though he uses not the name *equivocal article*, he first makes the word an *article*, and then *equivocal*—equivocal in etymology, and of course in meaning.[*] Nixon, in his English Parser, supposes it to be, *unequivocally*, the Greek article *tò*, *the*. See the work, p. 83. D. Booth says, "*To* is, by us, applied to Verbs; but it was the neuter Article (*the*) among the Greeks."—*Introd. to Analyt. Dict.* p. 60. According to Horne Tooke, "Minshew also distinguishes between the preposition TO, and the *sign* of the infinitive TO. Of the former he is silent, and of the latter he says: 'To, as *to* make, *to* walk, *to* do, a Græco articulo *tò*.' But Dr. Gregory Sharpe is persuaded, that our language has taken it from the *Hebrew*. And Vossius derives the correspondent Latin preposition AD from the same source."—*Diversions of Purley*, Vol. i, p. 293.

OBS. 3.—Tooke also says, "I observe, that Junius and Skinner and Johnson, have not chosen to give the slightest hint concerning the derivation of TO."—*Ibid.* But, certainly, of his *adverb* TO, Johnson gives this hint: "TO, Saxon; *te*, Dutch." And Webster, who calls it not an adverb, but a preposition, gives the same hint of the source from which it comes to us. This is as much as to say, it is etymologically the old Saxon preposition *to*—which, truly, it is—the very same word that, for a thousand years or more, has been used before nouns and pronouns to govern the objective case. Tooke himself does not deny this; but, conceiving that almost all particles, whether English or any other, can be traced back to ancient verbs or nouns, he hunts for the root of this, in a remoter region, where he pretends to find that *to* has the same origin as *do*; and though he detects the former in a *Gothic noun*, he scruples not to identify it with an *auxiliary verb*! Yet he elsewhere expressly denies, "that *any* words change their nature by use, so as to belong sometimes to one part of speech, and sometimes to another."—*Div. of Pur.* Vol. i, p. 68.

OBS. 4.—From this, the fair inference is, that he will have both *to* and *do* to be "*nouns substantive*" still! "Do (the *auxiliary* verb, as it has been called) is derived from the same root, and is indeed the same word as TO."—*Ib.* Vol. i, p. 290. "Since FROM means *commencement* or *beginning*, TO must mean *end* or *termination*."—*Ib.* i, 283. "The preposition TO (in Dutch written

* Nutting, I suppose did not imagine the Greek article, τò, *the*, and the English or Saxon verb *do*, to be equivalent or kindred words. But there is no knowing what terms conjectural etymology may not contrive to identify, or at least to approximate and ally. The ingenious David Booth, if he does not actually identify *do*, with τò, *the*, has discovered synonymes and cognates that are altogether as unapparent to common observers: as, "*It* and *the*," says he, "when Gender is not attended to, are *synonymous*. Each is expressive of Being in general, and when used Verbally, signifies to bring *forth*, or to add to what we already see. *The*, *it*, *and*, *add*, *at*, *to*, and *do*, are *kindred words*. They mark that an *addition* is made to some collected mass of existence. *To*, which literally signifies add, (like *at* and the Latin *ad*,) is merely a different pronunciation of *do*. It expresses the *junction* of an other thing, or circumstance, as appears more evidently from its varied orthography of *too*."—*Introd. to Analyt. Dict.* p. 45. Horne Tooke, it seems, could not persuade this author into his notion of the derivation and meaning of *the*, *it*, *to*, or *do*. But Lindley Murray, and his followers, have been more tractable. They were ready to be led without looking. "To," say they, "comes from *Saxon and Gothic words*, which signify action, effect, termination, to act, &c."—*Murray's Gram.* 8vo, p. 123; *Fisk's*, 92. What an admirable explanation is this! and how prettily the great Compiler says on the next leaf: "Etymology, when it is guided by *judgment*, and [when] *proper limits* are set to it, certainly merits great attention!"—*Ib.* p. 186. According to his own express rules for interpreting "a substantive *without any article to limit it*," and the "relative pronoun *with a comma before it*," he must have meant, that "*to* comes from Saxon and Gothic words" *of every sort*, and that *the words of these two languages* "signify action, effect, termination, to act, &c." The latter assertion is true enough; but, concerning the former, a man of sense may demur. Nor do I see how it is possible not to despise *such* etymology, be the interpretation of the words what it may. For, if *to* means *action* or *to act*, then our little *infinitive phrase*, *to be*, must mean, *action be*, or *to act be*; and what is this, but nonsense?

TOB and TOT, a little nearer to the original) is the Gothic substantive TΛΠI or TΛΠhTS, i. e. *act, effect, result, consummation.* Which Gothic substantive is indeed itself no other than the past participle of the verb TΛΠÇΛΠ, *agere.* And what is *done*, is *terminated, ended, finished.*"—*Ib.* i, 285. No wonder that Johnson, Skinner, and Junius, gave no hint of *this* derivation: it is not worth the ink it takes, if it cannot be made more sure. But, in showing its bearing on the verb, the author not unjustly complains of our grammarians, that, "Of all the points which they endeavour to *shuffle over*, there is none in which they do it more grossly than in this of the infinitive."—*Ib.* i, 287.

OBS. 5.—Many are content to call the word TO a *prefix*, a *particle*, a *little word*, a *sign of the infinitive*, a *part of the infinitive*, a *part of the verb*, and the like, without telling us whence it comes, how it differs from the preposition *to*, or to what part of speech it belongs. It certainly is not what we usually call a *prefix*, because we never *join it to* the verb; yet there are three instances in which it becomes such, before a noun: viz., *to-day, to-night, to-morrow.* If it is a "*particle*," so is any other preposition, as well as every small and invariable word. If it is a "*little word*," the whole bigness of a preposition is unquestionably found in it; and no "*word*" is so small but that it must belong to some one of the ten classes called parts of speech. If it is a "*sign of the infinitive*," because it is used before no other mood; so is it a *sign of the objective case*, or of what is Latin is called the dative, because it precedes no other case. If we suppose it to be a "*part of the infinitive*," or a "*part of the verb*," it is certainly no *necessary* part of either; because there is no verb which may not, in several different ways, be properly used in the infinitive without it. But if it be a part of the infinitive, it must be a *verb*, and ought to be classed with the *auxiliaries.* Dr. Ash accordingly placed it among the auxiliaries; but he says, (inaccurately, however,) "The auxiliary *sign seems* to have the nature of *adverbs.*"—*Grammatical Institutes*, p. 33. "The auxiliary [signs] are, *to, do, did, have, had, shall, will, may, can, must, might*," &c.—*Ib.* p. 31.

OBS. 6.—It is clear, as I have already shown, that the word *to* may be a *sign* of the infinitive, and yet not be a *part* of it. Dr. Ash supposes, it may even be a part of the *mood*, and yet not be a part of the *verb.* How this can be, I see not, unless the mood consists in something else than either the form or the parts of the verb. This grammarian says, "In parsing, every word should be considered as a *distinct part of speech*: for though two or more words may be united to form a *mode*, a tense, or a comparison; yet it seems quite improper to unite two or more words to make a noun, a *verb*, an adjective, &c."—*Gram. Inst.* p. 28. All the auxiliaries, therefore, and the particle *to* among them, he parses separately; but he follows not his own advice, to make these distinct parts of speech; for he calls them all *signs* only, and signs are not one of his ten parts of speech. And the participle too, which is one of the ten, and which he declares to be "no part of the verb," he parses separately; calling it a verb, and not a participle, as often as it accompanies any of his auxiliary signs. This is certainly a greater impropriety than there can be in supposing an auxiliary and a participle to constitute a verb; for the mood and tense are the properties of the compound, and ought not to be ascribed to the principal term only. Not so with the preposition *to* before the infinitive, any more than with the conjunction *if* before the subjunctive. These may well be parsed as separate parts of speech; for these moods are sometimes formed, and are completely distinguished in each of their tenses, without the adding of these signs.

OBS. 7.—After a careful examination of what others have taught respecting this disputed point in grammar, I have given, in the preceding rule, that explanation which I consider to be the most correct and the most simple, and also as well authorized as any. Who first parsed the infinitive in this manner, I know not; probably those who first called the *to* a *preposition*; among whom were Lowth and the author of the old British Grammar. The doctrine did not originate with me, or with Comly, or with any American author. In Coar's English Grammar, published in London in 1796, the phrase *to trample* is parsed thus: "*To*—A preposition, serving for a sign of the infinitive mood to the verb *Trample*—A verb neuter, infinitive mood, present tense, *governed by the preposition* TO before it. RULE. The preposition *to* before a verb, is the sign of the infinitive mood." See the work, p. 263. This was written by a gentleman who speaks of his "long habit of teaching the Latin Tongue," and who was certainly partial enough to the principles of Latin grammar, since he adopts in English the whole detail of Latin cases.

OBS. 8.—In Fisher's English Grammar, London, 1800, (of which there had been many earlier editions,) we find the following rule of syntax: "When two principal *Verbs* come together, the latter of them expresses an unlimited Sense, with the Preposition *to* before it; as *he loved to learn*; *I chuse to dance*: and is called the *infinitive Verb*, which may also follow a Name or Quality; as, *a Time to sing*; *a Book delightful to read.*" That this author supposed the infinitive to be *governed* by *to*, and not by the preceding verb, noun, or adjective, is plain from the following note, which he gives in his margin: "The Scholar will best understand this, by being told that *infinite or invariable Verbs*, having neither Number, Person, nor Nominative Word belonging to them, are known or *governed by the Preposition* TO coming before them. The Sign *to* is often understood; as, Bid Robert and his company (*to*) tarry."—*Fisher's New Gram.* p. 95.

OBS. 9.—The forms of parsing, and also the rules, which are given in the early English grammars, are so very defective, that it is often impossible to say positively, what their authors did, or did not, intend to teach. Dr. Lowth's specimen of "grammatical resolution" contains four infinitives. In his explanation of the first, the preposition and the verb are parsed separately, as above; except that he says nothing about government. In his account of the other three, the two words are taken together, and called a "*verb*, in the infinitive *mode.*" But as he elsewhere calls the particle *to* a preposition, and nowhere speaks of any thing else as governing the infinitive, it seems fair to infer, that he conceived the verb to be the regimen of this preposition.[*] If such was his idea, we have the learned Doctor's authority in opposition to that of his

_____

[*] So, from the following language of three modern authors, one cannot but infer, that they would parse the verb as *governed by the preposition*; but I do not perceive that they anywhere expressly say so:—
(1.) "The Infinitive is the form of the supplemental verb that always has, or admits, the preposition TO before

professed admirers and copyists. Of these, Lindley Murray is doubtless the most famous. But Murray's twelfth rule of syntax, while it expressly calls *to* before the infinitive a *preposition*, absurdly takes away from it this regimen, and leaves us a preposition that *governs nothing*, and has apparently nothing to do with the *relation* of the terms between which it occurs.

Obs. 10.—Many later grammarians, perceiving the absurdity of calling *to* before the infinitive a *preposition* without supposing it to govern the verb, have studiously avoided this name; and have either made the "*little word*" a supernumerary part of speech, or treated it as no part of speech at all. Among these, if I mistake not, are Allen, Lennie, Bullions, Alger, Guy, Churchill, Hiley, Nutting, and Wells. Except Comly, the numerous modifiers of Murray's Grammar are none of them more consistent, on this point, than was Murray himself. Such of them as do not follow him literally, either deny, or forbear to affirm, that *to* before a verb is a *preposition;* and consequently either tell us not what it is, or tell us falsely; some calling it "*a part of the verb*," while they neither join it to the verb as a prefix, nor include it among the auxiliaries. Thus Kirkham: "*To* is not a preposition when *joined to* a verb in this mood; thus, *to* ride, *to* rule; but it should be parsed *with the verb*, and *as a part* of it."—*Gram. in Familiar Lect.* p. 137. So R. C. Smith: "This little word *to*, when *used before* verbs in this manner, is not a preposition, but forms *a part of the verb*, and, in parsing, should be so considered."—*Productive Gram.* p. 65. How can that be "*a part of the verb*," which is *a word* used *before* it? or how is *to* "joined to the verb," or made a part of it, in the phrase, "*to ride?*" But Smith does not abide by his own doctrine; for, in an other part of his book, he adopts the phraseology of Murray, and makes *to* a preposition: saying, "The *preposition* TO, though generally used before the latter verb, is sometimes properly omitted; as, 'I heard him say it;' instead of '*to* say it.'"—*Productive Gram.* p. 156. See *Murray's Rule* 12th.

Obs. 11.—Most English grammarians have considered the word *to* as a part of the infinitive, a part *of the verb;* and, like the teachers of Latin, have referred the government of this mood to a preceding verb. But the rule which they give, is partial, and often inapplicable; and their exceptions to it, or the heterogeneous parts into which some of them divide it, are both numerous and puzzling. They teach that at least half of the ten different parts of speech "*frequently* govern the infinitive:" if so, there should be a distinct rule for each; for why should the government of one part of speech be made an exception to that of an other? and, if this be done, with respect to the infinitive, why not also with respect to the objective case? In all instances to which their rule is applicable, the rule which I have given, amounts to the same thing; and it obviates the necessity for their numerous exceptions, and the embarrassment arising from other constructions of the infinitive not noticed in them. Why then is the simplest solution imaginable still so frequently rejected for so much complexity and inconsistency? Or how can the more common rule in question be suitable for a child, if its applicability depends on a relation between the two verbs, which the preposition *to* sometimes expresses, and sometimes does not?

Obs. 12.—All authors admit that in some instances the sign *to* is "superfluous and improper," the construction and government appearing complete without it; and the "Rev. Peter Bullions, D.D., Professor of Languages in the Albany Academy," has recently published a grammar, in which he adopts the common rule, "One verb governs *another* in the infinitive mood; as, *I desire to learn;*" and then remarks, "The infinitive after a verb is governed by it *only when the attribute expressed by the infinitive is either the subject or* [the] *object of the other verb.* In such expressions as '*I read to learn*,' the infinitive is *not governed* by '*I read*,' but depends on the phrase '*in order to*' understood."—*Bullions's Prin. of E. Gram.* p. 110. But, "*I read 'in order to' to learn*," is not English; though it might be, if either *to* were any thing else than a preposition: as, "Now *set to to learn* your lesson." This broad exception therefore, which embraces well-nigh half the infinitives in the language, though it contains some obvious truth, is both carelessly stated, and badly resolved. The single particle *to* is quite sufficient, both to govern the infinitive, and to connect it to any antecedent term which can make sense with such an adjunct. But, in fact, the reverend author must have meant to use the "*little word*" but once; and also to deny that it is a preposition; for he elsewhere says expressly, though, beyond question, erroneously, "A preposition should *never* be used before the infinitive."—*Ib.* p. 92. And he also says, "The *Infinitive* mood expresses *a thing* in a general manner, without distinction of number, person, *or time*, and commonly has TO *before* it."—*Ib.* Second Edition, p. 35. Now if TO is "*before*" the mood, it is certainly not *a part* of it. And again, if this mood had no distinction of "*time*," our author's two tenses of it, and his two special rules for their application, would be as absurd as is his notion of its government. See his *Obs. 6 and* 7, *ib.* p. 124.

Obs. 13.—Richard Hiley, too, a grammarian of perhaps more merit, is equally faulty in his explanation of the infinitive mood. In the first place, he absurdly says, "TO *before the infinitive mood*, is considered as forming *part of the verb;* but in *every other* situation it is a preposition."—*Hiley's Gram.*, Third Edition, p. 28. To teach that a "*part of the verb*" stands "*before the mood*," is an absurdity manifestly greater, than the very opposite notion of Dr. Ash, that what is *not a part of the verb*, may yet be included *in the mood*. There is no need of either of these false suppositions; or of the other suggestion, doubly false, that *to*, "in *every other* situation, is a preposition." What does *preposition* mean? Is *to* a preposition when it is placed *after* a verb,

___

it; as, to *move.* Its general character is to represent the action in *prospect*, or *to do;* or in *retrospect*, as *to have done.* As a verb, it signifies *to do* the action; and as *object of the preposition* TO, it stands in the place of a noun for *the doing* of it. The infinitive verb and its prefix *to* are used much like a preposition and its noun object."—*Felch's Comprehensive Gram.* p. 62.

(2.) "The action or other signification of a verb may be expressed in its widest and most general sense, without any limitation by a person or agent, but *merely as the end or purpose* of some other action, state of being, quality, or thing; it is, from this want of limitation, said to be in the *Infinitive mode;* and is expressed by the verb with the *preposition* TO before it, to denote *this relation of end or purpose;* as, 'He came *to see* me;' 'The man is not fit *to die;*' 'It was not right for him *to do* thus.'"—*Dr. S. Webber's English Gram.* p. 35.

(3.) "RULE 3. A verb in the Infinitive Mode, is *the object* of the preposition TO, expressed or understood."—*S. W. Clark's Practical Gram.* p. 127.

and *not* a preposition when it is placed *before* it? For example: "I rise *to shut to the d* See *Luke*, xiii, 25.

OBS. 14.—In his syntax, this author further says, "When two verbs come together, the *must be in the infinitive mood, when it denotes the object* of the former; as, 'Study to *impr* This is his *Rule*. Now look at his *Notes*. "1. When the latter verb *does not express* the o *but the end*, or something remote, the word *for*, or the words *in order to*, are understood; a read *to learn;*' that is, 'I read *for* to learn,' or, '*in order* [TO] *to learn*.' The word *for*, hou is never, in such instances, expressed in good language. 2. The infinitive is *frequently* gover adjectives, substantives, and participles; but in *this instance* also, a preposition is understood, t *never expressed;* as, 'Eager *to learn;*' that is, 'eager *for* to learn;' or, '*for* learning;' 'A ce *improve;*' that is, '*for* to improve."—*Hiley's Gram.* p. 80. Here we see the origin of some a lions's blunders. *To* is so small a word, it slips through the fingers of these gentlemen. I utterly needless, and worse than needless, they foist into our language, in instances beyond ber, to explain infinitives that occur at almost every breath. Their students must see the *read to learn*," and, "*I study to improve*," with countless other examples of either sort, as *different constructions*, and not to be parsed by the same rule! And here the only govern the infinitive which Hiley affirms, is immediately contradicted by the supposition of a *for* "understood."

OBS. 15.—In all such examples as, "I *read* to *learn*,"—"I *strive* to *learn*,"—"Some *live*,"—"Some *live* to *eat*,"—"She *sings* to *cheer* him,"—"I *come* to *aid* you,"—"I *go* to *p* a place for you,"—*the action* and *its purpose* are connected by the word *to*; and if, in the c instances of this kind, the former verbs *do not govern* the latter, it is not because the phrase is elliptical, or ever was elliptical,* but because in no case is there any such government, in the construction of those verbs which take the infinitive after them without the prepo Professor Bullions will have the infinitive to be governed by a finite verb, "when the act *pressed by the infinitive is the subject* of the other verb." An infinitive may be made the *su* a finite verb; but this grammarian has mistaken the established meaning of *subject*, as w *attribute*, and therefore written nonsense. Dr. Johnson defines his *adverb* TO, "A particle between two verbs, and noting the second as the *object* of the first." But of all the word according to my opponents and their oracles, govern the infinitive, probably not more t quarter part are such verbs as usually *have an object* after them. Where then is the pr of their notion of infinitive government? And what advantage has it, even where it is lea jectionable?

OBS. 16.—Take for an example of this contrast the terms, "Strive to enter in—many w to enter in."—*Luke*, xiii, 24. Why should it be thought more eligible, to say, that the *strive* or *will seek* governs the infinitive verb *to enter;* than to say, that *to* is a preposition ing the relation between *strive* and *enter*, or between *will seek* and *enter*, and governing the verb? (See the exact and only needful form for parsing any such term, in the *Twelfth* P this work.) None, I presume, will deny, that in the Greek or the Latin of these phrase finite verbs govern the infinitive; or that, in the French, the infinitive *entrer* is governe one preposition, and then by an other. "*Contendite intrare—multi quærent intrare*."—Mt "Efforcez-vous d' entrer—plusieurs chercheront à y entrer."—*French Bible*. In my op before a verb is as fairly a preposition, as the French *de* or à; and it is the main design observations, while they candidly show the reader what others teach, *to prove it so*. The struction which makes it any thing else, is that which puts it after a verb or a particip sense of an adverbial supplement; as, "The infernal idol is bowed down *to*."—*Herod dom*. "Going *to* and fro."—*Bible*. "At length he came *to*."—"Tell him to heave t was ready to set *to*." With singular absurdness of opinion, some grammarians call *to* a j tion, when it thus *follows* a verb and governs nothing, who resolutely deny it that name, *precedes* the verb, and *requires it to be in the infinitive mood*, as in the last two examples. N this is not *government*, what is? And if *to*, without government, is not an *adverb*, what Obs. 2d on the List of Prepositions.

OBS. 17.—The infinitive thus admits a simpler solution in English, than in most ot guages; because we less frequently use it without a preposition, and seldom, if ever, a variety in this connecting and governing particle. And yet in no other language has its struction given rise to a tenth part of that variety of absurd opinions, which the defend true syntax must refute in ours. In French, the infinitive, though frequently placed in imm dependence on an other verb, may also be governed by several different prepositions, (as. *pour, sans, après,*) according to the sense.† In Spanish and Italian, the construction is s

---

* Rufus Nutting, A. M., a grammarian of some skill, supposes that in all such sentences there was an ellipsis, not of the phrase "*in order to*," but of the preposition *for*. He says, "Considering the merely a *verbal noun*, it might be observed, that the infinitive, when it expresses the *object*, is governed *sitive* verb; and, when it expresses the *final cause*, is governed by an *intransitive* verb, OR ANCIENTLY, E OSITION UNDERSTOOD. Of the former kind—'he learns *to read*.' Of the latter—'he reads *to learn*, learn.'"—*Practical Gram.* p. 101. If *for* was anciently understood in examples of this sort, it is underst and to a still greater extent; because we do not now insert the word *for*, as our ancestors sometimes di ellipsis can no otherwise grow obsolete, than by a continual use of what was once occasionally omitted

† (1.) "La préposition, est un mot indéclinable, placé devant les noms, les pronoms, et les verb *régis*."—" The preposition is an indeclinable word placed before the nouns, pronouns, and verbs, which it *—Perrin's Grammar*, p. 152.

(2.) "Every verb placed immediately after an *other verb*, or after *a preposition*, ought to be put in th *itive*; because it is then *the regimen* of the verb or preposition which precedes." See *La Grammai Grammaires, par Girault Du Vivier*, p. 774.

(3.) The American translator of the Elements of General Grammar, by the Baron De Sacy, is natura giving a version of his author's method of analysis, to parse the English infinitive mood essentia calling the word *to* a preposition, and the exponent, or sign, of a *relation* between the verb which fol some other word which is antecedent to it. Thus, in the phrase, "*commanding them to use his power*. that "'*to*' [is the] Exponent of a relation whose Antecedent is '*commanding*,' and [whose] Consequent,

Latin and Greek, the infinitive is, for the most part, immediately dependent on an other verb. But, according to the grammars, it may stand for a noun, in all the six cases; and many have called it an *indeclinable noun*. See the Port-Royal Latin and Greek grammars; in which several peculiar constructions of the infinitive are referred to the government of a *preposition*—constructions that occur frequently in Greek, and sometimes even in Latin.

OBS. 18.—It is from an improper extension of the principles of these "learned languages" to ours, that much of the false teaching which has so greatly and so long embarrassed this part of English grammar, has been, and continues to be, derived. A late author, who supposes every infinitive to be virtually a *noun*, and who thinks he finds in ours *all the cases* of an English noun, not excepting the possessive, gives the following account of its origin and nature: "This mood, with almost all its properties and uses, has been adopted into our language from the ancient Greek and Latin tongues. * * * * * * The definite article τὸ [,] *the*, which they [the Greeks] used before the infinitive, to mark, in an especial manner, its nature of a substantive, *is evidently the same word* that we use before our infinitive; thus, '*to write*,' signifies *the* writing; that is, the action of writing;—and when a verb governs an infinitive, it only governs it *as in the objective case*."—*Nixon's English Parser*, p. 83. But who will believe, that our old Saxon ancestors borrowed from Greek or Latin what is now our construction of the very *root* of the English verb, when, in all likelihood, they could not read a word in either of those languages, or scarcely knew the letters in their own, and while it is plain that they took not thence even the inflection of a *single branch* of any verb whatever?

OBS. 19.—The particle *to*, being a very common preposition in the Saxon tongue, has been generally used before the English infinitive, ever since the English language, or any thing like it, existed. And it has always *governed the verb*, not indeed "as in the *objective case*," for no verb is ever declined by cases, but simply as the *infinitive mood*. In the Anglo-Saxon version of the Gospels, which was made as early as the eleventh century, the infinitive mood is sometimes expressed in this manner, and sometimes by the termination *an* without the preposition. Dr. Johnson's History of the English Language, prefixed to his large Dictionary, contains, of this version, and of Wickliffe's, the whole of the first chapter of Luke; except that the latter omits the first four verses, so that the numbers for reference do not correspond. Putting, for convenience, English characters for the Saxon, I shall cite here three examples from each; and these, if he will, the reader may compare with the 19th, the 77th, and the 79th verse, in our common Bible. SAXON: "And ic eom asend with the *sprecan*. and the this *bodian*."—*Luce*, i, 19. WICKLIFFE: "And Y am sent to thee *to speke* and *to evangelise* to thee these thingis."—*Luk*, i, 15. SAXON: "To syllene his folce hæle gewit on hyra synna forgyfnesse."—*Luce*, i, 77. WICKLIFFE: "*To geve* science of heelth to his puple into remissioun of her synnes."—*Luk*, i, 73. SAXON: "Onlyhtan tham the on thystrum and on deathes sceade sittath. and to *gereccenne* on sibbe weg."—*Luce*, i, 79. WICKLIFFE: "*To geve* light to them that sitten in derknessis, and in schadowe of deeth, *to dresse* oure feet into the weye of pees."—*Luk*, i, 75.

OBS. 20.—Such, then, has ever been the usual construction of the *English* infinitive mood; and a wilder interpretation than that which supposes *to* an *article*, and says, "*to write* signifies *the writing*," cannot possibly be put upon it. On this supposition. "I am going to *write* a letter," is a pure Grecism; meaning, "I am going *the writing* a letter," which is *utter nonsense*. And further, the infinitive in Greek and Latin, as well as in Saxon and English, is always in fact governed as a *mood*, rather than as a *case*, notwithstanding that the Greek article in any of its four different cases may, in some instances, be put before it; for even with an article before it, the Greek infinitive usually retains its regimen as a verb, and is therefore not "a *substantive*," or noun. I am well aware that some learned critics, conceiving that the essence of the verb consists in predication, have plainly denied that the infinitive is a verb; and, because it may be made the subject of a finite verb, or may be governed by a verb or a preposition, have chosen to call it "a mere noun substantive." Among these is the erudite Richard Johnson, who, with so much ability and lost labour, exposed, in his Commentaries, the errors and defects of Lily's Grammar and others. This author adduces several reasons for his opinion; one of which is the following: "Thirdly, it is found to have a Preposition set before it, an other *sure sign of a Substantive*; as, '*Ille nihil præter loqui, et ipsum maledicte et maligne, didicit.*' Liv. l. 45, p. 888. [That is, "He learned nothing *but to speak*, and that slanderously and maliciously."] '*At si quis sibi beneficium dat, nihil interest inter dare et accipere.*' Seneca, de Ben. l. 5, c. 10." [That is, "If any one bestows a benefit on himself, there is no difference *between give* and *take*;"*—or, "*between bestowing and receiving.*"]—See Johnson's *Grammatical Com.* p. 342. But I deny that a preposition is a "sure sign of a substantive." (See Obs. 2d on the Prepositions, and also Obs. 1st on the List of Prepositions, in the tenth chapter of Etymology.) And if we appeal to philological authorities, to determine whether infinitives are nouns or verbs, there will certainly be found more for the latter name, than for the former; that is, more in number, if not in weight; though it must

---

—Fosdick's De Sacy, p. 181. In short, he expounds the word *to* in this relation, just as he does when it stands before the objective case. For example, in the phrase, "belonging to him alone: '*to*,' Exponent of a relation of which the Antecedent is '*belonging*,' and the Consequent, '*him alone*.' "—*Ib.* p. 126. My solution, in either case, differs from this in scarcely any thing else than the *choice of words* to express it.

(4.) It appears that, in sundry dialects of the north of Europe, the preposition *at* has been preferred for the governing of the infinitive: "The use of *at* for *to*, as the sign of the infinitive mode, is Norse, not Saxon. It is the regular prefix in Icelandic, Danish, Swedish, and Feroic. It is also found in the northern dialects of the Old English, and in the particular dialect of Westmoreland at the present day."—*Fowler, on the English Language*, 8vo, 1850, p. 46.

† Here is a literal version, in which two infinitives are governed by the preposition *between*; and, though such a construction is uncommon, I know not why it should be thought less accurate in the one language than in the other. In some exceptive phrases, also, it seems not improper to put the infinitive after some other preposition than *to*; as, "What can she do *besides sing*?"—"What has she done, *except rock* herself?" But such expressions, if allowable, are too unfrequent to be noticed in any general Rule of syntax. In the following example, the word *of* pretty evidently governs the infinitive: "Intemperance characterizes our discussions, that is calculated to embitter in stead *of conciliate*."—CINCINNATI HERALD: *Liberator*, No. 986.

be confessed, that many of the old Latin grammarians did, as Priscian tells us, consider the infinitive a noun, calling it *Nomen Verbi*, the Name of the Verb.* If we appeal to reasons, there are more also of these;—or at least as many, and most of them better: as, 1. That the infinitive is often transitive; 2. That it has tenses; 3. That it is qualified by adverbs, rather than by adjectives; 4. That it is never declined like a noun; 5. That the action or state expressed by it, is not commonly abstract, though it may be so sometimes; 6. That in some languages it is *the root* from which all other parts of the verb are derived, as it is in English.

OBS. 21.—So far as I know, it has not yet been denied, that *to* before a *participle* is a preposition, or that a preposition before a participle *governs* it; though there are not a few who erroneously suppose that participles, by virtue of such government, are necessarily converted into *nouns*. Against this latter idea, there are many sufficient reasons; but let them now pass, because they belong not here. I am only going to prove, in this place, that *to* before the infinitive is *just such a word* as it is before the participle; and this can be done, call either of them what you will. It is plain, that if the infinitive and the participle are ever *equivalent to each other*, the same word before them both must needs be equivalent *to itself*. Now I imagine there are some examples of such equivalence; as, "When we are habituated *to doing* [or *to do*] any thing wrong, we become blinded by it."—*Young Christian*, p. 326. "The lyre, or harp, was best adapted *to accompanying* [or *to accompany*] their declamations."—*Music of Nature*, p. 336. "The new beginner should be accustomed *to giving* [or *to give*] all the reasons for each part of speech."—*Nutting's Gram.* p. 85. "Which, from infecting our religion and morals, fell *to corrupt* [say, *to corrupting*] our language."— SWIFT: *Blair's Rhet.* p. 108. Besides these instances of *sameness in the particle*, there are some cases of *constructional ambiguity*, the noun and the verb having the same form, and the *to* not determining which is meant: as, "He was inclined *to sleep*."—"It must be a bitter experience, to be more accustomed *to hate* than *to love*." Here are *double* doubts for the discriminators of their "*sign of the infinitive*" fails, or becomes uncertain; *because they do not know it from a preposition*. Cannot my opponents see in these examples an argument against the distinction which they attempt to draw, between *to* and *to?* An other argument as good, is also afforded by the fact, that our ancestors often used the participle after *to*, in the very same texts in which we have since adopted the infinitive in its stead; as, "And if yee wolen resceyue, he is Elie that is *to comynge*."—*Matt.* xi, 14. "Ihesu that delyueride us fro wraththe *to comynge*."—1 *Thess.* i, 10. These, and seventeen other examples of the same kind, may be seen in *Tooke's Diversions of Purley*, Vol. ii, pp. 457 and 458.

OBS. 22.—Dr. James P. Wilson, speaking of the English infinitive, says: "But if the appella- tion of *mode* be denied it, it is then a *verbal noun*. This is indeed *its truest character*, because *its idea ever represents* an *object of approach*. *To* supplies the defect of a termination characteristic of the infinitive, precedes it, and marks it either as *that*,.*towards which* the preceding verb is directed; † or it signifies *act*, and shows the word to import an action. When the infinitive is the expression of an *immediate* action, which it must be, after the verbs, *bid, can, dare, do, feel, hear, let, make, may, must, need, see, shall*, and *will*, the preposition TO is omitted."—*Essay on Grammar*, p. 129. That the truest character of the infinitive is that of a verbal noun, is not to be conceded, in weak abandonment of all the reasons for a contrary opinion, until it can be shown that the action or being expressed by it, must needs assume a *substantive* character, in order to be "that *towards which* the preceding verb is directed." But this character is manifestly not supposable of any of those infinitives which, according to the foregoing quotation, must follow other verbs without the intervention of the preposition *to*: as, "Bid him *come*;"—"He can *walk*." And I see no reason to suppose it, where the relation of the infinitive to an other word *is not* "*immediate*," but marked by the preposition, as above described. For example: "And he laboured till the going-down of the sun TO *deliver* him."—*Dan.* vi, 14. Here *deliver* is governed by *to*, and connected by it to the finite verb *laboured*; but to tell us, it is to be understood *substan- tively* rather than *actively*, is an assumption as false, as it is needless.

---

* This doctrine has been lately revived in English by William B. Fowle, who quotes Dr. Rees, Beasnie, Harris, Tracy, and Crombie, as his authorities for it. He is right in supposing the English infinitive to be generally governed by the preposition *to*, but wrong in calling it a *noun*, or "the *name* of the verb," except this phrase be used in the sense in which every verb may be the name of itself. It is an error too, to suppose with Beasse, "that the infinitive never in any language *refers to a subject* or nominative;" or, as Harris has it, that infinitive "*have no reference at all to persons or substances*." See Fowle's *True English Gram* Part ii, pp. 74 and 75. For, though the infinitive verb never *agrees* with a subject or nominative, like a finite verb, it most commonly has a very obvious *reference* to something which is *the subject* of the being, action, or passion, which it expresses; and this reference is one of the chief points of difference between the infinitive and a noun. S. S. Greene, in a recent grammar, absurdly parses infinitives "*as nouns*," and by the common rules for nouns, though he begins with calling them *verbs*. Thus: "*Our honor is to be maintained*. To be maintained, is a regular passive verb, infin- itive mode, present tense, and is *used as a* NOUN *in the relation of predicate*; according to Rule II. A noun *or pronoun* used with the copula to form the *predicate*, must be in the *nominative case*."—*Greene's Gram*. 1848, p. 98. (See the Rule, ib. p. 26.) This author admits, "The '*to*' seems, like the preposition, to perform the office of a *connective*;" but then he ingeniously imagines, "The infinitive *differs from the preposition and its object*, in that the '*to*' is *the only preposition* used with the verb." And so he concludes, "The *two* [or more] *parts of the* infinitive are taken together, and, *thus* combined, may *become a* NOUN *in any relation*."—*Ib.*, 1st Edition, p. 51. S. S. Greene will also have the infinitive to make the verb before it *transitive*; for he says, "The only form [of phrase] used as the *direct object of a transitive verb* is the *infinitive*; as, 'We intend (What?) *to leave* [town] to-day;' 'They tried (What?) *to conceal* their fears.'"—*Ib.* p. 99. One might as well find transitive verbs in these equivalents: "*It is our purpose to leave* town to-day."—"They *endeavoured to conceal* their fears." Or in this "They blustered to conceal their fears."

† It is remarkable that the ingenious J. E. Worcester could discern nothing of the import of this particle before a verb. He expounds it, with very little consistency, thus: "Tō, or To, *ad*. A particle employed as the usual sign or prefix of the infinitive mood of the verb; and it might, in such use, be deemed *a syllable of the verb*. It is used *merely as a sign of the infinitive*, without having any distinct or separate meaning; as, 'He loves *to* read.'"—*Univ. and Crit. Dict.* Now is it not plain, that the action expressed by "*read*" is "that *towards* which" the affection signified by "*loves*" is directed? It is only because we can use no other word in lieu of this *to*, that its meaning is not readily seen. For calling it "a syllable of the verb," there is, I think, no reason or analogy whatever. There is absurdity in calling it even "a *part* of the verb."

OBS. 23.—To deny to the infinitive the appellation of *mood*, no more makes it a *verbal noun*, than does the Doctor's solecism about what "ITS IDEA *ever represents*." "The infinitive therefore," as Horne Tooke observes, "appears plainly to be what the Stoics called it, *the very verb itself*, pure and uncompounded."—*Diversions of Purley*, Vol. i, p. 296. Not indeed as including the particle *to*, or as it stands in the English perfect tense, but as it occurs in the *simple root*. But I cited Dr. Wilson, as above, not so much with a design of animadverting again on this point, as with reference to the *import* of the particle *to*; of which he furnishes a twofold explanation, leaving the reader to take which part he will of the contradiction. He at first conceives it to convey in general the idea of "*towards*," and to mark the infinitive as a term "*towards which*" something else "*is directed*." If this interpretation is the true one, it is plain that *to* before a verb is no other than the common preposition *to*; and this idea is confirmed by its ancient usage, and by all that is certainly known of its derivation. But if we take the second solution, and say, "it signifies *act*," we make it not a preposition, but either a noun or a verb; and then the question arises, *Which of these is it?* Besides, what sense can there be, in supposing *to go* to mean *act go*, or to be equivalent to *do go?*[*]

OBS. 24.—Though the infinitive is commonly made an adjunct to some finite verb, yet it may be connected to almost all the other parts of speech, or even to an other infinitive. The preposition *to* being its only and almost universal index, we seldom find any other preposition put before this; unless the word *about*, in such a situation, is a preposition, as I incline to think it is.[†] Anciently, the infinitive was sometimes preceded by *for* as well as *to*; as, "I went up to Jerusalem *for to* worship."—*Acts*, xxiv, 11. "What went ye out *for to* see?"—*Luke*, vii, 26. "And stood up *for to* read."—*Luke*, iv, 16. Here modern usage rejects the former preposition: the idiom is left to the uneducated. But it seems practicable to subjoin the infinitive to every one of the ten parts of speech, except the article: as,

1. To a noun; as, "If there is any *precept* to obtain felicity."—*Hawkesworth.* "It is high *time* to *awake* out of sleep."—*Rom.* xiii, 11. "To flee from the *wrath* to come."—*Matt.* iii, 7.
2. To an adjective; as, "He seemed *desirous* to speak, yet *unwilling* to offend."—*Hawkesworth.* "He who is the *slowest* to promise, is the *quickest* to perform."—*Art of Thinking*, p. 35.
3. To a pronoun; as, "I discovered *him* to be a scholar."—*W. Allen's Gram.* 166. "Is it lawful for *us* to give tribute to Cæsar?"—*Luke*, xx, 22. "Let me desire *you* to *reflect* impartially."—

---

[*] As there is no point of grammar on which our philologists are more at *variance*, so there seems to be none on which they are more at *fault*, than in their treatment of the infinitive mood, with its usual sign, or governing particle, *to*. For the information of the reader, I would gladly cite every explanation not consonant with my own, and show wherein it is objectionable; but so numerous are the forms of error under this head, that such as cannot be classed together, or are not likely to be repeated, must in general be left to run their course, exempt from any criticism of mine. Of these various forms of error, however, I may here add an example or two.

(1.) "What is the meaning of the word *to?* Ans. *To* means *act*. NOTE.—As our verbs and nouns *are spelled in the same manner*, it was formerly *thought best* to prefix the word TO, to words *when used as verbs*. For there is no difference between the NOUN, *love*; and the VERB, *to love*; but what is shown by the *prefix* TO, which *signifies act*; i. e. to act love."—*R. W. Green's Inductive Exercises in English Grammar*, N. Y. 1829, p. 52. Now all this, positive as the words are, is not only fanciful, but false, utterly false. To no more "means *act*," than *from* "means *act*." And if it did, it could not be a sign of the infinitive, or of a verb at all; for, "*act love*," is imperative, and makes the word "*love*" a *noun*; and so, "*to act love*," (where "*love*" is also a noun,) must mean "*act act love*," which is tautological nonsense. Our nouns and verbs are not, *in general*, spelled alike; nor are the latter, *in general*, preceded by *to*: nor could a particle which may govern *either*, have been *specifically intended*, at first, to mark their difference. By some, as we have seen, it is argued from this very sign, that the infinitive is always essentially a noun.

(2.) "The *infinitive mode* is the *root* or *simple form* of the verb, used to express an action or state *indefinitely*; as, *to hear, to speak*. It is generally distinguished by the sign *to*. When the particle *to* is employed in *forming* the infinitive, it is to be regarded as *a part of the verb*. In *every other case* it is a *preposition*."—*Wells's School Grammar*, 1st Ed. p. 80. "A *Preposition* is a word which is used to express the relation of a *noun* or *pronoun* depending upon it, to some other word in the sentence."—*Ib.* pp. 46 and 108. "The passive form of a verb is sometimes used in connection with a *preposition*, forming a *compound passive verb*. Examples :—' He *was listened to* without a murmur.'—A. H. EVERETT. 'Nor is this enterprise *to be scoffed at*.'—CHANNING."—*Ib.* p. 146. "A verb in the infinitive *usually relates* to some noun or pronoun. Thus, in the sentence, 'He *desires* to improve,' the verb *to improve* relates to the pronoun *he* while it is governed by *desires*."—*Ib.* p. 150. "' The *agent* to a verb in the infinitive *mode* must be in the *objective* case.'—NUTTING."—*Ib.* p. 148. These citations from Wells, the last of which he quotes approvingly, by way of authority, are in many respects self-contradictory, and in nearly all respects untrue. How can the infinitive be only "the *root* or *simple form* of the verb," and yet consist "generally" of two distinct words, and often of three, four, or five; as, "*to hear*,"—"*to have heard*,"—"*to be listened to*,"—"*to have been listened to?*" How can *to* be a "*preposition*" in the phrase, "*He was listened to*," and not so at all in "*to be listened to?*" How does the infinitive "express an action or state *indefinitely*," if it "*usually relates to some noun or pronoun?*" Why *must* its *agent* be in the *objective* case," if "*to improve* relates to the pronoun *he?*" Is *to* "in *every other case* a *preposition*," and not such before a verb or a participle? Must every preposition govern some "*noun or pronoun?*" And yet are there some prepositions which govern nothing, precede nothing?

(3.) "The *preposition* TO before a verb is the sign of the Infinitive."—*Weld's E. Gram.* 2d Ed. p. 74. "The *preposition* is *a part of speech* used to connect words, and show their relation."—*Ib.* p. 42. "The *perfect* infinitive is formed of the perfect participle and the auxiliary HAVE *preceded* by the *preposition* TO."—*Ib.* p. 96. "The infinitive mode *follows* a *verb, noun*, or *adjective*."—*Ib.* pp. 76 and 166. "A verb in the Infinitive *may follow:* 1. *Verbs* or *participles;* 2. *Nouns* or *pronouns;* 3. *Adjectives;* 4. *As* or *than;* 5. *Adverbs;* 6. *Prepositions;* 7. The *Expletive* is often used *independently;* 8. The Infinitive mode is often used in the office of a *verbal noun*, as the *nominative* case to the verb, and as the *objective* case after verbs and prepositions."—*Ib.* p. 167. These last two counts are absurdly included among what "the Infinitive *may follow;*" and is it not rather queer, that this mood should be found to "*follow*" every thing else, and *not* "the preposition TO," which comes "*before*" it, and by which it is "*preceded?*" This author adopts also the following absurd and needless rule: "The Infinitive mode has an objective case before it *when* [the word] THAT *is omitted;* as, I believe *the sun* to be the centre of the solar system; I know *him* to be a man of veracity."—*Ib.* p. 167; *Abridged Ed.* 124. (See Obs. 10th on Rule 2d, above.) "*Sun*" is here governed by "*believe;*" and "*him*," by "*know;*" and "*be*," in both instances, by "the preposition TO:" for this particle is not only "the *sign* of the Infinitive," but its *governing word*, answering well to the definition of a preposition above cited from Weld.

[†] "The infinitive is sometimes governed by a preposition; as, 'The shipmen were *about to flee*.'"—*Wells's School Gram.* 1st Ed. p. 149; 3d Ed. p. 158. Wells has altered this, and for "*preposition*" put "*adverb*."—*Ed. of 1850*, p. 163.

BLAIR: *Murray's Eng. Reader*, p. 77. "Whom hast thou then or *what I accuse?*"—*ton, P. L.* iv, 67.

4. To a finite verb; as, "Then Peter *began to rebuke* him."—*Matt.* xvi, 22. "The Son of a come *to seek and to save* that which was lost."—*Luke*, xix, 10.

5. To an other infinitive; as, "*To go to enter* into Egypt."—*Jer.* xli, 17. "We are not willing *to wait to consider.*"—*J. Abbott.* "For what had he *to do to chide* at me?"—

6. To a participle; as, "Still *threat'ning to devour* me."—*Milton.* "Or as a thief *bent to* the cash of some rich burgher."—*Id.*

7. To an adverb; as, "She is old *enough to go* to school."—"I know not *how to act.*"—*Nut Gram.* p. 106. "Tell me *when to come*, and *where to meet* you."—"He hath not *where* his head."

8. To a conjunction; as, "He knowes better *than to trust* you."—"It was so hot *as to* ornaments."—"Many who praise virtue, do no more *than praise* it."—*Dr. Johnson.*

9. To a preposition; as, "I was *about to write.*"—*Rev.* x, 4. "Not *for to hide* it in a *Burns's Poems*, p. 42. "Amatum iri, To be *about to be loved.*"—*Adam's Gram.* p. 9

10. To an interjection; as, "O *to forget* her!"—*Young's Night Thoughts.*

OBS. 25.—The infinitive is the mere verb, without affirmation, without person or number, therefore without the agreement peculiar to a finite verb. (See Obs. 8th on Rule 2d.) B most instances, it is not without *limitation* of the being, action, or passion, to some part person or persons, thing or things, that are said, supposed, or denied, to be, to act, or to be upon. Whenever it is not thus limited, it is taken *abstractly*, and has some resemblance noun; because it then suggests the being, action, or passion alone: though, even then, the infinitive may still govern the objective case; and it may also be easy to *imagine to whom* what the being, action, or passion, naturally pertains. The uses of the infinitive are so various, that it is no easy matter to classify them accurately. The following are unquestionably *the chief* of the things for which it may stand:—

1. For the *supplement* to an other verb, to complete the sense; as, "Loose him, and *let* go."—*John*, xi, 44. "They that *go to seek* mixed wine."—*Prov.* xxiii, 30. "His hands *refu labour*."—*Ib.* xxi, 25. "If you *choose to have* those terms."—*Tooke's D. P.*, ii, 374. "How old translators first *struggled to express* this."—*Ib.* ii, 456. "To any one who *will please to* our language."—*Ib.* ii, 444. "They *are forced to give up* at last."—*Ib.* ii, 375. "Which *be done*."—*Ib.* ii, 461. "Which *came to pass.*"—*Acts*, xi, 28. "I dare engage to *make* it *Swift.*

2. For the *purpose*, or end, of that to which it is added; as, "Each has employed his pains *to establish* a criterion."—*Tooke's D. P.*, ii, 374. "I shall not stop now, *to assist* elucidation."—*Ib.* ii, 75. "Our purposes are not endowed with words *to make* them kn *Ib.* ii, 74. [A] "TOOL is some instrument taken up *to work* with."—*Ib.* ii, 145. "Labo be rich."—*Prov.* xxiii, 4. "I flee unto thee *to hide* me."—*Ps.* cxliii, 9. "Evil shall *hunt* violent man *to overthrow* him."—*Ib.* cxl, 11.

3. For the *object* of an affection or passion; as, "He *loves to ride.*"—"I *desire to hear* her again."—*Shak.* "If we *wish to avoid* important error."—*Tooke's D. P.*, ii, 3. "Why do evil."—*Prov.* ii, 14. "All agreeing in earnestness *to see* him."—*Shak.* "Our *curiosity* to know what lies beyond."—*Kames, El. of Crit.* ii, 334.

4. For the *cause* of an affection or passion; as, "I rejoice *to hear* it."—"By which I have laid a foundation," &c.—*Blair's Rhet.* p. 34. "For he made me mad, *to see* him brisk, and *smell* so sweet."—*Beauties of Shak.* p. 118. "Thou didst eat strange flesh. some did die *to look* on."—*Ib.* p. 182. "They grieved *to see* their best allies at variance. *W. Allen's Gram.* p. 165.

5. For the *subject* of a proposition, or the chief term in such subject; as, "*To steal* is sinful "*To do* justice and judgement, is more acceptable to the Lord than sacrifice."—*Prov.* "*To do* RIGHT, is, to do that which is ordered to be done."—*Tooke's D. P.*, ii, 7. "*To* go to plague a neighbour, has in it more of malice, than of love to justice."—*Beattie's Mor.* N

6. For the *predicate* of a proposition, or the chief term in such predicate; as, "To *obey.*"—*Pope.* "The property of rain is *to wet*, and fire, *to burn.*"—*Beauties of Shak.* "*To die* is *to be banished* from myself."—*Ib.* p. 82. "The best way is, *to slander* Valentine p. 83. "The highway of the upright is *to depart* from evil."—*Prov.* xvi, 17.

7. For a *coming event*, or what *will* be; as, "A mutilated structure soon *to fall.*"—"He being dead, and I speedily *to follow* him."—*Tooke's D. P.*, ii, 111. "She shall re time *to come.*"—*Prov.* xxxi, 25. "Things present, or things *to come.*"—1 *Cor.* iii, 22.

8. For a *necessary event*, or what *ought* to be; as, "It is *to be remembered.*"—"It is *forgotten.*"—*Tooke's D. P.*, ii, 2. "An oversight much *to be deplored.*"—*Ib.* ii, 460. "The not *to be used* by itself, or *to stand* alone; but is *to be joined* to some other term."—*Ib.* "The Lord's name is *to be praised.*"—*Ps.* cxiii, 3.

9. For what is *previously suggested* by an other word; as, "I have *faith to believe.*"—"The sarist *did well* here not *to yield* to his inclination."—*Tooke's D. P.*, ii, 329. "*It is* a good *give* thanks unto the Lord."—*Ps.* xcii, 1. "*It is* as *sport* to a fool *to do* mischief."—*Prov.* "They have the *gift to know* it."—*Shak.* "We have no remaining *occupation* but *to take* the public."—*Art of Thinking*, p. 52.

10. For a term of *comparison* or *measure*; as, "He was so much affected as *to weep.*"— could do no less than *furnish* him."—*Tooke's D. P.*, ii, 408. "I shall venture no farther

* Some grammatists, being predetermined that no preposition shall control the infinitive, avoid the *con* by absurdly calling FOR, a *conjunction*; ABOUT, an *adverb*; and TO — no matter what — but generally Thus: "The *conjunction* FOR, is inelegantly used before verbs in the infinitive mood; as, 'He came Latin.' "—*Greenleaf's Gram.* p. 88. "The infinitive mood is sometimes *governed* by *conjunctions* or as, 'An object so high *as to be invisible*;' 'The army is *about to march.*'"—*Kirkham's Gram.* p. 188. note to that extra rule which Kirkham proposes for our use, "*if we reject the idea of government*, as app the verb in this mood!"—*Ib.*

explain the nature and convenience of these abbreviations."—*Ib.* ii, 439. "I have already said enough *to show* what sort of operation that is."—*Ib.* ii, 358.

OBS. 26.—After dismissing all the examples which may fairly be referred to one or other of the ten heads above enumerated, an observant reader may yet find *other uses* of the infinitive, and those so dissimilar that they can hardly be reduced to any one head or rule ; except that all are governed by the preposition *to,* which points *towards* or *to* the verb : as, "A great altar *to see to*."—*Joshua,* xxii, 10. "Βωμὸν μέγαν τοῦ ἰδεῖν."—*Septuagint.* That is, "An altar *great to behold*." "Altare infinitæ magnitudinis."—*Vulgate.* "Un fort grand autel."—*French Bible.* "Easy *to be entreated*." —*Jas.* iii, 17. "There was none *to help*."—*Ps.* cvii, 12. "He had rained down manna upon them *to eat*."—*Ps.* lxxviii, 24. "Remember his commandments *to do* them."—*Ps.* ciii, 18. "Preserve thou those that are appointed *to die*."—*Ps.* lxxix, 11. "As coals to burning coals, and as wood to fire ; so is a contentious man *to kindle* strife."—*Prov.* xxvi, 21. "These are far beyond the reach and power of any kings *to do* away."—*Tooke's D. P.,* ii, 126. "I know not indeed what *to do* with those words."—*Ib.* ii, 441. "They will be as little able *to justify* their innovation."—*Ib.* ii, 448. "I leave you *to compare* them."—*Ib.* ii, 458. "There is no occasion *to attribute* it."—*Ib.* ii, 376. "There is no day for me *to look* upon."—*Beauties of Shak.* p. 82. "Having no external thing *to lose*."—*Ib.* p. 100. "I'll never be a gosling *to obey* instinct."—*Ib.* p. 200. "Whereto serves mercy, but *to confront* the visage of offence ?"—*Ib.* p. 233. "If things do not go *to suit* him."— *Liberator,* ix, 182. "And, *to be* plain, I think there is not half a kiss *to choose,* who loves an other best."—*Shak.* p. 91. "But *to return* to R. Johnson's instance of *good man.*"—*Tooke's D. P.,* ii, 370. Our common Bibles have this text: and a certain woman cast a piece of a mill-stone upon Abimelech's head, and *all to break* his skull."—*Judges,* ix, 53. Perhaps the interpretation of this may be, "and *so as completely to break* his skull." The octavo edition stereotyped by "the Bible Association of Friends in America," has it, "and *all-to brake his scull*." This, most probably, was supposed by the editors to mean, "and *completely broke* his skull ;" but *all-to* is no proper compound word, and therefore the change is a perversion. The Septuagint, the Vulgate, and the common French version, all accord with the simple indicative construction, "and *broke* his skull."

OBS. 27.—According to Lindley Murray, "The infinitive mood is often *made absolute,* or used independently *on* [say *of*] the rest of the sentence, supplying the place of the conjunction *that* with the potential mood : as, '*To confess* the truth, I was in fault ;' '*To begin* with the first ;' '*To proceed ;*' '*To conclude ;*' that is, 'That I may confess,' &c."—*Murray's Gram.* 8vo, p. 184 ; *Ingersoll's Gram.* p. 244. Some other compilers have adopted the same doctrine. But on what ground the *substitution* of one mood for the other is imagined, I see not. The reader will observe that this potential mood is here just as much "*made absolute,*" as is the infinitive ; for there is nothing expressed to which the conjunction *that* connects the one phrase, or the preposition *to* the other. But possibly, in either case, there may be an ellipsis of some antecedent term ; and surely, if we imagine the construction to be complete without any such term, we make the conjunction the more anomalous word of the two. Confession of the truth, is here the aim of speaking, but not of what is spoken. The whole sentence may be, "*In order* to confess the truth, *I admit that* I was in fault." Or, "*In order* that I may confess the truth, *I admit that* I was in fault." I do not deny, that the infinitive, or a phrase of which the infinitive is a part, is sometimes put *absolute* ; for, if it is not so in any of the foregoing examples, it appears to be so in the following : "For every object has several faces, *so to speak,* by which it may be presented to us."—*Blair's Rhet.* p. 41. "*To declare* a thing shall be, long before it is in being, and then *to bring about* the accomplishment of that very thing, according to the same declaration ; this, or nothing, is the work of God."— *Justin Martyr.*

"*To be,* or *not to be ;*—that is the question."—*Shakspeare.*

"*To die ;—to sleep ;—To sleep !* perchance, *to dream !*"—*Id. Hamlet.*

OBS. 28.—The infinitive usually *follows* the word on which it depends, or to which the particle *to* connects it ; but this order is sometimes reversed : as, "*To beg* I am ashamed."—*Luke,* xvi, 3. "*To keep* them no longer in suspense, [I say plainly,] Sir Roger de Coverly is dead."—*Addison.* "*To suffer,* as to do, Our strength is equal."—*Milton.*

"*To catch* your vivid scenes, too gross her hand."—*Thomson.*

OBS. 29.—Though, in respect to its syntax, the infinitive is oftener connected with a verb, a participle, or an adjective, than with a noun or a pronoun, it should never be so placed that the reader will be liable to mistake the *person* to whom, or the *thing* to which, the being, action, or passion, pertains. Examples of error: "This system will require a long time to be executed as it should be."—*Journal of N. Y. Lit. Convention,* 1830, p. 91. It is not the *time,* that is to be executed ; therefore say, "This system, to be executed as it should be, will require a long time." "He spoke in a *manner distinct enough to be heard* by the whole assembly."—*Murray's Key,* 8vo, p. 192. This implies that the orator's *manner was heard !* But the grammarian interprets his own meaning, by the following alternative : "Or—*He spoke distinctly enough to be heard* by the whole assembly."—*Ibid.* This suggests that the man himself was heard. "When they hit upon a figure that pleases them, they are loth to part with it, and frequently continue it so long, as to become tedious and intricate."—*Murray's Gram.* p. 341. Is it the *authors,* or their *figure,* that becomes tedious and intricate ? If the latter, strike out, "*so long, as to become,*" and say, "*till it becomes.*" "Facts are always of the greatest consequence *to be remembered* during the course of the pleading."—*Blair's Rhet.* p. 272. The rhetorician here meant: "The facts stated in an argument, are always those parts of it, which it is most important that the hearers should be made to remember."

OBS. 30.—According to some grammarians, "The Infinitive of the verb *to be,* is often *understood ;* as, 'I considered it [*to be*] necessary to send the dispatches.'"—*W. Allen's Gram.* p. 166. In this example, as in thousands more, of various forms, the verb *to be* may be inserted without affecting the sense ; but I doubt the necessity of supposing an ellipsis in such sentences. The adjective or participle that follows, always relates to the preceding objective ; and if a noun is used, it is but an other objective in apposition with the former : as, "I considered *it* an *imposition.*"

This verb *to be*, with the perfect participle, forms the passive infinitive; and the supposition of such an ellipsis, extensively affects one's mode of parsing. Thus, "He considered himself insulted," "I will suppose the work *accomplished*," and many similar sentences, might be supposed to contain passive infinitives. Allen says, "In the following construction, the words in *italics* are (elliptically) passive infinitives; I saw the bird *caught*, and the hare *killed*; we heard the letters *read*."—*W. Allen's Gram.* p. 168. Dr. Priestley observes, "There is a remarkable ambiguity in the use of the participle *preterite*, as the same word may express a thing either doing, or done; as, I went to see the child *dressed*."—*Priestley's Gram.* p. 125. If the Doctor's participle is ambiguous, I imagine that Allen's infinitives are just as much so. "The *participle* which we denominate *past*, often means an action *whilst performing*: thus, I saw the *battle fought*, and the *standard lowered*."—*Wilson's Essay*, p. 158. Sometimes, especially in familiar conversation, an infinitive verb is suppressed, and the sign of it retained; as, "They might have aided us; they ought *to*" [have aided us].—*Herald of Freedom*. "We have tried to like it, but it's hard *to*."—*Lynn News*.

Obs. 31.—After the verb *make*, some writers insert the verb *be*, and suppress the preposition *to*; as, "He *must make* every syllable, and even every letter, in the word which he pronounces, *be heard* distinctly."—*Blair's Rhet.* p. 329; *Murray's E. Reader*, p. 9. "You *must make* yourself *be heard* with pleasure and attention."—*Duncan's Cicero*, p. 84. "To *make* himself *be heard* by all."—*Blair's Rhet.* p. 328. "To *make* ourselves *be heard* by one."—*Ibid.* "Clear enough to *make me be* understood."—*Locke, on Ed.* p. 198. In my opinion, it would be better, either to insert the *be*, or to use the participle only; as, "The information which he possessed, *made* his company *to be* courted."—*Dr. M'Rie.* "Which will both show the importance of this rule, and *make* the application of it *to be* understood."—*Blair's Rhet.* p. 103. Or, as in these brief forms: "To *make* himself *heard* by all."—"Clear enough to *make* me *understood*."

Obs. 32.—In those languages in which the infinitive is distinguished as such by its termination, this part of the verb may be used alone as the subject of a finite verb; but in English it is always necessary to retain the sign *to* before an abstract infinitive, because there is nothing else to distinguish the verb from a noun. Here we may see a difference between our language and the French, although it has been shown, that in their government of the infinitive they are in some degree analogous:—"HAIR est un tourment; AIMER est un besoin de l'ame."—*M. de Sigur.* "*To hate* is a torment; *to love* is a requisite of the soul." If from this any will argue that *to* is not here a preposition, the same argument will be as good, to prove that *for* is not a preposition when it governs the objective case; because that also may be used without any antecedent term of relation: as, "They are by no means points of equal importance, *for me to be deprived* of your affections, and *for him to be defeated* in his prosecution."—*Anon. in W. Allen's Gram.* p. 166. I said, the sign *to* must *always* be put before an abstract infinitive: but possibly a *repetition* of this sign may not always be necessary, when several such infinitives occur in the same construction: as, "But, *to fill* a heart with joy, *restore* content to the afflicted, or *relieve* the necessitous, these fall not within the reach of their five senses."—*Art of Thinking*, p. 66. It may be too much to affirm, that this is positively ungrammatical; yet it would be as well or better, to express it thus: "But *to relieve* the necessitous, *to restore* content to the afflicted, *and to fill* a heart with joy, these fall not within the reach of their five senses."

Obs. 33.—In the use of the English infinitive, as well as of the participle in *ing*, the distinction of *voice* is often disregarded; the active form being used in what, with respect to the noun before it, is a passive sense: as, "There's no time *to waste*."—*W. Allen's Gram.* p. 82. "You are *to blame*."—*Ib.* "The humming-bird is delightful *to look* upon."—*Ib.* "What pain it was *to drown*."—*Shak.* "The thing's *to do*."—*Id.* "When deed of danger was *to do*." —*Scott.* "The evil I bring upon myself, is the hardest *to bear*."—*Home's Art of Thinking*, p. 27. "Pride is worse *to bear* than cruelty."—*Ib.* p. 37. These are in fact active verbs, and not passive. We may suggest agents for them, if we please; as, "There is no time *for us* to waste." That the simple participle in *ing* may be used passively, has been proved elsewhere. It seems sometimes to have no distinction of voice; as, "What is worth *doing*, is worth *doing well*."—*Com. Maxim.* This is certainly much more agreeable, than to say, "What is worth *being done*, is worth *being done well*." In respect to the voice of the infinitive, and of this participle, many of our grammarians are obviously hypercritical. For example: "The active voice should not be used for the passive; as, I have work *to do*; a house *to sell, to let*, instead of *to be done, to be sold, to be let*."—*Sanborn's Gram.* p. 220. "Active verbs are often used *improperly* with a passive signification, as 'the house is *building*, lodgings *to let*, he has a house to *sell*, nothing is *wanting*;' in stead of 'the house is *being built*, lodgings *to be lett*, he has a house to *be sold*, nothing is *wanted*.'"—*Blair's Gram.* p. 64. In punctuation, orthography, and the use of capitals, here are more errors than it is worth while to particularize. With regard to such phraseology as, "The house is *being built*," see, in Part II, sundry Observations on the Compound Form of Conjugation. To say, "I have work *to do*,"—"I have a house *to sell*,"—or, "We have lodgings *to let*," is just as good English, as to say, "I have meat *to eat*."—John, iv, 32. And who, but some sciolist in grammar, would, in all such instances, prefer the passive voice?

IMPROPRIETIES FOR CORRECTION.

FALSE SYNTAX UNDER RULE XVIII.

INFINITIVES DEMANDING THE PARTICLE TO.

"William, please hand me that pencil."—*Smith's New Gram.* p. 12.

[FORMULE.—Not proper, because the infinitive verb *hand* is not preceded by the preposition *to*. But, according to Rule 18th, "The preposition *to* governs the infinitive mood, and commonly connects it to a finite verb." Therefore, *to* should be here inserted; thus, "William, please *to* hand me that pencil."]

"Please insert points so as to make sense."—*Davis's Gram.* p. 123. "I have known Lords abbreviate almost the half of their words."—*Cobbett's English Gram.* ¶ 153. "We shall find the practice perfectly accord with the theory."—*Knight, on the Greek Alphabet,* p. 23. "But it would tend to obscure, rather than elucidate the subject."—*L. Murray's Gram.* p. 95. "Please divide it for them as it should be."—*Willetts's Arith.* p. 193. "So as neither to embarrass, nor weaken the sentence."—*Blair's Rhet.* p. 116; *Murray's Gram.* 322. "Carry her to his table, to view his poor fare,* and hear his heavenly discourse."—SHERLOCK: *Blair's Rhet.* p. 157; *Murray's Gram.* 347. "That we need not be surprised to find this hold in eloquence."—*Blair's Rhet.* p. 174. "Where he has no occasion either to divide or explain."—*Ib.* p. 305. "And they will find their pupils improve by hasty and pleasant steps."—*Russell's Gram.* Pref. p. 4. "The teacher however will please observe," &c.—*Infant School Gram.* p. 8. "Please attend to a few rules in what is called syntax."—*Ib.* p. 128. "They may dispense with the laws to favor their friends, or secure their office."—*Webster's Essays,* p. 39. "To take back a gift, or break a contract, is a wanton abuse."—*Ib.* p. 41. "The legislature has nothing to do, but let it bear its own price."—*Ib.* p. 315. "He is not to form, but copy characters." —*Rambler,* No. 122. "I have known a woman make use of a shoeing-horn."—*Spect.* No. 536. "Finding this experiment answer, in every respect, their wishes."—*Sandford and Merton,* p. 51. "In fine let him cause his argument conclude in the term of the question."—*Barclay's Works,* Vol. iii, p. 443.

> "That he permitted not the winds of heaven
> Visit her face too roughly."—*Shakspeare, Hamlet.*

RULE XIX.—INFINITIVES.

The active verbs, *bid, dare, feel, hear, let, make, need, see,* and their participles, usually take the Infinitive after them without the preposition *to:* as, "If he *bade* thee *depart,* how *darest* thou *stay?*"—"I *dare* not *let* my mind *be* idle as I walk in the streets."—*Cotton Mather.*

> "Thy Hector, wrapt in everlasting sleep,
> Shall neither *hear* thee *sigh,* nor *see* thee *weep.*"—*Pope's Homer.*

OBSERVATIONS ON RULE XIX.

OBS. 1.—Respecting the syntax of the infinitive mood when the particle *to* is not expressed before it, our grammarians are almost as much at variance, as I have shown them to be, when they find the particle employed. Concerning *verbs governed by verbs,* Lindley Murray, and some others, are the most clear and positive, where their doctrine is the most obviously wrong; and, where they might have affirmed with truth, that the former verb *governs the latter,* they only tell us that "the preposition TO *is sometimes properly omitted,*"—or that such and such verbs "*have commonly other verbs following them* without the sign TO."—*Murray's Gram.* p. 183; *Alger's,* 63; *Allen's,* 167; and others. If these authors meant, that the preposition *to* is omitted *by ellipsis,* they ought to have said so. Then the many admirers and remodellers of Murray's Grammar might at least have understood him alike. Then, too, any proper definition of *ellipsis* must have proved both them and him to be clearly wrong about this construction also. If the word *to* is really "understood," whenever it is omitted after *bid, dare, feel,* &c., as some authors affirm, then is it here the governing word, if anywhere; and this nineteenth rule, however common, is useless to the parser. Then, too, does no English verb ever govern the infinitive without governing also a *preposition,* "expressed or understood." Whatever is omitted by ellipsis, and truly "*understood,*" really belongs to the grammatical construction; and therefore, if inserted, it cannot be actually *improper,* though it may be unnecessary. But all our grammarians admit, that *to* before the infinitive is sometimes "*superfluous and improper.*"—*Murray's Gram.* p. 183. I imagine, there cannot be any proper ellipsis of *to* before the infinitive, except in some forms of comparison; because, wherever else it is necessary, either to the sense or to the construction, it ought to be inserted. And wherever the *to* is rightly used, it is properly the governing word; but where it cannot be inserted without impropriety, it is absurd to say, that it is "*understood.*" The infinitive that is put after such a verb or participle as excludes the preposition *to,* is governed by this verb or participle, if it is governed by any thing: as,

> "To make them *do, undo, eat, drink, stand, move,*
> *Talk, think,* and *feel,* exactly as he chose."—*Pollok,* p. 69.

OBS. 2.—Ingersoll, who converted Murray's Grammar into "*Conversations,*" says, "I will just remark to you, that the verbs in the infinitive mood, that follow *make, need, see, bid, dare, feel, hear, let,* and their participles, are *always* GOVERNED by them."—*Conv. on Eng. Gram.* p. 120. Kirkham, who pretended to turn the same book into "*Familiar Lectures,*" says, "To, the sign of the infinitive mood, is *often understood* before the verb; as, 'Let me proceed;' that is, Let me *to* proceed."—*Gram. in Fam. Lect.* p. 137. The lecturer, however, does not suppose the infinitive to be here governed by the preposition *to,* or by the verb *let,* but rather by the pronoun *me.* For, in an other place, he avers, that the infinitive may be governed by a noun or a pronoun; as, "Let *him do* it."—*Ib.* p. 187. Now if the government of the infinitive is to be referred to the objective noun or pronoun that intervenes, none of those verbs that take the infinitive after them without the preposition, will usually be found to govern it, except *dare* and *need;* and if *need,* in such a

---

* After the word "*fare,*" Murray put a semicolon, which shows that he misunderstood the mood of the verb "*hear.*" It is not always necessary to repeat the particle *to,* when two or more infinitives are connected; and this fact is an other good argument against calling the preposition *to* "a part of the verb." But in this example, and some others here exhibited, the repetition is requisite.—G. B.

case, is an *auxiliary*, no government pertains to that. R. C. Smith, an other modifier of Mu having the same false notion of ellipsis, says, "*To*, the usual sign of this mood, is *sometime derstood* ; as, 'Let me go,' instead of, 'Let me to go.'"—*Smith's New Gram.* p. 85. Accord? Murray, whom these men profess to follow, *let*, in all these examples, is an *auxiliary*, and verb that follows it, is not in the *infinitive* mood, but in the *imperative*. So they severally co dict their oracle, and all are wrong, both he and they! The disciples pretend to correct master, by supposing "*Let me to go*," and "*Let me to proceed*," good English!

OBS. 3.—It is often impossible to say *by what* the infinitive is governed, according to the las tions of Murray, or according to any author who does not parse it as I do. Nutting says, " infinitive *mode* sometimes follows the comparative conjunctions, *as*, *than*, and *how*, wit GOVERNMENT."—*Practical Gram.* p. 106. Murray's uncertainty* may have led to some pa this notion, but the idea that *how* is a "comparative conjunction," is a blunder entire? Kirkham is so puzzled by "the language of that eminent philologist," that he bolts can from the course of his guide, and runs he knows not whither ; feigning that other able wr have well contended, "that this mood IS NOT GOVERNED by any particular word." Accord: he leaves his pupils at liberty to "*reject the idea of government*, as applied to the verb in mood ;" and even frames a rule which refers it always "to some noun or pronoun, as its sal or actor."—*Kirkham's Gram.* p. 188. Murray teaches, that the object of the active verb w times governs the infinitive that follows it ; as, "They have a *desire* to improve."—*Octavo G* p. 184. To what extent, in practice, he would carry this doctrine, nobody can tell ; proba? every sentence in which this object is the antecedent term to the preposition *to*, and pr further : as, "I *have a house to sell*."—*Nutting's Gram.* p. 106. "I *feel a desire* to exal? *felt my heart* within me *die*."—*Merrick*.

OBS. 4.—Nutting supposes, that the objective case before the infinitive always governs it w ever it denotes the agent of the infinitive action; as, "He commands *me* to *write* a lette *Practical Gram.* p. 96. Nixon, on the contrary, contends, that the finite verb, in such a sent can govern only one object, and that this object is the infinitive. "The objective case go ing it," he says, "is the subject or agent of that infinitive, and not governed by the prece verb." His example is, "Let *them* go."—*English Parser*, p. 97. "In the examples, 'H endeavouring *to persuade* them *to learn*,'—'It is pleasant *to see* the sun,'—the pronoun *the* adjective *pleasant*, and the participle *endeavouring*, I consider as *governing* the following ve the infinitive mode."—*Cooper's Plain and Pract. Gram.* p. 144. "Some erroneously say pronouns govern the infinitive mode in such examples as this : 'I expected *him* to be prese We will change the expression : 'He was expected to be present.' *All will admit* that a ? governed by *was expected*. The same verb that governs it in the passive voice, governs it in the tive."—*Sanborn's Gram.* p. 144. So do our *professed grammarians* differ about the government the infinitive, even in the *most common* constructions of it ! Often, however, it makes but ? difference in regard to the sense, which of the two words is considered the governing or cedent term ; but where the preposition is excluded, the construction seems to imply some mediate influence of the finite verb upon the infinitive.

OBS. 5.—The *extent* of this influence, or of such government, has never yet been clearly de mined. "This *irregularity*," says *Murray*, "extends only to *active or neuter* verbs : ['active neuter verbs,' says *Fisk* :] for all the verbs above mentioned, when made *passive*, require the pre tion *to* before the following verb : as, 'He was seen to go ;' 'He was heard to speak ;' 'The bidden *to* be upon their guard.'"—*Murray's Gram.* p. 183. Fisk adds, with no great accu "In the *past* and *future* tenses of the active voice also, these verbs generally require the *to* to be prefixed to the following verbs ; as, 'You *have dared to proceed* without authority ; '? *will* not *dare to attack* you.'"—*Gram. Simplified*, p. 125. What these gentlemen here call "*ne verbs*," are only the two words *dare* and *need*, which are, in most cases, active, though not al transitive; unless the infinitive itself can make them so—an inconsistent doctrine of th which I have elsewhere refuted. (See Obs. 3rd on Rule 5th.) These two verbs take the infin after them without the preposition, only when they are intransitive ; while all the rest we have this power, only when they are transitive. If there are any exceptions, they shall prec

---

* Lindley Murray, and several of his pretended improvers, say, "The infinitive sometimes *follows* the AS ; thus, 'An object so high *as to be* invisible.' The infinitive occasionally *follows* THAN *after* a comparis 'He desired *nothing more than to know* his own imperfections.'"—*Murray's Gram.* 8vo, p. 184 ; *Fisk* Alger's, 68 ; *Merchant's*, 92. See this second example in *Weld's Gram.* p. 167 ; *Abridg. 124. Mercha reliting the latter example, changes it thus : "I wish *nothing more, than to know* his fate." He puts a after *more*, and probably means, "I wish nothing *else* than to know his fate." So does Fisk, in the other wa and probably means, "He desired *nothing else* than to know his own imperfections." But Murray, A er? Weld, accord in punctuation, and their meaning seems rather to be, "He desired nothing *more hearts* [*he desired*] to know his own imperfections." And so is this or a similar text interpreted by both *Ingers* Weld, who suppose this infinitive to be "*governed by another verb, understood*: as, 'He *desired* nothing *than to see* his friends ;' 'than he *desired to see*,' &c."—*Ingersoll's Gram.* p. 244 ; *Weld's, Abridg* But, obvious as is the *ambiguity* of this fictitious example, in all its forms, not one of these five critics per the fault at all. Again, in their remark above cited, Ingersoll, Fisk, and Merchant, put a comma befo preposition "*after*," and thus make the phrase, "*after a comparison*," describe the place of the infinit. Murray and Alger probably meant that this phrase should denote the place of the conjunction "*than*" great "Compiler" seems to me to have misused the phrase "*a comparison*," for, "*an adjective or adverb comparative degree* ;" and the rest, I suppose, have blindly copied him, without thinking or knowing w ought to have said, or meant to say. Either this, or a worse error, is here apparent. Five learned gram severally represent either "*than*" or "*the infinitive*," as being "AFTER *a comparison*;" of which one copula, and the other but the beginning of the latter term! Palpable as is the *absurdity*, no one of perceives it! And, besides, no one of them says any thing about the *government of this infinitive* Ingersoll, and he supplies a verb. "*Than* and *as*," says Greenleaf, "sometimes *appear to govern* the in mood ; as, 'Nothing makes a man suspect *much more, than* to know little ;' 'An object so high *as* to ? ible.'"—*Gram. Simp.* p. 88. Here is an other fictitious and ambiguous example, in which the phrase." *little*," is the subject of *makes* understood. Nixon supposes the infinitive phrase after *as* to be always the of a finite verb *understood* after it ; as, "An object so high as to be *invisible is, or implies*." See *Parser*, p. 100.

be considered. A more particular examination of the construction proper for the infinitive after each of these eight verbs, seems necessary for a right understanding of the rule.

OBS. 6.—Of the verb BID. This verb, in any of its tenses, when it commands an action, usually governs an object and also an infinitive, which come together; as, "Thou *bidst* the *world adore.*"—Thomson. "If the prophet *had bid thee do* some great thing."—*2 Kings*, v, 13. But when it means, *to promise* or *offer*, the infinitive that follows, must be introduced by the preposition *to ;* as, "He *bids* fair *to* excel them all."—"Perhaps no person under heaven *bids* more unlikely *to* be saved."—*Brown's Divinity*, p. vii. "And each *bade* high *to* win him."—GRANVILLE: *Joh. Dict.* After the compound *forbid*, the preposition is also necessary; as, "Where honeysuckles *forbid* the sun *to* enter."—*Beauties of Shak.* p. 57. In poetry, if the measure happens to require it, the word *to* is sometimes allowed after the simple verb *bid*, denoting a command; as,

"*Bid* me *to* strike my dearest brother dead,
 To bring my aged father's hoary head."—*Rowe's Lucan*, B. i, l. 677.

OBS. 7.—Of the verb DARE. This verb, when used intransitively, and its irregular preterit *durst*, which is never transitive, usually take the infinitive after them without *to ;* as, "I *dare do* all that may become a man: Who *dares do* more, is none."—*Shakspeare.* "If he *durst steal* any thing adventurously."—*Id.* "Who *durst defy* th' Omnipotent to arms."—*Milton.* "Like one who *durst* his destiny *control.*"—*Dryden.* In these examples, the former verbs have some resemblance to auxiliaries, and the insertion of the preposition *to* would be improper. But when we take away this resemblance, by giving *dare* or *dared* an objective case, the preposition is requisite before the infinitive; as, "Time! I *dare thee to* discover Such a youth or such a lover."—*Dryden.* "He *dares me to* enter the lists."—*Fisk's Gram.* p. 125. So when *dare* itself is in the infinitive mood, or is put after an auxiliary, the preposition is not improper; as, "And *let* a private man *dare to say* that it will."—*Brown's Estimate*, ii, 147. "*Would* its compiler *dare to affront* the Deity ?"—*West's Letters*, p. 151. "What pow'r so great, *to dare to disobey* ?"—*Pope's Homer.* "Some *would* even *dare to* die."—*Bible.* "What *would* dare *to molest* him ?"—*Dr. Johnson.* "Do you *dare to prosecute* such a creature as Vaughan ?"—*Junius*, Let. xxxiii. Perhaps these examples might be considered good English, either with or without the *to ;* but the last one would be still better thus: "*Dare you prosecute* such a creature as Vaughan?" Dr. Priestley thinks the following sentence would have been better with the preposition inserted: "Who *have dared defy* the worst."—HARRIS: *Priestley's Gram.* p. 132. *To* is sometimes used after the simple verb, in the present tense; as, "Those whose words no one *dares to* repeat."—*Opie, on Lying*, p. 147.

"*Dare* I *to* leave of humble prose the shore ?"—*Young*, p. 377.
"Against heaven's endless mercies pour'd, how *dar'st* thou *to* rebel ?"—*Id.* p. 380.
"The man who *dares to* be a wretch, deserves still greater pain."—*Id.* p. 381.

OBS. 8.—Of the verb FEEL. This verb, in any of its tenses, may govern the infinitive without the sign *to ;* but it does this, only when it is used transitively, and that in regard to a bodily perception: as, "I *feel* it *move.*"—"I *felt* something *sting* me." If we speak of feeling any mental affection, or if we use the verb intransitively, the infinitive that follows, requires the preposition ; as, "I *feel* it *to* be my duty."—"I *felt* ashamed *to* ask."—"I *feel* afraid *to* go alone."—"I *felt* about, *to* find the door." One may say of what is painful to the body, "I *feel* it *to* be severe."

OBS. 9.—Of the verb HEAR. This verb is often intransitive, but it is usually followed by an objective case when it governs the infinitive; as, "To *hear* a bird *sing.*"—*Webster.* "You have never *heard me say* so." For this reason, I am inclined to think that those sentences in which it appears to govern the infinitive alone, are elliptical; as, "I *have heard tell* of such things."—"And I *have heard say* of thee, that thou canst understand a dream to interpret it."—*Gen.* xli, 15. Such examples may be the same as, "I have heard *people* tell,"—"I have heard *men* say," &c.

OBS. 10.—Of the verb LET. By many grammarians, this verb has been erroneously called an *auxiliary* of the *imperative* mood; or, as Dr. Johnson terms it, "a *sign* of the *optative* mood ;" though none deny, that it is sometimes also a principal verb. It is, in fact, always a principal verb; because, as we now apply it, it is always transitive. It commonly governs an objective noun or pronoun, and also an infinitive without the sign *to ;* as, "Rise up, *let us go.*"—*Mark.* "Thou *shalt let it rest.*"—*Exodus.* But sometimes the infinitive coalesces with it more nearly than the objective, so that the latter is placed after both verbs; as, "The solution *lets go* the mercury."—*Newton.* "One *lets slip* out of his account a good *part* of that duration."—*Locke.* "Back ! on your lives; *let be*, said he, my *prey.*"—*Dryden.* The phrase, *let go*, is sometimes spoken for, *let go your hold ;* and *let be*, for *let him be*, *let it be*, &c. In such instances, therefore, the verb *let* is not really intransitive. This verb, even in the passive form, may have the infinitive after it without the preposition *to ;* as, "Nothing *is let slip.*"—*Walker's English Particles*, p. 165. "They *were let go* in peace."—*Acts*, xv, 33. "The stage was never empty, nor the curtain *let fall.*"—*Blair's Rhet.* p. 469. "The pye's question was wisely *let fall* without a reply."—*L'Estrange.* With respect to other passives, Murray and Fisk appear to be right; and sometimes the preposition is used after this one: as, "There's a letter for you, sir, if your name be Horatio, as I *am let to know* it is."—*Shakspeare.* *Let*, when used intransitively, required the preposition *to* before the following infinitive; as, "He would not *let* [i. e. *forbear*] *to counsel* the king."—*Bacon.* But this use of *let* is now obsolete.

OBS. 11.—Of the verb MAKE. This verb, like most of the others, never immediately governs an infinitive, unless it also governs a noun or a pronoun which is the immediate *subject* of such infinitive; as, "You *make me blush.*"—"This only *made* the *youngster laugh.*"—*Webster's Spelling-Book.* "Which soon *made* the young *chap hasten* down."—*Ib.* But in very many instances it is quite proper to insert the preposition where this verb is transitive; as, "He *maketh* both the deaf *to* hear, and the dumb *to* speak."—*Mark*, vii, 37. "He *makes* the excellency of a sentence *to* consist in four things."—*Blair's Rhet.* p. 122; *Jamieson's*, 124. It is this that *makes* the observance of the dramatic unities *to* be of consequence."—*Blair's Rhet.* p. 464. "In *making* some tenses of the English verb *to* consist of principal and auxiliary."—*Murray's Gram.* p. 76. When *make* is intransitive, it has some qualifying word after it, besides the sign of the infinitive; as, "I think he *will make out to* pay his debts." Formerly, the preposition *to* was almost always in-

serted to govern the infinitive after *make* or *made*; as, " Let I *make* my brother *to* offend."—'
viii, 13. " He *made* many *to* fall."—*Jer.* xlvi, 16. Yet, in the following text, it is omitted.
where the verb is meant to be *passive*: "And it was lifted up from the earth, and *made stand*
the feet as a man."—*Dan.* vii, 4. This construction is improper, and not free from ambigu-
because *stand* may be a noun, and *made*, an active verb governing it. There may also be un-
tainty in the meaning, where the insertion of the preposition leaves none in the construct;
for *made* may signify either *created* or *compelled*, and the infinitive after it, may denote either
purpose of creation, or the *effect* of any temporary compulsion: as, " We *are made to be serv-
ble* to others."—*Murray's Key*, 8vo, p. 167. " Man *was made to mourn*."—*Burns*. " Taste
never *made to cater* for vanity."—*Blair.* The primitive word *make* seldom, if ever, produces a
struction that is thus equivocal. The infinitive following it without *to*, always denotes the ef-
of the making, and not the purpose of the maker. But the same meaning may be conv-
when the *to* is used; as,

			" The fear of God is freedom, joy, and peace;
			And *makes* all ills that vex us here *to* cease."—*Waller*, p. 56.

Obs. 12.—Of the verb NEED. I incline to think, that the word *need*, whenever it is rightly
lowed by the infinitive without *to*, is, in reality, an *auxiliary* of the potential mood; and th
like *may*, *can*, and *must*, it may properly be used, in both the present and the perfect tense, w
out personal inflection: as, " He *need* not *go*, He *need* not *have gone*;" where, if *need* is a prin-
pal verb, and governs the infinitive without *to*, the expressions must be, " He *needs* not *go*,
needed not *go*, or, He *has* not *needed go*." But none of these three forms is agreeable; and
last two are never used. Wherefore, in stead of placing in my code of false syntax the num-
ous examples of the former kind, with which the style of our grammarians and critics has f-
nished me, I have exhibited many of them, in contrast with others, in the eighth and ninth
servations on the Conjugation of Verbs; in which observations, the reader may see what reas
there are for supposing the word *need* to be sometimes an auxiliary and sometimes a prin-
verb. Because no other author has yet intentionally recognised the propriety of this distinct-
I have gone no farther than to show on what grounds, and with what authority from usage
might be acknowledged. If we adopt this distinction, perhaps it will be found that the reg-
or principal verb *need* always requires, or, at least, always admits, the preposition *to* before the
lowing infinitive; as, " They *need* not *to* be specially indicated."—*Adams's Rhet.* i, 302. "I
need only *to* remark."—*Ib.* ii, 224. " A young man *needed* only *to* ask himself," &c.—*Ib.* i, 1
" Nor is it conceivable to me, that the lightning of a Demosthenes *could need to* be sped upon
wings of a semiquaver."—*Ib.* ii, 226. " But these people *need to* be informed."—*Campbell's* Rh
p. 220. " No man *needed* less *to* be informed."—*Ib.* p. 175. " We *need* only *to* mention the d-
culty that arises."—*Kames, El. of Crit.* ii, 362. " *Can* there *need to* be argument to prove so p-
a point?"—*Graham's Lect.* " Moral instruction *needs to* have a more prominent place."—
Weeks. " Pride, ambition, and selfishness, *need to* be restrained."—*Id.* " Articles are somet-
omitted, where they *need to* be used."—*Sanborn's Gram.* p. 197. " Whose power *needs* not
dreaded."—*Wilson's Hebrew Gram.* p. 93. " A workman that *needeth* not *to* be ashamed."—2 T
ii, 15. " The small boys *may have needed to* be managed according to the school system."—
Woolsey. " The difficulty of making variety consistent, *needs* not *to* disturb him."—*Ram*
No. 122. " A more cogent proof *needs* not *to* be introduced."—*Wright's Gram.* p. 66. " No p-
son *needs to* be informed, that *you* is used in addressing a single person."—*Wilcox's Gram.* |
" I hope I *need* not *to* advise you further."—*Shak., All's Well*.

			" Nor me, nor other god, thou *needest to* fear,
			For thou to all the heavenly host art dear."—*Congreve*.

Obs. 13.—If *need* is ever an auxiliary, the essential difference between an auxiliary and a principal verb, will very well account for the otherwise puzzling facts, that good writers sometim-
inflect this verb, and sometimes do not; and that they sometimes use *to*, after it, and sometim-
do not. Nor do I see in what other way a grammarian can treat it, without condemning as g-
English a great number of very common phrases which he cannot change for the better. On th-
principle, such examples as, " He *need* not *proceed*," and " He *needs* not *to* proceed," may
perfectly right in either form; though Murray, Crombie,* Fisk, Ingersoll, Smith, C. Adams, a-
many others, pronounce both these forms to be wrong; and unanimously, (though contrary
what is perhaps the best usage,) prefer, " He *needs* not *proceed*."—*Murray's Key*, 8vo, p. 191

Obs. 14.—On questions of grammar, the *practice of authors* ought to be of more weight, th-
the *dogmatism of grammarians*; but it is often difficult to decide well by either; because err-
and contradictions abound in both. For example: Dr. Blair says, (in speaking of the pers-
represented by *I* and *thou*,) " Their sex *needs* not *be* marked."—*Rhet.* p. 79. Jamieson abridg-
the work, and says, " *needs* not *to* be marked."—*Gram. of Rhet.* p. 28. Dr. Lowth also say-
" *needs* not *be* marked."—*Gram.* p 21. Churchill enlarges the work, and says, " *needs* not *to*
marked."—*New Gram.* p. 72. Lindley Murray copies Lowth, and says, " *needs* not *be* marked

---

* Dr. Crombie, after copying the substance of Campbell's second Canon, that, " In doubtful cases such
should be regarded," remarks: " For the same reason, '*it needs*' and '*he dares*,' are better than '*he need* or
'*he dare*.'"—*On Etym. and Synt.* p. 326. Dr. Campbell's language is somewhat stronger: " In the verbs
dare and *to need*, many say, in the third person present singular, *dare* and *need*, as, '*he need* not *go*; he dar-
not do it.' Others say, *dares* and *needs*. As the first usage is *exceedingly irregular*, hardly any thing less th-
uniform practice could authorise it."—*Philosophy of Rhet.* p. 175. *Dare* for *dares* I suppose to be wrong; bu-
need is an auxiliary of the potential mood, to use it without inflection, is neither " irregular," nor at all inco-
sistent with the foregoing canon. But the former critic notices these verbs a second time, thus: " He d-
not,' '*he need* not,' may be justly pronounced *solecisms*, for '*he dares*,' '*he needs*.'"—*Crombie, on Etym. a-
Synt.* p. 273. He also says, " The verbs *bid*, *dare*, *need*, *make*, *see*, *hear*, *feel*, *let*, are not followed by the sign
the infinitive."—*Ib.* p. 277. And yet he writes thus: " These are truths, of which, I am persuaded, the auth-
to whom I allude, *needs* not *to* be reminded."—*Ib.* p. 123. So Dr. Bullions declares against *need* in the singul-
by putting down the following example as bad English: " He *need* not be in so much haste."—*Bullions' E.-
Gram.* p. 194. Yet he himself writes thus: " A name more appropriate than the term *neuter*, *need* not
desired."—*Ib.* p. 196. A school-boy may see the inconsistency of this.

m. 12mo, 2d Ed., p. 39; 23d Ed., p. 51; and perhaps all other editions. He afterwards goes his own work, and says, " *needs* not *to* be marked."—*Octavo Gram.* p. 51. But, according to Greenleaf they all express the idea ungrammatically; the only true form being, " Their need not be marked." See *Gram. Simplified*, p. 48. In the two places in which the etymology he syntax of this verb are examined, I have cited from proper sources more than twenty ples in which *to* is used after it, and more than twenty others in which the verb is not ted in the third person singular. In the latter, *need* is treated as an auxiliary; in the former, principal verb, of the regular construction. If the principal verb *need* can also govern the five without *to*, as all our grammarians have supposed, then there is a third form which is jectionable, and my pupils may take their choice of the three. But still there is a fourth which nobody approves, though the hands of some great men have furnished us with exam of it: as, "A figure of thought *need* not *to* detort the words from their literal sense."—*J. Q.* u's *Lectures*, Vol. ii, p. 254. " Which a man *need* only *to* appeal to his own feelings imme ly to evince."—*Clarkson's Prize-Essay on Slavery*, p. 106.

s. 15.—Webster and Greenleaf seem inclined to justify the use of *dare*, as well as of *need*, a third person singular. Their doctrine is this: " In *popular practice* it is used in the third n, without the personal termination. Thus, instead of saying, 'He *dares* not do it;' we why say, 'He *dare* not do it.' In like manner, *need*, when an active verb, is regular in its tions; as, 'A man *needs* more prudence.' But *when intransitive*, it drops the personal termi as in the present tense, and is followed by a verb without the prefix *to*; as, 'A man *need* not weary.'"—*Greenleaf's Grammar Simplified*, p. 38; *Webster's Philosophical Gram.* 178; *veed Gram.* 127. Each part of this explanation appears to me erroneous. In *popular prac se shall oftener hear, " He *dares* n't do it," or even, " You *dares* n't do it," than, "He *dare not* ." But it is only in the trained practice of the schools, that he shall ever hear, " He n't do it," or, " He *needs* not do it." If *need* is sometimes used without inflection, this larity, or the disuse of *to* before the subsequent infinitive, is not a necessary result of its renutive" character. And as to their latent *nominative*, "whereof there is no *account*," or, ereof there *needs* no *account*;" their *fact*, of which "there is no *evidence*," or of which re *needs* no *evidence* ;" I judge it a remarkable phenomenon, that authors of so high preten , could find, in these *transpositions*, a nominative to "*is*," but none to "*needs!*" See a final note under Rule 14th, at p. 546.

s. 16.—Of the verb SEE. This verb, whenever it governs the infinitive without *to*, governs an objective noun or pronoun; as, "*See* me do it."—"I saw *him* do it."—*Murray.* When it is intransitive, the following infinitive must be governed by *to*; as, "I will *see to have* it ."—*Comly's Gram.* p. 96; *Greenleaf's*, 38. "How could he *see to* do them?"—*Beauties of k* p. 43. In the following text, *see* is transitive, and governs the infinitive; but the two verbs at so far apart, that it requires some skill in the reader to make their relation apparent: hen ye therefore *shall see* the abomination of desolation, spoken of by Daniel the prophet, (in the holy place," &c.—*Matt.* xxiv, 15. An other scripturist uses the *participle*, and says— nding where it ought not," &c.—*Mark*, xiii, 14. The Greek word is the same in both; it is rticiple, agreeing with the noun for *abomination*. Sometimes the preposition *to* seems to be itted on purpose to protract the expression: as,

"Tranio, I *saw* her coral lips *to move*,
And with her breath she did perfume the air."—*Shak.*

s. 17.—A few other verbs, besides the eight which are mentioned in the foregoing rule and rks, sometimes have the infinitive after them without *to*. W. Allen teaches, that, "The sign generally omitted," not only after these eight, but also after eight others; namely, "*find, have, mark, observe, perceive, watch*, and the old preterit *gan*, for *began; and sometimes after behold know.*"—*Elements of Gram.* p. 167. Perhaps he may have found *some instances* of the omis of the preposition after all these, but in my opinion his rule gives a very unwarrantable nsion to this "irregularity," as Murray calls it. The usage belongs only to particular verbs, to them not in all their applications. Other verbs of the same import do not in general it the same idiom. But, by a license for the most part peculiar to the poets, the preposition occasionally omitted, especially after verbs equivalent to those which exclude it; as, "And them *sit*."—*Cowper's Task*, p. 46. That is, "And *make* them *sit*." According to Churchill, I use *ought* or *cause* in this manner, is a Scotticism: [as,] 'Won't you *cause* them *remove* the s?'—'You *ought* not *walk.*' SHAK.—*New Gram.* p. 317. The verbs, *behold, view, observe, watch*, and *spy*, are only other words for *see*; as, "There might you *behold* one joy *crown* her."—*Shak.* "There I sat, *viewing* the silver stream *glide* silently towards the tempestuous "—*Walton.* "I *beheld* Satan as lightning *fall* from heaven."—*Luke*, x, 18.

"Thy drowsy nurse hath sworn she did them *spy*
Come tripping to the room where thou didst lie,"—*Milton.*
————————"Nor with less dread the loud
Ethereal trumpet from on high 'gan *blow.*"—*Id. P. L.*, vi, 60.

s. 18.—After *have, help*, and *find*, the infinitive sometimes occurs without the preposition at much oftener with it; as, "When enumerating objects which we wish to *have appear* inct."—*Kirkham's Gram.* p. 222. " Certainly, it is heaven upon earth, to *have* a man's mind e in charity, *rest* in Providence, and *turn* upon the poles of truth."—*Ld. Bacon.* "What thou *have* me to do ?"—*Acts*, ix, 6. "He will *have* us *to* acknowledge him."—*Scougal*, p. "I *had to walk* all the way."—*Lennie's Gram.* p 85. "Would you *have* them *let go* then ? "—*Walker's Particles*, p. 248. According to Allen's rule, this question is ambiguous; but learned author explains it in Latin thus: "Placet igitur eos *dimitti?* Minime." That is, ould you have them *dismissed* then ? No." Had he meant, "Would you have them *to* let go n?'" he would doubtless have said so. Kirkham, by adding *help* to Murray's list, enumerates e verbs which he will have to exclude the sign of the infinitive; as, "*Help* me do it."—*Gram.* 186. But good writers sometimes use the particle *to* after this verb; as, "And Danby's match i impudence *helped to* support the knave."—DRYDEN : *Joh. Dict. w. Help.* Dr. Priestley says,

"It must, I suppose, be according to the *Scotch* idiom that Mrs. Macaulay omits it after the ve help : 'To *help carry* on the new measures of the court.' *History*, Vol. iv. p. 150."—*Priestley's Gram*. p. 133. "You will *find* the difficulty *disappear* in a short time."—*Cobbett's English Gram.* ¶ 16. "We shall always *find* this distinction *obtain*."—*Blair's Rhet*. p. 245. Here the pre osition *to* might have been inserted with propriety. Without it, a plural noun will render th construction equivocal. The sentence, "You will find the *difficulties disappear* in a short time, will probably be understood to mean, "You will find *that* the difficulties disappear in a sho time." "I do not *find* him *reject* his authority."—*Johnson's Gram. Com.* p. 167. Here too th preposition might as well have been inserted. But, as this use of the infinitive is a sort of Lati ism, some critics would choose to say, "I do not find *that he rejects* his authority." "Cyrus w extremely glad to find *them have* such sentiments of religion."—*Rollin*, ii, 117. Here th infinitive may be varied either by the participle or by the indicative ; as, "to find *them having,* or, "to find *they had.*" Of the three expressions, the last, I think, is rather the best.

OBS. 19.—When two or more infinitives are connected in the same construction, one preposition sometimes governs them both or all ; a repetition of the particle not being always necessary, unless we mean to make the terms severally emphatical. This fact is one evidence that *to* is not a necessary part of each infinitive verb, as some will have it to be. Examples: "Lord, suffer me first TO *go* and *bury* my father."—*Matt*. viii, 21. "To *shut* the door, means, TO *throw* or *cast* the door to."—*Tooke's D. P.*, ii, 105. "Most authors expect the printer TO *spell, point,* and *diges* their copy, that it may be intelligible to the reader."—*Printer's Grammar*.

"I'll not be made a soft and dull-eyed fool,
To *shake* the head, *relent,* and *sigh,* and *yield.*"—*Shak.*

OBS. 20.—An infinitive that explains an other, may sometimes be introduced without the prep osition *to* ; because, the former having it, the construction of the latter is made the same by this kind of apposition : as, "The most accomplished way of using books at present is, TO *serve* them as some do lords ; *learn* their *titles,* and then *brag* of their acquaintance."—SWIFT: *Kames, El. of Crit.* ii, 166.

OBS. 21.—After *than* or *as,* the sign of the infinitive is sometimes required, and sometimes excluded ; and in some instances we can either insert it or not, as we please. The latter term of a comparison is almost always more or less elliptical ; and as the nature of its ellipsis depends on the structure of the former term, so does the necessity of inserting or of omitting the sign of the infinitive. Examples: "No desire is more universal than [*is the desire*] to be exalted and honoured."—*Kames, El. of Crit.* i, 197. "The difficulty is not so great to die for a friend, as [*is the difficulty*] to find a friend worth dying for."—*Id. Art of Thinking*, p. 42. "It is no more in one's power to love or not to love, than [*it is in one's power*] to be in health or out of order."— *Ib.* p. 45. "Men are more likely to be praised into virtue, than [*they are likely*] to be railed out of vice."—*Ib.* p. 48. "It is more tolerable to be always alone, than [*it is tolerable*] never to be so."—*Ib.* p. 26. "Nothing [*is*] more easy than to do mischief [*is easy*]: nothing [*is*] more diffi cult than to suffer without complaining" [*is difficult*].—*Ib.* p. 46. Or: "than [*it is easy*] to do mischief :" &c., "than [*it is difficult*] to suffer" &c. "It is more agreeable to the nature of most men to follow than [*it is agreeable to their nature*] to lead."—*Ib.* p. 55. In all these examples, the preposition *to* is very properly inserted ; but what excludes it from the former term of a com parison, will exclude it from the latter, if such governing verb be understood there: as, "You so more heard me *say* those words, than [*you heard me*] *talk* Greek." It may be equally proper to say, "We choose rather to lead than *follow*," or, "We choose rather to lead than *to* follow."— *Art of Thinking*, p. 37. The meaning in either case is, "We choose to lead rather than *we choose to* follow." In the following example, there is perhaps an ellipsis of *to* before *cite*: "I need do nothing more than *simply* cite the explicit declarations," &c.—*Gurney's Peculiarities*, p. 4. So in these: "Nature did no more than *furnish* the power and means."—*Sheridan's Elocution*, p. 147.

"To beg, than *work,* he better understands ;
Or we perhaps might take him off thy hands."—*Pope's Odyssey*, xvii, 260.

OBS. 22.—It has been stated, in Obs. 16th on Rule 17th, that good writers are apt to shun a repetition of any part common to two or more verbs in the same sentence ; and among the examples there cited is this : "They mean *to,* and will, hear patiently."—*Salem Register*. So one might say, "Can a man arrive at excellence, who has no desire *to ?*"—"I do not wish to go, nor expect *to*."—"Open the door, if you are going *to.*" Answer : "We want *to,* and try *to,* but can't." Such ellipses of the infinitive after *to,* are by no means uncommon, especially in conversation ; nor do they appear to me to be always reprehensible, since they prevent repetition, and may con tribute to brevity without obscurity. But Dr. Bullions has lately thought proper to *condemn* them ; for such is presumed to have been the design of the following note : "*To,* the sign of the infinitive, should never be used for the infinitive itself. Thus, 'I have not written, and I do not intend *to,*' is a colloquial vulgarism for, 'I have not written, and I do not intend *to write.*'"— *Bullions's Analyt. and Pract. Gram*. p. 179. His "Exercises to be corrected," here, are these: "Be sure to write yourself and tell him to. And live as God designed me to."—*Ib.* 1st Ed. P. 180. It being manifest, that *to* cannot "be used *for*"—(that is, *in place of*—) what is implied *after* it, this is certainly a very awkward way of hinting "there should never be an ellipsis of the infini tive after *to.*" But, from the false syntax furnished, this appears to have been the meaning intended. The examples are severally faulty, but not for the reason suggested—not because "*to* " is used for "*write* " or "*live*"—not, indeed, for any one reason common to the three—but because, in the first, "*to write*" and "*have not written,*" have nothing in common which we can omit ; in the second, the mood of "*tell*" is doubtful, and, without a comma after "*yourself,*" we cannot precisely know the meaning ; in the third, the mood, the person, and the number of "*live,*" are all unknown. See Note 9th to Rule 17th, above ; and Note 2d to the General Rule, below.

OBS. 23.—Of some infinitives, it is hard to say whether they are transitive or intransitive ; as, "Well, then, let us proceed ; we have other forced marches to *make* ; other enemies to *subdue* ; more laurels to *acquire* ; and more injuries to *avenge.*"—BONAPARTE: *Columbian Orator*, p. 136. These, without ellipsis, are intransitive ; but relatives may be inserted.

IMPROPRIETIES FOR CORRECTION.

FALSE SYNTAX UNDER RULE XIX.

INFINITIVES AFTER BID, DARE, FEEL, HEAR, LET, &c.

"I dare not to proceed so hastily, lest I should give offence."—*Murray's Exercises*, p. 63.

[FORMULE.—Not proper, because the preposition *to* is inserted before *proceed*, which follows the active verb *dare*. But, according to Rule 19th, "The active verbs, *bid, dare, feel, hear, let, make, need, see*, and their participles, usually take the infinitive after them without the preposition *to*;" and this is an instance in which the finite verb should immediately govern the infinitive. Therefore, the *to* should be omitted; thus, "I *dare* not *proceed* so hastily," &c.]

"Their character is formed, and made appear."—*Butler's Analogy*, p. 115.

[FORMULE.—Not proper, because the preposition *to* is not inserted between *made* and *appear*, the verb is *made* being passive. But, according to Obs. 5th and 10th on Rule 19th, those verbs which in the active form govern the infinitive without *to*, do not so govern it when they are made passive, except the verb *let*. Therefore, *to* should be here inserted; thus, "Their character is formed, and made *to* appear."]

"Let there be but matter and opportunity offered, and you shall see them quickly to revive again."—*Wisdom of the Ancients*, p. 53. "It has been made appear, that there is no presumption against a revelation."—*Butler's Analogy*, p. 252. "MANIFEST, v. t. To reveal; to make to appear; to show plainly."—*Webster's American Dict.* "Let him to reign like unto good Aurelius, or let him to bleed like unto Socrates."—*Kirkham's Gram.* p. 169. "To sing I could not; to complain I durst not."—*S. Fothergill.* "If T. M. be not so frequently heard pray by them."—*Barclay's Works*, iii, 132. "How many of your own church members were never heard pray?"—*Ib.* iii, 133. "Yea, we are bidden pray one for another."—*Ib.* iii, 145. "He was made believe that neither the king's death, nor imprisonment would help him."—*Sheffield's Works*, ii, 291. "I felt a chilling sensation to creep over me."—*Inst.* p. 188. "I dare to say he has not got home yet."—*Ib.* "We sometimes see bad men to be honoured."—*Ib.* "I saw him to move."—*Felch's Comprehensive Gram.* p. 62. "For see thou, ah! see thou a hostile world to raise its terrours."—*Kirkham's Gram.* p. 167. "But that he make him to rehearse so."—*Lily's Gram.* p. xv. "Let us to rise."—*Fowle's True Eng. Gram.* p. 41.

> "Scripture, you know, exhorts us to it ;
> Bids us to 'seek peace, and ensue it.'"—*Swift's Poems*, p. 336.

> "Who bade the mud from Dives' wheel
> To spurn the rags of Lazarus?
> Come, brother, in that dust we'll kneel,
> Confessing Heaven that ruled it thus."—*Christmas Book.*

CHAPTER VII.—PARTICIPLES.

The true or regular syntax of the English Participle, as a part of speech distinct from the verb, and not converted into a noun or an adjective, is twofold; being sometimes that of simple *relation* to a noun or a pronoun that precedes it, and sometimes that of *government*, or the state of *being governed* by a preposition. In the former construction, the participle resembles an adjective; in the latter, it is more like a noun, or like the infinitive mood: for the participle after a preposition is governed *as a participle*, and not *as a case.*[*] To these two constructions, some add three others less regular, using the participle sometimes as the *subject* of a finite verb, sometimes as the *object* of a transitive verb, and sometimes as a *nominative* after a neuter verb. Of these five constructions, the first two, are the legitimate uses of this part of speech; the others are occasional, modern, and of doubtful propriety.

RULE XX.—PARTICIPLES.

Participles relate to nouns or pronouns, or else are governed by prepositions: as, "Elizabeth's tutor, at one time *paying* her a visit, found her *employed* in

---

[*] Some modern grammarians will have it, that a participle governed by a preposition is a "*participial noun*; and yet, when they come to parse an adverb or an objective following, their "noun" becomes a "*participle*" again, and *not* a "*noun.*" To allow words thus to *dodge* from one class to an other, is not only unphilosophical, but ridiculously absurd. Among those who thus treat this construction of the participle, the chief I think, are Butler, Hart, Wells, and S. S. Greene.

reading Plato."—*Hume.* "I have no more pleasure in *hearing* a attempting wit and *failing*, than in *seeing* a man *trying* to leap over a and *tumbling* into it."—*Dr. Johnson.*

"Now, *rais'd* on Tyre's sad ruins, Pharaoh's pride
Soar'd high, his legions *threat'ning* far and wide."—*Dryden.*

EXCEPTION FIRST.

A participle sometimes relates to a preceding *phrase* or *sentence*, of which it forms part; as, "I then quit the society; *to withdraw and leave them to themselves,* APPEAR me a duty."—"It is almost exclusively on the ground we have mentioned, that we heard *his being continued in office* DEFENDED."—*Professors' Reasons,* p. 23. (Better, *continuance* in office," or, "*the continuing of him* in office." See Obs. 13th on Rule 4th.

"But *ever to do ill* our sole delight,
As *being* the contrary to his high will."—*Milton.*

EXCEPTION SECOND.

With an infinitive denoting being or action in the abstract, a participle is sometimes taken *abstractly*; (that is, without reference to any particular noun, pronoun, or subject;) as, "To seem *compelled*, is disagreeable."—"To keep always *praying* alous plainly impossible."—"It must be disagreeable to be *left pausing* * on a word which not, by itself, produce any idea."—*Murray's Gram.* 8vo, p. 323.

"To praise him is to serve him, and fulfil,
Doing and *suff'ring*, his unquestion'd will."—*Cowper,* Vol. i, p. 86.

EXCEPTION THIRD.

The participle is often used irregularly in English, as a substitute for the infinitive to which it is sometimes equivalent without irregularity; as, "I saw him *enter*, or *enteri* —*Grant's Lat. Gram.* p. 230. "He is afraid *of trying*, or *to try.*"—*Ibid.* Examples irr lar: "Sir, said I, if the case stands thus, 'tis dangerous *drinking*:" i. e. to *drink.*—*Ca Tablet of Cebes.* "It will be but ill *venturing* thy soul upon that:" i. e. to venture *Bunyan's Law and Grace,* p. 27. "*Describing* a past event as present, has a fine effe language:" i. e. to describe.—*Kames, El. of Crit.* i, 93. "In English likewise it doe *remarking*:" i. e. to be remarked.—*Harris's Hermes,* p. 232. "Bishop Atterbury dee *being particularly mentioned*:" i. e. to be particularly mentioned.—*Blair's Rhet.* p. "This, however, is in effect no more than *enjoying* the sweet that predominates:" i. enjoy.—*Campbell's Rhet.* p. 43.

"Habits are soon assum'd; but when we strive
To strip them off, tis *being flay'd* alive."—*Cowper,* Vol. i, p. 44.

EXCEPTION FOURTH.

An other frequent irregularity in the construction of participles, is the practice of trea them essentially as nouns, without taking from them the regimen and adjuncts of part ples; as, "*Your having been well educated will be* a great recommendation."—*W. Allen's G* p. 171. (Better: "*Your excellent education*"—or, "*That you have been well educated,* will l &c.) "It arises from *sublimity's expressing* grandeur in its highest degree."—*Blair's* p. 29. "Concerning *the separating* by a circumstance, *words* intimately connected."—*Ka El. of Crit.* Vol. ii, p. 104. "As long as there is any hope of *their keeping pace* with th. —*Literary Convention,* p. 114. "Which could only arise from *his knowing the secrets* of hearts."—*West's Letters to a Young Lady,* p. 180. "But this again is *talking* quite a: dom."—*Butler's Analogy,* p. 146.

"*My being here* it is, that holds thee hence."—*Shak.*
"Such, but by foils, the clearest lustre see,
And deem *aspersing others, praising thee.*"—*Savage, to Walpole.*

OBSERVATIONS ON RULE XX.

OBS. 1.—To this rule, I incline to think, there are *properly* no other exceptions than the two above; or, at least, that we ought to avoid, when we can, any additional anomalies not to condemn with unbecoming positiveness what others receive for good English. I subjoined two items more, which include certain other irregularities now very common. when examples of a like form occur, the reader may *parse them as exceptions*, if he does not *to censure them as errors.* The mixed construction in which participles are made to govern possessive case, has already been largely considered in the observations on Rule 4th. M Allen, Churchill, and many other grammarians, great and small, admit that participles made the subjects or the objects of verbs, while they retain the nature, government, and adj. of participles; as, "Not *attending* to this rule, is the cause of a very common error."—*Mur*

* Dr. Blair, to whom Murray ought to have acknowledged himself indebted for this sentence, introductory noun, to which, in his work, this infinitive and these participles refer: thus, "It is disagreeable *for the* be *left pausing* on a word which does not, by itself, produce any idea."—*Blair's Rhetoric,* p. 126. See Obs. and 11th on Rule 14th.

Key, 8vo, p. 290; *Canby's Gram.* 188; *Weld's Gram.* 170. "*Polite* is employed to signify *their being highly civilized.*"—*Blair's Rhet.* p. 219. "One abhors *being* in debt."—*Ib.* p. 98; *Jamieson's Rhet.* 71; *Murray's Gram.* 144. "Who affected *being* a fine gentleman so unmercifully."—*Spect.* No. 496. "The minister's *being attached* to the project, prolonged their debate."—*Nixon's Parser*, p. 78. "It finds [i. e. *the* mind finds,] that *acting thus* would gratify one passion; *not acting*, or *acting otherwise*, would gratify another."—*Campbell's Rhet.* p. 109. "But further, *cavilling* and *objecting* upon any subject *is* much easier than *clearing up* difficulties."—*Bp. Butler's Charge to the Clergy of Durham*, 1751.

OBS. 2.—W. Allen observes, "The use of the participle as a nominative, is one of the *peculiarities* of our language."—*Elements of Gram.* p. 171. He might have added, that the use of the participle as an objective governed by a verb, as a nominative after a verb neuter, or as a word governing the possessive, is also one of the peculiarities of our language, or at least an idiom adopted by no few of its recent writers. But whether any one of these four modern departures from General Grammar ought to be countenanced by us, as an idiom that is either elegant or advantageous, I very much doubt. They are all however sufficiently common in the style of reputable authors; and, however questionable their character, some of our grammarians seem mightily attached to them all. It becomes me therefore to object with submission. These mixed and irregular constructions of the participle, ought, in my opinion, to be *generally* condemned as false syntax; and for this simple reason, that the ideas conveyed by them may *generally*, if not always, be expressed more briefly, and more elegantly, by other phraseology that is in no respect anomalous. Thus, for the examples above: "*Inattention* to this rule, is the cause of a very common error."—"*Polite* is employed to signify *a high degree of civilization;*" or, "*that they are* highly civilised."—"One abhors *debt.*"—"Who affected *the* fine gentleman so unmercifully."—"The minister's *partiality* to the project, prolonged their debate."—"It finds [i. e. *the* mind finds,] that *to act thus*, would gratify one passion; *and that not to act*, or *to act otherwise*, would gratify another."—"But further, *to cavil and object*, upon any subject, is much easier than *to clear up* difficulties." Are not these expressions much better English than the foregoing quotations? And if so, have we not reason to conclude that the adoption of participles in such instances is erroneous and ungrammatical?

OBS. 3.—In Obs. 17th on Rule 4th, it was suggested, that in English the participle, without governing the possessive case, is turned to a greater number and variety of uses, than in any other language. This remark applies mainly to the participle in *ing*. Whether it is expedient to make so much of one sort of derivative, and endeavour to justify every possible use of it which can be plausibly defended, is a question well worthy of consideration. We have already converted this participle to such a multiplicity of purposes, and into so many different parts of speech, that one can well-nigh write a chapter in it, without any other words. This practice may have added something to the copiousness and flexibility of the language, but it certainly has a tendency to impair its strength and clearness. Not every use of participles is good, for which there may be found precedents in good authors. One may run to great excess in the adoption of such derivatives, without becoming absolutely unintelligible, and without violating any rule of our common grammars. For example, I may say of somebody, "This very superficial grammatist, supposing empty criticism about the adoption of proper phraseology to be a show of extraordinary erudition, was displaying, in spite of ridicule, a very boastful turgid argument concerning the correction of false syntax, and about the detection of false logic in debate." Now, in what other language than ours, can a string of words anything like the following, come so near to a fair and literal translation of this long sentence? "This exceeding trifling witling, considering ranting criticising concerning adopting fitting wording being exhibiting transcending learning, was displaying, notwithstanding ridiculing, surpassing boasting swelling reasoning, respecting correcting erring writing, and touching detecting deceiving arguing during debating." Here are *not all* the uses to which our writers apply the participle in *ing*, but there would seem to be enough, without adding others that are less proper.

OBS. 4.—The active participles, *admitting, allowing, considering, granting, speaking, supposing*, and the like, are frequently used in discourse so independently, that they either relate to nothing, or to the pronoun *I* or *we* understood; as, "*Granting* this to be true, what is to be inferred from it?"—*Murray's Gram.* p. 195. This may be supposed to mean, "*I*, granting this to be true, *ask* what is to be inferred from it?" "The very chin was, *modestly speaking*, as long as my whole face."—*Addison.* Here the meaning may be, "*I*, modestly speaking, *say*." So of the following examples: "*Properly speaking*, there is no such thing as chance."—*W. Allen's Gram.* p. 172. "Because, *generally speaking*, the figurative sense of a word is derived from its proper sense."—*Kames, El. of Crit.* i, 190. "But, *admitting* that two or three of these offend less in their morals than in their writings, must poverty make nonsense sacred?"—*Pope's Works*, Vol. iii, p. 7. Some grammarians suppose such participles to be put absolute in themselves, so as to have no reference to any noun or pronoun; others, among whom are L. Murray and Dr. James P. Wilson, suppose them to be put absolute with a pronoun understood. On the former supposition, they form an other exception to the foregoing rule; on the latter, they do not: the participle relates to the pronoun, though both be independent of the rest of the sentence. If we supply the ellipsis as above, there is nothing put absolute.

OBS. 5.—Participles are almost always *placed after* the words on which their construction depends, and are distinguished from adjectives by this position; but when other words depend on the participle, or when several participles have the same construction, the whole phrase may come before the noun or pronoun: as, "*Leaning* my head upon my hand, *I* began to figure to myself the miseries of confinement."—*Sterne.*

"*Immur'd* in cypress shades, a *sorcerer* dwells."—*Milton.*

"*Brib'd, bought, and bound*, they banish shame and fear;
Tell you they're stanch, and have a soul sincere."—*Crabbe.*

OBS. 6.—When participles are compounded with something that does not belong to the verb, they become *adjectives*; and, as such, they cannot govern an object after them. The following construction is therefore inaccurate: "When Caius did any thing *unbecoming* his dignity."—

Jones's Church History, i, 87. "Costly and gaudy attire, *unbecoming* godliness."—*Extracts*, p. 185. Such errors are to be corrected by Note 15th to Rule 9th, or by changing the particle *un* to *not*; as, "Unbecoming *to* his dignity;" or, "*Not* becoming his dignity."

OBS. 7.—An imperfect or a preperfect participle, preceded by an article, an adjective, or a noun or pronoun of the possessive case, becomes a *verbal* or *participial noun;* and, as such, it cannot, with strict propriety, govern an object after it. A word which may be the object of the participle in its proper construction, requires the preposition *of*, to connect it with the verbal noun; as, 1. THE PARTICIPLE: "*Worshiping* idols, the Jews sinned."—"*Thus worshiping* idols,—*In worshiping* idols,—or, *By worshiping* idols, they sinned." 2. THE VERBAL NOUN: "*The worshiping of idols,* —*Such worshiping of* idols,—or, *Their worshiping of* idols, was sinful."—"*In the worshiping of* idols, there is sin.*"

OBS. 8.—It is commonly supposed that these two modes of expression are, in very many instances, equivalent to each other in meaning, and consequently interchangeable. How far they really are so, is a question to be considered. Example: "But if candour be *a confounding of* the distinctions between sin and holiness, *a depreciating* of the excellence of the latter, and at the same time *a diminishing of* the evil of the former; then it must be something openly at variance with the letter and the spirit of revelation."—*The Friend*, iv, 108. Here the nouns, *distinctions, excellence,* and *evil*, though governed by *of*, represent the *objects* of the forenamed actions; and therefore they might well be governed by *confounding, depreciating,* and *diminishing,* if these were participles. But if, to make them such, we remove the article and the preposition, the construction forsakes our meaning; for *be confounding*, (*be*) *depreciating*, and (*be*) *diminishing,* seem rather to be verbs of the compound form; and our uncertain nominatives after *be,* thus disappear in the shadow of a false sense. But some sensible critics tell us, that this preposition *of* should refer rather to the *agent* of the preceding action, than to its *passive object;* so that such a phrase as, "*the teaching of boys*," should signify rather the instruction which boys give, than that which they receive. If, for the sake of this principle, or for any other reason, we wish to avoid the foregoing phraseology, the meaning may be very well expressed thus: "But if your candour *confound* the distinctions between sin and holiness; *if it depreciate* the excellence of the latter, and at the same time *diminish* the evil of the former; then it must be something openly at variance with the letter and the spirit of revelation."

OBS. 9.—When the use of the preposition produces ambiguity or harshness, let a better expression be sought. Thus the sentence, "He mentions *Newton's writing of* a commentary," is not entirely free from either of these faults. If the preposition be omitted, the word *writing* will have a double construction, which is inadmissible, or at least objectionable. Some would say, "He mentions *Newton writing* a commentary." This, though not uncommon, is still more objectionable; because it makes the leading word in sense the adjunct in construction. The meaning may be correctly expressed thus: "He mentions *that Newton wrote* a commentary." "Mr. Dryden makes a very handsome observation on *Ovid's writing a letter* from Dido to Æneas." —*Spect.* No. 62; *Campbell's Rhet.* p. 265; *Murray's Key*, ii, 253. "Here the word *writing* is partly a noun and partly a participle. If we make it wholly a noun, by saying, "on *Ovid's writing of* a letter," or wholly a participle, by saying, "on *Ovid writing* a letter;" it may be doubted, whether we have effected any improvement. And again, if we adopt Dr. Lowth's advice, "Let it be either the one or the other, and abide by its proper construction;" we must make some change; and therefore ought perhaps to say, "on *Ovid's conceit of writing* a letter from Dido to Æneas." This is apparently what Addison meant, and what Dryden remarked upon: the latter did not speak of the letter itself, else the former would have said, "on *Ovid's letter* from Dido to Æneas."

OBS. 10.—When a needless possessive, or a needless article, is put before the participle, the correction is to be made, not by inserting *of*, but by expunging the article, according to Note 16th to Rule 1st, or the possessive, according to Note 5th to Rule 4th. Example: "By *his* studying the Scriptures he became wise."—*Lennie's Gram.* p. 91. Here *his* serves only to render the sentence incorrect; yet this spurious example is presented by Lennie, to *prove* that a participle may take the possessive case before it, when the preposition *of* is not admissible after it. So, in stead of expunging one useless word, our grammarians *often* add an other and call the twofold error a *correction;* as, "For *his* avoiding of that precipice, he is indebted to his friend's care."—*Murray's Key*, ii, 201. Or worse yet: "*It was from our* misunderstanding *of* the directions, *that* we lost our way."—*Ibid.* Here, not *our* and *of* only, but four other words, are worse than useless. Again: "By *the* exercising *of* our judgment, it is improved." Or thus: By *exercising* our judgment, it is improved."—*Comly's Key, in his Gram.* 12th Ed. p. 188. Each of these pretended corrections is wrong in more respects than one. Say, "By exercising our *judgment, we improve it.*" Or, "Our *judgement* is improved by *being exercised.*" Again: "*The loving of our* enemies is a divine *command;* Or, loving *our enemies* [is a divine command]."—*Ibid.* Both of these are also wrong. Say, "'Love *your enemies,*' is a divine command." Or, "*We are divinely commanded to love* our enemies." Some are apt to jumble together the active voice and the passive, and thus to destroy the unity even of a short sentence; as, "By *exercising* our memories, they *are improved.*"—*Kirkham's Gram.* p. 226 and 195. "The error *might have been avoided* by repeating the substantive."—*Murray's Gram.* p. 172. "By *admitting* such violations of established grammatical distinctions, confusion *would be introduced.*"—*Ib.* p. 187. In these instances, we have an active participle without an agent; and this, by the preposition *by*, is made an adjunct to a passive verb. Even the participial noun of this form, though it actually drops the distinction of voice, is awkward and apparently incongruous in such a relation.

OBS. 11.—When the verbal noun necessarily retains any adjunct of the verb or participle, it seems proper that the two words be made a compound by means of the hyphen; as, "Their hope shall be as the *giving-up* of the ghost."—*Job*, xi, 20. "For if the *casting-away* of them be the reconciling of the world."—*Rom.* xi, 15. "And the *gathering-together* of the waters called he seas."—*Gen.* i, 10. "If he should offer to stop the *runnings-out* of his justice."—*Law and Grace*, p. 26. "The *stopping-short* before the usual pause in the melody, aids the impression that is y the description of the stone's *stopping-short*."—*Kames, El. of Crit.* ii, 106. I do not find words united in the places referred to, but this is nevertheless their true figure. Our and printers are lamentably careless, as well as ignorant, respecting *the figure of words :* ch part of grammar, see the whole of the third chapter in Part First of this work; also tions on the fourth rule of syntax, from the 30th to the 35th. As certain other compounds netimes be broken by *tmesis*, so may some of these; as, "Not forsaking the *assembling* of es *together*, as the manner of some is."—*Heb.* x, 25. Adverbs may relate to participles, ms require adjectives. The following phrase is therefore inaccurate: "For the more *easily* of large numbers." Yet if we say, "For reading large numbers *the more easily*," the ction is different, and not inaccurate. Some calculator, I think, has it, "For the more eading large numbers." But Hutton says, "For the more *easy* reading *of* la*r*ge numbers." 's *Arith.* p. 5; so *Babcock's*, p. 12. It would be quite as well to say, "For the *greater ease* ing large numbers."

12.—Many words of a participial form are used directly as nouns, without any article, re, or possessive case before them, and without any object or adjunct after them. Such is nly the construction of the words *spelling, reading, writing, ciphering, surveying, drawing,* ., and many other such *names* of actions or exercises. They are rightly put by Johnson "*nouns* derived from *verbs ;*" for, "The [name of the] action is the same with the parti- resent, as *loving, frighting, fighting, striking*."—*Dr. Johnson's Gram.* p. 10. Thus : "I like ."—*W. Allen's Gram.* p. 171. "He supposed, with them, that *affirming* and *denying* were ons of the mind."—*Tooke's Diversions,* i, 35. " 'Not rendering,' said Polycarp the disciple a, 'evil for evil, or *railing* for *railing,* or *striking* for *striking,* or *cursing* for *cursing.*' "— *d. on War*. Against this practice, there is seldom any objection; the words are wholly both in sense and construction. We call them *participial* nouns, only because they resem- rticiples in their derivation; or if we call them *verbal* nouns, it is because they are derived rbs. But we too frequently find those which retain the government and the adjuncts of ples, used as nouns before or after verbs; or, more properly speaking, used as mongrels ndescripts, a doubtful species, for which there is seldom any necessity, since the infinitive, rbal or some other noun, or a clause introduced by the conjunction *that,* will generally the idea in a better manner: as, "*Exciting* such disturbances, is unlawful." Say rather, *cite* such disturbances,—*The exciting of* such disturbances,—*The excitation of* such disturb- —or, *That one should excite* such disturbances, is unlawful."

13.—Murray says, "The word *the,* before the *active participle,* in the following sentence, all others of a similar construction, is improper, and should be omitted : '*The* advising, or mpting, to excite such disturbances, is unlawful.' It should be, '*Advising* or *attempting* to listurbances.' "—*Octavo Gram.* p. 195. But, by his own showing, "the present participle, e definite article *the* before it, becomes a *substantive.*"—*Ib.* p. 192. And substantives, or by an other of his notes, can govern the infinitive mood, just as well as participles ; or just as the verbs which he thinks would be very proper here; namely, "To *advise* or *attempt* te such disturbances."—*Ib.* p. 196. It would be right to say, "*Any advice,* or *attempt,* to such disturbances, is unlawful." And I see not that he has improved the text at all, by ;ing the article. *Advising* and *attempting,* being disjunct nominatives to *is,* are nothing ins, whether the article be used or not; though they are rather less obviously such without therefore make the change is for the worse.

14.—Lennie observes, "When *a preposition* "—(he should have said, When *an other* pre- n—) " follows the participle, *of* is inadmissible; as, *His* depending *on* promises proved his *His* neglecting *to* study when young, rendered him ignorant all his life."—*Prin. of E.* 5th Ed. p. 65; 13th Ed. 91. Here *on* and *to,* of course, exclude *of*; but the latter may be d to *of*, which will turn the infinitive into a noun: as, "*His* neglecting *of study*," &c. *ding* " and "*neglecting,*" being equivalent to *dependence* and *neglect,* are participial nouns, t " participles." Professor Bullions, too, has the same faulty remark, examples and all; book, of the same title, is little else than a gross plagiarism from Lennie's ;) though he rgets his other erroneous doctrines, that, "*A preposition* should never be used before the re," and that, "Active verbs do not admit a preposition after them." See *Bullions' Prin. Gram.* pp. 91, 92, and 107.

15.—The participle in *ing* is, on many occasions, equivalent to the infinitive verb, so that aker or writer may adopt either, just as he pleases : as, "So their gerunds are sometimes *having* [or *to have*] an absolute or apparently neuter signification."—*Grant's Lat. Gram.* p. 'With tears that ceas'd not *flowing* " [or *to flow*].—*Milton.* "I would willingly have him ing [*produce,* or *to produce*] his credentials."—*Barclay's Works,* iii, 273. There are also es, and according to my notion not a few, in which the one is put *improperly* for the other. rticiple however is erroneously used for the infinitive much oftener than the infinitive for ticiple. The lawful uses of both are exceedingly numerous; though the syntax of the ple, strictly speaking, does not include its various *conversions* into other parts of speech. incipal instances of *regular* equivalence between infinitives and participles, may be reduced following heads :

fter the verbs *see, hear,* and *feel,* the participle in *ing,* relating to the objective, is often equiv- o the infinitive governed by the verb; as, "I saw him *running.*"—"I heard it *howling.*"— *en.* "I feel the wind *blowing.*" Here the verbs, *run, howl,* and *blow,* might be substituted. ter intransitive verbs signifying *to begin* or *to continue,* the participle in *ing,* relating nominative, may be used in stead of the infinitive connected to the verb; as, "The ass *galloping* with all his might."—*Sandford and Merton.* "It commenced *raining* very hard."— is. "The steamboats commenced *running* on Saturday."—*Daily Advertiser.* "It is now three years since he began *printing.*"—*Dr. Adam's Pref. to Rom. Antiq.* "So when they ned *asking* him."—*John,* viii, 7. Greek. " 'Ὡς δὲ ἐπέμενον ἐρωτῶντες αὐτὸν." Latin, "Cùm enseverarent *interrogantes* eum."—*Vulgate.* "Cùm autem preseverarent eum *interrogare.*" . "Then shall ye continue *following* the Lord your God."—1 *Sam.* xii, 14. "Eritis *sequentes* Dominam Deum vestrum."—*Vulgate.* "As she continued *praying* before the Lord."—1 Sam. i, 12. "Cùm illa *multiplicaret preces* coram Domino."—*Vulgate.* "And they went on *beating down* one an other."—2 Sam. xiv, 16. "Make the members of them go on *rising* and *growing* in their importance."—*Blair's Rhet.* p. 116. "Why do you keep *teasing* me?"

3. After *for, in, of,* or *to,* and perhaps some other prepositions, the participle may in most cases be varied by the infinitive, which is governed by *to* only; as, "We are better fitted *for receiving* the tenets and *obeying* the precepts of that faith which will make us wise unto salvation."—*West's Letters,* p. 51. That is,—"*to receive* the tenets and *obey* the precepts." "Men fit *for fighting,* practised in *fighting,* proud *of fighting,* accustomed *to fighting.*"—*Allen's Gram.* p. 172. That is,—"it *to fight,*" &c. "What is the right path, few take the trouble *of inquiring.*"—*Murray's Key,* 8vo, ii, 235. Better, perhaps:—"few take the trouble *to inquire.*"

OBS. 16.—One of our best grammarians says, "The infinitive, in the following sentences, *should be exchanged* for the participle: 'I am weary *to bear* them.' Is. i, 14. 'Hast thou, spirit, performed *to point* the tempest?' Shak."—*Allen's Gram.* p. 172. This suggestion implies, that the participle would be here not only equivalent to the infinitive in sense, but better in expression. It is true, the preposition *to* does not well express the relation between *weary* and *bear*; and, doubtless, some regard should be had to the meaning of this particle, whenever it is any thing more than an index of the mood. But the critic ought to have told us how he would make these corrections. For in neither case does the participle alone appear to be a fit substitute for the infinitive, either with or without the *to*; and the latter text will scarcely bear the participle at all, unless we change the former verb; as, "Hast thou, spirit, *done pointing* the tempest?" The true meaning of the other example seems somewhat uncertain. The Vulgate has it, "*Laborasti tinens,*" "I have laboured *bearing* them;" the French Bible, "*Je suis las de les souffrir,*" "I am tired *of bearing* them;" the Septuagint, "Ουκέτι ανήσω τὰς ἁμαρτίας ὑμῶν," "I will no more forgive your sins."

OBS. 17.—In the following text, the infinitive is used improperly, nor would the participle in its stead make pure English: "I will not reprove thee for thy sacrifices or thy burnt-offerings, *to have been* continually before me."—*Ps.* l, 8. According to the French version, "*to have been*" should be "*which are;*" but the Septuagint and the Vulgate take the preceding noun for the nominative, thus: "I will not reprove thee for thy sacrifices, *but thy burnt-offerings are* continually before me."

OBS. 18.—As the preposition *to* before the infinitive shows the latter to be "*that towards which* the preceding verb is directed," verbs of *desisting, omitting, preventing,* and *avoiding,* are generally found to take the participle after them, and not the infinitive: because, in such instances, the direction of effort seems not to be so properly *to,* or *towards,* as *from* the action.* Where the preposition *from* is inserted, (as it most commonly is, after some of these verbs,) there is no irregularity in the construction of the participle; but where the participle immediately follows the verb, it is perhaps questionable whether it ought to be considered the object of a verb, or a mere participle relating to the nominative which precedes. If we suppose the latter, the participle may be parsed by the common rule; if the former, it must be referred to the third exception above. For example:

1. After verbs of DESISTING; as, "The Cryer used to proclaim, DIXERUNT, i. e. They *have done speaking.*"—*Harris's Hermes,* p. 132. "A friend is advised to *put off making* love to Lalage."—*Philological Museum,* i, 446. "He *forbore doing* so, on the ground of expediency."—*The Friend,* iv, 35. "And yet architects never *give over attempting* to reconcile these two incompatibles."—*Kames, El. of Crit.* ii, 338. "Never to *give over seeking* and *praying* for it."—*N. Y. Observer.* "Do not *leave off seeking.*"—*President Edwards.* "Then Satan *hath done flattering* and *comforting.*"—*Baxter.* "The princes *refrained talking.*"—*Job,* xxix, 9. "Principes *cessabant loqui.*"—*Vulgate.* Here it would be better to say, "The princes refrained *from* talking." But Murray says, "*From* seems to be superfluous after *forbear*: as, 'He could not forbear *from* appointing the pope,' &c."—*Octavo Gram.* p. 203. But "*forbear to appoint*" would be a better correction; for this verb is often followed by the infinitive: as, "*Forbear to insinuate.*"—*West's Letters,* p. 62. "And he *forbare to go* forth."—1 Sam. xxiii, 13. The reader will observe, that, "*never to give over,*" or "*not to leave off,*" is in fact the same thing as *to continue*; and I have shown, by the analogy of other languages, that after verbs of *continuing* the participle is not an object of government; though possibly it may be so, in these instances, which are somewhat different.

2. After verbs of OMITTING: as, "He *omits giving* an account of them."—*Tooke's Diversions of Purley,* i, 261. I question the propriety of this construction; and yet, "*omits to give,*" seems still more objectionable. "Better, "He *omits all account* of them." Or, "He *neglects to give,* or *forbears to give,* any account of them." L. Murray twice speaks of apologizing, "for the use he has made of his predecessors' labours, and for *omitting to insert* their names."—*Octavo Gram. Pref.* p. vii; and *Note,* p. 73. The phrase, "*omitting to insert,*" appears to me a downright solecism; and the pronoun *their* is ambiguous, because there are well-known names both for the *men* and for their *labours,* and he ought not to have omitted either species wholly, as he did. "Yet they absolutely *refuse doing* so, one with another."—*Harris's Hermes,* p. 264. Better, "*refuse to do so.*" "I had as repeatedly *declined going.*"—*Leigh Hunt's Byron,* p. 15.

3. After verbs of PREVENTING; as, "Our sex are happily *prevented from engaging* in these turbulent scenes."—*West's Letters to a Lady,* p. 74. "To *prevent* our frail natures *from deviating* into bye paths [write *by-paths*] of error."—*Ib.* p 106. "Prudence, prevents our speaking or acting improperly."—*Blair's Rhet.* p. 99; *Murray's Gram.* p. 303; *Jamieson's Rhet.* p. 72. This construction,

---

* The perfect contrast between *from* and *to,* when the former governs the participle and the latter the infinitive, is an other proof that this *to* is the common preposition *to.* For example: "These are the four spirits of the heavens, which go forth *from standing* before the Lord of all the earth."—*Zech.* vi, 5. Now, if this were rendered, "which go forth *to stand,*" &c., it is plain that these prepositions would express quite opposite relations. Yet, probably from some obscurity in the original, the Greek version has been made to mean, "*going forth to stand;*" and the Latin, "which go forth, *that they may stand:*" while the French text conveys nearly the same sense as ours,—"which go forth *from the place where they stood.*"

though very common, is palpably wrong; because its most natural interpretation is, "Prudence improperly prevents our speech or action." These critics ought to have known enough to say, "Prudence prevents *us from* speaking or acting improperly." "This, however, doth not *hinder* pronunciation *to borrow* from singing."—*Kames, El. of Crit.* ii, 70. Here the infinitive is used, merely because it does not sound well to say, "*from borrowing from singing ;*" but the expression might very well be changed thus, "*from being indebted to singing.*" "'This by no means *hinders* the book *to be* a useful one.'—*Geddes.* It should be, '*from being.*'"—*Churchill's Gram.* p. 318.

4. After verbs of AVOIDING ; as, "He might have *avoided treating* of the origin of ideas."—*Tooke's Diversions*, i, 28. "We may *avoid talking* nonsense on these subjects."—*Campbell's Rhet.* p. 281. "But carefully *avoid being* at any time ostentatious and affected."—*Blair's Rhet.* p. 233. "Here I cannot *avoid mentioning* * the assistance I have received."—*Churchill's Gram.* p. iv. "It is our duty to *avoid leading* others into temptation."—*West's Letters*, p. 33. "Nay, such a garden should in some measure *avoid imitating* nature."—*Kames, El. of Crit.* ii, 251. "I can promise no entertainment to those who *shun thinking.*"—*Ib.* i, 36. "We cannot *help being* of opinion."—ENCYC. BRIT.: *Murray's Gram.* p. 76. "I cannot *help being* of opinion."—*Blair's Rhet.* p. 311. "I cannot *help mentioning* here one character more."—*Hughes, Spect.* No. 554. "These would sometimes very narrowly *miss being catched* away."—*Steele.* "Carleton very narrowly *escaped being taken.*"—*Grimshaw's Hist.* p. 111. Better, "escaped *from* being taken ;"—or, "*escaped capture.*"

OBS. 19.—In sentences like the following, the participle seems to be improperly made *the object* of the verb: "I intend *doing* it."—"I remember *meeting* him." Better, "I intend *to do* it."—"I remember *to have met* him." According to my notion, it is an error to suppose that verbs in general may govern participles. If there are any proper instances of such government, they would seem to be chiefly among verbs of *quitting* or *avoiding*. And even here the analogy of General Grammar gives countenance to a different solution; as, "They *left beating of* Paul."—*Acts*, xxi, 32. Better, "They *left beating* Paul ;"—or, "They *quit beating* Paul." Greek, "Ἐκαύσαντο τύπτοντες τὸν Παῦλον." Latin, "Cessaverunt *percutientes* Paulum."—*Montanus.* "Cessarunt *cedere* Paulum."—*Beza.* "Cessaverunt *percutere* Paulum."—*Vulgate.* It is true, the English participle in *ing* differs in some respects from that which usually corresponds to it in Latin or Greek ; it has more of a substantive character, and is commonly put for the Latin gerund. If this difference does not destroy the argument from analogy, the opinion is still just, that *left* and *quit* are here *intransitive*, and that the participle *beating* relates to the pronoun *they.* Such is unequivocally the construction of the Greek text, and also of the literal Latin of Arias Montanus. But, to the mere English grammarian, this method of parsing will not be apt to suggest itself ; because, at first sight, the verbs appear to be transitive, and the participle in *ing* has nothing to prove it an adjunct of the nominative, and not the object of the verb—unless, indeed, the mere fact that it is a participle, is proof of this.

OBS. 20.—Our great Compiler, Murray, not understanding this construction, or not observing what verbs admit of it, or require it, has very unskillfully laid it down as a rule, that, "The participle with its adjuncts, may be considered as a *substantive phrase* in the objective case, governed by the preposition or verb, *expressed or understood :* as, ' By *promising much, and performing but little*, we become despicable.' He studied to avoid *expressing himself too severely.*"—*Octavo Gram.* p. 194.† This very popular author seems never to have known that participles, as such, may be governed in English by prepositions. And yet he knew, and said, that "prepositions do not, *like articles and pronouns*, convert the participle itself into the nature of a substantive."—*Ibid.* This he avouches in the same breath in which he gives that "nature" to a participle and its adverb ! For, by a false comma after *much*, he cuts his first "*substantive phrase*" absurdly in two ; and doubtless supposes a false ellipsis of *by* before the participle *performing*. Of his method of resolving the second example, some notice has already been taken, in Observations 4th and 5th on Rule 5th. Though he pretends that the whole phrase is in the objective case, "the truth is, the assertion grammatically affects the first word only ;" which in one aspect he regards as a noun, and in an other as a participle : whereas he himself, on the preceding page, had adopted from Lowth a different doctrine, and cautioned the learner against treating words in *ing*, "as if they were of an *amphibious* species, partly nouns and partly *verbs ;*" that is, "partly nouns and partly *participles ;*" for, according to Murray, Lowth, and many others, participles are verbs. The term, "*substantive phrase*," itself a solecism, was invented merely to cloak this otherwise bald inconsistency. Copying Lowth again, the great Compiler defines a phrase to be "two or more words rightly put together ;" and, surely, if we have a well-digested system of grammar, whatsoever words are rightly put together, may be regularly parsed by it. But how can one indivisible word be consistently made two different parts of speech at once ? And is not this the situation of every transitive participle that is made either the *subject* or the *object* of a verb ? Adjuncts never alter either the nature or the construction of the words on which they depend ; and participial nouns differ from participles in both. The former express actions *as things* ; the latter generally attribute them *to their agents* or *recipients.*

OBS. 21.—The Latin gerund is "a kind of verbal noun, partaking of the nature of a participle."—*Webster's Dict.* "A gerund is a participial noun, of the neuter gender, and singular number, declinable like a substantive, having no vocative, construed like a substantive, and

---

* *Cannot*, with a verb of *avoiding*, or with the negative *but*, is equivalent to *must*. Such examples may therefore be varied thus : "I *cannot but mention ;*" i.e. "I *must* mention."—"I *cannot help exhorting* him to assume courage."—*Knox.* That is, "I *cannot but exhort* him."

† See the same thing in *Kirkham's Grammar*, p. 189; in *Ingersoll's*, p. 200; in *Smith's New Grammar*, p. 162 ; and in other modifications and mutilations of Murray's work. Kirkham, in an other place, adopts the doctrine, that, "*Participles* frequently govern nouns *and* pronouns in the possessive case; as, ' In case of his *majesty's dying* without issue, &c.; Upon *God's having* ended all his works, &c.; I remember *its being reckoned* a great exploit; At my *coming* in he said,' &c."—*Kirkham's Gram.* p. 181. None of these examples are written according to my notion of elegance, or of accuracy. Better : "In case his *Majesty die* without issue."—"*God having* ended all his works."—"I remember *it was* reckoned a great exploit."—"*At my entrance*, he said," &c.

governing the case of its verb."—*Grant's Lat. Gram.* p. 70. In the Latin gerund, thus defined, there is an appearance of ancient classical authority for that "amphibious species" of words of which so much notice has already been taken. Our participle in *ing*, when governed by a preposition, undoubtedly corresponds very nearly, both in sense and construction, to this Latin gerund; the principal difference being, that the one is declined, like a noun, and the other is not. The analogy, however, is but lamely maintained, when we come to those irregular constructions in which the participle is made a half-noun in English. It is true, the gerund of the nominative case may be made the subject of a verb in Latin; but we do not translate it by the English participle, but rather by the infinitive, or still oftener by the verb with the auxiliary *must*: as, "*Vivendum est mihi rectè,* I must live well."—*Grant's L. Gram.* p. 232. This is better English than the nearer version, "Living correctly is necessary for me;" and the exact imitation, "Living is to me correctly," is nonsense. Nor does the Latin gerund often govern the genitive like a noun, or ever stand as the direct object of a transitive verb, except in some few doubtful instances about which the grammarians dispute. For, in fact, to explain this species of words, has puzzled the Latin grammarians about as much as the English; though the former do not appear to have fallen into those palpable self-contradictions which embarrass the instructions of the latter.

OBS. 22.—Dr. Adam says, "The gerund in English becomes a substantive, by *prefixing* the article to it, and then it is always to be construed with the preposition *of*; as, 'He is employed *in writing* letters,' or, 'in *the writing of* letters:' but it is improper to say, 'in *the writing* letters,' or, 'in *writing of* letters.'"—*Latin and English Gram.* p. 184. This doctrine is also taught by Lowth, Priestley, Murray, Comly, Chandler, and many others; most of whom extend the principle to all participles that govern the possessive case; and they might as well have added all such as are made either the subjects or the objects of verbs, and such as are put for nominatives after verbs neuter. But Crombie, Allen, Churchill, S. S. Greene, Hiley, Wells, Weld, and some others, teach that participles may perform these several offices of a substantive, without dropping the regimen and adjuncts of participles. This doctrine, too, Murray and his copyists absurdly endeavour to reconcile with the other, by resorting to the idle fiction of "*substantive phrases*" endued with all these powers: as, "*His being at enmity with Cæsar* was the cause of perpetual discord."—*Crombie's Treatise,* p. 287; *Churchill's Gram.* p. 141. "Another fault is *allowing it to supersede* the use of a point."—*Churchill's Gram.* p. 372. "To be sure there is a possibility of some ignorant *reader's confounding the two vowels,* in pronunciation."—*Ib.* p. 375. It is much better to avoid all such English as this. Say rather, "His *enmity with Cæsar* was the cause of perpetual discord."—"An other fault is *the allowing of* it to supersede the use of a point."—"To be sure, there is a possibility *that* some ignorant *reader may confound* the two vowels, in pronunciation."

OBS. 23.—In French, the infinitive is governed by several different prepositions, and the gerundive by one only, the preposition *en*,—which, however, is sometimes suppressed; as, "*en passant, en faisant,—il alloit courant.*"—*Traité des Participes,* p. 2. In English, the gerundive is governed by several different prepositions, and the infinitive by one only, the preposition *to*,—which, in like manner, is sometimes suppressed; as, "*to pass, to do,—I saw him run.*" The difficulties in the syntax of the French participle in *ant,* which corresponds to ours in *ing,* are apparently as great in themselves, as those which the syntax of the English word presents; but they result from entirely different causes, and chiefly from the liability there is of confounding the participle with the verbal adjective, which is formed from it. The confounding of it with the gerundive is now, in either language, of little or no consequence, since in modern French, as well as in English, both are indeclinable. For this reason, I have framed the syntactical rule for participles so as to include under that name the gerund, or gerundive, which is a participle governed by a preposition. The great difficulty with us, is, to determine whether the participle ought, or ought not, to be allowed to assume *other* characteristics of a noun, without dropping those of a participle, and without becoming wholly a noun. The liability of confounding the English participle with the verbal or participial adjective, amounts to nothing more than the occasional misnaming of a word in parsing; or perhaps an occasional ambiguity in the style of some writer, as in the following citation: "I am resolved, 'let the newspapers say what they please of *canvassing* beauties, *haranguing* toasts, and *mobbing* demireps,' not to believe one syllable."—*Jane West's Letters to a Young Lady,* p. 74. From these words, it is scarcely possible to find out, even with the help of the context, whether these three sorts of ladies are spoken of as the canvassers, haranguers, and mobbers, or as being canvassed, harangued, and mobbed. If the prolixity and multiplicity of these observations transcend the reader's patience, let him consider that the questions at issue cannot be settled by the brief enunciation of loose individual opinions, but must be examined in the light of *all the analogies and facts* that bear upon them. So considerable are the difficulties of properly distinguishing the participle from the verbal adjective in French, that that indefatigable grammarian, Girault Du Vivier, after completing his *Grammaire des Grammaires* in two large octavo volumes, thought proper to *enlarge* his instructions on this head, and to publish them in a separate book, (*Traité des Participes,*) though we have it on his own authority, that the rule for participles had already given rise to a greater number of dissertations and particular treatises than any other point in French grammar.

OBS. 24.—A participle construed after the nominative or the objective case, is not in general equivalent to a verbal noun governing the possessive. There is sometimes a nice distinction to be observed in the application of these two constructions. For the leading word in sense, should not be made the adjunct in construction. The following sentences exhibit a disregard to this principle, and are both inaccurate: "He felt his *strength* declining."—"He was sensible of his *strength* declining." In the former sentence, the noun *strength* should be in the objective case, governed by *felt;* and in the latter, it should rather be in the possessive, governed by *declining.* Thus: "He felt his *strength* declining;" i. e. "*felt it decline.*"—"He was sensible of his *strength's* declining;" i. e. "*of its decline.*" These two sentences state the same fact, but, in construction, they are very different; nor does it appear, that where there is no difference of meaning, the two constructions are properly interchangeable. This point has already been briefly noticed in Obs. 12th and 13th on Rule 4th. But the false and discordant instructions which our grammarians deliver respecting possessives before participles; their strange neglect of this plain principle of reason, that the leading word in sense ought to be made the leading or governing word in the construction; and the difficulties which they and other writers are continually falling into, by taking their choice between two errors, in stead of avoiding both: these, as well as their suggestions of sameness or difference of import between the participle and the participial noun, require some further extension of my observations in this place.

Obs. 25.—Upon the classification of words, as parts of speech, distinguished according to their natures and uses, depends the whole scheme of grammatical science. And it is plain, that a bad distribution, or a confounding of such things as ought to be separated, must necessarily be attended with inconveniences to the student, for which no skill or learning in the expounder of such a system can ever compensate. The absurdity of supposing with Horne Tooke, that the same word can never be used so differently as to belong to different parts of speech, I have already alluded to more than once. The absolute necessity of classing words, not according to their derivation merely, but rather according to their sense and construction, is too evident to require any proof. Yet, different as are the natures and the uses of *verbs, participles,* and *nouns,* it is no uncommon thing to find these three parts of speech confounded together; and that too to a very great extent, and by some of our very best grammarians, without even an attempt on their part to distinguish them. For instances of this glaring fault and perplexing inconsistency, the reader may turn to the books of W. Allen and T. O. Churchill, two of the best authors that have ever written on English grammar. Of the participle the latter gives no formal definition, but he represents it as "*a form,* in which *the action* denoted by *the verb* is capable of being joined *to a noun as it's quality,* or accident."—*Churchill's New Gram.* p. 85. Again he says, "That the participle is *a mere mode of the verb* is manifest, if our definition of a verb be admitted."—*Ib.* p. 242. While he thus identifies the participle with the verb, this author scruples not to make what he calls the imperfect participle perform all the offices of a *noun:* saying, "Frequently too it is used as a noun, admits a preposition or article before it, becomes a plural by taking *s* at the end, and governs a possessive case: as, 'He who has *the comings* in of.a prince, may be ruined *by his* own *gaming,* or his *wife's squandering.*'"—*Ib.* p. 144. The plural here exhibited, if rightly written, would have the *s,* not at the end, but in the middle; for *comings-in,* (an obsolete expression for *revenues,*) is not two words, but one. Nor are *gaming* and *squandering,* to be here called participles, but nouns. Yet, among all his rules and annotations, I do not find that Churchill any where teaches that participles *become nouns* when they are used substantively. The following example he exhibits for the express purpose of showing that the nominatives to "*is*" and "*may be*" are not nouns, but participles: "*Walking is* the best exercise, though *riding may be* more pleasant."—*Ib.* p. 141. And, what is far worse, though his book is professedly an amplification of Lowth's brief grammar, he so completely annuls the advice of Lowth concerning the distinguishing of participles from participial nouns, that he not only misnames the latter when they are used correctly, but approves and adopts well-nigh all the various forms of error, with which the mixed and irregular construction of participles has filled our language: of these forms, there are, I think, not fewer than a dozen.

Obs. 26.—Allen's account of the participle is no better than Churchill's—and no worse than what the reader may find in many an English Grammar now in use. This author's fault is not so much a lack of learning or of comprehension, as of order and discrimination. We see in him, that it is possible for a man to be well acquainted with English authors, ancient as well as modern, and to read Greek and Latin, French and Saxon, and yet to falter miserably in describing the nature and uses of the English participle. Like many others, he does not acknowledge this sort of words to be one of the parts of speech; but commences his account of it by the following absurdity: "The participles *are adjectives* derived from the verb; as, *pursuing, pursued, having pursued.*"—*Elements of E. Gram.* p. 62. This definition not only confounds the participle with the participial adjective, but merges the whole of the former species in a part of speech of which he had not even recognised the latter as a subdivision: "An adjective shows *the quality* of a thing. Adjectives may be reduced to five classes: 1. Common—2. Proper—3. Numeral—4. Pronominal—5. Compound."—*Ib.* p. 47. Now, if "participles are adjectives," to which of these five classes do they belong? But there are participial or verbal adjectives, very many; a sixth class, without which this distribution is false and incomplete: as, "a *loving* father; an *approved* copy." The participle differs from these, as much as it does from a noun. But says our author, "Participles, as simple adjectives, belong to *a noun;* as, a *loving* father; an *approved* copy;— as parts of the verb, they have the same government *as* their verbs have; as, his father, *recalling the pleasures* of past years, joined their party."—*Ib.* p. 170. What confusion is this! a complete jumble of adjectives, participles, and "parts of verbs!" Again: "Present participles are often construed as substantives; as, early *rising* is conducive to health; I like *writing;* we depended on *seeing* you."—*Ib.* p. 171. Here *rising* and *writing* are nouns; but *seeing* is a participle, because it is active and governs *you.* Compare this second jumble with the definition above. Again he proceeds: "To participles thus used, many of our best authors prefix the article; as, '*The being chosen* did not prevent disorderly behaviour.' Bp. Tomline. '*The not knowing how to pass* our vacant hours.' Seed."—*Ib.* p. 171. These examples I take to be bad English. Say rather, "The *state of election* did not prevent disorderly behaviour."—"The *want of some entertainment for* our vacant hours." The author again proceeds: "If a noun limits the meaning of a participle thus used, that noun is put in the genitive; as, your *father's coming* was unexpected."—*Ib.* p. 171. Here *coming* is a noun, and no participle at all. But the author has a marginal note, "A possessive pronoun is equivalent to a genitive;" (*ibid.;*) and he means to approve of possessives before active participles: as, "Some of these irregularities arise from *our having received the words* through a French medium."—*Ib.* p. 116. This brings us again to that difficult and apparently unresolvable problem, whether participles as such, by virtue of their mixed gerundive character, can, or cannot, govern the possessive case; a question, about which, the more a man examines it, the more he may doubt.

Obs. 27.—But, before we say any thing more about the government of this case, let us look at our author's next paragraph on participles: "An active participle, preceded by *an article* or by *a genitive* is elegantly followed by the preposition *of*, before the substantive which follows it; as, *the compil*ing *of* that book occupied several years; *his* quitting *of* the army was unexpected."—*Allen's Gram* p. 171. Here the participial nouns *compiling* and *quitting* are improperly called active participles from which they are certainly as fairly distinguished by the construction, as they can be by any means whatever. And this complete distinction the author considers at least an elegance, if not an absolute requisite, in English composition. And he immediately adds: " When this construction produces *ambiguity,* the expression *must be varied.*"—*Ib.* p. 171. This suggestion is left without illustration; but it doubtless refers to one of Murray's remarks, in which it is said: "A phrase in which the article precedes the *present participle* and the possessive preposition follows it, will not, in every instance, convey the same meaning as would be conveyed by the participle without the article and preposition. ' He expressed the pleasure he had *in the hearing of* the philosopher,' is *capable of a different sense* from, ' He expressed the pleasure he had *in hearing* the philosopher.' —*Murray's Octavo Gram.* p. 193; *Smith's Gram.* 161; *Ingersoll's,* 199; and others. Here may be seen a manifest difference between the verbal or participial noun, and the participle or gerund; but Murray, in both instances, absurdly calls the word *hearing* a " present participle;" and, having robbed the former sentence of a needful comma, still more absurdly supposes it ambiguous: whereas the phrase, "in the hearing *of the philosopher,*" means only, "in the *philos*pher's hearing;" and not, "in hearing the philosopher," or, "in hearing *of* the philosopher." But the true question is, would it be right to say, "He expressed the pleasure he had in the *philosopher's* hearing *him?*" For here it would be *equivocal* to say, "in the philosopher's hearing *of* him;" and some aver, that *of* would be wrong, in any such instance, even if the sense were clear. But let us recur to the mixed example from Allen, and compare it with his own doctrines. To say, "from *our* having received *of* the words through a French medium," would certainly be no elegance; and if it be not an ambiguity, it is something worse. The expression, then, "must be varied." But varied how? Is it right without the *of*, though contrary to the author's rule for elegance?

Obs. 28.—The observations which have been made on this point, under the rule for the possessive case, while they show, to some extent, the inconsistencies in doctrine, and the improprieties of practice, into which the difficulties of the mixed participle have betrayed some of our principal grammarians, bring likewise the weight of much authority and reason against the custom of blending without distinction the characteristics of nouns and participles in the same word or words; but still they may not be thought sufficient to prove this custom to be altogether wrong, nor do they pretend to have fully established the dogma, that such a construction is in no instance admissible. They show, however, that possessives before participles are *seldom* to be approved, and perhaps, in the present instance, the meaning might be quite as well expressed by a common substantive, or the regular participial noun: as, "Some of these irregularities arise from *our reception of* the words—or *our receiving of* the words—through a French medium." But there are some examples which it is not easy to amend, either in this way, or in any other; as, "The miscarriages of youth have very much proceeded from *their being imprudently indulged,* or *left to* themselves."—*Friends' N. E. Discipline,* p. 13. And there are instances too, of a similar character, in which the possessive case cannot be used. For example: "Nobody will doubt of *this being* a sufficient proof."—*Campbell's Rhet.* p. 66. "But instead of *this being* the fact of the case, &c."—*Butler's Analogy,* p. 137. "There is express historical or traditional evidence, as ancient as history, of the *system of religion being taught* mankind by revelation."—*Ibid.* "From *things* in it *appearing* to men foolishness."—*Ib.* p. 175. "As to the consistency of the *members* of our society *joining* themselves to those called free-masons."—*N. E. Discip.* p. 51. "In *either of these cases happening,* the *person charging* is at liberty to bring the matter before the church, who are the only *judges* now *remaining.*"—*Ib.* p. 36; *Extracts,* p. 57. " Deriving its efficacy from the *power of God fulfilling* his purpose."—*Religious World,* Vol. ii, p. 235. " We have no idea of any certain *portion of time intervening* between the time of the action and the time of speaking of it."—*Priestley's Gram.* p. 38; *Murray's,* i, 70; *Emmons's,* 41; and others. The following example therefore, however the participle may seem to be the leading word in sense, is unquestionably wrong; and that in more respects than one: " The reason and time of the *Son of God's becoming* man."—*Brown's Divinity,* p. xxii. Many writers would here be satisfied with merely omitting the possessive sign; as does Churchill, in the following example: " The chief cause of this appears to me to lie in *grammarians having considered* them solely as the signs of tense."—*New Gram.* p. 243. But this sort of construction, too, whenever the noun before the participle is not the leading word in sense, is ungrammatical. In stead, therefore, of stickling for choice between two such errors, we ought to adopt some better expression; as, " The reason and time of the *Saviour's incarnation.*"—" The chief cause of this appears to me to *be, that* grammarians *have* considered them solely as signs of tense."

Obs. 29.—It is certain that the noun or pronoun which " limits the meaning of a participle," cannot always be " put in the *genitive* " or *possessive* case; for the sense intended sometimes positively forbids such a construction, and requires the objective: as, "A syllable consists of one or more *letters forming* one sound."—*Allen's Gram.* p. 29. The word *representing* or *denoting* would here be better than *forming,* because the letters do not, strictly speaking, *form* the sound. But chiefly let it be noticed, that the word *letters* could not with any propriety have been put in the possessive case. Nor is it always necessary or proper, to prefer that case, where the sense may be supposed to admit it; as, "' The example which Mr. Seyer has adduced, of the *gerund governing* the genitive of the agent.' Dr. Crombie."—*Grant's Lat. Gram.* p. 237. " Which possibly might have been prevented by *parents doing* their duty."—*N. E. Discipline,* p. 187. "As to the seeming contradiction of *One being* Three, and *Three* One."—*Religious World,* Vol. ii, p. 113. "You have watched them *climbing* from chair to chair."—PIERPONT: *Liberator,* Vol. x, p. 22. "Whether the world came into being as it is, by an intelligent *Agent forming* it thus, or not."—*Butler's Analogy,* p. 129. "In the farther supposition of necessary *agents being* thus rewarded and punished."—*Ib.* p. 140. "He grievously punished the *Israelites murmuring* for want of water."—*Leslie, on Tythes,* p. 21. Here too the words, *gerund, parents, One, Three, them, Agent, agents,* and *Israelites,* are rightly put in the objective case; yet doubtless some will think, though I do not, that they might as well have been put in the possessive. Respectable writers sometimes use the latter case, where the former would convey the same meaning, and be more regular; as, "Which is used, as active verbs often are, without its *regimen's* being expressed."—*Grant's Lat. Gram.* p. 302. Omit the apostrophe and *s*; and, if you please, the word *being* also. "The daily instances of *men's* dying around us."—*Butler's Analogy,* p. 113. Say rather,—"of *men* dying around us." "To prevent *our* rashly engaging in arduous or dangerous enterprises."—*Brown's Divinity,* p. 17. Say, "To prevent *us from*" &c. The following example is manifestly inconsistent with itself; and, in my opinion, the three possessives are all wrong: "The kitchen too now begins to give 'dreadful note of preparation;' not from *armourers* accomplishing the knights, but from the *shop maid's* chopping *force meat,* the *apprentice's* cleaning knives, and the *journeyman's* receiving a practical lesson in the art of waiting at table."—*West's Letters to a Lady,* p. 66. It should be—"not from *armorers* accomplishing the knights, but from the *shopmaid* chopping *forcemeat,* the *apprentice* cleaning knives, and the *journeyman* receiving," &c. The nouns are the principal words, and the participles are adjuncts. They might be separated by commas, if semicolons were put where the commas now are.

Obs. 30.—Our authors, good and bad, critics and no critics, with few exceptions, write sometimes the objective case before the participle, and sometimes the possessive, under precisely the same circumstances; as, "We should, presently, be sensible of the *melody* suffering."—*Blair's Rhet.* p. 122. "We should, presently, be sensible of the *melody's* suffering."—*Murray's Gram.* 8vo, p. 327. "We *shall* presently be sensible of the *melody* suffering."—*Murray's Exercises,* 8vo, p. 60. "We shall presently be sensible of the *melody's* suffering."—*Murray's Key,* 8vo, p. 195. "And I explain what is meant by the nominative *case governing* the verb, and by the *verb agreeing* with its nominative case."—*Rand's Gram.* p. 31. "Take the verb *study,* and speak of *John's studying* his lesson, at different times."—*Ib.* p. 53. "The following are examples of the nominative *case being used* instead of the objective."—*J. M. Putnam's Gram.* p. 112. "The following are examples of an *adverb's qualifying* a whole sentence."—*Ib.* p. 128. "Where the noun is the name of a *person,* the cases may also be distinguished by the *nominative's* answering to WHO, and the *objective* to WHOM."—*Hart's Gram.* p. 46. "This depends chiefly on *their* being more or less emphatic; and on the vowel *sound* being long or short."—*Churchill's Gram.* p. 182. "When they speak of a *monosyllable* having the grave or the acute accent."—*Walker's Key,* p. 328. Here some would erroneously prefer the possessive case before "*having*;" but, if any amendment can be effected it is only by inserting *as* there. "The *event of Maria's loving* her brother."—*O. B. Peirce's Gram.* p. 55. "Between that and the *man being* on it."—*Ib.* p. 59. "The fact of *James placing* himself."—*Ib.* p.166. "The event of the *persons' going.*"—*Ib.* p. 165. Here *persons* is carelessly put for *person's,* i. e. *James's*: the author was *parsing* the puerile text, "James went into a store and placed himself beside Horatio."—*Ib.* p. 164. And I may observe, in passing, that Murray and Blair are both wrong in using commas with the adverb *presently* above.

Obs. 31.—It would be easy to fill a page with instances of these two cases, the objective and the possessive, used, as I may say, indiscriminately; nor is there any other principle by which we can determine which of them is right, or which preferable, than that the leading word in sense ought not to be made the adjunct in the construction, and that the participle, if it remain such, ought rather to relate to its noun, as being the adjunct, than to govern it in the possessive, as being the principal term. To what extent either of these cases may properly be used before the participle, or in what instances either of them may be preferable to the other, it is not very easy to determine. Both are used a great deal too often, filling with blemishes the style of many authors: the possessive, because the participle is not the name of any thing that can be possessed; the objective, because no construction can be right in which the relation of the terms is not formed according to the sense. The former usage I have already criticised to a great extent. Let one example suffice here: "There can be no objection to a *syllable's being long,* on the ground of *its not being so long,* or so much protracted, as some other long syllables are."—*Murray's Gram.* 8vo, p. 242. Some would here prefer *syllable* to *syllable's,* but none would be apt to put *it* for *its,* without some other change. The sentence may be amended thus: "There can be no objection to a *syllable as being long,* on the ground *that it is not so long* as some other syllables."

Obs. 32.—It should be observed, that the use of *as* between the participle and the noun is *very often* better than either the adoption of the possessive sign, or the immediate connexion of the two words; as, "Another point constantly brought into the investigation now, is that of military *success as forming* a claim to civil position."—*Boston Daily Advertiser.* Concerning examples like the following, it may be questioned, whether the objective is proper or not; whether the possessive would be preferable or not; or whether a better construction than either may not be found: "There is scarce an instance of any *one being chosen* for a pattern."—*Kames, El. of Crit.* Vol. ii, p. 338. "Instead of its *authenticity being shaken,* it has been rendered more sure than ever." —*West's Letters,* p. 197. "When there is no longer a possibility of a proper *candidate being nominated* by either party."—*Liberator,* Vol. x, p. 9. "On the first *stone being thrown,* it was returned by a fire of musketry."—*Ib.* p. 16. "To raise a cry about an innocent *person being circumvented* by bribery."—*Blair's Rhet.* p. 276. "Whose principles forbid *them taking* part in the administration of the government."—*Liberator,* Vol. x, p. 15. "It can have no other ground than some such imagination, as that of our gross *bodies being* ourselves."—*Butler's Analogy,* p. 150. "In consequence of this *revelation being made.*"—*Ib.* p. 162. If such relations between the participle and the objective be disapproved, the substitution of the possessive case is liable to still stronger objections; but both may be avoided, by the use of the nominative, or otherwise: thus, "*Scarcely is* any one *ever* chosen for a pattern."—"*Its authenticity, in stead of being shaken,* has been rendered more sure than ever."—"When there is no longer a possibility *that* a proper candidate *will be* nominated by either party."—"*As soon as* the first stone *was* thrown, *there* was returned a fire of musketry."—"To raise a cry, *as if* an innocent person *had been* circumvented by bribery."—"Whose principles forbid them *to take* part in the administration of the government."

—"It can have no other ground than some such imagination, as that our gross bodies are our-selves."—"In consequence of this revelation *which is* made."

OBS. 33.—A recent grammarian quotes Dr. Crombie thus: "Some *late writers* have discarded a phraseology which appears unobjectionable, and substituted one that seems less correct; and instead of saying, 'Lady *Macbeth's* walking in her sleep is an incident full of tragic horror,' would say, 'Lady *Macbeth* walking in her sleep is an incident full of tragic horror.' This seems to me an idle affectation of the Latin idiom, less precise than the common mode of expression, and less consonant with the genius of our language: for, ask what was an incident full of tragic horror, and, according to this phraseology, the answer must be, *Lady Macbeth*; whereas the meaning is, not that *Lady Macbeth*, but her *walking in her sleep*, is an incident full of tragic horror. This phraseology also, in many instances, conveys not the intended idea; for, as Priestley remarks, if it is said, 'What think you of my *horse's running* to-day?' it is implied that the horse did actu-ally run. If it is said, 'What think you of my *horse running* to-day?' it is intended to ask whether it be proper for my horse to run to-day. This distinction, though frequently neglected, deserves attention; for it is obvious that ambiguity may arise from using the latter only of these phraseologies to express both meanings."—*Maunder's Compendious Eng. Gram.* p. 15. [See *Crombie's Treatise*, p. 288—290.] To this, before any comment is offered, let me add an other quotation: "RULE. *A noun before the present participle is put in the possessive case*; as, Much will depend on the *pupil's composing* frequently. Sometimes, however, the sense forbids it to be put in the possessive case; thus, What do you think of my *horse running* to-day? means, Do you think I should let him run? but, What do you think of my *horse's running?* means, he *has run*, do you think he ran well?—*Lennie's Gram.* p. 91; *Brace's Gram.* 94. See *Bullions's Gram.* p. 107; *Hiley's*, 94; *Murray's*, 8vo, 195; *Ingersoll's*, 201; and many others.

OBS. 34.—Any phraseology that conveys not the intended idea, or that involves such an absurd-ity as that of calling a lady an "incident," is doubtless sufficiently reprehensible; but, compared with a rule of grammar so ill-devised as to mislead the learner nine times in ten, an occasional ambiguity or solecism is a mere trifle. The word *walking*, preceded by a possessive and followed by a preposition, as above, is clearly *a noun*, and not a participle; but these authors probably in-tend to justify the use of possessives before *participles*, and even to hold all phraseology of this kind "unobjectionable." If such is not their design, they write as badly as they reason; and if it is, their doctrine is both false and inconsistent. That a verbal noun may govern the pos-sessive case, is certainly no proof that a participle may do so too; and, if these parts of speech are to be kept distinct, the latter position must be disallowed: each must "abide by its own con-struction," as says Lowth. But the practice which these authors speak of, as an innovation of "some late writers," and "an idle affectation of the Latin idiom," is in fact a practice as differ-ent from the blunder which they quote, as their just correction of that blunder is differ-ent from the thousand errors or irregularities which they intend to shelter under it. To call a lady an "incident," is just as far from any Latin idiom, as it is from good English; whereas the very thing which they thus object to at first, they afterwards approve in this text: "What think you of my *horse running* to-day?" This phraseology corresponds with "*the Latin idiom;*" and it is this, that, in fact, they begin with pronouncing to be "less correct" than, "What think you of my *horse's running* to-day?"

OBS. 35.—Between these expressions, too, they pretend to fix a distinction of signification; as if, "the *horse's running* to-day," must needs imply a *past* action, though, (they suppose,) "the *pupil's composing* frequently," or, "the *horse running* to-day," signifies a *future* one. This dis-tinction of time is altogether *imaginary*; and the notion, that to prefer the possessive case before participles, is merely to withstand an error of "*some late writers*," is altogether false. The in-structions above cited, therefore, determine nothing rightly, except the inaccuracy of one very uncommon form of expression. For, according to our best grammarians, the simple mode of cor-rection there adopted will scarcely be found applicable to any other text. It will not be right where the participle happens to be transitive, or even where it is qualified by an adverb. From their subsequent examples, it is plain that these gentlemen think otherwise; but still, who can understand what they mean by "*the common mode of expression?*" What, for instance, would they substitute for the following very inaccurate expression from the critical belles-lettres of Dr. Blair? "A *mother accusing* her son, and *accusing* him of such actions, as *having* first *bribed* judges to condemn her husband, and *having* afterwards *poisoned* him, *were circumstances* that naturally raised strong prejudices against Cicero's client."—*Blair's Lectures*, p. 274. Would they say, "A *mother's accusing* her son, &c., *were circumstances*," &c.? Is this their "common mode of expression?" and if it is, do they not make "common" what is no better English than the Doctor's? If, to accuse a son, and to accuse him greatly, can be considered different circum-stances of the same prosecution, the sentence may be corrected thus: "A *mother's accusing of* her son, and *her charging upon* him such actions, as *those of* having first bribed judges to condemn her husband, and having afterwards poisoned him, were circumstances that naturally raised strong prejudices against Cicero's client."

OBS. 36.—On several occasions, as in the tenth and twelfth observations on Rule 4th, and in certain parts of the present series, some notice has been taken of the equivalence or difference of meaning, real or supposed, between the construction of the possessive, and that of an other case, before the participle; or between the participial and the substantive use of words in *ing*. Dr. Priestley, to whom, as well as to Dr. Lowth, most of our grammarians are indebted for some of their doctrines respecting this sort of derivatives, pretends to distinguish them, both as consti-tuting different parts of speech, and as conveying different meanings. In one place, he says, "When a word ending in *ing* is preceded by an article, it seems to be used as a *noun*; and there-fore *ought not to govern an other word*, without the intervention of a preposition."—*Priestley's Gram.* p. 157. And in an other: "Many nouns are derived from verbs, and end in *ing*, like par-ticiples of the present tense. The difference between these nouns and participles is often over-looked, and the accurate distinction of the two senses not attended to. If I say ,What think you of my *horse's running* to-day, I use the NOUN *running*, and suppose the horse to have actually run; for it is the same thing as if I had said, What think you of *the running of* my horse. But if I say, What think you of my *horse running* to-day, I use the PARTICIPLE, and I mean to ask, whether it be proper that my horse should run or not; which, therefore, supposes that he had not then run.'—*Ib.* p. 132.   Whatever our other critics say about the *horse running* or the *horse's running*, they have in general borrowed from Priestley, with whom the remark originated, as it here stands.   It appears that Crombie, Murray, Maunder, Lennie, Bullions, Ingersoll, Barnard, Hiley, and others, approve the doctrine thus taught, or at least some part of it; though some of them, if not all, thereby contradict themselves.

OBS. 37.—By the two examples here contrasted, Priestley designed to establish a distinction, not for these texts only, but for *all similar expressions*—a distinction both of the noun from the participle, and of the different senses which he supposed these two constructions to exhibit.   In all this, there is a complete failure.   Yet with what remarkable ductility and implicitness do other professed critics take for granted what this superficial philologer so hastily prescribes!   By acknowledging, with reference to such an application of them, that the two constructions above are both *good English*, our grammarians do but the more puzzle their disciples respecting the choice between them; just as Priestley himself was puzzled, when he said, "So we *may either say*, I remember *it being reckoned* a great exploit; or, *perhaps more elegantly*, I remember *its being reckoned*, &c.".—*Gram.* p. 70.   Murray and others omit this "*perhaps*," and while they allow both forms to be good, decidedly prefer the latter; but neither Priestley, nor any of the rest, *ever* pretended to discern in these a difference of signification, or even of parts of speech.   For my part, in stead of approving either of these readings about the "*great exploit*," I have rejected both, for reasons which have already been given; and now as to the first two forms of the *horserace question*, so far as they may strictly be taken for models, I cannot but condemn them also, and for the same reasons: to which reasons may be joined the additional one, that neither expression is well adapted to the sense which the author himself gives to it in his interpretation.   If the Doctor designed to ask, "Do you think my horse ran well to-day?" or, "Do you think it proper for my horse to run to-day?" he ought to have used one or the other of these unequivocal and unobjectionable expressions.   There is in fact, between the others, no such difference of meaning as he imagines; nor does he well distinguish "the NOUN *running*" from the PARTICIPLE *running*; because he apparently allows the word, in both instances, to be qualified by the adverb *to-day*.*

OBS. 38.—It is clear, that the participle in *ing* partakes sometimes the nature of its verb and *an adjective*; so that it relates to a noun, like an adjective, and yet implies time, and, if transitive, governs an object, like a verb: as, "Horses *running* a race."   Hence, by dropping what here distinguishes it as a participle, the word may become an adjective, and stand before its noun; as, "A *running* brook."   So, too, this participle sometimes partakes the nature of its verb and *a noun*; so that it may be governed by a preposition, like a noun, though in itself it has no cases or numbers, but is indeclinable: as, "In *running* a race."   Hence, again, by dropping what distinguishes it as a participle, it may become a noun; as, "*Running* is a safer sport than *wrestling*."   Now, if to a participle we prefix something which makes it an adjective, we also take away its regimen, by inserting a preposition; as, "A doctrine *undeserving of* praise,"—"A man *uncompromising in* his principles."   So, if we put before it an article, an adjective, or a possessive, and thus give to the participle a substantive character or relation, there is reason to think, that we ought, in like manner, to take away its regimen, and its adverb too, if it have any, and be careful also to distinguish this noun from the participial adjective; as, "*The running of* a race,"—"*No racing of* horses,"—"*Your deserving of* praise,"—"A man's *compromising of* his principles."   With respect to the articles, or any adjectives, it seems now to be generally conceded, that these are signs of *substantives*; and that, if added to participles, they must cause them to be taken, in all respects, *substantively*.   But with respect to possessives before participles, the common prac-

---

* We have seen that Priestley's doctrine, as well as Lowth's, is, that when a participle is taken *substantively*, it "ought not to govern another word;" and, for the same reason, it ought not to have an *adverb* relating to it. But many of our modern grammarians disregard these principles, and do not restrict their "*participial nouns*" to the construction of nouns, in either of these respects.   For example: Because one may say, "To read *superficially*, is useless," Barnard supposes it right to say, "*Reading superficially* is useless."   "But the *participle*," says he, "will also take the adjective; as, '*Superficial* reading is useless.'"—*Analytic Gram.* p. 212.   In my opinion, this last construction ought to be preferred; and the second, which is both irregular and unnecessary, rejected.   Again, this author says: "We have laid it down as a rule, that the possessive case belongs, like an adjective, to a *noun*.   What shall be said of the following?   'Since the days of Samson, there has been no instance of *a man's* accomplishing a task so stupendous.'   The *entire clause* following man's, is taken as a noun. 'Of a man's *success* in a task so stupendous,' would present no difficulty.   A part of a sentence, or even a single participle, *thus* often stands *for a noun*.   'My going will depend on my father's giving his consent,' or 'on my father's consenting.'   A participle *thus used* as a noun, may be called a PARTICIPIAL NOUN."—*Ib.* p. 151.   I dislike this doctrine also.   In the first example, *man* may well be made the leading word in sense; and, as such, it must be in the objective case; thus: "There has been no instance of a man *accomplishing* a task so stupendous."   It is also proper to say, "*My going* will depend on my *father's consenting*." or, "on my *father's consent*."   But an action possessed by the agent, ought not to be transitive.   If, therefore, you make this the leading idea, insert *of*; thus, "There has been no instance of a man's *accomplishing* of a task so stupendous.'"—"*My going* will depend on my *father's giving* of his consent."—"My *brother's acquiring* [*of*] the French language will be a useful preparation for his travels."—*Barnard's Gram.* p. 227.   If participial nouns retain the power of participles, why is it wrong to say, "A superficial reading books is useless?"   Again, Barnard approves of the question, "What do you think of my *horse's running* to-day?" and adds, "Between this form of expression and the following, 'What do you think of my *horse running* to-day?' it is sometimes said, that we should make a distinction; because the former implies that the horse had actually run, and the latter, that it is in contemplation to have him do so.   The *difference of meaning certainly exists*; but it would seem more judicious to treat *the latter* as an improper mode of speaking.   What can be more uncouth than to say, 'What do you think of *me* going to Niagara?'   We should say *my going*, notwithstanding the ambiguity.   We ought, *therefore*, to introduce something explanatory; as, 'What do you think *of the propriety* of my going to Niagara?'"—*Analytic Gram.* p. 227.   The propriety of a past action is as proper a subject of remark as that of a future one; the explanatory phrase here introduced has therefore nothing to do with Priestley's distinction, or with the alleged ambiguity.   Nor does the uncouthness of an objective pronoun with the leading word in sense improperly taken as an adjunct, prove that a participle may properly take to itself a possessive adjunct, and still retain the active nature of a participle.

tice of our writers very extensively indulges the mixed construction of which I have said so much; and concerning the propriety of which, the opinions of our grammarians are so various, so confused, and so self-contradictory.

OBS. 39.—Though the participle with a nominative or an objective before it, is not in general equivalent to the verbal noun or the mixed participle with a possessive before it ; and though the significations of the two phrases are often so widely different as to make it palpably absurd to put either for the other ; yet the instances are not few in which it makes little or no difference to the sense, which of the two forms we prefer: and therefore, in these instances, I would certainly choose the more simple and regular construction; or, where a better than either can readily be found, reject both. It is also proper to have some regard to the structure of other languages, and to the analogy of General Grammar. If there be "some late writers" who are chargeable with "an idle affectation of the Latin idiom," there are perhaps more who as idly affect what they suppose "consonant with the genius of our language." I allude to those who would prefer the possessive case in a text like the following : "Wherefore is this noise of the *city being* in an uproar ?"—1 *Kings*, i, 41. "Quid sibi vult clamor civitatis tumultuantis ?"—*Vulgate*. "Τί ἡ φωνὴ τῆς πόλεως ἠχούσης ;"—*Septuagint*. Literally: "What [means] the clamour of the *city resounding ?*" "Que veut dire ce bruit de la ville qui est ainsi émue ?"—*French Bible*. Literally : "What means this noise of the *city which is so moved ?*" Better English : "What means this noise *with which the city rings ?*" In the following example, there is a seeming imitation of the foregoing Latin or Greek construction; but it may well be doubted whether it would be any improvement to put the word "*disciples*" in the possessive case; nor is it easy to find a third form which would be better than these : "Their difficulties will not be increased by the intended *disciples having ever resided* in a Christian country."—*West's Letters*, p. 119.

OBS. 40.—It may be observed of these different relations between participles and other words, that *nouns* are much more apt to be put in the nominative or the objective case, than are *pronouns*. For example : "There is no more of moral principle in the way of *abolitionists nominating* their own candidates, than in that of *their voting* for those nominated by others."—GERRIT SMITH : *Liberator*, Vol. x, p. 17. Indeed, a pronoun of the nominative or the objective case is hardly ever used in such a relation, unless it be so obviously the leading word in sense, as to preclude all question about the construction.* And this fact seems to make it the more doubtful, whether it be proper to use nouns in that manner. But it may safely be held, that if the noun can well be considered the leading word in sense, we are at least under no *necessity* of subjecting it to the government of a mere participle. If it be thought desirable to vary the foregoing example, it may easily be done, thus : "There is no more of moral principle *to prevent abolitionists from nominating* their own candidates, than *to prevent them from* voting for those nominated by others." The following example is much like the preceding, but less justifiable : "We see *comfort*, security, strength, pleasure, wealth, and prosperity, all flowing from *men combining together* ; and misery, weakness, and poverty, ensuing from *their acting separately* or in opposition to each other."—*West's Letters*, p. 133. Say rather,—"from *men's combining-together*," or, "from *the just combination of men in society* ;" and,—"from their *separate action*, or *their* opposition to one *an other*." Take an other example : "If *illorum* be governed here of *negotii*, it must be in this order, *gratiá negotii illorum videndi* ; and this is, for the sake of their *business* being seen, and not, for the sake of *them* being seen."—*Johnson's Grammatical Commentaries*, p. 352. Here the learned critic, in disputing Perizonius's resolution of the phrase, "*illorum videndi gratiá*," has written disputable English. But, had he *affected the Latin idiom*, a nearer imitation of it would have been,—"for the sake of their *business's being seen*, and not for the sake of *their being seen.*" Or nearer still,—"for the sake of *seeing of their business*, and not, for the sake of *seeing of them.*" An elegant writer would be apt to avoid all these forms, and say,—"for the sake of *seeing their business* ;" and,—"for the sake of *seeing them* :" though the former phrase, being but a version of bad Latin, makes no very good sense in any way.

OBS. 41.—Idioms, or peculiarities of expression, are never to be approved or valued, but according to their convenience, utility, or elegance. By this rule, some phrases that are not positively barbarous, may yet be ungrammatical ; and a construction that is sometimes allowable, may yet be quite unworthy to be made or reckoned, "the common mode of expression." Thus, in Latin, the infinitive verb is occasionally put for a noun, and taken to signify a property possessed ; as, "*Tuum scire*, [thy to know,] the same as *tua scientia*, thy knowledge. Pers."—*Adam's Gram.* p. 153. So, in English, the participle in *ing* is often taken substantively, when it does not actually become a substantive, or noun ; as, "Thy *knowing* this,"—"Our *doing* so."—*West*. Such forms of speech, because they are idiomatical, seldom admit of any literal translation, and are never naturalized by any transfer from one language or dialect into an other ; nor is it proper for grammarians to justify them, in vernacular speech, except as figures or anomalies that ought not to be generally imitated. It cannot be truly affirmed, that the genius of our language ever requires that participles, as such, should assume the relations of a noun, or govern the possessive case ; nor, on the other hand, can it be truly denied, that very excellent and learned writers do sometimes make use of such phraseology. Without disrespect to the many users and approvers of these anomalies, I set down for bad English every mixed construction of the participle, for which the language can furnish an equivalent expression that is more *simple* and more elegant. The extent to which these comparative barbarisms now abound in English

* The following is an example, but it is not very intelligible, nor would it be at all amended, if the pronoun were put in the possessive case. "I sympathize with my sable brethren, when I hear of *them being spared* even one lash of the cart-whip."—REV. DR. THOMSON : *Garrison, on Colonization*, p 89. And this is an other, in which the possessive pronoun would not be better : "But, if the slaves wish to return to slavery, let them do so ; not an abolitionist will turn out to stop *them going* back."—*Antislavery Reporter*, Vol. IV, p. 223. Yet it might be more accurate to say—"to stop them *from* going back." In the following example from the pen of Priestley, the objective is correctly used with *as*, where some would be apt to adopt the possessive : "It gives us an idea of *him, as being* the only person to whom it can be applied."—*Priestley's Gram.* p. 151. Is not this better English than to say, "*of his being* the only person ? "

ooks, and the ridiculous fondness for them, which has been shown by some writers on English rammar, in stead of amounting to any argument in their favour, are in fact plain proofs of the ecessity of an endeavour to arrest so obvious and so pernicious an innovation.

OBS. 42.—A late author observes as follows: "That the English gerund, participle, or verbal oun, in *ing*, has both an active and a passive signification, there can be little doubt.* Whether he Latin gerund has precisely a similar import, or whether it is only active, it may be difficult, ad, indeed, after all, it is not of much moment, to ascertain."—*Grant's Latin Gram.* p. 234. The gerund in Latin most commonly governs the case of its own verb, as does the active parti- iple, both in Latin and English: as, "Efferor studio *patres vestros videndi.* Cic. de sen. 23."— *Lily's Gram.* p. 96. That is, "I am transported with a desire *of seeing your fathers.*" But ometimes we find the gerund taken substantively and made to govern the genitive. Or,—to adopt the language of an old grammarian:—"Interdum *non invenustè* additur gerundiis in *di* tiam genitivus pluralis: ut, 'Quum *illorum videndi* gratiâ me in forum contulissem.'—'*Novarum* qui] *spectandi* faciunt copiam.' Ter. Heaut. prol. 29."—*Lily's Gram.* p. 97. That is, "To ge- unds in *di* there is sometimes *not inelegantly* added a genitive plural: as, 'When, for the sake f *seeing of them,* I went into the forum.'—'Who present an opportunity *of attending of new mas:*' i. e. new comedies." Here the *of* which is inserted after the participle to mark the geni- tive case which is added, forms rather an error than an elegance, though some English writers do now and then adopt this idiom. The gerund thus governing the genitive, is not analogous to our participle governing the possessive; because this genitive stands, not for *the subject* of the being or action, but for what would otherwise be *the object* of the gerund, or of the participle, as may be seen above. The objection to the participle as governing the possessive, is, that it retains its object or its adverb; for when it does not, it becomes fairly a noun, and the objection is re- moved. R. Johnson, like many others, erroneously thinks it a noun, even when it governs an objective, and has merely a preposition before it; as, "For the sake *of seeing them.* Where *see- ing* (says he) is a Substantive."—*Gram. Com.* p. 353.

OBS. 43.—If the Latin gerund were made to govern the genitive of the *agent*, and allowed at the same time to retain its government as a gerund, it would then correspond in every thing but declension, to the English participle when made to govern both the possessive case and the ob- jective. But I have before observed that no such analogy appears. The following example has been quoted by Seyer, as a proof that the gerund may govern the genitive of the agent: "*Cujus autem in dicendo aliquid reprehensum est*—Cic."—*Grant's Lat. Gram.* p. 236. That is, (as I un- derstand it,) "But in *whose speaking* something is reprehended." This seems to me a case in point; though Crombie and Grant will not allow it to be so. But a single example is not suffi- cient. If the doctrine is true, there must be others. In this solitary instance, it would be easier to doubt the accuracy even of Cicero, than to approve the notion of these two critics, that *cujus* is here governed by *aliquid*, and not by the gerund. "Here," says Grant, "I am inclined to concur in opinion with Dr. Crombie, whose words I take the liberty to use. ' That, *for the sake of eupho- ny*, the gerund is sometimes found governing the genitive of the patient, or *subject* [say *object*] of the action, is unquestionable: thus, *studio videndi patrum vestrorum.* [That is, literally, *By a desire of seeing of your fathers.*] But I recollect no example, where the gerund is joined with a possessive adjective, or genitive of a noun substantive, where the person is not the patient, but the agent; as, *dicendum meum, ejus dicendum, cujus dicendum.* [That is, *my speaking, his speak- ing, whose speaking.*] In truth, these phraseologies appear to me, not only repugnant to the idiom of the language, but also unfavourable to precision and perspicuity.'"—*Grant's Latin Gram.* 8vo, p. 236.

OBS. 44.—Of that particular distinction between the participle and the participial noun, which depends on the insertion or omission of the article and the preposition *of*, a recent grammarian of considerable merit adopts the following views: "This double nature of the participle has led to much irregularity in its use. Thus we find, 'indulging which,' 'indulging *of* which,' '*the* indulging which,' and '*the* indulging *of* which,' used indiscriminately. Lowth very properly instructs us, either to use both the article and the preposition with the participle; as, '*the* in- dulging *of* which:' or to reject both; as, 'indulging which:' thus keeping the verbal and sub- stantive forms distinct. But he is wrong, as Dr. Crombie justly remarks, in considering these two modes of expression as perfectly similar. Suppose I am told, 'Bloomfield spoke warmly of the pleasure he had *in hearing* Fawcet:' I understand at once, that the eloquence of Fawcet gave Bloomfield great pleasure. But were it said, 'Bloomfield spoke warmly of the pleasure he had *in the hearing of* Fawcet:' I should be led to conclude, merely that the orator was within hear- ing, when the poet spoke of the pleasure he felt from something, about which I have no infor- mation. Accordingly Dr. Crombie suggests as a general rule, conducive at least to perspicuity, and perhaps to elegance; that, when the noun connected with the participle is active, or doing something, the article should be inserted before the participle, and the preposition after it: and, when the noun is passive, or represents the object of an action, both the article and the preposi- tion should be omitted:† agreeably to the examples just adduced. It is true, that, when the noun following the participle denotes something incapable of the action the participle expresses, no mistake can arise *from using* either form: as, 'The middle condition seems to be the most ad- vantageously situate for *the gaining of* wisdom. Poverty turns our thoughts too much upon *the supplying of* our wants; and riches, upon *enjoying* our superfluities.' *Addison, Spect.*, 464. Yet

---

* Sometimes the passive form is adopted, when there is no real need of it, and when perhaps the active would be better, because it is simpler; as, "Those portions of the grammar are worth the trouble of *being committed to* memory."—*Dr. Barrow's Essays*, p. 109. Better, perhaps:—"worth the trouble of *committing* to memory:" or,—"worth the trouble of *committing them* to memory." Again: "What is worth *being uttered* at all, is worth *being spoken* in a proper manner."—*Kirkham's Elocution*, p. 68. Better, perhaps: "What is worth *uttering* at all, is worth *uttering* in a proper manner."—G. BROWN.

† "RULE.—When the participle expresses something of which the noun following is the DOER, it should have the article and preposition; as, 'It was said in *the hearing of* the witness.' When it expresses something of which the noun following is *not the doer*, but the OBJECT, both should be omitted; as, 'The court spent some time in *hearing the witness.*'"—BULLIONS, *Prin. of E. Gram.* p. 108; *Analyt. and Pract. Gram.* 181.

I cannot think it by any means a commendable practice, thus to jumble together different
and indeed it is certainly better, as *the two modes of expression have different significat*
confine each to its distinct and proper use, agreeably to Dr. Crombie's rule, even when
take could arise *from interchanging* them."—*Churchill's Gram.* p. 312.

Obs. 45.—The two modes of expression which these grammarians would thus apply con
to different uses, on the supposition that they have always different significations, *are t*
that Lindley Murray and his copyists suppose to be *generally equivalent*, and concerning
it is merely admitted by the latter, that they do " *not in every instance* convey the same me
(See Obs. 27th above.) If Dr. Lowth considered them "*as perfectly similar*," he was u
edly very wrong in this matter; though not more so than these gentlemen, who resolve t
pret them as being perfectly and constantly dissimilar. Dr. Adam says, "There are,
Latin and [in] English, substantives derived from the verb, which so much resemble the
in their signification, that *frequently* they may be substituted in its place. They are g
used, however, in a more undetermined sense than the Gerund, and in English have the
always * prefixed to them. Thus, with the gerund, *Delector legendo Ciceronem*, I am de
with reading Cicero. But with the substantive, *Delector lectione Ciceronis*, I am delight
the reading of Cicero."—*Lat. and Eng. Gram.* p. 142. " Gerunds are so called because the
were, signify the thing *in gerendo*, (anciently written *gerundo*,) *in doing*; and, along with
tion, convey an idea of the agent."—*Grant's Lat. Gram.* p. 70; *Johnson's Gram. Com.*
"*The reading of* Cicero," does not necessarily signify an action of which Cicero is the ag
Crombie, Churchill, and Hiley, choose to expound it; and, since the gerundive constru
words in *ing* ought to have a definite reference to the agent or subject of the action or bei
may perhaps amend even some of their own phraseology above, by preferring the part
noun: as, "No mistake can arise *from the using of* either form."—"And riches [ta
thoughts too much] *upon the enjoying of* our superfluities."—" Even when no mistake coul
from the interchanging of them." Where the agent of the action plainly appears, the ger
form is to be preferred on account of its brevity; as, "By *the* observing *of* truth, you w
mand respect;" or, "By *observing* truth, &c."—*Kirkham's Gram.* p. 189. Here the
phraseology is greatly preferable, though this author did not perceive it. "I thought m
was to be done by me before *the giving of* you thanks."—*Walker's Particles*, p. 69. Say,—"
giving you thanks;" for otherwise the word *thanks* has no proper construction, the pr
alone being governed by *of*—and here again is an error; for "*you*" ought to be the objec

Obs. 46.—In Hiley's Treatise, a work far more comprehensive than the generality of gra
" the *established principles* and *best usages* of the English" Participle are so adroitly summ
as to occupy only two pages, one in Etymology, and an other in Syntax. The author show
the participle differs from a verb, and how from an adjective; yet he neither makes it a sep
part of speech, nor tells us with what other it ought to be included. In lieu of a general ru
the parsing of *all participles*, he presents the remark, "Active transitive participles, like
verbs, govern the objective case; as, 'I am desirous of *hearing him*;' '*Having praised* th
eat down.'"—*Hiley's Gram.* p. 93. This is a rule by which one may parse the *few objective*
are governed by participles; but, for the usual construction of *participles themselves*, it is n
at all; neither does the grammar, full as it is, contain any. "*Hearing*" is here governed
and "*Having praised*" relates to *he*; but this author teaches neither of these facts, and the f
he expressly contradicts by his false definition of a preposition. In his first note, is exhib
two parts, the false and ill-written rule which Churchill quotes from Crombie. (1.) " Whe
noun, *connected with the participle*, is *active or doing* something, the *participle must have* an a
before it, and the preposition *of* after it; as, 'In the *hearing of* the philosopher;' or, '
philosopher's *hearing*;' ' By *the preaching of* Christ;' or, ' By Christ's *preaching*.' " In
instances," says Hiley, " the words *hearing* and *preaching* are *substantives*." If so, he coul
have corrected this rule, which twice calls them *participles*; but, in stead of doing that, he
adds, by way of alternative, two examples which expressly contradict what the rule asserts.
" But when the noun represents the *object* of an *action*, the article and the preposition *of* ar
omitted; as, 'In *hearing* the philosopher.'"—*Ib.* p. 94. If this principle is right, my second
below, and most of the corrections under it, are wrong. But I am persuaded that the ad
of this rule did not observe how common is the phraseology which it condemns; as, "For
casting-away of them be the *reconciling of the world*, what shall *the receiving of them* be, bu
from the dead?"—*Rom.* xi, 15. Finally, this author rejects the *of* which most critics
when a possessive precedes the verbal noun; justifies and prefers the mixed or double con
tion of the participle; and, consequently, neither wishes nor attempts to distinguish the part
from the verbal noun. Yet he does not fail to repeat, with some additional inaccurac
notion, that, " What do you think of my *horse's running*? is different to [say *from*,] What d
think of my *horse running*?"—*Ib.* p. 94.

Obs. 47.—That English books in general, and the style of even our best writers, should
be found exempt from errors in the construction of participles, will not be thought read
when we consider the multiplicity of uses to which words of this sort are put, and the str
inconsistencies into which all our grammarians have fallen in treating this part of syntax.
useless, and worse than useless, to teach for grammar any thing that is not true; and as dec
can be true of which one part palpably oversets an other. What has been taught on the
topic, has led me into a multitude of critical remarks, designed both for the refutation
principles which I reject, and for the elucidation and defence of those which are presen
summed up in notes, or special rules, for the correction of false syntax. If my decisions
agree with the teaching of our common grammarians, it is chiefly because these authors
dict themselves. Of this sort of teaching I shall here offer but one example more, and th
these strictures to a close: " When present participles are preceded by an article, or pr
adjective, they become nouns, and must not be followed by objective pronouns, or nouns

---

* This doctrine is far from being true. See Obs. 12th, in this series, above.—G. B.

a preposition; as, *the reading of many books wastes the health.* But such nouns, like all others, may be used without an article, being sufficiently discovered by the following preposition; as, *he was sent to prepare the way, by preaching of repentance.* Also an article, or pronoun adjective, may precede a clause, used as a noun, and commencing with a participle; as, *his teaching children was necessary.*"—*Dr. Wilson's Syllabus of English Gram.* p. xxx. Here the last position of the learned doctor, if it be true, completely annuls the first; or, if the first be true, the last must needs be false. And, according to Lowth, L. Murray, and many others, the second is as bad as either. The bishop says, concerning this very example, that by the use of the preposition *of* after the participle *preaching,* "the phrase is rendered *obscure* and *ambiguous:* for the obvious meaning of it, in its present form, is, 'by preaching *concerning* repentance, or on that subject;' whereas the sense intended is, 'by publishing the covenant of repentance, and declaring repentance to be a condition of acceptance with God.'"—*Lowth's Gram.* p. 82. "It ought to be, 'by *the* preaching *of* repentance;' or, by *preaching* repentance."—*Murray's Gram.* p. 193.

NOTES TO RULE XX.

NOTE I.—Active participles have the same government as the verbs from which they are derived; the preposition *of,* therefore, should never be used after the participle, when the verb does not require it. Thus, in phrases like the following, *of* is improper: "Keeping *of* one day in seven,"—"By preaching *of* repentance,"—"They left beating *of* Paul."

NOTE II.—When a transitive participle is converted into a noun, *of* must be inserted to govern the object following; as, "So that there was no *withstanding of* him."—*Walker's Particles,* p. 252. "The cause of their salvation doth not so much arise from *their embracing of* mercy, as from *God's exercising of* it."—*Penington's Works,* Vol. ii, p. 91. "Faith is *the receiving of* Christ with the whole soul." —*Baxter.* "In *thy pouring-out of* thy fury upon Jerusalem."—*Ezekiel,* ix, 8.

NOTE III.—When the insertion of the word *of,* to complete the conversion of the transitive participle into a noun, produces ambiguity or harshness, some better phraseology must be chosen. Example: "Because the action took *place prior to the taking place* of the other past action."—*Kirkham's Gram.* p. 140. Here the words *prior* and *place* have no regular construction; and if we say, "*prior* to the taking *of place of* the other," we make the jumble still worse. Say therefore, "Because the action took place *before* the other past action;"—or, "Because the action took place *previously to* the other past action."

NOTE IV.—When participles become nouns, their adverbs should either become adjectives, or be taken as parts of such nouns, written as compound words: or, if neither of these methods be agreeable, a greater change should be made. Examples of error: 1. "*Rightly* understanding a sentence depends very much on a knowledge of its grammatical construction."—*Comly's Gram.* 12th Ed. p. 3. Say, "*The right* understanding *of* a sentence," &c. 2. "Elopement is a running *away,* or private departure."—*Webster's El. Spelling-Book,* p. 102. Write "*running-away*" as one word. 3. "If they [Milton's descriptions] have any *faults,* it is their *alluding too frequently* to matters of learning, and to fables of antiquity."—*Blair's Rhet.* p. 451. Say, "If they have any *fault,* it is, *that they allude* too frequently," &c.

NOTE V.—When the participle is followed by an adjective, its conversion into a noun appears to be improper; because the construction of the adjective becomes anomalous, and its relation doubtful: as, "When we speak of '*ambition's being restless,*' or, 'a *disease's being deceitful.*'"—*Murray's Gram.* i, p. 346; *Kirkham's,* p. 224. This ought to be, "When we speak of *ambition as* being restless, or a *disease as* being deceitful;" but Dr. Blair, from whom the text originally came, appears to have written it thus: "When we speak of *ambition's* being restless, or a *disease* being deceitful."—*Lect.* xvi, p. 155. This is *inconsistent with itself;* for one noun is possessive, and the other, objective.

NOTE VI.—When a compound participle is converted into a noun, the hyphen seems to be necessary, to prevent ambiguity; but such compound nouns are never elegant, and it is in general better to avoid them, by some change in the expression. Example: "Even as *the being healed* of a wound, presupposeth the plaster or salve: but not, on the contrary; for the application of the plaster presupposeth not *the being healed.*"—*Barclay's Works,* Vol. i, p. 143. The phrase, "*the being healed,*" ought to mean only, *the creature healed ;* and not, *the being-healed*, or *the healing received*, which is what the writer intended. But the simple word *healing* might have been used in the latter sense ; for, in participial nouns, the distinctions of *voice* and of *tense* are commonly disregarded.

NOTE VII.—A participle should not be used where the infinitive mood, the verbal noun, a common substantive, or a phrase equivalent, will better express the meaning. Examples : 1. " But *placing* an accent on the second syllable of these words, would entirely derange them."—*Murray's Gram.* i, p. 239. Say rather, " But, *to place* an accent — But *the* placing *of* an accent — or, But an *accent placed* on the second syllable of these words, would entirely derange them." 2. " To require *their being* in that case."—*Ib.* ii, p. 21. Say, " To require *them to be* in that case." 3. " She regrets not having read it."—*West's Letters*, p. 216. Say, " She regrets *that she has not* read it." Or, " She *does not regret that she has* read it." For the text is equivocal, and admits either of these senses.

NOTE VIII.—A participle used for a nominative after *be, is, was*, &c., produces a construction which is more naturally understood to be a compound form of the verb ; and which is therefore not well adapted to the sense intended, when one tells what something is, was, or may be. Examples : 1. " Whose business *is shoeing* animals." —*O. B Peirce's Gram.* p. 365. Say, " Whose business *it* is, *to shoe* animals ;" —or, " Whose business is *the* shoeing *of* animals." 2. " This *was in fact converting* the deposite to his own use."—*Murray's Key*, ii, p. 200. Say rather, " This was in fact *a* converting *of* the deposite to his own use."—*Ib.*

NOTE IX.—Verbs of *preventing* should be made to govern, not the participle in *ing*, nor what are called substantive phrases, but the objective case of a noun or pronoun ; and if a participle follow, it ought to be governed by the preposition *from* : as, " But the admiration due to so eminent a poet, must not *prevent us from remarking* some other particulars in which he has failed."—*Blair's Rhet.* p. 438. Examples of error : 1. " I endeavoured to prevent *letting him* escape."—*Ingersoll's Gram.* p. 150. Say,—" to prevent *his escape.*" 2. " To prevent *its being connected* with the nearest noun."—*Churchill's Gram.* p. 367. Say, " To prevent *it from* being connected," &c. 3. " To prevent *it bursting* out with open violence."—*Robertson's America*, Vol. ii, p 146. Say, " To prevent it *from* bursting out," &c. 4. " To prevent *their injuring or murdering of* others."—*Brown's Divinity*, p. 26. Say rather, " To prevent *them from* injuring or murdering *others.*"

NOTE X.—In the use of participles and of verbal nouns, the leading word in sense should always be made the leading or governing word in the construction ; and where there is reason to doubt whether the possessive case or some other ought to come before the participle, it is better to reject both, and vary the expression. Examples : "Any person may easily convince himself of the truth of this, by listening to *foreigners conversing* in a language [which] he does not understand."—*Churchill's Gram.* p. 361. " It is a relic of the ancient *style abounding* with negatives."—*Ib.* p. 367. These forms are right ; though the latter might be varied, by the insertion of " *which abounds* " for " *abounding.*" But the celebrated examples before cited, about the " *lady holding up* her train," or the " *lady's holding up* her train," — the " *person dismissing* his servant," or the " *person's dismissing* his servant," — the " *horse running* to-day," or the " *horse's running* to-day," — and many others which some grammarians suppose to be interchangeable, are equally bad in both forms.

NOTE XI.—Participles, in general, however construed, should have a clear reference to the proper subject of the being, action, or passion. The following sentence is therefore faulty : " By *establishing* good laws, our *peace* is secured."—*Russell's Gram.* p. 88 ; *Folker's*, 27. Peace not being the *establisher* of the laws, these authors should have said, " By *establishing* good laws, *we* secure our peace." " There *will be no danger* of spoiling their faces, or of *gaining* converts."—*Murray's Key*, ii, p. 201. This sentence is to me utterly unintelligible. If the context were known, there might possibly be some sense in saying, " *They* will be *in* no danger of spoiling their faces," &c. " That law is annulled, in the very *act of its being made.*"—

O. B. Peirce's Gram. p 267. "The act of MAKING a law," is a phrase intelligible; but, "the act of its BEING MADE," is a downright solecism — a positive absurdity.

NOTE XII.—A needless or indiscriminate use of participles for nouns, or of nouns or participles, is inelegant, if not improper, and ought therefore to be avoided. Examples: "Of denotes possession or belonging."—Murray's Gram. i, p. 118; Ingersoll's, 71. "The preposition of, frequently implies possession, property, or belonging to."—Cooper's Pl. and Pr. Gram. p. 137. Say, "Of frequently denotes possession, or the relation of property." "England perceives the folly of the denying of such concessions."—Nixon's Parser, p. 149. Expunge the and the last of, that denying may stand as a participle.

NOTE XIII.—Perfect participles being variously formed, care should be taken to express them agreeably to the best usage, and also to distinguish them from the preterits of their verbs, where there is any difference of form. Example: "It would be well, if all writers who endeavour to be accurate, would be careful to avoid a corruption at present so prevalent, of saying, it was wrote, for, it was written; he was drove, for, he was driven; I have went, for, I have gone, &c. in all which instances a verb is absurdly used to supply the proper participle, without any necessity from the want of such word."—Harris's Hermes, p. 186.

IMPROPRIETIES FOR CORRECTION.

FALSE SYNTAX UNDER RULE XX.

EXAMPLES UNDER NOTE I.—EXPUNGE OF.

"In forming of his sentences, he was very exact."—Error noticed by Murray, i, p. 194.

[FORMULE.—Not proper, because the preposition of is used after the participle forming, whose verb does not require it. But, according to Note 1st under Rule 20th, "Active participles have the same government as the verbs from which they are derived; the preposition of, therefore, should not be used after the participle, when the verb does not require it." Therefore, of should be omitted; thus, "In forming his sentences, he was very exact."]

"For not believing of which I condemn them."—Barclay's Works, iii, 354. "To prohibit his hearers from reading of that book."—Ib. i, 223. "You will please them exceedingly, in crying down of ordinances."—MITCHELL: ib. i, 219. "The war-wolf subsequently became an engine for casting of stones."—Constable's Miscellany, xxi, 117. "The art of dressing of hides and working in leather was practised."—Ib. xxi, 101. "In the choice they had made of him, for restoring of order."—Rollin's Hist. ii, 37. "The Arabians exercised themselves by composing of orations and poems."—Sale's Koran, p. 17. "Behold, the widowwoman was there gathering of sticks."—1 Kings, xvii, 10. "The priests were busied in offering of burnt-offerings."—2 Chron. xxxv, 14. "But Asahel would not turn aside from following of him."—2 Sam. ii, 21. "He left off building of Ramah, and dwelt in Tirzah." —1 Kings, xv, 21. "Those who accuse us of denying of it, belie us."—Barclay's Works, iii, 280. "And breaking of bread from house to house."—Ib. i, 192. "Those that set about repairing of the walls."—Ib. i, 459. "And secretly begetting of divisions."—Ib. i, 521. "Whom he had made use of in gathering of his church."—Ib. i, 535. "In defining and distinguishing of the acceptions and uses of those particles."—Walker's Particles, p. 12.

"In punishing of this, we overthrow
The laws of nations and of nature too."—Dryden, p. 92.

UNDER NOTE II.—ARTICLES REQUIRE OF.

"The mixing them makes a miserable jumble of truth and fiction."—Kames, El. of Crit. ii, 357. "The same objection lies against the employing statues."—Ib. ii, 358. "More efficacious than the venting opulence upon the Fine Arts."—Ib. Vol. i, p. viii. "It is the giving different names to the same object."—Ib. ii, 19. "When we have in view the erecting a column."—Ib. ii, 56. "The straining an elevated subject beyond due bounds, is a vice not so frequent."—Ib. i, 206. "The cutting evergreens in the shape of animals is very ancient."—Ib. ii, 327. "The keeping juries, without meet, drink or fire, can be accounted for only on the same idea."—Webster's Essays, p. 301. "The writing the verbs at length on his slate, will be a very useful exercise."—Beck's Gram. p. 20. "The avoiding them is not an object of any moment."—Sheridan's Lect. p. 180. "Comparison is the increasing or decreasing the Signification of a Word by Degrees."—British Gram. p. 97. "Comparison is the Increasing or Decreasing the Quality by Degrees."—Buchanan's English Syntax, p. 27. "The placing a Circumstance before the Word with which it is connected, is the easiest of all Inversion."—Ib. p. 140. "What is emphasis? It is the emitting a stronger and fuller sound of voice," &c.—Bradley's Gram. p. 108. "Besides, the varying the terms will render the use of them more familiar."—Alex. Murray's Gram. p. 25. "And yet the confining themselves to this true principle, has misled them!"—Horne Tooke's Diversions, Vol. i, p. 15.

"What is here commanded, is merely the relieving his misery."—*Wayland's Moral Science*, p. 417. "The accumulating too great a quantity of knowledge at random, overloads the mind instead of adorning it."—*Formey's Belles-Lettres*, p. 5. "For the compassing his point."—*Rollin's Hist.* ii, 35. "To the introducing such an inverted order of things."—*Butler's Analogy*, p. 95. "Which require only the doing an external action."—*Ib.* p. 186. "The imprisoning my body is to satisfy your wills."—GEO. FOX: *Sewel's Hist.* p. 47. "Who oppose the conferring such extensive command on one person."—*Duncan's Cicero*, p. 130. "Luxury contributed not a little to the enervating their forces."—*Sale's Koran*, p. 49. "The keeping one day of the week for a sabbath."—*Barclay's Works*, i, 202. "The doing a thing is contrary to the forbearing of it."—*Ib.* i, 527. "The doubling the Sigma is, however, sometimes regular."—*Knight, on the Greek Alphabet*, p. 29. "The inserting the common aspirate too, is improper."—*Ib.* p. 134. "But in Spenser's time the pronouncing the *ed* seems already to have been something of an archaism."—*Philological Museum*, Vol. i, p. 656. "And to the reconciling the effect of their verses on the eye."—*Ib.* i, 659. "When it was not in their power to hinder the taking the whole."—*Brown's Estimate*, ii, 155. "He had indeed given the orders himself for the shutting the gates."—*Ibid.* "So his whole life was a doing the will of the Father."—*Penington*, iv, 99. "It signifies the suffering or receiving the action expressed."—*Priestley's Gram.* p. 37. "The pretended crime therefore was the declaring himself to be the Son of God."—*West's Letters*, p. 210. "Parsing is the resolving a sentence into its different parts of speech."—*Beck's Gram.* p. 26.

UNDER NOTE II.—ADJECTIVES REQUIRE OF.

"There is no expecting the admiration of beholders."—*Baxter*. "There is no hiding you in the house."—*Shakspeare*. "For the better regulating government in the province of Massachusetts."—*British Parliament*. "The precise marking the shadowy boundaries of a complex government."—*J. Q. Adams's Rhet.* Vol. ii, p. 6. "[This state of discipline] requires the voluntary foregoing many things which we desire, and setting ourselves to what we have no inclination to."—*Butler's Analogy*, p. 115. "This amounts to an active setting themselves against religion."—*Ib.* p. 264. "Which engaged our ancient friends to the orderly establishing our Christian discipline."—*N. E. Discip.* p. 117. "Some men are so unjust that there is no securing our own property or life, but by opposing force to force."—*Brown's Divinity*, p. 26. "An Act for the better securing the Rights and Liberties of the Subject."—*Geo. III*, 31st. "Miraculous curing the sick is discontinued."—*Barclay's Works*, iii, 137. "It would have been no transgressing the apostle's rule."—*Ib.* p. 146. "As far as consistent with the proper conducting the business of the House."—*Elmore, in Congress*, 1839. "Because he would have no quarrelling at the just condemning them at that day."—*Law and Grace*, p. 42. "That transferring this natural manner — will ensure propriety."—*Rush, on the Voice*, p. 372. "If a man were porter of hell-gate, he should have old turning the key."—*Macbeth*, Act ii, Sc. 3.

UNDER NOTE II.—POSSESSIVES REQUIRE OF.

"So very simple a thing as a man's wounding himself."—*Blair's Rhet.* p. 97; *Murray's Gram.* i, p. 317. "Or with that man's avowing his designs."—*Blair*, p. 104; *Murray*, p. 308; *Parker and Fox, Part III*, p. 88. "On his putting the question."—*Adams's Rhet.* Vol. ii. p. 111. "The importance of teachers' requiring their pupils to read each section many times over."—*Kirkham's Elocution*, p. 169. "Politeness is a kind of forgetting one's self in order to be agreeable to others."—*Ramsay's Cyrus*. "Much, therefore, of the merit, and the agreeableness of epistolary writing, will depend on its introducing us into some acquaintance with the writer."—*Blair's Rhet.* p. 370; *Mack's Dissertation in his Gram.* p. 175. "Richard's restoration to respectability, depends on his paying his debts."—*O. B. Peirce's Gram.* p. 176. "Their supplying ellipses where none ever existed; their parsing words, of sentences already full and perfect, as though depending on words understood."—*Ib.* p. 375. "Her veiling herself and shedding tears," &c., "her upbraiding Paris for his cowardice," &c.—*Blair's Rhet.* p. 433. "A preposition may be known by its admitting after it a personal pronoun, in the objective case."—*Murray's Gram.* p. 28; *Alger's*, 14; *Bacon's*, 16; *Merchant's*, 18; and others. "But this forms no just objection to its denoting time."—*Murray's Gram.* p. 65. "Of men's violating or disregarding the relations which God has placed them in here."—*Butler's Analogy*, p. 164. "Success, indeed, no more decides for the right, than a man's killing his antagonist in a duel."—*Campbell's Rhet.* p. 295. "His reminding them."—*Kirkham's Elocution*, p. 123. "This mistake was corrected by his preceptor's causing him to plant some beans."—*Ib.* p. 235. "Their neglecting this was ruinous."—*Frost's El. of Gram.* p. 82. "That he was serious, appears from his distinguishing the others as 'finite.'"—*Felch's Gram.* p. 10. "His hearers are not at all sensible of his doing it."—*Sheridan's Elocution*, p. 119.

UNDER NOTE III.—CHANGE THE EXPRESSION.

"An allegory is the saying one thing, and meaning another; a double-meaning or dilogy is the saying only one thing, but having two in view."—*Philological Museum*, Vol. i, p. 461.

"A verb may generally be distinguished, by its making sense with any of the personal pronouns, or the word *to* before it."—*Murray's Gram.* p. 28; *Alger's*, 13; *Bacon's*, 10; *Comly's*, and many others. "A noun may, in general, be distinguished by its taking an article before it, or by its making sense of itself."—*Merchant's Gram.* p. 17; *Murray's*, 27; &c. "An Adjective may usually be known by its making sense with the addition of the word *thing*: as, a *good* thing; a *bad* thing."—*Same Authors.* "It is seen in the objective case, from its denoting the object affected by the act of leaving."—*O. B. Peirce's Gram.* p. 44. "It is seen in the possessive case, from its denoting the *possessor* of something."—*Ibid.* "The name *man* is caused by the adname *whatever* to be twofold subjective case, from its denoting, of itself, one person as the subject of the two remarks."—*Ib.* p. 56. "*When*, as used in the last line, is a connective, from its joining that line to the other part of the sentence." —*Ib.* p. 59. "From their denoting reciprocation."—*Ib.* p. 64. "To allow them the making use of that liberty."—*Sale's Koran*, p. 116. "The worst effect of it is, the fixing on your mind a habit of indecision."—*Todd's Student's Manual*, p. 60. "And you groan the more deeply, as you reflect that there is no shaking it off."—*Ib.* p. 47. "I know of nothing that can justify the having recourse to a Latin translation of a Greek writer."—*Coleridge's Introduction*, p. 16. "Humour is the making others act or talk absurdly."—*Hazlitt's Lectures.* "There are remarkable instances of their not affecting each other."—*Butler's Analogy*, p. 150. "The leaving Cæsar out of the commission was not from any slight."—*Life of Cicero*, p. 44. "Of the receiving this toleration thankfully I shall say no more."—*Dryden's Works*, p. 88. "Henrietta was delighted with Julia's working lace so very well."—*O. B. Peirce's Gram.* p. 255. "And it is from their representing each two different words that the confusion has arisen."—*Booth's Introd.* p. 42. "Æschylus died of a fracture of his skull, caused by an eagle's letting fall a tortoise on his head."—*Biog. Dict.* "He doubted their having it."—*Felch's Comp. Gram.* p. 81. "The making ourselves clearly understood, is the chief end of speech."—*Sheridan's Elocution*, p. 68. "There is no discovering in their countenances, any signs which are the natural concomitants of the feelings of the heart."—*Ib.* p. 165. "Nothing can be more common or less proper than to speak of a *river's emptying itself*."—*Campbell's Rhet.* p. 186. "Our not using the former expression, is owing to this." —*Bullions's E. Gram.* p. 59.

UNDER NOTE IV.—DISPOSAL OF ADVERBS.

"To this generally succeeds the division, or the laying down the method of the discourse."—*Blair's Rhet.* p. 311. "To the pulling down of strong holds."—2 Cor. x, 4. "Can a mere buckling on a military weapon infuse courage?"—*Brown's Estimate*, i, 62. "Living expensively and luxuriously destroys health."—*Murray's Gram.* i, 234. "By living frugally and temperately, health is preserved."—*Ibid.* "By living temperately, our health is promoted."—*Ib.* p. 227. "By the doing away of the necessity."—*The Friend*, xiii, 157. "He recommended to them, however, the immediately calling of the whole community to the church."—*Gregory's Dict. w. Ventriloquism.* "The separation of large numbers in this manner certainly facilitates the reading them rightly."—*Churchill's Gram.* p. 303. "From their merely admitting of a twofold grammatical construction."—*Philol. Museum*, i, 463. "His gravely lecturing his friend about it."—*Ib.* i, 478. "For the blotting out of sin."— *Gurney's Evidences*, p. 140. "From the not using of water."—*Barclay's Works*, i, 189. "By the gentle dropping in of a pebble."—*Sheridan's Elocution*, p. 125. "To the carrying on a great part of that general course of nature."—*Butler's Analogy*, p. 127. "Then the not interposing is so far from being a ground of complaint."—*Ib.* p. 147. "The bare omission, or rather the not employing of what is used."—*Campbell's Rhet.* p. 180; *Jamieson's*, 48. "Bringing together incongruous adverbs is a very common fault."—*Churchill's Gram.* p. 329. "This is a presumptive proof of its not proceeding from them."—*Butler's Analogy*, p. 186. "It represents him in a character to which the acting unjustly is peculiarly unsuitable."—*Campbell's Rhet.* p. 372. "They will aim at something higher than merely the dealing out of harmonious sounds."—*Kirkham's Elocution*, p. 65. "This is intelligible and sufficient; and going farther seems beyond the reach of our faculties."—*Butler's Analogy*, p. 147. "Apostrophe is a turning off from the regular course of the subject."—*Murray's Gram.* p. 348; *Jamieson's Rhet.* 185. "Even Isabella was finally prevailed upon to assent to the sending out a commission to investigate his conduct."—*Life of Columbus.* "For the turning away of the simple shall slay them."—*Prov.* i, 32.

"Thick fingers always should command
Without the stretching out the hand."—*King's Poems*, p. 585.

UNDER NOTE V.—PARTICIPLES WITH ADJECTIVES.

"Is there any Scripture speaks of the light's being inward?"—*Barclay's Works*, i, 367. "For I believe not the being positive therein essential to salvation."—*Ib.* iii, 330. "Our not being able to act an uniform right part without some thought and care."—*Butler's Analogy*, p. 122. "Upon supposition of its being reconcileable with the constitution of nature."—*Ib.* p. 128. "Upon account of its not being discoverable by reason or experience."—*Ib.* p. 170. "Upon account of their being unlike the known course of nature."—

Ib. p. 171. "Our being able to discern reasons for them, gives a positive credibility to the history of them."—*Ib.* p. 174. "From its not being universal."—*Ib.* p. 175. "That they may be turned into the passive participle in *dus* is no decisive argument in favour of their being passive."—*Grant's Lat. Gram.* p. 233. "With the implied idea of St. Paul's being then *absent* from the Corinthians."—*Kirkham's Elocution,* p. 123. "On account of its becoming gradually weaker, until it finally dies away into silence."—*Ib.* p. 32. "Not without the author's being fully aware."—*Ib.* p. 84. "Being witty out of season, is one sort of folly."—*Sheffield's Works,* ii, 172. "Its being generally susceptible of a much stronger evidence."—*Campbell's Rhet.* p. 102. "At least their being such rarely enhanced our opinion, either of their abilities or of their virtues."—*Ib.* p. 162. "Which were the ground of our being one."—*Barclay's Works,* i, 513. "But they may be distinguished from it by their being intransitive."—*Murray's Gram.* i, 60. "To distinguish the higher degree of our persuasion of a thing's being possible."—*Churchill's Gram.* p. 234.

"His being idle, and dishonest too,
      Was that which caus'd his utter overthrow."—*Tobitt's Gram.* p. 61.

UNDER NOTE VI.—COMPOUND VERBAL NOUNS.

"When it denotes being subjected to the exertion of another."—*Booth's Introd.* p. 51. "In a passive sense, it signifies being subjected to the influence of the action."—*Felch's Comp. Gram.* p. 60. "The being abandoned by our friends is very deplorable."—*Goldsmith's Greece,* i, 181. "Without waiting for their being attacked by the Macedonians."—*Ib.* ii, 97. "In progress of time, words were wanted to express men's being connected with certain conditions of fortune."—*Blair's Rhet.* p. 135. "Our being made acquainted with pain and sorrow, has a tendency to bring us to a settled moderation."—*Butler's Analogy,* p. 121. "The chancellor's being attached to the king secured his crown; The general's having failed in this enterprise occasioned his disgrace; John's having been writing a long time had wearied him."—*Murray's Gram.* p. 66; *Sanborn's,* 171; *Cooper's,* 96; *Ingersoll's,* 46; *Fisk's,* 83; *and others.* "The sentence should be, 'John's having been writing a long time *has* wearied him.'"—*Wright's Gram.* p. 186. "Much depends on this rule's being observed."—*Murray's Key,* ii, 195. "He mentioned a boy's having been corrected for his faults; The boy's having been corrected is shameful to him."—*Alger's Gram.* p. 65; *Merchant's,* 93. "The greater the difficulty of remembrance is, and the more important the being remembered is to the attainment of the ultimate end."—*Campbell's Rhet.* p. 90. "If the parts in the composition of similar objects were always in equal quantity, their being compounded would make no odds."—*Ib.* p. 65. "Circumstances, not of such importance as that the scope of the relation is affected by their being known."—*Ib.* p. 379. "A passive verb expresses the receiving of an action or the being acted upon; as, 'John is beaten.'"—*Frost's El. of Gram.* p. 16. "So our Language has another great Advantage, namely its not being diversified by Genders."—*Buchanan's Gram.* p. 20. "The having been slandered is no fault of Peter."—*Frost's El. of Gram.* p. 82. "Without being Christ's friends, there is no being justified."—*William Penn.* "Being accustomed to danger, begets intrepidity, i. e. lessens fear."—*Butler's Analogy,* p. 112. "It is, not being affected so and so, but acting, which forms those habits."—*Ib.* p. 113. "In order to our being satisfied of the truth of the apparent paradox."—*Campbell's Rhet.* p. 164. "Tropes consist in a word's being employed to signify something that is different from its original and primitive meaning."—*Blair's Rhet.* p. 132; *Jamieson's,* 140; *Murray's Gram.* 337; *Kirkham's,* 222. "A Trope consists in a word's being employed," &c.—*Hiley's Gram.* p. 133. "The scriptural view of our being saved from punishment."—*Gurney's Evidences,* p. 124. "To submit and obey, is not a renouncing a being led by the Spirit."—*Barclay's Works,* i, 542.

UNDER NOTE VII.—PARTICIPLES FOR INFINITIVES, &c.

"Teaching little children is a pleasant employment."—*Bartlett's School Manual,* ii, 68. "Denying or compromising principles of truth is virtually denying their divine Author."—*Reformer,* i, 34. "A severe critic might point out some expressions that would bear being retrenched."—*Blair's Rhet.* p. 206. "Never attempt prolonging the pathetic too much."—*Ib.* p. 323. "I now recollect having mentioned a report of that nature."—*Whiting's Reader,* p. 132. "Nor of the necessity which there is for their being restrained in them."—*Butler's Analogy,* p. 116. "But doing what God commands, because he commands it, is obedience, though it proceeds from hope or fear."—*Ib.* p. 124. "Simply closing the nostrils does not so entirely prevent resonance."—*Music of Nature,* p. 484. "Yet they absolutely refuse doing so."—*Harris's Hermes,* p. 264. "But Artaxerxes could not refuse pardoning him."—*Goldsmith's Greece,* i, 173. "Doing them in the best manner is signified by the name of these arts."—*Rush, on the Voice,* p. 360. "Behaving well for the time to come, may be insufficient."—*Butler's Analogy,* p. 198. "The compiler proposed publishing that part by itself."—*Dr. Adam, Rom. Antiq.* p. v. "To smile upon those we should censure, is bringing guilt upon ourselves."—*Kirkham's Elocution,* p. 108. "But it would be doing great injustice to that illustrious orator to bring his genius down to the same level."—*Ib.* p. 28. "Doubting things go ill, often hurts more than to be sure they do."—*Beauties of Shak.* p. 203.

"This is called straining a metaphor."—*Blair's Rhet.* p. 150; *Murray's Gram.* i, 341. "This is what Aristotle calls giving manners to the poem."—*Blair's Rhet.* p. 427. "The painter's being entirely confined to that part of time which he has chosen, deprives him of the power of exhibiting various stages of the same action."—*Murray's Gram.* i, 195. "It imports retrenching all superfluities, and pruning the expression."—*Blair's Rhet.* p. 94; *Jamieson's,* 64; *Murray's Gram.* p. 301; *Kirkham's,* 220. "The necessity for our being thus exempted is further apparent."—*West's Letters,* p. 40. "Her situation in life does not allow of her being genteel in every thing."—*Ib.* p. 57. "Provided you do not dislike being dirty when you are invisible."—*Ib.* p. 58. "There is now an imperious necessity for her being acquainted with her title to eternity."—*Ib.* p. 120. "Discarding the restraints of virtue, is misnamed ingenuousness."—*Ib.* p. 105. "The legislature prohibits opening shop of a Sunday."—*Ib.* p. 66. "To attempt proving that any thing is right."—*O. B. Peirce's Gram.* p. 256. "The comma directs making a pause of a second in duration, or less."—*Ib.* p. 280. "The rule which directs putting other words into the place of it, is wrong."—*Ib.* p. 326. "They direct calling the specifying adjectives or adnames adjective pronouns."—*Ib.* p. 338. "William dislikes attending court."—*Frost's El. of Gram.* p. 82. "It may perhaps be worth while remarking that Milton makes a distinction."—*Philological Museum,* i, 659. "Professing regard, and acting differently, discover a base mind."—*Murray's Key,* p. 206; *Bullions's E. Gram.* pp. 82 and 112; *Lennie's,* 58. "You have proved beyond contradiction, that acting thus is the sure way to procure such an object."—*Campbell's Rhet.* p. 92.

UNDER NOTE VIII.—PARTICIPLES AFTER BE, IS, &c.

"Irony is expressing ourselves in a manner contrary to our thoughts."—*Murray's Gram.* p. 353; *Kirkham's,* 225; *Goldsbury's,* 90. "Irony is saying one thing and meaning the reverse of what that expression would represent."—*O. B. Peirce's Gram.* p. 303. "An Irony is dissembling or changing the proper signification of a word or sentence to quite the contrary."—*Fisher's Gram.* p. 151. "Irony is expressing ourselves contrary to what we mean."—*Sanborn's Gram.* p. 286. "This is in a great Measure delivering their own Compositions."—*Buchanan's Gram.* p. xxvi. "But purity is using rightly the words of the language."—*Jamieson's Rhet.* p. 59. "But the most important object is settling the English quantity."—*Walker's Key,* p. 17. "When there is no affinity, the transition from one meaning to another is taking a very wide step."—*Campbell's Rhet.* p. 293. "It would be losing time to attempt further to illustrate it."—*Ib.* p. 79. "This is leaving the sentence too bare, and making it to be, if not nonsense, hardly sense."—*Cobbett's Gram.* No. 227. "This is requiring more labours from every private member."—*West's Letters,* p. 120. "Is not this using one measure for our neighbours, and another for ourselves?"—*Ib.* p. 200. "Is it not charging God foolishly, when we give these dark colourings to human nature?" —*Ib.* p. 171. "This is not enduring the cross as a disciple of Jesus Christ, but snatching at it like a partizan of Swift's Jack."—*Ib.* p. 175. "What is Spelling? It is combining letters to form syllables and words."—*O. B. Peirce's Gram.* p. 18. "It is choosing such letters to compose words," &c.—*Ibid.* "What is Parsing? (1.) It is describing the nature, use, and powers of words."—*Ib.* pp. 22 and 192. (2.) "For parsing is describing the words of a sentence as they are used."—*Ib.* p. 10. (3.) "Parsing is only describing the nature and relations of words as they are used."—*Ib.* p. 11. (4.) "Parsing, let the pupil understand and remember, is describing facts concerning words; or representing them in their offices and relations as they are."—*Ib.* p. 34. (5.) "Parsing is resolving and explaining words according to the rules of grammar."—*Ib.* p. 326. (6.) "Parsing a word, remember, is enumerating and describing its various relations and qualities, and its grammatical relations to other words in the sentence."—*Ib.* p. 325. (7.) "For parsing a word is enumerating and describing its various properties and relations *to the* sentence."—*Ib.* p. 326. (8.) "Parsing a noun is telling of what person, number, gender, and case it is; and also telling all its grammatical relations in a sentence with respect to other words."— *Ingersoll's Gram.* p. 16. (9.) "Parsing any part of speech is telling all its properties and relations."—*Ibid.* (10.) "Parsing is resolving a sentence into its elements."—*Fowler's E. Gram.* 1850, § 588. "The highway of the righteous, is, departing from evil."—*O. B. Peirce's Gram.* p. 168. "Besides, the first step towards exhibiting truth should be removing the veil of error."—*Ib.* p. 377. "Punctuation is dividing sentences and the words of sentences, by pauses."—*Ib.* p. 280. "Another fault is using the preterimperfect *shook* instead of the participle *shaken.*"—*Churchill's Gram.* p. 259. "Her employment is drawing maps."— *Alger's Gram.* p. 65. "Going to the play, according to his notion, is leading a sensual life, and exposing ones self to the strongest temptations. This is begging the question, and therefor requires no answer."—*Formey's Belles-Lettres,* p. 217. "It is overvaluing ourselves to reduce every thing to the narrow measure of our capacities."—*Murray's Gram.* i, 193; *Ingersoll's,* 199. "What is vocal language? It is speaking; or expressing ideas by the human voice."—*Sanders, Spelling-Book,* p. 7.

UNDER NOTE IX.—VERBS OF PREVENTING.

"The annulling power of the constitution prevented that enactment's becoming a law." —*O. B. Peirce's Gram.* p. 267. "Which prevents the manner's being brief."—*Ib.* p. 365.

"This close prevents their bearing forward as nominatives."—*Rush, on the Voice*, p. 153. "Because this prevents its growing drowzy."—*Formey's Belles-Lettres*, p. 5. "Yet this does not prevent his being great."—*Ib.* p. 27. "To prevent its being insipid."—*Ib.* p. 112. "Or whose interruptions did not prevent its being continued."—*Ib.* p. 167. "This by no means prevents their being also punishments."—*Wayland's Moral Science*, p. 123. "This hinders not their being also, in the strictest sense, punishments."—*Ibid.* "The noise made by the rain and wind prevented their being heard."—*Goldsmith's Greece*, Vol. i, p. 118. "He endeavoured to prevent its taking effect."—*Ib.* i, 128. "So sequestered as to prevent their being explored."—*West's Letters*, p. 62. "Who prevented her making a more pleasant party."—*Ib.* p. 65. "To prevent our being tossed about by every wind of doctrine."—*Ib.* p. 123. "After the infirmities of age prevented his bearing his part of official duty."—*Religious World*, ii, 193. "Understanding the literal sense would have prevented their condemning the guiltless."—*Butler's Analogy*, p. 168. "To prevent splendid trifles passing for matters of importance."—*Kames, El. of Crit.* i, 310. "Which prevents his exerting himself to any good purpose."—*Beattie's Moral Science*, i, 146. "The want of the observance of this rule, very frequently prevents our being punctual in our duties."—*Student's Manual*, p. 65. "Nothing will prevent his being a student, and his possessing the means of study."—*Ib.* p. 127. "Does the present accident hinder your being honest and brave?"—*Collier's Antoninus*, p. 61. "The e is omitted to prevent two es coming together."—*Fowle's Gram.* p. 34. "A pronoun is used for or in place of a noun,—to prevent repeating the noun."—*Sanborn's Gram.* p. 13. "Diversity in the style relieves the ear, and prevents it being tired with the too frequent recurrence of the rhymes."—*Campbell's Rhet.* p. 166. "Diversity in the style relieves the ear, and prevents its being tired," &c.—*Murray's Gram.* i, p. 362. "Timidity and false shame prevent our opposing vicious customs."—*Murray's Key*, ii, 236 ; *Sanborn's Gram.* 171 ; *Merchant's*, 205. "To prevent their being moved by such."—*Campbell's Rhet.* p. 155. "Some obstacle or impediment, that prevents its taking place."—*Priestley's Gram.* p. 34. "Which prevents our making a progress towards perfection."—*Sheridan's Elocution*, p. 4. "This method of distinguishing words, must prevent any regular proportion of time being settled."—*Ib.* p. 67. "That nothing but affectation can prevent its always taking place."—*Ib.* p. 78. "This did not prevent John's being acknowledged and solemnly inaugurated Duke of Normandy."—HENRY: *Webster's Philos. Gram.* p. 182; his *Improved Gram.* 130; *Sanborn's Gram.* 189; *Fowler's*, 8vo, 1850, p. 541.

UNDER NOTE X.—THE LEADING WORD IN SENSE.

"This would preclude the possibility of a nouns' or any other word's ever being in the possessive case."—*O. B. Peirce's Gram.* p. 338. "A great part of our pleasure arises from the plan or story being well conducted."—*Blair's Rhet.* p. 18. "And we have no reason to wonder at this being the case."—*Ib.* p. 249. "She objected only, as Cicero says, to Oppianicus having two sons by his present wife."—*Ib.* p. 274. "The Britons being subdued by the Saxons, was a necessary consequence of their having called in these Saxons, to their assistance."—*Ib.* p. 329. "What he had there said, concerning the Saxons expelling the Britons, and changing the customs, the religion, and the language of the country, is a clear and good reason for our present language being Saxon rather than British."—*Ib.* p. 230. "The only material difference between them, besides the one being short and the other being prolonged, is, that a metaphor always explains itself by the words that are connected with it."—*Ib.* p. 151; *Murray's Gram.* p. 342. "The description of Death's advancing to meet Satan, on his arrival."—*Rush, on the Voice*, p. 156. "Is not the bare fact of God being the witness of it, sufficient ground for its credibility to rest upon ?"—*Chalmers, Serm.* p. 286. "As in the case of one entering upon a new study."—*Beattie's Moral Science*, i, 77. "The manner of these affecting the copula is called the imperative mode."—BP. WILKINS: *Lowth's Gram.* p. 43. "We are freed from the trouble, by our nouns having no diversity of endings."—*Buchanan's Syntax*, p. 20. "The Verb is rather indicative of the actions being *doing*, or *done*, than *the time when*, but indeed the ideas are undistinguishable."—*Booth's Introd.* p. 69. "Nobody would doubt of this being a sufficient proof."—*Campbell's Rhet.* p. 66. "Against the doctrine here maintained, of conscience being, as well as reason, a natural faculty."—*Beattie's M. Sci.* i, 263. "It is one cause of the Greek and English languages being much more easy to learn, than the Latin."—*Bucke's Classical Gram.* p. 26. "I have not been able to make out a solitary instance of such being the fact."—*Liberator, I,* 40. "An angel's forming the appearance of a hand, and writing the king's condemnation on the wall, checked their mirth, and filled them with terror."—*Wood's Dict. w. Belshazzar.* "The prisoners' having attempted to escape, aroused the keepers."—*O. B. Peirce's Gram.* p. 357. "I doubt not, in the least, of this having been one cause of the multiplication of divinities in the heathen world."—*Blair's Rhet.* p. 155. "From the general rule he lays down, of the verbs being the parent word of all language."—*Diversions of Purley*, Vol. i, p. 227. "He was accused of himself being idle."—*Felch's Comp. Gram.* p. 52. "Our meeting is generally dissatisfied with him so removing."—*Wm. Edmondson.* "The spectacle is too rare of men's deserving solid fame while not seeking it."—*Prof. Bush's Lecture on Swedenborg.* "What further need was there of an other priest rising?" See *Key.*

Under Note XI.—Reference of Participles.

"Viewing them separately, different emotions are produced."—*Kames, El. of Crit.* ii, 344. "But leaving this doubtful, another objection occurs."—*Ib.* ii, 358. "Proceeding from one particular to another, the subject grew under his hand."—*Ib.* i, 27. "But this is still an interruption, and a link of the chain broken."—*Ib.* ii, 314. "After some days hunting, Cyrus communicated his design to his officers."—*Rollin,* ii, 66. "But it is made, without the appearance of making it in form."—*Blair's Rhet.* p. 358. "These would have had a better effect disjoined thus."—*Ib.* p. 119; *Murray's Gram.* i, 309. "An improper diphthong has but one of the vowels sounded."—*Murray's Gram.* p. 9; *Alger's,* 12; *Merchant's,* 9; *Smith's,* 118; *Ingersoll's,* 4. "And being led to think of both together, my view is rendered unsteady."—*Blair's Rhet.* p. 95; *Murray's Gram.* 302; *Jamieson's Rhet.* 66. "By often doing the same thing, it becomes habitual."—*Murray's Key,* p. 257. "They remain with us in our dark and solitary hours, no less than when surrounded with friends and cheerful society." —*Ib.* p. 238. "Besides shewing what is right, the matter may be further explained by pointing out what is wrong."—*Lowth's Gram. Pref.* p. viii. "The former teaches the true pronunciation of words, comprising accent, quantity, emphasis, pause, and tone."—*Murray's Gram.* i, p. 235. "Persons may be reproved for their negligence, by saying; 'You have taken great care indeed.'"—*Ib.* i, 354. "The words preceding and following it, are in apposition to each other."—*Ib.* ii, p. 22. "Having finished his speech, the assembly dispersed." —*Cooper's Pract. Gram.* p. 97. "Were the voice to fall at the close of the last line, as many a reader is in the habit of doing."—*Kirkham's Elocution,* p. 101. "The misfortunes of his countrymen were but negatively the effects of his wrath, by depriving them of his assistance."—*Kames, El. of Crit.* ii, 299. "Taking them as nouns, this construction may be explained thus."—*Grant's Latin Gram.* p. 233. "These have an active signification, those which come from neuter verbs being excepted."—*Ib.* p. 233. "From the evidence of it not being universal."—*Butler's Analogy,* p. 84. "And this faith will continually grow, by acquainting ourselves with our own nature."—*Channing's Self-Culture,* p. 83. "Monosyllables ending with any consonant but *f, l,* or *s,* and preceded by a single vowel, never double the final consonant; excepting add, ebb," &c.—*Murray's Gram.* p. 23; *Picket's,* 10; *Merchant's,* 13; *Ingersoll's,* 8; *Fisk's,* 44; *Blair's,* 7. "The relation of being the object of the action is expressed by the change of the Noun *Maria* to *Mariam.*"—*Booth's Introd.* p. 38. "In analyzing a proposition, it is first to be divided into its logical subject and predicate." —*Andrews and Stoddard's Latin Gram.* p. 254. "In analyzing a simple sentence, it should first be resolved into its logical subject and logical predicate."—*Wells's School Gram.* 113th Ed. p. 189.

Under Note XII.—Of Participles and Nouns.

"The discovering passions instantly at their birth, is essential to our well being."—*Kames, El. of Crit.* i, 352. "I am now to enter on considering the sources of the pleasures of taste." —*Blair's Rhet.* p. 28. "The varieties in using them are, indeed many."—*Murray's Gram.* i, 319. "Changing times and seasons, removing and setting up kings, belong to Providence alone."—*Ib. Key,* ii, p. 200. "Adhering to the partitions seemed the cause of France, accepting the will that of the house of Bourbon."—*Bolingbroke, on Hist.* p. 246. "Another source of darkness in composing is, the injudicious introduction of technical words and phrases."—*Campbell's Rhet.* p. 247. "These are the rules of grammar, by the observing of which, you may avoid mistakes."—*Murray's Gram.* i, 192; *Merchant's,* 93; *Fisk's,* 135; *Ingersoll's,* 198. "By the observing of the rules, you may avoid mistakes."—*Alger's Gram.* 65. "By the observing of these rules he succeeded."—*Frost's El. of Gram.* p. 82. "Being praised was his ruin."—*Ibid.* "Deceiving is not convincing."—*Ibid.* "He never feared losing a friend."—*Ibid.* "Making books is his amusement."—*Alger's Gram.* p. 65. "We call it declining a noun."—*Ingersoll's Gram.* p. 22. "Washington, however, pursued the same policy of neutrality, and opposed firmly, taking any part in the wars of Europe."— *Hall and Baker's School Hist.* p. 294. "The following is a note of Interrogation, or asking a question (?)."—*Infant School Gram.* p. 132. "The following is a note of Admiration, or expressing wonder (!)."—*Ib.* "Omitting or using the article *a* forms a nice distinction in the sense."—*Murray's Gram.* ii, 284. "Placing the preposition before the word it governs is more graceful."—*Churchill's Gram.* p. 150. "Assistance is absolutely necessary to their recovery, and retrieving their affairs."—*Butler's Analogy,* p. 197. "Which termination, [*ish,*] when added to adjectives, imports diminution, or lessening the quality."—*Murray's Gram.* i, 131; *Kirkham's,* 172. "After what is said, will it be thought refining too much to suggest, that the different orders are qualified for different purposes?"—*Kames, El. of Crit.* ii, 114. "Who has nothing to think of but killing time."—*West's Letters,* p. 58. "It requires no nicety of ear, as in the distinguishing of tones, or measuring time."—*Sheridan's Elocution,* p. 65. "The *Possessive Case* denotes possession, or belonging to."—*Hall's Gram.* p. 7.

Under Note XIII.—Perfect Participles.

"Garcilasso was master of the language spoke by the Incas."—*Robertson's Amer.* ii, 459. "When an interesting story is broke off in the middle."—*Kames, El. of Crit.* i, 244. "Speaking of Hannibal's elephants drove back by the enemy."—*Ib.* ii, 32. "If Du Ryer had not wrote for bread, he would have equalled them."—*Formey's Belles-Lettres*, p. 166. "Pope describes a rock broke off from a mountain, and hurling to the plain."—*Kames*, ii, 106. "I have wrote *or* have written, Thou hast wrote *or* hast written, He hath *or* has wrote, *or* hath or has written;" &c.—*Dr. Ash's Gram.* p. 47; *Maltby's*, 47. "This was spoke by a pagan." —*Webster's Improved Gram.* p. 174. "But I have chose to follow the common arrangement."—*Ib.* p. 10. "The language spoke in Bengal."—*Ib.* p. 78. "And sound Sleep thus broke off, with sudden Alarms, is apt enough to discompose any one."—*Locke, on Ed.* p. 32. "This is not only the Case of those Open Sinners, before spoke of."—*Right of Tythes*, p. 26. "Some Grammarians have wrote a very perplexed and difficult doctrine on Punctuation." —*Ensell's Gram.* p. 340. "There hath a pity arose in me towards thee."—*Sewel's Hist. fol.* p. 324. "Abel is the only man that has underwent the awful change of death."—*Juvenile Theatre*, p. 4.

> "Meantime, on Afric's glowing sands,
> Smote with keen heat, the Trav'ler stands."—*Union Poems*, p. 88.

CHAPTER VIII.—ADVERBS.

The syntax of an Adverb consists in its simple relation to a verb, a participle, an adjective, or whatever else it qualifies; just as the syntax of an English Adjective, (except in a few instances,) consists in its simple relation to a noun or a pronoun.

RULE XXI.—ADVERBS.

Adverbs relate to verbs, participles, adjectives, or other adverbs: as, "Any passion that *habitually* discomposes our temper, or unfits us for *properly* discharging the duties of life, has *most certainly* gained a *very* dangerous ascendency."—*Blair.*

> "*How* bless'd this happy hour, should he appear,
> Dear to us all, to me *supremely* dear!"—*Pope's Homer.*

EXCEPTION FIRST.

The adverbs *yes*, *ay*, and *yea*, expressing a simple affirmation, and the adverbs *no* and *nay*, expressing a simple negation, are always independent. They generally answer a question, and are equivalent to a whole sentence. Is it clear, that they ought to be called adverbs? *No.* "Can honour set to a leg? *No.* Or an arm? *No.* Or take away the grief of a wound? *No.* Honour hath no skill in surgery then? *No.*"—SHAK.: *First Part of Hen. IV*, Act v, 1.

EXCEPTION SECOND.

The word *amen*, which is commonly called an adverb, is often used independently at the beginning or end of a declaration or a prayer; and is itself a prayer, meaning, *so let it be:* as, "Surely, I come quickly. *Amen:* Even so, come Lord Jesus."—*Rev.* xxii, 20. When it does not stand thus alone, it seems in general to be used substantively; as, "The strangers among them stood on Gerizim, and echoed *amen* to the blessings."—*Wood's Dict.* "These things saith the *Amen.*"—*Rev.* iii, 14.

EXCEPTION THIRD.

An adverb before a preposition seems sometimes to relate to the latter, rather than to the verb or participle to which the preposition connects its object; as, "This mode of pronunciation runs *considerably beyond* ordinary discourse."—*Blair's Rhet.* p. 334. "Yes, *all along* the times of the apostasy, this was the thing that preserved the witnesses."—*Penington's Works*, Vol. iv, p. 12. [See Obs. 8th on Rule 7th.]
> "*Right against* the eastern gate,
> Where the great sun begins his state."—*Milton, L'Allegro.*

EXCEPTION FOURTH.

The words *much, little, far*, and *all*, being originally adjectives, are sometimes preceded by the negative *not*, or (except the last) by such an adverb as *too, how, thus, so*, or *as*, when they are taken substantively; as, "*Not all* that glitters, is gold."—"*Too much* should not be offered at once."—*Murray's Gram.* p. 140. "*Thus far* is consistent."—*Ib.* p. 161. "*Thus far* is right."—*Lowth's Gram.* p. 101.

OBSERVATIONS ON RULE XXI.

OBS. 1.—On this rule of syntax, Dr. Adam remarks, "Adverbs sometimes likewise qualify *substantives;*" and gives Latin examples of the following import: "Homer *plainly* an orator;"—"*Truly* Metellus;"—"*To-morrow* moraing." But this doctrine is not well proved by such imperfect phrases, nor can it ever be very consistently admitted, because it destroys the characteristic difference between an adjective and an adverb. *To-morrow* is here an adjective; and as for *truly* and *plainly*, they are not such words as can make sense with nouns. I therefore imagine the phrases to be elliptical: "*Verè Metellus,*" may mean, "*This is truly* Metellus;" and "*Homerus plant orator,*" " Homer *was plainly* an orator." So, in the example, " Behold an Israelite *indeed,*" the true construction seems to be, " Behold, *hers is indeed* an Israelite;" for, in the Greek or Latin, the word *Israelite* is a nominative, thus: "*Ecce verè Israelita.*"—*Beza; also Montanus.* "Ἴδε ἀληθῶς Ἰσραηλίτης."—*Greek Testament.* Behold appears to be here an interjection, like *Ecce.* If we make it a transitive verb, the reading should be, " Behold *a true* Israelite;" for the text does not mean, "*Behold indeed* an Israelite." At least, this is not the meaning in our version. W. H. Wells, citing as authorities for the doctrine, "Bullions, Allen and Cornwell, Brace, Butler, and Webber," has the following remark: "There are, however, certain forms of expression in which *adverbs* bear a special relation to *nouns* or *pronouns; as,* ' Behold, I, *even I,* do bring a flood of waters.'—*Gen.* 6: 17. ' For our gospel came not unto you in *word only,* but also in power.'—1 *Thes.* 1: 5."—*Wells's School Gram.* 1st Ed. p. 156; late Ed. 168. And again, in his Punctuation, we find this: " When, however, the intervening word is an *adverb*, the comma is more commonly omitted; as, ' It is *labor only* which gives a relish to pleasure.' "—*Ib.* p. 176. From all this, the doctrine receives no better support than from Adam's suggestion above considered. The word "*only*" is often an *adjective*, and wherever its "special relation" is to a noun or a pronoun, it can be nothing else. "*Even,*" when it introduces a word repeated with emphasis, is a *conjunction*.

OBS. 2.—When participles become nouns, their adverbs are not unfrequently left standing with them in the original relation; as, " For the fall and *rising again* of many in Israel."—*Luke,* ii, 34. " To denote the *carrying forward* of the action."—*Barnard's Gram.* p. 52. But in instances like these, *the hyphen* seems to be necessary. This mark would make the terms *rising-again* and *carrying-forward* compound nouns, and not participial nouns with adverbs relating to them.

　　" There is no *flying hence,* nor *tarrying here.*"—*Shak.*, *Macbeth.*
　　" What! in ill thoughts again? men must endure
　　　Their *going hence,* ev'n as their *coming hither.*"—*Id.*

OBS. 3.—Whenever any of those words which are commonly used adverbially, are made to relate directly to nouns or pronouns, they must be reckoned *adjectives*, and parsed by Rule 9th. Examples: " The *above* verbs."—*Dr. Adam.* " To the *above* remarks."—*Campbell's Rhet.* p. 318. " The *above* instances."—*Ib.* p. 442. " After the *above* partial illustration."—*Dr. Murray's Hist. of Lang.* ii, 62. " The *above* explanation."—*Cobbett's Gram.* ¶ 22. " For *very* age."—*Zech.* viii, 4. " From its *very* greatness."—*Phil. Museum,* i, 431. " In his *then* situation."—*Johnson's Life of Goldsmith.* " This was the *then* state of Popery."—*Id. Life of Dryden,* p. 185. " The servant becomes the master of his *once* master."—*Shillitoe.* " Time *when* is put in the ablative, time how *long* is put in the accusative."—*Adam's Lat. Gram.* p. 201; *Gould's,* 198. " Nouns signifying the time *when* or how *long*, may be put in the objective case without a preposition."—*Wilbur and Livingston's Gram.* p. 24. " I hear the *far-off* curfew sound."—*Milton.* " Far on the *thither* side."—*Book of Thoughts,* p. 58. " My *hither* way."—" Since my *here* remain in England."—*Shak.* " But short and *seldom* truce."—*Fell.* "An *exceeding* knave."—*Pope.* "According to my *sometime* promise."—*Zenobia,* i, 176. " Thine *often* infirmities."—*Bible.* "A *far* country."—*Ib.* " No *wine*"—"*No* new thing"—"*No* greater joy."—*Ib.* " Nothing *else.*"—*Blair.* "*To-morrow* noon."—*Scott.* " Calamity *enough.*"—*Ty. Sallust.* " For thou *only* art holy."—*Rev.* xv, 4.

OBS. 4.—It is not my design to justify any uncouth substitution of adverbs for adjectives; nor do I affirm that all the foregoing examples are indisputably good English, though most of them are so; but merely, that the words, when they are thus used, *are adjectives*, and not adverbs. Lindley Murray, and his copyists, strongly condemn some of these expressions, and, by implication, most or all of them; but both he and they, as well as others, have repeatedly employed at least one of the very models they censure. They are too severe on all those which they specify. Their objections stand thus: "*Such expressions* as the following, though not destitute of authority, *are very inelegant*, and do *not suit the idiom* of our language; ' The *then* ministry,' for, ' the ministry of that time;' ' The *above* discourse,' for, ' the preceding discourse.' "—*Murray's Gram.* i, p. 196; *Crombie's,* 294; *Ingersoll's,* 206. " The following phrases are also exceptionable: ' The *then* ministry;' ' The *above* argument."—*Kirkham's Gram.* p. 190. "Adverbs used as adjectives, as, ' The *above* statement;' ' The *then* administration;' should be avoided."—*Barnard's Gram.* p. 285. "*When* and *then* must not be used for nouns *and pronouns*; thus, ' Since *when,*' ' since *then,*' ' the *then* ministry,' ought to be, ' Since *which time,*' ' since *that time,*' ' the ministry *of that period.*' "—*Hiley's Gram.* p. 96. Dr. Priestley, from whom Murray derived many of his critical remarks, noticed these expressions; and, (as I suppose,) *approvingly;* thus, "Adverbs are often put for adjectives, agreeably to the idiom of the Greek tongue: [as,] ' The action was *amiss.*'—' The *then* ministry.'—' The idea is *alike* in both.' Addison.— ' The *above* discourse.' Harris."—*Priestley's Gram.* p. 135. Dr. Johnson, as may be seen above, thought it not amiss to use *then* as Priestley here cites it; and for such a use of *above*, we may quote the objectors themselves: " To support the *above* construction."—*Murray's Gram.* i, p. 149; *Ingersoll's,* p. 238. " In all the *above* instances."—*Mur.* p. 202; *Ing.* 230. " To the *above* rule."—*Mur.* p. 270; *Ing.* 283. " The same as the *above.*"—*Mur.* p. 66; *Ing.* 46. " In such instances as the *above.*"—*Mur.* p. 24; *Ing.* 9; *Kirkham,* 23.*

* Dr. Webster considers the use of *then* and *above* as ADNOUNS. [i. e. adjectives,] to be ' well authorized and very convenient;' as, the *then* ministry ; the *above* remarks."—*Felch's Comp. Gram.* p. 108. Dr. Webster's remark is in the following words: " *Then* and *above* are often used as ATTRIBUTES; [i. e. adjectives; as,] the *then* min-

OBS. 5.—When words of an adverbial character are used after the manner of nouns, they be parsed as nouns, and not as adverbs; as, "The Son of God—was not yea and nay, but it was yea."—*Bible.* "For a great *while* to come."—*Ib.* "On this *perhaps,* this *paredexteri*mous for lies."—*Young.* "From the extremest *upward* of thine head."—*Shak.* "The *upwards* of fifteen millions of inhabitants."—*Murray's Key,* 8vo, p. 265. "Information has derived from *upwards* of two hundred volumes."—*Worcester's Hist.* p. v. "An eternal now always last."—*Cowley.* "Discourse requires an animated *no.*"—*Cowper.* "Their hea proud *hereafter* swelled."—*Sprague.* An adverb after a preposition is used substantively governed by the preposition; though perhaps it is not necessary to call it a common noun "For *upwards* of thirteen years."—*Hiley's Gram.* p. xvi. "That thou mayst curse me then *thence.*"—*Numb.* xxiii, 27. "Yet *for once* we'll try."—*Dr. Franklin.* But many take such together, calling them "*adverbial phrases.*" Allen says, "Two adverbs sometimes come tog as, 'Thou hast kept the good wine *until now.*'"—*Gram.* p. 174. But *until* is here more pr preposition, governing *now.*

OBS. 6.—It is plain, that when words of an adverbial form are used either adjectively a stantively, they cannot be parsed by the foregoing rule, or explained as having the ord relation of *adverbs;* and if the unusual relation or character which they thus assume, thought sufficient to fix them in the rank of adjectives or nouns, the parser may describe as adverbs used adjectively, or substantively, and apply the rule which their assumed construct requires. But let it be remembered, that adverbs, as such, neither relate to nouns, nor the nature of cases; but express the time, place, degree, or manner, of actions or qualities some instances in which their construction may seem not to be reconcilable with the c rule, there may be supposed an ellipsis of a verb or a participle;* as, "From Monday to S day *inclusively.*"—*Webster's Dict.* Here, the Doctor ought to have used a comma after Satu for the adverb relates, not to that noun, but to the word *reckoned,* understood. "It was we by Roscommon, '*too faithfully is pedantically.*'"—*Com. Sch. Journal,* i, 167. This saying pose to mean, "*To do a thing* too faithfully, is, *to do it* pedantically." "And, [I say] they had been mindful of that country from whence they came out, they might have had tunity to have returned."—*Heb.* xi, 15.

OBS. 7.—To abbreviate expressions, and give them vivacity, verbs of self-motion (such come, rise, get, &c.) are sometimes suppressed, being suggested to the mind by an em adverb, which seems to be put *for the verb,* but does in fact relate to it understood; as,

"I'll *hence* to London, on a serious matter."—*Shak.* Supply "*go.*"
"I'll *in.* I'll *in.* Follow your friend's counsel. I'll *in.*"—*Id.* Supply "*get.*"
"*Away,* old man; give me thy hand; *away.*"—*Id.* Supply "*come.*"
"Love hath wings, and will *away.*"—*Waller.* Supply "*fly.*"
"*Up, up,* Glentarkin! rouse thee, ho!"—*Scott.* Supply "*spring.*"
"Henry the Fifth is crowned; *up,* vanity!" Supply "*stand.*"
"*Down,* royal state! all you sage counsellors, *hence!*"—*Shak.* Supply "*fall,*" and "*get*
"But *up,* and enter now into full bliss."—*Milton.* Supply "*rise.*"

OBS. 8.—We have, on some occasions, a singular way of expressing a transitive action tively, or emphatically, by adding the preposition *with* to an adverb of direction; as, *up* w *down with it, in with it, out with it, over with it, away with it,* and the like; in which constr the adverb seems to be used elliptically as above, though the insertion of the verb would enervate or greatly alter the expression. Examples: "She *up with* her fist, and took h face."—*Sidney,* in *Joh. Dictionary.* "*Away with* him!"—*Acts,* xxi, 36. "*Away with* fellow from the earth."—*Ib.* xxii, 22. "The calling of assemblies I cannot *away with.*"—i i, 13. "*Hence with* denial vain, and coy excuse."—*Milton's Comus.* Ingersoll says, "Som a whole phrase is used as an interjection, and we call such *interjectional phrases;* as, *c him!—away with him!—Alas, what wonder! &c.*"—*Conversations on Gram.* p. 79. The m of lumping together several different parts of speech under the notion of one, and call whole an "*adverbial phrase,*" a "*substantive phrase,*" or an "*interjectional phrase,*" forced put, by which some grammarians would dodge certain difficulties which they know not to meet. It is directly repugnant to the idea of *parsing;* for the parser ever deals with the of speech as such, and not with whole phrases in the lump. The foregoing adverbs when imperatively, have some resemblance to interjections; but, in some of the examples above they certainly are not used in this manner.

OBS. 9.—A *conjunctive adverb* usually relates to two verbs at the same time, and thus co two clauses of a compound sentence; as, "And the rest will I set in order *when* I come."— xi, 34. Here *when* is a conjunctive adverb of time, and relates to the two verbs *will set* and the meaning being, "And the rest will I set in order *at the time at which* I come." This *when* is often used erroneously in lieu of a nominative after *is,* to which construction of the such an interpretation as the foregoing, would not be applicable; because the person mea tell, not *when,* but *what,* the thing is, of which he speaks; as, "Another cause of obscur *when* the structure of the sentence is too much complicated, or too artificial; or *when* the c is too long suspended by parentheses."—*Campbell's Rhet.* p. 246. Here the conjunct would be much better than *when,* but the sentence might advantageously spare them both; "An other cause of obscurity is too much *complication,* too artificial a *structure* of the sent or too long a *suspension* of the sense by *parenthesis.*"

istry; the above remarks; nor would I proscribe this use. It is well authorized and very convenient."— *Gram.* p. 245; *Improved Gram.* p. 176. Of this use of *them,* Dr. Crombie has expressed a very different opin "Here *them,*" says he, "the adverb equivalent to *at that time,* is solœcistically employed as an adjective, with *ministry.* This error seems to gain ground; it should therefore be vigilantly opposed, and caref avoided."—*On Etym. and Synt.* p. 405.

* W. Allen supposes, "An adverb sometimes qualifies a whole sentence; as, *Unfortunately for the lovers* tiquity, *no remains of Grecian paintings have been preserved.*"—*Elements of Eng. Gram.* p. 173 P example may be resolved thus: "*B happens unfortunately for the lovers of antiquity, that no rema Grecian paintings have been preserved.*"

OBS. 10.—For the *placing* of adverbs, no definite general rule can be given; yet is there no other part of speech so liable to be misplaced. Those which relate to adjectives, or to other adverbs, with very few exceptions, immediately precede them; and those which belong to compound verbs, are commonly placed after the first auxiliary; or, if they be emphatical, after the whole verb. Those which relate to simple verbs, or to simple participles, are placed sometimes before and sometimes after them. Examples are so very common, I shall cite but one: "A man may, in respect to grammatical purity, speak *unexceptionably*, and yet speak *obscurely*, or *ambiguously*; and though we cannot say, that a man may speak *properly*, and at the same time speak *unintelligibly*, yet this last case falls *more naturally* to be considered as an offence against perspicuity, than as a violation of propriety."—*Campbell's Rhet.* p. 239.

OBS. 11.—Of the infinitive verb and its preposition *to*, some grammarians say, that they must never be separated by an adverb. It is true, that the adverb is, in general, more elegantly placed before the preposition than after it; but, possibly, the latter position of it may sometimes contribute to perspicuity, which is more essential than elegance: as, "If any man refuse *so to implore*, and *to so receive* pardon, let him die the death."—*Fuller, on the Gospel*, p. 209. The latter word *so*, if placed like the former, might possibly be understood in a different sense from what it now bears. But perhaps it would be better to say, "If any man refuse so to implore, and *on such terms* to receive pardon, let him die the death." "Honour teaches us *properly* to respect ourselves."—*Murray's Key*, ii, 252. Here it is not quite clear, to which verb the adverb "*properly*" relates. Some change of the expression is therefore needful. The right to place an adverb sometimes between *to* and its verb, should, I think, be conceded to the poets: as,

"Who dared *to nobly stem* tyrannic pride."—BURNS: *C. Sat. N.*

OBS. 12.—The adverb *no* is used independently, only when it is equivalent to a whole sentence. This word is sometimes an adverb of *degree*; and as such it has this peculiarity, that it can relate only to comparatives: as, "*No* more,"—"*No* better,"—"*No* greater,"—"*No* sooner." When *no* is set before a noun, it is clearly an *adjective*, corresponding to the Latin *nullus*; as, "*No* clouds, *no* vapours intervene."—*Dyer*. Dr. Johnson, with no great accuracy, remarks, "It seems an *adjective* in these phrases, *no* longer, *no* more, *no* where; though sometimes it may be so commodiously changed to *not*, that it seems an adverb: as, 'The days are yet *no* shorter.'"—*Quarto Dict.* And his first example of what he calls the "*adverb* NO" is this: "'Our courteous Antony, Whom ne'er the word of *no* woman heard speak.' SHAKSPEARE."—*Ibid.* Dr. Webster says, "When it precedes *where*, as in *no where*, it may be considered as adverbial, though originally an adjective."—*Octavo Dict.* The truth is, that *no* is an adverb, whenever it relates to an adjective; an adjective, whenever it relates to a noun; and a noun, whenever it takes the relation of a case. Thus, in what Johnson cites from Shakspeare, it is a noun, and not an adverb; for the meaning is, that a woman never heard Antony speak the word *of no*—that is, *of negation*. And there ought to be a comma after this word, to make the text intelligible. To read it thus, "*the word of no woman*," makes *no* an adjective. So, to say, "There are *no abler* critics than these," is a very different thing from saying, "There are *critics no abler* than these;" because *no* is an adjective in the former sentence, and an adverb in the latter. *Somewhere*, *nowhere*, *anywhere*, *elsewhere*, and *everywhere*, are adverbs of place, each of which is composed of the noun *where* and an *adjective*; and it is absurd to write a part of them as compound words, and the rest as phrases, as many authors do.

OBS. 13.—In some languages, the more negatives one crowds into a sentence, the stronger is the negation; and this appears to have been formerly the case in English, or in what was anciently the language of Britain: as, "He *never* yet *no* vilanie *ne* sayde in alle his lif unto *no* manere wight."—*Chaucer*. "*Ne* I *ne* wol *non* reherce, yet that I may."—*Id.* "Give *not* me counsel; *nor* let *no* comforter delight mine ear."—*Shakspeare*. "She *cannot* love, *nor* take *no* shape *nor* project of affection."—*Id.* Among people of education, this manner of expression has now become wholly obsolete; though it still prevails, to some extent, in the conversation of the vulgar. It is to be observed, however, that the *repetition* of an independent negative word or clause yet strengthens the negation; as, "No, no, no."—"No, never."—"No, not for an hour."—*Gal. ii, 5.* "There is *none* righteous, no, *not* one."—*Rom.* iii, 10. But two negatives in the same clause, if they have any bearing on each other, destroy the negation, and render the meaning weakly affirmative; as, "*Nor* did they *not* perceive their evil plight."—*Milton*. That is, they *did* perceive it. "'His language, though inelegant, is *not ungrammatical*;' that is, it *is* grammatical."—*Murray's Gram.* p. 198. The term *not only*, or *not merely*, being a correspondent to *but* or *but also*, may be followed by an other negative without this effect, because the two negative words have no immediate bearing on each other; as, "Your brother is *not only not* present, and *not* assisting in prosecuting your injuries, *but* is now actually with Verres."—*Duncan's Cicero*, p. 19. "In the latter we have *not merely nothing*, to denote what the point should be; *but no* indication, that any point at all is wanting."—*Churchill's Gram.* p. 373. So the word *nothing*, when taken positively for nonentity, or that which does not exist, may be followed by an other negative; as,

"First, seat him somewhere, and derive his race,
Or else conclude that *nothing* has *no* place."—*Dryden*, p. 95.

OBS. 14.—The common rule of our grammars, "Two negatives, in English, destroy each other, or are equivalent to an affirmative," is far from being *true* of all possible examples. A sort of informal exception to it, (which is mostly confined to conversation,) is made by a *familiar* transfer of the word *neither* from the beginning of the clause to the end of it; as, "But here is *no* notice taken of that *neither*."—*Johnson's Gram. Com.* p. 336. That is, "But *neither* is any notice here taken of that." Indeed a negation may be repeated, by the same word or others, as often as we please, if no two of the terms in particular contradict each other; as, "He will *never* consent, *not* he, *no*, *never*, nor I *neither*." "He will *not* have time, *no*, nor capacity *neither*."—*Bolingbroke, on Hist.* p. 103. "Many terms and idioms may be common, which, nevertheless, have *not* the general sanction, *no*, nor even the sanction of those that use them."—*Campbell's Rhet.* p 160; *Murray's Gram.* 8vo, p. 358. And as to the equivalence spoken of in the common rule, such an expression as, " He did *not* say *nothing*," is in fact only a vulgar solecism, take it as you will ; whether for, " He did *not* say *anything*," or for, " He *did* say *something*." The latter indeed is what the contradiction amounts to ; but double negatives must be shunned, whenever they *seem like* blunders. The following examples have, for this reason, been thought objectionable ; though Allen says, " Two negatives destroy each other, or *elegantly* form an affirmation."—*Gram.* p. 174.

　　　　　　　　　　———————"Nor knew I not
　　　　To be both will and deed created free."—*Milton, P. L.*, B. v, l. 648.
　　"*Nor* doth the moon *no* nourishment exhale
　　　　From her moist continent to higher orbs."—*Ib.* B. v, l. 421.

OBS. 15.—Under this head of *double negatives*, there appears in our grammars a dispute of some importance, concerning the adoption of *or* or *nor*, when any other negative than *neither* or *nor* occurs in the preceding clause or phrase : as, " We will *not* serve thy gods, *nor* worship the golden image."—*Dan.* iii, 18. " Ye have *no* portion, nor right, *nor* memorial, in Jerusalem."—*Neh.* ii, 20. " There is *no* painsworthy difficulty *nor* dispute about them."—*Horne Tooke, Div.* Vol. i, p. 43. " So *as not* to cloud that principal object, *nor* to bury it."—*Blair's Rhet.* p. 116 ; *Murray's Gram.* p. 322. " He did *not* mention Leonora, nor her father's death."—*Murray's Key,* p. 264. " Thou canst *not* tell whence it cometh, *nor* whither it goeth."—*Ib.* p. 215. The form of this text, in John, iii, 8th, is—" But canst not tell whence it cometh, *and* whither it goeth;" which Murray inserted in his Exercises as bad English. I do not see that the copulative *and* is here ungrammatical ; but if we prefer a disjunctive, ought it not to be *or*, rather than *nor*? It appears to be the opinion of some, that in all these examples, and in similar instances innumerable, *nor* only is proper. Others suppose, that *or* only is justifiable ; and others again, that either *or* or *nor* is perfectly correct. Thus grammar, or what should be grammar, differs in the hands of different men ! The principle to be settled here, must determine the correctness or incorrectness of a vast number of very common expressions. I imagine that none of these opinions is warrantable, if taken in all that extent to which each of them has been, or may be, carried.

OBS. 16.—It was observed by Priestley, and after him by Lindley Murray, from whom others again have copied the remark : " Sometimes the particles *or* and *nor*, may, either of them, be used with nearly equal propriety ; [as,] ' The king, whose character was not sufficiently vigorous, *nor* decisive, assented to the measure.' *Hume. Or* would perhaps have been better, but *nor* seems to repeat the negation in the former part of the sentence, and therefore gives more emphasis to the expression."—*Priestley's Gram.* p. 138 ; *Murray's,* i, 212 ; *Ingersoll's,* 268 ; *R. C. Smith's*, 177. The conjunction *or* might doubtless have been used in this sentence, but *not with the same meaning* that is now conveyed ; for, if that connective had been employed, the adjective *decisive* would have been qualified by the adverb *sufficiently*, and would have seemed only an alternative for the former epithet, *vigorous*. As the text now stands, it not only implies a distinction between vigour of character and decision of character, but denies the latter to the king absolutely, the former, with qualification. If the author had meant to suggest such a distinction, and also to qualify his denial of both, he ought to have said—" not sufficiently vigorous, *nor sufficiently decisive*." With this meaning, however, he might have used *neither* for *not* ; or with the former, he might have used *or* for *nor*, had he transposed the terms—" was not decisive, *or* sufficiently vigorous."

OBS. 17.—In the tenth edition of John Burn's Practical Grammar, published at Glasgow in 1810, are the following suggestions : " It is not uncommon to find the conjunctions *or* and *nor* used indiscriminately ; but if there be any real distinction in the proper application of them, it is to be wished that it were settled. It is attempted thus :—Let the conjunction *or* be used simply to connect the members of a sentence, or to mark distribution, opposition, or choice, without any preceding negative particle ; and *nor* to mark the subsequent part of a negative sentence, with some negative particle in the preceding part of it. Examples of OR : ' Recreation of one kind *or* other is absolutely necessary to relieve the body *or* mind from too constant attention to labour *or* study.'—'After this life, succeeds a state of rewards *or* punishments.'—' Shall I come to you with a rod, *or* in love ? ' Examples of NOR : ' Let *no* man be too confident, *nor* too diffident of his own abilities.'—' *Never* calumniate any man, *nor* give the least encouragement to calumniators.' —' There is *not* a christian duty to which providence has not annexed a blessing, *nor* any affliction for which a remedy is not provided.' If the above distinction be just, the following passage seems to be faulty :

　　　　' Seasons return, but *not* to me returns
　　　　Day, *or* the sweet approach of ev'n *or* morn,
　　　　Or sight of vernal bloom, *or* summer's rose,
　　　　Or flocks, *or* herds, *or* human face divine.'
　　　　　　　　　　　　　Milton, P. L., B. iii, l. 40."—*Burn's Gr.* p. 108.

OBS. 18.—T. O. Churchill, whose Grammar first appeared in London in 1823, treats this matter thus ; " As *or* answers to *either*, *nor*, a compound of *not or* [*ne or*] by contraction, answers to *neither*, a similar compound of *not either* [*ne either*]. The latter however does not constitute that double use of the negative, in which one, agreeably to the principles of philosophical grammar, destroys the other ; for a part of the first word, *neither*, cannot be understood before the second, *nor* : and for the same reason a part of it could not be understood before *or*, which is sometimes improperly used in the second clause ; while the whole of it, *neither*, would be obviously improper before *or*. On the other hand, when *not* is used in the first clause, *nor* is improper in the second ; since it would involve the impropriety of understanding *not* before a compound of *not* [or *ne*] with *or*. ' I shall *not* attempt to convince, *nor* to persuade you.—What will you *not* attempt ?—To convince, *nor* to persuade you.' The impropriety of *nor* in this answer is clear : but the answer should certainly repeat the words not heard, or not understood."—*Churchill's New Gram.* p. 330.

OBS. 19.—" It is probable, that the use of *nor* after *not* has been introduced, in consequence of such improprieties as the following : ' The injustice of inflicting death for crimes, when *not* of the most heinous nature, *or* attended with extenuating circumstances.' Here it is obviously not the intention of the writer, to understand the negative in the last clause : and, if this were good

English, it would be not merely allowable to employ *nor* after *not*, to show the subsequent clause to be negative as well as the preceding, but it would always be necessary. In fact however, the sentence quoted is faulty, in not repeating the adverb *when* in the last clause; ' or *when* attended:' which would preclude the negative from being understood in it; for, if an adverb, conjunction, or auxiliary verb, preceding a negative, be understood in the succeeding clause, the negative is understood also; if it be repeated, the negative must be repeated likewise, or the clause becomes affirmative."—*Ib.* p. 331.

OBS. 20.—This author, proceeding with his remarks, suggests forms of correction for several other common modes of expression, which he conceives to be erroneous. For the information of the student, I shall briefly notice a little further the chief points of his criticism, though he teaches some principles which I have not thought it necessary always to observe in writing. "'And seemed *not* to understand ceremony, or to despise it.' *Goldsmith*. Here *either* ought to be inserted before *not*. 'It is *not* the business of virtue, to extirpate the affections of the mind, but to regulate them.' *Addison*. The sentence ought to have been: 'It is the business of virtue, *not* to extirpate the affections of the mind, but to regulate them.' 'I do *not* think, that he was averse to the office; *nor* do I believe, that it was unsuited to him.' How much better to say: 'I do not think, that he was averse to the office, *or* that it was unsuited to him!' For the same reason *nor* cannot follow *never*, the negative in the first clause affecting all the rest."—*Ib.* p. 332. "*Nor* is sometimes used improperly after *no:* [as,] 'I humbly however trust in God, that I have hazarded *no* conjecture, *nor* have given any explanation of obscure points, inconsistent with the general sense of Scripture, which must be our guide in all dubious passages.' *Gilpin*. It ought to be: '*and* have given *no* explanation;' or, 'I have *neither* hazarded any conjecture, *nor* given any explanation.' The use of *or* after *neither* is as common, as that of *nor* after *no* or *not*.[*] '*Neither* the pencil *or* poetry are adequate.' *Cove*. Properly, '*Neither* the pencil *nor* poetry *is* adequate.' 'The vow of poverty *allowed* the Jesuits individually, to have *no* idea of wealth.' *Dornford*. We cannot *allow* a *nonentity*. It should be: 'did *not* allow, to have *any* idea.'"—*Ib.* p. 333.

OBS. 21.—Thus we see that Churchill wholly and positively condemns *nor* after *not, no*, or *never;* while Burn totally disapproves of *or*, under the same circumstances. Both of these critics are wrong, because each carries his point too far; and yet it may not be right, to suppose both particles to be often equally good. Undoubtedly, a negation may be repeated in English without impropriety, and that in several different ways; as, "There is *no* living, *none*, if Bertram be away."—*Beauties of Shak.* p. 3. "Great men are *not* always wise, *neither* do the aged [always] understand judgement."—*Job*, xxxii. 9. "Will he esteem thy riches? *no, not* gold, *nor* all the forces of strength."—*Ib.* xxxiv, 19. Some sentences, too, require *or*, and others *nor*, even when a negative occurs in the preceding clause; as, "There was *none* of you that convinced Job, *or* that answered his words."—*Ib.* xxxii, 12. "How much less to him that accepteth *not* the persons of princes, *nor* regardeth the rich more than the poor."—*Ib.* xxxiv, 19. "This day is holy unto the Lord your God; mourn *not*, *nor* weep."—*Neh.* viii, 9. "Men's behaviour should be like their apparel, *not* too strait *or* point-de-vise, but free for exercise."—*Ld. Bacon*. Again, the mere repetition of a simple negative is, on some occasions, more agreeable than the insertion of any connective; as, "There is *no* darkness, *nor* shadow of death, where the workers of iniquity may hide themselves."—*Job*, xxxiv, 22. Better: "There is *no* darkness, *no* shadow of death, *wherein* the workers of iniquity may hide themselves." "*No* place *nor any* object appears to him void of beauty."—*Murray's Key*, 8vo, p. 255. Better: "*No* place, *no* object, appears to him void of beauty." That passage from Milton which Burn supposes to be faulty, and that expression of Addison's which Churchill dislikes, are, in my opinion, not incorrect as they stand; though, doubtless, the latter admits of the variation proposed. In the former, too, *or* may twice be changed to *nor*, where the following nouns are nominatives; but to change it throughout, would not be well, because the other nouns are objectives governed by *of:*

"Seasons return, but *not* to me returns
Day, *nor* the sweet approach of ev'n *or* morn,
Nor sight of vernal bloom, *or* summer's rose,
Or flocks, *or* herds, *or* human face divine."

OBS. 22.—*Ever* and *never* are directly opposite to each other in sense, and yet they are very frequently confounded and misapplied, and that by highly respectable writers; as, "Seldom, or *never* can we expect," &c.—*Blair's Lectures*, p. 305. "And seldom, or *ever*, did any one rise," &c. —*Ib.* p. 272. "Seldom, or *never*, is† there more than one accented syllable in any English word." —*Ib.* p. 329. "Which that of the present seldom or *ever* is understood to be."—*Dr. Murray's Hist. of Lang.* Vol. ii, p. 120. Here *never* is right, and *ever* is wrong. It is *time*, that is here spoken of; and the affirmative *ever*, meaning *always*, or *at any time*, in stead of being a fit alternative for *seldom*, makes nonsense of the sentence, and violates the rule respecting the order and fitness of time: unless we change *or* to *if*, and say, "seldom, *if* ever." But in sentences like the following, the adverb appears to express, not time, but *degree;* and for the latter sense *ever* is preferable to *never*, because the degree ought to be possible, rather than impossible: "*Ever so* little of the spirit of martyrdom is always a more favourable indication to civilisation, than *ever so* much dexterity of party management, or *ever so* turbulent protestation of immaculate patriotism."— *Wayland's Moral Science*, p. 411. "Now let man reflect but *never so* little on himself."—*Burlamaqui, on Law*, p. 29. "Which will *not* hearken to the voice of charmers, charming *never so* wisely."—*Ps.* lviii, 5. The phrase *ever so*, (which ought, I think, to be written as *one word*,) is now a very common expression to signify *in whatsoever degree;* as, "*everso* little,"—" *everso* much," —"*everso* wise,"—"*everso* wisely." And it is manifestly this, and not time, that is intended by the false phraseology above;—"a form of speech handed down by the best writers, but lately accused, I think with justice, of solecism. * * * It can only be defended by supplying a very harsh and unprecedented ellipsis."—*Johnson's Dict. w. Never*.

---

[*] This assertion of Churchill's is very far from the truth. I am confident that the latter construction occurs, even among reputable authors, ten times as often as the former can be found in any English books.—G. BROWN.
† Should not the Doctor have said, "*are there more*," since "*more than one*" must needs be plural? See Obs. 10th on Rule 17th.

OBS. 23.—Dr. Lowth seconds this opinion of Johnson, respecting the phrase, "*never so wisely*," and says, "It should be, '*ever so wisely*;' that is, '*how wisely soever*.'" To which he adds an other example somewhat different: "'Besides, a slave would *not* have been admitted into that society, had he had *never such* opportunities.' Bentley."—*Lowth's Gram.* p. 109. This should be. "had he had *everso excellent* opportunities." But Churchill, mistaking the common explanation of the meaning of *everso* for the manner of parsing or resolving it, questions the propriety of the term, and thinks it easier to defend the old phrase *never so*; in which he supposes *never* to be an adverb of time, and not to relate to *so*, which is an adverb of degree: saying, "'Be it *never so* true,' is resolvable into, 'Be it so true, *as never any thing was*.'[*] 'I have had *never* so much trouble on this occasion,' may be resolved into, 'I *have never had* so much trouble, *as on this* occasion:' while, 'I have had *ever* so much trouble on this occasion, cannot be resolved, without supplying some very harsh and unprecedented ellipsis indeed."—*New Gram.* p. 337. Why not! I see no occasion at all for supposing any ellipsis. *Ever* is here an adverb of degree, and relates to *so*; or, if we take *everso* as one word, this too is an adverb of degree, and relates to *much* because the meaning is—"*everso much* trouble." But the other phraseology, even as it stands in Churchill's explanations, is a solecism still; nor can any resolution which supposes *never* to be here an adverb of time, be otherwise. We cannot call that a grammatical resolution, which makes a different sense from that which the writer intended: as, "A slave would not have been admitted into that society, had he *never* had such opportunities." This would be Churchill's interpretation, but it is very unlike what Bentley says above. So, 'I have *never had so much* trouble,' and, 'I have had *everso much* trouble,' are very different assertions.

OBS. 24.—On the word *never*, Dr. Johnson remarks thus: "It seems in some phrases to have the sense of an *adjective*, [meaning,] *not any*; but in reality it is *not ever*: [as,] 'He answered him to *never* a word.' MATTHEW, xxvii, 14."—*Quarto Dict.* This mode of expression was formerly very common, and a contracted form of it is still frequently heard among the vulgar: as, "Because he'd *ne'er* an other tub."—*Hudibras*, p. 102. That is, "Because he had *no* other tub." "Letter nor line know I *never* a one."—*Scott's Lay of L. M.* p. 27. This is what the common people pronounce "*ne'er a one*," and use in stead of *neither* or *no one*. In like manner they contract *ever a one* into "*e'er a one*;" by which they mean *either* or *any one*. These phrases are the same that somebody—(I believe it is *Smith*, in his Inductive Grammar—) has ignorantly written "*ary one*" and "*nary one*," calling them vulgarisms.[†] Under this mode of spelling, the critic had an undoubted right to think the terms unauthorized! In the compounds *whoever* or *who'e*, *whichever* or *whiche'er*, *whatever* or *whate'er*, the word *ever* or *e'er*, which formerly stood separate, appears to be an adjective, rather than an adverb; though, by becoming part of the pronoun, it has now technically ceased to be either.

OBS. 25.—The same may be said of *soever* or *soe'er*, which is considered as only a part of an other word even when it is written separately; as, "On *which* side *soever* I cast my eyes." In Mark, iii, 28th, *wherewithsoever* is commonly printed as two words; but Alger, in his Pronouncing Bible, more properly makes it one. Dr. Webster, in his grammars, calls *soever* a WORD; but, in his dictionaries, he does not *define* it as such. "The word *soever* may be interposed between the attribute and the idea of unity; 'how clear soever this idea of infinity,'—'how remote soever it may seem.'—LOCKE."—*Webster's Philosophical Gram.*'p. 154; *Improved Gram.* p. 107. "SOEVER, *so* and *ever*, found in compounds, as in *whosoever*, *whatsoever*, *wheresoever*. See these words."—*Webster's Dict.* 8vo.

OBS. 26.—The word *only*, (i. e. *onely*, or *onelike*,) when it relates to a noun or a pronoun, is a definitive adjective, meaning *single*, *alone*, *exclusive of others*; as, "The *only* man,"—"The *only* men,"—"Man *only*,"—"Men *only*,"—"He *only*,"—"They *only*." When it relates to a verb or a participle, it is an adverb of manner, and means *simply*, *singly*, *merely*, *barely*; as, "We *hate* that we hate flattery, when we *only* hate the manner of it."—*Art of Thinking*, p. 38. "A disinterested love of one's country can *only* subsist in small republics."—*Ib.* p. 56. When it stands at the head of a clause, it is commonly a connective word, equivalent to *but*, or *except that*; in which sense, it must be called a conjunction, or at least a conjunctive adverb, which is nearly the same thing: as, "*Only* they would that we should remember the poor."—*Gal.* ii, 10. "For these signs are prepositions, *only* they are of more constant use than the rest."—*Ward's Gram.* p. 129.

OBS. 27.—Among our grammarians, the word "*only*" often passes for an adverb, when it is in fact an adjective. Such a mistake in this single word, has led Churchill to say of the adverb in

general, "It's place is for the most part before adjectives, after nouns, and after verbs;" &c.—
New Gram. p. 147. But, properly, the placing of adverbs has nothing to do with "nouns," because adverbs do not relate to nouns. In this author's example, "His *arm only* was bare," there
is no adverb; and, where he afterwards speaks of the latitude allowable in the placing of adverbs,
alleging, "It is indifferent whether we say, 'He bared his *arm only* ;" or, 'He bared *only* his
arm,'" the word *only* is an adjective, in one instance, if not in both. With this writer, and some
others, the syntax of an adverb centres mainly in the suggestion, that, "It's propriety and force
depend on *it's* position."—*Ib.* p. 147. Illustration : "Thus people commonly say; '*I only* spoke
three words:' which properly implies, that *I,* and *no other person,* spoke three words: when the
intention of the speaker requires; 'I spoke *only three* words; that is, *no more than three words.'* "
—*Ib.* p. 327. One might just as well say, "I spoke three words *only.*" But the interpretation
above is hypercritical, and contrary to that which the author himself gives in his note on the
other example, thus: "Any other situation of the adverb would make a difference. 'He *only*
bared his arm;' would imply, that he did *nothing more than* bare his arm. '*Only* he bared his
arm;' must refer to a preceding part of the sentence, stating something, to which the act of baring
his arm was an exception; as, 'He did it in the same manner, *only* he bared his arm.' If *only*
were placed immediately before *arm; as,* 'He bared his *only arm;*' it would be an adjective, and
signify, that he had but one arm."—*Ib.* p. 328. Now are not, "*I only spoke three words,*" and,
"*He only bared his arm,*" analogous expressions ? Is not the former as good English as the latter ?
Only, in both, is most naturally conceived to belong to the verb; but either may be read in such
a manner as to make it an adjective belonging to the pronoun.

OBS. 28.—The term *not but* is equivalent to two negatives that make an affirmative; as, "*Not
but* that it is a wide place."—*Walker's Particles,* p. 89. "*Non* quo *non* latus locus sit."—*Cic.* Ac.
iv, 12. It has already been stated, that *cannot but* is equal to *must; as,* "It is an affection which
cannot but be productive of some distress."—*Blair's Rhet.* p. 461. It seems questionable, whether
but is not here an adverb, rather than a conjunction. However this may be, by the customary
(but faulty) omission of the negative before *but,* in some other sentences, that conjunction has
acquired the adverbial sense of *only ;* and it may, when used with that signification, be called an
adverb. Thus, the text, "He hath *not* grieved me *but* in part, (2 *Cor.* ii, 5,) might drop the negative *not,* and still convey the same meaning : "He *hath* grieved me *but* in part ;" i. e. "*only* in
part." In the following examples, too, *but* appears to be an adverb, like *only :* "Things *but*
slightly connected should not be crowded into one sentence."—*Murray's Octavo Gram., Index.*
"The assertion, however, serves *but* to show their ignorance."—*Webster's Essays,* p. 96.
                    "Reason itself *but* gives it edge and power."—*Pope.*
                    "Born *but* to die, and reasoning *but* to err."—*Id.*

OBS. 29.—In some constructions of the word *but,* there is a remarkable ambiguity; as, "There
cannot be but one capital musical pause in a line."—*Kames, El. of Crit.* ii, 92. "A line admits *but
one* capital pause."—*Ibid.* Thus does a great critic, in the same paragraph, palpably contradict
himself, and not perceive it. Both expressions are equivocal. He ought rather to have said:
"A line admits *no more than* one capital pause."—"There cannot be *more than* one capital musical
pause in a line." Some would say—"admits *only* one "—"there can be *only* one." But here,
too, is some ambiguity; because *only* may relate either to *one,* or to the preceding verb. The
use of *only* for *but* or *except that,* is not noticed by our lexicographers; nor is it, in my opinion,
a practice much to be commended, though often adopted by men that pretend to write grammatically: as, "Interrogative pronouns are the same as *relative,* ONLY their antecedents cannot be
determined till the answer is *given to the question.*"—*Comly's Gram.* p. 16. "A diphthong is
always long; as, *Aurum, Cæsar,* &c. ONLY *præ* in composition before a vowel is commonly
short."—*Adam's Gram.* p. 254; *Gould's,* 246.

OBS. 30.—It is said by some grammarians, that, "The adverb *there* is often used as an *expletive,*
or as a word that adds nothing to the sense; in which case, it precedes the verb and the nominative; as, '*There* is a person at the door.'"—*Murray's Gram.* p. 197; *Ingersoll's,* 205; *Greenleaf's,*
33; *Nixon's Parser,* p. 53. It is true, that in our language the word *there* is thus used idiomatically, as an introductory term, when we tell what is taking, or has taken, *place ;* but still it is a
regular adverb *of place,* and relates to the verb agreeably to the common rule for adverbs. In
some instances it is even repeated in the same sentence, because, in its introductory sense, it is
always unemphatical; as, "Because *there* was pasture *there* for their flocks."—1 *Chron.* iv, 41.
"If *there* be indistinctness or disorder *there,* we can have no success."—*Blair's Rhet.* p. 271.
"*There, there* are schools adapted to every age."—*Woodbridge, Lit. Conv.* p. 78. The import of
the word is more definite, when emphasis is laid upon it; but this is no good reason for saying,
with Dr. Webster, that it is "without signification," when it is without emphasis; or, with Dr.
Priestley, that it "seems to have no meaning whatever, except it be thought to give a small
degree of emphasis."—*Rudiments of E. Gram.* p. 135.

OBS. 31.—The noun *place* itself is just as loose and variable in its meaning as the adverb *there.*
For example : "*There* is never any difference;" i. e. "No difference ever takes *place.*" Shall we
say that "*place,*" in this sense, is not a noun of place ? To *take place,* is, to occur *somewhere,* or
anywhere ; and the unemphatic word *there* is but as indefinite in respect to place, as these other
adverbs of place, or as the noun itself. S. B. Goodenow accounts it a *great error,* to say that *there*
is an adverb of place, when it is thus indefinite; and he chooses to call it an "*indefinite pronoun :*"
as, "'What is *there* here ?'—'*There* is no peace.'—'What need was *there* of it ?'" See his *Gram.*
p. 3 and p. 11. In treating of the various classes of adverbs, I have admitted and shown, that
here, there, and *where,* have sometimes the nature of pronouns, especially in such compounds as
hereof, thereof, whereof ; but, in this instance, I see not what advantage there is in calling *there*
a "pronoun:" we have just as much reason to call *here* and *where* pronouns — and that, perhaps,
on all occasions. Barnard says, "In the sentence, '*There* is one glory of the sun,' &c., the adverb *there* qualifies the verb *is,* and seems to have the force of an affirmation, like *truly.*"—*Analytic Gram.* p. 294. But an adverb of the latter kind may be used with the word *there,* and

perceive no particular similarity between them: as, "*Verily there is a reward for the righteous.*"—*Psal.* lviii, 11. "*Truly there is a glory of the sun.*"

OBS. 32.—There is a vulgar error of substituting the adverb *most* for *almost*, as in the phrases, "*most all,*"—"*most anywhere,*"—"*most every day,*" which we sometimes hear for "*almost all,*"—"*almost anywhere,*"—"*almost every day.*" The fault is gross, and chiefly colloquial, but it is sometimes met with in books; as, "But thinking he had replied *most* too rashly, he said, 'I won't answer your question.'"—*Wagstaff's History of Friends,* Vol. 1, p. 207.

NOTES TO RULE XXI.

NOTE I.—Adverbs must be placed in that position which will render the sentence the most perspicuous and agreeable. Example of error: "We are in no hazard of mistaking the sense of the author, though every word which he uses *be not precise* and exact."—*Blair's Rhet.* p. 95; *Jamieson's,* 66. Murray says,— "though every word which he uses *is not precise* and exact."—*Octavo Gram.* p. 302. Better:—"though *not every word* which he uses, *is precise* and exact."

NOTE II.—Adverbs should not be needlessly used for adjectives; nor should they be employed when quality is to be expressed, and not manner: as, "That the *now* copies of the original text are entire."—*S. Fisher.* Say, "the *present* copies," or, "the *existing* copies." "The arrows of calumny fall *harmlessly* at the feet of virtue." —*Murray's Key,* p. 167; *Merchant's Gram.* 186; *Ingersoll's,* 10; *Kirkham's,* 21. Say, "fall *harmless ;*" as in this example: "The impending black cloud, which is regarded with so much dread, may pass by *harmless.*"—*Murray's Key,* 8vo, p. 262.

NOTE III.—With a verb of motion, most grammarians prefer *hither, thither,* and *whither,* to *here, there,* and *where,* which are in common use, and perhaps allowable, though not so good; as, "Come *hither,* Charles,"—or, "Come *here.*"

NOTE IV.—"To the adverbs *hence, thence,* and *whence,* the preposition *from* is frequently (though not with strict propriety) prefixed; as, *from hence, from whence.*"—See *W. Allen's Gram.* p. 174. Some critics, however, think this construction allowable, notwithstanding the former word is implied in the latter. See *Priestley's Gram.* p. 134; and *L. Murray's,* p. 198. It is seldom elegant to use any word needlessly.

NOTE V.—The adverb *how* should not be used before the conjunction *that,* nor in stead of it; as, "He said *how* he would go."—"Ye see *how that* not many wise men are called." Expunge *how.* This is a vulgar error. Somewhat similar is the use of *how* for *lest* or *that not ;* as, "Be cautious *how* you offend him, i. e. *that* you *do not* offend him."—*W. Allen's Gram.* p. 175.

NOTE VI.—The adverb *when, while,* or *where,* is not fit to follow the verb *is* in a definition, or to introduce a clause taken substantively; because it expresses identity, not of being, but of time or place: as, "*Concord, is when* one word agrees with another in some accidents."—*Adam's Gram,* p. 151; *Gould's,* 155. Say, "Concord is *the agreement of* one word with *an other* in some *accident* or accidents."

NOTE VII.—The adverb *no* should not be used with reference to a *verb* or a *participle.* Such expressions as, "Tell me whether you will go or *no,*" are therefore improper: *no* should here be *not ;* because the verb *go* is understood after it. The meaning is, "Tell me whether you will go or *will not go ;*" but nobody would think of saying, "Whether you will go or *no go.*"

NOTE VIII.—A negation, in English, admits but one negative word; because two negatives in the same clause, usually contradict each other, and make the meaning affirmative. The following example is therefore ungrammatical: "For my part, I love him not, *nor* hate him *not.*"—*Beauties of Shakspeare,* p. 16. Expunge the last *not,* or else change *nor* to *and.*

NOTE IX.—The words *ever* and *never* should be carefully distinguished according to their sense, and not confounded with each other in their application. Example: "The Lord reigneth, be the earth *never so* unquiet."—*Experience of St. Paul,* p. 195. Here, I suppose, the sense to require *everso,* an adverb of degree: "Be the earth *everso* unquiet." That is,—"unquiet *in whatever degree.*"

NOTE X.—Adverbs that end in *ly,* are in general preferable to those forms which, for want of this distinction, may seem like adjectives misapplied. Example : " There would be *scarce* any such thing in nature as a folio."—*Addison*. Better :—"*scarcely*."

IMPROPRIETIES FOR CORRECTION.

FALSE SYNTAX UNDER RULE XXI.

EXAMPLES UNDER NOTE I.—THE PLACING OF ADVERBS.

"All that is favoured by good use, is not proper to be retained."—*Murray's Gram*. ii, p. 296.

[FORMULE.—Not proper, because the adverb *not* is not put in the most suitable place. But, according to Note 1st under Rule 21st, "Adverbs must be placed in that position which will render the sentence the most perspicuous and agreeable." The sentence will be improved by placing *not* before *all* ; thus, "*Not all* that is favoured by good use, is proper to be retained."]

" Every thing favoured by good use, [is] not on that account worthy to be retained."—*Ib*. i, 369 ; *Campbell's Rhet*. p. 179. " Most men dream, but all do not."—*Beattie's Moral Science*, i, 72. " By hasty composition, we shall acquire certainly a very bad style."—*Blair's Rhet*. p. 191. " The comparisons are short, touching on one point only of resemblance."—*Ib*. p. 416. " Having had once some considerable object set before us."—*Ib*. p. 116. " The positive seems improperly to be called a degree."—*Adam's Gram*. p. 69; *Gould's*, 68. " In some phrases the genitive is only used."—*Adam*, 159 ; *Gould*, 161. " This blunder is said actually to have occurred."—*Smith's Inductive Gram*. p. 5. " But every man is not called James, nor every woman Mary."—*Buchanan's Gram*. p. 15. " Crotchets are employed for the same purpose nearly as the parenthesis."—*Churchill's Gram*. p. 167. " There is still a greater impropriety in a double comparative."—*Priestley's Gram*. p. 78. " We have often occasion to speak of time."—*Lowth's Gram*. p. 39. " The following sentence cannot be possibly understood."—*Ib*. p. 104. " The words must be generally separated from the context."—*Comly's Gram*. p. 155. " Words ending in *ator* have the accent generally on the penultimate."—*Murray's Gram*. i, 239. " The learned languages, with respect to voices, moods, and tenses, are, in general, differently constructed from the English tongue."—*Ib*. i, 101. "Adverbs seem originally to have been contrived to express compendiously in one word, what must otherwise have required two or more."—*Ib*. i, 114. " But it is only so, when the expression can be converted into the regular form of the possessive case."—*Ib*. i, 174. " Enter, (says he) boldly, for here too there are gods."—*Harris's Hermes*, p. 8. " For none work for ever so little a pittance that some cannot be found to work for less."—*Sedgwick's Economy*, p. 190. " For sinners also lend to sinners, to receive as much again."—*Luke*, vi, 34. " They must be viewed exactly in the same light."—*Murray's Gram*. ii, 24. " If he does but speak to display his abilities, he is unworthy of attention."—*Ib. Key*, ii, 207.

UNDER NOTE II.—ADVERBS FOR ADJECTIVES.

"Motion upwards is commonly more agreeable than motion downwards."—*Blair's Rhet*. p. 48. " There are but two ways possibly of justification before God."—*Dr. Cox, on Quakerism*, p. 413. " This construction sounds rather harshly."—*Murray's Gram*. i, 194 ; *Ingersoll's*, 199. "A clear conception, in the mind of the learner, of regularly and well-formed letters."—*Com. School Journal*, i, 66. " He was a great hearer of * * * Attalus, Sotion, Papirius, Fabianus, of whom he makes often mention."—*Seneca's Morals*, p. xi. " It is only the Often doing of a thing that makes it a Custom."—*Divine Right of Tythes*, p. 72. " Because W. R. takes oft occasion to insinuate his jealousies of persons and things."—*Barclay's Works*, i, 570. " Yet often touching will wear gold."—*Beauties of Shak*. p. 18. " Uneducated persons frequently use an adjective, when they ought to use an adverb: as, ' The country looks *beautiful* ;' instead of *beautifully*."—*Bucke's Gram*. p. 84. " The adjective is put absolutely, or without its substantive."—*Ash's Gram*. p. 57. "A noun or pronoun in the second person, may be put absolutely in the nominative case."—*Harrison's Gram*. p. 45. "A noun or pronoun, when put absolutely with a participle," &c.—*Ib*. p. 44 ; *Jaudon's Gram*. 108. "A verb in the infinitive mood absolute, stands independently of the remaining part of the sentence."—*Wilbur and Livingston's Gram*. p. 24. "At my return lately into England, I met a book intituled, ' The Iron Age.' "—*Cowley's Preface*, p. v. " But he can discover no better foundation for any of them, than the practice merely of Homer and Virgil."—*Kames, El. of Criticism, Introd*. p. xxv.

UNDER NOTE III.—HERE FOR HITHER, &c.

"It is reported that the governour will come here to-morrow."—*Kirkham's Gram*. p. 196. " It *has been* reported that the governour will come here to-morrow."—*Ib. Key*, p. 227. "To catch a prospect of that lovely land where his steps are tending."—*Maturin's Sermons*, p. 244. " Plautus makes one of his characters ask another where he is going with that Vulcan shut up in a horn ; that is, with a lanthorn in his hand."—*Adams's Rhet*. ii, 331. " When we left Cambridge, we intended to return there in a few days."—*Anonym*. " Duncan comes here to-night."—*Shak., Macbeth*. " They talked of returning here last week."—*J. M. Putnam's Gram*. p. 116.

UNDER NOTE IV.—FROM HENCE, &c.

"From hence he concludes that no inference can be drawn from the meaning of the word, that a *constitution* has a higher authority than a law or statute."—*Webster's Essays*, p. 67. "From whence we may likewise date the period of this event."—*Murray's Key*, ii, p. 202. "From hence it becomes evident, that LANGUAGE, taken in the most comprehensive view, implies certain Sounds, having certain Meanings."—*Harris's Hermes*, p. 315. "They returned to the city from whence they came out."—*Alex. Murray's Gram.* p. 135. "Respecting ellipses, some grammarians differ strangely in their ideas; and from thence has arisen a very whimsical diversity in their systems of grammar."—*Author.* "What am I and from whence? i. e. what am I, and from whence *am* I?"—*Jaudon's Gram.* p. 171.

UNDER NOTE V.—THE ADVERB HOW.

"It is strange how a writer, so accurate as Dean Swift, should have stumbled on so improper an application of this particle."—*Blair's Rhet.* p. 112. "Ye know how that a good while ago God made choice among us," &c.—*Acts.* xv, 7. "Let us take care *how* we sin; i. e. *that* we *do not* sin."—*Priestley's Gram.* p. 135. "We see by these instances, how prepositions may be necessary to connect those words, which in their signification are not naturally connected."—*Murray's Gram.* i, p. 118. "Know ye not your own selves, how that Jesus Christ is in you, except ye be reprobates?"—2 *Cor.* xiii, 5. "That thou mayest know how that the earth is the Lord's."—*Exod.* ix, 29.

UNDER NOTE VI.—WHEN, WHILE, OR WHERE.

"Ellipsis is when one or more words are wanting to complete the sense."—*Adam's Gram.* p. 235; *Gould's*, p. 229; *B. F. Fisk's Greek Gram.* 184. "Pleonasm is when a word more is added than is absolutely necessary to express the sense."—*Same works.* "Hystĕron protĕron is when that is put in the former part of the sentence, which, according to the sense, should be in the latter."—*Adam*, p. 237; *Gould*, 230. "Hysteron proteron, n. A rhetorical figure, when that is said last which was done first."—*Webster's Dict.* "A Barbarism is when a foreign or strange word is *made use of.*"—*Adam's Gram.* p. 242; *Gould's*, 234. "A Solecism is when the rules of Syntax are transgressed."—*Iidem, ib.* "An Idiotism is when the manner of expression peculiar to one language is used in another."—*Iid. ib.* "Tautology is when we either uselessly repeat the same words, or repeat the same sense in different words."—*Adam*, p. 243; *Gould*, 235. "Bombast is when high sounding words are used without meaning, or upon a trifling occasion."—*Iid. ib.* "Amphibology is when, by the ambiguity of the construction, the meaning may be taken in two different senses."—*Iid. ib.* "Irony is when one means the contrary of what is said."—*Adam*, p. 247; *Gould*, 237. "The Periphrasis, or Circumlocution, is when several words are employed to express what might be expressed in fewer."—*Iid. ib.* "Hyperbole is when a thing is magnified above the truth."—*Adam*, p. 249; *Gould*, 240. "Personification is when we ascribe life, sentiments, or actions, to inanimate beings, or to abstract qualities."—*Iid. ib.* "Apostrophe, or Address, is when the speaker breaks off from the series of his discourse, and addresses himself to some person present or absent, living or dead, or to inanimate nature, as if endowed with sense and reason."—*Iid. ib.* "A Simile or Comparison is when the resemblance between two objects, whether *real* or *imaginary*, is expressed in form."—*Kirkham's Gram.* p. 223. "Simile, or Comparison, is when one thing is illustrated or heightened by comparing it to another."—*Adam's Gram.* p. 250; *Gould's*, 240. "Antithesis, or Opposition, is when things contrary or different are contrasted, to make them appear in the more striking light."—*Iid. ib.* "Description, or Imagery, [is] when any thing is painted in a lively manner, as if done before our eyes."—*Adam's Gram.* p. 250. "Emphasis is when a particular stress is laid on some word in a sentence."—*Ib.* "Epanorthosis, or Correction, is when the speaker either recalls or corrects what he had last said."—*Ib.* "Paralepsis, or Omission, is when one pretends to omit or pass by, what he at the same time declares."—*Ib.* "Incrementum, or Climax in sense, is when one member rises above another to the highest."—*Ib.* p. 251. "A Metonymy is where the cause is put for the effect, or the effect for the cause; the container for the thing contained; or the sign for the thing signified."—*Kirkham's Gram.* p. 223. "Agreement is when one word is like another in number, case, gender, or person."—*Frost's Gram.* p. 43; *Greenleaf's*, 32. "Government is when one word causes another to be in some particular number, person, or case."—*Webster's Imp. Gram.* p. 89; *Greenleaf's*, 32; *Frost's*, 43. "Fusion is while some solid substance is converted into a fluid by heat."—*B.* "A Proper Diphthong is where both the Vowels are sounded together; as, *oi* in *Voice, ou* in *House.*"—*Fisher's Gram.* p, 10. "An Improper Diphthong is where the Sound of but one of the two Vowels is heard; as *e* in *People.*"—*Ib.* p. 11.

UNDER NOTE VII.—THE ADVERB NO.

"An adverb is joined to a verb to show how, or whether or no, or when, or where one is, does, or suffers."—*Buchanan's Syntax*, p. 62. "We must be immortal, whether we will or no."—*Maturin's Sermons*, p. 33. "He cares not whether the world was made for Cæsar or no."—*American Quarterly Review.* "I do not know whether they are out or no."—*Byron's*

Letters. "Whether it can be proved or no, is not the thing."—*Butler's Analogy*, p. 84. "Whether or no he makes use of the means commanded by God."—*Ib.* p. 164. "Whether it pleases the world or no, the care is taken."—*L'Estrange's Seneca*, p. 5. "How comes this to be never heard of, nor in the least questioned, whether the Law was undoubtedly of Moses's writing or no ?"—*Bp. Tomline's Evidences*, p. 44. "Whether he be a sinner or no, I know not."—*John*, ix, 25. "Can I make men live, whether they will or no ?"—*Shak.*
"Can hearts, not free, be try'd whether they serve
Willing or no, who will but what they must ?"—*Milton, P. L.*

UNDER NOTE VIII.—OF DOUBLE NEGATIVES.

"We need not, nor do not, confine the purposes of God."—*Bentley.* "I cannot by no means allow him that."—*Idem.* "We must try whether or no we cannot increase the Attention by the Help of the Senses."—*Brightland's Gram.* p. 263. "There is nothing more admirable nor more useful."—*Horne Tooke*, Vol. i, p. 20. "And what in no time to come he can never be said to have done, he can never be supposed to do."—*Johnson's Gram. Com.* p. 345. "No skill could obviate, nor no remedy dispel, the terrible infection."—*Goldsmith's Greece*, i, 114. "Prudery cannot be an indication neither of sense nor of taste."—*Spurzheim, on Education*, p. 21. "But that scripture, nor no other, speaks not of imperfect faith."—*Barclay's Works*, i, 172. "But this scripture, nor none other, proves not that faith was or is always accompanied with doubting."—*Ibid.* "The light of Christ is not nor cannot be darkness."—*Ib.* p. 252. "Doth not the Scripture, which cannot lie, give none of the saints this testimony ?"—*Ib.* p. 379. "Which do not continue, nor are not binding."—*Ib.* Vol. iii, p. 79. "It not being perceived directly no more than the air."—*Campbell's Rhet.* p. 331. "Let's be no Stoics, nor no stocks, I pray."—*Shak., Shrew.* "Where there is no marked nor peculiar character in the style."—*Blair's Rhet.* p. 175. "There can be no rules laid down, nor no manner recommended."—*Sheridan's Lect.* p. 163.
"*Bates.* 'He hath not told his thought to the king ?'
K. Henry. 'No; nor it is not meet he should.'"—*Shak.*

UNDER NOTE IX.—EVER AND NEVER.

"The prayer of Christ is more than sufficient both to strengthen us, be we never so weak; and to overthrow all adversary power, be it never so strong."—*Hooker.* "He is like to have no share in it, or to be ever the better for it."—*Law and Grace*, p. 23. "In some parts of Chili, it seldom or ever rains."—*Willetts's Geog.* "If Pompey shall but never so little seem to like it."—*Walker's Particles*, p. 246. "Latin : 'Si Pompeius *paulum* modò ostenderit sibi placere.' *Cic.* i, 5."—*Ib.* "Though never such a power of dogs and hunters pursue him."—*Walker, ib.* "Latin : '*Quamlibet* magnà canum et venantium urgente vi.' *Plin.* l. 18, c. 16."—*Ib.* "Though you be never so excellent."—*Walker, ib.* "Latin : '*Quantumvis* licet excellas.' *Cic. de Amic.*"—*Ib.* "If you do amiss never so little."—*Walker, ib.* "Latin : 'Si *tantillum* peccàssis.' *Plaut. Rud.* 4, 4."—*Ib.* "If we cast our eyes never so little down."—*Walker, ib.* "Latin : 'Si *tantulum* oculos dejecerimus.' *Cic.* 7. *Ver.*"—*Ib.* "A wise man scorneth nothing, be it never so small or homely."—*Book of Thoughts*, p. 37. "Because they have seldom or ever an opportunity of learning them at all."—*Clarkson's Prize-Essay*, p. 170. "We seldom or ever see those forsaken who trust in God."—*Atterbury.*
"Where, playing with him at bo-peep,
He solved all problems, ne'er so deep."—*Hudibras.*

UNDER NOTE X.—OF THE FORM OF ADVERBS.

"One can scarce think that Pope was capable of epic or tragic poetry; but within a certain limited region, he has been outdone by no poet."—*Blair's Rhet.* p. 403. "I, who now read, have near finished this chapter."—*Harris's Hermes*, p. 82. "And yet, to refine our taste with respect to beauties of art or of nature, is scarce endeavoured in any seminary of learning."—*Kames, El. of Crit.* Vol. i, p. viii. "By the Numbers being confounded, and the Possessives wrong applied, the Passage is neither English nor Grammar."—*Buchanan's Syntax*, p. 123. "The letter G is wrong named *jee.*"—*Creighton's Dict.* p. viii. "Last; Remember that in science, as in morals, authority cannot make right, what, in itself, is wrong."—*O. B. Peirce's Gram.* p. 194. "They regulate our taste even where we are scarce sensible of them."—*Kames, El. of Crit.* ii, 96. "Slow action, for example, is imitated by words pronounced slow."—*Ib.* ii, 257. "Sure, if it be to profit withal, it must be in order to save."—*Barclay's Works*, i, 366. "Which is scarce possible at best."—*Sheridan's Elocution*, p. 57. "Our wealth being near finished."—HARRIS : *Priestley's Gram.* p. 80.

CHAPTER IX.— CONJUNCTIONS.

The syntax of Conjunctions consists, not (as L. Murray and others erroneously teach,) in "their power of determining the mood of verbs," or the "cases of nouns and pronouns," but in the simple fact, that they link together such and such terms, and thus " mark the connexions of human thought."—*Beattie.*

RULE XXII.—CONJUNCTIONS.

Conjunctions connect words, sentences, or parts of sentences: as, " Let there be no strife, I pray thee, between me *and* thee, *and* between my herdmen *and* thy herdmen ; *for* we are brethren."—*Gen.* xiii, 8.

"Ah! *if* she lend not arms *as well as* rules,
What can she more *than* tell us we are fools ?"—*Pope.*

EXCEPTION FIRST.

The conjunction *that* sometimes serves merely to introduce a sentence which is made the subject or the object of a finite verb ;* as, "*That* mind is not matter, is certain."
"*That* you have wronged me, doth appear in this."—*Shak.*
"*That* time is mine, O Mead ! to thee, I owe."—*Young.*

EXCEPTION SECOND.

When two corresponding conjunctions occur, in their usual order, the former should be parsed as referring to the latter, which is more properly the connecting word; as, "*Neither* sun *nor* stars in many days appeared."—*Acts,* xxvii, 20. "*Whether* that evidence has been afforded [*or* not,] is a matter of investigation."—*Keith's Evidences,* p. 18.

EXCEPTION THIRD.

Either, corresponding to *or,* and *neither,* corresponding to *nor* or *not,* are sometimes transposed, so as to repeat the disjunction or negation at the end of the sentence ; as, " Where then was their capacity of standing, or his *either?* "—*Barclay's Works,* iii, 359. " It is *not* dangerous *neither.*"—*Bolingbroke, on Hist.* p. 135. " He is very tall, but *not* too tall *neither.*"—*Spect.* No. 475.

OBSERVATIONS ON RULE XXII.

OBS. 1.—Conjunctions that connect particular *words,* generally join similar parts of speech in a common dependence on some other term. Hence, if the words connected be such as have *cases,* they will of course be in the same case; as, " For *me* and *thee.*"—*Matt.* xvii, 27. " Honour thy *father* and thy *mother.*"—*Ib.* xviii, 19. Here the latter noun or pronoun is connected by *and* to the former, and governed by the same preposition or verb. Conjunctions themselves have no government, unless the questionable phrase "*than whom*" may be reckoned an exception. See Obs. 17th below, and others that follow it.

OBS. 2.—Those conjunctions which connect *sentences* or *clauses,* commonly unite one sentence or clause to an other, either as an additional assertion, or as a condition, a cause, or an end, of what is asserted. The conjunction is placed *between* the terms which it connects, except there is a transposition, and then it stands before the dependent term, and consequently at the beginning of the whole sentence: as, " He taketh away the first, *that* he may establish the second."—*Heb.* x, 9. "*That* he may establish the second, he taketh away the first."

OBS. 3.—The term that follows a conjunction, is in some instances a *phrase* of several words, yet not therefore a whole clause or member, unless we suppose it elliptical, and supply what will make it such: as, "And whatsoever ye do, do it heartily, As *to the Lord,* AND *not unto men.*"—*Col.* iii, 23. If we say, this means, " *as doing it* to the Lord, and not *as doing it* unto men," the terms are still mere phrases ; but if we say, the sense is, " as *if ye did it* to the Lord, and not *as if ye did it* unto men," they are clauses, or sentences. Churchill says, " The office of the conjunction is, to connect one *word* with an other, or one *phrase* with an other."—*New Gram.* p. 152. But he uses the term *phrase* in a more extended sense than I suppose it will strictly bear: he means by it, a *clause,* or *member* ; that is, a sentence which forms a part of a greater sentence.

OBS. 4.—What is the office of this part of speech, according to Lennie, Bullions, Brace, Hart, Hiley, Smith, M'Culloch, Webster, Wells, and others, who say that it "joins *words and sentences* together," (see Errors on p. 415 of this work,) it is scarcely possible to conceive. If they imagine it to connect "*words*" on the one side, to "*sentences*" on the other ; this is plainly absurd, and contrary to facts. If they suppose it to join sentence to sentence, by merely connecting word to word, in a joint relation ; this also is absurd, and self-contradictory. Again, if they mean, that the conjunction sometimes connects word with word, and sometimes, sentence with sentence ; *this sense they have not expressed,* but have severally puzzled their readers by an ungrammatical use of the word "*and.*" One of the best among them says, " In *the sentence,* ' He *and* I must go,' the word *and* unites *two sentences,* and thus *avoids* an unnecessary repetition ; thus instead of saying, ' He must go,' ' I must go,' we connect *the words He, I,* as the same thing is affirmed of both, namely, *must go.*"—*Hiley's Gram.* p. 53. Here is the incongruous suggestion, that *by connecting words only,* the conjunction in fact *connects sentences* ; and the stranger blunder concerning *those words,* that " the same thing is affirmed of *both,* namely, [*that they*] *must go.*"

---

* The conjunction *that,* at the head of a sentence or clause, enables us to assume the whole proposition as one thing ; as, "All arguments whatever are directed to prove one or other of these *three things : that* something is true ; *that* it is morally right or fit ; or *that* it is profitable and good."—*Blair's Rhet.* p. 313. Here each *that* may be parsed as connecting its own clause to the first clause in the sentence ; or, to the word *things,* with which the three clauses are in a sort of apposition. If we conceive it to have no such connecting power, we must make this too an exception.

Whereas it is plain, that nothing is affirmed of either; for *"He and I must go,"* only affirms of *im* and *me*, that *"we must go."* And again it is plain, that *and* here connects nothing but the wo pronouns; for no one will say, that, *"He and I must go together,"* is a compound sentence, apable of being resolved into two; and if, *"He and I must go,"* is compound because it is equiv- lent to, "He must go, and I must go;" so is, *"We must go,"* for the same reason, though it has ut one nominative and one verb. *"He and I were present,"* is rightly given by Hiley as an exam- le of *two pronouns* connected together by *and.* (See *his Gram.* p. 105.) But, of *verbs* connected o each other, he absurdly supposes the following to be examples: "He spake, *and* it was done."— I know it, *and* I can prove it."—"Do you say so, *and* can you prove it ?"—*Ib.* Here *and* con- ects *sentences,* and not particular *words.*

OBS. 5.—Two or three conjunctions sometimes come together; as, "What rests, *but that* the iortal sentence pass ?"—*Milton.* "Nor yet *that* he should offer himself often."—*Heb.* ix, 25. 'hese may be severally parsed as "connecting what precedes and what follows," and the observ- nt reader will not fail to notice, that such combinations of connecting particles are sometimes equired by the sense; but, since nothing that is needless, is really proper, conjunctions should ot be unnecessarily accumulated: as, *"But* AND *if* that evil servant say in his heart," &c.— *Matt.* xxiv, 48. Greek, "Ἐὰν δὲ εἴπῃ ὁ κακὸς δοῦλος ἐκεῖνος," &c. Here is no *and.* *"But* AND *f* she depart."—1 *Cor.* vii, 11. This is almost a literal rendering of the Greek, "Ἐὰν δὲ καὶ χρονίσῃ,"—yet either *but* or *and* is certainly useless. "In several cases," says Priestley, " we ontent ourselves, now, with fewer conjunctive particles than our ancestors *did* [say *used*]. Ex- mple: *'So* AS *that* his doctrines were embraced by great numbers.' *Universal Hist.* Vol. 29, ι. 501. *So that* would have been much easier, and better."—*Priestley's Gram.* p. 139. Some of he poets have often used the word *that* as an expletive, to fill the measure of their verse; as,

"When *that* the poor have cried, Cæsar hath wept."—*Shakspeare.*
"If *that* he be a dog, beware his fangs."—*Id.*
"That made him pine away and moulder,
As though *that* he had been no soldier."—*Butler's Poems,* p. 164.

OBS. 6.—W. Allen remarks, that, *"And* is sometimes introduced to engage our attention to a ollowing word or phrase; as, 'Part pays, *and* justly, the deserving steer.' [*Pope.*] 'I see thee all, *and* by Achilles' hand.' [*Id.*]."—*Allen's E. Gram.* p. 184. The like idiom, he says, occurs n these passages of Latin: "'Forsan *et* hæc olim meminisse juvabit.' *Virg.* 'Mors *et* fugacem iersequitur virum.' *Hor.*"—*Allen's Gram.* p. 184. But it seems to me, that *and* and *et* are here egular connectives. The former implies a repetition of the preceding verb: as, "Part pays, *and ustly pays,* the deserving steer."—"I see thee fall, *and fall by Achilles' hand."* The latter refers iack to what was said before: thus, "Perhaps it will *also* hereafter delight you to recount these ivils."—*"And* death pursues the man that flees." In the following text, the conjunction is more ike an expletive; but even here it suggests an extension of the discourse then in progress: 'Lord, *and* what shall this man do ?"—*John,* xxi, 21. "Κύριε, οὗτος δὲ τί ;"—"Domine, hic utem quid ?"—*Beza.*

OBS. 7.—The conjunction *as* often unites words that are in *apposition,* or in *the same case;* as, 'He offered himself AS a *journeyman."*—"I assume *it* AS a *fact."*—*Webster's Essays,* p. 94. "In n other example of the same kind, the *earth,* AS a common *mother,* is animated to give refuge gainst a father's unkindness."—*Kames, El. of Crit.* Vol. ii, p. 168. "And then to offer *himself* P AS a *sacrifice* and *propitiation* for them."—*Scougal,* p. 99. So, likewise, when an intransitive erb takes the same case after as before it, by Rule 6th; as, *"Johnson* soon after engaged AS *usher* in a school."—*L. Murray.* *"He* was employed AS *usher."* In all these examples, the case hat follows *as,* is determined by that which precedes. If after the verb *"engaged"* we supply *imself, usher* becomes objective, and is in apposition with the pronoun, and not in agreement rith *Johnson:* "He engaged *himself* as usher." One late writer, ignorant or regardless of the nalogy of General Grammar, imagines this case to be an "objective governed by the conjunction *s,"* according to the following rule: "The conjunction *as,* when it takes the meaning of *for,* or u *the character of,* governs the objective case; as, Addison, *as* a *writer* of prose, is highly distin- uished."—*J. M. Putnam's Gram.* p. 113. S. W. Clark, in his grammar published in 1848, sets s in his list of *prepositions,* with this example: "'That England can spare from her service such ien *as* HIM."—*Lord Brougham."*—*Clark's Practical Gram.* p. 92. And again: "When the second erm of a *Comparison of equality* is a Noun, or Pronoun, the *Preposition* AS is commonly used. Example—'He hath died to redeem such a rebel *as* ME.'—*Wesley."* Undoubtedly, Wesley and Brougham here erroneously supposed the *as* to connect *words only,* and consequently to require hem to be in the same case, agreeably to OBS. 1st, above; but a moment's reflection on the sense, hould convince any one, that the construction requires the nominative forms *he* and *I,* with the erbs *is* and *am* understood.

OBS. 8.—The conjunction *as* may also be used between an adjective or a participle and the noun o which the adjective or participle relates; as, "It does not appear that brutes have the least eflex sense of *actions* AS *distinguished* from events; or that will and design, which constitute the ery nature of *actions* AS *such,* are at all an object of their perception."—*Butler's Analogy,* p. 277.

OBS. 9.—*As* frequently has the force of a *relative pronoun,* and when it evidently sustains the elation of a *case,* it ought to be called, and generally *is* called, a pronoun, rather than a conjunc- iom ; as, "Avoid such *as are* vicious."—*Anon.* "But as many *as received* him," &c.—*John,* i, 12. 'We have reduced the terms into as small a number *as was* consistent with perspicuity and dis- inction."—*Brightland's Gram.* p. ix. Here *as* represents a noun, and while it serves to connect he two parts of the sentence, it is also the subject of a verb. These being the true character- stics of a relative pronoun, it is proper to refer the word to that class. But when a clause or a entence is the antecedent, it is better to consider the *as* a conjunction, and to supply the pronoun *t,* if the writer has not used it; as, "He is angry, *as* [*it*] *appears* by this letter." Horne Tooke ays, "The truth is, that AS is *also* an *article;* and (however and whenever used in English) ieans the same as *It,* or *That,* or *Which."*—*Diversions of Purley,* Vol. i, p. 223. But what efinition he would give to *"an article,"* does not appear.

41

OBS. 10.—In some examples, it seems questionable whether *as* ought to be reckoned a noun, or ought rather to be parsed as a conjunction after which a nominative is understood. "He then read the conditions *as follow*."—"The conditions are *as follow*.—*Nutting's* G p. 106. "The principal evidences on which this assertion is grounded, are *as follow*."—*Gu Essays*, p. 166. "The Quiescent verbs are *as follow*."—*Pike's Heb. Lex.* p. 184. "The numbers are duplications of these, and proceed *as follow*."—*Dr. Murray's Hist. of Lang.* p. 35. "The most eminent of the kennel are bloodhounds, which lead the van, and are *low*."—*Steele, Tattler*, No. 62. "His words are *as follow*."—*Spect.* No. 62. "The words *follow*."—*Addison, Spect.* 513. "The objections that are raised against it as a tragedy, *follow*."—*Gay, Pref. to What d' ye call it*. "The particulars are *as follow*."—*Bucke's* p. 93. "The principal Interjections in English are *as follow*."—*Ward's Gram.* p. 81. In instances, one may suppose the final clause to mean, "*as they here* follow;"—or, supposing be a pronoun, one may conceive it to mean, "*such* as follow." But some critical wr appears, prefer the singular verb, "*as follows*." Hear Campbell: "When a verb is used *sonally*, it ought undoubtedly to be in the singular number, whether the neuter pron expressed or understood; and when no nominative in the sentence can regularly be co with the verb, it ought to be considered as impersonal. For this reason, analogy as well *favour* [say *favours*] this mode of expression, 'The conditions of the agreement were *as f* and not '*as follow*.' A few late writers have inconsiderately adopted this last form th mistake of the construction. For the same reason we ought to say, 'I shall consider his c so far only as *concerns* my friend's conduct;' and not 'so far as *concern*.'"—*Philosophy* p. 229. It is too much to say, at least of one of these sentences, that there is no nominat. w which the plural verb can be regularly construed. In the former, the word *as* may be said a plural nominative; or, if we will have this to be a conjunction, the pronoun *they*, repre *conditions*, may be regularly supplied, as above. In the latter, indeed, *as* is not a prono cause it refers to "*so far*," which is not a noun. But the sentence is *bad English*; beca verb *concern* or *concerns* is improperly left without a nominative. Say therefore, 'I shall his censures so far only as *they concern* my friend's conduct;'—or, 'so far only as my *conduct is concerned*.' The following is an other example which I conceive to be wrong: with an adverb for its antecedent, *as* is made a nominative: "They ought therefore to be *as quickly as is* consistent with distinct articulation."—*Sheridan's Elocution*, p. 76. Say "They ought therefore to be uttered *with as much rapidity* as is consistent with distinct art tion."

OBS. 11.—Lindley Murray was so much puzzled with Tooke's notion of *as*, and Campbe's trine of the *impersonal verb*, that he has expressly left his pupils to hesitate and doub himself, whether one ought to say "*as follows*" or "*as follow*," when the preceding plural; or—to furnish an alternative, (if they choose it,) he shows them at last how the *dodge the question*, by adopting some other phraseology. He begins thus: "*Grammarians* in opinion, respecting the propriety of the following modes of expression: 'The arg advanced were nearly *as follows*;' 'the positions were, *as appears*, incontrovertible.'"—M *Gram.* 8vo, p. 146. Then follows a detail of suggestions from Campbell and others, all the tations being anonymous, or at least without definite references. Omitting these, I wo say of the two examples given, that they are not parallel instances. For, "*as follow*," what the arguments were,—to the things themselves, considered plurally, and immediate exhibited; wherefore the expression ought rather to have been, "*as follow*," or, "*as th follow*." But, "*as appears*," means, "*as it appears*," or, "*as the case now appears*;" and these plain modes of expression would have been much preferable, because the *as* is here o nothing but a conjunction.

OBS. 12.—"The diversity of sentiment on this subject," says L. Murray, "and the v bility of the different opponents, will naturally induce *the readers* to pause and reflect, befo decide."—*Octavo Gram.* p. 147. The equivalent expressions by means of which he prop evade at last the dilemma, are the following: "The arguments advanced were nearly *such* low;"—"The arguments advanced were nearly of the following nature;"—"The follow nearly the arguments which were advanced;"—"The arguments advanced were nearly th follow;"—"These, or nearly these, were the arguments advanced:"—"The positions w as appear incontrovertible;"—"It appears that the positions were incontrovertible;"—"Th positions were incontrovertible, is apparent;"—"The positions were apparently incontrov —"In appearance, the positions were incontrovertible."—*Ibid*. If to shun the expression in our turn, surely here are ways enough! But to those who "pause and reflect" with the tion *to decide*, I would commend the following example: "Reconciliation was offered, as tions as moderate as *were* consistent with a permanent union."—*Murray's Key*, under Here Murray supposes "*was*" to be wrong, and accordingly changes it to "*were*," by the "A verb must agree with its nominative case in number and person." But the amendm pointed rejection of Campbell's "impersonal verb," or verb which "has no nominative." the singular is not right here, the rhetorician's respectable authority vouches only for a of errors. Again, if this verb must be *were* in order to agree with its nominative, it is still that *as*, is, or ought to be, the nominative; because the meaning may perhaps be better ex thus:—"on conditions as moderate *as any that were* consistent with a permanent union."

OBS. 13.—A late writer expresses his decision of the foregoing question thus: "Of all the ferent opinions on a grammatical subject, which have arisen in the literary world, there appears one more indefensible than that of supposing *as follows* to be an impersonal verb be correctly used in such sentences as this, 'The conditions were *as follows*.' Nay, we that, "A few late writers have adopted this form, 'The conditions were *as follow*,' imm *ately*;" and, to prove this charge of inconsiderateness, the following sentence is brought for 'I shall consider his censure [*censures* is the word used by Campbell and by Murray] so far *concern* my friend's conduct,' which should be, it is added, '*as concerns*, and not *as concern* analogy, simplicity, or syntactical authority, is of any value in our resolution of the sen

' The conditions were as follows,' the word *as* is as evident a relative as language can afford. It is undoubtedly equivalent to *that* or *which*, and relates to its antecedent *those* or *such* understood, and should have been the nominative to the verb *follow*; the sentence, in its present form, being inaccurate. The second sentence is by no means a parallel one. The word *as* is a conjunction; and though it has, as a relative, a reference to its antecedent *so*, yet in its capacity of a mere conjunction, it cannot possibly be the nominative case to any verb. It should be, ' *it concerns*.' Whenever *as* relates to an *adverbial* antecedent; as in the sentence, 'So far *as* it concerns me,' it is merely a conjunction; but when it refers to an *adjective* antecedent; as in the sentence, ' The business is *such as* concerns me;' it must be a relative, and susceptible of case, whether its antecedent is expressed or understood; being, in fact, the nominative to the verb *concerns*."—*Nixon's Parser*, p. 145. It will be perceived by the preceding remarks, that I do not cite what is here said, as believing it to be in all respects well said, though it is mainly so. In regard *to* the point at issue, I shall add but one critical authority more: "' The circumstances were as *follows*.' Several grammarians and critics have approved this phraseology: I am inclined, however, to concur with those who prefer ' *as follow*.' "—*Crombie, on Etym. and Synt*. p. 388.

Obs. 14.—The conjunction *that* is frequently understood; as, "*It* is seldom [*that*] their counsels are listened to."—*Robertson's Amer*. i, 318. "The truth is, [*that*] grammar is very much neglected among us."—*Lowth's Gram. Pref.* p. vi. "The Sportsman believes [*that*] there is Good in his Chace [chase]."—*Harris's Hermes*, p. 296.

"Thou warnst me [*that*] I have done amiss;
I should have earlier looked to this."—*Scott*.

Obs. 15.—After *than* or *as*, connecting the terms of a comparison, there is usually an ellipsis of some word or words. The construction of the words employed may be seen, when the ellipsis is supplied; as, "They are stronger *than we*" [are].—*Numb*. xiii, 31. "Wisdom is better *than weapons* of war" [are].—*Eccl*. ix, 18. "He does nothing who endeavours to do more *than* [what] *is allowed* to humanity."—*Dr. Johnson*. "My punishment is greater *than* [what] *I can bear*."—*Gen*. iv, 13. "Ralph gave him more *than I*" [gave him].—*Churchill's Gram*. p. 351. Ralph gave him more *than* [he gave] *me*."—*Ibid*. "Revelation, surely, was never intended for such *as he*" [is].—*Campbell's Four Gospels*, p. iv. "Let such as *him* sneer if they will."—*Liberator*, Vol. ix, p. 152. Here *him* ought to be *he*, according to Rule 2d, because the text speaks of such as *he is* or *was*. "' You were as innocent of it *as me :* ' ' He did it *as well as me*.' In both places it ought to be *I*: that is, *as I was, as I did*."—*Churchill's Gram*. p. 352.

"Rather let such poor souls *as you* and *I*
Say that the holidays are drawing nigh."—*Swift*.

Obs. 16.—The doctrine above stated, of ellipses after *than* and *as*, proceeds on the supposition that these words *are conjunctions*, and that they connect, not particular words merely, but sentences, or clauses. It is the common doctrine of nearly all our grammarians, and is doubtless liable to fewer objections than any other theory that ever has been, or ever can be, devised in lieu of it. Yet *as* is not always a conjunction; nor, when it is a conjunction, does it always connect sentences; nor, when it connects sentences, is there always an ellipsis; nor, when there is an ellipsis, is it always quite certain, what that ellipsis is. All these facts have been made plain, by observations that have already been bestowed on the word: and, according to some grammarians, the same things may severally be affirmed of the word *than*. But most authors consider *than* to be always a conjunction, and generally, if not always, to connect *sentences*. Johnson and Webster, in their dictionaries, mark it for an *adverb ;* and the latter says of it, "This word signifies also *then*, both in English and Dutch."—*Webster's Amer. Dict*. 8vo, *w*. Than. But what he means by "*also*," I know not; and surely, in no English of this age, is *than* equivalent to *then*, or *then* to *than*. The ancient practice of putting *then* for *than*, is now entirely obsolete ;[*] and, as we have no other term of the same import, most of our expositors merely explain *than* as "a particle used in comparison."—*Johnson, Worcester, Maunder*. Some absurdly define it thus: "THAN, *adv*. Placed in comparison."—*Walker*, (Rhym. Dict.) *Jones, Scott*. According to this definition, *than* should be a *participle!* But, since an express comparison necessarily implies a connexion between different terms, it cannot well be denied that *than* is a connective word; wherefore, not to detain the reader with any profitless controversy, I shall take it for granted that this word is always a conjunction. That it always connects sentences, I do not affirm; because there are instances in which it is difficult to suppose it to connect anything more than particular words: as, "Less judgement *than* wit is more sail *than* ballast."—*Penn's Maxims*. "With no less eloquence *than* freedom. ' Pari eloquentiâ ac libertate.' *Tacitus*."—*Walker's Particles*, p. 200. "Any comparison between th≥se two classes of writers, cannot be other *than* vague and loose."—*Blair's Rhet*. p. 347. "This *far more than* compensates all those little negligences."—*Ib*. p. 200.

"Remember Handel? Who, that was not born
Deaf as the dead to harmony, forgets,
Or can, *the more than* Homer of his age ?"—*Cowper*.

Obs. 17.—When any two declinable words are connected by *than* or *as*, they are almost always, according to the true idiom of our language, to be put in the *same case*, whether we suppose an ellipsis in the construction of the latter, or. not; as, "My *Father* is greater than *I*,"—*Bible*. "What do *ye* more than *others?*"—*Matt*. v, 47. "More *men* than *women* were there."—*Murray's Gram*. p. 114. "Entreat *him* as a *father*, and the younger *men* as *brethren*."—1 *Tim*. v, 1. "*I* would that all *men* were even as *I* myself."—1 *Cor*. vii, 7. "Simon, son of Jonas, lovest thou me more than these?"—*John*, xxi, 15. This last text is manifestly *ambiguous ;* so that some readers will doubt whether it means—"more than *thou lovest these*," or—"more than *these love me*." Is not this because there is an *ellipsis* in the sentence, and such a one as may be variously conceived and supplied? The original too is ambiguous, but not for the same reason: "Σιμων 'Ιωνᾶ, 'αγαπᾷς με πλεῖον τούτων ;"—And so is the Latin of the Vulgate and of Montanus: "Simon Jona,

---

[*] "*Note*, ⟨Then and then are distinct Particles, but use hath made the using of ther for than after a Comparative Degree at least passable. See Butler's Eng. Gram. Index.*"—*Walker's Eng. Particles*, Tenth Ed., 1691, p. 333.

diligis me *plus his?*" Wherefore Beza expressed it differently: "*Simon filii Jona*, diligis me *quàm hi?*" The French Bible has it: "Simon, fils de Jona, m'aimes-tu plus que *ne font* ci?" And the expression in English should rather have been, "Lovest thou me more the these?"

Obs. 18.—The comparative degree, in Greek, is said to govern the genitive case; in Latin ablative: that is, the genitive or the ablative is sometimes put after this degree without any necting particle corresponding to *than*, and without producing a compound sentence. have examples in the phrases, "πλεῖον τούτων" and "*plus his*," above. Of such a construct language admits no real example; that is, no exact parallel. But we have an imitation of the phrase *than whom*, as in this hackneyed example from Milton:

> "Which when Beëlzebub perceived, *than whom*,
> Satan except, none higher sat," &c.—*Paradise Lost*, B. ii, l. 300.

The objective, *whom*, is here preferred to the nominative, *who*, because the Latin ablative is monly rendered by the former case, rather than by the latter; but this phrase is no more a cable according to the usual principles of English grammar, than the error of putting the v tive case for a version of the ablative absolute. If the imitation is to be judged allowable us *a figure of syntax*—an obvious example of *Enallagè*, and of that form of Enallage, whi monly called *Antiptosis*, or the putting of one case for an other.

Obs. 19.—This use of *whom* after *than* has greatly puzzled and misled our grammarians. of whom have thence concluded that *than* must needs be, at least in this instance, a *prepo* and some have extended the principle beyond this, so as to include *than which, than wh* its following noun, and other nominatives which they will have to be objectives: as, "I seem guilty of ingratitude, *than which* nothing is more shameful." See *Russell's Gram.* "Washington, *than whose fame* naught earthly can be purer."—*Peirce's Gram.* p. 204. "Y given him more than *I.* You have sent her as much as *he.*"—*Buchanan's Eng. Syntax.* These last two sentences are erroneously called by their author, "*false syntax;*" not in a notion that *than* and *as* are prepositions, but on the false supposition that the prepo must necessarily be understood between them and the pronouns, as it is between the pr verbs and the pronouns *him* and *her.* But, in fact, "You have given him more than *I*, fectly good English; the last clause of which plainly means—"more than I *have given* him "You have sent her as much as *he,*" will of course be understood to mean—"as much as sent her;" but here, because the auxiliary implied is different from the one expressed. it have been as well to have inserted it: thus, "*You have* sent her as much as *he has.*" "Su you as much as *he,*" is also good English, though found, with the foregoing, among Bu examples of "false syntax."

Obs. 20.—Murray's twentieth Rule of syntax avers, that, "When the qualities of d things are compared, the latter noun or pronoun is *not governed* by the conjunction *than* or agrees with the verb," &c.—*Octavo Gram.* p. 214; *Russell's Gram.* 103; *Bacon's*, 51; *Al Smith's*, 179; *Fisk's*, 138. To this rule, the great Compiler and most of his followers *than whom* "is an exception," or, "*seems to form* an exception;" to which they add, that phrase is, however, avoided by the best modern writers."—*Murray*, i, 215. This latter as Russell conceives to be untrue: the former he adopts; and, calling *than whom* "an exce the general rule," says of it, (with no great consistency,) "Here the conjunction *than* tainly the force of a preposition, and supplies its place by governing the relative."—*R Abridgement of Murray's Gram.* p. 104. But this is hardly an instance to which one would the maxim elsewhere adopted by Murray: "*Exceptio probat regulam.*"—*Octavo Gram.* To ascribe to a conjunction the governing power of a preposition, is a very wide step, and too much like straddling the line which separates these parts of speech one from the other.

Obs. 21.—Churchill says, "If there be no ellipsis to supply, as sometimes happens whe noun relative occurs after than; the relative is to be put in the *objective case absolute:* as, "A *than whom* a greater king never reigned, deserves to be held up as a model to all future sove —*New Gram.* p. 153. Among his Notes, he has one with reference to this "*objective case* as follows: "It is not governed by the conjunction, for on no other occasion does a con govern any case; or by any word understood, for we can insert no word, or words, that oncile the phrase with any other rule of grammar: and if we employ a pronoun personal of the relative, as *he*, which will admit of being resolved elliptically, it must be put in the native case."—*Ib.* p. 352. Against this gentleman's doctrine, one may very well argue

---

* "When the relative *who* follows the preposition *than*, it must be used as in the accusative case."—
Gram. p. 98. Dr. Priestley seems to have imagined the word *than* to be always a preposition; for he c against the common doctrine and practice respecting the case after it: "It is, likewise, said, that the n case ought to follow the preposition *than*; because the verb *to be* is understood after it; As, *You are tall* and not *taller than him*; because at full length, it would be, *You are taller than he is*; but since it is allow the oblique case should follow prepositions; and since the comparative degree of an adjective, and the p *than* have, certainly, between them, the force *of a preposition*, expressing the relation of one word to anoth ought to require the oblique case of the pronoun following."—*Priestley's Gram.* p. 105. If *than* were a pr this reasoning would certainly be right; but the Doctor begs the question, by assuming that it is a pr William Ward, an other noted grammarian of the same age, supposes that, "*MB sapientior es*, may be tran *Thou art wiser* THAN ME." He also, in the same place, avers, that, "The best English Writers have co *than* as a Sign of an oblique Case; as, 'She suffers more THAN ME.' Swift. i. e. more than I suffer.
 'Thou art a Girl as much brighter THAN HER,
 As he was a Poet sublimer THAN ME.' Prior.
i. e. Thou art a Girl as much brighter *than she was*, as he was a Poet sublimer *than I am.*"—*Ward's P Gram.* p. 112. These examples of the objective case after *than*, were justly regarded by Lowth as bad Eng The construction, however, has a modern advocate in S. W. Clark, who will have the conjunctions *as, but saving*, and *than*, as well as the adjectives *like, unlike, near, next, nigh*, and *opposite*, to be prepositions a *Comparative* the *Preposition than* is commonly used. Example—Grammar is more interesting than other studies."—*Clark's Practical Gram.* p. 178. "*As, like, than*, &c., indicate a relation of comparison ample—'Thou hast been *wiser* all the while *than me.*' *Southey's Letters.*—*Ib.* p. 96. Here correct undoubtedly requires *I*, and not *me.* Such at least is my opinion.

himself does against that of Murray, Russell, and others; that on no other occasion do we speak of putting "the objective case absolute;" and if, agreeably to the analogy of our own tongue, our distinguished authors would condescend to say *than who,*[*] surely nobody would think of calling this an instance of the nominative case absolute,—except perhaps one swaggering *new theorist*, that most pedantic of all scoffers, Oliver B. Peirce.

OBS. 22.—The sum of the matter is this: the phrase, *than who*, is a more regular and more analogical expression than *than whom*; but both are of questionable propriety, and the former is seldom if ever found, except in some few grammars; while the latter, which is in some sort a Latinism, may be quoted from many of our most distinguished writers. And, since that which is irregular cannot be parsed by rule, if out of respect to authority we judge it allowable, it must be set down among the *figures* of grammar; which are, all of them, intentional deviations from the ordinary use of words. One late author treats the point pretty well, in this short hint: "After the conjunction *than*, contrary to analogy, *whom* is used in stead of *who.*"—*Nutting's Gram.* p. 106. An other gives his opinion in the following note: "When *who* immediately follows *than*, it is used *improperly* in the objective case; as, 'Alfred, *than whom* a greater king never reigned;'—*than whom* is not grammatical. It ought to be, *than who*; because *who* is the nominative to *was* understood.—*Than whom* is as bad a phrase as 'he is taller *than him.'* It is true that some of our best writers have used *than whom*; but it is also true, that they have used *other* phrases which we have rejected as ungrammatical; then why not reject this too?"—*Lennie's Grammar*, Edition of 1830, p. 105.

OBS. 23.—On this point, Bullions and Brace, two American copyists and plagiarists of Lennie, adopt opposite notions. The latter copies the foregoing note, without the last sentence; that is, without admitting that "*than whom*" has ever been used by good writers. See *Brace's Gram.* p. 90. The former says, "The relative *usually* follows *than* in the objective case, *even when the nominative goes before*; as, 'Alfred, than whom a greater king never reigned.' This anomaly it is difficult to explain. Most probably, *than*, at first had the force of a preposition, which it now retains only when followed by the relative."—*Bullions, E. Gram.* of 1843, p. 112. Again: "*A relative* after *than* is put in the objective case; as, 'Satan, than *whom* none higher sat.' This anomaly has not been satisfactorily explained. In this case, some regard *than* as a preposition. *It is* probably only a case of simple *enallage*."—*Bullions, Analyt. and Pract. Gram.* of 1849, p. 191. Prof. Fowler, in his great publication, of 1850, says of this example, "The expression should be, Satan, than *who* None higher sat."—*Fowler's E. Gram.* § 482, Note 2. Thus, by one single form of *antiptosis*, have our grammarians been as much divided and perplexed, as were the Latin grammarians by a vast number of such changes; and, since there were some among the latter, who insisted on a total rejection of the figure, there is no great presumption in discarding, if we please, the very little that remains of it in English.

OBS. 24.—Peirce's *new theory* of grammar rests mainly on the assumption, that no correct sentence ever is, or can be, in any wise, *elliptical*. This is one of the "TWO GRAND PRINCIPLES" on which the author says his "work is based."—*The Grammar*, p. 10. The other is, that grammar cannot possibly be taught without a thorough reformation of its nomenclature, a reformation involving a change of most of the names and technical terms heretofore used for its elucidation. I do not give precisely his own words, for one half of this author's system is expressed in such language as needs to be translated *into English* in order to be generally understood; but this is precisely his meaning, and in words more intelligible. In what estimation he holds these two positions, may be judged from the following assertion: "*Without these grand points*, no work, whatever may be its pretensions, can be A GRAMMAR of the LANGUAGE."—*Ib.* It follows, that no man who does not despise every other book that is called a grammar, can entertain any favourable opinion of Peirce's. The author however is tolerably consistent. He not only scorns to appeal, for the confirmation of his own assertions and rules, to the judgement or practice of any other writer, but counsels the learner to "spurn the idea of quoting, either as proof or for defence, the authority of any man." See p. 13. The notable results of these important premises are too numerous for detail even in this general pandect. But it is to be mentioned here, that, according to this theory, a nominative coming after *than* or *as*, is in general to be accounted a *nominative absolute*; that is, a nominative which is independent of any verb; or, (as the ingenious author himself expresses it,) "A word in the subjective case following another subjective, and immediately preceded by *than, as,* or *not*, may be used *without an* ASSERTER immediately depending on it for sense."—*Peirce's Gram.* p. 195. See also his "*Grammatical Chart*, Rule I, Part 2."

OBS. 25.—"Lowth, Priestley, Murray, and most grammarians say, that hypothetical, conditional, concessive, or exceptive conjunctions; as, *if, lest, though, unless, except; require*, or *govern* the subjunctive mood. But in this they are certainly wrong: for, as Dr. Crombie rightly observes, the verb is put in the subjunctive mood, because this mood expresses contingency, *not because it follows the conjunction*: for these writers themselves allow, that the same conjunctions are to be followed by the indicative mood, when the verb is not intended to express a contingency. In the following sentence: '*Though* he *be* displeased at it, I will bolt my door; and *let* him break it open, *if* he *dare*:' may we not as well affirm, that *and* governs the imperative mood, as that *though* and *if* govern the subjunctive?"—*Churchill's Gram.* p. 321.

OBS. 26.—In the list of *correspondents* contained in Note 7th below, there are some words which ought not to be called *conjunctions*, by the parser; for the relation of a word as the proper correspondent to an other word, does not necessarily determine its part of speech. Thus, *such is* to be parsed as an adjective; *as*, sometimes as a pronoun; *so*, as a conjunctive adverb. And *only*, *merely, also*, and *even*, are sometimes conjunctive adverbs; as, "*Nor* is this *only* a matter of convenience to the poet, it is *also* a source of gratification to the reader."—*Campbell's Rhet.* p. 166. *Murray's Gram.* i, 362. Professor Bullions will have it, that these adverbs may relate to *nouns*— a doctrine which I disapprove. "He says, "*Only, solely, chiefly, merely, too, also*, and perhaps

[*] In respect to the *case*, the phrase *than who* is similar to *than he, than they*, &c., as has been observed by many grammarians; but, since *than* is a conjunction, and *who* or *whom* is a relative, it is doubtful whether it can be strictly proper to set two such connectives together, be the case of the latter which it may. See Note 5th, in the present chapter, below.

a few others, are sometimes *joined to substantives;* as, "Not *only* the men, but the women *also* were present."—*English Gram.* p. 116. *Only* and *also* are here, I think, conjunctive adverbs; but it is not the office of adverbs to qualify nouns; and, that these words are adjuncts to the nouns *men* and *women*, rather than to the verb *were*, which is once expressed and once understood, I see no sufficient reason to suppose. Some teachers imagine, that an adverb of this kind qualifies the *whole clause* in which it stands. But it would seem, that the relation of such words to verbs, participles, or adjectives, according to the common rule for adverbs, is in general sufficiently obvious: as, "The perfect tense not *only refers* to what is past, but *also conveys* an allusion to the present time."—*Murray's Gram.* p. 70. Is there any question about the true mode of parsing "*only*" and "*also*" here? and have they not in the other sentence, a relation similar to what is seen here?

NOTES TO RULE XXII.

NOTE I.—When two terms connected are each to be extended and completed in sense by a third, they must both be such as will make sense with it. Thus, instead of saying, "He has made alterations and additions to the work," say, "He has made alterations *in* the work, and additions *to it;*" because the relation between *alterations* and *work* is not well expressed by *to*.

NOTE II.—In general, any two terms which we connect by a conjunction, should be the same in kind or quality, rather than different or heterogeneous. Example: "The assistance was welcome, and seasonably afforded."—*Murray's Key*, 8vo, p. 249. Better: "The assistance was welcome, and *it was* seasonably afforded." Or: "The assistance was *both seasonable and welcome.*"

NOTE III.—The conjunctions, copulative or disjunctive, affirmative or negative, must be used with a due regard to their own import, and to the true idiom of the language. Thus, say, "The general bent *or* turn of the language *is* towards the other form;" and not, with Lowth and Churchill, "The general bent *and* turn of the language *is* towards the other form."—*Short Introd.* p. 60; *New Gram.* p. 113. So, say, "I cannot deny *that* there are perverse jades;" and not, with Addison, "I cannot deny *but* there are perverse jades."—*Spect.* No. 457. Again, say, "I feared *that* I should be deserted;" not, "*lest* I should be deserted."

NOTE IV.—After *else, other,* * *otherwise, rather,* and all English *comparatives*, the latter term of an exclusive comparison should be introduced by the conjunction *than* — a word which is appropriated to this use solely: as, 'Style is nothing *else than* that sort of expression which our thoughts most readily assume."—*Blair's Rhet.* p. 92. "What we call fables or parables are no *other than* allegories."—*Ib.* p. 151; *Murray's Gram.* 8vo, p. 243. "We judge *otherwise* of them *than* of ourselves." —*R. Ainsworth.* "The premeditation should be of things *rather than* of words." —*Blair's Rhet.* p. 262. "Is not the life *more than* meat?"—*Com. Bible.* "Is not life a *greater* gift *than* food?"—*Campbell's Gospels.*

NOTE V.—Relative pronouns, being themselves a species of connective words, necessarily exclude conjunctions; except there be two or more relative clauses to be connected together; that is, one to the other. Example of error: "The principal and distinguishing excellence of Virgil, *and which*, in my opinion, he possesses

---

* After *else* or *other*, the preposition *besides* is sometimes used; and, when it recalls an idea previously suggested, it appears to be as good as *than*, or better: as, "*Other* words, *besides* the preceding, may begin with capitals."—*Murray's Gram.* Vol. i, p. 285. Or perhaps this preposition may be proper, whenever *else* or *other* denotes what is *additional* to the object of contrast, and not exclusive of it; as, "When we speak of any *other* quantity *besides* bare numbers."—*Tooke's Diversions*, Vol. i, p. 215. "Because he had no *other* father *besides* God."—*Milton, on Christianity*, p. 109. Though we sometimes express an addition by *more than*, the following example appears to me to be *bad English*, and its interpretation still worse: " 'The secret was communicated to *more men than him.*' That is, (when the ellipsis is duly supplied,) 'The secret was communicated to more *persons* than *to* him.' "—*Murray's Key*, 12mo, p. 61; his *Octavo Gram.* p. 215; *Ingersoll's Gram.* 252. Say rather,—"to *other* men *besides* him." Nor, again, does the following construction appear to be right: "Now *shew* me *another* Popish rhymester *but he.*"—DENNIS: *Notes to the Dunciad*, B. II, l. 268. Say rather, "Now *show* me an *other* popish rhymester *besides him.*" Or thus: "Now show me *any* popish rhymester *except him.*" This too is questionable: "Now pain must here be intended to signify something *else besides* warning."—*Wayland's Moral Science*, p. 121. If "warning" was here intended to be included with "something else," the expression is right; if not, *besides* should be *than*. Again: "There is seldom any *other* cardinal in Poland but him."—*Life of Charles XII.* Here "*but him*" should be either "*besides him*" or "*than he;*" for *but* never rightly governs the objective case, nor is it proper after *other*. "Many *more* examples, *besides* the foregoing, might have been adduced."—*Nesbit's English Parsing*, p. xv. Here, in fact, no comparison is expressed; and therefore it is questionable, whether this word "*more*" is allowably used. Like *else* and *other*, when construed with *besides*, it signifies *additional;* and, as this idea is implied in *besides*, any one of these adjectives going before is really pleonastic. In the sense above noticed, the word *beside* is sometimes written in stead of *besides*, though not very often; as, "There are *other* things which pass in the mind of man, *beside* ideas."—*Sheridan's Elocution*, p. 186.

beyond *all poets*, is tenderness."—*Blair's Rhet.* p. 439.   Better: "The principal and distinguishing excellence of Virgil, *an excellence* which, in my opinion, he possesses beyond all *other* poets, is tenderness."

NOTE VI.—The word *that*, (as was shown in the fifth chapter of Etymology,) is often made a pronoun in respect to what precedes it, and a conjunction in respect to what follows it—a construction which, for its anomaly, ought to be rejected.   For example : "*In the mean time* THAT the Muscovites were complaining to St. Nicholas, Charles returned thanks to God, and prepared for new victories."—*Life of Charles XII.*   Better thus : "*While* the Muscovites were *thus* complaining to St. Nicholas, Charles returned thanks to God, and prepared for new victories."

NOTE VII.—The words in each of the following pairs, are the proper *correspondents* to each other ; and care should be taken, to give them their right place in the sentence :

1.   To *though*, corresponds *yet ;* as, "*Though* he were dead, *yet* shall he live."—*John*, xi, 25.

2.   To *whether*, corresponds *or ;* as, "*Whether* it be greater *or* less."—*Butler's Analogy*, p. 77.

3.   To *either*, corresponds *or ;* as, "The constant indulgence of a declamatory manner, is not favourable *either* to good composition, *or* [to] good delivery."—*Blair's Rhet.* p. 334.

4.   To *neither*, corresponds *nor ;* as, "John the Baptist came *neither* eating bread *nor* drinking wine."—*Luke*, vii, 33.   "Thou shalt *neither* vex a stranger *nor* oppress him."—*Exod.* xxii, 21.

5.   To *both*, corresponds *and ;* as, "I am debtor *both* to the Greeks *and* to the Barbarians, *both* to the wise *and* to the unwise."—*Rom.* i, 14.

6.   To *such*, corresponds *as ;* (the former being a pronominal adjective, and the latter a relative pronoun ;) as, "An assembly *such as* earth saw never."—*Cowper*.

7.   To *such*, corresponds *that ;* with a finite verb following, to express a consequence : as, "The difference is *such that* all will perceive it."

8.   To *as*, corresponds *as ;* with an adjective or an adverb, to express equality of degree : as, "And he went out from his presence a leper *as* white *as* snow."—2 *Kings*, v, 27.

9.   To *as*, corresponds *so ;* with two verbs, to express proportion or sameness : as, "*As* two are to four, *so* are six to twelve."—"*As* the tree falls, *so* it must lie."

10.   *So* is used before *as ;* with an adjective or an adverb, to limit the degree by a comparison : as, "How can you descend to a thing *so* base *as* falsehood ?"

11.   *So* is used before *as ;* with a negative preceding, to deny equality of degree : as, "No lamb was e'er *so* mild *as* he."—*Langhorne*.   "Relatives are not *so* useful in language *as* conjunctions."—BEATTIE : *Murray's Gram.* p. 126.

12.   To *so*, corresponds *as ;* with an infinitive following, to express a consequence : as, "We ought, certainly, to read blank verse *so as* to make every line sensible to the ear."—*Blair's Rhet.* p. 382.

13.   To *so*, corresponds *that ;* with a finite verb following, to express a consequence : as, "No man was *so* poor *that* he could not make restitution."—*Milman's Jews*, i, 113.   "*So* run *that* ye may obtain."—1 *Cor.* ix, 24.

14.   To *not only*, or *not merely*, corresponds *but, but also*, or *but even ;* as, "In heroic times, smuggling and piracy were deemed *not only* not infamous, *but* [even] absolutely honourable."—*Maunder's Gram.* p. 15.   "These are questions, *not* of prudence *merely, but* of morals *also*."—*Dymond's Ess.* p. 82.

NOTE VIII.—"When correspondent conjunctions are used, the verb, or phrase, that precedes the first, applies [also] to the second ; but no word following the former, can [by virtue of this correspondence,] be understood after the latter."—*Churchill's Gram.* p. 353.   Such ellipses as the following ought therefore in general to be avoided : "Tones are different both from emphasis and [*from*] pauses."—*Murray's Gram.* 8vo, i, 250.   "Though both the intention and [*the*] purchase are now past."—*Ib.* ii, 24.

IMPROPRIETIES FOR CORRECTION.

FALSE SYNTAX UNDER RULE XXII.

EXAMPLES UNDER NOTE I.—TWO TERMS WITH ONE.

"The first proposal was essentially different and inferior to the second."—*Inst.* p. 171.

[FORMULA.—Not proper, because the preposition *to* is used with joint reference to the two adjectives *different* and *inferior*, which require different prepositions. But, according to Note 1st under Rule 22d, "When two terms connected are each to be extended and completed in sense by a third, they must both be such as will make sense with it." The sentence may be corrected thus: "The first proposal was essentially different *from* the second, and inferior *to* it."]

"A neuter verb implies the state a subject is in, without acting upon, or being acted upon, by another."—*Alex. Murray's Gram.* p. 30. "I answer, you may and ought to use stories and anecdotes."—*Student's Manual*, p. 220. "ORACLE, *n*. Any person or place where certain decisions are obtained."—*Webster's Dict.* "Forms of government may, and must be occasionally, changed."—*Ld. Lyttelton.* "I have, and pretend to be a tolerable judge." —*Spect.* No. 555. "Are we not lazy in our duties, or make a Christ of them ?"—*Baxter's Saints' Rest.* "They may not express that idea which the author intends, but some other which only resembles, or is a-kin to it."—*Blair's Rhet.* p. 94. "We may, we ought therefore to read them with a distinguishing eye."—*Ib.* p. 352. "Compare their poverty, with what they might, and ought to possess."—*Sedgwick's Econ.* p. 95. "He is a much better grammarian than they are."—*Murray's Key*, 8vo, p. 211. "He was more beloved, but not so much admired as Cinthio."—ADDISON, ON MEDALS: *in Priestley's Gram.* p. 200. "Will it be urged, that the four gospels are as old, or even older than tradition ?"—*Bolingb. Phi. Es.* iv, § 19. "The court of Chancery frequently mitigates, and breaks the teeth of the common law."—*Spectator*, No. 564; *Ware's Gram.* p. 16. "Antony, coming along side of her ship, entered is without seeing or being seen by her."—*Goldsmith's Rome*, p. 160. "In candid minds, truth finds an entrance, and a welcome too."—*Murray's Key*, ii, 168. "In many designs, we may succeed and be miserable."—*Ib.* p. 169. "In many pursuits, we embark with pleasure, and land sorrowfully."—*Ib.* p. 170. "They are much greater gainers than I am by this unexpected event."—*Ib.* p. 211.

UNDER NOTE II.—HETEROGENEOUS TERMS.

"Athens saw them entering her gates and fill her academies."—*Chazotte's Essay*, p. 30. "We have neither forgot his past, nor despair of his future success."—*Duncan's Cicero*, p. 121. "Her monuments and temples had long been shattered or crumbled into dust." —*Lit. Conv.* p. 15. "Competition is excellent, and the vital principle in all these things." —DR. LIEBER: *ib.* p. 64. "Whether provision should or not, be made to meet this exigency."—*Ib.* p. 128. "That our Saviour was divinely inspired, and endued with supernatural powers, are positions that are here taken for granted."—*Murray's Gram.* i, 206. "It would be much more eligible, to contract or enlarge their extent, by explanatory notes and observations, than by sweeping away our ancient landmarks, and setting up others."—*Ib.* i, p. 30. "It is certainly much better, to supply the defects and abridge superfluities, by occasional notes and observations, than by disorganizing, or altering a system which has been so long established."—*Ib.* i, 59. "To have only one tune, or measure, is not much better than having none at all."—*Blair's Rhet.* p. 126. "Facts too well known and obvious to be insisted on."—*Ib.* p. 233. "In proportion as all these circumstances are happily chosen, and of a sublime kind."—*Ib.* p. 41. "If the description be too general, and divested of circumstances."—*Ibid.* "He gained nothing further than to be commended."— *Murray's Key*, ii, 210. "I cannot but think its application somewhat strained, and out of place."—VETHAKE: *Lit. Conv.* p. 29. "Two negatives in the same clause, or referring to the same thing, destroy each other, and leave the sense affirmative."—*Maunder's Gram.* p. 15. "Slates are stones and used to cover roofs of houses."—*Webster's El. Spelling-Book*, p. 47. "Every man of taste, and possessing an elevated mind, ought to feel almost the necessity of apologizing for the power he possesses."—*Influence of Literature*, Vol. ii, p. 122. "They very seldom trouble themselves with Enquiries, or making useful observations of their own."—*Locke, on Ed.* p. 376.

"We've both the field and honour won;
The foe is profligate, and run."—*Hudibras*, p. 93.

UNDER NOTE III.—IMPORT OF CONJUNCTIONS.

"*The* is sometimes used before adverbs in the comparative and superlative degree."—*Lennie's Gram.* p. 6; *Bullions's*, 8; *Brace's*, 9. "The definite article *the* is frequently applied to adverbs in the comparative and superlative degree."—*Murray's Gram.* 8vo, p. 33; *Ingersoll's*, 33; *Lowth's*, 14; *Fisk's*, 53; *Merchant's*, 24; and others. "Conjunctions usually connect verbs in the same mode or tense."—*Sanborn's Gram.* p. 137. "Conjunctions connect verbs in the same style, and usually in the same mode, tense, or form."—*Ib.* "The ruins of Greece and Rome are but the monuments of her former greatness."—*Day's Gram.* p. 38. "In many of these cases, it is not improbable, but that the articles were used originally." —*Priestley's Gram.* p. 152. "I cannot doubt but that these objects are really what they appear to be."—*Kames, El. of Crit.* i, 85. "I question not but my reader will be as much pleased with it."—*Spect.* No. 535. "It is ten to one but my friend Peter is among them."—*Ib.* No. 457. "I doubt not but such objections as these will be made."—*Locke, on Education,* p. 169. "I doubt not but it will appear in the perusal of the following sheets."—*Buchanan's Syntax,* p. vi. "It is not improbable, but that, in time, these different constructions may be appropriated to different uses."—*Priestley's Gram.* p. 155. "But to forget or to remember at pleasure, are equally beyond the power of man."—*Idler,* No. 72. "The nominative case follows the verb, in interrogative and imperative sentences."—*Murray's Gram.* 8vo, Vol. ii, p. 290. "Can the fig-tree, my brethren, bear olive berries? either a vine, figs?"—*James,* iii, 12. "Whose characters are too profligate, that the managing of them should be of any consequence."—*Swift, Examiner,* No. 24. "You that are a step higher than a philosopher, a divine; yet have too much grace and wit than to be a bishop."—*Pope, to Swift,* Let. 80. "The terms rich or poor enter not into their language."—*Robertson's America,* Vol. i, p. 314. "This pause is but seldom or ever sufficiently dwelt upon."—*Music of Nature,* p. 181. "There would be no possibility of any such thing as human life and human happiness."—*Butler's Anal.* p. 110. "The multitude rebuked them, because they should hold their peace."—*Matt.* xx, 21.

UNDER NOTE IV.—OF THE CONJUNCTION THAN.

"A metaphor is nothing else but a short comparison."—*Adam's Gram.* p. 243; *Gould's,* 236. "There being no other dictator here but use."—*Campbell's Rhet.* p. 167. "This Construction is no otherwise known in English but by supplying the first or second Person Plural."—*Buchanan's Syntax,* p. xi. "Cyaxares was no sooner in the throne, but he was engaged in a terrible war."—*Rollin's Hist.* ii, 62. "Those classics contain little else but histories of murders."—*Am. Museum,* v, 526. "Ye shall not worship any other except God."—*Sale's Koran,* p. 15. "Their relation, therefore, is not otherwise to be ascertained but by their place."—*Campbell's Rhet.* p. 260. "For he no sooner accosted her, but he gained his point."—*Burder's Hist.* i, 6. "And all the modern writers on this subject have done little else but translate them."—*Blair's Rhet.* p. 336. "One who had no other aim, but to talk copiously and plausibly."—*Ib.* p. 317. "We can refer it to no other cause but the structure of the eye."—*Ib.* p. 46. "No more is required but singly an act of vision."—*Kames, El. of Crit.* i, 171. "We find no more in its composition, but the particulars now mentioned."—*Ib.* i, 48. "He pretends not to say, that it hath any other effect but to raise surprise."—*Ib.* ii, 61. "No sooner was the princess dead, but he freed himself."—*Johnson's Sketch of Morin.* "*Ought* is an imperfect verb, for it has no other modification besides this one."—*Priestley's Gram.* p. 113. "The verb is palpably nothing else but the tie."—*Neef's Sketch,* p. 66. "Does he mean that theism is capable of nothing else except being opposed to polytheism or atheism?"—*Blair's Rhet.* p. 104. "Is it meant that theism is capable of nothing else besides being opposed to polytheism, or atheism?"—*Murray's Gram.* 8vo, p. 307. "There is no other method of teaching that of which any one is ignorant, but by means of something already known."—DR. JOHNSON: *Murray's Gram.* i, 163; *Ingersoll's,* 214. "O fairest flower, no sooner blown but blasted!"—*Milton's Poems,* p. 132. "Architecture and gardening cannot otherwise entertain the mind, but by raising certain agreeable emotions or feelings."—*Kames, El. of Crit.* ii, 318. "Or, rather they are nothing else but nouns."—*British Gram.* p. 95.

"As if religion were intended
   For nothing else but to be mended."—*Hudibras,* p. 11.

UNDER NOTE V.—RELATIVES EXCLUDE CONJUNCTIONS.

"To prepare the Jews for the reception of a prophet mightier than him, and whose shoes he was not worthy to bear."—*Murray's Gram.* 8vo, p. 214. "Has this word which represents an action an object after it, and on which it terminates?"—*Osborn's Key,* p. 3. "The stores of literature lie before him, and from which he may collect, for use, many lessons of wisdom.—*Knapp's Lectures,* p. 31. "Many and various great advantages of this Grammar, and which are wanting in others, might be enumerated."—*Greenleaf's Gram.* p. 6. "About the time of Solon, the Athenian legislator, the custom is said to have been introduced, and which still prevails, of writing in lines from left to right."—*Jamieson's Rhet.* p. 19. "The fundamental rule of the construction of sentences, and into which all others might be resolved, undoubtedly is, to communicate, in the clearest and most natural order, the ideas which we mean to transfuse into the minds of others."—*Blair's Rhet.* p. 120; *Jamieson's,* 102. "He left a son of a singular character, and who behaved so ill that he was put in prison."—*Murray's Key,* 8vo, p. 221. "He discovered some qualities in the youth, of a disagreeable nature, and which to him were wholly unaccountable."—*Ib.* p. 213. "An emphatical pause is made, after something has been said of peculiar moment, and on which we want ['desire' M.] to fix the hearer's attention."—*Blair's Rhet.* p. 331; *Murray's Gram.* 8vo, p. 248. "But we have duplicates of each, agreeing in movement, though differing in measure, and which make different impressions on the ear."—*Murray's Gram.* 8vo, p. 259.

UNDER NOTE VI.—OF THE WORD THAT.

"It will greatly facilitate the labours of the teacher, at the same time that it will relieve the pupil of many difficulties."—*Frost's El. of E. Gram.* p. 4. "At the same time that the pupil is engaged in the exercises just mentioned, it will be a proper time to study the whole Grammar in course."—*Bullions, Prin. of E. Gram.*, Revised Ed., p. viii. "On the same ground that a participle and auxiliary are allowed to form a tense."—BEATTIE: *Murray's Gram.* 8vo, p. 76. "On the same ground that the voices, moods, and tenses, are admitted into the English tongue."—*Ib.* p. 101. "The five examples last mentioned, are corrected on the same principle that the preceding examples are corrected."—*Ib.* p. 186 ; *Ingersoll's Gram.* 254. "The brazen age began at the death of Trajan, and lasted till the time that Rome was taken by the Goths."—*Gould's Lat. Gram.* p. 277. "The introduction to the Duodecimo Edition, is retained in this volume, for the same reason that the original Introduction to the Grammar, is retained in the first volume."—*Murray's Gram.* 8vo, Vol. ii, p. iv. "The verb must also be of the same person that the nominative case is."—*Ingersoll's Gram.* p. 16. "The adjective pronoun *their*, is plural for the same reason that *who* is."—*Ib.* p. 34. "The Sabellians could not justly be called Patripassians, in the same sense that the Noetians were so called."—*Religious World*, Vol. ii, p. 122. "This is one reason that we pass over such smooth language, without suspecting that it contains little or no meaning."—*Murray's Gram.* 8vo, p. 298. "The first place that both armies came in sight of each other was on the opposite banks of the river Apsus."—*Goldsmith's Rome*, p. 118. "At the very time that the author gave him the first book for his perusal."—*Campbell's Rhetoric, Preface*, p. iv. "Peter will sup at the time that Paul will dine."—*Fosdick's De Sacy*, p. 81. "Peter will be supping at the time that Paul will enter."—*Ibid.* "These, at the same time that they may serve as models to those who may wish to imitate them, will give me an opportunity to cast more light upon the principles of this book."—*Ib.* p. 115.

"Time was, like thee, they life possest,
And time shall be, that thou shalt rest."—PARNELL: *Mur. Seq.* 241.

UNDER NOTE VII.—OF THE CORRESPONDENTS.

"Our manners should neither be gross, nor excessively refined."—*Merchant's Gram.* p. 11. "A neuter verb expresses neither action or passion, but being, or a state of being."—*O. B. Peirce's Gram.* p. 342. "The old books are neither *English* grammars, or *grammars*, in any sense of the English Language."—*Ib.* p. 378. "The author is apprehensive that his work is not yet as accurate and as much simplified as it may be."—*Kirkham's Gram.* p. 7. "The writer could not treat some topicks as extensively as was desirable."—*Ib.* p. 10. "Which would be a matter of such nicety, as no degree of human wisdom could regulate."—*Murray's Gram.* i, 26. "No undertaking is so great or difficult which he cannot direct."—*Duncan's Cic.* p. 126. "It is a good which neither depends on the will of others, nor on the affluence of external fortune."—*Harris's Hermes*, 299 ; *Murray's Gram.* i, 289. "Not only his estate, his reputation too has suffered by his misconduct."—*Murray's Gram.* i, 150 ; *Ingersoll's*, 233. "Neither do they extend as far as might be imagined at first view."—*Blair's Rhet.* p. 350. "There is no language so poor, but it hath two or three past tenses."—*Ib.* p. 82. "As far as this system is founded in truth, language appears to be not altogether arbitrary in its origin." —*Ib.* p. 56. "I have not that command of these convulsions as is necessary."—*Spect.* No. 474. "Conversation with such who know no arts which polish life."—*Ib.* No. 480. "And which can be neither very lively or very forcible."—*Jamieson's Rhet.* p. 78. "To that degree as to give proper names to rivers."—*Dr. Murray's Hist. of Lang.* i, 327. "In the utter overthrow of such who hate to be reformed."—*Barclay's Works*, i, 443. "But still so much of it is retained, as greatly injures the uniformity of the whole."—*Priestley's Gram. Pref.* p. vii. "Some of them have gone to that height of extravagance, as to assert," &c.—*Ib.* p. 91. "A teacher is confined—not more than a merchant, and probably not as much."—*Abbott's Teacher*, p. 27. "It shall not be forgiven him, neither in this world, neither in the world to come."— *Matt.* xii, 32. "Which no body presumes, or is so sanguine to hope."—*Swift, Drap. Let.* v. "For the torrent of the voice, left neither time or power in the organs, to shape the words properly."—*Sheridan's Elocution*, p. 118. "That he may neither unnecessarily waste his voice by throwing out too much, or diminish his power by using too little."—*Ib.* p. 123. "I have retained only such which appear most agreeable to the Measures of Analogy."— *Littleton's Dict. Pref.* "He is both a prudent and industrious man."—*Day's Gram.* p. 70. "Conjunctions either connect words or sentences."—*Ib.* pp. 81 and 101.

"Such silly girls who love to chat and play,
Deserve no care, their time is thrown away."—*Tobitt's Gram.* p. 20.
"Vice is a monster of so frightful mien,
As to be hated needs but to be seen."—POPE: *Mur. Gr.* ii, 17.
"Justice must punish the rebellious deed;
Yet punish so, as pity shall exceed."—DRYDEN: *in Joh. Dict.*

UNDER NOTE VIII.—IMPROPER ELLIPSES.

"That, whose, and as relate to either persons or things."—*Sanborn's Gram.* p. 93. "Which and what, as adjectives, relate either to persons or things."—*Ib.* p. 70. "Whether of a public or private nature."—*Adams's Rhet.* i, 43. "Which are included both among the public and private wrongs."—*Ib.* i, 308. "I might extract both from the old and new testament numberless examples of induction."—*Ib.* ii, 66. "Many verbs are used both in an active and neuter signification."—*Lowth's Gram.* p. 30; *Alger's*, 26; *Guy's*, 21; *Murray's*, 60.   " Its influence is likely to be considerable, both on the morals, and taste of a nation."—*Blair's Rhet.* p. 372.   " The subject afforded a variety of scenes, both of the awful and tender kind."—*Ib.* p. 439.   " Restlessness of mind disqualifies us, both for the enjoyment of peace, and the performance of our duty."—*Murray's Key,* ii, 166; *Ingersoll's Gram.* p. 10.   "Adjective Pronouns are of a mixed nature, participating the properties both of pronouns and adjectives."—*Murray's Gram.* i, 55; *Merchant's,* 43; *Flint's,* 22.   "Adjective Pronouns have the nature both of the adjective and the pronoun."—*Frost's El. of Gram.* p. 15.   "Pronominal adjectives are a kind of compound part of speech, partaking the nature both of pronouns and adjectives."—*Nutting's Gram.* p. 36.   " Nouns are used either in the singular or plural number."—*Blair's Gram.* p. 11.   "The question is not, whether the nominative or accusative ought to follow the particles *than* and *as*; but, whether these particles are, in such particular cases, to be regarded as conjunctions or prepositions."—*Campbell's Rhet.* p. 204.   " In English many verbs are used both as transitives and intransitives."—*Churchill's Gram.* p. 83.   " He sendeth rain both on the just and unjust."—*Guy's Gram.* p. 56.   "A foot consists either of two or three syllables."—*Blair's Gram.* p. 118.   "Because they participate the nature both of adverbs and conjunctions."—*Murray's Gram.* i, 116.   Surely, Romans, what I am now about to say, ought neither to be omitted nor pass without notice."—*Duncan's Cicero,* p. 196.   " Their language frequently amounts, not only to bad sense, but *non-sense*."—*Kirkham's Gram.* p. 14.   " Hence arises the necessity of a social state to man both for the unfolding, and exerting of his nobler faculties."—*Sheridan's Elocution,* p. 147.   " Whether the subject be of the real or feigned kind."—*Blair's Rhet.* p. 454.   " Not only was liberty entirely extinguished, but arbitrary power felt in its heaviest and most oppressive weight."—*Ib.* p. 249.   " This rule is applicable also both to verbal Critics and Grammarians."—*Hiley's Gram.* p. 144.   " Both the rules and exceptions of a language must have obtained the sanction of good usage."—*Ib.* p. 143.

CHAPTER X.—PREPOSITIONS.

The syntax of Prepositions consists, not solely or mainly in their power of governing the objective case, (though this alone is the scope which most grammarians have given it,) but in their adaptation to the other terms between which they express certain relations, such as appear by the sense of the words uttered.

RULE XXIII.—PREPOSITIONS.

Prepositions show the relations of words, and of the things or thoughts expressed by them: as, " He came *from* Rome *to* Paris, *in* the company *of* many eminent men, and passed *with* them *through* many cities."—*Analectic Magazine.*

"Ah! who can tell the triumphs *of* the mind,
By truth illumin'd, and *by* taste refin'd ? "—*Rogers.*

EXCEPTION FIRST.

The preposition *to*, before an abstract infinitive, and at the head of a phrase which is made the subject of a verb, has no proper antecedent term of relation; as, "*To* learn to die, is the great business of life."—*Dillwyn.* " Nevertheless, *to* abide in the flesh, is more needful for you."—ST. PAUL: *Phil.* i, 24. "*To* be reduced to poverty, is a great affliction."

" Too much *to* know, is, to know nought but fame ;
And every godfather can give a name."—*Shakspeare.*

EXCEPTION SECOND.

The preposition *for*, when it introduces its object before an infinitive, and the whole phrase is made the subject of a verb, has properly no antecedent term of relation; as, "*For* us to learn to die, is the great business of life."—" Nevertheless, *for* me to abide in the flesh, is more needful for you."—"*For* an old man to be reduced to poverty, is a very great affliction."

"*For* man to tell how human life began,
Is hard; for who himself beginning knew ? "—*Milton.*

OBSERVATIONS ON RULE XXIII.

OBS. 1.—In parsing a preposition, the learner should name the *two terms* of the relation, and apply the foregoing rule, after the manner prescribed in Praxis 12th of this work.   The principle is simple and etymological, being implied in the very definition of a preposition, yet not the less necessary to be given as a rule of syntax. Among tolerable writers, the prepositions exhibit more errors than any other equal number of words. This is probably owing to the careless manner in which they are usually slurred over in parsing. But the parsers, in general, have at least this excuse, that their text-books have taught them no better; they therefore call the preposition *a preposition*, and leave its use and meaning unexplained.

OBS. 2.—If the learner be at any loss to discover the two terms of relation, let him ask and answer *two questions :* first, with the interrogative *what* before the preposition, to find the antecedent ; and then, with the same pronoun after the preposition, to find the subsequent term. These questions answered according to the sense, will always give the true terms. For example : "They dashed that rapid torrent through."—*Scott.* Ques. *What* through ? Ans. *"Dashed through."* Ques. Through *what !* Ans. *"Through that torrent."* For the meaning is—"They dashed through that rapid torrent." If one term is perfectly obvious, (as it almost always is,) find the other in this way ; as, "Day unto day uttereth speech, and night unto night showeth knowledge."—*Psal.* xix, 2. Ques. *What* unto day ? Ans. *"Uttereth unto day."* Ques. *What* unto night ? Ans. *"Showeth unto night."* For the meaning is—"Day uttereth speech unto day, and night showeth knowledge unto night." To parse rightly, is, to understand rightly ; and what is well expressed, it is a shame to misunderstand or misinterpret. But sometimes the position of the two terms is such, that it may require some reflection to find either ; as,

> "Or that choice plant, so grateful to the nose,
> Which *in* I know not what far country grows."—*Churchill*, p. 18.

OBS. 3.—When a preposition *begins* or *ends* a sentence or clause, the terms of relation, if both are given, are transposed ; as, "To a studious *man*, action is a relief."—*Burgh.* That is, "Action is a relief *to* a studious man." "*Science* they [the ladies] do not *pretend* TO."—*Id.* That is, "They do not pretend *to* science." "Until I have done that *which I have spoken* to thee OF."—*Gen.* xxviii, 15. The word governed by the preposition is always the subsequent term of the relation, however it may be placed ; and if this be a relative pronoun, the transposition is permanent. The preposition, however, may be put before any relative, except *that* and *as ;* and this is commonly thought to be its most appropriate place: as, "Until I have done that *of which* I have spoken to thee." Of the placing of it last, Lowth says, "This is an idiom *which* our language is strongly inclined *to ;*" Murray and others, "This is an idiom *to which* our language is strongly inclined : " while they all add, "it prevails in common conversation, and suits very well with the familiar style in writing ; but the placing of the preposition before the relative, is more graceful, as well as more perspicuous, and agrees much better with the solemn and elevated style."—*Lowth's Gram.* p. 95 ; *Murray's*, 8vo, p. 200 ; *Fisk's*, 141 ; *R. C. Smith's*, 167 ; *Ingersoll's*, 227 ; *Churchill's*, 160.

OBS. 4.—The terms of relation between which a preposition may be used, are very various. The *former* or antecedent term may be a noun, an adjective, a pronoun, a verb, a participle, or an adverb : and, in some instances, we find not only one preposition put before an other, but even a conjunction or an interjection used on this side ; as, "*Because* OF offences,"—"*Alas* FOR him ! " The *latter* or *subsequent* term, which is the word governed by the preposition, may be a noun, a pronoun, a pronominal adjective, an infinitive verb, or an imperfect or preperfect participle : and, in some instances, prepositions appear to govern adverbs, or even whole phrases. See the observations in the tenth chapter of Etymology.

OBS. 5.—Both terms of the relation are usually expressed ; though either of them may, in some instances, be left out, the other being given: as, (1.) THE FORMER—"All shall know me, [reckoning] FROM the least to the greatest."—*Heb.* viii, 11. [*I say*] "IN a word, it would entirely defeat the purpose."—*Blair.* "When I speak of reputation, I mean not only [*reputation*] IN regard to knowledge, but [*reputation*] IN regard to the talent of communicating knowledge."—*Campbell's Rhet.* p. 163 ; *Murray's Gram.* i, 360. (2.) THE LATTER—"Opinions and ceremonies [*which*] they would die FOR."—*Locke.* "IN [*those*] who obtain defence, or [*in those*] who defend."—*Pope.* "Others are more modest than [*what*] this comes TO."—*Collier's Antoninus*, p. 66.

OBS. 6.—The only proper exceptions to the foregoing rule, are those which are inserted above, unless the abstract infinitive used as a predicate is also to be excepted ; as, "In both, to reason right, is *to* submit."—*Pope.* But here most if not all grammarians would say, the verb "*is*" is the antecedent term, or what their syntax takes to govern the infinitive. The relation, however, is not such as when we say, "He *is to submit ;*" that is, "He *must submit*, or *ought to submit :*" but, perhaps, to insist on a different mode of parsing the more separable infinitive or its preposition, would be a needless refinement. Yet some regard ought to be paid to the different relations which the infinitive may bear to this finite verb. For want of a due estimate of this difference, the following sentence is, I think, very faulty : "The great business of this life *is to prepare*, and *qualify us*, for the enjoyment of a better."—*Murray's Gram.* i, p. 373. If the author meant to tell what our great business in this life is, he should rather have said : "The great business of this life is, to prepare and qualify *ourselves* for the enjoyment of a better."

OBS. 7.—In relation to the infinitive, Dr. Adam remarks, that, "*To* in English is often taken *absolutely ; as, To* confess the truth, *To proceed ; To* conclude."—*Latin and Eng. Gram.* p. 182. But the assertion is not entirely true ; nor are his examples appropriate: for what he and many other grammarians call the *infinitive absolute*, evidently depends on something *understood ;* and the preposition is, surely, in no instance independent of what follows it, and is therefore never entirely absolute. Prepositions are not to be supposed to have no antecedent term, merely because they stand at the head of a phrase or sentence which is made the subject of a verb ; for the phrase or sentence itself often contains that term, as in the following example: "*In* what way mind acts upon matter, is unknown." Here *in* shows the relation between *acts* and *way ;* because the expression suggests, that mind *acts* IN *some way* upon matter.

OBS. 8.—The second exception above, wherever it is found applicable, cancels the first ; because it introduces an antecedent term before the preposition *to*, as may be seen by the examples given. It is questionable too, whether both of them may not also be cancelled in an other way ; that is, by transposition and the introduction of the pronoun *it* for the nominative: as, "*It is a great affliction*, TO *be reduced* to poverty."—"*It is hard* FOR *man* to tell how human life began."—"*Nevertheless it is more needful for you*, THAT *I should abide* in the flesh." We cannot so well say, "It is more needful *for you*, FOR *me to abide* in the flesh;" but we may say, "It is, *on your account*, more needful FOR *me to abide* in the flesh." If these, and other similar examples, are not to be accounted additional instances in which *to* and *for*, and also the conjunction *that*, are without any proper antecedent terms, we must suppose these particles to show the relation between what precedes and what follows them.

OBS. 9.—The preposition (as its name implies) *precedes* the word which it governs. Yet there are some exceptions. In the familiar style, a preposition governing a relative or an interrogative pronoun, is often separated from its object, and connected with the other term of relation; as, "*Whom* did he speak *to?*" But it is more dignified, and in general more graceful, to place the preposition before the pronoun; as, "*To whom* did he speak?" The relatives *that* and *as*, if governed by a preposition, must always precede it. In some instances, the pronoun must be supplied in parsing; as, "*To set off the banquet [that* or *which*] he gives notice *of*."—*Philological Museum*, i, 454. Sometimes the objective word is put first because it is emphatical; as, "*This* the great understand, *this* they pique themselves *upon*."—*Art of Thinking*, p. 66. Prepositions of more than one syllable, are sometimes put immediately after their objects, especially in poetry; as, "Known all the *world over*."—*Walker's Particles*, p. 291. "The thing is known all Lesbos over."—*Ibid.*

"Wild Carron's lonely *woods among*."—*Langhorne.*
"Thy deep *ravines* and *dells along*."—*Sir W. Scott.*

OBS. 10.—Two prepositions sometimes come together; as, "Lambeth is *over against* Westminster abbey."—*Murray's Gram.* i, 118. "And *from before* the lustre of her face, White break the clouds away."—*Thomson.* "And the meagre fiend Blows mildew *from between* his shrivell'd lips."—*Cowper.* These, in most instances, though they are not usually written as compounds, appear naturally to coalesce in their syntax, as was observed in the tenth chapter of Etymology, and to express a sort of compound relation between the other terms with which they are connected. When such is their character, they ought to be taken together in parsing; for, if we parse them separately, we must either call the first an adverb, or suppose some very awkward ellipsis. Some instances however occur, in which an object may easily be supplied to the former word, and perhaps ought to be; as, "He is at liberty to sell it *at* [a price] *above* a fair remuneration."—*Wayland's Moral Science*, p. 258. "And I wish they had been at the bottom of the ditch I pulled you out of, *instead of* [being] *upon* my back."—*Sandford and Merton*, p. 29. In such examples as the following, the first preposition, *of*, appears to me to govern the plural noun which ends the sentence; and the intermediate ones, *from* and *to*, to have both terms of their relation *understood*: "Iambic verse consists *of from* two *to* six feet; that is, *of from* four *to* twelve syllables."—*Blair's Gram.* p. 119. "Trochaic verse consists *of from* one *to* three feet."—*Ibid.* The meaning is—"Iambic verse consists *of feet* varying in number from two to six; or (it consists) *of syllables* varying from four to twelve."—"Trochaic verse consists *of feet* varying from one *foot* to three *feet*."

OBS. 11.—One antecedent term may have several prepositions depending on it, with one object after each, or more than one after any, or only one after both or all; as, "A declaration *for* virtue and *against* vice."—*Butler's Anal.* p. 157. "A positive law *against* all fraud, falsehood, *and* violence, and *for*, or *in* favour *of*, all justice *and* truth." "For *of* him, and *through* him, and *to* him, are all things."—*Bible.* In fact, not only may the relation be simple in regard to all or any of the words, but it may also be complex in regard to all or any of them. Hence several different prepositions, whether they have different antecedent terms or only one and the same, may refer either jointly or severally to one object or to more. This follows, because not only may either antecedents or objects be connected by conjunctions, but prepositions also admit of this construction, with or without a connecting of their antecedents. Examples: "They are capable *of*, and placed *in*, different stations in the society of mankind."—*Butler's Anal.* p. 115. "Our perception *of* vice *and* ill desert arises *from*, and is the result *of*, a comparison *of* actions *with* the nature and capacities *of* the agent."—*Ib.* p. 279. "And the design *of* this chapter is, *to* inquire how far this is the case; how far, *over and above* the moral nature which God has given us, and our natural notion *of* him, as righteous governor *of* those his creatures *to* whom he has given this nature; I say, how far, *besides* this, the principles *and* beginnings *of* a moral government *over* the world may be discerned, *notwithstanding and amidst* all the confusion and disorder *of* it."—*Ib.* p. 85.

OBS. 12.—The preposition *into*, expresses a relation produced by motion or change; and *in*, the same relation, without reference to motion as having produced it: hence, "to walk *into* the garden," and, "to walk *in* the garden," are very different in meaning. "It is disagreeable to find a word split *into* two by a pause."—*Kames, El. of Crit.* ii, 83. This appears to be right in sense, but because brevity is desirable in unemphatic particles, I suppose most persons would say, "split *in* two." In the Bible we have the phrases, "rent *in* twain,"—"cut *in* pieces,"—"brake *in* pieces the rocks,"—"brake all their bones *in* pieces,"—"brake them *to* pieces,"—"broken *to* pieces,"—"pulled *in* pieces." In all these, except the first, *to* may perhaps be considered preferable to *in*; and *into* would be objectionable only because it is longer and less simple. "Half of them dare not shake the snow from off their cassocks, lest they shake themselves *to* pieces."—SHAK.: *Kames*, ii, 246.

OBS. 13.—*Between*, or *betwixt*, is used in reference to two things or parties; *among*, or *amongst*, *amid*, or *amidst*, in reference to a greater number, or to something by which an other may be surrounded: as, "Thou pendulum *betwixt* a smile and tear."—*Byron.* "The host *between* the mountain and the shore."—*Id.* "To meditate *amongst* decay, and stand a ruin *amidst* ruins."—*Id.* In the following examples, the import of these prepositions is not very accurately regarded; "The Greeks wrote in capitals, and left no spaces *between* their words."—*Wilson's Essay*, p. 6. This construction may perhaps be allowed, because the spaces by which words are now divided, occur severally *between* one word and an other; but the author might as well have said, "and left no spaces to distinguish their words." "There was a hunting match agreed upon betwixt an ass, and a fox."—*L'Estrange.* Here *by* or *among* would, I think, be better than *betwixt*, be the partners were more than two. "*Between* two or more authors, different readers will exceedingly, as to the preference in point of merit."—*Campbell's Rhet.* p. 162; *Jamieson: Murray's Gram.* i, 360. Say, "*Concerning* two or more authors," because *between* is not co ent with the word *more.* "Rising *one among another* in the greatest confusion and disorder *Spect.* No. 476. Say, "Rising *promiscuously*," or, "Rising *all at once;*" for *among* is not sistent with the distributive term *one an other.*

OBS. 14.—Of two prepositions coming together between the same terms of relation, sometimes connected in the same construction, I have given several plain examples in this c ter, and in the tenth chapter of Etymology, a very great number, all from sources suffi respectable. But, in many of our English grammars, there is a stereotyped remark on this p originally written by Priestley, which it is proper here to cite, as an other specimen of the tor's hastiness, and of the blind confidence of certain compilers and copyists: "Two diff prepositions *must be improper* in the same construction, and in the same sentence ;a combat between *thirty Britons,* against *twenty English.* Smollett's Voltaire, Vol. 2, p. 2 *Priestley's Gram.* p. 156. Lindley Murray and others have the same remark, with the cla altered thus: "The combat *between* thirty *French against* twenty English."—*Murray's* 8vo, p. 200; *Smith's New Gram.* 167; *Fisk's,* 142; *Ingersoll's,* 228. W. Allen has it thus different prepositions in the *same construction* are improper; as, a combat *between twenty* Fr *against* thirty English."—*Elements of E. Gram.* p. 179. He gives the odds to the latter p Hiley, with no expense of thought, first takes from Murray, as he from Priestley, the ca remark, "Different relations, and different senses, must be expressed by different prepositi and then adds, "*One relation* must not, *therefore,* be expressed by two different prepos. the same clause; thus, 'The combat *between* thirty French *against* thirty English,' sh 'The combat *between* thirty French *and* thirty English.'"—*Hiley's E. Gram.* p. 97. It is ma that the error of this example is not in the use of *two prepositions,* nor is there any truth c in the note or notes made on it by all these critics; for had they said, "The combat *of* French *against* twenty English," there would still be two prepositions, but where would impropriety, or where the sameness of construction, which they speak of ? *Between* is c patible with *against,* only because it requires two parties or things for its own regimen; as combat *between* thirty *Frenchmen* and twenty *Englishmen.*" This is what Smollett should written, to make sense with the word "*between.*"

OBS. 15.—With like implicitness, Hiley excepted, these grammarians and others have al from Lowth an observation in which the learned doctor has censured quite too strongly ta reference of different prepositions to the same objective noun: to wit, "Some writers a the preposition from its noun, in order to connect different prepositions with the same as, 'To suppose the zodiac and planets to be efficient *of,* and antecedent *to,* themselves.' ley, Serm. 6. This [construction], whether in the familiar or the solemn style, *is always in* and *should never be admitted,* but in forms of law, and the like; where fulness and exac expression must take *place* of every other consideration."—*Lowth's Gram.* p. 96; *Murr* 200; *Smith's,* 167; *Fisk's,* 141; *Ingersoll's,* 228; *Alger's,* 67; *Picket's,* 207. Churchill even further, both strengthening the censure, and disallowing the exception: thus, "This, whe the solemn or in the familiar style, is *always* inelegant, and should *never be admitted.* I awkward *shift* for avoiding the repetition of a word, *which might be accomplished without* it person, who has the least command of language."—*New Gram.* p. 341. Yet, with all their mand of language, not one of these gentlemen has told us how the foregoing sentence Bentley may be *amended;* while many of their number not only venture to use different pr tions before the same noun, but even to add a phrase which puts that noun in the nom case: as, "Thus, the time of the infinitive may be *before, after,* or *the same as,* the tim governing verb, according as the *thing* signified by the infinitive is supposed to be *before, aft present with,* the *thing* denoted by the governing verb."—*Murray's Gram.* i, 191; *Ingersoll's* R. C. *Smith's,* 159.

OBS. 16.—The structure of this example not only contradicts palpably, and twice doctrine cited above, but one may say of the former part of it, as Lowth, Murray, and others (in no very accurate English,) of the text 1 Cor. ii, 9: "There seems to be an impropriety sentence, in which the same noun serves in a double capacity, performing at the same *offices both of the nominative and objective cases.*"—*Murray's Gram.* 8vo, p. 224. See also L *Gram.* p. 73; *Ingersoll's,* 277; *Fisk's,* 149; *Smith's,* 185. Two other examples, exactly which is so pointedly censured above, are placed by Murray under his thirteenth rule comma; and these likewise, with all faithfulness, are copied by Ingersoll, Smith, Alger, ham, Comly, Russell, and I know not how many more. In short, not only does this their punctuation include the construction in question; but the following exception to it, is remarkable for its various faults, or thorough faultiness, is applicable to *no other :* "Some when the *word* with which the *last* preposition *agrees,* is *single,* it is better to *omit* the on before it: as, 'Many states were in alliance *with,* and under the protection *of* Rome.'"—M *ray's Gram.* p. 272; *Smith's,* 190; *Ingersoll's,* 284; *Kirkham's,* 215; *Alger's,* 79; *Alden's Abel Flint's,* 103; *Russell's,* 115. But the blunders and contradictions on this point, here. Dr. Blair happened most unlearnedly to say, "What is called splitting of part separating a preposition from the noun which it governs, is *always to be avoided.* As if I say, 'Though virtue borrows no assistance from, yet it may often be accompanied by, the ad tages of fortune.'"—*Lect. XII,* p. 112. This too, though the author himself did not respect the rule, has been thought worthy to be copied, or stolen, with all its faults ! See son's *Rhetoric,* p. 93; and *Murray's Octavo Gram.* p. 319.

OBS. 17.—Dr. Lowth says, "The noun *aversion,* (that is, a turning away,) as likew adjective *averse,* seems to require the preposition *from* after it; and not so properly to a *to,* or *for,* which are often used with it."—*Gram.* p. 98. But this doctrine has not been later grammarians: "The words *averse* and *aversion* (says Dr. Campbell) are more properly used with *to* than with *from*. The examples in favour of the latter preposition, are beyond n outnumbered by those in favour of the former."—*Murray's Gram.* i, 201; *Fisk's*, 142; *s*, 229. This however must be understood only of mental aversion. The expression of i, "On the coast *averse from* entrance," would not be improved, if *from* were changed to the noun *exception*, and the verb to *except*, are sometimes followed by *from*, which has to the Latin particle *ex*, with which the word commences; but the noun at least is much frequently, and perhaps more properly, followed by *to*. Examples: "Objects of horror e *excepted from* the foregoing theory."—*Kames, El. of Crit.* ii, 268. "*From* which there i two *exceptions*, both of them rare."—*Ib.* ii, 89. "*To* the rule that fixes the pause after the rtion, there is one *exception*, and no more."—*Ib.* ii, 84. "No *exception* can be taken *to* the of the figure."—*Ib.* ii, 237. "Originally there was no *exception from* the rule."—*Lowth's* p. 58. "*From* this rule there is mostly an *exception*."—*Murray's Gram.* i, 269. "But *to* there are many *exceptions*."—*Ib.* i, 240. "They are not to be regarded as exceptions e rule."—*Campbell's Rhet.* p. 363.

18.—After correcting the example, "He *knows* nothing *on* [of] it," Churchill remarks, seems to be a strange perverseness among the *London vulgar* in perpetually substituting *f*, and *of* for *on*."—*New Gram.* p. 345. And among the expressions which Campbell under the name of *vulgarism*, are the following: "'Tis my humble request you will be lar in speaking *to* the following points."—*Guardian*, No. 57. "The preposition ought to en *on*. Precisely of the same stamp is the *on't* for *of it*, so much used by one class of ."—*Philosophy of Rhet.* p. 217. So far as I have observed, the use of *of* for *on* has never equent; and that of *on* for *of*, or *on't* for *of it*, though it may never have been a polite , is now a manifest *archaism*, or imitation of ancient usage. "And so my young Master, rer comes *on't*, must have a Wife look'd out for him."—*Locke, on Ed.* p. 378. In Saxon, i put for more than half a dozen of our present prepositions. The difference between *of* i, or *upon*, appears in general to be obvious enough; and yet there are some phrases in it is not easy to determine which of these words ought to be preferred: as, "Many things annot *lay hold on* at once."—HOOKER: *Joh. Dict.* "Ussah put forth his hand to the ark and *took hold of* it."—2 *Sam. ib.* "Rather thou shouldst *lay hold upon* him."—BEN x: *ib.* "Let them find courage to *lay hold on* the occasion."—MILTON: *ib.* "The hand d to *lay hold of* objects."—RAY: *ib.* "My soul *took hold on* thee."—ADDISON: *ib.* "To ld of this safe, this only method of cure."—ATTERBURY: *ib.* "And *give* fortune no more f him."—DRYDEN: *ib.* "And his laws *take* the surest *hold of* us."—TILLOTSON: *ib.* "It en be impossible you can *have* any *hold upon* him."—SWIFT: *ib.* "The court of Rome *laid hold on* all the opportunities."—*Murray's Key*, ii, p. 198. "Then did the officer *lay* f him and execute him."—*Ib.* ii, 219. "When one can *lay hold upon* some noted fact."— i *Rhet.* p. 311. "But when we would *lay* firm *hold of* them."—*Ib.* p. 28. "An advantage every one is glad to *lay hold of*."—*Ib.* p. 75. "To have *laid* fast *hold of* it in his mind."— 94. "I would advise them to lay aside their common-places, and to *think* closely *of* their t."—*Ib.* p. 317. "Did they not *take hold of* your fathers?"—*Zech.* i, 6. "Ten men shall old *of* the skirt of one that is a Jew."—*Ib.* viii, 23. "It is wrong to say, either 'to *lay* f a thing,' or 'to *take* hold *on* it.'"—*Blair's Gram.* p. 101. In the following couplet, *on* to have been preferred only for a rhyme:

> "Yet, lo! in me what authors have to *brag on!*
> Reduc'd at last to hiss in my own dragon."—*Pope.*

OBS. 19.—In the allowable uses of prepositions, there may perhaps be some room for choice; a that what to the mind of a critic may not appear the fittest word, may yet be judged not positively ungrammatical. In this light, I incline to view the following examples: "Homer's plan still more defective, *upon* another account."—*Kames, El. of Crit.* ii, 299. Say—"*on an other* account." "It was almost eight *of the* clock before I could leave that variety of objects."— *pectator*, No. 454. Present usage requires—"eight o'clock." "The Greek and Latin writers ad a considerable advantage *above* us."—*Blair's Rhet.* p. 114. "The study of oratory has this dvantage *above* that of poetry."—*Ib.* p. 338. "A metaphor has frequently an advantage *above* formal comparison."—*Jamieson's Rhet.* p. 150. This use of *above* seems to be a sort of Scotti- sm: an Englishman, I think, would say—"advantage *over* us," &c. "Hundreds have all these ruding *upon* them from morning *to* night."—*Abbott's Teacher*, p. 33. Better—"from morning night." But Horne Tooke observes, "We apply to indifferently to *place* or *time*; but TILL time only, and never to *place*. Thus we may say, 'From morn TO night th' eternal larum ang;' or, 'From morn TILL night,' &c."—*Diversions of Purley*, i, 284.

NOTES TO RULE XXIII.

NOTE I.—Prepositions must be chosen and employed agreeably to the usage and diom of the language, so as rightly to express the relations intended. Example of error: "By which we arrive *to* the last division."—*Richard W. Green's Gram.* p. ii. 8ay,—"arrive *at*."

NOTE II.—Those prepositions which are particularly adapted in meaning to *two* objects, or to *more*, ought to be confined strictly to the government of such terms only as suit them. Example of error: "What is *Person*? It is the *medium of* dis- tinction *between* the *speaker*, the *object* addressed or spoken *to*, and the *object* spoken of."—*O. B. Peirce's Gram.* p. 84. "*Between three*," is an incongruity; and the text here cited is bad in several other respects.

NOTE III.—An *ellipsis* or *omission* of the preposition is inelegant, except where long and general use has sanctioned it, and made the relation sufficiently intelligible. In the following sentence, *of* is needed: "I will not flatter you, that all I see in you is *worthy love.*"—*Shakspeare.* The following requires *from:* "Ridicule *is banished France,* and is losing ground in England."—*Kames, El. of Crit.* i, 106.

NOTE IV.—The *insertion* of a preposition is also inelegant, when the particle is needless, or when it only robs a transitive verb of its proper regimen; as, "The people of England may congratulate *to* themselves."—DRYDEN: *Priestley's Gram.* p. 168. "His servants ye are, *to* whom ye obey."—*Rom.* vi, 16.

NOTE V.—The preposition and its object should have that position in respect to other words, which will render the sentence the most perspicuous and agreeable. Examples of error: "Gratitude is a forcible and active principle in good and generous minds."—*Murray's Key,* 8vo, p. 169. Better: "In good and generous minds, gratitude is a forcible and active principle." "By a single stroke, he knows how to reach the heart."—*Blair's Rhet.* p. 439. Better: "He knows how to reach the heart by a single stroke."

IMPROPRIETIES FOR CORRECTION.

FALSE SYNTAX UNDER RULE XXIII.

EXAMPLES UNDER NOTE I.—CHOICE OF PREPOSITIONS.

"You have bestowed your favours to the most deserving persons."—*Swift, on E. Tongue.*

[FORMULE.—Not proper, because the relation between *have bestowed* and *persons* is not correctly expressed by the preposition *to*. But, according to Note 1st under Rule 23d, "Prepositions must be chosen and employed agreeably to the usage and idiom of the language, so as rightly to express the relations intended." This relation would be better expressed by *upon*; thus, "You have bestowed your favours upon the most deserving persons.]

"But to rise beyond that, and overtop the crowd, is given to few."—*Blair's Rhet.* p. 351. "This also is a good sentence, and gives occasion to no material remark."—*Ib.* p. 201. "Though Cicero endeavours to give some reputation of the elder Cato, and those who were his cotemporaries."—*Ib.* p. 245. "The change that was produced on eloquence, is beautifully described in the Dialogue."—*Ib.* p. 249. "Without carefully attending to the variation which they make upon the idea."—*Ib.* p. 367. "All of a sudden, you are transported into a lofty palace."—*Hazlitt's Lect.* p. 70. "Alike independent on one another."—*Campbell's Rhet.* p. 398. "You will not think of them as distinct processes going on independently on each other."—*Channing's Self-Culture,* p. 15. "Though we say, to *depend on, dependent on,* and *independent on,* we say, *independently of.*"—*Churchill's Gram.* p. 348. "Independently on the rest of the sentence."—*Lowth's Gram.* p. 78; *Guy's,* 88; *Murray's,* i, 145 and 184; *Ingersoll's,* 150; *Frost's,* 46; *Fisk's,* 125; *Smith's New Gram.* 156; *Gould's Lat. Gram.* 209; *Nixon's Parser,* 65. "Because they stand independent on the rest of the sentence."—*Fisk's Gram.* p. 111. "When a substantive is joined with a participle in English independently in the rest of the sentence."—*Adam's Lat. and Eng. Gram., Boston Ed. of 1803,* p. 213; *Albany Ed. of 1820,* p. 166. "Conjunction, comes of the two Latin words *con,* together, and *jungo,* to join."—*Merchant's School Gram.* p. 19. "How different to this is the life of Fulvia!"—*Addison, Spect.* No. 15. "*Loved* is a participle or adjective, derived of the word *love.*"—*Dr. Ash's Gram.* p. 27. "But I would inquire at him, what an office is?"—*Barclay's Works,* iii, 463. "For the capacity is brought unto action."—*Ib.* iii, 420. "In this period, language and taste arrive to purity."—*Webster's Essays,* p. 94. "And should you not aspire at distinction in the republick of letters?"—*Kirkham's Gram.* p. 13. "Delivering you up to the synagogues, and in prisons."—*Keith's Evidences,* p. 55. "One that is kept from falling in a ditch, is as truly saved, as he that is taken out of one."—*Barclay's Works,* i, 312. "The best on it is, they are but a sort of French Hugonots."—*Addison, Spect.* No. 62. "These last Ten Examples are indeed of a different Nature to the former."—*Johnson's Gram. Com.* p. 333. "For the initiation of students in the principles of the English language."—ANNUAL REVIEW: *Murray's Gram.* ii, 299. "Richelieu profited of every circumstance which the conjuncture afforded."—*Bolingbroke, on Hist.* p. 177. "In the names of drugs and plants, the mistake in a word may endanger life."—*Murray's Key,* ii, 165. "In order to the carrying on its several parts into execution."—*Butler's Analogy,* p. 192. "His abhorrence to the superstitious figure."—HUME: *Priestley's Gram.* p. 164. "Thy prejudice to my cause."—DRYDEN: *ib.* p. 164. "Which is found among every species of liberty."—HUME: *ib.* p. 169. "In a hilly region to the north of Jericho."—*Milman's Jews,* Vol. i. p. 8. "Two or more singular nouns, coupled with AND, require a verb and pronoun in the plural."—*Lennie's Gram.* p. 83.

"Books should to one of these four ends conduce,
For wisdom, piety, delight, or use."—*Denham,* p. 239.

UNDER NOTE II.—TWO OBJECTS OR MORE.

"The Anglo-Saxons, however, soon quarrelled between themselves for precedence."—*Con-stable's Miscellany*, xx, p. 69. "The distinctions between the principal parts of speech are sounded in nature."—*Webster's Essays*, p. 7. "I think I now understand the difference be-ween the active, passive, and neuter verbs."—*Ingersoll's Gram.* p. 124. "Thus a figure ncluding a space between three lines, is the real as well as nominal essence of a triangle." —*Locke's Essay*, p. 303. "We must distinguish between an imperfect phrase, a simple sentence, and a compound sentence."—*Lowth's Gram.* p. 117; *Murray's*, i, 267; *Ingersoll's*, !80; *Guy's*, 97. "The Jews are strictly forbidden by their law, to exercise usury among me another."—*Sale's Koran*, p. 177. "All the writers have distinguished themselves among one another."—*Addison*. "This expression also better secures the systematic uniformity between the three cases."—*Nutting's Gram.* p. 98. "When a disjunctive occurs between two or more Infinitive Modes, or clauses, the verb must be singular."—*Jaudon's Gram.* p. 15. "Several nouns or pronouns together in the same case, not united by *and*, require a comma between each."—*Blair's Gram.* p. 115. "The difference between the several vowels is produced by opening the mouth differently, and placing the tongue in a different manner for each."—*Churchill's Gram.* p. 2.. "Thus feet composed of syllables, being pro-nounced with a sensible interval between each, make a more lively impression than can be made by a continued sound."—*Kames, El. of Crit.* Vol. ii, p. 32. "The superlative degree implies a comparison between three or more."—*Smith's Productive Gram.* p. 51. "They are used to mark a distinction between several objects."—*Levizac's Gram.* p. 85.

UNDER NOTE III.—OMISSION OF PREPOSITIONS.

"This would have been less worthy notice."—*Churchill's Gram.* p. 197. "But I passed it, as a thing unworthy my notice."—*Werter*. "Which, in compliment to me, perhaps, you may, one day, think worthy your attention."—*Bucke's Gram.* p. 81. "To think this small present worthy an introduction to the young ladies of your very elegant establishment."— *Ib.* p. iv. "There are but a few miles portage."—*Jefferson's Notes on Virginia*, p. 17. "It is worthy notice, that our mountains are not solitary."—*Ib.* p. 26. "It is of about one hun-dred feet diameter."—*Ib.* p. 33. "Entering a hill a quarter or half a mile."—*Ib.* p. 47. "And herself seems passing to that awful dissolution, whose issue is not given human fore-sight to scan."—*Ib.* p. 160. "It was of a spheroidical form, of about forty feet diameter at the base, and had been of about twelve feet altitude."—*Ib.* p. 143. "Before this it was covered with trees of twelve inches diameter, and round the base was an excavation of five feet depth and width."—*Ibid.* "Then thou mayest eat grapes thy fill at thine own pleasure." —*Deut.* xxiii, 24. "Then he brought me back the way of the gate of the outward sanctu-ary."—*Ezekiel*, xliv, 1. "They will bless God that he has peopled one half the world with a race of freemen."—*Webster's Essays*, p. 94. "What use can these words be, till their meaning is known?"—*Town's Analysis*, p. 7. "The tents of the Arabs now are black, or a very dark colour."—*The Friend*, Vol. v, p. 265. "They may not be unworthy the attention of young men."—*Kirkham's Elocution*, p. 157. "The pronoun *that* is frequently applied to persons, as well as things."—*Merchant's Gram.* p. 87. "And *who* is in the same case that *man* is."—*Sanborn's Gram.* p. 148. "He saw a flaming stone, apparently about four feet diameter."—*The Friend*, vii, 409. "Pliny informs us, that this stone was the size of a cart."—*Ibid.* "Seneca was about twenty years of age in the fifth year of Tiberius, when the Jews were expelled Rome."—*Seneca's Morals*, p. 11. "I was prevented* reading a letter which would have undeceived me."—*Hawkesworth, Adv.* No. 54. "If the problem can be solved, we may be pardoned the inaccuracy of its demonstration."—*Booth's Introd.* p. 25. "The army must of necessity be the school, not of honour, but effeminacy."—*Brown's Estimate*, i, 65. "Afraid of the virtue of a nation, in its opposing bad measures."—*Ib.* i, 73. "The uniting them in various ways, so as to form words, would be easy."—*Music of Nature*, p. 34. "I might be excused taking any more notice of it."—*Watson's Apology*, p. 65. "Watch therefore; for ye know not what hour your Lord doth come."—*Matt.* xxiv, 42. "Here, not even infants were spared the sword."—*M'Ilvaine's Lectures*, p. 313. "To pre-vent men turning aside to corrupt modes of worship."—*Calvin's Institutes*, B. I, Ch. 12, Sec. 1. "God expelled them the Garden of Eden."—*Burder's Hist.* Vol. i, p. 10. "Nor could he refrain expressing to the senate the agonies of his mind."—*Art of Thinking*, p. 123. "Who now so strenuously opposes the granting him any new powers."—*Duncan's Cicero*, p. 127. "That the laws of the censors have banished him the forum."—*Ib.* p. 140. "We read not that he was degraded his office any other way."—*Barclay's Works*, iii, 149. "To all whom these presents shall come, Greeting."—*Hutchinson's Mass.* i, 459. "On the 1st, August, 1834."—*British Act for the Abolition of Slavery*.

"Whether you had not some time in your life
Err'd in this point which now you censure him."—*Shak.*

---

* A few of the examples under this head might be corrected equally well by some preceding note of a more specific character; for a general note against the improper omission of prepositions, of course includes those principles of grammar by which any particular prepositions are to be inserted. So the examples of error which were given in the tenth chapter of Etymology, might nearly all of them have been placed under the first note in

UNDER NOTE IV.—OF NEEDLESS PREPOSITIONS.

"And the apostles and elders came together to consider of this matter."—*Barclay's Works*, i, 481. "And the apostles and elders came together for to consider of this matter."—*Acts*, xv, 6. "Adjectives in our Language have neither Case, Gender, nor Number; the only Variation they have is by Comparison."—*Buchanan's Gram.* p. 27. " ' It is to you, that I am indebted for this privilege;' that is, 'to you am I indebted;' or, 'It is to you to whom I am indebted.' "—*Sanborn's Gram.* p. 232. "*Books* is a noun, of the third person, plural number, of neuter gender."—*Ingersoll's Gram.* p. 16. "*Brother's* is a common substantive, of the masculine gender, the third person, the singular number, and in the possessive case."—*Murray's Gram.* i, 229. "*Virtue's* is a common substantive, of the third person, the singular number, and in the possessive case."—*Ib.* i, 228. " When the authorities on one side greatly preponderate, it is in vain to oppose the prevailing usage."—*Campbell's Rhet.* p. 173; *Murray's Gram.* i, 367. "A captain of a troop of banditti, had a mind to be plundering of Rome."—*Collier's Antoninus*, p. 61. "And, notwithstanding of its Verbal power, we have added the *to* and other signs of exertion."—*Booth's Introd.* p. 38. " Some of these situations are termed CASES, and are expressed by additions to the Noun instead of by separate words."—*Ib.* p. 33. " Is it such a fast that I have chosen, that a man should afflict his soul for a day, and to bow down his head like a bulrush ?"—*Bacon's Wisdom*, p. 65. "And this first emotion comes at last to be awakened by the accidental, instead of, by the necessary antecedent."—*Wayland's Moral Science*, p. 17. "At about the same time, the subjugation of the Moors was completed."—*Balbi's Geog.* p. 269. " God divided between the light and between the darkness."—*Burder's Hist.* i, 1. " Notwithstanding of this, we are not against outward significations of honour."—*Barclay's Works*, i, 242. " Whether these words and practices of Job's friends, be for to be our rule."—*Ib.* i, 243. " Such verb cannot admit of an objective case after it."—*Lowth's Gram.* p. 73. " For which God is now visibly punishing of these Nations."—*Right of Tythes*, p. 139. " In this respect, Tasso yields to no poet, except to Homer."—*Blair's Rhet.* p. 444. " Notwithstanding of the numerous panegyrics on the ancient English liberty."—HUME: *Priestley's Gram.* p. 161. " Their efforts seemed to anticipate on the spirit, which became so general afterwards."—*Id. ib.* p. 167.

UNDER NOTE V.—THE PLACING OF THE WORDS.

" But how short are my expressions of its excellency ! "—*Baxter*. " There is a remarkable union in his style, of harmony with ease."—*Blair's Rhet.* p. 127. " It disposes in the most artificial manner, of the light and shade, for viewing every thing to the best advantage."—*Ib.* p. 139. "Aristotle too holds an eminent rank among didactic writers for his brevity."—*Ib.* p. 177. " In an introduction, correctness should be carefully studied in the expression."—*Ib.* p. 308. " Precision is to be studied, above all things in laying down a method."—*Ib.* p. 313. " Which shall make the impression on the mind of something that is one, whole and entire."—*Ib.* p. 353. "At the same time, there are some defects which must be acknowledged in the Odyssey."—*Ib.* p. 437. " Beauties, however, there are, in the concluding books, of the tragic kind."—*Ib.* p. 452. " These forms of conversation by degrees multiplied and grew troublesome."—*Spectator*, No. 119. " When she has made her own choice, for form's sake, she sends a congé-d'-élire to her friends."—*Ib.* No. 475. " Let us endeavour to establish to ourselves an interest in him who holds the reins of the whole creation in his hand."—*Ib.* No. 12. " Let us endeavour to establish to ourselves an interest in him, who, in his hand, holds the reins of the whole creation."—*Kames, El. of Crit.* ii, 63. " The most frequent measure next to this in English poetry is that of eight syllables."—*Blair's Gram.* p. 121. " To introduce as great a variety as possible of cadences."—*Jamieson's Rhet.* p. 80. " He addressed several exhortations to them suitable to their circumstances."—*Murray's Key*, ii, p. 191. " Habits must be acquired of temperance and self-denial."—*Ib.* p. 217. " In reducing the rules prescribed to practice."—*Murray's Gram.* Vol. ii, p. iv. " But these parts must be so closely bound together as to make the impression upon the mind, of one object, not of many."—*Ib.* Vol. i, p. 311; *Blair's Rhet.* p. 106. "Errors are sometimes committed by the most distinguished writers with respect to the use of *shall* and *will.*"—*Butler's Pract. Gram.* p. 106.

CHAPTER XI. — INTERJECTIONS.

Interjections, being seldom any thing more than natural sounds or short words uttered independently, can hardly be said to have any *syntax ;* but since some rule is necessary to show the learner how to dispose of them in parsing, a brief axiom for that purpose, is here added, which completes our

this tenth chapter of Syntax. But it was thought best to illustrate every part of this volume, by some examples of false grammar, out of the infinite number and variety with which our literature abounds.

series of rules : and, after several remarks on this canon, and on the common treatment of Interjections, this chapter is made to embrace *Exercises* upon all the other parts of speech, that the chapters in the Key may correspond to those of the Grammar.

RULE XXIV.—INTERJECTIONS.

Interjections have no dependent construction ; they are put absolute, either alone, or with other words : as, "*O !* let not thy heart despise me."—*Dr. Johnson.* "*O* cruel *thou !* "—*Pope, Odys.* B. xii, l. 383. "*Ah* wretched *we,* poets of earth ! "—*Cowley*, p. 28.

"*Ah Dennis ! Gildon ah !* what ill-starr'd rage
Divides a friendship long confirm'd by age ? "
Pope, Dunciad, B. iii, 1, 173.

OBSERVATIONS ON RULE XXIV.

OBS. 1.—To this rule, there are properly *no exceptions.* Though interjections are sometimes uttered in close connexion with other words, yet, being mere signs of passion or of feeling, they seem not to have any strict grammatical relation, or dependence according to the sense. Being destitute alike of relation, agreement, and government, they must be used independently, if used at all. Yet an emotion signified in this manner, not being causeless, may be accompanied by some object, expressed either by a nominative absolute, or by an objective after *for :* as, "*Alas !* poor *Yorick !* "—*Shak.* Here the grief denoted by *alas,* is certainly *for Yorick ;* as much so, as if the expression were, "Alas *for* poor Yorick ! " But, in either case, *alas,* I think, has no dependent construction ; neither has *Yorick,* in the former, unless we suppose an ellipsis of some governing word.

OBS. 2.—The interjection *O* is common to many languages, and is frequently uttered, in token of earnestness, before nouns or pronouns put absolute by direct address ; as, "Arise, *O Lord ; O God,* lift up thine hand."—*Psalms,* x, 12. "*O ye* of little faith ! "—*Matt.* vi, 30. The Latin and Greek grammarians, therefore, made this interjection the *sign* of the *vocative case ;* which case is the same as the nominative put absolute by address in English. But this particle is no positive index of the vocative ; because an independent address may be made without that sign, and the *O* may be used where there is no address : as, "*O* scandalous want! *O* shameful omission ! "— " Pray, *Sir,* don't be uneasy."—*Burgh's Speaker,* p. 86.

OBS. 3.—Some grammarians ascribe to two or three of our interjections the power of governing sometimes the nominative case, and sometimes the objective. First, NIXON ; in an exercise entitled, " NOMINATIVE GOVERNED BY AN INTERJECTION," thus : " The interjections O! Oh ! and Ah! *require* after them the nominative case of a *substantive* in the *second* person ; as, 'O thou *persecuter !* '—' O Alexander ! thou hast slain thy friend.' *O* is an interjection, *governing* the nominative case *Alexander.* "—*English Parser,* p. 61. Again, under the title, " OBJECTIVE CASE GOVERNED BY AN INTERJECTION," he says : " The interjections O! Oh ! and Ah! *require* after them the objective case of a *substantive* in the *first* or *third* person ; as, 'Oh *me!* ' 'Oh the *humiliations!* ' *Oh* is an interjection, *governing* the objective case *humiliations.* "—*Ib.* p. 63. These two rules are in fact contradictory, while each of them absurdly suggests that *O, oh,* and *ah,* are used only with nouns. So J. M. PUTNAM : "Interjections sometimes *govern* an objective case ; as, *Ah me! O* the tender *ties! O* the soft *enmity! O me* miserable! *O* wretched *prince! O* cruel *reverse* of fortune! When an address is made, the interjection does not perform the office of government."—*Putnam's Gram.* p. 113. So KIRKHAM ; who, under a rule quite different from these, extends the doctrine of government to *all* interjections: "According to the genius of the English language, transitive verbs and prepositions *require* the objective case of a noun or pronoun after them ; and this requisition is all that is meant by *government,* when we say that these parts of speech *govern the objective* case. THE SAME PRINCIPLE APPLIES TO THE INTERJECTION. 'Interjections *require* the objective case of a pronoun of the first person after them ; but the nominative of a noun or pronoun of the second or third person ; as, Ah *me!* Oh *thou!* O my *country !* ' To say, then, that interjections *require* particular cases after them, is synonymous with saying, that they *govern* those cases ; and this office of the interjection is in *perfect accordance* with that which it performs in the Latin, and many other languages."—*Kirkham's Gram.* p. 164. According to this, every interjection has as much need of an object after it, as has a transitive verb or a preposition ! The rule has, certainly, *no* "accordance" with what occurs in Latin, or in any other language ; it is wholly a fabrication, though found, in some shape or other, in well-nigh all English grammars.

OBS. 4.—L. MURRAY'S doctrine on this point is thus expressed : " The interjections *O! Oh!* and *Ah!* require the objective case of a pronoun in the first person after them : as, 'O me ! oh *me!* Ah me!' But the nominative case in the second person : as, 'O thou persecutor ! ' 'Oh ye hypocrites !' 'O thou, who dwellest,' &c."—*Octavo Gram.* p. 158. INGERSOLL copies this most faulty note literally, adding these words to its abrupt end,—i. e. to its inexplicable " &c.," used by Murray ; "because the first person *is governed by a preposition* understood: as, 'Ah *for* me !' or, 'O *what will become of* me !' &c.; and the second person is in the *nominative independent,* there being a direct address."—*Conversations on E. Gram.* p. 211. So we see that this grammarian and Kirkham, both modifiers of Murray, understand their master's false verb "*require*" very differently. LENNIE too, in renouncing a part of Murray's double or threefold error, "*Oh !* happy *us !*" for, "*O* happy *we !*" teaches thus ; "Interjections sometimes *require* the objective case

after them, but they never *govern* it. "In the first edition of this grammar," says he, "I follow
Mr. Murray and others, in leaving *we*, in the exercises to be turned into *us*; but that it shou
be *we*, and not *us*, is obvious; because it is the nominative to *are* understood; thus, *Oh ha*
are we, or, *Oh we are* happy, (being) surrounded with so many blessings."—*Lennie's Gram. Fi*
Edition, p. 84; *Twelfth*, p. 110. Here is an other solution of the construction of this pronoun
the first person, contradictory alike to Ingersoll's, to Kirkham's, and to Murray's; while all d
wrong, and this among the rest. The word should indeed be *we*, and not *us*; because we ha
both analogy and good authority for the former case, and nothing but the false conceit of such
grammatists for the latter. But it is a *nominative absolute*, like any other nominative which i
use in the same exclamatory manner. For the first person may just as well be put in the sam
native absolute, by exclamation, as any other; as, "Behold *I* and the *children* whom God has
given me!"—*Heb.* ii, 13. "Ecce *ego* et *pueri* quos mihi dedit Deus!"—*Bass.* "O brave we!".
Dr. *Johnson*, often. So Horace: "O *ego lævus*," &c.—*Ep. ad Pi.* 301.
    "Ah! luckless *I!* who purge in spring my spleen—
    Else sure the first of bards had Horace been."—*Francis's Hor.* ii, 209.

Obs. 5.—Whether Murray's remark above, on "O! Oh! and Ah!" was originally designed
a *rule of government* or not, it is hardly worth any one's while to inquire. It is too lame a
inaccurate every way, to deserve any notice, but that which should serve to explode it forev
Yet no few, who have since made English grammars, have copied the text literally; as they hav
for the public benefit, stolen a thousand other errors from the same quarter. The reader will fi
it, with little or no change, in Smith's New Grammar, p. 96 and 134; Alger's, 56; Alden's, 1?
Russell's, 92; Blair's, 100; Guy's, 89; Abel Flint's, 59; A Teacher's, 43; Picket's, 210; Coo
er's* Murray, 136; Wilcox's, 95; Bucke's, 87; Emmons's, 77; and probably in others. Len
varies it *indefinitely*, thus: "RULE. The interjections Oh! and Ah! &c. *generally* require th
objective case of the first personal pronoun, *and* the nominative of the second; as, Ah me! O th
fool! O ye hypocrites!"—*Lennie's Gram.* p. 110; *Brace's*, 88. M'Culloch, after Crombie, tha
"RULE XX. Interjections are joined with the objective case of the pronoun of the first pers
and with the nominative of the pronoun of the second; as, Ah me! O ye hypocrites."—*Man
of E. Gram.* p. 145; and *Crombie's Treatise*, p. 315; also *Fowler's E. Language*, p. 563. He
makes it a note, thus: "The interjections, O! Oh! Ah! *are followed by* the objective case of
pronoun of the first person; as, 'Oh me!' 'Ah me!' but by the nominative case of the pron
in the second person; as, 'O thou, who dwellest!'"—*Hiley's Gram.* p. 82.. This is what the sam
author elsewhere calls "THE GOVERNMENT OF INTERJECTIONS;" though, like some others,
had set it in the "Syntax of PRONOUNS." See *lb.* p. 106. Murray, in forming his own first
"Abridgment," omitted it altogether. In his other grammars, it is still a mere note, standin
where he at first absurdly put it, under his rule for the agreement of pronouns with their anter
dents. By many of his sage amenders, it has been placed in the catalogue of principal rule
But, that it is no adequate rule for interjections, is manifest; for, in its usual form, it
limited to *three*, and none of these can ever, with any propriety, be parsed by it. Murray hims
has not used it in any of his forms of parsing. He conceived, (as I hinted before in Chapter 1st,
that, "The syntax of the Interjection is of *so very limited a nature*, that it *does not require* a cl
tinct, appropriate rule."—*Octavo Gram.* i, 224.

Obs. 6.—Against this remark of Murray's, a good argument may be drawn from the ridicul
use which has been made of his own suggestion in the other place. For, though that suggestio
never had in it the least shadow of truth, and was never at all applicable either to the thre
interjections, or to pronouns, or to cases, or to the persons, or to any thing else of which it speak
it has not only been often copied literally, and called a "RULE" of syntax, but many have, ye
more absurdly, made it a *general canon* which imposes on all interjections a syntax that belon
to none of them. For example: "An *interjection must be followed* by the objective case of a *r*
noun in the first person; and by a nominative of the second person; as—Oh me! ah me! oh the
Ah hail, ye happy men!"—*Jaudon's Gram.* p. 116. This is as much as to say, that every int
jection must have a pronoun or two after it! Again: "*Interjections must be followed* by th
objective case of the pronoun in the first person; as, O me! Ah me! and by the nominative cas
of the second person; as, O thou persecutor! Oh ye hypocrites!"—*Merchant's Murray*, p. 9
Merchant's School Gram. p. 99. I imagine there is a difference between O and oh,† and that th
author, as well as Murray, in the first and the last of these examples, has misapplied them bot
Again: "*Interjections require* the objective case of a pronoun of the first person, and the seco
native case of the second; as, Ah me! O thou."—*Frost's El. of E. Gram.* p. 48. This, too,
general.

* "The Rev. Jacob Goldsmith Cooper, A. M.," was the author of two English grammars, as well as of what i
called "A New and Improved Latin Grammar," with "An Edition of the Works of Virgil, &c.," all published
Philadelphia. His first grammar, dated 1828, is entitled, "An *Abridgment of Murray's English Grammar, o*
Exercises." But it is no more an abridgment of Murray's work, than of mine; he having chosen to strike ou
the text of my Institutes, or supply matter of his own, about as often as to copy Murray. His second is the Lati
Grammar. His third, which is entitled, "A *Plain and Practical English Grammar*," and dated 1831, is a boo
very different from the first, but equally inaccurate and worthless. In this book, the syntax of interjectio
stands thus: "RULE 21. The interjections O, oh and ah are followed by the *objective case* of a noun or pronou
as: "O me! ah me! oh me! In the second person, they are a *mark* or *sign* of an address, made to a perso
thing, as: O thou persecutor! Oh, ye hypocrites! O virtue, how amiable thou art!"—Page 67. Th
inaccuracy of all this can scarcely be exceeded.

† "Oh is used to express the emotion of pain, sorrow, or surprise. O is used to express wishing, exclamatio
or a direct address to a person."—*Lennie's Gram.*, 12th Ed., p. 110. Of this distinction our grammarians i
general seem to have no conception; and, in fact, it is so often disregarded by other authors, that the propriet
of it may be disputed. Since O and oh are pronounced alike, or very nearly so, if there is no difference in the
application, they are only different modes of writing the same word, and one or the other of them is useless
there is a real difference, as I suppose there is, it ought to be better observed; and O me! and oh me! if I
believe are found only in grammars, should be regarded as bad English. Both O and oh, as well as ah, are
used in Latin by Terence, who was reckoned an elegant writer; and his manner of applying them favours th
distinction: and so do our own dictionaries, though Johnson and Walker do not draw it clearly, for ah be

OBS. 7.—Of *nouns*, or of the *third person*, the three rules last cited say nothing;[*] though it appears from other evidence, that their authors supposed them applicable at least to *some nouns* of the *second person*. The supposition however was quite needless, because each of their grammars contains an other Rule, that, " When an address is made, the noun or pronoun is in the nominative case *independent:*" which, by the by, is far from being universally true, either of the noun or of the pronoun. Russell imagines, " The words *depending* upon interjections, have so near a resemblance to those in a direct address, that they may very properly be classed under the same general head," and be parsed as being " in the nominative case *independent.*" See his *Abridgment of Murray's Gram.*" p. 91. He does not perceive that *depending* and *independent* are words that contradict each other. Into the same inconsistency, do nearly all those gentlemen fall, who ascribe to interjections a control over cases. Even Kirkham, who so earnestly contends that what any words *require* after them they must necessarily *govern*, forgets his whole argument, or justly disbelieves it, whenever he parses any noun that is uttered with an interjection. In short, he applies his principle to nothing but the word *me* in the phrases, "*Ah me!*" "*Oh me!*" and "*Me miserable!*" and even these he parses falsely. The second person used in the vocative, or the nominative put absolute by direct address, whether an interjection be used or not, he rightly explains as being " in the nominative case independent;" as, "*O Jerusalem, Jerusalem!*" —*Kirkham's Gram.* p. 130. "*O maid* of Inistore!"—*Ib.* p. 131. But he is wrong in saying that, " Whenever a noun is of the second person, it is in the nominative case independent;" (*Ib.* p. 130;) and still more so, in supposing that, " The principle contained in the note" [which tells what interjections *require*,] "*proves* that every noun of the second person is in the nominative case."—*Ib.* p. 164. A falsehood proves nothing but the ignorance or the wickedness of him who utters it. He is wrong too, as well as many others, in supposing that this nominative independent is not a nominative absolute; for, " The vocative is [*generally*, if not *always*,] absolute."—*W. Allen's Gram.* p. 142. But that nouns of the second person are not always absolute or independent, nor always in the nominative case, or the vocative, appears, I think, by the following example: "This is the stone which was set at nought *of you builders.*"—*Acts*, iv, 11. See Obs. 3d on Rule 8th.

OBS. 8.—The third person, when uttered in exclamation, with an interjection before it, is parsed by Kirkham, not as being governed by the interjection, either in the nominative case, according to his own argument and own rule above cited, or in the objective, according to Nixon's notion of the construction; nor yet as being put absolute in the nominative, as I believe it generally, if not always, is; but as being " the nominative to a verb understood; as, 'Lo,' *there is* ' the poor Indian!' 'O, the pain' *there is!* 'the bliss' *there is* 'IN dying!'"—*Kirkham's Gram.* p. 129. Pope's text is, "*Oh* the pain, the bliss *of* dying!" and, in all that is here changed, the grammarian has perverted it, if not in all that he has added. It is an other principle of Kirkham's Grammar, though a false one, that, " Nouns have but two persons, the second and [the] third."— P. 37. So that, these two being disposed of agreeably to his own methods above, which appear to include the second and third persons of pronouns also, there remains to him nothing but the objective of the pronoun of the first person to which he can suppose his other rule to apply; and I have shown that there is no truth in it even in regard to this. Yet, with the strongest professions of adhering to the principles, and even to " the language," of Lindley Murray, this gentleman, by copying somebody else in preference to " that eminent philologist," has made himself one of those by whom Murray's erroneous remark on *O, oh,* and *ah,* with pronouns of the first and second persons, is not only stretched into a rule for all interjections, but made to include nouns of the second person, and both nouns and pronouns of the third person: as, " Interjections require the objective case of a pronoun of the first person after them, but the nominative of a noun or pronoun of the second or third person; as, Ah! *me*; Oh! *thou*; O! *virtue.*"—*Kirkham's Gram.*, 2d Ed., p. 134; Stereotype Ed., p. 177. See the same rule, with examples and punctuation different, in his *Stereotype Edition*, p. 164; *Comly's Gram.* 116; *Greenleaf's*, 36; and *Fisk's*, 144. All these authors, except Comly, who comes much nearest to the thing, profess to present to us "*Murray's Grammar Simplified;*" and this is a sample of their work of *simplification!*—an ignorant piling of errors on errors!

　　"O imitatores servum pecus! ut mihi sæpe
　　　Bilem, sæpe jocum vestri movêre tumultus!"—*Horace.*

OBS. 9.—Since so many of our grammarians conceive that interjections require or govern cases, it may be proper to cite some who teach otherwise. "Interjections, in English, have no government."—*Lowth's Gram.* p. 111. " Interjections have no government, or admit of no construction." —*Coar's Gram.* p. 189. " Interjections have no connection with other words."—*Fuller's Gram.*

---

much an " *exclamation* " as O. In the works of Virgil, Ovid, and Horace, we find O or ô used frequently, but nowhere oh. Yet this is no evidence of their sameness, or of the uselessness of the latter; but rather of their difference, and of the impropriety of confounding them. O, oh, ho, and ah, are French words as well as English. Boyer, in his Quarto Dictionary, confounds them all; translating "O!" only by " Oh!" "OH! or HO!" by " Ho! Oh!" and "AH!" by " Oh! alas! well-a-day! ough! A! ah! hah! ho!" He would have done better to have made each one explain itself; and especially, not to have set down " ough!" and " A!" as English words which correspond to the French ah!

[*] This silence is sufficiently accounted for by *Murray's;* of whose work, most of the authors who have any such rule, are either piddling modifiers or servile copyists. And Murray's silence on these matters, is in part attributable to the fact, that when he wrote his remark, his system of grammar denied that nouns have any first person, or any objective case. Of course he supposed that all nouns that were uttered after interjections, whether they were of the second person or of the third, were in the nominative case; for he gave to nouns *two* cases only, the nominative and the possessive. And when he afterwards admitted the objective case of nouns, he did not alter his remark, but left all his pupils ignorant of the case of any noun that is used in exclamation or invocation. In his doctrine of two cases, he followed Dr. Ash; from whom also he copied the rule which I am criticising: " The *Interjections, O, Oh,* and *Ah,* require the *accusative* case of a pronoun in the *first* Person: as, O *me,* Oh *me,* Ah *me:* But the *Nominative* in the *second:* as, O *thou,* O *ye.*"—*Ash's Gram.* p. 60. Or perhaps he had Bicknell's book, which was later: "The *interjections O, oh,* and *ah,* require the accusative case of a pronoun in the *first* person after them; as, O, *me!* Oh, *me!* Ah, *me!* But the nominative case in the *second* person; as, O, *thou that rulest!* O, *ye rulers of this land!*"—*The Grammatical Wreath*, Part I, p. 106.

p. 71. "The interjection, in a grammatical sense, is totally unconnected with every other word in a sentence. Its arrangement, of course is altogether arbitrary, and cannot admit of any theory."—*Jamieson's Rhet.* p. 83. "Interjections cannot properly have either concord or government. They are only mere sounds excited by passion, and have no just connexion with any other part of a sentence. Whatever case, therefore, is joined with them, must depend on some other word understood, except the vocative, which is always placed absolutely."—*Adam's Latin Gram.* p. 196; *Gould's,* 193. If this is true of the Latin language, a slight variation will make it as true of ours. "Interjections, and phrases resembling them, are taken absolutely; as, *Oh,* world, *thy slippery turns!* But the phrases Oh *me!* and Ah *me!* frequently occur."—*W. Allen's Gram.* p. 188. This passage is, in several respects, wrong; yet the leading idea is true. The author entitles it, "SYNTAX OF INTERJECTIONS," yet absurdly includes in it I know not what *phrases!* In the phrase, "*thy slippery turns!*" no word is absolute, or "taken absolutely," but the noun "*turns;*" and this, without the least hint of its *case,* the learned author will have us understand to be absolute, because the phrase *resembles an interjection!* But the noun "*world,*" which is also absolute, and which still more resembles an interjection, he will have to be so for a different reason—because it is in what he chooses to call *the vocative case.* But, according to custom, he should rather have put his interjection absolute *with* the noun, and written it, "*O world,*" and not, "*Oh, world.*" What he meant to do with "*Oh me!* and *Ah me!*" is doubtful. If any phrases come fairly under his rule, these are the very ones; and yet he seems to introduce them as exceptions! Of these, it can hardly be said, that they "*frequently* occur." Lowth notices only the latter, which he supposes elliptical. The former I do not remember to have met with more than three or four times; except in grammars, which, in this case, are hardly to be called authorities: "*Oh! me,* how fared it with me then?"—*Job Scott.* "*Oh me!* all the host have got over the river, what shall we do?"—WALTON: *Joh. Dict.*

"But when he was first seen, *oh me!*
What shrieking and what misery!"—*Wordsworth's Works,* p. 114.

OBS. 10.—When a declinable word not in the nominative absolute, follows an interjection, as part of an imperfect exclamation, its construction (if the phrase be good English) depends on something understood; as, "Ah *me!*"—that is, "Ah! *pity* me;" or, "Ah! *it grieves* me:" or, as some will have it, (because the expression in Latin is "*Hei mihi!*") "Ah *for* me!"—*Ingersoll.* "Ah! *woo is to* me."—*Lowth.* "Ah! *sorrow is to* me."—*Coar.* So of "*oh me!*" for, in these expressions, if not generally, *oh* and *ah* are exactly equivalent the one to the other. As for "*O me,*" it is now seldom met with, though Shakspeare has it a few times. From these examples, O. B. Peirce erroneously imagines the "independent case" of the pronoun *I* to be *me,* and accordingly parses the word without supposing an ellipsis; but in the plural he makes that case to be *we,* and not *us.* So, having found an example of "Ah *Him!*" which, according to one half of our grammarians, is bad English, he conceives the independent case of *he* to be *him;* but in the plural, and in both numbers of the words *thou* and *she,* he makes it the nominative, or the same in form as the nominative. So builds he "the temple of Grammatical consistency!"—P. 7. Nixon and Cooper must of course approve of "*Ah him!*" because they assume that the interjection *ah* "requires" or "governs" the objective case of the third person. Others must condemn the expression, because they teach that *ah* requires the nominative case of this person. Thus Greenleaf sets down for false syntax, "O! happy *them,* surrounded with so many blessings!"—*Gram. Simplified,* p. 47. Here, undoubtedly, the word should be *they;* and, by analogy, (if indeed the instances are analogous,) it would seem more proper to say, "*Ah he!*" the nominative being our only case absolute. But if any will insist that "*Ah him!*" is good English, they must suppose that *him* is governed by something understood; as, "Ah! *I lament* him;" or, "Ah! *I mourn for* him." And possibly, on this principle, the example referred to may be most correct as it stands, with the pronoun in the objective case: "*Ah Him!* the first great martyr in this great cause!"—D. WEBSTER: *Peirce's Gram.* p. 199.

OBS. 11.—If we turn to the Latin syntax, to determine by analogy what case is used, or ought to be used, after our English interjections, in stead of finding a "perfect accordance" between that syntax and the rule for which such accordance has been claimed, we see at once an utter repugnance, and that the pretence of their agreement is only a sample of Kirkham's unconscionable pedantry. The rule, in all its modifications, is based on the principle, that the choice of *cases* depends on the distinction of *persons*—a principle plainly contrary to the usage of the Latin classics, and altogether untrue. In Latin, some interjections are construed with the nominative, the accusative, or the vocative; some, only with the dative; some, only with the vocative. But, in English, these four cases are all included in two, the nominative and the objective; and, the case independent or absolute being necessarily the nominative, it follows that the objective, if it occur after an interjection, must be the object of something which is capable of governing it. If any disputant, by supposing ellipses, will make objectives of what I call nominatives absolute, so be it; but I insist that interjections, in fact, never "require" or "govern" one case more than an other. So Peirce, and Kirkham, and Ingersoll, with pointed self-contradiction, may continue to make "the independent case," whether vocative or merely exclamatory, the subject of a verb, expressed or understood; but I will content myself with endeavouring to establish a syntax not liable to this sort of objection. In doing this, it is proper to look at all the facts which go to show what is right, or wrong. "*Lo, the poor Indian!*" is in Latin, "*Ecce pauper Indus!*" or, "*Ecce pauperem Indum!*" This use of either the nominative or the accusative after *ecce,* if it proves any thing concerning the case of the word *Indian,* proves it doubtful. Some, it seems, pronounce it an objective. Some, like Murray, say nothing about it. Following the analogy of our own language, I refer it to the nominative absolute, because there is nothing to determine it to be otherwise. In the examples, "*Heu me miserum!* Ah *wretch* that I am!"—(*Grant's Latin Gram.* p. 263,) and "*Miser ego homo!* O wretched *man* that I am!"—(*Rom.* vii, 24,) if the word *that* is a relative pronoun, as I incline to think it is, the case of the nouns *wretch* and *man* does not depend on any other words, either expressed or implied. They are therefore nominatives absolute, according to Rule 8th, though the Latin words may be most properly explained on the principle of ellipsis.

Obs. 12.—Of some impenetrable blockhead, Horace, telling how himself was vexed, says: "*O te, Bollane, cerebri Felicem! aiebam tacitus.*"—*Lib.* i, *Sat.* ix, 11. Literally: "*O thee, Bollanus, happy of brain! said I to myself.*" That is, "O! *I envy thee,*" &c. This shows that O does not "require the nominative case of the second person" after it, at least in Latin. Neither does *oh* or *ah*: for, if a governing word be suggested, the objective may be proper; as, "Whom did he injure? Ah! *thee,* my boy?"—or even the possessive; as, "Whose sobs do I hear? Oh! *thine,* my child?" Kirkham tells us truly, (Gram. p. 126,) that the exclamation "*O my,*" is frequently heard in conversation. These last resemble Lucan's use of the genitive, with an ellipsis of the governing noun: "*O misera sortis!*" i. e. "*O* [men] *of miserable lot!*" In short, all the Latin cases, as well as all the English, may possibly occur after one or other of the interjections. I have instanced all but the ablative, and the following is literally an example of that, though the word *quanto* is construed adverbially: "Ah, *quanto* satius est!"—*Ter. And.* ii, 1. "Ah, *how much* better it is!" I have also shown, by good authorities, that the nominative of the first person, both in English and in Latin, may be properly used after those interjections which have been supposed to require or govern the objective. But how far is analogy alone a justification? Is "*O thee*" good English, because "*O te*" is good Latin? No: nor is it bad for the reason which our grammarians assign, but because our best writers never use it, and because O is more properly the sign of the vocative. The literal version above should therefore be changed; as, "O Bollanus, *thou* happy numskull! said I to myself."

Obs. 13.—Allen Fisk, "author of Adam's Latin Grammar Simplified," and of "Murray's English Grammar Simplified," sets down for "*False Syntax,*" not only that hackneyed example, "Oh! happy we," &c., but, "O! You, who love iniquity," and, "Ah! you, who hate the light."—*Fisk's E. Gram.* p. 144. But, to imagine that either *you* or *we* is wrong here, is certainly no sign of a great linguist; and his punctuation is very inconsistent both with his own rule of syntax and with common practice. An interjection set off by a comma or an exclamation point, is of course put absolute *singly,* or by itself. If it is to be read as being put absolute with something else, the separation is improper. One might just as well divide a preposition from its object, as an interjection from the case which it is supposed to govern. Yet we find here not only such a division as Murray sometimes improperly adopted, but in one instance a total separation, with a capital following; as, "O! You, who love iniquity," for, "O you who love iniquity!" or, "O ye," &c. If a point be here set between the two pronouns, the speaker accuses all his hearers of loving iniquity; if this point be removed, he addresses only such as do love it. But an interjection and a pronoun, each put absolute singly, one after the other, seem to me not to constitute a very natural exclamation. The last example above should therefore be, "Ah! you hate the light." The first should be written, "*O happy we!*"

Obs. 14.—In other grammars, too, there are many instances of some of the errors here pointed out. R. C. Smith knows no difference between O and oh; takes "*Oh!* happy *us,*" to be accurate English; sees no impropriety in separating interjections from the pronouns which he supposes them to "govern;" writes the same examples variously, even on the same page; inserts or omits commas or exclamation points at random; yet makes the latter the means by which interjections are to be known! See his *New Gram.* pp. 40, 96, and 134. Kirkham, who lays claim to "a new system of punctuation," and also stoutly asserts the governing power of interjections, writes, and rewrites, and finally stereotypes, in one part of his book, "Ah me! *Oh* thou! O my country!" and in an other, "Ah! me; *Oh!* thou; O! virtue." See Obs. 3d and Obs. 8th above. From such hands, any thing "*new*" should be received with caution: this last specimen of his scholarship has more errors than words.

Obs. 15.—Some few of our interjections seem to admit of a connexion with other words by means of a preposition or the conjunction *that*; as, "O *to* forget her!"—*Young.* "O *for* that warning voice!"—*Milton.* "O *that* they were wise!"—*Deut.* xxxii, 29. "O *that* my people had hearkened unto me!"—*Ps.* lxxxi, 13. "Alas *for* Sicily!"—*Cowper.* "O *for* a world in principle as chaste As this is gross and selfish!"—*Id.* "Hurrah *for* Jackson!"—*Newspaper.* "A bawd, sir, fy *upon* him!"—*Shak.: Joh. Dict.* "And fy *on* fortune, mine avowed foe!"—*Spencer: ib.* This connexion, however, even if we parse all the words just as they stand, does not give to the interjection itself any dependent construction. It appears indeed to refute Jamieson's assertion, that, "The interjection is *totally unconnected* with every other word in a sentence;" but I did not quote this passage, with any averment of its accuracy; and, certainly, many nouns which are put absolute themselves, have in like manner a connexion with words that are not put absolute: as, "O *Lord* God of hosts, hear my prayer; give ear, O *God* of Jacob. Selah."—*Ps.* lxxxiv, 8. But if any will suppose, that in the foregoing examples something else than the interjection must be the antecedent term to the preposition or the conjunction, they may consider the expressions elliptical; though it must be confessed, that much of their vivacity will be lost, when the supposed ellipses are supplied: as, "O! *I desire* to forget her."—"O! *how I long* for that warning voice!"—"O! *how I wish* that they were wise!"—"Alas! *I wail* for Sicily."—"Hurrah! *I shout* for Jackson."—"Fy! *cry out* upon him." Lindley Murray has one example of this kind, and if his punctuation of it is not bad in all his editions, there must be an ellipsis in the expression: "O! *for* better times."—*Octavo Gram.* ii, 6; *Duodecimo Exercises,* p. 10. He also writes it thus: "O, *for* better times."—*Octavo Gram.* i, 120; *Ingersoll's Gram.* p. 47. According to common usage, it should be, "O for better times!"

Obs. 16.—The interjection may be placed at the *beginning* or the *end* of a simple sentence, and sometimes *between* its two intimate parts; but this part of speech is seldom, if ever, allowed to interrupt the connexion of any words which are closely united in sense. Murray's definition of an interjection, as I have elsewhere shown, is faulty, and directly contradicted by his example: "O virtue! how amiable thou art!"—*Octavo Gram.* i, 28 and 128; ii, 2. This was a favourite sentence with Murray, and he appears to have written it uniformly in this fashion; which, undoubtedly, is altogether right, except that the word "*virtue*" should have had a capital Vee, because the quality is here personified.

Obs. 17.—Misled by the false notion, that the term *interjection* is appropriate only to what is "thrown in between the parts of a *sentence*," and perceiving that this is in fact but rarely the situation of this part of speech, a recent critic, (to whom I should owe some acknowledgements, if he were not wrong in every thing in which he charges me with error,) not only denounces this name as "*barbarous*," preferring Webster's loose term, "*exclamation*;" but avers, that, "The words called *interjection* should *never* be so used—should *always stand alone*; as, 'Oh! virtue, how amiable thou art.' 'Oh? Absalom, my son.' G. Brown,"continues he, "drags one into the middle of a sentence, *where it never belonged*; thus, 'This enterprise, *alas!* will never compensate us for the trouble and expense with which it has been attended.' If G. B. meant the *enterprise of* studying grammar, in the old theories, his sentiment is very appropriate; but his *alas!* he should have known enough to have put into the right place:—before the sentence representing the fact that excites the emotion expressed by *alas!* See on the Chart part 3, of RULE XVII. An *exclamation* must *always precede* the phrase or sentence describing the fact that excites the emotion to be expressed by the *exclamation*; as, Alas! I have alienated my friend! *Oh!* Glorious hope of bliss secure!"—*Oliver B. Peirce's Gram.* p. 375. "*O* Glorious hope of bliss secure!"—*Ib.* p. 184. "O *glorious* hope!"—*Ib.* p. 304.

OBS. 18.—I see no reason to believe, that the class of words which have always, and almost universally, been called *interjections*, can ever be more conveniently explained under any other name; and, as for the term *exclamation*, which is preferred also by Cutler, Felton, and S. W. Clark, it appears to me much less suitable than the old one, because it is less specific. Any word uttered loudly in the same breath, is an *exclamation*. This name therefore is too general; it includes other parts of speech than interjections; and it was but a foolish whim in Dr. Webster, to prefer it in his dictionaries. When David "cried *with a loud voice*, O my son Absalom! O Absalom, my son, my son!"[*] he uttered *two* exclamations; but they included all his words. He did not, like my critic above, set off his first word with an interrogation point, or any other point. But, says Peirce, "These words are *used in exclaiming*, and are what all know them to be, *exclamations*; as I call them. May I not *call* them what they *are!*"—*Ibid.* Yes, truly. But to *exclaim* is to *cry out*, and consequently every *outcry* is an *exclamation*; though there are two chances to one, that *no interjection at all* be used by the bawler. As good an argument, or better, may be framed against every one of this gentleman's professed improvements in grammar; and as for his punctuation and orthography, any reader may be presumed capable of seeing that they are not fit to be proposed as models.

OBS. 19.—I like my position of the word "*alas*" better than that which Peirce supposes to be its only right place; and, certainly, his rule for the location of words of this sort, as well as his notion that they must always stand alone, is as false, as it is new. The obvious misstatement of Lowth, Adam, Gould, Murray, Churchill, Alger, Smith, Guy, Ingersoll, and others, that, "Interjections are words thrown in between the parts of *a sentence*," I had not only *excluded* from my grammars, but expressly censured in them. It was not, therefore, to prop any error of the old theorists, that I happened to set one interjection "*where*," according to this new oracle, "*it never belonged.*" And if any body but he has been practically misled by their mistake, it is not I, but more probably some of the following authors, here cited for his refutation: "I fear, *alas!* for my life."—*Fisk's Gram.* p. 89. "I have been occupied, *alas!* with trifles."—*Murray's Gr., Ex. for Parsing*, p. 6; *Guy's*, p. 56. "We eagerly pursue pleasure, but, *alas!* we often mistake the road."—*Smith's New Gram.* p. 40. "To-morrow, *alas!* thou mayest be comfortless!"—*Wright's Gram.* p. 35. "Time flies, *O!* how swiftly."—*Murray's Gram.* i, 226. "My friend, *alas!* is dead."—*J. Flint's Gram.* p. 21. "But John, *alas! he* is very idle."—*Merchant's Gram.* p. 22. "For pale and wan he was, *alas* the while!"—SPENSER: *Joh. Dict.* "But yet, *alas! O* but yet, *alas!* our haps be but hard haps."—SYDNEY: *ib.* "Nay, (what's incredible,) *alack!* I hardly hear a woman's clack."—SWIFT: *ib.* "Thus life is spent (*oh fie* upon't!) In being touch'd, and crying—Don't!"—*Cowper*, i, 231. "For whom, *alas!* dost thou prepare The sweets that I was wont to share?"—*Id.* i, 232. "But here, *alas!* the difference lies."—*Id.* i, 100. "Their names, *alas!* in vain reproach an age," &c.—*Id.* i, 88. "What nature, *alas!* has denied," &c.—*Id.* i, 235. "A. Hail Sternhold, then; and Hopkins, *hail!* B. Amen."—*Id.* i, 25.

"These Fate reserv'd to grace thy reign divine,
Foreseen by me, but *ah!* withheld from mine!"—*Pope, Dun.* iii, 275.

IMPROPRIETIES FOR CORRECTION.

FALSE SYNTAX PROMISCUOUS.

☞ [The following examples of bad grammar, being similar in their character to others already exhibited, are to be corrected, by the pupil, according to formules previously given.]

LESSON I.—ANY PARTS OF SPEECH.

"Such an one I believe yours will be proved to be."—PENT: *Farnum's Gram.* p. 1. "Of the distinction between the imperfect and the perfect tenses, it may be observed," &c.—*Ainsworth's Gram.* p. 122. "The subject is certainly worthy consideration."—*Ib.* p. 117. "By this means all ambiguity and controversy is avoided on this point."—*Bullions, Principles of Eng. Gram.*, 5th Ed., *Pref.* p. vi. "The perfect participle in English has both an active and passive signification."—*Ib.* p. 58. "The old house is at length fallen down."—*Ib.* p. 78. "The king, with the lords and commons, constitute the English form of government."—*Ib.* p. 93. "The verb in the singular agrees with the person next it."—*Ib.* p. 96. "Jane found Seth's gloves in James' hat."—*Felton's Gram.* p. 15. "Charles' task is too great."—*Ibid.* 15. "The conjugation of a verb is the naming, in regular order, its several modes tenses, numbers, and persons."—*Ib.* p. 24. "The long remembered beggar was his

---

[*] See 2 Sam. xix, 4; also xviii, 33. Peirce has many times *misquoted* this text, or some part of it; and, what is remarkable, he nowhere agrees either with himself or with the Bible! "O! Absalom! my son!"—*Gram.* p. 288. "O Absalom! my son, my son! would *to* God I had died for thee."—*Ib.* p. 304.

guest."—Ib., 1st Ed., p. 65. "Participles refer to nouns and pronouns."—Ib. p. 81. "F has an uniform sound in every position except in *of*."—*Hallock's Gram.*, 1st Ed., p. 15. "There are three genders; the masculine, the feminine and neuter."—Ib. p. 43. "When *so that* occur together, sometimes the particle *so* is taken as an adverb."—Ib. p. 124. "The definition of the articles show that they modify the words to which they belong."—Ib. p. 138. "The auxiliaries *shall, will* or *should* is implied."—Ib. p. 192. "Single rhyme trochaic omits the final short syllable."—Ib. p. 244. "Agreeable to this, we read of names being blotted out of God's book."—BURDER: *ib.* p. 156; *Webster's Philos. Gram.* 155; *Improved Gram.* 107. "The first person is the person speaking."—*Goldsbury's Common School Gram.* p. 10. "Accent is the laying a peculiar stress of the voice on a certain letter or syllable in a word."—Ib., Ed. of 1842, p. 75. "Thomas' horse was caught."—*Felton's Gram.* p. 64. "You was loved."—Ib. p. 45. "The nominative and objective end the same."—*Rev. T. Smith's Gram.* p. 18. "The number of pronouns, like those of substantives, are two, the singular and the plural."—Ib. p. 22. "*I* is called the pronoun of the *first* person, which is the person speaking."—*Frost's Practical Gram.* p. 32. "The essential elements of the phrase is an intransitive gerundive and an adjective."—*Hazen's Practical Gram.* p. 141. "Being rich is no justification for such impudence."—Ib. p. 141. "His having been a soldier in the revolution is not doubted."—Ib. p. 143. "Catching fish is the chief employment of the inhabitants. The chief employment of the inhabitants is catching fish."—Ib. p. 144. "The cold weather did not prevent the work's being finished at the time specified."— Ib. p. 145. "The former viciousness of that man caused his being suspected of this crime."—Ib. p. 145. "But person and number applied to verbs means, certain terminations."—*Barrett's Gram.* p. 69. "Robert fell a tree."—Ib. p. 64. "Charles raised up."—Ib. p. 64. "It might not be an useless waste of time."—Ib. p. 42. "Neither will you have that *implicit faith* in the writings and works of others which characterise the vulgar."—Ib. p. 5. "*I*, is the first person, because it denotes the speaker."—Ib. p. 46. "I would refer the student to Hedges' or Watts' Logic."—Ib. p. 15. "Hedge's, Watt's, Kirwin's, and Collard's Logic."—*Parker and Fox's Gram.*, Part III, p. 116. "Letters are called vowels which make a full and perfect sound of themselves."—*Cutler's Gram.* p. 10. "It has both a singular and plural construction."—Ib. p. 23. "For he beholdest thy beams no more."— Ib. p. 136. "To this sentiment the Committee has the candour to incline, as it will appear by their summing up."—*Macpherson's Ossian, Prelim. Disc.* p. xviii. "This is reducing the point at issue to a narrow compass."—Ib. p. xxv. "Since the English sat foot upon the soil."—*Exiles of Nova Scotia*, p. 12. "The arrangement of its different parts are easily retained by the memory."—*Hiley's Gram.*, 3d Ed., p. 262. "The words employed are the most appropriate which could have been selected."—Ib. p. 182. "To prevent it launching!"—Ib. p. 135. "Webster has been followed in preference to others, where it differs from them."—*Frazee's Gram.* p. 8. "Exclamation and Interrogation are often mistaken for one another."—*Buchanan's E. Syntax*, p. 160. "When all nature is hushed in sleep, and neither love nor guilt keep their vigils."—*Felton's Gram.* p. 96.

"When all nature's hushed asleep,
 Nor love, nor guilt, their vigils keep."—Ib. p. 95.

LESSON II.—ANY PARTS OF SPEECH.

"A VERSIFIER and POET are two different Things."—*Brightland's Gram.* p. 163. "Those Qualities will arise from the well expressing of the Subject."—Ib. p. 165. "Therefore the explanation of *network*, is taken no notice of here."—*Mason's Supplement*, p. vii. "When emphasis or pathos are necessary to be expressed."—*Humphrey's Punctuation*, p. 38. "Whether this mode of punctuation is correct, and whether it be proper to close the sentence with the mark of admiration, may be made a question."—Ib. p. 39. "But not every writer in those days were thus correct."—Ib. p. 59. "The sounds of A, in English orthoepy, are no less than four."—Ib. p. 69. "Our present code of rules are thought to be generally correct."—Ib. p. 70. "To prevent its running into another."—*Humphrey's Prosody*, p. 7. "Shakespeare, perhaps, the greatest poetical genius which England has produced."—Ib. p. 93. "This I will illustrate by example; but prior to which a few preliminary remarks may be necessary."—Ib. p. 107. "All such are entitled to two accents each, and some of which to two accents nearly equal."—Ib. p. 109. "But some cases of the kind are so plain that no one need to exercise his judgment therein."—Ib. p. 122. "I have forbore to use the word."—Ib. p. 127. "The propositions, 'He may study,' 'He might study,' 'He could study,' affirms an ability or power to study."—*Hallock's Gram. of 1842*, p. 76. "The divisions of the tenses has occasioned grammarians much trouble and perplexity."—Ib. p. 77. "By adopting a familiar, inductive method of presenting this subject, it may be rendered highly attractive to young learners."—*Wells's Sch. Gram.*, 1st Ed., p. 1; 3d, 9; 113th, 11. "The definitions and rules of different grammarians were carefully compared with each other."—Ib. *Preface*, p. iii. "So as not wholly to prevent some sounds issuing."—*Sheridan's Elements of English*, p. 64. "Letters of the Alphabet not yet taken notice of."—Ib. p. 11. "IT *is sad*, IT *is strange*, &c. seems to express only that *the thing* is sad, strange, &c."—*The Well-wishers' Gram.* p. 68. "THE WINNING is easier than THE PRESERVING a conquest."—Ib. p. 65. "The United States finds itself the owner of a vast region

of country at the West."—*Horace Mann in Congress*, 1848. "One or more letters pla
before a word, is a Prefix."—*S. W. Clark's Pract. Gram.* p. 42. "One or more letters ad
to a word, is a Suffix."—*Ib.* p. 42. "Two-thirds of my hair has fallen off."—*Ib.* p. 1
" 'Suspecting' describes 'we,' by expressing, incidentally, an act of 'we.' "—*Ib.* p. 1
"Daniel's predictions are now being fulfilled."—*Ib.* p. 136. "His being a scholar, entit
him to respect."—*Ib.* p. 141. "I doubted his having been a soldier."—*Ib.* p. 142. "Taki
a madman's sword to prevent his doing mischief, cannot be regarded as robbing him."—
p. 129. "I thought it to be him; but it was not him."—*Ib.* p. 149. "It was not me th
you saw."—*Ib.* p. 149. "Not to know what happened before you was born, is always to
a boy."—*Ib.* p. 149. "How long was you going? Three days."—*Ib.* p. 158. "The qu
ifying Adjective is placed next the Noun."—*Ib.* p. 165. "All went but me."—*Ib.* p. 1
"This is parsing their own language, and not the author's."—*Wells's School Gram.*, 1st E
p. 73. "Nouns which denote males, are of the masculine gender."—*Ib.* p. 49. "Nou
which denote females, are of the feminine gender."—*Ib.* p. 49. "When a comparison
expressed between more than two objects of the same class, the superlative degree is e
ployed."—*Ib.* p. 133. "Where *d* or *t* go before, the additional letter *d* or *t*, in this contrac
form, coalesce into one letter with the radical *d* or *t*."—*Dr. Johnson's Gram.* p. 9. "W
words which will show what kind of a house you live in—what kind of a book you h
in your hand—what kind of a day it is."—*Weld's Gram.* p. 7. "One word or more is ol
joined to nouns or pronouns to modify their meaning."—*Ib., 2d Ed.*, p. 30. "Good is
adjective; it explains the quality or character of every person or thing to which it
applied."—*Ib.* p. 33; *Abridg.* 32. "A great public as well as private advantage arises fr
every one's devoting himself to that occupation which he prefers, and for which he
specially fitted."—WAYLAND: *Wells's Gram.* p. 121; *Weld's*, 180. "There was a chance
his recovering his senses. Not thus: 'There was a chance of him recovering his sens
MACAULAY."—See *Wells's Gram.* 1st Ed. p. 121; 113th, 135. "This may be known by
not having any connecting word immediately preceding it."—*Weld's Gram.*, 2d Editi
p. 181. "There are *irregular* expressions occasionally to be met with, which usage or cu
tom rather than analogy, sanction."—*Ib.* p. 143. "He added an anecdote of Qui
relieving Thomson from prison."—*Ib.* p. 150. "The daily labor of her hands procure f
her all that is necessary."—*Ib.* p. 182. "Its being *me*, need make no change in your det
mination."—*Hart's Gram.* p. 128. "The classification of words into what is called th
Parts of Speech."—*Weld's Gram.* p. 5. "Such licenses may be explained under what
usually termed Figures."—*Ib.* p. 212.

"Liberal, not lavish, is kind nature's hands."—*Ib.* p. 196.

"They fall successive and successive live."—*Ib.* p. 213.

LESSON III.—ANY PARTS OF SPEECH.

"A figure of Etymology is the intentional deviation in the usual form of a word."—*Wel
Gram., 2d Edition*, p. 213. "A figure of Syntax is the intentional deviation in the usual con
struction of a word."—*Ib.* 213. "Synecdoche is putting the name of the whole of a
thing for a part, or a part for the whole."—*Ib.* p. 152. "Apostrophe is turning off fr
the regular course of the subject to address some person or thing."—*Ib.* 215. "Even your
pupils will perform such exercises with surprising interest and facility, and will une
sciously gain, in a little time, more knowledge of the structure of Language than he can ac
quire by a drilling of several years in the usual routine of parsing."—*Ib. Preface*, p. iv. "
few Rules of construction are employed in this Part, to guide in the exercise of parsing."—
Ibidem. "The name of every person, object, or thing, which can be thought of, or spoke
of, is a noun."—*Ib.* p. 18; *Abridged Ed.* 19. "A dot, resembling our period, is used betwe
every word, as well as at the close of the verses."—*W. Day's Punctuation*, p. 16: *London*, 184
"Casting types in matrices was invented by Peter Schoeffer, in 1452."—*Ib.* p. 23. "O
perusing it, he said, that, so far from it showing the prisoner's guilt, it positively establish
his innocence."—*Ib.* p. 37. "By printing the *nominative* and *verb* in *Italic* letters, the reade
will be able to distinguish them at a glance."—*Ib.* p. 77. "It is well, no doubt, to avo
using unnecessary words."—*Ib.* p. 99. "Meeting a friend the other day, he said to me
'Where are you going?' "—*Ib.* p. 124. "John was first denied *apples*, then he was promise
them, then he was offered *them*."—*Lennie's Gram.*, 5th Ed., p. 62. "He was denied ad
mission."—*Wells's School Gram.*, 1st. Ed., p. 146. "They were offered a pardon."—*Paul
Murray*, p. 118; *Wells*, 146. "I was this day shown a new potatoe."—DARWIN: *Webster's
Philos. Gram.* p. 179; *Imp. Gram.* 128; *Frazee's Gram.* 153; *Weld's*, 153. "Nouns o
pronouns which denote males are of the masculine gender."—*S. S. Greene's Gram.*, 1s
Ed., p. 211. "There are three degrees of comparison,—the positive, comparative, and
superlative."—*Ib.* p. 216; *First Les.* p. 49. "The first two refer to direction; the third, to
locality."—*Ib. Gr.* p. 103. "The following are some of the verbs which take a direct and
indirect object."—*Ib.* p. 62. "I was not aware of his being the judge of the Suprem
Court."—*Ib.* p. 86. "An indirect question may refer to either of the five elements of a
declarative sentence."—*Ib.* p. 123. "I am not sure *that he will be present—of his being pr
sent.*"—*Ib.* p. 169. "We left on Tuesday."—*Ib.* p. 103. "He left, as he told me, befor

the arrival of the steamer."—*Ib.* p. 146. "We told him *that he must leave*=We told him *to leave.*"—*Ib.* p. 168. "Because he was unable to persuade the multitude, he left in disgust."—*Ib.* p. 172. "He *left*, and *took* his brother with him."—*Ib.* p. 264. "This stating, or declaring, or denying any thing, is called the indicative mode, or manner of speaking."—*Weld's Gram.* p. 72; *Abridged Ed.* 59. "This took place at our friend Sir Joshua Reynold's." —*Weld's Gram.*, 2d. Ed., p. 150. "The manner of a young lady's employing herself usefully in reading will be the subject of another paper."—*Ib.* 150. "Very little time is necessary for Johnson's concluding a treaty with the bookseller."—*Ib.* 150. "My father is not now sick, but if he *was* your services would be welcome."—*Chandler's Grammar*, 1821, p. 54. "When we begin to write or speak, we ought previously to fix in our minds a clear conception of the end to be aimed at."—*Blair's Rhetoric*, p. 193. "Length of days are in her right hand, and in her left hand riches and honor."—*Bullions's Analytical and Practical Grammar*, 1849, p. 59. "The active and passive present express different ideas."—*Ib* p. 235. "An *Improper Diphthong*, or Digraph, is a diphthong in which only one of the vowels are sounded."—*Fowler's E. Gram.* 8vo, 1850, § 115. "The real origin of the words are to be sought in the Latin."—*Ib.* § 120. "What sort of an alphabet the Gothic languages possess, we know; what sort of alphabet they require, we can determine."—*Ib.* § 127. "The Runic Alphabet whether borrowed or invented by the early Goths, is of greater antiquity than either the oldest Teutonic or the Mœso-Gothic Alphabets."—*Ib.* § 129. "Common to the Masculine and the Neuter Genders."—*Ib.* § 222. "In the Anglo-Saxon *his* was common to both the Masculine and Neuter Genders."—*Ib.* § 222. "When time, number, or dimension are specified, the adjective follows the substantive."—*Ib.* § 459. "Nor pain, nor grief, nor anxious fear Invade thy bounds."—*Ib.* § 563. "To Brighton the Pavilion lends a *lath and plaster* grace."—*Ib.* § 590. "From this consideration nouns have been given but one person, the THIRD."—*D. C. Allen's Grammatic Guide*, p. 10.

"For it seems to guard and cherish
  Even the wayward dreamer—I."—*Home Journal.*

EXAMPLES FOR PARSING.

PRAXIS XIII. —SYNTACTICAL.

In the following Lessons, are exemplified most of the Exceptions, some of the Notes, and many of the Observations, under the preceding Rules of Syntax; to which Exceptions, Notes, or Observations, the learner may recur, for an explanation of whatsoever is difficult in the parsing, or peculiar in the construction, of these examples or others.

LESSON I.—PROSE.

"*The* higher a bird flies, *the* more out of danger he is; and *the* higher a Christian soars above the world, *the* safer are his comforts."—*Sparks.*

"*In* this point of view, and *with* this explanation, *it* is supposed, by some grammarians, that our language contains *a* few Impersonal Verbs; that is, *verbs* which declare the existence of some action or state, but *which* do not refer to any animate being, or any determinate particular subject."—*L. Murray's Gram.* 8vo, p. 109.

"Thus in England and France, a great landholder possesses *a* hundred *times* the property that is necessary for the subsistence of a family; and each landlord has perhaps *a* hundred families dependent on him for subsistence."—*Webster's Essays*, p. 87.

"*It* is as possible to become *pedantick* by fear of pedantry, as to be *troublesome* by ill-timed civility."—*Johnson's Rambler*, No. 178.

"*To* commence *author, is* to claim praise; and no man can justly aspire to honour, but at the hazard of disgrace."—*Ib.* No. 93.

"*For* ministers to be silent in the cause of Christ, *is* to renounce it; and to fly *is* to desert it."—SOUTH: *Crabb's Synonymes*, p. 7.

"Such instances shew how much *the sublime* depends upon a just selection of circumstances; and *with* how great care every circumstance must be avoided, which *by* bordering *in the least* upon *the mean*, or even upon *the gay* or *the trifling*, alters the tone of the emotion."—*Blair's Rhet.* p. 48.

"This great poet and philosopher, *the* more *he* contemplated the nature of the Deity, *found* that he waded *but the* more out of his depth, and that *he* lost *himself* in the thought *instead* of finding an end to it."—*Adaison.*

"*Odin, which* in Anglo-Saxon was *Woden*, was the supreme god of the Goths, answering to the Jupiter of the Greeks."—*Webster's Essays*, p. 262.

" Because confidence, that *charm* and *cement* of intimacy, *is* wholly wanting in the intercourse."—*Opie, on Lying*, p. 146.

" Objects of hearing may be compared together, as also *of* taste, *of* smell, and *of* touch : but the chief *fund* of comparison *are objects* of sight."—*Kames, El. of Crit.* Vol. ii, p. 136.

" The various relations of the various Objects exhibited by this (I mean *relations* of *near* and *distant, present* and *absent, same* and *different, definite* and *indefinite,* &c.) made it necessary that *here there* should not be one, but many Pronouns, such as *He, This, That, Other, Any, Some,* &c."—*Harris's Hermes*, p. 72.

" Mr. Pope's Ethical Epistles *deserve* to be mentioned with signal honour, *as* a *model,* next *to perfect, of* this kind of poetry."—*Blair's Rhet.* p. 402.

" The knowledge *of why* they so exist, must be the last act of favour *which* time and toil will bestow."—*Rush, on the Voice*, p. 253.

" *It* is unbelief, and *not faith, that* sinks the sinner into despondency.—Christianity disowns such characters."—*Fuller, on the Gospel*, p. 141.

" That God created the universe, [and] that men are accountable for their *actions, are frequently mentioned* by logicians, as instances of the mind judging."

Lesson II.—Prose.

" *To* censure works, *not men, is* the just *prerogative* of criticism ; and accordingly all personal censure is here avoided, unless *where necessary* to illustrate some general proposition."—*Kames, El. of Crit., Introduction,* p. 27.

" *There remains* to show by examples the manner of treating subjects, so as to give them a ridiculous appearance."—*Ib.* Vol. i, p. 303.

" The making of poetry, *like* any other *handicraft,* may be learned by industry."—*Macpherson's Preface to Ossian*, p. xlv.

" Whatever is found more strange or beautiful than *was expected,* is judged to be more strange or beautiful than it is in reality."—*Kames, El. of Crit.* Vol. i, p. 243.

" Thus the body of an animal, and of a plant, *are composed* of certain great vessels ; these [,] of *smaller ;* and these again [,] of still *smaller,* without end, *as far* as we can discover."—*Id. ib.* p. 270.

" This cause of beauty, is too extensive to be handled *as a branch* of any other subject : for *to* ascertain with accuracy even the proper meaning of words, *not to talk* of their figurative power, *would require* a large volume ; *an* useful *work* indeed, but not to be attempted without a large stock of time, study, and reflection."—*Id.* Vol. ii, p. 16.

" O the hourly *dangers* that we here walk *in !* Every sense, and member, *is* a snare ; every creature, and every duty, *is* a snare to us."—*Baxter, Saints' Rest.*

" *For* a man *to give* his opinion of what he sees *but* in part, *is* an unjustifiable *piece* of rashness and folly."—*Addison.*

" *That* the sentiments thus prevalent among the early Jews *respecting* the divine authority of the Old Testament were correct, *appears* from the testimony of Jesus Christ and his apostles."—*Gurney's Essays,* p. 69.

" So in Society we are not our *own,* but Christ's, and the church's, to good works and services, yet all in love."—*Barclay's Works,* Vol. i, p. 84.

" He [*Dr. Johnson*] sat up in his bed, *clapped* his hands, *and cried, '* O brave *we !* '—a peculiar *exclamation* of *his* when he rejoices."—*Boswell's Life of Johnson,* Vol. iii, p. 56.

" Single, double, and treble emphasis, *are* nothing but examples of antithesis."—*Knowles's Elocutionist,* p. xxviii.

" The curious *thing, and what,* I would almost say, *settles* the point, *is,* that we do *Horace* no service, even according to our view of the matter, by rejecting the scholiast's explanation. No two eggs can be *more like each other* than Horace's *Malthinus* and Seneca's *Mecenas.*"—*Philological Museum,* Vol. i, p. 477.

" *Acting, conduct, behaviour,* abstracted from all regard to what is, in fact and event, the consequence of *it, is itself* the natural object of this moral discernment, speculative truth *and* [say *or*] falsehood is *of* speculative reason."—*Butler's Analogy,* p. 277.

"*To* do what is *right,* with unperverted faculties, *is* ten *times easier* than to undo that is wrong."—*Porter's Analysis,* p. 37.

"Some *natures the* more *pains* a man takes to reclaim them, *the* worse they are."—*L'Estrange: Johnson's Dict. w. Pains.*

"Says *John Milton,* in that impassioned speech for the Liberty of Unlicensed Printing, where every word leaps with intellectual life, '*Who* kills a man, *kills* a reasonable creature, God's image ; but *who* destroys a good book, *kills* reason itself, kills the image of God, as it were, in the eye. Many a man lives a burden upon the earth; but a good book is the precious life-blood of a master spirit, embalmed and treasured up on purpose for a life beyond life ! ' "—*Louisville Examiner,* June, 1850.

LESSON III.—PROSE.

"The philosopher, the saint, or the hero—*the* wise, *the* good, or the great man—may often lies hid and concealed in a plebeian, *which* a proper education might have uninterred and *brought* to light."—*Addison.*

"The *year before,* he had so used the matter, that *what* by force, *what* by policy, he had taken from the Christians *above* thirty small castles."—*Knolles.*

"*It* is an important truth, that religion, vital *religion,* the *religion* of the heart, is the most powerful auxiliary of reason, in waging war with the passions, and promoting that sweet composure which constitutes the peace of God."—*Murray's Key,* p. 181.

"*Pray, sir, be pleased* to take the part of *us beauties* and *fortunes* into your consideration, and do not let us *be flattered* out of our senses. *Tell* people that *we* fair *ones* expect honest plain answers, as well as other folks."—*Spectator,* No. 584.

"*Unhappy it* would be *for* us, *did* not uniformity *prevail* in morals : *that* nor actions should uniformly be directed to what is *good* and against what is *ill, is*/the greatest *blessing* in society ; and *in* order to uniformity of action, uniformity of sentiment is indispensable."—*Kames, El. of Crit.* Vol. ii, p. 366.

"Thus the pleasure of all the senses is *the same* in *all, high* and *low, learned* and *unlearned.*"—*Burke, on Taste,* p. 39.

"*Upwards* of eight millions of acres *have,* I believe, been thus disposed of."—*Society in America,* Vol. i, p. 333.

"The Latin Grammar comes *something* nearer, but yet does not hit the mark neither."—*Johnson's Gram. Com.* p. 281.

"*Of* the like nature is the following inaccuracy *of Dean Swift's.*"—*Blair's Rhet.* p. 105. "Thus, Sir, I have given *you* my own opinion, relating to this weighty affair, as well as *that* of a great majority of both houses here."—*Ib.*

"A foot is just twelve *times* as long as an *inch ;* and an hour is sixty *times* the *length* of a minute."—*Murray's Gram.* p. 48.

"What can we expect, who come *a gleaning,* not after the first reapers, but after the *very* beggars ?"—*Cowley's Pref. to Poems,* p. x.

"In our *Lord's being betrayed* into the hands of the chief-priests and scribes, by Judas Iscariot ; in *his being* by them *delivered* to the Gentiles ; in *his being mocked, scourged, spitted on,* [say *spit upon,*] and *crucified ;* and in *his rising* from the dead after three days ; there was much that was singular, complicated, and not to be easily calculated on beforehand.' —*Gurney's Essays,* p. 40.

"*To* be *morose, implacable, inexorable,* and *revengeful,* is one of the greatest degeneracies of human nature."—*Dr. J. Owen.*

"Now, says *he,* if tragedy, which is in its nature *grand* and *lofty,* will not admit of this, *who can forbear laughing* to hear the historian Gorgias Leontinus styling Xerxes, that cowardly Persian king, *Jupiter ;* and vultures, living *sepulchres ?*"—*Holmes's Rhetoric,* Part II, p. 14.

"O let thy all-seeing eye, and not the eye of the world, be the star to steer my *course by ;* and let thy blessed favour, more than the liking of any sinful men, be ever my study and delight."—*Jenks's Prayers,* p. 156.

LESSON IV.—PROSE.

"O the Hope of Israel, the Saviour thereof in time of trouble, why shouldest thou be as a stranger in the land, and as a way-faring man, that turneth aside to tarry for a night?"—Jeremiah, xiv, 8.

"When once the long-suffering of God waited in the days of Noah, while the ark was a preparing, wherein few, that is, eight souls, were saved."—1 Peter, iii, 20.

"Mercy and truth are met together; righteousness and peace have kissed each other."—Psalms, lxxxv, 10.

"But in vain they do worship me, teaching for doctrines the commandments of men."—Matt. xv, 9.

"Knowest thou not this of old, since man was placed upon the earth, that the triumphing of the wicked is short, and the joy of the hypocrite but for a moment."—Job, xx, 4, 5.

"For now I see through a glass darkly; but then, face to face: now I know in part; but then shall I know even as also I am known."—1 Cor. xiii, 12.

"For then the king of Babylon's army besieged Jerusalem: and Jeremiah the Prophet was shut up in the court of the prison which was in the king of Judah's house."—Jer. xxxii, 2.

"For Herod had laid hold on John, and bound him, and put him in prison, for Herodias' sake, his brother Philip's wife."—Matt. xiv, 3.

"And now I have sent a cunning man, endued with understanding, of Huram my father's, the son of a woman of the daughters of Dan."—2 Chron. ii, 13.

"Bring no more vain oblations: incense is an abomination unto me; the new moons and sabbaths, the calling of assemblies, I cannot away with: it is iniquity even the solemn meeting."—Isaiah, i, 13.

"For I have heard the voice of the daughter of Zion, that bewaileth herself, that spreadeth her hands, saying, Woe is me now! for my soul is wearied because of murderers."—Jer. iv, 31.

"She saw men portrayed upon the wall, the images of the Chaldeans portrayed with vermilion, girded with girdles upon their loins, exceeding in dyed attire upon their heads, all of them princes to look to, after the manner of the Babylonians of Chaldea, the land of their nativity."—Ezekiel, xxiii, 15.

"And on them was written according to all the words which the Lord spake with you in the mount, out of the midst of the fire, in the day of the assembly."—Deut. ix, 10.

"And he charged them that they should tell no man: but the more he charged them. so much the more a great deal they published it."—Mark, vii, 36.

"The results which God has connected with actions, will inevitably occur, all the created power in the universe to the contrary notwithstanding."—Wayland's Moral Science, p. 5.

"Am I not an apostle? am I not free? have I not seen Jesus Christ our Lord? are not ye my work in the Lord? If I be not an apostle unto others, yet doubtless I am to you: for the seal of mine apostleship are ye in the Lord."—1 Cor. ix, 1, 2.

"Not to insist upon this, it is evident, that formality is a term of general import. It implies, that in religious exercises of all kinds the outward and [the] inward man are at diametrical variance."—Chapman's Sermons to Presbyterians, p. 354.

LESSON V.—VERSE.

"See the sole bliss Heaven could on all bestow,
  Which who but feels, can taste, but thinks, can know;
  Yet, poor with fortune, and with learning blind,
  The bad must miss, the good, untaught, will find."—Pope.
"There are, who, deaf to mad Ambition's call,
  Would shrink to hear th' obstrep'rous trump of fame;
  Supremely blest, if to their portion fall
  Health, competence, and peace."—Beattie.

" High stations *tumult*, but *not bliss*, create ;
None think *the great* unhappy, but *the great*.
Fools gaze and *envy :* envy darts a sting,
Which makes a swain as *wretched* as a king."—*Young.*

" Lo, earth receives him from the bending skies !
Sink down, ye *mountains ;* and, ye *valleys, rise ;*
With heads declin'd, *ye cedars*, homage *pay ;*
Be smooth, ye *rocks ;* ye rapid *floods, give* way."—*Pope.*

"Amid the forms which this full world presents
Like rivals to his choice, what human breast
E'er doubts, before the *transient* and *minute*,
To prize the *vast*, the *stable*, and *sublime ?* "—*Akenside.*

" Now fears in dire vicissitude invade ;
The rustling brake *alarms*, and quiv'ring *shade :*
Nor light nor darkness brings his *pain* relief ;
One shows the plunder, and one hides the thief."—*Johnson.*

" If Merab's choice could have complied with *mine*,
Merab, my elder comfort, had been *thine :*
And *hers*, at *last*, should have with *mine* complied,
Had I not *thine* and Michael's heart descried."—*Cowley.*

" The people have *as much* a negative voice
To hinder *making* war without their choice,
As kings of making laws in parliament :
'*No money*' is as *good* as '*No assent.*' "—*Butler.*

" Full *many a gem* of purest ray serene
The dark unfathom'd caves of ocean bear ;
Full *many a flower* is born to blush unseen,
And waste its sweetness on the desert air."—*Gray.*

"*Oh fool !* to think God hates the worthy *mind*,
The lover and the love of human kind,
Whose life is healthful, and *whose* conscience clear,
Because *he* wants *a* thousand pounds *a* year."—*Pope.*

" O *Freedom !* sovereign *boon* of Heav'n,
Great *charter*, with our being given ;
For *which* the patriot and the sage
Have plann'd, have bled thro' ev'ry age ! "—*Mallet.*

LESSON VI.—VERSE.

"Am I to set my life upon a throw,
Because a bear is rude and surly ? *No.*"—*Cowper.*

"*Poor, guiltless I !* and can I choose but *smile*,
When every coxcomb knows me by my style ? "—*Pope.*

" Remote from man, with God he pass'd his days,
Prayer all his *business*, all his *pleasure praise*."—*Parnell.*

" These are *thy* blessings, *Industry !* rough power ;
Whom labour still attends, and *sweat*, and *pain*."—*Thomson.*

"*What ho !* thou *genius* of the clime, *what ho !*
Liest thou *asleep* beneath these hills of snow ? "—*Dryden.*

" *What !* canst thou not forbear me *half an hour ?*
Then *get* thee gone, and *dig* my grave thyself."—*Shak.*

" Then palaces and lofty domes arose ;
These for devotion, and for pleasure *those*."—*Blackmore.*

" 'Tis very dangerous, *tampering* with a muse ;
The profit's small, and you have much to lose."—*Roscommon.*

"*Lucretius English'd !* 't was a work *might shake*
The power of English verse to undertake."—*Otway.*

"*The best* may slip, and *the most cautious fall*;
  He's *more* than *mortal*, that ne'er err'd *at all*."—*Pomfret*.
"*Poets* large *souls* heaven's noblest stamps do bear,
  Poets, the watchful angels' darling care."—*Stepney*.
" Sorrow breaks reasons, and reposing hours;
  Makes the night *morning*, and the noon-tide *night*."—*Shak*.
" Nor then the solemn nightingale *ceas'd warbling*."—*Milton*.
"And O, poor hapless *nightingale*, thought I,
  How *sweet* thou singst, how *near* the deadly *snare* !"—*Id*.
" He calls for *Famine*, and the meagre fiend
  Blows mildew *from between his* shrivell'd lips."—*Cowper*.
" If o'er their lives a refluent *glance* they cast,
  Theirs is *the present* who can praise *the past*."—*Shenstone*.
"*Who* wickedly is *wise*, or madly *brave*,
  Is but *the more* a fool, *the more* a knave."—*Pope*.
" Great *eldest-born* of Dullness, blind and bold !
  Tyrant ! more cruel than Procrustes old;
  Who, to his iron bed, by torture, fits,
  Their nobler *part*, the *souls* of suffering wits."—*Mallet*.
" Parthenia, *rise*.—What voice alarms my ear?
  Away. Approach not. Hah ! *Alexis* there !"—*Gay*.
" Nor is *it harsh* to make, nor *hard* to find
  A country *with*—*ay*, or without mankind."—*Byron*.
"A *frame* of adamant, a *soul* of fire,
  No dangers fright him, and *no* labours tire."—*Johnson*.
" Now *pall* the tasteless *meats*, and joyless *wines*,
  And *luxury* with sighs *her slave resigns*."—*Id*.
" *Seems?* madam ; nay, it is : I know not *seems*—
  For I have that within which passes show."—*Hamlet*.
"*Return ? said* Hector, fir'd with stern disdain :
  What ! coop whole armies in our walls again ?"—*Pope*.
"*He* whom the fortune of the field shall cast
  From forth his chariot, *mount* the next in haste."—*Id*.
" *Yet here, Laertes?* aboard, aboard, *for* shame !"—*Shak*.
"*Justice*, most gracious *Duke ; O grant me* justice !"—*Id*.
" But what *a vengeance* makes thee *fly*
  From me too, as thine enemy ?"—*Butler*.
"Immortal *Peter ! first* of monarchs ! He
  His stubborn *country* tam'd, *her* rocks, *her* fens,
  Her floods, *her* seas, *her* ill-submitting sons."—*Thomson*.
" O arrogance ! Thou liest, thou thread, thou thimble,
  Thou yard, three-quarters, half-yard, quarter, nail,
  Thou flea, thou nit, thou winter-cricket, thou :—
  Brav'd in mine own house with a skein of thread !
  Away, thou rag, thou quantity, thou remnant ;
  Or I shall so be-mete thee with thy yard,
  As thou shalt think on prating whilst thou liv'st."
        SHAK. : *Taming of the Shrew*, Act IV, Sc. 3.

CHAPTER XII.—REVIEW.

This twelfth chapter of Syntax is devoted to a series of lessons, methodically digested, wherein are reviewed and reapplied, mostly in. the order of the parts of speech, all those syntactical principles heretofore given which are useful for the correction of errors.

IMPROPRIETIES FOR CORRECTION.

FALSE SYNTAX FOR A GENERAL REVIEW.

☞ [The following examples of false syntax are arranged for a General Review of the doctrines contained in the preceding Rules and Notes. Being nearly all of them exact quotations, they are also a sort of syllabus of verbal criticism on the various works from which they are taken. What corrections they are supposed to need, may be seen by inspection of the twelfth chapter of the Key. It is here expected, that by recurring to the Instructions before given, the learner who takes them as an oral exercise, will ascertain for himself the proper, form of correcting each example, according to the particular Rule or Note under which it belongs. When two or more errors occur in the same example, they ought to be corrected successively, in their order. The erroneous sentence being read aloud as it stands, the pupil should say, "First, Not proper, because," &c. And when the first error has thus been duly corrected by a brief and regular syllogism, either the same pupil or an other should immediately proceed, and say, "Secondly, Not proper again, because," &c. And so of the third error, and the fourth, if there be so many. In this manner, a class may be taught to speak in succession without any loss of time, and, after some practice, with a near approach to that PERFECT ACCURACY which is the great end of grammatical instruction. When time cannot be allowed for this regular exercise, these examples may still be profitably rehearsed by a more rapid process, one pupil reading aloud the quoted false grammar, and an other responding to each example, by reading the intended correction from the Key.]

LESSON I.—ARTICLES.

"And they took stones, and made an heap."—*Com. Bibles; Gen.* xxxi, 46. "And I do know a many fools, that stand in better place."—*Beauties of Shak.* p. 44. "It is a strong antidote to the turbulence of passion, and violence of pursuit."—*Kames, El of Crit.* i, p. xxiii. "The word *news* may admit of either a singular or plural application."—*Wright's Gram.* p. 39. "He has gained a fair and a honorable reputation."—*Ib.* p. 140. "There are two general forms, called the solemn and familiar style."—*Sanborn's Gram.* p. 109. "Neither the article nor preposition can be omitted."—*Wright's Gram.* p. 190. "A close union is also observable between the Subjunctive and Potential Moods."—*Ib.* p. 72. "We should render service, equally, to a friend, neighbour, and an enemy."—*Ib.* p. 140. "Till an habit is obtained of aspirating strongly."—*Sheridan's Elocution,* p. 49. "There is an uniform, steady use of the same signs."—*Ib.* p. 163. "A traveller remarks the most objects he sees."—*Jamieson's Rhet.* p. 72. "What is the name of the river on which London stands? The Thames."— "We sometimes find the last line of a couplet or triplet stretched out to twelve syllables."—*Adam's Lat. and Eng. Gram.* p. 282. "Nouns which follow active verbs, are not in the nominative case."—*Blair's Gram.* p. 14. "It is a solemn duty to speak plainly of wrongs, which good men perpetrate."—*Channing's Emancip.* p. 71. "Gathering of riches is a pleasant torment."—*Treasury of Knowledge, Dict.* p. 446. "It [the lamentation of Helen for Hector] is worth the being quoted."—*Coleridge's Introd.* p. 100. "*Council* is a noun which admits of a singular and plural form."—*Wright's Gram.* p. 137. "To exhibit the connexion between the Old and the New Testaments."—*Keith's Evidences,* p. 25. "An apostrophe discovers the omission of a letter or letters."—*Guy's Gram.* p. 95. "He is immediately ordained, or rather acknowledged an hero."—*Pope, Preface to the Dunciad.* "Which is the same in both the leading and following State."—*Brightland's Gram.* p. 86. "Pronouns, as will be seen hereafter, have a distinct nominative, possessive, and objective case."—*Blair's Gram.* p. 15. "A word of many syllables is called polysyllable."—*Beck's Outline of E. Gram.* p. 2. "Nouns have two numbers, singular and plural."—*Ib.* p. 6. "They have three genders, masculine, feminine, and neuter."—*Ib.* p. 6. "They have three cases, nominative, possessive, and objective."—*Ib.* p. 6. "Personal Pronouns have, like Nouns, two numbers, singular and plural. Three genders, masculine, feminine, and neuter. Two cases, nominative and objective."—*Ib.* p. 10. "He must be wise enough to know the singular from plural."—*Ib.* p. 20. "Though they may be able to meet the every reproach which any one of their fellows may prefer."—*Chalmers, Sermons,* p. 104. "Yet for love's sake I rather beseech thee, being such an one as Paul the aged."—*Ep. to Philemon,* 9. "Being such one as Paul the aged."—*Dr. Webster's Bible.* "A people that jeoparded their lives unto the death."—*Judges,* v, 18. "By preventing the too great accumulation of seed within a too narrow compass."—*The Friend,* Vol. vii, p. 97. "Who fills up the middle space between the animal and intellectual nature, the visible and invisible world."—*Addison, Spect.* No. 519. "The Psalms abound with instances of an harmonious arrangement of the words."—*Murray's Gram.* i, p. 339. "On another table were an ewer and vase, likewise of gold."—*N. Y. Mirror,* xi, 307. "*Th* is said to have two sounds sharp, and flat."—*Wilson's Essay on Gram.* p. 33. "Section (§) is used in subdividing of a chapter into lesser parts."—*Brightland's Gram.* p. 152. "Try it in a Dog or an Horse or any other Creature."—*Locke, on Ed.* p. 46. "But particularly in learning of Languages there is least occasion for poseing of Children."—*Ib.* p. 296. "What kind of a noun is *river,* and why?"—*Smith's New Gram.* p. 10. "Is *William's* a proper or common noun?"—*Ib.* p. 12. "What kind of an article, then, shall we call *the?*"—*Ib.* p. 13.

"Each burns alike, who can, or cannot write,
    Or with a rival's or an eunuch's spite."—*Pope, on Crit.* l. 30.

LESSON II.—NOUNS, OR CASES.

"And there is stamped upon their Imaginations Idea's that follow them with Terror and Affrightment."—*Locke, on Ed.* p. 251. "There's not a wretch that lives on common charity, but 's happier than me."—VENICE PRESERVED: *Kames, El. of Crit.* i, 63. "But they overwhelm whomsoever is ignorant of them."—*Common School Journal*, i, 115. "I have received a letter from my cousin, she that was here last week."—*Inst.* p. 129. "Gentlemens Houses are seldom without Variety of Company."—*Locke, on Ed.* p. 107. "Because Fortune has laid them below the level of others, at their Masters feet."—*Ib.* p. 221. "We blamed neither John nor Mary's delay."—*Nixon's Parser*, p. 117. "The book was written by Luther the reformer's order."—*Ib.* p. 59. "I saw on the table of the saloon Blair's Sermons, and somebody else (I forget who's) sermons, and a set of noisy children."—*Lord Byron's Letters*. "Or saith he it altogether for our sakes?"—1 *Cor.* ix, 10. "He was not aware of the duke's being his competitor."—*Sanborn's Gram.* p. 190. "It is no condition of a word's being an adjective, that it must be placed before a noun."—FOWLE: *ib.* p. 190. "Though their Reason corrected the wrong Idea's they had taken in."—*Locke, on Ed.* p. 251. "It was him, who taught me to hate slavery."—*Morris, in Congress*, 1839. "It is him and his kindred, who live upon the labour of others."—*Id. ib.* "Payment of Tribute is an Acknowledgment of his being King to whom we think it Due."—*Right of Tythes*, p. 161. "When we comprehend what we are taught."—*Ingersoll's Gram.* p. 14. "The following words, and parts of words, must be taken notice of."—*Priestley's Gram.* p. 96. "Hence tears and commiseration are so often made use of."—*Blair's Rhet.* p. 269. "JOHN-A-NOKES. n. s. A fictitious name, made use of in law proceedings."—*Chalmers, Eng. Dict.* "The construction of Matter, and Part takes hold of."—*B. F. Fisk's Greek Gram.* p. x. "And such other names, as carry with them the Idea's of some thing terrible and hurtful."—*Locke, on Ed.* p. 250. "Every learner then would surely be glad to be spared the trouble and fatigue."—*Pike's Hebrew Lexicon*, p. iv. "Tis not the owning ones Dissent from another, that I speak against."—*Locke, on Ed.* p. 265. "A Man that cannot Fence will be more careful to keep out of Bullies and Gamesters Company, and will not be half so apt to stand upon Punctilio's."—*Ib.* p. 357. "From such Persons it is, one may learn more in one Day, than in a Years rambling from one Inn to another."—*Ib.* p. 377. "A long syllable is generally considered to be twice the length of a short one."—*Blair's Gram.* p. 117. "*I* is of the first person, and singular number; *Thou* is second per. sing.; *He, She*, or *It*, is third per. sing.; *We* is first per. plural; *Ye* or *You* is second per. plural; *They* is third per. plural."—*Kirkham's Gram.* p. 46. "The actor, doer, or producer of the action, is the nominative."—*Ib.* p. 43. "No Body can think a Boy of Three or Seven Years old, should be argued with, as a grown Man."—*Locke, on Ed.* p. 129. "This was in one of the Pharisees' houses, not, in Simon the leper's."—*Hammond.* "Impossible! it can't be me."—*Swift.* "Whose grey top shall tremble, Him descending." —*Dr. Bentley.* "What gender is *woman*, and why?"—*Smith's New Gram.* p. 8. "What gender, then, is *man*, and why?"—*Ibid.* "Who is *I*; who do you mean when you say I!" —*R. W. Green's Gram.* p. 19. "It [Parnassus] is a pleasant air, but a barren soil."—*Locke, on Ed.* p. 311. "You may, in three days time, go from Galilee to Jerusalem."—*Josephus, Vol.* 5, p. 174. "And that which is left of the meat-offering shall be Aaron's and his sons."— SCOTT'S BIBLE, and BRUCE'S: *Lev.* ii, 10. See also ii, 3.

<blockquote>"For none in all the world, without a lie,
Can say that this is mine, excepting I."—*Bunyan.*</blockquote>

LESSON III.—ADJECTIVES.

"When he can be their Remembrancer and Advocate every Assises and Sessions."— *Right of Tythes*, p. 244. "Doing, denotes all manner of action; as, to dance, to play, to write, to read, to teach, to fight, &c."—*Buchanan's Gram.* p. 33. "Seven foot long," — "eight foot long,"—"fifty foot long."—*Walker's Particles*, p. 205. "Nearly the whole of this twenty-five millions of dollars is a dead loss to the nation."—*Fowler, on Tobacco*, p. 16. "Two negatives destroy one another."—*R. W. Green's Gram.* p. 92. "We are warned against excusing sin in ourselves, or in each other."—*The Friend*, iv, 108. "The Russian empire is more extensive than any government in the world."—*School Geog.* "You will always have the Satisfaction to think it the Money of all other the best laid out."—*Locke, on Ed.* p. 145. "There is no one passion which all mankind so naturally give into as pride."—*Steele, Spect.* No. 462. "O, throw away the worser part of it."—*Beauties of Shak.* p. 237. "He showed us a more agreeable and easier way."—*Inst.* p. 134. "And the four last [are] to point out those further improvements."—*Jamieson's Rhet.* p. 52; *Campbell's*, 187. "Where he has not distinct and different clear Idea's."—*Locke, on Ed.* p. 353. "Oh, when shall we have such another Rector of Laracor!"—*Hazlitt's Lect.* "Speech must have been absolutely necessary previous to the formation of society."—*Jamieson's Rhet.* p. 2. "Go and tell them boys to be still."—*Inst.* p. 135. "Wrongs are engraved on marble; benefits, on sand: these are apt to be required; those, forgot."—*B.* "Neither of these several interpretations is the true one."—*B.* "My friend indulged himself in some freaks unbefitting the gravity of a clergyman."—*B.* "And their Pardon is All that either of their Impropriators will have to plead."—*Right of Tythes*, p. 196. "But the time usually chosen to send young Men abroad, is, I think, of all other, that which renders them least capable of reaping those Advantages."—*Locke, on Ed.* p. 372. "It is a mere figment of the human imagination, a rhapsody of the transcendent unintelligible."—*Jamieson's Rhet.* p. 120. "It contains a greater assemblage of sublime ideas, of bold and daring figures, than is perhaps any where to be met with."—*Blair's Rhet.* p. 163. "The order in which the two last words are placed, should have been reversed."—*Ib.* p. 204. "The *orders* in which the two last words are placed, should have been reversed."—*Murray's Gram.* 8vo, p. 310. "In Demosthenes, eloquence *shown* forth with higher splendour, than perhaps in any that ever bore the name of an orator."—*Blair's Rhet.* p. 242. "The circumstance of his being poor is decidedly favorable."—*Student's Manual,* p. 286. "The temptations to dissipation are greatly lessened by his being poor."—*Ib.* p. 287. "For with her death that tidings came."—*Beauties of Shak.* p. 257. "The next objection is, that these sort of authors are poor."—*Cleland.* "Presenting Emma as Miss Castlemain to these acquaintance."—*Opie's Temper.* "I doubt not but it will please more than the opera."—*Spect.* No. 28. "The world knows only two, that's Rome and I."—*Ben Johnson.* "I distinguish these two things from one another."—*Blair's Rhet.* p. 29. "And in this case, mankind reciprocally claim, and allow indulgence to each other."—*Sheridan's Lect.* p. 29. "The six last books are said not to have received the finishing hand of the author."—*Blair's Rhet.* p. 438. "The best executed part of the work, is the first six books."—*Ib.* p. 447.

"To reason how can we be said to rise?
So many cares attend the being wise."—*Sheffield.*

LESSON IV.—PRONOUNS.

"Once upon a time a goose fed its young by a pond side."—*Goldsmith's Essays,* p. 175. "If either [work] have a sufficient degree of merit to recommend them to the attention of the public."—*Walker's Rhyming Dict.* p. iii. "Now W. Mitchell his deceit is very remarkable."—*Barclay's Works,* i, 264. "My brother, I did not put the question to thee, for that I doubted of the truth of your belief."—*Bunyan's P. P.* p. 158. "I had two elder brothers, one of which was a lieutenant-colonel."—*Robinson Crusoe,* p. 2. "Though *James* is here the object of the action, yet, he is in the nominative case."—*Wright's Gram.* p. 64. "Here, *John* is the actor; and is known to be the nominative, by its answering to the question, 'Who struck Richard?'"—*Ib.* p. 43. "One of the most distinguished privileges which Providence has conferred upon mankind, is the power of communicating their thoughts to one another."—*Blair's Rhet.* p. 9. "With some of the most refined feelings which belong to our frame."—*Ib.* p. 13. "And the same instructions which assist others in composing, will assist them in judging of, and relishing, the beauties of composition."—*Ib.* p. 12. "To overthrow all which had been yielded in favour of the army."—*Mrs. Macaulay's Hist.* i, 335. "Let your faith stand in the Lord God who changes not, and that created all, and gives the increase of all."—*Friends' Advices,* 1676. "For it is, in truth, the sentiment or passion, which lies under the figured expression, that gives it any merit."—*Blair's Rhet.* p. 133. "Verbs are words which affirm the being, doing, or suffering of a thing, together with the time it happens."—*Al. Murray's Gram.* p. 29. "The Byass will always hang on that side, that nature first placed it."—*Locke, on Ed.* p. 177. "They should be brought to do the things are fit for them."—*Ib.* p. 178. "Various sources whence the English language is derived."—*Murray's Gram.* Vol. ii, p. 286. "This attention to the several cases, when it is proper to omit and when to redouble the copulative, is of considerable importance."—*Blair's Rhet.* p. 113. "Cicero, for instance, speaking of the cases where killing another is lawful in self defence, uses the following words."—*Ib.* p. 156. "But there is no nation, hardly any person so phlegmatic, as not to accompany their words with some actions and gesticulations, on all occasions, when they are much in earnest."—*Ib.* p. 335. "*William's* is said to be governed by *coat*, because it follows *William's*."—*Smith's New Gram.* p. 12. "There are many occasions in life, in which silence and simplicity are true wisdom."—*Murray's Key,* ii, 197. "In choosing umpires, the avarice of whom is excited."—*Nixon's Parser,* p. 153. "The boroughs sent representatives, which had been enacted."—*Ib.* p. 154. "No man believes but what there is some order in the universe."—*Anon.* "The moon is orderly in her changes, which she could not be by accident."—*Id.* "Of Sphynx her riddles, they are generally two kinds."—*Bacon's Wisdom,* p. 73. "They must generally find either their Friends or Enemies in Power."—*Brown's Estimate,* Vol. ii, p. 166. "For of old, every one took upon them to write what happened in their own time."—*Josephus's Jewish War, Pref.* p. 4. "The Almighty cut off the family of Eli the high priest, for its transgressions."—*See Key.* "The convention then resolved themselves into a committee of the whole."—*Inst.* p. 146. "The severity with which this denomination was treated, appeared rather to invite than to deter them from flocking to the colony."—*H. Adams's View,* p. 71. "Many Christians abuse the Scriptures and the traditions of the apostles, to uphold things quite contrary to it."—*Barclay's Works,* i, 461. "Thus, a circle, a square, a triangle, or a hexagon, please the eye, by their regularity, as beautiful figures."—*Blair's Rhet.* p. 46. "Elba is remarkable for its being the place to which Bonaparte was banished in 1814."—*See Sanborn's Gram.* p. 190. "The editor has the reputation of his being a good linguist and critic."—*See ib.* "'Tis a Pride should be cherished in them."—*Locke, on Ed.* p. 129. "And to restore us the Hopes of Fruits, to reward our Pains in its season."—*Ib.* p. 136. "The comick representation of

Death's victim relating its own tale."—*Wright's Gram.* p. 193.   "As for Scioppius his Grammar, that doth wholly concern the Latin Tongue."—Dr. Wilkins: *Tooke's D. P. i, i.*
"And chiefly thee, O Spirit, who dost prefer
Before all temples the upright heart and pure,
Instruct me, for Thou knowest."—*Burh's Classical Gram.* p. 45.

LESSON V.—VERBS.

"And there was in the same country shepherds abiding in the field."—Scott's Bible: *Luke*, ii, 8. "Whereof every one bear twins."—Com. Bible: *Sol. Song*, iv, 2. "Whereof every one bare twins."—Alger's Bible: *ib.* "Whereof every one beareth twins."—Scott's Bible: *ib.* "He strikes out of his nature one of the most divine principles, that is planted in it."—*Addison, Spect.* No. 181. "*Genii,* denote aerial spirits."—*Wright's Gram.* p. 40. "In proportion as the long and large prevalence of such corruptions have been obtained by force."—Bp. Halifax: *Butler's Analogy*, p. xvi. "Neither of these are fix'd to a Word of a general Signification, or proper Name."—*Brightland's Gram.* p. 95. "Of which a few of the opening lines is all I shall give."—*Moore's Life of Byron.* "The riches we had in England was the slow result of long industry and wisdom."—Davenant: *Webster's Imp. Gram.* p. 21; *Phil. Gram.* 29. "The following expression appears to be correct: —'Much publick thanks *is* due.'"—*Wright's Gram.* p. 201. "He hath been enabled to correct many mistakes."—*Lowth's Gram.* p. x. "Which road takest thou here?"—*Ingersoll's Gram.* p. 106. "Learnest thou thy lesson?"—*Ib.* p. 105. "Learned they their pieces perfectly?"—*Ibid.* "Thou learnedst thy task well."—*Ibid.* "There are some can't reach the town, and others can't away with the country."—Way of the World: *Kames, El. of Crit.* i, 304. "If thou meetest them, thou must put on an intrepid mien."—*Neef's Method of Ed.* p. 201. "Struck with terror, as if Philip was something more than human."—*Blair's Rhet.* p. 265. "If the personification of the form of Satan was admissible, it should certainly have been masculine."—*Jamieson's Rhet.* p. 176. "If only one follow, there seems to be a defect in the sentence."—*Priestley's Gram.* p. 104. "Sir, if thou have borne him hence, tell me where thou hast laid him."—*John*, xx, 15. "Blessed is the people that know the joyful sound."—*Psalms*, lxxxix, 15. "Every auditory take in good part those marks of respect and awe, which are paid to them by one who addresses them."—*Blair's Rhet.* p. 308. "Private causes were still pleaded [in the forum]; but the public was no longer interested; nor any general attention drawn to what passed there."—*Ib.* p. 246. "Nay, what evidence can be brought to show, that the Inflection of the Classic tongues were not originally formed out of obsolete auxiliary words?"—*Murray's Gram.* i, p. 112. "If the student reflects, that the principal and the auxiliary forms but one verb, he will have little or no difficulty, in the proper application of the present rule."—*Ib.* p. 183. "For the sword of the enemy and fear is on every side."—*Jeremiah*, vi, 25. "Even the Stoics agree that nature and certainty is very hard to come at."—*Collier's Antoninus*, p. 71. "His politeness and obliging behaviour was changed."—*Priestley's Gram.* p. 186. "His politeness and obliging behaviour were changed."—*Hume's Hist.* Vol. vi, p. 14. "War and its honours was their employment and ambition."—*Goldsmith.* "Does *a* and *an* mean the same thing?"—*R. W. Green's Gram.* p. 15. "When a number of words come in between the discordant parts, the ear does not detect the error."—*Cobbett's Gram.* ¶ 185. "The sentence should be, 'When a number of words comes in,' &c."—*Wright's Gram.* p. 170. "The nature of our language, the accent and pronunciation of it, inclines us to contract even all our regular verbs."—*Lowth's Gram.* p. 45. "The nature of our language, together with the accent and pronunciation of it, incline us to contract even all our Regular Verbs."—*Riley's Gram.* p. 45. "Prompt aid, and not promises, are what we ought to give."—*Author.* "The position of the several organs therefore, as well as their functions are ascertained."—*Medical Magazine*, 1833, p. 5. "Every private company, and almost every public assembly, afford opportunities of remarking the difference between a just and graceful, and a faulty and unnatural elocution."—*Enfield's Speaker*, p. 9. "Such submission, together with the active principle of obedience, make up the temper and character in us which answers to his sovereignty."—*Butler's Analogy*, p. 126. "In happiness, as in other things, there is a false and a true, an imaginary and a real."—*Fuller, on the Gospel*, p. 134. "To confound things that differ, and to make a distinction where there is no difference, is equally unphilosophical."—*Author.*

"I know a bank whereon the wild thyme blows,
Where ox-lips and the nodding violet grows."—*Beaut. of Shak.* p. 51.

LESSON VI.—VERBS.

"Whose business or profession prevent their attendance in the morning."—*Ogilby.* "And no church or officer have power over one another."—Lechford: *in Hutchinson's Hist.* i, 374. "While neither reason nor experience are sufficiently matured to protect them."—*Woodbridge.* "Among the Greeks and Romans, every syllable, or the far greatest number at least, was known to have a fixed and determined quantity."—*Blair's Rhet.* p. 383. "Among the Greeks and Romans, every syllable, or at least by far the greatest number of syllables, was known to have a fixed and determined quantity."—*Jamieson's Rhet.* p. 303. "Their vanity is awakened and their passions exalted by the irritation, which their self-love receives from contradiction."—*Influence of Literature*, Vol. ii, p. 218. "I and he was neither of us any great swimmer."—*Anon.* "Virtue, honour, nay, even self-interest, conspire to recommend the measure."—*Murray's Gram.* i, p. 150. "A correct plainness, and elegant simplicity, is the proper character of an introduction."—*Blair's Rhet.* p. 308. "In syntax there is what grammarians call concord or agreement, and government."—*Infant School Gram.* p. 122. "People find themselves able without much study to write and speak the English intelligibly, and thus have been led to think rules of no utility."—*Webster's Essays*, p. 6. "But the writer must be one who has studied to inform himself well, who has pondered his subject with care, and addresses himself to our judgment, rather than to our imagination."—*Blair's Rhet.* p. 353. "But practice hath determined it otherwise; and has, in all the languages with which we are much acquainted, supplied the place of an interrogative mode, either by particles of interrogation, or by a peculiar order of the words in the sentence."—*Lowth's Gram.* p. 84. "If the Lord have stirred thee up against me, let him accept an offering."—*1 Sam.* xxvi, 19. "But if the priest's daughter be a widow, or divorced, and have no child, and is returned unto her father's house, as in her youth, she shall eat of her father's meat."—*Levit.* xxii, 13. "Since we never have, nor ever shall study your sublime productions."—*Neef's Sketch*, p. 62. "Enabling us to form more distinct images of objects, than can be done with the utmost attention where these particulars are not found."—*Kames, El. of Crit.* Vol. i, p. 174. "I hope you will consider what is spoke comes from my love."—*Shak., Othello.* "We will then perceive how the designs of emphasis may be marred."—*Rush, on the Voice*, p. 406. "I knew it was Crab, and goes me to the fellow that whips the dogs."—SHAK.: *Joh. Dict. w.* ALL. "The youth was being consumed by a slow malady."—*Wright's Gram.* p. 192. "If all men thought, spoke, and wrote alike, something resembling a perfect adjustment of these points may be accomplished."—*Ib.* p. 240. "If you will replace what has been long since expunged from the language."—*Campbell's Rhet.* p. 167; *Murray's Gram.* i, 364. "As in all those faulty instances, I have now been giving."—*Blair's Rhet.* p. 149. "This mood has also been improperly used in the following places."—*Murray's Gram.* i, 184. "He [Milton] seems to have been well acquainted with his own genius, and to know what it was that nature had bestowed upon him."—*Johnson's Life of Milton.* "Of which I already gave one instance, the worst, indeed, that occurs in all the poem."—*Blair's Rhet.* p. 395. "It is strange he never commanded you to have done it."—*Anon.* "History painters would have found it difficult, to have invented such a species of beings."—ADDISON: see *Lowth's Gram.* p. 87. "Universal Grammar cannot be taught abstractedly, it must be done with reference to some language already known."—*Lowth's Preface*, p. viii. "And we might imagine, that if verbs had been so contrived, as simply to express these, no more was needful."—*Blair's Rhet.* p. 82. "To a writer of such a genius as Dean Swift, the plain style was most admirably fitted."—*Ib.* p. 181. "Please excuse my son's absence."—*Inst.* p. 188. "Bid the boys to come in immediately."—*Ib.*

"Gives us the secrets of his Pagan hell,
Where ghost with ghost in sad communion dwell."—*Crabbe's Bor.* p. 306.

"Alas! nor faith nor valour now remain;
Sighs are but wind, and I must bear my chain."—*Walpole's Catal.* p. 11.

LESSON VII.—PARTICIPLES.

"Of which the Author considers himself, in compiling the present work, as merely laying of the foundation-stone."—*Blair's Gram.* p. ix. "On the raising such lively and distinct images as are here described."—*Kames, El. of Crit.* i, 89. "They are necessary to the avoiding Ambiguities."—*Brightland's Gram.* p. 95. "There is no neglecting it without falling into a dangerous error."—*Burlamaqui, on Law*, p. 41. "The contest resembles Don Quixote's fighting windmills."—*Webster's Essays*, p. 67. "That these verbs associate with verbs in all the tenses, is no proof of their having no particular time of their own."—*Murray's Gram.* i, 190. "To justify my not following the tract of the ancient rhetoricians."—*Blair's Rhet.* p. 122. "The putting letters together, so as to make words, is called spelling."—*Infant School Gram.* p. 11. "What is the putting vowels and consonants together called."—*Ib.* p. 12. "Nobody knows of their being charitable but themselves."—*Fuller, on the Gospel*, p. 29. "Payment was at length made, but no reason assigned for its having been so long postponed."—*Murray's Gram.* i, 186; *Kirkham's*, 194; *Ingersoll's*, 254. "Which will bear being brought into comparison with any composition of the kind."—*Blair's Rhet.* p. 396. "To render vice ridiculous, is doing real service to the world."—*Ib.* p. 476. "It is copying directly from nature; giving a plain rehearsal of what passed, or was supposed to pass, in conversation."—*Ib.* p. 433. "Propriety of pronunciation is giving to every word that sound, which the most polite usage of the language appropriates to it."—*Murray's Key*, 8vo, p. 200. "To occupy the mind, and prevent our regretting the insipidity of an uniform plain."—*Kames, El. of Crit.* Vol. ii, p. 329. "There are a hundred ways of any thing happening."—*Steele.* "Tell me, signor, what was the cause of Antonio's sending Claudio to Venice, yesterday."—*Bucke's Gram.* p. 90. "Looking about for an outlet, some rich prospect unexpectedly opens to view."—*Kames, El. of Crit.* ii, 334. "A hundred volumes of modern novels may be read, without acquiring a new idea."—*Webster's Essays*, p. 20. "Poetry admits of greater latitude than prose, with respect to coining, or, at least, new compounding words."—*Blair's Rhet.* p. 93. "When laws were wrote on brazen tables inforced by the sword."—*Notes to the Dunciad.* "A pronoun, which saves the naming a person or thing a second time, ought to be placed as near as possible to the name of the person or thing."—*Kames, El. of Crit.* ii, 49. "The using a preposition in this case, is not always a matter of choice."—*Ib.* ii, 37. "To save multiplying words, I would be understood to comprehend both circumstances."—*Ib.* i, 219. "Immoderate grief is mute: complaining is struggling for consolation."—*Ib.* i, 398. "On the other hand, the accelerating or retarding the natural course, excites a pain."—*Ib.* i, 259. "Human affairs require the distributing our attention."—*Ib.* i, 264. "By neglecting this circumstance, the following example is defective in neatness."—*Ib.* ii, 29. "And therefore the suppressing copulatives must animate a description."—*Ib.* ii, 32. "If the laying aside copulatives give force and liveliness, a redundancy of them must render the period languid."—*Ib.* ii, 33. "It skills not asking my leave, said Richard."—*Scott's Crusaders.* "To redeem his credit, he proposed being sent once more to Sparta."—*Goldsmith's Greece*, i, 129. "Dumas relates his having given drink to a dog."—*Dr. Stone, on the Stomach*, p. 24. "Both are, in a like way, instruments of our receiving such ideas from external objects."—*Butler's Analogy*, p. 66. "In order to your proper handling such a subject."—*Spectator*, No. 533. "For I do not recollect its being preceded by an open vowel."—*Knight, on the Greek Alphabet*, p. 56. "Such is setting up the form above the power of godliness."—*Barclay's Works*, i, 72. "I remember walking once with my young acquaintance."—*Hunt's Byron*, p. 27. "He [Lord Byron] did not like paying a debt."—*Ib.* p. 74. "I do not remember seeing Coleridge when I was a child."—*Ib.* p. 318. "In consequence of the dry rot's having been discovered, the mansion has undergone a thorough repair."—*Maunder's Gram.* p. 17. "I would not advise the following entirely the German system."—*Dr. Lieber: Lit. Conv.* p. 66. "Would it not be making the students judges of the professors?"—*Id. ib.* p. 64. "Little time should intervene between their being proposed and decided upon."—*Prof. Vethake: ib.* p. 39. "It would be nothing less than finding fault with the Creator."—*Ib.* p. 116. "Having once been friends is a powerful reason, both of prudence and conscience, to restrain us from ever becoming enemies."—*Secker.* "By using the word as a conjunction, the ambiguity is prevented."—*Murray's Gram.* i, 216.

> "He forms his schemes the flood of vice to stem,
> But preaching Jesus is not one of them."—*J. Taylor.*

LESSON VIII.—ADVERBS.

"Auxiliaries cannot only be inserted, but are really understood."—*Wright's Gram.* p. 202. "He was since a hired Scribbler in the Daily Courant."—*Notes to the Dunciad*, ii, 299. "In gardening, luckily, relative beauty need never stand in opposition to intrinsic beauty."—*Kames, El. of Crit.* ii, 330. "I doubt much of the propriety of the following examples."—*Lowth's Gram.* p. 44. "And [we see] how far they have spread one of the worst Languages possibly in this part of the world."—*Locke, on Ed.* p. 341. "And in this manner to merely place him on a level with the beast of the forest."—*Smith's New Gram.* p. 5. "Where, ah! where, has my darling fled?"—*Anon.* "As for this fellow, we know not from whence he is."—*John*, ix, 29. "Ye see then how that by works a man is justified, and not by faith only."—*James*, ii, 24. "The Mixt kind is where the poet sometimes speaks in his own person, and sometimes makes other characters to speak."—*Adam's Lat. Gram.* p. 276; *Gould's*, 267. "Interrogation is, when the writer or orator raises questions and returns answers."—*Fisher's Gram.* p. 154. "Prevention is, when an author starts an objection which he foresees may be made, and gives an answer to it."—*Ib.* p. 154. "Will you let me alone, or no?"—*Walker's Particles.* p. 184. "Neither man nor woman cannot resist an engaging exterior."—*Chesterfield*, Let. lix. "Though the Cup be never so clean."—*Locke, on Ed.* p. 65. "Seldom, or ever, did any one rise to eminence, by being a witty lawyer."—*Blair's Rhet.* p. 272. "The second rule, which I give, respects the choice of objects, from whence metaphors, and other figures, are to be drawn."—*Blair's Rhet.* p. 144. "In the figures which it uses, it sets mirrors before us, where we may behold objects, a second time, in their likeness."—*Ib.* p. 139. "Whose Business is to seek the true measures of Right and Wrong, and not the Arts how to avoid doing the one, and secure himself in doing the other."—*Locke, on Ed.* p. 331. "The occasions when you ought to personify things, and when you ought not, cannot be stated in any precise rule."—*Cobbett's Eng. Gram.* ¶ 182. "They reflect that they have been much diverted, but scarce can say about what."—*Kames, El. of Crit.* i, 151. "The eyebrows and shoulders should seldom or ever be remarked by any perceptible motion."—*Adams's Rhet.* ii, 389. "And the left hand or arm should seldom or never attempt any motion by itself."—*Ib.* ii, 391. "Every speaker does not propose to please the imagination."—*Jamieson's Rhet.* p. 104. "And, like Gallio, they care little for none of these things."—*The Friend*, Vol. x, p. 351. "They may inadvertently be imitated, in cases where the meaning would be obscure."—*Murray's Gram. 8vo*, p. 172. "Nor a man cannot make him laugh."—*Shak.* "The Athenians, in their present distress, scarce knew

where to turn."—*Goldsmith's Gram.* i, 156. "I do not remember where ever God delivered his oracles by the multitude."—*Locke.* "The object of this government is twofold, outwards and inwards."—*Barclay's Works,* i, 553. "In order to rightly understand what we read."—*Johnson's Gram. Com.* p. 313. "That a design had been formed, to forcibly abduct or kidnap Morgan."—*Stone, on Masonry,* p. 410. "But such imposture can never maintain its ground long."—*Blair's Rhet.* p. 10. "But sure it is equally possible to apply the principles of reason and good sense to this art, as to any other that is cultivated among men."—*Ibid.* "It would have been better for you, to have remained illiterate, and to have been even hewers of wood."—*Murray's Gram.* i, 374. "Dissyllables that have two vowels, which are separated in the pronunciation, have always the accent on the first syllable."—*Ib.* i, 238. "And they all turned their backs without almost drawing a sword."—*Kames, El. of Crit.* i, 224. "The principle of duty takes naturally place of every other."—*Ib.* i, 342. "All that glitters is not gold."—*Maunder's Gram.* p. 13. "Whether now or never so many myriads of ages hence."—*Pres. Edwards.*
"England never did, nor never shall,
Lie at the proud foot of a conqueror."—*Beaut. of Shak.* p. 109.

LESSON IX.—CONJUNCTIONS.

"He readily comprehends the rules of Syntax, and their use and applicability in the examples before him."—*Greenleaf's Gram.* p. 6. "The works of Æschylus have suffered more by time, than any of the ancient tragedians."—*Blair's Rhet.* p. 470. "There is much more story, more bustle, and action, than on the French theatre."—*Ib.* p. 478. "Such an unremitted anxiety and perpetual application as engrosses our whole time and thoughts, are forbidden."—*Soame Jenyns: Tract,* p. 12. "It seems to be nothing else, but the simple form of the adjective."—*Wright's Gram.* p. 49. "But when I talk of *Reasoning,* I do not intend any other, but such as is suited to the Child's Capacity."—*Locke, on Ed.* p. 129. "Pronouns have no other use in language, but to represent nouns."—*Jamieson's Rhet.* p. 83. "The speculative relied no farther on their own judgment but to choose a leader, whom they implicitly followed."—*Kames, El. of Crit.* Vol. i, p. xxv. "Unaccommodated man is no more but such a poor, bare, forked animal as thou art."—*Beaut. of Shak.* p. 266. "A Parenthesis is a clause introduced into the body of a sentence obliquely, and which may be omitted without injuring the grammatical construction."—*Murray's Gram.* i, 280; *Ingersoll's,* 292; *Smith's,* 192; *Alden's,* 162; *A. Flint's,* 114; *Fisk's,* 158; *Cooper's,* 187; *Comly's,* 163. "A Caret, marked thus ʌ is placed where some word happens to be left *out in* writing, and which *is inserted over* the line."—*Murray's Gram.* i, 282; *Ingersoll's,* 293; *and others.* "At the time that I visit them they shall be cast down."—*Jer.* vi, 15. "Neither our virtues or vices are all our own."—*Dr. Johnson: Sanborn's Gram.* p. 167. "I could not give him an answer as early as he had desired."—*O. B. Peirce's Gram.* p. 200. "He is not as tall as his brother."—*Nixon's Parser,* p. 124. "It is difficult to judge when Lord Byron is serious or not."—*Lady Blessington.* "Some nouns are both of the second and third declension."—*Gould's Lat. Gram.* p. 48. "He was discouraged neither by danger or misfortune."—*Wells's Hist.* p. 161. "This is consistent neither with logic nor history."—*The Dial,* i, 62. "Parts of Sentences are simple and compound."—*Blair's Gram.* p. 114. "English verse is regulated rather by the number of syllables than of feet."—*Ib.* p. 120. "I know not what more he can do, but pray for him."—*Locke, on Ed.* p. 140. "Whilst they are learning; and apply themselves with Attention, they are to be kept in good Humour."—*Ib.* p. 295. "A Man cannot have too much of it, nor too perfectly."—*Ib.* p. 322. "That you may so run, as you may obtain; and so fight, as you may overcome."—*Wm. Penn.* "It is the case of some, to contrive false periods of business, because they may seem men of despatch."—*Lord Bacon.* "'A tall man and a woman.' In this sentence there is no ellipsis; the adjective or quality respect only the man."—*Dr. Ash's Gram.* p. 95. "An abandonment of the policy is neither to be expected or desired."—*Pres. Jackson's Message,* 1830. "Which can be acquired by no other means but frequent exercise in speaking."—*Blair's Rhet.* p. 344. "The chief and fundamental rules of syntax are common to the English as well as the Latin tongue."—*Ib.* p. 90. "Then I exclaim, that my antagonist either is void of all taste, or that his taste is corrupted in a miserable degree."—*Ib.* p. 21. "I cannot pity any one who is under no distress of body nor of mind."—*Kames, El. of Crit.* i, 44. "There was much genius in the world, before there were learning or arts to refine it."—*Blair's Rhet.* p. 391. "Such a Writer can have little else to do, but to new model the Paradoxes of ancient Scepticism."—*Brown's Estimate,* i, 102. "Our ideas of them being nothing else but a collection of the ordinary qualities observed in them."—*Duncan's Logic,* p. 25. "A *non-ens* or a negative can neither give pleasure nor pain."—*Kames, El. of Crit.* i, 63. "So as they shall not jostle and embarrass one another."—*Blair's Lectures,* p. 318. "He firmly refused to make use of any other voice but his own."—*Goldsmith's Greece,* i, 190. "Your marching regiments, Sir, will not make the guards their example, either as soldiers or subjects."—*Junius, Let.* 35. "Consequently, they had neither meaning, or beauty, to any but the natives of each country."—*Sheridan's Elocution,* p. 161.
"The man of worth, and has not left his peer,
Is in his narrow house for ever darkly laid."—*Burns.*

LESSON X.—PREPOSITIONS.

"These may be carried on progressively above any assignable limits."—*Kames, El. of Crit.* i, 296. "To crowd in a single member of a period different subjects, is still worse than to crowd them into one period."—*Ib.* ii, 27. "Nor do we rigidly insist for melodious prose."—*Ib.* ii, 76. "The aversion we have at those who differ from us."—*Ib.* ii, 366. "For we cannot bear his shifting the scene every line."—Ld. Halifax: *ib.* ii, 213. "We shall find that we come by it the same way."—*Locke.* "To this he has no better defense than that."—*Barnes's Red Book,* p. 347. "Searching the person whom he suspects for having stolen his casket."—*Blair's Rhet.* p. 479. "Who are elected as vacancies occur by the whole Board."—*Lit. Convention,* p. 81. "Almost the only field of ambition of a German, is science."—Dr. Lieber: *ib.* p. 66. "The plan of education is very different to the one pursued in the sister country."—Dr. Coley: *ib.* p. 197. "Some writers on grammar have contended that adjectives relate to, and modify the action of verbs."—*Wilcox's Gram.* p. 61. "They are therefore of a mixed nature, participating of the properties both of pronouns and adjectives."—*Ingersoll's Gram.* p. 57. "For there is no authority which can justify the inserting the aspirate or doubling the vowel."—*Knight, on Greek Alph.* p. 52. "The distinction and arrangement between active, passive, and neuter verbs."—*Wright's Gram.* p. 176. "And see thou a hostile world *to* spread its delusive snares."—*Kirkham's Gram.* p. 167. "He may be precaution'd, and be made see, how those joyn in the Contempt."—*Locke, on Ed.* p. 155. "The contenting themselves now in the want of what they wish'd for, is a vertue."—*Ib.* p. 185. "If the Complaint be of something really worthy your notice."—*Ib.* p. 198. "True Fortitude I take to be the quiet Possession of a Man's self, and an undisturb'd doing his Duty."—*Ib.* p. 204. "For the custom of tormenting and killing of Beasts will, by degrees, harden their Minds even towards Men."—*Ib.* p. 216. "Children are whip'd to 2 and made spend many Hours of their precious time uneasily in Latin."—*Ib.* p. 289. "The ancient rhetoricians have entered into a very minute and particular detail of this subject; more particular, indeed, than into any other that regards language."—*Jamieson's Rhet.* p. 123. "But the one should not be omitted without the other."—*Bullions's Eng. Gram.* p. 108. "In some of the common forms of speech, the relative pronoun is usually omitted."—*Murray's Gram.* i, 218; *Weld's,* 191. "There are a great variety of causes, which disqualify a witness from being received to testify in particular cases."—*J. Q. Adams's Rhet.* ii, 75. "Aside of all regard to interest, we should expect that," &c.—*Webster's Essays,* p. 92. "My opinion was given on a rather cursory perusal of the book."—*Murray's Key,* i, 202. "And the next day, he was put on board his ship."—*Ib.* ii, 201. "Having the command of no emotions but of what are raised by sight."—*Kames, El. of Crit.* ii, 318. "Did these moral attributes exist in some other being beside himself."—*Wayland's Moral Science,* p. 161. "He did not behave in that manner out of pride or contempt of the tribunal."—*Goldsmith's Greece,* i, 190. "These prosecutions of William seem to have been the most iniquitous measures pursued by the court."—*Murray's Key,* i, 199; *Priestley's Gram.* 126. "To restore myself into the good graces of my fair critics."—*Dryden.* "Objects denominated beautiful, please not in virtue of any one quality common to them all."—*Blair's Rhet.* p. 46. "This would have been less worthy notice, had not a writer or two of high rank lately adopted it."—*Churchill's Gram.* p. 197.

"A Grecian youth, with talents rare,
Whom Plato's philosophic care," &c.—*Felton's Gram.* p. 145.

LESSON XI.—PROMISCUOUS.

"To excel, is become a much less considerable object."—*Blair's Rhet.* p. 351. "My robe, and my integrity to heaven, is all I now dare call mine own."—*Beauties of Shak.* p. 173. "So thou the garland wear'st successively."—*Ib.* p. 134. "For thou the garland wear successively."—*Enfield's Speaker,* p. 341. "If that thou need'st a Roman's, take it forth."—*Ib.* p. 357. "If that thou be'st a Roman, take it forth."—*Beauties of Shak.* p. 356. "If thou provest this to be real, thou must be a smart lad, indeed."—*Neef's Method of Teaching,* p. 210. "And another Bridge of four hundred Foot in Length."—*Brightland's Gram.* p. 241. "*Metonymy* is putting one name for another on account of the near relation there is between them."—*Fisher's Gram.* p. 151. "An *Antonomasia* is putting an appellative or common name for a proper name."—*Ib.* p. 153. "Its being me needs make no difference in your determination."—*Bullions, E. Gram.* p. 82. "The first and second page are torn."—*Ib.* p. 145. "John's being from home occasioned the delay."—*Ib.* p. 81. "His having neglected opportunities of improvement, was the cause of his disgrace."—*Ib.* p. 81. "He will regret his having neglected opportunities of improvement when it may be too late."—*Ib.* p. 81. "His being an expert dancer does not entitle him to our regard."—*Ib.* p. 82. *

---

* Of this example, Professor Bullions says, "This will be allowed to be a *correct English sentence,* complete in itself, and requiring nothing to be supplied. The phrase, '*being an expert dancer,*' is the subject of the verb '*does entitle,*' but the word '*dancer*' in this phrase is neither the subject of any verb, nor is governed by any word in the sentence."—*Eng. Gram.* p. 82. It is because this word cannot have any regular construction after the participle when the possessive case precedes, that I deny his first proposition, and declare the sentence not "to be correct English." But the Professor at length reasons himself into the notion, that this indeterminate "predicate," as he erroneously calls it, "is properly in the *objective case,* and in parsing, may correctly be

"Cæsar went back to Rome to take possession of the public treasure, which his opponent, by a most unaccountable oversight, had neglected taking with him."—*Goldsmith's Rome*, p. 116. "And Cæsar took out of the treasury, to the amount of three thousand pound weight of gold, besides an immense quantity of silver."—*Ibid.* "Rules and definitions, which should always be clear and intelligible as possible, are thus rendered obscure."—*Greenleaf's Gram.* p. 5. "So much both of ability and merit is seldom found."—*Murray's Key*, ii, 179. "If such maxims, and such practices prevail, what is become of decency and virtue?"—*Ib.* ii, 196. "If such maxims and practices prevail, what is become of decency and virtue?"—*Bullions, E. Gram.* p. 78. "Especially if the subject require not so much pomp."—*Blair's Rhet.* p. 117. "However, the proper mixture of light and shade, in such compositions; the exact adjustment of all the figurative circumstances with the literal sense; have ever been considered as points of great nicety."—*Murray's Gram.* i, 343. "And adding to that hissing in our language, which is taken so much notice of by foreigners."—*Addison*: Dr. Coote: ii, i, 90. "Speaking impatiently to servants, or any thing that betrays unkindness or ill-humour, is certainly criminal."—*Murray's Key*, ii, 183; *Merchant's*, 190. "There is here a fulness and grandeur of expression well suited to the subject."—*Blair's Rhet.* p. 218. "I single Strada out among the moderns, because he had the foolish presumption to censure Tacitus."—*Murray's Key*, ii, 262. "I single him out among the moderns, because," &c.—*Bolingbroke, on Hist.* p. 116. "This is a rule not always observed, even by good writers, as strictly as it ought to be."—*Blair's Rhet.* p. 103. "But this gravity and assurance, which is beyond boyhood, being neither wisdom nor knowledge, do never reach to manhood."—*Notes to the Dunciad.* "The regularity and polish even of a turnpike-road has some influence upon the low people in the neighbourhood."—*Kames, El. of Crit.* ii, 358. "They become fond of regularity and neatness; which is displayed, first upon their yards and little enclosures, and next within doors."—*Ibid.* "The phrase, *it is impossible to exist*, gives us the idea of it's being impossible for men, or any body to exist."—*Priestley's Gram.* p. 85. "I'll give a thousand pound to look upon him."—*Beauties of Shak.* p. 151. "The reader's knowledge, as Dr. Campbell observes, may prevent his mistaking it."—*Murray's Gram.* i, 172; *Crombie's*, 253. "When two words are set in contrast, or in opposition to one another, they are both emphatic."—*Murray's Gram.* i, 243. "The number of persons, men, women, and children, who were lost in the sea, was very great."—*Ib.* ii, 20. "Nor is the resemblance between the primary and resembling object pointed out."—*Jamieson's Rhet.* p. 179. "I think it the best book of the kind which I have met with."—Dr. Mathews: *Greenleaf's Gram.* p. 2.

> "Why should not we their ancient rites restore,
> And be what Rome or Athens were before?"—*Roscommon*, p. 22.

LESSON XII.—TWO ERRORS.

"It is labour only which gives the relish to pleasure."—*Murray's Key*, ii, 234. "Groves are never so agreeable as in the opening of the spring."—*Ib.* p. 216. "His 'Philosophical Inquiry into the Origin of our Ideas on the Sublime and Beautiful' soon made him known to the literati."—*Biog. Dict. n. Burke.* "An awful precipice or tower whence we look down on the objects which lie below."—*Blair's Rhet.* p. 30. "This passage, though very poetical, is, however, harsh and obscure; owing to no other cause but this, that three distinct metaphors are crowded together."—*Ib.* p. 149. "I propose making some observations."—*Ib.* p. 280. "I shall follow the same method here which I have all along pursued."—*Ib.* p. 346. "Mankind never resemble each other so much as they do in the beginnings of society."—*Ib.* p. 380. "But no ear is sensible of the termination of each foot, in reading an hexameter line."—*Ib.* p. 383. "The first thing, says he, which either a writer of fables, or of heroic poems, does, is, to choose some maxim or point of morality."—*Ib.* p. 421. "The fourth book has been always most justly admired, and abounds with beauties of the highest kind."—*Ib.* p. 439. "There is no attempt towards painting characters in the poem."—*Ib.* p. 446. "But the artificial contrasting of characters, and the introducing them always in pairs, and by opposites, gives too theatrical and affected an air to the piece."—*Ib.* p. 479. "Neither of them are arbitrary nor local."—*Kames, El. of Crit.* p. xxi. "If crowding figures be bad, it is still worse to graft one figure upon another."—*Ib.* ii, 236. "The crowding withal so many objects together, lessens the pleasure."—*Ib.* ii, 324. "This therefore lies not in the putting off the Hat, nor making of Compliments."—*Locke, on Ed.* p. 149. "But the Samaritan Vau may have been used, as the Jews did the Chaldaic, both for a vowel and consonant."—*Wilson's Essay*, p. 19. "But if a solemn and familiar pronunciation really exists in our language, is it not the business of a grammarian to mark both?"—*Walker's Dict., Pref.* p. 4. "By making sounds follow each other agreeable to certain laws."—*Music*

<hr/>

called the *objective indefinite*;" of which one, he says, "The following are also examples: '*He* had the *honour* of being a *director* for life.' 'By being a diligent *student*, *he* soon acquired eminence in his profession.'"—*Ib.* p. 62. But "*director*" and "*students*" are here manifestly in the *nominative case*; each agreeing with the pronoun *he*, which denotes the same person. In the latter sentence, there is a very obvious transposition of the first five words.

of *Nature*, p. 406. "If there was no drinking intoxicating draughts, there could be
drunkards."—*O. B. Peirce's Gram.* p. 178. "Socrates knew his own defects, and if he
proud of any thing, it was in the being thought to have none."—*Goldsmith's Greece*, i,
"Lysander having brought his army to Ephesus, erected an arsenal for building of galli
—*Ib.* i, 161. "The use of these signs are worthy remark."—*Brightland's Gram.* p. 94.
received me in the same manner that I would you."—*Smith's New Gram.* p. 112. "C
sisting both of the direct and collateral evidence."—*Butler's Analogy*, p. 224. "If any
or woman that believeth have widows, let them relieve them, and let not the church
charged."—1 *Tim.* v, 16. "For mens sakes are beasts bred."—*Walker's Particles*, p.
"From three a clock there was drinking and gaming."—*Ib.* p. 141. "Is this he that I
seeking of, or no?"—*Ib.* p. 248. "And for the upholding every one his own opinion, the
is so much ado."—*Sewel's Hist.* p. 809. "Some of them however will be necessarily tak
notice of."—*Sale's Koran*, p. 71. "The boys conducted themselves exceedingly indiscreet.
Merchant's Key, p. 195. "Their example, their influence, their fortune, every talent th
possess, dispense blessings on all around them."—*Ib.* p. 197; *Murray's Key*, ii, 219. "T
two *Reynolds* reciprocally converted one another."—*Johnson's Lives*, p. 185. "The destroy
the two last Tacitus calls an attack upon virtue itself."—*Goldsmith's Rome*, p. 194. "Mo
is your suit."—*Beauties of Shak.* p. 38. "*Ch*, is commonly sounded like *tsh* ; as in chur
but in words derived from the Greek, has the sound of *k*."—*Murray's Gram.* i, 11. "W
one is obliged to make some utensil supply purposes to which they were not originally d
tined."—*Campbell's Rhet.* p. 222. "But that a being baptized with water, is a wash
away of sin, thou canst not from hence prove."—*Barclay's Works*, i, 190. "Being but sp
to one, it infers no universal command."—*Ibid.* "For if the laying aside Copulatives g
Force and Liveliness, a Redundancy of them must render the Period languid."—*Buchan
Syntax*, p. 134. "James used to compare him to a cat, who always fell upon her leg."
ADAM'S HIST. OF ENGLAND: *Crombie*, p. 384.

> "From the low earth aspiring genius springs,
> And sails triumphant born on eagles wings."—*Lloyd*, p. 162.

LESSON XIII.—TWO ERRORS.

"An ostentatious, a feeble, a harsh, or an obscure style, for instance, are always faul
—*Blair's Rhet.* p. 190. "Yet in this we find the English pronounce perfectly agreeable
rule."—*Walker's Dict.* p. 2. "But neither the perception of ideas, nor knowledge of
sort, are habits, though absolutely necessary to the forming of them."—*Butler's Anal
p. 111. "They were cast: and an heavy fine imposed upon them."—*Goldsmith's Gr
ii, 30. "Without making this reflection, he cannot enter into the spirit, nor relish
composition of the author."—*Blair's Rhet.* p. 450. "The scholar should be instruc
relative to finding his words."—*Osborn's Key*, p. 4. "And therefore they could neither h
forged, or reversified them."—*Knight, on the Greek Alph.* p. 30. "A dispensary is the pl
where medicines are dispensed."—*Murray's Key*, ii, 172. "Both the connexion and nu
ber of words is determined by general laws."—*Neef's Sketch*, p. 73. "An Anapest has
two first syllables unaccented, and the last accented : as, 'Contravene, acquiesce.'"—*M
ray's Gram.* i, 254. "An explicative sentence is, when a thing is said to be or not to be,
do or not to do, to suffer or not to suffer, in a direct manner."—*Ib.* i, 141; *Lowth's*
"BUT is a *conjunction*, in all cases when it is neither an adverb nor preposition."—*S
New Gram.* p. 109. "He wrote in the king Ahasuerus' name, and sealed it with the kin
ring."—*Esther*, viii, 10. "Camm and Audland were departed the town before this tim
—*Sewel's Hist.* p. 100. "Previous to their relinquishing the practice, they must be
viced."—*Dr. Webster, on Slavery*, p. 5. "Which he had thrown up previous to his sett
out."—*Grimshaw's Hist. U. S.* p. 84. "He left him to the value of an hundred drach
in Persian money."—*Spect.* No. 535. "All which the mind can ever contemplate conce
ing them, must be divided between the three."—*Cardell's Philol. Gram.* p. 88. "T
Puzzle is one of the most eminent immethodical disputants of any that has fallen un
my observation."—*Spect.* No 476. "When you have once got him to think himself
amends for his suffering, by the praise is given him for his courage."—*Locke, on Ed.*
"In all matters where simple reason, and mere speculation is concerned."—*Sheridan's E
cution*, p. 136. "And therefore he should be spared the trouble of attending to any th
else, but his meaning."—*Ib.* p. 105. "It is this kind of phraseology which is distingu
by the epithet *idiomatical*, and hath been originally the spawn, partly of ignorance,
partly of affectation."—*Campbell's Rhet.* p. 185. Murray has it—"and which has been
nally," &c.—*Octavo Gram.* i, 370. "That neither the letters nor inflection are such as
have been employed by the ancient inhabitants of Latium."—*Knight, Gr. Alph.* p. 13.
cases where the verb is intended to be applied to any one of the terms."—*Murray's Gr
i, 150. "But this people which know not the law, are accursed."—*John*, vii, 49. "A
the magnitude of the chorusses have weight and sublimity."—*Music of Nature*, p.
"Dare he deny but there are some of his fraternity guilty?"—*Barclay's Works*, i,
"Giving an account of most, if not all the papers had passed betwixt them."—*Ib.* i,

"In this manner, both as to parsing and correcting, all the rules of syntax should be treated, proceeding regularly according to their order."—*Murray's Exercises*, 12mo, p. x. "Ovando was allowed a brilliant retinue and a body guard."—*Sketch of Columbus.* "Is it I or he whom you requested to go?"—*Kirkham's Gram., Key*, p. 226. "Let thou and I go on."—*Bunyan's P. P.* p. 158. "This I no-where affirmed; and do wholly deny."—*Barclay's Works*, iii, 454. "But that I deny; and remains for him to prove."—*Ibid.* "Our country sinks beneath the yoke; It weeps, it bleeds, and each new day a gash Is added to her wounds."—*Shakspeare*: *Joh. Dict. w. Beneath.* "Thou art the Lord who didst choose Abraham, and broughtest him forth out of Ur of the Chaldees."—*Murray's Key*, ii, 189. "He is the exhaustless fountain, from which emanates all these attributes, that exists throughout this wide creation."—*Wayland's Moral Science*, 1st Ed. p. 155. "I am he who have communed with the son of Neocles; I am he who have entered the gardens of pleasure."—*Wright's Athens*, p. 66.

"Such was in ancient times the tales received,
Such by our good forefathers was believed."—*Rowe's Lucan*, B. ix, l. 605.

LESSON XIV.—TWO ERRORS.

"The noun or pronoun that stand before the active verb, may be called the agent."—*Alex. Murray's Gram.* p. 121. "Such seems to be the musings of our hero of the grammarquill, when he penned the first part of his grammar."—*Merchant's Criticisms.* "Two dots, the one placed above the other [:], is called Sheva, and represents a very short *e*."—*Wilson's Hebrew Gram.* p. 43. "Great has been, and is, the obscurity and difficulty, in the nature and application of them."—*Butler's Analogy*, p. 184. "As two is to four, so is four to eight."—*Everest's Gram.* p. 231. "The invention and use of it [arithmetic] reaches back to a period so remote as is beyond the knowledge of history."—*Robertson's America*, i, 288. "What it presents as objects of contemplation or enjoyment, fills and satisfies his mind."—*Ib.* i, 377. "If he dare not say they are, as I know he dare not, how must I then distinguish?"—*Barclay's Works*, iii, 311. "He was now grown so fond of solitude that all company was become uneasy to him."—*Life of Cicero*, p. 32. "Violence and spoil is heard in her; before me continually is grief and wounds."—*Jeremiah*, vi, 7. "Bayle's Intelligence from the Republic of Letters, which make eleven volumes in duodecimo, are truly a model in this kind."—*Formey's Belles-Lettres*, p. 168. "To render pauses pleasing and expressive, they must not only be made in the right place, but also accompanied with a proper tone of voice."—*Murray's Gram.* i, 249. "The opposing the opinions, and rectifying the mistakes of others, is what truth and sincerity sometimes require of us."—*Locke, on Ed.* p. 211. "It is very probable that this assembly was called, to clear some doubt which the king had, about the lawfulness of the Hollanders' throwing off the monarchy of Spain, and withdrawing, entirely, their allegiance to that crown."—*Murray's Key*, ii, 195. "Naming the cases and numbers of a noun in their order is called declining it."—*Frost's El. of Gram.* p. 10. "The embodying them is, therefore, only collecting such component parts of words."—*Town's Analysis*, p. 4. "The one is the voice heard at Christ's being baptized; the other, at his being transfigured."—*Barclay's Works*, i, 267. "Understanding the literal sense would not have prevented their condemning the guiltless."—*Butler's Analogy*, p. 165. "As if this were taking the execution of justice out of the hands of God, and giving it to nature."—*Ib.* p. 194. "They will say, you must conceal this good opinion of yourself; which yet is allowing the thing, though not the showing it."—*Sheffield's Works*, ii, 244. "So as to signify not only the doing an action, but the causing it to be done."—*Pike's Hebrew Lexicon*, p. 180. "This, certainly, was both dividing the unity of God, and limiting his immensity."—*Calvin's Institutes*, B. i, Ch. 13. "Tones being infinite in number, and varying in almost every individual, the arranging them under distinct heads, and reducing them to any fixed and permanent rules, may be considered as the last refinement in language."—*Knight, on Gr. Alph.* p. 16. "The fierce anger of the Lord shall not return, until he have done it, and until he have performed the intents of his heart."—*Jeremiah*, xxx, 24. "We seek for more heroic and illustrious deeds, for more diversified and surprising events."—*Blair's Rhet.* p. 373. "We distinguish the Genders, or Male and Female Sex, four different Ways."—*Buchanan's Gram.* p. 20. "Thus, ch and g, are ever hard. It is therefore proper to retain these sounds in Hebrew names, which have not been modernized, or changed by public use."—*Wilson's Essay on Gram.* p. 24. "The Substantive or noun is the name of any thing conceived to subsist, or of which we have any notion."—*Lindley Murray's Gram.*, 2d Ed., p. 26. "The Substantive, or Noun; being the name of any thing conceived to subsist, or of which we have any notion."—*Dr. Lowth's Gram.* p. 6. "The Noun is the name of any thing that exists, or of which we have, or can form, an idea."—*Maunder's Gram.* p. 1. "A noun is the name of any thing in existence, or of which we can form an idea."—*Ib.* p. 1. (See False Syntax under Note 7th to Rule 10th.) "The next thing to be taken Care of, is to keep him exactly to speaking of Truth."—*Locke, on Ed.* p. 254. "The material, vegetable, and animal world, receive this influence according to their several capacities."—*The Dial*, i, 59. "And yet, it is fairly defensible on the principles of the schoolmen; if that can be called principles which consists merely in words."—*Campbell's Rhet.* p. 274.

> "Art thou so bare and full of wretchedness,
> And fears to die? famine is in thy cheeks,
> Need and oppression starveth in thy eyes."—*Beaut. of Shak.* p. 317.

LESSON XV.—THREE ERRORS.

"The silver age is reckoned to have commenced on the death of Augustus, and continued to the end of Trajan's reign."—*Gould's Lat. Gram.* p. 277. "Language is become, in modern times, more correct, indeed, and accurate."—*Blair's Rhet.* p. 65. "It is evident, that words are most agreeable to the ear which are composed of smooth and liquid sounds, where there is a proper intermixture of vowels and consonants."—*Ib.* p. 121. See *Murray's Gram.* i, 325. "It would have had no other effect, but to add a word unnecessarily to the sentence."—*Blair's Rhet.* p. 194. "But as rumours arose of the judges having been corrupted by money in this cause, these gave occasions to much popular clamour, and had thrown a heavy odium on Cluentius."—*Ib.* p. 273. "A Participle is derived of a verb, and partakes of the nature both of the verb and the adjective."—*Dr. Ash's Gram.* p. 39; *E. Devis's,* 9. "I will have learned my grammar before you learn your's."—*Wilbur and Liv. Gram.* p. 14. "There is no earthly object capable of making such various and such forcible impressions upon the human mind as a complete speaker."—*Perry's Dict.,* Pref. "It was not the carrying the bag which made Judas a thief and an hireling."—*South.* "As the reasonable soul and flesh is one man, so God and man is one Christ."—*Athanasian Creed.* "And I will say to them which were not my people, Thou art my people; and they shall say, Thou art my God."—*Hosea,* ii, 23. "Where there is nothing in the sense which requires the last sound to be elevated or emphatical, an easy fall, sufficient to show that the sense is finished, will be proper."—*Murray's Gram.* i, 250. "Each party produces words where the letter *a* is sounded in the manner they contend for."—*Walker's Dict.* p. 1. "To countenance persons who are guilty of bad actions, is scarcely one remove from actually committing them."—*Murray's Gram.* i, 233. "'To countenance persons who are guilty of bad actions,' is part of a sentence, which is the nominative case to the verb 'is.'"—*Ibid.* "What is called splitting of particles, or separating a preposition from the noun which it governs, is always to be avoided."—*Blair's Rhet.* p. 112; *Jamieson's,* 93. See *Murray's Gram.* i, 319. "There is, properly, no more than one pause or rest in the sentence, falling betwixt the two members into which it is divided."—*Blair's Rhet.* p. 125; *Jamieson's,* 126; *Murray's Gram.* i, 329. "Going barefoot does not at all help on the way to heaven."—*Steele, Spect.* No. 497. "There is no Body but condemns this in others, though they overlook it in themselves."—*Locke, on Ed.* § 145. "In the same sentence, be careful not to use the same word too frequently, nor in different senses."—*Murray's Gram.* i, 296. "Nothing could have made her so unhappy, as marrying a man who possessed such principles."—*Murray's Key,* ii, 200. "A warlike, various, and a tragical age is best to write of, but worst to write in."—*Cowley's Pref.* p. vi. "When thou instances Peter his baptizing Cornelius."—*Barclay's Works,* i, 188. "To introduce two or more leading thoughts or agents, which have no natural relation to, or dependence on one another."—*Murray's Gram.* i, 313. "Animals, again, are fitted to one another, and to the elements where they live, and to which they are as appendices."—*Ibid.* "This melody, or varying the sound of each word so often, is a proof of nothing, however, but of the fine ear of that people."—*Jamieson's Rhet.* p. 5. "They can each in their turns be made use of upon occasion."—*Duncan's Logic,* p. 191. "In this reign lived the poet Chaucer, who, with Gower, are the first authors, who can properly be said to have written English."—*Bucke's Gram.* p. 144. "In the translating these kind of expressions, consider the IT IS, as if it were *they,* or *they are.*"—*Walker's Particles,* p. 179. "The chin has an important office to perform; for upon its activity we either disclose a polite or vulgar pronunciation."—*Music of Nature,* p. 27. "For no other reason, but his being found in bad company."—*Webster's Amer. Spelling-Book,* p. 96. "It is usual to compare them in the same manner as Polisyllables."—*Priestley's Gram.* p. 77. "The infinitive mood is recognised easier than any others, because the preposition *to* precedes it."—*Bucke's Gram.* p. 95. "Prepositions, you recollect, connect words as well as conjunctions: how, then, can you tell the one from the other?"—*Smith's New Gram.* p. 38.

> "No kind of work requires so nice a touch,
> And if well finish'd, nothing shines so much."—*Sheffield, Duke of Buck.*

LESSON XVI.—THREE ERRORS.

"It is the final pause which alone, on many occasions, marks the difference between prose and verse: which will be evident from the following arrangement of a few poetical lines."—*Murray's Gram.* i, 260. "I shall do all I can to persuade others to take the same measures for their cure which I have."—*Guardian :* see *Campbell's Rhet.* p. 207. "I shall do all I can, to persuade others to take the same measures for their cure which I have taken."—*Murray's Key,* ii, 215. "It is the nature of extreme self-lovers, as they will set an house on fire, and [or *an*] it were but to roast their eggs."—*Ld. Bacon.* "Did ever men struggle more earnestly in a cause where both his honour and life are concerned?"—*Duncan's Cicero*, p. 15. "So the rests and pauses, between sentences and their parts, are marked by points."—*Lowth's Gram.* p. 114. "Yet the case and mode is not influenced by him, but determined by the nature of the sentence."—*Ib.* p. 113. "By not attending to his rule, many errors have been committed: a number of which is subjoined, as a further notion and direction to the learner."—*Murray's Gram.* i, 214. "Though thou clothest hyself with crimson, though thou deckest thee with ornaments of gold, though thou rentest by face with painting, in vain shalt thou make thyself fair."—*Jeremiah*, iv, 30. "But that he doing good to others will make us happy, is not so evident; feeding the hungry, for sample, or clothing the naked."—*Kames, El. of Crit.* i, 161. "There is no other God but him, no other light but his."—*William Penn*. "How little reason to wonder, that a perfect and accomplished orator, should be one of the characters that is most rarely found?"—*Blair's Rhet.* p. 337. "Because they neither express doing nor receiving an action."—*Infant School Gram.* p. 53. "To find the answers, will require an effort of mind, and when given, will be the result of reflection, showing that the subject is understood."—*Ib.* p. vii. 'To say, that 'the sun rises,' is trite and common; but it becomes a magnificent image when expressed as Mr. Thomson has done."—*Blair's Rhet.* p. 137. "The declining a word is the giving it differing endings."—*Ware's Gram.* p. 7. "And so much are they for every men following their own mind."—*Barclay's Works*, i, 462. "More than one overture for a peace was made, but Cleon prevented their taking effect."—*Goldsmith's Greece*, i, 121. 'Neither in English or in any other language is this word, and that which corresponds to it in other languages, any more an article, than *two, three, four*."—*Dr. Webster: Knicker-bocker of 1836*. "But the most irksome conversation of all others I have met within the neighbourhood, has been among two or three of your travellers."—*Spect.* No. 474. "Set down the two first terms of supposition under each other in the first place."—*Smiley's Arithmetic*, p. 79. "It is an useful rule too, to fix our eye on some of the most distant persons in the assembly."—*Blair's Rhet.* p. 328. "He will generally please most, when pleasing is not his sole nor chief aim."—*Ib.* p. 336. "At length, the consuls return to the camp, and inform them they could receive no other terms but that of surrendering their arms, and passing under the yoke."—*Ib.* p. 360. "Nor is mankind so much to blame, in his choice thus determining him."—*Swift: Crombie's Treatise*, p. 360. "These forms are what is called Number."—*Fosdick's De Sacy*, p. 62. "In languages which admit but two Genders, all Nouns are either Masculine or Feminine, even though they designate beings which are neither male or female."—*Ib.* p. 66. "It is called a *Verb* or *Word* by way of eminence, because it is the most essential word in a sentence, without which the other parts of speech can form no complete sense."—*Gould's Adam's Gram.* p. 76. "The sentence will consist of two members, which are commonly separated from one another by a comma."—*Jamieson's Rhet.* p. 7. "Loud and soft in speaking, is like the *forte* and *piano* in music, it only refers to the different degrees of force used in the same key; whereas high and low imply a change of key."—*Sheridan's Elocution*, p. 116. "They are chiefly three: the acquisition of knowledge; the assisting the memory to treasure up this knowledge; or the communicating it to others."—*Ib.* p. 11.

"These kind of knaves I know, which in this plainness
Harbour more craft, and more corrupter ends,
Than twenty silly ducking observants."—*Beauties of Shak.* p. 261.

LESSON XVII.—MANY ERRORS.

"A man will be forgiven, even great errors, in a foreign language; but in his own, even the least slips are justly laid hold of, and ridiculed."—*American Chesterfield*, p. 83. "Let does not only express permission; but praying, exhorting, commanding."—*Lowth's Gram.* p. 41. "*Let*, not only expresses permission, but entreating, exhorting, commanding."—*Murray's Gram.* p. 88; *Ingersoll's*, 135. "That death which is our leaving this world, is nothing else but putting off these bodies."—*Sherlock*. "They differ from the saints recorded both in the Old and New Testaments."—*Newton*. "The nature therefore of relation consists in the referring or comparing two things one to another; from which comparison, one or both comes to be denominated."—*Locke's Essay*, i, 220. "It is not credible, that there hath been any one who through the whole course of their lives will say, that they have kept themselves undefiled with the least spot or stain of sin."—*Witsius*. "If acting conformably to the will of our Creator;—if promoting the welfare of mankind around us;—if securing our own happiness;—are objects of the highest moment:—then we are loudly called upon to cultivate and extend the great interests of religion and virtue."—*Murray's Gram.* i, 278; *Comly's*, 163; *Ingersoll's*, 291. "By the verb being in the plural number, it is supposed that it has a plural nominative, which is not the case. The only nominative to the verb, is, *the officer*: the expression *his guard*, are in the objective case, governed by the preposition *with*; and they cannot consequently form the nominative, or any part of it. The prominent subject, and the true nominative of the verb, and to which the verb peculiarly refers, is *the officer*."—*Murray's Parsing*, Gr. 8vo, ii, 22. "This is another use, that, in my opinion, contributes rather to make a man learned than wise; and is neither capable of pleasing the understanding, or imagination."—ADDISON: *Churchill's Gram.* p. 363. "The work is a dull performance; and is capable of pleasing neither the understanding, nor the imagination."—*Murray's Key,* ii, 210. "I would recommend the Elements of English Grammar, by Mr. Frost. Its plan is after Murray, but his definitions and language is simplified as far as the nature of the subject will admit, to meet the understanding of children. It also embraces more copious examples and exercises in Parsing, than is usual in elementary treatises."—*Hall's Lectures on School-Keeping,* 1st Ed., p. 37. "More rain falls in the first two summer months, than in the first two winter ones: but it makes a much greater show upon the earth, in these than in those; because there is a much slower evaporation." —*Murray's Key,* ii, 139. See *Priestley's Gram.* p. 90. "They often contribute also to the rendering some persons prosperous though wicked; and, which is still worse, to the rewarding some actions though vicious, and punishing other actions though virtuous."— *Butler's Analogy,* p. 92. "From hence, to such a man, arises naturally a secret satisfaction and sense of security, and implicit hope of somewhat further."—*Ib.* p. 93. "So much for the third and last cause of illusion that was taken notice of, arising from the abuse of very general and abstract terms, which is the principal source of all the nonsense that hath been vented by metaphysicians, mystagogues, and theologians."—*Campbell's Rhet.* p. 297. "As to those animals whose use is less common, or who on account of the place which they inhabit, fall less under our observation, as fishes and birds, or whom their diminutive size removes still further from our observation, we generally, in English, employ a single Noun to designate both Genders, Masculine and Feminine."—*Fosdick's De Sacy,* p. 67. "Adjectives may always be distinguished, by their being the word, or words, made use of to describe the quality, or condition, of whatever is mentioned."—*Emmons's Gram.* p. 20. "Adverb signifies a word added to a verb, participle, adjective, or other adverb, to describe or qualify their qualities."—*Ib.* p. 64. "The joining together two such grand objects, and the representing them both as subject, at one moment, to the command of God, produces a noble effect."—*Blair's Rhet.* p. 37. "Twisted columns, for instance, are undoubtedly ornamental; but as they have an appearance of weakness, they always displease when they are made use of to support any part of a building that is massy, and that seems to require a more substantial prop."—*Ib.* p. 49. "Upon a vast number of inscriptions, some upon rocks, some upon stones of a defined shape, is found an Alphabet different from the Greeks, Latins, and Hebrews, and also unlike that of any modern nation."—*Foster's E. Gram.* 8vo, 1850, p. 176.

LESSON XVIII.—MANY ERRORS.

"'The empire of Blefuscu is an island situated to the northeast side of Lilliput, from whence it is parted only by a channel of 800 yards wide.' *Gulliver's Travels.* The ambiguity may be removed thus:—'from whence it is parted by a channel of 800 yards wide only.'"—*Kames, El. of Crit.* ii, 44. "The nominative case is usually the agent or doer, and always the subject of the verb."—*Smith's New Gram.* p. 47. "There is an originality, richness, and variety in his [Spenser's] allegorical personages, which almost vies with the splendor of the ancient mythology."—*Hazlitt's Lect.* p. 68. "As neither the Jewish nor Christian revelation have been universal, and as they have been afforded to a greater or less part of the world at different times; so likewise, at different times, both revelations have had different degrees of evidence."—*Butler's Analogy,* p. 210. "Thus we see, that killing a man with a sword or a hatchet, are looked upon as no distinct species of action: but if the point of the sword first enter the body, it passes for a distinct species, called stabbing."—*Locke's Essay,* p. 314. "If a soul sin, and commit a trespass against the Lord, and lie unto his neighbour in that which was delivered him to keep, or hath deceived his neighbour, or have found that which was lost, and lieth concerning it, and sweareth falsely; in any of all these that a man doeth, sinning therein, then it shall be," &c.—*Lev.* vi, 2. "As the doing and teaching the commandments of God is the great proof of virtue, so the breaking them, and the teaching others to break them, is the great proof of vice."—*Wayland's Moral Science,* p. 281. "In Pope's terrific maltreatment of the latter simile, it is neither true to mind or eye."—*Coleridge's Introd.* p. 14. "And the two brothers were seen, transported with rage and fury, endeavouring like Eteocles and Polynices to plunge their swords into each others' hearts, and to assure themselves of the throne by the death of their rival." —*Goldsmith's Greece,* i, 176. "Is it not plain, therefore, that neither the castle, the planet, nor the cloud, which you see here, are those real ones, which you suppose exist at a distance?"—*Berkley's Alciphron,* p. 166. "I have often wondered how it comes to pass, that every Body should love themselves best, and yet value their neighbours Opinion about themselves more than their own."—*Collier's Antoninus,* p. 226. "VIRTUS ('*Áρετή Virtus*) as well as most of its Species, are all Feminine, perhaps from their Beauty and amiable Appearance."—*Harris's Hermes,* p. 55. "Virtue, with most of its Species, are all Feminine, from their Beauty and amiable Appearance; and so Vice becomes Feminine of Course, as being Virtue's natural opposite."—*British Gram.* p. 97. "Virtue, with most of its Species, is Feminine, and so is Vice, for being Virtue's opposite."—*Buchanan's Gram.* p. 22. "From this deduction, may be easily seen how it comes to pass, that personification makes so great a figure in all compositions, where imagination or passion have any concern."—*Blair's Rhet.* p. 155. "An Article is a word prefixed to a substantive to point them out, and to show how far their signification extends."—*Folker's Gram.* p. 4. 'All men have certain natural, essential, and inherent rights—among which are, the enjoying and defending life and liberty; acquiring, possessing, and protecting property; and, in a word, of seeking and obtaining happiness.'"—*Constitution of New Hampshire.* "From Grammarians who form their ideas, and make their decisions, respecting this part of English Grammar, on the principles and construction of languages, which, in these points, do not suit the peculiar nature of our own, but differ considerably from it, we may naturally expect grammatical schemes that are not very perspicuous, nor perfectly consistent, and which will tend more to perplex than inform the learner."—*Murray's Gram.* p. 68; *Hall's,* 15. "There are, indeed, but very few who know how to be idle and innocent, or have a relish of any pleasures that are not criminal; every diversion they take, is at the expense of some one virtue or another, and their very first step out of business is into vice or folly."—ADDISON: *Blair's Rhet.* p. 201.*

"Hail, holy love! thou word that sums all bliss!
Gives and receives all bliss; fullest when most
Thou givest; spring-head of all felicity!"—*Pollok, C. of T.*, B. v, l. 193.

CHAPTER XIII.—GENERAL RULE.

The following comprehensive canon for the correction of all sorts of nondescript errors in syntax, and the several critical or general notes under it, seem necessary for the completion of my design; which is, to furnish a thorough exposition of the various faults against which the student of English grammar has occasion to be put upon his guard.

GENERAL RULE OF SYNTAX.

In the formation of sentences, the consistency and adaptation of all the words should be carefully observed; and a regular, clear, and correspondent construction should be preserved throughout.

CRITICAL NOTES TO THE GENERAL RULE.

CRITICAL NOTE I.—OF THE PARTS OF SPEECH.

Words that may constitute different parts of speech, must not be left doubtful as to their classification, or to what part of speech they belong.

CRITICAL NOTE II.—OF DOUBTFUL REFERENCE.

The reference of words to other words, or their syntactical relation according to the sense, should never be left doubtful, by any one who means to be understood.

CRITICAL NOTE III.—OF DEFINITIONS.

A definition, in order to be perfect, must include the whole thing or class of things which it pretends to define, and exclude every thing which comes not under the name.

CRITICAL NOTE IV.—OF COMPARISONS.

A comparison is a form of speech which requires some similarity or common property in the things compared; without which, it becomes a solecism.

CRITICAL NOTE V.—OF FALSITIES.

Sentences that convey a meaning manifestly false, should be changed, rejected, or contradicted; because they distort language from its chief end, or only worthy use; which is, to state facts, and to tell the truth.

---

* Faulty as this example is, Dr. Blair says of it: "Nothing can be more elegant, or more finely turned, than this sentence. It is neat, *clear*, and musical. We could hardly *alter one word*, or disarrange one member, without *spoiling* it. Few sentences are to be found, more finished, or more happy."—*Lecture* XX, p. 201. See the six corrections suggested in my Key, and judge whether or not they *spoil* the sentence.—G. B.

CRITICAL NOTE VI.—OF ABSURDITIES.

Absurdities, of every kind, are contrary to grammar, because they are contrary to reason, or good sense, which is the foundation of grammar.

CRITICAL NOTE VII.—OF SELF-CONTRADICTION.

Every writer or speaker should be careful not to contradict himself; for what is self-contradictory, is both null in argument, and bad in style.

CRITICAL NOTE VIII.—OF SENSELESS JUMBLING.

To jumble together words without care for the sense, is an unpardonable negligence, and an abuse of the human understanding.

CRITICAL NOTE IX.—OF WORDS NEEDLESS.

Words that are entirely needless, and especially such as injure or encumber the expression, ought in general to be omitted.

CRITICAL NOTE X.—OF IMPROPER OMISSIONS.

Words necessary to the sense, or even to the melody or beauty of a sentence, ought seldom, if ever, to be omitted.

CRITICAL NOTE XI.—OF LITERARY BLUNDERS.

Grāve blunders made in the name of learning, are the strongest of all certificates against the books which contain them unreproved.

CRITICAL NOTE XII.—OF PERVERSIONS.

Proof-texts in grammar, if not in all argument, should be quoted literally; and even that which needs to be corrected, must never be perverted.

CRITICAL NOTE XIII.—OF AWKWARDNESS.

Awkwardness, or inelegance of expression, is a reprehensible defect in style, whether it violate any of the common rules of syntax or not.

CRITICAL NOTE XIV.—OF IGNORANCE.

Any use of words that implies ignorance of their meaning, or of their proper orthography, is particularly unscholarlike; and, in proportion to the author's pretensions to learning, disgraceful.

CRITICAL NOTE XV.—OF SILLINESS.

Silly remarks and idle truisms are traits of a feeble style, and, when their weakness is positive, or inherent, they ought to be entirely omitted.

CRITICAL NOTE XVI.—OF THE INCORRIGIBLE.

Passages too erroneous for correction, may be criticised, orally or otherwise, and then passed over without any attempt to amend them.*

---

* This Note, as well as all the others, will by-and-by be amply illustrated by citations from authors of sufficient repute to give it some value as a grammatical principle; but one cannot hope such language as is, in reality, incorrigibly bad, will always appear so to the generality of readers. Tastes, habits, principles, judgments, differ; and, where confidence is gained, many utterances are well received, that are neither well considered nor well understood. When a professed critic utters what is incorrect beyond amendment, the fact is the more noteworthy, as his professions are louder, or his standing is more eminent. In a recent preface, deliberately composed for a very comprehensive work on "English Grammar," and designed to allure both young and old to "a thorough and extensive acquaintance with their mother tongue,"—in the studied preface of a learned writer, who has aimed "to furnish not only a text-book for the higher institutions, but also a reference book for teachers, which may give breadth and exactness to their views,"—I find a paragraph of which the following is a part: "Unless men, at least occasionally, bestow their attention upon the science and the laws of the language, they are in some danger, amid the excitements of professional life, of losing the delicacy of their taste and giving sanction to vulgarisms, or to what is worse. On this point, listen to the recent declarations of two leading men in the Senate of the United States, both of whom understand the use of the English language in its power: 'In truth, I must say that, in my opinion, the vernacular tongue of the country has become greatly vitiated, depraved, and corrupted by the style of our Congressional debates.' And the other, in courteous response remarked, 'There is such a thing as an English and a parliamentary vocabulary, and I have never heard a worse, when circumstances called it out, on this side [of] Billingsgate!'"—Fowler's E. Gram. 8vo, 1850, Pref. p. iv.

Now, of these "two leading men," the former was Daniel Webster, who, in a senatorial speech, in the spring of 1850, made such a remark concerning the style of oratory used in Congress. But who replied, or what idea the "courteous response," as here given, can be said to convey, I do not know. The language seems to me both unintelligible and soloecistical; and, therefore, but a fair sample of the Incorrigible. Some intelligent persons,

GENERAL OBSERVATIONS ON THE SYNTAX.

OBS. 1.—In the foregoing code of syntax, the author has taken the parts of speech in their order, and comprised all the general principles of relation, agreement, and government, in twenty-four leading Rules. Of these rules, eight—(namely, the 1st, of *Articles*; the 4th, of *Possessives*; the 9th, of *Adjectives*; the 20th, of *Participles*; the 21st, of *Adverbs*; the 22d, of *Conjunctions*; the 23d, of *Prepositions*; and the 24th, of *Interjections*—) are used only in parsing. The remaining sixteen, because they embrace principles that are sometimes violated in practice, answer the double purpose of parsing and correcting. The Exceptions, of which there are thirty-two, (all occasionally applicable in parsing,) belong to nine different rules, and refer to all the parts of speech, except nouns and interjections. The Notes, of which there are one hundred and fifty-two, are subordinate rules of syntax, not designed to be used in parsing, but formed for the exposition and correction of so many different forms of false grammar. The Observations, of which there are, in this part of the work, without the present series, four hundred and ninety-seven, are designed not only to defend and confirm the doctrines adopted by the author, but to explain the arrangement of words, and whatever is difficult or peculiar in construction.

OBS. 2.—The rules in a system of syntax may be more or less comprehensive, as well as more or less simple or complex; consequently they may, without deficiency or redundance, be more or less numerous. But either complexity or vagueness, as well as redundance or deficiency, is a fault; and, when all these faults are properly avoided, and the two great ends of methodical syntax, *parsing* and *correcting*, are duly answered, perhaps the requisite number of syntactical rules, or grammatic canons, will no longer appear very indeterminate. In the preceding chapters, the essential principles of English syntax are supposed to be pretty fully developed; but there are yet to be exhibited some forms of error, which must be corrected under other heads or maxims, and for the treatment of which the several dogmas of this chapter are added. Completeness in the system, however, does not imply that it must have shown the pupil how to correct every form of language that is amiss; for there may be in composition many errors of such a nature that no rule of grammar can show, either what should be substituted for the faulty expression, or what fashion of amendment may be the most eligible. The inaccuracy may be gross and obvious, but the correction difficult or impossible. Because the sentence may require a change throughout; and a total change is not properly a correction; it is a substitution of something new, for what was, perhaps, in itself incorrigible.

OBS. 3.—The notes which are above denominated *Critical* or *General*, are not all of them obviously different in kind from the other notes; but they all are such as could not well have been placed in any of the earlier chapters of the book. The *General Rule of Syntax*, since it is not a canon to be used in parsing, but one that is to be applied only in the correcting of false syntax, might seem perhaps to belong rather to this order of notes; but I have chosen to treat it with some peculiar distinction, because it is not only more comprehensive than any other rule or note, but is in one respect more important; it is the rule which will be cited for the correction of the greatest number and variety of errors. Being designed to meet every possible form of inaccuracy in the mere construction of sentences,—or, at least, every corrigible solecism by which any principle of syntax can be violated,—it necessarily includes almost all the other rules and notes. It is too broad to convey very definite instruction, and therefore ought not in general to be applied where a more particular rule or note is clearly applicable. A few examples, not properly coming under any other head, will serve to show its use and application: such examples are given, in great abundance, in the false syntax below. If, in some of the instances selected, this rule is applied to faults that might as well have been corrected by some other, the choice, in such cases, is deemed of little or no importance.

OBS. 4.—The imperfection of *ancient* writing, especially in regard to division and punctuation, has left the syntactical relation of words, and also the sense of passages, in no few instances, uncertain; and has consequently made, where the text has been thought worthy of it, an abundance of difficult work for translators, critics, and commentators. Rules of grammar, now made and observed, as they ought to be, may free the compositions of this, or a future age, from similar embarrassments; and it is both just and useful, to test our authors by them, criticising or correcting their known blunders according to the present rules of accurate writing. But the readers and expounders of what has come to us from remote time, can be rightly guided only by such principles and facts as have the stamp of creditable antiquity. Hence there are, undoubtedly, in books, some errors and defects which have outlived the *time in which*, and the *authority by which*, they might have been corrected. As we have no right to make a man say that which he himself never said or intended to say, so we have in fact none to fix a positive meaning upon his language, without knowing for a certainty what he meant by it. Reason, or good sense, which, as I have suggested, is the foundation of grammar and of all good writing, is indeed a perpetual as well as a universal principle; but, since the exercises of our reason must, from the very

whom I have asked to interpret it, think, as Webster had accused our Congress of corrupting the English language, the respondent meant to accuse the British Parliament of doing the same thing in a greater degree,—of descending yet lower into the vileness of slang. But this is hardly a probable conjecture. Webster might be right in acknowledging a very depraving abuse of the tongue in the two Houses of Congress; but could it be "courteous," or proper, for the answerer to jump the Atlantic, and pounce upon the English Lords and Commons, as a set of worse corrupters?

The gentleman begins with saying, "There *is* such a *thing*"—as if he meant to describe some *one* thing; and proceeds with saying, "as *an* English *and* a parliamentary vocabulary," in which phrase, by repeating the article, he speaks of *two* "*things*"—*two vocabularies*; then goes on, "and I have never heard *a worse!*" A worse *what?* Does he mean "*a worse vocabulary?*" If so, what sense has "*vocabulary?*" And, again, "a worse" *than* what? Where and what is this "*thing*" which is so bad that the leading Senator has "never heard a worse?" Is it some "*vocabulary*," both "English and parliamentary?" If *so*, whose? If not, what else is it? Lest the wisdom of this oraculous "declaration" "be lost to the public through the defects of its syntax,—and lest more than one rhetorical critic seem hereby "in some danger" of "giving sanction to" *nonsense*,—it may be well for Professor Fowler, in his next edition, to present some elucidation of this short but remarkable passage, which he values so highly!

nature of the faculty, be limited to what we know and understand, we are not competent to positive correction, or to the sure translation, of what is obscure and disputable in the stand books of antiquity.

OBS 5.—Let me cite an example: "For all this I considered in my heart, even to declare this, that the righteous, and the wise, and their works, are in the hand of God: no man know either love or hatred *by* all *that is* before them. All *things come* alike to all."—*Ecclesiastes*, ii Here is, doubtless, *one* error which any English scholar may point out or correct. The pron: "*them*" should be *him*, because its intended antecedent appears to be "*man*," and not "*righteous and the wise*," going before. But are there not *other* faults in the version? The com mon French Bible, in this place, has the following import: "Surely I have applied my heart to that, and to unfold all this; *to wit*, that the righteous and the wise, and their actions, *are* at t hand of God and love and hatred; *and that* men know nothing of all *that which is* before the All *happens* equally to all." The Latin Vulgate gives this sense: "All these things have I a sidered in my heart, that I might understand them accurately: the righteous and the wise, a their works, *are* in the hand of God; and yet man doth not know, whether by love or by hr he may be worthy: but all things in the future are kept uncertain, so that all may happen : to the righteous man and to the wicked." In the Greek of the Septuagint, the introductory = bers of this passage are left at the end of the preceding chapter, and are literally thus: "that this I received into my heart, and my heart understood all this." The rest, commencing : chapter, is as follows: "For the righteous and the wise and their works *are* in the hand of (a and indeed both love and hatred man knoweth not: all things before their face *are* vanity to a Now, which of these several readings is the nearest to what Solomon meant by the original t or which is the farthest from it, and therefore the most faulty, I leave it to men more learned t myself to decide; but, certainly, there is no *inspired authority* in any of them, but *in so far* *they convey the sense which he really intended*. And if his meaning had not been, by some in fection in the oldest expression we have of it, *obscured and partly lost*, there could be n: cause nor excuse for these discrepancies. I say this with no willingness to depreciate the cre authority of the Holy Scriptures, which are for the most part clear in their import, and very translated into English, as well as into other languages.

IMPROPRIETIES FOR CORRECTION.
FALSE SYNTAX UNDER THE GENERAL RULE.
LESSON I.—ARTICLES.

(1.) "An article is a part of speech placed before nouns."—*Comly's Gram.* p. 11.

[FORMULE.—Not proper, because the article *an* is here inconsistent with the term "*part of speech*;" fr text declares one thing of a kind to be the whole kind. But, according to the General Rule of Syntax. "la formation of sentences, the consistency and adaptation of all the words should be carefully observed regular, clear, and correspondent construction should be preserved throughout." The sentence may be rected in two ways, thus: "*The article is a part of speech placed before nouns;*"—or better, "*An article word placed before nouns.*"*]

(2.) "An article is a part of speech used to limit nouns."—*Gilbert's Gram.* p.
(3.) "An article is a part of speech set before nouns to fix their vague Signification." *Ash's Gram.* p. 18. (4.) "An adjective is a part of speech used to describe a noun."—*G bert's Gram.* p. 19. (5.) "A pronoun is a part of speech used instead of a noun."—*J*. and *Weld's Gram.* pp. 30 and 50; *Abridg.* pp. 29 and 46. (6.) "A Pronoun is a Par Speech which is often used instead of a Noun Substantive common, and supplies the W of a Noun proper."—*British Gram.* p. 102; *Buchanan's Gram.* p. 29. (7.) "A verb i part of speech, which signifies *to be, to do*, or *to be acted upon.*"—*Merchant's School G* p. 17. (8.) "A verb is a part of speech, which signifies *to be, to act*, or *to receive* or *act* —*Comly's Gram.* p. 11. (9.) "A verb is a part of speech by which any thing is asserted. *Weld's Gram.* p. 50; *Abridg.* 46 and 58. (10.) "A verb is a part of speech which ex action, or existence, in a direct manner."—*Gilbert's Gram.* p. 20. (11.) "A participle part of speech derived from a verb, and expresses action or existence in an indirect ma ner."—*Ibid.* (12.) "A Participle is a Part of Speech derived from a Verb, and den being, doing, or suffering, and implies Time, as a Verb does."—*British Gram.* p. 139; F *chanan's*, p. 46. (13.) "An adverb is a part of speech used to add to the meaning of ve adjectives, and participles."—*Gilbert's Gram.* p. 20. (14.) "An adverb is an indeclina part of speech, added to a verb, adjective, or other adverb, to express some circumstan quality, or manner of their signification."—*Adam's Gram.* p. 142; *Gould's*, 147. (15.) " Adverb is a part of speech joined to a verb, an Adjective, a Participle, and sometime another Adverb, to express the quality or circumstance of it."—*Ash's Gram* p. 47. "An Adverb is a part of speech joined to a Verb, Adjective, Participle, and sometime another Adverb, to express some circumstances respecting it."—*Beck's Gram.* p. 23. "An Adverb is a Part of Speech which is joined to a Verb, Adjective, Participle, or to other Adverb to express some Modification, or Circumstance, Quality, or Manner of their

* As a mere assertion, this example is here sufficiently corrected; but, as a *definition*, (for which the so b probably intended it,) it is deficient; and consequently, in that sense, is still inaccurate. I would also ob that most of the subsequent examples under the present head, contain other errors than that for which the here introduced; and, of some of them, the faults are, in my opinion, very many: for example, the a definitions of an *adverb*, cited below. Lindley Murray's definition of this part of speech is not inserted a these, because I had elsewhere criticised that. So too of his faulty definition of a *conjunction*. See the I duction, Chap. X, paragraphs 26 and 28. See also *Corrections in the Key*, under Note 10th to Rule 1st.

fication."—*Buchanan's Gram.* p. 61. (18.) "An Adverb is a part of speech added to
a verb (whence the name), and sometimes even to another word."—*Bucke's Gram.* p. 7
.) "A conjunction is a part of speech used to connect words and sentences."—*Gilbert*
p. 29; *Weld's*, 51. (20.) "A Conjunction is a part of speech that joins words or
sentences together."—*Ask's Gram.* p. 48. (21.) "A Conjunction is that part of speech
which connect sentences, or parts of sentences, or single words."—*Blair's Gram.* p. 41
.) "A Conjunction is a part of speech, that is used principally to connect sentences, so
out of two, three, or more, sentences, to make one."—*Bucke's Gram.* p. 28. (23.) "A
conjunction is a part of speech that is chiefly used to connect sentences, joining two or more
simple sentences into one compound sentence: it sometimes connects only words."—*Kirk-*
's Gram. P. 118. (24.) "A Conjunction is a Part of Speech which joins Sentences
gether, and shews the Manner of their Dependance upon one another."—*British Gram.*
163; *Buchanan's*, P. 64; *E. Devis's*, 103. (25.) "A preposition is a part of Speech used to
how the relation between other words."—*Gilbert's Gram.* p. 20. (26.) "A Preposition is
part of speech which serves to connect words and show the relation between them."—
Bruce's El. of Gram. P. 42. (27.) "A preposition is a part of speech used to connect words
and show their relation."—*Weld's Gram.* p. 51; *Abridg.* 47. (28.) "A preposition is that
art of speech which shows the position of persons or things, or the relation that one noun
t pronoun bears toward another."—*Blair's Gram.* p. 40. (29.) "A Preposition is a Part of
Reference to each other."—*British Gram.* p. 165; *Buchanan's*, p. 65. (30.) "An interjection
a part of speech used to any other Parts of Speech serves to shew their State, Relation
an interjection is a part of speech used in giving utterance to some sudden feeling or emo-
speech, which being added to express sudden passion or emotion."—*Gilbert's Gram.* p. 20. (31.)
.)."—*Weld's Gram.* pp. 49 and 51; *Abridg.* 44 and 47. (32.) "An Interjection is that part of
speech which denotes any sudden affection or emotion of the mind."—*Blair's Gram.* p. 42.
.) "An Interjection is a Part of Speech thrown into Discourse, and denotes some sud-
en Passion or Emotion of the Soul."—*British Gram.* p. 172; *Buchanan's*, p. 67.
(34.) "A scene might tempt some peaceful sage
        To rear him a lone hermitage."—*Union Poems*, p. 89.
(35.) "Not all the storms that shake the pole
        Can e'er disturb thy halcyon soul,
        And smooth th' unaltered brow."—*Day's Gram.* p. 78; *E. Reader*, 230.

LESSON II.—NOUNS.

"The thrones of every monarchy felt the shock."—*Frelinghuysen.*

[FORMULE.—Not proper, because the plural noun *thrones* has not a clear and regular construction, adapted to
the author's meaning. But, according to the General Rule of Syntax, "In the formation of sentences, the
consistency and adaptation of all the words should be carefully observed; and a regular, clear, and correspondent construction should be preserved throughout." The sentence may be corrected thus: "The throne of
very monarchy felt the shock."]

"These principles ought to be deeply impressed upon the minds of every American."—
Webster's Essays, p. 44. "The word *church* and *shire* are radically the same."—*Ib.* p. 254.
They may not, in their present form, be readily accommodated to every circumstance belonging to the possessive cases of nouns."—*L. Murray's Gram.* 8vo, p. 53. "*Will*, in the
second and third person, only foretels."—*Ib.* p. 88. "Which seem to form the true distin-
tion between the subjunctive and the indicative moods."—*Ib.* P. 208. "The very general
approbation, which this performance of Walker has received from the public."—*Ib.* p. 261.
"Lest she carry her improvements this way too far."—*CAMPBELL*: *Ib.* p. 371. "These are
as extravagant, and by this means became poor and despicable."—*Murray's Key, Ivo. p.* ...
"We should entertain no prejudices against simple and rustic persons."—*Ib.* p. ...
"These are indeed the foundations of all solid merit."—*Blair's Rhet.* p. 175. "...
embellishment, by means of musical cadence, figures, or other parts of speech."—*Ib.* p. ...
"If he is at no pains to engage us by the employment of figures, musical arrangement, ...
any other art of writing."—*Ib.* p. 181. "The most eminent of the most ... ...
beautifully described than the death of old Priam."—*Ib.* P. 418. "...
... author of the book of Job, David and Isaiah."—*Ib.* P. ... "Nothing ... ...
Gram. p. 10. "How many *s* would goodness then end with ... ...
... a noun, the name of a thing or creature."—*Kirkham's Gram.*, Part ii, p. 5. ...
to every living creature."—*Bicknell's Gram.*, Part ii, p. 5. ...
be accommodated to the human figure."—*Kames, El. of Crit.* Vol. i. p. ...
"Whatever more than a simile has to be founded on low or familiar ... ...
... p. 450. "The mint and secretary of state's offices are near ... ...
emblem more than a simile has not from the Greek, it has from the ... ...
"The scenes of dead and still life are apt to pall upon ... ...
Thomas Aquinas and Duns Scotus, the angelical and the ... ...
... the scholastic constellation."—*Literary Hist.*—*Murray* p. 244. ...
... the angelical and ... ...
Bacon's, 13; *Fisk's*, 58; *Greenleaf's*, 21. "The ... ...
... distinguishing the sex."—*Murray's Gram.* ... ...
... sex."—*Smith's New Gram.* p. 44. "In English ... ...

methods of distinguishing sex."—*Jaudon's Gram.* p. 26. "There are three ways of distinguishing the sex."—*Lennie's Gram.* p. 10 ; *Picket's*, 26 ; *Bullions's*, 10. "There are three ways of distinguishing sex."—*Merchant's School Gram.* p. 26. "Gender is distinguished in three ways."—*Maunder's Gram.* p. 2. "Neither discourse in general, nor poetry in particular, can be called altogether imitative arts."—*Blair's Rhet.* p. 51.

"Do we for this the gods and conscience brave,
That one may rule and make the rest a slave ?"—*Rowe's Lucan,* B. ii, l. 96.

LESSON III.—ADJECTIVES.

"There is a deal of more heads, than either heart or horns."—*Barclay's Works,* i, 234.

[FORMULE.—Not proper, because the adjective *more* has not a clear and regular construction, adapted to the author's meaning. But, according to the General Rule of Syntax, "In the formation of sentences, the consistency and adaptation of all the words should be carefully observed ; and a regular, clear, and correspondent construction should be preserved throughout." The sentence may be corrected thus : "There is a deal more of heads, than *of* either heart or horns."]

"For, of all villains, I think he has the wrong name."—*Bunyan's P. P.* p. 86. "Of all the men that I met in my pilgrimage, he, I think bears the wrong name."—*Ib.* p. 84. "I am surprised to see so much of the distribution, and technical terms of the Latin grammar, retained in the grammar of our tongue."—*Priestley's Gram., Pref.,* p. vi. "Nor did the Duke of Burgundy bring him the smallest assistance."—HUME: *Priestley's Gram.* p. 178. "Else he will find it difficult to make one obstinate believe him."—*Brightland's Gram.* p. 243. "Are there any adjectives which form the degrees of comparison peculiar to themselves ?"—*Infant School Gram.* p. 46. "Yet the verbs are all of the indicative mood."—*Lowth's Gram.* p. 33. "The word *candidate* is in the absolute case."—*L. Murray's Gram.* 8vo, p. 155. "An Iambus has the first syllable unaccented, and the latter accented."—*Russell's Gram.* p. 108 ; *Smith's New Gram.* 188. "A Dactyl has the first syllable accented, and the two latter unaccented."—*L. Murray,* p. 253 ; *Bullions's E. Gram.* 170 ; *Smith's*, 188 ; *Kirkham's,* 219 ; *Guy's,* 120 ; *Blair's,* 118 ; *Merchant's,* 167 ; *Russell's,* 109. "It is proper to begin with a capital the first word of every book, chapter, letter, note, or any other piece of writing."—*L. Murray,* p. 284 ; *R. C. Smith's New Gram.* 192 ; *Ingersoll's,* 295 ; *Comly's,* 166 ; *Merchant's,* 14 ; *Greenleaf's,* 42 ; *D. C. Allen's,* 85 ; *Fisk's,* 159 ; *Bullions's,* 158 ; *Kirkham's,* 219 ; *Hiley's,* 119 ; *Weld's Abridged,* 16 ; *Bullions's Analyt. and Pract.,* 16 ; *Fowler's E. Gr.,* 674. "Five and seven make twelve, and one makes thirteen."—*Murray's Key,* 8vo, p. 227. "I wish to cultivate a farther acquaintance with you."—*Ib.* p. 272. "Let us consider the proper means to effect our purpose."—*Ib.* p. 276. "Yet they are of such a similar nature, as readily to mix and blend."—*Blair's Rhet.* p. 48. "The Latin is formed on the same model, but more imperfect."—*Ib.* p. 83. "I know very well how much pains have been taken."—*Sir W. Temple.* "The mananagement of the breath requires a good deal of care."—*Blair's Rhet.* p. 331. "Because the mind, during such a momentary stupefaction, is in a good measure, if not totally, insensible."—*Kames, El. of Crit.* Vol. i, p. 221. "Motives alone of reason and interest are not sufficient."—*Ib.* Vol. i, p. 232. "To render the composition distinct in its parts, and striking on the whole."—*Ib.* Vol. ii, p. 333. "*A* and *an* are named indefinite because they denote some one thing of a kind."—*Maunder's Gram.* p. 1. "*The* is named definite, because it points out some particular thing."—*Ibid.* "So much depends upon the proper construction of sentences, that, in every sort of composition, we cannot be too strict in our attention to it."—*Blair's Rhet.* p. 103. "All sort of declamation and public speaking, was carried on by them."—*Ib.* p. 123. "The first has on many occasions, a sublimity to which the latter never attains."—*Ib.* p. 440. "When the words *therefore, consequently, accordingly,* and the like are used in connexion with other conjunctions, they are adverbs."—*Kirkham's Gram.* p. 88. "Rude nations make little or no allusions to the productions of the arts."—*Jamieson's Rhet.* p. 10. "While two of her maids knelt on either side of her."—*Mirror,* xi, 307. "The third personal pronouns differ from each other in meaning and use, as follows."—*Bullions, Lat. Gram.* p. 65. "It was happy for the state, that Fabius continued in the command with Minucius: the former's phlegm was a check upon the latter's vivacity."—*L. Murray's Gram.* 8vo, p. 57. "If it should be objected that the words *must* and *ought,* in the preceding sentences, are all in the present tense."—*Ib.* p. 108. "But it will be well if you turn to them, every now and then."—*Bucke's Classical Gram.* p. 6. "That every part should have a dependence on, and mutually contribute to support each other."—*Rollin's Hist.* ii, 115. "The phrase, '*Good, my Lord,*' is not common, and low."—*Priestley's Gram.* p. 110.

"That brother should not war with brother,
And worry and devour each other."—*Cowper.*

LESSON IV.—PRONOUNS.

"If I can contribute to your and my country's glory."—*Goldsmith.*

[FORMULE.—Not proper, because the pronoun *your* has not a clear and regular construction, adapted to the author's meaning. But, according to the General Rule of Syntax, "In the formation of sentences, the consistency and adaptation of all the words should be carefully observed ; and a regular, clear, and correspondent construction should be preserved throughout." The sentence, having a doubtful or double meaning, may be corrected in two ways, thus : "If I can contribute to *our* country's glory ;"—or, "If I can contribute to *your* glory and that of my country."]

"As likewise of the several subjects, which have in effect each their verb."—*Lowth's Gram.* p. 120. "He is likewise required to make examples himself."—*J. Flint's Gram.* p. 3. "If the emphasis be placed wrong, we shall pervert and confound the meaning wholly."—*Murray's Gram.* 8vo, p. 242. "If the emphasis be placed wrong, we pervert and confound the meaning wholly."—*Blair's Rhet.* p. 330. "It was this that characterized the great men of antiquity; it is this, which must distinguish the moderns who would tread in their steps."—*Ib.* p. 341. "I am a great enemy to implicit faith, as well the Popish, as Presbyterian, who in that are much what alike."—*Barclay's Works,* iii, 280. "Will he thence dare to say the apostle held another Christ than he that died?"—*Ib.* iii, 414. "What need you be anxious about this event?"—*Collier's Antoninus,* p. 188. "If a substantive can be placed after the verb, it is active."—*Alex. Murray's Gram.* p. 31. "When we see bad men honoured and prosperous in the world, it is some discouragement to virtue."—*L. Murray's Key,* 8vo, p. 224. "It is a happiness to young persons, when they are preserved from the snares of the world, as in a garden enclosed."—*Ib.* p. 171. "The court of Queen Elizabeth, which was but another name for prudence and economy."—*Bullions, E. Gram.* p. 24. "It is no wonder if such a man did not shine at the court of Queen Elizabeth, *who* was but another name for prudence and economy. Here *which* ought to be used, and not *who.*"—*Priestley's Gram.* p. 99; *Fowler's,* §488. "Better thus; Whose name was but another word for prudence, &c."—*Murray's Gram.* p. 157; *Fisk's,* 115; *Ingersoll's,* 221; *Smith's,* 133; and others. "A Defective verb is one that wants some of its parts. They are chiefly the *Auxiliary* and *Impersonal* verbs."—*Bullions, E. Gram.* p. 31; *Old Editions,* 32. "Some writers have given our moods a much greater extent than we have assigned to them."—*Murray's Gram.* 8vo, p. 67. "The Personal Pronouns give information which no other words are capable of conveying."—*M'Culloch's Gram.* p. 37. "When the article *a, an,* or *the* precedes the participle, it also becomes a noun."—*Merchant's School Gram.* p. 93. "There is a preference to be given to some of these, which custom and judgment must determine."—*Murray's Gram.* 8vo, p. 107. "Many writers affect to subjoin to any word the preposition with which it is compounded, or the idea of which it implies."—*Ib.* p. 200; *Priestley's Gram.* 157.

"Say, dost thou know Vectidius?—Who, the wretch
Whose lands beyond the Sabines largely stretch?"—*Dryden's IV Sat. of Pers.*

LESSON V.—VERBS.

"We would naturally expect, that the word *depend,* would require *from* after it."—*Murray's Gram.* 8vo, p. 201. "A dish which they pretend to be made of emerald."—*Murray's Key,* 8vo, p. 198. "For the very nature of a sentence implies one proposition to be expressed."—*Blair's Rhet.* p. 106. "Without a careful attention to the sense, we would be naturally led, by the rules of syntax, to refer it to the rising and setting of the sun."—*Ib.* p. 105. "For any rules that can be given, on this subject, are very general."—*Ib.* p. 125. "He is in the right, if eloquence were what he conceives it to be."—*Ib.* p. 234. "There I would prefer a more free and diffuse manner."—*Ib.* p. 178. "Yet that they also agreed and resembled one another, in certain qualities."—*Ib.* p. 73. "But since he must restore her, he insists to have another in her place."—*Ib.* p. 431. "But these are far from being so frequent or so common as has been supposed."—*Ib.* p. 445. "We are not misled to assign a wrong place to the pleasant or painful feelings."—*Kames, El. of Crit.,* Introd., p. xviii. "Which are of greater importance than is commonly thought."—*Ib.* Vol. ii, p. 92. "Since these qualities are both coarse and common, lets find out the mark of a man of probity."—*Collier's Antoninus,* p. 40. "Cicero did what no man had ever done before him, draw up a treatise of consolation for himself."—*Life of Cicero.* "Then there can be no other Doubt remain of the Truth."—*Brightland's Gram.* p. 245. "I have observed some satirists use the term."—*Bullions's Prin. of E. Gram.* p. 79. "Such men are ready to despond, or commence enemies."—*Webster's Essays,* p. 83. "Common nouns express names common to many things."—*Infant School Gram.* p. 18. "To make ourselves be heard by one to whom we address ourselves."—*Blair's Rhet.* p. 328. "That, in reading poetry, he may be the better able to judge of its correctness, and relish its beauties."—*Murray's Gram.* p. 252. "On the stretch to comprehend, and keep pace with the author."—*Blair's Rhet.* p. 150. "For it might have been sold for more than three hundred pence, and have been given to the poor."—*Mark,* xiv, 5. "He is a beam that is departed, and left no streak of light behind."—OSSIAN: *Kames, El. of Crit.* ii, 262. "No part of this incident ought to have been represented, but reserved for a narrative."—*Kames, El. of Crit.* ii, 294. "The rulers and people debauching themselves, brings ruin on a country."—*Ware's Gram.* p. 9. "When *Doctor, Miss, Master,* &c. is prefixed to a name, the last of the two words is commonly made plural; as, the *Doctor Nettletons*—the two *Miss Hudsons.*"—*Alex. Murray's Gram.* p. 106. "Wherefore that field was called, The field of blood, unto this day."—*Matt.* xxvii, 8. "To comprehend the situations of other countries, which perhaps may be necessary for him to explore."—*Brown's Estimate,* ii, 111. "We content ourselves, now, with fewer conjunctive particles than our ancestors did."—*Priestley's Gram.* p. 139. "And who will be chiefly liable to make mistakes where others have been mistaken before them."

—*Ib.* p. 156. "The voice of nature and revelation unites."—*Wayland's Moral Science*, 3d Ed., p. 307.

"This adjective you see we can't admit,
But chang'd to *worse*, will make it just and fit."—*Tobitt's Gram.* p. 63.

LESSON VI.—PARTICIPLES.

"Its application is not arbitrary, depending on the caprice of readers."—*Murray's Gram.* 8vo, Vol. i, p. 246. "This is the more expedient, from the work's being designed for the benefit of private learners."—*Ib.* Vol. ii, p. 161. "A man, he tells us, ordered by his will, to have erected for him a statue."—*Blair's Rhet.* p. 106. "From some likeness too remote, and laying too far out of the road of ordinary thought."—*Ib.* p. 146. "Money is a fluid in the commercial world, rolling from hand to hand."—*Webster's Essays*, p. 123. "He pays much attention to learning and singing songs."—*Ib.* p. 246. "I would not be understood to consider singing songs as criminal."—*Ibid.* "It is a decided case by the Great Master of writing."—*Preface to Waller*, p. 5. "Did they ever bear a testimony against writing books?"—*Bates's Misc. Repository*. "Exclamations are sometimes mistaking for interrogations."—*Hist. of Printing*, 1770. "Which cannot fail proving of service."—*Smith's Printer's Gram.* "Hewn into such figures as would make them easily and firmly incorporated."—BEATTIE: *Murray's Gram.* i, 126. "Following the rule and example are practical inductive questions."—*J. Flint's Gram.* p. 3. "I think there will be an advantage in my having collected examples from modern writings."—*Priestley's Gram.*, Pref., p. xi. "He was eager of recommending it to his fellow-citizens."—HUME: *ib.* p. 160. "The good lady was careful of serving me of every thing."—*Ibid.* "No revelation would have been given, had the light of nature been sufficient in such a sense, as to render one not wanting and useless."—*Butler's Analogy*, p. 155. "Description, again is the raising in the mind the conception of an object by means of some arbitrary or instituted symbols."—*Blair's Rhet.* p. 52. "Disappointing the expectation of the hearers, when they look for our being done."—*Ib.* p. 326. "There is a distinction which, in the use of them, is deserving of attention."—*Maunder's Gram.* p. 15. "A model has been contrived, which is not very expensive, and easily managed."—*Education Reporter*. "The conspiracy was the more easily discovered, from its being known to many."—*Murray's Key*, ii, 191. "That celebrated work had been nearly ten years published, before its importance was at all understood."—*Ib.* p. 220. "The sceptre's being ostensibly grasped by a female hand, does not reverse the general order of government."—*West's Letters to a Lady*, p. 43. "I have hesitated signing the Declaration of Sentiments."—*Liberator*, x, 16. "The prolonging of men's lives when the world needed to be peopled, and now shortening them when that necessity hath ceased to exist."—*Brown's Divinity*, p. 7. "Before the performance commences, we have displayed the insipid formalities of the prelusive scene."—*Kirkham's Elocution*, p. 23. "It forbade the lending of money, or sending goods, or in any way embarking capital in transactions connected with that foreign traffic."—LORD BROUGHAM: *B. and F. Anti-Slavery Reporter*, Vol. ii, p. 218. "Even abstract ideas have sometimes conferred upon them the same important prerogative."—*Jamieson's Rhet.* p. 171. "Like other terminations, *ment* changes *y* into *i*, when preceded by a consonant."—*Walker's Rhyming Dict.* p. xiii; *Murray's Gram.* p. 24; *Ingersoll's*, 11. "The term *proper* is from being *proper*, that is, *peculiar* to the individual bearing the name. The term *common* is from being *common* to every individual comprised in the class."—*Fowler's E. Gram.* 8vo, 1850, § 139.

"Thus oft by mariners are shown (Unless the men of Kent are liars)
Earl Godwin's castles overflown, And palace-roofs, and steeple-spires."—*Swift*, p. 313.

LESSON VII.—ADVERBS.

"He spoke to every man and woman there."—*Murray's Gram.* p. 220; *Fisk's*, 147. "Thought and language act and react upon each other mutually."—*Blair's Rhet.* p. 120; *Murray's Exercises*, 133. "Thought and expression act upon each other mutually."—See *Murray's Key*, p. 264. "They have neither the leisure nor the means of attaining scarcely any knowledge, except what lies within the contracted circle of their several professions."—*Murray's Gram.* 8vo, p. 359. "Before they are capable of understanding but little, or indeed any thing of many other branches of education."—*Olney's Introd. to Geog.* p. 5. "There is not more beauty in one of them than in another."—*Murray's Key*, ii, 275. "Which appear not constructed according to any certain rule."—*Blair's Rhet.* p. 47. "The vehement manner of speaking became not so universal."—*Ib.* p. 61. "All languages, however, do not agree in this mode of expression."—*Ib.* p. 77. "The great occasion of setting aside this particular day."—ATTERBURY: *ib.* p. 294. "He is much more promising now than formerly."—*Murray's Gram.* Vol. ii, p. 4. "They are placed before a participle, independently on the rest of the sentence."—*Ib.* Vol. ii, p. 21. "This opinion appears to be not well considered."—*Ib.* Vol. i, p. 153; *Ingersoll's*, 249. "Precision in language merits a full explication; and the more, because distinct ideas are, perhaps, not commonly formed about it."—*Blair's Rhet.* p. 94. "In the more sublime parts of poetry, he [Pope] is not so distinguished."—*Ib.* p. 403. "How far the author was altogether happy in the choice of his subject, may be questioned."—*Ib.* p. 450. "But here also there s a great error in the common practice."—*Webster's Essays*, p. 7. "This order is the very order of the human mind, which makes things we are sensible of,‛ a means to come at those that are not so."—*Formey's Belles-Lettres, Foreman's Version*, p. 113. "Now, Who is not Discouraged, and Fears Want, when he has no Money?"—*Divine Right of Tythes*, p. 23. "Which the Authors of this work, consider of but little or no use."—*Wilbur and Livingston's Gram.* p. 6. "And here indeed the distinction between these two classes begins not to be clear."—*Blair's Rhet.* p. 152. "But this is a manner which deserves not to be imitated."—*Ib.* p. 180. "And in this department a person never effects so little, as when he attempts too much."—*Campbell's Rhet.* p. 173; *Murray's Gram.* 8vo, p. 367. "The verb that signifies merely being, is neuter."—*Dr. Ash's Gram.* p. 27. "I hope not much to tire those whom I shall not happen to please."—*Rambler*, No. 1. "Who were utterly unable to pronounce some letters, and others very indistinctly."—*Sheridan's Elocution*, p. 32. "The learner may point out the active, passive, and neuter verbs in the following examples, and state the reasons why."—*C. Adams's Gram.* p. 27. "These words are most always conjunctions."—*S. Barrett's Revised Gram.* p. 73.

"How fluent nonsense trickles from his tongue !
How sweet the periods, neither said, nor sung !"—*Dunciad.*

LESSON VIII.—CONJUNCTIONS.

"Who at least either knew not, nor loved to make, a distinction."—*Dr. Murray's Hist. of Europ. Lang.* i, 322. "It is childish in the last degree, if this become the ground of estranged affection."—*L. Murray's Key*, ii, 228. "When the regular or the irregular verb is to be preferred, p. 107."—*Murray's Index, Gram.* ii, 296. "The books were to have been sold, as this day."—*Priestley's E. Gram.* p. 138. "Do, an if you will."—*Beauties of Shak.* p. 105. "If a man had a positive idea of infinite, either duration or space, he could add two infinites together."—*Murray's Gram.* 8vo, p. 174. "None shall more willingly agree and advance the same nor I."—EARL OF MORTON : *Robertson's Scotland*, ii, 428. "That it cannot be but hurtful to continue it."—*Barclay's Works*, i, 192. "A conjunction joins words and sentences."—*Beck's Gram.* pp. 4 and 25. "The copulative conjunction connects words and sentences together and continues the sense."—*Frost's El. of Gram.* p. 42. "The Conjunction Copulative serves to connect or continue a sentence, by expressing an addition, a supposition, a cause, &c."—*Murray's Gram.* 8vo, i, 123. "All Construction is either true or apparent ; or in other Words just and figurative."—*Buchanan's Syntax*, p. 130 ; *British Gram.* 234. "But the divine character is such that none but a divine hand could draw."—*The Friend*, Vol. v, p. 72. "‛ Who is so mad, that, on inspecting the heavens, is insensible of a God ?'—CICERO :"—*Dr. Gibbons.* "It is now submitted to an enlightened public, with little desire on the part of the Author, than its general utility."—*Town's Analysis*, 9th Ed., p. 5. "This will sufficiently explain the reason that so many provincials have grown old in the capital, without making any change in their original dialect."—*Sheridan's Elocution*, p. 51. "Of these they had chiefly three in general use, which were denominated accents, and the term used in the plural number."—*Ib.* p. 55. "And this is one of the chief reasons, that dramatic representations have ever held the first rank amongst the diversions of mankind."—*Ib.* p. 95. "Which is the chief reason that public reading is in general so disgusting."—*Ib.* p. 96. "At the same time that they learn to read."—*Ib.* p. 96. "He is always to pronounce his words exactly with the same accent that he speaks them."—*Ib.* p. 98. "In order to know what another knows, and in the same manner that he knows it."—*Ib.* p. 136. "For the same reason that it is in a more limited state assigned to the several tribes of animals."—*Ib.* p. 145. "Were there masters to teach this, in the same manner as other arts are taught."—*Ib.* p. 169.

"Whose own example strengthens all his laws ;
And is himself that great Sublime he draws."—*Pope, on Crit.* l. 680.

LESSON IX.—PREPOSITIONS.

"The word *so* has, sometimes, the same meaning with *also, likewise, the same.*"—*Priestley's Gram.* p. 137. "The verb *use* relates not to pleasures of the imagination, but to the terms of fancy and imagination, which he was to employ as synonymous."—*Blair's Rhet.* p. 197. "It never can view, clearly and distinctly, above one object at a time."—*Ib.* p. 94. "This figure [Euphemism] is often the same with the Periphrasis."—*Adam's Gram.* p. 247 ; *Gould's*, 238. "All the between time of youth and old age."—*Walker's Particles*, p. 83. "When one thing is said to act upon, or do something to another."—*Lowth's Gram.* p. 70. "Such a composition has as much of meaning in it, as a mummy has life."—*Journal of Lit. Convention*, p. 91. "That young men of from fourteen to eighteen were not the best judges."—*Ib.* p. 130. "This day is a day of trouble, and of rebuke, and blasphemy."—*2 Kings*, xix, 3. "Blank verse has the same pauses and accents with rhyme."—*Kames, El. of Crit.* ii, 119. "In prosody, long syllables are distinguished by (¯), and short ones by what is called *breve* (˘)."—*Bucke's Gram.* p. 22. "Sometimes both articles are left out, especially in poetry."—*Ib.* p. 26. "In the following example, the pronoun and participle are omitted : [*He being*] ‛ Conscious of his own weight and importance, the aid of others was not solicited.'"—*Murray's Gram.* 8vo, p. 221. "He was an excellent person; a mirror of ancient faith in early youth."—*Murray's Key*, 8vo, p. 172. "The carrying on its several parts into execution."—*Butler's Analogy*, p. 192. "Concord, is the agreement which one word has over another, in gender, number, case and person."—*Folker's Gram.* p. 3. "It might perhaps have given me a greater taste of its antiquities."—ADDISON: *Priestley's Gram.* p. 160. "To call of a person, and to wait of him."—*Priestley, ib.* p. 161. "The great difficulty they found of fixing just sentiments."—HUME: *ib.* p. 161. "Developing the difference between the three."—*James Brown's first American Gram.* p. 12. "When the substantive singular ends in *s, ch soft, sh, ss,* or *s,* we add *es* in the plural."—*Murray's Gram.* p. 40. "We shall present him with a list or specimen of them."—*Ib.* p. 132. "It is very common to hear of the evils of pernicious reading, of how it enervates the mind, or how it depraves the principles."—*Dymond's Essays,* p. 168. "In this example, the verb 'arises' is understood before 'curiosity' and 'knowledge.'"—*Murray's Gram.* 8vo, p. 274; *Ingersoll's,* 286; *Comly's,* 155; and others. "The connective is frequently omitted between several words."—*Wilcox's Gram.* p. 81. "He shall expel them from before you, and drive them from out of your sight."—*Joshua,* xxiii, 5. "Who makes his sun shine and his rain to descend upon the just and the unjust."—*M'Ilvaine's Lectures,* p. 411.

LESSON X.—MIXED EXAMPLES.

"This sentence violates the rules of grammar."—*Murray's Gram.* 8vo, Vol. ii, pp. 19 and 21. "The words *thou* and *shalt,* are again reduced to short quantities."—*Ib.* Vol. i, p. 246. "Have the greater men always been the most popular? By no means."—DR. LIEBER: *Lit. Conv.* p. 64. "St. Paul positively stated that, 'he who loves one another has fulfilled the law.'"—*Spurzheim, on Education,* p. 248. "More than one organ is concerned in the utterance of almost every consonant."—*M'Culloch's Gram.* p. 18. "If the reader will pardon my descending so low."—*Campbell's Rhet.* p. 20. "To adjust them so, as shall consist equally with the perspicuity and the grace of the period."—*Blair's Rhet.* p. 118; *Murray's Gram.* 8vo, p. 324. "This class exhibits a lamentable want of simplicity and inefficiency."—*Gardiner's Music of Nature,* p. 481. "Whose style flows always like a limpid stream, where we see to the very bottom."—*Blair's Rhet.* p. 93. "Whose style flows always like a limpid stream, through which we see to the very bottom."—*Murray's Gram.* 8vo. p. 293. "We make use of the ellipsis."*—*Ib.* p. 217. "The ellipsis of the article is thus used."—*Ib.* p. 217. "Sometimes the ellipsis is improperly applied to nouns of different numbers: as, 'A magnificent house and gardens.'"—*Ib.* p. 218. "In some very emphatical expressions, the ellipsis should not be used."—*Ib.* 218. "The ellipsis of the adjective is used in the following manner."—*Ib.* 218. "The following is the ellipsis of the pronoun."—*Ib.* 218. "The ellipsis of the verb is used in the following instances."—*Ib.* p. 219. "The ellipsis of the adverb is used in the following manner."—*Ib.* 219. "The following instances, though short, contain much of the ellipsis."—*Ib.* 220. "If no emphasis be placed on any words, not only will discourse be rendered heavy and lifeless, but the meaning often less ambiguous."—*Ib.* p. 242. See *Hart's Gram.* p. 172. "If no emphasis be placed on any words, not only is discourse, rendered heavy and lifeless, but the meaning left often ambiguous."—*Blair's Rhet.* p. 330; *Murray's Eng. Reader,* p. xi. "He regards his word, but thou dost not regard it."—*Bullions's E. Gram.* p. 129; *his Analytical and Practical Gram.* p. 196. "He regards his word, but thou dost not: i. e. dost not regard it."—*Murray's Gram.* 8vo, p. 219; *Parker and Fox's,* p. 96; *Weld's,* 192. "I have learned my task, but you have not; i. e. have not learned."—*Ib. Mur.* 219; &c. "When the omission of words would obscure the sentence, weaken its force, or be attended with an impropriety, they must be expressed."—*Ib.* p. 217; *Weld's Gram.* 190. "And therefore the verb is correctly put in the singular number, and refers to the whole separately and individually considered."—*Murray's Gram.* 8vo, ii, 24 and 190. "I understood him the best of all who spoke on the subject."—*Murray's Key,* 8vo, p. 192. "I understood him better than any other who spoke on the subject."—*Ibid.* "The roughness found on our entrance into the paths of virtue and learning, grow smoother as we advance."—*Ib.* p. 171. "The roughnesses," &c.—*Murray's Key,* 12mo, p. 8. "Nothing promotes knowledge more than steady application, and a habit of observation."—*Murray's Key,* 8vo, p. 265. "Virtue confers supreme dignity on man: and should be his chief desire."—*Ib.* p. 192; *and Merchant's,* 192. "The Supreme author of our being has so formed the soul of man, that nothing but himself can be its last, adequate, and proper happiness."—*Addison, Spect.* No. 413; *Blair's Rhet.* p. 213. "The inhabitants of China laugh at the plantations of our Europeans; because, they say, any one may place trees in equal rows and uniform figures."—*Ad. Spect.* No. 414; *Blair's Rhet.* p. 222. "The divine laws are

* In his explanation of *Ellipsis,* Lindley Murray continually calls it "the ellipsis," and speaks of it as something that is "used,"—"made use of,"—"applied,"—"contained in" the examples; which expressions, referring, as they there do, to the mere absence of something, appear to me solecistical. The notion too, which this author and others have entertained of the figure itself, is in many respects erroneous; and nearly all their examples for its illustration are either questionable as to such an application, or obviously inappropriate. The absence of what is needless or unsuggested, is no ellipsis, though some grave men have not discerned this obvious fact. The nine solecisms here quoted concerning "the ellipsis," are all found in many other grammars. See *Fisk's E. Gram.* p. 144; *Guy's,* 91; *Ingersoll's,* 158; *J. M. Putnam's,* 157; *R. C. Smith's,* 120; *Weld's,* 189.

not reversible by those of men."—*Murray's Key*, ii, 167. "In both of these examples, the relative and the verb *which was*, are understood."—*Murray's Gram.* p. 273; *Comly's*, 152; *Ingersoll's*, 285. "The Greek and Latin languages, though, for many reasons, they cannot be called dialects of one another, are nevertheless closely connected."—*Dr. Murray's Hist. of European Lang.* Vol. ii, p. 51. "To ascertain and settle which, of a white rose or a red rose, breathes the sweetest fragrance."—*J. Q. Adams, Orat.* 1831. "To which he can afford to devote much less of his time and labour."—*Blair's Rhet.* p. 254.

"Avoid extremes; and shun the fault of such,
Who still are pleas'd too little or too much."—*Pope, on Crit.* l. 384.

LESSON XI.—BAD PHRASES.

"He had as good leave his vessel to the direction of the winds."—SOUTH: *in Joh. Dict.* "Without good nature and gratitude, men had as good live in a wilderness as in society."—L'ESTRANGE: *ib.* "And for this reason such lines almost never occur together."—*Blair's Rhet.* p. 385. "His being a great man did not make him a happy man."—*Crombie's Treatise*, p. 288. "Let that which tends to the making cold your love be judged in all."—*S. Crisp.* "It is worthy the observing, that there is no passion in the mind of man so weak but it mates and masters the fear of death."—*Bacon's Essays*, p. 4. "Accent dignifies the syllable on which it is laid, and makes it more distinguished by the ear than the rest."—*Sheridan's Lect.* p. 80; *Murray's Gram.* 8vo, p. 244. "Before he proceeds to argue either on one side or other."—*Blair's Rhet.* p. 313. "The change in general of manners throughout all Europe."—*Ib.* p. 375. "The sweetness and beauty of Virgil's numbers, throughout his whole works."—*Ib.* p. 440. "The French writers of sermons study neatness and elegance in laying down their heads."—*Ib.* p. 313. "This almost never fails to prove a refrigerant to passion."—*Ib.* p. 321. "At least their fathers, brothers, and uncles, cannot, as good relations and good citizens, dispense with their not standing forth to demand vengeance."—*Goldsmith's Greece*, Vol. i, p. 191. "Alleging, that their crying down the church of Rome, was a joining hand with the Turks."—*Barclay's Works*, i, 239. "To which is added the Assembly of Divines Catechism."—*New-England Primer*, p. 1. "This treachery was always present in both their thoughts."—*Dr. Robertson.* "Thus far both their words agree." ("*Conveniunt adhuc utriusque verba.* Plaut.")—*Walker's Particles*, p. 125. "Aparithmesia, or Enumeration, is the branching out into several parts of what might be expressed in fewer words."—*Gould's Gram.* p. 241. "Aparithmesis, or Enumeration, is when what might be expressed in a few words, is branched out into several parts."—*Adam's Gram.* p. 251. "Which may sit from time to time where you dwell or in the neighbouring vicinity."—*Taylor's District School*, 1st Ed., p. 281. "Place together a large and a small sized animal of the same species."—*Kames, El. of Crit.* i, 235. "The weight of the swimming body is equal to that of the weight, of the quantity of fluid displaced by it."—*Percival's Tales*, ii. 213. "The Subjunctive mood, in all its tenses, is similar to that of the Optative." *Gwilt's Saxon Gram.* p. 27. "No other feeling of obligation remains, except that of fidelity."—*Wayland's Moral Science*, 1st Ed., p. 82. "Who asked him, 'What could be the reason, that whole audiences should be moved to tears, at the representation of some story on the stage.' "—*Sheridan's Elocution*, p. 175. "Art not thou and you ashamed to affirm, that the best works of the Spirit of Christ in his saints are as filthy rags?"—*Barclay's Works*, i, 174. "A neuter verb becomes active, when followed by a noun of the same signification with its own."—*Sanborn's Gram.* p. 127. "But he has judged better, in omitting to repeat the article *the*."—*Blair's Rhet.* p. 194. "Many objects please us as highly beautiful, which have almost no variety at all."—*Ib.* p. 46. "Yet notwithstanding, they sometimes follow them."—*Emmons's Gram.* p. 21. "For I know of nothing more material in all the whole Subject, than this doctrine of Mood and Tense."—*Johnson's Gram. Com.* p. 292. "It is by no means impossible for an errour to be got rid of or supprest."—*Philological Museum*, Vol. i, p. 642. "These are things of the highest importance to the growing age."—*Murray's Key*, 8vo, p. 250. "He had better have omitted the word *many*."—*Blair's Rhet.* p. 205. "Which had better have been separated."—*Ib.* p. 225. "Figures and metaphors, therefore, should, on no occasion be stuck on too profusely."—*Ib.* p. 144; *Jamieson's Rhet.* 150. "Metaphors, as well as other figures, should on no occasion, be stuck on too profusely."—*Murray's Gram.* p. 338; *Russell's*, 136. "Something like this has been reproached to Tacitus."—BOLINGBROKE: *Priestley's Gram.* p. 164.

"O thou, whom all mankind in vain withstand,
Each of whose blood must one day stain thy hand!"—*Sheffield's Temple of Death.*

LESSON XII.—TWO ERRORS.*

"Pronouns are sometimes made to precede the things which they represent."—*Murray's Gram.* p. 160. "Most prepositions originally denote the relation of place."—*Lowth's Gram.*

---

* Some of these examples do, *in fact*, contain *more* than two errors; for mistakes in *punctuation*, or in the use of *capitals*, are not here reckoned. This remark may also be applicable to some of the other lessons. The reader may likewise perceive, that where two, three, or more improprieties occur in one sentence, some one or

p. 65. "*Which* is applied to inferior animals and things without life."—*Buffum's, E. Gram.* p. 24; *Pract. Lessons,* 30. "What noun do they describe or tell the kind?"—*Infant School Gram.* p. 41. "Iron cannon, as well as brass, is now universally cast solid."—*Jamieson's Dict.* "We have philosophers, eminent and conspicuous, perhaps, beyond any nation."— *Blair's Rhet.* p. 251. "This is a question about words alone, and which common sense easily determines."—*Ib.* p. 320. "The low [pitch of the voice] is, when he approaches to a whisper."—*Ib.* p. 328. "Which, as to the effect, is just the same with using no such distinctions at all."—*Ib.* p. 33. "These two systems, therefore, differ in reality very little from one another."—*Ib.* p. 23. "It were needless to give many instances, as they occur so often."— *Ib.* p. 109. "There are many occasions when this is neither requisite nor would be proper." —*Ib.* p. 311. "Dramatic poetry divides itself into the two forms, of comedy or tragedy."— *Ib.* p. 452. "No man ever rhymed truer and evener than he."—*Pref. to Walker,* p. 5. "The Doctor did not reap a profit from his poetical labours equal to those of his prose."— *Johnson's Life of Goldsmith.* "We will follow that which we found our father's practice." —*Sale's Koran,* i, 28. "And I would deeply regret having published them."—*Infant School Gram.* p. vii. "Figures exhibit ideas in a manner more vivid and impressive, than could be done by plain language."—*Kirkham's Gram.* p. 222. "The allegory is finely drawn, only the heads various."—*Spect.* No. 540. "I should not have thought it worthy a place here."— *Crombie's Treatise,* p. 219. "In this style, Tacitus excels all writers, ancient and modern." —*Kames, El. of Crit.* ii, 261. "No author, ancient or modern, possesses the art of dialogue equal to Shakspeare."—*Ib.* ii, 294. "The names of every thing we hear, see, smell, taste, and feel, are nouns."—*Infant School Gram.* p. 16. "What number are these boys? these pictures? &c."—*Ib.* p. 23. "This sentence is faulty, somewhat in the same manner with the last."—*Blair's Rhet.* p. 230. "Besides perspicuity, he pursues propriety, purity, and precision, in his language; which forms one degree, and no inconsiderable one, of beauty." —*Ib.* p. 181. "Many critical terms have unfortunately been employed in a sense too loose and vague; none more so, than that of the sublime."—*Ib.* p. 35. "Hence, no word in the language is used in a more vague signification than beauty."—*Ib.* p. 45. "But, still, he made use only of general terms in speech."—*Ib.* p. 73. "These give life, body, and colouring to the recital of facts, and enable us to behold them as present, and passing before our eyes."—*Ib.* p. 360. "Which carried an ideal chivalry to a still more extravagant height than it had risen in fact."—*Ib.* p. 374. "We write much more supinely, and at our ease, than the ancients."—*Ib.* p. 351. "This appears indeed to form the characteristical difference between the ancient poets, orators, and historians, compared with the moderns."—*Ib.* p. 350. "To violate this rule, as is too often done by the English, shews great incorrectness."—*Ib.* p. 463. "It is impossible, by means of any study to avoid their appearing stiff and forced."—*Ib.* p. 335. "Besides its giving the speaker the disagreeable appearance of one who endeavours to compel assent."—*Ib.* p. 328. "And, on occasions where a light or ludicrous anecdote is proper to be recorded, it is generally better to throw it into a note, than to hazard becoming too familiar."—*Ib.* p. 359. "The great business of this life is to prepare, and qualify us, for the enjoyment of a better."—*Murray's Gram.* 8vo, p. 373. "In some dictionaries, accordingly, it was omitted; and in others stigmatized as a barbarism." —*Crombie's Treatise,* p. 322. "You cannot see, or think of, a thing, unless it be a noun."— *Mack's Gram.* p. 65. "The fleet are all arrived and moored in safety."—*Murray's Key,* ii, 185.

LESSON XIII.—TWO ERRORS.

"They have each their distinct and exactly-limited relation to gravity."—*Hosler's Astronomy,* p. 219. "But in cases which would give too much of the hissing sound, the omission takes place even in prose."—*Murray's Gram.* 8vo, p. 175. "After *o* it [the *e*] is sometimes not sounded at all; sometimes like a single *u.*"—*Lowth's Gram.* p. 3. "It is situation chiefly which decides *of* the fortunes and characters of men."—*Hume: Priestley's Gram.* p. 159. "It is situation chiefly which decides the fortune (or, *concerning* the fortune) and characters of men."—*Murray's Gram.* 8vo, p. 201. "The vice of covetousness is what enters deeper into the soul than any other."—*Ib.* p. 167; *Ingersoll's,* 193; *Fisk's,* 103; *Campbell's Rhet.* 205. "Covetousness, of all vices, enters the deepest into the soul."— *Murray,* 167; *and others.* "Covetousness is what of all vices enters the deepest into the soul." —*Campbell's Rhet.* p. 205. "The vice of covetousness is what enters deepest into the soul of any other."—*Guardian,* No. 19. "*Would* primarily denotes inclination of will; and *should,* obligation: but they both vary their import, and are often used to express simple event."—*Lowth's Gram.* p. 43; *Murray's,* 89; *Fisk's,* 78; *Greenleaf's,* 27. "But they both vary their import, and are often used to express simple events."—*Comly's Gram.* p. 39; *Ingersoll's,* 137. "But they vary their import, and are often used to express simple event."—*Abel Flint's Gram.* p. 42. "A double conjunctive, in two correspondent clauses of

more of them may happen to be such, as he can, if he choose, correct by some rule or note belonging to a previous chapter. Great labour has been bestowed on the selection and arrangement of these syntactical exercises; but to give to so great a variety of literary faults, a distribution perfectly distinct, and perfectly adapted to all the heads assumed in this digest, is a work not only of great labour, but of great difficulty. I have come as near to these two points of perfection in the arrangement, as I well could.—G. BROWN.

a sentence, is sometimes made use of: as, 'Had he done this, he had escaped.'"—*Murray's Gram.* 8vo, p. 213; *Ingersoll's,* 269. "The pleasures of the understanding are preferable to those of the imagination, or of sense."—*Murray's Key,* 8vo, p. 191. "Claudian, in a fragment upon the wars of the giants, has contrived to render this idea of their throwing the mountains, which is in itself so grand, burlesque, and ridiculous."—*Blair's Rhet.* p. 42. "To which not only no other writings are to be preferred, but even in divers respects not comparable."—*Barclay's Works,* i, 53. "To distinguish them in the understanding, and treat of their several natures, in the same cool manner as we do with regard to other ideas."—*Sheridan's Elocution,* p. 137. "For it has nothing to do with parsing or analyzing language."—*Kirkham's Gram.* p. 19.　　Or: "For it has nothing to do with parsing, or analyzing, language."—*Id. Second Edition,* p. 16. "Neither was that language [the Latin] ever so vulgar in Britain."—SWIFT: see *Blair's Rhet.* p. 228. "All that I propose is to give some openings into the pleasures of taste."—*Ib.* p. 28. "But it would have been better omitted in the following sentences."—*Murray's Gram.* 8vo, p. 210. "But I think it had better be omitted in the following sentence."—*Priestley's Gram.* p. 162. "They appear, in this case, like excrescences jutting out from the body, which had better have been wanted."—*Blair's Rhet.* p. 326. "And therefore, the fable of the Harpies, in the third book of the Æneid, and the allegory of Sin and Death, in the second book of Paradise Lost, had been better omitted in these celebrated poems."—*Ib.* p. 430. "Ellipsis is an elegant Suppression (or the leaving out) of a Word, or Words in a Sentence."—*British Gram.* p. 234; *Buchanan's,* p. 131. "The article *a* or *an* had better be omitted in this construction."—*Blair's Rhet.* p. 67. "Now suppose the articles had not been left out in these passages."—*Bucke's Gram.* p. 27. "To give separate names to every one of those trees, would have been an endless and impracticable undertaking."—*Blair's Rhet.* p. 72. "Ei, in general, sounds the same as long and slender *a.*"—*Murray's Gram.* p. 12. "When a conjunction is used apparently redundant it is called Polysyndeton."—*Adam's Gram.* p. 236; *Gould's,* 229. "Each, every, either, neither, denote the persons or things which make up a number, as taken separately or distributively."—*M'Culloch's Gram.* p. 31. "The Principal Sentence must be expressed by verbs in the Indicative, Imperative, or Potential Modes."—*Clark's Pract. Gram.* p. 133. "Hence he is diffuse, where he ought to have been pressing."—*Blair's Rhet.* p. 246. "All manner of subjects admit of explaining comparisons."—*Ib.* p. 164; *Jamieson's Rhet.* 161. "The present or imperfect participle denotes action or being continued, but not perfected."—*Kirkham's Gram.* p. 78. "What are verbs? Those words which express what the nouns do."—*Fowle's True Eng. Gram.* p. 29.

"Of all those arts in which the wise excel,
Nature's chief masterpiece is writing well."—*J. Sheffield, Duke of Buck.*

"Such was that muse whose rules and practice tell
Nature's chief masterpiece is writing well."—*Pope, on Criticism.*

LESSON XIV.—THREE ERRORS.

"In some words the metaphorical sense has justled out the original sense altogether, so that in respect of it they are become obsolete."—*Campbell's Rhet.* p. 323. "Sure never any mortal was so overwhelmed with grief as I am at this present."—*Sheridan's Elocution,* p. 138. "All languages differ from each other in their mode of inflexion.—*Bullions, E. Gram.,* Pref., p. v. "Nouns and verbs are the only indispensable parts of speech—the one to express the subject spoken of, and the other the predicate or what is affirmed of it."—*M'Culloch's Gram.* p. 36. "The words in italics of the three latter examples, perform the office of substantives."—*L. Murray's Gram.* 8vo, p. 66. "Such a structure of a sentence is always the mark of careless writing."—*Blair's Rhet.* p. 231. "Nothing is frequently more hurtful to the grace or vivacity of a period, than superfluous dragging words at the conclusion."—*Ib.* p. 205. "When its substantive is not joined to it, but referred to, or understood."—*Lowth's Gram.* p. 24. "Yet they have always some substantive belonging to them, either referred to, or understood."—*Ib.* 24. "Because they define and limit the extent of the common name, or general term, to which they either refer, or are joined."—*Ib.* 24. "Every new object surprises, terrifies, and makes a strong impression on their mind."—*Blair's Rhet.* p. 136. "His argument required to have been more fully unfolded, in order to make it be distinctly apprehended, and to give it its due force."—*Ib.* p. 230. "Participles which are derived from active verbs, will govern the objective case, the same as the verbs from which they are derived."—*Emmons's Gram.* p. 61. "Whore, contrary to the rule, the nominative *I* precedes, and the objective case *whom* follows the verb."—*Murray's Gram.* 8vo, p. 181. "The same conjunction governing both the indicative and the subjunctive moods, in the same sentence, and in the same circumstances, seems to be a great impropriety."—*Ib.* p. 207; *Smith's New Gram.* 173: see *Lowth's Gram.* p. 105; *Fisk's,* 128; and *Ingersoll's,* 266. "A nice discernment, and accurate attention to the best usage, are necessary to direct us, on these occasions."—*Murray's Gram.* 8vo, p. 170. "The Greeks and Romans, the former especially, were, in truth, much more musical nations than we; their genius was more turned to delight in the melody of speech."—*Blair's Rhet.* p. 123. "When the sense admits it, the sooner a circumstance is introduced, the better, that the more important and significant words may possess the last place, quite disencumbered."—*Murray's Gram.* 8vo, i, p. 306; *Parker and Fox's*, Part. III, p. 88. "When the sense admits it, the sooner they are despatched, generally speaking, the better; that the more important and significant words may possess the last place, quite disencumbered."—*Blair's Rhet.* p. 118. See also *Jamieson's Rhet.* p. 101. "Thus we find it, both in the Greek and Latin tongues."—*Blair's Rhet.* p. 74. "A train of sentences, constructed in the same manner, and with the same number of members, should never be allowed to succeed one another."—*Ib.* p. 102; *Murray's Gram.* 8vo, Vol. i, p. 306; *Parker and Fox's Gram.*, Part III, p. 86. "I proceed to lay down the rules to be observed in the conduct of metaphors; and which are much the same for tropes of every kind."—*Blair's Rhet.* p. 143. "By a proper choice of words, we may produce a resemblance of other sounds which we mean to describe."—*Ib.* p. 129; *Murray's Gram.* 8vo, Vol. i, p. 331. "The disguise can almost never be so perfect, but it is discovered."—*Blair's Rhet.* p. 259. "The sense admits of no other pause than after the second syllable 'sit,' which therefore must be the only pause made in the reading."—*Ib.* p. 333. "Not that I believe North America to be peopled so late as the twelfth century, the period of Madoc's migration."—*Webster's Essays*, p. 212. "Money and commodities wil always flow to that country, when they are most wanted and wil command the most profit."—*Ib.* p. 308. "That it contains no visible marks, of articles, which are the most important of all others, to a just delivery."—*Sheridan's Elocution*, p. 13. "And of virtue, from its beauty, we call it a fair and favourite maid."—*Mack's Gram.* p. 66. "The definite article may agree with nouns in the singular and plural number."—*Infant School Gram.* p. 130.

LESSON XV. — MANY ERRORS.

(1.) "A compound word is included under the head of derivative words."—*Murray's Gram.* 8vo, p. 23. (2.) "An Apostrophe, marked thus ' is used to abbreviate or shorten a word. Its chief use is to show the genitive case of nouns."—*Ib.* p. 281.* (3.) "A Hyphen, marked thus - is employed in connecting compounded words. It is also used when a word is divided."—*Ib.* p. 282. (4.) "The Acute Accent, marked thus ': as, '*Fáncy*.' The Grave thus ` as, '*Fàvour*.' "—*Ib.* 282. (5.) "The stress is laid on long and short syllables indiscriminately. In order to distinguish the one from the other, some writers of dictionaries have placed the grave on the former, and the acute on the latter."—*Ib.* 282. (6.) "A Diæresis, thus marked ˙˙, consists of two points placed over one of the two vowels that would otherwise make a diphthong, and parts them into syllables."—*Ib.* 282. (7.) "A Section, marked thus §, is the division of a discourse, or chapter, into less parts or portions."—*Ib.* 282. (8.) "A Paragraph ¶ denotes the beginning of a new subject, or a sentence not connected with the foregoing. This character is chiefly used in the Old and in the New Testaments."—*Ib.* 282. (9.) "A Quotation " ". Two inverted commas are generally placed at the beginning of a phrase or a passage, which is quoted or transcribed from the speaker or author in his own words; and two commas in their direct position, are placed at the conclusion."—*Ib.* 282. (10.) "A Brace is used in poetry at the end of a triplet or three lines, which have the same rhyme. Braces are also used to connect a number of words with one common term, and are introduced to prevent a repetition in writing or printing."—*Ib.* p. 283. (11.) "Two or three asterisks generally denote the omission of some letters in a word, or ot some bold or indelicate expression, or some defect in the manuscript."—*Ib.* 283. (12.) "An Ellipsis ——— is also used, when some letters in a word, or some words in a verse, are omitted."—*Ib.* 283. (13.) "An Obelisk, which is marked thus †, and Parallels thus ‖, together with the letters of the Alphabet, and figures, are used as references to the margin, or bottom of the page."—*Ib.* 283. (14.) "A note of interrogation should not be employed, in cases where it is only said a question has been asked, and where the words are not used as a question. 'The Cyprians asked me why I wept.' "—*Ib.* p. 279; *Comly*, 163; *Ingersoll*, 291; *Fisk*, 157; *Flint*, 113. (15.) "A point of interrogation is improper after sentences which are not questions, but only expressions of admiration, or of some other emotion."—*Same authors and places*. (16.) "The parenthesis incloses in the body of a sentence a member inserted into it, which is neither necessary to the sense, nor at all affects the construction."—*Lowth's Gram.* p. 124. (17.) "Simple members connected by relatives, and comparatives, are for the most part distinguished by a comma."†—*Ib.* p. 121. (18.) "Simple members of sentences connected by comparatives, are, for the most

---

* In Murray's sixth chapter of Punctuation, from which this example, and eleven others that follow it, are taken, there is scarcely a single sentence that does not contain *many errors*; and yet the whole is literally copied in *Ingersoll's Grammar*, p. 298; in *Fisk's*, p. 159; in *Abel Flint's*, 116; and probably in some others. I have not always been careful to subjoin the great number of references which might be given for blunders selected from this hackneyed literature of the schools. For corrections, or improvements, see the Key.

† This example, or L. Murray's miserable modification of it, traced through the grammars of Alden, Alger, Bullions, Comly, Cooper, Flint, Hiley, Ingersoll, Jaudon, Merchant, Russell, Smith, and others, will be found to have a dozen different forms—all of them no less faulty than the original—all of them obscure, untrue, inconsistent, and almost incorrigible. It is plain, that "a comma," or *one* comma, cannot divide more than two "simple members;" and these, surely, cannot be connected by more than *one relative*, or by more than *one* "comparative;" if it be allowable to call *than*, *as*, or *so*, by this questionable name. Of the multitude of errors into which these pretended critics have so blindly fallen, I shall have space and time to point out only a *very small part*: this text, too justly, may be taken as a pretty fair sample of their scholarship!

part, distinguished by a comma."—*L. Murray's Gram.* p. 272; *Alden's*, 148; *Ingersoll's*, 284. See the same words without the last two commas, in *Comly's Gram.* p. 149; *Alger's*, 79; *Merchant's Murray*, 143:—and this again, with a *different sense*, made by a comma before "*connected*," in *Smith's New Gram.* 190; *Abel Flint's*, 102. (19.) "Simple members of sentences connected by comparatives, are for the most part distinguished by the comma."—*Russell's Gram.* p. 115. (20.) "Simple members of sentences, connected by comparatives, should generally be distinguished by a comma."—*Merchant's School Gram.* p. 150. (21.) "Simple members of sentences connected by *than* or *so*, or that express contrast or comparison, should, generally, be divided by a comma."—*Jaudon's Gram.* p. 185. (22.) "Simple members of sentences, connected by comparatives, if they be long, are separated by a comma."—*Cooper's New Gram.* p. 195. See the same without the first comma, in *Cooper's Murray*, p. 183. (23.) "Simple members of sentences connected by comparatives, and phrases placed in opposition to, or in contrast with, each other, are separated by commas." —*Bullions*, p. 153; *Hiley*, 113. (24.) "On which ever word we lay the emphasis, whether on the first, second, third, or fourth, it strikes out a different sense."—*Murray's Gram.* 8vo, p. 243. (25.) "To inform those who do not understand sea phrases, that, ' We tacked to the larboard, and stood off to sea,' would be expressing ourselves very obscurely."—*Ib.* p. 296; *and Hiley's Gram.* p. 151. (26.) "Of dissyllables, which are at once nouns and verbs, the verb has commonly the accent on the latter, and the noun, on the former syllable."— *Murray, ib.* p. 237. (27.) "And this gives our language a superior advantage to most others, in the poetical and rhetorical style."—*Id. ib.* p. 38; *Ingersoll*, 27; *Fisk*, 57. (28.) "And this gives the English an advantage above most other languages in the poetical and rhetorical style."—*Lowth's Gram.* p. 19. (29.) "The second and third scholar may read the same sentence; and as many, as it is necessary to learn it perfectly to the whole."— *Osborn's Key*, p. 4.

     (30.) " Bliss is the name in subject as a king,
         In who obtain defence, or who defend."—*Bullions, E. Gram.* p. 178.

LESSON XVI. — MANY ERRORS.

"The Japanese, the Tonquinese, and the Coreans, speak different languages from one another, and from the inhabitants of China, but use, with these last people, the same written characters; a proof that the Chinese characters are like hieroglyphics, independent of language."—*Jamieson's Rhet.* p. 18. "The Japanese, the Tonquinese, and the Coreans, who speak different languages from one another, and from the inhabitants of China, use, however, the same written characters with them; and by this means correspond intelligibly with each other in writing, though ignorant of the language spoken in their several countries; a plain proof," &c.—*Blair's Rhet.* p. 67. "The curved line is made square instead of round, for the reason beforementioned."—*Knight, on the Greek Alphabet*, p. 6. "Every one should content himself with the use of those tones only that he is habituated to in speech, and to give none other to emphasis, but what he would do to the same words in discourse. Thus whatever he utters will be done with ease, and appear natural."—*Sheridan's Elocution*, p. 103. "Stops, or pauses, are a total cessation of sound during a perceptible, and in numerous compositions, a measurable space of time."—*Ib.* p. 104. "Pauses or rests, in speaking and reading, are a total cessation of the voice during a perceptible, and, in many cases, a measurable space of time."—*Murray's Gram.* p. 248; *English Reader*, p. 13; *Goldsbury's Gr.* 76; *Kirkham's*, 208; *Felton's*, 133; *et al.* "Nouns which express a small one of the kind are called *Diminutive Nouns*; as, lambkin, hillock, satchel, gosling, from lamb, hill, sack, goose."—*Bullions, E. Gram.*, 1837, p. 9. "What is the cause that nonsense so often escapes being detected, both by the writer and by the reader ?"—*Campbell's Rhet.* p. xi, and 280. "An Interjection is a word used to express sudden emotion. They are so called, because they are generally thrown in between the parts of a sentence without reference to the structure of the other parts of it."—*M'Culloch's Gram.* p. 36. "*Ought* (in duty bound) *oughtest, oughtedst*, are it's only inflections."—*Mackintosh's Gram.* p. 165. "But the arrangment, government, agreement, and dependence of one word upon another, are referred to our reason."—*Osborn's Key, Pref.* p. 3. "*Me* is a personal pronoun, first person singular, and the accusative case."— *Guy's Gram.* p. 20. "The substantive *self* is added to a pronoun; as, herself, himself, &c.; and when thus united, is called a reciprocal pronoun."—*Ib.* p. 18. "One cannot avoid thinking that our author had done better to have begun the first of these three sentences, with saying, *it is novelty which bestows charms on a monster*, &c."—*Blair's Rhet.* p. 207. "The idea which they present to us of nature's resembling art, of art's being considered as an original, and nature as a copy,* seems not very distinct nor well brought out, nor indeed very material to our author's purpose."—*Ib.* p. 220. "The present construction of the

---

  * The " *idea* " which is here spoken of, Dr. Blair discovers in a passage of Addison's Spectator. It is, in fact, as here " *brought out* " by the critic, a bald and downright absurdity. Dr. Campbell has criticised, under the name of *marvellous nonsense*, a different display of the same " *idea*," cited from De Piles's Principles of Painting. The passage ends thus: " In this sense it may be asserted, that in Rubens' pieces, Art is above Nature, and Nature only a copy of that great master's works." Of this the critic says: " When the expression is stript of the absurd meaning, there remains nothing but balderdash."—*Philosophy of Rhet.* p. 278.

sentence, has plainly been owing to hasty and careless writing."—*Ib.* p. 220. "Adverbs serve to modify, or to denote some circumstance of an action, or of a quality, relative to its time, place, order, degree, and the other properties of it, which we have occasion to specify." —*Ib.* p. 84. "The more that any nation is improved by science, and the more perfect their language becomes, we may naturally expect that it will abound more with connective particles."—*Ib.* p. 85. "Mr. Greenleaf's book is by far the best adapted for learners of any that has yet appeared on the subject."—Dr. FELTUS and Bp. ONDERDONK: *Greenleaf's Gram.* p. 2. "Punctuation is the art of marking in writing the several pauses, or rests, between sentences, and the parts of sentences, according to their proper quantity or proportion, as they are expressed in a just and accurate pronunciation."—*Lowth's Gram.* p. 114. "A compound sentence must be resolved into simple ones, and separated by commas."—*Greenleaf's Gram.* p. 41; *Allen Fisk's,* 155.* "Simple sentences should be separated from each other by commas, unless such sentences are connected by a conjunction: as, ' Youth is passing away, age is approaching and death is near.' "—*Hall's Gram.* p. 36. "*V* has the sound of flat *f,* and bears the same relation to it, as *b* does to *p, d* to *t,* hard *g* to *k,* and *z* to *s.* It has also one uniform sound."—*Murray's Gram.* p. 17; *Fisk's,* 42. "*V* is flat *f,* and bears the same relation to it as *b* does to *p, d* to *t,* hard *g* to *k,* and *z* to *s.* It is never irregular."—*Walker's Dict.* p. 52. "*V* has the sound of flat *f;* and bears the same relation to it as *z* does to *s.* It has one uniform sound."—*Greenleaf's Gram.* p. 20. "The author is explaining the distinction, between the powers of sense and imagination in the human mind."—*Murray's Gram.* 8vo, Vol. i, p. 343. [The author is endeavouring] "to explain a very abstract point, the distinction between the powers of sense and imagination in the human mind."—*Blair's Rhet.* p. 164. "HE (Anglo-Saxon *he*) is a Personal pronoun, of the Third Person, Masculine Gender (Decline he), of the singular number, in the nominative case."—*Fowler's E. Gram.* 8vo, 1850, § 589.

FALSE SYNTAX UNDER THE CRITICAL NOTES.

UNDER CRITICAL NOTE I.—OF THE PARTS OF SPEECH.

"The passive voice denotes a being acted upon."—*Maunder's Gram.* p. 6.

[FORMULA.—Not proper, because the term "being acted upon," as here used, suggests a doubt concerning its classification in parsing. But, according to Critical Note 1st, "Words that may constitute different parts of speech, must not be left doubtful as to their classification, or to what part of speech they belong." Therefore, the phraseology should be altered; thus, "The passive voice denotes an *action received.*" Or: "The passive voice denotes *the receiving of an action.*"]

"Milton, in some of his prose works, has very finely turned periods."—*Blair's Rhet.* p. 127; *Jamieson's,* 129. "These will be found to be all, or chiefly, of that class."—*Blair's Rhet.* p. 32. "All appearances of an author's affecting harmony, are disagreeable."—*Ib.* p. 127; *Jamieson,* 128. "Some nouns have a double increase, that is, increase by more syllables than one; as, *iter, itineris.*"—*Adam's Gram.* p. 255; *Gould's,* 247. "The powers of man are enlarged by advancing cultivation."—*Gurney's Essays,* p. 62. "It is always important to begin well; to make a favourable impression at first setting out."—*Blair's Rhet.* p. 307. "For if one take a wrong method at first setting out, it will lead him astray in all that follows."—*Ib.* p. 313. "His mind is full of his subject, and his words are all expressive."—*Ib.* p. 179. "How exquisitely is this all performed in Greek!"—*Harris's Hermes,* p. 422. "How little is all this to satisfy the ambition of an immortal soul!"—*Murray's Key,* 8vo, p. 253. "So as to exhibit the object in its full and most striking point of view."—*Blair's Rhet.* p. 41. "And that the author know how to descend with propriety to the plain, as well as how to rise to the bold and figured style."—*Ib.* p. 401. "The heart can only answer to the heart."—*Ib.* p. 259. "Upon its first being perceived."—*Harris's Hermes,* p. 229. "Call for Samson, that he may make us sport."—*Judges,* xvi, 25. "And he made them sport."—*Ibid.* "The term *suffer* in this definition is used in a technical sense, and means simply the receiving of an action, or the being acted upon."—*Bullions,* p. 29. "The Text is what is only meant to be taught in Schools."—*Brightland, Pref.* p. ix. "The perfect participle denotes action or being perfected or finished."—*Kirkham's Gram.* p. 78. "From the intricacy and confusion which are produced by their being blended together."—*Murray's Gram.* 8vo, p. 66. "This very circumstance of a word's being employed antithetically, renders it important in the sentence."—*Kirkham's Elocution,* p. 121. "It [the pronoun *that,*] is applied to both persons and things."—*Murray's Gram.* p. 53. "Concerning us, as being every where evil spoken of."—*Barclay's Works,* Vol. ii, p. vi. "Every thing beside was buried in a profound silence."—*Steele.* "They raise more full conviction than any reasonings produce."—*Blair's Rhet.* p. 367. "It appears to me no more than a fanciful refinement."—*Ib.* p. 436. "The regular resolution throughout of a complete passage."—*Churchill's Gram.* p. vii. "The infinitive is known by its being immediately preceded by the word *to.*"—*Maunder's Gram.* p. 6. "It will not be gaining much ground to urge that the basket, or vase, is understood to be the capital."—*Kames, El. of Crit.* Vol. ii, p. 356. "The disgust one has to drink ink in reality, is not to the purpose where the

---

* All his rules for the comma, Fisk appears to have taken unjustly from Greenleaf. It is a *double shame,* for a grammarian to *steal* what is so badly *written!*—G. BROWN.

that is drinking ink figuratively."—*Ib.* ii, 231. "That we run not into the extreme of being so very close."—*Blair's Rhet.* p. 111. "Being obliged to rest for a little on the preposition by itself."—*Ib.* p. 112; *Jamieson's Rhet.* 93. "Being obliged to rest a little on a preposition by itself."—*Murray's Gram.* p. 319. "Our days on the earth are as a shadow, and there is none abiding."—1 *Chron.* xxix, 15. "There may be a more particular passion attempted, of certain objects, by means of resembling sounds."—*Blair's Rhet.* 129; *Jamieson's,* 130; *Murray's Gram.* 331. "The right disposition of the shade, makes the light and colouring strike the more."—*Blair's Rhet.* 144. "I observed that a diffuse style inclines most to long periods."—*Ib.* p. 178. "Their poor Arguments, which they only skit up and down the Highway."—*Divine Right of Tythes,* p. iii. "Which must be little, as transcribing out of their writings."—*Barclay's Works,* iii, 353. "That single impulse a forcing out of almost all the breath."—*Rush, on the Voice,* p. 254. "Picini compares modulation to the turning off from a road."—*Gardiner's Music of Nature,* p. 405. "So much has been written, on and off, of almost every subject."—*The Friend,* ii, 117. "By reading books written by the best authors, his mind became highly improved."—*Murray's Key,* 8vo, 201. "For I never made the being richly provided a token of a spiritual ministry."—*Barclay's Works,* iii, 470.

Under Critical Note II.—Of Doubtful Reference.

"However disagreeable, we must resolutely perform our duty."—*Murray's Key,* 8vo, p. 171.

Perple.—Not proper, because the adjective *disagreeable* appears to relate to the pronoun *we,* though such relation was probably not intended by the author. But, according to Critical Note 2d, "The reference of *we* to other words, or their syntactical relation according to the sense, should never be left doubtful, by any *we* who means to be understood." The sentence may be amended thus: "However disagreeable *the task,* we must resolutely perform our duty."]

"The formation of verbs in English, both regular and irregular, is derived from the Saxon."—*Lowth's Gram.* p. 47. "Time and chance have an influence on all things human, and on nothing more remarkably than on language."—*Campbell's Rhet.* p. 180. "Time and chance have an influence on all things human, and on nothing more remarkable than on language."—*Jamieson's Rhet.* p. 47. "Archytases being a virtuous man, who happened to wish once upon a time, is with him a sufficient ground," &c.—*Philological Museum,* i, 466. He will be the better qualified to understand, with accuracy, the meaning of a numerous class of words, in which they form a material part."—*Murray's Gram.* 8vo, p. 120. "We should continually have the goal in view, which would direct us in the race."—*Murray's Key,* 8vo, p. 172. "But [Addison's figures] seem to rise of their own accord from the subject, and constantly embellish it."—*Blair's Rhet.* p. 150; *Jamieson's,* 157. "As far as persons and other animals and things that we can see go, it is very easy to distinguish Nouns."—*Abbott's Gram.* ¶ 14. "Dissyllables ending in *y, e* mute, or accented on the last syllable, may be sometimes compared like monosyllables."—*Frost's El. of Gram.* p. 12. "Admitting the above objection, it will not overrule the design."—*Rush, on the Voice,* p. 140. "These philosophical innovators forget, that objects are like men, known only by their actions."—*Dr. Murray's Hist. of Lang.* i, 326. "The connexion between words and ideas is arbitrary and conventional, owing to the agreement of men among themselves."—*Jamieson's Rhet.* p.

"The connexion between words and ideas may, in general, be considered as arbitrary and conventional, owing to the agreement of men among themselves."—*Blair's Rhet.* p. 53. A man whose inclinations led him to be corrupt, and had great abilities to manage and multiply and defend his corruptions."—*Swift.* "They have no more control over him than any other men."—*Wayland's Moral Science,* 1st Ed., p. 372. "His old words are all true English, and numbers exquisite."—*Spectator,* No. 540. "It has been said, that not only suits can equivocate."—*Murray's Exercises,* 8vo, p. 121. "It has been said, that Jesuits can not only equivocate."—*Murray's Key,* 8vo, p. 253. "The nominative of the first and second person in Latin is seldom expressed."—*Adam's Gram.* p. 154; *Gould's,* 157. "Some words are the same in both numbers."—*Murray's Gram.* 8vo, p. 40; *Ingersoll's,* 18; *Fisk's,* ; *Kirkham's,* 39; *W. Allen's,* 42; *et al.* "Some nouns are the same in both numbers."—*Merchant's Gram.* p. 29; *Smith's,* 45; *et al.* "Others are the same in both numbers; as, *sw, swine,* &c."—*Frost's El. of Gram.* p. 8. "The following list denotes the sounds of the consonants, being in number twenty-two."—*Murray's Gram.* p. 6; *Fisk's,* 36. "And is the ignorance of these peasants a reason for others to remain ignorant; or to render the subject less becoming inquiry?"—*Harris Hermes,* p. 293; *Murray's Gram.* 8vo, p. 288. "He is one of the most correct, and perhaps the best, of our prose writers."—*Lowth's Gram. Pref.* iv. "The motions of a vortex and a whirlwind are perfectly similar."—*Jamieson's Rhet.* 131. "What I have been saying throws light upon one important verse in the Bible, which I should like to have read."—*Abbott's Teacher,* p. 182. "When there are any circumstances of time, place, or other limitations, which the principal object of our sentence requires to have connected with it."—*Blair's Rhet.* p. 115; *Jamieson's Rhet.* 98; *Murray's Gram.* i, 322. "Interjections are words used to express emotion, affection, or passion, and imply suddenness."—*Bucke's Gram.* p. 77. "But the genitive is only used to express the measure of things in the plural number."—*Adam's Gram.* p. 200; *Gould's,* 198. "The buildings of the institution have been enlarged; the expense of which, added to the in-

creased price of provisions, renders it necessary to advance the terms of admission."—
Murray's Key, 8vo, p. 183.　"These sentences are far less difficult than complex."—S. &
Greene's Analysis, or Grammar, 1st Ed., p. 179.

" Far from the madding crowd's ignoble strife,
Their sober wishes never learn'd to stray."—*Gray's Elegy*.

UNDER CRITICAL NOTE III.—OF DEFINITIONS.

(1.) "*Definition* is such a description of things as exactly describes the thing and the
thing only."—*Blair's Gram.* p. 135.

[FORMULE.—Not proper, because this definition of a *definition* is not accurately adapted to the thing. Is,
according to Critical Note 3d, "A definition, in order to be perfect, must include the whole thing or class of
things which it pretends to define, and exclude every thing which comes not under the name."* The example
may be amended thus : "A definition is a *short and lucid* description of *a thing, or species, according to its
nature and properties.*"]

(2.) " Language, in general, signifies the expression of our ideas by certain articulate
sounds, which are used as the signs of those ideas."—*Blair's Rhet.* p. 53.　(3.) "A WORD
is an articulate *sound* used by common consent as the sign of an idea."—*Bullions, Analyt. and
Pract. Gr.* p. 17.　(4.) "A word is a sound, or combination of sounds, which is used in the
expression of thought."—*Hazen's Gram.* p. 12.　(5.) "*Words* are articulate sounds, used as
signs to convey our ideas."—*Hiley's Gram.* p. 5.　(6.) "A *word* is a number of letters used
together to represent some idea."—*Hart's E. Gram.* p. 28.　(7.) "A *Word* is a combination
of letters, used as the sign of an idea."—*S. W. Clark's Practical Gram.* p. 9.　(8.) "A *word*
is a letter or a combination of letters, used as the sign of an idea."—*Wells's School Gram.* p.
41.　(9.) " Words are articulate sounds, by which ideas are communicated."—*Wright's
Gram.* p. 28.　(10.) " Words are certain articulate sounds used by common consent as signs
of our ideas."—*Bullions, Principles of E. Gram.* p. 6 ; *Lat. Gram.* 6 : see *Lowth, Murray, Smith,
et al.*　(11.) " Words are sounds used as signs of our ideas."—*W. Allen's Gram.* p. 30.
(12.) " Orthography means *word-making, or spelling.*"—*Kirkham's Gram.* p. 19 ; *Smith's
New Gram.* p. 41.　(13.) "A vowel is a letter, the name of which constitutes a full, open
sound."—*Hazen's Gram.* p. 10 ; *Lennie's,* 5 ; *Brace's,* 7.　(14.) " Spelling is the art of reading by naming the letters singly, and rightly dividing words into their syllables.　Or, in
writing, it is the expressing of a word by its proper letters."—*Lowth's Gram.* p. 5 ; *Churchill's,* 20.　(15.) " Spelling is the art of rightly dividing words into their syllables, or of
expressing a word by its proper letters."—*Murray's Gram.* p. 21 ; *Ingersoll's,* 6 ; *Merchant's,*
10 ; *Alger's,* 12 ; *Greenleaf's,* 20 ; and others.　(16.) " Spelling is the art of expressing words
by their proper letters ; or of rightly dividing words into syllables."—*Comly's Gram.* p. 1.
(17.) " Spelling is the art of expressing a word by its proper letters, and rightly dividing
it into syllables."—*Bullions's Prin. of E. Gram.* p. 2.　(18.) " Spelling is the art of expressing a word by its proper letters."—*Kirkham's Gram.* p. 23 ; *Sanborn's,* p. 259.　(19.) "A
Syllable is a sound either simple or compounded, pronounced by a single impulse of the
voice, and constituting a word or part of a word."—*Lowth,* p. 5 ; *Murray,* 21 ; *Ingersoll, 6 ;
Fisk,* 11 ; *Greenleaf,* 20 ; *Merchant,* 9 ; *Alger,* 12 ; *Bucke,* 15 ; *Smith,* 118 ; *et al.*　(20.) "A
Syllable is a complete Sound uttered in one Breath."—*British Gram.* p. 32 ; *Buchanan's,* 5.
(21.) "A syllable is a distinct sound, uttered by a single impulse of the voice."—*Kirkham's
Gram.* p. 20.　(22.) "A *Syllable* is a distinct sound forming the whole of a word, or so much
of it as can be sounded at once."—*Bullions, E. Gr.* p. 2.　(23.) "A *syllable* is a word, or part
of a word, or as much as can be sounded at once."—*Picket's Gram.* p. 10.　(24.) "A diphthong is the union of two Vowels, both of which are pronounced as one : as in Bear and beat."
—*Bucke's Gram.* p. 15.　(25.) "A diphthong consists of two vowels, forming one syllable ; as,
ea, in *beat.*"—*Guy's Gram.* p. 2.　(26.) "A triphthong consists of three vowels forming one
syllable ; as, *eau* in *beauty.*"—*Ib.*　(27.) " But the Triphthong is the union of three Vowels,
pronounced as one."—*Bucke's Gram.* p. 15.　(28.) " What is a Noun Substantive ? A Noun
Substantive is the thing itself ; as, a Man, a Boy."—*British Gram.* p. 85 ; *Buchanan's,* 25.
(29.) "An adjective is a word added to nouns to describe them."—*Maunder's Gram.* p. 1.
(30.) "An adjective is a word joined to a noun, to describe or define it."—*Smith's New
Gram.* p. 51.　(31.) "An adjective is a word used to describe or define a noun."—*Wilcox's
Gram.* p. 2.　(32.) " The adjective is added to the noun, to express the quality of it."—
Murray's Gram. 12mo, 2d Ed., p. 27 ; *Lowth,* p. 6.　(33.) "An Adjective expresses the quality

* Bad definitions may have other faults than to include or exclude what they should not, but this is their
great and peculiar vice.　For example : "*Person* is *that property of nouns and pronouns which distinguishes the
speaker, the person or thing addressed, and the person or thing spoken of.*"—*Wells's School Gram.* 1st Ed. p.
51 ; 113th Ed. p. 57.　See nearly the same words, in *Weld's English Gram.* p. 67 ; and in his *Abridgment,*
p. 49.　The three persons of *verbs* are all improperly excluded from this definition ; which absurdly takes
" *person* " to be *one* property *that has all the effect of all the persons*; so that each person, in its turn, since each
cannot have all this effect, is seen to be excluded also : that is, it is not such a property as is described !　Again :
"An *intransitive verb* is a verb which *does not have* a noun or pronoun for its object."—*Wells, 1st Ed.* p. 73.
According to Dr. Johnson, " *does not have,*" is not a scholarly phrase ; but the adoption of a puerile expression
is a trifling fault, compared with that of including here all passive verbs, and some transitives, which the author
meant to exclude ; to say nothing of the inconsistency of excluding here the two classes of verbs which he
absurdly calls " intransitive," though he finds them " followed by objectives depending upon them !"—*Id.* p.
145.　Weld imitates these errors too, on pp. 70 and 153.

of the noun to which it is applied; and may generally be known by its making sense in connection with it; as, 'A *good* man,' 'A *genteel* woman.'"—*Wright's Gram.* p. 34. (34.) "An adverb is a word used to modify the sense of other words."—*Wilcox's Gram.* p. 2. (35.) "An Adverb is a word joined to a verb, an adjective, or another adverb, to modify or denote some circumstance respecting it."—*Bullions, E. Gram.* p. 66; *Lat. Gram.* 185. (36.) "A Substantive or Noun is a name given to every object which the senses can perceive; the understanding comprehend; or the imagination entertain."—*Wright's Gram.* p. 34. (37.) "GENDER means the distinction of nouns with regard to sex."—*Bullions, Prin. of E. Gram.*, 2d Ed., p. 9. (38.) "Gender is a distinction of nouns with regard to sex."—*Frost's Gram.* p. 7. (39.) "Gender is a distinction of nouns in regard to sex."—*Perley's Gram.* p. 10. (40.) "Gender is the distinction of nouns, in regard to sex."—*Cooper's Murray*, 24; *Practical Gram.* 21. (41.) "Gender is the distinction of nouns with regard to sex." —*Murray's Gram.* p. 37; *Alger's*, 16; *Bacon's*, 12; *R. G. Greene's*, 16; *Bullions, Prin., 5th Ed.*, 9; *his New Gr.* 22; *Fisk's*, 19; *Hull's*, 9; *Ingersoll's*, 15. (42.) "Gender is the distinction of sex."—*Alden's Gram.* 9; *Comly's*, 20; *Dalton's*, 11; *Davenport's*, 15; *J. Flint's*, 28; *A. Flint's*, 11; *Greenleaf's*, 21; *Guy's*, 4; *Hart's*, 36; *Hiley's*, 12; *Kirkham's*, 34; *Lennie's*, 11; *Picket's*, 25; *Smith's*, 43; *Sanborn's*, 25; *Wilcox's*, 8. (43.) "Gender is the Distinction of Sex, or the Difference betwixt Male and Female."—*British Gram.* p. 94; *Buchanan's*, 18. (44.) "Why are nouns divided into genders? To distinguish their sexes."—*Fowle's True Eng. Gram.* p. 10. (45.) "What is meant by *Gender?* The different sexes."—*Burn's Gram.* p. 34. (46.) "Gender, in grammar, is a difference of termination, to express distinction of sex." — *Webster's Philos. Gram.* p. 30; *Improved Gram.* 22. (47.) "Gender signifies a distinction of nouns, according to the different sexes of things they denote."—*Coar's Gram.* p. 32. (48.) "Gender is the distinction occasioned by sex. Though there are but two sexes, still nouns necessarily admit of *four distinctions*[*] of gender."—*Hall's Gram.* p. 6. (49.) "Gender is a term which is employed for the distinction of nouns with regard to sex and species." — *Wright's Gram.* p. 41 .(50.) "Gender is a Distinction of Sex."—*Fisher's Gram.* p. 53. (51.) "GENDER marks the distinction of Sex."—*W. Allen's Gram.* p. 37. (52.) "*Gender* means the kind, or sex. There are four genders."—*Parker and Fox's Part I*, p. 7. (53.) "Gender is a property of the noun which distinguishes sex."—*Weld's Gram.*, 2d Ed., p. 57. (54.) "Gender is a property of the noun or pronoun by which it distinguishes sex."—*Weld's Grammar Abridged*, p. 49. (55.) "Case is the state or condition of a noun with respect to the other words in a sentence."—*Bullions's E. Gram.* p. 16; *his Analyt. and Pract. Gram.* p. 31. (56.) "*Case* means the different state or situation of nouns with regard to other words." —*Kirkham's Gram.* p. 55. (57.) "The cases of substantives signify their different terminations, which serve to express the relations of one thing to another."—*L. Murray's Gram.* 12mo, 2d Ed., p. 35. (58.) "Government is the power which one *part of speech* has over *another*, when it causes it or requires it to be of some particular person, number, gender, case, style, or mode."—*Sanborn's Gram.* p. 126: see *Murray's Gram.* 142; *Smith's*, 119; *Pond's*, 88; *et al.* (59.) "A simple sentence is a sentence which contains only one nominative case and one verb to agree with it."—*Sanborn, ib.:* see *Murray's Gram. et al.* (60.) "Declension means putting a noun through the different cases."—*Kirkham's Gram.* p. 58. (61.) "Zeugma is when two or more substantives have a verb in common which is applicable only to one of them."—*B. F. Fisk's Greek Gram.* p. 185. (62.) "An Irregular Verb is that which has its passed tense and perfect participle terminating differently; as, smite, smote, smitten." —*Wright's Gram.* p. 92. (63.) "*Personal* pronouns are employed as substitutes for nouns that denote *persons.*"—*Hiley's Gram.* p. 23.

UNDER CRITICAL NOTE IV.—OF COMPARISONS.

"We abound more in vowel and diphthong sounds, than most languages."—*Blair's Rhet.* p. 39.

[FORMULE.—Not proper, because the terms *we* and *languages*, which are here used to form a comparison, express things which are totally unlike. But, according to Critical Note 4th, "A comparison is a form of speech which requires some similarity or common property in the things compared; without which, it becomes a solecism." Therefore, the expression ought to be changed; thus, "*Our language* abounds more in vowel and diphthong sounds, than most *other tongues*." Or: "We abound more in vowel and *diphthongal* sounds, than most *nations*."]

"A line thus accented, has a more spirited air, than when the accent is placed on any other syllable."—*Kames, El. of Crit.* Vol. ii, p. 86. "Homer introduceth his deities with no

---

[*] S. R. Hall thinks it necessary to recognize "*four distinctions*" of "*the distinction* occasioned by sex." In general, the other authors here quoted, suppose that we have only "*three distinctions*" of "*the distinction* of *sex*." And, as no philosopher has yet discovered more than two sexes, some have thence stoutly argued, that it is absurd to speak of more than two genders. Lily makes it out, that in Latin there are *seven:* yet, with no great consistency, he will have *a gender* to be a or *the* distinction *of sex.* "GENUS est sexus discretio. Et sunt genera numero septem."—*Lilii Gram.* p. 10. That is, "GENDER is the distinction *of sex.* And *the genders* are *seven* in number." Ruddiman says, "GENUS est, discrimen *nominis* secundum sexum, vel *ejus* in structurâ grammaticâ imitatio. Genera nominum sunt *tria.*"—*Ruddimanni Gram.* p. 4. That is, "GENDER is the diversity of *the noun* according to sex, or [it is] the imitation *of it* in grammatical structure. The genders of nouns are *three.*" These old definitions are no better than the newer ones cited above. All of them are miserable failures, full of faults and absurdities. Both the nature and the cause of their defects are in some degree explained near the close of the tenth chapter of my Introduction. Their most prominent errors are

greater ceremony than as mortals; and Virgil has still less moderation."—*Ib.* Vol. ii, p. 287. "Which the more refined taste of later writers, who had far inferior genius to them, would have taught them to avoid."—*Blair's Rhet.* p. 28. "The poetry, however, of the Book of Job, is not only equal to that of any other of the sacred writings, but is superior to them all, except those of Isaiah alone."—*Ib.* p. 419. "On the whole, Paradise Lost is a poem that abounds with beauties of every kind, and that justly entitles its author to a degree of fame not inferior to any poet."—*Ib.* p. 452. "Most of the French writers compose in short sentences; though their style in general, is not concise; commonly less so than the bulk of English writers, whose sentences are much longer."—*Ib.* p. 178. "The principles of the Reformation were deeper in the prince's mind than to be easily eradicated."—HUME: *Cobbett's E. Gram.* ¶ 217. "Whether they do not create jealousy and animosity more hurtful than the benefit derived from them."—DR. J. LEO WOLF: *Lit. Conv.* p. 250. "The Scotch have preserved the ancient character of their music more entire than any other country."—*Music of Nature,* p. 461. "When the time or quantity of one syllable exceeds the rest, that syllable readily receives the accent."—*Rush, on the Voice,* p. 277. "What then can be more obviously true than that it should be made as just as we can?"—*Dymond's Essays,* p. 198. "It was not likely that they would criminate themselves more than they could avoid."—*Clarkson's Hist. Abridged,* p. 76. "Their understandings were the most acute of any people who have ever lived."—*Knapp's Lectures,* p. 32. "The patentees have printed it with neat types, and upon better paper than was done formerly."—*Lily's Gram., Pref.,* p. xiii. "In reality, its relative use is not exactly like any other word."—*Felch's Comprehensive Gram.* p. 62. "Thus, instead of two books, which are required, (the grammar and the exercises,) the learner finds both in one, for a price at least not greater than the others."—*Bullions's E. Gram.,* Recom., p. iii; *New Ed.,* Recom., p. 6. "They are not improperly regarded as pronouns, though in a sense less strict than the others."—*Ib.* p. 199. "We have had the opportunity, as will readily be believed, of becoming conversant with the case much more particularly, than the generality of our readers can be supposed to have had."—*The British Friend,* 11mo. 29th, 1845.

UNDER CRITICAL NOTE V.—OF FALSITIES.

"The long sound of *i* is compounded of the sound of *a*, as heard in *ball*, and that of *e*, as heard in *be*."—*Churchill's Gram.* p. 3.

[FORMULE.—Not proper, because the sentence falsely teaches, that the long sound of *i* is that of the diphthong heard in *oil* or *boy*. But, according to Critical Note 5th, "Sentences that convey a meaning manifestly false, should be changed, rejected, or contradicted; because they distort language from its chief end, or only worthy use; which is, to state facts, and to tell the truth." The error may be corrected thus: "The long sound of *i* is *like a very quick union* of the sound of *a*, as heard in *bar*, and that of *e*, as heard in *be*."]

"The omission of a word necessary to grammatical propriety, is called ELLIPSIS."— *Priestley's Gram.* p. 45. "Every substantive is of the third person."—*Alexander Murray's Gram.* p. 91. "A noun, when the subject is spoken *to*, is in the second person; and when spoken *of*, it is in the third person; but never in the first."—*Nutting's Gram.* p. 17. "With us, no substantive nouns have gender, or are masculine and feminine, except the proper names of male and female creatures."—*Blair's Rhet.* p. 156. "Apostrophe is a little mark signifying that something is shortened; as, for William his hat, we say, William's hat."— *Infant School Gram.* p. 30. "When a word beginning with a vowel is coupled with one beginning with a consonant, the indefinite article must be repeated; thus, 'Sir Matthew Hale was *a* noble and *an* impartial judge;' 'Pope was *an* elegant and *a* nervous writer.'" —*Maunder's Gram.* p. 11. "*W* and *y* are consonants, when they begin a word or syllable; but in every other situation they are vowels."—*Murray's Gram.* p. 7: *Bacon, Comly, Cooper, Fisk, Ingersoll, Kirkham, Smith, et al.* "*The* is used before all adjectives and substantives, let them begin as they will."—*Bucke's Gram.* p. 26. "Prepositions are also prefixed to words in such manner, as to coalesce with them, and to become a part of them."— *Lowth's Gram.* p. 66. "But *h* is entirely silent at the beginning of syllables not accented, as *historian*."—*Blair's Gram.* p. 5. "Any word that will make sense with *to* before it, is a verb."—*Kirkham's Gram.* p. 44. "Verbs do not, in reality, express actions; but they are intrinsically the mere *names* of actions."—*Ib.* p. 37. "The nominative is the actor or subject, and the active verb is the action performed by the nominative."—*Ib.* p. 45. "If, therefore, only one creature or thing acts, only one action, at the same instant, can be done; as, the *girl writes*."—*Ib.* 45. "The verb *writes* denotes but one action, which the girl performs; therefore the verb *writes* is of the singular number."—*Ib.* 45. "And when I say,

these: 1. They all assume, that *gender*, taken as one thing, is in fact two, three, or more, *genders*. 2. Nearly all of them seem to say or imply, that *words* differ from one another in *sex*, like animals. 3. Many of them expressly confine *gender*, or *the genders*, to *nouns* only. 4. Many of them confessedly *exclude the neuter gender*, though their authors afterwards admit this gender. 5. That of Dr. Webster supposes, that words differing in gender never have the same "*termination*." The absurdity of this may be shown by a multitude of examples; as, *man* and *woman, male* and *female, father* and *mother, brother* and *sister*. In his Dictionary, the Doctor calls GENDER, "In grammar, a difference *in words* to express distinction *of sex*." This is better, but still not free from some other faults which I have mentioned. For the correction of all this great batch of errors, I shall simply substitute in the Key one short definition, which appears to me to be exempt from each of these inaccuracies.

Two men *walk*, is it not equally apparent, that *walk* is plural, because it expresses *two* actions?"—*Ib.* p. 47. "The subjunctive mood is formed by adding a conjunction to the indicative mood."—*Beck's Gram.* p. 16. "The possessive case should always be distinguished by the apostrophe."—*Frost's El. of Gram.*, Rule 44th, p. 49. "'At these proceedings of the commons,'—Here *of* is the sign of the genitive or possessive case, and *commons* is of that case, governed of proceedings."—*Alex. Murray's Gram.* p. 95. "Here let it be observed again that, strictly speaking, no verbs have numbers nor persons, neither have nouns nor pronouns persons, when they refer to irrational creatures and inanimate things." —*S. Barrett's Gram.* p. 136. "The noun or pronoun denoting the person or thing addressed or spoken to, is in the nominative case independent."—*Frost's El. of Gram.*, Rule 8th, p. 44. "Every noun, when addressed, becomes of the second person, and is in the nominative case absolute; as—'*Paul*, thou art beside thyself.'"—*Jaudon's Gram.*, Rule 19th, p. 108. "Does the Conjunction join Words together? No; only Sentences."—*British Gram.* p. 103. "No; the Conjunction only joins Sentences together."—*Buchanan's Gram.* p. 64. "Every Genitive has a Noun to govern it, expressed or understood; as, St. James's, *Palace* is understood; therefore one Genitive cannot govern another."—*Ib.* p. 111. "Every adjective, and every adjective pronoun, belongs to a substantive, expressed or understood."—*Murray's Gram.* p. 161; *Bacon's*, 48; *Alger's*, 57; *et al.* "Every adjective qualifies a substantive expressed or understood."—*Bullions, E. Gram.* p. 97. "Every adjective belongs to some noun, expressed or understood."—*Ingersoll's Gram.* p. 36. "'Adjectives belong to the nouns which they describe."—*Smith's New Gram.* p. 137. "Adjectives must agree with the nouns, which they qualify."—*Fisk's Murray*, p. 101. "The Adjective must agree with its Substantive in Number."—*Buchanan's Gram.* p. 94. "Every adjective and participle belongs to some noun or pronoun expressed or understood."—*Frost's El. of Gram.* p. 44. "Every Verb of the Infinitive Mood, supposes a Verb before it expressed or understood."—*Buchanan's Gram.* p. 94. "Every Adverb has its Verb expressed or understood." —*Ib.* p. 94. "Conjunctions which connect Sentence to Sentence, are always placed betwixt the two Propositions or Sentences which they unite."—*Ib.* p. 88. "The words *for all that*, seem to be too low."—*Murray's Gram.* p. 213. "*For all that* seems to be too low and vulgar."—*Priestley's Gram.* p. 139. "The reader, or hearer, then, understands from *and*, that he is to add something."—*J. Brown's Eng. Syntax*, p. 124. "But *and* never, never connects one *thing* with another thing, nor one *word* with another word."—*Ib.* p. 122. "'Six, and six are twelve.' Here it is affirmed that, *six is twelve!*"—*Ib.* p. 120. "'John, and his wife have six children.' This is an instance of gross *catachresis*. It is here affirmed that John has six children, and that his wife has six children."—*Ib.* p. 122. "Nothing which is not right can be great."—*Murray's Exercises*, 8vo, p. 146: see *Rambler*, No. 185. "Nothing can be great which is not right."—*Murray's Key*, 8vo, p. 277. "The highest degree of reverence should be paid to youth."—*Ib.* p. 278. "There is, in many minds, neither knowledge nor understanding."—*Murray's Gram.* 8vo, p. 151; *Russell's*, 84; *Alger's*, 54; *Bacon's*, 47; *et al.* "Formerly, what we call the objective cases of our pronouns, were employed in the same manner as our present nominatives are."—*Kirkham's Gram.* p. 164. "As it respects a choice of words and expressions, no rules of grammar can materially aid the learner."—*S. S. Greene's Gram.*, 1st Ed., p. 202. "Whatever exists, or is conceived to exist, is a Noun." —*Fowler's E. Gram.* 8vo, 1850, § 137. "As all men are not brave, *brave* is itself comparative."—*Ib.* § 190.

UNDER CRITICAL NOTE VI.—OF ABSURDITIES.

(1.) "And sometimes two unaccented syllables follow each other."—*Blair's Rhet.* p. 384.

[FORMULE.—Not proper, because the phrase, "*follow each other*," is here an absurdity; it being impossible for two things to "follow each other," except they alternate, or whirl round. But, according to Critical Note 6th, "Absurdities, of every kind, are contrary to grammar; because they are contrary to reason, or good sense, which is the foundation of grammar." Therefore, a different expression should here be chosen; thus: "And sometimes two unaccented syllables *come together*." Or: "And sometimes *one* unaccented *syllable follows an other*."]

(2.) "What nouns frequently succeed each other?"—*Sanborn's Gram.* p. 66. (3.) "Words are derived from one another in various ways."—*Ib.* p. 288; *Merchant's Gram.* 78; *Weld's*, 2d Edition, 222. (4.) "Prepositions are derived from the two Latin words *præ* and *pono*, which signify before and place."—*Maak's Gram.* p. 86. (5.) "He was sadly laughed at for such conduct."—*Bullions, E. Gram.* p. 79. (6.) "Every adjective pronoun belongs to some noun or pronoun expressed or understood."—*Ingersoll's Gram.* p. 212. (7.) "If he [Addison] fails in any thing, it is in want of strength and precision, which renders his manner not altogether a proper model."—*Blair's Rhet.* p. 187. (8.) "Indeed, if Horace be deficient in any thing, it is in this, of not being sufficiently attentive to juncture and connexion of parts."—*Ib.* p. 401. (9.) "The pupil is now supposed to be acquainted with the nine sorts of speech, and their most usual modifications."—*Taylor's District School*, p. 204. (10.) "I could see, hear, taste, and smell the rose."—*Sanborn's Gram.* p. 156. (11.) "The triphthong *iou* is sometimes pronounced distinctly in two syllables; as in bilious, various, abstemious."—*L. Murray's Gram.* p. 13; *Walker's Dict.*, Prin. 292, p. 37. (12.) "The diphthong *aa* generally sounds like *a* short in proper names; as in Balaam, Canaan,

Isaac; but not in Baal, Gaal."—*Murray's Gram.* p. 10. (13.) "Participles are sometimes governed by the article; for the present participle, with the definite article *the* before it, becomes a substantive."—*Ib.* p. 192. (14.) "Words ending with *y*, preceded by a consonant, form the plurals of nouns, the persons of verbs, verbal nouns, past participles, comparatives, and superlatives, by changing *y* into *i*."—*Walker's Rhyming Dict.* p. viii; *Murray's Gram.* 23; *Merchant's Murray*, 13; *Fisk's*, 44; *Kirkham's*, 23; *Greenleaf's*, 20; *Wright's Gram.* 28; *et al.* (15.) "But *y* preceded by a vowel, *in such instances as the above*, is not changed; as, boy, boys."—*Murray's Gram.* p. 24; *Merchant's*, *Fisk's*, *Kirkham's*, *Greenleaf's*, *et al.* (16.) "But when *y* is preceded by a vowel, it is very rarely* changed in the additional syllable: as, coy, coyly."—*Murray's Gram. again*, p. 24; *Merchant's*, 14; *Fisk's*, 45; *Greenleaf's*, 20; *Wright's*, 29; *et al.* (17.) "But when *y* is preceded by a vowel, *in such instances*, it is very rarely changed to *i*; as, *coy*, COYLESS."—*Kirkham's Gram.* p. 24. (18.) "Sentences are of a twofold nature : Simple and Compound."—*Wright's Gram.* p. 122. (19.) "The neuter pronoun *it* is applied to all nouns and pronouns: as, *It is he*; *it is she*; *it is they*; *it is the land*."—*Bucke's Gram.* p. 92. (20.) "*It is* and *it was*, are often used in a plural construction; as, '*It was* the heretics who first began to rail.'"—*Merchant's Gram.* p. 87. (21.) "*It is*, and *it was*, are often, after the manner of the French, used in a plural construction, by some of our best writers: as, '*It was the heretics that* first began to rail.' Smollett."—*Priestley's Gram.* p. 190; *Murray's*, 158; *Smith's*, 134; *Ingersoll's*, 210; *Fisk's*, 115; *et al.* (22.) "w and y, as consonants, have one sound."—*Town's Spelling-Book*, p. 9. (23.) "The conjunction *as* is frequently used as a relative."—*Bucke's Gram.* p. 93. (24.) "When several clauses succeed each other, the conjunction may be omitted with propriety."—*Merchant's Gram.* p. 97. (25.) "If, however, the members succeeding each other, are very closely connected, the comma is unnecessary: as, 'Revelation tells us how we may attain happiness.'"—*Murray's Gram.* p. 273; *Merchant's*, 151; *Russell's*, 115; *Comly's*, 152; *Alger's*, 80; *Smith's*, 190; *et al.* (26.) "The mind has difficulty in passing readily through so many different views given it, in quick succession, of the same object."—*Blair's Rhet.* p. 149. (27.) "The mind has difficulty in passing readily through many different views of the same object, presented in quick succession."—*Murray's Gram.* 8vo, p. 341. (28.) "Adjective Pronouns are a kind of adjectives which point out nouns by some distinct specification."—*Kirkham's Gram., the Compend, or Table.* (29.) "A noun of multitude conveying plurality of idea,† must have a verb or pronoun agreeing with it in the plural."—*Ib.* pp. 59 and 181: see also *Lowth's Gram.* p. 74; *L. Murray's*, 152; *Comly's*, 80; *Lennie's*, 87; *Alger's*, 54; *Jaudon's*, 96; *Alden's*, 81; *Parker and Fox's*, I, 76; II, 26; *and others*. (30.) "A noun or pronoun, signifying possession, is governed by the noun it possesses."—*Greenleaf's Gram.* p. 35. (31.) "A noun signifying possession is governed by the noun which it possesses."—*Wilbur and Livingston's Gram.* p. 24. (32.) "A noun or pronoun in the possessive case, is governed by the noun it possesses."—*Goldsbury's Gram.* p. 68. (33.) "The possessive case is governed by the person or thing possessed; as, 'this is *his* book.'" —*P. E. Day's Gram.* p. 81. (34.) "A noun or pronoun in the possessive case, is governed by the noun which it possesses."—*Kirkham's Gram., Rule 12th*, pp. 52 and 181; *Frazee's Gram.*, 1844, p. 25; *F. H. Miller's*, 21. (35.) "Here the boy is represented as acting. He is, therefore, in the nominative case."—*Kirkham's Gram.* p. 41. (36.) "Some of the auxiliaries are themselves principal verbs, as: *have, do, will*, and *am*, or *be*."—*Cooper's Gram. both*, p. 50. (37.) "Nouns of the male kind are masculine. Those of the female kind are feminine."—*Beck's Gram.* p. 6. (38.) "'To-day's lesson is longer than yesterday's :' here *to-day* and *yesterday* are substantives."—*Murray's Gram.* p. 114; *Ingersoll's*, 50; *et al.* (39.) "In this example, *to-day* and *yesterday* are nouns in the possessive case."—*Kirkham's Gram.* p. 88. (40.) "An Indian in Britain would be much surprised to stumble upon an elephant feeding at large in the open fields."—*Kames, El. of Crit.* Vol. i. p. 219. (41.) "If we were to contrive a new language, we might make any articulate sound the sign of any idea : there would be no impropriety in calling oxen *men*, or rational beings by the name of *oxen*."—

---

* Walker states this differently, and even repeats his remark, thus : "But *y* preceded by a vowel is never changed ; as *coy, coyly, gay, gayly*."—*Walker's Rhyming Dict.* p. x. "Y preceded by a vowel is never changed, as boy, boys, I cloy, he cloys, &c."—*Ib.* p. viii. Walker's twelve "Orthographical Aphorisms," which Murray and others republish as their "Rules for Spelling," and which in stead of amending they merely corrupt, happened through some carelessness to contain *two* which should have been condensed into *one*. For "words ending with *y* preceded by a consonant," he has not only the absurd rule or assertion above recited, but an other which is better, with an exception or remark under each, respecting "*y* preceded by a vowel." The grammarians follow him in his errors, and add to their number : hence the repetition, or similarity, in the absurdities here quoted. By the term "*verbal nouns*," Walker meant nouns denoting agents, as *carrier* from *carry*; but Kirkham understood him to mean "*participial nouns*," as *the carrying*. Or rather, he so mistook "that able philologist" Murray; for he probably knew nothing of Walker in the matter; and accordingly changed the word "*verbal*" to "*participial*;" thus teaching, through all his hundred editions, except a few of the first, that participial nouns from verbs ending in *y* preceded by a consonant, are formed by merely "changing the *y* into *i*." But he seems to have known, that this is not the way to form the participle ; though he did not know, that "*coyless*" is not a proper English word.

† The idea of *plurality* is not "*plurality of idea*," any more than the idea of *wickedness*, or the idea of *absurdity*, is absurdity or wickedness of idea ; yet, behold, how our grammarians copy the blunder, which Lowth (perhaps) first fell into, of putting the one phrase for the other! Even Professor Fowler, (as well as Murray, Kirkham, and others,) talks of having regard "*to unity or plurality of idea!*"—*Fowler's E. Gram.* 8vo, 1850, § 513.—G. BROWN.

Murray's Gram. p. 139. "All the parts of a sentence should correspond to each other."—*Ib.* p. 222; *Kirkham's,* 193; *Ingersoll's,* 275; *Goldsbury's,* 74; *Hiley's,* 110; *Weld's,* 193; *Alger's,* 71; *Fisk's,* 148; *S. Putnam's,* 95; *Merchant's,* 101; *Merchant's Murray,* 95.

"Full through his neck the weighty falchion sped,
　Along the pavement roll'd the mutt'ring head."—*Odyssey,* xxii, 365.

UNDER CRITICAL NOTE VII.— OF SELF-CONTRADICTION.

(1.) "Though the construction will not admit of a *plural verb,* the sentence would certainly stand better thus : 'The king, the lords, and the commons, *form* an excellent constitution.' "—*Murray's Gram.* p. 151; *Ingersoll's,* 239.

[FORMULE.—Not proper, because the first clause here quoted is contradicted by the last. But, according to Critical Note 7th, "Every writer or speaker should be careful not to contradict himself; for what is self-contradictory, is both null in argument, and bad in style." The following change may remove the discrepance : "Though 'the king *with* the lords and commons,' *must have a singular rather than* a plural verb, the sentence would certainly stand better thus : 'The king, the lords, *and* the commons, *form* an excellent constitution.' "]

(2.) "*L* has always a soft liquid sound ; as in love, billow, quarrel. It is sometimes mute ; as in half, talk, psalm."—*Murray's Gram.* p. 14; *Fisk's,* 40. (3.) "*L* has always a soft liquid sound ; as in *love, billow.* It is often silent ; as in *half, talk, almond.*"—*Kirkham's Gram.* p. 22. (4.) "The words *means* and *amends,* though formerly used in the singular, as well as in the plural number, are now, by polite writers, restricted to the latter. Our most distinguished modern authors say, 'by *this means,*' as well as, 'by *these means.*' "—*Wright's Gram.* p. 150. (5.) " 'A friend exaggerates a man's virtues : an enemy inflames his crimes.' Better thus : 'A friend exaggerates a man's virtues : an enemy his crimes.' "—*Murray's Gram.* i, p. 325. "A friend exaggerates a man's virtues, an enemy inflames his crimes."—*Ib. Key,* ii, p. 173. (6.) "The auxiliary *have,* in the perfect tense of the subjunctive mood, should be avoided."—*Merchant's Gram.* p. 97. "Subjunctive Mood, Perfect Tense, If I *have* loved, If thou hast loved," &c.—*Ib.* p. 51. (7.) "There is also an impropriety in governing both the indicative and subjunctive moods, with the same conjunction ; as, 'If a man *have* a hundred sheep, and *if* one of them *be* gone astray,' &c. It should be, and one of them *is* gone astray, &c."—*Ib.* p. 97. (8.) "The rising series of contrasts convey inexpressible dignity and energy to the conclusion."—*Jamieson's Rhet.* p. 79. (9.) "A groan or a shriek is instantly understood, as a language extorted by distress, a language which no art can counterfeit, and which conveys a meaning that words are utterly inadequate to express."—*Porter's Analysis,* p. 127. "A groan or shriek speaks to the ear, as the language of distress, with far more thrilling effect than words. Yet these may be counterfeited by art."—*Ib.* p. 147. (10.) "These words [*book* and *pen*] cannot be put together in such a way as will constitute plurality."—*James Brown's English Syntax,* p. 125. (11.) "Nor can the real *pen,* and the real *book* be expressed in two words in such a manner as will constitute *plurality* in grammar."—*Ibid.* (12.) "*Our* is an adjective pronoun of the possessive kind. Decline it."—*Murray's Gram.* p. 227. (13.) "*This* and *that,* and likewise their Plurals, are always opposed to each other in a Sentence."—*Buchanan's Syntax,* p. 103. "When *this* or *that* is used alone, i. e. not opposed to each other, *this* is written or spoken of Persons or Things immediately present, and as it were before our Eyes, or nearest with relation to Place or Time. *That* is spoken or written of Persons or Things passed, absent and distant in relation to Time and Place."—*Ibid.* (14.) "Active and neuter verbs may be conjugated by adding their present participle to the auxiliary verb *to be,* through all its variations."—*Kirkham's Gram.* p. 159. "*Be* is an auxiliary whenever it is placed before the perfect participle of another verb, but in every other situation, it is a *principal* verb."—*Ib.* p. 155. (15.) "A verb in the imperative mood, is always of the second person."—*Kirkham's Gram.* p. 136. "The verbs, according to an idiom of our language, or the poet's license, are used in the *imperative,* agreeing with a nominative of the first or third person."—*Ib.* p. 164. (16.) "Personal Pronouns are distinguished from the relative, by their denoting the *person* of the nouns for which they stand."—*Kirkham's Gram.* p. 97. "Pronouns of the first person, do not agree in person with the nouns they represent."—*Ib.* p. 98. (17.) "Nouns have three cases, nominative, possessive, and objective."—*Beck's Gram.* p. 6. "Personal pronouns have, like nouns, two cases, nominative and objective."—*Ib.* p. 10. (18.) "In some instances the preposition suffers no change, but becomes an adverb merely by its application : as, 'He was *near* falling.' "—*Murray's Gram.* p. 116. (19.) "Some nouns are used only in the plural ; as, *ashes, literati, minutiæ,* SHEEP, DEER."—*Blair's Gram.* p. 43. "Some nouns are the same in both numbers, as *alms, couple,* DEER, *series, species, pair,* SHEEP."—*Ibid.* "Among the inferior parts of speech there are some *pairs* or *couples.*"—*Ib.* p. 94. (20.) "Concerning the pronominal *adjectives,* that *can* and *can not, may* and *may not,* represents *its* noun."—*O. B. Peirce's Gram.* p. 336. (21.) "The *article a* is in a few instances employed in the sense of a *preposition* ; as, Simon Peter said I go a [to] fishing."—*Weld's Gram.,* 2d Ed., p. 177; Abridg. 128. " 'To go a fishing ;' i. e. to go on a fishing voyage or business."—*Weld's Gram.* p. 192. (22.) "So also verbs, really transitive, are used intransitively, when they have no object."—*Bullions, Analyt. and Pract. Gram.* p. 60.

(23.) "When first young Maro, in his boundless mind,
　A work t'outlast immortal Rome design'd."—*Pope, on Crit.* l. 130.

UNDER CRITICAL NOTE VIII.—OF SENSELESS JUMBLING.

"Number distinguishes them [viz., *nouns*], as one, or many, of the same kind, called the singular and plural."—*Dr. Blair's Lectures on Rhetoric*, p. 74.

[FORMULE.—Not proper, because the words of this text appear to be so carelessly put together, as to make nothing but jargon, or a sort of scholastic balderdash. But, according to Critical Note 8th, "To jumble together words without care for the sense, is an unpardonable negligence, and an abuse of the human understanding." I think the learned author should rather have said: "*There are two members*, called the singular and *the plural, which distinguish nouns as signifying either* one *thing*, or many of the same kind."]

"Here the noun *James Munroe* is addressed, he is spoken to, it is here a noun of the second person."—*Mack's Gram.* p. 66. "The number and case of a verb can never be ascertained until its nominative is known."—*Emmons's Gram.* p. 36. "A noun of multitude, or signifying many, may have the verb and pronoun agreeing with it either in the singular or plural number; yet not without regard to the import of the word, as conveying unity or plurality of idea."—*Lowth's Gram.* p. 75; *Murray's*, 152; *Alger's*, 54; *Russell's*, 55; *Ingersoll's*, 248; *et al.* "To express the present and past imperfect of the active and neuter verb, the auxiliary *do* is sometimes used: I *do* (now) love; I *did* (then) love."—*Lowth's Gram.* p. 40. "If these are perfectly committed, they will be able to take twenty lines for a lesson on the second day; and may be increased each day."—*Osborn's Key*, p. 4. "When *o* is joined with *h* (*oh*), they are generally sounded in the same manner: as in *Charles*, church, cheerfulness, and cheese. But foreign words (except in those derived from the French, as *chagrin*, *chicanery*, and *chaise*, in which *ch* are sounded like *sh*) are pronounced like *k*: as in Chaos, character, chorus, and chimera."—*Bucke's Classical Gram.* p. 10. "Some substantives, naturally neuter, are, by a figure of speech, converted into the masculine or feminine gender."—*Murray's Gram.* p. 37; *Comly's*, 20; *Bacon's*, 13; *A Teacher's*, 9; *Alger's*, 16; *Lennie's*, 11; *Fisk's*, 56; *Merchant's*, 27; *Kirkham's*, 35; *et al.* "Words in the English language may be classified under ten general heads, the names of which classes are usually termed the ten parts of speech."—*Nutting's Gram.* p. 14. "'Mercy is the true badge of nobility.' *Nobility* is a noun of multitude, mas. and fem. gender, third person, sing. and in the obj. case, and governed by 'of:' RULE 31."—*Kirkham's Gram.* p. 161. "'gh, are either silent, or have the sound of f, as in laugh."—*Town's Spelling-Book*, p. 10. "As many people as were destroyed, were as many languages or dialects lost and blotted out from the general catalogue."—*Chazotte's Essay*, p. 25. "The grammars of some languages contain a greater number of *the* moods, than *others*, and exhibit *them* in different forms."—*Murray's Gram.* 8vo, i, p. 95. "A COMPARISON or SIMILE, is, *when* the resemblance between two objects *is expressed in form*, and *generally pursued* more fully than the nature of a metaphor admits."—*Ib.* p. 343. "In *some dialects*, the word *what* is improperly used for *that*, and sometimes we find it in *this sense* in writing."—*Ib.* p. 156; *Priestley's Gram.* 93; *Smith's*, 132; *Merchant's*, 87; *Fisk's*, 114; *Ingersoll's*, 220; *et al.* "Brown makes great ado concerning the *sameness* principles of preceding works, in relation to the *gender* of pronouns."—*O. B. Peirce's Gram.* p. 323. "The nominative precedes and performs the action of the verb."—*Beck's Gram.* p. 8. "The Primitive are those which cannot receive more simple forms than those which they already possess."—*Wright's Gram.* p. 28. "The long sound [of *i*] is always marked by the *e* final in monosyllables: as, thin, thine; except give, live."—*Murray's Gram.* p. 13; *Fisk's*, 39; *et al.* "But the third person or thing spoken of, being absent, and in many respects unknown, it is necessary that it should be marked by a distinction of gender."—*Lowth's Gram.* p. 21; *L. Murray's*, 51; *et al.* "Each of the diphthongal letters was, doubtless, originally heard in pronouncing the words which contain them. Though this is not the case at present, with respect to many of them, these combinations still retain the name of diphthongs; but, to distinguish them, they are marked by the term *improper*."—*L. Murray's Gram.* p. 9; *Fisk's*, 37; *et al.* "A Mode is the form of, or manner of using a verb, by which the being, action, or passion is expressed."—*Alex. Murray's Gram.* p. 32. "The word *that* is a demonstrative pronoun when it is followed immediately by a substantive, to which it is either joined, or refers, and which it limits or qualifies."—*Lindley Murray's Gram.* p. 54.

"The guiltless woe of being past,
Is future glory's deathless heir."—*Sumner L. Fairfield.*

UNDER CRITICAL NOTE IX.—OF WORDS NEEDLESS.

"A knowledge of grammar enables us to express ourselves better in conversation and in writing composition."—*Sanborn's Gram.* p. 7.

[FORMULE.—Not proper, because the word *composition* is here needless. But, according to Critical Note 9th, "Words that are entirely needless, and especially such as injure or encumber the expression, ought in general to be omitted." The sentence would be better without this word, thus: "A knowledge of grammar enables us to express ourselves better in conversation, and in writing."]

"And hence we infer, that there is no other dictator here but use."—*Jamieson's Rhet.* p. 42. "Whence little else is gained, except correct spelling and pronunciation."—*Town's Spelling-Book*, p. 5. "The man who is faithfully attached to religion, may be relied on, with humble confidence."—*Merchant's School Gram.* p. 76. "Shalt thou build me an house for me to dwell in?"—*2 Sam.* vii, 5. "The house was deemed polluted which was entered into by so abandoned a woman."—*Blair's Rhet.* p. 279. "The farther that he searches, the firmer will be his belief."—*Keith's Evidences*, p. 4. "I deny not, but that religion consists in these things."—*Barclay's Works*, i, 321. "Except the king delighted in her, and that she were called by name."—*Esther*, ii, 14. "The proper method of reading these lines, is to read them according as the sense dictates."—*Blair's Rhet.* p. 386. "When any words become obsolete, or at least are never used, except as constituting part of particular phrases, it is better to dispense with their service entirely, and give up the phrases."—*Campbell's Rhet.* p. 185; *Murray's Gram.* p. 370. "Those savage people seemed to have no element but that of war."—*Murray's Key*, 8vo, p. 211. "*Man* is a common noun, of the third person, singular number, masculine gender, and in the nominative case."—*J. Flint's Gram.* p. 33. "The orator, according as circumstances require, will employ them all."—*Blair's Rhet.* p. 247. "By deferring our repentance, we accumulate our sorrows."—*Murray's Key*, ii, p. 166. "There is no doubt but that public speaking became early an engine of government."—*Blair's Rhet.* p. 245. "The different meaning of these two first words may not at first occur."—*Ib.* p. 225. "The sentiment is well expressed by Plato, but much better by Solomon than him."—*Murray's Gram.* p. 214; *Ingersoll's*, 251; *Smith's*, 179; *et al.* "They have had a greater privilege than we have had."—*Murray's Key*, 8vo, p. 211. "Every thing should be so arranged, as that what goes before may give light and force to what follows." —*Blair's Rhet.* p. 311. "So as that his doctrines were embraced by great numbers."— UNIV. HIST.: *Priestley's Gram.* p. 139. "They have taken another and a shorter cut."— SOUTH: *Joh. Dict.* "The Imperfect Tense of a regular verb is formed from the present by adding *d* or *ed* to the present; as, 'I *loved.*' "—*Frost's El. of Gram.* p. 32. "The pronoun *their* does not agree in gender or number with the noun 'man,' for which it stands."—*Kirkham's Gram.* p. 182. "This mark denotes any thing of wonder, surprise, joy, grief, or sudden emotion."—*Bucke's Gram.* p. 19. "We are all accountable creatures, each for himself."— *Murray's Key*, p. 204; *Merchant's*, 195. "If he has commanded it, then I must obey."— *Smith's New Gram.* pp. 110 and 112. "I now present him with a form of the diatonic scale."—*Dr. John Barber's Elocution*, p. xi. "One after another of their favourite rivers have been reluctantly abandoned."—*Hodgson's Tour.* "*Particular* and *peculiar* are words of different import from each other."—*Blair's Rhet.* p. 196. "Some adverbs admit rules of comparison: as, Soon, sooner, soonest."—*Bucke's Gram.* p. 76. "From having exposed himself too freely in different climates, he entirely lost his health."—*Murray's Key*, p. 200. "The Verb must agree with its Nominative before it in Number and Person."—*Buchanan's Syntax*, p. 93. "Write twenty short sentences containing only adjectives."—*Abbott's Teacher*, p. 102. "This general inclination and tendency of the language seems to have given occasion to the introducing of a very great corruption."—*Lowth's Gram.* p. 60. "The second requisite of a perfect sentence, is its *Unity.*"—*Murray's Gram.* p. 311. "It is scarcely necessary to apologize for omitting to insert their names."—*Ib.* p. vii. "The letters of the English language, called the English Alphabet, are twenty-six in number."—*Ib.* p. 2; *T. Smith's*, 5; *Fisk's*, 10; *Alger's*, 9; *et al.* "A writer who employs antiquated or novel phraseology, must do it with design: he cannot err from inadvertence as he may do it with respect to provincial or vulgar expressions."—*Jamieson's Rhet.* p. 56. "The *Vocative* case, in some Grammars, is wholly omitted; why, if we must have cases, I could never understand the propriety of."—*Bucke's Classical Gram.* p. 45. "Active verbs are conjugated with the auxiliary verb *I have*; passive verbs are conjugated with the auxiliary verb *I am.*"—*Ib.* p. 57. "What word, then, may *and* be called? A Conjunction."—*Smith's New Gram.* p. 37. "Have they ascertained the person who gave the information?"—*Bullions's E. Gram.* p. 81.

UNDER CRITICAL NOTE X.—OF IMPROPER OMISSIONS.

"All qualities of things are called adnouns, or adjectives."—*Blair's Gram.* p. 10.

[FORMULE.—Not proper, because this expression lacks two or three words which are necessary to the sense intended. But according to Critical Note 10th, "Words necessary to the sense, or even to the melody or beauty of a sentence, ought seldom, if ever, to be omitted." The sentence may be amended thus: "All *words signifying concrete* qualities of things, are called adnouns, or adjectives."]

"The - signifies the long or accented syllable, and the breve indicates a short or unaccented syllable."—*Blair's Gram.* p. 118. "Whose duty is to help young ministers."—*N. E. Discipline*, p. 78. "The passage is closely connected with what precedes and follows." —*Philological Museum*, Vol. i, p. 255. "The work is not completed, but soon will be."— *Smith's Productive Gram.* p. 113. "Of whom hast thou been afraid or feared?"—*Isaiah*, lvii, 11. "There is a God who made and governs the world."—*Butler's Analogy*, p. 263. "It was this made them so haughty."—*Goldsmith's Greece*, Vol. ii, p. 102. "How far the whole charge affected him is not easy to determine."—*Ib.* i, p. 189. "They saw, and worshipped the God, that made them."—*Bucke's Gram.* p. 157. "The errors frequent in the use of hyperboles, arise either from overstraining, or introducing them on unsuitable occasions."—*Murray's Gram.* 8vo, p. 256. "The preposition *in* is set before countries, cities, and large towns: as, 'He lives *in* France, *in* London, or *in* Birmingham.' But before villages, single houses, and cities which are in distant countries, *at* is used: as, 'He lives *at* Hackney.'"—*Ib.* p. 204; *Dr. Ash's Gram.* 60; *Ingersoll's*, 232; *Smith's*, 170; *Fisk's*, 143; *et al.* "And, in such recollection, the thing is not figured as in our view, nor any image formed."—*Kames, El. of Crit.* Vol. i, p. 86. "Intrinsic and relative beauty must be handled separately."—*Ib.* Vol. ii, p. 336. "He should be on his guard not to do them injustice, by disguising, or placing them in a false light."—*Blair's Rhet.* p. 272. "In that work, we are frequently interrupted by unnatural thoughts."—*Murray's Key,* 8vo, p. 275. "To this point have tended all the rules I have given."—*Blair's Rhet.* p. 120. "To these points have tended all the rules which have been given."—*Murray's Gram.* 8vo, p. 356. "Language, as written, or oral, is addressed to the eye, or to the ear."—*Lit. Conv.* p. 184. "He will learn, Sir, that to accuse and prove are very different."—*Walpole.* "They crowded around the door so as to prevent others going out."—*Abbott's Teacher,* p. 17. "One person or thing is singular number; more than one person or thing is plural number."—*John Flint's Gram.* p. 27. "According to the sense or relation in which nouns are used, they are in the NOMINATIVE OF POSSESSIVE CASE, thus, *nom.* man ; *poss.* man's."—*Blair's Gram.* p. 11. "Nouns or pronouns in the possessive case are placed before the nouns which govern them, to which they belong."—*Sanborn's Gram.* p. 130. "A teacher is explaining the difference between a noun and verb."—*Abbott's Teacher,* p. 72. "And therefore the two ends, or extremities, must directly answer to the north and south pole."—HARRIS : *Joh. Dict. w. Gnomon.* "*Walks* or *walketh, rides* or *rideth, stands* or *standeth,* are of the third person singular."—*Kirkham's Gram.* p. 47. "I grew immediately roguish and pleasant to a degree, in the same strain."—SWIFT : *Tattler,* 31. "An Anapæst has the first syllables unaccented, and the last accented."—*Blair's Gram.* p. 119. "An Anapæst has the first two syllables unaccented, and the last accented."—*Kirkham's Gram.* p. 219; *Bullions's Principles,* 170. "An Anapæst has the two first syllables unaccented, and the last accented."—*L. Murray's Gram.* p. 254; *Jamieson's Rhet.* 305; *Smith's New Gram.* 188; *Guy's Gram.* 120; *Merchant's,* 167; *Russell's,* 109; *Picket's,* 226. "But hearing and vision differ not more than words spoken and written."—*Wilson's Essay on Gram.* p. 21. "They are considered by some prepositions."—*Cooper's Pl. and Pr. Gram.* p. 102. "When those powers have been deluded and gone astray."—*Philological Museum,* i, 642. "They will soon understand this, and like it."—*Abbott's Teacher,* p. 92. "They had been expelled their native country Romagna."—*Leigh Hunt, on Byron,* p. 18. "Future time is expressed two different ways."—*Adam's Gram.* p. 80; *Gould's,* 78. "Such as the borrowing from history some noted event."—*Kames, El. of Crit.* Vol. ii, p. 280. "Every Verb must agree with its Nominative in Number and Person."—*Bucke's Gram.* p. 94. "We are struck, we know not how, with the symmetry of any thing we see."—*Murray's Key,* 8vo, p. 268. "Under this head, I shall consider every thing necessary to a good delivery."—*Sheridan's Lect.* p. 26. "A good ear is the gift of nature; it may be much improved, but not acquired by art."—*Murray's Gram.* p. 298. "'Truth,' A noun, neuter, singular, the nominative."—*Bullions, E. Gram.* p. 73. "'Possess,' A verb transitive, present, indicative active,—third person, plural."—*Ibid.* 73. "*Fear* is a noun, neuter, singular, and is the nominative to (or subject of) *is.*"—*Id. ib.* p. 133. "*Is* is a verb, intrans., irregular—am, was, been; it is in the present, indicative, third person singular, and agrees with its nominative *fear.* Rule I. 'A verb agrees,' &c."—*Ibid.* 133. "*As* in Gaelic, has the sound of long *a.*"—*Wells's School Gram.,* 1st. Ed., p. 29.

UNDER CRITICAL NOTE XL.—OF LITERARY BLUNDERS.

"Repeat some [adverb] that are composed of the article *a* and nouns."—*Kirkham's Gram.* p. 89.

[FORMULE.—Not proper, because the grammatist here mistakes for the article *a,* the prefix or preposition *a;* as in "*aside, ashore, afoot, astray,*" &c. But, according to Critical Note 11th, "Grave blunders made in the name of learning, are the strongest of all certificates against the books which contain them unreproved." The error should be corrected thus : "Repeat some adverbs that are composed of the *prefix a,* or *preposition a,* and nouns."]

"Participles are so called, because derived from the Latin word *participium,* which signifies *to partake.*"—*Merchant's School Gram.* p. 18. "The possessive *follows* another noun, and is known by the sign '*s* or *of.*"—*Beck's Gram.* p. 8. "Reciprocal pronouns are formed by adding *self* or *selves* to the possessive ; as, my*self,* your*selves.*"—*Ib.* p. 19. "The word *self,* and its plural *selves,* must be considered nouns, as they occupy the places of nouns, and stand for the names of them."—*Wright's Gram.* p. 61. "The Dactyl, *rolls round,* expresses beautifully the majesty of the sun in his course."—*Webster's Philos. Gram.* p. 231; *Webster's Imp. Gram.* p. 165; *Frazee's Imp. Gram.* p. 192. "Prepositions govern the objective case ; as, John learned his lesson."—*Frazee's Gram.* p. 153. "Prosody primarily signified punctuation ; and as the name implies, related to stopping *by the way.*"—*Hendrick's Gram.* p. 103. "On such a principle of forming modes, there would be as many modes as verbs ; and instead of four modes, we should have forty-three thousand, which is the number of verbs in the English language, according to Lowth."—*Hallock's Gram.* p. 76. "The following phrases are elliptical : 'To let *out* blood.' 'To go a hunting;' that is, 'To go a hunting excursion.'"—*Bullions, E. Gram.* p. 129. "In Rhyme, the last syllable of two lines has the same sound."—*Id. Practical Lessons,* p. 129. "The possessive case ending in *es,* has the apostrophe, but omits the *s*; as, *Eagles'* wings."—*Weld's Gram.* p. 6 *Abridg.* p. 54. "Horses (plural) -mane. [should be written] horses' mane."—*Weld, ib.* pp.

and 54. "W takes its written form from the union of two v's, this being the form of the Roman capital letter which we call V."—*Fowler's E. Gram.*, 1850, p. 157. "In the sentence, 'I saw the lady who sings,' what *word* do I say sings?'"—*J. Flint's Gram.* p. 12. "In the sentence. 'this is the pen which John made,' what *word* do I say John made?'"—*Ibid.* "'That we fall into *no* sin:' *no*, an adverb used idiomatically, instead of we do not fall into any sin."—*Blair's Gram.* p. 54. "'That *all* our doings may be ordered by thy governance:' *all*, a pronoun used for *the whole*."—*Ibid.* "'Let him be made *to* study.' What causes the sign *to* to be expressed before *study?* Its being used in the passive voice after *be made*."—*Sanborn's Gram.* p. 145. "The following Verbs have neither Preter-Tense nor Passive-Participle, viz. Cast, cut, cost, shut, let, bid, shed, hurt, hit, put, &c."—*Buchanan's Gram.* p. 60. "The agreement, which *every* word has with *the* others in person, gender, *and* case, is called CONCORD; and that power, which one *person of speech* has over *another*, in respect to ruling its case, mood, or *tense*, is called GOVERNMENT."—*Bucke's Classical Gram.* p. 83. "The word *ticks* tells what the noun *watch* does."—*Sanborn's Gram.* p. 15. "*Breve* (ˇ) *marks a short* vowel or syllable, and the dash (—) a long."—*Bullions, E. Gram.* p. 157; *Lennie*, 137. "'Charles, you, by your diligence, make easy work of the task given you by your preceptor.' The first *you* is used in the nom. poss. and obj. case."—*Kirkham's Gram.* p. 103. "*Ouy* in *bouy* is a proper tripthong. *Eau* in flambeau is an improper tripthong."—*Sanborn's Gram.* p. 255. "'While I of things to come, As past rehearsing, sing.' POLLOK. That is, 'While I sing of things which are to come, as one sings of things which are past rehearsing.'"—*Kirkham's Gram.* p. 169. "A simple sentence has in it but one nominative, and one neuter verb."—*Folker's Gram.* p. 14. "An Irregular Verb is that which has its passed tense and perfect participle terminating differently; as, smite, smote, smitten."—*Wright's Gram.* p. 92. "But when the antecedent is used in a general sense, a comma is properly inserted before the relative; as, 'There is no *charm* in the female sex, *which* can supply the place of virtue.'"—*Kirkham's Gram.* p. 213. "Two capitals in this way denote the plural number; as, L. D. *Legis Doctor*; LL. D. *Legum Doctor*."—*Gould's Lat. Gram.* p. 274. "Was any person besides the mercer present? Yes, both he and his clerk."—*Murray's Key*, 8vo, p. 188. "*Adnoun*, or *Adjective*, comes from the Latin, *ad* and *jicio*, to *add to*."—*Kirkham's Gram.* p. 69. "Another figure of speech, proper only to animated and warm composition, is what some critical writers call vision; when, *in place* of relating *some thing that is past*, we use the *present tense*, and describe *it* as actually *passing* before our eyes. Thus Cicero, in his fourth oration against Cataline: 'I seem to myself to behold this city, the ornament of the earth, and the capital of all nations, suddenly involved in one conflagration. I see before me the slaughtered heaps of citizens lying unburied in the midst of their ruined country. The furious countenance of Cethegus rises to my view, while with a savage joy he is triumphing in *your* miseries.'"—*Blair's Rhet.* p. 171. "Vision is another figure of speech, which is proper only in animated and warm composition. It is produced when, *instead* of relating *something that is past*, we use the present tense," &c.—*Murray's Gram.* 8vo, p. 352. "When *several* verbs *follow one another*, having the same nominative, the auxiliary is frequently *omitted after the first* through an ellipsis, and understood *to the rest*: as, 'He has gone and left me;' that is, 'He has gone, and *has* left me.'"—*Comly's Gram.* p. 94. "When I use the word *pillar* as supporting an edifice, I employ it literally,"—*Hiley's Gram.*, 3d Ed., p. 133. "The conjunction *nor* is often used for *neither*; as, 'Simois *nor* Xanthus shall be wanting there.'"—*Ib.* p. 129.

UNDER CRITICAL NOTE XII. — OF PERVERSIONS.

"In the beginning, God created the heavens and the earth."—*Murray's Gram.* 8vo, Vol. i, p. 330; *Hallock's Gram.* p. 179; *Melmoth, on Scripture*, p. 16.

[FORMULE.—Not proper, because this reading is false in relation to the word "*heavens;*" nor is it usual to put a comma after the word "*beginning.*" But, according to Critical Note 12th, "Proof-texts in grammar, if met in all argument, should be quoted literally; and even that which needs to be corrected, must never be perverted." The authorised text is this: "In the beginning God created the *heaven* and the earth."—*Gen.* i, 1.]

"Canst thou, by searching, find out the Lord?"—*Murray's Gram.* p. 335. "Great is the Lord, just and true are thy ways, thou king of saints."—*Priestley's Gram.* p. 171; *L. Murray's*, 168; *Merchant's*, 90; *R. C. Smith's*, 145; *Ingersoll's*, 194; *Enoll's*, 330; *Fisk's*, 104; *et al.* "Every one that saith unto me, Lord, Lord, shall not enter into the kingdom of heaven."—*Alex. Murray's Gram.* p. 137. "Though he was rich, yet for our sakes he became poor."—*L. Murray's Gram.* p. 211; *Bullions's*, 111 and 113; *Everest's*, 230; *Smith's*, 177; *et al.* "Whose foundation was overflown with a flood."—FRIENDS' BIBLE: *Job*, xxii, 16. "Take my yoke upon ye, for my yoke is easy."—*The Friend*, Vol. iv, p. 150. "I will to prepare a place for you."—*Weld's E. Gram.*, 2d Ed., p. 67. "Ye who are dead hath he quickened."—*Ib.* p. 189. "Go, flee thee away into the land of Judea."—*Hart's Gram.* p. 115. "Hitherto shalt thou come, and no farther."—*Murray's Key*, 8vo, p. 222. "Thine is the day and night."—*Brown's Concordance*, p. 82. "Faith worketh patience; and patience, experience; and experience, hope."—*O. B. Peirce's Gram.* p. 282. "Soon shall the dust return to dust, and the soul, to God who gave it. BIBLE."—*Ib.* p. 166. "For, in the end, it biteth like a serpent, and stingeth like an adder. It will lead thee into destruction, and cause thee to utter perverse things. Thou wilt be like him who lieth down in the midst of the sea. BIBLE."

—*Ib.* p. 167. "The memory of the just shall be honored: but the name of the wicked shall rot. BIBLE."—*Ib.* p. 168. "He that is slow in anger, is better than the mighty. He that ruleth his spirit, is better than he that taketh a city. BIBLE."—*Ib.* p. 72. "The Lord loveth whomsoever he correcteth; as the father correcteth the son in whom he delighteth. BIBLE."—*Ib.* p. 72. "The first future tense represents what is to take place hereafter. G. B."—*Ib.* p. 366. "Teach me to feel another's wo; [and] To hide what faults I see."—*Ib.* p. 197. "Thy speech bewrayeth thee; for thou art a Gallilean."—*Murray's Ex.* ii, p. 118. "Thy speech *betrays* thee; for thou art a Gallilean."—*Murray's Key,* 8vo, p. 250. "Strait is the gate, and narrow the way, that lead to life eternal."—*Ib. Key,* p. 172. "Straight is the gate," &c.—*Ib. Ex.* p. 36. "'Thou buildest the wall, that thou *mayst* be their king.' *Neh.* vi. 6."—*Murray's Gram.* 8vo, p. 210. "'There is forgiveness with thee, that thou *mayst* be feared.' *Psalms* cxxx. 4."—*Ib.* p. 210. "But yesterday the word, *Cæsar,* might Have stood against the world."—*Kirkham's Elocution,* p. 316. "The north-east spends its rage. THOMSON."—*Joh. Dict. w. Effusive.* "Tells how the drudging goblet swet. MILTON."—*Churchill's Gram.* p. 263. "And to his faithful servant hath in place *Bore* witness gloriously. SAM. AGON."—*Ib.* p. 266. "Then, if thou fallest, O, Cromwell, Thou fallest a blessed martyr."—*Kirkham's Elocution,* p. 190. "I see the dagger-crest of Mar, I see the *Moray's* silver star, *Waves* o'er the cloud of Saxon war, That up the lake *came* winding far!—SCOTT."—*Merchant's School Gram.* p. 143. "Each *bird, and* each insect, *is* happy in its *kind.*"—*Ib.* p. 85. "*They who are* learning to *compose and* arrange *their* sentences with accuracy and order, *are* learning, at the same time, to think with accuracy and order. BLAIR."—*Ib.* p. 176; *L. Murray's Gram.,* Title-page, 8vo and 12mo. "We, then, as workers together with *you,* beseech you also, that ye receive not the grace of God in vain."—*James Brown's Eng. Syntax,* p. 129. "And on the *bounty* of thy goodness calls."—*O. B. Peirce's Gram.* p. 245. "Knowledge dwells In heads replete with thoughts of other men; Wisdom, in *minds retentive* to their own. COWPER."—*Merchant's School Gram.* p. 172. "*Oh!* let me listen to the *word* of life. THOMSON."—*Ib.* p. 155. "Save that from yonder ivy-mantled *bower,* &c. GRAY'S ELEGY."—*Tooke's Div. of Purley,* Vol. i, p. 116. "*Weigh* the *mens* wits against the *ladies hairs.* POPE."—*Dr. Johnson's Gram.* p. 6. "*Weigh* the men's wits against the *woman's hairs.* POPE."—*Churchill's Gram.* p. 214. "*Prior to* the publication of Lowth's excellent *little grammar,* the grammatical study of our *own* language, formed no part of the ordinary method of instruction. HILEY'S PREFACE."—*Dr. Bullions's E. Gram.,* 1843, p. 189. "Let there be no strife betwixt me and thee."—*Weld's Gram.* p. 143.

"What! canst thou not bear with me half an hour?—SHARP."—*Ib.* p. 185.

"Till then who knew the force of those dire dreams.—MILTON."—*Ib.* p. 186.

"In words, as fashions, the rule will hold,
Alike fantastic, if too new or old:"—*Murray's Gram.* p. 136.

"Be not the first, by whom the new *is* tried,
Nor yet the last, to lay the old aside."—*Bucke's Gram.* p. 104.

UNDER CRITICAL NOTE XIII.—OF AWKWARDNESS.

"They slew Varus, who was he that I mentioned before."—*Murray's Key,* 8vo, p. 194.

[FORMULE.—Not proper, because the phrase, "*who was he that,*" is here prolix and awkward. But, according to Critical Note 13th, "Awkwardness, or inelegance of expression, is a reprehensible defect in style, whether it violate any of the common rules of syntax or not." This example may be improved thus: "They slew Varus, *whom* I mentioned before."]

"Maria rejected Valerius, who was he that she had rejected before."—*Murray's Gram.* 8vo, p. 174. "The English in its substantives has but two different terminations for cases." —*Lowth's Gram.* p. 18. "Socrates and Plato were wise; they were the most eminent philosophers of Greece."—*Ib.* p. 175; *Murray's Gram.* 149; *et al.* "Whether one person or more than one, were concerned in the business, does not yet appear."—*Murray's Key,* 8vo, p. 184. "And that, consequently, the verb and pronoun agreeing with it, cannot with propriety, be ever used in the plural number."—*Murray's Gram.* p. 153; *Ingersoll's,* 249; *et al.* "A second help may be the conversing frequently and freely with those of your own sex who are like minded."—*John Wesley.* "Four of the semi-vowels, namely, *l, m, n, r,* are also distinguished by the name of *liquids,* from their readily uniting with other consonants, and flowing as it were into their sounds."—*Murray's Gram.* p. 8; *Churchill's,* 5; *Alger's,* 11; *et al.* "Some conjunctions have *their* correspondent conjunctions *belonging to them;* so that, in the subsequent member of the sentence the *latter answers* to the former."—*Lowth's Gram.* p. 109; *Adam's,* 209; *Gould's,* 205; *L. Murray's,* 211; *Ingersoll's,* 268; *Fisk's,* 137; *Churchill's,* 153; *Fowler's,* 562; *et al.* "The mutes are those consonants, whose sounds cannot be protracted. The *semi-vowels; such whose* sounds can be continued *at pleasure, partaking* of the nature of vowels, from *which* they derive their name."—*Murray's Gram.* p. 9; *et al.* "The pronoun of the third person, of the masculine and feminine gender, is sometimes used as a noun, and regularly declined: as, 'The *hes* in birds.' BACON. 'The *shes* of Italy.' SHAK."—*Churchill's Gram.* p. 73. "The following *examples* also *of* separation of a preposition from the word which it governs, *is* improper *in common writings.*"—*C. Adams's Gram.* p. 103. "The word *whose* begins likewise to be restricted to persons, but *it* is not *done* so generally but that good writers, and even in prose, use it when speaking of things."—*Priestley's Gram.* p. 99;

L. Murray's, 157 ; *Fisk's*, 115; *et al.* "There are new and surpassing wonders present themselves to our views."—*Sherlock.* "Inaccuracies are often found in the way wherein the degrees of comparison are applied and construed."—*Campbell's Rhet.* p. 202. "Inaccuracies are often found in the way in which the degrees of comparison are applied and construed."—*Murray's Gram.* p. 167; *Smith's*, 144; *Ingersoll's*, 193 ; *et al.* "The connecting circumstance is placed too remotely, to be either perspicuous or agreeable."—*Murray's Gram.* p. 177. "Those tenses are called simple tenses, which are formed of the principal without an auxiliary verb."—*Ib.* p. 91. "The nearer *that* men approach to *each other,* the more numerous are their points of contact and the greater will be their pleasures or their pains."—*Murray's Key.* 8vo, p. 275. "This is the machine that he is the inventor of."—*Nixon's Parser,* p. 124. "To give this sentence the interrogative form, it should be expressed thus."—*Murray's Gram.* 8vo, p. 279. "Never employ those words which may be susceptible of a sense different from the sense you intend to be conveyed."—*Hiley's Gram.* p. 152. "Sixty pages are occupied in explaining what would not require more than ten or twelve to be explained according to the ordinary method."—*Ib., Pref.,* p. ix. "The present participle in *-ing* always expresses an action, or the suffering of an action, or the being, state, or condition of a thing as *continuing* and *progressive.*"—*Bullions, E. Gram.* p. 57. "The *Present participle of all active verbs*[*] has an active signification ; as, James *is building* the house. In *many of these,* however, *it has also* a passive *signification ; as, the* house *was building when the wall fell.*"—*Id. ib.,* 2d or 4th Ed., p. 57. "Previous to parsing this sentence, it may be analyzed to the young pupil by such questions as the following, viz."—*Id. ib.* p. 73. "Subsequent to that period, however, attention has been paid to this important subject."—*Ib.,* New Ed., p. 189 ; *Hiley's Preface,* p. vi. "A definition of a word is an explanation in what sense the word is used, or what idea or object we mean by it, and which may be expressed by any one or more of the properties, effects, or circumstances of that object, so as sufficiently to distinguish it from other objects."—*Hiley's Gram.* p. 245.

UNDER CRITICAL NOTE XIV.—OF IGNORANCE.

"What is an Asserter ? It is *the part of speech* which asserts."—*O. B. Peirce's Gram.* p. 20.

[FORMULE.—Not proper, because the term "*Asserter,*" which is here put for *Verb,* is both ignorantly misspelled, and whimsically misapplied. But, according to Critical Note 14th, "Any use of words that implies ignorance of their meaning, or of their proper orthography, is particularly unscholarlike ; and, in proportion to the author's pretensions to learning, disgraceful." The errors here committed might have been avoided thus : "What is *a verb ?* It is *a word* which signifies *to be, to act,* or *to be acted upon.*" Or thus : "What is an *assertor ?* Ans. 'One who affirms positively ; an affirmer, supporter, or vindicator.'—*Webster's Dict.*"]

"Virgil wrote the Æneod."—*Kirkham's Gram.* p. 56. "Which, to a supercilious or inconsiderate Japaner, would seem very idle and impertinent."—*Locke, on Ed.* p. 225. "Will not a look of disdain cast upon you, throw you into a foment ?"—*Life of Th. Say,* p. 146. "It may be of use to the scholar, to remark in this place, that though only the conjunction *if* is affixed to the verb, any other conjunction proper for the subjunctive mood, may, with equal propriety, be occasionally annexed."—*L. Murray's Gram.* p. 93. "When proper names have an article annexed to them, they are used as common names."—*Ib.* p. 36 ; *Ingersoll's,* 25 ; *et al.* "When a proper noun has an article annexed to it, it is used as a common noun."—*Merchant's Gram.* p. 25. "Seeming to disenthral the death-field of its terrors."—*Ib.* p. 109. "For the same reason, we might, without any disparagement to the language, dispense with the terminations of our verbs in the singular."—*Kirkham's Gram.* p. 50. "It diminishes all possibility of being misunderstood."—*Abbott's Teacher,* p. 175. "Approximation to excellence is all that we can expect."—*Ib.* p. 42. "I have often joined in singing with musicianists at Norwich."—*Music of Nature,* p. 274. "When not standing in regular prosic order."—*O. B. Peirce's Gram.* p. 281. "Disregardless of the dogmas and edicts of the philosophical umpire."—*Kirkham's Gram.* p. 75. "Others begin to talk before their mouths are open, affixing the mouth-closing M to most of their words—as M-yes for Yes."—*Music of Nature,* p. 28. "That noted close of his, *esse videatur,* exposed him to censure among his cotemporaries."—*Blair's Rhet.* p. 127. "OWN. Formerly, a man's *own* was what he *worked for, own* being a past participle of a verb signifying to *work.*"—*Kirkham's Gram.* p. 71. "As [requires] so : expressing a comparison of quality : as, '*As* the one dieth, *so* dieth the other.'"—*Murray's Gram.* p. 212; *R. C. Smith's,* 177 ; *and many others.* "To obey our parents is a solemn duty."—*Parker and Fox's Gram.,* Part I, p. 67. "Most all the political papers of the kingdom have touched upon these things."—H. C. WRIGHT: *Liberator,* Vol. xiv, p. 22. "I shall take leave to make a few observations on the subject." —*Hiley's Gram.* p. iii. "His loss I have endeavoured to supply, as far as additional vigilance and industry would allow."—*Ib.* p. xi. "That they should make vegetation so exhuberant as to anticipate every want."—*Frazee's Gram.* p. 43. "The quotors " " which

---

[*] In the Doctor's "New Edition, Revised and Corrected," the text stands thus : "The *Present participle* of THE ACTIVE VOICE has an active signification ; as, James is *building* the house. In *many of these,* however, it has," &c. Here the first sentence is but an idle truism ; and the phrase, "In *many of these,*" for lack of an antecedent to *these,* is utter nonsense. What is in "the active voice," ought of course to be *active* in "signification ;" but, in this author's present scheme of the verb, we find "the active voice," in direct violation of his own definition of it, ascribed not only to verbs and participles either neuter or intransitive, but also, as it would seem by this passage, to "many" that are *passive !*—G. BROWN.

denote that one or more words are extracted from another author."—*Day's District School Gram.* p. 112. "Ninevah and Assyria were two of the most noted cities of ancient history." —*Ib.* p. 32 and p. 88. "Ninevah, the capital of Assyria, *is* a celebrated ancient city."— *Ib.* p. 88. "It may, however, be rendered definite by introducing some definition of time; as, yesterday, last week, &c."—*Bullions, E. Gram.* p. 40. "The last is called heroic measure, and is the same that is used by Milton, Young, Thompson. Pollock, &c."— *Id., Practical Lessons,* p. 129. "Perrenial ones must be sought in the delightful regions above."—*Hallock's Gram.* p. 194. "Intransitive verbs are those which are inseperable from the effect produced."—*Cutler's Gram.* p. 31. "Femenine gender, belongs to women, and animals of the female kind."—*Ib.* p. 15. "*Woe!* unto you scribes and pharasees."—*Day's Gram.* p. 74. "A pyrrick, which has both its syllables short."—*Ib.* p. 114. "What kind of Jesamine? a Jesamine in flower, or a flowery Jesamine."—*Barrett's Gram.,* 10th Ed., p. 53. "*Language,* derived from '*linguæ,*' the tongue, is the *faculty* of communicating our thoughts to *each* other, by proper words, used by common consent, as signs of our ideas."— *Ib.* p. 9. "Say *none* not *nara.*"—*Staniford's Gram.* p. 81. "ABY ONE, for either."—*Pond's Larger Gram.* p. 194. (See Obs. 24th, on the Syntax of Adverbs, and the Note at the bottom of the page.)

> "Earth loses thy *patron* for ever and aye;
> O sailor boy! sailor boy! peace to thy soul."—*S. Barrett's Gram.,* 1837, p. 116.
> "His brow was sad, his eye beneath,
> Flashed like a halcyon from its sheath."—*Liberator,* Vol. xii, p. 24.

UNDER CRITICAL NOTE XV.—OF SILLINESS AND TRUISMS.

"Such is the state of man, that he is never at rest."—*L. Murray's Gram.* p. 57.

[FORMULE.—This is a remark of no wisdom or force, because it would be nearer the truth, to say, "Such is the state of man, that he *must often* rest." But, according to Critical Note 15th, "Silly remarks and idle truisms are traits of a feeble style, and when their weakness is positive, or inherent, they ought to be entirely omitted." It is useless to attempt a correction of this example, for it is not susceptible of any form worth preserving.]

"Participles belong to the nouns or pronouns to which they relate."—*Wells's Gram.,* 1st Ed., p. 153. "Though the measure is mysterious, it is worthy of attention."—*Murray's Key.* 8vo, p. 221. "Though the measure is *mysterious,* it is not unworthy your attention." —*Kirkham's Gram.* pp. 197 and 227. "The inquietude of his mind made his station and wealth far from being enviable."—*Murray's Key,* 8vo, p. 260. "By rules so general and comprehensive as these are [,] the clearest ideas are conveyed."—*Ib.* p. 273. "The mind of man cannot be long without some food to nourish the activity of its thoughts."—*Ib.* p. 185. "Not having known, or not having considered, the measures proposed, he failed of success." —*Ib.* p. 202. "Not having known or considered the subject, he made a crude decision."— *Ib.* p. 275. "Not to exasperate him, I spoke only a very few words."—*Ib.* p. 257. "These are points too trivial, to be noticed. They are objects with which I am totally unacquainted."—*Ib.* p. 275. "Before we close this section, it may afford instruction to the learners, to be informed, more particularly than they have been."—*Murray's Gram.* p. 110. "The articles are often properly omitted: when used, they should be justly applied, according to their distinct nature."—*Ib.* p. 170; *Alger's,* 60. "Any thing, which is done now, is supposed to be done at the present time."—*Sanborn's Gram.* p. 34. "Any thing which was done yesterday is supposed to be done in past time."—*Ib.* 34. "Any thing which may be done hereafter, is supposed to be done in future time."—*Ib.* 34. "When the mind compares two things in reference to each other, it performs the operation of comparing."—*Ib.* p. 244. "The persons, with whom you dispute, are not of your opinion."—*Cooper's Pl. and Pr. Gram.* p. 124. "But the preposition *at* is *always used* when it *follows the neuter Verb* in the same Case: as, 'I have been *at* London.'"—*Dr. Ash's Gram.* p. 60. "But the preposition *at* is *generally used* after the neuter verb *to be:* as, 'I have been *at* London.'"—*L. Murray's Gram.* p. 203; *Ingersoll's,* 231; *Fisk's,* 143; *et al.* "The article *the* has sometimes a *differ*ent effect, in distinguishing a person by an epithet."—*Murray's Gram.* p. 172. "The article *the* has, sometimes, a *fine* effect, in distinguishing a person by an epithet."—*Priestley's Gram.* p. 151. "Some nouns have plurals belonging only to themselves."—*Infant School Gram.* p. 26. "Sentences are either simple or compounded."—*Lowth's Gram.* p. 68. "All sentences are either simple or compound."—*Gould's Adam's Gram.* p. 155. "The definite article *the* belongs to nouns in the singular or plural number."—*Kirkham's Gram.,* Rule 24, p. 176. "Where a riddle is not intended, it is *always a fault* in allegory to be *too dark.*"— *Blair's Rhet.* p. 151; *Murray's Gram.* 343. "There may be an *excess in too many* short sentences *also*; by *which* the sense is split and broken."—*Blair's Rhet.* p. 101. "Are there any nouns you cannot see, hear, or feel, but only think of? Name such a noun."—*Infant School Gram.* p. 17. "*Flock* is of the singular number, it denotes but one flock—and in the nominative case, it is the *active agent* of the verb."—*Kirkham's Gram.* p. 58. "The article THE *agrees* with nouns of *the singular or plural* number."—*Parker and Fox's Gram.* p. 8. "The admiral bombarded Algiers, which has been continued."—*Nixon's Parser,* p. 128. "The world demanded freedom, which might have been expected."—*Ibid.* "The past tense represents an action as past and finished, either with or without respect to the time when."— *Felton's Gram.* p. 22. "That boy rode the *wicked* horse."—*Butler's Practical Gram.* p. 42.

The snake *swallowed itself*."—*Ib*. p. 87. "*Do* is sometimes used when *shall* or *should* is omitted; as, 'If thou *do* repent.'"—*Ib*. p. 85. "SUBJUNCTIVE MOOD. This mood *has the uses of the indicative*."—*Ib*. p. 87. "As *nouns never speak*, they are never in the first person." —*Davis's Practical Gram.* p. 148. "Nearly *all parts* of speech are *used more or less* in an *elliptical sense*."—*Day's District School Gram.* p. 80. "RULE. No word in a period can have any greater *extension* than the *other* words *or sections* in the same sentence *will give* it."— *Barrett's Revised Gram.* p. 38 and p. 43. "Words used exclusively as Adverbs, should not be used as Adjectives."—*Clark's Practical Gram.* p. 166. "Adjectives used in Predication, should not take the Adverbial form."—*Ib*. pp. 167 and 173.

UNDER CRITICAL NOTE XVI. — OF THE INCORRIGIBLE.

"And this state of things belonging to the painter governs it in the possessive case."— *Murray's Gram.* p. 195; *Ingersoll's,* 201; *et al.*

[FORMULE.—This composition is incorrigibly bad. The participle "*belonging*," which seems to relate to '*things*," is improperly meant to qualify "*state*." And the "*state of things*," (which *state* really belongs *only to the things*,) is absurdly supposed to belong to a *person*—i. e., "*to the painter*." Then this man, to whom he "*state of things*" is said to belong, is forthwith called "*it*," and nonsensically declared to be "in the *possessive case*." But, according to Critical Note 16th, "Passages too erroneous for correction, may be criticised, *orally* or otherwise, and then passed over without any attempt to amend them." Therefore, no correction is *attempted* here.]

"Nouns or pronouns, following the verb *to be*; or the words *than, but, as*; or that answer the question *who*? have the same case *after as preceded* them."—*Beck's Gram.* p. 29. "The common gender is *when* the noun may be either masculine or feminine."—*Frost's Gram.* p. 8. "The possessive is generally pronounced the same as if the *s* were added."—*Alden's Gram.* p. 11. "For, assuredly, as soon as men *had got* beyond simple interjections, *and began* to communicate *themselves* by discourse, they *would be* under a necessity of assigning names to the objects they *saw around* them, *which* in grammatical language, *is called* the invention of substantive nouns."—*Blair's Rhet.* p. 72. "Young children will learn to form letters as *soon*, if not *readier*, than *they* will when *older*."—*Taylor's District School*, p. 159. "This *comparing* words with one another, constitutes what *is* called the *degrees* of comparison."— *Sanborn's Gram.* p. 29. "Whenever a noun is *immediately annexed* to a *preceding neuter* verb, *it expresses either* the same notion *with* the verb, or denotes only *the* circumstance of the *action*."—*Lowth's Gram.* p. 73. "Two or more nouns or pronouns joined *singular* together by the conjunction *and, must have verbs* agreeing with them in the plural number."—*Infant School Gram.* p. 129. "Possessive and demonstrative pronouns agree with their nouns in number and case; as, 'my brother,' 'this slate,' 'these slates.'"—*Ib*. p. 130. "Participles which have no relation to time are used either as adjectives or as substantives."—*Maunder's Gram.* p. 1. "They are in use only in some of their times and modes; and in some of them are a composition of times of several defective verbs, having the same signification." —*Lowth's Gram.* p. 59. "When *words* of the possessive case *that are* in apposition, *follow one another* in quick succession, the possessive sign should be annexed to the *last only*, and *understood* to the rest; as, 'For David, my servant's sake.'"—*Comly's Gram.* p. 92. "By *this order*, the first nine *rules* accord with *those* which respect the *rules* of concord; and the *remainder include*, though *they* extend beyond the *rules* of government."—*Murray's Gram.* p. 143. "*Own* and *self* in the plural *selves*, are joined to the possessives, my, our, thy, your, his, her, their; as, my *own* hand, myself, yourselves; both of them expressing emphasis or opposition, as, 'I did it *my own self*,' that is, *and* no one else; the latter also forming the reciprocal pronoun, as, 'he hurt *himself*.'"—*Lowth's Gram.* p. 25. "A *flowing* copious style, therefore, is required *in* all public speakers; *guarding*, at the *same time*, against such a degree of *diffusion*, as renders *them* languid and tiresome; *which* will always *prove the case*, when they *inculcate too much*, and present the *same thought* under *too many* different views."— *Blair's Rhet.* p. 177. "As sentences should be cleared of redundant words, so also of redundant members. As every word ought to present a new idea, so every member ought to contain a new thought. Opposed to *this*, stands the fault we sometimes meet with, of the *last* member of a period *being* no other than *the* echo of the *former*, or *the* repetition of it in *somewhat* a different form."[*]—*Ib*. p. 111. "*Which* always refers grammatically to the substantive *immediately preceding*: [as,] 'It is folly to pretend, by heaping up treasures, to arm ourselves against the accidents of *life, which* nothing can protect us against, but the good providence of our heavenly Father.'"—*Murray's Gram.* p. 311; *Maunder's,* p. 18; *Blair's Rhet.* p. 105. "The English *adjectives*, having but a very limited syntax, *is classed* with *its* kindred *article*, the adjective pronoun, under the eighth rule."—*L. Murray's Gram.* 8vo, p. 143. "When a *substantive* is put *absolutely*, and does *not agree* with the following verb, it *remains independent* on the participle, and *is called* the *case* absolute, or the *nominative* absolute."—*Ib*. p. 195. "It will, doubtless, *sometimes* happen, that, on *this occasion*, as well as on many *other occasions*, a strict adherence to grammatical rules, *would* render *the* language stiff and formal: but when *cases of this sort* occur, it is better to give the expression a

[*] One objection to these passages is, that they are *examples* of the very construction which they describe as a *fault*. The first and second sentences ought to have been separated only by a semicolon. This would have made them "*members*" of one and the same sentence. Can it be supposed that one "*thought*" is sufficient for two periods, or for what one chooses to point as such, but not for two members of the same period?—G BROWN.

different turn, than to violate *grammar* for the sake of *ease*, or even of *elegance*."—*Ib.* p. "Number, which distinguishes *objects as singly* or *collectively*, must have been coeval the very infancy of language."—*Jamieson's Rhet.* p. 25. "The article *a* or *an agrees* nouns *in* the singular number *only*, *individually* or *collectively*."—*L. Murray's Gram.* p. *and others.* "No language is perfect *because it is a human* invention."—*Parker and Grammar*, Part III, p. 112. "The *participles*, or as they may properly be termed, *for* the verb in the *second infinitive*, usually *precedes another* verb, and *states* some fact, or from which an *inference* is drawn *by that verb ; as,* "the sun *having arisen*, they —*Day's Grammar*, 2nd Ed., p. 36. "They must describe *what has happened* as he so in the past *or the present* time, or as *likely to occur* in the future."—*The W Grammar, Introd.*, p. 5. "Nouns are either male, female, or neither."—*Fowle's School Grammar*, Part Second, p. 12. "Possessive *Adjectives* express possession, and guish *nouns* from *each* other by showing to *what they* belong ; as, my hat, John's hat." *Ib.* p. 31.

PROMISCUOUS EXAMPLES OF FALSE SYNTAX.
LESSON I.—VARIOUS RULES.

"What is the reason that our language is less refined than that of Italy, Spain, France?"—*Murray's Key*, 8vo, p. 185. "What is the reason that our language is less fined than that of France?"—*Ingersoll's Gram.* p. 152. "'I believe your Lordship will with me, in the reason why our language is less refined than those of Italy, Spain France.' DEAN SWIFT. Even in this short sentence, we may discern an inaccuracy—' our language is less refined than *those* of Italy, Spain, or France ;' putting the pronoun in the plural, when the antecedent substantive to which it refers is in the singular, *or* *guage.*"—*Blair's Rhet.* p. 228. "The sentence might have been made to run much in this way; ' why our language is less refined than the Italian, Spanish, or French.'" "But when arranged in an entire sentence, which they must be to make a complete they show it still more evidently."—*L. Murray's Gram.* p. 65. "This is a more and refined construction than that, in which the common connective is simply made *a* —*Ib.* p. 127. "We shall present the reader with a list of Prepositions, which are d from the Latin and Greek languages."—*Ib.* p. 120. "Relatives comprehend the meani a pronoun and conjunction copulative."—*Ib.* p. 126. "Personal pronouns being used *to* ply the place of the noun, are not employed in the same part of the sentence *as the* which they represent."—*Ib.* p. 155 ; *R. C. Smith's Gram.* 131. "There is very seldom occasion for a substitute in the same part where the principal word is present."—*M Gram.* p. 155. "We hardly consider little children as persons, because that term *g* the idea of reason and reflection."—*Priestley's Gram.* p. 98 ; *Murray's*, 157 ; *Smith's and others.* "The occasion of exerting each of these qualities is different."—*Blair' p. 95 ; *Murray's Gram.* 302 ; *Jamieson's Rhet.* 66. "I'll tell you who time ambles who time trots withal, who time gallops withal, and who he stands still withal. I pray who doth he trot withal?"—*Shakspeare.* "By greatness, I do not only mean the bulk single object, but the largeness of a whole view."—*Addison.* "The question may be put, What does he more than mean?"—*Blair's Rhet.* p. 103. "The question m put, what more does he than only mean?"—*Ib.* p. 204. "He is surprised to find got to so great a distance, from the object with which he at first set out."—*Ib.* p. 108. is surprised to find himself at so great a distance from the object with which he sets *Murray's Gram.* p. 313. "Few precise rules can be given, which will hold without tion in all cases."—*Ib.* p. 267 ; *Lowth's Gram.* p. 115. "Versification is the arrangeme a certain number of syllables according to certain laws."—*Dr. Johnson's Gram.* p. 13. " sification is the arrangement of a certain number and variety of syllables, according to tain laws."—*L. Murray's Gram.* p. 252 ; *R. C. Smith's*, 187 ; and others. "Charlotte, friend of Amelia, to whom no one imputed blame, was too prompt in her own ton."—*Murray's Key*, 8vo, p. 273. "Mr. Pitt, joining the war party in 1793, t striking and the most fatal instance of this offence, is the one which at once itself."—*Brougham's Sketches*, Vol. i, p. 57. "To the framing such a sound constitution mind."—*The American Lady*, p. 132. "'I beseech you,' said St. Paul to his Ephesian converts, 'that ye walk worthy the vocation wherewith ye are called.'"—*Ib.* p. 208. "So as to prevent its being equal to that."—*Booth's Introd.* p. 88. "When speaking of an a tion's being performed."—*Ib.* p. 89. "And, in all questions of an action's being so per formed, *est* is added to the second person."—*Ib.* p. 72. "No account can be given of this than that custom has blinded their eyes."—*Dymond's Essays*, p. 269.

"Design, or chance, make others wive;
But nature did this match contrive."—*Waller*, p. 24.

LESSON II.—VARIOUS RULES.

"I suppose each of you think it is your own nail."—*Abbott's Teacher*, p. 58. "They are useless, from their being apparently based upon this supposition."—*Ib.* p. 71. "The form tal manner, in which this plan may be adopted; is various."—*Ib.* p. 83. "Making intellectual effort, and acquiring knowledge, are always pleasant to the human mind."—*Ib.* p. 85. "This will do more than the best lecture which ever was delivered."—*Ib.* p. 90. "Doing my things is generally dull work."—*Ib.* p. 92. "Such is the tone and manner of some teachers."—*Ib.* p. 118. "Well, the fault is, being disorderly at prayer time."—*Ib.* p. 153. "Do you remember speaking on this subject in school?"—*Ib.* p. 154. "The course above recommended, is not trying lax and inefficient measures."—*Ib.* p. 156. "Our community agreed that there is a God."—*Ib.* p. 163. "It prevents their being interested in what is said."—*Ib.* p. 175. "We will also suppose that I call another boy to me, who I have reason believe to be a sincere Christian."—*Ib.* p. 180. "Five minutes notice is given by the ell."—*Ib.* p. 211. "The Annals of Education gives notice of it."—*Ib.* p. 240. "Teacher's meetings will be interesting and useful."—*Ib.* p. 243. "She thought an half hour's study would conquer all the difficulties."—*Ib.* p. 257. "The difference between an honest and a hypocritical confession."—*Ib.* p. 263. "There is no point of attainment where we must stop."—*Ib.* p. 267. "Now six hours is as much as is expected of teachers."—*Ib.* p. 268. How much is seven times nine ?"—*Ib.* p. 292. "Then the reckoning proceeds till it come a ten hundred."—*Frost's Practical Gram.* p. 170. "Your success will depend on your own exertions; see, then, that you are diligent."—*Ib.* p. 142. "Subjunctive Mood, Present tense: If I am known, If thou art known, If he is known;" &c.—*Ib.* p. 91. "If I be loved, If thou be loved, If he be loved;" &c.—*Ib.* p. 85. "An Interjection is a word used to express sudden emotion. They are so called, because they are generally thrown in between the parts of a sentence without any reference to the structure of the other parts of it."—*Ib.* p. 35. "The Cardinals are those which simplify or denote number; as one, two, three."—*Ib.* p. 31. "More than one organ is concerned in the utterance of almost every consonant."—*Ib.* p. 21. "To extract from them all the Terms we make use in our Divisions and Subdivisions of the Art."—*Holmes's Rhetoric,* Pref. "And there was written therein lamentations, and mourning, and woe."—*Ezekiel,* ii, 10. "If I were to be judged as to my behaviour, compared with that of John's."—*Josephus,* Vol. 5, p. 172. "When the preposition *to* signifies *in order to,* it used to be preceded by *for,* which is now almost obsolete; What went ye out *for* to see."—*Priestley's Gram.* p. 132. "This makes the proper perfect tense, which, in English, is always expressed by the help of the auxiliary verb, 'I have written.'"—*Blair's Rhet.* p. 82. "Indeed, in the formation of character, personal exertion is the first, the second, and the third virtues."—*Sanders, Spelling-Book,* p. 93. "The reducing them to the condition of the beasts that perish."—*Dymond's Essays,* p. 67. "Yet this affords no reason to deny that the nature of the gift is not the same, or that both are not divine."—*Ib.* p. 68. "If God have made known his will."—*Ib.* p. 98. "If Christ have prohibited them, [i. e., oaths,] nothing else can prove them right."—*Ib.* p. 150. "That the taking them is wrong, every man who simply consults his own heart, will know."—*Ib.* p. 53. "These evils would be spared the world, if one did not write."—*Ib.* p. 188. "It is to a great degree our own faults."—*Ib.* p. 200. "It is worthy observation that lesson-learning is nearly excluded."—*Ib.* p. 212. "Who spares the aggressor's life even to the endangering his own."—*Ib.* p. 227. "Who advocates the taking the life of an aggressor."—*Ib.* p. 229. "And thence up to the intentionally and voluntary fraudulent."—*Ib.* p. 318. "And the contention was so great among them, that they departed asunder, one from another."—*Acts* xv. 39."—*Rev. Matt. Harrison's English Lang.* p. 235. "Here the man is John, and John is the man; so the words are *the imagination and the fancy,* and *the imagination and the fancy* are the words."—*Harrison's E. Lang.* p. 227. "The article, which is here so emphatic in the Greek, is lost sight of in our translation."—*Ib.* p. 223. "We have no less than thirty pronouns."—*Ib.* p. 166. "It will admit of a pronoun being joined to it."—*Ib.* p. 57. "From intercourse and from conquest, all the languages of Europe participate with each other."—*Ib.* p. 104. "It is not always necessity, therefore, that has been the cause of our introducing terms derived from the classical languages."—*Ib.* p. 100. "The man of genius stamps upon it any impression that he pleases."—*Ib.* p. 90. "The proportion of names ending in *son* preponderate greatly among the Dano-Saxon population of the North."—*Ib.* p. 43. "As a proof of the strong similarity between the English and the Danish languages."—*Ib.* p. 37. "A century from the time that Hengist and Horsa landed on the isle of Thanet."—*Ib.* p. 27.

"I saw the colours waving in the wind,
And they within, to mischief how combin'd."—*Bunyan.*

LESSON III.—VARIOUS RULES.

"A ship excepted : of whom we say, *she* sails well."—*Ben Jonson's Gram.* Chap 10. "Honesty is reckoned little worth."—*Paul's Accidence,* p. 58. "Learn to esteem life as it ought."—*Economy of Human Life,* p. 118. "As the soundest health is less perceived than the lightest malady, so the highest joy toucheth us less deep than the smallest sorrow."—*Ib.* p. 152. "Being young is no apology for being frivolous."—*Whiting's Elementary Reader,* p. 117. "The porch was the same width with the temple."—*Milman's Jews,* Vol. i, p. 208. The other tribes neither contributed to his rise or downfall."—*Ib.* i, p. 165. "His whole laws and religion would have been shaken to its foundation."—*Ib.* i, p. 109. "The English has most commonly been neglected, and children taught only the Latin syntax."—*Lily's Gram.*, Pref., p. xi. "They are not taken notice of in the notes."—*Ib.* p. x. "He walks in righteousness, doing what he would be done to."—*S. Fisher's Works*, p. 14. "They stand independently on the rest of the sentence."—*Ingersoll's Gram.* p. 151. "My uncle, with his son, were in town yesterday."—*Lennie's Gram.* p. 142. "She with her sisters are well."—*Ib.* p. 143. "His purse, with its contents, were abstracted from his pocket."—*Ib.* 143. "The great constitutional feature of this institution being, that directly the acrimony of the last election is over, the acrimony of the next begins."—*Dickens's Notes*, p. 27. "His disregarding his parents' advice has brought him into disgrace."—*Farnum's Pract. Gram.*, 2d Ed., p. 19. "Error: Can you tell me the reason of his father making that remark ?—*Ib.* p. 93. Cor.: Can you tell me the reason of his father's making that remark?" —See *Farnum's Gram.*, Rule 12th, p. 76. "Error: What is the reason of our teacher detaining us so long ?—*Ib.* p. 76. Cor.: What is the reason of our *teacher's* detaining us so long?" —See *Ib.* "Error: I am certain of the boy having said so. Correction: I am certain of the *boy's* having said so."—*Exercises in Farnum's Gram.* p. 76. "*Which* means any thing or things before named; and *that* may represent any person or persons, thing or things, which have been speaking, spoken to or spoken of."—*Dr. Perley's Gram.* p. 9. "A certain number of syllables connected, form a foot. They are called *feet*, because it is by their aid that the voice, as it were, steps along."—*L. Murray's Gram.* p. 252; *C. Adams's*, 121. "Asking questions with a principal verb—as, *Teach I? Burns he*, &c. are barbarisms, and carefully to be avoided."—*Alex. Murray's Gram.* p. 122. "Tell whether the 18th, 19th, 20th, 21st, 22d, or 23d Rules are to be used, and repeat the Rule."—*Parker and Fox's Gram.*, Part I, p. 4. "The resolution was adopted without much deliberation, which caused great dissatisfaction."—*Ib.* p. 71. "The man is now taken much notice of by the people thereabouts."—*Edward's First Lessons in Gram.* p. 42. "The sand prevents their sticking to one another."—*Ib.* p. 84. "Defective Verbs are those which are used only in some of their moods and tenses."—*Murray's Gram.* p. 108; *Guy's*, 42; *Russell's*, 46; *Bacon's*, 42; *Frost's*, 40; *Alger's*, 47; *S. Putnam's*, 47; *Goldsbury's*, 54; *Felton's*, 59; and *others*. "Defective verbs are those which want some of their moods and tenses."—*Lennie's Gram.* p. 47; *Bullions, E. Gram.* 65; *Practical Lessons*, 75. "Defective Verbs want some of their parts."—*Bullions, Lat. Gram.* p. 78. "A Defective verb is one that wants some of its parts."—*Bullions, Analyt. and Pract. Gram.*, 1849, p. 101. "To the irregular verbs are to be added the defective; which are not only for the most part irregular, but also wanting in some of their parts."—*Lowth's Gram.* p. 59. "To the irregular verbs are to be added the defective; which are not only wanting in some of their parts, but are, when inflected, irregular."—*Churchill's Gram.* p. 112. "When two or more nouns succeed each other in the possessive case."—*Farnum's Gram.*, 2d Ed., pp. 20 and 63. "When several short sentences succeed each other."—*Ib.* p. 113. "Words are divided into ten Classes, and are called PARTS OF SPEECH."—*Ainsworth's Gram.* p. 8. "A Passive Verb has its *agent* or *doer* always in the objective case, and is governed by a preposition."—*Ib.* p. 40. "I am surprised at your negligent attention."—*Ib.* p. 43. "SINGULAR: Thou lovest or you love. *You* has always a plural verb."—*Bullions, E. Gram.* p. 43. "How do you know that *love* is the first person ? *Ans.* Because *we* is the first personal pronoun."—*Id. ib.* p. 47; *Lennie's Gram.* p. 26. "The lowing herd wind slowly round the lea."—*Bullions, E. Gram.* p. 96. "Iambic verses have every second, fourth, and other even syllables accented."—*Ib.* p. 170. "Contractions are often made in poetry, which are not allowable in prose."—*Ib.* p. 179. "Yet to their general's voice they all obeyed."—*Ib.* p. 179. "It never presents to his mind but one new subject at the same time."—*Felton's Gram.*, 1st Edition, p. 6. "When the name of a quality is abstracted, that is separated from its substance, it is called an abstract noun."—*Ib.* p. 9. "Nouns are in the *first* person when speaking."—*Ib.* p. 9. "Which of the two brothers are graduates ?"—*Hallock's Gram.* p. 59. "I am a linen draper bold, as you and all the world doth know."—*Ib.* p. 60. "O the bliss, the pain of dying !"—*Ib.* p. 127. "This do; take you censers, Korah, and all his company."—*Numbers*, xvi, 6. "There are two participles,—the *present* and *perfect*; as, *reading, having read*. Transitive verbs have an *active* and *passive* participle. Examples: ACTIVE, *Present*, Loving; *Perfect*, Having loved: PASSIVE, *Present*, Loved or being loved; *Perfect*, Having been loved."—*S. S. Greene's Analysis*, 1st Ed., p. 225.

> "O heav'n, in my connubial hour decree
> This man my spouse, or such a spouse as he."—*Pope.*

LESSON IV.—VARIOUS RULES.

"The *Past Tenses* represent a conditional past fact or event, and of which the speaker is uncertain."—*Hiley's Gram.* p. 89. "Care also should be taken that they are not introduced too abundantly."—*Ib.* p. 134. "Till they are become familiar to the mind."—*Ib.*, Pref., p. v. "When once a particular arrangement and phraseology are become familiar to the mind."—*Ib.* p. vii. "I have furnished the student with the plainest and most practical directions which I could devise."—*Ib.* p. xiv. "When you are become conversant with the Rules of Grammar, you will then be qualified to commence the study of Style."—*Ib.* p. xxii. "*C* has a soft sound like *s* before *e, i,* and *y,* generally."—*Murray's Gram.* p. 10. "*G* before *e, i,* and *y,* is soft; as in genius, ginger, Egypt."—*Ib.* p. 12. "*C* before *e, i,* and *y,* generally sounds soft like *s.*"—*Hiley's Gram.* p. 4. "*G* is soft before *e, i,* and *y,* as in genius, ginger, Egypt."—*Ib.* p. 4. "As a perfect Alphabet must always contain as many letters as there are elementary sounds in the language, the English Alphabet is therefore both defective and redundant."—*Hiley's Gram.* p. 5. " Common Nouns are the names given to a whole class or species, and are applicable to every individual of that class."—*Ib.* p. 11. "Thus an adjective has always a noun either expressed or understood."—*Ib.* p. 20. " First, let us consider emphasis ; by *this,* is meant a *stronger* and *fuller* sound of voice, by which we distinguish *the accented syllable* of some word, on *which* we *design to lay* particular stress, *and to shew* how *it effects* the rest of the sentence."—*Blair's Rhet.* p. 330. " By emphasis is meant a *stronger* and *fuller* sound of voice, by which we distinguish some word or words on which we *design to lay* particular stress, *and to show* how *they affect* the rest of the sentence."—*Murray's Gram.* p. 242. " Such a simple question as this : ' Do you ride to town to-day,' is capable of *no fewer than* four different acceptations, *according as* the emphasis is differently placed *on the words.*"—*Blair's Rhet.* p. 330 ; *Murray's Gram.* p. 242. " Thus, *bravely,* or ' in a brave manner,' is derived from *brave-like.*"—*Hiley's Gram.* p. 51. " In the same manner, the different parts of speech are formed from each other generally by means of some affix."—*Ib.* p. 60. " Words derived from each other, are always, more or less, allied in signification."—*Ib.* p. 60. " When a noun of multitude conveys unity of idea the verb and pronoun should be singular. But when it conveys plurality of idea, the verb and pronoun must be plural."—*Hiley's Gram.* p. 71. " They have spent their whole time to make the sacred chronology agree with that of the profane."—*Ib.* p. 87. " ' I have studied my lesson, but you *have* not ; ' that is, ' but you have not *studied* it.' "—*Ib.* p. 109. " When words follow each other in pairs, there is a comma between each pair."—*Ib.* p. 112 ; *Bullions,* 152; *Lennie,* 132. " When words follow each other in pairs, the pairs should be marked by the comma."—*Farnum's Gram.* p. 111. " His ' Studies of Nature,' is deservedly a popular work."—*Univ. Biog. Dict. n. St. Pierre.* " ' Here lies *his* head, a *youth* to fortune and to fame unknown.' ' Youth,' here is in the *possessive* (the sign being omitted), and is *in apposition* with ' his.' The meaning is ' the head of him, a youth,' &c."—*Hart's E. Gram.* p. 124. " The pronoun I, and the interjection O, should be written with a capital."—*Weld's E. Gram.,* 2d Ed., p. 16. " The pronoun *I* always should be written with a capital letter."—*Ib.* p. 68. " He went from England to York."—*Ib.* p. 41. "An adverb is a part of speech joined to verbs, adjectives and other adverbs, to modify their meaning."—*Ib.* p. 51; "*Abridged Ed.*" 46. "*Singular,* signifies ' one person or thing.' *Plural,* (Latin *plus,*) signifies ' more than one.' "—*Weld's Gr.* p. 55. " When the present ends in e, *d* only is added to form the Imperfect and Perfect participle."—*Ib.* p. 82. " SYNÆRESIS is the contraction of two syllables into one; as, *Seest* for *see-est, drowned* for *drown-ed.*"—*Ib.* p. 213. " Words ending in *ee* drop the final *e* on receiving an additional syllable beginning with *e* ; as, *see, seest, agree, agreed.*"—*Ib.* p. 227. " Monosyllables in *f, l.* or *s.* preceded by a single vowel are doubled ; as, staff, grass, mill."—*Ib.* p. 226. " Words ending *ie* drop the *e* and take *y;* as die, dying."—*Ib.* p. 226. " One number may be used for another; as, *we* for *I,* you for *thou.*"—*S. S. Greene's Gram.,* 1st Ed., p. 198. " STROB'ILE, n. A pericarp made up of scales that lie over each other. SMART."—*Worcester's Univ. and Crit. Dict.*

" Yet ever from the clearest source have ran
Some gross allay, some tincture of the man."—*Dr. Lowth.*

LESSON V.—VARIOUS RULES.

" The possessive case is always followed by the noun which is the name of the thing possessed, expressed or understood."—*Felton's Gram.* p. 61; *Revised Edition,* pp. 64 and 86. " Hadmer of Aggstein was as pious, devout, and praying a Christian, as were Nelson, Washington, or Jefferson; or as are Wellington, Tyler, Clay, or Polk."—H. C. WRIGHT: *Liberator,* Vol. xv, p. 21. "A word in the possessive case is not an independent noun, and cannot stand by its self."—*Wright's Gram.* p. 130. " Mary is not handsome, but she is good-natured, which is better than beauty."—*St. Quentin's Gram.* p. 9. "After the practice of joining words together had ceased, notes of distinction were placed at the end of every word."—*Murray's Gram.* p. 267 ; *Hallock's,* 224. " Neither Henry nor Charles dissipate his time."—*Hallock's Gram.* p. 166. " ' He had taken from the Christians' abode thirty small castles.'—*Knowles.*"—*Ib.* p. 61. " In *whatever* character Butler was admitted, is unknown." —*Ib.* p. 62. " How is the agent of a passive, and the object of an active verb often left ? " —*Ib.* p. 88. " By *subject* is meant the word of which something is declared of its object." —*Chandler's Gram.,* 1821, p. 103. " Care should also be taken that an intransitive verb is not used instead of a transitive: as, I lay, (the bricks) for, I lie down ; I raise the house, for, I rise; I sit down, for, I set the chair down, &c."—*Ib.* p. 114. " On them depend the duration of our Constitution and our country."—*J. C. Calhoun at Memphis.* " In the present sentence neither the sense nor the measure require *what.*"—*Chandler's Gram.,* 1821, p. 164. " The Irish thought themselves oppress'd by the Law that forbid them to draw with their

Horses Tails."—*Brightland's Gram.*, Pref., p. iii. "*So willingly* are adverbs, qualifying deceives."—*Cutler's Gram.* p. 90. "Epicurus for experiment sake confined himself to a narrower diet than that of the severest prisons."—*Ib.* p. 116. "Derivative words are such as are compounded of other words, as common-wealth, good-ness, false-hood."—*Ib.* p. 12. "The distinction here insisted on is as old as Aristotle, and should not be lost sight of."—*Hart's Gram.* p. 61. "The Tenses of the Subjunctive and the Potential Moods."—*Ib.* p. 80. "A triphthong is a union of three vowels uttered in like manner : as, *uoy* in buoy."—*P. Davis's Practical Gram.* p. xvi. "Common nouns are the names of a species or kind."—*Ib.* p. 8. "The superlative degree is a comparison between three or more."—*Ib.* p. 14. "An adverb is a word or phrase serving to give an additional idea of a verb, and adjective, article, or another adverb."—*Ib.* p. 36. "When several nouns in the possessive case succeed each other, each showing possession of the same noun, it is only necessary to add the *sign* of the possessive to the last : as, He sells men, women, and *children's* shoes. Dog, cat, and *tiger's* feet are digitated."—*Ib.* p. 72. "A rail-road is making *should be* A rail-road is *being made*. A school-house is building, *should be* A school-house is *being* built."—*Ib.* p. 111. "Auxiliaries are not of themselves verbs ; they resemble in their character and use *those* terminational or other inflections in other languages, *which we are obliged to use in ours to* express the action in the mode, tense, &c., desired."—*Ib.* p. 158. "Please hold my horse while I speak to my friend."—*Ib.* p. 159. "If I say, ' Give me *the* book,' I ask for some *particular* book."—*Butler's Practical Gram.* p. 39. "There are five men here."—*Ib.* p. 134. "In the active the object may be omitted ; in the passive the name of the agent may be omitted."—*Ib.* p. 63. "The Progressive and the Emphatic forms give in each case a *different* shade of meaning to the verb."—*Hart's Gram.* p. 80. "*That* is a Kind of a Redditive Conjunction, when it answers to *so* and *such*."—*W. Ward's Gram.* p. 152. "He attributes to negligence your failing to succeed in that business."—*Smart's Accidence,* p. 36. "*Does will* and *go* express but *our* action ?"—*S. Barrett's Revised Gram.* p. 58. "Language is the *principle* vehicle of thought. G. BROWN."—*James Brown's English Syntax,* p. 3. "*Much* is applied to things weighed or measured ; *many*, to those that are numbered. *Elder* and *oldest*, to persons only ; *older* and *oldest*, either to persons or things."—*Bullions, E. Gram.* p. 20 ; *Pract. Les.* 25. "If there are any old maids still extant, while mysogonists are so rare, the fault must be attributable to themselves."—*Kirkham's Elocution,* p. 286. "The second method used by the Greeks, has never been the practice of any part of Europe."—*Sheridan's Elocution,* p. 64. "Neither consonant, nor vowel, are to be dwelt upon beyond their common quantity, when they close a sentence."—*Sheridan's Rhetorical Gram.* p. 54. "IRONY is a mode of speech expressing *a sense contrary* to that which the speaker or writer intends to convey."—*Wells's School Gram.*, 1st Ed., p. 196 ; 113th Ed., p. 212. "IRONY is *the intentional* use of words *in a sense contrary* to that which the writer or speaker *intends* to convey."—*Weld's Gram.*, 2d Ed., p. 215. "The persons speaking, or spoken to, are supposed to be present."—*Wells*, p. 68. "The persons speaking and spoken to are supposed to be present."—*Murray's Gram.* p. 51. "A *Noun* is a word used to express the *name of* an object."—*Wells's School Gram.* pp. 46 and 47. "A *syllable* is a word, or such a part of a word as is uttered by one articulation."—*Weld's English Gram.* p. 15 ; "*Abridged Ed.*" p. 16.

 "Thus wondrous fair ; thyself how wondrous then !
Unspeakable, who sits above these heavens."—*Cutler's Gram.* p. 131.
"And feel thy sovereign vital lamp ; but thou
 Revisitest not these eyes, that roll in vain."—*Felton's Gram.* p. 133.
"Before all temples the upright and pure."—*Butler's Gram.* p. 195.
"In forest wild, in thicket, break or den."—*Cutler's Gram.* p. 130.
"The rogue and fool by fits is fair and wise ;
And e'en the best, by fits, what they despise."—*Pope's Ess.* iii, 233.

CHAPTER XIV.—QUESTIONS.

ORDER OF REHEARSAL, AND METHOD OF EXAMINATION.

PART THIRD, SYNTAX.

☞ [The following questions, which embrace nearly all the important particulars of the foregoing code of Syntax, are designed not only to direct and facilitate class rehearsals, but also to develop the acquirements of those who may answer them at examinations more public.]

LESSON I.—DEFINITIONS.

1. Of what does Syntax treat ? 2. What is the *relation* of words ? 3. What is the *agreement* of words ? 4. What is the *government* of words ? 5. What is the *arrangement* of words ? 6. What is a *sentence* ? 7. How many and what are the *principal parts* of a sentence ? 8. What are the other parts called ? 9. How many kinds of *sentences* are there ? 10. What is a *simple* sentence ? 11. What is a *compound* sentence ? 12. What is a *clause*, or *member* ? 13. What is a *phrase* ? 14. What words must be supplied in parsing ? 15. How

are the leading principles of syntax presented? 16. In what order are the rules of syntax arranged in this work?

LESSON II. — THE RULES.

1. To what do articles relate? 2. What case is employed as the subject of a finite verb? 3. What agreement is required between words in apposition? 4. By what is the possessive case governed? 5. What case does an active-transitive verb or participle govern? 6. What case is put after a verb or participle not transitive? 7. What case do prepositions govern? 8. When, and in what case, is a noun or pronoun put absolute in English? 9. To what do adjectives relate? 10. How does a pronoun agree with its antecedent? 11. How does a pronoun agree with a collective noun? 12. How does a pronoun agree with joint antecedents? 13. How does a pronoun agree with disjunct antecedents?

LESSON III. — THE RULES.

14. How does a finite verb agree with its subject, or nominative? 15. How does a verb agree with a collective noun? 16. How does a verb agree with joint nominatives? 17. How does a verb agree with disjunct nominatives? 18. What governs the infinitive mood? 19. What verbs take the infinitive after them without the preposition *to*? 20. What is the regular construction of participles, as such? 21. To what do adverbs relate? 22. What do conjunctions connect? 23. What is the use of prepositions? 24. What is the syntax of interjections?

LESSON IV. — THE RULES.

1. What are the several titles, or subjects, of the twenty-four rules of syntax? 2. What says Rule 1st of *Articles*? 3. What says Rule 2d of *Nominatives*? 4. What says Rule 3d of *Apposition*? 5. What says Rule 4th of *Possessives*? 6. What says Rule 5th of *Objectives*? 7. What says Rule 6th of *Same Cases*? 8. What says Rule 7th of *Objectives*? 9. What says Rule 8th of *the Nominative Absolute*? 10. What says Rule 9th of *Adjectives*? 11. What says Rule 10th of *Pronouns*? 12. What says Rule 11th of *Pronouns*? 13. What says Rule 12th of *Pronouns*? 14. What says Rule 13th of *Pronouns*? 15. What says Rule 14th of *Finite Verbs*? 16. What says Rule 15th of *Finite Verbs*? 17. What says Rule 16th of *Finite Verbs*? 18. What says Rule 17th of *Finite Verbs*? 19. What says Rule 18th of *Infinitives*? 20. What says Rule 19th of *Infinitives*? 21. What says Rule 20th of *Participles*? 22. What says Rule 21st of *Adverbs*? 23. What says Rule 22d of *Conjunctions*? 24. What says Rule 23d of *Prepositions*? 25. What says Rule 24th of *Interjections*?

LESSON V. — THE ANALYZING OF SENTENCES.

1. What is it, "to analyze a sentence?" 2. What are the component parts of a sentence? 3. Can all sentences be divided into clauses? 4. Are there different methods of analysis, which may be useful? 5. What is the first method of analysis, according to this code of syntax? 6. How is the following example analyzed by this method? "Even the Atheist, who tells us that the universe is self-existent and indestructible—even he, who, instead of seeing the traces of a manifold wisdom in its manifold varieties, sees nothing in them all but the exquisite structures and the lofty dimensions of materialism—even he, who would despoil creation of its God, cannot look upon its golden suns, and their accompanying systems, without the solemn impression of a magnificence that fixes and overpowers him." 7. What is the second method of analysis? 8. How is the following example analyzed by this method? "Fear naturally quickens the flight of guilt. Rasselas could not catch the fugitive, with his utmost efforts; but, resolving to weary, by perseverance, him whom he could not surpass in speed, he pressed on till the foot of the mountain stopped his course." 9. What is the third method of analysis? 10. How is the following example analyzed by this method? "Such is the emptiness of human enjoyment, that we are always impatient of the present. Attainment is followed by neglect, and possession, by disgust. Few moments are more pleasing than those in which the mind is concerting measures for a new undertaking. From the first hint that wakens the fancy, to the hour of actual execution, all is improvement and progress, triumph and felicity." 11. What is the fourth method of analysis? 12. How are the following sentences analyzed by this method? (1.) "Swift would say, 'The thing has not life enough in it to keep it sweet;' Johnson, 'The creature possesses not vitality sufficient to preserve it from putrefaction.'" (2.) "There is one Being to whom we can look with a perfect conviction of finding that security, which nothing about us can give, and which nothing about us can take away." 13. What is said of the fifth method of analysis?

[Now, if the teacher choose to make use of any other method of analysis than full syntactical parsing, he may direct his pupils to turn to the next selection of examples, or to any other accurate sentences, and analyze them according to the method chosen.]

LESSON VI. — OF PARSING.

1. Why is it necessary to observe *the sense*, or *meaning*, of what we parse? 2. What is required of the pupil in syntactical parsing? 3. How is the following long example parsed in Praxis XII? "A young man studious to know his duty, and honestly bent on doing it,

will find himself led away from the sin or folly in which the multitude thoughtlessly indulge themselves; but, ah! poor fallen human nature! what conflicts are thy portion, when inclination and habit — a rebel and a traitor — exert their sway against our only saving principle!"

[Now parse, in like manner, and with no needless deviations from the prescribed forms, the ten lessons of the Twelfth Praxis; or such parts of those lessons as the teacher may choose.]

LESSON VII. — THE RULES.

1. In what chapter are the rules of syntax first presented? 2. In what praxis are these rules first applied in parsing? 3. Which of the ten parts of speech is left without any rule of syntax? 4. How many and which of the ten have but one rule apiece? 5. Then, of the twenty-four rules, how many remain for the other three parts,—nouns, pronouns, and verbs? 6. How many of these seventeen speak of *cases*, and therefore apply equally to nouns and pronouns? 7. Which are these seven? 8. How many rules are there for the agreement of pronouns with their antecedents, and which are they? 9. How many rules are there for finite verbs, and which are they? 10. How many are there for infinitives, and which are they? 11. What ten chapters of the foregoing code of syntax treat of the ten parts of speech in their order? 12. Besides the rules and their examples, what sorts of matters are introduced into these chapters? 13. How many of the twenty-four rules of syntax are used both in parsing and in correcting? 14. Of what use are those rules which cannot be violated in practice? 15. How many such rules are there among the twenty-four? 16. How many and what parts of speech are usually parsed by such rules only?

LESSON VIII. — THE NOTES.

1. What is the essential character of the *Notes* which are placed under the rules of syntax? 2. Are the different forms of false construction as numerous as these notes? 3. Which exercise brings into use the greater number of grammatical principles, parsing or correcting? 4. Are the principles or doctrines which are applied in these different exercises usually the same, or are they different? 5. In etymological parsing, we use about seventy *definitions*; can these be used also in the correcting of errors? 6. For the correcting of false syntax, we have a hundred and fifty-two *notes*; can these be used also in parsing? 7. How many of the rules have no such notes under them? 8. What order is observed in the placing of these notes, if some rules have many, and others few or none? 9. How many of them are under the rule for *articles*? 10. How many of them refer to the construction of *nouns*? 11. How many of them belong to the syntax of *adjectives*? 12. How many of them treat of *pronouns*? 13. How many of them regard the use of *verbs*? 14. How many of them pertain to the syntax of *participles*? 15. How many of them relate to the construction of *adverbs*? 16. How many of them show the application of *conjunctions*? 17. How many of them expose errors in the use of *prepositions*? 18. How many of them speak of *interjections*?

[Now correct orally the examples of *False Syntax* placed under the several Rules and Notes; or so many texts under each head as the teacher may think sufficient.]

LESSON IX. — THE EXCEPTIONS.

1. In what exercise can there be occasion to cite and apply the *Exceptions* to the rules of syntax? 2. Are there exceptions to all the rules, or to how many? 3. Are there exceptions in reference to all the parts of speech, or to how many of the ten? 4. Do articles always relate to nouns? 5. Can the subject of a finite verb be in any other case than the nominative? 6. Are words in apposition always supposed to be in the same case? 7. Is the possessive case always governed by the name of the thing possessed? 8. Can an active-transitive verb govern any other case than the objective? 9. Can a verb or participle not transitive take any other case after it than that which precedes it? 10. Can a preposition, in English, govern any other case than the objective? 11. Can "the case absolute," in English, be any other than the nominative? 12. Does every adjective "belong to a substantive, expressed or understood," as Murray avers? 13. Can an adjective ever relate to any thing else than a noun or pronoun? 14. Can an adjective ever be used without relation to any noun, pronoun, or other subject? 15. Can an adjective ever be substituted for its kindred abstract noun? 16. Are the person, number, and gender of a pronoun always determined by an antecedent? 17. What pronoun is sometimes applied to animals so as not to distinguish their sex? 18. What pronoun is sometimes an expletive, and sometimes used with reference to an infinitive following it?

LESSON X. — THE EXCEPTIONS.

19. Does a singular antecedent ever admit of a plural pronoun? 20. Can a pronoun agree with its antecedent in one sense and not in an other? 21. If the antecedent is a collective noun conveying the idea of plurality, must the pronoun always be plural? 22. If there are two or more antecedents connected by *and*, must the pronoun always be plural? 23. If there are antecedents connected by *or* or *nor*, is the pronoun always to take them separately? 24. Must a finite verb always agree with its nominative in number and person? 25. If the nominative is a collective noun conveying the idea of plurality, must the verb always be plural? 26. If there are two or more nominatives connected by *and*, must

the verb always be plural? 27. If there are nominatives connected by *or* or *nor*, is the verb always to refer to them separately? 28. Does the preposition *to* before the infinitive always govern the verb? 29. Can the preposition *to* govern or precede any other mood than the infinitive? 30. Is the preposition *to* "understood" after *bid, dare, feel*, and so forth, where it is "superfluous and improper?" 31. How many and what exceptions are there to rule 20th, concerning participles? 32. How many and what exceptions are there to the rule for adverbs? 33. How many and what exceptions are there to the rule for conjunctions? 34. How many and what exceptions are there to the rule for prepositions? 35. Is there any exception to the 24th rule, concerning interjections?

Lesson XI.—The Observations.

1. How many of the ten parts of speech in English are in general incapable of any agreement? 2. Can there be a syntactical relation of words without either agreement or government? 3. Is there ever any needful agreement between unrelated words? 4. Is the mere relation of words according to the sense an element of much importance in English syntax? 5. What parts of speech have no other syntactical property than that of simple relation? 6. What rules of relation are commonly found in grammars? 7. Of what parts is syntax commonly said to consist? 8. Is it common to find in grammars, the rules of syntax well adapted to their purpose? 9. Can you specify some that appear to be faulty? 10. Wherein consists *the truth* of grammatical doctrine, and how can one judge of what others teach? 11. Do those who speak of syntax as being divided into two parts, Concord and Government, commonly adhere to such division? 12. What false concords and false governments are cited in Obs. 7th of the first chapter? 13. Is it often expedient to join in the same rule such principles as must always be applied separately? 14. When one can condense several different principles into one rule, is it not expedient to do so? 15. Is it ever convenient to have one and the same rule applicable to different parts of speech? 16. Is it ever convenient to have rules divided into parts, so as to be double or triple in their form? 17. What instance of extravagant innovation is given in Obs. 12th of the first chapter?

Lesson XII.—The Observations.

18. Can a uniform series of good grammars, Latin, Greek, English, &c., be produced by a mere revising of one defective book for each language? 19. Whose are "The Principles of English Grammar" which Dr. Bullions has republished with alterations, "on the plan of Murray's Grammar?" 20. Can praise and success entitle to critical notice works in themselves unworthy of it? 21. Do the Latin grammarians agree in their enumeration of the concords in Latin? 22. What is said in Obs. 16th, of the plan of mixing syntax with etymology? 23. Do not the principles of etymology affect those of syntax? 24. Can any words agree, or disagree, except in something that belongs to each of them? 25. How many and what parts of speech are concerned in government? 26. Are rules of government to be applied to the governing words, or to the governed? 27. What are gerundives? 28. How many and what are the principles of syntax which belong to the head of simple relation? 29. How many agreements, or concords, are there in English syntax? 30. How many rules of government are there in the best Latin grammars? 31. What fault is there in the usual distribution of these rules? 32. How many and what are the governments in English syntax? 33. Can the parsing of words be varied by any transposition which does not change their import? 34. Can the parsing of words be affected by the parser's notion of what constitutes a simple sentence? 35. What explanation of simple and compound sentences is cited from Dr. Wilson, in Obs. 25? 36. What notion had Dr. Adam of simple and compound sentences? 37. Is this doctrine consistent either with itself or with Wilson's? 38. How can one's notion of *ellipsis* affect his mode of parsing, and his distinction of sentences as simple or compound?

Lesson XIII.—Articles.

1. Can one noun have more than one article? 2. Can one article relate to more than one noun? 3. Why cannot the omission of an article constitute a proper ellipsis? 4. What is the position of the article with respect to its noun? 5. What is the usual position of the article with respect to an adjective and a noun? 6. Can the relative position of the article and adjective be a matter of indifference? 7. What adjectives exclude, or supersede, the article? 8. What adjectives precede the article? 9. What four adverbs affect the position of the article and adjective? 10. Do other adverbs come between the article and the adjective? 11. Can any of the definitives which preclude *an* or *a*, be used with the adjective *one?* 12. When the adjective follows its noun, where stands the article? 13. Can the article, in English, ever be placed after its noun? 14. What is the effect of the word *the* before comparatives and superlatives? 15. What article may sometimes be used in lieu of a possessive pronoun? 16. Is the article *an* or *a* always supposed to imply unity? 17. Respecting *an* or *a*, how does present usage differ from the usage of ancient writers? 18. Can the insertion or omission of an article greatly affect the import of a sentence? 19. By a repetition of the article before two or more adjectives, what other repetition is implied? 20. How

do we sometimes avoid such repetition? 21. Can there ever be an implied repetition of a noun when no article is used?

LESSON XIV.—NOUNS, OR CASES.

1. In how many different ways can the nominative case be used? 2. What is the usual position of the nominative and verb, and when is it varied? 3. With what nominative in the second person, does the imperative verb agree? 4. Why is it thought improper to put a noun in two cases at once? 5. What case in Latin and Greek is reckoned *the subject* of the infinitive mood? 6. Can this, in general, be literally imitated in English? 7. Do our English authors adopt the Latin doctrine of the accusative (or objective) before the infinitive? 8. Is the objective, when it occurs before the infinitive in English, usually governed by some verb, participle, or preposition? 9. What is our nearest approach to the Latin construction of the accusative before the infinitive? 10. What is *apposition*, and from what did it receive this name? 11. Is there a construction of like cases, that is not apposition? 12. To which of the apposite terms is the rule for apposition to be applied? 13. Are words in apposition always to be parsed separately? 14. Wherein are the common rule and definition of apposition faulty? 15. Can the explanatory word ever be placed first? 16. If ever indifferent, which word be called the principal, and which the explanatory, term? 17. Why cannot two nouns, each having the possessive sign, be put in apposition with each other? 18. Where must the sign of possession be put, when two or more possessives are in apposition? 19. Is it compatible with apposition to supply between the words a relative and a verb; as, "At Mr. Smith's [*who is*] the bookseller?" 20. How can a noun be, or seem to be, in apposition with a possessive pronoun? 21. What construction is produced by the *repetition* of a noun or pronoun? 22. What is the construction of a noun, when it emphatically repeats the idea suggested by a preceding sentence?

LESSON XV.—NOUNS, OR CASES.

23. Can words differing in number be in apposition with each other? 24. What is the usual construction of *each other* and *one an other*? 25. Is there any argument from analogy for taking *each other* and *one an other* as compounds? 26. Do we often put proper nouns in apposition with appellatives? 27. What preposition is often put between nouns that signify the same thing? 28. When is an active verb followed by two words in apposition? 29. Does apposition require any other agreement than that of case? 30. What three modes of construction appear like exceptions to Rule 4th? 31. In the phrase, "For *David my servant's* sake," which word is governed by *sake*, and which is to be parsed by the rule of apposition? 32. In the sentence, "It is *man's* to err," what is supposed to govern *man's*? 33. Does the possessive case admit of any abstract sense or construction? 34. Why is it reasonable to limit the government of the possessive to nouns only, or to words taken substantively? 35. Does the possessive case before a real participle denote the possessor of something? 36. What two great authors differ in regard to the correctness of the phrases, "*upon the rule's being observed*," and "*of its being neglected?*" 37. Is either of them right in his argument? 38. Is the distinction between the participial noun and the participle well preserved by Murray and his amenders? 39. Who invented the doctrine, that the participle and its adjuncts may be used as "*one name*," and in that capacity govern the possessive? 40. Have any popular authors adopted this doctrine? 41. Is the doctrine well sustained by its adopters, or is it consistent with the analogy of general grammar? 42. When one doubts whether a participle ought to be the governing word or the adjunct,— that is, whether he ought to use the possessive case before it or the objective,— what shall he do? 43. What is objected to the sentences in which participles govern the possessive case, and particularly to the examples given by Priestley, Murray, and others, to prove such a construction right? 44. Do the teachers of this doctrine agree among themselves? 45. How does the author of this work generally dispose of such government? 46. Does he positively determine, that the participle should *never* be allowed to govern the possessive case?

LESSON XVI.—NOUNS, OR CASES.

47. Are the distinctions of voice and of time as much regarded in participial nouns as in participles? 48. Why cannot an omission of the possessive sign be accounted a true *ellipsis?* 49. What is the usual position of the possessive case, and what exceptions are there? 50. In what other form can the meaning of the possessive case be expressed? 51. Is the possessive often governed by what is not expressed? 52. Does every possessive sign imply a separate governing noun? 53. How do compounds take the sign of possession? 54. Do we put the sign of possession always and only where the two terms of the possessive relation meet? 55. Can the possessive sign ever be rightly added to a separate adjective? 56. What is said of the omission of *s* from the possessive singular on account of its hissing sound? 57. What errors do Kirkham, Smith, and others, teach concerning the possessive singular? 58. Why is Murray's rule for the possessive case objectionable? 59. Do compounds embracing the possessive case appear to be written with sufficient uniformity? 60. What rules for nouns coming together are inserted in Obs. 31st on Rule 4th? 61. Does

compounding of words necessarily preclude their separate use? 62. Is there a differ-
ce worth notice, between such terms or things as *heart-ease* and *heart's-ease*; a *hardship* and
lar's lip; a *headsman* and a *headsman*; a *lady's-slipper* and a *lady's slipper*? 63. Where
ge is utterly unsettled, what guidance should be sought? 64. What peculiarities are
ticed in regard to the noun *side*? 65. What peculiarities has the possessive case in
gard to correlatives? 66. What is remarked of the possessive relation between time and
ion? 67. What is observed of nouns of weight, measure, or time, coming immediately
gether?

LESSON XVII. — NOUNS, OR CASES.

8. Are there any exceptions or objections to the old rule, "Active verbs govern the ob-
tive case?" 69. Of how many different constructions is the objective case susceptible?
What is the usual position of the objective case, and what exceptions are there? 71.
a any thing but the governing of an objective noun or pronoun make an active verb
nsitive? 72. In the sentence, "What *have* I to *do* with thee?" how are *have* and *do* to
parsed? 73. Can infinitives, participles, phrases, sentences, and parts of sentences, be
lly "in the objective case?" 74. In the sentence, "I *know why* she blushed," how is
w to be parsed? 75. In the sentence, "I *know that* Messias cometh," how are *know* and
t to be parsed? 76. In the sentence, "And *Simon* he surnamed *Peter*," how are *Simon*
l *Peter* to be parsed? 77. In such sentences as, "I paid *him* the *money*,"—"He asked
m the *question*," how are the two objectives to be parsed? 78. Does any verb in English
r govern two objectives that are not coupled? 79. Are there any of our passive verbs
it can properly govern the objective case? 80. Is not our language like the Latin, in
pect to verbs governing two cases, and passives retaining the latter? 81. How do our
mmarians now dispose of what remains to us of the old Saxon dative case? 82. Do any
utable writers allow passive verbs to govern the objective case? 83. What says Lindley
urray about this passive government? 84. Why is the position, "Active verbs govern
i objective case," of no use to the composer? 85. On what is the construction of *same*
s founded? 86. Does this construction admit of any variety in the position of the
rds? 87. Does an ellipsis of the verb or participle change this construction into appo-
on? 88. Is it ever right to put both terms before the verb? 89. What kinds of words
i take different cases after them? 90. Can a participle which is governed by a preposi-
n, have a case after it which is governed by neither? 91. How is the word *man* to be
ved in the following example? "The atrocious *crime of being* a young *man*, I shall neither
empt to palliate, nor deny."

LESSON XVIII. — NOUNS, OR CASES.

2. In what kinds of examples do we meet with a doubtful case after a participle? 93.
he case after the verb reckoned doubtful, when the subject going before is a sentence, or
mething not declinable by cases? 94. In the sentence, "It is certainly as easy to be a
ler, as a *gamester*," what is the case of *scholar* and *gamester*, and why? 95. Are there
t verbs that sometimes connect like cases, and sometimes govern the objective? 96.
ut faults are there in the rules given by *Lowth*, *Murray*, *Smith*, and others, for the con-
iction of *like cases*? 97. Can a preposition ever govern any thing else than a noun or a
noun? 98. Is every thing that a preposition governs, necessarily supposed to have cases,
l to be in the objective? 99. Why or wherein is the common rule, "Prepositions govern
objective case," defective or insufficient? 100. In such phrases as *in vain*, *at first*, *in
ticular*, how is the adjective to be parsed? 101. In such expressions as, "I give it up
lost,"—"I take it *for granted*," how is the participle to be parsed? 102. In such phrases
at once*, *from thence*, *till now*, how is the latter word to be parsed? 103. What peculiarity
here in the construction of nouns of time, measure, distance, or value? 104. What is
rved of the words *like*, *near*, and *nigh*? 105. What is observed of the word *worth*?
. According to Johnson and Tooke, what is *worth*, in such phrases as, "Wo *worth* the
?" 107. After verbs of *giving*, *paying*, and the like, what ellipsis is apt to occur?
. What is observed of the nouns used in dates? 109. What defect is observable in the
mon rules for "the case absolute," or "the nominative independent?" 110. In
r many ways is the nominative case put absolute? 111. What participle is often under-
d after nouns put absolute? 112. In how many ways can nouns of the second person
mployed? 113. What is said of nouns used in exclamations, or in mottoes and abbre-
led sayings? 114. What is observed of such phrases as, "*hand to hand*,"—"*face to
e?" 115. What authors deny the existence of "the case absolute?"

LESSON XIX. — ADJECTIVES.

. Does the adjective frequently relate to what is not uttered with it? 2. What is ob-
ved of those rules which suppose every adjective to relate to some noun? 3. To what
s the adjective usually relate, when it stands alone after a finite verb? 4. Where is the
n or pronoun, when an adjective follows an infinitive or a participle? 5. What is ob-
ved of adjectives preceded by *the* and used elliptically? 6. What is said of the position
he adjective? 7. In what instances is the adjective placed after its noun? 8. In what

instances may the adjective either precede or follow the noun? 9. What are the construction and import of the phrases, *in particular*, *in general*, and the like? 10. What is said of adjectives as agreeing or disagreeing with their nouns in number? 11. What is observed of *this* and *that* as referring to two nouns connected? 12. What is remarked of the use of adjectives for adverbs? 13. How can one determine whether an adjective or an adverb is required? 14. What is remarked of the placing of two or more adjectives before one noun? 15. How can one avoid the ambiguity which Dr. Priestley notices in the use of the adjective *no*?

LESSON XX. — PRONOUNS.

1. Can such pronouns as stand for things not named, be said to agree with the nouns for which they are substituted? 2. Is the pronoun *we* singular when it is used in lieu of *I*? 3. Is the pronoun *you* singular when used in lieu of *thou* or *thee*? 4. What is there remarkable in the construction of *ourself* and *yourself*? 5. Of what person, number, and gender, is the relative, when put after such terms of address as, *your Majesty*, *your Highness*, *your Lordship*, *your Honour*? 6. How does the English fashion of putting *you* for *thou*, compare with the usage of the French, and of other nations? 7. Do any imagine these fashionable substitutions to be morally objectionable? 8. What figures of rhetoric are liable to affect the agreement of pronouns with their antecedents? 9. How does the pronoun agree with its noun in cases of personification? 10. How does the pronoun agree with its noun in cases of metaphor? 11. How does the pronoun agree with its noun in cases of metonymy? 12. How does the pronoun agree with its noun in cases of synecdoche? 13. What is the usual position of pronouns, and what exceptions are there? 14. When a pronoun represents a phrase or sentence, of what person, number, and gender is it? 15. Under what circumstances can a pronoun agree with either of two antecedents? 16. With what does the relative agree when an other word is introduced by the pronoun *it*? 17. In the sentence, "*It* is useless to complain," what does *it* represent? 18. How are relative and interrogative pronouns placed? 19. What are the chief constructional peculiarities of the relative pronouns? 20. Why does the author discard the two special rules commonly given for the construction of relatives?

LESSON XXI. — PRONOUNS.

21. To what part of speech is the greatest number of rules applied in parsing? 22. Of the twenty-four rules in this work, how many are applicable to pronouns? 23. Of the seven rules for cases, how many are applicable to relatives and interrogatives? 24. What is remarked of the ellipsis or omission of the relative? 25. What is said of the suppression of the antecedent? 26. What is noted of the word *which*, as applied to persons? 27. What relative is applied to a proper noun taken merely as a name? 28. When do we employ the same relative in successive clauses? 29. What odd use is sometimes made of the pronoun *your*? 30. Under what *figure* of syntax did the old grammarians rank the plural construction of a noun of multitude? 31. Does a collective noun with a singular definitive before it ever admit of a plural verb or pronoun? 32. Do collective nouns generally admit of being made literally plural? 33. When joint antecedents are of different persons, with which person does the pronoun agree? 34. When joint antecedents differ in gender, of what gender is the pronoun? 35. Why is it wrong to say, "The first has a lenis, *and the* other an asper over *them*?" 36. Can nouns without *and* be taken jointly, as if they had it? 37. Can singular antecedents be so suggested as to require a plural pronoun, when only one of them is uttered? 38. Why do singular antecedents connected by *or* or *nor* appear to require a singular pronoun? 39. Can differing antecedents connected by *or* be accurately represented by differing pronouns connected in the same way? 40. Why are we apt to use a plural pronoun after antecedents of different genders? 41. Do the Latin grammars teach the same doctrine as the English, concerning nominatives or antecedents connected disjunctively?

LESSON XXII. — VERBS.

1. What is necessary to every finite verb? 2. What is remarked of such examples as this: "The *Pleasures* of Memory *was published* in 1792?" 3. What is to be done with "*Thinks I* to myself," and the like? 4. Is it right to say with Smith, "Every hundred *years constitutes* a century?" 5. What needless ellipses both of nominatives and of verbs are commonly supposed by our grammarians? 6. What actual ellipsis usually occurs with the imperative mood? 7. What is observed concerning the place of the verb? 8. What besides a noun or a pronoun may be made the subject of a verb? 9. What is remarked of the faulty omission of the pronoun *it* before the verb? 10. When an infinitive phrase is made the subject of a verb, do the words remain adjuncts, or are they abstract? 11. How can we introduce a noun or pronoun before the infinitive, and still make the whole phrase the subject of a finite verb? 12. Can an objective before the infinitive become "the subject of the affirmation?" 13. In making a phrase the subject of a verb, do we produce an exception to Rule 14th? 14. Why is it wrong to say, with Dr. Ash, "The king and queen appearing in public *was* the cause of my going?" 15. What inconsistency is found in

Murray, with reference to his "*nominative sentences?*" 16. What is Dr. Webster's ninth rule of syntax? 17. Why did Murray think all Webster's examples under this rule bad English? 18. Why are both parties wrong in this instance? 19. What strange error is taught by Cobbett, and by Wright, in regard to the relative and its verb? 20. Is it demonstrable that verbs often agree with relatives? 21. What is observed of the agreement of verbs in interrogative sentences? 22. Do we ever find the subjunctive mood put after a relative pronoun? 23. What is remarked of the difference between the indicative and the subjunctive mood, and of the limits of the latter?

LESSON XXIII. — VERBS.

24. In respect to collective nouns, how is it generally determined, whether they convey the idea of plurality or not? 25. What is stated of the rules of Adam, Lowth, Murray, and Kirkham, concerning collective nouns? 26. What is Nixon's notion of the construction of the verb and collective noun? 27. Does this author appear to have gained "a *clear idea* of the nature of a collective noun?" 28. What great difficulty does Murray acknowledge concerning "nouns of multitude?" 29. Does Murray's notion, that collective nouns are of different sorts, appear to be consistent or warrantable? 30. Can words that agree with the same collective noun, be of different numbers? 31. What is observed of collective nouns used partitively? 32. Which are the most apt to be taken plurally, collections of persons, or collections of things? 33. Can a collective noun, as such, take a plural adjective before it? 34. What is observed of the expressions, *these people, these gentry, these folk?* 35. What is observed of sentences like the following, in which there seems to be no nominative: "There *are* from eight to twelve professors?" 36. What rule does Dr. Webster give for such examples as the following: "There *was* more than a hundred and fifty thousand pounds?" 37. What grammarians teach, that two or more nouns connected by *and*, "always require the verb or pronoun to which they refer, to be in the plural number?" 38. Does Murray acknowledge or furnish any exceptions to this doctrine? 39. On what principle can one justify such an example as this: "*All work and no play, makes* Jack a dull boy?" 40. What is remarked of instances like the following: "Prior's *Henry and Emma contains* an other beautiful example?" 41. What is said of the suppression of the conjunction *and?* 42. When the speaker changes his nominative, to take a stronger one, what concord has the verb? 43. When two or more nominatives connected by *and* explain a preceding one, what agreement has the verb? 44. What grammarian approves of such expressions as, "Two and two *is* four?" 45. What is observed of verbs that agree with the nearest nominative, and are understood to the rest? 46. When the nominatives connected are of different persons, of what person is the verb?

LESSON XXIV. —VERBS.

47. What is the syntax of the verb, when one of its nominatives is expressed, and an other or others implied? 48. What is the syntax of the verb, when there are nominatives connected by *as?* 49. What is the construction when two nominatives are connected by *as well as, but,* or *save?* 50. Can words connected by *with* be properly used as joint nominatives? 51. Does the analogy of other languages with ours prove any thing on this point? 52. What does Cobbett say about *with* put for *and?* 53. What is the construction of such expressions as this: "A torch, *muff* and *all, goes* out in a moment?" 54. Does our rule for the verb and disjunct nominatives derive confirmation from the Latin and Greek syntax? 55. Why do collective nouns singular, when connected by *or* or *nor,* admit of a plural verb? 56. In the expression, "*I, thou,* or *he, may affirm,*" of what person and number is the verb? 57. Who says, "the verb agrees with *the last nominative?*" 58. What authors prefer "*the nearest person,*" and "*the plural number?*" 59. What authors prefer "the *nearest nominative,* whether singular or plural?" 60. What author declares it improper ever to connect by *or* or *nor* any nominatives that require different forms of the verb? 61. What is Cobbett's '*clear principle*" on this head? 62. Can a zeugma of the verb be proved to be right, in spite of these authorities? 63. When a verb has nominatives of different persons or numbers, connected by *or* or *nor,* with which of them does it *commonly* agree? 64. When does it agree with the remoter nominative? 65. When a noun is implied in an adjective of a different number, which word is regarded in the formation of the verb? 66. What is remarked concerning the place of the pronoun of the first person singular? 67. When verbs are connected by *and, or,* or *nor,* do they necessarily agree with the same nominative? 68. Why is the thirteenth rule of the author's Institutes and First Lines not retained as a rule in this work? 69. Are verbs often connected without agreeing in mood, tense, and form?

LESSON XXV.—VERBS.

70. What particular convenience do we find in having most of our tenses composed of separable words? 71. Is the connecting of verbs elliptically, or by parts, any thing peculiar to our language? 72. What faults appear in the teaching of our grammarians concerning *do* used as a "substitute for other verbs?" 73. What notions have been entertained concerning the word *to* as used before the infinitive verb? 74. How does Dr. Ash parse *to* before the infinitive? 75. What grammarians have taught that the preposition *to* governs

the infinitive mood? 76. Does Lowth agree with Murray in the anomaly of supposing *to* a preposition that governs nothing? 77. Why do those teach just as inconsistently, who forbear to call the *to* a preposition? 78. What objections are there to the rule, with its exceptions, "One verb governs an other in the infinitive mood?" 79. What large exception to this rule has been recently discovered by Dr. Bullions? 80. Are the countless examples of this exception truly elliptical? 81. Is the infinitive ever governed by a preposition in French, Spanish, or Italian? 82. What whimsical account of the English infinitive is given by Nixon? 83. How was the infinitive expressed in the Anglo-Saxon of the eleventh century? 84. What does Richard Johnson infer from the fact that the Latin infinitive is sometimes governed by a preposition? 85. What reasons can be adduced to show that the infinitive is not a noun? 86. How can it be proved that *to* before the infinitive is a preposition? 87. What does Dr. Wilson say of the character and *import* of the infinitive? 88. To what other terms can the infinitive be connected? 89. What is the infinitive, and for what things may it stand? 90. Do these ten heads embrace all the uses of the infinitive? 91. What is observed of Murray's "*infinitive made absolute?*" 92. What is said of the position of the infinitive? 93. Is the infinitive ever liable to be misplaced?

Lesson XXVI.—Verbs.

94. What is observed of the frequent ellipses of the verb *to be*, supposed by Allen and others? 95. What is said of the suppression of *to* and the insertion of *be*; as, "To make himself *be* heard?" 96. Why is it necessary to use the sign *to* before an abstract infinitive, where it shows no relation? 97. What is observed concerning the distinction of *voice* in the simple infinitive and the first participle? 98. What do our grammarians teach concerning the omission of *to* before the infinitive, after *bid, dare, feel*, &c.? 99. How do Ingersoll, Kirkham, and Smith, agree with their master Murray, concerning such examples as, "*Let me go?*" 100. What is affirmed of the difficulties of parsing the infinitive according to the code of Murray? 101. How do Nutting, Kirkham, Nixon, Cooper, and Sanborn, agree with Murray, or with one an other, in pointing out what governs the infinitive? 102. What do Murray and others mean by "*neuter verbs,*" when they tell us that the taking of the infinitive without *to* "extends only to active and neuter verbs?" 103. How is the infinitive used after *bid*? 104. How, after *dare*? 105. How, after *feel*? 106. How, after *hear*? 107. How, after *let*? 108. How, after *make*? 109. How, after *need*? 110. Is *need* ever an auxiliary? 111. What errors are taught by Greenleaf concerning *dare* and *need* or *needs*? 112. What is said of *see*, as governing the infinitive? 113. Do any other verbs, besides these eight, take the infinitive after them without *to*? 114. How is the infinitive used after *have, help*, and *find*? 115. When two or more infinitives occur in the same construction, must *to* be used with each? 116. What is said of the sign *to* after *than* or *as*?

Lesson XXVII.—Participles.

1. What questionable uses of participles are commonly admitted by grammarians? 2. Why does the author incline to condemn these peculiarities? 3. What is observed of the multiplicity of uses to which the participle in *ing* may be turned? 4. What is said of the participles which some suppose to be put absolute? 5. How are participles placed? 6. What is said of the transitive use of such words as *unbecoming*? 7. What distinction, in respect to government, is to be observed between a participle and a participial noun? 8. What shall we do when *of* after the participial noun is objectionable? 9. What is said of the correction of those examples in which a needless article or possessive is put before the participle? 10. What is stated of the retaining of adverbs with participial nouns? 11. Can words having the form of the first participle be nouns, and clearly known to be such, when they have no adjuncts? 12. What strictures are made on Murray, Lennie, and Bullions, with reference to examples in which an infinitive follows the participial noun? 13. In what instances is the first participle equivalent to the infinitive? 14. What is said of certain infinitives supposed to be erroneously put for participles? 15. What verbs take the participle after them, and not the infinitive? 16. What is said of those examples in which participles seem to be made the objects of verbs? 17. What is said of the teaching of Murray and others, that, "The participle with its adjuncts may be considered as a *substantive phrase?*" 18. How does the English participle compare with the Latin gerund? 19. How do Dr. Adam and others suppose "the gerund in English" to become a "substantive," or noun? 20. How does the French construction of participles and infinitives compare with the English?

Lesson XXVIII.—Participles.

21. What difference does it make, whether we use the possessive case before words in *ing*, or not? 22. What is said of the distinguishing or confounding of different parts of speech, such as verbs, participles, and nouns? 23. With how many other parts of speech does W. Allen confound the participle? 24. How is the distinguishing of the participle from the verbal noun inculcated by Allen, and their difference of meaning by Murray? 25. Is it pretended that the authorities and reasons which oppose the mixed construction of participles, are sufficient to prove such usage altogether inadmissible? 26. Is it proper to teach, in general terms, that the noun or pronoun which limits the meaning of a participle

;hould be put in the possessive case? 27. What is remarked of different cases used indis-
:riminately before the participle or verbal noun? 28. What say Crombie and others about
:his disputable phraseology? 29. What says Brown of this their teaching? 30. How do
Priestley and others pretend to distinguish between the participial and the substantive use
)f verbals in *ing?* 31. What does Brown say of this doctrine? 32. If when a participle be-
:omes an adjective it drops its regimen, should it not also drop it on becoming a noun?
!3. Where the sense admits of a choice of construction in respect to the participle, is not
ittention due to the analogy of general grammar? 34. Does it appear that nouns before
participles are less frequently subjected to their government than pronouns? 35. Why must
ι grammarian discriminate between idioms, or peculiarities, and the common mode of expres-
iion? 36. Is the Latin gerund, like the verbal in *ing,* sometimes active, sometimes pas-
iive; and when the former governs the genitive, do we imitate the idiom in English?
!7. Is it agreed among grammarians, that the Latin gerund may govern the genitive of the
ιgent? 38. What distinction between the participial and the substantive use of verbals in
ing do Crombie and others propose to make? 39. How does this accord with the views of
Murray, Lowth, Adam, and Brown? 40. How does Hiley treat the English participle?
ι1. What further is remarked concerning false teaching in relation to participles?

LESSON XXIX.—ADVERBS.

1. What is replied to Dr. Adam's suggestion, that, "Adverbs sometimes qualify substan-
ives?" 2. Do not adverbs sometimes relate to participial nouns? 3. If an adverbial word
:elates directly to a noun or pronoun, does not that fact constitute it an adjective? 4. Are
iuch expressions as, "the *then* ministry," "the *above* discourse," good English, or bad—well
authorized, or not? 5. When words commonly used as adverbs assume the construction of
ιouns, how are they to be parsed? 6. Must not the parser be careful to distinguish
ιbverbs used substantively or adjectively, from such as may be better resolved by the suppos-
ng of an ellipsis? 7. How is an adverb to be parsed, when it seems to be put for a verb?
!. How are adverbs to be parsed in such expressions as, "*Away with him?*" 9. What is
ibserved of the relation of conjunctive adverbs, and of the misuse of *when?* 10. What is
iaid in regard to the placing of adverbs? 11. What suggestions are made concerning the
word *no?* 12. What is remarked of two or more negatives in the same sentence? 13. Is
:hat a correct rule which says, "Two negatives, in English, destroy each other, or are equiv-
ιlent to an affirmative?" 14. What is the dispute among grammarians concerning the
ιdoption of *or* or *nor* after *not* or *no?* 15. What fault is found with the opinion of Priestley,
Murray, Ingersoll, and Smith, that "either of them may be used with nearly equal propriety?" 16. How does John Burn propose to settle this dispute? 17. How does Churchill
:reat the matter? 18. What does he say of the manner in which "the use of *nor* after *not*
has been introduced?" 19. What other common modes of expression are censured by this
ιuthor under the same head? 20. How does Brown review these criticisms, and attempt
:o settle the question? 21. What critical remark is made on the misuse of *ever* and *never?*
!2. How does Churchill differ from Lowth respecting the phrase, "*ever so wisely,*" or "*never
io wisely?*" 23. What is observed of *never* and *ever* as seeming to be adjectives, and being
iable to contraction? 24. What strictures are made on the classification and placing of the
word *only?* 25. What is observed of the term *not but,* and of the adverbial use of *but?* 26.
What is noted of the ambiguous use of *but* or *only?* 27. What notions are inculcated by
lifferent grammarians about the introductory word *there?*

LESSON XXX.—CONJUNCTIONS.

1. When two declinable words are connected by a conjunction, why are they of the same
:ase? 2. What is the power, and what the position, of a conjunction that connects sentences
)r clauses? 3. What further is added concerning the terms which conjunctions connect?
ι. What is remarked of two or more conjunctions coming together? 5. What is said of
ιnd as supposed to be used to call attention? 6. What relation of case occurs between
ιouns connected by *as?* 7. Between what other related terms can *as* be employed? 8.
What is *as* when it is made the subject or the object of a verb? 9. What questions are
aised among grammarians, about the construction of *as follow* or *as follows,* and other
imilar phrases? 10. What is said of Murray's mode of treating this subject? 11. Has
Murray written any thing which goes to show whether *as follows* can be right or not, when
he preceding noun is plural? 12. What is the opinion of Nixon, and of Crombie? 13.
What conjunction is frequently understood? 14. What is said of ellipsis after *than* or *as?*
5. What is suggested concerning the character and import of *than* and *as?* 16. Does *than*
ιs well as *as* usually take the same case after it that occurs before it? 17. Is the Greek or
Latin construction of the latter term in a comparison usually such as ours? 18. What
nferences have our grammarians made from the phrase *than whom?* 19. Is *than* supposed
iy Murray to be capable of governing any other objective than *whom?* 20. What gram-
narian supposes *whom* after *than* to be "in the objective case *absolute?*" 21. How does
he author of this work dispose of the example? 22. What notice is taken of O. B. Peirce's
Frammar, with reference to his manner of parsing words after *than* or *as?* 23. What says
:hurchill about the notion that certain conjunctions govern the subjunctive mood? 24.
What is said of the different parts of speech contained in the list of correspondents?

thought and well expressed."—*Ib.* p. 297. "The mayor of Newyork's portrait."—*Ware's English Grammar*, p. 9.

  "Calm Temperance, whose blessings those partake
  Who hunger, and who thirst, for scribbling sake."—*Pope, Dunciad, i, 50.*

EXERCISE III.—ADJECTIVES.

"Plumb down he drops ten thousand fathom deep."—*Milton, P. L.*, B. ii, l. 933. "In his Night Thoughts, there is much energy of expression : in the three first, there are several pathetic passages."—*Blair's Rhet.* p. 403. "Learn to pray, to pray greatly and strong."—*The Dial*, Vol. ii, p. 215. "The good and the bad genius are struggling with one another."—*Philological Museum*, i, 490. "The definitions of the parts of speech, and application of syntax, should be given almost simultaneous."—*Wilbur and Livingston's Gram.* p. 6. "I had studied grammar previous to his instructing me."—*Ib.* p. 13. "So difficult it is to separate these two things from one another."—*Blair's Rhet.* p. 92. "New words should never be ventured upon, except by such whose established reputation gives them some degree of dictatorial power over language."—*Ib.* p. 94. "The verses necessarily succeed each other."—*O. B. Peirce's Gram.* p. 142. "They saw that it would be practicable to express, in writing, the whole combinations of sounds which our words require."—*Blair's Rhet.* p. 68. "There are some Events, the Truth of which cannot appear to any, but such whose Minds are first qualify'd by some certain Knowledge."—*Brightland's Gram.* p. 242. "These Sort of Feet are in Latin called Iambics."—*Fisher's Gram.* p. 134. "And the Words are mostly so disposed, that the Accents may fall on every 2d, 4th, 6th, 8th, and 10th Syllables."—*Ib.* p. 135. "If the verse does not sound well and harmonious to the ear."—*Ib.* p. 136. "I gat me men-singers and women-singers, and the delights of the sons of men, as musical instruments, and that of all sorts."—*Ecclesiastes*, ii, 8. "No people have so studiously avoided the collision of consonants as the Italians."—*Campbell's Rhet.* p. 181. "And these two subjects must destroy one another."—*Ib.* p. 42. "Duration and space are two things in some respects the most like, and in some respects the most unlike to one another."—*Ib.* p. 103. "Nothing ever affected him so much, as this misconduct of his friend."—*Sanborn's Gram.* p. 155. "To see the bearing of the several parts of speech on each other."—*Greenleaf's Gram.* p. 2. "Two or more adjectives following each other, either with or without a conjunction, qualify the same word."—*Bullions, E. Gram.* p. 75. "The two chapters which now remain, are by far the most important of any."—*Student's Manual*, p. 293. "That has been the subject of no less than six negotiations."—*Pres. Jackson's Message*, 1830. "His gravity makes him work cautious."—*Steele, Spect.* No. 534. "Grandeur, being an extreme vivid emotion, is not readily produced in perfection but by reiterated impressions."—*Kames, El. of Crit.* i, 203. "Every object appears less than when viewed separately and independent of the series."—*Ib.* ii, 14. "An Organ is the best of all other musical instruments."—*Dilworth's English Tongue*, p. 94.

  "Let such teach others who themselves excel,
  And censure freely who have written well."—*Pope, on Crit.* l. 15.

EXERCISE IV.—PRONOUNS.

"You had musty victuals, and he hath holp to eat it."—*Shak.: Joh. Dict. w. Victual.* "Sometime am I all wound with adders, who, with cloven tongues, do hiss me into madness."—*Beauties of Shak.* p. 68. "When a letter or syllable is transposed, it is called METATHESIS."—*Adam's Lat. Gram.* p. 275. "When a letter or syllable is added to the beginning of a word, it is called PROSTHESIS."—*Ib.* "If a letter or syllable be taken from the beginning of a word, it is called APHÆRESIS."—*Ib.* "We can examine few, or rather no Substances, so far, as to assure ourselves that we have a certain Knowledge of most of its Properties."—*Brightland's Gram.* p. 244. "Who do you dine with ?"—*Fisher's Gram.* p. 99. "Who do you speak to ?"—*Shakspeare.* "All the objects of prayer are calculated to excite the most active and vivid sentiments, which can arise in the heart of man."—*Adams's Rhet.* i, 328. "It has been my endeavour to furnish you with the most useful materials, which contribute to the purposes of eloquence."—*Ib.* ii, 28. "All paraphrases are vicious : it is not translating, it is commenting."—*Formey's Belles-Lettres*, p. 163. "Did you never bear false witness against thy neighbour ?"—*Sir W. Draper: Junius*, p. 40. "And they shall eat up thine harvest and thy bread : they shall eat up thy flocks and thine herds."—*Jer.* v, 17. "He was the spiritual rock who miraculously supplied the wants of the Israelites."—*Gurney's Evidences*, p. 53. "To cull from the mass of mankind those individuals upon which the attention ought to be most employed."—*Rambler*, No. 4. "His speech contains one of the grossest and most infamous calumnies which ever was uttered."—*Merchant's Gram., Key*, p. 198. "STROMBUS, i. m. A shell-fish of the sea, that has a leader whom they follow as their king. Plin."—*Ainsworth's Dict.* 4to. "Whomsoever will, let him come."—*Morning Star: Lib.* xi, 13. "Thy own words have convinced me (stand a little more out of the sun if you please) that thou hast not the least notion of true honour."—*Fielding.* "Whither art going, pretty Annette ? Your little feet you'll surely wet."—*L. M. Child.* "Metellus, who conquered Macedon, was carried to the funeral pile by his four sons, one of which was the prætor."—*Kennett's Roman Ant.* p. 332. "That not a soldier

·hich they did not know, should mingle himself among them."—*Josephus*, Vol. v, p. 170. The Neuter Gender denotes objects which are neither males nor females."—*Murray's 'ram.* 8vo, p. 37. "And hence it is, that the most important precept, which a rhetorical :acher can inculcate respecting this part of discourse, is negative."—*Adams's Rhet.* ii, 97. The meanest and most contemptible person whom we behold, is the offspring of heaven, ne of the children of the Most High."—*Scougal*, p. 102. "He shall sit next to Darius, ecause of his wisdom, and shall be called Darius his cousin."—1 *Esdras*, iii, 7. "In 1757, e published his ' Fleece;' but he did not long survive it."—*L. Murray, Seq.* p. 252.

"The sun upon the calmest sea
Appears not half so bright as thee."—*Prior.*

EXERCISE V. — VERBS.

"The want of connexion here, as well as in the description of the prodigies that accom-·anied the death of Cæsar, are scarce pardonable."—*Kames, El. of Crit.* Vol. i, p. 38. "The auses of the original beauty of language, considered as significant, which is a branch of the ɪresent subject, will be explained in their order."—*Ib.* Vol. ii, p. 6. "Neither of these two)efinitions do rightly adjust the Genuine signification of this Tense."—*Johnson's Gram. ɔm.* p. 280. "In the earnest hope that they may prove as beneficial to other teachers as hey have to the author."—*John Flint's Gram.* p. 3. "And then an example is given show-ɪg the manner in which the pupil should be required to classify."—*Ib.* p. 3. "*Qu* in ₪nglish words are equivalent to *kw.*"—*Sanborn's Gram.* p. 258. "*Qu* has the power of *kw*, herefore quit doubles the final consonant in forming its preterite."—*Ib.* p. 103. "The ɪord pronoun or substantive can be substituted, should any teacher prefer to do it."—*Ib.*). 132. "The three angles of a right-angled triangle were equal to two right angles in the lays of Moses, as well as now."—GOODELL: *Liberator*, Vol. xi, p. 4. "But now two paces ɪf the vilest earth is room enough."—*Beaut. of Shak.* p. 126. "Latin and French, as the World now goes, is by every one acknowledged to be necessary."—*Locke, on Ed.* p. 351. 'These things, that he will thus learn by sight, and have by roat in his Memory, is not all, I confess, that he is to learn upon the Globes."—*Ib.* p. 321. "Henry: if John shall meet ne, I will hand him your note."—*O. B. Peirce's Gram.* p. 261. "They pronounce the syl-ables in a different manner from what they do at other times."—*Blair's Rhet.* p. 329. 'Cato reminded him of many warnings he had gave him."—*Goldsmith's Rome*, i, 114. "The Wages is small. The Compasses is broken."—*Fisher's Gram.* p. 95. "Prepare thy heart for prayer, lest thou temptest God."—*Life of Luther*, p. 83. "That a soldier should ɖy is a shameful thing."—*Adam's Lat. Gram.* p. 155. "When there is two verbs which are together."—*Woodworth's Gram.* p. 27. "Interjections are words used to express some passion of the mind; and is followed by a note of admiration!"—*Infant School Gram.* p. 126. "And the king said, If he be alone, there is tidings in his mouth."—2 *Samuel*, xviii, 25. "The opinions of the few must be overruled, and submit to the opinions of the many."—*Webster's Essays*, p. 56. "One of the principal difficulties which here occurs, has been already hinted."—*Blair's Rhet.* p. 391. "With milky blood the heart is overflown."—*Thomson, Castle of Ind.* "No man dare solicit for the votes of his nabors."—*Webster's Es-\ays*, p. 344. "Yet they cannot, and they have no right to exercise it."—*Ib.* p. 56. "In order to make it be heard over their vast theatres."—*Blair's Rhet.* p. 471. "Sometimes, however, the relative and its clause is placed before the antecedent and its clause."—*Bul-lions, Lat. Gram.* p. 200.

"Here thou, great Anna! whom three realms obey,
Does sometimes counsel take—and sometimes tea."—*Kames, El. of Crit.* i, 321.

EXERCISE VI. — PARTICIPLES.

"On the other hand, the degrading or vilifying an object, is done successfully by ranking it with one that is really low."—*Kames, El. of Crit.* ii, 50. "The magnifying or diminishing objects by means of comparison, proceeds from the same cause."—*Ib.* i, 239. "Gratifying the affection will also contribute to my own happiness."—*Ib.* i, 53. "The pronouncing syllables in a high or a low tone."—*Ib.* ii, 77. "The crowding into one period or thought different figures of speech, is not less faulty than crowding metaphors in that manner."—*Ib.* ii, 234. "To approve is acknowledging we ought to do a thing; and to condemn is own-ing we ought not to do it."—*Burlamaqui, on Law*, p. 39. "To be provoked that God suffers men to act thus, is claiming to govern the word in his stead."—*Secker.* "Let every subject be well understood before passing on to another."—*Infant School Gram.* p. 18. "Doubling the *t* in *bigotted* is apt to lead to an erroneous accentuation of the word or the second sylla-ble."—*Churchill's Gram.* p. 22. "Their compelling the man to serve was an act of tyranny."—*Webster's Essays*, p. 54. "One of the greatest misfortunes of the French tragedy is, its being always written in rhyme."—*Blair's Rhet.* p. 469. "Horace entitles his satire ' Sermones,' and seems not to have intended rising much higher than prose put into numbers."—*Ib.* p. 492. "Feeding the hungry, clothing the naked, comforting the afflicted, yield more pleas-ure than we receive from those actions which respect only ourselves."—*Murray's Key*, 8vo, p. 238. "But when we attempt to go a step beyond this, and inquire what is the cause of regularity and variety producing in our minds the sensation of beauty, any reason we can assign is extremely imperfect."—*Blair's Rhet.* p. 29. "In an author's writing with propriety, his being free of the two former faults seems implied."—*Ib.* p. 94. "To prevent our being carried away by that torrent of false and frivolous taste."—*Ib.* p. 12. "When we are unable to assign the reasons of our being pleased."—*Ib.* p. 15. "An adjective will not make good sense without joining it to a noun."—*Sanborn's Gram.* p. 12. "What is said respecting sentences being inverted?"—*Ib.* p. 71. "Though he admits of all the other cases, made use of by the Latins."—*Bicknell's Gram.* p. viii. "This indeed, is accounting but feebly for its use in this instance."—*Wright's Gram.* p. 148. "The Knowledge of what passes in the Mind is necessary for the understanding the Principles of Grammar."—*Brightland's Gram.* p. 73. "By *than's* being used instead of *as,* it is not asserted that the former has as much fruit as the latter."—*O. B. Peirce's Gram.* p. 207. "Thus much for the Settling your Authority over your Children."—*Locke, on Ed.* p. 58.

EXERCISE VII.—ADVERBS.

"There can scarce be a greater Defect in a Gentleman, than not to express himself well either in Writing or Speaking."—*Locke, on Ed.* p. 335. "She seldom or ever wore a thing twice in the same way."—*Castle Rackrent,* p. 84. "So can I give no reason, nor I will not."—*Beauties of Shak.* p. 45. "Nor I know not where I did lodge last night."—*Ib.* p. 270. "It is to be presumed they would become soonest proficient in Latin."—*Burn's Gram.* p. xi. "The difficulty of which has not been a little increased by that variety."—*Ward's Pref. to Lily's Gram.* p. xi. "That full endeavours be used in every monthly meeting to seasonably end all business or cases that come before them."—*N. E. Discipline,* p. 44. "In minds where they had scarce any footing before."—*Spectator,* No. 566. "The negative form is when the adverb *not* is used."—*Sanborn's Gram.* p. 61. "The interrogative form is when a question is asked."—*Ibid.* "The finding out the Truth ought to be his whole Aim."—*Brightland's Gram.* p. 239. "Mention the first instance when *that* is used in preference to *who, whom,* or *which.*"—*Sanborn's Gram.* p. 96. "The plot was always exceeding simple. It admitted of few incidents."—*Blair's Rhet.* p. 470. "Their best tragedies make not a deep enough impression on the heart."—*Ib.* p. 472. "The greatest genius on earth, not even a Bacon, can be a perfect master of every branch."—*Webster's Essays,* p. 13. "The verb OUGHT is only used in the indicative [and subjunctive moods]."—*Dr. Ash's Gram.* p. 70. "It is still a greater deviation from congruity, to affect not only variety in the words, but also in the construction."—*Kames, El. of Crit.* ii, 28. "It has besides been found that, generally, students attend those lectures more carefully for which they pay."—*Dr. Lieber. Lit. Conv.* p. 65. "This book I obtained through a friend, it being not exposed for sale."—*Woolsey, ib.* p. 76. "Here there is no manner of resemblance but in the word *drown.*"—*Kames, El. of Crit.* ii, 163. "We have had often occasion to inculcate, that the mind passeth easily and sweetly along a train of connected objects."—*Ib.* ii, 197. "Observe the periods when the most illustrious persons flourished."—*Worcester's Hist.* p. iv. "For every horse is not called Bucephalus, nor every dog Turk."—*Buchanan's Gram.* p. 15. "One can scarce avoid smiling at the blindness of a certain critic."—*Kames, El. of Crit.* ii, 257. "Provided always, that we run not into the extreme of pruning so very close, so as to give a hardness and dryness to style."—*Jamieson's Rhet.* p. 92; *Blair's,* 111. "Agreement is when one word is like another in number, case gender or person."—*Frost's Gram.* p. 41. "Government is when one word causes another to be in some particular number, person or case."—*Ibid.* "It seems to be nothing more than the simple form of the adjective, and to imply not either comparison or degree."—*Murray's Gram.,* 2d Ed., p. 47.

EXERCISE VIII.—CONJUNCTIONS.

"The Indians had neither cows, horses, oxen, or sheep."—*Olney's Introd. to Geog.* p. 46. "Who have no other object in view, but, to make a shew of their supposed talents."—*Blair's Rhet.* p. 344. "No other but these, could draw the attention of men in their rude uncivilized state."—*Ib.* p. 379. "That he shall stick at nothing, nor nothing stick with him."—*Pope.* "To enliven it into a passion, no more is required but the real or ideal presence of the object."—*Kames, El. of Crit.* i, 110. "I see no more to be made of it but to rest upon the final cause first mentioned."—*Ib.* i, 175. "No quality nor circumstance contributes more to grandeur than force."—*Ib.* i, 215. "It being a quotation, not from a poet nor orator, but from a grave author, writing an institute of law."—*Ib.* i, 233. "And our sympathy cannot be otherwise gratified but by giving all the succour in our power."—*Ib.* i, 362. "And to no verse, as far as I know, is a greater variety of time necessary."—*Ib.* ii, 79. "English Heroic verse admits no more but four capital pauses."—*Ib.* ii, 105. "The former serves for no other purpose but to make harmony."—*Ib.* ii. 231. "But the plan was not perhaps as new as some might think it."—*Literary Conv.* p. 85. "The impression received would probably be neither confirmed or corrected."—*Ib.* p. 183. "Right is nothing else but what reason acknowledges."—*Burlamaqui, on Law,* p. 32. "Though it should be of no other use but this."—BP. WILKINS: *Tooke's D. P.,* ii, 27. "One hope no sooner dies in us but another rises up."—*Spect.* No. 535. "This rule implies nothing else but the agreement of an adjective with a substantive."—*Adam's Lat. Gram.* p. 156; *Gould's,* 159. "There can be no doubt but the plan of exercise pointed out at page 132, is the best that be adopted."—*Blair's Gram.* p. viii. "The exertions of this gentleman have done more than any other writer on the subject."—DR. ABERCROMBIE: *Rec. in Murray's Gram.* Vol. ii, p. 306. "No accidental nor unaccountable event ought to be admitted."—*Kames, El. of Crit.* ii, 272. "Wherever there was much fire and vivacity in the genius of nations."—*Jamieson's Rhet.* p. 5. "I am at nothing else but your safety."—*Walker's Particles,* p. 90. "There are pains inflicted upon man for other purposes except warning."—*Wayland's Moral Sci.* p. 122. "Of whom we have no more but a single letter remaining."—*Campbell's Pref. to Matthew.* "The publisher meant no more but that W. Ames was the author."—*Sewel's History, Preface,* p. xii. "Be neether bashful, nor discover uncommon solicitude."—*Webster's Essays,* p. 403. "They put Minos to death, by detaining him so long in a bath, till he fainted."—*Lempriere's Dict.* "For who could be so hard-hearted to be severe."—*Cowley.* "He must neither be a panegyrist nor a satirist."—*Blair's Rhet.* p. 353. "No man unbiassed by philosophical opinions, thinks that life, air, or motion, are precisely the same things."—*Dr. Murray's Hist. of Lang.* i, 426. "Which I had no sooner drank, but I found a pimple rising in my forehead."—ADDISON: *Sanborn's Gram.* p. 182. "This I view very important, and ought to be well understood."—*Osborn's Key,* p. 5. "So that neither emphases, tones, or cadences should be the same."—*Sheridan's Elocution,* p. 5.

"You said no more but that yourselves must be
The judges of the scripture sense, not we."—*Dryden,* p. 96.

EXERCISE IX.—PREPOSITIONS.

"To be entirely devoid of relish for eloquence, poetry, or any of the fine arts, is justly construed to be an unpromising symptom of youth."—*Blair's Rhet.* p. 14. "Well met, George, for I was looking of you."—*Walker's Particles,* p. 441. "There is another fact worthy attention."—*Channing's Emancip.* p. 49. "They did not gather of a Lord's-day, in costly temples."—*The Dial,* No. ii, p. 209. "But certain ideas have, by convention between those who speak the same language, been agreed to be represented by certain articulate sounds."—*Adams's Rhet.* ii, 271. "A careful study of the language is previously requisite, in all who aim at writing it properly."—*Blair's Rhet.* p. 91. "He received his reward in a small place, which he enjoyed to his death."—*Notes to the Dunciad,* B. ii, l. 283. "Gaddi, the pupil of Cimabue, was not unworthy his master."—*Literary History,* p. 268. "It is a new, and picturesque, and glowing image, altogether worthy the talents of the great poet who conceived it."—*Kirkham's Elocution,* p. 100. "If the right does exist, it is paramount his title."—*Angell, on Tide Waters,* p. 237. "The most appropriate adjective should be placed nearest the noun."—*Sanborn's Gram.* p. 194. "Is not Mr. Murray's octavo grammar more worthy the dignified title of a 'Philosophical Grammar?'"—*Kirkham's Gram.* p. 39. "If it shall be found unworthy the approbation and patronage of the literary public."—*Perley's Gram.* p. 3. "When the relative is preceded by two words referring to the same thing, its proper antecedent is the one next it."—*Bullions's E. Gram.* p. 101. "The magistrates commanded them to depart the city."—*Sewel's Hist.* p. 97. "Mankind act oftener from caprice than reason."—*Murray's Gram.* i, 272. "It can never view, clearly and distinctly, above one object at a time."—*Jamieson's Rhet.* p. 65. "The theory of speech, or systematic grammar, was never regularly treated as a science till under the Macedonian kings."—*Knight, on Greek Alph.* p. 106. "I have been at London a year, and I saw the king last summer."—*Murray's Key,* 8vo, p. 198. "This is a crucifying of Christ, and a rebelling of Christ."—*Waldenfield.* "There is another advantage worthy our observation."—*Bolingbroke, on Hist.* p. 26. "Certain conjunctions also require the subjunctive mood after them, independently on the sense."—*Grant's Lat. Gram.* p. 77. "If the critical reader will think proper to admit of it at all."—*Priestley's Gram.* p. 191. "It is the business of an epic poet to copy after nature."—*Blair's Rhet.* p. 427. "Good as the cause is, 'tis one from which numbers have deserted."—*Murray's Key,* 8vo, p. 222. "In respect of the images it will receive from matter."—*Spectator,* No. 413. "Instead of following on to hither morality would conduct it."—*Dymond's Essays,* p. 85. "A variety of questions upon subjects on which their feelings, and wishes, and interests, are involved."—*Ib.* p. 147. In the Greek, Latin, Saxon, and German tongues, some of these situations are termed cases, and are expressed by additions to the Noun instead of by separate words and phrases."—*Booth's Introd.* p. 33. "Every teacher is bound during three times each week, to deliver a public lecture, gratis."—*Howitt's Student-Life of Germany,* p. 35. "But the professors of every political as well as religious creed move amongst each other in manifold circles."—*Ib.* p. 113.

EXERCISE X.—PROMISCUOUS.

"The inseparable Prepositions making no Sense alone, they are used only in Composition."—*Buchanan's Gram.* p. 66. "The English Scholar learns little from the two last tables."—*Ib. Pref.* p. xi. "To prevent the body being stolen by the disciples."—*Watson's Apology,* p. 123. "To prevent the Jews rejoicing at his death."—*Wood's Dict.* p. 584. "After he had wrote the chronicles of the priesthood of John Hyrcanus."—*Whiston's Josephus,* v, 95. "Such words are sometimes parsed as a direct address, than which, nothing could be further from the truth."—*Goodenow's Gram.* p. 89. "The signs of the tenses in these

51

modes are as follows."—*C. Adams's Gram.* p. 33. "The signs of the tenses in the Potential mode are as follows."—*Ibid.* "And, if more promiscuous examples be found necessary, they may be taken from Mr. Murray's English Exercises."—*Nesbit's Parsing,* p. xvi. "One is a numeral adjective, the same as *ten.*"—*Ib.* p. 95. "Nothing so much distinguishes a little mind as to stop at words."—MONTAGUE: *Letter-Writer,* p. 129. "But I say, again, What signifies words?"—*Id. ib.* "Obedience to parents is a divine command, given in both the Old and the New Testaments."—*Nesbit's Parsing,* p. 207. "A Compound Subject is a union of several Subjects to all which belong the same Attribute."—*Fosdick's De Sacy, on General Gram.* p. 22. "There are other languages in which the Conjunctive does not prevent our expressing the subject of the Conjunctive Proposition by a Pronoun."—*Ib.* p. 58. "This distinction must necessarily be expressed by language, but there are several different modes of doing it."—*Ib.* p. 64. "This action may be considered with reference to the person or thing upon whom the action falls."—*Ib.* p. 97. "There is nothing in the nature of things to prevent our coining suitable words."—*Barnard's Gram.* p. 41. "What kind of a book is this?"—*Ib.* p. 43. "Whence all but him had fled."—*Ib.* p. 58. "Person is a distinction between individuals, as speaking, spoken to, or spoken of."—*Ib.* p. 114. "He repented his having neglected his studies at college."—*Emmons's Gram.* p. 19. "What avails the taking so much medicine, when you are so careless about taking cold?"—*Ib.* p. 29. "Active transitive verbs are those where the action passes from the agent to the object." —*Ib.* p. 33. "Active intransitive verbs, are those where the action is wholly confined to the agent or actor."—*Ibid.* "Passive verbs express the receiving, or suffering, the action." —*Ib.* p. 34. "The pluperfect tense expresses an action or event that passed prior or before some other period of time specified in the sentence."—*Ib.* p. 42. "There is no doubt of his being a great statesman."—*Ib.* p. 64. "Herschell is the fartherest from the sun of any of the planets."—*Fuller's Gram.* p. 66. "There has not been introduced into the foregoing pages any reasons for the classifications therein adopted."—*Ib.* p. 80. "There must be a comma before the verb, as well as between each nominative case."—*Ib.* p. 98. "*You,* with *former* and *latter,* are also adjectives."—*Brace's Gram.* p. 17. "You was."—*Ib.* p. 32. "If you was."—*Ib.* p. 39. "Two words which end in *ly* succeeding each other are indeed a little offensive to the ear."—*Ib.* p. 85; *Lennie's Gram.* p. 102.

"Is endless life and happiness despis'd?
  Or both wish'd here, where neither can be found?"—*Young,* p. 124.

EXERCISE XI.—PROMISCUOUS.

"Because any one of them is placed before a noun or pronoun, as you observe I have done in every sentence."—*Rand's Gram.* p. 74. "*Might accompany* is a transitive verb, because it expresses an action which effects the object *me.*"—*Gilbert's Gram.* p. 94. "*Intend* is an intransitive verb because it expresses an action which does not effect any object." —*Ib.* p. 93. "Charles and Eliza were jealous of one another."—*J. M. Putnam's Gram.* p. 44. "Thus *one another* include both nouns."—*Ibid.* "When the antecedent is a child, *that* is elegantly used in preference to *who, whom,* or *which.*"—*Sanborn's Gram.* p. 94. "He can do no more in words, but make out the expression of his will."—*Bp. Wilkins.* "The form of the first person plural of the imperative, *love we,* is grown obsolete."—*Lowth's Gram.* p. 38. "Excluding those verbs which are become obsolete."—*Priestley's Gram.* p. 47. "He who sighs for pleasure, the voice of wisdom can never reach, nor the power of virtue touch." —*Wright's Athens,* p. 64. "The other branch of wit in the thought, is that only which is taken notice of by Addison."—*Kames, El. of Crit.* i, 312. "When any measure of the Chancellor was found fault with."—*Professors' Reasons,* p. 14. "*Whether* was formerly made use of to signify interrogation."—*Murray's Gram.* p. 54. "Under the article of *Pronouns* the following words must be taken notice of."—*Priestley's Gram.* p. 95. "In a word, we are afforded much pleasure, to be enabled to bestow our most unqualified approbation on this excellent work."—*Wright's Gram., Rec.,* p. 4. "For Recreation is not being Idle, as every one may observe."—*Locke, on Ed.* p. 365. "In the easier valuing and expressing that sum." —*Dilworth's Arith.* p. 3. "Addition is the putting together of two or more numbers."— *Alexander's Arith.* p. 8. "The reigns of some of our British Queens may fairly be urged in proof of woman being capable of discharging the most arduous and complicated duties of government."—*West's Letters to Y. L.,* p. 43. "What is the import of that command to love such an one as ourselves?"—*Wayland's Moral Science,* p. 206. "It should seem then the grand question was, What is good?"—*Harris's Hermes,* p. 297. "The rectifying bad habits depends upon our consciousness of them."—*Sheridan's Elocution,* p. 32. "To prevent our being misled by a mere name."—*Campbell's Rhet.* p. 168. "I was refused an opportunity of replying in the latter review."—*Fowle's True English Gram.* p. 10. "But how rare is such generosity and excellence as Howard displayed!"—*M'Culloch's Gram.* p. 39. "The noun is in the Nominative case when it is the name of the person or thing which acts or is spoken of."—*Ib.* p. 54. "The noun is in the Objective case when it is the name of the person or thing which is the object or end of an action or movement."—*Ib.* p. 54. "To prevent their being erased from your memory."—*Mack's Gram.* p. 17. "Pleonasm, is when a superfluous word is introduced abruptly."—*Ib.* p. 69.

"Man feels his weakness, and to numbers run,
  Himself to strengthen, or himself to shun."—*Crabbe, Borough,* p. 137.

EXERCISE XII.—TWO ERRORS.

"Independent on the conjunction, the sense requires the subjunctive mood."—*Grant's Latin Gram.* p. 77. "A Verb in past time without a sign is Imperfect tense."—*C. Adams's Gram.* p. 33. "New modelling your household and personal ornaments is, I grant, an indispensable duty."—*West's Letters to Y. L.*, p. 58. "For grown ladies and gentlemen earning to dance, sing, draw, or even walk, is now too frequent to excite ridicule."—*Ib.* p. 123. "It is recorded that a physician let his horse blood on one of the evil days, and it soon lay dead."—*Constable's Miscellany*, xxi, 99. "As to the apostrophe, it was seldom used to distinguish the genitive case till about the beginning of the present century, and then seems to have been introduced by mistake."—*Dr. Ash's Gram.* p. 23. "One of the relatives only is varied to express the three cases."—*Lowth's Gram.* p. 24. "What! does every body take their mornings draught of this liquor?"—*Collier's Cebes.* "Here, all things come round, and bring the same appearances a long with them."—*Collier's Antoninus*, p. 102. 'Most commonly both the relative and verb are elegantly left out in the second member." —*Buchanan's Gram.* p. ix. "A fair receipt of water, of some thirty or forty foot square."— *Bacon's Essays*, p. 127. "The old know more indirect ways of outwiting others, than the young."—*Burgh's Dignity*, i, 60. "The pronoun singular of the third person hath three genders."—*Lowth's Gram.* p. 21. "The preposition *to* is made use of before nouns of place, when they follow verbs and participles of motion."—*Murray's Gram.* p. 203. "It is called, understanding human nature, knowing the weak sides of men, &c."—*Wayland's Moral Science*, p. 284. "Neither of which are taken notice of by this Grammar."—*Johnson's Gram. Com.* p. 279. "But certainly no invention is entitled to such degree of admiration as that of language."—*Blair's Rhet.* p. 54. "The Indians, the Persians, and Arabians, were all famous for their tales."—*Ib.* p. 374. "Such a leading word is the preposition and the conjunction."—*Felch's Comp. Gram.* p. 21. "This, of all others, is the most encouraging circumstance in these times."—*Sheridan's Elocution*, p. 37. "The putting any constraint on the organs of speech, or urging them to a more rapid action than they can easily perform in their tender state, must be productive of indistinctness in utterance."—*Ib.* p. 35. "Good articulation is the foundation of a good delivery, in the same manner as the sounding the simple notes in music, is the foundation of good singing."—*Ib.* p. 33. "The offering praise and thanks to God, implies our having a lively and devout sense of his excellencies and of his benefits."—ATTERBURY: *Blair's Rhet.* p. 295. "The pause should not be made till the fourth or sixth syllable."—*Blair, ib.* p. 333. "Shenstone's pastoral ballad, in four parts, may justly be reckoned one of the most elegant poems of this kind, which we have in English."—*Ib.* p. 394. "What need Christ to have died, if heaven could have contained imperfect souls?"—*Baxter.* "Every person is not a man of genius, nor is it necessary that he should."—*Beattie's Moral Science*, i, 69. "They were alarmed from a quarter where they least expected."—*Goldsmith's Greece*, ii, 6.

"If thou more murmur'st, I will rend an oak,
And peg thee in his knotty intrails."—SHAK.: *White's Verb*, p. 94.

EXERCISE XIII.—TWO ERRORS.

"In consequence of this, much time and labor are unprofitably expended, and a confusion of ideas introduced into the mind, which, by never so wise a method of subsequent instruction, it is very difficult completely to remove."—*Grenville's Gram.* p. 3. "So that the restoring a natural manner of delivery, would be bringing about an entire revolution, in its most essential parts."—*Sheridan's Elocution*, p. 170. "'Thou who loves us, wilt protect us still:' here *who* agrees with *thou*, and is nominative to the verb loves."—*Alex. Murray's Gram.* p. 67. "The Active voice signifies action; the Passive, suffering, or being the object of an action."—*Adam's Latin Gram.* p. 80; *Gould's*, 77. "They sudden set upon him, fearing no such thing."—*Walker's Particles*, p. 252. "*That* may be used as a pronoun, an adjective, and a conjunction, depending on the office which it performs in the sentence." —*Kirkham's Gram.* p. 110. "This is the distinguishing property of the church of Christ from all other antichristian assemblies or churches."—*Barclay's Works*, i, 533. "My words, the course which the legislature formerly took with respect to the slave-trade, appears to me to be well deserving the attention both of the government and your lordships."— BROUGHAM: *Antislavery Reporter*, Vol. ii, p. 218. "We speak that we do know, and testify that we have seen."—*John*, iii, 11. "This is a consequence I deny, and remains for him to prove."—*Barclay's Works*, iii, 329. "To back this, He brings in the Authority of Accursius, and Consensius Romanus, to the latter of which, he confesses himself beholding for this Doctrine."—*Johnson's Gram. Com.* p. 343. "The compound tenses of the second order, or those in which the participle present is made use of."—*Priestley's Gram.* p. 24. 'To lay the accent always on the same syllable, and the same letter of the syllable, which they do in common discourse."—*Sheridan's Elocution*, p. 78. "Though the converting the *o* into a *v* is not so common as the changing the *v* into a *w*."—*Ib.* p. 46. "Nor is this all; or by means of accent, the times of pauses also are rendered quicker, and their proportions more easily to be adjusted and observed."—*Ib.* p. 72. "By mouthing, is meant, dwelling upon syllables that have no accent; or prolonging the sounds of the accented syllables, beyond their due proportion of time."—*Ib.* p. 76. "Taunt him with the licence of ink; if thou thou'st him some thrice, it shall not be amiss."—SHAX.: *Joh. Dict. w. Thou.* "The eye that mocketh at his father, and despiseth to obey his mother, the ravens of the valley shall pick it out, and the young eagles shall eat it."—*Prov.* xxx, 17. "Copying, or merely imitating others, is the death of arts and sciences."—*Spurzheim, on Ed.* p. 170. "He arrived at that degree of perfection, as to surprise all his acquaintance."—*Ensell's Gram.* p. 296. "Neither the King nor Queen are gone."—*Buchanan's E. Syntax,* p. 155. "Many pronounced as if it were wrote *manny.*"—*Dr. Johnson's Gram. with Dict.* p. 2.

"And as the music on the waters float,
Some bolder shore returns the soften'd note."—*Crabbe, Borough,* p. 118.

EXERCISE XIV. — THREE ERRORS.

"It appears that the Temple was then a building, because these Tiles must be supposed to be for the covering it."—*Johnson's Gram. Com.* p. 281. "It was common for sheriffs to omit or excuse the not making returns for several of the boroughs within their counties."— *Brown's Estimate,* Vol. ii, p. 132. "The conjunction *as* when it is connected with the pronoun, such, many, or same, is sometimes called a relative pronoun."—*Kirkham's Gram. & Compend.* "Mr. Addison has also much harmony in his style; more easy and smooth, but less varied than Lord Shaftesbury."—*Blair's Rhet.* p. 127; *Jamieson's,* 129. "A number of uniform lines having all the same pause, are extremely fatiguing; which is remarkable is French versification."—*Kames, El. of Crit.* Vol. ii, p. 104. "Adjectives qualify or distinguish one noun from another."—*Fowle's True Eng. Gram.* p. 18. "The words *one, other,* and *same* are used in both numbers."—*Kirkham's Gram.* p. 107. "A compound word is made up of two or more words, usually joined by an hyphen, as summer-house, spirit-less, school-master."—*Blair's Gram.* p. 7. "There is an inconvenience in introducing new words by composition which nearly resembles others in use before; as, *disserve,* which is too much like *deserve.*"—*Priestley's Gram.* p. 145. "For even in that case, the transgressing the limits in the least, will scarce be pardoned."—*Sheridan's Lect.* p. 119. "What other are the foregoing instances but describing the passion another feels."—*Kames, El. of Crit.* i, 238. "'Two and three are five.' If each *substantive* is to be taken separately as a subject, then 'two *is* five,' and 'three *is* five.'"—*Goodenow's Gram.* p. 87. "The article *a* joined to the simple *pronoun other* makes *it* the compound *another.*"—*Priestley's Gram.* p. 96. "The word *another* is composed of the indefinite *article prefixed* to the *word other.*"—*Murray's Gram.* p. 57; *et al.* "In relating things that were formerly expressed by another person, we often meet with modes of expression similar to the following."—*Ib.* p. 191. "Dropping one *l* prevents the recurrence of three very near each other."—*Churchill's Gram.* p. 202. "Sometimes two or more genitive cases succeed each other; as, 'John's wife's father.'"—*Duke's Gram.* p. 14. "Sometimes, though rarely, two nouns in the possessive case immediately succeed each other, in the following form: 'My friend's wife's sister.'"—*Murray's Gram.* p. 45.

EXERCISE XV. — MANY ERRORS.

"Number is of a two fold nature,—Singular and Plural: and comprehends, accordingly to its application, the distinction between them."—*Wright's Gram.* p. 37. "The former, Figures of Words, are commonly called Tropes, and *consists* in a word's being employed to signify something, *which* is different from its original and primitive meaning."—*Murray's Gram.* 8vo, p. 337. "The former, figures of words, are commonly called tropes, and *consists* in a word's being employed to signify something *that* is different from its original and primitive meaning."—*Blair's Rhet.* p. 132. "A particular number of connected syllables are called feet, or measured paces."—*Blair's Gram.* p. 118. "Many poems, and especially songs, are written in the dactyl or anapæstic measure, some consisting of eleven or twelve syllables, and some of less."—*Ib.* p. 121. "A Diphthong makes always a long Syllable, unless one of the Vowels be droped."—*British Gram.* p. 34. "An Adverb is generally employed as an attributive, to denote some peculiarity or manner of action, with respect to the time, place, or order, of the noun or circumstance to which it is connected."—*Wright's Definition, Philos. Gram.* pp. 35 and 114. "A Verb expresses the action, the suffering or enduring, or the existence or condition of a noun."—*Ib.* pp. 35 and 64. "These three adjectives should be written our's, your's, their's."—*Fowle's True Eng. Gram.* p. 22. "Never was man so teized, or suffered half the uneasiness as I have done this evening."—*Tattler,* No. 168; *Priestley's Gram.* p. 200; *Murray's,* i, 223. "There may be reckoned in English four different cases, or relations of a substantive, called the subjective, the possessive, the objective, and the absolute cases."—*Goodenow's Gram.* p. 31. "To avoid the too often repeating the Names of other Persons or Things of which we discourse, the words *he, she, it, who, what, were* invented."—*Brightland's Gram.* p. 85. "Names which denote a number of the same things, are called nouns of multitude."—*Infant School Gram.* p. 21. "But lest he should think, this were too slightly a passing over his matter, I will propose to him to be considered these things following."—*Barclay's Works,* Vol. iii, p. 472. "In the pronunciation of the letters of the Hebrew proper names, we find nearly the same rules prevail as in those of Greek and Latin."—*Walker's Key,* p. 223. "The distributive pronominal adjectives *each, every, either*, agree with *the* nouns, *pronouns, and* verbs of the singular number only."—*Lowth's Gram.* p. 89. "*Having treated* of the different *sorts* of *words*, and *their* various modifications, *which is* the first part of Etymology, *it* is now proper to explain the *methods* by which *one word* is derived from another."—*L. Murray's Gram.* p. 130.

EXERCISE XVI.—MANY ERRORS.

"A Noun with its Adjectives (or any governing Word with its Attendants) is as one compound Word, whence the Noun and Adjectives so joined, do often admit another Adjective, and sometimes a third, and so on; as, a Man, an old Man, a very good old Man, a very learned, judicious, sober Man."—*British Gram.* p. 195; *Buchanan's*, 79. "A substantive *with* its adjective *is* reckoned as one *compounded* word; whence *they* often take *another* adjective, and sometimes a third, and so on: as, 'An old man; a good old man; a very learned, judicious, good old man.'"—*L. Murray's Gram.* p. 169; *Ingersoll's*, 195; *and others.* "But though this elliptical style *be* intelligible, and *is* allowable in conversation *and* epistolary *writing*, yet in all *writings* of a serious or dignified kind, *is* ungraceful."—*Blair's Rhet.* p. 112. "There is no talent *so useful* towards rising in the world, *or which* puts men more out of the reach of fortune, than that quality generally possessed by the dullest sort of people, and is, in common language, called discretion."—SWIFT: *Blair's Rhet.* p. 113. "Which to allow, is just as reasonable as to own, that 'tis the greatest ill of a body to be in the utmost *manner* maimed or distorted; but *that* to lose the use *only* of one limb, or to be impaired in some single organ or member, is no ill worthy the least notice."—SHAFTESBURY: *ib.* p. 115; *Murray's Gram.* p. 322. "If the singular nouns *and* pronouns, which *are joined* together by a copulative conjunction, *be* of *several* persons, in *making* the plural pronoun *agree* with them in person, the second person takes *place of* the third, and the *first of* both."—*Murray's Gram.* p. 151; *et al.* "'The painter * * * cannot exhibit various stages of the same action.' *In* this sentence we see that *the* painter *governs*, or agrees with, the verb *can*, as *its nominative* case."—*Ib.* p. 195. "It expresses *also* facts *which* exist *generally*, at *all times*, general truths, attributes *which* are permanent, habits, customary actions, and the like, without the reference to a specific time."—*Ib.* p. 73; *Webster's Philos. Gram.* p. 71. "The different species of animals may therefore be considered, as so many different nations speaking different languages, *that have* no commerce with *each* other; each of *which* consequently understands *none* but *their* own."—*Sheridan's Elocution*, p. 142. "It is also important to *understand and* apply the principles of grammar in our common conversation; not only because *it* enables us to make our language *understood by educated* persons, but because it furnishes the readiest evidence *of our* having received a good education *ourselves*."—*Frost's Practical Gram.* p. 16.

EXERCISE XVII.—MANY ERRORS.

"This faulty Tumour in Stile is like an huge unpleasant Rock in a Champion Country, that's difficult to be transcended."—*Holmes's Rhet.*, Book ii, p. 16. "For there are no Pelops's, nor Cadmus's, nor Danaus's dwell among us."—*Ib.* p. 51. "None of these, except *will*, is ever used as a principal verb, but as an auxiliary to some principal, either expressed or understood."—*Ingersoll's Gram.* p. 134. "Nouns which signify either the male or female are common gender."—*Perley's Gram.* p. 11. "An Adjective expresses the kind, number, or quality of a noun."—*Parker and Fox's Gram.*, Part I, p. 9. "There are six tenses; the Present, the Imperfect, the Perfect, the Pluperfect, the Future, and the Future Perfect tenses."—*Ib.* p. 18. "*My* refers to the first person singular, either gender. *Our* refers to the first person plural, either gender. *Thy* refers to the second person singular, either gender. *Your* refers to the second person plural, either gender. *Their* refers to the third person plural, either gender."—*Parker and Fox's Gram.*, Part II, p. 14. "Good use, which for brevity's sake, shall hereafter include reputable, national, and present use, is not always uniform in her decisions."—*Jamieson's Rhet.* p. 44. "Nouns which denote but one object are considered in the singular number."—*Edward's First Lessons in Gram.* p. 35. "If, therefore, the example of Jesus should be plead to authorize accepting an invitation to dine on the sabbath, it should be plead just as it was."—*Barnes's Notes: on Luke*, xiv, 1. "The teacher will readily dictate what part may be omitted, the first time going through it."—*Ainsworth's Gram.* p. 4. "The contents of the following pages have been drawn chiefly, with various modification, from the same source which has supplied most modern writers on this subject, viz. LINDLEY MURRAY'S GRAMMAR."—*Felton's Gram.* p. 3. "The term *person* in grammar distinguishes between the speaker, the person or thing spoken to, and the person or thing spoken of."—*Ib.* p. 9. "In my father's garden grow the Maiden's Blush and the Prince' Feather."—*Felton, ib.* p. 15. "A preposition is a word used to connect words with one another, and show the relation between them. They generally stand before nouns and pronouns."—*Ib.* p. 60. "Nouns or pronouns addressed are always either in the second person, singular or plural."—*Hallock's Gram.* p. 154. "The plural MEN not ending in s, is the reason for adding the apostrophic's."—*T. Smith's Gram.* p. 19. "*Pennies* denote real coin; *pence*, their value in computation."—*Hazen's Gram.* p. 24. "We commence, first, with *letters*, which is termed *Orthography*; secondly, with *words*, denominated *Etymology*; thirdly, with *sentences*, styled *Syntax*; fourthly, with *orations* and *poems*, called *Prosody*."—

Barrett's Gram. p. 22. "Care must be taken, that sentences of proper construction and obvious import be not rendered obscure by the too free use of the ellipsis."—*Felton's Grammar, Stereotype Edition,* p. 80.

EXERCISE XVIII.—PROMISCUOUS.

"Tropes and metaphors so closely resemble *each* other that it is not always easy, nor is it important to *be able to* distinguish the *one* from the *other*."—*Parker and Fox,* Part III, p. 66. "With regard to *relatives,* it may be further observed, that obscurity often arises from *the* too frequent repetition of them, particularly of the pronouns who, and they, and them, and theirs. When we find *these personal pronouns* crowding too fast upon us, we have often no method left, but to throw the whole sentence into some other form."—*Ib.* p. 90; *Murray's Gram.* p. 311; *Blair's Rhet.* p. 106. "Do scholars acquire any valuable knowledge, by learning to repeat long strings of words, without any definite ideas, or *several* jumbled together like rubbish in a corner, and apparently with no application, *either for the* improvement of mind *or of* language?"—*Cutler's Gram., Pref.,* p. 5. "The being officiously good natured and civil are things so uncommon in the world, that one cannot hear a man make professions of them without being surprised, or at least, suspecting the disinterestedness of his intentions."—Fables: *Cutler's Gram.* p. 125. "Irony is the intentional use of words to express a sense contrary to that which the speaker or writer means to convey."—*Parker and Fox's Gram.,* Part III, p. 68. "The term *Substantive* is derived from *substare,* to stand, to distinguish it from an adjective, which cannot, like the noun, stand alone."—*Hiley's Gram.* p. 11. "They have two numbers, *like nouns,* the singular and plural; and three persons in each number, namely, *I,* the first person, represents the speaker. *Thou,* the second person, represents the person spoken to. *He, she, it,* the third person, represents the person or thing spoken of."—*Ib.* p. 23. "*He, She, It,* is the Third Person singular; but *he with others, she with others,* or *it with others,* make each of them *they,* which is the Third Person plural."—*White, on the English Verb,* p. 97. "The words *had I been,* that is, the Third Past Tense of the Verb, marks the Supposition, as referring itself, not to the Present, but to some former period of time."—*Ib.* p. 88. "A pronoun is a word used instead of a noun, to avoid a too frequent repetition of the same word."—*Frazee's Improved Gram.* p. 122.

"That which he cannot use, and dare not show,
And will not give—why longer should he owe?"—*Crabbe.*

PART IV.
PROSODY.

Prosody treats of punctuation, utterance, figures, and versification.

OBSERVATIONS.

Obs. 1.—The word *prosody,* (from the Greek πρὸς, *to,* and ᾠδὴ, *song,*) is, with regard to its derivation, exactly equivalent to *accent,* or the Latin *accentus,* which is formed from *ad, to,* and *cantus, song:* both terms, perhaps, originally signifying a *singing with,* or *sounding to,* some instrument or voice. Prosodia, as a Latin word, is defined by Littleton, "Pars Grammaticæ quæ docet *accentus.* h. e. rationem attollendi et depremendi syllabas, tum quantitatem earundem." And in English, "*The art of* accenting, *or the rule of pronouncing syllables truly,* long *or* short."—*Litt. Dict.* 4to. This is a little varied by Ainsworth thus: "*The rule of* accenting, *or pronouncing syllables truly, whether* long *or* short."—*Ains. Dict.* 4to. Accent, in English, belongs as much to prose as to poetry; but some deny that in Latin it belongs to either. There is also much difficulty about the import of the word; since some prosodists identify accent with *tone;* some take it for the *inflections* of voice; and some, like the authors just cited, seem to confound it with *quantity,*—"long *or* short."*

*(1.) "*Accent* is the *tone* of the voice with which a syllable is pronounced."—*Dr. Adam's Latin and English Gram.* p. 266.
(2.) "*Accent* is a peculiar *stress* of the voice on some syllable in a word to distinguish it from the others."—*Gould's Adam's Lat. Gram.* p. 243.
(3.) "The *tone* by which one syllable is distinguished from another is the *accent;* which is a greater *stress and elevation* of voice on that particular syllable."—*Bicknell's Eng. Gram.,* Part II, p. 111.
(4.) "*Quantity* is the Length or Shortness of Syllables; and the Proportion, generally speaking, betwixt a long and [a] short Syllable, is two to one; as in *Music,* two *Quavers* to one *Crotchet.—Accent* is the rising and falling of the Voice, above or under its usual Tone, but an Art of which we have little Use, and know less, in the English Tongue; nor are we like to improve our Knowledge in this Particular, unless the Art of *Delivery* or *Utterance* were a little more study'd."—*Brightland's Gram.* p. 156.
(5.) "accent, *s. m. (inflexion de la voix.)* Accent, *tone,* pronunciation."—*Nouveau Dictionnaire Universel,* 4to, Tome Premier, sous le mot *Accent.*
"accent, *subst. (tone or inflection of the voice.)* Accent, *ton* ou *inflexion de voix.*"—*Same Work, Garner's New Universal Dictionary,* 4to, under the word *Accent.*
(6.) "The word *accent* is derived from the Latin language and signifies *the tone of the voice.*"—*Parker and Fox's English Gram.,* Part III, p. 82.
(7.) "The unity of the word consists in the *tone* or *accent,* which binds together the two parts of the composition."—*Fowler's E. Gram.* § 360.
(8.) "The accent of the ancients is the opprobrium of modern criticism. Nothing can show more evidently

Obs. 2.—"*Prosody*," says a late writer, "strictly denotes only that *musical tone or melody* which accompanies speech. But the usage of modern grammarians justifies an extremely general application of the term."—*Frost's Practical Grammar*, p. 160. This remark is a note upon the following definition: "PROSODY is that part of grammar which treats of the structure of Poetical Composition."—*Ibid.* Agreeably to this definition, Frost's Prosody, with all the generality the author claims for it, embraces only a brief account of Versification, with a few remarks on "Poetical License." Of Pronunciation and the Figures of Speech, he takes no notice; and Punctuation, which some place with Orthography, and others distinguish as one of the chief parts of grammar, he exhibits as a portion of Syntax. Not more comprehensive is this part of grammar, as exhibited in the works of several other authors; but, by Lindley Murray, R. C. Smith, and some others, both Punctuation and Pronunciation are placed here; though no mention is made of the former in their subdivision of Prosody, which, they not very aptly say, "consists of *two* parts, Pronunciation and Versification." Dr. Bullions, no less deficient in method, begins with saying, "PROSODY consists of two parts; Elocution and Versification;" (*Principles of E. Gram.* p. 163;) and then absurdly proceeds to treat of it under the following *six* principal heads: viz., Elocution, Versification, Figures of Speech, Poetic License, Hints for Correct and Elegant Writing, and Composition.

Obs. 3.—If, in regard to the subjects which may be treated under the name of *Prosody*, "the usage of *modern* grammarians justifies an extremely general application of the term," such an application is certainly not *less* warranted by the usage of *old* authors. But, by the practice of neither, can it be *easily* determined how many and what things *ought* to be embraced under this head. Of the different kinds of verse, or "the structure of Poetical Composition," some of the old prosodists took little or no notice; because they thought it their chief business, to treat of syllables, and determine the orthoëpy of words. The Prosody of Smetius, dated 1599, (my edition of which was published in Germany in 1691,) is in fact a *pronouncing dictionary* of the Latin language. After a brief abstract of the old rules of George Fabricius concerning quantity and accent, it exhibits, in alphabetical order, and with all their syllables marked, about twenty-eight thousand words, with a poetic line quoted against each, to prove the pronunciation just. The Prosody of John Genuensis, an other immense work, concluded by its author in 1286, improved by Badius in 1506, and printed at Lyons in 1514, is also mainly a *Latin dictionary*, with derivations and definitions as in other dictionaries. It is a folio volume of seven hundred and thirty closely-printed pages; six hundred of which are devoted to the vocabulary, the rest to orthography, accent, etymology, syntax, figures, points—almost everything *but versification*. Yet this vast sum of grammar has been entitled *Prosody*—"*Prosodia seu Catholicon*,"—"*Catholicon seu Universale Vocabularium ac Summa Grammatices*."—See pp. 1 and 5.

CHAPTER I. — PUNCTUATION.

Punctuation is the art of dividing literary composition, by points, or stops, for the purpose of showing more clearly the sense and relation of the words, and of noting the different pauses and inflections required in reading.

The following are the principal points, or marks; namely, the Comma [,], the Semicolon [;], the Colon [:], the Period [.], the Dash [—], the Eroteme, or Note of Interrogation [?], the Ecphoneme, or Note of Exclamation [!], and the Curves, or Parenthesis, [( )].

The Comma denotes the shortest pause; the Semicolon, a pause double that of the comma; the Colon, a pause double that of the semicolon; and the Period, or Full Stop, a pause double that of the colon. The pauses required by the other four, vary according to the structure of the sentence, and their place in it. They may be equal to any of the foregoing.

OBSERVATIONS.

Obs. 1.—The pauses that are made in the natural flow of speech, have, in reality, no definite and invariable proportions. Children are often told to pause at a comma while they might count *one*; at a semicolon, *one, two*; at a colon, *one, two, three*; at a period, *one, two, three, four*. This may be of some use, as teaching them to observe the necessary stops, that they may catch the sense; but the standard itself is variable, and so are the times which good sense gives to the points. As a final stop, the period is immeasurable; and so may be the pause after a question or an exclamation.

Obs. 2.—The first four points take their names from the parts of discourse, or of a sentence, which are distinguished by them. The *Period*, or *circuit*, is a complete *round* of words, often consisting of several clauses or members, and always bringing out full sense at the close. The *Colon*, or *member*, is the greatest division or *limb* of a period, and is the chief constructive part of a compound sentence. The *Semicolon*, *half member*, or *half limb*, is the greatest division of a colon, and is properly a smaller constructive part of a compound sentence. The *Comma*, or *seg-*

the fallibility of the human faculties, than the *total ignorance* we are in at present of the nature of the Latin and Greek accent."—*Walker's Principles*, No. 486; Dict. p. 58.

(9.) "It is not surprising, that the accent and quantity of the ancients should be so obscure and mysterious, when two such learned men of our own nation as Mr. Forster and Dr. Gally, differ about the very existence of quantity in our own language."—*Walker's Observations on Accent*, &c.; Key, p. 811.

(10.) "What these accents are has puzzled the learned so much that they seem neither to understand each other nor themselves."—*Walker's Octavo Dict. w. Barytone.*

ment, is a small part or clause *out off*, and is properly the least constructive part of a compound sentence. A *simple sentence* is sometimes a whole period, sometimes a chief member, sometimes a half member, sometimes a segment, and sometimes perhaps even less. Hence it may require the period, the colon, the semicolon, the comma, or even no point, according to the manner in which it is used. A sentence whose relatives and adjuncts are all taken in a restrictive sense, may be considerably complex, and yet require no division by points; as,

"Thank him who puts me loath to this revenge
On you who wrong me not for him who wrong'd."—*Milton.*

OBS. 3.—The system of punctuation now used in English, is, in its main features, common to very many languages. It is used in Latin, French, Spanish, Italian, Portuguese, Dutch, German, and perhaps most of the tongues in which books are now written or printed. The Germans, however, make less frequent use of the comma than we; and the Spaniards usually mark a question or an exclamation *doubly*, inverting the point at the beginning of the sentence. In Greek, the difference is greater: the colon, expressed by the upper dot alone, is the only point between the comma and the period; the ecphoneme, or note of exclamation, is hardly recognised, though some printers of the classics have occasionally introduced it; and the eroteme, or note of interrogation, retains in that language its pristine form, which is that of our semicolon. In Hebrew, a full stop is denoted by a heavy colon, or something like it; and this is the only pointing adopted, when the vowel points and the accents are not used.

OBS. 4.—Though the points in use, and the principles on which they ought to be applied, are in general well fixed, and common to almost all sorts of books; yet, through the negligence of editors, the imperfections of copy, the carelessness of printers, or some other means, it happens, that different editions and different versions of the same book are often found pointed very variously. This circumstance, provided the sense is still preserved, is commonly thought to be of little moment. But all *writers* will do well to remember, that they owe it to their readers, to show them at once how they mean to be read; and, since the punctuation of the early printers was unquestionably very *defective*, the republishers of ancient books should not be over scrupulous about an exact imitation of it: they may, with proper caution, correct obvious faults.

OBS. 5.—The precise origin of the points, it is not easy to trace in the depth of antiquity. It appears probable, from ancient manuscripts and inscriptions, that the period is the oldest of them; and it is said by some, that the first system of punctuation consisted in the different positions of this dot alone. But after the adoption of the small letters, which improvement is referred to the ninth century, both the comma and the colon came into use, and also the Greek note of interrogation. In old books, however, the comma is often found, not in its present form, but in that of a straight stroke, drawn up and down, obliquely between the words. Though the colon is of Greek origin, the practice of writing it with two dots we owe to the Latin authors, or perhaps to the early printers of Latin books. The semicolon was first used in Italy, and was not adopted in England till about the year 1600. Our marks for questions and exclamations were also derived from the same source, probably at a date somewhat earlier. The curves of the parenthesis have likewise been in use for several centuries. But the dash is a more recent invention: Lowth, Ash, and Ward,—Buchanan, Bicknell, and Burn,—though they name all the rest, make no mention of this mark; but it appears by their books, that they all occasionally *used* it.

OBS. 6.—Of the *colon* it may be observed, that it is now much less frequently used than it was formerly; its place being usurped, sometimes by the semicolon, and sometimes by the period. For this ill reason, some late grammarians have discarded it altogether. Thus Felton: "The COLON is now so seldom used by good writers, that rules for its use are unnecessary."—*Concise Manual of English Gram.* p. 140. So Nutting: "It will be noticed, that the *colon* is omitted in this system; because it is omitted by the writers of the present age; three points, with the *dash*, being considered sufficient to mark the different lengths of the pauses."—*Practical Grammar,* p. 120. These critics, whenever they have occasion to copy such authors as Milton and Pope, do not scruple to mutilate their punctuation by putting semicolons or periods for all the colons they find. But who cannot perceive, that without the colon, the semicolon becomes an absurdity? It can no longer be a *semicolon*, unless the half can remain when the whole is taken away! The colon, being the older point of the two, and once very fashionable, is doubtless on record in more instances than the semicolon; and, if now, after both have been in common use for some hundreds of years, it be found out that only one is needed, perhaps it would be more reasonable to prefer the former. Should public opinion ever be found to coincide with the suggestions of the two authors last quoted, there will be reason to regret that Caxton, the old English typographer of the fifteenth century, who for a while successfully withstood, in his own country, the introduction of the semicolon, had not the power to prevent it forever. In short, to leave no literary extravagance unbroached, the latter point also has not lacked a modern impugner. "One of the greatest improvements in punctuation," says Justin Brenan, "is the rejection of the eternal semicolons of our ancestors. In latter times, the semicolon has been gradually disappearing, not only from the newspapers, but from books."—*Brenan's "Composition and Punctuation familiarly Explained,"* p. 100; London, 1830. The colon and the semicolon are both useful, and, not unfrequently, necessary; and all correct writers will, I doubt not, continue to use both.

OBS. 7.—Since Dr. Blair published his emphatic caution against too frequent a use of *parentheses*, there has been, if not an abatement of the kind of error which he intended to censure, at least a diminution in the use of the *curves*, the sign of a parenthesis. These, too, some inconsiderate grammarians now pronounce to be out of vogue. "The parenthesis is now generally exploded as a deformity."—*Churchill's Gram.* p. 362. "The Parenthesis, ( ) has become nearly obsolete, except in mere references, and the like; its place, by modern writers, being usually supplied by the use of the comma, and the dash."—*Nutting's Practical Grammar,* p. 126; *Fraser's Improved Grammar,* p. 187. More use may have been made of the curves than was necessary, and more of the parenthesis itself than was agreeable to good taste; but, the sign being well adapted to the construction, and the construction being sometimes sprightly and elegant, there are no good reasons for wishing to discard either of them; nor is it true, that the former "has become nearly obsolete."

OBS. 8.—The name *parenthesis*, which literally means *a putting-in-between*, is usually applied both to the *curves*, and to the incidental *clause* which they enclose. This twofold application of the term involves some inconvenience, if not impropriety. According to Dr. Johnson, the enclosed '*sentence*" alone is the *parenthesis* ; but Worcester, agreeably to common usage, defines the word as meaning also "the *mark* thus ( )." But, as this again consists of two distinct parts, two corresponding curves, it seems more natural to use a plural name : hence L. Murray, when he would designate the sign only, adopted a plural expression ; as, "*the parenthetical characters*,"—'*the parenthetical marks*." So, in an other case, which is similar : "the *hooks* in which words are included," are commonly called *crotchets* or *brackets* ; though Bucke, in his Classical Grammar, I know not why, calls the two "[ ] *a Crotchet* ;" (p. 23 ;) and Webster, in his octavo Dictionary, defines *a* "*Bracket*, in printing," as Johnson does *a* "*Crotchet*," by a plural noun : "*hooks* ; thus,]." Again, in his grammars, Dr. Webster rather confusedly says : "The parenthesis ( ) and hooks [ ] include a remark or clause, not essential to the sentence in construction."—*Philosophical Gram.* p. 219 ; *Improved Gram.* p. 154. But, in his Dictionary, he forgets both the hooks and the parenthesis that are here spoken of ; and, with still worse confusion or inaccuracy, says : '*The parenthesis* is usually included in *hooks* or curved lines, thus, ( )." Here he either improperly calls these regular little curves "*hooks*," or erroneously suggests that both the hooks and the curves are usual and appropriate signs of "*the parenthesis*." In Garner's quarto Dictionary, the French word *Crochet*, as used by printers, is translated, "*A brace, a crotchet, a parenthesis* ;" and the English word *Crotchet* is defined, "The *mark* of a *parenthesis*, in printing, *thus* [ ]." But Webster defines *Crotchet*, "In printing, a *hook* including words, a *sentence* or a *passage* distinguished from the rest, thus [ ]." This again is both ambiguous and otherwise inaccurate. It conveys no clear idea of what a crotchet is. *One* hook *includes* nothing. Therefore Johnson said : "*Hooks* in which words are included [thus]." But if each of the hooks is a crotchet, as Webster suggests, and almost every body supposes, then both lexicographers are wrong in not making the whole expression plural : thus, "*Crotchets*, in printing, are angular *hooks* usually including some explanatory words." But is this all that Webster meant ? I cannot tell. He may be understood as saying also, that a *Crotchet* is " *a sentence* or *a passage* distinguished from the rest, thus [ ] ;" and doubtless it would be much better to call a hint thus marked, a *crotchet*, than to call it a *parenthesis*, as some have done. In Parker and Fox's Grammar, and also in Parker's Aids to English Composition, the term *Brackets* only is applied to these angular hooks ; and, contrary to all usage of other authors, so far as I know, the name of *Crotchets* is there given to the *Curves*. And then, as if this application of the word were general, and its propriety indisputable, the pupil is simply told : "The *curved lines* between which a parenthesis is enclosed are called *Crotchets*."—*Gram.*, Part III, p. 30 ; *Aids*, p. 40. "Called *Crotchets*" by whom ? That not even Mr. Parker himself knows them by that name, the following most inaccurate passage is a proof : "The *note* of admiration *and* interrogation, as also the *parenthesis*, the *bracket*, and the reference marks, [are noted in the margin] in the same manner as the apostrophe."—*Aids*, p. 314. In some late grammars, (for example, *Hazen's*, and *Day's*,) the parenthetic curves are called "*the Parentheses*." From this the student must understand that it always takes *two parentheses* to mark *one parenthesis !* If then it is objectionable, to call the two marks *a parenthesis* ;" it is much more so, to call each of them by that name, or both "*the parentheses*." And since Murray's phrases are both entirely too long for common use, what better name can be given them than this very simple one, *the Curves?*

OBS. 9.—The words *eroteme* and *ecphoneme*, which, like *aposteme* and *philosopheme*, are orderly derivatives from Greek roots,[*] I have ventured to suggest as fitter names for the two marks to which they are applied above, than are any of the long catalogue which other grammarians, each choosing for himself, have presented. These marks have not unfrequently been called "*the interrogation* and *the exclamation* ;" which names are not very suitable, because they have other uses in grammar. According to Dr. Blair, as well as L. Murray and others, interrogation and exclamation are "passionate *figures*" of rhetoric, and oftentimes also plain "unfigured" expressions. The former however are frequently and more fitly called by their Greek names *erotesis* and *ecphonesis*, terms to which those above have a happy correspondence. By Dr. Webster and some others, all *interjections* are called "*exclamations* ;" and, as each of these is usually followed by the mark of emotion, it cannot but be inconvenient to call both by the same name.

OBS. 10.—For things so common as the marks of asking and exclaiming, it is desirable to have simple and appropriate *names*, or at least some settled mode of denomination ; but, it is remarkable, that Lindley Murray, in mentioning these characters six times, uses six different modes of expression, and all of them complex : (1.) "Notes of Interrogation and Exclamation." (2.) "The point of Interrogation, ?"—"The point of Exclamation, !" (3.) "The Interrogatory Point."—'The Exclamatory Point." (4.) "A note of interrogation,"—"The note of exclamation." (5.) 'The interrogation and exclamation points." (6.) "The points of Interrogation and Exclamation."—*Murray, Flint, Ingersoll, Alden, Pond.* With much better taste, some writers denote them uniformly thus : (7.) "The Note of Interrogation,"—"The Note of Exclamation."—*Churchill, Hiley.* In addition to these names, all of which are too long, there may be cited many others, though none that are unobjectionable : (8.) "The Interrogative sign,"—"The Exclamatory sign."—*Peirce, Hazen.* (9.) "The Mark of Interrogation,"—"The Mark of Exclamation."—*Ward, Felton, Hendrick.* (10.) "The Interrogative point,"—"The Exclamation point."—*T. Smith, Alger.* (11.) 'The interrogation point,"—"The exclamation point."—*Webster, St. Quentin, S. Putnam.* (12.) 'A Note of Interrogation,"—"A Note of Admiration."—*Coar, Nutting.* (13.) "The Interrogative point,"—"The Note of Admiration, or of vocation."—*Bucke.* (14.) "Interrogation (?),"—"Admiration (!) or Exclamation."—*Lennie, Bullions.* (15.) "A Point of Interrogation,"—"A Point of Admiration or Exclamation."—*Buchanan.* (16.) "The Interrogation point (?),"—"The Admiration point (!)."—*Perley.* (17.) "An interrogation (?),"—"An exclamation (!)."—*Cutler.* (18.) "The interrogator ?"—"The exclaimor !"—*Day's Gram.* p. 112. [The putting of "ex-

---

*[*] "Interrogatio, Græcé *Erotema*, Accentum quoque transfert ; ut, Ter. *Siccine ais Parmeno?* Voss jussębæ."—*Prat's Latin Grammar*, 8vo, Part II, p. 190.

claimor" for *exclaimer*, like this author's changing of *quoters* to "*quotors*," as a name for th guillemets, is probably a mere sample of ignorance.] (19.) "Question point,"—"Exclamati point."—*Sanborn*, p. 272.

SECTION I.—THE COMMA.

The Comma is used to separate those parts of a sentence, which are so nearly connected in sense, as to be only one degree removed from that clos connexion which admits no point.

RULE I.—SIMPLE SENTENCES.

A simple sentence does not, in general, admit the comma; as, "The weakest reasoners are the most positive."—*W. Allen's Gram.* p. 202. "Theology has not hesitated to make or support a doctrine by the position of a comma."—*Tract on Tone*, p. 4.
"Then pain compels the impatient soul to seize
On promis'd hopes of instantaneous ease."—*Crabbe*.

EXCEPTION.—LONG SIMPLE SENTENCES.

When the nominative in a long simple sentence is accompanied by inseparable adjuncts, or when several words together are used in stead of a nominative, a comma should be placed immediately before the verb; as, "Confession of sin without amendment, obtains no pardon."—*Dillwyn's Reflections*, p. 6. "To be totally indifferent to praise or censure, is a real defect in character."—*Murray's Gram.* p. 268.
"O that the tenor of my just complaint,*
Were sculpt with steel in rocks of adamant!"—*Sandys*.

RULE II.—SIMPLE MEMBERS.

The simple members of a compound sentence, whether successive or involved, elliptical or complete, are generally divided by the comma; as,
1. "Here stand we both, and aim we at the best."—*Shak.*
2. "I, that did never weep, now melt in woe."—*Id.*
3. "Tide life, tide death, I come without delay."—*Id.*
4. "I am their mother, who shall bar me from them?"—*Id.*
5. "How wretched, were I mortal, were my state!"—*Pope.*
6. "Go; while thou mayst, avoid the dreadful fate."—*Id.*
7. "Grief aids disease, remember'd folly stings,
And his last sighs reproach the faith of kings."—*Johnson*.

EXCEPTION I.—RESTRICTIVE RELATIVES.

When a relative immediately follows its antecedent, and is taken in a restrictive sense, the comma should not be introduced *before* it; as, "For the things *which* are seen, are temporal; but the things *which* are not seen, are eternal."—*2 Cor.* iv, 18. "A letter is a character *that* expresses a sound without any meaning."—*St. Quentin's General Gram.* p. 3.

EXCEPTION II.—SHORT TERMS CLOSELY CONNECTED.

When the simple members are short, and closely connected by a conjunction or a conjunctive adverb, the comma is generally omitted; as, "Honest poverty is better than wealthy fraud."—*Dillwyn's Ref.* p. 11. "Let him tell me *whether* the number of the stars be even or odd."—TAYLOR: *Joh. Dict. w. Even.* "It is impossible *that* our knowledge of words should outstrip our knowledge of things."—CAMPBELL: *Murray's Gram.* p. 359.

EXCEPTION III.—ELLIPTICAL MEMBERS UNITED.

When two simple members are immediately united, through ellipsis of the relative, the antecedent, or the conjunction *that*, the comma is not inserted; as, "Make an experiment on the first man you meet."—*Berkley's Alciphron*, p. 125. "Our philosophers do infinitely despise and pity whoever shall propose or accept any other motive to virtue."—*Ib.* p. 136. "It is certain we imagine before we reflect."—*Ib.* p. 359.
"The same good sense that makes a man excel,
Still makes him doubt he ne'er has written well."—*Young*.

---

* In regard to the admission of a comma before the verb, by the foregoing exception, neither the practice of authors nor the doctrine of punctuators is entirely uniform; but, where a considerable pause is, and must be made in the reading, I judge it not only allowable, but necessary, to mark it in writing. In W. Day's "Punctuation Reduced to a System," a work of no inconsiderable merit, this principle is disallowed; and even when the adjunct of the nominative is a *relative clause*, which, by Rule 3d below and its first exception, requires a comma after it but none before it, this author excludes both, putting no comma before the principal verb. The following is an example: "But it frequently happens, that punctuation is not made a prominent exercise in schools; and the brief *manner* in which the subject is there *dismissed has proved* insufficient to impress upon the minds of youth a due sense of its importance."—*Day's Punctuation*, p. 32. A pupil of mine would here have put a comma after the word *dismissed*. So, in the following examples, after *sake*, and after *dispense*: "The comely that would accept power for its own sake *is* the pettiest of human passions."—*Ib.* p. 75. "The generous delight of beholding the happiness he dispenses *is* the highest enjoyment of man."—*Ib.* p. 100.

RULE III. — MORE THAN TWO WORDS.

When more than two words or terms are connected in the same construction, or in joint dependence on some other term, by conjunctions expressed or understood, the comma should be inserted after every one of them but the last; and, if they are nominatives before a verb, the comma should follow the last also :* as,

1. " Who, to the enraptur'd heart, and ear, and eye,
   Teach beauty, virtue, truth, and love, and melody."—*Beattie.*
2. " Ah ! what avails * * * * * * * *
   All that art, fortune, enterprise, can bring,
   If envy, scorn, remorse, or pride, the bosom wring ? "—*Id.*
3. " Women are soft, mild, pitiful, and flexible ;
   Thou, stern, obdurate, flinty, rough, remorseless."—*Shak.*
4. " She plans, provides, expatiates, triumphs there."—*Young.*
5. ————————" So eagerly the Fiend
   O'er bog, or steep, through strait, rough, dense, or rare,
   With head, hands, wings, or feet, pursues his way,
   And swims, or sinks, or wades, or creeps, or flies."—*Milton.*

RULE IV. — ONLY TWO WORDS.

When only two words or terms are connected by a conjunction, they should not be separated by the comma; as, " It is a *stupid and barbarous* way to extend dominion by arms ; for true power is to be got by *arts and industry*."—*Spectator*, No. 2.
"*Despair and anguish* fled the struggling soul."—*Goldsmith.*

EXCEPTION I.—TWO WORDS WITH ADJUNCTS.

When the two words connected have several adjuncts, or when one of them has an adjunct that relates not to both, the comma is inserted; as, " I shall spare no pains to make their instruction agreeable, and their diversion useful."—*Spectator*, No. 10. " *Who* is applied to persons, or things personified."—*Bullions.*
" With listless eyes the dotard views the store,
He views, and wonders that they please no more."—*Johnson.*

EXCEPTION II.—TWO TERMS CONTRASTED.

When two connected words or phrases are contrasted, or emphatically distinguished, the comma is inserted; as, "The vain are easily obliged, and easily disobliged."—*Kames.*
" Liberal, not lavish, is kind Nature's hand."—*Beattie.*
" 'T is certain he could write, and cipher too."—*Goldsmith.*

EXCEPTION III.—ALTERNATIVE OF WORDS.

When there is merely an alternative of names, or an explanatory change of terms, the comma is usually inserted; as, " We saw a large opening, or inlet."—*W. Allen.* " Have we not power to lead about a sister, a wife, as well as other apostles ? "—1 *Cor.* ix, 5.

EXCEPTION IV.—CONJUNCTION UNDERSTOOD.

When the conjunction is understood, the comma is inserted; and, if two separated words or terms refer alike to a third term, the second requires a second comma : as, " Reason, virtue, answer one great aim."—*L. Murray, Gram.* p. 269.
" To him the church, the realm, their pow'rs consign."—*Johnson.*
" She thought the isle that gave her birth,
The sweetest, wildest land on earth."—*Hogg.*

RULE V. — WORDS IN PAIRS.

When successive words are joined in pairs by conjunctions, they should be separated in pairs by the comma; as, " Interest and ambition, honour and shame, friendship and enmity, gratitude and revenge, are the prime movers in public transactions."—*W. Allen.* " But, whether ingenious or dull, learned or ignorant, clownish or polite,

---

* When several nominatives are connected, some authors and printers put the comma only where the conjunction is omitted. W. Day separates them all, one from an other; but after the last, when this is singular before a plural verb, he inserts no point. Example : " Imagination is one of the principal ingredients which enter into the complex idea of genius ; but *judgment, memory, understanding, enthusiasm,* and *sensibility* are also included."—*Day's Punctuation,* p. 52. If the points are to be put where the pauses naturally occur, here should be a comma after *sensibility ;* and, if I mistake not, it would be more consonant with current usage to set one there. John Wilson, however, in a later work, which is for the most part a very good one, prefers the doctrine of Day, as in the following instance : " *Reputation, virtue,* and *happiness* depend greatly on the choice of companions."—*Wilson's Treatise on Punctuation,* p. 30.

every innocent man, without exception, has as good a right to liberty as to life."—
Beattie's Moral Science, p. 313.

> "Then say how hope and fear, desire and hate,
> O'erspread with snares the crowded maze of fate."—*Dr. Johnson.*

RULE VI. — WORDS PUT ABSOLUTE.

Nouns or pronouns put absolute, should, with their adjuncts, be set off by the comma; as, "The prince, *his father being dead*, succeeded."—"*This done*, we parted."—"*Zaccheus*, make haste and come down."—"*His prætorship in Sicily*, what did it produce ?"—*Cicero.*

> "Wing'd with his fears, on foot he strove to fly,
> *His steeds too distant*, and *the foe too nigh*."—*Pope, Iliad*, xi, 440.

RULE VII.—WORDS IN APPOSITION.

Words in apposition, (especially if they have adjuncts,) are generally set off by the comma; as, "He that now calls upon thee, is Theodore, *the hermit of Teneriffe*."—*Johnson.* "LOWTH, *Dr. Robert, bishop of London*, born in 1710, died in 1787."—*Biog. Dict.* "HOME, *Henry, lord Kames*."—*Ib.*

> "What next I bring shall please thee, be assur'd,
> Thy *likeness*, thy *fit help*, thy other *self*,
> Thy *wish* exactly to thy heart's desire."—*Milton, P. L.*, viii, 450.

"And he, their prince, shall rank among my peers."—*Byron.*

EXCEPTION I.—COMPLEX NAMES.

When several words, in their common order, are used as one compound name, the comma is not inserted; as, "Dr. Samuel Johnson,"—"Publius Gavius Cosanus."

EXCEPTION II.—CLOSE APPOSITION.

When a common and a proper name are closely united, the comma is not inserted; as, "The brook Kidron,"—"The river Don,"—"The empress Catharine,"—"Paul the Apostle."

EXCEPTION III.—PRONOUN WITHOUT PAUSE.

When a pronoun is added to an other word merely for emphasis and distinction, the comma is not inserted; as, "Ye men of Athens,"—"I myself,"—"Thou flaming minister,"—"You princes."

EXCEPTION IV.—NAMES ACQUIRED.

When a name acquired by some action or relation, is put in apposition with a preceding noun or pronoun, the comma is not inserted: as, "I made the *ground* my *bed*;"—"To make *him king*;"—"*Whom* they revered as *God*;"—"With *modesty* thy *guide*."—*Pope.*

RULE VIII.—ADJECTIVES.

Adjectives, when something depends on them, or when they have the import of a dependent clause, should, with their adjuncts, be set off by the comma; as,

> 1. ———————————"Among the roots
> Of hazel, *pendent o'er the plaintive stream*,
> They frame the first foundation of their domes."—*Thomson.*
> 2. ———————————" Up springs the lark,
> *Shrill-voic'd* and *loud*, the messenger of morn."—*Id.*

EXCEPTION.—ADJECTIVES RESTRICTIVE.

When an adjective immediately follows its noun, and is taken in a restrictive sense, the comma should not be used before it; as,

> ———————————"And on the coast *averse*
> From entrance or cherubic watch."—*Milton, P. L.*, B. ix, l. 68.

RULE IX.—FINITE VERBS.

Where a finite verb is understood, a comma is generally required : as, "From law arises security; from security, curiosity; from curiosity, knowledge."—*Murray.*

> "Else all my prose and verse were much the same;
> This, prose on stilts; that, poetry fallen lame."—*Pope.*

EXCEPTION.—VERY SLIGHT PAUSE.

As the semicolon must separate the clauses when the comma is inserted by this rule, if the pause for the omitted verb be very slight, it may be left unmarked, and the comma be used for the clauses; as, "When the profligate speaks of piety, the miser of generosity, the coward of valour, and the corrupt of integrity, they are only the more despised by those who know them."—*Comstock's Elocution*, p. 132.

RULE X.—INFINITIVES.

The infinitive mood, when it follows a verb from which it must be separated, or when it depends on something remote or understood, is generally, with its adjuncts, set off by the comma; as, "*One* of the greatest secrets in composition is, *to know* when to be simple."—*Jamieson's Rhet.* p. 151. "*To confess the truth*, I was much in fault."—*Murray's Gram.* p. 271.

  " The Governor of all—has interposed,
  Not seldom, his avenging arm, *to smite*
  The injurious trampler upon nature's law."—*Cowper.*

RULE XI.—PARTICIPLES.

Participles, when something depends on them, when they have the import of a dependent clause, or when they relate to something understood, should, with their adjuncts, be set off by the comma; as, 1. " Law is a rule of civil conduct, *prescribed* by the supreme power in a state, *commanding* what is right, and *prohibiting* what is wrong."—BLACKSTONE: *Beattie's Moral Science*, p. 346.

  2. "Young Edwin, *lighted by the evening star*,
  Ling'ring and listning, wander'd down the vale."—*Beattie.*
  3. "*United*, we stand; *divided*, we fall."—*Motto.*
  4. "*Properly speaking*, there is no such thing as chance."

EXCEPTION.—PARTICIPLES RESTRICTIVE.

When a participle immediately follows its noun, and is taken in a restrictive sense, the comma should not be used before it; as,
  "A man *renown'd for repartee*,
  Will seldom scruple to make free
  With friendship's finest feeling."—*Cowper.*

RULE XII.—ADVERBS.

Adverbs, when they break the connexion of a simple sentence, or when they have not a close dependence on some particular word in the context, should, with their adjuncts, be set off by the comma; as, "We must not, *however*, confound this gentleness with the artificial courtesy of the world."—"*Besides*, the mind must be employed."—*Gilpin.* "*Most unquestionably*, no fraud was equal to all this."—*Lyttelton.* " But, *unfortunately for us*, the tide was ebbing already."

  " When buttress and buttress, *alternately*,
  Seem framed of ebon and ivory."—*Scott's Lay*, p. 33.

RULE XIII.—CONJUNCTIONS.

Conjunctions, when they are separated from the principal clauses that depend on them, or when they introduce examples, are generally set off by the comma; *as,* "*But*, by a timely call upon Religion, the force of Habit was eluded."—*Johnson.*

  " They know the neck that joins the shore and sea,
  Or, ah! how chang'd that fearless laugh would be."—*Crabbe.*

RULE XIV.—PREPOSITIONS.

Prepositions and their objects, when they break the connexion of a simple sentence, or when they do not closely follow the words on which they depend, are generally set off by the comma; as, " Fashion is, *for the most part*, nothing but the ostentation of riches."—"*By reading*, we add the experience of others to our own."

  " In vain the sage, *with retrospective eye*,
  Would from th' apparent What conclude the Why."—*Pope.*

RULE XV.—INTERJECTIONS.

Interjections that require a pause, though more commonly emphatic and followed by the ecphoneme, are sometimes set off by the comma; as, " For, *lo*, I will call all the families of the kingdoms of the north."—*Jeremiah*, i, 15. "*O*, 'twas about some-

thing you would not understand."—*Columbian Orator*, p. 221. "Ha, ha!
were finely taken in, then!"—*Aikin*. "Ha, ha, ha! A facetious gentle
truly!"—*Id*.

> "*Oh*, when shall Britain, conscious of her claim,
> Stand emulous of Greek and Roman fame?"—*Pope*.

RULE XVI.—WORDS REPEATED.

A word emphatically repeated, is generally set off by the comma; as, "Hap
happy, happy pair!"—*Dryden*. "Ay, ay, there is some comfort in that."—*Sh*
"Ah! no, no, no."—*Id*.

> "The old oaken bucket, the iron-bound bucket,
> The moss-covered bucket, which hung in the well!"—*Woodworth*.

RULE XVII.—DEPENDENT QUOTATIONS.

A quotation, observation, or description, when it is introduced in close depend
on a verb, (as, *shy*, *reply*, *cry*, or the like,) is generally separated from the res
the sentence by the comma; as, "'The book of nature,' said he, 'is before thee'".
Hawkesworth. "I say unto all, Watch."—*Mark*. "'The boy has become a mu
means, 'he has *grown to be* a man.' 'Such conduct becomes a man,' means, 'su
conduct *befits* him.'"—*Hart's Gram.* p. 116.

> "While man exclaims, 'See all things for my use!'
> 'See man for mine!' replies a pamper'd goose."—*Pope*.

IMPROPRIETIES FOR CORRECTION.

FALSE PUNCTUATION.—ERRORS CONCERNING THE COMMA.

UNDER RULE I.—OF SIMPLE SENTENCES.

"Short, simple sentences should not be separated by a comma."—*Felton's Gram.*, 1st E
p. 135; 3d Ed., Stereotyped, p. 137.

[FORMULE.—Not proper, because a needless comma is put after *short*, the sentence being simple. But, accord
ing to Rule 1st for the Comma, "A simple sentence does not, in general, admit the comma." Therefore t
comma should be omitted; thus, "Short simple sentences should not be separated by a comma." Or, sti
better: "A short simple sentence should rarely be divided by the comma." For such sentences, construe
form a period, should generally be separated; and even a single one may have some phrase that must be set of.]

"A regular and virtuous education, is an inestimable blessing."—*Murray's Key*, 8vo,
174. "Such equivocal expressions, mark an intention to deceive."—*Ib*. p. 256. "Th
are, *This* and *that*, with their plurals *these* and *those*."—*Bullions, E. Gram.* p. 26; Pract.
Lessons, p. 33. "A nominative case and a verb, sometimes make a complete sentence; a
He sleeps."—*Felton's Gram.* p. 78. "*Tense*, expresses the action connected with certa
relations of time; *mood*, represents it as farther modified by circumstances of continger
conditionality, &c."—*Bullions, E. Gram.* p. 37. "The word Noun, means name."—*Ras
soll's Gram.* p. 14. "The present, or active participle, I explained then."—*Ib*. p. 97. "A
some verbs used, both transitively and intransitively?"—*Cooper's Pl. and Pract. Gram.*
54. "Blank verse, is verse without rhyme."—*Hallock's Gram.* p. 242. "A distributi
adjective, denotes each one of a number considered separately."—*Ib*. p. 51.

> "And may at last my weary age,
> Find out the peaceful hermitage."—*Murray's Gr.*, 12mo, p. 205; 8vo, 255.

UNDER THE EXCEPTION CONCERNING SIMPLE SENTENCES.

"A noun without an Article to limit it is taken in its widest sense."—*Bullions, E. Gra*
p. 8; *Practical Lessons*, p. 10.

[FORMULE.—Not proper, because no comma is here set before the verb *is taken*. But, according to the Exce
tion to Rule 1st for the Comma, "When the nominative in a long simple sentence is accompanied by inerten
adjuncts, or when several words together are used in stead of a nominative, a comma should be placed imme
ately before the verb." Therefore, a comma should be here inserted; thus, "A noun without an article to li
it, is taken in its widest sense."—*Lennie's Gram.* p. 6.]

"To maintain a steady course amid all the adversities of life marks a great mind."—*Dex
District School Gram.* p. 84. "To love our Maker supremely and our neighbor as our
selves comprehends the whole moral law."—*Ibid*. "To be afraid to do wrong is tr
courage."—*Ib*. p. 85. "A great fortune in the hands of a fool is a great misfortune."
Bullions, Practical Lessons, p. 89. "That he should make such a remark is indeed strang
—*Farnum, Practical Gram.* p. 30. "To walk in the fields and groves is delightful."—*i
ib*. "That he committed the fault is most certain."—*Id. ib*. "Names common to
things of the same sort or class are called *Common nouns*: as, *man*, *woman*, *day*."—*Buls
Pract. Les.* p. 12. "That it is our duty to be pious *admits* not of any doubt."—*Id. E. Gra*
p. 118. "To endure misfortune with resignation is the characteristic of a great mind."

Id. ib. p. 81.   "The assisting of a friend in such circumstances was certainly a duty."—*Id. ib.* 81.   "That a life of virtue is the safest is certain."—*Hallock's Gram.* p. 169.   "A collective noun denoting the idea of unity should be represented by a pronoun of the singular number."—*Ib.* p. 167.

UNDER RULE II.—OF SIMPLE MEMBERS.

"When the sun had arisen the enemy retreated."—*Day's District School Gram.* p. 85.

[FORMULE.—Not proper, because no comma here separates the two simple members which compose the sentence. But, according to Rule 2d, "The simple members of a compound sentence, whether successive or avolved, elliptical or complete, are generally divided by the comma." Therefore, a comma should be inserted *fter arisen;* thus, "When the sun had arisen, the enemy retreated."]

"If he *become* rich he may be less industrious."—*Bullions, E. Gram.* p. 118.   "The more I study grammar the better I like it."—*Id. ib.* p. 127.   "There is much truth in the old adage that fire is a better servant than master."—*Id. ib.* p. 128.   "The verb *do,* when used as an auxiliary gives force or emphasis to the expression."—*Day's Gram.* p. 39.   "Whatsoever it is incumbent upon a man to do it is surely expedient to do well."—*J. Q. Adams's Rhetoric,* Vol. i, p. 46.   "The soul which our philosophy divides into various capacities, is still one essence."—*Channing, on Self-Culture,* p. 15.   "Put the following words in the plural and give the rule for forming it."—*Bullions, Practical Lessons,* p. 19.   "We will do it if you wish."—*Id. ib.* p. 29. "He who does well will be rewarded."—*Id. ib.* 29. "That which is always true is expressed in the present tense."—*Id. ib.* p. 119.   "An observation which is always true must be expressed in the present tense."—*Id. Prin. of E. Gram.* p. 123. 'That part of orthography which treats of combining letters to form syllables and words is called SPELLING."—*Day's Gram.* p. 8.   "A noun can never be of the first person except it is in apposition with a pronoun of that person."—*Ib.* p. 14.   "When two or more singular nouns or pronouns refer to the same object they require a singular verb and pronoun."—*Ib.* p. 89.   "James has gone but he will return in a few days."—*Ib.* 89.   "A pronoun should have the same person, number, and gender as the noun for which it stands."—*Ib.* 39 and 80.   "Though he is out of danger he is still afraid."—*Bullions, E. Gram.* p. 80. 'She is his inferior in sense but his equal in prudence."—*Ib.* p. 81.   "The man who has no sense of religion is little to be trusted."—*Ib.* 81.   "He who does the most good has the most pleasure."—*Ib.* 81.   "They were not in the most prosperous circumstances when we last saw them."—*Ib.* 81.   "If the day continue pleasant I shall return."—*Felton's Gram.* 1st Ed., p. 22 ; Ster. Ed., 24.   "The days that are past are gone forever."—*Ib.* pp. 89 and 92.   "As many as are friendly to the cause will sustain it."—*Ib.* 89 and 92.   "Such as desire aid will receive it."—*Ib.* 89 and 92.   "Who gave you that book which you prize so much ?"—*Bullions, Pract. Lessons,* p. 32.   "He who made it now preserves and governs it." —*Bullions, E. Gram.* p. 83.

> "Shall he alone, whom rational we call,
> Be pleased with nothing if not blessed with all ?"—*Felton's Gram.* p. 126.

UNDER THE EXCEPTIONS CONCERNING SIMPLE MEMBERS.

"Newcastle is the town, in which Akenside was born."—*Bucke's Classical Gram.* p. 54.

[FORMULE.—Not proper, because a needless comma here separates the restrictive relative *which* from its antecedent *town.* But, according to Exception 1st to Rule 2d, "When a relative immediately follows its antecedent, and is taken in a restrictive sense, the comma should not be introduced before it." Therefore, this comma should be omitted ; thus, "Newcastle is the town in which Akenside was born."]

"The remorse, which issues in reformation, is true repentance."—*Campbell's Philos. of Rhet.* p. 255.   "Men, who are intemperate, are destructive members of community."— *Alexander's Gram.* p. 93.   "An active-transitive verb expresses an action, which extends to an object."—*Felton's Gram.* pp. 16 and 22.   "They, to whom much is given, will have much to answer for."—*Murray's Key,* 8vo, p. 188.   "The prospect, which we have, is charming."—*Cooper's Pl. and Pr. Gram.* p. 143.   "He is the person, who informed me of the matter."—*Ib.* p. 134 ; *Cooper's Murray,* 120.   "These are the trees, that produce no fruit."—*Ib.* 134 ; and 120.   "This is the book, which treats of the subject."—*Ib.* 134 ; and 120.   "The proposal was such, as pleased me."—*Cooper, Pl. and Pr. Gram.* p. 134.   "Those, that sow in tears, shall reap in joy."—*Id. ib.* pp. 118 and 124 ; and *Cooper's Murray,* p. 141. 'The pen, with which I write, makes too large a mark."—*Ingersoll's Gram.* p. 71. 'Modesty makes large amends for the pain, it gives the persons, who labour under it, by the prejudice, it affords every worthy person in their favour."—*Ib.* p. 80.   "Irony is a figure, whereby we plainly intend something very different from what our words express."— *Bucke's Gram.* p. 108.   "Catachresis is a figure, whereby an improper word is used instead of a proper one."—*Ib.* p. 109.   "The man, whom you met at the party, is a Frenchman."— *Frost's Practical Gram.* p. 155.

UNDER RULE III.—OF MORE THAN TWO WORDS.

"John, James and Thomas are here : that is, John *and* James, &c."—*Cooper's Plain and Practical Grammar,* p. 153.

[FORMULE.—Not proper, because no comma is here used after *James,* or after *Thomas,* or again after *John,* in the latter clause ; the three nouns being supposed to be in the same construction, and all of them nominatives to the verb *are.* But, according to Rule 3d for the Comma, "When more than two words or terms are connected in the same construction, or in a joint dependence on some other term, by conjunctions expressed or under-stood, the comma should be inserted after every one of them but the last; and, if they are nominatives before a verb, the comma should follow the last also." Therefore, the comma should be inserted after each; thus, "John, James, and Thomas, are here: that is, John, and James, and Thomas, are here."] *

"Adverbs modify verbs adjectives and other adverbs."—*Bullions, E. Gram.* p. 97. "Nouns belong Person, Gender, Number and Case."—*Id. Practical Lessons,* p. 12. "Wheat, corn, rye, and oats are extensively cultivated."—*Id. ib.* p. 13. "In many, the definitions, rules and leading facts are prolix, inaccurate and confused."—*Finch's Report on Gram.* p. "Most people consider it mysterious, difficult and useless."—*Ib.* p. 3. "His father and mother, and uncle reside at Rome."—*Farnum's Gram.* p. 11. "The relative pronouns are *who, which* and *that*."—*Bullions, Practical Lessons,* p. 29. "*That* is sometimes a demonstrative, sometimes a relative and sometimes a conjunction."—*Id. ib.* p. 33. "Our reputation, virtue, and happiness greatly depend on the choice of our companions."—*Day's Gram.* p. "The spirit of true religion is social, kind and cheerful."—*Felton's Gram.* p. 81. "*Do, have* and *will* are sometimes principal verbs."—*Ib.* p. 26. "John and Thomas and Peter reside at Oxford."—*Webster, Philos. Gram.* p. 142; *Improved Gram.* p. 96. "The most innocent pleasures are the most rational, the most delightful and the most durable."—*Id.* pp. 215 and 151. "Love, joy, peace and blessedness are reserved for the good."—*Id.* 215 and 151. "The husband, wife and children, suffered extremely."—*Murray's Gram.* 4th Am. Ed., 8vo, p. 269. "The husband, wife, and children suffer extremely."—*Sanborn, Analytical Gram.* p. 268. "He, you, and I have our parts assigned us."—*Ibid.*

"He moaned, lamented, tugged and tried,
Repented, promised, wept and sighed."—*Felton's Gr.* p. 108.

UNDER RULE IV.—OF ONLY TWO WORDS.

"Disappointments derange, and overcome, vulgar minds."—*Murray's Exercises,* p. 15.

[FORMULE.—Not proper, because the two verbs here connected by *and*, are needlessly separated from each other, and from their object following. But, according to Rule 4th, "When only two words or terms are connected by a conjunction, they should not be separated by the comma." Therefore, these two commas should be omitted; thus, "Disappointments derange and overcome vulgar minds."]

"The hive of a city, or kingdom, is in the best condition, when there is the least noise or buzz in it."—*Murray's Key,* 8vo, p. 171. "When a direct address is made, the noun, or pronoun, is in the nominative case independent."—*Ingersoll's Gram.* p. 88. "The verbs *love* and *teach,* make *loved,* and *taught,* in the imperfect and participle."—*Ib.* p. 97. "Neither poverty, nor riches were injurious to him."—*Cooper's Pl. and Pr. Gram.* p. 133. "Thou or I am in fault."—*Wright's Gram.* p. 136. "A verb is a word that expresses action, or being."—*Day's District School Gram.* pp. 11 and 61. "The Objective Case denotes the object of a verb, or a preposition."—*Ib.* pp. 17 and 19. "Verbs of the second conjugation may be either transitive, or intransitive."—*Ib.* p. 41. "Verbs of the fourth conjugation may be either transitive, or intransitive."—*Ib.* 41. "If a verb does not form its past indicative by adding d, or ed to the indicative present, it is said to be *irregular*."—*Ib.* 41. "The young lady is studying rhetoric, and logic."—*Cooper's Pl. and Pr. Gram.* p. 143. "He writes, and speaks the language very correctly."—*Ib.* p. 148. "Man's happiness, or misery, is, in great measure, put into his own hands."—*Murray's Key,* 8vo, p. 183. "This accident, so characteristic of nouns, is called their *Gender*."—*Bullions, E. Gram.,* 1843, p. 195.

"Grant that the powerful still the weak controul;
Be Man the Wit, and Tyrant of the whole."—POPE: *Brit. Poets,* vi, 375.

UNDER EXCEPTION I. — TWO WORDS WITH ADJUNCTS.

"Franklin is justly considered the ornament of the new world and the pride of modern philosophy."—*Day's District School Gram.* p. 88.

[FORMULE.—Not proper, because the words *ornament* and *pride,* each of which has adjuncts, are here connected by *and* without a comma before it. But, according to Exception 1st to Rule 4th, "When the two words connected have several adjuncts, or when one of them has an adjunct that relates not to both, the comma is inserted." Therefore, a comma should be set before *and;* thus, "Franklin is justly considered the ornament of the New World, and the pride of modern philosophy."]

"Levity and attachment to wordly pleasures, destroy the sense of gratitude to him."—*Murray's Key,* 8vo, p. 183. "In the following Exercise, point out the adjectives and the substantives which they qualify."—*Bullions, Practical Lessons,* p. 100. "When a noun ...

* Some printers, and likewise some authors, suppose a series of words to require the comma, only where the conjunction is suppressed. This is certainly a great error. It gives us such punctuation as comports neither with the *sense* of three or more words in the same construction, nor with the pauses which they require in reading. "John, James and Thomas are here," is a sentence which plainly tells John that James and Thomas are here; and which, if read according to this pointing, cannot possibly have any other meaning. Yet this is the way in which the rules of *Cooper, Felton, Frost, Webster,* and perhaps others, teach us to point it, when we mean to tell somebody else that all three are here! In his pretended "Abridgment of Murray's English Grammar," (a work abounding in small thefts from Brown's Institutes,) Cooper has the following example: "John, James or Joseph intends to accompany me."—Page 120. Here, John being addressed, the punctuation is right; but, to make this noun a nominative to the verb, a comma must be put after each *of the others.* In Cooper's "Plain and Practical Grammar," the passage is found in this form: "John, James, or Joseph intends to accompany us."—Page 182. This pointing is doubly wrong; because it is adapted to neither sense. If the three nouns have the same construction, the principal pause will be immediately before the verb; and surely a comma is as much required by that pause, as by the second. See the Note on Rule 3d, above.

ronoun is used to explain or give emphasis to a preceding noun or pronoun."—*Day's Gram.* p. 87. "Superior talents and *briliancy* of intellect do not always constitute a great man."—*Ib.* p. 92. "A word that makes sense after an *article* or the phrase *speak of*, is a noun."—*Bullions, Practical Lessons*, p. 12. "All feet used in poetry, are reducible to eight kinds; four of two syllables and four of three."—*Hiley's Gram.* p. 123. "He would not do himself nor let me do it."—*Bullions, E. Gram.* p. 113.* "The old writers give examples in the subjunctive mode and give other modes to explain what is meant by the words in the subjunctive."—*O. B. Peirce's Gram.* p. 352.

UNDER EXCEPTION II.—TWO TERMS CONTRASTED.

"We often commend as well as censure imprudently."—*Murray's Key*, 8vo, p. 214. "It is truly a violation of the right of property, to take little as to take much; to purloin a book, or a penknife, as to steal money; to steal fruit as to steal a horse; to defraud the revenue as to rob my neighbour; to overcharge the public as to overcharge my brother; to cheat the postoffice as to cheat my friend."—*Wayland's Moral Science*, 1st Edition, p. 254. The classification of verbs has been and still is a vexed question."—*Bullions, E. Grammar*, revised Edition, p. 200. "Names applied only to individuals of a sort or class and not common to all, are called *Proper nouns*."—*Id. Practical Lessons*, p. 12. "A hero would aspire to be loved as well as to be reverenced."—*Day's Gram.* p. 108. "Death or some worse misfortune now divides them."—*Cooper's Pl. and Pr. Gram.* p. 133. "Alexander replied, 'The world will not permit two suns nor two sovereigns.'"—*Goldsmith's Greece*, Vol. ii, p. 113.

> "From nature's chain, whatever link you strike,
> Tenth or ten thousandth, breaks the chain alike."—*Felton's Gram.* p. 131.

UNDER EXCEPTION III.—ALTERNATIVE OF WORDS.

"*Metre* or *Measure* is the number of poetical feet which a verse contains."—*Hiley's Gram.* 123. "The *Cæsura* or *division*, is the pause which takes place in a verse, and which divides it into two parts."—*Ib.* 123. "It is six feet or one fathom deep."—*Bullions, E. Gram.* p. 113. "A BRACE is used in poetry at the end of a triplet or three lines which rhyme together."—*Felton's Gram.* p. 142. "There are four principal kinds of English verse poetical feet."—*Ib.* p. 143. "The period or full stop denotes the end of a complete sentence."—*Sanborn's Analytical Gram.* p. 271. "The scholar is to receive as many *jetons* or counters as there are words in the sentence."—*St. Quentin's Gram.* p. 16. "*That* [thing] the thing which purifies, fortifies also the heart."—*Peirce's Gram.* p. 74. "*That thing* or thing which would induce a laxity in public or private morals, or indifference to guilt and wretchedness, should be regarded as the deadly Sirocco."—*Ib.* 74. "What is elliptically *what thing* or *that thing which*."—*Sanborn's Gram.* p. 99. "*Demonstrate* means *show* or point out precisely."—*Ib.* p. 139. "*The* man or *that* man, who endures to the end, shall be saved."—*Hiley's Gram.* p. 73.

UNDER EXCEPTION IV.—A SECOND COMMA.

"Reason, passion answer one great end."—*Bullions's E. Gram.* p. 152; *Hiley's*, p. 112. "Reason, virtue answer one great aim."—*Cooper's Pl. and Pract. Gram.* p. 194; *Butler's*, &c. "Every good gift, and every perfect gift is from above."—*Felton's Gram.* p. 90. "Every plant, and every tree produces others after its kind."—*Day's Gram.* p. 91. "James, and not John was paid for his services."—*Ib.* 91. "The single dagger, or obelisk † is the second."—*Ib.* p. 113. "It was I, not he that did it."—*St. Quentin's Gram.* p. 152. "Each ant, (and) each cousin hath her speculation."—*Sanborn's Gram.* p. 139. "'I shall see you *when* you come,' is equivalent to 'I shall see you *then*, or *at that time* when you come.'"—*Butler's Pract. Gram.* p. 121.

> "Let wealth, let honour wait the wedded dame,
> August her deed, and sacred be her fame."—*Pope*, p. 334.

UNDER RULE V.—OF WORDS IN PAIRS.

'My hopes and fears, joys and sorrows centre in you."—B. GREENLEAF: *Sanborn's Gram.* p. 268.

[FORMULE.—Not proper, because no comma here separates the second pair of nominatives from the verb. But, according to Rule 5th, "When successive words are joined in pairs by conjunctions, they should be separated in pairs by the comma." Therefore, an other comma should be inserted after *sorrows*; thus, "My hopes and fears, and sorrows, centre in you."]

'This mood implies possibility, or liberty, will, or obligation."—*Ingersoll's Gram.* p. 113. "Substance is divided into Body, and Spirit into Extended and Thinking."—*Brightland's Gram.* p. 253. "These consonants, [*d* and *t*,] like *p*, and *b*, *f*, and *v*, *k*, and hard *g*, and *s*, and *z*, are letters of the same organ."—*Walker's Dict.* p. 41; *Principles*, No. 358. "Neither nor twist pigtail nor cavendish have passed my lips since, nor ever shall they again."—*Boston Cultivator*, Vol. vii, p. 36. "The words WHOEVER, or WHOSOEVER, WHICHEVER, or

In punctuation, the grammar here cited is unaccountably defective. This is the more strange, because many of its errors are mere *perversions* of what was accurately pointed by an other hand. On the page above referred to, Dr. Bullions, in copying from Lennie's syntactical exercises a *dozen consecutive lines*, has omitted a useful *commas*, which Lennie had been careful to insert!

WHICHSOEVER, and WHATEVER, or WHATSOEVER are called COMPOUND RELATIVE PRONOUNS."—*Day's Gram.* p. 23. "Adjectives signifying profit or disprofit, likeness or unlikeness govern the dative."—*Bullions, Lat. Gram.*, 12th Ed., 215.

UNDER RULE VI.—OF WORDS ABSOLUTE.

"Thy rod and thy staff they comfort me."—*Bullions, E. Gram.* p. 135.

[FORMULE.—Not proper, because no comma is here set after *staff*, which, with the noun *rod*, is put absolute by pleonasm. But, according to Rule 6th, "Nouns or pronouns put absolute, should, with their adjuncts, be set off by the comma." Therefore, a comma should be here inserted; thus, "Thy rod and thy staff, they comfort me."—*Psalm* xxiii, 4.]

"Depart ye wicked."—*Wright's Gram.* p. 70. "He saith to his mother, Woman behold thy son."—*Gurney's Portable Evidences*, p. 44. "Thou God seest me."—*Bullions, E. Gram.* p. 9; *Practical Lessons*, p. 13. "Thou, God seest me."—*Id. E. Gram.*, Revised Ed., p. 195. "John write me a letter. Henry go home."—*O. B. Peirce's Gram.* p. 356. "John; write a letter. Henry; go home."—*Ib.* p. 317. "Now, G. Brown; let us reason together."—*Ib.* p. 326. "Smith: You say on page 11, the objective case denotes the object."—*Ib.* p. 344. "Gentlemen: will you always speak as you mean?"—*Ib.* p. 352. "John: I said my books to William for his brothers."—*Ib.* p. 47. "Walter and Seth: I will take my things, and leave yours."—*Ib.* p. 69. "Henry: Julia and Jane left their umbrella, and took yours."—*Ib.* p. 73. "John; harness the horses and go to the mine for some coal. William; run to the store for a few pounds of tea."—*Ib.* p. 160. "The king being dead the parliament was dissolved."—*Chandler's Gram.* p. 119.

> "Cease fond nature, cease thy strife,
> And let me languish into life."—*Bullions's E. Gram.* p. 173.

"Forbear great man, in arms renown'd, forbear."—*Ib.* p. 174.

> "Eternal sunshine of the spotless mind,
> Each prayer accepted and each wish resign'd."—*Hiley's Gr.* p. 123.

UNDER RULE VII.—WORDS IN APPOSITION.

"We, the people of the United States, in order to form a more perfect union, establish justice," &c.—*Hallock's Gram.* p. 200.

[FORMULE.—Not proper, because no comma is here set after the pronoun *We*, with which the word *people*, which has adjuncts, is in apposition. But, according to Rule 7th, "Words in apposition, (especially if they have adjuncts,) are generally set off by the comma." Therefore, an other comma should be here inserted; thus, "We, the people of the United States," &c.]

"The Lord, the covenant God of his people requires it."—*Anti-Slavery Magazine*, Vol. i, p. 73. "He as a patriot deserves praise."—*Hallock's Gram.* p. 124. "Thomson the watchmaker and jeweller from London, was of the party."—*Bullions, E. Gram.* p. 128. "Every body knows that the person here spoken of by the name of *the conqueror*, is William duke of Normandy."—*Murray's Gram.* 8vo, p. 33. "The words *myself, thyself, himself, herself*, and their plurals *ourselves, yourselves*, and *themselves* are called Compound Personal Pronouns."—*Day's Gram.* p. 22.

> "For who to dumb forgetfulness a prey,
> This pleasing anxious being e'er resign'd,
> Left the warm precincts of the cheerful day,
> Nor cast one longing, ling'ring look behind?"—*U. Poems*, p. 68.

UNDER EXCEPTIONS CONCERNING APPOSITION.

"Smith and Williams' store; Nicholas, the emperor's army."—*Day's Gram.* p. 17. "He was named William, the conquerer."—*Ib.* p. 80. "John, the Baptist, was beheaded."—*Ib.* p. 87. "Alexander, the coppersmith, did me great harm."—*Hart's Gram.* p. 126. "A nominative in immediate apposition; as 'The boy, Henry, speaks.' "—*Smart's Accidence*, p. 29. "A noun objective can be in apposition with some other; as, 'I teach the boy, Henry.' "—*Ib.* p. 30.

UNDER RULE VIII.—OF ADJECTIVES.

"But he found me, not singing at my work ruddy with health vivid with cheerfulness; but pale and dejected, sitting on the ground, and chewing opium."

[FORMULE.—Not proper, because the phrases, "ruddy with health," and "vivid with cheerfulness," which begin with adjectives, are not here commaed. But, according to Rule 8th, "Adjectives, when something depends on them, or when they have the import of a dependent clause, should, with their adjuncts, be set off by the comma." Therefore, two other commas should be here inserted; thus, "But he found me, not singing at my work, ruddy with health, vivid with cheerfulness; but pale," &c.—*Dr. Johnson.*]

"I looked up, and beheld an inclosure beautiful as the gardens of paradise, but of a small extent."—*See Key.* "A is an article, indefinite and belongs to 'book.' "—*Bullions, Practical Lessons*, p. 10. "The first expresses the rapid movement of a troop of horse over the plain eager for the combat."—*Id. Lat. Gram.* p. 296. "He [, the Indian chieftain, King Philip,] was a patriot, attached to his native soil; a prince true to his subjects and indignant of their wrongs; a soldier daring in battle firm in adversity patient of fatigue, of hunger,

of every variety of bodily suffering and ready to perish in the cause he had espoused."
—*See Key.*

> " For thee, who mindful of th' unhonour'd dead
> Dost in these lines their artless tale relate."—*Union Poems*, p. 68.
> " Some mute inglorious Milton here may rest:
> Some Cromwell guiltless of his country's blood."—*Day's Gram.* p. 117.
> " Idle after dinner in his chair
> Sat a farmer ruddy, fat, and fair."—*Hiley's Gram.* p. 125.

UNDER THE EXCEPTION CONCERNING ADJECTIVES.

" When an attribute becomes a title, or is emphatically applied to a name, it follows it; as Charles, the Great; Henry, the First; Lewis, the Gross."—*Webster's Philos. Gram.* p. 153; *Improved Gram.* p. 107. " Feed me with food, convenient for me."—*Cooper's Practical Gram.* p. 118. " The words and phrases, necessary to exemplify every principle progressively laid down, will be found strictly and exclusively adapted to the illustration of the principles to which they are referred."—*Ingersoll's Gram.*, *Pref.*, p. x. " The *Infinitive Mode* is that form of the verb which expresses action or being, unlimited by person, or number."—*Day's Gram.* p. 35. " A man, diligent in his business, prospers."—*Frost's Practical Gram.* p. 113.

> " O wretched state! oh bosom, black as death! "—*Halloch's Gram.* p. 118.
> " O, wretched state! O, bosom, black as death! "—*Singer's Shak.* Vol. ii, p. 494.

UNDER RULE IX.—OF FINITE VERBS.

" The Singular denotes *one*; the Plural *more* than one."—*Bullions, E. Gram.* p. 12; *Pract. Lessons*, p. 16; *Lennie's Gram.* p. 7.

[FORMULE.—Not proper, because no comma is here set after *Plural*, where the verb *denotes* is understood. But, according to Rule 9th, " Where a finite verb is understood, a comma is generally required." Therefore, a comma should be inserted at the place mentioned; thus, " The Singular denotes *one*; the Plural, *more* than one."]

" The *comma* represents the shortest pause; the *semicolon* a pause longer than the comma; the *colon* longer than the semicolon; and the *period* longer than the colon."—*Hiley's Gram.* p. 111. " The comma represents the shortest pause; the semicolon a pause double that of the comma; the colon, double that of the semicolon; and the period, double that of the colon."—*Bullions, E. Gram.* p. 151; *Pract. Lessons*, p. 127. " Who is applied only to persons; which to animals and things; what to things only; and that to persons, animals, and things."—*Day's Gram.* p. 23. " A or an is used before the singular number only; *the* before either singular or plural."—*Bullions, Practical Lessons*, p. 10. " Homer was the greater genius; Virgil the better artist."—*Day's Gram.* p. 96. " Homer was the greater genius, Virgil the better artist."—POPE'S PREFACE : *British Poets*, Vol. vi, p. viii. " Words are formed of syllables; syllables of letters."—*St. Quentin's General Gram.* p. 2. " The conjugation of an active verb is styled the ACTIVE VOICE; and that of a passive verb the PASSIVE VOICE."—*Frost's El. of E. Gram.* p. 19. " The CONJUGATION of an active verb is styled the ACTIVE VOICE, and that of a passive verb the PASSIVE VOICE."—*Smith's New Gram.* p. 71. " The possessive is sometimes called the genitive case; and the objective the accusative."—*L. Murray's Gram.* 12mo, p. 44. " Benevolence is allied to few vices; selfishness to fewer virtues."—*Kames, Art of Thinking*, p. 40. " Orthography treats of Letters, Etymology of Words, Syntax of Sentences, and Prosody of Versification."—*Hart's English Gram.* p. 21.

> " Earth praises conquerors for shedding blood;
> Heaven those that love their foes, and do them good."—*See Key.*

UNDER RULE X.—OF INFINITIVES.

" His business is to observe the agreement or disagreement of words."—*Bullions, E. Grammar*, Revised Edition, p. 189.

[FORMULE.—Not proper, because no comma here divides *to observe* from the preceding verb. But, according to Rule 10th, " The infinitive mood, when it follows a verb from which it must be separated, or when it depends on something remote or understood, is generally, with its adjuncts, set off by the comma." Therefore, a comma could be inserted after *is*; thus, " His business is, to observe the agreement or disagreement of words."]

" It is a mark of distinction to be made a member of this society."—*Farnum's Gram.*, 1st Ed., p. 25; 2d Ed., p. 23. " To distinguish the conjugations let the pupil observe the following rules."—*Day's D. S. Gram.* p. 40. " He was now sent for to preach before the parliament."—*Life of Dr. J. Owen*, p. 18. " It is incumbent on the young to love and honour their parents."—*Bullions, E. Gram.* p. 83. " It is the business of every man to prepare for death."—*Id. ib.* 83. " It argued the sincerest candor to make such an acknowledgement."—*Id. ib.* p. 115. " The proper way is to complete the construction of the first member, and leave that of the second understood."—*Ib. ib.* p. 125. " ENEMY is a name. It a term of distinction given to a certain person to show the character in which he is represented."—*O. B. Peirce's Gram.* p. 23. " The object of this is to preserve the soft sound c and g."—*Hart's Gram.* p. 29. " The design of grammar is to facilitate the *reading, writing*, and *speaking* of a language."—*Barrett's Gram.*, 10th Ed., *Pref.*, p. iii. " Four kinds type are used in the following pages to indicate the portions that are considered more less elementary."—*Hart's Gram.* p. 3.

UNDER RULE XI.—OF PARTICIPLES.

"The chancellor being attached to the king secured his crown."—*Wright's Gram.* p. 114.

[FORMULE.—Not proper, because the phrase, "being attached to the king," is not *commed.* But, according to Rule 11th, "Participles, when something depends on them, when they have the import of a dependent clause, or when they relate to something understood, should, with their adjuncts, be set off by the comma." There-fore, two commas should be here inserted; thus, "The chancellor, being attached to the king, secured his crown."—*Murray's Gram.* p. 66.]

"The officer having received his orders, proceeded to execute them."—*Day's Gram.* p. 108. "Thus used it is in the present tense."—*Bullions, E. Gram.*, Revised Ed., p. 33. "The *Imperfect* tense has three distinct forms corresponding to those of the present tense."—*Id. ib.* p. 40. "Every possessive case is governed by some noun denoting the thing possessed." —*Id. ib.* p. 87. "The word *that* used as a conjunction is preceded by a comma."—*Id. ib.* p. 154. "His narrative being composed upon such good authority, deserves credit."— *Cooper's Pl. and Pr. Gram.* p. 97. "The hen being in her nest, was killed and eaten there by the eagle."—*Murray's Key*, 8vo, p. 252. "Pronouns being used instead of nouns are subject to the same modifications."—*Sanborn's Gram.* p. 92. "When placed at the begin-ning of words they are consonants."—*Hallock's Gram.* p. 14. "Man starting from his coach, shall sleep no more."—*Ib.* p. 222. "*His* and *her* followed by a noun are possessive pronouns; not followed by a noun they are personal pronouns."—*Bullions, Practical Lessons,* p. 33.
   "He with viny crown advancing,
   First to the lively pipe his hand addressed."—*Id. E. Gram.* p. 83.

UNDER THE EXCEPTION CONCERNING PARTICIPLES.

"But when they convey the idea of many, acting individually, or separately, they are of the plural number."—*Day's Gram.* p. 15. "Two or more singular antecedents, connected by *and* require verbs and pronouns of the plural number."—*Ib.* pp. 80 and 91. "Words ending in y, preceded by a consonant, change y into *i* when a termination is added."— *Butler's Gram.* p. 11. "A noun, used without an article to limit it, is generally taken in its widest sense."—*Ingersoll's Gram.* p. 30. "Two nouns, meaning the same person or thing, frequently come together."—*Bucke's Gram.* p. 89. "Each one must give an account to God for the use, or the abuse of the talents, committed to him."—*Cooper's Pl. and Pract. Gram.* p. 133. "Two vowels, united in one sound, form a diphthong."—*Frost's El. of E. Gram.* p. 6. "Three vowels, united in one sound, form a triphthong."—*Ib.* "Any word, joined to an adverb, is a secondary adverb."—*Barrett's Revised Gram.* p. 68. "The person, spoken to, is put in the Second person. The person, spoken of, in the Third person."— *Cutler's Gram.* p. 14. "A man, devoted to his business, prospers."—*Frost's Pr. Gram.* p. 131.

UNDER RULE XII.—OF ADVERBS.

"So in indirect questions; as, 'Tell me *when* he will come.'"—*Butler's Gram.* p. 121.

[FORMULE.—Not proper, because the adverb *So* is not set off by the comma. But, according to Rule 12th, "Ad-verbs, when they break the connexion of a simple sentence, or when they have not a close dependence on some particular word in the context, should, with their adjuncts, be set off by the comma." Therefore, a comma should be inserted after *So*; thus, "So, in indirect questions; as," &c.]

"Now when the verb tells what one person or thing does to another, the verb is transi-tive."—*Bullions, Pract. Les.* p. 37. "Agreeably to your request I send this letter."—*Id. E. Gram.* p. 141. "There seems therefore, to be no good reason for giving them a different classification."—*Id. E. Gram.* p. 199. "Again the kingdom of heaven is like unto a mer-chantman, seeking goodly pearls."—*ALGER'S BIBLE : Matt.* xiii, 45. "Again the kingdom of heaven is like unto a net, that was cast into the sea."—*Ib. ib.* verse 47. "*Cease* how-ever, is used as a transitive verb by our best writers."—*Webster's Philos. Gram.* p. 171. "Time admits of three natural divisions, namely : Present, Past, and Future."—*Day's Gram.* p. 37. "There are three kinds of comparison, namely : regular, irregular, and adverbial."—*Ib.* p. 31. "There are five Personal Pronouns namely : *I, thou, he, she,* and *it.*"—*Ib.* p. 22. "Nouns have three cases, viz. the Nominative, Possessive, and Objective." —*Bullions, E. Gram.* p. 16; *P. Lessons,* p. 19. "Hence in studying Grammar, we have to study words."—*Frazee's Gram.* p. 18. "Participles like Verbs relate to Nouns and Pro-nouns."—*Miller's Ready Grammarian,* p. 23. "The time of the participle like that of the infinitive is estimated from the time of the leading verb."—*Bullions, Lat. Gram.* p. 97.
   "The dumb shall sing the lame his crutch forego,
   And leap exulting like the bounding roe."—*Hiley's Gram.* p. 123.

UNDER RULE XIII.—OF CONJUNCTIONS.

"But he said, Nay; lest while ye gather up the tares, ye root up also the wheat with them."—*FRIENDS' BIBLE,* and *SMITH'S : Matt.* xiii, 29.

[FORMULE.—Not proper, because no comma is inserted after *lest.* But, according to Rule 13th, "Conjunctions, when they are separated from the principal clauses that depend on them, or when they introduce examples, are generally set off by the comma." Therefore, a comma should be put after the word *lest*; thus, "But he said, Nay; lest, while ye gather up the tares, ye root up also the wheat with them."—*SCOTT'S BIBLE, ALGER'S, BRUCE'S.*]

"Their intentions were good; but wanting prudence, they missed the mark at which they aimed."—*Murray's Key*, 8vo, Vol. ii, p. 221. "The verb *be* often separates the name from its attribute; as war is expensive."—*Webster's Philos. Gram.* p. 153. "*Either* and *or* denote an alternative; as 'I will take *either* road at your pleasure.'"—*Ib.* p. 63; *Imp.*

Gram. 45. "*Either* is also a substitute for a name; as '*Either* of the roads is good.'"—*Webster, both Grams.* 63 and 45. "But alas! I fear the consequence."—*Day's Gram.* p. 74. "Or if he ask a fish, will he for a fish give him a serpent?"—*Scott's Bible, and Smith's* "Or if he shall ask an egg, will he offer him a scorpion?"—*Smith's Bible.* "The infinitive sometimes performs the office of a nominative case, as 'To enjoy is to obey.'—POPE."—*Cutler's Gram.* p. 62. "The plural is commonly formed by adding *s* to the singular, as *book, books.*"—*Bullions, E. Gram.* p. 12. "As 'I *were* to blame, if I did it.'"—*Smart's Accidence,* p. 16. "Or if it be thy will and pleasure Direct my plough to find a treasure."—*Hiley's Gram.* p. 124. "Or if it be thy will and pleasure, Direct my plough to find a treasure."—*Hart's Gram.* p. 185.

UNDER RULE XIV.—OF PREPOSITIONS.

"Pronouns agree with the nouns for which they stand in gender, number, and person."—*Butler's Practical Gram.* pp. 141 and 148; *Bullions's Analyt. and Pract. Gram.* p. 150.

[FORMULE.—Not proper, because the preposition *in* has not the comma before it, as the text requires. But, according to Rule 14th, "Prepositions and their objects, when they break the connexion of a simple sentence, or when they do not closely follow the words on which they depend, are generally set off by the comma." Therefore, a comma should be here inserted; thus, "Pronouns agree with the nouns for which they stand, in gender, number, and person." Or the words may be transposed, and the comma set before *with*; thus, "Pronouns agree *in* gender, number, and person, *with* the nouns for which they stand."]

"In the first two examples the antecedent is *person,* or something equivalent; in the last it is *thing.*"—*Butler, ib.* p. 53. "In what character he was admitted is unknown."—*Ib.* p. 55. "To what place he was going is not known."—*Ib.* p. 55. "In the preceding examples *John, Cæsar,* and *James* are the subjects."—*Ib.* p. 59. "*Yes* is generally used to denote assent in the answer to a question."—*Ib.* p. 120. "*That* in its origin is the passive participle of the Anglo-Saxon verb *thean, to take.*"—*Ib.* p. 127. "But in all these sentences *as* and *so* are *adverbs.*"—*Ib.* p. 127. "After an interjection or exclamatory sentence is placed the mark of exclamation."—*Blair's Gram.* p. 116. "Intransitive verbs from their nature can have no distinction of voice."—*Bullions, E. Gram.* p. 30. "To the inflection of verbs belong Voices, Moods, Tenses, Numbers, and Persons."—*Id. ib.* p. 33; *Pract. Lessons,* p. 41. "*As* and *so* in the antecedent member of a comparison are properly adverbs."—*Id. E. Gram.* p. 113. "In the following Exercise point out the words in apposition."—*Id. P. Lessons,* p. 103. "In the following Exercise point out the noun or pronoun denoting the possessor."—*Id. ib.* p. 105. "*Its* is not found in the Bible except by misprint."—*Hallock's Gram.* p. 68. "No one's interest is concerned except mine."—*Ib.* p. 70. "In most of the modern languages there are four concords."—*St. Quentin's Gen. Gram.* p. 143. "In illustration of these remarks let us suppose a case."—*Hart's Gram.* p. 104. "On the right management of the emphasis depends the life of pronunciation."—*Ib.* p. 172; *Murray's,* 8vo, p. 242.

UNDER RULE XV.—OF INTERJECTIONS.

"Behold he is in the desert."—SCOTT'S BIBLE: *Matt.* xxiv, 26.

[FORMULE.—Not proper, because the interjection *Behold,* which has usually a comma after it in Scripture, has here no point. But, according to Rule 15th, "Interjections that require a pause, though more commonly emphatic and followed by the ecphoneme, are sometimes set off by the comma." In this instance, a comma should be used; thus, "Behold, he is in the desert."—*Common Bible.*]

"And Lot said unto them, Oh not so my Lord."—SCOTT'S BIBLE: *Gen.* xix, 18. "Oh let me escape thither, (is it not a little one?) and my soul shall live."—SCOTT: *Gen.* xix, 20. "Behold! I come quickly.—BIBLE."—*Day's Gram.* p. 74. "Lo! I am with you always."—*Day's Gram.* pp. 10 and 73. "And lo! I am with you always."—*Ib.* pp. 78 and 110. "And lo, I am with you alway."—SCOTT'S BIBLE, and BRUCE'S: *Matt.* xxviii, 20. "Ha! ha! ha! how laughable that is."—*Bullions, Pract. Les.* p. 83. "Interjections of Laughter,—Ha! he! hi! ho!"—*Wright's Gram.* p. 121.

UNDER RULE XVI.—OF WORDS REPEATED.

"Lend lend your wings! I mount! I fly!"—*Example varied.*

[FORMULE.—Not proper, because the repeated word *lend* has here no comma. But, according to Rule 16th, "A word emphatically repeated, is generally set off by the comma." In this instance, a comma is required after the former *lend,* but not after the latter; thus,

'Lend, lend your wings! I mount! I fly!'"—*Pope's Poems,* p. 817.]

"To bed to bed to bed. There is a knocking at the gate. Come come come. What is done cannot be undone. To bed to bed to bed."—See *Burgh's Speaker,* p. 130. "I will roar, that the duke shall cry, Encore encore let him roar let him roar once more once more."—See *ib.* p. 136.

"Vital spark of heav'nly flame, Quit oh quit this mortal frame!"—*Hiley's Gram.* p. 126. "Vital spark of heav'nly flame, Quit, oh, quit, this mortal frame!"—*Bullions, E. Gr.* p. 172. "O the pleasing pleasing Anguish, When we love, and when we languish."—*Ward's Gram.* p. 161. "Praise to God immortal praise For the love that crowns your das!"—*Hiley's Gram.* p. 124.

UNDER RULE XVII.—OF DEPENDENT QUOTATIONS.

"Thus, of an infant, we say '*It* is a lovely creature.'"—*Bullions, Prin. of E. Gram.* p. 12.

[FORMULE.—Not proper, because no comma is here inserted between *say* and the citation which follows. But, according to Rule 17th, "A quotation, observation, or description, when it is introduced in close dependence on a verb, (as, *say, reply, cry,* or the like,) is generally separated from the rest of the sentence by the comma." Therefore, a comma should be put after *say*; as, "Thus, of an infant, we say, '*It* is a lovely creature.'"]

"No being can state a falsehood in saying *I am*; for no one can utter it, if it is not true."—*Cardell's Gram.* 18mo, p. 118. "I know they will cry out against this and say 'should he pay,' means if he should pay.'"—*O. B. Peirce's Gram.* p. 352. "For instance, when we say '*the house is building,*' the advocates of the new theory ask, 'building *what?*' We might ask in turn, when you say 'the field ploughs well,' ploughs *what?* 'Wheat sells well,' sells *what?* If *usage* allows us to say 'wheat *sells* at a dollar' in a sense that is not active, why may it not also allow us to say 'wheat *is selling* at a dollar' in a sense that is not active?"—*Hart's English Gram.* p. 76. "*Man* is accountable, equals *mankind* are accountable."—*S. Barrett's Revised Gram.* p. 37. "Thus, when we say 'He may be reading,' *may* is the real verb; the other parts are verbs by name only."—*Smart's English Accidence,* p. 6. "Thus we say *an apple, an hour,* that two vowel sounds may not come together."—*Ib.* p. 27. "It would be as improper to say *an unit,* as to say *an youth*; to say *an one,* as to say *an wonder.*"—*Ib.* p. 27. "When we say 'He died for the truth,' *for* is a preposition."—*Ib.* p. 28. "We do not say 'I might go yesterday,' but 'I might have gone yesterday.'"—*Ib.* p. 11. "By student, we understand one who has by matriculation acquired the rights of academical citizenship; but, by bursché, we understand one who has already spent a certain time at the university."—*Howitt's Student-Life of Germany,* p. 27.

SECTION II.—THE SEMICOLON.

The Semicolon is used to separate those parts of a compound sentence, which are neither so closely connected as those which are distinguished by the comma, nor so little dependent as those which require the colon.

RULE I.—COMPLEX MEMBERS.

When two or more complex members, or such clauses as require the comma in themselves, are constructed into a period, they are generally separated by the semicolon: as, "In the regions inhabited by angelic natures, unmingled felicity forever blooms; joy flows there with a perpetual and abundant stream, nor needs any mound to check its course."—*Carter.* "When the voice rises, the gesture naturally ascends; and when the voice makes the falling inflection, or lowers its pitch, the gesture follows it by a corresponding descent; and, in the level and monotonous pronunciation of the voice, the gesture seems to observe a similar limitation, by moving rather in the horizontal direction, without much varying its elevation."—*Comstock's Elocution,* p. 107.

"The wide, the unbounded prospect lies before me;
But shadows, clouds, and darkness, rest upon it."—*Addison.*

RULE II.—SIMPLE MEMBERS.

When two or more simple members, or such clauses as complete their sense without subdivision, are constructed into a period; if they require a pause greater than that of the comma, they are usually separated by the semicolon: as, "Straws swim upon the surface; but pearls lie at the bottom."—*Murray's Gram.* p. 276. "Every thing grows old; every thing passes away; every thing disappears."—*Hiley's Gram.* p. 115. "Alexander asked them the distance of the Persian capital; what forces the king of Persia could bring into the field; what the Persian government was; what was the character of the king; how he treated his enemies; what were the most direct ways into Persia."—*Whelpley's Lectures,* p. 175.

"A longer care man's helpless kind demands;
That longer care contracts more lasting bands."—*Pope.*

RULE III.—OF APPOSITION, &c.

Words in apposition, in disjunct pairs, or in any other construction, if they require a pause greater than that of the comma, and less than that of the colon, may be separated by the semicolon: as, "Pronouns have three cases; the nominative, the possessive, and the objective."—*Murray's Gram.* p. 51. "Judge, judgement;

lge, lodgement; acknowledge, acknowledgement."—*Butler's Gram.* p. 11. " Do
t the eyes discover humility, pride; cruelty, compassion; reflection, dissipation;
ndness, resentment?"—*Sheridan's Elocution*, p. 159. " This rule forbids parents
lie to children, and children to parents; instructors to pupils, and pupils to in-
·uctors; the old to the young, and the young to the old; attorneys to jurors, and
rors to attorneys; buyers to sellers, and sellers to buyers."—*Wayland's Moral
·tence*, p. 304.

"*Make· made; have, had; pay, paid; say, said; leave, left;*
    Dream, dreamt; mean, meant; reave and *bereave* have *reft*."—*Ward's Gr.* p. 66.

IMPROPRIETIES FOR CORRECTION.

FALSE PUNCTUATION.—ERRORS CONCERNING THE SEMICOLON.

UNDER RULE I.—OF COMPLEX MEMBERS.

"The buds spread into leaves, and the blossoms swell to fruit, but they know not how
ey grow, nor who causes them to spring up from the bosom of the earth."—*Day's Gr.* p. 72.
FORMULA.—Not proper, because the two chief members which compose this period, are separated only by the
ama after "*fruit*." But, according to Rule 1st for the Semicolon, " When two or more complex members, or
h clauses as require the comma in themselves, are constructed into a period, they are generally separated
the semicolon." Therefore, the pause after "*fruit*" should be marked by a semicolon.]

"But he used his eloquence chiefly against Philip, king of Macedon, and, in several ora-
ns, he stirred up the Athenians to make war against him."—*Bullions, E. Gram.* p. 84.
For the sake of euphony, the *n* is dropped before a consonant, and because most words
gin with a consonant, this of course is its more common form."—*Ib.* p. 192. " But if I say
Vill *a* man be able to carry this burden?' it is manifest the idea is entirely changed, the
ference is not to number, but to the species, and the answer might be 'No; but a horse
ll.'"—*Ib.* p. 193. "In direct discourse, a noun used by a speaker or writer to designate
mself, is said to be of the *first* person—used to designate the person addressed, it is said to
· of the *second* person, and when used to designate a person or thing spoken of, it is said
be of the *third* person."—*Ib.* p. 195. " Vice stings us, even in our pleasures, but virtue
nsoles us, even in our pains."—*Day's Gram.* p. 84. " Vice is infamous though in a prince,
d virtue honorable though in a peasant."—*Ib.* p. 72. "Every word that is the name
a person or thing, is a *Noun*, because 'A noun is the name of any person, place, or thing."
·*Bullions, Pract. Les.* p. 83.

"This is the sword, with which he did the deed,
    And that the shield by which he was defended."—*Bucke's Gram.* p. 56.

UNDER RULE II.—OF SIMPLE MEMBERS.

"A deathlike paleness was diffused over his countenance, a chilling terror convulsed his
me; his voice burst out at intervals into broken accents."—*Principles of Eloquence*, p. 73.
FORMULA.—Not proper, because the first pause in this sentence is not marked by a suitable point. But,
ording to Rule 2d for the Semicolon, " When two or more simple members, or such clauses as complete their
se without subdivision, are constructed into a period; if they require a pause greater than that of the comma,
y are usually separated by the semicolon." Therefore, the comma after "*countenance*" should be changed
a semicolon.]

"The Lacedemonians never traded—they knew no luxury—they lived in houses built of
ugh materials—they lived at public tables—fed on black broth, and despised every thing
feminate or luxurious."—*Whelpley's Lectures*, p. 167. " Government is the agent. Society
the principal."—*Wayland's Moral Science*, 1st Ed., p. 377. "The essentials of speech were
ciently supposed to be sufficiently designated by the *Noun* and the *Verb*, to which was
bsequently added, the *Conjunction*."—*Bullions, E. Gram.* p. 191. "The first faint gleam-
gs of thought in its mind are but the reflections from the parents' own intellect,—the first
anifestations of temperament are from the contagious parental fountain,—the first as-
rations of soul are but the warnings and promptings of the parental spirit."—*Jocelyn's
·ize Essay*, p. 4. "*Older* and *oldest* refer to maturity of age, *elder* and *eldest* to priority of
ght by birth. *Father* and *farthest* denote place or distance: *Further* and *furthest*, quantity
addition."—*Bullions, E. Gram.* p. 148. Let the divisions be *natural*, such as obviously
ggest themselves to the mind, and as may aid your main design, and be easily re-
embered."—*Goldsbury's Manual of Gram.* p. 91.

"Gently make haste, of labour not afraid:
    A hundred times consider what you've said."—*Dryden's Art of Poetry.*

UNDER RULE III.—OF APPOSITION, &c.

(1.) "Adjectives are divided into two classes: *Adjectives denoting quality*, and *Adjectives
noting number*."—*Frost's Practical Gram.* p. 31.
FORMULA.—Not proper, because the colon after the word " classes," is not the most suitable sign of the pause
quired. But, according to Rule 3d for the Semicolon, " Words in apposition, in disjunct pairs, or in any other
nstruction, if they require a pause greater than that of the comma, and less than that of the colon, may be
parated by the semicolon." In this case, the semicolon should have been preferred to the colon.]

(2.) "There are two classes of adjectives—*qualifying* adjectives, and *limiting* adjectives." —*Butler's Practical Gram.* p. 33. (3.) "There are three Genders, the *Masculine*, the *Feminine*, and the *Neuter*."—*Frost's Pract. Gram.* p. 51; *Hiley's Gram.* p. 12; *Alger's*, 16; *S. Putnam's*, 14; *Murray's*, 8vo, 37; *and others.* (4.) "There are three genders: the MASCULINE, the FEMININE, and the NEUTER."—*Murray's Gram.* 12mo, p. 39; *Jaudon's*, 25. (5.) "There are three Genders: The *Masculine*, the *Feminine*, and the *Neuter*."—*Hendrick's Gram.* p. 15. (6.) "The Singular denotes ONE, and the Plural MORE THAN ONE."—*Hart's Gram.* p. 40. (7.) "There are three Cases viz. the *Nominative*, the *Possessive*, and the *Objective*."—*Hendrick's Gram.* p. 7. (8.) "Nouns have three cases, the nominative, the possessive, and the objective." —*Kirkham's Gram.* p. 41. (9.) "In English, nouns have three cases—the nominative, the possessive, and the objective."—*R. C. Smith's New Gram.* p. 47. (10.) "Grammar is divided into four parts, namely, ORTHOGRAPHY, ETYMOLOGY, SYNTAX, and PROSODY."—*Ib.* p. 41. (11.) "It is divided into four parts, viz. ORTHOGRAPHY, ETYMOLOGY, SYNTAX, and PROSODY."—*L. Murray's Grammars all; T. Smith's Gram.* p. 5. (12.) "It is divided into four parts: viz. Orthography—Etymology—Syntax—Prosody."—*Bucke's Gram.* p. 3. (13.) "It is divided into four parts, namely: Orthography, Etymology, Syntax and Prosody."—*Day's Gram.* p. 5. (14.) "It is divided into four parts: viz. *Orthography, Etymology, Syntax,* and *Prosody.*"—*Hendrick's Gram.* p. 11. (15.) "Grammar is divided into four parts: viz. Orthography, Etymology, Syntax and Prosody."—*Chandler's Gram.* p. 13. (16.) "It is divided into four parts: Orthography, Etymology, Syntax, and Prosody."—*Cooper's Pl. and Pract. Gram.* p. 1; *Frost's Pract. Gram.* 19. (17.) "English grammar has been usually divided into four parts, viz. Orthography, Etymology, Syntax and Prosody."—*Nutting's Gram.* p. 13. (18.) "Temperance leads to happiness, intemperance to misery."—*Hiley's Gram.* p. 137; *Hart's*, 188. (19.) "A friend exaggerates a man's virtues, an enemy his crimes."—*Hiley's Gram.* p. 137. (20.) "A friend exaggerates a man's virtues: an enemy his crimes."—*Murray's Gram.* 8vo, p. 325. (21.) "Many writers use a *plural noun* after the second of two numeral adjectives, thus, 'The first and second pages are torn.'"—*Bullions, E. Gram.*, 5th Ed., p. 145. (22.) "Of these, the Latin has six, the Greek, five, the German, four, the Saxon, six, the French, three, &c."—*Id. ib.* p. 196.

"In (*ing*) it ends, when *doing* is express'd,
In *d, t, n*, when *suffering's* confess'd."—*Brightland's Gram.* p. 93.

MIXED EXAMPLES OF ERROR.

"In old books *i* is often used for *j*, *v* for *u*, *vv* for *w*, and *ii* or *ij* for *y*."—*Hart's E. Gram.* p. 22. "The forming of letters into words and syllables is also called *Spelling.*"—*Ib.* p. 21. "Labials are formed chiefly by the *lips*, dentals by the *teeth*, palatals by the *palate*, gutturals by the *throat*, nasals by the *nose*, and linguals by the *tongue*."—*Ib.* p. 25. "The labials are *p, b, f, v*; the dentals *t, d, s, z*; the palatals *g* soft and *j*; the gutturals *k, q,* and *c* and *g* hard; the nasals *m* and *n*; and the linguals *l* and *r*."—*Ib.* p. 25. "Thus, 'the man having *finished* his letter, will carry it to the post office.'"—*Ib.* p. 75. "Thus, in the sentence 'he had a dagger *concealed* under his cloak,' *concealed* is passive, signifying *being* concealed; but in the former combination, it goes to make up a form, the force of which is active."—*Ib.* p. 75. "Thus, in Latin, 'he had concealed the dagger' would be '*pugionem abdiderat*;' but 'he had the dagger concealed' would be '*pugionem abditum habebat.*'" —*Ib.* p. 75. "*Here*, for instance, means 'in this place,' *now*, 'at this time,' &c."—*Ib.* p. 90. "Here *when* both declares the *time* of the action, and so is an adverb, and also *connects* the two verbs, and so is a conjunction."—*Ib.* p. 91. "These words were all no doubt originally other parts of speech, viz.: verbs, nouns, and adjectives."—*Ib.* p. 92. "The principal parts of a sentence are the subject, the attribute, and the object, in other words the nominative, the verb, and the objective."—*Ib.* p. 104. "Thus, the adjective is connected with the noun, the adverb with the verb or adjective, pronouns with their antecedents, &c."— *Ib.* p. 104. "*Between* refers to two, *among* to more than two."—*Ib.* p. 120. "*At* is used after a verb of *rest, to* after a verb of motion."—*Ib.* p. 120. "Verbs are of three kinds, Active, Passive, and Neuter."—*Lennie's Gram.* p. 19; *Bullions, Prin.*, 2d Ed., p. 29. "Verbs are divided into two classes: Transitive and Intransitive."—*Hendrick's Gram.* p. 28. "The Parts of Speech in the English language are nine, viz. The Article, Noun, Adjective, Pronoun, Verb, Adverb, Preposition, Interjection and Conjunction."—*Bullions, Prin. of E. Gram.* p. 7. "Of these the Noun, Pronoun, and Verb are declined, the rest are indeclinable."—*Id. ib.* p. 7; *Practical Lessons*, p. 9. "The first expression is called the 'Active form.' The second the 'Passive form.'"—*Weld's Gram.*, 2d Ed., p. 83; Abridged, p. 66.

"O 'tis a godlike privilege to save,
And he that scorns it is himself a slave."—*Cowper*, Vol. i, p. 123.

SECTION III.—THE COLON.

The Colon is used to separate those parts of a compound sentence, which are neither so closely connected as those which are distinguished by the semicolon, nor so little dependent as those which require the period.

RULE I.—ADDITIONAL REMARKS.

'hen the preceding clause is complete in itself, but is followed by some additional irk or illustration, especially if no conjunction is used, the colon is generally and erly inserted : as, "Avoid evil doers : in such society, an honest man may become med of himself."—" See that moth fluttering incessantly round the candle : man leasure, behold thy image!"—*Art of Thinking*, p. 94. "Some things we can, others we cannot do: we can walk, but we cannot fly."—*Beattie's Moral nce*, p. 112.

" Remember Heav'n has an avenging rod :
To smite the poor is treason against God."—*Cowper*.

RULE II.—GREATER PAUSES.

'hen the semicolon has been introduced, or when it must be used in a subsequent ber, and a still greater pause is required within the period, the colon should be oyed : as, " Princes have courtiers, and merchants have partners ; the voluptu- have companions, and the wicked have accomplices : none but the virtuous can friends."—" Unless the truth of our religion be granted, a Christian must be greatest monster in nature : he must at the same time be eminently wise, and riously foolish ; a wise man in his practice, and a fool in his belief : his reasoning rs must be deranged by a constant delirium, while his conduct never swerves the path of propriety."—*Principles of Eloquence*, p. 80.

"A decent competence we fully taste ;
It strikes our sense, and gives a constant feast :
More we perceive by dint of thought alone ;
The rich must labour to possess their own."—*Young*.

RULE III.—INDEPENDENT QUOTATIONS.

quotation introduced without a close dependence on a verb or a conjunction, is rally preceded by the colon ; as, " In his last moments, he uttered these words : ill a sacrifice to sloth and luxury.' "—"At this the king hastily retorted : ' No ffs, my lord ; answer me presently.' "—*Churchill's Gram.* p. 367. "The r addressed himself to them to this effect : ' O my sons, behold the power of :!' "—*Rippingham's Art of Speaking*, p. 85.

IMPROPRIETIES FOR CORRECTION.

FALSE PUNCTUATION.—ERRORS CONCERNING THE COLON.

UNDER RULE I. — ADDITIONAL REMARKS.

f is a preposition, it expresses the relation between *fear* and *Lord*."—*Bullions*, E. ᴸ p. 133.

ᴿᵁᴸᴱ.—Not proper, because the additional remark in this sentence is not sufficiently separated from the 'lause, by the comma after the word *preposition*. But, according to Rule 1st for the Colon, " When the ing clause is complete in itself, but is followed by some additional remark or illustration, especially if no ction is used, the colon is generally and properly inserted." Therefore, the colon should here be substi- 'or the comma.)

Vealth and poverty are both temptations to man; *that* tends to excite pride, *this* dis- ntment."—*Id. ib.* p. 98 : see also *Lennie's Gram.* p. 81; *Murray's*, 56 ; *Ingersoll's*, 61 ; 's, 25 ; *Merchant's*, 44 ; *Hart's*, 137 ; *et al.* " Religion raises men above themselves, gion sinks them beneath the brutes ; *this* binds them down to a poor pitiable speck of iable earth, that opens for them a prospect to the skies."—*Bullions, E. Gram.* p. 98 ; i's Gram.* p. 81. " Love not idleness, it destroys many."—*Ingersoll's Gram.* p. 71. ldren, obey your parents; honor thy father and mother, is the first commandment promise."—*Bullions, Pract. Lessons*, p. 88. " Thou art my hiding place, and my shield. e in thy promises."—*O. B. Peirce's Gram.* p. 56. " The sun shall not smite me by ior the moon by night. The Lord will preserve from evil. He will save my soul.— t."—*Ib.* p. 67. " Here Greece is assigned the highest place in the class of objects 7 *which* she is numbered—the nations of antiquity—she is one of them."—*Lennie's* ᴸ p. 79.

"From short (as usual) and disturb'd repose
I wake; how happy they who wake no more!"—*Hallock's Gram.* p. 216.

UNDER RULE II.—GREATER PAUSES.

. taste *of* a thing, implies actual enjoyment of it ; but a taste for it, implies only capacity for enjoyment; as, 'When we have had a true taste of the pleasures of virtue, we a have no relish for those of vice.'"—*Bullions, E. Gram.* p. 147.

[FORMULE.—Not proper, because the pause after *enjoyment* is marked only by a semicolon. But, according to Rule 2d for the Colon, "When the semicolon has been introduced, or when it must be used in a subsequent member, and a still greater pause is required within the period, the colon should be employed." Therefore, second semicolon here should be changed to a colon.]

"The Indicative mood simply declares a thing; as, He *loves;* He *is loved;* Or, it ask question; as, *Lovest* thou me?'"—*Id. ib.* p. 35; *Pract. Lessons,* p. 43; *Lennie's Gr.* p.
"The Indicative Mood simply indicates or declares a thing: as, 'He loves, he is loved or it asks a question: as, 'Does he love?' 'Is he loved?'"—*L. Murray's Gram.* 8vo, 63; 12mo, p. 63. "The Imperfect (or Past) tense represents an action or event indefinite as past; as, Cæsar *came,* and *saw,* and *conquered;* or it represents the action definitely unfinished and continuing at a certain time, now entirely past; as, My father *was* coming home when I met him."—*Bullions, P. L.* p. 45; *E. Gr.* 39. "Some nouns have no plural as, *gold, silver, wisdom, health;* others have no singular; as, *ashes, shears, tongs;* others alike in both numbers; as, *sheep, deer, means, news.*"—*Day's School Gram.* p. 15. "The same verb may be transitive in one sense, and intransitive in another; thus, in the sentence 'He believes my story,' *believes* is transitive; but in this phrase, 'He believes in God,' it i intransitive."—*Butler's Gram.* p. 61. "Let the divisions be *distinct;* one part should no include another, but each should have its proper place, and be of importance in the place, and all the parts well fitted together and united, should present a whole."—*Goldsbury's C. S. Gram.* p. 91. "In the use of the transitive verb there are always three thing implied,—the *actor,* the *act,* and the *object* acted upon. In the use of the intransitive there are only *two*—the *subject* or thing spoken of, and the *state,* or *action* attributed to it."—*Bullions, E. Gram.* p. 30.

　　　"Why labours reason? instinct were as well;
　　Instinct far better; what can choose, can err."—*Brit. Poets,* Vol. viii, p. 336.

UNDER RULE III.—INDEPENDENT QUOTATIONS.

"The sentence may run thus; 'He is related to the same person, and is governed by him.'"—*Hart's Gram.* p. 118.

[FORMULE.—Not proper, because the semicolon is here inserted, in an unusual manner, before a quotation not closely dependent. But, according to Rule 3d for the Colon, "A quotation introduced without a close dependence on a verb or a conjunction, is generally preceded by the colon." Therefore, the colon should be preferred.]

"Always remember this ancient proverb, 'Know thyself.'"—*Hallock's Gram.* p. 26
"Consider this sentence. The boy runs swiftly."—*Frazee's Gram.,* Stereotype Ed., p. 16; 1st Ed., 110. "The comparative is used thus; 'Greece was more polished than any other nation of antiquity.' The same idea is expressed by the superlative when the word *other* is left out. Thus. 'Greece was the most polished nation of antiquity.'"—*Bullions, E. Gram.* p. 114; see *Lennie's Gram.* p. 78. "Burke, in his speech on the Carnatic war, makes the following allusion to the well known fable of Cadmus's sowing dragon's teeth;—'Every day you are fatigued and disgusted with this cant, the Carnatic is a country that will soon recover, and become instantly as prosperous as ever. They think they are talking to innocents, who believe that by the sowing of dragon's teeth, men may come up ready grown and ready made.'"—*Hiley's Gram.* p. 137; see also *Hart's,* 180.

　　　"For sects he car'd not, 'they are not of us,
　　Nor need we, brethren, their concerns discuss.'"—*Crabbe.*
　　"Habit with him was all the test of truth,
　　'It must be right: I've done it from my youth.'
　　Questions he answer'd in as brief a way,
　　'It must be wrong—it was of yesterday.'"—*Id. Borough,* p. 33.

MIXED EXAMPLES OF ERROR.

"This would seem to say, 'I doubt nothing save one thing, namely, that he will fulfil his promise;' whereas, that is the very thing not doubted."—*Bullions, E. Gram.* p. 16.
"The common use of language requires that a distinction be made between *morals* and *manners,* the former depend upon internal dispositions, the latter on outward and visible accomplishments."—*Beattie's Moral Science,* p. 233. "Though I detest war in each particular fibre of my heart yet I honor the Heroes among our fathers who fought with bloody hand: Peacemakers in a savage way they were faithful to their light; the most inspired can be no more, and we, with greater light, do, it may be, far less."—*Parker's Idea of a Church,* p. 21. "The Article *the,* like *a,* must have a substantive joined with it, whereas *that,* like *one,* may have it understood; thus, speaking of books, I may select one, and say, 'give me that;' but not, 'give me *the;*' 'give me *one;*' but not 'give me *a.*'"—*Bullions, E. Gram.* p. 194. "The Present tense has three distinct forms—the *simple;* as, I read; the *emphatic;* as, I do read; and the *progressive;* as, I am reading."—*Ib.* p. 39. "The tenses in English are usually reckoned six. The *Present,* the *Imperfect,* the *Perfect,* the *Pluperfect,* the *Future,* and the *Future Perfect.*"—*Ib.* p. 38. "There are three participles, the *Present* or *Active,* the *Perfect* or *Passive,* and the *Compound Perfect;* as, 'loving, loved, having

'"—*L. Murray's Gram.*, 2d Edition, p. 52; *Alger's*, 28; *Fisk's*, 82; *Bacon's*, 24. "The iples are three, the Present, the Perfect, and the Compound Perfect; as, *loving, loved, loved.*"—*Hart's Gram.* p. 74. "*Will* is conjugated regularly, when it is a principal is, present, I will, past, I willed, &c."—*Frazee's Gram.*, Ster. Ed., p. 42; Old Ed., p. 40. both sounds of *s* are compound, one is that of *gz*, and the other, that of *ks.*"—*Ib.* Ed., p. 16. "The man is happy: he is benevolent: he is useful."—*Cooper's Murray, Pl. and Pract. Gr.* 33. "The Pronoun stands instead of the noun; as, The man is '; *he* is benevolent; *he* is useful."—*L. Murray's Gram.*, 2d Ed., p. 27. "A Pronoun is i used instead of a noun, to avoid the too frequent repetition of the same word: as, man is happy,' '*he* is benevolent,' '*he* is useful.' "—*Ib.* p. 37. "A pronoun is a word, n the room of a noun, or as a substitute for one or more words, as : the man is happy; enevolent; *he* is useful."—*Cooper's Pl. and Pr. Gram.* p. 14; *his Abridg. of Mur.* 34. mmon noun is the name of a sort, kind, or class of beings, or things, as : animal; tree; ; fish; fowl."—*Cooper's Pl. and Pr. Gram.* p. 17. "Nouns have three persons: the the second; and the third."—*Ib.* 17.

> "(Eve) so saying, her rash hand in evil hour
> Forth reaching to the fruit; she pluck'd, she ate !
> Earth felt the wound : and nature from her seat,
> Sighing through all her works, gave signs of wo,
> That all was lost."—*Cooper's Pl. and Pr. Gram.* p. 175.

SECTION IV.—THE PERIOD.

e Period, or Full Stop, is used to mark an entire and independent sen-, whether simple or compound.

RULE I.—DISTINCT SENTENCES.

en a sentence, whether long or short, is complete in respect to sense, and endent in respect to construction, it should be marked with the period: as, ry deviation from truth is criminal. Abhor a falsehood. Let your words be ous. Sincerity possesses the most powerful charm."—"The force of a true dual is felt through every clause and part of a right book; the commas and s are alive with it."—*R. W. Emerson.*

> "By frequent trying, TROY was won.
> All things, by trying, may be done."—*Lloyd*, p. 183.

RULE II.—ALLIED SENTENCES.

) period is often employed between two sentences which have a general con-, expressed by a personal pronoun, a conjunction, or a conjunctive adverb: as, selfish man languishes in *his* narrow circle of pleasures. *They* are confined to ffects his own interests. *He* is obliged to repeat the same gratifications, till ecome insipid. *But* the man of virtuous sensibility moves in a wider sphere of "—*Blair.*

> "And whether we shall meet again, I know not.
> *Therefore* our everlasting farewell take."—*Shak.*, J. C.

RULE III.—ABBREVIATIONS.

) period is generally used after abbreviations, and very often to the exclusion of points ; but, as in this case it is not a constant sign of pause, other points may ly follow it, if the words written in full would demand them: as, A. D. for *Domini* ; Pro tem. for *pro tempore* ; Ult. for *ultimo* ; i. e. for *id est*, that is ; Spect., No. 285 ;—i. e., *Addison, in the Spectator, Number 285th.*

> "Consult the statute ; ' quart.' I think, it is,
> ' Edwardi sext.,' or ' prim. et quint. Eliz.' "—*Pope*, p. 399.

OBSERVATIONS.

1.—It seems to be commonly supposed, whether correctly or not, that short sentences are in themselves distinct, and which in their stated use must be separated by the period, metimes be rehearsed as examples, in so close succession as not to require this point: as, f thou wilt enter into life, keep the commandments. He saith unto him, Which ? Jesus hou shalt do no murder, Thou shalt not commit adultery, Thou shalt not steal, Thou ot bear false witness, Honour thy father and thy mother: and, Thou shalt love thy neigh- thyself."—SCOTT, ALGER, AND OTHERS: *Matt.* xix, 17, 18, 19. "The following sentences ify the possessive pronouns :—'*My* lesson is finished; *Thy* books are defaced; He loves dies ; She performs *her* duty ; We own *our* faults ; *Your* situation is distressing ; I admire *their virtues.' "—L. Murray's Gram.* 8vo, p. 55. What mode of pointing is best adapted to examples like these, is made a very difficult question by the great diversity of practice in such cases. The semicolon, with guillemets, or the semicolon and a dash, with the quotation marks may sometimes be sufficient; but I see no good reason why the *period* should not in general be preferred to the comma, the semicolon, or the colon, where full and distinct sentences are thus recited. The foregoing passage of Scripture I have examined in five different languages, ten different translations, and seventeen different editions, which happened to be at hand. In these, it is found pointed in twelve different ways. In Leusden's, Griesbach's, and Aitton's Greek, it has nine colons; in Leusden's Latin from Montanus, eight; in the common French version, six, in the old Dutch, five; in our Bibles, usually one, but not always. In some books, these commandments are mostly or wholly divided by periods; in others, by colons; in others, by semicolons; in others, as above, by commas. The first four are negative, or prohibitory; the other two, positive, or mandatory. Hence some make a greater pause after the fourth, than elsewhere between any two. This greater pause is variously marked by the semicolon, the colon, or the period; and the others, at the same time, as variously, by the comma, the semicolon, or the colon. Dr. Campbell, in his Four Gospels, renders and points the latter part of this passage thus: " Jesus answered, ' Thou shalt not commit murder. Thou shalt not commit adultery. Thou shalt not steal. Thou shalt not give false testimony. Honour thy father and mother; and love thy neighbour as thyself.' " But the corresponding passage in Luke, xviii, 20, he exhibits thus: " Thou knowest the commandments. Do not commit adultery; do not commit murder; do not steal; do not give false testimony; honour thy father and thy mother." This is here given as present advice, *referring to* the commandments, but not actually *quoting* them; and, in this view of the matter, semicolons, not followed by capitals, may be right. See the common reading under Rule XIV for Capitals, on page 155.

OBS. 2.—Letters written for *numbers,* after the manner of the Romans, though read as words, are never words in themselves; nor are they, except perhaps in one or two instances, abbreviations of words. C, a hundred, comes probably from *Centum;* and M, a thousand, is the first letter of *Mille;* but the others, I, V, X, L, D, and the various combinations of them all, are direct numerical signs, as are the Arabic figures. Hence it is not really necessary that the period should all be set after them, except at the end of a sentence, or where it is suitable as a sign of pause. It is, however, and always has been, a prevalent custom, to mark numbers of this kind with a period, as if they were abbreviations; as, " While pope Sixtus V. who succeeded Gregory XIII. fulminated the thunder of the church against the king of Navarre."—*Smollett's Eng.* iii, 32. The period is here inserted where the reading requires only the comma; and, in my opinion, the latter point should have been preferred. Sometimes, of late, we find other points set after this period, as, " Otho II., surnamed the Bloody, was son and successor of Otho I.; he died in 983."—*Univ. Biog. Dict.* This may be an improvement on the former practice, but double points are not yet *generally* used, even where they are proper; and, if the period is not indispensable, a simple change of the point would perhaps sooner gain the sanction of general usage.

OBS. 3.—Some writers, judging the period to be wrong or needless in such cases, omit it, and insert only such points as the reading requires; as, "For want of doing this, Judge Blackstone has, in Book IV, Chap. 17, committed some most ludicrous errors."—*Cobbett's Gram.,* Let. XII. ¶ 251. To insert points needlessly, is as bad a fault as to omit them when they are requisite. In Wm. Day's " Punctuation Reduced to a System," (London, 1847,) we have the following obscure and questionable RULE: "*Besides denoting a grammatical pause, the full point is used to mark contractions, and is requisite after every abbreviated word, as well as after numeral letters.*" —Page 102. This seems to suggest that both a pause and a contraction may be denoted by the same point. But what are properly called "*contractions,*" are marked, not by the period, but by the apostrophe, which is no sign of pause; and the confounding of these with words "*abbreviated,*" makes this rule utterly absurd. As for the period " after *numeral letters,*" if they really *needed* it at all, they would need it *severally,* as do the abbreviations; but there are none of them, which do not uniformly dispense with it, when not final to the number; and they may as well dispense with it, in like manner, whenever they are not final to the sentence.

OBS. 4.—Of these letters, Day gives this account: "*M.* denotes *mille,* 1,000; *D.,* dimidium *mille,* half a thousand, or 500; *C. centum,* 100; *L.* represents the lower half of *C.,* and expresses 50; *X.* resembles *V. V.,* the one upright, the other inverted, and signifies 10; *V.* stands for 5, because its sister letter U is the fifth vowel; and *I.* signifies 1, probably because it is the plainest and simplest character in the alphabet."—*Day's Punctuation,* p. 103. There is some fancy in this. Dr. Adam says, " The Letters employed for this purpose [i. e. to express *numbers,*] were C. I. L. V. X."—*Latin and Eng. Gram.* p. 288. And again: "A thousand is marked thus CIↃ, which in later times was *contracted* into M. *Five hundred* is marked thus, IↃ, or by *contraction,* D."— *Ib.* Day inserts periods thus: " IV. means 4; IX., 9; XL., 40; XC., 90; CD., 400; CM., 900." —Page 103. And again: " 4to. *quarto,* the fourth of a sheet of paper; 8vo., *octavo,* the eighth of a sheet of paper; 12mo., *duodecimo,* the twelfth of a sheet of paper; N. L., 8°., 9'., 10″., North latitude, eight degrees, nine minutes, ten seconds."—Page 104. But IV may mean 4, without the period; 4to or 8vo has no more need of it than 4th or 8th; and N. L. 8° 9' 10″ is an expression little to be mended by commas, and not at all by additional periods.

OBS. 5.—To allow the period of abbreviation to supersede all other points wherever it occurs, as authors generally have done, is sometimes plainly objectionable; but, on the other hand, to suppose double points to be always necessary wherever abbreviations or Roman numbers have pauses less than final, would sometimes seem more nice than wise, as in the case of Biblical and other references. A concordance or a reference Bible pointed on this principle, would differ greatly from any now extant. In such references, *numbers* are very frequently pointed with the period, with scarcely any regard to the pauses required in the reading; as, " DIADEM, Job 29. 14. Isa. 28. 5. and 62. 3. Ezek. 21. 26."—*Brown's Concordance.* " Where no vision is, the people perish, Prov. xxix. 18. Acts iv. 12. Rom. x. 14."—*Brown's Catechism,* p. 104. " What I urge from 1. Pet. 3. 21. in my Apology."—*Barclay's Works,* iii, 498. " I. Kings—II. Kings."—*Alger's Bible,* p. iv. " Compare iii. 45. with 1. Cor. iv. 13."—*Scott's Bible, Pref. to Lam. Jer.* " Hen. v.

c. 5."—*Butler's Gram.* p. 41.   "See Rule iii. Rem. 10."—*Ib.* p. 162.   Some set a *colon*
in the number of the chapter and that of the verse; which mark serves well for distinction,
both numbers are in Arabic figures: as, "'He that formed the eye, shall he not see?'—
: 9."—*Wells's Gram.* p. 126.   "He had only a lease-hold title to his service. Lev. 25: 29,
21: 2."—*True Amer.* 1, 29.   Others adopt the following method, which seems preferable
of the foregoing: "Isa. lv, 3; Ezek. xviii, 20; Mic. vi, 7."—*Gurney's Essays*, p. 133.
hill, who is uncommonly nice about his punctuation, writes as follows: "*Luke*, vi, 41, 42.
so Chap. xv, 8; and *Phil.*, iii, 12."—*New Gram.* p. 353.

6.—Arabic figures used as ordinals, or used for the ,numeral adverbs, *first*, or *firstly*, *sec-*
thirdly, &c., are very commonly pointed with the period, even where the pause required
hem is less than a full stop; as, "We shall consider these words, 1. as expressing *resolution ;*
as expressing *futurity*."—*Butler's Gram.* p. 106.   But the period thus followed by a small
has not an agreeable appearance, and some would here prefer the comma, which is, un-
edly, better suited to the pause.   A fitter practice, however, would be, to change the
sion thus: "We shall consider these words, 1st, as expressing *resolution ;* and, 2dly, as
sing *futurity.*"

7.—Names vulgarly shortened, then written as they are spoken, are not commonly marked
period; as, *Ben* for *Benjamin:* "O RARE BEN JOHNSON!"—*Biog. Dict.*

> "From whence the inference is plain,
> Your friend MAT PRIOR wrote with pain."—LLOYD: *B. P.*, Vol. viii, p. 188.

IMPROPRIETIES FOR CORRECTION.

FALSE PUNCTUATION. — ERRORS CONCERNING THE PERIOD.

UNDER RULE I.—DISTINCT SENTENCES.

he third person is the position of the name spoken of; as, Paul and Silas were im-
ied, the earth thirsts, the sun shines."—*Frazee's Gram.*, 1st Ed., p. 21; Ster. Ed., p. 23.

[RULE.—Not proper, because three totally distinct sentences are here thrown together as examples, with
r distinction than what is made by two commas. But, according to Rule 1st for the Period, "When a
e, whether long or short, is complete in respect to sense, and independent in respect to construction, it
be marked with the period." Therefore, these commas should be periods; and, of course, the first
f each example must be a capital.]

wo and three and four make nine; if he were here, he would assist his father and
er, for he is a dutiful son; they live together, and are happy, because they enjoy each
's society; they went to Roxbury, and tarried all night, and came back the next day."
dsbury's Parsing Lessons in his Manual of E. Gram. p. 64.

Ve often resolve, but seldom perform; she is wiser than her sister; though he is often
ed, yet he does not reform; reproof either softens or hardens its object; he is as old
classmates, but not so learned; neither prosperity, nor adversity, has improved him;
m that standeth, take heed lest he fall; he can acquire no virtue, unless he make
sacrifices."—*Ibid.*

> "Down from his neck, with blazing gems array'd,"
> Thy image, lovely Anna! hung portray'd,
> Th' unconscious figure, smiling all serene,
> Suspended in a golden chain was seen."—*S. Barrett's E. Gr.* p. 92.

UNDER RULE II.—ALLIED SENTENCES.

his life is a mere prelude to another, which has no limits, it is a little portion of du-
. As death leaves us, so the day of judgment will find us."—*Merchant's School*
p. 76.

[RULE.—Not proper, because the pause after *limits,* which is sufficient for the period, is marked only by the
. But, according to Rule 2d, "The period is often employed between two sentences which have a general
don, expressed by a personal pronoun, a conjunction, or a conjunctive adverb." It would improve the
e, to omit the first comma, change the second to a period, and write the pronoun *it* with a capital. *Judg-*
lso might be bettered with an *e,* and *another* is properly two words.]

le went from Boston to New York; he went from Boston; he went to New York; in
ng across the floor, he stumbled over a chair."—*Goldsbury's Manual of E. Gram.* p. 62.
saw him on the spot, going along the road, looking towards the house; during the
of the day, he sat on the ground, under the shade of a tree."—*Id. ib.*
leorge came home, I saw *him* yesterday, here; the word him, can extend only to the
idual *George.*"—*S. Barrett's E. Gram.*, 10th Ed., p. 45.
lommas are often used now, where parentheses were formerly; I cannot, however,
m this an improvement."—See the *Key.*

> "Thou, like a sleeping, faithless sentinel
> Didst let them pass unnoticed, unimproved,
> And know, for that thou slumb'rest on the guard,
> Thou shalt be made to answer at the bar
> For every fugitive."—*Hallock's Gram.* p. 222; *Enfield's Sp.* p. 380.

UNDER RULE III.—OF ABBREVIATIONS.

The term pronoun (Lat *pronomen*) strictly means a word used for, or instead of a noun."
llions, E. Gram. p. 198.

[RULE.—Not proper, because the syllable here put for the word *Latin,* is not marked with a period. But,
ling to Rule 3d, "The period is generally used after abbreviations, and very often to the exclusion of other

points; but, as in this case it is not a constant sign of pause, other points may properly follow it, if the words written in full would demand them." In this instance, a period should mark the abbreviation, and a comma be set after *of.* , By analogy, *in stead* is also more properly two words than one.]

"The period is also used after abbreviations; as, A. D. P. S. G. W. Johnson."—*Butler's Pract. Gram.* p. 211.   "On this principle of classification, the later Greek grammarians divided words into eight classes or parts of speech, viz: the Article, Noun, Pronoun, Verb, Participle, Adverb, Preposition, and Conjunction."—*Bullions, E. Gram.* p. 191.

"'*Metre* is not confined to verse: there is a tune in all good prose; and Shakspeare's was a sweet one.'—*Epea Pter*, II, 61.   Mr. H. Tooke's idea was probably just, agreeing with Aristotle's; but not accurately expressed."—*Churchill's New Gram.* p. 385.

"Mr. J. H. Tooke was educated at Eton and at Cambridge, in which latter college he took the degree of A. M; being intended for the established church of England, he entered into holy orders when young, and obtained the living of Brentford, near London, which he held ten or twelve years."—*Div. of Purley*, 1st Amer. Edition, Vol. i, p. 60.

"I, nor your plan, nor book condemn,
But why your name. and why A. M!"—*Lloyd.*

MIXED EXAMPLES OF ERROR.

"'If thou *turn* away thy foot from the sabbath, &c. *Isaiah.* lviii. 7."—*Butler's Gram.* p. 67.   "'He that hath eeris of herynge, *here he. Wiclif.* Matt xi."—*Butler's Gram.* p. 71.   "See General Rules for Spelling, iii., v., and vii."—*Butler's Gram.* p. 81.   "'False witnesses did rise up.' *Ps.* xxxv. ii."—*Butler's Gram.* p. 105.

"An *explicative* sentence is used for explaining. An *interrogative* sentence for enquiring. An *imperative* sentence for commanding."—*S. Barrett's Prin. of Language*, p. 87.   "In October, corn is gathered in the field by men, who go from hill to hill with baskets, into which they put the ears; Susan labors with her needle for a livelihood; notwithstanding his poverty, he is a man of integrity."—*Goldsbury's Parsing, Manual of E. Gram.* p. 62.

"A word of one syllable, is called a monosyllable.   A word of two syllables; a dissyllable. A word of three syllables; a trissyllable. A word of four or more syllables; a polysyllable."—*Frazee's Improved Gram.*, 1st Ed., p. 15.   "A word of one syllable, is called a monosyllable.   A word of two syllables, a dissyllable.   A word of three syllables, a trissyllable.   A word of four or more syllables, a polysyllable."—*Frazee's Improved Gram.*, Ster. Ed., p. 17.

"If I say, '*if it did not rain*, I would take a walk;' I convey the idea that it does rain, at the time of speaking, *If it rained*, or *did it rain*, in the present time, implies, it does not rain; *if it did not rain*, or *did it not rain*, in present time, implies that *it does rain*; thus in this peculiarity, an *affirmative* sentence always implies a *negation*, and a *negative* sentence an *affirmation*."—*Frazee's Gram.*, 1st Ed., p. 61; Ster. Ed., 62.   "*If I were loved*, and, *were I loved*, imply, I am *not* loved; *if I were not loved*, and, *were I not loved*, imply, I am loved; a negative sentence implies an affirmation; and an affirmative sentence implies a negation, in these forms of the subjunctive."—*Ib.*, Old Ed., p. 73; Ster. Ed., 72.

"What is Rule III.?"—*Hart's Gram.* p. 114.   "How is Rule III. violated?"—*Ib.* p. 115.   "How do you parse 'letter' in the sentence, 'James writes a *letter*'?   *Ans.*—'*Letter* is a noun com., of the MASC. gend., in the 3d p., sing. num., and *objective case*, and is governed by the verb 'writes,' according to Rule III., which says. 'A transitive verb,' &c."—*Ib.* p. 114.*

"Creation sleeps.   'T is as the general pulse
Of life stood still, and nature made a pause;
An awful pause! prophetic of her end,
And let her prophecy be soon fulfilled;
Fate drop the curtain; I can lose no more."—*Hallock's Gram.* p. 216.

SECTION V.—THE DASH.

The Dash is mostly used to denote an unexpected or emphatic pause, of variable length; but sometimes it is a sign of faltering, or of the irregular stops of one who hesitates in speaking: as, "Then, after many pauses, and inarticulate sounds, he said : 'He was very sorry for it, was extremely concerned it should happen so — but — a — it was necessary — a —'   Here lord E—— stopped him short, and bluntly demanded, if his post were destined for an other."—See *Churchill's Gram.* p. 170.

RULE I.—ABRUPT PAUSES.

A sudden interruption, break, or transition, should be marked with the dash; as,
1. "'I must inquire into the affair; and if'—'And *if!*' interrupted the farmer."
2. "Whom I—But first 't is fit the billows to restrain."—*Dryd. Virg.*
3. "HERE LIES THE GREAT—False marble! where?
    Nothing but sordid dust lies here."—*Young.*

* Needless abbreviations, like most that occur in this example, are in *bad taste*, and *ought to be avoided.* The great faultiness of this text as a model for learners, compels me to vary the words considerably in suggesting the correction. See the *Key.*—G. B.

RULE II.—EMPHATIC PAUSES.

To mark a considerable pause, greater than the structure of the sentence or the points inserted would seem to require, the dash may be employed; as, 1. "I pause for a reply.—None?—Then none have I offended.—I have done no more to Cæsar, than you should do to Brutus."—SHAKSPEARE: *Enfield's Speaker*, p. 182. 2. "Tarry a little. There is something else.—
This bond—doth give thee here—no jot of blood."—ID. *Burgh's Sp.* p. 167. 3. "It thunders;—but it thunders to preserve."—*Young*. 4. "Behold the picture!—Is it like?—Like whom?"—*Cowper*.

RULE III.—FAULTY DASHES.

Dashes needlessly inserted, or substituted for other stops more definite, are in general to be treated as errors in punctuation; as, "Here Greece stands by *itself* as opposed to the *other* nations of antiquity—She was none of the *other nations*—She was more polished than they."—*Lennie's Gram.* p. 78. "Here Greece stands by *herself*, as opposed to the *other* nations of antiquity. She was none of the *other nations*: She was more polished than they."—*Bullions, E. Gram.* p. 114. If this colon is sufficient, the capital after it is needless: a period would, perhaps, be better.

OBSERVATIONS.

OBS. 1.—The dash does not appear to be always a rhetorical stop, or always intended to lengthen the pause signified by an other mark before it. As one instance of a different design, we may notice, that it is now very often employed between a text and a reference;—i. e., between a quotation and the name of the author or of the book quoted;—in which case, as Wm. Day suggests, "it serves as a *connecting mark* for the two."—*Day's Punctuation*, p. 131. But this usage, being comparatively recent, is, perhaps, not so general or so necessary, that a neglect of it may properly be censured as false punctuation.

OBS. 2.—An other peculiar use of the dash, is its application to *side-titles*, to set them off from other words in the same line, as is seen often in this Grammar as well as in other works. Day says of this, "When the *substance* of a paragraph is given as a side-head, a dash is *necessary* to *connect* it with its relative matter."—*Ibid*. Wilson also approves of this usage, as well as of the others here named; saying, "The dash should be inserted between a title and the subject-matter, and also between the subject-matter, and the authority from which it is taken, when they occur in the same paragraph."—*Wilson's Punctuation*, Ed. of 1850, p. 139.

OBS. 3.—The dash is often used to signify the omission of something; and, when set between the two extremes of a series of numbers, it may represent all the intermediate ones; as, "Page 10—15;" i. e. "Page 10, 11, 12, &c. to 15."—"Matt. vi, 9—14."

IMPROPRIETIES FOR CORRECTION.

FALSE PUNCTUATION.—ERRORS CONCERNING THE DASH.

UNDER RULE I.—ABRUPT PAUSES.

"And there is something in your very strange story, that resembles . . . Does Mr. Bevil know your history particularly?"—See *Key*.

[FORMULE.—Not proper, because the abrupt pause after *resembles* is here marked by three periods. But, according to Rule 1st for the Dash, "A sudden interruption, break, or transition, should be marked with the dash." Therefore, the dash should be preferred to these points.]

"Sir, Mr. Myrtle, Gentlemen! You are friends; I am but a servant. But."—See *Key*. "Another man now would have given plump into this foolish story; but I? No, no, your humble servant for that."—See *Key*. "Do not plunge thyself too far in anger, lest thou hasten thy trial; which if Lord have mercy on thee for a hen!"—See *Key*.
"But ere they came, O, let me say no more!
Gather the sequel by that went before."—See *Key*.

UNDER RULE II.—EMPHATIC PAUSES.

"*M*, Malvolio; *M*, why, that begins my name."

[FORMULE.—Not proper, because the pauses after *M* and *Malvolio* seem not to be sufficiently indicated here. But, according to Rule 2d for the Dash, "To mark a considerable pause, greater than the structure of the sentence or the points inserted would seem to require, the dash may be employed." Therefore, a dash may be set after the commas and the semicolon, in this sentence.]

"Thus, by the creative influence of the Eternal Spirit, were the heavens and the earth finished in the space of six days, so admirably finished, an unformed chaos changed into a system of perfect order and beauty, that the adorable Architect himself pronounced it very good, and all the sons of God shouted for joy."—See *Key*.
"If I were an American, as I am an Englishman, while a foreign troop remained in my

country, I NEVER would lay down my arms; NEVER, NEVER NEVER."—*Columbian Orator*, p. 265.

"Madam, yourself are not exempt in this,
Nor your son Dorset, Buckingham, nor you."—*See Key.*

UNDER RULE III.—FAULTY DASHES.

"— You shall go home directly, Le Fevre, said my uncle Toby, to my house,—and we send for a doctor to see what's the matter,—and we'll have an apothecary,—and the corporal shall be your nurse;—and I'll be your servant, Le Fevre."—STERNE: *Enfield Speaker*, p. 306.

[FORMULE.—Not proper, because all the dashes here quoted, except perhaps the last, are useless, or obviously substituted for more definite marks. But, according to Rule 3d, "Dashes needlessly inserted, or substituted for other stops more definite, are in general to be treated as errors in punctuation." Therefore, the first of the should be simply expunged; the second, third, and fourth, with their commas, should be changed to semicolons; and the last, with its semicolon, may well be made a colon.]

"He continued—Inferior artists may be at a stand, because they want materials."—HARRIS: *Enfield's Speaker*, p. 191. "Thus, then, continued he—The end in other arts ever distant and removed."—*Id. ib.*

"The nouns must be coupled with *and*, and when a pronoun is used it must be plural. In the example—When the nouns are *disjoined* the pronoun must be singular."—*Lennie's Grammar*, 5th Ed., p. 57.

"*Opinion* is a noun or substantive common,—of the singular number,—neuter gender,—nominative case,—and third person."—*Wright's Philos. Gram.* p. 228.

"The mountain—thy pall and thy prison—may keep thee;
I shall see thee no more; but till death I will weep thee."—*Felton's Gram.* p. 14

MIXED EXAMPLES OF ERROR.

"If to accommodate man and beast, heaven and earth; if this be beyond me, 'tis not possible.—What consequence then follows? or can there be any other than this—If I seek an interest of my own, detached from that of others; I seek an interest which is chimerical, and can never have existence."—HARRIS: *Enfield's Speaker*, p. 139.

"Again—I must have food and clothing—Without a proper genial warmth, I instantly perish—Am I not related, in this view, to the very earth itself? To the distant sun, from whose beams I derive vigour?"—*Id. ib.* p. 140.

"Nature instantly ebb'd again—the film returned to its place—the pulse flutter'd—stopp'd—went on—throbb'd—stopp'd again—mov'd—stopp'd—shall I go on?—No."—STERNE: *ib.* p. 307.

"Write ten nouns of the masculine gender. Ten of the feminine. Ten of the neuter. Ten indefinite in gender."—*Pardon Davis's Gram.* p. 9.

"The Infinitive Mode has two tenses—the Indicative, six—the Potential, two—the Subjunctive, six, and the Imperative, one."—*Frazee's Gram.*, Ster. Ed., p. 39; 1st Ed., 37. "Now notice the following sentences. John runs,—boys run—thou runnest."—*Ib.*, Ster. Ed., 50; 1st Ed., p. 48.

"The Pronoun sometimes stands for a name—sometimes for an adjective—a sentence—a part of a sentence—and, sometimes for a whole series of propositions."—*O. B. Peirce's Gram.*, 1st Ed., 12mo, p. 321.

"The self-applauding bird, the peacock, see—
"Mark what a sumptuous pharisee is he!"—*Cowper*, i, 49.

SECTION VI. — THE EROTEME.

The Eroteme, or Note of Interrogation, is used to designate a question.

RULE I.—QUESTIONS DIRECT.

Questions expressed directly as such, if finished, should always be followed by the note of interrogation; as, "Was it possible that virtue so exalted should be erected upon injustice? that the proudest and the most ambitious of mankind should be the great master and accomplished pattern of humility? that a doctrine so pure as the Gospel should be the work of an uncommissioned pretender? that so perfect a system of morals should be established on blasphemy?"—*Jerningham's Essay*, p. 81.

"In life, can love be bought with gold?
Are friendship's pleasures to be sold?"—*Johnson.*

RULE II.—QUESTIONS UNITED.

When two or more questions are united in one compound sentence, the comma, semicolon, or dash, is sometimes used to separate them, and the eroteme occurs at the last only; as, 1. "When—under what administration—under what exigence

war or peace—did the Senate ever before deal with such a measure in such a man-
? Never, sir, never."—*D. Webster, in Congress*, 1846.

   2. " Canst thou, and honour'd with a Christian name,
      Buy what is woman-born, and feel no shame ;
      Trade in the blood of innocence, and plead
      Expedience as a warrant for the deed ? "—*Cowper*.

   3. " Truths would you teach, or save a sinking land?
      All fear, none aid you, and few understand."—*Pope*.

Rule III.—Questions Indirect.

When a question is mentioned, but not put directly as a question, it loses both the
ility and the sign of interrogation ; as, " The Cyprians asked me *why I wept*."—
rray.

OBSERVATIONS.

bs. 1.—The value of the eroteme as a sign of pause, is stated very differently by different
amarians; while many of the vast multitude, by a strange oversight, say nothing about it.
unquestionably *variable*, like that of the dash, or of the ecphoneme. W. H. Wells says,
ie comma requires a momentary pause; the semicolon, a pause somewhat longer than the
ma; the colon, a pause somewhat longer than the semicolon; and the period, a full stop.
note of interrogation, or the note of exclamation, *may take the place* of EITHER *of these*, and
rdingly requires a pause of the same length as the point for which it is substituted."—*Wells's
ol Gram.* p. 175. This appears to be accurate in idea, though perhaps hardly so in language.
lley Murray has stated it thus : " The interrogation and exclamation points are *indeterminate*
) their quantity or time, and may be equivalent in that respect to a semicolon, a colon, or a
od, as the sense may require."—*Octavo Gram.* p. 280. But Sanborn, in regard to his "*Ques-
Point*," awkwardly says: "*This pause* is generally *some longer* than that of a period."—
lytical Gram. p. 271. Buchanan, as long ago as 1767, taught as follows : " The Pause after
two Points of Interrogation and Admiration ought to be equal to that of the Period, or a Colon
`ast."—English Syntax*, p. 160. And J. S. Hart avers, that, "A question is reckoned as equal
complete sentence, and the mark of interrogation as equal to a period."—*Hart's English
m.* p. 166. He says also, that, " the first word after a note of interrogation should begin with
pital."—*Ib.* p. 162. In some instances, however, he, like others, has not adhered to these
ptionable principles, as may be seen by the false grammar cited below.

bs. 2.—Sometimes a series of questions may be severally complete in sense, so that each
require the interrogative sign, though some or all of them may be so united in construction,
ot to admit either a long intermediate pause or an initial capital; as, " Is there no honor in
rosity ? nor in preferring the lessons of conscience to the impulses of passion ? nor in main-
ng the supremacy of moral principle, and in paying reverence to Christian truth ?"—*Gannett*.
ue honour is manifested in a steady, uniform train of actions, attended by justice, and directed
rudence. Is this the conduct of the duellist ? will justice support him in robbing the com-
ity of an able and useful member ? and in depriving the poor of a benefactor ? will it support
in preparing affliction for the widow's heart ? in filling the orphan's eyes with tears ?"—
ingham's Essay, p. 113. But, in this latter example, perhaps, commas might be substituted
he second and fourth erotemes ; and the word *will* might, in both instances, begin with a
tal.

bs. 3.—When a question is mentioned in its due form, it commonly retains the sign of inter-
tion, though not actually asked by the writer ; and, except perhaps when it consists of some
interrogative word or phrase, requires the initial capital : as, " To know when this point
t to be used, do not say : [,] ' Is a question asked ? ' but, ' Does the sentence ask a question ? ' "
urchill's Gram. p. 368. " They put their huge inarticulate question, ' What do you mean to
ith us ? ' in a manner audible to every reflective soul in this kingdom."—*Carlyle's Past and
ent*, p. 16. "An Adverb may be generally known, by its answering to the question, How ?
much ? when? or where ? as, in the phrase, ' He reads *correctly*,' the answer to the question,
does he read ? is *correctly*."—*L. Murray's Gram.* p. 28. This passage, which, without ever
ing at great accuracy, has been altered by Murray and others in ways innumerable, is every-
c exhibited with five interrogation points. But, as to capitals and commas, as well as the
truction of words, it would seem no easy matter to determine what impression of it is nearest
. In Flint's Murray, it stands thus : "An adverb may generally be known by its answering
uestion, How ? How much ? When ? or Where ? As in the phrase, ' He reads *correctly*,'
answer to the question, ' How does he read ? ' is, ' *correctly*.' " Such questions, when the
e is slight, do not however, in all cases, require capitals: as,

    "*Rosal.* Which of the visors was it, that you wore ?
     Biron. Where ? when ? what visor ? why demand you this ? "
              Shakspeare, Love's Labour Lost, Act V, Sc. 2.

bs. 4.—A question is sometimes put in the form of a mere declaration; its interrogative
icter depending solely on the eroteme, and the tone, or inflection of voice, adopted in the
ance : as, " I suppose, Sir, you are his apothecary ?"—*Swift: Burgh's Speaker*, p. 85. "I
, you have, upon no account, promoted sternutation by hellebore ?"—*Id. ib.* "This priest
io pride in him ?"—*Singer's Shak., Henry* VIII, ii, 2.

IMPROPRIETIES FOR CORRECTION.

FALSE PUNCTUATION.—ERRORS CONCERNING THE EROTEME.

UNDER RULE I.—QUESTIONS DIRECT.

"When will his ear delight in the sound of arms."—*O. B. Peirce's Gram.* 12mo, p. 59.

[FORMULE.—Not proper, because here is a finished question with a period set after it. But, according to let for the Eroteme, "Questions expressed directly as such, if finished, should always be followed by the so interrogation." Therefore, the eroteme, or note of interrogation, should here be substituted for the period.]

"When shall I, like Oscar, travel in the light of my steel."—*Ib.* p. 59. "Will H call on me while he shall be journeying South."—*Peirce, ib.* p. 133.

"An Interrogative Pronoun is one that is used in asking a question; as, '*who* is he, *what* does he want?' "—*Day's School Gram.* p. 21. "*Who* is generally used when we inquire for some unknown person or persons; as, *who* is that man."—*Ib.* p. 24. ' fathers, where are they, and the prophets, do they live forever?"—*Ib.* p. 109.

"It is true, that some of our best writers have used *than whom*; but it is also true they have used *other* phrases which we have rejected as ungrammatical: then why not this too.—The sentences in the Exercises [with *than who*] are correct as they stand."—*Lei Gram.*, 5th Ed., 1819, p. 79.

"When the perfect participle of an active-intransitive verb is annexed to the neuter *to be?* What does the combination form?"—*Hallock's Gram.* p. 88. "Those adverbs w answer to the question *where, whither* or *whence,* are called adverbs of *place.*"—*Ib.* p. 116

"Canst thou, by searching, find out God; Canst thou find out the Almighty to tion; It is high as heaven, what canst thou do? deeper than hell, what canst thou know? —*Blair's Rhet.* p. 132.

"Where, where, for shelter shall the guilty fly,
When consternation turns the good man pale."—*Ib.* p. 222.

UNDER RULE II.—QUESTIONS UNITED.

"Who knows what resources are in store? and what the power of God may do for thee?"

[FORMULE.—Not proper, because an eroteme is set after *store*, where a comma would be sufficient. But, according to Rule 2d for the Eroteme, "When two or more questions are united in one compound sentence, the comma, semicolon, or dash, is sometimes used to separate them, and the eroteme occurs after the last only." Therefore, the comma should here be preferred, as the author probably wrote the text. See Key.]

"The Lord is not a man that he should lie, neither the son of man that he should repent. Hath he said it? and shall he not do it? Hath he spoken it? and shall he not make it good?"—*Murray's Gram.* 8vo, p. 353; 12mo, 277; *Hiley's,* 139; *Hart's,* 181. "*Hath the Lord said it? and shall he not do it? Hath he spoken it? and shall he not make it good!*"— Lennie's Gram. p. 113; Bullions's, 176.

"Who calls the council, states the certain day?
Who forms the phalanx, and who points the way."—*Brit. Poets,* vi, 376.

UNDER RULE III.—QUESTIONS INDIRECT.

"To be, or not to be?—that is the question."—*Enfield's Sp.* p. 367; *Kirkham's Eloc.* 123.*

[FORMULE.—Not proper, because the note of interrogation is here set after an expression which has neither the form nor the nature of a direct question. But, according to Rule 3d for the Eroteme, "When a question is mentioned, but not put directly as a question, it loses both the quality and the sign of interrogation." Therefore, the semicolon, which seems adapted to the pause, should here be preferred.]

"If it be asked, why a pause should any more be necessary to emphasis than to an accent? or why an emphasis alone, will not sufficiently distinguish the members of sentences from each other, without pauses, as accent does words? the answer is obvious; that we are pre-acquainted with the sound of words, and cannot mistake them when distinctly pronounced, however rapidly; but we are not pre-acquainted with the meaning of sentences, which must be pointed out to us by the reader or speaker."—*Sheridan's Rhet. Gram.* p. 171.

"Cry, By your Priesthood tell me what you are?"—
POPE: *British Poets,* London, 1800, Vol. vi, p. 411.

MIXED EXAMPLES OF ERROR.

"Who else can he be. Where else can he go."—*S. Barrett's Gram.,* 1846, p. 71. "In familiar language *here, there* and *where* are used for *hither, thither* and *whither.*"—*N. Butler's Gram.* p. 183. "Take, for instance, this sentence, 'Indolence undermines the foundation of virtue.' "—*Hart's Gram.* p. 106. "Take, for instance, the sentence before quoted. '*Indolence* undermines the foundation of virtue.' "—*Ib.* p. 110. "Under the same head are considered such sentences as these, '*he* that heareth, let him hear,' 'Gad, a troop shall overcome him.' &c."—*Ib.* p. 108.

"TENSES are certain modifications of the verb which point out the distinctions of time." —*Bullions, E. Gram.* p. 38; *Pract. Les.* p. 44. "Calm was the day and the scene delight-

* "To be, or not to be?—that's the question."—*Hallock's Gram.* p. 520. "To be, or not to be, that is the question."—*Singer's Shak.* ii 4-8. "To be, or not to be; that is the Question."—*Ward's Gram.* p. 160. "To be, or not to be; that is the Question."—*Brightland's Gram.* p. 200.

ful."—*Id. E. Gr.* p. 80. " The capital letters used by the Romans to denote numbers, were C. I. L. V. X. which are therefore called Numeral Letters. I, denotes *one* ; V, *five* ; X, *ten*; L, *fifty* ; and C, a hundred."—*Id. Lat. Gram.* p. 56. " ' I shall have written ;' viz, at or before some future time or event."—*Id. ib.* p. 89. " In Latin words the liquids are *l* and *r* only. In Greek words *l, r, m, n.*"—*Id. ib.* p. 277. " Each legion was divided into ten cohorts, each cohort into three maniples, and each maniple into two centuries."—*Id. ib.* p. 309. " Of the Roman literature previous to A. U. 514 scarcely a vestige remains."—*Id. ib.* p. 312.

"And that, which He delights in must be happy.
But when !—or where !—This world was made for Cæsar."—*Burgh's Sp.* p. 122.
"And that which he delights in must be happy.
But when, or where ? This world was made for Cæsar."—*Enfield's Sp.* p. 321.
" Look next on greatness. Say, where greatness lies ?
Where but among the heroes and the wise."—*Burgh's Sp.* p. 91.
" Look next on greatness ! say where greatness lies.
Where, but among the heroes and the wise ?"—*Essay on Man*, p. 51.
" Look next on Greatness ; say where Greatness lies :
Where, but among the Heroes and the Wise ?"—*Brit. Poets*, vi, 380.

SECTION VII.—THE ECPHONEME.

The Ecphoneme, or Note of Exclamation, is used to denote a pause with some strong emotion of admiration, joy, grief, or other feeling ; and, as a sign of great wonder, it is sometimes, though not very elegantly, repeated : as, " Grammatical consistency ! ! !   What a gem ! "—*Peirce's Gram.* p. 352.

RULE I.—INTERJECTIONS, &c.

Emphatic interjections, and other expressions of great emotion, are generally followed by the note of exclamation ; as, " Hold ! hold ! Is the devil in you ?   Oh ! I am bruised all over."—MOLIERE: *Burgh's Sp.* p. 250.

"And O ! till earth, and seas, and heav'n, decay,
Ne'er may that fair creation fade away !"—*Dr. Lowth.*

RULE II.—INVOCATIONS.

After an earnest address or solemn invocation, the note of exclamation is now generally preferred to any other point ; as, " Whereupon, O king Agrippa ! I was not disobedient unto the heavenly vision."—*Acts*, xxvi, 19.

" Be witness thou, immortal Lord of all !
Whose thunder shakes the dark aërial hall."—*Pope.*

RULE III.—EXCLAMATORY QUESTIONS.

Words uttered with vehemence in the form of a question, but without reference to an answer, should be followed by the note of exclamation ; as, " How madly have I talked ! "— *Young.*

"An Author ! 'Tis a venerable name !
How few deserve it, and what numbers claim ! "—*Id. Br. Po.* viii, 401.

IMPROPRIETIES FOR CORRECTION.

FALSE PUNCTUATION.—ERRORS CONCERNING THE ECPHONEME.

UNDER RULE I.—OF INTERJECTIONS, &c.

(1.) " O that he were wise."—*Bullions, E. Gram.* p. 111.

[FORMULE—Not proper, because this strong wish, introduced by " O," is merely marked with a period. But, according to Rule 1st for the Ecphoneme, " Emphatic interjections, and other expressions of great emotion, are generally followed by the note of exclamation." Therefore, the pause after this sentence, should be marked with the latter sign ; and, if the " O " be read with a pause, the same sign may be there also.]

(2.) " O that his heart was tender."—*Exercises, ib.* p. 111. (3.) "*Oh*, what a sight is here ! "—*Lennie's Gram.* p. 48. (4.) " Oh ! what a sight is here."—*Bullions, E. Gram.* p. 71 ; (Obs. 2 ;) *Pract. Les.* p. 83. (5.) " O virtue ! How amiable thou art."—*Id. ib.* p. 71 ; *Pract. Les.* p. 82. (6.) " O *virtue ! how* amiable thou art."—*Day's Gram.* p. 109. (7.) " O, virtue ! how amiable thou art."—*S. Putnam's Gram.* p. 53. (8.) "*Oh!* virtue, how amiable thou art."—*Hart's Gram.* p. 191 ; *O. B. Peirce's*, 375. (9.) "*O* virtue ! how amiable thou art ! "—*Bullock's Gram.* p. 126. (10.) " Oh ! that I had been more diligent."—*Hart's Gram.* p. 167 ; see *Hiley's*, 117. (11.) " O ! the humiliation to which vice reduces us."—*Farnum's Gram.* p. 12 ; *Murray's Ex.* p. 5. (12.) " O ! that he were more prudent."—*Farnum's*

Gram. p. 81. (13.) "Ah! me."—*P. Davis's Gram.* p. 79. (14.) "Ah me!"—*Ib.* p. 12[
(15.) "Lately alas I knew a gentle boy," &c.—*The Dial,* Vol. i, p. 71.
(16.) " Wo is me Alhama."—*Wells's School Gram.* 1st Ed. p. 190.
(17.) " Wo is me, Alhama."—*Ibid.,* "113th Thousand," p. 206.

UNDER RULE II.—OF INVOCATIONS.

"Weep on the rocks of roaring winds, O *maid* of Inistore."—*Kirkham's Gram.* p. 191;
Cooper's, 158.

[FORMULE.—Not proper, because the emphatic address in this sentence, is marked with a period after it. But,
according to Rule 2d for the Ecphoneme, "After an earnest address or solemn invocation, the note of exclamation is now generally preferred to any other point." Therefore, this period should be changed to the last
sign.]

"Cease a little while, O wind; stream, be thou silent a while; let my voice be heard
around. Let my wanderer hear me. Salgar, it is Colma who calls. Here is the tree, an]
the rock. Salgar, my love, I am here. Why delayest thou thy coming? Lo, the clear
moon comes forth. The flood is bright in the vale."—*See Key.*
      "Ah, stay not, stay not, guardless and alone;
      Hector, my lov'd, my dearest, bravest son."—*See Key.*

UNDER RULE III.—EXCLAMATORY QUESTIONS.

"How much better is wisdom than gold."—*Bullions, E. Gram.* p. 153; *Hiley,* p. 113.

[FORMULE.—Not proper, because this exclamatory sentence is pointed with a period at the end. But, according to Rule 3d for the Ecphoneme, "Words uttered with vehemence in the form of a question, but with
reference to an answer, should be followed by the note of exclamation." Therefore, this period should be
changed to the latter sign.]

"O virtue! how amiable art thou."—*Flint's Murray,* p. 51. "At that hour, O how was
all sublunary happiness."—*Day's Gram.* p. 74. "Alas! how few and transitory are the
joys which this world affords to man."—*Ib.* p. 12. "Oh! how vain and transitory are all
things here below."—*Ib.* p. 110.
      "And oh! what change of state, what change of rank,
      In that assembly everywhere was seen."—*Day's Gram.* p. 12.
      "And O! what change of state! what change of rank!
      In that assembly every where was seen!"—*Pollok,* B. ix, l. 781.

MIXED EXAMPLES OF ERROR.

"O shame! where is thy blush."—*S. Barrett's Principles of Language,* p. 86. "O shame,
where is thy blush; John, give me my hat."—*Ib.* p. 98. "What! is Moscow in flames,"
—*Ib.* p. 86. "Ah! what happiness awaits the virtuous."—*Ib.* 86.
"Ah welladay,—do what we can for him, said Trim, maintaining his point,—the poor
soul will die."—STERNE: *Enfield's Speaker,* p. 306. "A well o'day! do what we can for
him, said Trim, maintaining his point: the poor soul will *die*."—*Kirkham's Elocution,* p. 14
"*Will* John return to-morrow."—*S. Barrett's Gram.,* Tenth Ed., p. 55. "*Will* not J—
return to-morrow."—*Ib.* 55. "John! *return* to-morrow; Soldiers! *stand* firm."—*Ib.*
"If *mea* which means *my* is an adjective in *Latin,* why may not *my* be so called *in Engli*s
and if *my* is an adjective, why not *Barrett's*"—*Ib.* p. 50.
"Oh? Absalom, my son."—*O. B. Peirce's Gram.* p. 375. "Oh! STAR-EYED SCIENCE
whither hast thou fled?"—*Ib.* p. 366. "Why do you tolerate your own inconsistency,
calling it the present tense!"—*Ib.* p. 360. "Thus the declarative mode may be use in
asking a question; as, *what* man *is* frail."—*Ib.* p. 358. " What connexion has motive with
or supposition, with the term subjunctive!"—*Ib.* p. 348. "A grand reason, truly '
calling it a golden key."—*Ib.* p. 347. "What '*suffering* '/ the man who can say this, will
be ' *enduring*.' "—*Ib.* p. 345. " What is Brown's Rule! in relation to this matter?"—*Ib.* p. 2
"*Alas!* how short is life." "*Thomas,* study your book."—*Day's District School Gram.*
109. "As, ' *alas!* how short is life; *Thomas,* study your book.' "—*Ib.* p. 82. "Who can tell
us who they are."—*Sanborn's Gram.* p. 178. " Lord have mercy on my son; for he is
lunatic, etc."—*Felton's Gram.,* 1st Ed., p. 138; Ster. Ed., 140. " O, ye wild groves, O, where
is now your bloom!"—*Ib.* p. 88; Ster. Ed., 91.
      "O who of man the story will unfold!"—*Farnum's Gr.,* 2d Ed., p. 104.
      "Methought I heard Horatio say to-morrow.
      Go to I will not hear of it—to-morrow."—*Hallock's Gr.,* 1st Ed., p. 221.
      "How his eyes languish? how his thoughts adore
      That painted coat which Joseph never wore? "—*Love of Fame,* p. 66.

SECTION VIII. — THE CURVES.

The Curves, or Marks of Parenthesis, are used to distinguish a clause or
hint that is hastily thrown in between the parts of a sentence to which it does

t properly belong ; as, " Their enemies (and enemies they will always
ve) would have a handle for exposing their measures."—*Walpole*.

> " To others do (the law is not severe)
> What to thyself thou wishest to be done."—*Beattie*.

Bs.—The incidental clause should be uttered in a lower tone, and faster, than the principal
stence. It always requires a pause as great as that of a comma, or greater.

RULE I.—THE PARENTHESIS.

A clause that breaks the unity of a sentence or passage too much to be incorporated
h it, and only such, should be enclosed within curves, as a parenthesis ; as, " For
now that in me, (that is, in my flesh,) dwelleth no good thing."—*Rom.* vii, 18.

> " Know then this truth, (enough for man to know,)
> Virtue alone is happiness below."—*Pope*.

RULE II.—INCLUDED POINTS.

The curves do not supersede other stops ; and, as the parenthesis terminates with a
se equal to that which precedes it, the same point should be included, except when
sentences differ in form : as, 1. " Now, for a recompense in the same, (I speak
unto my children,) be ye also enlarged."—*2 Cor.* vi, 13.

> 2. " Man's thirst of happiness declares it is :
> (For nature never gravitates to nought :)
> That thirst unquench'd, declares it is not here."—*Young*.

> 3. " Night visions may befriend : (as sung above :)
> Our waking dreams are fatal. How I dreamt
> Of things impossible ! (could sleep do more ?)
> Of joys perpetual in perpetual change ! "—*Young*.

IMPROPRIETIES FOR CORRECTION.

FALSE PUNCTUATION.—ERRORS CONCERNING THE CURVES.

UNDER RULE I.—OF THE PARENTHESIS.

Another is composed of the indefinite article *an*, which etymologically means *one* and
r, and denotes *one other*."—*Hallock's Gram.* p. 63.

ANULE.—Not proper, because the parenthetic expression, " which etymologically means *one*," is not suffi-
ly separated from the rest of the passage. But, according to Rule 1st for the Curves, " A clause that
is the unity of a sentence or passage too much to be incorporated with it, and only such, should be enclosed
n curves, as a parenthesis." Therefore, the curves should be here inserted ; and also, by Rule 2d, a
ma at the word *one*.]

Each mood has its peculiar Tense, Tenses (or Times)."—*Bucke's Gram.* p. 58.

ANULE.—Not proper, because the expression, " or Times," which has not the nature of a parenthesis, is
marked with curves. But, according to Rule 1st for the Curves, " A clause that breaks the unity of a
nce or passage too much to be incorporated with it, *and only such*, should be enclosed within curves, as a
rthesis." Therefore, these marks should be omitted ; and a comma should be set after the word " *Tenses*,"
ule 2d]

In some very ancient languages, as the Hebrew, which have been employed chiefly for
essing plain sentiments in the plainest manner, without aiming at any elaborate length
armony of periods, this pronoun [the relative] occurs not so often."—*L. Murray's Gram.*
p. 127.

Before I shall say those Things, (O conscript Fathers) about the Public Affairs, which
o be spoken at this Time ; I shall lay before you, in few Words, the Motives of the
ney, and the Return."—*Brightland's Gram.* p. 149.

> " Of well-chose Words some take not care enough,
> And think they shou'd be (like the Subject) rough."—*Ib.* p. 173.

" Then, having shewed his wounds, *he'd* sit (him) down."—*Bullions, E. Gr.* p. 32.

UNDER RULE II.—OF INCLUDED POINTS.

Then Jael smote the Nail into his Temples, and fastened it to the Ground : (for he was
asleep, and weary) so he died. OLD TEST."—*Ward's Gram.* p. 17.

ANULE.—Not proper, because this parenthesis is not marked as terminating with a pause equal to that
t precedes it. But, according to Rule 2d above, " The curves do not supersede other stops ; and, as the
thesis terminates with a pause equal to that which precedes it, the same point should be included, except
the sentences differ in form." Therefore, a colon should be inserted within the curve after *weary*.]

Every thing in the Iliad has manners (as Aristotle expresses it) that is, every thing is
l or spoken."—*Pope, Pref. to Homer*, p. vi.

Those nouns, that end in *f*, or *fe* (except some few I shall mention presently), form
als by changing those letters into *ves* : as, thief, *thieves* ; wife, *wives*."—*Bucke's Gram.* p. 35.

"*As*, requires *as*; (expressing equality) Mine is as good as yours. *As*, —— so; (expressing equality) As the stars, so shall thy seed be. *So*, —— *as*; (with a negative expressing inequality) He is not so wise as his brother. *So*, —— *that*; (expressing consequence) I am so weak that I cannot walk."—*Bullions, E. Gram.* p. 113; *Pract. Les.* p. 112.

> "A captious question, sir (and yours is one,)
> Deserves an answer similar, or none."—*Cowper*, ii, 228.

MIXED EXAMPLES OF ERROR.

"Whatever words the verb to BE serves to unite referring to the same thing, must be of the same case; § 61, as, *Alexander* is a *student*."—*Bullions, E. Gram.* p. 75. "When the objective is a relative or interrogative, it comes before the verb that governs it. § 40, R. 2. (Murray's 6th rule is unnecessary.)"—*Id. ib.* p. 90. "It is generally improper (except in poetry,) to omit the antecedent to a relative; and always to omit a relative when of the nominative case."—*Id. ib.* p. 130. "In every sentence there must be a *verb* and a *nominative* (or subject) expressed or understood."—*Id. ib.* p. 87; *Pract. Lessons*, p. 91. "Nouns and pronouns, and especially words denoting time, are often governed by prepositions understood; or are used to restrict verbs or adjectives without a governing word, § 50. Rem. 6 and Rule; as, He gave (to) me a full account of the whole affair."—*Bullions, E. Gram.* p. 80. "When *should* is used instead of *ought*, to express *present* duty, § 20, 4, it may be followed by the present; as, "You *should* study that you *may* become learned."—*Id. ib.* p. 123. "The indicative present is frequently used after the words, *when, till, before, as soon as, after*, to express the relative time of a future action; (§ 24, I, 4,) as, 'When he comes, he will be welcome.'"—*Id. ib.* p. 124. "The relative is parsed by stating its gender, number, case, and antecedent, (the gender and number being always the same as those of the antecedent) thus, 'The boy who.' '*Who*' is a relative pronoun, masculine, singular, the nominative, and refers to '*boy*' as its antecedent."—*Bullions, Pract. Les.* p. 31.

> "Now, now I seize, I clasp *thy* charms,
> And now *you* burst; ah! cruel from my arms.

Here is an unnecessary change from the second person singular to the second plural. It would have been better, thus,

> Now, now I seize, I clasp *your* charms,
> And now *you* burst; ah! cruel from my arms."—*J. Burn's Gram.* p. 193.

SECTION IX.—THE OTHER MARKS.

There are also several other marks, which are occasionally used for various purposes, as follow:—

I. ['] The APOSTROPHE usually denotes either the possessive case of a noun, or the elision of one or more letters of a word: as, "The *girl's* regard to her *parents'* advice;"—*'gan, lov'd, e'en, thro'*; for *began, loved, even, through*. It is sometimes used in pluralizing a mere letter or sign; as, Two *a's*—three 6's.*

II. [-] The HYPHEN connects the parts of many compound words, especially such as have two accents; as, *ever-living*. It is also frequently inserted where a word is divided into syllables; as, *con-tem-plate*. Placed at the end of a line, it shows that one or more syllables of a word are carried forward to the next line.

III. [··] The DIÆRESIS, or DIALYSIS, placed over either of two contiguous vowels, shows that they are not a diphthong; as, *Danäe, aërial*.

IV. ['] The ACUTE ACCENT marks the syllable which requires the principal stress in pronunciation; as, *e'qual, equal'ity*. It is sometimes used in opposition to the grave accent, to distinguish a close or short vowel; as, "*Fáncy:*" (*Murray:*) or to denote the rising inflection of the voice; as, "Is it *hé*?"

V. [`] The GRAVE ACCENT is used in opposition to the acute, to distinguish an open or long vowel; as, "*Fàvour:*" (*Murray:*) or to denote the falling inflection of the voice; as, "*Yès*; it is *hè*." It is sometimes placed over a vowel to show that it is not to be suppressed in pronunciation; as,

> "Let me, though in humble speech,
> Thy refinèd maxims teach."—*Amer. Review*, May, 1848.

---

* In the works of some of our older poets, the apostrophe is sometimes irregularly inserted, and perhaps needlessly, to mark a prosodial synæresis, or synalepha, where no letter is cut off or left out; as,

> "Retire, or taste thy *folly*', and learn by proof,
> Hell-born, not to contend with *spir'its* of Heaven "—*Milton, P. L.*, ii, 696.

In the following example, it seems to denote nothing more than the open or long sound of the preceding vowel *e*:

> "That sleep and feeding may prorogue his honour,
> Even till a *lethe'd* dulness."—*Singer's Shakspeare*, ii, p. 280.

VI. [^] The CIRCUMFLEX generally denotes either the broad sound of *a* or an unusual sound given to some other vowel; as in *âll, hêir, machîne*. Some use it to mark a peculiar *wave* of the voice, and when occasion requires, reverse it; as, " If you said *só*, then I said *sô*."

VII. [˘] The BREVE, or STENOTONE, is used to denote either the close, short, *shut* sound of a vowel, or a syllable of short quantity; as, *lĭve*, to have life—*răv'en*, to devour*—călămŭs*, a reed.

VIII. [¯] The MACRON, or MACROTONE,† is used to denote either the open, long, *primal* sound of a vowel, or a syllable of long quantity; as, *līve*, having life—*rā'ven*, a bird—*ē'quīne*, of a horse.

IX. [——] or [* * * *] or [. . . .] The ELLIPSIS, or SUPPRESSION, denotes the omission of some letters or words: as, *K—g*, for *King*; *c****d*, for *coward*; *d....d*, for *damned*.

X. [ʌ] The CARET, used only in writing, shows where to insert words or letters that have been accidentally omitted.

XI. [⌒] The BRACE serves to unite a triplet; or, more frequently, to connect several terms with something to which they are all related.

XII. [§] The SECTION marks the smaller divisions of a book or chapter; and, with the help of numbers, serves to abridge references.

XIII. [¶] The PARAGRAPH (chiefly used in the Bible) denotes the commencement of a new subject. The parts of discourse which are called paragraphs, are, in general, sufficiently distinguished by beginning a new line, and carrying the first word a little forwards or backwards. The paragraphs of books being in some instances numbered, this character may occasionally be used, in lieu of the word *paragraph*, to shorten references.

XIV. [" "] The GUILLEMETS, or QUOTATION POINTS, distinguish words that are exhibited as those of an other author or speaker. A quotation within a quotation is usually marked with single points; which, when both are employed, are placed within the others: as, "And again he saith, ' Rejoice, ye Gentiles, with his people.' "— *Rom.* xv, 10.

XV. [[]] The CROTCHETS, or BRACKETS, generally inclose some correction or explanation, but sometimes the sign or subject to be explained; as, " He [Mr. Maurice] was of a different opinion."—*Allen's Gram.* p. 213.

XVI. [☞] The INDEX, or HAND, points out something remarkable, or what the reader should particularly observe.

XVII. [*] The ASTERISK, or STAR, [†] the OBELISK, or DAGGER, [‡] the DIESIS, or DOUBLE DAGGER, and [‖] the PARALLELS, refer to marginal notes. The SECTION also [§], and the PARAGRAPH [¶], are often used for marks of reference, the former being usually applied to the fourth, and the latter to the sixth note on a page; for, by the usage

---

* The breve is properly a mark of *short quantity*, only when it is set over an unaccented syllable or an unemphatic monosyllable, as it often is in the scanning of verses. In the examples above, it marks the close or short power of the *vowels*; but, *under the accent*, even this power may become part of a *long syllable*; as it does in the word *rav'en*, where the syllable *rav*, having twice the length of that which follows, must be reckoned *long*. In poetry, *räv-en* and *rä-ven* are both *trochees*, the former syllable in each being long, and the latter short.

† 1. The signs of long and short sounds, and especially of the former, have been singularly slow in acquiring *appropriate names*—or any appellatives suited to their nature, or such as could obtain the sanction of general use. The name *breve*, from the French *brève*, (which latter word came, doubtless, originally from the neuter of the Latin adjective *brevis*, short,) is now pretty generally applied to the one; and the Greek term *macron*, long, (also originally a neuter adjective,) is perhaps as common as any name for the other. But these are not quite so well adapted to each other, and to the things named, as are the substitutes added above.

2. These signs are explained in our grammars under various names, and often very unfit ones, to say the least; and, in many instances, their use is, in some way, awkwardly stated, without any attempt to name them, or more than one, if either. The Rev. T. Smith names them " Long (¯), and Short (˘)."—*Smith's Murray*, p. 72. Churchill calls them " The long ¯ and the short ˘."—*New Gram.* p. 170. Gould calls them ' a horizontal line " and " a curved line."—*Gould's Adam's Gram.* p. 3. Coar says, " Quantity is distinguished by the characters of ¯ long, and ˘ short."—*Eng. Gram.* p. 197. But, in speaking of the *signs*, he calls them, "*A long syllable* ¯," and "*A short syllable* ˘."—*Gram.* pp. 222 and 228. S. S. Greene calls them " the *long sound*," and " the *breve* or short sound."—*Gram.* p. 257. W. Allen says, " The *long-syllable mark*, (¯) and the *breve*, or *short-syllable mark*, (˘) denote the quantity of *words* poetically employed."—*Gram.* p. 215. Some call them, " the *Long Accent*," and "the *Short Accent*;" as does *Guy's Gram.* p. 96. This naming seems to confound accent with quantity. By some, the *Macron* is improperly called " a *Dash*;" as by *Lennie*, p. 137; by *Bullions*, p. 157; by *Hiley*, p. 128; by *Butler*, p. 215 Some call it " a *small dash*;" as does *Wells*, p. 183; so *Hiley*, p. 117. By some it is absurdly named "*Hyphen*;" as by *Buchanan*, p. 162; by *Alden*, p. 165; by *Chandler*, 180; by *Parker and Fox*, iii, 96; by *Jaudon*, 193. Sanborn calls it " the *hyphen*, or *macron* "—*Analyt. Gr.* p. 279 Many, who name it not, introduce it to their readers by a " *this*-," or " *thus*-;" as do *Alger, Blair, Dr. Adam, Comly, Cooper, Ingersoll, L. Murray, Sanders, Wright*, and others !

of printers, these signs are now commonly introduced in the following order : 1 *, 2 †, 3 ‡, 4 §, 5 ‖, 6 ¶, 7 **, 8 ††, &c.   Where many references are to be made, the *small letters* of the alphabet, or the *numerical figures*, in their order, may be conveniently used for the same purpose.

XVIII. [*₊*] The ASTERISM, or THE THREE STARS, a sign not very often used, is placed before a long note, without a particular reference.

XIX. [,] The CEDILLA is a mark borrowed from the French, by whom it is placed under the letter *c*, to give it the sound of *s* before *a* or *o ;* as in the words, " façade," "Alençon."   In Worcester's Dictionary, it is attached to three other letters, to denote their *soft* sounds : viz., " Ç as J ; Ş as Z ; ҳ as gz."

☞ [Oral exercises in punctuation should not be confined to the correction of errors. An application of its principles to points rightly inserted, is as easy a process as that of ordinary syntactical parsing, and perhaps as useful. For this purpose, the teacher may select a portion of this grammar, or of any well-pointed book, to which the foregoing rules and explanations may be applied by the pupil, as reasons for the points that occur.]

IMPROPRIETIES FOR CORRECTION.

FALSE PUNCTUATION. — MIXED EXAMPLES OF ERROR.

" The principal stops are the following :—
The Comma (,) the semicolon (;) the colon (:) the period, or full stop (.) the note of interrogation (?) the note of exclamation (!) the parenthesis () and the dash (—) [.] "—*Bullions, E. Gram.* p. 151 ; *Pract. Les.* p. 127.   "The modern punctuation in Latin is the same as in English.   The marks employed, are the *Comma* (,); *Semicolon* (:); *Colon* (:); *Period* (.); *Interrogation* (?); *Exclamation* (!)."—*Bullions, Lat. Gram.* p. 3.

" Plato reproving a young man for playing at some childish game ; you chide me, says the youth, for a trifling fault.   Custom, replied the philosopher, is no trifle.   And, adds Montagnie, he was in the right ; for our vices begin in infancy."—*Home's Art of Thinking*, (N. Y. 1818,) p. 54.

"A merchant at sea asked the skipper what death his father died ?   ' My father,' says the skipper, my grandfather, and my great-grandfather, were all drowned.   ' Well,' replies the merchant, and are not you afraid of being drowned too ? ' "—*Ib.* p. 135.

" The use of inverted comma's derives from France, where one Guillemet was the author of them ; [and] as an acknowledgement for the improvement his countrymen call them after his name GUILLEMETS."—*History of Printing*, (London, 1770,) p. 266.

" This, however, is seldom if ever done unless the word following the possessive begins with *s ;* thus we do not say, ' the prince' feather,' but, ' the prince's feather.' "—*Bullions, E. Gram.* p. 17.   "And this phrase must mean *the feather of the prince* but *princesfeather* written as one word is the name of a plant : a species of amaranth."—See *Key.*

" Boëthius soon had the satisfaction of obtaining the highest honour his country could bestow."—*Ingersoll's Gram.* 12mo, p. 279.   "Boethius soon had," &c.—*Murray's Gram.* 8vo, Vol. ii, p. 83.

" When an example, a quotation, or a speech is introduced, it is separated from the rest of the sentence either by a semicolon or a colon ; as, ' The scriptures give us an amiable representation of the Deity, in these words ; *God is love.*' "—*Hiley's Gram.* p. 116.   " Either the colon or semicolon may be used when an example, a quotation, or a speech is introduced ; as, 'Always remember this ancient maxim ; *Know thyself.*'   ' The scriptures give us an amiable representation of the Deity, in these words : *God is love.*' "—*Bullions, E. Gram.* p. 155.

" The first word of a quotation, introduced after a colon [, must begin with a capital] ; as, always remember this ancient maxim : '*Know* thyself.' "—*Bullions, E. Gram.* p. 159 ; *Lennie's Gram.* p. 106.   [Lennie has "*Always*" with a capital.]   "The first word of a quotation, introduced after a colon, or *when it is* in a direct form : as, 'Always remember this ancient maxim : *Know thyself.*'   ' Our great lawgiver says, Take up thy cross daily, and follow me.' "—*Murray's Gram.* 8vo, p. 284.   " 8. The first word of a quotation, *introduced after a colon,* or *when it is* in a direct form.   EXAMPLES.—'Always remember this ancient maxim, ' Know thyself.''   ' Our great Lawgiver says, Take up thy cross daily, and follow me. ' "—*Weld's Gram. Abridged*, p. 17.

" Tell me in whose house do you live."—*N. Butler's Gram.* p. 55.   " He, that acts wisely, deserves praise."—*Ib.* p. 50.   " He, who steals my purse, steals trash."—*Ib* p. 51.   " The antecedent is sometimes omitted, as, ' Who steals my purse, steals trash ; ' that is, *he who*, or the *person* who."—*Ib.* p. 51.   " Thus, ' Whoever steals my purse steals trash ; ' ' Whoever does no good does harm.' "—*Ib.* p. 53.   "Thus, ' Whoever sins will suffer.'   This means that any one without exception who sins will suffer."—*Ib.* 53.

" Letters form syllables, syllables words, words sentences, and sentences, combined and connected form discourse."—*Cooper's Plain and Practical Gram.* p. 1.   "A letter, which forms a perfect sound, when uttered by itself, is called a vowel, as : *a, e, i.*"—*Ib.* p. 1.   "A proper noun is the name of an individual, as : John ; Boston : Hudson ; America."—*Ib.* p. 17.

" Many men have been capable of doing a wise thing, more a cunning thing, but very few a generous thing."—*P. Davis's Gram.* p. 96. "In the place of an ellipsis of the verb a comma must be inserted."—*Ib.* p. 121. "A common noun unlimited by an article is sometimes understood in its broadest acceptation : thus, '*Fishes* swim' is understood to mean *all* fishes. '*Man* is mortal,' *all* men."—*Ib.* p. 13.

"Thus those sounds formed principally by the throat are called *gutturals.* Those formed principally by the palate are called *palatals.* Those formed by the teeth, *dentals*—those by the lips, *labials*—those by the nose, *nasals,* &c."—*P. Davis's Gram.* p. 13. "Some adjectives are compared irregularly ; as, *Good, better, best. Bad, worse, worst. Little, less, least.*"—*Felton's Gram.*, 1st Ed., p. 63 ; Ster. Ed., p. 66.

"Under the fourth head of grammar, therefore, four topics will be considered, viz. PUNCTUATION, ORTHOEPY, FIGURES, and VERSIFICATION."—*Hart's Gram.* p. 161.

"Direct her onward to that peaceful shore,
Where peril, pain and death are felt no more ! "
                              Falconer's Poems, p. 136 : *Barrett's New Gram.* 94.

BAD ENGLISH BADLY POINTED.

LESSON I.—UNDER VARIOUS RULES.

"Discoveries of such a character are sometimes made in grammar also, and such, too, is often their origin and their end."—*Bullions, E. Gram.* p. 191.

"*Traverse,* (to cross.) To deny what the opposite party has alleged. To traverse an indictment, &c. is to deny it."—*Id. ib.* p. 216.

"The *Ordinal* [numerals] denote the *order* or *succession* in which any number of persons or things is mentioned, as *first, second, third, fourth,* &c."—*Hiley's Gram.* p. 22.

"Nouns have three persons, FIRST, SECOND, and THIRD. The First person is the speaker, the Second is the one spoken to, the Third is the one spoken of."—*Hart's Gram.* p. 44.

"Nouns have three cases, NOMINATIVE, POSSESSIVE, and OBJECTIVE. The relation indicated by the case of a noun includes three ideas, viz : those of *subject, object,* and *ownership.*"—*Ib.* p. 45.

"In speaking of animals that are of inferior size, or whose sex is not known or not regarded, they are often considered as without sex : thus, we say of a *cat* '*it* is treacherous,' of an infant '*it* is beautiful,' of a *deer* '*it* was killed.'"—*Ib.* p. 39.

"When *this* or *these, that* or *those,* refers to a preceding sentence ; *this,* or *these,* refers to the latter member or term ; *that,* or *those,* to the former."—*Churchill's Gram.* p. 136 ; see *Lowth's Gram.* p. 102.

"The rearing of them [i. e. of plants] became his first care, their fruit his first food, and marking their kinds his first knowledge."—*N. Butler's Gram.* p. 44.

"After the period used with abbreviations we should employ other points, if the construction demands it ; thus, after Esq. in the last example, there should be, besides a period, a comma."—*Ib.* p. 212.

"In the plural, the verb is the same in all the persons ; and hence the principle in *Rem.* 5, under Rule iii. [that the first or second person takes precedence,] is not applicable to verbs."—*Ib.* p. 158.

"Rex and Tyrannus are of very different characters. The one rules his people by laws to which they consent ; the other, by his absolute will and power : *that* is called freedom, *this,* tyranny."—*Murray's Key,* 8vo, p. 190.

"A noun is the name of any person, place, or thing, which can be known, or mentioned, as : George ; London ; America ; goodness ; charity."—*Cooper's Plain & Pract. Gram.* p. 17.

"Etymology treats of the classification of words ; their various modifications and derivations."—*Day's School Gram.* p. 9.

"To punctuate correctly implies a thorough acquaintance with the meaning of words and phrases, as well as of all their corresponding connexions."—*W. Day's Punctuation,* p. 31.

"All objects which belong to neither the male nor female kind are called *neuter.*"—*Weld's Gram.,* 2d Ed., p. 57. "All objects, which belong to neither the male nor female kind, are said to be of the neuter gender."—*Weld's Gram. Abridged,* p. 51.

"The Analysis of the Sounds in the English language presented in the preceding statements are sufficiently exact for the purpose in hand. Those who wish to pursue it further can consult Dr. Rush's admirable work, 'The Philosophy of the Human Voice.'"—*Fowler's E. Gram.* 1850, § 65. "Nobody confounds the name of *w* or *y* with their sound or phonetic import."—*Ib.* § 74.

"Order is Heaven's first law ; and this confest.
Some are and must be greater than the rest."—*Ib.* p. 96.

LESSON II.—UNDER VARIOUS RULES.

"In adjectives of *one* syllable, the Comparative is formed by adding—*er* to the positive ; and the Superlative by adding—*est* ; as, *sweet, sweeter, sweetest.*"—*Bullions, Prin of E. Gram.* p. 19.

"In monosyllables the comparative is formed by adding *er* or *r* to the positive, and the superlative by adding *est* or *st* ; as, *tall, taller, tallest ; wise, wiser, wisest.*"—*Id. Pract. Les.* p. 24.

"By this method the confusion and unnecessary labor occasioned by studying grammars, in these languages, constructed on different principles is avoided, the study of one is rendered a profitable introduction to the study of another, and an opportunity is furnished to the enquiring student of comparing the languages in their grammatical structure, and seeing at once wherein they agree, and wherein they differ."—*Bullions, Prin. of E. Gram.*, Pref. to 5th Ed., p. vii.

"No larger portion should be assigned for each recitation than the class can easily master, and till this is done, a new portion should not be given out."—*Id. ib.* p. viii. "The acquisitions made in every new lesson should be rivetted and secured by repeated *revisals.*"—*Id. ib.* p. viii.

"The personal pronouns may be parsed briefly thus; *I*, the first personal pronoun, masculine (or feminine), singular, the nominative. *His*, the third personal pronoun, masculine, singular, the possessive, &c."—*Bullions, E. Gram.* p. 23; *Pract. Les.* p. 28.

"When the male and female are expressed by distinct terms; as, *shepherd, shepherdess,* the masculine term has also a general meaning, expressing both male and female, and is always to be used when the office, occupation, profession, &c., and not the sex of the individual, is chiefly to be expressed. The feminine term is used only when the discrimination of sex is indispensably necessary. Thus, when it is said 'the Poets of this country are distinguished by correctness of taste,' the term 'Poet' clearly includes both *male* and *female* writers of poetry."—*Id. E. Gram.* p. 12; *his Analyt. and Pract. Gram.* 24.

"Nouns and pronouns, connected by conjunctions, must be in the same cases."—*Ingersoll's Gram.* p. 78. "Verbs, connected by conjunctions, must be in the same moods and tenses, and, when in the subjunctive present, they must be in the same form."—*Ib.* p. 112.

"This will habituate him to reflection—exercise his judgment on the meaning of the author, and without any great effort on his part, impress indelibly on his memory, the rules which he is required to give. After the exercises under the rule have been gone through as directed in the note page 96, they may be read over again in a corrected state the pupil making an emphasis on the correction made, or they may be presented in writing at the next recitation."—*Bullions, Prin. of E. Gram.*, 2d Ed. Revised and Cor., p. viii.

"Man, but for *that*, no action *could* attend
And but for *this*, be *thoughtful* to no end."—*O. B. Peirce's Gram.*, Pref., p. 5.

LESSON III.—UNDER VARIOUS RULES.

"'Johnson the bookseller and stationer,' indicates that the bookseller and the stationer are epithets belonging to the same person; 'the bookseller and the stationer' would indicate that they belong to different persons."—*Bullions, E. Gram.* p. 127.

"*Past* is an adjective; *passed*, the past tense or perfect participle of the verb, and they ought not, as is frequently done, to be confounded with each other."—*Id. ib.* p. 148.

"Not only the nature of the thoughts and sentiments, but the very selection and arrangement of the words, gives English poetry a character, which separates it widely from common prose."—*Id. ib.* p. 178.

"Men of sound, discriminating, and philosophical minds—men prepared for the work by long study, patient investigation, and extensive acquirements, have labored for ages to improve and perfect it, and nothing is hazarded in asserting, that should it be unwisely abandoned, it will be long before another equal in beauty, stability and usefulness, be produced in its stead."—*Id. ib.* p. 191.

"The Article *The*, on the other hand is used to restrict, and is therefore termed *Definite.* Its proper office is to call the attention to a particular individual or class, or to any number of such, and is used with nouns in either the singular or plural number."—*Id. ib.* p. 193.

"Hence also the infinitive mood, a participle, a member of a sentence, or a proposition, forming together the subject of discourse, or the object of a verb or preposition, and being the name of an act or circumstance, are in construction, regarded as nouns, and are usually called 'substantive phrases;' as '*To play* is pleasant,' '*His being an expert dancer* is no recommendation,' 'Let your motto be *Honesty is the best policy.*'"—*Id. ib.* p. 194.

"In accordance with his definition, Murray has divided verbs into three classes, *Active, Passive,* and *Neuter,* and includes in the first class *transitive* verbs only, and in the last all verbs used *intransitively.*"—*Id. ib.* p. 200.

"Moreover, as the name of the speaker or the person spoken to is seldom expressed, (the pronouns *I* and *thou* being used in its stead,) a noun is very seldom in the first person, not often in the second, and almost never in either, unless it be a proper noun, or a common noun personified."—*Bullions, Pract. Les.* p. 13.

"In using the above exercises it will save much time, which is all important, if the pupil be taught to say every thing belonging to the nouns in the fewest words possible, and to say them always in the same order as above."—*Id. ib.* p. 21.

"In any phrase or sentence the adjectives qualifying a noun may generally be found by prefixing the phrase 'What kind of,' to the noun in the form of a question; as, What kind of a horse? What kind of a stone? What kind of a way? The word containing the answer to the question is an adjective."—*Id. ib.* p. 22.

"In the following exercise let the pupil first point out the nouns, and then the adjectives; and tell how he knows them to be so."—*Id. ib.* p. 23.

"In the following sentences point out the improper ellipsis. Show why it is improper, and correct it."—*Id. ib.* p. 124.

"Singular Pronouns.	Plural Pronouns.
1. I—am being smitten.	1. We—are being smitten.
2. Thou—art being smitten.	2. Ye *or* you—are being smitten.
3. He—is being smitten.	3. They—are being smitten."

Wright's Philos. Gram. p. 98.

CHAPTER II. — UTTERANCE.

Utterance is the art or act of vocal expression. It includes the principles of articulation, of pronunciation, and of elocution.

SECTION I. — OF ARTICULATION.

Articulation is the forming of words, by the voice, with reference to their component letters and sounds.

ARTICLE I. — OF THE DEFINITION.

Articulation differs from pronunciation, in having more particular regard to the elements of words, and in not embracing accent.* A recent author defines it thus: "ARTICULATION is the act of forming, with the organs of speech, the elements of vocal language."—*Comstock's Elocution,* p. 16. And again: "A good articulation is the *perfect* utterance of the elements of vocal language."—*Ibid.*

An other describes it more elaborately thus: "ARTICULATION, in language, is the forming of the human voice, accompanied by the breath, in some few consonants, into the simple and compound sounds, called vowels, consonants, and diphthongs, by the assistance of the organs of speech; and the uniting of those vowels, consonants, and diphthongs, together, so as to form syllables and words, and constitute spoken language."—*Bolles's Dict., Introd.,* p. 7.

ARTICLE II. — OF GOOD ARTICULATION.

Correctness in articulation is of such importance, that without it speech or reading becomes not only inelegant, but often absolutely unintelligible. The opposite faults are mumbling, muttering, mincing, lisping, slurring, mouthing, drawling, hesitating, stammering, misreading, and the like.

"A good articulation consists in giving every letter in a syllable its due proportion of sound, according to the most approved custom of pronouncing it; and in making such a distinction between the syllables of which words are composed, that the ear shall without difficulty acknowledge their number; and perceive, at once, to which syllable each letter belongs. Where these points are not observed, the articulation is proportionably defective."—*Sheridan's Rhetorical Grammar,* p. 50.

Distinctness of articulation depends, primarily, upon the ability to form the simple elements, or sounds of letters, by the organs of speech, in the manner which the custom of the language demands; and, in the next place, upon the avoidance of that precipitancy of utterance, which is greater than the full and accurate play of the organs will allow. If time be not given for the full enunciation of any word which we attempt to speak, some of the syllables will of course be either lost by elision or sounded confusedly.

Just articulation gives even to a feeble voice greater power and reach than the loudest vociferation can attain without it. It delivers words from the lips, not mutilated, distorted, or corrupted, but as the acknowledged sterling currency of thought; —"as beautiful coins newly issued from the mint, deeply and accurately impressed, perfectly finished, neatly struck by the proper organs, distinct, sharp, in due succession, and of due weight."—*Austin's Chironomia,* p. 38.

* "As soon as language proceeds, from mere *articulation,* to coherency, and connection, *accent* becomes the guide of the voice. It is founded upon an obscure perception of symmetry, and proportion, between the different sounds that are uttered."—*Noehden's Grammar of the German Language,* p. 66.

OBS.—The principles of articulation constitute the chief exercise of all those who learning either to speak or to read. So far as they are specifically taught in this, they will be found in those sections which treat of the powers of the letters.

SECTION II. — OF PRONUNCIATION.

Pronunciation, as distinguished from elocution, or delivery, is the utterance of words taken separately. The correct pronunciation of words, or that part of grammar which teaches it, is frequently called *Orthoëpy.*

Pronunciation, or orthoëpy, requires a knowledge of the just powers of the letters in all their combinations; of the distinction of quantity in vowels and syllables; and of the force and seat of the accent.

ARTICLE I. — OF THE POWERS OF LETTERS.

The JUST POWERS of the letters, are those sounds which are given to them by the best readers. These are to be learned, as reading is learned, partly from example, and partly from such books as show or aid the pronunciation of words.

It is to be observed, however, that considerable variety, even in the powers of the letters, is produced by the character and occasion of what is uttered. It is noticed by Walker, that, "Some of the vowels, when neither under the accent, nor closed by a consonant, have a longer or a shorter, an opener or a closer sound, according to the solemnity or familiarity, the deliberation or rapidity of our delivery."—*Pronouncing Dict., Preface*, p. 4. In cursory speech, or in such reading as imitates it, even the best scholars utter many letters with quicker and obscurer sounds than ought ever to be given them in solemn discourse. "In public speaking," says Rippingham, "every word should be uttered, as though it were spoken singly. The solemnity of an oration justifies and demands such scrupulous distinctness. That careful pronunciation which would be ridiculously pedantic in colloquial intercourse, is an essential requisite of good elocution."—*Art of Public Speaking*, p. xxxvii.

ARTICLE II. — OF QUANTITY.

QUANTITY, or TIME, in pronunciation, is the measure of sounds or syllables in regard to their duration; and, by way of distinction, is supposed ever to determine them to be either *long* or *short.**

The absolute time in which syllables are uttered, is very variable, and must be different to suit different subjects, passions, and occasions; but their relative length or shortness may nevertheless be preserved, and generally must be, especially in reciting poetry.

Our long syllables are chiefly those which, having sounds naturally capable of being lengthened at pleasure, are made long by falling under some stress either of accent or of emphasis. Our short syllables are the weaker sounds, which, being the less significant words, or parts of words, are uttered without peculiar stress

OBS.—As quantity is chiefly to be regarded in the utterance of poetical compositions, this subject will be further considered under the head of Versification.

* According to Johnson, Walker, Webster, Worcester, and perhaps all other lexicographers, *Quantity*, in grammar, is—"The measure of *time* in pronouncing a *syllable.*" And, to this main idea, are conformed, so far as I know, all the different definitions ever given of it by grammarians and critics, except that which appeared in Asa Humphrey's English Prosody, published in 1847. In this work—the most elaborate and the most comprehensive, though not the most accurate or consistent treatise we have on the subject—*Time* and *Quantity* are explained separately, as being "*two distinct things;*" and the latter is supposed not to have regard to *duration*, but solely to the *amount* of sound given to each syllable.

This is not only a fanciful distinction, but a radical innovation—and one which, in any view, has little to recommend it. The author's explanations of both *time* and *quantity*—of their characteristics, differences, and subdivisions—of their relations to each other, to poetic numbers, to emphasis and cadence, or to accent and non-accent—as well as his derivation and history of "these technical terms, *time* and *quantity*"—are hardly just or clear enough to be satisfactory. According to his theory, "Poetic numbers are composed of *long* and *short* syllables alternately;" (page 5;) but the difference or proportion between the times of these classes of syllables he holds to be *indeterminable*, "because their lengths are various." He began with destroying the proper distinction of quantity, or time, as being *either long or short*, by the useless recognition of an indefinite number of "*intermediate lengths;*" saying of our syllables at large, "some are LONG, some SHORT, and some are of INTERMEDIATE LENGTHS; as, *mat, not, con*, &c. are short sounds; *mate, note, cone*, and *grave* are long. Some of our diphthongal sounds are LONGER STILL; as, *voice, noise, sound, bound*, &c. OTHERS are seen to be of INTERMEDIATE length."—*Humphrey's Prosody*, p. 4.

On a scheme like this, it must evidently be impossible to determine, with any certainty, either what syllables are *long* and what *short*, or what is the difference or ratio between *any two* of the innumerable "lengths" of *that* time, or quantity, which is *long, short, variously intermediate*, or *longer still*, and again *variously intermediate!* No marvel then that the ingenious author scans some lines in a manner peculiar to himself.

ARTICLE III.—OF ACCENT.

ACCENT, as commonly understood, is the peculiar stress which we lay upon some particular syllable of a word, whereby that syllable is distinguished from and above the rest; as, *gram'-mar, gram-ma'-ri-an.*

Every word of more than one syllable, has one of its syllables accented; and sometimes a compound word has two accents, nearly equal in force; as, *e'ven-hand'ed, home'-depart'ment.*[*]

Besides the chief or *primary* accent, when the word is long, for the sake of harmony or distinctness, we often give a *secondary* or less forcible accent to an other syllable; as, to the last of *tem'-per-a-ture',* and to the second of *in dem'-ni-fi-ca'-tion.*

"Accent seems to be regulated, in a great measure, by etymology. In words from the Saxon, the accent is generally on the root; in words from the learned languages, it is generally on the termination; and if to these we add the different accent we lay on some words, to distinguish them from others, we seem to have the three great principles of accentuation; namely, the radical, the terminational, and the distinctive."— *Walker's Principles,* No. 491 ; *L. Murray's Grammar,* 8vo, p. 236.

A full and open pronunciation of the long vowel sounds, a clear articulation of the consonants, a forcible and well-placed accent, and a distinct utterance of the unaccented syllables, distinguish the elegant speaker.

OBSERVATIONS.

OBS. 1.—The pronunciation of the English language is confessedly very difficult to be mastered. Its rules and their exceptions are so numerous, that few become thoroughly acquainted with any general system of them. Nor, among the different systems which have been published, is there any which is worthy in all respects to be accounted a STANDARD. And, if we appeal to custom, the custom even of the best speakers is far from an entire uniformity. Perhaps the most popular directory on this subject is Walker's Critical Pronouncing Dictionary. The "Principles of English Pronunciation," which this author has furnished, occupy fifty-six closely-printed octavo pages, and are still insufficient for the purpose of teaching our orthoëpy by rule. They are, however, highly valuable, and ought to be consulted by every one who wishes to be master of this subject. In its vocabulary, or stock of words, this Dictionary is likewise deficient. Other lexicographers have produced several later works, of high value to the student; and, though no one has treated the subject of pronunciation so elaborately as did Walker, some may have given the results of their diligence in a form more useful to the generality of their consulters. Among the good ones, is the Universal and Critical Dictionary of Joseph E. Worcester.

OBS. 2.—Our modern accentuation of Greek or Latin words is regulated almost wholly by the noted rule of Sanctius, which Walker has copied and Englished in the Introduction to his Key, and of which the following is a new version or paraphrase, never before printed:

> RULE FOR THE ACCENTING OF LATIN.
>
> *One* syllable has stress of course,
> And words of *two* the *first* enforce;
> In *longer* words the *penult* guides,
> Its *quantity* the point decides;
> If *long,* 'tis *there* the accent's due,
> If *short,* accent the *last but two ;*
> For accent, in a Latin word,
> Should ne'er go higher than the third.

This rule, or the substance of it, has become very important by long and extensive use; but it should be observed, that stress on monosyllables is more properly *emphasis* than *accent;* and that, in English, the accent governs quantity, rather than quantity the accent.

---

[*] It was the doctrine of Sheridan, and perhaps of our old lexicographers in general, that no English word can have more than one *full accent;* but, in some modern dictionaries, as Bolles's, and Worcester's, many words are marked as if they had two; and a few are given by Bolles as having three. Sheridan erroneously affirmed, that "*every word has an accent,*" even "all monosyllables, the particles alone excepted."—*Lectures on Elocution,* pp. 61 and 71. And again, yet more erroneously: "The *essence* of English words consisting in accent, as that of syllables in articulation; we know that there are *as many syllables as we hear articulate sounds,* and *as many words as we hear accents.*"—*Ib.* p. 70. Yet he had said before, in the same lecture: "The longer polysyllables, have frequently *two accents,* but one is so much stronger than the other, as to shew that it is but one word; and the inferior accent is always less forcible, than any accent that is the single one in a word."—*Ib.* p. 61. Wells defines accent as if it might lie on *many* syllables of a word; but, in his examples, he places it on no more than one: "*Accent is the stress* which is laid on *one or more syllables* of a word, in pronunciation; as, *reverberate,* undertake."—*Wells's School Gram.* p. 185. According to this loose definition, he might as well have accented at least one other syllable in each of these examples; for there seems, certainly, to be some little stress on *ate* and *un.* For sundry other definitions of accent, see Chap. IV, Section 2d, of *Versification;* and the marginal note referring to Obs. 1st on *Prosody.*

SECTION III. — OF ELOCUTION.

Elocution is the graceful utterance of words that are arranged into sentences, and form discourse.

Elocution requires a knowledge, and right application, of emphasis, pauses, inflections, and tones.

ARTICLE I. — OF EMPHASIS.

EMPHASIS is the peculiar stress of voice which we lay upon some particular word or words in a sentence, which are thereby distinguished from the rest as being more especially significant.*

As accent enforces a syllable, and gives character to a word; so emphasis distinguishes a word, and often determines the import of a sentence. The right placing of accent, in the utterance of words, is therefore not more important, than the right placing of emphasis, in the utterance of sentences. If no emphasis be used, discourse becomes vapid and inane; if no accent, words can hardly be recognized as English.

"Emphasis, besides its other offices, is the great regulator of quantity. Though the quantity of our syllables is fixed, in words separately pronounced, yet it is mutable, when [the] words are [ar]ranged in[to] sentences; the long being changed into short, the short into long, according to the importance of the words with regard to meaning: and, as it is by emphasis only, that the meaning can be pointed out, emphasis must be the regulator of the quantity."—*L. Murray's Gram.* p. 246.†

"Emphasis changes, not only the quantity of words and syllables, but also, in particular cases, the seat of the accent. This is demonstrable from the following examples: 'He shall *increase*, but I shall *decrease*.' 'There is a difference between giving and *forgiving*.' 'In this species of composition, *plausibility* is much more essential than *probability*.' In these examples, the emphasis requires the accent to be placed on syllables to which it does not commonly belong."—*Ib.* p. 247.

In order to know what words are to be made emphatic, the speaker or reader must give constant heed to *the sense* of what he utters; his only sure guide, in this matter, being a just conception of the force and spirit of the sentiments which he is about to pronounce. He must also guard against the error of multiplying emphatic words too much; for, to overdo in this way, defeats the very purpose for which emphasis is used. To manage this stress with exact propriety, is therefore one of the surest evidences both of a quick understanding, and of a delicate and just taste.

ARTICLE II. — OF PAUSES.

PAUSES are cessations in utterance, which serve equally to relieve the speaker, and to render language intelligible and pleasing.

Pauses are of three kinds: first, *distinctive* or *sentential* pauses,—such as form the divisions required by the sense; secondly, *emphatic* or *rhetorical* pauses,—such as

---

* According to Dr. Rush, Emphasis is—" a stress of voice on one or more words of a sentence, distinguishing them by intensity or peculiarity of meaning."—*Philosophy of the Voice*, p. 282. Again, he defines thus: "Accent is the fixed but inexpressive distinction of syllables *by quantity and stress*: alike both in place and nature, whether the words are pronounced singly from the columns of a vocabulary, or connectedly in the series of discourse. Emphasis may be defined to be the *expressive* but occasional distinction of a syllable, and consequently of the whole word, by one or more of the specific modes of *time, quality, force*, or *pitch*."—*Ibid*.

† 1. This doctrine, though true in its main intent, and especially applicable to the poetic quantity of monosyllables, (the class of words most frequently used in English poetry,) is, perhaps, rather too strongly stated by Murray; because it agrees not with other statements of his, concerning the power of *accent* over quantity; and because the effect of accent, as a "regulator of quantity," *may*, on the whole, be as great as that of emphasis. Sheridan contradicts himself yet more pointedly on this subject; and his discrepancies may have been the efficients of Murray's. " The *quantity* of our syllables is perpetually varying with the sense, and is *for the most part regulated by* EMPHASIS."—*Sheridan's Rhetorical Gram.* p. 65. Again: " It is by the ACCENT *chiefly* that the quantity of our syllables is regulated."—*Sheridan's Lectures on Elocution*, p. 57. See Chap. IV, Sec. 2d, Obs 1 and marginal note on Obs. 8.

2. Some writers erroneously confound *emphasis* with *accent*; especially those who make accent, and not quantity, the foundation of verse. Contrary to common usage, and to his own definition of accent, Wells takes it upon him to say, " The term *accent* is also applied, in poetry, to the stress laid on monosyllabic words; as,

'Content is *wealth*, the riches of the *mind*.'—*Dryden*."—*Wells's School Grammar*, p. 185.

It does not appear that stress laid on monosyllables is any more fitly termed *accent*, when it occurs in the reading of poetry, than when in the utterance of prose. Churchill, who makes no such distinction, thinks accent essential alike to emphasis and to the quantity of a long vowel, and yet, as regards monosyllables, dependent on their both.' His words are these: " Monosyllables are sometimes accented, sometimes not. This depends entirely on their being *more* or *less emphatic*; and on the vowel sound being *long* or *short*. We can, or give *emphasis* to any word, or to [its] proper duration to a *long* vowel, without *accenting*)."—*Churchill's New Gram.* p. 182.

particularly call the hearer's attention to something which has been, or is about to be, uttered ; and lastly, *poetical* or *harmonic* pauses,—such as are peculiar to the utterance of metrical compositions.

The duration of the distinctive pauses should be proportionate to the degree of connexion between the parts of the discourse.   The shortest are long enough for the taking of some breath ; and it is proper, thus to relieve the voice at every stop, if needful.   This we may do, slightly at a comma, more leisurely at a semicolon, still more so at a colon, and completely at a period.

Pauses, whether in reading or in public discourse, ought always to be formed after the manner in which we naturally form them in ordinary, sensible conversation ; and not after the stiff, artificial manner which many acquire at school, by a mere mechanical attention to the common punctuation.

Forced, unintentional pauses, which accidentally divide words that ought to be spoken in close connexion, are always disagreeable ; and, whether they arise from exhaustion of breath, from a habit of faltering, or from unacquaintance with the text, they are errors of a kind utterly incompatible with graceful elocution. .

Emphatic or rhetorical pauses, the kind least frequently used, may be made immediately before, or immediately after, something which the speaker thinks particularly important, and on which he would fix the attention of his audience.   Their effect is similar to that of a strong emphasis ; and, like this, they must not be employed too often.

The harmonic pauses, or those which are peculiar to poetry, are of three kinds : the *final pause*, which marks the end of each line ; the *cæsural* or *divisional pause*, which commonly divides the line near the middle ; and the *minor rests*, or *demi-cæsuras*, which often divide it still further.

In the reading of poetry, these pauses ought to be observed, as well as those which have reference to the sense ; for, to read verse exactly as if it were prose, will often rob it of what chiefly distinguishes it from prose.   Yet, at the same time, all appearance of singsong, or affected tone, ought to be carefully guarded against.

ARTICLE III. — OF INFLECTIONS.

INFLECTIONS are those peculiar variations of the human voice, by which a continuous sound is made to pass from one note, key, or pitch, into an other.   The passage of the voice from a lower to a higher or shriller note, is called the *rising* or *upward* inflection.   The passage of the voice from a higher to a lower or graver note, is called the *falling* or *downward* inflection.   These two opposite inflections may be heard in the following examples : 1. The rising, "Do you mean to *go* ?"   2. The falling, "*When* will you *go* ? "

In general, questions that may be answered by *yes* or *no*, require the rising inflection ; while those which demand any other answer, must be uttered with the falling inflection.   These slides of the voice are not commonly marked in writing, or in our printed books ; but, when there is occasion to note them, we apply the acute accent to the former, and the grave accent to the latter.*

A union of these two inflections upon the same syllable, is called a *circumflex*, a *wave*, or a "*circumflex inflection.*"   When the slide is first downward and then

* Not only are these inflections denoted occasionally by the accentual marks, but they are sometimes expressly *identified with accents*, being called by that name.   This practice, however, is plainly objectionable. It confounds things known to be different,—mere stress with elevation or depression,—and may lead to the supposition, that to accent a syllable, is to inflect the voice upon it.   Such indeed has been the guess of many concerning the nature of Greek and Latin accents, but of the English accent, the common idea is, that it is only a greater force distinguishing some one syllable of a word from the rest.   Walker, however, in the strange account he gives in his Key, of "what we mean by *the accent and quantity* of our own language," charges this current opinion with error, dissenting from Sheridan and Nares, who held it ; and, having asserted, that, "in speaking, the voice is continually *sliding* upwards or downwards," proceeds to contradict himself thus : "As high and low, loud and soft, forcible and feeble, are comparative terms, words of one syllable pronounced alone, and without relation to other words or syllables, *cannot be said to have any* ACCENT.   The only distinction to which such words are liable, is an *elevation or depression* of voice, when we compare the beginning with the end of the word or syllable.   Thus a monosyllable, considered singly, rises from a lower to a higher tone in the question *Nó ? which* may therefore be called *the acute* ACCENT ; and falls from a higher to a lower tone upon the same word in the answer *Nṍ, which* may therefore be called *the grave* [ACCENT.]'—*Walker's Key,* p. 316   Thus he tells of different accents on "a monosyllable,' which, by his own showing, "cannot be said to have any accent' ' and others read and copy the text with as little suspicion of its inconsistency !   See *Worcester's Universal and Critical Dictionary,* p. 134.

upward, it is called the *rising circumflex*, or "the *gravo-acute circumflex*;" wh*
first upward and then downward, it is denominated the *falling circumflex*, or "th
acuto-grave circumflex." Of these complex inflections of the voice, the emph*
words in the following sentences may be uttered as examples : "And it shall go h*
but I will *úse* the information."—"*Ò!* but be *paúsed* upon the brink."

When a passage is read without any inflection, the words are uttered in wh* i
called a *monotone ;* the voice being commonly pitched at a grum note, and ma*
move for the time, slowly and gravely, on a perfect level.

" Rising inflections are far more numerous than falling inflections : the former *
stitute the main body of oral language, while the latter are employed for the purp*
of emphasis, and in the formation of cadences. Rising inflections are often emp*
but their emphasis is weaker than that of falling inflections."—*Comstock's El*
tion, p. 50.

" Writers on Elocution have given numerous rules for the regulation of inflecti*
but most of these rules are better calculated to make *bad* readers than good *
Those founded on the construction of sentences might, perhaps, do credit to a m*
chanic, but they certainly do none to an *elocutionist*."—*Ib.* p. 51.

" The reader should bear in mind that a falling inflection gives more importance *
a word than a rising inflection. Hence it should never be employed merely f* th
sake of *variety ;* but for *emphasis* and *cadences*. Neither should a rising inflect*
be used for the sake of mere ' *harmony*,' where a falling inflection would better *
press the meaning of the author. The *sense* should, in *all* cases, determine the dire*
tion of inflections."—*Ib.*

Cadence is a fall of the voice, which has reference not so much to pitch as to fr*
though it may depress both ; for it seems to be generally contrasted with emp***
and by some is reprehended as a fault. "Support your voice steadily and firm*
says Rippingham, " and pronounce the concluding words of the sentence with fir*
and vivacity, rather than with a languid cadence."—*Art of Speaking*, p. 17.

The pauses which L. Murray denominates the suspending and the closing p*
he seems to have discriminated chiefly by the inflections preceding them, if he c* h
said to have distinguished them at all. For he not only teaches that the form* m*
sometimes be used at the close of a sentence, and the latter sometimes where "*
sense is not completed;" but, treating cadence mainly as a defect, add* the fol*
lowing caution : " The closing pause must not be confounded with that fall of th*
voice, or *cadence*, with which many readers uniformly finish a sentence. Nothing i*
more destructive of propriety and energy than this habit. The tones and inflection*
of the voice at the close of a sentence, ought to be diversified, according to the gene*
nature of the discourse, and the particular construction and meaning of the sentence*
—*Murray's Gram.* 8vo, p. 250 ; 12mo, p. 200.

ARTICLE IV.—OF TONES.

TONES are those modulations of the voice, which depend upon the feelings of *
speaker. They are what Sheridan denominates "the language of emotions." A*
it is of the utmost importance, that they be natural, unaffected, and rightly adapt* *
the subject and to the occasion ; for upon them, in a great measure, depends a* th*
is pleasing or interesting in elocution.

" How much of the propriety, the force, and [the] grace of discourse, must dep*
on these, will appear from this single consideration ; that to almost every senti*
we utter, more especially to every strong emotion, nature has adapted some pec*
tone of voice ; insomuch, that he who should tell another that he was very ang*

* In Humphrey's English Prosody, *cadence* is taken for the reverse of *accent*, and is obviously ident*
confounded with *short quantity*, or what the author inclines to call "*small quantity*." He defines it a* fo*
" Cadence is the reverse or counterpart *to* accent ; a falling or depression of voice on syllables unaccent*
by which the sound is shortened and depressed."—P. 3. This is not exactly what is generally understoo* *
word *cadence*. Lord Kames also contrasts *cadence* with *accent* ; but, by the latter term, he seems to have m*
something different from our ordinary accent. "Sometimes to humour the sense," says he, " and sometim* *
melody, a particular syllable is sounded *in a higher tone* ; and this is termed *accenting a syllable*, or gi* *
with an accent. Opposed to the accent, is the *cadence*, which I have not mentioned as one of the requi* *
verse, because it is entirely regulated by the sense, and hath no peculiar relation to verse."—*Elements of Cr*
Vol. ii, p. 78.

much grieved, in a tone which did not suit such emotions, instead of being believed, would be laughed at."—*Blair's Rhet.* p. 333.

" The different passions of the mind must be expressed by different tones of the voice. *Love*, by a soft, smooth, languishing voice ; *anger*, by a strong, vehement, and ele-vated voice ; *joy*, by a quick, sweet, and clear voice ; *sorrow*, by a low, flexible, in-terrupted voice ; *fear*, by a dejected, tremulous, hesitating voice ; *courage*, by a full, bold, and loud voice ; and *perplexity*, by a grave and earnest voice. In *exordiums*, the voice should be low, yet clear ; in *narrations*, distinct ; in *reasoning*, slow ; in *persuasions*, strong : it should thunder in *anger*, soften in *sorrow*, tremble in *fear*, and melt in *love*."—*Hiley's Gram.* p. 121.

Obs.—Walker observes, in his remarks on the nature of Accent and Quantity, "As to the tones of the passions, which are so many and various, these, in the opinion of one of the best judges in the kingdom, are *qualities* of sound, occasioned by certain vibrations of the organs of speech, independent *on* [say *of*] high, low, loud, soft, quick, slow, forcible, or feeble : which last may not improperly be called different *quantities* of sound."—*Walker's Key*, p. 305.

CHAPTER III.—FIGURES.

A Figure, in grammar, is an intentional deviation from the ordinary spel-ling, formation, construction, or application, of words. There are, accord-ingly, figures of Orthography, figures of Etymology, figures of Syntax, and figures of Rhetoric. When figures are judiciously employed, they both strengthen and adorn expression. They occur more frequently in poetry than in prose ; and several of them are merely poetic licenses.

SECTION I.—FIGURES OF ORTHOGRAPHY.

A Figure of Orthography is an intentional deviation from the ordinary or true spelling of a word. The principal figures of Orthography are two ; namely, *Mi-me'-sis* and *Ar'-cha-ism*.

EXPLANATIONS.

I. *Mimesis* is a ludicrous imitation of some mistake or mispronunciation of a word, in which the error is mimicked by a false spelling ; as, "*Maister*, says he, have you any *very* good *weal* in your *vâllet ?*"—*Columbian Orator*, p. 292. "Ay, he was *porn* at Monmouth, captain Gower."—*Shak.*

"*Perdigious !* I can hardly stand."—LLOYD : *Brit. Poets*, Vol. viii, p. 184.

II. An *Archaism* is a word or phrase expressed according to ancient usage, and not according to our modern orthography ; as, "*Newe grene chese* of *smalle clam-meynes comfortethe* a *hotte stomake.*"—T. PAYNEL : *Tooke's Diversions*, ii, 132.—" He *hath holpen* his servant Israel."—*Luke*, i, 54.

" With him was rev'rend Contemplation *pight*,
   Bow-bent with *eld*, his beard of snowy hue."—*Beattie.*

Obs.—Among the figures of this section, perhaps we might include the *foreign* words or phrases which individual authors now and then adopt in writing English ; namely, the *Scotticisms*, the *Gallicisms*, the *Latinisms*, the *Grecisms*, and the like, with which they too *often* garnish their English style. But these, except they stand as foreign quotations, in which case they are exempt from our rules, are in general offences against the *purity* of our *language* ; and it may therefore be sufficient, just to mention them here, without expressly *putting* any of them into the category of grammatical figures.

SECTION II.—FIGURES OF ETYMOLOGY.

A Figure of Etymology is an intentional deviation from the ordinary forma-*tion* of a word. The principal figures of Etymology are eight ; namely, *A-phær'-e-sis*, *Pros'-the-sis*, *Syn'-co-pe*, *A-poc'-o-pe*, *Par-a-go'-ge*, *Di-œr'-e-sis*, *Syn-œr'-e-sis*, and *Tme'-sis*.

EXPLANATIONS.

I. *Aphæresis* is the elision of some of the initial letters of a word : as, *'gainst*, for *against ; 'gan*, for *began ; 'neath*, for *beneath ; 'thout*, for *without*.

II. *Prosthesis* is the prefixing of an expletive syllable to a word : as, *adown*, for *down ; appaid*, for *paid ; bestrown*, for *strown ; evanished*, for *vanished ; yclad*, for *clad*.

III. *Syn'copè* is the elision of some of the middle letters of a word ; as, *med'cine*, for *medicine ; e'en*, for *even ; o'er*, for *over ; conq'ring*, for *conquering ; se'nnight*, for *sevennight*.

IV. *Apoc'opè* is the elision of some of the final letters of a word : as, *tho'*, for *though ; th'*, for *the ; t'other*, for *the other ; thro'*, for *through*.

V. *Parago'gè* is the annexing of an expletive syllable to a word : as, *Johnny*, for *John ; deary*, for *dear ; withouten*, for *without*.

VI. *Diæresis* is the separating of two vowels that might be supposed to form a diphthong : as, *coöperate*, not *cooperate ; aëronaut*, not *æronaut ; or'thoëpy*, not *orthæpy*.

VII. *Synæresis* is the sinking of two syllables into one : as, *seëst*, for *seëst ; tackèd*, for *tack-ed ; drowned*, for *drown-ed ; spok'st*, for *spok-est ; show'dst*, for *show-edst ; 'tis*, for *it is ; I'll*, for *I will*.

VIII. *Tmesis* is the inserting of a word between the parts of a compound, or between two words which should be united if they stood together : as, " On *which* side *soever*."—*Rolla*. " To *us ward* ; "—" To God *ward*."—*Bible*. " The *assembling* of ourselves *together*."—*Id*. " With *what* charms soe'er she will."—*Cowps*. " So *new* a *fashion'd* robe."—*Shak*. " Lament the *live* day *long*."—*Burns*.

OBS.—In all our pronunciation, except that of the solemn style, such verbal or participial terminations as can be so uttered, are usually sunk by *synæresis* into mere modifications of preceding syllables. The terminational consonants, if not uttered with one vowel, must be uttered with an other. When, therefore, a vowel is entirely suppressed in pronunciation, (whether retained in writing or not,) the consonants connected with it, necessarily fall into an other syllable : thus, *tried, triest, sued, suest, loved, lovest, mov'd, mov'st*, are monosyllables ; and *studied, studiest, studi'dst, argued, arguest, argu'dst*, are dissyllables ; except in solemn discourse, in which the *e* is generally retained and made vocal.

SECTION III.—FIGURES OF SYNTAX.

A Figure of Syntax is an intentional deviation from the ordinary construction of words. The principal figures of syntax are five ; namely, *El-lip'-sis, Ple'-o-nasm, Syl-lep'-sis, En-al'-la-ge*, and *Hy-per'-ba-ton*.

EXPLANATIONS.

I. *Ellipsis* is the omission of some word or words which are necessary to complete the construction, but not necessary to convey the meaning. Such words are said, in technical phrase, to be *understood ;*[*] because they are received as belonging to the sentence, though they are not uttered.

Of compound sentences, a vast many are more or less elliptical ; and sometimes, for brevity's sake, even the most essential parts of a simple sentence, are suppressed :[†] as, " But more of this hereafter."—*Harris's Hermes*, p. 77. This means, "But *I shall say* more of this hereafter." " Prythee, peace."—*Shak*. That is, "*I pray* thee, *hold thou thy* peace."

There may be an omission of any of the parts of speech, or even of a whole clause, when this repeats what precedes ; but the omission of mere articles or interjections can scarcely constitute a proper ellipsis, because these parts of speech, wherever they are really necessary to be recognized, ought to be expressed.

EXAMPLES OF ELLIPSIS SUPPLIED.

1. Of the ARTICLE :— "A man and [a] woman."—"The day, [the] month, and [the

* The Latin term, (made plural to agree with *verba, words*,) is *subaudita, underheard*—the perfect participle of *subaudio*, to *underhear*. Hence the noun, *subauditio, subauditum*, the recognition of ellipses.
† " Thus, in the Proverbs of all Languages, many Words are usually left to be supplied from the trite obvious Nature of what they express ; as, *out of Sight out of Mind ; the more the merrier*, &c."—*W. Ward's Pract Gram*. p. 147.

"—" She gave me an appple and [a] pear, for a fig and [an] orange."—*Jaudon's n.* p. 170.

Of the NOUN:— " The common [*law*] and the statute law."—" The twelve [*apostles*]." The same [*man*] is he."—" One [*book*] of my books."—"A dozen [*bottles*] of wine."— nscience, I say; not thine own [*conscience*], but [*the conscience*] of the other."—1 *Cor.* x, " Every moment subtracts *from* [*our lives*] what it adds *to* our lives."—*Dillwyn's Ref.* . " Bad actions mostly lead to worse " [*actions*].—*Ib.* p. 5.

Of the ADJECTIVE:— "There are subjects proper for the one, and not [*proper*] for the r."—*Kames.* "A just weight and [*a just*] balance are the Lord's."—*Prov.* xvi, 11. True ses of the adjective alone, are but seldom met with.

. Of the PRONOUN:— " Leave [*thou*] there thy gift before the altar, and go [*thou*] thy ;; first be [*thou*] reconciled to thy brother, and then come [*thou*] and offer [*thou*] thy gift." [*att.* v, 24. " Love [*ye*] your enemies, bless [*ye*] them that curse you, do [*ye*] good to them ; hate you."—*Ib.* v, 44. "Chastisement does not always immediately follow error, but sometimes comes when [*it is*] least expected."—*Dillwyn, Ref.* p. 31. "Men generally a greater value upon the favours [*which*] they bestow, than upon those [*which*] they re- e."—*Art of Thinking,* p. 48. " Wisdom and worth were all [*that*] he had."—*Allen's m.* p. 294.

Of the VERB:— " The world is crucified unto me, and I [*am crucified*] unto the ld."—*Gal.* vi, 14. " Hearts should not [*differ*], though heads may, differ."—*Dillwyn,* p. "Are ye not much better than they " [*are*]?—*Matt.* vi, 26. "Tribulation worketh ence ; and patience [*worketh*] experience ; and experience [*worketh*] hope."—*Rom.* v, 4. 'rongs are engraved on marble ; benefits [*are engraved*] on sand."—*Art of Thinking,* p. 41. > whom thus Eve, yet sinless " [*spoke*].—*Milton.*

. Of the PARTICIPLE:— " That [*being*] o'er, they part."—"Animals of various natures, e adapted to the wood, and some [*adapted*] to the wave."—*Melmoth, on Scripture,* p. 13. " His knowledge [*being*] measured to his state and place,
    His time [*being*] a moment, and a point [*being*] his space."—*Pope.*

. Of the ADVERB:— " He can do this independently of me, if not [*independently*] of you." " She shows a body rather than a life;
    A statue, [*rather*] than a breather."—*Shak., Ant. and Cleop.,* iii, 3.

. Of the CONJUNCTION:— " But the fruit of the Spirit is love, [*and*] joy, [*and*] peace, i] long-suffering, [*and*] gentleness, [*and*] goodness, [*and*] faith, [*and*] meekness, [*and*] perance."—*Gal.* v, 22. The repetition of the conjunction is called *Polysyndeton*; and omission of it, *Asyndeton.*

Of the PREPOSITION:— " It shall be done [*on*] this very day."—"We shall set off some time [*in*] next month."—"He departed [*from*] this life."—"He gave [*to*] me a L."—"We walked [*through*] a mile."—"He was banished [*from*] the kingdom."—*W.* n. "He lived like [*to*] a prince."—*Wells.*

). Of the INTERJECTION:— "Oh! the frailty, [*oh !*] the wickedness of men."—"Alas Mexico! and [*alas*] for many of her invaders !"

l. Of PHRASES or CLAUSES:— " The active commonly do more than they are bound to the indolent [*commonly do*] less " [*than they are bound to do*].—"Young men, angry, n less than they say ; old men, [*angry, mean*] more" [*than they say*].—"It is the duty astice, not to injure men ; [*it is the duty*] of modesty, not to offend them."—*W. Allen.*

OBSERVATIONS.

ss. 1.—Grammarians in general treat of ellipsis without *defining* it ; and exhibit such s and examples as suppose our language to be a hundred-fold more elliptical than it really This is a great error, and only paralleled by that of a certain writer elsewhere noticed, denies the existence of all ellipsis whatever.   (See Syntax, Obs. 24th on Rule 22d.) e have defined this figure in a way that betrays a very inaccurate notion of what it is : 'ELLIPSIS is *when* one or more words are wanting *to complete the sense.*"—*Adam's Lat. Eng. Gram.* p. 235 ; *Gould's,* 229. "ELLIPSIS, is the omission of one or more words ssary *to complete the sense.*"—*Bullions, Lat. Gram.* p. 265. These definitions are decid- worse than none ; because, if they have any effect, they can only mislead. They rdly suggest that every elliptical sentence lacks a part of its own meaning ! Ellipsis i fact, the mere omission or absence of certain *suggested words;* or of words that may be ed from utterance, *without defect in the sense.*   There never can be an ellipsis of any g which is either unnecessary to the construction or necessary to the sense ; for to say t we mean and nothing more, never can constitute a deviation from the ordinary gram- cal construction of words.   As a figure of syntax, therefore, the *ellipsis* can only be of words as are so evidently suggested to the reader, that the writer is as fully answer- for them as if he had written them.

ss. 2.—To suppose an ellipsis where there is none, or to overlook one where it really

indley Murray and some others say, "As the ellipsis occurs in almost every sentence in the English language, rous examples of it[might] be given."—*Murray's Gram.* p. 230 ; *Weld's,* 292 ; *Fisk's,* 147. They could, without , have exhibited many true specimens of Ellipsis ; but most of those which they have given, are only fanci- d false ones ; and their notion of the frequency of the figure, is monstrously hyperbolical.

occurs, is to pervert or mutilate the text, in order to accommodate it to the parser's or reader's ignorance of the principles of syntax. There never can be either a general uniformity or a self-consistency in our methods of parsing, or in our notions of grammar, till the true nature of an ellipsis is clearly ascertained; so that the writer shall distinguish it from a *blundering omission* that impairs the sense, and the reader or parser be barred from an *arbitrary insertion* of what would be cumbrous and useless. By adopting loose and extravagant ideas of the nature of this figure, some pretenders to learning and philosophy have been led into the most whimsical and opposite notions concerning the grammatical construction of language. Thus, with equal absurdity, *Cardell* and *Sherman*, in their *Philosophic Grammars*, attempt to confute the doctrines of their predecessors, by supposing *ellipses* at pleasure. And while the former teaches, that prepositions do not govern the objective case, but that every verb is transitive, and governs at least two objects, expressed or *understood*, its own and that of a preposition; the latter, with just as good an argument, contends that no verb is transitive, but that every objective case is governed by a preposition expressed or *understood*. A world of nonsense for lack of a *definition!*

II. PLEONASM is the introduction of superfluous words; as, "But of the tree of the knowledge of good and evil, thou shalt not eat *of it.*"—*Gen.* ii, 17. This figure is allowable only, when, in animated discourse, it abruptly introduces an emphatic word, or repeats an idea to impress it more strongly; as, "*He* that hath ears to hear, let him hear."—*Bible.* "All ye inhabitants of the world, and *dwellers on the earth.*" —*Id.* "There shall not be left one stone upon an other *that shall not be thrown down.*"—*Id.* "I know thee *who thou art.*"—*Id.* A Pleonasm, as perhaps in these instances, is sometimes impressive and elegant; but an unemphatic repetition of the same idea, is one of the worst faults of bad writing.

OBS.—Strong passion is not always satisfied with saying a thing once, and in the fewest words possible; nor is it natural that it should be. Hence repetitions indicative of intense feeling may constitute a beauty of the highest kind, when, if the feeling were wanting, or supposed to be so, they would be reckoned intolerable tautologies. The following is an example, which the reader may appreciate the better, if he remembers the context: "At her feet he bowed, he fell, he lay down; at her feet he bowed, he fell; where he bowed, there he fell down dead."—*Judges,* v, 27.

III. SYLLEPSIS is agreement formed according to the figurative sense of a word, or the mental conception of the thing spoken of, and not according to the literal or common use of the term; it is therefore in general connected with some figure of rhetoric: as, "The *Word* was made flesh, and dwelt amongst us, and we beheld *his* glory."— *John,* i, 14. "Then Philip went down to the *city* of Samaria, and preached Christ unto *them.*"—*Acts,* viii, 5. "The *city* of London *have* expressed *their* sentiments with freedom and firmness."—*Junius,* p. 159. "And I said [to backsliding *Israel,*] after *she* had done all these things, Turn *thou* unto me; but *she* returned not: and *her* treacherous *sister Judah* saw it."—*Jer.* iii, 7. "And he surnamed them *Boanerges, which is,* The sons of thunder."—*Mark,* iii, 17.

"While *Evening* draws *her* crimson curtains round."—*Thomson,* p. 68.
"The *Thunder* raises *his* tremendous voice."—*Id.* p. 113.

OBSERVATIONS.

OBS. 1.—To the parser, some explanation of that agreement which is controlled by tropes, is often absolutely necessary; yet, of our modern grammarians, none appear to have noticed it; and, of the older writers, few, if any, have given it the rank which it deserves among the figures of syntax. The term *Syllepsis* literally signifies *conception, comprehension,* or *taking-together.* Under this name, have been arranged, by the grammarians and rhetoricians, many different forms of unusual or irregular agreement; some of which are quite too unlike to be embraced in the same class, and not a few, perhaps, too unimportant or too ordinary to deserve any classification as figures. I therefore omit some forms of expression which others have treated as examples of *Syllepsis,* and define the term with reference to such as seem more worthy to be noticed as deviations from the ordinary construction of words. Dr. Webster, allowing the word two meanings, explains it thus: "SYLLEPSIS, n. [Gr. συλληψις.] 1. In *grammar,* a figure by which we conceive the sense of words otherwise than the words import, and construe them according to the intention of the author; otherwise called *substitution.*[*] 2. The agreement of a verb or adjective, not with the word next to it, but with the most worthy in the sentence."—*American Dict.*

___
[*] Who besides Webster has called syllepsis "*substitution,*" I do not know. *Substitution* and *conception* are terms of quite different import, and many authors have explained syllepsis by the latter word. Dr. Webster gives to "SUBSTITUTION" two meanings, thus: "1. The act of putting one person or thing in the place of another to

OBS. 2.—In short, *Syllepsis* is a *conception* of which grammarians have *conceived* so variously, that it has become doubtful, what definition or what application of the term is now the most appropriate. Dr. Prat, in defining it, cites one notion from Sanctius, and adds an other of his own, thus: "SYLLEPSIS, id est, *Conceptio*, est quoties Generibus, aut Numeris videntur voces discrepare. Sanct. l. 4. c. 10. Vel sit Comprehensio indignioris sub digniore."—*Prat's Lat. Gram.*, Part ii, p. 164. John Grant ranks it as a mere form or species of *Ellipsis*, and expounds it thus: "*Syllepsis* is *when* the adjective or verb, joined to different substantives, agrees with the more worthy."—*Institutes of Lat. Gram.* p. 321. Dr. Littleton describes it thus: "SYLLEPSIS,—A Grammatical figure *where* two Nominative Cases singular of different persons are joined to a Verb plural."—*Latin Dict.* 4to. By Dr. Morell it is explained as follows: "SYLLEPSIS,—A grammatical figure, *where* one is put for many, and many for one, Lat. *Conceptio*."—*Morell's Ainsworth's Dict.* 4to, Idex Vitand.

IV. *Enállagè* is the use of one part of speech, or of one modification, for an other. This figure borders closely upon solecism; and, for the stability of the language, it should be sparingly indulged. There are, however, several forms of it which can appeal to good authority: as,

1. "*You know* that *you are* Brutus, that *say* this."—*Shak.*
2. "They fall *successive*[ly], and *successive*[ly] rise."—*Pope.*
3. "Than *whom* [who] a fiend more fell is nowhere found."—*Thomson.*
4. "Sure some disaster has *befell*" [befallen].—*Gay.*
5. "So furious was that onset's shock,
    Destruction's gates at once *unlock*" [unlocked].—*Hogg.*

OBSERVATIONS.

OBS. 1.—*Enallage* is a Greek word, signifying *commutation, change,* or *exchange.* "*Enallage,* in a general sense, is the change of words, or of their accidents, one for another."—*Grant's Latin Gram.* p. 322. The word *Antimeria,* which literally expresses *change of parts,* was often used by the old grammarians as synonymous with *Enallage;* though, sometimes, the former was taken only for the substitution of one *part of speech* for an other, and the latter, only, or more particularly, for a change of *modification*—as of mood for mood, tense for tense, or number for number. The putting of one *case* for an other, has also been thought worthy of a particular name, and been called *Antiptosis.* But *Enallage,* the most comprehensive of these terms, having been often of old applied to all such changes, reducing them to one head, may well be now defined as above, and still applied, in this way, to all that we need recognize as figures. The word *Enallaxis,* preferred by some, is of the same import. "ENALLAXIS, so called by *Longinus,* or ENALLAGE, is an *Exchange of Cases, Tenses, Persons, Numbers,* or *Genders.*"—*Holmes's Rhet.* Book i, p. 57.

"An ANALLAXIS changes, when it pleases,
Tenses, or Persons, Genders, Numbers, Cases."—*Ib.* B. ii, p. 60.

OBS. 2.—Our most common form of *Enallage* is that by which a single person is addressed in the plural number. This is so fashionable in our civil intercourse, that some very polite grammarians improperly dispute its claims to be called a *figure;* and represent it as being more ordinary, and even more literal, than the regular phraseology; which a few of them, as we have seen, would place among *archaisms.* The next in frequency, (if indeed it can be called a different form,) is the practice of putting *we* for *I,* or the plural for the singular in the *first* person. This has never yet been claimed as literal and regular syntax, though the usages differ in nothing but commonness; both being honourably authorized, both still improper on some occasions, and, in both, the *Enallage* being alike obvious. Other varieties of this figure, not uncommon in English, are the putting of adjectives for adverbs, of adverbs for nouns, of the present tense for the preterit, and of the preterit for the perfect participle. But, in the use of such liberties, elegance and error sometimes approximate so nearly, there is scarcely an obvious line betwixt them, and grammarians consequently disagree in making the distinction.

OBS. 3.—Deviations of this kind are, *in general,* to be considered solecisms; otherwise, the rules of grammar would be of no use or authority. *Despauter,* an ancient Latin grammarian, gave an improper latitude to this figure, or to a species of it, under the name of *Antiptosis;* and *Behourt* and others extended it still further. But *Sanctius* says, "*Antiptosi grammaticorum nihil imperitius, quod figmentum si esset verum, frustra quaereretur, quem casum verba regerent.*" And the *Messieurs De Port Royal* reject the figure altogether. There are, however, some changes of this kind, which the grammarian is not competent to condemn, though they do not accord with the ordinary principles of construction.

V. *Hyperbaton* is the transposition of words; as, "He wanders *earth around.*" —*Cowper.* "*Rings the world* with the vain stir."—*Id.* "*Whom* therefore ye igno-

---

supply [his or] *its place.*—2. In *grammar,* syllepsis, or the use of one word for another."—*American Dict.* 8vo. This explanation seems to me inaccurate; because it confounds both substitution and syllepsis with *enallage.* It has signs of carelessness throughout; the former sentence being both tautological and ungrammatical.—G. B.

rantly worship, *him declare I* unto you."—*Acts*, xvii, 23.   "'*Happy*,' says *Montesquieu*, '*is that nation* whose annals are tiresome.'"—*Corwin, in Congress*, 1847. This figure is much employed in poetry.   A judicious use of it confers harmony, variety, strength, and vivacity upon composition.   But care should be taken lest it produce ambiguity or obscurity, absurdity or solecism.

OBS.—A confused and intricate arrangement of words, received from some of the ancients the name of *Syn'chysis*, and was reckoned by them among the figures of grammar. By some authors, this has been improperly identified with *Hyper'baton*, or elegant inversion; as may be seen under the word *Synchysis* in Littleton's Dictionary, or in Holmes's Rhetoric, at page 58th. *Synchysis* literally means *confusion*, or *commixtion*; and, in grammar, is significant only of some poetical jumble of words, some verbal *kink* or *snarl*, which cannot be grammatically resolved or disentangled: as,
    "*Is piety* thus *and* pure *devotion* paid?"—*Milton, P. L.*, B. xi, l. 452.
        "An ass will with his long ears fray
         The flies that tickle him, away;
         But man delights to have *his ears*
         Blown maggots in by flatterers."—*Butler's Poems*, p. 161.

SECTION IV.—FIGURES OF RHETORIC.

A Figure of Rhetoric is an intentional deviation from the ordinary application of words.   Several of this kind of figures are commonly called *Tropes*, i. e., *turns;* because certain words are turned from their original signification to an other.[*]

Numerous departures from perfect simplicity of diction, occur in almost every kind of composition.   They are mostly founded on some similitude or relation of things, which, by the power of imagination, is rendered conducive to ornament or illustration.

The principal figures of Rhetoric are sixteen; namely, *Sim'-i-lè, Met-a-phor, Al'-le-go-ry, Me-ton'-y-my, Syn-ec'-do-che, Hy-per'-bo-le, Vis'-ion, A-pos-tro-phe, Per-son'-i-fi-ca'-tion, Er-o-te'sis, Ec-pho-ne'-sis, An-tith'-e-sis, Cli'-max, I'-ro-ny, A-poph'-a-sis,* and *On-o-ma-to-pœ'-ia.*

EXPLANATIONS.

1. A *Simile* is a simple and express comparison; and is generally introduced by *like, as,* or *so: as,* "Such a passion is *like falling in love with a sparrow flying over your head;* you have but one glimpse of her, and she is out of sight."—*Collier's Antoninus*, p. 89.   "Therefore they shall be *as the morning cloud,* and *as the early dew* that passeth away; *as the chaff* that is driven with the whirlwind out of the floor, and *as the smoke* out of the chimney."—*Hosea*, xiii, 3.
        "At first, *like thunder's distant tone,*
         The rattling din came rolling on."—*Hogg*.
        "Man, *like the generous vine,* supported lives;
         The strength he gains, is from th' embrace he gives."—*Pope*.

OBS.—Comparisons are sometimes made in a manner sufficiently intelligible, without any express term to point them out.   In the following passage, we have a triple example of what seems the *Simile*, without the usual sign—without *like, as,* or *so:* "Away with all tampering with such a question!   Away with all trifling with the man in fetters! *Give a hungry man a stone, and tell what beautiful houses are made of it;—give ice to a freezing man,*

---

[*] Between Tropes and Figures, some writers attempt a full distinction; but this, if practicable, is of little use. According to Holmes, "TROPES affect only single *Words*; but FIGURES, whole *Sentences*."—*Rhetoric*, B. i, p. 29. "The CHIEF TROPES in Language," says this author, "are seven; a *Metaphor*, an *Allegory*, a *Metonymy*, a *Synecdoche*, an *Irony*, an *Hyperbole*, and a *Catachresis*."—Ib. p. 30. The term *Figure* or *Figures* is more comprehensive than *Trope* or *Tropes;* I have therefore not thought it expedient to make much use of the latter, in either the singular or the plural form. Holmes's seven tropes are all of them defined in the main text of this section, except *Catachresis,* which is commonly explained to be "an *abuse* of a trope."   According to this sense, it seems in general to differ but little from Impropriety. At best, a Catachresis is a forced expression, though sometimes, perhaps, to be indulged where there is great excitement. It is a sort of figure by which a word is used in a sense different from, yet connected with, or analogous to, its own; as,
        "And pity, like a naked new-born babe,
         Striding the blast, as heaven's cherubim
         Hors'd upon the sightless couriers of the air,
         Shall blow the horrid deed in every eye,
         That tears shall drown the wind."—*Shak., Macbeth*, Act i, Sc. 7.

and tell him of its good properties in hot weather; — throw a drowning man a dollar, as a mark of your good will; — but do not mock the bondman in his misery, by giving him a Bible when he cannot read it."—FREDERICK DOUGLASS: *Liberty Bell*, 1848.

II. A *Metaphor* is a figure that expresses or suggests the resemblance of two objects by applying either the name, or some attribute, adjunct, or action, of the one, directly to the other; as,

1.   " The LORD is my *rock*, and my *fortress*."—*Psal.* xviii. 1.
2.   " His eye was *morning's brightest ray.*"—*Hogg.*
3.   " An *angler* in the *tides* of fame."—*Id.*, *Q. W.*, p. 30.
4.   " Beside him *sleeps* the warrior's bow."—*Langhorne.*
5.   " Wild fancies in his moody brain
        Gambol'd unbridled and unbound."—*Hogg, Q. W.*, p. 90.
6.   " Speechless, and fix'd in all the *death* of wo."—*Thomson.*

OBS.—A *Metaphor* is commonly understood to be only the tropical use of some *single word* or *short phrase;* but there seem to be occasional instances of one *sentence*, or *action*, being used metaphorically to represent an other. The following extract from the London Examiner has several figurative expressions, which perhaps belong to this head: "In the present age, nearly all people are critics, even to the pen, and treat the gravest writers with a sort of *taproom* familiarity. If they are dissatisfied, *they throw a short and spent cigar in the face of the offender:* if they are pleased, *they lift the candidate off his legs, and send him away with a hearty slap on the shoulder.* Some of the shorter, when they are bent to mischief, *dip a twig in the gutter, and drag it across our polished boots:* on the contrary, when they are inclined to be gentle and generous, *they leap boisterously upon our knees, and kiss us* with bread-and-butter in their mouths."—WALTER SAVAGE LANDOR.

III. An *Allegory* is a continued narration of fictitious events, designed to represent and illustrate important realities. Thus the Psalmist represents the *Jewish nation* under the symbol of a *vine:* "Thou hast brought a vine out of Egypt: thou hast cast out the heathen, and planted it. Thou preparedst room before it, and didst cause it to take deep root, and it filled the land. The hills were covered with the shadow of it, and the boughs thereof were like the goodly cedars."—*Psalms*, lxxx, 8—10.

OBS.—The *Allegory*, agreeably to the foregoing definition of it, includes most of those similitudes which in the Scriptures are called *parables;* it includes also the better sort of *fables.* The term *allegory* is sometimes applied to a *true history* in which something else is intended, than is contained in the words literally taken. See an instance in *Galatians*, iv, 24. In the *Scriptures*, the term *fable* denotes an idle and groundless story: as in 1 *Timothy*, iv, 7; and 2 *Peter*, i, 16. It is now commonly used in a better sense. "A *fable* may be defined to be an analogical narrative, intended to convey some moral lesson, in which irrational animals or objects are introduced as speaking."—*Philological Museum*, Vol. i, p. 280.

IV. A *Metonymy* is a change of names between things related. It is founded, not on resemblance, but on some such relation as that of *cause* and *effect*, of *progenitor* and *posterity*, of *subject* and *adjunct*, of *place* and *inhabitant*, of *container* and *thing contained*, or of *sign* and *thing signified:* as, (1.) "God is our *salvation;*" i. e., *Saviour.* (2.) "Hear, O *Israel;*" i. e., O *ye descendants of* Israel. (3.) "He was the *sigh* of her secret soul;" i. e., the *youth* she loved. (4.) "They smote the *city;*" i. e., the *citizens.* (5.) "My son, give me thy *heart;*" i. e., *affection.* (6.) "The *sceptre* shall not depart from Judah;" i. e., *kingly power.* (7.) "They have *Moses and the prophets;*" i. e., *their writings.* See *Luke*, xvi, 29.

V. *Synecdoche*, (that is, *Comprehension*,) is the naming of a part for the whole, as of the whole for a part; as, (1.) "This *roof* [i. e., house] protects you." (2.) "Now the *year* [i. e., summer] is beautiful." (3.) "A *sail* [i. e., a ship or vessel] passed at a distance." (4.) "Give us this day our daily *bread;*" i. e., food. (5.) "Because they have taken away *my Lord*, [i. e., the body of Jesus,] and I know not where they have laid him."—*John.* (6.) "The same day there were added unto them about three thousand *souls;*" i. e., persons.—*Acts.* (7.) "There went out a decree from Cæsar Augustus, that all *the world* [i. e., the Roman empire] should be taxed."—*Luke*, ii, 1.

VI. *Hyperbole* is extravagant exaggeration, in which the imagination is indulged beyond the sobriety of truth; as, "My little finger *shall be thicker* than my father's loins."—2 *Chron.* x, 10.   "When I washed my *steps* *with* *butter*, and the rock poured me out *rivers of oil*."—*Job*, xxix, 6.

"The sky *shrunk upward with unusual dread*,
And trembling Tiber *div'd beneath his bed*."—*Dryden*.

VII. *Vision*, or *Imagery*, is a figure by which the speaker represents the objects of his imagination, as actually before his eyes, and present to his senses; as,

"I see the dagger-crest of Mar!
I see the Moray's silver star
Wave o'er the cloud of Saxon war,
That up the lake comes winding far!"—*Scott, L. L.*, vi, 15.

VIII. *Apostrophe* is a turning from the regular course of the subject, into an animated address; as, "Death is swallowed up in victory.   O Death! where is thy sting? O Grave! where is thy victory?"—1 *Cor.* xv, 55.

IX. *Personification* is a figure by which, in imagination, we ascribe intelligence and personality to unintelligent beings or abstract qualities; as,

1. "The *Worm*, aware of his intent,
Harangued him thus, right eloquent."—*Cowper*.
2. "Lo, steel-clad *War* his gorgeous standard rears!"—*Rogers*.
3. "Hark! *Truth* proclaims, thy triumphs cease!"—*Idem*.

X. *Erotesis* is a figure in which the speaker adopts the form of interrogation, not to express a doubt, but, in general, confidently to assert the reverse of what is asked; as, "Hast thou an arm like God? or canst thou thunder with a voice like him?"— *Job*. xl, 9.   "He that planted the ear, shall he not hear? he that formed the eye, shall he not see?"—*Psalms*, xciv, 9.

XI. *Ecphonesis* is a pathetic exclamation, denoting some violent emotion of the mind; as, "O liberty!—O sound once delightful to every Roman ear!—O sacred privilege of Roman citizenship!—once sacred—now trampled upon."—*Cicero*.   "And I said, O that I had wings like a dove! for then would I fly away, and be at rest."— *Psalms*, lv, 6.

XII. *Antithesis* is a placing of things in opposition, to heighten their effect by contrast; as, "I will talk of things *heavenly*, or things *earthly*; things *moral*, or things *evangelical*; things *sacred*, or things *profane*; things *past*, or things *to come*; things *foreign*, or things *at home*; things more *essential*, or things *circumstantial*; provided that all be done to our profit."—*Bunyan, P. P.*, p. 90.

"Contrasted faults through all his manners reign;
Though *poor, luxurious*; though *submissive*, vain;
Though *grave*, yet *trifling*; *zealous*, yet *untrue*;
And e'en *in penance, planning sins* anew."—*Goldsmith*.

XIII. *Climax* is a figure in which the sense is made to advance by successive steps, to rise gradually to what is more and more important and interesting, or to descend to what is more and more minute and particular; as, "And besides this, giving all diligence, add to your faith, virtue; and to virtue, knowledge; and to knowledge, temperance; and to temperance, patience; and to patience, godliness; and to godliness, brotherly kindness; and to brotherly kindness, charity."—2 *Peter*, i, 5.

XIV. *Irony* is a figure in which the speaker sneeringly utters the direct reverse of what he intends shall be understood; as, "We have, to be sure, great reason to believe the modest man would not ask him for a debt, when he pursues his life."— *Cicero*.   "No doubt but ye are the people, and wisdom shall die with you."—*Job*, xii, 2.   "They must esteem learning *very much*, when they see its professors used with such little ceremony!"—*Goldsmith's Essays*, p. 150.

XV. *Apophasis*, or *Paralipsis*,* is a figure in which the speaker or writer pretends to omit what at the same time he really mentions; as, "I Paul have written it with

* Holmes, in his Art of Rhetoric, writes this word "Paraleipsis," retaining the Greek orthography.   So does Fowler in his recent "English Grammar," § 646.   Webster, Adam, and some others, write it "Paralepsis."   I write it as above on the authority of Littleton, Ainsworth, and some others; and this is according to the analogy of the kindred word *ellipsis*, which we never write either *elleipsis*, or, as the Greek, *ellepsis*.

mine own hand, I will repay it; albeit *I do not say to thee*, how thou owest unto me even thine own self besides."—*Philemon*, 19.

XVI. *Onomatopœia* is the use of a word, phrase, or sentence, the sound of which resembles, or intentionally imitates, the sound of the thing signified or spoken of: as, " Of a knocking at the door, *Rat a tat tat*."—*Fowler's Gram.* p. 334. "*Ding-dong! ding-dong!* Merry, merry, go the bells, *Ding-dong! ding-dong!* "—*H. K. White*. " Bow'wow, *n.* The loud bark of a dog. *Booth.*"—*Worcester's Dict.* This is often written separately; as, "*Bow wow*."—*Fowler's Gram.* p. 334. The imitation is better with three sounds: "*Bow wow wow*." The following verses have been said to exhibit this figure :—

> " But when loud surges lash the sounding shore,
> The hoarse rough verse should like the torrent roar."—*Pope, on Crit.* l. 369.

OBS.—The whole number of figures, which I have thought it needful to define and illustrate in this work, is only about thirty. These are the *chief* of what have sometimes been made a very long and minute catalogue. In the hands of some authors, Rhetoric is scarcely anything else than a detail of figures ; the number of which, being made to include almost every possible form of expression, is, according to these authors, not less than two hundred and forty. Of their *names*, John Holmes gives, in his index, two hundred and fifty-three ; and he has not all that might be quoted, though he has more than there are of the forms named, or the figures themselves. To find a learned name for every particular mode of expression, is not necessarily conducive to the right use of language. It is easy to see the inutility of such pedantry : and Butler has made it sufficiently ridiculous by this caricature :

> " For all a rhetorician's rules
> Teach nothing but to name his tools."—*Hudibras*, P. i, C. i, l. 90.

SECTION V.— EXAMPLES FOR PARSING.

PRAXIS XIV. — PROSODICAL.

In the Fourteenth Praxis, are exemplified the several Figures of Orthography, of Etymology, of Syntax, and of Rhetoric, which the parser may name and define ; and by it the pupil may also be exercised in relation to the principles of Punctuation, Utterance, Analysis, or whatever else of Grammar the examples contain.

LESSON I.—FIGURES OF ORTHOGRAPHY.

MIMESIS AND ARCHAISM.

" I *ax'd* you what you had to sell. I am fitting out a *wessel* for *Wenice*, loading her with *warious keinds* of *prowisions*, and *wittualling* her for a long *woyage;* and I want several *undred* weight of *weal, wenison*, &c., with plenty of *inyons* and *winegar*, for the *preservation* of *ealth*."—*Columbian Orator*, p. 292

" God bless you, and lie still quiet (*says* I) a bit longer, for my *shister's* afraid of ghosts, and would die on the spot with the fright, *was* she to see you come to life all on a sudden this way without the least preparation."—*Edgeworth's Castle Rackrent*, p. 143.

" None [else are] so desperately *evill*, as they that may *bee* good and will not : or have *beene* good and are not."—*Rev. John Rogers*, 1620. "A Carpenter finds his work as *hee* left it, but a minister shall find his *sett* back. You need preach continually."—*Id.*

> " Here *whilom ligg'd* th' Esopus of his age,
> But call'd by Fame, in soul *ypricked* deep."—*Thomson.*

> " It was a fountain of Nepenthe rare,
> Whence, as Dan Homer sings, huge *pleasaunce* grew."—*Id.*

LESSON II.—FIGURES OF ETYMOLOGY.

APHÆRESIS, PROSTHESIS, SYNCOPE, APOCOPE, PARAGOGE, DIERESIS, SYNÆRESIS, AND TMESIS.

> " Bend '*gainst* the steepy hill thy breast,
> Burst down like torrent from its crest."—*Scott.*

> " '*Tis* mine to teach *th*' inactive hand to reap
> Kind nature's bounties, *o'er* the globe *diffus'd*."—*Dyer.*

56

"Alas ! alas ! how impotently true
   Th' aërial pencil forms the scene anew."—*Cawthorne.*
" Here a deformed monster *joy'd* to won,
   Which on fell rancour ever was *ybent.*"—*Lloyd.*
" *Withouten* trump was proclamation made."—*Thomson.*
" The gentle knight, who saw their rueful case,
   Let fall *adown* his silver beard some tears.
   ' Certes,' quoth he, ' it is not *e'en* in grace,
   T' undo the past and eke your broken years."—*Id.*
" Vain *tamp'ring* has but *foster'd* his disease ;
   'Tis desp'rate, and he sleeps the sleep of death."—*Cowper.*
" ' I have a pain upon my forehead here '—
   ' Why *that's* with watching ; *'twill* away again.' "—*Shakspeare.*
" I'll to the woods, among the happier brutes;
   Come, *let's* away ; hark ! the shrill horn resounds."—*Smith.*
" *What* prayer and supplication *soever* be made."—*Bible.* " By the grace of G
we have had our conversation in the world, and more abundantly *to* you *ward.*"—

LESSON III.—FIGURES OF SYNTAX.
FIGURE I.—ELLIPSIS.

"And now he faintly kens the bounding fawn,
   And [—] villager [—] abroad at early toil."—*Beattie.*
" The cottage curs at [—] early pilgrim bark."—*Id.*
" 'Tis granted, and no plainer truth appears,
   Our most important [—] are our earliest years."—*Cowper.*
" To earn her aid, with fix'd and anxious eye,
   He looks on nature's [—] and on fortune's course."—*Akenside.*
" For longer in that paradise to dwell,
   The law [—] I gave to nature him forbids."—*Milton.*
" So little mercy shows [—] who needs so much."—*Cowper.*
" Bliss is the same [—] in subject, as [—] in king ;
   In [—] who obtain defence, and [—] who defend."—*Pope.*
" Man made for kings ! those optics are but dim
   That tell you so—say rather, they [—] for him."—*Cowper.*
" Man may dismiss compassion from his heart,
   But God will never [———————]."—*Id.*
" Vigour [—] from toil, from trouble patience grows."—*Beattie.*
" Where now the rill melodious, [—] pure, and cool,
   And meads, with life, and mirth, and beauty crown'd ?"—*Id.*
" How dead the vegetable kingdom lies !
   How dumb the tuneful [———————] !"—*Thomson.*
" Self-love and Reason to one end aspire,
   Pain [—] their aversion, pleasure [—] their desire ;
   But greedy that its object would devour,
   This [—] taste the honey, and not wound the flower."—*Pope.*

LESSON IV.—FIGURES OF SYNTAX.
FIGURE II.—PLEONASM.

"*According* to their deeds, *accordingly* he will *repay,* fury to his adversaries. re
ompense to his enemies ; to the islands he will repay recompense."—*Isaiah,* lix. :
" Open to me, my sister, my love, my dove, my undefiled : for my head is filled w
dew, *and my locks with the drops of the night.*"—*Song of Sol.* v, 2. " Thou
chastised me, *and I was chastised,* as a bullock unaccustomed to the yoke : turn :
me, *and I shall be turned ;* for thou art the Lord my God."—*Jer.* xxx, 18. " C
sider the *lilies* of the field how *they* grow."—*Matt.* vi, 28. "*He* that glorieth
him glory in the Lord."—2 *Cor.* x, 17.
    "*He* too is witness, noblest of the train
      That wait on man, the flight-performing horse."—*Cowper.*

FIGURE III.—SYLLEPSIS.

" ' Thou art Simon the son of Jona : thou shalt be called *Cephas ;* ' *which* is, by interpretation, a stone."—*John*, i, 42. " Thus saith the Lord of hosts, ' Behold, I will break the bow of *Elam*, the chief of *their* might.' "—*Jer.* xlix, 35. " Behold, I lay in Sion a *stumbling-stone* and *rock* of offence : and whosoever believeth on *him* shall not be ashamed."—*Rom.* ix, 33.

" Thus *Conscience* pleads *her* cause within the breast,
Though long rebell'd against, not yet suppress'd."—*Cowper.*

"*Knowledge* is proud that *he* has learn'd so much ;
Wisdom is humble that *he* knows no more."—*Id.*

" For those the *race* of Israel oft forsook
Their living *strength*, and unfrequented left
His righteous altar, bowing lowly down
To bestial gods."—*Milton, Paradise Lost,* B. i, l. 432.

LESSON V.—FIGURES OF SYNTAX.

FIGURE IV.—ENALLAGE.

" Let me tell *you*, Cassius, *you* yourself
Are much condemned to have an itching palm,
To sell and mart *your* offices for gold."—*Shakspeare.*

" Come, Philomelus ; let us *instant* go,
O'erturn his bow'rs, and lay his castle low."—*Thomson.*

" Then palaces shall rise ; the joyful son
Shall finish what the short-liv'd sire *begun.*"—*Pope.*

" Such was that temple built by Solomon,
Than *whom* none richer reign'd o'er Israel."—*Author.*

" He spoke : with fatal eagerness we *burn*,
And *quit* the shores, undestin'd to return."—*Day.*

" Still as he pass'd, the nations he *sublimes.*"—*Thomson.*

" Sometimes, with early morn, he mounted *gay.*"—*Id.*

" ' I've lost a day '—the prince who nobly cried,
Had been an emperor without his crown."—*Young.*

FIGURE V.—HYPERBATON.

" Such *resting* found *the sole* of unblest feet."—*Milton.*

" Yet, though successless, *will the toil* delight."—*Thomson.*

" Where, 'midst the changeful scen'ry ever new,
Fancy a thousand wondrous *forms* descries."—*Beattie.*

" Yet so much bounty is in God, such grace,
That who advance his glory, not their own,
Them he himself to glory will advance."—*Milton.*

" No quick *reply* to dubious questions make ;
Suspense and caution still prevent mistake."—*Denham.*

LESSON VI.—FIGURES OF RHETORIC.

FIGURE I.—SIMILE.

" Human greatness is short and transitory, *as the odour of incense in the fire.*"—r. *Johnson.* " Terrestrial happiness is of short continuance : *the brightness of the xme is wasting its fuel, the fragrant flower is passing away in its own odours.*"—" Thy nod is *as the earthquake that shakes the mountains ;* and thy smile, *as* e *dawn of the vernal day.*"—*Id.*

"*Plants rais'd with tenderness are seldom strong ;*
Man's coltish disposition asks the thong ;
And, without discipline, the fav'rite child,
Like a neglected forester, runs wild."—*Cowper.*

"As turns a flock of geese, and, on the green,
Poke out their foolish necks in awkward spleen,
(Ridiculous in rage !) to *hiss,* not *bite,*
So war their quills, when sons of *dulness* write."—*Young.*

" Who can unpitying see the flowery race,
    Shed by the morn, their new-flush'd bloom resign,
    Before th' unbating beam ? *So fade the fair,*
    When fevers revel through their azure veins."—*Thomson.*

FIGURE II.—METAPHOR.

" Cathmon, thy name is a pleasant *gale.*"—*Ossian.*   " Rolled into himself he
flew, wide on the *bosom of winds.* The old *oak felt* his departure, and *shook* its
whistling *head.*"—*Id.*   " Carazan gradually lost the inclination to do good, as he
acquired the power ; as the *hand of time* scattered *snow* upon his head, the *freezing
influence* extended to his bosom."—*Hawkesworth.*   " The sun *grew weary* of gilding the palaces of Morad ; the *clouds of sorrow* gathered round his head ; and *the
tempest of hatred* roared about his dwelling."—*Dr. Johnson.*

LESSON VII.—FIGURES OF RHETORIC.

FIGURE III.—ALLEGORY.

" But what think ye ? A certain man had two sons; and he came to the first, and
said, ' Son, go work to-day in my vineyard.'   He answered and said, ' I will not;'
but afterward he repented, and went.   And he came to the second, and said likewise.
And he answered and said, ' I go, sir ;' and went not.   Whether of them twain did
the will of his father ? They say unto him, ' The first. ' "—*Matt.* xxi, 28—31.

FIGURE IV.—METONYMY.

" Swifter than a whirlwind, flies the leaden *death.*"—*Hervey.*   " ' Be all the dead
forgot,' said Foldath's bursting *wrath.*   ' Did not I fail in the field ?' "—*Ossian.*

" Their *furrow* oft the stubborn glebe has broke."—*Gray.*

" Firm in his love, resistless in his hate,
    His arm is *conquest,* and his frown is *fate.*"—*Day.*

"At length the *world,* renew'd by calm repose,
    Was strong for toil ; the dappled morn arose."—*Parnell.*

" What modes of sight betwixt each wide extreme,
    The mole's dim curtain and the lynx's *beam !*
    Of hearing, from the *life* that fills the flood,
    To *that* which warbles through the vernal wood !"—*Pope.*

FIGURE V.—SYNECDOCHE.

" 'Twas then his *threshold* first receiv'd a guest."—*Parnell.*

" For yet by swains alone the world he knew,
    Whose *feet* came wand'ring o'er the nightly dew."—*Id.*

" Flush'd by the spirit of the genial *year,*
    Now from the virgin's cheek a fresher bloom
    Shoots, less and less, the live carnation round."—*Thomson.*

LESSON VIII.—FIGURES OF RHETORIC.

FIGURE VI.—HYPERBOLE.

" I saw their chief, tall as a rock of ice ; his spear, the blasted fir ; his shield the
rising moon ; he sat on the shore, like a cloud of mist on the hill."—*Ossian.*

"At which the universal host up sent
    A shout, that tore Hell's concave, and beyond
    Frighted the reign of Chaos and old Night."—*Milton.*

" Will all great Neptune's ocean wash this blood
    Clean from my hand ? No ; this my hand will rather
    The multitudinous seas incarnadine,
    Making the green one red ! "—*Shakspeare.*

FIGURE VII.—VISION.

" How mighty is their defence who reverently trust in the arm of God ! How powerfully do they contend who fight with lawful weapons ! Hark ! 'Tis the voice of
eloquence, pouring forth the living energies of the soul ; pleading, with generous
indignation and holy emotion, the cause of injured humanity against lawless might.

and reading the awful destiny that awaits the oppressor !—I see the stern countenance of despotism overawed ! I see the eye fallen, that kindled the elements of war ! I see the brow relaxed, that scowled defiance at hostile thousands ! I see the knees tremble, that trod with firmness the embattled field ! Fear has entered that heart which ambition had betrayed into violence ! The tyrant feels himself a man, and subject to the weakness of humanity !—Behold ! and tell me, is that power contemptible which can thus find access to the sternest hearts ? "—*Author.*

FIGURE VIII.—APOSTROPHE.

" Yet still they breathe destruction, still go on,
  Inhumanly ingenious to find out
  New pains for life, new terrors for the grave ;
  Artificers of death ! Still monarchs dream
  Of universal empire growing up
  From universal ruin. *Blast the design,*
  Great God of Hosts ! nor let thy creatures fall
  Unpitied victims at Ambition's shrine."—*Porteus.*

LESSON IX.—FIGURES OF RHETORIC.

FIGURE IX.—PERSONIFICATION.

" Hail, sacred *Polity*, by *Freedom* rear'd !
  Hail, sacred *Freedom*, when by *Law* restrain'd !
  Without you, what were man ? A grov'ling herd,
  In darkness, wretchedness, and want, enchain'd."—*Beattie.*

" Let cheerful *Mem'ry*, from her purest cells,
  Lead forth a goodly train of *Virtues* fair,
  Cherish'd in early youth, now paying back
  With tenfold usury the pious care."—*Porteus.*

FIGURE X.—EROTESIS.

" He that chastiseth the heathen, shall not he correct ? He that teacheth man knowledge, shall not he know ? "—*Psal.* xciv, 10. " Can the Ethiopian change his skin, or the leopard his spots ? then may ye also do good, that are accustomed to do evil."—*Jeremiah,* xiii, 23.

FIGURE XI.—ECPHONESIS.

" O that my head were waters, and mine eyes a fountain of tears, that I might weep day and night for the slain of the daughter of my people ! O that I had in the wilderness a lodging place of way-faring men, that I might leave my people, and go from them ! "—*Jeremiah,* ix, 1.

FIGURE XII.—ANTITHESIS.

" On this side, modesty is engaged ; on that, impudence : on this, chastity ; on that, lewdness : on this, integrity ; on that, fraud : on this, piety ; on that, profaneness : on this, constancy ; on that, fickleness : on this, honour ; on that, baseness : on this, moderation ; on that, unbridled passion."—*Cicero.*

" She, from the rending earth, and bursting skies,
  Saw gods descend, and fiends infernal rise ;
  Here fix'd the dreadful, there the blest abodes ;
  Fear made her devils, and weak hope her gods."—*Pope.*

LESSON X.—FIGURES OF RHETORIC.

FIGURE XIII.—CLIMAX.

" Virtuous actions are necessarily approved by the awakened conscience ; and when they are approved, they are commended to practice ; and when they are practised, they become easy ; and when they become easy, they afford pleasure ; and when they afford pleasure, they are done frequently ; and when they are done frequently, they are confirmed by habit : and confirmed habit is a kind of second nature."—*Inst.* p. 246.

" Weep all of every name : begin the wo,
  Ye woods, and tell it to the doleful winds ;

And doleful winds, wail to the howling hills;
And howling hills, mourn to the dismal vales;
And dismal vales, sigh to the sorrowing brooks;
And sorrowing brooks, weep to the weeping stream;
And weeping stream, awake the groaning deep;
And let the instrument take up the song,
Responsive to the voice—harmonious wo!"—*Pollok*, B. vi, l. 115.

FIGURE XIV.—IRONY.

"And it came to pass at noon, that Elijah mocked them, and said, ' Cry aloud; for he is a god: either he is talking, or he is pursuing, or he is in [*on*] a journey, or peradventure he sleepeth, and must be awaked!'"—1 *Kings*, xviii, 27.

"After the number of the days in which ye searched the land, even forty days, each day for a year, shall ye bear your iniquities, even forty years; and ye shall know my breach of promise."—*Numbers*, xiv, 34.

" Some lead a life unblamable and just,
Their own dear virtue their unshaken trust;
They never sin—or if (as all offend)
Some trivial slips their daily walk attend,
The poor are near at hand, the charge is small,
A slight gratuity atones for all."—*Cowper*.

FIGURE XV.—APOPHASIS, OR PARALIPSIS.

I say nothing of the notorious profligacy of his character; nothing of the reckless extravagance with which he has wasted an ample fortune; nothing of the disgusting intemperance which has sometimes caused him to reel in our streets;—but I aver that he has not been faithful to our interests,—has not exhibited either probity or ability in the important office which he holds.

FIGURE XVI.—ONOMATOPŒIA.

☞ [The following lines, from Swift's Poems, satirically mimick the imitative music of a violin.]

" Now slowly move your fiddle-stick;
Now, tantan, tantantivi, quick;
Now trembling, shivering, quivering, quaking,
Set hoping hearts of Lovers aching."

" Now sweep, sweep the deep.
See Celia, Celia dies,
While true Lovers' eyes
Weeping sleep, Sleeping weep,
Weeping sleep, Bo-peep, bo-peep."

CHAPTER IV.—VERSIFICATION.

Versification is the forming of that species of literary composition which is called *verse;* that is, *poetry*, or *poetic numbers*.

SECTION I.—OF VERSE.

Verse, in opposition to prose, is language arranged into metrical lines of some determinate length and rhythm—language so ordered as to produce harmony, by a due succession of poetic feet, or of syllables differing in quantity or stress.

DEFINITIONS AND PRINCIPLES.

The *rhythm* of verse is its relation of quantities; the modulation of its numbers; or, the kind of metre, measure, or movement, of which it consists, or by which it is particularly distinguished.

The *quantity* of a syllable, as commonly explained, is the relative portion of time occupied in uttering it. In poetry, every syllable is considered to be either long or short. A long syllable is usually reckoned to be equal to two short ones.

In the construction of English verse, long quantity coincides always with the primary accent, generally also with the secondary, as well as with emphasis; and short quantity, as reckoned by the poets, is found only in unaccented syllables, and unemphatical monosyllabic words.*

The quantity of a syllable, whether long or short, does not depend on what is called the long or the short sound of a vowel or diphthong, or on a supposed distinction of accent as affecting vowels in some cases and consonants in others, but principally on the degree of energy or loudness with which the syllable is uttered, whereby a greater or less portion of time is employed.

The open vowel sounds, which are commonly but not very accurately termed *long,* are those which are the most easily protracted, yet they often occur in the shortest and feeblest syllables; while, on the other hand, no vowel sound, that occurs under the usual stress of accent or of emphasis, is either so short in its own nature, or is so "quickly joined to the succeeding letter," that the syllable is not one of long quantity.

Most monosyllables, in English, are variable in quantity, and may be made either long or short, as strong or weak sounds suit the sense and rhythm; but words of greater length are, for the most part, fixed, their accented syllables being always long, and a syllable immediately before or after the accent almost always short.

One of the most obvious distinctions in poetry, is that of rhyme and blank verse. *Rhyme* is a similarity of sound, combined with a difference; occurring usually between the last syllables of different lines, but sometimes at other intervals; and so ordered that the rhyming syllables begin differently and end alike. *Blank verse* is verse without rhyme.

The principal rhyming syllables are almost always long. Double rhyme adds one short syllable; triple rhyme, two. Such syllables are redundant in iambic and anapestic verses; in lines of any other sort, they are generally, if not always, included in the measure.

A *Stanza* is a combination of several verses, or lines, which, taken together, make a regular division of a poem. It is the common practice of good versifiers, to form all stanzas of the same poem after one model. The possible variety of stanzas is infinite; and the actual variety met with in print is far too great for detail.

OBSERVATIONS.

OBS. 1.—*Verse,* in the broadest acceptation of the term, is poetry, or metrical language, in general. This, to the eye, is usually distinguished from prose by the manner in which it is written and printed. For, in very many instances, if this were not the case, the reader would be puzzled to discern the difference. The division of poetry into its peculiar lines, is therefore not a mere accident. The word *verse,* from the Latin *versus,* literally signifies a *turning.* Each full line of metre is accordingly called *a verse;* because, when its measure is complete, the writer *turns* to place an other under it. A *verse,* then, in the primary sense of the word with us, is, "A *line* consisting of a certain succession of sounds, and number of syllables."—*Johnson, Walker, Todd, Bolles,* and others. Or, according to *Webster,* it is, "A poetic *line,* consisting of a certain number of long and short syllables, disposed according to the rules of the species of poetry which the author intends to compose."—See *American Dict.* 8vo.

OBS. 2.—If to settle the theory of English verse on true and consistent principles, is as difficult a matter, as the manifold contrarieties of doctrine among our prosodists would indicate, there can be no great hope of any scheme entirely satisfactory to the intelligent examiner. The very elements of the subject are much perplexed by the incompatible dogmas of authors deemed skilful to elucidate it. It will scarcely be thought a hard matter to distinguish true verse from prose, yet is it not well agreed wherein the difference consists: what the generality regard as the most essential elements or characteristics of the former, some respectable authors dismiss entirely from their definitions of both verse and versification. The existence of quantity in our language; the dependence of our rhythms on the division of syllables into long and short; the concurrence of our accent, (except in some rare and questionable instances,) with long quantity only; the constant effect of emphasis to lengthen quantity; the limitation of quantity to mere duration of sound; the doctrine that quantity

---

* To this principle there seems to be now and then an exception, as when a weak dissyllable begins a foot in an anapestic line, as in the following examples:

      "I think—let me see—yes, it is, I declare,
       As long *ago now* as that Buckingham there."—*Leigh Hunt.*
      "And Thomson, though best in his indolent fits,
       Either slept blumself weary, or blasted his wits."—*Id.*

Here, if we reckon the feet in question to be anapests, we have dissyllables with both parts short. But some, accenting "*ago*" on the latter syllable, and "*Either*" on the former, will call "*ago now*" a bacchy, and "*Either slept*" an amphimac: because *they make them such* by their manner of reading.—G. B.

pertains to all *syllables* as such, and not merely to vowel sounds; the recognition of the same general principles of syllabication in poetry as in prose; the supposition that accent pertains, not to certain *letters* in particular, but to certain *syllables* as such; the limitation of accent to stress, or percussion, only; the conversion of short syllables into long, and long into short, by a change of accent; our frequent formation of long syllables with what are called short vowels; our more frequent formation of short syllables with what are called long or open vowels; the necessity of some order in the succession of feet or syllables, to form rhythm; the need of framing each line to correspond with some other line or lines in length; the propriety of always making each line susceptible of scansion by itself: all these points, so essential to a true explanation of the nature of English verse, though, for the most part, well maintained by some prosodists, are nevertheless denied by some, so that opposite opinions may be cited concerning them all. I would not suggest that all or any of these points are thereby made *doubtful;* for there may be opposite judgements in a dozen cases, and yet concurrence enough (if concurrence *can* do it) to establish them every one.

OBS. 3.—An ingenious poet and prosodist now living,[*] Edgar Allan Poe, (to whom I owe a word or two of reply) in his "Notes upon English Verse," with great self-complacency, represents, that, "While much has been written upon the structure of the Greek and Latin rhythms, comparatively *nothing* has been done as regards the English;" that, "It may be said, indeed, we are *without a treatise* upon our own versification;" that, "The very best" *definition* of versification[†] to be found in any of "*our ordinary treatises* on the topic," has "*not a single point* which does not involve an error;" that, "A *leading defect* in each of these treatises is the confining of the subject to mere *versification*, while metre, or rhythm, in general, is the real question at issue;" that, "Versification is *not* the *art*, but the *act*," of making verses; that, "A correspondence in the *length* of lines is by no means essential;" that, '*Harmony*," produced "by the regular alternation of syllables differing in quantity," does not include "*melody;*" that, "A *regular alternation*, as described, forms *no part* of the principle of metre;" that, "There is no necessity of *any regularity* in the succession of *feet;*" that, "By consequence," he ventures to "dispute the *essentiality* of any alternation, regular or irregular, of *syllables* long and short;" that, "For *anything more intelligible* or more *satisfactory* than this definition, [i. e., Brown's former definition of versification,] we shall look in vain in any *published treatise* upon the subject;" that, "So general and *so total a failure* can be referred only to some *radical misconception;*" that, "The word *verse* is derived (through *versus*) from the Latin *verto, I turn,* and • • • it can be nothing but *this derivation*, which has led to the *error* of our writers upon prosody;" that, "*It is this* which *has seduced them* into regarding the *line* itself—the *versus*, or turning—as an essential, or principle of metre;" that, "Hence the term *versification* has been employed as sufficiently general, or inclusive, for treatises upon rhythm in general;" that, "Hence, also, [comes] the precise catalogue of a few varieties of English *lines*, when these varieties are, in fact, almost without limit;" that, "*I*," the aforesaid Edgar Allan Poe," *shall dismiss entirely*, from the consideration of the principle of *rhythm*, the idea of *versification*, or the construction of verse;" that, "In so doing, *we* shall avoid *a world of confusion;*" that, "Few is, indeed, an *afterthought* or an *embellishment*, or an *improvement*, rather than an element of rhythm;" that, "*This fact* has induced the easy admission, into the realms of Poesy, of such works as the 'Télémaque' of Fenelon;" because, forsooth, "In the elaborate modulation of their sentences, THEY FULFIL THE IDEA OF METRE."—*The Pioneer, a Literary and Critical Magazine*, (Boston, March, 1843,) Vol. I, p. 102 to 105.

OBS. 4.—"Holding these things in view," continues this sharp connoisseur, "the prosodist who rightly examines that which constitutes the external, or most immediately recognisable, form of Poetry, will commence with the definition of *Rhythm*. Now *rhythm*, from the Greek ὑρϑμος, *number*, is a term which, in its present application, very nearly conveys *its own idea*. No more *proper* word could be employed to present *the conception intended, but rhythm*, in prosody, is, in its *last analysis*, identical with *time* in music. For this reason," says he, "I have used, throughout this article, as synonymous with *rhythm*, the word *met* from μετρον, *measure*. Either the one or the other may be defined as *the arrangement of words into two or more consecutive, equal, pulsations of time.* These pulsations are *feet*. Two feet, at least, are requisite to constitute a *rhythm;* just as, in mathematics, two units are necessary to form [a] *number*.[‡] The syllables of which the foot consists, when the foot is

---

[*] " Edgar A. Poe, the author, died at Baltimore on Sunday " [the 7th].—*Daily Evening Traveller*, Boston, Oct. 8, 1849. This was eight or ten months after the writing of these observations.—†] B.

[†] " Versification is the art of arranging words into lines of correspondent length, so as to produce harmony by the regular alternation of syllables differing in quantity."—*Brown's Institutes of E. Gram.* p. 236.

[‡] This appears to be an error; for, according to Dilworth, and other arithmeticians, "*a unit is a number;*" and so is it expounded by Johnson, Walker, Webster, and Worcester. See, in the *Introduction*, a note at the foot of p. 101. Some prosodists have taught the absurdity, that two feet are necessary to constitute a *metre*, and have accordingly applied the terms, *monometer, dimeter, trimeter, tetrameter, pentameter*, and *hexameter*,—or so many of them as they could so misapply.—In a sense very different from the usual acceptation. The proper principle, that, " One foot constitutes a metre."—*Dr. P. Wilson's Greek Prosody*, p. 58. And verses are to be denominated *Monometer, Dimeter, Trimeter*, &c., according to "THE NUMBER OF FEET"—See ib. p. 6. But Worcester's Universal and Critical Dictionary has the following not very consistent explanations: "MONOMETER, n. One measure. Beck. DIMETER, n. A poetic measure of four feet; a series of two metres. Beck. TRIMETER, n. Consisting of three poetical measures, forming an iambic of six feet. Tyrwhitt. TETRAMETER, n. A Latin or Greek verse con-

not a syllable in itself, are subdivisions of the pulsations. No equality is demanded in these subdivisions. It is only required that, so far as regards two consecutive feet at least, the sum of the times of the syllables in one, shall be equal to the sum of the times of the syllables in the other. Beyond two pulsations there is no necessity for equality of time. All beyond is arbitrary or conventional. A third and fourth pulsation may embody half, or double, or any proportion of the time occupied in the two first. Rhythm being thus understood, the prosodist should proceed to define *versification* as *the making of verses*, and *verse* as *the arbitrary or conventional isolation of rhythms into masses of greater or less extent*."—*Ib.* p. 105.

Obs. 5.—No marvel that all usual conceptions and definitions of rhythm, of versification, and of verse, should be found dissatisfactory to the critic whose idea of *metre* is fulfilled by the pompous *prose* of Fenelon's Té'émaque. No right or real examination of this matter can ever make the most immediately *recognizable* form of poetry to be any thing else than the form of *verse*—the form of writing in *specific lines*, ordered by number and chime of syllables, and not squared by gage of the composing-stick. And as to the derivation and primitive signification of *rhythm*, it is plain that in the extract above, both are misrepresented. The etymology there given is a gross error; for, " the Greek ἀριθμος, *number*," would make, in English, not *rhythm*, but *arithm*, as in *arithmetic*. Between the two combinations, there is the palpable difference of three or four letters in either six; for neither of these forms can be varied to the other, but by dropping one letter, and adding an other, and changing a third, and moving a fourth. *Rhythm* is d rived, not thence, but from the Greek 'ρυθμος; which, according to the lexicons, is a primitive word, and means, *rhythmus, rhythm, concinnity modulation, measured tune*, or *regular flow*, and *not* " *number*."

Obs. 6.—*Rhythm*, of course, like every other word not misapplied, "conveys *its own idea*;" and that, not qualifiedly, or "*very nearly*," but *exactly*. That this idea, however, was originally that of arithmetical *number*, or is nearly so now, is about as fanciful a notion, as the happy suggestion added above, that *rhythm* in lieu of *arithm* or *number*, is the fittest of words, *because* " rhythm in prosody is *time* in music!" Without dispute, it is important to the prosodist, and also to the poet or versifier, to have as accurate an idea as possible of the import of this common term, though it is observable that many of our grammarians make little or no use of it. That it has some relation to *numbers*, is undeniable. But what is it ? Poetic numbers, and numbers in arithmetic. and numbers in grammar, are three totally different sorts of things. *Rhythm* is related only to the first. Of the signification of this word, a recent expositor gives the following brief explanation : " RHYTHM, *n.* Metre ; verse ; *numbers*. Proportion applied to any motion whatever."—*Bolles's Dictionary*, 8vo. To this definition, Worcester prefixes the following: "The consonance of measure and time in poetry. *prose composition*, and music;—also in dancing."—*Universal and Critical Dict.* In verse, the proportion which forms rhythm—that is, the chime of quantities—is applied to the *sounds* of syllables. Sounds, however, may be considered as a species of *motion*, especially those which are rhythmical or musical.* It seems more strictly correct, to regard rhythm as a *property* of poetic numbers, than to identify it with them. It is their proportion or modulation, rather than the numbers themselves. According to Dr. Webster, " RHYTHM, or RHYTHMUS, in *music*, [is] variety in the movement as to quickness or slowness, or length and shortness of the notes; or *rather* the proportion which the parts of the motion have to each other."—*American Dict.* The "*last analysis*" of rhythm can be nothing else than the reduction of it to its *least parts*. And if, in this reduction, it is " identical with *time*," then it is here the same thing as *quantity*, whether prosodical or musical; for, "The *time* of a note, or syllable, is called *quantity*. The time of a rest is also called quantity; because *rests*, as well as notes are a constituent of rhythm."—*Comstock's Elocution*, p. 61. But rhythm is, in fact, neither time nor quantity; for the analysis which would make it such, destroys the relation in which the thing consists.

SECTION II.— OF ACCENT AND QUANTITY.

Accent and Quantity have already been briefly explained in the second chapter of Prosody, as items coming under the head of Pronunciation. What we have to say of them here, will be thrown into the form of *critical observa-*

---

isting of *four feet*: a series of four metres. TETRAMETER, *a.* Having *four* metrical *feet*. *Twichitt.* PENTAMETER, *a.* A Greek or Latin verse of *five feet*; a series of five metres. PENTAMETER, *a.* Having *five* metrical *feet*. *Warton.* HEXAMETER, *n.* A verse or line of poetry. having *six feet*, either dactyls or spondees ; the heroic. and most important, verse among the Greeks and Romans:—a rhythmical series of six metres. HEXAMETER, *a.* Having *six* metrical *feet*. *Dr. Warton.*" According to these definitions, Dimeter has as many feet as Tetrameter ; and Trimeter has as many as Hexameter !

* It is common, at any rate, for prosodists to speak of " the *movement* of the voice," as do Sheridan, Murray, Humphrey, and Everett ; but Kames, in treating of the Beauty of Language from resemblance, says, " There is no resemblance or of sound to motion, nor of sound to sentiment."—*Elements of Criticism*, Vol. II, p 68 This image, however, is admitted by the critic, and cited to show how, " causes that have no resemblance may produce resembling effects."— *Ib.* II, 64. " By a number of syllables in succession, an emotion is sometimes raised extremely similar to that raised by successive motion ; which may be evident even to those who are defective in taste, from the following feet, that the term *movement* in all languages is equally applied to both."—*Ib.* II, 66.

tions; in the progress of which, many quotations from other writers on these subjects, will be presented, showing what has been most popularly taught.

OBSERVATIONS.

OBS. 1.—Accent and quantity are distinct things;[*] the former being the stress, force, loudness, or percussion of voice, that distinguishes certain syllables from others; and the latter, the *time,* distinguished as *long* or *short,* in which a syllable is uttered. But, as the great sounds which we utter, naturally take more time than the *small* ones, there is a necessary connexion between quantity and accent in English,—a connexion which is sometimes expounded as being the mere relation of *cause and effect;* nor is it in fact much different from that. "As no utterance can be agreeable to the ear, which is void of proportion; as *all quantity,* or proportion of time in utterance, depends upon a due observation of *accent;* it is a matter of absolute necessity to all, who would arrive at a good and graceful delivery, to be master of that point. Nor is the use of *accent* in our language confined to *quantity* alone; but it is also the chief mark by which words are distinguished from syllables. Or rather I may say, it is *the very essence* of words, which without that, would be only so many collections of syllables."—*Sheridan's Lectures on Elocution,* p. 61. "As no utterance *which is void of proportion,* can be agreeable to the ear; and as quantity, or proportion of time in utterance, *greatly* depends *on* a due *attention to* the *accent;* it is absolutely *necessary for every person,* who would attain a *just* and *pleasing* delivery, to be master of that point."—*Murray's Gram.* 8vo, p. 241; 12mo, 194.

OBS. 2.—In the first observation on Prosody, at page 742, and in its marginal note, was reference made to the fact, that the nature and principles of *accent* and *quantity* are involved in difficulty, by reason of the different views of authors concerning them. To this source of embarrassment, it seems necessary here again to advert; because it is upon this distinction of syllables in respect to quantity, or accent, or both, that every system of versification, except his who merely counts, is based. And further, it is not only requisite that the principle of distinction which we adopt should be clearly made known, but also proper to consider which of these three modes is the best or most popular foundation for a theory of versification. Whether or wherein the accent and quantity of the ancient languages, Latin or Greek, differed from those of our present English, we need not now inquire. From the definitions which the learned lexicographers Littleton and Ainsworth give to *prosodia,* prosody, it would seem that, with them, "the art of *accenting*" was nothing else than the art of giving to syllables their right *quantity,* "whether *long* or *short*." And some have charged it as a glaring error, long prevalent among English grammarians, and still a fruitful source of disputes, to confound accent with quantity in our language.[†] This charge, however, there is reason to believe, is sometimes, if not in most cases, made on grounds rather fanciful than real; for some have evidently mistaken the notion of concurrence or coincidence for that of identity. But, to affirm that the stress which we call accent, coincides always and only with long quantity, does not necessarily make accent and quantity to be one and the same thing. The greater force or loudness which causes the accented syllable to occupy more time than any other, is in itself something different from time. Besides, quantity is divisible,—is either *long* or *short:* these two species of it are acknowleged on all sides, and some

* "From what has been said of accent and quantity in our own language, we may conclude them to be essentially distinct *and perfectly separable:* nor is it to be doubted that they were *equally separable* in the learned languages."—*Walker's Observations* on *Gr. and Lat. Accent and Quantity,* § 20; Key, p. 326. In the short essay here cited, Walker meant by *accent* the rising or the falling *inflection,*—an upward or a downward slide of the voice; and by *quantity,* nothing but the open or close sound of some vowel; as of "the *a* in *scatter*" and "*skater,*" the initial syllables of which words he supposed to differ in quantity as much as any two syllables.—*Ib* § 24; Key, p. 331. With these views of *the things,* it is perhaps the less to be wondered at, that he who appears to have been a candid and courteous writer, charges "that excellent scholar Mr. Forster" with "*ignorance* of the accent and quantity of his own language;" (*Ib. Note on* § 8; Key, p. 317;) and, in his next accent, ancient or modern, elsewhere confesses his own ignorance, and that of every body else, to be as—See marginal note on Obs 4th. below.

† (1.) "We shall now take a view of sounds when united into *syllables.* Here a beautiful variation of presents itself as the next object of our attention. The knowledge of *long* and *short* syllables, is the most neglected quality in the whole art of pronunciation. The disputes of our modern writers on this subject, have arisen chiefly from an absurd notion that has prevailed; viz. that there is no difference between the *accent* and the *quantity,* in the English language; that accented syllables are always *long,* and the unaccented always *short.* An absurdity so glaring, does not need refutation Pronounce any one line from Milton, and the ear will mine whether or not the accent and quantity always coincide. Very seldom they do."—*HARRIS Gram.,* Part ii, p. 108.

(2.) "Some of our Moderns (especially Mr. *Bishe,* in his *Art of Poetry*) and lately Mr. *Mattaire,* in what is *The English Grammar,* erroneously use *Accent* for *Quantity,* one signifying the Length or Shortness of a the other the raising or falling of the Voice in *Discourse.*"—*Brightland's Gram,* London, 1746, p 156

(3.) "Tempus cum accentu a nonnullis male confunditur; quasi idem sit acui et produci. Cum brevi syllaba acuitur, elevatur quidem vox in eå proferenda, sed tempus non augetur. Sic in voce *hominibus* mi; at ni quæ sequitur, æquam in efferendo moram postulat."—*Lily's Gram.* p. 125. Version: "By acute sons, *time* is improperly confounded with *accent;* as if to acute and to lengthen were the same. For a short syllable is acuted, the voice indeed is raised in pronouncing it, but the time is not increased The word *hominibus,* mi has the acute accent; but ni, which follows, demands equal slowness in the pronunciation To English ears, this can hardly seem a correct representation; for, in pronouncing *hominibus,* it is not min, that we accent; and this syllable is manifestly as much longer than the rest, as it is louder.

lists will have a third, which they call "*common*."● But, of our English accent, the
being taken in its usual acceptation, no *such* division is ever, with any propriety,
; for even the stress which we call *secondary accent*, pertains to *long* syllables rather
:o short ones; and the mere absence of stress, which produces short quantity, we do
ll *accent*.

.. 3.—The impropriety of affirming *quantity* to be the same as *accent*, when its most
ent species occurs only in the absence of accent, must be obvious to every body; and
writers who anywhere suggest this identity, must either have written absurdly, or
taken *accent* in some sense which includes the sounds of our *unaccented* syllables. The
sometimes means, "The *modulation* of the voice in speaking."—*Worcester's Dict. w.
t.* In this sense, the lighter as well as the more impressive sounds are included; but
whether both together, considered as accents, can be reckoned the same as long and
quantities, is questionable. Some say, they cannot; and insist that they are yet
ferent, as the variable tones of a *trumpet*, which swell and fall, are different from the
y loud and soft notes of the monotonous *drum*. This illustration of the "easy Distinc-
etwixt *Quantity* and *Accent*," is cited, with commendation, in Brightland's Grammar,
ge 157th;† the author of which grammar, *seems* to have understood *Accent*, or *Accents*,
the same as *Inflections*—though these are still unlike to quantities, if he did so. (See
planation of Inflections in Chap II, Sec. iii, Art. 3, above.) His exposition is this:
nt is the *rising* and *falling* of the Voice, above or under its usual *Tone*. There are three
of Accents, an *Acute*, a *Grave*, and an *Inflex*, is also call'd a *Circumflex*. The *Acute*,
irp, naturally *raises* the Voice; and the *Grave*, or *Base*, as naturally *falls* it. The
nflex is a kind of *Undulation*, or *Waving* of the Voice."—*Brightland's Gram.*, Seventh
ond. 1746, p. 156.

.. 4.—Dr. Johnson, whose great authority could not fail to carry some others with
too evidently identifies accent with quantity, at the commencement of his Prosody.
:NUNCIATION is just," says he, "when every letter has its proper sound, and when every
le has its proper accent, or which in English versification is *the same*, its proper quan-
—*Johnson's Gram.* before Dict. 4to, p. 13; *John Burn's Gram.* p. 240; *Jones's Prosodial
.* before Dict. p. 10. Now our most common notion of *accent*—the sole notion with
—and that which the accentuation of Johnson himself everywhere inculcates—is, that
ings *not* to "*every syllable*," but only to some particular syllables, being either "a *stress
c* on a certain syllable," or a *small mark* to denote such stress.—See *Scott's Dict.* or
ter's. But Dr. Johnson, in the passage above, must have understood the word *accent*
ibly to his own imperfect definition of it; to wit, as "*the sound given to the syllable
unced.*"—*Joh. Dict.* An *unaccented* syllable must have been to him a syllable unpro-
:ed. In short he does not appear to have recognized any syllables as being unaccented.
vord *unaccented* had no place in his lexicography, nor could have any without incon-
cy. It was unaptly added to his text, after sixty years, by one of his amenders, Todd
.imers; who still blindly neglected to mend his definition of *accent*. In these particu-
Walker's dictionaries exhibit the same deficiencies as Johnson's; and yet no author
iore frequently used the words *accent* and *unaccented*, than did Walker.‡ Mason's Sup-

) "Syllables, with respect to their *quantity*, are either *long*, *short*, or *common*."—*Gould's Adam's Lat.*
p 243. "Some syllables are *common*; that is, sometimes long, and sometimes short."—*Adam's Lat. and
Gram.* p 252. *Common* is here put for *variable*, or *not permanently settled in respect to quantity* : in this
from which no third species ought to be inferred, our language is, perhaps, more extensively "common"
n other.

"Most of our Monosyllables either take this Stress or not, according as they are more or less emphatical;
erefore English Words of one Syllable may be considered as *common*; i. e either as long or short in certain
ons. These Situations are chiefly determined by the Pause, or Cesure, of the Verse, and this Pause by the
And as the English abounds in Monosyllables, there is probably no Language in which the Quantity of
es is more regulated by the Sense than in English."—*W. Ward's Gram.*, Ed. of 1765, p. 156.
Bicknell's theory of quantity, for which he refers to Herries, is this: "The English *quantity* is divided into
hort, and *common*. The longest species of syllables are those that end in a vowel, and are under the accent;
in harmonious, *sole* in *console*, &c. When a monosyllable, which is unemphatic, ends in a vowel, it is
hort; but when the emphasis is placed upon it, it is always long. *Short* syllables are such as end in any
six mutes; as *cut*, *stop*, *rapid*, *rugged*, *lock*. In *all* such *syllables* the sound cannot be lengthened: they
essarily and invariably *short*. If another consonant intervenes between the vowel and mute, as *rend*, *soft*,
he syllable is rendered *somewhat longer*. The other species of syllables called *common*, are such as termi-
a half-vowel or aspirate. For instance, in the words *run*, *swim*, *crush*, *purl*, the concluding sound can be
ir! or shortened, as we please. This scheme of quantity," it is added, "is founded on fact and experience."
nell's Gram., Part ii, p 109. But is it not a *fact*, that *such* words as *cuttest*, *stopping*, *rapid*, *rugged*, are
., in verse? and is not *unlock* an *iambus*? And what becomes of syllables that end with vowels or l.quids
e not accented?

‡ *lan* used the same comparison, "To illustrate the difference between the accent of the ancients and that
[our tongue] Our accent be supposed, with Nares and others, to have "no reference to *inflections* of
ce.'—See *Art of Reading*, p. 75; *Lectures on Elocution*, p 56; *Walker's Key*, p. 313
.it may in some measure account for these remarkable omissions, to observe that Walker, in his lexicography,
.d Johnson in almost every thing but pronunciation. On this latter subject, his own authority is perhaps
t as that of any single author. And here I am led to introduce a remark or two touching *the accent and
ty* with which he was chiefly concerned; though the suggestions may have no immediate connexion with
or of confounding these properties
Walker, in his theory, regarded the *inflections* of the voice as pertaining to *accent*, and as affording a satis-
solu-tion of the difficulties in which this subject has been involved; but, as an English orthoepist, he treats
nt in no other sense, than as *stress laid on a particular syllable of a word*—a sense implying contrast, and

plement, first published in 1801, must have suggested to the revisers of Johnson the addi of the latter term, as appears by the authority cited for it : " UNA'CCENTED, *adj.* N accented. 'It being enough to make a syllable long, if it be accented; and short, if it be *unaccented.*' *Harris's Philological Inquiries.*"—*Mason's Sup.*

OBS. 5.—This doctrine of Harris's, that long quantity accompanies the accent, and unaccented syllables are short, is far from confounding or identifying accent with quantity, has already been shown; and, though it plainly contradicts some of the elementary teachings of Johnson, Sheridan, Walker, Murray, Webster, Fowler, and others, in regard to the length or shortness of certain syllables, it has been clearly maintained by many excellent authors, so that no opposite theory is better supported by authority. On this point, our language stands not alone; for the accent controls quantity in some others.* G H. Noehden, a writer of uncommon ability, in his German Grammar for Englishmen, defines accent to be, as we see it is in English, "that *stress* which marks a particular syllable in speaking;" and recognizing, as we also do, both a full accent and a partial one, or "demi-accent," presents the syllables of his language as being of three conditions : the "*accented,*" which "cannot be used otherwise than as *long;*" the "*half-accented,*" which "must be regarded as ambiguous, or common;" and the "*accentless,*" which "are in their nature *short.*"—*See Noehden's Gram.* p. 87. His middle class, however, our prosodists in general very properly dispense with. In Fiske's History of Greek Literature, which is among the additions to the Manual of Classical Literature from the German of E-chenburg, are the following passages: "The *tone* [i. e. accent] in Greek is placed upon short syllables as well as long ; in German, it accompanies regularly only long syllables."—"In giving an accent to a syllable in an English word we *thereby* render it a long syllable, whatever may be the sound given to its vowel. and in whatever way the syllable may be composed ; so that as above stated in relation to the German, an English accent, or stress in pronunciation, accompanies only a long syllable."—*Manual of Class. Lit.* p. 437. With these extracts, accords the doctrine of some of the ablest of our English grammarians. "In the English Pronunciation," says William Ward, " there is a certain Stress of the Voice laid on some one Syllable at least, of every Word of two or more Syllables ; and that Syllable on which the Stress is laid may be considered *long.* Our Grammarians have agreed to consider this Stress of the Voice as the *Accent* in English ; and therefore the Accent and long Quantity coincide in our Language."

necessarily dividing all syllables into accented and unaccented, except monosyllables Having acknowledged "*total ignorance* of the nature of the Latin and Greek accent." he adds : " The accent of the English language, which is constantly sounding in our ears, and every moment open to investigation, seems *as much a mystery* as that accent which is removed almost two thousand years from our view Obscurity, perplexity, and confusion, run through every trea se on the subject, and nothing could be so hopeless as an attempt to explain it. the unit circumstance pre-ent itself, which at once accounts for the confusion, and affords a clew to lead us out of it No one writer on accent has given such a definition of the voice as acquaints us with its essential properties ** But let us once divide the voice into its rising and falling inflections, the obscurity vanishes, and accent becomes as intelligible as any other part of language. * * * On the present occasion it will be sufficient to observe, that *the stress* or *call accent* is as well understood as is necessary for the pronunciation of single words, which is the object of this treatise."—*Walker's Dict.* p. 53, *Princip.* 486. 487. 488.

(3.) Afterwards, on introducing *quantity,* as an orthoëpical topic, he has the following remark : " In treating this part of pronunciation, it will not be necessary to enter into the nature of *that quantity which constitutes poetry* the quantity here considered will be that which relates to words taken singly ; and this is *nothing more than the length or shortness of the vowels,* either as they stand alone, or as they are differently combined with the vowels or consonants."—*Ib.* p. 62, *Princip.* 529. Here is suggested a distinction which has not been so well observed by grammarians and prosodists, or even by Walker himself as it ought to have been So long as the practice continues of denominating certain mere *vowel sounds,* the *long* and the *short,* it will be very necessary to notice that these are not the same as the *syllabic quantities,* long and short, which constitute English verse.

* (1) In the Latin and Greek languages this is not commonly supposed to be the case ; but, on the contrary, the quantity of syllables is professedly adjusted by its own rules independently of what we call accent ; and in our English pronunciation of these languages the accentuation of all long words is regulated by the quantity of the last syllable but one Walker, in the introduction to his Key, speaks of " The English pronunciation of Greek and Latin [as] injurious to quantity " And no one can deny, that we often accent what are called our short syllables, and perhaps oftener leave unaccented such as are called long ; but, after all, were the quantity of all our long syllables always judged of by their actual time. and not with reference to the vowel sounds called long and short, there our violations of the old quantities would be found much fewer than some suppose they are.

(2) Dr. Adam's view of the accents, acute and grave, appears to be peculiar ; and of a nature which may perhaps come nearer to an actual identity with the quantities, long and short, than any other. He says,
"1. The *acute* or *sharp* accent raises the voice in pronunciation, and is thus marked [']; *préfero, préfer* the English word is written, not thus, but with two E.'s, *proffer* —O. B.)
"2 The *grave* or *base* accent depresses the voice, or keeps it in i's natural tone ; and is thus marked [']; *doci'.* This accent properly belongs to all syllables which have no other.
"The accents are hardly ever marked in English books except in dictionaries, grammars, spelling-books, & the like, where the acute accent only is used The accents are likewise seldom marked in Latin books, except for the sake of distinction ; as in these adverbs, *aliquò, continù, docté, unà,* &c."—*Adam's Latin and English Grammar.* p 266.

(3.) As stress naturally lengthens the syllables on which it falls, if we suppose the grave accent to be the mark of this, and to belong to all syllables which have no peculiar stress,—are not enforced, not acuted, not irregularly not emphasized ; then shall we truly have an accent which our short quantity may fairly coincide. I have said, " the mere absence of stress, which produces short quantity, we do not call *accent ;*" and it may be observed, that the learned improver of Dr. Adam's Grammar, B A Gould. has totally rejected all that this deceased 'augh' concerning *accent,* and has given an entirely different definition of the thing see mine on page 742 above. Dr. Johnson also cites from Holder a very different explanation of it, as follows : " the accent, as in the Greek names and usage, seems to have regarded the tune of the voice ; the acute accent, raising the voice in some certain syllables, to a higher. (i. e. more acute) pitch or tone ; and the grave, depressing it more or voice in some certain syllables, to a higher. (i. e. more acute) pitch or tone ; and the grave, depressing it and both having some *emphasis,* i. e. more *vigorous* pronunciation. HOLDER."—*Johnson's Quarto 4to.* B Accent.

rd's Practical Gram. p. 155. As to the vowel sounds, with the quantity of which prosodists have greatly puzzled both themselves and their readers, this writer says, *y* may be made as long, or as short, as the Speaker pleases."—*Ib.* p. 4.

s. 6.—From the absurd and contradictory nature of many of the *principles usually laid* by our grammarians, for the discrimination of long quantity and short, it is quite *ent,* that but very few of them have well understood either the distinction itself or own rules concerning it. Take Fisher for an example. In Fisher's Practical Gram- first published in London in 1753,—a work not unsuccessful, since Well's quotes the *i edition*" as appearing in 1795, and this was not the last,—we find, in the first place, owel sounds distinguished as long or short thus : "*Q.* How many Sounds has a Vowel ? wo in general, viz. 1. A LONG SOUND, When the Syllable ends with a Vowel, either *mosyllables,* or in Words of more Syllables ; as, *tăke, wĕ, I, gō, nū ;* or, as, *Nāture, Nĭtre, Nŏvice, Nŭisance.* 2. A SHORT SOUND, When the Syllable ends with a Conso- either in Monosyllables, or others ; as *Hŭt, hĕr, bĭt, rŏb, Tŭn ;* or, as *Bŭrber, bĭtten, n.*"—See p. 5. To this rule, the author makes needless exceptions of all such words *ance* and *banish,* wherein a single consonant between two vowels goes to the former ; *se,* like Johnson, Murray, and most of our old grammarians, he divides on the vowel ; *y* calls the accented syllable short ; and imagines the consonant to be heard *twice,* or *'e* "*a double Accent.*" On page 35th, he tells us that, "*Long and short Vowels,* and *long and Syllables,* are *synonimous* [—*synonymous,* from *συνώνυμος—*] Terms ;" and so indeed have been most erroneously considered by sundry subsequent writers ; and the consequence it all who judge by their criteria, mistake the poetic quantity, or prosodical value, of *ps* one half the syllables in the language. Let each syllable be reckoned long that *s* with a Vowel," and each short that "ends with a Consonant," and the decision will *bly* be oftener wrong than right ; for more syllables end with consonants than with *is,* and of the latter class a majority are without stress and therefore short. Thus the *ping* principle, contrary to the universal practice of the poets, determines many *accented iles* to be "*short ;*" as the first in "*barber, bitten, button, balance, banish ;*—" and many *ented* ones to be "*long ;*" as the last in *sofa, specie, noble, metre, sorrow, daisy, valley, *, native ;* or the first in *around, before, delay, divide, remove, seclude, obey, cocoon, presume, ie,* and other words innumerable.

s. 7.—Fisher's conceptions of accent and quantity, as constituting prosody, were much to the original and etymological sense of the words, than to any just or useful view of *sh* versification : in short, this latter subject was not even mentioned by him ; for *dy,* in his scheme, was nothing but the right pronunciation of words, or what we now *rthoĕpy.* This part of his Grammar commences with the following questions and ers :

. What is the Meaning of the Word PROSODY ? *A.* It is a Word borrowed from the *c* ; which, in Latin, is rendered *Accentus,* and in English *Accent.*

. What do you mean by *Accent ? A.* Accent originally signified a Modulation of *'oice,* or chanting to a musical Instrument ; but is now generally used to signify *Due inciation,* i. e. the pronouncing [of] a syllable according to its Quantity, (whether it be or short,) with a stronger Force or Stress of Voice than the other Syllables in the Word ; as, *a* in *ăble, o* in *abŏve,* &c.

. What is *Quantity ? A.* Quantity is the different Measure of *Time* in pronouncing bles, from whence they are called long or short.

. What is the *Proportion* between a long and a short Syllable ? *A.* Two to one ; that ong Syllable is twice as long in pronouncing as a short one ; as, *Hate, Hat.* This mark *t* over a Syllable, shows that it is long, and this (ˇ) that it is short ; as, *rēcord, rĕcord.*

. How do you *know* long and short Syllables ? *A.* A Syllable is long or short accord- *s* the Situation of the Vowel, i. e. it is generally long when it ends with a Vowel, hort when with a Consonant ; as, *Fā-* in *Favour,* and *Măn-* in *Manner.*"—*Fisher's ical Gram.* p. 34.

w one grand mistake of this is, that it supposes syllabication to fix the quantity, and *:ity* to determine the accent ; whereas it is plain, that accent controls quantity, so far *st* that, in the construction of verse, a syllable fully accented cannot be reckoned short. this mistake is practical ; for we see, that, in three of his examples, out of the four *,* the author himself misstates the quantity, because he disregards the accent : the *re-cord',* being accented on the second syllable, is an *iambus ;* and the nouns *rec'-ord ian'-ner,* being accented on the first, are *trochees ;* and just as plainly so, as is the word *r.* But a still greater blunder here observable is, that, as a "*due pronunciation*" neces- includes the utterance of every syllable, the explanation above stolidly supposes *all* yllables to be *accented,* each "according to its Quantity, (whether it be long or short,)" ach "*with a stronger Force or Stress of Voice,* than *the other* Syllables !" Absurdity akin *s,* and still more worthy to be criticised, has since been propagated by Sheridan, by *.er,* and by Lindley Murray, with a host of followers, as Alger, D. Blair, Comly, er, Cutler, Davenport, Felton, Fowler, Frost, Guy, Jaudon, Parker and Fox, Picket, , Putnam, Russell, Smith, and others.

OBS. 8.—Sheridan was an able and practical teacher of *English pronunciation*, and on
who appears to have gained reputation by all he undertook, whether as an actor, as a
elocutionist, or as a lexicographer. His publications that refer to that subject, though two
mostly superseded by others of later date, are still worthy to be consulted. The chief of
them are, his Lectures on Elocution, his Lectures on the Art of Reading, his Rhetor. a
Grammar, his Elements of English, and his English Dictionary. His third lecture on Fl
cution, and many pages of the Rhetorical Grammar, are devoted to *accent* and *quant* —
subjects which he conceived to have been greatly misrepresented by other writers up to
his time.* To this author, as it would seem, we owe the invention of that absurd doctrine,
since copied into a great multitude of our English grammars, that the accent on a syll
of two or more letters, belongs, *not to the whole of it, but only to some* ONE LETTER; and a
according to the character of this letter, as vowel or consonant, the same stress serve to
lengthen or shorten the syllable's quantity! Of this matter, he speaks thus: "The *s*
distinction of our accent depends upon its *seat*; which may be either upon a vowel or a
sonant. Upon a vowel, as in the words, gló'ry, fá'ther, hó'ly. Upon a consonant, as in th
words, hab'it, bor'row, bat'tle. When the accent is on the vowel, the syllable is long
because the accent is *made by dwelling* upon the vowel. When it is on the consonant, th
syllable is short ;† because the accent is *made by passing rapidly* over the vowel, and giving
smart stroke of the voice to the following consonant. *Obvious as this point is*, it has yet
escaped the observation of all our grammarians and compilers of dictionaries; who, instead
examining the peculiar genius of our tongue, implicitly and pedantically have followed th
Greek method, of always placing the accentual mark over a vowel."—*Sheridan's Rhetor.*
Gram. p. 51. The author's reprehension of the old mode of accentuation, is not without
reason; but his "great distinction" of short and long syllables is only fit to puzzle or m
lead the reader. For it is plain, that the first syllables of *hab'it, bor'row*, and *bat'tle*, are
twice as long as the last; and, in poetry, these words are trochees, as well as the oth
three, *glo'ry, fa'ther*, and *ho'ly*.

OBS. 9.—The only important distinction in our accent, is that of the *primary* and th
secondary, the latter species occurring when it is necessary to enforce more syllables of a w
than one; but Sheridan, as we see above, after rejecting all the old distinctions of *rising* a
falling, raising and *depressing*, *acute* and *grave*, *sharp* and *base*, *long* and *short*, contrived a ne
one still more vain, which he founded on that of vowels and consonants, but "referred to
or *quantity*." He recognized, in fact, a *vowel accent* and a *consonant accent*; or, in reference
quantity, a *lengthening accent* and a *shortening accent*. The discrimination of these was wi
him "THE GREAT DISTINCTION of our accent." He has accordingly mentioned it in sever
different places of his works, and not always with that regard to consistency which becom
precise theorist. It led him to new and variant ways of *defining* accent; some of which
to imply a division of consonants from their vowels in utterance, or to suggest that sylla
are not the least parts of spoken words. And no sooner has he told us that our accent is
one single mode of distinguishing a syllable, than he proceeds to declare it two. Consid
the following citations: "As the pronunciation of English words is chiefly regulated by
cent, it will be necessary in the first place to have a *precise idea* of that term. Accent wi
us means *no more* than *a certain stress* of the voice upon *one letter* of a syllable, which
tinguishes it from all the *other letters* in a word."—*Sheridan's Rhetorical Gram.* p. 39. Ag
"Accent, in the English language, means *a certain stress* of the voice upon a *particular l*
of a syllable which distinguishes it from the rest, and, at the same time, *distinguish*
syllable itself to which it belongs from the others which compose the word."—*Same* wo
50. Again: "But as *our accent consists in stress only*, it can just as well be placed on a
sonant as [on] a vowel."—*Same*, p. 51. Again: "By the word *accent*, is meant *the str*
the voice on *one letter* in a syllable."—*Sheridan's Elements of English*, p. 55. Again: "Th

---

* (1.) "Amongst them [the ancients,] we know that accents were marked by certain *inflexions* [inflect.
the voice like musical notes; and the grammarians to this day, with great formality inform their pupils, that t
acute accent, is the raising [of] the voice on a certain syllable; the grave, a depression of it; and the circumfl
raising and depression both, in one and the same syllable. *This jargon they constantly preserve*, though
have no sort of ideas annexed to these words; for if they are asked to shew how this is to be done, they canno
tell, and their practice always belies their precept."—*Sheridan's Lectures on Eloc.* p. 54.
　(2.) "It is by the accent chiefly that the quantity of our syllables is regulated; but not according to the
taken rule laid down by *all who have written* on the subject, that the accent *always makes the syllable* long th
which *there cannot be any thing more false*."—*Ib.* p. 57.
　(3.) "And here I cannot help taking notice of a circumstance, which shews in the strongest light, the *sor*
deficiency of those, who have hitherto employed their labours on that subject, [accent, or pronunciation,] a
of knowledge of the true genius and constitution of our tongue. Several of the compilers of dictionaries, gra
laries, and spelling books, have undertaken to mark the accents of our words; but so *little acquainted* wer
with the nature of our accent, that they thought it necessary only to mark *the syllable* on which the stress is
be laid, without marking the *particular letter* of the syllable to which the accent belongs."—*Ib.* p. 59.
　(4.) "The mind thus taking a bias under the prejudice of false rules, never arrives at a knowledge of the tru
nature of *quantity*: and accordingly we find that *all attempts hitherto* to settle the prosody of our language, hav
been vain and fruitless."—*Sheridan's Rhetorical Gram.* p. 52.
　† In the following extract, this matter is stated somewhat differently: "The *quantity* depends upon the us
the accent, whether it be on the vowel or [on the] consonant; if on the vowel, the syllable is necessarily *long*
it makes the vowel long; if on the consonant, *it may be either long or short*, according to the nature of the co
nant, or *the time taken up* in dwelling upon it."—*Sheridan's Lectures on Eloc.* p. 57. This last clause shews th
"distinction" to be a very weak one.—G. BROWN.

term [*accent*] with us has no reference to *inflexions* of the voice, or musical notes, but only means *a peculiar manner of distinguishing one syllable of a word from the rest*, denominated by us accent; and the term for that reason [is] used by us in the singular number.—This distinction is made by us in *two ways;* either by *dwelling longer upon one syllable* than the rest; or by *giving it a smarter percussion* of the voice in utterance. Of the first of these, we have instances in the words, *glōry, fäther, hŏly;* of the last, in *bat'tle, hab'it, bor'row.* So that accent, with us, is not referred to tune, but to *time;* to *quantity,* not quality; to the more *equable* or *precipitate* motion of the voice, not to the variation of notes or *inflexions.*"—*Sheridan's Lectures on Elocution,* p. 56; *Flint's Murray's Gram.* p. 85.

OBS. 10.—How "precise" was Sheridan's idea of accent, the reader may well judge from the foregoing quotations; in four of which, he describes it as "*a certain stress,*" "*the stress,*" and "*stress only,*" which enforces some "*letter;*" while, in the other, it is whimsically made to consist in two different modes of pronouncing "*syllables*"—namely, with *equability,* and with *precipitance*—with "*dwelling longer,*" and with "*smarter percussion*"—which terms the author very improperly supposes to be *opposites:* saying, "For the two ways of distinguishing syllables by accent, as mentioned before, are *directly opposite,* and produce *quite contrary effects;* the one, by *dwelling* on the syllable, necessarily makes it long; the other, by the *smart percussion* of the voice, as necessarily *makes it short.*"—*Ib.* p. 57. Now it is all a mistake, however common, to suppose that our accent, consisting as it does, in stress, enforcement, or "percussion of voice," can ever *shorten* the syllable on which it is laid; because what increases the quantum of a vocal sound, cannot diminish its length; and a syllable accented will always be found *longer* as well as *louder,* than any unaccented one immediately before or after it. Though weak sounds may possibly be protracted, and shorter ones be exploded loudly, it is not the custom of our speech, so to deal with the sounds of syllables.

OBS. 11.—Sheridan admitted that some syllables are naturally and necessarily short, but denied that any are naturally and necessarily long. In this, since syllabic length and shortness are relative to each other, and to the cause of each, he was, perhaps, hardly consistent. He might have done better, to have denied both, or neither. Bating his new division of accent to subject it sometimes to short quantity, he recognized very fully the dependence of quantity, long or short, whether in syllables or only in vowels, upon the presence or absence of accent or emphasis. In this he differed considerably from most of the grammarians of his day; and many since have continued to uphold other views. He says, "It is an *infallible rule* in our tongue that no vowel ever has a long sound in an unaccented syllable."—*Lectures on Elocution,* p. 60. Again: "In treating of the simple elements or letters, I have shown that some, both vowels and consonants, are *naturally short;* that is, whose sounds *cannot possibly* be prolonged; and these are the [short or shut] sounds of ĕ, I, and ŭ, of vocal sounds; and three pure mutes, k, p, t, of the consonant; as in the words *beck, lip, cut.* I have shown also, that the sounds of all the other vowels, and of the consonant semivowels, may be prolonged to what degree we please; but at the same time it is to be observed, that all these may also be reduced to a short quantity, and are capable of being uttered in as short a space of time as those which are naturally short. So that they who speak of syllables as absolutely in their own nature long, *the common cant of prosodians,* speak of a nonentity: for though, as I have shown above, there are syllables absolutely short, which cannot possibly be prolonged by any effort of the speaker, yet it is in his power to shorten or prolong the others to what degree he pleases."—*Sheridan's Rhetorical Gram.* p. 52. And again: "I have already mentioned that when the accent is on the vowel, it of course makes the syllable *long;* and when the accent is on the consonant, the syllable may be *either long or short,* according to the nature of the consonant, or *will of the speakers.* And as *all unaccented syllables are short,* the quantity of our syllables is adjusted by the easiest and simplest rule in the world, and in the exactest proportion."—*Lect. on Elocution,* p. 66.

OBS. 12.—This praise of our rule for the adjustment of quantity, would have been much more appropriate, had not the rule itself been greatly mistaken, perplexed, and misrepresented by the author. If it appear, on inspection, that "*beck, lip, cut,*" and the like syllables, are twice as long when under the accent, as they are when not accented, so that, with a short syllable annexed or a long one prefixed, they may form *trochees;* then is it *not true,* that such syllables are either always necessarily and *inherently* short, or always, "by the smart percussion of the voice, as necessarily *made* short;" both of which inconsistent ideas are above affirmed of them. They may not be so long as some other long syllables; but, if they are twice as long as the accompanying short ones, they are not short. And, if not short, then that remarkable distinction in accent, which assumes that they are so, is as needless as it is absurd and perplexing. Now let the words, *beck'on, lip'ping, cut'ter,* be properly pronounced, and their syllables be compared with each other, or with those of *lim'beck, fil'lip, Drā'cut;* and it cannot but be perceived, that *beck, lip,* and *cut,* like other syllables in general, are *lengthened* by the accent, and shortened only in its absence; so that all these words are manifestly trochees, as all similar words are found to be, in our versification. To suppose "as many words as we hear accents," or that "it is the laying of an accent on *one* syllable, which *constitutes a word,*" and then say, that "no unaccented sylla-ble or vowel is ever to be accounted long," as this enthusiastic author does in fact, is to make strange scansion of a very large portion of the trissyllables and polysyllables which occur in verse.   An other great error in Sheridan's doctrine of quantity, is his notion that all monosyllables, except a few small particles, are *accented ;* and that their quantity is de-termined to be long or short by the *seat* or the *mode* of the accent, as before stated. Now, as our poetry abounds with monosyllables, the relative time of which is adjusted by emphasis and cadence, according to the nature and importance of the terms, and according to the requirements of rhythm, with no reference to this factitious principle, no conformity thereto but what is accidental, it cannot but be a puzzling exercise, when these difficulties come to be summed up, to attempt the application of a doctrine so vainly conceived to be " the easiest and simplest rule in the world ! "

OBS. 13.—Lindley Murray's principles of accent and quantity, which later grammarians have so extensively copied, were mostly extracted from Sheridan's ; and, as the compiler appears to have been aware of but few, if any, of his predecessor's errors, he has adopted and greatly spread well-nigh all that have just been pointed out ; while, in regard to some points, he has considerably increased the number. His scheme, as he at last fixed it, appears to consist essentially of propositions already refuted, or objected to, above ; as any reader may see, who will turn to his definition of accent, and his rules for the determina-tion of quantity. In opposition to Sheridan, who not very consistently says, that, "all unaccented syllables are *short,*" this author appears to have adopted the greater error of Fisher, who supposed that the *vowel sounds* called long and short, are just the same as the long and short *syllabic quantities.* By this rule, thousands of syllables will be called long, which are in fact short, being always so uttered in both prose and poetry ; and, by the other, some will occasionally be called short, which are in fact long, being made so by the poet, under a slight secondary accent, or perhaps none. Again, in supposing our numer-ous monosyllables to be accented, and their quantity to be thereby fixed, without excepting " the *particles,* such as *a, the, to, in,* &c.," which were excepted by Sheridan, Murray has much augmented the multitude of errors which necessarily flow from the original rule. This principle, indeed, he adopted timidly ; saying, as though he hardly believed the assertion true : "And *some writers assert,* that every monosyllable of two or more letters, has *one* of its letters thus distinguished."— *Murray's Gram.* 8vo, p. 236 ; 12mo, 189. But still he *adopted* it, and adopted it *fully,* in his section on Quantity ; for, of his twelve words, exemplifying syllabic time so regulated, no fewer than nine are monosyllables. It is observable, however, that, in some instances, it is not *one* letter, but *two,* that he marks ; as in the words, "mōŏd, hoüse."—*Ib.* p. 239 ; 12mo, 192. And again, it should be observed, that generally, wherever he marks accent, he follows the *old mode,* which Sheridan and Webster so justly condemn ; so that, even when he is speaking of "the accent on the *consonant,*" the sign of stress, as that of time, is set over a *vowel :* as, "Sádly, róbber."—*Ib.* 8vo, 240 ; 12mo, 193. So in his Spelling-Book, where words are often falsely divided : as, "Vé nice," for Ven'-ice ; "Há no ver," for Han'o-ver ; &c.—See p. 101.

OBS. 14.—In consideration of the great authority of this grammarian, now backed by a a score or two of copyists and modifiers, it may be expedient to be yet more explicit. Of *accent* Murray published about as many different definitions, as did Sheridan ; which, as they show what notions he had at different times, it may not be amiss for some, who hold him always in the right, to compare.   In one, he describes it thus : "Accent *signifies that stress* of the voice, which is laid on *one syllable,* to distinguish it from the rest."—*Murray's Spelling-Book,* p. 138. He should here have said, (as by his examples it would appear he meant,) "on one syllable *of a word ;*" for, as the phrase now stands, it may put stress on a *monosyllable in a sentence ;* and it is a matter of dispute, whether this can properly be called accent. Walker and Webster say, it is emphasis, and not accent.   Again, an other definition, which was written before he adopted the notion of accent on consonants, of accent on monosyllables, or of accent for quantity in the formation of verse, he gives in these words : "Accent is *the laying of* a peculiar stress of the voice on a certain *vowel* or syllable in a word, that it may be better heard than the rest, or distinguished from the others ; as, in the word *presúme,* the stress of the voice must be on the second syllable, *súme,* which takes the accent."—*Murray's Gram., Second Edition,* 12mo, p. 161. In this edition, which was published at York, in 1796, his chief rules of quantity say nothing about accent, but are thus expressed : [1.] "A *vowel or syllable* is long, when *the vowel or vowels contained in it* are slowly joined in pronunciation with the *following letters ;* as, ' Fāll, bāle, mōōd, hōū: fēature.' [2.] A syllable is short, when the vowel is quickly joined to the succeeding letter as, ' ärt, bŏnnĕt, hŭngĕr.'"—*Ib.* p. 166. Besides the absurdity of representing " *a vowel* as having " *vowels* contained in it," these rules are *made up* of great faults. They confound syllabic quantities with vowel sounds. They suppose quantity to be, not the time of whole syllable, but the quick or slow junction of *some* of its parts. They apply to no sylla-ble that ends with a vowel sound. The former applies to none that ends with one conso-nant only ; as, " mood," or the first of " feat-ure." In fact, it does not apply to *any* of the examples given ; the final letter in each of the other words being *silent.* The latter rule yet: it misrepresents the examples; for "*bonnet*" and "*hunger*" are trochees, and with any stress on it, is long.

15.—In all late editions of L. Murray's Grammar, and many modifications of it, accent ned thus: "Accent is *the laying of* a peculiar stress of the voice, on a certain *letter* or *e* in a word, that *it* may be better heard than *the rest*, or distinguished from *them*: as, word *presúme*, the stress of the voice must be on the *letter u*, AND [the] *second syllable*, which take the accent."—*Murray's Gram.* 8vo, p. 235; 12mo, 188; 18mo, 57; *Alger's, lacon's*, 52; *Comly's*, 168; *Cooper's*, 176; *Davenport's*, 121; *Felton's*, 134; *Frost's El. 'isk's*, 32; *Merchant's*, 145; *Parker and Fox's*, iii, 44; *Pond's*, 197; *Putnam's*, 96; *Rus-* 106; *R. C. Smith's*, 186. Here we see a curious jumble of the common idea of accent, .ress laid on some particular *syllable* of a *word*," with Sheridan's doctrine of accenting s "a particular *letter* of a *syllable*,"—an idle doctrine, contrived solely for the accom- .ion of short quantity with long, *under the accent*. When this definition was adopted, .y's scheme of quantity was also revised, and materially altered. The principles of .in text, to which his copiers all confine themselves, then took the following form: .ie quantity of a syllable, is *that* time which is occupied in pronouncing it. It is con- .d as LONG or SHORT.

vowel or syllable is long, when the accent is on the vowel; *which* occasions it to be joined in pronunciation with the following *letters*: as, 'Fàll, bàle, mòod, hòuse, e.'

.yllable is short. when the accent is on the consonant; *which* occasions the vowel to .ckly joined to the succeeding *letter*: as, 'ànt, bònnĕt, hŭngĕr.'

long syllable generally requires double the time of a short one *in pronouncing it*: 'Màte' and 'Nòte' should be pronounced as slowly again as 'Măt' and 'Nŏt.'"— *y's Gram.* 8vo, p. 239; 12mo, 192; 18mo, 57; *Alger's*, 72; *D. C. Allen's*, 86; *Bacon's, omly's*, 168; *Cooper's*, 176; *Cutler's*, 165; *Davenport's*, 121; *Felton's*, 134; *Frost's El. isk's*, 32; *Maltby's*, 115; *Parker and Fox's*, iii, 47; *Pond's*, 198; *S. Putnam's*, 96; *R. C. s*, 187; *Rev. T. Smith's*, 68.

e we see a revival and an abundant propagation of Sheridan's erroneous doctrine, that cent produces both short quantity and long, according to its seat; and since none of se grammars, but the first two of Murray's, give any *other* rules for the discrimination ntities, we must infer, that these were judged sufficient. Now, of all the principles ich any have ever pretended to determine the quantity of syllables, none, so far as I are more defective or fallacious than these. They are liable to more objections than orth while to specify. Suffice it to observe, that they divide certain accented syllables ng and short, and say nothing of the unaccented; whereas it is plain, and acknowl- even by Murray and Sheridan themselves, that in "*ant, bonnĕt, hungĕr*," and the like, accented syllables are the *only short ones*: the rest can be, and here are, lengthened.[*]

16.—The foregoing principles, differently expressed, and perchance in some instances fitly, are found in many other grammars, and in some of the very latest; but they erywhere a *mere dead letter*, a record which, if it is not always untrue, is seldom .tood. and never applied in any way to practice. The following are some examples:

"In a long syllable, the vowel is accented; in a short syllable [,] the consonant; *ŏll, pŏll; tŏp, cŭt*."—*Rev. W. Allen's Gram.* p. 222.

"A syllable *or word* is long, when the accent is on the vowel: as nŏ, lìne, là, mè; and when on the consonant: as nŏt, lĭn, Làtin, mĕt."—*S. Barrett's Grammar*, ("*Principles guage*,") p. 112.

"A syllable is long when the accent is on the vowel, as Pàll, sàle, mòuse, crèature. .ble is short when the accent is placed on the consonant; as great', let'ter, mas'ter." *D. Blair's Practical Gram.* p. 117.

"When the stress is on the *vowel*, the measure of quantity is *long*: as, Màte, fàte, .in, plàyful, un der mìne. When the stress is on a *consonant*, the quantity is *short*: as, .t', com pel', prog'ress, dis man'tle."—*Pardon Davis's Practical Gram.* p. 125.

"The quantity of a syllable is considered as *long* or *short*. It is long when the accent .e vowel; as, Fàll, bàle, mòod, hòuse, fèature. It is short when the accent is placed .consonant; as, Mas'ter, let'ter."—*Guy's School Gram.* p. 118; *Picket's Analytical Gram.*, 2d Ed., p. 224.

"A syllable is *long* when the accent is on the vowel; and *short*, when the accent is .consonant. A *long* syllable requires twice the time in pronouncing it that a *short* .q. Long syllables are marked thus –; as, tùbe; short syllables, thus ˘; as, măn."— *English Gram.* p. 120.

"When the accent is on a vowel, the syllable is generally long; as àlehòuse, amùse- .ntures. But when the accent is on a consonant, the syllable is mostly short; as,

---

the consonant be in its nature a short one, the syllable is necessarily short. If it be a long one, that is, e sound is capable of being lengthened, it *may be long or short* at the will of the speaker. By a short con- mean one whose sound cannot be continued after a vowel, such as c or k p t, as ac, ap, at—whilst that onsonants can, as, al em en er ev, &c."—*Sheridan's Lectures on Elocution*, p. 58. Sheridan here forgets '*row* is one of his examples of short quantity.

r admits that "accent on a *semi vowel*" may make the syllable long; and his semivowels are these: n, r, v, s z, x, and c and g soft." See his *Octavo Gram.* p. 240 and p. 8.

hăp'py, măn'ner. A long syllable requires twice as much time in the pronunciation. as short one; as, *hāte, hŭt; nōte, nŏt; cāne, căn; fĭne, fĭn."—Jaudon's Union Gram.* p. 17.

(8.) "If the syllable *be long,* the accent is on the vowel; as, in *bāle, mōōd, educátion.* If *short,* the accent is on the consonant; as, in *ŭnt, bŏnnet, hŭnger,* &c."—*Merchant's Am can School Gram.* p. 145.

The quantity of our unaccented syllables, none of these authors, except Allen, thoug it worth his while to notice. But among their accented syllables, they all include *every one syllable,* though most of them thereby pointedly contradict their own definitions accent. To find in our language no short syllables but such as are accented, is certainly very strange and very great oversight. Frazee says, "The pronunciation of an accent syllable *requires double the time* of that of an unaccented one."—*Frazee's Improved Gram.* 180. If so, our poetical quantities are greatly misrepresented by the rules above cited Allen truly says, "Unaccented syllables are generally short; as, *rĕtŭrn, tŭrnĕr."—Elem of E. Gram.* p. 222. But how it was ever found out, that in these words we accent only t vowel *u,* and in such as *hunter* and *bluntly,* some one of the consonants only, he does a inform us.

OBS. 17.—As might be expected, it is not well agreed among those who accent single con senants and vowels, *what particular letter* should receive the stress and the mark. The word or syllable "*ant,*" for example, is marked "an't" by Alger, Bacon, and others enforce the *n;* "ant'" by Frost, Putnam, and others, to enforce the *t;* "ănt" by Mur Russell, and others, to show, as they say, "*the accent on the consonant!*" But, in "A'NTLER Dr. Johnson accented the *a;* and, to mark the same pronunciation, Worcester now writ "ÂNT'LER;" while almost any prosodist, in scanning, would mark this word "ânt'lĕr." s call it a *trochee.** Churchill, who is in general a judicious observer, writes thus: "T *leading feature* in the English language, on which *it's* melody both in prose and verse ver *depends,* is *it's accent.* Every word in it of *more than one syllable* has one of *it's* syllable tinguished by this from the rest; the accent being in some cases on the vowel, in others *consonant that closes the syllable:* on the vowel, when it has *it's* long sound; on the cons when the vowel is short."—*Churchill's New Gram.* p. 181. But to this, as a rule of accent tion, no attention is in fact paid nowadays. Syllables that have long vowels not very properly take the sign of stress on or after a consonant or a mute vowel; as, *air'y chăm'ber, slāy'er, bĕad'rōll, slēa'zy, slēĕp'er, slēĕve'less, live'ly, mind'fŭl, slight'y, sil'ts bōld'ness, grōss'ly, whōl'ly, ūse'less."—See Worcester's Dict.*

OBS. 18.—It has been seen, that Murray's principles of quantity were greatly altered himself, after the first appearance of his grammar. To have a full and correct view of this it is necessary to notice something more than his main text, as revised, with which a amenders content themselves, and which he himself thought sufficient for his *Abridgem* The following positions, which, in some of his revisals, he added to the large grammar, therefore cited :—

(1.) "Unaccented syllables are generally short: as, 'ădmīre, bōldnĕss, sĭnnĕr.' But this rule there are *many* exceptions: as, 'ălsō, éxīle, gángrēne, úmpīre, fóretáste,' &c.

(2.) "When the accent is on the consonant, the syllable is often *more or less short,* ends with a *single consonant,* or with more than *one:* as, 'Săd'ly, róbber; persist, mai

(3.) "When the accent is on a *semi-vowel,* the time of the syllable *may be protract* dwelling upon the *semi-vowel:* as, 'Cur', can', fulfil' :' but when the accent falls on a the syllable *cannot be lengthened in the same manner:* as, 'Búbble, cáptain, tótter.'"—L ray's Gram. 8vo, p. 240; 12mo, 193.

(4.) "In this work, and in the author's Spelling-book, the vowels *e* and *o,* in the : syllable of such words as, behave, prejudge, domain, propose; and in the second syl of such as pulley, turkey, borrow, follow; are considered as *long vowels.* The syllables in such words as, baby, spicy, holy, fury, are also considered as *long syllab* Ib. 8vo, p. 241.

(5.) "In the words *scarecrow, wherefore,* both the syllables are *unquestionably* not of equal length. *We* presume *therefore,* that the syllables under consideration, those which end with the sound of *e* or *o* without accent,] may also be properly *long syllables,* though their length is not equal to that of some others."—*Murray's Gram.* p. 241.

OBS. 19.—Sheridan's "*infallible rule,*" that no vowel ever has a long sound in an unaccent ed syllable," is in striking contrast with three of these positions, and the exact truth of matter is with neither author. But, for the accuracy of his doctrine, Murray appeal "the authority of the judicious Walker," which he seems to think sufficient to prove syllable long whose vowel is called so; while the important distinction suggested

---

* On account of the different uses made of the breve, the macron, and the accents, one grammarian has posed a new mode of marking poetic quantities. Something of the kind might be useful; but there were reversal of order in this scheme, the macrotone being here made light, and the stenotone dark and heav

" Long and short syllables have *sometimes* been designated by the same marks which are used for accent and the quality of the vowels; but it will be better [.] to prevent confusion [,] to use different marks. The may represent a long syllable, and this * a short syllable; as,

'At the close of the day when the hamlet is still.' "—*Perley's Gram.* p. 78.

Walker, in his Principles, No. 529, between "the lengt   ness of the vowels," and "that quantity which constitutes poetry," is entirely overl   is safe to affirm, that all the accented syllables occurring in the examples above, are   nd all the unaccented ones, *short*; for Murray's long syllables vary in length, and his   ort ones in shortness, till not only the just proportion, but the actual relation, of long and short, is evidently lost with some of them. Does not *match* in "*match'less*," *sad* in "*sad'ly*," or *bub* in "*bub'ble*," require more time, than *so* in "*al'so*," *key* in "*tur'key*," or *ly* in "*ho'ly*"? If so, four of the preceding positions are very faulty. And so, indeed, is the remaining one; for where is the sense of saying, that "when the accent falls *on a mute*, the syllable cannot be lengthened *by dwelling upon the semi-vowel*"? This is an apparent truism, and yet not true. For a semivowel in the middle or at the beginning of a syllable, may lengthen it as much as if it stood at the end. "*Cur*" and "*can*," here given as protracted syllables, are certainly no longer by usage, and no more susceptible of protraction, than "*mat*" and "*not*," "*art*" and "*ant*," which are among the author's examples of short quantity. And if a semivowel accented will make the syllable long, was it not both an error and a self-contradiction, to give "*bŏnnĕt*" and "*hŭngĕr*" as examples of quantity *shortened* by the accent? The syllable *man* has two semivowels; and the letter *l*, as in "*fulfil*," is the most sonorous of consonants; yet, as we see above, among their false examples of short syllables accented, different authors have given the words "*man*" and "*man'ner*," "*dis-man'-tle*" and "*com-pel*," "*mas'ter*" and "*let'ter*," with sundry other sounds which may easily be lengthened. Sanborn says, "The *breve* distinguishes a *short syllable*; as, *mŭnner*."—*Analytical Gram.* p. 273. Parker and Fox say, "The Breve (thus ˘) is placed over a vowel to indicate *its short sound*; as, St. Hĕlena."—*English Gram.* Part iii, p. 31. Both explanations of this sign are defective; and neither has a suitable example. The name "*St. Hĕlĕ'nă*," as pronounced by Worcester, and as commonly heard, is two trochees; but "*Hĕl'ĕna*," for *Helen*, having the penult short, takes the accent on the first syllable, which is thereby *made long*, though the vowel sound is *called short*. Even Dr. Webster, who expressly notes the difference between "long and short *vowels*" and "long and short *syllables*," allows himself, on the very same page, to confound them: so that, of his three examples of a *short syllable*,—"*thŭt, not', mĕlon*,"— all are erroneous; two being monosyllables, which any emphasis must lengthen; and the third,—the word "*mĕl'on*,"—with the first syllable marked short, and not the last! See *Webster's Improved Gram.* p. 157.

OBS. 20.—Among the latest of our English grammars, is Chandler's new one of 1847. The Prosody of this work is fresh from the mint; the author's old grammar of 1821, which is the nucleus of this, being "confined to Etymology and Syntax." If from any body the public has a right to expect correctness in the details of grammar, it is from one who has had the subject so long and so habitually before him. "*Accent*," says this author, "is *the* stress on a syllable, *or letter*."—*Chandler's Common School Gram.* p. 188. Now, if our less prominent words and syllables require *any* force at all, a definition so loose as this, may give accent to some words, or to all; to some syllables, or to all; to some letters, or to all— except those which are *silent!* And, indeed, whether the stress which distinguishes some monosyllables from others, is supposed by the writer to be accent, or emphasis, or both, it is scarcely possible to ascertain from his elucidations. "The term *emphasis*," says he, "is used to denote a fuller sound of voice *after* certain words that come in *antithesis*; that is, contrast. ' He can *write*, but he cannot *read*.' Here, *read* and *write* are *antithetical* (that is, in contrast), and are *accented*, or *emphasized*."—P. 189. The word "*after*" here may possibly be a misprint for *upon*; but no preposition really suits the connexion : the participle *impressing* or *affecting* would be better. Of *quantity*, this work gives the following account : "The *quantity* of a *syllable* is that time which is required to pronounce it. A syllable may be *long* or *short*. *Hate* is long, as the vowel *a* is elongated by the final *e*; *hat* is short, and requires about half the time for pronunciation which is used in pronouncing *hate*. So of *ate*, *at*; *bate*, *bat*; *cure*, *cur*. Though unaccented syllables are usually short, yet *many* of those which are accented are short also. The following are short: *ădvent*, *sin'ner*, *sup'per*. In the following, the unaccented syllables are long: *ălso*, *ĕxile*, *găngrene*, *ŭmpire*. It may be remarked, that the quantity of a syllable is short when the accent is on the consonant; as, art', bon'net, hun'ger. The *hyphen* (-), placed over a syllable, denotes that it is long: nā'ture. The breve (˘) over a syllable, denotes that it is short; as, dĕtrăct."—*Chandler's Common School Gram.* p. 189. This scheme of quantity is truly remarkable for its absurdity and confusion. What becomes of the elongating power of *e*, without accent or emphasis, as in *jun'cate*, *pal'ate*, *prel'ate*? Who does not know that such syllables as "*at*, *bat*, and *cur*," are often long in poetry? What more absurd, than to suppose both syllables short in such words as, "*ădvent*, *sin'ner*, *sup'per*," and then give "sĕrmŏn, filtĕr, spĭrĭt, găthĕr," and the like, for regular trochees, with "the first syllable long, and the second short," as does this author? What more contradictory and confused, than to pretend that the primal sound of a vowel lengthens an unaccented syllable, and accent on the consonant shortens an accented one, as if in "*ăl'so*" the first syllable must be short and the second long, and then be compelled, by the evidence of one's senses to mark "ēchŏ" as a trochee, and "dĕtrăct" as an iambus? What less pardonable misnomer, than for a great critic to call the sign of long quantity a "*hyphen*"?

OBS. 21.—The following suggestions found in two of Dr. Webster's grammars, are no far from the truth : "Most prosodians who have treated particularly of this subject, have been guilty of a fundamental error, in considering the movement of English verse as depending on long and short syllables, formed by long and short vowels. This hypothesis h led them into capital mistakes. The truth is, many of those syllables which are consider as *long* in verse, are formed by the shortest vowels in the language; as, *strength, health, grand.* The doctrine, that long vowels are necessary to form long syllables in poetry at length exploded, and the principles which regulate the movement of our verse, a explained ; viz. *accent* and *emphasis.* Every emphatical word, and every accented syll ble, will form what is called in verse, a long syllable. The unaccented syllables, m unemphatical monosyllabic words, are considered as short syllables."—*Webster's Philosophi Gram.* p. 222 ; *Improved Gram.* 158. Is it not remarkable, that, on the same page wi this passage, the author should have given the first syllable of "*melon*" as an example *short* quantity ?

OBS. 22.—If the principle is true, which every body now takes for granted, that the fore dation of versifying is some distinction pertaining to syllables ; it is plain, that nothing co be done towards teaching the Art of Measuring Verses, till it be known *upon what distincti* in syllables our scheme of versification is based, and by what rule or rules the discrimin tion is, or ought to be, made. Errors here are central, radical, fundamental. Hence th necessity of these present disquisitions. Without some effectual criticism on their num false positions, prosodists may continue to theorize, dogmatize, plagiarize, and blund on, as they have done, indefinitely, and knowledge of the rhythmic art be in no degr advanced by their productions, new or old. For the supposition is, that in general th consulters of these various oracles are persons more fallible still, and therefore likely to b misled by any errors that are not expressly pointed out to them. In this work, it is a sumed, that *quantity,* not laboriously ascertained by "a great variety of rules applied fro the Greek and Latin prosody," but discriminated on principles of our own—*quantity, in* pendent in some degree on the nature and number of the letters in a syllable, but sti more on the presence or absence of stress—is the true foundation of our metre. It ha already been stated, and perhaps proved, that this theory is as well supported by authori as any ; but, since Lindley Murray, persuaded wrong by the positiveness of Sheridan, ex changed his scheme of feet formed by quantities, for a new one of "feet formed by accent" —or, rather, for an impracticable mixture of both, a scheme of supposed "*duplicates* o each foot"—it has been becoming more and more common for grammarians to repres the basis of English versification to be, not the distinction of long and short quantiti, but the recurrence of *accent* at certain intervals. Such is the doctrine of Butler, Febi, Fowler, S. S. Greene, Hart, Hiley, R. C. Smith, Weld, Wells, and perhaps others. But, in this, all these writers contradict themselves ; disregard their own definitions of accent; count monosyllables to be accented or unaccented ; displace emphasis from the rank which Murray and others give it, as "the great regulator of quantity ;" and suppose the length or shortness of syllables not to depend on the presence or absence of either accent or emphe sis ; and not to be of much account in the construction of English verse. As these stricture are running to a great length, it may be well now to introduce the poetic feet, and t reserve, for notes under that head, any further examination of opinions as to what constitute the *foundation* of verse.

SECTION III.—OF POETIC FEET.

A verse, or line of poetry, consists of successive combinations of called *feet.* A poetic *foot,* in English, consists either of two or syllables, as in the following examples :

1. "Căn tў | -rănts bŭt | bў tў | -rănts cōn | -quĕred bē ? "—
2. "Hōlў, | hōlў, | hōlў ! | āll thĕ | sāints ă | -dōre thĕe."—*Heber.*
3. "Aňd thĕ brēath | ŏf thĕ Dē | -ĭtў cīr | -clĕd thĕ roōm."—*Hunt.*
4. "Hāil tŏ thĕ | chiĕf whŏ ĭn | triŭmph ăd | -vāncĕs ! "—*Scott.*

EXPLANATIONS AND DEFINITIONS.

Poetic feet being arbitrary combinations, contrived merely for the verses, and the ready ascertainment of the syllables that suit each rhythm, among prosodists a perplexing diversity of opinion, as to the *number* which w to recognize in our language. Some will have only two or three ; others, four: eight ; and others, twelve. The dozen are all that can be made of two syllabl of three. Latinists sometimes make feet of four syllables, and admit sixteen these, acknowledging and naming twenty-eight in all. The *principal* are the *Iambus,* the *Trochee,* the *Anapest,* and the *Dactyl.*

1. The *Iambus*, or *Iamb*, is a poetic foot consisting of a short syllable and a long one ; as, *bĕtrāy, cŏnfēss, dĕmānd, ĭntent, dĕgrēe.*

2. The *Trochee*, or *Choree*, is a poetic foot consisting of a long syllable and a short one; as, *hātefŭl, pēttĭsh, lēgăl, mĕasŭre, hōlȳ.*

3. The *Anapest* is a poetic foot consisting of two short syllables and one long one ; as, *cŏntrăvēne, ăcquĭēsce, ĭmpŏrtūne.*

4. The *Dactyl* is a poetic foot consisting of one long syllable and two short ones; as, *lābŏurĕr, pŏssĭblĕ, wŏndĕrfŭl.*

These are our principal feet, not only because they are oftenest used, but because each kind, with little or no mixture, forms a distinct order of numbers, having a peculiar rhythm. Of verse, or poetic measure, we have, accordingly, four principal kinds, or orders ; namely, *Iambic, Trochaic, Anapestic,* and *Dactylic ;* as in the four lines cited above.

The more pure these several kinds are preserved, the more exact and complete is the chime of the verse. But, exactness being difficult, and its sameness sometimes irksome, the poets generally indulge some variety ; not so much, however, as to confound the drift of the rhythmical pulsations : or, if ever these be not made obvious to the reader, there is a grave fault in the versification.

The *secondary* feet, if admitted at all, are to be admitted only, or chiefly, as occasional diversifications. Of this class of feet, many grammarians adopt four ; but they lack agreement about the selection. Brightland took the *Spondee,* the *Pyrrhic,* the *Moloss,* and the *Tribrach.* To these, some now add the other four ; namely, the *Amphibrach,* the *Amphimac,* the *Bacchy,* and the *Antibacchy.*

Few, if any, of these feet are really *necessary* to a sufficient explanation of English verse ; and the adopting of so many is liable to the great objection, that we thereby produce different modes of measuring the same lines. But, by naming them all, we avoid the difficulty of selecting the most important ; and it is proper that the student should know the import of all these prosodical terms.

5. A *Spondee* is a poetic foot consisting of two long syllables ; as, *cōld nīght, pōōr sōuls, āmēn, shrōvetīde.*

6. A *Pyrrhic* is a poetic foot consisting of two short syllables ; as, presumpt- | *ŭoŭs,* perpet- | *ŭăl,* unhap- | *pĭlȳ,* inglo- | *rĭoŭs.*

7. A *Moloss* is a poetic foot consisting of three long syllables ; as, *Dĕath's pāle hōrse,—grĕat whīte thrōne,—dēep dāmp vāūlt.*

8. A *Tribrach* is a poetic foot consisting of three short syllables ; as, prohib- | *ĭtŏrȳ,* innat- | *ŭrăllȳ,* author- | *ĭtătĭve,* innum- | *ĕrăblĕ.*

9. An *Amphibrach* is a poetic foot of three syllables, having both sides short, the middle long ; as, *ĭmprŭdĕnt, cŏnsĭdĕr, trănspŏrtĕd.*

10. An *Amphimac, Amphimacer,* or *Cretic,* is a poetic foot of three syllables, having both sides long, the middle short ; as, *wīndĭngshēet, līfe-ĕstāte, sōul-dĭsēased.*

11. A *Bacchy* is a poetic foot consisting of one short syllable and two long ones ; as, *thĕ whōle wōrld,—ă grĕat vāse,—ŏf pūre gold.*

12. An *Antibacchy,* or *Hypobacchy,* is a poetic foot consisting of two long syllables and a short one ; as, *knĭght-sērvĭce, glōbe-dāisȳ, grāpe-flŏwĕr, gōld-bĕatĕr.*

Among the variegations of verse, one emphatic syllable is sometimes counted for a foot. "When a single syllable is [thus] taken by itself, it is called a *Cæsura,* which is commonly a long syllable."*

For Example :—"Keeping | *time,* | *time,* | *time,*
In a | sort of | Runic | *rhyme,*
To the | tintin | -nabu | -lation | that so | musi | -cally | *wells*
From the | *bells,* | *bells,* | *bells,* | *bells,*
Bells,* | *bells,* | *bells.*"—Edgar A. Poe : *Union Magazine, for Nov.* 1849 ; *Literary World, No.* 143.

* Dr. Adam's Gram. p. 287 ; B. A. Gould's, 257. The Latin word *cæsura* signifies "*a cutting,* or *division.*" The name is sometimes Anglicized, and written "*Cesure.*" See Brightland's Gram. p. 161 ; or Worcester's Dict. *Cesure.*

OBSERVATIONS.

Obs. 1.—In defining our poetic feet, many late grammarians substitute the terms *accented* and *unaccented* for *long* and *short*, as did Murray, after some of the earlier editions of his grammar; the only feet recognized in his *second* edition being the *Iambus*, the *Trochee*, the *Dactyl*, and the *Anapest*, and all these being formed by *quantities* only. This change has been made on the supposition, that accent and long quantity, as well as their opposites, nonaccent and short quantity, may oppose each other; and that the basis of English verse is not, like that of Latin or Greek poetry, a distinction in the *time* of syllables, not a difference in *quantity*, but such a successive accenting and nonaccenting as overrides all relations of this sort, and makes both length and shortness compatible alike with stress or no stress. Such a theory, I am persuaded, is untenable. Great authority, however, may be quoted for it, or for its principal features. Besides the several later grammarians who give it countenance, even "the judicious Walker," who, in his Pronouncing Dictionary, as before cited, very properly suggests a difference between "*that quantity which constitutes poetry,*" and the mere "*length or shortness of vowels,*" when he comes to explain our English accent and quantity, in his "*Observations on the Greek and Latin Accent and Quantity,*" finds "accent perfectly compatible with either long or short quantity;" (*Key*, p. 312;) repudiates that vulgar accent of Sheridan and others, which "is only a greater force upon one syllable than another;" (*Key*, p. 313;) prefers the doctrine which "makes the elevation or depression of the voice inseparable from accent;" (*Key*, p. 314;) holds that, "unaccented vowels are frequently pronounced long when the accented vowels are short;" (*Key*, p. 312;) takes long or short *vowels* and long or short *syllables* to be things everywhere tantamount; saying, "We have *no conception* of quantity arising from any thing but the nature of the vowels, as they are pronounced long or short;" (*ibid.*;) and again: "Such long quantity" as consonants may produce with a close or short vowel, "an English ear *has not the least idea of.* Unless the sound of the vowel be altered, we have *not any conception* of a long or short syllable."— *Walker's Key*, p. 322; and *Worcester's Octavo Dict.* p. 935.

Obs. 2.—In the opinion of Murray, Walker's authority should be thought sufficient to settle any question of prosodial quantities. "But," it is added, "there are some critical writers, who dispute the propriety of his arrangement."—*Murray's Octavo Gram.* p. 241. And well there may be; not only by reason of the obvious incorrectness of the foregoing positions, but because the great orthoëpist is not entirely consistent with himself. In his "*Preparatory Observations,*" which introduce the very essay above cited, he avers that, "the different states of the voice," which are indicated by the comparative terms *high* and *low*, *loud* and *soft*, *quick* and *slow*, *forcible* and *feeble*, "may not improperly be called *quantities* of sound."—*Walker's Key*, p. 305. Whoever thinks this, certainly conceives of quantity as arising from *several other things* than "the nature of the vowels." Even Humphrey, with whom, "Quantity differs materially from time," and who defines it, "the weight, or aggregate quantum of sounds," may find his questionable and unusual "conception" of it included among these.

Obs. 3.—Walker must have seen, as have the generality of prosodists since, that such a distinction as he makes between long syllables and short, could not possibly be the basis of English versification, or determine the elements of English feet; yet, without the analogy of any known usage, and contrary to our customary mode of reading the languages, he proposes it as applicable—and as the only doctrine conceived to be applicable—to Greek or Latin verse. Ignoring all long or short quantity not formed by what are called long or short vowels,[*] he suggests, "*as a last refuge,*" (§ 25,) the very doubtful scheme of reading Latin and Greek poetry with the vowels conformed, agreeably to this English sense of *long* and *short* vowel sounds, to the ancient rules of quantity. Of such words as *fallo* and *ambo*, pronounced as we usually utter them, he says, "*nothing can be more evident* than the long quantity of the final vowel though without the accent, and the short quantity of the initial and accented syllable."—*Obs. on Greek and Lat. Accent.* § 23; Key, p. 331. Now the very reverse of this appears to me to be "evident." The *a*, indeed, may be close or short, while the *o*, having its primal or *name* sound, is *called long*; but the first *syllable*, if fully accented, will have *twice the time* of the second; nor can the proportion be reversed but by changing the accent, and misplacing it on the latter syllable. Were the principle *true*, which the learned author pronounces so "evident," these, and all similar words, would constitute *iambic feet*; whereas it is plain, that in English they are *trochees*; and in Latin,—where "*o* final is *common*,"—either *trochees* or *spondees*. The word *ambo*, as every accurate scholar knows, is always a *trochee*, whether it be the Latin adjective for "*both*," or the English noun for "*a reading desk*, or *pulpit*."

[*] "As to the long quantity arising from the succession of two consonants, which the ancients are uniform in asserting, if it did not mean that the preceding vowel was to lengthen its sound, *as we should do* by pronouncing the *a* in *scatter* as we do in *skater*, (one who skates,) *I have no conception of what is meant;* for if it meant that only the *time of the syllable* was prolonged, the vowel retaining the same sound, I must confess as utter an inability of comprehending *this source* of quantity in the Greek and Latin as in English."—*Walker on Gr. and L. Accent*, § 24; Key, p. 331. This distinguished author seems unwilling to admit, that the consonants occupy time in their utterance, or that other vowel sounds than those which *name* the vowels can be protracted and become long; but these are *truths*, nevertheless; and, since every letter adds *something* to the syllable in which it is uttered, it is by consequence a "*source of quantity,*" whether the syllable be long or short.

OBS. 4.—The names of our poetic feet are all of them derived, by change of endings, from similar names used in Greek, and thence also in Latin; and, of course, English words and Greek or Latin, so related, are presumed to stand for things somewhat similar. This reasonable presumption is an argument, too often disregarded by late grammarians, for considering our poetic feet to be quantitative, as were the ancient,—not accentual only, as some will have them,—nor separately both, as some others absurdly teach. But, whatever may be the difference or the coincidence between English verse and Greek or Latin, it is certain, that, in *our* poetic division of syllables, strength and length must always concur, and any scheme which so contrasts accent with long quantity, as to confound the different species of feet, or give contradictory names to the same foot, must be radically and grossly defective. In the preceding section it has been shown, that the principles of quantity adopted by Sheridan, Murray, and others, being so erroneous as to be wholly nugatory, were as unfit to be the basis of English verse, as are Walker's, which have just been spoken of. But the puzzled authors, instead of reforming these their elementary principles, so as to adapt them to the quantities and rhythms actually found in our English verse, have all chosen to assume, that our poetical feet in general *differ radically* from those which the ancients called by the same names; and yet the *coincidence* found—the *"exact sameness of nature"* acknowledged—is sagely said by some of them *to duplicate each foot into two distinct sorts for our special advantage;* while the *difference*, which they presume to exist, or which their false principles of accent and quantity would create, between feet quantitative and feet accentual, (both of which are allowed to us,) would *implicate different names,* and convert foot into foot—iambs, trochees, spondees, pyrrhics, each species into some other—till all were confusion!

OBS. 5.—In Lindley Murray's revised scheme of feet, we have first a paragraph from Sheridan's Rhetorical Grammar, suggesting that the ancient poetic measures were formed of syllables divided " into *long* and *short*," and affirming, what is not very true, that, for the forming of ours, " In English, syllables are divided into *accented* and *unaccented*."—*Rhet. Gram.* p. 64 ; *Murray's Gram.* 8vo, 253 ; *Hart's Gram.* 182; and others. Now *some* syllables are accented, and others are unaccented ; but syllables singly significant, i. e. monosyllables, which are very numerous, belong to neither of these classes. The contrast is also comparatively new : our language had much good poetry, long before *accented* and *unaccented* were ever thus misapplied in it. Murray proceeds thus : " When the feet are formed by *accent on vowels,* they are *exactly of the same nature as the ancient feet*, and have the same just quantity in their syllables. So that, in this respect, *we have all that the ancients had,* and something which they had not. We have in fact *duplicates of each foot,* yet with such a *difference*, as to fit them for *different purposes,* to be applied at our pleasure."—*Ib.* p. 253. Again : " *We* have observed, that *English verse is composed of feet formed by accent*; and that when the accent falls on *vowels,* the feet are equivalent to those formed by quantity."—*Ib.* p. 258. And again : " From the preceding view of English versification, we may see *what a copious stock of materials* it possesses. For *we are not only allowed the use of all the ancient poetic feet*, in our *heroic measure,* but we have, as before observed, *duplicates of each,* agreeing in movement, though differing in measure,* *and which* make different impressions on the ear; *an opulence peculiar* to our language, *and which* may be the source of a boundless variety."—*Ib.* p. 259.

OBS. 6.—If it were not dullness to overlook the many errors and inconsistencies of this scheme, there should be thought a rare ingenuity in thus turning them all to the great advantage and peculiar riches of the English tongue! Besides several grammatical faults, elsewhere noticed, these extracts exhibit, first, the inconsistent notion—of " *duplicates with a difference ;*" or, as Churchill expresses it, of " *two distinct species of each foot ;*" (*New Gram.* p. 189 ;) and here we are gravely assured withal, that these *different sorts*, which have no separate names, are, sometimes forsooth, " *exactly of the same nature" !* Secondly, it is incompatibly urged, that, " English verse *is composed of feet formed by accent,*" and at the same time shown, that it partakes largely of *feet* " *formed by quantity.*" Thirdly, if " *we have all that the ancients had,*" of poetic feet, and " *duplicates of each,*" " *which they had not,*" we are *encumbered* with an enormous surplus ; for, of the twenty-eight Latin feet,† mentioned by

---

* Murray has here a marginal note, as follows : " Movement and measure are thus distinguished. *Movement* expresses the progressive order of sounds, whether from strong to weak, from long to short, or vice versa. *Measure* signifies the proportion of time, both in sounds *and pauses.*"—*Octavo Gram.* p 259. This distinction is neither usual nor accurate; though Humphrey adopts it, with slight variations Without some species of *measure*,— Iambic, Trochaic, Anapestic, Dactylic, or some other,—there can be no regular *movement*, no " progressive order of sounds." Measure is therefore too essential to movement to be in contrast with it. And the movement " from *strong* to *weak*, from *long* to *short*," is but one and the same, a *trochaic* movement; its reverse, the movement, " *vice versa*," from *weak* to *strong*, or from *short* to *long*, is, of course, that of *iambic* measure. But Murray's doctrine is, that *strong* and *long*, *weak* and *short*, may be separated ; that *strong* may be *short*, and *weak* be *long* ; so that the movement from *weak* to *strong* may be from *long* to *short*, and *vice versa* : as if a trochaic movement might arise from iambic measure, and an iambic movement from trochaic feet ! This absurdity comes of attempting to regulate the *movement* of verse by accent, and not by quantity, while it is admitted that quantity, and not accent, forms the *measure*, which " signifies *the proportion of time.*" The idea that pauses *belong to measure*, is an other radical error of the foregoing note. There are more pauses in poetry than in prose, but none of them are properly " *parts* " of either. Humphrey says truly, " *Feet* are the *constituent parts* of verse."—*English Prosody*, p 8. But L Murray says, " *Feet and pauses* are the constituent parts of verse."— *Octavo Gram* p. 252. Here Sheridan gave bias. Intending to treat of verse, and " the pauses peculiarly belonging to it," the " *Cæsural* pause and the "*Final*," the rhetorician had *improperly* said, " The constituent *parts* of verse are, feet, and pauses." —*Sheridan's Rhetorical Gram.* p. 64.

† " But as many Ways as Quantities may be varied by Composition and Transposition, so many different Feet have the *Greek* Poets contriv'd, and that under distinct Names, from two to six Syllables, to the Number of 124.

Dr. Adam and others, Murray never gave the names of more than eight, and his early editions acknowledged *but four*, and these *single*, not "*duplicates*"—*unigenous*, not severally of "*two species*." Fourthly, to suppose a multiplicity of feet to be "*a copious stock of materials*" for versification, is as absurd as to imagine, in any other case, a variety of *measures* to be materials for producing the thing measured. Fifthly, "*our heroic measure*" is *iambic pentameter*, as Murray himself shows; and, to give to this, "*all the ancient poetic feet*," is to bestow most of them where they are least needed. Sixthly, "feet *differing in measures*," so as to "*make different impressions on the ear*," cannot well be said to "*agree in movement*," or to be "*exactly of the same nature!*"

OBS. 7.—Of the foundation of metre, *Wells* has the following account : "The *quantity of* a syllable is the relative time occupied in its pronunciation. A syllable may be *long* in quantity, as *fate ;* or *short*, as *let*. The Greeks and Romans based their poetry on the quantity of syllables ; but modern versification depends chiefly upon accent, the quantity of syllables being almost wholly disregarded."—*School Gram.*, 1st Ed., p. 185. Again : "*Versification* is a measured arrangement of words [,] in which the *accent* is made to recur at certain regular intervals. This definition applies only to modern verse. In Greek and Latin poetry, it is the regular recurrence of *long syllables*, according to settled laws, which constitutes verse."—*Ib.* p. 186. The contrasting of ancient and modern versification, since Sheridan and Murray each contrived an example of it, has become very common in our grammars, though not in principle very uniform ; and, however needless where a correct theory prevails, it is, to such views of accent and quantity as were adopted by these authors, and by Walker, or their followers, but a necessary counterpart. The notion, however, that English verse has less regard to quantity than had that of the old Greeks or Romans, is a mere assumption, originating in a false idea of what quantity is ; and, that Greek or Latin verse was less accentual than is ours, is another assumption, left proofless too, of what many authors disbelieve and contradict. Wells's definition of quantity is similar to mine, and perhaps unexceptionable ; and yet his idea of the thing, as he gives us reason to think, was very different, and very erroneous. His examples imply, that, like Walker, he had "no conception of quantity arising from any thing but the nature of the vowels,"—no conception of a long or a short *syllable* without what is called a long or a short *vowel sound*. That "the Greeks and Romans based their poetry on quantity " of that restricted sort,—on *such* "*quantity*" as "*fate*" and "*let*" may serve to discriminate,—is by no means probable ; nor would it be more so, were a hundred great modern masters to declare themselves ignorant of any other. The words do not distinguish at all the long and short quantities even of our own language ; much less can we rely on them for an idea of what is long or short in other tongues. Being monosyllables, both are long with emphasis, both short without it ; and, could they be accented, accent too would lengthen, as its absence would shorten, both. In the words *phosphate* and *streamlet*, we have the same sounds, both short ; in *lettuce* and *fateful*, the same, both long. This cannot be disproved. And, in the scansion of the following stanza from Byron, the word " *Let*," twice used, is to be reckoned a *long* syllable, and not (as Wells would have it) a *short* one :

> " Cavalier ! and man of worth !
> *Let* these words of mine go forth ;
> *Let* the Moorish Monarch know,
> That to him I nothing owe :
> Wo is me, Alhama !"

OBS. 8.—In the English grammars of Allen H. Weld, works remarkable for their egregious inaccuracy and worthlessness, yet honoured by the Boston school committee of 1845 and '9, the author is careful to say, "Accent should not be confounded with emphasis. Emphasis is a stress of voice on a word in a sentence, to mark its importance. *Accent* is a stress of voice on a syllable in a word." Yet, within seven lines of this, we are told, that, "A *verse* consists of a certain number of *accented and unaccented syllables*, arranged according to certain rules."—*Weld's English Grammar*, 2d Edition, p. 207 ; "Abridged Edition," p. 137. A doctrine cannot be contrived, which will more evidently or more extensively confound accent with emphasis, than does this ! In English verse, on an average, about three quarters of the words are monosyllables, which, according to Walker, " have no accent," certainly none distinguishable from emphasis ; hence, in fact, our syllables are no more " divided into *accented* and *unaccented*," as Sheridan and Murray would have them, than into *emphasized* and *unemphasized*, as some others have thought to class them. Nor is this confounding of accent with emphasis at all lessened or palliated by teaching with Walk. in its justification, that, "The term *accent* is also applied, in poetry, to *the* stress laid on monosyllabic words."—*Wells's School Gram.* p. 185 ; 113th Ed., § 273. What better is this than to apply the term *emphasis* to the accenting of syllables in poetry, or to all the stress in question, as is virtually done in the following citation ? " In English, verse is regulated by the *emphasis*, as there should be one *emphatick* syllable in every foot ; for it is by the interchange of *emphatick* and *non-emphatick* syllables, that verse grateful to the ear is formed." —*Thomas Coar's E. Gram.* p. 196. In Latin poetry, the longer words predominate, so that, in Virgil's verse, not one word in five is a monosyllable; hence accent, if our use of it were adjusted to the Latin quantities, might have much more to do with Latin verse than with English. With the following lines of Shakspeare, for example, accent has, properly speaking, no connexion:

> " Good friend, thou hast no cause to say so yet:
> But thou shalt have; and creep time ne'er so slow,
> Yet it shall come, for me to do thee good.
> I had a thing to say,—But let it go."—*King John*, Act iii, Sc. 3.

Obs. 9.—T. O. Churchill, after stating that the Greek and Latin rhythms are composed of syllables long and short, sets ours in contrast with them thus: "These terms are commonly employed also in speaking of English verse, though it is marked, *not by long and short*, but by accented and unaccented syllables; the accented syllables being *accounted* long; the unaccented, short."—*Churchill's New Gram.* p. 183. This, though far from being right, is very different from the doctrine of Murray or Sheridan; because, in practice, or the scansion of verses, it comes to the *same results* as to suppose all our feet to be "formed by quantity." To *account* syllables long or short and not *believe* them to be so, is a ridiculous inconsistency: it is a shuffle in the name of science.

Obs. 10.—Churchill, though not apt to be misled by others' errors, and though his own scanning has no regard to the principle, could not rid himself of the notion, that the quantity of a syllable must depend on the "vowel sound." Accordingly he says, "Mr. Murray *justly observes*, that our accented syllables, or those reckoned long, may have either *a long or [a] short vowel sound*, so that we have *two distinct species* of each foot."—*New Gram.* p. 189. The obvious impossibility of "two distinct species" in one,—or, as Murray has it, of "duplicates fitted for different purposes,"—should have prevented the teaching and repeating of this nonsense, propound it who might. The commender himself had not such faith in it as is here implied. In a note, too plainly incompatible with this praise, he comments thus: "Mr. Murray adds, that this is 'an opulence *peculiar* to our language, and which may be the source of a boundless variety:' a point, on which, I confess, *I have long entertained doubts*. I am inclined to suspect, that the English mode of reading verse *is analogous* to that of the ancient Greeks and Romans. Dion. Hal., *de Comp. Verb.*, § xi, speaks of the *rhythm of verse differing* from the proper measure of the syllables, and often reversing it: does not this imply, that the ancients, contrary to the opinion of the learned author of Metronariston, read verse as we do?"—*Churchill's New Gram.* p. 393, note 329.

Obs. 11.—The nature, chief sources, and true distinction of *quantity*, at least as it pertains to our language, I have set forth with clearness, first in the short chapter on Utterance, and again, more fully, in this, which treats of Versification; but that the syllables, long and short, of the old Greek and Latin poets, or the feet they made of them, are to be expounded on precisely the same principles that apply to ours, I have not deemed it necessary to affirm or to deny. So far as the same laws are applicable, let them be applied. This important property of syllables,—their *quantity*, or relative time,—which is the basis of all rhythm, is, as my readers have seen, very variously treated, and in general but ill appreciated, by our English prosodists, who ought, at least in this their own province, to understand it alike, and as it is; and so common among the erudite is the confession of Walker, that "the accent and quantity of the ancients" are, to modern readers, "obscure and mysterious," that it will be taken as a sign of arrogance and superficiality, to pretend to a very certain knowledge of them. Nor is the difficulty confined to Latin and Greek verse: the poetry of our own ancestors, from any remote period, is not easy of scansion. Dr. Johnson, in his History of the English Language, gave examples, with this remark: "Of the *Saxon* poetry some specimen is necessary, though our ignorance of the laws of their metre and the quantities of their syllables, *which it would be very difficult, perhaps impossible, to recover*, excludes us from that pleasure which the old bards undoubtedly gave to their contemporaries."

Obs. 12.—The imperfect measures of "the father of English poetry," are said by Dryden to have been *adapted to the ears* of the rude age which produced them. "The verse of Chaucer," says he, "I confess, is not harmonious to us; but it is like the eloquence of one whom Tacitus commends, it was ' *auribus istius temporis accommodata:* ' they who lived with him, and sometime after him, thought it musical; and it continues so even in our judgment, if compared with the numbers of Lidgate and Gower, his contemporaries: there is the rude sweetness of a Scotch tune in it, which is natural and pleasing, though not perfect. It is true, I cannot go so far as he who published the last edition of him; for he would make us believe the fault is in *our ears*, and that there were really ten syllables in a verse where we find but nine: but this opinion is not worth confuting; it is so gross and obvious an error, that common sense (which is a rule in every thing but matters of faith and revelation) must convince the reader that equality of numbers in every verse, which we call Heroic, was either not known, or not always practised in Chaucer's age. It were an easy matter to produce some thousands of his verses, which are lame for want of half a foot, and sometimes a whole one, and which no pronunciation can make otherwise. We can only say, that he lived in the infancy of our poetry, and that nothing is brought to perfection at the first."—*British Poets*, Vol. iii, p. 171.

OBS. 13.—Dryden appears to have had more faith in the ears of his own age than in those of an earlier one; but Poe, of our time, himself an ingenious versifier, in his Notes upon English Verse, conveys the idea that all ears are alike competent to appreciate the elements of metre. "Quantity," according to his dogmatism, "is a point in the investigation of which the lumber of mere learning may be dispensed with, if ever in any. *Its appreciation*," says he, "*is universal.* It appertains to no region, nor race, nor era in especial. To melody and to harmony the Greeks hearkened with ears precisely similar to those which we employ, for similar purposes, at present; and a pendulum at Athens would have vibrated much after the same fashion as does a pendulum in the city of Penn." —*The Pioneer*, Vol. i, p. 103. Supposing here not even the oscillations of a pendulum to be more uniform than are the nature and just estimation of quantity the world over, this author soon after expounds his idea of the thing as follows: "I have already said that all syllables, in metre, are either long or short. Our usual prosodies maintain that a long syllable is equal, in its time, to two short ones; this, however, is but an approach to the truth. It should be here observed that the quantity of an English syllable *has no dependence upon* the sound of its vowel or dipthong [diphthong], but [depends] chiefly upon *accentuation.* Monosyllables are exceedingly variable, and, for the most part, may be either long or short, to suit the demand of the rhythm. In polysyllables, the accented *ones* [say, *syllables*] are always long, while those which immediately precede or succeed them, are always short. *Emphasis* will render any short syllable long."—*Ibid.* p. 105. In penning the last four sentences, the writer must have had Brown's Institutes of English Grammar before him, and open at page 235.

OBS. 14.—Sheridan, in his Rhetorical Grammar, written about 1780, after asserting that a distinction of accent, and not of quantity, marks the movement of English verse, proceeds as follows: "From not having examined the peculiar genius of our tongue, our Prosodians have fallen into a variety of errors; some having adopted the rules of our neighbours, the French; and others having had recourse to those of the ancients; though neither of them, in reality, would square with our tongue, on account of an essential difference *between them.* [He means, "*between each language and ours,*" and should have said so.] With regard to the French, they measured verses by the number of syllables whereof they were composed, on account of a constitutional defect in their tongue, which rendered it incapable of numbers formed by poetic feet. For it has neither accent nor quantity suited to the purpose; the syllables of their words being for the most part equally accented; and the number of long syllables being out of all proportion greater than that of the short. Hence for a long time it was supposed, *as it is by most people at present,* that our verses were composed, not of feet, but syllables; and accordingly they *are denominated* verses of ten, eight, six, or four syllables, *even to this day.* Thus have we lost sight of the great advantage which our language has given us over the French, in point of poetic numbers, by its being capable of a geometrical proportion, on which the harmony of versification depends; and blindly reduced ourselves to that of the arithmetical kind which contains no natural power of pleasing the ear. And hence, like the French, our chief pleasure in verse arises from the poor ornament of rhyme."—*Sheridan's Rhetorical Gram.* p. 64.

OBS. 15.—In a recent work on this subject, Sheridan is particularly excepted, and he alone, where Hallam, Johnson, Lord Kames, and other "Prosodians" in general, are charged with "astonishing ignorance of the first principles of our verse;" and, at the same time, he is as particularly commended for having "especially insisted on the subject of Quantity."—*Everett's English Versification*, Preface, p. 6. That the rhetorician was but slenderly entitled to these compliments, may plainly appear from the next paragraph of his Grammar, just cited; for therein he mistakingly represents it as a central error, to regard our poetic feet as being "formed by quantity" at all. "Some few of our Prosodians," says he, "finding this to be an error, and that our verses were really composed of feet, not syllables, without farther examination, boldly applied all the rules of the Latin prosody to our versification; though scarce any of them answered exactly, and some of them were utterly incompatible with the genius of our tongue. *Thus because the Roman feet were formed by quantity, they asserted the same of ours, denominating all the accented syllables long; whereas I have formerly shewn, that the accent, in some cases, as certainly makes the syllable on which it is laid, short, as in others it makes it long.* And their whole theory of quantity, borrowed from the Roman, in which they endeavour to establish the proportion of long and short, as immutably fixed in the syllables of words constructed in a certain way, at once falls to the ground; when it is shewn, that the quantity of our syllables is *perpetually varying with the sense,* and is *for the most part regulated by* EMPHASIS: which has been fully proved in the course of Lectures on the Art of reading Verse; where it has been also shewn, that *this very circumstance* has given us *an amazing advantage over the ancients* in the point of poetic numbers."—*Sheridan's Rhet. Gram.* p. 64.

OBS. 16.—The lexicographer here claims to have "*shewn,*" or "*proved,*" what he had only *affirmed,* or *asserted.* Erroneously taking the quality of the vowel for the quantity of the syllable, he had suggested, in his confident way, that short quantity springs from the accenting of *consonants,* and long quantity, from the accenting of *vowels*—a doctrine which has been amply noticed and refuted in a preceding section of the present chapter. Nor is he, in what is here cited, consistent with himself. For, in the first place, nothing comes nearer than this doctrince of his, to an "endeavour to establish the proportion of long and short, as immutably fixed to the syllables of words constructed in a certain way"! Next, although he elsewhere contrasts accent and emphasis, and supposes them different, he either confounds them in reference to verse, or contradicts himself by ascribing to each the chief control over quantity. And, lastly, if our poetic feet are not quantitative, not formed of syllables long and short, as were the Roman, what "advantage over the ancients," can we derive from the fact, that quantity is regulated by stress, whether accent or emphasis?

Obs. 17.—We have, I think, no prosodial treatise of higher pretensions than Erastus Everett's "System of English Versification," first published in 1848. This gentleman professes to have borrowed no idea but what he has regularly quoted. "He mentions this, that it may not be supposed that this work is a compilation. It will be seen," says he, "how great a share of it is original; and the author, having deduced his rules from the usage of the great poets, has the best reason for being confident of their correctness."—*Preface*, p. 5. Of the place to be filled by this System, he has the following conception: "It is thought to supply an important desideratum. It is a matter of surprise to the foreign student, who attempts the study of English poetry and the structure of its verse, to find that *we have no work on which he can rely as authority on this subject*. In the other modern languages, the most learned philologers have treated of the subject of versification, in all its parts. In English alone, in a language which possesses a body of poetical literature more extensive, as well as more valuable than any other modern language, not excepting the Italian, *the student has no rules to guide him*, but a few meagre and incorrect outlines appended to elementary text-books." Then follows this singularly inconsistent exception: "We must except from this remark two works, published in the latter part of the sixteenth century. But as they were written before the poetical language of the English tongue was fixed, and as the rules of verse were not then settled, these works can be of little practical utility."—*Preface*, p. 1. The works thus excepted as of *reliable authority without practical utility*, are "a short tract by *Gasc yne*," doubtless *George Gascoigne's* 'Notes of Instruction concerning the making of Verse or Rhyme in English,' published in 1575, and Webbe's 'Discourse of English Poetry,' dated 1586, neither of which does the kind exceptor appear to have ever seen! Mention is next made, successively, of Dr. Carey, of Dryden, of Dr. Johnson, of Blair, and of Lord Kames. "To these *guides*," or at least to the last two, "the author is indebted for many valuable hints;" yet he scruples not to say, "Blair betrays a paucity of knowledge on this subject;"—"Lord Kames has slurred over the subject of Quantity," and "shown an unpardonable ignorance of the first principles of Quantity in our verse;"—and, "Even Dr. Johnson speaks of syllables in such a manner as would lead us to suppose that he was in the same error as Kames. These inaccuracies," it is added, "can be accounted for only from the fact that Prosodians have not thought *Quantity* of sufficient importance to merit their attention."—See *Preface*, p. 4—6.

Obs. 18.—Everett's Versification consists of seventeen chapters, numbered consecutively, but divided into two parts, under the two titles Quantity and Construction. Its specimens of verse are numerous, various, and beautiful. Its modes of scansion—the things chiefly to be taught—though perhaps generally correct, are sometimes questionable, and not always consonant with the writer's own rules of quantity. From the citations above, one might expect from this author such an exposition of quantity, as nobody could either mistake or gainsay; but, as the following platform will show, his treatment of this point is singularly curt and incomplete. He is so sparing of words as not even to have given a *definition* of quantity. He opens his subject thus: "VERSIFICATION is the proper arrangement of words in *a line* according to *their quantity*, and the disposition of *these lines in* couplets, stanzas, or in blank verse, in such order, and according to such rules, as are sanctioned by usage.—A FOOT is a combination of two or *more* syllables, whether long or short.—A LINE is one foot, or more than one.—The QUANTITY of each *word* depends on its *accent*. In words of more than one syllable, all accented syllables are long, and all unaccented syllables are short. Monosyllables are long or short, according to the following Rules:—1st. All Nouns, Adjectives, Verbs and Participles are long.—2nd. The articles are always short.—3rd. The Pronouns are long or short, according to *emphasis*.—4th. Interjections and Adverbs are generally *long*, but sometimes *made short* by *emphasis*.—5th. Prepositions and Conjunctions are almost always *short*, but sometimes *made long by emphasis*."—*English Versification*, p. 13. None of these principles of quantity are unexceptionable; and whoever follows them implicitly, will often differ not only from what is right, but from their author himself, in the analysis of verses. Nor are they free from important antagonisms. "Emphasis," as here spoken of, not only clashes with "accent," but contradicts itself, by making some syllables long and some short; and, what is more mysteriously absurd, the author says, "It *frequently happens* that syllables *long by* QUANTITY become *short by* EMPHASIS."—*Everett's Eng. Versif.*, 1st Ed., p. 99. Of this, he takes the first syllable of the following line, namely, "the word *bids*," to be an example:

"Bĭds mĕ lĭve bŭt tŏ hŏpe fŏr pŏstĕrĭty's prāise."

Obs. 19.—In the American Review, for May, 1848, Everett's System of Versification is named as "an apology and occasion"—not for a critical examination of this or any other scheme of prosody—but for the promulgation of a new one, a rival theory of English metres, "the principles and laws" of which the writer promises, "at an other time" more fully "to develop." The article referred to is entitled, "*The Art of Measuring Verse.*" The writer, being designated by his initials, "J. D. W.," is understood to be James D. Whelpley, editor of the Review. Believing Everett's principal doctrines to be radically erroneous, this critic nevertheless excuses them, because he thinks we have nothing better! "The views supported in the work itself," says his closing paragraph, "*are not, indeed, such as we would subscribe to, nor can we admit the numerous analyses of English metres which it contains to be correct; yet, as it* is as complete in design and execution as anything that has yet appeared on the subject, and well calculated to excite the attention, and direct the inquiries, of English scholars, to the study of our own metres, we shall even pass it by without a word of criticism."—*American Review, New Series,* Vol. I, p. 492.

OBS. 20.—Everett, although, as we have seen, he thought proper to deny that the student of English versification had any well authorized "rules to guide him," still argues that, "The laws of our verse are just as fixed, and may be as clearly laid down, if we but attend to the usage of the great Poets, as are the laws of our syntax."—*Preface,* p. 7. But this critic, of the American Review, ingenious though he is in many of his remarks, flippantly denies that our English prosody has either authorities or principles which one ought to respect; and accordingly cares so little whom he contradicts, that he is often inconsistent with himself. Here is a sample: "As there are *no established authorities* in this art, and, indeed, *no acknowledged principles*—every rhymester being permitted to *invent* his own *method,* and write by *instinct* or *imitation*—the critic feels quite at liberty to say just what he pleases, and *offer his private observations* as though these were really of some moment."—*Am. Rev.* Vol. i, p. 494. In respect to writing, "*to invent,*" and *to* "*imitate,*" are repugnant ideas; and so are, *after* a "*method,*" and, "*by instinct.*" Again, what sense is there in making the "liberty" of publishing one's "private observations" to depend on the presumed absence of rivals? That the author did not lack confidence in the general applicability of his speculations, subversive though they are of the best and most popular teaching on this subject, is evident from the following sentence: "We intend, also, that if these principles, with the others previously expressed, are true in the given instances, *they are equally true for all languages and all varieties of metre,* even to the denial that *any* poetic metres, founded on other principles, can properly exist."—*Ib.* p. 491.

OBS. 21.—J. D. W. is not one of those who discard quantity and supply accent in expounding the nature of metre; and yet he does not coincide very nearly with any of those who have heretofore made quantity the basis of poetic numbers. His views of the rythmical elements being in several respects *peculiar,* I purpose briefly to notice them here, though some of the peculiarities of this new "*Art of Measuring Verses,*" should rather be quoted under the head of *Scanning,* to which they more properly belong. "Of every species of beauty," says this author, "and more especially of the beauty of sounds, *continuousness* is the *first element;* a succession of *pulses* of sound becomes agreeable, only when the breaks, or intervals, cease to be heard." Again: "Quantity, or the *division into measures of time,* is a *second element* of verse; each line must be *stuffed out with sounds,* to a certain fullness and plumpness, that will sustain the voice, and force it to dwell upon the sounds."—*Rev.* p. 486. The first of these positions is subsequently contradicted, or very largely qualified, by the following: "So, the line of significant sounds, in a verse, is also marked by *accents,* or *pulses,* and divided into portions called *feet.* These are necessary and natural for the very simple reason that *continuity by itself is tedious;* and the greatest pleasure arises from the union of continuity with *variety.* [That is, with "*interruption,*" as he elsewhere calls it!] In the line,

'Full mány a tàle thèir mùsic tèlls,'

there are at least four accents or stresses of the voice, with faint *pauses* after them, just enough to separate the continuous stream of sound into these four parts, to be read thus:

Fullman—yataleth—eirmus—ictells,*

by which, new combinations of sound are produced, of a singularly musical character. It is evident from the inspection of the above line, that the division of the feet by the accents is quite independent of the division of words by the sense. The sounds are melted into continuity, and *re-divided again* in a manner agreeable to the musical ear."—*Ib.* p. 486. Undoubtedly, the due formation of our poetic feet occasions both a blending of some words and a dividing of others, in a manner unknown to prose; but still we have the authority of this writer, as well as of earlier ones, for saying, "Good verse requires to be read *with the natural quantities of the syllables,*" (p. 487,) a doctrine with which that of the

* "THE BELLS OF ST. PETERSBURGH."
"Those ev'ning bells, those ev'ning bells,
How many a tale their music tells!"—*Moore's Melodies,* p. 283.
This couplet, like all the rest of the piece from which it is taken, is iambic verse, and to be divided into feet thus:—

"Those ev' | -ning bells, | those ev' | -ning bells,
How man | -y a tale | their mu | -sic tells!"

redivision appears to clash. If the example given be read with any regard to the *cæsural pause*, as undoubtedly it should be, the *th* of *their* cannot be joined, as above, to the word *tale ;* nor do I see any propriety in joining the *s* of *music* to the third foot rather than to the fourth. Can a theory which turns topsyturvy the whole plan of syllabication, fail to affect " the *natural quantities* of syllables ? "

OBS. 22.—Different modes of reading verse, may, without doubt, change the quantities of very many syllables. Hence a correct mode of reading, as well as a just theory of measure, is essential to correct scansion, or a just discrimination of the poetic feet. It is a very common opinion, that English verse has but few spondees ; and the doctrine of Brightland has been rarely disputed, that, " *Heroic Verses* consist of five *short,* and *five long* Syllables *intermixt,* but not so very strictly as never to alter that order."—*Gram.,* 7th Ed., p. 160.[*] J. D. W., being a heavy reader, will have each line so " *stuffed out with sounds,*" and the consonants so syllabled after the vowels, as to give to our heroics three spondees for every two iambuses ; and lines like the following, which, with the elisions, I should resolve into four iambuses, and without them, into three iambuses and one anapest, he supposes to consist severally of four spondees :

> " ' When coldness wraps this suffering clay,
> Ah ! whither strays the immortal mind ? ' "

[These are] to be read," according to this prosodian,

> " Whencoldn—esswrapeth—issuff'r—ingclay,
> Ah ! whith—erstraysth'—immort—almind ? "

" The verse," he contends, " is perceived to consist of *six* [probably he meant to say *eight*] heavy syllables, each composed of a vowel followed by a group of consonantal sounds, the whole measured into four equal feet. The movement is what is called spondaic, a spondee being a foot of two heavy sounds. The absence of short syllables gives the line a peculiar weight and solemnity suited to the sentiment, and doubtless prompted by it."—*Am. Rev.* Vol. i, p. 437. Of his theory, he subsequently says : " It maintains that good English verse is as thoroughly quantitative as the Greek, though it be *much more heavy and spondaic.*"—*Ib.* p. 491.[†]

OBS. 23.—For the determining of quantities and feet, this author borrows from some old Latin grammar three or four rules, commonly thought inapplicable to our tongue, and, mixing them up with other speculations, satisfies himself with stating that the " Art of Measuring Verses " requires yet the production of many more such ! But, these things being the essence of his principles, it is proper to state them *in his own words :* " A short vowel sound followed by a double consonantal sound, usually makes a *long* quantity ;[‡] so also does a long vowel like *y* in *beauty,* before a consonant. The *metrical accents,* which *often differ from the prosaic,* mostly fall upon the heavy sounds ; *which must also be prolonged in reading,* and never slurred or lightened, unless to help out a bad verse. In our language *the groupings of the consonants furnish a great number of spondaic feet,* and give the language, especially its more ancient forms, as in the verse of Milton and the prose of Lord Bacon, a grand and solemn character. One vowel followed by another, unless the first be *naturally made long* in the reading, makes a short quantity, as in *thē old.* So, also, a short vowel followed by a single short consonant, gives a short *time* or *quantity,* as in *tŏ give.* ☞ A great variety of rules for the detection of long and short quantities *have yet to be invented,* or applied from the Greek and Latin prosody. *In all languages they are of course the same,* making due allowance for difference of organization ; but it is as absurd to suppose that the Greeks should have a system of prosody differing in principle from our own, as that their rules of musical harmony should be different from the modern. Both result from the nature of the ear and of *the organ of speech,* and are consequently *the same* in all ages and nations."—*Am. Rev.* Vol. i, p. 488.

OBS. 24.—QUANTITY is here represented as " *time* " only. In this author's first mention of it, it is called, rather less accurately, " *the division into measures of time.*" With too little regard for either of these conceptions, he next speaks of it as including both " *time and accent.*" But I have already shown that " *accents* or *stresses* " cannot pertain to *short* syllables, and therefore cannot be ingredients of quantity. The whole article lacks that *clearness* which is a prime requisite of a sound theory. Take all of the writer's next paragraph as an example of this defect : " The two elements of musical metre, *time* and *accent,* both together constituting *quantity,* are *equally* elements of the metre of verse. Each *iambic* foot or metre, is marked by a swell of the voice, concluding abruptly in an *accent,* or *interruption,* on the *last sound* of the foot ; or, [omit this ' or :' it is improper,] in metres of the *trochaic* order, in such words as *dandy, handy, bottle, favor, labor,* it [the foot]

[*] Lord Kames, too, speaking of " English Heroic verse," says : " Every line consists of ten syllables, *five short and five long ;* from which [rule] there are but two exceptions, both of them rare."—*Elements of Criticism,* Vol. ii, p. 89.

[†] " The Latin is a far more *stately* tongue than our own. It is essentially *spondaic ;* the English is as essentially *dactylic.* The *long* syllable is the spirit of the Roman (and Greek) verse ; the *short* syllable is the essence of ours."—*Poe's Notes upon English Verse ; Pioneer,* Vol. i, p. 110. " We must search for spondaic *words,* which, in English, are rare indeed."—*Ib.* p. 111.

[‡] " There is a rule, in Latin prosody, that a vowel *before two consonants* is long. We moderns have not only no such rule, but profess inability to comprehend its *rationale.*"—*Poe's Notes ; Pioneer,* p. 112.

begins with a heavy accented sound, and declines to a faint or light one at the close. The line is thus composed of a series of swells or waves of sound, *concluding and beginning alike.* The *accents,* or points at which the voice is most forcibly exerted in the feet, *being the divisions of time,* by which a part of its musical character is given to the verse, are *usually made to coincide,* in our language, with the accents of the words as they are spoken; which [coincidence] diminishes the musical character of our verse. In Greek hexameters and Latin hexameters, on the contrary, this coincidence is avoided, as tending to monotony and a prosaic character."—*Ibid.*

OBS. 25.—The passage just cited represents "*accent*" or "*accents*" not only as partly constituting *quantity,* but as being, in its or their turn, "*the divisions of time;*"—as being also stops, pauses, or "*interruptions*" of sound else continuous;—as being of two sorts, "*metrical*" and "*prosaic,*" which "usually coincide," though it is said, they "often differ," and their "interference" is "very frequent;"—as being "the points" of stress "in the *feet,*" but not always such in "the *words,*" of verse;—as striking different feet differently, "each *iambic* foot" on the latter syllable and every *trochee* on the former, yet causing, in each line, only such waves of sound as conclude and begin "*alike;*"—as coinciding with the long quantities and "*the prosaic accents,*" in iambics and trochaics, yet not coinciding with these always;—as giving to verse "a part of its musical character," yet *diminishing* that character, by their usual coincidence with "*the prose accents;*"—as being kept distinct in Latin and Greek, "*the metrical*" *from* "*the prosaic,*" and their "coincidence avoided," to make poetry more poetical,—though the old prosodists, in all they say of accents, acute, grave, and circumflex, give no hint of this primary distinction! In all this elementary teaching, there seems to be a want of a clear, steady, and consistent notion of the things spoken of. The author's theory led him to several strange combinations of words, some of which it is not easy, even with his whole explanation before us, to regard as other than *absurd.* With a few examples of his new phraseology, Italicized by myself, I dismiss the subject: "It frequently happens that *word and verse accent* fall differently."—P. 489. "The *verse syllables,* like *the verse feet,* differ *in the prosaic and* [the] *metrical reading* of the line."—*Ib.* "If we read it by *the prosaic syllabication,* there will be no possibility of measuring the quantities." —*Ib.* "The metrical are perfectly distinct from the *prosaic properties of verse.*"—*Ib.* "It may be called *an iambic dactyl,* formed by the substitution of two short for one long time in the last portion of the foot. *Iambic spondees and dactyls* are to be distinguished by the *metrical accent* falling on the last syllable."—p. 491.

SECTION IV.—THE KINDS OF VERSE.

The principal kinds of verse, or orders of poetic numbers, as has already been stated, are four; namely, *Iambic, Trochaic, Anapestic,* and *Dactylic.* Besides these, which are sometimes called "*the simple orders,*" being un-mixed, or nearly so, some recognize several "*Composite orders,*" or (with a better view of the matter) several kinds of mixed verse, which are said to constitute "*the Composite order.*" In these, one of the four principal kinds of feet must still be used as the basis, some other species being inserted therewith, in each line or stanza, with more or less regularity.

PRINCIPLES AND NAMES.

The diversification of any species of metre, by the occasional change of a foot, or, in certain cases, by the addition or omission of a short syllable, is not usually regarded as sufficient to change the denomination, or stated order, of the verse; and many critics suppose some variety of feet, as well as a studied diversity in the position of the cæsural pause, essential to the highest excellence of poetic composition.

The dividing of verses into the feet which compose them, is called *Scanning,* or *Scansion.* In this, according to the technical language of the old prosodists, when a syllable is wanting, the verse is said to be *catalectic;* when the measure is exact, the line is *acatalectic;* when there is a redundant syllable, it forms *hypermeter.*

Since the equal recognition of so many feet as twelve, or even as eight, will often produce different modes of measuring the same lines; and since it is desirable to measure verses with uniformity, and always by the simplest process that will well answer the purpose; we usually scan by the principal feet, in preference to the secondary, where the syllables give us a choice of measures, or may be divided in different ways.

A single foot, especially a foot of only two syllables, can hardly be said to constitute a line, or to have rhythm in itself; yet we sometimes see a foot so placed, and rhyming as a line.   Lines of two, three, four, five, six, or seven feet, are common ; and these have received the technical denominations of *dim'eter, trim'eter, tetram'eter, pentam'eter, hexam'eter,* and *heptam'eter.*   On a wide page, iambics and trochaics may possibly be written in *octom'eter ;* but lines of this measure, being very long, are mostly abandoned for alternate tetrameters.

ORDER I. — IAMBIC VERSE.

In Iambic verse, the stress is laid on the even syllables, and the odd ones are short. Any short syllable added to a line of this order, is supernumerary ; iambic lines, which are naturally single, being made double by one, and triple by two.   But the adding of one short syllable, which is much practised in dramatic poetry, may be reckoned to convert the last foot into an amphibrach, though the adding of two cannot.   Iambics consist of the following measures :

MEASURE I.—IAMBIC OF EIGHT FEET, OR OCTOMETER.
Psalm XLVII, 1 *and* 2.

" O all | yĕ pĕo | -plĕ, clăp | yŏur hănds, | ănd wĭth | trĭūm | -phănt vŏic | -ĕs sĭng ; ꓶ
No force | the might | -y power | withstands | of God, | the u | -nivers | -al King."
See the "Psalms of David, in Metre," p. 54.

Each couplet of this verse is now commonly reduced to, or exchanged for, a simple stanza of four tetrameter lines, rhyming alternately, and each commencing with a capital ; but, sometimes, the second line and the fourth are still commenced with a small letter : as,

" Your ut | -most skill | in praise | be shown,
for Him | who all | the world | commands,
Who sits | upon | his right | -eous throne,
and spreads | his sway | o'er heath | -en lands."
Ib., verses 7 and 8 ; Edition bound with Com. Prayer, N. Y. 1819.

An other Example.

" The hour | is come | —the cher | -ish'd hour,
When from | the bus | -y world | set free,
I seek | at length | my lone | -ly bower,
And muse | in si | -lent thought | on thee."
Theodore Hook's Remains : The Examiner, No. 82.

MEASURE II.—IAMBIC OF SEVEN FEET, OR HEPTAMETER.
Example I.— Hat-Brims.

" It's odd | how hats | expand | their brims | as youth | begins | to fade,
As if | when life | had reached | its noon, | it want | -ed them | for shade."
Oliver Wendell Holmes : From a Newspaper.

Example II.—Psalm XLII, 1.

"As pants | the hart | for cool | -ing streams, | when heat | -ed in | the chase ;
So longs | my soul, | O God, | for thee, | and thy | refresh | -ing grace."
Episcopal Psalm-Book : The Rev. W. Allen's Eng. Gram. p. 227.

Example III.—The Shepherd's Hymn.

" Oh, when | I rove | the des | -ert waste, | and 'neath | the hot | sun pant,
The Lord | shall be | my Shep | -herd then, | he will | not let | me want ;
He'll lead | me where | the past | -ures are | of soft | and shad | -y green,
And where | the gen | -tle wa | -ters rove, | the qui | -et hills | between.
And when | the sav | -age shall | pursue, | and in | his grasp | I sink,
He will | prepare | the feast | for me, | and bring | the cool | -ing drink.
And save | me harm | -less from | his hands, | and strength | -en me | in toil,
And bless | my home | and cot | -tage lands, | and crown | my head | with oil.
With such | a Shep | -herd to | protect, | to guide | and guard | me still,
And bless | my heart | with ev | -'ry good, | and keep | from ev | -'ry ill,
Surely | I shall | not turn | aside, | and scorn | his kind | -ly care,
But keep | the path | he points | me out, | and dwell | for ev | -er there."
W. Gilmore Simms : North American Reader, p. 376.

Example IV.—"The Far, Far East."— First six Lines.

" It was | a dream | of earl | -y years, | the long | -est and | the last,
. And still | it ling | -ers bright | and lone | amid | the drear | -y past ;
When I | was sick | and sad | at heart | and faint | with grief | and care,
It threw | its ra | -diant smile | athwart | the shad | -ows of | despair :

And still | when falls | the hour | of gloom | upon | this way | -ward breast,
Unto | THE FAR, | FAR EAST | I turn | for sol | -ace and | for rest."
Edinburgh Journal; and *The Examiner.*

Example V.—"Lament of the Slave."— Eight Lines from thirty-four.

"Behold | the sun‚ which gilds | yon *heaven*, | how love | -ly it | appears !
And must | it shine | to light | a world | of war | -fare and | of tears ?
Shall hu | -man pas | -sion ov | -er sway | this glo | -*rious world* | of God,
And beau | -ty, wis | -dom, hap | -piness, | sleep with | the tram | -pled sod ?
Shall peace | ne'er lift | her ban | -ner up, | shall truth | and rea | -son cry,
And men | oppress | them down | with worse | than an | -cient tyr | -anny ?
Shall all | the les | -sons time | has taught, | be so | long taught | in vain ;
And earth | be steeped | in hu | -man tears, | and groan | with hu | -man pain ?"
ALONZO LEWIS: *Freedom's Amulet*, Dec. 6, 1848.

Example VI.—"Greek Funeral Chant."— First four of sixty-four Lines.

"A wail | was heard | around | the bed, | the death | -bed of | the young ;
Amidst | her tears, | the Fu | -*neral Chant* | a mourn | -ful moth | -er sung.
'I-an | -this! dost | thou sleep ?— | Thou sleepst !— | but this | is not | the rest,
The breath | -ing, warm, | and ros | -y calm, | I've pil | -low'd on | my breast !'"
FELICIA HEMANS: *Poetical Works*, Vol. ii, p. 37.

Everett observes, "The *Iliad* was translated into this measure by CHAPMAN, and the *Æneid* by PHAER."—*Eng. Versif.* p. 68. Prior, who has a ballad of one hundred and eighty such lines, intimates in a note the great antiquity of the verse. Measures of this length, though not very uncommon, are much less frequently used than shorter ones A practice has long prevailed of dividing this kind of verse into alternate lines of four and of three feet, thus :—

"To such | as fear | thy ho | -ly name,
myself | I close | -ly join ;
To all | who their | obe | -dient wills
to thy | commands | resign."
Psalms with Com. Prayer: Psalm cxix, 63.

This, according to the critics, is the most soft and pleasing of our lyric measures. With the slight change of setting a capital at the head of each line, it becomes the regular ballad-metre of our language. Being also adapted to hymns, as well as to lighter songs, and, more particularly, to quaint details of no great length, this stanza, or a similar one more ornamented with rhymes, is found in many choice pieces of English poetry. The following are a few popular examples :—

"When all | thy mer | -cies, O | my God !
My ris | -ing soul | surveys,
Transport | -ed with | the view | I'm lost
In won | -der, love, | and praise."
Addison's Hymn of Gratitude.

"God pros | -per long | our no | -ble king,
Our lives | and safe | -ties all ;
A wo | -ful hunt | -ing once | there did
In Chev | -y Chase | befall."
Later Reading of Chevy Chase.

"John Gil | -pin was | a cit | -izen
Of cred | -it and | renown,
A train | -band cap | -tain eke | was he
Of fam | -ous Lon | -don town."
Cowper's Poems, Vol. i, p. 275.

"Turn, An | -geli | -na, ev | -er dear,
My charm | -er, turn | to see
Thy own, | thy long | -lost Ed | -win here,
Restored | to love | and thee."
Goldsmith's Poems, p. 67.

"'Come back ! | come back !' | he cried | in grief,
Across | this storm | -y wa*ter :*
'And I'll | forgive | your High | -land chief,
My daugh | -ter !—oh | my daugh*ter !'*
'Twas vain : | the loud | waves lashed | the shore,
Return | or aid | prevent*ing—*
The wa | -ters wild | went o'er | his child,—
And he | was left | lament*ing.*"—*Campbell's Poems*, p. 110.

The rhyming of this last stanza is irregular and remarkable, yet not unpleasant. It is contrary to rule, to omit any rhyme which the current of the verse leads the reader to expect. Yet here the word "*shore*," ending the first line, has no correspondent sound, where twelve examples of such correspondence had just preceded ; while the third line, without previous example, is so rhymed within itself that one scarcely perceives the omission. Double rhymes are said by some to unfit this metre for serious subjects, and to adapt it only to what is meant to be burlesque, humorous, or satiric. The example above does not confirm this opinion, yet the rule, as a general one, may still be just. Ballad verse may in some degree imitate the language of a simpleton, and become popular by clownishness, more than by elegance : as,

'Father | and I | went down | to the camp   And there | we saw | a thun | -dering gun,—
Along | with cap | -tain Goodwin,   It took | a horn | of powder,—
And there | we saw | the men | and boys   It made | a noise | like fa | -ther's gun,
As thick | as hast | -y pudding;   Only | a na | -tion louder."
                                                        Original Song of Yankee Doodle.

Even the line of seven feet may still be lengthened a little by a double rhyme: as,
How gay | -ly, o | -ver fell | and fen, | yon sports | -man light | is *dashing!*
And gay | -ly, in | the sun | -beams bright, | the mow | -er's blade | is *flashing!*

Of this length, T. O. Churchill reckons the following couplet; but, by the general usage
of the day, the final *ed* is not made a separate syllable:—
" With *hic* | and *hæc*, | as Pris | -cian tells, | *sacer* | -*dos* was | decli | -*nĕd*;
But now | its gen | -der by | the pope | far bet | -ter is | *dĕft* | -*nĕd*."
                                                        Churchill's New Grammar, p. 183.

MEASURE III.—IAMBIC OF SIX FEET, OR HEXAMETER.

Example I.— A Couplet.

"Sŏ vă | -*rÿing still* | their moods, | ŏbsĕrv | -ĭng ÿet | ĭn all
Their quan | -tities, | their rests, | their cen | -sures met | -rical."
                    MICHAEL DRAYTON: *Johnson's Quarto Dict. w. Quantity.*

Example II.— From a Description of a Stag-Hunt.

"And through | the cumb | -rous thicks, | as fear | -fully | he makes,
He with | his branch | -ed head | the ten | -der sap | -lings shakes,
That sprink | -ling their | moist pearl | do seem | for him | to weep;
When aft | -er goes | the cry, | with yell | -ings loud | and deep,
That all | the for | -est rings, | and ev | -ery neigh | -bouring place:
And there | is not | a hound | but fall | -eth to | the chase."
                DRAYTON: *Three Couplets from twenty-three in Everett's Versif.* p. 66.

Example III.—An Extract from Shakspeare.

" If love | make me | forsworn, | how shall | I swear | to love?
O, nev | -er faith | could hold, | if not | to beau | -ty vow'd:
Though to | myself | forsworn, | to thee | I'll con | -stant prove;
Those thoughts, | to me | like oaks, | to thee | like o | -siers bow'd.
Stŭdÿ | his bi | -as leaves, | and makes | his book | thine eyes,
Where all | those pleas | -ures live, | that art | can com | -prehend.
If knowl | -edge be | the mark, | to know | thee shall | suffice;
Well learn | -ed is | that tongue | that well | can thee | commend;
All ig | -norant | that soul | that sees | thee with' | -*oŭt wonder;*
Which is | to me | some praise, | that I | thy parts | admire:
Thine eye | Jove's light | -ning seems, | thy voice | his dread | -*ful thunder,*
Which (not | to an | -ger bent) | is mu | -sic and | sweet fire.
Celes | -tial as | thou art, | O, do | not love | that wrong,
To sing | the heav | -ens' praise | with such | an earth | -ly tongue."
                The Passionate Pilgrim, Stanza IX; SINGER'S SHAK., Vol. ii, p. 594.

Example IV.— The Ten Commandments Versified.

" Adore | no God | besides | me, to | provoke | mine eyes;
Nor wor | -ship me | in shapes | and forms | that men | devise;
With rev | 'rence use | my name, | nor turn | my words | to jest;
Observe | my sab | -bath well, | nor dare | profane | my rest;
Honor | and due | obe | -dience to | thy pa | -rents give;
Nor spill | the guilt | -less blood, | nor let | the guilt | -y live; *
Preserve | thy bod | -y chaste, | and flee | th' unlaw | -ful bed;
Nor steal | thy neigh | -bor's gold, | his gar | -ment, or | his bread;
Forbear | to blast | his name | with false | -hood or | deceit;
Nor let | thy wish | -es loose | upon | his large | estate."
                        DR. ISAAC WATTS: *Lyric Poems*, p. 46.

This verse, consisting, when entirely regular, of twelve syllables in six iambs, is the
Alexandrine; said to have been so named because it was " first used in a poem called *Alexander."—Worcester's Dict.* Such metre has sometimes been written, with little diversity,
through an entire English poem, as in Drayton's Polyolbion; but, couplets of this
length being generally esteemed too clumsy for our language, the Alexandrine has been
little used by English versifiers, except to complete certain stanzas beginning with shorter
iambics, or, occasionally, to close a period in heroic rhyme. French heroics are similar to
this; and if, as some assert, we have obtained it thence, the original poem was doubtless a

* The opponents of capital punishment will hardly take this for a fair version of the sixth commandment.—G. B.

58

French one, detailing the exploits of the hero "*Alexandre.*" The phrase, "*an Alexandrine verse,*" is, in French, "*un vers Alexandrin.*" Dr. Gregory, in his Dictionary of Arts and Sciences, copies Johnson's Quarto Dictionary, which says, "ALEXANDRINE, a kind of verse borrowed from the French, first used in a poem called Alexander. They [Alexandrines] consist, among the French, of twelve and thirteen syllables, in alternate couplets; and, among us, of twelve." Dr. Webster, in his American Dictionary, *improperly* (as I think) gives to the name two forms, and seems also to acknowledge two sorts of the English verse: "ALEXAN'DRINE, or ALEXAN'DRIAN, *n.* A kind of verse, consisting of twelve syllables, or of twelve and thirteen alternately." "The Pet-Lamb," a modern pastoral, by Wordsworth, has sixty-eight lines, all probably meant for Alexandrines; most of which have twelve syllables, though some have thirteen, and others, fourteen. But it were a great pity, that versification so faulty and unsuitable should ever be imitated. About half of the said lines, as they appear in the poet's royal octavo, or "the First Complete American, from the Last London Edition," are as sheer prose as can be written, it being quite impossible to read them into any proper rhythm. The poem being designed for children, the measure should have been reduced to iambic trimeter, and made exact at that. The story commences thus :—

" The dew | was fall | -ing fast, | the stars | began | to blink;
I heard | a voice; | it said, | ' Drink, pret | -ty crea | -ture, drink ! '
And, look | -ing o'er | the hedge, | before | me I | espied
A snow | -white moun | -tain Lamb | *with ă Măid* | -en at | its side."

All this is regular, with the exception of one foot; but who can make anything but *prose* of the following?

" Thy limbs will shortly be twice as stout as they are now,
Then I'll yoke thee to my cart like a pony in the plough."
" Here thou needest not dread the raven in the sky;
Night and day thou art safe,—our cottage is hard by."
WORDSWORTH's *Poems*, New-Haven Ed., 1836, p. 4.

In some very ancient English poetry, we find lines of twelve syllables combined in couplets with others of fourteen; that is, six iambic feet are alternated with seven, in lines that rhyme. The following is an example, taken from a piece of fifty lines, which Dr. Johnson ascribes to the *Earl of Surry*, one of the wits that flourished in the reign of Henry VIII :—

" Such way | -ward wayes | hath Love, | that most | part in | discord,
Our willes | do stand, | whereby | our hartes | but sel | -dom do | accord:
Decyte | is hys | delighte, | and to | begyle | and mocke,
The aim | -ple hartes | which he | doth strike | with fro | -ward di | -vers stroke.
He caus | -eth th' one | to rage | with gold | -en burn | -ing darte,
And doth | alay | with lead | -en cold, | again | the oth | -er's harte :
Whose gleames | of burn | -ing fyre | and eas | -y sparkes | of flame,
In bal | -ance of | ūnē | -qual weyght | he pon | -dereth | by ame."
See *Johnson's Quarto Dict., History of the Eng. Lang.* p. 41.

MEASURE IV.—IAMBIC OF FIVE FEET, OR PENTAMETER.

Example I.— Hector to Andromache.

"Andrōm | -āchē ! | my soul's | fär bēt | -tĕr pärt,
Why with | untime | -ly sor | -rows heaves | thy heart ?
No hos | -tile hand | can an | -tedate | my doom,
Till fate | condemns | me to | the si | -lent tomb.
Fix'd is | the term | to all | the race | of earth ;
And such | the hard | conditi | -on of | our birth,
No force | can then | resist, | no flight | can save ;
All sink | alike, | the fear | -ful and | the brave."
POPE's HOMER : *Iliad*, B. vi, l. 624—632.

Example II.— Angels' Worship.

" No soon | -er had | th' Almight | -y ceas'd | *but* all
The mul | -titude | of an | -gels with | a shout
Loud as | from num | -bers with' | -out num | -ber, sweet
As from | blest voi | -ces ut | -*tĕring jŏy,* | heav'n rung
With ju | -bilee, | and loud | hosan | -nas fill'd
Th' eter | -nal | re | -gions: low | -ly rev | -erent
Tow'rds ei | -ther throne | they bow, | and to | the ground
With sol | -emn ad | -ora | -tion down | they cast
Their crowns | inwove | with am | -arant | and gold."
MILTON : *Paradise Lost*, B. iii, l. 344.

Example III.— Deceptive Glosses.

" The world | is still | deceiv'd | with or | -nament.
In law, | what plea | so taint | -ed and | corrupt,
But, be | -ing sea | -son'd with | a gra | -cious voice,

Obscures | the show | of e | -vil? In | *religiŏn,*
What dam | -nĕd er | -ror, but | some so | -ber brow
Will bless | it, and | approve | it with | a text,
Hiding | the gross | -ness with | fair or | -nament?"
SHAKSPEARE: Merch. of Venice, Act iii, Sc. 2.

Example IV.— Praise God.

" Ye head | -long tor | -rents, rap | -id, and | profound;
Ye soft | -er floods, | that lead | the hu | -mid maze
Along | the vale ; | and thou, | majes | -tic main,
A se | -cret world | of won | -ders in | thyself,
Sound His | -stupen | -dous | praise ; | whose great | -er voice
Or bids | you roar, | or bids | your roar | -ings fall."
THOMSON : Hymn to the Seasons.

Example V.— The Christian Spirit.

" Like him | the soul, | thus kin | -dled from | above,
Spreads wide | her arms | of u | -niver | -sal love;
And, still | enlarg'd | as she | receives | the grace,
Includes | crĕā | -tion in | her close | embrace.
Behold | a Chris | -tian! and | without | the fires
The found | -ĕr ŏf | that name | alone | inspires,
Though all | accom | -plishment, | all knowl | -edge meet,
To make | the shin | -ing prod | -igy | complete,
Whoev | -er boasts | that name— | behold | a cheat !"
COWPER : Charity; Poems, Vol. i, p. 135.

Example VI.—To London.

" Ten right | -eous would | have sav'd | a cit | -y once,
And thou | hast man | -y right | -eous.—Well | for thee—
That salt | preserves | thee; more | corrupt | -ed else,
And there | -fore more | obnox | -ious, at | this hour,
Than Sod | -om in | her day | had pow'r | to be,
For whom | God heard | his Abr' | -ham plead | in vain."
IDEM : The Task, Book iii, at the end.

verse, the iambic pentameter, is the regular English *heroic*—a stately species, and
which most of our great poems are composed, whether epic, dramatic, or descriptive.
ell adapted to rhyme, to the composition of sonnets, to the formation of stanzas of
sorts ; and yet is, perhaps, the only measure suitable for blank verse—which latter
ways demands a subject of some dignity or sublimity.

Elegiac Stanza, or the form of verse most commonly used by elegists, consists of four
rhyming alternately ; as,

" Thou knowst | how trans | -port thrills | the ten | -der breast,
Where love | and fan | -cy fix | their ope | -ning reign ;
How na | -ture shines | -in live | -lier col | -ours dress'd,
To bless | their un | -ion, and | to grace | their train."
SHENSTONE : British Poets, Vol. vii, p. 106.

ic verse is seldom continued perfectly pure through a long succession of lines.
: its most frequent diversifications, are the following; and others may perhaps be
l hereafter :—

The first foot is often varied by a substitutional trochee; as,

" *Bacchus,* | that first | from out | the pur | -ple grape
Crush'd the | sweet poi | -son of | mis-ūs | -ĕd wine,
After | the Tus | -can mar | -iners | transform'd,
Coasting | the Tyr | -rhene shore, | ăs thĕ | winds listĕd,
On Cir | -ce's isl | -and fell. | Who knows | not Circĕ,
The daugh | -ter of | the sun? | whose charm | -ĕd cup
Whoev | -er tast | -ed, lost | his up | -right shape,
And down | -ward fell | īntŏ | a grov | -elling swine."
MILTON : Comus ; British Poets, Vol. ii, p. 147.

By a synæresis of the two short syllables, an anapest may sometimes be employed
iambus ; or a dactyl, for a trochee. This occurs chiefly where one unaccented vowel
es an other in what we usually regard as separate syllables, and both are clearly
though uttered perhaps in so quick succession that both syllables may occupy only
e time of a long one. Some prosodists, however, choose to regard these substitutions
ances of trissyllabic feet mixed with the others ; and, doubtless, it is in general
make them such, by an utterance that avoids, rather than favours, the coalescence.
llowing are examples:—

"No rest: | through man | -y a dark | and drear | -y vale
They pass d, | and man | -y a re | -gion dol | -orous,
O'er man | -y a fro | -zen, man | -y a fi | -ery Alp."—MILTON: P. L., B. ii, l. 618

"Rejoice | ye na | -tions, vin | -dicate | the sway
Ordain'd | for com | -mon hap | -piness. | Wide, o'er
The globe | terra | -queous, let | Britan | -nia pour
The fruits | of plen | -ty from | her co | -pious horn."—DYER: Fleece, B. iv, l. 651

"Myriads | of souls | that knew | one pa | -rent mold,
See sad | -ly sev | -er'd by | the laws | of chance!
Myriads, | in time's | peren | -nial list | enroll'd,
Forbid | by fate | to change | one | tran | -sient glance!"
         SHENSTONE: British Poets, Vol. vii, p. 109.

(3.) In plays, and light or humorous descriptions, the last foot of an iambic line is often varied or followed by an additional short syllable; and, sometimes, in verses of triple rhyme, there is an addition of two short syllables, after the principal rhyming syllable. Some prosodists call the variant foot, in the former instance, an amphibrach, and would probably, in the latter, suppose either an additional pyrrhic, or an amphibrach with still a surplus syllable; but others scan, in these cases, by the iambus only, calling what remains after the last long syllable hypermeter; and this is, I think, the better way. The following examples show these and some other variations from pure iambic measure:—

Example I.— Grief.

"Each sub | stance of | a grief | hath twen | -ty shadōws,
Which show | like grief | itself, | but are | not so:
For sor | -row's eye, | glazed | with blind | -ing tears,
Divides | one thing | entire | to man | -y objects;
Like per | -spectives, | which, right | -ly gaz'd | upon,
Show noth | -ing but | confu | -sion; ey'd | awry,
Distin | -guish form: | so your | sweet maj | -esty,
Looking | awry | upon | your lord's | departūre,
Finds shapes | of grief, | more than | himself, | to wail;
Which, look'd | on as | it is, | is nought | but shadōws."
         SHAKSPEARE: Richard II, Act ii, Sc. 2.

Example II.—A Wish to Please.

"O, that | I had | the art | of eas | -y writing
What should | be eas | -y read | -ing! could | I scale
Parnas | -sus, where | the Mus | -es sit | inditing
Those pret | -ty po | -ems nev | -er known | to fail,
How quick | -ly would | I print | (the world | delighting)
A Gre | -cian, Syr | -ian, or | Assyrian tale;
And sell | you, mix'd | with west | -ern sen | -timentalism,
Some sam | -ples of | the fin | -est O | -rientalism."
         LORD BYRON: Beppo, Stanza XLVIII.

MEASURE V.—IAMBIC OF FOUR FEET, OR TETRAMETER.

Example I.—Presidents of the United States of America.

"First stands | the loft | -y Wash | -ington,   And Jack | -son, sev | -enth in | the train;
That no | -ble, great, | immor | -tal one;   Van Bu | -ren, eighth | upon | the line;
The eld | -er Ad | -ams next | we see;   And Har | -rison | counts num | -ber nine;
And Jef | -ferson | comes num | -ber three;   The tenth | is Ty | -ler, in | his turn;
Then Mad | -ison | is fourth, | you know;   And Polk, | elev | -enth, as | we learn;
The fifth | one on | the list, | Monroe;   The twelfth | is Tay | -lor, peo | -ple say;
The sixth | an Ad | -ams comes | again;   The next | we learn | some fu | -ture day."
         ANONYMOUS: From Newspaper, 1849.

Example II.—The Shepherd Bard.

"The bard | on Ett | -rick's moun | -tain green
In Na | -ture's bo | -som nursed | had been,
And oft | had marked | in for | -est lone
Her beau | -ties on | her moun | -tain throne;
Had seen | her deck | the wild | -wood tree,
And star | with snow | -y gems | the lea;
In love | -liest col | -ours paint | the plain,
And sow | the moor | with pur | -ple grain;
By gold | -en mead | and moun | -tain sheer,
Had viewed | the Ett | -rick wav | -ing clear,
Where shad | -owy flocks | of pur | -est snow
Seemed graz | -ing in | a world | below."
         JAMES HOGG: The Queen's Wake, p. 76.

xample III.—Two Stanzas from Eighteen, Addressed to the Ettrick Shepherd.

ep | -herd ! since | 'tis thine | to boast
e fas | -cinat | -ing pow'rs | of song,
ar | above | the count | -less host,
10 swell | the Mus | -es' sup | -*pliant*
   throng,

The GIFT | of GOD | distrust | no more,
His in | -spira | -tion be | thy guide ;
Be heard | thy harp | from shore | to shore,
Thy song's | reward | thy coun | -try's
   pride."

B. BARTON : Verses prefixed to the Queen's Wake.

Example IV.—"Elegiac Stanzas," in Iambics of Four feet and Three.

| a dirge ! | But why | complain ?
ath | -er a | trium | -phal strain
hen FER | -MOR's race | is run ;
| -land of | immor | -tal boughs
1d | around | the Chris | -tian's brows,
10sc glo | -*rious work* | is done.

We pay | a high | and ho | -ly debt;
No tears | of pas | -sionate | regret
   Shall stain | this vo | -tive lay ; [grief
Ill-wor | -thy, Beau | -mont ! were | the
That flings | itself | on wild | relief
   When Saints | have passed | away."

W. WORDSWORTH : Poetical Works, First complete Amer. Ed., p. 208.

line, the iambic tetrameter, is a favourite one, with many writers of English verse,
been much used, both in couplets and in stanzas. Butler's Hudibras, Gay's Fables,
ny allegories, most of Scott's poetical works, and some of Byron's, are written in
s of this measure. It is liable to the same diversifications as the preceding metre.
equent admission of an additional short syllable, forming double rhyme, seems
bly to adapt it to a familiar, humorous, or burlesque style. The following may suffice
example :—

"First, this | large par | -cel brings | you *tidings*
Of our | good Dean's | eter | -nal *chidings ;*
Of Nel | -ly's pert | -ness, Rob | -in's *leasings,*
And Sher | -idan's | perpet | -ual *teasings.*
This box | is cramm'd | on ev | -ery side
With Stel | -la's mag | -iste | -rial pride."

DEAN SWIFT : British Poets, Vol. v, p. 334.

'ollowing lines have *ten syllables* in each, yet the measure is not iambic of five feet,
t of four with hypermeter :—

"There was | ăn ăn | -cient sage | phi*losopher,*
Who had | read Al | -exan | -der *Ross over."—Butler's Hudibras.*

"I'll make | them serve | for per | -pendiculars,
As true | as e'er | wĕre us'd | by *bricklayers."—Ib.,* Part ii, C. iii, l. 1020.

MEASURE VI.—IAMBIC OF THREE FEET, OR TRIMETER.

Example.—To Evening.

"Now teach | me, maid | compos'd,
To breathe | some soft | -en'd strain."—*Collins,* p. 39.

short measure has seldom, if ever, been used alone in many successive couplets;
s often found in stanzas, sometimes without other lengths, but most commonly with
The following are a few examples :—

Example I.—Two ancient Stanzas, out of Many.

is while | we are | abroad,
3hall we | not touch | our lyre ?
all we | not sing | an ode ?
3hall now | that ho | -ly fire,
us, | that strong | -ly glow'd,
n this | cold air, | expire ?

Though in | the ut | -most peak,
A while | we do | remain,
Amongst | the moun | -tains bleak,
Expos'd | to sleet | and rain,
No sport | our hours | shall break,
To ex | -ercise | our vein."

DRAYTON : Dr. Johnson's Gram. p. 13 ; John Burn's, p. 244.

Example II.—Acis and Galatea.

r us | the zeph | -yr blows,
?or us | distils | the dew,
r us | unfolds | the rose,
And flow'rs | display | their hue ;

For us | the win | -ters rain,
For us | the sum | -mers shine,
Spring swells | for us | the grain,
And au | -tumn bleeds | the vine."

JOHN GAY : British Poets, Vol. vii, p. 376.

Example III.—"Mene, Mene, Tekel, Upharsin."

e king | was on | his throne,
The sa | -traps thronged | the hall ;
thou | -sand bright | lamps shone
O'er that | high fes | -tival.
thou | -sand cups | of gold,
In Ju | -dah deemed | divine—
10 | -vah's ves | -sels, hold
The god | -less Hea | -then's wine !

In that | same hour | and hall,
The fin | -gers of | a hand
Came forth | against | the wall,
And wrote | as if | on sand :
The fin | -gers of | a man,—
A sol | -ita | -ry hand
Along | the let | -ters ran,
And traced | them like | a wand."

LORD BYRON : Vision of Belshazzar.

Example IV.—Lyric Stanzas.

" Descend, | celes | -tial fire,
   And seize | me from | above,
Melt me | in flames | of pure | desire,
   A sac | -rifice | to love.'

Let joy | and wor | -ship spend
   The rem | -nant of | my days,
And to | my God, | my soul | ascend,
   In sweet | perfumes | of praise."
WATTS : *Poems sacred to Devotion,* p. 56.

Example V.—Lyric Stanzas.

" I would | begin | the mu | -sic here,
   And so | my soul | should rise:
O for | some heav'n | -ly notes | to bear
   My spir | -it to | the skies !

There, ye | that love | my sav | -iour, sit,
   There I | would fain | have place
Amongst | your thrones, | or at | your feet,
   So I | might see | his face."
WATTS : *Same work,* "*Horæ Lyricæ,*" p. 71.

Example VI.—England's Dead.

" The hur | -ricane | hath might
   Along | the In | -dian shore,
And far, | by Gan | -ges' banks | at night,
Is heard | the ti | -ger's roar.

But let | the sound | roll on !
   It hath | no tone | of dread
For those | that from | their toils | are gone;
   — *There* slum | -ber Eng | -land's dead.''
HEMANS : *Poetical Works,* Vol. ii, p. 61.

The following examples have some of the common diversifications already noticed under the longer measures:—

Example I.—"Languedocian Air."

"*Love is* | a hunt | -er boy,
   Who makes | young hearts | his prey;
And in | his nets | of joy
   Ensnares | them night | and day.

But 'tis | his joy | most sweet,
   At earl | -y dawn | to trace
The print | of Beau | -ty's feet,
   And give | the trem | -bler chase.

In vain | conceal'd | they lie,
   Love tracks | them ev' | -ry where;
In vain | aloft | they fly,
   Love shoots | them fly | -ing there.

And most | he loves | through snow
   To track | those foot | -steps fair,
For then | the boy | doth know,
   None track'd | before | him there."
MOORE's *Melodies and National Airs,* p. 274.

Example II.—From a "Portuguese Air."

" Flow on, | thou shin | -ing *river,*
   But ere | thou reach | the sea,
Seek El | -la's bower, | and *give her*
   The wreaths | I fling | o'er thee.

But *if* | in wand' | -ring *thither,*
   Thou find | she mocks | my pray'r,
Then leave | those wreaths | to *wither*
   Upon | the cold | bank there."
MOORE: *Same Volume,* p. 261.

Example III.—Resignation.

" O Res | -igna | -tion ! yet | unsung,
Untouch'd | by for | -mer strains ;
Though claim | -ing ev | -*ery mu* | -*se's*
And ev | -*ery po* | -et's pains ! [smile,

All oth | -er du | -ties cres | -cents are
Of vir | -tue faint | -ly bright ;
The glo | -*rious con* | -summa | -tion, thou,
Which fills | her orb | with light !"
YOUNG: *British Poets,* Vol. viii, p. 377.

MEASURE VII.—IAMBIC OF TWO FEET, OR DIMETER.
Example.—A Scolding Wife.

1.

" There was | a man
Whose name | was Dan,
Who sel | -dom spoke,
His part | -ner sweet
He thus | did greet,
Without | a joke :

2.

My love | -ly wife,
Thou art | the life
Of all | my joys ;
Without | thee, I
Should sure | -ly die
For want | of noise.

3.

O, prec | -ious one,
Let thy | tongue run
In a | sweet fret ;
And this | will give
A chance | to live,
A long | time yet.

4.

When thou | dost scold
So loud | and bold,
I'm kept | awake ;
But if | thou leave,
It will | me grieve,
Till life | forsake.

5.

Then said | his wife,
I'll have | no strife
With you, | sweet Dan ;
As 'tis | your mind,
I'll let | you find
I am | your man.

6.

And fret | I will,
To keep | you still
Enjoy | -ing life ;
So you | may be
Content | with me,
A scold | -ing wife."
ANONYMOUS : *Cincinnati Herald,* 1844.

Iambic dimeter, like the metre of three iambs, is much less frequently used alone than in stanzas with longer lines; but the preceding example is a refutation of the idea, that no piece is ever composed wholly of this measure, or that the two feet cannot constitute a line. In Humphrey's English Prosody, on page 16th, is the following paragraph ; which is not only defective in style, but erroneous in all its averments :—

" Poems are never composed of lines of two [-] feet metre, in succession : they [combina-
tions of two feet] are only used occasionally in poems, hymns, odes, &c. to diversify the
metre ; and are, in no case, lines of poetry, or verses ; but hemistics, [*hemistichs*,] or half
lines. The shortest metre of which iambic verse is composed, in lines successively, is that
of three feet ; and this is the shortest metre *which* can be denominated lines, or verses ; and
this is not frequently used."

In ballads, ditties, hymns, and versified psalms, scarcely any line is *more common* than the
iambic trimeter, here denied to be "frequently used ;" of which species, there are about
seventy lines among the examples above. Dr. Young's poem entitled "Resignation," has
eight hundred and twenty such lines, and as many more of iambic tetrameter. His
" Ocean " has one hundred and forty-five of the latter, and two hundred and ninety-two of
the species now under consideration ; i. e., iambic dimeter. But how can the metre which
predominates by two to one, be called, in such a case, an occasional diversification of that
which is less frequent ?

Lines of two iambs are not very uncommon, even in psalmody ; and, since we have some
lines *yet shorter*, and the lengths of all are determined only by the act of measuring, there
is, surely, no propriety in calling dimeters "hemistichs," merely because they are short. The
following are some examples of this measure combined with longer ones :—

Example I.—From Psalm CXLVIII.

1, 2.

" Ye bound | -less realms | of joy,
Exalt | your Ma | -ker's fame ;
His praise | your songs | employ
Above | the star | -ry frame :
Your voi | -ces raise,
Ye Cher | -ubim,
And Ser | -aphim,
To sing | his praise.

3, 4.

Thou moon, | that rul'st | the night,
And sun, | that guid'st | the day,
Ye glitt' | -ring stars | of light,
To him | your hom | -age pay :
His praise | declare,
Ye heavens | above,
And clouds | that move
In liq | -uid air."

The Book of Psalms in Metre, (with Com. Prayer,) 1819.

Example II.— From Psalm CXXXVI.

" To God | the might | -y Lord,
your joy | -ful thanks | repeat ;
To him | due praise | afford,
as good | as he | is great :
For God | does prove
Our con | -stant friend,
His bound | -less love
Shall nev | -er end."—*Ib.* p. 164.

Example III.— Gloria Patri.

"To God | the Fa | -ther, Son,
And Spir | -it ev | -er bless'd,
Eter | -nal Three | in One,
All wor | -ship be | address'd ;
As here | -tofore
It was, | is now,
And shall | be so
For ev | -ermore."—*Ib.* p. 179.

Example IV.— Part of Psalm III.

[O] " Lord, | how man | -y are | my foes !
How man | -y those
That [now] | in arms | against | me rise !
Many | are they
That of | my life | distrust | -fully | thus say :
' No help | for him | in God | there lies.'

But thou, | Lord, art | my shield | my glory ;
Thee, through | my story,
Th' exalt | -er of | my head | I count ;
Aloud | I cried
Unto | Jeho | -vah, he | full soon | replied,
And heard | me from | his ho | -ly mount."

MILTON : *Psalms Versified ; British Poets*, Vol. ii, p. 161.

Example V.—Six Lines of an "Air."

"As when | the dove
Laments | her love
All on | the na | -ked spray ;

When he | returns,
No more | she mourns,
But loves | the live | -long day."

JOHN GAY : *British Poets*, Vol. vii, p. 377.

Example VI.—Four Stanzas of an Ode.

XXVIII.

Gold pleas | -ure buys ;
But pleas | -ure dies,
Too soon | the gross | fruiti | -on cloys :
Though rapt | -ures court,
The sense | is short ;
But vir | -tue kin | -dles liv | -ing joys :

XXIX.

Joys felt | alone !
Joys ask'd | of none !   [miss ;
Which Time's | and For | -tune's ar | -rows
Joys that | subsist,
Though fates | resist,
An un | -preca | -rious, end | -less bliss !

XXX.

The soul | refin'd
Is most | inclin'd
To ev | -*erў mŏr* | -al ex | -cellence ;
All vice | is dull,
A knave's | a fool ;
And Vir | -tue is | the child | of Sense.

XXXI.

The vir | -*tuous mind*
Nor wave, | nor wind,
Nor civ | -il rage, | nor ty | -rant's frown,
The shak | -en ball,
Nor plan | -ets' fall,
From its | firm ba | -sis can | dethrone."

YOUNG'S " OCEAN :" *British Poets*, Vol. viii, p. 277.

There is a line of five syllables and double rhyme, which is commonly regarded as iambic dimeter with a supernumerary short syllable; and which, though it is susceptible of two other divisions into two feet, we prefer to scan in this manner, because it usually alternates with pure iambics. Twelve such lines occur in the following extract:—

LOVE TRANSITORY.

" Could Love | for ever	But since | our sighing
Run like | a river,	Ends not | in dying,
And Time's | endeavour	And, formed | for flying,
Be tried | in vain,—	Love plumes | his wing;
No oth | -er pleasure	Then for | this reason
With this | could measure;	Let's love | a season;
And like | a treasure	But let | that season
We'd hug | the chain.	Be on | -ly spring."

LORD BYRON: See *Everett's Versification*, p. 19; *Fowler's E. Gram.* p. 656.

MEASURE VIII.—IAMBIC OF ONE FOOT, OR MONOMETER.

"The shortest form of the English Iambic," says Lindley Murray, "consists of an Iambus, with an additional short syllable: as,

Disdaining,	Consenting,
Complaining,	Repenting.

We have no poem of this measure, but it may be met with in stanzas. The Iambus, with this addition, coincides with the Amphibrach."—*Murray's Gram.* 12mo, p. 204; 8vo, p. 254. This, or the substance of it, has been repeated by many other authors. Everett varies the language and illustration, but teaches the same doctrine. See *E. Versif.* p. 15.

Now there are sundry examples which may be cited to show, that the iambus, without any additional syllable, and without the liability of being confounded with an other foot, may, and sometimes does, stand as a line, and sustain a regular rhyme. The following pieces contain instances of this sort:—

Example I.—"How to Keep Lent."

" Is this | a Fast, | to keep	No:—'Tis | a Fast | to dole
The lard | -er lean	Thy sheaf | of wheat,
And clean	And meat,
From fat | of neats | and sheep ?	Unto | the hun | -gry soul.
Is it | to quit | the dish	It is | to fast | from strife,
Of flesh, | yet still	From old | debate,
To fill	And hate ;
The plat | -ter high | with fish ?	To cir | -cumcise | thy life ;
Is it | to fast | an hour,	To show | a *heart* | grief-rent ;
Or ragg'd | to go,	To starve | thy sin,
Or show	Not *bin* :
A down | -cast look | and sour ?	Ay, that's | to keep | thy Lent."

ROBERT HERRICK: *Clapp's Pioneer*, p. 48.

Example II.—"To Mary Ann."

[This singular arrangement of seventy-two separate iambic feet, I find *without intermediate points*, and leave it so. It seems intended to be read in three or more different ways, and the punctuation required by one mode of reading would not wholly suit an other.]

" Your face	Your tongue	Your wit
So fair	So sweet	So sharp
First bent	Then drew	Then hit
Mine eye	Mine ear	Mine heart
Mine eye	Mine ear	Mine heart
To like	To learn	To love
Your face	Your tongue	Your wit
Doth lead	Doth teach	Doth move
Your face	Your tongue	Your wit
With beams	With sound	With art
Doth blind	Doth charm	Doth rule
Mine eye	Mine ear	Mine heart
Mine eye	Mine ear	Mine heart
With life	With hope	With skill
Your face	Your tongue	Your wit
Doth feed	Doth feast	Doth fill

O face	O tongue	O wit
With frowns	With check	With smart
Wrong not	Vex not	Wound not
Mine eye	Mine ear	Mine heart
This eye	This ear	This heart
Shall joy	Shall bend	Shall swear
Your face	Your tongue	Your wit
To serve	To trust	To fear."

ANONYMOUS: *Sundry American Newspapers*, in 1849.

Example III.—Umbrellas.

"The late George Canning, of whom Byron said that 'it was his happiness to be at once a wit, poet, orator, and statesman, and excellent in all,' is the author of the following clever *jeu d'esprit*:" [except three lines here added in brackets:]

"I saw | a man | with two | umbrellas,
(One of | the lon | -gest kind | of fellows,)
  When it rained,
  Mēet ă | lādy
  On the | shady
  Side of | thirty | -three,
Minus | one of | these rain | -dispellers.
   'I see,'
  Says she,
'Your qual | -ity | of mer | -cy is | not strain-
ed.'

[Not slow | to comprehend | an inkling,
His eye | with wag | -gish hu | -mour
 twinkling,]
  Replied | he, 'Ma'am,
  Be calm;
  This one | under | my arm
  Is rotten,   [ling.]
[And can | -not save | you from | a sprink-
  Besides, | to keep | you dry,
'Tis plain | that you | as well | as I,
  'Can lift | your cotton.'"

See *The Essex County Freeman*, Vol. i, No. 1.

Example IV.—Shreds of a Song.

1. SPRING.

"The cuck | -oo then, | on ev | -ery tree,
Mocks mar | -ried men, | for thus | sings he,
  Cuckoo';
Cuckoo', | cuckoo',— | O word | of fear,
Unpleas | -ing to | a mar | -ried ear!"

2. WINTER.

"When blood | is nipp'd, | and ways | be foul,
Then night | -ly sings | the star | -ing owl,
  To-who;
To-whit, | to-who, | a mer | -ry note,
While greas | -y Joan | doth keel | the pot."

SHAKSPEARE: *Love's Labour's Lost*, Act v, Sc. 2.

Example V.—Puck's Charm.

[*When he has uttered the fifth line, he squeezes a juice on Lysander's eyes.*]

"On the ground,
Sleep sound:
I'll apply
To your eye,
Gentle | lover, | remedy.

When thou wak'st,
Thou tak'st
True delight
In the sight
Of thy | former | lady's eye."*

IDEM: *Midsummer-Night's Dream*, Act iii, Sc. 2.

ORDER II.—TROCHAIC VERSE.

In Trochaic verse, the stress is laid on the odd syllables, and the even ones are short. Single-rhymed trochaic omits the final short syllable, that it may end with a long one; for the common doctrine of Murray, Chandler, Churchill, Bullions, Butler, Everett, Fowler, Weld, Wells, and others, that this chief rhyming syllable is "*additional*" to the real number of feet in the line, is manifestly incorrect. One long syllable is, in some instances, used *as a foot;* but it is one or more *short syllables only*, that we can properly admit *as hypermeter.* Iambics and trochaics often occur in the same poem; but, in either order, written with exactness, the number of feet is always the number of the long syllables.

Examples from Gray's Bard.

(1.)

"*Ruin* | *seize thee,* | *ruthless* | *king!*
Confu | -sion on | thy ban | -ners wait,
Though, fann'd | by Con | -quest's crim |
 -son wing,
They mock | the air | with i | -dle state.
Helm, nor | *hauberk's* | *twisted* | *mail,*
Nor e'en | thy vir | -tues, ty | -rant, shall |
 avail."

(2.)

"*Weave the* | *warp, and* | *weave the* | *woof,*
The wind | -ing-sheet | of Ed | -ward's
 race.
Give am | -ple room, | and verge | enough,
The char | -acters | of hell | to trace.
Mark the | *year, and* | *mark the* | *night,*
When Sev | -ern shall | re-ech | -o with |
 affright."

"*The Bard, a Pindaric Ode:*" *British Poets*, Vol. vii, p. 281 and 282.

* These versicles, except the two which are Italicised, are *not iambic.* The others are partly trochaic; and, according to many of our prosodists, wholly so; but it is questionable whether they are not as properly amphimacric, or Cretic.

OBSERVATIONS.

OBS. 1.—Trochaic verse without the *final* short syllable, is the same as iambic would be without the *initial* short syllable;—it being quite plain, that iambic, so changed, *becomes trochaic*, and is iambic no longer. But trochaic, retrenched of its last short syllable, is trochaic still; and can no otherwise be made iambic, than by the prefixing of a short syllable to the line. Feet, and the orders of verse, are distinguished one from an other by two things, and in general by two only; the number of syllables taken as a foot, and the order of their quantities. Trochaic verse is always as distinguishable from iambic, as iambic is from any other. Yet have we several grammarians and prosodists who contrive to confound them—or who, at least, mistake catalectic trochaic for catalectic iambic; and that too, where the syllable wanting affects only the last foot, and makes a perhaps but a common and needful cæsura.

OBS. 2.—To suppose that iambic verse may drop its initial short syllable, and still be iambic, still be measured as before, is not only to take a single long syllable for a foot, not only to recognize a pedal cæsura at the *beginning* of each line, but utterly to destroy the only principles on which iambics and trochaics can be discriminated. Yet Hiley, of Leeds, and Wells, of Audover, while they are careful to treat separately of these two orders of verse, not only teach that any order may take at the end "an additional syllable," but also suggest that the iambic *may drop* a syllable "from the first foot," without diminishing the number of feet.—without changing the succession of quantities,—without disturbing the mode of scansion! "Sometimes," say they, (in treating of iambics,) "a syllable is cut off from the first foot; as,

Práise | to Gód, | immór | -tal práise,
Fòr | the lóve | that crówns | our dáys."[—BARBAULD.]

Hiley's E. Gram., Third Edition, London, p. 124; *Wells's*, Third Edition, p. 198.

OBS. 3.—Now this couplet is the precise exemplar, not only of the thirty-six lines of which it is a part, but also of the most common of our trochaic metres; and if this may be thus scanned into iambic verse, so may all other trochaic lines in existence: distinction between the two orders must then be worse than useless. But I reject the doctrine, and trust that most readers will easily see its absurdity. A prosodist might just as well scan all iambics into trochaics, by pronouncing each initial short syllable to be hypermeter. For, surely, if deficiency may be discovered at the *beginning* of measurement, so may redundance. But if neither is to be looked for before the measurement ends, (which supposition is certainly more reasonable,) then is the distinction already vindicated, and the scansion above-cited is shown to be erroneous.

OBS. 4.—But there are yet other objections to this doctrine, other errors and inconsistencies in the teaching of it. Exactly the same kind of verse as this, which is said to consist of "*four iambuses*," from one of which "a syllable *is cut off*," is subsequently scanned by the same authors as being composed of "*three trochees* and an *additional* syllable; as,

'Haste thee, | Nymph, | and | bring with | *thee*
Jest and | youthful | Jolli | -ty.'—MILTON."

Wells's School Grammar, p. 208.

"Vităl | spărk ŏf | heăv'nly | *flăme*,
Quĭt ŏh | quĭt thĭs | mŏrtăl | *frăme*."*[—POPE.]

Hiley's English Grammar, p. 126.

There is, in the works here cited, not only the inconsistency of teaching two very different modes of scanning the same species of verse, but in each instance the scansion is wrong; for all the lines in question are *trochaic of four feet*,—single-rhymed, and, of course, catalectic, and ending with a cæsura, or elision. In no metre that lacks but one syllable, can this sort of foot occur *at the beginning* of a line; yet, as we see, it is sometimes *imagined* to be there, by those who have never been able to find it *at the end*, where it oftenest exists!

OBS. 5.—I have hinted, in the main paragraph above, that it is a common error of our prosodists, to underrate, by one foot, the measure of all trochaic lines, when they terminate with single rhyme; an error into which they are led by an other as gross, that of taking for hypermeter, or mere surplus, the whole rhyme itself, the sound or syllable most indispensable to the verse.

" (For rhyme the *rudder* is of verses,
With which, like ships, they steer their courses.)"—*Hudibras*.

Iambics and trochaics, of corresponding metres, and exact in them, agree of course in both the number of feet and the number of syllables; but as the former are slightly redundant with double rhyme, so the latter are deficient as much, with single rhyme; yet, the number of feet may, and should, in these cases, be reckoned the same. An estimable author now living says, "Trochaic verse, with an additional long syllable, is the same as iambic verse, without the initial short syllable."—*N. Butler's Practical Gram.* p. 193. This instruction is not quite accurate. Nor would it be so, even if there could be "iambic verse without the initial short syllable," and if it were universally *true*, that, "Trochaic verse may take an additional *long* syllable."—*Ibid*. For the addition and subtraction here suggested, will inevitably make the difference of a foot, between the measures or verses said to be the same!

OBS. 6.—"I doubt," says T. O. Churchill, "whether the *trochaic* can be considered as a legitimate English measure. All the examples of it given by Johnson have an additional long syllable at the end: but these are *iambics*, if we look upon the additional syllable to be at the beginning, which is much more agreeable to the analogy of music."—*Churchill's New Gram.* p. 390. This doubt, ridiculous as must be all reasoning in support of it, the author seriously endeavours to raise into a general conviction *that we have no trochaic order of verse!* It can hardly be worth while to notice here all his remarks. "*An additional long syllable*" Johnson never dreamed of—" at the end "— "at the beginning"—or anywhere else. For he discriminated metres, not by the number of feet, as he ought to have done, but by the number of *syllables* he found in each line. His doctrine is this: " Our *iambick* measure comprises verses—Of four syllables,—Of six,—Of eight,—Of ten. Our *trochaick* measures are—Of three syllables,—Of five,—Of seven. These are the measures which are now in use, and above the rest those of seven, eight and ten syllables. Our ancient poets wrote verses sometimes of twelve syllables, as Drayton's Polyolbion; and of fourteen, as Chapman's

---

* See exercises in Punctuation, on page 757, of this work.—G. B.

Homer." " We have another measure very quick and lively, and therefore much used in songs, which may be called the *anapestick.*

> ' May I góvern my pássion with ábsolute swáy,
> And grow wiser and bétter as life wears away.' *Dr. Pope.*

" In this measure a syllable is often retrenched from the first foot, [:] as [,]

> ' When present we lóve, and when ábsent agrée,
> I think not of I'ris [,] nor I'ris of me.'　*Dryden.*

" These measures are varied by many combinations, and sometimes by *double endings*, either with or without rhyme, as in the *heroick* measure.

> ' 'Tis the divinity that stirs *within us,*
> 'Tis heaven itself that points out an *hereafter.'*　*Addison.*

" So in that of eight syllables,

> ' They neither added nor confounded,
> They neither wanted nor abounded.'　*Prior.*

" In that of seven,

> ' For resistance I could *fear none,*
> But with twenty ships had done,
> What thou, brave and happy *Vernon,*
> Hast achieved with six alone.'　*Glover.*

" To these measures and their laws, may be reduced every species of English verse."—*Dr. Johnson's Grammar of the English Tongue,* p. 14. See his *Quarto Dict.* Here, except a few less important remarks, and sundry examples of the metres named, is Johnson's *whole scheme* of versification.

OBS. 7.—How, when a prosodist judges certain examples to " have an additional long syllable at the end," he can " look upon the additional syllable to be at the beginning," is a matter of marvel; yet, to abolish trochaics, Churchill not only does and advises this, but imagines short syllables removed sometimes from the beginning of lines; while sometimes he couples final short syllables with initial long ones, to make iambs, and yet does not always count these as feet in the verse, when he has done so! Johnson's instructions are both misunderstood and misrepresented by this grammarian. I have therefore cited them the more fully. The first syllable being retrenched from an *anapest,* there remains an *iambus.* But what countenance has Johnson lent to the gross error of reckoning such a foot an anapest still?—or to that of commencing the measurement of a line by including a syllable not used by the poet? The preceding stanza from Glover, is *trochaic of four feet;* the odd lines full, and of course making double rhyme; the even lines catalectic, and of course ending with a long syllable counted as a foot. Johnson cited it merely as an example of " *double endings,"* imagining in it no " additional syllable," except perhaps the two which terminate the two trochees, " fear none " and " Vernon." These, it may be inferred, he improperly conceived to be additional to the regular measure; because he reckoned measures by the number of syllables, and probably supposed single rhyme to be the normal form of all rhyming verse.

OBS. 8.—There is false scansion in many a school grammar, but perhaps none more uncouthly false, than Churchill's pretended amendments of Johnson's. The second of these—wherein " the old *seven*[-]*foot iambic* " is professedly found in two lines of Glover's *trochaic tetrameter*—I shall quote :—

" In the anapæstic measure, Johnson himself allows, that a syllable is often retrenched from the first foot; yet he gives *as an example of trochaics with an additional syllable at the end of the even lines* a stanza, which, by adopting the *same principle,* would be in the iambic measure:

> ˇ Fŏr | rĕsĭs- | tănce I | coŭld feăr | nŏne,
> Bŭt | wĭth twĕn | tў shĭps | hăd dŏne,
> ˇ Whăt | thŏu, brăve | ănd hắp | pў Vĕr- | nŏn,
> Hăst | ăchiĕv'd | wĭth sĭx | ălŏne.

In fact, *the second and fourth lines* here stamp the character of the measure ; [☞] *which is the old seven* [-] *foot iambic broken into four and three,* WITH AN ADDITIONAL SYLLABLE AT THE BEGINNING."—*Churchill's New Gram.* p. 391.

After these observations and criticisms concerning the trochaic order of verse, I proceed to say, trochaics consist of the following measures, or metres : —

MEASURE I.—TROCHAIC OF EIGHT FEET, OR OCTOMETER.

Example I.—"The Raven."—First Two out of Eighteen Stanzas.

1.

> " Once up | -on a | midnight | dreary, | while I | pondered, | weak and | weary,
> Over | mӑnў ӑ | quaint and | cūriŏŭs | volume | of for | -gotten | lore,
> While I | nodded, | nearly | napping, | sudden | -ly there | came a | tapping,
> As of | some one | gently rapping, | rapping | at my | chamber | door.
> ' 'Tis some | visit | -or,' I | muttered, | ' tapping | at my | chamber | door—
> Only | this, and | nothing | more.'

2.

> Ah ! dis | -tinctly | I re | -member | it was | in the | bleak De | -cember,
> And each | sēpŭrӑte | dying | ember | wrought its | ghost up | -on the | floor ;
> Eager | -ly I | wished the | morrow ;— | vainly | had I | tried to | borrow
> From my | books sur | -cease of | sorrow— | sorrow | for the | lost Le | -nore—
> For the | rare and | rӑdiӑnt | maiden, | whom the | angels | name Le | -nore—
> Nameless | here for | ever | -more."

EDGAR A. POE : *American Review for February,* 1845.

Double rhymes being less common than single ones, in the same proportion, is this long verse less frequently terminated with a full trochee, than with a single long syllable counted as a foot. The species of measure is, however, to be reckoned the same, though catalectic. By Lindley Murray, and a number who implicitly re-utter what he teaches, the verse of *six trochees*, in which are *twelve syllables* only, is said "to be *the longest* Trochaic line that our language admits."—*Murray's Octavo Gram.* p. 257; *Weld's E. Gram.* p. 211. The examples produced here will sufficiently show the inaccuracy of their assertion.

Example II.— "The Shadow of the Obelisk."—Last two Stanzas.

8.

"Herds are | feeding | in the | Forum, | as in | old E | -vander's | time:
Tumbled | from the | steep Tar | -peian | every | pile that | sprang sub | -lime.
Strange! that | what seemed | most in | -constant | should the | most a | -biding | prove;
Strange! that | what is | hourly | moving | no mu | -tation | can re | -move:
Ruined | lies the | cirque! the | *chariots,* | long a | -go, have | ceased to | roll—
E'en the | Obe | -lisk is | broken | —but the | shadow | still is | whole.

9.

Out a | -las! if | *mightiest* | empires | leave so | little | mark be | -hind,
How much | less must | heroes | hope for, | in the | wreck of | human | kind!
Less than | e'en this | darksome | picture, | which I | tread be | -neath my | feet,
Copied | by a | lifeless | moonbeam | on the | pebbles | of the | street;
Since if | Cæsar's | best am | -bition, | living, | was, to | be re | -nowned,
What shall | Cæsar | leave be | -hind him, | save the | shadow | of a | sound?"
            T. W. PARSONS: *Lowell and Carter's "Pioneer,"* Vol. i, p. 120.

Example III.—"The Slaves of Martinique."—Nine Couplets out of Thirty-six.

"Beams of | noon, like | burning | lances, | through the | tree-tops | flash and | glisten,
As she | stands be | -fore her | lover, | with raised | face to | look and | listen.

Dark, but | comely, | like the | maiden | in the | ancient | Jewish | song,
Scarcely | has the | toil of | task-fields | done her | graceful | beauty | wrong.

He, the | strong one, | and the | manly, | with the | vassal's | garb and | hue,
Holding | still his | spirit's | birthright, | to his | higher | nature | true;

Hiding | deep the | *strengthening* | purpose | of a | freeman | in his | heart,
As the | Greegree | holds his | Fetish | from the | white man's | gaze a | -part.

Ever | foremost | of the | toilers, | when the | driver's | morning | horn
Calls a | -way to | stifling | millhouse, | or to | fields of | cane and | corn;

Fall the | keen and | burning | lashes | never | on his | back or | limb;
Scarce with | look or | word of | censure, | turns the | driver | unto | him.

Yet his | brow is | always | thoughtful, | and his | eye is | hard and | stern;
Slavery's | last and | humblest | lesson | he has | never | deigned to | learn."

"And, at | evening | when his | comrades | dance be | -fore their | master's | door,
Folding | arms and | knitting | forehead, | stands he | silent | ever | -more.

God be | praised for | *every* | instinct | which re | -bels a | -gainst a | lot
Where the | brute sur | -vives the | human, | and man's | upright | form is | not!"
            J. G. WHITTIER: *National Era, and other Newspapers,* Jan. 1848.

Example IV.—"The Present Crisis."—Two Stanzas out of sixteen.

"Once to | *every* | man and | nation | comes the | moment | to de | -cide,
In the | strife of | Truth with | Falsehood, | for the | good or | evil | side;
Some great | cause, God's | new Mes | -siah, | *offering* | each the | bloom or | blight,
Parts the | goats up | -on the | left hand, | and the | sheep up | -on the | right,
And the | choice goes | by for | -ever | 'twixt that | darkness | and that | light.

Have ye | chosen, | O my | people, | on whose | party | ye shall | stand,
Ere the | Doom from | *its* worn | sandals | shakes the | dust a | -gainst our | land?
Though the | cause of | evil | prosper, | yet the | Truth a | -lone is | strong,
And, al | -*beit she* | wander | outcast | now, I | see a | -round her | throng
Troops of | beauti | -ful tall | angels | to en | -shield her | from all | wrong."
            JAMES RUSSELL LOWELL: *Liberator,* September 4th, 1846.

Example V.—The Season of Love.—A short Extract.

"In the | Spring, a | fuller | crimson | comes up | -on the | robin's | breast;
In the | Spring, the | wanton | lapwing | gets him | -self an | other | crest;
In the | Spring, a | *livelier* | iris | changes | on the | burnished | dove;
In the | Spring, a | young man's | fancy | lightly | turns to | thoughts of | love.

Then her | cheek was | pale, and | thinner | than should | be for | one so | young;
And her | eyes on | all my | motions, | with a | mute ob | -servance, | hung.
And I | said, 'My | cousin | Amy, | speak, and | speak the | truth to | me;
Trust me, | cousin, | all the | current | of my | being | sets to | thee.'"

Poems by ALFRED TENNYSON, Vol. ii, p. 35.

Trochaic of eight feet, as these sundry examples will suggest, is much oftener met with than iambic of the same number; and yet it is not a form very frequently adopted. The reader will observe that it requires a considerable pause after the fourth foot; at which place, one might divide it, and so reduce each couplet to a stanza of four lines, similar to the following examples:—

PART OF A SONG, IN DIALOGUE.

SYLVIA.

"Corin, | cease this | idle | teasing;
 Love that's | forc'd is | harsh and | sour:
If the | lover | be dis | -pleasing,
 To per | -sist dis | -gusts the | more."

CORIN.

"'Tis in | vain, in | vain to | fly me,
 Sylvia, | I will | still pur | -sue;
Twenty thousand | times de | -ny me,
 I will | kneel and | weep a | -new."

SYLVIA.

"Cupid | ne'er shall | make me | languish,
 I was | born a | -verse to | love;
Lovers' | sighs, and | tears, and | anguish,
 Mirth and | pastime | to me | prove."

CORIN.

"Still I | vow with | patient | duty
 Thus to | meet your | proudest | scorn;
You for | unre | -lenting | beauty,
 I for | constant | love was | born."

Poems by ANNA LÆTITIA BARBAULD, p. 56.

PART OF A CHARITY HYMN.

1.

"Lord of | life, all | praise ex | -celling,
 thou, in | glory | uncon | -fin'd,
Deign'st to | make thy | humble | dwelling
 with the | poor of | humble | mind.

2.

As thy | love, through | all cre | -ation,
 beams like | thy dif | -fusive | light;
So the | scorn'd and | humble | station
 shrinks be | -fore thine | equal | sight.

3.

Thus thy | care, for | all pro | -viding,
 warm'd thy | faithful | prophet's | tongue;
Who, the | lot of | all de | -ciding,
 to thy | chos en | *Israel* | sung:

4.

'When thine | harvest | yields thee | pleas-
 thou the | golden | sheaf shalt | bind; |ure,
To 'he | poor be | -longs the | treasure
 of the | scatter'd | ears be | -hind.'"

Psalms and Hymns of the Protestant Episcopal Church, Hymn LV.

A still more common form is that which reduces all these tetrameters to single rhymes, preserving their alternate succession. In such metre and stanza, is Montgomery's "Wanderer of Switzerland, a Poem, in Six Parts," and with an aggregate of eight hundred and forty-four lines. Example:—

1.

"'*Wanderer*, | whither | wouldst thou | roam?
 To what | region | far a | -way,
Bend thy | steps to | find a | home,
 In the | twilight | of thy | day?'

2.

'In the | twilight | of my | day,
 I am | hastening | to the | west;
There my | weary | limbs to | lay,
 Where the | sun re | -tires to | rest.

3.

Far be | -yond the At | -lantic | floods,
 Stretched be | -neath the | evening | sky,
Realms of | mountains, | dark with | woods,
 In Co | -lumbia's | bosom | lie.

4.

There, in | glens and | caverns | rude,
 Silent | since the | world be | -gan,
Dwells the | virgin | Soli | -tude,
 Unbe | -trayed by | faithless | man:

5.

Where a | tyrant | never | trod,
 Where a | slave was | never | known,
But where | nature | worships | God
 In the | wilder | -ness a | -lone.

6.

Thither, | thither | would I | roam;
 There my | children | may be | free:
I for | them will | find a | home;
 They shall | find a | grave for | me.'"

First six stanzas of Part VI, pp. 71 and 72.

MEASURE II.—TROCHAIC OF SEVEN FEET, OR HEPTAMETER.

Example.—Psalm LXX, * *Versified.*

Hasten, | Lord, to | rescue | me, and | set me | safe from | trouble;
Shame thou | those who | seek my | soul, re | -ward their | mischief | double.
Turn the | taunting | scorners | back, who | cry, 'A | -ha! | so | loudly;
Backward | in con | -fusion | hurl the | foe that | mocks me | proudly.
Then in | thee let | those re | -joice, who | seek thee, | self-de | -nying;
All who | thy sal | -vation | love, thy | name be | glory | -fying.
So let | God be | magni | -fied. But | I am | poor and | needy:
Hasten, | Lord, who | art my | Helper; | let thine | aid be | speedy.

* The Seventieth Psalm is the same as the last five verses of the Fortieth, except a few unimportant differences of words or points.

This verse, like all other that is written in very long lines, requires a cæsural pause of proportionate length; and it would scarcely differ at all to the ear, if it were cut in two at the place of this pause—provided the place were never varied. Such metre does not appear to have been at any time much used, though there seems to be no positive reason why it might not have a share of popularity. To commend our versification for its "boundless variety," and at the same time exclude from it forms either unobjectionable or well authorized, as some have done, is plainly inconsistent. Full trochaics have some inconvenience, because all their rhymes must be double; and, as this inconvenience becomes twice as much when any long line of this sort is reduced to two short ones, there may be a reason why a stanza precisely corresponding to the foregoing couplets is seldom seen. If such lines be divided and rhymed at the middle of the fourth foot, where the cæsural pause is apt to fall, the first part of each will be a trochaic line of four feet, single-rhymed and catalectic, while the rest of it will become an *iambic* line of three feet, with double rhyme and hypermeter. Such are the prosodial characteristics of the following lines; which, if two were written as one, would make exactly our full trochaic of seven feet, the metre exhibited above:—

" Whisp'ring, | heard by | wakeful | maids,
    To whom | the night | stars *guide* | us,
Stolen | walk, through | moonlight | shades,
    With those | we love | be*side* | us."—*Moore's Melodies*, p. 276.

But trochaic of seven feet may also terminate with single rhyme, as in the following couplet, which is given anonymously, and, after a false custom, erroneously, in N. Butler's recent Grammar, as " trochaic of *six feet, with an additional long syllable :*"—

" Night and | morning | were at | meeting | over | Water | -loo;
Cocks had | sung their | *earliest* | greeting; | faint and | low they | crew."*

In Frazee's Grammar, a separate line or two, similar in metre to these, are rightly reckoned to have *seven feet*, and many lines, (including those above from Tennyson, which W. C. Fowler erroneously gives for *Heptameter*,) being a foot longer, are presented as trochaics of *eight* feet; but Everett, the surest of our prosodists, remaining, like most others, a total stranger to our octometers, and too little acquainted with trochaic heptameters to believe the species genuine, on finding a couple of stanzas in which two such lines are set with shorter ones of different sorts, and with some which are defective in metre, sagely concludes that all lines of more than "*six trochees*" must necessarily be condemned as prosodial anomalies. It may be worth while to repeat the said stanzas here, adding such corrections and marks as may suggest their proper form and scansion. But since they commence with the shorter metre of six trochees only, and are already placed under that head, I too may take them in the like connexion, by now introducing my third species of trochaics, which is Everett's tenth.

MEASURE III.—TROCHAIC OF SIX FEET, OR HEXAMETER.

Example.—Health.

" Up the | dewy | mountain, | Health is | bounding | lightly;
On her | brows a | garland, | twin'd with | richest | posies :
Gay is | she, e | -late with | hope, and | smiling | sprightly;
Redder | is her | cheek, and | sweeter | than the | rose is."
    G. BROWN : *The Institutes of English Grammar*, p. 258.

This metre appears to be no less rare than the preceding ; though, as in that case, I know no good reason why it may not be brought into vogue. Professor John S. Hart says of it: " This is the *longest* Trochaic verse that seems *to have been cultivated.*"—*Hart's English Gram.* p. 187. The seeming of its cultivation he doubtless found only in sundry modern grammars. Johnson, Bicknell, Burn, Coar, Ward, Adam,—old grammarians, who vainly profess to have illustrated " every species of English verse,"—make no mention of it ; and, with all the grammarians who notice it, *one anonymous couplet*, passing from hand to hand, has everywhere served to exemplify it.

Of this, " the line of six Trochees," Everett says : " This measure is *languishing*, and rarely used. The following example is often cited :—

' On a | mountain, | stretched be | -neath a | hoary | willow,
Lay a | shepherd | swain, and | view'd the | rolling | billow.' "†

Again : " We have the following from BISHOP HEBER :—

' Hōlȳ, | hŏlȳ, | hŏlȳ ! | āll thē | sāints ă | -dōre thĕe,
    Cāstĭng | dŏwn thēir | gŏldĕn | crŏwns ă | -rŏund thĕ | glāssȳ | sēa;
Chĕrŭ | -bĭm ănd | sĕră | -phĭm [*ŭre*] | fāllĭng | dŏwn bĕ | -fŏre thĕe,
Whĭch wĕrt, | ănd ārt, | ănd ēv | -ērmōre | shălt bĕ !

---

* It is obvious, that these two lines may easily be reduced to an agreeable stanza, by simply dividing each after the fourth foot.—G. B.

† In Sanborn's Analytical Grammar, on page 279th, this couplet is ascribed to "*Pope ;*" but I have sought in vain for this quotation, or any example of similar verse, in the works of that poet. The lines, one or both of them, appear, *without reference*, in L. *Murray's Grammar, Second Edition*, 1796, p. 176, and in subsequent editions ; in *W. Allen's*, p. 225; *Bullions's*, 178 ; *N. Butler's*, 192 ; *Chandler's New*, 196 ; *Clark's*, 201 ; *Churchill's*. 187; *Cooper's Practical*, 185; *Davis's*, 187 ; *Farnum's*, 100 ; *Felton's*, 142 ; *Frazee's*, 184 ; *Frost's*, 164 ; *S. S Greene's*, 230 ; *Hallock's*, 244 ; *Hart's*, 187 ; *Hiley's*, 127 ; *Humphrey's Prosody*. 17 ; *Parker and Fox's Gram.*, Part III, p. 60 ; *Weld's*, 211 ; *Ditto Abridged*, 188 ; *Wells's*, 200 ; *Fowler's*, 658 ; and doubtless in many other such books.

Holy, | holy, | holy ! | though the | darkness | hide thee,
    Though the | eye of | sinful | man thy | glory | may not | see,
Only | thou, [O | God,] art | holy ; | there is | none be | -side thee,
    Pĕrfĕct | ĭn pōw'r, | ĭn lŏve, | ănd pū | -rĭty.'

Only the first *and the third* lines of these stanzas are to our purpose," remarks the prosodist. That is, only these he conceived to be " lines of six Trochees." But it is plain, that the third line of the first stanza, having seven long syllables, must have seven feet, and cannot be a trochaic hexameter; and, since the third below should be like it in metre, one can hardly forbear to think the words which I have inserted in brackets, were accidentally omitted.

Further : " It is worthy of remark," says he, "that the second line of each of these stanzas is composed of *six Trochees* and an *additional long syllable.* As its corresponding line is an Iambic, and as the piece has some licenses in its construction, it is *far safer* to conclude that this line is an *anomaly* than that it forms a distinct species of verse. We must therefore conclude that the tenth [the metre of six trochees] is the longest species of Trochaic line known to English verse."—*Everett's Versification,* pp. 95 and 96.

This, in view of the examples above, of our longer trochaics, may serve as a comment on the author's boast, that, " having deduced his rules from the usage of the great poets, he has the best reason for being confident of their correctness."—*Ibid.* Pref. p. 5.

Trochaic hexameter, too, may easily be written with *single rhyme ;* perhaps more easily than a specimen suited to the purpose can be cited from any thing already written. Let me try :—

Example I.—The Sorcerer.

Lonely | in the | forest, | subtle | from his | birth,
Lived a | necro | -mancer, | wondrous | son of | earth.
More of | him in | -quire not, | than I | choose to | say :
Nymph or | dryad | bore him— | else 'twas | witch or | fay :
Ask you | who his | father?— | haply | he might | be
Wood-god | satyr, | sylvan : | —such his | pedi | -gree.
Reared mid | fauns and | faries, | knew he | no com | -peers ;
Neither | cared he | for them, | saving | ghostly | seers.
Mistress | of the | black-art, | " wizard | gaunt and | grim,"
Nightly | on the | hill-top, | " read the | stars to | him."
These were | welcome | teachers ; | drank he | in their | lore ;
Witchcraft | so en | -ticed him, | still to | thirst for | more.
Spectres | he would | play with, | phantoms | raise or | quell ;
Gnomes from | earth's deep | centre | knew his | potent | spell.
Augur | or a | -ruspex | had not | half his | art ;
Master | deep of | magic, | spirits | played his | part :
Demons, | imps in | -fernal, | conjured | from be | -low,
Shaped his | grand en | -chantments | with im | -posing | show.

Example II.—An Example of Hart's, Corrected.

" Where the | wood is | waving, | *shady,* | green, and | high,
    Fauns and | dryads, | *nightly,* | watch the | starry | sky."

See *Hart's E. Gram.* p. 187 ; or *the citation thence below.*

A couplet of this sort might easily be reduced to a pleasant little stanza, by severing each line after the third foot, thus :—

Hearken !	hearken !	hear ye ;	Friends ! " So	-ho !" they're	shouting.—
Voices	meet my	ear.	" Ho ! so	-ho, a	-hoy ! "—
Listen,	never	fear ye ;	'Tis no	Indian,	scouting.
Friends—or	foes—are	near.	Cry, *so*	-*ho !* with	joy.

But a similar succession of eleven syllables, six long and five short, divided after the seventh, leaving two iambs to form the second or shorter line,—(since such a division produces different orders and metres both,—) will, I think, retain but little resemblance in rhythm to the foregoing, though the actual sequence of quantities long and short is the same. If this be so, the particular measure or correspondent length of lines is more essential to the character of a poetic strain than some have supposed. The first four lines of the following extract are an example relevant to this point :—

Ariel's Song.

" Cŏme ŭn | -tŏ'thĕse | yĕllŏw | sănds,
    Ănd thĕn | tăke hănds :
Court'sied | when you | have and | kiss'd,
    (The wild | waves whist,)
Foot it | featly | here and | there ;
And, sweet | spritos, the | burden | bear."

SINGER'S SHAKSPEARE : *Tempest,* Act i, Sc. 2.

MEASURE IV.—TROCHAIC OF FIVE FEET, OR PENTAMETER.

Example 1.—Double Rhymes and Single, Alternated.

"Mountain | winds! oh! | whither | do ye | call me?
Vainly, | vainly, | would my | steps pur | -sue :
Chains of | care to | lower | earth en | -thrall me,
Wherefore | thus my | weary | spirit | woo?

Oh! the | strife of | this di | -vided | being !
Is there | peace where | ye are | borne, on | high?
Could we | soar to | your proud | eyries | fleeing,
In our | hearts, would | haunting | *mĕmōrĭes* | die?"
FELICIA HEMANS: *"To the Mountain Winds:" Everett's Versif.* p. 91.

Example II.—Rhymes Otherwise Arranged.

"Then, me | -thought, I | heard a | hollow | sound,
Gāthĕrĭng | up from | all the | lower | ground :
Nārrŏwĭng | in to | where they | sat as | -sembled,
Low vo | -*lŭptŭoŭs* | music, | winding, | trembled."
ALFRED TENNYSON: *Frazee's Improved Gram.* p. 184 ; *Fowler's*, 657.

This measure, whether with the final short syllable or without it, is said, by Murray, Everett, and others, to be "*very uncommon.*" Dr. Johnson, and the other old prosodists named with him above, knew nothing of it. Two couplets, exemplifying it, now to be found in sundry grammars, and erroneously reckoned to *differ as to the number of their feet,* were either selected or composed by Murray, for his Grammar, at its origin—or, if not then, at its first reprint, in 1796. They are these:—

"All that | walk on | foot or | ride in | *chariots*,
All that | dwell in | pala | -ces or | garrets."
L. Murray's Gram., 12mo, 175 ; 8vo, 257 ; *Chandler's*, 196 ; *Churchill's*, 187 ; *Hiley's*, 126 ; *et al.*

"Idle | after | dinner, | in his | chair,
Sat a | farmer, | ruddy, | fat, and | fair."
Murray, same places ; N. Butler's Gr. p. 193 ; *Hallock's*, 244 ; *Hart's*, 187 ; *Weld's*, 211 ; *et al.*

Richard Hiley most absurdly scans this last couplet, and all verse like it, into "*the Heroic measure,*" or a form of our *iambic pentameter ;* saying, "Sometimes a syllable is cut off from the *first* foot ; as,

Ĭ | dlĕ ăf | -tĕr dĭn | -nĕr ĭn | hĭs chāir [.]
Sāt | ă făr | -mĕr [,] rŭd | -dȳ, făt, | ănd fāir."
Hiley's English Grammar, Third Edition, p. 122.

J. S. Hart, who, like many others, has mistaken the metre of this last example for "*Tro-chaic Tetrameter,*" with a surplus "syllable," after repeating the current though rather questionable assertion, that "this measure is very uncommon," proceeds with our "*Tro-chaic Pentameter,*" thus : "This species is likewise uncommon. It is composed of *five* trochees ; as,

Ĭn thĕ | dărk ănd | grēen ănd | glōomȳ | vāllĕy,
Sātȳrs | bȳ thĕ | brōoklĕt | lōve tŭ | dāllȳ."

And again : [☞] "*The* SAME *with an* ADDITIONAL *accented syllable ;* as,
Whĕre thĕ | wōod ĭs | grēen ănd | hĭgh,
Fāuns ănd | Drȳăds | wătch thĕ | stārrȳ | skȳ."
Hart's English Grammar, First Edition, p. 187.

These examples appear to have been made for the occasion ; and the latter, together with its introduction, made unskillfully. The lines are of five feet, and so are those about the ruddy farmer ; but there is nothing "*additional,*" in either case ; for, as pentameter, they are all *catalectic,* the final short syllable being dispensed with, and a cæsura preferred, for the sake of single rhyme, otherwise not attainable. "Five trochees" and a rhyming "syllable" will make trochaic *hexameter,* a measure perhaps more pleasant than this. See examples above.

MEASURE V.—TROCHAIC OF FOUR FEET, OR TETRAMETER.

Example I.—A Mournful Song.

1.

"Raving | winds a | -round her | blowing,
Yellow | leaves the | woodlands | strowing,
By a | river | hoarsely | roaring,
Isa | -bella | strayed de | -ploring.
' Farewell | hours that | late did | measure
Sunshine | days of | joy and | pleasure ;
Hail, thou | gloomy | night of | sorrow,
Cheerless | night that | knows no | morrow.

2.

O'er the | past too | fondly | *wandering*,
On the | hopeless | future | *pondering*,
Chilly | grief my | life-blood | *freezes*,
Fell de | -spair my | fancy | *seizes*.
Life, thou | soul of | *every* | blessing,
Load to | *misery* | most dis | -*tressing*,
O how | gladly | I'd re | -sign thee,
And to | dark ob | -*livion* | join thee !'"
ROBERT BURNS : *Select Works,* Vol. ii, p. 131.

Example II.—A Song Petitionary.

"*Powers ce* | -lestial, | whose pro | -tection |Make the | gales you | waft a | -round her
Ever | guards the | *virtuous* | fair,   Soft and | peaceful | as her | breast;
While in | distant | climes I | wander,   Breathing | in the | breeze that | fans her,
Let my | Mary | be your | care :   Soothe her | bosom | into | rest :
Let her | form so | fair and | faultless,   *Guardian* | angels, | O pro | -tect her,
Fair and | faultless | as your | own ;   When in | distant | lands I | roam ;
Let my | Mary's | kindred | spirit   *To realms | unknown | while fate | exiles me,*
Draw your | choicest | *influence* | down.   Make her | bosom | still my | home."

BURNS'S SONGS, *Same Volume,* p. 165.

Example III.—Song of Juno and Ceres.

Ju. " Honour, | riches, marriage | -blessing, |Vines with | clust'ring | bunches | grow-
Long con | -tinuance, | and in | -creas-   ing ;
   ing,   Plants with | goodly | burden | bowing;
Hourly | joys be | still up | -on you !   Spring come | to you, | at the | far-
Juno | sings her | blessings | on you."   thest,
Cer. " Earth's in | -crease, and | foison | In the | very | end of | harvest !
   plenty ;   Scarci | -ty and | want shall | shun you;
Barns and | garners | never | empty ;   Ceres' | blessing | so is | on you."

SHAKSPEARE : *Tempest,* Act iv, Sc. 1.

Example IV.—On the Vowels.

" We are | little | airy | creatures,   T' other | you may | see in | tin,
All of | diff'rent | voice and | features :   And the | fourth a | box with | -in;
One of | us in | glass is | set,   If the | fifth you | should pur | -sue,
One of | us you'll | find in | jet ;   It can | never | fly from | you."

SWIFT : *Johnson's British Poets,* Vol. v, p. 343.

Example V.—Use Time for Good.

" Life is | short, and | time is | swift;   Bard ! not | vainly | heaves the | ocean ;
Roses | fade, and | shadows | shift ;   Bard ! not | vainly | flows the | river;
But the | ocean | and the | river   Be thy | song, then, | like their | motion,
Rise and | fall and | flow for | ever :   Blessing | now, and | blessing | ever."

EBENEZER ELLIOT : *From a Newspaper.*

Example VI.—"The Turkish Lady."—First Four Stanzas.

1.   **3.**

" 'Twas the | hour when | rites un | -holy   Then 'twas | from an | Emir's | palace
Called each | Paynim | voice to | pray'r,   Came an | eastern | lady | bright;
And the | star that | faded | slowly,   She, in | spite of | tyrants | jealous,
Left to | dews the | freshened | air.   Saw and | loved an | English | knight.

2.   **4.**

Day her | sultry | fires had | wasted,   ' Tell me, | captive, | why in | anguish
Calm and | sweet the | moonlight | rose;   Foes have | dragged thee | here to | dwell,
E'en a | captive's | spirit | tasted   Where poor | Christians, | as they | languish,
Half ob | -livion | of his | woes.   Hear no | sound of | sabbath | bell ? ' "

THOMAS CAMPBELL : *Poetical Works,* p. 115.

Example VII.—The Palmer's Morning Hymn.

" Lauded | be thy | name for | ever,   I have | seen thy | wondrous | might
Thou, of | life the | guard and | giver !   Through the | shadows | of this | night !
Thou canst | guard thy | creatures | sleeping,   Thou, who | slumber'st | not, nor | sleepest !
Heal the | heart long | broke with | weeping,   Blest are | they thou | kindly | keepest !
Rŭle thĕ | ōuphes ănd | ĕlves ăt | will   Spirits, | from the | ocean | under,
Thăt vĕx | thĕ āir | ŏr hāunt | thĕ hĭll,   Liquid | flame, and | levell'd | thunder,
Ānd ăll | thĕ fū | -rў sŭb | -jĕct kĕep   Need not | waken | nor a | -larm them—
Ŏf bŏil | -ing clŏud | ănd chăf | -ĕd dĕep   All com | -bined, they | cannot | harm them.
I hăve | sĕen, ănd | wĕll I | knŏw ĭt !   God of | evening's | yellow | ray,
Thou hast | done, and | Thou wilt | do it !   God of | yonder | dawning | day,
God of | stillness | and of | motion !   Thine the | flaming | sphere of | light !
Of the | rainbow | and the | ocean !   Thine the | darkness | of the | night !
Of the | mountain, | rock, and | river !   Thine are | all the | gems of | even,
Blessed | be Thy | name for | ever !   God of | angels ! | God of | heaven ! "

JAMES HOGG : *Mador of the Moor, Poems,* p. 206.

59

Example VIII.—A Short Song, of Two Stanzas.

1.

"Stay, my | charmer, | can you | leave me ?
Cruel, | cruel, | to de | -ceive me !   [me :
Well you | know how | much you | grieve
  Cruel | charmer, | can you | go?
  Cruel | charmer, | can you | go?

2.

By my | love, so | ill re | -quited ;
By the | faith you | fondly | plighted ;
By the | pangs of | lovers | slighted ;
  Do not, | do not | leave me | so !
  Do not, | do not | leave me | so ! "

ROBERT BURNS: *Select Works*, Vol. ii, p. 129.

Example IX.—Lingering Courtship.

1.

"Never | wedding, | ever | wooing,
Still a | lovelorn | heart pur | -suing,
Read you | not the | wrong you're | doing,
  In my | cheek's pale | hue ?
All my | life with | sorrow | strewing,
  Wed, or | cease to | woo.

2.

Rivals | banish'd, | bosoms | plighted,
Still our | days are | disu | -nited ;
Now the | lamp of | hope is | lighted,

Now half | quench'd ap | -pears,
Damp'd, and | *wavering*, | and be | -nighted.
  Midst my | sighs and | tears.

3.

Charms you | call your | dearest | blessing.
Lips that | thrill at | your ca | -ressing.
Eyes a | *mutual* | soul con | -fessing.
  Soon you'll | make them | grow
Dim, and | worthless | your pos | -sessing.
  Not with | age, but | woe ! "

CAMPBELL: *Everett's System of Versification*, p. 91.

Example X.—"Boadicea."—Four Stanzas from Eleven.

1.

"When the | British | warrior | queen,
  Bleeding | from the | Roman | rods,
Sought, with | an in | -dignant | mien,
  Counsel | of her | country's | gods,

2.

Sage be | -neath the | spreading | oak,
  Sat the | Druid, | hoary | chief ;
Every |·burning | word he | spoke
  Full of | rage, and | full of | grief.

3.

Princess ! | if our | aged | eyes
  Weep up | -on thy | matchless | wrongs,
'Tis be | -cause re | -sentment | ties
  All the | terrors | of our | tongues.

4.

ROME SHALL | PERISH— | write that | word
  In the | blood that | she hath | spilt ;
Perish, | hopeless | and ab | -horr'd,
  Deep in | ruin | as in | guilt."

WILLIAM COWPER: *Poems*, Vol. ii, p. 344.

Example XI.—"The Thunder Storm."—Two Stanzas from Ten.

"Now in | deep and | dreadful | gloom,
  Clouds on | clouds por | -tentous | spread,
Black as | if the | day of | doom
Hung o'er | Nature's | shrinking | head :
Lo ! the | lightning | breaks from | high,
God is | coming ! | —God is | nigh !

Hear ye | not his | *chariot* | wheels,
  As the | mighty | thunder | rolls ?
Nature, | startled | Nature | reels,
  From the | centre | to the | poles :
Tremble ! | —Ocean, | Earth, and | Sky !
Tremble ! | —God is | passing | by ! "

J. MONTGOMERY: *Wanderer of Switzerland, and other Poems*, p. 130.

*Example XII.—"The Triumphs of Owen," King of North Wales.**

"Owen's | praise de | -mands my song,
Owen | swift and | Owen | strong ;
Fairest | flow'r of | *Roderic's* | stem,
Gwyneth's | shield, and | Britain's | gem.
He nor | heaps his | brooded | stores,
Nor the | whole pro | -fusely | pours ;
Lord of | *every* | regal | art,
Liberal | hand and | open | heart.
Big with | hosts of | mighty | name,
Squadrons | three a | -gainst him | came ;
This the | force of | Eirin | hiding,
Side by | side as | proudly | riding,
On her | shadow | long and | gay,
Lochlin | ploughs the | *watery* | way :
There the | Norman | sails a | -far
Catch the | winds, and | join the | war ;
Black and | huge, a | -long they | sweep,
Burthens | of the | angry | deep.

Dauntless | on his | native | sands,
The Drag | -on-son | *of Mo* | -na stands ;†
In glit | -tering arms | and glo | -ry drest,
High he | rears his | ruby | crest.
There the | *thundering* | strokes be | -gin,
There the | press, and | there the | din ;
Taly | -malfra's | rocky | shore
Echoing | to the | battle's | roar ;
Where his | glowing | eyeballs | turn,
Thousand | banners | round him | burn.
Where he | points his | purple | spear,
Hasty, | hasty | rout is | there,
Marking | with in | -dignant | eye
Fear to | stop, and | shame to | fly.
There Con | -fusion, | Terror's | child,
Conflict | fierce, and | Ruin | wild,
Ago | -ny, that | pants for | breath,
Despair, | *and how* | -OURA | -BLE DEATH."

THOMAS GRAY: *Johnson's British Poets*, Vol. vii, p. 284.

Example XIII.—"Grongar Hill."—First Twenty-six Lines.

" Silent | Nymph, with | *curious* | eye,
Who, the | purple | eve, dost | lie
On the | mountain's | lonely | van,
Beyond | *the noise* | *of bus* | *-y man ;*
Painting | fair the | form of | things,
While the | yellow | linnet | sings;
Or the | tuneful | nightin | -gale
Charms the | forest | with her | tale;
Come, with | all thy | *various* | hues,
Come, and | aid thy | sister | Muse.
Now, while | Phœbus, | riding | high,
Gives lus | *-tre to* | *the land* | *and sky,*
Grongar | Hill in | -vites my | song ;

Draw the | landscape | bright and | strong ;
Grongar, | in whose | mossy | cells,
Sweetly | -musing | Quiet | dwells ;
Grongar, | in whose | silent | shade,
For the | modest | Muses | made,
So oft | *I have,* | *the eve* | *-ning still,*
At the | fountain | of a | rill,
Sat up | -on a | *flowery* | bed,
With my | hand be | -neath my | head,
While stray'd | *my eyes* | *o'er Tow* | *-y's flood,*
Over | mead and | over | wood,
From house | *to house,* | *from hill* | *to hill,*
Till Con | *-templa* | *-tion had* | *her fill.*"

JOHN DYER: *Johnson's British Poets*, Vol. vii, p. 65.

OBSERVATIONS.

OBS. 1.—This is the most common of our trochaic measures; and it seems to be equally popular, whether written with single rhyme, or with double; in stanzas, or in couplets; alone, or with some intentional intermixture. By a careful choice of words and style, it may be adapted to all sorts of subjects, grave, or gay; quaint, or pathetic; as may the corresponding iambic metre, with which it is often more or less mingled, as we see in some of the examples above. Milton's *L'Allegro,* or *Gay Mood,* has one hundred and fifty-two lines; ninety-eight of which are iambics; fifty-four, trochaic tetrameters; a very few of each order having double rhymes. These orders the poet has *not*—" very ingeniously *alternated*," as Everett avers; but has simply interspersed, or commingled, with little or no regard to alternation. His *Il Penseroso,* or *Grave Mood,* has twenty-seven trochaic tetrameters, mixed irregularly with one hundred and forty-nine iambics.

OBS. 2.—Everett, who divides our trochaic tetrameters into two species of metre, imagines that the catalectic form, or that which is single-rhymed, " has a *solemn* effect,"—" imparts to all pieces *more dignity* than any of the other short measures,"—" and not of trivial or humorous subject should be treated in this measure,"—and that, " besides dignity, it imparts an air of *sadness* to the subject."—*English Versif.* p. 87. Our " line of four trochees " he supposes to be " *difficult* of construction,"—" not of very *frequent* occurrence,"—" the most *agreeable* of all the trochaic measures," —" remarkably well adapted to *lively* subjects,"—and " peculiarly expressive of the eagerness and fickleness of the passion of love."—*Ib.* p. 90. These pretended metrical characteristics seem scarcely more worthy of reliance, than astrological predictions, or the oracular guessings of our modern craniologists.

OBS. 3.—Dr. Campbell repeats a suggestion of the older critics, that gayety belongs naturally to all trochaics, as such, and gravity or grandeur, as naturally, to iambics; and he attempts to find a reason for the fact; while, perhaps, even here—more plausible though the supposition is—the fact may be at least half imaginary. " The iambus," says he, " is expressive of dignity and grandeur; the trochee, on the contrary, according to Aristotle, (Rhet. Lib. III.,) is frolicsome and gay. It were difficult to assign a reason of this difference that would be satisfactory; but of the thing itself, I imagine, most people will be sensible on comparing the two kinds together. I know not whether it will be admitted as a sufficient reason, that the distinction into metrical feet hath a much greater influence in poetry on the rise and fall of the voice, than the distinction into words; and if so, when the cadences happen mostly after the long syllables, the verse will naturally have an air of greater gravity than when they happen mostly after the short."—*Campbell's Philosophy of Rhetoric*, p. 354.

MEASURE VI.—TROCHAIC OF THREE FEET, OR TRIMETER.

Example I.—Youth and Age Contrasted.

" Crabbed | age and | youth
Cannot | live to | -gether ;
Youth is | full of | pleasance,
Age is | full of | care:
Youth, like | summer | morn,
Age, like | winter | weather ;
Youth, like | summer, | brave ;

Age, like | winter, | bare.
Youth is | full of | sport,
Age's | breath is | short,
Youth is | nimble, | age is | lame;
Youth is | hot and | bold,
Age is | weak and | cold;
Youth is | wild, and | age is | tame."

The Passionate Pilgrim; SINGER'S SHAKSPEARE, Vol. ii, p. 594.

Example II.—Common Sense and Genius.

3.

" While I | touch the | string,
Wreathe my | brows with | laurel ;
For the | tale I | sing,
Has, for | once, a | moral !

4.

Common | Sense went | on,
Many | wise things | saying;
While the | light that | shone,
Soon set | Genius | straying.

5.

One his | eye ne'er | rais'd
From the | path be | -fore him ;
T' other | idly | gaz'd
On each | night-cloud | o'er him.

6.

While I | touch the | string,
Wreathe my | brows with | laurel ;
For the | tale I | sing,
Has, for | once, a | moral !

7.

So they | came, at | last,
To a | shady | river ;
Common | Sense soon | pass'd
Safe,—as | he doth | ever.

8.

While the | boy whose | look
Was in | heav'n that | minute,
Never | saw the | brook,—
But turn | -bled head | -long in it !"

Six Stanzas from Twelve.—MOORE'S MELODIES, p. 271.

This short measure is much oftener used in stanzas, than in couplets. It is, in many instances, combined with some different order or metre of verse, as in the following :—

Example III.—Part of a Song.

" Go where | glory | waits thee,
But while | fame e | -lates thee,
Oh! still | remem | -ber me.
When the | praise thou | meetest,
To thine | ear is | sweetest,
Oh! then | remem | -ber me.
Other | arms may | press thee,
Dearer | friends ca | -ress thee,
All the | joys that | bless thee,
Sweeter | far may | be :
But when | friends are | nearest,
And when | joys are | dearest,
Oh! then | remem | -ber me.

When, at | eve, thou | rovest,
By the | star thou | lovest,
Oh! then | remem | -ber me.
Think when | home re | -turning,
Bright we've | seen it | burning ;
Oh! thus | remem | -ber me.
Oft as | summer | closes,
When thine | eye re | -poses
On its | ling'ring | roses,
Once so | loved by | thee,
Think of | her who | wove them,
Her who | made thee | love them ;
Oh! then | remem | -ber me."

MOORE'S *Melodies, Songs, and Airs,* p. 107.

Example IV.—From an Ode to the Thames.

" On thy | shady | margin,
Care its | load dis | -charging,
Is lull'd | to gen | -tle rest :

Britain | thus dis | -arming,
Nothing | her a | -larming,
Shall sleep | on Cæ | -sar's breast."

See ROWE'S POEMS : *Johnson's British Poets,* Vol. iv, p. 58.

Example V.—"The True Poet."—First Two of Nine Stanzas.

1.

" Poet | of the | heart,
Delving | in its | mine,
From man | -kind a | -part,
Yet where | jewels | shine ;
Heaving | upward | to the | light,
Precious | wealth that | charms the | sight ;

2.

Toil thou | still, deep | down,
For earth's | hidden | gems ;
They shall | deck a | crown,
Blaze in | dia | -dems ;
And when | thy hand | shall fall | to rest,
Brightly | jewel | beauty's | breast."

JANE E. LOCKE : *N. Y. Evening Post ; The Examiner,* No. 98.

Example VI.—"Summer Longings."—First Two of Five Stanzas.

1.

"Ah ! my | heart is | ever | waiting,
Waiting | for the | May,—
Waiting | for the | pleasant | rambles,
Where the | fragrant | hawthorn | brambles,
With the | woodbine | alter | -nating,
Scent the | dewy | way.
Ah ! my | heart is | weary | waiting,
Waiting | for the | May.

2.

Ah ! my | heart is | sick with | longing,
Longing | for the | May,—
Longing | to e | -scape from | study,
To the | young face | fair and | ruddy,
And the | thousand | charms be | -longing
To the | Summer's | day.
Ah ! my | heart is | sick with | longing,
Longing | for the | May."

" D. F. M. C. :" *Dublin University Magazine ; Liberator,* No. 952.

MEASURE VII.—TROCHAIC OF TWO FEET, OR DIMETER.

Example I.—Three Short Excerpts.

1.

" My flocks | feed not,
My ewes | breed not,
My rams | speed not,
All is | amiss :
Love's de | -nying,
Faith's de | -fying,
Heart's re | -nying,
Causer | of this."

2.

" In black | mourn I,
All fears | scorn I,
Love hath | lorn me,
Living | in thrall :
Heart is | bleeding,
All help | needing,
(Cruel | speeding,)
Fraughted | with gall."

3.

" Clear wells | spring not,
Sweet birds | sing not,
Loud bells | ring not
Cheerfully ;
Herd- stand | weeping,
Flocks all | sleeping,
Nymphs back | creeping
Fearfully."

SHAKSPEARE : *The Passionate Pilgrim.* See Sec. xv.

Example II.—Specimen with Single Rhyme.

"*To Quinbus Flestrin, the Man-Mountain.*"

A LILLIPUTIAN ODE.

I.	II.	III.
"In a | -maze,	"See him | stride	"Turn'd a | -side
Lost, I | gaze.	Valleys | wide:	From his | hide,
Can our | eyes	Over | woods,	Safe from | wound,
Reach thy | size?	Over | floods,	Darts re | -bound.
May my | lays	When he | treads,	From his | nose,
Swell with | praise,	Mountains' | heads	Clouds he | blows;
Worthy | thee,	Groan and | shake:	When he | speaks,
Worthy | me!	Armies | quake,	Thunder | breaks !
Muse, in | -spire	Lest his | spurn	When he | eats,
All thy | fire !	Over | -turn	Famine | threats !
Bards of | old	Man and | steed:	When he | drinks,
Of him | told,	Troops, take | heed !	Neptune | shrinks !
When they | said	Left and | right	Nigh thy | ear,
Atlas' | head	Speed your | flight !	In mid | air,
Propp'd the | skies:	Lest an | host	On thy | hand,
See ! and | *believe* | *your eyes !*	*Beneath* | *his foot* | *be lost.*	Let me | stand.
		So shall | I [sky."
		(Lofty | poet !) touch the

JOHN GAY: *Johnson's British Poets*, Vol. vii, p. 376.

Example III.—Two Feet with Four.

"Oh, the | pleasing, | pleasing | anguish,	Charms trans | -porting !
When we | love, and | when we | languish!	Fancy | viewing
Wishes | rising !	Joys en | -suing !
Thoughts sur | -prising !	Oh, the | pleasing, | pleasing | anguish ! "
Pleasure | courting !	ADDISON's *Rosamond*, Act i, Scene 6.

Example IV.—Lines of Three Syllables with Longer Metres.

1. WITH TROCHAICS.	2. WITH IAMBICS.
"Or we | sometimes | pass an | hour	"What sounds | were heard,
Under | a green | willow,	What scenes | appear'd,
That de | -fends us | from the | shower,	O'er all | the drear | -y coasts !
Making | earth our | pillow;	Dreadful | gleams,
Where we | may	Dismal | screams,
Think and | pray,	Fires that | glow,
Be'fore | death	Shrieks of | wo,
Stops our | breath:	Sullen | moans,
Other | joys,	Hollow | groans,
Are but | toys,	And cries | of tor | -tur'd ghosts !"
And to | be la | -mented."*	POPE: *Johnson's Brit. Poets*, Vol. vi, p. 315.

Example V.—"The Shower."—In Four Regular Stanzas.

1.

"In a \| valley \| that I \| know—
   Happy \| scene !
There are \| meadows \| sloping \| low,
There the \| fairest \| flowers \| blow,
And the \| brightest \| waters \| flow,
   All se \| -rene;
But the \| sweetest \| thing to \| see,
If you \| ask the \| dripping \| tree,
Or the \| harvest \| -hoping \| swain,
   Is the \| Rain.

When the \| cloud-king \| shakes his \| crown,
And the \| pearls come \| pouring \| down
   From the \| sky !
They de \| -scry no \| charm at \| all
Where the \| sparkling \| jewels \| fall,
And each \| moment \| of the \| shower,
   Seems an \| hour !

3.

Yet there's \| something \| very \| sweet
   In the \| sight,
When the \| crystal \| currents \| meet
In the \| dry and \| dusty \| street,
And they \| wrestle \| with the \| heat,
   In their \| might !

2.

Ah, the \| dwellers \| of the \| town,
   How they \| sigh,—
How un \| -grateful \| -ly their \| frown,

---

* This passage, or some part of it, is given as a trochaic example, in many different systems of prosody. Everett ascribes it entire to "*John Chalkhill;*" and Nutting, more than twenty years before, had attached the name of "*Chalkhill*" to a part of it. But the six lines "of three syllables," Dr. Johnson, in his Grammar, credits to "*Walton's Angler;*" and Bicknell, too, ascribes the same to "*Walton*" The readings also have become various. Johnson, Bicknell, Burn, Churchill, and Nutting, have "*Here*" for "*Where,*" in the fifth line above; and Bicknell and Burn have "*Stop,*" in the eighth line, where the rest read "*Stops.*" Nutting has, for the ninth line, "*Others' joys,*" and not, "*Other joys,*" as have the rest.—G. B.

While they | seem to | hold a | talk
With the | stones a | -long the | walk,
And re | -mind them | of the | rule,
To 'keep | cool ! '
        4.
Ay, but | in that | quiet | dell,
Ever | fair,
Still the | Lord doth | all things | well,

When h's | clouds with | blessings |
   swell,
And they | break a | brimming | shell
   On the | air ;
There the | shower | hath its | charms,
Sweet and | welcome | to the | farms
As they | listen | to its | voice,
And re | -joice ! "
    Rev. RALPH HOYT's *Poems : The Examiner*, Nov. 6, 1847.

Example VI.—"A Good Name."—Two Beautiful Little Stanzas.

1.
" Children, | choose it,
Don't re | -fuse it,
'Tis a | precious | dia | -dem ;
Highly | prize it,
Don't de | -spise it,
You will | need it | when you're | men.

2.
Love and | cherish,
Keep and | nourish,
'Tis more | precious | far than | gold ;
Watch and | guard it,
Don't dis | -card it,
You will | need it | when you're | old."
    The Family Christian Almanac for 1850, p. 20.

OBSERVATIONS.

OBS. 1.—Trochaics of two feet, like those of three, are, more frequently than otherwise, found in connexion with longer lines, as in some of the examples above cited. The trochaic line of three syllables, which our prosodists in general describe as consisting, not of two feet, but " of one Trochee and a long syllable," may, when it stands alone, be supposed to consist of one *amphimac*; but, since this species of foot is not admitted by all, and is reckoned a secondary one by those who do admit it, the better practice is, to divide even the three syllables into two feet, as above.

OBS. 2.—Murray, Hart, Weld, and many others, erroneously affirm, that, " The *shortest* Trochaic verse in our language, consists of one Trochee and a long syllable."—*Murray's Gram.* p. 256 ; *Hart's, First Edition*, p. 186 ; *Weld's, Second Edition*, p. 210. The error of this will be shown by examples below—examples of *true "Trochaic Monometer,"* and not of Dimeter mistaken for it. like Weld's, Hart's, or Murray's.

OBS. 3.—These authors also aver, that, " This measure is *defective in dignity*, and can seldom be used on serious occasions."—*Same places.* " Trochaic of *two feet*—is likewise so *brief*, that," in their opinion, " it is rarely used for any very serious purpose."—*Same places.* Whether the expression of love, or of its disappointment, is " any very serious purpose " or not, I leave to the decision of the reader. What lack of dignity or seriousness there is, in several of the foregoing examples, especially the last two, I think it not easy to discover.

MEASURE VIII.—TROCHAIC OF ONE FOOT, OR MONOMETER.

Examples with Longer Metres.

1. WITH IAMBICS.
" Fróm wălk | tŏ wălk, | frŏm shăde | tŏ
   shăde,   [vey'd,
From stream | to purl | -ing stream | con-
Through all | the ma | -zes of | the grove,
Through all | the ming | -ling tracks | I
   Turning,   [rove,
   Burning,
   Changing,
   Ranging,
Fúll ŏf | grief ănd | fúll ŏf | lóve."
   ADDISON's *Rosamond*, Act I, Sc. 4 :
   Everett's Versification, p. 81.

2. WITH ANAPESTICS, &c.
" Tŏ lŏve ănd tŏ lănguĭsh,
   Tŏ sigh | ănd cŏmplăin,
How crŭĕl's thĕ ănguĭsh !
How tŏrmĕnt | -ĭng thĕ păin !
   Suing,
   Pursuing,
   Flying,
   Denying,
O the curse | of disdain !
How torment | -ing's the pain ! "
GEO. GRANVILLE : *Br. Poets*, Vol. v, p. 31.

OBSERVATIONS.

OBS. 1.—The metres acknowledged in our ordinary schemes of prosody, scarcely amount, with all their " boundless variety," to more than one half, or three quarters, of what may be found in *actual use* somewhere. Among the foregoing examples, are some which are longer, and some which are shorter, than what are commonly known to our grammarians ; and some also, which seem easily practicable, though perhaps not so easily quotable. This last trochaic metre, so far as I know, has not been used alone,—that is, without longer lines,—except where grammarians so set examples of it in their prosodies.

OBS. 2.—" Trochaic of One foot," as well as " Iambic of One foot," was, I believe, first recognised, prosodically, in Brown's Institutes of English Grammar, a work first published in 1823. Since that time, both have obtained acknowledgement in sundry schemes of versification, contained in the new grammars ; as in Farnum's, and Hallock's, of 1842 ; in Pardon Davis's, of 1845 ; in S. W. Clark's, and S. S. Greene's, of 1848 ; in Professor Fowler's, of 1850. Wells, in his School Grammar, of 1846, and D. C. Allen, in an other, of 1847, give to the *length of lines* a laxity positively absurd : " *Rhymed* verses," say they, " may consist of *any number* of syllables."—*Wells*, 1st Ed. p. 187 ; late Ed., 204 ; *Allen*, p. 88. Everett has recognized " *The line of a single Trochee*," though he repudiates some long measures that are much more extensively authorized.

ORDER III. — ANAPESTIC VERSE.

In full Anapestic verse, the stress is laid on every third syllable, the first two syllables of each foot being short. The first foot of an anapestic line, may be an iambus. This is the most frequent diversification of the order. But, as a diversification, it is, of course, not *regular* or *uniform*. The stated or uniform adoption of the iambus for a part of each line, and of the anapest for the residue of it, produces verse of the *Composite Order*. As the anapest ends with a long syllable, its rhymes are naturally single; and a short syllable after this, producing double rhyme, is, of course, supernumerary: so are the two, when the rhyme is triple. Some prosodists suppose, a surplus at the end of a line may compensate for a deficiency at the beginning of the next line; but this I judge to be an error, or at least the indulgence of a questionable license. The following passage has two examples of what may have been *meant* for such compensation, the author having used a dash where I have inserted what seems to be a necessary word:—

" Apol | -lo smil'd shrewd | -ly, and bade | him sit down,
With ' Well, | Mr. Scott, | you have man | -aged the town;
·Now pray, | copy less— | have a lit | -tle temer | -*itў*—
[And] Try | if you can't | also man | -age poster | -*ity.*
[For] All | you add now | only les | -sens your cred | -*it ;*
And how | could you think, | too, of tak | -ing to ed | -*ite?* ' "

LEIGH HUNT'S Feast of the Poets, page 20.

The anapestic measures are few; because their feet are long, and no poet has chosen to set a great many in a line. Possibly lines of five anapests, or of four and an initial iambus, might be written; for these would scarcely equal in length some of the iambics and trochaics already exhibited. But I do not find any examples of such metre. The longest anapestics that have gained my notice, are of fourteen syllables, being tetrameters with triple rhyme, or lines of four anapests and two short surplus syllables. This order consists therefore of measures reducible to the following heads:—

MEASURE I.—ANAPESTIC OF FOUR FEET, OR TETRAMETER.

Example I.—A "Postscript."—An Example with Hypermeter.

" Lean Tom, | when I saw | him, last week, | on his *horse* | *awry,*
Threaten'd loud | -ly to turn | me to stone | with his *sor* | *-cery.*
But, I think, | little Dan, | that, in spite | of what *our* | *foe says,*
He will find | I read Ov | -id and his | *Metamor* | *-phoses.*
For, omit | -ting the first, | (where I make | a compar | *-ison,*
With a sort | of allu | -sion to Put | -land or *Har* | *-rison,*)
Yet, by | my descrip | -tion, you'll find | he in *short* | *is*
A pack | and a gar | -ran, a top | and a *tor* | *-toise.*
So I hope | from hencefor | -ward you ne'er | will ask, *can* | *I maul*
This teas | -ing, conceit | -ed, rude, in | -solent *an* | *-imal?*
And, if | this rebuke | might be turn'd | to his *ben* | *-efit,*
(For I pit | -y the man,) | I should | be glad *then* | *of it.*"

SWIFT'S POEMS: Johnson's British Poets, Vol. v, p. 324.

Example II.—"The Feast of the Poets."—First Twelve Lines.

" T' other day, | as Apol | -lo sat pitch | -ing his darts
Through the clouds | of Novem | -ber, by fits | and by starts,
He began | to consid | -er how long | it had been
Since the bards | of Old Eng | -land had all | been rung in.
' I think,' | said the god, | recollect | -ing, (and then
He fell twid | -dling a sun | -beam as I | may my | pen,)
' I think— | let me see— | yes, it is, | I declare,
As long | ago now | as that Buck | -ingham there:
And yet | I can't see | why I've been | so remiss,
Unless | it may be— | and it cer | -tainly is,
That since Dry | -den's fine ver | -ses and Mil | -ton's sublime,
I have fair | -ly been sick | of their sing | -song and rhyme.' "

LEIGH HUNT: Poems, New-York Edition, of 1814.

Example III.—The Crowning of Four Favourites.

" Then, ' Come,' | cried the god | in his el | -egant mirth,
' Let us make | us a heav'n | of our own | upon earth,

And wake, | with the lips | that we dip | in our bowls,
That divin | -est of mu | -sic—conge | -nial souls.'
So say | -ing, he led | through the din | -ing-room door,
And, seat | -ing the po | -ets, cried, 'Lau | -rels for four!'
No soon | -er demand | -ed, than, lo ! | they were there,
And each | of the bards | had a wreath | in his hair.
Tom Camp | -bell's with wil | -low and pop | -lar was twin'd,
And South | -ey's, with moun | -tain-ash, pluck'd | in the wind ;
And Scott's, | with a heath | from his old | garden stores,
And, with vine | -leaves and jump | -up-and-kiss | -me, Tom Moore's."
                        LEIGH HUNT : *ib.* from line 330 to line 342.

Example IV.—"Glenara."—First Two of Eight Stanzas.

" O heard | ye yon pi | -broch sound sad | in the gale,
Where a band | cometh slow | -ly with weep | -ing and wail !
'Tis the chief | of Glena | -ra laments | for his dear ;
And her sire, | and the peo | -ple, are called | to her bier.

Glena | -ra came first | with the mourn | -ers and shroud ;
Her kins | -men, they fol | -lowed, but mourned | not aloud :
Their plaids | all their bo | -soms were fold | -ed around :
They marched | all in si | -lence—they looked | on the ground."
                        T. CAMPBELL'S *Poetical Works,* p. 105.

Example V.—"Lochiel's Warning."—Ten Lines from Eighty-six.

" 'Tis the sun | -set of life | gives me mys | -tical lore,
And com | -ing events | cast their shad | -ows before.
I tell | thee, Cullo | -den's dread ech | -oes shall ring
With the blood | -hounds that bark | for thy fu | -gitive king.
Lo ! anoint | -ed by Heav'n | with the vi | -als of wrath,
Behold, | where he flies | on his des | -olate path !
Now, in dark | -ness and bil | -lows he sweeps | from my sight :
Rise ! rise ! | ye wild tem | -pests, and cov | -er his flight !
'Tis fin | -ished. Their thun | -ders are hushed | on the moors ;
Cullo | -den is lost, | and my coun | -try deplores."—*Ib.* p. 89.

Example VI.—"The Exile of Erin."—The First of Five Stanzas.

" There came | to the beach | a poor Ex | -ile of E | -rĭn,
The dew | on his thin | robe was heav | -y and chill :
For his coun | -try he sighed, | when at twi | -light repair | -ĭng
To wan | -der alone | by the wind | -beaten hill.
But the day | -star attract | -ed his eye's | sad devo | -tĭon,
For it rose | o'er his own | native isle | of the o | -cĕan,
Where once, | in the fire | of his youth | -ful emo | -tĭon,
He sang | the bold an | -them of E | -rin go bragh."—*Ib.* p. 116.

Example VII.—"The Poplar Field."

"*The pop* | -lars are fell'd, | *farewell* | to the shade,
And the whis | -pering sound | of the cool | colonnade ;
The winds | play no lon | -ger and sing | in the leaves,
Nor Ouse | on his bo | -som their im | -age receives.
Twelve years | have elaps'd, | since I last | took a view
Of my fa | -vourite field, | and the bank | where they grew ;
And now | in the grass | *behold* | they are laid,
And the tree | is my seat | that once lent | me a shade.
The black | -bird has fled | to anoth | -er retreat,
Where the ha | -zels afford | him a screen | from the heat,
And the scene, | where his mel | -ody charm'd | me before,
Resounds | with his sweet | -flowing dit | -ty no more.
My fu | -gitive years | are all hast | -ing away,
And I | must ere long | lie as low | -ly as they,
With a turf | on my breast, | and a stone | at my head,
Ere anoth | -er such grove | shall arise | in its stead.
'Tis a sight | to engage | me, if an | -y thing can,
To muse | on the per | -ishing pleas | -ures of man ;
Though his life | be a dream, | his enjoy | -ments, I see,
Have a be | -ing less dur | -able e | -ven than he."
                        COWPER'S *Poems,* Vol. i, p. 257.

OBSERVATIONS.

OBS. 1.—Everett avers, that, " The purely Anapestic measure is more easily constructed than the Trochee, [Trochaic,] and of much more frequent occurrence."—*English Versification,* p. 97.

Both parts of this assertion are at least very questionable; and so are this author's other suggestions, that, "The Anapest is [necessarily] the vehicle of *gayety and joy;* " that, "Whenever this measure is employed in the treating of *sad* subjects, *the effect is destroyed;* " that, "Whoever should attempt to write an elegy in this measure, would be *sure to fail;* " that, "The words might express grief, but the measure *would express joy;* " that, "The Anapest should never be employed throughout a *long piece;* " because "buoyancy of spirits can never be supposed to last," —"sadness *never leaves us,* BUT joy remains but for a moment;" and, again, because, "the measure is *exceedingly monotonous.*"—*Ibid.* pp. 97 and 98.

OBS. 2.—Most anapestic poetry, so far as I know, is in pieces of no great length; but Leigh Hunt's "Feast of the Poets," which is thrice cited above, though not a long *poem,* may certainly be regarded as "*a long piece,*" since it extends through fifteen pages, and contains four hundred and thirty-one lines, all, or nearly all, of anapestic tetrameter. And, surely, no poet had ever more need of a metre well suited to his purpose, than he. who, intending a critical as well as a descriptive poem, has found so much fault with the versification of others. Pope, as a versifier, was regarded by this author, "not only as no master of his art, but as a very indifferent practiser." —*Notes on the Feast of the Poets,* p. 35. His "*monotonous and cloying*" use of numbers, with that of Darwin, Goldsmith, Johnson, Haley, and others of the same "school," is alleged to have wrought a general corruption of taste in respect to versification—a fashion that has prevailed, not temporarily,

> "*But ever since Pope spoil'd the ears of the town*
> *With his cuckoo-song verses, half up and half down.*"—*Ib.*

OBS. 3.—Excessive monotony is thus charged by one critic upon all verse of "the purely Anapestic measure;" and, by an other, the same fault is alleged in general terms against all the poetry "of the school of Pope," well-nigh the whole of which is iambic. The defect is probably, in either case, at least half imaginary; and, as for the inherent joyousness of anapestics, that is perhaps not less ideal. Father Humphrey says, "Anapestic and amphibrachic verse, being similar in measure and movement, are pleasing to the ear, and well adapted to cheerful and humourous compositions; and *sometimes to elegiac compositions,* and subjects important and solemn."— *Humphrey's English Prosody,* p. 17.

OBS. 4.—The anapest, the dactyl, and the amphibrach, have this in common,—that each, with one long syllable, takes two short ones. Hence there is a degree of similarity in their rhythms, or in their several effects upon the ear; and consequently lines of each order, (or of any two, if the amphibrachic be accounted a separate order,) are sometimes commingled. But the propriety of acknowledging an order of "*Amphibrachic verse,*" as does Humphrey, is more than doubtful; because, by so doing, we not only recognize the amphibrach as one of the principal feet, but make a vast number of lines ambiguous in their scansion. For our Amphibrachic order will be *made up* of lines that are commonly scanned as anapestics—such anapestics as are diversified by an iambus at the beginning, and sometimes also by a surplus short syllable at the end; as in the following verses, better divided as in the sixth example above :—

> "Thĕre cáme tŏ | thĕ bĕach ă | pŏor Exĭle | ŏf Erĭn,
> The dew on | his thin robe | was heavy | and chill:
> Fŏr hĭs coŭn | -trў hĕ sĭghed, | whĕn ăt twĭ | -lĭght rĕpâir | -ĭng
> To wander | alone by | the wind-beat | -en hill."

MEASURE II.—ANAPESTIC OF THREE FEET, OR TRIMETER.

Example I.—"*Alexander Selkirk.*"—First Two Stanzas.

I.

" I am mon | -arch of all | I survey,
My right | there is none | to dispute;
From the cen | -tre all round | to the sea,
I am lord | of the fowl | and the brute.
O Sol | -itude! where | are the charms
That sa | -ges have seen | in thy face?
Better dwell | in the midst | of alarms,
Than reign | in this hor | -rible place.

II.

I am out | of human | -ity's reach,
I must fin | -ish my jour | -ney alone,
Never hear | the sweet mu | -sic of speech,
I start | at the sound | of my own.
The beasts | that roam o | -ver the plain,
My form | with indif | ference see;
They are so | unacquaint | -ed with man,
Their tame | -ness is shock | -ing to me."
COWPER's *Poems,* Vol. i, p. 199.

Example II.—"*Catharina.*"—Two Stanzas from Seven.

IV.

" Though the pleas | -ures of Lon | -don exceed
In num | -ber the days | of the year,
Cathari | -na, did noth | -ing impede,
Would feel | herself hap | -pier here;
For the close | -woven arch | -es of limes
On the banks | of our riv | -er, I know,
Are sweet | -er to her | many times
Than aught | that the cit | -y can show.

V.

So it is, | when the mind | is endued
With a well | -judging taste | from above;
Then, wheth | -er embel | -lish'd or rude,
'Tis na | -ture alone | that we love.
The achieve | -ments of art | may amuse,
May e | -ven our won- | der excite,
But groves, | hills, and val | -leys, diffuse
A last | -ing, a sa | -cred delight."
COWPER's *Poems,* Vol. ii, p. 232.

Example III.—"*A Pastoral Ballad.*"—Two Stanzas from Twenty-seven.

(8.)

Not a pine | in my grove | is there seen,
But with ten | -drils of wood | -bine is bound;

Not a beech | 's more beau | -tiful green,
But a sweet | -briar twines | it around.
Not my fields | in the prime | of the year
More charms | than my cat | -tle unfold;

Not a brook | that is lim | -pid and clear,
  But it glit | -ters with fish | -es of gold.
           (9.)
One would think | she might like | to retire
  To the bow'r | I have la | -bour'd to rear;
Not a shrub | that I heard | her admire,

  But I hast | -ed and plant | -ed it there.
O how sud | -den the jes | -samine strove
  With the li | -lac to ren | -der it gay!
Alread | -y it calls | for my love,
  To prune | the wild branch | -es away."
  SHENSTONE: *British Poets*, Vol. vii, p. 139.

Anapestic lines of four feet and of three are sometimes alternated in a stanza, as in the following instance :—

Example IV.—"The Rose."

"The rose | had been wash'd, | just wash'd | in a show'r,
  Which Ma | -ry to An | -na convey'd;
The plen | -tiful moist | -ure encum | -ber'd the flow'r,
  And weigh'd | down its beau | -tiful head.

The cup | was all fill'd, | and the leaves | were all wet,
  And it seem'd | to a fan | -ciful view,
To weep | for the buds | it had left, | with regret,
  On the flour | -ishing bush | where it grew.

I hast | -ily seized | it, unfit | as it was
  For a nose | -gay, so drip | -ping and drown'd,
And, swing | -ing it rude | -ly, too rude | -ly, alas!
  I snapp'd | it,—it fell | to the ground.

And such, | I exclaim'd, | is the pit | -iless part
  Some act | by the del | -icate mind,
Regard | -less of wring | -ing and break | -ing a heart
  Alread | -y to sor | -row resign'd.

This el | -egant rose, | had I shak | -en it less,
  Might have bloom'd | with its own | -er a while;
And the tear | that is wip'd | with a lit | -tle address,
  May be fol | low'd perhaps | by a smile."
        COWPER: *Poems*, Vol. i, p. 216; *English Reader*, p. 211.

MEASURE III.—ANAPESTIC OF TWO FEET, OR DIMETER.

Example I.—Lines with Hypermeter and Double Rhyme.

"CORONACH," OR FUNERAL SONG.

1.

"He is gone | on the moun | -tain
  He is lost | to the for | -est
Like a sum | -mer-dried foun | -tain
  When our need | was the sor | -est.
The font, | reappear | -ing,
  From the rain | -drops shall bor | -row,
But to us | comes no cheer | -ing,
  To Dun | -can no mor | -row!

2.

The hand | of the reap | -er
  Takes the ears | that are hoar | -y,
But the voice | of the weep | -er
  Wails man | -hood in glo | -ry;
The au | -tumn winds rush | -ing,
  Waft the leaves | that are sear | -est,
But our flow'r | was in flush | -ing,
  When blight | -ing was near | -est."
    WALTER SCOTT: *Lady of the Lake*, Canto iii, St. 16.

Example II.—Exact Lines of Two Anapests.

"Prithee, Cu | -pid, no more
Hurl thy darts | at threescore;
To thy girls | and thy boys,

Give thy pains | and thy joys;
Let Sir Trust | -y and me
From thy frol | -ics be free."
  ADDISON: *Rosamond*, Act ii, Scene 2; *Ev. Versif.* p. 166.

Example III.—An Ode, from the French of Malherbe.

"This An | -na so fair,
  So talk'd | of by fame,
Why dont | she appear?
  Indeed, | she's to blame!
Lewis sighs | for the sake
  Of her charms, | as they say;
What excuse | can she make
  For not com | -ing away?
If he does | not possess,
  He dies | with despair;
Let's give | him redress,
  And go find | out the fair."

"Cette Anne si belle,
  Qu'on vante si fort,
Pourquoi ne vient elle?
  Vraiment, elle a tort!
Son Louis soupire
  Après ses appas;
Que veut elle dire,
  Qu'elle ne vient pas?
S'il ne la posséde,
  Il s'en va mourir;
Donnons y reméde,
  Allons la quérir."
    WILLIAM KING, LL. D.: *Johnson's British Poets*, Vol. iii, p. 590.

Example IV.—'Tis the Last Rose of Summer.

1.

.s the last | rose of sum | -mĕr,
Left bloom | -ing alone ;
l her love | -ly compan | -iŏns
Are fad | -ed and gone ;
flow'r | of her kin | -drĕd,
No rose | -bud is nigh,
reflect | back her blush | -ĕs,
Or give | sigh for sigh.

2.

l not leave | thee, thou lone | ŏne !
To pine | on the stem !
ice the love | -ly are sleep | -ĭng,
Go, sleep | thou with them ;

Thus kind | -ly I scat | -tĕr
Thy leaves | o'er thy bed,
Where thy mates | of the gar | -dĕn
Lie scent | -less and dead.

3.

So, soon | may I fol | -lŏw,
When friend | -ships decay,
And, from love's | shining cir | -clĕ,
The gems | drop away ;
When true | hearts lie with | -ĕr'd,
And fond | ones are flown,
Oh ! who | would inhab | -it
This bleak | world alone ? "
T. MOORE : *Melodies, Songs, and Airs*, p. 171.

Example V.—Nemesis Calling up the Dead Astarte.

Shadow ! | or spir | -ĭt !
Whatev | -er thou art,
Which still | doth inher | -ĭt
The whole | or a part
Of the form | of thy birth,
Of the mould | of thy clay,
Which return'd | to the earth,

Re-appear | to the day !
Bear what | thou bor | -ĕst
The heart | and the form,
And the as | -pect thou wor | -ĕst
Redeem | from the worm !
Appear !—Appear !—Appear ! "
LORD BYRON : *Manfred*, Act ii, Sc. 4.

Example VI.—Anapestic Dimeter with Trimeter.

FIRST VOICE.

e room | for the com | -bat, make room;
und the trum | -pet and drum ;
r | -er than Ve | -nus prepares
ncoun | -ter a great | -er than Mars.
e room | for the com | -bat, make room;
und the trum | -pet and drum."

SECOND VOICE.

" Give the word | to begin,
Let the com | -batants in,
The chal | -lenger en | -ters all *glo* | -*riŏŭs ;*
But Love | has decreed,
Though Beau | -ty may bleed,
Yet Beau | -ty shall still | be *victo* | -*riŏŭs."*
GEORGE GRANVILLE : *Johnson's British Poets*, Vol. v, p. 58.

Example VII.—Anapestic Dimeter with Tetrameter.

AIR.

" Let the pipe's | merry notes | aid the skill | of the voice ;
For our wish | -es are crown'd, | and our hearts | shall rejoice.
Rejoice, | and be glad ;
For, sure, | he is mad,
Who, where mirth, | and good hu | -mour, and har | -mony's found,
Never catch | -es the smile, | nor lets pleas | -ure go round.
Let the stu | -pid be grave,
'Tis the vice | of the slave ;
But can nev | -er agree
With a maid | -en like me,
Who is born | in a coun | -try that's hap | -py and free."
LLOYD : *Johnson's British Poets*, Vol. viii, p. 178.

MEASURE IV.—ANAPESTIC OF ONE FOOT, OR MONOMETER.

measure is rarely if ever used except in connexion with longer lines. The follow-
imple has six anapestics of two feet, and two of one ; but the latter, being verses of
rhyme, have each a suplus short syllable ; and four of the former commence with
ibus :—

Example I.—A Song in a Drama.

" Now, mor | -tal, prepare,
For thy fate | is at hand ;
Now, mor | -tal, prepare,
And surrĕn | -dĕr.

For Love | shall arise,
Whom no pow'r | can withstand,
Who rules | from the skies
Tŏ thĕ cĕn | -trĕ."

GRANVILLE, VISCOUNT LANSDOWNE : *Joh. Brit. Poets*, Vol. v, p. 49.
following extract, (which is most properly to be scanned as anapestic, though con-
ly diversified,) has two lines, each of which is pretty evidently composed of a single
t :—

Example II.—A Chorus in the Same.

t trum | -pets and tym | -băls,
t atŭ | -bals and cym | -băls,
ims | and let haut | -boys give o | -vĕr;
But lĕt flūtes,

And lĕt lūtes
Our pas | -sions excite
To gent | -ler delight,
And ev | -ery Mars | be a lov | -ĕr."—*Ib.* p 56.

OBSERVATIONS.

OBS. 1.—That a single anapest, a single foot of any kind, or even a single long syllable, ma be, and sometimes is, in certain rather uncommon instances, set as a line, is not to be denied "Dr. Caustic," or T. G. Fessenden, in his satirical "Directions for *Doing* Poetry," uses in thi manner the monosyllables, "*Whew,*" "*Say,*" and "*Dress,*" and also the iambs, "*The gay,*" and "*All such,*" rhyming them with something less isolated.

OBS. 2.—Many of our grammarians give anonymous examples of what they conceive to be "*Anapestic Monometer,*" or "*the line of one anapest,*" while others—(as Allen, Bullions, Churchill and Hiley—) will have the length of *two* anapests to be *the shortest* measure of this order. Prof. Hart says, "The shortest anapæstic verse is a *single* anapæst; as,

'In ǎ swēet   Āll thěir fēet   Āll thě night
    Rěsōnánce,   In thě dánce   Tinklěd light.'

This measure," it is added, "is, however, *ambiguous;* for by laying an accent on the first, as well as the third syllable, we may generally make it a trochaic."—*Hart's English Gram.* p. 183. The same six versicles are used as an example by Prof. Fowler, who, without admitting any ambiguity in the measure, introduces them, rather solecistically, thus: "*Each* of the following lines consist of a single Anapest."—*Fowler's E. Gram.* 8vo, 1850, § 694.

OBS. 3.—Verses of three syllables, with the second short. the last long, and the first common, or *variable,* are, it would seem, *doubly doubtful* in scansion; for, while the first syllable, if made short, gives us an anapest, to make it long. gives either an ambimac or what is virtually two trochees. For reasons of choice in the latter case, see Observation 1st on Trochaic Dimeter. For the *fixing of variable quantities,* since the case admits no other rule, regard should be had to the *analogy of the verse,* and also to the common principles of accentuation. It is doubtless possible to read the six short lines above, into the measure of so many *anapests;* but, since the two intermediate syllables "*In*" and "*All*" are as easily made long as short, whoever considers the common pronunciation of the longer words, "*Resonance*" and "*Tinkled,*" may well doubt whether the learned professors have, in this instance, hit upon the right mode of scansion. The example may quite as well be regarded either as Trochaic Dimeter, catalectic, or as Amphimacric Monometer, acatalectic. But the word *resonance,* being accented usually on the first syllable only, is naturally a *dactyl;* and, since the other five little verses end severally with a monosyllable, which can be varied in quantity, it is possible to read them all as being *dactylics;* and so the whole may be regarded as *trebly doubtful* with respect to the measure.

OBS. 4.—L. Murray says, "*The shortest anapæstic verse must be a single anapæst:* as,
                But in váin,
              They complain."

And then he adds, "This measure is, however, ambiguous; for, by laying the stress of the voice on the first and third syllables, we *might make* a trochaic. And *therefore* the first and simplest form of our genuine Anapæstic verse, is made up of *two Anapæsts.*"—*Murray's Gram.* 8vo. p. 257; 12mo, p. 207. This conclusion is utterly absurd, as well as completely contradictory to his first assertion. The genuineness of this small metre depends not at all on what may be made of the same words by other pronunciation; nor can it be a very natural reading of this passage, that gives to "*But*" and "*They*" such emphasis as will make them long.

OBS. 5.—Yet Chandler, in his improved grammar of 1847, has not failed to repeat the substance of all this absurdity and self-contradiction, carefully dressing it up in other language thus: "Verses composed of single Anapæsts are *frequently found* in stanzas of songs; and the same is true of several of the other kinds of feet; *but we may consider the first* [i. e., shortest] *form* of anapæstic verse as consisting of *two* Anapæsts."—*Chandler's Common School Gram.* p. 196.

OBS. 6.—Everett, speaking of anapestic lines, says. "The first and shortest of these is composed of *a single Anapest following an Iambus.*"—*English Versification,* p. 99. This not only denies the existence of *Anapestic Monometer,* but improperly takes for Anapestic verse what is, by the statement itself, half Iambic, and therefore of the Composite Order. But the false assertion is plainly refuted even by the author himself, and on the same page. For, at the bottom of this page, he has this contradictory note: "It has been remarked (§ 15) that though the Iambus with an additional short syllable *is the shortest line that is known* to Iambic verse, *there are isolated instances of a single Iambus,* and even of a *single long syllable.* There are examples of *lines made up of a single Anapest,* as the following example will show:—

'Jove in his chair,	Cock of the school,	His bald pate
Of the sky lord mayor,	He bears despotic rule;	Jove would cuff,
With his nods	His word,	He's so bluff,
Men and gods	Though absurd,	For a straw.
Keeps in awe;	Must be law.	Cowed deities,
When he winks,	Even Fate,	Like mice in cheese,
Heaven shrinks;	Though so great,	To stir must cease
* * * *	Must not prate;	Or gnaw.'

O'HARA:—*Midas,* Act i, Sc. 1."—*Everett's Versification,* p. 99.

ORDER IV. — DACTYLIC VERSE.

In pure Dactylic verse, the stress is laid on the first syllable of each successive three; that is, on the first, the fourth, the seventh, and the tenth syllable of each line of four feet. Full dactylic generally forms triple rhyme. When one of the final short syllables is omitted, the rhyme is double; when both, single. These omissions are here essential to the formation of such rhymes. Dactylic with double rhyme, ends virtually with a *trochee;* dactylic with single rhyme, commonly ends with a *cæsura;* that is, with a long syllable taken for a foot. Dactylic with single rhyme is the same

anapestic would be without its initial short syllables. Dactylic verse is rather un-
mmon; and, when employed, is seldom perfectly pure and regular.

MEASURE I.—DACTYLIC OF EIGHT FEET, OR OCTOMETER.

Example.—Nimrod.

mrod the | hunter was | mighty in | hunting, and | famed as the | ruler of | cities of |
    yore;
,bel, and | Erech, and | Accad, and | Calneh, from | Shinar's fair | region his | name
afar | bore.

MEASURE II.—DACTYLIC OF SEVEN FEET, OR HEPTAMETER.

Example.—Christ's Kingdom.

ut of the | kingdom of | Christ shall be | gathered, by | angels o'er | Satan vic | -torious,
ll that of | -fendeth, that | lieth, that | faileth to | honour his | name ever | glorious.

MEASURE III.—DACTYLIC OF SIX FEET, OR HEXAMETER.

Example I.—Time in Motion.

Time, thou art | ever in | motion, on | wheels of the | days, years, and | ages;
Restless as | waves of the | ocean, when | Eurus or | Boreas | rages.

Example II.—Where is Grand-Pré?

" This is the | forest pri | -meval; but | where are the | hearts that be | -neath it
Leap'd like the | roe, when he | hears in the | woodland the | voice of the | huntsman?
Where is the | thatch-roofèd | village, the | home of A | -cadian | farmers? "
    H. W. LONGFELLOW: *Evangeline*, Part i, l. 7—9.

MEASURE IV. — DACTYLIC OF FIVE FEET, OR PENTAMETER.

Example.—Salutation to America.

" Land of the | beautiful, | beautiful, | land of the | free,
Land of the | negro-slave, | negro-slave, | land of the | chivalry,
Often my | heart had turned, | heart had turned, | longing to | thee;
Often had | mountain-side, | mountain-side, | broad lake, and | stream,
Gleamed on my | waking thought, | waking thought, | crowded my | dream.
Now thou dost | welcome me, | welcome me, | from the dark | sea,
Land of the | beautiful, | beautiful, | land of the | free,
Land of the | negro-slave, | negro-slave, | land of the | chivalry."

MEASURE V.—DACTYLIC OF FOUR FEET, OR TETRAMETER.

Example I.—The Soldier's Wife.

" Weary way | -wanderer, | languid and | sick at heart,
Travelling | painfully | over the | rugged road,
Wild-visaged | Wanderer! | God help thee, | wretched one!

Sorely thy | little one | drags by thee | barefooted;
Cold is the | baby that | hangs at thy | bending back,
Meagre, and | livid, and | screaming for | misery.

Woe-begone | mother, half | anger, half | agony,
Over thy | shoulder thou | lookest to | hush the babe,
Bleakly the | blinding snow | beats in thy | haggard face.

Ne'er will thy | husband re | -turn from the | war again,
Cold is thy | heart, and as | frozen as | Charity!
Cold are thy | children.—Now | God be thy | comforter! "
    ROBERT SOUTHEY: *Poems*, Philad. 1843, p. 250.

Example II.—Boys.—A Dactylic Stanza.

" Boys will an | -ticipate, | lavish, and | dissipate
All that your | busy pate | hoarded with | care;
And, in their | foolishness, | passion, and | mulishness,
Charge you with | churlishness, | spurning your pray'r."

Example III.—"Labour."—The First of Five Stanzas.

" Pause not to | dream of the | future be | -fore us;
Pause not to | weep the wild | cares that come | o'er us:
Hark, how Cre | -ation's deep, | musical | chorus,
Uninter | -mitting, goes | up into | Heaven!
Never the | ocean-wave | falters in | flowing;
Never the | little seed | stops in its | growing;
More and more | richly the | rose-heart keeps | glowing,
Till from its | nourishing | stem it is | riven."
    FRANCES S. OSGOOD: *Clapp's Pioneer*, p. 94.

Example IV.—"Boat Song."—First Stanza of Four.

" Hail to the | chief who in | triumph ad | -vances !
Honour'd and | bless'd be the | ever-green | pine !
Long may the | tree in his | banner that | glances,
Flourish the | shelter and | grace of our | line !
Heaven send it happy dew,
Earth lend it sap anew,
Gayly to | bourgeon, and | broadly to | grow,
While ev'ry | Highland glen
Sends our shout | back agen,
' Roderigh Vich Alpine Dhu, ho ! ieroe ! ' "
WALTER SCOTT: *Lady of the Lake,* C. ii, St. 19.

MEASURE VI.—DACTYLIC OF THREE FEET, OR TRIMETER.

Example.—To the Catydid.

" Ca-ty-did, | Ca-ty-did, | sweetly sing,—
Sing to thy | loving mates | near to thee ;
Summer is | come, and the | trees are green,—
Summer's glad | season so | dear to thee.

Cheerily, | cheerily, | insect, sing ;
Blithe be thy | notes in the | hickory :
Every | bough shall an | answer ring,
Sweeter than | trumpet of | victory."

MEASURE VII.—DACTYLIC OF TWO FEET, OR DIMETER.

Example I.—The Bachelor.—Four Lines from Many.

" Free from sa | -tiety,
Care, and anx | -iety,
Charms in va | -riety,
Fall to his | share."—ANON. : *Newspaper.*

Example II.—The Pibroch.—Sixteen Lines from Forty.

" Pibroch of | Donuil Dhu,
Pibroch of | Donuil,
Wake thy wild | voice anew,
Summon Clan | -Conuil.
Come away, | come away !
Hark to the | summons !
Come in your | war-array,
Gentles and | commons !

" Come as the | winds come, when
Forests are | rended ;
Come as the | waves come, when
Navies are | stranded :
Faster come, | faster come,
Faster and | faster !
Chief, vassal, | page, and groom,
Tenant and | master."—W. SCOTT.

Example III.—"My Boy."

'*There is even a happiness that makes the heart afraid.*'—HOOD.

1.

" One more new | claimant for
Human fra | -ternity,
Swelling the | flood that sweeps
On to e | -ternity !
I who have | filled the cup,
Tremble to | think of it ;
For, be it | what it may,
I must yet | drink of it.

2.

Room for him | into the
Ranks of hu | -manity ;
Give him a | place in your
Kingdom of | vanity !
Welcome the | stranger with
Kindly af | -fection ;
Hopefully, | trustfully,
Not with de | -jection.

3.

See, in his | waywardness,
How his fist | doubles ;
Thus pugi | -listical,
Daring life's | troubles :
Strange that the | neophyte
Enters ex | -istence
In such an | attitude,
Feigning re | -sistance.

4.

Could he but | have a glimpse
Into fu | -turity,
Well might he | fight against
Farther ma | -turity ;
Yet does it | seem to me
As if his | purity
Were against | sinfulness
Ample se | -curity.

5.

Incompre | -hensible,
Budding im | -mortal,
Thrust all a | -mazedly
Under life's | portal ;
Born to a | destiny
Clouded in | mystery,
Wisdom it | -self cannot
Guess at its | history.

6.

Something too | much of this
Timon-like | croaking,
See his face | wrinkle now,
Laughter pro | -voking.
Now he cries | lustily—
Bravo, my | hearty one !
Lungs like an | orator
Cheering his | party on.

7.

. how his | merry eyes
rn to me | pleadingly !
we help | loving him—
ving ex | -ceedingly ?
y with | hopefulness,
rtly with | fears,
, as I | look at him,
isten with | tears.

8.

then to | find a name ;—
iere shall we | search for it ?
to his | ancestry,
to the | church for it ?

Shall we en | -dow him with
    Title he | -roic,
After some | warrior,
    Poet, or | stoic ?

9.

One aunty | says he will
    Soon 'lisp in | numbers,'
Turning his | thoughts to rhyme,
    E'en in his | slumbers ;
Watts rhymed in | babyhood,
    No blemish | spots his fame—
Christen him | even so :
    · Young Mr. | Watts his name."

ANONYMOUS : *Knickerbocker*, and *Newspapers*, 1849.

ASURE VIII.—DACTYLIC OF ONE FOOT, OR MONOMETER.

" Fearfully,
    Tearfully."

OBSERVATIONS.

single dactyl, set as a line, can scarcely be used otherwise than as part of a stanza, ion with longer verses. The initial accent and triple rhyme make it necessary to ig else with it. Hence this short measure is much less common than the others, inted differently. Besides, the line of three syllables, as was noticed in the obser-apestic Monometer, is often peculiarly uncertain in regard to the measure which it

A little difference in the laying of emphasis or accent may, in many instances, one species of verse to an other. Even that which seems to be dactylic of two feet, able be sufficiently lengthened to admit of single rhyme with the full metre, becomes btful in its scansion ; because, in such case, the last foot may be reckoned an *amphi-nacer*. Of this, the following stanzas from Barton's lines " to the Gallic Eagle," (or in St. Helena,) though different from all the rest of the piece, may serve as a

im the | *battle's shock,*
hath fast | bound thee ;
l to the | *rugged rock,*
is warring | round thee.

[Now, for] the | *trumpet's sound,*
    Sea-birds are | shrieking ;
Hoarse on thy | *rampart's bound,*
    Billows are | breaking."

s may be regarded as verse of the Composite Order ; and, perhaps, more properly tylic with mere incidental variations. Lines like those in which the questionable licized, may be united with longer dactylics, and thus produce a stanza of great mony. The following is a specimen. It is a song, written by I know not whom, by Dempster. The twelfth line is varied to a different measure.

"ADDRESS TO THE SKYLARK."

of the | wilderness,
some and | cumberless,
natin o'er | moorland and | lea ;
im of | happiness,
is thy | dwelling-place ;
n the | desert with | thee!

" O'er moor and | mountain green,
    O'er fell and | fountain sheen,
O'er the red | streamer that | heralds the | day ;
    Over the | cloudlet dim,
    Over the | rainbow's rim,
Musical | cherub, hie, | hie thee a | -way.

is thy | lay, and loud,
i the | downy cloud ;
nergy, | love gave it | birth :
', on thy | dewy wing,
art thou | journeying ?
eav | -en, thy love | is on earth.

" Then, when the | gloamin comes,
    Low in the | heather blooms,
Sweet will thy | welcome and | bed of love | be.
    Emblem of | happiness,
    Blest is thy | dwelling-place ;
O ! to a | -bide in the | desert with | thee !"

observed by Churchill, (*New Gram.* p. 387,) that, Shakspeare has used the dac-te to mournful occasions." The chief example which he cites, is the following :—

as | -sist our moan,
| sigh and groan
ly, | heavily.

Graves, yawn and | yield your dead,
    Till death be | uttered
    Heavily, | heavily."—*Much Ado,* V, 3.

six lines of Dactylic (or Composite) Dimeter are subjoined by the poet to four of iter. There does not appear to me to be any particular adaptation of either iful subjects, more than to others ; but later instances of this metre may be cited, the character of the topic treated. The following long example consists of lines of them dactylic only ; but, of the seventy-six, there are twelve which *may* be l, and as many more which *must* be, because they commence with a short

" THE BRIDGE OF SIGHS."—BY THOMAS HOOD.

fortunate,
eath,
tunate,
death !

Take her up | tenderly,
Lift her with | care ;
Fashioned so | slenderly,
Young, and so | fair !

Look at her | garments
Clinging like | cerements,
Whilst the wave | constantly
Drips from her | clothing ;

Take her up | instantly,
  Loving, not | loathing.

Touch her not | scornfully;
Think of her | mournfully,
  Gently, and | humanly;
Not of the | stains of her:
All that re | -mains of her
  Now, is pure | womanly.

Make no deep | scrutiny
Into her | mutiny,
  Rash and un |-dutiful;
Past all dis | honour,
Death has left | on her
  Only the | beautiful.

Still, for all | slips of hers,—
  One of Eve's | family,—
Wipe those poor | lips of hers,
  Oozing so | clammily.
Loop up her | tresses,
  Escaped from the comb,—
Her fair auburn tresses:

Whilst wonderment guesses,
  Where was her | home?

Who was her | father?
  Who was her | mother?
Had she a | sister?
  Had she a | brother?
Was there a | dearer one
  Yet, than all | other?

Alas, for the rarity
Of Christian charity
  Under the | sun!
O, it was | pitiful!
Near a whole | city full,
  Home she had | none.

Sisterly, | brotherly,
Fatherly, | motherly
  Feelings had | changed:
Love, by harsh | evidence,
Thrown from its | eminence;
  Even God's | providence
  Seeming e | -stranged.

Where the lamps | quiver
So far in the river,
  With many a | light,
From window and casement,
From garret to basement,
She stood, with amazement,
  Houseless, by | night.

The bleak wind of March
  Made her tremble and shiver:
But not the dark arch,
  Or the black-flowing river:
Mad from life's | history,
Glad to death's | mystery,
  Swift to be | hurled,—
Anywhere, | anywhere,
  Out of the | world!

In she plung'd | boldly,—
No matter how coldly
  The rough | river ran,—
Over the | brink of it:
Picture it, | think of it,
  Dissolute | man!"
            Clapp's Pioneer, p. 54.

OBS. 5.—As each of our principal feet,—the Iambus, the Trochee, the Anapest, and the Dactyl.—has always one, and only one long syllable; it should follow, that, in each of our principal orders of verse,—the Iambic, the Trochaic, the Anapestic, and the Dactylic,—any line, not diversified by a secondary foot, must be reckoned to contain just as many feet as long syllables. So, too, of the Amphibrach, and any line reckoned Amphibrachic. But it happens, that the common error by which single-rhymed Trochaics have so often been counted a foot *shorter* than they are, is also extended by some writers to single-rhymed Dactylics—the rhyming syllable, if long, being esteemed *supernumerary!* For example, three dactylic stanzas, in each of which a pentameter couplet is followed by a hexameter line, and this again by a heptameter, are introduced by Prof. Hart thus: "The *Dactylic Tetrameter, Pentameter,* and *Hexameter,* with *the additional* or *hypermeter syllable,* are all found combined in the following extraordinary specimen of versification. *** This is the only specimen of Dactylic *hexameter* or even *pentameter* verse that the author recollects to have seen."

LAMENT OF ADAM.

"Glad was our | meeting: thy | glittering | bosom I | *heard,*
  Beating on | mine, like the | heart of a | timorous | *bird;*
Bright were thine | eyes as the | stars, and their | glances were | radiant as | *gleams*
  Falling from | eyes of the | angels, when | singing by | Eden's pur | -pureal | *streams.*

"Happy as | seraphs were | we, for we | wander'd a | *-lone,*
  Trembling with | passionate | thrills, when the | twilight had | *flown:*
Even the | echo was | silent: our | kisses and | whispers of | love
  Languish'd un | -heard and un | -known, like the | breath of the | blossoming | buds of the | *grove.*

"Life hath its | pleasures, but | fading are | they as the | *flowers:*
  Sin hath its | sorrows, and | sadly we | turn'd from those | *bowers:*
Bright were the | angels be | -hind with their | falchions of | heavenly | *flame!*
  Dark was the | desolate | desert be | -fore us, and | darker the | depth of our | *shame."*
            HENRY B. HIRST: *Hart's English Grammar,* p. 190.

OBS. 6.—Of Dactylic verse, our prosodists and grammarians in general have taken but very little notice; a majority of them appearing by their silence, to have been utterly ignorant of the whole species. By many, the dactyl is expressly set down as an inferior foot, which they imagine is used only for the occasional diversification of an iambic, trochaic, or anapestic line. Says Everett: "It is *never used* except as a *secondary foot,* and then in the *first place* of the line."—*English Versification,* p. 122. On this order of verse, Lindley Murray bestowed only the following words: "The DACTYLIC measure being very uncommon, we shall give only one example of one species of it:—

    From the low pleasures of this fallen nature,
      Rise we to higher, &c."—*Gram.* 12mo, p. 207; 8vo, p. 257.

Read this example with "*we rise*" for "*Rise we,*" and all the poetry of it is gone! Humphrey says, "*Dactyle* verse is seldom used, as remarked heretofore; but *is used occasionally,* and has three metres; viz. of 2, 3, and 4 feet. Specimens follow. 2 feet. Free from anxiety. 3 feet. Singing most sweetly and merrily. 4 feet. Dactylic measures are wanting in energy."—*English Prosody,* p. 18. Here the prosodist has made his own examples; and the last one, which unjustly impeaches all dactylics, he has made very badly—very prosaically; for the word "*Dactylic,*" though it has three syllables, is properly no dactyl, but rather an amphibrach.

OBS. 7.—By the Rev. David Blair, this order of poetic numbers is utterly misconceived and misrepresented. He says of it, "DACTYLIC verse consists of *a short syllable,* with one, two, or three feet, *and a long syllable;* as,

    'Distracted with woe,
      I'll rush on the foe.' ADDISON."—*Blair's Pract. Gram.* p. 119.
    "'Ye shepherds so cheerful and gay,
      'Whose flocks never carelessly roam;
    'Should Corydon's happen to stray,
      'Oh! call the poor wanderers home.' SHENSTONE."—*Ib.* p. 120.

It is manifest, that these lines are not dactylic at all. There is not a dactyl in them. They are composed of iambs and anapests. The order of the versification is Anapestic; but it is here varied by the very common diversification of dropping the first short syllable. The longer example is from a ballad of 216 lines, of which 99 are thus varied, and 117 are full anapestics.

OBS. 8.—The makers of school-books are quite as apt to copy blunders, as to originate them; and, when an error is once started in a grammar, as it passes with the user for good learning, no one can guess where it will stop. It seems worth while, therefore, in a work of this nature, to be liberal in the citation of such faults as have linked themselves, from time to time, with the several topics of our great subject. It is not probable, that the false scansion just criticised originated with Blair; for the Comprehensive Grammar, a British work, republished, in its third edition, by Dobson, of Philadelphia, in 1789, teaches the same doctrine, thus: "Dactylic measure may consist of one, two, or three Dactyls, introduced by a feeble syllable, and terminated by a strong one; as,

Mȳ | dĕar Irīsh | fŏlks,   Sŏ | fáir ănd sŏ | bright,
Cŏme | lĕave ŏff yŏur | jŏkes,   Thĕy'll | gĭve yŏu dĕ | -light:
And | búy ŭp mȳ | hálfpĕnce sŏ | fíne;   Ob | -sĕrvĕ'hŏw thĕy | glĭstĕr ănd | shĭne. SWIFT.
A | cŏblĕr thĕre | wăs ănd hĕ | lĭv'd ĭn ă | stăll,
Whĭch | sĕrv'd hĭm fŏr | kĭtchĕn fŏr | párlŏur ănd | hall;
Nŏ | cŏĭn ĭn hĭs | pŏckĕt, nŏ | cáre ĭn hĭs | páte;
Nŏ ăm | -bĭtĭon hĕ | hăd, ănd nŏ | dŭns ăt hĭs | gáte."—*Comp. Gram.* p. 150.

To this, the author adds, "Dactylic measure becomes Anapestic by setting off an Iambic foot in the beginning of the line."—*Ib.* These verses, all but the last one, unquestionably have an iambic foot at the beginning; and, for that reason, they are not, and by no measurement can be, dactylics. The last one is purely anapestic. All the divisional bars, in either example, are placed wrong.

ORDER V. — COMPOSITE VERSE.

Composite verse is that which consists of various metres, or different feet, combined,—not accidentally, or promiscuously, but by design, and with some regularity. In Composite verse, of any form, the stress must be laid rhythmically, as in the simple orders, else the composition will be nothing better than unnatural prose. The possible variety of combinations in this sort of numbers is unlimited; but, the pure and simple kinds being generally preferred, any stated mixture of feet is comparatively uncommon. Certain forms which may be scanned by other methods, are susceptible also of division as Composites. Hence there cannot be an exact enumeration of the measures of this order, but instances, as they occur, may be cited to exemplify it.

Example I.—From Swift's Irish Feast.

"O'Rourk's | noble fare | will ne'er | be forgot,
By those | who were there, | or those | who were not.
His rev | -els to keep, | we sup | and we dine
On sev | -en score sheep, | fat bul | -locks, and swine.
Usquebaugh | to our feast | in pails | was brought up,
An hun | -dred at least, | and a mad | -der our cup.
O there | is the sport! | we rise | with the light,
In disor | -derly sort, | from snor | -ing all night.
O how | was I trick'd! | my pipe | it was broke,
My pock | -et was pick'd, | I lost | my new cloak.
I'm ri | -fled, quoth Nell, | of man | -tle and kerch | -er:
Why then | fare them well, | the de'il | take the search | -er."

Johnson's Works of the Poets, Vol. v, p. 310.

Here the measure is tetrameter; and it seems to have been the design of the poet, that each hemistich should consist of one iamb and one anapest. Such, with a few exceptions, is the arrangement throughout the peice; but the hemistichs which have double rhyme, may each be divided into two amphibrachs. In Everett's Versification, at p. 100, the first six lines of this example are broken into twelve, and set in three stanzas, being given to exemplify "*The Line of a single Anapest preceded by an Iambus,*" or what he improperly calls "The first and shortest species of Anapestic lines." His other instance of the same metre is also *Composite* verse, rather than *Anapestic,* even by his own showing. "In the following example," says he, "we have this measure alternating with Amphibrachic lines:"

Example II.—From Byron's Manfred.

"The Captive Usurper,   I broke through his slumbers,
  Hurl'd down | from the throne,   I shiv | -er'd his chain,
Lay buried in torpor,   I leagued him with numbers—
  Forgotten and lone;   He's Ty | -rant again!
With the blood | of a mill | -ion he'll an | -swer my care,
With a na | -tion's destruc | -tion—his flight | and despair."—Act ii, Sc. 3.

Here the last two lines, which are not cited by Everett, are pure anapestic tetrameters; and it may be observed, that, if each two of the short lines were printed as one, the eight, which are here scanned otherwise, would become four of the same sort, except that these would each begin with an iambus. Hence the specimen *sounds* essentially as anapestic verse.

Example III.—*Woman on the Field of Battle.*

"Gentle and | lovely form,
　　What didst | thou here,
When the fierce | battle storm
　　Bore down | the spear ?

Banner and | shiver'd crest,
　　Beside | thee strown,
Tell, that a | -midst the best
　　Thy work | was done !

Low lies the | stately head,
　　Earth-bound | the free :
How gave those | haughty dead
　　A place | to thee ?

Slumb'rer ! thine | early bier
　　Friends should | have crown'd,
Many a | flow'r and tear
　　Shedding | around.

Soft voices, | dear and young,
　　Mingling | their swell,
Should o'er thy | dust have sung
　　Earth's last | farewell.

Sisters a | -bove the grave
　　Of thy | repose
Should have bid | vi'lets wave
　　With the | white rose.

Now must the | trumpet's note,
　　Savage | and shrill,
For requi'm | o'er thee float,
　　Thou fair | and still !

And the swift | charger sweep,
　　In full | career,
Trampling thy | place of sleep—
　　Why cam'st | thou here ?

Why ?—Ask the | true heart why
　　Woman | hath been
Ever, where | brave men die,
　　Unshrink | -ing seen.

Unto this | harvest ground,
　　Proud reap | -ers came,
Some for that | stirring sound,
　　A warr | -ior's name :

Some for the | stormy play,
　　And joy | of strife,
And some to | fling away
　　A wea | -ry life.

But thou, pale | sleeper, thou,
　　With the | slight frame,
And the rich | locks, whose glow
　　Death can | -not tame ;

Only one | thought, one pow'r,
　　Thee could | have led,
So through the | tempest's hour
　　To lift | thy head !

Only the | true, the strong,
　　The love | whose trust
Woman's deep | soul too long
　　Pours on | the dust."

HEMANS : *Poetical Works,* Vol. ii, p. 157.

Here are fourteen stanzas of composite dimeter, each having two sorts of lines ; the first sort consisting, with a few exceptions, of a dactyl and an amphimac ; the second, mostly, of two iambs ; but, in some instances, of a trochee and an iamb ;—the latter being, in such a connexion, much the more harmonious and agreeable combination of quantities.

Example IV.—*Airs from a "Serenata."*

AIR 1.

" Love sounds | the alarm,
　　And fear | is a fly | -ing :
When beau | -ty's the prize,
　　What mor | -tal fears dy | -ing ?
In defence | of my treas | -ure,
　　I'd bleed | at each | vein :
Without | her no pleas | -ure ;
　　For life | is a pain."

AIR 2.

" Consid | -er, fond shep | -herd,
　　How fleet | -ing's the pleas | -ure,
That flat | -ters our hopes
　　In pursuit | of the fair :
The joys | that attend | It,
　　By mo | -ments we meas | -ure ;
But life | is too lit | -tle
　　To meas | -ure our care."

GAY'S POEMS : *Johnson's Works of the Poets,* Vol. vii, p. 378.

These verses are essentially either anapestic or amphibrachic. The anapest divides two of them in the middle ; the amphibrach will so divide eight. But either division will give many iambs. By the present scansion, the *first foot* is an iamb in all of them but the two anapestics.

Example V.—*"The Last Leaf."*

1.

" I saw | him once | before
As he pass | -ĕd by | the door,
　　And again
The pave | -ment stones | resound
As he tot | -ters o'er | the ground
　　With his cane.

2.

They say | that in | his prime,
Ere the prun | -ing-knife | of Time
　　Cut him down,

Not a bet | -ter man | was found
By the cri | -er on | his round
　　Through the town.

3.

But now | he walks | the streets,
And he looks | at all | he meets
　　So forlorn ;
And he shakes | his fee | -ble head,
That it seems | as if | he said,
　　They are gone.

          4.
mos | -sy mar | -bles rest
the lips | that he | has press'd
    In their bloom ;
  the names | he lov'd | to hear
e been carv'd | for man | -y a year
    On the tomb.
          5.
rand | -mamma | has said,—
 old La | -dy ! she | is dead
    Long ago,—
he had | a Ro | -man nose,
his cheek | was like | a rose
    In the snow.
          6.
ow | his nose | is thin,
it rests | upon | his chin
    Like a staff ;

And a crook | is in | his back,
And a mel | -anchol | -y crack
    In his laugh.
          7.
I know | it is | a sin
For me [thus] | to sit | and grin
    At him here ;
But the old | three-cor | -ner'd hat,
And the breech | -es, and | all that,
    Are so queer !
          8.
And if I | should live | to be
The last leaf | upon | the tree
    In the spring,—
Let them smile, | as I | do now,
At the old | forsak | -en bough
    Where I cling."

OLIVER W. HOLMES : *The Pioneer*, 1843, p. 108.

OBSERVATIONS.

Composite verse, especially if the lines be short, is peculiarly liable to uncertainty,
ty of scansion ; and that which does not always abide by one chosen order of quantities,
 be found agreeable : it must be more apt to puzzle than to please the reader. The
 is of this last example, have eight lines of *iambic trimeter* ; and, since, seven times in
netre holds the first place in the stanza, it is a double fault, that one such line seems
a its proper position. It would be better to prefix the word *Now* to the fourth line,
l the forty-third thus :—

        " And should | I live | to be "—

ibic feet of this piece, as I scan it, are numerous ; being the sixteen short lines of
and the twenty-four initial feet of the lines of seven syllables. Every one of the forty
e thirty-sixth, " *The* last leaf "—) begins with a monosyllable which may be varied
so that, with stress laid on this monosyllable, the foot becomes an *amphimac* ; with-
ess, an *anapest*.
incline to read this piece as composed of iambs and anapests ; but B. A. Poe, who
ded " the effective harmony of these lines," and called the example " an excellently
d and well managed specimen of versification," counts many syllables long, which
ig makes short, and he also divides all but the iambics in a way quite different from
" Let us scan the first stanza.

  saw | him once | before   The pave- | ment stones | resound
s he | passed | by the | door,   As he | totters | o'er the | ground
   And a- | gain   With his | cane.'

e, " is the general scansion of the poem. We have first three iambuses. The sec-
 the rhythm into the *trochaic*, giving us three trochees, with a caesura equivalent, in
 trochees. The third line is a trochee and equivalent caesura."—Poe's Notes
H Verse : *Pioneer*, p. 109. These quantities are the same as those by which the
made to consist of iambs and amphimacs.
its *rhythmical effect* upon the ear, a supernumerary short syllable at the end of a
times, perhaps, compensate for the want of such a syllable at the beginning of the
iay be seen in the fourth example above ; but still it is unusual, and seems im-
iose such syllable to belong to the scansion of the subsequent line ; for the division of
r harmonic pauses, is greater than the division of feet, and implies that no foot can
e split by it. Poe has suggested that the division into lines may be disregarded in
sometimes must be. He cites for an example the beginning of Byron's " Bride of
issage which has been admired for its easy flow, and which, he says, has greatly
who have attempted to scan it. Regarding it as essentially anapestic tetrame-
ing some initial iambs, and the first and fifth lines dactylic, I shall here divide it
us :—

   " Know ye the | land where the | cypress and | myrtle
    Are em | -blems of deeds | that are done | in their clime—
   Where the rage | of the vul | -ture, the love | of the tur | -tle,
   Now melt | into soft | -ness, now mad | -den to crime ?
   Know ye the | land of the | cedar and | vine,
   Where the flow'rs | ever blos | -som, the beams | ever shine,
   And the light | wings of Zeph | -yr, oppress'd | with perfume,
   Wax faint | o'er the gar | -dens of Gul | in her bloom ?
   Where the cit | -ron and ol | -ive are fair | -est of fruit,
   And the voice | of the night | -ingale nev | -er is mute ?
   Where the vir | -gins are soft | as the ros | -es they twine,
   And all, | save the spir | -it of man, | is divine ?
   'Tis the land | of the East— | 'tis the clime | of the Sun—
   Can he smile | on such deeds | as his chil | -dren have done ?
   Oh, wild | as the ac | -cents of lov | -ers' farewell,
   Are the hearts | that they bear, | and the tales | that they tell."

Obs. 4.—These lines this ingenious prosodist divides not thus, but, throwing them together like prose unpunctuated, finds in them "a regular succession of *dactylic rhythms*, varied only at three points by equivalent *spondees*, and separated into two distinct divisions by equivalent terminating *cæsuras.*" He imagines that, "By all who have ears—not over long—this will be acknowledged as the true and the sole true scansion."—*E. A. Poe, Pioneer*, p. 107. So it may, for aught I know; but, having dared to show there is an other way quite as simple and plain, and less objectionable, I submit both to the judgement of the reader :—

"Knŏw yĕ thĕ | lănd whĕre thĕ | cýprĕss ănd | mýrtlĕ ăre | ĕmblĕms ŏf | dĕeds thăt ăre | dŏne ĭn thĕir | clĭme whĕre thĕ | răge ŏf thĕ | vŭltŭre thĕ | lŏve ŏf thĕ | tŭrtlĕ nŏw | mĕlt ĭntŏ | sŏftnĕss nŏw | mădden tŏ | crime. Knŏw yĕ thĕ | lănd ŏf thĕ | cĕdăr ănd | vĭne whĕre thĕ | flŏw'rs ĕvĕr | blŏssŏm thĕ | bĕams ĕvĕr | shĭne whĕre thĕ | lĭght wĭngs ŏf | zĕphўr ŏp- | prĕss'd wĭth pĕr- | fŭme wăx | făint ŏ'er thĕ | gărdĕns ŏf | Gŭl ĭn hĕr | blŏom whĕre thĕ | cĭtrŏn ănd | ŏlĭve ăre făirĕst ŏf | frŭit ănd thĕ | vŏice ŏf thĕ | nĭghtĭngăle | nĕvĕr ĭs | mŭte whĕre thĕ | vĭrgĭns ăre sŏft ăs thĕ | rŏsĕs thĕy | twine ănd | ăll săve thĕ | spĭrĭt ŏf | măn ĭs dĭ- | vĭne 'tĭs thĕ | lănd ŏf thĕ | Ĕast 'tĭs.thĕ | clĭme ŏf thĕ | Sŭn căn hĕ | smĭle ŏn sŭch | dĕeds ăs hĭs | chĭldrĕn hăve | dŏne ăs | wĭld ăs thĕ | ăccĕnts ŏf | lŏvĕrs' făre- | wĕll ăre thĕ | hĕarts thăt thĕy | bĕar ănd thĕ | tălĕs thăt thĕy | tell."—*Ib.*

Obs. 5.—In the sum and proportion of their quantities, the anapest, the dactyl, and the amphibrach, are equal, each having two syllables short to one long; and, with two short quantities between two long ones, lines may be tolerably accordant in rhythm, though the order, at the commencement, be varied, and their number of syllables be not equal. Of the following sixteen lines, nine are pure anapestic tetrameters; one *may* be reckoned dactylic, but it may quite as well be said to have a trochee, an iambus, and two anapests or two amphimacs; one is a spondee and three anapests; and the rest *may* be scanned as amphibrachics ending with an iambus, but are more properly anapestics commencing with an iambus. Like the preceding example from Byron, they lack the uniformity of proper composites, and are rather to be regarded as anapestics irregularly diversified.

THE ALBATROSS.

"'Tis said the Albatross never rests."—*Buffon.*

"Whĕre thĕ făth | -ŏmlĕss wăves | ĭn magnĭf | -ĭcence toss,
Hŏmelĕss | ănd hĭgh | soars the wild | Albatross;
Unwea | ried, undaunt | -ed, unshrink | -ing, alone,
The o | -cean his em | -pire, the tem | -pest his throne.
When the ter | -rible whirl | -wind raves wild | o'er the surge,
And the hur | -ricane howls | out the mar | -iner's dirge,
In thy glo | -ry thou spurn | -est the dark | -heaving sea,
Prŏud bird | of the o | -cean-world. home | -less and free.
When the winds | are at rest, | and the sun | in his glow,
And the glit | -tering tide | sleeps in beau | -ty below,
In the pride | of thy pow | -er trium | -phant above,
With thy mate | thou art hold | -ing thy rev | -els of love.
Untir | -ed, unfet | -tered, unwatched, | unconfined,
Be my spir | -it like thee. | in the world | of the mind;
No lean | -ing for earth, | e'er to wea | -ry its flight,
And fresh | as thy pin | -ions in re | -gions of light."

SAMUEL DALY LANGTREE: *North American Reader*, p. 443.

Obs. 6.—It appears that the most noted measures of the Greek and Latin poets were not of any simple order, but either composites, or mixtures too various to be called composites. It is not to be denied, that we have much difficulty in reading them rhythmically, according to their stated feet and scansion; and so we should have, in reading our own language rhythmically, in any similar succession of feet. Noticing this in respect to the Latin Hexameter, or Heroic verse. Poe says, "Now the discrepancy in question is not observable in English metres; where the scansion coincides with the reading, *so far as the rhythm is concerned*—that is to say, if we pay no attention to the *sense* of the passage. But these facts indicate a *radical difference* in the genius of the two languages, as regards their capacity for modulation. In truth, * * * the Latin is a far more *stately* tongue than our own. It is essentially spondaic; the English is as essentially dactylic."—*Pioneer*, p. 110. (See the marginal note in Section 3d, at Obs. 22d, above.) Notwithstanding this difference, discrepance, or difficulty, whatever it may be, some of our poets have, in a few instances, attempted imitations of certain Latin metres; which imitations it may be proper briefly to notice under the present head. The Greek or Latin Hexameter line has, of course, six feet, or pulsations. According to the Prosodies, the first four of these may be either dactyls or spondees; the fifth is always, or nearly always, a dactyl; and the sixth, or last, is always a spondee: as,

"Lūdĕrĕ | quæ vĕl | -lĕm călă | -mō pĕr | -mĭsĭt ă | -grĕstĭ."—*Virg.*
"Infăn- | dŭm, Rē | -gĭnă, jŭ | -bĕs rĕnŏ | -vărĕ dŏ | -lōrĕm."—*Id.*

Of this sort of verse, in English, somebody has framed the following very fair example :—

"Măn ĭs ă | cŏmplĕx, | cŏmpŏund | cŏmpŏst, | yĕt ĭs hĕ | Gŏd-bŏrn."

Obs. 7.—Of this species of versification, which may be called Mixed or Composite Hexameter, the most considerable specimen that I have seen in English, is Longfellow's Evangeline, a poem of one thousand three hundred and eighty-two of these long lines, or verses. This work has found admirers, and not a few; for, of these, nothing written by so distinguished a scholar could fail but, surely, not many of the verses in question exhibit truly the feet of the ancient Hexameters; or,if they do, the ancients contented themselves with very imperfect rhythms, even in their noblest heroics. In short, I incline to the opinion of Poe, that, "Nothing less than the deservedly high reputation of Professor Longfellow, could have sufficed to give currency to his lines as to Greek Hexameters. In general, they are neither one thing nor another. Some few of them are dactylic verses.—English dactylics. But do away with the division into lines, and the most astute critic would never have suspected them of any thing more than prose."—*Pioneer*, p. 111. The following are the last ten lines of the volume, with such a division into feet as the poet is presumed to have contemplated:—

"Still stands the | forest pri | -meval; but | under the | shade of its | branches
Dwells an | -other | race, with | other | customs and | language.
Only a | -long the | shore of the | mournful and | misty At | -lantic
Linger a | few A | -cadian | peasants, whose | fathers from | exile
Wandered | back to their | native | land to | die in its | bosom.
In the | fisherman's | cot the | wheel and the | loom are still | busy;
Maidens still | wear their | Norman | caps and their | kirtles of | homespun,
And by the | evening | fire re | -peat E | -vangeline's | story,
While from its | rocky | caverns the | deep-voiced, | neighbouring | ocean
Speaks, and in | accents dis | -consolate | answers the | wail of the | forest."
HENRY W. LONGFELLOW: *Evangeline*, p. 162.

OBS. 8.—An other form of verse, common to the Greeks and Romans, which has sometimes been imitated—or, rather, which some writers have *attempted to imitate*—in English, is the line or stanza called Sapphic, from the inventress, Sappho, a Greek poetess. The Sapphic verse, according to Fabricius, Smetius, and all good authorities, has eleven syllables, making "five feet—the first a trochee, the second a spondee, the third a dactyl, and the fourth and fifth trochees." The Sapphic stanza, or what is sometimes so called, consists of three Sapphic lines and an Adonian, or Adonic,—this last being a short line composed of "a dactyl and a spondee." Example from Horace:—

"Intĕ | -gĕr vī | -tæ, scĕlĕ | -rīsquĕ | pūrŭs
Non e | -get Mau | -ri jacu | -lis ne | -qu' arcu,
Nec ven | -ena | -tis gravi | -dâ sa | -gittis,
Fusce, pha | -retra."

OBS. 9.—To arrange eleven syllables in a line, and have half or more of them to form trochees, is no difficult matter; but, to find *rhythm* in the succession of "a trochee, a spondee, and a dactyl," as we read words, seems hardly practicable. Hence few are the English Sapphics, if there be any, which abide by the foregoing formule of quantities and feet. Those which I have seen, are generally, if not in every instance, susceptible of a more natural scansion as being composed of trochees, with a dactyl, or some other foot of three syllables, at the *beginning* of each line. The cæsural pause falls sometimes after the fourth syllable, but more generally, and much more agreeably, after the fifth. Let the reader inspect the following example, and see if he do not agree with me in laying the accent on only the first syllable of each foot, as the feet are here divided. The accent, too, must be carefully laid. Without considerable care in the reading, the hearer will not suppose the composition to be any thing but prose:—

"THE WIDOW."—(IN "SAPPHICS.")

" Cold was the | night-wind, | drifting | fast the | snow fell,
Wide were the | downs, and | shelter | -less and | naked,
When a poor | Wanderer | struggled | on her | journey,
Weary and | way-sore.

Drear were the | downs, more | dreary | her re | -flections;
Cold was the | night-wind, | colder | was her | bosom;
She had no | home, the | world was | all be | -fore her;
She had no | shelter.

Fast o'er the | heath a | chariot | rattled | by her;
' Pity me!' | feebly | cried the | lonely | wanderer;
' Pity me, | strangers! | lest, with | cold and | hunger,
Here I should | perish.

' Once I had | friends,—though | now by | all for | -saken!
' Once I had | parents, | —they are | now in | heaven!
' I had a | home once, | —I had | once a | husband—
Pity me, | strangers!

' I had a | home once, | —I had | once a | husband—
' I am a | widow, | poor and | broken | -hearted!'
Loud blew the | wind; un | -heard was | her oom | -plaining;
On drove the | chariot.

Then on the | snow she | laid her | down to | rest her;
She heard a | horseman; | ' Pity | me!' she | groan'd out;
Loud was the | wind; un | -heard was | her com | -plaining;
On went the | horseman.

Worn out with | anguish, | toil, and | cold, and | hunger,
Down sunk the | Wanderer; | sleep had | seized her | senses;
There did the | traveller | find her | in the | morning;
God had re | -leased her."
ROBERT SOUTHEY: *Poems*, Philad. 1843, p. 251.

OBS. 10.—Among the lyric poems of Dr. Watts, is one, entitled, "THE DAY OF JUDGEMENT; *an Ode, attempted in English Sapphic.*" It is perhaps as good an example as we have of the species. It consists of nine stanzas, of which I shall here cite the first three, dividing them into feet as above:—

" When the fierce | North Wind, | with his | airy | forces,
Rears up the | Baltic | to a | foaming | fury;
And the red | lightning | with a | storm of | hail comes
Rushing a | -main down;

How the poor | sailors | stand a | -maz'd and | tremble !
While the hoarse | thunder, | like a | bloody | trumpet,
Roars a loud | onset | to the | gaping | waters,
    Quick to de | -vour them.

Such shall the | noise be, | and the | wild dis | -order,
(If things e | -ternal | may be | like these | earthly,)
Such the dire | terror, | when the | great Arch | -angel
    Shakes the cre | -ation."—*Horæ Lyricæ*, p. 67.

OBS. 11.—"These lines," says Humphrey, who had cited the first four, "are good English Sapphics, and contain the essential traits of the original as nearly as the two languages, Greek and English, correspond to each other. This stanza, together with the poem, from which this was taken, may stand for a model, in our English compositions."—*Humphrey's E. Prosody*, p. 19. This author erroneously supposed, that the trissyllabic foot, in any line of the Sapphic stanza, must occupy the second place : and, judging of the ancient feet and quantities by what he found, or supposed he found, in the English imitations, and not by what the ancient prosodists say of them, yet knowing that the ancient and the modern Sapphics are in several respects unlike, he presented forms of scansion for both, which are not only peculiar to himself, but not well adapted to either. "We have," says he, "no established rule for this kind of verse, in our English compositions, which has been uniformly adhered to. The rule for which, in Greek and Latin verse, *as far as I can ascertain*, was this : ˉ ˘ | ˉ ˘ | ˉ ˘ ˘ | ˉ ˘ | ˉ ˘ a trochee, a *moloss*, a *pyrrhic*, a trochee, and [a] *spondee ;* and *sometimes, occasionally*, a trochee, instead of a poem, at the end. But as our language is not favourable to the use of the spondee and moloss, the moloss is seldom or never used in our English Sapphics ; but, instead of which, some other *trissyllable* foot is used. Also, instead of the spondee, a trochee is commonly used ; and sometimes a trochee instead of the pyrrhic, in the third place. As some prescribed rule, or model for imitation. may be necessary, in this case, I will cite a stanza from one of our best English poets, which may serve for a model.

'Whĕn thĕ | fiĕrce nôrth-wĭnd, | wĭth hĭs | áirў | fôrcĕs [,]
Reărs ŭp | thĕ Băltĭc | tŏ ă | fôamĭng | fûrў ;
And thĕ | rĕd lĭghtnĭng | wĭth ă | stôrm ŏf | hâil cŏmes
    Rûshĭng | ămăin dŏwn.'—Watts."—*Ib.* p. 19.

OBS. 12.—In "the Works of George Canning," a small book published in 1829, there is a poetical dialogue of nine stanzas, entitled, "The Friend of Humanity and the Knife-Grinder," said to be "a burlesque on Mr. Southey's Sapphics." The metre appears to be near enough like to the foregoing. But these verses I divide, as I have divided the others, into trochees with initial dactyls. At the commencement, the luckier party salutes the other thus :—

"'Needy knife | -grinder ! | whither | are you | going ?
Rough is the | road, your | wheel is | out of | order—
Bleak blows the | blast ;—your | hat has | got a | hole in't,
    So have your | breeches !
'Weary knife | -grinder ! | little | think the | proud ones
Who in their | coaches | roll a | -long the | turnpike-
Road, what hard | work 'tis, | crying | all day, | 'Knives and
    Scissors to | grind O !' "—P. 44.

OBS. 13.—Among the humorous poems of Thomas Green Fessenden, published under the sobriquet of Dr. Caustic, or "Christopher Caustic, M. D.," may be seen an other comical example of Sapphics, which extends to eleven stanzas. It describes a contra-dance, and is entitled, "Horace Surpassed." The conclusion is as follows :—

"Willy Wagnimble dancing with Flirtilla,
Almost as light as air-balloon inflated,
Rigadoons around her, 'till the lady's heart is
    Forced to surrender.

Benny Bamboozle cuts the drollest capers,
Just like a camel, or a hippopot'mus ;
Jolly Jack Jumble makes as big a rout as
    Forty Dutch horses.

See Angelina lead the mazy dance down ;
Never did fairy trip it so fantastic ;
How my heart flutters, while my tongue pronounces,
    'Sweet little seraph !'

Such are the joys that flow from contra-dancing,
Pure as the primal happiness of Eden,
Love, mirth, and music, kindle in accordance
    Raptures extatic."—*Poems*, p. 208.

SECTION V.—ORAL EXERCISES.

IMPROPRIETIES FOR CORRECTION.

FALSE PROSODY, OR ERRORS OF METRE.

LESSON I.—RESTORE THE RHYTHM.

"The lion is laid down in his lair."—*O. B. Peirce's Gram.* p. 134.

[FORMULE.—Not proper, because the word "*lion*," here put for Cowper's word "*beast*," destroys the metre, and changes the line to prose. But, according to the definition given on p. 798, "Verse, in opposition to prose, *is lan-*

guage arranged into metrical lines of some determinate length and rhythm—language so ordered as to produce harmony, by a due succession of poetic feet." This line was composed of one iamb and two anapests; and, to such form, it should be restored, thus: "The *beast* is laid down in his lair."—*Cowper's Poems*, Vol. i, p. 201.]

" Where is thy true treasure? Gold says, not in me."—*Hallock's Gram.*, 1842, p. 66.
" Canst thou grow sad, thou sayest, as earth grows bright? "—*Frazee's Gram.*, 1845, p. 140.
" It must be so, Plato, thou reasonest well."— *Wells's Gram.*, 1846, p. 122.
" Slow rises merit, when by poverty depressed."—*Ib.* p. 195 ; *Hiley*, 132 ; *Hart*, 179.
" Rapt in future times, the bard begun."—*Wells's Gram.*, 1846, p. 153.
" Is there not rain enough in the sweet heavens
   To wash it white as snow? Whereunto serves mercy,
   But to confront the visage of offence! "—*Hallock's Gram.*, 1842, p. 118.
"Look ! in this place ran Cassius's dagger through."—*Kames, El. of Cr.*, Vol. i, p. 74.
" ——— When they list their lean and flashy songs,
   Harsh grate on their scrannel pipes of wretched straw."—*Jamieson's Rhet.* p. 135.
" Did not great Julius bleed for justice's sake ? "—*Dodd's Beauties of Shak.* p. 253.
" Did not great Julius bleed for justice sake ?"—*Singer's Shakspeare*, Vol. ii, p. 266.
" May I, unblam'd, express thee ? Since God is light."—*O. B, Peirce's Gram.* p. 290.
" Or hearest thou, rather, pure ethereal stream ! "—*2d Perversion, ib.*
" Republics ; kingdoms ; empires, may decay ;
   Princes, heroes, sages, sink to nought."—*O. B. Peirce's Gram.* p. 287.
"Thou bringest, gay creature as thou art,
   A solemn image to my heart."—*E. J. Hallock's Gram.* p. 197.
" Know thyself, presume not God to scan ;
   The proper study of mankind is Man."—*O. B. Peirce's Gram.* p. 285.
" Raised on a hundred pilasters of gold."—*Charlemagne*, C. i, St. 40.
" Love in Adalgise's breast has fixed his sting."—*Ib.* C. i, St. 30.

| " Thirty days hath September, | February twenty-eight alone, |
| April, June, and November, | All the rest thirty and one." |

Colet's Grammar, or Paul's Accidence, Lond. 1793, p. 75.

LESSON II.—RESTORE THE RHYTHM.

" 'Twas not the fame of what he once had been,
   Or tales in old records and annals seen."—*Rowe's Lucan*, B. i, l. 274.
"And Asia now and Afric are explor'd,
   For high-priced dainties, and citron board."—*Eng. Poets: ib.* B. i, l. 311.
" Who knows not, how the trembling judge beheld
   The peaceful court with arm'd legions fill'd ?"—*Eng. Poets: ib.* B. i, l. 578.
" With thee the Scythian wilds we'll wander o'er,
   With thee burning Libyan sands explore."—*Eng. Poets: ib.* B. i, l. 661.
" Hasty and headlong different paths they tread,
   As blind impulse and wild distraction lead."—*Eng. Poets: ib.* B. i, l. 858.
" But Fate reserv'd to perform its doom,
   And be the minister of wrath to Rome."—*Eng. Poets: ib.* B. ii, l. 136.
" Thus spoke the youth. When Cato thus exprest
   The sacred counsels of his most inmost breast."—*Eng. Poets: ib.* B. ii, l. 435.
" These were the strict manners of the man,
   And this the stubborn course in which they ran ;
   The golden mean unchanging to pursue,
   Constant to keep the proposed end in view."—*Eng. Poets: ib.* B. ii, l. 586.
" What greater grief can a Roman seize,
   Than to be forc'd to live on terms like these ! "—*Eng. Poets: ib.* B. ii, l. 782.
" He views the naked town with joyful eyes,
   While from his rage an arm'd people flies."—*Eng. Poets: ib.* B. ii, l. 880.
" For planks and beams he ravages the wood,
   And the tough bottom extends across the flood."—*Eng. Poets: ib.* B. ii, l. 1040.
" A narrow pass the horned mole divides,
   Narrow as that where Euripus' strong tides
   Beat on Eubœan Chalcis' rocky sides."—*Eng. Poets: ib.* B. ii, l. 1095.
" No force, no fears their hands unarm'd bear,
   But looks of peace and gentleness they wear."—*Eng. Poets, ib.* B. iii, l. 112.
" The ready warriors all aboard them ride,
   And wait the return of the retiring tide."—*Eng. Poets: ib.* B. iv, l. 716.
" He saw those troops that long had faithful stood,
   Friends to his cause, and enemies to good,
   Grown weary of their chief, and satiated with blood."—*Eng. Poets: ib.* B. v, l. 337.

CHAPTER V.—QUESTIONS.
ORDER OF REHEARSAL, AND METHOD OF EXAMINATION.
PART FOURTH, PROSODY.

☞ [The following questions call the attention of the student to the main doctrines in the foregoing code of Prosody, and embrace or demand those facts which it is most important for him to fix in his memory; they may, therefore, serve not only to aid the teacher in the process of examining his classes, but also to direct the learner in his manner of preparation for recital.]

LESSON I.—OF PUNCTUATION.

1. Of what does Prosody treat? 2. What is *Punctuation?* 3. What are the principal points, or marks? 4. What pauses are denoted by the first four points? 5. What pauses are required by the other four? 6. What is the general use of the Comma? 7. How many rules for the Comma are there, and what are their heads? 8. What says Rule 1st of *Simple Sentences?* 9. What says Rule 2d of *Simple Members?* 10. What says Rule 3d of *More than Two Words?* 11. What says Rule 4th of *Only Two Words?* 12. What says Rule 5th of *Words in Pairs?* 13. What says Rule 6th of *Words put Absolute?* 14. What says Rule 7th of *Words in Apposition?* 15. What says Rule 8th of *Adjectives?* 16. What says Rule 9th of *Finite Verbs?* 17. What says Rule 10th of *Infinitives?* 18. What says Rule 11th of *Participles?* 19. What says Rule 12th of *Adverbs?* 20. What says Rule 13th of *Conjunctions?* 21. What says Rule 14th of *Prepositions?* 22. What says Rule 15th of *Interjections?* 23. What says Rule 16th of *Words Repeated?* 24. What says Rule 17th of *Dependent Quotations?*

LESSON II.—OF THE COMMA.

1. How many exceptions, or forms of exception, are there to Rule 1st for the comma? 2.—to Rule 2d? 3.—to Rule 3d? 4.—to Rule 4th? 5.—to Rule 5th? 6.—to Rule 6th? 7.—to Rule 7th? 8.—to Rule 8th? 9.—to Rule 9th? 10.—to Rule 10th? 11.—to Rule 11th? 12.—to Rule 12th? 13.—to Rule 13th? 14.—to Rule 14th? 15.—to Rule 15th? 16.—to Rule 16th? 17.—to Rule 17th? 18. What says the Exception to Rule 1st of a *Long Simple Sentence?* 19. What says Exception 1st to Rule 2d of *Restrictive Relatives?* 20. What says Exception 2d to Rule 2d of *Short Terms closely Connected?* 21. What says Exception 3d to Rule 2d of *Elliptical Members United?* 22. What says Exception 1st to Rule 4th of *Two Words with Adjuncts?* 23. What says Exception 2d to Rule 4th of *Two Terms Contrasted?* 24. What says Exception 3d to Rule 4th of a mere *Alternative of Words?* 25. What says Exception 4th to Rule 4th of *Conjunctions Understood?*

LESSON III.—OF THE COMMA.

1. What rule speaks of the separation of *Words in Apposition?* 2. What says Exception 1st to Rule 7th of *Complex Names?* 3. What says Exception 2d to Rule 7th of *Close Apposition?* 4. What says Exception 3d to Rule 7th of a *Pronoun without a Pause?* 5. What says Exception 4th to Rule 7th of *Names Acquired?* 6. What says the Exception to Rule 8th of *Adjectives Restrictive?* 7. What is the rule which speaks of a finite *Verb Understood?* 8. What says the Exception to Rule 9th of a *Very Slight Pause?* 9. What is the Rule for the pointing of *Participles?* 10. What says the Exception to Rule 11th of *Participles Restrictive?*

[Now, if you please, you may correct orally, according to the formules given, some or all of the various examples of *False Punctuation*, which are arranged under the rules for the Comma in Section First.]

LESSON IV.—OF THE SEMICOLON.

1. What is the general use of the Semicolon? 2. How many rules are there for the Semicolon? 3. What are their heads? 4. What says Rule 1st of *Complex Members?* 5. What says Rule 2d of *Simple Members?* 6. What says Rule 3d of *Apposition, &c.?*

[Now, if you please, you may correct orally, according to the formules given, some or all of the various examples of *False Punctuation*, which are arranged under the rules for the Semicolon in Section Second.]

LESSON V.—OF THE COLON.

1. What is the general use of the Colon? 2. How many rules are there for the Colon? 3. What are their heads? 4. What says Rule 1st of *Additional Remarks?* 5. What says Rule 2d of *Greater Pauses?* 6. What says Rule 3d of *Independent Quotations?*

[Now, if you please, you may correct orally, according to the formules given, some or all of the various examples of *False Punctuation*, which are arranged under the rules for the Colon in Section Third.]

LESSON VI.—OF THE PERIOD.

1. What is the general use of the Period? 2. How many rules are there for the Period? 3. What are their heads? 4. What says Rule 1st of *Distinct Sentences?* 5. What says Rule 2d of *Allied Sentences?* 6. What says Rule 3d of *Abbreviations?*

[Now, if you please, you may correct orally, according to the formules given, some or all of the various examples of *False Punctuation*, which are arranged under the rules for the Period in Section Fourth.]

LESSON VII.—OF THE DASH.

1. What is the general use of the Dash? 2. How many rules are there for the Dash?

.t are their heads? 4. What says Rule 1st of *Abrupt Pauses?* 5. What says Rule
nphatic Pauses? 6. What says Rule 3d of *Faulty Dashes?*

f you please, you may correct orally, according to the formules given, some or all of the various exam-
ile *Punctuation*, which are arranged under the rules for the Dash in Section Fifth.]

Lesson VIII.—Of the Eroteme.

hat is the use of the Eroteme, or Note of Interrogation? 2. How many rules
·e for this mark? 3. What are their heads? 4. What says Rule 1st of *Questions*
5. What says Rule 2d of *Questions United?* 6. What says Rule 3d of *Questions*
f

f you please, you may correct orally, according to the formules given, of the various exam-
ile *Punctuation*, which are arranged under the rules for the Eroteme in Section Sixth]

Lesson IX.—Of the Ecphoneme.

hat is the use of the Ecphoneme, or Note of Exclamation? 2. How many rules are
r this mark? 3. What are their heads? 4. What says Rule 1st of *Interjections?* 5.
nys Rule 2d of *Invocations?* 6. What says Rule 3d of *Exclamatory Questions?*

f you please, you may correct orally, according to the formules given, some or all of the various exam-
ile *Punctuation*, which are arranged under the rules for the Ecphoneme in Section Seventh.]

Lesson X.—Of the Curves.

hat is the use of the Curves, or Marks of Parenthesis? 2. How many rules are
r the Curves? 3. What are their titles, or heads? 4. What says Rule 1st of *the*
esis? 5. What says Rule 2d of *Included Points?*

f you please, you may correct orally, according to the formules given, some or all of the various exam-
ile *Punctuation*, which are arranged under the rules for the Curves in Section Eighth]

Lesson XI.—Of the Other Marks.

hat is the use of the Apostrophe? 2. What is the use of the Hyphen? 3. What
se of the Diæresis, or Dialysis? 4. What is the use of the Acute Accent? 5. What
se of the Grave Accent? 6. What is the use of the Circumflex? 7. What is the use
|reve, or Stenotone? 8. What is the use of the Macron or Macrotone? 9. What
se of the Ellipsis, or Suppression? 10. What is the use of the Caret? 11. What is
of the Brace? 12. What is the use of the Section? 13. What is the use of the
,ph? 14. What is the use of the Guillemets, or Quotation Points? 15. How do
k a quotation within a quotation? 16. What is the use of the Crotchets, or Brack-
7. What is the use of the Index, or Hand? 18. What are the six Marks of Refer-
their usual order? 19. How can references be otherwise made? 20. What is the
he Asterism, or the Three Stars? 21. What is the use of the Cedilla?

f correctly answered the foregoing questions, the pupil should be taught to apply the principles of punc-
and, for this purpose, he may be required to read a portion of some accurately pointed book,—or may be
o turn to the *Fourteenth Praxis*, beginning on p. 783,—and to assign a reason for every mark he finds.]

Lesson XII.—Of Utterance.

hat is *Utterance?* 2. What does it include? 3. What is articulation? 4. How
iculation differ from pronunciation? 5. How does Comstock define it? 6. What,
iew, is a good articulation? 7. How does Bolles define articulation? 8. Is a good
tion important? 9. What are the faults opposite to it? 10. What says Sheridan,
d articulation? 11. Upon what does distinctness depend? 12. Why is just articu-
etter than mere loudness? 13. Do we learn to articulate in learning to speak or read?

Lesson XIII.—Of Pronunciation.

hat is pronunciation? 2. What is it that is called *Orthoëpy?* 3. What knowledge
onunciation require? 4. What are the just powers of the letters? 5. How are these
? 6. Are the just powers of the letters in any degree variable? 7. What is quan-
. Are all long syllables equally long, and all short ones equally short? 9. What
ss of voice to do with quantity? 10. What is accent? 11. Is every word accented?
we ever lay two equal accents on one word? 13. Have we more than one sort of
14. Can any word have the secondary accent, and not the primary? 15. Can
llables have either? 16. What regulates accent? 17. What four things distinguish
ant speaker?

· Lesson XIV.—Of Elocution.

hat is elocution? 2. What does elocution require? 3. What is emphasis? 4.
omparative view is taken of accent and emphasis? 5. How does L. Murray connect
is with quantity? 6. Does emphasis ever affect accent? 7. What is the guide to a
nphasis? 8. Can one read with too many emphases? 9. What are pauses? 10. How
nd what kinds of pauses are there? 11. What is said of the duration of pauses, and
ng of breath? 12. After what manner should pauses be made? 13. What pauses
icularly ungraceful? 14. What is said of rhetorical pauses? 15. How are the har-
auses divided? 16. Are such pauses essential to verse?

LESSON XV.—OF ELOCUTION.

17. What are inflections? 18. What is called the rising or upward inflection? 19. What is called the falling or downward inflection? 20. How are these inflections exemplified? 21. How are they used in asking questions? 22. What is said of the notation of them? 23. What constitutes a circumflex? 24. What constitutes the rising, and what the falling, circumflex? 25. Can you give examples? 26. What constitutes a monotone, in elocution? 27. Which kind of inflection is said to be most common? 28. Which is best adapted to strong emphasis? 29. What says Comstock of rules for inflections? 30. Is the voice to be varied for variety's sake? 31. What should regulate the inflections? 32. What is cadence? 33. What says Rippingham about it? 34. What says Murray? 35. What are tones? 36. Why do they deserve particular attention? 37. What says Blair about tones? 38. What says Hiley?

LESSON XVI.—OF FIGURES.

1. What is a *Figure* in grammar? 2. How many kinds of figures are there? 3. What is a figure of orthography? 4. What are the principal figures of orthography? 5. What is Mimesis? 6. What is an Archaism? 7. What is a figure of etymology? 8. How many and what are the figures of etymology? 9. What is Aphæresis? 10. What is Prosthesis? 11. What is Syncope? 12. What is Apocope? 13. What is Paragoge? 14. What is Diæresis? 15. What is Synæresis? 16. What is Tmesis? 17. What is a figure of syntax? 18. How many and what are the figures of syntax? 19. What is Ellipsis, in grammar? 20. Are sentences often elliptical? 21. What parts of speech can be omitted, by ellipsis? 22. What is Pleonasm? 23. When is this figure allowable? 24. What is Syllepsis? 25. What is Enallage? 26. What is Hyperbaton? 27. What is said of this figure?

LESSON XVII.—OF FIGURES.

28. What is a figure of rhetoric? 29. What peculiar name have some of these? 30. Do figures of rhetoric often occur? 31. On what are they founded? 32. How many and what are the principal figures of rhetoric? 33. What is a Simile? 34. What is a Metaphor? 35. What is an Allegory? 36. What is a Metonymy? 37. What is Synecdoche? 38. What is Hyperbole? 39. What is Vision? 40. What is Apostrophe? 41. What is Personification? 42. What is Erotesis? 43. What is Ecphonesis? 44. What is Antithesis? 45. What is Climax? 46. What is Irony? 47. What is Apophasis, or Paralipsis? 48. What is Onomatopœia?

[Now, if you please, you may examine the quotations adopted for the *Fourteenth Praxis*, and may name and define the various figures of grammar which are contained therein.]

LESSON XVIII.—OF VERSIFICATION.

1. What is *Versification?* 2. What is verse, as distinguished from prose? 3. What is the rhythm of verse? 4. What is the quantity of a syllable? 5. How are the poetic quantities denominated? 6. How are they proportioned? 7. What quantity coincides with accent or emphasis? 8. On what but the vowel sound does quantity depend? 9. Does syllabic quantity always follow the quality of the vowels? 10. Where is quantity variable, and where fixed, in English? 11. What is rhyme? 12. What is blank verse? 13. What is remarked concerning the rhyming syllables? 14. What is a stanza? 15. What uniformity have stanzas? 16. What variety have they?

LESSON XIX.—OF VERSIFICATION.

17. Of what does a verse consist? 18. Of what does a poetic foot consist? 19. How many feet do prosodists recognize? 20. What are the principal feet in English? 21. What is an Iambus? 22. What is a Trochee? 23. What is an Anapest? 24. What is a Dactyl? 25. Why are these feet principal? 26. What orders of verse arise from these? 27. Are these kinds to be kept separate? 28. What is said of the secondary feet? 29. How many and what secondary feet are explained in this code? 30. What is a Spondee? 31. What is a Pyrrhic? 32. What is a Moloss? 33. What is a Tribrach? 34. What is an Amphibrach? 35. What is an Amphimac? 36. What is a Bacchy? 37. What is an Antibacchy? 38. What is a Cæsura?

LESSON XX.—OF VERSIFICATION.

39. What are the principal kinds, or orders, of verse? 40. What other orders are there? 41. Does the composite order demand any uniformity? 42. Do the simple orders admit any diversity? 43. What is meant by *scanning* or *scansion?* 44. What mean the technical words *catalectic, acatalectic,* and *hypermeter?* 45. In scansion, why are the principal feet to be preferred to the secondary? 46. Can a single foot be a line? 47. What are the several combinations that form dimeter, trimeter, tetrameter, pentameter, hexameter, heptameter, and octometer? 48. What syllables have stress in a pure iambic line? 49. What are the several measures of iambic verse? 50. What syllables have stress in a pure trochaic line? 51. Can it be right, to regard as hypermeter the long rhyming syllable of a line? 52. Is the number of feet in a line to be generally counted by that of the long syllables? 53. What are the several measures of trochaic verse?

LESSON XXI.—OF VERSIFICATION.

What syllables have stress in a pure anapestic line? 55. What variation may occur rst foot? 56. Is this frequent? 57. Is it ever uniform? 58. What is the result of a mixture? 59. Is the anapest adapted to single rhyme? 60. May a surplus ever p for a deficiency? 61. Why are the anapestic measures few? 62. How many syl- re found in the longest? 63. What are the several measures of anapestic verse? at syllables have stress in a pure dactylic line? 65. With what does single-rhymed end? 66. Is dactylic verse very common? 67. What are the several measures of verse? 68. What is composite verse? 69. Must composites have rhythm? 70. kinds of composite verse numerous? 71. Why have we no exact enumeration of sures of this order? 72. Does this work contain specimens of different kinds of te verse?

now be required of the pupil to determine, by reading and scansion, the metrical elements of any good oetry which may be selected for the purpose—the feet being marked by pauses, and the long syllables f voice. He may also correct orally the few *Errors of Metre* which are given in the Fifth Section of V.]

CHAPTER VI.—FOR WRITING.
EXERCISES IN PROSODY.

hen the pupil can readily answer all the questions on Prosody, and apply the rules of punctuation to any n in which the points are rightly inserted, he should *write out* the following exercises, supplying what 1, and correcting what is amiss. Or, if any teacher choose to exercise his classes *orally*, by means of these he can very well do it; because, to read words, is always easier than to write them, and even points or may be quite as readily named as written.]

EXERCISE I.—PUNCTUATION.
the following sentences, and insert the COMMA *where it is requisite.*

EXAMPLES UNDER RULE I.—OF SIMPLE SENTENCES.

dogmatist's assurance is paramount to argument." "The whole course of his ntation comes to nothing." "The fieldmouse builds her garner under ground." —"The first principles of almost all sciences are few." "What he gave me to publish a small part." "To remain insensible to such provocation is apathy." "Minds 1 of poverty would be proud of affluence." "To be totally indifferent to praise or is a real defect in character."—*Wilson's Punctuation*, p. 38.

UNDER RULE II.—OF SIMPLE MEMBERS.

is eyes to the blind and feet was I to the lame." "They are gone but the remem-)f them is sweet." "He has passed it is likely through varieties of fortune." "The ough free has a governor within itself." "They I doubt not oppose the bill on pub- iples." "Be silent be grateful and adore." "He is an adept in language who always he truth." "The race is not to the swift nor the battle to the strong." I.—"He that has far to go should not hurry." "Hobbes believed the eternal truths e opposed." "Feeble are all pleasures in which the heart has no share." "The ich survives the tomb is one of the noblest attributes of the soul."—*Wilson's Punc-* p. 38. II.—"A good name is better than precious ointment." "Thinkst thou that duty ve dread to speak?" "The spleen is seldom felt where Flora reigns."

UNDER RULE III.—OF MORE THAN TWO WORDS.

city army court espouse my cause." "Wars pestilences and diseases are terrible ors." "Walk daily in a pleasant airy and umbrageous garden." Wit spirits facul- make it worse." "Men wives and children stare cry out and run." "Industry, and temperance are essential to happiness."—*Wilson's Punctuation*, p. 29. "Honor, , and pleasure seduce the heart."—*Ib.* p. 31.

UNDER RULE IV.—OF TWO TERMS CONNECTED.

e and fear are essentials in religion." "Praise and adoration are perfective of s." "We know bodies and their properties most perfectly." "Satisfy yourselves at is rational and attainable." "Slowly and sadly we laid him down." I.—"God will rather look to the inward motions of the mind than to the outward the body." "Gentleness is unassuming in opinion and temperate in zeal." II.—"He has experienced prosperity and adversity." "All sin essentially is and mortal." "Reprove vice but pity the offender." II.—"One person is chosen chairman or moderator." "Duration or time is meas- motion." "The governor or viceroy is chosen annually." V.—"Reflection reason still the ties improve." "His neat plain parlour wants our style." "We are fearfully wonderfully made."

UNDER RULE V.—OF WORDS IN PAIRS.

quired and rejected consulted and deliberated." "Seed-time and harvest cold and mer and winter day and night shall not cease."

EXERCISE II. — PUNCTUATION.

Copy the following sentences, and insert the COMMA *where it is requisite.*

EXAMPLES UNDER RULE VI.—OF WORDS PUT ABSOLUTE.

"The night being dark they did not proceed." "There being no other coach we h no alternative." "Remember my son that human life is the journey of a day." "All cumstances considered it seems right." "He that overcometh to him will I give pow-r "Your land strangers devour it in your presence." "Ah sinful nation a people laden with iniquity!"

"With heads declin'd ye cedars homage pay;
Be smooth ye rocks ye rapid floods give way!"

UNDER RULE VII.—OF WORDS IN APPOSITION.

"Now Philomel sweet songstress charms the night." "'Tis chanticleer the shepherd's clock announcing day." "The evening star love's harbinger appears." "The queen of night fair Dian smiles serene." "There is yet one man Micaiah the son of Imlah." "Our whole company man by man ventured down." "As a work of wit the Dunciad has few equals."

"In the same temple the resounding wood
All vocal beings hymned their equal God."

Exc. I.—"The last king of Rome was Tarquinius Superbus." "Bossuet highly eulogizes Maria Theresa of Austria." "No emperor has been more praised than Marcus Aurelius Antoninus."

Exc. II.—"For he went and dwelt by the brook Cherith." "Remember the example of the patriarch Joseph." "The poet, Milton, excelled in prose as well as in verse."

Exc. III.—"I wisdom dwell with prudence." "Ye fools be ye of an understanding heart." "I tell you that which you yourselves do know."

Exc. IV.—"I crown thee king of intimate delights." "I count the world a stranger for thy sake." "And this makes friends such miracles below." "God has pronounced it death to taste-that tree." "Grace makes the slave a freeman."

UNDER RULE VIII.—OF ADJECTIVES.

"Deaf with the noise I took my hasty flight." "Him piteous of his youth soft disengage." "I played a while obedient to the fair." "Love free as air spreads his light wings and flies." "Physical science separate from morals parts with its chief dignity."

"Then active still and unconfined his mind
Explores the vast extent of ages past."
"But there is yet a liberty unsung
By poets and by senators unpraised."

Exc.—"I will marry a wife beautiful as the Houries." "He was a man able to speak upon doubtful questions." "These are the persons, anxious for the change." "Are they men worthy of confidence and support?" "A man, charitable beyond his means, is scarcely honest."

UNDER RULE IX.—OF FINITE VERBS.

"Poverty wants some things—avarice all things." "Honesty has one face—flattery two." "One king is too soft and easy—an other too fiery."

"Mankind's esteem they court—and he his own:
Theirs the wild chase of false felicities;
His the compos'd possession of the true."

EXERCISE III. — PUNCTUATION.

Copy the following sentences, and insert the COMMA *where it is requisite.*

EXAMPLES UNDER RULE X.—OF INFINITIVES.

"My desire is to live in peace." "The great difficulty was to compel them to pay their debts." "To strengthen our virtue God bids us trust in him." "I made no bargain with you to live always drudging." "To sum up all her tongue confessed the shrew." "To proceed my own adventure was still more laughable."

"We come not with design of wasteful prey
To drive the country force the swains away."

UNDER RULE XI.—OF PARTICIPLES.

"Having given this answer he departed." "Some sunk to beasts find pleasure end in pain." "Eased of her load subjection grows more light." "Death still draws nearer never seeming near." "He lies full low gored with wounds and weltering in his blood." "Kind is fell Lucifer compared to thee." "Man considered in himself is helpless and wretched." "Like scattered down by howling Eurus blown." "He with wide nostrils snorting skims the wave." "Youth is properly speaking introductory to manhood."

Exc.—"He kept his eye fixed on the country before him." "They have their part assigned them to act." "Years will not repair the injuries, done by him."

UNDER RULE XII.—OF ADVERBS.

"Yes we both were philosophers." "However Providence saw fit to cross our design." "Besides I know that the eye of the public is upon me." "The fact certainly is much otherwise." "For nothing surely can be more inconsistent."

UNDER RULE XIII.—OF CONJUNCTIONS.

"For in such retirement the soul is strengthened." "It engages our desires; and in some degree satisfies them also." "But of every Christian virtue piety is an essential part." "The English verb is variable; as *love lovest loves.*"

UNDER RULE XIV.—OF PREPOSITIONS.

"In a word charity is the soul of social life." "By the bowstring I can repress violence and fraud." "Some by being too artful forfeit the reputation of probity." "With regard to morality I was not indifferent." "Of all our senses sight is the most perfect and delightful."

UNDER RULE XV.—OF INTERJECTIONS.

"Behold I am against thee O inhabitant of the valley!" "O it is more like a dream than a reality." "Some wine ho!" "Ha ha ha; some wine eh?'"
"When lo the dying breeze begins to fail,
And flutters on the mast the flagging sail."

UNDER RULE XVI.—OF WORDS REPEATED.

"I would never consent never never never." "His teeth did chatter chatter chatter still." "Come come come come—to bed to bed to bed."

UNDER RULE XVII.—OF DEPENDENT QUOTATIONS.

"He cried ' Cause every man to go out from me.'" "'Almet' said he ' remember what thou hast seen.'" "I answered ' Mock not thy servant who is but a worm before thee.'"

EXERCISE IV. — PUNCTUATION.

I. THE SEMICOLON.—*Copy the following sentences, and insert the Comma and the* SEMICOLON *where they are requisite.*

EXAMPLES UNDER RULE I.—OF COMPOUND MEMBERS.

"' Man is weak' answered his companion ' knowledge is more than equivalent to force.'" "To judge rightly of the present we must oppose it to the past for all judgement is comparative and of the future nothing can be known." "' Content is natural wealth' says Socrates to which I shall add 'luxury is artificial poverty.'"
"Converse and love mankind might strongly draw
When love was liberty and nature law."

UNDER RULE II.—OF SIMPLE MEMBERS.

"Be wise to-day 'tis madness to defer." "The present all their care the future his." "Wit makes an enterpriser sense a man." "Ask thought for joy grow rich and hoard within." "Song soothes our pains and age has pains to soothe." "Here an enemy encounters there a rival supplants him." "Our answer to their reasons is ' No' to their scoffs nothing."
"Here subterranean works and cities see
There towns aërial on the waving tree."

UNDER RULE III.—OF APPOSITION.

"In Latin there are six cases namely the nominative the genitive the dative the accusative the vocative and the ablative." "Most English nouns form the plural by taking *s* : as *boy boys nation nations king kings bay bays.*" "Bodies are such as are endued with a vegetable soul as plants a sensitive soul as animals or a rational soul as the body of man."

II. THE COLON.—*Copy the following sentences, and insert the Comma, the Semicolon, and the* COLON, *where they are requisite.*

UNDER RULE I.—OF ADDITIONAL REMARKS.

"Indulge not desire at the expense of the slightest article of virtue pass once its limits and you fall headlong into vice." "Death wounds to cure we fall we rise we reign." "Beware of usurpation God is the judge of all."
"Bliss !—there is none but unprecarious bliss
That is the gem sell all and purchase that."

UNDER RULE II.—OF GREATER PAUSES.

"I have the world here before me I will review it at leisure surely happiness is somewhere to be found." "A melancholy enthusiast courts persecution and when he cannot obtain it afflicts himself with absurd penances but the holiness of St. Paul consisted in the simplicity of a pious life."
"Observe his awful portrait and admire
Nor stop at wonder imitate and live."

UNDER RULE III.—OF INDEPENDENT QUOTATIONS.

"Such is our Lord's injunction ' Watch and pray.' "   " He died praying for his cutors ' Father forgive them they know not what they do.' "   " On the old gentleman' cane was inscribed this motto 'Festina lentè.' "

III. THE PERIOD.—*Copy the following sentences, and insert the Comma, the Semicolon, the Colon, and the* PERIOD, *where they are requisite.*

UNDER RULE I.—OF DISTINCT SENTENCES.

" Then appeared the sea and the dry land the mountains rose and the rivers flowed the sun and moon began their course in the skies herbs and plants clothed the ground the xr the earth and the waters were stored with their respective inhabitants at last man was made in the image of God"

" In general those parents have most reverence who most deserve it for he that lives well cannot be despised"

UNDER RULE II.—OF ALLIED SENTENCES.

" Civil accomplishments frequently give rise to fame but a distinction is to be made between fame and true honour the statesman the orator or the poet may be famous while yet the man himself is far from being honoured"

UNDER RULE III.—OF ABBREVIATIONS.

" Glass was invented in England by Benalt a monk A D 664 "   "The Roman era C C commenced A C 1753 years "   " Here is the Literary Life of S T Coleridge Esq "   " PLAT a most illustrious philosopher of antiquity died at Athens 348 B C aged 81 his writings are very valuable his language beautiful and correct and his philosophy sublime "—See Uni Biog Dict

EXERCISE V.—PUNCTUATION.

I. THE DASH.—*Copy the following sentences, and insert, in their proper places, the* DASH, *and such other points as are necessary.*

EXAMPLES UNDER RULE I.—OF ABRUPT PAUSES.

" You say *famous* very often and I don't know exactly what it means a *famous* uniform *famous* doings What does *famous* mean' "

" O why *famous* means Now don't you know what *famous* means It means It is a word that people say It is the fashion to say it It means it means *famous* "

UNDER RULE II.—OF EMPHATIC PAUSES.

" But this life is not all there is there is full surely an other state abiding us And if there is what is thy prospect O remorseless obdurate Thou shalt hear it would be thy wisdom to think thou now hearest the sound of that trumpet which shall awake the dead Return O yet return to the Father of mercies and live "

"The future pleases Why The present pains
But that's a secret yes which all men know "

II. THE EROTEME.—*Copy the following sentences, and insert rightly the* EROTEME, *or* NOTE OF INTERROGATION, *and such other points as are necessary.*

UNDER RULE I.—OF QUESTIONS DIRECT.

"Does Nature bear a tyrant's breast │ Wears she the despot's purple vest
Is she the friend of stern control   │ Or fetters she the freeborn soul "

" Why should a man whose blood is warm within
Sit like his grandsire cut in alabaster"

" Who art thou courteous stranger and from whence
Why roam thy steps to this abandon'd dale "

UNDER RULE II.—OF QUESTIONS UNITED.

" Who bid the stork Columbus-like explore
Heav'ns not his own and worlds unknown before
Who calls the council states the certain day
Who forms the phalanx and who points the way"

UNDER RULE III.—OF QUESTIONS INDIRECT.

" They asked me who I was and whither I was going."   " St. Paul asked king Agrippa if he believed the prophets? But he did not wait for an answer."

" Ask of thy mother Earth why oaks are made
Taller and stronger than the weeds they shade"

III. THE ECPHONEME.—*Copy the following sentences, and insert rightly the* ECPHONEME, *or* NOTE OF EXCLAMATION, *and such other points as are necessary.*

UNDER RULE I.—OF INTERJECTIONS.

" Oh talk of hypocrisy after this Most consummate of all hypocrites After instructing your chosen official advocate to stand forward with such a defence such an exposition of your motives to dare utter the word hypocrisy and complain of those who charged you with it " *Brougham*

"Alas how is that rugged heart forlorn"
" Behold the victor vanquish'd by the worm"
" Bliss sublunary Bliss proud word and vain"

UNDER RULE II.—OF INVOCATIONS.

" O Popular Applause what heart of man
Is proof against thy sweet seducing charms"
"More than thy balm O Gilead heals the wound"

UNDER RULE III.—OF EXCLAMATORY QUESTIONS.

" With what transports of joy shall I be received In what honour in what delightful repose shall I pass the remainder of my life What immortal glory shall I have acquired" *Hooke's Roman History*

" How often have I loiter'd o'er thy green
Where humble happiness endear'd each scene"

IV. THE CURVES.—*Copy the following sentences, and insert rightly the* CURVES, *or* MARKS OF PARENTHESIS, *and such other points as are necessary.*

UNDER RULE I.—OF THE PARENTHESIS.

"And all the question wrangle e'er so long
Is only this If God has plac'd him wrong"
"And who what God foretells who speaks in things
Still louder than in words shall dare deny"

UNDER RULE II.—OF INCLUDED POINTS.

" Say was it virtue more though Heav'n ne'er gave
Lamented Digby sunk thee to the grave"
" Where is that thrift that avarice of time
O glorious avarice thought of death inspires"
"And oh the last last what can words express
Thought reach the last last silence of a friend"

EXERCISE VI.—PUNCTUATION.

Copy the following MIXED EXAMPLES, *and insert the points which they require.*

"As one of them opened his sack he espied his money" "They cried out the more exceedingly Crucify him" " The soldiers' counsel was to kill the prisoners" " Great injury these vermin mice and rats do in the field" " It is my son's coat an evil beast hath devoured him" " Peace of all worldly blessings is the most valuable" " By this time the very foundation was removed" " The only words he uttered were I am a Roman citizen" " Some distress either felt or feared gnaws like a worm" " How then must I determine Have I no interest If I have not I am stationed here to no purpose" *Harris* " In the fire the destruction was so swift sudden vast and miserable as to have no parallel in story" " Dionysius the tyrant of Sicily was far from being happy" "I ask now Verres what thou hast to advance" " Excess began and sloth sustains the trade" " Fame can never reconcile a man to a death bed" "They that sail on the sea tell of the danger" " Be doers of the word and not hearers only" " The storms of wintry time will quickly pass" " Here Hope that smiling angel stands" " Disguise I see thou art a wickedness" "There are no tricks in plain and simple faith" " True love strikes root in reason passion's foe" " Two gods divide them all Pleasure and Gain" "I am satisfied My son has done his duty" " Remember Almet the vision which thou hast seen" " I beheld an enclosure beautiful as the gardens of paradise" "The knowledge which I have received I will communicate" " But I am not yet happy and therefore I despair" Wretched mortals said I to what purpose are you busy" " Bad as the world is respect is always paid to virtue" " In a word he views men in the clear sunshine of charity" "This being the case I am astonished and amazed" " These men approached him and saluted him king" " Excellent and obliging sages these undoubtedly" " Yet at the same time the man himself undergoes a change" " One constant effect of idleness is to nourish the passions" " You heroes regard nothing but glory" " Take care lest while you strive to reach the top you fall " " Proud and presumptuous they can brook no opposition" " Nay some awe of religion may still subsist" " Then said he Lo I come to do thy will O God" *Bible* "As for me behold I am in your hand" *Ib.* " Can any hide himself in secret places that I shall not see him saith the Lord" *Jer* xxiii 24 " Now I Paul myself beseech you" " Now for a recompense in the same I speak as unto my children be ye also enlarged" 2 *Cor* vi 13 " He who lives always in public cannot live to his own soul whereas he who retires remains calm " "Therefore behold I even I will utterly forget you" " This text speaks only of those to whom it speaks" " Yea he warmeth himself and saith Aha I am warm " " King Agrippa believest thou the prophets"

EXERCISE VII. — PUNCTUATION.

Copy the following MIXED EXAMPLES, *and insert the points which they require.*

To whom can riches give repute or trust
Content or pleasure but the good and just *Pope*
To him no high no low no great no small
He fills he bounds connects and equals all *Id*
Reasons whole pleasure all the joys of sense
Lie in three words health peace and competence *Id*
Not so for once indulgd they sweep the main
Deaf to the call or hearing hear in vain *Anon*
Say will the falcon stooping from above
Smit with her varying plumage spare the dove *Pope*
Throw Egypts by and offer in its stead
Offer the crown on Berenices head *Id*
Falsely luxurious will not man awake
And springing from the bed of sloth enjoy
The cool the fragrant and the silent hour *Thomson*
Yet thus it is nor otherwise can be
So far from aught romantic what I sing *Young*
Thyself first know then love a self there is
Of virtue fond that kindles at her charms *Id*
How far that little candle throws his beams
So shines a good deed in a naughty world *Shakspeare*
You have too much respect upon the world
They lose it that do buy it with much care *Id*
How many things by season seasond are
To their right praise and true perfection *Id*
Canst thou descend from converse with the skies
And seize thy brothers throat For what a clod *Young*
In two short precepts all your business lies
Would you be great *be virtuous* and *be wise Denham*
But sometimes virtue starves while vice is fed
What then is the reward of virtue bread *Pope*
A life all turbulence and noise may seem
To him that leads it wise and to be praisd
But wisdom is a pearl with most success
Sought in still waters and beneath clear skies *Cowper*
All but the swellings of the softend heart
That waken not disturb the tranquil mind *Thomson*
Inspiring God who boundless spirit all
And unremitting energy pervades
Adjusts sustains and agitates the whole *Id*
Ye ladies for indifferent in your cause
I should deserve to forfeit all applause
Whatever shocks or gives the least offence
To virtue delicacy truth or sense
Try the criterion tis a faithful guide
Nor has nor can have Scripture on its side. *Cowper*

EXERCISE VIII. — SCANNING.

Divide the following VERSES *into the feet which compose them, and distinguish by marks the long and the short syllables.*

Example I.—"Our Daily Paths."—By F. Hemans.

" There's Beauty all around our paths, if but our watchful eyes
Can trace it 'midst familiar things, and through their lowly guise ;
We may find it where a hedgerow showers its blossoms o'er our way,
Or a cottage-window sparkles forth in the last red light of day."

Example II.—"Fetching Water."—Anonymous.

" Early on a sunny morning, while the lark was singing sweet,
Came, beyond the ancient farmhouse, sounds of lightly-tripping feet.
'Twas a lowly cottage maiden, going,—why, let young hearts tell,—
With her homely pitcher laden, fetching water from the well."

Example III.—Deity.

Alone thou sitst above the everlasting hills,
And all immensity of space thy presence fills :
For thou alone art God ;—as God thy saints adore thee ;
Jehovah is thy name ;—they have no gods before thee.—*G. Brown.*

Example IV.—Impenitence.

The impenitent sinner whom mercy empowers,
  Dishonours that goodness which seeks to restore;
As the sands of the desert are water'd by showers,
  Yet barren and fruitless remain as before.—*G. Brown.*

Example V.—Piety.

Holy and pure are the pleasures of piety,
  Drawn from the fountain of mercy and love;
Endless, exhaustless, exempt from satiety,
  Rising unearthly, and soaring above.—*G. Brown.*

Example VI.—A Simile.

The bolt that strikes the tow'ring cedar dead,
Oft passes harmless o'er the hazel's head.—*G. Brown.*

Example VII.—A Simile.

" Yet to their general's voice they soon obey'd
Innumerable. As when the potent rod
Of Amram's son, in Egypt's evil day,
Wav'd round the coast, up call'd a pitchy cloud
Of locusts, warping on the eastern wind,
That o'er the realm of impious Pharaoh hung
Like night, and darken'd all the land of Nile."—*Milton.*

Example VIII.—Elegiac Stanza.

Thy name is dear—'tis virtue balm'd in love;
  Yet e'en thy name a pensive sadness brings.
Ah! wo the day, our hearts were doom'd to prove,
  That fondest love but points affliction's stings!—*G. Brown.*

Example IX.—Cupid.

Zephyrs, moving bland, and breathing fragrant
  With the sweetest odours of the spring,
O'er the winged boy, a thoughtless vagrant,
  Slumb'ring in the grove, their perfumes fling.—*G. Brown.*

Example X.—Divine Power.

When the winds o'er Gennesaret roar'd,
  And the billows tremendously rose,
The Saviour but utter'd the word,
  They were hush'd to the calmest repose.—*G. Brown.*

Example XI.—Invitation.

Come from the mount of the leopard, spouse,
  Come from the den of the lion;
Come to the tent of thy shepherd, spouse,
  Come to the mountain of Zion.—*G. Brown.*

Example XII.—Admonition.

| In the days of thy youth, | O! forsake not his truth, |
| Remember thy God: | Incur not his rod.—*G. Brown.* |

Example XIII.—Commendation.

| Constant and duteous, | How art thou beauteous, |
| Meek as the dove, | Daughter of love!—*G. Brown.* |

EXERCISE IX. — SCANNING.

Mark the feet and syllables which compose the following lines—or mark a sample of each metre.

Edwin, an Ode.

I. STROPHE.

Led by the pow'r of song, and nature's love,
Which raise the soul all vulgar themes above,
    The mountain grove
    Would Edwin rove
  In pensive mood, alone;
  And seek the woody dell,
  Where noontide shadows fell,
      Cheering,
      Veering,
    Mov'd by the sephyr's swell.
Here nurs'd he thoughts to genius only known

61

When nought was heard around
But sooth'd the rest profound
Of rural beauty on her mountain throne.
Nor less he lov'd (rude nature's child)
The elemental conflict wild ;
When, fold on fold, above was pil'd
The watery swathe, careering on the wind.
Such scenes he saw
With solemn awe,
As in the presence of the Eternal Mind.
Fix'd he gaz'd,
Tranc'd and rais'd,
Sublimely rapt in awful pleasure undefin'd.

II. ANTISTROPHE.

Reckless of dainty joys, he finds delight
Where feebler souls but tremble with affright.
Lo ! now, within the deep ravine,
A black impending cloud
Infolds him in its shroud,
And dark and darker glooms the scene.
Through the thicket streaming,
Lightnings now are gleaming ;
Thunders rolling dread,
Shake the mountain's head ;
Nature's war
Echoes far,
O'er ether borne.
That flash
The ash
Has scoth'd and torn !
Now it rages ;
Oaks of ages,
Writhing in the furious blast,
Wide their leafy honours cast ;
Their gnarled arms do force to force oppose :
Deep rooted in the crevic'd rock,
The sturdy trunk sustains the shock,
Like dauntless hero firm against assailing foes.

III. EPODE.

' O Thou who sitst above these vapours dense,
And rul'st the storm by thine omnipotence !
Making the collied cloud thy car,
Coursing the winds, thou rid'st afar,
Thy blessings to dispense.
The early and the latter rain,
Which fertilize the dusty plain,
Thy bounteous goodness pours.
Dumb be the atheist tongue abhorr'd !
All nature owns thee, sovereign Lord !
And works thy gracious will ;
At thy command the tempest roars,
At thy command is still.
Thy mercy o'er this scene sublime presides ;
'Tis mercy forms the veil that hides
The ardent solar beam ;
While, from the volley'd breast of heaven,
Transient gleams of dazzling light,
Flashing on the balls of sight,
Make darkness darker seem.
Thou mov'st the quick and sulph'rous leven—
The tempest-driven
Cloud is riven ;
And the thirsty mountain-side
Drinks gladly of the gushing tide.'
So breath'd young Edwin, when the summer shower,
From out that dark o'erchamb'ring cloud,
With lightning flash and thunder loud,
Burst in wild grandeur o'er his solitary bower.—*G. Bross.*

THE END OF PART FOURTH.

KEY

IMPROPRIETIES FOR CORRECTION,

CONTAINED IN

THE GRAMMAR OF ENGLISH GRAMMARS,

AND

DESIGNED FOR ORAL EXERCISES

UNDER

ALL THE RULES AND NOTES OF THE WORK.

☞ [The various examples of error which are exhibited for oral correction, in the Grammar of English Grammars, are all here explained, in their order, by full amended readings, sometimes with authorities specified, and generally with references of some sort. They are intended to be corrected orally by the pupil, according to the formules given under corresponding heads in the Grammar. Some portion, at least, under each rule or note, should be used in this way; and the rest, perhaps, may be read and compared more simply.]

THE KEY.—PART I.—ORTHOGRAPHY.

CHAPTER I.—OF LETTERS.

CORRECTIONS RESPECTING CAPITALS.

UNDER RULE I.—OF BOOKS.

"Many a reader of the *Bible* knows not who wrote the *Acts* of the *Apostles*."—G. B. "The sons of Levi, the chief of the fathers, were written in the book of the *Chronicles*."—ALGER'S BIBLE: *Neh.* xii, 23. "Are they not written in the book of the *Acts* of Solomon?"—FRIENDS' BIBLE: 1 *Kings*, xi, 41. "Are they not written in the book of the Chronicles of the *Kings* of Israel?"—ALGER CORRECTED: 1 *Kings*, xxii, 39. "Are they not written in the book of the *Chronicles* of the *Kings* of Judah."—See ALGER: *ib. ver.* 45. "Which were written in the law of Moses, and in the prophets, and in the *Psalms*."—ALGER, ET AL.: *Luke*, xxiv, 44. "The narrative of which may be seen in Josephus's History of the Jewish *War*."—Dr. Scott cor. [OBS.—The word in Josephus is "*War*," not "*Wars*."—G. Brown.] "This *History* of the Jewish *War* was Josephus's first work, and published about A. D. 75."—*Whiston cor.* "'I have read,' says Photius, 'the *Chronology* of Justus of Tiberias.'"—*Id.* "*A Philosophical Grammar*, written by James Harris, Esquire."—*Murray cor.* "The reader is referred to Stroud's *Sketch* of the *Slave Laws*."—A. S. *Mag. cor.* "But God has so made the *Bible* that it interprets itself."—*Idem.* "In 1562, with the help of Hopkins, he completed the *Psalter*."—*Gardiner cor.* "Gardiner says this of Sternhold; of whom the *Universal Biographical Dictionary* and the American *Encyclopedia* affirm, that he died in 1549."—G. B. "The title of a book, to wit: 'English Grammar in *Familiar Lectures*,'" &c.—*Kirkham cor.* "We had not, at that time, seen Mr. Kirkham's 'Grammar in *Familiar Lectures*.'"—*Id.* "When you parse, you may spread the Compendium before you."—*Id.** "Whenever you parse, you may spread the *Compendium* before you."—*Id.* "Adelung was the author of a *Grammatical* and *Critical Dictionary* of the German *Language*, and other works."—*Biog. Dict. cor.* "Alley, William, author of '*The Poor Man's Library*,' and a translation of the Pentateuch, died in 1570."—*Id.*

UNDER RULE II.—OF FIRST WORDS.

"Depart instantly;"—"*Improve* your time;"—"*Forgive* us our sins."—*Murray corrected.* EXAMPLES:—"Gold is corrupting;"—"*The* sea is green;"—"*A* lion is bold."—*Mur. et al. cor.* Again: "It may rain;"—"*He* may go or stay;"—"*He* would walk;"—"*They* should learn."—*Iidem.* Again: "Oh! I have alienated my friend;"—"*Alas!* I fear for life."—*Iidem.* See *Alger's Gram.* p. 50. Again: "He went from London to York;"—"*She* is above disguise;"—"*They* are supported by industry."—*Iidem.* "On the foregoing examples, I have a word to say. *They* are better than a fair specimen of their kind. *Our* grammars abound with worse illustra-

---

* OBS.—Of this, and of every other example which requires no amendment, let the learner simply say, after reading the passage, "This sentence is correct as it stands."—G. BROWN.

tions. *Their* models of English are generally spurious quotations. *Few* of their proof-texts have any just parentage. *Goose-eyes* are abundant, but names scarce. *Who* fathers the foundlings? *Nobody.* Then let their merit be nobody's, and their defects his who could write no better."—*Author.* "*Goose-eyes!*" says a bright boy; "pray, what are they? *Does* this Mr. Author make new words when he pleases? *Dead-eyes* are in a ship. *They* are blocks, with holes in them. *But* what are goose-eyes in grammar?" ANSWER: "*Goose-eyes* are quotation points. *Some* of the Germans gave them this name, making a jest of their form. *The* French call them *guillemets*, from the name of their inventor."—*Author.* "*It* is a personal pronoun, of the third person singular."—*Comly cor.* "*Ourselves* is a personal pronoun, of the first person plural."—*Id.* "*Thou* is a personal pronoun, of the second person singular."—*Id.* "*Contentment* is a common *noun*, of the third person singular."—*Id.* "*Were* is a neuter verb, of the indicative mood, imperfect tense."—*Id.*

UNDER RULE III.—OF DEITY.

"O thou *Dispenser* of life! thy mercies are boundless."—*Allen cor.* "Shall not the *Judge* of all the earth do right?"—ALGER, FRIENDS, ET AL.: *Gen.* xviii, 25. "And the *Spirit* of God moved upon the face of the waters."—SCOTT, ALGER, FRIENDS, ET AL.: *Gen.* i, 2. "It is the gift of *Him*, who is the great *Author* of good, and the Father of mercies."—*Murray cor.* "This is thy *God* that brought thee up out of Egypt."—FRIENDS' BIBLE: *Neh.* ix, 18. "For the LORD is our defence; and the *Holy One* of Israel is our *King*."—*Psal.* lxxxix, 18. "By making him the responsible steward of *Heaven's* bounties."—*A. S. Mag. cor.* "Which the Lord, the righteous *Judge*, shall give me at that day."—ALGER: 2 *Tim.* iv, 8. "The cries of them * * * entered into the ears of the Lord of *Sabaoth*."—ALGER, FRIENDS: *James*, v, 4. "In Horeb, the *Deity* revealed himself to Moses, as the *Eternal* 'I AM,' the *Self-existent One*; and, after the first discouraging interview of his messengers with Pharaoh, he renewed his promise to them, by the awful name, JEHOVAH—a name till then unknown, and one which the Jews always held it a fearful profanation to pronounce."—*G. Brown.* "And God spake unto Moses, and said unto him, I am the LORD: and I appeared unto Abraham, unto Isaac, and unto Jacob, by the name of God Almighty; but by my name JEHOVAH was I not known to them."—SCOTT, ALGER, FRIENDS: *Exod.* vi, 2. "Thus saith the LORD* the *King* of Israel, and his *Redeemer* the LORD of hosts; I am the *First*, and I am the *Last*; and besides me there is no *God*."—See *Isa.* xliv, 6.

"His impious race their blasphemy renew'd,
And nature's *King*, through nature's optics view'd."—*Dryden cor.*

UNDER RULE IV.—OF PROPER NAMES.

"Islamism prescribes fasting during the month *Ramadan*."—*Balbi cor.* "Near Mecca, in Arabia, is *Jebel Nor*, or the *Mountain of Light*, on the top of which the *Musulmans* erected a mosque, that they might perform their devotions where, according to their belief, *Mohammed* received from the angel *Gabriel* the first chapter of the Koran."—*G. Brown.* "In the *Kaaba* at *Mecca* there is a celebrated block of volcanic basalt, which the *Mohammedans* venerate as the gift of *Gabriel* to *Abraham*, but their ancestors once held it to be an image of *Remphan*, or *Saturn*; so 'the image which fell down from *Jupiter*,' to share with *Diana* the homage of the *Ephesians*, was probably nothing more than a meteoric stone."—*Id.* "When the *Lycaonians* at *Lystra* took *Paul* and *Barnabas* to be gods, they called the former *Mercury*, on account of his eloquence, and the latter *Jupiter*, for the greater dignity of his appearance."—*Id.* "Of the writings of the apostolical fathers of the first century, but few have come down to us; yet we have in those of *Barnabas*, *Clement* of *Rome*, *Hermas*, *Ignatius*, and *Polycarp*, very certain evidence of the authenticity of the New Testament, and the New Testament is a voucher for the Old."—*Id.* "It is said by *Tatian*, that *Theagenes* of *Rhegium*, in the time of *Cambyses*, *Stesimbrotus* the Thracian, *Antimachus* the Colophonian, *Herodotus* of Halicarnassus, *Dionysius* the Olynthian, *Ephorus* of *Cumæ*, *Philochorus* the Athenian, *Metaclides* and *Chameleon* the Peripatetics, and *Zenodotus*, *Aristophanes*, *Callimachus*, *Crates*, *Eratosthenes*, *Aristarchus*, and *Apollodorus*, the grammarians, all wrote concerning the poetry, the birth, and the age of *Homer*."—See *Coleridge's Introd.* p. 57. "Yet, for aught that now appears, the life of *Homer* is as fabulous as that of *Hercules*; and some have even suspected, that, as the son of *Jupiter* and *Alcmena* has fathered the deeds of forty other *Herculeses*, so this unfathered son of *Critheis*, *Themisto*, or whatever dame—this *Melesigenes*, *Mæonides*, *Homer*—the blind schoolmaster, and poet, of *Smyrna*, *Chios*, *Colophon*, *Salamis*, *Rhodes*, *Argos*, *Athens*, or whatever place—has, by the help of *Lycurgus*, *Solon*, *Pisistratus*, and other learned ancients, been made up of many poets or *Homers*, and set so far aloft and aloof on old *Parnassus*, as to become a god in the eyes of all *Greece*, a wonder in those of all *Christendom*."—*G. Brown.*

"Why so sagacious in your guesses?
Your *Effs*, and *Tees*, and *Ars*, and *Esses?*"—*Swift corrected.*

UNDER RULE V.—OF TITLES.

"The king has conferred on him the title of *Duke*."—*Murray cor.* "At the court of Queen Elisabeth."—*Priestley's E. Gram.* p. 99; see *Bullions's*, p. 24. "The laws of nature are, truly, what *Lord* Bacon styles his aphorisms, laws of laws."—*Murray cor.* "Sixtus the *Fourth* was, if I mistake not, a great collector of books."—*Id.* "Who at that time made up the court of *King* Charles the *Second*."—*Id.* "In case of his *Majesty's* dying without issue."—*Kirkham cor.* "King Charles the *First* was beheaded in 1649."—*W. Allen cor.* "He can no more impart, or (to use *Lord* Bacon's word) *transmit* convictions."—*Kirkham cor.* "I reside at *Lord* Stormont's, my old patron and benefactor." Better: "I reside *with Lord* Stormont, my old patron and bene-

---

* OBSERVATION.—In our Bible, the word LORD, whenever it stands for the Hebrew name JEHOVAH, not only commences with a full capital, but has small or half capitals for the other letters; and I have thought proper to print both words in that manner here. In correcting the last example, I follow Dr. Scott's Bible, except in the word "*God*," which he writes with a small *g*. Several other copies have "*first*" and "*last*" with small initials, which I think not so correct; and some distinguish the word "*hosts*" with a capital, which seems to be needless. The sentence here has eleven capitals: in the Latin Vulgate, it has but six, and one of them is for the last word, "*Deus*," God.—G. B.

factor."—*Murray cor.*   "We staid a month at *Lord Lyttelton's*, the ornament of his country." Much better: "We *stayed* a month at *the seat of Lord Lyttelton, who is* the ornament of his country."—*Id.*   "Whose prerogative is it ?   It is the *King-of-Great-Britain's* ; *"—"* That is the *Duke* of-Bridgewater's canal ; "—"The *Bishop*-of-Landaff's excellent book ; "—"The Lord *Mayor*-of-London's authority."—*Id.*   (See Murray's Note 4th on his Rule 10th.)   "Why call ye me, *Lord, Lord*, and do not the things which I say ? "—*Luke*, vi, 46.   "And of them he chose twelve, whom also he named *Apostles*."—ALGER, FRIENDS, ET AL. : *Luke*, vi, 13.   "And forthwith he came to Jesus, and said, Hail, *Master ;* and kissed him."—*Matt.* xxvi, 49.   "And he said, Nay, *Father* Abraham : but if one went unto them from the dead, they *would* repent."—*Bible cor.*

UNDER RULE VI.—OF ONE CAPITAL.

"*Fallriver*, a village in Massachusetts, population (in 1830) 3,431."—*Williams cor.*   " Dr. Anderson died at *Westham*, in Essex, in 1808."—*Biog. Dict. cor.*   "*Madriver*, the name of two towns in Clark and Champaign counties, Ohio."—*Williams cor.* "*Whitecreek*, a town of Washington county, New York."—*Id.*   "*Saltcreek*, the name of four towns in different parts of Ohio." —*Id.*   "*Saltlick*, a town of Fayette county, Pennsylvania."—*Id.*   "*Yellowcreek*, a town of Columbiana county, Ohio."—*Id.* "*Whiteclay*, a hundred of Newcastle county, Delaware."—*Id.* "*Newcastle, a* town and *half-shire* of Newcastle county, Delaware."—*Id.*   "*Singsing*, a village of *Westchester* county, New York. situated in the town of *Mountpleasant*."—*Id.*   "*Westchester*, a county of New York: *East Chester* and *West Chester are towns* in Westchester county."—*Id.* "*Westtown*, a village of Orange county, New York."—*Id.*   "*Whitewater*, a town of Hamilton county, Ohio."—*Worcester's Gaz.*   "*Whitewater* River, a considerable stream that rises in Indiana, and flowing southeasterly unites with the Miami in Ohio."—See *ib.*   "*Blackwater*, a village of Hampshire, in England, and a town in Ireland."—See *ib.*   "*Blackwater*, the name of seven different rivers, in England, Ireland, and the United States."—See *ib.*   "*Redhook*, a town of Dutchess county, New York, on the Hudson."—*Williams cor.*   "*Kinderhook*, a town of Columbia county, New York, on the Hudson."—*Williams right.* " *Newfane*, a town of Niagara county. New York."—*Williams cor.*   "*Lakeport*, a town of Chicot county, Arkansas."—*Id.*   "*Moosehead* Lake, the chief source of the Kennebeck, in Maine."—*Id.* (See *Worcester's Gaz.*)   "*Macdonough*, a county of Illinois, population (in 1830) 2,959."—*Williams's Univ. Gaz.* p. 408.   "*Macdonough*, a county of Illinois, with a *court-house* at Macomb."—*Williams cor.* "*Halfmoon*, the name of two towns, in New York and Pennsylvania; also of two bays in the West Indies."—*S. Williams's Univ. Gaz.*   "*Lebœuf*, a town of Erie county, Pennsylvania, near a small lake of the same name."—See *ib.*   "*Charlescity, Jamescity, Elizabethcity*, names of counties in Virginia, not cities, nor towns."—See *Univ. Gaz.* p. 404.† " The superior qualities of the waters of the Frome, here called *Stroudwater*."—*Balbi cor.*

UNDER RULE VII.—OF TWO CAPITALS.

" The Forth rises on the north side of *Ben Lomond*, and runs easterly."—*Glasgow Geog.* 8vo, *corrected.*   " The red granite of *Ben Nevis* is said to be the finest in the world."—*Id.*   "*Ben More*, in Perthshire, is 3,915 feet above the level of the sea."—*Id.*   " The height of *Ben Cleugh* is 2,420 feet."—*Id.*   " In Sutherland and Caithness, are Ben Ormod, Ben Clibeg, Ben Grin, Ben Hope, and Ben Lugal."—*Glas. Geog. right.*   "*Ben Vracky* is 2,756 feet high; *Ben Ledi*, 3,009; and *Ben Voirlich*, 3,300."—*Glas. Geog. cor.*   " The river Dochart gives the name of *Glen Dochart* to the vale through which it runs."—*Id.*   " About ten miles from its source, it [the Tay] diffuses itself into *Loch Dochart*."—*Glasgow Geog.* Vol. ii, p. 314.   LAKES :—"*Loch Ard,* Loch Achray, Loch Con, Loch Doine, Loch Katrine, Loch Lomond, Loch Voil."—*Scott corrected.* GLENS :—"*Glen Finlas*, Glen Fruin, Glen Luss, Ross Dhu, Leven Glen, Strath Endrick, Strath Gartney, Strath Ire."—*Id.*   MOUNTAINS :—"*Ben An*, Ben Harrow, *Ben Ledi*, Ben Lomond, *Ben Voirlich, Ben Venue*, or, (as some spell it,) *Ben Ivenew*."—*Id.*‡   "Fenelon died in 1715, deeply lamented by all the inhabitants of the *Low Countries*."—*Murray cor.*   "And *Pharaoh Nechoj* made Eliakim. the son of Josiah, king."—See ALGER: 2 *Kings*, xxiii, 34.   "Those who seem so merry and well pleased, call her *Good Fortune*; but the others, who weep and wring their hands, *Bad Fortune*."—*Collier cor.*

UNDER RULE VIII.—OF COMPOUNDS.

" When Joab returned, and smote Edom in the *Valley* of *Salt*."—FRIENDS' BIBLE : *Ps.* lx, title. " Then Paul stood in the midst of *Mars Hill*, and said," &c.—*Scott cor.*   "And at night he went out, and abode in the mount that is called the *Mount* of Olives."—*Bible cor.*   "Abgillus, son of the king of the Frisii, surnamed Prester John, was in the Holy *Land* with Charlemagne."—*U. Biog. Dict. cor.*   "Cape Palmas, in Africa, divides the Grain *Coast* from the Ivory *Coast.*"—*Dict. of Geog. cor.*   " The North Esk, flowing from Loch *Lee*, falls into the sea three miles north of Montrose."—*Id.*   "At Queen's *Ferry*, the channel of the Forth is contracted by promontories on both coasts."—*Id.*   " The Chestnut *Ridge* is about twenty-five miles west of the Alleghanies, and Laurel *Ridge*, ten miles further West."—*Balbi cor.*   " Washington City, the metropolis of the United States of America."—*Williams, U. Gaz.* p. 380.   " Washington *City*, in the District of

---

* OBS.—This construction I dislike.   Without hyphens, it is improper ; and with them it is not to be commended.   See Syntax, Obs. 24th on Rule IV.—G. B.

† On the page here referred to, the author of the *Gazetteer* has written "*Charles city*," &c.   Analogy requires that the words be compounded, because they constitute three names which are applied to *counties*, and not to cities.

‡ OBS.—The following words, *as names of towns*, come under Rule 6th, and are commonly found correctly compounded in the books of Scotch geography and statistics : "Strathaven, Stonehaven, Strathdon, Glenluce, Greenlaw, Coldstream, Lochwinnoch, Lochcarron, Lochmaber, Prestonpans, Prestonkirk, Peterhead, Queensferry, Newmills," and many more like them.

§ OBS.—This name, in both the Vulgate and the Septuagint, is *Pharao Nechao*, with two capitals and no hyphen.   Walker gives the two words separately in his Key, and spells the *latter* Necho, and not *Nechoh*.   See the same orthography in *Jer.* xlvi, 2.   In our common Bibles, many such names are needlessly, if not improperly, compounded ; sometimes with one capital, and sometimes with two.   The proper manner of writing Scripture names, is too little regarded even by good men and biblical critics.

Columbia, population (in 1830) 18,826."—*Williams cor.* "The loftiest peak of the *White Mountains*, in *New* Hampshire, is called *Mount* Washington."—*G. Brown.* "Mount's Bay, in the west of England, lies between the *Land's End* and *Lizard Point.*"—*Id.* "Salamis, an island of the Egean Sea, off the southern coast of the ancient Attica."—*Dict. of Geog.* "Rhodes, an island of the Egean *Sea*, the largest and most easterly of the Cyclades."—*Id. cor.* "But he overthrew Pharaoh and his host in the Red *Sea.*"—SCOTT: *Ps.* cxxxvi, 15. "But they provoked him at the sea, even at the Red *Sea.*"—ALGER, FRIENDS: *Ps.* cvi, 7

UNDER RULE IX.—OF APPOSITION.

"At that time, Herod the *tetrarch* heard of the fame of Jesus."—SCOTT, FRIENDS, ET AL. *Matt.* xiv, 1. "Who has been more detested than Judas the *traitor?*"—*G. Brown.* "St. Luke the *evangelist* was a physician of Antioch, and one of the converts of St. Paul."—*Id.* "Luther, the *reformer*, began his bold career by preaching against papal indulgences."—*Id.* "The *poet* Lydgate was a disciple and admirer of Chaucer: he died in 1440."—*Id.* "The *grammarian* Varro, * the most learned of the Romans,* wrote three books when he was eighty years old."—*K.* "John Despauter, the great *grammarian* of Flanders, whose works are still valued, died in 1520." —*Id.* "Nero, the *emperor* and *tyrant* of Rome, slew himself to avoid a worse death."—*Id.* "Cicero the *orator*, 'the Father of his Country,' was assassinated at the age of 64."—*Id.* "Euripides, the Greek *tragedian*, was born in the *island* of Salamis, B. C. 476."—*Id.* "I will say unto God my *rock*, Why hast thou forgotten me?"—ALGER, ET AL.: *Ps.* xlii, 9. "Staten Island, an island of New York, nine miles below New York *city.*"—*Williams cor.* "When the son of Atreus, *king* of *men*, and the noble Achilles first separated."—*Coleridge cor.*
"Hermes, his *patron-god*, those gifts bestow'd,
Whose shrine with *weanling* lambs he wont to load."—*Pope cor.*

UNDER RULE X.—OF PERSONIFICATIONS.

"But *Wisdom* is justified of all her children."—FRIENDS' BIBLE: *Luke*, vii, 35. "*Fortune* and the *Church* are generally put in the feminine gender: that is, when personified." "Go to your *Natural Religion*; lay before her Mahomet and his disciples."—*Bp. Sherlock.* "O *Death!* where is thy sting? O *Grave!* where is thy victory."—*Pope:* 1 *Cor.* xv, 55; *Merchant's Gram.* 172. "Ye cannot serve God and Mammon."—*Matt.* vi, 24. "Ye cannot serve God and *Mammon.*"—See *Luke*, xvi, 13. "This house was built as if *Suspicion* herself had dictated the plan." —*Rasselas.* "Poetry distinguishes herself from *Prose*, by yielding to a musical law."—*Music of Nature*, p. 501. "My beauteous deliverer thus uttered her divine instructions: 'My name is *Religion*. I am the offspring of *Truth* and *Love*, and the parent of *Benevolence, Hope*, and *Joy*. That monster, from whose power I have freed you, is called *Superstition*: she is called the child of *Discontent*, and her followers are *Fear* and *Sorrow.*'"—*E. Carter.* "Neither *Hope* nor *Fear* could enter the retreats; and *Habit* had so absolute a power, that even *Conscience*, if *Religion* had employed her in their favour, would not have been able to force an entrance."—*Dr. Johnson.*
"In colleges and halls in ancient days,
There dwelt a sage called *Discipline.*"—*Cowper.*

UNDER RULE XI.—OF DERIVATIVES.

"In English, I would have *Gallicisms* avoided."—*Felton.* "Sallust was born in Italy, 85 years before the *Christian* era."—*Murray cor.* "Dr. Doddridge was not only a great man, but one of the most excellent and useful *Christians*, and *Christian* ministers."—*Id.* "They corrupt their style with untutored *Anglicisms.*"—*Milton.* "Albert of Stade, author of a chronicle from the creation to 1286, a *Benedictine* of the 13th century."—*Biog. Dict. cor.* "Graffio, a *Jesuit* of Capua in the 16th century, author of two volumes on moral subjects."—*Id.* "They *Frenchify* and *Italianize* words whenever they can."—*Bucke's Gram.* p. 86. "He who sells a *Christian*, sells the grace of God."—*Mag. cor.* "The first persecution against the *Christians*, under Nero, began A. D. 64."—*Gregory cor.* "P. Rapin, the *Jesuit*, uniformly decides in favour of the Roman writers."—*Blair's Rhet.* p. 248. "The Roman poet and *Epicurean* philosopher Lucretius has said," &c.—*Cohen cor.* Spell "*Calvinistic, Atticism, Gothicism, Epicurism, Jesuitism, Sabianism, Socinianism, Anglican, Anglicism, Anglicize, Vandalism, Gallicism*, and *Romanize.*"—*Webster cor.* "The large *Ternate* bat."—*Id. and Bolles cor.*
"Church-ladders are not always mounted best
By learned clerks, and *Latinists* profess'd."—*Cowper cor.*

UNDER RULE XII.—OF I AND O.

"Fall back, fall back; *I* have not room—*O!* methinks *I* see a couple whom *I* should know." —*Lucian.* "Nay, *I* live as *I* did, *I* think as *I* did, *I* love you as *I* did; but all these are to no purpose; the world will not live, think, or love, as *I* do."—*Swift to Pope.* "Whither, *O!* whither shall *I* fly? *O* wretched prince! *O* cruel reverse of fortune! *O* father Micipsa! is this the consequence of thy generosity?"—*Tr. of Sallust.* "When I was a child, I spake as a child, I understood as a child, I thought as a child; but when *I* became a man, *I* put away childish things."—1 *Cor.* xiii, 11. "And *I* heard, but *I* understood not: then said *I*, *O* my Lord, what shall be the end of these things?"—*Dan.* xii, 8. "Here am *I*; *I* think *I* am very good, and *I* am quite sure *I* am very happy, yet *I* never wrote a treatise in my life."—*Few Days in Athens*, p. 127. "Singular, Vocative, *O master!* Plural, Vocative, *O masters!*"—*Bicknell cor.*
"I, I am he; O father! rise, behold
Thy son, with twenty winters now grown old!"—*Pope's Odyssey*, B. 24, l. 375.

UNDER RULE XIII.—OF POETRY.

"Reason's whole pleasure, all the joys of sense,
Lie in three words—health, peace, and competence;
But health consists with temperance alone,
And peace, O Virtue! peace is all thy own."—*Pope.*

* "*Marcus*] Terentius Varro, vir Romanorum eruditissimus."—QUINTILIAN. Lib. x, Cap. 1.

"Observe the language well in all you write,
And swerve not from it in your loftiest flight.
The smoothest verse and the exactest sense
Displease us, if ill English give offence:
A barbarous phrase no reader can approve;
Nor bombast, noise, or affectation love.
In short, without pure language, what you write
Can never yield us profit or delight.
Take time for thinking; never work in haste;
And value not yourself for writing fast."—*Dryden.*

UNDER RULE XIV.—OF EXAMPLES.

" The word *rather* is very properly used to express a small degree or excess of a quality; as, *She is rather* profuse in her expenses.' "—*Murray cor.* "*Neither* imports *not either ;* that is, not ne nor the other : as, '*Neither* of my friends was there.' "—*Id.* " When we say, '*He* is a tall an,'—'*This* is a fair day,' we make some reference to the ordinary size of men, and to different *eather.*"—*Id.* " We more readily say, ' A million of men,' than, '*A* thousand of men.' "—*Id.* So in the instances, '*Two* and two are four ; '—'*The* fifth and sixth volumes will complete the et of books.' "—*Id.* " The adjective may frequently either precede or follow the verb : as, '*The* an is *happy ;*' or, '*Happy* is the man ; '—' The interview was *delightful ;*' or, '*Delightful* was the terview.' "—*Id.* " If we say, '*He* writes a pen ; '—'*They* ran the river ; '—'*The* tower fell the reeks ; '—' Lambeth is Westminster *Abbey ;* '—[we speak absurdly ;] and, it is evident, there is vacancy which must be filled up by some connecting word : as thus, ' He writes *with* a pen ; '— *They* ran *towards* the river ; '—'*The* tower fell *upon* the Greeks ; '—' Lambeth is *over against* Westminister *Abbey.*' "—*Id.* " Let me repeat it ;—*He* only is great, who has the habits of great- ess."—*Id.* " I say not unto thee, *Until* seven times ; but, *Until* seventy times seven."—*Matt.* viii, 22.

" The Panther smil'd at this ; and, '*When,*' said she,
' Were those first councils disallow'd by me ? ' "—*Dryd. cor.*

UNDER RULE XV.—OF CHIEF WORDS.

" The supreme council of the nation is called the *Divan.*"—*Balbi cor.* " The British *Parlia- ent* is composed of *King, Lords,* and *Commons.*"—*Comly's Gram.* 129 ; and *Jaudon's,* 127. " A opular orator in the House of Commons has a sort of patent for coining as many new terms as e pleases."—See *Campbell's Rhet.* p. 169 ; *Murray's Gram.* 364. " They may all be taken togeth- r, as one name ; as, '*The House of Commons.*'"—*Merchant cor.* " Intrusted to persons in whom he *Parliament* could confide."—*Murray cor.* " For ' The Lords' House,' it were certainly better o say, ' *The House of Lords ;* ' and, in stead of ' The *Commons*' vote,' to say, ' The *vote of the Commons.*' "—*Id, and Priestley cor.* " The *House of Lords* were so much influenced by these rea- ons."—*Iidem.* " Rhetoricians commonly divide them into two great classes ; *Figures of Words,* nd *Figures of Thought.* The former, *Figures of Words,* are commonly called *Tropes.*"—*Murray's Gram.* p. 337. " Perhaps, *Figures of Imagination,* and *Figures of Passion,* might be a more use- l distribution."—*Ib.* " Hitherto we have considered sentences, under the heads of *Perspicuity, nity,* and *Strength.*"—See *Murray's Gram.* p. 356.

" The word is then depos'd ; and, in this view,
You rule the *Scripture,* not the *Scripture* you."—*Dryd. cor.*

UNDER RULE XVI.—OF NEEDLESS CAPITALS.

" Be of good cheer ; *it* is I ; be not afraid."—FRIENDS' BIBLE, AND SCOTT's : *Matt.* xiv, 27. Between passion and lying, there is not a *finger's* breadth."—*Mur. cor.* " Can our *solicitude* lter the course, or unravel the intricacy, of human events ? "—*Id.* " The last edition was care- ully compared with the *original manuscript.*"—*Id.* " And the governor asked him, saying, Art hou the *king* of the Jews ? "—SCOTT: *Matt.* xxvii, 11. " Let them be turned back for a reward f their *shame,* that say, Aha, *aha !* "—SCOTT ET AL. : *Ps.* lxx, 3. " Let them be desolate for a eward of their *shame,* that say unto me, Aha, aha!"—IIDEM : *Ps.* xl, 15. " What think ye f Christ ? whose *son* is he ? They say unto him, The *son* of David. He saith unto them, How hen doth David in *spirit* call him Lord ? "—ALGER: *Matt.* xxii, 42, 43. " Among all *things* in he *universe,* direct your *worship* to the *greatest.* And which is that ? *It* is that Being *who manages* nd *governs* all the rest."—*Collier's Antoninus cor.* "As for *modesty* and *good faith, truth* and *justice,* hey have left this wicked *world* and retired to *heaven : and* now what is it that can keep you ere ? "—*Idem.*

" If pulse of verse a nation's temper shows,
In keen iambics English metre flows."—*Brightland cor.*

PROMISCUOUS CORRECTIONS RESPECTING CAPITALS.

LESSON I.—MIXED EXAMPLES.

" Come, gentle *Spring, ethereal* mildness, come."—*Thomson's Seasons,* p. 29. As, " He is the Cicero of his age ; "—"*He* is reading the *Lives* of the Twelve Cæsars : "—or, if no particular book s meant,—" the *lives* of the *twelve* Cæsars ; " (as it is in *Fisk's Grammar,* p. 57 ;) for the sentence, s it stands in Murray, is ambiguous. " In the *History* of Henry the *Fourth,* by *Father* Daniel, re are *surprised* at not finding him the great man."—*Smollett's Voltaire,* Vol. v, p. 82. " Do not hose same poor peasants use the *lever,* and the *wedge,* and many other instruments ? "—*Harris* nd *Mur. cor.* " Arithmetic is excellent for the gauging of *liquors ; geometry,* for the measuring f *estates ; astronomy,* for the making of *almanacs ;* and *grammar,* perhaps, for the drawing of onds and *conveyances.*"—See *Murray's Gram.* p. 288. " The [*History of the*] *Wars* of Flanders, ritten in Latin by Famianus Strada, is a book of some note."—*Blair cor.* " *William* is a noun. *Why ? Was* is a verb. *Why ? A* is an article. *Why ? Very* is an adverb. *Why ?*" &c.— *Merchant cor.* " In the beginning was the *Word,* and that *Word* was with God, and God was

that *Word*."—See *Gospel of John*, i, 1. "The *Greeks* are numerous in *Thessaly, Macedonia, Romelia*, and *Albania*."—*Balbi's Geog.* p. 360. "He [the Grand Seignior] is styled by the Turks, Sultan, Mighty, or Padishah, *Lord*."—*Balbi cor.* "I will ransom them from the power of the grave; I will redeem them from death. O *Death!* I will be thy *plague*; O *Grave!* I will be thy destruction."—*Bible cor.* "Silver and *gold* have I none; but such as I have, give I [unto] thee."—See *Acts*, iii, 6. "Return, we beseech thee, O God of *hosts!* look down from heaven, and behold and visit this vine."—See *Psalm*, lxxx, 14. "In the Attic *commonwealth*, it was the privilege of every citizen to rail in public."—*Murray's Gram.* i, p. 316. "They assert, that in the phrases, 'GIVE me *that*,'—'*This* is John's,'—and, '*Such* were *some* of you,—the words in *Italics* are pronouns; but that, in the following phrases, they are not pronouns: '*This* book is instructive;'—'*Some* boys are ingenious;'—'*My* health is declining;'—'*Our* hearts are deceitful.'"—*Murray partly corrected.* "And the coast bends again to the northwest, as far as *Farout Head*."—*Geog. cor.* "Dr. Webster, and other makers of spelling-books, very improperly write *Sunday, Monday, Tuesday, Wednesday, Thursday, Friday*, and *Saturday*, without capitals."—*G. Brown.* "The commander in chief of the Turkish navy is styled the *Capitan Pacha*."—*Balbi cor.* "Shall we not much rather be in subjection unto the *Father* of spirits, and live?"—ALGER'S BIBLE: *Heb.* xii, 9. "He [Dr. Beattie] was more anxious to attain the character of a *Christian* hero."—*Murray cor.* "Beautiful for situation, the joy of the whole earth, is *Mount* Zion."—*W. Allen's Gram.* p. 393. The Lord is my *helper*, and I will not fear what man shall do unto me."—ALGER, FRIENDS, ET AL.: *Heb.* xiii, 6. "Make haste to help me, O LORD my *salvation*."—IDEM: *Psalms*, xxxviii, 22.
            "The *city* which *thou* seest, no other deem
            Than great and glorious Rome, *queen* of the *earth*."—*Paradise Regained*, B. iv.

LESSON II.—MIXED EXAMPLES.

"That range of hills, known under the general name of *Mount* Jura."—*Account of Geneva.* "He rebuked the Red *Sea* also, and it was dried up."—FRIENDS' BIBLE: *Ps.* cvi, 9. "Jesus went unto the *Mount* of Olives."—*Bible cor.* "Milton's book in reply to the *Defence of the King*, by Salmasius, gained him a thousand pounds from the *Parliament*, and killed his antagonist with vexation."—*G. B.* "Mandeville, Sir John, an Englishman famous for his travels, born about 1300, died in 1372."—*B. Dict. cor.* "Ettrick *Pen*, a mountain in Selkirkshire, Scotland, height 2,200 feet."—*G. Geog. cor.* "The coast bends from *Dungsby Head*, in a northwest direction, to the promontory of *Dunnet Head*.—*Id.* "General Gaines ordered a detachment of *nearly* 300 men, under the command of Major Twiggs, to surround and take an Indian *village* called *Fowltown*, about fourteen miles from *Fort* Scott."—*Cohen cor.* "And he took the damsel by the hand, and said unto her, 'Talitha, *cumi*.'"—*Bible Editors cor.* "On religious subjects, a frequent *adoption* of *Scripture* language is attended with peculiar force."—*Murray cor.* "Contemplated with gratitude to their Author, the Giver of all *good*."—*Id.* "When he, the Spirit of *truth*, is come, he will guide you into all [the] truth."—SCOTT, ALGER, ET AL.: *John*, xvi, 13. "See the *Lecture* on Verbs, Rule XV, Note 4th."—*Fisk cor.* "At the commencement of *Lecture* 2d, I informed you that Etymology treats, *thirdly*, of derivation."—*Kirkham cor.* "This *8th Lecture* is a very important one."—*Id.* "Now read the 11*th* and 12*th* lectures, four or five times over."—*Id.* "In 1752, he [Henry Home] was advanced to the bench, under the title of *Lord Kames*."—*Murray cor.* "One of his maxims was, 'Know thyself.'"—*Lempriere cor.* "Good *Master*, what good thing shall I do, that I may have eternal life?"—FRIENDS' BIBLE: *Matt.* xix, 16. "His best known works, however, [John Almon's] are, '*Anecdotes of the Life of the Earl of Chatham*,' 2 vols. 4to, 3 vols. 8vo; and '*Biographical, Literary*, and *Political Anecdotes* of several of the *Most Eminent Persons* of the *Present Age*; never before printed,' 3 vols. 8vo, 1797."—*Biog. Dict. cor.* "O gentle *Sleep*, Nature's soft nurse, how have I frighted thee?"—SHAK.: *Kames, El. of Crit.* Vol. ii, p. 175. "And peace, O *Virtue!* peace is all thy own."—*Pope et al. cor.*

LESSON III.—MIXED EXAMPLES.

"Fenelon united the characters of a nobleman and a *Christian* pastor. His book entitled, 'An *Explication* of the Maxims of the Saints, concerning the *Interior Life*,' gave considerable offence to the guardians of orthodoxy."—*Murray cor.* "When *Natural Religion*, who before was only a spectator, is introduced as speaking by the *Centurion's* voice."—*Murray's Gram.* Vol. i, p. 347. "You cannot deny, that the great *Mover* and *Author* of nature constantly explaineth himself to the eyes of men, by the sensible intervention of arbitrary signs, which have no similitude to, or connexion with, the things signified."—*Berkley cor.* "The name of this letter is *Double-u*, in form, that of a double V."—*Dr. Wilson cor.* "Murray, in his *Spelling-Book*, wrote *Charleston* with a *hyphen* and two capitals."—*G. Brown.* "He also wrote *European* without a capital."—*Id.* "They profess themselves to be *Pharisees*, who are to be heard and not imitated."—*Calvin cor.* "Dr. Webster wrote both *Newhaven* and *New York* with single capitals."—*G. Brown.* "*Gay Head*, the west point of Martha's Vineyard."—*Williams cor.* "Write *Crab Orchard, Egg Harbour, Long Island, Perth Amboy, West Hampton, Little Compton, New Paltz, Crown Point, Fell's Point, Sandy Hook, Port Penn, Port Royal, Porto Bello*, and *Porto Rico*."—*G. Brown.* "Write the names of the months: *January, February, March, April, May, June, July, August, September, October, November, December*."—*Id.* "Write the following names and words properly: *Tuesday, Wednesday, Thursday, Friday, Saturday, Saturn;—Christ, Christian, Christmas, Christendom, Michaelmas, Indian, Bacchanals;—East Hampton, Omega, Johannes, Aonian, Levitical, Deuteronomy, European*."—*Id.*
            "Eight *letters* in some *syllables* we find,
            And no more *syllables* in *words* are join'd."—*Brightland cor.*

_____

* NOTE.—By this amendment, we remove a multitude of errors, but the passage is still very faulty. What Murray here calls "*phrases*," are properly *sentences*; and, in his second clause, he deserts the terms of the first to bring in "*my*," "*our*," and also "*&c.*," which seem to be out of place there.—G. BROWN.

CHAPTER II. — OF SYLLABLES.

CORRECTIONS OF FALSE SYLLABICATION.

LESSON I.—CONSONANTS.

1. Correction of *Murray*, in words of two syllables : civ-il, col-our, cop-y, dam-ask, doz-en, ev-er, feath-er, gath-er, heav-en, heav-y, hon-ey, lem-on, lin-en, mead-ow, mon-ey, nev-er, ol-ive, -ange, oth-er, pheas-ant, pleas-ant, pun-ish, rath-er, read-y, riv-er, rob-in, schol-ar, shov-el, om-ach, tim-id, whith-er.

2. Correction of *Murray*, in words of three syllables : ben-e-fit, cab-i-net, can-is-ter, cat-a-logue, iar-ac-ter, char-i-ty, cov-et-ous, dil-i-gence, dim-i-ty, el-e-phant, ev-i-dent, ev-er-green, friv-o-us, gath-er-ing, gen-er-ous, gov-ern-ess, gov-ern-or, hon-est-y, kal-en-dar, lav-en-der, lev-er-, lib-er-al, mem-or-y, min-is-ter, mod-est-ly, nov-el-ty, no-bod-y, par-a-dise, pov-er-ty, pres-ent-, prov-i-dence, prop-er-ly, pris-on-er, rav-en-ous, sat-is-fy, sev-er-al, sep-ar-ate, trav-el-ler, vag-bond ;—con-sid-er, con-tin-ue, de-liv-er, dis-cov-er, dis-fig-ure, dis-hon-est, dis-trib-ute, in-hab-, me-chan-ic, what-ev-er ;—rec-om-mend, ref-u-gee, rep-ri-mand.

3. Correction of *Murray*, in words of four syllables : cat-er-pil-lar, char-i-ta-ble, dil-i-gent-ly, iis-er-a-ble, prof-it-a-ble, tol-er-a-ble ;—be-nev-o-lent, con-sid-er-ate, di-min-u-tive, ex-per-i-ment, x-trav-a-gant, in-hab-i-tant, no-bil-i-ty, par-tic-u-lar, pros-per-i-ty, ri-dic-u-lous, sin-cer-i-ty ;—em-on-stra-tion, ed-u-ca-tion, em-u-la-tion, ep-i-dem-ic, mal-e-fac-tor, man-u-fac-ture, mem-o-an-dum, mod-er-a-tor, par-a-lyt-ic, pen-i-ten-tial, res-ig-na-tion, sat-is-fac-tion, sem-i-co-lon.

4. Correction of *Murray*, in words of five syllables : a-bom-i-na-ble, a-poth-e-ca-ry, con-sid-er--ble, ex-plan-a-to-ry, prep-ar-a-to-ry ;—ac-a-dem-i-cal, cu-ri-os-i-ty, ge-o-graph-i-cal, man-u-fac-or-y, sat-is-fac-tor-y, mer-i-to-ri-ous ;—char-ac-ter-is-tic, ep-i-gram-mat-ic, ex-per-i-ment-al, iol-y-syl-la-ble, con-sid-er-a-tion.

5. Correction of *Murray*, in the division of proper names : Hel-en, Leon-ard, Phil-ip, Rob-ert, Hor-ace, Thom-as ;—Car-o-line, Cath-a-rine, Dan-i-el, Deb-o-rah, Dor-o-thy, Fred-er-ick, Is-a-bel, Jon-a-than, Lyd-i-a, Nich-o-las, Ol-i-ver, Sam-u-el, Sim-e-on, Sol-o-mon, Tim-o-thy, Val-en-ine ;—A-mer-i-ca, Bar-thol-o-mew, E-liz-a-beth, Na-than-i-el, Pe-nel-o-pe, The-oph-i-lus.

LESSON II.—MIXED EXAMPLES.

1. Correction of *Webster*, by Rule 1st :—ca-price, e-steem, dis-e-steem, o-blige ;—a-zure, ma-tron, pa-tron, pha-lanx, si-ren, trai-tor, tren-cher, bar-ber, bur-nish, gar-nish, tar-nish, var-nish, mar-ket, mus-ket, pam-phlet ;—bra-ver-y, kna-ver-y, sla-ver-y, e-ven-ing, sce-ner-y, bri-ber-y, ni-ce-ty, chi-ca-ner-y, ma-chin-er-y, im-a-ger-y ;—a-sy-lum, ho-ri-zon,—fin-an-cier, her-o-ism,—sar-do-nyx, scur-ri-lous,—co-me-di-an, pos-te-ri-or.

2. Correction of *Webster*, by Rule 2d : o-yer, fo-li-o, ge-ni-al, ge-ni-us, ju-ni-or, sa-ti-ate, vi-ti-ate ;—am-bro-si-a, cha-me-*le*-on, par-he-li-on, con-ve-ni-ent, in-ge-ni-ous, om-nis-ci-ence, pe-cu-li-ar, so-ci-a-ble, par-ti-al-i-ty, pe-cu-ni-a-ry ;—an-nun-ci-ate, e-nun-ci-ate, ap-pre-ci-ate, as-so-ci-ate, ex-pa-ti-ate, in-gra-ti-ate, in-i-ti-ate, li-cen-ti-ate, ne-go-ti-ate, no-vi-ti-ate, of-fi-ci-ate, pro-pi-ti-ate, sub-stan-ti-ate.

3. Correction of *Cobb* and *Webster*, by each other, under Rule 3d : "dress-er, hast-y, past-ry, seiz-ure, roll-er, jest-er, weav-er, vamp-er, hand-y, dross-y, gloss-y, mov-er, mov-ing, ooz-y, full-er, trust-y, weight-y, nois-y, drows-y, swarth-y."—*Webster.* Again : "east-ern, ful-ly, pul-let, ril-let, scant-y, need-y."—*Cobb.*

4. Correction of *Webster* and *Cobb*, under Rule 4th : a-wry, a-thwart', pro-spect'-ive, pa-ren'-the-sis, re-sist-i-bil'-i-ty, hem-i-spher'-ic, mon'-o-stich, hem'-i-stich, to'-wards.

5. Correction of the words under Rule 5th : Eng-land, an oth-er,* Beth-es'-da, Beth-ab'-a-ra.

LESSON III.—MIXED EXAMPLES.

1. Correction of *Cobb*, by Rule 3d : bend-er, bless-ing, brass-y, chaff-y, chant-er, clasp-er, craft-y, curd-y, fend-er, film-y, fust-y, glass-y, graft-er, grass-y, gust-y, hand-ed, mass-y, musk-y, rust-y, swell-ing, tell-er, test-ed, thrift-y, vest-ure.

2. Corrections of *Webster*, mostly by Rule 1st : bar-ber, bur-nish, bris-ket, can-ker, char-ter, cnc-koo, fur-nish, gar-nish, guilt-y, han-ker, lus-ty, por-tal, tar-nish, tes-tate, tes-ty, trai-tor, trea-ty, var-nish, ves-tal, di-ur-nal, e-ter-nal, in-fer-nal, in-ter-nal, ma-ter-nal, noc-tur-nal, pa-ter-nal.

3. Corrections of *Webster*, mostly by Rule 1st : ar-mor-y, ar-ter-y, *butch-er-y*, cook-er-y, eb-on-y, em-er-y, ev-er-y, fel-on-y, fop-per-y, frip-per-y, gal-ler-y, his-tor-y, liv-er-y, lot-ter-y, mock-er-y,' mys-*ter-y*,† nun-ner-y, or-rer-y, pil-lor-y, quack-er-y, sor-cer-y, witch-er-y.

4. Corrections of *Cobb*, mostly by Rule 1st : an-kle, bas-ket, blan-ket, buc-kle, cac-kle, cran-kle, crin-kle, Eas-ter, fic-kle, free-kle, knuc-kle, mar-ket, mon-key, por-tress, pic-kle, poul-tice, pun-cheon, quad-rant, quad-rate, squad-ron, ran-kle, shac-kle, sprin-kle, tin-kle, twin-kle, wrin-kle.

5. Corrections of *Emerson*, by Rules 1st and 3d : as-cribe, blan-dish, branch-y, cloud-y, dust-y, drear-y, e-ven-ing, fault-y, filth-y, frost-y, gaud-y, gloom-y, health-y, heark-en, heart-y, hoar-y, leak-y, loun-ger, marsh-y, might-y, milk-y, naught-y, pass-ing, pitch-er, read-y, rock-y, speed-y, stead-y, storm-y, thirst-y, thorn-y, trust-y, vest-ry, west-ern, wealth-y.

CHAPTER III. — OF WORDS.

CORRECTIONS RESPECTING THE FIGURE, OR FORM, OF WORDS.

RULE I.—COMPOUNDS.

" Professing to imitate Timon, the *manhater*."—*Goldsmith corrected.* "Men load hay with a pitchfork."—*Webster cor.* "A *peartree* grows from the seed of a pear."—*Id.* "A *toothbrush* is

---

* *An other* is a phrase of two words, which ought to be written separately. The transferring of the *n* to the latter word, is a gross vulgarism. Separate the words, and it will be avoided.

† *Mys-ter-y*, according to Scott and Cobb ; *mys-te-ry*, according to Walker and Worcester.

good to brush your teeth."—*Id.*   "The mail is opened at the *post-office*."—*Id.*   "The error seems to me *twofold*."—*Sanborn cor.*   "To *preëngage* means to engage *beforehand*."—*Webster cor.* "It is a mean act to deface the figures on a *milestone*."—*Id.*   "A grange is a farm, *with its farmhouse*."—*Id.*   "It is no more right to steal apples or *watermelons*, than [to steal] money."—*Id.* "The awl is a tool used by shoemakers and *harness-makers*."—*Id.*   "*Twenty-five* cents are equal to one quarter of a dollar."—*Id.*   "The *blowing-up* of the Fulton at New York, was a terrible disaster."—*Id.*   "The elders also, and the *bringers-up* of the children, sent to Jehu."—ALGER, FRIENDS, ET AL.: 2 *Kings*, x, 5.   "Not with *eyeservice*, as *menpleasers*."—*Col.* iii, 22.   "A *good-natured* and equitable construction of cases."—*Ash cor.*   "And purify your hearts, ye *double-minded*."—*James*, iv, 8.   "It is a *mean-spirited* action to steal; i. e., To steal is a *mean-spirited* action."—*A. Murray cor.*   "There is, indeed, one form of orthography which is *akin* to the subjunctive mood of the Latin tongue."—*Booth cor.*   "To bring him into nearer connexion with real and everyday life."—*Philological Museum*, Vol. i, p. 459.   "The *commonplace*, stale declamation of its revilers would be silenced."—*Id cor.*   "She [Cleopatra] formed a very singular and unheard-of project."—*Goldsmith cor.*   "He [William Penn] had many vigilant, though *forbidtalented* and *mean-spirited* enemies."—*R. Vaux cor.*   "These *old-fashioned* people would level our psalmody," &c.—*Gardiner cor.*   "This *slow-shifting* scenery in the theatre of harmony."—*Id.* "So we are assured from Scripture *itself*."—*Harris cor.*   "The mind, being disheartened, then betakes *itself* to trifling."—*R. Johnson cor.*   "*Whosoever* sins ye remit, they are remitted unto them."—*Bible cor.*   "Tarry we *ourselves* how we will."—*W. Walker cor.*   "Manage your credit so, that you need neither swear *yourself*, nor *seek* a voucher."—*Collier cor.*   "Whereas *song* never conveys any of the *abovenamed* sentiments."—*Dr. Rush cor.*   "I go on *horseback*."—*Gay cor.*   "This requires purity, in opposition to barbarous, obsolete, or *new-coined* words."—*Adam cor.*   "May the *ploughshare* shine."—*White cor.*   "*Whichever* way we consider it."—*Locke cor.*

"*Where'er* the silent *e* a place obtains,
The *voice* foregoing, *length* and softness gains."—*Brightland cor.*

RULE II.—SIMPLES.

"It qualifies any of the four parts of speech *above* named."—*Kirkham cor.*   "After a *while* they put us out among the rude multitude."—*Fox cor.*   "It would be a *shame*, if your *mind* should falter and give in."—*Collier cor.*   "They stared a *while* in silence one upon *an other*."— *Johnson cor.*   "After passion has for a *while* exercised its tyrannical sway."—*Murray cor.* "Though set within the same *general frame* of intonation."—*Rush cor.*   "Which do not carry any of the natural *vocal signs* of expression."—*Id.*   "The measurable *constructive powers* of a few associable constituents."—*Id.*   "Before each accented syllable or emphatic *monosyllabic word*."—*Id.*   "One should not think *too* favorably of *one's self*."—*Murray's Gram.* i, 154. "Know ye not your *own selves*, how that Jesus Christ is in you?"—2 *Cor.* xiii, 5.   "I judge not my *own self*, for I know nothing of my *own self*."—*Sep* 1 *Cor.* iv, 3.   "Though they were in such a rage, I desired them to tarry a *while*."—*Josephus cor.*   "A, *in stead* of an, is now used before words beginning with *u* long."—*Murray cor.*   "John will have earned his wages *by* next *new year's* day."—*Id.*   "A *new year's gift* is a present made on the first day of the year."—*Johnson et al. cor.*   "When he sat on the throne, distributing *new year's gifts*."—*Id.*   "St. Paul admonishes Timothy to refuse *old wives' fables*."—See 1 *Tim.* iv, 7.   "The world, take it *all together*, is but one."—*Collier cor.*   "In writings of this stamp, we must accept of sound *in stead of* sense."—*Murray cor.*   "A *male* child, a *female* child ; *male* descendants, *female* descendants."— *Goldsbury et al. cor.*   "*Male* servants, *female* servants ; *male* relations, *female* relations."—*Fulton cor.*

"Reserved and cautious, with no partial aim,
My muse e'er sought to blast *an other's* fame."—*Lloyd cor.*

RULE III.—THE SENSE.

"Our discriminations of this matter have been but *four-footed* instincts."—*Rush cor.*   "He is in the right, (says Clytus,) not to bear *free-born* men at his table."—*Goldsmith cor.*   "To the *short-seeing* eye of man, the progress may appear little."—*The Friend cor.*   "Knowledge and virtue are, emphatically, the *stepping-stones* to individual distinction."—*Town cor.*   "A *tin-peddler* will sell tin vessels as he travels."—*Webster cor.*   "The beams of a *wooden house* are held up by the posts and joists."—*Id.*   "What you mean by *future-tense* adjective, I can easily understand."—*Tooke cor.*   "The town has been for several days very *well-behaved*."—*Spectator cor.* "A *rounce* is the handle of a *printing-press*."—*Webster cor.*   "The phraseology [which] we call *thee-and-thouing* [or, better, *thoutheeing*,] is not in so common use with us, as the *tutoyant* among the French."—*Walker cor.*   "Hunting and other *outdoor* sports, are generally pursued." —*Balbi cor.*   "Come unto me, all ye that labor and are *heavy-laden*."—*Scott et al. cor.*   "God so loved the world, that he gave his *only-begotten* Son to save it."—See ALGER'S BIBLE, and FRIENDS': *John*, iii, 16.   "Jehovah is a *prayer-hearing* God: Nineveh repented, and was spared." —*Observer cor.*   "These are *well-pleasing* to God, in all ranks and relations."—*Barclay cor.* "Whosoever cometh *anything* near unto the tabernacle."—*Bible cor.*   "The words *coalesce*, when they have a *long-established* association."—*Mur. cor.*   "Open to me the gates of righteousness: I will go *into* them."—MODERN BIBLE: *Ps.* cxviii, 19.   "He saw an angel of God, coming *in to* him."—*Acts*, x, 3.   "The consequences of any action are to be considered in a *twofold* light."—*Wayland cor.*   "We commonly write *twofold*, *threefold*, *fourfold*, and so on up to *tenfold*, without a hyphen; and, after that, we use one."—*G. Brown.*   "When the first mark is going off, he cries, Turn! the *glassholder* answers, Done!"—*Bowditch cor.*   "It is a kind of familiar *shaking-hands* (or *shaking of hands*) with all the vices."—*Maturin cor.*   "She is a *good-natured* woman;"—"James is *self-opinionated*;"—"He is *broken-hearted*."—*Wright cor.*   "These three examples apply to the *present-tense* construction only."—*Id.*   "So that it was like a game of *hide-and-go-seek*."—*Gram. cor.*

"That lowliness is young ambition's ladder,
Whereto the *climber-upward* turns his face."—*Shak.*

RULE IV.—ELLIPSES.

"This building serves yet for a *schoolhouse* and a meeting-house."—*G. Brown.* "Schoolmasters and *schoolmistresses, if* honest friends, are to be encouraged."—*Discip. cor.* · "We never assumed to ourselves a *faith-making* or a *worship-making* power."—*Barclay cor.* "*Potash* and *pearlash* are made from common ashes."—*Webster cor.* "Both the *ten-syllable* and the *eight-syllable* verses are iambics."—*Blair cor.* "I say to myself, thou *sayst to thyself,* he says to *himself,* &c."—*Dr. Murray cor.* "Or those who have esteemed themselves *skilful,* have tried for the mastery in *two-horse* or *four-horse* chariots."—*Ware cor.* "I remember him barefooted and *bareheaded,* running through the streets."—*Edgeworth cor.* "Friends have the entire control of the *schoolhouse* and *dwelling-house.*" Or :—"of the *schoolhouses* and *dwelling-houses.*" Or :—"of the *schoolhouse* and the *dwelling-houses.*" Or :—"of the *schoolhouses* and the *dwelling-house.*" Or :— "of the *school,* and *of the dwelling-houses.*" [For the sentence here to be corrected is so ambiguous, that any of these may have been the meaning intended by it.]—*The Friend cor.* "The meeting is held at the *first-mentioned* place in *Firstmonth;* at the *last-mentioned,* in *Secondmonth;* and so on."—*Id.* "Meetings for worship are held, at the same hour, on *Firstday* and *Fourthday.*" Or :— "on *Firstdays* and *Fourthdays.*"—*Id.* "Every part of it, inside and *outside,* is covered with gold leaf."—*Id.* "The Eastern Quarterly Meeting is held on the last *Seventhday* in *Secondmonth, Fifthmonth. Eighthmonth,* and *Eleventhmonth.*"—*Id.* "Trenton Preparative Meeting is held on the third *Fifthday* in each month, at ten o'clock; meetings for worship [are held,] at the same hour, on *Firstdays* and *Fifthdays.*"—*Id.* "Ketch, a vessel with two masts, a *mainmast* and a *mizzenmast.*"—*Webster cor.* "I only mean to suggest a doubt, whether nature has enlisted herself [either] as a *Cis-Atlantic* or [as a] *Trans-Atlantic* partisan."—*Jefferson cor.* "By large hammers, like those used for *paper-mills* and fulling-mills, they beat their hemp."—*Johnson cor.* "ANT-HILL, or ANT-HILLOCK, *n. A* small *protuberance* of earth, *formed by* ants, *for* their *habitation.*" —*Id.* "It became necessary to substitute simple indicative terms called *pronames* or *pronouns.*"

"Obscur'd, where highest woods, impenetrable
To *light of star or sun,* their umbrage spread."—*Milton cor.*

RULE V.—THE HYPHEN.

"*Evil-thinking;* a noun. compounded of the noun *evil* and the imperfect participle *thinking;* singular number;" &c.—*Churchill cor.* "*Evil-speaking;* a noun, compounded of the noun *evil* and the imperfect participle *speaking.*"—*Id.* "I am a tall, *broad-shouldered,* impudent, black fellow."—*Spect.* or *Joh. cor.* "Ingratitude! thou *marble-hearted* fiend."—*Shak.* or *Joh. cor.* "A popular *license* is indeed the *many-headed* tyranny."—*Sidney* or *Joh. cor.* "He from the *many-peopled* city flies."—*Sandys* or *Joh. cor.* "He *many-languaged* nations has surveyed."—*Pope* or *Joh. cor* "The *horse-cucumber* is the large green cucumber, and the best for the table."—*Mort* or *Joh. cor.* "The bird of night did sit, even at *noon-day,* upon the market-place."—*Shak.* or *Joh. cor.* "These make a general *gaol-delivery* of souls not for punishment "—*South* or *Joh. cor.* "Thy air, thou other *gold-bound* brow, is like the first."—*Shak.* or *Joh. cor* "His person was deformed to the highest degree; *flat-nosed* and *blobber-lipped.*"—*L'Estr.* or *Joh. cor.* "He that defraudeth the labourer of his hire, is a *blood-shedder.*"—*Ecclus.* xxxiv, 22. "*Bloody-minded, adj.,* from *bloody* and *mind;* Cruel, inclined to *bloodshed.*"—*Johnson cor.* "*Blunt-witted* lord, ignoble in demeanour."—*Shak.* or *Joh. cor.* "A young fellow, with a *bob-wig* and a black silken bag tied to it."—*Spect.* or *Joh. cor.* "I have seen enough to confute all the *bold-faced* atheists of this age."—*Bramhall* or *Joh. cor.* "Before *milk-white,* now purple with love's wound."—*Shak. Dict. w. Bolt.* "For what else is a *red-hot* iron than fire? and what else is a burning coal than *red-hot* wood?"—*Newton* or *Joh. cor.* "*Poll-evil* is a large swelling, inflammation, or imposthume, in the horse's poll, or nape of the neck, just between the ears."—*Far.* or *Joh. cor.*

"Quick-witted, *brazen-fac'd,* with fluent tongues,
Patient of labours, and dissembling wrongs."—*Dryden cor.*

RULE VI.—NO HYPHEN.

"From his fond parent's eye a *teardrop* fell."—*Snelling cor.* "How great, poor *jackdaw,* would thy sufferings be!"—*Id.* "Placed, like a *scarecrow* in a field of corn."—*Id.* "Soup for the *almshouse* at a cent a quart."—*Id.* "Up into the *watchtower* get, and see all things despoiled of fallacies."—*Donne* or *Joh. cor.* "In the *daytime* she [Fame] sitteth in a *watchtower,* and flieth most by night."—*Bacon* or *Joh. cor.* "The moral is the first business of the poet, as being the *groundwork* of his instruction."—*Dryd.* or *Joh. cor.* "Madam's own hand the *mousetrap* baited."—*Prior* or *Joh cor.* "By the sinking of the *airshaft,* the air has liberty to circulate."—*Ray* or *Joh. cor.* "The multiform and amazing operations of the *airpump* and the loadstone."—*Watts* or *Joh. cor.* "Many of the *firearms* are named from animals."—*Johnson cor.* "You might have trussed him and all his apparel into an *eelskin.*"—*Shak.* or *Joh. cor.* "They may serve as *landmarks,* to show what lies in the direct way of truth."—*Locke* or *Joh cor.* "A *packhorse* is driven constantly in a narrow lane and dirty road."—*Locke* or *Joh. cor.* "A *millhorse,* still bound to go in one circle."—*Sidney* or *Joh. cor.* "Of singing birds, they have linnets, *goldfinches,* ruddocks, Canary birds, blackbirds, thrushes, and divers others."—*Carew* or *Joh. cor.* "Cartridge, a case of paper or parchment filled with *gunpowder;* [or, rather, containing the *entire charge* of a gun]."—*Joh cor.*

"Deep night, dark night, the silent of the night,
The time of night when Troy was set on fire,
The time when *screechowls* cry, and *bandogs* howl."

SHAKSPEARE: in *Johnson's Dict. w. Screechowl.*

PROMISCUOUS CORRECTIONS IN THE FIGURE OF WORDS.

LESSON I.—MIXED EXAMPLES.

"They that live in *glass houses,* should not throw stones."—*Adage.* "If a man profess Christianity in any manner or form *whatsoever.*"—*Watts cor.* "For Cassius is *aweary* of the world." Better: "For Cassius is *weary* of the world."—*Shak. cor.* "By the *coming-together* of more, the chains were fastened on."—*W. Walker cor.* "Unto the *carrying-away* of Jerusalem captive in the fifth month."—*Bible cor.* "And the *goings-forth* of the border shall be to Zedad."—*Id.* "And the *goings-out* of it shall be at *Hazar Enan.*"—See *Walker's Key.* "For the *taking-place* of effects, in a certain particular series "—*West cor.* "The *letting go* of which was the occasion of all that corruption."—*Owen cor.* "A *falling-off* at the end, is always injurious."—*Jamieson cor.* "As all *holdings-forth* were courteously supposed to be trains of reasoning."—*Dr. Murray cor.* "Whose *goings-forth* have been from of old, from everlasting."—*Bible cor.* "Sometimes the adjective becomes a substantive."—*Bradley cor.* "It is very plain, *that* I consider man as viewed anew."—*Barclay cor.* "Nor do I *anywhere* say, as he falsely insinuates."—*Id.* "*Everywhere, anywhere, elsewhere, somewhere, nowhere.*"—*L. Murray's Gram.* Vol. i, p. 115. "The world burns off *apace,* and time is like a rapid river."—*Collier cor.* "But to *new-model* the paradoxes of ancient skepticism."—*Dr. Brown cor.* "The *southeast* winds from the ocean invariably produce rain."—*Webster cor.* "*Northwest* winds from the *highlands* produce cold clear weather."—*Id.* "The greatest part of such tables would be of little use to *Englishmen.*"—*Priestley cor.* "The *ground-floor* of the east wing of *Mulberry-street meeting-house* was filled."—*The Friend cor.* "Prince Rupert's Drop. This singular production is made at the *glasshouses.*"—*Barnes cor.*

> "The lights and shades, whose *well-accorded* strife
> Gives all the strength and colour of our life."—*Pope.*

LESSON II.—MIXED EXAMPLES.

"In the *twenty-seventh* year of Asa king of Judah, did Zimri reign seven days in Tirzah."—*Bible cor.* "In the *thirty-first* year of Asa king of Judah, began Omri to reign over Israel."—*Id.* "He cannot so deceive himself as to fancy that he is able to do a *rule-of-three* sum." Better—"a sum in the rule of three."—*Qr. Rev. cor.* "The best cod are those known under the name of *Isle-of-Shoals dun-fish.*"—*Babli cor.* "The soldiers, with *downcast* eyes, seemed to beg for mercy."—*Goldsmith cor.* "His head was covered with a coarse, *wornout* piece of cloth."—*Id.* "Though had lately received a reinforcement of a thousand *heavy-armed* Spartans."—*Id.* "But he laid them by unopened; and, with a smile, said, ' Business *to-morrow.* ' "—*Id.* "Chester *Monthly Meeting* is held at Moorestown, on the *Thirdday* following the second *Secondday.*"—*The Friend cor.* "Egg-harbour *Monthly Meeting* is held on the first *Secondday.*"—*Id.* "*Little-Egg-harbour* Monthly Meeting is held at Tuckerton on the second *Fifthday* in each month."—*Id.* "At three o'clock, on *Firstday* morning, the 24th of *Eleventhmonth,* 1834," &c.—*Id.* "In less than *one fourth* part of the time usually devoted."—*Kirkham cor.* "The pupil will not have occasion to use it *one tenth* part *so much.*"—*Id.* "The painter dips his *paintbrush* in paint, to paint the carriage."—*Id.* "In an ancient English version of the *New Testament.*"—*Id.* "The little boy was *bareheaded.*"—*Red Book cor.* "The man, being a little *short-sighted,* did not immediately know him."—*Id.* "*Picture-frames* are gilt with gold "—*Id.* "The *parkkeeper* killed one of the deer."—*Id.* "The fox was killed near the *brickkiln.*"—*Id.* "Here comes Esther, with her *milkpail.*"—*Id.* "The *cabinet-maker* would not tell us."—*Id.* "A fine *thorn-hedge* extended along the edge of the hill."—*Id.* "If their private interests should be *everso* little affected."—*Id.* "Unios are *fresh-water* shells, vulgarly called *fresh-water* clams."—*Id. cor.*

> "Did not each poet mourn his luckless doom,
> Jostled by pedants out of *elbow-room.*"—*Lloyd cor.*

LESSON III.—MIXED EXAMPLES.

"The captive hovers *a while* upon the sad remains."—*Johnson cor.* "Constantia saw that the *hand-writing* agreed with the contents of the letter."—*Id.* "They have put me in a silk *nightgown,* and a gaudy *foolscap.*"—*Id.* "Have you no more manners than to rail at Hocus, that has saved that clod-pated, *numb-skulled ninny-hammer* of yours from ruin, and all his family?"—*Id.* "A noble, (that is, six shillings and *eight pence,*) is [paid], and usually hath been paid."—*Id.* "The king of birds, *thick-feathered,* and with full-summed wings, fastened his talons east and west."—*Id.* "*To-morrow.* This—supposing *morrow* to mean *morning,* as it did originally—is an idiom of the same kind as *to-night, to-day.*"—*Johnson cor.* "To-day goes away, and to-morrow comes."—*Id.* "Young children, who are tried in gocarts, to keep their steps from sliding."—*Id.* "Which, followed well, would demonstrate them but *goers-backward.*"—*Id.* "Heaven's *gold-winged* herald late he saw, to a poor Galilean virgin sent."—*Id.* "My *pent-house* eyebrows and my shaggy beard offend your sight."—*Id.* "The hungry lion would fain have been dealing with good *horseflesh.*"—*Id.* "A *broad-brimmed* hat ensconced each careful head."—*Snelling cor.* "With harsh vibrations of his *three-stringed* lute."—*Id.* "They magnify a *hundred-fold* an author's merit."—*Id.* "I'll nail them fast to some *oft-opened* door."—*Id.* Glossed over only with *saintlike* show, still thou art bound to vice."—*Johnson's Dict. w. Saintlike.* "Take of aqua-fortis two ounces, of *quicksilver* two drachms."—*Id. cor.* "This rainbow never appears but when it rains in the *sunshine.*"—*Id. cor.*

> "Not but there are, who merit other palms;
> Hopkins and *Sternhold* glad the heart with *psalms.*"—*Pope.*

CHAPTER IV.—OF SPELLING.

CORRECTIONS OF FALSE SPELLING.

RULE I.—FINAL F, L, OR S.

"He *will* observe the moral law, in *his* conduct."—*Webster corrected.* "A *cliff* is a steep bank, or a precipitous rock."—*Walker cor.* "A needy man's budget is *full* of schemes."—*Maria cor.* "Few large publications, in this country, *will* pay a printer."—*N. Webster cor.* "I *shall,* with cheerfulness, resign my other papers to oblivion."—*Id.* "The proposition *was* suspended till the next session of the legislature."—*Id.* "Tenants for life *will* make the most of lands for themselves."—*Id.* "While every thing *is* left to lazy negroes, a state *will* never be *well* cultivated."—*Id.* "The heirs of the original proprietors *still* hold the soil."—*Id.* "Say my *answer*

n money loaned *shall* be six per cent."—*Id.* "No man would submit to the drudgery of
s, if he could make money *as* fast by lying *still*."—*Id.* "A man may *as well* feed himself
odkin, *as* with a knife of the present fashion."—*Id.* "The clothes *will* be ill washed, the
ll be badly cooked; you *will* be ashamed of your wife, if she *is* not ashamed of herself."
He *will* submit to the laws of the state while he *is* a member of it."—*Id.* "But *will* our
iters on law forever think by tradition ?"—*Id.* "Some *still* retain a sovereign power in
rritories."—*Id.* "They *sell* images, prayers, the sound of *bells*, remission of sins, &c."—
i *cor.* "And the law had sacrifices offered every day, for the sins of *all* the people."—*Id.*
it may please the Lord, they *shall* find it to be a restorative."—*Id.* "Perdition is repent-
t *off till* a future day."—*Maxim cor.* "The angels of God, who *will* good and cannot
l, have nevertheless perfect liberty of *will.*"—*Perkins cor.* "Secondly, this doctrine
the excuse of *all* sin."—*Id.* "*Knell*, the sound of a bell rung at a funeral."—*Dict. cor.*

"If gold with *dross* or grain with *chaff* you find,
　Select—and leave the *chaff* and *dross* behind."—*G. Brown.*

RULE II.—OTHER FINALS.

i *mob* hath many heads, but no brains."—*Maxim cor.* "*Clam ;* to clog with any glutinous
ous matter."—See *Webster's Dict.* "*Whur ;* to pronounce the letter *r* with too much
—See *ib.* "*Flip ;* a mixed liquor, consisting of beer and spirit sweetened."—See *ib.* "*Glyn ;*
r between two mountains, a glen."—See *Walker's Dict.* "*Lam*, or *belam ;* to beat soundly
:udgel or bludgeon."—See *Red Book.* "*Bun ;* a small cake, a simnel, a kind of sweet
—See *Webster's Dict.* "*Brunet.* or *Brunette ;* a woman with a brown complexion."—See
Scott's Dict. "*Wadset ;* an ancient tenure or lease of land in the Highlands of Scotland."
ter cor. "To *dod* sheep, is to cut the wool away about their tails."—*Id.* "In aliquem
. *Cic.* To run full *butt* at one."—*W. Walker cor.* "Neither your policy nor your tem-
ild *permit* you to kill me."—*Phil. Mu. cor.* "And *admit* none but his own offspring to
iem."—*Id.* "The *sum* of all this dispute is, that some make them Participles."—*R.*
i *cor.* "As, the *whistling* of winds, the *buzz* and *hum* of insects, the *hiss* of serpents,
h of falling timber."—*Murray's Gram.* p. 331. "*Van ;* to winnow, or a fan for winnow-
See *Scott.* "Creatures that *buzz*, are very commonly such as will sting."—*G. Brown.*
uy, or borrow; *but* beware how you find."—*Id.* "It is better to have a house to *let*, than
to *get*."—*Id.* "Let not your tongue *cut* your throat."—*Precept cor.* "A little *wit* will
'ortunate man."—*Adage cor.* "There is many a *slip* 'twixt the cup and the *lip*."—*Id.*
ers' darlings make but *milksop* heroes."—*Id.* "One eye-witness is worth *ten* hearsays."

"The judge shall *job*, the bishop bite the town,
　And mighty dukes pack cards for half a crown."
　　　　　　　　　　　POPE: *in Johnson's Dict. w. Job.*

RULE III.—DOUBLING.

i, to curl; *frizzed*, curled; *frizzing*, curling."—*Webster cor.* "The commercial interests
o foster the principles of *Whiggism*."—*Payne cor.* "Their extreme indolence *shunned*
pecies of labour."—*Robertson cor* "In poverty and *strippedness*, they attend their little
:s."—*The Friend cor.* "In guiding and *controlling* the power you have thus obtained."
t cor. "I began, Thou *beganned* or *beganst*, He began, &c."—*A. Murray cor.* "Why
van change its ending; as, I began, Thou *beganned* or *beganst ?*"—*Id.* "Truth and con-
cannot be *controlled* by any methods of coercion."—*Hints cor.* "Dr. Webster *nodded*,
e wrote *knit*, *knitter*, and *knitting-needle*, without doubling the *t*."—*G. Brown.* "A wag
have wit enough to know when other wags are *quizzing* him."—*Id.* "*Bonny ;* handsome,
ll, merry."—*Walker cor.* "*Coquettish ; practising* coquetry; after the manner of a jilt."
Worcester. "*Pottage ;* a species of food made of meat and vegetables boiled to softness in
—See *Johnson's Dict.* "*Pottager ;* (from *pottage ;*) a porringer, a small vessel for chil-
ood."—See *ib.* "Compromit, *compromitted, compromitting ;* manumit, manumitted, manu-
."—*Webster cor.* "*Inferrible ;* that may be inferred or deduced from premises."—*Walker.*
are either solid, liquid, or *gasseous.*"—*Gregory cor.* "The spark will pass through the
oted space between the two wires, and explode the *gasses*."—*Id.* "Do we sound *gasses* and
r like *cases* and *caseous ?* No: they are more like *glasses* and *osseous.*"—*G. Brown.* "I
ot need here to mention *Swimming*, when he is of an age able to learn."—*Locke cor.*
do lexicographers spell *thinnish* and *mannish* with two Ens, and *dimmish* and *rammish*
e Em, each ?"—*G. Brown.* "*Gas* forms the plural regularly, *gasses.*"—*Peirce cor.* "Sin-
as ; Plural, *gasses*."—*Clark cor.* "These are contractions from *shedded, bursted*."—*Hi-
i. "The Present Tense denotes what is *occurring* at the present time."—*Day cor.* "The
ding in *eth* is of the solemn or antiquated style; as, He loveth, He walketh, He run-
-*Davis cor.*

"Thro' Freedom's sons no more remonstrance rings,
　Degrading nobles and *controlling* kings."—*Johnson.*

RULE IV.—NO DOUBLING.

goted* and tyrannical clergy will be feared."—See *Johnson, Walker,* &c. "Jacob *worshiped*
ator, leaning on the top of his staff."—*Murray's Key*, 8vo, p. 165. "For it is all *marvel*-
estitute of interest."—See *Johnson, Walker,* and *Worcester.* "As, box, boxes ; church,
:s ; lash, lashes ; kiss, kisses ; rebuk, rebuses."—*Murray's Gram.* 8vo, p. 40. "*Gossiping*
ig go hand in hand."—See *Webster's Dict., and Worcester's, w. Gossiping.* "The substance
:riticisms on the Diversions of Purley was, with singular industry, *gossiped* by the present
e Secretary *at* [of] war, in Payne the bookseller's shop."—*Tooke's Diversions*, Vol. i, p. 187.
uip makes *worshiped, worshiper, worshiping; gossip, gossiped, gossiper, gossiping; fillip,*
filliper, filliping."—*Web. Dict.* "I became a *fidgety* as a fly in a milk-jug."—See *ib.* "That
us error seems to be *riveted* in popular opinion."—See *ib.* "Whose mind *is* not *biased* by
.l attachments to a sovereign."—See *ib.* "Laws against usury originated in a *bigoted*

prejudice against the Jews."—*Webster cor.* "The most *critical* period of life *is* usually between thirteen and seventeen."—*Id.* "*Generalissimo*, the chief commander of an army or military force."—*Every Dict.* "*Tranquilize*, to quiet, to make calm and peaceful."—*Webster's Dict.* "*Pommelled*, beaten, bruised; having pommels, as a sword-hilt."—*Webster et al. cor.* "From what a height does the *jeweller* look down upon his shoemaker!"—*Red Book cor.* "You will have a verbal account from my friend and fellow-*traveller*."—*Id.* "I observe that you have written the word *counselled* with one *l* only."—*Ib.* "They were offended at such as *combated* these notions."—*Robertson cor.* "From *libel*, come *libelled, libeller, libelling, libellous*; from *gravel, grovelled, groveller, grovelling*; from *gravel, gravelled* and *gravelling*."—*Webster cor.* "*Woolliness*, the state of being woolly."—*Worcester's Dict.* "Yet he has spelled chapelling, bordeller, *medalist, metaline, metalist, metalize*, clavellated, &c., with *ll*, contrary to his rule."—*Webster cor.* "Again, he has spelled *cancellation* and *snivelly* with single *l*, and cupellation, pannellation, wittolly, with *ll*."—*Id.* "*Oily*, fatty, greasy, containing oil, glib."—*Walker cor.* "*Medalist*, one curious in medals; *Metalist*, one skilled in metals."—*Walker's Rhym. Dict.* "He is *benefited*." —*Webster.* "They *travelled* for pleasure."—*Clark cor.*

"Without you, what were man? A *grovelling* herd,
In darkness, wretchedness, and want enchain'd."—*Beattie cor.*

RULE V.—FINAL CK.

"He hopes, therefore, to be pardoned by the *critic*."—*Kirkham corrected.* "The leading object of every *public* speaker should be, to persuade."—*Id.* "May not four feet be as *poetic* as five; or fifteen feet, as *poetic* as fifty?"—*Id.* "Avoid all theatrical trick and *mimicry*, and especially all *scholastic* stiffness."—*Id.* "No one thinks of becoming skilled in dancing, or in *music*, or in *mathematics*, or in *logic*, without long and close application to the subject."—*Id.* "Casper's sense of feeling, and susceptibility of *metallic* and *magnetic* excitement, were also very extraordinary."—*Id.* "Authorship has become a mania, or, perhaps I should say, an *epidemic*."—*Id.* "What can prevent this *republic* from soon raising a literary standard?"—*Id.* "Courteous reader, you may think me garrulous upon *topics* quite foreign to the subject before me."—*Id.* "Of the *Tonic, Subtonic*, and *Atonic* elements."—*Id.* "The *subtonic* elements are *inferior* to the *tonics*, in all the *emphatic* and elegant purposes of speech."—*Id.* "The nine *atonics* and the three abrupt *subtonics* cause an interruption to the continuity of the *syllabic* impulse."*—Id.* "On *scientific* principles, conjunctions and prepositions are [*not*] one [and the same] part of speech."—*Id.* "That some inferior animals should be able to *mimick* human articulation, will not seem wonderful."—*L. Murray cor.*

"When young, you led a life *monastic*,
And wore a vest *ecclesiastic*;
Now, in your age, you grow *fantastic*."—*Denham's Poems*, p. 235.

RULE VI.—RETAINING.

"*Fearlessness*; exemption from fear, intrepidity."—*Johnson cor.* "*Dreadlessness; fearlessness*, intrepidity, undauntedness."—*Id.* "*Regardlessly*, without heed; *Regardlessness*, heedlessness."—*Id.* "*Blamelessly*, innocently; *Blamelessness*, innocence."—*Id.* "That is better than to be flattered into pride and *carelessness*."—*Id.* "Good fortunes began to breed a proud *recklessness* in them." —*Id.* "See whether he lazily and *listlessly* dreams away his time."—*Id.* "It may be, the palate of the soul is indisposed by *listlessness* or sorrow."—*Id.* "*Pitilessly*, without mercy; *Pitilessness*, unmercifulness."—*Id.* "What say you to such as these? abominable, accordable, *agreeable*, &c." —*Tooke cor.* "*Artlessly*; naturally, sincerely, without craft."—*Johnson cor.* "A *chillness*, or shivering of the body, generally precedes a fever."—*See Webster.* "*Smallness*; littleness, minuteness, weakness."—*Walker's Dict. et al.* "*Galless*, adj. Free from gall or bitterness."—*Webster cor.* "*Tallness*; height of stature, upright length with comparative slenderness"—*Webster's Dict.* "*Willful*; stubborn, contumacious, perverse, inflexible."—*See ib.* "He guided them by the *skilfulness* of his hands."—*See ib.* "The earth is the Lord's, and the *fullness* thereof."—*Friend's* BIBLE: Ps. xxiv, 1. "What is now, is but an *amassment* of imaginary conceptions."—*Glanville cor.* "*Embarrassment*; perplexity, entanglement."—*Walker.* "The second is slothfulness, whereby they are performed slackly and *carelessly*."—*Perkins cor.* "*Installment*; induction into office, part of a large sum of money, to be paid at a particular time."—*See Webster's Dict.* "*Inthrallment*; servitude, slavery, bondage."—*Ib.*

"I, who at some times spend, at others spare,
Divided between *carelessness* and care."—*Pope cor.*

RULE VII.—RETAINING.

"*Shall*, on the contrary, in the first person, simply *foretells*."—*Lowth's Gram.* p. 41; *Comly's*, 38; *Cooper's*, 51; *Lennie's*, 26. "There are a few compound irregular verbs, as *befall, bespeak, &c.*" —*Ash cor.* "That we might frequently *recall* it to our memory."—*Calvin cor.* "The angels exercise a constant solicitude that no evil *befall* us."—*Id.* "*Inthrall*; to enslave, to shackle, to reduce to servitude."—*Johnson.* "He makes resolutions, and *fulfills* them by new ones."—*See Webster.* "To *enroll* my humble name upon the list of authors on Elocution."—*See Webster.* "*Forestall*; to anticipate, to take up beforehand."—*Johnson.* "*Miscall*; to call wrong, to name improperly."—*Webster.* "*Bethrall*; to enslave, to reduce to bondage."—*Id.* "*Befall*; to happen to, to come to pass."—*Walker's Dict.* "*Unroll*; to open what is rolled or convolved."—*Webster's Dict.* "*Counterroll*; to keep copies of accounts to prevent frauds."—*See ib.* "As Sisyphus *uprolls* a rock, which constantly overpowers him at the summit."—*G. Brown.* "*Unwell*; not well, indisposed, not in good health."—*Webster.* "*Undersell*; to defeat by selling for less, to sell cheaper than an other."—*Johnson.* "*Inwall*; to enclose or fortify with a wall."—*Id.* "*Twibill*; an instrument with two bills, or with a point and a blade; a pickaxe, a mattock, a halberd, a battleaxe."—*Dict. cor.* "What you *miscall* their folly, is their care."—*Dryden cor.* "My heart

---

* Kirkham borrowed this doctrine of "Tonics, Subtonics, and Atonics," from Rush; and dressed it up in his own worse bombast. See Obs. 13 and 14, on the Powers of the Letters.—G. B.

will sigh when I *miscall* it so."—*Shak. cor.* "But if the arrangement *recalls* one set of ideas more readily than an other."—*Murray's Gram.* Vol. i, p. 334.

"'Tis done; and since 'tis done, 'tis past *recall;*
And since 'tis past *recall*, must be forgotten."—*Dryden cor.*

RULE VIII.—FINAL LL.

"The righteous is taken away from the *evil* to come."—*Isaiah*, lvii, 1. "*Patrol;* to go the rounds in a camp or garrison, to march about and observe what passes."—See *Joh. Dict.* "*Marshal;* the chief officer of arms, one who regulates rank and order."—See *ib.* "*Weevil;* a destructive grub that gets among corn."—See *ib.* "It much *excels* all other studies and arts."—*W. Walker cor.* "It is *essential* to all magnitudes, to be in one place."—*Perkins cor.* "By nature was thy *vassal*, but Christ hath redeemed me."—*Id.* "Some, being in want, pray for *temporal* blessings."—*Id.* "And this the Lord doth, either in *temporal* or in *spiritual* benefits."—*Id.* "He makes an *idol* of them, by setting his heart on them."—*Id.* "This *trial* by desertion serveth or two purposes."—*Id.* "Moreover, this destruction is both *perpetual* and terrible."—*Id.* "Giving to *several* men several gifts, according to his good pleasure."—*Id.* "*Until;* to some time, place, or degree, mentioned."—See *Dict.* "*Annul;* to make void, to nullify, to abrogate, to abolish."—See *Dict.* "Nitric acid combined with *argil*, forms the nitrate of *argil*."—*Gregory cor.*

"Let modest Foster, if he will, *excel*
Ten metropolitans in preaching well."—*Pope cor.*

RULE IX.—FINAL E.

"Adjectives ending in *able* signify capacity; as, *comfortable, tenable, improvable.*"—*Priestley cor.* "Their mildness and hospitality are *ascribable* to a general administration of religious ordinances."—*Webster cor.* "Retrench as much as possible without *obscuring* the sense."—*J. Brown cor.* "*Changeable*, subject to change; *Unchangeable*, immutable."—*Walker cor.* "*Tamable*, susceptive of taming; *Untamable*, not to be tamed."—*Id.* "*Reconcilable, Unreconcilable, Reconcilableness;* Irreconcilable, Irreconcilably, Irreconcilableness."—*Johnson cor.* "We have thought it most *advisable* to pay him some little attention."—*Merchant cor.* "*Provable*, that may be proved; Reprovable, *blamable*, worthy of reprehension."—*Walker cor.* "*Movable* and Immovable, *Movably* and Immovably, *Movables* and Removal, *Movableness* and Improvableness, *Unremovable* and Unimprovable, *Unremovably* and Removable, *Provable* and Approvable, *Irreprovable* and Reprovable, *Unreprovable* and Improvable, *Unimprovableness* and Improvably."—*Johnson cor.* "And with this cruelty you are *chargeable* in some measure yourself."—*Collier cor.* "Mothers would certainly resent it, as *judging* it proceeded from a low opinion of the genius of their sex."—*Brit. Gram. cor.* "*Tithable*, subject to the payment of tithes; *Salable*, vendible, fit for sale; *Losable*, possible to be lost; *Sizable*, of reasonable bulk or size."—See *Webster's Dict.* "When he began this custom, he was *puling* and very tender."—*Locke cor.*

"The plate, coin, revenues, and *movables*,
Whereof our uncle Gaunt did stand possess'd."—*Shak. cor.*

RULE X.—FINAL E.

"*Diversely;* in different ways, differently, variously."—See *Walker's Dict.* "The event thereof contains a *wholesome* instruction."—*Bacon cor.* "Whence Scaliger *falsely* concluded that Articles were useless."—*Brightland cor.* "The child that we have just seen, is *wholesomely* fed."—*Murray cor.* "Indeed, *falsehood* and legerdemain sink the character of a prince."—*Collier cor.* "In earnest, at this rate of *management*, thou usest thyself very *coarsely*."—*Id.* "To give them in *arrangement* and a diversity, as agreeable as the nature of the subject would admit."—*Murray cor.* "Alger's Grammar is only a trifling *enlargement* of Murray's little *Abridgement*."—*G. Brown.* "You ask whether you are to retain or to omit the mute *e* in the *words, judgement, abridgement, acknowledgement, lodgement, adjudgement,* and *prejudgement*."—*Red Book cor.* "Fertileness, fruitfulness; *fertilely*, fruitfully, abundantly."—*Johnson cor.* "*Chastely*, purely, without contamination; *Chasteness*, chastity, purity."—*Id.* "*Rhymester*, n. One who makes rhymes; a versifier; a mean poet."—*Walker, Chalmers, Maunder, Worcester.* "It is therefore *a* heroical *achievement* to dispossess this imaginary monarch."—*Berkley cor.* "Whereby is not meant the present time, as he *imagines*, but the time past."—*R. Johnson cor.* "So far is this word from affecting the noun, in regard to its *definiteness*, that its own character of *definiteness* or *indefiniteness*, depends upon the name to which it is prefixed."—*Webster cor.*

"Satire, by *wholesome* lessons, would reclaim,
And heal their vices to secure their fame."—*Brightland cor.*

RULE XI.—FINAL Y.

"Solon's the *veriest* fool in all the play."—*Dryden cor.* "Our author prides himself upon his great *shiness* and shrewdness."—*Merchant cor.* "This tense, then, *implies* also the signification of *debeo*."—*R. Johnson cor.* "That may be *applied* to a subject, with respect to something accidental."—*Id.* "This latter author *accompanies* his note with a distinction."—*Id.* "This rule is *defective*, and none of the annotators have sufficiently *supplied its deficiencies*."—*Id.* "Though he *fancied* supplement of Sanctius, Scioppius, Vossius, and Mariangelus, may take place."—*Ib.* "Yet, as to the commutableness of these two tenses, which is *denied* likewise, they [the foregoing *examples*] are *all one* [; i. e., *exactly equivalent*."]—*Id.* "Both these tenses may represent a futurity, *implied* by the dependence of the clause."—*Id.* "Cry, cries, crying, cried, crier, decrial; shy, *shier*, *shiest*, *shily*, *shiness*; Fly, flies, flying, flier, high-flier; Sly, *slier*, *sliest*, *slily*, *sliness*; spy, spies, spying, spied, espial; Dry, drier, driest, *drily, driness*."—*Cobb, Webster, and Chalmers cor.* "I would sooner listen to the thrumming of a *dandizette* at her piano."—*Kirkham cor.* "Send her away: for she *crieth* after us."—*Matt.* xv, 23. "IVIED, *a.* overgrown with ivy."—*Cobb's Dict.*, and *Maunder's.*

"Some *drily* plain, without invention's aid,
Write dull receipts how poems may be made."—*Pope cor.*

RULE XII.—FINAL Y.

"The *gayety* of youth should be tempered by the precepts of age."—*Murray cor.* "In the

storm of 1703, two thousand stacks of *chimneys* were blown down, in and about London."—*Red Book cor.* "And the vexation was not abated by the *hackneyed* plea of haste."—*Id.* "The fourth sin of our *days*, is lukewarmness."—*Perkins cor.* "God hates the workers of iniquity, and *destroys* them that speak lies."—*Id.* "For, when he *lays* his hand upon us, we may not fret."—*Id.* "Care not for it; but if thou *mayst* be free, choose it rather."—*Id.* "Alexander Severus saith, 'He that *buyeth*, must sell: I will not suffer buyers and sellers of offices.'"—*Id.* "With these measures, fell in all *moneyed* men."—See *Johnson's Dict.* "But rattling nonsense in full *volleys* breaks."—*Murray's Reader, q. Pope.* "*Valleys* are the intervals betwixt mountains."—*Woodward cor.* "The Hebrews had fifty-two *journeys*, or marches."—*Wood cor.* "It was not possible to mannge or steer the *galleys* thus fastened together."—*Goldsmith cor.* "*Turkeys* were not known to naturalists till after the discovery of America."—*Gregory cor.* "I would not have given it for a wilderness of *monkeys*."—SHAK.: *in Johnson's Dict.* "Men worked at embroidery, especially in *abbeys*."—*Constable cor.* "By which all purchasers or mortgagees may be secured of all *moneys* they lay out."—*Temple cor.* "He would fly to the mines or the *galleys*, for his recreation."—*South cor.* "Here *pulleys* make the pon'drous oak ascend."—*Gay cor.*
————"You need my help, and you say,
Shylock, we would have *moneys*."—*Shak. cor.*

RULE XIII.—IZE AND ISE.

"Will any able writer *authorise* other men to *revise* his works?"—*G. B.* "It can be made as strong and expressive as this *Latinized* English."—*Murray cor.* "Governed by the success or failure of an *enterprise*."—*Id.* "Who have *patronized* the cause of justice against powerful oppressors."—*Id. et al.* "Yet custom *authorizes* this use of it."—*Priestley cor.* "They *surprise* myself,**** ; and I even think the writers themselves will be *surprised*."—*Id.* "Let the interest *rise* to any sum which can be obtained."—*Webster cor.* "To *determine* what interest shall *arise* on the use of money."—*Id.* "To direct the popular councils and check *any rising* opposition."—*Id.* "Five were appointed to the immediate *exercise* of the office."—*Id.* "No man ever offers himself as a candidate by *advertising*."—*Id.* "They are honest and economical, but indolent, and destitute of *enterprise*."—*Id.* "I would, however, *advise* you to be cautious."—*Id.* "We are accountable for what we *patronize* in others."—*Murray cor.* "After he was *baptized*, and was solemnly admitted into the office."—*Perkins cor.* "He will find all, or most, of them, *comprised* in the Exercises."—*Brit. Gram. cor.* "A quick and ready habit of *methodizing* and regulating their thoughts."—*Id.* "To *tyrannize* over the time and patience of his reader."—*Kirkham cor.* "Writers of dull books, however, if *patronized* at all, are rewarded beyond their deserts."—*Id.* "A little reflection will show the reader the reason for *emphasizing* the words marked."—*Id.* "The English Chronicle contains an account of a *surprising* cure."—*Red Book cor.* "*Dogmatize*, to assert positively; Dogmatizer, an *assertor*, a magisterial teacher."—*Chalmers cor.* "And their inflections might now have been easily *analyzed*."—*Murray cor.* "Authorize, *disauthorize*, and unauthorized; Temporize, *contemporize*, and extemporize."—*Walker cor.* "Legalize, *equalize*, methodize, sluggardize, *womanize*, humanize, patronize, cantonize, gluttonize, epitomize, anatomize, phlebotomize, sanctuarize, characterize, *synonymize*, recognize, detonize, colonize."—*Id. cor.*
"This beauty sweetness always must *comprise*,
Which from the subject, well express'd, will rise."—*Brightland cor.*

RULE XIV.—COMPOUNDS.

"The glory of the Lord shall be thy *rear-ward*."—SCOTT, ALGER: *Isa.* lviii. 8. "A mere *vant-courier* to announce the coming of his master."—*Tooke cor.* "The *party-coloured* shutter appeared to come close up before him."—*Kirkham cor.* "When the day broke upon this *handful* of forlorn but dauntless spirits."—*Id.* "If, upon a *plumtree*, peaches and apricots are ingrafted, nobody will say they are the natural growth of the *plumtree*."—*Berkley cor.* "The channel between Newfoundland and Labrador is called the Straits of *Belleisle*."—*Worcester cor.* "There being nothing that more exposes to *the headache*:"—or, (perhaps more accurately,) "*headaks*."—*Locke cor.* "And, by a sleep, to say we end the *heartach*:"—or, "*heartake*."—*Shak. cor.* "He that sleeps, feels not the *toothache*:"—or, "*toothake*."—*Id.* "That the shoe must fit him, because it fitted his father and *grandfather*."—*Phil. Museum cor.* "A single word, *misspelled* [or *misspelt*] in a letter, is sufficient to show that you have received a defective education."—*C. Bucke cor.* "Which *misstatement* the committee attributed to a failure of memory."—*Professors cor.* "Then he went through the *Banqueting-House* to the scaffold."—*Smollet cor.* "For the purpose of maintaining a clergyman and a *schoolmaster*."—*Webster cor.* "They however knew that the lands were claimed by *Pennsylvania*."—*Id.* "But if you ask a reason, they immediately bid *farewell* to argument."—*Barnes cor.* "Whom resist, *steadfast* in the faith."—*Alger's Bible.* "And they continued *steadfastly* in the apostles' doctrine."—*Ib.* "Beware lest ye also fall from your own *steadfastness*."—*Ib.* "*Galiot*, or *Galliot*, a Dutch vessel carrying a main-mast and a *mizzen-mast*."—*Webster cor.* "Infinitive, to overflow; Preterit, overflowed; Participle, *overflowed*."—*Cobbett cor.* "After they have *misspent* so much precious time."—*Brit. Gram. cor.* "Some say, 'two *handsful*;' some, 'two *handfuls*;' and others, 'two *handful*.' The second expression is right."—*G. Brown.* "*Lapful*, as much as the lap can contain."—*Webster cor.* "*Dareful*, full of defiance."—*Walker cor.* "The road to the *blissful* regions, is as open to the peasant as to the king."—*Mur. cor.* "*Misspell* is *misspelled* [or *misspelt*] in every dictionary which I have seen."—*Barnes cor.* "*Downfall*; ruin, calamity, fall from rank or state."—*Johnson cor.* "The whole legislature *likewise* acts as a court."—*Webster cor.* "It were better, a *millstone* were hanged about his neck."—*Perkins cor.* "*Plumtree*, a tree that produces plums; *Hogplumtree*, a tree."—*Webster cor.* "*Trissyllables* ending in re or *le*, accent the first syllable."—*Murray cor.*
"It happen'd on a summer's *holyday*,
That to the greenwood shade he took his way."—*Dryden.*

RULE XV.—USAGE.

"Nor are the *moods* of the Greek tongue more uniform."—*Murray cor.* "If we *analyze* a conjunctive *preterit*, the rule will not appear to hold."—*Priestley cor.* "No landholder would have been at that *expense.*"—*Id.* "I went to see the child whilst they were putting on its *clothes.*"—*Id.* "This *style* is ostentatious, and *does* not suit grave writing."—*Id.* "The king of Israel, and *Jehoshaphat* the king of Judah, sat each on his throne."—1 *Kings,* xxii. 10 ; 2 *Chron.* xviii, 9. "*Lysias,* speaking of his friends, promised to his father, never to abandon them."—*Murray cor.* "Some, to avoid this *error,* run into *its* opposite."—*Churchill cor.* "Hope the balm of life *soothes* us under every misfortune."—*Jaudon's Gram.* p. 182. "Any judgement or decree might be *heard* and reversed by the legislature."—*N. Webster cor.* "A pathetic *harangue will screen* from punishment any knave."—*Id.* "For the same *reason,* the *women* would be improper judges."—*Id.* "Every person *is* indulged in worshiping *as* he *pleases.*"—*Id.* "Most or all *teachers* are excluded from genteel company."—*Id.* "The *Christian* religion, in its purity, *is* the best institution on *earth.*"—*Id.* "*Neither* clergymen nor human laws *have* the *least* authority over the conscience."—*Id.* "A *guild* is a society, fraternity, or corporation."—*Barnes cor.* "Phillis was not able to *untie* the knot, and so she cut it."—*Id.* "An *acre* of land is the quantity of one hundred and sixty perches."—*Id.* "*Ochre* is a fossil earth combined with the *oxyd* of some metal."—*Id.* "*Genii,* when denoting *atrial* spirits ; *geniuses,* when signifying persons of genius."—*Murray cor. ;* also *Frost ;* also *Nutting.* "Acrisius. king of Argos. had a beautiful daughter, whose name was *Danäe.*"—*Classic Tales cor.* "*Phäeton* was the son of Apollo and Clymene."—*Id.* "But, after all, I may not have reached the intended *goal.*"—*Buchanan cor.* "'*Pittacus* was offered a large sum.' Better : 'To *Pittacus* was offered a large sum.'"—*Kirkham cor.* "King *Micipsa* charged his sons to respect the senate and people of Rome."—*Id.* "For example : '*Galileo* greatly improved the telescope.'"—*Id.* "*Cathmor's warriors* sleep in death."—*Macpherson's Ossian.* "For parsing will enable you to detect and correct *errors* in composition."—*Kirkham cor.*

> "O'er barren mountains, o'er the flow'ry plain,
> Extends thy *uncontroll'd* and boundless reign."—*Dryden cor.*

PROMISCUOUS CORRECTIONS OF FALSE SPELLING.
LESSON I.—MIXED EXAMPLES.

"A bad author deserves better usage than a bad *critic.*"—*Pope (or Johnson) cor.* "Produce a single passage, *superior* to the speech of Logan, a Mingo chief, to Lord Dunmore, *governor* of this state."—*Jefferson's Notes,* p. 94. "We have none *synonymous* to supply its place."—*Jamieson cor.* "There is a probability that the effect will be *accelerated.*"—*Id.* "Nay, a regard to sound *has controlled* the public choice."—*Id.* "Though learnt [better, *learned*] from the uninterrupted use of *guttural* sounds."—*Id.* "It is by carefully filing off all roughness and *all inequalities,* that languages, like metals, must be polished."—*Id.* "That I have not *misspent* my time in the service of the community."—*Buchanan cor.* "The leaves of *maize* are also called blades."—*Webster cor.* "Who boast that they know what is past, and can *foretell* what is to come."—*Robertson cor.* "Its tasteless *dullness* is interrupted by nothing but its perplexities."—*Abbott, right.* "Sentences constructed with the Johnsonian *fullness* and swell."—*Jamieson, right.* "The privilege of escaping from his prefatory *dullness* and prolixity."—*Kirkham, right.* "But, in poetry, this *characteristic* of *dullness* attains its full growth."—*Id. corrected.* "The leading *characteristic* consists in an increase of the force and fullness."—*Id. cor.* "The character of this opening *fullness* and feebler vanish."—*Id. cor.* "Who, in the *fullness* of *unequalled* power, would not believe himself the favourite of Heaven ?"—*Id. right.* "They *mar* one *an* other, and distract him."—*Philol. Mus. cor.* "Let a deaf *worshiper* of antiquity and an English prosodist settle this."—*Rush cor.* "This *Philippic* gave rise to my satirical reply in self-defence."—*Merchant cor.* "We here saw no *innuendoes,* no new sophistry, no falsehoods."—*Id.* "A witty and *humorous* vein has often produced enemies."—*Murray cor.* "Cry *hollo !* to thy tongue, I pray thee :*" it *curvets* unseasonably."—*Shak. cor.* "I said, in my *sliest* manner, 'Your health, sir.'"—*Blackwood cor.* "And *attorneys* also travel the circuit in *pursuit* of business."—*Barnes cor.* "Some whole counties in Virginia would hardly *sell* for the *value* of the *debts due* from the inhabitants."—*Webster cor.* "They were called the Court of Assistants, and *exercised* all powers, *legislative* and judicial."—*Id.* "Arithmetic is excellent for the *gauging* of liquors."—*Harris's Hermes,* p. 295. "Most of the inflections may be *analyzed* in a way somewhat similar."—*Murray cor.*

> "To epithets allots emphatic state,
> While principals, *ungrac'd,* like *lackeys* wait."—*T. O. Churchill's Gram.* p. 326.

LESSON II.—MIXED EXAMPLES.

"Hence *less* is a privative *suffix,* denoting destitution ; as in *fatherless, faithless, penniless.*"—*Webster cor.* "*Bay ;* red, or reddish, inclining to a *chestnut colour.*"—*Id.* "*To mimick,* to imitate or ape for sport ; *a mimic,* one who imitates or *mimicks.*"—*Id.* "Counterroll, a counterpart or copy of the rolls ; *Counterrollment,* a counter account."—*Id.* "*Millennium,* [from *mille* and *annus,*] the thousand years during which Satan shall be bound."—*See Johnson's Dict.* "*Millennial,* [like *septennial, decennial,* &c.,] pertaining to the *millennium,* or to a thousand years."—*See Worcester's Dict.* "*Thralldom ;* slavery, bondage, a state of servitude."—*Webster's Dict.* "Brier, a prickly bush ; Briery, rough, prickly, full of briers ; *Sweetbrier,* a fragrant shrub."—*See Ainsworth's Dict. Scott's, Cobb's,* and others. "*Will,* in the second and third persons, barely *foretells.*"—*Brit. Gram. cor.* "And *therefore* there is no word false, but what is distinguished by Italics."—*Id.* "What should be *repeated,* is left to their discretion."—*Id.* "Because they are abstracted or *separated* from material substances."—*Id.* "All motion is in time, and *therefore, wherever* it exists, implies time as its *concomitant.*"—*Harris's Hermes,* p. 95. "And illiterate grown persons are guilty of *blamable* spelling."—*Brit. Gram. cor.* "They *will* always be ignorant, and of rough,

---

* There is, in most English dictionaries, a contracted form of this phrase, written *prithee,* or *I prithee ;* but Dr. Johnson censures it as "a familiar *corruption,* which some writers have *injudiciously* used ;" and, as the abbreviation amounted to nothing but the slurring of one vowel sound into an other, it has now, I think, very *deservedly* become obsolete.—G. BROWN.

uncivil manners."—*Webster cor.* "This fact *will* hardly be *believed* in the northern states."—*Id.* "The province, however, *was harassed* with disputes."—*Id.* "So little concern *has* the legislature for the interests of *learning.*"—*Id.* "The gentlemen *will* not admit that a *schoolmaster* can be a gentleman."—*Id.* "Such absurd *quid-pro-quoes* cannot be too strenuously avoided."—*Churchill cor.* "When we say of a man, 'He looks *slily;*' we signify, that he takes a sly glance or peep at something."—*Id.* "*Peep;* to look through a crevice; to look narrowly, closely, or *slily.*"—*Webster cor.* "Hence the confession has become a *hackneyed* proverb."—*Wayland cor.* "Not to mention the more ornamental parts of *gilding,* varnish, &c."—*Tooke cor.* "After this system of self-interest had been *riveted.*"—*Dr. Brown cor.* "Prejudice might have prevented the cordial approbation of a *bigoted* Jew."—*Dr. Scott cor.*

"All twinkling with the *dewdrop* sheen,
The *brier-rose* fell in streamers green."—*Sir W. Scott cor.*

LESSON III.—MIXED EXAMPLES.

"The infinitive *mood* has, commonly, the sign *to* before it."—*Harrison cor.* "Thus, it is *advisable* to write *singeing,* from the verb to *singe,* by way of distinction from *singing,* the participle of the verb to *sing.*"—*Id.* "Many verbs form both the *preterit* tense and the *preterit* participle irregularly."—*Id.* "Much must be left to every one's taste and *judgement.*"—*Id.* "Verses of different lengths, intermixed, form a *Pindaric* poem."—*Priestley cor.* "He'll *surprise* you."—*Frost cor.* "Unequalled archer! why was this concealed?"—*Knowles.* "So *gayly* curl the waves before each dashing prow."—*Byron cor.* "When is a *diphthong* called a proper *diphthong?*"—*Inf. S. Gram. cor.* "How many *Esses* would *the word* then end with? Three; for it would be *goodness's.*"—*Id.* "*Qu.* What is a *triphthong?* *Ans.* A triphthong is a *coalition* of three vowels *in one syllable.*"—*Bacon cor.* "The verb, noun, or pronoun, is referred to the preceding terms taken *separately.*"—*Murray.* "The cubic foot of matter which occupies the *centre* of the globe."—*Cardell cor.* "The wine imbibes *oxygen,* or the acidifying principle, from the air."—*Id.* "Charcoal, sulphur, and nitre, make *gunpowder.*"—*Id.* "It would be readily understood, that the thing so *labelled* was a bottle of Madeira wine."—*Id.* "They went their ways, one to his farm, an other to his *merchandise.*"—*Matt. xxii,* 5. "A *diphthong* is the union of two vowels, *both in one syllable.*"—*Russell cor.* "The professors of the *Mohammedan* religion are called Mussulmans."—*Maltby cor.* "This shows that *let* is not a *mere* sign of the imperative mood, but a real verb."—*Id.* "Those *preterits* and participles which are first mentioned in the list, seem to be the most eligible."—*Murray's Gram.* 107; *Fisk's,* 81; *Ingersoll's,* 103. "Monosyllables, for the most part, are compared by *er* and *est;* and *dissyllables,* by *more* and *most.*"—*Murray's Gram.* p. 47. "This termination, added to a noun or an adjective, changes it into a verb: as, *modern,* to *modernize;* a *symbol,* to *symbolize.*"—*Churchill cor.* "An *Abridgement* of Murray's Grammar, with additions from Webster, Ash, Tooke, and others."—*Maltby's Gram.* p. 2. "For the sake of occupying the room more *advantageously,* the subject of Orthography is merely glanced at."—*Nutting cor.* "So contended the accusers of Galileo."—*O. B. Peirce cor.* Murray says, "They were *travelling post* when he met them."—*Murray's Gram.* 8vo, p. 69. "They *fulfil* the only purposes for which they were designed."—*Peirce cor.*—See *Webster's Dict.* "On the *fulfilment* of the event."—*Peirce, right.* "*Fullness* consists in expressing every idea."—*Id.* "Consistently with *fullness* and perspicuity."—*Peirce cor.* "The word *veriest* is a *regular adjective;* as, 'He is the *veriest* fool on earth.'"—*Wright cor.* "The sound will *recall* the idea of the object."—*Hiley cor.* "Formed for great *enterprises.*"—*Hiley's Gram.* p. 113. "The most important rules and definitions are printed in large type, *Italicized.*"—*Hart cor.* "HAMLETED, *a.,* accustomed to a hamlet, countrified."—*Webster,* and *Worcester.* "Singular, *spoonful, cupful, coachful, handful;* plural, *spoonfuls, cupfuls, coachfuls, handfuls.*"—*Worcester's Universal and Critical Dict.*

"Between superlatives and following names,
Of, by *grammatic* right, a station claims."—*Brightland cor.*

THE KEY.—PART II.—ETYMOLOGY.

CHAPTER I.—PARTS OF SPEECH.

The first chapter of Etymology, as it exhibits only the distribution of words into the ten Parts of Speech, contains no false grammar for correction. And it may be here observed, that as mistakes concerning the forms, classes, or modifications of words, are chiefly to be found in *sentences,* rather than in any separate exhibition of the terms; the quotations of this kind, with which I have illustrated the principles of etymology, are many of them such as might perhaps with more propriety be denominated *false syntax.* But, having examples enough at hand to show the ignorance and carelessness of authors in every part of grammar, I have thought it most advisable, so to distribute them as to leave no part destitute of this most impressive kind of illustration. The examples exhibited as *false etymology,* are as distinct from those which are called *false syntax,* as the nature of the case will admit.

CHAPTER II.—ARTICLES.

CORRECTIONS RESPECTING A, AN, AND THE.

LESSON I.—ARTICLES ADAPTED.

"Honour is *a* useful distinction in life."—*Milnes cor.* "No writer, therefore, ought to foment *a* humour of innovation."—*Jamieson cor.* "Conjunctions [generally] require a situation between the things of which they form *a* union."—*Id.* "Nothing is more easy than to mistake *a* u for an *a*."—*Tooke cor.* "From making so ill *a* use of our innocent expressions."—*Penn cor.* "To grant thee *a* heavenly and incorruptible c.own of glory."—*Sewel cor.* "It in no wise follows, that such *a* one was able to predict."—*Id.* "With *a* harmless patience, they have borne most heavy oppressions."—*Id.* "My attendance was to make me *a* happier man."—*Spect. cor.* "On the wonderful nature of *a* human mind."—*Id.* "I have got *a* hussy of a maid. who is most craftily given to this."—*Id.* "Argus is said to have had *a* hundred eyes, some of which were always awake."—*Stories cor.* "Centiped, having *a* hundred feet; centennial, consisting of *a* hundred years."—*Town cor.* "No good man, he thought, could be *a* heretic."— *Gilpin cor.* "As, a Christian, an infidel, *a* heathen."—*Ash cor.* "Of two or more words, usually joined by *a* hyphen."—*Blair cor.* "We may consider the whole space of *a* hundred years as time present."—*Ingersoll's Gram.* p. 138. "In guarding against such *a* use of meats and drinks."—*Ash cor.* "Worship is *a* homage due from man to his Creator."—*Monitor cor.* "Then *a* eulogium on the deceased was pronounced."—*Grimshaw cor.* "But for Adam there was not found *a* help meet for him."—*Bible cor.* "My days are consumed like smoke, and my bones are burned as *a* hearth."—*Id.* "A foreigner and *a* hired servant shall not eat thereof."— *Id.* "The hill of God is as the hill of Bashan; *a* high hill, as the hill of Bashan."—*Id.* "But I do declare it to have been *a* holy offering, and such *a* one too as was to be once for all."—*Penn cor.* "*A* hope that does not make ashamed those that have it."—*Barclay cor.* "Where there is not *a* unity, we may exercise true charity."—*Id.* "Tell me, if in any of these such *a* union can be found?"—*Dr. Brown cor.*

"Such holy drops her tresses steeped,
　　Though 'twas *a* hero's eye that weeped."—*Sir W. Scott cor.*

LESSON II.—ARTICLES INSERTED.

"This veil of flesh parts the visible and *the* invisible world."—*Sherlock cor.* "The copulative and *the* disjunctive conjunctions operate differently on the verb."—*L. Murray cor.* "Every combination of *a* preposition and *an* article with the noun."—*Id.* "*Either* signifies, 'the one or the other:' *neither* imports, 'not either;' that is, 'not *the* one nor the other.'"—*Id.* "A noun of multitude may have a pronoun or *a* verb agreeing with it. either of the singular number or *of the* plural."—*Bucke cor.* "*The* principal copulative conjunctions are, *and, as, both, because, for, if, that, then, since.*"—*Id.* "The two real genders are the masculine and *the* feminine."—*Id.* "In which a mute and a liquid are represented by the same character, *th.*"—*Gardiner cor.* "They said, John *the* Baptist hath sent us unto thee."—*Bible cor.* "They indeed remember the names of *an* abundance of places."—*Spect. cor.* "Which created a great dispute between the young and *the* old men."—*Goldsmith cor.* "Then shall be read the Apostles' or *the* Nicene Creed."— *Com. Prayer cor.* "The rules concerning the perfect tenses and *the* supines of verbs are Lily's." —*K. Henry's Gr. cor.* "It was read by the high and the low, the learned and *the* illiterate."— *Dr. Johnson cor.* "Most commonly, both the pronoun and *the* verb are understood."—*Buchanan cor.* "To signify the thick and *the* slender enunciation of tone."—*Knight cor.* "The difference between a palatial and *a* guttural aspirate is very small."—*Id.* "Leaving it to waver between the figurative and *the* literal sense."—*Jamieson cor.* "Whatever verb will not admit of both an active and *a* passive signification."—*Alex. Murray cor.* "*The* is often set before adverbs in the comparative or *the* superlative degree."—*Id. and Kirkham cor.* "Lest any should fear the effect of such a change, upon the present or *the* succeeding age of writers."—*Fowle cor.* "In all these measures, the accents are to be placed on *the* even syllables; and every line is, in general, *the* more melodious, as this rule is *the* more strictly observed."—*L. Murray et al. cor.* "How many numbers do nouns appear to have? Two; the singular and *the* plural."—*R. C. Smith cor.* "How many persons? Three; the first, *the* second, and *the* third."—*Id.* "How many cases? Three; the nominative, *the* possessive, and *the* objective."—*Id.*

"Ah! what avails it me, the flocks to keep,
　Who lost my heart while I preserv'd *the* sheep:"—or, "*my sheep.*"

LESSON III.—ARTICLES OMITTED.

"The negroes are all *descendants* of Africans."—*Morse cor.* "*Sybarite* was applied as a term of reproach to a man of dissolute manners."—*Id.* "The original signification of *knave* was *boy.*" —*Webster cor.* "The meaning of these will be explained, for greater clearness and precision."— *Bucke cor.* "What sort of *noun* is *man?* A noun substantive, common."—*Buchanan cor.* "Is *what* ever used as three kinds of *pronoun?*"—*Kirkham's Question cor.* [Answer: "No; as a pronoun, it is either relative or interrogative."—*G. Brown.*] "They delighted in *having done it,* as well as in the doing of it."—*R. Johnson cor.* "*Both parts* of this rule are exemplified in the following sentences."—*Murray cor.* "He has taught them to hope for *an other and better* world." —*Knapp cor.* "It was itself only preparatory to a future, *better,* and perfect revelation."—*Keith cor.* "*Es* then makes *an other and distinct* syllable."—*Brightland cor.* "The eternal clamours of a *selfish and factious* people."—*Dr. Brown cor.* "To those whose taste in elocution is *but little* cultivated."—*Kirkham cor.* "They considered they had but a *sort of gourd* to rejoice in."—*Bennet cor.* "Now there was *but one such bough,* in a spacious and shady grove."—*Bacon cor.* "Now the absurdity of this latter supposition will go a great way *towards making* a man easy."—*Collier cor.* "This is true of *mathematics, with which taste* has but little to do."—*Todd cor.* "To stand prompter to a *pausing yet ready* comprehension."—*Rush cor.* "Such an obedience as the *yoked and tortured* negro is compelled to yield to the whip of the overseer."—*Chalmers cor.* "For the gratification of a *momentary and unholy* desire."—*Wayland cor.* "The body is slenderly put together; the mind, a rambling *sort of thing.*"—*Collier cor.* "The only nominative to the verb, is *officer.*"—*Murray cor.* "And though *in general* it ought to be admitted, &c."—*Blair cor.* "Philosophical writing admits of a polished, *neat,* and elegant style."—*Id.* "But notwithstanding this defect, Thomson is a strong *and beautiful* describer."—*Id.* "So should he be sure to be ransomed, *and many* poor men's lives *should be* saved."—*Shak. cor.*

"Who felt the wrong, or feared it, *took* alarm,
　　Appealed to law. and Justice lent her arm."—*Pope cor.*

LESSON IV.—ARTICLES CHANGED.

"To enable us to avoid too frequent *a* repetition of the same word."—*Bucke cor.* "The former is commonly acquired in *a* third part of the time."—*Burn cor.* "Sometimes *an* adjective becomes a substantive ; and, *like other substantives, it may have an* adjective *relating* to it: as, '*The chief good.*'"—*L. Murray cor.* "An articulate sound is *a* sound of the human voice, formed by the organs of speech."—*Id.* "*A tense* is a distinction of time : there are six tenses."—*Maunder cor.* "In this case, *an* ellipsis of the last article would be improper."—*L. Murray cor.* "Contrast *always* has the effect to make each of the contrasted objects appear in *a* stronger light."—*Id. et al.* "These remarks may serve to show the great importance of *a* proper use of the *articles*."—*Lowth et al. cor.* "'Archbishop Tillotson,' says *the* author of *a* history of England, ' died in this year.'"—*Dr. Blair cor.* "Pronouns are used in stead of substantives, to prevent too frequent *a* repetition of them."—*A. Murray cor.* "THAT, as a relative, seems to be introduced to *prevent* too frequent a repetition of WHO and WHICH."—*Id.* "A pronoun is a word used in stead of a noun, to *prevent* too frequent a repetition of it."—*L. Murray cor.* "THAT is often used as a relative, to prevent too frequent a repetition of WHO and WHICH."—*Id. et al. cor.* "His knees smote one against *the* other."—*Logan cor.* "They stand now on one foot, then on *the* other."—*W. Walker cor.* "The Lord watch between thee and me, when we are absent one from *the* other."—*Bible cor.* "Some have enumerated ten parts of speech, making *the* participle a distinct part."—*L. Murray cor.* "Nemesis rides upon *a* hart because *the* hart is a most lively creature."—*Bacon cor.* "The transition of the voice from one vowel of the diphthong to *the* other."—*Dr. Wilson cor.* "So difficult it is, to separate these two things one from *the* other."—*Dr. Blair cor.* "Without *a* material breach of any rule."—*Id.* "The great source of *looseness* of style, in opposition to precision, is *an* injudicious use of *what* are termed *synonymous words.*" —*Blair cor.* ; also *Murray.* "Sometimes one article is improperly used for *the* other."—*Sanborn cor.*

> "Satire of sense, alas! can Sporus feel ?
> Who breaks a butterfly upon *the* wheel ?"—*Pope cor.*

LESSON V.—MIXED EXAMPLES.

"He hath no delight in the strength of *a* horse."—*Maturin cor.* "The head of it would be *a* universal monarch."—*Butler cor.* "Here they confound the material and the formal object of faith."—*Barclay cor.* "The Irish [Celtic] and *the Scottish* Celtic are one language ; the Welsh, *the* Cornish, and *the* Armorican, are *an* other."—*Dr. Murray cor.* "In *a* uniform and perspicuous manner."—*Id.* "SCRIPTURE, *n.* Appropriately, and by way of distinction, the books of the Old and *the* New Testament ; the Bible.'"—*Webster cor.* "In two separate volumes, entitled, 'The Old and New Testaments.'"—*Wayland cor.* "The Scriptures of the Old and *the* New Testament, contain a revelation from God."—*Id.* "Q has *always* a u after it ; which, in words of French origin, is not sounded."—*Wilson cor.* "What should we say of such *a* one ? that he is regenerate ? No."—*Hopkins cor.* "Some grammarians subdivide *the* vowels into simple and compound."—*L. Murray cor.* "Emphasis has been *divided* into the weaker and *the* stronger emphasis."—*Id.* "Emphasis has also been divided into *the* superior and the inferior emphasis."—*Id.* "Pronouns must agree with their antecedents, or *the* nouns which they represent, in gender, number, and person."—*Merchant cor.* "The adverb *where* is often used improperly, for *a* relative pronoun and *a* preposition" : as, "Words *where* [in which] the *h* is not silent."—*Murray.* p. 31. "The termination *ish* imports diminution, or a lessening *of* the quality."—*Merchant cor.* "In this train, all their verses proceed : one half of *a* line always answering to the other."—*Dr. Blair cor.* "To a height of prosperity and glory, unknown to any former age."—*L. Murray cor.* "*Hwilc*, who, which, such as, such *a* one, is declined as follows."—*Gwilt cor.* "When a vowel precedes *the* y, *s* only is required to form *the* plural ; as, *day, days.*"—*Bucke cor.* "He is asked what sort of *word* each is ; whether a primitive, *a* derivative, or *a* compound."—*British Gram. cor.* "It *is* obvious, that neither the second, *the* third, nor *the* fourth chapter of Matthew, is the first ; consequently, there are not '*four first* chapters.'"—*Churchill cor.* "Some thought, which a writer wants *the* art to introduce in its proper place."—*Dr. Blair cor.* "Groves and meadows are *the* most pleasing in the spring."—*Id.* "The conflict between the carnal and *the* spiritual mind, is often long."—*Gurney cor.* "A Philosophical Inquiry into the Origin of our Ideas of the Sublime and *the* Beautiful."—*Burke cor.*

> "Silence, my muse ! make not these jewels cheap,
> Exposing to the world too large *a* heap."—*Waller cor.*

CHAPTER III.—NOUNS.

CORRECTIONS IN THE MODIFICATIONS OF NOUNS.

LESSON I.—NUMBERS.

"All *the* ablest of the Jewish *rabbies* acknowledge it."—*Wilson cor.* "Who has thoroughly imbibed the system of one or other of our Christian *rabbies.*"—*Campbell cor.* "The seeming *singularities* of reason soon wear off."—*Collier cor.* "The chiefs and *arikies,* or priests, have the power of declaring a place or object taboo."—*Balbi cor.* "Among the various tribes of this family' are the Pottawatomies, the *Sauks* and Foxes, or *Saukies* and Ottogamies."—*Id.* "The Shawnees, Kickapoos, Menom'onies, *Miamies,* and Delawares, are of the same region."—*Id.* "The Mohegans and *Abenaquies* belonged also to this family."—*Id.* "One tribe of this family, the *Winnebagoes,* formerly resided near lake Michigan."—*Id.* "The other tribes are the Ioways, the Ottoes, the *Missouries,* the Quapaws."—*Id.* "The great Mexican family comprises the Aztecs, the Toltecs, and the *Tarascoes.*"—*Id.* "The Mulattoes are born of negro and white parents ; the *Zamboes,* of Indians and Negroes."—*Id.* "To have a place among the Alexanders, the Cæsars, the *Louises,* or the *Charleses,*—the scourges and butchers of their fellow-creatures." —*Burgh cor.* "Which was the notion of the Platonic philosophers and the Jewish *rabbies.*"—*Id.*

" That they should relate to the whole body of *virtuosoes*."—*Cobbett cor*. " What *thanks* have ye ? for sinners also love those that love them."—*Bible cor*. " There are five ranks of nobility ; dukes, *marquises*, earls, viscounts, and barons."—*Balbi cor*. "Acts which were so well known to the two *Charleses*."—*Payne cor*. "*Courts-martial* are held in all parts, for the trial of the blacks."—*Observer cor*. " It becomes a common noun, and may have the plural number ; as, the two *Davids*, the two *Scipios*, the two *Pompeys*."—*Staniford cor*. " The food of the rattlesnake is birds, squirrels, *hares*, rats, and reptiles."—*Balbi cor*. "And let *fowls* multiply in the earth."—*Bible cor*. " Then we reached the *hillside*, where eight *buffaloes* were grazing."—*Martineau cor*. " CORSET, *n*. a *bodice* for a woman."—*Worcester cor*. "As, the *Bees*, the *Cees*, the *Double-ues*."—*Peirce cor*. " Simplicity is the *mean* between ostentation and rusticity."—*Pope cor*. " You have disguised yourselves like *tipstaffs*."—*Gil Blas cor*. " But who, that *has* any taste, can endure the incessant quick returns of the *alsoes*, and the *likewises*, and the *moreovers*, and the *howevers*, and the *notwithstandings* ! "—*Campbell cor*.

" Sometimes, in mutual sly disguise,
Let *ays* seem *noes*, and *noes* seem *ays*."—*Gay cor*.

LESSON II.—CASES.

" For whose *name's* sake, I have been made willing."—*Penn cor*. " Be governed by your conscience, and never ask any *body's* leave to be honest."—*Collier cor*. " To overlook *nobody's* merit or misbehaviour."—*Id*. "And Hector at last fights his way to the stern of *Ajax's* ship."—*Coleridge cor*. " Nothing is lazier, than to keep *one's* eye upon words without heeding their meaning."—*Museum cor*. " Sir William *Jones's* division of the day."—*Id*. "I need only refer here to *Voss's* excellent account of it."—*Id*. " The beginning of *Stesichorus's* palinode has been preserved."—*Id*. " Though we have *Tibullus's* elegies, there is not a word in them about Glycĕra."—*Id*. " That Horace was at *Thaliarchus's* country-house."—*Id*. " That *Sisyphus's* foot-tub should have been still in existence."—*Id*. " How everything went on in Horace's closet, and in *Mecenas's* antechamber."—*Id*. " Who, for elegant *brevity's* sake, put a participle for a verb."—*W. Walker cor*. " The *country's* liberty being oppressed, we have no more to hope."—*Id*. "A brief but true account of this *people's* principles."—*Barclay cor*. "As, The *Church's* peace, or, The peace of the Church ; *Virgil's* Æneid, or, The Æneid of Virgil."—*Brit. Gram. cor*. " Which, with Hubner's Compend, and *Wells's* Geographia Classica, will be sufficient."—*Burgh cor*. " Witness Homer's speaking horses, scolding goddesses, and Jupiter enchanted with *Venus's* girdle."—*Id*. Dr. *Watts's* Logic may with success be read to them and commented on."—*Id*. " Potter's Greek, and Kennet's Roman Antiquities, *Strauchius's* and *Helvicus's* Chronology."—*Id*. " SING. *Alice's* friends, *Felix's* property ; PLUR. The Alices' friends, The Felixes' property."—*Peirce cor*. " Such as *Bacchus's* company—at *Bacchus's* festivals."—*Ainsworth cor*. "*Burns's* inimitable *Tam o' Shanter* turns entirely upon such a circumstance."—*Scott cor*. " Nominative, men ; Genitive, [or Possessive,] *men's* ; Objective, men."—*Cutler cor*. "*Men's* happiness or misery is *mostly* of their own making."—*Locke cor*. " That your *son's clothes* be never made strait, especially about the breast."—*Id*. "*Children's* minds are narrow and weak."—*Id*. " I would not have little children much tormented about *punctilios*, or niceties of breeding."—*Id*. " To fill his head with suitable *ideas*."—*Id*. " The *Burgusdisciuses* and the Scheiblers did not swarm in those days, as they do now."—*Id*. " To see the various ways of dressing—a *calf's* head ! "—*Shenstone cor*.

" He puts it on, and for *decorum's* sake
Can wear it e'en as gracefully as she."—*Cowper cor*.

LESSON III.—MIXED EXAMPLES.

" Simon the *wizard* was of this religion too."—*Bunyan cor*. " MAMMODIES, *n*. Coarse, plain, India muslins."—*Webster cor*. " Go on from single persons to families, that of the *Pompeys* for instance."—*Collier cor*. " By which the ancients were not able to account for *phenomena*."—*Bailey cor*. "After this I married a *woman* who had lived at Crete, but a *Jewess* by birth."—*Josephus cor*. " The very *heathens* are inexcusable for not *worshiping* him."—*Todd cor*. " Such poems as *Camoens's* Lusiad, Voltaire's Henriade, &c."—*Dr. Blair cor*. " My learned correspondent writes a word in defence of large *scarfs*."—*Spect. cor*. " The forerunners of an apoplexy are *dullness*, *vertigoes*, tremblings."—*Arbuthnot cor*. " *Vertigo*, [in Latin,] changes the *o* into *inēs*, making the plural *vertignēs* : " [not so, in English.]—*Churchill cor*. "*Noctambulo*, [in Latin,] changes the *o* into *ōnēs*, making the plural *noctambulōnēs* : " [not so, in English.]—*Id*. " What shall we say of *noctambuloes*? It is the regular English plural."—*G. Brown*. " In the curious fretwork of rocks and *grottoes*."—*Blair cor*. "*Wharf* makes the plural *wharfs*, according to the best usage."—*G. Brown*. "A few *cents'* worth of *macaroni* supplies all their wants."—*Balbi cor*. " C sounds hard, like *k*, at the end of a word or *syllable*."—*Blair cor*. " By which the *virtuosoes* try The magnitude of every lie."—*Butler cor*. "*Quartoes*, *octavoes*, shape the lessening pyre."—*Pope cor*. " Perching within square royal *roofs*."—*Sidney cor*. "*Similes* should, even in poetry, be used with moderation."—*Dr. Blair cor*. "*Similes* should never be taken from low or mean objects."—*Id*. " It were certainly better to say, ' The *House of Lords*,' than, ' The *Lords' House*.'"—*Murray cor*. " Read your answers. *Units'* figure ? ' Five.' *Tens'* ? ' Six.' *Hundreds'* ? ' Seven.'"—*Abbott cor*. "Alexander conquered *Darius's* army."—*Kirkham cor*. " Three *days'* time was requisite, to prepare matters."—*Dr. Brown cor*. " So we say, that *Cicero's* style and *Sallust's* were not one ; nor *Cæsar's* and *Livy's* ; nor *Homer's* and *Hesiod's* ; nor *Herodotus's* and *Thucydides's* ; nor *Euripides's* and *Aristophanes's* ; nor *Erasmus's* and *Budæus's*."—*Puttenham cor*. " LEX (i. e. *legs*, a *law*,) is no other than our *ancestors'* past participle *læg*, laid *down*."—*Tooke cor*. "*Achaia's* sons at Ilium slain for the *Atridæ's* sake."—*Cowper cor*. " The *corpses* of her senate manure the fields of Thessaly."—*Addison cor*.

" Poisoning, without regard of fame or fear :
And spotted *corpses* load the frequent bier."—*Dryden cor*.

CHAPTER IV. —ADJECTIVES.
CORRECTIONS IN THE FORMS OF COMPARISON, &c.
LESSON I.—DEGREES.

" I have the real excuse of the *most honest* sort of bankrupts."—*Cowley corrected.* " The *most honourable* part of talk, is, to give him one of the *most modest* of his own proverbs."—*Barclay cor.* " Our language is now, certainly, *more proper* and more natural, than it was formerly."—*Burnet cor.* " Which will be of the *greatest* and *most frequent* use to him in the world."—*Locke cor.* " The same is notified in the *most considerable* places in the diocese."—*Whitgift cor.* " But it was the *most dreadful* sight that ever I saw."—*Bunyan cor.* " Four of the *oldest*, soberest, and discreetest of the brethren, chosen for the occasion, shall regulate it."—*Locke cor.* " Nor can there be any clear understanding of any Roman author, especially of *more ancient* time, without this skill."—*W. Walker cor.* " Far the *most learned* of the Greeks." —*Id.* " The *more learned* thou art, the humbler be thou."—*Id.* " He is none of the best, or *most honest*."—*Id.* " The *most proper* methods of communicating it to others."—*Burn cor.* " What heaven's great King hath *mightiest* to send against us."—*Milton cor.* " Benedict is not the *most unhopeful* husband that I know."—*Shakspeare cor.* " That he should immediately do all the meanest and *most trifling* things himself."—*Ray cor.* " I shall be named among the *most renown'd* of women."—*Milton cor.* " Those have the *most inventive* heads for all purposes."— *Ascham cor.* " The *more wretched* are the contemners of all helps."—*B. Johnson cor.* " I will now deliver a few of the *most proper* and *most natural* considerations that belong to this piece."— *Wotton cor.* " The *most mortal* poisons practised by the West Indians, have some mixture of the blood, fat, or flesh of man."—*Bacon cor.* " He so won upon him, that he rendered him one of the *most faithful* and most affectionate allies the Medes ever had."—*Rollin cor.* " ' You see before you,' says he to him, ' the most devoted servant, and the *most faithful* ally, you ever had.' " —*Id.* " I chose the *most flourishing* tree in all the park."—*Cowley cor.* " Which he placed, I think, some centuries *earlier* than *did* Julius Africanus afterwards."—*Bolingbroke cor.* " The Tiber, the *most noted* river of Italy."—*Littleton cor.*

" To *farthest* shores th' ambrosial spirit flies."—*Pope.*
——" That what she wills to do or say,
Seems wisest, *worthiest*, discreetest, best."—*Milton cor.*

LESSON II.—MIXED EXAMPLES.

" During the *first three or four* years of its existence."—*Taylor cor.* " To the first of these divisions, my *last ten* lectures have been devoted."—*Adams cor.* " There are, in the twenty-four states, not *fewer* than sixty thousand common schools."—*J. O. Taylor cor.* " I know of nothing which gives teachers *more* trouble, *than* this want of firmness."—*Id.* " I know of nothing *else* that throws such darkness over the line which separates right from wrong."—*Id.* " None need this purity and *this* simplicity of language and thought, *more than does the instructor of a common school.*"—*Id.* " I know of no *other* periodical that is so valuable to the teacher, as the Annals of Education."—*Id.* " Are not these schools of the highest importance ? Should not every individual feel *a deep* interest in their character and condition ? "—*Id.* " If instruction were made a *liberal* profession, teachers would feel more sympathy for one an *other*."—*Id.* " Nothing is *more interesting to* children, *than* novelty, *or* change."—*Id.* " I know of no *other* labour which affords so much happiness as the teacher's."—*Id.* " Their school exercises are the most pleasant and agreeable *duties*, that they engage in."—*Id.* " I know of no exercise *more* beneficial to the pupil *than* that of drawing maps."—*Id.* " I know of nothing in which our district schools are *more* defective, *than* they are in the art of teaching grammar."—*Id.* " I know of *no other branch of knowledge*, so easily acquired, as history."—*Id.* " I know of *no other school exercise* for which pupils usually have such an abhorrence, as *for* composition."—*Id.* " There is nothing *belonging to* our fellow-men, which we should respect *more sacredly than* their good name."—*Id.* " *Surely*, never any *other creature* was so unbred as that odious man."—*Congreve cor.* " In the dialogue between the mariner and the shade of the *deceased*."—*Phil. Museum cor.* " These master-works would still be less excellent and *finished*."—*Id.* " Every attempt to staylace the language of *polished* conversation, renders our phraseology inelegant and clumsy."—*Id.* " Here are a few of the *most unpleasant* words that ever blotted paper."—*Shakspeare cor.* " With the most easy *and obliging* transitions."—*Broome cor.* " Fear is, of all affections, the *least apt* to admit any conference with reason."—*Hooker cor.* " Most chymists think glass a body *less destructible* than gold itself."—*Boyle cor.* " To part with *unhacked* edges, and bear back our barge undinted."— *Shak. cor.* " Erasmus, who was an *unbigoted* Roman Catholic, was transported with this passage." —*Addison cor.* " There are no *fewer* than five words, with any of which the sentence might have terminated."—*Campbell cor.* " The *ones* preach Christ of contention ; but the *others*, of love." Or, " The *one party* preach," &c.—*Bible cor.* " Hence we find less discontent and *fewer* heart-burnings, than where the subjects are unequally burdened."—*H. Home, Ld. Kames, cor.*

" The serpent, *subtlest* beast of all the field."—*Milton, P. L., B. ix, l. 86.*
" Thee, Serpent, *subtlest* beast of all the field,
I knew, but not with human voice indued."—*Id. P. L., B. ix, l. 560.*
" How much more grievous would our lives appear,
To reach th' *eight-hundreth*, than the eightieth year ! "—*Denham cor.*

LESSON III.—MIXED EXAMPLES.

" Brutus engaged with Aruns ; and so fierce was the attack, that they pierced *each other* at the same time."—*Lempriere cor.* " Her two brothers were, one after *the other*, turned into stone."— *Kames cor.* " Nouns are often used as adjectives ; as, A *gold* ring, a *silver* cup."—*Lennie cor.* " Fire and water destroy *each other*."—*Wanostrocht cor.* " Two negatives, in English, destroy *each other*, or are equivalent to an affirmative."—*Lowth, Murray, et al. cor.* " Two negatives destroy *each other*, and are generally equivalent to an affirmative."—*Kirkham and Felton cor.* " Two negatives destroy *each other*, and make an affirmative."—*Flint cor.*   "Two negatives destroy *each other*, being equivalent to an affirmative."—*Frost cor.*   "Two objects, resembling *each other*, are presented to the imagination."—*Parker cor.*   "Mankind, in order to hold converse with *one an other*, found it necessary to give names to objects."—*Kirkham cor.*   "*Derivative* words are *formed* from *their primitives* in various ways."—*Cooper cor.*   "There are many *different* ways of deriving words *one from an other*."—*Murray cor.*   "When several verbs *have a joint construction* in a sentence, the auxiliary is usually *expressed* with the first *only*."—*Frost cor.*   "Two or more verbs, having the same nominative case, and *coming in immediate succession*, are also separated by *the comma*."— *Murray et al. cor.*   "Two or more adverbs, *coming in immediate succession*, must be separated by *the comma*."—*Iidem.*   "If, however, the *two* members are very closely connected, the comma is *unnecessary*."—*Iidem.*   "Gratitude, when exerted towards *others*, naturally produces a very pleasing sensation in the mind of a *generous* man."—*L. Murray cor.*   "Several verbs in the infinitive mood, *coming in succession*, and having a common dependence, are also divided by commas."— *Comly cor.*   "The several words of which it consists, have so near a relation *one to an other*."— *Murray et al. cor.*   "When two or more verbs, or two or more adverbs,* *occur in immediate succession*, and have a common dependence, they must be separated by *the comma*."—*Comly cor.*   "*One noun* frequently *follows an other*, both meaning the same thing."—*Sanborn cor.*   "And these two tenses may thus answer *each other*."—*R. Johnson cor.*   "Or some other relation which two objects bear to *each other*."—*Jamieson cor.*   "That the heathens tolerated *one an other*, is allowed."—*A. Fuller cor.*   "And yet these two persons love *each other* tenderly."—*E. Reader cor.*   "In the six *hundred* and first year."—*Bible cor.*   "Nor is this arguing of his, *any thing* but a *reiterated* clamour."—*Barclay cor.*   "In *several* of them the inward life of Christianity is to be found."—*Id.*   "Though Alvarez, *Despauter*, and *others, do not allow it* to be plural."—*R. Johnson cor.*   "Even the most *dissipated* and shameless blushed at the sight."—*Lempriere cor.*   "We feel a *higher* satisfaction in surveying the life of animals, *than* [in *contemplating*] that of vegetables."—*Jamieson cor.*   "But this man is so *full-fraught* with malice."—*Barclay cor.*   "That I suggest some things concerning the *most proper* means."—*Dr. Blair cor.*

"So, hand in hand, they passed, the loveliest pair
    That ever *yet* in love's embraces met."—*Milton cor.*
"Aim at *supremacy; without such height*,
    Will be for thee no sitting, or not long."—*Id. cor.*

CHAPTER V.— PRONOUNS.
CORRECTIONS IN THE FORMS AND USES OF PRONOUNS.
LESSON I.—RELATIVES.

"*While* we attend to this pause, every appearance of *singsong* must be carefully *avoided*."— *Murray cor.*   "For thou shalt go to all *to whom* I shall send thee."—*Bible cor.*   "Ah! how happy would it have been for me, had I spent in retirement these twenty-three years *during which* I have possessed my kingdom."—*Sanborn cor.*   "In the same manner *in which* relative pronouns and their antecedents are usually parsed."—*Id.*   "Parse or *explain* all the other nouns *contained in the examples, after the very* manner *of* the word *which is parsed for you*."—*Id.*   "The passive verb will always *have* the person and number that *belong to* the verb *be*, of which it is in part composed."—*Id.*   "You have been taught that a verb must always *agree in* person and number *with its* subject or nominative."—*Id.*   "A relative pronoun, also, must always *agree in* person, *in* number, and even *in* gender, *with* its antecedent."—*Id.*   "The *answer* always *agrees* in case *with the pronoun* which asks the question."—*Id.*   "One sometimes represents an antecedent noun, in the definite manner of a personal pronoun." †—*Id.*   "The mind, being carried forward to the time *at which* the event *is to happen*, easily conceives it to be present."—*Id.*   "SAVE and SAVING are [*seldom to be*] parsed in the manner *in which* EXCEPT and EXCEPTING are [commonly explained]."— *Id.*   "Adverbs qualify *verbs*, or modify *their* meaning, *as* adjectives *qualify* nouns [and describe things.]"—*Id.*   "The third person singular of verbs, *terminates in s* or *es, like* the plural number of nouns."—*Id.*   "He saith further: that, 'The apostles did not baptize anew such persons *as* had been baptized with the baptism of John.'"—*Barclay cor.*   "For we *who* live,"—or, "For we *that are alive*, are always delivered unto death for Jesus' sake."—*Bible cor.*   "For they *who* believe in God, must be careful to maintain good works."—*Barclay cor.*   "Nor yet of those *who* teach things *that* they ought not, for filthy lucre's sake."—*Id*   "So as to hold such bound in heaven *as* they bind on earth, and such loosed in heaven *as* they loose on earth."—*Id.*   "Now, if it be an evil, to do any thing out of strife; then such things *as* are seen so to be done, are they not to be avoided and forsaken?"—*Id.*   "All such *as* do not satisfy themselves with the superficies of religion."—*Id.*   "And he is the same in subs^tance, *that* he was upon earth,—*the same* in spirit, soul, and body."—*Id.*   "And those that do not thus, are such, *as* the Church of Rome can have no charity *for*."   Or: "And those that do not thus, are *persons toward* whom the Church of Rome can have no charity."—*Id.*   "Before his book, he *places* a great list of *what* he accounts the blasphemous assertions of the Quakers."—*Id.*   "And this is *what* he should have proved."—*Id.*   "Three of *whom* were at that time actual students of philosophy in the university."—*Id.*   "Therefore it is not lawful for any *whomsoever* * * * to force the consciences of others."—*Id.*   "*Why were* the former days better than these?"—*Bible cor.*   "In the same manner *in which*"—or, better, "*Just as*—the term *my* depends on the name *books*."—*Peirce cor.*   "*Just as* the term HOUSE depends on the [preposition *to*, understood after the *adjective*] NEAR."—*Id.*   "James died on the day *on which* Henry returned."—*Id.*

* This is the doctrine of Murray, and his hundred copyists; but it is by no means generally true. It is true of adverbs, only when they are connected by conjunctions; and seldom applies to *two* words, unless the conjunction which may be said to connect them, be suppressed and understood.—G. BROWN.

† Example: "Imperfect articulation comes not so much from bad *organs*, as from the abuse of good *ones*."— *Porter's Analysis.* Here *ones* represents *organs*, and prevents unpleasant repetition.—G. BROWN.

LESSON II.—DECLENSIONS.

"OTHER makes the plural OTHERS, when it is found without *its* substantive."—*Priestley cor.* "But *his, hers, ours, yours,* and *theirs,* have evidently the form of the possessive case."—*Lowth cor.* "To the Saxon possessive cases, *hire, ure, eower, hira,* (that is, *hers, ours, yours, theirs,*) we have added the *s,* the characteristic of the possessive case of nouns."—*Id.* "Upon the name of Jesus Christ our Lord, both *theirs* and *ours.*"—*Friends cor.* "In this place, *His* is clearly preferable either to *Her* or to *Its.*"—*Harris cor.* "That roguish leer of *yours* makes a pretty woman's heart ache."—*Addison cor.* "Lest by any means this liberty of *yours* become a stumbling-block." *Bible cor.* "First person: Sing. I, *my* or mine, me; Plur. we, *our* or ours, us."—*Wilbur and Livingston cor.* "Second person: Sing. thou, *thy* or thine, thee; Plur. ye or you, *your* or yours, you."—*Iid.* "Third person: Sing. she, *her* or hers, her; Plur. they, *their* or theirs, them."—*Iid.* "So shall ye serve strangers in a land that is not *yours.*"—*ALGER, BRUCE, ET AL.: Jer.* v, 19. "Second person, Singular: Nom. *thou,* Poss. *thy* or thine, Obj. *thee.*"—*Frost cor.* "Second person, Dual: Nom. Gyt, ye two; Gen. Incer, of *you* two; Dat. Inc, incrum, to *you* two; Acc. Inc, *you* two; Voc. Eala inc, O ye two; Abl. Inc, incrum, from *you* two."—*Gwilt cor.* "Second person, Plural: Nom. Ge, ye; Gen. Eower, of *you;* Dat. Eow, to *you;* Acc. Eow, *you;* Voc. Eala ge, O ye; Abl. Eow, from *you.*"—*Id.* "These words are, *mine, thine, his, hers, ours, yours, theirs,* and *whose.*"—*Cardell cor.* "This house is *ours,* and that is *yours. Theirs* is very commodious."—*Murray's Gram.* p. 55. "And they shall eat up *thy* harvest, and thy bread: they shall eat up thy flocks and *thy* herds." *Bible cor.* "*Whoever* and *Whichever* are thus declined: Sing. Nom. whoever, Poss. *whosever,* Obj. whomever; Plur. Nom. whoever, Poss. *whosever,* Obj. whomever. Sing. Nom. whichever, Poss. (*wanting,*) Obj. whichever; Plur. Nom. whichever, Poss. (*wanting,*) Obj. whichever."— *Cooper cor.* "The compound personal pronouns are thus declined: Sing. Nom. myself, Poss. (*wanting,*) Obj. myself; Plur. Nom. ourselves, Poss. (*wanting,*) Obj. ourselves. Sing. Nom. thyself or yourself, Poss. (*wanting,*) Obj. thyself, &c."—*Perley cor.* "Every one of us, each for *himself,* laboured to recover him."—*Sidney cor.* "Unless when ideas of their opposites manifestly suggest *themselves.*"—*Wright cor.* "It not only exists in time, but is *itself* time."—*Id.* "A position which the action *itself* will palpably *confute.*"—*Id.* "A difficulty sometimes presents *itself.*"— *Id.* "They are sometimes explanations in *themselves.*"—*Id.* "*Ours, Yours, Theirs, Hers, Its.*"— *Barrett cor.*

"*Theirs,* the wild *chase* of false felicities ;
His, the composed possession of the true."—*Young, N. Th.,* N. viii, l. 1100.

LESSON III.—MIXED EXAMPLES.

"It is the boast of Americans, without distinction of parties, that their government is the most free and perfect *that* exists on the earth."—*Dr. Allen cor.* "Children *that* are dutiful to their parents, enjoy great prosperity."—*Sanborn cor.* "The scholar *that* improves his time, sets an example worthy of imitation."—*Id.* "Nouns and pronouns *that* signify the same person, place, or thing, agree in case."—*Cooper cor.* "An interrogative sentence is one *that* asks a question."—*Id.* "In the use of words and phrases *that* in point of time relate to each other, *the order of time* should be *duly regarded.*"—*Id.* "The same observations *that show* the effect of the article *upon* the participle, appear to be applicable [also] to the pronoun and participle."—*Murray cor.* "The reason *why* they have not the same use of them in reading, may be traced to the very defective and erroneous method in which the art of reading is taught."—*Id.* "*Ever since* reason began to exert her powers, thought, during our waking hours, has been active in every breast, without a moment's suspension or pause."—*Id. et al. cor.* "In speaking of *such as* greatly delight in the same."—*Pope cor.* "Except *him* to *whom* the king shall hold out the golden sceptre, that he may live."—*Bible cor.* "But the same day on *which* Lot went out of Sodom, it rained fire and brimstone from heaven, and destroyed them all."—*Bible cor.* "In the next place, I will explain several *constructions* of nouns and pronouns, *that* have not yet come under our notice"—*Kirkham cor.* "Three natural distinctions of time are all *that* can exist."—*Hall cor.* "We have exhibited such only as are obviously distinct ; and *thew* seem to be sufficient, and not more than sufficient."—*Murray et al. cor.* "*The parenthesis* encloses a *phrase or clause that* may be omitted without materially injuring the connexion of the other members."—*Hall cor.* "Consonants are letters *that* cannot be sounded without the aid of a vowel."—*Bucke cor.* "Words are not *mere* sounds, but sounds *that* convey a meaning to the mind."—*Id.* "Nature's postures are always easy ; and, *what* is more, nothing but your own will can put you out of them."—*Collier cor.* "Therefore ought we to examine our *own selves,* and prove our *own selves.*"—*Barclay cor.* "Certainly, it had been much more natural, to have divided Active verbs into *Immanent,* or those *whose* action is terminated *within itself,* and *Transient,* or those *whose* action is terminated in something without *itself.*"—*R. Johnson cor.* "This is such an advantage as no other lexicon will afford."—*Dr. Taylor cor.* "For these reasons, such liberties are taken in the Hebrew tongue, with those words *which* are of the most general and frequent use."—*Pike cor.* "While we object to the *laws which* the antiquarian in language would impose on us, we must *also* enter our protest against those *authors who* are too fond of innovations."— *L. Murray cor.*

CHAPTER VI. — VERBS.

CORRECTIONS IN THE FORMS OF VERBS.

LESSON I.—PRETERITS.

"In speaking on a matter which *touched* their hearts."—*Phil. Museum cor.* "Though Horace *published* it some time after."—*Id.* "The best subjects with which the Greek models *furnished* him."—*Id.* "Since he *attached* no thought to it."—*Id.* "By what slow steps the Greek alphabet *reached* its perfection."—*Id.* "Because Goethe *wished* to erect an affectionate memorial."—*Id.* "But the Saxon forms soon *dropped* away."—*Id.* "It speaks of all the towns that *perished* in the ge of Philip."—*Id.* "This *enriched* the written language with new words."—*Id.* "He merely *furnished* his friend with matter for laughter."—*Id.* "A cloud arose, and *stopped* the light."—*Swift* or. "She *slipped* spadillo in her breast."—*Id.* "I *guessed* the hand."—*Id.* "The tyrant *stripped* me to the skin; My skin he *flayed*, my hair he *cropped*; At head and foot my body *lopped.*" —*Id.* "I see the greatest owls in you, That ever *screeched* or ever flew."—*Id.* "I *sat* with delight, From morning till night."—*Id.* "Dick nimbly *skipped* the gutter."—*Id.* "In at the pantry door this morn I *slipped.*"—*Id.* "Nobody living ever *touched* me, but you."—*W. Walker cor.* 'Present, I ship; *Preterit*, I shipped; *Perf. Participle*, shipped."—*A. Murray cor.* "Then the :ing arose, and *tore* his garments."—*Bible cor.* "When he *lifted* up his foot, he knew not where ıe should set it next."—*Bunyan cor.* "He *lifted* up his spear against eight hundred, whom he lew at one time."—*Bible cor.* "Upon this chaos *rode* the distressed ark."—*Burnet cor.* "On vhose foolish honesty, my practices *rode* easy."—*Shakspeare cor.* "That form of the first or rimogenial Earth, which *rose* immediately out of chaos."—*Burnet cor.* "Sir, how *came* it, you ıave *helped* to make this rescue ?"—*Shak. cor.* "He *swore* he *would* rather lose all his father's mages, than that table."—*Peacham cor.* "When our language *dropped* its ancient terminations." —*Dr. Murray cor.* "When themselves they *vilified.*"—*Milton cor.* "But I *chose* rather to do hus."—*Barclay cor.* "When he *pleaded* (or *pled*) against the parsons."—*Hist. cor.* "And he hat saw it, *bore* record." Or : "And he that saw it, *bare* record."—*John*, xix, 35. "An irreguar verb has one more variation ; as, drive, drivest, [*driveth*,] drives, drove, *drovest*, driving, driven." —*Matt. Harrison cor.* "Beside that village, Hannibal *pitched* his camp."—*W. Walker cor.* "He *etched* it from Tmolus."—*Id.* "He *supped* with his morning-gown on."—*Id.* "There *stamped* ıer sacred name."—*Barlow cor.*

"*Fix'd* on the view the great discoverer stood,
And thus *address'd* the messenger of good."—*Barlow cor.*

LESSON II.—MIXED EXAMPLES.

"Three freemen *were on trial*"—or, "*were receiving their trial*—at the date of our last information."—*Editor cor.* "While the house *was building*, many of the tribe arrived."—*Cox cor.* 'But a foundation has been laid in Zion, and the church *is built*—(or, *continues to be built*—) ıpon it."—*The Friend cor.* "And one fourth of the people are *receiving education.*"—*E. I. Mag.* or. "The present [*tense*,] or that [*form of the verb*] which [*expresses what*] is now *doing.*"—*Beck* or. "A new church, called the Pantheon, is *about* being completed, in an expensive style."— *Thompson cor.* "When I last saw him, he *had* grown considerably."—*Murray cor.* "I know vhat a rugged and dangerous path I *have* got into."—*Duncan cor.* "You *might as well* preach ease o one on the rack."—*Locke cor.* "Thou hast heard me, and *hast* become my salvation."—*Bible* or. "While the Elementary Spelling-Book *was preparing* (or, *was in progress of preparation*) for ıhe press."—*Cobb cor.* "Language *has* become, in modern times, more correct."—*Jamieson cor.* 'If the plan *has* been executed in any measure answerable to the author's wishes."—*Robbins cor.* 'The vial of wrath is still *pouring* out on the seat of the beast."—*Christian Ex. cor.* "Christianity ıad become the generally-adopted and established religion of the whole Roman Empire."—*Gurey cor.* "Who wrote before the first century *had* elapsed."—*Id.* "The original and analogical 'orm *has* grown quite obsolete."—*Louth cor.* "Their love, and their hatred, and their envy, *have* ıerished."—*Murray cor.* "The poems *had* got abroad, and *were* in a great many hands."— *Waller cor.* "It is more harmonious, as well as more correct, to say, ' The bubble *is ready to* ·urst.' "—*Cobbett cor.* "I *drove* my suitor from his mad humour of love."—*Shak. cor.* "Se viriiter expedivit.—*Cic.* He *has played* the man."—*Walker cor.* "Wilt thou kill me, as thou *didst* he Egyptian yesterday ?"—*Bible cor.* "And we, *methought*, [or *thought I*,] looked up to him from ur hill."—*Cowley cor.* "I fear thou *dost* not think *so* much of the best things as thou *ought.*"— *Memoir cor.* "When this work was commenced."—*Wright cor.* "Exercises and *a* Key to this vork are *about* being prepared."—*Id.* "James is loved by John."—*Id.* "Or that which is ex- ·ibited."—*Id.* "He *was* smitten."—*Id.* "In the passive *voice* we say, ' I am loved.' "—*Id.* ' Subjunctive Mood: If I *be* smitten, If thou *be* smitten, If he *be* smitten."—*Id.* "I *shall* not be ·ble to convince you how superficial the reformation is."—*Chalmers cor.* "I said to myself, I *hall* be obliged to expose the folly."—*Chazotte cor.* "When Clodius, had he meant to return hat day to Rome, must have arrived."—*J. Q. Adams cor.* "That the fact has been done, *is* ·oing, or will be done."—*Peirce cor.* "Am I *to* be instructed ?"—*Wright cor.* "I *choose* him." —*Id.* "John, who *respected* his father, was obedient to his commands."—*Barrett cor.*

"The region *echoes* to the clash of arms."—*Beattie cor.*
"And *sitst* on high, and mak'st creation's top
Thy footstool ; and *beholdst* below thee—all."—*Pollok cor.*
"And see if thou *canst* punish sin and let
Mankind go free. Thou *failst*—be not surprised."—*Idem.*

LESSON III.—MIXED EXAMPLES.

"What follows, *might better have been* wanting altogether."—*Dr. Blair cor.* "This member of he sentence *might* much.better have been omitted altogether."—*Id.* "One or *the* other of them, herefore, *might* better have been omitted."—*Id.* "The whole of this last member of the senence *might* better have been dropped."—*Id.* "In this case, they *might* much better be omitted." —*Id.* "He *might* better have said ' the *productions.*'"—*Id.* "The Greeks *ascribed* the origin ıf poetry to Orpheus, Linus, and Musæus."—*Id.* "It *was* noticed long ago, that all these ıctitious names have the same number of syllables."—*Phil. Museum cor.* "When I found that ıe had committed nothing worthy of death, I *determined* to send him."—*Bible cor.* "I *would* ·ather be a door-keeper in the house of my God."—*Id.* "As for such, I wish the Lord *would open*

* From the force of habit, or to prevent the possibility of a false pronunciation, these ocular contractions are ıtill sometimes carefully made in printing poetry ; but they are not very important, and some modern authors, or ıeir printers, disregard them altogether. In correcting short poetical examples, I shall in general take no particu- lar pains to distinguish them from prose. All needful contractions however will be preserved, and sometimes lso a capital letter, to show where the author commenced a line.

their eyes." Or, better: "*May* the Lord *open* (or, I *pray* the Lord *to* open) their *eyes.*"—*Barclay cor.* "It would *have* made our *passage* over the river very difficult."—*Walley cor.* "We should not *have* been able to *carry* our great guns."—*Id.* "Others would *have* questioned our prudence, if we had."—*Id.* "Beware thou *be* not BECESARED; i. e., Beware that thou *do not* dwindle—or, *lest thou dwindle*—into a mere Cæsar."—*Harris cor.* "Thou *raisedst* (or, familiarly, thou *raised*) thy voice to record the stratagems of needy heroes."—*Arbuthnot cor.* "Life *hurries* off apace; thine is almost *gone* already."—*Collier cor.* "'How unfortunate has this accident made me!' *cries* such a one."—*Id.* "The muse that soft and sickly *woos* the ear."—*Pollok cor.* "A man *might* better relate himself to a statue."—*Bacon cor.* "I heard thee say but now, thou *liked* not that."—*Shak. cor.* "In my whole course of wooing, thou *criedst*, (or, familiarly, thou *cried*,) Indeed!'"—*Id.* "But our ears *have* grown familiar with '*I have wrote,*' '*I have drank,*' &c., which are altogether as ungrammatical."—*Lowth et al. cor.* "The court was in session before Sir Roger came."—*Addison cor.* "She *needs*—(or, if you please, *need*—) be no more with the jaundice *possessed.*"—*Swift cor.* "Besides, you found fault with our victuals one day when you *were* here."—*Id.* "If spirit of other sort, So minded, *hath* (or *has*) o'erleaped these earthy bounds."—*Milton cor.* "It *would* have been more rational to have *forborne* this."—*Barclay cor.* "A student is not master of it till he *has* seen all these."—*Dr. Murray cor.* "The said justice shall *summon* the party."—*Brevard cor.* "Now what *has* become of thy former wit and humour?"—*Spect. cor.* "Young stranger, whither *wanderst* thou?"—*Burns cor.* "Subj. Pres. If I love, If thou *love*, If he love. Imp. If I loved, If thou *loved*, If he loved."—*Merchant cor.* "Subj. If I do not love, If thou *do* not love, If he *do* not love."—*Id.* "If he *has* committed sins, they shall be forgiven him."—*Bible cor.* "Subjunctive Mood of the verb *to call*, second person singular: If thou *call*, (rarely, If thou *do call*,) If thou *called*."—*Hiley cor.* "Subjunctive Mood of the verb *to love*, second person singular: If thou love, (rarely, If thou do love,) If thou *loved*."—*Bullions cor.* "I *was*; thou wast; he, she, or it, was: We, you or ye, they, were."—*White cor.* "I taught, thou *taughtest*, (familiarly, thou *taught*,) he taught."—*Coar cor.* "We say, 'If it rain,' 'Suppose it rain,' 'Lest it rain,' 'Unless it rain.' This manner of speaking is called the SUBJUNCTIVE MOOD."—*Weld cor.* "He *has* arrived at what is deemed the age of manhood."—*Priestley cor.* "He *might* much better have let it alone."—*Tooke cor.* "He were better without it. Or: He *would* be better without it."—*Locke cor.* "*Hadst* thou not been by. Or: *If* thou *hadst* not been by. Or, in the familiar style: *Had* not thou been by."—*Shak. cor.* "I learned geography. Thou *learned* arithmetic. He learned grammar."—*Fuller cor.* "Till the sound *has* ceased."—*Sheridan cor.* "Present, die; Preterit, died; Perf. Participle *died.*"—*Six English Grammars corrected.*

> "Thou *bow'dst* thy glorious head to none, *fear'dst* none." Or:—
> "Thou *bowed* thy glorious head to none, *feared* none."—*Pollok cor.*
> "Thou *lookst* upon thy boy as though thou *guess'd* it."—*Knowles cor.*
> "As once thou *slept*, while she to lite was formed."—*Milton cor.*
> "Who finds the partridge in the puttock's nest,
> But may imagine how the bird was *killed?*"—*Shak. cor.*
> "Which might have well *become* the best of men."—*Idem cor.*

CHAPTER VII. — PARTICIPLES.

CORRECTIONS IN THE FORMS OF PARTICIPLES.

LESSON I.—IRREGULARS.

"Many of your readers have *mistaken* that passage."—*Steele cor.* "Had not my dog of a steward *run* away."—*Addison cor.* "None should be admitted, except he had *broken* his collar-bone thrice."—*Id.* "We could not know what was *written* at twenty."—*Waller cor.* "I have *written*, thou hast *written*, he has *written*; we have *written*, you have *written*, they have *written*."—*Ash cor.* "As if God had *spoken* his last words there to his people."—*Barclay cor.* "I had like to have *come* in that ship myself."—*Observer cor.* "Our ships and vessels being *driven* out of the harbour by a storm."—*Hutchinson cor.* "He will endeavour to write as the ancient author would have *written*, had he *written* in the same language."—*Bolingbroke cor.* "When his doctrines grew too strong to be *shaken* by his enemies."—*Atterbury cor.* "The immortal mind that hath *forsaken* her mansion."—*Milton cor.* "Grease that's *sweated* (or *sweat*) from the murderer's gibbet, throw into the flame."—*Shak. cor.* "The court also was *chidden* (or *chid*) for allowing such questions to be put."—*Stone cor.* "He would have *spoken.*"—*Milton cor.* "Words *interwoven* (or *interweaved*) with sighs found out their way."—*Id.* "Those kings and potentates who have *strived* (or *striven*.)"—*Id.* "That even Silence was *taken.*"—*Id.* "And envious Darkness, ere they could return, had *stolen* them from me."—*Id.* "I have *chosen* this perfect man."—*Id.* "I *shall* scarcely think you have *swum* in a gondola."—*Shak. cor.* "The fragrant brier was *woven* (or *weaved*) between."—*Dryden cor.* "Then finish what you have *begun.*"—*Id.* "But now the years a numerous train have *run.*"—*Pope cor.* "Repeats your verses *written* (or *writ*) on glasses."—*Prior cor.* "Who by turns have *risen.*"—*Id.* "Which from great authors I have *taken.*"—*Id.* "Even there he should have *fallen.*"—*Id.*

> "The sun has *ris'n*, and gone to bed,
> Just as if Partridge were not dead."—*Swift cor.*
> "And, though no marriage words are *spoken*,
> They part not till the ring is *broken.*"—*Swift cor.*

LESSON II.—REGULARS.

"When the word is *stripped* of all the terminations."—*Dr. Murray cor.* "Forgive him, Tom; his head is *cracked.*"—*Swift cor.* "For 'tis the sport, to have the engineer *hoised* (or *hoisted*) with his own petar."—*Shak. cor.* "As great as they are, I was *nursed* by their mother."—*Swift cor.* "If he should now be *cried* down since his change."—*Id.* "*Dipped* over head and ears—in

ebt.''—*Id.* "We see the nation's credit *cracked.*"—*Id.* "Because they find their pockets *picked.*"
—*Id.* "O what a pleasure *mixed* with pain!"—*Id.* "And only with her brother *linked.*"—*Id.*
"Because he ne'er a thought allowed, That might not be *confessed.*"—*Id.* "My love to Sheelah
more firmly *fixed.*"—*Id.* "The observations *annexed* to them will be intelligible."—*Phil.*
fusserum cor. "Those eyes are always *fixed* on the general principles."—*Id.* "Laborious conjectures will be *banished* from our commentaries."—*Id.* "Tiridates was dethroned, and Phraates
was *reestablished,* in his stead."—*Id.* "A Roman who was *attached* to Augustus."—*Id.* "Nor
should I have spoken of it, unless Baxter had *talked* about two such."—*Id.* "And the reformers
of language have generally *rushed* on."—*Id.* "Three centuries and a half had then *elapsed* since
the date."—*Ib.* "Of such criteria, as has been *remarked* already, there is an abundance."—*Id.*
"The English have *surpassed* every other nation in their services."—*Id.* "The party *addressed* is
next in dignity to the speaker."—*Harris cor.* "To which we are many times *helped.*"—*W. Walk-*
r cor. "But for him, I should have *looked* well enough to myself."—*Id.* "Why are you
vexed, Lady? why do frown?"—*Milton cor.* "Obtruding false rules *pranked* in reason's garb."
—*Id.* "But, like David *equipped* in Saul's armour, it is encumbered and oppressed."—*Camp-*
bell cor.

> "And when their merchants are blown up, and *cracked,*
> Whole towns are cast away in storms, and *wrecked.*"—*Butler cor.*

LESSON III.—MIXED EXAMPLES.

"The lands are *held* in free and common soccage."—*Trumbull cor.* "A stroke is *drawn* under
such words."—*Cobbett's Gr.,* 1st Ed. "It is *struck* even, with a strickle."—*W. Walker cor.* "Whilst
I was *wandering,* without any care, beyond my bounds."—*Id.* "When one would do something,
unless *hindered* by something present."—*R. Johnson cor.* "It is used potentially, but not so as
to be *rendered* by these signs."—*Id.* "Now who would dote upon things *hurried* down the stream
thus fast?"—*Collier cor.* "Heaven hath timely *tried* their growth."—*Milton cor.* "O! ye mistook, ye should have *matched* his wand."—*Id.* "Of true virgin here *distressed.*"—*Id.* "So that
they have at last come to be *substituted* in the stead of it."—*Barclay cor.* "Though ye have *lain*
among the pots."—*Bible cor.* "And, lo, in her mouth was an olive leaf *plucked* off."—*Scott's
Bible, and Alger's.* "Brutus and Cassius *Have ridden,* (or *rode,*) like madmen, through the gates
of Rome."—*Shak. cor.* "He shall be *spit upon.*"—*Bible cor.* "And are not the countries so over-
flowed still *situated* between the tropics?"—*Bentley.* "Not *tricked* and *frounced* as she was wont,
But *kerchiefed* in a comely cloud."—*Milton cor.* "To satisfy his rigour, *Satisfied* never."—*Id.*
"With him there *crucified.*"—*Id* "Th' earth cumbered, and the wing'd air *darked* with plumes."
—*Id.* "And now their way to Earth they had *descried.*"—*Id.* "Not so thick swarmed once the soil
Bedropped with blood of Gorgon."—*Id.* "And in a troubled sea of passion *tossed.*"—*Id.* "The
cause, alas! is quickly *guessed.*"—*Swift cor.* "The kettle to the top was *hoised,* or *hoisted.*"—*Id.*
"In chains thy syllables are *linked.*"—*Id.* "Rather than thus be *overtopped,* Would you not wish
their laurels *cropped?*"—*Id.* "The HYPHEN, or CONJOINER, is a little line *drawn* to connect
words, or parts of words."—*Cobbett cor.* "In the other manners of dependence, this general rule
is sometimes *broken.*"—*R. Johnson cor.* "Some intransitive verbs may be rendered transitive by
means of a preposition *prefixed* to them."—*Grant cor.* "Whoever now should place the accent
on the first syllable of *Valerius,* would set every body *a laughing.*"—*J. Walker cor.* "Being
mocked, scourged, *spit upon,* and crucified."—*Gurney cor.*

> "For rhyme in Greece or Rome was never known,
> Till barb'rous hordes those states had *overthrown.*"—*Roscommon cor.*

> "In my own Thames may I be *drowned,*
> If e'er I stoop beneath *the crowned.*"   Or thus:—

> "In my own Thames may I be *drown'd dead,*
> If e'er I stoop beneath a crown'd head."—*Swift cor.*

CHAPTER VIII.—ADVERBS.
CORRECTIONS RESPECTING THE FORMS OF ADVERBS.

"We can much *more easily* form the conception of a fierce combat."—*Blair corrected.* "When
he was restored *agreeably* to the treaty, he was a perfect savage."—*Webster cor.* "How I shall
acquit myself *suitably* to the importance of the trial."—*Duncan cor.* "Can any thing show your
Holiness how *unworthily* you treat mankind?"—*Spect. cor.* "In what other, *consistently* with
reason and common sense, can you go about to explain it to him?"—*Lowth cor.* "*Agreeably* to
this rule, the short vowel Sheva has two characters."—*Wilson cor.* "We shall give a *remarkably*
fine example of this figure."—See *Blair's Rhet.* p. 156. "All of which is most *abominably* false."
—*Barclay cor.* "He heaped up great riches, but passed his time *miserably.*"—*Murray cor.* "He
is never satisfied with expressing any thing clearly and *simply.*"—*Dr. Blair cor.* "Attentive only to
exhibit his ideas *clearly* and *exactly,* he appears dry."—*Id.* "Such words as have the most liquids
and vowels, glide the *most softly.*" Or: "Where liquids and vowels most abound, the utterance
is softest."—*Id.* "The simplest points, such as are *most easily* apprehended."—*Id.* "Too historical to be accounted a *perfectly* regular epic poem."—*Id.* "Putting after them the oblique
case, *agreeably* to the French construction."—*Priestley cor.* "Where the train proceeds with an
extremely slow pace."—*Kames cor.* "So as *scarcely* to give an appearance of succession."—*Id.*
"That concord between sound and sense, which is perceived in some expressions, *independently*
of artful pronunciation."—*Id.* "Cornaro had become very corpulent, *previously* to the adoption
of his temperate habits."—*Hitchcock cor.* "Bread, which is a solid, and *tolerably* hard, substance."—*Day cor.* "To command every body that was not dressed as *finely* as himself."—*Id.*
"Many of them have *scarcely* outlived their authors."—*J. Ward cor.* "Their labour, indeed, did
not penetrate very *deeply.*"—*Wilson cor.* "The people are *miserably* poor, and subsist on fish."
—*Hume cor.* "A scale, which I took great pains, some years *ago,* to make."—*Bucke cor.* "There

is no truth on earth *better* established *than* the truth of the Bible."—*Taylor cor.* " I know of no work *more* wanted *than* the one *which* Mr. Taylor has now furnished."—*Dr. Nott cor.* " And therefore their requests are *unfrequent* and reasonable."—*Taylor cor.* " Questions are *more easily* proposed, than answered rightly."—*Dillwyn cor.* " Often reflect on the advantages you possess, and on the source *from which* they are all derived."—*Murray cor.* " If there be no special rule which requires it to be put *further forward*."—*Milnes cor.* " The masculine and *the* neuter have the same dialect in all *the* numbers, especially when they end *alike*."—*Id.*

> "And children are more busy in their play
> Than those that *wiseliest* pass their time away."—*Butler cor.*

CHAPTER IX.—CONJUNCTIONS.
CORRECTIONS IN THE USE OF CONJUNCTIONS.

"A *Verb* is so called from the Latin *verbum*, a word."—*Bucke cor.* " References are often marked by letters *or* figures."—*Adam and Gould cor.* (1.) "A Conjunction is a word which joins words *or* sentences together."—*Lennie, Bullions, and Brace, cor.* (2.) "A Conjunction is used to connect words *or* sentences together."—*R. C. Smith cor.* (3.) "A Conjunction is used to connect words *or* sentences."—*Maunder cor.* (4.) " Conjunctions are words used to join words *or* sentences."—*Wilcox cor.* (5.) "A Conjunction is a word used to connect words *or* sentences."—*M'Culloch, Hart, and Day, cor.* (6.) "A Conjunction joins words *or* sentences together."—*Mackintosh and Hiley cor.* (7.) " The Conjunction joins words *or* sentences together."—*L. Murray cor.* (8.) " Conjunctions connect words *or* sentences to each other."—*Wright cor.* (9.) " Conjunctions connect words *or* sentences."—*Wells and Wilcox cor.* (10.) " The conjunction is a part of speech, used to connect words *or* sentences."—*Weld cor.* (11.) "A conjunction is a word used to connect words *or* sentences together."—*Fowler cor.* (12.) " Connectives are *particles that unite* words *or* sentences in construction."—*Webster cor.* " English Grammar is miserably taught in our district schools; the teachers know *little or nothing* about it."—*J. O. Taylor cor.* "Let, in stead of preventing *diseases*, you draw *them* on."—*Locke cor.* " The definite article *the* is frequently applied to adverbs in the comparative *or the* superlative degree."—*Murray et al. cor.* " When nouns naturally neuter are *assumed to be* masculine *or* feminine."—*Murray cor.* " This form of the perfect tense represents an action *as* completely past, *though* often *as done* at no great distance *of time, or at a time* not specified."—*Id.* " The *Copulative Conjunction* serves to connect *words or clauses, so as* to continue a sentence, by expressing an addition, a supposition, a cause, or a consequence."—*Id.* " The *Disjunctive Conjunction* serves, not only to continue a sentence by connecting its parts, but also to express opposition of meaning, *either real or nominal*."—*Id.* "*If* we open the volumes of our divines, philosophers, historians, or artists, we shall find that they abound with all the terms necessary to communicate *the* observations and discoveries *of their authors*."—*Id.* " When a disjunctive *conjunction* occurs between a singular noun or pronoun and a plural one, the verb is made to agree with the plural noun or pronoun."—*Murray et al. cor.* " Pronouns must always agree with their antecedents, *or* the nouns for which they stand, in gender and number."—*Murray cor.* " Neuter verbs do not *express action, and consequently do not* govern nouns *or* pronouns."—*Id.* "And the auxiliary of the past imperfect *as well as of the* present *tense*."—*Id.* " If this rule should not appear to apply to every example *that* has been produced, or to others which might be cited."—*Id.* "An emphatical pause is made, after something of peculiar moment has been said, *on* which we desire to fix the hearer's attention."—*Murray and Hart cor.* "An imperfect* phrase contains no assertion, *and* does not amount to a proposition, or sentence."—*Murray cor.* " The word was in the mouth of every one, *yet* its meaning may still be a secret."—*Id.* " This word was in the mouth of every one, *and yet*, as to its precise and definite idea, this may still be a secret."—*Harris cor.* " It cannot be otherwise, *because* the French prosody differs from that of every other European language."—*Smollett cor.* " So gradually *that it may be* engrafted on a subtonic."—*Rush cor.* " Where the Chelsea *and* Malden bridges now are." Or better : " Where the Chelsea *or the* Malden *bridge* now *is*."—*Judge Parker cor.* "Adverbs are words *added* to verbs, *to* participles, *to* adjectives, *or to* other adverbs."—*R. C. Smith cor.* " I could not have told you who the hermit was, *or* on what mountain he lived."—*Bucke cor.* "As and Be (for they are the same *verb*) naturally, or in themselves, signify *being*."—*Brightland cor.* " Words are *signs, either oral or written*, by which we express our thoughts, *or* ideas."—*Mrs. Bethune cor.* " His fears will detect him, *that* he shall not escape."—*Comly cor.* " *Whose* is equally applicable to persons *and to* things."—*Webster cor.* " One negative destroys an other, *so that two are* equivalent to an affirmative."—*Bullions cor.*

> " No sooner does he peep into the world,
> Than he has done his do."—*Hudibras cor.*

CHAPTER X.—PREPOSITIONS.
CORRECTIONS IN THE USE OF PREPOSITIONS.

" Nouns are often formed *from* participles."—*L. Murray corrected.* " What tenses are formed *from* the perfect participle ?"—*Ingersoll cor.* " Which tense is formed *from* the *present*, or root of the verb ?"—*Id.* " When a noun or a pronoun is placed before a participle, independently of the rest of the sentence."—*Churchill's Gram.* p. 348. " If the addition consists *of* two or more *words*."—*Mur. et al. cor.* " The infinitive mood is often made absolute, or used independently *of* the rest of the sentence."—*Lowth's Gram.* 80; *Churchill's*, 143; *Bucke's*, 96; *Merchant's*, 92. " For

---

* The word " *imperfect* " is not really necessary here ; for the declaration is true of *any phrase*, as this *name* is commonly applied.—G. Brown.

he great satisfaction of the reader, we *shall present a variety* of false constructions."—*Murray* or. "For your satisfaction, I *shall present you a variety* of false constructions."—*Ingersoll cor.* ' I shall here *present [to] you a scale* of derivation."—*Bucke cor.* "These two manners of representation in respect *to* number."—*Lowth and Churchill cor.* "There are certain adjectives which eem to be derived *from verbs, without* any variation."—*Lowth cor.* "Or disqualify us for receiving mstruction or reproof *from* others."—*Murray cor.* "For being more studious than any other pupil *m* the school."—*Id.* "Misunderstanding the directions, we lost our way."—*Id.* "These people educed the greater part of the island *under* their own power."—*Id.* "The principal accent distinguishes one syllable *of* a word from the rest."—*Id.* "Just numbers are in unison *with* the human mind."—*Id.* "We must accept of sound *in stead* of sense."—*Id.* "Also, *in stead of consultation*, he uses *consult.*"—*Priestley cor.* "This ablative seems to be governed *by* a preposition mderstood."—*W. Walker cor.* "*Lest* my father *hear of it*, by some means or other."—*Id.* "And, *besides*, my wife would hear *of it* by some means."—*Id.* "For insisting *on* a requisition so odious o them."—*Robertson cor.* "Based *on* the great self-evident truths of liberty and equality."—*Manual cor.* "Very little knowledge of their nature is acquired *from* the spelling-book."—*Murray cor.* "They do not cut it off: except *from* a few words; as, *due, duty,* &c."—*Id.* "Whether *passing at* such time, or then finished."—*Lowth cor.* "It hath disgusted hundreds *with* that confession."—*Barclay cor.* "But they have egregiously fallen *into* that inconveniency."—*Id.* "For *s* not this, to set nature *at* work ?"—*Id.* "And, surely, that which should set all its springs *at* work, *s* God."—*Atterbury cor.* "He could not end his treatise without a panegyric *on* modern learning." —*Temple cor.* "These are entirely independent *of* the modulation of the voice."—*J. Walker cor.* ' It is dear *at* a penny. It is cheap *at* twenty pounds."—*W. Walker cor.* "It will be despatched, *on* most occasions, without resting."—*Locke cor.* "*Oh* the pain, the bliss *of* dying!"—*Pope.* ' When the objects or the facts are presented *to him.*"—*R. C. Smith cor.* "I will now present you *a* synopsis."—*Id.* "The disjunctive conjunction connects *words or* sentences, *and suggests* an opposition of meaning, *more or less* direct."—*Id.* "I shall now present *to* you a few lines."—*Bucke cor.* "Common names, or substantives, are those which stand for things *assorted.*"—*Id.* "Adjectives, in the English language, *are not varied by* genders, numbers, or cases; *their only inflection is for* the degrees of comparison."—*Id.* "Participles are [little more than] adjectives formed *from* verbs."—*Id.* "I do love to walk out *on* a fine *summer* evening."—*Id.* "*Ellipsis,* when applied to grammar, is the elegant omission of one or more words *of* a sentence."—*Merchant cor.* "The *preposition to* is generally *required* before verbs in the infinitive mood, but *after* the following verbs it is properly omitted; namely, *bid, dare, feel, need, let, make, hear, see:* as, ' He *bid* me *do* it;' not, ' He *bid* me to do it.'"—*Id.* "The infinitive sometimes follows *than, for the latter term* of a comparison; as, [' Murray should have known *better than to write,* and Merchant, *better than to copy,* the text here corrected, or the ambiguous example they appended to it.']"—*Id.* "Or, by prefixing the *adverb more* or *less, for* the comparative, and *most* or *least, for* the superlative."—*Id.* "A pronoun is a word used *in stead* of a noun."—*Id.* "*From* monosyllables, the comparative is regularly formed by adding *r* or *er.*"—*Perley cor.* "He has particularly named these, in distinction *from* others."—*Harris cor.* "To revive the decaying taste *for* *ancient* literature."—*Id.* "He found the greatest difficulty *in* writing."—*Hume cor.*

"And the tear, that is wiped with a little address,
May be followed perhaps *by* a smile."—*Cowper, i, 216.*

CHAPTER XI.— INTERJECTIONS.
CORRECTIONS IN THE USE OF INTERJECTIONS.

"Of chance or change, *O* let not man complain."—*Beattie's Minstrel, B. ii, l. 1.* "O thou persecutor! *O* ye hypocrites!"—*Russell's Gram.* p. 92. "*O* thou my voice inspire, Who *touch'd* Isaiah's hallow'd lips with fire!"—*Pope's Messiah.* "*O happy we!* surrounded by so many blessings!"—*Merchant cor.* "*O thou who* art so unmindful of thy duty!"—*Id.* "If I am wrong, *O* teach my heart To find that better way."—*Murray's Reader,* p. 248. "*Heus!* evocate huc Davum."—*Ter.* "Ho! call Davus out hither."—*W. Walker cor.* "It was represented by an analogy (*O* how inadequate!) which was borrowed from the *ceremonies* of paganism."—*Murray cor.* "*O* that Ishmael might live before thee!"—*Friends' Bible;* and *Scott's.* "And he said unto him, *O* let not the Lord be angry, and I will speak."—*Alger's Bible;* and *Scott's.* "And he said *O* let not the Lord be angry."—*Alger; Gen.* xviii, 32. "*O* my Lord, let thy servant, I pray thee, speak a word."—*Scott's Bible.* "*O* Virtue! how amiable thou art!"—*Murray's Gram.* p. 128. "*Alas!* I fear for life."—See *Ib.* "*Ah* me! they little know How dearly I abide that boast so vain!"—See *Bucke's Gram.* p. 87. "*O* that I had digged myself a cave!"—*Fletcher cor.* "*Oh,* my good lord! thy comfort comes too late."—*Shak. cor.* "The vocative takes no article; it is distinguished thus: *O Pedro! O* Peter! *O Dios! O* God!"—*Bucke cor.* "*Oho!* But, the relative is always the same."—*Cobbett cor.* "*All-hail,* ye happy men!"—*Jaudon cor.* "*O* that I had wings like a dove!"—*Scott's Bible.* "*O glorious* hope! O *bless'd* abode!"—*O. B. Peirce's Gram.* p. 304. "*Welcome,* friends! how joyous is your presence!"—*T. Smith cor.* "*O* blissful days!—*but, ah!* how soon ye pass!"—*Parker and Fox cor.*

"*O* golden days! *O* bright unvalued hours!—
What bliss, did ye but know that bliss, were yours!"—*Barbauld cor.*

"*Ah* me! what perils do environ
The man that meddles with cold iron!"—*Hudibras cor.*

THE KEY.—PART III.—SYNTAX.

CHAPTER I.—SENTENCES.

The first chapter of Syntax, being appropriated to general views of this part of grammar, to an exhibition of its leading doctrines, and to the several forms of sentential analysis, with an application of the principal rules in parsing, contains no false grammar for correction; and has, of course, nothing to correspond to it, in this Key, except the title, which is here inserted for form's sake.

CHAPTER II.—ARTICLES.

CORRECTIONS UNDER THE NOTES TO RULE I.

UNDER NOTE I.—AN OR A.

"I have seen a horrible thing in the house of Israel."—*Bible cor.* "There is a harshness in the following sentences."—*Murray's Gram.*, 8vo. p. 152. "Indeed, such a one is not to be looked for."—*Dr. Blair cor.* "If each of you will be disposed to approve himself a useful citizen."—*Id.* "Land with them had acquired almost a European value."—*Webster cor.* "He endeavoured to find out a wholesome remedy."—*Neef cor.* "At no time have we attended a yearly meeting more to our own satisfaction."—*The Friend cor.* "Addison was not a humorist in character."—*Kames cor.* "Ah me! what a one was he!"—*Lily cor.* "He was such a one as I never saw before."—*Id.* "No man can be a good preacher, who is not a useful one."—*Dr. Blair cor.* "A usage which is too frequent with Mr. Addison."—*Id.* "Nobody joins the voice of a sheep with the shape of a horse."—*Locke cor.* "A universality seems to be aimed at by the omission of the article."—*Priestley cor.* "Architecture is a useful as well as a fine art."—*Kames cor.* "Because the same individual conjunctions do not preserve a uniform signification."—*Nutting cor.* "Such a work required the patience and assiduity of a hermit."—*Johnson cor.* "Resentment is a union of sorrow with malignity."—*Id.* "His bravery, we know, was a high courage of blasphemy."—*Pope cor.* "HYSSOP; an herb of bitter taste."—*Pike cor.*
    "On each enervate string they taught the note
    To pant, or tremble through a eunuch's throat."—*Pope cor.*

UNDER NOTE II.—AN OR A WITH PLURALS.

"At a *session* of the court, in March, it was moved," &c.—*Hutchinson cor.* "I shall relate my conversations, of which I kept memoranda."—*D. D'Ab. cor.* "I took an *other* dictionary, and with a *pair of* scissors cut out, for instance, the word ABACUS."—*A. B. Johnson cor.* "A person very meet seemed he for the purpose, *and about* forty-five years old."—*Gardiner cor.* "And it came to pass, about eight days after these sayings."—*Bible cor.* "There were slain of them about three thousand men."—*1 Macc. cor.* "Until I had gained the top of these white mountains, which seemed *other* Alps of snow."—*Addison cor.* "To make them satisfactory amends for all the losses they had sustained."—*Goldsmith cor.* "As a *first-fruit* of many that shall be gathered."—*Barclay cor.* "It makes indeed a little *amend*, (or *some amends*,) by inciting us to oblige people."—*Sheffield cor.* "A large and lightsome *back stairway* (or *flight of backstairs*) leads up to an entry above."—*Id.* "Peace of mind is an *abundant recompense* for *any* sacrifices of interest."—*Murray et al. cor.* "With such a spirit, and *such* sentiments, were hostilities carried on."—*Robertson cor.* "In the midst of a thick *wood*, he had long lived a voluntary recluse."—*G. B.* "The flats look almost like a young *forest*."—*Chronicle cor.* "As we went on, the country for a little *way* improved, but scantily."—*Freeman cor.* "Whereby the Jews were permitted to return into their own country, after a *captiv... of seventy years* at Babylon."—*Rollin cor.* "He did not go a great *way* into the country."—*Gilbert cor.*
    "A large *amend* by fortune's hand is made,
    And the lost Punic blood is well repay'd."—*Rowe cor.*

UNDER NOTE III.—NOUNS CONNECTED.

"As where a landscape is conjoined with the music of birds, and *the* odour of flowers."—*Kames cor.* "The last order resembles the second in the mildness of its accent, and *the* softness of its pause."—*Id.* "Before the use of the loadstone, or *the* knowledge of the compass."—*Dryden cor.* "The perfect participle and *the* imperfect tense ought not to be confounded."—*Murray cor.* "In proportion as the taste of a poet or *an* orator becomes more refined."—*Blair cor.* "A situation can never be intricate. *so* long as there is an angel, a devil, or a musician, to lend a helping hand."—*Kames cor.* "Avoid rude sports: an eye is soon lost, or *a* bone broken."—*Inst. p. 30.* "Not a word was uttered, nor a sign given."—*Ib.* "I despise not the doer, but *the* deed."—*Ib.* "For the sake of an easier pronunciation and *a* more agreeable sound."—*Lowth cor.* "The levity as well as *the* loquacity of the Greeks made them incapable of keeping up the true standard of history."—*Bolingbroke cor.*

UNDER NOTE IV.—ADJECTIVES CONNECTED.

"It is proper that the vowels be a long and *a* short one."—*Murray cor.* "Whether the person mentioned was seen by the speaker a long or *a* short time before."—*Id. et al.* "There are three genders; the masculine, *the* feminine, and *the* neuter."—*Adam cor.* "The numbers are two; *the* singular and *the* plural."—*Id. et al.* "The persons are three; *the* first, *the* second, and *the* third."—*Iidem.* "Nouns and pronouns have three cases; the nominative, *the* possessive, and *the* objective."—*Comly and Ing. cor.* "Verbs have five moods; namely, the infinitive, *the* indicative, *the* potential, *the* subjunctive, and *the* imperative."—*Bullions et al. cor.* "How many numbers have pronouns? Two, the singular and *the* plural."—*Bradley cor.* "To distinguish between an interrogative and *an* exclamatory sentence."—*Murray et al. cor.* "The first and *the* last of which are *compound* members."—*Lowth cor.* "In the last lecture, I treated of the concise and *the* diffuse, the nervous and *the* feeble manner."—*Blair cor.* "The passive and *the* neuter verbs I shall reserve for some future conversation."—*Ingersoll cor.* "There are two voices; the active and *the* passive."—*Adam et al. cor.* "WHOSE is rather the poetical than *the* regular genitive of WHICH." —*Johnson cor.* "To feel the force of a compound or *a* derivative word."—*Town cor.* "To preserve the distinctive uses of the copulative and *the* disjunctive conjunctions."—*Murray et al. cor.* "E has a long and *a* short sound, in most languages."—*Bicknell cor.* "When the figurative and *the* literal sense are mixed and jumbled together."—*Dr. Blair cor.* "The Hebrew, with which the Canaanitish and *the* Phœnician stand in connexion."—*Conant and Fowler cor.* "The languages of Scandinavia proper, the Norwegian and *the* Swedish."—*Fowler cor.*

UNDER NOTE V.—ADJECTIVES CONNECTED.

"The path of truth is a plain and safe path."—*Murray cor.* "Directions for acquiring a just and happy elocution."—*Kirkham cor.* "Its leading object is, to adopt a correct and easy method."—*Id.* "How can it choose but wither in a long and sharp winter?"—*Cowley cor.* "Into a dark and distant unknown."—*Dr. Chalmers cor.* "When the bold and strong, enslaved his fellow man."—*Chazotte cor.* "We now proceed to consider the things most essential to an accurate and perfect sentence."—*Murray cor.* "And hence arises a second and very considerable source of the improvement of taste."—*Dr. Blair cor.* "Novelty produces in the mind a vivid and agreeable emotion."—*Id.* "The deepest and bitterest feeling still is *that of* the separation."— *Dr. M'Rie cor.* "A great and good man looks beyond time."—See *Brown's Inst.* p. 283. "They made but a weak and ineffectual resistance."—*Ib.* "The light and worthless kernels will float." —*Ib.* "I rejoice that there is an other and better world."—*Ib.* "For he is determined to revise his work, and present to the *public an other and better* edition."—*Kirkham cor.* "He hoped that this title would secure *to* him an ample and independent authority."—*L. Murray cor. et al.* "There is, however, *an other and more limited* sense."—*J. Q. Adams cor.*

UNDER NOTE VI.—ARTICLES OR PLURALS.

"This distinction forms what are called the diffuse *style* and the concise."—*Dr. Blair cor.* "Two different modes of speaking, distinguished at first by the denominations of *the Attic manner* and *the Asiatic.*"—*Adams cor.* "But the great design of uniting the Spanish and French monarchies under the former, was laid."—*Bolingbroke cor.* "In the solemn and poetic styles, it [*do* or *did*] is often rejected."—*Allen cor.* "They cannot be, at the same time, in *both* the objective *case* and the nominative." Or: "They cannot be, at the same time, in *both* the objective and the nominative *case.*" Or: "They cannot be, at the same time, in the nominative *case,* and *also in the* objective." Or: "They cannot be, at the same time, in the nominative and objective cases."—*Murray's Gram.* 8vo, p. 148. Or, better: "They cannot be, at the same time, in *both* cases, the nominative and *the* objective."—*Murray et al. cor.* "They are named the positive, comparative, and superlative *degrees.*"—*Smart cor.* "Certain adverbs are capable of taking an inflection; namely, that of the comparative and superlative *degrees.*"—*Fowler cor.* "In the subjunctive mood, the present and imperfect tenses often carry with them a future sense."—*Murray et al. cor.* "The imperfect, the perfect, the pluperfect, and the first-future *tense,* of this mood, are conjugated like the same tenses of the indicative."—*Kirkham bettered.* "What rules apply in parsing personal pronouns of the second and third *persons?*"—*Id.* "Nouns are sometimes in the nominative or *the* objective case after the neuter verb *be,* or after an active-intransitive or *a* passive verb."—*Id.* "The verb varies its *ending* in the singular, in order to agree with its nominative, in the first, second, and third *persons.*"—*Id.* "They are identical in effect, with the radical and the vanishing *stress.*"—*Rush cor.* "In a sonnet, the first, *the* fourth, *the* fifth, and *the* eighth line, *usually* rhyme to *one an* other: so do the second, third, sixth, and seventh *lines;* the ninth,eleventh, and thirteenth *lines;* and the tenth, twelfth, and fourteenth *lines.*"—*Churchill cor.* "The iron and golden ages are run; youth and manhood are departed."—*Wright cor.* "If, as you say, the iron and the golden *age* are past, the youth and the manhood of the world."—*Id.* "An Exposition of the Old and New *Testaments.*"—*Henry cor.* "The names and order of the books of the Old and *the* New Testament."—*Bible cor.* "In the second and third *persons* of that tense." —*Murray cor.* "And who still unites in himself the human and the divine *nature.*"—*Gurney cor.* "Among whom arose the Italian, Spanish, French, and English languages."—*Murray cor.* "Whence arise these two *numbers,* the singular and the plural."—*Burn cor.*

UNDER NOTE VII.—CORRESPONDENT TERMS.

"Neither the definitions nor *the* examples are entirely the same *as* his."—*Ward cor.* "Because it makes a discordance between the thought and *the* expression."—*Kames cor.* "Between the adjective and *the* following substantive."—*Id.* "Thus Athens became both the repository and *the* nursery of learning."—*Chazotte cor.* "But the French pilfered from both the Greek and *the* Latin." —*Id.* "He shows that Christ is both the power and *the* wisdom of God."—*The Friend cor.* "That he might be Lord both of the dead and *of* the living."—*Bible cor.* "This is neither the obvious nor *the* grammatical meaning of his words."—*Blair cor.* "Sometimes both the accusative and *the* infinitive are understood."—*Adam and Gould cor.* "In some cases, we can use either the nominative or *the* accusative, promiscuously."—*Iidem.* "Both the former and *the* latter substantive are sometimes to be understood."—*Iidem.* "Many of *which* have escaped both the commentator and *the* poet himself."—*Pope cor.* "The verbs MUST and OUGHT, have both a present and *a* past signification."—*L. Murray cor.* "How shall we distinguish between the friends and *the* enemies of the government?"—*Dr. Webster cor.* "Both the *ecclesiastical* and *the* secular powers concurred in those measures."—*Dr. Campbell cor.* "As the period has a beginning and *an* end within itself, it implies an *inflection.*"—*J. Q. Adams cor.* "Such as ought to subsist between a principal and *an* accessory."—*Ld. Kames cor.*

UNDER NOTE VIII.—CORRESPONDENCE PECULIAR.

"When both the upward and the downward *slide* occur in *the sound of one* syllable, they are called a CIRCUMFLEX, or WAVE."—*Kirkham cor.* "The word THAT is used both in the nominative and in *the* objective *case.*"—*Sanborn cor.* "But, *in* all the other moods and tenses, both of the active and *of the* passive *voice,* [the verbs] are conjugated at large."—*Murray cor.* "Some writers on grammar, admitting the second-future *tense into* the indicative mood, *reject it from the* subjunctive."—*Id.* "*After* the same conjunction, *to use* both the indicative and the subjunctive *mood* in the same sentence, and *under* the same circumstances, seems to be a great impropriety."—*Id.* "The true distinction between the subjunctive and the indicative *mood* in this tense."—*Id.* "I doubt of his capacity to teach either the French or *the* English *language.*"—*Chazotte cor.* "It is as necessary to make a distinction between the active-transitive and the active-intransitive verb, as between the active and *the* passive."—*Nixon cor.*

UNDER NOTE IX.—A SERIES OF TERMS.

"As comprehending the terms uttered by the artist, the mechanic, and *the* husbandman."—*Chazotte cor.* "They may be divided into four classes ; the Humanists, *the* Philanthropists, *the* Pestalozzians and the *Productives.*"—*Smith cor.* "Verbs have six tenses ; the present, the imperfect, the perfect, the pluperfect, the *first-future,* and *the second-future.*"—*Murray et al. cor.* "Is is an irregular *neuter* verb, [from *be, was, being, been ;* found in] *the* indicative mood, present tense, third person, and singular number."—*Murray cor.* "SHOULD GIVE is an irregular *active-transitive* verb, [from *give, gave, giving, given ;* found] in the potential mood, imperfect tense, first person, and plural number."—*Id.* "Us is a personal pronoun, *of the* first person, plural number, *masculine gender,* and objective case."—*Id.* "THEM is a personal pronoun, of the third person, plural number, *masculine gender,* and objective case."—*Id.* "It is surprising that the Jewish critics, with all their skill in dots, points, and accents, never had the ingenuity to invent a *point* of interrogation, *a point* of admiration, or a parenthesis."—*Dr. Wilson cor.* "The fifth, sixth, seventh, and eighth *verses.*" Or : "The fifth, *the* sixth, *the* seventh, and the eighth *verse.*"—*O. B. Peirce cor.* "Substitutes have three persons ; the First, *the* Second, and the Third."—*Id.* "JOHN's is a proper noun, of the third person, singular number, masculine gender, and possessive case: and *is* governed by ' WIFE,' *according to* Rule " [4th, *which says,* &c.]—*Smith cor.* "Nouns, in the English language, have three cases ; the nominative, the possessive, and *the* objective."—*Bar. and Alex. cor.* "The potential mood has four tenses ; viz., the present, the imperfect, the perfect, and *the* pluperfect."—*Ingersoll cor.*

"Where Science, Law, and Liberty depend,
And own the patron, patriot, and friend."—*Savage cor.*

UNDER NOTE X.—SPECIES AND GENUS.

"*The* pronoun is a part of speech* put for *the* noun."—*Paul's Ac. cor.* "*The* verb is a part of speech declined with mood and tense."—*Id.* "*The* participle is a part of speech derived *from the* verb."—*Id.* "*The* adverb is a part of speech joined to verbs, [participles, adjectives, or other adverbs,] to declare their signification."—*Id.* "*The* conjunction is a part of speech *that joins words or* sentences together."—*Id.* "*The* preposition is a part of speech most commonly set before other parts."—*Id.* "*The* interjection is a part of speech which *betokens* a *sudden* emotion or passion of the mind."—*Id.* "*The* enigma, or riddle, is also a species of *allegory.*"—*Blair and Murray cor.* "We may take from the Scriptures a very fine example of *the* allegory."—*Iidem.* "And thus have you exhibited a sort of sketch of art."—*Harris cor.* "We may ' imagine a subtle kind of reasoning,' as Mr. Harris acutely observes."—*Churchill cor.* "But, before entering on these, I shall give one instance *of metaphor, very beautiful,* (or, one very *beautiful* instance of metaphor,) that I may show the figure to full advantage."—*Blair cor.* "Aristotle, in his Poetics, uses *metaphor* in this extended sense, for any figurative meaning *imposed* upon a word; as, *the* whole put for *a* part, or a part for *the* whole ; *a* species for the genus, or *the* genus for *a* species."—*Id.* "It shows what kind of apple it is of which we are speaking."—*Kirkham cor.* "Cleon was *an other* sort of man."—*Goldsmith cor.* "To keep off his right wing, as a kind of reserved body."—*Id.* "This part of speech is called *the* verb."—*Mack cor.* "What *sort* of thing is it ? "—*Hiley cor.* "What sort of charm do they possess ? "—*Bullions cor.*

"Dear Welsted, mark, in dirty hole,
That painful animal, the mole."—*Dunciad cor.*

UNDER NOTE XI.—ARTICLES NOT REQUISITE.

"Either thou or the boys were in fault."—*Comly cor.* "It may, at first view, appear to be too general."—*Murray et al. cor.* "When the verb has reference to future time."—*Iidem.* "No, they are the language of imagination, rather than of passion."—*Blair cor.* "The dislike of English Grammar, which has so generally prevailed, can be attributed only to the intricacy of [our] syntax."—*Russell cor.* "Is that ornament in good taste ? "—*Kames cor.* "There are not *many* fountains in good taste." Or : "Not many fountains are [ornamented] in good taste."—*Id.* "And I persecuted this way unto death."—*Bible cor.* "The sense of feeling can, indeed, give us a *notion* of extension."—*Addison, Spect. No. 411.* "The distributive *adjectives, each, every, either,* agree with nouns, pronouns, *or* verbs, of the singular number only."—*Murray cor.* "Expressing by one word, what might, by a circumlocution, be resolved into two or more words belonging to other parts of speech."—*Blair cor.* "By certain muscles which operate [in harmony, and] all at the same time."—*Murray cor.* "It is sufficient here to have observed thus much in general concerning them."—*Campbell cor.* "Nothing disgusts us sooner than empty pomp of language." —*Murray cor.*

UNDER NOTE XII.—TITLES AND NAMES.

"He is entitled to the appellation of *gentleman.*"—*G. Brown.* "Cromwell assumed the title of

---

* A part *of speech* is a *sort of words,* and not *one word only.* We cannot say, that every pronoun, or *every verb,* is a part *of speech,* because the parts of speech are *only ten.* But every pronoun, verb, or other word, is *a word ;* and, if we will refer to this genus, there is no difficulty in defining all the parts of speech in the *singular ;* as, "*A* pronoun is *a word* put for *a noun.*" Murray and others say, "*An Adverb is a part of speech,*" &c. "*A Conjunction is a part of speech,*" &c., which is the same as to say, "*One adverb is a sort of words,*" &c. This is a palpable absurdity.—G. BROWN.

Protector."—Id. "Her father is honoured with the title of *Earl."—Id.* "The chief magistrate is styled *President."—Id.* "The highest title in the state is that of *Governor."—Id.* "That boy is known by the name of *Idler."—Murray cor.* "The one styled *Mufti*, is the head of the ministers of law and religion."—*Balbi cor.* "Ranging all that possessed them under one class, he called that whole class *tree."—Blair cor.* "For *oak, pine,* and *ash*, were names of whole classes of objects."—*Id.* "It is of little importance whether we give to some particular mode of expression the name of *trope*, or of *figure."—Id.* "The collision of a vowel with itself is the most ungracious of all combinations, and has been doomed to peculiar reprobation under the name of *hiatus."—Adams cor.* "We hesitate to determine, whether *Tyrant* alone is the nominative, or whether the nominative includes the *word Spy."—Cobbett cor.* "Hence originated the customary abbreviation of *twelve months* into *twelvemonth;* of *seven nights* into *sennight;* of *fourteen nights* into *fortnight."—Webster cor.*

UNDER NOTE XIII.—COMPARISONS AND ALTERNATIVES.

"He is a better writer than reader."—*Allen.* "He was an abler mathematician than linguist." —*Id.* "I should rather have an orange than an apple."—*G. Brown.* "He was no less able *as* a negotiator, than courageous *as* a warrior."—*Smollett cor.* "In an epic poem, we pardon many negligences that would not be permitted in a sonnet or *an* epigram."—*Kames cor.* "That figure is a sphere, globe, or ball."—*Churchill's Gram.* p. 357.

UNDER NOTE XIV.—ANTECEDENTS TO WHO OR WHICH.

"*The* carriages which were formerly in use, were very clumsy."—"The place is not mentioned by *the* geographers who wrote at that time."—"*Those* questions which a person *puts to* himself in contemplation, ought to be terminated *with* points of interrogation."—*Mur. et al. cor.* "The work is designed for the use of *those* persons who may think it merits a place in their libraries." —*Mur. cor.* "That *those* who think confusedly, should express themselves obscurely, is not to be wondered at."—*Id.* "*Those* grammarians who limit the number to two, or three, do not reflect." —*Id.* "*The* substantives which end in *ian*, are those that signify profession." Or : "*Those* substantives which end in *ian*, are *such as* signify profession."—*Id.* "To these may be added *those* verbs which, among the poets, *usually* govern the dative."—*Adam and Gould cor.* "*The* consonants are *those* letters which cannot be sounded without the aid of a vowel."—*Bucke cor.* "To employ the curiosity of *persons skilled* in grammar : "—"of *those* who are skilled in grammar : "— "of *persons that* are skilled in grammar : "—"of *such* persons *as* are skilled in grammar : " or— "of *those* persons *who* are skilled in grammar."—*L. Murray cor.* "This rule refers only to *those* nouns and pronouns which have the same bearing, or relation."—*Id.* "So that *the* things which are seen, were not made of things *that* do appear."—*Bible cor.* "Man is an imitative creature ; he may utter *the* sounds which he has heard."—*Dr. Wilson cor.* "But *those* men whose business is wholly domestic, have little or no use for any language but their own."—*Dr. Webster cor.*

UNDER NOTE XV.—PARTICIPIAL NOUNS.

"Great benefit may be reaped from *the* reading of histories."—*Sewel cor.* "And some attempts were made towards *the* writing of history."—*Bolingbroke cor.* "It is *an* invading of the priest's office, for any other to offer it."—*Leslie cor.* "And thus far of *the* forming of verbs."— *W. Walker cor.* "And without *the* shedding of blood *there* is no remission."—*Bible cor.* "For *the* making of measures, we have the best method here in England."—*Printer's Gram. cor.* "This is really both *an* admitting and *a* denying at once."—*Butler cor.* "And hence the origin of *the* making of parliaments."—*Dr. Brown cor.* "Next thou objectest, that *the* having of saving light and grace presupposes conversion. But that I deny : for, on the contrary, conversion *presupposes the having of* light and grace."—*Barclay cor.* "They cried down *the* wearing of rings and other superfluities, as we do."—*Id.* "Whose adorning, let it not be that outward adorning, of *the* plaiting *of* the hair, and of *the* wearing of gold, or of *the* putting-on of apparel."—*Bible cor.* "In *the* spelling of derivative words, the *primitives* must be kept whole."—*Brit. Gr. and Buchanan's cor.* "And the princes offered for *the* dedicating of the altar."—*Numb. cor.* "Boasting is not only *a* telling of lies, but also *of* many unseemly truths."—*Sheffield cor.* "We freely confess that *the* forbearing of prayer in the wicked is sinful."—*Barclay cor.* "For *the* revealing of a secret, there is no remedy."—*G. Brown.* "He turned all his thoughts to *the* composing of laws for the good of the State."—*Rollin cor.*

UNDER NOTE XVI.—PARTICIPLES, NOT NOUNS.

"It is salvation to be kept from falling into a pit, as truly as to be taken out of it after falling in."—*Barclay cor.* "For in receiving and embracing the testimony of truth, they felt their souls eased."—*Id.* "True regularity does not consist in having but a single rule, and forcing every thing to conform to it."—*Phil. Museum cor.* "To the man of the world, this sound of glad tidings appears only an idle tale, and not worth attending to."—*Say cor.* "To be the deliverer of the captive Jews, by ordering their temple to be rebuilt," *&c.—Rollin cor.* "And for preserving them from being defiled."—*Discip. cor.* "A wise man will *forbear to show* any excellence in trifles."—*Kames cor.* "Hirsutus had no other reason for valuing a book."—*Johnson, and Wright, cor.* "To being heard with satisfaction, it is necessary that the speaker should deliver himself with ease." Perhaps better : "*To be* heard, &c." Or : "*In order to be* heard, &c."—*Sheridan cor.* "And, to the *end of* being well heard and clearly understood, a good and distinct articulation contributes more, than *can even the greatest* power of voice."—*Id.;*
"*Potential* purports, *having power or will;*
As, If you *would* improve you *should* be still."—*Tobitt cor.*

UNDER NOTE XVII.—VARIOUS ERRORS.

"For the same reason, a neuter verb cannot become passive."—*Lowth cor.* "A period is *a* whole sentence complete in itself."—*Id.* "A colon, or member, is a chief constructive part, or *the greatest* division, of *a* sentence."—*Id.* "A semicolon, or half-member, is a *smaller* constructive part, or a subdivision, of a sentence or of a member."—*Id.* "A sentence or a member is again subdivided into commas, or segments."—*Id.* "The first error that I would mention, is, too general an attention to the dead languages, with a neglect of our own tongue."—*Webster cor.* "One third of the importations would supply the demands of the people."—*Id.* "And especially in a grave style."—*Murray's Gram.* i, 178. "By too eager a pursuit, he ran a great risk of being disappointed."—*Murray cor.* "The letters are divided into vowels and consonants."—*Mur. et al. cor.* "The consonants are divided into mutes and semivowels."—*Iidem.* "The first of these forms is the most agreeable to the English idiom."—*Murray cor.* "If they gain, it is at too dear a rate."—*Barclay cor.* "A pronoun is a word used in stead of a noun, to prevent too frequent a repetition of it."—*Maunder cor.* "This vulgar error might perhaps arise from too partial a fondness for the Latin."—*Ash cor.* "The groans which too heavy a load extorts from her."—*Hitchcock cor.* "The numbers of a verb are, of course, the singular and the plural."—*Bucke cor.* "To brook no meanness, and to stoop to no dissimulation, are indications of a great mind."—*Murray cor.* "This mode of expression rather suits the familiar than the grave style."—*Id.* "This use of the word best suits a familiar and low style."—*Priestley cor.* "According to the nature of the composition, the one or the other may be predominant."—*Blair cor.* "Yet the commonness of such sentences prevents in a great measure too early an expectation of the end."—*Campbell cor.* "A eulogy or a philippic may be pronounced by an individual of one nation upon a subject of an other."—*J. Q. Adams cor.* "A French sermon is, for the most part, a warm animated exhortation."—*Blair cor.* "I do not envy those who think slavery no very pitiable lot."—*Channing cor.* "The auxiliary and the principal united constitute a tense."—*Murray cor.* "There are some verbs which are defective with respect to the persons."—*Id.* "In youth, habits of industry are the most easily acquired."—*Id.* "The apostrophe (') is used in place of a letter left out."—*Bullions cor.*

CHAPTER III.—CASES, OR NOUNS.

CORRECTIONS UNDER RULE II; OF NOMINATIVES.

"The whole need not a physician, but they that are sick."—*Bunyan cor.* "He will in no wise cast out whosoever cometh unto him." Better: "He will in no wise cast out any that come unto him."—*Hall cor.* "He feared the enemy might fall upon his men, who, he saw, were of their guard."—*Hutchinson cor.* "Whosoever shall compel thee to go a mile, go with him twain."—*Matt.* v, 41. "The ideas of the author have been conversant with the faults of other writers."—*Swift cor.* "You are a much greater loser than I, by his death." Or: "Thou art a much greater loser by his death than I."—*Id.* "Such peccadilloes pass with him for pious frauds."—*Barclay cor.* "In whom I am nearly concerned, and who, I know, would be very apt to justify my whole procedure."—*Id.* "Do not think such a man as I contemptible for my garb."—*Addison cor.* "His wealth and he bid adieu to each other."—*Priestley cor.* "So that, 'He is greater than I,' will be more grammatical than, 'He is greater than me.'"—*Id.* "The Jesuits had more interests at court than he."—*Id. and Smollett cor.* "Tell the Cardinal that I understand poetry better than he."—*Iid.* "An inhabitant of Crim Tartary was far more happy than he."—*Iid.* "My father and he have been very intimate since."—*Fair Am. cor.* "Who was the agent, and who, the object struck or kissed?"—*Mrs. Bethune cor.* "To find the person who, he imagined, was concealed there."—*Kirkham cor.* "He offered a great recompense to whosoever would help him." Better: "He offered a great recompense to any one who would help him."—*Hume and Pr. cor.* "They would be under the dominion, absolute and unlimited, of whosoever (or any one who) might exercise the right of judgement."—*Haynes cor.* "They had promised to accept whosoever (or any one who) should be born in Wales."—*Croker cor.* "We sorrow not as they that have no hope."—*Merwin cor.* "If he suffers, he suffers as they that have no hope."—*Id.* "We acknowledge that he, and he only, hath been our peacemaker."—*Gratton cor.* "And what can be better than he that made it?"—*Jenks cor.* "None of his school-fellows is more beloved than he."—*Cooper cor.* "Solomon, who was wiser than they all."—*Watson cor.* "Those who the Jews thought were the last to be saved, first entered the kingdom of God."—*Tract cor.* "A stone is heavy, and the sand weighty; but a fool's wrath is heavier than both."—*Bible cor.* "A man of business, in good company, is hardly more insupportable, than she whom they call a notable woman."—*Steele cor.* "The king of the Sarmatians, who we may imagine was no small prince, restored to him a hundred thousand Roman prisoners."—*Life of Anton. cor.* "Such notions would be avowed at this time by none but rosicrucians, and fanatics as mad as they."—*Campbell's Rhet.* p. 203. "Unless, as I said, Messieurs, you are the masters, and not I."—*Hall cor.* "We had drawn up against peaceable travellers, who must have been as glad as we to escape."—*Burnes cor.* "Stimulated, in turn, by their approbation and that of better judges than they, she turned to their literature with redoubled energy."—*Quarterly Rev. cor.* "I know not who else are expected."—*Scott cor.* "He is great, but truth is greater than we all." Or: "He is great, but truth is greater than any of us."—*H. Mann cor.* "He I accuse has entered." Or, by ellipsis of the antecedent, thus: "Whom I accuse has entered."—*Fowler cor.; also Shakspeare.*

> "Scotland and thou did each in other live."—*Dryden cor.*
> "We are alone; here's none but thou and I."—*Shak. cor.*
> "I rather would, my heart might feel your love,
> Than my unpleas'd eye see your courtesy."—*Shak. cor.*
> "Tell me, in sadness, who is she you love?"—*Shak. cor.*
> "Better leave undone, than by our deeds acquire
> Too high a fame, when he we serve 's away."—*Shak. cor.*

CORRECTIONS UNDER RULE III; OF APPOSITION.

"Now, therefore, come thou, let us make a covenant, thee and me."—*Bible cor.* "Now, therefore, come thou, we will make a covenant, thou and I."—*Variation corrected.* "The word came

Esau, the hunter, that stayed not at home; but to Jacob, the plain man, *him* that dwelt
."—*Penn cor.* " Not to every man, but to the man of God, (i. e.,) *him* that is led by the
f God."—*Barclay cor.* " For, admitting God to be a creditor, or *him* to whom the debt
be paid, and Christ *him* that satisfies or pays it on behalf of man the debtor, this question
se, whether he paid that debt as God, or man, or both ? "—*Penn cor.* " This Lord Jesus
the heavenly Man, the Emmanuel, God with us, we own and believe in : *him* whom the
iests raged against," &c.—*Fox cor.* " Christ, and *He* crucified, was the Alpha and Omega
is addresses, the fountain and foundation of his hope and trust."—*Exp. cor.* " Christ,
crucified, is the head, and the only head, of the church."—*Denison cor.* " But if Christ,
crucified, *is* the burden of the ministry, such disastrous results are all avoided."—*Id.* " He
et fall the least intimation, that himself, or any other person *whosoever*, was the object of
)."—*View cor.* " Let the elders that rule well, be counted worthy of double honour, espe-
hem who labour in the word and doctrine."—*Bible cor.* " Our Shepherd, *he* who is styled
f saints, will assuredly give his saints the victory."—*Sermon cor.* " It may seem odd, to
us subscribers."—*Fowle cor.* "And they shall have none to bury them ; *they*, their wives,
ir sons, nor[*] their daughters ; for I will pour their wickedness upon them."—*Bible cor.*
supposed it necessary to send to you Epaphroditus, my brother, and companion in labour,
low-soldier, but your messenger, and *him* that ministered to my wants."—*Bible cor.*

> "Amidst the tumult of the routed train,
> The sons of false Antimachus were slain ;
> *Him* who for bribes his faithless counsels sold,
> And voted Helen's stay for Paris' gold."—*Pope cor.*
> " See the vile King his iron sceptre bear—
> His only praise attends the pious heir ;
> *Him* in whose soul the virtues all conspire,
> The best good son, from the worst wicked sire."—*Lowth cor.*
> " Then from thy lips poured forth a joyful song
> To thy Redeemer !—yea, it poured along
> In most melodious energy of praise,
> To God, the Saviour, *him* of ancient days."—*Arm Chair cor.*

CORRECTIONS UNDER RULE IV; OF POSSESSIVES.

UNDER NOTE I.—THE POSSESSIVE FORM.

n's chief good is an upright mind."—" The translator of *Mallet's* History *has* the follow-
:e."—*Webster cor.* " The act, while it gave five *years'* full pay to the officers, allowed but
ir's pay to the privates."—*Id.* " For the study of English is preceded by several *years'*
on to Latin and Greek."—*Id.* " The first, the *Court-Baron*, is the *freeholders'* or *freemen's*
—*Coke cor.* " I affirm, that *Vaugelas's* definition labours under an essential defect."—
ell *cor.; and also Murray.* " There is a chorus in *Aristophanes's* plays."—*Blair cor.* " It
s the same perception in my mind as in *theirs*."—*Duncan cor.* " This afterwards enabled
read *Hickes's* Saxon Grammar."—*Life of Dr. Mur. cor.* " I will not do it for *ten's* sake."
or. Or : " I will not *destroy* it for *ten's* sake."—*Gen.* xviii, 32. " I arose, and asked if those
ng infants were *hers*."—*Worter cor.* " They divide their time between *milliners'* shops
taverns."—*Dr. Brown cor.* " The *angels'* adoring of Adam is also mentioned in the Tal-
—*Sale cor.* " Quarrels arose from the *winners'* insulting of those who lost."—*Id.* " The va-
occasioned by Mr. *Adams's* resignation."—*Adv. to Adams's Rhet. cor.* " Read, for in-
Junius's address, commonly called his *Letter to the King.*"—*Adams cor.* "A perpetual
e against the tide of *Hortensius's* influence."—*Id.* " Which, for *distinction's* sake, I shall
wn severally."—*R. Johnson cor.* " The fifth case is in a clause signifying the matter of
ar."—*Id.* "And they took counsel, and bought with them the *potter's* field."—*Alger cor.*
for thy *servants'* help, and redeem them for thy mercy's sake."—*Jenks cor.* " Shall not
ittle, their substance, and every beast of *theirs*, be ours ?"—COM. BIBLE : *Gen.* xxxiv, 23.
gular plural, *bullaces*, is used by Bacon."—*Churchill cor.* " Mordecai walked every day be-
e court of the *women's* house."—*Scott cor.* " Behold, they that wear soft clothing, are in
houses."—*Alger's Bible.* " Then Jethro, *Moses's* father-in-law, took Zipporah, *Moses's* wife,
r two sons: and Jethro, *Moses's* father-in-law, came, with his sons and his wife, unto
"—*Scott's Bible.* " King *James's* translators merely revised former translations."—*Frasse*
May they be like corn on *houses'* tops."—*White cor.*

> "And for his Maker's *image'* sake exempt."—*Milton cor.*
> " By all the fame acquired in ten *years'* war."—*Rowe cor.*
> " Nor glad vile poets with true *critics'* gore."—*Pope cor.*
> "Man only of a softer mold is made,
> Not for his *fellows'* ruin, but their aid."—*Dryden cor.*

UNDER NOTE II.—POSSESSIVES CONNECTED.

vas necessary to have both the *physician's* and the surgeon's advice."—*L. Murray's False*
, RULE x. "This *outside* fashionableness of the *tailor's* or *the tirewoman's* making."—
or. " Some pretending to be of Paul's party, others of *Apollos's*, others of *Cephas's*, and
(pretending yet higher,) to be of Christ's."—*Wood cor.* "Nor is it less certain, that
' and Milton's spelling agrees better with our pronunciation."—*Phil. Museum cor.* " Law's,
is's, and *Watts's Survey* of the Divine Dispensations." Or thus: "*Law, Edwards*, and
s, Surveys of the Divine Dispensations."—*Burgh cor.* "And who was Enoch's Saviour,
prophets' ?"—*Bayly cor.* " Without any impediment but his own, his *parents'*, or his
n's will."—*Journal corrected.* " James relieves neither the *boy's* nor the girl's distress."

propriety of this conjunction, "nor," is questionable : the reading in both the Vulgate and the Septuagint
ry, and their wives, and their sons, and their daughters."

—*Nixon cor.* "John regards neither the *master's* nor the pupil's advantage."—*Id.* "You reward neither the *man's* nor the woman's labours."—*Id.* "She examines neither *James's* nor John's conduct."—*Id.* "Thou pitiest neither the *servant's* nor the master's injuries."—*Id.* "We promote *England's* or Ireland's happiness."—*Id.* "Were *Cain's* and Abel's occupation the same ?"—*G. Brown.* "Were *Cain* and Abel's occupations the same ?"—*Id.* "What was *Simon* and Andrew's employment ?"—*Id.* "Till he can read *for* himself *Sanctius's* Minerva with *Scioppius's* and Perizonius's Notes."—*Locke cor.*

"And *love* and friendship's finely-pointed dart
Falls blunted from each indurated heart." Or :—
"And *love's* and friendship's finely-pointed dart
Fall blunted from each indurated heart."—*Goldsmith cor.*

UNDER NOTE III.—CHOICE OF FORMS.

"But some degree of trouble is the portion *of all men.*"—*Murray et al. cor.* "With the *names* of his father and mother upon the blank leaf."—*Abbott cor.* "The general, in the name *of the* army, published a declaration."—*Hume cor.* "The vote *of the Commons.*"—*Id.* "The *House of Lords.*"—*Id.* "A collection of *the faults of writers ;* "—or, "A collection *of literary faults.*"—*Swift cor.* "After ten *years of wars.*"—*Id.* "Professing his detestation of such practices as *those of* his predecessors."—*Pope cor.* "By that time I shall have ended my *year of office.*"—*W. Walker cor.* "For the sake *of Herodias,* the wife of *his brother Philip.*"—*Bible and Mur. cor.* "I endure all things for *the sake of the elect,* that they may also obtain salvation."—*Bible cor.* "He was *heir to the son of* Louis the Sixteenth."—*W. Allen.* "The throne we honour is the people's choice."—*Rolla.* "An account of the proceedings of *Alexander's court.*"—*"An excellent taste for the child of a person of fashion !*"—*Gil Blas cor.* "It is curious enough, that this *sentence of* the Bishop's is, itself, ungrammatical."—*Cobbett cor.* "The troops broke into the palace *of the Emperor* Leopold."—*Nixon cor.* "The meeting was called by desire of Eldon the *judge.*"—*Id.* "The occupation *of Peter, John,* and *Andrew,* was that of fishermen."—*Murray's Key.* B. lt. "The *debility of* the venerable president of the Royal *Academy,* has lately increased."—*Maunder cor.*

UNDER NOTE IV.—NOUNS WITH POSSESSIVES PLURAL.

"God hath not given us our *reason* to no purpose."—*Barclay cor.* "For our *sake,* no doubt, this is written."—*Bible cor.* "Are not health and strength of body desirable for their own *sake?*"—*Harris and Murray cor.* "Some sailors who were boiling their *dinner* upon the shore."—*Day cor.* "And they, in their *turn,* were subdued by others."—*Pinnock cor.* "Industry on our *part* is not superseded by God's grace."—*Arrowsmith cor.* "Their *health* perhaps may be pretty well secured."—*Locke cor.* "Though he was rich, yet for *your sake* he became poor."—See 2 *Cor.* viii, 9. "It were to be wished, his correctors had been as wise on their *part.*"—*Harris cor.* "The Arabs are commended by the ancients for being most exact to their *word,* and respectful to their kindred."—*Sale cor.* "That is, as a reward of some exertion on our *part.*"—*Gurney cor.* "So that it went ill with Moses for their *sake.*"—*Ps. cor.* "All liars shall have their *part* in the burning lake."—*Watts cor.* "For our own *sake* as well as for thine."—*Pref. to Waller cor.* "By discovering their *ability* to detect and amend errors."—*L. Murray cor.*

"This world I do renounce ; and, in your *sight,*
Shake patiently my great affliction off."—*Shak. cor.*
"If your relenting *anger* yield to treat,
Pompey and thou, in safety, here may meet."—*Rowe cor.*

UNDER NOTE V.—POSSESSIVES WITH PARTICIPLES.

"This will encourage him to proceed without acquiring the prejudice."—*Smith cor.* "And the notice which they give of an *action as* being completed or not completed."—*Mur. et al. cor.* "Some obstacle, or impediment, that prevents *it from* taking place."—*Priestley and A. Mur. cor.* "They have apostolical authority for so frequently urging the seeking of the Spirit."—*The Friend cor.* "Here then is a wide field for *reason to exert* its powers in relation to the objects of taste."—*Blair cor.* "Now this they derive altogether from their greater capacity of imitation and description."—*Id.* "This is one clear reason *why they paid* a greater attention to that construction."—*Id.* "The dialogue part had also a modulation of its own, which was capable of being set to notes."—*Id.* "*Why are we so often* frigid and unpersuasive in public discourse?"—*Id.* "Which is only a preparation for leading his forces directly upon us."—*Id.* "The nonsense about *which,* as relating to things only, and having no declension, needs no refutation."—*Fowle cor.* "Who, upon breaking it open, found nothing but the following inscription."—*Rollin cor.* "A prince will quickly have reason to repent *of* having exalted one person so high."—*Id.* "Notwithstanding *it is* the immediate subject of his discourse."—*Churchill cor.* "With our definition of *it, as* being synonymous with *time.*"—*Booth cor.* "It will considerably increase our *danger of* being deceived."—*Campbell cor.* "His beauties can never be mentioned without suggesting his blemishes also."—*Blair cor.* "No example has ever been adduced, of a *man conscientiously approving* an action, because of its badness." Or :—"of a *man who conscientiously approved of an* action because of its badness."—*Gurney cor.* "The last episode, of the *angel showing to Adam* the fate of his posterity, is happily imagined."—*Blair cor.* "And the news came to my son, that *he* and the bride *were* in Dublin."—*M. Edgeworth cor.* "There is no room for the *mind to exert* any great effort."—*Blair cor.* "One would imagine, that these *critics* never so much as heard that Homer wrote first."—*Pope cor.* "Condemn the book, for not being a geography : or,—"because it is not a geography."—*Peirce cor.* "There will be in many words a transition from being the figurative to being the proper signs of certain ideas."—*Campbell cor.* "The doctrine *that the Pope is* the only source of ecclesiastical power."—*Rel. W. cor.* "This *was* the more expedient, *because* the work *was* designed for the benefit of private learners."—*L. Murray cor.* "This was *done, because* the Grammar, *being already in type,* did not admit of enlargement."—*Id.*

CORRECTIONS UNDER RULE V; OF OBJECTIVES.

UNDER THE RULE ITSELF.—THE OBJECTIVE FORM.

hom should I meet the other day but my old friend!"—*Spect. cor.* "Let not him boast
uts on his armour, but *him* that takes it off."—*Barclay cor.* "Let none touch it, but *them*
re clean."—*Sale cor.* "Let the sea roar, and the fullness thereof; the world, and *them*
.well therein."—*Ps. cor.* "Pray be private, and careful *whom* you trust."—*Mrs. Goffe cor.*
w shall the people know *whom* to entrust with their property and their liberties?"—*J. O.
r cor.* "The chaplain entreated my comrade and *me* to dress as well as possible."—*World*
"And *him* that cometh *to* me, I will in no wise cast out."—*John,* vi, 37. "*Whom,* during
reparation, they constantly and solemnly invoke."—*Hope of Is. cor.* "Whoever or what-
wes us, is Debtor; *and whomever* or whatever we owe, is Creditor."—*Marsh cor.* "De-
g the curricle was his, and he should have *in it whom* he chose."—*A. Ross cor.* "The
, Burke is the only one of all the host of brilliant contemporaries, *whom* we can rank as a
ate orator."—*Knickerb. cor.* "Thus you see, how naturally the Fribbles and the Daffodils
roduced the *Messalinas* of our time."—*Dr. Brown cor.* "They would find in the Roman
th the *Scipios.*"—*Id.* "He found his wife's clothes on fire, and *her* just expiring."—*Ob-
cor.* "To present you holy, and *unblamable,* and *unreprovable* in his sight."—*Colossians,* i,
' Let the distributer do his duty with simplicity; the superintendent, with diligence; *him*
erforms offices of compassion, with cheerfulness."—*Stuart cor.* "If the crew rail at the
r of the vessel, *whom* will they mind?"—*Collier cor.* "He having none but them, they
g none but *him.*"—*Drayton cor.*

"*Thee,* Nature, partial Nature, I arraign;
Of thy caprice maternal I complain."—*Burns cor.*
"Nor *weens* he who it is, *whose charms* consume
His *longing soul,* but loves he knows not *whom.*"—*Addison cor.*

UNDER NOTE I.—OF VERBS TRANSITIVE.

hen it gives that sense, and also connects *sentences,* it is a conjunction."—*L. Murray cor.*
ugh thou wilt not acknowledge *thyself to be guilty,* thou canst not deny the fact *stated.*"—
' They specify *some object,* like many other adjectives, and *also* connect sentences."—*Kirk-*
or. "*A* violation of this rule tends so much to perplex *the reader* and obscure *the sense,* that
afer to err by *using* too many short sentences."—*L. Murray cor.* "A few exercises are sub-
. to each important definition, for him [the pupil] to practise upon as he proceeds in com-
g the grammar to memory."—*Nutting cor.* "A verb signifying *an action directly transitive,*
ns the accusative."—*Adam et al. cor.* "Or, any word that *can be conjugated,* is a verb."—
am cor. "In these two concluding sentences, the author, hastening to *a close,* appears to
rather carelessly."—*Dr. Blair cor.* "He simply reasons on one side of the question, and
eaves it."—*Id.* "Praise to God teaches *us* to be humble and lowly ourselves."—*Atterbury*
This author has endeavoured to surpass *his rivals.*"—*R. W. Green cor.* "Idleness and *pleas-
tigue a man as soon as business.*"—*Webster cor.* "And, in conjugating *any verb,*"—or, "And
ning the conjugations, you must pay particular attention to the manner in which these signs
plied."—*Kirkham cor.* "He said Virginia would have emancipated *her slaves* long ago."—
or. "And having a readiness"—or, "And *holding ourselves* in readiness"—or, "And *being* in
.ess—to revenge all disobedience."—*Bible cor.* "However, in these cases, custom generally
aines *what is right.*"—*Wright cor.* "In proof, let the following *cases be taken.*"—*Id.* "We
marvel that he should so speedily have forgotten his first principles."—*Id.* "How should
nder at the expression, 'This is a *soft* question!'"—*Id.* "And such as prefer *this course,*
arse it as a possessive adjective."—*Goodenow cor.* "To assign all the reasons that induced
thor to deviate from other grammarians, would lead to a needless prolixity."—*Alexander cor.*
Indicative Mood simply indicates or declares *a thing.*"—*L. Murray's Gram.* p. 63.

UNDER NOTE II.—OF VERBS INTRANSITIVE.

his seventh chapter he *expatiates* at great length."—*Barclay cor.* "He *quarrels with me*
during some *ancient* testimonies agreeing with what I say."—*Id.* "Repenting of his de-
—*Hume cor.* "Henry knew, that an excommunication could not fail to *produce* the most
rous effects."—*Id.* "The popular lords did not fail to enlarge on the subject."—*Mrs. Ma-*
' *cor.* "He is always master of his subject, and seems to *play* with it:" or,—"seems to
imself with it."—*Blair cor.* "But as soon as it *amounts to real* disease, all his secret infirm-
how themselves."—*Id.* "No man repented of his wickedness."—*Bible cor.* "Go one
r other, either on the right hand, or on the left."—*Id.* "He lies down by the *river's edge.*"
He *lays himself* down *on the river's brink.*"—*W. Walker cor.* "For some years past, *I have*
ardent *wish* to retire to some of our American plantations."—*Cowley cor.* "I fear thou
rink from the payment of it."—*Ware cor.* "We never *retain* an idea, without acquiring
:ombination."—*Rippingham cor.*

"Yet more; the stroke of death he must abide,
Then lies *he* meekly down, fast by his brethren's side."—*Milton cor.*

UNDER NOTE III.—OF VERBS MISAPPLIED.

e parliament *confiscated the property* of all those who had borne arms against the king."—
cor.* "The practice of *confiscating* ships *that* had been wrecked."—*Id.* "The nearer his
ry successes *brought* him to the throne." Or: "The nearer, *through* his military successes,
roached the throne."—*Id.* "In the next example, '*you*' *represents* ' *ladies* ;' therefore it is
."—*Kirkham cor.* "The first '*its*' *stands for* ' *vale* ;' the second ' *its*' represents ' *stream.*'"
"Pronouns do not always *prevent* the repetition of nouns."—*Id.* "*Very* is an adverb of de-
it *relates* to the adjective *good.*"—*Id.* "You will please to commit *to memory* the following
.aph."—*Id.* "Even the Greek and Latin passive verbs *form* some of their tenses *by means*

of auxiliaries."—*Mur. cor.* "The deponent verbs in Latin also *employ auxiliaries* to *form sev*-eral of their tenses."—*Id.* "I have no doubt he made as wise and true proverbs, as any body has made since."—*Id.* "*Monotonous delivery* assumes as many set forms, as *ever* Proteus *did of fleet*-ing shapes."—*Kirkham cor.* "When words in apposition *are uttered* in quick succession."—*Nix-on cor.* "Where *many* such sentences *occur in succession.*"—*L. Mur. cor.* "Wisdom leads us to speak and *do* what is most proper."—*Blair and Mur. cor.*

"*Jul.* Art thou not Romeo, and a Montague?
Rom. Neither, fair saint, if either thee *displease.*" Or :—
"Neither, fair saint, if either *thou* dislike."—*Shak. cor.*

UNDER NOTE IV.—OF PASSIVE VERBS.

"*To us,* too, must be allowed the privilege of forming our own laws." Or : "*We* too *must have* the privilege," &c.—*Murray cor.* "*For* not only *is* the use of all the ancient poetic *feet* allowed [to] us," &c.—*Id. et al.* "By what code of morals *is the right or privilege denied me?*"—*Bartlett cor.* "*To* the children of Israel alone, *has* the possession of it been denied."—*Keith cor.* "At York, all quarter *was refused to* fifteen hundred Jews."—*Id.* "He would teach the French language in three lessons, provided *there were paid him* fifty-five dollars in advance."—*Prof. Chazotte cor.* "And when *it* was demanded of *him by* the Pharisees, when the kingdom of God should come." Or : "And when *the Pharisees demanded* of him," &c.—*Bible cor.* "A book *has been shown* me."—*Dr. Campbell cor.* "*To* John Horne Tooke *admission was refused,* only because he had been in holy orders."—"Mr. Horne Tooke having taken orders, admission to the bar was refused him."—*Churchill cor.* "Its reference to place is *disregarded.*"—*Dr. Bullions cor.* "What striking lesson *is taught* by the tenor of this history?"—*Bush cor.* "No less *a sum* than eighty thousand pounds had been left *him* by a friend."—*Dr. Priestley cor.* "Where there are many things to be done, *there* must be allowed to *each* its share of time and labour."—*Dr. Johnson cor.* "Presenting the subject in a far more practical form, than *has heretofore been given it.*"—*Kirkham cor.* "If *to* a being of entire impartiality should be shown the two companies."—*Dr. Scott cor.* "The command of the British army was offered *to him.*"—*Grimshaw cor.* "*To whom* a considerable sum had been unexpectedly left."—*Johnson cor.* "Whether such a privilege may be granted *to* a maid or a widow."—*Spect. cor.* "Happily, *to* all these affected terms, the public suffrage *has* been denied."—*Campbell cor.* "Let *the parsing table* next be *shown him.*"—*Nutting cor.* "Then the use of the *analyzing table* may be *explained to* him."—*Id.* "*To* Pittacus *there* was offered a great sum of money."—*Sanborn cor.* "More time for study had *been allowed him.*"—*Id.* "If a little care were *bestowed on the walks* that lie between them."—*Blair's Rhet.* p. 222. "Suppose an office or a bribe *be* offered *me.*"—*Pierpont cor.*

"*Is then* one chaste, one last embrace *denied?*
Shall I not lay me by his clay-cold side?"—*Rowe cor.*

UNDER NOTE V.—OF PASSIVE VERBS TRANSITIVE.

"The preposition TO is *used* before nouns of place, when they follow verbs *or participles of mo*-tion."—*Murray et al. cor.* "They were *not allowed to enter* the house."—*Mur. cor.* "Their sepa-rate signification has been *overlooked.*"—*Tooke cor.* "But, whenever TH is *used,* it must be in the nominative case, and *not* in the objective."—*Cobbett cor.* "It is said, that more persons than one *receive* handsome salaries, to see *that* acts of parliament *are* properly worded."—*Churchill cor.* "The following Rudiments of English Grammar have been *used* in the University of Pennsylva-nia."—*Dr. Rogers cor.* "It never should be *forgotten.*"—*Newman cor.* "A very curious fact *has been noticed* by those expert metaphysicians."—*Campbell cor.* "The archbishop interfered, that Michelet's lectures might be *stopped.*"—*The Friend cor.* "The disturbances in Gottengen have been entirely *quelled.*"—*Daily Adv. cor.* "Besides those *which are noticed in these exceptions.*"—*Priestley cor.* "As one, two, or three auxiliary verbs are *employed.*"—*Id.* "The *arguments which* have been *used.*"—*Addison cor.* "The circumstance is properly *noticed* by the author."—*Blair cor.* "Patagonia has never been taken *into possession* by any European nation."—*Cumming cor.* "He will be *censured* no more."—*Walker cor.* "The thing was to be *terminated somehow.*"—*Hunt cor.* "In 1796, the Papal Territory was *seised* by the French."—*Pinnock cor.* "The idea has not for a moment *escaped the attention of* the Board."—*C. S. Journal cor.* "I shall easily be excused *from* the labour of more transcription."—*Johnson cor.* "If I may be allowed *to use* that expression."—*Campbell cor.* "If without offence I may *make* the observation."—*Id.* "There are other characters, which are frequently *used* in composition."—*Mur. et al. cor.* "Such unaccount-able infirmities might be *overcome,* in many cases, *and* perhaps in most."—*Beattie cor.* "Which ought never to be *employed,* or *resorted to.*"—*Id.* "That *care* may be *noticed of the widows.*" Or : "That the widows may be *provided for.*"—*Barclay cor.* "Other cavils will yet be *noticed.*"—*Pope cor.* "Which implies, that *to* all Christians *is* eternal salvation *offered.*"—*West cor.* "Yet even the dogs are allowed *to eat* the crumbs fallen from their master's table."—*Campbell cor.* "For we say, the light within must be *heeded.*"—*Barclay cor.* "This sound of *a is noticed in* Steele's Grammar."—*J. Walker cor.* "One came to *receive* ten guineas for a pair of silver buckles."—*M. Edgeworth cor.* "Let therefore the application of the several questions in the table be carefully *shown* [to] *him.*"—*Nutting cor.* "After a few times, it is no longer *noticed by* the hearers."—*Sheridan cor.* "It will not admit of the same excuse, nor *receive* the same indul-gence, *from* people of any discernment."—*Id.* "Of inanimate things, property may be *made.*" Or : "Inanimate things may be made property;" i. e., "may *become* property."—*Beattie cor.*

"And, when *some rival bids a higher* price,
Will not be sluggish in the work, *or* nice."—*Butler cor.*

UNDER NOTE VI.—OF PERFECT PARTICIPLES.

"All the words *employed* to denote spiritual *or* intellectual things, are in their origin *metaphors.*"—*Dr. Campbell cor.* "A reply to an argument commonly *brought forward* by unbelievers."—*Dr. Blair cor.* "It was *once* the only form *used* in the *past* tenses."—*Dr. Ash cor.* "Of the *points* and other characters used in writing."—*Id.* "If THY be the personal pronoun *adopted*."—*Walker cor.* "The Conjunction is a word *used* to connect [words or] sentences."—*Burn cor.* "The points *which* answer these purposes, are the four following."—*Harrison cor.* "INCENSE signifies *perfume* exhaled by fire, and *used* in religious ceremonies."—*L. Mur. cor.* "In most of his orations, there is too much art; *he carries it even to* ostentation."—*Blair cor.* "To illustrate the great truth, so often *overlooked* in our times."—*C. S. German cor.* "The principal figures *calculated* to affect the heart, are Exclamation, Confession, Deprecation, Commination, and Imprecation."—*Formey cor.* "Disgusted at the odious artifices *employed* by the judge."—*Junius cor.* "*All the reasons for which there was allotted to us* a condition out of which so much wickedness and misery would in fact arise."—*Bp. Butler cor.* "Some characteristical circumstance being *generally* invented or *seized upon.*"—*Ld. Kames cor.*

"And BY is likewise used with names that shew
The method or the means *of what we do.*"—*Ward cor.*

UNDER NOTE VII.—OF CONSTRUCTIONS AMBIGUOUS.

"Many adverbs admit of degrees of comparison, as *do* adjectives."—*Priestley cor.* "But the author who, by the number and reputation of his works, *did* more than any one *else, to bring* our language into its present state, *was* Dryden."—*Blair cor.* "In some states, courts of admiralty have no juries, nor *do* courts of chancery *employ* any at all."—*Webster cor.* "I feel grateful to my friend."—*Murray cor.* "This requires a writer to have *in his own* mind a very clear apprehension of the object which he means to present to us."—*Blair cor.* "Sense has its own harmony, *which naturally contributes something to the harmony of* sound."—*Id.* "The apostrophe denotes the omission of an *i*, which was formerly inserted, and *which gave to the word an additional* syllable."—*Priestley cor.* "There are few *to whom* I can refer with more advantage than *to* Mr. Addison."—*Blair cor.* "DEATH, (in *theology,*) is a perpetual separation from God, *a state of* eternal torments."—*Webster cor.* "That could inform the *traveller* as well as *could* the old man himself!"—*O. B. Peirce cor.*

UNDER NOTE VIII.—OF YE AND YOU IN SCRIPTURE.

"Ye daughters of Rabbah, gird *you* with sackcloth."—SCOTT, FRIENDS, and the COMPREHENSIVE BIBLE: *Jer.* xlix, 3. "Wash *you*, make you clean."—SCOTT, ALGER, FRIENDS, ET AL.: *Isaiah*, i, 16. "Strip *you*, and make *you* bare, and gird sackcloth upon your loins."—SCOTT, FRIENDS, ET AL.: *Isaiah*, xxxii, 11. "*Ye* are not ashamed that *ye* make yourselves strange to me."—SCOTT, BRUCE, and BLAYNEY: *Job*, xix, 3. "If *ye* knew the gift of God." Or: "If *thou* knew the gift of God."—See *John*, iv, 10. "Depart from me, ye workers of iniquity; I know *you* not."—*Penington cor.*

CORRECTIONS UNDER RULE VI; OF SAME CASES.

UNDER THE RULE ITSELF.—OF PROPER IDENTITY.

"Who would not say, 'If it be *I*,' rather than, 'If it be *me?*'"—*Priestley cor.* "Who is there? It is *I*."—*Id.* "It is *he*."—*Id.* "Are these the houses you were speaking of? Yes; they are *the same*."—*Id.* "It is not *I, that* you are in love with."—*Addison cor.* "It cannot be *I*."—*Swift cor.* "To that which once was *thou*."—*Prior cor.* "There is but one man that she can have, and that man is *myself*."—*Priestley cor.* "We enter, as it were, into his body, and become in some measure *he*." Or, better:—"and become in some measure *identified with* him."—*A. Smith and Pr. cor.* "Art thou proud yet? Ay, that I am not *thou*."—*Shak. cor.* "He knew not *who* they were."—*Milnes cor.* "*Whom* do you think me to be?"—*Dr. Lowth's Gram.* p. 77. "*Who* do men say that I, the Son of man, am?"—*Bible cor.* "But *who* say ye that I am?"—*Id.* "*Who* think ye that I am? I am not he."—*Id.* "No; I am in error; I perceive it is not the person *that* I supposed it was."—*Winter in London cor.* "And while it is He *that* I serve, life is not without value."—*Ware cor.* "Without ever dreaming it was *he*."—*Charles XII cor.* "Or he was not the illiterate personage *that* he affected to be."—*Montgom. cor.* "Yet was he *the man* who was to be the greatest apostle of the Gentiles."—*Barclay cor.* "Sweet was the thrilling ecstasy; I know not if 'twas love, or *thou*."—*J. Hogg cor.* "Time was, when none would cry, that oaf was *I*."—*Dryden cor.* "No matter where the vanquished be, or *who*."—*Rowe cor.* "No; I little thought it had been *he*."—*Gratton cor.* "That reverence, that godly fear *which is ever due* to 'Him who can destroy both body and soul in hell.'"—*Maturin cor.* "It is *we* that they seek to please, or rather to astonish."—*J. West cor.* "Let the same be *her* that thou hast appointed for thy servant Isaac."—*Bible cor.* "Although I knew it to be *him*."—*Dickens cor.* "Dear gentle youth, is 't none but *thou?*"—*Dorset cor.* "*Who* do they say it is?"—*Fowler cor.*

"These are her garb, not *she*; they but express
Her form, her semblance, her appropriate dress."—*More cor.*

UNDER NOTE I.—OF THE CASE DOUBTFUL.

"I had no knowledge of *any connexion* between them."—*Col. Stone cor.* "To promote iniquity in others, is nearly the same *thing*, as *to be* the actors of it ourselves." (That is, "*For us* to promote iniquity in others, is nearly the same *thing* as *for us* to be the actors of it ourselves.")—*Murray cor.* "It must arise from *a delicate* feeling in ourselves."—*Blair and Murray cor.* "Because there has *not* been exercised a competent physical power for their enforcement."—*Mass. Legisl. cor.* "PUPILAGE, n. The state of a *pupil*, or scholar."—*Dictionaries cor.* "Then the other *part*, being the *definition, would include* all verbs, of every description."—*Peirce cor.* "John's *friendship for me* saved me from inconvenience."—*Id.* "William's *judgeship*"—or, "William's appointment *to the office* of judge,"—changed his whole demeanour."—*Id.* "William's *practical acquaintance with teaching*, was the cause of the interest he felt."—*Id.* "To be but one among many, stifleth the chidings of conscience."—*Tupper cor.* "As for *the opinion that it is* a close translation, I doubt not many have been led into that error by the shortness of it."—*Pope cor.* "All presumption *that death is* the destruction of living bodies, must go upon *the* supposition that they are compounded, and *therefore* discerptible."—*Butler cor.* "This argues rather *that they are* proper names."—*Churchill cor.* "But may it not be retorted, that *this gratification itself,* is that which excites our resentment?"—*Campbell cor.* "Under the common notion, *that it is* a system of the whole poetical art."—*Blair cor.* "Whose *want of* time, or *whose* other circumstances, forbid *them to become* classical scholars."—*Lit. Journal cor.* "It would *prove him not to have been a mere* fictitious personage." Or: "It would preclude the notion *that he was merely a* fictitious personage."—*Phil. Mu. cor.* "For *heresy,* or under pretence *that they are* heretics or infidels." —*Oath cor.* "We may here add Dr. Horne's sermon on *Christ, as being* the Object of religious adoration."—*Rel. World cor.* "To say nothing of Dr. *Priestley, as being* a strenuous advocate," &c.—*Id.* "*Through the agency of Adam, as being* their public head." Or: "*Because Adam was* their public head."—*Id.* "Objections against *the existence of* any such moral plan as this."— *Butler cor.* "A greater instance of a *man being* a blockhead."—*Spect. cor.* "We may insure or promote *what will make it* a happy state of existence to ourselves."—*Gurney cor.* "Since it often undergoes the same kind of unnatural treatment."—*Kirkham cor.* "Their *apparent* foolishness"—"Their *appearance of* foolishness"—or, "*That they appear* foolishness,—is no presumption against this."—*Butler cor.* "But what arises from *them as* being offences; *i. e.,* from their *liability* to be perverted."—*Id.* "And he *went into the* house of a certain man named Justus, one that *worshiped* God."—*Acts cor.*

Under Note II.—Of False Identification.

"But *popular,* he observes, is an ambiguous word."—*Blair cor.* "The infinitive mood, *a phrase, or a sentence,* is often *made the subject of* a verb."—*Murray cor.* "When any person, in speaking, introduces his name *after the pronoun I,* it is *of* the first person; as, 'I, James, of the city of Boston.'"—*R. C. Smith cor.* "The name of the person spoken to, is *of* the second person; as, 'James, come to me.'"—*Id.* "The name of the person or thing *merely* spoken of, or about, is *of* the third person; as, 'James has come.'"—*Id.* "The passive verb *has no object, because* its subject or nominative always represents *what is acted upon,* and the *object* of a verb must needs be in the *objective* case."—*Id.* "When a noun is the nominative to an active verb, it *denotes* the actor."—*Kirkham cor.* "And *the pronoun* THOU *or* YE, *standing for the name* of the person *or persons* commanded, is its nominative."—*Ingersoll cor.* "The first person is that *which denotes the speaker.*" —*Brown's Institutes,* p. 32. "The conjugation of a verb is *a regular arrangement of* its different variations or inflections throughout the moods and tenses."—*Wright cor.* "The first person is *that which denotes* the speaker *or writer.*"—G. BROWN: for the correction of *Parker and Fox, Hiley,* and *Sanborn.* "The second person is *that which denotes the hearer, or the person addressed.*"—*Id.*: for the same. "The third person is *that which denotes the person or thing merely* spoken of."—*Id.*: for the same. "*I* is *of* the first person, singular; WE, *of* the first person, plural."—*Mur. et al. cor.* "THOU is *of* the second person, singular; YE or YOU, *of* the second person, plural."—*Id.* "HE, SHE, or IT, is *of* the third person, singular; THEY, *of* the third person, plural."—*Id.* "The nominative case *denotes* the actor, *and is the* subject of the verb."—*Kirkham cor.* "John is the actor, therefore the noun JOHN is in the nominative case."—*Id.* "The actor is always *expressed by* the nominative case, *unless the verb be passive.*"—*Smith cor.* "The nominative case *does not* always *denote an* agent or actor."—*Mack cor.* "In mentioning each name, tell the part of speech."—*Flint cor.* "*Of* what number is *boy?* Why?"—*Id.* "*Of* what number is *pens?* Why?" —*Id.* "The speaker is *denoted by* the first person; the person spoken to *is denoted by* the second person; and the person or thing spoken of *is denoted by* the third person."—*Id.* "What nouns are *of the* masculine gender? *The names of* all males are *of the* masculine gender."—*Id.* "An interjection is a *word that is uttered merely to indicate some strong or* sudden emotion of the mind."—*G. Brown's Grammars.*

CORRECTIONS UNDER RULE VII; OF OBJECTIVES.

Under the Rule itself.—Of the Objective in Form.

"But I do not remember *whom* they were for."—*Abbott cor.* "But if you can't help it, *whom* do you complain of?"—*Collier cor.* "*Whom* was it from? and what was it about?"—*M. Edgeworth cor.* "I have plenty of victuals, and, between you and *me,* something in a corner."—*Day cor.* "The upper one, *whom* I am now about to speak of."—*Leigh Hunt cor.* "And to poor us, thy enmity *is* most capital."—*Shak. cor.* "Which, thou dost confess, '*twere* fit for thee to use, as *them* to claim." That is,—"as *for them* to claim."—*Id.* "To beg of thee, it is my more dishonour, than *thee* of them." That is,—"as *for them* to beg of them."—*Id.* "There are still a few, who, like *thee* and *me,* drink nothing but water."—*Gil Blas cor.* "Thus, 'I *shall* fall,'— 'Thou *shalt* love thy neighbour,'—'He *shall* be rewarded,'—express no resolution on the part of *me, thee,* or *him.*" Or better:—"on the part of *the persons signified by the nominatives, I, Thou, He.*"—*Lennie and Bullions cor.* "So saucy with the hand of *her* here—what's her name?"— *Shak. cor.* "All debts are cleared between you and *me.*"—*Id.* "Her price is paid, and she is sold like *thee.*"—HARRISON'S *E. Lang.* p. 172. "Search through all the most flourishing *eras of* Greece."—*Dr. Brown cor.* "The family of the *Rudolphs* had been long distinguished."—*The Friend cor.* "It will do well enough for you and *me.*"—*Edgeworth cor.* "The public will soon discriminate between him who is the sycophant, and *him* who is the teacher."—*Chazotte cor.* "We are still much at a loss *to determine whom* civil power belongs to."—*Locke cor.* "What do you call it? and *to whom* does it belong?"—*Collier cor.* "He had received no lessons from the *Socrateses,* the *Platoes,* and the *Confuciuses* of the age."—*Haller cor.* "I cannot tell *whom* to compare them to."—*Bunyan cor.* "I see there was some resemblance betwixt this good man and *me.*" —*Id.* "They, by those means, have brought themselves into the hands and house of I do not know *whom.*"—*Id.* "But at length she said, there was a great deal of difference between Mr. Cotton and *us.*"—*Hutch. Hist. cor.* "So you must ride on horseback after *us.*"—*Mrs. Gilpin cor.* "A separation must soon take place between our minister and *me.*"—*Werter cor.* "When she exclaimed on Hastings, you, and *me*."—*Shak. cor.* "To *whom?* to thee? What art thou?"—*Id.* "That they should always bear the certain marks *of him from whom* they came."—*Bp. Butler cor.* "This life has joys for you and *me*, And joys that riches ne'er could buy."—*Burns cor.*

UNDER THE NOTE.—OF TIME OR MEASURE.

"Such as almost every child, ten years old, knows."—*Town cor.* "*Four months' schooling* will carry any industrious scholar, of ten or twelve years *of age*, completely through this book."—*Id.* "A boy of six years *of age* may be taught to speak as correctly, as Cicero did before the Roman senate."—*Webster cor.* "A lad about twelve years old, who was taken captive by the Indians."—*Id.* "Of nothing else *than* that individual white figure of five inches *in length*, which is before him."—*Campbell cor.* "Where lies the fault, that boys of eight or ten years *of age* are with great difficulty made to understand any of its principles?"—*Guy cor.* "Where language three centuries old is employed."—*Booth cor.* "Let a gallows be made, of fifty cubits *in height*." Or: "Let a gallows *fifty cubits high* be made."—*Bible cor.* "I say to this child, nine years old, ' Bring me that hat. He hastens, and brings it me."—*Osborn cor.* " ' He laid a floor, twelve feet long, and nine feet wide : ' that is, *the floor was* long *to* the extent of twelve feet, and wide *to the extent* of nine feet."—*Merchant cor.* "The Goulah people are a tribe of about fifty thousand *in strength*." Or: "The Goulah people are a tribe about fifty thousand strong."—*Examiner cor.*

CORRECTIONS UNDER RULE VIII; NOM. ABSOLUTE.

"*He* having ended his discourse, the assembly dispersed."—*Inst. of E. G.* p. 190. "*I* being young, they deceived me."—*Id.* p. 279. "*They* refusing to comply, I withdrew."—*Ib.* "*Thou* being present, he would not tell what he knew."—*Ib.* "The child is lost ; and *I*, whither shall I go?"—*Ib.* "O happy *we!* surrounded with so many blessings."—*Ib.* " ' *Thou* too ! Brutus, my son !' cried Cæsar, overcome."—*Ib.* "*Thou!* Maria! and so late! and who is thy companion?'" —*Mirror cor.* "How swiftly our time passes away! and ah! *we*, how little concerned to improve it!"—*Greenleaf's False Syntax, Gram.* p. 47.

"There all thy gifts and graces we display,
Thou, only *thou*, directing all our way."—*Pope, Dunciad.*

CHAPTER IV.—ADJECTIVES.

CORRECTIONS UNDER THE NOTES TO RULE IX.

UNDER NOTE I.—OF AGREEMENT.

"I am not recommending *this* kind of sufferings to your liking."—*Sherlock cor.* "I have not been to London *these* five years."—*Webster cor.* "*Verbs of this kind* are more expressive than their radicals."—*Dr. Murray cor.* "Few of us would be less corrupted than kings are, were we, like them, beset with flatterers, and poisoned with *those* vermin."—*Kames cor.* "But it seems *these* literati had been very ill rewarded for their ingenious labours."—*R. Random cor.* "If I had not left off troubling myself about *things of that kind*."—*Swift cor.* "For *things of this sort* are usually joined to the most noted fortune."—*Bacon cor.* "The nature of *those* riches and *that* long-suffering, is, to lead to repentance."—*Barclay cor.* "I fancy *it is this* kind of gods, *that* Horace mentions."—*Addison cor.* "During *those* eight days, they are prohibited from touching the skin."—*Hope of Is. cor.* "Besides, he had *but a small quantity of* provisions left for his army."— *Goldsmith cor.* "Are you not ashamed to have no other thoughts than *those* of amassing wealth, and of acquiring glory, credit, and dignities?"—*Murray's Sequel*, p. 115. "It *distinguishes* still more remarkably the feelings of the former from *those* of the latter."—*Kames cor.* "And *these* good tidings of the reign shall be published through all the world."—*Campbell cor.* "*These* twenty years have I been with thee."—*Gen. cor.* "In *this* kind of expressions, some words seem to be understood."—*W. Walker cor.* "He thought *this* kind of excesses indicative of greatness."— *Hunt cor.* "*This* sort of fellows *is* very numerous." Or thus: "*Fellows of this sort are* very numerous."—*Spect. cor.* "Whereas *men of this sort* cannot give account of their faith." Or: "Whereas *these* men cannot give account of their faith."—*Barclay cor.* "But the question is, whether *those are* the words."—*Id.* "So that *expressions of this sort* are not properly optative." —*R. Johnson cor.* "Many things are not *such as* they appear to be."—*Sanborn cor.* "So that *all* possible means are used."—*Formey cor.*

"We have strict statutes, and most biting laws,
Which, for *these* nineteen years, we have let sleep."—*Shak. cor.*

"They could not speak ; and so I left them both,
To bear *these* tidings to the bloody king."—*Shak. cor.*

UNDER NOTE II.—OF FIXED NUMBERS.

"Why, I think she cannot be above six *feet* two inches high."—*Spect. cor.* "The world is pretty regular for about forty *rods* east and ten west."—*Id.* "The standard being more than two *feet* above it."—*Bacon cor.* "Supposing, among other things, *that* he saw two suns, and two *Thebeses*."—*Id.* "On the right hand we go into a parlour *thirty-three feet* by *thirty-nine*."—*Shaffield cor.* "Three *pounds* of gold went to one shield."—*1 Kings cor.* "Such an assemblage of men as there appears to have been at that *session*."—*The Friend cor.* "And, truly, he *has* saved me from this *labour*."—*Barclay cor.* "Within *these* three *miles* may you see it coming."—*Shak. cor.* "Most of the churches, not all, had one *ruling elder or more*."—*Hutch. cor.* "While a Minute Philosopher, not six *feet* high, attempts to dethrone the Monarch of the universe."—*Berkley cor.* "The wall is ten *feet* high."—*Harrison cor.* "The stalls must be ten *feet* broad."—*Walker cor.* "A close prisoner in a room twenty *feet* square, being at the north side of his chamber, is at liberty to walk twenty *feet* southward, not to walk twenty *feet* northward."—*Locke cor.* "Nor, after all this *care* and industry, did they think themselves qualified."—*C. Orator cor.* "No *fewer* than thirteen *Gypsies* were condemned at one Suffolk *assize*, and executed."—*Webster cor.* "The king was petitioned to appoint *one person or more*."—*Mrs. Macaulay cor.* "He carries weight! he rides a race! 'Tis for a thousand *pounds*."—*Cowper cor.* "They carry three *tiers* of guns at the head, and at the stern, *two tiers*."—*Joh. Dict. cor.* "The verses consist of two *sorts of* rhymes."—*Formey cor.* "A present of forty *camel-loads* of the most precious things of Syria." —*Wood's Dict. cor.* "A large grammar, that shall extend to every *minutia*."—*S. Barrett cor.*

> "So many spots, like nævus on Venus' soil,
> One gem set off with *many a glitt'ring* foil."—*Dryden cor.*
> "For, *off the end, a double* handful
> It had devour'd, it was so manful."—*Butler cor.*

UNDER NOTE III.—OF RECIPROCALS.

"That *shall* and *will* might be substituted *one for the other*."—*Priestley cor.* "We use *not shall* and *will* promiscuously *the one for the other*."—*Brightland cor.* "But I wish to distinguish the three high ones from *one an* other also."—*Fowle cor.* "Or on some other relation which two objects bear to *each other*."—*Blair cor.* "Yet the two words lie so near to *each other* in meaning, that, in the present case, *perhaps either* of them would have been sufficient."—*Id.* "Both orators use great liberties *in their treatment of each other*."—*Id.* "That greater separation of the two sexes from *each other*."—*Id.* "Most of whom live remote from *one an other*."—*Webster cor.* "Teachers like to see their pupils polite to *one an other*."—*Id.* "In a little time, he and I must keep company with *each other* only."—*Spect. cor.* "Thoughts and circumstances crowd upon *one an other*."—*Kames cor.* "They cannot *perceive* how the ancient Greeks could understand *one an other*."—*Lit. Conv. cor.* "The poet, the patriot, and the prophet, vied with *one an other* in his breast."—*Hazlitt cor.* "Athamas and Ino loved *each other*."—*C. Tales cor.* "Where two things are compared or contrasted *one with the other*." Or: "Where two things are compared or contrasted with *each other*."—*Blair and Mur. cor.* "In the classification of words, almost all writers differ from *one an other*."—*Bullions cor.*

> "I will not trouble thee, my child.   Farewell;
> We'll no more meet; *we'll* no more see *each other*."—*Shak. cor.*

UNDER NOTE IV.—OF COMPARATIVES.

"*Errors* in education should be less indulged than any *others*."—*Locke cor.* "This was less his case than any *other* man's that ever wrote."—*Pref. to Waller cor.* "This trade enriched some *other* people, more than it enriched them."—*Mur. cor.* "The Chaldee alphabet, in which the Old Testament has reached us, is more beautiful than any *other* ancient character known."— *Wilson cor.* "The Christian religion gives a more lovely character of God, than any *other* religion ever did."—*Murray cor.* "The temple of Cholula was deemed more holy than any *other* in New Spain."—*Robertson cor.* "Cibber grants it to be a better poem of its kind, than *any other that* ever was *written*."—*Pope cor.* "Shakspeare is more faithful to the true language of nature, than any *other* writer."—*Blair cor.* "One son I had—one, more than all my *other* sons, the strength of Troy." Or: "One son I had—one, *the most of all my sons*, the strength of Troy."— *Cowper cor.* "Now Israel loved Joseph more than all his *other* children, because he was the son of his old age."—*Bible cor.*

UNDER NOTE V.—OF SUPERLATIVES.

"Of *all simpletons*, he was the greatest."—*Nutting cor.* "Of *all beings*, man has certainly the greatest reason for gratitude."—*Id.* "This lady is *prettier than any* of her sisters."—*Payton cor.* "The relation which, of all *the class*, is by far the most fruitful of tropes, I have not yet mentioned."—*Blair cor.* "He studied Greek the most of *all noblemen*."—*W. Walker cor.* "And indeed that was the qualification *which was* most wanted at that time."—*Goldsmith cor.* "Yet we deny that the knowledge of him as outwardly crucified, is the best of all knowledge of him."— *Barclay cor.* "Our ideas of numbers are, of all *our conceptions*, the most accurate and distinct." —*Duncan cor.* "This indeed is, of all *cases, the one in which it is* least necessary to name the agent."—*J. Q. Adams cor.* "The period to which you have arrived, is perhaps the most critical and important moment of your lives."—*Id.* "Perry's royal octavo is esteemed the best of *all the* pronouncing dictionaries yet known."—*D. H. Barnes cor.* "This is the tenth persecution, and, of all the *ten*, the most bloody."—*Sammes cor.* "The English tongue is the most susceptible of sublime imagery, of *all the languages* in the world."—*Buck cor.* "Of *all writers* whatever, Homer is universally allowed to have had the greatest Invention."—*Pope cor.* "In a version of this particular work, which, *more than* any other, seems to require a venerable antique cast."—*Id.* "Because I think him the *best-informed* naturalist *that* has ever written."—*Jefferson cor.* "Man is capable of being the most social of *all animals*."—*Sheridan cor.* "It is, of all *signs* (or *expressions*) that which most moves us."—*Id.* "Which, of all *articles*, is the most necessary."—*Id.*

> "Quoth he, 'This gambol thou advisest,
> Is, of all *projects*, the unwisest.'"—*S. Butler cor.*

UNDER NOTE VI.—OF INCLUSIVE TERMS.

"Noah and his family *were the only antediluvians* who *survived* the flood."—*Webster cor.* "I think it superior to any *other grammar that* we have yet had."—*Blair cor.* "We have had no *other* grammarian who has employed so much labour and *judgement* upon our native language, as *has* the author of these volumes."—*British Critic cor.* "*Those* persons feel *most* for the distresses of others, who have experienced distress themselves."—*L. Murray cor.* "Never was any *other* people so much infatuated as the Jewish nation."—*Id. et al.* "No *other* tongue is so full of connective particles as the Greek."—*Blair cor.* "Never *was sovereign* so much beloved by the people." Or: "*Never was any other* sovereign so much beloved by *his* people."—*L. Murray cor.* "Nothing *else* ever affected her so much as this misconduct of her child."—*Id. et al.* "Of *all the* figures of speech, *no other* comes so near to painting as *does* metaphor."—*Blair et al. cor.* "I know *no other writer* so happy in his metaphors as *is* Mr. Addison."—*Blair cor.* "Of all the English authors, none is *more* happy in his metaphors *than* Addison."—*Jamieson cor.* "Perhaps no *other* writer in the world was ever so frugal of his words as Aristotle."—*Blair and Jamieson cor.* "Never was any *other* writer so happy, in that concise *and* spirited style, as Mr. Pope."—*Blair cor.* "In the harmonious structure and disposition of *his* periods, no *other* writer whatever, ancient or modern, equals Cicero."—*Blair and Jamieson cor.* "Nothing *else* delights me so much as the works of nature."—*Mur. cor.* "No person was ever *more* perplexed *than* he has been to-day."—*Id.* "In no *other* case are writers so apt to err, as in the position of the word *only*."—*Maunder cor.* "For nothing is *more* tiresome *than* perpetual uniformity."—*Blair cor.*

"Naught else sublimes the spirit, sets it free,
Like sacred and soul-moving poesy."—Sheffield cor.

Under Note VII.—Extra Comparisons.

"How much *better are ye* than the fowls!"—*Bible cor.* "Do not thou hasten above the Most High."—*Esdras cor.* "This word, PEER, is principally used for the nobility of the realm."—*Cowell cor.* "Because the same is not only most *generally* received, &c."—*Barclay cor.* "This is, I say, not the best and most *important* evidence."—*Id.* "Offer unto God thanksgiving, and pay thy vows unto the Most High"—*The Psalter cor.* "The holy place of the tabernacle of the Most High."—*Id.* "As boys should be educated with temperance, so the first *great* lesson that should be taught them, is, to admire frugality."—*Goldsmith cor.* "More *general* terms are put for such as are more restricted."—*Rev. J. Brown cor.* "This, *this* was the unkindest cut of all."—*Enfield's Speaker*, p. 353. "To take the basest and most *squalid* shape."—*Shak. cor.* "I'll forbear: *I have* fallen out with my more *heady* will."—*Id.* "The power of the Most *High* guard thee from sin."—*Percival cor.* "Which title had been more *true*, if the dictionary had been in Latin and Welsh."—*Verstegan cor.* "The waters are frozen sooner and harder, than further upward, within the inlands."—*Id.* "At every descent, the worst may become more *depraved*."—*Mann cor.*

"Or as a moat defensive to a house
Against the envy of less *happy* lands."—*Shak. cor.*
"A dreadful quiet felt, and *worse by* far
Than arms, a sullen interval of war."—*Dryden cor.*

Under Note VIII.—Adjectives Connected.

"It breaks forth in its *highest, most energetic*, and *most impassioned* strain."—*Kirkham cor.* "He has fallen into the *vilest and grossest* sort of railing."—*Barclay cor.* "To receive that *higher and more general* instruction which the public affords."—*J. O. Taylor cor.* "If the best things have the *best and most perfect* operations."—*Hooker cor.* "It became the plainest and most elegant, the *richest* and most splendid, of all languages."—*Bucke cor.* "But the *principal and most frequent* use of pauses, is, to mark the divisions of the sense."—*Blair cor.* "That every thing belonging to ourselves is *the best and the most perfect*."—*Clarkson cor.* "And to instruct their pupils in the *best and most thorough* manner."—*School Committee cor.*

Under Note IX.—Adjectives Superadded.

"The Father is figured out as a *venerable old* man."—*Brownlee cor.* "There never was exhibited *an other such* masterpiece of ghostly assurance."—*Id.* "After the *first three* sentences, the question is entirely lost."—*Spect. cor.* "The *last four* parts of speech are commonly called particles."—*Al. Murray cor.* "The *last two* chapters will not be found deficient, in this respect."—*Todd cor.* "Write upon your slates a list of the *first ten* nouns."—*J. Abbott cor.* "We have a few remains of *two other* Greek poets in the pastoral style, Moschus and Bion."—*Blair cor.* "The *first nine* chapters of the book of Proverbs are highly poetical."—*Id.* "For, of these five heads, only the *first two* have any particular relation to the sublime."—*Id.* "The resembling sounds of the *last two* syllables, give a ludicrous air to the whole."—*Kames cor.* "The *last three* are arbitrary."—*Id.* "But in the *sentence*, 'She hangs the curtains,' *hangs* is an *active-transitive* verb."—*Comly cor.* "If our definition of a verb, and the arrangement of *active-transitive, active-intransitive*, passive, and neuter verbs, are properly understood."—*Id.* "These *last two* lines have an embarrassing construction."—*Rush cor.* "God was provoked to drown them all, but Noah and *seven other* persons."—*Wood cor.* "The *first six* books of the Æneid are extremely beautiful."—*Formey cor.* "Only a few instances *more* can *here* be given."—*Murray cor.* "A few years *more* will obliterate every vestige of a subjunctive form."—*Nutting cor.* "Some define them to be verbs devoid of the *first two* persons."—*Crombie cor.* "In *an other such* Essay-tract as this." —*White cor.* "But we fear that not *an other such* man is to be found."—*Ed. Irving cor.* "O *for an other such* sleep, that I might see *an other such* man!" Or, to preserve poetic measure, say:—

"O *for such sleep again*, that I might see
An other such man, *though but in a dream!*"—*Shak. cor.*

Under Note X.—Adjectives for Adverbs.

"*The* is an article, relating to the noun *balm, agreeably* to Rule 11th."—*Comly cor.* "*Wise* is an adjective, relating to the noun *man's, agreeably* to Rule 11th."—*Id.* "To whom I observed, that the beer was *extremely* good."—*Goldsmith cor.* "He writes *very elegantly*." Or: "He writes *with remarkable elegance*."—*O. B. Peirce cor.* "John behaves *very civilly* (or, *with true civility*) to all men."—*Id.* "All the sorts of words hitherto considered, have each of them some meaning, even when taken *separately*."—*Beattie cor.* "He behaved himself *conformably* to that blessed example."—*Sprat cor.* "*Marvellously* graceful."—*Clarendon cor.* "The Queen having changed her ministry, *suitably* to her wisdom."—*Swift cor.* "The assertions of this author are *more easily* detected."—*Id.* "The characteristic of his sect allowed him to affirm no *more strongly* than that."—*Bentley cor.* "If one author had spoken *more nobly* and *loftily* than an other."—*Id.* "Xenophon says *expressly*."—*Id.* "I can never think so very *meanly* of him."—*Id.* "To convince all that are ungodly among them, of all their ungodly deeds, which they have *impiously* committed."—*Bible cor.* "I think it *very ably* written." Or: "I think it written *in a very mas-*

terly *manner.*"—*Swift cor.* "The whole design must refer to the golden age, which it represents *in a* lively *manner.*"—*Addison cor.* "*Agreeably* to this, we read of names being blotted out of God's book."—*Burder et al. cor.* "*Agreeably* to the law of nature, children are bound to support their indigent parents."—*Paley.* "Words taken *independently* of their meaning, are parsed as nouns of the neuter gender."—*Maltby cor.*
                "Conceit in weakest bodies *strongliest* works."—*Shak. cor.*

UNDER NOTE XI.—THEM FOR THOSE.

"Though he was not known by *those* letters, or the name CHRIST."—*Bayly cor.* "In a gig, or some of *those* things." Better: "In a gig, or *some such vehicle.*"—*M. Edgeworth cor.* "When cross-examined by *those* lawyers."—*Same.* "As the custom in *those* cases is."—*Same.* "If you had listened to *those* slanders."—*Same.* "The old people were telling stories about *those* fairies: but, to the best of my *judgement,* there is nothing in *them.*"—*Same.* "And is it not a pity that the Quakers have no better authority to substantiate their principles, than the testimony of *those* old Pharisees?"—*Hibbard cor.*

UNDER NOTE XII.—THIS AND THAT.

"Hope is as strong an incentive to action, as fear: *that* is the anticipation of good, *this* of evil."—*Inst.* p. 265. "The poor want some advantages which the rich enjoy; but we should not therefore account *these* happy, and *those* miserable."—*Inst.* p. 266.

"Ellen and Margaret, fearfully, | Then turned their ghastly look each one,
.Sought comfort in each other's eye; | *That* to her sire, *this* to her son."—*Scott cor.*
                "Six youthful sons, as many blooming maids,
                In one sad day beheld the Stygian shades;
                Those by Apollo's silver bow were slain,
                These Cynthia's arrows stretch'd upon the plain."—*Pope cor.*
            "Memory and forecast just returns engage,
            That pointing back to youth, *this* on to age."—*Pope, on Man.*

UNDER NOTE XIII.—EITHER AND NEITHER.

"These make the three great subjects of discussion among mankind; *namely,* truth, duty' and interest: but the arguments directed towards *any* of them are generally distinct."—*Dr. Blair cor.* "A thousand other deviations may be made, and still *any of the accounts* may be correct in principle; for *all* these divisions, and their technical terms, are arbitrary."—*Green cor.* "Thus it appears, that our alphabet is deficient; as it has but seven vowels to represent thirteen different sounds; and has no letter to represent *any* of five simple consonant sounds."—*Churchill cor.* "Then *none* of these five verbs can be neuter."—*Peirce cor.* "And the *assertor** is in *none* of the four already mentioned."—*Id.* "As it is not in *any* of these four."—*Id.* "See whether or not the word comes within the definition of *any* of the other three simple cases."—*Id.* "*No* one of the ten was there."—*Frazee cor.* "Here are ten oranges, take *any one* of them."—*Id.* "There are three modes, by *any* of which recollection will generally be supplied; inclination, practice, and association."—*Rippingham cor.* "Words not reducible to *any* of the three preceding heads."—*Fowler cor.* "Now a sentence may be analyzed in reference to *any* of these four classes."—*Id.*

UNDER NOTE XIV.—WHOLE, LESS, MORE, AND MOST.

"Does not all proceed from the law, which regulates *all the* departments of the state?"—*Blair cor.* "A messenger relates to Theseus *all the* particulars."—*Ld. Kames cor.* "There are no *fewer* than twenty-*nine* diphthongs in the English language."—*Ash cor.* "The Redcross Knight runs through *all the* steps of the Christian life."—*Spect. cor.* "There were not *fewer* than fifty or sixty persons present."—*Mills and Merchant cor.* "Greater experience, and *a* more cultivated state *of* society, abate the warmth of imagination, and chasten the manner of expression."—*Blair and Murray cor.* "By which means, knowledge, *rather* than oratory, *has* become the principal requisite."—*Blair cor.* "No *fewer* than seven illustrious cities disputed the right of having given birth to the greatest of poets."—*Lempriere cor.* "Temperance, *rather* than medicines, is the proper means of curing many diseases."—*Murray cor.* "I do not suppose, that we Britons *are* more *deficient* in genius than our neighbours."—*Id.* "In which, he *says,* he has found no *fewer* than twelve untruths."—*Barclay cor.* "The several places of rendezvous were concerted, and *all the* operations *were* fixed."—*Hume cor.* "In these rigid opinions, *all the* sectaries concurred."—*Id.* "Out of whose modifications have been made *nearly all* complex modes."—*Locke cor.* "The Chinese vary each of their words on no *fewer* than five different tones."—*Blair cor.* "These people, though they possess *brighter* qualities, are not so proud as he is, nor so vain as she."—*Murray cor.* "It is certain, *that* we believe *our own judgements* more *firmly,* after we have made a thorough inquiry into the *things.*"—*Brightland cor.* "As well as the whole course and *all the* reasons of the operation."—*Id.* "Those rules and principles which are of *the greatest* practical advantage."—*Newman cor.* "And *all* curse shall be *no more.*"— *Rev. cor.*—(See *the Greek.*) "And death shall be *no more.*"—*Id.* "But, in recompense, we have pleasanter pictures of ancient manners."—*Blair cor.* "Our language has suffered *a greater number of* injurious changes in America, since the British army landed on our shores, than it had suffered before, in the period of three centuries."—*Webster cor.* "*All the* conveniences of life are derived from mutual aid and support in society."—*Ld. Kames cor.*

---

* All our lexicographers, and all accurate authors, spell this word with an *o;* but the gentleman who has furnished us with the last set of *new terms* for the science of grammar, writes it with an *e,* and applies it to the end and the *participle.* With him, every verb or participle is an "*asserter;*" except when he forgets his creed, as he did in writing the preceding example about certain "*verbs.*" As he changes the names of all the parts of speech, and denounces the entire technology of grammar, perhaps his innovation would have been sufficiently broad, had he for THE VERB, the most important class of all, adopted some name which he knew how to spell.—G. B.

UNDER NOTE XV.—PARTICIPIAL ADJECTIVES.

"To such as think the nature of it *deserving of* their attention."—*Butler cor.* "In all points, *more deserving of* the approbation of their readers."—*Keepsake cor.* "But to give way to childish sensations, was *unbecoming to* our nature."—*Lempriere cor.* "The following extracts are *deserving of* the serious perusal of all."—*The Friend cor.* "No inquiry into wisdom, however superficial, is *undeserving of* attention."—*Bulwer cor.* "The opinions of illustrious men are *deserving of* great consideration."—*Porter cor.* "And resolutely keep its laws, *Uncaring for* consequences." Or :—"*Not heeding* consequences."—*Burns cor.* "This is an item that is *deserving of* more attention."—*Goodell cor.*

"Leave then thy joys, *unsuiting to* such age :"—Or,
"Leave then thy joys *not suiting* such an age,
To a fresh comer, and resign the stage."—*Dryden cor.*

UNDER NOTE XVI.—FIGURE OF ADJECTIVES.

"The tall dark mountains and the *deep-toned* seas."—*Dana.* "O! learn from him To station *quick-eyed* Prudence at the helm."—*Frost cor.* "He went in a *one-horse* chaise."—*Dr. Blair cor.* "It ought to be, 'in a *one-horse* chaise.'"—*Crombie cor.* "These are marked with the *above-mentioned* letters."—*Folker cor.* "A *many-headed* faction."—*Ware cor.* "Lest there should be no authority in any popular grammar, for the perhaps *heaven-inspired* effort."—*Fowle cor.* "*Common-metre* stanzas consist of four iambic lines ; one of eight, and the next of six syllables. They were formerly written in two *fourteen-syllable* lines."—*Goodenow cor.* "*Short-metre* stanzas consist of four iambic lines ; the third of eight, the rest of six syllables."—*Id.* "*Particular-metre* stanzas consist of six iambic lines ; the third and sixth of six syllables, the rest of eight."—*Id.* "*Hallelu'ah-metre* stanzas consist of six iambic lines ; the last two of eight syllables, and the rest of six."—*Id.* "*Long-metre* stanzas are merely the union of four iambic lines, of ten syllables each."—*Id.* "A majesty more commanding than is to be found among the rest of the *Old-Testament* poets."—*Blair cor.*

"You, sulphurous and *thought-executed* fires,
Vaunt-couriers to *oak-cleaving* thunderbolts,
Singe my white head! And thou, *all-shaking* thunder,
Strike flat the thick rotundity o' th' world !"—*Lear*, Act iii, Sc. 2.

CHAPTER V.— PRONOUNS.

CORRECTIONS UNDER RULE X AND ITS NOTES.

UNDER THE RULE ITSELF.—OF AGREEMENT.

"The subject is to be joined with *its* predicate."—*Wilkins cor.* "Every one must judge of *his* own feelings."—*Byron cor.* "Every one in the family should know *his or her* duty."—*Penn cor.* "To introduce its possessor into that way in which *he* should go."—*Inf. S. Gram. cor.* "Do not they say, *that* every true believer has the Spirit of God in *him?*"—*Barclay cor.* "There is none in *his* natural state righteous; no, not one."—*Wood cor.* "If ye were of the world, the world would love *its* own."—*Bible cor.* "His form had not yet lost all *its* original brightness."—*Milton cor.* "No one will answer as if I were *his* friend or companion."—*Steele cor.* "But, in lowliness of mind, let each esteem *others* better than *himself.*"—*Bible cor.* "And let none of you imagine evil in *his* heart against his neighbour."—*Id.* "For every tree is known by *its* own fruit."—*Id.* "But she fell to laughing, like one out of *his* right mind."—*M. Edgeworth cor.* "Now these systems, so far from having any tendency to make men better, have a manifest tendency to make *them* worse."—*Wayland cor.* "And nobody else would make that city *his* refuge any more."—*Josephus cor.* "What is quantity, as it respects syllables or words ? It is *the* time which a *speaker* occupies in pronouncing *them.*"—*Bradley cor.* "In such expressions, the adjective so much resembles an adverb in its meaning, that *it is* usually parsed as such."—*Bullions cor.* "The tongue is like a racehorse; which runs the faster, the less weight *he* carries." Or thus : "The tongue is like a racehorse; the less weight *it* carries, the faster *it* runs."—*Addison, Murray, et al. cor.* "As two thoughtless boys were trying to see which could lift the greatest weight with *his* jaws, one of them had several of his firm-set teeth wrenched from their sockets."—*Newspaper cor.* "Every body nowadays publishes memoirs ; every body has recollections which *he* thinks worthy of recording."—*Duchess D'Ab. cor.* "Every body trembled, for *himself,* or *for his* friends."—*Goldsmith cor.*

"A steed comes at morning : no rider is there ;
But *his* bridle is red with the sign of despair."—*Campbell cor.*

UNDER NOTE I.—PRONOUNS WRONG OR NEEDLESS.

"Charles loves to study ; but John, alas ! is very idle."—*Merchant cor.* "Or what man is there of you, *who,* if his son ask bread, will give him a stone ?"—*Bible cor.* "Who, in stead of going about doing good, are perpetually intent upon doing mischief."—*Tillotson cor.* "Whom ye delivered up, and denied in the presence of Pontius Pilate."—*Bible cor.* "Whom, when they had washed *her,* they laid in an upper chamber."—*Id.* "Then Manasseh knew that the Lord was God."—*Id.* "Whatever a man conceives clearly, he may, if he will be at the trouble, put into distinct propositions, and express clearly to others."—*See Blair's Rhet.* p. 93. "But the painter, being entirely confined to that part of time which he has chosen, cannot exhibit various stages of the same action."—*Murray's Gram.* i, 195. "What he subjoins, is without any proof at all."—*Barclay cor.* "George Fox's Testimony concerning Robert Barclay."—*Title cor.* "According to the *advice of the* author of the Postcript."—*Barclay cor.* "These things seem as ugly to the eye of their meditations, as those Ethiopians *that were* pictured *on Nemesis's* pitcher."—*Bacon cor.* "Moreover, there is always a twofold condition propounded with *the Sphynx's enigmas.*"

—*Id.* " Whoever believeth not therein, shall perish."—*Koran cor.* " When, at *Sestius's* entreaty, I had been at his house."—*W. Walker cor.*

" There high on *Sipylus's* shaggy brow,
　　She stands, her own sad monument of wo."—*Pope cor.*

UNDER NOTE II.—CHANGE OF NUMBER.

" So will I send upon you famine, and evil beasts, and they shall bereave *you.*"—*Bible cor.*
" Why do you plead so much for it? why do *you* preach it up?" Or: " Why do *ye* plead so much for it? why do *ye* preach it up?"—*Barclay cor.* " Since thou hast decreed that I shall bear man, *thy* darling."—*Edward's Gram. cor.* " You have my book, and I have *yours;* i. e., *your* book." Or thus: "*Thou hast* my book, and I have *thine;* i. e., *thy* book."—*Chandler cor.*
" Neither art thou such a one as to be ignorant of what *thou art.*"—*Bullions cor.* " Return, thou backsliding Israel, saith the Lord, and I will not cause mine anger to fall upon *thee.*"
—*Bible cor.* " The Almighty, unwilling to cut thee off in the fullness of iniquity, has sent me to give *thee* warning."—*Ld. Kames cor.* " *Wast* thou born only for pleasure? *wast thou* never to do any thing?"—*Collier cor.* " Thou shalt be required to go to God, to die, and *to* give up *thy* account."—*Barnes cor.* " And canst thou expect to behold the resplendent glory of the Creator? would not such a sight annihilate *thee?*"—*Milton cor.* " If the prophet had commanded thee to do some great thing, *wouldst thou* have refused?"—*C. S. Journal cor.* " Art thou a penitent? evince *thy* sincerity, by bringing forth fruits meet for repentance."—*Vade-Mecum cor.* " I will call thee my dear son: I remember all *thy* tenderness."—*C. Tales cor.* " So do thou, my son: open *thy* ears, and *thy* eyes."—*Wright cor.* " I promise you, this was enough to discourage *you.*"
—*Bunyan cor.* " Ere you remark an other's sin, Bid *your* own conscience look within."—*Gay cor.*
" Permit that I share in thy wo, The privilege *canst thou* refuse?"—*Perfect cor.* " Ah! Strephon, how *canst thou* despise Her who, without thy pity, *diest?*"—*Swift cor.*

" Thy verses, friend, are Kidderminster stuff;
　　And I must own, thou'st measured out enough."—*Shenst. cor.*

" This day, dear Bee, is thy nativity;
　　Had Fate a luckier one, she'd give it *thee.*"—*Swift cor.*

UNDER NOTE III.—WHO AND WHICH.

" Exactly like so many puppets, *which* are moved by wires."—*Blair cor.* " They are my servants, *whom* I brought forth* out of the land of Egypt."—*Leviticus,* xxv, 55. " Behold, I and the children *whom* God hath given me."—See *Isaiah,* viii, 18. " And he sent Eliakim, *who* was over the household, and Shebna the scribe."—*Isaiah,* xxxvii, 2. " In a short time the streets were cleared of the corpses *which* filled them."—*M'Ilvaine cor.* " They are not of those *who* teach things *that* they ought not, for filthy lucre's sake."—*Barclay cor.* " As a lion among the beasts of the forest, as a young lion among the flocks of sheep; *which,* if he go through, both treadeth down and teareth in pieces."—*Bible cor.* " Frequented by every fowl *which* nature has taught to dip the wing in water."—*Johnson cor.* " He had two sons, one of *whom* was adopted by the family of Maximus."—*Lempriere cor.* " And the ants, *which* are collected by the smell, are burned *with* fire."—*The Friend cor.* " They being the agents to *whom* this thing was trusted."—*Nixon cor.* " A packhorse *which* is driven constantly *one way and the other,* to *and from* market."—*Locke cor.* " By instructing children, *whose* affection will be increased."—*Nixon cor.*
" He had a comely young woman, *who* travelled with him."—*Hutchinson cor.* " A butterfly, *who* thought himself an accomplished traveller, happened to light upon a beehive."—*Inst.* p. 267. " It is an enormous elephant of stone, *which* disgorges from his uplifted trunk a vast but graceful shower."—*Ware cor.* " He was met by a dolphin, *which* sometimes swam before him, and sometimes behind him."—*Edward's Gram. cor.*

" That Cæsar's horse, *which,* as fame goes,| Was not by half so tender-hoof'd,
　　Had corns upon his feet and toes,| Nor trod upon the ground so soft."—*Butler cor.*

UNDER NOTE IV.—NOUNS OF MULTITUDE.

" He instructed and fed the crowds *that* surrounded him."—*Murray's Key.* " The court, *which* gives currency to manners, ought to be exemplary."—*Ib.* p. 187. " Nor does he describe classes of sinners *that* do not exist."—*Mag. cor.* " Because the nations among *which* they took their rise, were not savage."—*Murray cor.* " Among nations *that* are in the first and rude periods of society."—*Blair cor.* " The martial spirit of those nations among *which* the feudal government prevailed."—*Id.* " France, *which* was in alliance with Sweden."—*Priestley's Gram.* p. 97.
" That faction, in England, *which* most powerfully opposed his arbitrary pretensions."—*Ib.* " We may say, 'the crowd *which* was going up the street.'"—*Cobbett's E. Gram.* ¶ 204. " Such members of the Convention *which* formed this Lyceum, as have subscribed this Constitution."—*N. Y. Lyceum cor.*

UNDER NOTE V.—CONFUSION OF SENSES.

"*The name of* the possessor shall take a particular form to show its case."—*Kirkham cor.*
" Of which reasons, the principal one is, that no noun, properly so called, implies *the presence of the thing named.*"—*Harris cor.* " *Boston* is a proper noun, which distinguishes *the city of Boston* from other cities."—*Sanborn cor.* "*The word* CONJUNCTION means union, or *the act of* joining together. *Conjunctions are* used to join or connect either words or sentences."—*Id.* " The word INTERJECTION means *the act of throwing between. Interjections are* interspersed among other words, to express *strong or sudden* emotion."—*Id.* " *Indeed* is composed of *in* and *deed. The words* may better be written separately, as they formerly were."—*Cardell cor.* " *Alexander,* on the contrary, is a particular name; and is *employed* to distinguish *an individual only.*"—*Jamieson cor.* " As an indication that nature itself had changed *its* course." Or:—" that *Nature herself* had changed her course."—*History cor.* " Of removing from the United States and *their* territories

---

* It would be better to omit the word "*forth,*" or else to say—" whom I *brought forth from* the land of Egypt." The phrase, "*forth out of,*" is neither a very common nor a very terse one.—G. BROWN.

free people of colour."—*Jenifer cor.* "So that *gh* may be said not to have *its* proper sound."
hus: "So that *the letters, g* and *h*, may be said not to have their proper *sounds.*"—*Webster*
"Are we to welcome the loathsome harlot, and introduce *her* to our children ?"—*Maturin*
"The first question is this: 'Is reputable, national, and present use, *which*, for brevity's
', I shall hereafter simply denominate *good use*, always uniform, [i. e., undivided, and unequiv-
.] in *its* decisions?'"—*Campbell cor.* "In *personifications*, Time is always masculine, on ac-
it of *his* mighty efficacy; Virtue, feminine, *by reason of her* beauty and *loveliness.*"—*Murray,*
r, et al. cor.* "When you speak to a person or thing, the *noun or pronoun* is in the second
on."—*Bartlett cor.* "You now know the noun; for *noun* means *name.*"—*Id.* "T. What
ou see ? *P. A book. T. Spell *book.*"—R. W. Green cor.* "T. What do you see now ? *P.
books. T. Spell *books.*"—Id.* "If the United States lose *their* rights as a nation."—*Lib-
or cor.* "When a person or thing is addressed or spoken to, the *noun or pronoun* is in the
nd person."—*Frost cor.* "When a person or thing is *merely* spoken of, the *noun or pronoun*
the third person."—*Id.* "The *word* ox *also, taking* the same plural termination, *makes
x."—*Bucke cor.*

> "Hail, happy States! *yours* is the blissful seat
> Where nature's gifts and art's improvements meet."—*Everett cor.*

UNDER NOTE VI.—THE RELATIVE THAT.

.) "This is the most useful art *that* men possess."—*L. Murray cor.* "The earliest accounts
history gives us, concerning all nations, bear testimony to these facts."—*Blair et al. cor.*
r. Addison was the first *that* attempted a regular inquiry [into the pleasures of taste]."—*Blair*
"One of the first *that* introduced it, was Montesquieu."—*Murray cor.* "Massillon is per-
the most eloquent *sermonizer that* modern times have produced."—*Blair cor.* "The greatest
er *that* ever lived, is our guiding star and prototype."—*Hart cor.*
.) "When prepositions are subjoined to nouns, they are generally the same *that* are subjoined
he verbs from which the nouns are derived."—*Murray's Gram.* p. 200. Better thus: "*The
ositions which* are subjoined to nouns, *are generally the same that,*" &c.—*Priestley cor.* "The
e proportions *that* are agreeable in a model, are not agreeable in a large building."—*Kames*
"The same ornaments *that* we admire in a private apartment, are unseemly in a temple."
urray cor. "The same *that* John saw also in the sun."—*Milton cor.*
.) "Who can ever be easy, *that* is reproached with his own ill conduct ?"—*T. à Kempis cor.*
ho is she *that* comes clothed in a robe of green ?"—*Inst.* p. 267. "Who *that* has either sense
vility, does not perceive the vileness of profanity ?"—*G. Brown.*
.) "The second person denotes the person or thing *that* is spoken to."—*Kirkham cor.* "The
d person denotes the person or thing *that* is spoken of."—*Id.* "A passive verb denotes ac-
received or endured by the person or thing *that* is *signified by* its nominative."—*Id.* "The
ces and states *that* had neglected or favoured the growth of this power."—*Bolingbroke cor.*
he nominative expresses the name of the person or thing *that* acts, or *that* is the subject of
ourse."—*Hiley cor.*
.) "Authors *that* deal in long sentences, are very apt to be faulty."—*Blair cor.* "Writers
deal," &c.—*Murray cor.* "The neuter gender denotes objects *that* are neither male nor
ale."—*Merchant cor.* "The neuter gender denotes things *that* have no sex."—*Kirkham cor.*
ouns *that* denote objects neither male nor female, are of the neuter gender."—*Wells's Gram.*
ate, p. 55. Better thus: "*Those* nouns *which* denote objects *that are* neither male nor
ale, are of the neuter gender."—*Wells cor.* "Objects and ideas *that* have been long familiar,
e too faint an impression to give an agreeable exercise to our faculties."—*Blair cor.* "Cases
custom has left dubious, are certainly within the grammarian's province."—*L. Murray cor.*
ubstantives *that* end in *ery*, signify action or habit."—*Id.* "After all *that* can be done to
der the definitions and rules of grammar accurate."—*Id.* "Possibly, all *that* I have said, is
wn and taught."—*A. B. Johnson cor.*
.) "It is a strong and manly style *that* should chiefly be studied."—*Blair cor.* "It is this
, *precision*] *that* chiefly makes a division appear neat and elegant."—*Id.* "I hope it is not I
he is displeased with."—*L. Murray cor.* "When it is this alone *that* renders the sentence
ure."—*Campbell cor.* "This sort of full and ample assertion, '*It is this that,*' is to be
l when a proposition of importance is laid down."—*Blair cor.* "She is the person *that* I un-
tood it to have been."—*L. Murray cor.* "Was it thou, or the wind, *that* shut the door ?"—
. p. 267. "It was not I *that* shut it."—*Ib.*
.) "He is not the person *that* he seemed to be."—*Murray and Ingersoll cor.* "He is really
person *that* he appeared to be."—*Iid.* "She is not now the woman *that* they represented her
ave been."—*Iid.* "An *only child* is one *that* has neither brother nor sister; a *child alone* is
that is left by itself, *or unaccompanied.*"—*Blair, Jam. and Mur. cor.*

UNDER NOTE VII.—RELATIVE CLAUSES CONNECTED.

.) "A Substantive, or Noun, is the name of a thing; (i. e.,) of whatever we conceive to sub-
, or *of whatever* we *merely imagine.*"—*Lowth cor.* (2.) "A Substantive, or Noun, is the name
ny thing *which* exists, or of which we have any notion."—*Murray et al. cor.* (3.) "A Sub-
itive, or Noun, is the name of any person, place, or thing, that exists, or *that* we can have
idea *of.*"—*Frost cor.* (4.) "A Noun is the name of any thing *which* exists, or of which we
n an idea."—*Hallock cor.* (5.) "A Noun is the name of any person, place, object, or thing,
: exists, or *that* we may conceive to exist."—*D. C. Allen cor.* (6.) "The name of every
ig *which* exists, or of which we can form any notion, is a noun."—*Fisk cor.* (7.) "An alle-
y is the representation of some one thing by an other that resembles it, and *that* is made to
d for it."—*Blair's Rhet.* p. 150. (8.) "Had he exhibited such sentences as contained ideas
pplicable to young minds, or *such as* were of a trivial or injurious nature."—*L. Murray cor.*
"Man would have others obey him, even his own kind; but he will not obey God, *who* is
much above him, and who made him."—*Penn cor.* (10.) "But what we may consider here,

and *what* few persons have *noticed*, is," &c.—*Brightland cor.* (11.) "The compiler has **not** inserted *those* verbs *which* are irregular only in familiar writing or discourse, and which are improperly terminated by *t in stead* of *ed.*"—*Murray, Fisk, Hart, Ingersoll, et al. cor.* (12.) " The remaining parts of speech, which are called the indeclinable parts, *and which* admit of no variations, (or, *being words that* admit of no variations,) will not detain us long."—*Dr. Blair cor.*

UNDER NOTE VIII.—THE RELATIVE AND PREPOSITION.

"In the temper of mind *in which* he was then."—*Lowth's Gram.* p. 102. "To bring them into the condition *in which* I am at present."—*Add. cor.* "In the posture *in which* I lay."—*Lowth's Gram.* p. 102. "In the sense *in which* it is sometimes taken."—*Barclay cor.* "Tools and utensils are said to be right, when they *answer well* the uses *for which* they were made."—*Collier cor.* "If, in the extreme danger *in which* I now am," &c. Or: "If, in *my present* extreme danger," &c.—*Murray's Sequel*, p. 116. "News was brought, that Darius was but twenty miles from the place *in which* they then were."—*Goldsmith cor.* "Alexander, upon hearing this news, continued four days *where* he then was: " or—"*in the place in which* he then was."—*Id.* "To read in the best manner *in which* reading is now taught."—*L. Murray cor.* "It may be expedient to give a few directions as to the manner *in which* it should be studied."—*Hallock cor.* " Participles are words derived from verbs, and convey an idea of the acting of an agent, or the suffering of an object, with the time *at which* it happens."*—A. Murray cor.*

"Had I but serv'd my God with half the zeal
With which I serv'd my king, he would not *thus*,
In age, have left me naked to *my foes.*"—*Shak. cor.*

UNDER NOTE IX.—ADVERBS FOR RELATIVES.

"In compositions *that are not designed to be delivered in public.*"—*Blair cor.* "They framed a protestation *in which* they repeated their claims."—*Priestley's Gram.* p. 133; *Murray's*, 197. "Which have reference to *inanimate* substances, *in which* sex *has no* existence."—*Harris cor.* "Which denote substances *in which* sex never had existence."—*Ingersoll's Gram.* p. 26. "There is no rule given *by which* the truth may be found out."—*W. Walker cor.* " The nature of the objects *from which* they are taken."—*Blair cor.* "That darkness of character, *through which* we can see no heart :" [i. e., generous emotion.]—*L. Murray cor.* "The states *with which* [or *between which*] they negotiated."—*Formey cor.* " Till the motives *from which* men act, be known." —*Beattie cor.* " He assigns the principles *from which* their power of pleasing flows."—*Blair cor.* "But I went on, and so finished this History, in that form *in which* it now appears."—*Sewel cor.* " By prepositions we express the cause *for which*, the instrument by which, *and* the manner *in* which, a thing is done."—*A. Murray cor.* " They are not such in the language *from which* they are derived."—*Town cor.* " I find it very hard to persuade several, that their passions are affected by words from *which* they have no ideas."—*Burke cor.* "The known end, then, *for which* we are placed in a state of so much affliction, hazard, and difficulty, is our improvement in virtue and piety."—*Bp. Butler cor.*

"Yet such his acts as Greeks unborn shall tell,
And curse the *strife in which* their fathers fell."—*Pope cor.*

UNDER NOTE X.—REPEAT THE NOUN.

"Youth may be thoughtful, but *thoughtfulness in the young* is not very common."—*Webster cor.* "A proper name is *a name* given to one person or thing."—*Bartlett cor.* "A common name is *a name* given to many things of the same sort."—*Id.* " This rule is often violated ; some instances of *its violation* are annexed."—*L. Murray et al. cor.* " This is altogether careless writing. Such negligence respecting *the pronouns*, renders style often obscure, and always inelegant."—*Blair cor.* "Every inversion which is not governed by this rule, will be disrelished by *every person* of taste." —*Kames cor.* "A proper diphthong, is *a diphthong* in which both the vowels are sounded."— *Brown's Institutes*, p. 18. "An improper diphthong, is *a diphthong* in which only one of the vowels is sounded."—*Ib.* "Abraham, Isaac, Jacob, and the descendants *of Jacob*, are called Hebrews."—*Wood cor.* " In our language, *every word* of more than one syllable, has one *of its syllables* distinguished from the rest in this manner."—*L. Murray cor.* "Two consonants *proper* to begin a word, must not be separated; as, fa-ble, sti-fle. But when *two consonants* come between two vowels, and are such as cannot begin a word, they must be divided; as, ut-most, under."—*Id.* " Shall the intellect alone feel no pleasures in its energy, when we allow *pleasures* to the grossest relations of appetite and sense ?"—*Harris and Murray cor.* "No man has a propensity to vice as such : on the contrary, a wicked deed disgusts *every one*, and makes *him* abhor the author."—*Ld. Kames cor.* " The same *grammatical properties* that belong to *nouns*, belong also to pronouns."—*Greenleaf cor.* "What is language ? It is the means of communicating thoughts from one *person* to an other."—*Peirce cor.* "A simple word is *a word which* is not made up of *other words.*"—*Adam and Gould cor.* " A compound word is *a word* which is made up of two or more words."—*Iid.* " When a conjunction is to be supplied, *the ellipsis* is called Asyndeton."—*Adam cor.*

UNDER NOTE XI.—PLACE OF THE RELATIVE.

" It gives *to words a meaning which* they would not have."—*L. Murray cor.* "There are in the English language many *words, that* are sometimes used as adjectives, and sometimes as adverbs."—*Id.* "Which do not more effectually show the varied intentions of the mind, than do the *auxiliaries which* are used to form the potential mood."—*Id.* " These *accents, which will be* the subject of a following speculation, make different impressions on the mind."—*Ld. Kames cor.* "And others differed very much from the words *of the writers to whom* they were ascribed."— *John Ward cor.* " Where there is in the sense *nothing which* requires the last sound to be elevated, an easy fall will be proper."—*Murray and Bullions cor.* "In the last clause, there is an *ellipsis*

---

* This *doctrine*, that participles divide and specify time, I have elsewhere shown to be erroneous.—G. Brown.

e verb ; and, when you supply *it*, you find it necessary to use the adverb *not in lieu of no*."
—*Campbell and Mur. cor.* "Study is *of the* singular number, because *the* nominative *I, with which* it agrees, *is singular*."—*R. C. Smith cor.* " John is the *person who* is in error, or thou art."
—*right cor.* "For he hath made him, who knew no sin, to be sin for us."—*Harrison's E. G.* p. 197.

　　" My friend, take that of *me, who* have the power
　　To seal th' accuser's lips."—*Shakspeare cor.*

Under Note XII.—WHAT for THAT.

I had no idea but *that* the story was true."—*Brown's Inst.* p. 268. "The postboy is not so *fly* but *that* he can whistle."—*Ib.* "He had no intimation but *that* the men were honest."—
" Neither Lady Haversham nor Miss Mildmay will ever believe but *that* I have been entirely same."—*Priestley cor.* "I am not satisfied but *that* the integrity of our friends is more essential to our welfare than their knowledge of the world."—*Id.* "Indeed, there is in poetry
being so entertaining or descriptive. but *that an ingenious* didactic writer may introduce *it* in some of his work."—*Blair cor.* "Brasidas, being bit by a mouse he had catched, let it slip out of his fingers : ' No creature,' says he, ' is so contemptible but *that it* may provide for its own safety, if it have courage.' "—*Ld. Kames cor.*

Under Note XIII.—ADJECTIVES FOR ANTECEDENTS.

In narration, Homer is, at all times, remarkably concise, *and therefore* lively and agreeable."
—*Blair cor.* "It is usual to talk of a nervous, a feeble, or a spirited style ; which *epithets* plainly *indicate the* writer's manner of thinking."—*Id.* "It is too violent an alteration, if any alterations were necessary, *whereas* none is."—*Knight cor.* "Some men are too ignorant to be humble ;
without *humility* there can be no docility."—*Berkley cor.* "Judas declared him innocent ;
innocent he could not be, had he in any respect deceived the disciples."—*Porteus cor.* "They
used him to be innocent, *but* he certainly was not so."—*Murray el al. cor.* "They accounted
honest, *but* he certainly was not *so*."—*Felch cor.* "Be accurate in all you say or do ; for accuracy is important in all the concerns of life."—*Brown's Inst.* p. 268. "Every law supposes
a transgressor to be wicked ; *and* indeed he is *so*, if the law is just."—*Ib.* "To be pure in
heart, pious, and benevolent, (*and* all may be *so*,) constitutes human happiness."—*Murray cor.*
" be dexterous in danger, is a virtue ; but to court danger to show *our dexterity, is a weakness.*"
—Same cor.

Under Note XIV.—SENTENCES FOR ANTECEDENTS.

This seems not so allowable in prose ; which *fact* the following erroneous examples will demonstrate."—*L. Murray cor.* "The accent is laid upon the last syllable of a word ; which *circumstance* is favourable to the melody."—*Kames cor.* "Every line consists of ten syllables, five short and five long ; from which *rule* there are but two exceptions, both of them rare."—*Id.* "The soldiers refused obedience, *as* has been explained."—*Nixon cor.* "Cæsar overcame Pompey—*a
circumstance* which was lamented."—*Id.* "The crowd hailed William, *agreeably to the expectations
of his friends*."—*Id.* "The tribunes resisted Scipio, *who knew their malevolence towards him*."—
"The censors reproved vice, *and were held in great honour*."—*Id.* "The generals neglected *discipline, which fact* has been proved."—*Id.* "There would be two nominatives to the verb *was*,
which a construction is improper."—*Adam and Gould cor.* "His friend bore the abuse very patiently ; *whose forbearance, however,* served only to increase his rudeness : it produced, at length, contempt and insolence."—*Murray and Emmons cor.* "Almost all *compound* sentences are more or less elliptical ; *and some* examples of *ellipsis* may be *found*, under *nearly all* the different parts of speech."—*Murray, Guy, Smith, &c. cor.*

Under Note XV.—REPEAT THE PRONOUN.

In things of Nature's workmanship, whether we regard their internal or *their* external structure, beauty and design are equally conspicuous."—*Kames cor.* "It puzzles the reader, by making him doubt whether the word ought to be taken in its proper, or *in its* figurative sense."—*Id.*
"Neither my obligations to the muses, nor *my* expectations from them, are so great."—*Cowley cor.* "The Fifth Annual Report of the *Antislavery* Society of Ferrisburgh and *its* vicinity."—
Extr. cor. "Meaning taste in its figurative as well as *its* proper sense."—*Kames cor.* "Every
care in which either your personal or *your* political character is concerned."—*Junius cor.* "A
jealous and righteous God has often punished such in themselves or *in their* offspring."—*Extr.*
" Hence their civil and *their* religious history are inseparable."—*Milman cor.* "Esau thus
easily threw away both his civil and *his* religious inheritance."—*Id.* "This intelligence excites not only our hopes, but *our* fears likewise."—*Jaudon cor.* "In what *way* our defect of principle, and *our* ruling manners, have completed the ruin of the national spirit of union."—*Dr.
Mason cor.* "Considering her descent, her connexion, and *her* present intercourse."—*Webster cor.* "His own and *his* wife's wardrobe are packed up in a firkin."—*Parker and Fox cor.*

Under Note XVI.—CHANGE THE ANTECEDENT.

The *sounds* of *e* and *o* long, in *their* due degrees, will be preserved, and clearly distinguished."
—*Murray cor.* "If any *persons* should be inclined to think," &c., "the author takes the liberty to suggest to *them*," &c.—*Id.* "And he walked in all the *way* of Asa his father ; he turned not aside from *it*."—*Bible cor.* "If ye from your hearts forgive not every one his *brethren their*
trespasses."—*Id.* "None ever fancied *they* were slighted by him, or had the courage to think *themselves* his *betters*."—*Collier cor.* "And *Rebecca* took *some very good clothes* of her eldest son *Esau's*, which *were* with her in the house, and put *them* upon Jacob her younger son."—*Gen. cor.*
There all the attention of *men* is given to *their* own indulgence."—*Maturin cor.* "The idea *of a father* is a notion superinduced to *that of* the substance, or man—let *one's idea of* man be *as* it will."—*Locke cor.* "Leaving *all* to do as they list."—*Barclay cor.* "Each *person* performed his part handsomely."—*Flint cor.* "This block of marble rests on two layers of *stones*,

bound together with lead, which, however, has not prevented the Arabs from forcing out several of them."—*Parker and Fox cor.*
  " Love gives to *all our powers* a double power,
    Above their functions and their offices." Or :—
  " Love gives to every power a double power,
    Exalts all functions and *all* offices."—*Shak. cor.*

CORRECTIONS UNDER RULE XI; OF PRONOUNS.

UNDER THE RULE ITSELF.—THE IDEA OF PLURALITY.

" The jury will be confined till *they* agree on a verdict."—*Brown's Inst.* p. 145. " And mankind directed *their* first cares towards the needful."—*Formey cor.* " It is difficult to deceive a free people respecting *their* true interest."—*Life of Charles XII cor.* " All the virtues of mankind are to be counted upon a few fingers, but *their* follies and vices are innumerable."—*Swift cor.* " Every sect saith, ' Give *us* liberty : ' but give it *them*, and to *their* power, *and they* will not yield it to any body else."—*Cromwell cor.* " Behold, the people shall rise up as a great lion, and lift up *themselves* as a young lion."—*Bible cor.* " For all flesh had corrupted *their* way upon the earth."—*Id.* " There happened to the army a very strange accident, which put *them* in great consternation."—*Goldsmith cor.*

UNDER NOTE I.—THE IDEA OF UNITY.

" The meeting went on *with its* business as a united body."—*Foster cor.* " Every religious association has an undoubted right to adopt a creed for *itself*."—*Gould cor.* " It would therefore be extremely difficult to raise an insurrection in that state against *its* own government."—*Dr. Webster cor.* " The mode in which a lyceum can apply *itself* in effecting a reform in commerce schools."—*N. Y. Lyc. cor.* " Hath a nation changed *its* gods, which yet are no gods ?"—*Jer. cor.* " In the holy Scriptures, each of the twelve tribes of Israel is often called by the name of its patriarch from whom *it* descended." Or better :—" from whom *the tribe* descended."—*Adams cor.*

UNDER NOTE II.—UNIFORMITY OF NUMBER.

" A nation, by the reparation of *the wrongs which it has done*, achieves a triumph more glorious than any field of blood can ever give."—*Adams cor.* " The English nation, from *whom we descended*, have been gaining their liberties inch by inch."—*Webster cor.* " If a Yearly Meeting should undertake to alter *its* fundamental doctrines, is there any power in the society to prevent *it from* doing so ?"—*Foster's Rep. cor.* " There is [*] a generation that *curse* their father, and do not bless their mother."—*Bible cor.* " There is [*] a generation that are pure in their own eyes, and yet *are* not washed from their filthiness."—*Id.* " He hath not beheld iniquity in Jacob, neither hath he seen perverseness in Israel : the Lord *their* God is with *them*, and the shout of a king is among them."—*Id.* " My people *have* forgotten me, they have burnt incense to vanity."—*Id.* " When a quarterly meeting *has* come to a *judgement* respecting any difference, relative to any monthly meeting belonging to *it*," &c.—*Discip. cor.* " The number of such compositions is every day increasing, and *it appears* to be limited only by the pleasure or *the convenience of writers*."—*Booth cor.* " The Church of Christ *has* the same power now as ever, and is led by the same Spirit into the same practices."—*Barclay cor.* " The army, whose *their* chief had thus abandoned, pursued meanwhile their miserable march." Or thus: " The army, *which its* chief had thus abandoned, pursued meanwhile *its* miserable march."—*Lockhart cor.*

CORRECTIONS UNDER RULE XII; OF PRONOUNS.

ANTECEDENTS CONNECTED BY AND.

" Discontent and sorrow manifested *themselves* in his countenance."—*Brown's Inst.* p. 184. " Both conversation and public speaking became more simple and plain, such as we now find them."—*Blair cor.* " Idleness and ignorance, if *they* be suffered to proceed, &c."—*Johnson and Priestley cor.* " Avoid questions and strife : *they show* a busy and contentious disposition."—*Prus cor.* " To receive the gifts and benefits of God with thanksgiving, and witness *them* blessed and sanctified to us by the word and prayer, is owned by us."—*Barclay cor.* " Both minister and magistrate are compelled to choose between *their* duty and *their* reputation."—*Junius cor.* " All the sincerity, truth, and faithfulness, or disposition of heart or conscience to approve them, found among rational creatures, necessarily originate from God."—*Rev. J. Brown cor.* " Your levity and heedlessness, if *they* continue, will prevent all substantial improvement."—*Brown's Inst.* p. 269. " Poverty and obscurity will oppress him only who esteems *them* oppressive."—*Ib.* " Good sense and refined policy are obvious to few, because *they* cannot be discovered but by a train of reflection."—*Ib.* " Avoid haughtiness of behaviour, and affectation of manners : *they* imply a want of solid merit."—*Ib.* " If love and unity continue, *they* will make you partakers of one an other's joy."—*Ib.* " Suffer not jealousy and distrust to enter : *they* will destroy. like a canker, every germ of friendship."—*Ib.* " Hatred and animosity are inconsistent with Christian charity : guard, therefore, against the slightest indulgence of *them*."—*Ib.* " Every man is entitled to liberty of conscience, and freedom of opinion, if he does not pervert *them* to the injury of others."—*Ib.*
  " With the azure and vermilion
    Which are mix'd for my pavilion."—*Byron cor.*

---

[*] Perhaps it would be as well or better, in correcting these two examples, to say, " There *are* a generation.' But the article *a*, as well as the literal form of the noun, is a sign of unity ; and a complete uniformity of number is not here practicable."

CORRECTIONS UNDER RULE XIII; OF PRONOUNS.

ANTECEDENTS CONNECTED BY OR OR NOR.

"Neither prelate nor priest can give *his* [flock or] flocks any decisive evidence that you are lawful pastors."—*Brownlee cor.* "And is there a heart of parent or of child, that does not beat and burn within *him?*"—*Maturin cor.* "This is just as if an eye or a foot should demand a salary for *its* service to the body."—*Collier cor.* "If thy hand or thy foot offend thee, cut *it* off, and cast *it* from thee."—*Bible cor.* "The same might as well be said of Virgil, or any great author; whose general character will infallibly raise many casual additions to *his* reputation."—*Pope cor.* "Either James or John,—one *or the other,*—will come."—*Smith cor.* "Even a rugged rock or *a* barren heath, though in *itself* disagreeable, *contributes,* by contrast, to the beauty of the whole."—*Kames cor.* "That neither Count Rechteren nor Monsieur Mesnager had behaved *himself* right in this affair."—*Spect. cor.* "If an Aristotle, a Pythagoras, or a Galileo, *suffers* for *his* opinions, *he is a* 'martyr.'"—*Fuller cor.* "If an ox gore a man or a woman, that *he or she* die; then the ox *shall surely* be stoned."—*Exod. cor.* "She was calling out to one or an other, at every step, that a Habit was ensnaring him."—*Johnson cor.* "Here is a task put upon children, *which* neither this author *himself,* nor any other, has yet undergone."—*R. Johnson cor.* "Hence, if an adjective or *a* participle be subjoined to the verb when *the construction is singular, it* will agree both in gender and *in* number with the collective noun."—*Adam and Gould cor.* "And if you can find a diphthong or a triphthong, be pleased to point *that* out too."—*Bucke cor.* "And if you can find a trisyllable or a polysyllable, point *it* out."—*Id.* "The false refuges in which the atheist or the sceptic *has* intrenched *himself.*"—*Chr. Spect. cor.* "While the man or woman thus assisted by art, expects *his* charms *or hers* will be imputed to nature alone."—*Opie cor.* "When you press a watch, or pull a clock, *it answers* your question with precision; for *it repents* exactly the hour of the day, and tells you neither more nor less than you desire to know."—*Bolingbroke cor.*

"Not the Mogul, or Czar of Muscovy,
Not Prester John, or Cham of Tartary,
Is in *his mansion* monarch more than I."—*King cor.*

CHAPTER VI.—VERBS.

CORRECTIONS UNDER RULE XIV AND ITS NOTES.

UNDER THE RULE ITSELF.—VERB AFTER THE NOMINATIVE.

"Before you left Sicily, you *were reconciled* to Verres."—*Duncan cor.* "Knowing that you *were* my old master's good friend."—*Spect. cor.* "When the judge *dares* not act, where is the loser's remedy?"—*Webster cor.* "Which extends it no farther than the variation of the verb *extends.*"—*Mur. cor.* "They presently dry without hurt, as myself *have* often proved."—*R. Williams cor.* "Whose goings-forth *have* been from of old, from everlasting."—*Micah,* v, 2. "You *were* paid to fight against Alexander, not to rail at him."—*Porter cor.* "Where more than one part of speech *are* almost always concerned."—*Churchill cor.* "Nothing less than murders, rapines, and conflagrations, *employs* their thoughts." Or: "*No less things* than murders, rapines, and conflagrations, *employ* their thoughts."—*Duncan cor.* "I wondered where you *were,* my dear."—*Lloyd cor.* "When thou most sweetly *singst.*"—*Drummond cor.* "Who *dares,* at the present day, avow himself equal to the task?"—*Gardiner cor.* "Every body *is* very kind to her, and not discourteous to me."—*Byron cor.* "As to what thou *sayst* respecting the diversity of opinions."—*M. B. cor.* "Thy nature, Immortality, who *knows?*"—*Everest cor.* "The natural distinction of sex in animals, *gives* rise to what, in grammar, *are* called genders."—*Id.* "Some pains *have* likewise been taken."—*Scott cor.* "And many a steed in his stables *was* seen."—*Penwarne cor.* "They *were* forced to eat what never was esteemed food."—*Josephus cor.* "This that *you* yourself *have* spoken, I desire that they may take their oaths upon."—*Hutchinson cor.* "By men whose experience best *qualifies* them to judge."—*Committee cor.* "He *dares* venture to kill and destroy several other kinds of fish."—*Walton cor.* "If a gudgeon meet a roach, He ne'er *will* venture to approach." Or thus: "If a gudgeon *meets* a roach, He *dares* not venture to approach."—*Swift cor.* "Which thou *endeavourst* to establish to thyself."—*Barclay cor.* "But they pray together much oftener than thou *insinuat'st.*"—*Id.* "Of people of all denominations, over whom thou *presidest.*"—*N. Waln cor.* "I can produce ladies and gentlemen whose progress *has* been astonishing."—*Chazotte cor.* "Which of these two kinds of vice *is the* more criminal?"—*Dr. Brown cor.* "Every twenty-four hours *afford* to us the vicissitudes of day and night."—*Smith's False Syntax, New Gram.* p. 103. Or thus: "Every *period of* twenty-four hours *affords* to us the vicissitudes of day and night."—*Smith cor.* "Every four years *add* an other day."—*Smith's False Syntax, Gram.* p. 103. Better thus: "Every *fourth year adds* an other day."—*Smith cor.* "Every error I could find, *Has* my busy muse employed."—*Swift cor.* "A studious scholar *deserves* the approbation of his teacher."—*Sanborn cor.* "Perfect submission to the rules of a school *indicates* good breeding."—*Id.* "A comparison in which more than two *are* concerned."—*Lennie's Gram.* p. 78. "By the facilities which artificial language *affords* them."—*O. B. Peirce cor.* "Now thyself *hast* lost both lop and top."—*Spencer cor.* "Glad tidings *are* brought to the poor."—*Campb. cor.* "Upon which, all that is pleasurable or affecting in elocution, chiefly *depends.*"—*Sher. cor.* "No pains *have* been spared to render this work complete."—*Bullions cor.* "The United States *contain* more than a twentieth part of the land of this globe."—*Clinton cor.* "I am mindful that myself *am* strong."—*Fowler cor.* "Myself *am* (not *is*) weak;"—"Thyself *art* (not *is*) weak."—*Id.*

"How pale each worshipful and reverend guest
Rises from *clerical* or city feast!"—*Pope cor.*

UNDER THE RULE ITSELF.—VERB BEFORE THE NOMINATIVE.

"Where *were* you bo:n? In London."—*Buchanan cor.* "There *are* frequent occasions for commas."—*Ingersoll cor.* "There necessarily *follow* from thence these plain and unquestionable consequences."—*Priestley cor.* "And to this impression *contributes* the redoubled effort."—*Kames cor.* "Or, if he was, *were* there no spiritual men then?"—*Barclay cor.* "So, by these two also, *are* signified their contrary principles."—*Id.* "In the motions made with the hands, *consists* the chief part of gesture in speaking."—*Blair cor.* "*Dares* he assume the name of a popular magistrate?"—*Duncan cor.* "There *were* no damages as in England, and so Scott lost his wager."—*Byron cor.* "In fact, there *exist* such resemblances."—*Kames cor.* "To him *give all* the prophets witness."—*Acts*, x, 43. "That there *were* so many witnesses and actors."—*Addison cor.* "How *do* this man's definitions stand affected?"—*Collier cor.* "Whence *come* all the powers and prerogatives of rational beings?"—*Id.* "Nor *do* the scriptures cited by thee prove thy intent."—*Barclay cor.* "Nor *does* the scripture cited by thee prove the contrary."—*Id.* "Why then *citest* thou a scripture which is so plain and clear for it?"—*Id.* "But what *say* the Scriptures as to respect of persons among Christians?"—*Id.* "But in the mind of man, while in the savage state, there *seem* to be hardly any ideas but what enter by the senses."—*Robertson cor.* "What sounds *has* each of the vowels?"—*Griscom cor.* "Out of this *have* grown up aristocracies, monarchies, despotisms, tyrannies."—*Brownson cor.* "And there *were* taken up, of fragments that remained to them, twelve baskets."—*Bible cor.* "There *seem* to be but two general classes."—*Day cor.* "Hence *arise* the six forms of expressing time."—*Id.* "There *seem* to be no other words required."—*Chandler cor.* "If there *are* two, the second increment is the syllable next *to* the last."—*Bullions cor.* "Hence *arise* the following advantages."—*Id.* "There *are* no data by which it can be estimated."—*Calhoun cor.* "To this class, *belongs* the Chinese language, in which we have nothing but naked *primitives.*"—*Fowler cor.* [☞ "Nothing but naked *roots,*" is faulty; because no word is a *root*, except some derivative spring from it.—G. B.] "There *were* several other grotesque figures that presented themselves."—*Spect. cor.* "In these *consist* that sovereign good which ancient sages so much extol."—*Percival cor.* "Here *come* those I have done good to against my will."—*Shak. cor.* "Where there *are* more than one auxiliary." Or: "Where there *are* more auxiliaries than one."—*O. B. Peirce cor.*

"On me to cast those eyes where *shines* nobility."—*Sidney cor.*

"Here *are* half-pence in plenty, for one you'll have twenty."—*Swift cor.*

"Ah, Jockey, ill *advisest* thou, I wis,
 To think of songs at such a time as this."—*Churchill cor.*

UNDER NOTE I.—THE RELATIVE AND VERB.

"Thou, who *lovest* us, wilt protect us still."—*A. Murray cor.* "To use that endearing language, 'Our Father, who *art* in heaven.'"—*Bates cor.* "Resembling the passions that *produce* these actions."—*Kames cor.* "Except *dwarf, grief, hoof, muff,* &c., which *take* s to make the plural."—*Ash cor.* "As the cattle that *go* before me, and the children, be able to endure."—*Gen. cor.* "Where is the man who *dares* affirm that such an action is mad?"—*Dr. Pratt cor.* "The ninth book of Livy affords one of the most beautiful exemplifications of historical painting, that *are* anywhere to be met with."—*Dr. Blair cor.* "In some studies, too, that relate to taste and fine writing, which *are* our object," &c.—*Id.* "Of those affecting situations which *make* man's heart feel for man."—*Id.* "We see very plainly, that it is neither Osmyn nor Jane Shore that *speaks.*"—*Id.* "It should assume that briskness and ease which *are* suited to the freedom of dialogue."—*Id.* "Yet they grant, that none ought to be admitted into the ministry, but such as *are* truly *pious.*"—*Barclay cor.* "This letter is one of the best that *have* been written about Lord Byron."—*Hunt cor.* "Thus, besides what *were* sunk, the Athenians took above two hundred ships."—*Goldsmith cor.* "To have made and declared such orders as *were* necessary."—*Hutchinson cor.* "The idea of such a collection of men as *makes* an army."—*Locke cor.* "I'm not the first that *has* been wretched."—*Southern cor.* "And the faint sparks of it which *are* in the angels, are concealed from our view."—*Calvin cor.* "The subjects are of such a nature, as *allows* room (or, as *to allow* room) for much diversity of taste and sentiment."—*Dr. Blair cor.* "It is in order to propose examples of such perfection, as *is* not to be found in the real examples of society"—*Formey cor.* "I do not believe that he would amuse himself with such fooleries as *have* been attributed to him."—*Id.* "That shepherd, who first *taught* the chosen seed."—*Milton, P. L.,* B. i, l. 8. "With respect to the vehemence and warmth which *are* allowed in popular eloquence."—*Dr. Blair cor.* "Ambition is one of those passions that *are* never to be satisfied."—*Home cor.* "Thou wast he that *led* out and *brought* in Israel."—*Bible cor.* "Art thou the man of God, that *came* from Judah?"—*Id.*

"How beauty is excell'd by manly grace
 And wisdom, which alone *are* truly fair."—*Milton cor.*
"What art thou, speak, that on designs unknown,
 While others sleep, thus *roamest* the camp alone?"—*Pope cor.*

UNDER NOTE II.—NOMINATIVE WITH ADJUNCTS.

"The literal sense of the words *is*, that the action had been done."—*Dr. Murray cor.* "The rapidity of his movements *was* beyond example."—*Wells cor.* "Murray's Grammar, together with his Exercises and Key, *has* nearly superseded every thing else of the kind."—*Murray's Rev. cor.* "The mechanism of clocks and watches *was* totally unknown."—*Hume cor.* "The *it*, together with the verb *to be, expresses a state* of being."—*Cobbett cor.* "Hence it is, that the profuse variety of objects in some natural landscapes, *occasions* neither confusion nor fatigue."—*Kames cor.* "Such a clatter of sounds *indicates* rage and ferocity."—*Gardiner cor.* "One of the fields made threescore square yards, and the other, only fifty-five."—*Duncan cor.* "The happy effects of this fable *are* worth attending to."—*Bailey cor.* "Yet the glorious serenity of its parting rays, *still* lingers with us."—*Gould cor.* "Enough of its form and force *is* retained to render them *uneasy.*"—*Maturin cor.* "The works of nature, in this respect, *are* extremely regular."—*Pratt cor.* "No

ll addition of exotic and foreign words and phrases, *has* been made by commerce."—*Bicknell*
"The dialect of some nouns *is noticed* in the notes."—*Milnes cor.* "It has been said, that
scovery of the full resources of the arts, *affords* the means of debasement, or of perversion."
ush cor. "By which means, the order of the words *is* disturbed."—*Holmes cor.* "The two-
influence of these and the others, *requires* the *verb* to be in the plural form."—*Peirce cor.*
id each of these *affords* employment."—*Percival cor.* "The pronunciation of the vowels *is*
explained under the rules relative to the consonants."—*Coar cor.* "The judicial power of
e courts *extends* to all cases in law and equity."—*Hall and Baker cor.* "One of you *has* stolen
money."—*Humorist cor.* "Such redundancy of epithets, in stead of pleasing, *produces* sa-
y and disgust."—*Kames cor.* "It has been alleged, that a compliance with the rules of Rhet-
, *tends* to cramp the mind."—*Hiley cor.* "Each of these *is* presented to us in different rela-
s."—*Hendrick cor.* "The past tense of these verbs, (*should, would, might, could,*) *is* very
:finite with respect to time."—*Bullions cor.* "The power of the words which are said to gov-
this mood, *is* distinctly understood."—*Chandler cor.*
    "And now, at length, the fated term of years
    The world's desire *hath* brought, and lo! the God appears."—*Lowth cor.*
    "Variety of numbers still *belongs*
    To the soft melody of *odes,* or *songs.*"—*Brightland cor.*

UNDER NOTE III.—COMPOSITE OR CONVERTED SUBJECTS.

Many are the works of human industry, which to begin and finish, *is* hardly granted to the
e man."—*Johnson cor.* "To lay down rules for these, *is* inefficacious."—*Pratt cor.* "To pro-
regard and act *injuriously, discovers* a base mind."—*L. Murray et al. cor.* "To magnify to the
;ht of wonder things great, new, and admirable, extremely *pleases* the mind of man."—*Fisher*
"In this passage, '*according as*' *is* used in a manner which is very common."—*Webster cor.*
CAUSE DE, *is* called a preposition; A CAUSE QUE, a conjunction."—*Webster cor.* "To these
given to speak in the name of the Lord."—*The Friend cor.* "While *wheat* has no plural,
has seldom any singular."—*Cobbett cor.* "He cannot assert that *ll* (i. e., *double Ell*) *is* ined in *fullness* to denote the sound of *u.*"—*Cobb cor.* "*Ch,* in Latin, *has* the power of *k.*"—
ld cor. "*Ti,* before a vowel, and unaccented, *has* the sound of *si* or *ci.*"—*Id.* "In words de-
d from French, as *chagrin, chicanery,* and *chaise, ch is sounded* like *sh.*"—*Bucke cor.* "But, in
words schism, schismatic, &c., the *ch is* silent."—*Id.* "*Ph,* at the beginning of words, *is* always
nded like *f.*"—*Bucke cor.* "*Ph has* the sound of *f,* as in *philosophy.*"—*Webster cor.* "*Sh*
one sound only, as in *shall.*"—*Id.* "*Th has* two sounds."—*Id.* "*Sc,* before *a, o, u,* or *r, has*
sound of *sk.*"—*Id.* "*Aw has* the sound of *a* in *hall.*"—*Bolles cor.* "*Ew sounds* like *u.*"—*Id.*
c, when both *vowels are* sounded, *has* the *power* of *ou* in *thou.*"—*Id.* "*Ui,* when both *vowels*
pronounced in one syllable, *sounds* like *wi* short, as in *languid.*"—*Id.*
    "*Ui* three *other sounds at least expresses,*
    As *who hears* GUILE, REBUILD, and BRUISE, *confesses.*"—*Brightland cor.*

UNDER NOTE IV.—EACH, ONE, EITHER, AND NEITHER.

When each of the letters which compose this word, *has* been learned."—*Dr. Weeks cor.* "As
her of us *denies* that both Homer and Virgil have great beauties."—*Dr. Blair cor.* "Yet
her of them *is* remarkable for precision."—*Id.* "How far each of the three great epic poets
distinguished *himself.*"—*Id.* "Each of these *produces* a separate, agreeable sensation."—*Id.*
n the Lord's day, every one of us Christians *keeps* the sabbath."—*Tr. of Iren. cor.* "And each
hem *bears* the image of purity and holiness."—*Hope of Is. cor.* "*Was* either of these meet-
i ever acknowledged or recognized?"—*Foster cor.* "Whilst neither of these letters *exists* in
Eugubian inscription."—*Knight cor.* "And neither of them *is* properly termed indefinite."
r. Wilson cor. "As likewise of the several subjects, which have in effect *their several verbs:*"
—"*each of which has* in effect *its own verb.*"—*Lowth cor.* "Sometimes, when the word ends
, neither of the signs *is* used."—*A. Mur. cor.* "And as neither of these manners *offends* the
"—*J. Walker cor.* "Neither of these two tenses *is* confined to this signification only."—*R. John-*
cor. "But neither of these circumstances *is* intended here."—*Tooke cor.* "So that all are
ebted to each, and each *is* dependent upon all."—*Bible Rep. cor.* "And yet neither of them *ex-*
uses any more action in this case, than *it* did in the other."—*Bullions cor.* "Each of these ex-
usions denotes action."—*Hallock cor.* "Neither of these moods *seems* to be defined by distinct
ndaries."—*Butler cor.* "Neither of these solutions *is* correct."—*Bullions cor.* "Neither
rs any sign of case at all."—*Fowler cor.*
    "Each in *his* turn, like Banquo's monarchs, *stalks.*" Or:—
    "*All* in *their* turn, like Banquo's monarchs, *stalk.*"—*Byron cor.*
    "And tell what each *doth* by *the* other lose."—*Shak. cor.*

UNDER NOTE V.—VERB BETWEEN TWO NOMINATIVES.

The quarrels of lovers *are but* a renewal of love."—*Adam et al. cor.* "Two dots, one placed
ve the other, *are* called *a Sheva.*"—*Wilson cor.* "A few centuries more or less *are* a matter of
ll consequence."—*Id.* "Pictures were the first step towards the art of writing; *hieroglyph-*
were the second step."—*Parker cor.* "The comeliness of youth *is* modesty and frankness;
ige, condescension and dignity." Or, much better: "The *great ornaments* of youth *are,*" &c.
Murray cor. "Merit and good works *are* the end of man's motion."—*Bacon cor.* "Divers
losophers hold, that the lips *are* parcel of the mind."—*Shak. cor.* "The clothing of the na-
es *was* the skins of wild beasts." Or thus: "The *clothes* of the natives *were* skins of wild
sts."—*Hist. cor.* "Prepossessions in *favour* of our *native* town, *are* not a matter of surprise."
Webster cor. "Two shillings and sixpence *are* half a crown, but not a half crown."—*Priestley*
l Bicknell cor. "Two vowels, pronounced by a single impulse of the voice, and uniting in one
nd, *are* called a *diphthong.*"—*Cooper cor.* "Two or more sentences united together *are* called
ompound Sentence."—*Day cor.* "Two or more words rightly put together, but not com-

pleting an entire proposition, *are* called a Phrase."—*Id.* "But the common number of times is five." Or, to state the matter truly: "But the common number of *tenses is six.*"—*Brit. Gram. cor.* "Technical terms, injudiciously introduced, *are an other* source of darkness in composition."—*Jamieson cor.* "The United States *are* the great middle division of North America."—*Mons cor.* "A great cause of the low state of industry, *was* the restraints put upon it."—*Priestley's Gram.* p. 190; *Churchill's*, 314. "Here two tall ships *become* the victor's prey."—*Rowe cor.* "The expenses incident to an outfit *are* surely no object."—*The Friend cor.*

> "Perhaps their loves, or else their sheep,
> *Were* all that did their silly thoughts so busy keep."—*Milt. cor.*

UNDER NOTE VI.—CHANGE OF THE NOMINATIVE.

"Much *care* has been taken, to explain all the kinds of words."—*Inf. S. Gr. cor.* "Not *four* [years] than three years, are spent in attaining this faculty." Or, perhaps better: "Not less than three *years' time, is* spent in attaining this faculty." Or thus: "Not less *time* than three years, *is* spent," &c.—*Gardiner cor.* "Where this night are met in state Many *friends* to gratulate His wish'd presence."—*Milton cor.* "Peace! my darling, here's no danger, Here's *no ox anear* thy bed."—*Watts cor.* "But *all* of these are mere conjectures, and some of them very unhappy ones."—*Coleridge cor.* "The old theorists' *practice of* calling the Interrogatives and Repliers ADVERBS, is only a part of their regular system of naming words."—*Peirce cor.* "When *several sentences* occur, place them in the order *of the facts.*"—*Id.* "And that *all the events* in conjunction make a regular chain of causes and effects."—*Kames cor.* "*In regard to their* origin. the Grecian and Roman republics, though equally involved in the obscurities and uncertainties of fabulous events, present one remarkable distinction."—*Adams cor.* "In these respects, *man* is left by nature an unformed, unfinished creature."—*Bp. Butler cor.* "The *Scriptures* are the oracles of God himself."—*Hooker cor.* "And at our gates are all *kinds* of pleasant fruits."—*S. Say cor.* "The *preterits of pluck, look,* and *toss,* are, in speech, pronounced *pluckt, lookt, toast.*"—*Fowler corrected.*

> "Severe the doom that *days prolong'd* impose,
> To stand sad witness of unnumbered woes!"—*Melmoth cor.*

UNDER NOTE VII.—FORMS ADAPTED TO DIFFERENT STYLES.

1. *Forms adapted to the Common or Familiar Style.*

"Was it thou* that *built* that house?"—*Brown's Institutes,* Key, p. 270. "That boy *writes* very elegantly."—*Ib.* "*Could* not thou write without blotting thy book?"—*Ib.* "*Dost* not thou think—or, *Don't* thou think, it will rain to-day?"—*Ib.* "*Does* not—or, *Don't* your cousin intend to visit you?"—*Ib.* "That boy *has* torn my book."—*Ib.* "Was it thou that *spread* the hay?"—*Ib.* "Was it James, or thou, that *let* him in?"—*Ib.* "He *dares* not say a word."—*Ib.* "Thou *stood* in my way and *hindered* me."—*Ib.*

"Whom *do I see?*—Whom *dost* thou *see* now?—Whom *does* he *see?*—Whom *dost* thou *love* most? —What *art* thou *doing* to-day?—What person *dost* thou *see* teaching that boy?—He *has* two new knives.—Which road *dost* thou *take?*—What child is he *teaching?*"—*Ingersoll cor.* "Thou, who *mak'st* my shoes, *sellst* many more." Or thus: "*You*, who *make* my shoes, *sell* many more."—*Id.* "The English language *has* been much cultivated during the last two hundred years. It *has* been considerably polished and refined."—*Lowth cor.* "This *style* is ostentatious, and does not suit grave writing."—*Priestley cor.* "But custom *has* now appropriated *who* to persons, and *which* to things" [and brute animals.]—*Id.* "The indicative mood *shows* or *declares something*, as. *Ego amo,* I love: or else *asks* a question; as, *Amas tu?* Dost thou love?"—*Paul's Ac. cor.* "Though thou *cannot* do much for the cause, thou *may* and *should* do something."—*Murray cor.* "The support of so many of his relations, was a heavy tax; but thou *knowst* (or, *you know*) he paid it cheerfully."—*Id.* "It may, and often *does*, come short of it."—*Murray's Gram.* p. 359.

> "'Twas thou, who, while thou *seem'd* to chide,
> To give me all thy pittance *tried*."—*Mitford cor.*

2. *Forms adapted to the Solemn or Biblical Style.*

"The Lord *hath prepared* his throne in the heavens; and his kingdom *ruleth* over all."—*Psalms,* ciii. 19. "Thou *answeredst* them, O Lord our God: thou *wast* a God that forgavest them, though thou *tookest* vengeance of their inventions."—See *Psalms,* xcix. 8. "Then thou *spakest* in vision to thy Holy One, and *saidst,* I have laid help upon one that is mighty."—*Ps.* lxxxix. 19. "'So then, it is not of him that *willeth,* nor of him that *runneth,* but of God that *showeth* mercy;' who *dispenseth* his blessings, whether temporal or spiritual, as *seemeth* good in his sight."—*Christian Experience of St. Paul,* p. 344; see *Rom.* ix, 16.

> "Thou, the mean while, *wast* blending with my thought;
> Yea, with my life, and life's own secret joy."—*Coleridge cor.*

UNDER NOTE VIII.—EXPRESS THE NOMINATIVE.

"Who is here so base, that *he* would be a bondman?"—*Shak. cor.* "Who is here so rude, *he* would not be a *Roman?*"—*Id.* "There is not a sparrow *which* falls to the ground without his notice." Or, better: "*Not a sparrow* falls to the ground, without his notice."—*Murray cor.* "In order to adjust them *in such a manner* as shall consist equally with the perspicuity and the strength of the period."—*Id.* and *Blair cor.* "But sometimes there is a verb *which* comes in." Better: "But sometimes there is a verb *introduced.*"—*Cobbett cor.* "Mr. Prince has a genius

---

* Though the pronoun *thou* is not much used in *common discourse,* it is as proper for the grammarian to consider and show, what form of the verb belongs to it *when it is so used,* as it is for him to determine what form is adapted to any other pronoun, when a difference of style affects the question.

† "*Forgavest,*" as the reading is in our common Bible, appears to be wrong; because the relative *that* and its antecedent *God* are of the third person, and not of the second.

:A would prompt him to better things."—*Spect. cor.* "It is this *that* removes that impenetrability."—*Harris cor.* "By the praise *which* is given him for his courage."—*Locke cor.* "There o man *who* would be more welcome here."—*Steele cor.* "Between an antecedent and a consent, or what goes before, and *what* immediately follows."—*Blair cor.* "And as connected i what goes before and *what* follows."—*Id.* "No man doth a wrong for the wrong's sake."—on *cor.* "All the various miseries of life, which people bring upon themselves by negligence olly, and *which* might have been avoided by proper care, are instances of this."—*Bp. But-or.* "Ancient philosophers have taught many things in *favour* of morality, so far at least as spects justice and goodness towards our fellow-creatures."—*Fuller cor.* "Indeed, if there ny such, *who* have been, or *who* appear to be of us, as suppose there is not a wise man among .ll, nor an honest man, that is able to judge betwixt his brethren; we shall not covet to med. in their *matters*."—*Barclay cor.* "There were *some* that drew back; there were *some* that le shipwreck of faith; yea, there were *some* that brought in damnable heresies."—*Id.* "The ire of the cause rendered this plan altogether proper; and, *under* similar *circumstances, the 'or's method* is fit to be imitated."—*Blair cor.* "This is an idiom to which our language is ngly inclined, and *which* was formerly very prevalent."—*Churchill cor.* "His roots are pped about the heap, and *he* seeth the place of stones."—*Bible cor.*

"New York, Fifthmonth 3d, 1823.

r friend,
am sorry to hear of thy loss; but *I* hope it may be retrieved. I should be happy to render : any assistance in my power. *I* shall call to see thee to-morrow morning. Accept assurances ny regard.
A. B."

"New York, May 3d, P. M., 1823.

r sir,
have just received the kind note *you* favoured me with this morning; and *I* cannot forbear to ress my gratitude to you. On further information, *I* find *I* have not lost so much as *I* at : supposed; and *I* believe *I* shall still be able to meet all my engagements. *I* should, however, lappy to see you. Accept, dear sir, my most cordial thanks.
C. D."
Brown's Institutes, p. 271.

"Will martial flames forever fire thy mind,
And *wilt thou* never be to Heaven resign'd?"—*Pope cor.*

UNDER NOTE IX.—APPLICATION OF MOODS.
First Clause of the Note.—The Subjunctive Present.

He will not be pardoned unless he *repent*."—*Inst.* p. 191. "If thou *find* any kernelwort in i marshy meadow, bring it to me."—*Neef cor.* "If thou *leave* the room, do not forget to shut t drawer."—*Id.* "If thou *grasp* it stoutly, thou wilt not be hurt:" or, (familiarly,)—"thou ! not be hurt."—*Id.* "On condition that he *come*, I will consent to stay."—*Murray's Key,* p. . "If he *be* but discreet, he will succeed."—*Inst.* p. 280. "Take heed that thou *speak* not !acob "—*Gen.* xxxi, 24. "If thou *cast* me off, I shall be miserable."—*Inst.* p. 280. "Send n to me, if thou *please*."—*Ib.* "Watch the door of thy lips, lest thou *utter* folly."—*Ib.* hough a liar *speak* the truth, he will hardly be believed."—*Bartlett cor.* "I will go, unless I ll."—*L. Murray cor.* "If the word or words understood *be* supplied, the true construction be apparent."—*Id.* "Unless thou *see* the propriety of the measure, we shall not desire thy port."—*Id.* "Unless thou *make* a timely retreat, the danger will be unavoidable."—*Id.* 'e may live happily, though our possessions *be* small."—*Id.* "If they *be* carefully studied, y will enable the student to parse all the exercises."—*Id.* "If the accent *be* fairly preserved ihe proper syllable, this drawling sound will never be heard."—*Id.* "One phrase may, in it of sense, be equivalent to an other, though its grammatical nature *be* essentially different." d. "If any man *obey* not our word by this epistle, note that man."—*2 Thess.* iii, 14. "Thy ll will be the greater, if thou *hit* it."—*Put., Cobb, or Knowles cor.* "We shall overtake him, ugh he *run*."—*Priestley et al. cor.* "We shall be disgusted, if he *give* us too much."—*Blair cor.*
"What is't to thee, if he *neglect* thy urn,
Or without spices *let* thy body burn?"—*Dryden cor.*

Second Clause of Note IX.—The Subjunctive Imperfect.[*]

And so would I, if I *were* he."—*Inst.* p. 191. "If I *were* a Greek, I should resist Turkish potism."—*Cardell cor.* "If he *were* to go, he would attend to your business."—*Id.* "If u *felt* as I do, we should soon decide."—*Inst.* p. 280. "Though thou *shed* thy blood in the se, it would but prove thee sincerely a fool."—*Ib.* "If thou *loved* him, there would be more ience of it."—*Ib.* "If thou *convinced* him, he would not act accordingly."—*Murray cor.* "If re *were* no liberty, there would be no real crime."—*Formey cor.* "If the house *were* burnt rn, the case would be the same."—*Foster cor.* "As if the mind *were* not always in action, :n it prefers any thing."—*West cor.* "Suppose I *were* to say, 'Light is a body.'"—*Harris* "If either oxygen or azote *were* omitted, life would be destroyed."—*Gurney cor.* "The b *dare* is sometimes used as if it *were* an auxiliary."—*Priestley cor.* "A certain lady, whom I ld name, if it *were* necessary."—*Spect. cor.* "If the *e were* dropped, *c* and *g* would assume ir hard sounds."—*Buchanan cor.* "He would no more comprehend it, than if it *were* the ech of a Hottentot."—*Neef cor.* "If thou *knew* the gift of God," &c.—*Bible cor.* "I wish I r at home."—*O. B. Peirce cor.* "Fact alone does not constitute right: if it *did*, general rants were lawful."—*Junius cor.* "Thou *lookst* upon thy boy, as though thou *guessed* it."—

All the corrections under this head are directly contrary to the teaching of William S. Cardell, Oliver B. re, and perhaps some other such writers on grammar; and some of them are contrary also to Murray's late ions. But I am confident that these authors teach erroneously; that their use of indicative forms for mere positions that are contrary to the facts, is positively ungrammatical; and that the potential imperfect is less ant, in such instances, than the simple subjunctive, which they reject or distort.

Putnam, Cobb, or Knowles cor. "He fought as if he *contended* for life."—*Hiley cor.* "He fought as if he *were contending* for his life."—*Id.*

"The dewdrop glistens on thy leaf, | As if thou *knew* my tale of grief,
As if thou *shed* for me a tear ; | Felt all my sufferings severe."—*Latham cor.*

Last Clause of Note IX.—The Indicative Mood.

"If he *knows* the way, he does not need a guide."—*Inst.* p. 191. "And if there *is* no difference, one of them must be superfluous, and ought to be rejected."—*Murray cor.* "I cannot say that I admire this construction, though it *is* much used."—*Priestley cor.* "We are disappointed, if the verb *does* not immediately follow it."—*Id.* "If it *was* they, *that* acted so ungratefully, they are doubly in fault."—*Murray cor.* "If art *becomes* apparent, it disgusts the reader."—*Jamieson cor.* "Though perspicuity *is* more properly a rhetorical than a grammatical quality, I thought it better to include it in this book."—*Campbell cor.* "Although the efficient cause *is* obscure, the final cause of those sensations lies open."—*Blair cor.* "Although the barrenness of language, or the want of words, *is* doubtless one cause of the invention of tropes."—*Id.* "Though it *enforces* not its instructions, yet it furnishes a greater variety."—*Id.* "In other cases, though the idea *is* one, the words remain quite separate."—*Priestley cor.* "Though the form of our language *is* more simple, and has that peculiar beauty."—*Buchanan cor.* "Human works are of no significancy till they *are* completed."—*Kames cor.* "Our disgust lessens gradually till it *vanishes* altogether."—*Id.* "And our relish improves by use, till it *arrives* at perfection."—*Id.* "So long as he *keeps* himself in his own proper element."—*Coke cor.* "Whether this translation *was* ever published or not, I am wholly ignorant."—*Sale cor.* "It is false to affirm, 'As it is day, it is light,' unless it actually *is* day."—*Harris cor.* "But we may at midnight affirm, 'If it *is* day, it is light.' "—*Id.* "If the Bible *is* true, it is a volume of unspeakable interest."—*Dickinson cor.* "Though he *was* a son, yet learned he obedience by the things which he suffered."—*Bible cor.* "If David then *calleth* (or *calls*) him Lord, how is he his son ? "—*Id.*

"'Tis hard to say, if greater want of skill
Appears in writing, or in judging, ill."—*Pope cor.*

UNDER NOTE X.—FALSE SUBJUNCTIVES.

"If a man *has built* a house, the house is his."—*Wayland cor.* "If God *has required* them of him, as is the fact, he has time."—*Id.* "Unless a previous understanding to the contrary *has been had* with the principal."—*Berrian cor.* "O! if thou *hast hid* them in some flowery cave."—*Milton cor.* "O! if Jove's will *has linked* that amorous power to thy soft lay."—*Id.* "SUBJUNCTIVE MOOD: If thou love, If thou loved."—*Dr. Priestley, Dr. Murray, John Burn, David Blair, Harrison, and others.* "Till religion, the pilot of the soul, *hath* lent thee her unfathomable coil."—*Tupper cor.* "Whether nature or art *contributes* most to form an orator, is a trifling inquiry."—*Blair cor.* "Year after year steals something from us, till the decaying fabric *totters* of itself, and *at length crumbles* into dust."—*Murray cor.* "If spiritual pride *has* not entirely vanquished humility."—*West cor.* "Whether he *has* gored a son, or *has* gored a daughter."—*Bible cor.* "It is doubtful whether the object introduced by way of simile, *relates* to what goes before or to what follows."—*Kames cor.*

"And bridle in thy headlong wave, | "And bridle in thy headlong wave,
Till thou our summons answer'd *hast*." Or :— | Till thou *hast granted what we crave.*"—*Mir. cor.*

CORRECTIONS UNDER RULE XV AND ITS NOTE.

UNDER THE RULE ITSELF.—THE IDEA OF PLURALITY.

"The gentry *are* punctilious in their etiquette."—*G. B.* "In France, the peasantry *go* barefoot, and the middle sort *make* use of wooden shoes."—*Harvey cor.* "The people *rejoice* in that which should cause sorrow."—*Murray varied.* "My people are foolish, they have not known me."—*Bible and Lowth cor.* "For the people *speak,* but *do* not write."—*Phil. Mu. cor.* "So that all the people that *were* in the camp, trembled."—*Bible cor.* "No company *like* to confess that they are ignorant."—*Todd cor.* "Far the greater part of their captives *were* anciently sacrificed."—*Robertson cor.* "More than one half of them *were* cut off before the return of spring."—*Id.* "The other class, termed Figures of Thought, *suppose* the words to be used in their proper and literal meaning."—*Blair and Mur. cor.* "A multitude of words in their dialect *approach* to the Teutonic form, and therefore afford excellent assistance."—*Dr. Murray cor.* "A great majority of our authors *are* defective in manner."—*J. Brown cor.* "The greater part of these new-coined words *have* been rejected."—*Tooke cor.* "The greater part of the words it contains, *are* subject to certain modifications *or* inflections."—*The Friend cor.* "While all our youth *prefer* her to the rest."—*Waller cor.* "Mankind *are* appointed to live in a future state."—*Butler cor.* "The greater part of human kind *speak* and *act* wholly by imitation."—*Rambler,* No. 146. "The greatest part of human gratifications *approach* so nearly to vice."—*Ib.* No. 160.

"While still the busy world *are* treading o'er
The paths they trod five thousand years before."—*Young cor.*

UNDER THE NOTE.—THE IDEA OF UNITY.

"In old English, this species of words *was* numerous."—*Dr. Murray cor.* "And a series of exercises in false grammar *is* introduced towards the end."—*Frost cor.* "And a jury, in conformity with the same idea, *was* anciently called *homagium,* the homage, or manhood."—*Webster cor.* "With respect to the former, there *is* indeed *a* plenty of means."—*Kames cor.* "The number of school districts *has* increased since the last year."—*Throop cor.* "The Yearly Meeting *has* purchased with its funds these publications."—*Foster cor.* "*Has* the legislature power to prohibit assemblies ? "—*Sullivan cor.* "So that the whole number of the streets *was* fifty."—*Rollin cor.* "The number of inhabitants *was* not more than four millions."—*Smollett cor.* "The house of Commons *was* of small weight."—*Hume cor.* "The assembly of the wicked *hath* (or *has*)

osed me."—*Psal. cor.* "Every kind of convenience and comfort *is* provided."—*C. S. Journal*
"Amidst the great decrease of the inhabitants in Spain, the body of the clergy *has* suffered
.iminution; but *it* has rather been gradually increasing."—*Payne cor.* "Small as the num-
of inhabitants *is*, yet their poverty is extreme."—*Id.* "The number of the names *was* about
hundred and twenty."—*Ware and Acts cor.*

CORRECTIONS UNDER RULE XVI AND ITS NOTES.

Under the Rule itself.—The Verb after Joint Nominatives.

So much ability and [so much] merit *are* seldom found."—*Mur. et al. cor.* "The *etymology and
ax* of the language *are* thus spread before the learner."—*Bullions cor.* "Dr. Johnson tells us,
, in English poetry, the accent and the quantity of syllables *are* the same thing."—*Adams*
"Their general scope and tendency, having never been clearly apprehended, *are* not remem-
d at all."—*L. Murray cor.* "The soil and sovereignty *were* not purchased of the natives."
napp cor. "The boldness, freedom, and variety, of our blank verse, *are* infinitely more favour-
to *sublimity of style*, than [are the constraint and uniformity of] rhyme."—*Blair cor.* "The
city and sensibility of the Greeks *seem* to have been much greater than ours."—*Id.* "For
etimes the mood and tense *are* signified by the verb, sometimes they are signified of the verb by
ething else."—*R Johnson cor.* "The verb and the noun making a complete sense, *whereas* the
.iciple and the noun *do* not."—*Id.* "The growth and decay of passions and emotions, traced
ugh all their mazes, *are* a subject too extensive for an undertaking like the present."—*Kames*
"The true meaning and etymology of some of his words *were* lost."—*Knight cor.* "When
force and direction of personal satire *are* no longer understood."—*Junius cor.* "The frame
condition of man *admit* of no other principle."—*Dr. Brown cor.* "Some considerable time
care *were* necessary."—*Id.* "In consequence of this idea, much ridicule and censure *have*
1 thrown upon Milton."—*Blair cor.* "With rational beings, nature and reason *are* the same
ug."—*Collier cor.* "And the flax and the barley *were* smitten."—*Bible cor.* "The colon and
.icolon *divide* a period; this with, and that without, a connective."—*Ware cor.* "Consequently,
rever space and time *are* found, there God must also be."—*Newton cor.* "As the past tense
perfect participle of LOVE *end* in ED, it is regular."—*Chandler cor.* "But the usual arrange-
it and nomenclature *prevent* this from being readily seen."—*Butler cor.* "Do and *did* simply
ly opposition or emphasis."—*A. Murray cor.* "*I* and *an other* make the plural WE; *thou* and
ther are *equivalent* to YE; *he, she,* or *it,* and *an other,* make THEY."—*Id.* "*I* and *an other* or
rs are the same as WE, the first person plural; *thou* and *an other* or *others are* the same as YE,
second person plural; *he, she,* or *it.* and *an other* or *others, are* the same as THEY, the third
son plural."—*Buchanan and Brit. Gram. cor.* "God and thou *are* two, and thou and thy
ghbour are two."—*Love Conquest cor.* "Just as AN and A *have* arisen out of the numeral ONE."
owler cor. "The tone and style of *all* of them, particularly of the first and the last, *are* very
erent."—*Blair cor.* "Even as the roebuck and the hart *are* eaten."—*Bible cor.* "Then I may
clude that two and three *do not make* five."—*Barclay cor.* "Which, at sundry times, thou
thy brethren *have* received from us."—*Id.* "Two and two *are* four, and one is five:" i. e.,
id one, added to four, *is* five."—*Pope cor.* "Humility and knowledge with poor apparel, *excel*
le and ignorance under costly array."—See *Murray's Key,* Rule 2d. "A page and a half *have*
n added to the section on composition."—*Bullions cor.* "Accuracy and expertness in this ex-
se *are* an important acquisition."—*Id.*

> "Woods and groves are of thy dressing,
> Hill and dale *proclaim* thy blessing." Or thus :—
> "Hill and *valley* boast thy blessing."—*Milton cor.*

Under the Rule itself.—The Verb before Joint Nominatives.

There *are* a good and a bad, a right and a wrong, in taste, as in other things."—*Blair cor.*
Vhence *have* arisen much stiffness and affectation."—*Id.* "To this error, *are* owing, in a great
.sure, that intricacy and [that] harshness, in his figurative language, which I before *noticed.*"
Blair and Jamieson cor. "Hence, in his Night Thoughts, there *prevail* an obscurity and a
dness of style."—*Blair cor.* See *Jamieson's Rhet.* p. 157. "There *are,* however, in that work,
ch good sense and excellent criticism."—*Blair cor.* "There *are* too much low wit and scur-
y in Plautus." Or : "There *is, in Plautus,* too much *of* low wit and scurrility."—*Id.* "There
too much reasoning and refinement, too much pomp and studied beauty, in them." Or :
here *is* too much *of* reasoning and refinement, too much *of* pomp and studied beauty, in them."
d. "Hence *arise* the structure and characteristic expression of exclamation."—*Rush cor.*
nd such pilots *are* he and his brethren, according to their own confession."—*Barclay cor.*
f whom *are* Hymeneus and Philetus; who concerning the truth have erred."—*Bible cor.* "Of
m *are* Hymeneus and Alexander; whom I have delivered unto Satan."—*Id.* "And so *were*
ies and John, the sons of Zebedee."—*Id.* "Out of the same mouth, *proceed* blessing and curs-
."—*Id.* "Out of the mouth of the Most High, *proceed* not evil and good."—*Id.* "In which
re *are* most plainly a right and a wrong."—*Bp. Butler cor.* "In this sentence, there *are* both
actor and an object."—*R. C. Smith cor.* "In the breastplate, *were* placed the mysterious
m and Thummim."—*Milman cor.* "What *are* the gender, number, and person, *of the pronoun**
he first *example?*"—*R. C. Smith cor.* "There *seem* to be a familiarity and *a* want of dignity
t."—*Priestley cor.* "It has been often asked, what *are* Latin and Greek ?"—*Lit. Journal cor.*
or where *do* beauty and high wit, But in your constellation, meet ?"—*Butler cor.* "Thence
he land where *flow* Ganges and Indus."—*Milton cor.* "On these foundations, *seem* to rest the
Inight riot and dissipation of modern assemblies."—*Dr. Brown cor.* "But what *have* disease,

This is what Smith must have *meant* by the inaccurate phrase, "*those* in the first." For his first example is,
e went to school;" which contains only the *one* pronoun " He."—See *Smith's New Gram.* p. 19.

deformity, and filth, upon which the thoughts can be allured to dwell?"—*Dr. Johnson cor.*
"How *are* the gender and number of the relative known?"—*Bullions cor.*
"High rides the sun, thick rolls the dust,
And feebler *speed* the blow and thrust."—*Scott cor.*

UNDER NOTE I.—CHANGE THE CONNECTIVE.

"In every language, there prevails a certain structure, *or* analogy of parts, which is understood to give foundation to the most reputable usage."—*Blair cor.* "There runs through his whole manner a stiffness, *an* affectation, which renders him [Shaftsbury] very unfit to be considered a general model."—*Id.* "But where declamation *for* improvement in speech is the sole aim."—*Id.* "For it is by these, chiefly, that the train of thought, the course of reasoning, the whole progress of the mind, in continued discourse of *any* kind, is laid open."—*Lowth cor.* "In all writing and discourse, the proper composition *or* structure of sentences is of the highest importance."—*Blair cor.* "Here the wishful *and* expectant look of the beggar naturally leads to a vivid conception of that which was the object of his thoughts."—*Campbell cor.* "Who say, that the outward names of Christ, *with the sign* of the cross, puts away devils."—*Barclay cor.* "By which an oath with a penalty was to be imposed *on* the members."—*Junius cor.* "Light, *or* knowledge, in what manner soever afforded us, is equally from God."—*Bp. Butler cor.* "For instance, sickness *or* untimely death is the consequence of intemperance."—*Id.* "When grief *or* blood ill-tempered vexeth him." Or: "When grief, *with* blood ill-tempered. *vexes* him."—*Shak. cor.* "Does continuity, *or* connexion, create sympathy and relation in the parts of the body?"—*Collier cor.* "His greatest concern, *his* highest enjoyment, was, to be approved in the sight of his Creator."—*Murray cor.* "Know ye not that there is *a* prince, a great man, fallen this day in Israel?"—*Bible cor.* "What is vice, *or* wickedness? No rarity, you may depend on it."—*Collier cor.* "There is also the fear *or* apprehension of it."—*Bp. Butler cor.* "The apostrophe *with s* ('s) is an abbreviation for *is*, the termination of the old English genitive."—*Bullions cor.* "*T̄, c̄, or c,* when followed by a vowel, usually has the sound of *sh*; as in *partial, ocean, special.*"—*Weld cor.*
"Bitter constraint *of* sad occasion dear
Compels me to disturb your season due."—*Milton cor.*
"*Debauch'ry*, or excess, though with less noise,
As great a portion of mankind destroys."—*Waller cor.*

UNDER NOTE II.—AFFIRMATION WITH NEGATION.

"Wisdom, and not wealth, *procures* esteem."—*Key, Inst.* p. 272. "Prudence, and not pomp, *is* the basis of his fame."—*Ib.* "Not fear, but labour *has* overcome him."—*Ib.* "The decency, and not the abstinence, *makes* the difference."—*Ib.* "Not her beauty, but her talents *attract* attention."—*Ib.* "It is her talents, and not her beauty, *that attract* attention."—*Ib.* "It is her beauty, and not her talents, *that attracts* attention."—*Ib.*
"His belly, not his brains, this impulse *gives*:
He'll grow immortal; for he cannot live" Or thus:—
"His *bowels*, not his brains, this impulse give:
He'll grow immortal; for he cannot live."—*Young cor.*

UNDER NOTE III.—AS WELL AS, BUT, OR SAVE.

"Common sense, as well as piety, *tells* us these are proper."—*Fam. Com. cor.* "For without it the critic, as well as the undertaker, ignorant of any rule, *has* nothing left but to abandon himself to chance."—*Kames cor.* "And accordingly hatred, as well as love, *is* extinguished by long absence."—*Id.* "But at every turn the richest melody, as well as the sublimest sentiment, is conspicuous."—*Id.* "But it, as well as the lines immediately subsequent, *defies* all translation."—*Coleridge cor.* "But their religion, as well as their customs and manners, *was* strangely misrepresented."—*Bolingbroke, on History*, Paris Edition of 1808, p. 93. "But his jealous policy, as well as the fatal antipathy of Fonseca, *was* conspicuous."—*Robertson cor.* "When their extent, as well as their value, *was* unknown."—*Id.* "The etymology, as well as the syntax, of the more difficult parts of speech, *is* reserved for his attention at a later period."—*Parker and Fox cor.* "What I myself owe to him, no one but myself *knows*."—*Wright cor.* "None, but thou, O mighty prince! can avert the blow."—*Inst. Key,* p. 272. "Nothing, but frivolous amusements, *pleases* the indolent."—*Ib.*
"Nought, save the gurglings of the rill, *was* heard."—*G. B.*
"All songsters, save the hooting owl, *were* mute."—*G. B.*

UNDER NOTE IV.—EACH, EVERY, OR NO.

"Give every word, and every member, *its* due weight and force."—*Murray's Gram.* Vol. i. p. 316. "And to one of these *belongs* every noun, and every third person of every verb."—*Dr. Wilson cor.* "No law, no restraint, no regulation, *is* required to keep him *within* bounds."—*Ld. Journal cor.* "By that time, every window and every door in the street *was* full of heads."—*Observer cor.* "Every system of religion, and every school of philosophy, *stands* back from this field, and *leaves* Jesus Christ alone, the solitary example." Or: "*All systems* of religion, and *all schools* of philosophy, *stand* back from this field, and *leave* Jesus Christ alone, the solitary example."—*Abbott cor.* "Each day, and each hour, *brings its* portion of duty."—*Inst. Key,* p. 272. "And every one that was in distress, and every one that was in debt, and every one that was discontented, *resorted* unto him."—*Bible cor.* "Every private Christian, *every* member of the church, ought to read and peruse the Scriptures, that *he* may know *his* faith and belief is founded upon them."—*Barclay cor.* "And every mountain and *every* island *was* moved out of its place."—*Bible cor.*
"No bandit fierce, no tyrant mad with pride,
No cavern'd hermit *rests* self-satisfied."—*Pope.*

* According to modern usage, *has* would here be better than *is*,—though *is fallen* is still allowable.—G. Brown

UNDER NOTE V.—WITH, OR, &c., FOR AND.

'The *sides*, A, B, *and* C, compose the triangle."—*Tobitt, Felch*, and *Ware cor.* "The stream, : rock, *and* the tree, must each of them stand forth, so as to make a figure in the imagination."—*:ir cor.* "While this, with euphony, *constitutes*, finally, the whole "—*O. B. Peirce cor.* "The :, with the guineas and dollars in it, *was* stolen."—*Cobbett cor.* "Sobriety, with great indus- 'and talent, *enables* a man to perform great deeds." Or: "Sobriety, industry, and talent, *ible* a man to perform great deeds."—*Id.* "The *it*, together with the verb, *expresses a state of* :ng."—*Id.* "Where Leonidas the Spartan king, *and* his chosen band, fighting for their coun- :, were cut off to the last man."—*Kames cor.* "And Leah also, *and* her children, came near d bowed themselves."—*Bible cor.* "The First *and the* Second will either of them, by *itself*, :lesce with the Third, but *they do* not *coalesce* with each other."—*Harris cor.* "The whole :st centre in the query, whether Tragedy *and* Comedy are hurtful and dangerous representa- :ns."—*Formey cor.* "Both grief *and* joy are infectious : the emotions *which* they raise in the :ctator, resemble them perfectly."—*Kames cor.* "But, in all other words, the *q and u* are :th sounded."—*Ensell cor.* "*Q and u* (which are always together) have the sound of *kw*, as in :en ; or *of k only*, as in *opaque.*" Or, better : "*Q* has always the sound of *k* ; and the *u* which :lows it, that of *w* ; except in French words, in which the *u* is silent."—*Goodenow cor.* "In :s selection, the *a and i* form distinct syllables."—*Walker cor.* "And a considerable village, :th gardens, fields, &c., *extends* around on each side of the square."—*Lib. cor.* "Affection *and* :terest guide our notions and behaviour in the affairs of life ; imagination and passion affect the :timents that we entertain in matters of taste."—*Jamieson cor.* " She heard none of those :imations of her *defects*, which envy, petulance, *and* anger, produce among children."—*John- :* cor. " The King, Lords, and Commons, *constitute* an excellent form of government."—*:ombie et al. cor.* "If we say, ' I am the man who commands you,' the relative clause, with : antecedent *man*, *forms* the predicate."—*Crombie cor.*

"The spacious firmament on high, | And spangled heav'ns, a shining frame,
The blue ethereal *vault of* sky, | Their great Original proclaim."—*Addison cor.*

UNDER NOTE VI.—ELLIPTICAL CONSTRUCTIONS.

"There *are* a reputable and a disreputable practice." Or : " There is a reputable, and *there is* disreputable practice "—*Adams cor.* "This *man* and this *were* born in her."—*Milton cor.* This *man* and that *were* born in her."—*Bible cor.* "This and that man *were* born there."—*:ndrick cor.* "Thus *le* in *lego*, and *le* in *legi*, seem to be sounded equally long."—*Adam and :uld cor.* "A distinct and an accurate articulation *form* the groundwork of good delivery." : "A distinct and accurate articulation *forms* the groundwork of good delivery."—*Kirkham* :. " How *are* vocal and written language understood ?"—*Sanders cor.* "The good, the wise, d the learned man, *are ornaments* to human society." Or : " The good, wise, and learned man an ornament to human society."—*Bartlett cor.* "*In* some points, the expression of song and *xt of* speech *are* identical."—*Rush cor.* " To every room, there *were* an open and a secret pass- :."—*Johnson cor.* " There are such *things as a true* and a false taste ; and the latter *as* often :ects fashion, as the former."—*Webster cor.* " There *are* such *things* as a prudent and an impru- :nt institution of life, with regard to our health and our affairs."—*Bp. Butler cor.* " The lot of : outcasts of Israel, and *that of* the dispersed of Judah, however different in one respect, have an other corresponded with wonderful exactness."—*Hope of Israel cor.* " On these final sylla- :s, the radical and *the* vanishing movement *are* performed."—*Rush cor.* " To be young or old, d *to be* good, just, or the contrary, are physical or moral events."—*Spurzheim cor., and Felch.* The eloquence of George Whitfield and *that of* John Wesley *were* very different *in* character :ch from the other."—*Dr. Sharp cor.* "The affinity of *m* for the series *beginning with b*, and *xt of n* for the series *beginning with t*, give occasion for other euphonic changes."—*Fowler cor.*

"Pylades' soul, and mad Orestes', *were*
   In these, if *right the Greek philosopher.*" Or thus :—
"Pylades' and Orestes' *soul did pass*
   To these, if we believe Pythagoras."   Or, without ellipsis :—
"Pylades and Orestes' *souls did pass*
   To these, if we believe Pythagoras."—*Cowley corrected.*

UNDER NOTE VII.—DISTINCT SUBJECT PHRASES.

" To be moderate in our views, and to proceed temperately in the pursuit of them, *are* the :st *ways* to ensure success."—*Murray cor.* " To be of any species, and to have a right to the me of that species, *are* both one."—*Locke cor.* " With whom, to will, and to do, *are* the same." *Dr. Jamieson cor.* " To profess, and to possess, *are* very different things."—*Inst. Key.* p. 272. To do justly, to love mercy, and to walk humbly with God, *are* duties of universal obligation." *Ib.* " To be round or square, to be solid or fluid, to be large or small, and to be moved :iftly or slowly, *are* all equally alien from the nature of thought."—*Dr. Johnson.* " The resolv- g of a sentence into its elements, or parts of speech, and [*a*] stating [*of*] the accidents which :long to these, *are* called PARSING." Or, according to Note 1st above : "The resolving of a :ntence into its elements, or parts of speech, *with* [a] stating [of] the accidents which belong to :se, *is* called PARSING."—*Bullions cor.* " To spin and to weave, to knit and to sew, *were* once : girl's *employments* ; but now, to dress, and *to* catch a beau, *are* all she calls enjoyments."—*:mball cor.*

CORRECTIONS UNDER RULE XVII AND ITS NOTES.

UNDER THE RULE ITSELF.—NOMINATIVES CONNECTED BY OR.

" We do not know in what either reason or instinct *consists.*"—*Johnson corrected.* "A noun or pronoun joined with a participle, *constitutes* a nominative case absolute."—*Bicknell cor.* "The :ative will be of that case which the verb or noun following, or the preposition going before, :s to govern :" or,—" usually *governs.*"—*Adam, Gould, et al. cor.* " In the different modes of pronunciation, which habit or caprice *gives* rise to."—*Knight cor.* " By which he, or his *deputy, was* authorized to cut down any trees in Whittlebury forest."—*Junius cor.* " Wherever objects were named, in which sound, noise, or motion, *was* concerned, the imitation by words was *abundantly* obvious."—*Blair cor.* " The pleasure or pain resulting from a train of perceptions in *different* circumstances, *is* a beautiful contrivance of nature for valuable purposes."—*Kames cor.* " Because their foolish vanity, or their criminal ambition, *represents* the principles by which they *are* influenced, as absolutely perfect."—*D. Boileau cor.* " Hence naturally *arises* indifference *or* aversion between the parties."—*Dr. Brown cor.* "A penitent unbeliever, or an *impenitent* believer, *is a character nowhere* to be found."—*Tract cor.* " Copying whatever is peculiar in the *talk* of all those whose birth or fortune *entitles* them to imitation."—*Johnson cor.* " Where *love,* hatred, fear, or contempt, *is* often of decisive influence."—*Duncan cor.* "A lucky *anecdote, a* an enlivening tale, *relieves* the folio page."—*D'Israeli cor.* " For outward matter or *event fashions* not the character within." Or: (according to the antique style of this modern book of proverbs:) —"*fashioneth* not the character within"—*Tupper cor.* " Yet sometimes we have seen that wine, or chance, *has* warmed cold brains."—*Dryden cor.* " Motion is a genus; flight, a species; this flight or that flight *is an individual.*"—*Harris cor.* " When *et, aut, vel, sive,* or *nec, is repeated before* different members of the same sentence."—*Adam, Gould, and Grant cor.* " Wisdom or *folly governs* us."—*Fisk cor.* "A or an is styled *the* indefinite *article.*"—*Folker cor.* "A rusty nail, *or* a crooked pin, *shoots* up into *a prodigy.*"—*Spect. cor.* "*Is* either the subject or the *predicate in* the second sentence modified?"—*Prof. Fowler cor.*

> " Praise from a friend, or censure from a foe,
> *Is* lost on hearers that our merits know."—*Pope cor.*

UNDER THE RULE ITSELF.—NOMINATIVES CONNECTED BY NOR.

" Neither he nor she *has* spoken to him."—*Perrin cor.* " For want of a process of events, neither knowledge nor elegance *preserves* the reader from weariness."—*Johnson cor.* " Neither history nor tradition *furnishes* such information."—*Robertson cor.* " Neither the form nor *the* power of the liquids *has* varied materially."—*Knight cor.* " Where neither noise nor motion *is* concerned."—*Blair cor.* " Neither Charles nor his brother *was* qualified to support such a system."—*Junius cor.* " When, therefore, neither the liveliness of representation, nor the warmth of passion, *serves,* as it were, to cover the trespass, it is not safe to leave the beaten track."—*Campbell cor.* " In many countries called Christian, neither Christianity, nor its evidence, *is* fairly laid before men."—*Butler cor.* " Neither the intellect nor the heart *is* capable of being driven." —*Abbott cor.* " Throughout this hymn, neither Apollo nor Diana *is* in any way connected with the Sun or Moon."—*Coleridge cor.* " Of which, neither he, nor this grammar, *takes* any notice." —*R. Johnson cor.* " Neither their solicitude nor their foresight *extends* so far."—*Robertson cor.* " Neither Gomara, nor Oviedo, nor Herrera, *considers* Ojeda, or his companion Vespucci, as the first *discoverer* of the continent of America."—*Id.* " Neither the general situation of our colonies, nor that particular distress which forced the inhabitants of Boston to take up arms, *has* been thought worthy of a moment's consideration."—*Junius cor.*

> " Nor war nor wisdom *yields* our Jews delight,
> They will not study, and they dare not fight."—*Crabbe cor.*
> " Nor time nor chance *breeds* such confusions yet,
> Nor are the mean so rais'd, nor sunk the great."—*Rowe cor.*

UNDER NOTE I.—NOMINATIVES THAT DISAGREE.

" The definite article, *the,* designates what particular thing or things *are* meant."—*Merchant cor.* " Sometimes a word, or *several* words, necessary to complete the grammatical construction of a sentence, *are* not expressed, but *are* omitted by ellipsis."—*Burr cor.* " Ellipsis, (better, *Ellipses,*) or abbreviations, *are* the wheels of language."—*Maunder cor.* " The conditions or tenor of none of them *appears* at this day." Or : " The *tenor or conditions* of none of them *appear* at this day."—*Hutchinson cor.* " Neither men nor money *was* wanting for the service." Or : " Neither *money* nor *men were* wanting for the service."—*Id.* " Either our own feelings, or the representation of those of others, *requires* emphatic distinction *to be frequent.*"—*Dr. Barber cor.* " Either Atoms and Chance, or Nature, *is* uppermost : now I am for the latter part of the disjunction."—*Collier cor.* " Their riches or poverty *is* generally proportioned to their activity *or* indolence."—*Cox cor.* " Concerning the other part of him, neither *he nor you* seem to have entertained an idea."—*Horne cor.* " Whose earnings or income *is* so small."—*Discip. cor.* " Neither riches nor fame *renders* a man happy."—*Day cor.* " The references to the pages always point to the first volume, unless the Exercises or Key *is* mentioned." Or, better:—"unless *mention is made of* the Exercises or Key." Or :—"unless the Exercises or Key *be named.*"—*L. Murray cor.*

UNDER NOTE II.—COMPLETE THE CONCORD.

" My lord, you wrong my father ; *neither is* he, nor *am* I, capable of harbouring a thought against your peace."—*Walpole cor.* " There was no division of acts ; *there were* no pauses, or *intervals, in the performance;* but the stage was continually full; occupied either by the actors, or *by* the chorus."—*Blair cor.* " Every word ending in *b, p,* or *f, is* of this order, as also *are* many *that end* in *v.*"—*Dr. Murray cor.* " Proud as we are of human reason, nothing can be more absurd than *is* the general system of human life and human knowledge."—*Bolingbroke cor.* " By which the body of sin and death is done away, and we *are* cleansed."—*Barclay cor.* "And those *were* already converted, and regeneration *was* begun in them."—*Id.* " For I am an old man, and my wife *is* well *advanced* in years."—*Bible cor.* " Who is my mother ? or *who are* my brethren ?"—*See Matt.* xii, 48. " Lebanon is not sufficient to burn, nor *are* the beasts thereof sufficient for a burnt-offering."—*Bible cor.* " Information has been obtained, and some trials *have been made.*" —*Martineau cor.* " It is as obvious, and its causes *are* more easily understood."—*Webster cor.* "All languages furnish examples of this kind, and the English *contains* as many as any other." —*Priestley cor.* " The winters are long, and the cold *is* intense."—*Morse cor.* " How have I hated instruction, and how *hath* my heart despised reproof !"—*Prov. cor.* " The vestals were plished by Theodosius the Great, and the fire of Vesta *was* extinguished."—*Lempriere cor.* Riches beget pride; pride *begets* impatience."—*Bullions cor.* "Grammar is not reasoning, any re than organization is thought, or letters *are* sounds."—*Enclytica cor.* "Words are imple- nts, and grammar *is* a machine."—*Id.*

UNDER NOTE III.—PLACE OF THE FIRST PERSON.

'*Thou or I* must undertake the business."—*L. Murray cor.* "*He and I* were there."—*Ash cor.* nd we dreamed a dream in one night, *he and I*."—*Bible cor.* "If my views remain the same *his and mine* were in 1833."—*Goodell cor.* "*My father and I* were riding out."—*Inst. Key,* p. i. "The premiums were given to *George and me.*"—*Ib.* "*Jane and I* are invited."—*Ib.* They ought to invite *my sister and me.*"—*Ib.* "*You and I* intend to go."—*Guy cor.* "*John and* re going to town."—*Brit. Gram. cor.* "*He and I* are sick."—*James Brown cor.* "*Thou and I* well."—*Id.* "*He and I are.*"—*Id.* "*Thou and I are.*"—*Id.* "*He and I write.*"—*Id.* "*They i I* are well."—*Id.* "*She, and thou, and I,* were walking."—*Id.*

UNDER NOTE IV.—DISTINCT SUBJECT PHRASES.

'To practise tale-bearing, or even to countenance it, *is* great injustice."—*Inst. Key,* p. 273. 'o reveal secrets, or to betray one's friends, *is* contemptible perfidy."—*Ib.* "To write all sub- ntives with capital letters, or to exclude *capitals* from adjectives derived from proper names, y perhaps be thought *an offence* too small for animadversion; but the evil of innovation is ays something."—*Dr. Barrow cor.* "To live in such families, or to have such servants, *is a* using from God."—*Fam. Com. cor.* "How they portioned out the country, what revolutions y experienced, or what wars they maintained, *is* utterly unknown." Or: "How they por- ned out the country, what revolutions they experienced, *and* what wars they maintained, *are ngs* utterly unknown."—*Goldsmith cor.* "To speak or to write perspicuously and agreeably, *is attainment* of the utmost consequence to all who purpose, either by speech or by writing, to dress the public."—*Dr. Blair cor.*

UNDER NOTE V.—MAKE THE VERBS AGREE.

' Doth he not leave the ninety and nine, and *go* into the mountains, and *seek* that which is gone ray?"—*Bible cor.* "Did he not fear the Lord, and *beseech* the Lord, and *did not* the Lord re- u of the evil which he had pronounced?"—*Id.* "And dost thou open thine eyes upon such a :, and *bring* me into judgement with thee?"—*Id.* "If any man among you *seemeth* to be reli- us, and bridleth not his tongue, but deceiveth his own heart, this man's religion is vain."—*Id.* f thou sell aught unto thy neighbour, or *buy* aught of thy neighbour's hand, ye shall not oppress e an other."—*Id.* "And if thy brother that dwelleth by thee, *become* poor, and be sold to thee, u shalt not compel him to serve as a bond-servant."—*Id.* "If thou bring thy gift to the altar, l there *remember* that thy brother hath aught against thee," &c.—*Id.* "Anthea was content call a coach, and *so to cross* the brook." Or:—"and *in that she crossed* the brook."—*Johnson* . "It is either totally suppressed, or *manifested only* in its lowest and most imperfect form." *Blair cor.* "But if any man *is* a worshiper of God, and doeth his will, him he heareth." Or: f any man *be* a worshiper of God, and *do* his will, him *will* he *hear.*"—*Bible cor.* "Whereby righteousness and obedience, death and sufferings without, become profitable unto us, and *are* de ours."—*Barclay cor.* "Who ought to have been here before thee, and *to have objected,* if y had *any thing* against me."—*Bible cor.*

"Yes! thy proud lords, unpitied land, shall see, That man *has* yet a soul, and *dares* be free."—*Campbell cor.*

UNDER NOTE VI.—USE SEPARATE NOMINATIVES.

'H is only an aspiration, or breathing; and sometimes, at the beginning of a word, *it* is not nded at all."—*Lowth cor.* "Man was made for society, and *he* ought to extend his good will all men."—*Id.* "There is, and must be, a Supreme Being, of infinite goodness, power, and dom, who created, and *who* supports them."—*Beattie cor.* "Were you not affrighted, and *did i not mistake* a spirit for a body?"—*Bp. Watson cor.* "The latter noun or pronoun is not gov- ed by the conjunction *than* or *as,* but *it either* agrees with the verb, or is governed by the verb the preposition, expressed or understood."—*Mur. et al. cor.* "He had mistaken his true inter- and *he* found himself forsaken."—*Murray cor.* "The amputation was exceedingly well per- med, and *it* saved the patient's life."—*Id.* "The intentions of some of these philosophers, r, of many, might have been, and probably *they* were, good."—*Id.* "This may be true, and *it* will not justify the practice."—*Webster cor.* "From the practice of those who have had a 'ral education, and *who* are therefore presumed to be best acquainted with men and things."— *mpbell cor.* "For those energies and bounties which created, and *which* preserve, the uni- se."—*J. Q. Adams cor.* "I shall make it once for all, and *I* hope it will be remembered." *Blair cor.* "This consequence is drawn too abruptly. *The argument* needed more explana- n." Or: "This consequence is drawn too abruptly, and *without sufficient* explanation."—*Id.* They must be used with more caution, and *they* require more preparation."—*Id.* "The apos- phe denotes the omission of an *i,* which was formerly inserted, and *which* made an addition of yllable to the word."—*Priestley cor.* "The succession may be rendered more various or more form, but, in one shape or an other, *it* is unavoidable."—*Kames cor.* "It excites neither terror · compassion; nor is *it* agreeable in any respect."—*Id.*

"Cheap vulgar arts, whose narrowness affords No flight for thoughts,—*they* poorly stick at words."—*Denham cor.*

UNDER NOTE VII.—MIXTURE OF DIFFERENT STYLES.

' Let us read the living page, whose every character *delights* and instructs us."—*Maunder cor.* 'or if it *is* in any degree obscure, it puzzles, and *does* not please."—*Kames cor.* "When a aker *addresses* himself to the understanding, he proposes the instruction of his hearers."—

Campbell cor. "As the wine which strengthens and *refreshes* the heart."—*H. Adams cor.* "This truth he *wraps* in an allegory, and feigns that one of the goddesses had taken up her abode with the other."—*Pope cor.* "God searcheth and *understandeth* the heart." Or: "God *searches* and *understands* the heart."—*T. à Kempis cor.* "The grace of God, that *bringeth* salvation, hath appeared to all men."—*Titus,* ii, 11. "Which things also we speak, not in the words which man's wisdom *teacheth,* but which the Holy Ghost teacheth."—1 *Cor.* ii, 13. "But he *has* an objection, which he *urges,* and by which he thinks to overturn all."—*Barclay cor.* "In that it gives them not that comfort and joy which it *gives to* them who love it."—*Id.* "Thou here misunderstood the place and *misapplied* it." Or: "Thou here *misunderstoodst* the place and *misappliedst* it." Or: (as many of our grammarians will have it:) "Thou here *misunderstoodest* the place and *misappliedst* it."—*Id.* "Like the barren heath in the desert, which knoweth not when good *cometh.* —See *Jer.* xvii, 6. "It *speaks* of the time past, *and shows* that something was then doing, but not quite finished."—*Devis cor.* "It subsists in spite of them; it *advances* unobserved."—*Pascal cor.*

    "But where is he, the Pilgrim of my song?—
    Methinks he *lingers* late and tarries long."—*Byron cor.*

UNDER NOTE VIII.—CONFUSION OF MOODS.

"If a man *have* a hundred sheep, and one of them go (or *be gone*) astray," &c.—*Matt.* xviii, 12. Or: "If a man *has* a hundred sheep, and one of them *goes* (or *is gone*) astray," &c. Or: "If a man *hath* a hundred sheep, and one of them *goeth* (or *is gone*) astray," &c.—*Kirkham cor.* "As a speaker *advances* in his discourse, and *increases* in energy and earnestness, a higher and louder tone will naturally steal upon him."—*Id.* "If one man *esteem one* day above an other, and an other *esteem* every day alike; let every man be fully persuaded in his own mind."—*Barclay cor.* See *Rom.* xiv, 5. "If there be but one body of legislators, it *will be* no better than a tyranny; if there be only two, there will want a casting voice."—*Addison cor.* "Should you come up this way, and I be still here, you need not be assured how glad I *should* be to see you."—*Byron cor.* "If he repent and *become* holy, let him enjoy God and heaven."—*Brownson cor.* "If thy fellow approach thee, naked and destitute, and thou *say* unto him, ' Depart in peace, be warmed and filled, and yet thou *give* him not those things *which* are needful to him, what benevolence is there in thy conduct?'"—*Kirkham cor.*

    "Get on your nightgown, lest occasion *call* us,
    And *show* us to be watchers."—*Singer's Shakspeare.*
    "But if it *climb,* with your assisting *hand,*
    The Trojan walls, and in the city *stand.*"—*Dryden cor.*
    ———————"Though Heaven's King
    Ride on thy wings, and thou with thy compeers,
    Used to the yoke, *draw* his triumphant wheels."—*Milton cor.*

UNDER NOTE IX.—IMPROPER ELLIPSES.

"Indeed we have seriously wondered that Murray should leave some things as he has left them."—*Reporter cor.* "Which they neither have *done* nor can do."—*Barclay cor.* "The Lord hath *revealed,* and doth and will reveal, his will to his people; and hath *raised up,* and doth raise up, members of his body," &c.—*Id.* "We see, then, that the Lord hath *given,* and doth *give,* such."—*Id.* "Towards those that have *declared,* or do declare, themselves. members."—*Id.* "For which we can *give,* and have given, our sufficient reasons."—*Id.* "When we mention the several properties of the different words in sentences, as we have *mentioned* those of the word *William's* above, what is the exercise called?"—*R. C. Smith cor.* "It is however to be doubted, whether this Greek idiom ever has *obtained,* or *ever* will obtain, extensively, in English."—*Nutting cor.* "Why did not the Greeks and Romans abound in auxiliary words as much as we do?" —*Murray cor.* "Who delivers his sentiments in earnest, as they ought to be *delivered* in order to move and persuade."—*Kirkham cor.*

UNDER NOTE X.—DO, USED AS A SUBSTITUTE.

"And I would avoid it altogether, if it could be *avoided.*" Or: "I would avoid it altogether, if to *avoid* it *were* practicable."—*Kames cor.* "Such a sentiment from a man expiring of his wounds, is truly heroic; and *it* must elevate the mind to the greatest height *to which it can be raised* by a single expression."—*Id.* "Successive images, *thus* making deeper and deeper impressions, must elevate *the mind* more than any single image *can.*"—*Id.* "Besides making a deeper impression than can be *made* by cool reasoning."—*Id.* "Yet a poet, by the force of genius alone, *may* rise higher than a public speaker *can.*" Or:—"than *can* a public speaker."— *Blair cor.* "And the very same reason that has induced several grammarians to go so far as they have *gone,* should have induced them to go farther."—*Priestley cor.* "The pupil should commit the first section *to memory* perfectly, before he *attempts* (or *enters upon*) the second part of grammar."—*Bradley cor.* "The Greek *ch* was pronounced hard, as we now *pronounce it* in *chord*"— *Booth cor.* "They pronounce the syllables in a different manner from what they *adopt* (or, is a manner *different* from *that which* they are accustomed to use) at other times."—*Murray cor.* "And give him the *cool and formal* reception that Simon had *given.*"—*Scott cor.* "I do not say, as *some* have said."—*Bolingbroke cor.* "If he suppose the first, he may the last."—*Barclay cor.* "We are now despising Christ in his inward appearance, as the Jews of old *despised* him in his outward [advent]."—*Id.* "That text of Revelations must not be understood as he *understands* it."— *Id.* "Till the mode of parsing the noun is so familiar to him that he can *parse* it readily"—*R. C. Smith cor.* "Perhaps it is running the same course *that* Rome had *run* before."—*Middleton or* "It ought even on this ground to be avoided; *and it* easily *may be,* by a different construction." —*Churchill cor.* "These two languages are now pronounced in England as no other nation in Europe *pronounces them.*"—*Creighton cor.* "Germany ran the same risk that Italy had run"— *Bolingbroke, Murray, et al. cor.*

UNDER NOTE XI.—PRETERITS AND PARTICIPLES.

The beggars themselves will be *broken* in a trice."—*Swift cor.* "The hoop is *hoisted* above nose."—*Id.* "And *his* heart was *lifted* up in the ways of the Lord."—*2 Chron.* xvii. 6. "Who to oft have mourned, Yet to temptation *run.*"—*Burns cor.* "Who would not have let them *var.*"—*Steele cor.* "He would have had you *seek* for ease at the hands of Mr. Legality."—*yan cor.* "From me his madding mind is *turned ; He woos* the widow's daughter, of the *i.*"—*Spenser cor.* "The man has *spoken,* and *he* still speaks."—*Ash cor.* "For you have but *'aken* me all this while."—*Shak. cor.* "And will you *rend* our ancient love asunder ?"—*Id.* r. Birney has *pled* (or *pleaded*) the inexpediency of passing such resolutions."—*Liberator cor.* *Tho* have *worn* out their years in such most painful labours."—*Littleton cor.* "And in the con- ion you were *chosen* probationer."—*Spectator cor.*

"How she was lost, *ta'en* captive, made a slave ;
And how against him set that should her save."—*Bunyan cor.*

UNDER NOTE XII.—OF VERBS CONFOUNDED.

But Moses preferred to *while* away his time."—*Parker cor.* "His face *shone* with the rays of sun."—*John Allen cor.* "Whom they had *set* at defiance so lately."—*Bolingbroke cor.* "And n he *had sat down,* his disciples came unto him."—*Bible cor.* "When he *had sat down* on judgement-seat." Or: "*While* he *was sitting* on the judgement-seat."—*Id.* "And, *they ing kindled* a fire in the midst of the hall, and *sat* down together, Peter sat down among n."—*Id.* "So after he had washed their feet, and had taken his garments, and *had* down again, [or, literally, '*sitting down again,*'] he said *to* them, Do ye *know* what I have e to you ?"—*Id.* "Even as I also overcame, and *sat* down with my Father in his throne."— Or : (rather less literally :) "Even as I *have* overcome, and *am sitting* with my Father *on* his *one.*"—*Id.* "We have such *a* high priest, who *sitteth* on the right hand of the throne of the esty in the heavens."—*Id.* "And *is now sitting* at the right hand of the throne of God."—*Id.* e *set* on foot a furious persecution."—*Payne cor.* "There *lieth* (or *lies*) an obligation upon saints to help such."—*Barclay cor.* "There let him *lie.*"—*Byron cor.* "Nothing but moss, shrubs, and *stunted* trees, can grow upon it."—*Morse cor.* "Who had *laid* out considerable is purely to distinguish themselves."—*Goldsmith cor.* "Whereunto the righteous *flee,* and are *.*"—*Barclay cor.* "He *rose* from supper, and laid aside his garments."—*Id.* "Whither—*oh !* ther—shall I *flee* ?"—*Murray cor.* "*Fleeing* from an adopted murderer."—*Id.* "To you I *flee* refuge."—*Id.* "The sign that should warn his disciples to *flee* from *the* approaching ruin."— *th cor.* "In one she *sits* as a prototype for exact imitation."—*Rush cor.* "In which some only it, bark, mew, *whinny,* and bray, a little better than others."—*Id.* "Who represented to him unreasonableness of being *affected* with such unmanly fears."—*Rollin cor.* "Thou *sawest* every on." Or, familiarly : "Thou *saw* every action."—*Guy cor.* "I taught, thou *taughtest* or *taught,* or she taught."—*Coar cor.* "Valerian *was* taken by Sapor and *flayed* alive, A. D. 260."—*Lem- rs cor.* "What a fine vehicle *has* it now become, for all conceptions of the mind !"—*Blair cor.* *That has* become of so many productions ?"—*Volney cor.* "What *has* become of those ages of ndance and of life ?"—*Keith cor.* "The Spartan admiral *had* sailed to the Hellespont."—*Gold- th cor.* "As soon as he *landed,* the multitude thronged about him."—*Id.* "Cyrus *had* arrived lardia."—*Id.* "Whose year *had* expired."—*Id.* "It *might* better have been, ' that faction ch.' " Or : "'That faction which,' *would* have been better."—*Murray's Gram.* p. 157. "This ple *has* become a great nation."—*Murray and Ingersoll cor.* "And here we *enter* the region of iment."—*Blair cor.* "The ungraceful parenthesis which follows, *might* far better have been ided."—*Id.* "Who forced him under water, and there held him until *he was drowned.*"— *. cor.*

"I *would* much rather be myself the slave,
And wear the bonds, than fasten them on him."—*Cowper cor.*

UNDER NOTE XIII.—WORDS THAT EXPRESS TIME.

[I *finished* my letter *before* my brother arrived." Or : "I *had finished* my letter *when* my brother ved "—*Kirkham cor.* "I *wrote* before I received his letter."—*Blair cor.* "From what *was* nerly delivered."—*Id.* "Arts *were at length* introduced among them." Or : "Arts *have been* late introduced among them."—*Id.* [But the latter reading suits not the Doctor's context.] am not of opinion, that such rules *can be* of much use, unless persons *see* them exemplified.] —"*could be* " and "*saw.*"—*Id.* "If we *use* the noun itself, we *say,* (or *must say,*) ' This com- tion is John's.' " Or : "If we *used* the noun itself, we *should say,*" &c.—*Murray cor.* "But e assertion *refer* to something that *was transient,* or to *something that is not* supposed to be *ays the same,* the past tense must be preferred " [as,] " They told him, that Jesus of Nazareth *passing by.*"—*Murray cor.* "There is no particular intimation but that I *have continued* to k, even to the present moment."—*Green cor.* "Generally, as *has been* observed already, it *ut* hinted in a single word or phrase."—*Campbell cor.* "The wittiness of the passage *has* i already illustrated."—*Id.* "As was observed *before.*" Or : "As *has been* observed *already.*" *i.* "It *has been* said already in general *terms.*"—*Id.* "As I hinted *before.*" Or : "As I *have 'ed already.*"—*Id.* "What, I believe, was hinted once *before.*"—*Id.* "It is obvious, as *was* *'ed* formerly, that this is but an artificial and arbitrary connexion."—*Id.* "They *did* anciently eat deal of hurt."—*Bolingbroke cor.* "Then said Paul, I knew not, brethren, that he *was* high priest."—See *Acts,* xxiii. 5 : *Webster cor.* "Most prepositions originally *denoted* the tions of place; and *from those* they *were* transferred, to denote, by similitude, other relations." *owth and Ch. cor.* "His gift was but a poor offering, *in comparison with* his *great* estate."— *Murray cor.* "If he should succeed, and obtain his end, he *would* not be the happier for it." better : "If he *succeed,* and *fully attain* his end, he will not be the happier for it."—*Id.* *ese* are torrents that swell to-day, and *that* will have spent themselves by to-morrow."— *ir cor.* "Who have called that wheat *on one day,* which they have called tares *on the next.*" *arclay cor.* "He thought it *was* one of his tenants."—*Id.* "But if one went unto them i the dead, *they would* repent."—*Bible cor.* "Neither *would* they be persuaded, though one

rose from the dead."—*Id.* "But it is while men *sleep*, that the archenemy always *sows* his tares." —*The Friend cor.* "Crescens would not *have failed* to *expose* him."—*Addison cor.*
"Bent *is* his bow, the Grecian hearts to wound;
Fierce as he *moves*, his silver shafts resound."—*Pope cor.*

UNDER NOTE XIV.—VERBS OF COMMANDING, &c.

"Had I commanded you to *do* this, you would have thought hard of it."—*G. B.* "I *found* him better than I expected to *find* him."—*Murray's Gram.* i, 187. "There are several small faults, which I at first intended to *enumerate*."—*Webster cor.* "Antithesis, therefore, may, on many occasions, be employed to advantage, in order to strengthen the impression which we intend that any object *shall* make."—*Blair cor.* "The girl said, if her master would but have let her *have* money, she might have been well long ago."—*Priestley et al. cor.* "Nor is there the least ground to fear that we *shall here* be cramped within too narrow limits."—*Campbell cor.* "The Romans, flushed with success, expected to *retake* it."—*Hooke cor.* "I would not have let *fall* an unseasonable pleasantry in the venerable presence of Misery, to be entitled to all the wit that ever Rabelais scattered."—*Sterne cor.* "We expected that he *would arrive* last night."— *Brown's Inst.* p. 282. "Our friends intended to *meet* us."—*Ib.* "We hoped to *see* you."—*A* "He would not have been allowed to *enter*."—*Ib.*

UNDER NOTE XV.—PERMANENT PROPOSITIONS.

"Cicero maintained, that whatsoever *is* useful *is* good."—"I observed, that love *constitutes* the whole moral character of God."—*Dwight cor.* "Thinking that one *gains* nothing by being a good man."—*Voltaire cor.* "I have already told you, that I *am* a gentleman."—*Fontaine cor.* "If I should ask, whether ice and water *are* two distinct species of things."—*Locke cor.* "A stranger to the poem would not easily discover that this *is* verse."—*Murray's Gram.* 8vo, i, 292. "The doctor affirmed, that fever always *produces* thirst."—*Brown's Inst.* p. 282 "The ancients asserted, that virtue *is* its own reward."—*Ib.* "They should not have repeated the error, of insisting that the infinitive *is* a mere noun."—*Tooke cor.* "It was observed in Chap. III, that the distinctive OR *has* a double use."—*Churchill cor.* "Two young gentlemen, who have made a discovery that there *is* no God."—*Campbell's Rhet.* p. 206.

CORRECTIONS UNDER RULE XVIII; OF INFINITIVES.
INSTANCES DEMANDING THE PARTICLE To.

"William, please *to* hand me that pencil."—*Smith cor.* "Please *to* insert points so as to make sense."—*P. Davis cor.* "I have known lords *to* abbreviate almost half of their words."— *Cobbett cor.* "We shall find the practice perfectly *to* accord with the theory."—*Knight cor.* "But it would tend to obscure, rather than *to* elucidate, the subject."—*L. Murray cor.* "Please *to* divide it for them, as it should be *divided*."—*J. Willetts cor.* "So as neither to embarrass nor to weaken the sentence."—*Blair and Mur. cor.* "Carry her to his table, to view his poor fare, and *to* hear his heavenly discourse."—*Same.* "That we need not be surprised to find this to hold [i. e., to find *the same to be true*, or to find *it so*] in eloquence."—*Blair cor.* "Where he has no occasion either to divide or *to* explain" [*the topic in debate*.]—*Id.* "And they will find their pupils *to* improve by hasty and pleasant steps."—*Russell cor.* "The teacher however will please *to* observe," &c.—*Inf. S. Gr. cor.* "Please *to* attend to a few rules in what is called syntax."—*Id.* "They may dispense with the laws, to favour their friends, or *to* secure their office."—*Webster cor.* "To take back a gift, or *to* break a contract, is a wanton abuse."—*Id.* "The legislature *has* nothing to do, but *to* let it bear its own price."—*Id.* "He is not to turn, but to copy characters."—*Rambler cor.* "I have known a woman to make use of a shoeing-horn."—*Spect. cor.* "Finding this experiment *to* answer, in every respect, their wishes."—*Day cor.* "In fine, let him cause his argument *to* conclude in the term of the question."—*Barclay corrected.*

"That he permitted not the winds of heaven
To visit her too roughly." [Omit "*face*," to keep the measure: or say.]
"That he *did never let* the winds of heaven
Visit her face too roughly."—*Shak. cor.*

CORRECTIONS UNDER RULE XIX; OF INFINITIVES.
INSTANCES AFTER BID, DARE, FEEL, HEAR, LET, MAKE, NEED, SEE.

"I dare not proceed so hastily, lest I give offence."—See *Murray's Key*, Rule xii. "Their character is formed, and made *to* appear."—*Butler cor.* "Let there be but matter and opportunity offered, and you shall see them quickly revive again."—*Bacon cor.* "It has been made to appear, that there is no presumption against a revelation."—*Butler cor.* "MANIFEST, *v. t.* To reveal; to make appear; to show plainly."—*Webster cor.* "Let him reign, like good Aurelian, or let him bleed, like *Seneca:*" [Socrates did not bleed, he was poisoned.]—*Kirkham's translation of Pope cor.* "Sing I could not; *complain* I durst not."—*Fotherγill cor.* "If T. M. be not so frequently heard *to* pray by them."—*Barclay cor.* "How many of your own church members were never heard *to* pray?"—*Id.* "Yea, we are bidden to pray one for an other."—*Id.* "He was made *to* believe that neither the king's death nor *his* imprisonment would help him."—*Shuffield cor.* "I felt a chilling sensation creep over me."—*Inst.* p 279. "I dare say he has not got home yet."—*Ib.* "We sometimes see bad men honoured."—*Ib.* "I saw him move."—*Felch cor.* "For see thou, ah! see thou, a hostile world its *terrors* raise."—*Kirkham cor.* "But that he make him rehearse so."—*Lily cor.* "Let us rise."—*Fowle cor.*

"Scripture, you know, exhorts us to it;
It bids us 'seek peace, and ensue it.'"—*Swift cor.*
"Who bade the mud from Dives' wheel
Bedash the rags of Lazarus?
Come, brother, in that dust we'll kneel,
Confessing Heaven that ruled it thus."—*Christmas Book cor.*

CHAPTER VII. — PARTICIPLES.

CORRECTIONS UNDER THE NOTES TO RULE XX.

UNDER NOTE I.—EXPUNGE OF.

"In forming his sentences, he was very exact."—*L. Murray.* "For not believing which, I con-mn them."—*Barclay cor.* "To prohibit his hearers from reading that book."—*Id.* "You will ease them exceedingly in crying down ordinances."—*Mitchell cor.* "The warwolf subsequent-became an engine for casting stones." Or :—"for *the* casting *of* stones."—*Cons. Misc. cor.* The art of dressing hides and working in leather was practised."—*Id.* " In the choice they had ade of him for restoring order."—*Rollin cor.* "The Arabians exercised themselves by compos-g orations and poems."—*Sale cor.* "Behold, the widow-woman was there, gathering sticks." *Bible cor.* "The priests were busied in offering burnt-offerings."—*Id.* "But Asahel would it turn aside from following him."—*Id.* "He left off building Ramah, and dwelt in Tirzah."—*Id.* Those who accuse us of denying it, belie us."—*Barclay cor.* "And breaking bread from house to ouse."—*Acts,* iv, 46. "Those that set about repairing the walls."—*Barclay cor.* "And secretly getting divisions."—*Id.* "Whom he had made use of in gathering his church."—*Id.* " In ining and distinguishing the *acceptations* and uses of those particles."—*W. Walker cor.*

" In *making this a crime,* we overthrow
The laws of nations and of nature too."—*Dryden cor.*

UNDER NOTE II.—ARTICLES REQUIRE OF.

"The mixing *of* them makes a miserable jumble of truth and fiction."—*Kames cor.* "The same jection lies against the employing *of* statues."—*Id.* "More efficacious than the venting *of* ulence upon the fine arts."—*Id.* "It is the giving *of* different names to the same object."—*Id.* When we have in view the erecting *of* a column."—*Id.* " The straining *of* an elevated subject yond due bounds, is a vice not so frequent."—*Id.* "The cutting *of* evergreens in the shape of iimals, is very ancient."—*Id.* " The keeping *of* juries without *meat,* drink, or fire, can be ac-ounted for only on the same idea."—*Webster cor.* "The writing *of* the verbs at length on his ate, will be a very useful exercise."—*Beck cor.* "The avoiding *of* them is not an object of any oment."—*Sheridan cor.* "Comparison is the increasing or decreasing *of* the signification of a ord by degrees."—*Brit. Gram. cor.* "Comparison is the increasing or decreasing *of* the quality by grees."—*Buchanan cor.* "The placing *of* a circumstance before the word with which it is con-ected is the easiest of all inversion."—*Id.* "What is emphasis? It is the emitting *of* a stronger id fuller sound of voice," &c.—*Bradley cor.* "Besides, the varying *of* the terms will render the ie of them more familiar."—*A. Mur. cor.* "And yet the confining *of* themselves to this true rinciple, has misled them."—*Tooke cor.* "What is here commanded, is merely the relieving *of* is misery."—*Wayland cor.* "The accumulating *of* too great a quantity of knowledge at ran-om, overloads the mind *in stead of* adorning it."—*Formey cor.* "For the compassing *of* his int."—*Rollin cor.* "To the introducing *of* such an inverted order of things."—*Butler cor.* Which require only the doing *of* an external action."—*Id.* "The imprisoning *of* my body is to itisfy your wills."—*Fox cor.* "Who oppose the conferring *of* such extensive command on one rson."—*Duncan cor.* "Luxury contributed not a little to the enervating *of* their forces."—*Sale r.* "The keeping *of* one day of the week for a sabbath."—*Barclay cor.* "The doing *of* a thing contrary to the forbearing of it."—*Id.* "The doubling *of* the Sigma is, however, sometimes gular."—*Knight cor.* "The inserting *of* the common aspirate too, is improper."—*Id.* "But in enser's time the pronouncing *of* the *ed* [as a separate syllable,] seems already to have been mething of an archaism."—*Phil. Mu. cor.* "And to the reconciling *of* the effect of their verses i the eye."—*Id.* "When it was not in their power to hinder the taking *of* the whole."—*Dr.* rown cor. "He had indeed given the orders himself for the shutting *of* the gates."—*Id.* "So a whole life was a doing *of* the will of the Father."—*Pennington cor.* "It signifies the suffering receiving *of* the action expressed."—*Priestley cor.* "The pretended crime therefore was the de-aring *of* himself to be the Son of God."—*West cor.* "Parsing is the resolving *of* a sentence into i different parts of speech."—*Beck cor.*

UNDER NOTE II.—ADJECTIVES REQUIRE OF.

"There is *no* expecting *of* the admiration of beholders."—*Baxter cor.* "There is no hiding *of* u in the house."—*Shak. cor.* "For the better regulating *of* government in the province of assachusetts."—*Brit. Parl. cor.* "The precise marking *of* the shadowy boundaries of a com-ex government."—*Adams cor.* "This state of discipline requires the voluntary foregoing *of* any things which we desire, and *the* setting *of* ourselves to what we have no inclination to." *Butler cor.* "This amounts to an active setting *of* themselves against religion."—*Id.* "Which gaged our ancient friends to the orderly establishing *of* our Christian discipline."—*Friends cor.* Some men are so unjust that there is no securing *of* our own property or life, but by opposing rce to force."—*Rev. John Brown cor.* "An Act for the better securing *of* the Rights and Lib-ties of the Subject."—*Geo. III cor.* "Miraculous curing *of* the sick is discontinued."—*Barclay r.* "It would have been no transgressing *of* the apostle's rule."—*Id.* "As far as consistent th the proper conducting *of* the business of the House."—*Elmore cor.* "Because he would ive no quarrelling at the just condemning *of* them at that day." Or :—"at *their just condemna-*m at that day."—*Bunyan cor.* "That transferring *of* this natural manner will insure propri-y."—*Rush cor.* "If a man were porter of hell-gate, he should have old [i. e., frequent] turning the key."—*Singer's Shakspeare.*

UNDER NOTE II.—POSSESSIVES REQUIRE OF.

"So very simple a thing as a man's wounding *of* himself."—*Dr. Blair cor., and Murray.* "Or ith that man's avowing *of* his designs."—*Blair, Mur., et al. cor.* "On his putting *of* the question."—*Adams cor.*   " The importance of teachers' requiring *of* their pupils to read each section many times over."—*Kirkham cor.*   " Politeness is a kind of forgetting *of* one's self, in order to be agreeable to others."—*Ramsay cor.*   "Much, therefore, of the merit and the agreeableness of epistolary writing, will depend on its introducing *of* us into some acquaintance with the writer." —*Blair and Mack cor.*   "Richard's restoration to respectability depends on his paying *of* his debts."—*O. B. Peirce cor.*   " Their supplying *of* ellipses where none ever existed ; their parsing *of the* words of sentences already full and perfect, as though depending on words understood."— *Id.*   " Her veiling *of* herself, and shedding *of* tears, &c., her upbraiding of Paris for his cowardice," &c.—*Blair cor.*   "A preposition may be made known by its admitting *of* a personal pronoun after it, in the objective case."—*Murray et al. cor.*   " But this forms no just objection to its denoting *of* time."—*Mur. cor.*   " Of men's violating or disregarding *of* the relations *in which* God has *here* placed them."—*Butler cor.*   " Success, indeed, no more decides for the right, than a man's killing *of* his antagonist in a duel."—*Campbell cor.*   " His reminding *of* them."—*Kirkham cor.*   " This mistake was corrected by his preceptor's causing *of* him to plant some beans."—*Id.*   "Their neglecting *of* this was ruinous."—*Frost cor.*   " That he was serious, appears from his distinguishing *of* the others as 'finite.' "—*Felch cor.*   " His hearers are not at all sensible of his doing *of* it."   Or :—" *that he does* it."—*Sheridan cor.*

UNDER NOTE III.—CHANGE THE EXPRESSION.

"An allegory is *a fictitious story the meaning of which is figurative, not literal ;* a double meaning, or dilogy, is the saying *of* only one thing, *when we have two* in view."—*Phil. Mu. cor.*   "A verb may generally be distinguished by *the sense which it makes* with any of the personal pronouns, or *with* the word TO, before it."—*Murray et al. cor.*   "A noun may in general be distinguished by *the article which comes* before it, or by *the sense which it makes* of *itself.*"—*Merchant et al. cor.*   "An adjective may usually be known by *the sense which it makes* with the word *thing ;* as, *a good* thing, a *bad* thing."—*Iid.*   " It is seen *to be* in the objective case, *because it denotes* the object affected by the act of leaving."—*Peirce cor.*   " It is seen *to be* in the possessive case, *because it denotes* the possessor of something."—*Id.*   " The noun MAN is caused by the *adjective* WHATEVER to *seem like* a twofold *nominative, as if it denoted,* of itself, one person as the subject of the two remarks."—*Id.*   " WHEN, as used in the last line, is a connective, *because it joins* that line to the other part of the sentence."—*Id.*   "*Because they denote* reciprocation."—*Id.*   " To allow them *to make* use of that liberty ;"—" To allow them *to use* that liberty ;"—or, " To allow them that liberty."—*Sale cor.*   " The worst effect of it is, *that it fixes* on your mind a habit of indecision."—*Todd cor.*   "And you groan the more deeply, as you reflect that *you have not power to* shake it off."—*Id.*   " I know of nothing that can justify the *student in* having recourse to a Latin translation of a Greek writer."—*Coleridge cor.*   "Humour is the *conceit of* making others act or talk absurdly."—*Hazlitt cor.*   " There are remarkable instances *in which they do not affect each* other."—*Butler cor.*   " *That Cæsar was left out* of the commission, was not from any alight."— *Life cor.*   "Of the *thankful reception of* this toleration, I shall say no more," Or : " Of the *propriety of* receiving this toleration thankfully, I shall say no more."—*Dryden cor.*   " Henrietta was delighted with Julia's *skill in* working lace."—*Peirce cor.*   "And it is *because each of them represents* two different words, that the confusion has arisen."—*Booth cor.*   "Æschylus died of a fracture of his skull, caused by an eagle's *dropping of* a tortoise on his head."   Or :—" *caused by* a tortoise *which an eagle let fall* on his head."—*Biog. Dict. cor.*   " He doubted *whether they had* it."—*Felch cor.*   "*To make* ourselves clearly understood, is the chief end of speech."—*Sheridan cor.*   "*One cannot discover* in their countenances any signs which are the natural concomitants of the feelings of the heart."—*Id.*   " Nothing can be more common or less proper, than to speak of a *river as emptying itself.*"—*Campbell cor.*   " Our *non-use of* the former expression, is owing to this."—*Bullions cor.*

UNDER NOTE IV.—DISPOSAL OF ADVERBS.

" To this generally succeeds the division, or the *laying-down of* the method of the discourse."— *Blair cor.*   " To the *pulling-down* of strong holds."—*Bible cor.*   " Can a mere *buckling-on* of a military weapon infuse courage ?"—*Dr. Brown cor.*   "*Expensive* and *luxurious* living *destroys* health."—*Murray cor.*   " By *frugal* and *temperate* living, health is preserved."   Or : " By *living* frugally and temperately, *we preserve our* health."—*Id.*   " By the *doing-away* of the necessity." —*The Friend cor.*   " He recommended to them, however, the *immediate* calling of—(or, *immediately to call*—) the whole community to the church."—*Gregory cor.*   " The separation of large numbers in this manner, certainly facilitates the *right* reading *of* them."—*Churchill cor.*   " From their *mere* admitting of a twofold grammatical construction."—*Phil. Mu. cor.*   " His *grave* lecturing *of* his friend about it."—*Id.*   " For the *blotting-out* of sin."—*Gurney cor.*   " From the *setting* of water."—*Barclay cor.*   " By the gentle *dropping-in* of a pebble."—*Sheridan cor.*   " To the *carrying-on* of a great part of that general course of nature."—*Butler cor.*   " Then the *setting interposing* is so far from being a ground of complaint."—*Id.*   " The bare omission, (or rather, the *not-employing,*) of what is used."—*Campbell cor.*   " The *bringing-together* of incongruous adverbs is a very common fault."—*Churchill cor.*   " This is a presumptive proof *that it does* not *proceed* from them."—*Butler cor.*   " It represents him in a character to which *any injustice* is peculiarly unsuitable."—*Campbell cor.*   " They will aim at something higher than *a mere dealing-out* of harmonious sounds."—*Kirkham cor.*   " This is intelligible and sufficient ; and *any further account of the matter* seems beyond the reach of our faculties."—*Butler cor.*   "Apostrophe is a *turning-off* from the regular course of the subject."—*Mur. et al. cor.*   "Even Isabella was finally prevailed upon to assent to the *sending-out of* a commission to investigate his conduct."—*Life of Col. cor.*   " For the *turning-away* of the simple shall slay them."—*Bible cor.*

  " Thick fingers always should command
  Without *extension of* the hand."—*King cor.*

UNDER NOTE V.—OF PARTICIPLES WITH ADJECTIVES.

"Is there any Scripture *which* speaks of the *light as* being inward ?"—*Barclay cor.*   " For I believe not *positiveness* therein essential to salvation."—*Id.*   " Our *inability* to act a *uniformly*

right part without some thought and care."—*Butler cor.* "*On the* supposition *that it is reconcilable* with the constitution of nature."—*Id.* "*On the ground that it is* not discoverable by reason or experience."—*Id.* "*On the ground that they are* unlike the known course of nature."—*Id.* "Our *power* to discern reasons for them, gives a positive credibility to the history of them."—*Id.* "From its *lack of universality.*"—*Id.* "That they may be turned into passive *participles* in *dus*, is no decisive argument *to prove them* passive."—*Grant cor.* "With the implied idea *that St. Paul was* then absent from the Corinthians."—*Kirkham cor.* "*Because it becomes* gradually weaker, until it finally dies away into silence."—*Id.* "Not without the author's *full knowledge.*"—*Id.* "*Wit* out of season is one sort of folly."—*Sheffield cor.* "Its *general susceptibility* of a much stronger evidence."—*Campbell cor.* "At least, *that they are* such, rarely enhances our opinion, either of their abilities or of their virtues."—*Id.* "Which were the ground of our *unity.*" —*Barclay cor.* "But they may be distinguished from it by their *intransitiveness.*"—*Murray cor.* "To distinguish the higher degree of our persuasion of a thing's *possibility.*"—*Churchill cor.* "*That he was* idle, and dishonest too,
Was that which caus'd his utter overthrow."—*Tobitt cor.*

UNDER NOTE VI.—OF COMPOUND VERBAL NOUNS.

"When it denotes *subjection* to the exertion of an other."—*Booth cor.* "In a passive sense, it signifies *a subjection* to the influence of the action."—*Felch cor.* "*To be* abandoned by our friends, is very deplorable."—*Goldsmith cor.* "Without waiting *to be* attacked by the Macedonians."— *Id.* "In progress of time, words were wanted to express men's *connexion* with certain conditions of fortune."—*Blair cor.* "Our *acquaintance* with pain and sorrow has a tendency to bring us to a settled moderation."—*Butler cor.* "The chancellor's *attachment* to the king, secured *to the monarch* his crown."—*L. Murray et al. cor.* "The general's *failure* in this enterprise occasioned his disgrace."—*Iid.* "John's *long application to writing* had wearied him."—*Iid.* "The sentence *may* be. ‘John's *long application to writing* has wearied him."—*Wright cor.* "Much depends on *the observance of* this rule."—*Murray cor.* He mentioned *that a boy had been* corrected for his faults."—*Alger and Merchant cor.* "The boy's *punishment* is shameful to him." —*Iid.* "The greater the difficulty of remembrance is, and the more important the *being-remembered* is to the attainment of the ultimate end."—*Campbell cor.* "If the parts in the composition of similar objects were always in equal quantity, their *being-compounded* (or their *compounding*) would make no odds."—*Id.* "Circumstances, not of such importance as that the scope of the relation is affected by their *being-known*—or, "by the *mention of them.*"—*Id.* "A passive verb expresses the receiving of an action, or *represents its subject as* being acted upon; as, ‘John is beaten.'"—*Frost cor.* "So our language has an other great advantage; namely, *that it is little* diversified by genders."—*Buchanan cor.* "The *slander concerning Peter* is no fault of *his.*"— *Frost cor.* "Without *faith in Christ,* there is no *justification.*"—*Penn cor.* "*Habituation* to danger begets intrepidity; i. e., lessens fear."—*Butler cor.* "It is not *affection of any kind,* but *action that* forms those habits."—*Id.* "In order *that we may* be satisfied of the truth of the apparent paradox."—*Campbell cor.* "*A trope consists* in *the employing of a word* to signify something that is different from its original *or usual* meaning."—*Blair, Jamieson, Murray, and Kirkham cor. ;* also *Hiley.* "The scriptural view of our *salvation* from punishment."—*Gurney cor.* "To submit and obey, is not renouncing *of the Spirit's leading.*"—*Barclay cor.*

UNDER NOTE VII.—PARTICIPLES FOR INFINITIVES, &c.

"*To teach* little children, is a pleasant employment." Or: "*The teaching of* little children," &c.—*Bartlett cor.* "*To deny* or compromise *the* principles of truth, is virtually *to deny* their divine Author."—*Reformer cor.* "A severe critic might point out some expressions that would bear *retrenching*"—*retrenchment*—or, "*to be* retrenched."—*Blair cor.* "Never attempt *to prolong* the pathetic too much."—*Id.* "I now recollect *to have* mentioned—(or, *that I* mentioned—) a report of that nature."—*Whiting cor.* "Nor of the necessity which there is, for their *restraint*— (or, for *them to be* restrained—) in them."—*Butler cor.* "But, *to do* what God commands because he commands it, is obedience, though it proceeds from hope or fear."—*Id.* "Simply *to close* the nostrils, does not so entirely prevent resonance."—*Gardiner cor.* "Yet they absolutely refuse *to do so.*"—*Harris cor.* "But Artaxerxes could not refuse *to pardon* him."—*Goldsmith cor.* "The doing of them in the best manner, is signified by the *names* of these arts."—*Rush cor.* "To *be have* well for the time to come, may be insufficient."—*Butler cor.* "The compiler proposed *to publish* that part by itself."—*Adam cor.* "To smile *on* those *whom* we should censure, is, *to bring* guilt upon ourselves."—*Kirkham cor.* "But it would be great injustice to that illustrious orator, to bring his genius down to the same level."—*Id.* "*The doubt that* things go ill, often hurts more, than to be sure they do."—*Shak. cor.* "This is called the straining *of* a metaphor."—*Blair and Murray cor.* "This is what Aristotle calls *the* giving *of* manners to the poem."—*Blair cor.* "The painter's *entire confinement* to that part of time which he has chosen, deprives him of the power of exhibiting various stages of the same action."—*Mur. cor.* "It imports *the retrenchment of* all superfluities, and a pruning *of* the expression."—*Blair et al. cor.* "The necessity for *us to be* thus exempted, is further apparent."—*Jane West cor.* "Her situation in life does not allow *her to be* genteel in every thing."—*Same.* "Provided you do not dislike *to be* dirty when you are invisible."—*Same.* "There is now an imperious necessity for her *to be* acquainted with her title to eternity."—*Same.* "*Disregard to the* restraints of virtue, is misnamed ingenuousness."—*Same.* "The legislature prohibits *the* opening *of shops on* Sunday."—*Same.* "To attempt *to prove* that any thing is right."—*O. B. Peirce cor.* "The comma directs *us to make* a pause of a second in duration, or less."—*Id.* "The rule which directs *us to put* other words into the place of it, is wrong." —*Id.* "They direct *us to* call the specifying adjectives, or adnames, adjective pronouns."—*Id.* "William dislikes *to attend* court."—*Frost cor.* "It may perhaps be worth while *to remark,* that Milton makes a distinction."—*Phil. Mu. cor.* "*To profess* regard and *act injuriously, discovers* a base mind."—*Murray et al. cor.* "You have proved beyond contradiction, that *this course of action* is the sure way to procure such an object."—*Campbell cor.*

UNDER NOTE VIII.—PARTICIPLES AFTER BE, IS, &c.

"Irony is *a figure in which the speaker sneeringly utters the direct reverse of what he intends shall be understood.*"—*Brown's Inst.* p. 235. [Correct by this the four false definitions of "Irony" cited from Murray, Peirce, Fisher, and Sanborn.] "This is, in a great measure, a *delivering of* their own compositions."—*Buchanan cor.* "But purity is *a right use of* the words of the language."—*Jamieson cor.* "But the most important object is *the settling of* the English quantity."—*Walker cor.* "When there is no affinity, the transition from one meaning to another is a very wide step *taken.*"—*Campbell cor.* "It would be *a loss of* time, to attempt further to illustrate it."—*Id.* "This *leaves* the sentence too bare, and *makes* it to be, if not nonsense, hardly sense."—*Cobbett cor.* "This is a requiring *of* more labours from every private member."—*J. West cor.* "Is not this, *to use* one measure for our neighbours and *an other* for ourselves?"—*Same.* "*Do we* not *charge* God foolishly, when we give these dark colourings to human nature?"—*Same.* "This is not, *to endure* the cross, as a disciple of Jesus Christ; *to snatch* at it, like a *partisan* of Swift's Jack."—*Same.* "What is spelling? It is *the combining of* letters to form syllables and words."—*O. B. Peirce cor.* "It is *the choosing of such letters* to compose words," &c.—*Id.* "What is Parsing? (1.) It is a *describing of* the nature, use, and powers of words."—*Id.* (2.) "For Parsing is *a describing of* the words of a sentence as they are used."—*Id.* (3.) "Parsing is only a *describing of* the nature and relations of words as they are used."—*Id.* (4.) "Parsing, let the pupil understand and remember, is a *statement of facts concerning words*; or a *describing of words* in their offices and relations, as they are."—*Id.* (5.) "Parsing is *the* resolving and explaining *of* words according to the rules of grammar."—*Id.* Better: "Parsing is the resolving or explaining *of a sentence* according to the *definitions and rules* of grammar."—*Brown's Inst.* p. 28. (6.) "*The* parsing *of* a word, remember, is *an enumerating* and describing *of* its various qualities, and its grammatical relations to other words in the sentence."—*Peirce cor.* (7.) "For the parsing *of* a word is an enumerating and describing *of* its various properties, and [its] relations to [other words in] the sentence."—*Id.* (8.) "*The parsing of* a noun is *an explanation of its* person, number, gender, and case; and also *of* its grammatical *relation* in a sentence, with respect to *some other word* or words."—*Ingersoll cor.* (9.) "*The* parsing *of* any part of speech is *an explanation of* all its properties and relations."—*Id.* (10.) "Parsing is *the* resolving *of* a sentence into its elements."—*Fowler cor.* "The highway *of* the upright is, *to depart* from evil."—*Prov.* xvi, 17. "Besides, the first step towards exhibiting the truth, should be, *to remove* the veil of error."—*Peirce cor.* "Punctuation is *the* dividing *of* sentences, and the words of sentences, by *points for* pauses."—*Id.* "*An other* fault is *the using of* the imperfect *tense* SHOOK *in stead of* the participle SHAKEN."—*Churchill cor.* "Her employment is *the* drawing *of* maps."—*Alger cor.* "*To go* to the play, according to his notion, is, *to lead* a sensual life, and *to expose one's* self to the strongest temptations. This is *a begging of the* question, and *therefore* requires no answer."—*Formey cor.* "It is *an overvaluing of ourselves, to* reduce every thing to the narrow measure of our capacities."—*Comly's Key, in his Gram.* p. 188; *Fisk's Gram.* p. 135. "What is vocal language? It is *speech*, or *the* expressing *of* ideas by the human voice."—*C. W. Sanders cor.*

UNDER NOTE IX.—VERBS OF PREVENTING.

"The annulling power of the constitution prevented that *enactment from* becoming a law."—*O. B. Peirce cor.* "Which prevents the *manner from* being brief."—*Id.* "This close *prevents them from* bearing forward as nominatives."—*Rush cor.* "Because this prevents *it from growing drowsy.*"—*Formey cor.* "Yet this does not prevent *him from* being great."—*Id.* "To prevent *it from* being insipid."—*Id.* "Or whose interruptions did not prevent its *continuance.*" Or thus: "Whose interruptions did not prevent *it from* being continued."—*Id.* "This by no means prevents *them from* being also punishments."—*Wayland cor.* "This hinders *them* not *from being* also, in the strictest sense, punishments."—*Id.* "The noise made by the rain and wind, prevented *them from* being heard."—*Goldsmith cor.* "He endeavoured to prevent *it from* taking effect."—*Id.* "So sequestered as to prevent *them from* being explored."—*Jane West cor.* "Who prevented her *from* making a more pleasant party."—*Same.* "To prevent *us from* being tossed about by every wind of doctrine."—*Same.* "After the infirmities of age prevented *him from* bearing his part of official duty."—*R. Adam cor.* "*An* understanding *of* the literal sense"—*et.* "*To have understood* the literal sense, would not have prevented *them from* condemning the guiltless."—*Butler cor.* "To prevent splendid trifles *from* passing for matters of importance."—*Kames cor.* "Which prevents *him from* exerting himself to any good purpose."—*Beattie cor.* "The *nonobservance* of this rule very frequently prevents *us from* being punctual in *the performance of* our duties."—*Todd cor.* "Nothing will prevent *him from* being a student, and possessing the means of study."—*Id.* "Does the present accident hinder *you from* being honest and brave?"—*Collier cor.* "The e is omitted, to prevent two *Ees from* coming together."—*Fisk cor.* "A pronoun is used for, or in place of, a noun,—to prevent *a repetition of* the noun."—*Sanborn cor.* "Diversity in the style relieves the ear, and prevents *it from* being tired with the frequent recurrence of the rhymes."—*Campbell cor.*; also *Murray.* "Timidity and false shame prevent *us from* opposing vicious customs."—*Mur. et al. cor.* "To prevent *them from* being moved by such."—*Campbell cor.* "Some obstacle, or impediment, that prevents *it from* taking place."—*Priestley cor.* "Which prevents *us from* making a progress towards perfection."—*Sheridan cor.* "This method of distinguishing words, must prevent any regular proportion of time *from* being settled."—*Id.* "That nothing but affectation can prevent *it from* always taking place."—*Id.* "This did not prevent *John from* being acknowledged and solemnly inaugurated Duke of Normandy." Or: "*Notwithstanding* this, *John was* acknowledged and solemnly inaugurated Duke of Normandy."—*Henry, Webster, Sanborn, and Fowler cor.*

UNDER NOTE X.—THE LEADING WORD IN SENSE.

"This would *make it impossible for* a *noun*, or any other *word*, ever *to be* in the possessive case."—*O. B. Peirce cor.* "A great part of our pleasure arises from *finding* the plan or story well con-ted."—*Blair cor.* "And we have no reason to wonder *that this was* the case."—*Id.* "She ected only, (as Cicero says,) to Oppianicus *as* having two sons by his present wife."—*Id.* le *subjugation of* the Britons by the Saxons, was a necessary consequence of their *calling of* se Saxons to their assistance."—*Id.* "What he had there said concerning the Saxons, *that* y *expelled* the Britons, and *changed* the customs, the religion, and the language of the coun- is a clear and good reason *why* our present language is Saxon, rather than British."—*Id.* he only material difference between them, *except that* the one *is* short and the other *more* longed, is, that a metaphor *is always explained* by the words that are connected with it."— *et Mur. cor.* "The description of *Death,* advancing to meet Satan on his arrival."—*Rush cor.* s not the bare fact, *that* God *is* the witness of it, sufficient ground for its credibility to rest n?"—*Chalmers cor.* "As in the case of one *who is* entering upon a new study."—*Beattie cor.* he manner *in which* these *affect* the copula, is called the imperative *mood.*"—*Wilkins cor.* Ve are freed from the trouble, *because* our nouns *have scarcely* any diversity of endings."— *hanan cor.* "The verb is rather indicative of the *action as* being doing, or done, than *of* the e *of the event;* but indeed the ideas are undistinguishable."—*Booth cor.* "Nobody would bt *that* this *is* a sufficient proof."—*Campbell cor.* "Against the doctrine here maintained, t conscience, as well as reason, *is* a natural faculty."—*Beattie cor.* "It is one cause *why* the rk and English languages *are* much more easy to learn, than the Latin."—*Bucks cor.* "I e not been able to make out a solitary instance *in which* such *has been* the fact."—*Lib. cor.* n *angel,* forming the appearance of a hand, and writing the king's condemnation on the wall, cked their mirth, and filled them with terror."—*Wood cor.* "The *prisoners, in attempting* to tpe, aroused the keepers."—*Peirce cor.* "I doubt not, in the least, *that* this *has* been one se of the multiplication of divinities in the heathen world."—*Blair cor.* "From the general : he lays down, *that the verb is* the parent word of all language."—*Tooke cor.* "He was ac- ed of being idle." Or: "He was accused of *idleness.*"—*Felch cor.* "Our meeting is generally atisfied with him *for* so removing." Or:—"with *the circumstances of his removal.*"—*Edmond- cor.* "The spectacle is too rare, of *men* deserving solid fame while not seeking it."—*Bush cor.* "What further need was there *that* an other priest *should rise?*"—*Heb.* vii, 11.

UNDER NOTE XI.—REFERENCE OF PARTICIPLES.

Viewing them separately, *we experience* different emotions." Or: "*Viewed* separately, *they* luce different emotions."—*Kames cor.* "But, *this being left* doubtful, an other objection urs."—*Id.* "As he proceeded from one particular to an other, the subject grew under his d."—*Id.* "But this is still an interruption, and a link of the chain *is* broken."—*Id.* "After le *days'* hunting,—(or, After some days *spent in* hunting,—) Cyrus communicated his design lis officers."—*Rollin cor.* "But it is made, without the appearance of *being made* in form." ir cor. "These would have had a better effect, *had they been* disjoined, thus."—*Blair and* rray cor. "*In* an improper diphthong, but one of the vowels *is* sounded."—*Murray, Alger, et* or." "And *I* being led to think of both together, my view is rendered unsteady."—*Blair, Mur.* I Jam. cor. "By often doing the same thing, *we make the action* habitual." Or: "*What is* m *done,* becomes habitual."—*Murray cor.* "They remain with us in our dark and solitary irs, no less than when *we are* surrounded with friends and cheerful society."—*Id.* "Besides ving what is right, *one may further explain* the matter by pointing out what is wrong."—*Lowth* "The former teaches the true pronunciation of words, *and comprises* accent, quantity, em- ais, *pauses,* and *tones.*"—*Murray cor.* "*A person may reprove others* for their negligence, by say- ' You have taken great care indeed.'"—*Id.* "The *word* preceding and *the word* following ure in apposition to each other."—*Id.* "*He* having finished his speech, the assembly dispersed. *'ooper cor.* "Were the voice to fall at the close of the last line, as many a reader is in the habit illowing *it to do.*"—*Kirkham cor.* "The misfortune of his countrymen were but negatively effects of his wrath, *which only deprived* them of his assistance."—*Kames cor.* "Taking them louns, *we may explain* this construction thus."—*Grant cor.* "These have an active significa- i, *except* those which come from neuter verbs."—*Id.* "From *its* evidence not being universal." "From the *fact that its evidence is* not universal."—*Butler cor.* "And this faith will con- tally grow, *as we acquaint* ourselves with our own nature."—*Channing cor.* "Monosyllables ing with any consonant but *f, l,* or *s,* never double the final consonant, *when it is preceded by* ngle vowel; except *add, ebb,*" &c.—*Kirkham's Gram.* p. 23. Or: "*Words* ending with any con- ant except *f, l,* or *s,* do not double the final letter. Exceptions. Add, ebb, &c."—*Bullions's Gram.* p. 3. (See my 2d Rule for Spelling, of which this is a partial copy.) "The relation of ria *as* being the object of the action, is expressed by the change of the noun *Maria* to *Mariam:*" ., in the *Latin* language."—*Booth cor.* "In analysing a proposition, *one must* first *divide* it i its logical subject and predicate."—*Andrews and Stoddard cor.* "In analysing a simple sen- :e, *one* should first *resolve it* into its logical subject and logical predicate."—*Wells cor.*

UNDER NOTE XII.—OF PARTICIPLES AND NOUNS.

The *instant discovery of* passions at their birth, is essential to our well-being."—*Kames cor.* am now to enter on *a consideration of* the sources of the pleasures of taste."—*Blair cor.* he varieties in *the use of* them are indeed many."—*Murray cor.* "*The changing of* times and lons, *the removing* and *the setting up of* kings, belong to Providence alone."—*Id.* "*Adher- :* to the partitions, seemed the cause of France; *acceptance of* the will. that of the house of irbon "—*Bolingbroke cor.* "An other source of darkness in *composition,* is the injudicious intro- tion of technical words and phrases."—*Campbell cor.* "These are the rules of grammar; by rring which, you may avoid mistakes."—*Mur. et al. cor.* "By observing the rules, you y avoid mistakes."—*Alger cor.* "By observing these rules, he succeeded."—*Frost cor.* "*The* ise *bestowed on him* was his ruin."—*Id.* "*Deception* is not *convincement.*"—*Id.* "He never ed the *loss of* a friend."—*Id.* "*The making of* books is his amusement."—*Alger cor.* "We it *the declining—*(or, *the declension—*) of a noun."—*Ingersoll cor.* "Washington, however, sued the same policy of neutrality, and opposed firmly *the taking of* any part in the wars of

Europe."—*Hall and Baker cor.* " The following is a note of Interrogation, or *of a question* : (?)."
—*Inf. S. Gram. cor.* " The following is a note of Admiration, or *of wonder* : (!)."—*Id.* "The
use or *omission* of the article A forms a nice distinction in the sense."—*Murray cor.* "The
placing *of* the preposition before the word *which* it governs, is more graceful."—*Churchill cor.*
(See *Lowth's Gram.* p. 96 ; *Murray's,* i, 200 ; *Fisk's,* 141 ; *Smith's,* 167.) "Assistance is absolutely necessary to their recovery, and *the* retrieving *of* their affairs."—*Butler cor.* " Which termination, [*ish,*] when added to adjectives, imports diminution, or *a* lessening *of* the quality."—
Mur. and Kirkham cor. "After what *has been* said, will it be thought *an excess of refinement,* to
suggest that the different orders are qualified for different purposes ?"—*Kames cor.* " Who has
nothing to think of, but *the* killing *of* time."—*West cor.* " It requires no nicety of ear, as in the
distinguishing of tones, or *the* measuring *of* time."—*Sheridan cor.* " The *possessive case* [is that
form or state of a noun or pronoun, which] denotes possession, or *the relation of property.*"—*S.
R. Hall cor.*

UNDER NOTE XIII.—PERFECT PARTICIPLES.

" Garcilasso was master of the language *spoken* by the Incas."—*Robertson cor.* " When an interesting story is *broken* off in the middle."—*Kames cor.* " Speaking of Hannibal's elephants driven
back by the enemy."—*Id.* " If Du Ryer had not *written* for bread, he would have equalled them."
—*Formey cor.* " Pope describes a rock *broken* off from a mountain, and hurling to the plain."—
Kames cor. " I have written, Thou hast written, He hath or has written ; &c."—*Ash and Maltby
cor.* "This was *spoken* by a pagan."—*Webster cor.* "But I have *chosen* to follow the common
arrangement."—*Id.* "The language *spoken* in Bengal."—*Id.* "And sound sleep thus *broken* of
with *sudden* alarms, is apt enough to discompose any one."—*Locke cor.* " This is not only the
case of those open sinners before *spoken* of."—*Leslie cor.* " Some grammarians have *written* a
very perplexed and difficult doctrine on Punctuation."—*Ensell cor.* " There hath a pity *arisen* in
me towards thee."—*G. Fox Jun. cor.* "Abel is the only man that has *undergone* the awful change
of death."—*De Genlis, Death of Adam.*

" Meantime, on Afric's glowing sands,
Smit with keen heat, the traveller stands."—*Ode cor.*

CHAPTER VIII. — ADVERBS.

CORRECTIONS UNDER THE NOTES TO RULE XXI.

UNDER NOTE I.—THE PLACING OF ADVERBS.

"*Not* all that is favoured by good use, is proper to be retained."—*L. Murray corrected.* "*Not* every
thing favoured by good use, is on that account worthy to be retained."—*Campbell cor.* " Most
men dream, but *not* all."—*Beattie cor.* " By hasty composition, we shall *certainly* acquire a very
bad style."—*Blair cor.* " The comparisons are short, touching on *only* one point of resemblance."
—*Id.* " Having *once* had some considerable object set before us."—*Id.* " The *positive* seems
to be *improperly* called a degree."*—*Adam and Gould cor.* " In some phrases, the *genitive only*
is used."—*Iid.* " This blunder is said to have *actually* occurred."—*Smith cor.* " But *not every*
man is called James, nor every woman, Mary."—*Buchanan cor.* " Crotchets are employed *for
nearly* the same purpose as the parenthesis."—*Churchill cor.* " There is a *still* greater impropriety
in a double comparative."—*Priestley cor.* " We *often* have occasion to speak of time."—*Lowth
cor.* " The following sentence cannot *possibly* be understood."—*Id.* " The words *must generally*
be separated from the context."—*Comly cor.* " Words ending in *ator, generally* have the accent
on the penultimate."—*L. Mur. cor.* " The learned languages, with respect to voices, moods, and
tenses, are, in general, constructed *differently* from the English tongue."—*Id.* "Adverbs seem to
have been *originally* contrived to express compendiously, in one word, what must otherwise have
required two or more."—*Id.* " But it is so, *only* when the expression can be converted into the
regular form of the possessive case."—*Id.* " '*Enter boldly,*' says he, ' for here too there are
gods.' "—*Harris cor.* " For none *ever* work for so little a pittance that some cannot be found to
work for less."—*Sedgwick cor.* " For sinners also lend to sinners, to receive *again* as much."—
Bible cor. Or, as Campbell has it in his version :—' *that they* may receive as much in return."—
Luke, vi, 34. " They must be viewed in *exactly* the same light."—*Murray cor.* " If he *speaks* but
to display his abilities, he is unworthy of attention."—*Id.*

UNDER NOTE II.—ADVERBS FOR ADJECTIVES.

"*Upward* motion is commonly more agreeable than motion *downward.*"—*Blair cor.* "There
are but two *possible* ways of justification before God."—*Cas cor.* " This construction *sounds*
rather *harsh.*"—*Mur. cor.* "A clear conception, in the mind of the learner, of *regular* and well-
formed letters."—*C. S. Jour. cor.* " He was a great hearer of * * * Attalus, Sotion, Papirius, Fabianus, of whom he makes *frequent* mention."—*L'Estrange cor.* " It is only the *frequent doing* of
a thing, that makes it a custom."—*Leslie cor.* " Because W. R. takes *frequent* occasion to insinuate his jealousies of persons and things."—*Barclay cor.* " Yet *frequent* touching will wear
gold."—*Shak. cor.* " Uneducated persons frequently use an *adverb,* when they ought to use an
adjective : as, ' The country looks *beautifully* ;' in stead of *beautiful.*"†—*Bucke cor.* " The adjective is put *absolute,* or without its substantive."—*Ash cor.* "A noun or *a* pronoun in the
second person, may be put *absolute* in the nominative case."—*Harrison cor.* "A noun or a pro-

---

* From this opinion, I dissent. See Obs. 1st on the Degrees of Comparison, and Obs. 4th on Regular Comparison, in the Etymology of this work, at pp. 266 and 272.—G. BROWN.

† " The country looks *beautiful* ;" that is, *appears* beautiful—*is* beautiful. This is right, and therefore the one
which Bucke makes of it, may be fairly reversed. But the example was ill chosen ; and I incline to think, it may
also be right to say, " The country *looks beautifully* ;" for the *quality* expressed by *beautiful,* is nothing else than
the *manner* in which the thing *shows* to the eye. See Obs. 11th on Rule 9th.—G. BROWN.

n, when *put absolute* with a participle," &c.—*Id. and Jaudon cor.* "A verb in the infinitive
d absolute, stands *independent* of the remaining part of the sentence."—*Wilbur and Liv. cor.*
my *late* return into England, I met a book *entitled*, 'The Iron Age.' "—*Cowley cor.* "But he
discover *no* better foundation for any of them, than the *mere* practice of Homer and Virgil."
ames cor.

UNDER NOTE III.—HERE FOR HITHER, &c.

It is reported, that the *governor* will come *hither* to-morrow."—*Kirkham cor.* "It has been
rted that the *governor* will come *hither* to-morrow."—*Id.* "To catch a prospect of that
ly land *whither* his steps are tending."—*Maturin cor.* "Plautus makes one of his characters
an other, whither he is going with that Vulcan shut up in a horn; that is, with a *lantern* in
hand."—*Adams cor.* "When we left Cambridge, we intended to return *thither* in a few
s."—*Anon. cor.* "Duncan comes *hither* to-night."—*Churchill's Gram.* p. 323. "They talked
eturning hither last week."—See *J. M. Putnam's Gram.* p. 129.

UNDER NOTE IV.—FROM HENCE, &c.

Hence he concludes, that no inference can be drawn from the meaning of the word, that a
titution has a higher authority than a law or statute."—*Webster cor.* "Whence we may like-
: date the period of this event."—*Murray cor.* "Hence it becomes evident, that LANGUAGE,
:n in the most comprehensive view, implies certain sounds, [or certain written signs,] having
ain meanings."—*Harris cor.* "They returned to the city whence they came out."—*A. Mur-
cor.* "Respecting ellipses, some grammarians differ strangely in their ideas; and thence
arisen a very whimsical diversity in their systems of grammar."—*G. Brown.* "What am I,
whence? That is, What am I, and whence *am I?*"—*Jaudon cor.*

UNDER NOTE V.—THE ADVERB HOW.

It is strange, *that* a writer so accurate as Dean Swift, should have stumbled on so improper
application of this particle "—*Blair cor.* "Ye know *that* a good while ago God made choice
ing us," &c.—*Bible cor.* "Let us take care *lest* we sin; i. e.—*that* we do not sin."—*Priestley*
"We see by these instances, *that* prepositions may be necessary, to connect *such* words as
not naturally connected *by* their *own* signification."—*L. Murray cor.* "Know ye not your
i selves, that Jesus Christ is in you, except ye be reprobates?"—*Bible cor.* "That thou *mayst*
w that the earth is the Lord's."—*Id.*

UNDER NOTE VI.—WHEN, WHILE, or WHERE.

ELLIPSIS is *the omission of some word or words which are necessary to complete the construc-
, but not wanting to complete the sense.*"—*G. B.* "PLEONASM is *the insertion of some word or
ds more than are absolutely necessary, either to complete the construction, or to express the
se.*"—*G. B.* "HYSTERON-PROTERON is *a figure in which* that is put in the former part of the
tence, which, according to the sense, should be in the latter."—*Adam and Gould cor.* "HYS-
.ON-PROTERON is a rhetorical figure *in which* that is said last, which was done first."—*Webster*
"A BARBARISM is a foreign or strange word, *an expression contrary to the pure idiom of the
nuage.*"—*G. B.* "A SOLECISM is *an impropriety in respect to* syntax, *an absurdity or incon-
ty in speech.*"—*G. B.* "An IDIOTISM is *a* manner of expression peculiar to one language
dishly *transferred to an other.*"—*G. B.* "TAUTOLOGY is *a disagreeable repetition, either of
same words, or of the same sense in different words.*"—*G. B.* "BOMBAST, or FUSTIAN, is *an
zted or ambitious style, in which high-sounding words are used, with little or no meaning, or
n a trifling occasion.*"—*G. B.* "AMPHIBOLOGY is ambiguity of construction, *phraseology
ch may be taken in two different senses.*"—*G. B.* "IRONY is *a figure in which* one means
contrary of what is said."—*Adam and Gould cor.* "PERIPHRASIS, or CIRCUMLOCUTION, is
use of several words, to express what might be *said* in fewer."—*Iid.* "HYPERBOLE is *a figure
:hich* a thing is magnified above the truth."—*Iid.* "PERSONIFICATION is *a figure which as-
es human life, sentiments, or actions, to inanimate beings, or to abstract qualities.*"—*G. B.*
POSTROPHE is a turning from the tenor of one's discourse, *into an animated address to some
on, present or absent, living or dead, or to some object personified.*"—*G. B.* "A SIMILE
simple and express comparison; and is generally introduced by LIKE, AS, or SO."—*G. B., Inst.*
33. "ANTITHESIS is *a placing of things in opposition, to heighten their effect by contrast.*"—*Ib.*
34. "VISION, or IMAGERY, is *a figure in which what is present only to the mind, is represented
actually before one's eyes, and present to the* senses."—*G. B.* "EMPHASIS is a particular
as of voice laid on some *word* in a sentence."—*Gould's Adam's Gram.* p. 241. "EPANOR-
sis, or CORRECTION, is *the recalling or correcting by the speaker,* of what he last said."—*Ibid.*
ARALIPSIS, or OMISSION, is *the pretending* to omit or pass by, what one at the same time dees."—*Ibid.* "INCREMENTUM, or CLIMAX in sense, is *the rising* of one member above an other
he highest."—*Ibid.* "METONYMY is *a change of names: as when* the cause is *mentioned* for
effect, or the effect for the cause; the container for the thing contained, or the sign for the
ig signified."—*Kirkham cor.* "*The* Agreement *of words is their similarity* in person, number,
der, case, *mood, tense, or form.*"—*Brown's Inst.* p. 104. "*The* Government *of words is that
er which one* word has *over an other, to cause it to assume some particular modification.*"—*Ib.*
usion is *the converting of* some solid substance into a fluid by heat."—*G. B.* "A proper
hthong is *a diphthong in which* both the vowels are *sounded* together; as, *oi* in *voice, ou* in
se."—*Fisher cor.* "An improper diphthong is *a diphthong in which* the sound of but one of
two vowels is heard; as, *eo* in *people.*"—*Id.*

UNDER NOTE VII.—THE ADVERB NO FOR NOT.

An adverb is *added* to a verb to show how, or when, or where, or whether or *not*, one is, does,
suffers."—*Buchanan cor.* "We must be immortal, whether we will or *not.*"—*Maturin cor.*
:e cares *not* whether the world was made for Cæsar or *not.*"—*A. Q. Rev. cor.* "I do not know
:ther they *are* out or *not.*"—*Byron cor.* "Whether it can be proved or *not*, is not the thing."—

Butler cor. " Whether he makes use of the means commanded by God, or *not*."—*Id.* " Whether it pleases the world or *not*, the care is taken."—*L'Estrange cor.* " How comes this to be never heard of, nor in the least questioned, whether the Law was undoubtedly of Moses's writing or *not?*"—*Tomline cor.* " Whether he be a sinner or *not*, I *do not know.*" Or, as the text is more literally translated by Campbell : " Whether he be a sinner, I know not."—*Bible cor.* " Can I make men live, whether they will or *not?*"—*Shak. cor.*

" Can hearts not free, be tried whether they serve
Willing or <i>not</i>, who will but what they must ? "—<i>Milton cor.</i></div>

UNDER NOTE VIII —OF DOUBLE NEGATIVES.

" We need not, nor do *we*, confine the purposes of God." Or : " We need not, *and* do not, confine," &c.—*Bentley cor.* " I cannot by *any* means allow him that."—*Id.* " We must try whether or *not* we can increase the attention by the help of the senses."—*Brightland cor.* " There is nothing more admirable *or* more useful."—*Tooke cor.* "And what in time to come he can never be said to have done, he can never be supposed to do."—*R. Johnson cor.* " No skill could obviate, no remedy dispel, the terrible infection."—*Goldsmith cor.* " Prudery cannot be an indication *either* of sense *or* of taste."—*Spurzheim cor.* " But *neither* that scripture, nor *any* other, speaks of imperfect faith."—*Barclay cor.* " But *neither* this scripture, nor *any* other, proves that faith was or is always accompanied with doubting."—*Id.* " The light of Christ is not, *and* cannot be, darkness."—*Id.* " Doth not the Scripture, which cannot lie, give *some* of the saints this testimony ?"—*Id.* " Which do not continue, *and* are not binding."—*Id.* " It not being perceived directly, *any* more than the air."—*Campbell cor.* " Let us be no Stoics, *and* no stocks, I pray." —*Shak. cor.* " Where there is no marked *or* peculiar character in the style."—*Blair cor.* " There can be no rules laid down, nor *any* manner recommended."—*Sheridan cor.*

"Bates. ' He hath not told his thought to the king ?'
K. Henry. ' No; and it is not meet he should.' "
Or thus: " ' No; nor <i>is it</i> meet he should.' "—<i>Shak. cor.</i></div>

UNDER NOTE IX.—EVER AND NEVER.

" The prayer of Christ is more than sufficient both to strengthen us, be we *everso* weak ; and to overthrow all adversary power, be it *everso* strong."—*Hooker cor.* " He is like to have no share in it, or to be *never* the better for it." Or : " He is *not likely* to have *any* share in it, or to be *ever* the better for it."—*Bunyan cor.* " In some parts of Chili, it seldom or *never* rains."—*Willetts cor.* " If Pompey shall but *everso* little seem to like it."—*W. Walker cor.* " Though *everso* great a *posse* of dogs and hunters pursue him."—*Id.* " Though you be *everso* excellent."—*Id.* " If you do amiss *everso* little."—*Id.* " If we cast our eyes *everso* little down."—*Id.* " A wise man scorneth nothing, be it *everso* small or homely."—*M. F. Tupper cor.* " Because they have seldom *if* ever an opportunity of learning them at all."—*Clarkson cor.* " We seldom or *never* see those forsaken who trust in God."—*Atterbury cor.*

" Where, playing with him at bo-peep,
He solved all problems, e'erso deep."—<i>Butler cor.</i></div>

UNDER NOTE X.—OF THE FORM OF ADVERBS.

" One can *scarcely* think that Pope was capable of epic or tragic poetry ; but, within a certain limited region, he has been outdone by no poet."—*Blair cor.* " I, who now read, have *nearly* finished this chapter."—*Harris cor.* "And yet, to refine our taste with respect to beauties of art or of nature, is *scarcely* endeavoured in any seminary of learning."—*Kames cor.* " The numbers being confounded, and the possessives *wrongly* applied, the passage is neither English nor grammar."—*Buchanan cor.* " The letter G is *wrongly* named *Jee.*"—*Creighton cor.* "*Lastly*, remember that in science, as in morals, authority cannot make right what in itself is wrong."—*Penn cor.* " They regulate our taste even where we are *scarcely* sensible of them."—*Kames cor.* " Slow action, for example, is imitated by words pronounced *slowly.*"—*Id.* "*Surely*, if it be to profit withal, it must be in order to save."—*Barclay cor.* " Which is *scarcely* possible at best."—*Sheridan cor.* " Our wealth being *nearly* finished."—*Harris cor.*

CHAPTER IX. — CONJUNCTIONS.

CORRECTIONS UNDER THE NOTES TO RULE XXII.

UNDER NOTE I.—OF TWO TERMS WITH ONE.

" The first proposal was essentially different *from* the second, and inferior *to it.*"—"A *neuter* verb *expresses* the state *which* a subject is in, without acting upon *any other thing*, or being acted upon by an other."—*A. Murray cor.* " I answer, You *may use* stories and anecdotes, and *ought* to do so."—*Todd cor.* "ORACLE, *n.* Any person *from whom*, or place *at which*, certain *decisions* are obtained."—*Webster cor.* " Forms of government may, and *occasionally must, be changed.*" —*Lyttelton cor.* " I have *been*, and *I still* pretend to be, a tolerable judge."—*Spect. cor.* " Are we not lazy in our duties, or *do we not* make a Christ of them ? "—*Baxter cor.* " They may not express that idea which the author intends, but some other which only resembles *it*, or is *akin* to it."—*Blair cor.* " We may *therefore read them*, we ought to read them, with a distinguishing eye."—*Id.* " Compare their poverty with what they might *possess*, and ought to *possess.*"— *Sedgwick cor.* " He is much better *acquainted with grammar* than they are."—*L. Murray cor.* " He was more beloved *than Cinthio*, but [he was] not so much admired."—*Murray's Gram.* i. 222. " Will it be urged, that the four gospels are as old *as tradition, and even older ?* "—*Campbell's Rhet.* p. 207. " The court of chancery frequently mitigates and *disarms* the common law."— *Spect. and Ware cor.* "Antony, coming along side of her ship, entered it without *seeing her, or* being seen by her."—*Goldsmith cor.* "*Into* candid minds, truth *enters as* a welcome *guest.*"—

. *Murray cor.* "*There are* many designs *in which* we may succeed, *to our ultimate ruin.*"—*Id.* From many pursuits *in which* we embark with pleasure, *we are destined to* land sorrowfully."— . "They *gain* much *more* than I, by this unexpected event."—*Id.*

UNDER NOTE II.—OF HETEROGENEOUS TERMS.

"Athens saw them entering her gates and *filling* her academies."—*Chazotte cor.* "*Neither* we we forgot his past *achievements,* nor *do we* despair of his future success."—*Duncan cor.* Her monuments and temples had long been shattered, or *had* crumbled into dust."—*Journal* r "Competition is excellent; *it is* the vital principle in all these things."—*Id.* "Whether ovision should. or *should* not, be made, *in order* to meet this exigency."—*Id.* "That our Saour was divinely inspired, and *that he was* endued with supernatural powers, are positions that e here taken for granted."—*L. Mur. cor.* "It would be much more eligible, to contract or large their extent by explanatory notes and observations, than *to sweep* away our ancient landarks and *set* up others."—*Id.* "It is certainly much better to supply defects and abridge surfluities by occasional notes and observations, than *to disorganize* or *greatly alter* a system which is been so long established."—*Id.* "To have only one tune, or measure, is not much better an *to have* none at all."—*Blair cor.* "Facts too well known and *too* obvious to be insisted —*Id.* "In proportion as all these circumstances are happily chosen, and *are* of a sublime nd."—*Id.* "If the description be too general, and *be* divested of circumstances."—*Id.* "He ined nothing *but commendation.*"—*L. Mur. cor.* "I cannot but think its application somewhat rained and *misplaced.*"—*Vethake cor.* "Two negatives *standing* in the same clause, or referring the same thing, destroy each other, and leave the sense affirmative."—*Maunder cor.* "Slates e *thin plates of stone,* and *are often* used to cover *the* roofs of houses."—*Webster cor.* "Every an of taste, and *of* an elevated mind, ought to feel almost the necessity of apologizing for the wer he possesses."—*Translator of De Stael cor.* "They very seldom trouble themselves with *quiries,* or *make any* useful observations of their own."—*Locke cor.*
"We've both the field and honour won;
    Our foes are profligate, and run."—*Butler cor.*

UNDER NOTE III.—IMPORT OF CONJUNCTIONS.

"THE is sometimes used before adverbs in the comparative *or the* superlative degree."—*Lennie,* *ullions, and Brace cor.* "The definite article THE is frequently applied to adverbs in the comparare *or the* superlative degree."—*Lowth, Murray, et al. cor.* "Conjunctions usually connect verbs the same mood *and* tense." Or, more truly : "Verbs connected by *a conjunction. are* usually the same mood *and* tense."—*Sanborn cor.* "Conjunctions connect verbs in the same style, and nually in the same mood, tense, *and* form." Or better: "Verbs connected by *a conjunction,* are nually *of the* same mood, tense, *and* form, *as well as* style."—*Id.* "The ruins of Greece *or* Rome e but the monuments of her former greatness."—*P. E Day cor.* "It is not improbable, *that in any of these cases* the articles were used originally."—*Priestley cor.* "I cannot doubt that these jects are really what they appear to be."—*Kames cor.* "I question not *that* my reader will be much pleased with it."—*Spect. cor.* "It is ten to one *that* my friend Peter is among them." *Id* "I doubt not *that* such objections as these will be made."—*Locke cor.* "I doubt not *that* will appear in the perusal of the following sheets."—*Buchanan cor.* "It is not improbable, at in time these different constructions may be appropriated to different uses."—*Priestley cor.* But to forget *and* to remember at pleasure, are equally beyond the power of man."—*Idler cor.* The nominative case follows the verb, in interrogative *or* imperative sentences."—*L. Mur. cor.* Can the fig-tree, my brethren, bear olive berries ? or a vine, figs ?"—*Bible cor.* "Whose charters are too profligate *for* the managing of them to be of any consequence."—*Swift cor.* "You, at are a step higher than a philosopher, a divine, yet have too much grace and wit to be a shop."—*Pope cor.* "The terms *rich and poor* enter not into their language."—*Robertson cor.* This pause is but seldom, *if* ever, sufficiently dwelt upon." Or : "This pause is seldom *or never* fficiently dwelt upon."—*Gardiner cor.* "There would be no possibility of any such thing as man life *or* human happiness."—*Butler cor.* "The multitude rebuked them, *that* they should ld their peace."—*Bible cor.*

UNDER NOTE IV.—THE CONJUNCTION THAN.

"A metaphor is nothing *else than* a short comparison." Or : "A metaphor is nothing *but* a ort comparison."—*Adam and Gould cor.* "There being no other dictator here *than* use."— *'urray's Gram.* i, 364. "This construction is no otherwise known in English, *than* by supplyg the first or *the* second person plural."—*Buchanan cor.* "Cyaxares was no sooner on the rone, *than* he was engaged in a terrible war."—*Rollin cor.* "Those classics contain little else an histories of murders."—*Am. Mu. cor.* "Ye shall not worship any other *than* God."—*Sale* r. "Their relation, therefore, is not otherwise to be ascertained, *than* by their place."—*Campbell* r. "For he no sooner accosted her, *than* he gained his point."—*Burder cor.* "And all the odern writers on this subject, have done little else *than* translate them."—*Blair cor.* "One who ld no other aim *than* to talk copiously and plausibly."—*Id.* "We can refer it to no other cause an the structure of the eye."—*Id.* "No more is required *than* singly an act of vision."—*Kames* r. "We find no more in its composition, *than* the particulars now mentioned."—*Id.* "He does t pretend to say, that it *has* any other effect *than* to raise surprise."—*Id.* "No sooner was e princess dead, *than* he freed himself !"—*Johnson cor.* "OUGHT is an imperfect verb, for it is no modification besides this one."—*Priestley cor.* "The verb is palpably nothing else *than* e tie."—*Neef cor.* "Does he mean that theism is capable of nothing else *than of* being opsed to polytheism or atheism ?"—*Blair cor.* "Is it meant that theism is capable of nothing se *than of* being opposed to polytheism or atheism ?"—*L. Murray cor.* "There is no other ethod of teaching that of which any one is ignorant, *than* by means of something already nown."—*Ingersoll's Grammar, Titlepage.* "O fairest flower, no sooner blown *than* blasted !"— *'ilton cor.* "Architecture and gardening cannot otherwise entertain the mind, *than* by raising certain agreeable emotions or feelings."—*Kames cor.* "Or, rather, they are nothing else than nouns."—*Br. Gram. cor.*

"As if religion were intended
For nothing else *than* to be mended."—*Butler cor.*

UNDER NOTE V.—RELATIVES EXCLUDE CONJUNCTIONS.

"To prepare the Jews for the reception of a prophet mightier than *himself, a teacher* whose shoes he was not worthy to bear."—*Anon. or Mur. cor.* "Has this word, which represents an action, an object after it, on which *the action* terminates ?"—*Osborne cor.* "The stores of literature lie before him, from which he may collect for use many lessons of wisdom."—*Knapp cor.* "Many and various great advantages of this grammar *over* others, might be enumerated."—*Greenleaf cor.* "The custom which still prevails, of writing in lines from left to right, is said to have been introduced about the time of Solon, the Athenian legislator."—*Jamieson cor.* "The fundamental rule *for* the construction of sentences, *the rule* into which all others might be resolved, undoubtedly is, to communicate, in the clearest and most natural order, the ideas which we mean to express."—*Blair and Jamieson cor.* "He left a son of a singular character, who behaved so ill that he was put in prison."—*L. Murray cor.* "He discovered in the youth some disagreeable qualities which to him were wholly unaccountable."—*Id.* "An emphatical pause is made after something *of* peculiar moment has been said, on which we *wish* to fix the hearer's attention." Or: "An emphatical pause is made after something has been said *which is* of peculiar moment, and on which we *wish* to fix the hearer's attention."—*Blair and Murray cor.* "But we have duplicates of each, agreeing in movement, though differing in measure, and *making* different impressions on the ear."—*Murray cor.*

UNDER NOTE VI.—OF THE WORD THAT.

"It will greatly facilitate the labours of the teacher, *and*, at the same time, it will relieve the pupil *from* many difficulties."—*Frost cor.* "*While* the pupil is engaged in the exercises just mentioned, it will be proper *for him* to study the whole grammar in course."—*Bullions cor.* "On the same ground *on which* a participle and *an* auxiliary are allowed to form a tense."—*Beattie and Murray cor.* "On the same ground *on which* the voices, moods, and tenses, are admitted into the English tongue."—*Murray cor.* "The five examples last mentioned, are corrected on the same principle that *is applied to the* errors preceding *them.*"—*Murray and Ingersoll cor.* " The brazen age began at the death of Trajan, and lasted till Rome was taken by the Goths."—*Gould cor.* "The introduction to the duodecimo edition is retained in this volume, for the same reason *for which* the original introduction to the Grammar is retained in the first volume."—*L. Murray cor.* "The verb must also *agree in person with its subject or* nominative."—*Ingersoll cor.* " The *personal* pronoun ' THEIR' is plural for the same reason *for which* ' WHO' is plural."—*Id.* " The Sabellians could not justly be called Patripassians, in the same sense *in which* the Noetians were so called."—*R. Adam cor.* "This is one reason *why* we pass over such smooth language without suspecting that it contains little or no meaning."—*Murray cor.* "The first place *at which the two* armies came *within* sight of each other, was on the opposite banks of the river Apsus."—*Goldsmith cor.* "At the very time *at which* the author gave him the first book for his perusal."—*Campbell cor.* "Peter will sup at the time *at which* Paul will dine."—*Fosdick cor.* " Peter will be supping *when* Paul will enter."—*Id.* " These, *while* they may serve as models to those who may wish to imitate them, will give me an opportunity to cast more light upon the principles of this book."—*Id.*

"Time was, like thee, they life possess'd,
And time shall be, *when* thou shalt rest."—*Parnell cor.*

UNDER NOTE VII.—OF THE CORRESPONDENTS.

"Our manners should be *neither* gross nor excessively refined."—*Murray's Key*, ii, 165. "A neuter verb expresses neither action *nor* passion, but being, or a state of being."—*Peirce cor.* "The old books are neither English grammars, nor *in any sense* grammars of the English language."—*Id.* " The author is apprehensive that his work is not yet so accurate and so much simplified as it may be."—*Kirkham cor.* "The writer could not treat some *topics so* extensively as [it] was desirable [to treat them]."—*Id.* "Which would be a matter of such nicety, *that* no degree of human wisdom could regulate *it.*"—*L. Murray cor.* "No undertaking is so great or difficult, *that* he cannot direct *it.*"—*Duncan cor.* " It is a good which depends *neither* on the will of others, nor on the affluence of external fortune."—*Harris cor.* "Not only his estate, but his reputation too, has suffered by his misconduct."—*Murray and Ingersoll cor.* " Neither do they extend *so* far as might be imagined at first view."—*Blair cor.* "There is no language so poor, but *that* it *has* (or, *as not to have*) two or three past tenses."—*Id.* "So far as this system is founded in truth, language appears to be not altogether arbitrary in its origin."—*Id.* " I have not *and* command of these convulsions *as* is necessary." Or: " I have not *that* command of these convulsions *which* is necessary."—*Spect. cor.* "Conversation with such as (or, *those who*) know so arts *that* polish life."—*Id.* "And which cannot be *either* very lively or very forcible."—*Jamieson cor.* "To *such* a degree as to give proper names to rivers."—*Dr. Murray cor.* " In the same overthrow of such *as* hate to be reformed."—*Barclay cor.* "But still so much of it is retained, *that it* greatly injures the uniformity of the whole."—*Priestley cor.* "Some of them have gone to *such* a height of extravagance, as to assert," &c.—*Id.* "A teacher is confined, not more than a merchant, and probably not *so* much."—*Abbott cor.* "It shall not be forgiven him, neither in this world, nor in the world to come." Or: "It shall not be forgiven him, *either* in this world, or in the world to come."—*Bible cor.* "Which *nobody* presumes, or is so sanguine *as* to hope."—*Swift cor.* "For the torrent of the voice left neither time, *nor* power in the organs, to shape the words properly."—*Sheridan cor.* "That he may neither unnecessarily waste his voice by throwing out too much, *nor* diminish his power by using too little."—*Id.* " I have retained only *such* *as* appear most agreeable to the measures of analogy."—*Littleton cor.* "He is a man

adent and industrious."—*Day cor.*   "Conjunctions connect either words or sentences."—
own's Inst. p. 169.

> " Such silly girls *as* love to chat and play,
> Deserve no care; their time is thrown away."—*Tobitt cor.*
> " Vice is a monster of so frightful mien,
> *That* to be hated *she* but needs be seen."—*Pope cor.*
> " Justice must punish the rebellious deed ;
> Yet punish so *that* pity shall exceed."—*Dryden cor.*

Under Note VIII.—Improper Ellipses.

"That, whose, and as, relate either to persons or *to* things." Or better :—"relate *as well to*
rsons *as* to things."—*Sanborn cor.* "Which and what, as adjectives, relate either to persons
to things." Or better :—"relate to persons *as well as to* things."—*Id.* "Whether of a public
of a private nature."—*Adams cor.* "Which are included *among both* the public and *the* private
ongs."—*Id.* " I might extract, both from the Old and *from the* New Testament, numberless
amples of induction."—*Id.* "Many verbs are used both in an active and *in* a neuter significa-
m."   Or thus: "Many verbs are used *in both* an active and *a* neuter signification."—*Lowth,*
ur. et al. cor. " Its influence is likely to be considerable, both on the morals and *on the* taste
a nation."—*Blair cor.* " The subject afforded a variety of scenes, both of the awful and *of the*
oder kind."—*Id.* " Restlessness of mind disqualifies us, both for the enjoyment of peace, and
· the performance of our duty."—*Mur. and Ing. cor.* "*Pronominal adjectives* are of a mixed
ture, participating the properties both of pronouns and *of* adjectives."—*Mur. et al. cor.* "*Pro-*
minal adjectives have the nature both of the adjective and *of* the pronoun."—*Frost cor.* Or:
[Pronominal adjectives] partake of the properties *of both* adjectives *and* pronouns."—*Bucke's*
ram. p. 55. " Pronominal adjectives are a kind of compound part of speech, partaking the
.ture both of pronouns and *of* adjectives."—*Nutting cor.* "Nouns are used either in the singu-
r or *in the* plural number." Or perhaps better : "Nouns are used *in either* the singular or *the*
ural number."—*D. Blair cor.* " The question is not, whether the nominative or *the* accusative
ght to follow the particles than and as ; but, whether these particles are, in such particular
ses, to be regarded as conjunctions or *as* prepositions."—*Campbell cor.* " In English, many
rbs are used both as transitives and as intransitives."—*Churchill cor.* " He sendeth rain both
i the just and *on the* unjust."—*See Matt.* v, 45. "A foot consists either of two or *of* three sylla-
es "—*D. Blair cor.* " Because they participate the nature both of adverbs and *of* conjunc-
ms."—*L. Murray cor.* " Surely, Romans, what I am now about to say, ought neither to be
aitted, nor to pass without notice."—*Duncan cor.* " Their language frequently amounts, not
ily to bad sense, but *to nonsense.*"—*Kirkham cor.* " Hence arises the necessity of a social
ate to man, both for the unfolding, and *for the* exerting, of his nobler faculties."—*Sheridan*
r. " Whether the subject be of the real or *of the* feigned kind."—*Blair cor.* " Not only was
erty entirely extinguished, but arbitrary power *was* felt in its heaviest and most oppressive
:ight."—*Id.* " This rule is *also* applicable both to verbal Critics and *to* Grammarians."—*Hiley*
r. " Both the rules and *the* exceptions of a language must have obtained the sanction of good
age."—*Id.*

CHAPTER X. — PREPOSITIONS.

CORRECTIONS UNDER THE NOTES TO RULE XXIII.

Under Note I.—Choice of Prepositions.

" You have bestowed your favours *upon* the most deserving persons."—*Swift corrected.* " But,
rise *above* that, and overtop the crowd, is given to few."—*Dr. Blair cor.* " This [also is a
od] sentence [, and] gives occasion *for* no material remark."—*Blair's Rhet.* p. 203. ·"Though
cero endeavours to give some reputation *to* the elder Cato, and those who were his *contempo-*
ries." Or :—" to give some *favourable account* of the elder Cato," &c.—*Blair cor.* " The change
at was produced in eloquence, is beautifully described in the dialogue."—*Id.* " Without care-
lly attending to the variation which they make *in* the idea."—*Id.* " All on a sudden, you are
insported into a lofty palace."—*Hazlitt cor.* "Alike independent *of* one *an* other." Or : "Alike
iependent one *of an* other."—*Campbell cor;* " You will not think of them as distinct processes
ing on independently *of* each other."—*Channing cor.* " Though we say to *depend on, dependent*
, and *dependence on,* we say, independent *of,* and independently *of.*"—*Churchill cor.* "Independ-
tly *of* the rest of the sentence."—*Lowth's Gram.* p. 80; *Buchanan's,* 83; *Bullions's,* 110;
urchill's, 348.[a] " Because they stand independent *of* the rest of the sentence."—*Fisk cor.*
When a substantive is joined with a participle, in English, independently *of* the rest of the
stence."—*Dr. Adam cor.* "Conjunction comes *from* the two Latin words con, together, and
igo, to join."—*Merchant cor.* "How different *from* this is the life of Fulvia ! "—*Addison cor.*
Loved is a participle or adjective, derived *from* the word *love.*"—*Ash cor.* "But I would
juire *of* him, what an office is."—*Barclay cor.* " For the capacity is brought *into* action."—*Id.*
In this period, language and taste arrive *at* purity."—*Webster cor.* "And, should you not aspire
(or *after*) distinction in the *republic* of letters."—*Kirkham cor.* " Delivering you up to the
nagogues, and *into* prisons."—*Luke,* xxi, 12. "He that is kept from falling *into* a ditch, is as

---

[a] Many examples and authorities may be cited in favour of these corrections; as, "He acted independently *of*
eign assistance."—*Murray's Key,* ii, p. 222. " Independently *of* any necessary relation."—*Murray's Gram.* i,
225. " Independently *of* this peculiar mode of construction."—*Blair's Rhet.* p. 413. " Independent *of* the
ll of the people."— *Webster's Essays,* p. 13. "Independent one *of* an other."—*Barclay's Works,* i, 84. " The
initive is often independent *of* the rest of the sentence."—*Lennie's Gram.* p. 85. " Some sentences are inde-
ndent *of* each other."—*Murray's Gram.* i, 277. "As if it were independent *of* it."—*Priestley's Gram.* p. 186.
ndependent *of* appearance and show."—*Blair's Rhet.* p. 19.

truly saved, as he that is taken out of one."—*Barclay cor.* "The best *of* it is, they are but a sort of French Huguenots."—*Addison cor.* "These last ten examples are indeed of a different nature *from* the former."—*R. Johnson cor.* "For the initiation of students *into* the principles of the English language."—*Ann. Rev. cor.* "Richelieu profited *by* every circumstance which the conjuncture afforded"—*Bolingbroke cor.* "In the names of drugs and plants, the mistake *of* a word may endanger life."—*Merchant's Key,* p. 185. Or better: "In *naming* drugs *or* plants, *to* mistake a word, may endanger life."—*Murray cor.* "In order to the carrying *of* its several parts into execution."—*Butler cor.* "His abhorrence *of* the superstitious figure."—*Priestley.* "Thy prejudice *against* my cause."—*Id.* "Which is found *in* every species of liberty."—*Hume cor.* "In a hilly region *on* the north of Jericho."—*Milman cor.* "Two or more singular nouns coupled *by* AND require a verb *or* pronoun in the plural."—*Lennie cor.*

"Books should to one of these four ends conduce,
    To wisdom, piety, delight, or use."—*Denham cor.*

UNDER NOTE II.—TWO OBJECTS OR MORE.

"The Anglo-Saxons, however, soon quarrelled *among* themselves for precedence."—*Const. Misc. cor.* "The distinctions *among* the principal parts of speech are founded *in* nature."—*Webster cor.* "I think I now understand the difference between the active verbs and *those which are* passive or neuter."—*Ingersoll cor.* "Thus a figure including a space *within* three lines, is the real as well as nominal essence of a triangle."—*Locke cor.* "We must distinguish between an imperfect phrase and a simple sentence, *and between a simple sentence* and a compound sentence."—*Lowth, Murray, et al. cor.* "The Jews are strictly forbidden by their law, to exercise usury *towards one an* other."—*Sale cor.* "All the writers have distinguished themselves among themselves."—*Addison cor.* "This expression also better secures the systematic uniformity *of* the three cases."—*Nutting cor.* "When two or more *infinitives* or clauses *are connected disjunctively as the subjects* of an *affirmation,* the verb must be singular."—*Jaudon cor.* "Several nouns or pronouns together in the same case, require a comma *after* each; [except the last, which must sometimes be followed by a greater point.]"—*D. Blair cor.* "The difference between *one vowel and an other* is produced by opening the mouth differently, and placing the tongue in a different manner for each."—*Churchill cor.* "Thus feet composed of syllables, being pronounced with a sensible interval between *one foot and an other,* make a more lively impression than can be made by a continued sound."—*Kames cor.* "The superlative degree implies a comparison, *sometimes* between *two, but generally among* three or more."—*Smith cor.* "They are used to mark a distinction *among* several objects."—*Levizac cor.*

UNDER NOTE III.—OMISSION OF PREPOSITIONS.

"This would have been less worthy *of* notice."—*Churchill cor.* "But I passed it, as a thing unworthy *of* my notice."—*Werter cor.* "Which, in compliment to me, perhaps you may one day think worthy *of* your attention."—*Bucke cor.* "To think this small present worthy *of* an introduction to the young ladies of your very elegant establishment."—*Id.* "There are but a few miles *of* portage."—*Jefferson cor.* "It is worthy *of* notice, that our mountains are not solitary."—*Id.* "It is *about* one hundred feet *in* diameter."*—*Id.* "Entering a hill a quarter or half *of* a mile."—*Id.* "And herself seems passing to *an* awful dissolution, whose issue *it* is not given to human foresight to scan."—*Id.* "It was of a spheroidical form, *about* forty feet *in* diameter at the base, and had been *about* twelve feet *in* altitude."—*Id.* "Before this, it was covered with trees of twelve inches *in* diameter; and, round the base, *there* was an excavation of five feet *in* depth and *five in* width."—*Id.* "Then thou *mayst* eat grapes *to* thy fill, at thine own pleasure." —*Bible cor.* "Then he brought me back *by* the way of the gate of the outward sanctuary."—*Id.* "They will bless God, that he has peopled one half *of* the world with a race of freemen."—*Webster cor.* "*Of* what use can these words be, till their meaning *is* known?"—*Town cor.* "The tents of the Arabs now are black, or *of* a very dark colour."—*The Friend cor.* "They may not be unworthy *of* the attention of young men."—*Kirkham cor.* "The pronoun THAT is frequently applied to persons as well as *to* things."—*Merchant cor.* "And '*who*' is in the same case that '*man*' is in."—*Sanborn cor.* "He saw a flaming stone, apparently about four feet *in* diameter."— *The Friend cor.* "Pliny informs us, that this stone was *of* the size of a cart."—*Id.* "Seneca was about twenty years of age in the fifth year of Tiberius, when the Jews were expelled *from* Rome."—*L'Estrange cor.* "I was prevented *from* reading a letter which would have undeceived me."—*Hawkesworth cor.* "If the problem can be solved, we may be pardoned *for* the inaccuracy of its demonstration."—*Booth cor.* "The army must of necessity be the school, not of honour, but *of* effeminacy."—*Dr. Brown cor.* "Afraid of the virtue of a nation in its opposing *of* bad measures:" or,—"in its *opposition to* bad measures."—*Id.* "The uniting *of* them in various ways, so as to form words, would be easy."—*Gardiner cor.* "I might be excused *from* taking any more notice of it."—*Watson cor.* "Watch therefore; for ye know not *at* what hour your Lord *will* come."—*Bible cor.* "Here, not even infants were spared *from* the sword."—*M'Ilvaine cor.* "To prevent men *from* turning aside to *false* modes of worship."—*John Allen cor.* "God expelled them *from* the garden of Eden."—*Burder cor.* "Nor could he refrain *from* expressing to the senate the agonies of his mind."—*Home cor.* "Who now so strenuously opposes the granting *to* him *of* any new powers."—*Duncan cor.* "That the laws of the censors have banished him *from* the forum."—*Id.* "We read not that he was degraded *from* his office *in* any other way."—*Barclay cor.* "To all *to* whom these presents shall come, greeting."—*Hutchinson cor.* "On the 1st *of* August, 1834."—*Brit. Parl. cor.*

"Whether you had not some time in your life
    Err'd in this point *on* which you censure him."—*Shak. cor.*

---

* The preposition *of* which Jefferson uses before *about,* appears to me to be useless. It does not govern the noun *diameter,* and is therefore no substitute for the *in* which I suppose to be wanting; and, as the preposition *about* seems to be sufficient between *is* and *feet,* I omit the *of.* So in other instances below.—G. BROWN.

UNDER NOTE IV.—OF NEEDLESS PREPOSITIONS.

"And the apostles and elders came together to consider this matter."—*Barclay cor.*; also *lcts.* "Adjectives, in our language, have neither case, *nor* gender, nor number; the only variation they have, is comparison."—*Buchanan cor.* "' It is to you that I am indebted for this privilege ;' that is, ' To you am I indebted ;' or, ' It is you to whom I am indebted.'"—*Sanborn cor.* ' BOOKS is a *common* noun, of the third person, plural number, *and* neuter gender."—*Ingersoll* or " BROTHER's is a common *noun*, of the third person, singular number, masculine gender, nd possessive case."—*Murray cor.* " VIRTUE's is a common *noun*, of the third person, singular umber, [neuter gender,] and possessive case."—*Id.* " When the authorities on one side greatly reponderate, it is vain to oppose the prevailing usage."—*Campbell and Murray cor.* "A captain f a troop of banditti, had a mind to be plundering Rome."—*Collier cor.* "And, notwithstanding ts verbal power, we have added the TO and other signs of exertion."—*Booth cor.* " Some of these ituations are termed CASES, and are expressed by additions to the noun, *in stead of* separate vords :" or,—" *and not by* separate words."—*Id.* " Is it such a fast that I have chosen, that a nan should afflict his soul for a day, and bow down his head like a bulrush ?"—*Bacon cor.* Comare *Isa.* lviii, 5. "And this first emotion comes at last to be awakened by the accidental *in tead of* the necessary antecedent."—*Wayland cor.* "About the same time, the subjugation of he Moors was completed."—*Balbi cor.* " God divided between the light and the darkness "—*3urder cor.* " Notwithstanding this, we are not against outward significations of honour."—*3arclay cor.* " Whether these words and practices of Job's friends, *ought* to be our rule."—*Id.* ' Such verb cannot admit an objective case after it."—*Lowth cor.* " For which, God is now visibly unishing these nations."—*C. Leslie cor.* " In this respect, Tasso yields to no poet, except fomer "—*Blair cor.* " Notwithstanding the numerous panegyrics on the ancient English iberty."—*Hume cor.* " Their efforts seemed to anticipate the spirit which became so general fterwards."—*Id.*

UNDER NOTE V.—THE PLACING OF THE WORDS.

" But how short *of* its excellency are my expressions ! "—*Baxter cor.* "*In* his style, there is a emarkable union *of* harmony with ease."—*Blair cor.* " It disposes *of* the light and shade *in the* nost artificial manner, *that* every thing *may be viewed* to the best advantage."—*Id.* "*For* revity, Aristotle too holds an eminent rank among didactic writers."—*Id.* "In an introducion, correctness *of* expression should be carefully studied."—*Id.* "*In* laying down a method, *ne ought* above all things *to study* precision."—*Id.* " Which shall make *on* the mind the imression *of* something that is one, whole, and entire."—*Id.* "At the same time, there are *in* the)dyssey some defects which must be acknowledged." Or : "At the same time, *it* must be acnowledged *that* there are some defects in the Odyssey."—*Id.* "*In* the concluding books, howver, there are beauties *of* the tragic kind."—*Id.* " These forms of conversation multiplied *by* legrees, and grew troublesome."—*Kames, El. of Crit.* ii. 44. " When she has made her own hoice, she sends, *for* form's sake, a congé-d'élire to her friends."—*Ib.* ii, 46. " Let us endeavour o establish to ourselves an interest in him who holds *in* his hand the reins of the whole creation."—*Spectator cor.* ; also *Kames.* " Next to this, the measure most frequent *in* English poetry, is h.at of eight syllables."—*Blair cor.* " To introduce as great a variety *of* cadences as possible." —*Jamieson cor.* " He addressed *to* them several exhortations, suitable to their circumstances." —*Murray cor.* " Habits *of* temperance and self-denial must be acquired."—*Id.* " In reducing o practice the rules prescribed."—*Id.* " But these parts must be so closely bound together, as o make *upon* the mind the impression *of* one object, not of many."—*Blair and Mur. cor.* " Errors *rith* respect to the use of *shall* and *will*, are sometimes committed by the most distinguished rriters."—*N. Butler cor.*

CHAPTER XI.—PROMISCUOUS EXERCISES.

CORRECTIONS OF THE PROMISCUOUS EXAMPLES.

LESSON I.—ANY PARTS OF SPEECH.

" Such *a* one, I believe, yours will be proved to be."—*Peet and Farnum cor.* " Of the distinction etween the imperfect and the perfect *tense*, it may be observed," &c.—*L. Ainsworth cor.* " The ubject is certainly worthy *of* consideration."—*Id.* " By this means, all ambiguity and controersy *on this point are avoided.*"—*Bullions cor.* " The perfect participle, in English, has both n active and *a* passive signification." Better: " The perfect participle, in English, has *somemes* an active, and *sometimes* a passive, signification."—*Id.* " The old house *has* at length illen down."—*Id.* " The king, the lords, and *the* commons, constitute the English form of govrnment."—*Id.* " The verb in the singular agrees with the person next *to* it." Better: " The erb agrees *in* person with *that which is* next *to* it."—*Id.* " Jane found Seth's gloves in *James's* iat."—*O. C. Felton cor.* " *Charles's* task is too great."—*Id.* " The conjugation of a verb is he naming *of* its several *moods*, tenses, numbers, and persons, *in regular order.*"—*Id.* " The onq-*remembered* beggar was his guest "—*Id.* " Participles refer to nouns or pronouns."—*Id.* ' F has *a* uniform sound, in every position, except in OF." Better: " F has *one unvaried* sound, n every position, except in OF."—*E. J. Hallock cor.* " There are three genders ; the masculine, the eminine, and *the* neuter."—*Id.* " When so *and* THAT occur together, sometimes the particle so s taken as an adverb."—*Id.* " The definition of the articles *shows* that they modify [the import f] the words to which they belong."—*Id.* " The *auxiliary*, SHALL, WILL, or SHOULD is implied." —*Id.* "*Single-rhymed* trochaic omits the final short syllable "—*Brown's Inst.* p. 237. "*Agreeibly* to this, we read of names being blotted out of God's book."—*Burder, Hallock, and Webster or.* " The first person is *that which denotes the speaker.*"—*Inst.* p. 32. "Accent is the laying *of* peculiar stress of the voice, on a certain letter or syllable in a word."—*L. Murray's Gram.* p. 35; *Felton's*, 134. "*Thomas's* horse was caught."—*Felton cor.* " You *were* loved."—*Id.* " The nominative and the objective end alike."—T. Smith cor.   "The numbers of pronouns, like those of substantives, are two, the singular and the plural."—Id.   "I is called the pronoun of the first person, because it represents the person speaking."—Frost cor.   "The essential elements of the phrase are an intransitive gerundive and an adjective."—Hazen cor.   "Wealth is no justification for such impudence."—Id.   "That he was a soldier in the revolution, is not doubted."—Id.   "Fishing is the chief employment of the inhabitants."—Id.   "The chief employment of the inhabitants, is the catching of fish."—Id.   "The cold weather did not prevent the work from being finished at the time specified."—Id.   "The man's former viciousness caused him to be suspected of this crime."—Id.   "But person and number, applied to verbs, mean certain terminations."—Barrett cor.   "Robert felled a tree."—Id.   "Charles raised himself up."—Id.   "It might not be a useless waste of time."—Id   "Neither will you have that implicit faith in the writings and works of others, which characterises the vulgar."—Id.   "I is of the first person, because it denotes the speaker."—Id.   "I would refer the student to Hedge's or Watts's Logic."—Id.   "Hedge's, Watts's, Kirwin's, and Collard's Logic."—Parker and Fox cor.   "Letters that make a full and perfect sound of themselves, are called vowels."   Or: "The letters which make," &c.—Cutler cor.   "It has both a singular and a plural construction."—Id.   "For he beholds (or beholdeth) thy beams no more."—Id. Carthon.   "To this sentiment the Committee have the candour to incline, as it will appear by their summing-up."—Macpherson cor.   "This reduces the point at issue to a narrow compass."—Id.   "Since the English set foot upon the soil."—Exiles cor.   "The arrangement of its different parts is easily retained by the memory."—Hiley cor.   "The words employed are the most appropriate that could have been selected."—Id.   "To prevent it from launching!"—Id.   "Webster has been followed in preference to others, where he differs from them."   Or: "Webster's Grammar has been followed in preference to others, where it differs from them."—Frazee cor.   "Exclamation and interrogation are often mistaken the one for the other."—Buchanan cor.   "When all nature is hushed in sleep, and neither love nor guilt keeps its vigils."—Felton cor.   Or thus :—

"When all nature's hush'd asleep,
Nor love, nor guilt, doth vigils keep."

LESSON II.—ANY PARTS OF SPEECH.

"A Versifier and a Poet are two different things."—Brightland cor.   "Those qualities will arise from the well-expressing of the subject."—Id.   "Therefore the explanation of NETWORK is not noticed here."—Mason cor.   "When emphasis or pathos is necessary to be expressed."—Humphrey cor.   "Whether this mode of punctuation is correct, or whether it is proper to close the sentence with the mark of admiration, may be made a question."—Id.   "But not every writer in those days was thus correct."—Id.   "The sounds of A, in English orthoepy, are no fewer than four."—Id.   "Our present code of rules is thought to be generally correct."   Or: "The rules in our present code are thought to be generally correct."—Id.   "To prevent it from running into an other."—Id.   "Shakspeare, perhaps, the greatest poetical genius that England has produced."—Id.   "This I will illustrate by example; but, before doing so, a few preliminary remarks may be necessary."—Id.   "All such are entitled to two accents each, and some of them to two accents nearly equal."—Id.   "But some cases of the kind are so plain, that no one needs to exercise (or, need exercise) his judgement therein."—Id.   "I have forborne to use the word."—Id.   "The propositions, 'He may study,' 'He might study,' 'He could study,' affirm an ability or power to study."—E. J. Hallock cor.   "The divisions of the tenses have occasioned grammarians much trouble and perplexity."—Id.   "By adopting a familiar, inductive method of presenting this subject, one may render it highly attractive to young learners."—Wells cor.   "The definitions and rules of different grammarians were carefully compared with one an other : "   or—"one with an other."—Id.   "So as not wholly to prevent some sound from issuing."—Sheridan cor.   "Letters of the Alphabet, not yet noticed."—Id.   "'It is sad,' 'It is strange,' &c., seem to express only that well-thing is sad, strange, &c."—Well-wishers cor.   "The winning is easier than the preserving of a conquest."—Same.   "The United States find themselves the owners of a vast region of country at the west."—H. Mann cor.   "One or more letters placed before a word are a prefix "—S. W. Clark cor.   "One or more letters added to a word, are a Suffix."—Id.   "Two thirds of my hair have fallen off."   Or: "My hair has, two thirds of it, fallen off."—Id.   "'Suspecting' describes us, the speakers, by expressing, incidentally, an act of ours."—Id.   "Daniel's predictions are now about being fulfilled."   Or thus: "Daniel's predictions are now receiving their fulfillment."—Id.   "His scholarship entitles him to respect."—Id.   "I doubted whether he had been a soldier."—Id.   "The taking of a madman's sword to prevent him from doing mischief, cannot be regarded as a robbery."—Id.   "I thought it to be him; but it was not he."—Id.   "It was not I that you saw."—Id.   "Not to know what happened before you were born, is always to be a boy."—Id.   "How long were you going? Three days."—Id.   "The qualifying adjective is placed next to the noun."—Id.   "All went but I."—Id.   "This is a parsing of their own language, and not of the author's "—Wells cor.   "Those nouns which denote males, are of the masculine gender."   Or: "Nouns that denote males, are of the masculine gender."—Wells, late Ed.   "Those nouns which denote females, are of the feminine gender."   Or: "Nouns that denote females, are of the feminine gender."—Wells, late Ed.   "When a comparison among more than two objects of the same class is expressed, the superlative degree is employed."—Wells cor.   "Where d or t goes before, the additional letter d or t, in this contracted form, coalesces into one letter with the radical d or t."—Dr. Johnson cor.   "Write words which will show what kind of house you live in—what kind of book you hold in your hand—what kind of day it is."—Weld cor.   "One word or more are often joined to nouns or pronouns to modify their meaning."—Id.   "Good is an adjective; it explains the quality or character of every person to whom, or thing to which, it is applied."   Or :—"of every person or thing that it is applied to."—Id.   "A great public as well as private advantage arises from every one's devoting of himself to that occupation which he prefers, and for which he is specially fitted."—Wayland, Wells, and Weld cor.   "There was a chance for him to recover his senses."   Or: "There was a chance that he might recover his senses."—

Wells and Macaulay cor. "This may be known by *the absence of* any connecting word immediately preceding it."—*Weld cor.* "There are irregular expressions occasionally to be met with, which usage, or custom, rather than analogy, *sanctions*."—*Id.* "He added an anecdote of *Quin* relieving Thomson from prison." Or: "He added an anecdote of *Quin as* relieving Thomson from prison." Or: "He added an anecdote of Quin's relieving *of* Thomson from prison." Or better: "He *also told how Quin relieved* Thomson from prison."—*Id.* "The daily labour of her hands *procures* for her all that is necessary."—*Id.* "*That it is I, should* make no change in your determination."—*Hart cor.* "The classification of words into what *are* called the Parts of Speech." —*Weld cor.* "Such licenses may be explained *among* what *are* usually termed Figures."—*Id.*
"Liberal, not lavish, is kind Nature's *hand*."—*Beattie.*
"They fall successive, and successive rise."—*Pope.*

LESSON III.—ANY PARTS OF SPEECH.

"A Figure of Etymology is *an* intentional deviation *from* the usual form of a word."—*See Brown's Institutes,* p. 229. "A Figure of Syntax is *an* intentional deviation *from* the usual construction of a word."—*See Brown's Inst.* p. 230. "Synecdoche is *the naming* of the whole of *any thing* for a part, or a part for the whole."—*Weld cor.* "Apostrophe is *a turning-off* from the regular course of the subject, to address some person or thing."—*Id.* "Even young pupils will perform such exercises with surprising interest and facility, and will unconsciously gain, in a little time, more knowledge of the structure of *language*, than *they* can acquire by a drilling of several years in the usual routine of parsing."—*Id.* "A few *rules* of construction are employed in this *part*, to guide *the pupil* in the exercise of parsing."—*Id.* "The name of *any* person, object, or thing, *that* can be thought of, or spoken of, is a noun."—*Id.* "A dot, resembling our period, is used between every *two words*, as well as at the close of *each verse*."—*W. Day cor.* "*The* casting *of* types in matrices was invented by Peter Schoeffer, in 1452."—*Id.* "On perusing it, he said, that, so far [*was it*] *from* showing the prisoner's guilt, [that] it positively established his innocence."—*Id.* "By printing the nominative and verb in Italic letters, *we shall enable* the reader to distinguish them at a glance."—*Id.* "It is well, no doubt, to avoid unnecessary words."—*Id.* "*I* meeting a friend the other day, he said to me, 'Where are you going?'"—*Id.* "To John, apples *were* first denied; then *they were* promised *to him*; then *they were* offered *to him*."—*Lennie cor.* "Admission was denied *him*."—*Wells cor.* "A pardon *was* offered *to them*."—*L. Murray's Grammar,* 8vo, p. 183. "A new *potato* was this day shown *me*."—*Darwin, Webster, Frazee,* and *Weld, cor.* "*Those* nouns or pronouns which denote males, are of the masculine gender."—*S. S. Greene cor.* "There are three degrees of comparison; the positive, *the* comparative, and *the* superlative."—*Id.* "The first two refer to direction; the third *refers* to locality."—*Id.* "The following are some of the verbs which take a direct and *an* indirect object." —*Id.* "I was not aware *that he was* the judge of the supreme court."—*Id.* "An indirect question may refer to *any* of the five elements of a declarative sentence."—*Id.* "I am not sure that he will be present."—*Id.* "We left *New York* on Tuesday."—*Id.* "He left *the city*, as he told me, before the arrival of the steamer."—*Id.* "We told him that he must leave *us*;"—"We told him to leave *us*."—*Id.* "Because he was unable to persuade the multitude, he left *the place*, in disgust." —*Id.* "He left *the company*, and took his brother with him."—*Id.* "This stating, or declaring, or denying *of* any thing, is called the indicative mood, or manner of speaking."—*Weld cor.* "This took place at our friend Sir Joshua *Reynolds's*."—*Id.* "The manner *in which* a young *lady may employ* herself usefully in reading, will be the subject of *an other* paper."—*Id.* "Very little time is necessary for *Johnson to conclude* a treaty with the bookseller."—*Id.* "My father is not now sick; but if he *were*, your services would be welcome."—*Chandler's Common School Gram.*, Ed. *of* 1847, p. 79. "*Before* we begin to write or speak, we ought to fix in our minds a clear conception of the end to be aimed at."—*Blair cor.* "Length of days *is* in her right hand; and, in her left hand, *are* riches and honour."—See *Proverbs*, iii, 16. "The active and *the* passive present express different ideas."—*Bullions cor.* "An *Improper Diphthong, (sometimes called a* Digraph,) is a diphthong in which only one of the vowels *is* sounded."—*Fowler cor.* (See G. Brown's definition.) "The real origin of the words *is* to be sought in the Latin."—*Fowler cor.* "What sort of alphabet the Gothic languages possess, we know; what sort of alphabet they require, we can determine."—*Id.* "The Runic alphabet, whether borrowed or invented by the early Goths, is of greater antiquity than either the oldest Teutonic or the Mœso-Gothic *alphabet*."—*Id.* "Common to the Masculine and Neuter Genders."—*Id.* "In the Anglo-Saxon, HIS was common to both the Masculine and *the* Neuter *Gender*."—*Id.* "When time, number, or dimension, *is* specified, the adjective follows the substantive."—*Id.* "Nor pain, nor grief, nor anxious fear, *Invades* thy bounds."—*Id.* "To Brighton, the Pavilion lends a *lath-and-plaster* grace"—*Fowler cor.* "From this consideration, *I have given to nouns* but one person, the THIRD."—*D. C. Allen cor.*
"For it seems to guard and cherish
E'en the wayward dreamer—*me*."—*Anon. cor.*

CHAPTER XII. — GENERAL REVIEW.

CORRECTIONS UNDER ALL THE PRECEDING RULES AND NOTES.
LESSON I.—ARTICLES.

"And they took stones, and made *a* heap."—ALGER'S BIBLE: *Gen.* xxxi, 46. "And I do know many fools, that stand in better place."—*Shak. cor.* "It is a strong antidote to the turbulence of passion, and *the* violence of pursuit."—*Kames cor.* "The word NEWS may admit of either a singular or *a* plural application."—*Wright cor.* "He has gained a fair and honourable reputa-

* Murray, Jamieson, and others, have this definition with the article "*a*," and the comma, but without the hyphen: "*Apostrophe is a turning off* from the regular course," &c. See errors under Note 4th to Rule 20th.

tion."—*Id.* "There are two general forms, called the solemn and *the* familiar style." Or :—"called the solemn and familiar *styles.*"—*Sanborn cor.* "Neither the article nor *the* preposition can be omitted."—*Wright cor.* "A close union is also observable between the subjunctive and *the* potential *mood.*"—*Id.* "Should we render service equally to a friend, *a* neighbour, and an enemy ?"—*Id.* "Till *a* habit is obtained, of aspirating strongly."—*Sheridan cor.* "There is *a* uniform, steady use of the same signs."—*Id.* "A traveller remarks most *of the* objects *which* he sees."—*Jamieson cor.* "What is the name of the river on which London stands ? *Thames.*"—*G. B.* "We sometimes find the last line of *a* couplet or *a* triplet stretched out to twelve syllables."—*Adam cor.* "*The* nouns which follow active verbs, are not in the nominative case."—*Blair cor.* "It is a solemn duty to speak plainly of *the* wrongs which good men perpetrate."—*Channing cor.* "*The* gathering of riches is a pleasant torment."—*L. Cobb cor.* "It is *worth* being quoted." Or better : "It is worth quoting."—*Coleridge cor.* "COUNCIL is a noun which admits of a singular and *a* plural form."—*Wright cor.* "To exhibit the connexion between the Old *Testament* and the New."—*Keith cor.* "An apostrophe discovers the omission of a letter or *of* letters."—*Guy cor.* "He is immediately ordained, or rather acknowledged, *a* hero."—*Pope cor.* "Which is the same in both the leading and *the* following state."—*Brightland cor.* "Pronouns, as will be seen hereafter, have *three* distinct *cases; the* nominative, *the* possessive, and *the* objective."—*D. Blair cor.* "A word of many syllables is called *a* polysyllable."—*Beck cor.* "Nouns have two numbers ; *the* singular and *the* plural."—*Id.* "They have three gendera; *the* masculine, *the* feminine, and *the* neuter."—*Id.* "They have three cases; *the* nominative, *the* possessive, and *the* objective."—*Id.* "Personal pronouns have, like nouns, two numbers; *the* singular and *the* plural ;—three genders; *the* masculine, *the* feminine, and *the* neuter ;—three cases ; *the* nominative, *the* possessive, and *the* objective."—*Id.* "He must be wise enough to know the singular from *the* plural."—*Id.* "Though they may be able to meet every reproach which any one of their fellows may prefer."—*Chalmers cor.* "Yet for love's sake I rather beseech thee, being such *a* one as Paul the aged."—*Bible cor.*; also *Webster.* "A people that jeoparded their lives unto death."—*Bible cor.* "By preventing too great *an* accumulation of seed within too narrow *a* compass."—*The Friend cor.* "Who fills up the middle space between the animal and *the* intellectual nature, the visible and *the* invisible world."—*Addison cor.* "The Psalms abound with instances of *the* harmonious arrangement of words."—*Murray cor.* "On *an* other table, were *a* ewer and *a* vane, likewise of gold."—*Mirror cor.* "TH is said to have two sounds, *a* sharp and *a* flat."—*Wilson cor.* "*The* SECTION (§) is *sometimes* used in *the* subdividing of a chapter into lesser parts."—*Brightland cor.* "Try it in a dog, or *a* horse, or any other creature."—*Locke cor.* "But particularly in *the* learning of languages, there is *the* least *oc* :asion *to pose* children."—*Id.* "*Of* what kind is *the* noun RIVER, and why ?"—*R. C. Smith cor.* "Is WILLIAM'S a proper or *a* common noun ?"—*Id.* What kind of article, then, shall we call *the?*" Or better : "What then shall we call the article *the?*"—*Id.*

> "Each burns alike, who can, or cannot write,
> Or with a rival's, or a eunuch's spite."—*Pope cor.*

LESSON II.—NOUNS, OR CASES.

"And there *are* stamped upon their imaginations *ideas* that follow them with terror and *affright.*"—*Locke cor.* "There's not a wretch that lives on common charity, but's happier than *I.*"—*Ves. Pres. cor.* "But they overwhelm *every one who* is ignorant of them."—*H. Mann cor.* "I have received a letter from my cousin, *her* that was here last week."—*Inst.* p. 129. "*Gentlemen's* houses are seldom without variety of company."—*Locke cor.* "Because Fortune has laid them below the level of others, at their *masters'* feet."—*Id.* "We blamed neither *John's* nor Mary's delay."—*Nixon cor.* "The book was written by order of *Luther the reformer.*"—*Id.* "I saw at the table of the saloon Blair's Sermons, and *somebody's* else, (I forget *whose,*) and [*about the* room] a set of noisy children."—*Byron cor.* "Or saith he it altogether for our *sake?*"—*Bible cor.* "He was not aware *that the Duke was* his competitor."—*Sanborn cor.* "It is no condition of an adjective, that *the word* must be placed before a noun." Or : "It is no condition on which a word becomes an adjective, that it must be placed before a noun."—*Id. and Fowle cor.* "Though their reason corrected the wrong *ideas which* they had taken in."—*Locke cor.* "It was *he that* taught me to hate slavery."—*Morris cor.* "It is *he* and his kindred, who live upon the labour of others."—*Id.* "Payment of tribute is an acknowledgement of *him as* being King —(of *him as* King—or, *that he is* King—) to whom we think it due."—*C. Leslie cor.* "When we comprehend what *is taught us.*"—*Ingersoll cor.* "The following words, and parts of *words,* must be *noticed.*"—*Priestley cor.* "Hence tears and commiseration are so often *employed.*"—*Blair cor.* "JOHN-A NOKES, *n.* A fictitious name used in law proceedings."—*A. Chalmers cor.* "The construction of *words denoting* matter, and *the* part *grasped.*"—*Fisk cor.* "And such other names as carry with them the *idea* of *something* terrible and hurtful."—*Locke cor.* "Every learner then would surely be glad to be spared *from* the trouble and fatigue"—*Pike cor.* "It is not the owning *of one's* dissent from *an other,* that I speak against "—*Locke cor.* "A man that cannot fence, will be more careful to keep out of bullies and *gamesters'* company, and will not be half *so* apt to stand upon *punctilios.*"—*Id.* "From such persons it is, *that* one may learn more in one day, than in a *year's* rambling from one inn to *an other.*"—*Id.* "A long syllable is generally considered to be twice *as long as* a short one."—*D. Blair cor.* "I is of the first person, and *the* singular number. THOU is *of the* second person singular. HE, SHE, or IT, is *of the* third person singular. WE is *of the* first person plural. YE or YOU is *of the* second person plural. THEY is *of the* third person plural."—*Kirkham cor.* "This actor, doer, or producer of the action, is denoted by some word in the nominative *case.*"—*Id.* "Nobody can think, *that* a boy of three or seven years *of age* should be argued with as a grown man."—*Locke cor.* "This was in the *house of* one of the Pharisees, not in Simon the leper's."—*Hammond cor.* "Impossible ! it can't be *I*"—*Swift cor.* "Whose grey top shall tremble, He descending"—*Milton, P. L.,* xii, 227. "*Of* what gender is *woman,* and why ?"—*R. C. Smith cor.* "*Of* what gender, then, is *man,* and why?"—*Id.* "Who is *this I; whom* do you mean, when you say *I?*"—*Green cor.* "It *has* a pleasant air, but *the soil is* barren."—*Locke cor.* "You may, in three *days'* time, go from Galilee to Jerusalem."—*W. Whiston cor.* "And that which is left of the meat-offering, shall be Aaron's and his *sons'*."—FRIENDS' BIBLE.

"For none in all the world, without a lie,
　　Can say *of* this, ''*T*is mine,' but *Bunyan, I*."—*Bunyan cor.*

LESSON III.—ADJECTIVES.

"When he can be their remembrancer and advocate *at all assizes* and sessions."—*Leslie cor.* "DOING denotes *every* manner of action; as, to dance, to play, to write, &c."—*Buchanan cor.* "Seven *feet* long,"—"eight *feet* long,"—"fifty *feet* long."—*W. Walker cor.* "Nearly the whole of *these* twenty-five millions of dollars is a dead loss to the nation."—*Fowler cor.* "Two negatives destroy *each* other."—*Green cor.* "We are warned against excusing sin in ourselves, or in *one an* other."—*Friend cor.* "The Russian empire is more extensive than any *other* government in the world."—*Inst.* p. 265. "You will always have the satisfaction to think it, of all *your expenses*, the money best laid out."—*Locke cor.* "There is no *other* passion which all mankind so naturally *indulge*, as pride."—*Steele cor.* "O, throw away the *viler* part of it."—*Shak. cor.* "He showed us *an easier* and *more agreeable* way."—*Inst.* p. 265. "And the *last four* are to point out those further improvements."—*Jamieson and Campbell cor.* "Where he has not clear *ideas*, distinct and different."—*Locke cor.* "Oh, when shall we have *an other such* Rector of Laracor!"—*Hazlitt cor.* "Speech must have been absolutely necessary *previously* to the formation of society." Or better thus: "Speech must have been absolutely necessary to the formation of society."—*Jamieson cor.* "Go and tell *those* boys to be still."—*Inst.* p. 265. "Wrongs are engraved on marble; benefits, on sand : *those* are apt to be requited : *these*, forgot."—*G. B.* "*None* of these several interpretations is the true one."—*G. B.* "My friend indulged himself in some freaks *not befitting* the gravity of a clergyman."—*G. B.* "And their pardon is all that *any* of their impropriators will have to plead."—*Leslie cor.* "But the time usually chosen to send young men abroad, is, I think, of all *periods*, that *at* which *they are* least capable of reaping those advantages."—*Locke cor.* "It is a mere figment of the human imagination, a rhapsody of the *transcendently* unintelligible."—*Jamieson cor.* "It contains a greater assemblage of sublime ideas, of bold and daring figures, than is perhaps *anywhere else* to be met with."—*Blair cor.* "The order in which the *last two* words are placed, should have been reversed."—*Blair cor.* ; also *Murray.* "In Demosthenes, eloquence *shone* forth with higher splendour, than perhaps in any *other* that ever bore the name of *orator*."—*Id.* "The circumstance of his *poverty* (or, *that he is* poor) is decidedly favourable."—*Todd cor.* "The temptations to dissipation are greatly lessened by his *poverty*."—*Id.* "For, with her death, *those* tidings came."—*Shak. cor.* "The next objection is, that *authors of this sort* are poor."—*Cleland cor.* "Presenting Emma, as Miss Castlemain, to these *acquaintances* :" or,—"to these *persons of her* acquaintance."—*Opie cor.* "I doubt not *that* it will please more *persons* than the opera :" or,—"that it will be *more pleasing* than the opera."—*Spect. cor.* "The world knows only two; *these are*, Rome and I."—*Ben Johnson cor.* "I distinguish these two things from *each* other."—*Blair cor.* "And, in this case, mankind reciprocally claim and allow indulgence to *one an* other."—*Sheridan cor.* "The *last six* books are said not to have received the finishing hand of the author."—*Blair cor.* "The *best-executed* part of the work, is the first six books."—*Id.*

"To reason how can we be said to rise?
　So *hard the task for mortals to be* wise !"—*Sheffield cor.*

LESSON IV.—PRONOUNS.

"Once upon a time, a goose fed *her* young by a *pond's* side :" or—"by a *pondside*."—*Goldsmith cor.* (See OBS. 33d on Rule 4th.) "If either *has* a sufficient degree of merit to recommend *it* to the attention of the public."—*J. Walker cor.* "Now W. *Mitchell's* deceit is very remarkable."—*Barclay cor.* "My brother, I did not put the question to thee, for that I doubted of the truth of *thy* belief."—*Bunyan cor.* "I had two elder brothers, one of *whom* was a lieutenant-colonel."—*De Foe cor.* "Though James is here the object of the action, yet *the word James* is in the nominative case."—*Wright cor.* "Here John is the actor; and *the word John* is known to be *in* the nominative, by its answering to the question, '*Who* struck Richard?'"—*Id.* "One of the most distinguished privileges *that* Providence has conferred upon mankind, is the power of communicating their thoughts to one *an other*."—*Blair cor.* "With some of the most refined feelings *that* belong to our frame."—*Id.* "And the same instructions *that* assist others in composing *works of elegance*, will assist them in judging of, and relishing, the beauties of composition."—*Id.* "To overthrow all *that* had been yielded in favour of the army."—*Macaulay cor.* "Let your faith stand in the Lord God, who changes not, *who* created all, and *who* gives the increase of all."—*Friends cor.* "For it is, in truth, the sentiment or passion which lies under the figured expression, that gives it *all its* merit."—*Blair cor.* "Verbs are words *that* affirm the being, doing, or suffering of a thing, together with the time *at which* it happens."—*A. Murray cor.* "The *bias* will always hang on that side on *which* nature first placed it."—*Locke cor.* "They should be brought to do the things *which* are fit for them."—*Id.* "The various sources *from which* the English language is derived."—*L. Murray cor.* "This attention to the several cases *in which* it is proper to omit *or* to redouble the copulative, is of considerable importance."—*Blair cor.* "Cicero, for instance, speaking of the cases *in which it* is lawful *to kill an other in* self-defence, uses the following words."—*Id.* "But there is no nation, hardly *are there* any *persons*, so phlegmatic, as not to accompany their words with some actions, or gesticulations, *whenever* they are much in earnest."—*Id.* "*William's* is said to be governed by *coat*, because *coat* follows *William's*." Or better:—"because *coat* is the name of the thing possessed by William."—*Smith cor.* "In life, there are many *occasions on which* silence and simplicity are *marks of* true wisdom."—*L. Murray cor.* "In chosing umpires *whose* avarice is excited."—*Nixon cor.* "The boroughs sent representatives, *according to law*."—*Id.* "No man believes but *that* there is some order in the universe."—*G. B.* "The moon is orderly in her changes, *and* she could not be *so* by accident."—*Id.* "*The riddles of the Sphynx* (or, The *Sphynx's* riddles) are generally *of* two kinds."—*Bacon cor.* "They must generally find either their friends or *their* enemies in power."—*Dr. Brown cor.* "Far, of old, very many took upon them to write what happened in their own time."—*Whiston cor.* "The Almighty cut off the family of Eli the high priest, for *their* transgressions."—*The Friend*, vii. 109. "The convention then resoved *itself* into a committee of the whole."—*Inst.* p. 269. "The severity with which *persons* of this denomination *were* treated, appeared rather to invite *them to the colony*, than to deter them from flocking *thither*."—*H. Adams cor.* "Many Christians abuse the Scriptures and the traditions of the apostles, to uphold things quite contrary to *them*."—*Barclay cor.* "Thus, a circle, a square, a triangle, or a hexagon, *pleases* the eye by *its* regularity, *and is a* beautiful *figure*."—*Blair cor.* "Elba is remarkable for being the place to which Bonaparte was banished in 1814."—*Olney's Geog.* "The editor has the reputation of being a good linguist and critic."—*Rel. Herald.* "It is a pride *which* should be cherished in them."—*Locke cor.* "And to restore *to us the hope of* fruits, to reward our pains in *their* season."—*Id.* "The comic representation of death's victim relating *his* own tale."—*Wright cor.* "As for *Scioppius's* Grammar, that wholly *concerns the* Latin tongue."—*Wilkins cor.*

> "And chiefly *Thou*, O Spirit, *that* dost prefer
> Before all temples *th'* upright heart and pure,
> Instruct me, for Thou *knowest*."—*Milton, P. L.*, B. i, l. 17.

LESSON V.—VERBS.

"And there *were* in the same country shepherds abiding in the field."—*Friends' Bible*; also *Bruce's*, and *Alger's*. "Whereof every one *bears* [or *beareth*] twins."—BIBLE COR.: *Song*, vi. 6. "He strikes out of his nature one of the most divine principles that *are* planted in it."—*Addison cor.* "GENII [i. e., the *word* GENII] *denotes aërial* spirits."—*Wright cor.* "In proportion as the long and large prevalence of such corruptions *has* been obtained by force."—*Halifax cor.* "Neither of these *is set before* any word of a general signification, or *before a* proper name."—*Brightland cor.* "Of which, a few of the opening lines *are* all I shall give."—*Moore cor.* "The *wealth* we had in England, was the slow result of long industry and wisdom." Or: "The *riches* we had in England *were*," &c.—*Davenant cor.* "The following expression appears to be correct: 'Much *public gratitude* is due.'" Or this: "'*Great public* thanks *are* due.'"—*Wright cor.* "He *has* been enabled to correct many mistakes."—*Lowth cor.* "Which road *dost* thou *take* here?"—*Ingersoll cor.* "*Dost* thou *learn* thy lesson?"—*Id.* "*Did* they *learn* their pieces perfectly?"—*Id.* "Thou *learned* thy task well."—*Id.* "There are some *who* can't relish the town, and others can't bear with the country."—*Sir Wilful cor.* "If thou *meet* them, thou must put on an intrepid mien."—*Neef cor.* "Struck with terror, as if Philip *were* something more than human."—*Blair cor.* "If the personification of the form of Satan *were* admissible, *the pronouns* should certainly have been masculine."—*Jamieson cor.* "If only one *follows*, there seems to be a defect in the sentence."—*Priestley cor.* "Sir, if thou *hast* borne him hence, tell me where thou hast laid him."—*Bible cor.* "Blessed *are* the people that know the joyful sound."—*Id.* "Every auditory *takes* in good part those marks of respect and awe *with which a modest speaker naturally commences a public discourse*."—*Blair cor.* "Private causes were still pleaded in the forum; but the public *was* no longer interested, nor *was* any general attention drawn to what passed there."—*Id.* "Nay, what evidence can be brought to show, that the *inflections* of the *classic* tongues were *not* originally formed out of obsolete auxiliary words?"—*L. Murray cor.* "If the student *observe* that the principal and the auxiliary *form* but one verb, he will have little or no difficulty in the proper application of the present rule."—*Id.* "For the sword of the enemy, and fear, *are* on every side."—*Bolingbroke cor.* "Even the Stoics agree that nature, or certainty, is very hard to come at."—*Collier cor.* "His politeness, *his* obliging behaviour, *was* changed." Or thus: "His *polite* and obliging behaviour was changed."—*Priestley and Hume cor.* "War and its honours *were* their employment and ambition." Or thus: "War *was* their employment; its honours *were their* ambition."—*Goldsmith cor.* "*Do* A and AN mean the same thing?"—*Green cor.* "When *several* words *come* in between the discordant parts, the ear does not detect the error."—*Cobbett cor.* "The sentence should be, 'When *several* words *come* in,' &c."—*Wright cor.* "The nature of our language, the accent and pronunciation of it, *incline* us to contract even all our regular verbs."—*Churchill's New Gram.* p. 104. Or thus: "The nature of our language,—(*that is*, the accent and pronunciation of it,—) inclines us to contract even all our regular verbs."—*Lowth cor.* "The nature of our language, together with the accent and pronunciation of it, *inclines* us to contract even all our regular verbs."—*Hiley cor.* "Prompt aid, and not promises, *is* what we ought to give."—*G. B.* "The position of the several organs, therefore, as well as their functions, *is* ascertained."—*Mad. Mag. cor.* "Every private company, and almost every public assembly, *affords* opportunities of remarking the difference between a just and graceful, and a faulty and unnatural elocution."—*Enfield cor.* "Such submission, together with the active principle of obedience, *makes* up *in us the* temper or character which answers to his sovereignty."—*Butler cor.* "In happiness, as in other things, there *are* a false and a true, an imaginary and a real."—*A. Fuller cor.* "To confound things that differ, and to make a distinction where there is no difference, *are* equally unphilosophical."—*G. Brown.*

> "I know a bank whereon *doth* wild thyme blow,
> Where oxlips and the nodding violet *grow*."—*Shak. cor.*

LESSON VI.—VERBS.

"*Whose* business or profession *prevents* their attendance in the morning."—*Ogilby cor.* "And no church or officer *has* power over *an other*."—*Lechford cor.* "While neither reason nor experience *is* sufficiently matured to protect them."—*Woodbridge cor.* "Among the Greeks and Romans, almost every syllable was known to have a fixed and determined quantity." Or thus: "Among the Greeks and Romans, *all syllables*, (or at least the far *greater* number,) *were* known to have *severally* a fixed and determined quantity."—*Blair and Jamieson cor.* "Their vanity *is* awakened, and their passions *are* exalted, by the irritation which their self-love receives from contradiction."—*Tr. of Mad. De Staël cor.* "He and I *were* neither of us any great *swimmer*."—*Anon.* "Virtue, honour—nay, even self-interest *recommends* the measure."—*Murray cor.* (See

Obs. 6th on Rule 16th.) "A correct plainness, *an* elegant simplicity, is the proper character of an introduction."—*Blair cor.* "In syntax, there is what grammarians call concord, or agreement, and *there is* government."—*Inf. S. Gram. cor.* "People find themselves able, without much study, to write and speak English intelligibly, and thus *are* led to think *that* rules *are* of no utility."—*Webster cor.* "But the writer must be one who has studied to inform himself well, who has pondered his subject with care, and *who* addresses himself to our *judgement*, rather than to our imagination."—*Blair cor.* "But practice *has* determined it otherwise; and has, in all the languages with which we are much acquainted, supplied the place of an interrogative *mood*, either by particles of interrogation, or by a peculiar order of the words in the sentence."—*Lowth cor.* "If the Lord *hath* stirred thee up against me, let him accept an offering."—*Bible cor.* "But if the priest's daughter be a widow, or divorced, and have no child, and *she return* unto her father's house, as in her youth, she shall eat of her father's meat."—*Id.* "Since we never have *studied, and never* shall study, your sublime productions."—*Neef cor.* "Enabling us to form *distincter* images of objects, than can be *formed*, with the utmost attention, where these particulars are not found."—*Kames cor.* "I hope you will consider *that* what is *spoken* comes from my love."—*Shak. cor.* "We *shall* then perceive how the designs of emphasis may be marred."—*Rush cor.* "I knew it was Crab, and *went* to the fellow that whips the dogs."—*Shak. cor.* "The youth *was consuming* by a slow malady."—*Murray's Gram.* p. 64; *Ingersoll's*, 45; *Fisk's*, 82. "If all men thought, spoke, and wrote alike, something resembling a perfect adjustment of these points *might* be accomplished."—*Wright cor.* "If you will replace what has been, *for* a long *time*, expunged from the language." Or: "If you will replace what *was* long *ago* expunged from the language."—*Campbell cor.* "As in all those faulty instances *which* I have *just* been giving."—*Blair cor.* "This mood *is* also used *improperly* in the following places."—*Murray cor.* "He seems to have been well acquainted with his own genius, and to *have known* what it was that nature had bestowed upon him."—*Johnson cor.* "Of which I *have* already *given* one instance, the worst indeed that occurs in the poem."—*Blair cor.* "It is strange he never commanded you to *do* it."—*Anon.* "History painters would have found it difficult, to *invent* such a species of beings."—*Addison cor.* "Universal Grammar cannot be taught abstractedly; it must be *explained* with reference to some language already known."—*Lowth cor.* "And we might imagine, that if verbs had been so contrived as simply to express these, no *other tenses would have been* needful."—*Blair cor.* "To a writer of such a genius as *Dean Swift's*, the plain style is most admirably fitted."—*Id.* "Please *to* excuse my son's absence."—*Inst.* p. 279. "Bid the boys come in immediately."—*Ib.*

"Gives us the secrets of his pagan hell,
Where *restless ghosts* in sad communion dwell."—*Crabbe cor.*

"Alas! nor faith nor valour now *remains*;
Sighs are but wind, and I must bear my *chains*."—*Walpole cor.*

LESSON VII.—PARTICIPLES.

"Of which the author considers himself, in compiling the present work, as merely laying the foundation-stone."—*D. Blair cor.* "On the raising of such lively and distinct images as are here described."—*Kames cor.* "They are necessary to the avoiding of ambiguities."—*Brightland cor.* "There is no neglecting *of* it without falling into a dangerous error." Or better: "*None can neglect* it without falling," &c.—*Burlamaqui cor.* "The contest resembles Don Quixote's fighting of (or *with*) windmills."—*Webster cor.* "That these verbs associate with *other* verbs in all the tenses, is no proof *that they have* no particular time of their own."—*Murray cor.* "To justify *myself in* not following the *track* of the ancient rhetoricians."—*Blair cor.* "The *putting-together of* letters, so as to make words, is called Spelling."—*Inf. S. Gram. cor.* "What is the *putting-together of* vowels and consonants called?"—*Id.* "Nobody knows of their *charitableness*, but themselves." Or: "Nobody knows *that they are* charitable, but themselves."—*Fuller cor.* "Payment was at length made, but no reason *was* assigned for so long a *postponement of it.*"—*Murray et al. cor.* "Which will bear to *be* brought into comparison with any composition of the kind."—*Blair cor.* "To render vice ridiculous, is to *do* real service to the world."—*Id.* "It is *a direct* copying from nature, a plain rehearsal of what passed, or was supposed to pass, in conversation."—*Id.* "Propriety of pronunciation *consists in* giving to every word that sound which the most polite usage of the language appropriates to it."—*Murray's Key*, 8vo, p. 200; and again, p. 219. "To occupy the mind, and prevent *us from* regretting the insipidity of *a* uniform plain."—*Kames cor.* "There are a hundred ways in *which* any thing may happen."—*Steele cor.* "Tell me, *seignior, for* what cause (or *why*) Antonio *sent* Claudio to Venice yesterday."—*Bucke cor.* "*As you are* looking about for an outlet, some rich prospect unexpectedly opens to view."—*Kames cor.* "A hundred volumes of modern novels may be read without *communicating* a new idea." Or thus: "*A person may read* a hundred volumes of modern novels without acquiring a new idea."—*Webster cor.* "Poetry admits of greater latitude than prose, with respect to *the* coining, or at least *the* new compounding, of words."—*Blair cor.* "When laws were *written* on brazen tablets, *and enforced* by the sword."—*Pope cor.* "A pronoun, which saves the naming of a person or thing a second time, ought to be placed as near as possible to the name of that person or thing."—*Kames cor.* "The using of a preposition in this case, is not always a matter of choice."—*Id.* "To save *the* multiplying *of* words, I would be understood to comprehend both circumstances."—*Id.* "Immoderate grief is mute: *complaint* is a *struggle* for consolation."—*Id.* "On the other hand, the accelerating or *the* retarding *of* the natural course, excites a pain."—*Id.* "Human affairs require the distributing *of* our attention."—*Id.* "By neglecting this circumstance, *the author* of the following example *has made it* defective in neatness."—*Id.* "And therefore the suppressing *of* copulatives must animate a description."—*Id.* "If the *omission of* copulatives *gives* force and liveliness, a redundancy of them must render the period languid."—*Id.* "It skills not, *to ask* my leave, said Richard."—*Scott cor.* "To redeem his credit, he proposed *to be* sent once more to Sparta."—*Goldsmith cor.* "Dumas relates *that he gave* drink to a dog."—*Stone cor.* "Both are, in a like way, instruments of our *reception of* such ideas from external objects."—*Butler cor.* "In order to your proper handling *of* such a subject."—*Spect. cor.* "For I do not recollect *it* preceded by an open vowel."—*Knight cor.* "Such is *the setting-up of* the form above the power of godliness."—*Barclay cor.* " I remember *that I was* walking once with my young acquaintance."—*Hunt cor.* " He did not like *to pay* a debt."—*Id.* " I do not remember *to have seen* Coleridge when I was a child."—*Id.* " In consequence of the dry *rot discovered in it, the* mansion has undergone a thorough repair."—*Maunder cor.* " I would not advise the following of the German system *in all its parts.*"—*Lieber cor.* " Would it not be, *to make* the students judges of the professors ?*"—*Id.* " Little time should intervene between *the proposing of them* and *the deciding* upon *them.*"—*Vethake cor.* " It would be nothing less than *to find* fault with the Creator."—*Lit. Journal cor.* *"That we were once friends,* is a powerful reason, both of prudence and *of* conscience, to restrain us from ever becoming enemies."—*Secker cor.* " By using the word as a conjunction, *we prevent* the ambiguity."—*Murray cor.*

" He forms his schemes the flood of vice to stem,
But *faith in Jesus has no part in* them."—*J. Taylor cor.*

LESSON VIII.—ADVERBS.

"*Auxiliaries not only can* be inserted, but are really understood."—*Wright cor.* " He was *afterwards* a hired scribbler in the Daily Courant."—*Pope's Annotator cor.* " In gardening, luckily, relative beauty *never need stand* (or, perhaps better, *never needs to stand*) in opposition to relative beauty."—*Kames cor.* " I *much* doubt the propriety of the following examples."—*Lowth cor.* "And [we see] how far they have spread, in this part of the world, one of the worst languages *possible.*"—*Locke cor.* "And, in this manner, *merely to place* him on a level with the beast of the forest."—*Smith cor.* *"Whither,* ah ! *whither,* has my darling fled."—*Anon.* "As for this fellow, we know not whence he is."—*Bible cor.* " Ye see then, that by works a man is justified, and not by faith only."—*Id.* " The *Mixed* kind is *that in which* the poet sometimes speaks in his own person, and sometimes makes other characters speak."—*Adam and Gould cor.* " Interrogation is *a rhetorical figure in which* the writer or orator raises questions, and, *if he pleases,* returns answers."—*Fisher cor.* " Prevention is *a figure in which* an author starts an objection which he foresees may be made, and gives an answer to it."—*Id.* " Will you let me alone, or *not ?*"—*W. Walker cor.* " Neither man nor woman *can* resist an engaging exterior."—*Chesterfield cor.* " Though the cup be *everso* clean."—*Locke cor.* " Seldom, or *never,* did any one rise to eminence, by being a witty lawyer." Or thus : "Seldom, *if ever, has* any one *risen* to eminence, by being a witty lawyer."—*Blair cor.* " The second rule which I give, respects the choice of *the* objects from *which* metaphors, and other figures, are to be drawn."—*Id.* " In the figures which it uses, it sets mirrors before us, *in which* we may behold objects *reflected* in their likeness."—*Id.* " Whose business *it* is, to seek the true measures of right and wrong, and not the arts *by which he may* avoid doing the one, and secure himself in doing the other."—*Locke cor.* " The occasions *on which* you ought to personify things, and *those on which* you ought not, cannot be stated in any precise rule."—*Cobbett cor.* " They reflect that they have been much diverted, but *scarcely can they* say about what."—*Kames cor.* " The eyebrows and shoulders should seldom or *never* be remarked by any perceptible motion."—*J. Q. Adams cor.* "And the left hand or arm should seldom or never attempt any motion by itself."—*Id. right.* "Not every speaker *purposes* to please the imagination."—*Jamieson cor.* "And, like Gallio, they care for none of these things." Or : "And, like Gallio, they care *little* for *any* of these things."—*S. cor.* " They may inadvertently be *used* where *their* meaning would be obscure."—*L. Murray cor.* " Nor can a man make him laugh."—*Shak. cor.* " The Athenians, in their present distress, *scarcely* knew *whither* to turn."—*Goldsmith cor.* " I do not remember where God *ever* delivered his oracles by the multitude."—*Locke cor.* " The object of this government is twofold, *outward* and *inward.*"—*Barclay cor.* "In order *rightly* to understand what we read."—*R. Johnson cor.* " That a design had been formed, to *kidnap* or *forcibly abduct* Morgan."—*Col. Stone cor.* " But such imposture can never *long* maintain its ground."—*Blair cor.* " But *surely* it is *as* possible to apply the principles of reason and good sense to this art, as to any other that is cultivated among men."—*Id.* "It would have been better for you, to have remained illiterate, and *even* to have been hewers of wood."—*L. Murray cor.* " Dissyllables that have two vowels which are separated in the pronunciation, *always* have the accent on the *first* syllable."—*Id.* "And they all turned their backs, *almost* without drawing a sword." Or : "And they all turned their backs, *scarcely venturing to draw* a sword."—*Kames cor.* " The principle of duty *naturally* takes *precedence* of every other." —*Id.* "*Not* all that glitters, is gold."—*Maunder cor.* " Whether now, or *everso* many myriads of ages hence."—*Edwards cor.*

" England never did, nor *ever* shall,
Lie at the proud foot of a conqueror."—*Shak cor.*

LESSON IX.—CONJUNCTIONS.

" He readily comprehends the rules of syntax, their use in *the constructing of sentences,* and *their* applicability *to* the examples before him."—*Greenleaf cor.* " The works of Æschylus have suffered more by time, than *those of* any *other* ancient *tragedian.*"—*Blair cor.* " There is much more story, more bustle, and *more* action, than on the French theatre."—*Id.* (See Obs. 8th on Rule 16th.) " Such an unremitted anxiety, *or such* a perpetual application, as engrosses *all* our time and thoughts, *is* forbidden."—*Jenyns cor.* " It seems to be nothing else *than* the simple form of the adjective."—*Wright cor.* " But when I talk of *reasoning,* I do not intend any other *than* such as is suited to the child's capacity."—*Locke cor.* " Pronouns have no other use in language, *than* to represent nouns."—*Jamieson cor.* " The speculative relied no farther on their own judgement, *than* to choose a leader, whom they implicitly followed."—*Kames cor.* " Unaccommodated man is no more *than* such a poor, bare, forked animal as thou art."—*Shak. cor.* "A Parenthesis is a *suggestion which is* introduced into the body of a sentence obliquely, *and which* may be omitted without injuring the grammatical construction."—*Mur. et al. cor.* "The Caret (marked thus ∧) is placed where *something that happened* to be left out, *is to be put into* the line."—*Iid.* "*When* I visit them, they shall be cast down."—*Bible cor.* " Neither our *virtues* nor our vices are all our own."—*Johnson and Sanborn cor.* " I could not give him *so early* an answer as he had desired."—*Peirce cor.* " He is not *so* tall as his brother."—*Nixon cor.* " It is lge *whether* Lord Byron is serious or not."—*L. Blessington cor.* " Some nouns are cond and *the* third declension."—*Gould cor.* " He was discouraged neither by dan-ifortune."—*Wells cor.* " This is consistent neither with logic nor *with* history."—?arts of sentences are *either* simple *or* compound."—*D. Blair cor.* " English verse ither by the number of syllables, than *by* feet:" or,—" than by the number of feet." iow not what more he can do, *than* pray for him."—*Locke cor.* " Whilst they are *are applying* themselves with attention, they are to be kept in good humour."—*Id.* ot have too much of it, nor *have it* too perfectly."—*Id.* " That you may so run, as i so fight, as *to* overcome." Or thus: " That you may so run, *that* you may obtain ; *that* you may overcome."—*Penn cor.* " It is the *artifice* of some, to contrive false .iness, *that* they may seem men of despatch."—*Bacon cor.* " 'A tall man and a this *phrase*, there is no ellipsis ; *the* adjective *belongs only to the former noun ;* the *'s* only the man."—*Ash cor.* " An abandonment of the policy is neither to be ex-*be* desired."—*Jackson cor.* " Which can be acquired by no other means *than by* :ise in speaking."—*Blair cor.* " The chief *or* fundamental rules of syntax are com-nglish *and* the Latin tongue." Or:—" are *applicable* to the English as well as *to* gue."—*Id.* " Then I exclaim, *either* that my antagonist is void of all taste, or that rrupted in a miserable degree." Or thus : " Then I exclaim, that my antagonist is all taste, or *has a taste that* is *miserably* corrupted."—*Id.* " I cannot pity any one no distress *either* of body *or* of mind."—*Kames cor.* " There was much genius in ore there were learning *and* arts to refine it."—*Blair cor.* " Such a writer can have do, *than* to *new-model* the paradoxes of ancient scepticism."—*Dr. Brown cor.* f them being nothing else *than collections* of the ordinary qualities observed in can cor. " A *non-ens*, or negative, can give *neither* pleasure nor pain."—*Kames cor.* · shall not justle and embarrass one an other."—*Blair cor.* " He firmly refused to any other voice *than* his own."—*Murray's Sequel*, p. 113. " Your marching regi-ll not make the guards their example, either as soldiers or *as* subjects."—*Jamieson* :quently they had neither meaning *nor* beauty, to any but the natives of each *eridan cor.*

> " The man of worth, *who* has not left his peer,
> Is in his narrow house forever darkly laid."—*Burns cor.*

LESSON X.—PREPOSITIONS.

ıy be carried on progressively *beyond* any assignable limits."—*Kames cor.* " To .t subjects *into* a single member of a period, is still worse than to crowd them into —*Id.* " Nor do we rigidly insist *on having* melodious prose."—*Id.* " The aversion ose who differ from us."—*Id.* " For we cannot bear his shifting *of* the scene *at* -Halifax cor. " We shall find that we come by it *in* the same way."—*Locke cor.* ı he has no better *defence* than that."—*Barnes cor.* " Searching the person whom *′* having stolen his casket."—*Blair cor.* " Who, as vacancies occur, are elected *by* ard."—*Lit. Journal cor.* "Almost the only field of ambition *for* a German, is sci-*r cor.* " The plan of education is very different *from* the one pursued in the sister *bley cor.* " Some writers on grammar have contended, that adjectives *sometimes* ı, and modify *their* action."—*Wilcox cor.* " They are therefore of a mixed nature, the properties both of pronouns and *of* adjectives."—*Ingersoll cor.* " For there is which can justify the inserting *of* the aspirate or *the* doubling *of* the vowel."—" The distinction and arrangement *of* active, passive, and neuter verbs."—*Wright* ıe thou a hostile world spread its delusive snares."—*Kirkham cor.* " He may be and be made *to* see how those *join* in the contempt."—*Locke cor.* " The contenting in the *present* want of what they wished for, is a *virtue*."—*Id.* " If the complaint be ng really worthy *of* your notice."—*Id.* " True fortitude I take to be the quiet pos-ıan's self, and an undisturbed doing *of* his duty."—*Id.* " For the custom of torment-g beasts, will, by degrees, harden their minds even towards men."—*Id.* " Children o it, and made *to* spend many hours of their precious time uneasily *at* Latin."—*Id.* ject, [the Harmony of Periods,] the ancient rhetoricians have entered into a very articular detail ; more particular, indeed, than *on* any other *head* that regards lan-*Blair's Rhet.* p. 122. " But the one should not be omitted, *and the other retained.*" ı one should not be *used without* the other."—*Bullions cor.* "*From* some common ch, the relative pronoun is usually omitted."—*Murray and Weld cor.* " There are uses which disqualify a witness *for* being received to testify in particular cases."—"Aside *from* all regard to interest, we should expect that," &c.—*Webster cor.* was given *after* a rather cursory perusal of the book."—*Murray cor.* "And, [on] ', he was put on board *of* his ship." Or thus: "And, the next day, he was put ip."—*Id.* " Having the command of no emotions, but what are raised by sight."—'Did these moral attributes exist in some other being *besides* himself." Or :—" in :ing *than* himself."—*Wayland cor.* " He did not behave in that manner *from* pride, ıtempt of the tribunal."—*Murray's Sequel*, p. 113. " These prosecutions *against* ı to have been the most iniquitous measures pursued by the court."—*Murray and* " To restore myself *to* the good graces of my fair critics."—*Dryden cor.* " Objects beautiful, please not *by* virtue of any one quality common to them all."—*Blair cor.* have been less worthy *of* notice, had not a writer or two of high rank lately adopted *ill cor.*

> "A Grecian youth, *of* talents rare,
> Whom Plato's philosophic care," &c.—WHITEHEAD: E. R. p. 196.

LESSON XI.—PROMISCUOUS.

has become a much less considerable object."—*Blair cor.* " My robe, and my in-av'n, *are* all I dare now call *my* own."—*Enfield's Speaker*, p. 347. "*For* thou the garland *wearst* successively."—*Shak. cor.*; also *Enfield.* "If *then* thou *art* a *Roman, take it* forth."—*Id.* "If thou *prove* this to be real, thou must be a smart lad indeed."—*Neef cor.* "And an *other* bridge of four hundred *feet* in length."—*Brightland cor.* "METONYMY is *the putting of* one name for *an other*, on account of the near relation *which* there is between them."—*Fisher cor.* "ANTONOMASIA is *the* putting *of* an appellative or common name for a proper name."—*Id.* "That it is I, *should* make no difference in your determination."—*Bullions cor.* "The first and second *pages* are torn." Or: "The first and *the* second *page* are torn." Or: "The first *page* and *the* second are torn."—*Id.* "John's *absence* from home occasioned the delay."—*Id.* "His *neglect of* opportunities *for* improvement, was the cause of his disgrace."—*Id.* "He will *regret* his *neglect of his* opportunities *for* improvement, when it *is* too late."—*Id.* "His *eagerness at* dancing does not entitle him to our regard."—*Id.* "Cæsar went back to Rome, to take possession of the public treasure, which his opponent, by a most unaccountable oversight, had neglected *to carry away* with him."—*Goldsmith cor.* "And Cæsar took out of the treasury, *gold* to *the amount of* three thousand *pounds'* weight, besides an immense quantity of silver."*—Id.* "Rules and definitions, which should always be *as* clear and intelligible as possible, are thus rendered obscure." —*Greenleaf cor.* "So much both of ability and *of* merit is seldom found." Or thus: "So much *of* both ability and merit is seldom found."†—*Murray cor.* "If such maxims, and such practices prevail, what *has* become of decency and virtue?"‡—*Murray's False Syntax*, ii, 62. Or: "If such maxims and practices prevail, what *will* become of decency and virtue?"—*Murray and Bullions cor.* "Especially if the subject *does not require* so much pomp."—*Blair cor.* "However, the proper mixture of light and shade in such compositions,—the exact adjustment of all the figurative circumstances with the literal sense,—*has* ever been *found an affair* of great nicety." —*Blair's Rhet.* p. 151. "And adding to that hissing in our language, which is so much *noticed* by foreigners."—*Addison, Coote, and Murray cor.* "To speak *impatiently* to servants, or *to do* any thing that betrays unkindness or ill-humour, is certainly criminal." Or better: "Impatience, unkindness, or ill-humour, is certainly criminal."—*Mur. et al. cor.* "Here *are* a *fullness and* grandeur* of expression, well suited to the subject."—*Blair cor.* "I *single out* Strada *from among* the moderns, because he had the foolish presumption to censure Tacitus."—*Murray cor.* "I single him out *from* among the moderns, because," &c.—*Bolingbroke cor.* "This *rule is not* always observed, even by good writers, *so* strictly as it ought to be."—*Blair cor.* "But this gravity and assurance, which *are* beyond boyhood, being neither wisdom nor knowledge, do never reach to manhood."—*Pope cor.* "The regularity and polish even of a turnpike-road, *have* some influence upon the low people in the neighbourhood."—*Kames cor.* "They become fond of regularity and neatness; *and this improvement of their taste* is displayed, first upon their yards and little enclosures, and next within doors."—*Id.* "The phrase, '*it is impossible to exist*,' gives us the idea, *that it is* impossible for men, or any body, to exist."—*Priestley cor.* "I'll give a thousand *pounds* to look upon him."—*Shak. cor.* "The reader's knowledge, as Dr. Campbell observes, may prevent *him from* mistaking it."—*Crombie and Murray cor.* "When two words are set in contrast, or in opposition to *each* other, they are both emphatic."—*L. Murray cor.* "The *number* of *the* persons—men, women, and children—who were lost in the sea, was very great." Or thus: "The number of persons—men, women, and children—*that* were lost in the sea, was very great."—*Id.* "Nor is the resemblance between the primary and *the* resembling object pointed out."—*Jamieson cor.* "I think it the best book of the kind, *that* I have met with."—*Mathews cor.* "Why should not we their ancient rites restore, And be what Rome or Athens *was* before?"—*Roscommon cor.*

LESSON XII.—TWO ERRORS.

"It is labour only *that* gives relish to pleasure."—*L. Murray cor.* "Groves are never *more* agreeable *than* in the opening of spring."—*Id.* "His Philosophical Inquiry into the Origin of our Ideas *of* the Sublime *and the* Beautiful, soon made him known to the literati."—See *Blair's Lect.* pp. 34 and 45. "An awful precipice or tower *from which* we look down on the objects which are below."—*Blair cor.* "This passage, though very poetical, is, however, harsh and obscure: and *for* no other cause *than* this, that three distinct metaphors are crowded together."—*Id.* "I *purpose to make* some observations."—*Id.* "I shall *here* follow the same method *that* I have all along pursued."—*Id.* "Mankind *at no other time* resemble *one an* other so much as they do in the beginnings of society."—*Id.* "But no ear is sensible of the termination of each foot, in *the* reading *of* a hexameter line."—*Id.* "The first thing, says he, *that* a writer *either* of fables or of heroic poems does, is, to choose some maxim or point of morality."—*Id.* "The fourth book has *always* been most justly admired, and *indeed it* abounds with beauties of the highest kind."—*Id.* "There is *in* the poem no attempt towards *the* p*i*inting *of* characters."—*Id.* "But the artificial contrasting of characters, and the *constant* introducing *of* them in pairs and by opposites, *give* too theatrical and affected an air to the piece."—*Id.* "Neither of them *is* arbitrary *or* local."— *Kames cor.* "If *the* crowding *of* figures *is* bad, it is still worse to graft one figure upon *an other*." —*Id.* "The *crowding-together of* so many objects lessens the pleasure."—*Id.* "This therefore lies not in the *putting-off of* the hat, nor *in the* making of compliments."—*Locke cor.* "But the Samaritan Vau may have been used, as the Jews *used* the Chaldaic, both for a vowel and *for a* consonant."—*Wilson cor.* "But if a solemn and *a* familiar pronunciation really *assist* in our language, is it not the business of a grammarian to mark both?"—*J. Walker cor.* "By *making*

---

* This sentence may be written correctly in a dozen different ways, with *precisely the same meaning, and very* nearly the same words. I have here made the noun *gold* the object of the verb *took*, which *in the original appears* to govern the noun *treasure*, or *money*, understood. The noun *amount* might about as well be made *its object, by* a suppression of the preposition *to.* And again, for "*pounds' weight,*" we may say, "*pounds in weight.*" The words will also admit of many different positions.—G. BROWN.

† See a different reading of this example, cited as the first item of false syntax under Rule 16th above, and *there* corrected differently. The words "*both of*," which make the difference, were probably added by L. Murray in some of his *revisals*; and yet it does not appear that this popular critic ever got the sentence *right.*—G. BROWN.

‡ "If such maxims, and such practices prevail, what *has become* of national liberty?"—*Hume's History*, Vol. VI, p. 254; *Priestley's Gram.* p. 128.

w one an other *agreeably* to certain laws."—*Gardiner cor.* " If there were no drink-
.cating draughts, there could be no drunkards."—*Peirce cor.* " Socrates knew his
, and if he was proud of any thing, it was *of* being thought to have none."—*Goldsmith
.nder, having brought his army to Ephesus, erected an arsenal for *the* building of *gal-
*" The use of these signs *is* worthy *of* remark."—*Brightland cor.* " He received me
manner in *which* I would *receive* you." Or thus: " He received me *as* I would re-
.-R. C. Smith cor.* " Consisting of *both* the direct and *the* collateral evidence."—*But-
*f any man or woman that believeth *hath* widows, let *him or her* relieve them, and let
.ch be charged."—*Bible cor.* " For *men's sake* are beasts bred."—*W. Walker cor.*
e o'clock, there *were* drinking and gaming."—*Id.* " Is this he that I am seeking.
.d. "And for the upholding *of every one's* own opinion, there is so much ado."—*Sncol
e of them, however, will *necessarily* be *noticed.*"—*Sale cor.* " The boys conducted
.*very indiscreetly.*"—*Merchant cor.* " Their example, their influence, their fortune,—
they possess,—*dispenses* blessings on all *persons* around them."—*Id. and Murray cor.*
.*eyeseldeess* reciprocally converted *each* other."—*Johnson cor.* " The destroying of the
.itus calls an attack upon virtue itself."—*Goldsmith cor.* "*Moneys are* your suit."—
.*'Ch* is commonly sounded like *tch*, as in *church* ; but, in words derived from Greek,
.und of *k*."—*Murray cor.* " When one is obliged to make some utensil *serve for* pur-
.ch *it was* not *originally* destined."—*Campbell cor.* " But that a *baptism* with water
.*away* of sin, then canst not hence prove."—*Barclay cor.* " Being *spoken* to *but* one,
.miversal command."—*Id.* " For if the *laying-aside of* copulatives gives force and
.redundancy of them must render the period languid."—*Buchanan cor.* " James used
.im to a cat, *which* always *falls* upon her legs."—*Adam cor.*
 " From the low earth aspiring genius springs,
 And sails triumphant, *borne* on *eagle's* wings."—*Lloyd cor.*

LESSON XIII.—TWO ERRORS.

.*tatious*, a feeble, a harsh, or an obscure style, for instance, *is* always *faulty.*"—*Blair
this we find *that* the English pronounce *quite agreeably* to rule." Or thus: " Yet in
.ne English *pronunciation* perfectly agreeable to rule." Or thus: " Yet in this we find
.lish pronounce *in a manner* perfectly agreeable to rule."—*J. Walker cor.* " But
.erception of ideas, nor knowledge of any sort, *is a habit*, though absolutely neces-
.orming of *habits.*"—*Butler cor.* " They were cast ; and a heavy fine *was* imposed
.—*Goldsmith cor.* " Without making this reflection, he cannot enter into the spirit
., or relish the composition."—*Blair cor.* " The scholar should be instructed *in
.ne finding *of* his words." Or thus: " The scholar should be *told how* to *find* his
.born cor.* " And therefore they could neither have forged, *nor have* reversified them."
.. "A dispensary is a place *at which* medicines are dispensed *to the poor.*"—*Mur cor.*
.onnexion and *the* number of words *are* determined by general laws."—*Neef cor.* "An
.the *first two* syllables unaccented, and the last *one* accented ; as, cóntravéne, aequi-
.. cor.* "An explicative sentence is *one in which* a thing is said, *in a direct manner*,
.o be, to do or not to do, to suffer or not to suffer."—*Lowth and Mur. cor.* " But
.ion *whenever* it is neither an adverb nor a preposition."*⚫*—*Smith cor.* " He wrote
.*of* king *Ahasuerus*, and sealed *the writing* with the king's ring."—*Bible cor.*
.Andland *had* departed *from* the town before this time."—*Sewel cor.* " Be-
.*l relinquish* the practice,' they must be convinced."—*Webster cor.* " Which he
.*p before he set* out."—*Grimshaw cor.* " He left *to him* the value of a hundred
.Persian money."—*Spect. cor.* "All *that* the mind can contemplate concerning them,
.led *among* the three."—*Cardell cor.* " Tom Puzzle is one of the most eminent im-
.isputants, of *all* that *have* fallen under my observation."—*Spect. cor.* " When you
.t him to think himself *compensated* for his suffering, by the praise *which* is given
.eurage."—*Locke cor.* " In all matters *in which* simple reason, or mere speculation,
."—*Sheridan cor.* "And therefore he should be spared *from* the trouble of attend-
.ing else *than* his meaning."—*Id.* " It is this kind of phraseology *that* is distin-
.ne epithet *idiomatical ; a species that was* originally the spawn, partly of ignorance,
.' affectation."—*Campbell and Murray cor.* " That neither the inflection nor *the let-
.as* could have been employed by the ancient inhabitants of Latium."—*Knight cor.*
.ses *in which* the verb is intended to be applied to any one of the terms."—*Murray
.these* people *who* know not the law, are accursed."—*Bible cor.* "And the magni-
.*horuses has* weight and sublimity."—*Gardiner cor.* "*Dares* he deny *that* there are
.raternity guilty ? "—*Barclay cor.* "Giving an account of most, if not all, *of* the
.had passed betwixt them."—*Id.* " In this manner, *as to both* parsing and correct-
.l the rules of syntax be treated, *being taken up* regularly according to their order."
.. "To Ovando *were* allowed a brilliant retinue and a *body-guard.*"—*Sketch cor.*
.he, *that* you requested to go ? "—*Kirkham cor.* " Let *thee* and *me* go on."—*Bunyan
.I nowhere affirmed ; and *I* do wholly deny *it.*"—*Barclay cor.* " But that I deny ;
.s for him to prove *it.*"—*Id.* " Our country sinks beneath the yoke ; *She* weeps, *she
.ich* new day a gash Is added to her wounds."—*Shak. cor.* " Thou art the Lord who
.n, and *brought* him forth out of Ur of the Chaldees."—*Bible and Mur. cor.* " He
.tless fountain, from which *emanate* all these attributes that *exist* throughout this
.."—*Wayland cor.* " I am he who *has* communed with the son of Neocles ; I am he
.red the gardens of pleasure."—*Wright cor.*
 " Such *were* in ancient times the tales received,
 Such by our good forefathers *were* believed."—*Rowe cor.*

LESSON XIV.—TWO ERRORS.

.or pronoun that *stands* before the active verb, *usually represents* the agent."—*A
.* " Such *seem* to *have been* the musings of our hero of the grammar-quill, when he
.to my notion, *but* is never a preposition ; but there are some who think otherwise.—*G. Brown.*

penned the first part of his grammar."—*Merchant cor.* "Two dots, the one placed above the other [:] are called Sheva, and *are used to represent* a very short *e.*"—*Wilson cor.* "Great *have* been, and *are*, the obscurity and difficulty, in the nature and application of them" [: i. e.—of natural remedies].—*Butler cor.* "As two *are* to four, so *are* four to eight."—*Everest cor.* "The invention and use of arithmetic, *reach* back to a period so remote, as *to be* beyond the knowledge of history."—*Robertson cor.* "What it presents as objects of contemplation or enjoyment, *fill* and *satisfy* his mind."—*Id.* "If he *dares* not say they are, as I know he *dares* not, how *must* I then distinguish?"—*Barclay cor.* "He *had* now grown so fond of solitude, that all *company had* become uneasy to him."—*Life of Cic. cor.* "Violence and spoil *are* heard in *her*; *before* me continually *are* grief and wounds."—*Bible cor.* "Bayle's Intelligence from the *Republic* of Letters, which *makes* eleven volumes in duodecimo, *is* truly a model in this kind."—*Formey cor.* "Pauses, to *be rendered* pleasing and expressive, must not only be made in the right place, but also *be* accompanied with a proper tone of voice."—*Murray cor.* "*To oppose* the opinions and *rectify* the mistakes of others, is what truth and sincerity sometimes require of us."—*Locke cor.* "It is very probable, that this assembly was called, to clear some doubt which the king had, *whether it were lawful for the Hollanders to throw off* the monarchy of Spain, and *withdraw* entirely their allegiance to that crown." Or :—"about the lawfulness of the Hollanders' *rejection of* the monarchy of Spain, and *entire withdrawment of their* allegiance to that crown."—*Murray cor.* "*A naming of* the numbers and cases of a noun in their order, is called *the declining of* it, or *its declension.*"—*Frost cor.* "The embodying *of them is,* therefore, only *a* collecting *of* such component parts of words."—*Town cor.* "The one is the voice heard *when Christ was* baptized; the other, *when he was* transfigured."—*Barclay cor.* "An understanding *of* the literal sense"—or, "*To have understood* the literal sense, would not have prevented *them from* condemning the guiltless."—*Butler cor.* "As if this were, *to take* the execution of justice out of the hands of God, and *to give* it to nature."—*Id.* "They will say, you must conceal this good opinion of yourself; which yet is *an* allowing *of* the thing, though not of the showing of it." Or :—"which yet is, *to allow* the thing, though not the *showing of* it."—*Sheffield cor.* "So as to signify not only the doing *of* an action, but the causing *of* it to be done."—*Pike cor.* "This, certainly, was both *a* dividing *of* the unity of God, and *a limiting of* his immensity."—*Calvin cor.* "Tones being infinite in number, and varying in almost every individual, the arranging *of* them under distinct heads, and *the* reducing *of* them to any fixed and permanent rules, may be considered as the last refinement in language."—*Knight cor.* "The fierce anger of the Lord shall not return, until he *hath* done it, and until he *hath* performed the intents of his heart." —*Bible cor.* "We seek for deeds *more* illustrious and heroic, for events more diversified and surprising."—*Blair cor.* "We distinguish the genders, or the male and *the* female sex, *in four* different ways."—*Buchanan cor.* "Thus, *ch* and *g* are ever hard. It is therefore proper to retain these sounds in *those* Hebrew names which have not been *modernised*, or changed by public use." —*Dr. Wilson cor.* "*A* Substantive, or Noun, is the name of any thing *which is* conceived to subsist, or of which we have any notion."—*Murray and Lowth cor.* "*A* Noun is the name of any thing *which* exists, or of which we have, or can form, an idea."—*Maunder cor.* "A Noun *is* the name of any thing in existence, or of *any thing* of which we can form an idea."—*Id.* "The next thing to be *attended to*, is, to keep him exactly to *the* speaking of truth."—*Locke cor.* "The material, *the* vegetable, and *the* animal world, receive this influence according to their several capacities."—*Dial cor.* "And yet it is fairly defensible on the principles of the schoolmen; *if those* things can be called principles, which *consist* merely in words."—*Campbell cor.*

> "Art thou so bare, and full of wretchedness,
> And *fearst* to die? Famine is in thy cheeks,
> Need and oppression *starve* in thy *sunk* eyes."—*Shak. cor.*

LESSON XV.—THREE ERRORS.

"The silver age is reckoned to have commenced *at* the death of Augustus, and *to have* continued *till* the end of Trajan's reign."—*Gould cor.* "Language *has indeed* become, in modern times, more correct, and *more determinate.*"—*Dr. Blair cor.* "It is evident, that *those* words are *the* most agreeable to the ear, which are composed of smooth and liquid sounds, *and in which* there is a proper intermixture of vowels and consonants."—*Id.* "It would have had no other effect, *than* to add *to* the sentence *an unnecessary* word."—*Id.* "But as rumours arose, *that* the *judges had* been corrupted by money in this cause, these gave *occasion* to much popular clamour, and *threw* a heavy odium on Cluentius."—*Id.* "A Participle is derived *from* a verb, and partakes of the nature both of the verb and *of an* adjective."—*Ash and Devis cor.* "I *shall* have learned my grammar before you *will have learned* yours."—*Wilbur and Livingston cor.* "There is no *other* earthly object capable of making *so* various and *so* forcible impressions upon the human mind, as a complete speaker."—*Perry cor.* "It was not the carrying *of* the bag, *that* made Judas *a thief* and *a* hireling."—*South cor.* "As the reasonable soul and *the* flesh *are* one man, so God and man are one Christ."—*Creed cor.* "And I will say to them *who* were not my people, *Ye are* my people; and they shall say, Thou art *our* God."—*Bible cor.* "Where there is *in the sense* nothing *that* requires the last sound to be elevated or *suspended*, an easy fall, sufficient to show that the sense is finished, will be proper."—*L. Mur. cor.* "Each party *produce* words *in which* the letter *a* is sounded in the manner *for which* they contend."—*J. Walker cor.* "To countenance persons *that* are guilty of bad actions, is scarcely one remove from *an actual commission of the same crimes.*"—*L. Mur. cor.* "'To countenance persons *that* are guilty of bad actions,' is *a phrase or clause* which is *made the subject of* the verb '*is.*'"—*Id.* "What is called *the* splitting of particles,—*that is, the* separating *of* a preposition from the noun which it governs,—is always *to be* avoided."—*Blair et al. cor.* (See Obs. 16th on Rule 23d.) "There is properly *but* one pause, or rest, in the sentence; *and this falls* betwixt the two members into which *the sentence is* divided." —*Iid.* "*To go* barefoot does not at all help *a man* on, in the way to heaven."—*Steele cor.* "There is *nobody who does not condemn* this in others, though *many* overlook it in themselves."— *Locke cor.* "Be careful not to use the same word *in* the same sentence *either* too frequently *or* in different senses."—*Murray cor.* "Nothing could have made her *more* unhappy, *than to have*

n *of* such principles."—*Id.* "A warlike, various, and tragical age is *the* best to
the worst to write in."—*Cowley cor.* "When thou *instancest Peter's* baptising *of* Cor-
clay cor. "To introduce two or more leading thoughts or *topics*, which have no
y or *mutual* dependence."—*Murray cor.* "Animals, again, are fitted to one *an*
the elements *or regions in which* they live, and to which they are as appendices."—
elody, however, or so *frequent* varying of the sound of each word, is a proof of noth-
fine ear of that people."—*Jamieson cor.* "They can, each in *its* turn, be *used* upon
Duncan cor. "In this reign, lived the *poets* Gower *and* Chaucer, who are the first
an properly be said to have written English."—*Bucke cor.* "In translating ex-
is kind, consider the [phrase] '*it is*,' as if it were *they are*."—*W. Walker cor.* "The
important office to perform ; for, *by the degree of* its activity, we disclose *either* a polite
pronunciation."—*Gardiner cor.* "For no other reason, *than that he was* found in
it."—*Webster cor.* "It is usual to compare them *after* the manner *of polysyllables*."—
"The infinitive mood is *recognized more easily* than any *other*, because the preposition it."—*Bucke cor.* "Prepositions, you recollect, connect words, *and so do* con-
new, then, can you tell *a conjunction* from *a preposition* ?" Or :—"how, then, can you
former from the *latter* ?"—*R. C. Smith cor.*
"No kind of work requires *a nicer* touch,
 And, *this* well finish'd, *none else* shines so much."—*Sheffield cor.*

LESSON XVI.—THREE ERRORS.

occasions, it is the final pause alone, *that* marks the difference between prose and
will be evident from the following arrangement of a few poetical lines."—*L. Murray*
do all I can to persuade others to take *for their cure* the same measures *that* I have
made."—*Guardian cor.* ; also *Murray.* "It is the nature of extreme self-lovers, *that*
house on fire, *as* it were, but to roast their eggs."—*Bacon cor.* "Did ever man
earnestly in a cause *in which* both his honour and *his* life *were* concerned ?"—*Dun-
the* rests, *or* pauses, *which separate* sentences *or* their parts, are marked by points."
"Yet the case and *mood are* not influenced by them, but *are* determined by the
sentence."—*Id.* "*Through inattention* to this rule, many errors have been com-
mitted of which *are here* subjoined, *as* a further caution and direction to the learner."—
"Though thou *clothe* thyself with crimson, though thou *deck* thee with ornaments
though thou *polish* thy face with painting, in vain shalt thou make thyself fair." ●—
But that the doing *of* good to others will make us happy, is not so evident ;
for the hungry, for example, or *the* clothing *of* the naked." Or : "But that, *to*
others, will make us happy, is not so evident ; *to feed* the hungry, for example, or *to*
feed."—*Kames cor.* "There is no other God *than he*, no other light *than* his." Or :
"*God but he*, no light *but* his."—*Penn cor.* "How little reason *is there* to wonder,
that and accomplished orator should be one of the characters that *are* most rarely
their cor. "Because they express *neither the* doing nor *the* receiving *of* an action."—
cor. "To find the answers, will require an effort of mind ; and, when *right answers*
will be the result of reflection, *and show* that the subject is understood."—*Id.*
cases,' is *an expression* trite and common ; but *the same idea* becomes a magnificent im-
age, essed in the language of Mr. Thomson."—*Blair cor.* "The declining *of* a word is the
different endings." Or : "*To decline* a word, is, *to give* it different endings."—*Ware*
so much are they for *allowing* every one *to follow his* own mind."—*Barclay cor.*
The overture for peace *were* made, but Cleon prevented *them from* taking effect."—
"Neither in English, *nor* in any other language, is this word, *or* that which cor-
in meaning, any more an article, than TWO, THREE, or FOUR."—*Webster cor.* "But
some conversation of all *that* I have met *with in* the neighbourhood, has been *with*
your travellers."—*Spect. cor.* "Set down the *first two* terms of *the* supposition,
either, in the first place."—*Smiley cor.* "It is a useful *practice* too, to fix *one's* eye
most distant persons in the assembly."—*Blair cor.* "He will generally please *his*
when to please them is not his sole *or his* chief aim."—*Id.* "At length, the consuls
camp, and inform *the soldiers, that* they could *obtain for them* no other terms *than*
rendering their arms and passing under the yoke."—*Id.* "Nor *are* mankind so much
their choice thus determining *them*."—*Swift cor.* "These forms are what are called
Or : "These forms are called *Numbers*."—*Fosdick cor.* "In *those* languages
that two genders, all nouns are either masculine *or* feminine, even though they de-
note that are neither male *nor* female."—*Id.* "It is called *Verb* or *Word* by way of
use it is the most essential word in a sentence, *and one* without which the other
cannot form *any* complete sense."—*Gould cor.* "The sentence will consist of two
these will commonly *be* separated from *each* other by a comma."—*Jamieson cor.*
that in speaking *are* like the *forté* and *piano* in music ; *they* only *refer* to the different
e used in the same key : whereas high and low imply a change of key."—*Sheridan*
are chiefly three : the acquisition of knowledge ; the assisting *of* the memory *to*
this knowledge ; *and* the communicating *of* it to others."—*Id.*
"*This* kind of knaves I know, *who* in this plainness
Harbour more craft, and *hide* corrupter ends,
Than twenty silly ducking observants."—*Shak. cor.*

LESSON XVII.—MANY ERRORS.

be forgiven, even *for* great errors, *committed* in a foreign language ; but, in *the use*

is te coccino, cùm ornata fueris monili aureo, et *pinzeris stibio* oculos tuos, frustra componèris."—
'περιβάλῃ κόκκινον, καὶ κοσμήσῃ κόσμῳ χρυσῷ ἐὰν ἐγχρίσῃ στίβι τοὺς ὀφθαλμούς σου,
ἴσμός σου."—*Septuagint.* "Quoique tu te revêtes de pourpre, que tu te pares d'ornemens d'or,
et les yeux avec du fard, tu t'emballis en vain."—*French Bible.*

he makes of his own, even the least slips are justly *pointed out* and ridiculed."—*Amer. Chesterfield cor.* " LET expresses *not only* permission, but *entreaty, exhortation, and command.*"—*Lowth cor.*; also *Murray, et al.* " That death which is our leaving of this world, is nothing else *than the putting-off* of these bodies."—*Sherlock.* " They differ from the saints recorded *in either* the Old or *the* New Testament."—*Newton cor.* " The nature of relation, *therefore,* consists in the *referring or comparing of* two things to *each* other ; from which comparison, one or both *come* to be denominated."—*Locke cor.* " It is not credible, that there *is* any one who will say, that *through* the whole course of *his life he* has kept *himself entirely* undefiled, *without* the least spot or stain of sin."—*Witsius cor.* " If *to act* conformably to the will of our Creator,—if *to promote* the welfare of mankind around us,—*if to secure* our own happiness, *is an object* of the highest moment ; then are we loudly called upon to cultivate and extend the great interests of religion and virtue." Or : " If, to act conformably to the will of our Creator, to promote the welfare of mankind around us, and to secure our own happiness, *are objects* of the highest moment ; then," &c.—*Murray et al. cor.* " The verb being in the plural number, it is supposed, that *the officer and his guard are joint agents. But this* is not the case : the only nominative to the verb is *'officer.'* In the expression, ' *with his guard,*' the noun '*guard*' *is* in the objective case, *being* governed by the preposition *with ;* and *consequently it* cannot form the nominative, or any part of it. The prominent subject *for the agreement,* the true nominative *to* the verb, *or the term* to which the verb peculiarly refers, is the *word '* officer.'"—*L. Murray cor.* " This is *an other* use, that, in my opinion, contributes to make a man learned *rather* than wise ; and is *incapable* of pleasing *either* the understanding or *the* imagination."—*Addison cor.* " The work is a dull performance ; and is *incapable* of pleasing *either* the understanding or the imagination."—*Murray cor.* " I would recommend the ' Elements of English Grammar,' by Mr. Frost. *The* plan *of this little work* is *similar to that of* Mr. L. *Murray's smallest Grammar ;* but, *in order* to meet the understanding of children, *its* definitions and language *are* simplified, *so* far as the nature of the subject will admit. It also embraces more examples *for* Parsing, than *are* usual in elementary treatises."—*S. R. Hall cor.* " More rain falls in the first two summer months, than in the first two *months of* winter ; but *what falls,* makes a much greater show upon the earth, in *winter* than in *summer,* because there is a much slower evaporation."—*Murray cor.* " They often contribute also *to render* some persons prosperous, though wicked ; and, *what* is still worse, *to reward* some actions, though vicious ; and *punish* other actions, though virtuous."—*Butler cor.* " Hence, to such a man, *arise* naturally a secret satisfaction, *a* sense of security, and an implicit hope of somewhat further."—*Id.* " So much for the third and last cause of illusion, that was *noticed above ; which arises* from the abuse of very general and abstract terms ; *and* which is the principal source of the *abundant* nonsense that *has* been vented by metaphysicians, mystagogues, and theologians."—*Campbell cor.* " As to those animals *which are* less common, or *which,* on account of the places they inhabit, fall less under our observation, as *fishes* and birds, or *which* their diminutive size removes still further from our observation, we generally, in English, employ a single noun to designate both genders, *the* masculine and *the* feminine."—*Fosdick cor.* "Adjectives may always be distinguished by their *relation to other words : they* express the quality, condition *or number,* of whatever *things are* mentioned."—*Emmons cor.* "An adverb *is* a word added to a verb, a participle, an adjective, or an other adverb ; *and generally expresses time, place, degree, or manner.*"—*Brown's Inst.* p. 29. "The *joining-together* of two objects *so* grand, and the representing of them both, as subject at one moment to the command of God, *produce* a noble effect."—*Blair cor.* " Twisted columns, for instance, are undoubtedly ornamental ; but, as they have the appearance of weakness, they displease *the eye, whenever* they are *used* to support any *mass* part of a building, or *what seems* to require a more substantial prop."—*Id.* " *In* a vast number of inscriptions, some upon rocks, some upon stones of a defined shape, is found an Alphabet different from the *Greeks', the Latins',* and *the Hebrews',* and also unlike that of any modern nation."—*W. C. Fowler cor.*

LESSON XVIII.—MANY ERRORS.

" The empire of Blefuscu is an island, situated *on* the northeast side of Lilliput, from *which it is* parted by a channel of *only* 800 yards *in width.*"—*Swift and Kames cor.* " The nominative *case* usually *denotes* the agent or doer ; and *any noun or pronoun which is* the subject of *a finite verb, is always in this case.*"—*Smith cor.* " There are, *in* his allegorical personages, an originality, a richness, and *a* variety, which almost *vie* with the splendours of the ancient mythology."—*Hazlitt cor.* "As neither the Jewish nor *the* Christian revelation *has* been universal, and as *each has* been afforded to a greater or *a* less part of the world at different times ; so likewise, at different times, both revelations have had different degrees of evidence."—*Butler cor.* " Thus we see, that, *to kill* a man with a sword, *and to kill one* with a hatchet, are looked upon as no distinct species of action ; but, if the point of the sword first enter the body, *the action* passes for a distinct species, called *stabbing.*"—*Locke cor.* " If a soul sin, and commit a trespass against the Lord, and lie unto his neighbour *concerning* that which was delivered him to keep, or *deceive* his neighbour, or *find* that which was lost, and *lie* concerning it, and *swear* falsely ; in any of all these that a man doeth, sinning therein, then it shall be," &c.—*Bible cor.* "As, to do and *teach* the commandments of God, is the great proof of virtue ; so, *to break* them, and *to teach* others to break them, *are* the great *proofs of* vice." —*Wayland cor.* " The latter simile, *in* Pope's terrific maltreatment of *it,* is true *neither to the* mind *nor* to the eye."—*Coleridge cor.* "And the two brothers were seen, transported with rage and fury, like Eteocles and Polynices, *each endeavouring* to plunge *his sword* into *the other's heart,* and to assure *himself* of the throne by the death of *his* rival."—*Goldsmith cor.* " Is it not plain, therefore, that neither the castle, nor the planet, nor the cloud, which you *here* see, *is that real one* which you suppose *to* exist at a distance ? "—*Berkley cor.* " I have often wondered, how it comes to pass, that every body should love *himself* best, and yet value *his neighbours'* opinion about *himself* more than his own."—*Collier cor.* " Virtue, ('Αρετὴ, *Virtus,*) as well as most of its *species, when sex is figuratively ascribed to it, is made* feminine, perhaps from *its* beauty and amiable appearance."—*Harris cor.* " Virtue, with most of its species, is *made* feminine *when personified ;* and so is Vice, *perhaps* for being Virtue's opposite."—*Brit. Gram. cor. ;* also *Buchanan.* " From this deduction, *it* may *easily* be seen, how it comes to pass, that personification makes *so* great a figure in all compositions *in which* imagination or passion *has* any concern."—*Blair cor.* "An Article is a word *placed before* a noun, to point *it* out *as such*, and to show how far *its* signification extends."—*Folker cor.* "All men have certain natural, essential, and inherent rights ;—among which are the *rights of* enjoying and defending life and liberty ; *of* acquiring, possessing, and protecting property ; and, in a word, of seeking and obtaining happiness."—*N. H. cor.* " From *those* grammarians who form their ideas and make their decisions, respecting this part of English grammar, *from* the principles and construction of *other* languages,—*of languages* which do not in these points accord *with* our own, but *which* differ considerably from it,—we may naturally expect grammatical schemes that *will be neither* perspicuous nor consistent, and *that* will tend *rather* to perplex than *to* inform the learner."—*Murray and Hall cor.* "*Indeed* there are but very few who know how to be idle and innocent, or *who* have a relish *for* any pleasures that are not criminal ; every diversion *which the majority* take, is at the expense of some one virtue or *other*, and their very first step out of business is into vice or folly."—*Addison cor.*

" Hail, holy Love ! thou *bliss* that *sumst* all bliss !
Giv'st and *receiv'st* all bliss ; fullest when most
Thou *giv'st;* spring-head of all felicity !"—*Pollok cor.*

CHAPTER XIII. — GENERAL RULE.

CORRECTIONS UNDER THE GENERAL RULE.

LESSON I.—ARTICLES.

(1.) "*The* article is a part of speech placed before nouns." Or thus : "*An* article is a *word* placed before nouns."—*Comly cor.* (2.) "*The* article is a part of speech used to limit nouns."—*Gilbert cor.* (3.) "An article is a *word* set before nouns to fix their vague signification."—*Ash cor.* (4.) "*The* adjective is a part of speech used to describe *something named by* a noun."—*Gilbert cor.* (5.) "A pronoun is a *word* used *in stead* of a noun."—*Id. and Weld cor. : Inst.* p. 45. (6.) "*The* pronoun is a part of speech which is often used *in stead* of a noun."—*Brit. Gram. and Buchanan cor.* (7.) "A verb is a *word* which signifies *to be, to do,* or *to be acted upon.*"—*Merchant cor.* (8.) "*The* verb is a part of speech which signifies *to be, to act,* or *to receive an action.*"—*Comly cor.* (9.) "*The* verb is *the* part of speech by which any thing is asserted."—*Weld cor.* (10.) "*The* verb is a part of speech, which expresses action or existence in a direct manner."—*Gilbert cor.* (11.) "A participle is a *word* derived from a verb, and expresses action or existence in an indirect manner."—*Id.* (12.) "*The* participle is a part of speech derived from *the* verb, and denotes being, doing, or suffering, and implies time, as a verb does."—*Brit. Gram. and Buchanan cor.* (13.) "*The* adverb is a part of speech used to add *some modification* to the meaning of verbs, adjectives, and participles."—*Gilbert cor.* (14.) "An adverb is an indeclinable *word* added to a verb, [*a participle*,] an adjective, or *an* other adverb, to express some circumstance, *accident*, or manner of *its* signification."—*Adam and Gould cor.* (15.) "An adverb is a *word added* to a verb, an adjective, a participle, or *an* other adverb, to express the circumstance of *time, place, degree, or manner.*"—*Dr. Ash cor.* (16.) "An adverb is a *word added* to a verb, an adjective, a participle, or, sometimes, an other adverb, to express some *circumstance* respecting *the sense.*"—*Beck cor.* (17.) "*The* adverb is a part of speech, which is *added* to *verbs, adjectives, participles*, or to other *adverbs*, to express some modification or circumstance, quality or manner, of their signification."—*Buchanan cor.* (18.) "*The* adverb is a part of speech *which we add* to the verb, (whence the name,) *to the adjective or participle likewise*, and sometimes even to *an* other adverb."—*Bucke cor.* (19.) "A conjunction is a *word* used to connect words *or* sentences."—*Gilbert and Weld cor.* (20.) "*The* conjunction is a part of speech that joins words or sentences together."—*Ash cor.* (21.) "*The* conjunction is that part of speech which *connects* sentences, or parts of sentences, or single words."—*D. Blair cor.* (22.) "*The* conjunction is a part of speech that is used principally to connect sentences, so as, out of two, three, or more sentences, to make one."—*Bucke cor.* (23.) "*The* conjunction is a part of speech that is used to connect *words or* sentences *together ; but*, chiefly, *to join* simple sentences into *such as are* compound."—*Kirkham cor.* (24.) "A conjunction is a *word* which joins *words or* sentences together, and *shows* the manner of their *dependence, as they stand in connexion.*"—*Brit. Gram. et al. cor.* (25.) "A preposition is a *word* used to show the relation between other words, *and govern the subsequent term.*"—*Gilbert cor.* (26.) "A preposition is a *governing word* which serves to connect *other* words, and *to* show the relation between them."—*Frost cor.* (27.) "A preposition is a *governing particle* used to connect words and show their relation."—*Weld cor.* (28.) "*The* preposition is that part of speech which shows the *various positions* of persons or things, *and* the *consequent relations* that certain *words* bear toward *one an* other."—*Blair cor.* (29.) "*The* preposition is a part of speech, which, being added to *certain* other parts of speech, serves to *show* their state *of* relation, or *their* reference to each other."—*Brit. Gram. and Buchanan cor.* (30.) "*The* interjection is a part of speech used to express sudden passion or *strong* emotion."—*Gilbert cor.* (31.) "An interjection is an *unconnected word* used in giving utterance to some sudden feeling or *strong* emotion."—*Weld cor.* (32.) "*The* interjection is that part of speech which denotes any sudden affection or *strong* emotion of the mind."—*Blair cor.* (33.) "An interjection is *an independent word or sound* thrown into discourse, and denotes some sudden passion or *strong* emotion of the soul."—*Brit. Gram. and Buchanan cor.*

(34.) "*The* scene might tempt some peaceful *sage*
To rear a *lonely* hermitage."—*Gent. of Aberdeen cor.*
(35.) "Not all the storms that shake the pole,
Can e'er disturb thy halcyon soul,
And *smooth unalter'd* brow."—*Barbauld's Poems*, p. 42.

LESSON II.—NOUNS.

" The *throne* of every monarchy felt the shock."—*Frelinghuysen cor.* " These principles ought to be deeply impressed upon the *mind* of every American."—*Dr. N. Webster cor.* " The *words*

CHURCH and SHIRE are radically the same."—*Id.* "They may not, in their present form, be readily accommodated to every circumstance belonging to the possessive *case* of nouns."—*L. Murray cor.* "Will, in the second and third *persons*, only *foretells*."—*Id. : Lowth's Gram.* p. 41. "Which seem to form the true distinction between the subjunctive and the indicative *mood*." —*Murray cor.* "The very general approbation which this performance of *Walker's* has received from the public."—*Id.* "Lest she carry her improvements *of this kind* too far." Or thus : "Lest she carry her improvements *in* this way too far."—*Id. and Campbell cor.* "Charles was extravagant, and by *his prodigality* became poor and despicable."—*Murray cor.* "We should entertain no *prejudice* against simple and rustic persons."—*Id.* "These are indeed the *foundation* of all solid merit."—*Dr. Blair cor.* "And his embellishment, by means of *figures, musical cadences*, or other *ornaments* of speech."—*Id.* "If he is at no pains to engage us by the employment of figures, musical arrangement, or any other *ornament* of *style*."—*Id.* "The most eminent of the sacred poets, are, *David, Isaiah*, and the *author* of the Book of Job."—*Id.* "Nothing, in any *poem*, is more beautifully described than the death of old Priam."—*Id.* "When two vowels meet together, and are *joined in one syllable*, they are called a *diphthong*."—*Inf. S. Gram. cor.* "How many *Esses* would *goodness'* then end with ? Three ; as *goodness's*."—*Id.* "Birds is a noun ; it is the common name of *feathered animals*."—*Kirkham cor.* "Adam gave names to all living *creatures*." Or thus: "Adam gave *a name* to every living creature."—*Bicknell cor.* "The steps of a *flight of stairs* ought to be accommodated to the human figure." Or thus : "*Stairs* ought to be accommodated to the *ease of the users*."—*Kames cor:* "Nor ought an emblem, more than a simile, to be founded on *a low or familiar object*."—*Id.* "Whatever the Latin has not from the Greek, it has from the Gothic."—*Tooke cor.* "The mint, and *the office of* the *secretary of state*, are neat buildings."—*The Friend cor.* "The scenes of dead and still *existence* are apt to fall upon us."— *Blair cor.* "And Thomas Aquinas and Duns Scotus, the angelical *doctor* and the subtle, are the brightest stars in the scholastic constellation."—*Lit. Hist. cor.* "The English language has three methods of distinguishing the *sexes*."—*Murray et al. cor.*; also *Smith.* "In English, there are the three following methods of distinguishing *the sexes*."—*Jaudon cor.* "There are three ways of distinguishing the *sexes*."—*Lennie et al. cor.*; also *Merchant.* "*The sexes are* distinguished in three ways."—*Maunder cor.* "Neither discourse in general, nor poetry in particular, can be called altogether *an* imitative *art*."—*Blair cor.*

"Do we for this the gods and conscience brave,
   That one may rule and *all* the rest *enslave!*"—*Rowe cor.*

LESSON III.—ADJECTIVES.

"There is a deal *more* of heads, than *of* either heart or horns."—*Barclay cor.* "For, of all villains, I think he has the *most improper* name."—*Bunyan cor.* "Of all the men that I met in my pilgrimage, he, I think, bears the *wrongest* name."—*Id.* "I am *surprised* to see so much of the distribution, and *so many of the* technical terms, of the Latin grammar, retained in the grammar of our tongue."—*Priestley cor.* "Nor did the Duke of Burgundy bring him *any* assistance." —*Hume and Priestley cor.* "Else he will find it difficult to make *an* obstinate *person* believe him."—*Brightland cor.* "Are there any adjectives which form the degrees of comparison in *a* manner peculiar to themselves ?"—*Inf. S. Gram. cor.* "Yet *all* the verbs are of the indicative mood."—*Lowth cor.* "The word *candidate* is *absolute*, in the *nominative case*."—*Murray cor.* "An Iambus has the first syllable unaccented, and the *last* accented."—*L. Murray, D. Blair, Jamieson, Kirkham, Bullions, Guy, Merchant*, and others. "A Dactyl has the first syllable accented, and the *last two* [*syllables*] unaccented."—*Murray et al. cor.* "It is proper to begin with a capital the first word of every book, chapter, letter, note, or* other piece of writing."—*Jaudon's Gram.* p. 195 ; *John Flint's*, 105. "Five and seven make twelve, and one *more* makes thirteen." —*Murray cor.* "I wish to cultivate a *nearer* acquaintance with you."—*Id.* "Let us consider the means *which are proper* to effect our purpose." Or thus : "Let us consider *what* means are proper to effect our purpose."—*Id.* "Yet they are of *so* similar *a* nature as readily to mix and blend."—*Blair cor.* "The Latin is formed on the same model, but *is* more imperfect."—*Id.* "I know very well how *great* pains have been taken." Or thus : "I know very well how much *care* has been taken."—*Temple cor.* "The management of the breath requires a *great* deal of care." —*Blair cor.* "Because the mind, during such a momentary stupefaction, is, in a *great* measure, if not totally, insensible."—*Kames cor.* "Motives of reason and interest *alone* are not sufficient." —*Id.* "To render the composition distinct in its parts, and on the whole *impressive*."—*Id.* "*A* and *an* are named *the* Indefinite *article*, because they denote *indifferently any* one thing of a kind." —*Maunder cor.* "*The* is named the Definite *article*, because it points out some particular thing or things."—*Id.* "So much depends upon the proper construction of sentences, that, in *any* sort of composition, we cannot be too strict in our attention to it." Or :—"that, in *every* sort of composition, we *ought to be very* strict in our attention to it." Or :—"that, in *no* sort of composition, can *we be* too strict," &c.—*Blair cor.* "*Every* sort of declamation and public speaking, was carried on by them." Or thus : "All *sorts* of declamation and public speaking, *were* carried on by them."—*Id.* "The *former* has, on many occasions, a sublimity to which the latter never attains." —*Id.* "When the words, *therefore, consequently, accordingly*, and the like are used in connexion with conjunctions, they are adverbs."—*Kirkham cor.* "Rude nations make *few* or no allusions to the productions of the arts."—*Jamieson cor.* "While two of her maids knelt on *each* side of her." Or, if there were only two maids kneeling, and not four : "While two of her maids knelt, one on *each* side of her."—*Mirror cor.* "The personal pronouns *of the third person*, differ from *one* or other in meaning and use, as follows."—*Bullions cor.* "It was happy for the state, that Fabius continued in the command with *Minutius* : the phlegm *of the former* was a check on the vivacity *of the latter*."—*L. Murray and others cor.*: see *Maunder's Gram.* p. 4. "If it be objected, that the words *must* and *ought*, in the preceding sentences, are *both* in the present tense." Or thus : "If it be

---

* The word "*any*" is here omitted, not merely because it is *unnecessary*, but because "*every any other piece*," —with which a score of our grammarians have pleased themselves,—is not good English. The impropriety might perhaps be avoided, though less elegantly, by *repeating the preposition*, and saying,—" or *of* any *other piece* of writing."—G. BROWN.

in *all* the preceding sentences the words *must* and *ought* are in the present tense."
"But it will be well, if you turn to them now and then." Or:—"if you turn to
ally."—*Bucke cor.* "That every part should have a dependence on, and mutually
support, *every* other."—*Rollin cor.* "The phrase, '*Good, my lord,*' is not common,
Or :—" is *uncommon*, and low."—*Priestley cor.*
"That brother should not war with brother,
And *one* devour *or vex an* other."—*Cowper cor.*

LESSON IV.—PRONOUNS.

)ntribute to *our* country's glory." Or :—"to *your* glory and *that* of my country."—
. "As likewise of the several subjects, which have in effect each *its* verb."—*Lowth*
likewise required to make examples *for* himself." Or: "He *himself* is likewise re-
:e examples."—*J. Flint cor.* "If the emphasis be placed wrong, *it will* pervert and
meaning wholly." Or: "If the emphasis be placed wrong, the meaning *will be per-
founded* wholly." Or: "If *we place* the emphasis wrong, we pervert and confound
wholly."—*Blair cor.; also Murray.* "It was this, that characterized the great men
it is this, *that* must distinguish the moderns who would tread in their steps."—*Id.*
: enemy to implicit faith, as well the Popish as *the* Presbyterian ; *for,* in that, *the*
ie *Presbyterians* are *very* much alike."—*Barclay cor.* "Will he thence dare to say,
ild *an other* Christ than *him* that died ? "—*Id.* "*Why* need you be anxious about
Or : "What need *have* you *to* be anxious about this event."—*Collier cor.* "If a
.n be placed after the verb, *the latter* is active."—*A. Murray cor.* "To *see* bad men
prosperous in the world, is some discouragement to virtue." Or: "*It* is some discour-
rtue, *to see* bad men," &c.—*L. Murray cor.* "It is a happiness to young persons,
1 from the snares of the world, as in a garden enclosed."—*Id.* "*At* the court of
:th, *where all* was prudence and economy."—*Bullions cor.* "It is no wonder, if
d not shine at the court of Queen Elizabeth, who was *so remarkable* for *her* prudence
"—*Priestley, Murray, et al. cor.* "A defective verb is *a verb* that wants some parts.
verbs are chiefly the *auxiliaries* and the impersonal verbs."—*Bullions cor.* "Some
:iven *to the* moods a much greater extent than *I* have assigned to them."—*L. Murray*
irsonal pronouns give *such* information *as* no other words are capable of conveying."
or. "When the article *a, an,* or *the,* precedes the participle, *the latter* also becomes
rchant cor. "To some of these, there is a preference to be given, which custom
.t must determine."—*L. Murray cor.* "Many writers affect to subjoin to any word
n with which it is compounded, or *that* of which it *literally* implies the idea."—*Id.*
"Say, dost thou know Vectidius ? *Whom,* the wretch
Whose lands beyond the Sabines largely stretch ?"—*Dryden cor.*

LESSON V.—VERBS.

1 naturally expect, that the word *depend* would require *from* after it."—*Priestley's*
"A dish which they pretend *is* made of emerald."—*Murray cor.* "For the very
entence implies *that* one proposition *is* expressed."—*Murray's Gram.* 8vo, p. 311.
ireful attention to the sense, we *should* be naturally led, by the rules of syntax, to
rising and setting of the sun."—*Blair cor.* "For any rules that can be given, on
.ust *be* very general."—*Id.* "He *would be* in the right, if eloquence were what he
. be."—*Id.* "There I *should* prefer a more free and diffuse manner."—*Id.* "Yet
resembled one an other, and agreed in certain qualities."—*Id.* "But, since he must
e insists *on having an other* in her place."—*Id.* "But these are far from being so
) common, as *they have* been supposed *to be.*"—*Id.* "We are not *led* to assign a
o the pleasant or *the* painful feelings."—*Kames cor.* "Which are of greater im-
they are commonly thought."—*Id.* "Since these qualities are both coarse and
us find out the mark of a man of probity."—*Collier cor.* "Cicero did what no
r done before him ; *he drew* up a treatise of consolation for himself."—*Biographer*
there can *remain* no other doubt of the truth."—*Brightland cor.* "I have observed
rists use the term." Or : "I have observed some satirists *to* use the term."—*Bul-
luch men are ready to despond, or *to become* enemies."—*Webster cor.* "Common
nes common to many things."—*Inf. S. Gram. cor.* "To make ourselves *heard* by
we address ourselves."—*Blair cor.* "That, in reading poetry, he may be the better
of its correctness, and *may* relish its beauties." Or :—"and *to* relish its beauties."
"On the stretch to keep pace with the author, and *comprehend his meaning.*"—
For it might have been sold for more than three hundred pence, and *the money*
ven to the poor."—*Bible cor.* "He is a beam that *has* departed, and *has* left no
t behind."—*Ossian cor.* "No part of this incident ought to have been represented.
should have been reserved for a narrative."—*Kames cor.* "The rulers and people
iemselves, *a country is brought to ruin.*" Or: "*When* the rulers and people de-
lves, *they bring* ruin on a country."—*Ware cor.* "When *a title,* (as Doctor, Miss,
is prefixed to a name, the *latter only,* of the two words, is commonly *varied to form*
, 'The Doctor *Nettletons,*'— The two-*Miss Hudsons.*' "—*A. Murray cor.* "Where-
has been called, '*The Field of Blood,*' unto this day."—*Bible cor.* "To compre-
ations of other countries, which perhaps *it* may be necessary for him to explore."—
:. "We content ourselves now with fewer conjunctive particles than our ancestors
tley cor. "And who will be chiefly liable to make mistakes where others have *erred*
—*Id.* "The voice of nature and *that of* revelation *unite.*" Or: "*Revelation and*
ature *unite.*" Or : "The voice of nature *unites with revelation.*" Or : "The voice
.es *with that of* revelation."—*Wayland cor.*
"This adjective, you see, we can't admit ;
But, changed to '*WORSE,*' *the word is* just and fit."—*Tobitt cor.*

LESSON VI.—PARTICIPLES.

"Its application is not arbitrary, *or dependent* on the caprice of readers."—*Murray cor.* "This is the more expedient, *because the work is designed* for the benefit of private learners."—*Id.* "A man, he tells us, ordered by his will, to have a *statue erected* for him."—*Dr. Blair cor.* "From some likeness too remote, and *lying* too far out of the road of ordinary thought."—*Id.* "In the commercial world, money is a *fluid, running* from hand to hand."—*Dr. Webster cor.* "He pays much attention to *the* learning and singing *of* songs."—*Id.* "I would not be understood to consider *the* singing *of* songs as criminal."—*Id.* "It is a *case decided by* Cicero, the great master *of* writing."—*Editor of Waller cor.* "Did they ever bear a testimony against *the writing of* books?"—*Bates's Rep. cor.* "Exclamations are sometimes *mistaken* for interrogations."—*Ent. of Print. cor.* "Which cannot fail *to prove* of service."—*Smith cor.* "Hewn into such figures as would make them *incorporate* easily and firmly."—*Beat. or Mur. cor.* "*After* the rule and example, *there* are practical inductive questions."—*J. Flint cor.* "I think *it* will be an advantage, *that I have* collected *my* examples from modern writings."—*Priestley cor.* "He was eager *to* recommend it to his fellow-citizens."—*Id. and Hume cor.* "The good lady was careful *to serve* me *with* every thing."—*Id.* "No revelation would have been given, had the light of nature been sufficient, in such a sense as to render one *superfluous* and useless."—*Butler cor.* "Description, again, is *a representation which raises* in the mind the conception of an object, by means of some arbitrary or instituted symbols."—*Blair cor.* "Disappointing the expectation of the hearers, when they look for *an end.*" Or:—"for *the termination of* our discourse."—*Id.* "There is a distinction, which, in the use of them, is *worthy of* attention."—*Maunder cor.* "A model has been contrived, which is not very expensive, and *which is* easily managed."—*Ed. Reporter cor.* "The conspiracy was the more easily discovered, *because the conspirators were* many."—*Murray cor.* "Nearly ten years *had* that celebrated work *been published,* before its importance was at all understood."—*Id.* "*That the sceptre is* ostensibly grasped by a female hand, does not reverse the general order of government."—*West cor.* "I have hesitated *about* signing the Declaration of Sentiments."—*Lib. cor.* "The prolonging of men's lives when the world needed to be peopled, and *the subsequent* shortening *of* them when that necessity *had* ceased."—*Brown cor.* "Before the performance commences, we *see* displayed the insipid formalities of the prelusive scene."—*Kirkham cor.* "It forbade the lending of money, or *the* sending of goods, or *the* embarking of capital in any way, in transactions connected with that foreign traffic."—*Brougham cor.* "Even abstract ideas have sometimes the same important *prerogative conferred* upon them."—*Jamieson cor.* "*Ment,* like other terminations, changes *y* into *i,* when *the y is preceded* by a consonant."—*Kirkham's Gram.* p. 25. "The term PROPER is from the French *propre,* own, or the Latin *proprius,* and *a* Proper noun is *so called, because it* is peculiar to the individual *or family* bearing the name. The term COMMON is from the Latin *communis,* pertaining equally to several or many; and *a* Common noun is *so called, because it is* common to every individual comprised in the class."—*Fowler cor.*

> "Thus oft by mariners are *showed* (Unless the men of Kent are liars)
> Earl Godwin's castles *overflowed,* And palace-roofs, and steeple-spires."—*Swift cor.*

LESSON VII.—ADVERBS.

"He spoke to every man and woman *who was* there."—*Murray cor.* "Thought and language act and react upon each other."—*Murray's Key,* p. 264. "Thought and expression act *and react* upon each other."—*Murray's Gram.* 8vo, p. 356. "They have neither the leisure nor the means of attaining any knowledge, except what lies within the contracted circle of their several professions."—*Campbell's Rhet.* p. 160. "Before they are capable of understanding *much,* or indeed any thing, of *most* other branches of education."—*Olney cor.* "There is *no* more beauty in one of them, than in *an other.*"—*Murray cor.* "Which appear *to be* constructed according to *no* certain rule."—*Blair cor.* "The vehement manner of speaking became *less* universal." Or better:—"*less general.*"—*Id.* "*Not* all languages, however, agree in this mode of expression." Or: "This mode of expression, however, *is not common to all* languages."—*Id.* "The great occasion of setting *apart* this particular day."—*Atterbury cor.* "He is much more promising now, than *he was* formerly."—*L. Murray cor.* "They are placed before a participle, *without dependence* on the rest of the sentence."—*Id.* "This opinion *does not appear to have been* well considered." Or: "This opinion appears *to have been formed without due consideration.*"—*Id.* "Precision in language merits a full explication; and *merits it* the more, because distinct ideas are, perhaps, *but rarely* formed concerning it."—*Blair cor.* "In the more sublime parts of poetry, he is *less* distinguished." Or:—"he is not so *highly* distinguished."—*Id.* "*Whether* the author was altogether happy in the choice of his subject, may be questioned."—*Id.* "But, *with regard to this matter* also, there is a great error in the common practice."—*Webster cor.* "This order is the very order of the human mind, which makes things we are sensible of, a means to come at those that are not *known.*" Or:—"which makes things *that* are *already known,* its means *of finding out* those that are not so."—*Foreman cor.* "Now, who is not discouraged, and *does not fear* want, when he has no money?"—*C. Leslie cor.* "Which the authors of this work consider of little or no use."—*Wilbur and Liv. cor.* "And here indeed the distinction between these two classes begins to be *obscure.*"—*Blair cor.* "But this is a manner which deserves to be *avoided.*" Or:—"which *does not deserve* to be imitated."—*Id.* "And, in this department, a person effects *very* little, *whenever* he attempts too much."—*Campbell and Murray cor.* "The verb that signifies *mere* being, is neuter."—*Ash cor.* "I hope to tire *but little* those whom I shall not happen to please."—*Rambler cor.* "Who were utterly unable to pronounce some letters, and *who pronounced* others very indistinctly."—*Sheridan cor.* "The learner may point out the active, passive, and neuter verbs in the following examples, and state the reasons *for thus distinguishing them.*" Or: "The learner may point out the active, *the* passive, and *the* neuter verbs in the following examples, and state the reasons for calling them *so.*"—*C. Adams cor.* "These words are *almost* always conjunctions."—*Barrett cor.*

> "*How glibly* nonsense trickles from his tongue!
> How sweet the periods, neither said nor sung!"—*Pope cor.*

LESSON VIII.—CONJUNCTIONS.

least, either knew not, *or did not love* to make, a distinction." Or better thus : ast, either knew *no distinction,* or *did not like* to make *any."—Dr. Murray cor.* "It ι the last degree, *to let* this become the ground of estranged affection."—*L. Murray* n the regular, *and when* the irregular verb, is to be preferred, p. 107."—*Id.* "The o have been sold this day." Or :—" *on* this day."—*Priestley cor.* "Do, *as* you will." ᵣ you will."—*Shak. cor.* "If a man had a positive idea *either* of infinite duration or ᵢace, he could add two infinites together." Or : "If a man had a positive idea of ite, either *in* duration or *in* space, he could," &c.—*Murray's proof-text cor.* "None illingly agree *to* and advance the same *than* I."—*Morton cor.* "That it cannot *but* be ontinue it."—*Barclay cor.* "A conjunction joins words *or* sentences."—*Beck cor.* ιtive conjunction connects words *or* sentences together, and continues the sense."— ᶜ The *copulative* conjunction serves to connect [*words or clauses,*] *and* continue a sen- pressing an addition, a cause, *or* a supposition."—*Murray cor.* "All construction is ᵣ apparent ; or, in other words, *either literal or* figurative."—*Buchanan and Brit.* " But the divine character is such *as* none but a divine hand could draw." Or : "But ιaracter is such, *that* none but a divine hand could draw *it.*"—*A. Keith cor.* "Who ιat, on inspecting the heavens, *he* is insensible of a God ?"—*Gibbons cor.* "It is now o an enlightened public, with little *further* desire on the part of the *author,* than *for* utility."—*Town cor.* "This will sufficiently explain *why* so many provincials have ι the capital without making any change in their original dialect."—*Sheridan cor.* they had chiefly three in general use, which were denominated ACCENTS, the term ι the plural number."—*Id.* "And this is one of the chief reasons *why* dramatic rep- ι have ever held the first rank amongst the diversions of mankind."—*Id.* "Which reason *why* public reading is in general so disgusting."—*Id.* "At the same time *in* learn to read." Or : "*While* they learn to read."—*Id.* "He is always to pronounce ith exactly the same accent that he uses *in speaking."—Id.* "In order to know what ows, and in the same manner *in which* he knows it."—*Id.* "For the same reason *for* in a more limited state, assigned to the several tribes of animals."—*Id.* "Were there teach this, in the same manner *in which* other arts are taught." Or : "Were there each this, *as* other arts are taught."—*Id.*

" Whose own example strengthens all his laws ;
Who is himself that great sublime he draws."—*Pope cor.*

LESSON IX.—PREPOSITIONS.

ᵣd so has sometimes the same meaning *as* ALSO, LIKEWISE, or THE SAME."—*Priestley* verb *use* relates not to 'pleasures of the imagination ;' but to the terms *fancy* and ι, which he was to employ as synonymous."—*Blair cor.* "It never can view, clearly ᵢly, *more than* one object at a time."—*Id.* "This figure [Euphemism] is often the same ᵢhrasis."—*Adam and Gould cor.* "All the *intermediate* time *between* youth and old *Walker cor.* "When one thing is said to act *upon an other,* or do something to *it.*" ᵣ. "Such a composition has as much of meaning in it, as a mummy has *of* life." ι a composition has as much meaning in it, as a mummy has life."—*Lit. Conv. cor.* ng men, from fourteen to eighteen *years of age,* were not the best judges."—*Id.* is a day of trouble, and of rebuke, and *of* blasphemy."—*Isaiah,* xxxvii, 3. "Blank he same pauses and accents *that occur in* rhyme."—*Kames cor.* "In prosody, long re distinguished by *the macron* (‾) ; and short ones, by what is called *the breve* (˘)." ᵣ. "Sometimes both articles are left out, especially *from* poetry."—*Id.* "*From* the ᵢample, the pronoun and participle are omitted." Or : "In the following example, ᵢn and participle are *not expressed."—Murray cor.* [But the example was faulty. ᵢscious of his weight and importance,"—or, "*Being* conscious of his own weight and ι, he did not *solicit* the aid of others."—*Id.* "He was an excellent person ; *even in his* ι, a mirror of *the* ancient faith."—*Id.* " The carrying of its several parts into execu- ιtler cor.* "Concord is the agreement which one word has *with* an other, in gender, ιse *or* person."—*L. Murray's Gram.* p. 142. "It might perhaps have given me a te *for* its antiquities."—*Addison cor.* "To call *on* a person, and to wait *on* him."— ᶜor.* "The great difficulty they found *in* fixing just sentiments."—*Id. and Hume cor.* ng the *differences of* the three."—*J. Brown cor.* "When the singular ends in x, ch , or s, we add *es to* form the plural."—*Murray cor.* "We shall present him a list or ᵢf them."—*Id.* "It is very common to hear of the evils of pernicious reading, how it the mind, or how it depraves the principles."—*Dymond cor.* "In this example, the is understood before 'curiosity' and *before* 'knowledge.'"—*Murray et al. cor.* "The ι is frequently omitted, *when* several words *have the same construction."—Wilcox cor.* l expel them from before you, and drive them *out from* your sight."—*Bible cor.* ιkes his sun *to* shine, and his rain to descend, upon the just and the unjust." Or ᶜho makes his sun shine, and his rain descend, upon the just and the unjust."—*M'Il-*

LESSON X.—MIXED EXAMPLES.

entence violates *an established rule* of grammar."—*Murray cor.* " The words *thou* and gain reduced to *syllables of* short *quantity."—Id.* "Have the *greatest* men always been popular ? By no means."—*Lieber cor.* "St. Paul positively stated, that, 'He *that* ιther, *hath* fulfilled the law.' "—*Rom.* xiii, 8. "More *organs* than one *are* concerned in nce of almost every consonant."—*M'Culloch cor.* "If the reader will pardon *me for* g so low."—*Campbell cor.* "To adjust them in *such a manner* as shall consist equally ᵢerspicuity and the grace of the period." Or : "To adjust them so, *that they* shall con- ly," &c.—*Blair and Mur. cor.* "This class exhibits a lamentable inefficiency, and *a* ᵗ of simplicity."—*Gardiner cor.* "Whose style, *in all its course,* flows like a limpid stream, *through which* we see to the very bottom."—*Blair cor.; also Murray.* "We admit various ellipsis." Or thus: "An *ellipsis,* or *omission,* of some words, is frequently admitted."—*Lennie's Gram.* p. 116. "The ellipsis of *articles may occur* thus."—*Murray cor.* "Sometimes the article a is improperly applied to nouns of different numbers; as, 'A magnificent house and gardens.'"—*Id.* "In some very emphatical expressions, *no* ellipsis should be *allowed.*"—*Id.* "Ellipses of the adjective *may happen* in the following manner."—*Id.* "The following *examples show* that *there may be an* ellipsis of the pronoun."—*Id.* "*Ellipsis* of the verb *occur* in the following instances."—*Id.* "*Ellipses* of the adverb *may occur* in the following manner."—*Id.* "The following *brief expressions are all of them* elliptical."*—*Id.* "If no emphasis be placed on any word, not only will discourse be rendered heavy and lifeless, but the meaning *will* often be *left* ambiguous." —*Id.; also Hart and Blair cor.* "He regards his word, but thou dost not *regard thine.*"—*Bullions, Murray et al. cor.* "I have learned my task, but you have not *learned yours.*"—*Id.* "When the omission of words would obscure the *sense,* weaken *the expression,* or be attended with impropriety, *no ellipsis* must be *indulged.*"—*Murray and Weld cor.* "And therefore the verb is correctly put in the singular number, and refers to *them all,* separately and individually considered."—*Murray cor.* "*He was to me the most intelligible* of all who spoke on the subject."—*Id.* "I understood him better than *I did* any other who spoke on the subject."—*Id.* "The roughness found on our entrance into the paths of virtue and learning, *decreases* as we advance." Or: "The *roughnesses encountered in* the paths of virtue and learning *diminish* as we advance."—*Id.* "*There is* nothing *which* more promotes knowledge, than *do* steady application and *habitual* observation."—*Id.* "Virtue confers *on man the highest* dignity *of which he is capable; it* should *therefore* be *the chief object of* his desire."—*Id. and Merchant cor.* "The supreme Author of our being has so formed the *human soul,* that nothing but himself can be its last, adequate, and proper happiness."—*Addison and Blair cor.* "The inhabitants of China laugh at the plantations of our Europeans: 'Because,' *say they,* 'any one may place trees in equal rows and uniform figures.'"—*Id.* "The divine laws are not *to be reversed* by those of men."—*Murray cor.* "In both of these examples, the relative *which* and the verb *was* are understood."—*Id. et al. cor.* "The Greek and Latin languages, though for many reasons they cannot be called dialects of one *and the same tongue,* are nevertheless closely connected."—*Dr. Murray cor.* "To ascertain and settle *whether* a white rose or a red breathes the sweetest fragrance." Or thus: "To ascertain and settle which *of the two* breathes the *sweeter* fragrance, a white rose or a red *one.*"—*J. Q. Adams cor.* "To which he can afford to devote *but little* of his time and labour."—*Blair cor.*

> "Avoid extremes; and shun the fault of such
> *As* still are pleased too little or too much."—*Pope cor.*

LESSON XI.—OF BAD PHRASES.

"He *might as well* leave his vessel to the direction of the winds."—*South cor.* "Without good-nature and gratitude, men *might as well* live in a wilderness as in society."—*L'Estrange cor.* "And, for this reason, such lines *very seldom* occur together."—*Blair cor.* "His *greatness* did not make him *happy.*"—*Crombie cor.* "Let that which tends to *cool* your love, be judged in all."—*Crisp cor.* "It *is worth* observing, that there is no passion in the mind of man so weak but it mates and masters the fear of death."—*Bacon cor.* "Accent dignifies the syllable on which it is laid, and makes it more *audible* than the rest."—*Sheridan and Murray cor.* "Before he proceeds to argue on *either* side."—*Blair cor.* "The *general* change of manners, throughout Europe."—*Id.* "The sweetness and beauty of Virgil's numbers, *through all* his works."—*Id.* "The French writers of sermons, study neatness and elegance in *the division of their discourses.*" —*Id.* "This *seldom* fails to prove a refrigerant to passion."—*Id.* "But their fathers, brothers, and uncles, cannot, as good relations and good citizens, *excuse themselves for* not standing forth to demand vengeance."—*Murray's Sequel,* p. 114. "Alleging, that their *decrial of* the church of Rome, was a *uniting* with the Turks."—*Barclay cor.* "To which is added the Catechism *by* the Assembly of Divines."—*N. E. Prim. cor.* "This treachery was always present in *the thoughts* of both of them."—*Robertson cor.* "Thus far their words agree." Or: "Thus far *the words of both* agree."—*W. Walker cor.* "Aparithmesis is *an* enumeration *of* the several parts of what, *as a whole,* might be expressed in few words."—*Gould cor.* "Aparithmesis, or Enumeration, is *a figure in which* what might be expressed in a few words, is branched out into several parts." — *Dr. Adam cor.* "Which may sit from time to time, where you dwell, or in the vicinity."—*J. O. Taylor cor.* "Place together a *large-sized animal and a small one,* of the same *species.*" Or: "Place together a large and a small animal of the same species."—*Kames cor.* "The *weight of* the swimming body is equal to that of the quantity of fluid displaced by it."—*Percival cor.* "The Subjunctive mood, in all its tenses, is similar to the Optative."—*Gwilt cor.* "No feeling of obligation remains, except that of *an obligation to* fidelity."—*Wayland cor.* "Who asked him *why* whole audiences should be moved to tears at the representation of some story on the stage." —*Sheridan cor.* "*Are you not ashamed* to affirm, that the best works of the Spirit of Christ in his saints, are as filthy rags?"—*Barclay cor.* "A neuter verb becomes active, when followed by a noun of *kindred* signification."—*Sanborn cor.* "But he has judged better, in *forbearing to* repeat the article *the.*"—*Blair cor.* "Many objects please us, *and are thought* highly beautiful, which have *scarcely any* variety at all."—*Id.* "Yet they sometimes follow *them.*"—*Emmons cor.* "For I know of nothing more *important* in the whole subject, than this doctrine of *mood* and tense."—*R. Johnson cor.* "It is by no means impossible for an *error* to be *avoided* or *suppressed.*" —*Philol. Museum cor.* "These are things of the highest importance to *children and youth.*"— *Murray cor.* "He *ought to* have omitted the word *many.*" Or: "He *might* better have *omitted* the word many."—*Blair cor.* "Which *might* better have been separated." Or: "Which *ought* rather *to* have been separated."—*Id.* "Figures and metaphors, therefore, should *never* be *used*

---

* This correction, as well as the others which relate to what Murray says of the several forms of ellipsis, doubtless conveys the sense which he intended to express; but, as an assertion, it is by no means true of all the examples which he subjoins, neither indeed are the rest. But that is a fault of his which I cannot correct.—G. Brown.

rofusely."—*Id. and Jam. cor.*   "Metaphors, *or other figures, should never be used in too great* bundance."—*Murray and Russell cor.*   "Something like this has been *alleged against* Tacitus."
—*Bolingbroke cor.*

"O thou, whom all mankind in vain withstand,
Who with the blood of each must one day stain thy hand!"—*Sheffield cor.*

LESSON XII.—OF TWO ERRORS.

"Pronouns sometimes precede the *terms* which they represent."—*L. Murray cor.*   "Most prepositions originally *denoted relations* of place."—*Lowth cor.*   "WHICH is applied to *brute* animals, and 'o things without life."—*Bullions cor.*   "What *thing* do they describe, or *of what do they* tell the :ind?"—*Inf. S. Gram. cor.*   "Iron *cannons,* as well as brass, *are* now universally cast solid."—*Jamieson cor.*   "We have philosophers, *more* eminent perhaps *than those of any other* nation."—*Blair cor.*   "This is a question about words *only,* and *one* which common sense easily determines."
—*Id.*   "The low pitch of the voice, is *that which* approaches to a whisper."—*Id.*   "Which, as to the effect, is just the same *as to use* no such distinctions at all."—*Id.*   "These two systems, therefore, *really* differ from *each* other *but* very little."—*Id.*   "It *is* needless to give many nstances, *as examples* occur so often."—*Id.*   "There are many occasions *on which* this is neither requisite nor proper."—*Id.*   "Dramatic poetry divides itself into the two forms, comedy *and* tragedy."—*Id.*   "No man ever rhymed *with more exactness* than he." [I. e., than Roscommon.]
—*Editor of Waller cor.*   "The Doctor did not reap from his poetical labours a *profit* equal to *that* of his prose."—*Johnson cor.*   "We will follow that which we *find* our fathers *practised.*" Or:
"We will follow that which we *find to have been* our *fathers'* practice."—*Sale cor.*   "And I *should* deeply regret *that I had* published them."—*Inf. S. Gram. cor.*   "Figures exhibit ideas *with more riridness and power,* than could be *given them* by plain language."—*Kirkham cor.*   "The allegory is finely drawn, *though* the heads *are* various."—*Spect. cor.*   "I should not have thought it worthy *of this* place." Or: "I should not have thought it worthy *of being placed* here."—*Crombie cor.*
"In this style, Tacitus excels all *other* writers, ancient *or* modern."—*Kames cor.*   "No *other* author, ancient or modern, possesses the art of dialogue *so completely as* Shakspeare."—*Id.*   "The names of *all the things* we see, hear, smell, taste, or feel, are nouns."—*Inf. S. Gram. cor.*   "Of what number are *the expressions,* 'these boys,' 'these pictures,' &c.?"—*Id.*   "This *sentence has* faults somewhat *like those of* the last."—*Blair cor.*   "Besides perspicuity, he pursues propriety, purity, and precision, in his language; which *qualities form* one degree, and no inconsiderable one, of beauty."—*Id.*   "Many critical terms have unfortunately been employed in a sense too loose and vague; none *with less precision,* than *the word* sublime."—*Id.*   "Hence no word in the language is used *with* a more vague signification, than *the word* beauty."—*Id.*   "But still, *in speech,* he made use of general *terms only.*"—*Id.*   "These give life, body, and colouring, to the *facts recited;* and enable us to *conceive of* them as present, and passing before our eyes."—*Id.*   "Which carried an ideal chivalry to a still more extravagant height, than *the adventurous spirit of knighthood* had *ever attained* in fact."—*Id.*   "We write much more supinely, and *with far less labour,* than *did* the ancients."—*Id.*   "This appears indeed to form the characteristical difference between the ancient poets, orators, and historians, *and the* modern."—*Id.*   "To violate this rule, as the English too often do, *shows* great incorrectness."—*Id.*   "It is impossible, by means of any *training, to prevent them from* appearing stiff and forced."—*Id.*   "*And it also gives to* the speaker the disagreeable *semblance* of one who endeavours to compel assent."—*Id.*   "And, *whenever* a light or ludicrous anecdote is proper to be recorded, it is generally better to throw it into a note, than to run the hazard *of* becoming too familiar."—*Id.*   "*It is* the great business of this life, to prepare and qualify *ourselves* for the enjoyment of a better."—*Murray cor.*   "*From* some dictionaries, accordingly, it was omitted; and in others *it is* stigmatised as a barbarism."—*Crombie cor.*   "You cannot see a thing, or think of *one, the name of which is not* a noun."—*Mack cor.*   "*All* the fleet *have* arrived, and *are* moored in safety." Or better: "The *whole* fleet *has* arrived, and *is* moored n safety."—*Murray cor.*

LESSON XIII.—OF TWO ERRORS.

"They have *severally* their distinct and exactly-limited *relations* to gravity."—*Hasler cor.*   "But *where the additional s* would give too much of the hissing sound, the omission takes place even in prose."—*Murray cor.*   "After o, it [the *w*] is sometimes not sounded at all; *and* sometimes *it is* sounded like a single u."—*Lowth cor.*   "It is situation chiefly, *that* decides the *fortunes* and characters of men."—*Hume cor.;* also *Murray.*   "The vice of covetousness is *that* [vice] *which* enters more *deeply* into the soul than any other."—*Murray et al. cor.*   "*Of* all vices, covetousness enters the *most deeply* into the soul."—*Iid.*   "*Of all vices,* covetousness is *that which* enters the *most deeply* into the soul."—*Campbell cor.*   "The vice of covetousness is *a fault which* enters *more deeply* into the soul *than* any other."—*Guardian cor.*   "WOULD primarily denotes inclination of will; and SHOULD, obligation: but *they* vary their import, and are often used to express simple *events.*" Or:—"but *both of them* vary their import," &c. Or:—"but *both* vary their import, and are used to express simple *events.*"—*Lowth, Murray, et al. cor.*   "A double *condition,* in two correspondent clauses of a sentence, is sometimes made *by the word* HAD; as, 'Had he done this, he *had* escaped.'"—*Murray et al. cor.*   "The pleasures of the understanding are preferable to those of the imagination, *as well as to those* of sense."—*Murray cor.*   "Claudian, in a fragment upon the wars of the giants, has contrived to render this idea of their throwing *of* the mountains, which in itself *has so much grandeur,* burlesque and ridiculous."—*Blair cor.*   "To which not only no other writings are to be preferred, but *to which,* even in divers respects, *none are* comparable."—*Barclay cor.*   "To distinguish them in the understanding, and treat of their several natures, in the same cool manner *that we use* with regard to other ideas."—*Sheridan cor.*   "For it has nothing to do with parsing, or *the analyzing of* language."—*Kirkham cor.*   Or: "For it has nothing to do with *the* parsing, or analyzing, *of* language."—*Id.*   "Neither *has* that language [the Latin] *ever been* in common in Britain."—*Swift cor.*   "All that I *purpose,* is, *to give* some openings into the pleasures of taste."—*Blair cor.*   "But the following sentences would have been better *without it.*"—*Murray cor.*   "But I think the following sentence *would* be better *without it.*" Or: "But I think it *should be expunged from* the following sentence."—*Priestley cor.* "They appear, in this case, like *ugly* excrescences jutting out from the body."—*Blair cor.* "And therefore the fable of the Harpies, in the third book of the Æneid, and the allegory of Sin and Death, in the second book of *Paradise* Lost, *ought not to have been inserted* in these celebrated poems."—*Id.* "Ellipsis is an elegant suppression, or *omission*, of *some* word or words, *belonging to* a sentence."—*Brit. Gram. and Buchanan cor.* "The article A or AN *is not very proper* in this construction."—*D. Blair cor.* "Now suppose the articles had not been *dropped from* these passages."—*Bucke cor.* "To *have given* a separate name to every one of those trees, would have been an endless and impracticable undertaking."—*Blair cor.* "*Ei*, in general, *has the same sound* as long and slender *a.*" Or better: "*Ei generally has the sound of* long *or* slender *a.*"—*Murray cor.* "When a conjunction is used *with apparent redundance, the insertion of it* is called Polysyndeton."—*Adam and Gould cor.* "EACH, EVERY, EITHER and NEITHER, denote the persons or things *that* make up a number, as taken separately or distributively."—*M'Culloch cor.* "The principal sentence must be expressed by a *verb* in the indicative, imperative, or potential *mood.*"—*Clark cor.* "Hence he is diffuse, where he ought to be *urgent.*"—*Blair cor.* "All *sorts* of subjects admit of *explanatory* comparisons."—*Id. et al. cor.* "The present or imperfect participle denotes being, action, *or passion*, continued, *and* not perfected."—*Kirkham cor.* "What are verbs? Those words which *chiefly* express what *is said of things.*"—*Fowle cor.*

"Of all those arts in which the wise excel,
The *very* masterpiece is *writing-well.*"—*Sheffield cor.*
"Such was that muse whose rules and practice tell,
That art's chief masterpiece is *writing-well.*"—*Pope cor.*

LESSON XIV.—OF THREE ERRORS.

"*From some* words, the metaphorical sense has justled out the original sense altogether; or that, in respect *to the latter*, they *have* become obsolete."—*Campbell cor.* "*Surely*, never any other mortal was so overwhelmed with grief, as I am at this present *moment.*"—*Sheridan cor.* "All languages differ from *one an* other in their *modes of inflection.*"—*Bullions cor.* "The *noun* and *the verb* are the only indispensable parts of speech; the one, to express the subject spoken of; and the other, the predicate, or what is affirmed of *the subject.*"—*M'Culloch cor.* "The words Italicised in the *last three* examples, perform the office of substantives."—*Murray cor.* "A sentence *so constructed* is always *a* mark of *carelessness in the writer.*"—*Blair cor.* "Nothing is more hurtful to the grace or *the* vivacity of a period, than superfluous *and* dragging words at the conclusion."—*Id.* "When its substantive is not *expressed with* it, but *is* referred to, *being understood.*"—*Lowth cor.* "Yet they *always* have *substantives* belonging to them, either *expressed* or understood."—*Id.* "Because they define and limit the *import* of the common *names*, or *general terms*, to which they refer."—*Id.* "Every new object surprises *them*, terrifies *them*, and makes a strong impression on their *minds.*"—*Blair cor.* "His argument required *a* more *full development*, in order to be distinctly apprehended, and to *have* its due force."—*Id.* "*Those* participles which are derived from *active-transitive* verbs, will govern the objective case, as *do* the verbs from which they are derived."—*Emmons cor.* "Where, *in violation of* the rule, the objective case *when* follows the verb, *while* the nominative *I* precedes *it.*"—*Murray cor.* "*To use, after* the same conjunction, both the indicative and the subjunctive *mood*, in the same sentence, and *under the same* circumstances, seems to be a great impropriety."—*Lowth, Murray, et al. cor.* "A nice discernment *of the import of words*, and *an* accurate attention to the best usage, are necessary on these occasions."—*Murray cor.* "The Greeks and Romans, the former especially, were, in truth, much more musical than we *are*; their genius was more turned to *take* delight in the melody of speech."—*Blair cor.* "*In general, if* the sense admits it *early*, the sooner *a circumstance is introduced*, the better; that the more important and significant words may possess the last place, *and be* quite disencumbered."—*Murray et al. cor.*; also *Blair and Jamieson.* "Thus we find it in *both* the Greek and *the* Latin *tongue.*"—*Blair cor.* "*Several* sentences, constructed in the same manner, and *having* the same number of members, should never be allowed to *come in succession.*"—*Blair et al. cor.* "I proceed to lay down the rules to be observed in the conduct of metaphors; and *these, with little variation, will* be applicable to tropes of every kind."—*Blair cor.* "By *selecting* words *with a* proper *regard to their sounds*, we may *often imitate* other sounds which we mean *to* describe."—*Blair and Mur. cor.* "The disguise can *scarcely* be so perfect *as to deceive.*"—*Blair cor.* "The sense *does not admit* of *any* other pause, than *one* after the second syllable 'sit;' *this* therefore must be the only pause made in the reading."—*Id.* "Not that I believe North America to *have been first* peopled so *lately* as *in* the twelfth century, the period of Madoc's migration."—*Webster cor.* "Money and commodities *will* always flow to that country *in which* they are most wanted, and *in which they will* command the most profit."—*Id.* "That it contains no visible marks of certain articles which are of the *utmost* importance to a just delivery."—*Sheridan cor.* "And *Virtue*, from *her* beauty, we call a fair and favourite maid."—*Mack. cor.* "The definite article may *relate* to nouns *of either* number."—*Inf. S. Gram. cor.*

LESSON XV.—OF MANY ERRORS.

(1.) "Compound *words are* [, by Murray and others, improperly] included *among the derivatives.*"—*Murray corrected.* (2.) "*The* Apostrophe, *placed above the line*, thus ', is used to abbreviate or shorten *words.* But its chief use is, to *denote* the *possessive* case of nouns."—*Id.* (3.) "*The* Hyphen, *made* thus -, *connects* the parts of compound words. It is also used when a word is divided."—*Id.* (4.) "The Acute Accent, *made* thus ', denotes *the syllable on which stress is laid, and sometimes also, that the vowel is short:* as, '*Fancy.*' The Grave Accent, made thus ', *usually* denotes, (*when applied to English words,*) that the stress is laid *where a vowel ends the syllable*: as, '*Favour.*'"—*Id.* (5.) "The stress is laid on long *vowels or* syllables, and *on* short ones, *indiscriminately.* In order to distinguish the *long or open* vowels from the *close or short ones*, *some* writers of dictionaries have placed the grave *accent* on the former, and the acute on the latter."—*Id.* (6.) "*The* Diæresis, thus *made* ¨, *is* placed over one of two *contiguous* vowels, *to show that they are not* a diphthong."—*Id.* (7.) "*The* Section, *made thus* §, *is sometimes used to mark the ubdivisions* of a discourse or chapter."—*Id.* (8.) "*The* Paragraph, *made thus* ¶, *sometimes* de-' lotes the beginning of a new subject, or *of* a *passage* not connected with the *text preceding.* This haracter is *now seldom* used [*for such a purpose*], *except* in the Old and New Testaments." Or etter:—"except in the *Bible.*"—*Id.* (9.) "*The* Quotation *Points, written thus* " ", mark the be-rinning *and the end of what* is quoted or transcribed from *some* speaker or author, in his own words. n type, they are inverted commas at the beginning, *apostrophes* at the conclusion."—*Id.* (10.) '*The* Brace *was formerly* used in poetry at the end of a triplet, or *where* three lines *rhymed* to-*ether in heroic verse; it also serves* to connect *several terms* with one, *when the one is common to ill,* and *thus* to prevent a repetition *of the* common term."—*Id.* (11.) "*Several* asterisks *put* to-*ether,* generally denote the omission *of* some letters *belonging to* a word, or of some bold or in-lelicate expression; *but sometimes they imply a* defect in the manuscript *from which the text is opied.*"—*Id.* (12.) "*The* Ellipsis, *made thus* ———, or *thus* ****, is used *where* some letters *f* a word, or some words *of* a verse, are omitted."—*Id.* (13.) "*The* Obelisk, which is *made* thus '; and *the* Parallels, *which are made* thus ‖; *and sometimes* the letters of the alphabet; and *also he Arabic* figures; are used as references to *notes in* the margin, or *at the* bottom, of the page." —*Id.* (14.) "*The* note of interrogation should not be employed, where it is only said *that* a ques-ion has been asked, and where the words are not used as a question; *as,* 'The Cyprians asked ne why I wept.'"—*Id. et al. cor.* (15.) "*The* note of interrogation is improper after *mere* expres-ions of admiration, or of *any* other emotion, *though they may bear the form of* questions."—*Iid.* 16.) "*The* parenthesis incloses *something which is thrown* into the body of a sentence, *in an ender tone; and* which affects neither the sense, nor the construction, *of the main text.*"—*Lowth* or. (17.) "Simple members connected by a *relative not used restrictively, or by a conjunction that mplies comparison,* are for the most part *divided* by *the* comma."—*Id.* (18.) "Simple members, r *sentences,* connected *as terms of comparison,* are for the most part *separated* by *the* comma."— *Murray et al. cor.* (19.) "Simple sentences connected by *a comparative particle,* are for the most art *divided* by the comma."—*Russell cor.* (20.) "Simple sentences *or clauses* connected *to form a omparison,* should generally be *parted* by *the* comma."—*Merchant cor.* (21.) "*The* simple mem-ers of sentences that express contrast or comparison, should generally be divided by *the* comma." —*Jaudon cor.* (22.) "*The* simple members of *a comparative sentence, when* they are long, are eparated by a comma."—*Cooper cor.* (23.) "Simple sentences connected *to form a comparison,* r phrases placed in opposition, or contrast, are *usually* separated by *the comma.*"—*Hiley and ullions cor.* (24.) "On *whichever* word we lay the emphasis,—whether on the first, *the* second, *he* third, or *the* fourth,—*every change of it* strikes out a different sense."—*Murray cor.* (25.) "To ny to those who do not understand sea phrases, 'We tacked to the larboard, and stood off to ea,' would *give them little or no information.*"—*Murray and Hiley cor.* (26.) "Of *those* dissyl-ables which are *sometimes* nouns and *sometimes* verbs, *it may be observed, that* the verb *is* com-nonly *accented* on the latter *syllable,* and the noun, on *the* former."—*Murray cor.* (27.) "And his gives *to* our language *an* advantage *over* most others, in the poetical *or* rhetorical style."— *d. et al. cor.* (28.) "And this gives *to* the English *language an* advantage *over* most *others,* in he poetical and *the* rhetorical style."—*Lowth cor.* (29.) "The second and *the* third scholar may ead the same sentence; or as many *may repeat the text,* as are necessary to *teach* it perfectly to he whole *class.*"—*Osborn cor.*

   30. "Bliss is the *same,* in subject, *or in* king,
      In who obtain defence, or who defend."—*Pope's Essay on Man,* IV, 56.

LESSON XVI.—OF MANY ERRORS.

"The Japanese, the Tonquinese, and the Coreans, speak languages *differing* from one *an other,* nd from *that of* the inhabitants of China; *while all* use the same written characters, and, by ieans *of them,* correspond intelligibly with *one* an other in writing, though ignorant of the lan-uage spoken *by their correspondents:* a plain proof, that the Chinese characters are like hieru-lyphics, *and essentially* independent of language."—*Jamieson cor.*; also *Blair.* "The curved .ne, *in stead* of *remaining* round, is *changed to a* square one, for the reason *before mentioned.*"— *Cnight cor.* '"Every *reader* should content himself with the use of those tones only, that he is abituated to in speech; and *should* give *to the words no* other emphasis, *than* what he would *ive* to the same words, in discourse. [Or, perhaps the author meant:—and *should* give *to the mphatic words no* other intonation, *than* what he would *give,* &c.] Thus, whatever he utters, ill be *delivered* with ease, and *will* appear natural."—*Sheridan cor.* "A stop, or *pause, is* a total essation of sound, during a perceptible, and, in *musical or poetical* compositions, a measurable pace of time."—*Id.* "Pauses, or rests, in speaking *or* reading, are total *cessations* of the voice, uring perceptible, and, in many cases, measurable *spaces* of time."—*Murray et al. cor.* "*Those erivative* nouns which *denote* small *things* of the kind *named by their primitives,* are called *iminutive* Nouns: as, lambkin, hillock, satchel, gosling; from lamb, hill, sack, goose."—*Bul-ons cor.* "*Why is it,* that nonsense so often escapes *detection, its character not being perceived :ther* by the writer *or* by the reader?"—*Campbell cor.* "An Interjection is a word used to ex-ress sudden emotion. *Interjections* are so called, because they are generally thrown in between 1e parts of *discourse, and have no* reference to the structure of *those* parts."—*M'Culloch cor. The verb* OUGHT *has no other inflection than* OUGHTEST, *and this is nearly obsolete.*"—*Macintosh* ir. " But the *arrangement,* government, *and* agreement *of words,* and *also their* dependence 1e upon *an other,* are referred to our reason."—*Osborn cor.* "ME is a personal pronoun, *of* ie first person, singular *number,* and *objective* case."—*Guy cor.* "The noun SELF is *usually* dded to a pronoun; as, herself, himself, &c. *The* compounds thus *formed are* called reciprocal *ronouns.*"—*Id.* "One cannot *but* think, that our author *would have* done better, *had he* begun 1e first of these three sentences, with saying, '*It is* novelty, *that* bestows charms on a monster.'" -*Blair cor.* "The idea which they present to ûs, of *nature* resembling art, of *art* considered as n original, and nature as a copy, seems not very distinct, *or* well *conceived,* nor indeed very ma-rial to our author's purpose."—*Id.* "*This faulty* construction of the sentence, *evidently arose om haste* and *carelessness.*"—*Id.* "Adverbs serve to modify *terms* of action or quality, or to denote time, place, order, degree, *or some other circumstance* which we have occasion to specify."—*Id.* "We may naturally expect. *that* the more any nation is improved by science, and the more perfect *its* language becomes, *the* more will *that language* abound with connective particles."—*Id.* "Mr. Greenleaf's book is *far better* adapted *to the capacity of* learners, *than* any *other* that has yet appeared, on the subject."—*Feltus and Onderdonk's false praise English-ed.* "Punctuation is the art of marking, in writing *or in print,* the several pauses, or rests, *which separate* sentences, *or* the parts of sentences : *so as to denote* their proper quantity or proportion, as *it is exhibited* in a just and accurate *delivery.*"—*Lowth cor.* "A compound sentence must *generally* be resolved into simple ones, and *these* be separated by *the comma.*" Or better : "A compound sentence *is generally divided,* by *the comma,* into *its* simple *members.*"—*Greenleaf and Fisk cor.* "Simple sentences should *in general* be separated from *one* an other by *the comma,* unless *a greater point is required ;* as, ' Youth is passing away, age is approaching, and death is near.' "—*Hall cor.* "*V* has *always* one uniform sound, *which is that of f flattened,* as in *these* from *thief : thus v* bears to *f* the same relation *that b* does to *p, d* to *t,* hard *g* to *k,* or *z* to *s.*"—*Murray and Fisk cor. ;* also *Walker ;* also *Greenleaf.* "The author is explaining the *difference* between sense and imagination, *as powers of* the human mind."—*Murray cor.* Or, if *this was* the critic's meaning : "The author is endeavouring to explain a very abstract point, the distinction between the powers of sense and *those of* imagination, *as two different faculties of* the human mind.'"—*Id. ;* also *Blair cor.* "HE—*(from the* Anglo-Saxon HE—) is a personal pronoun, of the third person, singular number, masculine gender, *and* nominative case. Decline HE."—*Fowler cor.*

CORRECTIONS UNDER THE CRITICAL NOTES.

UNDER CRITICAL NOTE I.—OF THE PARTS OF SPEECH.

"The passive voice denotes *an action received.*" Or : "The passive voice denotes *the receiving of an action.*"—*Maunder corrected.* "Milton, in some of his prose works, has *many* very *finely-turned* periods."—*Blair and Jam. cor.* "These will be found to be *wholly,* or *chiefly,* of that class."—*Blair cor.* "All appearances of an author's *affecting of* harmony, are disagreeable."—*Id. and Jam. cor.* "Some nouns have a double increase ; that is, *they increase* by more syllables than one : as *iter, itinĕris.*"—*Adam et al. cor.* "The powers of man are enlarged by *progressive* cultivation."—*Gurney cor.* "It is always important to begin well ; to make a favourable impression at *the first setting-out.*"—*Blair cor.* "For if one take a wrong method at *his first setting-out,* it will lead him astray in all that follows."—*Id.* "His mind is full of his subject, and *all* his words are expressive."—*Id.* "How exquisitely is *all* this performed in Greek ! "—*Harris cor.* "How *unworthy* is all this to satisfy the ambition of an immortal soul ! "—*Murray cor.* "So as to exhibit the object in its *full grandeur,* and *its* most striking point of view."—*Blair cor.* "And that the author know how to descend with propriety to the *plain style,* as well as how to rise to the bold and figured."—*Id.* "The heart *alone* can answer to the heart."—*Id.* "Upon *the* first *perception of it.*" Or : "*As it is* first perceived."—*Harris cor.* "Call for Samson, that he may make *sport for us.*"—*Bible cor.* "And he made sport *before them.*"—*Id.* "The term '*to suffer,*' in this definition, is used in a technical sense ; and means simply, *to receive* an action, or *to be* acted upon."—*Bullions cor.* "The text *only* is what is meant to be taught in schools."—*Brightland cor.* "The perfect participle denotes action or *existence* perfected or finished."—*Kirkham cor.* "From the intricacy and confusion which are produced *when they are* blended together."—*Murray cor.* "This very circumstance, *that the word* is employed antithetically, renders it important in the sentence."—*Kirkham cor.* "It [the pronoun *that,*] is applied *both to* persons and *to* things."—*Murray cor.* "Concerning us, as being *everywhere traduced.*"—*Barclay cor.* "Every thing *else* was buried in a profound silence."—*Steele cor.* "They raise *fuller* conviction, than any reasonings produce."—*Blair cor.* "It appears to me *nothing* but a fanciful refinement." Or : "It appears to me *nothing* more than a fanciful refinement."—*Id.* "The regular *and thorough* resolution of a complete passage."—*Churchill cor.* "The infinitive is *distinguished* by the word TO, *which* immediately *precedes it.*"—*Maunder cor.* "It will not be a *gain of* much ground, to urge that the basket, or vase, is understood to be the capital."—*Kames cor.* "The disgust one has to drink ink in reality, is not to the purpose, where *the drinking of it is merely figurative.*"—*Id.* "That we run not into the extreme of pruning so very *closely.*"—See *Murray's Gram.* 8vo, p. 318. "Being obliged to rest for a *little while* on the preposition itself." Or : "Being obliged to rest a *while* on the preposition itself." Or : "Being obliged to rest [for] a *moment* on the preposition *alone.*"—*Blair and Jam. cor.* "Our days on the earth are as a shadow, and there is no abiding."—*Bible cor.* "There *may be attempted* a more particular expression of certain objects, by means of *imitative* sounds."—*Blair, Jam. and Mur. cor.* "The right disposition of the shade, makes the light and colouring *the more apparent.*"—*Blair cor.* "I *observe* that a diffuse style *is apt to run into* long periods."—*Id.* "Their poor arguments, which they only *picked up in the highways.*"—*Leslie cor.* "Which must be little *else than* a transcribing of their writings."—*Barclay cor.* "That single impulse is *a forcing-out of* almost all the breath." Or : "That single impulse *forces* out almost all the breath."—*Rush cor.* "Picini compares modulation to the *turning-off* from a road."—*Gardiner cor.* "So much has been written on and off almost every subject."—*Sophist cor.* "By *the* reading *of* books written by the best authors, his mind became highly improved." Or : "By *the study of the most instructive* books, his mind became highly improved."—*Mur. cor.* "For I never made a *rich provision* a token of a spiritual ministry."—*Barclay cor.*

UNDER CRITICAL NOTE II.—OF DOUBTFUL REFERENCE.

"However disagreeable *the task,* we must resolutely perform our duty."—*Murray cor.* "The formation of *all* English verbs, *whether they be* regular or irregular, is derived from the Saxon *tongue.*"—*Lowth cor.* "Time and chance have an influence on all things human, and nothing *do they affect* more remarkably than language."—*Campbell cor.* "Time and chance have an influence on all things human, and on nothing *a* more remarkable *influence* than on language."—

amieson cor. "That Archytases, who was a virtuous man, happened to perish once upon a time, with him a sufficient ground," &c.—Phil. Mu. cor. "He will be the better qualified to understand the meaning of the numerous words into which they enter as material parts."—Murray cor. We should continually have the goal in view, that it may direct us in the race."—Id. "But ddison's figures seem to rise of their own accord from the subject, and constantly to embellish ." Or :—"and they constantly embellish it."—Blair and Jam. cor. "So far as they signify persons, animals, and things that we can see, it is very easy to distinguish nouns."—Cobbett cor. Dissyllables ending in y or mute e, or accented on the final syllable, may sometimes be compared like monosyllables."—Frost cor. "If the foregoing objection be admitted, it will not overrule the design."—Rush cor. "These philosophical innovators forget, that objects, like men, re known only by their actions."—Dr. Murray cor. "The connexion between words and ideas, arbitrary and conventional; it has arisen mainly from the agreement of men among themselves."—Jamieson cor. "The connexion between words and ideas, may in general be considered as arbitrary and conventional, or as arising from the agreement of men among themselves." -Blair cor. "A man whose inclinations led him to be corrupt, and who had great abilities to anage and multiply and defend his corruptions."—Swift cor. "They have no more control ver him, than have any other men."—Wayland cor. "All his old words are true English, and is numbers are exquisite."—Spect. cor. "It has been said, that not Jesuits only can equivocate." -Mur. in Ex. and Key, cor. "In Latin, the nominative of the first or second person, is seldom xpressed."—Adam and Gould cor. "Some words have the same form in both numbers."—Murry et al. cor. "Some nouns have the same form in both numbers."—Merchant et al. cor. "Others ave the same form in both numbers; as, deer, sheep, swine."—Frost cor. "The following st denotes the consonant sounds, of which there are twenty-two." Or: "The following list enotes the twenty-two simple sounds of the consonants."—Mur. et al. cor. "And is the ignorance of these peasants a reason for other persons to remain ignorant; or does it render the subject the less worthy of our inquiry?"—Harris and Mur. cor. "He is one of the most correct, nd perhaps he is the best, of our prose writers."—Lowth cor. "The motions of a vortex and f a whirlwind are perfectly similar." Or: "The motion of a vortex and that of a whirlwind are erfectly similar."—Jamieson cor. "What I have been saying, throws light upon one important erse in the Bible; which verse I should like to hear some one read."—Abbott cor. "When ere are any circumstances of time, place, and the like, by which the principal terms of our sentence must be limited or qualified."—Blair, Jam. and Mur. cor. "Interjections are words that xpress emotion, affection, or passion, and that imply suddenness." Or: "Interjections express notion, affection, or passion, and imply suddenness."—Bucke cor. "But the genitive expressing e measure of things, is used in the plural number only."—Adam and Gould cor. "The buildgs of the institution have been enlarged; and an expense has been incurred, which, with the creased price of provisions, renders it necessary to advance the terms of admission."—Murray r. "These sentences are far less difficult than complex ones."—S. S. Greene cor.

"Far from the madding crowd's ignoble strife
They sober lived, nor ever wished to stray."—Gray cor.

UNDER CRITICAL NOTE III.—OF DEFINITIONS.

(1.) "A definition is a short and lucid description of a thing, or species, according to its nature and operties."—G. Brown: Rev. David Blair cor. (2.) "Language, in general, signifies the exression of our ideas by certain articulate sounds, or written words, which are used as the signs those ideas."—Dr. Hugh Blair cor. (3.) "A word is one or more syllables used by common conmt as the sign of an idea."—Bullions cor. (4.) "A word is one or more syllables used as the sign of a idea, or of some manner of thought."—Hazen cor. (5.) "Words are articulate sounds, or eir written signs, used to convey ideas."—Hiley cor. (6.) "A word is one or more syllables used ally or in writing, to represent some idea."—Hart cor. (7.) "A word is one or more syllables sed as the sign of an idea."—S. W. Clark cor. (8.) "A word is a letter or a combination of tters, a sound or a combination of sounds, used as the sign of an idea."—Wells cor. (9.) Words are articulate sounds, or their written signs, by which ideas are communicated."—Wright r. (10.) "Words are certain articulate sounds, or their written representatives, used by common onsent as signs of our ideas."—Bullions, Lowth, Murray, et al. cor. (11.) "Words are sounds written symbols used as signs of our ideas."—W. Allen cor. (12.) "Orthography literally means rrect writing."—Kirkham and Smith cor. [The word orthography stands for different things : , 1. The art or practice of writing words with their proper letters; 2. That part of grammar hich treats of letters, syllables, separate words, and spelling.] (13.) "A vowel is a letter which rms a perfect sound when uttered alone."—Inst. p. 16. (14—18.) "Spelling is the art of exressing words by their proper letters." (19.) "A syllable is one or more letters, pronounced r a single impulse of the voice, and constituting a word, or part of a word."—Lowth, Mur. et al. r. (20.) "A syllable is a letter or a combination of letters, uttered in one complete sound."— rit. Gram. and Buch. cor. (21.) "A syllable is one or more letters representing a distinct sound, or hat is uttered by a single impulse of the voice."—Kirkham cor. (22.) "A syllable is so much of a ord as is sounded at once, whether it be the whole or a part."—Bullions cor. (23.) "A syllable so many letters as are sounded at once; and is either a word, or a part of a word."—Picket cor. 4.) "A diphthong is a union of two vowels in one syllable, as in bear and beat."—Bucke cor. r: "A diphthong is the meeting of two vowels in one syllable."—Brit. Gram. p. 15; Buchanan's, (25.) "A diphthong consists of two vowels put together in one syllable; as, ea in beat, oi in oice."—Guy cor. (26.) "A triphthong consists of three vowels put together in one syllable; as, eu in beauty."—Id. (27.) "But a triphthong is the union of three vowels in one syllable."— ucke cor. Or: "A triphthong is the meeting of three vowels in one syllable."—British Gram. 21; Buchanan's, 3. (28.) "What is a noun? A noun is the name of something; as, a man, a oy."—Brit. Gram. and Buchanan cor. (29.) "An adjective is a word added to a noun or proun, to describe the object named or referred to."—Maunder cor. (30.) "An adjective is a word ded to a noun or pronoun, to describe or define the object mentioned."—R. C. Smith cor. (31.) An adjective is a word which, without assertion or time, serves to describe or define something;

as, a good man, every boy."—*Wilcox cor.* (32.) "*An* adjective *is a word* added to *a* noun *or pronoun, and generally expresses* a quality."—*Mur. and Lowth cor.* (33.) "An adjective *expresses* the quality, *not* of the noun or pronoun to which it is applied, *but of the person or thing spoken of;* and *it* may generally be known by *the* sense *which it thus makes* in connexion with *its noun; as,* 'A *good* man,' 'A *genteel* woman.' "—*Wright cor.* (34.) "An adverb is a word used to modify the sense of *a verb, a participle, an adjective, or an other adverb.*"—*Wilcox cor.* (35.) "An adverb *is* a word *added* to a verb, *a participle,* an adjective, or an other adverb, to modify *the sense, or denote* some circumstance."—*Bullions cor.* (36.) "A *substantive,* or noun, is a name given to *some* object which the senses can perceive, the understanding comprehend, or the imagination entertain."—*Wright cor.* (37—54.) "*Genders are modifications that* distinguish *objects* in regard to sex."—*Brown's Inst.* p. 35. (55 and 56.) "*A* case, in *grammar,* is the state or condition of *a* noun *or pronoun,* with respect to *some* other *word in the* sentence."—*Bullions and Kirkham cor.* (57.) "*Cases* are modifications that distinguish the relations of nouns and pronouns *to other words.*"—*Brown's Inst.* p. 36. (58.) "Government is the power which one *word* has over an other, *to cause* it to *assume* some particular *modification.*"—*Sanborn et al. cor.* See *Inst.* p. 104. (59.) "A simple sentence is a sentence which contains only one *assertion, command, or question.*"—*Sanborn et al. cor.* (60.) "Declension means *the* putting *of* a noun *or pronoun* through the different cases *and numbers.*"—*Kirkham cor.* Or better: "The declension of a *word* is a regular arrangement of its numbers and cases."—See *Inst.* p. 37. (61.) "Zeugma *is a figure in which* two or more *words refer* in common *to an* other which *literally agrees with* only one of them."—*Fisk cor.* (62.) "An irregular verb is *a verb that does not form the preterit* and *the* perfect participle *by assuming* d or *ed ; as,* smite, smote, smitten."—*Inst.* p. 75. (63.) "*A* personal *pronoun is a pronoun that shows, by its form, of what person it is.*"—*Inst.* p. 46.

UNDER CRITICAL NOTE IV.—OF COMPARISONS.

"*Our language* abounds more in vowel and diphthong sounds, than most *other tongues.*" Or: "We abound more in vowel and *diphthongal* sounds, than most *nations.*"—*Blair cor.* "A line thus accented has a more spirited air, than *one which takes* the accent on any other syllable."—*Kames cor.* "Homer *introduces* his deities with no greater ceremony, than [*what*] *he uses towards* mortals ; and Virgil has still less moderation *than he.*"—*Id.* "Which the more *refined* taste of later writers, *whose* genius *was* far inferior to *theirs,* would have taught them to avoid."—*Blair cor.* "*As* a poetical composition, however, the Book of Job is not only equal to any other *of the* sacred writings, but is superior to them all, except those of Isaiah alone."—*Id.* "On the whole, Paradise Lost is a poem *which* abounds with beauties of every kind, and *which* justly entitles its author to *be equalled in* fame *with* any poet."—*Id.* "Most of the French writers compose in short sentences ; though their style, in general, is not concise ; commonly less so than *that of most* English writers, whose sentences are much longer."—*Id.* "The principles of the Reformation were *too deeply fixed* in the prince's mind, to be easily eradicated."—*Hume cor.* "Whether they do not create jealousy and animosity, more than *sufficient to counterbalance* the benefit derived from them."—*Leo Wolf cor.* "The Scotch have preserved the ancient character of their music more entire, than *have the inhabitants of* any other country."—*Gardiner cor.* "When the time or quantity of one syllable exceeds *that of* the rest, that syllable readily receives the accent."—*Rush cor.* "What then can be more obviously true, than that it should be made as just as *we* can *make it.*"—*Dymond cor.* "It was not likely that they would criminate themselves more than they could *not* avoid."—*Clarkson cor.* "*In* their understandings *they* were the most acute people *that* have ever lived."—*Knapp cor.* "The patentees have printed it with neat types, and upon better paper than was *used* formerly."—*John Ward cor.* "In reality, its relative use is not exactly like *that of* any other word."—*Felch cor.* "Thus, *in stead of having to purchase* two books,—the Grammar and the Exercises,—the learner finds both in one, for a price at *most* not greater than *that of* the others."—*Alb. Argus cor.* "They are not improperly regarded as pronouns, though *they are* less *strictly* such than the others."—*Bullions cor.* "We have had, as will readily be believed, *a much better* opportunity of becoming conversant with the case, than the generality of our readers can be supposed to have had."—*Brit. Friend cor.*

UNDER CRITICAL NOTE V.—OF FALSITIES.

"The long sound of i is *like a very quick union* of the sound of *a,* as heard in *bar,* and that *of e,* as heard in *be.*"—*Churchill cor.* "The omission of a word necessary to grammatical propriety, is *of course an impropriety, and not a true* ellipsis."—*Priestley cor.* "*Not* every substantive, *or* noun, is *necessarily* of the third person."—*A. Murray cor.* "A noun is in the third person, when the subject is *merely* spoken *of ;* and in the second person, when the subject is spoken *to ; and* in the first person, *when it names the speaker as such.*"—*Nutting cor.* "With us, no nouns are *literally of the* masculine *or* the feminine gender, except the names of male and female creatures." —*Dr. Blair cor.* "*The* apostrophe is a little mark, *either denoting the possessive case of nouns,* or signifying that something is shortened : as, '*William's* hat ;'—'*the learn'd,*' for '*the learned.*'"— *Inf. S. Gram. cor.* "When a word beginning with a vowel is coupled with one beginning with a consonant, the indefinite article must *not* be repeated, *if the two words be adjectives belonging to one and the same noun ;* thus, 'Sir Matthew Hale was a noble and impartial judge ;'—'Pope was an elegant and nervous writer."—*Maunder cor.*[•] "*W* and y are consonants, when they *precede* a vowel *heard in the same* syllable : in every other situation, they are vowels."—*Mur. et al. cor.* See *Inst.* p. 16. "*The* is *not varied* before adjectives and substantives, let them begin as they will."— *Bucke cor.* "*A few English* prepositions, *and many* which *we have borrowed from other languages,* are *often* prefixed to words, in such a manner as to coalesce with them, and to become *parts* of the compounds *or derivatives thus formed.*"—*Lowth cor.* "H, at the beginning of syllables not accented, is *weaker,* but *not* entirely silent ; as in *historian, widowhood.*"—*D. Blair cor.* "*Not* every word that will make sense with *to* before it, is a verb ; for *to* may govern nouns, pronouns,

---

[•] The article *may* be repeated in examples like these, without producing *impropriety ;* but then it will alter the construction of the adjectives, and render the expression more *formal* and emphatic, by suggesting *a repetition of* the noun."—G. BROWN.

or participles."—*Kirkham cor.* "*Most* verbs do, in reality, express actions; but they are *not* intrinsically the mere names of actions: *these must of course be nouns.*"—*Id.* "The nominative *denotes* the actor or subject; and the verb, the action *which is* performed *or received by this actor or subject.*"—*Id.* "*But,* if only one creature or thing acts, *more than* one action may, at the same instant, be done; as, 'The girl not only *holds* her pen badly, but *scowls,* and *distorts* her features, while she *writes.*'"—*Id.* "*Nor is each of these verbs of the singular number because it* denotes but one action which the girl performs, *but because the subject or nominative* is of the singular number, *and the words must agree.*"—*Id.* "And when I say, '*Two men walk,*' is it not equally apparent, that *walk* is plural because it *agrees with men?*"—*Id.* "The subjunctive mood is formed by *using the simple verb in a suppositive sense, and without personal inflection.*"—*Beck cor.* "The possessive case *of nouns, except in instances of apposition or close connexion,* should always be distinguished by the apostrophe."—*Frost cor.* "'At these proceedings *of the Commons :*' Here *of* is a sign *of the objective* case; and '*Commons*' is of that case, *being governed by this preposition.*" —*A. Murray cor.* "Here let it be observed again, that, strictly speaking, *all finite* verbs have numbers *and* persons; *and so* have *nearly all* nouns *and* pronouns, *even* when they refer to irrational creatures and inanimate things."—*Barrett cor.* "The noun denoting the person or *persons* addressed or spoken to, is in the nominative case independent : *except it be put in apposition with a pronoun of the second person;* as, 'Woe to *you* lawyers;'—'*You* political men are constantly manœuvring.'"—*Frost cor.* "Every noun, when *used in a direct address and set off by a comma,* becomes of the second person, and is in the nominative case absolute; as, '*Paul,* thou art beside thyself.'"—*Jaudon cor.* "Does the conjunction *ever* join words together ? *Yes;* the conjunction *sometimes* joins *words* together, *and sometimes* sentences, *or certain parts of sentences.*"— *Brit. Gram. cor.;* also *Buchanan.* "Every *noun of the possessive form* has a *governing* noun, expressed or understood; as, *St. James's.* Here *Palace* is understood. But one *possessive may* govern an other; as, '*William's father's* house.'"—*Buchanan cor.* "Every adjective (*with the exceptions noticed under Rule* 9th) belongs to a *noun or pronoun,* expressed or understood."—*Murray et al. cor.* "*Not* every adjective qualifies a substantive, expressed or understood."—*Bullions cor.* "*Not* every adjective belongs to *a* noun, expressed or understood."—*Ingersoll cor.* "Adjectives belong to nouns *or pronouns, and serve to describe things.*"—*R. C. Smith cor.* "*English* adjectives, *in general,* have *no modifications in which they can* agree with the nouns *to* which they *relate.*"—*Fisk cor.* "The adjective, *if it denote unity or plurality,* must agree with its substantive in number."— *Buchanan cor.* "*Not* every adjective and participle, *by a vast many,* belongs to some noun or pronoun, expressed or understood."—*Frost cor.* "*Not* every verb of the infinitive mood, supposes a verb before it, expressed or understood."—*Buchanan cor.* "*Nor* has every adverb its verb, expressed or understood; *for some adverbs relate to participles, to adjectives, or to other adverbs.*" —*Id.* "*A conjunction that connects one* sentence to an other, *is not* always placed betwixt the two propositions or sentences which *it unites.*"—*Id.* "The words *for all that,* are by no means '*low;*' but the putting of this phrase for *yet* or *still,* is neither necessary nor elegant."—*Mur. and Pr. cor.* "The reader or hearer then understands from AND, that *the author adds one proposition, number, or thing, to an other.* Thus AND *often, very often,* connects one thing with an other thing, *or* one word with an other word."—*James Brown cor.* "'Six AND six are twelve.' Here it is affirmed, that *the two sixes added together are* twelve."—*Id.* "'John AND his wife *have six* children.' This is an instance *in which* AND *connects two nominatives in a simple sentence.* It is *not* here affirmed that John has six children, and that his wife has six *other* children."—*Id.* "That 'Nothing can be great which is not right,' is itself a *great falsity:* there are great blunders, great evils, great sins."—*L. Murray cor.* "The highest degree of reverence should be paid to *the most exalted virtue or goodness.*"—*Id.* "There is in *all* minds *some* knowledge, *or* understanding."—*Murray et al. cor.* "Formerly, the nominative and objective cases of our pronouns, were *more generally distinguished in practice,* than they now are."—*Kirkham cor.* "As it respects a choice of words and expressions, *the just* rules of grammar *may* materially aid the learner."—*S. S. Greene cor.* "The *name of* whatever exists, or is conceived to exist, is a noun."—*Fowler cor.* "*As not all* men are brave, *brave* is itself *distinctive.*"—*Id.*

UNDER CRITICAL NOTE VI.—OF ABSURDITIES.

(1.) "And sometimes two unaccented syllables *come together.*"—*Blair cor.* (2.) "What nouns frequently *stand together?*" Or : "What nouns *are* frequently *used one after an other?*"—*Sanborn cor.* (3.) "*Words* are derived from *other words* in various ways."—*Idem et al. cor.* (4.) "*The name* PREPOSITION *is* derived from the two Latin words *præ* and *pono,* which signify *before* and *place.*"—*Mack cor.* (5.) "He was *much* laughed at for such conduct."—*Bullions cor.* (6.) "*Every pronominal adjective* belongs to some noun, expressed or understood."—*Ingersoll cor.* (7.) "If he [Addison] fails in any thing, it is in strength and precision; *the want of* which renders his manner not altogether a proper model."—*Blair cor.* (8.) "Indeed, if Horace *is* deficient in any thing, *his fault* is this, of not being sufficiently attentive to juncture, *or the* connexion of parts."—*Id.* (9.) "The pupil is now supposed to be acquainted with the *ten parts* of speech, and their most *usual* modifications."—*Taylor cor.* (10.) "I could see, *feel,* taste, and smell the rose."—*Sanborn cor.* (11.) "The *vowels iou are* sometimes pronounced distinctly in two syllables; as in *various, abstemious;* but not in *bilious.*"—*Murray and Walker cor.* (12.) "The diphthong *aa* generally sounds like *a* short; as in *Balaam, Canaan, Isaac:* in *Baal* and *Gaal,* we make no diphthong."—*Mur. cor.* (13.) "Participles *cannot be said to be* 'governed by the article;' for *any* participle, with *an* article before it, becomes a substantive, or an adjective used substantively: as, *the learning, the learned.*"—*Id.* (14.) "From words ending with *y* preceded by a consonant, *we* form the plurals of nouns, the persons of verbs, *agent* nouns, *perfect* participles, comparatives, and superlatives, by changing the *y* into *i,* and adding *es, ed, er, eth,* or *est.*"—*Walker, Murray, et al. cor.* (15.) "But *y* preceded by a vowel, *remains unchanged,* in the derivatives above named; as, *boy, boys.*"—*Murray et al. cor.* (16.) "But when *the final y* is preceded by a vowel, it *remains unchanged before an* additional syllable; as, *coy, coyly.*"—*Iid.* (17.) "But *y* preceded by a vowel, *remains unchanged,* in *almost all* instances; as, coy, *coyly.*"—*Kirkham cor.* (18.) "Sentences are of *two kinds,* simple and compound."—*Wright cor.* (19.) "The neuter pronoun *it* may be employed to *introduce a nominative* of any person, number, or gender; as, '*It is he*;'—'*It is she*;'—'*It is they*;'—'*It is the land.*'"—*Bucke cor.* (20 and 21.) "*It is*, and *it was*, are *always singular*; but they *may introduce words of* a plural construction: as, '*It was the heretics that* first began to rail.' SMOLLETT."—*Merchant cor.*; also *Priestley et al.* (22.) "*W* and *y*, as consonants, have *each of* them one sound."—*Town cor.* (23.) "The *word as* is frequently a relative *pronoun.*"—*Bucke cor.* (24.) "*From a series of* clauses, the conjunction may *sometimes* be omitted with propriety."—*Merchant cor.* (25.) "If, however, the *two* members are very closely connected, the comma is unnecessary; as, 'Revelation tells us how we may attain happiness.'"—*Murray et al. cor.* (26—7.) "The mind has difficulty in *taking effectually*, in quick succession, so many different views of the same object."—*Blair cor.*; also *Mur.* (28.) "*Pronominal adjectives* are a kind of *definitive*, which *may either accompany their* nouns, or *represent them understood.*"—*Kirkham cor.* (29.) "*When the nominative or antecedent is a collective noun* conveying *the idea of plurality, the* verb or pronoun *must agree* with it in the plural *number.*"—*Id. et al. cor.* (30—34.) "A noun or a pronoun in the possessive case, is governed by the *name of the thing possessed.*"—*Brown's Inst.* p. 175. (35.) "Here the boy is represented as acting: *the word boy* is therefore in the nominative *case.*" —*Kirkham cor.* (36.) "*Do, be, have,* and *will,* are *sometimes* auxiliaries, *and sometimes* principal verbs."—*Cooper cor.* (37.) "*Names of males* are masculine. *Names* of *females* are feminine."— *Adam's Gram.* p. 10. (38.) "'*To-day's* lesson is longer than yesterday's.' Here *to-day's* and *yesterday's* are substantives."—*Murray et al. cor.* (39.) "In this example, *to-day's* and *yesterday's* are nouns in the possessive case."—*Kirkham cor.* (40.) "An Indian in Britain would be much surprised to *find by chance* an elephant feeding at large in the open fields."—*Kames cor.* (41.) "If we were to contrive a new language, we might make any articulate sound the sign of any idea: *apart from previous usage,* there would be no impropriety in calling oxen *men,* or rational beings *oxen.*"—*Murray cor.* (42.) "All the parts of a sentence should *form a consistent whole.*"—*Id. et al. cor.*

(43.) "Full through his neck the weighty falchion sped,
Along the pavement roll'd the *culprit's* head."—*Pope cor.*

UNDER CRITICAL NOTE VII.—OF SELF-CONTRADICTION.

(1.) "Though 'The king, *with* the lords and commons,' *must have a singular rather than* a plural verb, the sentence would certainly stand better thus: 'The king, the lords, *and* the commons, form an excellent constitution.'"—*Mur. and Ing. cor.* (2—3.) "*L* has a soft liquid sound; as in *love, billow, quarrel.* This *letter* is sometimes silent; as in *half, talk, psalm.*"—*Mur. and Fisk cor.*; also *Kirkham.* (4.) "The words *means* and *amends,* though regularly derived from the singulars *mean* and *amend,* are *not* now, *even* by polite writers, restricted to the plural number. Our most distinguished modern authors *often* say, '*by this means,*' as well as, '*by these means.*'"— *Wright cor.* (5.) "A friend exaggerates a man's virtues; an enemy, his crimes."—*Mur. cor.* (6.) "The auxiliary *have,* or *any form of* the perfect tense, *belongs not properly to* the subjunctive mood. *We suppose past facts by the indicative*; as, If I *have loved,* If thou *hast loved,* &c."—*Merchant cor.* (7.) "There is also an impropriety in *using* both the indicative and the subjunctive *mood,* with the same conjunction; as, '*If* a man *have* a hundred sheep, and one of them *is* gone astray,' &c. [This is Merchant's perversion of the text. It should be, 'and one of them *go* astray;' or, '*be* gone astray,' as in Matt. xviii, 12.]"—*Id.* (8.) "The rising series of contrasts *conveys transcendent* dignity and energy to the conclusion."—*Jamieson cor.* (9.) "A groan or a shriek is instantly understood, as a language extorted by distress, a *natural* language which conveys a meaning that *words* are *not adequate* to express. A groan or a shriek speaks to the ear with a far more thrilling effect than words; yet *even this natural* language of distress may be counterfeited by art."—*Dr. Porter cor.* (10.) "*If* these words [*book* and *pen*] cannot be put together in such a way as will constitute plurality, then they cannot be '*these words*;' and then, also, *one and one* cannot be *two.*"—*James Brown cor.* (11.) "Nor can the real pen and the real book be *added or counted together* in words, in such a manner as will *not* constitute plurality in grammar."—*Id.* (12.) "*Our* is *a personal* pronoun, of the possessive *case. Murray does not* decline it."—*Mur. cor.* (13.) "*This* and *that,* and their plurals *these* and *those,* are *often* opposed to each other in a sentence. When *this* or *that* is used alone, i. e., *without contrast, this* is *applied* to *what is* present or near; *that,* to *what is* absent or distant."—*Buchanan cor.* (14.) "Active and neuter verbs may be conjugated by adding their *imperfect* participle to the auxiliary verb *be,* through all its variations."—'*Be* is an auxiliary whenever it is placed before either the perfect *or the imperfect* participle of an other verb; but, in every other situation, it is a principal verb."—*Kirkham cor.* (15.) "A verb in the imperative mood is *almost* always of the second person."—'The verbs, according to *a foreign idiom,* or the poet's license, are used in the imperative, agreeing with a nominative of the first or third person."—*Id.* (16.) "*A personal pronoun, is a pronoun that shows, by its form, of what person it is.*"—'Pronouns of the first person do not *disagree* in person with the nouns they represent."— *Id.* (17.) "Nouns have three cases; *the* nominative, *the* possessive, and *the* objective."—"Personal pronouns have, like nouns, *three* cases; *the* nominative, *the possessive,* and *the* objective."— *Beck cor.* (18.) "In *many* instances the preposition suffers a change *and* becomes an adverb by its *mere* application."—*Murray cor.* (19.) "Some nouns are used only in the plural; as, *ashes, literati, minutiæ.* Some nouns *have* the same *form* in both numbers; as, *sheep, deer, series, species.* Among the inferior parts of speech, there are some *pairs* or *couples.*"—*D. Blair cor.* (20.) "Concerning the pronominal adjectives, that may, or may not, represent *their nouns.*"—*B. Peirce cor.* (21.) "The *word a* is in a few instances employed in the sense of a preposition; as, 'Simon Peter *saith unto* them, I go *a* fishing;' i. e., I go to fishing."—*Weld cor.* (22.) "So, too, verbs *that are* commonly transitive, are used intransitively, when they have no object."—*Bullions cor.*

(23.) "When first young Maro, in his boundless mind,
A work t' outlast *imperial* Rome design'd."—*Pope cor.*

UNDER CRITICAL NOTE VIII.—OF SENSELESS JUMBLING.

"*There are two numbers,* called the singular and *the* plural, *which* distinguish nouns as *signifying either* one *thing,* or many of the same kind."—*Blair cor.* "Here James Monroe is addressed, he is spoken to; *the name is therefore* a noun of the second person."—*Mack cor.* "The number and *person* of *an English* verb can *seldom* be ascertained until its nominative is known."—*Emmons cor.* "A noun of multitude, or *a singular noun* signifying many, may have *a* verb *or a* pronoun agreeing with it in *either* number; yet not without regard to the import of the *noun*, as conveying *the idea of*, unity or plurality."—*Lowth et al. cor.* "To *form* the present *tense* and *the* past imperfect of *our* active or neuter *verbs*, the auxiliary *do, and its preterit did, are* sometimes used: *as,* I do now love; I *did* then love."—*Lowth cor.* "If these *be* perfectly committed *to memory, the learner* will be able to take twenty lines for *his second* lesson, and *the task* may be increased each day."—*Osborn cor.* "*Ch is* generally sounded in the same manner *as if it were* t*ch*: as in *Charles,'church, cheerfulness,* and *cheese.* But, *in Latin or Greek* words, *ch is* pronounced like *k*: as in *Chaos, character, chorus,* and *chimera. And,* in *words* derived from the French, *ch is* sounded like *sh*: as *in Chagrin, chicanery,* and *chaise.*"—*Bucke cor.* "Some *nouns literally* neuter, are *made* masculine or feminine by a figure of speech."—*Murray et al. cor.* "In the English language, words may be classified under ten general heads: the *sorts, or chief classes, of words,* are usually termed the ten parts of speech."—*Nutting cor.* "'Mercy is the true badge of nobility.' *Nobility* is a *common* noun, *of the* third person, singular number, *neuter* gender, and objective case; and is governed by *of*."—*Kirkham cor.* "*Gh is* either silent, *as in* plough, or *has the* sound of *f*, as in *laugh.*"—*Town cor.* "Many *nations* were destroyed, and as many languages or dialects were lost and blotted out from the general catalogue."—*Chazotte cor.* "Some languages contain a greater number of moods than others, and *each* exhibits *its own as* forms *peculiar to itself.*"—*Murray cor.* "A SIMILE is a simple and express comparison; and is generally introduced by *like, as,* or *so.*"—*Id.* See *Inst.* p. 233. "The word *what* is sometimes improperly used for the conjunction *that.*"—*Priestley, Murray, et al. cor.* "Brown makes *no* ado *in condemning* the *absurd* principles of preceding works, in relation to the gender of pronouns."—*Peirce cor.* "The nominative *usually* precedes the verb, and *denotes the agent of* the action."—*Beck cor.* "Primitive *words* are those which *are not formed from other words* more simple."—*Wright cor.* "In monosyllables, the single vowel *i* always preserves its long sound before a single consonant with *e* final; as in *thine, strive:* except in *give* and *live*, which are short; and in *shire*, which has the sound of long *e.*"—*Murray et al. cor.* "But the person or thing *that is merely* spoken of, being *frequently* absent, and *perhaps* in many respects unknown *to the hearer*, it is *thought more* necessary, that *the third person* should be marked by a distinction of gender."—*Lowth, Mur. et al. cor.* "*Both vowels of every diphthong were,* doubtless, originally *vocal.* Though in many instances *they are* not *so* at present, *the* combinations *in which one only is* heard, still retain the name of diphthongs, *being distinguished from others* by the term *improper.*"—*Mur. et al. cor.* "*Moods are different forms* of the verb, *each of which expresses* the being, action, or passion, *in some particular* manner."—*Inst.* p. 33; *A. Mur. cor.* "The word THAT is a demonstrative *adjective, whenever* it is followed by a *noun* to which it refers."—*L. Mur. cor.*

"The *guilty soul* by Jesus *wash'd,*
Is future glory's deathless heir.'"—*Fairfield cor.*

UNDER CRITICAL NOTE IX.—OF WORDS NEEDLESS.

"A knowledge of grammar enables us to express ourselves better in conversation and in writing."—*Sanborn cor.* "And hence we infer, that there is no dictator here but use."—*Jamieson cor.* "Whence little is gained, except correct spelling and pronunciation."—*Town cor.* "The man who is faithfully attached to religion, may be relied on with confidence."—*Merchant cor.* "Shalt thou build me *a* house to dwell in?" Or: "Shalt thou build *a* house for me to dwell in?"—*Bible cor.* "The house was deemed polluted which was entered by so abandoned a woman."—*Blair cor.* "The farther he searches, the firmer will be his belief."—*Keith cor.* "I deny not that religion consists in these things."—*Barclay cor.* "Except the king delighted in her, and she were called by name."—*Bible cor.* "The proper method of reading these lines, is, to read them as the sense dictates."—*Blair cor.* "When any words become obsolete, or are used *only in* particular phrases, it is better to dispense with their service entirely, and give up the phrases."—*Campbell and Mur. cor.* "Those savage people seemed to have no element but war."—*Mur. cor.* "*Man* is a common noun, of the third person, singular number, masculine gender, and nominative case."—*Flint cor.* "The orator, as circumstances require, will employ them all."—*Blair cor.* "By deferring repentance, we accumulate our sorrows."—*Murray cor.* "There is no doubt that public speaking became early an engine of government."—*Blair cor.* "The different *meanings* of these w*o*rds, may not at first occur."—*Id.* "The sentiment is well expressed by Plato, but much better by Solomon."—*Murray et al. cor.* "They have had a greater privilege than we."—*Mur. cor.* "Every thing should be so arranged, that what goes before, may give light and force to what follows."—*Blair cor.* "So that his doctrines were embraced by great numbers."—*Hist. cor.* "They have taken *an other* and shorter cut."—*South cor.* "The imperfect tense of a regular verb is formed from the present by adding *d* or *ed;* as, *love, loved.*"—*Frost cor.* "The pronoun *their* does not agree in number with the noun '*man,*' for which it stands."—*Kirkham cor.* "This mark [!] denotes wonder, surprise, joy, grief, or sudden emotion."—*Bucke cor.* "We all are accountable, each for himself."—*Mur. et al. cor.* "If he has commanded it, I must obey."—*Smith cor.* "I now present him a form of the diatonic scale."—*Barber cor.* "One after an other, their favourite rivers have been reluctantly abandoned." Or: "One after an other *of* their favourite rivers have *they* reluctantly abandoned."—*Hodgson cor.* "*Particular* and *peculiar* are words of different import."—*Blair cor.* "Some adverbs admit of comparison; as, *soon, sooner, soonest.*"—*Bucke cor.* "Having exposed himself too freely in different climates, he entirely lost his health."—*Mur. cor.* "The verb must agree with its nominative in number and person."—*Buchanan cor.* "Write twenty short sentences containing adjectives."—*Abbott cor.* "This general tendency of the language seems to have given occasion to a very great corruption."—*Churchill's Gram.* p. 113. "The second requisite of a perfect sentence is *unity.*"—*Murray cor.* "It is scarcely necessary to apologize for omitting their names."—*Id.* "The letters of the English alphabet are twenty-six."—*Id. et al. cor.* "He who employs antiquated or novel phraseology, must do it with design; he cannot err from inadvertence, as he may with respect to provincial or vulgar expressions."—*Jamieson cor.* "The vocative case, in some grammars, is wholly omitted; why, if we must have cases, I could never understand."—*Bucke cor.* "Active verbs are conjugated with the auxiliary verb *have*; passive verbs, with the auxiliary *am* or *be*."—*Id.* "What then may AND be called? A conjunction."—*Smith cor.* "Have they ascertained who gave the information?"—*Bullions cor.*

UNDER CRITICAL NOTE X.—OF IMPROPER OMISSIONS.

"All *words signifying concrete* qualities of things, are called adnouns, or adjectives."—*D. Blair cor.* "The *macron* [¯] signifies a long or accented syllable, and the breve [˘] indicates a short or unaccented syllable."—*Id.* "Whose duty *it* is, to help young ministers."—*Friends cor.* "The passage is closely connected with what precedes and *what* follows."—*Phil. Mu. cor.* "The work is not completed, but *it* soon will be."—*R. C. Smith cor.* "Of whom hast thou been afraid, or *whom* hast thou feared?"—*Bible cor.* "There is a God who made, and *who* governs the world."—*Butler cor.* "It was this *that* made them so haughty."—*Goldsmith cor.* "How far the whole charge affected him, *it* is not easy to determine."—*Id.* "They saw *these wonders of nature*, and *worshiped the* God that made them."—*Bucke cor.* "The errors frequent in the use of hyperboles, arise either from overstraining *them*, or *from* introducing them on unsuitable occasions."—*Mur. cor.* "The preposition *in* is set before *the names of* countries, cities, and large towns; as, 'He lives *in* France, *in* London, or *in* Birmingham.' But, before *the names of* villages, single houses, or foreign cities, *at* is used; as, 'He lives *at* Hackney.'"—*Id. et al. cor.* "And, in such recollection, the thing is not figured as in our view, nor *is* any image formed."—*Kames cor.* "Intrinsic beauty and relative beauty must be handled separately."—*Id.* "He should be on his guard not to do them injustice by disguising *them* or placing them in a false light."—*Blair cor.* "In *pursuing that* work, we are frequently interrupted by *the author's* unnatural thoughts."—*Murray cor.* "To this point have tended all the rules *which* I have *just* given."—*Blair cor.* "To *this point* have tended all the rules which have *just* been given."—*Murray cor.* "Language, as written, or *as oral*, is addressed to the eye, or to the ear."—*Journal cor.* "He will learn, Sir, that to accuse *and to prove* are very different."—*Walpole cor.* "They crowded around the door so as to prevent others *from* going out."—*Abbott cor.* "*A word denoting* one person or thing, is *of the singular* number; *a word denoting* more than one person or thing, is *of the plural number.*"—*J. Flint cor.* "Nouns, according to the sense or relation in which they are used, are in the nominative, *the* possessive, or *the objective* case: thus, Nom. man, Poss. man's, Obj. man."—*D. Blair cor.* "Nouns or pronouns in the possessive case are placed before the nouns which govern them, *and* to which they belong."—*Sanborn cor.* "A teacher is explaining the difference between a noun *and a* verb."—*Abbott cor.* "And therefore the two ends, or extremities, must directly answer to the north and *the* south pole."—*Harris cor.* "WALKS or WALKETH, RIDES or RIDETH, *and* STANDS or STANDETH, are of the third person singular."—*Kirkham cor.* "I grew immediately roguish and pleasant, to a *high* degree, in the same strain."—*Swift cor.* "An *Anapest* has the first *two* syllables unaccented, and the last *one* accented."—*Blair cor.; also Kirkham et al.; also Mur. et al.* "But hearing and vision differ not more than words spoken and *words written.*" Or: "But hearing and vision *do not differ* more than *spoken words* and written."—*Wilson cor.* "They are considered as some *authors to be* prepositions."—*Cooper cor.* "When those powers have been deluded and *have* gone astray."—*Phil. Mu. cor.* "They will understand this, and *will like* it."—*Abbott cor.* "They had been expelled *from* their native country Romagna."—*Hunt cor.* "Future time is expressed *in* two different ways."—*Adam and Gould cor.* "Such as the borrowing *of some noted event* from history."—*Kames cor.* "Every *finite* verb must agree with its nominative in number and person."—*Bucke cor.* "We are struck, we know not how, with the symmetry of any *handsome* thing we see."—*Murray cor.* "Under this head, I shall consider every thing *that is* necessary to a good delivery."—*Sheridan cor.* "A good ear is the gift of nature; it may be much improved, but *it* cannot *be* acquired, by art."—*Murray cor.* "'Truth' is *a common* noun, *of the third person,* singular *number*, neuter *gender*, and nominative *case.*"—*Bullions cor. by Brown's Form.* "*Possess is a regular* active-transitive verb, *found in the* indicative mood, present *tense*, third person, *and* plural *number*."—*Id.* "'*Fear*' is *a* common noun, *of the third person,* singular *number*, neuter *gender*, and nominative *case:* and is the subject of *is; according to the Rule which* says, 'A noun or a pronoun which *is the subject of a finite verb, must be in the nominative case.'* Because the meaning is—'*fear is*,'"—*Id.* "'*Is*' is an irregular *neuter* verb, *from be, was, being,* been; *found* in the indicative mood, present *tense*, third person, *and* singular *number:* and agrees with its nominative *fear; according to the* Rule *which says,* '*Every finite* verb *must agree with its subject, or nominative, in person and number.'* Because the meaning is—'*fear is.'*"—*Id.* "*As in the word* Gaelic, has the sound of long *a.*"—*Wells cor.*

UNDER CRITICAL NOTE XI.—OF LITERARY BLUNDERS.

"Repeat some adverbs that are composed of the *prefix or preposition a* and nouns."—*Kirkham cor.* "Participles are so called, because *they participate or partake the properties of verbs and of adjectives or nouns.* The Latin word *participium*, which signifies *a participle, is* derived from *participo*, to partake."—*Merchant cor.* "The possessive *precedes* an other noun, and is known by the sign '*s*, or by this', the apostrophe only."—*Back cor.* "Reciprocal pronouns, *or compound personal* pronouns, are formed by adding *self or selves* to the *simple possessives of the first and second persons, and to the objectives of the third person;* as, *myself, yourselves, himself, themselves.*"—*Id.* "The word SELF, and its plural SELVES, *when used separately as names*, must be considered nouns; but *when* joined to the simple pronouns, *they are not nouns, but parts of the compound personal pronouns.*"—*Wright cor.* "The Spondee, 'rolls round,' expresses beautifully the majesty of the sun in his course."—*Webster and Frazee cor.* "*Active-transitive verbs* govern the objective case; as, 'John *learned* his *lesson.'*"—*Frazee cor.* "Prosody primarily signified *accent, or the modulation of the voice;* and, as the name implies, related *to poetry, or song.*"—*Hendrick cor.* "On such a principle of forming *them*, there would be as many *moods* as verbs; and, *in stead of* four *moods,* we should have *four thousand three hundred*, which is the number of verbs in the English language, according to Lowth."—*Hallock cor.* "The phrases, 'To let *out* blood,'—'To go a hunt-ing,' are *not* elliptical; for *out* is needless, and *a* is a preposition, governing *hunting.*"—*Bullions cor.* "In Rhyme, the last syllable of every *line corresponds in* sound *with that of some other line or lines.*"—*Id.* "The possessive case plural, *where the nominative ends in s*, has the apostrophe *only* ; as, 'Eagles' wings,'—'lions' whelps,'—'bears' claws.'"—*Weld cor.* "'Horses-masses,' plu-ral, should be written *possessively*, 'horses' manes :'" [one "*mane*" is never possessed by many "*horses.*"]—*Id.* "W takes its *usual* form from the union of two Vees, V being the *figure* of the Roman capital letter which was anciently called *U.*"—*Fowler cor.* "In the sentence, 'I saw the lady who sings,' what word is *nominative* to SINGS?"—*Flint cor.* "In the sentence, 'This is the pen which John made,' what word *expresses the object of* MADE?"—*Id.* "'That we fall into *no* sin :' *no* is a definitive or pronominal *adjective*, not compared, and relates to *sin.*"—*D. Blair cor.* "'That *all* our doings may be ordered by thy governance:' *all* is a pronominal adjective, not compared, and relates to *doings.*"—*Id.* "'Let him be made *to* study.' *Why is* the sign *to* ex-pressed before *study*? Because *be made* is passive; and passive verbs do not take the infinitive after them without the preposition *to.*"—*Sanborn cor.* "The following verbs have *both the pre-terit tense and the perfect participle like the present :* viz., Cast, cut, cost, shut, let, bid, shed, hurt, hit, put, &c."—*Buchanan cor.* "The agreement which *any word* has with *an other* in person, *number, gender, or case*, is called CONCORD; and *the* power which one *word* has over *an other*, in respect to ruling its *case*, mood, or *form*, is called GOVERNMENT."—*Bucks cor.* "The word *ticks* tells what the watch *is doing.*"—*Sanborn cor.* "*The* Breve (ˇ) marks a short vowel or syllable, and the *Macron* (¯), a long *one.*"—*Bullions and Lennie cor.* "'Charles, you, by your diligence, make easy work of the task given you by your preceptor.' The first *you* is in the *nominative* case, being the subject of the verb *make.*"—*Kirkham cor.* "*Uoy* in *buoy* is a proper *triphthong ; eau* in *flambeau* is an improper *triphthong.*"—*Sanborn cor.* "'While I of things to come, As past rehears-ing, sing.'—POLLOK. That is, 'While I sing of things to come, as *if I were rehearsing things that are past.*'"—*Kirkham cor.* "A simple sentence *usually* has in it but one nominative, and *but* one *finite* verb."—*Folker cor.* "An irregular verb is *a verb that does not form the preterit* and *the* per-fect participle *by assuming d or ed.*"—*Brown's Inst.* p. 76. "But, when the antecedent is used in a *restricted* sense, a comma is *sometimes* inserted before the relative; as, 'There is no *charm* in the female sex, *which* can supply the place of virtue."—*Murray's Gram.* p. 273. Or: "But, when the antecedent is used in a *restricted* sense, no comma is *usually* inserted before the relative ; as, 'There is in the female sex no *charm which* can supply the place of virtue.'"—*Kirkham cor.* "Two capitals *used* in this way, denote *different words* ; but *one repeated, marks* the plural number: as, L. D. *Legis Doctor* ; LL. D. *Legum Doctor.*"—*Gould cor.* "'Was any person *present besides* the mercer? Yes; his clerk.'"—*Murray cor.* "The word *adjective* comes from the Latin *adjec-tivum* ; and this, from *ad*, to, and *jacio*, I cast."—*Kirkham cor.* "Vision, or *Imagery*, is a figure by *which* the speaker represents the objects of his imagination, as actually before his eyes, and *present to his senses.* Thus Cicero, in his fourth oration against Cataline: 'I seem to myself to behold this city, the ornament of the earth, and the capital of all nations, suddenly involved in one conflagration. I see before me the slaughtered heaps of citizens lying unburied in the midst of their ruined country. The furious countenance of Cethe'gus rises to my view, while with savage joy he is triumphing in your miseries.'"—*Blair cor.* ; also *Murray.* "When *two or more* verbs fol-low the same nominative, *an* auxiliary *that is common to them both or all*, is *usually expressed to the* first, and understood to the rest : as, 'He *has gone* and *left* me ;' that is, 'He *has gone* and *has left* me.'"—*Comly cor.* "When I use the word *pillar* to denote *a column that supports* an edifice, I employ it literally."—*Hiley cor.* "*In poetry*, the conjunction *nor* is often used for *neither* ; as,

'A stately superstructure, that *nor* wind,
Nor wave, nor shock of falling years, could move.'—POLLOK."—*Id.*

UNDER CRITICAL NOTE XII.—OF PERVERSIONS.

[a] "In the beginning God created the *heaven* and the earth."—*Genesis*, i, 1. "Canst thou *by* searching find out *God* ?"—*Job*, xi, 7. "Great *and marvellous are thy works*, Lord *God Almighty* ; just and true are thy ways, thou King of saints."—*Rev.* xv, 3. "*Not* every one that saith unto me, Lord, Lord, shall enter into the kingdom of heaven."—*Matt.* vii, 21. "Though he was rich, yet for *your* sakes he became poor."—*2 Cor.* viii, 9. "Whose foundation was *overthrown* with a flood."—SCOTT'S BIBLE: *Job*, xxii, 16. "Take my yoke upon *you, and learn of me* ;" &c.—*Matt.* xi, 29. "I *go* to prepare a place for you."—*John*, xiv, 2. "*And* you hath he quickened, who *were dead in* trespasses and *sins.*"—*Ephesians*, ii, 1. "Go, flee thee away into the land of Ju-dah."—*Amos*, vii, 12; *Lowth's Gram.* p. 44. Or: "Go, flee away into the land of *Judah.*"—*Hart cor.* "Hitherto shalt thou come, *but* no *further.*"—*Job*, xxxviii, 11. "The day is thine, the *night* also is thine."—*Psal.* lxxiv, 16. "*Tribulation* worketh patience ; and patience, experience ; and experience, hope."—*Romans*, v, 4. "*Then* shall the dust return to *the earth as it was* ; and the *spirit shall return unto* God who gave it."—*Ecclesiastes*, xii, 7. "*At the last* it biteth like a ser-pent, and stingeth like an adder. *Thine eyes shall behold strange women*, and *thine heart shall* utter perverse things : *Yea*, thou *shalt* be *as he that* lieth down in the midst of the sea."—*Prov.* xxiii, 32, 33, 34. "The memory of the just *is* blessed : but the name of the wicked shall rot."—*Prov.* x, 7. "He that is slow *to* anger, is *better* than the mighty ; *and* he that ruleth his spirit, than he that taketh a city."—*Prov.* xvi, 32. "*For whom the Lord loveth* he correcteth ; *even as a* father the son in whom he delighteth."—*Prov.* iii, 12. "The *first-future* tense *is that which ex-presses* what *will* take place hereafter."—*Brown's Inst. of E. Gram.* p. 64. "Teach me to feel another's woe, To hide *the fault* I see."—*Pope's Univ. Prayer.* "Surely thou art one of them ; for thou art a *Galilean.*"—*Mark*, xiv, 70. "Surely thou also art one of them ; for thy speech be-wrayeth thee."—*Matt.* xxvi, 73. "Strait is the gate, and narrow *is* the way, *which leadeth* unto

*"The whole number of verbs in the English language, regular and irregular, simple and compounded, taken together, is about 4300."—Lowth's Gram. p. 59 ; Murray's, Duo., p. 96 ; 8vo, p. 109 ; et al.

life."—*Matt.* vii, 14. "Thou buildest the wall, that thou *mayest* be their king."—*Nehemiah, vi, 6.* "There is forgiveness with thee, that thou mayest be feared."—*Psal.* cxxx, 4. "But yesterday, the word *of Cæsar* might Have stood against the world."—*Beauties of Shakspeare,* p. 200. "The North-east spends *his* rage."—*Thomson's Seasons,* p. 34. "Tells how the drudging *golis* swet."—*Milton's Allegro,* l. 105. "And to his faithful *champion* hath in place Borne witness gloriously."—*Milton's Sam. Agon.* l. 1752. "Then if thou *fall'st,* O Cromwell, Thou *fall'st* a blessed martyr."—*Beauties of Shakspeare,* p. 173. Better: "Then if thou *fall,* O Cromwell! thou *fallst* a blessed martyr."—*K. cor.* "I see the dagger-crest of Mar, I see the *Moray's* silver star, *Wave o'er the* cloud of Saxon war, That up the lake *comes* winding far!"—*Scott's Lady of the Lake,* p. 142. "Each *beast,* each insect, happy in its own."—*Pope, on Man,* Ep. i, l. 185. "And *he that is learning* to arrange *his* sentences with accuracy and order, *is* learning, at the same time, to think with accuracy and order."—*Blair's Lect.* p. 120. "We then, as workers together with *him,* beseech you also that ye receive not the grace of God in vain."—*2 Cor.* vi, 1. "And on the *boundless* of thy goodness calls."—*Young's Last Day,* B. ii, l. 320. "Knowledge dwells In heads replete with thoughts of other men; Wisdom, in minds *attentive* to their own."—*Cowper's Task,* B. vi, l. 99. "O! let me listen to the *words* of life!"—*Thomson's Paraphrase on Matt.* vi. "Save that, from *yonder* ivy-mantled *tower,*" &c.—*Gray's Elegy,* l. 9. "*Weighs* the men's wits against the *Lady's hair.*"—*Pope's Rape of the Lock,* Canto v, l. 72. "*Till* the publication of *Dr. Lowth's small Introduction,* the grammatical study of our language formed no part of the ordinary method of instruction."—*Hiley's Preface,* p. vi. "Let there be no strife, *I pray thee, between* me and thee." —*Gen.* xiii, 8.

> "What! canst thou not *forbear* me half an hour?"—*Shakspeare.*
> "Till then who knew the force of those dire *arms?*"—*Milton.*
> "In words, as fashions, the *same* rule will hold;
> Alike fantastic, if too new or old:
> Be not the first by whom the new *are* tried
> Nor yet the last to lay the old aside."—*Pope, on Criticism,* l. 333.

UNDER CRITICAL NOTE XIII.—OF AWKWARDNESS.

"They slew Varus, *whom* I mentioned before."—*Murray cor.* "Maria rejected Valerius, *whom* she had rejected before." Or: "Maria rejected Valerius *a second time.*"—*Id.* "In the English *language,* nouns *have* but two different terminations for cases."—*Churchill's Gram.* p. 64. "Socrates and Plato were *the wisest men, and* the most eminent philosophers in Greece."—*Buchanan's Gram.,* Pref., p. viii. "Whether more than one were concerned in the business, does not yet appear." Or: "*How many* were concerned in the business, does not yet appear."—*Murray cor.* "And that, consequently, the verb *or* pronoun agreeing with it, can never with propriety be used in the plural number."—*Id. et al. cor.* "A second help may be, *frequent* and *free converse* with *others* of your own sex who are like minded."—*Wesley cor.* "Four of the *semivowels,* namely, *l, m, n,* and *r,* are *termed* LIQUIDS, *on account of the fluency* of their sounds."—See *Brown's Inst.* p. 16. "Some conjunctions *are used in pairs,* so that *one* answers to *an other, as its regular* correspondent."—*Lowth et al. cor.* "The mutes are those consonants whose sounds cannot be protracted; the *semivowels have imperfect* sounds *of their own,* which can be continued at pleasure."—*Murray et al. cor.* "HE *and* SHE *are* sometimes used as *nouns,* and, *as such,* are regularly declined: as, 'The *hes* in birds.'—BACON. 'The *shes* of Italy.'—SHAK."—*Churchill cor.* "The separation of a preposition from the *word* which it governs, is [censured by some writers, as being] improper."—*C. Adams cor.* "The word WHOSE, *according to some critics, should* be restricted to persons; but good writers *still occasionally* use it *with reference to* things."—*Priestley et al. cor.* "New and surpassing wonders present themselves to our *view.*"—*Sherlock cor.* "The degrees of comparison are often *inaccurately* applied and construed."—*Alger's Murray.* Or: "*Passages* are often found in which the degrees of comparison *have not an accurate construction.*"—*Campbell cor.;* also Murray. "The *sign of expression* is placed too *far from the name,* to *form a construction that is* either perspicuous or agreeable."—*Murray cor.* "*The simple tenses* are those which are formed *by* the principal verb without an auxiliary."—*Id.* "The *more intimate* men are, the more *they affect one an other's happiness.*" —*Id.* "This is the machine that he *invented.*"—*Nixon cor.* "To give this sentence the interrogative form, *we must express* it thus." Or: "This sentence, *to have* the interrogative form, should be expressed thus."—*Murray cor.* "Never employ words *that are* susceptible of a sense different from *that which* you intend to convey."—*Hiley cor.* "Sixty pages are occupied in explaining what, according to the ordinary method, would not require more than ten or twelve."— *Id.* "The participle in *ing* always expresses action, suffering, or being, as continuing, *or in progress.*"—*Bullions cor.* "The *first* participle of all active verbs, has *usually* an active signification; as, 'James is *building* the house.' Often, however, it *takes* a passive *meaning*; as, '*The house is building.*'"—*Id.* "*Previously* to parsing this sentence, the young pupil may be *taught to analyze* it, by such questions as the following: viz."—*Id.* "*Since* that period, however, attention has been paid to this important subject."—*Id. and Hiley cor.* "A definition of a word is *a brief* explanation *of* what *it means.*"—G. BROWN: *Hiley cor.*

UNDER CRITICAL NOTE XIV.—OF IGNORANCE.

"What is *a verb?* It is *a word* which signifies *to be, to act,* or *to be acted upon.*" Or thus: "What is an *assertor?* Ans. 'One who affirms positively; an affirmer, supporter, or vindicator'" —WEBSTER's DICT.—*Peirce cor.* "Virgil wrote the *Æneid.*"—*Kirkham cor.* "Which, to a supercilious or inconsiderate *native of Japan,* would seem very idle and impertinent."—*Locke cor.* "Will not a look of disdain cast upon you throw you into a *ferment?*"—*Say cor.* "Though only the conjunction *if is here set before* the verb, there are several others, (as *that, though, lest, unless, except,*) which may be *used with* the subjunctive mood."—*Murray cor.* "When proper names have an article *before* them, they are used as common names."—*Id. et al. cor.* "When a proper noun has an article *before* it, it is used as a common noun."—*Merchant cor.* "Seeming to *rob* the death-field of its terrors."—*Id.* "For the same reason, we might, without any *detriment* to the language, dispense with the terminations of our verbs in the singular."—*Kirkham cor.* "It *removes* all possibility of being misunderstood."—*Abbott cor.* "Approximation to *perfection* is all that we can expect."—*Id.* "I have often joined in singing with *musicians* at Norwich."—*Gardiner cor.* "When not standing in regular *prosaic* order." Or:—"in *the* regular order *of prose.*"—*Peirce cor.* "*Regardless* of the dogmas and edicts of the philosophical umpire."—*Kirkham cor.* "Others begin to talk before their mouths are open, *prefixing* the mouth-closing M to most of their words; as, ' *M-yes*,' for ' *Yes.*' "—*Gardiner cor.* "That noted close of his ' *esse videatur*,' exposed him to censure among his *contemporaries.*"—*Blair cor.* "A man's *own is* what he *has, or possesses by right ; the word own* being a past participle of *the* verb *to owe*, which formerly signified *to have* or *possess.*"—*Kirkham cor.* "As requires so ; expressing a comparison of *manner : as, 'As* one dieth, *so* dieth the other.' "—*Mur. et al. cor.* "To obey our parents, *is an obvious* duty."—*Parker and Fox cor.* "Almost all the political papers of the kingdom have touched upon these things."—*Wright cor.* "I shall take *the liberty* to make a few observations on the subject."—*Hiley cor.* "His loss I have endeavoured to supply, *so* far as *by* additional vigilance and industry *I could.*"—*Id.* "That they should make vegetation so *exuberant* as to anticipate every want."—*Frazee cor.* "The *guillemets,* or *quotation points,* [" "] denote that one or more words are extracted from an other author."—*P. E. Day cor.* "*Nineveh, the capital of* Assyria, *was* one of the most noted cities of ancient *times.*"—*Id.* "It may, however, be rendered definite by *the mention of* some *particular* time; as, yesterday, last week, &c."—*Bullions cor.* "The last is called heroic measure, and is the same that is used by Milton, Young, Thomson, Pollok, &c."—*Id.* "*Perennial* ones must be sought in the delightful regions above."—*Hallock cor.* "Intransitive verbs are those which are *inseparable* from the effect produced." Or better: "Intransitive verbs are those which *express action without governing an object.*"—*Cutler cor.* "*The Feminine* gender belongs to women, and animals of the female kind."—*Id.* "Wo unto you, scribes and *Pharisees,* hypocrites !"—*ALGER'S BIBLE: Luke,* xi, 44. "A *pyrrhic,* which has both its syllables short."—*Day cor.* "What kind of *jessamine ?* A *jessamine* in flower, or a flowery *jessamine.*"—*Barrett cor.* "LANGUAGE, *a word* derived from LINGUA, the tongue, *now signifies, any series of sounds or letters formed into words, and used for the expression of thought.*"—*Id.* See the *Gram. of E. Gram.* p. 132. "Say '*none,*' not '*ne'er a one.*' "—*Staniford cor.* " ' *E'er a one,*' [is sometimes used for '*any* '] or ' *either.*' "—*Pond cor.*

"Earth loses thy *pattern* for ever and aye ;
O sailor-boy ! sailor-boy ! peace to thy soul."—*Dymond.*
"His brow was sad ; his eye beneath
Flashed like a *falchion* from its sheath."—*Longfellow's Ballads,* p. 129.

☞[The examples exhibited for exercises under Critical Notes 15th and 16th, being judged either incapable of correction, or unworthy of the endeavour, are submitted to the criticism of the reader, without any attempt to amend them, or to offer substitutes in this place.]

PROMISCUOUS CORRECTIONS OF FALSE SYNTAX.

LESSON I.—UNDER VARIOUS RULES.

"*Why is* our language less *refined* than that of Italy, Spain, or France ? "—*Murray cor.* "*Why is* our language less refined than *the French ?*"—*Ingersoll cor.* "I believe your Lordship will agree with me, in the reason why our language is less refined than *that* of Italy, Spain, or France."—*Swift cor.* "Even in this short sentence, ' why our language is less refined than *those* of Italy, Spain, or France,' we may discern an inaccuracy ; the *pronominal adjective* ' *those* ' is made plural, when the substantive to which it refers, or the thing for which it stands, ' the *language* of Italy, Spain, or France,' is singular."—*Blair cor.* "The sentence *would* have run much better in this way :—' why our language is less refined, than the Italian, *the* Spanish, or *the* French.' "—*Id.* "But when arranged in an entire sentence, *as* they must be to make a complete sense, they show it still more evidently."—*Murray cor.* "This is a more artificial and refined construction, than that in which the common connective is simply *used.*"—*Id.* "I shall present *to* the reader a list of *certain* prepositions, *or prefixes,* which are derived from the Latin and Greek languages."—*Id.* "*A relative sometimes comprehends* the meaning of a *personal* pronoun and a copulative conjunction."—*Id.* "Personal pronouns, being used to supply the *places* of *nouns,* are not *often* employed in the same *clauses with the* nouns which they represent."—*Id. and Smith cor.* "There is very seldom any occasion for a substitute where the principal word is present."—*Mur. cor.* "We hardly consider little children as persons, because the term *person* gives us the idea of reason, *or intelligence.*"—*Priestley et al. cor.* "The *occasions for* exerting these *two* qualities *are* different."—*Blair et al. cor.* "I'll tell you *with whom* time ambles withal, *with whom* time trots withal, *with whom* time gallops withal, and *with whom* he stands still withal. I pray thee, *with whom* doth he trot withal ?"—*Buchanan's Gram.* p. 122. "By greatness, I mean, *not* the bulk of any single object *only,* but the largeness of a whole view."—*Addison cor.* "The question may then be put, What *more* does he than mean ?"—*Blair cor.* "The question might be put, What *more* does he than mean ?"—*Id.* "He is surprised to find himself at so great a distance from the object with which he *set* out."—*Id.* ; also *Murray cor.* "Few rules can be given which will hold *good* in all cases."—*Lowth and Mur. cor.* "Versification is the arrangement *of words into metrical lines* according to the laws *of verse.*"—*Johnson cor.* "Versification is the arrangement *of words into rhythmical lines of some particular length, so as to produce harmony by the regular alternation of syllables differing in quantity.*"—*Murray et al. cor.* "*Amelia's* friend Charlotte, to whom no one imputed blame, was too prompt in her own vindication."—*Murray cor.* "Mr. Pitt's joining *of the* war party in 1793, the most striking and the most fatal instance of this offence, is the one which at once presents itself."—*Brougham cor.* "To the framing *of* such a sound constitution of mind."—*Lady cor.* " ' I beseech you,' said St. Paul to his Ephesian converts, ' that ye walk worthy *of* the vocation wherewith ye are called.' "—*See Eph.*

iv, 1. "So as to prevent it from being equal to that."—*Booth cor.* "When speaking of an action as being performed." Or: "When speaking of the performance of an action."—*Id.* "And, in all questions of actions being so performed, est is added for the second person.'—*Id.* "No account can be given of this, but that custom has blinded their eyes." Or: "No other account can be given of this, than that custom has blinded their eyes."—*Dymond cor.*

"Design, or chance, makes others wive;
But nature did this match contrive."—*Waller cor.*

LESSON II.—UNDER VARIOUS RULES.

"I suppose each of you thinks it is his own nail."—*Abbott cor.* "They are useless, because they are apparently based upon this supposition."—*Id.* "The form, or manner, in which this plan may be adopted, is various."—*Id.* "The making of intellectual effort, and the acquiring of knowledge, are always pleasant to the human mind."—*Id.* "This will do more than the best lecture that ever was delivered."—*Id.* "The doing of easy things is generally dull work."—*Id.* "Such as the tone and manner of some teachers."—*Id.* "Well, the fault is, that some one was disorderly at prayer time."—*Id.* "Do you remember to have spoken on this subject in school?"—*Id.* "The course above recommended, is not the trying of lax and inefficient measures."—*Id.* "Our community agree that there is a God."—*Id.* "It prevents them from being interested in what is said." —*Id.* "We will also suppose that I call an other boy to me, whom I have reason to believe to be a sincere Christian."—*Id.* "Five minutes' notice is given by the bell."—*Id.* "The Annals of Education give notice of it." Or: "The work entitled 'Annals of Education' gives notice of it."—*Id.* "Teachers' meetings will be interesting and useful."—*Id.* "She thought a half hour's study would conquer all the difficulties."—*Id.* "The difference between an honest and a hypocritical confession."—*Id.* "There is no point of attainment at which we must stop."—*Id.* "Now six hours' service is as much as is expected of teachers."—*Id.* "How many are seven times nine?" —*Id.* "Then the reckoning proceeds till it comes to ten hundred."—*Frost cor.* "Your success will depend on your own exertions; see, then, that you be diligent."—*Id.* "Subjunctive Mood, Present Tense: If I be known, If thou be known, If he be known; " &c.—*Id.* "If I be loved, If thou be loved, If he be loved;" &c.—*Fr. right.* "An Interjection is a word used to express sudden emotion. Interjections are so called because they are generally thrown in between the parts of discourse, without any reference to the structure of those parts."—*Frost cor.* "The Cardinal numbers are those which simply tell how many; as, one, two, three."—*Id.* "More than one organ are concerned in the utterance of almost every consonant." Or thus: "More organs than one are concerned in the utterance of almost any consonant."—*Id.* "To extract from them all the terms which we use in our divisions and subdivisions of the art."—*Holmes cor.* "And there were written therein lamentations, and mourning, and woe."—*Bible cor.* "If I were to be judged as to my behaviour, compared with that of John."—*Whiston's Jos. cor.* "The preposition to, signifying in order to, was anciently preceded by for; as, ' What went ye out for to see?' "—*Murray's Gram.* p. 184. "This makes the proper perfect tense, which, in English, is always expressed by the auxiliary verb have; as, ' I have written.' "—*Dr. Blair cor.* "Indeed, in the formation of character, personal exertion is the first, the second, and the third virtue."—*Sanders cor.* "The reducing of them to the condition of the beasts that perish."—*Dymond cor.* "Yet this affords no reason to deny that the nature of the gift is the same, or that both are divine." Or: "Yet this affords no reason to aver that the nature of the gift is not the same, or that both are not divine."—*Id.* "If God has made known his will."—*Id.* "If Christ has prohibited them, nothing else can prove them right."—*Id.* "That the taking of them is wrong, every man who simply consults his own heart, will know."—*Id.* "From these evils the world would be spared, if one did not write."—*Id.* "It is in a great degree our own fault."—*Id.* "It is worthy of observation, that lesson-learning is nearly excluded."—*Id.* "Who spares the aggressor's life even to the endangering of his own." —*Id.* "Who advocates the taking of the life of an aggressor."—*Id.* "And thence up to the intentionally and voluntarily fraudulent."—*Id.* "And the contention was so sharp between them, that they departed asunder one from the other."—*Scott's, Friends', Alger's, Bruce's Bible, and Others: Acts,* xv, 39. "Here the man is John, and John is the man; so the words are imagination and fancy; but the imagination and the fancy are not words: they are intellectual powers." —*Rev. M. Harrison cor.* "The article, which is here so emphatic in the Greek, is quite forgotten in our translation."—*Id.* "We have no fewer than twenty-four pronouns."—*Id.* "It will admit of a pronoun joined to it."—*Id.* "From intercourse and from conquest, all the languages of Europe participate one with an other."—*Id.* "It is not always necessity, therefore, that has been the cause of our introducing of terms derived from the classical languages."—*Id.* "The man of genius stamps upon it any impression that pleases him." Or:—"any impression that chooses." —*Id.* "The proportion of names ending in son preponderates greatly among the Dane-Saxon population of the North."—*Id.* "As a proof of the strong similarity between the English language and the Danish."—*Id.* "A century from the time when (or at which) Hengist and Horsa landed on the Isle of Thanet."—*Id.*

"I saw the colours waving in the wind,
And them within, to mischief how combin'd."—*Bunyan cor.*

LESSON III.—UNDER VARIOUS RULES.

"A ship excepted: of which we say, 'She sails well.' "—*Jonson cor.* "Honesty is reckoned of little worth."—*Lily cor.* "Learn to esteem life as you ought."—*Dodsley cor.* "As the soundest health is less perceived than the lightest malady, so the highest joy toucheth us less sensibly than the smallest sorrow."—*Id.* "Youth is no apology for frivolousness."—*Whiting cor.* "The porch was of the same width as the temple "—*Milman cor.* "The other tribes contributed neither to his rise nor to his downfall."—*Id.* "His whole religion, with all its laws, would have been shaken to its foundation."—*Id.* "The English has most commonly been neglected, and children have been taught only in the Latin syntax."—*J. Ward* cor.   "They are not *noticed* in the notes."—*Id.* "He walks in righteousness, doing what he would *have others do to him*."—*Fisher* cor.   "They stand *independent* of the rest of the sentence."—*Ingersoll* cor.   "My uncle *and* his son were in town yesterday."—*Lennie* cor.   "She *and* her sisters are well."—*Id.*   " His purse, with its contents, *was* abstracted from his pocket."—*Id.*   " The great constitutional feature of this institution being, that directly *after* the acrimony of the last election is over, the acrimony of the next begins."—*Dickens* cor.   "His disregarding *of* his parents' advice has brought him into disgrace." —*Farnum* cor.   "Can you tell me *why* his father *made* that remark ?"—*Id.*   "*Why does* our teacher *detain* us so long ?"—*Id.*   "I am certain *that* the boy said so."—*Id.*   "WHICH means any thing or things before named; and THAT may represent any person or persons, thing or things, *that* have been speaking, spoken to, or spoken of."—*Perley* cor.   "A certain number of syllables *occurring in a particular order,* form a foot.   *Poetic feet* are so called, because it is by their aid that the voice, as it were, steps along."—*Mur. et al.* cor.   "*Questions asked by* a principal verb *only*—as, ' Teach I ? ' ' Burns he ? ' &c.,—are *archaisms,* and now *peculiar to the poets*."—*A. Mur.* cor.   "Tell whether the 18th, *the* 19th, *the* 20th, *the* 21st, *the* 22d, or *the* 23d *rule is* to be used, and repeat the rule."—*Parker and Fox* cor.   " The resolution was adopted without much deliberation, *and consequently* caused great dissatisfaction."   Or : " The resolution, *which* caused great dissatisfaction, was adopted without much deliberation."—*Iid.*   " The man is now much *noticed* by the people thereabouts."—*Webb's Gram.* cor.   " The sand prevents *them from* sticking to one an other."—*Id.*   " Defective verbs are those which are used only in some of *the* moods and tenses." —*Greenleaf's Gram.* p. 29; *Ingersoll's,* 121; *Smith's,* 90; *Merchant's,* 64; *Nutting's,* 68.   " Defective verbs are those which want some of *the* moods or tenses."—*Lennie et al.* cor.   " Defective verbs want some of *the* parts *common to other verbs*."—*Bullions* cor.   "A Defective verb is one that wants some of *the* parts *common to verbs*."—*Id.*   "To the irregular verbs *may* be added the defective ; which are not only irregular, but also wanting in some parts."—*Lowth* cor.   "To the irregular verbs *may* be added the defective ; which are not only wanting in some parts, but are, when inflected, irregular."—*Churchill* cor.   "When two or more nouns *occur together* in the possessive case."—*Farnum* cor.   "When several short sentences *come together*."—*Id.*   "Words are divided into ten classes, called Parts of Speech."—*L. Ainsworth* cor.   "A passive verb has its agent or doer always in the objective case, governed by a preposition."—*Id.*   "I am surprised at your *inattention*."—*Id.*   "SINGULAR: Thou lovest, *not* You love.   *You* has always a plural verb." —*Bullions* cor.   "How do you know that love is *of* the first person ?   Ans.   Because *we, the pronoun,* is *of* the first person."—*Id. and Lennie* cor.   " The lowing herd *winds* slowly o'er the lea."— *Gray's Elegy,* l. 2.   "Iambic verses have *their* second, fourth, and other even syllables accented." —*Bullions* cor.   "Contractions *that* are not allowable in prose, are often made in poetry."—*Id.* "Yet to their general's voice they *soon obey'd.*"—*Milton.*   "It never presents to his mind *more than* one new subject at the same time."—*Felton* cor.   "An *abstract noun* is the name of some particular quality considered apart from its substance."—*Brown's Inst. of E. Gram.* p. 32.   "*A noun* is of the first person when it denotes the speaker."—*Felton* cor.   "Which of the two brothers *is a graduate ?*"—*Hallock* cor.   "I am a linen-draper bold, As all the world doth know."—*Cowper.* "*Oh the pain, the bliss* of dying!"—*Pope.*   "This do ; take *to* you censers, *thou, Korah,* and all *thy* company."—*Bible* cor.   " There are *three* participles ; the *imperfect, the perfect,* and *the preperfect* : as, reading, read, having read.   Transitive verbs have an *active and passive* participle : that is, their form for the perfect is sometimes active, and sometimes passive ; as, *read,* or *loved.*"—*Greene* cor.

"O Heav'n, in my connubial hour decree
My *spouse this man,* or such a *man* as he."—*Pope* cor.

LESSON IV.—UNDER VARIOUS RULES.

"The past tenses (of Hiley's subjunctive mood) represent conditional past *facts* or *events,* of which the speaker is uncertain."—*Hiley* cor.   "Care also should be taken that they *be* not introduced too abundantly."—*Id.*   "Till they *have* become familiar to the mind."   Or : "Till they *become* familiar to the mind."—*Id.*   "When once a particular arrangement and phraseology *have* become familiar to the mind."—*Id.*   "I have furnished the student with the plainest and most practical directions *that* I could devise."—*Id.*   "When you are conversant with the Rules of Grammar, you will be qualified to commence the study of Style."—*Id.*   "*C before e, i, or y, always* has a soft sound, like *s.*"—*L. Murray* cor.   "*G* before *e, i, or y,* is *generally* soft; as in *genius, ginger, Egypt.*"—*Id.*   "*C* before *e, i, or y, always* sounds soft, like *s.*"—*Hiley* cor.   "*G* is *generally* soft before *e, i, or y ;* as in *genius, ginger, Egypt.*"—*Id.*   "A perfect alphabet must always contain *just* as many letters as *there* are elementary sounds in the language: the English alphabet, *having fewer letters than sounds,* and sometimes more than one letter for the same sound, is both defective and redundant."—*Id.*   "A common *noun is a name* given to a whole class or species, and *is* applicable to every individual of that class."—*Id.*   "Thus an adjective has *usually* a noun either expressed or understood."—*Id.*   "Emphasis is *extraordinary force used in the enunciation of such words as we wish to make prominent in discourse*."   Or : "Emphasis is a *peculiar stress of voice, used in the utterance of words specially significant.*"—*Blair* cor. ; also *L. Murray.*   "So simple a question as, ' Do you ride to town to-day ? ' is capable of *as many as* four different acceptations, *the sense varying* as the emphasis is differently placed."—*Iid.*   "Thus, *bravely, for* ' in a brave manner,' is derived from *brave-like.*"—*Hiley* cor.   "In *this* manner, *several different* parts of speech are *often* formed from *one root* by means of *different affixes.*"—*Id.*   "Words derived from *the same root,* are always more or less allied in signification."—*Id.*   "When a noun of multitude *conveys the idea of unity,* the verb and pronoun should be singular; but when it conveys *the idea of plurality,* the verb and pronoun must be plural."—*Id.*   "They have spent their whole time to make the sacred chronology agree with the profane."—*Id.*   "I have studied my lesson, but you have not *looked at yours.*"—*Id.*   "When words *are connected* in pairs, there is *usually* a comma *after* each pair."—*Hiley, Bullions, and Lennie* cor.   "When words *are connected* in pairs, the pairs should be marked by the comma."—*Farnum cor.*   "His *book entitled, 'Studies of Nature,'* is deservedly a popular work."—*Biog. Dict.*

"Here *rests* his head *upon the lap of earth,*
A youth to Fortune and to Fame unknown."—GRAY.

" '*Youth,*' here, is in the *nominative case,* (the verb '*rests*' being, in this instance, *transitive,*) and is *the subject of the sentence.* The meaning is, '*A youth here rests his head,*' &c."—*Hart cor.*   "The pronoun *I, as well as* the interjection *O,* should be written with a capital."   Or :   "The pronoun *I, and* the interjection *O,* should be written with *capitals.*"—*Weld cor.*   "The pronoun *I* should *always* be written with a capital."—*Id.*   "He went from *London* to York."—*Id.*   "An adverb is a *word added to a verb, a participle, an adjective, or an other adverb,* to modify *its* meaning."—*Id.* (See Lesson 1st under the General Rule.)   "SINGULAR signifies, '*expressing only one* ; ' *denoting but* one person or thing. PLURAL, (Latin, *pluralis,* from *plus,* more,) signifies, '*expressing* more than one.' "—*Weld cor.*   "When the present ends in *e, d* only is added to form the imperfect *tense* and the perfect participle of regular verbs."—*Id.*   "Synæresis is the contraction of two syllables into one; as, *seest* for *seest, drowned* for *drown-ed.*"—*Id.* (See *Brown's Inst.* p. 230.)   "Words ending in *ee* are often *inflected by mere consonants, and without* receiving an additional syllable beginning with *e* : as, *see, seest. sees* ; *agree, agreed, agrees.*"—*Weld cor.*   "In monosyllables, final *f, l,* or *s,* preceded by a single vowel, *is* doubled ; as in *staff, mill, grass.*"—*Id.*   "Before *ing,* words ending in *ie* drop the *e,* and *change the i into y* ; as, *die, dying.*"—*Id.*   "One number may be used for the other—*er,* rather, the plural may be used for the singular* ; as, *we* for *I, you* for *thou.*"—*Greene cor.*   "STROBILE, *n.* A pericarp made up of scales that lie *one over an other.*"—*Worcester cor.*

"Yet ever, from the clearest source, *hath run*
Some gross allay, some tincture of the man."—*Lowth cor.*

LESSON V.—UNDER VARIOUS RULES.

"The possessive case is *usually* followed by *a* noun, *expressed or understood,* which is the *name* of the thing possessed."—*Felton cor.*   "Hadmer of Aggstein was as pious, devout, and praying a Christian, as *was* Nelson, Washington, or Jefferson; or as *is* Wellington, Tyler, Clay, or Polk."—*H. C. Wright cor.*   "A word in the possessive case is not an independent noun, and cannot stand by *itself.*"—*J. W. Wright cor.*   "Mary is not handsome, but she is good-natured, *and good-nature* is better than beauty."—*St. Quentin cor.*   "After the practice of joining *all* words together had ceased, *a note* of distinction *was placed* at the end of every word."—*Mur. et al. cor.*   "Neither Henry nor Charles *dissipates* his time."—*Hallock cor.*   "He had taken from the *Christians above* thirty small castles.' KNOLLES :"—*Brown's Institutes,* p. 200; *Johnson's Quarto Dict. w. What.* "In *what* character Butler was admitted, is unknown."   Or : "In *whatever* character Butler was admitted, *that character* is unknown."—*Hallock cor.*   "How *are* the agent of a passive and the object of an active verb often left ?"—*Id.*   "By SUBJECT, is meant the word of *whose object* something is declared."   Or : "By SUBJECT, is meant the word *which has* something declared of *the thing signified.*"—*Chandler cor.*   "Care should also be taken that a *transitive* verb *be* not used *in stead* of a *neuter or intransitive* ; as, *lay* for *lie, raise* for *rise, set* for *sit,* &c."—*Id.*   "On *them depends* the duration of our Constitution and our country."—*Calhoun cor.*   "In the present sentence, neither the sense nor the measure *requires* WHAT."—*Chandler cor.*   "The Irish thought themselves oppressed by the *law* that forbid them to draw with their *horses' tails.*"—*Brightland cor.*   "*So and willingly* are adverbs.   So is an adverb of *degree,* and qualifies *willingly. Willingly* is an adverb of *manner,* and qualifies *deceives.*"—*Cutler cor.*   "Epicurus, for *experiment's* sake, confined himself to a narrower diet than that of the severest prisons."—*Id.*   "Derivative words are such as are *formed from other* words *by prefixes or suffixes* ; as, *injustice, goodness, falsehood.*"—*Id.*   "The distinction here insisted on is as old as Aristotle, and should not be lost *from* sight." Or :—" and *it* should *still* be *kept in view.*"—*Hart cor.*   "The Tenses of the Subjunctive and Potential Moods."   Or : "The Tenses of the Subjunctive and the Potential Mood."—*Id.*   "A triphthong is a union of three vowels, uttered *by a single impulse of the voice* ; as, *uoy* in *buoy.*"—*Davis cor.*   "A common noun *is* the *name* of a species or kind."—*Id.*   "The superlative degree *implies* a comparison *either* between *two* or among* more."—*Id.*   "An adverb is a word serving to give an additional idea *to* a verb, *a participle,* an adjective, or *an other* adverb."—*Id.*   When several nouns in the possessive case *occur in succession,* each showing possession *of things* of the same *sort,* it is *generally* necessary to add the sign of the possessive to *each of them* ; as, 'He sells *men's, women's,* and children's shoes.'—*Dogs', cats',* and *tigers'* feet are digitated.' "—*Id.* " 'A *rail-road is being made,*' should be, 'A *railroad is making* ; ' 'A *school-house is being built,*' should be, 'A *school-house is building.*' "—*Id.*   "Auxiliaries *are* of themselves verbs ; *yet* they resemble, in their character and use, those terminational or other inflections *which,* in other languages, *serve* to express the action in the mood, tense, *person,* and *number* desired."—*Id.* "Please *to* hold my horse while I speak to my friend."—*Id.*   "If I say, 'Give me *the* book,' I *demand* some particular book."—*Butler cor.*   "Here are five men."—*Id.*   "*After* the active *verb,* the object may be omitted ; *after* the passive, the name of the agent may be *omitted.*"—*Id.*   "The Progressive and Emphatic forms give, in each case, a different shade of meaning to the verb."—*Hart cor.*   "THAT *may be called* a Redditive Conjunction, when it answers to so or SUCH."—*Ward cor.*   "He attributes to negligence your *want of success* in that business."—*Smart cor.,* "Do WILL and GO express but one action ?"   Or : "Does *' will go* ' express but *one* action ?"—*Barrett cor.*   "Language is the *principal* vehicle of thought."—*G. Brown's Inst., Pref.,* p. iii.   "*Much* is applied to things weighed or measured ; *many,* to those that are numbered.   *Elder* and *eldest* are *applied* to persons only ; *older* and *oldest,* to *either* persons *or* things."—*Bullions cor.*   "If there are any old maids still extant, while *mysogynists* are so rare, the fault must be attributable to themselves."—*Kirkham cor.*   "The second method, used by the Greeks, has never been the practice of any *other people* of Europe."—*Sheridan cor.*   "Neither consonant nor vowel *is* to be dwelt upon beyond *its* common quantity, when *it closes* a sentence."   Or : "Neither *consonants* nor *vowels* are to be dwelt upon beyond their common quantity, when they close a sentence."   Or, better thus : "Neither *a* consonant nor *a* vowel, when *it closes* a sentence, to be *protracted* beyond *its usual length*."—*Id*. " Irony is a mode of speech, in which what is said, the opposite of what is meant."—*McElligott's Manual*, p. 103. " The *person speaking, and the person or persons* spoken to, are supposed to be present."—*Wells cor*.; also *Murray*. "A *Noun a name*, a word used to express the *idea* of an object."—*Wells cor*. "A syllable is *such* a word, *a part* of a word, as is uttered by one articulation."—*Weld cor*.

"Thus wond'rous fair ; thyself how wond'rous then !
Unspeakable, who *sitst* above these heavens."—*Milton*, B. v, l. 156.
"And feel thy *sovran* vital lamp ; but thou
Revisitst not these eyes, that roll in vain."—*Id*. iii, 22.
" Before all temples *th'* upright *heart* and pure."—*Id*. i, 18.
" In forest wild, in thicket, *brake*, or den."—*Id*. vii, 458.
" The rogue and fool by fits *are* fair and wise ;
And e'en the best, by fits, what they despise."—*Pope cor*.

THE KEY.—PART IV.—PROSODY.

CHAPTER I.—PUNCTUATION.

SECTION I.—THE COMMA.

CORRECTIONS UNDER RULE I.—OF SIMPLE SENTENCES.

"*A* short simple *sentence* should *rarely* be *divided* by *the* comma."—*Felton cor*. "A regular nd virtuous education is an inestimable blessing."—*Mur. cor*. " Such equivocal expressions mark an intention to deceive."—*Id*. "They are *this* and *that*, with their plurals *these* and *those*."—*Bullions cor*. "A nominative and a verb sometimes make a complete sentence ; as, He sleeps."—*Felton cor*. "TENSE expresses the action *as* connected with certain relations of time ; MOOD represents it as *further* modified by circumstances of contingency, conditionality, &c."—*Bullions or*. " The word *noun* means *name*."—*Ingersoll cor*. " The present or active participle I explained hen."—*Id*. "Are some verbs used both transitively and intransitively ?"—*Cooper cor*. " Blank erse is verse without rhyme."—*Brown's Institutes*, p. 235. "A distributive adjective denotes each ne of a number considered separately."—*Hallock cor*.
"And may at last my weary age
Find out the peaceful hermitage."—MILTON: *Ward's Gr*. 158 ; *Hiley's*, 124.

UNDER THE EXCEPTION CONCERNING SIMPLE SENTENCES.

"A noun without an *article* to limit it, is taken in its widest sense."—*Lennie*, p. 6. " To main-in a steady course amid all the adversities of life, marks a great mind."—*Day cor*. " To love ur Maker supremely and our neighbour as ourselves, comprehends the whole moral law."—*Id*. To be afraid to do wrong, is true courage."—*Id*. "A great fortune in the hands of a fool, is a reat misfortune."—*Bullions cor*. " That he should make such a remark, is indeed strange."—*arnum cor*. " To walk in the fields and groves, is delightful."—*Id*. " That he committed the ult, is most certain."—*Id*. " Names common to all things of the same sort or class, are called *common nouns* ; as, man, woman, day."—*Bullions cor*. " That it is our duty to be pious, admits ot of any doubt."—*Id*. " To endure misfortune with resignation, is the characteristic of a great ind."—*Id*. " The assisting of a friend in such circumstances, was certainly a duty."—*Id*. That a life of virtue is the safest, is certain."—*Hallock cor*. "A collective noun denoting the lea of unity, should be represented by a pronoun of the singular number."—*Id*.

UNDER RULE II.—OF SIMPLE MEMBERS.

" When the sun had arisen, the enemy retreated."—*Day cor*. " If he *become* rich, he may be as industrious."—*Bullions cor*. " The more I study grammar, the better I like it."—*Id*. " There much truth in the old adage, that fire is a better servant than master."—*Id*. " The verb *do*, hen used as an auxiliary, gives force or emphasis to the expression."—*P. E. Day cor*. " What-ever it is incumbent upon a man to do, it is surely expedient to do well."—*Adams cor*. " The ul, which our philosophy divides into various capacities, is still one essence."—*Channing cor*. Put the following words in the plural, and give the rule for forming it."—*Bullions cor*. " We ill do it, if you wish."—*Id*. " He who does well, will be rewarded."—*Id*. " That which is lways true, is expressed in the present tense."—*Id*. "An observation which is always true, ust be expressed in the present tense."—*Id*. " That part of orthography which treats of com-ining letters to form syllables and words, is called SPELLING."—*Day cor*. "A noun can never e of the first person, except it is in apposition with a pronoun of that person."—*Id*. " When wo or more singular nouns or pronouns refer to the same object, they require a singular verb ad pronoun."—*Id*. "James has gone, but he will return in a few days."—*Id*. "A pronoun iould have the same person, number, and gender, as the noun for which it stands."—*Id*. Though he is out of danger, he is still afraid."—*Bullions cor*. " She is his inferior in sense, but is equal in prudence."—*Murray's Exercises*, p. 6. " The man who has no sense of religion, is ttle to be trusted."—*Bullions cor*. " He who does the most good, has the most pleasure."—*Id*. They were not in the most prosperous circumstances, when we last saw them."—*Id*. " If the ay continue pleasant, I shall return."—*Felton cor*. " The days that are past, are gone forever."—*Id*. " As many as are friendly to the cause, will sustain it."—*Id*. " Such as desire aid, will ceive it."—*Id*. " Who gave you that book, which you prize so much ?"—*Bullions cor*. " He ho made it, now preserves and governs it."—*Id*.
" Shall he alone, whom rational we call,
Be pleas'd with nothing, if not *blest* with all ?"—*Pope*.

UNDER THE EXCEPTIONS CONCERNING SIMPLE MEMBERS.

"Newcastle is the town in which Akenside was born."—*Bucke cor.* "The remorse which issues in reformation, is true repentance."—*Campbell cor.* "Men who are intemperate, are destructive members of community."—*Alexander cor.* "An active-transitive verb expresses an action which extends to an object."—*Felton cor.* "They to whom much is given, will have much to answer for."—*Murray cor.* "The prospect which we have, is charming."—*Cooper cor.* "He is the person who informed me of the matter."—*Id.* "These are the trees that produce no fruit."—*Id.* "This is the book which treats of the subject."—*Id.* "The proposal was such as pleased me."—*Id.* "Those that sow in tears, shall reap in joy."—*Id.* "The pen with which I write, makes too large a mark."—*Ingersoll cor.* "Modesty makes large amends for the pain it gives the persons who labour under it, by the prejudice it affords every worthy person, in their favour."—*Id.* "Irony is a figure whereby we plainly intend something very different from what our words express."—*Bucke cor.* "Catachresis is a figure whereby an improper word is used in stead of a proper one."—*Id.* "The man whom you met at the party, is a Frenchman."—*Frost cor.*

UNDER RULE III.—OF MORE THAN TWO WORDS.

"John, James, and Thomas, are here : that is, John, *and* James, and Thomas, are here."—*Cooper cor.* "Adverbs modify verbs, adjectives, and other adverbs."—*Bullions, E. Gram.* p. 116. "To Nouns belong Person, Gender, Number, and Case."—*Id. ib.* p. 9. "Wheat, corn, rye, and oats, are extensively cultivated."—*Id.* "In many, the definitions, rules, and leading facts, are prolix, inaccurate, and confused."—*Finch cor.* "Most people consider it mysterious, difficult, and useless."—*Id.* "His father, and mother, and uncle, reside at Rome."—*Farnum cor.* "The relative pronouns are *who, which,* and *that.*"—*Bullions, E. Gram.* p. 23. "*That* is sometimes a demonstrative, sometimes a relative, and sometimes a conjunction."—*Bullions cor.* "Our reputation, virtue, and happiness, greatly depend on the choice of our companions."—*Day cor.* "The spirit of true religion is social, kind, and cheerful."—*Felton cor.* "*Do, be, have,* and *will,* are sometimes principal verbs."—*Id.* "John, and Thomas, and Peter, reside at Oxford."—*Webster cor.* "The most innocent pleasures are the most rational, the most delightful, and the most durable."—*Id.* "Love, joy, peace, and blessedness, are reserved for the good."—*Id.* "The husband, wife, and children, suffered extremely."—*Murray cor.* "The husband, wife, and children, suffer extremely."—*Sanborn cor.* "He, you, and I, have our parts assigned us."—*Id.*

"He moaned, lamented, tugged, and tried.
Repented, promised, wept, and sighed."—*Cowper.*

UNDER RULE IV.—OF ONLY TWO WORDS.

"Disappointments derange and overcome vulgar minds."—*Murray cor.* "The hive of a city or kingdom, is in the best condition, when there is the least noise or buzz in it."—*Id.* "When a direct address is made, the noun or pronoun is in the nominative case, independent."—*Ingersoll cor.* "The verbs *love* and *teach,* make *loved* and *taught,* in the imperfect and participle."—*Id.* "Neither poverty nor riches were injurious to him."—*Murray's Gram.* 8vo, p. 152. "Thou or I am in fault."—*Ib.* p. 152. "A verb is a word that expresses action or being."—*P. E. Day cor.* "The Objective Case denotes the object of a verb or a preposition."—*Id.* "Verbs of the second conjugation may be either transitive or intransitive."—*Id.* "Verbs of the fourth conjugation may be either transitive or intransitive."—*Id.* "If a verb does not form its past indicative by adding *d* or *ed* to the indicative present, it is said to be *irregular.*"—*Id.* "The young lady is studying rhetoric and logic."—*Cooper cor.* "He writes and speaks the language very correctly."—*Id.* "Man's happiness or misery is, in a great measure, put into his own hands."—*Mur. cor.* "This accident or characteristic of nouns, is called their *Gender.*"—*Bullions cor.*

"Grant that the powerful still the weak *control*;
Be *man* the *wit* and *tyrant* of the whole."—*Pope cor.*

UNDER EXCEPTION I.—TWO WORDS WITH ADJUNCTS.

"Franklin is justly considered the ornament of the New World, and the pride of modern philosophy."—*Day cor.* "Levity, and attachment to worldly pleasures, destroy the sense of gratitude to Him."—*Mur. cor.* "In the following Exercise, point out the adjectives, and the substantives which they qualify."—*Bullions cor.* "When a noun or pronoun is used to explain, or give emphasis to, a preceding noun or pronoun."—*Day cor.* "Superior talents, and *brilliancy* of intellect, do not always constitute a great man."—*Id.* "A word that makes sense after an article, or the phrase *speak of,* is a noun."—*Bullions cor.* "All feet used in poetry, are reducible to eight kinds ; four of two syllables, and four of three."—*Hiley cor.* "He would not do it himself, nor let me do it."—*Lennie's Gram.* p. 84. "The old writers give examples of the subjunctive *mood,* and give other *moods* to explain what is meant by the words in the subjunctive."—*Peirce cor.*

UNDER EXCEPTION II.—TWO TERMS CONTRASTED.

"We often commend, as well as censure, imprudently."—*Mur. cor.* "It is as truly a violation of the right of property, to take little, as to take much ; to purloin a book or a penknife, as to steal money ; to steal fruit, as to steal a horse ; to defraud the revenue, as to rob my neighbour ; to overcharge the public, as to overcharge my brother ; to cheat the post-office, as to cheat my friend."—*Wayland cor.* "The classification of verbs has been, and still is, a vexed question."—*Bullions cor.* "Names applied only to individuals of a sort or class, and not common to all, are called *Proper nouns.*"—*Id.* "A hero would desire to be loved, as well as to be reverenced."—*Day cor.* "Death, or some worse misfortune, now divides them." Better : "Death, or some *other* misfortune, soon divides them."—*Murray's Gram.* p. 151. "Alexander replied, 'The world will not permit two suns, nor two sovereigns.'"—*Goldsmith cor.*

"From nature's chain, whatever link you strike,
Tenth, or *ten-thousandth,* breaks the chain alike."—*Pope.*

UNDER EXCEPTION III.—OF AN ALTERNATIVE OF WORDS.

"*Metre*, or *Measure*, is the number of poetical feet which a verse contains."—*Hiley cor.* "The *Cæsura*, or *division*, is the pause which takes place in a verse, and which divides it into two parts."—*Id.* "It is six feet, or one fathom, deep."—*Bullions cor.* "A *Brace* is used in poetry, at the end of a triplet, or three lines which rhyme together."—*Felton cor.* "There are four principal kinds of English verse, or poetical feet."—*Id.* "The period, or full stop, denotes the end of a complete sentence."—*Sanborn cor.* "The scholar is to receive as many *jetons*, or counters, as there are words in the sentence."—*St. Quentin cor.* "*That* [thing], or *the thing, which* purifies, fortifies also the heart."—*Peirce cor.* "*That thing*, or *the thing*, which would induce a laxity in public or private morals, or indifference to guilt and wretchedness, should be regarded as the deadly Sirocco."—*Id.* "*What is*, elliptically, *what thing*, or *that thing which*."—*Sanborn cor.* "*Demonstrate* means *show*, or *point out precisely*."—*Id.* "*The* man, or *that* man, who endures to the end, shall be saved."—*Hiley cor.*

UNDER EXCEPTION IV.—OF A SECOND COMMA.

"That reason, passion, answer one great aim."—POPE: *Bullions and Hiley cor.* "Reason, virtue, answer one great aim."—*L. Murray's Gram.* p 269; *Cooper's Murray*, 182; *Comly*, 145; *Ingersoll*, 282; *Sanborn*, 268; *Kirkham*, 212; *et al.* "Every good gift, and every perfect gift, is from above."—*James*, i, 17. "Every plant, and every tree, produces others after its kind."—*Day cor.* "James, and not John, was paid for his services."—*Id.* "The single dagger, or obelisk †, is the second."—*Id.* "It was I, not he, that did it."—*St. Quentin cor.* "Each aunt, each cousin, hath her speculation."—*Byron.* "'I shall see you *when* you come,' is equivalent to, 'I shall see you *then*, or *at that time*, when you come.'"—*Butler cor.*

"Let wealth, let honour, wait the wedded dame;
August her deed, and sacred be her fame."—*Pope cor.*

UNDER RULE V.—OF WORDS IN PAIRS.

"My hopes and fears, joys and sorrows, centre in you."—*Greenleaf or Sanborn cor.* "This mood implies possibility or liberty, will or obligation."—*Ingersoll cor.* "Substance is divided into *body* and *spirit*, into *extended* and *thinking*."—*Brightland cor.* "These consonants, [d and t,]. like *p* and *b*, *f* and *v*, *k* and hard *g*, and *s* and *z*, are letters of the same organ."—*Walker cor.* "Neither fig nor twist, pigtail nor Cavendish, *has* passed my lips since; nor ever shall again."—*Cultivator cor.* "The words *whoever* or *whosoever*, *whichever* or *whichsoever*, and *whatever* or *whatsoever*, are called Compound Relative Pronouns."—*Day cor.* "Adjectives signifying profit or disprofit, likeness or unlikeness, govern the dative."—*Bullions cor.*

UNDER RULE VI.—OF WORDS ABSOLUTE.

"Thy rod and thy staff, they comfort me."—*Psalm* xxiii, 4. "Depart, ye wicked."—*Wright cor.* "He saith unto his mother, Woman, behold thy son!"—*John*, xix, 26. "Thou, God, seest me."—*Bullions cor.* "John, write me a letter. Henry, go home."—*Peirce cor. twice.* "Now, G. Brown, let us reason together."—*Id.* "*Mr.* Smith, *you* say, on page 11th, '*The* objective case denotes the object.'"—*Id.* "Gentlemen, will you always speak as you mean?"—*Id.* "John, I sold my books to William, for his brothers."—*Id.* "Walter, and Seth, I will take my things, and leave yours."—*Id.* "Henry, Julia and Jane left their umbrella, and took yours."—*Id.* "John, harness the horses, and go to the mine for some coal."—*Id.* "William, run to the store, for a few pounds of tea."—*Id.* "The king being dead, the parliament was dissolved."—*Chandler cor.*

"Cease, fond Nature, cease thy strife,
And let me languish into life."—*Pope, Brit. Poets,* vi, 317.

"Forbear, great man, in arms renown'd, forbear."—*Hiley's Grammar,* p. 127.

"Eternal sunshine of the spotless mind!
Each prayer accepted, and each wish resign'd."—*Pope, Brit. Poets,* vi, 335.

UNDER RULE VII.—OF WORDS IN APPOSITION.

"We, the people of the United States, in order to form a more perfect union, establish justice," &c.—*Constit. of U. S.* "The Lord, the covenant God of his people, requires it."—*A. S. Mag. cor.* "He, as a patriot, deserves praise."—*Hallock cor.* "Thomson, the watchmaker and jeweller from London, was of the party."—*Bullions cor.* "Every body knows that the person here spoken of by the name of '*the Conqueror*,' is William, duke of Normandy."—*Mur. cor.* "The words *myself, thyself, himself, herself, itself*, and their plurals, *ourselves, yourselves*, and *themselves*, are called Compound Personal Pronouns."—*Day cor.*

"For who, to dumb forgetfulness a prey,
This pleasing, anxious being e'er resign'd,
Left the warm precincts of the cheerful day,
Nor cast one longing, ling'ring look behind?"—GRAY: *M. Seq.*

UNDER THE EXCEPTIONS CONCERNING APPOSITION.

"Smith & Williams's store: Nicholas the emperor's army."—*Day cor.* "He was named William the Conqueror."—*Id.* "John the Baptist was beheaded."—*Id.* "Alexander the coppersmith did me *much evil*."—2 *Tim.* iv, 14. "A nominative in immediate apposition; as, 'The boy *Henry* speaks.'"—*Smart cor.* "A noun objective can be in apposition with some other: as, 'I teach the boy *Henry*.'"—*Id.*

UNDER RULE VIII.—OF ADJECTIVES.

"But he found me, not singing at my work, ruddy with health, vivid with cheerfulness; but pale," &c.—DR. JOHNSON: *Murray's Sequel,* p. 4. "I looked up, and beheld an inclosure, beautiful as the gardens of paradise, but of a small extent."—HAWKESWORTH: *ib.* p. 20. "*A* is an article, indefinite, and belongs to '*book*.'"—*Bullions cor.* "The first expresses the rapid move-

ment of a troop of horse over the plain, eager for the combat."—*Id.* "He [, the Indian chieftain, King Philip,] was a patriot, attached to his native soil ; a prince, true to his subjects, and
indignant of their wrongs ; a soldier, daring in battle, firm in adversity, patient of fatigue, of
hunger, of every variety of bodily suffering, and ready to perish in the cause he had espoused."
—*W. Irving.*

"For thee, who, mindful of th' unhonour'd dead,
Dost in these lines their artless tale relate."—GRAY : *Mur. Seq.* p. 258.
"Some mute inglorious Milton here may rest ;
Some Cromwell, guiltless of his country's blood."—GRAY : *Enf. Sp.* p. 245.
"Idle after dinner [,] in his chair,
Sat a farmer, ruddy, fat, and fair."—*Murray's Gram.* p. 257.

UNDER THE EXCEPTION CONCERNING ADJECTIVES.

"When an attribute becomes a title, or is emphatically applied to a name, it follows it : as,
Charles the Great ; Henry the First ; Lewis the Gross."—*Webster cor.* "Feed me with food convenient for me."—*Prov.* xxx, 8. "The words and phrases necessary to exemplify every principle progressively laid down, will be found strictly and exclusively adapted to the illustration of
the principles to which they are referred."—*Ingersoll cor.* "The Infinitive *Mood* is that form of
the verb which expresses *being or action* unlimited by person or number."—*Day cor.* "A man
diligent in his business, prospers."—*Frost cor.*
"*Oh* wretched state ! oh bosom black as death !"—SHAK. : *Enfield,* p. 368.

UNDER RULE IX.—OF FINITE VERBS.

"The Singular denotes *one ;* the Plural, *more* than one."—*Bullions and Lennie cor.* "The
Comma represents the shortest pause ; the *Semicolon,* a pause longer than the comma ; the
Colon, longer than the semicolon ; and the *Period,* longer than the colon."—*Hiley cor.* "The
Comma represents the shortest pause ; the Semicolon, a pause double that of the Comma ; the
Colon, double that of the semicolon ; and the Period, double that of the colon."—*L. Murray's
Gram.* p. 266. "WHO is applied only to persons ; WHICH, to animals and things ; WHAT, to
things only ; and THAT, to persons, animals, and things."—*Day cor.* "*A* or *an* is used before
the singular number only ; *the,* before either singular or plural."—*Bullions cor.* "Homer was
the greater genius ; Virgil, the better artist."—*Day cor. ;* also *Pope.* "Words are formed of syllables ; syllables, of letters."—*St. Quentin cor.* "The conjugation of an active verb is styled the
ACTIVE VOICE ; and that of a passive verb, the PASSIVE VOICE."—*Frost cor. ;* also *Smith : L.
Murray's Gram.* p. 77. "The possessive is sometimes called the *genitive* case ; and the objective, the *accusative.*"—*Murray cor.* "Benevolence is allied to few vices ; selfishness, to fewer
virtues."—*Kames cor.* "Orthography treats of Letters ; Etymology, of Words ; Syntax, of Sentences ; and Prosody, of Versification."—*Hart cor.*
"Earth praises conquerors for shedding blood ;
Heaven, those that love their foes, and do them good."—*Waller.*

UNDER RULE X.—OF INFINITIVES.

"His business is, to observe the agreement or disagreement of words."—*Bullions cor.* "It is
a mark of distinction, to be made a member of this society."—*Farnum cor.* "To distinguish the
conjugations, let the pupil observe the following rules."—*Day cor.* "He was now sent for, to
preach before the Parliament."—*E. Williams cor.* "It is incumbent on the young, to love and
honour their parents."—*Bullions cor.* "It is the business of every man, to prepare for death."—
Id. "It argued the sincerest candor, to make such an acknowledgement."—*Id.* "The proper
way is, to complete the construction of the first member, and leave that of the second *elliptical.*"
—*Id.* "ENEMY is a name. It is a term of distinction, given to a certain person, to show the
character in which he is represented."—*Peirce cor.* "The object of this is, to preserve the soft
sounds of c and g."—*Hart cor.* "The design of grammar is, to facilitate the reading, writing,
and speaking of a language."—*Barrett cor.* "Four kinds of type are used in the following pages,
to indicate the portions that are considered more or less elementary."—*Hart cor.*

UNDER RULE XI.—OF PARTICIPLES.

"The chancellor, being attached to the king, secured his crown."—*Murray's Grammar,* p. 66.
"The officer, having received his orders, proceeded to execute them."—*Day cor.* "Thus used,
it is in the present tense."—*Bullions, E. Gr.,* 2d Ed., p. 35. "The imperfect tense has three
distinct forms, corresponding to those of the present tense."—*Bullions cor.* "Every possessive
case is governed by some noun, denoting the thing possessed."—*Id.* "The word *that,* used as
a conjunction, is [generally] preceded by a comma."—*Hiley's Gram.* p. 114. "His narrative,
being composed upon *so* good authority, deserves credit."—*Cooper cor.* "The hen, being in her
nest, was killed and eaten there by the eagle."—*Murray cor.* "Pronouns, being used *in stead*
of nouns, are subject to the same modifications."—*Sanborn cor.* "When placed at the beginning
of words, they are consonants."—*Hallock cor.* "Man, starting from his couch, shall sleep no
more."—*Young.* "*His* and *her,* followed by a noun, are possessive pronouns ; not followed by a
noun, they are personal pronouns."—*Bullions cor.*
"He, with viny crown advancing,
First to the lively pipe his hand address'd."—*Collins.*

UNDER THE EXCEPTION CONCERNING PARTICIPLES.

"But when they convey the idea of many acting individually, or separately, they are of the
plural number."—*Day cor.* "Two or more singular antecedents connected by *and,* [when they
happen to introduce more than one verb and more than one pronoun,] require verbs and pronouns of the plural number."—*Id.* "Words ending in *y* preceded by a consonant, change *y* into
i, when a termination is added."—*Butler cor.* "A noun used without an article to limit it, is

generally taken in its widest sense."—*Ingersoll cor.* "Two nouns meaning the same person or thing, frequently come together."—*Bucke cor.* "Each one must give an account to God for the use, or abuse, of the talents committed to him."—*Cooper cor.* "Two vowels united in one sound, form a diphthong."—*Frost cor.* "Three vowels united in one sound, form a triphthong."—*Id.* "Any word joined to an adverb, is a secondary adverb."—*Barrett cor.* "The person spoken *to*, is put in the *Second* person; the person spoken *of*, in the *Third* person."—*Cutler cor.* "A man devoted to his business, prospers."—*Frost cor.*

UNDER RULE XII.—OF ADVERBS.

"So, in indirect questions; as, 'Tell me *when* he will come.'"—*Butler cor.* "Now, when the verb tells what one person or thing does to an *other*, *it* is transitive."—*Bullions cor.* "Agreeably to your request, I send this letter."—*Id.* "There seems, therefore, to be no good reason for giving them a different classification."—*Id.* "Again, the kingdom of heaven is like unto a merchant-man seeking goodly pearls."—*Scott's Bible, Smith's, and Bruce's.* "Again, the kingdom of heaven is like unto a net that was cast into the sea."—*Same.* "Cease, however, is used as a transitive verb by our best writers."—*Webster cor.* "Time admits of three natural divisions; namely, Present, Past, and Future."—*Day cor.* "There are three kinds of comparison; namely, Regular, Irregular, and Adverbial."—*Id.* "There are five personal pronouns; namely, *I, thou, he, she,* and *it.*"—*Id.* "Nouns have three cases; viz., the Nominative, *the* Possessive, and *the* Objective."—*Bullions cor.* "Hence, in studying Grammar, we have to study words."—*Frazee cor.* "Participles, like verbs, relate to nouns and pronouns."—*Miller cor.* "The time of the participle, like that of the infinitive, is estimated from the time of the leading verb."—*Bullions cor.*

> "The dumb shall sing, the lame his crutch forego,
> And leap exulting, like the bounding roe."—*Pope.*

UNDER RULE XIII.—OF CONJUNCTIONS.

"But he said, Nay; lest, while ye gather up the tares, ye root up also the wheat with them."—*Scott's Bible, et al.* "Their intentions were good; but, wanting prudence, they missed the mark at which they aimed."—*Mur. cor.* "The verb *be* often separates the name from its attribute; as, '*War* is expensive.'"—*Webster cor.* "*Either* and *or* denote an alternative; as, 'I will take *either* road at your pleasure.'"—*Id.* "*Either* is also a substitute for a name; as, '*Either* of the roads is good.'"—*Id.* "But, alas! I fear the consequence."—*Day cor.* "Or, if he ask a fish, will he for a fish give him a serpent?"—*Luke*, xi, 11. "Or, if he shall ask an egg, will he offer him a scorpion?"—*ALGER'S BIBLE: Luke*, xi, 12. "The infinitive sometimes performs the office of a nominative case; as, 'To enjoy is to obey.'—*POPE.*"—*Cutler cor.* "The plural is commonly formed by adding *s* to the singular; as, *book,* books."—*Bullions, P. Lessons,* p. 16. "As, 'I *were* to blame, if I did it.'"—*Smart cor.*

> "Or, if it be thy will and pleasure,
> Direct my plough to find a treasure."

UNDER RULE XIV.—OF PREPOSITIONS.

"Pronouns agree with the nouns for which they stand, in gender, number, and person."—*Butler and Bullions cor.* "In the first two examples, the antecedent is *person*, or something equivalent; in the last [*one*], it *is thing*."—*Butler cor.* "In what character he was admitted, is unknown."—*Id.* "To what place he was going, is not known."—*Id.* "In the preceding examples, *John, Cæsar,* and *James,* are the subjects."—*Id.* "*Yes* is generally used to denote assent, *in answer* to a question."—*Id.* "*That,* in its origin, is the passive participle of the Anglo-Saxon verb *thean,* [*thegan, thicgan, thicgean,* or *thigan,*] to *take.*"—*Id.* "But, in all these sentences, *as* and *so* are adverbs."—*Id.* "After an interjection or an exclamatory sentence, is *usually* placed the mark of exclamation."—*D. Blair cor.* "Intransitive verbs, from their nature, can have no distinction of voice."—*Bullions cor.* "To the inflection of verbs, belong Voices, Moods, Tenses, Numbers, and Persons."—*Id.* "*As* and *so,* in the antecedent member of a comparison, are properly Adverbs." Better: "*As* or *so,* in the antecedent member of a comparison, *is* properly *an adverb.*"—*Id.* "In the following Exercise, point out the words in apposition."—*Id.* "In the following Exercise, point out the noun or pronoun denoting the possessor."—*Id.* "*Its* is not found in the Bible, except by misprint."—*Brown's Institutes,* p. 49. "N*o* one's interest is concerned, except mine."—*Hallock cor.* "In most of the modern languages, there are four concords."—*St. Quentin cor.* "In illustration of these remarks, let us suppose a case."—*Hart cor.* "On the right management of the emphasis, depends the life of pronunciation."—*See Blair's Rhet.* p. 330.

UNDER RULE XV.—OF INTERJECTIONS.

"Behold, he is in the desert."—*Friends' Bible.* "And Lot said unto them, Oh, not so, my Lord."—*Alger's Bible.* "Oh, let me escape thither, (is it not a little one?) and my soul shall live."—*Friends' Bible, and Alger's.* "Behold, I come quickly."—*Rev.* xxii, 7. "Lo, I am with you always."—*Day cor.* "And, lo, I am with you alway."—*Alger's Bible.* "Ha, ha, ha; how laughable that is!"—*Bullions cor.* "Interjections of laughter; *ha, ha, ha.*"—*Wright cor.*

UNDER RULE XVI.—OF WORDS REPEATED.

"Lend, lend your wings!" &c.—*Pope.* "To bed, to bed, to bed. There is a knocking at the gate. Come, come, come. What is done, cannot be undone. To bed, to bed, to bed."—*SHAKSPEARE: Burgh's Speaker,* p. 130. "I will roar, that the duke shall cry, Encore, encore, let him roar, let him roar, once more, once more."—*Id. ib.* p. 136.

> "Vital spark of heavenly flame!
> Quit, oh quit this mortal frame!"—*Pope.*

> "O the pleasing, pleasing anguish,
> When we love, and when we languish."—*Addison.*

> "Praise to God, immortal praise,
> For the love that crowns our days!"—*Barbauld.*

UNDER RULE XVII.—OF DEPENDENT QUOTATIONS.

"Thus, of an infant, we say, '*It is a lovely creature.*'"—*Bullions cor.* "No being can state a falsehood in saying, '*I am ;*' for no one can utter *this*, if it is not true."—*Cardell cor.* "I know they will cry out against this, and say, 'Should he pay,' means, 'If he should pay.'"—*Priw cor.* "For instance, when we say, '*The house is building*,' the advocates of the new theory ask, —'building *what?*' We might ask in turn, When you say, 'The field *ploughs* well,'—ploughs *what?* 'Wheat *sells* well,'—sells *what?* If *usage* allows us to say, 'Wheat *sells* at a dollar,' in a sense that is not active; why may it not also allow us to say, 'Wheat *is selling* at a dollar,' in a sense that is not active?"—*Hart cor.* "'*Man* is accountable,' equals, '*Mankind* are accountable.'"—*Barrett cor.* "Thus, when we say, 'He may be reading,' *may* is the real verb; the other parts are verbs by name only."—*Id.* "Thus we say, *an apple, an hour*, that two vowel sounds may not come together."—*Id.* "It would be as improper to say, *an unit*, as to say, *an youth*, to say, *an one*, as to say, *an wonder*."—*Id.* "When we say, 'He died for the truth,' *for* is a preposition."—*Id.* "We do not say, 'I might go yesterday;' but, 'I might have gone yesterday.'"—*Id.* "By *student*, we understand, one who has by matriculation acquired the rights of academical citizenship; but, by *bursch*, we understand, one who has already spent a certain time at the university."—*Howitt cor.*

SECTION II.—THE SEMICOLON.

CORRECTIONS UNDER RULE I.—OF COMPLEX MEMBERS.

"The buds spread into leaves, and the blossoms swell to fruit; but they know not how they grow, nor who causes them to spring up from the bosom of the earth."—*Day cor.* "But he used his eloquence chiefly against Philip, king of Macedon; and, in several orations, he stirred up the Athenians to make war against him."—*Bullions cor.* "For the sake of euphony, the *n* is dropped before a consonant; and, because most words begin with a consonant, this of course is its more common form."—*Id.* "But if I say, 'Will *a* man be able to carry this burden?' it is manifest the idea is entirely changed; the reference is not to number, but to the species; and the answer might be, 'No; but a horse will.'"—*Id.* "In direct discourse, a noun used by the speaker or writer to designate himself [in the special relation of speaker or writer], is said to be of the *first* person; used to designate the person addressed, it is said to be of the second person; and, when used to designate a person or thing [merely] spoken of, it is said to be of the *third* person."—*Id.* "Vice stings us, even in our pleasures; but virtue consoles us, even in our pains."—*Day cor.* "Vice is infamous, though in a prince; and virtue, honourable, though in a peasant."—*Id.* "Every word that is the name of a person or thing, is a *noun*; because, 'A noun is the name of any person, place, or thing.'"—*Bullions cor.*

"This is the sword with which he did the deed;
And that, the shield by which he was defended."—*Bucke cor.*

UNDER RULE II.—OF SIMPLE MEMBERS.

"A deathlike paleness was diffused over his countenance; a chilling terror convulsed his frame; his voice burst out at intervals into broken accents."—*Jerningham cor.* "The Lacedemonians never traded; they knew no luxury; they lived in houses built of rough materials; they ate at public tables; fed on black broth; and despised every thing effeminate or luxurious."—*Whelpley cor.* "Government is the agent; society is the principal."—*Wayland cor.* "The essentials of speech were anciently supposed to be sufficiently designated by the *Noun* and the *Verb*; to which was subsequently added the *Conjunction*."—*Bullions cor.* "The first faint gleamings of thought in its mind, are but reflections from the parents' own intellect; the first manifestations of temperament, are from the contagious parental fountain; the first aspirations of soul, are but the warnings and promptings of the parental spirit."—*Jocelyn cor.* "*Older* and *oldest* refer to maturity of age; *elder* and *eldest*, to priority of right by birth. *Farther* and *farthest* denote place or distance; *further* and *furthest*, quantity or addition."—*Bullions cor.* "Let the divisions be *natural*; such as obviously suggest themselves to the mind; *such* as may aid your main design; and *such* as may be easily remembered."—*Goldsbury cor.*

"Gently make haste, of labour not afraid;
A hundred times consider what you've said."—*Dryden cor.*

UNDER RULE III.—OF APPOSITION, &c.

(1.) "Adjectives are divided [, in Frost's Practical Grammar,] into two classes; adjectives denoting *quality*, and adjectives denoting *number*."—*Frost cor.* (2.) "There are [, according to some authors,] two classes of adjectives; *qualifying* adjectives, and *limiting* adjectives."—*Butler cor.* (3–5.) "There are three genders; the *masculine*, the *feminine*, and the *neuter*."—*Frost et al. cor.*; also *Mur. et al.*; also *Hendrick: Inst.* p. 35. (6.) "The Singular denotes *one*; the Plural, *more* than one."—*Hart cor.* (7.) "There are three cases; viz., the Nominative, the Possessive, and the Objective."—*Hendrick cor.* (8.) "Nouns have three cases; the *nominative*, the *possessive*, and the *objective*."—*Kirkham cor.* (9.) "In English, nouns have three cases; the *nominative*, the *possessive*, and the *objective*."—*Smith cor.* (10.) "Grammar is divided into four parts; namely, Orthography, Etymology, Syntax, Prosody."—*Hazen.* (11.) "It is divided into four parts; viz., Orthography, Etymology, Syntax, and Prosody."—*Mur. et al. cor.* (12.) "It is divided into four parts; viz., Orthography, Etymology, Syntax, Prosody."—*Bucks cor.* (13.) "It is divided into four parts; namely, Orthography, Etymology, Syntax, and Prosody."—*Lennie, Bullions, et al.* (14.) "It is divided into four parts; viz., Orthography, Etymology, Syntax, and Prosody."—*Hendrick cor.* (15.) "Grammar is divided into four parts; viz., Orthography, Etymology, Syntax, and Prosody."—*Chandler cor.* (16.) "It is divided into four parts; Orthography, Etymology, Syntax, and Prosody."—*Cooper and Frost cor.* (17.) "English Grammar has been usually divided into four parts; viz., Orthography, Etymology, Syntax, and Prosody."—*Nutting cor.* (18.) "Temperance leads to happiness; intemperance, to misery."—*Riley and Hart cor.* (19, 20.) "A friend exaggerates a man's virtues; an enemy, his crimes."—*Hiley cor.*; also *Murray.* (21.) "Many writers use a plural noun after the second of two numeral adjectives; thus, 'The first and second *pages* are torn.'"—*Bullions cor.* (22.) "Of these, [i. e., of *Cases*,] the Latin has six; the Greek, five; the German, four; the Saxon, six; the French, three; &c."—*Id.*

"In *ing* it ends, when doing is expressed;
In *d, t, n,* when suffering's confessed."—*Brightland cor.*

MIXED EXAMPLES CORRECTED.

"In old books, *i* is often used for *j*; *v*, for *u*; *vv*, for *w*; and *ii* or *ij*, for *y*."—*Hart cor.* "The forming of letters into words and syllables, is also called *Spelling.*"—*Id.* "Labials are formed chiefly by the *lips*; dentals, by the *teeth*; palatals, by the palate; gutturals, by the *throat*; nasals, by the *nose*; and linguals, by the *tongue*."—*Id.* "The labials are *p, b, f, v*; the dentals, *t, d, s, z*; the palatals, *g* soft and *j*; the gutturals, *k, q*, and *c* and *g* hard; the nasals, *m* and *n*; and the linguals, *l* and *r*."—*Id.* "Thus, 'The man, *having finished* his letter, will carry it to the *post-office.*'"—*Id.* "Thus, in the sentence, '*He* had a dagger concealed under his cloak,' *concealed* is passive, signifying *being concealed*; but, in the former combination, it goes to make up a form the force of which is active."—*Id.* "Thus, in Latin, '*He* had concealed the dagger,' would be, '*Pugionem abdiderat*;' but, '*He* had the dagger concealed,' would be, '*Pugionem abditum habebat.*'"—*Id.* "Here, for instance, means, 'in this place;' now, 'at this time;' &c."—*Id.* "Here *when* both declares the *time* of the action, and so is an adverb; and also connects the two verbs, and so *resembles* a conjunction."—*Id.* "These words were all, no doubt, originally other parts of speech; viz., verbs, nouns, and adjectives."—*Id.* "The principal parts of a sentence, are the subject, the attribute, and the object; in other words, the nominative, the verb, and the objective."—*Id.* "Thus, the adjective is connected with the noun; the adverb, with the verb or adjective; *the pronoun*, with *its antecedent*; &c."—*Id.* "*Between* refers to two; *among*, to more than two."—*Id.* "*At* is used after a verb of rest; *to*, after a verb of motion."—*Id.* "Verbs are of three kinds; Active, Passive, and Neuter."—*L. Murray.* [Active] "Verbs are divided into two classes; Transitive and Intransitive."—*Hendrick cor.* "The Parts of Speech, in the English language, are nine; viz., the Article, Noun, Adjective, Pronoun, Verb, Adverb, Preposition, Interjection, and Conjunction."—*Bullions cor.* See *Lennie.* "Of these, the Noun, Pronoun, and Verb, are declined; the rest are indeclinable."—*Bullions, Analyt. and Pract. Gram.* p. 18. "The first expression is called 'the *Active* form;' the second, 'the *Passive* form.'"—*Weld cor.*

"O, 'tis a godlike privilege to save;
And he that scorns it, is himself a slave."—*Cowper cor.*

SECTION III.—THE COLON.

CORRECTIONS UNDER RULE I.—OF ADDITIONAL REMARKS.

"*Of* is a preposition: it expresses the relation between *fear* and *Lord*."—*Bullions cor.* "Wealth and poverty are both temptations to man: *that* tends to excite pride; *this*, discontentment."—*Id. et al. cor.* "Religion raises men above themselves; irreligion sinks them beneath the brutes: *this* binds them down to a poor pitiable speck of perishable earth; *that* opens for them a prospect to the skies."—*Murray's Key*, 8vo, p. 189. "Love not idleness: it destroys many." —*Ingersoll cor.* "Children, obey your parents: 'Honour thy father and mother,' is the first commandment with promise.'"—*Bullions cor.* "Thou art my *hiding-place* and my shield: I hope in thy *word*."—*Psalm cxix*, 114. "The sun shall not smite *thee* by day, nor the moon by night. The Lord *shall* preserve *thee* from *all* evil: *he shall preserve thy* soul."—*Psalm cxxi*, 6. "Here *to* Greece is assigned the highest place in the class of objects among which she is numbered—the nations of antiquity: she is one of them."—*Bullions, E. Gram.* p. 114.

"From short (as usual) and disturb'd repose,
I wake: how happy they who wake no more!"—*Young, N. T.*, p. 3.

UNDER RULE II.—OF GREATER PAUSES.

"A taste *of* a thing, implies actual enjoyment of it; but a taste *for* it, implies only capacity for enjoyment: as, 'When we have had a true taste *of* the pleasures of virtue, we can have no relish *for* those of vice.'"—*Bullions cor.* "The Indicative mood simply declares a thing: as, 'He *loves*;' 'He *is* loved;' or it asks a question; as, '*Lovest* thou me?'"—*Id. and Lennie cor.*; also *Murray.* "The Imperfect (or Past) tense represents an action or event indefinitely as past; as, '*Cæsar came*, and *saw*, and *conquered*:' or it represents the action definitely as unfinished and continuing at a certain time now entirely past; as, 'My father *was coming* home when I met him.'" —*Bullions cor.* "Some nouns have no plural; as, *gold, silver, wisdom*: others have no singular; as, *ashes, shears, tongs*: others are alike in both numbers; as, *sheep, deer, means, news*."—*Day cor.* "The same verb may be transitive in one sense, and intransitive in an other: thus, in the sentence, 'He believes my story,' *believes* is transitive; but, in this phrase, 'He believes in God,' it is intransitive."—*Butler cor.* "Let the divisions be *distinct*: one part should not include *an other*, but each should have its proper place, and be of importance in that place; and all the parts, well fitted together and united, should present a *perfect* whole."—*Goldsbury cor.* "In the use of the transitive verb, there are always *three* things implied; the *actor*, the *act*, and the *object* acted upon: in the use of the intransitive, there are only *two*; the *subject*, or *the thing* spoken of, and the *state* or *action* attributed to it."—*Bullions cor.*

"Why labours reason? instinct were as well;
Instinct, far better: what can choose, can err."—*Young, vii, 622.*

UNDER RULE III.—OF INDEPENDENT QUOTATIONS.

"The *sentence* may run thus: 'He is related to the same person, and is governed by him.'"— *Hart cor.* "Always remember this ancient proverb: 'Know thyself.'"—*Hallock cor.* "Consider this sentence: 'The boy runs swiftly.' "—*Frazee cor.* "The comparative is used thus: 'Greece was more polished than any other nation of antiquity.' The same idea is expressed by the superlative, when the word *other* is left out: thus, 'Greece was the most polished nation of antiquity.' "—*Bullions and Lennie cor.* " Burke, in his speech on the Carnatic war, makes the following allusion to the well known fable of *Cadmus* sowing dragon's teeth :—' Every day you are fatigued and disgusted with this cant: 'The Carnatic is a country that will soon recover, and become instantly as prosperous as ever.' They think they are talking to innocents, who believe that by the sowing of dragon's teeth, men may come up ready grown and ready made.' "—*Hiley and Hart cor.*

> " For sects he car'd not: ' They are not of us,
> Nor need we, brethren, their concerns discuss.' "—*Crabbe cor.*
> " Habit, with him, was all the test of truth :
> ' It must be right ; l've done it from my youth.'
> Questions he answer'd in as brief a way :
> ' It must be wrong ; it was of yesterday.' "—*Id.*

MIXED EXAMPLES CORRECTED.

" This would seem to say, 'I doubt nothing, save one thing ; namely, that he will *fulfil his* promise :' whereas that is the very thing not doubted."—*Bullions cor.* " The common use of language requires, that a distinction be made between *morals* and *manners* : the former depend upon internal dispositions ; the latter, *upon* outward and visible accomplishments."—*Beattie cor.* " Though I detest war in each particular fibre of my heart, yet I honour the heroes among our fathers, who fought with bloody hand. Peacemakers in a savage way, they were faithful to their light: the most inspired can be no more ; and we, with greater light, do, it may be, far less."— *T. Parker cor.* " The article *the*, like *a*, must have a substantive joined with it; whereas *that*, like *one*, may have it understood : thus, speaking of books, I may select one, and say, ' Give me *that* ;' but not, ' Give me *the* ;'—[so I may say,] ' Give me *one* ;' but not, ' Give me *a*.' "—*Bullions cor.* " The Present tense has three distinct forms : the *simple* ; as, I read : the *emphatic* ; as, I do read : and the *progressive* ; as, I am reading." Or thus: " The Present tense has three distinct forms ;—the *simple* ; as, ' I read ;'—the *emphatic* ; as, ' I do read ;'—and the *progressive* ; as, ' I am reading.' "—*Id.* " The tenses in English are usually reckoned six ; the *Present*, the *Imperfect*, the *Perfect*, the *Pluperfect*, the *First-future*, and the *Second-future*."—*Id.* " There are three participles ; the Present or Active, the Perfect or Passive, and the Compound Perfect : as, *loving*, *loved*, *having loved*." Or, better: " There are three participles from each verb ; namely, the *Imperfect*, the *Perfect*, and the *Preperfect* : as, *turning*, *turned*, *having turned*."—*Murray et al. cor.* " The participles are three ; the Present, the Perfect, and the Compound Perfect : as, *loving*, *loved*, *having loved*." Better : " The participles of each verb are three ; the *Imperfect*, the *Perfect*, and the *Preperfect* : as, *turning*, *turned*, *having turned*."—*Hart cor.* " *Will* is conjugated regularly, when it is a principal verb: as, present, I *will* ; past, I *willed* ; &c."—*Frazee cor.* " And both sounds of *x* are compound : one is that of *gs*, and the other, that of *ks*."—*Id.* " The man is happy ; he is benevolent ; he is useful."—*Mur.* 28 : *Cooper cor.* " The Pronoun stands in *stead* of the noun : as, ' The man is happy ; *he* is benevolent; *he* is useful.' "—*Murray cor.* " A Pronoun is a word used *in stead* of a noun, to *prevent* too frequent *a* repetition of it: as, ' The man is happy ; *he* is benevolent ; *he is* useful.' "—*Id.* " A Pronoun is a word used in the room of a noun, or as a substitute for one or more words : as, ' The man is happy ; *he* is benevolent; *he* is useful.' "—*Cooper cor.* " A common noun is the name of a sort, kind, or class, of beings or things ; as, *Animal*, *tree*, *insect*, *fish*, *fowl*."—*Id.* " Nouns have three persons ; the *first*, the *second*, and the *third*."—*Id.*

> "So saying, her rash hand in evil hour
> Forth reaching to the fruit, she pluck'd, she *eat* :
> Earth felt the wound ; and *Nature* from her seat,
> Sighing through all her works, gave signs of *woe*,
> That all was lost."—MILTON, P. L., Book ix, l. 780.

SECTION IV.—THE PERIOD.

CORRECTIONS UNDER RULE I.—OF DISTINCT SENTENCES.

" The third person is the position of *a word by which an object is merely* spoken of; as, ' Paul and Silas were imprisoned.'—' The earth thirsts.'—' The sun shines.' "—*Frazee cor.*

" Two, and three, and four, make nine. If he were here, he would assist his father and mother; for he is a dutiful son. They live together, and are happy, because they enjoy each other's society. They went to Roxbury, and tarried all night, and came back the next day."—*Goldsbury cor.*

" We often resolve, but seldom perform. She is wiser than her sister. Though he is often advised, yet he does not reform. Reproof either softens or hardens its object. He is as old as his classmates, but not so learned. Neither prosperity, nor adversity, has improved him. Let him that standeth, take heed lest he fall. He can acquire no virtue, unless he make some sacrifices."—*Id.*

> " Down from his neck, with blazing gems array'd,
> Thy image, lovely Anna ! hung portray'd;
> Th' unconscious figure smiling all serene,
> Suspended in a golden chain was seen."—*Falconer.*

UNDER RULE II.—OF ALLIED SENTENCES.

" This life is a mere prelude to *an other* which has no limits. *It* is a little portion of duration. As death leaves us, so the day of *judgement* will find us."—*Merchant cor.*

" He went from Boston to New York.—He went (I say) from Boston ; he went to New York. In walking across the floor, he stumbled over a chair."—*Goldsbury corrected.*

"' I saw him on the spot, going along the road, looking towards the house. During the heat of the day, he sat on the ground, under the shade of a tree."—*Goldsbury corrected.*

"' George came home; I saw him yesterday.' *Here* the word *him* can extend only to the individual George."—*Barrett corrected.*

"Commas are often used now, where parentheses were [adopted] formerly. I cannot, however, esteem this an improvement."—*Bucke's Classical Grammar,* p. 20.

> "Thou, like a sleeping, faithless sentinel,
> Didst let them pass unnotic'd, unimprov'd.
> And know, for that thou *slumberst* on the guard,
> Thou shalt be made to answer at the bar
> For every fugitive."—COTTON: *Hallock and Enfield cor.*

UNDER RULE III.—OF ABBREVIATIONS.

"The term *pronoun* (Lat. *pronomen*) strictly means a word used *for,* or *in stead of,* a noun."—*Bullions corrected.*

"The period is also used after abbreviations; as, A. D., P. S., G. W. Johnson."—*Butler cor.*

"On this principle of classification, the later Greek grammarians divided words into eight classes, or parts of speech: viz., the Article, Noun, Pronoun, Verb, Participle, Adverb, Preposition, and Conjunction."—*Bullions cor.*

"'*Metre* [*Melody*] is not confined to verse: there is a tune in all good prose; and Shakspeare's was a sweet one.'—*Epea Pter.*, ii, 61. [*First American Ed.*, ii, 50.] Mr. H. Tooke's idea was probably just, agreeing with Aristotle's; but [,if so, it is] not accurately expressed."—*Churchill cor.*

"Mr. J. H. Tooke was educated at Eton and at Cambridge, in which latter college he took the degree of A. M. Being intended for the established church of England, he entered into holy orders when young; and obtained the living of Brentford, near London, which he held ten or twelve years."—*Tooke's Annotator cor.*

> "I, nor your plan, nor book condemn;
> But why your name? and why A. M.?"—*Lloyd cor.*

MIXED EXAMPLES CORRECTED.

"If thou turn away thy foot from the sabbath," &c.—*Isaiah,* lviii, 13.   "He that hath eeris of herynge, *here he.*"—WICKLIFFE: *Matt.* xi, 15.   "See General Rules for Spelling, iii, v, and vii."—*Butler cor.*   "False witnesses did rise up."—*Ps.* xxxv, 11.

"An *explicative* sentence is used for explaining; an *interrogative* sentence, for inquiring; an *imperative* sentence, for commanding."—*Barrett cor.*   "In October, corn is gathered in the field by men, who go from hill to hill with baskets, into which they put the ears.—Susan labours with her needle for a livelihood.—Notwithstanding his poverty, he is a man of integrity."—*Golds. cor.*

"A word of one syllable is called a monosyllable; a word of two syllables, a dissyllable; a word of three syllables, a trissyllable; a word of four or more syllables, a polysyllable."—*Frazee cor.*

"If I say, '*If it did not rain,* I would take a walk:' I convey the idea that it *does* rain at the time of speaking. '*If it rained,*' or, '*Did it rain,*' in [reference to] the present time, implies *that* it does *not* rain. '*If it did not rain,*' or, '*Did it not rain,*' in [reference to the] present time, implies that it *does* rain. Thus, in this peculiar *application,* an affirmative sentence always implies a negation; and a negative sentence, an affirmation."—*Id.*   "'*If I were loved,*' and, '*Were I loved;*' imply I am *not* loved; '*If I were not loved,*' and, '*Were I not loved,*' imply I am loved. A negative sentence implies an affirmation, and an affirmative sentence implies a negation, in these forms of the subjunctive."—*Id.*

"What is Rule III?"—*Hart cor.*   "How is Rule III violated?"—*Id.*   "How do you parse *letter* in the sentence, 'James writes a letter?' Ans. *Letter* is a common noun, of the third person, singular number, *neuter* gender, and objective case; and is governed by the verb *writes,* according to Rule III, which says, 'A transitive verb governs the objective case.'"—*Id.*

> "Creation sleeps. 'Tis as the gen'ral pulse
> Of life stood still, and nature made a pause;
> An awful pause! prophetic of her end.
> And let her prophecy be soon fulfill'd:
> Fate, drop the curtain; I can lose no more."—*Young.*

SECTION V.—THE DASH.

CORRECTIONS UNDER RULE I.—OF ABRUPT PAUSES.

"And there is something in your very strange story, that resembles—Does Mr. Bevil know your history particularly?"—*Burgh's Speaker,* p. 149.   "Sir,—Mr. Myrtle—Gentlemen—You are friends—I am but a servant—But—"—*Ib.* p. 118.

"An other man now would have given plump into this foolish story; but I—No, no, your humble servant for that."—GARRICK, *Neck or Nothing.*

"Do not plunge thyself too far in anger, lest thou hasten thy trial; which if—Lord have mercy on thee for a hen!"—SHAKSPEARE, *All's Well.*

> "But ere they came,—O, let me say no more!
> Gather the sequel by that went before."—IDEM, *Com. of Errors.*

UNDER RULE II.—OF EMPHATIC PAUSES.

"*M,*—Malvolio; — *M,*—why, that begins my name."—SINGER'S SHAK., *Twelfth Night.*

"Thus, by the creative influence of the Eternal Spirit, were the heavens and the earth finished in the space of six days—so admirably finished—an unformed chaos changed into a system of perfect order and beauty—that the adorable Architect himself pronounced it *very good*, and *all the sons of God shouted for joy*."—*Historical Reader*, p. 10.

"If I were an American, as I am an Englishman, while a foreign troop remained in my country, I never would lay down my arms—never, never, never."—*Pitt's Speech*.

"Madam, yourself are not exempt in this,—
Nor your son Dorset ;—Buckingham, nor you."—SHAK.

UNDER RULE III.—OF FAULTY DASHES.

"'You shall go home directly, Le Fevre,' said my uncle Toby, 'to my house; and we'll send for a doctor to see what's the matter; and we'll have an apothecary; and the corporal shall be your nurse: and I'll be your servant, Le Fevre.'"—*Sterne cor.*

"He continued: 'Inferior artists may be at a stand, because they want materials.'"—*Harris cor.* "Thus, then, continued he: 'The end, in other arts, is ever distant and removed.'"—*Id.*

"The nouns must be coupled with *and;* and when a pronoun is used, it must be plural, as in the example. When the nouns are *disjoined*, the pronoun must be singular."—*Lennie cor.*

"*Opinion* is a common noun, or substantive, of the third person, singular number, neuter gender, and nominative case."—*Wright cor.*

"The mountain, thy pall and thy prison, may keep thee ;
I shall see thee no more, but till death I will weep thee."—
See *Felton's Gram.* p. 93.

MIXED EXAMPLES CORRECTED.

"If to accommodate man and beast, heaven and earth—if this be beyond me, 'tis not possible.—What consequence then follows? Or can there be any other than this ?—*if* I seek an interest of my own, detached from that of others, I seek an interest which is chimerical, and can never have existence."—*Harris.*

"Again: I must have food and clothing. Without a proper genial warmth, I instantly perish. Am I not related, in this view, to the very earth itself?—*to* the distant sun, from whose beams I derive vigour?"—*Id.*

"Nature instantly ebbed again; the film returned to its place; the pulse fluttered—stopped —went on—throbbed—stopped again—moved—stopped.—Shall I go on?—No."—*Sterne cor.*

"Write ten nouns of the masculine gender ;—ten of the feminine ;—ten of the neuter ;— ten indefinite in gender."—*Davis cor.*

"The infinitive *mood* has two tenses ; the indicative, six ; the potential, *four ;* the subjunctive, *two ;* and the imperative, one."—*Frazee cor.* "Now notice the following sentences : 'John runs.' —'Boys run.'—'Thou runnest.'"—*Id.*

"The Pronoun sometimes stands for a name ; sometimes, for an adjective, a sentence, *or* a part of a sentence ; and, sometimes, for a whole series of propositions."—*Peirce cor.*

"The self-applauding bird, the peacock, see ;
Mark what a sumptuous pharisee is he !"—*Cowper cor.*

SECTION VI. — THE EROTEME.

CORRECTIONS UNDER RULE I.—OF QUESTIONS DIRECT.

"When will his ear delight in the sound of arms ? When shall I, like Oscar, travel in the light of my steel ?"—*Ossian*, Vol. i, p. 357. "Will Henry call on me, while he shall be journeying south ?"—*Peirce cor.*

"An Interrogative Pronoun is one that is used in asking a question ; as, '*Who* is he ? and *what* does he want ?'"—*Day cor.* "*Who* is generally used when we would inquire *about* some unknown person or persons ; as, '*Who* is that man ?'"—*Id.* "*Your* fathers, where are they ? and the prophets, do they live forever ?"—*Zech.* i, 5.

"It is true, that some of our best writers have used *than whom ;* but it is also true, that they have used *other* phrases which we have rejected as ungrammatical : then why not reject this too ? —The sentences in the exercises, with *than who*, are correct as they stand."—*Lennie cor.*

"When the perfect participle of an active intransitive verb is annexed to the neuter verb *to be*, what does the combination form ?"—*Hallock cor.* "Those adverbs which answer to the question *where? whither?* or *whence?* are called adverbs of *place*."—*Id.* "Canst thou by searching find out God? canst thou find out the Almighty unto perfection ? It is as high as heaven ; what canst thou do? deeper than hell ; what canst thou know?"—SCOTT, ALGER, BRUCE, AND OTHERS : *Job*, xi, 7 and 8.

"Where, where, for shelter shall the guilty fly,
When consternation turns the good man pale ?"—*Young.*

UNDER RULE II.—OF QUESTIONS UNITED.

"Who knows what resources are in store, and what the power of God may do for thee ?"— STERNE: *Enfield's Speaker*, p. 307.

'God is not a man, that he should lie ; neither the son of man, that he should repent : hath he said, and shall he not do it ? or hath he spoken, and shall he not make it good ?'—SCOTT'S BIBLE, ALGER'S, FRIENDS', BRUCE'S, AND OTHERS: *Numb.* xxiii, 19. "Hath the Lord said it, and shall he not do it ? hath he spoken it, and shall he not make it good ?"—*Lennie and Bullions cor.*

"Who calls the council, states the certain day,
Who forms the phalanx, and who points the way ?"—*Pope's Essay.*

UNDER RULE III.—OF QUESTIONS INDIRECT.

"To be, or not to be ;—that is the question."—*Shak. et al. cor.* "If it be asked, why a pause should any more be necessary to emphasis than to an accent,—or why an emphasis alone will not

sufficiently distinguish the members of sentences from each other, without pauses, as accent does words,—the answer is obvious : that we are preacquainted with the sound of words, and cannot mistake them when distinctly pronounced, however rapidly ; but we are not preacquainted with the meaning of sentences, which must be pointed out to us by the reader or speaker.—*Sheridan cor.*
    " Cry, ' By your priesthood, tell me what you are.' "—*Pope cor.*

MIXED EXAMPLES CORRECTED.

" Who else can he be ? "—*Barrett cor.* " Where else can he go ? "—*Id.* " In familiar language, *here, there,* and *where,* are used for *hither, thither,* and *whither.*"—*Butler cor.* " Take, for instance, this sentence : ' Indolence undermines the foundation of virtue.' "—*Hart cor.* " Take, for instance, the sentence before quoted: ' Indolence undermines the foundation of virtue.' "—*Id.* " Under the same head, are considered such sentences as these : '*He that hath ears to hear,* let him hear.'—'*Gad,* a troop shall overcome him.' "—*Id.*
" Tenses are certain modifications of the verb, which point out the distinctions of time."—*Bullions cor.* " Calm was the day, and the scene, delightful."—*Id.* See *Murray's Exercises,* p. 5. " The capital letters used by the Romans to denote numbers, were C, I, L, V, X ; which are therefore called Numeral Letters. I denotes *one ;* V, *five ;* X, *ten ;* L, *fifty ;* and C, *a hundred.*"—*Bullions cor.* " ' I shall have written ;' viz., at or before some future time or event."—*Id.* " In Latin words, the liquids are *l* and *r* only ; in Greek words, *l, r, m,* and *n.*"—*Id.* " Each legion was divided into ten cohorts ; each cohort, into three maniples ; and each maniple, into two centuries."—*Id.* " Of the Roman literature previous to A. U. 514, scarcely a vestige remains."—*Id.*
    "And that which He delights in, must be happy.
    But when ? or where ? This world was made for Cæsar."—CATO.
    " Look next on greatness. Say where greatness lies.
    Where, but among the heroes and the wise ? "—*Pope.*

SECTION VII.—THE ECPHONEME.

CORRECTIONS UNDER RULE I.—OF INTERJECTIONS, &c.

(1.) " O ! that he were wise ! "—*Bullions cor.* (2.) " O ! that his heart *were* tender ! "—See *Murray's Ex. or Key,* under Rule xix. (3 and 4.) " Oh ! what a sight is here ! "—*Bullions, E. Gram.* p. 71 ; (§ 37 ;) *Pract. Les.* p. 82 ; *Analyt. and Pract. Gram.* p. 111. (5—9.) " O Virtue ! how amiable thou art ! "—*Farnum's Gram.* p.12 ; *Bullions's Analyt. and Pract. Gram.* p .111. (10.) " Oh ! that I had been more diligent ! "—*Hart cor. ;* and *Hiley.* (11.) " O ! the humiliation to which vice reduces us ! "—*Farnum* and *Mur. cor.* (12.) " O ! that he were more prudent ! "—*Farnum cor.* (13 and 14.) " Ah me ! "—*Davis cor.*
    (15.) " Lately, alas ! I knew a gentle boy," &c.—*Dial cor.*
    (16 and 17.) " Wo is me, Alhama ! "—*Byron's Poems : Wells cor.*

UNDER RULE II.—OF INVOCATIONS.

" Weep on the rocks of roaring winds, O maid of Inistore ! "—*Ossian.* " Cease a little while, O wind ! stream, be thou silent a while ! let my voice be heard around. Let my wanderer hear me ! Salgar ! it is Colma who calls. Here is the tree, and the rock. Salgar, my love ! I am here. Why delayest thou thy coming ? Lo ! the calm moon comes forth. The flood is bright in the vale."—*Id.* Vol. i, p. 369.
    "Ah, stay not, stay not ! guardless and alone :
    Hector ! my lov'd, my dearest, bravest son ! "—*Pope,* Il. xxii, 51.

UNDER RULE III.—OF EXCLAMATORY QUESTIONS.

" How much better is wisdom than gold ! "—See *Murray's Gram.* 8vo, p. 272. " O Virtue ! how amiable art thou ! "—See *Murray's Grammar,* 2d Edition, p. 95. " At that hour, O how vain was all sublunary happiness ! "—*Brown's Institutes,* p. 117 ; see *English Reader,* p. 135. " Alas ! how few and transitory are the joys which this world affords to man ! "—*Day cor.* " Oh ! how vain and transitory are all things here below ! "—*Id.*
    "And O ! what change of state, what change of rank,
    In that assembly everywhere was seen ! "—*Pollok cor. ;* also *Day.*

MIXED EXAMPLES CORRECTED.

" O *Shame !* where is thy blush."—*Shak.* " *John,* give me my hat."—*Barrett cor.* " What ! is Moscow in flames ? "—*Id.* " *O !* what happiness awaits the virtuous ! "—*Id.*
"*Ah, welladay !* do what we can for him, said Trim, maintaining his point,—the poor soul will die."—*Sterne* or *Enfield cor. ;* also *Kirkham.*
" Will John return to-morrow ? "—*Barrett cor.* " Will not John return to-morrow ? "—*Id.* " John, return to-morrow."—*Id.* " Soldiers, stand firm."—*Id.* " If *mea,* which means *my,* is an adjective in Latin, why may not *my* be so called in English ? and if my is an adjective, why not *Barrett's* ? "—*Id.*
" O Absalom, my son ! "—See 2 Sam. xix, 4. " O star-eyed Science ! whither hast thou fled ? "—*Peirce cor.* " Why do you tolerate your own inconsistency, by calling it the present tense ? "—*Id.* " Thus the declarative mode [i. e., the indicative mood] may be used in asking a question ; as, ' *What* man *is* frail ? ' "—*Id.* " What connexion has motive, wish, or supposition, with the term *subjunctive* ? "—*Id.* " A grand reason, truly, for calling it a golden key ! "—*Id.* " What ' *suffering*' the man who can say this, must be enduring ! "—*Id.* " What is Brown's Rule in relation to this matter ? "—*Id.*

---

  * In Singer's Shakspeare, Vol. ii, p. 495, this sentence is expressed and pointed thus : "O, shame ! where is thy blush ? "—*Hamlet,* Act iii, Sc. 4. This is as if the speaker meant, "O ! it is a shame ! where is thy blush ?" Such is not the sense above ; for there " *Shame* " is the person addressed.

"Alas! how short is life!"—*Day cor.*   "Thomas, study your book."—*Id.*   "Who can tell us who they are?"—*Sanborn cor.*   "Lord, have mercy on my son; for he is lunatic, and sorely vexed."—*See Matt.* xvii, 15.   "O ye wild groves!   O, where is now your bloom?"—*Felton cor.*
"O who of man the story will unfold?"—*Farnum cor.*
"Methought I heard Horatio say, To-morrow.
Go to—I will not hear of it—to-morrow!"—Colton.
"How his eyes languish! how his thoughts adore
That painted coat which Joseph never wore!"

SECTION VIII.—THE CURVES.

Corrections under Rule I.—Of Parentheses.

"*Another* [, better written as a phrase, *An other*,] is composed of the indefinite article *an*, (which etymologically means *one*,) and *other;* and denotes *one other.*"—*Hallock cor.*
"Each mood has its peculiar Tense, Tenses. or Times."—*Bucke cor.*
"In some very ancient languages, (as the Hebrew,) which have been employed chiefly for expressing plain sentiments in the plainest manner, without aiming at any elaborate length or harmony of periods, this pronoun [the relative] occurs not so often."—*Murray cor.*
"Before I shall say those things, O Conscript Fathers! about the public affairs, which are to be spoken at this time; I shall lay before you, in few words, the motives of the journey and the return."—*Brightland cor.*
"Of well-chose words some take not care enough,
And think they should be, like the subject, rough."—*Id.*
"Then, having *showed* his wounds, he'd sit him down."—*Bullions cor.*

Under Rule II.—Of Included Points.

"Then Jael smote the nail into his temples, and fastened it *into* the ground: (for he was fast asleep, and weary:) so he died."—Scott's Bible: *Judges,* iv, 21.
"Every thing in the Iliad has manners, (as Aristotle expresses it,) that is, every thing is acted or spoken."—*Pope cor.*
"Those nouns that end in *f* or *fe*, (except some few *which* I shall mention presently,) form plurals by changing those letters into *ves*: as, thief, *thieves;* wife, *wives.*"—*Bucke cor.*
"*As* requires *as;* (expressing equality *of degree;*) thus, 'Mine is *as* good *as* yours.'   As [requires] *so;* (expressing equality *or proportion;*) thus, '*As* the stars, *so* shall thy seed be.'   So [requires] *as;* (with a negative expressing inequality;) *as*, 'He is *not so* wise *as* his brother.' So [requires] *that;* (expressing *a consequence;*) *as*, 'I am *so* weak *that* I cannot walk.'"*—Bullions cor.*   "A captious question, sir, (and yours is one,)
Deserves an answer similar, or none."—*Cowper cor.*

MIXED EXAMPLES CORRECTED.

"Whatever words the verb TO BE serves to unite, referring to the same thing, must be of the same case; (§ 61;) as, '*Alexander* is a *student.*'"—*Bullions cor.*   "When the objective is a relative or [an] interrogative, it comes before the verb that governs it: (§ 40, R. 9:) Murray's 6th rule is unnecessary."—*Id.*   "It is generally improper, except in poetry, to omit the antecedent to a relative; and always, to omit a relative, when of the nominative case."—*Id.*   "In every sentence, there must be a verb and a nominative or subject, expressed or understood."—*Id.*   "Nouns and pronouns, and especially words denoting time, are often governed by prepositions understood; or are used to restrict verbs or adjectives, without a governing word: (§ 50, Rem. 6 and Rule:) as, 'He gave [to] me a full account of the affair.'"—*Id.*   "When *should* is used in stead of *ought,* to express *present* duty, (§ 20, 4,) it may be followed by the present; as, 'You *should* study that you *may* become learned.'"—*Id.*   "The indicative present is frequently used after the words *when, till, before, as soon as, after,* to express the relative time of a future action; (§ 24, I, 4;) as, 'When he *comes,* he will be welcome.'"—*Id.*   "The relative is parsed [, *according to Bullions,*] by stating its gender, number, case, and antecedent; (the gender and number being always the same as those of the antecedent;) thus, 'The boy who'—'*Who*' is a relative pronoun, masculine, singular, the nominative; and refers to '*boy*' as its antecedent."—*Id.*
"'Now, now, I seize, I clasp *thy* charms;
And now *you* burst, ah cruel! from my arms.'—*Pope.*
Here is an unnecessary change from the second person singular to the second *person* plural. *The text* would have been better, thus:—
'Now, now, I seize, I clasp *your* charms;
And now *you* burst, ah cruel! from my arms.'"—*John Burn cor.*
See *Lowth's Gram.* p. 35; *Churchill's,* 293.

SECTION IX.—ALL POINTS.

MIXED EXAMPLES CORRECTED.

"The principal stops are the following: the Comma [,], the Semicolon [;], the Colon [:], the Period, or Full Stop [.], the Note of Interrogation [?], the Note of Exclamation [!], the Paren-

---

* If, in each of these sentences, the colon were substituted for the latter semicolon, the curves might well be spared. Lowth has a similar passage, which (bating a needful variation of guillemets) he pointed thus: " *as* ——, *as* expressing a comparison of equality; '*as* white as snow:' as ——, *so*; expressing a comparison sometimes of equality; '*as* the stars, *so* shall thy seed be;' that is, equal in number: but" &c.—*Lowth's Gram.* p. 109. Murray, who broke this passage into paragraphs, retained at first these semicolons, but afterwards changed them *all* to colons. Of later grammarians, some retain the former colon in each sentence; some, the latter; and some, neither. Hiley points thus: "*As* requires *as*, expressing *equality;* as, 'He is *as* good *as* she.'"—*Hiley's E. Gram.* p. 107.

thesis [( )], and the Dash [—]."—*Bullions cor.* "The modern punctuation in Latin is the same as in English. The *chief* marks employed, are the Comma [,], *the* Semicolon [;], *the* Colon [:], *the* Period [.], *the Note of* Interrogation [?], *the Note of* Exclamation [!], *the Parenthesis* [( )], *and the Dash* [—]."—*Id.*

"Plato reproving a young man for playing at some childish game, 'You chide me,' says the youth, 'for a trifling fault.' 'Custom,' replied the philosopher, 'is no trifle.' 'And,' adds *Montaigne,* 'he was in the right; for our vices begin in infancy.'"—*Home cor.*

"A merchant at sea asked the skipper what death his father died. 'My father,' says the skipper, 'my grandfather, and my great-grandfather, were all drowned.' 'Well,' replies the merchant, 'and are not you afraid of being drowned too?'"—*Id.*

"The use of inverted commas derives from France, where one Guillemet was the author of them; [and,] as an acknowledgement for the improvement, his countrymen call them after his name, GUILLEMETS."—*Hist. cor.*

"This, however, is seldom if ever done, unless the word following the possessive begins with *s* : thus, we do not say, 'the *prince'* feather;' but, 'the *prince's* feather.'"—*Bullions cor.* "And this phrase must mean, '*the feather of the prince;* ' but '*prince's-feather,*' written as one word, [and with both apostrophe and hyphen,] is the name of a plant, a species of amaranth."—*G. Brown.*

"Boëthius soon had the satisfaction of obtaining the highest honour his country could bestow." —*Ingersoll cor.* ; also *Murray.*

"When an example, a quotation, or a speech, is introduced, it is separated from the rest of the sentence either by a *comma* or *by* a colon; as, 'The Scriptures give us an amiable representation of the Deity, in these words: *God is love.'*"—*Riley cor.* "Either the colon or *the comma* may be used, [according to the nature of the case,] when an example, a quotation, or a speech, is introduced; as, 'Always remember this ancient maxim: *Know thyself.'*—'The Scriptures give us an amiable representation of the Deity, in these words: *God is love.'*"—*Bullions cor.*

"The first word of a quotation introduced after a colon, or *of any sentence quoted* in a direct form, must begin with a capital: as, 'Always remember this ancient maxim: *Know thyself.'*— 'Our great lawgiver says, *Take* up thy cross daily, and follow me.'"—*Bullions and Lennie cor.* ; also *Murray*; also *Weld.* See *Luke,* ix. 23.

"Tell me, in whose house do you live?"—*N. Butler cor.* "He that acts wisely, deserves praise."—*Id.* "He who steals my purse, steals trash."—*Id.* "The antecedent is *sometimes* omitted; as, 'Who steals my purse, steals trash.'—[*Shak.*] That is, '*He* who,' or, 'The *person* who.'"—*Id.* "Thus, 'Whoever steals my purse, steals trash;'—' Whoever does no good, does harm.'"—*Id.* "Thus, 'Whoever sins, will suffer.' This means, that any one, without exception, who sins, will suffer."—*Id.*

"Letters form syllables; syllables, words; words, sentences; and sentences, combined and connected, form discourse."—*Cooper cor.* "A letter which forms a perfect sound when uttered by itself, is called a vowel; as, *a, e, i.*"—*Id.* "A proper noun is the name of an individual, [or of a particular people or place]; as, John, Boston, Hudson, America."—*Id.*

"Many men have been capable of doing a wise thing; more, a cunning thing; but very few, a generous thing."—*Davis cor.* "In the place of an ellipsis of the verb, a comma must be inserted." —*Id.* "A common noun unlimited by an article, is sometimes understood in its broadest acceptation: thus, '*Fishes* swim,' is understood to mean *all* fishes; '*Man* is mortal,' *all* men."—*Id.*

"Thus, those sounds formed principally by the throat, are called *gutturals* ; those formed principally by the palate, *palatals* ; those formed by the teeth, *dentals* ; those by the lips, *labials* ; and those by the nose, *nasals.*"—*Davis cor.*

"Some adjectives are compared irregularly: as, Good, better, best ; Bad, worse, worst ; Little less, least."—*Felton cor.*

"Under the fourth head of grammar, therefore, four topics will be considered; viz., PUNCTUATION, ORTHOEPY, FIGURES, and VERSIFICATION."—*Hart cor.*

"Direct her onward to that peaceful shore,
Where peril, pain, and death, are felt no more!"—*Falconer cor.*

GOOD ENGLISH RIGHTLY POINTED.

LESSON I.—UNDER VARIOUS RULES.

"Discoveries of such a character are sometimes made in grammar also; and such, too, *are* often their origin and their end."—*Bullions cor.*

"TRAVERSE, [literally, *to cross.*] To deny what the opposite party has alleged. To traverse an indictment, *or the like,* is to deny it."—*Id.*

"The *Ordinal* numerals denote the *order,* or *succession,* in which any number of persons or things *are* mentioned; as, *first, second, third, fourth,* &c."—*Hiley cor.*

"Nouns have three persons; *the* First, *the* Second, and *the* Third. The First person is *that which denotes* the speaker; the Second is *that which denotes* the *person or thing* spoken to; the Third is *that which denotes* the *person or thing* merely spoken of."—*Hart cor.*

"Nouns have three cases; *the* Nominative, *the* Possessive, and *the* Objective. The *relations* indicated by the *cases* of a noun, *include* three *distinct* ideas; viz., those of subject, object, and ownership."—*Id.*

"In speaking of animals that are of inferior size, or whose sex is not known or not regarded, *we* often *treat them* as without sex: thus, we say of a cat, '*It* is treacherous;' of an infant, '*It* is beautiful;' of a deer, '*It* was killed.'"—*Id.*

"When THIS *and* THAT, or THESE *and* THOSE, refer to a preceding sentence; THIS or THESE *represents* the latter member or term, *and* THAT or THOSE, the former."—*Churchill cor.* ; and *Lowth.*

"The rearing of them became his first care; their fruit, his first food; and *the* marking *of* their kinds, his first knowledge."—*Butler cor.*

"After the period used with abbreviations, we should employ other points, if the construction demands *them* : thus, after ' Esq.,' in the last example, there should be, besides *the* period, a comma."—*Id.*

"In the plural, the verb *has* the same *form* in all the persons; *but still* the principle in *Rem. 5.* under Rule iii, that the first or second person takes precedence, is applicable to verbs, in *parsing.*"—*Id.*

"Rex and Tyrannus are of very different characters. The one rules his people by laws to which they consent; the other, by his absolute will and power: that *government* is called *freedom;* this, tyranny."—*Murray cor.*

"A Noun is the name of any person, place, or thing, *that* can be known or mentioned: as, George, London, America, goodness, charity."—See *Brown's Institutes,* p. 31.

"Etymology treats of the classification of words, their various modifications, and *their derivation.*"—*P. E. Day cor.*

"To punctuate correctly, implies a thorough acquaintance with the meaning of words and phrases, as well as *with* all their corresponding connexions."—*W. Day cor.*

"All objects *that* belong to neither the male nor *the* female kind, are said to be of the neuter gender, *except certain things personified.*"—*Weld cor. twice.*

"The Analysis of the Sounds in the English language, presented in the preceding statement, *is* sufficiently exact for the purpose in hand. Those who wish to pursue *the subject* further, can consult Dr. Rush's admirable work, 'The Philosophy of the Human Voice.'"—*Fowler cor.* "Nobody confounds the name of *w* or *y* with *the* sound *of the letter,* or *with its* phonetic import."—*Id.* [☞ This assertion is hardly true. Strange as such a blunder is, it has actually occurred. See, in Orthography, Obs. 5, on the Classes of the Letters, at p. 143.—G. B.]

"Order is Heav'n's first law; and, this *confess'd,*
    Some are, and must be, greater than the rest."—*Pope.*

LESSON II.—UNDER VARIOUS RULES.

"*From* adjectives of one syllable, *and some of two,* the comparative is formed by adding *r* or *d* to the positive; and the superlative, by adding *st* or *est:* as, *sweet, sweeter, sweetest; able, abler, ablest.*"—*Bullions cor.*

"From monosyllables, *or from dissyllables ending with a vowel or the accent,* the comparative is formed by adding *er* or *r* to the positive; and the superlative, by adding *est* or *st:* as, *tall, taller, tallest; wise, wiser, wisest; holy, holier, holiest; complete, completer, completest.*"—*Id.*

"By this method, the confusion and unnecessary labour occasioned by studying grammars, in these languages, constructed on different principles, *are* avoided; the study of one is rendered a profitable introduction to the study of an other; and an opportunity is furnished to the *inquiring* student, of comparing the languages in their grammatical structure, and *of* seeing at once wherein they agree, and wherein they differ."—*Id.*

"No larger portion should be assigned for each recitation, than the class can easily master; and, till *the previous lessons are well learned,* a new portion should not be given out."—*Id.* "The acquisitions made in every new lesson, should be *riveted* and secured by repeated revisals."—*Id.*

"The personal pronouns may be parsed briefly thus: '*I is* a personal pronoun, *of* the first *person,* singular *number,* masculine *gender,* (feminine, if the speaker is a female,) *and* nominative *case.*' '*His is a* personal pronoun, *of* the third *person,* singular *number,* masculine *gender, and* possessive *case.*'"—*Id.*

"When the male and *the* female are expressed by distinct terms, as, *shepherd, shepherdess,* the masculine term has also a general meaning, expressing both male and female; and is always to be used when the office, occupation, *or* profession, and not the sex, of the individual, is chiefly to be expressed; the feminine term *being* used only when the discrimination of sex is indispensably necessary. Thus, when it is said, 'The poets of this country are distinguished *for* correctness of taste,' the term 'poets' clearly includes both male and female writers of poetry."—*Id.*

"Nouns and pronouns connected by conjunctions, must be in the same *case.*"—*Ingersoll cor.* "Verbs connected by *and, or,* or *nor,* must *generally* be in the same *mood* and *tense;* and, when *the tense has different forms,* they must be in the same form."—*Id.*

"This will habituate him to reflection; exercise his *judgement* on the meaning of the author; and, without any great effort on his part, impress indelibly on his memory the rules which he is required to give. After the exercises under *any* rule have been gone through, *agreeably to the direction* in the note *at the bottom of* page 88*th,* they may be read over again in a corrected state, the pupil making an emphasis on the correction made; or they may be presented in writing, at the next recitation."—*Bullions cor.*

"Man, but for that, no action could attend;
    And, but for this, *were active* to no end."—*Pope.*

LESSON III.—UNDER VARIOUS RULES.

"'Johnson, the bookseller and stationer,' indicates that *bookseller* and *stationer* are *terms* belonging to the same person; 'the bookseller and the stationer,' would indicate that they belong to different persons."—*Bullions cor.*

"*Past* is [commonly] an adjective; *passed,* the past tense or perfect participle of the verb: and they ought not (as *they* frequently *are*) to be confounded with each other."—*Id.*

"Not only the nature of the thoughts and sentiments, but the very selection *or* arrangement of the words, gives English poetry a character which separates it widely from common prose."—*Id.*

"Men of sound, discriminating, and philosophical minds—men prepared for the work by long study, patient investigation, and extensive acquirements—have laboured for ages to improve and perfect it; and nothing is hazarded in asserting, that, should it be unwisely abandoned, it will be long before an other, equal in beauty, stability, and usefulness, *will* be produced in its stead."—*Id.,* on the common "system of English Grammar."

"The article *the,* on the other hand, is used to restrict; and is therefore termed *Definite.* Its proper office is, to call the attention to a particular individual or class, or to any number of such; and *accordingly it* is used with nouns *of* either number, singular or plural."—*Id.*

"Hence, also, the infinitive mood, a participle *with its adjuncts,* a member of a sentence, or a *whole* proposition, forming the subject of discourse, or the object of a verb or preposition, and being the name of an act or circumstance, *is,* in construction, regarded as *a noun;* and *is* usually called, '*a* substantive phrase : ' as, '*To play,* is pleasant.' —'*That he is an expert dancer,* is no recommendation.'—' Let your motto be, *Honesty is the best policy.*' "—*Id.*

" In accordance with his definition, Murray has divided verbs into three classes ; *Active, Passive,* and *Neuter ;—*and *included* in the first class transitive verbs only; and, in the last, all verbs used intransitively."—*Id.*

"Moreover, as the name of the speaker or *that of* the person spoken to is seldom expressed, (the *pronoun* I being used *for the former,* and Thou or You *for the latter,*) a noun is very *rarely* in the first person; not often in the second; and *hardly ever* is either, unless it *is* a proper noun, or a common noun *denoting an object* personified."—*Id.*

" In using the *parsing* exercises, it will save much time, (*and this saving is all-important,*) if the pupil be taught to say *all things* belonging to the noun, in the fewest words possible; and to say them always in the same order, *after the example* above."—*Id.*

" In any phrase or sentence, the adjectives qualifying a noun may generally be found by prefixing the phrase, ' What kind of,' to the noun, in the form of a question; as, ' What kind of horse ? ' ' What kind of stone ?' ' What kind of way ?' The word containing the answer to the question, is an adjective."—*Id.*

" In the following exercise, let the pupil first point out the nouns, and then the adjectives; and tell how he knows them to be *such.*"—*Id.*

" In the following sentences, point out the improper *ellipses; show* why *they are* improper; and correct *them.*"—*Id.*

	"SINGULAR.		PLURAL.
1.	I am smitten,	1.	We are smitten,
2.	Thou art smitten,	2.	You are smitten,
3.	He is smitten;	3.	They are smitten."—*Wright cor.*

CHAPTER II.—UTTERANCE.

The second chapter of Prosody, treating of articulation, pronunciation, elocution and the minor topics that come under Utterance, contains no exercises demanding correction in this Key.

CHAPTER III.—FIGURES.

In the third chapter of Prosody, the several Figures of speech are explained; and, as the illustrations embrace no errors for correction, nothing here corresponds to the chapter, but the title.

CHAPTER IV.—VERSIFICATION.

FALSE PROSODY, OR ERRORS OF METRE, CORRECTED.

LESSON I.—RHYTHM RESTORED.

" Where thy true treasure ? Gold says, ' Not in me.' "—*Young.*

"Canst thou grow sad, thou *say'st,* as earth grows bright."—*Dana.*

" It must be so ;—Plato, thou *reason'st* well."—CATO: *Enfield,* p. 321.

" Slow rises *worth* by poverty depressed."—*Wells's Gram., Late Ed.,* p. 211.

" Rapt *into* future times, the bard begun."—POPE.—*Ib.* p. 165.

" Is there not rain enough in the sweet heavens
To wash it white as snow ?   *Whereto* serves mercy
But to confront the visage of offence ?"—*Shak., Hamlet.*

" Look ! in this place ran *Cassius'* dagger through."—*Id., J. Cæsar.*

" *And* when they list, their lean and flashy songs
Grate on their scrannel pipes of wretched straw."—*Milton, Lycidas.*

" Did not great Julius bleed for *justice'* sake ? "—*Dodd* and *Shak. cor.*

" May I *express thee' unblam'd ? since* God is light."—*Milton,* B. iii, l. 3.

" Or *hear'st* thou rather pure ethereal stream ?"—*Id.* B. iii, l. 7.

" Republics, kingdoms, empires, may decay;
Great princes, heroes, sages, sink to nought."—*Peirce or La-Rue cor.*

" Thou *bringst,* gay creature as thou art,
A solemn image to my heart."—*Hallock cor.*

"Know *then* thyself, presume not God to scan ;
The proper study of mankind is Man."—*Pope, on Man,* Ep. ii, l. 1.

" Raised on *pilasters high* of *burnished* gold."—*Dr. S. Butler cor.*

" Love in *Adalgise'* breast has fixed his sting."—*Id.*

"Thirty days *each have* September,
April, June, and *old* November;
Each of the rest *has* thirty-one,
Bating February alone,
Which has twenty-eight in fine,
Till leap-year gives it twenty-nine."
—*Dean Colet cor.*

LESSON II.—RHYTHM RESTORED.

" 'Twas not the fame of what he once had been,
Or tales in *records old* and annals seen."—*Rowe cor.*

" And Asia now and Afric are explored
For high-priced dainties and *the* citron board."—*Rowe cor.*

" Who knows not how the trembling judge beheld
The peaceful court with *arméd* legions fill'd ? "—*Rowe cor.*

" With thee the Scythian wilds we'll wander o'er,
With thee *the* burning Libyan sands explore."—*Rowe cor.*

" Hasty and headlong, different paths they tread,
As *impulse blind* and wild distraction lead."—*Rowe cor.*

" But Fate reserv'd *him* to perform its doom,
And be the minister of wrath to Rome."—*Rowe cor.*

" Thus spoke the youth.   When Cato thus *express'd*
The sacred counsels of his inmost breast."—*Rowe cor.*

" These were the *rigid* manners of the man,
This *was* the stubborn course in which they ran ;
The golden mean unchanging to pursue,
Constant to keep the *purpos'd* end in view."—*Rowe cor.*

" What greater grief can *on* a Roman seize,
Than to be forced to live on terms like these! "—*Rowe cor.*

" He views the naked town with joyful eyes,
While from his rage an *arméd* people flies."—*Rowe cor.*

" For planks and beams, he ravages the wood,
And the tough *oak* extends across the flood."—*Rowe cor.*

"A narrow pass the hornéd mole divides,
Narrow as that where *strong Euripus'* tides
Beat on Eubœan Chalcis' rocky sides."—*Rowe cor.*

" No force, no fears their hands *unarméd* bear,"—or,
" No force, no fears their hands unarm'd *now* bear,
But looks of peace and gentleness they wear."—*Rowe cor.*

" The ready warriors all aboard them ride,
And wait return of the retiring tide."—*Rowe cor.*

" He saw those troops that long had faithful stood,
Friends to his cause, and enemies to good,
Grown weary of their chief, and *satiate* with blood."—*Rowe cor.*

END OF THE KEY.

APPENDIX I.

TO PART FIRST, OR ORTHOGRAPHY.

OF THE SOUNDS OF THE LETTERS.

In the first chapter of Part I, the powers of the letters, or the elementary sounds of the English language, were duly enumerated and explained; for these, as well as the letters themselves, are few, and may be fully stated in few words: but, since we often express the same sound in many different ways, and also, in some instances, give to the same letter several different sounds,—or, it may be, no sound at all,—any adequate account of the powers of the letters considered severally according to usage,—that is, of the sound or sounds of each letter, with its mute positions, as these occur in practice,—must, it was thought, descend to a minuteness of detail not desirable in the first chapter of Orthography. For this reason, the following particulars have been reserved to be given here as an Appendix, pertaining to the First Part of this English Grammar.

OBSERVATIONS.

Obs. 1.—A proper discrimination of the different vowel sounds by the epithets most commonly used for this purpose,—such as *long* and *short*, *broad* and *slender*, *open* and *close*, or *open* and *shut*,—is made difficult, if not impossible, by reason of the different, and sometimes directly contradictory senses in which certain orthoepists have employed such terms. Wells says, " Vowel sounds are called *open* or *close*, according to the *relative size of the opening* through which the voice passes in forming them. Thus, *a* in *father*, and *o* in *nor*, are called *open* sounds, because they are formed by a *wide opening* of the organs of speech; while *e* in *me*, and *u* in *rule*, are called *close* sounds, because the organs are *nearly closed* in uttering them."—*School Grammar*, 1850, p. 32. Good use should fix the import of words. How does the passage here cited comport with this hint of Pope?

> " These, equal syllables alone require,
> Though *oft* the ear the open vowels tire."—*Essay on Criticism*, l. 344.

Obs. 2.—Walker, too, in his Principles, 64 and 65, on page 19th of his Critical Pronouncing Dictionary, mentions a similar distinction of vowels, " which arises from *the different apertures* of the mouth in forming them; " and says, " We accordingly find vowels denominated by the French, *ouvert* and *fermé*; by the Italians, *aperto* and *chiuso*; and by the English (.) *open* and *shut*. But whatever propriety there may be in the use of these terms in other languages, it is certain they must be used with caution in English for fear of confounding them with *long* and *short*. Dr. Johnson and other grammarians call the *a* in *father* the *open a*: which may, indeed, distinguish it from the *slender a* in *paper*; but not from the *broad a* in *water*, which is still more open. Each of these letters [the seven vowels] has a *short* sound, which may be called a *shut* sound; but the *long* sounds cannot be so properly denominated *open* as more or less *broad*; that is, the *a* in *paper*, the slender sound; the *a* in *father*, the broadish or middle sound; and the *a* in *water*, the broad sound. The same may be observed of the *o*. This letter has three long sounds, heard in *move*, *note*, *nor*; which graduate from slender to broadish, and broad [,] like [those three sounds of] the *a*. The ı also in *mine* may be called the broad ı, and that in *machine* the slender *i*; though each of them is equally *long*: and though these vowels that are *long* [,] may be said to be more or less *open* according to the different apertures of the mouth in forming them, yet the *short* vowels cannot be said to be more or less *shut*; for as *short* always implies *shut* (except in verse,) though *long* does not always imply *open*, we must be careful not to confound *long* and *open*, and *close* and *shut*, when we speak of the quantity and quality of the vowels. The truth of it is," continues he, " all vowels either terminate a syllable, or are united with a consonant. In the first case, if the accent be on the syllable, the vowel is *long*,though it may not be *open*: in the second case, where a syllable is terminated by a consonant, except that consonant be r, whether the accent be on the syllable or not, the vowel has its *short* sound, which, compared with its long one, may be called *shut*: but [,] as no vowel can be said to be *shut* that is not joined to a consonant, *all vowels that end syllables* may be said to be *open*, whether the accent be on them or not."—*Crit. Pron. Dict.*, New York, 1827, p. 19.

Obs. 3.—These suggestions of Walker's, though each in itself may seem clear and plausible, are, undoubtedly, in several respects, confused and self-contradictory. *Open* and *shut* are here inconsistently referred first to one principle of distinction, and then to an other:—first, (as are " *open* and *close* " by Wells,) to " the *relative size* of the opening," or to " the *different apertures* of the mouth; " and then, in the conclusion, to the *relative position* of the vowels with respect to other letters. These principles improperly give to each of the contrasted epithets two very different senses: as, with respect to aperture, *wide* and *narrow*; with respect to position, *closed* and *unclosed*. Now, that *open* may mean *unclosed*, or *close* be put for *closed*, is not to be questioned; but that *open* is a good word for *wide*, or that *shut* (not to say *close*) can well mean *narrow*, is an assumption hardly scholarlike. According to Walker, " *we must be careful* not to confound " *open* with *long*, or *shut* with *short*, or *close* with *shut*; and yet, if he himself does not, in the very paragraph above quoted, confound them all,—does not identify in sense, or fail to distinguish, the two words in each of these pairs,—I know not who can need his " caution." If there are vowel sounds which graduate through several degrees of openness or broadness, it would seem most natural to express these by regularly comparing the epithet preferred; as, *open*, *opener*, *openest*; or *broad*, *broader*, *broadest*. And again, if " all vowels that end syllables may be said to be open," then it is not true, that " the long sounds " of *a* in *paper*, *father*, *water*, cannot be so " denominated; " or that to " call the *a* in *father* the *open a*, may, indeed, distinguish it from the slender *a* in *paper*." Nor, on this principle, can it be said that " the broad *a* in *water* is still *more open*; " for this *a* no more " ends a syllable " than the others. If any vowel sound is to be called the *open* sound because the letter ends a syllable, or is not shut by a consonant, it is, undoubtedly, the *primal* and *most usual* sound, as found in the letter when accented, and not some other of rare occurrence.

Obs. 4.—Dr. Perley says, " It is greatly to be regretted that the different sounds of a vowel should be called by the names *long*, *short*, *slender*, and *broad*, which convey no idea of the nature of the sound, for *mat* and *not* are as long in poetry as *mate* and *note*. The first sound of a vowel [,] as [that of *a* in] *fate* [,] may be called *open*, because it is the sound which the vowel generally has when it ends a syllable; the second sound as [that of *a* in] *fat*, may be called *close*, because it is the sound which the vowel generally has when it is joined with a consonant following in the same syllable, as *fat-ten*; when there are more than two sounds of any vowel [,] they may be numbered onward; as *3 far*, *4 fall*."—*Perley's Gram.* p. 73.

Obs. 5.—Perley thought a long or short vowel sound essential to a long or short quantity in any syllable. By this, if he was wrong in it, (as, in the chapter on Versification, I have argued that he was,) he probably disturbed more the proper distinction of quantities, than that of vowel sounds. As regards *long* and *short*, therefore, Perley's regret seems to have cause; but, in making the same objection to " *slender*, and *broad*," he reasons illogically. So far as his view is right, however, it coincides with the following earlier suggestion: " The terms *long* and *short*, which are often used to denote certain vowel sounds, being also used, with a different import, to distinguish the quantity of syllables, are frequently misunderstood; for which reason, we have substituted for them the terms *open* and *close ;*—the former, to denote the sound usually given to a vowel when it *forms* or *ends* an accented syllable ; as, *ba, be, bi, bo, bu, by ;*—the latter, to denote the sound which the vowel commonly takes when *closed by a consonant ;* as, *ab, eb, ib, ob, ub.*"—*Brown's Institutes,* p. 285.

I. OF THE LETTER A.

The vowel *A* has *four* sounds properly its own ; they are named by various epithets : as,
1. The English, open, full, long, or slender *a ;* as in *aid, fame, favour, efficacious.*
2. The French, close, curt, short, or stopped *a ;* as in *bat, banner, balance, carrying.*
3. The Italian, broadish, grave, or middle *a ;* as in *far, father, aha, comma, scoria, sofa.*
4. The Dutch, German, Old-Saxon, or broad *a ;* as in *wall, haul, walk, warm, water.*

OBSERVATIONS.

OBS. 1.—Concerning the number of sounds pertaining to the vowel *a,* or to certain other particular letters, and consequently in regard to the whole number of the sounds which constitute the oral elements of the English language, our educational literati,—the grammarians, orthoepists, orthographers, elocutionists, phonographers, and lexicographers,—are found to have entertained and inculcated a great variety of opinions. In their different countings, the number of our phonical elements varies from twenty-six to more than forty. Wells says 'here are "*about forty* elementary sounds."—*School Gram.* § 64. His first edition was more positive, and stated them at "*forty-one.*" See the last and very erroneous passage which I have cited at the foot of page 149. In Worcester's Universal and Critical Dictionary, there appear to be noted several *more* than *forty-one ;* but I know not whether this author, or Walker either, has anywhere told us how many of his marked sounds he considered to be severally different from all others. Sheridan and Jones admitted *twenty-eight.* Churchill acknowledges, as undisputed and indisputable, only *twenty-six ;* though he enumerates, "Of simple vowel sounds, *twelve,* or perhaps *thirteen,*" (New Grammar, p. 5,) and says, "The consonant sounds in the English language are *seventeen,* or rather *twenty.*"—P. 13.

OBS. 2.—Thus, while Pitman, Comstock, and others, are amusing themselves with the folly of inventing new "Phonetic Alphabets," or of overturning all orthography to furnish "a character for each of the 38 elementary sounds," more or fewer, one of the acutest observers among our grammarians can fix on no number more definite or more considerable than *thirty-one,* *thirty-two,* or *thirty-three ;* and the finding of these he announces with a "*perhaps,*" and the admission that other writers object to as many as *five* of the questionable number. Churchill's vowel sounds, he says, "may be found in the following words : 1. Bate, 2. Bat, 3. Ball ; 4. Bat, 5. Be ; 6 Bit ; 7. Bot, 8. Bone, 9. Boon ; 10. But, 11. Bull ; 12. Lovely ; 13. Wool."—*New Grammar,* p. 5. To this he adds : "Many of the writers on orthoepy, however, consider the first and fourth of the sounds above distinguished as actually the same, the former differing from the latter only by being lengthened in the pronunciation. They also reckon the seventh sound, to be the third shortened ; the twelfth, the fifth shortened ; and the eleventh, the ninth shortened. Some consider the fifth and sixth as differing only in length ; and most esteem the eleventh and thirteenth as identical."—*Ib.*

OBS. 3.—Now, it is plain, that these six identifications, or so many of them as are admitted, must diminish by six, or by the less number allowed, the thirteen vowel sounds enumerated by this author. By the best authorities, *W* initial, as in "*Wool,*" is reckoned a *consonant ;* and, of course, its sound is supposed to differ in some degree from that of *oo* in "Boon," or that of *u* in "Bull,"—the ninth sound or the eleventh in the foregoing series. By Walker, Murray, and other popular writers, the sound of *y* in "Lovely" is accounted to be essentially the same as that of *e* in "Be." The twelfth and the thirteenth, then, of this list, being removed, and three others added,—namely, the *a* heard in *far,* the *i* in *fine,* and the *u* in *fuse,*—we shall have the *fourteen vowel sounds* which are enumerated by L. Murray and others, and adopted by the author of the present work.

OBS. 4.—Wells says, "*A* has *six* sounds :—1. Long ; as in *late.* 2. Grave ; as in *father.* 3. Broad ; as in *fall.* 4. Short ; as in *man.* 5. The sound heard in *care, hare.* 6 Intermediate between a in *man* and *a* in *father ;* as in *grass, pass, branch.*"—*School Gram.,* 1850, p. 33. Besides these six, Worcester recognizes a seventh sound,—the "*A obscure ;* as in *war, rival.*"—*Univ. and Crit. Dict.* p. ix. Such a multiplication of the oral elements of our first vowel,—or, indeed, any extension of them beyond four,—appears to me to be unadvisable : because it not only makes our alphabet the more defective, but is unnecessary, and not sustained by our best and most popular orthoepical authorities. The sound of *a* in *har,* (and in *rival* too, if made "*obscure,*") is a borrowed one, pertaining more properly to the letter *u.* In *grass, pass,* and *branch,* properly uttered, the *a* is essentially the same as in *man.* In *care* and *hare,* we have the first sound of *a,* made as slender as the *r* will admit.

OBS. 5.—Concerning his fifth sound of *a,* Wells cites authorities thus : "Walker, Webster, Sheridan, Fulton and Knight, Kenrick, Jones, and Nares, give *a* in *care* the *long* sound of *a,* as in *late.* Page and Day give it the *short* sound of *a,* as in *mat.* See Page's Normal Chart, and Day's Art of Elocution. Worcester and Perry make the sound of *a* in *care* a separate element ; and this distinction is also recognized by Russell, Mandeville, and Wright. See Russell's Lessons in Enunciation, Mandeville's Elements of Reading and Oratory, and Wright's Orthography."—*Wells's School Grammar,* p. 34. Now the opinion that *a* in *care* has its long, primal sound, and is not properly "a separate element," is maintained also by Murray, Hiley, Bullions, Scott, and Cobb ; and is, undoubtedly, much more prevalent than any other. It accords, too, with the scheme of Johnson. To count this *a* by itself, seems too much like a distinction without a difference.

OBS. 6.—On his sixth sound of *a,* Wells remarks as follows : "Many persons pronounce this *a* incorrectly, giving it either the grave or the short sound. Perry, Jones, Nares, Webster, and Day, give to *a* in *grass* the grave sound, as in *father ;* while Walker, Jamieson, and Russell, give it the short sound, as in *man.* But good speakers generally pronounce *a* in *grass, plant,* etc., as a distinct element, intermediate between the grave and the short sound."—*School Gram.* p. 34. He also cites Worcester and Smart to the same effect ; and thinks, with the latter, "*There can be no harm* in avoiding the censure of both parties by *shunning the extreme* that offends the taste of each."—*Ib.* p 35. But I say, that a needless multiplication of questionable vowel powers, difficult to be discriminated, *is* "harm," or a fault in teaching ; and, where intelligent orthoepists dispute whether words have "the *grave* or the *short* sound " of *a,* how can others, who condemn both parties, acceptably split the difference, and form "a distinct element" in the interval? Words are often mispronounced, and the French or close *a* may be mistaken for the Italian or broadish *a,* and *vice versa ;* but, between the two, there does not appear to be room for an other distinguishable from both. Dr. Johnson says, (inaccurately indeed,) "*A* has *three* sounds, the slender, [the] open, and [the] broad. *A* slender is found in *most words,* as *face, mane. A* open is the *a* of the Italian, or nearly resembles it ; as *father, congratulate, fancy, glass. A* broad resembles the *a* of the German ; as *all, wall, call.* ☞ The *short a* approaches to the *a* open, as *grass.*"—*Johnson's Grammar, in his Quarto Dictionary,* p. 1. Thus the same word, *grass,* that serves Johnson for an example of "the *short a,*" is used by Wells and Worcester to exemplify the "*a intermediate ;*" while of the Doctor's five instances of what he calls the "*a open,*" three, if not four, are evidently such as nearly all readers nowadays would call close or short !

OBS. 7.—There are several grammarians who agree in ascribing to our first vowel *five* sounds, but who nevertheless oppose one an other in making up the five. Thus, according to Hart, "A has five sounds of its own, as in fate, fare, far, fall, fat."—*Hart's E. Gram.* p. 26. According to W. Allen, "A has five sounds :—the long or slender, as in *cane ;* the short or open, as in *can ;* the middle, as in *arm ;* the broad, as in *all ;* and the *broad* contracted, as in *want.*"—*Allen's E. Gram.* p. 6. P. Davis has the same sounds in a different order, thus : "A [as in] mane, mar, fall, mat, what."—*Davis's E. Gram.* p. xvi. Mennye says, "A has five sounds : as, 1 fame, 2 fat, 3 false, 4 farm, 5 beggar."—*Mennye's E. Gram.* p. 55. Here the fifth sound is the seventh of Worcester, —the "A *obscure.*"

DIPHTHONGS BEGINNING WITH A.

The only proper diphthong in which *a* is put first, is the word *ay,* meaning *yes :* in which *a* has its *middle* sound, as in *ah,* and *y* is like *open e,* or *ee,* uttered feebly—*ah-ee.*

Aa, when pronounced as an improper diphthong, and not as pertaining to two syllables, usually takes the sound of *close a;* as in *Balaam, Canaan, Isaac.* In many words, as in *Baäl, Gaäl, Gaäsh,* the diæresis occurs. In *baa,* the cry of a sheep, we hear the Italian sound of *a;* and, since we hear it but once, one *a* or the other must be silent.

Æ, a Latin improper diphthong. common also in the Anglo-Saxon, generally has, according to modern orthoëpists, the sound of *open e* or *ee;* as in *Cæsar, ænigma, pæan;*— sometimes that of *close* or *short e;* as in *apheresis, diæresis, et cætera.* Some authors, judging the *a* of this diphthong to be needless, reject it, and write *Cesar, enigma,* &c.

Ai, an improper diphthong, generally has the sound of *open* or *long a;* as in *sail, avail, vainly.* In a final unaccented syllable, it sometimes preserves the first sound of *a;* as in *chilblain, mortmain:* but oftener takes the sound of *close* or *short i;* as in *certain, curtain, mountain, villain.* In *said, saith, again,* and *against,* it takes the sound of *close* or *short e;* and in the name *Britain,* that of *close* or *short u.*

Ao, an improper diphthong, occurs in the word *gaol,* now frequently written as it is pronounced, *jail;* also in *gaoler,* which may be written *jailer;* and in the compounds of *gaol:* and, again, it is found in the adjective *extraordinary,* and its derivatives, in which, according to nearly all our orthoëpists, the *a* is silent. The name *Pharaoh,* is pronounced *Fā'rō.*

Au, an improper diphthong, is generally sounded like *broad a;* as in *cause, caught, applause.* Before *n* and an other consonant, it usually has the sound of *grave* or *middle a;* as in *aunt, flaunt, gaunt, launch, laundry.* So in *laugh, laughter,* and their derivatives. *Gauge* and *gauger* are pronounced *gage* and *gager,* and sometimes written so.

Aw, an improper diphthong, is always sounded like *broad a;* as in *draw, drawn, drawl.*

Ay, an improper diphthong, like *ai,* has usually the sound of *open* or *long a;* as in *day, pay, delay:* in *sayst* and *says,* it has the sound of *close* or *short e.*

TRIPHTHONGS BEGINNING WITH A.

Awe is sounded *au,* like *broad a. Aye,* an adverb signifying *always,* has the sound of *open* or *long a* only; being different, both in sound and in spelling, from the adverb *ay, yes,* with which it is often carelessly confounded. The distinction is maintained by Johnson, Walker, Todd, Chalmers, Jones, Cobb, Maunder, Bolles, and others; but Webster and Worcester give it up, and write "*ay,* or *aye,*" each sounded *ah-ee,* for the affirmation, and "*aye,*" sounded *ā,* for the adverb of time: Ainsworth, on the contrary, has *ay* only, for either sense, and does not note the pronunciation.

II. OF THE LETTER B.

The consonant *B* has but one sound; as in *boy, robber, cub. B* is silent before *t* or after *m* in the same syllable; as in *debt, debtor, doubt, dumb, lamb, climb, tomb.* It is heard in *subtile,* fine; but not in *subtle,* cunning.

III. OF THE LETTER C.

The consonant *C* has two sounds, neither of them peculiar to this letter; the one *hard,* like that of *k,* the other *soft,* or rather *hissing,* like that of *s. C* before *a, o, u, l, r, t,* or when it ends a syllable, is generally hard, like *k;* as in *can, come, curb, clay, crab, act, action, accent, flaccid. C* before *e, i,* or *y,* is always soft, like *s;* as in *cent, civil, decency, acid.*

In a few words, *c* takes the *flat* sound of *s,* like that of *z;* as in *discern, suffice, sacrifice, sice. C* before *ea, ia, ie, io,* or *eou,* when the accent precedes, sounds like *sh;* as in *ocean, special, species, gracious, cetaceous. C* is silent in *czar, czarina, victuals, indict, muscle, corpuscle,* and the second syllable of *Connecticut.*

Ch is generally sounded like *tch,* or *tsh,* which is the same to the ear; as in *church, chance, child.* But, in words derived from the learned languages, it has the sound of *k;* as in *character, scheme, catechise, chorus, choir, chyle, patriarch, drachma, magna charta:* except in *chart, charter, charity. Ch,* in words derived from the French, takes the sound of *sh;* as in *chaise, machine.* In Hebrew words or names, in general, *ch* sounds like *k;* as in *Chebar, Sirach, Enoch:* but in *Rachel, cherub,* and *cherubim,* we have Anglicized the sound by uttering it as *tch. Loch,* a Scottish word, sometimes also a medical term, is heard as *lok.*

"*Arch,* before a vowel, is pronounced *ark;* as in *archives, archangel, archipelago:* except in *arched, archer, archery, archenemy.* Before a consonant, it is pronounced *artch;* as in *archbishop, archduke, archfiend.*"—See *W. Allen's Gram.* p. 10. *Ch* is silent in *schism, yacht,* and *drachm.* In *schedule,* some utter it as *k;* others, as *sh;* and many make it mute: I like the first practice.

IV. OF THE LETTER D.

The general sound of the consonant *D,* is that which is heard in *dog, eddy, did. D,* in the termination *ed,* preceded by a sharp consonant, takes the sound of *t,* when the *e* is suppressed or unheard: as in *faced, stuffed, cracked, tripped, passed;* pronounced *faste, stuft, cract, tript, past. D* before *ia, ie, io,* or *eou,* when the accent precedes, generally sounds like *j;* as in *Indian, soldier, tedious, hideous.* So in *verdure, arduous, education.*

V. OF THE LETTER E.

The vowel *E* has *two* sounds properly its own,—and I incline to think, *three*:—
1. The open, long, full, or primal *e*; as in *me, mere, menial, melodious.*
2. The close, curt, short, or stopped *e*; as in *men, merry, ebony, strength.*
3. The obscure or faint *e*; as in *open, garden, shovel, able.* This third sound is scarcely perceptible, and barely sufficient to articulate the consonant and form a syllable.

E final is mute, and belongs to the syllable formed by the preceding vowel or diphthong; as in *age, eve, ice, ore.* Except—1. In the words, *be, he, me, we, she,* in which it has the open sound; and the article *the,* wherein it is open before a vowel, and obscure before a consonant. 2. In Greek and Latin words, in which it has its open sound, and forms a distinct syllable, or the basis of one; as in *Penelope, Pasiphaë, Cyaneë, Gargaphië, Arsinoë, apostrophe, catastrophe, simile, extempore, epitome.* 3. In the terminations *cre, gre, tre,* in which it has the sound of *close* or *curt u,* heard before the *r;* as in *acre, meagre, centre.*

Mute *e,* after a single consonant, or after *st* or *th,* generally preserves the open or long sound of the preceding vowel; as in *cane, here, pine, cone, tune, thyme, baste, waste, lathe, clothe:* except in syllables unaccented; as in the last of *genuine;*—and in a few monosyllables; as *bade, are, were, gone, shone, one, done, give, live, shove, love.*

DIPHTHONGS BEGINNING WITH E.

E before an other vowel, in general, either forms with it an *improper* diphthong, or else belongs to a separate syllable. We do not hear both vowels in one syllable, except perhaps in *eu* or *ew.*

Ea, an improper diphthong, mostly sounds like *open* or *long e;* as in *ear, fear, tea:* frequently, like *close* or *curt e;* as in *head, health, leather:* sometimes, like *open* or *long a;* as in *steak, bear, forswear:* rarely, like *middle a;* as in *heart, hearth, hearken.* *Ea* in an unaccented syllable, sounds like *close* or *curt u;* as in *vengeance, pageant.*

Ee, an improper diphthong, mostly sounds like one *open* or *long e;* as in *eel, sheep, tree, trustee, referee.* The contractions *e'er* and *ne'er,* are pronounced *air* and *nair,* and not like *ear* and *near.* *E'en,* however, preserves the sound of *open e.* *Been* is most commonly heard with the curt sound of *i, bin.*

Ei, an improper diphthong, mostly sounds like the *primal* or *long a;* as in *reign, veil:* frequently, like *open* or *long e;* as in *deceit, either, neither, seize:* sometimes, like *open* or *long i;* as in *height, sleight, heigh-ho:* often, in unaccented syllables, like *close* or *curt i;* as in *foreign, forfeit, surfeit, sovereign:* rarely, like *close e;* as in *heifer, nonpareil.*

Eo, an improper diphthong, in *people,* sounds like *open* or *long e;* in *leopard* and *jeopardy,* like *close* or *curt e;* in *yeoman,* according to the best usage, like *open* or *long o;* in *George, Georgia, georgic,* like *close o;* in *dungeon, puncheon, sturgeon, &c.,* like *close u.* In *feoff,* and its derivatives, the *close* or *short* sound of *e* is most fashionable; but some prefer the long sound of *e;* and some write the word *"fief."* *Feod, feodal, feodary,* and *feodatory,* are now commonly written as they are pronounced, *feud, feudal, feudary, feudatory.*

Eu and *ew* are sounded alike, and almost always with the diphthongal sound of *open* or *long u;* as in *feud, deuce, jewel, dew, few, new.* These diphthongs, when initial, sound like *yu.* Nouns beginning with this sound, require the article *a,* and not *an,* before them; as, *A European, a ewer.* After *r* or *rh, eu* and *ew* are commonly sounded like *oo;* as in *drew, grew, screw, rheumatism.* In *sew* and *Shrewsbury, ew* sounds like *open o:* Worcester, however, prefers the sound of *oo* in the latter word. *Shew* and *strew,* having the same meaning as *show* and *strow,* are sometimes, by sameness of pronunciation, made to be the same words; and sometimes distinguished as different words, by taking the sounds *shu* and *stroo.*

Ey, accented, has the sound of *open* or *long a;* as in *bey, prey, survey:* unaccented, it has the sound of *open e;* as in *alley, valley, money.* *Key* and *ley* are pronounced, *kee, lee.*

TRIPHTHONGS BEGINNING WITH E.

Eau, a French triphthong, sounds like *open o;* as in *beau, flambeau, portmanteau, bureau:* except in *beauty,* and its compounds, in which it is pronounced like *open u,* as if the word were written *buty.*

Eou is a combination of vowels sometimes heard in one syllable, especially after *c* or *g;* as in *crus-ta-ceous, gor-geous.* Walker, in his Rhyming Dictionary, gives one hundred and twenty words ending in *eous,* in all of which he separates these vowels; as in *ex-tra-ne-ous.* And why, in his Pronouncing Dictionary, he gave us several such anomalies as *fa-ba-ce-ous* in four syllables and *her-ba-ceous* in three, it is not easy to tell. The best rule is this: after *c* or *g,* unite these vowels; after the other consonants, separate them.

Ewe is a triphthong having the sound of *yu,* and forming a word. The vulgar pronunciation *yoo* should be carefully avoided.

Eye is an improper triphthong which also forms a word, and is pronounced like *open i,* or the pronoun *I.*

VI. OF THE LETTER F.

The consonant *F* has one unvaried sound, which is heard in *fan, effort, staff:* except *of,* which, when simple, is pronounced *ov.*

VII. OF THE LETTER G.

The consonant *G* has two sounds;—the one *hard*, guttural, and peculiar to this letter; the other *soft*, like that of *j*. *G* before *a, o, u, l, r*, or at the end of a word, is hard; as in *game, gone, gull, glory, grace, log, bog*: except in *goal*. *G* before *e, i*, or *y*, is soft; as in *gem, ginger, elegy*. Except—1. In *get, give, gewgaw, finger*, and a few other words. 2. When a syllable is added to a word ending in *g*: as, *long, longer; fog, foggy*.

G is silent before *m* or *n* in the same syllable; as in *phlegm, apothegm, gnaw, design. G*, when silent, usually lengthens the preceding vowel; as in *resign, impregn, impugn*.

Gh at the beginning of a word has the sound of *g hard;* as in *ghastly, gherkin, Ghibelline, ghost, ghoul, ghyll:* in other situations, it is generally silent; as in *high, mighty, plough, bough, though, through, fight, night, bought. Gh final* sometimes sounds like *f;* as in *laugh, rough, tough;* and sometimes, like *g hard;* as in *burgh*. In *hough, lough, shough*, it sounds like *k*, or *ck;* thus, *hock, lock, shock*.

VIII. OF THE LETTER H.

The sound of the consonant *H*, (though articulate and audible when properly uttered,) is little more than an aspirate breathing. It is heard in *hat, hit, hot, hut, adhere*.

H at the beginning of a word, is always sounded; except in *heir, herb, honest, honour, hospital, hostler, hour, humble, humour*, with their compounds and derivatives. *H* after *r*, is always silent; as in *rhapsody, rhetoric, rheum, rhubarb. H final*, immediately following a vowel, is always silent; as in *ah, Sarah, Nineveh, Shiloh*.

IX. OF THE LETTER I.

The vowel *I* has *three* sounds, each very common to it, and perhaps properly its own :—

1. The open, long, full, or primal *i ;* as in *life, fine, final, time, bind, child, sigh, pint, resign*. This is a diphthongal sound, equivalent to the sounds of *middle a* and *open e* quickly united.

2. The close, curt, short, or stopped *i ;* as in *ink, limit, disfigure, mimicking*.

3. The feeble, faint, or slender *i*, accentless; as in *divest, doctrinal, diversity*.

This third sound is equivalent to that of *open e*, or *ee*, uttered feebly. *I* generally has this sound when it occurs at the end of an unaccented syllable : except at the end of Latin words, or of ancient names, where it is *open* or *long ;* as in *literati, Nervii, Eli, Levi*.

In some words, (principally from other modern languages,) *i* has the full sound of *open e*, under the accent ; as in *Porto Rico, machine, magazine, antique, shire*.

Accented *i* followed by a vowel, has its open or primal sound ; and the vowels belong to separate syllables ; as in *pliant, diet, satiety, violet, pious*. Unaccented *i* followed by a vowel, has its feeble sound ; as in *expatiate, obedient, various, abstemious*.

DIPHTHONGS BEGINNING WITH I.

I, in the situation last described, readily coalesces with the vowel which follows, and is often sunk into the same syllable, forming a proper diphthong ; as in *fustian, quotient, question*. The terminations *cion, sion*, and *tion*, are generally pronounced *shun;* and *cious* and *tious* are pronounced *shus*.

Ie is commonly an improper diphthong. *Ie* in *die, hie, lie, pie, tie, vie*, and their derivatives, has the sound of *open i. Ie* in words from the French, (as *cap-a-pie, ecurie, grenadier, siege, bier*,) has the sound of *open e*. So, generally, in the middle of English roots; as in *chief, grief, thief;* but, in *sieve*, it has the sound of *close* or *short i*. In *friend*, and its derivatives or compounds, it takes the sound of *close e*.

TRIPHTHONGS BEGINNING WITH I.

The triphthongs *ieu* and *iew* both sound like *open* or *long u ;* as in *lieu, adieu, view*.

The three vowels *iou*, in the termination *ious*, often fall into one syllable, and form a triphthong. There are two hundred and forty-five words of this ending; and more than two hundred derivatives from them. Walker has several puzzling inconsistencies in their pronunciation ; such as *fas-tid-i-ous* and *per-fid-ious, con-ta-gi-ous* and *sac-ri-le-gious*. After *c, g, t*, or *x*, these vowels should coalesce ; as in *gra-cious, re-li-gious, vex-a-tious, ob-nox-ious*, and about two hundred other words. After the other consonants, let them form two syllables ; (except when there is a synæresis in poetry ;) as in *du-bi-ous, o-di-ous, va-ri-ous, en-vi-ous*.

X. OF THE LETTER J.

The consonant *J*, the tenth letter of the English alphabet, has invariably the sound of *soft g*, like the *g* in *giant*, which some say is equivalent to the complex sound *dzh ;* as, *jade, jet, jilt, joy, justice, jewel, prejudice*.

XI. OF THE LETTER K.

The consonant *K*, not silent, has uniformly the sound of *c hard;* and occurs where *c* would have its soft sound : as in *keep, looking, kind, smoky*.

K before *n* is silent ; as in *knave, know, knuckle*. In stead of doubling *c final*, we write *ck ;* as in *lack, lock, luck, attac'k*. In English words, *k* is never doubled, though two Kays may come together in certain compounds ; as in *brickkiln, jackknife*. Two Kays, belonging to different syllables, also stand together in a few Scripture names ; as in *Akkub*, *Bakbakkar*, *Bukki*, *Bukkiah*. *Habakkuk*, *Hakkoz*, *Ikkesh*, *Sukkiims*.   C before *k*, though it does not always double the sound which *c* or *k* in such a situation must represent, always shuts or shortens the preceding vowel ; as in *rack*, *speck*, *freckle*, *cockle*, *wicked*.

XII. OF THE LETTER L.

The consonant *L*, the plainest of the semivowels, has a soft, liquid sound ; as in *line*, *lily*, *roll*, *follow*. *L* is sometimes silent ; as in *Holmes*, *alms*, *almond*, *calm*, *chalk*, *walk*, *calf*, *half*, *could*, *would*, *should*. *L*, too, is frequently doubled where it is heard but once ; as in *hill*, *full*, *travelled:* and any letter that is written twice, and not twice sounded, must there be once mute ; as the last in *baa*, *ebb*, *add*, *see*, *staff*, *egg*, *all*, *inn*, *coo*, *err*, *less*, *buzz*.

XIII. OF THE LETTER M.

The consonant *M* is a semivowel and a liquid, capable of an audible, humming sound through the nose, when the mouth is closed. It is heard in *map*, *murmur*, *mammon*. In the old words, *compt*, *accompt*, *comptroller*, (for *count*, *account*, *controller*,) the *m* is sounded as *n*. *M* before *n*, at the beginning of a word, is silent ; as in *Mnason*, *Mnemosyne*, *mnemonics*.

XIV. OF THE LETTER N.

The consonant *N*, which is also a semivowel and a liquid, has two sounds ;—the first, the pure and natural sound of *n* ; as in *nun*, *banner*, *cannon* ;—the second, the ringing sound of *ng*, heard before certain gutturals ; as in *think*, *mangle*, *conquer*, *congress*, *singing*, *twinkling*, *Cen'chreä*. The latter sound should be carefully preserved in all words ending in *ing*, and in such others as require it. The sounding of the syllable *ing* as if it were *in*, is a vulgarism in utterance ; and the writing of it so, is, as it would seem by the usage of Burns, a Scotticism.

N final preceded by *m*, is silent ; as in *hymn*, *solemn*, *column*, *damn*, *condemn*, *autumn*. But this *n* becomes audible in an additional syllable ; as in *autumnal*, *condemnable*, *damning*.

XV. OF THE LETTER O.

The vowel *O* has *three* different sounds, which are properly its own :—
1. The open, full, primal, or long *o* ; as in *no*, *note*, *opiate*, *opacity*, *Roman*.
2. The close, curt, short, or stopped *o* ; as in *not*, *nor*, *torrid*, *dollar*, *fond'e*.
3. The slender or narrow *o*, like *oo* ; as in *prove*, *move*, *who*, *to*, *do*, *tomb*.

O, in many words, sounds like *close* or *curt u* ; as in *love*, *shove*, *son*, *come*, *nothing*, *dost*, *attorney*, *gallon*, *dragon*, *comfit*, *comfort*, *coloration*. One is pronounced *wun* ; and *once*, *wunce*. In the termination *on* immediately after the accent, *o* is often sunk into a sound scarcely perceptible, like that of *obscure e* ; as in *mason*, *person*, *lesson*.

DIPHTHONGS BEGINNING WITH O.

Oa, an improper diphthong, has the sound of *open* or *long o* ; as in *boat*, *coal*, *roach*, *coast*, *coastwise:* except in *broad* and *groat*, which have the sound of *broad a*.

Oe, an improper diphthong, when *final*, has the sound of *open* or *long o* ; as in *doe*, *foe*, *throe:* except in *canoe*, *shoe*, pronounced *canoo*, *shoo*. *Œ*, a Latin diphthong, generally sounds like *open e* ; as in *Antœci*, *fœtus:* sometimes, like *close* or *curt e* ; as in *fœtid*, *fœticide*. But the English word *fétid* is often, and perhaps generally, written without the *o*.

Oi is generally a proper diphthong, uniting the sound of *close o* or *broad a*, and that of *open e* ; as in *boil*, *coil*, *soil*, *rejoice*. But the vowels, when they appear together, sometimes belong to separate syllables ; as in *Stoic*, *Stoicism*. *Oi* unaccented, sometimes has the sound of *close* or *curt i* ; as in *avoirdupois*, *connoisseur*, *tortoise*.

Oo, an improper diphthong, generally has the slender sound of *o* ; as in *coo*, *too*, *woo*, *fool*, *room*. It has, in some words, a shorter or closer sound, (like that of *u* in *bull*,) as in *foot*, *good*, *wood*, *stood*, *wool* ;—that of *close u*, in *blood* and *flood* ;—and that of *open o*, in *door* and *floor*. Derivatives from any of these, sound as their primitives.

Ou is generally a proper diphthong, uniting the sound of *close* or *curt o*, and that of *u* as heard in *bull*,—or *u* sounded as *oo* ; as in *bound*, *found*, *sound*, *ounce*, *thou*. *Ou* is also, in certain instances, an improper diphthong ; and, as such, it has *six* different sounds :—(1.) That of *close* or *curt u* ; as in *rough*, *tough*, *young*, *flourish*. (2.) That of *broad a* ; as in *ought*, *bought*, *thought*. (3.) That of *open* or *long o* ; as in *court*, *dough*, *four*, *though*. (4.) That of *close* or *curt o* ; as in *cough*, *trough*, *lough*, *shough:* which are, I believe, the only examples. (5.) That of *slender o*, or *oo* ; as in *soup*, *you*, *through*. (6.) That of *u* in *bull*, or of *oo* shortened ; only in *would*, *could*, *should*.

Ow generally sounds like the proper diphthong *ou*,—or like a union of *short o* with *oo* ; as in *brown*, *dowry*, *now*, *shower:* but it is often an improper diphthong, having only the sound of *open* or *long o* ; as in *know*, *show*, *stow*.

Oy is a proper diphthong, equivalent in sound to *oi* ; as in *joy*, *toy*, *oyster*.

TRIPHTHÓNGS BEGINNING WITH O.

Œu is a French triphthong, pronounced in English as *oo*, and occurring in the word *manœuvre*, with its several derivatives. *Owe* is an improper triphthong, and an English word, in which the *o* only is heard, and heard always with its long or open sound.

XVI. OF THE LETTER P.

The consonant *P*, when not written before *h*, has commonly one peculiar sound; which is heard in *pen, pine, sup, supper*. The word *cupboard* is usually pronounced *kubburd*. *P*, written with an audible consonant, is sometimes itself silent; as in *psalm, psalter, pseudography, psychology, ptarmigan, ptyalism, receipt, corps*.

Ph generally sounds like *f*; as in *philosophy*. In *Stephen* and *nephew*, *ph* has the sound of *v*. The *h* after *p*, is silent in *diphthong, triphthong, naphtha, ophthalmic;* and both the *p* and the *h* are silent in *apophthegm, phthisis, phthisical*. From the last three words, *ph* is sometimes dropped.

XVII. OF THE LETTER Q.

The consonant *Q*, being never silent, never final, never doubled, and not having a sound peculiar to itself, is invariably heard, in English, with the power of *k;* and is always followed by the vowel *u*, which, in words *purely English*, is sounded like the narrow *o*, or *oo*,—or, perhaps, is squeezed into the consonantal sound of *w;*—as in *queen, quaver, quiver, quarter, request*. In some words of *French* origin, the *u* after *q* is silent; as in *coquet, liquor, burlesque, etiquette*.

XVIII. OF THE LETTER R.

The consonant *R*, called also a semivowel and a liquid, has usually, at the beginning of a word, or before a vowel, a rough or pretty strong sound; as in *roll, rose, roam, proudly, prorogue*. "In other positions," it is said by many to be "smooth" or "soft;" " as in *hard, ford, word*."—*W. Allen*.

OBSERVATIONS.

OBS. 1.—The letter *R* turns the tip of the tongue up against or towards the roof of the mouth, where the sound may be lengthened, roughened, trilled, or quavered. Consequently, this element may, at the will of the speaker, have more or less—little or nothing, or even very much—of that peculiar roughness, jar, or whur, which is commonly said to constitute the sound. The extremes should here be avoided. Some readers very improperly omit the sound of *r* from many words to which it pertains; pronouncing *or* as *awe*, *nor* as *knaw*, *for* as *fawgh*, and *war* as the first syllable of *water*. On the other hand, "The excessive *trilling* of the *r*, as practised by some speakers, is a great fault."—*D. P. Page*.

OBS. 2.—Dr. Johnson, in his "Grammar of the English Tongue," says, "*R* has the same *rough snarling sound* as in other tongues."—P. 3. Again, in his Quarto Dictionary, under this letter, he says, "*R* is called the *canine letter*, because it is uttered *with some resemblance to the growl or snarl of a cur;* it has *one constant sound* in English, such as it has in other languages; as, *red, rose, more, muriatick*." Walker, however, who has a greater reputation as an orthoepist, teaches that, "There is a distinction in the sound of this letter, which is," says he, "in my opinion, *of no small importance;* and that is, the [distinction of] the rough and [the] smooth *r*. Ben Jonson," continues he, " in his Grammar, says, ' It is sounded firm in the beginning of words, and more liquid in the middle and ends, as in *rarer, riper;* and so in the Latin.' The rough *r* is formed by jarring the tip of the tongue against the roof of the mouth near the fore teeth : the smooth *r* is a vibration of the lower part of the tongue, near the root, against the inward region of the palate, near the entrance of the throat."—*Walker's Principles*, No. 419 ; *Octavo Dict.* p. 48.

OBS. 3.—Wells, with his characteristic indecision, forbears all recognition of this difference, and all intimation of the quality of the sound, whether smooth or rough; saying, in his own text, only this: "*R* has the sound heard in *rare*."—*School Grammar*, p. 40. Then, referring the student to sundry authorities, he adds in a footnote certain "quotations," that are said to "present a general view of the different opinions which exist among orthoepists respecting this letter." And so admirably are these authorities or opinions balanced and offset, one class against an other, that it is hard to tell which has the odds. First, though it is not at all probable that Wells's utterance of "*rare*" exhibits twice over the *rough snarl* of Johnson's *r*, the "general view" seems intended to confirm the indefinite teaching above, thus : "'*R* has one constant sound in English.'—*Johnson*. The same view is adopted by Webster, Perry, Kenrick, Sheridan, Jones, Jameson, Knowles, and others."—*School Grammar*, p. 40. In counterpoise of these, Wells next cites about as many more—namely, Frazee, Page, Russell, Walker, Rush, Barber, Comstock, and Smart,—as maintaining or admitting that *r* has sometimes a rough sound, and sometimes a smoother one.

XIX. OF THE LETTER S.

The consonant *S* has a sharp, hissing, or hard sound ; as in *sad, sister, thus :* and a flat, buzzing, or soft sound, like that of *z ;* as in *rose, dismal, bosom, husband*. *S*, at the beginning of words, or after any of the sharp consonants, is always sharp; as in *see, steps, cliffs, sits, stocks, smiths*. *S*, after any of the flat mutes, or at the end of words when not preceded by a sharp consonant, is generally flat; as in *eyes, trees, beds, bags, calves*. But in the English termination *ous*, or in the Latin *us*, it is sharp; as *joyous, vigorous, hiatus*.

Ss is generally sharp; as in *pass, kiss, harass, assuage, basset, cassock, remissness*. But the first two Esses in *possess*, or any of its regular derivatives, as well as the two in *dissolve*, or its proximate kin, sound like two Zees; and the soft or flat sound is commonly given to each *s* in *hyssop, hussy*, and *hussar*. In *scissel, scissible*, and *scissile*, all the Esses hiss ;—in *scissors*, the last three of the four are flat, like *z ;*—but in the middle of *scissure* and *scission* we hear the sound of *zh*.

S, in the termination *sion*, takes the sound of *sh*, after a consonant; as in *aspersion, session, passion, mission, compulsion :* and that of *zh*, after a vowel; as in *invasion, elision, confusion*.

In the verb *assure*, and each of its derivatives, also in the nouns *pressure* and *fissure*, with their derivatives, we hear, according to Walker, the sound of *sh* for each *s*, or twice in each

word; but, according to the orthoëpy of Worcester, that sound is heard only in the accented syllable of each word, and the vowel in each unaccented syllable is *obscure*.
S is silent or mute in the words, *isle, island, aisle, demesne, corps,* and *viscount*.

XX. OF THE LETTER T.

The general sound of the consonant *T*, is heard in *time, letter, set*. *T*, immediately after
the accent, takes the sound of *tch*, before *u*, and generally also before *eou*; as in *nature, feature, virtue, righteous, courteous*: when *s* or *x* precedes, it takes this sound before *ia* or *io*; as
in *fustian, bastion, mixtion*. But the general or most usual sound of *t* after the accent, when
followed by *i* and an other vowel, is that of *sh*; as in *creation, patient, cautious*.

In English, *t* is seldom, if ever, silent or powerless. In *depot*, however, a word borrowed
from the French, we do not sound it; and in *chestnut*, which is a compound of our own, it
is much oftener written than heard. In *often* and *soften*, some think it silent; but it seems
rather to take here the sound of *f*. In *chasten, hasten, fasten, castle, nestle, whistle, apostle,
epistle, bustle*, and similar words, with their sundry derivatives, the *t* is said by some to be
mute; but here it seems to take the sound of *s*; for, according to the best authorities, this
sound is heard twice in such words.

Th, written in Greek by the character called *Theta*, (Θ or ϴ capital, ϑ or θ small,)
represents an elementary sound; or, rather, two distinct elementary sounds, for which the
Anglo-Saxons had different characters, supposed by Dr. Bosworth to have been applied
with accurate discrimination of "the *hard* or *sharp* sound of *th*," from "the *soft* or *flat*
sound."—(See *Bosworth's Compendious Anglo-Saxon Dictionary*, p. 268.) The English *th* is
either sharp, as in *thing, ethical, thinketh*; or flat, as in *this, whither, thither*.

"*Th* initial is sharp; as in *thought*: except in *than, that, the, thee, their, them, then, thence,
there, these, they, thine, this, thither, those, thou, thus, thy*, and their compounds."—*W. Allen's
Grammar*, p. 22.

Th final is also sharp; as in *south*: except in *beneath, booth, with*, and several verbs formerly with *th* last, but now frequently (and more properly) written with final *e*; as *loathe,
mouthe, seethe, soothe, smoothe, clothe, wreathe, bequeathe, uncloathe*.

Th medial is sharp, too, when preceded or followed by a consonant; as in *Arthur, ethnic,
swarthy, athwart*: except in *brethren, burthen, farther, farthing, murther, northern, worthy*.
But "*th* between two vowels, is generally flat in words purely English; as in *gather, neither,
whither*: and sharp in words from the learned languages; as in *atheist, ether, method*."—See
W. Allen's Gram. p. 22.

"*Th*, in *Thames, Thomas, thyme, asthma, phthisis*, and their compounds, is pronounced like
t."—*Ib*.

XXI. OF THE LETTER U.

The vowel *U* has three sounds which may be considered to be properly its own :—
1. The open, long, full, primal, or diphthongal *u*; as in *tube, cubic, juvenile*.
2. The close, curt, short, or stopped *u*; as in *tub, butter, justice, unhung*.
3. The middle *u*, resembling a short or quick *oo*; as in *pull, pulpit, artful*.

U forming a syllable by itself, or *U* as naming itself, is nearly equivalent in sound to
you, and requires the article *a*, and not *ah*, before it; as, *a U, a union*.

U sometimes borrows the sound of some other vowel; for *bury* is pronounced *berry*, and
busy is pronounced *bizzy*. So in the derivatives, *buried, burial, busied, busily*, and the like.

The long or diphthongal *u*, commonly sounded as *yu*, or as *ew* in *ewer*,—or any equivalent
diphthong or digraph, as *ue, ui, eu*, or *ew*,—when it follows *r* or *rh*, assumes the sound of
slender *o* or *oo*; as in *rude, rhubarb, rue, rueful, rheum, fruit, truth, brewer*.

DIPHTHONGS BEGINNING WITH U.

U, in the proper diphthongs, *ua, ue, ui, uo, uy*, has the sound of *w* or of *oo feeble*; as in
persuade, query, quell, quiet, languid, quote, obloquy.

Ua, an improper diphthong, has the sound—1. Of *middle a*; as in *guard, guardian*. 2.
Of *close a*; as in *guarantee, piquant*. 3. Of *obscure e*; as in *victuals* and its compounds or
kindred. 4. Of *open u*; as in *mantuamaker*.

Ue, an improper diphthong, has the sound—1. Of *open u*; as in *blue, ensue, ague*. 2. Of
close e; as in *guest, guesser*. 3. Of *close u*; as in *leaguer*. *Ue final* is sometimes silent; as
in *league, antique*.

Ui, an improper diphthong, has the sound—1. Of *open i*; as in *guide, guile*. 2. Of *close
i*; as in *conduit, circuit*. 3. Of *open u*; as in *juice, sluice, suit*.

Uo can scarcely be called an improper diphthong, except, perhaps, after *q* in *liquor,
liquorice, liquorish*, where *uor* is heard as *ur*.

Uy, an improper diphthong, has the sound—1. Of *open y*; as in *buy, buyer*. 2. Of *feeble
y*, or of *ee feeble*; as in *plaguy, roguy*.

TRIPHTHONGS BEGINNING WITH U.

Uai is pronounced nearly, if not exactly, like *way*; as in *guai-a-cum, quail, quaint*. *Uaw*
is sounded like *wa* in *water*; as in *squaw*, a female Indian. *Uay* has the sound of *way*; as

in *Par-a-guay:* except in *guay,* which nearly all our orthoepists pronounce *kee. Uea* and *uee* are each sounded *wee;* as in *queasy, queer, squeal, squeeze. Uoi* and *uoy* are each sounded *woi;* as in *quoit, buoy.* Some say, that, as *u,* in these combinations, sounds like *w,* it is a consonant; others allege, that *w* itself has only the sound of *oo,* and is therefore in all cases a vowel. *U* has, certainly, in these connexions, as much of the sound of *oo,* as has *w;* and perhaps a little more.

XXII. OF THE LETTER V.

The consonant *V* always has a sound like that of *f flattened;* as in *love, vulture, viva cious.* It is never silent, never final, never doubled.

XXIII. OF THE LETTER W.

W, when reckoned a *consonant,* (as it usually is when uttered with a vowel that follows it,) has the sound heard at the beginning of *wine, win, woman, woody;* being a sound less vocal than that of *oo,* and depending more upon the lips.

W before *h,* is usually pronounced as if it followed the *h;* as in *what, when, where, while:* but, in *who, whose, whom, whole, whoop,* and words formed from these, it is silent. Before *r,* in the same syllable, it is also silent; as in *wrath, wrench, wrong.* So in a few other cases; as in *sword, answer, two.*

W is never used alone as a *vowel;* except in some Welsh or foreign names, in which it is equivalent to *oo:* as in " *Cwm Cothy,*" the name of a mountain in Wales; " *Wkra,*" the name of a small river in Poland.—See *Lockhart's Napoleon,* Vol. ii, p. 15. In a diphthong, when heard, it has the power of *u* in *bull,* or nearly that of *oo;* as in *new, now, brow, fr n. Aw* and *ow* are frequently improper diphthongs, the *w* being silent, the *a* broad, and the *o* long; as in *law, flaw,—tow, snow. W,* when sounded before vowels, being reckoned a *consonant,* we have no diphthongs or triphthongs beginning with this letter.

XXIV. OF THE LETTER X.

The consonant " X has a *sharp* sound, like *ks;* as in *ox:* and a *flat* one, like *gz;* as in *example.* X is sharp, when its ends an accented syllable; as in *exercise, exit, excellence:* or when it precedes an accented syllable beginning with a consonant; as in *expand, extreme, expunge.* X unaccented is generally flat, when the next syllable begins with a vowel; as in *exist, exemption, exotic.* X initial, in Greek proper names, has the sound of *z;* as in *Xanthus, Xantippe, Xenophon, Xerxes.*"—See *W. Allen's Gram.* p. 25.

XXV. OF THE LETTER Y.

Y, as a *consonant,* has the sound heard at the beginning of *yarn, young, youth;* being rather less vocal than the feeble sound of *i,* or of the vowel *y,* and serving merely to modify that of a succeeding vowel, with which it is quickly united. *Y,* as a *vowel,* has the same sounds as *i:*—

1. The open, long, full, or primal *y;* as in *cry, crying, thyme, cycle.*
2. The close, curt, short, or stopped *y;* as in *system, symptom, cynic.*
3. The feeble or faint *y,* accentless; (like *open e feeble;*) as in *cymar, cycloidal, mercy.*

The vowels *i* and *y* have, in general, exactly the same sound under similar circumstances; and, in forming derivatives, we often change one for the other: as in *city, cities; tie, tying easy, easily.*

Y, before a vowel heard in the same syllable, is reckoned a *consonant;* we have, therefore, no diphthongs or triphthongs *commencing* with this letter.

XXVI. OF THE LETTER Z.

The consonant *Z,* the last letter of our alphabet, has usually a soft or buzzing sound, the same as that of *s flat;* as in *Zeno, zenith, breeze, dizzy.* Before *u primal* or *i feeble, z,* as well as *s flat,* sometimes takes the sound of *zh,* which, in the enumeration of consonantal sounds, is reckoned a distinct element; as in *azure, seizure, glazier; osier, measure, pleasure.*

END OF THE FIRST APPENDIX.

APPENDIX II.

TO PART SECOND, OR ETYMOLOGY.

OF THE DERIVATION OF WORDS.

Derivation, as a topic to be treated by the grammarian, is a species of Etymology, which explains the various methods by which those derivative words which are not formed by mere grammatical inflections, are deduced from their primitives. Most of those words which are regarded as primitives in English, may be traced to ulterior sources, and many of them are found to be compounds or derivatives in the other languages from which they have come to us. To show the composition, origin, and literal sense of these, is also a part, and a highly useful part, of this general inquiry, or theme of instruction.

This species of information, though insignificant in those whose studies reach to nothing better,—to nothing valuable and available in life,—is nevertheless essential to education and to science ; because it is essential to a right understanding of the import and just application of such words. All reliable etymology, all authentic derivation of words, has ever been highly valued by the wise. The learned James Harris has a remark as follows : " How useful to Ethic Science, and indeed to Knowledge in general, a Grammatical Disquisition into the *Etymology* and *Meaning* of Words was esteemed by the chief and ablest Philosophers, may be seen by consulting *Plato* in his *Cratylus ; Xenophon's Memorabilia,* IV, 5, 6 ; *Arrian. Epict.* I, 17 ; II, 10 ; *Marc. Anton.* III, 11 ; " &c.—See *Harris's Hermes,* p. 407.

A knowledge of the *Saxon, Latin, Greek,* and *French* languages, will throw much light on this subject, the derivation of our modern English : nor is it a weak argument in favour of studying these, that our acquaintance with them, whether deep or slight, tends to a better understanding of what is borrowed, and what is vernacular, in our own tongue. But etymological analysis may extensively teach the origin of English words, their composition, and the import of their parts, without demanding of the student the power of reading foreign or ancient languages, or of discoursing at all on General Grammar. And, since many of the users of this work may be but readers of our current English, to whom an unknown letter or a foreign word is a particularly uncouth and repulsive thing, we shall here forbear the use of Saxon characters, and, in our explanations, not go beyond the precincts of our own language, except to show the origin and primitive import of some of our definitive and connecting particles, and to explain the prefixes and terminations which are frequently employed to form English derivatives.

The rude and cursory languages of barbarous nations, to whom literature is unknown, are among those transitory things which, by the hand of time, are irrecoverably buried in oblivion. The fabric of the English language is undoubtedly of *Saxon* origin ; but what was the particular form of the language spoken by the *Saxons,* when about the year 450 they entered Britain, cannot now be accurately known. It was probably a dialect of the *Gothic* or *Teutonic.* This *Anglo-Saxon* dialect, being the nucleus, received large accessions from other tongues of the north, from the *Norman French,* and from the more polished languages of *Rome* and *Greece,* to form the modern *English.* The speech of our rude and warlike ancestors thus gradually improved, as christianity, civilization, and knowledge, advanced the arts of life in Britain ; and, as early as the tenth century, it became a language capable of expressing all the sentiments of a civilized people. From the time of *Al red,* its progress may be traced by means of writings which remain ; but it can scarcely be called *English,* as I have shown in the Introduction to this work, till about the thirteenth century. And for two or three centuries later, it was so different from the modern English, as to be scarcely intelligible at all to the mere English reader ; but, gradually improving by means upon which we need not here dilate, it at length became what we now find it, a language copious, strong, refined, impressive, and capable, if properly used, of a great degree of beauty and harmony.

SECTION I.—DERIVATION OF THE ARTICLES.

1. For the derivation of our article The, which he calls " *an adjective,*" Dr. Webster was satisfied with giving this hint : " Sax. *the ;* Dutch, *de.*"—*Amer. Dict.* According to Horne Tooke, this definite article of ours, is the Saxon *verb* "the," imperative, from thean, *to take ;* and is nearly equivalent in meaning to *that* or *those,* because our *that* is " the past

participle of THEAN," and "means *taken*."—*Diversions of Purley*, Vol. ii, p. 49. But this is not very satisfactory. Examining ancient works, we find the word, or something resembling it, or akin to it, written in various forms, as *se, see, ye, te, de, the, thã*, and others that cannot be shown by our modern letters; and, tracing it as one article, or one and the same word, through what we suppose to be the oldest of these forms, in stead of accounting the forms as signs of different roots, we should sooner regard it as originating in the imperative of SEON, *to see*.

2. AN, our indefinite article, is the Saxon *æn, ane, an,* ONE; and, by dropping *n* before a consonant, becomes *a*. Gawin Douglas, an ancient English writer, wrote *ane*, even before a consonant; as, "*Ane* book,"—"*Ane* lang spere,"—"*Ane* volume."

OBSERVATIONS.

OBS 1.—The words of Tooke, concerning the derivation of *That* and *The*, as nearly as they can be given in our letters, are these : " THAT (in the Anglo-Saxon Thæt, i. e. Thead, Theat) means *taken, assumed*; being merely the past participle of the Anglo-Saxon verb Thean, Thagan, Thion, Thihan, Thicgan, Thigian ; sumere, assumere, accipere; to THE, to *get*, to *take*, to *assume*.

'Ill mote he THE That caused me
To make myselfe a frere.'—*Sir T. More's Workes, pag* 4.

THE (our *article*, as it is called) is the imperative of the same verb Thean : which may very well supply the place of the correspondent Anglo-Saxon article Se, which is the imperative of Seon, videre : for it answers the same purpose in discourse, to say ... *see* man, or *take* man."—*Diversions of Purley*, Vol. ii, p. 49.

OBS 2.—Now, between *That* and *Theat*, there is a considerable difference of form, for *æ* and *ea* are not the same diphthong; and, in the identifying of so many infinitives, as forming but one verb, there is room for error. Nor is it half so probable that these are truly one root, as that our article *The* is the same, in its origin, as the old Anglo-Saxon *Se*. Dr. Bosworth, in his Anglo-Saxon Dictionary, gives no such word as *Thean* or *Thegan*, no such participle as *Thead* or *Theat*, which derivative is perhaps imaginary ; but he has inserted together " Thicgan, thicgean, thigan, *to receive, or take*;" and, separately, "Theon, *to thrive, or flourish*,"—" Thihan, *to thrive*,"—and " Thion, *to flourish*;" as well as the preterit "Theat, *howled*," from "Theotan, *to howl*." And is it not plain, that the old verb " THE," as used by More, is from Theon, *to thrive*, rather than from Thicgan, *to take* ? " Ill mote he THE "—" Ill might he *thrive*," not, " Ill might he *take*."

OBS 3.—Professor Hart says, " The word *the* was originally *thaet*, or *that*. In course of time [,] it became abbreviated, and the short form acquired, in usage, a shade of meaning different from the original long one. *That* is demonstrative with emphasis; *the* is demonstrative without emphasis."—*Hart's E. Grammar*, p. 32. This derivation of *The* is quite improbable : because the shortening of a monosyllable of five letters by striking out the third and the fifth, is no usual mode of abbreviation. Bosworth's Dictionary explains THE as " An indeclinable article, often used for all the cases of Se, seó, thæt, especially in adverbial expressions and in corrupt Anglo-Saxon, as in the *Chronicle* after the year 1158."

SECTION II. — DERIVATION OF NOUNS.

In *English*, Nouns are derived from nouns, from adjectives, from verbs, or from participles.

I. Nouns are derived from *Nouns* in several different ways :—

1. By the adding of *ship, dom, ric, wick, or, ate, hood,* or *head* : as, *fellow, fellowship* ; *king, kingdom* ; *bishop, bishopric* ; *bailiff,* or *baily, bailiwick* ; *senate, senator* ; *tetrarch, tetrarchate* ; *child, childhood* ; *God, Godhead.* These generally denote dominion, office, or character.

2. By the adding of *ian* : as, *music, musician* ; *physic, physician* ; *theology, theologian* ; *grammar, grammarian* ; *college, collegian.* These generally denote profession.

3. By the adding of *y, ry,* or *ery* : as, *grocer, grocery* ; *cutler, cutlery* ; *slave, slavery* ; *scene, scenery* ; *fool, foolery.* These sometimes denote state or habit ; sometimes, an artificer's wares or shop.

4. By the adding of *age* or *ade* : as, *patron, patronage* ; *porter, porterage* ; *band, bandage* ; *lemon, lemonade* ; *baluster, balustrade* ; *wharf, wharfage* ; *vassal, vassalage.*

5. By the adding of *kin, let, ling, ock, el, erel,* or *et* : as, *lamb, lambkin* ; *ring, ringlet* ; *cross, crosslet* ; *duck, duckling* ; *hill, hillock* ; *run, runnel* ; *cock, cockerel* ; *pistol, pistolet* ; *eagle, eaglet* ; *circle, circlet.* All these denote little things, and are called diminutives.

6. By the adding of *ist* : as, *psalm, psalmist* ; *botany, botanist* ; *dial, dialist* ; *journal, journalist.* These denote persons devoted to, or skilled in, the subject expressed by the primitive.

7. By the prefixing of an adjective, or an other noun, so as to form a compound word : as, *foreman, broadsword, statesman, tradesman* ; *bedside, hillside, seaside* ; *bear-berry, bear-fly, bear-garden* ; *bear's-ear, bear's-foot, goat's-beard.*

8. By the adoption of a negative prefix to reverse the meaning : as, *order, disorder* ; *pleasure, displeasure* ; *consistency, inconsistency* ; *capacity, incapacity* ; *observance, nonobservance* ; *resistance, nonresistance* ; *truth, untruth* ; *constraint, unconstraint.*

9. By the use of the prefix *counter*, signifying *against* or *opposite* : as, *attraction, counter-attraction* ; *bond, counter-bond* ; *current, counter-current* ; *movement, counter-movement.*

10. By the addition of *ess, ix,* or *ine,* or the changing of masculines to feminines so terminating : as, *heir, heiress* ; *prophet, prophetess* ; *abbot, abbess* ; *governor, governess* ; *testator, testatrix* ; *hero, heroine.*

II. Nouns are derived from *Adjectives* in several different ways : —

1. By the adding of *ness, ity, ship, dom,* or *hood* : as, *good, goodness* ; *real, reality* ; *hard, hardship* ; *wise, wisdom* ; *free, freedom* ; *false, falsehood.*

2. By the changing of *t* into *ce* or *cy* : as, *radiant, radiance* ; *consequent, consequence* ; *flagrant, flagrancy* ; *current, currency* ; *discrepant, discrepance,* or *discrepancy.*

3. By the changing of some of the letters, and the adding of *t* or *th* : as, *long, length* ;

broad, breadth; wide, width; high, height. The nouns included under these three heads, generally denote abstract qualities, and are called abstract nouns.

4. By the adding of *ard:* as, *drunk, drunkard; dull, dullard.* These denote ill character.

5. By the adding of *ist:* as, *sensual, sensualist; separate, separatist; royal, royalist; fatal, fatalist.* These denote persons devoted, addicted, or attached, to something.

6. By the adding of *a,* the Latin ending of neuter plurals, to certain proper adjectives: as, *Miltonian, Miltoniana; Johnsonian, Johnsoniana.* These literally mean, *Miltonian things, sayings,* or *anecdotes,* &c.; and are words somewhat fashionable with the journalists, and are sometimes used for titles of books that refer to table-talk.

III. Nouns are derived from *Verbs* in several different ways :—

1. By the adding of *ment, ance, ence, ure,* or *age:* as, *punish, punishment; abate, abatement; repent, repentance; condole, condolence; forfeit, forfeiture; stow, stowage; equip, equipage; truck, truckage.*

2. By a change of the termination of the verb, into *se, ce, sion, tion, ation,* or *ition:* as, *expand, expanse, expansion; pretend, pretence, pretension; invent, invention; create, creation; omit, omission; provide, provision; reform, reformation; oppose, opposition.* These denote either the act of doing or the thing done.

3. By the adding of *er* or *or:* as, *hunt, hunter; write, writer; collect, collector; assert, assertor; instruct, instructer,* or *instructor.* These generally denote the doer. To denote the person to whom something is done, we sometimes form a derivative ending in *ee:* as, *promisee, mortgagee, appellee, consignee.*

4. Nouns and Verbs are sometimes alike in orthography, but different in pronunciation: as, a *house,* to *house;* a *use,* to *use;* a *reb'el,* to *rebel';* a *rec'ord,* to *record';* a *cem'ent,* to *cement'.* Of such pairs, it may often be difficult to say which word is the primitive.

5. In many instances, nouns and verbs are wholly alike as to form and sound, and are distinguished by their sense and construction only: as, *love,* to *love; fear,* to *fear; sleep,* to *sleep;*—to *revise,* a *revise;* to *rebuke,* a *rebuke.* In these, we have but the same word used differently.

IV. Nouns are often derived from *Participles* in *ing;* as, a *meeting,* the *understanding, murmurings, disputings, sayings,* and *doings:* and, occasionally, one is formed from such a word and an adverb or a perfect participle joined with it; as, "The *turning-away,*"—"His *goings-forth,*"—"Your *having-boasted* of it."

SECTION III.—DERIVATION OF ADJECTIVES.

In *English,* Adjectives are derived from nouns, from adjectives, from verbs, or from participles.

I. Adjectives are derived from *Nouns* in several different ways :—

1. By the adding of *ous, ious, eous, y, ey, ic, al, ical,* or *ine:* (sometimes with an omission or change of some of the final letters :) as, *danger, dangerous; glory, glorious; right, righteous; rock, rocky; clay, clayey; poet, poetic,* or *poetical; nation, national; method, methodical; vertex, vertical; clergy, clerical; adamant, adamantine.* Adjectives thus formed, generally apply the properties of their primitives, to the nouns to which they relate.

2. By the adding of *ful:* as, *fear, fearful; cheer, cheerful; grace, graceful; shame, shameful; power, powerful.* These come almost entirely from personal qualities or feelings, and denote abundance.

3. By the adding of *some:* as, *burden, burdensome; game, gamesome; toil, toilsome.* These denote plenty, but do not exaggerate.

4. By the adding of *en:* as, *oak, oaken; silk, silken; wheat, wheaten; oat, oaten; hemp, hempen.* Here the derivative denotes the matter of which something is made.

5. By the adding of *ly* or *ish:* as, *friend, friendly; gentleman, gentlemanly; child, childish; prude, prudish.* These denote resemblance. The termination *ly* signifies *like.*

6. By the adding of *able* or *ible:* as, *fashion, fashionable; access, accessible.* But these terminations are generally, and more properly, added to verbs. See Obs. 17th, 18th, &c., on the Rules for Spelling.

7. By the adding of *less:* as, *house, houseless; death, deathless; sleep, sleepless; bottom, bottomless.* These denote privation or exemption—the absence of what is named by the primitive.

8. By the adding of *ed:* as, *saint, sainted; bigot, bigoted; mast, masted; wit, witted.* These have a resemblance to participles, and some of them are rarely used, except when joined with some other word to form a compound adjective: as, *three-sided, bare-footed, long-eared, hundred-handed, flat-nosed, hard-hearted, marble-hearted, chicken-hearted.*

9. Adjectives coming from proper names, take various terminations : as, *America, American; England, English; Dane, Danish; Portugal, Portuguese; Plato, Platonic.*

10. Nouns are often converted into adjectives, without change of termination: as, *paper* currency; a *gold* chain; *silver* knee-buckles.

II. Adjectives are derived from *Adjectives* in several different ways :—

1. By the adding of *ish* or *some:* as, *white, whitish; green, greenish; lone, lonesome; glad, gladsome.* These denote quality with some diminution.

2. By the prefixing of *dis, in,* or *un:* as, *honest, dishonest; consistent, inconsistent; wise, unwise.* These express a negation of the quality denoted by their primitives.

3. By the adding of *y* or *ly:* as, *mearth, swarthy; good, goodly.* Of these there are but few; for almost all derivatives of the latter form are adverbs.

III. Adjectives are derived from *Verbs* in several different ways :—

1. By the adding of *able* or *ible:* (sometimes with a change of some of the final letters :) as, *perish, perishable; vary, variable; convert, convertible; divide, divisible,* or *dividable.* These, according to their analogy, have usually a passive import, and denote susceptibility of receiving action.

2. By the adding of *ive* or *ory:* (sometimes with a change of some of the final letters :) as, *elect, elective; interrogate, interrogative, interrogatory; defend, defensive; defame, defamatory; explain, explanatory.*

3. Words ending in *ate,* are mostly verbs; but some of them may be employed as adjectives, in the same form, especially in poetry; as, *reprobate, complicate.*

IV. Adjectives are derived from *Participles,* not by suffixes, but in these ways :—

1. By the prefixing of *un,* meaning *not;* as, *unyielding, unregarded, undeserved, unendowed, unendeared, unendorsed, unencountered, unencumbered, undisheartened, undishonoured.* Of this sort there are very many.

2. By a combining of the participle with some word which does not belong to the verb; as, *way-faring, hollow-sounding, long-drawn, deep-laid, dear-purchased, down-trodden.* These, too, are numerous.

3. Participles often become adjectives without change of form. Such adjectives are distinguished from participles by their construction alone: as, "A *lasting* ornament;"—"The *starving* chymist;"—"Words of *learned* length;"—"With *counterfeited* glee."

SECTION IV.—DERIVATION OF THE PRONOUNS.

I. The *English* Pronouns are all of *Saxon* origin; but, in them, our language differs very strikingly from that of the Anglo-Saxons. The following table compares the simple personal forms :—

Eng. I,	My or Mine,		Me;	We,	Our or Ours,		Us.
Sax. Ic,		Min, Me or Mec;		We,	Ure or User,		Us.
Eng. Thou,	Thy or Thine,		Thee;	Ye,	Your or Yours,		You.
Sax. Thu,		Thin, The or Thec;		Ge,	Eower,	Eow or Eowic.	
Eng. He,	His,		Him;	They,	Their or Theirs,		Them.
Sax. He,	His or Hys,	Him or Hine;		Hi or Hig,	Hira or Heora,	Heom or Hi.	
Eng. She,	Her or Hers,		Her;	They,	Their or Theirs,		Them.
Sax. Heo,	Hire or Hyre,		Hi;	Hi or Hig,	Hira or Heora,	Heom or Hi.	
Eng. It,	Its,		It;	They,	Their or Theirs,		Them.
Sax. Hit,	His or Hys,		Hit;	Hi or Hig,	Hira or Heora,	Heom or Hi.	

Here, as in the personal pronouns of other languages, the plurals and oblique cases do not all appear to be regular derivatives from the nominative singular. Many of these pronouns, perhaps all, as well as a vast number of other words of frequent use in our language, and in that from which it chiefly comes, were very variously written by the Middle English, Old English, Semi-Saxon, and Anglo-Saxon authors. He who traces the history of our language, will meet with them under all the following forms, (or such as these would be with Saxon characters for the Saxon forms,) and perhaps in more :—

1. I, J, Y, y, i, ic, che, ich, Ic;—MY, mi, min, MINE, myne, myn;—ME, mee, me, meh, mec, mech :—WE, wee, ve;—OUR or OURS, oure, ure, user, usse, usser, usses, ussum;—US, ous, vs, uss, usic, usich, usig, usih.

2. THOU, thoue, thow, thowe, thu;—THY or THINE, thi, thyne, thyn, thin;—THEE, the, theh, thee :—YE, yee, ze, zee, ge ;—YOUR or YOURS, youre, zour, gour, goure, eower;—YOU, youe, yow, gou, zou, iu, iuh, eow, iow, geow, eowih, eowic, iowih.

3. HE, hee, se ;—HIS, hise, is, hys, ys, hyse;—HIM, hine, hen, hyne, hym, im :—THEY, thay, thei, the, tha, thai, thii, yai, hi, hie, heo, hig, hyg, hy ;—THEIR or THEIRS, ther, theyr, theyrs, thair, thare, theora, hare, here, her, hire, hira, hiora, hiera, heora, hyra ;—THEM, theym, thaym, thaim, thame, tham, em, hem, heom, hom, him, hi, hig.

4. SHE, shee, sche, scho, sho, scæ, seo, heo, hio, hiu ;—HER, (possessive,) hur, hir, hire, hyr, hyre, hyra, hera ;—HER, (objective,) hire, hyre, hir, hi. The plural forms of this feminine pronoun are like those of the masculine *He;* but the "*Well-Wishers to Knowledge,*" in their small Grammar, (erroneously, as I suppose,) make *hire* masculine only, and *heora* feminine only. See their *Principles of Grammar,* p. 38.

5. IT, yt, itt, hit, hyt, hyt. The possessive *Its* is a modern derivative; *His* or *Hys* was formerly used in lieu of it. The plural forms of this neuter pronoun, *It,* are like those of *He* and *She.* According to Horne Tooke, who declares *het* to have been one of its ancient forms, "this pronoun was merely the past participle of the verb HAITAN, *hætan,* nominare," to *name,* and literally signifies "*the said;*" (*Diversions of Purley,* Vol. ii, p. 46 ; *W. Allen's Gram.* p. 57 ;) but Dr. Alexander Murray, exhibiting it in an other form, not adapted to this opinion,

makes it the neuter of a declinable adjective, or pronoun, inflected from the masculine, thus : " He, heo hita, *this.*"—*Hist. of Lang.* Vol. i, p. 315.

II. The relatives are derived from the same source, the Anglo-Saxon tongue, and have passed through similar changes, or varieties in orthography. They have been found in all the following forms :—

1. WHO, ho, wha, hwa, hus, wua, qua, quha ;—WHOSE, who's, whos, quhois, quhais, quhase, hwæs;—WHOM, whome, quhum, quhome, hwom, hwam, hwæm, hwæne, hwone.

2. WHICH, whiche, whyche, whilch, wych, quilch. quilk, quhilk, hwilc, hwylc, hwelc, whilk, huilic, hvilc. For the Anglo-Saxon forms, Dr. Bosworth's Dictionary gives " *hwilc, hwylc,* and *hwelc* ;" but Professor Fowler's E. Grammar makes them " *huilic* and *hvilc.*"—See p. 240. *Whilk* is a Scotch form.

3. WHAT, hwat, hwet, quhat, hwæt. This pronoun, whether relative or interrogative, is regarded by Bosworth and others as a neuter derivative from the masculine or feminine *hwa,* who. It may have been thence derived, but, in modern English, it is not always of the neuter gender. See the last note on page 297.

4. THAT, Anglo-Saxon Thæt. Tooke's notion of the derivation of this word is noticed above in the section on Articles. There is no certainty of its truth ; and our lexicographers make no allusion to it. W. Allen reaffirms it. See his *Gram.* p. 54.

OBSERVATIONS.

OBS. 1.—In the Well-Wishers' Grammar, (p. 39,) as also in L. Murray's and some others, the pronoun *Which* is very strangely and erroneously represented as being always " of the *neuter* gender." (See what is said of this word in the Introduction, Chap. ix, ¶ 32.) Whereas it is the relative most generally applied to *brute animals,* and, in our common version of the Bible, its application to *persons* is peculiarly frequent. Fowler says. " In its origin it is a Compound."—*E. Gram.* p. 240. Taking its first Anglo-Saxon form to be " *Huilic,*" he thinks it traceable to " hwa, who," or its " ablative *hwi,*" and " *hic,* like."—*Ib.* If this is right, the neuter sense is not its primitive import, or any part of it.

OBS. 2.—From its various uses, the word *That* is called sometimes a pronoun, sometimes an adjective, and sometimes a conjunction ; but, in respect to derivation, it is, doubtless, one and the same. As a relative pronoun, it is of either number, and has no plural form different from the singular; as, " Blessed is the *man that* heareth me."—*Prov.* viii, 34. " Blessed are *they that* mourn."—*Matt.* v, 4. As an adjective, it is said by Tooke to have been formerly " applied indifferently to plural nouns and to singular; as, ' Into *that* holy ordres.'—*Ir. Martin.* ' At *that* dayes.'—*Id.* ' *That* euyll aungels the deuilles.'—*Sir Tho. More.* ' This pleasure undoubtedly farre excelleth all *that* pleasures that in this life male be obtained.'—*Id.*"—*Diversions of Purley,* Vol. ii, pp. 47 and 48. The introduction of the plural form *those,* must have rendered this usage bad English.

SECTION V. — DERIVATION OF VERBS.

In English, Verbs are derived from nouns, from adjectives, or from verbs.

I. Verbs are derived from *Nouns* in the following different ways :—

1. By the adding of *ize, ise, en,* or *ate :* as, *author, authorize ; critic, criticise ; length, lengthen; origin, originate.* The termination *ize* is of Greek origin, and *ise* is most probably of French : the former is generally preferable in forming English derivatives ; but both are sometimes to be used, and they should be applied according to Rule 13th for Spelling.

2. Some few verbs are derived from nouns by the changing of a sharp or hard consonant to a flat or soft one, or by the adding of a mute *e,* to soften a hard sound : as, *advice, advise ; price, prize ; bath, bathe ; cloth, clothe ; breath, breathe ; wreth, wreathe ; sheath, sheathe ; grass, graze.*

II. Verbs are derived from *Adjectives* in the following different ways:—

1. By the adding of *ize* or *en :* as, *legal, legalize ; immortal, immortalize ; civil, civilize; human, humanize ; familiar, familiarize ; particular, particularize ; deaf, deafen ; stiff, stiffen; rough, roughen ; deep, deepen ; weak, weaken.*

2. Many adjectives become verbs by being merely used and inflected as verbs : as, *warm,* to *warm,* he *warms ; dry,* to *dry,* he *dries ; dull,* to *dull,* he *dulls ; slack,* to *slack,* he *slacks; forward,* to *forward,* he *forwards.*

III. Verbs are derived from *Verbs* in the following modes, or ways:—

1. By the prefixing of *dis* or *un* to reverse the meaning : as, *please, displease ; qualify, disqualify ; organize, disorganize ; fasten, unfasten ; muzzle, unmuzzle ; nerve, unnerve.*

2. By the prefixing of *a, be, for, fore, mis, over, out, under, up,* or *with :* as, *rise, arise ; sprinkle, besprinkle ; bid, forbid ; see, foresee ; take, mistake ; look, overlook ; run, outrun ; go, undergo ; hold, uphold ; draw, withdraw.*

SECTION VI. — DERIVATION OF PARTICIPLES.

All *English* Participles are derived from *English* verbs, in the manner explained in Chapter 7th, under the general head of Etymology ; and when foreign participles are introduced into our language, they are not participles with us, but belong to some other class of words, or part of speech.

SECTION VII. — DERIVATION OF ADVERBS.

1. In *English,* many Adverbs are derived from adjectives by the addition of *ly ;* which is an abbreviation for *like,* and which, though the addition of it to a noun forms an adjective, is the most distinctive as well as the most common termination of our adverbs : as,

candid, candidly ; sordid, sordidly ; presumptuous, presumptuously. Most adverbs of manner are thus formed.

2. Many adverbs are compounds formed from two or more English words ; as, *herein, thereby, to-day, always, already, elsewhere, sometimes, wherewithal.* The formation and the meaning of these are, in general, sufficiently obvious.

3. About seventy adverbs are formed by means of the prefix, or inseparable preposition, *a ;* as, *Abreast, abroach, abroad, across, afar, afield, ago, agog, aland, along, amiss, atilt.*

4. *Needs,* as an adverb, is a contraction of *need is ; prithee,* or *pr'ythee,* of *I pray thee ; alone,* of *all one ; only,* of *one-like ; anon,* of the Saxon *an on ;* i. e., *in one* [instant] ; *never,* of *ne ever ;* i. e., *not* ever. Gibbs, in Fowler's Grammar, makes *needs* "the Genitive case."—P. 311.

5. *Very* is from the French *veray,* or *vrai,* true ; and this, probably, from the Latin *verus. Rather* appears to be the regular comparative of the ancient *rath,* soon, quickly, willingly ; which comes from the Anglo-Saxon *"Rathe,* or *Hrathe,* of one's own accord."—*Bosworth.* But the parent language had also *"Hrathre,* to a mind."—*Id.* That is, to *one's* mind, or, perhaps, *more willingly.*

OBSERVATIONS.

Obs. 1.—Many of our most common adverbs are of Anglo-Saxon derivation, being plainly traceable to certain very old forms, of the same import, which the etymologist regards but as the same words differently spelled : as, *All,* eall, eal, or æll ; *Almost,* calmæst, or ælmæst ; *Also,* ealswa, or ælswa ; *Else,* elles ; *Elsewhere,* elles-hwær ; *Enough,* genog, or genoh ; *Even,* euen, efen, or æfen ; *Ever,* euer, æfer, or efre ; *Downward,* dune-weard ; *Forward,* forweard, or foreweard ; *Homeward,* hamweard ; *Homewards,* hamweardes ; *How,* hu ; *Little,* lytel ; *Less,* læs ; *Least,* læst ; *No,* na ; *Not,* noht, or nocht ; *Out,* ut, or ute ; *So,* swa ; *Still,* stille, or stylle ; *Then,* thenne ; *There,* ther, thar, thær ; *Thither,* thider, or thyder ; *Thus,* thuss, or thus ; *Together,* togædere, or togædre ; *Too,* to ; *When,* hwenne, or hwænne ; *Where,* hwær ; *Whither,* hwider, hwyder, or hwyther ; *Yea,* is, gea, or gee ; *Yes,* gese, gise, or gyse.

Obs. 2.—According to Horne Tooke, *"Still* and *Else* are the imperatives *Stell* and *Ales* of their respective verbs *Stellan,* to put, and *Alesan,* to dismiss."—*Diversions,* Vol. i, p. 111. He afterwards repeats the doctrine thus : *"Still* is only the imperative *Stell* or *Steall,* of *Stellan* or *Steallian,* ponere."—*Ib.* p. 146. "This word *Else,* formerly written *alles, alys, alyse, elles, ellus, ellis, ells, els,* and now *else ;* is, as I have said, no other than *Ales* or *Alys,* the imperative of *Alesan* or *Alysan,* dimittere."—*Ib.* p. 148. These ulterior and remote etymologies are perhaps too conjectural.

SECTION VIII. — DERIVATION OF CONJUNCTIONS.

The *English* Conjunctions are mostly of Anglo-Saxon origin. The best etymological vocabularies of our language give us, for the most part, the same words in Anglo-Saxon characters ; but Horne Tooke, in his *Diversions of Purley,* (a learned and curious work which the advanced student may peruse with advantage,) traces, or professes to trace, these and many other English particles, to *Saxon verbs* or *participles.* The following derivations, so far as they partake of such speculations, are offered principally on his authority :—

1. ALTHOUGH, signifying *admit, allow,* is from *all* and *though ;* the latter being supposed the imperative of Thafian, or Thafigan, *to allow, to concede, to yield.*

2. AN, an obsolete or antiquated conjunction, signifying *if,* or *grant,* is the imperative of the Anglo-Saxon verb Anan or Unan, *to grant, to give.*

3. AND, [Saxon, And,] *add,* is said by Tooke to come from "An-ad, the imperative of Anan-ad, *Dare congeriem.*"—*D. of P.,* Vol. i, p. 111. That is, *"To give the heap."* The truth of this, if unapparent, I must leave so.

4. AS, according to Dr. Johnson, is from the Teutonic *als ;* but Tooke says that *als* itself is a contraction for *all* and the original particle *es* or *as,* meaning *it, that,* or *which.*

5. BECAUSE, from *be* and *cause,* means *by cause ;* the *be* being written for *by.*

6. BOTH, *the two,* is from the pronominal adjective *both ;* which, according to Dr. Alexander Murray, is a contraction of the Visigothic *Bagoth,* signifying *doubled.* The Anglo-Saxons wrote for it *butu, butwu, buta,* and *batwa ;* i. e., *ba,* both, *twa,* two.

7. BUT,—(in Saxon, *bute, butan, buton,* or *butun,*—) meaning *except, yet, now, only, else than, that not,* or *on the contrary,*—is referred by Tooke and some others, to two roots,—each of them but a conjectural etymon for it. " BUT, implying *addition,*" say they, is from Bot, the imperative of Botan, *to boot, to add ;* BUT, denoting *exception,* is from Be-utan, the imperative of Beon-utan, *to be out.*"—See *D. of P.,* Vol. i, pp. 111 and 155.

8. EITHER, *one of the two,* like the pronominal adjective EITHER, is from the Anglo-Saxon Ægther, or Egther, a word of the same uses, and the same import.

9. EKE, *also,* (now nearly obsolete,) is from " Eac, the imperative of Eacan, *to add.*"

10. EVEN, whether a noun, an adjective, an adverb, or a conjunction, appears to come from the same source, the Anglo-Saxon word Efen or Æfen.

11. EXCEPT, which, when used as a conjunction, means *unless,* is the imperative, or (according to Dr. Johnson) an ancient perfect participle, of the verb *to except.*

12. FOR, *because,* is from the Saxon preposition *For ;* which, to express this meaning, our ancestors combined with something else, reducing to one word some such phrase as, *For that, For this, For this that ;* as, " Fortha, Fortham, Forthan, Forthamthe, Forthan the."—See *Bosworth's Dict.*

13. IF, *give, grant, allow,* is from " Gif, the imperative of the Anglo-Saxon Gifan, *to give.*"—*Tooke's Diversions,* Vol. i, p. 111.

14. LEST, *that not, dismissed,* is from " Lesed, the perfect participle of Lesan, *to dismiss.*"

15. NEITHER, *not either,* is a union and contraction of *ne either :* our old writers frequently

used *ne* for *not;* the Anglo-Saxons likewise repeated it, using *ne—ne,* in lieu of our corresponsives *neither—nor;* and our modern lexicographers still note the word, in some of these senses.

16. Nor, *not other, not else,* is supposed to be a union and contraction of *ne or.*

17. Notwithstanding, *not hindering,* is an English compound of obvious formation.

18. Or, an alternative conjunction, seems to be a word of no great antiquity. It is supposed to be a contraction of *other,* which Johnson and his followers give, in Saxon characters, either as its source, or as its equivalent.

19. Provided, the perfect participle of the verb *provide,* becomes occasionally a disjunctive conjunction, by being used alone or with the particle *that,* to introduce a condition, a saving clause, a proviso.

20. Save, anciently used with some frequency as a conjunction, in the sense of *but,* or except, is from the imperative of the English verb *save,* and is still occasionally turned to such a use by the poets.

21. Seeing, sometimes made a copulative conjunction, is the imperfect participle of the verb *see.* Used at the head of a clause, and without reference to an agent, it assumes a conjunctive nature.

22. Since is conjectured by Tooke to be "the participle of Seon, *to see,*" and to mean "*seeing, seeing that, seen that,* or *seen as.*"—*D. of P.,* Vol. i, pp. 111 and 220. But Johnson and others say, it has been formed "by contraction from *sithence,* or *sith thence,* from *sithe,* Sax."—*Joh. Dict.*

23. Than, which introduces the latter term of a comparison, is from the Gothic *than,* or the Anglo-Saxon *thanne,* which was used for the same purpose.

24. That, when called a conjunction, is said by Tooke to be etymologically the same as the adjective or pronoun That, the derivation of which is twice spoken of above; but, in Todd's Johnson's Dictionary, as abridged by Chalmers, That, the *conjunction,* is referred to "*thatei,* Gothic; That, the *pronoun,* to "*that, thata,* Gothic; *thet,* Saxon; *dat,* Dutch."

25. Then, used as a conjunction, is doubtless the same word as the Anglo-Saxon *Thenne,* taken as an illative, or word of inference.

26. "Though, *allow,* is [from] the imperative Thaf, or Thafig, of the verb Thafian or Thafigan, *to allow.*"—*Tooke's Diversions,* Vol. i, pp. 111 and 150.

27. "Unless, *except, dismiss,* is [from] Onles, the imperative of Onlesan, *to dismiss.*"—*Ib.*

28. Whether, a corresponsive conjunction, which introduces the first term of an alternative, is from the Anglo-Saxon *hwether,* which was used for the same purpose.

29. Yet, *nevertheless,* is from "Get, the imperative of Getan, *to get.*"—*Tooke.*

SECTION IX.—DERIVATION OF PREPOSITIONS.

The following are the principal *English* Prepositions, explained in the order of the list:—

1. Aboard, meaning *on board of,* is from the prefix or preposition *a* and the noun *board,* which here means "*the deck* of a ship" or vessel. *Abord,* in French, is *approach, arrival,* or a *landing.*

2. About, [Sax. Abútan, or Abúton,] meaning *around, at circuit,* or *doing,* is from the prefix *a,* meaning *at,* and the noun *bout,* meaning a *turn,* a *circuit,* or a *trial.* In French, *bout* means end; and *about, end,* or *but-end.*

3. Above, [Sax. Abufan, Abufon, A-be-ufan,] meaning *over,* or, literally, *at-by-over,* or *at-by-top,* is from the Saxon or Old English *a, be,* and *ufa,* or *ufan,* said to mean "*high, upwards,* or *the top.*"

4. Across, *at cross, athwart, traverse,* is from the prefix *a* and the word *cross.*

5. After, [Sax. Æfter, or Æftan,] meaning *behind, subsequent to,* is, in form, the comparative of *aft,* a word common to seamen, and it may have been thence derived.

6. Against, *opposite to,* is probably from the Anglo-Saxon, Ongean, or Ongegen, each of which forms means *again* or *against.* As prefixes, *on* and *a* are often equivalent.

7. Along, [i. e., *at-long,*] meaning *lengthwise of, near to,* is formed from *a* and *long.*

8. Amid, [, i. e., *at mid* or *middle,*] is from *a* and *mid;* and Amidst [, i. e., *at midst,*] is from *a* and *midst,* contracted from *middest,* the superlative of *mid.*

9. Among, *mixed with,* is probably an abbreviation of *amongst;* and Amongst, according to Tooke, is from *a* and *mongst,* or the older "Ge-menced," Saxon for "*mixed, mingled.*"

10. Around, *about, encircling,* is from *a* and *round,* a circle, or circuit.

11. At, *gone to,* is supposed by some to come from the Latin *ad;* but Dr. Murray says, "We have in Teutonic At for Agt, touching or touched, joined, *at.*"—*Hist. of Lang.* i, 349.

12. Athwart, *across,* is from *a* and *thwart,* cross; and this from the Saxon Thweor.

13. Bating, a preposition for *except,* is the imperfect participle of *bate,* to abate.

14. Before, [i. e., *by-fore,*] in front of, is from the prefix *be* and the adjective *fore.*

15. Behind, [i. e., *by-hind,*] in rear of, is from the prefix *be* and the adjective *hind.*

16. Below, [i. e., *by-low,*] meaning *under,* or *beneath,* is from *be* and the adjective *low.*

17. Beneath [, Sax. or Old Eng. Beneoth.] is from *be* and *neath,* or Sax. Neothe, *low.*

18. Beside [, i. e., *by-side,*] is from *be* and the noun or adjective *side.*

19. Besides [, i. e., *by-sides,*] is probably from *be* and the plural noun *sides.*

20. BETWEEN, [Sax. Betweonan, or Betwynan,] literally, *by-twain*, seems to have been formed from *be*, by, and *twain*, two,—or the Saxon Twegen, which also means *two*, *twain*.

21. BETWIXT, meaning *between*, [Sax. Betweox, Betwux, Betwyx, Betwyxt, &c.,] is from *be*, by, and *twyx*, originally a "Gothic" word signifying "*two*, or *twain*."—See *Tooke*, Vol. i, p. 329.

22. BEYOND, *past*, [Sax. Begeond,] is from the prefix *be*, by, and *yond*, [Sax. Geond,] *past*, *far*.

23. BY [, Sax. Be, Bi, or Big,] is affirmed by Tooke to be "the imperative Byth, of the Anglo-Saxon verb Beon, *to be*."—*D. of P.*, Vol. i, p. 326. This seems to be rather questionable.

24. CONCERNING, the preposition, is from the first participle of the verb *concern*.

25. DOWN, the preposition, is from the Anglo-Saxon Dune, down.

26. DURING, prep. of time, is from the first participle of an old verb *dure*, to last, formerly in use; as, "While the world may *dure*."—*Chaucer's Knight's Tale*.

27. ERE, *before*, prep. of time, is from the Anglo-Saxon Ær, a word of like sort.

28. EXCEPT, *bating*, is from the imperative, or (according to Dr. Johnson) the ancient perfect participle of the verb *to except*; and EXCEPTING, when a preposition, is from the first participle of the same verb.

29. FOR, *because of*, is the Anglo-Saxon preposition For, a word of like import, and supposed by Tooke to have come from a Gothic noun signifying *cause*, or *sake*.

30. FROM, in Saxon, *Fram*, is probably derived from the old adjective Frum, *original*.

31. IN, or the Saxon In, is the same as the Latin *in* : the Greek is *ev*; and the French, *en*.

32. INTO, like the Saxon Into, noting entrance, is a compound of *in* and *to*.

33. MID and MIDST, as English prepositions, are poetical forms used for *Amid* and *Amidst*.

34. NOTWITHSTANDING, *not hindering*, is from the adverb *not*, and the participle *withstanding*.

35. OF is from the Saxon Of, or Af; which is supposed by Tooke to come from a noun signifying *offspring*.

36. OFF, opposed to *on*, Dr. Johnson derives from the "Dutch *af*."

37. ON, a word very often used in Anglo-Saxon, is traced by some etymologists to the Gothic *ana*, the German *an*, the Dutch *aan*; but no such derivation fixes its meaning.

38. OUT, [Sax. Ut, Ute, or Utan,] when made a preposition, is probably from the adverb or adjective *Out*, or the earlier *Ut*; and OUT-OF, [Sax. Ut-of,] opposed to *Into*, is but the adverb *Out* and the preposition *Of*—usually written separately, but better joined, in some instances.

39. OVER, *above*, is from the Anglo-Saxon Ofer, *over*; and this, probably, from Ufa, *above*, *high*, or from the comparative, Ufera, *higher*.

40. OVERTHWART, meaning *across*, is a compound of *over* and *thwart*, cross.

41. PAST, *beyond*, *gone by*, is a contraction from the perfect participle *passed*.

42. PENDING, *during* or *hanging*, has a participial form, but is either an adjective or a preposition : we do not use *pend* alone as a verb, though we have it in *depend*.

43. RESPECTING, *concerning*, is from the first participle of the verb *respect*.

44. ROUND, a preposition for *about* or *around*, is from the noun or adjective *round*.

45. SINCE is most probably a contraction of the old word *Sithence*; but is conjectured by Tooke to have been formed from the phrase, "*Seen as*."

46. THROUGH [, Sax. Thurh, or Thurch,] seems related to *Thorough*, Sax. Thuruh; and this again to Thuru, or Duru, a *Door*.

47. THROUGHOUT, *quite through*, is an obvious compound of *through* and *out*.

48. TILL, [Sax. Til or Tille,] *to*, *until*, is from the Saxon Til or Till, *an end*, *a station*.

49. TO, whether a preposition or an adverb, is from the Anglo-Saxon particle To.

50. TOUCHING, *with regard to*, is from the first participle of the verb *touch*.

51. TOWARD or TOWARDS, written by the Anglo-Saxons *Toweard* or *Toweardes*, is a compound of *To* and *Ward* or *Weard*, a guard, a look-out; "Used in composition to express *situation* or *direction*."—*Bosworth*.

52. UNDER, [Gothic, Undar; Dutch, Onder,] *beneath*, *below*, is a common Anglo-Saxon word, and very frequent prefix, affirmed by Tooke to be "nothing but *on-neder*," a Dutch compound—*on lower*.—See *Diversions of Purley*, Vol. i, p. 331.

53. UNDERNEATH is a compound of *under* and *neath*, low ; whence *nether*, lower.

54. UNTIL is a compound from *on* or *un*, and till, or *til*, the end.

55. UNTO, now somewhat antiquated, is formed, not very analogically, from *un* and *to*.

56. UP is from the Anglo-Saxon adjective, "Up or Upp, *high*, *lofty*."

57. UPON, which appears literally to mean *high on*, is from the two words *up* and *on*.

58. WITH comes to us from the Anglo-Saxon With, a word of like sort and import ; which Tooke says is an imperative verb, sometimes from "Withan, *to join*," and sometimes from "Wyrthan, *to be*."—See his *Diversions*, Vol. i, p. 262.

59. WITHIN [, i. e., *by-in*,] is from *with* and *in* : Sax. Withinnan, Binnan, or Binnon.

60. WITHOUT [, i. e., *by-out*,] is from *with* and *out* : Sax. Withútan,-úten,-úton ; Bútan, Búton, Bútun.

OBSERVATION.

In regard to some of our minor or simpler prepositions, as of sundry other particles, to go beyond the forms and constructions which present or former usage has at some period given them as particles, and to ascertain their actual origin in something ulterior, if such they had, is no very easy matter; nor can there be either satisfaction or profit in studying what one suspects to be mere guesswork. "How do you account for IN, OUT, ON, OFF, and AT?" says the friend of Tooke, in an etymological dialogue at Purley. The substance of his answer is, "The explanation and etymology of these words require a degree of knowledge in all the *antient* northern languages, and a skill in the application of that knowledge, which I am very far from assuming: and though I am almost persuaded by some of my own conjectures concerning them, I am not willing, by an apparently forced and far-fetched derivation, to justify your imputation of etymological legerdemain."—*Diversions*, Vol. i, p. 370.

SECTION X.—DERIVATION OF INTERJECTIONS.

Those significant and constructive words which are occasionally used as Interjections, (such as *Good! Strange! Indeed!*,) do not require an explanation here; and those mere sounds which are in no wise expressive of thought, scarcely admit of definition or derivation. The interjection HEY is probably a corruption of the adjective *High ;*—ALAS is from the French *Hélas ;*—ALACK is probably a corruption of *Alas ;*—WELAWAY, or WELLAWAY, (which is now corrupted into WELLADAY,) is said by some to be from the Anglo-Saxon *Wä-lä-wä*, i. e., *Wo-lo-wo ;*—"FIE," says Tooke, "is the imperative of the Gothic and Anglo-Saxon verb *Fian*, to hate;"—*Heyday* is probably from *high day ;*—AVAUNT, perhaps from the French *avant*, before ;—LO, from *look ;*—BEGONE, from *be* and *gone ;*—WELCOME, from *well* and *come ;*—FAREWELL, from *fare* and *well.*

SECTION XI.—EXPLANATION OF THE PREFIXES.

In the formation of English words, certain particles are often employed as prefixes; which, as they generally have some peculiar import, may be separately explained. A few of them are of Anglo-Saxon origin, or character; and the greater part of these are still employed as separate words in our language. The rest are Latin, Greek, or French prepositions. The *roots* to which they are prefixed, are not always proper English words. Those which are such, are called SEPARABLE RADICALS; those which are not such, INSEPARABLE RADICALS.

CLASS I.—THE ENGLISH OR ANGLO-SAXON PREFIXES.

1. A, as an English prefix, signifies *on, in, at,* or *to :* as in *a-board, a-shore, a-foot, a-bed, a-soak, a-tilt, a-slant, a-far, a-field;* which are equal to the phrases, *on board, on shore, on foot, in bed, in soak, at tilt, at slant, to a distance, to the fields.* The French *à,* to, is probably the same particle. This prefix is sometimes redundant, adding little or nothing to the meaning; as in *awake, arise, amend.*

2. BE, as a prefix, signifies *upon, over, by, to, at,* or *for :* as in *be-spatter, be-cloud, be-times, be-tide, be-howl, be-speak.* It is sometimes redundant, or merely intensive; as in *be-gird, be-deck, be-loved, be-dazzle, be-moisten, be-praise, be-quote.*

3. COUNTER, an English prefix, allied to the French *Contre,* and the Latin *Contra,* means *against,* or *opposite ;* as in *counter-poise, counter-evidence, counter-natural.*

4. FOR, as a prefix, unlike the common preposition *For,* seems generally to signify from: it is found in the irregular verbs *for-bear, for-bid, for-get, for-give, for-sake, for-swear ;* and in *for-bathe, for-do, for-pass, for-pine, for-say, for-think, for-waste,* which last are now disused, the *for* in several being merely intensive.

5. FORE, prefixed to a verb, signifies *before ;* as in *fore-know, fore-tell :* prefixed to a noun, it is usually an adjective, and signifies anterior ; as in *fore-side, fore-part.*

6. HALF, signifying *one of two equal parts,* is much used in composition ; and, often, merely to denote imperfection : as, *half-sighted,* seeing imperfectly.

7. MIS signifies *wrong* or *ill ;* as in *mis-cite, mis-print, mis-spell, mis-chance, mis-hap.*

8. OVER denotes superiority or excess ; as in *over-power, over-strain, over-large.*

9. OUT, prefixed to a verb, generally denotes excess ; as in *out-do, out-leap, out-poise :* prefixed to a noun, it is an adjective, and signifies *exterior ;* as in *out-side, out-parish.*

10. SELF generally signifies one's own person, or belonging to one's own person ; but, in *self-same,* it means *very.* We have many words beginning with *Self,* but most of them seem to be compounds rather than derivatives ; as, *self-love, self-abasement, self-abuse, self-affairs, self-willed, self-accusing.*

11. UN denotes negation or contrariety ; as in *un-kind, un-load, un-truth, un-coif.*

12. UNDER denotes inferiority ; as in *under-value, under-clerk, under-growth.*

13. UP denotes motion upwards ; as in *up-lift :* sometimes subversion ; as in *up-set.*

14. WITH, as a prefix, unlike the common preposition *With,* signifies *against, from,* or *back ;* as in *with-stand, with-hold, with-draw, with-stander, with-holdment, with-drawal.*

CLASS II.—THE LATIN PREFIXES.

The primitives or radicals to which these are prefixed, are not many of them employed separately in English. The final letter of the prefix *Ad, Con, Ex, In, Ob,* or *Sub,* is often changed before certain consonants; not capriciously, but with uniformity, to adapt or assimilate it to the sound which follows.

1. A, AB, or ABS, means From, or Away: as, *a-vert*, to turn from, or away; *ab-duce*, to lead from; *ab-duction*, a carrying-away; *abs-tract*, to draw from, or away.

2. AD,—forming *ac, af, al, an, ap, as, at,*—means To, or At: as, *ad-vert*, to turn to; *ac-cede*, to yield to; *af-flux*, a flowing-to; *al-ly*, to bind to; *an-nex*, to link to; *ap-ply*, to put to; *as-sume*, to take to; *at-test*, to witness to; *ad-mire*, to wonder at.

3. ANTE means Fore, or Before: as, *ante-past*, a fore-taste; *ante-cedent*, foregoing, or going before; *ante-mundane*, before the world; *ante-date*, to date before.

4. CIRCUM means Round, Around, or About: as *circum-volve*, to roll round; *circum-scribe*, to write around; *cirum-vent*, to come around; *circum-spect*, looking about one's self.

5. CON,—which forms *com, co, col, cor,*—means Together: as, *con-tract*, to draw together; *com-pel*, to drive together; *co-erce*, to force together; *col-lect*, to gather together; *cor-rade*, to rub or scrape together; *con-junction*, a joining-together.

6. CONTRA, or CONTRO, means Against, or Counter: as, *contra-dict*, to speak against; *contra-vene*, to come against; *contra-mure*, countermure; *contro-vert*, to turn against.

7. DE means Of, From, or Down: as *de-note*, to be a sign of; *de-tract*, to draw from; *de-pend*, to hang down; *de-press*, to press down; *de-crease*, to grow down, to grow less.

8. DIS, or DI, means Away or Apart: as, *dis-pel*, to drive away; *dis-sect*, to cut apart; *di-vert*, to turn away.

9. E or EX,—making also *ec, ef,*—means Out: as, *e-ject*, to cast out; *e-lect*, to choose out; *ex-clude*, to shut out; *ex-cite*, to summon out; *ec-stacy*, a raising-out; *ef-face*, to blot out.

10. EXTRA means Beyond, or Out Of: as, *extra-vagant*, syllabled *ex-trav'a-gant*, roving beyond; *extra-vasate, ex-trav'a-sate*, to flow out of the vessels; *extra-territorial*, being out of the territory.

11. IN,—which makes also *il, im, ir,*—means In, Into, or Upon: as, *in-spire*, to breathe in; *il-lude*, to draw in by deceit; *im-mure*, to wall in; *ir-ruption*, a rushing-in; *in-spect*, to look into; *in-scribe*, to write upon; *in-sult*, to jump upon. These syllables, prefixed to English nouns or adjectives, generally reverse their meaning; as in *in-justice, il-legality, im-partiality, ir-religion, ir-rational, in-secure, in-sane.*

12. INTER means Between, or In between: as *inter-sperse*, to scatter in between; *inter-jection*, something thrown in between; *inter-jacent*, lying between; *inter-communication*, communication between.

13. INTRO means In, Inwards, or Within: as, *intro-duce*, to lead in; *intro-vert*, to turn inwards; *intro-spect*, to look within; *intro-mission*, a sending-in.

14. OB,—which makes also *oc, of, op,*—means Against: as, *ob-trude*, to thrust against; *oc-cur*, to run against; *of-fer*, to bring against; *op-pose*, to place against; *ob-ject*, to cast against.

15. PER means Through or By: as, *per-vade*, to go through; *per-chance*, by chance; *per-cent*, by the hundred; *per-plex*, to tangle through, or to entangle thoroughly.

16. POST means After: as, *post-pone*, to place after; *post-date*, to date after.

17. PRÆ, or PRE, means Before: as, *pre-sume*, to take before: *pre-position*, a placing-before, or thing placed before; *præ-cognita*, things known before.

18. PRO means For, Forth, or Forwards: as, *pro-vide*, to take care for; *pro-duce*, to bring forth; *pro-trude*, to thrust forwards; *pro-ceed*, to go forward; *pro-noun*, for a noun.

19. PRETER means By, Past, or Beyond: as, *preter-it*, bygone, or gone by; *preter-imperfect*, past imperfect; *preter-natural*, beyond what is natural; *preter-mit*, to put by, to omit.

20. RE means Again or Back: as, *re-view*, to view again; *re-pel*, to drive back.

21. RETRO means Backwards, Backward, or Back: as, *retro-active*, acting backwards; *retro-grade*, going backward; *retro-cede*, to cede back again.

22. SE means Aside or Apart: as, *se-duce*, to lead aside; *se-cede*, to go apart.

23. SEMI means Half: as, *semi-colon*, half a colon; *semi-circle*, half a circle.

24. SUB,—which makes *suf, sug, sup, sur,* and *sus,*—means Under, and sometimes Up: as, *sub-scribe*, to write under; *suf-fossion*, an undermining; *sug-gest*, to convey under; *sup-ply*, to put under; *sur-reption*, a creeping-under; *sus-tain*, to hold up; *sub-ject*, cast under.

25. SUBTER means Beneath: as, *subter-fluous*, flowing beneath.

26. SUPER means Over or Above: as, *super-fluous*, flowing over; *super-natant*, swimming above; *super-lative*, carried over, or carrying over; *super-vise*, to overlook, to oversee.

27. TRANS,—whence TRAN and TRA,—means Beyond, Over, To another state or place: as, *trans-gress*, to pass beyond or over; *tran-scend*, to climb over; *trans-mit*, to send to another place; *trans-form*, to change to another shape; *tra-montane*, from beyond the mountains; i. e., *Trans-Alpine*, as opposed to *Cis-Alpine.*

CLASS III.—THE GREEK PREFIXES.

1. A and AN, in Greek derivatives, denote privation: as, *a-nomalous*, wanting rule; *an-onymous*, wanting name; *an-archy*, want of government; *a-cephalous*, headless.

2. AMPHI means Two, Both, or Double: as, *amphi-bious*, living in two elements; *amphi-brach*, both [sides] short; *amphi-theatre*, a double theatre.

3. ANTI means Against: as, *anti-slavery*, against slavery; *anti-acid*, against acidity; *anti-febrile*, against fever; *anti-thesis*, a placing-against.

4. APO, APH,—From : as, *apo-strophe*, a turning-from ; *aph-eresis*, a taking-from.

5. DIA,—Through : as, *dia-gonal*, through the corners ; *dia-meter*, measure through.

6. EPI, EPH,—Upon : as, *epi-demic*, upon the people ; *eph-emera*, upon a day.

7. HEMI means Half : as, *hemi-sphere*, half a sphere ; *hemi-stich*, half a verse.

8. HYPER means Over : as, *hyper-critical*, over-critical ; *hyper-meter*, over-measure.

9. HYPO means Under : as, *hypo-stasis*, substance, or that which stands under ; *hypo-thesis*, supposition, or a placing-under ; *hypo-phyllous*, under the leaf.

10. META means Beyond, Over, To an other state or place : as, *meta-morphose*, to change to an other shape ; *meta-physics*, mental science, as beyond or over physics.

11. PARA means Against : as, *para-dox*, something contrary to common opinion.

12. PERI means Around : as, *peri-phery*, the circumference, or measure round.

13. SYN,—whence *Sym, Syl*,—means Together : as, *syn-tax*,[1] a putting-together ; *sym-pathy*, a suffering-together ; *syl-lable*, what we take together ; *syn-thesis*, a placing-together.

CLASS IV.—THE FRENCH PREFIXES.

1. A is a preposition of very frequent use in French, and generally means *To*. I have suggested above that it is probably the same as the Anglo-Saxon prefix *a*. It is found in a few English compounds or derivatives that are of French, and not of Saxon origin : as, *a-dieu*, to God ; i. e., I commend you to God ; *a-larm*, from *alarme*, i. e., à *l'arme*, to arms.

2. DE means Of or From : as in *de-mure*, of manners ; *de-liver*, to ease from or of.

3. DEMI means Half : as, *demi-man*, half a man ; *demi-god*, half a god ; *demi-devil*, half a devil.

4. EN,—which sometimes becomes *em*,—means In, Into, or Upon : as, *en-chain*, to hold in chains ; *em-brace*, to clasp in the arms ; *en-tomb*, to put into a tomb ; *em-boss*, to stud upon. Many words are yet wavering between the French and the Latin orthography of this prefix : as *embody*, or *imbody* ; *ensurance*, or *insurance* ; *ensnare*, or *insnare* ; *enquire*, or *inquire*.

5. SUR, as a French prefix, means Upon, Over, or After : as, *sur-name*, a name upon a name ; *sur-vey*, to look over ; *sur-mount*, to mount over or upon ; *sur-render*, to deliver over to others ; *sur-feit*, to overdo in eating ; *sur-vive*, to live after, to over-live, to outlive.

END OF THE SECOND APPENDIX.

APPENDIX III.

TO PART THIRD, OR SYNTAX.

OF THE QUALITIES OF STYLE.

Style, as a topic connected with syntax, is the particular manner in which a person expresses his conceptions by means of language. It is different from mere words, different from mere grammar, in any limited sense, and is not to be regulated altogether by rules of construction. It always has some relation to the author's peculiar manner of thinking; involves, to some extent, and shows his literary, if not his moral, character; is, in general, that sort of expression which his thoughts most readily assume; and, sometimes, partakes not only of what is characteristic of the man, of his profession, sect, clan, or province, but even of national peculiarity, or some marked feature of the age. The words which an author employs, may be proper in themselves, and so constructed as to violate no rule of syntax, and yet his style may have great faults.

In reviews and critical essays, the general characters of style are usually designated by such epithets as these;—concise, diffuse,—neat, negligent,—terse, bungling,—nervous, weak,—forcible, feeble,—vehement, languid,—simple, affected,—easy, stiff,—pure, barbarous,—perspicuous, obscure,—elegant, uncouth,—florid, plain,—flowery, artless,—fluent, dry,—piquant, dull,—stately, flippant,—majestic, mean,—pompuous, modest,—ancient, modern. A considerable diversity of style, may be found in compositions all equally excellent in their kind. And, indeed, different subjects, as well as the different endowments by which genius is distinguished, require this diversity. But, in forming his style, the learner should remember, that a negligent, feeble, affected, stiff, uncouth, barbarous, or obscure style is always faulty; and that perspicuity, ease, simplicity, strength, neatness, and purity, are qualities always to be aimed at.

In order to acquire a good style, the frequent practice of composing and writing something, is indispensably necessary. Without exercise and diligent attention, rules or precepts for the attainment of this object, will be of no avail. When the learner has acquired such a knowledge of grammar, as to be in some degree qualified for the undertaking, he should devote a stated portion of his time to composition. This exercise will bring the powers of his mind into requisition, in a way that is well calculated to strengthen them. And if he has opportunity for reading, he may, by a diligent perusal of the best authors, acquire both language and taste as well as sentiment;—and these three are the essential qualifications of a good writer.

In regard to the qualities which constitute a good style, we can here offer nothing more than a few brief hints. With respect to words and phrases, particular attention should be paid to three things,—*purity, propriety,* and *precision;* and, with respect to sentences, to three others,—*perspicuity, unity,* and *strength.* Under each of these six heads, we shall arrange, in the form of short *precepts,* a few of the most important directions for the forming of a good style.

SECTION I.—OF PURITY.

Purity of style consists in the use of such words and phrases only, as belong to the language which we write or speak. Its opposites are the faults aimed at in the following precepts.

PRECEPT I.—Avoid the unnecessary use of foreign words or idioms : such as the French words *fraicheur, hauteur, delicatesse, politesse, noblesse;*—the expression, "He *repented himself;*"—or, "It *serves* to an excellent purpose."

PRECEPT II.—Avoid obsolete or antiquated words, except there be some special reason for their use : that is, such words as *acception, addressful, administrate, affamish, affrontiveness, belikely, blusterous, clergical, cruciate, rutilate, timidous.*

PRECEPT III.—Avoid strange or unauthorized words : such as, *flutteration, inspectator, judgematical, incumberment, connexity, electerized, martyrised, reunition, marvelize, limpitude, affectated, adorement, absquatulate.* Of this sort is O. B. Peirce's "*assimilarity,*" used on page 19th of his *English Grammar;* and still worse is Jocelyn's "*irradicable,*" for *uneradicable,* used on page 5th of his *Prize Essay on Education.*

PRECEPT IV.—Avoid bombast, or affectation of fine writing. It is ridiculous, however serious the subject. The following is an example: "Personifications, however rich the depictions, and unconstrained their latitude; analogies, however imposing the objects of parallel, and the media of comparison; can never expose the consequences of sin to the extent of fact, or the range of demonstration."—*Anonymous.*

SECTION II. — OF PROPRIETY.

Propriety of language consists in the selection and right construction of such words as the best usage has appropriated to those ideas which we intend to express by them. Impropriety embraces all those forms of error, which, for the purposes of illustration, exercise, and special criticism, have been so methodically and so copiously posted up under the various heads, rules, and notes, of this extensive Grammar. A few suggestions, however, are here to be set down in the form of precepts.

PRECEPT I.—Avoid low and provincial expressions: such as, "Now, *says I*, boys;"— "*Thinks I to myself;*"—"*To get into a scrape;*"—"Stay here *while* I come back;"—"*By jinkers;*"—"*By the living jingoes.*"

PRECEPT II.—In writing prose, avoid words and phrases that are merely poetical: such as, *morn, eve, plaint, corse, weal, drear, amid, oft, steepy;*—"*what time* the winds arise."

PRECEPT III.—Avoid technical terms: except where they are necessary in treating of a particular art or science. In technology, they are proper.

PRECEPT IV.—Avoid the recurrence of a word in different senses, or such a repetition of words as denotes paucity of language: as, "His own *reason* might have suggested better *reasons.*"—"Gregory *favoured* the undertaking, for no other *reason* than this; that the manager, in countenance, *favoured* his friend."—"I *want* to go and see what he *wants.*"

PRECEPT V.—Supply words that are wanting: thus, instead of saying, "This action increased his former services," say, "This action increased *the merit of* his former services." —"How many [*kinds of*] substantives are there? Two; proper and common."—See E. *Devis's Gram.* p. 14. "These changes should not be left to be settled by chance or by caprice, but [*should be determined*] by the judicious application of the principles of Orthography."—See *Fowler's E. Gram.,* 1850, p. 170.

PRECEPT VI.—Avoid equivocal or ambiguous expressions: as, "His *memory* shall be lost on the earth."—"I long since learned to like nothing but what you *do.*"

PRECEPT VII.—Avoid unintelligible, inconsistent, or inappropriate expressions: such as, "I have observed that the superiority among these coffee-house politicians proceeds from an *opinion* of gallantry and fashion."—"These words do not convey even an *opaque* idea of the author's meaning."

PRECEPT VIII.—Observe the natural order of things or events, and do not *put the cart before the horse:* as, "The scribes *taught and studied* the Law of Moses."—"They can neither *return* to nor *leave* their houses."—"He tumbled, *head over heels*, into the water."—"'Pat, how did you carry that quarter of beef?' 'Why, I thrust *it through a stick*, and threw *my shoulder over it.*'"

SECTION III. — OF PRECISION.

Precision consists in avoiding all superfluous words, and adapting the expression exactly to the thought, so as to say, with no deficiency or surplus of terms, whatever is intended by the author. Its opposites are noticed in the following precepts.

PRECEPT I.—Avoid a useless tautology, either of expression or of sentiment: as, "When will you return *again?*"—"We returned *back* home *again.*"—"On entering *into* the room, I saw *and discovered* he had fallen *down* on the floor and could not *rise* up."—"They have a *mutual* dislike to each other."—"Whenever I go, he *always* meets me there."—"Where is he *at?* In there."—"His faithfulness *and fidelity* should be rewarded."

PRECEPT II.—Repeat words as often as an exact exhibition of your meaning requires them; for repetition may be elegant, if it be not useless. The following example does not appear faulty: "Moral *precepts* are *precepts* the reasons of which we see; positive *precepts* are *precepts* the reasons of which we do not see."—*Butler's Analogy*, p. 165.

PRECEPT III.—Observe the exact meaning of words accounted synonymous, and employ those which are the most suitable; as, "A diligent scholar may *acquire* knowledge, *gain* celebrity, *obtain* rewards, *win* prizes, and *get* high honour, though he *earn* no money." These six verbs have nearly the same meaning, and yet no two of them can here be correctly interchanged.

PRECEPT IV.—Observe the proper form of each word, and do not confound such as resemble each other. "Professor J. W. Gibbs, of Yale College," in treating of the "Peculiarities of the Cockney Dialect," says, "The Londoner sometimes confounds two different forms; as, *contagious* for *contiguous; eminent* for *imminent; humorous* for *humorsome; ingeniously* for *ingenuously; luxurious* for *luxuriant; scrupulosity* for *scruple; successfully* for *successively.*"—See *Fowler's E. Gram.* p. 87; and Pref., p. vi.

PRECEPT V.—Think clearly, and avoid absurd or incompatible expressions. Example of error: "To pursue *those* remarks, would, *probably*, be of no further *service* to the learner than *that of* burdening *his memory* with a catalogue of dry and *uninteresting* peculiarities; *which*

may gratify curiosity, without affording information adequate to the trouble of the perusal."
—*Wright's Gram.* p. 122.

PRECEPT VI.—Avoid words that are useless ; and, especially, a multiplication of them into sentences, members, or clauses, that may well be spared. Example : " If one could *really* be a spectator of what is passing in the world *around us* without taking part in the events, *or sharing in the passions and actual performance on the stage ; if we could set ourselves down, as it were, in a private box of the world's great theatre, and quietly look on at the piece that is playing, no more moved than is absolutely implied by sympathy with our fellow-creatures, what a curious, what amusing*, what an interesting spectacle would life present."—G. P. R. JAMES : *"The Forger,"* commencement of Chap. xxxi. This sentence contains *eighty-seven* words, " of which *sixty-one* are entirely unnecessary to the expression of the author's idea, if idea it can be called."—*Holden's Review.*

OBSERVATION.

Verbosity, as well as tautology, is not so directly opposite to precision, as to conciseness, or brevity. From the manner in which lawyers usually multiply terms in order to express their facts *precisely*, it would seem that, with them, precision consists rather in the use of *many* words than of *few*. But the ordinary style of legal instruments no popular writer can imitate without becoming ridiculous. A terse or concise style is very apt to be elliptical ; and, in some particular instances, must be so ; but, at the same time, the full expression, perhaps, may have more *precision*, though it be less agreeable. For example : "A word of one syllable, is called a monosyllable ; a word of two syllables, *is called* a dissyllable : a word of three syllables, *is called a trisyllable : a* word of four or more syllables, *is called* a polysyllable."—*O. B. Peirce's Gram.* p. 19 Better, perhaps, thus : "A word of one syllable is called a *monosyllable* ; a word of two syllables, a *dissyllable* ; a word of three syllables, a *trissyllable* ; and a word of four or more syllables, a *polysyllable.*"—*Brown's Institutes*, p. 17.

SECTION IV.—OF PERSPICUITY.

Perspicuity consists in freedom from obscurity or ambiguity. It is a quality so essential to every kind of writing, that for the want of it no merit of other name can compensate. " Without this, the richest ornaments of style, only glimmer through the dark, and puzzle in stead of pleasing the reader."—*Dr. Blair.* Perspicuity, being the most important property of language, and an exemption from the most embarrassing defects, seems even to rise to a degree of positive beauty. We are naturally pleased with a style that frees us from all suspense in regard to the meaning ; that carries us through the subject without embarrassment or confusion ; and that always flows like a limpid stream, through which we can " see to the very bottom." Many of the errors which have heretofore been pointed out to the reader, are offences against perspicuity. Only three or four hints will here be added.

PRECEPT I.—Place adjectives, relative pronouns, participles, adverbs, and explanatory phrases near enough to the words to which they relate, and in a position which will make their reference clear. The following sentences are deficient in perspicuity : " Reverence is the veneration paid to superior sanctity, *intermixed* with a certain degree of awe."—*Unknown.* " The Romans understood liberty, *at least*, as well as we."—See *Murray's Gram.* p. 307. " Taste was never *made to cater* for vanity."—*J. Q. Adams's Rhet.*, Vol. i, p. 119.

PRECEPT II.—In prose, avoid a poetic collocation of words. For example : " Guard your weak side from being known. If it be attacked, the best way is, to join in the attack."— KAMES : *Art of Thinking*, p. 75. This maxim of prudence might be expressed more poetically, but with some loss of perspicuity, thus : " Your weak side guard from being known. Attacked in this, the assailants join."

PRECEPT III.—Avoid faulty ellipses, and repeat all words necessary to preserve the sense. The following sentences require the words which are inserted in crotchets : " Restlessness of mind disqualifies us, both for the enjoyment of peace, and [*for*] the performance of our duty."—*Murray's Key*, 8vo, p. 166. " Double Comparatives and [*Double*] Superlatives should be avoided."—*Fowler's E. Gram.*, 1850, p. 489.

PRECEPT IV.—Avoid the pedantic and sense-dimming style of charlatans and new theorists, which often demands either a translation or a tedious study, to make it at all intelligible to the ordinary reader. For example : " RULE XI. Part 3. An intransitive or receptive *asserter* in the unlimited mode, depending on a word in the possessive case, may have, after it, a word in the subjective case, denoting the same thing : And, when it acts the part of an assertive name, depending on a relative, it may have after it a word in the subjective case. EXAMPLES :—John's being my *friend*, saved me from inconvenience. Seth Hamilton was unhappy in being a *slave* to party prejudice."—*O. B. Peirce's Gram.*, 1839, p. 201. The meaning of this *third part of a Rule* of syntax, is, in proper English, as follows : "A participle not transitive, with the possessive case before it, may have after it a nominative denoting the same thing ; and also, when a preposition governs the participle, a nominative may follow, in agreement with one which precedes." In doctrine, the former clause of the sentence is erroneous : it serves only to propagate false syntax by rule. See the former example, and a note of mine, referring to it, on page 509 of this work.

SECTION V.—OF UNITY.

Unity consists in avoiding needless pauses, and keeping one object predominant throughout a sentence or paragraph. Every sentence, whether its parts be few or many, requires strict unity. The chief faults, opposite to this quality of style, are suggested in the following precepts.

PRECEPT I.—Avoid brokenness, hitching, or the unnecessary separation of parts that naturally come together. Examples: "I was, soon after my arrival, taken out of my Indian habit."—*Addison, Tattler*, No. 249. Better: "Soon after my arrival, I was taken out of my Indian habit."—*Churchill's Gram.* p. 326. "Who can, either in opposition, or in the ministry, act alone?"—*Ib.* Better: "Who can act alone, either in opposition, or in the ministry?"—*Ib.* "I, like others, have, in my youth, trifled with my health, and old age now prematurely assails me."—*Ib.* p. 327. Better: "Like others, I have trifled with my health, and old age now prematurely assails me."

PRECEPT II.—Treat different topics in separate paragraphs, and distinct sentiments in separate sentences. Error: "The two volumes are, indeed, intimately connected, and constitute one uniform system of English Grammar."—*Murray's Preface*, p. iv. Better thus: "The two volumes are, indeed, intimately connected. *They* constitute one uniform system of English *grammar*."

PRECEPT III.—In the progress of a sentence, do not desert the principal subject in favour of adjuncts, or change the scene unnecessarily. Example: "After we came to anchor, they put me on shore, where I was welcomed by all my friends, who received me with the greatest kindness, which was not then expected." Better: "The vessel having come to anchor, I was put on shore; where I was unexpectedly welcomed by all my friends, and received with the greatest kindness."—See *Blair's Rhet.* p. 107.

PRECEPT IV.—Do not introduce parentheses, except when a lively remark may be thrown in without diverting the mind too long from the principal subject. Example: "But (saith he) since I take upon me to teach the whole world, (it is strange, it should be so natural for this man to write untruths, since I direct my *Theses* only to the Christian world : but if it may render me odious, such *Peccadillo's* pass with him, it seems, but for *Pia Fraudes :*) I intended never to write of those things, concerning which we do not differ from others."—*R. Barclay's Works*, Vol. iii, p. 279. The parts of this sentence are so put together, that, as a whole, it is scarcely intelligible.

SECTION VI.—OF STRENGTH.

Strength consists in giving to the several words and members of a sentence, such an arrangement as shall bring out the sense to the best advantage, and present every idea in its due importance. Perhaps it is essential to this quality of style, that there be animation, spirit, and *vigour of thought*, in all that is uttered. A few hints concerning the Strength of sentences, will here be given in the form of precepts.

PRECEPT I.—Avoid verbosity: a concise style is the most favourable to strength. Examples: "No human happiness is so pure as not to contain *any* alloy."—*Murray's Key*, 8vo, p. 270. Better: "No human happiness is *unalloyed*." "He was so much skilled in the exercise of the oar, that few could equal him."—*Ib.* p. 271. Better: "He was so *skilful at* the oar, that few could *match* him." Or thus: "At the oar, he was *rarely equalled*." "The reason why they [the pronouns] are considered separately is, because there is something particular in their inflections."—*Priestley's Gram.* p. 81. Better: "The pronouns are considered separately, because there is something peculiar in their inflections."

PRECEPT II.—Place the most important words in the situation in which they will make the strongest impression. Inversion of terms sometimes increases the strength and vivacity of an expression: as, "All these things will I give thee, if thou wilt fall down and worship me."—*Matt.* iv, 9. "Righteous art thou, O Lord, and upright are thy judgements."—*Psalms*, cxix, 137. "Precious in the sight of the Lord is the death of his saints."—*Ps.* cxvi, 15.

PRECEPT III.—Have regard also to the relative position of clauses, or members; for a weaker assertion should not follow a stronger; and, when the sentence consists of two members, the longer should be the concluding one. Example: "We flatter ourselves with the belief that we have forsaken our passions, when they have forsaken us." Better: "When our passions have forsaken us, we flatter ourselves with the belief that we have forsaken them."—See *Blair's Rhet.* p. 117; *Murray's Gram.* p. 323.

PRECEPT IV.—When things are to be compared or contrasted, their resemblance or opposition will be rendered more striking, if a pretty near resemblance in the language and construction of the two members, be preserved. Example: "The wise man is happy, when he gains his own approbation; the fool, when he recommends himself to the applause of those about him." Better: "The wise man is happy, when he gains his own approbation; the fool, when he gains the applause of others."—See *Murray's Gram.* p. 324.

PRECEPT V.—Remember that it is, in general, ungraceful to end a sentence with an adverb, a preposition, or any inconsiderable word or phrase, which may either be omitted or be introduced earlier. "For instance, it is a great deal better to say, 'Avarice is a crime of which wise men are often guilty,' than to say, 'Avarice is a crime which wise men are often guilty of.'"—*Blair's Rhet.* p. 117; *Murray's Gram.* p. 323.

END OF THE THIRD APPENDIX.

APPENDIX IV.

TO PART FOURTH, OR PROSODY.

OF POETIC DICTION.

Poetry, as defined by Dr. Blair, " is the language of passion, or of enlivened imagination, formed, most commonly, into regular numbers."—*Rhet.* p. 377. The style of poetry differs, in many respects, from that which is commonly adopted in prose. Poetic diction abounds in bold figures of speech, and unusual collocations of words. A great part of the figures, which have been treated of in one of the chapters of Prosody, are purely poetical. The primary aim of a poet, is, to please and to move; and, therefore, it is to the imagination, and the passions, that he speaks. He may also, and he should, have it in his view, to instruct and to reform; but it is indirectly, and by pleasing and moving, that such a writer accomplishes this end. The exterior and most obvious distinction of poetry, is versification : yet there are some forms of verse so loose and familiar, as to be hardly distinguishable from prose; and there is also a species of prose, so measured in its cadences, and so much raised in its tone, as to approach very nearly to poetic numbers.

This double approximation of some poetry to prose, and of some prose to poetry, not only makes it a matter of acknowledged difficulty to distinguish, by satisfactory definitions, the two species of composition, but, in many instances, embarrasses with like difficulty the attempt to show, by statements and examples, what usages or licenses, found in English works, are proper to be regarded as peculiarities of poetic diction. It is purposed here, to enumerate sundry deviations from the common style of prose; and perhaps all of them, or nearly all, may be justly considered as pertaining only to poetry.

POETICAL PECULIARITIES.

The following are among the chief peculiarities in which the poets indulge, and are indulged :—

I. They not unfrequently omit the ARTICLES, for the sake of brevity or metre; as,

"What dreadful pleasure ! there to stand sublime,
Like *shipwreck'd mariner* on *desert* coast ! "—*Beattie's Minstrel*, p. 12.

"*Sky lour'd*, and, muttering thunder, some sad drops
Wept at *completing* of the mortal sin."—*Milton, P. L.*, B. ix, l. 1002.

II. They sometimes abbreviate common NOUNS, after a manner of their own : as, *amaze*, for *amazement*; *acclaim*, for *acclamation*; *consult*, for *consultation*; *corse*, for *corpse*; *eve*, or *even*, for *evening*; *fount*, for *fountain*; *helm*, for *helmet*; *lament*, for *lamentation*; *morn*, for *morning*; *plaint*, for *complaint*; *targe*, for *target*; *weal*, for *wealth*.

III. By *enallage*, they use verbal forms substantively, or put verbs for nouns; perhaps for brevity, as above : thus,

1. "Instant, without *disturb*, they took alarm."—*P. Lost : Joh. Dict. w. Aware.*
2. "The gracious Judge, without *revile* reply'd."—*P. Lost*, B. x, l. 118.
3. "If they were known, as the *suspect* is great."—*Shakspeare.*
4. "Mark, and perform it; *seest* thou? for the *fail*
Of any point in't shall be death."—*Shakspeare.*

IV. They employ several nouns that are not used in prose, or are used but rarely; as, *benison, boon, emprise, fane, guerdon, guise, ire, ken, lore, meed, sire, steed, welkin, yore.*

V. They introduce the noun *self* after an other noun of the possessive case; as,

1. "Affliction's semblance bends not o'er thy tomb,
Affliction's *self* deplores thy youthful doom."—*Byron.*
2. "Thoughtless of beauty, she was beauty's *self*."—*Thomson.*

VI. They place before the verb nouns, or other words, that usually come after it; and, after it, those that usually come before it : as,

1. "No jealousy *their dawn of love* o'ercast,
Nor *blasted* were *their wedded days* with strife."—*Beattie.*
2. "No *hive* hast *thou* of hoarded sweets."—*W. Allen's Gram.*
3. "Thy chain *a wretched weight* shall prove."—*Langhorne.*
4. "Follows the loosen'd aggravated *roar*."—*Thomson.*
5. "That *purple* grows *the primrose pale*."—*Langhorne.*

VII. They more frequently place ADJECTIVES after their nouns, than do prose writers; as,

    1. "Or where the gorgeous East, with richest hand,
        Show'rs on her kings *barbaric*, pearl and gold."—*Milton, P. L.*, B. ii, l. 2.
    2. "Come, nymph *demure*, with mantle *blue*."—*W. Allen's Gram.* p. 189.
    3. "This truth *sublime* his simple sire had taught."—*Beattie's Minstrel*, p. 14.

VIII. They ascribe qualities to things to which they do not literally belong; as,
    1. "The ploughman homeward plods his *weary way*."—*Gray's Elegy*, l. 3.
    2. "Or *drowsy tinklings* lull the distant folds."—*Ibidem*, l. 8.
    3. "Imbitter'd more and more from *peevish day* to day."—*Thomson*.
    4. "All thin and naked, to the numb cold *night*."—*Shakspeare*.

IX. They use concrete terms to express abstract qualities; (i. e., adjectives for nouns;) as,
    1. "Earth's meanest son, all trembling, prostrate falls,
        And on the *boundless* of thy goodness calls."—*Young*.
    2. "Meanwhile, whate'er of *beautiful* or *new*,
        Sublime or *dreadful*, in earth, sea, or sky,
        By chance or search, was offer'd to his view,
        He scann'd with curious and romantic eye."—*Beattie*.
    3. "Won from the void and formless *infinite*."—*Milton*.
    4. "To thy large heart give utterance due; thy heart
        Contains of *good, wise, just*, the perfect shape."—*Id. P. R.*, B. iii, l. 10.

X. They substitute quality for manner; (i. e., adjectives for adverbs;) as,
    1. —————— "The stately-sailing swan
        Gives out his snowy plumage to the gale,
        And, arching *proud* his neck, with oary feet,
        Bears forward *fierce*, and guards his osier isle."—*Thomson*.
    2. "Thither *continual* pilgrims crowded still."—*Id. Cas. of Ind.* i, 8.
    3. "Level at beauty, and at wit;
        The fairest mark is *easiest* hit."—*Butler's Hudibras*.

XI. They form new compound epithets, oftener than do prose writers; as,
    1. "In *world-rejoicing* state, it moves sublime."—*Thomson*.
    2. "The *dewy-skirted* clouds imbibe the sun."—*Idem*.
    3. "By brooks and groves in *hollow-whispering* gales."—*Idem*.
    4. "The violet of *sky-woven* vest."—*Langhorne*.
    5. "A league from Epidamnum had we sail'd,
        Before the *always wind-obeying* deep
        Gave any tragic instance of our harm."—*Shakspeare*.
    6. "'*Blue-eyed, strange-voiced, sharp-beaked, ill-omened* fowl,
        What art thou?' 'What I ought to be, an owl.'"—*Day's Punctuation*, p. 139.

XII. They connect the comparative degree to the positive, before a verb; as,
    1. "*Near and more near* the billows rise."—*Merrick*.
    2. "*Wide and wider* spreads the vale."—*Dyer's Grongar Hill*.
    3. "*Wide and more wide*, the o'erflowings of the mind
        Take every creature in, of every kind."—*Pope*.
    4. "*Thick and more thick* the black blockade extends,
        A hundred head of Aristotle's friends."—*Id., Dunciad.*

XIII. They form many adjectives in *y*, which are not common in prose; as, The *dimply* flood,—*dusky* veil,—a *gleamy* ray,—*heapy* harvests,—*moony* shield,—*paly* circlet,—*sheety* lake, —*stilly* lake,—*spiry* temples,—*steely* casque,—*steepy* hill,—*towery* height,—*vasty* deep,— *writhy* snake.

XIV. They employ adjectives of an abbreviated form: as, *dread*, for *dreadful; drear*, for *dreary; ebon*, for *ebony; hoar*, for *hoary; lone*, for *lonely; scant*, for *scanty; slope*, for *sloping; submiss*, for *submissive; vermil*, for *vermilion; yon*, for *yonder*.

XV. They employ several adjectives that are not used in prose, or are used but seldom; as, *azure, blithe, boon, dank, darkling, darksome, doughty, dun, fell, rife, rapt, rueful, sear, sylven, twain, wan.*

XVI. They employ the personal PRONOUNS, and introduce their nouns afterwards; as,
    1. "*It* curl'd not Tweed alone, that *breeze*."—*Sir W. Scott.*
    2. "What may *it* be, the heavy *sound*
        That moans old Branksome's turrets round?"—*Idem, Lay*, p. 21.
    3. "Is it the lightning's quivering glance,
        That on the thicket streams;
        Or do *they* flash on spear and lance,
        The sun's retiring *beams?*"—*Idem, L. of L.*, vi, 15.

XVII. They use the forms of the second person singular oftener than do others; as,
    1. "Yet I had rather, if I were to chuse,
        Thy service in some graver subject use,
        Such as may make *thee* search thy coffers round,
        Before *thou clothe* my fancy in fit sound."—*Milton's Works*, p. 132.
    2. "But *thou*, of temples old, or altars new,
        Standest alone—with nothing like to thee."—*Byron, Pilg.*, iv, 154.

3. "*Thou seest* not all; but piecemeal *thou* must break,
To separate contemplation, the great whole."—*Id. ib.*, iv, 157.

4. "*Thou* rightly *deemst*, fair youth, began the bard;
The form *thou sawst* was Virtue ever fair."—*Pollok, C. of T.*, p. 16.

XVIII. They sometimes omit relatives that are nominatives; (see Obs. 22, at p. 532;) as,
"For is there aught in sleep *can charm* the wise?"—*Thomson.*

XIX. They omit the antecedent, or introduce it after the relative; as,
1. "*Who* never fasts, no banquet e'er enjoys,
Who never toils or watches, never sleeps."—*Armstrong.*
2. "*Who* dares think one thing and an other tell,
My soul detests *him* as the gates of hell."—*Pope's Homer.*

XX. They remove relatives, or other connectives, into the body of their clauses; as,
1. "Parts the fine locks, her graceful head *that* deck."—*Darwin.*
2. "Not half so dreadful rises to the sight
Orion's dog, the year *when* autumn weighs."—*Pope, Iliad*, B. xxii, l. 37.

XXI. They make intransitive VERBS transitive, changing their class; as,
1. ———— "A while he stands,
Gazing the inverted landscape, half afraid
To *meditate* the blue profound below."—*Thomson.*
2. "Still in harmonious intercourse, they *liv'd*
The rural day, and *talk'd* the flowing heart."—*Idem*
3. ———" I saw and heard, for we sometimes   [l. 330.
Who *dwell* this wild, constrain'd by want, come forth."—*Milton, P. R.*, B. i,

XXII. They make transitive verbs intransitive, giving them no regimen; as,
1. "The soldiers should have toss'd me on their pikes,
Before I would have *granted* to that act."—*Shakspeare.*
2. "This ministrel-god, well-pleased, amid the quire
Stood proud to *hymn*, and tune his youthful lyre."—*Pope.*

XXIII. They give to the imperative mood the first and the third person; as,
1. "*Turn we* a moment fancy's rapid flight."—*Thomson.*
2. "*Be* man's peculiar *work* his sole delight."—*Beattie.*
3. "And what is reason? *Be she* thus *defin'd:*
Reason is upright stature in the soul."—*Young.*

XXIV. They employ *can, could,* and *would,* as principal verbs transitive; as,
1. "*What* for ourselves we *can,* is always ours."—*Anon.*
2. "Who does the best his circumstance allows,
Does well, acts nobly:—angels *could* no *more.*"—*Young.*
3. "*What would* this man? Now upward will he soar,
And, little less than angel, would be more."—*Pope.*

XXV. They place the infinitive before the word on which it depends; as,
1. "When first thy sire *to send* on earth
Virtue, his darling child, *design'd.*"—*Gray.*
2. "As oft as I, *to kiss* the flood, *decline;*
So oft his lips ascend, to close with mine."—*Sandys.*
3. "Besides, Minerva, *to secure* her care,
Diffus'd around a veil of thicken'd air."—*Pope.*

XXVI. They place the auxiliary verb after its principal, by hyperbaton; as,
1. "No longer *heed* the sunbeam bright
That plays on Carron's breast he *can.*"—*Langhorne.*
2. "*Follow* I *must,* I cannot go before."—*Beauties of Shakspeare*, p. 147.
3. "The man who suffers, loudly may complain;
And *rage* he *may,* but he shall rage in vain."—*Pope.*

XXVII. Before verbs, they sometimes arbitrarily employ or omit prefixes: as, *bide,* or *abide; dim,* or *bedim; gird,* or *begird; lure,* or *allure; move,* or *emove; reave,* or *bereave; vails,* or *avails; vanish,* or *evanish; wail,* or *bewail; weep,* or *beweep; wilder,* or *bewilder:*—
1. "All knees to thee shall bow, of them that *bide*
In heav'n, or earth, or under earth in hell."—*Milton, P. L.*, B. iii, l. 321.
2. "Of a horse, *ware* the heels; of a bull-dog, the jaws;
Of a bear, the embrace; of a lion, the paws."—*Churchill's Gram.* p. 215.

XXVIII. Some few verbs they abbreviate: as, *list,* for *listen; ope,* for *open; hark,* for *hearken; dark,* for *darken; threat,* for *threaten; sharp,* for *sharpen.*

XXIX. They employ several verbs that are not used in prose, or are used but rarely; as, *appal, astound, brook, cower, doff, ken, wend, ween, trow.*

XXX. They sometimes imitate a Greek construction of the infinitive; as,
1. "Who would not sing for Lycidas? he knew
Himself *to sing,* and *build* the lofty rhyme."—*Milton.*
2. "For not, *to have been dipp'd* in Lethe lake,
Could save the son of Thetis *from to die.*"—*Spenser.*

XXXI. They employ the PARTICIPLES more frequently than prose writers, and in a construction somewhat peculiar; often, intensive by accumulation : as,
    1. " He came, and, standing in the midst, explain'd
        The peace *rejected*, but the truce *obtain'd.*"—*Pope.*
    2. " As a poor miserable captive thrall
        Comes to the place where he before had sat
        Among the prime in splendor, now *depos'd*,
        Ejected, emptied, gaz'd, unpitied, shunn'd,
        A spectacle of ruin or of scorn."—*Milton*, P. R., B. i, L. 411.
    3. " Though from our birth the faculty divine
        Is chain'd and *tortured—cabin'd, cribb'd,confined.*"—*Byron*, Pilg. C. iv, St. 127.
XXXII. In turning participles to adjectives, they sometimes ascribe actions, or active properties, to things to which they do not literally belong; as,
    " The green leaf quivering in the gale,
      The *warbling hill*, the *lowing vale.*"—MALLET : *Union Poems*, p. 26.
XXXIII. They employ several ADVERBS that are not used in prose, or are used but seldom ; as, *oft, haply, inly.*
XXXIV. They give to adverbs a peculiar location in respect to other words ; as,
    1. " Peeping from *forth* their alleys green."—*Collins.*
    2. " Erect the standard *there* of ancient Night."—*Milton.*
    3. " The silence *often* of pure innocence
        Persuades, when speaking fails."—*Shakspeare.*
    4. " Where Universal Love *not* smiles around."—*Thomson.*
    5. " Robs me of that which *not* enriches him."—*Shakspeare.*
XXXV. They sometimes omit the introductory adverb *there ;* as,
    " *Was* nought around but images of rest."—*Thomson.*
XXXVI. They briefly compare actions by a kind of compound adverbs, ending in *like ;* as,
    " Who bid the stork, *Columbus-like,* explore
      Heavens not his own, and worlds unknown before ? "—*Pope.*
XXXVII. They employ the CONJUNCTIONS, *or—or,* and *nor—nor,* as correspondents ; as,
    1. " *Or* by the lazy Scheldt *or* wandering Po."—*Goldsmith.*
    2. " Wealth heap'd on wealth, *nor* truth *nor* safety buys."—*Johnson.*
    3. " Who by repentance is not satisfied,
        Is *nor* of earth, *nor* heaven."—*Shakspeare.*
    4. " Toss it, *or* to the fowls, *or* to the flames."—*Young*, N. T., p. 157.
    5. " *Nor* shall the pow'rs of hell, *nor* wastes of time,
        Or vanquish, *or* destroy."—*Gibbon's Elegy on Davies.*
XXXVIII. They oftener place PREPOSITIONS and their adjuncts, before the words on which they depend, than do prose writers; as,
    "*Against* your fame *with* fondness hate *combines ;*
    The rival batters, and the lover mines."—*Dr. Johnson.*
XXXIX. They sometimes place a disyllabic preposition after its object ; as,
    1. " When beauty, *Eden's bowers within,*
        First stretched the arm to deeds of sin,
        When passion burn'd and prudence slept,
        The pitying angels bent and wept."—*James Hogg.*
    2. " The Muses fair, *these peaceful shades among,*
        With skillful fingers sweep the trembling strings."—*Lloyd.*
    3. " Where Echo walks *steep hills among,*
        List'ning to the shepherd's song."—*J. Warton*, U. Poems, p. 33.
XL. They have occasionally employed certain prepositions for which, perhaps, it would not be easy to cite prosaic authority ; as, *adown, aloft, aloof, anear, aneath, askant, aslant, aslope, atween, atwixt, besouth, traverse, thorough, sans.* (See Obs. 10th, and others, at p. 423.)
XLI. They oftener employ INTERJECTIONS than do prose writers; as,
    "*O* let me gaze !—Of gazing there's no end.
    O let me think !—Thought too is wilder'd here."—*Young.*
XLII. They oftener employ ANTIQUATED WORDS and modes of expression ; as,
    1. " *Withouten* that, would come *an* heavier bale."—*Thomson.*
    2. " He was *too weet*, a little roguish page,
        Save sleep and play, who minded nought at all."—*Id.*
    3. " Not one *eftsoons* in view was to be found."—*Id.*
    4. " To number up the thousands dwelling here,
        An useless were, and *eke* an endless task."—*Id.*
    5. " Of clerks good plenty here you *mote espy*."—*Id.*
    6. " But these I *passen* by with nameless numbers *moe*."—*Id.*

THE END OF APPENDIX FOURTH,

AND

THE END OF THE GRAMMAR.